DIRECTORY OF GEOSCIENCE DEPARTMENTS

51st Edition

Carolyn Wilson, Editor

American Geosciences Institute
Alexandria, Virginia

Directory of Geoscience Departments 2016, 51st Edition

Edited by Carolyn Wilson

ISBN-13: 978-0-913312-64-3
ISBN-10: 0-9133-1264-9
ISSN: 0364-7811

Typeset in Times New Roman and Arial using Adobe InDesign CC.
Layout and programming: Christopher M. Keane
Advertising: John P. Rasanen

For more information on the American Geosciences Institute and its publications check us out at www.americangeosciences.org

Cover
Cross-bedding structures in the Navajo Sandstone of Zion National Park. The large-scale cross bedding developed in the Jurassic as successive layers of fine dune sand, blowing up gentle windward dune slopes, were deposited on steeper leeward slopes where wind velocity lessened. The Navajo Sandstone was deposited in an ancient desert about the size of today's Sahara. Copyright © Marli Miller.

Introduction

Thank you for using the 51st edition of the Directory of Geoscience Departments. The American Geosciences Institute (AGI) continues to be grateful to all the departments who took the time this year to update their information and provide additional historical data of enrollments and awarded degrees for their department.

We would also like to thank Jordan Ellington, the AGI Workforce Program fall intern, for her work updating the international listings and further enhancing the completeness and quality of the department listings. Thanks to the efforts of all of the data interns hired by the AGI Workforce Program since 2013 for their major enhancement of the international department listings.

For this edition, departments were able to provide social media contacts and indicate whether they host a field camp. The field camp listings are categorized as either open enrollment to students outside the department or department-only enrollment. This edition also has two different faculty indexes sorting the department faculty by their specialization and alphabetically.

This edition includes a listing of U.S. and Canadian student theses and dissertations from 2013 that have been reported to GeoRef Information Services. We would like to thank GeoRef for their diligent work compiling this list for use in this edition.

The data used to compile the directory is provided by the individuals and departments listed. AGI only edits the information for consistency and format. Any errors or omissions most likely reflect the entries of the individuals or the primary department contact. If you identify any issues, please email dgd@americangeosciences.org with information about a current responsible contact for the department in question, so that we may further encourage updates to the next edition.

The American Geosciences Institute does not warrant the accuracy of any of the self-reported information, but we do encourage individuals and departments to update the material they believe is out-of-date.

Some basic statistics for the 51st edition of the Directory of Geoscience Departments: 1990 academic departments and programs globally, with 970 of those departments in the United States. Three hundred thirty departments in the United States are two-year institutions. The U.S. numbers increased slightly due to an increase in the number of two-year institutions found with geoscience programs and faculty.

Carolyn Wilson
Editor

DIRECTORY OF GEOSCIENCE DEPARTMENTS
51st Edition 2016

Table of Contents

Usage Key

Degrees Offered
A - Associate's or 2-year degree
B - Bachelor's or equivalent undergraduate degree
M - Master's Degree
D - Doctorate

Basic enrollment and degrees-granted data for the most recent year reported are shown below department information: degree level, enrollment, and degrees granted (in parentheses).

⬚ indicates thesis and dissertations were provided.
● indicates department offers a field camp only for their majors.
○ indicates department offers a field camp with open enrollment.

The letters following individual faculty listings indicates their research specialties. Capital letters indicate general area, lowercase letters indicate subspecialty. Two or more consecutive lowercase letters refer to multiple subspecialties in the same major focus area referred to by the preceding capital letter.

DEPARTMENTS AND FACULTIES

This section contains a global listing of academic geoscience departments. Universities and colleges in the United States are arranged alphabetically by state. Non-U.S. institutions are listed alphabetically by country following the U.S. section.

All data is as reported by the departments and faculty themselves and current as of January 28, 2016. If you are aware of updates, corrections, or other means to ensure continued improvement of this listing, please email dgd@agiweb.org with the appropriate information so that it can be addressed during the next revision.

Alabama

Alabama A&M University
Dept of Biological and Environmental Sciences (A,B,M,D) (2015)
P.O. Box 1208
Normal, AL 35762
  p. (256) 372-4214
  anthony.overton@aamu.edu
  http://www.aamu.edu
  Enrollment: No data reported since 1999
Chair:
  Anthony Overton
Professor:
  Tommy L. Coleman, (D), Iowa State, 1980, So
  Florence A. Okafor, (D), Nigeria, 1995, OnEn
  Govind Sharma, (D), Kansas State, 1970, On
  James W. Shuford, (D), Penn State, 1975, So
Associate Professor:
  Monday O. Mbila, (D), Iowa State, 2000, Sd
Secretary:
  Martha Palmer

Auburn University
Dept of Agronomy & Soils (M,D) (2014)
201 Funchess Hall
Auburn University, AL 36849
  p. (334) 844-4100
  touchjt@auburn.edu
  Enrollment (2006): M: 8 (2) D: 6 (3)
Head:
  Joseph T. Touchton, (D), Illinois, 1977, Sc
Extension Agronomist-Soils:
  Charles C. Mitchell, (D), Florida, 1980, Sc
Professor:
  Elizabeth A. Guertal, (D), Oklahoma State, 1993, Sc
  Joey N. Shaw, (D), Georgia, 1997, Sd
  Charles W. Wood, (D), Colorado State, 1990, Sc
Associate Professor:
  Yucheng Feng, (D), Penn State, 1995, Sb
  John W. Odom, (D), Purdue, 1977, Sc
Assistant Professor:
  Julie Howe, Wisconsin, 2005, Sc

Dept of Geology & Geography (B,M) (2014)
210 Petrie Hall
Auburn University, AL 36849-5305
  p. (334) 844-4282
  bdm0018@auburn.edu
  http://www.auburn.edu/academic/science_math/geology/docs
  Enrollment (2013): B: 93 (17) M: 28 (4)
Chair:
  Mark G. Steltenpohl, (D), North Carolina, 1985, Gtc
Professor:
  Willis E. Hames, (D), Virginia Tech, 1990, GpCc
  David T. King, Jr., (D), Missouri, 1980, GrOn
  Ming-Kuo Lee, (D), Illinois, 1993, Hw
  James A. Saunders, (D), Colorado Mines, 1986, Cl
  Charles E. Savrda, (D), S California, 1986, Gd
  Lorraine W. Wolf, (D), Alaska (Fairbanks), 1989, Ysg
Associate Professor:
  Phil L. Chaney, (D), Louisiana State, 1999, OynOn
  Ronald D. Lewis, (D), Texas, 1982, Pi

Luke J. Marzen, (D), Kansas State, 2001, Oir
Ashraf Uddin, (D), Florida State, 1996, GdOn
Assistant Professor:
  Chandana Mitra, (D)
  Stephanie Shepherd, (D), GmOi
  Haibo Zou, (D), Florida State, 1999, GiCa
Instructor:
  Richard R. Greene, (M), On
  James Norwood, Oy
Lecturer:
  John Hawkins, Gg
  Daniel McGowin, (D)
Emeritus:
  Robert B. Cook, (D), Georgia, 1971, Eg
  Cyrus B. Dawsey, (D), Florida, 1975, Oy
  Tom L. Martinson, (D), Kansas, 1969, Oy

Dauphin Island Sea Lab
Marine Science Program (M,D) (2014)
P.O. Box 369
101 Bienville Boulevard
Dauphin Island, AL 36528
  p. (334) 861-7528
  langelo@disl.org
  http://www.disl.org/aboutus.html
  Department Secretary: Carolyn F. Wood
  Enrollment: No data reported since 1999
Director:
  William W. Schroeder, (D), Texas A&M, 1971, Og
Professor:
  Thomas S. Hopkins, (D), California (San Diego), 1967, Ob
Associate Professor:
  Jonathan R. Pennock, (D), Delaware, 1983, Oc
Librarian:
  Dennis Patronas, On
Cooperating Faculty:
  George F. Crozier, (D), California (San Diego), 1966, On

University of Alabama 🗋
Dept of Geological Sciences (B,M,D) ⭕ (2015)
Box 870338
201 7th Avenue
Room 2003 Bevill Bldg.
Tuscaloosa, AL 35487-0338
  p. (205) 348-5095
  geology@geo.ua.edu
  http://www.geo.ua.edu
  Enrollment (2015): B: 94 (22) M: 44 (14) D: 17 (3)
Professor:
  Paul Aharon, (D), Australian National, 1980, Ge
  Ibrahim Çemen, (D), Penn State, 1983, Gct
  Rona J. Donahoe, (D), Stanford, 1984, Cl
  Harold H. Stowell, (D), Princeton, 1987, Gp
  Chunmiao Zheng, (D), Wisconsin, 1988, Hw
Chair:
  C. Fred T. Andrus, (D), Georgia, 2000, PeGaCs
Associate Professor:
  Andrew Goodliffe, (D), Hawaii, 1998, Yg
  Samantha E. Hansen, (D), California (Santa Cruz), 2007, YsGt
  Alberto Perez-Huerta, (D), Oregon, 2004, PgClGz
  Delores Robinson, (D), Arizona, 2001, Gc
  Geoffrey Tick, (D), Arizona, 2003, Hw
  Yong Zhang, (D), Nanjing, 1998, Hqw

Assistant Professor:
  Natasha T Dimova, (D), Florida State, 2010, HwCcm
  Kimberly Genareau, (D), Arizona State, 2009, Gvi
  Deborah A. Keene, (D), Georgia, 2002, Gga
  Yuehan Lu, (D), Michigan, 2008, GgOuGe
  Rezene Mahatsente, (D), Clausthal Tech, 1998, YgmYv
  Tom S. Tobin, (D), Washington, 2014, PsCsPe
  Bo Zhang, (D), Oklahoma, 2014, YeGoEo
Stable Isotope Research Scientist:
  W. Joseph Lambert, (D), Alabama, 2010, CsPeCg
Emeritus:
  Donald J. Benson, (D), Cincinnati, 1976, Gd
  Richard H. Groshong, Jr., (D), Brown, 1971, Gc
  W. Gary Hooks, (D), North Carolina, 1961, Gm
  Ernest A. Mancini, (D), Texas A&M, 1974, Pe
  Carl W. Stock, (D), North Carolina, 1977, Pi
Geochemical Research Lab Manager:
  Sidhartha Bhattacharyya, (D), Alabama, 2010, CatGe

University of South Alabama
Dept of Earth Sciences (B) O (2016)
5871 USA Dr. N.
Room 136
Mobile, AL 36688-0002
  p. (251) 460-6381
  dhaywick@southalabama.edu
  http://www.usouthal.edu/earthsci
  Enrollment (2015): B: 53 (15)
Chair:
  Sytske K. Kimball, (D), Penn State, 2000, Ow
Professor:
  Roy Ryder, (D), Florida, 1989, SdOry
Associate Professor:
  David T. Allison, (D), Florida State, 1992, Gc
  Keith G. Blackwell, (D), Texas A&M, 1990, Ow
  Murlene W. Clark, (D), Florida State, 1983, PiGrg
  Douglas W. Haywick, (D), James Cook, 1990, Gs
  Carol F. Sawyer, (D), Texas State, 2007, GmOye
  Aaron Williams, (D), Oklahoma, 1971, Ow
Assistant Professor:
  Alex Beebe, (D), Clemson, 2013, Ge
  Wes Terwey, (D), Colorado State, 2007, Ow
Instructor:
  Karen J. Jordan, (M), Alabama, 2005, Oyr
  Andrew Murray, Florida State, 2010, Ow
  Diana Sturm, (D), Alabama, 2000, Geg
  Sam Stutsman, (M), Alabama, 1996, Oiy

Dept of Marine Sciences (M,D) (2015)
307 University Drive
Mobile, AL 36688-0002
  p. (334) 460-7136
  keyser@southalabama.edu
  Administrative Assistant: Jan Keyser
  Enrollment: No data reported since 1999
Chair:
  Sean Powers, (D), Ob
Professor:
  Ronald P. Kiene, (D), SUNY (Stony Brook), 1986, Oc
Adjunct Professor:
  Douglas W. Haywick, (D), James Cook, 1990, Gs
  Erich M. Mueller, (D), Miami, 1983, Ob

University of West Alabama
Dept of Biological & Environmental Sciences (B,M) (2015)
UWA Station 7
Livingston, AL 35470
  p. (205) 652-3416
  arindsberg@uwa.edu
  http://www.uwa.edu/Biological_and_Environmental_Sci-
  ences.aspx
  Enrollment: No data reported since 1999
Associate Professor:
  Andrew K. Rindsberg, (D), Colorado Mines, 1986, PeGePi
Curator, Black Belt Museum:
  John C. Hall, (D), Alabama, 1985, Og

James P. Lamb, (B), Alabama, PvePg

Prince William Sound Community College
Dept of Natural Sciences (2011)
P.O. Box 97
Valdez, AK 99686
  p. (907) 822-3673
  rsbenda@pwscc.edu
  http://www.pwscc.edu

University of Alaska Fairbanks
Dept of Geosciences (B,M,D) O (2016)
900 Yukon Drive
P.O. Box 755780
Fairbanks, AK 99775-5780
  p. (907) 474-7565
  pjmccarthy@alaska.edu
  http://www.uaf.edu/geology/
  Enrollment (2010): B: 48 (11) M: 30 (9) D: 37 (6)
Dean, CNSM:
  Paul Layer, (D), Stanford, 1986, Ym
Chair:
  Paul McCarthy, (D), Guelph, 1995, Gs
Associate Dean, CNSM :
  Anupma Prakash, (D), Roorkee (India), 1966, Or
Professor:
  James E. Beget, (D), Washington, 1981, Gm
  Douglas Christensen, (D), Michigan, 1987, Ys
  Hajo Eicken, (D), Bremen, 1990, Og
  Jeffrey T. Freymueller, (D), South Carolina, 1991, Yd
  Catherine L. Hanks, (D), Alaska (Fairbanks), 1991, Go
  Regine M. Hock, (D), Swiss Fed Inst Tech, 1997, Ol
  Jessica F. Larsen, (D), California (Santa Cruz), 1996, Gv
  Rainer J. Newberry, (D), Stanford, 1980, Em
  Vladimir Romanovsky, (D), Alaska (Fairbanks), 1996, Yg
  Michael T. Whalen, (D), Syracuse, 1993, Gs
Associate Professor:
  Bernard Coakley, (D), Columbia, 1991, Yg
  Cary de Wit, (D), Kansas, 1997, Og
  Patrick S. Druckenmiller, (D), Calgary, 2006, Pv
  Sarah Fowell, (D), Columbia, 1994, Pl
  Mary J. Keskinen, (D), Stanford, 1979, Gx
  Dan Mann, (D), Washington, 1983, Oy
  Franz J. Meyer, (D), Tech (Munich), 2004, Or
  Erin C. Pettit, (D), Washington, 2003, Ol
Assistant Professor:
  Chris Maio, (D), Massachusetts (Boston), 2014, Oy
  Elisabeth Nadin, (D), Caltech, 2007, Gt
  Carl Tape, (D), Caltech, 2009, Ys
Instructor:
  Jochen Mezger, (D), Alberta, Gg
Emeritus:
  Kenneth P. Severin, (D), California (Davis), 1987
  David B. Stone, (D), Newcastle, 1963, Ym
  Donald M. Triplehorn, (D), Illinois, 1961, Gs

University of Alaska, Anchorage
Dept of Geological Sciences (B) ● (2015)
3211 Providence Drive
CPISB 101
Anchorage, AK 99508-4670
  p. (907) 786-1298
  uaa_mns@uaa.alaska.edu
  http://www.uaa.alaska.edu/geology/
  f: www.facebook.com/UAAGeologicalSciences
  t: @UAAGeology
  Enrollment (2015): B: 60 (8)
Chair:
  Kristine J. Crossen, (D), Washington, 1997, Gl
Professor:
  LeeAnn Munk, (D), Ohio State, 2001, Cle
Associate Professor:
  Jennifer Aschoff, (D), Colorado Mines, 2008, GrdGo
  Donald Matt Reeves, (D), Nevada, 2006, GeHgOn

Term Assistant Professor:
    Terry R. Naumann, (D), Idaho, 1998, Gi
Assistant Professor:
    Erin Shea, (D), MIT, 2014, CcGcCg
Term Instructor:
    Peter J. Oswald, (M), Idaho, Gg
    Mark Rivera, (M), New Mexico State, 2000, Gg

University of Alaska, Fairbanks 🗋
Alaska Quaternary Center (2014)
907 Yukon Drive
Fairbanks, AK 99775-1200
    p. (907) 474-7758
    rmtopp@alaska.edu
    Administrative Assistant: Leicha Welton
    Enrollment: No data reported since 1999
Professor:
    W. Scott Ambruster, (D), California (Davis), 1981, On
    Bruce P. Finney, (D), Oregon State, 1987, Ou
    David M. Hopkins, (D), Harvard, 1955, Gg
    Roger W. Powers, (D), Wisconsin, 1973, On
    Dan L. Wetzel, (B), Alaska (Fairbanks), 1975, On
Research Associate:
    Wendy H. Arundale, (D), Michigan State, 1976, On
    Peter Bowers, (M), Washington State, 1980, Ga
    Owen Mason, (D), Alaska, 1990, Ga
Adjunct Professor:
    Daniel H. Mann, (D), Washington, 1983, Pe
Geology Librarian:
    Judy Triplehorn, On

Dept of Mining & Geological Engineering (B,M,D) (2014)
P.O. Box 755800
Fairbanks, AK 99775-5800
    p. (907) 474-7388
    fnedw@uaf.edu
    http://www.alaska.edu/uaf/cem/ge/
    Administrative Assistant: Judy L. Johnson
    Enrollment (2011): B: 10 (10) M: 2 (2) D: 2 (2)
Professor:
    Sukumar Bandopadhyay, (D), Penn State, 1982, Nm
    Gang Chen, (D), Virginia Tech, 1989, Nm
    Scott L. Huang, (D), Missouri (Rolla), 1981
    Hsing K. Lin, (D), Utah, 1985, On
    Paul A. Metz, (D), Imperial Coll (UK), 1991
    Daniel E. Walsh, (D), Alaska (Fairbanks), 1984, On
Associate Professor:
    Debsmita Misra, (D), Onn
Assistant Professor:
    Margaret M. Darrow, (D), Onn
    Sabry Sabour Hafez, (D), Nm
Emeritus:
    Rajive Ganguli, (D), Kentucky, 1999, Nm

Museum (1999)
Box 756960
Fairbanks, AK 99775-6960
    p. (907) 474-7505
    museum@uaf.edu
    Administrative Assistant: Marie D. Ward
Curator:
    Roland A. Gangloff, (D), California (Berkeley), 1975, Pi
Associate Scientist:
    Paul E. Mattheus, (D), Alaska, 1997, Po
Adjunct Professor:
    William A. Clemens, (D), California (Berkeley), 1960, Pv
    Dale Guthrie, (D), Chicago, 1963, Pv
    Donald M. Triplehorn, (D), Illinois, 1961, Gs

University of Alaska, Southeast
Dept of Natural Sciences (2015)
11120 Glacier Hwy
Juneau, AK 99801
    p. (907) 796-6163
    cathy.connor@uas.alaska.edu
    http://www.uas.alaska.edu

Arizona State University 🗋
School of Earth and Space Exploration (B,M,D) (2014)
Box 871404
Tempe, AZ 85287-1404
    p. (480) 965-5081
    sese@asu.edu
    http://sese.asu.edu
    Enrollment (2007): B: 84 (0) M: 37 (0) D: 43 (0)
Director:
    Kip V. Hodges, (D), MIT, 1982, Gc
Director, Astrobiology Program:
    Jack D. Farmer, (D), California (Davis), 1978, Py
Professor:
    Donald M. Burt, (D), Harvard, 1972, Eg
    Peter R. Buseck, (D), Columbia, 1962, Cg
    Philip R. Christensen, (D), California (Los Angeles), 1981, Xg
    Edward Garnero, (D), Caltech, 1994, Ys
    Richard Hervig, (D), Chicago, 1979, Cg
    L. Paul Knauth, (D), Caltech, 1973, Cs
    Lawrence Krauss, (D), MIT, 1982, On
    Stephen J. Reynolds, (D), Arizona, 1982, Gt
    Mark Robinson, (D), Hawaii, 1993, On
    Everett Shock, (D), California (Berkeley), 1987, On
    Sumner Starrfield, (D), California (Los Angeles), On
    James A. Tyburczy, (D), Oregon, 1983, Yx
    Meenakshi Wadhwa, (D), Washington, 1994, On
    Kelin Whipple, (D), Washington, 1999, Gt
    Stanley N. Williams, (D), Dartmouth, 1983, Gv
Associate Professor:
    Ariel Anbar, (D), Caltech, 1996, Cg
    Ramon Arrowsmith, (D), Stanford, 1995, Gc
    Steven Desch, (D), Illinois (Urbana Champaign), 1998, On
    Arjun Heimsath, (D), California (Berkeley), 1999, Gc
    James Rhoads, (D), Princeton, 1997, On
    Thomas G. Sharp, (D), Arizona State, 1990, Gz
Assistant Professor:
    Amanda Clarke, (D), Penn State, 2002, Gv
    Christopher Groppi, (D), Arizona, 2003, On
    Hilairy Hartnett, (D), Washington, 1998, Cg
    Allen McNamara, (D), Michigan, 2002, Yx
    Srikanth Saripalli, (D), S California, 2007, On
    Evan Scannapieco, (D), California (Berkeley), 2001, On
    Steven Semken, (D), MIT, 1989, Gg
    Patrick Young, (D), Arizona, 2004, On
Research Associate:
    Mikhail Y. Zolotov, (D), Vernadsky Inst (Russia), 1990, Cg
Emeritus:
    Robert F. Lundin, (D), Illinois, 1962, Pm

Arizona Western College
Dept of Geosciences (A) (2015)
2020 S. Avenue 8E
Yuma, AZ 85365
    p. (928) 317-6000
    fred.croxen@azwestern.edu
    Enrollment (2015): A: 3 (0)
Professor:
    Fred W. Croxen III, (M), N Arizona, 1977, HwPvOi
    Catherine B. Hill, (M)
Adjunct Professor:
    Earl E. Burnett, (B), Arizona, 1965, HwGc
    Kelly L. Esslinger, (M), OapGg
    Maureen Garrett, (M), Gg
    Tia McCraley, (M), Gg
    Todd Pinnt, (M), Oyi

Central Arizona College
Dvision of Science (2011)
Coolidge, AZ 85228
    p. (602) 426-4444
    diane.beecroft@centralaz.edu
Instructor:
    Allan E. Morton, (M), Brigham Young, 1975, Oe

3

Cochise College
Geology Dept (A) (2016)
901 North Colombo Avenue
Sierra Vista, AZ 85635
>p. (520) 515-5425
>deakinj@cochise.edu
>http://skywalker.cochise.edu/wellerr/aawellerweb.htm
Instructor:
>Joann Deakin, (M), Mast, Ggg

Dine' College
Science Dept (A,B) (2015)
#1 Circle Drive
Tsaile, Navajo Nation, AZ 86556
>p. 928-724-6721
>cacate@dinecollege.edu
>http://www.dinecollege.edu
>*Enrollment (2002): A: 18 (0)*
Chair:
>Don Robinson, (D), Maharishi Management
Instructor:
>Margaret Mayer, (M), Rhode Island, GeOn

Mesa Community College
Dept of Physical Science (A) (2011)
1833 W. Southern Avenue
Mesa, AZ 85202
>p. (480) 461-7015
>santistevan@mesacc.edu
>http://www.mesacc.edu/dept/d43/glg/
>*Enrollment: No data reported since 1999*
Professor:
>Donna M. Benson, (M), Arizona State, 1996, Gg
>Robert S. Leighty, (D), Arizona State, 1997, Og
Adjunct Professor:
>Zack Bowles, (M), Arizona State, Gg
>Chloe Branciforte, (M), SD Mines, Gg
>Mike Grivois, (M), Texas Christian
>Steve Guggino
>Jack Kepper
>Jill Lockard
>Tony Occhiuzzi, (M), Arizona State, On
>Donna Pollard, (M)
>Joanna Scheffler, (M), Washington State, Gg
>Melinda Shimizu, (M), Arizona State, 2008, Gg
>Carolyn Taylor, (M), Georgia State, Gg
>Kelli Wakefield, (M), Arizona State, Gg
Emeritus:
>Armand J. Lombard, (M), Arizona, 1977, Gg

Northern Arizona University 📄
Dept of Geography, Planning, and Recreation (B,M) (2013)
P.O. Box 15016
Flagstaff, AZ 86011
>p. (928) 523-2650
>geog@nau.edu
>http://nau.edu/sbs/gpr/
>*Enrollment (2013): B: 39 (15) M: 44 (17)*
Park Ranger Training Program Director:
>Mark J. Maciha, (M), N Arizona, 2009, OnnOn
Professor and Chair:
>Pamela Foti, (D), Wisconsin, 1988, On
Coordinator, Parks and Recreation Management Program:
>Charles Hammersley, (D), New Mexico, 1988, On
Professor:
>Alan A. Lew, (D), Oregon, 1986, Oy
Associate Professor:
>Rebecca D. Hawley, (D), Arizona State, 1994, On
>Ruihong Huang, (D), Wisconsin (Milwaukee), 2003
Assistant Professor:
>Erik Schiefer, (D), British Columbia, 2004, GmOyi
Senior Lecturer:
>Judith Montoya, (M), New Mexico, 1985, Oy

Lecturer - Outdoor Leadership and Education:
>Aaron Divine, (M), N Arizona, 2004, OnnOn
Distance Learning Lecturer:
>R. Marieke Taney, (M), N Arizona, 2002, OnnOn
Emeritus:
>Graydon L. Berlin, (D), Tennessee, 1970, Or
>Robert O. Clark, (D), Denver, 1970, On
>Carolyn M. Daugherty, (D), Arizona State, 1987, On
>Leland R. Dexter, (D), Colorado, 1986, Oy
>Christina B. Kennedy, (D), Arizona, 1989, On
>Stanley W. Swarts, (D), California (Los Angeles), 1975, Oy
>George A. Van Otten, (D), Oregon State, 1977, On

Dept of Geology (B,M) (2014)
P O Box 4099
Building 12, Room 100
Knoles Drive
Flagstaff, AZ 86011-4099
>p. (928) 523-4561
>mary.reid@nau.edu
>http://www.cefns.nau.edu/Academic/Geology
>*Enrollment (2009): B: 108 (15) M: 29 (8)*
Chair:
>Mary R. Reid, (D), MIT, 1987, Gi
Professor:
>Ronald C. Blakey, (D), Iowa, 1973, Gr
>David S. Brumbaugh, (D), Indiana, 1972, Ys
>Ernest M. Duebendorfer, (D), Wyoming, 1986, Gc
>David K. Elliott, (D), Bristol (UK), 1979, Pv
>Thomas D. Hoisch, (D), S California, 1985, Gp
>Darrell S. Kaufman, (D), Colorado, 1991, Gm
>Michael H. Ort, (D), California (Santa Barbara), 1991, Gv
>Roderic A. Parnell, (D), Dartmouth, 1982, Cl
>Nancy Riggs, (D), California (Santa Barbara), 1991, Gv
>James C. Sample, (D), California (Santa Cruz), 1986, Cl
>Abraham E. Springer, (D), Ohio State, 1994, Hw
>Paul J. Umhoefer, (D), Washington, 1989, Gt
Associate Professor:
>Larry T. Middleton, (D), Wyoming, 1979, Gs
Research Associate:
>Joseph E. Hazel, Jr., (M), N Arizona, 1991, Gs
>Matthew A. Kaplinski, (M), N Arizona, 1990, Yg
Adjunct Professor:
>Wendell A. Duffield, (D), Stanford, 1967, Gv
>David D. Gillette, (D), S Methodist, 1974, Pv
>John H. Sass, (D), Australian National, 1965, Yg
>Wesley Ward, (D), Washington, 1978, Gs
Emeritus:
>Charles W. Barnes, (D), Wisconsin, 1965, Gc
>Stanley S. Beus, (D), California (Los Angeles), 1963, Pi
>Augustus S. Cotera, Jr., (D), Texas, 1962, Gg
>Richard F. Holm, (D), Washington, 1969, Gv
>James I. Mead, (D), Arizona, 1983, Po
>Paul Morgan, (D), London, 1973, Yh
>Jack D. Nations, (D), California (Berkeley), 1969, Pm
Laboratory Director:
>James Wittke, (D), Texas, 1984, Gi
Office Manager:
>Susan M. Sabala-Foreman, (A), N Arizona, 1981, On

Phoenix College
Dept of Physical Sciences (A) (2016)
1202 West Thomas Road
Phoenix, AZ 85013
>p. (602) 285-7244
>abeer.hamdan@phoenixcollege.edu
Chair:
>James J. White, (D), Arizona, 1986
Professor:
>Richard Cups, (M), Arizona State, 1983, Gg
>Don Speed, (M), Arizona, 1980, Gg

Pima Community College - Community Campus
Geology Dept (1999)
401 North Bonita Ave.
Tucson, AZ 85709-5000

p. (520) 206-4500
wrcavanaugh@pima.edu
http://www.pima.edu

Pima Community College - West Campus
Geology Dept (1999)
2202 West Anklam Rd.
Tucson, AZ 85709-0001
p. (520) 206-4500
jrasmussen@pima.edu
http://www.pima.edu

Prescott College
Dept of Environmental Studies (B) (2014)
220 Grove Avenue
Prescott, AZ 86301
p. (928) 350-2256
kurt.refsnider@prescott.edu
http://www.prescott.edu
Professor:
Kurt Refsnider, (D), Colorado, 2012, GmlPe

Scottsdale Community College
Dept of Mathematics and Sciences (1999)
9000 East Chaparral Road
Scottsdale, AZ 85256-2626
p. (480) 423-6111
merry.wilson@scottsdalecc.edu
http://www.scottsdalecc.edu/geology/index.html

South Mountain Community College
Math, Science, and Engineering Div (1999)
7050 South 24th Street
Phoenix, AZ 85042-5806
p. (602) 243-8290
jean.slack@smcmail.maricopa.edu

University of Arizona
Dept of Geosciences (B,M,D) O (2015)
Gould-Simpson Building
1040 E. Fourth Street
Tucson, AZ 85721-0077
p. (520) 621-6000
achase@email.arizona.edu
http://www.geo.arizona.edu
Administrative Assistant: Anne Chase
Administrative Assistant: Sylvia Quintero
Enrollment (2006): B: 70 (0) M: 23 (0) D: 52 (0)
Head:
Peter Reiners, (D), Washington, Cg
Professor:
Victor R. Baker, (D), Colorado, 1971, Gm
Mark D. Barton, (D), Chicago, 1981, Eg
Susan L. Beck, (D), Michigan, 1987, Ys
Richard Bennett, (D), MIT, 1995, Yd
Jon Chorover, California (Berkeley), 1993, Sc
Andrew S. Cohen, (D), California (Davis), 1982, Ps
Julia E. Cole, (D), Columbia, 1992, Pe
Owen K. Davis, (D), Minnesota, 1981, Pl
Peter G. DeCelles, (D), Indiana, 1984, Gd
Robert T. Downs, (D), Virginia Tech, 1992, Gi
Mihai N. Ducea, (D), Caltech, 1998, Gt
Karl W. Flessa, (D), Brown, 1973, Po
Jiba Ganguly, (D), Chicago, 1967, Gx
George E. Gehrels, (D), Caltech, 1986, Gt
Vance Holliday, (D), Colorado, 1982, Ga
Roy A. Johnson, (D), Wyoming, 1984, Ys
A. J. Timothy Jull, (D), Bristol, 1976, Cg
Paul Kapp, (D), California (Los Angeles), 2001, Gc
Alfred S. McEwen, (D), Arizona State, 1988, Xg
Jonathan T. Overpeck, (D), Brown, 1985, Oa
Jon D. Pelletier, (D), Cornell, 1997, Gm
Mary Poulton, (D), Arizona, 1990, Ng
Jay Quade, (D), Utah, 1990, Sc
Randall M. Richardson, (D), MIT, 1978, Yg

Joaquin Ruiz, (D), Michigan, 1983, Cg
Timothy Swindle, (D), Washington, 1986, Xc
Connie Woodhouse, (D), Arizona, 1996, Pe
Associate Professor:
Barbara Carrapa, (D), Vrije (Amsterdam), 2002, Gs
Joellen Russell, (D), Scripps, 1999, Oc
Eric Seedorff, (D), Stanford, 1987, Eg
Jessica Tierney, (D), Brown, 2010, Co
Marek Zreda, (D), New Mexico Tech, 1994, Cc
Assistant Professor:
Jennifer McIntosh, (D), Michigan, 2004, Hy
Matthew Steele-MacInnes, (D), Virginia Tech, 2013, Eg
Jianjun Yin, (D), Illinois (Urbana-Champaign), Og
Lecturer:
Paul Goodman, Washington, 2000, Oa
Jessica Kapp, (D), California (Los Angeles), Gg
Adjunct Professor:
Robert J. Kamilli, (D), Harvard, 1976, Eg
Charles Prewitt, (D), MIT, 1969, On
Marc Sbar
Emeritus:
William B. Bull, (D), Stanford, 1960, Gm
Robert Butler, (D), Stanford, 1972, Yg
Clement G. Chase, (D), California (San Diego), 1970, Yg
George H. Davis, (D), Michigan, 1971, Gc
William R. Dickinson, (D), Stanford, 1958, Gt
John M. Guilbert, (D), Wisconsin, 1962, Em
DeVerle P. Harris, (D), Penn State, 1965, Eg
C. Vance Haynes, Jr., (D), Arizona, 1965, Ga
Everett H. Lindsay, (D), California (Berkeley), 1967, Pv
Edgar J. McCullough, Jr., (D), Arizona, 1963, Ge
Jonathan Patchett, (D), Edinburgh, 1976
Joseph Schreiber, (D)
Spencer R. Titley, (D), Arizona, 1958, Eg
George Zandt, (D), MIT, 1978, Ys
Researcher:
David Dettman, (D), Michigan, 1994, Cs
Christopher J. Eastoe, (D), Tasmania, 1979, Cs

Dept of Hydrology & Water Resources (B,M,D) ● (2014)
226A Harshbarger Building #11
PO Box 210011
Tucson, AZ 85721-0011
p. (520) 621-5082
programs@hwr.arizona.edu
http://www.hwr.arizona.edu
Administrative Assistant: Erma Santander
Enrollment (2014): B: 0 (2) M: 23 (2) D: 27 (1)
Head:
Thomas Maddock, III, (D), Harvard, 1972, Hq
Regents Professor:
Victor R. Baker, (D), Colorado, 1971, Gm
Shlomo P. Neuman, (D), California (Berkeley), 1968, Hq
W. James Shuttleworth, (D), Manchester (UK), 1971, Hs
Director, SAHRA Center:
Juan B. Valdes, (D), MIT, 1976, Hs
Professor:
Paul D. Brooks, (D), Colorado, 1995, Cg
Paul A. Ferre, (D), Waterloo, 1997, Hw
Hoshin V. Gupta, (D), Case Western, 1984, Hs
Thomas Meixner, (D), Arizona, 1999, Cg
Peter A. Troch, (D), Ghent, 1993, Hs
Tian-Chyi Jim Yeh, (D), New Mexico Tech, 1983, Hq
Marek G. Zreda, (D), New Mexico Tech, 1994, Hw
Associate Professor:
Michael D. Bradley, (D), Michigan, 1971, On
Jennifer C. McIntosh, (D), Michigan, 2004, Cg
Associate Director, SAHRA Center:
James C. Washburne, (D), Arizona, 1994, Hs
Gary C. Woodard, (D), Michigan, 1981, On
Adjunct Associate Professor:
David C. Goodrich, (D), Arizona, 1990, Hs
Robert H. Webb, (D), Arizona, 1985, Gm
Adjunct Assistant Professor:
James E. Smith, (D), Waterloo, 1995, Hw
Adjunct Professor:
Roger C. Bales, (D), Caltech, 1984, Cg

5

David Hargis, (D), Arizona, Hwq
Leo S. Leonhart, (D), Arizona, 1978, Hw
Robert MacNish, (D), Michigan, 1966, Hw
Soroosh Sorooshian, (D), California (Los Angeles), 1978, Hq
Donald W. Young, (D), Arizona, 1994, On
Emeritus:
Robert A. Clark, (D), Texas A&M, 1964, Hs
Lucien Duckstein, (D), Colorado State, 1962, Hq
Simon Ince, (D), Iowa, 1953, Hs
Austin Long, (D), Arizona State, 1966, Cl
Ernest T. Smerdon, (D), Missouri State, 1959, Hs
Arthur W. Warrick, (D), Iowa State, 1967, Sp
Peter J. Wierenga, (D), California (Davis), 1968, Sp
Lorne G. Wilson, (D), California (Davis), 1962, Hw
Cooperating Faculty:
Mark L. Brusseau, (D), Florida, 1989, Hw
Jonathan D. Chorover, (D), California (Berkeley), 1993, Cg
Bonnie C. Colby, (D), Wisconsin, 1983, On
R. B. Hawkins, (D), Colorado State, 1968, Hs
Katherine K. Hirschboeck, (D), Arizona, 1985, Pe
Katharine L. Jacobs, (M), California (Berkeley), 1981, Hg
Kevin E. Lansey, (D), Texas, 1987, Hs
Sharon B. Megdal, (D), Princeton, 1981, Hg
Steven L. Mullen, (D), Washington, 1985, Oa
Ferenc Szidarovszky, (D), K Marx Univ of Econ, 1977, Hq
Robert G. Varady, (D), Arizona, 1981, On
Marvin Waterstone, (D), Rutgers, 1983, On

Dept of Mining & Geological Engineering (B,M,D) (2015)
1235 E. James E. Rogers Way
Mines Building, Room 229
PO Box 210012
Tucson, AZ 85721-0012
    p. (520) 621-6063
    ENGR-Mining@email.arizona.edu
    http://www.mge.arizona.edu
    Enrollment (2012): B: 75 (18) M: 25 (12) D: 20 (4)
Head:
John M. Kemeny, (D), California (Berkeley), 1986, Nr
Director, Lab for Advanced Subsurface Imaging:
Ben K. Sternberg, (D), Wisconsin, 1977, Ye
Professor:
J. Brent Hiskey, (D), Utah, 1973, Nx
Pinnaduwa H. S. W. Kulatilake, (D), Ohio State, 1981, Nr
Mary M. Poulton, (D), Arizona, 1990, Ng
Associate Professor:
Sean Dessureault, (D), British Columbia, 2002, Nx
Jaeheon Lee, (D), Arizona, 2004, Nx
Moe Momayez, (D), McGill, NmYeNr
Jinhong Zhang, (D), Virginia Tech, 2006, Nm
Assistant Professor:
Kwangmin Kim, (D), Arizona, 2012, NmrNx
Professor of Practice:
Victor Tenorio, (D), Arizona, 2012, Nmx

Dept of Planetary Sciences (M,D) (2010)
1629 E. University Boulevard
Tucson, AZ 85721-0092
    p. (520) 621-6963
    acad_info@lpl.arizona.edu
    http://www.lpl.arizona.edu
    Administrative Assistant: Pamela S. Streett
    Enrollment (2001): D: 33 (6)
Head:
Michael J. Drake, (D), Oregon, 1972, Xc
Research Professor:
Martin G. Tomasko, (D), Princeton, 1969, Oa
Professor:
Victor R. Baker, (D), Colorado, 1971, Xg
William V. Boynton, (D), Carnegie Mellon, 1971, Xc
Robert H. Brown, (D), Hawaii, 1982, Xc
Uwe Fink, (D), Penn State, 1965, Oa
Tom Gehrels, (D), Chicago, 1956, On
Richard J. Greenberg, (D), MIT, 1972, Xy
William B. Hubbard, (D), California (Berkeley), 1967, Xy
Donald M. Hunten, (D), McGill, 1950, Oa
Jack R. Jokipii, (D), Caltech, 1965, Xy

Harold P. Larson, (D), Purdue, 1967, On
John S. Lewis, (D), California (San Diego), 1968, Xc
Jonathan I. Lunine, (D), Caltech, 1985, Xc
Renu Malhotra, (D), Cornell, 1988, On
Alfred McEwen, (D), Arizona State, 1988, Xg
Henry J. Melosh, (D), Caltech, 1972, Gt
George H. Rieke, (D), Harvard, 1969, On
Timothy D. Swindle, (D), Washington (St. Louis), 1986, Xm
Roger Yelle, (D), Wisconsin, 1984, On
Senior Scientist:
Jozsef Kota, (D), Roland Eotvos, 1980, Oa
Associate Professor:
Caitlin Griffith, (D), SUNY (Stony Brook), 1991, On
David Kring, (D), Harvard, 1989, Xc
Robert Kursinski, (D), Caltech, 1997, Oa
Assistant Professor:
Joe Giacalone, (D), Kansas, 1991, Xy
Dante Lauretta, (D), Washington (St. Louis), 1997, On
Adam Showman, (D), Caltech, 1998, On
Senior Research Scientist:
Lyle A. Broadfoot, (D), Saskatchewan, 1963, Or
Jay B. Holberg, (D), California (Berkeley), 1974, Oa
Lonnie L. Hood, (D), California (Los Angeles), 1979, Xy
Larry A. Lebofsky, (D), MIT, 1974, Og
Bill R. Sandel, (D), Rice, 1972, Oa
Research Associate:
Alexander Dessler, (D), Duke, 1956, On
Ralph Lorenz, (D), Kent (UK), 1994, Xg
Elizabeth Turtle, (D), Arizona, 1998, Xg
Associate Research Scientist:
Robert S. McMillan, (D), Texas, 1977, On
Peter Smith, (M), Arizona, 1977, Or
Emeritus:
Elizabeth Roemer, (D), California (Berkeley), 1955, On
Charles P. Sonett, (D), California (Los Angeles), 1954, Yg
Robert G. Strom, (M), Stanford, 1957, Xg
Manager, Academic Affairs:
Joan M. Weinberg, (B), Hunter, 1963, On

Dept of Soil, Water & Environmental Science (B,M,D) (2014)
PO Box 210038
Shantz 429
Tucson, AZ 85721-0038
    p. (520) 621-1646
    sleavitt@ltrr.arizona.edu
    https://swes.cals.arizona.edu
    Enrollment (2001): B: 49 (18) M: 17 (3) D: 42 (15)
Head:
Jonathan Chorover, (D), California (Berkeley), 1993, Sb
Adjunct Professor:
Paul (Ty) Ferre, (D), So
Jim Yeh, (D), Sp
Professor:
Mark L. Brusseau, (D), Florida, 1989, Hw
Kevin Fitzsimmons, (D), Arizona, 1999, On
Charles P. Gerba, (D), Miami, 1973, Sb
Martha C. Hawes, (D)
Raina M. Maier, (D), Rutgers, 1988, On
Ian L. Pepper, (D), Ohio State, 1975, On
Charles Sanchez, (D), Iowa State, 1986, On
Jeffrey C. Silvertooth, (D), Oklahoma State, 1986, So
Markus Tuller, (D), On
James Walworth, (D), Georgia, 1985, So
Arthur W. Warrick, (D), Iowa State, 1967, Sp
Associate Professor:
Joan E. Curry, (D), California (Davis), 1992, Sc
Craig Rasmussen, (D), So
Marcel Schaap, (D), So
Adjunct Assistant Professor:
Susan Moran, So
Assistant Professor:
Karletta Chief, (D), Arizona, 2007, On
Associate Specialist:
Michael Crimmins, (D), Arizona, On
Associate Research Scientist:
Janick F. Artiola, (D), Arizona, 1980, Sc

Associate Professor of Practice:
 Thomas B. Wilson, (D), On
Adjunct Professor:
 Floyd Adamsen, (D), Colorado State, 1983, So
Emeritus:
 Ed Glenn, (D), Hawaii, 1978, On
 Donald F. Post, (D), Purdue, 1967, Sd
 James Riley, (D), Arizona, 1968, On
 Peter J. Wierenga, (D), California, 1968, Sp
Extension Specialist:
 Paul W. Brown, (D), Wisconsin, 1981, Ow

Laboratory of Tree Ring Research (2015)
Bryant Bannister Tree-Ring Bldg
1215 E. Lowell St.
Tucson, AZ 85721
 p. (520) 621-1608
 webmaster@ltrr.arizona.edu
 http://ltrr.arizona.edu/
 f: Laboratory of Tree-Ring Research
 t: @TreeRingLabUA
Professor:
 Malcolm K. Hughes, (D), Durham (UK), 1970, Pe
 Steven W. Leavitt, (D), Arizona, 1982, Cs
 Russ Monson, (D), Washington State, 1982
Associate Professor:
 Katherine K. Hirschboeck, (D), Arizona, 1985, Oa
 Paul Sheppard, (D), 1995
 Ronald Towner, (D), Arizona, 1997
 Valerie Trouet, (D), KULeuven, Belgium, 2004
Assistant Professor:
 Charlotte Pearson, (D), Reading, 2003
Research Associate:
 Richard L. Warren, (B), Arizona, 1962, On
Emeritus:
 Bryant Bannister, (D), Arizona, 1960, On
 Jeffrey S. Dean, (D), Arizona, 1967, On
 Harold C. Fritts, (D), Ohio State, 1956, Pe
 Charles W. Stockton, (D), Arizona, 1971, Hq
 Thomas W. Swetnam, (D), Arizona, 1987, Pe
Research Professor:
 David M. Meko, (D), Arizona, 1981, Hq
 Ramzi Touchan, (D), Arizona, 1991
Research Associate:
 Peter Brewer, (D), Reading, 2004
 Matt Salzer, (D), 2000
Curator:
 Pearce Paul Creasman, (D), Texas A&M, 2008
Assoc. Research Professor:
 Irina Panyushkina, (D), Sukachev Inst of Forest, 1997
 Tomasz Wazny, (D), Hamburg, 1990
Asistant Research Professor:
 Margaret Evans, (D), Arizona, 2003

School of Geography and Development (B,M,D) (2014)
Harvill Building
PO Box 210076
Tucson, AZ 85721
 p. (520) 621-1652
 robbins@email.arizona.edu
 http://geog.arizona.edu/
 Enrollment (2010): B: 350 (0) M: 20 (0) D: 54 (0)
Director:
 Paul Robbins, (D), Clark, 1996
Dean:
 John Paul Jones, III, (D), Ohio State, 1984, On
Co-Director of the University of Arizona Institute of the Environment:
 Diana Liverman, (D), California (Los Angeles), 1984
Professor:
 Michael E. Bonine, (D), Texas, 1975, Ou
 Andrew Comrie, (D), Pennsylvania, 1992, Oy
 Stuart E. Marsh, (D), Stanford, 1978, Or
 Sallie A. Marston, (D), Colorado, 1986, Ou
 Beth A. Mitchneck, (D), Columbia, 1990, On
 David A. Plane, (D), Pennsylvania, 1981, On
 Stephen R. Yool, (D), California (Santa Barbara), 1985, Or

Associate Professor:
 Keiron D. Bailey, (D), Kentucky, 2002, Oi
 Carl J. Bauer, (D), California (Berkeley), 1995, Hs
 Sandy Dall'Erba, (D), Pau, 2004
 Elizabeth Oglesby, (D), California (Berkeley), 2002, On
 Christopher A. Scott, (D), Cornell, 1998, Hw
 Willem van Leeuwen, (D), Arizona, 1995, Oy
 Marvin Waterstone, (D), Rutgers, 1983, On
 Margaret Wilder, (D), Arizona, 2002, On
Director of GIST:
 Christopher Lukinbeal, (D), San Diego State, 2000, Oi
Assistant Professor:
 Jeffrey Banister, (D), Arizona, 2010
 Gary Christopherson, (D), Arizona, 2000, Oi
 Sarah Moore, (D), Kentucky, 2006
 Tracey Osborne, (D), California (Berkeley), 2010
 Daoqin Tong, (D), Ohio State, 2007, Oi
Adjunct Professor:
 Julio Betancourt, (D), Arizona, 1989, On
 Katherine Hirschboeck, (D), Arizona, 1985, Oa
 Vance Holliday, (D), Colorado, 1982, Ga
 Laura Huntoon, (D), Pennsylvania, 1991, On
 Charles F. Hutchinson, (D), California (Riverside), 1978, Or
 Miranda Joseph, (D), Stanford, 1995, On
 Barbara Morehouse, (D), Arizona, 1993, On
 Thomas W. Swetnam, (D), Arizona, 1987, On
Director, International Studies-External Affairs:
 Wayne Decker, (D), Johns Hopkins, 1979

Arkansas

Arkansas Tech University
Dept of Physical Sciences-Geology (B) (2015)
1701 N. Boulder Ave
McEver Science Building
Russellville, AR 72801
 p. (479) 968-0293
 jmusser@atu.edu
 http://www.atu.edu/physci
 Enrollment (2014): B: 44 (10)
Professor:
 Cathy Baker, (D), Iowa, 1986, Gg
Assistant Professor:
 Genet Duke, (D), South Dakota Mines
 Jason A. Patton, (D), Arkansas, 2008, GgeGc

Northwest Arkansas Community College
Northwest Arkansas Community College (1999)
One College Drive
Bentonville, AR 72712
 p. (479) 631-8661
 dandroes@nwacc.edu
 http://www.nwacc.edu

Ozarka College
Math, Science, and Education (1999)
218 College Drive
Melbourne, AR 72556
 hayers@ozarka.edu
 http://www.ozarka.edu/

University of Arkansas at Little Rock
Dept of Earth Sciences (B) O (2015)
2801 South University Avenue
Little Rock, AR 72204-1099
 p. (501) 569-3546
 jbconnelly@ualr.edu
 http://www.ualr.edu/earthsciences/
 f: https://www.facebook.com/pages/UALR-Earth-Sci-
 ence/176341909085754
 Administrative Assistant: Ginny L. Oswalt
 Enrollment (2015): B: 56 (11)
Chair:
 Jeffrey B. Connelly, (D), Tennessee, 1993, GcNg

Professor:
  Margaret E. McMillan, (D), Wyoming, 2003, Gm
Assistant Professor:
  Michael T. DeAngelis, (D), Tennessee, 2011, GpCp
  Laura S. Ruhl, (D), Duke, 2012, GeClGb
  Rene A. Shroat-Lewis, (D), Tennessee, 2011, PeOe
Instructor:
  Joshua C. Spinler, (D), Arizona, 2014, YdGt
Emeritus:
  Philip L. Kehler, (D), S Methodist, 1970, Gr
  Michael T. Ledbetter, (D), Rhode Island, 1978, Og

University of Arkansas, Fayetteville
Arkansas Water Resources Center (2004)
113 Ozark Hall
Fayetteville, AR 72701
  p. (501) 575-4403
  ralphd@mail.uark.edu
  http://www.uark.edu/depts/awrc
  Administrative Assistant: Theresa J. Russell
Director:
  Kenneth F. Steele, (D), North Carolina, 1971, Cg
Research Associate:
  Terry E. Nichols, (D), Chicago, 1973, On
Laboratory Director:
  Marc A. Nelson, (D), Arkansas, 1992, Cl

Dept of Geosciences (B,M,D) O (2016)
340 N. Campus Drive
216 Gearhart Hall
Fayetteville, AR 72701
  p. (479) 575-3355
  lmilliga@uark.edu
  http://fulbright.uark.edu/departments/geosciences/
  f: https://www.facebook.com/groups/90439940396/
  Enrollment (2015): M: 88 (13) D: 12 (0)
Maurice Storm Endowed Chair:
  Christopher Liner, (D), Colorado Mines, 1989, YseGg
Distinguished Professor:
  David W. Stahle, (D), Arizona State, 1990, GegGg
Professor:
  Stephen K. Boss, (D), North Carolina, 1994, GeYgGg
  John C. Dixon, (D), Colorado, 1983, GmSdGg
  Margaret J. Guccione, (D), Colorado, 1982, GmaGg
  John G. Hehr, (D), Michigan State, 1971, Owy
  Thomas R. Paradise, (D), Arizona State, 1993, Ogy
  Doy L. Zachry, (D), Texas, 1969, Gr
University Professor:
  W. Fred Limp, (D), Indiana, 1983, Oi
Director of the Center for Advanced Spatial Technologies:
  Jackson D. Cothren, (D), Ohio State, 2004, Oi
Chair:
  Ralph K. Davis, (D), Nebraska, 1992, HwGgg
Associate Professor:
  Fiona M. Davidson, (D), Nebraska, 1991, Ou
  Jason A. Tullis, (D), South Carolina, 2003, Ori
Assistant Professor:
  Mohamed H. Aly, (D), Texas A&M, 2006, OriGg
  Matthew Covington, (D), California, 2008, HqGmg
  Gregory Dumond, (D), Massachusetts (Amherst), 2008, GtcGg
  Song Feng, (D), Chinese Acad of Sci, 1999, OaGgg
  Adriana Potra, (D), Florida International, 2011, EgCcGg
  John B. Shaw, (D), Texas (Austin), 2013, GsrGg
  Xuan Shi, (D), West Virginia, 2007, Ori
  Celina Suarez, (D), Kansas, ClPeGg
Associate Research Professor:
  Phillip D. Hays, (D), Texas A&M, 1996, HwCsGg
Instructor:
  Paula Anderson, (M), Arkansas, 2012, Gg
  Rashauna Hintz, (M), Arkansas, Ou
  Henry Turner, III, (D), Arkansas, Gg
  Jamie Woolsey, (M), Arkansas, Gg
Emeritus:
  Malcolm Cleaveland, (D), Arizona, 1982, Og
  Thomas O. Graff, (D), Kansas, 1973, Ou
  Walter Manger, (D), Iowa, Gr
  Ken Steele, (D), North Carolina, HgCgGg

8

California

American River College
Dept of Earth Science (A) (2014)
4700 College Oak Drive
Sacramento, CA 95841
  p. (916) 484-8107
  aubertj@arc.losrios.edu
  http://arc.losrios.edu/~earthsci/
  Enrollment: No data reported since 1999
Chair:
  Melissa H. Levy, (M), E Tennessee State, 1994, GgOgy
Professor:
  John E. Aubert, (M), California (Davis), 1994, Oy
  Charles E. Thomsen, (M), Cal State (Chico), 1994, Oy
GIS Coordinator:
  Hugh H. Howard, (D), Kansas, 2003, Oi
Assistant Professor:
  Glenn Jaecks, (D), California (Davis), 2002, GgOgPg
Adjunct:
  Paul M. Veisze, (M), California (Berkeley), 1985, Oi
Adjunct Professor:
  Terry J. Boroughs, (M), Ohio State, 1992, GgXgCg
  Beth Dushman, (M), California (Davis), 2007, Gg
  Robert Earle, (M), Oi
  Nathan Jennings, (M), Oi
  Tom Lupo, (M), Oi
  Richard L. Oldham, (M), Nevada, 1972, Gg
  Kimberly Olson, (M), Cal State (Chico), 2008, Oye
  Steven C. Smith, (M), Cal State (Chico), 1994, OynOn

Antelope Valley College
Math, Science, and Engineering Div-Geosciences Prog (2013)
3041 West Avenue K
Lancaster, CA 93536
  p. (661) 722-6300 x6415
  luhazy@avc.edu
  http://www.avc.edu/academics/ms/geosciences.html
Professor:
  Richard S. Balogh, (M), California (Los Angeles), 1976, Gl
Instructor:
  Michael Pesses, (M), Cal State (Northridge), 2002, Oyi

Bakersfield College
Physical Science Dept (2010)
1801 Panorama Drive
Bakersfield, CA 93305
  p. (661) 395-4391
  kvaughan@bakersfieldcollege.edu
Acting Chair:
  Robert A. Schiffman, (M), California (Santa Barbara), 1971, Ga
Professor:
  John C. Lyman, (B), Cal State (San Diego), 1962, Gg
Instructor:
  Robert Lewy, (M), Cal State (Bakersfield), 1992, Gx
  Michael Oldershaw, (M), California (Davis), 1987, Eo

Cabrillo College
Dept of Earth Science (A) (2015)
6500 Soquel Drive
Aptos, CA 95003
  p. (408) 479-6495
  daschwar@cabrillo.edu
  http://www.cabrillo.edu/academics/earthscience/
  Enrollment (2015): A: 35 (0)
Chair:
  David Schwartz, (M), San Jose State, 1983, Gu

California Institute of Technology ⬚
Div of Geological & Planetary Sciences (B,M,D) (2015)
1200 East California Boulevard
MC 170-25
Pasadena, CA 91125
  p. (626) 395-6111

marcia@gps.caltech.edu
http://www.gps.caltech.edu
Enrollment (2015): B: 19 (4) M: 0 (16) D: 113 (11)
Chair:
John P. Grotzinger, (D), Virginia Tech, 1985, GsPeXg
Professor:
Jess F. Adkins, (D), MIT, 1997, Cm
Paul D. Asimow, (D), Caltech, 1997, Cp
Jean-Philippe Avouac, (D), Inst Physique du Globe de Paris, 1991, GtYs
Geoffrey A. Blake, (D), Caltech, 1985, Xc
Michael E. Brown, (D), California (Berkeley), 1994, Xy
Robert W. Clayton, (D), Stanford, 1981, Ye
John M. Eiler, (D), Wisconsin, 1994, Cg
Charles Elachi, (D), Caltech, 1971, Xg
Kenneth A. Farley, (D), California (San Diego), 1991, Cg
Woodward W. Fischer, (D), Harvard, 2007, Py
Michael C. Gurnis, (D), Australian National, 1987, Ys
Thomas H. Heaton, (D), Caltech, 1979, Ne
Donald V. Helmberger, (D), California (San Diego), 1967, Ys
Andrew P. Ingersoll, (D), Harvard, 1966, Oa
Jennifer M. Jackson, (D), Illinois, 2005, Gy
Joseph L. Kirschvink, (D), Princeton, 1979, Pg
Shrinivas R. Kulkarni, (D), California (Berkeley), 1983, Xy
Michael P. Lamb, (D), California (Berkeley), 2008, Gm
Nadia Lapusta, (D), Harvard, 2001, GcYs
Jared R. Leadbetter, (D), Michigan State, 1997, Pm
Dianne K. Newman, (D), MIT, 1997, Py
Victoria Orphan, (D), California (Santa Barbara), 2001, Py
George R. Rossman, (D), Caltech, 1971, Gz
Tapio Schneider, (D), Princeton, 2001, PeOg
Alex L. Sessions, (D), Indiana, 2001, Co
Mark Simons, (D), MIT, 1995, Ys
David J. Stevenson, (D), Cornell, 1976, Xy
Joann M. Stock, (D), MIT, 1988, Gt
Edward M. Stolper, (D), Harvard, 1979, Cp
Paul O. Wennberg, (D), Harvard, 1994, Oa
Brian P. Wernicke, (D), MIT, 1982, Gc
Yuk L. Yung, (D), Harvard, 1974, Oa
Associate Professor:
Christian Frankenberg, (D), Ruprecht-Karls Univ, 2005, Or
Assistant Professor:
Jean-Paul Ampuero, (D), Paris VII, 2002, Ys
Konstantin Batygin, (D), Caltech, 2012, Xg
Simona Bordoni, (D), California (Los Angeles), 2007, Op
Bethany Ehlmann, (D), Brown, 2010, Xg
Heather Knutson, (D), Harvard, 2009, Xg
Andrew F. Thompson, Scripps, 2006, Op
Victor Tsai, (D), Harvard, 2009, Yg
Zhongwen Zhan, Caltech, 2013, Ys
Research Professor:
Egill Hauksson, (D), Columbia, 1981, Ys
Research Associate:
D.A. (Dimitri) Papanastassiou, (D), Caltech, 1970, Cg
Emeritus:
Arden L. Albee, (D), Harvard, 1957, GizXg
Clarence R. Allen, (D), Caltech, 1954, Ys
Donald S. Burnett, (D), California (Berkeley), 1963, Xc
Peter M. Goldreich, (D), Cornell, 1963, Xy
David G. Harkrider, (D), Caltech, 1963, Ys
Hiroo Kanamori, (D), Tokyo, 1964, Ys
Duane O. Muhleman, (D), Harvard, 1963, Xy
Jason B. Saleeby, (D), California (Santa Barbara), 1975, Gc
Leon T. Silver, (D), Caltech, 1955, Cc
Hugh P. Taylor, (D), Caltech, 1959, Cs
Gerald J. Wasserburg, (D), Chicago, 1954, Cc
Peter J. Wyllie, (D), St. Andrews, 1958, Cp

California Lutheran University
Dept of Geology (B) (2015)
60 West Olsen Road #3700
Thousand Oaks, CA 91360-2787
p. (805) 493-3264
bilodeau@callutheran.edu
http://www.callutheran.edu/admission/undergraduate/majors/geology/
Enrollment (2015): B: 15 (1)

Chair:
William L. Bilodeau, (D), Stanford, 1979, GcsGg
Professor:
Linda A. Ritterbush, (D), California (Santa Barbara), 1990, Pi

California Polytechnic State University
Earth & Soil Sciences Dept (B,M) (2014)
One Grand Avenue
San Luis Obispo, CA 93407
p. (805) 756-2261
jstevens@calpoly.edu
http://www.earth.soils.calpoly.edu
Enrollment (2002): B: 126 (19) M: 3 (0)
Chair:
Thomas J. Rice, (D), North Carolina State, 1981, Sd
Professor:
Delmar D. Dingus, (D), Oregon State, 1975, So
Brent G. Hallock, (D), California (Davis), 1979, Sf
William L. Preston, (D), Oregon, 1979, Oe
Thomas A. Ruehr, (D), Colorado State, 1975, Sb
Terry L. Smith, (D), Nebraska, 1980, So
Associate Professor:
Antonio Garcia, (D), California (Santa Cruz), 2001, Gg
Assistant Professor:
Christopher (Chip) S. Appel, (D), Florida, 2001, Sc
Emeritus:
Ronald D. Taskey, (D), Oregon State, 1977, Sf
Administrative Coordinator:
Joan M. Stevens, On
Instructional Tech:
Craig Stubler, (B), California Polytech, 1996, So

Physics Dept (B) (2014)
1 Grand Ave
180 204
San Luis Obispo, CA 93407
p. (805) 756-2448
physics@calpoly.edu
http://www.physics.calpoly.edu
Administrative Assistant: Kathy Simon
Professor:
Antonio F. Garcia, (D), California (Santa Barbara), 2001, GmrGs
Associate Professor:
John J. Jasbinsek, (D), Wyoming, 2008, Ysg
Scott Johnston, (D), California (Santa Barbara), 2006, GcpCc
Emeritus:
David H. Chipping, (D), Stanford, 1970, Grt

California State Polytechnic University, Pomona
Dept of Geological Sciences (B,M) (2015)
3801 West Temple Avenue
Pomona, CA 91768
p. (909) 869-3454
janourse@csupomona.edu
http://geology.csupomona.edu
Administrative Assistant: Monica Baez
Enrollment (2014): B: 130 (18) M: 28 (5)
Chair:
Jonathan A. Nourse, (D), Caltech, 1989, GctEm
Professor:
Jeffrey S. Marshall, (D), Penn State, 2000, GmtHs
Jascha Polet, (D), Caltech, 1999, Ysg
Associate Professor:
Stephen G. Osborn, (D), Arizona, 2010, HwClSp
Assistant Professor:
Nicholas J. Van Buer, (D), Stanford, 2012, GxtGz
Emeritus:
David R. Berry, (D), California (Los Angeles), 1983, PgGo
David R. Jessey, (D), Missouri (Rolla), 1981, Eg
John A. Klasik, (D), Louisiana State, 1976, Gu
Equipment Technician:
Mike McAtee, (B), Cal Poly Pomona, 1978, On

California State University, Bakersfield
Dept of Geological Sciences (B,M) (2015)
9001 Stockdale Hwy, 62 Sci

California

9

Bakersfield, CA 93311
  p. (661) 654-3027
  dbaron@csub.edu
  http://www.csub.edu/Geology/
  f: https://www.facebook.com/groups/103146842589/
  Administrative Assistant: Sue Holt
  Enrollment (2014): B: 102 (24) M: 23 (5)
Professor:
  Dirk Baron, (D), Oregon Inst of Tech, 1995, Cl
  Janice Gillespie, (D), Wyoming, 1991, Go
  Robert A. Horton, Jr., (D), Colorado Mines, 1985, GdsGo
  Robert M. Negrini, (D), California (Davis), 1986, Ymg
Assistant Professor:
  Graham D. M. Andrews, (D), Leicester, 2006, GtvGx
  Junhua "Adam" Guo, (D), Missouri, Gs
  W Chris Krugh, Swiss Fed Inst Tech, 2008, GcmCc
Lecturer:
  David Miller, (D), Stanford, GgzGs
Adjunct Professor:
  Sarah Brown, (D), Simon Fraser, 2010, GtCac
Department IT Support:
  Elizabeth Powers, (B), N Arizona, 1998, Pe

California State University, Chico
Dept of Geological and Environmental Sciences (B,M) (2014)
400 W First Street
Chico, CA 95929-0205
  p. (530) 898-5262
  geos@csuchico.edu
  http://www.csuchico.edu/geos/
  Enrollment (2014): B: 200 (50) M: 30 (6)
Chair:
  Russell Shapiro, (D), California (Santa Barbara), 1998, Ps
Professor:
  David L. Brown, (D), California (Berkeley), 1995, Hg
  Ann Bykerk-Kauffman, (D), Arizona, 1990, GcOe
  Julie Monet, (D), Rutgers, 2006, GgNg
  Gregory R. Taylor, (D), Washington, 1987, Oa
Associate Professor:
  Todd Greene, (D), Stanford, 2000, Gsr
  Karin A. Hoover, (D), Johns Hopkins, 1998, Hw
  Randy S. Senock, (D), Kansas State, 1994, Sf
  Rachel Teasdale, (D), Idaho, 2001, Gv
Assistant Professor:
  Shane D. Mayor, (D), Wisconsin, 2001, Oa
Lecturer:
  John L. McMurtry, (M), Chico State, 1991, Hw
Emeritus:
  Jerold J. Behnke, (D), Nevada (Reno), 1968, Hw
  Victor A. Fisher, (D), Florida State, 1968, Gr
  Richard A. Flory, (D), Oregon State, 1975, Ps
  Rolland K. Hauser, (D), Chicago, 1967, Oa
  K. R. Gina Johnston, (D), Florida, 1970, Hs
  Terence T. Kato, (D), California (Los Angeles), 1976, Gt
  William M. Murphy, (D), California (Berkeley), 1985, Cl
  James L. Regas, (D), Harvard, 1969, Xg
  Howard L. Stensrud, (D), Washington, 1970, Em

California State University, Dominguez Hills
Earth Sciences (B) (2014)
1000 E. Victoria Street
NSM B202
Carson, CA 90747
  p. (310) 243-3377
  cmtrujillo@csudh.edu
  Administrative Assistant: Virginia L. Knauss
  Enrollment (2014): B: 55 (9)
Dean, Natural & Behavioral Sciences:
  Rodrick Hay, (D), Arizona State, 1996, Or
Professor:
  Brendan A. McNulty, (D), California (Santa Cruz), 1996, Gc
  Ralph Saunders, (D), Arizona, 1996, Oy
Chair:
  Ashish Sinha, (D), S California, 1997, Gg
Associate Professor:
  John Keyantash, (D), California (Los Angeles), 2001, Hg

Lecturer:
  Michael H. Ferris, (M), Cal State (Long Beach), 2012, Or
  Judith A. King-Rundel, (M), California (Los Angeles), 2003, Oe
Emeritus:
  David Sigurdson, (D), California (Riverside), 1974, GizEg

California State University, East Bay
Dept of Anthropology, Geography, and Environmental Studies (2010)
25800 Carlos Bee Blvd
Hayward, CA 94542
  p. (510) 885-3193
  david.larson@csueastbay.edu
  http://class.csueastbay.edu/geography
  Enrollment (2005): B: 0 (22) M: 14 (2)
Chair:
  David J. Larson, (D), California (Berkeley), 1994, Ou
Professor:
  Scott W. Stine, (D), California (Berkeley), 1987, Gm
Associate Professor:
  Karina Garbesi, (D), California (Berkeley), 1994, Cg
  Michael D. Lee, (D), London Schl of Econ, 1990, Hg
  Gary Li, (D), SUNY (Buffalo), 1997, Oi
  David Woo, (D), California (Santa Barbara), 1991, Or

Dept of Earth & Environmental Sciences (B,M) (2015)
25800 Carlos Bee Blvd.
Hayward, CA 94542-3088
  p. (510) 885-3486
  geology@csueastbay.edu
  http://www.sci.csueastbay.edu/earth
  Enrollment (2015): B: 68 (15) M: 17 (6)
Associate Professor:
  Jean Moran, (D), Rochester, 1994, HwCl
Professor:
  Mitchell S. Craig, (D), Georgia Tech, 1990, Yg
  Jeffery C. Seitz, (D), Virginia Tech, 1994, CgOeGx
Associate Professor:
  Luther M. Strayer, (D), Minnesota, 1998, Gc
Assistant Professor:
  Michael Massey, (D), Stanford, 2013, OnGeCg

California State University, Fresno 🗗
Dept of Earth & Environmental Sciences (B,M) (2014)
2345 E. San Ramon Avenue
MH24
Fresno, CA 93740-8031
  p. (559) 278-3086
  slewis@csufresno.edu
  http://www.csufresno.edu/ees/
  Enrollment (2009): B: 51 (13) M: 30 (5)
Chair:
  Stephen D. Lewis, (D), Columbia, 1982, Yg
Professor:
  Keith D. Putirka, (D), Columbia, 1997, GviGp
Associate Professor:
  John Wakabayashi, (D), California (Berkeley), GmcGt
  Zhi (Luke) Wang, (D), Leuven (Belgium), 1997, GeHwOr
Assistant Professor:
  Robert G. Dundas, (D), California (Berkeley), 1994, PvGr
  Chris Pluhar, (D), California (Santa Cruz), 2007, NgGe
  Mathieu Richaud, (D), Bordeaux, 2007, GusCs
  Peter Van de Water, (D), Arizona, GrPbGf
Lecturer:
  Jeff Anglen, (M), Texas Tech, 2001, GsdPg
  Susan Bratcher, (M), Cal State (Fresno), 2008, Hw
  Kerry Workman-Ford, (M), Cal State (Fresno), 2003, Gc
Adjunct Professor:
  Jerry DeGraff, (M), Utah State, 1976, On
  Dong Wang, (D), HwSpOr
Emeritus:
  Jon C. Avent
  Bruce A. Blackerby, (D), California (Los Angeles), Giz
  Roland H. Brady, (D), California (Davis), 1986, NgOuGa
  Seymour Mack, YrHgOn
  Robert D. Merrill, (D), Texas, 1974, GsmPe

C. John Suen, (D), MIT, 1978, Hw

California State University, Fullerton
Dept of Geological Sciences (B,M) ● (2015)
800 N. State College Boulevard
Geological Sciences, MH 254
Fullerton, CA 92831
    p. (657) 278-3882
    geology@fullerton.edu
    http://geology.fullerton.edu
    f: https://www.facebook.com/CalStateFullerton.Geology
    Enrollment (2014): B: 145 (9) M: 16 (0)
Chair:
    Phillip A. Armstrong, (D), Utah, 1996, GcYg
Professor:
    David D. Bowman, (D), S California, 1999, Ys
    Diane Clemens-Knott, (D), Caltech, 1992, Gig
    Jeffrey R. Knott, (D), California (Riverside), 1998, Gmg
    Brady P. Rhodes, (D), Montana, 1984, Gcg
Associate Professor:
    Nicole Bonuso, (D), S California, 2005, Pie
    Matthew E. Kirby, (D), Syracuse, 2001, GnPeGg
    W. Richard Laton, (D), W Michigan, 1997, HwGg
    Adam D. Woods, (D), S California, 1998, Gsg
Assistant Professor:
    Joe Carlin, (D), Texas A&M, Og
    Sean Loyd, (D), S California, 2010, CgGe
    Valbone Memeti, (D), S California, GvEgGx
    James Parham, (D), California (Berkeley), 2003, PvoGg
Lecturer:
    Freddi Jo Bruschke, (D), Gg
    Patricia M. Butcher, (M), Utah, 1993, Oeg
    Robert deGroot, (D), Gg
    Joanna Fantozzi, (M), Gg
    Emily Hamecher, (D), Gg
    Wayne G. Henderson, (M), George Washington, 1997, PgGg
    Scott Mata, (D), Gg
    Carolyn Rath, (M), Gg
    Kelly R. Ruppert, (M), California (Riverside), 2001, Gg
    Mike Van Ry, (M), Gg
    Kristin Weaver Bowman, (M), S California, 1999, Oe
Emeritus:
    Galen R. Carlson, (D), Og
    John H. Foster, (D)
    Prem K. Saint, (D), Minnesota, 1973, Hw
    Margaret S. Woyski, (D), Minnesota, 1946, Gi

California State University, Long Beach
Dept of Geological Sciences (B,M) (2013)
1250 Bellflower Boulevard
Long Beach, CA 90840-3902
    p. (562) 985-4809
    rfrancis@csulb.edu
    http://www.csulb.edu/colleges/cnsm/departments/geology/
    Administrative Assistant: Margaret Costello
    Enrollment (2009): B: 67 (11) M: 16 (3)
Chair:
    Stanley C. Finney, (D), Ohio State, 1977, Ps
Conrey Endowed Chair:
    Matthew Becker, (D), Texas, 1996, Hwg
Professor:
    Richard J. Behl, (D), California (Santa Cruz), 1992, Gs
    Robert D. Francis, (D), California (San Diego), 1980, Co
    Roswitha B. Grannell, (D), California (Riverside), 1969, Yv
    Jack Green, (D), Columbia, 1953, Gv
Associate Professor:
    Gregory J. Holk, (D), Caltech, 1997, CsGxEm
Assistant Professor:
    Thomas Kelty, (D), California (Los Angeles), 1998, Gc
    Nate Onderdonk, (D), California (Santa Barbara), 2003, Gtm
    Lora R. Stevens (Landon), (D), Minnesota, 1997, Gn
Lecturer:
    Bruce Perry, (M), Cal State (Long Beach), 1993, Gc
Emeritus:
    Kwan M. Chan, (D), Liverpool, 1966, Oc
    Paul J. Fritts, (D), Colorado, 1969, Pm

Charles T. Walker, (D), Leeds, 1952, Cl
Robert E. Winchell, (D), Ohio State, 1963, Gz

California State University, Los Angeles
Dept of Geological Sciences (B,M) (2014)
5151 State University Drive
Los Angeles, CA 90032
    p. (323) 343-2400
    geology@calstatela.edu
    http://www.calstatela.edu/dept/geology/
    Enrollment (2006): B: 23 (4) M: 23 (4)
Chair:
    Pedro C. Ramirez, (D), California (Santa Cruz), 1990, Gs
Professor:
    Kim Bishop, (D), S California, 1994, Gc
    Richard W. Hurst, (D), California (Los Angeles), 1975, Cc
Associate Professor:
    Barry Hibbs, (D), Texas, 1993, Hw
Assistant Professor:
    Andre Ellis, (D), HwCg
    Jennifer Garrison, (D), California (Los Angeles), 2004, Giv
    Nathan Onderdonk, (D), California (Santa Barbara), 2003, Gt
Adjunct Professor:
    Mohammad Hassan Rezaie-Boroon, (D), Erlangen (Nuremberg), 1997, GeCg
Emeritus:
    Ivan P. Colburn, (D), Stanford, 1961, Gs
    Terry E. Davis, (D), California (Santa Barbara), 1969, Cc
    Gary A. Novak, (D), Virginia Tech, 1970, Gz
    Robert J. Stull, (D), Washington, 1969, Gi

California State University, Northridge
Dept of Geography (B,M) (2015)
18111 Nordhoff Street
Northridge, CA 91330-8249
    p. (818) 677-3532
    geography@csun.edu
    http://www.csun.edu/social-behavioral-sciences/geography
Institute for Social and Behavioral Sciences:
    Shawna J. Dark, (D), California (Los Angeles), 2003, Oi
Professor:
    Helen M. Cox, (D), California (Los Angeles), 1998, OwgOr
    Julie E. Laity, (D), California (Los Angeles), 1982, Oy
    Amalie Orme, (D), California (Los Angeles), 1983, Gm
    Yifei Sun, (D), SUNY (Buffalo), 2000, Oi
Assistant Professor:
    Sanchayeeta Adhikari, (D), Florida, 2011, Oi
    Soheil Boroushaki, (D), UWO, 2010, Oi
    Mario A. Giraldo, (D), Georgia, 2007, OrHgOg
    Regan Maas, (D), California (Los Angeles), 2010, Oi
Emeritus:
    Gong-yuh Lin, (D), Hawaii, 1974, Oa
    Eugene Turner, (D), Washington, 1977, Or

Dept of Geological Sciences (B,M) (2013)
18111 Nordhoff Street
MD: 8266
Northridge, CA 91330-8266
    p. (818) 677-3541
    doug.yule@csun.edu
    http://www.csun.edu/geology/
    Administrative Assistant: Mari C. Flores-Garcia
    Enrollment (2012): B: 72 (0) M: 23 (0)
Chair:
    Vicki A. Pedone, (D), SUNY (Stony Brook), 1990, GdCs
Professor:
    Kathleen M. Marsaglia, (D), California (Los Angeles), 1989, Gs
    Gerald W. Simila, (D), California (Berkeley), 1979, Yg
    Richard L. Squires, (D), Caltech, 1973, Pg
    M. Ali Tabidian, (D), Nebraska, 1987, Hw
    J. Douglas Yule, (D), Caltech, 1996, Gt
Associate Professor:
    Elena A. Miranda, (D), Wyoming, 2006, Gc
    Jon R. Sloan, (D), California (Davis), 1980, Pm
    Dayanthie Weeraratne, (D), Carnegie Inst, 2005, Yg

Assistant Professor:
  M. Robinson Cecil, (D), Arizona, 2009, GiCcGz
  Matthew d'Alessio, (D), California (Berkeley), 2004, OeGt
  Richard V. Heermance, (D), California (Santa Barbara), 2007, GrCc
  Joshua J. Schwartz, (D), Wyoming, 2007, GiCc
Emeritus:
  Herbert G. Adams, (D), California (Los Angeles), 1971, Ng
  Lorence G. Collins, (D), Illinois, 1959, Gz
  George C. Dunne, (D), Rice, 1972, Gc
  A. Eugene Fritsche, (D), California (Los Angeles), 1969, Gd

California State University, Sacramento

Dept of Geology (B,M) ○ (2015)
6000 J Street
Placer Hall
Sacramento, CA 95819-6043
  p. (916) 278-6337
  geology@csus.edu
  http://www.csus.edu/geology/
  Enrollment (2010): B: 77 (16) M: 18 (3)
Chair:
  Tim C. Horner, (D), Ohio State, 1992, HwGs
Professor:
  Kevin J. Cornwell, (D), Nebraska, 1994, Gm
  Lisa Hammersley, (D), California (Berkeley), 2003, Gig
  Brian Hausback, (D), California (Berkeley), 1984, Gv
  Judith E. Kusnick, (D), California (Davis), 1996, Oe
Lecturer:
  Barbara J. Munn, (D), Virginia Tech, 1997, Ggp
Adjunct Professor:
  Brian Bergamaschi, (D), Washington, 1995, HwOc
Emeritus:
  Diane H. Carlson, (D), Washington State, 1984, Gc
  Charles C. Plummer, (D), Washington, 1969, Gp
  Greg Wheeler, (D), Washington, Em
On Leave:
  David G. Evans, (D), Louisiana State, 1989, HwYg
Secretary:
  Stacy Sinz, (B), California (Sacramento), 2010, On
Instructional Support Tech:
  Steven W. Rounds, (B), Cal State (Sacramento), 1990, Gg

California State University, San Bernardino

Dept of Geological Sciences (B,M) (2015)
5500 University Parkway
San Bernardino, CA 92407-2397
  p. (909) 537-5336
  smcgill@csusb.edu
  http://www.geology.csusb.edu
  Administrative Assistant: Christina Palmer
  Enrollment (2014): B: 45 (8) M: 1 (1)
Acting Chair:
  Sally F. McGill, (D), Caltech, 1992, Gt
Professor:
  Joan E. Fryxell, (D), North Carolina, 1984, Gct
  Erik Melchiorre, (D), Washington, 1997, EmHwCl
  Alan L. Smith, (D), California (Berkeley), 1969, GviGz
Associate Professor:
  W. Britt Leatham, (D), Ohio State, 1987, Ps
Assistant Professor:
  Codi Lazar, (D), California (Los Angeles), 2010
Emeritus:
  Louis A. Fernandez, (D), Syracuse, 1969, Gi
Cooperating Faculty:
  Stuart S. Sumida, (D), California (Los Angeles), 1987, Pv

California State University, Stanislaus

Dept of Physics and Geology (B) ● (2015)
One University Circle
Turlock, CA 95382
  p. (209) 667-3466
  HFerriz@csustan.edu
  http://geology.csustan.edu
  Administrative Assistant: Dawn McCulley
  Enrollment (2015): B: 37 (3)

Chair:
  Horacio Ferriz, (D), Stanford, 1985, NgHwYe
Professor:
  Mario J. Giaramita, (D), California (Davis), 1989, Gpz
  Julia Sankey, (D), Louisiana State, 1998, Pve
Associate Professor:
  Robert D. Rogers, (D), Texas, 2003, GcmGt
Lecturer:
  Garry F. Hayes, (M), Nevada (Reno), 1988, Gg
  Roger Putnam, (M), North Carolina (Chapel Hill), 2013, Ggi
  Marilyn Vogel, (D), Stanford, 2003, GgCgPy
  Michael Whittier, (M), CSU Stanislaus, 2005, Ggz

Cerritos College

Earth Science Dept (A) (2013)
11110 E. Alondra Boulevard
Norwalk, CA 90650
  p. (562) 860-2451
  ddekraker@cerritos.edu
  http://www.cerritos.edu/earth-science/
  Enrollment (2012): A: 9 (0)
Earth Science Dept Chair:
  Crystal LoVetere, (D), S California, Oy
Assistant Professor:
  Dan DeKraker, (M), Cal State (Fullerton), 2004, Oe
  Aline Gregorio, (M), Cal State (Fullerton), 2011
  Tor Lacy, (M), Cal State (Long Beach), 2005, Gg
Instructor:
  Gary D. Johnpeer, (M), Arizona State, 1977, Ng

Chabot College

Div of Mathematics & Science (A) (2004)
25555 Hesperian Boulevard
Hayward, CA 94545
  p. (415) 786-6865
Instructor:
  Adolph A. Oliver, (M), Stanford, 1974, Ys
  David J. Perry, (M), San Jose State, 1967, Op

Chaffey College

Earth Science/Geology Dept (2010)
5885 Haven Avenue
Rancho Cucamonga, CA 91737-3002
  p. (909) 652-6402
  henry.shannon@chaffey.edu
  http://www.chaffey.edu/mathandscience/
  Enrollment: No data reported since 1999
Professor:
  Jane Warger, (M), Columbia, 1990, OgGg

City College of San Francisco

Earth Sciences Dept (A) (2014)
Box S50
50 Phelan Avenue
San Francisco, CA 94112
  p. (415) 452-7014
  cjlewis@ccsf.edu
  http://www.ccsf.edu/Earth
  Enrollment (2011): A: 10 (0)
Chair:
  Katryn Wiese, (M), Oregon State, 1992, GgOg
Professor:
  Darrel E. Hess, (M), California (Los Angeles), 1990, Oy
  Chris Lewis, (M), California (Berkeley), 1993, GgEmOs
Adjunct Professor:
  Ian Duncan, (D), San Francisco State, Oy
  James Kuwabara, (D), Caltech, 1980, Og
  Joyce Lucas-Clark, (D), Stanford, PgGg
  Russell McArthur, (M), California (Berkeley), Gg
  Elizabeth Proctor, (M), San Francisco State, Oi
  Kirstie L. Stramler, (D), Columbia, OagGg
  Gordon Ye, (M), California (Berkeley), 1993, Oi

College of Marin

Geology Dept (A) (2014)
835 College Ave
SC 192, Phone Ext: 7523
Kentfield, CA 94904
  p. (415) 457-8811
  dfoss@marin.edu
  http://marin.edu/~geology
  Enrollment: No data reported since 1999
Professor:
  Donald J. Foss, (M), Boise State, 1980, Og
Emeritus:
  James L. Locke, (M), San Jose State, 1971, Og

College of San Mateo

Geological Sciences (A) (2014)
1700 W. Hillsdale Blvd.
San Mateo, CA 94402
  p. (650) 574-6633
  hand@smccd.edu
  http://www.collegeofsanmateo.edu/geologicalsciences/
  Enrollment (2014): A: 12 (0)
Professor:
  Linda M. Hand, (M), Texas A&M, 1988, GgPgOg

College of the Canyons

Dept of Earth, Space, and Environmental Sciences (A) (2014)
26455 Rockwell Canyon Road
Santa Clarita, CA 91355
  p. (661) 362-3658
  Vincent.Devlahovich@canyons.edu
  http://www.canyons.edu/departments/ESES/
  Enrollment (2012): A: 4 (0)
Chair:
  Vincent A. Devlahovich, (D), Cal State (Northridge), 2012, GgOye
Professor:
  Mary Bates, (M), Cal State (Northridge), Oyg

College of the Desert

Dept of Science (A) (2015)
43-500 Monterey Avenue
Palm Desert, CA 92260
  p. (760) 776-7272
  nmoll@collegeofthedesert.edu
  http://www.collegeofthedesert.edu/students/ss/ap/physsci/
  Pages/Geology.aspx
  Enrollment (2013): A: 3 (1)
Professor:
  Nancy E. Moll, (D), Washington, 1981, Gge
Adjunct Professor:
  Brian Koenig, (M), Arizona, 1978, Gge
  Robert Pellenbarg, (D), OgGg

College of the Sequoias

Science Div (A) (2004)
Visalia, CA 93277
  p. (209) 730-3812
  erich@giant.sequoias.cc.ca.us
  Enrollment (2000): A: 2 (0)
Chair:
  Eric D. Hetherington, (D), Minnesota, 1991, Gc
Emeritus:
  John R. Crain, (M), Nevada, 1961, Gg

College of the Siskiyous

Dept of Biological & Physical Sciences (A) (2016)
800 College Avenue
Weed, CA 96094
  p. (530) 938-5255
  hirt@siskiyous.edu
  http://www.siskiyous.edu/class/ess/
  Enrollment (2015): A: 1 (0)
Instructor:
  William H. Hirt, (D), California (Santa Barbara), 1989, Gi

Contra Costa College

Astronomy/Engineering/Geology/Physics Dept (A) (2015)
2600 Misson Bell Drive
San Pablo, CA 94806
  p. (510) 235-7800
  jsmithson@contracosta.edu
  http://www.contracosta.edu/home/programs-departments/
  engineering/
Professor:
  Mary Lewis, Gg
  Jayne Smithson, Gg

Cosumnes River College

Dept of Science, Mathematics & Engineering (A) (2015)
8401 Center Parkway
Sacramento, CA 95823
  p. (916) 691-7210
  MuranaB@crc.losrios.edu
  Department Secretary: Sue McCoy
Chair:
  Debra Sharkey, (M), California (Davis), 1994, Oy
Assistant Professor:
  Hiram Jackson, (M), California (Davis), 1992, Gg
Adjunct Professor:
  Gerry Drobny, (M), Washington State, 1981, Gg

Crafton Hills College

Geology Dept (A) (2014)
11711 Sand Canyon Road
Yucaipa, CA 92399
  p. (909) 794-2161
  rihughes@craftonhills.edu
  http://www.craftonhills.edu/courses_&_programs/Physi-
  cal_Science/Geology/
  Enrollment (2013): A: 16 (4)
Professor:
  Richard O. Hughes III, (M), Ohio, 1994, GlOe

Cuesta College

Physical Sciences Div (A) (2014)
P. O. Box 8106
San Luis Obispo, CA 93403
  p. (805) 546-3230
  jgrover@cuesta.edu
  http://academic.cuesta.edu/physci/Geology/
  Enrollment (2014): A: 6 (0)
Professor:
  Jeff Grover, Gg
  Debra Stakes, (D), Gg

Cuyamaca College

Dept of Science and Engineering (A) (2014)
900 Rancho San Diego Parkway
El Cajon, CA 92019
  p. (619) 660-4345
  Glenn.Thurman@gcccd.edu
  http://www.cuyamaca.edu/
Instructor:
  Lisa Chaddock, Oy
  Michael Farrell, Gg
  Bryan Miller-Hicks, Gg
  Agatha Wein, Gg
  Ray Wolcott, Og
Emeritus:
  Waverly Ray, Gg

Cypress College

Geology Dept (A) (2010)
9200 Valley View Street
Cypress, CA 90630
  p. (714) 484-7153
  RArmale@CypressCollege.edu
  Enrollment: No data reported since 1999

Professor:
    Russell L. Flynn, (M), San Diego State, 1971, Op
Adjunct Professor:
    Hank Wadleigh, (B), Cal State (Long Beach), 1957, Gg
Visiting Professor:
    Curtis J. Williams, (M), Cal State (Los Angeles), 1996, Gg
Emeritus:
    Keith E. Green, (M), S California, 1958, Pg
    Altus Simpson, (M), S California, 1958, Go

Diablo Valley College
Div. of Physical Sciences (A) (2013)
321 Golf Club Road
Pleasant Hill, CA 94523
    p. (925) 685-1230 x46
    JHetherington@dvc.edu
    http://www.dvc.edu/org/departments/physics/
Chair:
    Jean Hetherington, (M), Washington, 1983, Gg

East Los Angeles College
Dept of Anthropology/Geography/Geology (2010)
Monterey Park, CA 91754
    p. (213) 265-8838
    mirettd@elac.edu
Chair:
    Gerald R. Licari, (D), California (Los Angeles), 1971, Pm
Professor:
    John Grant, (M), North Carolina, 1958, On
    Domenick Miretti, (D), California (Los Angeles), 1979, Oy
    James D. Sullivan, (M), California (Riverside), 1966, Oy

El Camino College
Dept of Earth Sciences (A) (2014)
16007 Crenshaw Blvd.
Torrance, CA 90506
    p. (310) 660-3593
    jholliday@elcamino.edu
    http://www.elcamino.edu/academics/naturalsciences/earth/
    Enrollment: No data reported since 1999
Professor:
    Jerry Brothen, (M), California (Los Angeles), Oy
    Sara Di Fiori, (M), California (Los Angeles), GgOg
    Matt Ebiner, (M), California (Los Angeles), Oy
    Joseph W. Holliday, (M), Oregon State, 1982, Og
Associate Professor:
    Chuck Herzig, (D), California (Riverside), GgOg
Instructor:
    Gary Booher, Og
    Robin Bouse, Gg
    Charles Dong, Og
    Lynn Fielding, Og
    Patricia Neumann, Og
    Douglas Neves, Og
    Jim Noyes, (D), Scripps, Og
    Ebenezer Peprah, Og

Feather River College
Feather River College (A) (2010)
570 Golden Eagle Ave.
Quincy, CA 95971
    dlerch@frc.edu
    http://www.frc.edu/
Instructor:
    Derek Lerch, Og

Folsom Lake College
Geosciences (A) ● (2015)
10 College Parkway
Folsom, CA 95630
    p. (916) 608-6668
    pittmaj@flc.losrios.edu
    http://www.flc.losrios.edu/Academics/Geology.htm
    Enrollment (2015): A: 7 (1)

Professor:
    Jason Pittman, (M), Oregon State, 1999, OgiOi

Fresno City College
Earth & Physical Science Dept (A) (2016)
Math, Science & Engineering Div
1101 E. University Avenue
Fresno, CA 93741
    p. (559) 442-4600
    craig.poole@fresnocitycollege.edu
    Enrollment (2015): A: 15 (0)
Instructor:
    Brandy Anglen, (D), Indiana, 2005, Gg
    T. Craig Poole, (M), Cal State (Fresno), 1987, Gg

Fullerton College
Div of Natural Sciences (Geology) (A) (2014)
321 E. Chapman Ave
Fullerton, CA 92832
    p. (714) 992-7445
    rlozinsky@fullcoll.edu
    http://natsci.fullcoll.edu/
    Enrollment (2014): A: 5 (3)
Professor:
    Sean Chamberlin, (D), S California, OgcOb
    Carolyn Heath, (D), California (Santa Cruz), Ob
    Richard P. Lozinsky, (D), New Mexico Tech, 1988, GreGm
Assistant Professor:
    Marc Willis, (M), Gg

Gavilan College
Dept of Physical Sciences (2011)
5055 Santa Theresa Boulevard
Gilroy, CA 95020
    p. (408) 848-4701
    rlee@gavilan.edu
    http://www.gavilan.edu/natural_sciences/
Instructor:
    Duane Willahan, (M), Santa Fe State, 1992, Gg

Golden West College
Physical Science Program (A) (2011)
15744 Golden West Street
Huntington Beach, CA 92647
    p. (714) 892-7711 x51116
    msouto@gwc.cccd.edu
    http://www.goldenwestcollege.edu/campus/physicalscience.html
    Enrollment (2005): A: 2 (0)
Professor:
    Ronald C. Gibson, (M), California (Riverside), 1964, Gc
    Bernard J. Gilpin, (M), California (Riverside), 1976, Ys

Grossmont College
Dept of Earth Sciences (A) (2013)
8800 Grossmont College Drive
El Cajon, CA 92020
    p. (714) 644-7887
    gary.jacobson@gcccd.edu
    http://www.grossmont.edu/earthsciences/
    Enrollment (2004): A: 15 (0)
Professor:
    Chris Hill, (D), Gg
Instructor:
    Gary L. Jacobson, (M), San Diego State, 1982, GucEm

Hartnell College
Div of Math and Science (A) (2014)
411 Central Avenue
Salinas, CA 93901
    aramirez@hartnell.edu
    http://www.hartnell.edu/academics/math.html
Instructor:
    Robert Barminski, (M), Moss Landing Marine Lab, GgOg

Humboldt State University
Dept of Geology (B,M) O (2015)
1 Harpst Street
Arcata, CA 95521-8299
   p. (707) 826-3931
   geology@humboldt.edu
   http://www.humboldt.edu/geology/
   Enrollment (2015): B: 90 (24) M: 9 (1)
Chair:
   Mark Hemphill-Haley, (D), Oregon, 2000, Gt
Professor:
   Susan M. Cashman, (D), Washington, 1977, Gc
   Andre K. Lehre, (D), California (Berkeley), 1982, Gm
   William C. Miller, (D), Tulane, 1984, Pi
Associate Professor:
   Brandon L. Browne, (D), Alaska (Fairbanks), 2005, Gi
Assistant Professor:
   Melanie Michalak, (D), California (Santa Cruz), 2013
   Jasper Oshun, (D), California (Berkeley), 2015, HyGmg
Research Associate:
   Eileen Hemphill-Haley, (D), California (Santa Cruz), 1991, Pm
   Robert C. McPherson, (M), Humboldt State, 1989, Gt
   Dallas D. Rhodes, (D), Syracuse, 1973
Lecturer:
   Amanda R. Admire, (M), Humboldt State, 2013, Og
   Jason R. Patton, (D), Oregon State, 2014, GuOg
Adjunct Professor:
   David Bazard, (D), Arizona, 1991
   Alan Gillespie, (D), Caltech, 1982, GmlOr
   Angela S. Jayko, (D), California (Santa Cruz), Gt
   Harvey M. Kelsey, (D), California (Santa Cruz), 1976, Gm
   Thomas Lisle, (D), California (Berkeley), 1976, Hs
   Mary Ann Madej, (D), Washington, Gm
   Jon R. Pedicino, (D), Arizona, 1996
   Silvio K. Pezzopane, (D), Oregon, 1993, Gt
   Carol S. Prentice, (D), Caltech, 1989, Gt
   Leslie Reid, (D), Washington, 1989, Gm
   Brandon E. Schwab, (D), Oregon, 2000, Gi
   William E. Weaver, (D), 1986
   Robert Ziemer, (D), Colorado State, 1978, HgGm
Emeritus:
   Kenneth R. Aalto, (D), Wisconsin, 1970, Gr
   Raymond M. Burke, (D), Colorado, 1976, Gm
   Gary A. Carver, (D), Washington, 1972, Gmt
   Lorinda Dengler, (D), California (Berkeley), 1978, Yg
   Alistair W. McCrone, (D), Kansas, 1961, Gs

Imperial Valley College
Science, Math & Engineering Div (A) (2015)
380 E. Aten Rd.
Imperial, CA 92251
   p. (760) 355-6304
   ofelia.duarte@imperial.edu
   http://www.imperial.edu/
Professor:
   Kevin G. Marty, (M), New Orleans, 1994, GcOg
Instructor:
   Kevin Marty, Gg

Irvine Valley College
Dept of Environnmental Sciences (A) (2010)
5500 Irvine Center Drive
Irvine, CA 92618
   p. (949) 451-5561
   astinson@ivc.edu
   http://www.ivc.edu
   Administrative Assistant: Liz Nichols
   Enrollment (2007): A: 20 (5)
Professor:
   George Brogan, (M), San Diego State, Gc
   Amy L. Stinson, (M), San Diego State, 1990, Gc
Adjunct Professor:
   Mark Bordelon, (M)

Laney College
Dept of Geography/Geology (A) (2010)
900 Fallon Street
Oakland, CA 94607
   p. (510) 464-3233
   lsanford@peralta.edu
   http://www.laney.peralta.edu/apps/comm.asp?Q=30123

Las Positas College
Dept of Geology (2010)
3033 Collier Canyon Road
Livermore, CA 94550
   p. (925) 424-1319
   rhanna@laspositascollege.edu
   http://www.laspositascollege.edu/geology/
Instructor:
   Ruth L. Hanna, (M), California (Davis), 1988, Gg
Geology Lab Technician:
   Carol Edson, Gg

Loma Linda University
Dept of Earth and Biological Sciences (B,M,D) (2014)
Loma Linda University
Loma Linda, CA 92350
   p. (909) 824-4530
   pbuchheim@llu.edu
   Enrollment (2013): B: 7 (4) M: 16 (4) D: 21 (1)
Director:
   H. Paul Buchheim, (D), Wyoming, 1978, GnsGr
Professor:
   Leonard R. Brand, (D), Cornell, 1970, Pv
Associate Professor:
   Leroy Leggitt, (D), Loma Linda, 2001, Pi
   Kevin Nick, (D), Oklahoma, Gdb
Assistant Professor:
   Ben Clausen, (D), Colorado, 1987, CtGiYg
   Raul Esperante, (D), Loma Linda, 2003, Pv
   Ronny Nalin, (D), Gsr

Los Angeles County Museum of Natural History
Research and Collections Branch (2004)
900 Exposition Boulevard
Los Angeles, CA 90007
   p. (213) 763-3361
   kjohnson@nhm.org
Chief Curator:
   John M. Harris, (D), Bristol, 1970, Pv
Curator:
   Lawrence G. Barnes, (D), California (Berkeley), 1972, Pv
   Kenneth E. Campbell, (D), Florida, 1973, Pv
   Anthony R. Kampf, (D), Chicago, 1976, Gz
Associate Curator:
   Luis M. Chiappe, (D), Buenos Aires, 1992, Pv
Assistant Curator:
   Joe D. Stewart, (D), Kansas, 1984, Pv
Emeritus:
   Lou Ella R. Saul, (M), California (Los Angeles), 1959, Pi
   David P. Whistler, (D), California (Berkeley), 1969, Pv
Curatorial Assistant:
   Shelley M. Cox, (B), California (Los Angeles), 1972, Pv
   Cathy McNassor, (M), Cal State (Los Angeles), 1981, Pv
Collections Manager:
   Dorothy Ettensohn, (M), Illinois, 1989, Gz
   Samuel A. McLeod, (D), California (Berkeley), 1981, Pv
   Christopher A. Shaw, (M), Cal State (Long Beach), 1981, Pv

Los Angeles Harbor College
Dept of Earth Science (A) (2013)
1111 Figueroa Place
Wilmington, CA 90744
   p. (310) 233-4000
   munasit@lahc.edu
   http://www.lahc.cc.ca.us/
Instructor:
   Patricia Kellner, (D), Og

John Mack, Og
Tissa Munasinghe, (D), Og
Melanie Renfrew, (D), Og
Susan White, Og

Los Angeles Pierce College
Physics and Planetary Sciences (A) (2013)
6201 Winnetka Ave
Woodland Hills, CA 91371
   p. (818) 710-2218
   zayacjm@piercecollege.edu
   Enrollment (2012): A: 11 (0)
Professor:
John M. Zayac, (M), California (Santa Barbara), 2006, Ggv
Professor:
Jason P. Finley, (M), California (Los Angeles), Ow
Stephen C. Lee, (B), Illinois, 1971, Og
W. Craig Meyer, (M), S California, 1973, GePm
Adjunct Professor:
Harry Filkorn, (D), Kent State, GgPi
James Krohn, (M), S California, 1974, Ng
Donald Prothero, (D), Columbia, Gg
Emeritus:
Ruth Y. Lebow, (M), Chicago, 1941, Op
Mark L. Powell, (M), Cal State (Northridge), 1967, Oa
William H. Russell, (M), Cal State (Northridge), 1970, Ow
James Y. Vernon, (M), California (Los Angeles), 1951, Ow

Los Angeles Southwest College
Geology Dept (A) (2011)
1600 West Imperial Highway
Los Angeles, CA 90047
   p. (323) 241-5297
   doosepr@lasc.edu
   http://www.lasc.edu
Chair:
Glenn Yoshida, Gg
Professor:
Paul R. Doose, (D), California (Los Angeles), 1980

Los Angeles Valley College
Earth Science (A) (2015)
5800 Fulton Ave.
Valley Glen, CA 91401
   p. (818) 778-5566
   hamsje@lavc.edu
   http://lavc.edu/earthscience/index.aspx
   Enrollment (2014): A: 3 (0)
Chair:
Jacquelyn E. Hams, (M), Cal State Los Angeles, 1987, GgOue
Academic Senate President:
Donald J. Gauthier, (M), California (Los Angeles), 1993, OiyOw
Assistant Professor:
Meredith L. Leonard, (M), Cal State (Northridge), OweOi

Mendocino College
Earth Science (A) (2014)
1000 Hensley Creek Road
Ukiah, CA 95482
   p. (707) 468-3002
   scardimo@mendocino.edu
   Enrollment (2010): A: 29 (3)
Professor:
Steve Cardimona, (D), Texas, 1992, Ys

Merced College
Science, Mathematics & Engineering Div (A) (2010)
3600 M Street
Merced, CA 95348
   p. (209) 384-6293
   gargova.s@mccd.edu
   Enrollment: No data reported since 1999
Chair:
Terry L. Eyrich, (D), California (Davis), 1973, On

MiraCosta College
Dept of Geography (A) (2010)
1 Barnard Drive
Oceanside, CA 92056
   p. (760) 757-2121 x6247
   hstern@miracosta.edu
   https://www.miracosta.edu/Instruction/Geography/
Chair:
Herschel I. Stern, (D), Oregon, 1988, Oy

Dept of Physical Sciences (A) (2013)
1 Barnard Drive
Oceanside, CA 92056
   p. (760) 944-4449 x7738
   lmiller@miracosta.edu
   https://www.miracosta.edu/Instruction/Geology/
Professor:
Keith H. Meldahl, (D), Arizona, 1990, Gg
Christopher V. Metzler, (D), California (San Diego), 1987, Gg
John Turbeville, GgOg
Adjunct Professor:
Phil Farquharson, Gg
Laboratory Director:
Larry Hernandez, Gg

Modesto Junior College
Dept of Science, Mathematics & Engineering (A) (2010)
435 College Avenue
Modesto, CA 95350
   p. (209) 575-6172
   vierraro@yosemite.edu
   Enrollment (1999): A: 9 (5)
Instructor:
Donald C. Ahrens, (D), N Colorado, Og
Garry F. Hayes, (M), Nevada (Reno), 1985, Gg

Monterey Peninsula College
Earth Sciences Dept (A) (2014)
980 Fremont St.
Monterey, CA 93940
   p. (831) 646-4000
   ahochstaedter@mpc.edu
   http://www.mpc.edu/academics/academic-divisions/physi-
   cal-science/earth-science-eart
Chair:
Alfred Hochstaedter, (D), California (Santa Cruz), 1991, GgOgg

Moorpark College
Geology Program (A) (2015)
7075 Campus Road
Moorpark, CA 93021
   p. (805) 553-4161
   rharma@vcccd.edu
   http://www.moorparkcollege.edu/geology
   Enrollment (2014): A: 20 (0)
Instructor:
Roberta L. Harma, (M), Hawaii, 1982, Gg

Moss Landing Marine Laboratories
Geological Oceanography (M) O (2014)
8272 Moss Landing Road
Moss Landing, CA 95039
   p. (831) 771-4400
   frontdesk@mlml.calstate.edu
   http://www.mlml.calstate.edu
   Enrollment (2014): M: 7 (25)
Director:
James T. Harvey, (D), Oregon, 1987, Ob
Librarian:
Joan Parker, (M), California (Los Angeles), 1986, On
Professor:
Kenneth H. Coale, (D), California (Santa Cruz), 1988, CmcOc
Jonathan Geller, (D), California (Berkeley), 1988, On
Michael Graham, (D), Scripps, 2000, Ob
Nicholas A. Welschmeyer, (D), Washington, 1982, Ob

Research Faculty:
John S. Oliver, (D), Scripps, 1980, Ob
Associate Professor:
Ivano Aiello, (D), Bologna, 1997, Gu
Assistant Professor:
Scott Hamilton, (D), California (Santa Barbara), 2008
Birgitte McDonald, (D)
Research Faculty:
Simona Bartl, (D), California (San Diego), 1989, On
Laurence Breaker, (D), Naval Postgrad Sch, 1983, Op
David Ebert, (D), Rhodes, 1990, On
Stacy Kim, (D), WHOI, 1996, On
Valerie Loeb, (D), Scripps, 1979, On
Richard Starr, (D), Autó Baja California Sur, 2002, On
Emeritus:
Gregor M. Cailliet, (D), California (Santa Barbara), 1972, On
Michael Foster, (D), California (Santa Barbara), 1971, On
H. Gary Greene, (D), Stanford, 1977, Gu
Diving Safety Officer:
Diana Steller, (D), California (Santa Cruz), 2003, On

Mt. San Antonio College
Dept of Earth Sciences & Astronomy (A) (2015)
1100 North Grand Avenue
Walnut, CA 91789
p. (909) 594-5611
cwebb@mtsac.edu
Enrollment (2010): A: 16 (0)
Acting Chair:
Julie Ali-Bray, (M), S California, 1999, On
Professor:
Micol Christopher, (D), Caltech, 2007, On
Craig A. Webb, (M), Duke, 1996, OgwOg
Part-time Instructor-Oceanography:
Larry Mendenhall, (D), Oregon State, 1961, Ow
Part-time Instructor-Earth Sciences:
Barbara Grubb, (M), Cal State (Long Beach), 1991, Ps
Charles Roberts, (M), Ohio, 1972, Pm
Instructor:
Mark Boryta, (D), New Mexico Tech, 1997
Emeritus:
Hallock J. Bender, (D), San Gabriel, 1959, Gg
John W. Burns, (M), Pittsburgh, 1960, On
Damon P. Day, (M), Michigan Tech, 1965, Gg
Ron N. Hartman, (M), Cal State (Los Angeles), 1973, Xm
Kazimierz M. Pohopien, (M), McGill, 1951, Ge
Harold V. Thurman, (M), Cal State (Los Angeles), 1966, Og
Geotechnician:
Mark Koestel, (B), Arizona, 1978, Em

Naval Postgraduate School
Dept of Meteorology (M,D) (2013)
589 Dyer Road
Root Hall, Room 254
Monterey, CA 93943-5114
p. (831) 656-2516
nuss@nps.edu
http://www.nps.edu/Academics/Schools/GSEAS/Departments/Meteorology/
Enrollment (2012): M: 45 (36) D: 9 (2)
Chair:
Wendell A. Nuss, (D), Washington, 1986, Ow
Distinguished Professor:
Michael T. Montgomery, (D), Harvard, 1990, Ow
Dean:
Philip A. Durkee, (D), Colorado State, 1984, Owr
Professor:
Patrick A. Harr, (D), Naval Postgrad Sch, 1993, Ow
Qing Wang, (D), Penn State, 1993, Ow
Associate Professor:
Joshua P. Hacker, (D), British Columbia, 2001, Ow
Assistant Professor:
Richard W. Moore, (D), Colorado State, 2004, Ow
Barbara V. Scarnato, (D), ETH, 2008, Ow
Research Associate:
Hway-Jen Chen, (M), California (Los Angeles), 1993, Ow

Paul A. Frederickson, (M), Maryland, 1989, Ow
Mary S. Jordan, (M), Naval Postgrad Sch, 1985, Ow
Kurt E. Nielsen, (M), Oklahoma, 1988, Ow
Andrew Penny, (M), Arizona, 2009, Ow
Emeritus:
Robert Haney, (D), California (Los Angeles), 1971, Ow
Robert J. Renard, (D), Ow
Carlyle H. Wash, (D), Wisconsin, 1978, Ow
Forrest Williams, (M), MIT, 1972, Ow
Roger T. Williams, (D), California (Los Angeles), 1963, Ow
Research Professor:
Kenneth L. Davidson, (D), Michigan, 1970, Ow
Peter S. Guest, (D), Naval Postgrad Sch, 1992, Ow
Research Associate Professor:
James Thomas Murphree, (D), California (Davis), 1989, Ow
NRC Postdoctoral Fellow:
Myung-Sook Park, (D), Ow
Distinguished Research Professor:
Russell L. Elsberry, (D), Colorado State, 1968, Ow
Distinguished Professor:
Chih-Pei Chang, (D), Washington, 1972, Ow
Meteorologist:
Robert L. Creasey, (M), Ow

Dept of Oceanography (M,D) (2014)
833 Dyer Road, Room 328
Monterey, CA 93943-5122
p. (831) 656-2673
pcchu@nps.edu
http://www.nps.edu/Academics/GSEAS/Oceanography/
Enrollment (2014): M: 14 (14) D: 2 (2)
Chair:
Peter C. Chu, (D), Chicago, 1985, Op
Professor:
Ching-Sang Chiu, (D), MIT/WHOI, 1985, Op
Jeffrey D. Paduan, (D), Oregon State, 1987, Op
Associate Professor:
Jamie MacMahan, (D), Onp
Timour Radko, Florida State, Op
Emeritus:
Robert H. Bourke, (D), Oregon State, 1972, Op
Curtis A. Collins, (D), Oregon State, 1967, Op
Roland W. Garwood, (D), Washington, 1976, Op
Eugene C. Haderlie, (D), California (Berkeley), 1950, Ob
Thomas H. Herbers, (D), California (San Diego), 1990, Op
Albert J. Semtner, (D), Princeton, 1973, Op
Edward B. Thornton, (D), Florida, 1970, On
Eugene D. Traganza, (D), Miami, 1966, Oc
Stevens P. Tucker, (D), Oregon State, 1972, Og
Joseph J. Von Schwind, (D), Texas A&M, 1968, Op
Jacob B. Wickham, (M), Scripps, 1949, Op
Research Professor:
Wieslaw Maslowski, (D), Alaska (Fairbanks), 1994, Op
Timothy P. Stanton, (M), Auckland, 1978, Op
Research Associate Professor:
Robin T. Tokmakian, (D), Naval Postgrad Sch, 1997, Op

Occidental College
Dept of Geology (B) (2016)
1600 Campus Road
Los Angeles, CA 90041
p. (323) 259-2823
jangarcia@oxy.edu
http://www.oxy.edu/Geology.xml
Administrative Assistant: Tracy Mikuriya
Enrollment (2015): B: 15 (8)
Professor:
Scott W. Bogue, (D), California (Santa Cruz), 1982, Ym
Margaret E. Rusmore, (D), Washington, 1985, Gc
James L. Sadd, (D), South Carolina, 1987, Oi
Related Staff:
Jan Garcia, On

Ohlone College
Dept of Geology (A) (2014)
43600 Mission Boulevard

Fremont, CA 94539
    p. (510) 979-7938
    pbelasky@ohlone.edu
    http://www.ohlone.edu/instr/geology/
Professor:
    Paul Belasky, (D), California (Los Angeles), 1994, PqiGs

Orange Coast College
Div of Mathematics & Science (A) (2015)
2701 Fairview Road
Box 5005
Costa Mesa, CA 92626-5005
    p. (714) 432-5647
    ebender@occ.cccd.edu
    Enrollment (2015): A: 13 (1)
Chair:
    E. Erik Bender, (D), S California, 1994, Giz
Instructor:
    Jim Schneider, (M), Cal State (Sacramento), Geu
Lecturer:
    Scott Mata, Pg
    Diana Pomeroy, (M), Cal State (Long Beach), 2013, Pv
    Michael Van Ry, (M), Cal State (Fullerton), 2010, Gv

Palomar College
Dept of Earth Sciences (A) (2015)
1140 West Mission Road
San Marcos, CA 92069
    p. (760) 744-1150
    sfigg@palomar.edu
    http://www.palomar.edu/earthscience/
    Administrative Assistant: Brenda Morris
    Enrollment (2014): A: 35 (0)
Professor:
    Doug Key, (M), San Diego State, Oy
    Lisa Yon, (D), Brown, 1996, Ogg
Associate Professor:
    Wing Cheung, (M), Indiana, Oyi
    Patricia A. Deen, (M), San Diego State, 1984, Ogg
    Cathy Jain, (M), San Diego State, 2000, Oy
    Mark Lane, (M), San Diego State, 1996, On
    Alan P. Trujillo, (M), N Arizona, 1984, Og
Assistant Professor:
    Sean Figg, (M), N Colorado, 2012, Gg
Emeritus:
    Jim Pesavento, GgOg

Pasadena City College
Dept of Physical Science (Geology) (2010)
1570 E. Colorado Boulevard
Pasadena, CA 91106
    p. (626) 585-7138
    dacantarero@paccd.cc.ca.us
    Enrollment (1999): A: 7 (0)
Chair:
    David N. Douglass, (D), Dartmouth, 1987, Ym
Instructor:
    Martha House, (D), MIT, Gg
    Gerald L. Lewis, (M), Cal State (Long Beach), 1965, Ps
    Yuet-Ling O'Connor, (D), S California, Gg
Geology Lab Tech:
    Debra A. Cantarero, (A), Pasadena City Coll, 2000, On

Pomona College
Geology Dept (B) (2015)
185 East Sixth Street
Claremont, CA 91711-6339
    p. (909) 621-8675
    LKeala@pomona.edu
    http://www.geology.pomona.edu
    Administrative Assistant: Lori Keala
    Enrollment (2014): B: 21 (9)
Professor:
    Eric B. Grosfils, (D), Brown, 1995, Xg

Chair:
    Jade Star Lackey, (D), Wisconsin, 2005, GipCs
Associate Professor:
    Robert R. Gaines, (D), California (Riverside), 2003, Gs
    Linda A. Reinen, (D), Brown, 1993, Gct
Emeritus:
    Richard W. Hazlett, (D), S California, 1986, Gv
    Donald H. Zenger, (D), Cornell, 1962, Gr

Riverside City College
Dept of Physical Science: Geology (A) (2016)
4800 Magnolia Avenue
Riverside, CA 92506-1299
    p. (951) 222-8350
    william.phelps@rcc.edu
    Enrollment (2015): A: 8 (5)
Assistant Professor:
    William Phelps, (D), GgOpPe

Sacramento City College
Dept of Physics, Astronomy, & Geology (A) (2015)
3835 Freeport Blvd.
Sacramento, CA 95822
    p. (916) 558-2343
    stantok@scc.losrios.edu
    http://wserver.scc.losrios.edu/~sah/physics/
    Enrollment (2015): A: 10 (0)
Professor:
    Kathryn Stanton, (D), California (Davis), 2006, GgPg

Saddleback Community College
Dept of Earth and Ocean Sciences (A) (2015)
28000 Marguerite Parkway
Mission Viejo, CA 92692
    p. (949) 582-4820
    jrepka@saddleback.edu
    http://www.saddleback.edu/mse/geo/
    f: https://www.facebook.com/Saddleback-College-Geolo-
    gy-731491460197935/
    Enrollment (2015): A: 7 (1)
Chair:
    James Repka, (D), California (Santa Cruz), 1998, GgmOe
Professor:
    Kalon Morris, (M), Scripps, 2001, OgpOw

San Bernardino County Museum
Geological Sciences Div (2014)
2024 Orange Tree Lane
Redlands, CA 92374
    p. (909) 307-2669
    kspringer@sbcm.sbcounty.gov
    http://www.co.san-bernardino.ca.us/museum/
Senior Curator:
    Kathleen B. Springer, (M), California (Riverside), Og
Curator:
    J. Chris Sagebiel, (M), Texas, 1998, Pv

San Bernardino Valley College
Earth and Spatial Sciences Program (A) (2010)
701 South Mount Vernon Ave.
San Bernardino, CA 92410
    p. (909) 384-8638
    theibel@valleycollege.edu
Head:
    Todd Heibel, Oyi
Professor:
    Stephen H. Sandlin, Oy
Instructor:
    Gary M. Croft, Oy
    Vanessa Engstrom, Oy
    Walter Grossman, Og
    Jeffrey Krizek, Oi
    William Muir, Og
    Solomon Nana Kwaku Nimako, Oi
    Edmund Jekwu Ogbuchiekwe, Oy

Lisa Schmidt, Oy
Adjunct Professor:
Donald G. Buchanan, (M), Naval Postgrad Sch, 1975, Og

San Diego State University
Dept of Geological Sciences (B,M,D) ● (2015)
5500 Campanile Drive
San Diego, CA 92182-1020
p. (619) 594-5586
dkimbrough@mail.sdsu.edu
http://www.geology.sdsu.edu
f: https://www.facebook.com/SDSU.Geology
t: @sdsugeology
Administrative Assistant: Irene Occhiello
Administrative Assistant: Pia Parrish
Enrollment (2015): B: 72 (9) M: 25 (12) D: 9 (0)
Chairman:
David L. Kimbrough, (D), California (Santa Barbara), 1982, Cc
Associate Dean, Division of Undergraduate Studies:
Stephen A. Schellenberg, (D), S California, 2000, Pe
Professor:
Eric G. Frost, (D), S California, 1983, Or
Gary H. Girty, (D), Columbia, 1983, Gc
Kim B. Olsen, (D), Utah, 1994, Ye
Thomas K. Rockwell, (D), California (Santa Barbara), 1983, Gm
Senior Scientist:
Barry B. Hanan, (D), Virginia Tech, 1980, Cc
Associate Professor:
Shuo Ma, (D), California (Santa Barbara), 2006, Ys
Kathryn W. Thorbjarnarson, (D), California (Los Angeles), 1990, Hq
Lecturer:
Victor E. Camp, (D), Washington State, 1976, Gv
Kevin Robinson, (M), San Diego State, 1996, Gc
Isabelle Sacramentogrilo, (M), San Diego State, 1999, Gg
Adjunct Professor:
Mario V. Caputo, (D), Cincinnati, 1988, GsdOn
Emeritus:
Patrick L. Abbott, (D), Texas, 1973, Gs
Kathe K. Bertine, (D), Yale, 1970, Cl
Steven M. Day, (D), California (San Diego), 1977, Ys
Clive E. Dorman, (D), Oregon State, 1974, Op
George R. Jiracek, (D), California (Berkeley), 1972, Ye
J. Philip Kern, (D), California (Los Angeles), 1968, Pg
Daniel Krummenacher, (D), Geneva, 1959, Cc
Claude Monte Marshall, (D), Stanford, 1971, Ym
Richard H. Miller, (D), California (Los Angeles), 1975, Ps
Gary L. Peterson, (D), Washington, 1963, Gr
Anton D. Ptacek, (D), Washington (St. Louis), 1965, Gx

San Francisco State University
Dept of Earth & Climate Sciences (B,M) (2013)
1600 Holloway Avenue TH 509
San Francisco, CA 94132
p. (415) 338-2061
geosci@sfsu.edu
http://tornado.sfsu.edu
Enrollment (2013): B: 56 (0) M: 22 (0)
Chair:
Karen Grove, (D), Stanford, 1989, Gs
Professor:
David P. Dempsey, (D), Washington, 1985, Oa
Oswaldo Garcia, (D), SUNY (Albany), 1976, Oa
John P. Monteverdi, (D), California (Berkeley), 1977, Oa
David A. Mustart, (D), Stanford, 1972, Gg
Raymond Pestrong, (D), Stanford, 1965, Ng
Associate Professor:
John Caskey, (D), Nevada (Reno), 1996, Gc
Petra Dekens, (D), California (Santa Cruz), Pe
Newell (Toby) Garfield, (D), Rhode Island, 1990, Op
Mary Leech, (D), Stanford, 1999, Go
Leonard Sklar, (D), California (Berkeley), 2003, Gm
Assistant Professor:
Jason Gurdak, (D), Colorado, 2006, Hw
Alexander Stine, (D), California (Berkeley), Gg

Adjunct Professor:
E. Jan Null, (D), California (Davis), 1974, Ge
Emeritus:
Charles E. Bickel, (D), Harvard, 1971, Gx
York T. Mandra, (D), Stanford, 1958, Pg
Erwin Seibel, (D), Michigan, 1972, On
Raymond Sullivan, (D), Glasgow, 1960, Go
Lisa D. White, (D), California (Santa Cruz), 1989, Pg
Geosciences Tech:
Russell McArthur, On

San Joaquin Delta College
Dept of Geology (A) (2013)
Stockton, CA 95204
p. (209) 954-5354
gfrost@deltacollege.edu
http://www.deltacollege.edu/div/scimath/geology.html
Enrollment: No data reported since 1999
Professor:
Gina Marie Frost, (D), California (Santa Cruz), Gg

San Jose City College
Dept of Physical Science (2010)
San Jose, CA 95128
p. (408) 288-3716
jessica.smay@sjcc.edu
Department Secretary: Marlene Underwood
Director:
D. James Samuelson, (M), California (Santa Barbara), 1969, On
Instructor:
Judy Mariant, (M), San Jose State, 1994, Gg
Emeritus:
John W. Martin, (M), San Jose State, 1959, Og

San Jose State University
Dept of Geology (B,M) ○ (2015)
One Washington Square
San Jose, CA 95192-0102
p. (408) 924-5050
leslie.blum@sjsu.edu
http://www.sjsu.edu/geology/
Enrollment (2009): B: 26 (7) M: 24 (6)
Emeritus Professor:
Calvin H. Stevens, (D), S California, 1963, Ps
John W. Williams, (D), Stanford, 1970, Ng
Chair:
Robert B. Miller, (D), Washington, 1980, Gct
Professor:
David W. Andersen, (D), Utah, 1973, GsCl
Emmanuel Gabet, (D), California (Santa Barbara), 2002, Gm
Paula Messina, (D), CUNY, 1998, OeGm
Ellen P. Metzger, (D), Syracuse, 1984, GpOe
Jonathan S. Miller, (D), North Carolina, 1994, GiCc
June A. Oberdorfer, (D), Hawaii, 1983, Hw
Donald L. Reed, (D), California (San Diego), 1985, GuYg
Associate Professor:
Jonathan Hendricks, (D), Cornell, 2005, Pio

Santa Barbara City College
Dept of Earth & Planetary Sciences (A) (2015)
721 Cliff Drive
Santa Barbara, CA 93109
p. (805) 965-0581
schultz@sbcc.edu
Enrollment (2000): A: 47 (12)
Chair:
Michael A. Robinson, (D), California (Santa Barbara), 2009, OyiOw
Professor:
Jeffrey W. Meyer, (D), California (Santa Barbara), 1992, GgzGx
Jan Schultz, (M), California (Santa Barbara), 1991, GgePg
Assistant Professor:
William Dinklage, (D), California (Santa Barbara), Gge
Emeritus:
Robert S. Gray, (D), Arizona, 1965, PvGzx

Santa Monica College
Earth Science Dept (A) O (2015)
1900 Pico Blvd.
Santa Monica, CA 90405
p. (310) 434-8652
drake_vicki@smc.edu
http://www.smc.edu/AcademicPrograms/EarthScience/
Pages/default.aspx
Assistant Professor:
Cara Thompson, (D), Tennessee, 2011
Adjunct Professor:
Alessandro Grippo, (D), Gs
Jenney Hall, (D), LSU, 2002
Michelle Hopkins, (D), Colorado (Boulder), 2014
Bryan Murray, (D), California (Santa Barbara), 2013
Richard Robinson, (M), Gg

Santa Rosa Junior College
Earth and Space Sciences (A) (2011)
1501 Mendocino Avenue
Santa Rosa, CA 95401-4395
p. (707) 527-4365
llupa@santarosa.edu
http://online.santarosa.edu/presentation/?2992

Santiago Canyon College
Dept of Earth, Space, & Physical Sciences (2010)
8045 East Chapman Avenue
Orange, CA 92869-4512
p. (714) 564-4788
hannes_susan@sccollege.edu
Chair:
Debra A. Brooks, (M), Texas A&M, 1989, Yg
Adjunct Professor:
Gail F. Montwill, (M), Cal State (Los Angeles), 1988, Gg
Lizanne V. Simmons, (B), Brigham Young, 1979, Gr
Amy L. Stinson, (M), San Diego State, 1990, Gc
Adam D. Woods, (D), S California, 1998, Gs

Solano Community College
School of Mathematics and Science (1999)
4000 Suisun Valley Road
Fairfield, CA 94534
p. (707) 864-7211
John.Yu@solano.edu
http://www.solano.edu/

Sonoma State University
Dept of Geology (B) (2015)
1801 East Cotati Avenue
Rohnert Park, CA 94928
p. (707) 664-2334
james@sonoma.edu
http://www.sonoma.edu/geology/
Administrative Assistant: Elizabeth Kettmann
Enrollment (2015): B: 70 (12)
Department Chair:
Matthew J. James, (D), California (Berkeley), 1987, PiGhPo
Professor:
Matty Mookerjee, (D), Rochester, 2005, GcYgOi
Assistant Professor:
Owen Anfinson, (D), Calgary, 2012, GsdGg
Emeritus:
Thomas B. Anderson, (D), Colorado, 1969, GsrGd
Rolfe C. Erickson, (D), Arizona, 1968, Gx
Walt Vennum, (D), Stanford, 1971, Gi
Retired:
Daniel B. Karner, (D), California (Berkeley), 1997, Cc
Instructional Support Technician:
Phillip Mooney, (M), California (Davis), 2010, OnGc

Stanford University
Dept of Geological and Environmental Sciences (B,M,D) (2014)
Stanford, CA 94305-2115
p. (650) 723-0847

maslin@stanford.edu
http://pangea.stanford.edu/GES/
Administrative Assistant: Elaine Andersen
Enrollment (2010): B: 21 (9) M: 11 (5) D: 45 (8)
Chair:
Jonathan F. Stebbins, (D), California (Berkeley), 1983, Cg
Research Professor:
J. Michael Moldowan, (D), Michigan, 1972, Co
Consulting Professor:
Richard Bernknopf, (D), George Washington, 1980, On
Alan K. Cooper, Yr
Francois Farges, Yr
Professor:
Atilla Aydin, (D), Stanford, 1978, Gc
Dennis K. Bird, (D), California (Berkeley), 1978, Cg
Gordon E. Brown, Jr., (D), Virginia Tech, 1970, Gz
C. Page Chamberlain, (D), Harvard, 1985, Yr
Robert B. Dunbar, (D), California (San Diego), 1981, On
Marco T. Einaudi, (D), Harvard, 1969, Em
W. Gary Ernst, (D), Johns Hopkins, 1959, Cp
Steven M. Gorelick, (D), Stanford, 1981, Hw
Stephan A. Graham, (D), Stanford, 1976, Go
James C. Ingle, Jr., (D), S California, 1966, Pm
Andre G. Journel, (D), Nancy (France), 1977, Gq
Juhn G. Liou, (D), California (Los Angeles), 1970, Gp
Keith Loague, (D), British Columbia, 1986, Hq
Donald R. Lowe, (D), Illinois, 1967, Gd
Gail A. Mahood, (D), California (Berkeley), 1979, Gi
Pamela A. Matson, (D), Oregon State, 1983, Sb
Michael O. McWilliams, (D), Australian National, 1978, Ym
Elizabeth L. Miller, (D), Rice, 1977, Gc
David D. Pollard, (D), Stanford, 1969, Gc
Paul Switzer, (D), Harvard, 1965, Gq
Consulting Associate Professor:
Trevor Dumitru, (D), Melbourne, 1990, Gc
Thomas Holzer, (D), Stanford, 1970, Ng
Joseph W. Ruetz, (M), Stanford, 1977, Gg
Joseph Wooden, (D), North Carolina, 1975, Cg
Associate Professor:
Christopher F. Chyba, (D), Cornell, 1991, Gh
Assistant Professor:
Scott E. Fendorf, (D), Delaware, 1992, Sc
Adina Paytan, (D), California (San Diego), 1996, Oc
Courtesy Professor:
Peter G. Brewer, (D), Liverpool, 1967, Oc
David A. Clague, (D), California (San Diego), 1974, Ob
Peter K. Kitanidis, (D), Yr
Stephen G. Monismith, Yr
Courtesy Associate Professor:
James P. Barry, Yr
Ronaldo I. Borja, Yr
David L. Freyberg, Yr
Simon L. Klemperer, (D), Cornell, 1985, Yr
Anders Nilsson, Yr
Alfred Spormann, Yr
Debra S. Stakes, (D), Oregon State, 1978, Ob
Courtesy Assistant Professor:
Kevin Arrigo, (D), S California, 1992, Og
Courtesy Professor:
James O. Leckie, (D), Harvard, 1970, Cl
Emeritus:
Robert G. Coleman, (D), Stanford, 1957, Gi
Robert R. Compton, (D), Stanford, 1949, Gx
John W. Harbaugh, (D), Wisconsin, 1955, Gq
Ronald J. P. Lyon, (D), California (Berkeley), 1954, Or
Irwin Remson, (D), Columbia, 1954, Hw
Tjeerd H. Van Andel, (D), Groningen (Neth), 1950, Gu

Dept of Geophysics (B,M,D) (2015)
397 Panama Mall
Stanford, CA 94305-2215
p. (650) 497-3498
mbrunner@stanford.edu
https://earth.stanford.edu/geophysics/
Enrollment (2013): B: 2 (1) M: 2 (1) D: 67 (7)
Chair:
Howard A. Zebker, (D), Stanford, 1984, Yx

20

Professor:
Gregory C. Beroza, (D), MIT, 1989, Ys
Biondo L. Biondi, (D), Stanford, 1990, Ye
Jerry M. Harris, (D), Caltech, 1980, Ys
Simon L. Klemperer, (D), Cornell, 1985, Gt
Rosemary J. Knight, (D), Stanford, 1985, Hy
Gerald M. Mavko, (D), Stanford, 1977, Yg
Paul Segall, (D), Stanford, 1981, Yg
Norman H. Sleep, (D), MIT, 1972, Yg
Mark D. Zoback, (D), Stanford, 1975, Yg
Associate Professor:
Tapan Mukerji, (D), Yg
Assistant Professor:
Eric M. Dunham, (D), California (Santa Barbara), 2005, Ys
Jenny Suckale, (D), Yg
Tiziana Vanorio, (D), Yx
Adjunct Professor:
Steven Gorelick, Yr
Emeritus:
Jon F. Claerbout, (D), MIT, 1967, Ye
Antony C. Fraser-Smith, (D), Auckland, 1966, Ym
Robert L. Kovach, (D), Caltech, 1962, Ys
Amos M. Nur, (D), MIT, 1969, Yg
Joan Roughgarden, (D), Harvard, 1971, Ob
George A. Thompson, (D), Stanford, 1949, Yg
Department Manager:
Csilla Csaplar, On

Taft College
Math/Science Div (1999)
29 Emmons Park Drive
Taft, CA 93268
p. (661) 763-7932
ggolling@taftcollege.edu

University of California, Berkeley
Dept of Earth & Planetary Science (B,M,D) (2015)
307 McCone
Berkeley, CA 94720-4767
p. (510) 642-3993
bbuffett@berkeley.edu
http://eps.berkeley.edu
Enrollment (2002): B: 43 (18) M: 1 (1) D: 6 (6)
Chair:
Hans-Rudolf Wenk, (D), Zurich, 1965, Gz
Professor:
Walter Alvarez, (D), Princeton, 1967, Grh
Jillian Banfield, (D), Johns Hopkins, 1990, CoGz
James K. Bishop, (D), MIT/WHOI, 1977, Oc
George H. Brimhall, (D), California (Berkeley), 1972, Eg
Roland Burgmann, (D), Stanford, 1993, Gt
Donald J. DePaolo, (D), Caltech, 1978, Cc
William E. Dietrich, (D), Washington, 1982, Gm
Inez Fung, (D), MIT, 1977, Oa
B. Lynn Ingram, (D), Stanford, 1992, Cs
Raymond Jeanloz, (D), Caltech, 1979, Gy
James W. Kirchner, (D), California (Berkeley), 1990, Ge
Michael Manga, (D), Harvard, 1994, GvXy
Mark A. Richards, (D), Caltech, 1986, Yg
Barbara A. Romanowicz, (D), Paris, 1979, Ys
Associate Professor:
Kristie Boering, (D), Stanford, 1991, Oa
Douglas S. Dreger, (D), Caltech, 1992, Ys
Assistant Professor:
Richard M. Allen, (D), Princeton, 2001, Ys
Burkhard Militzer, (D), Illinois (Urbana), 2000, Gy
Adjunct Associate Professor:
David L. Alumbaugh, (D), California (Berkeley), 1993, Ye
Paul Renne, (D), California (Berkeley), 1987, Cc
Adjunct Professor:
Steven Pride, (D), Texas A&M, 1991, Ys
Visiting Professor:
William D. Collins, (D), Chicago, 1988, Oa
Emeritus:
Mark S. Bukowinski, (D), California (Los Angeles), 1975, Gy
Ian S. Carmichael, (D), London, 1958, Gi

Garniss H. Curtis, (D), California (Berkeley), 1951, Cc
Lane R. Johnson, (D), Caltech, 1966, Ys
Chi-Yuen Wang, (D), Harvard, 1964, Yg
Related Staff:
Doris Sloan, (D), California (Berkeley), 1981, Ge

Dept of Environmental Science, Policy and Management
(B,M,D) (2012)
140 Mulford Hall
Berkeley, CA 94720-3110
p. (510) 643-3788
earthy@berkeley.edu
http://espm.berkeley.edu/

Dept of Integrative Biology (B,M,D) (2014)
3040 Valley Life Sciences Building #3140
Berkeley, CA 94720-3140
p. (510) 642-3281
johnh@berkeley.edu
http://ib.berkeley.edu/
Administrative Assistant: Derek Maskell
Administrative Assistant: Mona Radice
Enrollment: No data reported since 1999
Vice Chair:
Robert J. Full, (D), SUNY (Buffalo), 1984, Pi
Professor:
Roy L. Caldwell, (D), Iowa, 1969, Pi
F. Stuart Chapin, (D), Stanford, 1973, Pe
William A. Clemens, (D), California (Berkeley), 1960, Pv
Harry W. Green, (D), Tennessee, 1977, Pv
Carole S. Hickman, (D), Stanford, 1975, Po
Ned K. Johnson, (D), California (Berkeley), 1961, Pv
Mimi A. R. Koehl, (D), Duke, 1976, Po
David R. Lindberg, (D), California (Santa Cruz), Pi
Jere H. Lipps, (D), California (Los Angeles), 1966, Po
Brent Mishler, (D), Harvard, 1984, Pe
James L. Patton, (D), Arizona, 1968, Pv
Thomas M. Powell, (D), California (Berkeley), 1970, Op
Montgomery Slatkin, (D), Harvard, 1970, Po
Glennis Thompson, (D), Melbourne, 1974, On
David B. Wake, (D), S California, 1964, Po
Marvalee H. Wake, (D), S California, 1968, Po
Associate Professor:
Anthony D. Barnosky, (D), Washington, 1983, Pv
Thomas Duncan, (D), Michigan, 1976, Pb
Kevin Padian, (D), Yale, 1980, Pv
Mary E. Power, (D), Washington, 1981, Pe
Wayne P. Sousa, (D), California (Santa Barbara), 1977, Ob
Assistant Professor:
Nan Arens, (D), Harvard, Pb
Carla D'Antonio, (D), California (Santa Barbara), 1990, Pe
Deborah L. Penry, (D), Washington, 1988, Ob
Adjunct Professor:
Donald Weston, (D), William & Mary, 1983, Ob
Emeritus:
William Z. Lidicker, Jr., (D), Illinois, 1957, Pv
Robert Ornduff, (D), California (Berkeley), 1961, Pb
Thelma Rowell, (D), Cambridge, 1959, Pv
James W. Valentine, (D), California (Los Angeles), 1958, Po

Dept of Materials Science and Engineering (B,M,D) (2014)
577 Evans Hall
Berkeley, CA 94720-1760
p. (510) 642-3801
hfmorrison@berkeley.edu
http://www.mse.berkeley.edu/
Enrollment: No data reported since 1999
Chair:
Robert O. Ritchie, (D), Cambridge, 1973, Om
Professor:
Alex Becker, (D), McGill, 1963, Yg
George A. Cooper, (D), Cambridge, 1967, Np
Didier deFontaine, (D), Northwestern, 1967, Om
Lutgard DeJonghe, (D), California (Berkeley), 1970, Om
Thomas M. Devine, (D), MIT, 1974, Om
Fiona M. Doyle, (D), Imperial Coll (UK), 1983, Nx
James W. Evans, (D), SUNY (Buffalo), 1970, Nx

Douglas W. Fuerstenau, (D), MIT, 1953, Nx
Andreas Glaeser, (D), MIT, 1981, Om
Ronald Gronsky, (D), California (Berkeley), 1977, Om
Eugene Haller, (D), Basel, 1970, Om
J. W. Morris, Jr., (D), MIT, 1969, Om
H. Frank Morrison, (D), California (Berkeley), 1967, Yg
T. N. Narasimhan, (D), California (Berkeley), 1975, Hw
Timothy Sands, (D), California (Berkeley), 1984, Om
Kalanadh V. S. Sastry, (D), California (Berkeley), 1970, Nx
Eicke Weber, (D), Cologne, 1976, Om
Associate Professor:
Tad W. Patzek, (D), Silesian Tech, 1979, Np
James W. Rector, III, (D), Stanford, 1990, Ys
Assistant Professor:
Daryl Chrzan, (D), California (Berkeley), 1989, Om
Mauro Ferrari, (D), California (Berkeley), 1989, Om

GeoEngineering Program (B,M,D) (2011)
Berkeley, CA 94720
p. (510) 642-3157
pestana@ce.berkeley.edu
http://www.ce.berkeley.edu/geo/
Enrollment (1997): M: 5 (2) D: 7 (0)
Chair:
Lisa Alvarez-Cohen
Professor:
Alex Becker, (D), McGill, 1964, Ye
Huntly Frank Morrison, (D), California (Berkeley), 1967, Ye
Senior Scientist:
Ki Ha Lee, (D), California (Berkeley), 1978, Ye
Assistant Professor:
James W. Rector, (D), Stanford, 1990, Ye

Museum of Paleontology (2014)
1101 Valley Life Sciences Bldg #4780
Berkeley, CA 94720-4780
p. (510) 642-1821
rlcaldwell@berkeley.edu
http://www.ucmp.berkeley.edu
Enrollment (1995): B: 2 (2) D: 4 (4)
Director:
Roy Caldwell, (D), Iowa, 1969, Po
Curatorial Associate:
Walter Alvarez, (D), Princeton, 1967, Gr
Curator:
Carole S. Hickman, (D), Stanford, 1975, Po
David R. Lindberg, (D), California (Santa Cruz), 1983, Po
Jere H. Lipps, (D), California (Los Angeles), 1966, Po
Kevin Padian, (D), Yale, 1980, Pv
Tim White, (D), Michigan, Pv
Principal Museum Scientist:
Mark B. Goodwin, (D), California (Davis), 2008, Pv
Museum Scientist:
Diane Erwin, (D), Alberta, 1990, Pb
Pat Holroyd, (D), Duke, 1994, Pv
Curator:
Leslea Hlusko, (D), Penn State, 2000, Onn
Associate Curator:
Anthony D. Barnosky, (D), Washington, 1983, Pv
Curator:
William A. Clemens, (D), California (Berkeley), 1960, Pv
Assistant Director, Education & Public Programs:
Judith Scotchmoor, (B), California (Berkeley), Pg
Emeritus:
James W. Valentine, (D), California (Los Angeles), 1958, Po

University of California, Davis

Dept of Earth and Planetary Sciences (B,M,D) ● (2015)
2119 Earth & Physical Sciences Building
One Shields Ave.
Davis, CA 95616-5270
p. (530) 752-0350
geology@ucdavis.edu
http://geology.ucdavis.edu
f: https://www.facebook.com/pages/Geology-Department-
at-UC-Davis/87869598212
Enrollment (2014): B: 93 (30) M: 17 (7) D: 32 (3)

Chair:
Dawn Y. Sumner, (D), MIT, 1995, Gs
Professor:
Magali I. Billen, (D), Caltech, 2001, Yg
Sandra J. Carlson, (D), Michigan, 1986, Po
Kari M. Cooper, (D), California (Los Angeles), 2001, Gi
Eric S. Cowgill, (D), California (Los Angeles), 2001, Gc
Louise H. Kellogg, (D), Cornell, 1988, Yg
Charles E. Lesher, (D), Harvard, 1985, Gi
James S. McClain, (D), Washington, 1979, Yr
Isabel P. Montañez, (D), Virginia Tech, 1990, Gd
Ryosuke Motani, (D), Toronto, 1997, Pv
Sujoy Mukhopadhyay, (D), Caltech, 2002, Cg
Michael Oskin, (D), Caltech, 2002, GmtGc
Nicholas Pinter, (D), California (Santa Barbara), 1992, Gm
John Rundle, (D), California (Los Angeles), 1976, Yd
Howard J. Spero, (D), California (Santa Barbara), 1986, PeCs
Sarah T. Stewart, (D), Caltech, 2002
Geerat J. Vermeij, (D), Yale, 1971, Pe
Kenneth L. Verosub, (D), Stanford, 1973, Ym
Qing-zhu Yin, (D), Max Planck, 1995, Cc
Robert A. Zierenberg, (D), Wisconsin, 1983, Cs
Associate Professor:
Tessa M. Hill, (D), California (Santa Barbara), 2004, Pe
Research Associate:
Irina Delusina, (D), Tallinn Inst of Geology (Estonia), 1989, Pl
Oliver Kreylos, (D), California (Davis), 2003, Ng
Ann D. Russell, (D), Washington, 1994, Cm
Peter Thy, (D), Aarhus (Denmark), 1982, Gx
Burak Yikilmaz, California (Davis), 2010, Gc
Vice-Chair:
David A. Osleger, (D), Virginia Tech, 1990, Gr
Emeritus:
Cathy J. Busby, (D), Princeton, 1983, Gt
Richard Cowen, (D), Cambridge, 1966, Po
Howard W. Day, (D), Brown, 1971, Gp
John Dewey, (D), London (UK), 1960, Gt
James A. Doyle, (D), Harvard, 1970, Pb
Charles G. Higgins, (D), California (Berkeley), 1950, Gm
Eldridge M. Moores, (D), Princeton, Gt
Jeffrey F. Mount, (D), California (Santa Cruz), 1980, Gm
Sarah M. Roeske, (D), California (Santa Cruz), 1988, Gc
James R. Rustad, (D), Minnesota, 1992, Cl
Peter Schiffman, (D), Stanford, 1978, Gp
Donald L. Turcotte, (D), Caltech, 1958, Yg
Robert J. Twiss, (D), Princeton, 1970, Gc
Cooperating Faculty:
William H. Casey, (D), Penn State, 1985, Cl
Graham E. Fogg, (D), Texas, 1986, Hw
Alexandra Navrotsky, (D), Chicago, 1967, Om

Dept of Land, Air & Water Resources (B,M,D) O (2015)
1110 Plant and Environmental Sciences Building
One Shields Avenue
Davis, CA 95616
p. (530) 752-1130
rjsouthard@ucdavis.edu
http://lawr.ucdavis.edu/
Enrollment (2014): B: 5 (5) M: 54 (19) D: 55 (8)
Specialist in Cooperative Extension:
Toby O'Geen, (D), Idaho, 2002, Os
Professor:
Cort Anastasio, (D), Duke, 1994, Oa
Shu-Hua Chen, (D), Purdue, 1999, OraOw
Randy A. Dahlgren, (D), Washington, 1987, Os
Graham E. Fogg, (D), Texas, 1986, Hw
Mark E. Grismer, (D), Colorado State, 1971, Hw
Richard Grotjahn, (D), Florida State, 1979, Oa
Peter J. Hernes, (D), Washington, 1999, Hg
Jan W. Hopmans, (D), Auburn, Os
William R. Horwath, (D), Michigan State, 1993, Os
Louise E. Jackson, (D), Washington, 1982, Os
Terrence R. Nathan, (D), Univat Albany, 1985, Oa
Kate Scow, (D), Cornell, 1988, Os
Randal J. Southard, (D), North Carolina State, 1983, Os
Susan L. Ustin, (D), California (Davis), 1983, Or

Associate Professor:
Ben Houlton, (D), Princeton, So
Sanjai Parikh, (D), Arizona, Os
Assoc Proj Scientist:
Martin Burger, (D), California (Davis), 2002, Spb
Specialist in Cooperative Extension:
Daniel Geisseler, (D), California (Davis), 2009, Os
20% Cooperative Extension:
Samuel Sandoval Solis, (D), Texas (Austin), 2011, Hg
Assistant Professor:
Helen E. Dahlke, (D), Cornell, 2011, Hg
Yufang Jin, (D), Boston, 2002, Or
Adjunct Professor:
Minghua Zhang, (D), California (Davis), 1993, Hg
Emeritus:
James H. Richards, (D), Alberta, 1981, Os
Asst Proj Scientist:
Michael L. Grieneisen, (D), North Carolina (Chapel Hill), 1992, Hg
Asst Professional Researcher:
Lucas CR Silva, (D), Guelph, 2011, Sb
Cooperating Faculty:
Stephen R. Grattan, (D), California (Riverside), 1984, Sp
Thomas Harter, (D), University of Arizona, 1994, Hg
Richard L. Snyder, (D), Iowa State, 1980, Oa
Daniele Zaccaria, (D), Utah State, 2011, Hg

Dept of Land, Air, & Water Resources - Hydrology Program
(B,M,D) (2013)
1110A Plant Environmental Sciences
One Shields Avenue
Davis, CA 95616-8628
p. (530) 752-3060
radahlgren@ucdavis.edu
http://lawr.ucdavis.edu/
Enrollment (2012): B: 25 (0) M: 16 (0) D: 21 (0)
Chair:
Randy Dahlgran, (D), Washington, 1987, Sc
Jan W. Hopmans, (D), Auburn, 1985, Sp
Professor:
William H. Casey, (D), Penn State, 1985, Sc
Graham E. Fogg, (D), Texas, 1986, Hy
Mark E. Grismer, (D), Colorado State, 1984, Sp
Theodore C. Hsiao, (D), Illinois, 1963, Sb
Miguel A. Marino, (D), California (Los Angeles), 1972, Hw
Gregory B. Pasternack, (D), Johns Hopkins, 1998, Sp
Carlos E. Puente, (D), MIT, 1984, Hq
Susan L. Ustin, (D), California (Davis), 1983, Or
Wesley W. Wallender, (D), Utah State, 1982, Hg
Water Management Specialist:
Terry L. Prichard, (D), California (Davis), 1975, On
Plant-Water Relations Specialist:
Stephen R. Grattan, (D), California (Riverside), 1984, On
Irrigation Specialist:
Larry J. Schwankl, (D), California (Davis), 1991, On
Irrigation & Soil Specialist:
David A. Goldhamer, (D), California (Davis), 1980, On
Groundwater Hydrology Specialist:
Thomas L. Harter, (D), Arizona, 1993, Hw
Associate Professor:
Peter Hernes, (D), Washington, Og
Assistant Professor:
Samuel Sandoval, (D), Texas, 2011, Hg
Irrigation & Drainage Specialist:
Blaine R. Hanson, (D), Colorado State, 1977, Hg
Emeritus:
Robert M. Hagan, California (Davis), 1948, Hg
Allen W. Knight, (D), Utah, 1965, Hs
Donald R. Nielsen, (D), Iowa State, 1958, Sp
Verne H. Scott, Colorado State, 1959, Hs

Graduate Group in Hydrologic Sciences (M,D) (2013)
1152 PES
One Shields Ave
Davis, CA 95616
p. (530) 752-1669
lawrgradadvising@ucdavis.edu
http://hydscigrad.ucdavis.edu/

Administrative Assistant: Diane Swindall
Enrollment (2010): M: 14 (1) D: 14 (0)
Chair:
Graham E. Fogg, (D), Texas, 1986, Hy
Professor:
William H. Casey, (D), Pennsylvania, 1985, Cl
Jeannie Darby, (D), Texas, 1988, Hg
Mark E. Grismer, (D), Colorado State, 1984, Hw
Jan W. Hopmans, (D), Auburn, 1985, So
Theodore C. Hsiao, (D), Illinois, 1964, On
B. E. Larock, (D), Stanford, 1966, On
Jay R. Lund, (D), Washington, 1986, Hs
M. A. Marino, (D), California (Los Angeles), 1972, Hw
James S. McClain, (D), Washington, 1979, Yr
Eldridge M. Moores, (D), Princeton, 1963, Gt
Jeffrey F. Mount, (D), California (Santa Cruz), 1980, Gs
Dennis E. Rolston, (D), California (Davis), 1971, So
K. K. Tanji, (M), California (Davis), 1961, On
Wes W. Wallender, (D), Utah State, 1982, Hg
B. C. Weare, (D), SUNY (Buffalo), 1974, Oa
Associate Professor:
Bruce Kutter, (D), Cambridge, 1983, Ne
Carlos E. Puente, (D), MIT, 1984, Hg
Emeritus:
Robert A. Matthews, (B), California (Berkeley), 1953, Ge

University of California, Irvine
Dept of Earth System Science (B,D) (2015)
School of Physical Sciences
Irvine, CA 92697-3100
p. (949) 824-8794
essinfo@ess.uci.edu
http://www.ess.uci.edu
Enrollment (2013): B: 166 (64) D: 49 (5)
Chair:
Michael L. Goulden, (D), Stanford, 1992, Og
Advance Professor:
Ellen R. M. Druffel, (D), California (San Diego), 1980, Oc
Professor:
James Famiglietti, (D), Princeton, Hw
Gudrun Magnusdottir, (D), Colorado State, 1989, Oa
Michael J. Prather, (D), Yale, 1975, Oa
Eric Rignot, (D), S California, 1991, Ol
Eric S. Saltzman, (D), Rosenstiel, 1986, Oa
Soroosh Sorooshian, (D), California (Los Angeles), 1978, Hg
Susan E. Trumbore, (D), Columbia, 1989, Sc
Jin-Yi Yu, (D), Washington, Og
Charles Zender, (D), Colorado, 1996, Oa
Associate Professor:
Jefferson Keith Moore, (D), Oregon State, 1999, Op
Francois Primeau, (D), MIT/WHOI, 1998, Op
Assistant Professor:
Claudia Czimczik, (D)
Steven J. Davis, (D), Stanford, 2008, Ge
Todd Dupont, (D), Penn State, 2004, Ol
Julie Ferguson, (D), Oxford, 2008, Oe
Kathleen Johnson, (D), California (Berkeley), 2004, Og
Saewung Kim, (D), Georgia Tech, 2007, Oa
Adam Martiny, (D), Tech (Denmark), 2003, Ob
Michael Pritchard, (D)
Isabella Velicogna, (D), Trieste, 1999, Or
Laboratory Director:
John Southon, (D), Og

University of California, Los Angeles
Dept of Atmospheric and Oceanic Sciences (B,M,D) (2015)
7127 Math Sciences
Box 951565
Los Angeles, CA 90095
p. (310) 825-1217
deptinfo@atmos.ucla.edu
http://www.atmos.ucla.edu
f: https://www.facebook.com/AOS.UCLA
Chair:
Jochen P. Stutz, (D), Heidelberg, 1996, Oa

Professor:
  Kuo Nan Liou, (D), New York, 1970, Oa
  Lawrence Lyons, (D), California (Los Angeles), 1972, Oa
  James McWilliams, (D), Harvard, 1971, Oa
  Carlos R. Mechoso, (D), Princeton, 1978, Oa
  J. David Neelin, (D), Princeton, 1987, Oa
  Suzanne Paulson, (D), Caltech, 1991, Oa
  Richard M. Thorne, (D), MIT, 1968, Oa
  Yongkang Xue, (D)
Associate Professor:
  Jacob Bortnik, (D)
  Alex Hall, (D)
  Qinbin Li
Assistant Professor:
  Daniele Bianchi , (D)
  Jasper Kok , (D)
  Ulli Seibt , (D)
  Andrew Stewart, (D)
  Arahdna Tripati, (D)
Lecturer:
  Jeffrey Lew, (D), California (Los Angeles), 1985, Oa
Emeritus:
  Akio Arakawa, (D), Tokyo, 1961, Oa
  Robert Fovell, (D), Illinois, 1988, Oa
  Michael Ghil, (D), Courant Inst, 1975, Oa
  Richard Turco, (D), Illinois, 1971, Oa

Dept of Earth, Planetary, and Space Sciences (B,M,D) O (2015)
595 Charles E Young Drive East
3806 Geology Building, Box 951567
Los Angeles, CA 90095-1567
  p. (310) 825-3880
  info@epss.ucla.edu
  http://epss.ucla.edu
  Enrollment (2011): B: 69 (17) M: 11 (14) D: 61 (15)
Chair:
  Kevin D. McKeegan, (D), Washington Univ (St. Louis), 1987, XcCsc
Professor:
  Vassilis Angelopoulos, (D), California (Los Angeles), 1993, XyOa
  Jonathan M. Aurnou, (D), Johns Hopkins, 1999, XyYmg
  Paul M. Davis, (D), Queensland, 1974, YsmYg
  T. Mark Harrison, (D), Australian National, 1981, CcGt
  Raymond V. Ingersoll, (D), Stanford, 1976, Gst
  David Jewitt, (D), Caltech, 1983, XyOnn
  Abby Kavner, (D), California (Berkeley), 1997, GyYg
  Craig E. Manning, (D), Stanford, 1989, GxCp
  Jean-Luc Margot, (D), Cornell, 1999, XyOn
  William I. Newman, (D), Cornell, 1979, Xy
  David A. Paige, (D), Caltech, 1985, Xy
  Gilles Peltzer, (D), Paris VII, 1987, OrGt
  Edward J. Rhodes, (D), Oxford, 1990, CcGma
  Christopher T. Russell, (D), California (Los Angeles), 1968, Xy
  J. William Schopf, (D), Harvard, 1968, Po
  Laurence C. Smith, (D), Cornell, 1996, Hs
  Marco Velli, (D), Pisa, 1985, Yg
  An Yin, (D), S California, 1988, Gt
  Edward D. Young, (D), S California, 1990, CsXc
Associate Professor:
  Caroline Beghein, (D), Utrecht, 2003, Ysg
  Jonathan Mitchell, (D), Chicago, 2007, OaXg
  Edwin A. Schauble, (D), Caltech, 2002, Cgs
  Axel K. Schmitt, (D), Giessen (Germany), 1999, GiCc
  Tina Treude, (D), Max Planck Inst, 2004, GuPy
  Aradhna Tripati, (D), California (Santa Cruz), 2002, CmPeCs
Assistant Professor:
  Lingsen Meng, (D), Caltech, 2012, Ys
  Ulrike Seibt, (D), Hamburg, 2003, PyCg
Instructor:
  Stephen L. Salyards, (D), Caltech, 1989, Ys
Adjunct Professor:
  Sinan Akciz, MIT, Gt
  Robert C. Newton, (D), California (Los Angeles), 1963, CpGp
Visiting Professor:
  Friedrich H. Busse, (D), Munich, 1962, Yg
Emeritus:
  Orson L. Anderson, (D), Utah, 1951, Gy
  G. Peter Bird, (D), MIT, 1976, YgGtg

Donald Carlisle, (D), Wisconsin, 1950, Eg
Paul J. Coleman, (D), California (Los Angeles), 1966, Xy
Wayne A. Dollase, (D), MIT, 1966, Gz
Clarence A. Hall, (D), Stanford, 1956, Gt
David D. Jackson, (D), MIT, 1969, YsdYg
Isaac R. Kaplan, (D), S California, 1962, Csg
Margaret G. Kivelson, (D), Radcliffe, 1957, Xy
Robert L. McPherron, (D), California (Berkeley), 1968, Xy
Paul M. Merifield, (D), Colorado, 1963, Ng
Art Montana, (D), Penn State, 1966, Cp
Gerhard Oertel, (D), Bonn, 1945, Gc
John L. Rosenfeld, (D), Harvard, 1954, Gp
Bruce Runnegar, (D), Queensland, 1967, Po
Gerald Schubert, (D), California (Berkeley), 1964, YgXy
Ronald Shreve, (D), Caltech, 1958, Gm
Raymond J. Walker, (D), California (Los Angeles), 1973, Xy
John T. Wasson, (D), MIT, 1958, Xmc

Inst of Geophysics & Planetary Physics (2014)
3845 Slichter Hall
Los Angeles, CA 90095-1567
  p. (310) 825-1664
  kolwin@igpp.ucla.edu
  http://www.igpp.ucla.edu
Director:
  Michael Ghil, (D), New York, 1975, Oa
Professor:
  Vassilis Angelopoulos, (D), California (Los Angeles), 1993, Yg
  Maha Ashour-Abdalla, (D), Imperial Coll (UK), 1971, On
  Friedrich H. Busse, (D), Munich, 1967, On
  Richard E. Dickerson, (D), Minnesota, 1957, On
  T. Mark Harrison, (D), Australian National, 1980, Cc
  Charles F. Kennel, (D), Princeton, 1964, On
  Margaret G. Kivelson, (D), Radcliffe, 1957, Xy
  Robert L. McPherron, (D), California (Berkeley), 1968, Xy
  James C. McWilliams, (D), Harvard, 1971, Oa
  Paul H. Roberts, (D), Cambridge, 1967, Ym
  Bruce Runnegar, (D), Queensland, 1967, Po
  Christopher T. Russell, (D), California (Los Angeles), 1968, Yg
  J. William Schopf, (D), Harvard, 1968, Po
  Gerald Schubert, (D), California (Berkeley), 1964, Yg
  Karl O. Stetter, (D), Tech (Munich), 1973, Po
  Richard Turco, (D), Illinois, 1971, Oa
  Raymond J. Walker, (D), California (Los Angeles), 1973, On
  John T. Wasson, (D), MIT, 1958, Xm
  Edward Young
Senior Scientist:
  Stanislav I. Braginsky, (D), Moscow Inst, 1948, Ym
  Robert J. Strangeway, (D), London, 1978, On
  M I. Venkatesan, (D), Madras, 1973, Co
  Paul Warren, (D), California (Los Angeles), 1979, Xm
Associate Professor:
  Abby Kavner, (D), California (Berkeley), 1997, Yg
  J. David Neelin, (D), Princeton, 1987, Oa
Associate Research Scientist:
  Jean Berchem, (D), California (Los Angeles), 1986, On
  Gregory Kallemeyn, (D), California (Los Angeles), 1982, Cg
  Frank T. Kyte, (D), California (Los Angeles), 1983, Ct
  Alan E. Rubin, (D), New Mexico, 1982, Xm
  David Schriver, (D), California (Los Angeles), 1988, Yg
  Fred Schwab, (B), California (Los Angeles), 1960, Ys
Assistant Research Scientist:
  Kayo Ide, (D), Caltech, 1990, Og
  Krishan Khurana, (D), Durham, 1984, On
  Robert Richard, (D), California (Los Angeles), 1988, Yg
  William Smythe, (D), California (Los Angeles), 1979, Ys
  Ferenc D. Varadi, (D), California (Los Angeles), 1989, On
Emeritus:
  Orson L. Anderson, (D), Utah, 1951, Yx
  Paul J. Coleman, Jr., (D), California (Los Angeles), 1966, Gc
  Isaac R. Kaplan, (D), S California, 1962, Cg
  Leon Knopoff, (D), Caltech, 1949, Ys
  Ronald L. Shreve, (D), Caltech, 1958, Gm
Department Manager:
  James Nakatsuka, On

University of California, Riverside

Dept. of Earth Sciences (B,M,D) ● (2015)
University of California Riverside
Earth Sciences Department
Riverside, CA 92521
  p. (951) 827-3182
  david.oglesby@ucr.edu
  http://earthscience.ucr.edu
  Enrollment (2013): B: 51 (13) M: 15 (8) D: 38 (4)
Chair:
  David D. Oglesby, (D), California (Santa Barbara), 1999, Ys
Distinguished Professor:
  Timothy Lyons, (D), Yale, Cg
Professor:
  Mary L. Droser, (D), S California, 1987, Po
  Nigel C. Hughes, (D), Bristol (UK), 1990, Po
  Gordon Love, (D), Strathclyde, 1995, Co
  Richard A. Minnich, (D), California (Los Angeles), 1978, Oy
  Andy Ridgwell, (D), East Anglia, 2001, On
  Peter M. Sadler, (D), Bristol (UK), 1973, GrPs
Associate Professor:
  Gareth Funning, (D), Oxford, 2005, YdgYs
  Michael A. McKibben, (D), Penn State, 1984, Cg
Assistant Professor:
  Robert J. Allen, (D), Yale, 2009, Oa
  Nicolas Barth, (D), Otago, 2013, Gt
  Andrey Bekker, (D), Virginia Tech, 2001, GsrCg
  Heather Ford, (D), Ys
  Abhijit Ghosh, (D), Washington, Ys
  Sandra Kirtland Turner, (D), Scripps, Cs
Adjunct Assistant Professor:
  Katherine J. Kendrick, (D), California (Riverside), 1999, Gm
  Thomas A. Scott, (D), California (Berkeley), 1987, Oy
Adjunct Professor:
  Elizabeth Cochran, California (Los Angeles), 2005, Ys
  Larissa F. Dobrzhinetskaya, (D), Inst of Physics of Earth (Moscow), 1978, Gx
  Douglas M. Morton, (D), California (Los Angeles), 1966, Gp
Professor of the Graduate Division:
  James H. Dieterich, (D), Yale, 1968, Yg
  Harry W. Green, II, (D), California (Los Angeles), 1968, Yx
Emeritus:
  Wilfred A. Elders, (D), Durham, 1961, Gi
  Michael A. Murphy, (D), California (Los Angeles), 1954, Ps
  Stephen K. Park, (D), MIT, 1984, Ym
  Michael O. Woodburne, (D), California (Berkeley), 1966, Pv

University of California, San Diego

Scripps Institution of Oceanography (B,M,D) (2015)
Graduate Office
9500 Gilman Dr.
Mail Code 0208
La Jolla, CA 92093-0208
  p. (858) 534-3206
  siodept@sio.ucsd.edu
  https://scripps.ucsd.edu/education/
  Enrollment (2012): M: 7 (0) D: 62 (13)
Vice Chancellor:
  Margaret Leinen, (D), Rhode Island, 1980, OgPe
Chair:
  Lisa Tauxe, (D), Columbia, 1983, Ym
Director, Inst of Geophys & Planetary Phys:
  Catherine G. Constable, (D), California (San Diego), 1987, Ym
Professor:
  Duncan C. Agnew, (D), California (San Diego), 1979, Ys
  Laurence Armi, (D), California (Berkeley), 1975, Op
  Farooq Azam, (D), Czech Acad of Sci, 1968, Ob
  Jeffrey L. Bada, (D), California (San Diego), 1968, Co
  Douglas H. Bartlett, (D), Illinois, 1985, Ob
  Kevin M. Brown, (D), Durham (UK), 1987, Gu
  Michael J. Buckingham, (D), Reading, 1971, Op
  Ronald S. Burton, (D), Stanford, 1981, Ob
  Steven C. Cande, (D), Columbia, 1976, Yr
  Paterno R. Castillo, (D), Washington (St. Louis), 1987, Gi
  Paola Cessi, (D), MIT, 1987, Op
  Christopher D. Charles, (D), Columbia, 1991, Pe

David M. Checkley, (D), California (San Diego), 1978, Ob
Steven C. Constable, (D), Australian National, 1983, Yr
Paul K. Dayton, (D), Washington, 1970, Ob
Andrew G. Dickson, (D), Liverpool (UK), 1978, Cm
Leroy M. Dorman, (D), Wisconsin, 1970, Yg
Neal W. Driscoll, (D), Columbia, 1992, Gu
Horst Felbeck, (D), Muenster, 1979, Ob
William H. Fenical, (D), California (Riverside), 1968, Oc
Peter J. S. Franks, (D), MIT/WHOI, 1990, Ob
Terry Gaasterland, (D), Maryland, 1992, Ob
Jeffrey S. Gee, (D), California (San Diego), 1991, Gu
William H. Gerwick, (D), California (San Diego), 1981, Cm
Carl H. Gibson, (D), Stanford, 1962, Oo
Sarah T. Gille, (D), MIT/WHOI, 1995, Op
Robert T. Guza, (D), California (San Diego), 1974, On
Philip A. Hastings, (D), Arizona, 1987, Ob
Anthony DJ Haymet, (D), Chicago, 1981, On
Myrl C. Hendershott, (D), Harvard, 1966, Op
John A. Hildebrand, (D), Stanford, 1983, Yr
David R. Hilton, (D), Cambridge, 1985, Cs
William S. Hodgkiss, Jr., (D), Duke, 1975, Oo
Nicholas D. Holland, (D), Stanford, 1965, Ob
Glenn R. Ierley, (D), MIT, 1982, Op
Jeremy B. C. Jackson, (D), Yale, 1971, Po
Miriam Kastner, (D), Harvard, 1970, Cl
William A. Kuperman, (D), Maryland, 1972, Op
Devendra Lal, (D), Bombay, 1958, Xc
Michael R. Landry, (D), Washington, 1976, Ob
Lisa A. Levin, (D), California (San Diego), 1982, Ob
Peter F. Lonsdale, (D), California (San Diego), 1974, Gu
T. Guy Masters, (D), Cambridge, 1979, Ys
W. Kendall Melville, (D), Southampton (UK), 1974, Op
J. Bernard H. Minster, (D), Caltech, 1974, Ys
Mario J. Molina, (D), California (Berkeley), 1972, Oa
Bradley S. Moore, (D), Zurich, 1995, Cm
Richard D. Norris, (D), Harvard, 1990, Gu
Mark D. Ohman, (D), Washington, 1983, Ob
John A. Orcutt, (D), California (San Diego), 1976, Yr
Brian Palenik, (D), MIT/WHOI, 1989, Ob
Robert Pinkel, (D), California (San Diego), 1974, Op
Kimberly A. Prather, (D), California (Davis), 1990, Oa
V. Ramanathan, (D), SUNY (Stony Brook), 1973, Oa
Dean H. Roemmich, (D), MIT/WHOI, 1980, Op
Gregory W. Rouse, (D), Sydney, 1991, Ob
Daniel L. Rudnick, (D), California (San Diego), 1987, Op
Lynn M. Russell, (D), Caltech, 1995, Oa
Richard L. Salmon, (D), California (San Diego), 1976, Op
David T. Sandwell, (D), California (Los Angeles), 1981, Yr
John G. Sclater, (D), Cambridge, 1966, Yh
Uwe Send, (D), California (San Diego), 1988, Op
Jeffrey P. Severinghaus, (D), Columbia, 1995, Pe
Peter M. Shearer, (D), California (San Diego), 1986, Ys
Dariusz Stramski, (D), Gdansk (Poland), 1985, Op
George Sugihara, (D), Princeton, 1983, Ob
Lynne D. Talley, (D), MIT/WHOI, 1982, Op
Martin Wahlen, (D), Bern, 1969, Cs
Ray F. Weiss, (D), California (San Diego), 1970, Cm
Bradley T. Werner, (D), Caltech, 1987, Gm
Clinton D. Winant, (D), S California, 1972, On
William R. Young, (D), MIT/WHOI, 1981, Op
Associate Professor:
  Lihini I. Aluwihare, (D), MIT/WHOI, 1999, Gu
  Katherine A. Barbeau, (D), MIT/WHOI, 1998, Oc
  Yuri A. Fialko, (D), Princeton, 1998, Gu
  Helen A. Fricker, (D), Tasmania, 1999, Yr
  Ralph F. Keeling, (D), Harvard, 1988, Oa
  James J. Leichter, (D), Stanford, 1997, Ob
  Joel R. Norris, (D), Washington, 1997, Oa
Assistant Professor:
  Eric E. Allen, (D), California (San Diego), 2002, Ob
  Todd Martz, (D), Montana, 2005, Gg
  Jennifer E. Smith, (D), Hawaii, 2003, Ob
Adjunct Professor:
  Jay P. Barlow, (D), California (San Diego), 1982, Ob
  Nancy Knowlton, (D), California (Berkeley), 1978, Ob
  William F. Perrin, (D), California (Los Angeles), 1972, Ob
  Paul E. Smith, (D), Iowa, 1962, Ob

Detlef B. Stammer, (D), Kiel, 1992, Ow
Research Professor:
 John A. McGowan, (D), California (San Diego), 1960, Ob
Emeritus:
 Gustaf Arrhenius, (D), Stockholm, 1952, Cg
 George E. Backus, (D), Chicago, 1956, Yg
 Wolfgang H. Berger, (D), California (San Diego), 1968, Gs
 Charles S. Cox, (D), Scripps, 1954, Op
 Joseph R. Curray, (D), Scripps, 1959, Gu
 Edward A. Frieman, (D), Brooklyn Polytech, 1951, On
 Joris M. Gieskes, (D), Manitoba, 1965, Oc
 J. Freeman Gilbert, (D), MIT, 1956, Ys
 James W. Hawkins, (D), Washington, 1963, Gp
 Robert R. Hessler, (D), Chicago, 1960, Ob
 Douglas L. Inman, (D), Scripps, 1953, On
 Charles F. Kennel, (D), Princeton, 1964, Oa
 Gerald L. Kooyman, (D), Arizona, 1966, Ob
 J. Douglas Macdougall, (D), California (San Diego), 1972, Cm
 Walter H. Munk, (D), Scripps, 1947, Op
 William A. Newman, (D), California (Berkeley), 1962, Ob
 Pearn P. Niiler, (D), Brown, 1964, Op
 Robert L. Parker, (D), Cambridge, 1966, Ym
 Joseph L. Reid, (M), Scripps, 1950, Op
 Richard H. Rosenblatt, (D), California (Los Angeles), 1959, Ob
 Richard C. Somerville, (D), New York, 1966, Oa
 Victor D. Vacquier, (D), California (Berkeley), 1968, Ob
 Edward L Winterer, (D), California (Los Angeles), 1954, Gd

University of California, Santa Barbara
Dept of Earth Science (B,M,D) (2014)
Room 1006
Webb Hall
Santa Barbara, CA 93106-9630
 p. (805) 893-4688
 gs-mso@geol.ucsb.edu
 http://www.geol.ucsb.edu
 Administrative Assistant: Hannah Smit
 Enrollment (2012): B: 81 (22) M: 12 (2) D: 36 (3)
Chair:
 Doug Burbank, (D), Dartmouth, 1982, Gmt
Professor:
 Ralph J. Archuleta, (D), California (San Diego), 1976, Ys
 Stanley M. Awramik, (D), Harvard, 1973, Po
 Cathy J. Busby, (D), Princeton, 1983, Gs
 Jordan Clark, (D), Columbia, 1995, Hg
 Bradley R. Hacker, (D), California (Los Angeles), 1998, Gp
 Edward A. Keller, (D), Purdue, 1973, Gm
 David W. Lea, (D), MIT, 1990, Oc
 Frank J. Spera, (D), California (Berkeley), 1977, Gi
 Toshiro Tanimoto, (D), California (Berkeley), 1982, Ys
 Bruce H. Tiffney, (D), Harvard, 1977, Pb
 David Valentine, (D), Cm
 Andre R. Wyss, (D), Columbia, 1989, Pv
Associate Professor:
 Phillip B. Gans, (D), Stanford, 1987, Gt
 Chen Ji, (D), Caltech, 2002, Ys
 Lorraine Lisiecki, (D), Brown, 2005, Gn
 Susannah Porter, (D), Harvard, 2002, Gn
Assistant Professor:
 John Cottle, (D), Oxford, 2007, Gi
 Alex Simms, (D), Rice, 2006, Gu
 Syee Weldeab, (D), Tubingen, 2002, PeCm
Undergraduate Staff Advisor:
 Alice MaCall, (B)

Inst for Crustal Studies (2015)
Mail Code 1100
Santa Barbara, CA 93106-1100
 p. (805) 893-8231
 davey@eri.ucsb.edu
 http://www.crustal.ucsb.edu
 Administrative Assistant: Kathy J. Scheidemen
Director:
 Douglas W. Burbank, (D), Dartmouth, 1982, Gm
Associate Director:
 Bradley R. Hacker, (D), California (Los Angeles), 1988, Gx

Professor:
 Ralph J. Archuleta, (D), California (San Diego), 1976, Ys
 Cathy Busby, (D), Princeton, 1983, Gs
 Edward A. Keller, (D), Purdue, 1973, Gt
 Bruce P. Luyendyk, (D), California (San Diego), 1969, Yr
 Frank J. Spera, (D), California (Berkeley), 1977, Cp
 Toshiro Tanimoto, (D), California (Berkeley), 1982, Ys
Associate Professor:
 Jordan Clark, (D), Columbia, 1995, Cg
 Phillip B. Gans, (D), Stanford, 1987, Gt
Research Seismologist:
 Jamison H. Steidl, (D), California (Santa Barbara), 1995, Ys
Assistant Research Scientist:
 Christopher C. Sorlien, (D), California (Santa Barbara), 1994, Yr
Assistant Professor:
 Bodo Bookhagen, (D), Potsdam, 2005, Gm

University of California, Santa Cruz
Center for the Dynamics & Evolution of the Land-Sea Interface
(2014)
1156 High Street
Room A234, Earth & Marine Sciences Building
Santa Cruz, CA 95064
 p. (831) 459-4089
 acr@es.ucsc.edu
Professor:
 Robert S. Anderson, (D), Washington, 1986, Gm
 Kenneth W. Bruland, (D), California (San Diego), 1974, Oc
 Daniel P. Costa, (D), California (Santa Cruz), 1978, Ob
 Margaret L. Delaney, (D), MIT/WHOI, 1983, Oc
 Russell Flegal, (D), Oregon State, Cg
 Laurel R. Fox, (D), California (Santa Barbara), On
 Dianne Gifford-Gonzalez, (D), California (Berkeley), On
 Mark S. Mangel, (D), British Columbia, 1978, On
 Donald C. Potts, (D), California (Santa Barbara), Ob
 Mary W. Silver, (D), California (San Diego), 1971, Ob
 Jonathan P. Zehr, (D), California (Davis), 1985, Ob
Associate Professor:
 Mark Carr, (D), California (Santa Barbara), Ob
 Brent Haddad, (D), California (Berkeley), 1996, On
 Karen D. Holl, (D), Virginia Tech, 1994, Ou
 Christina Ravelo, (D), Columbia, 1991, Cs
 Donald R. Smith, (D), California (Santa Cruz), On
Assistant Professor:
 Don Croll, (D), California (Santa Cruz), Ob
 Raphael M. Kudela, (D), S California, 1995, Or
 Margaret A. McManus, (D), Old Dominion, 1996, On

Center for the Origin, Dynamics, & Evolution of Planets (2010)
1156 High Street
Room A234, Earth & Marine Sciences Building
Santa Cruz, CA 95064
 p. (831) 459-4089
 dkorycan@ucsc.edu
Professor:
 Robert S. Anderson, (D), Washington, 1986, Gm
 Peter Bodenheimer, (D), California (Berkeley), 1965, Xc
 Frank Bridges, (D), California (San Diego), 1968, Yx
 Douglas Lin, (D), Cambridge, 1976, Xc
 Steven Vogt, (D), Texas, 1978, Xc
Associate Professor:
 Erik Asphaug, (D), Arizona, 1993, Xg
Other:
 Don Korycansky, (D), California (Santa Cruz), Xc

Center for the Study of Imaging & Dynamics of the Earth (2015)
1156 High Street
Room A234, Earth & Marine Sciences Building
Santa Cruz, CA 95064
 p. (831) 459-4089
 judy@ucsc.edu
 http://cside.ucsc.edu/
Research Geophysicist:
 Steven N. Ward, (D), Princeton, 1978, Ys
 Ru-shan Wu, (D), MIT, 1984, Ys
Associate Professor:
 Jeremy K. Hourigan, (D), Stanford, 2003, Gt

Research Geophysicist:
    Xiao-bi Xie, (D), Chinese Acad of Sci, 1988, Ys
    Xixi Zhao, (D), California (Santa Cruz), 1987, Ym
Emeritus:
    Erik Asphaug, (D), Arizona, 1993, Xy
    J. Casey Moore, (D), Princeton, 1971, Gc

Earth & Planetary Sciences Dept (B,M,D) ● (2015)
1156 High Street
Earth & Marine Sciences Bldg, Rm A232
Santa Cruz, CA 95064
    p. (831) 459-4089
    qwilliams@pmc.ucsc.edu
    http://www.eps.ucsc.edu
    f: https://www.facebook.com/UcscEPS
    t: @EpsUcsc
    Enrollment (2013): B: 180 (80) M: 7 (4) D: 53 (9)
Distinguished Professor, Department Chair:
    Quentin Williams, (D), California (Berkeley), 1988, Gy
Distinguished Professor:
    Gary B. Griggs, (D), Oregon State, 1968, On
    Thorne Lay, (D), Caltech, 1983, Ys
Professor:
    Emily Brodsky, (D), Caltech, 2000, Ys
    Patrick Y. Chuang, (D), Caltech, 1999, Oa
    Andrew T. Fisher, (D), Miami, 1989, Hw
    Elise Knittle, (D), California (Berkeley), 1988, Gy
    Paul L. Koch, (D), Michigan, 1989, Pv
    Susan Y. Schwartz, (D), Michigan, 1988, Ys
    Eli A. Silver, (D), California (San Diego), 1969, Yr
    Slawek Tulaczyk, (D), Caltech, 1998, Gl
    James C. Zachos, (D), Rhode Island, 1988, Cm
Associate Professor:
    Matthew E. Clapham, (D), S California, 2006, Pe
    Jeremy Hourigan, (D), Stanford, 2002, Cc
Assistant Professor:
    Terrence Blackburn, (D), MIT, 2012, Cc
    Noah J. Finnegan, (D), Washington, 2007, Gm
    Ian Garrick-Bethell, (D), MIT, 2009, Xy
    Xi Zhang, (D), CalTech, 2013, OaXy
Senior Lecturer:
    Hilde Schwartz, (D), California (Santa Cruz), 1983, Pv
Emeritus:
    Erik Asphaug, (D), Arizona, 1993, Xg
    Kenneth L. Cameron, (D), Virginia Tech, 1971, Gx
    Robert S. Coe, (D), California (Berkeley), 1966, Ym
    Robert E. Garrison, (D), Princeton, 1964, Gs
    James B. Gill, (D), Australian National, 1972, Gi
    Gary A. Glatzmaier, (D), Colorado, 1980, Xy
    Leo F. Laporte, (D), Columbia, 1960, Pg
    Karen C. McNally, (D), California (Berkeley), 1976, Ys
    J. Casey Moore, (D), Princeton, 1971, Gc
    Lisa C. Sloan, (D), Penn State, 1990, Pe
    Othmar T. Tobisch, (D), London (UK), 1963, Gc
    Gerald E. Weber, (D), California (Santa Cruz), 1980, Ng
Graduate Program Advisor:
    Jennifer M. Fish, (B), California (Santa Cruz), On
Department Manager:
    Judy Van Leuven, On

Inst of Geophysics & Planetary Physics (2010)
1156 High Street
Earth & Marine Sciences Building, Room A234
Santa Cruz, CA 95064
    p. (831) 459-4089
    tgoebel@ucsc.edu
    http://igpp.ucsc.edu
    Enrollment: No data reported since 1999
Director:
    Ana Christina Ravelo, (D), OcGe

University of San Diego
Dept of Marine Science & Environmental Studies (B,M) (2014)
Alcala Park
San Diego, CA 92110
    p. (619) 260-4795
    boum@sandiego.edu

http://www.sandiego.edu/mars_envi/
    Enrollment: No data reported since 1999
Chair:
    Michel A. Boudrias, (D), California (San Diego), 1992, Ob
Professor:
    Hugh I. Ellis, (D), Florida, 1976, Ob
Associate Professor:
    Ronald S. Kaufmann, (D), California (San Diego), 1992, Ob
    Anne A. Sturz, (D), California (San Diego), 1991, Cm
Assistant Professor:
    Richard Gonzalez, (D), Penn State, On
    Sarah Gray, (D), California (Santa Cruz), On
Adjunct Professor:
    Ann B. Bowles, (D), California (San Diego), On
    Joseph R. Jehl, (D), Michigan, 1967, Ob
    Donald B. Kent, (M), San Diego State, 1980, Ob
    Brent S. Stewart, (D), California (Los Angeles), 1988, Ob
    Pam Yochem, (D), California (Davis), 1992, On
Cooperating Faculty:
    Gerald N. Estberg, (D), Cornell, 1966, Ow
    Mary Sue Lowery, (D), California (San Diego), 1987, Ob
    LeeAnn Otto, (D), British Columbia, 1981, On
    Marie Simovich, (D), California (Riverside), 1985, On

University of Southern California
Dept of Earth Sciences (B,M,D) ● (2015)
3651 Trousdale Parkway ,ZHS117
Los Angeles, CA 90089-0740
    p. (213) 740-6106
    waite@usc.edu
    http://www.usc.edu/dept/earth
    Administrative Assistant: Vardui Ter-Simonian
    Administrative Assistant: Cynthia Waite
    Enrollment (2010): B: 26 (0) M: 2 (0) D: 48 (0)
Chair:
    William M. Berelson, (D), S California, 1986, Cm
Research Professor:
    David A. Okaya, (D), Stanford, 1985, Ys
Professor:
    Jan Amend, (D), California (Berkeley), 1995, Cm
    Thorsten W. Becker, (D), Harvard, 2002, Ys
    Yehuda Ben-Zion, (D), S California, 1990, Ys
    David J. Bottjer, (D), Indiana, 1978, Pe
    Frank A. Corsetti, (D), California (Santa Barbara), 1998, Gs
    Gregory A. Davis, (D), California (Berkeley), 1961, Gc
    James F. Dolan, (D), California (Santa Cruz), 1988, Gt
    Douglas E. Hammond, (D), Columbia, 1975, Cm
    Thomas H. Jordan, (D), Caltech, 1972, Ys
    Steven P. Lund, (D), Minnesota, 1981, Ym
    James Moffett, (D), Miami, 1986, Oc
    Kenneth Nealson, (D), Chicago, 1969, Py
    Scott R. Paterson, (D), California (Santa Cruz), 1986, Gc
    John Platt, (D), California (Santa Barbara), 1973, Gc
    Charles G. Sammis, (D), Caltech, 1971, Yg
    Sergio Sanudo, (D), California (Santa Cruz), 1993, Py
    Lowell D. Stott, (D), Rhode Island, 1989, Pm
Research Associate Professor:
    Yong-Gang Li, (D), S California, 1988, Ys
    Ellen S. Platzman, (D), ETH, 1990
Assistant Professor:
    Julien Emile-Geay, (D), Columbia, 2006, Oc
    Sarah Feakins, (D), Columbia, 2006, Oc
    Meghan Miller, (D), Australian National, 2006, Gt
    Josh West, (D), Cambridge, 2005, Cg
Emeritus:
    Robert G. Douglas, (D), California (Los Angeles), 1966, Pe
    Alfred G. Fischer, (D), Columbia, 1950, Gs
    Thomas L. Henyey, (D), Caltech, 1968, Yg
    Teh-Lung Ku, (D), Columbia, 1966, Cg
    Bernard W. Pipkin, (D), Arizona, 1964, Ng
    Ta-liang Teng, (D), Caltech, 1966, Ys

University of the Pacific
Dept of Geological & Environmental Sciences (B) (2015)
3601 Pacific Avenue
Stockton, CA 95211

p. (209) 946-2482
lrademacher@pacific.edu
http://pacific.edu/EES
Enrollment (2014): B: 41 (12)
Chair:
Laura K. Rademacher, (D), California (Santa Barbara), 2002, ClHyOs
Professor:
Eugene F. Pearson, (D), Wyoming, 1972, GsPgOg
Associate Professor:
Kurtis C. Burmeister, (D), Illinois, 2005, GctEg
Lydia K. Fox, (D), California (Santa Barbara), 1989, GizOe
Emeritus:
Roger T. Barnett, (D), California (Berkeley), 1973, Oy
J. Curtis Kramer, (D), California (Davis), 1976, Gg

Ventura College

Dept of Geology (2015)
4667 Telegraph Road
Ventura, CA 93003
p. (805) 289-6000
spalladino@vcccd.edu
Chair:
Luke D. Hall, (M), W Kentucky, 1975, Oy
Assistant Professor:
Steve D. Palladino, (M), California (Santa Barbara), 1994, Oi
Instructor:
William Budke, (M), California Polytech, 2001, Os

Victor Valley College

Victor Valley College (2014)
18422 Bear Valley Road
Victorville, CA 92395
p. (415) 506-0234
carol.delong@vvc.edu
http://www.vvc.edu/

West Valley College

Dept of Geology (A) (2014)
14000 Fruitvale Avenue
Saratoga, CA 95070-5698
p. (408) 741-2437
robert_lopez@westvalley.edu
Instructor:
Harry Shade, (M), Miami (Ohio), 1959, Gg
Emeritus:
Theodore C. Herman, (M), Michigan, 1961, Oe

Whittier College

Environmental Science Program (B) (2011)
Whittier, CA 90608
p. (562) 907-4220
cswift@whittier.edu
http://www.whittier.edu/Academics/EnvironmentalSciences/
Enrollment (1999): B: 23 (3)
Chair:
Cheryl Swift
Visiting Professor:
Andrew H. Wulff, (D), Massachusetts, 1998, Gi
Emeritus:
William B. Wadsworth, (D), Northwestern, 1966, Gi

Colorado

Adams State University

Biology and Earth Sciences (B) O (2014)
208 Edgemont Blvd
Suite 3060
Alamosa, CO 81101
p. (719) 587-7256
babrink@adams.edu
http://www.adams.edu/academics/earthscience
f: https://www.facebook.com/groups/231799753584196/
Enrollment (2014): B: 34 (7)

Chair:
Benita A. Brink, (D), Marquette, 1989
Professor:
Robert G. Benson, (D), Colorado Mines, 1997, Gg
Associate Professor:
Jared M. Beeton, (D), Kansas, 2007, OySd

Aims Community College

Dept of Sciences (A) (2013)
5401 West 20th Street
Greeley, CO 80634
p. (970) 339-6637
jim.stone@aims.edu
http://www.aims.edu/academics/sciences/index.php
Instructor:
Jim Stone, Og

Arapahoe Community College

Geology Program (A) (2015)
5900 South Santa Fe Drive
Littleton, CO 80120
p. (303) 797-5831
henry.weigel@arapahoe.edu
http://www.arapahoe.edu/departments-and-programs/a-z-offerings/geology
Program Chair:
Henry Weigel

Colorado College

Geology Dept (B) (2015)
14 E Cache La Poudre
Colorado Springs, CO 80903
p. (719) 389-6621
geology@coloradocollege.edu
http://www.coloradocollege.edu/academics/dept/geology
f: https://www.facebook.com/geodept.coloradocollege
Enrollment (2015): B: 30 (22)
Professor:
Eric M. Leonard, (D), Colorado, 1981, Gl
Paul M. Myrow, (D), Memorial, 1987, Gs
Jeffrey B. Noblett, (D), Stanford, 1980, Gx
Christine S. Siddoway, (D), California (Santa Barbara), 1993, Gc
Department Chair:
Henry C. Fricke, (D), Michigan, 1997, Cs
Associate Professor:
Megan L. Anderson, (D), Arizona, 2005, YgGt
Technical Director:
Stephen G. Weaver, (D), Colorado Mines, 1988, Gx

Colorado Mesa University

Dept of Physical & Environmental Sciences (A,B) O (2016)
1100 North Avenue
Grand Junction, CO 81501-3122
p. (970) 248-1993
rwalker@coloradomesa.edu
http://www.coloradomesa.edu/geosciences/
Enrollment (2015): A: 21 (3) B: 83 (13)
Professor:
Andres Aslan, (D), Colorado, 1994, Gm
Rex D. Cole, (D), Utah, 1975, Gs
Verner C. Johnson, (D), Tennessee, 1975, Yg
Richard F. Livaccari, (D), New Mexico, 1994, Gc
Gigi Richard, (D), Colorado State, 2001, Hsg
Lecturer:
Harold W. Hase, (M), Michigan Tech, 1973, Em
Lawrence Jones, (D), Gs
Adjunct Professor:
William C. Hood, (D), Montana, 1964, Gg
Julia McHugh, (D), Iowa, 2012, Pgv
Dave Wolny, (B), Mesa State, 1992, Ys
Emeritus:
James B. Johnson, (D), Colorado, 1979, Gl
Jack E. Roadifer, (D), Arizona, 1966, Gx

Colorado Mountain College

Geology Div (A) (2004)
3000 County Road 114
Glenwood Springs, CO 81601
  p. (303) 945-7481 x263
Professor:
  Garrett E. Zabel, (M), Houston, 1977, Gg

Colorado School of Mines

Dept of Chemistry & Geochemistry (B,M,D) (2015)
1012 14th Street, CO 204
Golden, CO 80401
  p. (303) 273-3610
  chemistry@mines.edu
  http://chemistry.mines.edu/
  f: https://www.facebook.com/csmchemistry/
  Enrollment (2015): M: 2 (0) D: 7 (0)
Head:
  David T. Wu, (D), California (Berkeley), 1991, On
Professor:
  Mark E. Eberhart, (D), MIT, 1983, Om
  Mark Jensen, (D), Florida State, 1994
  Daniel M. Knauss, (D), Virginia Tech, 1994
  James Ranville, (D), Colorado Mines, Ca
  Ryan M. Richards, (D), Michigan State, 2000
  Bettina Voelker, (D), Swiss Fed Inst Tech, 1994, Ca
  Kim R. Williams, (D), Michigan State, 1986, Ca
Associate Professor:
  Stephen G. Boyes, (D), New South Wales (Australia), 2000
  Renee L. Falconer, (D), South Carolina, 1994
  Matthew C. Posewitz, (D), Dartmouth, 1995
  Mark R. Seger, (D), Colorado State
  Alan Sellinger, (D), Michigan, 1997
  Angela C. Sower, (D), New Mexico
Assistant Professor:
  Jenifer C. Braley, (D), Washington State, 2010
  Allison Caster, (D), California (Berkeley), 2010
  Svitlana Pylypenko, (D), New Mexico
  Brian G. Trewyn, (D), Iowa State, 2006
  Shubham Vyas, (D), Ohio State
  Yongan Yang, (D), Chinese Acad of Sci, 1999
Emeritus:
  Scott W. Cowley, (D), S Illinois, 1975
  Dean W. Dickerhoof, (D), Illinois, 1961
  Donald L. Macalady, (D), Wisconsin, 1969, Cl
  Patrick MacCarthy, (D), Cincinnati, 1975, Co
  Craig Simmons, (D), SUNY (Stony Brook), 1976, Cp
  Kent J. Voorhees, (D), Utah State, 1970, Co
  Thomas R. Wildeman, (D), Wisconsin, 1967, Ct

Dept of Geology & Geological Engineering (B,M,D) ● (2016)
1516 Illinois Street
Golden, CO 80401-1887
  p. (303) 273-3800
  psanti@mines.edu
  http://geology.mines.edu/
  Enrollment (2015): B: 131 (36) M: 121 (44) D: 54 (10)
Head:
  Paul M. Santi, (D), Colorado Mines, 1995, Ng
Professor:
  Wendy J. Harrison, (D), Manchester, 1979, Cl
  Murray W. Hitzman, (D), Stanford, 1983, Em
  Reed M. Maxwell, (D), California (Berkeley), 1998, Hs
  Stephen A. Sonnenberg, (D), Colorado Mines, 1981, Go
  Richard F. Wendlandt, (D), Penn State, 1978, Gx
  Lesli Wood, (D), Colorado State, 1992, Go
Associate Professor:
  David A. Benson, (D), Nevada (Reno), 1998, Hq
  Thomas Monecke, (D), Germany, 2003, Em
  Piret Plink-Bjorklund, (D), Goteborg, 1998, Gs
  Kamini Singha, (D), Stanford, 2005, Hw
  Bruce D. Trudgill, (D), Imperial Coll (UK), 1989, Gc
  Wei (Wendy) Zhou, (D), Missouri (Rolla), 2001, Or
Assistant Professor:
  Alex Gysi, (D), Iceland, 2011, Cg
  Yvette D. Kuiper, (D), New Brunswick, 2003, Gc

Alexis Navarre-Sitchler, (D), Penn State, 2008, Ca
Gabriel Walton, (D), Queens, 2014, NgrYg
Lecturer:
  Christian V. Shorey, (D), Iowa, 2002, Gg
Emeritus:
  L. Graham Closs, (D), Queen's, 1973, Ce
  John B. Curtis, (D), Ohio State, 1989, Go
  L. Trowbridge Grose, (D), Stanford, 1955, Gt
  John D. Haun, (D), Wyoming, 1953, Go
  Jerry D. Higgins, (D), Missouri (Rolla), 1980, Ng
  Gregory S. Holden, (D), Wyoming, 1978, Gx
  Richard W. Hutchinson, (D), Wisconsin, 1954, Em
  Keenan Lee, (D), Stanford, 1969, Or
  Eileen P. Poeter, (D), Washington State, 1980, Ng
  Samuel B. Romberger, (D), Penn State, 1968, Em
  A. Keith Turner, (D), Purdue, 1969, Ng
  John E. Warme, (D), California (Los Angeles), 1966, Pi
  Robert J. Weimer, (D), Stanford, 1953, Gr

Dept of Geophysics (B,M,D) (2010)
1500 Illinois Street
Golden, CO 80401
  p. (303) 273-3450
  mszobody@mines.edu
  http://geophysics.mines.edu/
  Enrollment (2009): B: 69 (0) M: 26 (0) D: 25 (0)
Professor:
  Michael L. Batzle, (D), MIT, 1978, Yg
  Thomas L. Davis, (D), Colorado Mines, 1974, Ye
  Dave Hale, (D), Stanford, 1997, Ye
  Gary R. Olhoeft, (D), Toronto, 1975, Yg
  Roel Snieder, (D), Utrecht (Neth), 1987, Ye
  Ilya D. Tsvankin, (D), Moscow State, 1982, Ye
Senior Scientist:
  Warren Hamilton, (D), California (Los Angeles), 1951, Ys
  Misac Nabighian, (D), Columbia, 1967, Nm
Associate Research Professor:
  Robert D. Benson, (M), Colorado Mines, 1984, Ye
Associate Professor:
  Yaoguo Li, (D), British Columbia, 1992, Yv
Assistant Professor:
  Paul Sava, (D), Stanford, 2005, Ye
Emeritus:
  Kenneth L. Larner, (D), MIT, 1970, Ye
Research Professor:
  Norman Bleistein, (D), Courant Inst, 1965, Yg

Dept of Mining Engineering (B,M,D) ● (2016)
1600 Illinois
Golden, CO 80401
  p. (303) 273-3700
  csmmining@mines.edu
  http://mining.mines.edu/
  Enrollment (2015): B: 100 (41) M: 18 (18) D: 14 (6)
Head:
  Priscilla Nelson, (D), Cornell, 1983, Nm
Research Professor:
  Karl Zipf, (D), Penn State, 1988, Nm
Professor:
  Kadri Dagdelen, (D), Colorado Mines, 1985, Nm
  M. Ugur Ozbay, (D), Witwatersrand, 1988, Nr
Associate Professor:
  Mark Kuchta, (D), Lulea Univ of Tech, 1990, Nm
  Hugh Miller, (D), Colorado Mines, 1996, Nm
  Masami Nakagawa, (D), Cornell, 1988, Oe
Assistant Professor:
  Elizabeth Holley, (D), Colorado Mines, 2012, Eg
  Rennie Kaunda, (D), W Michigan, 2007, Nm
  Eunhye Kim, (D), Penn State, 2010, Nm
Research Assistant Professor:
  Vilem Petr, (D), Colorado Mines, 2000, Nm
Manager of Earth Mechanics Institute:
  Brian Asbury, Nr
Research Associate:
  Jürgen Brune, (D), Technische Univ Clausthal, 1994, Nm

Colorado State University
Dept of Atmospheric Science (M,D) (2012)
1371 Campus Delivery
Fort Collins, CO 80523-1371
Fort Collins, CO 80523-1371
    p. (970) 491-8360
    info@atmos.colostate.edu
    http://www.atmos.colostate.edu
    Enrollment (2013): M: 39 (19) D: 49 (6)
Head:
    Jeffrey L. Collett, Jr., (D), Caltech, 1989, Oa
Professor:
    Richard H. Johnson, (D), Washington, 1975, Oa
    Sonia M. Kreidenweis, (D), Caltech, 1989, Oa
    David A. Randall, (D), California (Los Angeles), 1976, Oa
    Steven A. Rutledge, (D), Washington, 1983, Oa
    Wayne H. Schubert, (D), California (Los Angeles), 1973, Oa
    Thomas H. Vonder Haar, (D), Wisconsin, 1968, Oa
Associate Professor:
    A.Scott Denning, (D), Colorado State, 1994, Oa
    Christian D. Kummerow, (D), Minnesota, 1987, Yr
    Eric Maloney, (D), Washington, 2000, Oa
Assistant Professor:
    Thomas Birner, (D), Muenchen, 2003, Oa
    Colette Heald, (D), Oa
    Takamitsu Ito, (D), Cambridge, 2005, Oa
    David W. J. Thompson, (D), Washington, 2000, Yr
    Sue van den Heever, (D), Colorado State, 2001, Oa

Dept of Geosciences (B,M,D) O (2015)
1482 Campus Delivery
Fort Collins, CO 80523-1482
    p. (970) 491-5661
    WCNR_GEO_Info@mail.colostate.edu
    http://warnercnr.colostate.edu/departments/geosciences
    Administrative Assistant: Sharon Gale
    Enrollment (2015): B: 164 (36) M: 43 (11) D: 32 (1)
Head:
    Richard Aster, (D), Scripps, Ys
Professor:
    Judith L. Hannah, (D), California (Davis), 1980, GiCc
    Dennis L. Harry, (D), Texas (Dallas), 1989, Yg
    Ellen E. Wohl, (D), Arizona, 1988, Gm
Senior Scientist:
    Holly J. Stein, (D), North Carolina, 1985, EmCc
Associate Professor:
    Sven O. Egenhoff, (D), Tech (Berlin), 2000, Gs
    Jerry F. Magloughlin, (D), Minnesota, 1993, Gpz
    Sara L. Rathburn, (D), Colorado State, 2001, Ggm
    John R. Ridley, (D), Edinburgh, 1982, Eg
    Michael J. Ronayne, (D), Stanford, 2008, Hwq
    William E. Sanford, (D), Cornell, 1992, Hw
    Derek L. Schutt, (D), Oregon, 2000, Ysg
    Sally J. Sutton, (D), Cincinnati, 1987, GdCl
Assistant Professor:
    John Singleton, (D), Texas, 2011, Gc
    Lisa Stright, (D), Stanford, 2011, Go
Research Associate:
    James R. Chappell, (B), Colorado State, 2000, Ge
    Svetoslav Georgiev, (D), ETH (Switzerland), 2008, CcGo
    Ronald J. Karpilo, Jr, (M), Denver, 2004, Oy
    Richard Markey, (M), N Illinois, 1990, Cca
    Stephanie O'Meara, (M), Colorado State, 1997, Gc
    Trista L. Thornberry-Ehrlich, (M), Colorado State, 2001, Gg
    Gang Yang, (D), Sci & Tech (China), 2005, Cc
    Aaron Zimmerman, (M), Colorado State, 2006, Cc
Emeritus:
    Eric A. Erslev, (D), Harvard, 1981, Gc
    Frank G. Ethridge, (D), Texas A&M, 1970, Gs
Academic Success Coordinator:
    Jill Putman, (M), Georgia, 2009

Community College of Aurora
Dept of Science (1999)
16000 East Centretech Parkway
Aurora, CO 80011

    p. (303) 361-7398
    jim.weedin@ccaurora.edu
    http://www.ccaurora.edu

Denver Museum of Nature & Science
Dept of Earth Sciences (2015)
2001 Colorado Boulevard
Denver, CO 80205-5798
    p. (303) 370-6000
    Carla.Bradmon@dmns.org
    http://www.dmns.org
Director of Earth and Space Sciences Branch, Department Chair of
Earth Sciences, Curator of Paleobotany:
    Ian Miller, (D), Yale, 2007, PbGg
Tim and Kathryn Ryan Curator of Geology:
    James W. Hagadorn, (D), S California, 1998, GgsPg
Curator of Vertebrate Paleontology:
    Tyler Lyson, (D), Yale, 2012, Pv
    Joseph Sertich, (D), Stony Brook, 2011, Pv
Collections Manager:
    Logan D. Ivy, (D), Colorado, 1993, Pv
Chief Preparator:
    Mike Getty, (M), Calgary, Pv

Fort Lewis College
Dept of Geosciences (B) (2013)
1000 Rim Drive
Durango, CO 81301
    p. (970) 247-7278
    gonzales_d@fortlewis.edu
    http://geo.fortlewis.edu
    Enrollment (2012): B: 120 (22)
Chair:
    David A. Gonzales, (D), Kansas, 1997, Gx
Professor:
    James D. Collier, (D), Colorado Mines, 1982, Cg
    Gary Gianniny, (D), Wisconsin, 1995, Gs
    Kimberly Hannula, (D), Stanford, 1993, Gc
    Ray Kenny, (D), Arizona State, 1991, Gm
Associate Professor:
    Scott White, (D), Utah, 2001, Oy
Instructor:
    Lauren Heerschap, (M), Colorado, GgEgGt
Adjunct Professor:
    Charles Burnham, (D), MIT, 1961, Gz
    Mary L. Gillam, (D), Colorado, 1998, Gm
Laboratory Director:
    Andrea J. Kirkpatrick,

Front Range Community College - Larimer
Natural Sciences (A) (2014)
4616 S. Shields Street
Fort Collins, CO 80526
    p. (970) 204-8607
    stephanie.irwin@frontrange.edu
    http://www.frontrange.edu/Academics/Academic-Depart-
    ments/Larimer-Campus/Natural-Applied-Environment-
    Science/
Instructor:
    Andy Caldwell, (M), N Colorado, 1999, Gg
    Mike Smith, (M), N Colorado, 1998, GgOe

Front Range Community College - Westminster
Science (A) (2015)
3645 West 112th Avenue
Westminster, CO 80031
    p. (303) 404-5279
    Fran.Goszdak@frontrange.edu
    http://www.frontrange.edu/programs-and-courses/
    academic-departments/westminster-campus-departments/
    westminster-science

Metropolitan State College of Denver
Earth & Atmospheric Sciences Dept (B) (2014)
P.O. Box 173362, Campus Box 22

Colorado

Denver, CO 80217-3362
p. (303) 556-3143
cronoblj@mscd.edu
Administrative Assistant: Diane Hollenbeck
Enrollment: No data reported since 1999
Chair:
James M. Cronoble, (D), Colorado Mines, 1977, Gg
Ken Engelbrecht
Professor:
John R. Kilcoyne, (D), Washington, 1973, Oy
Anthony A. Rockwood, (M), Colorado State, 1976, Ow
Roberta A. Smilnak, (D), Clark, 1973, Og
Associate Professor:
Thomas J. Corona, (M), Colorado State, 1978, Ow
Assistant Professor:
Robert E. Leitz, (M), California (Berkeley), 1974, Gz
Rafael Moreno, (D), Colorado State, 1992, Og
Emeritus:
James MacLachlan, (D), Princeton, Gg
H. Dixon Smith, (D), Minnesota, 1960, Og

Northeastern Junior College
Math, Science, and Health (1999)
100 College Avenue
Sterling, CO 80751
p. (970) 521-6753
david.coles@njc.edu
http://njc.edu

Red Rocks Community College
Geology Program, Science Dept (A) (2015)
13300 West Sixth Avenue
Campus Box 20
Lakewood, CO 80228
p. (303) 914-6290
eleanor.camann@rrcc.edu
http://rrcc.edu/geology/
Associate Professor:
Eleanor J. Camann, (D), North Carolina, 2005, OneGs

United States Air Force Academy
Dept of Economics & Geosciences (B) (2014)
HQ USAFA/DFEG
2354 Fairchild Drive, Suite 6K110
USAF Academy, CO 80840-5701
p. (719) 333-3080
matthew.tracy@usafa.edu
http://www.usafa.edu/df/dfeg/?catname=dfeg
Enrollment (2013): B: 90 (27)
Professor:
Terry W. Haverluk, (D), Minnesota, 1993, Og
Associate Professor:
Steven J. Gordon, (D), Arizona State, 1999, Gm
Thomas Koehler, (D), Wisconsin, Oa
Lt Col :
Matthew Tracy, (D), Arizona State, 2008, On
Assistant Professor:
Glen Gibson, (D), Virginia Tech, 2012, Ori
Brett Machovina, (D), Denver, 2010, Oir
Evan Palmer, (D), Arizona State, 2014, Oig
Sarah Robinson, (D), Arizona State, GgOi
Instructor:
Scott Dubsky, (M), North Dakota, 2006, OyGm
Related Staff:
Danny Portillo, (B), Oi

University of Colorado 📄
Dept of Geography (B,M,D) (2010)
Campus Box 260
Boulder, CO 80309-0260
p. (303) 492-8312
Suzanne.Anderson@colorado.edu
Administrative Assistant: Marcia Signer
Enrollment (2010): B: 213 (67) M: 32 (10) D: 51 (6)

Chair:
Susan W. Beatty, (D), Cornell, 1981, So
Professor:
Roger G. Barry, (D), Southampton, 1965, Oa
T. Nelson Caine, (D), Australian National, 1966, Gm
Konrad Steffem, (D), ETH (Switzerland), 1983, Or
Thomas T. Veblen, (D), California (Berkeley), 1975, Og
Mark W. Williams, (D), California (Santa Barbara), 1990, Og
Associate Professor:
John Pitlick, (D), Colorado State, 1988, Gm
Assistant Professor:
Suzanne Anderson, (D), California (Berkeley), 1995, Gm
Geology Librarian:
Suzanne Larsen, (M), Denver, 1973, On

Dept of Geological Sciences (B,M,D) (2015)
Campus Box 399
Boulder, CO 80309-0399
p. (303) 492-8141
shemin.ge@Colorado.edu
http://www.colorado.edu/geolsci/
Administrative Assistant: Carmen Juszczyk
Enrollment (2014): B: 248 (29) M: 13 (7) D: 45 (10)
Chair:
Shemin Ge, (D), Johns Hopkins, 1990, Hw
Associate Dean:
Mary J. Kraus, (D), Colorado, 1983, GsSa
Professor:
Robert Anderson, (D), Washington, 1986, Gm
David A. Budd, (D), Texas, 1984, Gd
G. Lang Farmer, (D), California (Los Angeles), 1983, Cg
Bruce M. Jakosky, (D), Caltech, 1982, Xg
Craig H. Jones, (D), MIT, 1987, Ys
Gifford H. Miller, (D), Colorado, 1975, Cc
Stephen J. Mojzsis, (D), California (San Diego), 1997, Xc
Peter Molnar, (D), Columbia, 1970, Gt
Karl J. Mueller, (D), Wyoming, 1992, Gc
Anne F. Sheehan, (D), MIT, 1991, Ys
Joseph R. Smyth, (D), Chicago, 1970, Gz
Charles R. Stern, (D), Chicago, 1973, Gi
James P. Syvitski, (D), British Columbia, 1978, Gs
Eric E. Tilton, (D), California (Santa Cruz), 1998, Hw
Greg E. Tucker, (D), Penn State, 1996, Gm
Paul Weimer, (D), Texas, 1989, Go
James W. C. White, (D), Columbia, 1983, Cs
Associate Professor:
Karen Chin, (D), California (Santa Barbara), 1996, Po
Jaelyn J. Eberle, (D), Wyoming, 1996, Pv
Brian M. Hynek, (D), Washington, 2003, Xg
Thomas M. Marchitto, (D), MIT, 1999, Oc
Dena M. Smith, (D), Arizona, 2000, Pg
Alexis Templeton, (D), Stanford, 2002, ClGe
Assistant Professor:
Rebecca Flowers, (D), MIT, 2005, CgcGt
Kevin H. Mahan, (D), Massachusetts, 2005, Gpc
Julio C. Sepúlveda, (D), Bremen, 2008, Co
Instructor:
Lon Abbott, (D), California (Santa Cruz), 1993, Gg
Emeritus:
John T. Andrews, (D), Nottingham (UK), 1965, Gl
William W. Atkinson, Jr., (D), Harvard, 1973, Em
Roger Bilham, (D), Cambridge, 1970, YsGt
Peter W. Birkeland, (D), Stanford, 1961, Sd
William C. Bradley, (D), Stanford, 1956, Gm
Don L. Eicher, (D), Yale, 1958, Pm
Alexander Goetz, (D), Caltech, 1967, Or
Edwin E. Larson, (D), Colorado, 1965, Ym
James L. Munoz, (D), Johns Hopkins, 1966, Cp
Peter Robinson, (D), Yale, 1960, Pv
Donald D. Runnells, (D), Harvard, 1964, Cl
Hartmut A. Spetzler, (D), Caltech, 1969, Ys
Theodore R. Walker, (D), Wisconsin, 1952, Gd

Univ of Colorado Museum (2014)
Campus Box 265
Boulder, CO 80309-265
p. (303) 492-6165

31

linda.cordell@colorado.edu
http://cumuseum.colorado.edu/
Assistant Professor:
  Karen Chin, (D), California (Santa Barbara), 1996, Po
  Jaelyn J. Eberle, (D), Wyoming, 1996, Pv
  Dena M. Smith, (D), Arizona, 2000, Po
Adjunct Curator:
  Kenneth Carpenter, Pv
  Mary Dawson, Pv
  Trihn Dzanh, Pv
  Emmett Evanoff, Pi
  Jeff Indeck, Pv
  Jonathan Marcot, Pv
  Greg McDonald, Pv
  Karen Sears, Pv
Emeritus:
  Judith A. Harris, (D), Cambridge, 1972, Pv
  Peter Robinson, (D), Yale, 1960, Pv
Museum Associate:
  Emily Bray, Pg
  Frank Fisher, Pg
  Pat Monaco, Pg
  Steve Wallace, Pg
Collection Manager:
  Amy P. Moe-Hoffman, (M), Colorado, 2002, Pg
  Tonia Superchi-Culver, (M), SD Mines, 2001, Pg
Associate Curator, Micropaleontology:
  Donald Eicher, (D), Yale, 1958, Pm
Associate Curator, Fossil Primates:
  Herbert Covert, Pv

University of Colorado, Denver
Dept of Geography, & Environmental Science (2015)
CB 172
P.O. Box 173364
Denver, CO 80217-3364
  p. (303) 556-2276
  sue.eddleman@ucdenver.edu
  Enrollment: No data reported since 1999
Associate Professor:
  John W. Wyckoff, (D), Utah, 1980, Oy
Emeritus:
  Wesley E. LeMasurier, (D), Stanford, 1965, Gv
  Martin G. Lockley, (D), Birmingham (UK), 1977, Pi

University of Denver
Dept of Geography and the Environment (B,M,D) (2015)
2050 E. Iliff Avenue
Boettcher Center West, Room 120
Denver, CO 80208
  p. (303) 871-2654
  agoetz@du.edu
  http://www.du.edu/geography
  f: https://www.facebook.com/DUGeography/
  Enrollment (2015): B: 175 (53) M: 69 (26) D: 12 (2)
Chair:
  Andrew R. Goetz, (D), Ohio State, 1987, Og
Director, Graduate Program:
  Matthew Taylor, (D), Arizona State, 2003, Og
Professor:
  Paul C. Sutton, (D), California (Santa Barbara), 1999, Oi
Director, Undergraduate Program:
  Donald G. Sullivan, (D), California (Berkeley), 1988, Og
Director, Environmental Science:
  Michael W. Kerwin, (D), Colorado, 2000, Gg
Associate Professor:
  Eric Boschmann, (D), Ohio State, 2008
  Michael Daniels, (D), Wisconsin, 2002
  Michael J. Keables, (D), Wisconsin, 1986, Oa
  Rebecca Powell, (D), California (Santa Barbara), 2006
Assistant Professor:
  Jing Li, (D), George Mason, 2012
Adjunct Professor:
  Joseph Berry, (D), Colorado State, 1976
  Andrea Gelfuso, (D), Denver, 1992
  Michelle Moran-Taylor, (D), Arizona State, 2003

Martha A. Narey, (D), Denver, 1999, Og
Sean Tierney, (D), Denver, 2009
Emeritus:
  David Longbrake, (D), Iowa, 1972
  Terrence J. Toy, (D), Denver, 1973, Gm

University of Northern Colorado
Earth and Atmospheric Sciences (B,M) (2015)
Campus Box 100
Greeley, CO 80639
  p. (970) 351-2647
  william.hoyt@unco.edu
  http://esci.unco.edu
  Administrative Assistant: Vicki Ouellette
  Enrollment (2015): B: 60 (12) M: 12 (1)
Director, Mathematics & Science Teaching Inst.:
  Steve Anderson, (D), Arizona, 1990, GvgOe
Chair:
  William H. Hoyt, (D), Delaware, 1982, OgGsOe
Associate Professor:
  Graham Baird, (D), Minnesota, 2006, GcgGz
  Joe T. Elkins, (D), Georgia, 2002, OeGgCl
  Emmett Evanoff, (D), Colorado, 1990, GrPgGs
  Lucinda Shellito, (D), California (Santa Cruz), 2004, OaPeOw
Assistant Professor:
  Wendilyn Flynn, (D), Illinois, 2012, Owa
  David G. Lerach, (D), Colorado State, 2012, Owa
Lecturer:
  Sarah M. Hirner, (M), Colorado, 2013, Gg
  Carolyn D. Lambert, (M), Arizona, 2003, Hw
  Amy Nicholl, (M), N Colorado, 2004, GgOge
  Andrea Smith, (M), Illinois, 2010, Owa
  Byron Straw, (M), N Colorado, 2010, GglOg
Adjunct Professor:
  Todd A. Dallegge, (D), Alaska (Fairbanks), 2002, GosGr
  Walter A. Lyons, (D), Chicago, 1970, Oaw
Emeritus:
  Richard D. Dietz, (D), Colorado, 1965, Xg
  Kenneth D. Hopkins, (D), Washington, 1976, Gm
  William D. Nesse, (D), Colorado, 1977, Gxz
  K. Lee Shropshire, (D), Colorado, 1974, Pg

Western State Colorado University
Dept of Geology (B) O (2015)
Gunnison, CO 81231
  p. (303) 943-2015
  astork@western.edu
  http://www.western.edu/geology
  Enrollment (2015): B: 98 (15)
Professor:
  Robert P. Fillmore, (D), Kansas, 1994, Gs
  Allen L. Stork, (D), California (Santa Cruz), 1984, Giv
Associate Professor:
  David W. Marchetti, (D), Utah, 2006, GmCl
Rady Chair:
  Bradford R. Burton, (D), Wyoming, 1997, GocGt
Moncrief Chair:
  Elizabeth S. Petrie, (D), Utah State, 2014, GcoYe
Lecturer:
  Holly Brunkal, (D), Colorado Mines, 2015, NgGm
Adjunct Professor:
  James Coogan, (D), Wyoming, 1992, Gc

Connecticut

Central Connecticut State University
Dept of Physics & Earth Sciences (B,M) (2014)
1615 Stanley Street
New Britain, CT 06050-4010
  p. (860) 832-2930
  antar@CCSU.EDU
  http://www.physics.ccsu.edu/
  Department Secretary: Sandra O'Day
  Enrollment: No data reported since 1999
Chair:
  Ali A. Antar, (D), Connecticut, On

Professor:

Sandra Burns, (D), Connecticut, 1972, Oe

Steven B. Newman, (D), SUNY (Albany), Oa

Associate Professor:

Marsha Bednarski, (D), Connecticut, 1997, Oe

Mark Evans, (D), Pittsburgh, 1989, GciGz

Kristine Larsen, (D), Connecticut, 1988, Xy

Jennifer L. Piatex, (D), Pittsburgh, XgOr

Michael Wizevich, (D), Virginia Tech

Emeritus:

Charles W. Dimmick, (D), Tulane, 1969, Ge

Related Staff:

R. Craig Robinson, (B), Millersville, 1971, Xy

Eastern Connecticut State University

Environmental Earth Science Dept (B) ● (2015)

83 Windham Street

Willimantic, CT 06226

p. (860) 465-4317

drzewieckip@easternct.edu

http://www1.easternct.edu/environmentalearthscience/

f: https://www.facebook.com/groups/181927638678890/

Enrollment (2010): B: 102 (22)

Chair:

Peter A. Drzewiecki, (D), Wisconsin, 1996, GrsGd

Professor:

Catherine A. Carlson, (D), Michigan State, 1994, Hwg

William D. Cunningham, (D), Texas (Austin), 1993, GtcGp

James A. Hyatt, Queens, 1993, Gml

Associate Professor:

Paul Torcellini, (D), Purdue, 1993, On

Assistant Professor:

Meredith Metcalf, (D), Connecticut, 2013, OirHw

Stephen Nathan , (D), Massachusetts (Amherst), 2005, PmEo

Bryan Oakley, (D), Rhode Island, 2012, OnGml

Adjunct Professor:

Susan Bruening, (M), Eastern Connecticut State, 1988, Og

Heath Carlson, (M), Eastern Connecticut State, 2013, Og

Lynn-Ann DeLima, (M), S Connecticut State, 2000, Og

Vishnu R. Khade, (D), Cincinnati, 1987, Og

Emile Levasseur, (M), Sacred Heart, 1992, Og

Bruce Morton, (M), Connecticut, 1983, Og

James Motyka, (M), Eastern Connecticut State, 1987, Og

Julie Sandeen, (M), Connecticut, 1991

Wesley Winterbottom, (M), Connecticut, 1988, Og

Emeritus:

Sherman M. Clebnik, (D), Massachusetts, 1975, Gl

Fred Loxsom, (D), Dartmouth, 1969, On

Henry I. Snider, (D), New Mexico, 1966, Ge

Roy R. Wilson, (D), Oregon State, 1984, Oi

Middlesex Community College

Div of Science, Allied Health and Engineering (A) (2013)

100 Training Hill Road

Middletown, CT 06457

p. (860) 343-5779

MBusa@mxcc.commnet.edu

http://www.mxcc.commnet.edu/Content/Environmental_Science_1.asp

Professor:

Mark Busa, (D), Connecticut, OgEgYg

Assistant Professor:

Christine Witkowski, (M), Connecticut, Og

Naugatuck Valley Community College

Science, Technology, Engineering, and Mathematics (STEM) (1999)

750 Chase Parkway

Waterbury, CT 06708

p. (203) 596-8690

cdonaldson@nv.edu

http://www.nvcc.commnet.edu

Norwalk Community College

Sciences Deptartment (2014)

188 Richards Avenue

Norwalk, CT 06854

p. (203) 857-7275

mbarber@ncc.commnet.edu

http://www.ncc.commnet.edu/dept/science/

Quinebaug Valley Community College

Dept of Environmental Science (1999)

742 Upper Maple Street

Danielson, CT 06239

p. (860) 412-7230

mvesligaj@gvcc.commnet.edu

http://www.qvcc.commnet.edu

Southern Connecticut State University

Dept of Earth Sciences (B) O (2015)

501 Crescent Street

New Haven, CT 06515

p. (203) 392-5835

flemingt1@southernct.edu

http://www.southernct.edu/earthscience/

Enrollment (2014): B: 46 (7)

Professor:

Cynthia R. Coron, (D), Toronto, 1982, Eg

Thomas H. Fleming, (D), Ohio State, 1995, GiCgc

Associate Professor:

James W. Fullmer, (D), MIT, 1979, Ow

Assistant Professor:

Michael Knell, (D), Montana State, 2012, PvGg

Instructor:

Christopher Balsley, (M), Wesleyan, 1972, Gg

Daniel Coburn, (M), C Connecticut State, 2003, Oe

Jennifer Cooper, (M), Missouri (Columbia), 2006, Ggi

Yolanda Lee-Gorishti, (M), Connecticut, 2006, GaOe

Julie Rumrill, (M), Vermont, 2009, GgeGl

Emeritus:

John W. Drobnyk, (D), Rutgers, 1962, Ghs

Robert Radulski, (D), Rhode Island, Og

William Tolley, (M), Syracuse, Gg

University of Connecticut

Center for Integrative Geosciences (B,M,D) (2014)

354 Mansfield Road

U-1045

Storrs, CT 06269-1045

p. (860) 486-4432

geology@uconn.edu

http://www.geosciences.uconn.edu

Enrollment (2012): B: 31 (0) M: 10 (0) D: 7 (0)

Program Director:

Pieter Visscher, (D), Groningen, 1991, Co

Professor:

Vernon F. Cormier, (D), Columbia, 1976, Ys

William F. Fitzgerald, (D), MIT/WHOI, 1970, Oc

Gary A. Robbins, (D), Texas A&M, 1983, Hw

Robert M. Thorson, (D), Washington, 1970, Gm

Associate Professor:

Timothy Byrne, (D), California (Santa Cruz), 1981, Gc

Jean M. Crespi, (D), Colorado, 1985, Gc

Lanbo Liu, (D), Stanford, 1993, Yg

Assistant Professor:

Andrew M. Bush, (D), Harvard, 2005, Pg

Christophe Dupraz, (D), Fribourg, 1999, Py

Michael Hren, (D), Stanford, 2007, CslCo

William Ouimet, (D), MIT, 2007, GmOy

Emeritus:

Larry Frankel, (D), Nebraska, 1956, Pm

Alfred J. Frueh, (D), MIT, 1949, Gz

Norman H. Gray, (D), McGill, 1971, Gx

Raymond Joesten, (D), Caltech, 1970, Gp

Homer C. Liese, (D), Utah, 1962, Ct

Anthony R. Philpotts, (D), Cambridge, 1963, Gi

Dept of Marine Sciences (B,M,D) (2015)

1080 Shennecossett Road

Groton, CT 06340

p. (860) 405-9152
marinesciences@uconn.edu
http://www.marinesciences.uconn.edu/
Enrollment (2011): B: 47 (11) M: 7 (1) D: 31 (3)
Head:
James Edson, (D), Penn State, 1989, Op
Professor:
Ann Bucklin, (D), California (Berkeley), 1980, Ob
Hans G. Dam, (D), SUNY (Stony Brook), 1989, Ob
Senjie Lin, (D), SUNY (Stony Brook), 1995, Ob
Robert Mason, (D), Connecticut, 1991, Oc
George B. McManus, (D), SUNY (Stony Brook), 1986, Ob
James O'Donnell, (D), Delaware, 1986, Op
Sandra Shumway, (D), Coll of North Wales, 1976, Ob
Pieter T. Visscher, (D), Groningen, 1991, Co
J. Evan Ward, (D), Delaware, 1989, Ob
Associate Professor:
Peter Auster, (D), National (Ireland), 2000, Ob
Timothy Byrne, (D), California (Santa Cruz), 1981, Ou
Heidi Dierssen, (D), California, 2000, Op
David Lund, (D), MIT/WHOI, 2006, Oc
Annelie Skoog, (D), Göteborg (Sweden), Oc
Craig Tobias, (D), William & Mary, 1999, Oc
Penny Vlahos, (D), Massachusetts, Oc
Michael Whitney, (D), Delaware, 2003, Op
Huan Zhang, (D), Tokyo Fisheries, 1995, Ob
Assistant Professor:
Hannes Baumann, (D), Hamburg, 2006, Ob
Zofia Baumann, (D), Stony Brook, 2011, Oc
Melanie Fewings, (D), MIT/WHOI, 2007, Op
Julie Granger, (D), British Columbia, 2006, Oc
Kelly Lombardo, (D), Stony Brook, 2011, Op
Jamie Vaudrey, (D), Connecticut, 2007, Ob
Emeritus:
Walter F. Bohlen, (D), MIT/WHOI, 1969, Op
William F. Fitzgerald, (D), MIT/WHOI, 1970, Oc
Edward C. Monahan, (D), MIT, 1966, Oa

University of New Haven
Dept of Biology & Environmental Sciences (B,M) (2015)
300 Boston Post Rd
West Haven, CT 06516
p. (203) 932-7101
rldavis@newhaven.edu
http://www.newhaven.edu
Enrollment (2014): B: 39 (10) M: 23 (8)
Undergraduate Director:
R. Laurence Davis, (D), Rochester, 1980, GemHg
Graduate Director:
Roman N. Zajac, (D), Connecticut, 1985, On
Provost and Senior Vice President of Academic Affairs:
Daniel J. May, (D), California (Santa Barbara), GtxGe
Associate Professor:
Carmela Cuomo, (D), Yale, CmmGu
John Kelly, (D), California (Davis), Obn
Assistant Professor:
Amy L. Carlile, (D), Washington, Obn
Lecturer:
Jean-Paul Simjouw, (D), Old Dominion, 2004, OcCma
Practitioner-in-Residence:
Paul Bartholemew, (D), British Columbia, GeOiGz

Wesleyan University
Dept of Earth & Environmental Sciences (B,M) (2016)
265 Church Street
Room 455
Middletown, CT 06459-0139
p. (860) 685-2244
vharris@wesleyan.edu
http://www.wesleyan.edu/ees
Administrative Assistant: Virginia M.. Harris
Enrollment (2015): B: 42 (24) M: 5 (4)
Chair:
Martha S. Gilmore, (D), Brown, 1997, XgGmOr
Professor:
Barry Chernoff, (D), Michigan, 1983, Ge

Suzanne B. O'Connell, (D), Columbia, 1986, GsuGe
Peter C. Patton, (D), Texas, 1976, Gm
Dana Royer, (D), Yale, 2002, PeoPb
Johan C. Varekamp, (D), Utrecht (Neth), 1979, CgGzv
Associate Professor:
Timothy C.W. Ku, (D), Michigan, 2001, Cl
Phillip G. Resor, (D), Stanford, 2003, Gct
Assistant Professor:
James P. Greenwood, (D), Brown, 1997, Xc
Emeritus:
Jelle Z. De Boer, (D), Utrecht (Neth), 1963, YmGta
James T. Gutmann, (D), Stanford, 1972, Gv
Facilities Manager:
Joel LaBella, (B), S Connecticut, 1987, On

Yale University
Dept of Geology & Geophysics (B,D) (2014)
210 Whitney Avenue
P.O. Box 208109
New Haven, CT 06520-8109
p. (203) 432-3114
rebecca.pocock@yale.edu
http://earth.yale.edu
Enrollment (2009): B: 13 (7) D: 55 (5)
Professor:
Jay J. Ague, (D), California (Berkeley), 1987, Gx
David Bercovici, (D), California (Los Angeles), 1989, Yg
Robert A. Berner, (D), Harvard, 1962, Cl
Ruth E. Blake, (D), Michigan, 1997, Cg
Mark T. Brandon, (D), Washington, 1984, Gc
Derek E G Briggs, (D), Cambridge, 1976, Yg
David A D Evans, (D), Caltech, 1998, Ym
Alexey V. Fedorov, (D), Scripps, 1997, Op
Jacques Gauthier, (D), California (Berkeley), 1984, Pv
Shun-ichiro Karato, (D), Tokyo, 1977, Gy
Jun Korenaga, (D), MIT, 2000, Yg
Mark Pagani, (D), Penn State, 1998, Pe
Jeffrey J. Park, (D), California (San Diego), 1985, Ys
Danny M. Rye, (D), Minnesota, 1972, Cs
Brian J. Skinner, (D), Harvard, 1955, Cg
Ronald B. Smith, (D), Johns Hopkins, 1975, Oa
George Veronis, (D), Brown, 1954, Op
Elisabeth S. Vrba, (D), Cape Town, 1974, Pv
John S. Wettlaufer, (D), Washington, 1991, Yg
Senior Research Scientist:
Edward W. Bolton, (D), California (Los Angeles), 1985, Gq
Ellen Thomas, (D), Utrecht (Neth), 1979, Pm
Associate Professor:
Hagit P. Affek, (D), Weizmann Inst, 2003, Cg
Assistant Professor:
William Boos, (D), MIT, 2008
Kanani K.M. Lee, (D), California (Berkeley), 2003, Gy
Maureen D. Long, (D), MIT, 2006, Ys
Trude Storelvmo, (D), Oslo, 2006
Mary-Louise Timmermans, (D), Cambridge, 2000, Oc
Zhengrong Wang, (D), Caltech, 2005, Cg
Adjunct Professor:
Leo W. Buss, (D), Johns Hopkins, 1979, Po
Thomas E. Graedel, (D), Michigan, 1969, Cl
Emeritus:
Elizabeth K. Berner, (D), Radcliffe, 1959, Cl
Robert B. Gordon, (D), Yale, 1955, Nr
Research Affiliate:
William C. Graustein, (D), Yale, 1981, Cl
Related Staff:
Laurent Bonneau, (M), Connecticut, 1997, Oa
James O. Eckert, (D), Texas A&M, 1988, Gp
Francis J. Robinson, (D), Hong Kong Sci & Tech, 1999, Gg
H. Catherine W. Skinner, (D), Adelaide, 1959, Gz

Peabody Museum of Natural History (2014)
PO Box 208118
170 Whitney Avenue
New Haven, CT 06520-8118
p. (203) 432-3752
peabody.director@yale.edu
http://www.peabody.yale.edu/

Curator:
    Jay J. Ague, (D), California (Berkeley), 1987, Gzx
    Derek E. G Briggs, (D), Cambridge, 1976, Pi
    Leo W. Buss, (D), Johns Hopkins, 1979, Pi
    Peter Crane, (D), Reading, 1981, Pbo
    Michael J. Donoghue, (D), Harvard, 1982, Pbo
    Jacques A. Gauthier, (D), California (Berkeley), 1984, Pv
    Andrew Hill, (D), London, 1975, Pve
    Elisabeth S. Vrba, (D), Cape Town, 1974, Pvo
Senior Collections Manager:
    Susan H. Butts, (D), Idaho, 2003, PiGsPe
    Christopher A. Norris, (D), Oxford, 1992, Pv
Collections Manager:
    Shusheng Hu, (D), Florida, 2006, PblGs
    Stefan Nicolescu, (D), Gothenburg, 1998, CtGpz

Delaware

University of Delaware 🗇
Dept of Geological Sciences (B,M,D) ● (2016)
103 Penny Hall
Newark, DE 19716
    p. (302) 831-2569
    smcgeary@udel.edu
    http://www.ceoe.udel.edu/schools-departments/depart-
    ment-of-geological-sciences
    f: https://www.facebook.com/UDCEOE
    t: @udceoe
    Administrative Assistant: Cheryl Doherty
    Enrollment (2015): B: 43 (14) M: 13 (6) D: 12 (3)
Chair:
    Neil Sturchio, (D), Washington Univ (St. Louis), Cl
Professor:
    Ronald E. Martin, (D), California (Berkeley), 1981, Pm
    James E. Pizzuto, (D), Minnesota, 1982, Gm
Associate Professor:
    Clara Chan, (D), California (Berkeley), 2006, PyCmGz
    John A. Madsen, (D), Rhode Island, 1987, Yr
    Susan McGeary, (D), Stanford, 1984, Yg
    Holly Michael, (D), MIT, 2005, Hw
    Michael ONeal, (D), Washington, 2005, Gm
    Arthur C. Trembanis, (D), William & Mary, 2004, On
Assistant Professor:
    Adam F. Wallace, (D), Virginia Tech, 2008, ClGzCg
    Jessica Warren, (D), MIT/WHOI, 2007, GxCpGt
Visiting Professor:
    Ed Kohut, (D), Oregon State, GvxGg
Emeritus:
    Billy P. Glass, (D), Columbia, 1968, Xm
    Robert R. Jordan, (D), Bryn Mawr, 1964, Gr
    John C. Kraft, (D), Minnesota, 1955, Gs
    Peter B. Leavens, (D), Harvard, 1967, Gz
    Allan M. Thompson, (D), Brown, 1968, Gx
    John F. Wehmiller, (D), Columbia, 1971, Cl
Laboratory Director:
    Bill Parnella, (B), Buffalo, 1984, Gg
Cooperating Faculty:
    A. Scott Andres, (M), Lehigh, 1984, Hy
    Katharina Billups, (D), California (Santa Cruz), 1998, Ou
    Shreeram Inamdar, (D), Virginia Tech, 1996, Hg
    Thomas E. McKenna, (D), Texas, 1997, Hy
    Peter P. McLaughlin, Jr., (D), Louisiana State, 1989, Gr
    Kelvin W. Ramsey, (D), Delaware, 1988, Gs
    William S. Schenck, (M), Delaware, 1997, Gg
    Christopher K. Sommerfield, (D), SUNY (Stony Brook), 1997, On
    John H. Talley, (M), Franklin & Marshall, 1974, Eg
    William J. Ullman, (D), Chicago, 1982, Oc

Oceanography Program (M,D) (2014)
700 Pilottown Road
Lewes, DE 19958
    p. (302) 645-4279
    kbillups@udel.edu
    http://www.ocean.udel.edu
    Enrollment (2000): M: 21 (2) D: 16 (5)
Professor:
    Thomas M. Church, (D), California (San Diego), 1970, Cm

Victor Klemas, (D), Braunschweig (Germany), 1965, Or
    George W. Luther, III, (D), Pittsburgh, 1972, Cm
    Jonathan H. Sharp, (D), Dalhousie, 1972, Oc
    William J. Ullman, (D), Chicago, 1982, Cm
    Ferris Webster, (D), MIT, 1961, Op
    Xiao-Hai Yan, (D), SUNY (Stony Brook), 1989, Or
Associate Professor:
    Katharina Billups, (D), California (Santa Cruz), 1998, Pe
    Douglas C. Miller, (D), Washington, 1985, Ob
Associate Scientist:
    Charles H. Culberson, (D), Oregon State, 1972, Oc
    Richard T. Field, (D), Delaware, 1994, Og
Assistant Professor:
    Matthew J. Oliver, (D), Rutgers, 2006, ObrOg
    Christopher K. Sommerfield, (D), SUNY (Stony Brook), 1997, Gs
Adjunct Professor:
    Richard B. Coffin, (D), Delaware, 1986, On
    James Crease, (D), Cambridge, 1951, Op
    Marilyn L. Fogel, (D), Texas, 1977, Oc
    Norden E. Huang, (D), Johns Hopkins, 1967, On
    David E. Krantz, (D), South Carolina, Cs
    Kamlesh Lulla, (D), Indiana State, 1963, Or
    Donald B. Nuzzio, (D), Rutgers, 1982, Oc
    Manmohan Sarin, (D), Gujarat (India), 1984, On
    Alain J. Veron, (D), Paris, 1988, Oc
    John F. Wehmiller, (D), Columbia, Gu
Emeritus:
    Jin Wu, (D), Iowa, 1964, Op

District of Columbia

Carnegie Institution of Washington
Dept of Terrestrial Magnetism (2015)
5241 Broad Branch Road, N.W.
Washington, DC 20015-1305
    p. (202) 478-8820
    jdunlap@carnegiescience.edu
    https://dtm.carnegiescience.edu
Director:
    Richard W. Carlson, (D), California (San Diego), 1980, Cc
Senior Scientist:
    Conel M. O'D Alexander, (D), Essex (UK), 1987, Xc
    Alan P. Boss, (D), California (Santa Barbara), 1979, On
    R. Paul Butler, (D), Maryland, 1993, On
    John E. Chambers, (D), Manchester, 1994, On
    Peter E. Driscoll, (D), Johns Hopkins, 2010, GtYm
    Erik H. Hauri, (D), MIT/WHOI, 1992, Cc
    Larry R. Nittler, (D), Washington (St. Louis), 1996, Xc
    Diana C. Roman, (D), Oregon, 2004, Gv
    Scott S. Sheppard, (D), Hawaii, 2004, Xg
    Steven B. Shirey, (D), SUNY (Stony Brook), 1984, Cc
    Peter E. vanKeken, (D), Utrecht, 1993, GtYsCg
    Lara S. Wagner, (D), Arizona, 2005, YsgGt
    Alycia J. Weinberger, (D), Caltech, 1998, Xg
Emeritus:
    David E. James, (D), Stanford, 1967, YsGtYg
    Alan T. Linde, (D), Queensland, 1972, Ys
    Fouad Tera, (D), Vienna, 1962, Cc
Senior Scientist and former Director on Leave:
    Sean C. Solomon, (D), MIT, 1971, YgsGt
Senior Research Scientist and SIMS Lab Manager:
    Jianhua Wang, (D), Chicago, 1995, Cs
Senior Fellow:
    I. Selwyn Sacks, (D), Witwatersrand, 1961, Ys
Mass Spectrometry Laboratory Manager:
    Timothy D. Mock, (M), Vermont, 1989, Cc
Geochemistry Laboratory Manager:
    Mary F. Horan, (M), SUNY (Stony Brook), 1984, Cc
Fiscal Officer:
    Terry L. Stahl, On
Cooperating Faculty:
    Shaun J. Hardy, (M), SUNY (Buffalo), 1987, On

Geophysical Laboratory (2015)
5251 Broad Branch Road, N.W.
Washington, DC 20015-1305
    p. (202) 478-8900

cody@gl.ciw.edu
http://www.gl.ciw.edu/
Senior Scientist:
    Ronald E. Cohen, (D), Harvard, 1985, Gy
    Yingwei Fei, (D), City Univ of New York, 1989, Cp
    Alexander F. Goncharov, (D), Russian Academy of Sci 1983, Gy
    Robert M. Hazen, (D), Harvard, 1975, Gz
    Russell J. Hemley, (D), Harvard, 1983, Yx
    Ho-kwang Mao, (D), Rochester, 1968, Yx
    Bjorn O. Mysen, (D), Penn State, 1974, Cp
    Douglas Rumble, III, (D), Harvard, 1969, Gp
    Anat Shahar, (D), California (Los Angeles), 2008, Cg
    Andrew Steele, (D), Portsmouth, 1996, Xy
    Timothy A. Strobel, (D), Colorado Mines, 2008, Om
    Viktor V. Struzhkin, (D), Moscow Inst of Physics & Tech, 1991, Gy
Senior Scientist:
    T. Neil Irvine, (D), Caltech, 1959, Gi
Director:
    Wesley T. Huntress, Jr., (D), Stanford, 1968, Xc
Research Scientist:
    Muhetaer Aihaiti, (D), Electrocommunications Tokyo, 1996, Yg
    John Armstrong, (D), Arizona State, Yg
    Reinhard Boehler, (D), Tubingen, 1974, Yg
    Xiaojia Chen, (D), Zhejiang, 1997, Ym
    Dionysis Foustoukos, (D), Minnesota, 2005, Cg
    Stephen Gramsch, (D), Chicago, 1994, Yg
    Jinfu Shu, (M), Wuhan, 1981, Yx
    Maddury Somayazulu, (D), Bombay, 1992, Yx
    Changsheng Zha, (D), Beijing Inst Tech, 1969, YgOm
Director, HPCAT:
    Guoyin Shen, (D), Uppsala, 1994, GzCg
Beamline Scientist, NSLS:
    Zhenxian Liu, (D), Jilian (China), 1990, Gy
Beamline Scientist:
    Paul Chow, (D), Illinois, 1988, Yg
    Yue Meng, (D), Yg
    Changyong Park, (D), Tohoku, 1998, Yg
    Yuming Xiao, (D), California (Davis), 2007, Yg
Associate Director, HPCAT:
    Stanislav Sinogeikin, (D), Yg
Acting Director:
    George D. Cody, (D), Penn State, 1992, Co
Cooperating Faculty:
    Shaun J. Hardy, On

George Washington University
Dept of Geography (B,M) (2011)
619 21st Street, NW
Washington, DC 20052
    p. (202) 994-6185
    mprice@gwu.edu
    Department Secretary: Karin Johnston
Chair:
    Elizabeth Chacko, (D), California (Los Angeles), 1997, Oy
Professor:
    John C. Lowe, (D), Clark, 1969, Og
    Dorn C. McGrath, Jr., (M), Harvard, 1959, Oy
Assistant Professor:
    Doult O. Fuller, (D), Maryland, 1994, Oy
    Marie D. Price, (D), Syracuse, 1990, Oy
Visiting Professor:
    Micheal Brewer, (D), Delaware, 1997, Or
    Thomas Foltltin, (D), Montana, 1980, Oy

National Academy of Sciences/
National Research Council
Board on Earth Sciences and Resources (2015)
The National Academies Keck Center-6th Floor
500 5th Street, NW
Washington, DC 20001
    p. (202) 334-2744
    besr@nas.edu
    http://dels.nas.edu/besr
Director:
    Elizabeth A. Eide, (D), Stanford, 1993, GoEgo

Senior Program Officer:
    Sammantha L. Magsino, (M), Florida Intl, 1993, GvNg
Scholar:
    Anne M. Linn, (D), California (Los Angeles), 1991, Gs

Smithsonian Institution /
National Air & Space Museum
Center for Earth & Planetary Studies (2015)
MRC 315, P.O. Box 37012
6th and Independence Ave., SW
Washington, DC 20013-7012
    p. (202) 633-2470
    campbellb@si.edu
    http://airandspace.si.edu/research/earth-and-planetary/
    Enrollment: No data reported since 1999
Geophysicist:
    Bruce A. Campbell, (D), Hawaii, 1991, Or
Planetary Geologist:
    James R. Zimbelman, (D), Arizona State, 1984, Xg
Geologist:
    Robert A. Craddock, (D), Virginia, 1999, Xg
    John A. Grant, (D), Brown, 1990, Xg
    Rossman P. Irwin, (D), Virginia, 2005
    Thomas R. Watters, (D), George Washington, 1985, Xg
Geographer:
    Andrew K. Johnston, (D), Maryland, 2013, Oy
Geologist:
    Ted A. Maxwell, (D), Utah, 1977, Xg
Program Manager:
    Priscilla L. Strain, (B), Smith, 1974, Or
Photo Librarian:
    Rosemary Aiello

Smithsonian Institution /
National Museum of Natural History
Dept of Mineral Sciences (2015)
NHB MRC 119
10th & Constitution Avenue, NW
PO Box 37012
Washington, DC 20013-7012
    p. (202) 633-1860
    gvp@si.edu
    http://mineralsciences.si.edu/
Chair:
    Timothy J. McCoy, (D), Hawaii, 1994, Xmg
Research Geologist:
    Benjamin Andrews, (D), Texas, 2009, Gv
    Catherine Corrigan, (D), Case Western, 2004, Xmg
    Elizabeth Cottrell, (D), Columbia, 2004, Cp
    Glenn J. MacPherson, (D), Princeton, 1981, XcGi
    Jeffrey E. Post, (D), Arizona State, 1981, Gz
    Cara Santelli, (D), MIT/WHOI, 2007, Py
    Sorena S. Sorensen, (D), California (Los Angeles), 1984, Gp
    Michael A. Wise, (D), Manitoba, 1987, Gz
Museum Specialist (Labs):
    Timothy Gooding, (B), Hampshire Coll, 1990
Museum Specialist (IT):
    Adam Mansur, (M), Maryland, 2008
Museum Specialist (GVP):
    Sally K. Sennert, (M), Pittsburgh, 2003, GvOr
    Edward Venzke, (M), Minnesota (Duluth), 1993, Gv
    Richard Wunderman, (D), Michigan Tech, 1988, Gv
Museum Specialist (Education):
    Adam Blankenbicker, (M), Michigan Tech, 2009, Oe
Geochemist:
    Emma Bullock, (D), Open, 2006, Xm
    Yulia Goreva, (D), Xm
Collection Manager:
    Cathe Brown, (M), Maryland, 1996, Gz
    Russell Feather, (B), George Mason, 1982, Gz
    Leslie Hale, (B), Maryland, 1989, Gg
    Linda Welzenbach, (M), Bowling Green, 1992, Xm
Analytical Laboratories - Manager:
    Timothy Rose, (M), Maryland, 1991, CaGv

Research Collaborator:
  Steve Lynton, (D), Maryland, 2003
Postdoctoral Fellow:
  Andrew Beck, (D), Tennessee, 2011, Xm
  Karen R. Cahill, (D), Tennessee, 2005, Xg
  Dominique Chaput, (D), Oxford, 2011, Py
  Fred Davis, (D), Minnesota, 2012, Gv
  Kathryn Gardner-Vandy, (D), Arizona, 2012, Xm
  Brent Grocholski, (D), California (Berkeley), 2008, Xm
  Marion Le Voyer, (D), Blaise Pascal, 2009, Gz
  Christoph Popp, (D), Bern, 2008, Gv
Contract Geologist:
  Rob Dennen, (M), SUNY (Buffalo), 2011, Gv
  Carter Hearn, (D), Johns Hopkins, 1959, Gi
  Julie Herrick, (M), Michigan Tech, 2011, Gv
  Sheryl Singerling, (M), Tennessee, 2012, Xm
Research Associate:
  Maryjo Brounce, (B), Penn State, 2009
Emeritus:
  Roy S. Clarke, Jr., (D), George Washington, 1976, Xm
  Richard S. Fiske, (D), Johns Hopkins, 1960, Gv
  William G. Melson, (D), Princeton, 1964, GvtGa
Management Support:
  Phyllis McKenzie, On

Dept of Paleobiology (2010)
Dept. of Paleobiology, MRC121
NMNH, Smithsonian Institution
P.O. Box 37012
Washington, DC 20013-7012
  p. (202) 633-1320
  paleodept@si.edu
  http://www.nmnh.si.edu/paleo/
Curator:
  Scott L. Wing, (D), Yale, 1981, Pb
Curator:
  Anna K. Behrensmeyer, (D), Harvard, 1973, Pv
  William A. DiMichele, (D), Illinois, 1979, Pb
  Brian T. Huber, (D), Ohio State, 1988, Pm
  Conrad C. Labandeira, (D), Chicago, 1991, Pi
  Ian G. Macintyre, (D), McGill, 1967, Gs
Curator:
  Martin A. Buzas, (D), Yale, 1963, Pm
  Douglas H. Erwin, (D), California (Santa Barbara), 1985, Pi
  Daniel J. Stanley, (D), Grenoble, 1964, Ou
Curator:
  Matthew T. Carrano, (D), Chicago, 1998, Pv
Curator:
  Gene Hunt, (D), Chicago, 2003, Pm
Geologist:
  Thomas Dutro, (D), Pi
  Bevan French, (D), Xm
  John Pojeta, (D), Cincinnati, 1963, Pi
Curator:
  Alan H. Cheetham, (D), Columbia, 1959, Po
  Robert Emry, (D), Columbia, 1970, Pv
  Clayton E. Ray, (D), Harvard, 1962, Pv
  Thomas R. Waller, (D), Columbia, 1966, Pi
Associate Chair & Collections Manager:
  Jann W. M. Thompson, (B), George Washington, 1970, Pg

Florida

Broward College
Natural Science Dept (A) (2010)
111 East Las Olas Boulevard
Fort Lauderdale, FL 33301
  p. (954) 201-7650
  bmemari@broward.edu
Instructor:
  Xenia Conquy, (M), Florida Atlantic, Gg
  Henri L. Liauw, (M), South Florida, Gg
  William Opperman, (M), Florida, Gg

Broward College, Central Campus
Dept of Physical Sciences (Oceanography & Geology) (A,B)

(2015)
3501 SW Davie Road
Davie, FL 33314
  p. (954) 201-6771
  jmuza@broward.edu
  http://www.broward.edu/academics/programs/Pages/
  science-technology-math-engineering-STEM
  Administrative Assistant: Nicki Pickett
  Enrollment (2005): A: 10 (10)
Chair:
  Valerio Bartolucci, (M), Bologna, Ge
Professor:
  Lewis Fox, (D), Delaware, 1981, Oc
  Jay P. Muza, (D), Florida State, 1996, OuPme
  Laura Precedo, (D), Emory, 1993, Oc
Lab Manager:
  Lynn A. Curtis, (B), Florida Atlantic, 1997, Gg

Chipola College
Dept of Natural Science (A) (2010)
3094 Indian Circle
Mariana, FL 32446
  p. (850) 526-2761
  tidwella@chipola.edu
  http://www.chipola.edu/instruct/science/index.htm
Professor:
  Allan Tidwell, (M), Troy State, Og

Daytona State College
School of Biological and Physical Sciences (A) (2014)
1200 W. International Speedway Blvd.
Daytona Beach, FL 32114
  p. (386)506-3000 x3769
  horikas@daytonastate.edu
  http://www.daytonastate.edu/CampusDirectory/deptInfo.
  jsp?dept=SCI
Instructor:
  Debra W. Woodall, GgOg

Eckerd College
Dept of Geosciences (B) (2013)
4200 54th Avenue South
St. Petersburg, FL 33711
  p. (727) 864-8200
  wetzellr@eckerd.edu
  http://www.eckerd.edu/academics/marinescience/
  Enrollment (2013): B: 8 (3)
Professor:
  Gregg R. Brooks, (D), S Florida, 1986, Gu
  Joel B. Thompson, (D), Syracuse, 1989, Py
  Laura R. Wetzel, (D), Washington (St. Louis), 1997, Yr

Florida Atlantic University
Dept of Geosciences (B,M,D) O (2014)
777 Glades Road
Boca Raton, FL 33431
  p. (561) 297-3250
  croberts@fau.edu
  http://www.geosciences.fau.edu
  Enrollment (2014): B: 129 (35) M: 17 (4) D: 26 (4)
Interim Dean:
  Russell L. Ivy, (D), Florida, 1992, On
Professor:
  Leonard Berry, (D), Bristol, 1969, Og
  Edward J. Petuch, (D), Miami, 1980, Pg
  Zhixiao Xie, (D), SUNY (Buffalo), 2002, Oir
Interim Chair:
  Charles E. Roberts, (D), Penn State, 1991, Or
Assistant Chair:
  Scott H. Markwith, (D), Georgia, 2007, Oy
  David L. Warburton, (D), Chicago, 1978, CgGe
Associate Professor:
  Xavier Comas, (D), Rutgers, 2005, Yg
  Maria Fadiman, (D), Texas, 2003, On
  Anton Oleinik, (D), Purdue, 1998, Pe

Tara L. Root, (D), Wisconsin, 2005, Hg
Associate Scientist:
    Tobin Hindle, (D), Florida Atlantic, 2006, HwOi
Assistant Professor:
    Tiffany M. Roberts Briggs, (D), South Florida, 2012, On
    Caiyun Zhang, (D), Texas (Dallas), 2010, Or
Instructor:
    James Gammack-Clark, (M), Florida Atlantic, 2001, Ori
Emeritus:
    Howard Hanson, (D), Miami, 1979, Oag
    Jorge I. Restrepo, (D), Colorado State, 1987, Hq

Florida Gateway College
Mathematics/Science Div (A,B) (2015)
149 SE College Place
Lake City, FL 32025
    p. (386) 752-1822
    mustapha.kane@fgc.edu
    https://www.fgc.edu/academics/liberal-arts--sciences/math-and-science.aspx
Professor:
    Mustapha Kane, (D), Og
Instructor:
    Avo Oymayan, Og

Florida Institute of Technology
Dept of Marine & Env Systems-Environmental Science Program (B,M,D) (2014)
150 West University Boulevard
Melbourne, FL 32901
    p. (321) 674-8096
    dmes@fit.edu
    http://www.fit.edu/dmes
    Staff Assistant: Carmen Serrano
    Enrollment: No data reported since 1999
Head:
    George A. Maul, (D), Miami, 1974, Op
Chair:
    John G. Windsor, Jr., (D), William & Mary, 1976, Oc
Professor:
    Thomas V. Belanger, (D), Florida, 1979, On
    John H. Trefry, (D), Texas A&M, 1977, Cm
Associate Professor:
    Charles R. Bostater, (D), Delaware, 1990, Op
Assistant Professor:
    Steven Lazarus, (D), Oklahoma, Oa
Adjunct Professor:
    Joseph A. Angelo, (D), Arizona, 1976, Og
    Diane Barile, (M), Florida Inst of Tech, Ou
    Michael F. Helmletter, (D), Old Dominion, Oc
    J. J. Keaffaber, (D), Florida, Oc
    Carlton R. Parks, (M), Oklahoma, 1981, Ow
    D. R. Resio, (D), Virginia, Op
    Ned P. Smith, (D), Wisconsin, 1972, Op

Dept of Marine & Env Systems-Ocean Engineering Program (B,M,D) (2015)
150 West University Boulevard
Melbourne, FL 32901
    p. (321) 674-8096
    dmes@fit.edu
    http://www.fit.edu/dmes
    f: https://www.facebook.com/FloridaTechOceanEngineering/?ref=bookmarks
    Enrollment: No data reported since 1999
Head:
    Stephen L. Wood, (D), Oregon State, 1995, Oo
Professor:
    Ronnal Reichard, (D), Oo
    Geoffry Swain, (D), Southampton, 1981, Oo
Associate Professor:
    Prasanta Sahoo, (D), Oo
    Robert Weaver, (D), Oo

Dept of Marine & Env Systems-Oceanography Program (B,M,D) (2014)

150 West University Boulevard
Melbourne, FL 32901
    p. (321) 674-8096
    jwindsor@marine.fit.edu
    http://www.fit.edu/dmes
    Staff Assistant: Carmen Serrano
    Enrollment: No data reported since 1999
Head:
    George A. Maul, (D), Miami, 1974, Op
Acting Chair:
    John G. Windsor, (D), William & Mary, 1976, Oc
Professor:
    Thomas V. Belanger, (D), Florida, Hw
    Iver W. Duedall, (D), Dalhousie, 1973, Oc
    Geoffrey W.J Swain, (D), Southampton, 1981, Ob
    John H. Trefry, (D), Texas A&M, 1977, Cm
    Gary A. Zarillo, (D), Georgia, 1979, Ou
Associate Professor:
    Charles R. Bostater, (D), Delaware, 1990, Op
    Lee E. Harris, (D), Florida Atlantic, 1995, On
Assistant Professor:
    Elizabeth A. Irlandi, (D), North Carolina, 1993, Ob
    Eric D. Thosteson, (D), Florida, On
Research Associate:
    Simone Metz, (D), Florida Inst of Tech, 1986, Cm
    Chih-Shin Shieh, (D), Florida Inst of Tech, 1988, Oc
    Robert P. Trocine, (M), Florida Inst of Tech, 1979, Cm
Adjunct Professor:
    Diane D. Barile, (M), Florida Inst of Tech, 1975, Ou
    Michael F. Helmstetter, (D), Old Dominion, 1992, Oc
    Ned P. Smith, (D), Wisconsin, 1972, Op
Emeritus:
    Dean R. Norris, (D), Texas A&M, 1969, Ob

Meteorology Program (B,M) (2014)
150 West University Boulevard
Melbourne, FL 32901
    p. (321) 674-8096
    dmes@fit.edu
    http://coe.fit.edu/dmes/
    Enrollment (2014): B: 100 (25) M: 60 (20)
Head:
    George A. Maul, (D), Miami, 1974, Op
Professor:
    Thomas V. Belanger, (D), Florida, Hw
    Joseph R. Dwyer, (D), Chicago, 1994, Oa
    Steven M. Lazarus, (D), Oklahoma, Oa
    John G. Windsor, Jr., (D), William & Mary, Oc
Associate Professor:
    Tom Utley, (D), Florida Inst of Tech, 1996, Ow
Assistant Professor:
    Pallav Ray, (D), Miami, 2009, Oa

Florida International University
Center for the Study of Matter at Extreme Conditions (M,D) (2013)
VH-150
Miami, FL 33199
    p. (305) 348-3030
    saxenas@fiu.edu
    http://cesmec.fiu.edu
    Enrollment (2012): D: 2 (2)
Director:
    Surendra K. Saxena, (D), Uppsala, 1967, Gy
Associate Professor:
    Jiuhua Chen, (D), Japan Grad Univ Adv Studies, 1994, Gyz

Dept of Earth & Environment (B,M,D) (2014)
Miami, FL 33199
    p. (305) 348-2365
    geology@fiu.edu
    http://www.fiu.edu/orgs/geology
    Enrollment (2007): B: 30 (7) M: 11 (5) D: 20 (5)
Professor:
    Grenville Draper, (D), West Indies, 1979, Gc
    Rosemary Hickey-Vargas, (D), MIT, 1983, Cg
    Jose F. Longoria, (D), Texas (Dallas), 1972, Ps
    Florentin J-M. R. Maurrasse, (D), Columbia, 1973, Ps

Gautam Sen, (D), Texas (Dallas), 1981, Gi
Associate Professor:
William T. Anderson, (D), ETH (Switzerland), 2000, Cs
Laurel S. Collins, (D), Yale, 1988, Po
Michael Gross, (D), Penn State, 1993, Gc
Andrew W. Macfarlane, (D), Harvard, 1989, Em
Dean Whitman, (D), Cornell, 1993, Yg
Assistant Professor:
Rene Price, (D), Miami, 2001, Hw
Michael Sukop, (D), Kentucky, 2001, Hq
Ping Zhu, (D), Miami, 2002, Oa
Distinguished Research Professor:
Hugh E. Willoughby, (D), Miami, 1977, Oa
Lecturer:
Neptune Srimal, (D), Rochester, 1986, Gt
Adjunct Professor:
Jose Antonio Barros, (D), Miami, 1995, Or
Michael Wacker, (M), Florida Intl, Gg
Research Scientist:
Edward Robinson, (D), London, 1969, Pm
Distinguished Research Professor:
Stephen E. Haggerty, (D), London, 1968, Gz
Research Lab Manager:
Diane H. Pirie, (B), Florida Intl, 1980, Gg
Cooperating Faculty:
Gabriel Guitierrez-Alonso, (D), Oviedo, 1992, Gc

Florida State University 🗂

Dept of Earth, Ocean, and Atmospheric Science (B,M,D) (2005)
108 Carraway Building
Tallahassee, FL 32306-4100
p. (850) 644-5861
odom@gly.fsu.edu
http://www.gly.fsu.edu
Program Assistant: Tami S. Karl
Enrollment: No data reported since 1999
Chair:
LeRoy A. Odom, (D), North Carolina, 1971, Cg
Professor:
James B. Cowart, (D), Florida State, 1974, Cc
Lynn M. Dudley, (D), Washington State, 1983, Sc
Philip Froelich, (D), Rhode Island, 1979, Og
Bill X. Hu, (D), Purdue, 1996, Hw
James F. Tull, (D), Rice, 1973, Gc
Sherwood W. Wise, Jr, (D), Illinois, 1970, Pm
Associate Professor:
Anthony J. Arnold, (D), Harvard, 1983, Pm
Joseph F. Donoghue, (D), S California, 1981, Gu
Munir Humayan, (D), Chicago, 1994, XcCg
Stephen A. Kish, (D), North Carolina, 1983, Eg
William C. Parker, (D), Chicago, 1980, Pi
Vincent J. Salters, (D), MIT, 1989, Cg
Associate Scientist:
Yang Wang, (D), Utah, 1992, Cg
Assistant Professor:
Jennifer Georgen, (D), MIT/WHOI, 2001, Gu
Ming Ye, (D), Arizona, 2002, Hg
Emeritus:
George W. Devore, (D), Chicago, 1952, Gp
John K. Osmond, (D), Wisconsin, 1954, Cc
Paul C. Ragland, (D), Rice, 1962, Ca

Hillsborough Community College

Earth Science (A) (2011)
2112 North 15th St.
Tampa, FL 33605
p. (813) 253-7647
jolney2@hccfl.edu
http://www.hccfl.edu
Enrollment: No data reported since 1999
Instructor:
Marianne O. Caldwell, Og
James W. Fatherree, Og
Thomas M. Klee, (M), S Illinois, 1986, Gg
Jessica L. Olney, (D), N Illinois, 2006, OgGg
Matthew J. Werhner, (M), Adelphi, 1974, Gg

James F. Wysong, Jr., (M), S Florida, 1989, Ow
Adjunct Professor:
Joseph D. Brod, Og
Kyle M. Champion, Og
James R. Douthat, Jr., Og
Van E. Hayes, Og
James E. MacNeil, Og
Brian W. Marlowe, Og
Matthew P. Olney, (D), N Illinois, 2006, OgGg
Leonard T. Roth, Og
Norman E. Soash, Og
Poetchanaporn Tongdee, Og
Kevan A. Van Cleave, Og
William V. Wills, Og

Jacksonville University

Dept of Biology & Marine Science (B) (2010)
2800 University Boulevard North
Jacksonville, FL 32211
p. (904) 256-7302
web@ju.edu
Enrollment (2001): B: 39 (6)
Professor:
Ted T. Allen, (D), Florida, Og
Lee Ann J. Clements, (D), South Carolina, 1988, Ob
Kenneth D. Hoover, (D), New Mexico State, Og
Assistant Professor:
Karen E. Jackson, (D), Florida, Og
Daniel McCarthy, (D), Kings College, Og
Curtis Small, (D), North Carolina, Og

Miami Dade College (Kendall Campus)

Chemistry-Physics & Earth Science Dept (A) (2014)
11011 S.W. 104 St.
Room 3291
Miami, FL 33176
p. (305) 237-2492
sorbon@mdc.edu
http://www.mdc.edu/kendall/chmphy/
Enrollment (2010): A: 100 (0)
Assistant Professor:
Michael G. McGauley, (M), Miami, 2003, Owp
Emeritus:
John M. Steger, (D), Naval Postgrad Sch, 1997, OgwOg

Miami-Dade Community College (Wolfson Campus)

Dept of Natural Sciences, Health & Wellness (A) (2010)
300 NE 2nd Avenue
Miami, FL 33132
p. (305) 237-3658
sjoseph4@mdc.edu
Administrative Assistant: Ileana Baldizon
Enrollment (2000): A: 4 (0)
Professor:
Tony Barros, (D), Miami, 1995, Og
Michael Kaldor, (M), SUNY (Buffalo), 1969, Gg

Palm Beach Community College

Environmental Science (1999)
MS #56 4200 Congress Avenue
Lake Worth, FL 33467
p. (561) 868-3475
milesj@palmbeachstate.edu
http://www.pbcc.edu

Pensacola Junior College

Dept of Physical Sciences (2014)
1000 Collge Blvd
Pensacola, FL 32504-8998
p. (850) 484-1189
estout@pensacolastate.edu
Administrative Assistant: Kimberly LaFlamme
District Academic Department Head:
Edwin Stout

Professor:
  Lois Dixon
  Brooke L. Towery, (M), Ball State, 1969, Gg
  Wayne Wooten
  Joseph Zayas
Assistant Professor:
  Thor Garber
  Timothy Hathaway
Instructor:
  Bobby Roberson
  Michael Stumpe
Emeritus:
  Thomas Gee
Science Lab Specialist:
  Darrell Kelly

Saint Petersburg College, Clearwater
Dept of Natural Sciences (A) (2013)
2465 Drew Street
Clearwater, FL 33765
  p. (727) 791-2534
  williams.john@spcollege.edu
  http://www.spcollege.edu/clw/science/
Professor:
  Carl Opper, (M), Florida, 1982, Hw
Adjunct Professor:
  Neva Duncan Tabb, Ow
  Hilary Flower, (M), California (Santa Barbara), Gg
  Joseph C. Gould, (D), Nova, Gg
  Heather L. Judkins, (D), South Florida, Og

Sante Fe Community College
Physical Science Dept (1999)
3000 NW 83rd Street
Gainesville, FL 32606
  p. (505) 428-1307
  david.johnson@sfcc.edu
  http://www.sfcollege.edu

University of Florida 🗎
Dept of Geological Sciences (B,M,D) O (2015)
P.O. Box 112120
241 Williamson Hall
1843 Stadium Road
Gainesville, FL 32611-2120
  p. (352) 392-2231
  info@geology.ufl.edu
  http://web.geology.ufl.edu/
  Enrollment (2015): B: 100 (20) M: 16 (6) D: 30 (1)
Chair:
  David A. Foster, (D), SUNY (Albany), 1989, GtCc
Professor:
  Thomas S. Bianchi, (D), Maryland, 1987, Co
  Mark Brenner, (D), Florida, 1983, Gn
  James E T Channell, (D), Newcastle upon Tyne, 1975, YmGt
  Ellen E. Martin, (D), California (San Diego), 1993, Cl
  Jonathan B. Martin, (D), California (San Diego), 1993, ClHg
  Joseph G. Meert, (D), 1993, YgGt
  Paul A. Mueller, (D), Rice, 1971, Cc
  Michael R. Perfit, (D), Columbia, 1977, Giu
  Elizabeth J. Screaton, (D), Lehigh, 1995, Hg
Associate Professor:
  Peter N. Adams, (D), California (Santa Cruz), 2004, Gm
  Paul J. Ciesielski, (D), Florida State, 1978, Pm
  John M. Jaeger, (D), SUNY (Stony Brook), 1998, Gs
  Raymond Russo, (D), Northwestern, 1990, Yg
  Andrew Zimmerman, (D), William & Mary, 2000, Co
Associate Scientist:
  Kyoungwon Min, (D), California (Berkeley), 2002, Cc
Assistant Professor:
  Andrea Dutton, (D), Michigan, 2003, CgGsPe
  Mark Panning, (D), California (Berkeley), 2004, Ys
Research Associate:
  Ray G. Thomas, (B), Florida, 1990, Og
Lecturer:
  Matthew C. Smith, (D), Gi

Jim Vogl, (D), California (Santa Barbara), 2000, Gct
Emeritus:
  Frank N. Blanchard, (D), Michigan, 1960, Gz
  Guerry H. McClellan, (D), Illinois, 1964, En
  Neil D. Opdyke, (D), Durham (UK), 1958, Ym
  Anthony F. Randazzo, (D), North Carolina, 1968, Gd
  Douglas L. Smith, (D), Minnesota, 1972, Yh
  Daniel P. Spangler, (D), Arizona, 1969, Hw
Laboratory Director:
  Jason H. Curtis, (D), Florida, 1997, Pe
  Ann L. Heatherington, (D), Washington (St. Louis), 1988, Cc
  George D. Kamenov, (D), Florida, 2004, Cg
Geologist:
  Kainian Huang, (D), Acad Sinica, 1986, Ym
Assistant Curator:
  Jonathan Bloch, (D), Michigan, 2001, Pv
Affiliate Faculty:
  Micheal W. Binford, (D), Indiana, 1980, Or
  Joann Mossa, (D), Louisiana State, 1990, Gm
Cooperating Faculty:
  David L. Dilcher, (D), Yale, 1964, Pb
  Douglas S. Jones, (D), Princeton, 1980, Pg
  Steven R. Manchester, (D), Indiana, 1981, Pb
  Bruce J. McFadden, (D), Columbia, 1976, Pv
  Claire L. Schelske, (D), Michigan, 1961, Pe

Florida Museum of Natural History (2014)
PO Box 117800
Gainesville, FL 32611-7800
  p. (352) 846-2000
  bmacfadd@flmnh.ufl.edu
  http://www.flmnh.ufl.edu
  Administrative Assistant: Pam Dennis
Director:
  Douglas S. Jones, (D), Princeton, 1980, Pg
Associate Director:
  Graig D. Shaak, (D), Pittsburgh, 1972, Pe
Associate Curator:
  Bruce J. MacFadden, (D), Columbia, 1976, Pv
  Steven R. Manchester, (D), Indiana, 1981, Pb
  David W. Steadman, (D), Arizona, 1982, Pq
Graduate Research Professor:
  David L. Dilcher, (D), Yale, 1964, Pb
Research Associate:
  Ann S. Cordell, (M), Florida, 1983, Gx
  David M. Jarzen, (D), Toronto, 1973, Pb
  Roger W. Portell, (B), Florida, 1985, Pi
Emeritus:
  Sylvia J. Scudder, (M), Florida, 1993, Pg

Soil & Water Science Dept (B,M,D) (2014)
PO Box 110290
2181 McCarty Hall A
Gainesville, FL 32611-0290
  p. (352) 294-3151
  krr@ufl.edu
  http://soils.ifas.ufl.edu
  Enrollment (2001): B: 34 (6) M: 28 (5) D: 26 (1)
Professor and Center Director:
  Charley Wesley Wood, (D), Os
Chair:
  K Ramesh Reddy, (D), Louisiana State, 1976, Sf
Professor and Center Director:
  Nicholas B. Comerford, (D), SUNY (Syracuse), 1980, Sf
  John E. Rechcigl, (D), Virginia Tech, 1986, So
Professor:
  Teri Balser, (D), Oss
  Mary E. Collins, (D), Iowa State, 1980, Sd
  James H. Graham, Jr., (D), Oregon State, 1980, Sb
  Willie G. Harris, Jr., (D), Virginia Tech, 1984, Sc
  George J. Hochmuth, (D), Wisconsin, 1980, So
  Yuncong Li, (D), Maryland, 1993, ScOs
  Lena Q. Ma, (D), Colorado State, 1991, Sc
  Peter Nkedi-Kizza, (D), California, 1979, Sp
  George A. O'Connor, (D), Colorado State, 1970, Sc
  Thomas A. Obreza, (D), Florida, 1983, So
  Andrew V. Ogram, (D), Tennessee, 1988, Sb

Jerry B. Sartain, (D), North Carolina, 1973, So
Associate Professor:
Sabine Grunwald, (D), Giessen, 1996, OisOr
Zhenli He, (D), Zhejang Ag, 1988, Sc
James W. Jawitz, (D), Florida, 1999, SpHsw
Marc Kramer, (D), Os
S Rao Mylavarapu, (D), Clemson, 1996, Sc
Arnold W. Schumann, (D), Georgia, 1997, So
P. Christopher Wilson, (D), Clemson, 1999, So
Assistant Professor:
Mark W. Clark, (D), Florida, 2000, Sf
Samira H. Daroub, (D), Michigan State, 1994, So
Stefan Gerber, (D), Os
Patrick Inglett, (D), Florida, 2005, Sf
Cheryl Mackowiak, (D), Utah State, 2001, So
Kelly Morgan, (D), So
Maria Silveira, (D), Sao Paulo, 2003, Sc
Max Teplitski, (D), Ohio State, 2002, On
Gurpal Toor, (D), Lincoln, 2002, Sc
Alan Wright, (D), Sc
Research Associate Professor:
Vimala D. Nair, (D), Gottingen, 1978, Sc
Ann C. Wilkie, (D), Univ Coll (Ireland), 1984, Sb
Lecturer:
James Bonczek, (D), OsHsg
Susan Curry, (D), Os
Research Assistant Professor:
Todd Osborne, (D), Sf
John Thomas, (D), Sp
Assistant In:
Mengsheng Gao, (D), On

University of Miami
Dept of Geological Sciences (B,M,D) (2013)
1301 Memorial Drive
43 Cox Science Building
Coral Gables, FL 33124
p. (305) 284-4253
ruthgoodin@miami.edu
http://www.as.miami.edu/geology/
Administrative Assistant: Ruth Goodin
Enrollment (2013): B: 42 (0)
Chair:
Harold R. Wanless, (D), Johns Hopkins, 1971, Gs
Professor:
Larry C. Peterson, (D), Brown, 1984, Gr
Peter Swart
Senior Lecturer:
Teresa A. Hood, (D), Miami, 1991, Gg
Assistant Professor:
James S. Klaus, (D), Illinois, 2005, Gg
Emeritus:
David E. Fisher, (D), Florida, 1958, Cs
John R. Southam, (D), Illinois, 1974, Op
Scientist:
Donald F. McNeill, (D), Miami, 1989, Gg

Div of Marine Geology & Geophysics (M,D) (2013)
RSMAS
4600 Rickenbacker Causeway
Miami, FL 33149-1098
p. (305) 421-4663
mgg@rsmas.miami.edu
http://rsmas.miami.edu/divs/mgg/
Enrollment (2013): M: 2 (0) D: 6 (0)
Professor:
Peter K. Swart, (D), London, 1980, ClPs
Professor:
Falk Amelung, (D), Lous Pasteur, 1996, On
Keir Becker, (D), Scripps, 1981, Yr
Gregor P. Eberli, (D), ETH, 1985, Gr
Christopher G.A. Harrison, (D), 1964, Yr
James Natland, (D), Scripps, 1975, Gi
Larry C. Peterson, (D), Brown, 1984, Gu
Ruth P. Reid, (D), Miami, 1979, Gs
Associate Professor:
Mark Grasmueck, (D), ETH, 1995, Yr

Shimon Wdowinski, (D), Harvard, 1990, Yd
Assistant Professor:
Guochin Lin, (D), Scripps, 2005, Yg
Ali Pourmand, (D), Tulane, 2005, Cga
Emeritus:
Tim Dixon, (D), Scripps, 1979, Or
Robert N. Ginsburg, (D), Chicago, 1953, Gs
Cooperating Faculty:
Patricia L. Blackwelder, (D), South Carolina, 1976, Po

University of South Florida
College of Marine Science (M,D) (2015)
140 7th Avenue South
St. Petersburg, FL 33701
p. (727) 553-1130
Mitchum@usf.edu
http://www.marine.usf.edu
Enrollment (2009): M: 30 (13) D: 50 (6)
Distinguished Research Professor:
Robert H. Byrne, (D), Rhode Island, 1974, Cm
John H. Paul, (D), Miami, 1980, Ob
John J. Walsh, (D), Miami, 1969, Ob
Robert H. Weisberg, (D), Rhode Island, 1975, Op
Professor:
Kent A. Fanning, (D), Rhode Island, 1973, Oc
Luis H. Garcia-Rubio, (D), McMaster, 1981, Oc
Pamela Hallock-Muller, (D), Hawaii, 1977, Pm
Albert C. Hine, (D), South Carolina, 1975, Gs
Gary T. Mitchum, (D), Florida State, 1984, Op
Frank E. Muller-Karger, (D), Maryland, 1988, Or
Joseph J. Torres, (D), California, 1980, Ob
Edward S. Van Vleet, (D), Rhode Island, 1978, Co
Associate Professor:
Paula G. Coble, (D), MIT/WHOI, 1992, Cm
Kendra Lee Daly, (D), Tennessee, 1995, Ob
Boris Galperin, (D), Israel Inst of Tech, 1982, Op
David J. Hollander, (D), Swiss Fed Inst Tech, 1989, Oc
Mark E. Luther, (D), North Carolina, 1982, Op
David F. Naar, (D), Scripps, 1990, Ou
Assistant Professor:
Mya Breitbart, (D), California (San Diego), 2006, Ob
Ernst B. Peebles, (D), South Florida, 1996, Ob
Ashanti J. Pyrtle, (D), Texas A&M, 1999, Oc
Research Associate:
Rick Cole, (B), Florida Inst of Tech, 1983, Op
Dwight A. Dieterle, (M), San Jose, 1979, Ob
Jeff C. Donovan, (B), Florida, 1985, Op
Debra E. Huffman, (D), S Florida, 1994, On
Stanley D. Locker, (D), Rhode Island, 1989, Ou
Wensheng Yao, (D), Miami, 1995, Oc
Research Assistant:
David C. English, (M), Washington, 1983, Op
Adjunct Professor:
Serge Andrefouet, (D), Polynesie Francaise, 1998, Opr
Bruce Barber, (D), Ob
Leonard Ciaccio, (D)
Thomas Cuba, (D), USF, Ob
Christopher D'Elia, (D), Georgia, 1974, Ob
George Denton, (D), Og
Cynthia Heil, (D), USF, Ob
Brian Keller, (D)
John Lisle, (D)
Anne Meylan, (D), Florida, 1984, Ob
Terrence Quinn, (D), Ou
Harunur Rashid, (D)
Eugene Shinn, (B), Miami, 1957, Gg
Randy Wells, (D), California (Santa Cruz), 1986, Ob
Emeritus:
Peter R. Betzer, (D), Rhode Island, 1970, Cm
Norman J. Blake, (D), Rhode Island, 1972, Ob
John C. Briggs, (D), Stanford, 1951, Ob
Kendall L. Carder, (D), Oregon State, 1970, Op
Thomas L. Hopkins, (D), Florida State, 1964, Ob
Harold J. Humm, (D), Duke, 1945, Ob
Gabriel A. Vargo, (D), Rhode Island, 1976, Ob

University of South Florida, Saint Petersburg

Center for Ocean Technology (2014)
140 7th Avenue South, MSL 119
St. Petersburg, FL 33701-5016
    p. (727) 553-1280
    jpatten@marine.usf.edu
    http://cot.marine.usf.edu/
    Administrative Assistant: Antoinette Flournoy
Director:
    Larry C. Langebrake, (M), S Florida, 1990, Oo
Research Assistant:
    David P. Fries, (M), S Florida, 1999, Oo
    Eric A. Kaltenbacher, (M), Dayton, 1996, Oo
    Chad E. Lembke, (B), S Florida, 1995, Oo
    James T. Patten, (B), West Florida, 1981, Oo
    D. Randy Russell, (M), S Florida, 1990, Oo
    Scott A. Samson, (D), Iowa, 1994, Oo
    R. Timothy Short, (D), Tennessee, 1987, Oo
Mechanical Engineer:
    Michael Hall, (B), North Carolina State, 1996, Oo
Field Support Engineer:
    Graham Tilbury, (B), Natal (Durban), 1996, Oo
Business Development Manager:
    Carol S. Steele, (D), Fielding Inst, 2000, On

University of South Florida, Tampa

Dept of Geology (B,M,D) (2014)
SCA 528
4202 East Fowler Avenue
Tampa, FL 33620-5201
    p. (813) 974-2236
    mhaney@chuma1.cas.usf.edu
    Administrative Assistant: Mary Haney
    Enrollment (2003): B: 54 (15) M: 31 (9) D: 11 (2)
Chair:
    Charles B. Connor, (D), Dartmouth, 1987, Gv
Professor:
    Mark T. Stewart, (D), Wisconsin, 1976, Hw
    H. Leonard Vacher, (D), Northwestern, 1971, Hw
Associate Professor:
    Peter J. Harries, (D), Colorado, 1993, Pg
    Jeffrey G. Ryan, (D), Columbia, 1989, Ct
Assistant Professor:
    Sarah E. Kruse, (D), MIT, 1989, Yg
    Thomas Pichler, (D), Ottawa, 1998, Cl
    Mark C. Rains, (D), California (Davis), 2002, Hw
    Ping Wang, (D), S Florida, 1995, Gs
Instructor:
    Thomas C. Juster, (D), S Florida, 1995, Hw
    Eleanour Snow, (D), Brown, 1987, Gz
Emeritus:
    Richard A. Davis, Jr., (D), Illinois, 1964, Gs
Assistant Curator:
    Raymond Denicourt, Gz
Cooperating Faculty:
    Jeffrey Heikoop, Cl
    Lisa Robbins, (D), Miami, 1987, Py
    James E. Sorauf, (D), Kansas, 1962, Pg
    Barbara W. Leyden, (D), Indiana, 1982, Pl
    Robert Morton, (D), West Virginia, 1972, Gs
    Thomas M. Scott, (D), Florida State, Gr
    Sam B. Upchurch, (D), Northwestern, 1970, Hw

University of West Florida

Dept of Earth and Environmental Sciences (B,M) (2015)
11000 University Parkway
Pensacola, FL 32514
    p. (850) 474-3377
    environmental@uwf.edu
    http://uwf.edu/cse/departments/earth-and-environmental-sciences/
    Enrollment (2015): B: 171 (29) M: 14 (15)
Professor:
    Johan Liebens, (D), Michigan State, 1995, So
    Klaus J. Meyer-Arendt, (D), Louisiana State, 1987, On

Chairperson:
    Matthew C. Schwartz, (D), Delaware, 2002, OcCl
Associate Professor:
    Zhiyong Hu, (D), Georgia, 2003, Or
Assistant Professor:
    John D. Morgan, (D), Florida State, 2010, Oi
    Jason Ortegren, (D), North Carolina (Greensboro), 2008, PeOu
    Phillip P. Schmutz, (D), Louisiana State, 2014, Gm
Instructor:
    Chasidy Hobbs, (M), West Florida, 2005, Oy
    Taylor Kirschenfeld, (M), West Florida, 1988, Ob
Adjunct Professor:
    Wilbur G. Hugli, (D), West Florida, 2001, Oa
    Hilde Snoeckx, (D), Michigan, 1995, Ou
Online GIS Program Coordinator:
    Amber Bloechle, (M), West Florida, 2007, Oi
GeoData Center Coordinator:
    Nathan McKinney, (M), West Florida, 2011, Oi

Valencia Community College

Valencia Community College (2014)
P.O. Box 3028
Orlando, FL 32802
    p. (407) 299-5000
    abosley@valenciacollege.edu
    http://www.valenciacc.edu

Georgia

Columbus State University

Dept. of Earth & Space Sciences (B,M) ● (2015)
4225 University Avenue
Columbus, GA 31907-5645
    p. (706) 507-8091
    barineau_clinton@columbusstate.edu
    http://ess.columbusstate.edu/
    f: https://www.facebook.com/pages/Earth-and-Space-Sciences-at-Columbus-State-University-GA/347767372234
    Enrollment (2015): B: 42 (14) M: 6 (4)
Professor:
    William J. Frazier, (D), North Carolina, 1973, GsrGd
    David R. Schwimmer, (D), SUNY (Stony Brook), 1973, Pv
Interim Chair:
    Clinton I. Barineau, (D), Florida State, 2009, GctGx
Emeritus:
    Thomas B. Hanley, (D), Indiana, 1975, Gc

Dalton State Community College

Dept of Natural Sciences (B) (2015)
650 College Drive
Dalton, GA 30720
    p. (706) 272-4440
    jmjohnson@daltonstate.edu
    http://www.daltonstate.edu/natural-sciences/
Associate Professor:
    Jean M. Johnson, (D), Og

East Georgia State College

Science & Mathematics (A,B) (2015)
131 College Circle
Swainsboro, GA 30401
    p. (478) 289-2073
    stracher@ega.edu
    http://faculty.ega.edu/facweb/stracher/stracher.html
    Enrollment (2015): A: 3 (1)
Professor Emeritus:
    Glenn B. Stracher, (D), Nebraska, 1989, GycEc

Emory University

Dept of Environmental Studies (B) (2014)
Mathematics & Science Center
400 Dowman Drive
Atlanta, GA 30322
    p. (404) 727-4216
    jwegner@emory.edu

http://www.envs.emory.edu/
Enrollment (2000): D: 1 (0)
Head:
  Joy Budensiek, (D)
Chair:
  Lance Gunderson, (D), Florida, 1992, Sf
Associate Professor:
  William B. Size, (D), Illinois, 1971, Gi
Assistant Professor:
  Thomas Gillespie, (D), Florida, On
  Tracy Yandle, (D), Indiana, 2001, Ob
Instructor:
  Anne M. Hall, (M), Georgia Tech, 1985, Gz
Senior Lecturer:
  C Woodbridge Hickcox, (D), Rice, 1971, Gg
Campus Env Officer:
  John Wegner, (D), Carleton, 1995, Sf
Lecturer:
  Anthony J. Martin, (D), Georgia, 1991, Pe
Adjunct Professor:
  Pamela J. W. Gore, (D), George Washington, 1983, Gs
Visiting Professor:
  Ellen Spears, (D), Emory, On
Emeritus:
  Howard R. Cramer, (D), Northwestern, 1954, Pg
  Willard H. Grant, (D), Johns Hopkins, 1955, Cg
  Lore Ruttan, (D), California (Davis), 1999, Ob

Fort Valley State University
Cooperative Developmental Energy Program (2014)
Box 5800 FVSU
1005 State University Drive
Fort Valley, GA 31030
  p. (912) 825-6454
  crumblyi@fvsu.edu
  http://www.fvsu.edu/academics/cdep
  Enrollment: No data reported since 1999
Director:
  Isaac J. Crumbly, (D), North Dakota State, 1970, On
Assistant Director:
  Jackie Hodges, (B), Georgia Southern, 1983, On
Associate Professor:
  Aditya Kar, (D), Oklahoma, 1997, Ct

Georgia Highlands College
Div of Science and Physical Education (A,B) (2010)
Main Campus 3175 Hwy 27 South
P.O. Box 1864
Rome, GA 30162
  p. (706) 368-7528
  geology@highlands.edu
  http://www.highlands.edu/site/geology
Associate Professor:
  Billy Morris, Gg
Instructor:
  Tracy Hall, Gg

Georgia Institute of Technology
School of Earth & Atmospheric Sciences (B,M,D) (2014)
311 Ferst Drive
Atlanta, GA 30332-0340
  p. (404) 894-3893
  rita.anderson@eas.gatech.edu
  http://www.eas.gatech.edu
  Enrollment (2011): B: 63 (21) M: 34 (19) D: 76 (13)
Chair:
  Judith A. Curry, (D), Chicago, 1992, OarOn
Professor:
  Gregory L. Huey, (D), Wisconsin, 1992, Oa
  Edward Michael Perdue, (D), Georgia Tech, 1973, Co
  Irina Sokolik, (D), Russian Acad of Sci, 1989, Oar
  Rodney J. Weber, (D), Minnesota, 1995, Oa
  Peter J. Webster, (D), MIT, 1972, Oap
  Paul H. Wine, (D), Florida State, 1974, Oa
Senior Scientist:
  Hai-ru Chang, (D), Oa

Robert Stickel, (D), Rice, 1979, Oa
Viatcheslav Tatarskii, (D), Oa
Hsiang-Jui Wang, (D), Georgia Tech, 1995, Oa
Associate Professor:
  Michael H. Bergin, (D), Carnegie Mellon, 1995, Oa
  Robert X. Black, (D), MIT, 1990, Oa
  Emanuele Di Lorenzo, (D), Scripps, 2003, OpnOn
  Christian Huber, (D), California (Berkeley), 2009
  Ellery D. Ingall, (D), Yale, 1991, Cm
  Takamitsu Ito, (D), MIT, 2005
  Jean Lynch-Stieglitz, (D), Columbia, 1995, PeCmOc
  Athanasios Nenes, (D), Caltech, 2002, Oa
  Marc Stieglitz, (D), Columbia, 1995, Hsg
  Martial Taillefert, (D), Northwestern, 1997, Cmg
  Yuhang Wang, (D), Harvard, 1997, Oa
  James Wray, (D), Cornell, 2010
Assistant Professor:
  Annalisa Bracco, (D), Genova (Italy), 2000, OpnOn
  Kim M. Cobb, (D), Scripps, 2002, PeCsOn
  Yi Deng, (D), Illinois, 2005, OanOn
  Josef Dufek, (D), Washington, 2006, GvOnn
  Andrew V. Newman, (D), Northwestern, 2000, YsOn
  Carol M. Paty, (D), Washington, 2006, YmgOn
  Zhigang Peng, (D), S California, 2004, YsgOn
  Andrew Stack, (D), Wyoming, 2002, Cg
Research Scientist:
  Carlos Hoyos, (D), Georgia Tech, 2008, Oa
  Hyemi Kim, (D), Oa
  Jiping Liu, (D), Columbia, Oa
  Chao Luo, (D), Peking, 1990, Oa
  James C. St. John, (D), Georgia Tech, 1997, Oa
  Henian Zhang, (D), Oa
Adjunct Associate Professor:
  Jay Brandes, (D), Washington, Og
  Carmen Nappo, (D), Georgia Tech, 1989, Oa
  Valerie Thomas, (D), Cornell, 1987, Ou
Adjunct Assistant Professor:
  Karim Sabra, (D), Michigan, 2003, Yg
Adjunct Professor:
  Clark R. Alexander, (D), North Carolina State, 1990, Cl
  Dominic Assimaki, (D)
  Jackson O. Blanton, (D), Oregon State, 1968, Cl
  Thomas D. Christina, (D), Caltech, 1989, Cl
  James Crawford, (D), Georgia Tech, Oa
  Heidi Cullen, (D), Columbia, Ow
  Herman Fritz, (D), ETH, 2002
  Rong Fu, (D)
  Leonid Germanovich, (D), Moscow State Mining (Russia), 1982, NrYg
  Gary Gimmestad, (D), Colorado, 1978, Oa
  Richard Jahnke, (D), Washington, 1976, Cl
  Yongqiang Liu, (D), Ow
  Joseph Montoya, (D), Harvard, 1990, Cm
  Armistead G. Russell, (D), Caltech, 1985, Oa
  Stuart G. Wakeham, (D), Washington, 1976, Co
  Herbert L. Windom, (D), California (San Diego), 1968, Cm

Georgia Perimeter College
Dept of Geology, Newton Campus (A) (2013)
239 Cedar Lane
Covington, GA 30014
  p. (770) 278-1263
  Polly.bouker@gpc.edu
  http://www.gpc.edu/~newsci/
Associate Professor:
  Polly A. Bouker, (M), Georgia, Gg

Dept of Life & Earth Science, Clarkston Campus (A) (2015)
555 North Indian Creek Drive
Clarkston, GA 30021
  p. (678) 891-3754
  Pamela.Gore@gpc.edu
  http://depts.gpc.edu/~gpcsci/
  Enrollment (2007): A: 3 (0)
Professor:
  Pamela J. W. Gore, (D), George Washington, 1983, GsOeGn

Associate Professor:
  E. Lynn Zeigler, (M), Emory, 1989, Gd
Lecturer:
  Stephan Fitzpatrick, (M), Georgia, HwGg
  Robin John McDowell, (D), Kentucky, Geg
Adjunct Professor:
  Debia F. McCulloch, (M), Emory, 1987, Gg

Dept of Life and Earth Science (A) (2015)
Dunwoody Campus
2101 Womack Road
Dunwoody, GA 30338-4497
  p. (770) 274-5050
  http://www.gpc.edu/~dunsci/depthp.htm
  Administrative Assistant: Kristopher Chandler
  Enrollment (2011): A: 4 (0)
Lecturer:
  Rob J. McDowell, (D), Kentucky, 1992, Gts
  Kimberly Schulte, (M), Tulsa, 1997, Ge

Georgia Perimeter College - Decatur
Dept of Science (A) (2015)
3251 Panthersville Road
Decatur, GA 30034-3897
  p. (678) 891-2600
  Pamela.Leggett-Robinson@gpc.edu
  http://www.gpc.edu/~decsci/
Instructor:
  Daniel E. Bulger, (M), NE Illinois, GgOn
Adjunct Professor:
  Chad Hall, Gg

Georgia Perimeter College - Online
Dept of Science (A) (2015)
555 North Indian Creek Drive
Clarkston, GA 30021
  p. (678) 212-7523
  Solomon.Fesseha@gpc.edu
  http://depts.gpc.edu/~olsci/
Assistant Professor:
  Deniz Z. Ballero, (M), Montclair State, Gg
Adjunct Professor:
  Edward Albin, (D), Georgia, Xm

Georgia Perimeter College at Alpharetta Center
Dept of Science (A) (2015)
3705 Brookside Parkway
Alpharetta, GA 30022
  p. (678) 240-6035
  laura.whitlock@gpc.edu
  http://depts.gpc.edu/~alpmsbpe/science.html
Associate Professor:
  Dion C. Stewart, (D), Gg

Georgia Southern University
Applied Coastal Research Laboratory (2015)
10 Ocean Science Circle
Savannah, GA 31411
  p. (912) 598-2329
  clarkalexander@georgiasouthern.edu
  http://cosm.georgiasouthern.edu/icps/acrl/
Director:
  Clark R. Alexander, (D), North Carolina State, 1990, OuGsOn
Assistant Professor:
  Chester M. Jackson, (D), Georgia, 2010, OnGs
Research Associate:
  Michael Robinson, (B), Georgia Southern, 2002, Oin

Dept of Geology and Geography (B) (2014)
68 Georgia Avenue
Building 201
PO Box 8149
Statesboro, GA 30460-8149
  p. (912) 478-5361
  sjunderwood@georgiasouthern.edu

http://cost.georgiasouthern.edu/geo/
  Enrollment (2014): B: 90 (16)
Chair:
  Stephen J. Underwood, (D), Georgia, 1999, Ow
Professor:
  James S. Reichard, (D), Purdue, 1995, Hw
  Fredrick J. Rich, (D), Penn State, 1979, Pl
  Mark R. Welford, (D), Illinois, 1993, Oy
Associate Professor:
  Charles H. Trupe, (D), North Carolina, 1997, Gc
  Wei Tu, (D), Texas A&M, 2004, Oi
  R. Kelly Vance, (D), New Mexico Tech, 1989, Eg
  Robert A. Yarbrough, (D), Georgia, 2006, On
Assistant Professor:
  Christine Hladik, (D)
  Chester W. Jackson, (D), Georgia, 2010, GsmGu
  Jacque L. Kelly, (D), Hawaii, 2012, Cl
  Kathlyn M. Smith, (D), Michigan, 2010, Pv
  John Van Stan, (D), Delaware, 2011, Oy
  Xiaolu Zhou, (D)
Emeritus:
  Gale A. Bishop, (D), Texas, 1971, Pi
  James H. Darrell, (D), Louisiana State, 1973, Pl
  Daniel B. Good, (D), Tennessee, 1973, On
  Dallas D. Rhodes, (D), Syracuse, 1973, Gm

Georgia Southwestern State University
Dept of Geology & Physics (B) (2014)
800 GSW State University Drive
Americus, GA 31709
  p. (229) 931-2353
  Deborah.Standridge@gsw.edu
  http://www.gsw.edu/%7Egeology/
  Administrative Assistant: Debbie Standridge
  Enrollment (2004): B: 15 (2)
Professor:
  Burchard D. Carter, (D), West Virginia, 1981, Ps
  Thomas J. Weiland, (D), North Carolina, 1988, Gi
Associate Professor:
  Samuel T. Peavy, (D), Virginia Tech, 1997, Yg
Assistant Professor:
  Svilen Kostov, (D), CUNY, 1992, On
Emeritus:
  Daniel D. Arden, (D), California (Berkeley), 1961, Ps
  Harland E. Cofer, (D), Illinois, 1957, Gz
  John P. Manker, (D), Rice, 1975, Gs

Georgia State University 🗋
Dept of Geosciences (B,M,D) O (2015)
340 Kell Hall
PO Box 3965
24 Peachtree Center Avenue
Atlanta, GA 30302-3965
  p. (404) 413-5750
  deocampo@gsu.edu
  geosciences.gsu.edu
  f: https://www.facebook.com/gsugeosciences
  t: @FromWater2Rocks
  Administrative Assistant: Basirat Lawal
  Enrollment (2015): B: 120 (15) M: 42 (5) D: 3 (0)
Chair:
  Daniel M. Deocampo, (D), Rutgers, 2001, Gsn
VPAA-Provost:
  Risa I. Palm, (D), Minnesota, 1972, On
Associate Professor:
  Hassan A. Babaie, (D), Northwestern, 1984, Gc
  Dajun Dai, (D), S Illinois, 2007, Oi
  Jeremy E. Diem, (D), Arizona, 2000, Oa
  W. Crawford Elliott, (D), Case Western, 1988, Cl
  Katherine B. Hankins, (D), Georgia, 2004, On
  Lawrence M. Kiage, (D), Louisiana State, 2007, OyPlOr
Assistant Professor:
  Timothy Hawthorne, (D), Ohio State, Oi
  Nadine Kabengi, (D), Florida, ScClGe
  Luke Pangle, (D), Oregon State, 2013, HqCs
  Katie Price, (D), Georgia, HsGm

Lecturer:
Paulo Hidalgo, (D), Michigan State, 2011, GiCg
Brian Meyer, (D), Georgia State, 2013, GesHw
Ricardo Nogueira, (D), Louisiana State, 2009, Oaw
Christy Visaggi, (D), North Carolina (Wilmington), 2011, PiOe
Adjunct Professor:
J. Marion Wampler, (D), Columbia, 1963, Cc
Emeritus:
Sanford H. Bederman, (D), Minnesota, 1973, On
Timothy E. La Tour, (D), W Ontario, 1979, Gp
W. Robert Power, (D), Johns Hopkins, 1959, En
Seth E. Rose, (D), Arizona, 1987, Hw
Related Staff:
Atieh Tajik, (M), Georgia State, 2005, Gg

Mercer University
Dept of Environmental Engineering (B,M) (2004)
1400 Coleman Avenue
Macon, GA 31207
p. (912) 744-2597
lackey_l@mercer.edu
Department Secretary: Brenda Walraven
Enrollment: No data reported since 1999
Professor:
Bruce D. Dod, (D), S Mississippi, 1973, Og
Dan R. Quisenberry, (D), World Open, 1980, Or
Assistant Professor:
Geoffrey W. Hayden, (D), Pennsylvania, 1987, Om
Robert L. Huffman, (D), Massachusetts, 1985, On
Research Associate:
Paul P. Sipiera, (D), Otago (NZ), 1985, Xm
Instructor:
Barbara D. Henley, (M), Mercer, 1978, Gg

Middle Georgia College
Geology Dept (A) (2010)
1100 Second Street
Cochran, GA 31014
tmahaffee@mgc.edu
http://www.mgc.edu
Associate Professor:
Tina Mahaffee, (M), Georgia State, Gg
Assistant Professor:
Daniel Snyder, (D), Iowa, Gg

University of Georgia
Dept of Crop & Soil Science (B,M,D) (2011)
311 Plant Sciences Building
Athens, GA 30602-7272
p. (706) 542-2461
dgs@uga.edu
http://www.cropsoil.uga.edu/
Enrollment: No data reported since 1999
Chair:
Don Shilling
Professor:
Domy C. Adriano, (D), Kansas State, 1970, Sc
Paul M. Bertsch, (D), Kentucky, 1983, Sc
Gary J. Gascho, (D), Michigan State, 1968, Sc
James E. Hook, (D), Penn State, 1975, Sp
Edward T. Kanemasu, (D), Wisconsin, 1969, Sp
David E. Kissel, (D), Kentucky, 1969, Sc
William P. Miller, (D), Virginia Tech, 1981, Sc
David E. Radcliffe, (D), Kentucky, 1984, Sp
William P. Segars, (D), Clemson, 1972, Sc
Larry M. Shuman, (D), Penn State, 1970, Sc
Associate Professor:
Miguel L. Cabrera, (D), Kansas State, 1986, So
Peter G. Hartel, (D), Oregon State, 1984, Sb
Owen C. Plank, (D), Virginia Tech, 1973, Sc
Larry T. West, (D), Texas A&M, 1986, Sd
Assistant Professor:
Glendon H. Harris, (D), Michigan State, 1993, Sb

Dept of Geology (B,M,D) ● (2015)
210 Field Street

Room 308
Athens, GA 30602
p. (706) 542-2652
ashleym@uga.edu
http://www.gly.uga.edu/
Enrollment (2011): B: 69 (9) M: 32 (11) D: 6 (0)
Head:
Douglas E. Crowe, (D), Wisconsin, 1990, Em
Grad Coordinator:
Susan T. Goldstein, (D), California (Berkeley), 1984, Pm
Professor:
Ervan G. Garrison, (D), Missouri, 1979, Ga
Robert B. Hawman, (D), Princeton, 1988, Ys
Steven M. Holland, (D), Chicago, 1990, Gr
John E. Noakes, (D), Texas A&M, 1962, Cc
Valentine A. Nzengung, (D), Georgia Tech, 1993, Cl
Alberto E. Patino-Douce, (D), Oregon, 1990, Gp
L. Bruce Railsback, (D), Illinois, 1989, Gd
Michael F. Roden, (D), MIT, 1982, Gi
Paul A. Schroeder, (D), Yale, 1992, Gz
Sally E. Walker, (D), California (Berkeley), 1988, Pm
James (Jim) E. Wright, (D), California (Santa Barbara), 1981, Gt
Associate Head:
Raymond Freeman-Lynde, (D), Columbia, 1980, Gu
Assistant Professor:
John F. Dowd, (D), Yale, 1984, Hy
Christian Klimczak, (D), Gc
Adam Milewski, (D), W Michigan, 2008, Hw
Senior Lecturer:
Patino Douce Marta, (D), Buenos Aires, 1990, Gi
Adjunct Assistant Professor:
Roger A. Burke, (D), S Florida, 1985, Cl
Adjunct Professor:
Elizabeth J. Reitz, (D), Florida, 1979, Ga
Sandra Whitney, (D), Georgia, 1992, Ga
Emeritus:
Gilles O. Allard, (D), Johns Hopkins, 1956, Eg
R. David Dallmeyer, (D), SUNY (Stony Brook), 1972, Gt
Sam Swanson , (D)
David B. Wenner, (D), Caltech, 1971, Cs
James A. Whitney, (D), Stanford, 1972, Gi

University of West Georgia
Dept of Geosciences (B) (2015)
1601 Maple Street
Callaway Building, Room 150
Carrollton, GA 30118
p. (678) 839-4051
jmayer@westga.edu
http://www.westga.edu/geosci/
Administrative Assistant: Anita M. Bryant
Enrollment (2015): B: 45 (10)
Chair:
James R. Mayer, (D), Texas, 1995, Hw
Professor:
David M. Bush, (D), Duke, 1991, Ou
Curtis L. Hollabaugh, (D), Washington State, 1980, GzCg
Randal L. Kath, (D), SD Mines, 1990, Gc
Jeong C. Seong, (D), Georgia, 1999, Oi
Associate Professor:
Brad Deline, (D), Cincinnati, 2009, Pi
Georgina G. DeWeese, (D), Tennessee, 2007, Oy
Hannes Gerhardt, (D), Arizona, 2007, On
I. Shea Rose, (D), Florida State, 2008, OyaOw
Karen S. Tefend, (D), Michigan State, 2005, CgGe
Nathan A. Walter, (D), Florida State, 2005, Og
Assistant Professor:
Christopher A. Berg, (D), Texas, 2007, Gpi
Jessie Hong, (D), Colorado, 2012, OieOy
Research Associate:
Randa R. Harris, (M), Tennessee, 2001, Hs
Emeritus:
Timothy M. Chowns, (D), Newcastle, 1968, Gs
Thomas J. Crawford, (M), Emory, 1957, Eg
Lab Coordinator:
John D. Congleton, (M), S Methodist, 1990, Pv

Valdosta State University
Dept of Physics, Astronomy & Geosciences (B) (2013)
1500 North Patterson Street
Valdosta, GA 31698-0055
> p. (229) 333-5752
> echatela@valdosta.edu
> http://www.valdosta.edu/phy/
> *Enrollment (2010): B: 77 (10)*

Head:
> Edward E. Chatelain, (D), Iowa, 1984, Pi

Professor:
> Cecilia S. Barnbaum, (D), California (Los Angeles), 1992, On
> Frank A. Flaherty, (D), Fordham, 1983, On
> Martha A. Leake, (D), Arizona, 1982, Xg
> Kenneth S. Rumstay, (D), Ohio State, 1984, On

Associate Professor:
> Can Denizman, (D), Florida, 1998, Hw
> Mary A. Fares, (D), Tennessee Tech, 1992, On
> Judy Grable, (D), Tennessee, 2001, Hs
> Mark S. Groszos, (D), Florida State, 1996, Gc
> Michael G. Noll, (D), Kansas, 2000, On
> Paul Vincent, (D), Texas A&M, 2004, Oig

Pre-Engineering Director:
> Barry Hojjatie, (D), Florida, 1990, Om

Assistant Professor:
> Jason Allard, (D), Penn State, 2006, Oag

Instructor:
> Perry A. Baskin, (M), Valdosta State, 1972, On
> Donald Thieme, (D), Georgia, 2003, GaSdGm

Emeritus:
> Dennis W. Marks, (D), Michigan, 1970, On
> Arnold E. Somers, Jr., (D), Virginia Tech, 1975, On

Guam

University of Guam
College of Natural and Applied Sciences (B,M) (2013)
Mohammad H. Golabi, PhD
Mangilao, GU 96923
> p. (671) 734-9305
> mgolabi@uguam.uog.edu
> *Enrollment: No data reported since 1999*

Associate Professor:
> Mohammad H. Golabi, (M), OsSpc

Water & Environmental Research Institute of the Western Pacific
(M) (2014)
UOG Station
Mangilao, GU 96923
> p. (671) 735-2685
> jjenson@uguamlive.uog.edu
> http://www.weriguam.org/
> *Enrollment (2014): M: 4 (1)*

Director:
> Shahram Khosrowpanah, (D), Colorado State, 1984, Hs

Professor:
> Gary R. W. Denton, (D), London, 1974, Ob
> John W. Jenson, (D), Oregon State, 1993, HwGel

Associate Professor:
> Joseph D. Rouse, (D), Hg
> Yuming Wen, (D), Rhode Island, 2004, Oir

Assistant Professor:
> Mark A. Lander, (D), Hawaii, 1990, Ow

Research Associate:
> Nathan C. Habana, (M), Guam, 2009, Hw

Professor of Hydrology:
> Leroy F. Heitz, (D), Idaho, Hg

Professor of Geology:
> Henry Galt Siegrist, jr, (D), Penn State, 1961, GdzHy

Hawaii

Honolulu Community College
Natural Sciences (A) (2015)
874 Dillingham Blvd.
Honolulu, HI 96817

> p. (808) 845-9488
> brill@hawaii.edu
> http://libart.honolulu.hawaii.edu/natsci/geology.php

Professor:
> Richard C. Brill, Jr., (M), Hawaii, Gg

University of Hawai'i, Hilo
Dept of Geology (B) (2014)
200 W. Kawili Street
Hilo, HI 96720-4091
> p. (808) 933-3383
> kenhon@hawaii.edu
> *Enrollment: No data reported since 1999*

Chair:
> Ken Hon, (D), Colorado, 1987, Gvi

Professor:
> Jene D. Michaud, (D), Arizona, 1992, HqwGm

Associate Professor:
> James L. Anderson, (D), S California, 1987, GctYd

Assistant Professor:
> Steven P. Lundblad, (D), North Carolina, 1994, GraGe

Emeritus:
> Joseph B. Halbig, (D), Penn State, 1969, Ca

Cooperating Faculty:
> Christina C. Heliker, (M), W Washington, 1984, Gv
> John P. Lockwood, (D), Princeton, 1966, Gv

Affiliate Faculty:
> Cheryl A. Gansecki, (D), Stanford, 1998, Cc

University of Hawai'i, Manoa ⬚
Dept of Atmospheric Sciences (B,M,D) (2015)
2525 Correa Road, HIG 350
Honolulu, HI 96822
> p. (808) 956-8775
> metdept@hawaii.edu
> http://www.soest.hawaii.edu/MET
> *Enrollment (2013): B: 18 (5) M: 12 (2) D: 18 (4)*

Chair:
> Gary M. Barnes, (D), Virginia, 1980, Ow

Professor:
> Steven Businger, (D), Washington, 1986, Ow
> Yi-Leng Chen, (D), Illinois, 1980, Ow
> Pao-Shin Chu, (D), Wisconsin, 1981, Oa
> Tim Li, (D), Hawaii, 1993, Oa
> Duane E. Stevens, (D), Harvard, 1977, Ow
> Bin Wang, (D), Florida State, 1984, Ow
> Yuqing Wang, (D), Monash, 1995, Oa

Associate Professor:
> Michael Bell, (D), Naval Postgrad Sch, Owr
> Jennifer Griswold, (D), California (Santa Cruz), Owr

Cooperating Faculty:
> Antony D. Clarke, (D), Washington, 1983, Oc

Dept of Geology & Geophysics (B,M,D) (2015)
1680 East-West Road, POST 701
Honolulu, HI 96822
> p. (808) 956-7640
> krubin@hawaii.edu
> http://www.soest.hawaii.edu/gg
> *Enrollment (2015): B: 47 (8) M: 20 (10) D: 31 (3)*

Chair:
> Kenneth H. Rubin, (D), California (San Diego), 1991, CcGvCg

Dean:
> Brian Taylor, (D), Columbia, 1982, Gt

Assoc. Dean:
> Charles H. Fletcher, (D), Delaware, 1986, GsOnu

Professor:
> Aly I. El-Kadi, (D), Cornell, 1983, Hw
> L. Neil Frazer, (D), Princeton, 1978, Ys
> Eric J. Gaidos, (D), MIT, 1996, Po
> Michael O. Garcia, (D), California (Los Angeles), 1976, Gi
> Craig R. Glenn, (D), Rhode Island, 1987, Gs
> Julia E. Hammer, (D), Oregon, 1998, GiCpGv
> Bruce F. Houghton, (D), Otago (NZ), 1977, Gv
> Garrett T. Ito, (D), MIT/WHOI, 1996, Yr
> A. Hope Jahren, (D), California (Berkeley), 1992, CsOs

Kevin T. M. Johnson, (D), MIT, 1990, Gi
Stephen J. Martel, (D), Stanford, 1987, Ng
Gregory F. Moore, (D), Cornell, 1977, Gt
Brian N. Popp, (D), Illinois, 1986, Cs
Scott K. Rowland, (D), Hawaii, 1987, On
Paul Wessel, (D), Columbia, 1989, Yr
Associate Professor:
Janet M. Becker, (D), California (San Diego), 1989, Oo
Clint Conrad, (D), MIT, 1999, Gt
Henrietta Dulai, (D), Florida State, 2005, CcHw
Robert A. Dunn, (D), Oregon, 1999, Yr
Gregory Ravizza, (D), Yale, 1991, Cm
Kathleen Ruttenberg, (D), Yale, 1990, Cg
Assistant Researcher:
Thomas Shea, (D), Hawaii, 2010, Gv
Assistant Professor:
Jasper G. Konter, (D), California (San Diego), 2007, CcGiCt
Christian A. Miller, (D), MIT/WHOI, 2009, CslCm
Bridget R. Smith-Konter, (D), California (San Diego), 2005, YdXy
Emeritus:
Frederick K. Duennebier, (D), Hawaii, 1972, Yr
Loren W. Kroenke, (D), Hawaii, 1972, Gu
Ralph Moberly, (D), Princeton, 1956, Gu
John M. Sinton, (D), Otago (NZ), 1976, Gi
Jr. Specialist:
Jennifer Engels, (D), Hawaii, 2001, Oe
Director of Student Services:
Leona M. Anthony, (B), 1986, On
Cooperating Faculty:
David A. Clague, (D), California (San Diego), 1974, Gi
Eric H. De Carlo, (D), Hawaii, 1982, Ca
Margo H. Edwards, (D), Columbia, 1992, Gu
Sarah Fagents, (D), Lancaster (UK), 1994, Gv
Luke P. Flynn, (D), Hawaii, 1992, Or
Patricia B. Fryer, (D), Hawaii, 1981, Gu
Milton A. Garces, (D), California (San Diego), 1995, Ys
Emilio Herrero-Bervera, (D), Hawaii, 1984, Ym
Richard N. Hey, (D), Princeton, 1975, Yr
Klaus Keil, (D), Johannes-Gutenberg (Germany), 1961, Xm
Alexander N. Krot, (D), Moscow State (Russia), 1989, Xm
Paul G. Lucey, (D), Hawaii, 1986, Xy
Fred T. Mackenzie, (D), Lehigh, 1962, Cm
Murli H. Manghnani, (D), Montana State, 1962, Yx
Fernando Martinez, (D), Columbia, 1988, Yr
Floyd W. McCoy, Jr., (D), Harvard, 1974, Gu
Peter J. Mouginis-Mark, (D), Lancaster (UK), 1977, Xg
Jane E. Schoonmaker, (D), Northwestern, 1981, Cl
Edward R. Scott, (D), Cambridge, 1971, Xm
Shiv K. Sharma, (D), Indian Inst of Tech, 1973, Gx
G. Jeffrey Taylor, (D), Rice, 1970, Xm
Donald M. Thomas, (D), Hawaii, 1977, Ca
Affiliate Graduate Faculty:
James P. Kauahikaua, (D), Hawaii, 1982, Gv
Donald A. Swanson, (D), Johns Hopkins, 1964, Gv

Dept of Oceanography (B,M,D) (2015)
1000 Pope Road
Honolulu, HI 96822
   p. (808) 956-7633
   ocean@soest.hawaii.edu
   http://www.soest.hawaii.edu/oceanography/
   Administrative Assistant: Kristin Momohara
   Enrollment (2001): B: 56 (0) M: 41 (3) D: 26 (0)
Chair:
Michael J. Mottl, (D), Harvard, 1976, Ou
Professor:
Barbara Bruno, (D), Hawaii, 1994, Ob
Eric H. De Carlo, (D), Hawaii, 1982, Cm
Jeffrey C. Drazen, (D), San Diego, 2000, Ob
Eric Firing, (D), MIT, 1978, Op
Pierre J. Flament, (D), California (San Diego), 1986, Op
David Ho, (D), Columbia, 2001, Ou
David M. Karl, (D), California (San Diego), 1978, Ob
Paul Kemp, (D), Oregon State, 1985, Ob
Rudolf C. Kloosterziel, (D), Utrecht (Neth), 1990, Op
Douglas S. Luther, (D), MIT, 1980, Op
Julian P. McCreary, (D), California (San Diego), 1977, Op

Margaret Anne McManus, (D), Old Dominion, 1996, Op
Christopher Measures, (D), Southampton, 1978, Oc
Mark A. Merrifield, (D), California (San Diego), 1989, Op
Bo Qiu, (D), Kyoto, 1990, Op
Kelvin J. Richards, (D), Southampton, 1978, Op
Kathleen C. Ruttenberg, (D), Yale, Cg
Francis J. Sansone, (D), North Carolina, 1980, Cm
Niklas Schneider, (D), Hawaii, 1992, Og
Craig R. Smith, (D), California (San Diego), 1983, Ob
Grieg F. Steward, (D), California (San Diego), 1996, Ob
Axel Timmermann, (D), Hamburg, 1998, Op
Richard E. Zeebe, (D), Bremen, 1998, Ou
Associate Professor:
Glenn Carter, (D), Washington, 2005, Op
Matthew Church, (D), William & Mary, 2003, Ob
Brian Glazer, (D), Cm
Erica Goetze, (D), California (San Diego), 2004, Ob
Christopher Kelley, (D), Hawaii, 1995, Ob
Gary M. McMurtry, (D), Hawaii, 1979, Cm
Brian Powell, (D), Colorado, 2005, Op
Karen E. Selph, (D), Hawaii, 1999, Ob
Emeritus:
Paul K. Bienfang, (D), Hawaii, 1977, Ob
Antony D. Clarke, (D), Washington, 1983, Oa
Richard W. Grigg, (D), California (San Diego), 1969, Ob
Barry J. Huebert, (D), Northwestern, 1970, Oc
Yuan-Hui Li, (D), Columbia, 1967, Cm
Roger Lukas, (D), Hawaii, 1981, Op
Fred T. Mackenzie, (D), Lehigh, 1962, Cm
Lorenz Magaard, (D), Kiel, 1963, Op
Alexander Malahoff, (D), Hawaii, 1965, Cm
Peter Muller, (D), Hamburg, 1974, Op
Jane E. Schoonmaker, (D), Northwestern, 1981, Cm
Stephen V. Smith, (D), Hawaii, 1970, Ou
Richard E. Young, (D), Miami, 1968, Ob
Affiliate Graduate Faculty:
Allen Andrews, (D), Rhodes, 2009
Russell E. Brainard, (D), Naval Postgrad Sch, 1994
Paul G. Falkowski, (D), British Columbia, 1975, Og
Carolyn Jones, (D), Georgia Tech, 2004
Dennis Moore, (D), Harvard, 1968, Og
Jaromir Ruzicka, (D), Tech (Czech), 1963, On
John R. Sibert, (D), Columbia, 1968, Ob
Kevin Weng, (D), Stanford, 2007, Ob
Cooperating Faculty:
Marlin J. Atkinson, (D), Hawaii, 1981, Ob
Whitlow W L. Au, (D), Washington State, 1970, On
Janet M. Becker, (D), California (San Diego), 1989, Og
Robert R. Bidigare, (D), Texas A&M, 1981, Og
Michael Cooney, (D), California (Davis), 1992, Og
Walter Dudley, (D), Hawaii, 1976, Ou
Eric J. Gaidos, (D), MIT, 1996, Yg
Ruth D. Gates, (D), Newcastle (UK), 1990, Ob
Petra H. Lenz, (D), California (Santa Barbara), 1983, Og
Jeffrey J. Polovina, (D), California (Berkeley), 1974, On
Brian N. Popp, (D), Illinois, 1986, Cm
Michael S. Rappe, (D), Oregon State, 1997, Og
Florence Thomas, (D), California (Berkeley), 1992, Ob
Robert Toonen, (D), California (Davis), 2001, Ob
John C. Wiltshire, (D), Hawaii, 1983, Og

Windward Community College
Natural Sciences (A) (2014)
45-720 Kea'ahala Rd.
Kane'ohe, HI 96744
   p. (808) 236-9115
   fmccoy@hawaii.edu
   http://windward.hawaii.edu
   Enrollment (2014): A: 6 (1)
Professor:
Floyd W. McCoy, (D), Harvard, 1974, GgaGu

Idaho

Boise State University
Dept of Geosciences (B,M,D) ● (2016)

1910 University Drive
Mail Stop 1535
Boise, ID 83725
    p. (208) 426-1631
    geosciences@boisestate.edu
    http://earth.boisestate.edu/
    Administrative Assistant: Liz Johansen
    Enrollment (2014): B: 143 (11) M: 29 (6) D: 20 (7)
University Distinguished Professor:
    Matthew Kohn, (D), Rensselaer, 1991, CsGpPv
Dean Graduate College:
    John R. Pelton, (D), Utah, 1979, Ysg
Chair:
    James P. McNamara, (D), Alaska (Fairbanks), 1997, Hg
Associate Dean/College of Arts & Sciences:
    Clyde J. Northrup, (D), MIT, 1996, Gc
Professor:
    Shawn Benner, (D), Waterloo, 2000, Clt
    John Bradford, (D), Rice, 1999, Yeg
    Nancy Glenn, (D), Nevada (Reno), 2000, OrNgOi
    Paul Michaels, (D), Utah, 1993, Ne
    Mark D. Schmitz, (D), MIT, 2001, CcaCg
Senior Scientist:
    Jim Crowley, (D), Carleton, 1997, Ccg
    Samantha Evans, (D), Florida Intl, 2009, Cs
Associate Professor:
    Alejandro N. Flores, (D), MIT, 2009, HqOa
    Jeffrey Johnson, (D), Washington, 2000, YsGv
    Hans-Peter Marshall, (D), Colorado, YxOl
    Jen Pierce, (D), New Mexico, 2004, GmPe
    David E. Wilkins, (D), Utah, 1997, OyGm
Research Professor:
    Vladimir I. Davydov, (D), St. Petersburg, 1982, Pg
Program Director:
    Karen Viskupic, (D), MIT, 2002, OeGc
Clinical Assistant Professor:
    Sam Matson, (D), Minnesota, 2010, GrPv
Assistant Professor:
    Brittany Brand, (D), Arizona State, 2008, Gsv
Research Professor:
    Lee M. Liberty, (M), Wyoming, 1992, Ys
Adjunct Professor:
    Virginia S. Gillerman, (D), California (Berkeley), 1982, Eg
Emeritus Research Professor:
    Warren Barrash, (D), Idaho, 1986, HwYx
Emeritus:
    Paul R. Donaldson, (D), Colorado Mines, 1974, Ye
    Kenneth M. Hollenbaugh, (D), Idaho, 1968, Eg
    Walter S. Snyder, (D), Stanford, 1977, Gr
    Claude Spinosa, (D), Iowa, 1968, Pi
    Charles J. Waag, (D), Arizona, 1968, Gc
    Mont M. Warner, (D), Iowa, 1963, Gs
    Craig M. White, (D), Oregon, 1980, Giv
    Monte D. Wilson, (D), Idaho, 1969, Gm
    Spencer H. Wood, (D), Caltech, 1975, Gmm

Brigham Young University - Idaho

Dept of Geology (B) ● (2015)
525 South Center Street
Rexburg, ID 83460-0510
    p. (208) 496-7670
    willisj@byui.edu
    http://www.byui.edu/Geology
    Enrollment (2015): B: 143 (26)
Chair:
    Julie B. Willis, (D), Utah, 2009, GtOri
Professor:
    Daniel K. Moore, (D), Rensselaer, 1997, GxiCp
    Robert W. Clayton, (D), S California, 1993, GcYgNg
    Forest J. Gahn, (D), Michigan, 2004, PogGs
    William W. Little, (D), Colorado, 1995, GsdGm
    Mark D. Lovell, (M), Idaho, 1998, HyOie
Associate Professor:
    Gregory T. Roselle, (D), Wisconsin, 1997, GpCaHg
Assistant Professor:
    Megan Pickard, (D), Penn State, 2008, GiOeGe

College of Southern Idaho

Dept of Physical Science (A) (2013)
Box 1238
315 Falls Avenue
Twin Falls, ID 83301
    p. (208) 732-6400
    swillsey@csi.edu
    http://physsci.csi.edu/geology/
    Enrollment (2013): A: 8 (0)
Professor:
    Shawn P. Willsey, (M), N Arizona, 2000, GgcGv

College of Western Idaho

Math and Sciences (A) (2010)
5500 E Opportunity Drive
Nampa, ID 83687
    natashaferney@cwidaho.cc
    http://cwidaho.cc
Adjunct Professor:
    Natasha Ferney, Gg
    Bob Frank, Gg
    Ander Sundell, Gg
    Clay Wright, Gg

Idaho State University

Dept of Geosciences (B,M,D) ○ (2015)
921 S. 8th Ave STOP 8072
Pocatello, ID 83209-8072
    p. (208) 282-3365
    geology@isu.edu
    http://geology.isu.edu/
    f: https://www.facebook.com/idahostategeosciences/
    t: @ISUGeoscience
    Enrollment (2015): B: 103 (11) M: 34 (8) D: 4 (1)
Chair:
    Leif Tapanila, (D), Utah, 2005, Pi
Professor:
    Paul K. Link, (D), California (Santa Barbara), 1982, Gs
    Michael O. McCurry, (D), California (Los Angeles), 1985, Gz
    David W. Rodgers, (D), Stanford, 1987, Gc
    Glenn D. Thackray, (D), Oregon State, 1989, Gl
Associate Professor:
    Benjamin T. Crosby, (D), MIT, 2006, GmtHs
Assistant Professor:
    Donna M. Delparte, (D), Calgary, 2008, Oi
    Sarah E. Godsey, (D), California (Berkeley), 2009, HwGm
    Shannon E. Kobs-Nawotniak, (D), Buffalo, 2007, Gv
    David M. Pearson, (D), Arizona, 2012, Gc
Research Associate:
    Diana L. Boyack, (M), Idaho State, 2012, Oi
Lecturer:
    H. Carrie Bottenberg, (D), Missouri S&T, 2012, OiGtc
    Lori Tapanila, (M), Utah, 2006, Gg
Emeritus:
    Scott S. Hughes, (D), Oregon State, 1983, Gx
GIS Director:
    Keith Weber, (M), Montana, Oi
Financial Tech:
    Melissa Neiers
Related Staff:
    Kate Anthony-Zajanc, (M), Idaho State, 2013, Oi
Cooperating Faculty:
    John A. Welhan, (D), California, 1981, Hw

Lewis-Clark State College

Earth Sciences (B) (2015)
Div of Natural Science & Mathematics
500 8th Ave
Lewiston, ID 83501
    p. (208) 792-2283
    klschmidt@lcsc.edu
    http://www.lcsc.edu/science/degree-programs/earth-science/
    Enrollment (2015): B: 15 (2)

Professor:
    Keegan L. Schmidt, (D), S California, 2000, Gc

North Idaho College
Dept of Geology and Geography (1999)
1000 West Garden Avenue
Coeur d'Alene, ID 83814
    p. (208) 769-3477
    Bill_Richards@nic.edu
    http://www.nic.edu/

University of Idaho 🖻
Geological Sciences (B,M,D) ◯ (2015)
875 Perimeter Drive
MS 3022
Moscow, ID 83844-3022
    p. (208) 885-6192
    geology@uidaho.edu
    http://www.uidaho.edu/sci/geology
    Enrollment (2015): B: 72 (17) M: 8 (9) D: 16 (1)
Chair:
    Mickey E. Gunter, (D), Virginia Tech, 1987, Gz
Professor:
    Jerry P. Fairley, (D), California (Berkeley), 2000, Hw
    Dennis J. Geist, (D), Oregon, 1985, Gi
    Peter E. Isaacson, (D), Oregon State, 1974, Pi
    Kenneth F. Sprenke, (D), Alberta, 1983, Ye
Associate Professor:
    Thomas R. Wood, (D), Idaho, 2005, Hw
Assistant Professor:
    Elizabeth J. Cassel, (D), Stanford, 2010, Gs
    Jeffrey Langman, (D), Texas, 2008, Hwy
    Eric L. Mittelstaedt, (D), Hawaii, 2008, Yr
    Brian J. Yanites, (D), Colorado, 2009, Gm

Soil Science Div (B,M,D) (2010)
Dept of Plant, Soil, & Entomological Sciences
Moscow, ID 83844-2339
    p. (208) 885-7012
    pses@uidaho.edu
    Enrollment: No data reported since 1999
Professor:
    Guy Knudsen, (D), Cornell, 1984, Sb
    Robert L. Mahler, (D), North Carolina State, 1980, On
Associate Professor:
    Bradford D. Brown, (D), Utah State, 1985, On
    Matthew J. Morra, (D), Ohio State, 1986, Sb
Assistant Professor:
    Jodi Johnson-Maynard, (D), California (Riverside), 1999, Sd
    Paul A. McDaniel, (D), North Carolina State, 1989, Sd
    Daniel G. Strawn, (D), Delaware, 1999, Sc

Illinois

Augustana College
Dept of Geology (B) (2015)
639 38th St.
Rock Island, IL 61201
    p. (309) 794-7318
    jeffreystrasser@augustana.edu
    http://www.augustana.edu/geology
    Administrative Assistant: Gail Parsons
    Enrollment (2015): B: 19 (13)
Professor:
    William R. Hammer, (D), Wayne State, 1979, Pv
    Jeffrey C. Strasser, (D), Lehigh, 1996, Gm
    Michael B. Wolf, (D), Caltech, 1992, Gi
Geology Lab Technician:
    Sallie Heine, (M), W Illinois, 2008, Oe
Assistant Curator:
    John Oostenryk
Museum Educational Programs Coordinator:
    Susan Kornreich Wolf, (B), Hamilton, 1987, Oe

Black Hawk College
Dept of Natural Science & Engineering (A) (2013)
6600 34th Avenue
Moline, IL 61265
    p. (309) 796-5000
    harwoodr@bhc.edu
    http://www.bhc.edu/academics/departments/natural-science-and-engineering/
    Administrative Assistant: Tara Carey
Chair:
    Brian Glaser, (D), N Iowa, 1996, On
Professor:
    Richard D. Harwood, (M), N Arizona, 1989, Gv

College of Lake County
Earth Science Dept (A) (2013)
19351 W. Washington Steet
Grayslake, IL 60030-1198
    p. (847) 543-2504
    eng499@clcillinois.edu
    http://www.clcillinois.edu/programs/esc/
    Enrollment: No data reported since 1999
Professor:
    Eric Priest, (M), Creighton, 1986, Owe
    Xiaoming Zhai, (D), California (Davis), 1997, Gp

Columbia College Chicago
Dept of Science & Mathematics (2013)
600 South Michigan Avenue
Chicago, IL 60605
    p. (312) 369-7396
    crasinariu@colum.edu
    http://www.colum.edu
Professor:
    Gerald E. Adams, (D), Northwestern, 1985, Gi
    Robin L. Whatley, (D), California (Santa Barbara), 2004, Gg

Eastern Illinois University
Dept of Geology/Geography (B) (2014)
600 Lincoln Avenue
Charleston, IL 61920-3099
    p. (217) 581-2626
    geoscience@eiu.edu
    http://www.eiu.edu/~geoscience/
    Administrative Assistant: Susan Kile
    Enrollment (2014): B: 74 (23)
Chair:
    Michael W. Cornebise, (D), Tennessee, 2003, Og
Professor:
    Craig A. Chesner, (D), Michigan Tech, 1988, Gx
    Betty E. Smith, (D), SUNY (Buffalo), 1994, Oi
Associate Professor:
    Diane M. Burns, (D), Wyoming, 2006, Gs
    James A. Davis, (D), Kansas State, 2001, Og
    Belayet H. Khan, (D), Pittsburgh, 1985, Oyw
    John P. Stimac, (D), Oregon, 1996, Gct
    Dave Viertel, (D), Texas State, 2008, Or
Assistant Professor:
    Katherine Johnson, (D), Ohio State, 2008, Pmi
    Barry J. Kronenfeld, (D), SUNY (Buffalo), 2004, Oig
    Christopher R. Laingen, (D), Kansas State, 2009, SfOn
Instructor:
    Robert Cataneo, (M), E Illinois, 2003, Oa
Emeritus:
    Alan Baharlou, (D), Tulsa, 1973, Cg
    Kathleen M. Bower, (D), New Mexico, 1993, Ng
    Vincent P. Gutowski, (D), Pittsburgh, 1986, GmOy
    Godson C. Obia, (D), Oklahoma, 1986, On
    Raymond N. Pheifer, (D), Indiana, 1979, EcPg
    James F. Stratton, (D), Indiana, 1975, Pg
Related Staff:
    Steven DiNaso, (M), Indiana State, 2009, Oi

Elgin Community College
Dept of Geology (2010)

49

1700 Spartan Drive
Elgin, IL 60123
   p. (847) 214-7359
   jhillier@ghc.edu
   http://www.elgin.edu/employeelisting/faculty/
Adjunct Professor:
   Mark R. Kuntz, Gg
   Timothy M. Millen, (M), N Illinois, 1982, Gg
   Joseph E. Peterson, Gg

Field Museum of Natural History
Dept of Geology (2014)
1400 S. Lake Shore Drive
Chicago, IL 60605-2496
   p. (312) 665-7621
   klawson@fieldmuseum.org
   http://www.fieldmuseum.org
   Administrative Assistant: Karsten L.. Lawson
   Administrative Assistant: Elaine Zeiger
Chair:
   Olivier C. Rieppel, (D), Basel, 1978, Pv
Curator, Meteoritics:
   Meenakshi Wadhwa, (D), Washington (St. Louis), 1994, Xm
Curator, Fossil Fishes:
   Lance Grande, (D), CUNY, 1983, Pv
Curator, Fossil Amphibians & Reptiles:
   John R. Bolt, (D), Chicago, 1968, Pv
Associate Curator, Fossil Invertebrates:
   Scott H. Lidgard, (D), Johns Hopkins, 1984, Pi
Emeritus:
   Matthew H. Nitecki, (D), Chicago, 1968, Pi
   William D. Turnbull, (D), Chicago, 1967, Pv
   Bertram G. Woodland, (D), Chicago, 1962, Gp
Associate Curator, Fossil Invertebrates:
   Peter J. Wagner, (D), Chicago, 1995, Pi

Harold Washington College
Physcial Science Dept (A) (2014)
30 E. Lake Street
Room 903
Chicago, IL 60601
   p. (312) 553-5791
   pvargas21@ccc.edu
   http://www.ccc.edu/colleges/washington/departments/
   Pages/Physical-Sciences.aspx
   Enrollment (2012): A: 17 (0)

Heartland Community College
Math And Science Div (A) (2010)
2400 Instructional Commons Building
1500 W Raab Road
Normal, IL 61761
   p. (309) 268-8640
   mark.finley@heartland.edu
   http://www.heartland.edu/ms/easc/
Professor:
   Mark Finley, (M), Iowa State, Gg
Associate Professor:
   Robert Dennison, (M), S Mississippi, Og
Adjunct Professor:
   Janet Beach Davis, (B), Illinois (Springfield), Og
   Paul Ritter, (M), E Illinois, Og
   Steven Travers, (M), Illinois State, Og
   Mark Yacucci, (B), Youngstown State, Og

Illinois Central College
Math, Science, and Engineering Dept (A) (2010)
One College Drive
East Peoria, IL 61611
   p. (309) 694-5364
   sdunham@icc.edu
   Administrative Assistant: Diane Weber
   Enrollment: No data reported since 1999
Professor:
   Martin A. Petit, (M), Illinois State, 1967, Oe

Associate Professor:
   Cheryl R. Emerson, (M), N Arizona, 1989, Oe
Assistant Professor:
   Ed Stermer, (M), Iowa, Og
Adjunct Professor:
   Linda Aylward, (B), Bradley, 1980, Oe
   Sean Mulkey, (M), Iowa, 1994, Oe

Illinois State University 🗋
Dept of Geography-Geology (B,M) O (2016)
101 South School Street
Campus Box 4400
206 Felmley Hall of Science
Normal, IL 61790-4400
   p. (309) 438-7649
   geo@ilstu.edu
   http://www.geo.ilstu.edu/contactus/
   Enrollment (2015): B: 61 (17) M: 15 (8)
Chair:
   Dagmar Budikova, (D), Calgary, 2001, Ge
Professor:
   James E. Day, (D), Iowa, 1988, Pi
   David H. Malone, (D), Wisconsin, 1994, Gc
   Eric W. Peterson, (D), Missouri, 2002, Hws
Associate Professor:
   John Kostelnick, (D), Kansas, 2006, Oi
   Catherine M. O'Reilly, (D), Arizona, 2001, HgCgGg
   Jonathan B. Thayn, (D), Kansas, 2009, Oir
Assistant Professor:
   Tenley Banik, (D), Vanderbilt, 2015, GvzGl
   Rex J. Rowley, (D), Kansas, 2009, Oi
   Lisa Tranel, (D), Virginia Tech, 2010, Gm
Adjunct Professor:
   Toby J. Dogwiler, (D), Missouri (Colombia), 2002, Gm
   Walton R. Kelly, (D), Virginia, 1993, HgCg
   Edward Mehnert, (D), Illinois, 1998, Hg
   Andrew Stumpf, (D), New Brunswick, 2001, GgsCg
   Steve Van Der Hoven, (D), Utah, 2000, HwSpYg
Emeritus:
   Robert S. Nelson, (D), Iowa, 1970, Gm
Geographic Tech:
   William Shields, (M), Illinois State, 2001, Gg

Illinois Valley Community College
Dept of Geology (A) (2015)
Natural Sciences & Business Division
815 North Orlando Smith Road
Oglesby, IL 61348-9692
   p. (815) 224-0394
   Mike_Phillips@ivcc.edu
   http://www.ivcc.edu/geology.aspx?id=534
   Enrollment (2015): A: 4 (4)
Professor:
   Michael Phillips, (M), S Illinois, 1990, GgeGm

Kaskaskia College
Life and Physical Sciences Dept (A) (2013)
27210 College Road
Centralia, IL 62801
   pvig@kaskaskia.edu
   http://www.kaskaskia.edu/LPDept/Default.aspx
Instructor:
   Pradeep K. Vig, Gg

Lincoln Land Community College
Math and Sciences (A) (2010)
Springfield, IL 62794-9256
   p. (217) 786-4923
   dean.butzow@llcc.edu
   http://www.llcc.edu/mtsc/Sciences/tabid/3280/Default.aspx
   Enrollment (2006): A: 7 (0)
Professor:
   Dean G. Butzow, (M), W Michigan, Oy
Instructor:
   Samantha Reif, (M), Michigan Tech, Gg

McHenry County College
Geography, Geology and Earth Science (A) (2015)
8900 US Hwy 14
Crystal Lake, IL 60012
  p. (815) 455-3700
  pstahmann@mchenry.edu
  http://www.mchenry.edu/EarthScience/index.asp
Instructor:
  Theodore Erski, (M), Akron, Og
  Paul Hamill, (M), Wisconsin, Owg
  Kate Kramer, (M), Indiana-Purdue, 2008, GgOg
  Paul Stahmann, (M), Brigham Young, 2000, Oyg

Moraine Valley Community College
Physical Sciences Dept (A) (2015)
9000 W. College Pwky
Palos Hills, IL 60465-2478
  p. 708-974-5615
  syrup@morainevalley.edu
Professor:
  Krista Syrup, (M), 2002, Cs

Northeastern Illinois University
Dept of Earth Science (B) ● (2015)
5500 N. St. Louis Avenue
Chicago, IL 60625
  p. (773) 442-6050
  K-Voglesonger@neiu.edu
  http://www.neiu.edu/academics/college-of-arts-and-scienc-
  es/departments/earth-science
  f: https://www.facebook.com/pages/NEIU-Earth-
  Science/178754214181?ref=hl
  Administrative Assistant: Dwan Buetow
  Enrollment (2015): B: 50 (12)
Professor:
  Laura L. Sanders, (D), Kent State, 1986, HwGe
Assistant Professor:
  Elisabet M. Head, (D), GvOrCg
  Nadja Insel, (D), Michigan, 2011, Gt
  Kenneth M. Voglesonger, (D), Arizona State, 2004, ClGe
Instructor:
  Mohammad Fariduddin, (D), N Illinois, 1999, Pe
  Rebekah Fitchett, (M), Illinois (Chicago), 2006, GgCg
  Jean M. Hemzacek Laukant, (M), N Illinois, 1986, Sc

Northern Illinois University 🗋
Dept of Geology and Environmental Geosciences (B,M,D)
○ (2015)
Davis Hall 312, Normal Rd.
De Kalb, IL 60115-2854
  p. (815) 753-1943
  askgeology@niu.edu
  http://www.niu.edu/geology/
  Enrollment (2015): B: 65 (40) M: 43 (15) D: 7 (1)
Chair:
  Mark P. Fischer, (D), Penn State, 1994, Gco
Professor:
  Phillip J. Carpenter, (D), New Mexico Tech, 1984, Yg
  Ross D. Powell, (D), Ohio State, 1980, Gs
  Reed P. Scherer, (D), Ohio State, 1991, Pm
  James A. Walker, (D), Rutgers, 1982, Gi
Graduate Program Director:
  Mark R. Frank, (D), Maryland, 2001, Cp
Associate Professor:
  Melissa E. Lenczewski, (D), Tennessee, 2001, Ge
  Paul R. Stoddard, (D), Northwestern, 1989, Gt
Assistant Professor:
  Justin P. Dodd, (D), New Mexico, 2011, Cs
  Nicole D. LaDue, (D), Michigan State, 2013, Oe
  Nathan D. Stansell, (D), Pittsburgh, 2009, Gl
Adjunct Professor:
  B. Brandon Curry, (D), Illinois, 1995, GelPs
  Virginia Naples, (D), Massachusetts, 1980, Pv
  Karen Samonds, (D), Stony Brook, 2006, Pv

Emeritus:
  Jonathan H. Berg, (D), Massachusetts, 1976, Gp
  Colin J. Booth, (D), Penn State, 1984, Hw
  C. Patrick Ervin, (D), Wisconsin, 1972, Yv
  Hsin-Yi Ling, (D), Washington (St. Louis), 1963, Pm
  Carla W. Montgomery, (D), MIT, 1977, Cc
  Eugene C. Perry, (D), MIT, 1963, Cs

Northwestern University 🗋
Earth and Planetary Sciences (B,D) (2015)
2145 Sheridan Rd
Technological Institute
Office F374
Evanston, IL 60208-3130
  p. (847) 491-3238
  earth@northwestern.edu
  http://www.earth.northwestern.edu/
  t: @DepEarthandPlan
  Administrative Assistant: Lisa Collins
  Administrative Assistant: Alexis McAdams
  Administrative Assistant: Benjamin Rice
  Enrollment (2015): B: 27 (5) D: 23 (3)
Chair:
  Bradley B. Sageman, (D), Colorado, 1991, PsGsPe
Professor:
  Craig R. Bina, (D), Northwestern, 1987, YgOmGy
  Neal E. Blair, (D), Stanford, 1980, CoSbOc
  Donna M. Jurdy, (D), Michigan, 1974, YgXyg
  Emile A. Okal, (D), Caltech, 1978, YsgYr
  Seth Stein, (D), Caltech, 1978, YsdYg
Associate Professor:
  Matthew T. Hurtgen, (D), Penn State, 2003, GsPoGr
  Steven D. Jacobsen, (D), Colorado, 2001, GyzOm
  Andrew D. Jacobson, (D), Michigan, 2001, ClPeCa
  Suzan van der Lee, (D), Princeton, 1996, YsxYg
Assistant Professor:
  Daniel Horton, (D), Michigan, 2011, OaPeOn
  Magdalena Osburn, (D), Caltech, 2013, Py
Assistant Chair:
  Patricia A. Beddows, (D), Bristol, 2004, HyGma
Visiting Professor:
  Gilbert Klapper, (D), Iowa, 1962, PgiPo
  Wayne Marko, (D), Texas Tech, 2012, Gp
  Matthew Rossi, (D), Arizona State, 2014, Gm
Adjunct Professor Emeritus:
  Johannes Weertman, (D), Carnegie Inst, 1951, Om
Emeritus:
  Abraham Lerman, (D), Harvard, 1964, CgGnCm

Oakton Community College
Earth Science (A) (2013)
1600 E. Golf Road
Des Plaines, IL 60016
  p. (847) 376-7042
  cumpston@oakton.edu
  http://www.oakton.edu/academics/academic_departments/
  earth_science/
Chair:
  John Carzoli, (D), Oklahoma, 2000, On
Professor:
  Thomas R. Brehman, (M), NE Illinois, 1974, Po
Assistant Professor:
  Jennifer Cumpston, (M), Og

Olivet Nazarene University
Dept of Chemistry and Geosciences (B) (2014)
One University Avenue
Bourbonnais, IL 60914
  p. (815) 939-5394
  mreams@olivet.edu
  http://geology.olivet.edu/
  f: https://www.facebook.com/pages/Olivet-Nazarene-Uni-
  versity-Geosciences/50458842809
  Enrollment (2014): B: 37 (5)
Chair:
  Max W. Reams, (D), Washington (St. Louis), 1968, GsmPg

Professor:
    Kevin E. Brewer, (D), Nevada (Reno), 1994, HwOiNg
    Charles W. Carrigan, (D), Michigan, 2005, GzCgGc
Director, Strickler Planetarium:
    Stephen Case, (D), Notre Dame, 2014, GhXg
Assistant Professor:
    Priscilla Skalac, (M), Olivet Nazarene, 2005, Oe

Prarie State College
Dept of Physical Science, Earth Science, and Geology (1999)
202 S. Halsted St
Chicago Heights, IL 60411
    p. (708) 709-3674
    lburrough@prairiestate.edu
    http://www.prairie.cc.il.us

Principia College
Dept of Geology (2014)
1 Maybeck Place
Elsah, IL 62028
    p. (618) 374-5294
    Chrissy.mcallister@principia.edu
    http://principia.edu/mammoth
    Enrollment: No data reported since 1999
Chair:
    Janis D. Treworgy, (D), Illinois (Urbana), 1985, GgPvGe

Richard J. Daley Community College
Physical Sciences (1999)
7500 South Pulaski Rd
Chciago, IL 60652
    p. (773) 838-7636
    gguerra@ccc.edu
    http://daley.ccc.edu/

Richland Community College
Richland Community College (1999)
One College Park
Decatur, IL 62521
    p. (217) 875-7211
    jsmith@richland.edu
    http://www.richland.edu/

Rock Valley College
Rock Valley College (1999)
3301 North Mulford Road
Rockford, IL 61114
    J.Hankins@RockValleyCollege.edu
    http://ednet.rockvalleycollege.edu/

Sauk Valley Community College
Earth Science (2014)
173 IL Rt. 2
Dixon, IL 61021
    michael.j.bates@svcc.edu
    http://www.svcc.edu

South Suburban College
Dept of Physical Science (1999)
15800 South State Street
South Holland, IL 60473
    p. (708) 596-2000 x2417
    ahelwig@ssc.edu
    http://www.ssc.edu

Southern Illinois University Carbondale ▯
Dept of Geology (B,M,D) ○ (2015)
1259 Lincoln Drive, Mailcode 4324
Parkinson 102
Carbondale, IL 62901
    p. (618) 453-3351
    geology@geo.siu.edu
    http://www.geology.siu.edu/
    f: Geology at Southern Illinois University

Administrative Assistant: Richard A. Black
Administrative Assistant: Mona Martin
    Enrollment (2015): B: 54 (20) M: 30 (12) D: 6 (1)
Chair:
    Steven P. Esling, (D), Iowa, 1983, HwGl
Professor:
    Ken B. Anderson, (D), Melbourne, 1989, Co
    Eric C. Ferre, (D), Toulouse, 1989, Gc
    Scott E. Ishman, (D), Ohio, 1990, Pe
    Susan M. Rimmer, (D), Penn State, 1985, EcCgGo
    John L. Sexton, (D), Indiana, 1974, Ye
Associate Professor:
    James Conder, (D), Brown, 2001, Ysr
    Liliana Lefticariu, (D), N Illinois, 2004, CsgGe
Assistant Professor:
    Justin Filiberto, (D), Stony Brook, 2006, Gi
    Sally Potter-McIntyre, (D), Utah, 2013, Gs
Research Associate:
    Harvey Henson, (M), S Illinois, 1989, Yg
    William Huggett, (M), S Illinois, 1981, Ec
Leader, Coal Characterization Lab:
    John C. Crelling, (D), Penn State, 1973, Ec
Emeritus:
    Richard Fifarek, (D), Oregon State, 1985, Em
    Charles O. Frank, (D), Syracuse, 1973, Gx
    Stanley E. Harris, Jr., (D), Iowa, 1947, Ge
    John E. Marzolf, (D), California (Los Angeles), 1970, Gs
    Paul D. Robinson, (M), S Illinois, 1963, Gz
    Jay Zimmerman, Jr., (D), Princeton, 1968, Gc

Southwestern Illinois College-Belleville Campus
Dept of Earth Science (1999)
2500 Carlyle Avenue
Belleville, IL 62221
    p. (618) 235-2700
    http://www.swic.edu

Southwestern Illinois College-Sam Wolf Granite City Campus
Physical Science (A) (2013)
4950 Maryville Road
Granite City, IL 62040
    p. (618) 235-2700
    http://www.swic.edu
Professor:
    Joy Branlund, (D), Washington Univ (St. Louis), 2008, Og

Triton College
Triton College (2014)
2000 Fifth Ave.
River Grove, IL 60171
    p. (708) 456-0300
    austinweinstock@triton.edu
    http://www.triton.edu

University of Chicago
Dept of the Geophysical Sciences (B,M,D) (2015)
5734 S. Ellis Avenue
Chicago, IL 60637
    p. (773) 702-8101
    info@geosci.uchicago.edu
    http://geosci.uchicago.edu
    Administrative Assistant: David J. Taylor
    Enrollment (2009): B: 20 (9) D: 31 (4)
Professor:
    David Archer, (D), Washington, 1990, Yr
    Peter R. Crane, (D), Reading, 1981, Po
    Andrew Davis, (D), Yale, 1977, Xc
    Michael J. Foote, (D), Chicago, 1989, Pg
    John E. Frederick, (D), Colorado, 1975, Oa
    Lawrence Grossman, (D), Yale, 1972, Xc
    David Jablonski, (D), Yale, 1979, Pi
    Michael C. LaBarbera, (D), Duke, 1976, Po
    Douglas R. MacAyeal, (D), Princeton, 1983, Yr
    Raymond T. Pierrehumbert, (D), MIT, 1980, Oa

Frank M. Richter, (D), Chicago, 1972, Gt
David B. Rowley, (D), SUNY (Albany), 1983, Gc
Associate Professor:
Dion L. Heinz, (D), California (Berkeley), 1986, Yx
Noboru Nakamura, (D), Princeton, 1989, Oa
Assistant Professor:
Charles Kevin Boyce, (D), Harvard, 2001, Pb
Fred Ciesla, (D), Arizona, 2003, Xcg
Albert Colman, (D), Yale, 2002, PyCs
Nicolas Dauphas, (D), Centre Pétro et Géochimiques, 2002, Xc
Pamela Martin, (D), California (Santa Barbara), 2000, Pe
Elisabeth Moyer, (D), Caltech, 2001, Oa
Mark Webster, (D), California (Riverside), 2003, Pi
Visiting Professor:
Ho-kwang (David) Mao, (D), Rochester, 1968, Yg
Emeritus:
Alfred T. Anderson, Jr., (D), Princeton, 1963, Gv
Robert N. Clayton, (D), Caltech, 1955, Cs
Dave Fultz, (D), Chicago, 1947, Oa
Susan M. Kidwell, (D), Yale, 1982, Gs
David M. Raup, (D), Harvard, 1957, Po
Ramesh C. Srivastava, (D), McGill, 1964, Oa

University of Illinois at Chicago
Dept of Earth and Environmental Sciences (B,M,D) (2015)
845 W. Taylor Street
2440 SES
MC 186
Chicago, IL 60607-7059
p. (312) 996-3155
klnagy@uic.edu
http://eaes.uic.edu/
Enrollment (2015): B: 72 (13) M: 7 (3) D: 11 (1)
Head:
Kathryn L. Nagy, (D), Texas A&M, 1988, Cg
Professor:
Stephen J. Guggenheim, (D), Wisconsin, 1976, Gz
Fabien Kenig, (D), Orleans (France), 1991, Co
Roy E. Plotnick, (D), Chicago, 1983, Pi
Carol A. Stein, (D), Columbia, 1984, Yg
Associate Professor:
Andrew J. Dombard, (D), Washington (St. Louis), 2000, Xy
DArcy Meyer Dombard, (D), Washington (St. Louis), 2004, Py
Assistant Professor:
Max Berkelhammer, (D), S California, 2010, Cg
Adjunct Professor:
Peter T. Doran, (D), Nevada (Reno), 1996, Hw
Paul Fenter, (D), Pennsylvania, 1990, Gy
Barry Lesht, (D), Chicago, 1977, Op
Neil C. Sturchio, (D), Washington (St. Louis), 1983, Cg
Eugene Yan, (D), Ohio State, 1998, Hg
Reika Yokochi, (D), Nancy (France), 2005, Ct
Emeritus:
Jean Bogner, (D), N Illinois, 1996, Hw
Martin F. J. Flower, (D), Manchester, 1971, Gi
August F. Koster Van Groos, (D), Leiden (Neth), 1966, Cp
Kelvin S. Rodolfo, (D), S California, 1967, Gu
Clinical Assistant Professor:
Stefany Sit, (D), Miami, 2013, Ygs
Research Specialist:
Kenneth Kearney, (M), Illinois (Chicago), 2013, Cg
Office Support Specialist:
Minnie O. Jones, On
Asst to the Head/Business Manager:
Edna L. Rivera, (B), Illinois (Chicago), 2004, On

University of Illinois, Urbana-Champaign 🗇
Dept of Atmospheric Sciences (B,M,D) (2015)
105 S. Gregory Street
Urbana, IL 61801-3070
p. (217) 333-2046
atmos-sci@illinois.edu
http://www.atmos.illinois.edu
Administrative Assistant: Tammy R. Warf
Enrollment (2015): B: 95 (26) M: 23 (5) D: 30 (4)

Head:
Robert M. Rauber, (D), Colorado State, 1985, Oa
Professor:
Larry Di Girolamo, (D), McGill, 1996, Or
Atul K. Jain, (D), India, 1988, Oa
Sonia Lasher-Trapp, (D), Oklahoma, 1998, Oa
Greg M. McFarquhar, (D), Toronto, 1992, Or
Michael E. Schlesinger, (D), California (Los Angeles), 1976, Oa
Robert J. Trapp, (D), Oklahoma, 1994, Oa
Donald J. Wuebbles, (D), California (Davis), 1983, Oa
Associate Professor:
Stephen W. Nesbitt, (D), Utah, 2003, Oa
Nicole Riemer, (D), Karlsruhe, 2002, Oa
Zhuo Wang, (D), Hawaii, 2004, Oa
Assistant Professor:
Francina Dominguez, (D), Illinois, 2006, Oa
Deanna Hence, (D), Washington, 2011, Oa
Ryan Sriver, (D), Purdue, 2008, Oa
Research Scientist:
Brian Jewett, (D), Illinois, 1996, Oa
Jun shik Um, (D), Illinois, 2009
Research Associate:
Guangyu Zhao, (D), Illinois, 2006
Lecturer:
Donna J. Charlevoix, (M), California (Davis), 1996, Oa
Emeritus:
Kenneth V. Beard, (D), California (Los Angeles), 1970, Oa
Mankin Mak, (D), MIT, 1968, Oa
Walter A. Robinson, (D), Columbia, 1985, Oa
John E. Walsh, (D), MIT, 1974, Oa
Robert B. Wilhelmson, (D), Illinois, 1972, Oa
Director of Undergraduate Study:
Eric R. Snodgrass, (M), Illinois, 2006, Oa
Clinical Assistant Professor:
Jeffrey Frame, (D), Penn State, 2008, Oaw
Chief Clerk:
Karen Eichelberger

Dept of Geology (B,M,D) ● (2016)
605 E. Springfield Avenue
152 Computing Applications Bldg.
Champaign, IL 61820
p. (217) 333-3540
geology@illinois.edu
http://www.geology.illinois.edu
Enrollment (2013): B: 43 (7) M: 15 (8) D: 15 (2)
Threet Professor:
James L. Best, (D), London, 1985, Gs
Johnson Professor:
Gary Parker, (D), Minnesota, 1974, Gm
Head:
Thomas M. Johnson, (D), California (Berkeley), 1995, Hw
Grim Professor:
Jay D. Bass, (D), SUNY (Stony Brook), 1982, Gy
Feng-Sheng Hu, (D), Washington, 1994, Pe
Affiliate Faculty:
Stanley Ambrose, (D), California (Santa Barbara)
Kenneth T. Christensen, (D), Illinois
Marcelo Garcia, (D), Minnesota, 1989, Gm
Bruce Rhoads, (D), Arizona, Gm
Charles J. Werth, (D), Stanford
Professor:
Bruce W. Fouke, (D), SUNY (Stony Brook), 1993, Gs
Craig C. Lundstrom, (D), California (Santa Cruz), 1996, Cp
Stephen Marshak, (D), Columbia, 1983, Gc
Xiaodong Song, (D), Caltech, 1994, Ys
Associate Head:
Stephen P. Altaner, (D), Illinois, 1985, Gz
Affiliate Faculty:
Scott Olson, (D), Illinois
Associate Professor:
Alison M. Anders, (D), Washington, 2005, Gm
Affiliate Faculty:
Surangi Punyasena, (D), Chicago, Ge
Assistant Professor:
Jessica Conroy, (D), Arizona, 2011, Cs
Jennifer Druhan, (D), California (Berkeley), 2012, HwCs

Patricia Gregg, (D), MIT/WHOI, 2008, YgCg
Lijun Liu, (D), Caltech, 2010, Yg
Wendy Yang, (D), California (Berkeley), 2010
Adjunct Professor:
Ercan Alp, (D), S Illinois, 1984
Kurtis Burmeister, (D), Illinois, 2005
Brandon Curry, Illinois, 1995
Przemyslaw Dera, (D), Mickiewicz (Poland), 2000
Robert J. Finley, (D), South Carolina, 1975, Go
Leon R. Follmer, (D), Illinois, 1970, Sa
Hannes E. Leetaru, (D), Illinois, 1997, Go
Morris W. Leighton, (D), Chicago, 1951, Eo
George Roadcap, (D), Illinois, 2004
William W. Shilts, (D), Syracuse, 1970, Gs
M. Scott Wilkerson, (D), Illinois, 1991, Gc
Walgreen Chair Emeritus Professor:
Susan W. Kieffer, (D), Caltech, 1971, Gv
Grim Emeritus Professor:
Craig M. Bethke, (D), Illinois, 1984, Hw
Emeritus:
Thomas F. Anderson, (D), Cs
Daniel B. Blake, (D), California (Berkeley), 1966, Pi
Albert V. Carozzi, (D), Geneva, 1948, Gd
Chu-Yung Chen, (D), MIT, 1983, Cg
Wang-Ping Chen, (D), MIT, 1979, Ys
Donald L. Graf, (D), Columbia, 1950, Cl
Ralph L. Langenheim, Jr., (D), Minnesota, 1951, Gr
Alberto S. Nieto, (D), Illinois, 1974, Ng
Philip A. Sandberg, (D), Stockholm, 1965, Gd
Teaching Specialist:
Eileen A. Herrstrom, (D), Iowa, 1995, Gi
Ann D. Long, (M), Leeds, 1981, Gm
Research Scientist:
Jonathan H. Tomkin, (D), Australian National, 2002, Gm
Research Programmer:
Stephen D. Hurst, (D), California (Davis), 1991, Gc
Research Associate Professor:
Robert A. Sanford, (D), Michigan State, 1996, Py
Assistant Research Professor:
J. Cory Pettijohn, (D), Boston, 2008, Hg
Assistant Clinical Professor:
Michael A. Stewart, (D), Duke, 2000, Gi

Dept of Natural Resources & Environmental Sciences
(B,M,D) (2014)
W-503 Turner Hall
1102 South Goodwin Avenue
Urbana, IL 61801-4798
p. (217) 333-2770
g-rolfe@uiuc.edu
http://nres.illinois.edu/
Enrollment: No data reported since 1999
Chair:
Jeffrey Brawn
Professor:
Charles W. Boast, (D), Iowa State, 1970, Sp
Mark B. David, (D), New York, 1983, Sf
John J. Hassett, (D), Utah State, 1970, Sc
Robert L. Jones, (D), Illinois, 1962, Sc
Richard L. Mulvaney, (D), Illinois, 1983, Sc
Theodore R. Peck, (D), Wisconsin, 1962, Sc
Joseph W. Stucki, (D), Purdue, 1975, Sc
Associate Professor:
Robert G. Darmody, (D), Maryland, 1980, Sd
Timothy R. Ellsworth, (D), California, 1989, Sp
Kenneth R. Olson, (D), Cornell, 1983, Sc
F. William Simmons, (D), North Carolina State, 1987, Sp
Assistant Professor:
Robert J. M. Hudson, (D), MIT, 1989, Cg
Gregory F. McIsaac, (D), Illinois, 1994, Hs

Waubonsee Community College
Earth Sciences (A) (2015)
Rt. 47 at Waubonsee Dr.
Sugar Grove, IL 60554
p. (630) 466-2783
dvoorhees@waubonsee.edu

https://www.waubonsee.edu/learning/academics/disci-plines/science/earth/
Enrollment (2015): A: 8 (0)
Associate Professor:
David H. Voorhees, (M), Rensselaer, 1982, OgGg
Assistant Professor:
Karl Schulze, (M), Texas A&M, 2003, Ogw
Instructor:
Alfred W. Weiss, (M), S Illinois, 2000, Oiy

Western Illinois University
Dept of Geology (B) O (2015)
1 University Circle
Macomb, IL 61455
p. (309) 298-1151
pl-calengas@wiu.edu
http://www.wiu.edu/cas/geology/
Administrative Assistant: Diane Edwards
Enrollment (2013): B: 41 (7)
Chair:
Peter L. Calengas, (D), Indiana, 1977, En
Professor:
Kyle R. Mayborn, (D), California (Davis), 2000, Gp
Leslie A. Melim, (D), S Methodist, 1991, Gd
Associate Professor:
Steven W. Bennett, (D), Indiana, 1994, Hw
Assistant Professor:
Thomas A. Hegna, (D), Yale, Pi
Instructor:
Sara Bennett, (M), Indiana, Gg
Emeritus:
Jack B. Bailey, (D), Illinois, 1975, Pg
Cooperating Faculty:
Robert E. Johnson, (B), W Illinois, 1978, On

Wheaton College
Dept of Geology & Environmental Science (B) (2015)
501 E. College Ave.
Wheaton, IL 60187
p. (630) 752-5063
geology@wheaton.edu
http://www.wheaton.edu/geology/
Administrative Assistant: Jamie L. Fearon
Enrollment (2015): B: 50 (12)
Chair:
Stephen O. Moshier, (D), Louisiana State, 1986, Gd
Professor:
James A. Clark, (D), Colorado, 1977, GmHy
Jeffrey K. Greenberg, (D), North Carolina, 1978, Gt
Charles Keil, (D), Illinois (Chicago), 1994, On
Instructor:
Lisa Heidlauf, (M), Illinois (Urbana), 1986, Gg
Emeritus:
Gerald H. Haddock, (D), Oregon, 1967, Gi

Indiana

Ball State University
Dept of Geology (B,M,D) O (2014)
2000 University Avenue
AR117
Muncie, IN 47306
p. (765) 285-8270
geology@bsu.edu
http://www.bsu.edu/geology
Administrative Assistant: Brenda J. Rathel
Enrollment (2014): B: 47 (15) M: 10 (3) D: 2 (0)
Chair:
Richard H. Fluegeman, (D), Cincinnati, 1987, Pm
Associate Dean:
Jeffry D. Grigsby, (D), Cincinnati, 1989, Gs
Professor:
Kirsten N. Nicholson, (D), Joseph Fourier, 1999, Gi
R. Scott Rice-Snow, (D), Penn State, 1983, Gm
Associate Professor:
Carolyn B. Dowling, (D), Rochester, 2002

Klaus Neumann, (D), Alabama, 1999, Cl
Assistant Professor:
   Lee J. Florea, (D), S Florida, 2006, Ge
   Yi-Hua Weng, (D), Texas, 1997, Gip
Emeritus:
   Alan C. Samuelson, (D), Penn State, 1972, Hw
Geological Tech:
   Michael Kutis, (B), Wisconsin (Platteville), 1989, Gg

College of the Holy Cross
Dept of Geosciences (A,B) (2010)
P.O. Box 308
Notre Dame, IN 46556
   p. (219) 239-8417
   wcaponigri@hcc-nd.edu
   Enrollment: No data reported since 1999
Professor:
   Winifred Caponigri Farquhar, (M), Notre Dame, 1971, GrcGe

DePauw University
Dept of Geosciences (B) (2015)
602 South College Avenue
Julian Science Center
Greencastle, IN 46135
   p. (765) 658-4654
   jmills@depauw.edu
   http://www.depauw.edu/acad/geosciences/
   f: https://www.facebook.com/DePauw-University-Geosci-
   ences-118662514879623/?ref=aymt_homepage_panel
   Administrative Assistant: Mary M.. Donohue
   Enrollment (2015): B: 32 (17)
Professor:
   James G. Mills, (D), Michigan State, 1991, Gi
   Frederick M. Soster, (D), Case Western, 1984, Gs
   M. Scott Wilkerson, (D), Illinois, 1991, Gct
Associate Professor:
   Tim D. Cope, (D), Stanford, 2003, GsOi
   Jeanette K. Pope, (D), Virginia Tech, 2002, Ge
Emeritus:
   James A. Madison, (D), Washington (St. Louis), 1968, Gz

Earlham College
Geology Dept (B) (2015)
801 National Road West
Richmond, IN 47374-4095
   p. (765) 983-1429
   streeme@earlham.edu
   http://www.earlham.edu/geology/
   Administrative Assistant: Jayne H. Arnold
   Enrollment (2006): B: 18 (4)
Associate Professor:
   Cynthia Fadem, (D), Washington, 2009, Ga
   Andrew Moore, (D), Washington, 1999, Gm
   Meg Streepey Smith, (D), Michigan, 2001, Gt
Emeritus:
   Jon W. Branstrator, (D), Cincinnati, 1975, Pg
   Charles W. Martin, (D), Wisconsin, 1962, Gg

Hanover College
Dept of Geology (B) (2011)
PO Box 890
Hanover, IN 47243-0890
   p. (812) 866-7306
   worcestr@hanover.edu
   Enrollment (2007): B: 12 (5)
Chair:
   Peter A. Worcester, (D), Miami (Ohio), 1976, Gi
Professor:
   Heyo Van Iten, (D), Michigan, 1989, Pg
Associate Professor:
   Kenneth A. Bevis, (D), Oregon State, 1998, Gl
Emeritus:
   Stanley M. Totten, (D), Illinois, 1962, Gl

Indiana State University

Dept of Earth and Environmental Systems (B,M,D) (2014)
159 Science Building
Terre Haute, IN 47809
   p. (812) 237-2444
   isu-ees@mail.indstate.edu
   http://www.indstate.edu/ess/
   f: www.facebook.com/isu.ees
   Enrollment (2009): B: 87 (13) M: 16 (7) D: 6 (2)
Professor:
   Gregory Bierly, (D), Michigan State, Oaw
   Sandra S. Brake, (D), Colorado Mines, 1989, Ge
   Anthony Rathbun, (D), Duke, 1992, PyOu
   James Speer, (D), Tennessee, 2001, Pe
   C. Russell Stafford, (D), Arizona State, 1981, Gam
   Qihao Weng, (D), Georgia, Oru
Associate Professor:
   Susan Berta, (D), Oklahoma, 1986, GmOr
   Kathleen M. Heath, (D), Utah, 2001, Pb
   Jennifer Latimer, (D), Indiana, 2004, CmGe
   Nancy J. Obermeyer, (D), Chicago, 1987, Oi
   Shawn Phillips, (D), New York, 2001
Emeritus:
   William Dando, (D)
   Prodip K. Dutta, (D), Indiana, 1983, Gs

Indiana University / Purdue University, Fort Wayne
Dept of Geosciences (B) (2015)
2101 East Coliseum Boulevard
Fort Wayne, IN 46805-1499
   p. (260) 481-6249
   argast@ipfw.edu
   http://www.geosci.ipfw.edu/
   Enrollment (2011): B: 27 (3)
Vice Chancellor for Academic Affairs:
   Carl N. Drummond, (D), Michigan, 1994, Gs
Chair:
   Anne S. Argast, (D), SUNY (Binghamton), 1986, Gdz
Professor:
   Solomon A. Isiorho, (D), Case Western, 1987, HwGeOy
Associate Professor:
   Benjamin F. Dattilo, (D), Cincinnati, 1994, GrPiGs
   Aranzazu Pinan-Llamas, (D), Boston, 2007, GcdGp
LTL:
   Mick Cseri, (M), W Michigan, 1990, Oiy
Lecturer:
   Raynond F. Gildner, (D), Cornell, 1990, GgPq
Emeritus:
   Dipak K. Chowdhury, (D), Texas A&M, 1961, Ys
   James O. Farlow, (D), Yale, 1980, PvoPe
Department Secretary:
   Diana Weber
Dept. Technician:
   Clarence Tennis

Indiana University / Purdue University, Indianapolis
Dept of Earth Sciences (B,M) (2014)
723 West Michigan Street
Indianapolis, IN 46202-5132
   p. (317) 274-7484
   ibsz100@iupui.edu
   http://www.geology.iupui.edu
   Enrollment: No data reported since 1999
Chair:
   Gabriel M. Filippelli, (D), California (Santa Cruz), 1994, Cm
Professor:
   Andrew P. Barth, (D), S California, 1989, Gi
Associate Professor:
   Kathy J. Licht, (D), Colorado, 1999, Gl
   Joseph F. Pachut, Jr., (D), Michigan State, 1977, Po
   Gary D. Rosenberg, (D), California (Los Angeles), 1972, Po
   Lenore P. Tedesco, (D), Miami, 1991, Gs
Assistant Professor:
   Pierre-Andre Jacinthe, (D), Ohio State, 1995, Cl

Lin Li, (D), Brown, 2002, Xg
Lecturer:
  R. Jeffrey Swope, (D), Colorado, 1997, Gz
Adjunct Professor:
  Timothy S. Brothers, (D), California (Los Angeles), 1985, Oy
  Timothy G. Fisher, (D), Calgary, 1993, Gl
  Swapan K. Ghosh, (D), Syracuse, 1975, Cl
  Hendrik M. Haitjema, (D), Minnesota, 1982, Hy
  Frederick W. Kleinhans, (D), Ohio State, 1971, Xg

Indiana University Northwest
Dept of Geosciences (A,B) (2015)
3400 Broadway
Gary, IN 46408
  p. (219) 980-6738
  zkilibar@iun.edu
  http://www.iun.edu/~geos/
  Enrollment (2015): B: 19 (4)
Chair:
  Zoran Kilibarda, (D), Nebraska, 1994, GsmGd
Associate Professor:
  Erin Argyilan, (D), Illinois (Chicago), 2004, GeHwOw
  Kristin Huysken, (D), Michigan State, 1996, GizGc
Emeritus:
  Robert Votaw, (D), PiGrs

Indiana University, Bloomington
Dept of Geological Sciences (B,M,D) O (2015)
1001 E. Tenth Street
Bloomington, IN 47405
  p. (812) 855-5582
  geoinfo@indiana.edu
  http://geology.indiana.edu/
  Enrollment (2014): B: 67 (20) M: 33 (0) D: 39 (0)
Chair:
  Lisa M. Pratt, (D), Princeton, 1981, Co
Professor:
  Abhijit Basu, (D), Indiana, 1975, Gd
  David L. Bish, (D), Penn State, 1977, Gz
  Simon C. Brassell, (D), Bristol, 1980, Co
  James G. Brophy, (D), Johns Hopkins, 1984, Gi
  Michael W. Hamburger, (D), Cornell, 1986, Ys
  Gary L. Pavlis, (D), Washington, 1982, Ys
  P David Polly, (D), California (Berkeley), 1993, PvgPq
  Edward M. Ripley, (D), Penn State, 1976, Em
  Juergen Schieber, (D), Oregon, 1985, Gs
  Robert P. Wintsch, (D), Brown, 1975, Gp
  Chen Zhu, (D), Johns Hopkins, 1992, On
Academic Director Judson Mead Geologic Field Station:
  Bruce Douglas, (D), Princeton, 1983, Gc
Senior Scientist:
  Chusi Li, (D), Toronto, 1993, Ce
  Arndt Schimmelmann, (D), California (Los Angeles), 1985, Cs
Associate Professor:
  Claudia C. Johnson, (D), Colorado, 1993, Pe
  Kaj Johnson, (D), Stanford, 2004, Yg
Associate Scientist:
  Erika R. Elswick, (D), Cincinnati, 1998, Cl
  Edward W. Herrmann, (D), Indiana, 2013, Sa
  Peter Sauer, (D), Colorado, 1997, Pe
Assistant Professor:
  Douglas A. Edmonds, (D), Penn State, 2009, Gsm
  Julie C. Fosdick, (D), Stanford, 2011, Gt
  Chanh Q. Kieu, (D), Maryland, 2008, Oa
  Jackson K. Njau, (D), Rutgers, 2006, Pv
  Paul W. Staten, (D), Utah, 2013, Oa
  Laura E. Wasylenki, (D), Caltech, 1999, Cl
Lab Manager - SIRF:
  Ben Underwood, (B), Indiana, 2009, Ca
Lab Manager - SESAME:
  Alice Hui, (M), Indiana, 2013, Cl
Lecturer:
  Cody Kirkpatrick, (D), Alabama (Huntsville), 2010, Oa
Adjunct Professor:
  Brian D. Keith, (D), Rensselaer, 1974, Gs
  Maria D. Mastalerz, (D), Poland, 1988, Ec

Jeffrey White, (D), Syracuse, 1984, Hs
Emeritus:
  Robert F. Blakely, (D), Indiana, 1973, Ys
  J. Robert Dodd, (D), Caltech, 1961, Po
  John B. Droste, (D), Illinois, 1956, Gs
  Jeremy D. Dunning, (D), North Carolina, 1978, Gc
  Donald E. Hattin, (D), Kansas, 1954, Gr
  John M. Hayes, (D), MIT, 1966, Co
  Erle G. Kauffman, (D), Michigan, 1961, Po
  Enrique Merino, (D), California (Berkeley), 1973, Cl
  Greg A. Olyphant, (D), Iowa, 1979, Hw
  Lee J. Suttner, (D), Wisconsin, 1966, Gd
Senior Lecturer:
  Bruce Douglas, (D), Princeton, 1983, Gc
Facilities Administrator:
  John L. Hettle Jr.

School of Public & Environmental Affairs (B,M,D) (2015)
SPEA Building
Bloomington, IN 47408
  p. (812) 855-7485
  spea@indiana.edu
  http://www.spea.indiana.edu/home/
Geology Librarian:
  Christina Sheley, On
Professor:
  Ronald A. Hites, (D), MIT, 1968, Co
  Jeffrey R. White, (D), Syracuse, 1984, Hg
Chair:
  Philip S. Stevens, (D), Harvard, 1990, Oa
Associate Professor:
  Diane S. Henshel, (D), Washington, 1987, On
  Todd Royer, (D), Idaho State, 1999, HsOg
Assistant Professor:
  Vicky J. Meretsky, (D), Arizona, 1995, Sf
  Flynn W. Picardal, (D), Arizona, 1992, So
Lecturer:
  Melissa Clark, (M), Indiana, 1999, SfOg

Indiana University, Indianapolis
Dept of Geography (A,B) (2011)
213 Cavanaugh Hall
Indianapolis, IN 46202
  p. (317) 274-8877
  tbrother@iupui.edu
  http://www.iupui.edu/~geogdept/
  Enrollment: No data reported since 1999
Chair:
  Jeffey S. Wilson, (D), Indiana State, 1998, Oy
Professor:
  F. L. Bein, (D), Florida, 1974, Oy
Associate Professor:
  Timothy S. Brothers, (D), California (Los Angeles), 1985, Oy
  Catherine J. Souch, (D), British Columbia, 1990, Gm

Purdue University
Dept of Earth, Atmospheric, and Planetary Sciences (B,M,D)
(2014)
550 Stadium Mall Drive
West Lafayette, IN 47907-2051
  p. (765) 494-3258
  eas-info@purdue.edu
  http://www.eaps.purdue.edu
  Enrollment (2014): M: 13 (13) D: 58 (6)
Department Head:
  Indrajeet Chaubey, (D), Oklahoma State, 1997, Hg
University Distinguished Professor:
  H. Jay Melosh, (D), Caltech, 1972, XmgXy
Distinguished Professor:
  John Cushman, (D), Iowa State, 1978, Sp
  Paul B. Shepson, (D), Penn State, 1982, Oa
Associate Department Head:
  Darryl E. Granger, (D), California (Berkeley), 1996, Oa
  Harshvardhan, (D), SUNY (Stony Brook), 1976, Oa
Professor:
  Ernest M. Agee, (D), Missouri, 1968, Oa

Indiana

Lawrence W. Braile, (D), Utah, 1973, Ys
Maarten de Hoop, (D), Delft (Neth), 1992, Gq
Timothy R. Filley, (D), Penn State, 1997, Co
Andrew M. Freed, (D), Arizona, 1998, Gg
Andrei Gabrielov, (D), Moscow State, 1973, Ys
Alexander Gluhovsky, (D), USSR Acad of Sci, Oa
Jon M. Harbor, (D), Washington, 1990, HwGlm
Robert L. Nowack, (D), MIT, 1985, Ys
James G. Ogg, (D), California (San Diego), 1981, Gs
Kenneth D. Ridgway, (D), Rochester, 1992, Gs
Daniel Shepardson, (D), Iowa, 1990, Oe
Yuch-Ning Shieh, (D), Caltech, 1968, Cs
Wen-Yih Sun, (D), Chicago, 1975, Oa
Terry R. West, (D), Purdue, 1966, Ng
William J. Zinsmeister, (D), California (Riverside), 1974, Ps
Indiana State Climatologist:
Dev Niyogi, (D), North Carolina State, 2000, Oa
Associate Professor:
Chris Andronicos, (D), Princeton, 1999, Gg
Michael Baldwin, (D), Oklahoma, 2003, Oa
Lucy M. Flesch, (D), Carnegie Inst, 2005, Yg
Hersh Gilbert, (D), Colorado, 2001, Ys
Greg Michalski, (D), California (San Diego), 2003, Cs
Wen-wen Tung, (D), California (Los Angeles), 2002, Oa
Qianlai Zhuang, (D), Alaska (Fairbanks), On
Assistant Professor:
Julie Elliott, (D), Alaska (Fairbanks), 2011, Yd
Marty Frisbee, (D), New Mexico Inst of Technology, 2010, Hws
Saad Haq, (D), SUNY (Stony Brook), 2004, Gt
Briony Horgan, (D), Cornell, 2010, Xg
Nathaniel A. Lifton, (D), Arizona, 1997, GmCc
David Minton, (D), Arizona, 2009, Xg
Lisa Welp, (D), Caltech, 2006, Cs
Yutian Wu, (D), Columbia, 2011, Oa
Emeritus:
William J. Hinze, (D), Wisconsin, 1957, Ye
Arvid M. Johnson, (D), Penn State, 1965, Gc
Gerald H. Krockover, (D), Iowa, 1970, Oe
Darrell I. Leap, (D), Penn State, 1974, Hy
Phillip J. Smith, (D), Wisconsin, 1967, Oa
Thomas M. Tharp, (D), Wisconsin, 1978, Nm
Dayton G. Vincent, (D), MIT, 1969, Oa

University of Notre Dame
Dept of Civil & Environmental Engineering & Earth Sciences
(B,M,D) (2015)
156 Fitzpatrick Hall
Notre Dame, IN 46556
   p. (219) 631-5380
   ceees@nd.edu
   http://www.nd.edu/~ceees
   Enrollment (2001): B: 12 (11) M: 1 (1) D: 16 (5)
Chair:
Joannes J. Westerink, (D), MIT, 1984, On
Professor:
Peter C. Burns, (D), Manitoba, 1994, Gz
Jeremy B. Fein, (D), Northwestern, 1989, Cl
Joe Fernando, (D), Johns Hopkins, 1983, Oa
Patricia Maurice, (D), Stanford, 1994, Cl
Clive R. Neal, (D), Leeds (UK), 1985, Gi
Associate Professor:
Andrew Kennedy, (D), Monash, 1998, On
Tony Simonetti, (D), Carleton, 1994, Ct
Assistant Professor:
Melissa Berke, (D), Minnesota, 2011, Cs
Diogo Bolster, (D), Calfornia (San Diego), 2007, Hw
Alan Hamlet, (D), Washington, 2006, Hs
Amy Hixon, (D), Clemson, 2013, Cl
David Richter, (D), Stanford, 2011, Oa
Instructor:
Stephanie Simonetti, (D), McGill, 2002, On

University of Southern Indiana
Dept of Geology & Physics (B) (2015)
8600 University Boulevard
Evansville, IN 47712

   p. (812) 464-1701
   wselliott@usi.edu
   http://www.usi.edu/science/geology-and-physics
   Administrative Assistant: Kim E.. Schauss
   Enrollment (2015): B: 47 (11)
Professor:
Joseph A. DiPietro, (D), Oregon State, 1990, Gc
Paul K. Doss, (D), N Illinois, 1991, Hw
Chair:
William S. Elliott, Jr., (D), Indiana, 2002, GsrCl
Associate Professor:
James Durbin, (D), Nebraska, 1999, Gm
Tony Maria, (D), Rhode Island, 2000, Gv
Instructor:
Carrie L. Wright, (M), Wright State, 2006, Oe
Emeritus:
Norman R. King, (D), Indiana, 1973, Gr

Iowa

Cornell College
Dept of Geology (B) ● (2015)
600 First Street SW
Mount Vernon, IA 52314
   p. (319) 895-4306
   rdenniston@cornellcollege.edu
   http://www.cornellcollege.edu/geology
   Enrollment (2014): B: 25 (10)
Chair:
Emily O. Walsh, (D), California (Santa Barbara), 2003, GptCc
Professor:
Rhawn F. Denniston, (D), Iowa, 2000, GeCs
Benjamin J. Greenstein, (D), Cincinnati, 1990, GuPie

Drake University
Dept of Environmental Science and Policy (B) (2005)
Des Moines, IA 50311
   p. (515) 271-2803
   thomas.rosburg@drake.edu
   Enrollment: No data reported since 1999

Iowa State University of Science & Technology
Dept of Agronomy (B,M,D) (2014)
2101 Agronomy Hall
Ames, IA 50011-1010
   p. (515) 294-1360
   slf@iastate.edu
   http://www.agron.iastate.edu/
   Department Secretary: Pam Hinderaker
   Enrollment (1999): B: 35 (9) M: 31 (10) D: 16 (5)
Director:
Dennis R. Keeney, (D), Iowa, 1965, So
Chair:
Kendall Lamkey, (D)
Associate Dean, College of Agriculture:
Gerald A. Miller, (D), Iowa State, 1974, So
Professor:
Raymond W. Arritt, (D), Colorado State, 1985, Ow
Richard E. Carlson, (D), Iowa State, 1971, Ow
Richard M. Cruse, (D), Minnesota, 1978, So
V. P. (Bill) Evangelou, (D), California (Davis), 1981, Sc
William J. Gutowski, (D), MIT, 1984, Ow
Robert Horton, (D), New Mexico State, 1981, Sp
Douglas L. Karlen, (D), Kansas State, 1978, So
Randy J. Killorn, (D), Idaho, 1983, So
Thomas E. Loynachan, (D), North Carolina State, 1975, So
Thomas B. Mooreman, (D), Washington State, 1983, So
Jonathan A. Sandor, (D), California (Berkeley), 1983, Sd
John W. Schafer, Jr., (D), Michigan State, 1968, So
Eugene S. Takle, (D), Iowa State, 1971, Oa
M. Ali Tatabatai, (D), Iowa State, 1965, Sc
Elwynn Taylor, (D), Washington (St. Louis), 1970, Oa
Regis D. Voss, (D), Iowa State, 1962, So
Douglas N. Yarger, (D), Arizona, 1967, Oa
Associate Professor:
Cynthia Cambardella, (D), Colorado, 1991, So

Thomas A. Kaspar, (D), Iowa State, 1982, So
David A. Laird, (D), Iowa State, 1987, Sc
Antonio W. Mallarino, (D), Iowa State, 1991, So
Michael L. Thompson, (D), Ohio State, 1980, Sd
Assistant Professor:
Lee Burras, (D), Ohio State, 1992, Sd
Larry Halverson, (D), Wisconsin, 1991, So
Stanley J. Henning, (D), Oregon State, 1975, So
Thomas A. Polito, (D), Iowa State, 1987, So
Emeritus:
Jerry K. Radke, (D), Wisconsin, 1965, Sp
Geology Librarian:
Peter A. Peterson, (D), Illinois, 1953, On

Dept of Geological & Atmospheric Sciences (B,M,D) ○ (2015)
253 Science I
2237 Osborn Drive
Ames, IA 50011-3212
p. (515) 294-4477
geology@iastate.edu
http://www.ge-at.iastate.edu/
f: https://www.facebook.com/ISUgeology
Administrative Assistant: DeAnn Frisk
Enrollment (2015): B: 166 (30) M: 23 (5) D: 20 (0)
Chair:
William W. Simpkins, (D), Wisconsin, 1989, Hw
Professor:
Igor A. Beresnev, (D), USSR Acad of Sci, 1986, Yg
Cinzia C. Cervato, (D), ETH (Switzerland), 1990, Gg
Tsing-Chang Chen, (D), Michigan, 1975, Oa
William A. Gallus, (D), Colorado State, 1993, Oa
William J. Gutowski, (D), MIT, 1984, Oa
Neal R. Iverson, (D), Minnesota, 1989, Gl
Paul G. Spry, (D), Toronto, 1984, Em
Eugene S. Takle, (D), Iowa State, 1971, Oa
Xiaoqing Wu, (D), California (Los Angeles), 1992, Oa
Associate Professor:
Kristie Franz, (D), California (Irvine), 2006, Hs
Chris Harding, (D), Houston, 2001, Gq
Alan D. Wanamaker, (D), Maine, 2007, CsPe
Assistant Professor:
Beth E. Caissie, (D), Massachusetts, 2012, Pe
Franciszek J. Hasiuk, (D), Michigan, 2008, Gs
Jacqueline Reber, (D), Oslo, 2012, Gct
Yuyu Zhou, (D), Rhode Island, 2008, Oyi
Senior Lecturer:
James V. Aanstoos, (D), Purdue, 1996, Or
Jane P. Dawson, (D), New Mexico, 1995, Gp
David M. Flory, (M), Iowa State, 2003, Ow
Lecturer:
Aaron R. Wood, (D), Michigan, 2009, Po
Adjunct Professor:
Michael R. Burkart, (D), Iowa, 1976, Hy
Emeritus:
Robert Cody, (D), Colorado, 1968, Gz
Carl E. Jacobson, (D), California (Los Angeles), 1980, Gc
Karl E. Seifert, (D), Wisconsin, 1963, Ct
Carl F. Vondra, (D), Nebraska, 1963, Gr
Kenneth E. Windom, (D), Penn State, 1976, Cp
Douglas N. Yarger, (D), Arizona, 1967, Oa
Teaching Lab Coordinator:
Mark E. Mathison, (M), Iowa State, 2000, Oe

Scott Community College
Environmental Science (2014)
500 Belmont Road
Bettendorf, IA 52722
p. 563-441-4001
eiccinfo@eicc.edu
http://www.eicc.edu

University of Iowa 🗐
Earth & Environmental Sciences (B,M,D) ● (2015)
115 Trowbridge Hall
123 N. Capitol Street
Iowa City, IA 52242

p. (319) 335-1818
geology@uiowa.edu
http://clas.uiowa.edu/ees/
Administrative Assistant: Angela Bellew
Enrollment (2015): B: 55 (14) M: 15 (5) D: 20 (0)
Chair:
Charles T. Foster Jr., (D), Johns Hopkins, 1975, Gp
Professor:
Jonathan M. Adrain, (D), Alberta, 1993, Pi
E. Arthur Bettis III, (D), Iowa, 1995, On
Christopher A. Brochu, (D), Texas, 1997, Pv
Jane A. Gilotti, (D), Johns Hopkins, 1987, Gc
William C. McClelland, (D), Arizona, 1990, GctCc
David W. Peate, (D), Open, 1989, CgGi
Mark K. Reagan, (D), California (Santa Cruz), 1987, Gi
Associate Professor:
Jeffrey A. Dorale, (D), Minnesota, 2001, Cs
Ingrid Ukstins Peate, (D), Royal Holloway, 2003, GviXg
Frank H. Weirich, (D), Toronto, 1982, Gm
Assistant Professor:
William Barnhart, (D), Cornell, 2013, Gt
Bradley D. Cramer, (D), Ohio State, 2009, GrPsGs
Emily S. Finzel, (D), Purdue, 2010, Gsr
Hallie J. Sims, (D), Chicago, 2000, Pe
Adjunct Associate Professor:
Brian J. Witzke, (D), Iowa, 1981, Ps
Adjunct Assistant Professor:
Raymond R. Anderson, (D), Iowa, 1992, Gr
Rhawn F. Denniston, (D), Iowa, 2000, Cs
Douglas J. Schnoebelen, (D), Indiana, 1999, Hg
Emily O. Walsh, (D), California (Santa Barbara), 2003, Ggi
Adjunct Professor:
David L. Campbell, (D), California (Berkeley), 1969, Yg
Emeritus:
Richard G. Baker, (D), Colorado, 1969, Pl
Ann F. Budd, (D), Johns Hopkins, 1978, Po
Robert S. Carmichael, (D), Pittsburgh, 1967, Ye
Lon D. Drake, (D), Ohio State, 1968, Hy
Philip H. Heckel, (D), Rice, 1966, Gd
Gilbert Klapper, (D), Iowa, 1962, Pm
George R. McCormick, (D), Ohio State, 1964, Gz
Holmes A. Semken, Jr., (D), Michigan, 1965, Pv
Keene Swett, (D), Edinburgh, 1965, Gs
You-Kuan Zhang, (D), Arizona, 1990, Hw
Rock Lab Manager:
Matthew J. Wortel, (M), Iowa, 2007, On
Collections Manager, Paleontology:
Tiffany S. Adrain, (M), Iowa, 2003, On
Department Secretary:
Christine Harms

University of Northern Iowa
Dept of Earth Science (B) (2015)
121 Latham Hall
Cedar Falls, IA 50614-0335
p. (319) 273-2759
siobahn.morgan@uni.edu
http://www.earth.uni.edu/
f: https://www.facebook.com/pages/University-of-Northern-
Iowa-Earth-and-Environmental-Science/56860203682
t: @uni_earthsci
Administrative Assistant: Nora Janssen
Enrollment (2015): B: 77 (25)
Head:
Siobahn M. Morgan, (D), Washington, 1991, On
Professor:
Alan C. Czarnetzki, (D), Wisconsin, 1992, Ow
Thomas A. Hockey, (D), New Mexico State, 1988, On
Mohammad Z. Iqbal, (D), Indiana, 1994, Hw
Associate Professor:
Kyle R. Gray, (D), Akron, 2009, OeGg
Chad E. Heinzel, (D), N Illinois, 2005, Gag
Assistant Professor:
Alexa Sedlacek, (D), Ohio State, 2013, Cs
Xinhua Shen, (D), Colorado State, 2011, Oaw
Instructor:
Paula Even, (M), N Iowa, 2005, On

Lee S. Potter, (D), Texas, 1996, Gz
Aaron Spurr, (M), N Iowa, 1997, Oe
Michael Stevens, (M), N Iowa, 1992, Oe
Emeritus:
Wayne I. Anderson, (D), Iowa, 1964, Pg
Lynn A. Brant, (D), Penn State, 1980, Gn
Timothy M. Cooney, (D), N Colorado, 1976, Oe
Walter E. De Kock, (D), Ohio State, 1972, Oe
Kenneth J. De Nault, (D), Stanford, 1974, Gz
James C. Walters, (D), Rutgers, 1975, Gm
Lab Tech:
Steven J. Smith, (M), N Iowa, 2000, Og

Kansas

Emporia State University
Earth Science Dept (B,M) (2014)
1 Kellogg Circle
Emporia, KS 66801-5087
p. (620) 341-5330
mschulme@emporia.edu
http://www.emporia.edu/earthsci/
Enrollment (2014): B: 30 (7) M: 22 (6)
Professor:
James S. Aber, (D), Kansas, 1978, Gl
Kenneth W. Thompson, (D), Iowa State, 1991, Oe
Head:
Marcia K. Schulmeister, (D), Kansas, 2000, HwClGe
Associate Professor:
Michael Morales, (D), California (Berkeley), 1987, Pv
Richard O. Sleezer, (D), Kansas, 2001, Os
Assistant Professor:
Alivia J. Allison, (D), Missouri (Kansas City), 2013, GgaGm
Lecturer:
Susan W. Aber, (D), Emporia State, 2005, Gz
Emeritus:
Paul J. Johnston, (M), Kansas, Gg

Fort Hays State University 🗂
Dept of Geosciences (B,M) ● (2016)
600 Park Street
Tomanek Hall
Hays, KS 67601-4099
p. (785) 628-5389
geosciences@fhsu.edu
http://www.fhsu.edu/geo
f: https://www.facebook.com/GeoFHSU/
t: @GeoFHSU
Administrative Assistant: Patricia Duffey
Enrollment (2015): B: 154 (18) M: 43 (3)
Emeritus:
Paul Phillips, (D), Kansas, 1977, Oe
Richard J. Zakrzewski, (D), Michigan, 1968, Pv
Professor:
Kenneth R. Neuhauser, (D), South Carolina, 1973, Gc
Chair:
P. Grady Dixon, (D), Arizona State, 2005, OwyOa
Associate Professor:
Richard Lisichenko, (D), Kansas State, 2000, Oi
Tom Schafer, (D), Kansas State, 2000, Oyi
Assistant Professor:
Hendratta N. Ali, (D), Oklahoma State, 2010, GogYs
Keith Bremer, (D), Texas State, 2011, Oun
Laura E. Wilson, (D), Colorado (Boulder), 2012, PgGgOn
Chunfu Zhang, (D), Florida State, 2011, Ggz
Instructor:
Eamonn Coveney, (M), Fort Hays State, 2006, Oyn
Amelia A. Fox, (D), Mississippi State, 2015, Or
William H. Heimann, (M), Fort Hays State, 1987, Hgw
Kara Kuntz, (M), Kansas State, 1990, On
Cooperating Faculty:
Joseph R. Thomasson, (D), Iowa State, 1976, Pb

Johnson County Community College
Science Div (A) (2015)
12345 College Blvd
Overland Park, KS 66210
p. (913) 469-3826
csilla@jccc.edu
http://www.jccc.edu/academics/math-science/index.html
Enrollment (2015): A: 7 (2)
Professor:
Lynne Beatty, GgOy
Assistant Professor:
John P. Harty, (D), Oy
Adjunct Professor:
John Maher, (D), Oy

Kansas State University
Dept of Agronomy (B,M,D) (2016)
2004 Throckmorton
Manhattan, KS 66506
p. (785) 532-6101
agronomy@ksu.edu
http://www.agronomy.k-state.edu/
f: https://www.facebook.com/kstate.agronomy
t: @KStateAgron
Enrollment (2014): B: 70 (33) M: 41 (9) D: 43 (10)
Deparment Head:
Gary M. Pierzynski, (D), Ohio State, 1989, Sc
Professor:
Stewart Duncan, (D), Kansas State, 1991, So
Dale Fjell, (D), Kansas State, 1982, So
Allan Fritz, (D), Kansas State, 1994, So
Mary Beth Kirkham, (D), Wisconsin, Sp
Gerard J. Kluitenberg, (D), Iowa State, 1989, Sp
David Mengel, (D), Purdue, 1975, So
Clenton E. Owensby, (D), Kansas State, 1969, Sf
Dallas Peterson, (D), North Dakota State, 1987, So
Vara Prasad, (D), Reading (United Kingdom), 1999, So
Mickey D. Ransom, (D), Ohio State, 1984, Sd
Chuck W. Rice, (D), Kentucky, 1983, Sb
Bill T. Schapaugh, (D), Purdue, 1979, So
Alan Schlegel, (D), Purdue, 1985, So
Phillip Stahlman, (D), Wyoming, 1989, So
Daniel Sweeny, (D), Florida, So
Curtis Thompson, (D), Idaho, 1993, So
Steve M. Welch, (D), Michigan State, 1977, Sp
Associate Professor:
Robert Aiken, (D), Michigan State, 1992, So
Ignacio Ciampitti, (D), Purdue, 2012, So
Gary Cramer, (D), Nebraska, 1998, So
Walter H. Fick, (D), Texas Tech, 1978, Sf
Ganga Hettiarachchi, (D), Kansas State, 2000, Sc
John Holman, (D), Idaho, 2005, So
Doo-Hong Min, (D), Maryland, 1998, So
Nathan Nelson, (D), North Carolina State, 2004, So
DeAnn Presley, (D), Kansas State, 2007, So
Kraig Roozeboom, (D), Kansas State, 2006, So
Dorivar Ruiz-Diaz, (D), Iowa State, 2007, So
Tesfaye Tesso, (D), Kansas State, 2002, So
Assistant Professor:
Eric Adee, (D), Wisconsin, 1993, So
Lucas Haag, (D), Kansas State, 2013, So
Mithila Jugulam, (D), Guelph, 2004, So
Xiaomao Lin, (D), Nebraska, 1999, On
Colby Moorberg, (D), North Carolina, 2014, So
Geoffrey Morris, (D), Chicago, 2007, So
Augustine Obour, (D), Florida, 2010, So
Ram Perumal, (D), Tamil Nadu Ag Univ, 1993, So
Eduardo Santos, (D), Guelph, 2011, So
Gretchen Sassenrath, (D), Illinois, 1988, So
Peter Tomlinson, (D), Arkansas, 2006, So
Guorong Zhang, (D), North Dakota State, 2007, So
Emeritus:
Mark Claassen, (D), Iowa State, 1971, So
Bill Eberle, (D), So
Stan Ehler, (D), Missouri, 1975, So
Barney Gordon, (D), South Dakota, 1990, So
Keith Janssen, (D), Michigan State, 1973, So
George Liang, (D), Wisconsin, 1965, So
Gerry L. Posler, (D), Iowa State, 1969, Sf
Kevin Price, (D), Utah, 1987, Or

David Regehr, (D), Illinois, 1975, So
Jim Shroyer, (D), Iowa State, 1980, So
Loyd Stone, (D), South Dakota, 1973, Sp
Steve J. Thien, (D), Purdue, 1971, Sc
Richard Vanderlip, (D), So
D.A. Whitney, (D), Iowa State, 1966, So
Agronomist:
Doug Shoup, (D), Kansas State, 2006, So

Dept of Geology (B,M) (2013)
108 Thompson Hall
Manhattan, KS 66506-3201
  p. (785) 532-6724
  rocknrat@ksu.edu
  http://www.k-state.edu/geology/
  Administrative Assistant: Lori Page-Willyard
  Enrollment (2013): B: 69 (15) M: 27 (5)
Department Head:
Pamela D. Kempton, (D), S Methodist, 1984, GiCt
Professor:
Sambhudas Chaudhuri, (D), Ohio State, 1966, Cc
George R. Clark, II, (D), Caltech, 1969, Poy
Charles G. Oviatt, (D), Utah, 1984, Gm
Associate Professor:
Allen W. Archer, (D), Indiana, 1983, Gr
Matthew W. Totten, (D), Oklahoma, 1992, Gso
Assistant Professor:
Matthew E. Brueseke, (D), Miami (Ohio), 2006, GivGt
Saugata Datta, (D), W Ontario, 2001, ClHwGe
Keith B. Miller, (D), Rochester, 1988, Pe
Abdelmoneam E. Raef, (D), AGH (Poland), 2001, YesGf
Joel Q.G. Spencer, (D), Glasgow (UK), 1996, CcGs
Emeritus:
Robert L. Cullers, (D), Wisconsin, 1971, Ct
Ronald R. West, (D), Oklahoma, 1970, Po

University of Kansas 🗐
Dept of Geology (B,M,D) (2014)
1475 Jayhawk Boulevard
Room 120
Lindley Hall
Lawrence, KS 66045-7613
  p. (785) 864-4974
  geology@ku.edu
  http://geo.ku.edu/
  f: https://www.facebook.com/KUGeology?ref=hl
  Enrollment (2013): B: 72 (14) M: 50 (17) D: 34 (9)
Chair:
Luis A. Gonzalez, (D), Michigan, 1989, CsGd
Union Pacific Distinguished Professor:
J. Douglas Walker, (D), MIT, 1985, Gc
Ritchie Distinguished Professor:
Michael D. Blum, (D), Texas (Austin), 1997, GsrGm
Gulf-Hedberg Distinguished Professor:
Paul A. Selden, (D), Cambridge
Associate Dean of Mathematics and Natural Sciences:
Robert H. Goldstein, (D), Wisconsin, 1986, Gs
Professor:
J. Rick Devlin, (D), Waterloo, 1994, Hw
Evan K. Franseen, (D), Wisconsin, 1989, Gd
Stephen T. Hasiotis, (D), Colorado, 1997, Pe
Mary C. Hill, (D), Princeton, 1985, Hgq
Hubert H. and Kathleen M. Hall Professor of Geology:
Gene Rankey, (D), Kansas, 1996, Gs
Associate Professor:
Ross A. Black, (D), Wyoming, 1989, Ye
David A. Fowle, (D), Notre Dame, 2000, Py
Diane Kamola, (D), Georgia, 1989, Gs
Gwen L. Macpherson, (D), Texas, 1989, Hw
Craig Marshall, (D), Tech (Sidney), 2001, Py
Jennifer A. Roberts, (D), Texas, 2000, Py
Michael H. Taylor, (D), California (Los Angeles), 2004, Gt
George P. Tsoflias, (D), Texas, 1999, Yg
Anthony W. Walton, (D), Texas, 1972, Gs
Assistant Professor:
Noah McLean, (D), MIT, 2012, Cc
Andreas Möller, (D), Christian-Albrechts (Germany), 1996, Gt

Alison Olcott Marshall, (D), S California, 2006, Py
Leigh Stearns, (D), Maine, 2007, Ol
Randy Stotler, (D), Waterloo, 2008, Hw
Chi Zhang, (D), Rutgers, 2012, Ygx
Courtesy Professor:
James M. Butler, (D), Stanford, 1986, Hw
John H. Doveton, (D), Edinburgh, 1969, Gq
William C. Johnson, (D), Wsconsin, 1976, Grm
Leonard Krishtalka, (D), Kansas, 1976, Pv
Bruce S. Lieberman, (D), Columbia, 1994, Po
Gregory A. Ludvigson, (D), Iowa, 1988, Gs
Rolfe Mandel, (D), Kansas, 1991, Ga
Richard D. Miller, (M), Kansas, 1983, Ye
Edith Taylor, (D), Ohio State, 1983, Pb
Thomas N. Taylor, (D), Illinois, 1964, Pb
W. Lynn Watney, (D), Kansas, 1985, Gr
Donald O. Whittemore, (D), Penn State, 1973, Cl
Courtesy Associate Professor:
Geoff Bohling, (D), Kansas, 1999, Hw
Gaisheng Liu, (D), Alabama, 2004, Hg
Courtesy Assistant Professor:
Andrea Brookfield, (D), Waterloo, 2009, Hw
Jon Smith, (D), Kansas, 2008, GsPe
Adjunct Professor:
Timothy R. Carr, (D), Wisconsin, 1981, Go
John Gosse, (D), Lehigh, 1994, Gm
Daniel F. Stockli, (D), Stanford, 1999, Gc
Visiting Professor:
Kelsey S. Bitting, (D), Rutgers, 2013, Oe
Emeritus:
Ernest E. Angino, (D), Kansas, 1961, Cl
Wakefield Dort, Jr., (D), Stanford, 1955, Gm
Gisela Dreschoff, (D), Tech (Braunschweig), 1972, Ce
Paul Enos, (D), Yale, 1965, Gs
Lee C. Gerhard, (D), Kansas, 1964, Gs
Carl D. McElwee, (D), Kansas, 1970, Hg
Richard A. Robinson, (D), Texas, 1962, Pg
Albert J. Rowell, (D), Leeds, 1953, Pi
Donald W. Steeples, (D), Stanford, 1975, Ys
W. Randall Van Schmus, (D), California (Los Angeles), 1964, Cc

Wichita State University
Dept of Geology (B,M) (2011)
1845 Fairmount
Wichita, KS 67260-0027
  p. (316) 978-3140
  john.gries@wichita.edu
  Administrative Assistant: K. L. Smith
  Enrollment (1997): B: 41 (6) M: 28 (3)
Chair:
William C. Parcell, (D), Alabama, 2000, Gr
Professor:
William D. Bischoff, (D), Northwestern, 1985, Cl
John C. Gries, (D), Texas, 1970, Gt
Salvatore J. Mazzullo, (D), Rensselaer, 1974, Go
Associate Professor:
Collette D. Burke, (D), Wisconsin (Milwaukee), 1983, Pm
Assistant Professor:
Hongsheng Cao, (D), Florida State, 2001, Cl
Wan Yang, (D), Texas, 1999, Gs
Lecturer:
Toni K. Jackman, (M), Wichita State, 1984, Ge
David L. Schaffer, (B), Utah, 1982, Ow
Emeritus:
James N. Gundersen, (D), Minnesota, 1958, Ga
Daniel F. Merriam, (D), Kansas, 1961, Gr
Peter G. Sutterlin, (D), Northwestern, 1958, Gd

Kentucky

Alice Lloyd College
Div of Natural Sciences & Mathematics (2004)
Pippa Passes, KY 41844-9701
  p. (606) 368-2101 x5405

Bluegrass Community and Technical College
Environmental Science Technology Program (2015)
470 Cooper Dr
Lexington, KY 40506
    p. (859) 246-6448
    jean.watts@kctcs.edu
    http://www.bluegrass.kctcs.edu/Natural_Sciences/Environ-
    mental_Science_Technology.aspx

Eastern Kentucky University
Dept of Geosciences (B) (2015)
521 Lancaster Avenue
Roark 103
Richmond, KY 40475-3102
    p. (859) 622-1273
    melissa.dieckmann@eku.edu
    http://www.geoscience.eku.edu
    Enrollment (2013): B: 102 (22)
Chair:
    Melissa S. Dieckmann, (D), Notre Dame, 1995, OeCg
Professor:
    Walter S. Borowski, (D), North Carolina, 1998, CgGo
    Stewart S. Farrar, (D), SUNY (Binghamton), 1976, Gp
    John C. White, (D), Baylor, 2002, GiCgt
    David Zurick, (D), Hawaii, 1986, On
Associate Professor:
    French T. Huffman, (D), Connecticut, 2006, Oi
    Donald M. Yow, (D), South Carolina, 2003, Owy
Assistant Professor:
    Robert T. Lierman, (D), George Washington, 1995, Gsr
    Kelly Watson, (D), Florida State, 2012, Or
Lecturer:
    Glenn A. Campbell, (M), Marshall, 1995, Oy
    Sonja H. Yow, (D), Kentucky, 2008, On
Emeritus:
    Gary L. Kuhnhenn, (D), Illinois, 1976, Gd

Morehead State University
Dept of Earth and Space Sciences (B) (2014)
235 Martindale Drive
Morehead, KY 40351
    p. (606) 783-2381
    c.mason@moreheadstate.edu
    http://www.moreheadstate.edu/physsci/
    Administrative Assistant: Amanda Holbrook
    Enrollment (2014): B: 40 (4)
Department Chair:
    Benjamin K. Malphrus, (D), West Virginia, 1990
Professor:
    Charles E. Mason, (M), George Washington, 1981, PiGrs
Associate Professor:
    Marshall Chapman, (D), Massachusetts, 1996, Gv
    Eric Jerde, (D), California (Los Angeles), 1991, Cg
    Jennifer O'Keefe, (D), Kentucky, 2008, PlEcOe
    Steven K. Reid, (D), Texas A&M, 1991, Gs

Murray State University
Dept of Geosciences (B,M) O (2014)
334 Blackburn Hall
Murray, KY 42071
    p. (270) 809-2591
    george.kipphut@murraystate.edu
    http://www.murraystate.edu/geosciences
    Enrollment (2012): B: 44 (9) M: 8 (4)
Chair:
    George W. Kipphut, (D), Columbia, 1978, GeOg
Professor:
    Haluk Cetin, (D), Purdue, 1993, OiGe
    Kit W. Wesler, (D), North Carolina, 1981, Oni
Associate Professor:
    Qiaofeng (Robin) Zhang, (D), W Ontario, 2002, Oi
Assistant Professor:
    Sung-ho Hong, (D), New Mexico Tech, 2008, HyGe
Research Associate:
    Jane L. Benson, (M), Murray State, 1986, Oi

Instructor:
    Anthony L. Ortmann, (D), Tulane, 2007, OnYg
Adjunct Professor:
    Michael R. Busby, (M), Murray State, 1996, Oi

Northern Kentucky University
Dept of Geology (B) O (2015)
204H Natural Sciences Center
Highland Heights, KY 41099
    p. (859) 572-5309
    rockawayj@nku.edu
    http://nku.edu/
    Enrollment (2015): B: 60 (14)
Associate Professor:
    Janet Bertog, (D), Cincinnati, 2002, Gd
    Samuel Boateng, (D), Missouri (Rolla), 1996, Hw
    John D. Rockaway, (D), Purdue, 1968, Ng
Lecturer:
    Reuben G. Bullard, (M), Cincinnati, 2000, Gd
    Sarah E. Johnson, (M), Purdue, 1997, Ng

Owensboro Community and Technical College
Owensboro Community and Technical College (1999)
4800 New Hartford Road
Owensboro, KY 42303
    http://www.owensboro.kctcs.edu/

University of Kentucky 📖
Dept of Earth and Environmental Sciences (B,M,D) O (2015)
101 Slone Research Building
121 Washington St.
Lexington, KY 40506-0053
    p. (859) 257-3758
    moker@uky.edu
    http://ees.as.uky.edu
    Enrollment (2015): B: 57 (14) M: 29 (6) D: 12 (0)
Chair:
    David P. Moecher, (D), Michigan, 1988, GxtCg
Professor:
    Frank R. Ettensohn, (D), Illinois, 1975, Ps
    Dhananjay Ravat, (D), Purdue, 1989, YgmYv
    Edward W. Woolery, (D), Kentucky, 1998, Ys
Associate Professor:
    Alan E. Fryar, (D), Alberta, 1992, Hw
    Kevin Yeager, (D), Texas A&M, 2002, GsCm
Assistant Professor:
    Sean Bemis, (D), Oregon, 2010, GctYs
    Rebecca Freeman, (D), Tulane, 2011, GrPi
    Michael M. McGlue, (D), Arizona, 2011, Gso
    Ryan Thigpen, (D), Virginia Tech, 2009, Gtc
Lecturer:
    Kent Ratajeski, (D), North Carolina, 1999, Gi
Adjunct Professor:
    J. Richard Bowersox, (D), South Florida, 2006, Go
    Cortland F. Eble, (D), West Virginia, 1988, Pl
    Stephen F. Greb, (D), Kentucky, 1992, Ec
    Christopher Groves, (D), Virginia, 1993, Hg
    James C. Hower, (D), Penn State, 1978, Ec
    Hickman B. John, (D), Kentucky, 2011, Gto
    Thomas M. Parris, (D), California (Santa Barbara), 1998, Cg
    Thomas Robl, (D), Kentucky, 1977, EcCo
    Zhenming Wang, (D), Kentucky, 1998, Ys
    Gerald A. Weisenfluh, (D), South Carolina, 1982, Ec
    Junfeng Zhu, (D), Arizona, 2005
Emeritus:
    William H. Blackburn, (D), MIT, 1967, GxCg
    Bruce R. Moore, (D), Melbourne, 1967, Gd
    Kieran D. O'Hara, (D), Brown, 1984, Gc
    Lyle V. A. Sendlein, (D), Iowa State, 1964, Hw
    Ronald L. Street, (D), St. Louis, 1975, Ys
    William A. Thomas, (D), Virginia Tech, 1960, Gt
Laboratory Director:
    Peter J. Idstein, (M), Eastern Kentucky, 1992, Gg

Dept of Mining Engineering (B,M,D) (2015)
230 Mining & Mineral Resources Building

Lexington, KY 40506-0107
p. (859) 257-8026
rick.honaker@uky.edu
http://www.engr.uky.edu/mng/
t: @UK_Mining
Enrollment (2015): B: 125 (36) M: 14 (7) D: 17 (3)
Chair:
Rick Honkaer, (D), Virginia Tech, 1992, Nm
Professor:
Zach Agioutantis, (D), Virginia Tech, 1987, Nr
Braden Lusk, (D), Missouri (Rolla), 2006, Nm
Thomas Novak, (D), Penn State, 1984, Nm
Joseph Sottile, Jr., (D), Penn State, 1991, Nm
Assistant Professor:
Kyle Perry , (D), Kentucky, 2010, Nr
Jhon Silva-Castro, (D), Kentucky, 2012, Nm
William Chad Wedding, (D), Kentucky, 2014, Nm
Emeritus:
Kot F. Unrug, (D), Academy of Mining-Metallurgy, 1966, Nr
Andrew M. Wala, (D), Academy of Mining-Metallurgy, 1972, Nm

Western Kentucky University
Dept of Geography & Geology (B,M) O (2015)
1906 College Heights Blvd
#31066
Bowling Green, KY 42101-1066
p. (270) 745-4555
david.keeling@wku.edu
http://www.wku.edu/geoweb
Enrollment (2015): B: 140 (18) M: 26 (7)
Head:
David Keeling, (D), Oregon, 1992, Og
Professor:
Catherine Algeo, (D), Louisiana State, 1997, Oi
Stuart Foster, (D), Ohio State, 1988, Oa
Christopher Groves, (D), Virginia, 1993, Hg
Rezaul Mahmood, (D), Oklahoma, 2000, Oa
Michael May, (D), Indiana, 1993, Ge
Associate Professor:
John All, (D), Arizona, 2001, Oyr
Josh Durkee, (D), Georgia, Oa
Greg Goodrich, (D), Arizona, Oa
Margaret "Peggy" Gripshover, (D), Tennessee, On
Fredrick D. Siewers, (D), Illinois, 1995, Pg
Andrew Wulff, (D), Massachusetts, 1993, Gv
Jun Yan, (D), Buffalo, 2004, Oi
Assistant Professor:
Xingang Fan, (D), Lanzhou, Oa
Nahid Gani, (D), Texas, Gc
Leslie North, (D), South Florida, Og
Jason Polk, (D), South Florida, Gm
Instructor:
William Blackburn, (M), W Kentucky, 2002, Oy
Kevin Cary, (M), W Kentucky, 2000, Oi
Margaret Crowder, (D), WKU, 2012, Oe
Scott Dobler, (M), Bowling Green, 1996, Oa
Patricia Kambesis, (D), Mississippi State, 2014, OigHw
Instructor:
Amy Nemon, (M), WKU, 2005, Oig
Emeritus:
Nicholas Crawford, (D), Clark, 1977, Hg
Kenneth W. Kuehn, (D), Penn State, 1982, Ec
Louis M. Trapasso, (D), Indiana State, 1978, Oa

Louisiana

Centenary College of Louisiana
Dept of Geology (B) (2014)
2911 Centenary Boulevard
Shreveport, LA 71104
p. (318) 869-5234
dbieler@centenary.edu
Enrollment (2014): B: 19 (0)
Professor:
Scott K. Vetter, (D), South Carolina, 1989, Gi

Associate Professor:
David B. Bieler, (D), Illinois, 1983, GtrYe

Delgado Community College
Science & Math Div (A) (2014)
615 City Park Avenue
New Orleans, LA 70119
p. (504) 671-6480
jwood@dcc.edu
http://www.dcc.edu/divisions/sciencemath/
Professor:
Jacqueline Wood, (M), New Orleans, Gg

Louisiana State University
Dept of Agronomy (B,M,D) (2014)
104 M. B. Sturgis Hall
Baton Rouge, LA 70803
p. (225) 578-2110
Fmartin@agcenter.lsu.edu
http://www.agronomy.lsu.edu
Enrollment: No data reported since 1999
Head:
Freddie A. Martin, (D), Cornell, 1970, On
Professor:
Gary A. Breitenbeck, (D), Iowa State, 1984, Sb
Hussein M. Selim, (D), Iowa State, 1971, Sp
Assistant Professor:
Lewis A. Gaston, (D), Florida, 1987, Sc
Maud Walsh, (D), Louisiana State, 1989, Ge
Jim Wang, (D), Iowa State, 1990, Sc
Instructor:
Michal Lindsey, (M), Louisiana State, 1998, So

Dept of Geography & Anthropology (B,M,D) (2011)
227 Howe-Russell Geoscience Complex
Baton Rouge, LA 70803
p. (225) 578-5942
gachair@lsu.edu
http://www.ga.lsu.edu
Enrollment (2006): B: 54 (23) M: 12 (6) D: 22 (7)
Chair:
Kevin Robbins
Professor:
Patrick A. Hesp, (D), Sydney, 1981, Gm
Richard H. Kesel, (D), Maryland, 1971, Hg
Associate Professor:
Steven Namikas, (D), S California, 1999, Gm

Dept of Geology & Geophysics (B,M,D) O (2015)
E235 Howe Russell Kniffen Geoscience Complex
Baton Rouge, LA 70803-4101
p. (225) 578-3353
geology@lsu.edu
www.lsu.edu/science/geology/
f: http://www.facebook.com/LSUGeology
t: @LSUGeology
Enrollment (2015): B: 158 (26) M: 38 (7) D: 29 (4)
Chair:
Carol M. Wicks, (D), Virginia, 1992, HwClHy
Professor:
Huiming Bao, (D), Princeton, 1998, Cs
Samuel J. Bentley, (D), SUNY (Stony Brook), 1998, Gu
Peter Clift, (D), Edinburgh, 1993, GsuGo
Peter Doran, (D), Hgs
Barbara L. Dutrow, (D), S Methodist, 1985, Gz
Brooks B. Ellwood, (D), Rhode Island, 1977, Ym
Darrell J. Henry, (D), Wisconsin, 1981, Gp
Associate Professor:
Philip J. Bart, (D), Rice, 1998, Gr
Juan M. Lorenzo, (D), Columbia, 1991, Ys
Sophie Warny, (D), Catholic (Belgium), 1999, Pl
Field Camp Director:
Amy Luther, (D), New Mexico Tech, Gc
Assistant Professor:
Achim Herrmann, (D), Penn State, 2005, PeGd
Suniti Karuntillake, (D), Cornell, 2008, Xg

Karen Luttrell, (D), Scripps, Yg
Jianwei Wang, (D), Illinois (Urbana-Champaign), CgGz
Carol A. Wilson, (D), Boston, 2003, GsOnCc
Guangsheng Zhuang, (D), California (Santa Cruz), 2011, CccCo
Instructor:
Yanxia Ma, (D), Og
Associate Curator, LSU Museum of Natural Science:
Judith A. Schiebout, (D), Texas, 1973, Pv
Emeritus:
Ajoy K. Baksi, (D), Toronto, 1970, Cc
Gary R. Byerly, (D), Michigan State, 1974, Gi
Ray E. Ferrell, Jr., (D), Illinois, 1966, Cl
Jeffrey S. Hanor, (D), Harvard, 1967, Cl
George Hart, (D), Sheffield, 1961, Gg
Clyde Moore, On
Jeffrey A. Nunn, (D), Northwestern, 1981, Yg
James E. Roche, (D), Illinois, 1969, Gg
Barun K. Sen Gupta, (D), Indian Inst of Tech, 1963, Pm

Dept of Oceanography & Coastal Sciences (M,D) (2014)
1002 Energy Coast and Environment Building
Baton Rouge, LA 70803
p. (225) 578-6308
ocean@lsu.edu
http://www.ocean.lsu.edu
Administrative Assistant: Gaynell Gibbs
Enrollment (2010): M: 63 (11) D: 92 (11)
Professor:
Robert P. Gambrell, (D), North Carolina State, 1974, Cg
Paul A. LaRock, (D), Rensselaer, 1968, Ob
Irving A. Mendelssohn, (D), North Carolina State, 1974, Ob
Richard F. Shaw, (D), Maine, 1981, Ob
Robert E. Turner, (D), Georgia, 1974, Ob
Associate Professor:
Donald M. Baltz, (D), California (Davis), 1980, Ob
Robert S. Carney, (D), Oregon State, 1977, Ob
Lawrence J. Rouse, Jr., (D), Louisiana State, 1969, Op
Assistant Professor:
Mark C. Benfield, (D), Texas A&M, 1991, Ob
Adjunct Professor:
Dubravko Justic, (D), Zagreb, 1989, Op
Nancy N. Rabalais, (D), Texas, 1983, Ob
Harry H. Roberts, (D), Louisiana State, 1969, Gs
Paul W. Sammarco, (D), SUNY, 1978, On
Nan D. Walker, (D), Cape Town, 1989, Og

Louisiana Tech University
Geosciences Program (B,M) (2011)
600 W. Arizona Street
Ruston, LA 71272
p. (318) 257-3972
mm@engr.latech.edu
http://www.coes.latech.edu/geo/
Department Secretary: Connie McKenzie
Enrollment: No data reported since 1999
Chair:
Gary S. Zumwalt, (D), California (Davis), 1976, Pi
Associate Professor:
Maureen McCurdy, (D), Wisconsin, 1990, Hw
Emeritus:
Leo A. Herrmann, (D), Johns Hopkins, 1951, Go

Nicholls State University
Dept of Physical Sciences (2015)
P.O. Box 2022
Thibodaux, LA 70310
p. (985) 448-4502
marguerite.moloney@nicholls.edu
http://www.nicholls.edu/phsc
Enrollment: No data reported since 1999
Instructor:
Adam Beyer, (M), S Illinois, Gg
Marguerite M. Moloney, (M), S Illinois, 2004, GeOnn

Northwestern State University
Dept of Chemistry and Physics (B) (2015)

Natchitoches, LA 71497
p. (318) 357-5501
chinc@nsula.edu
Enrollment: No data reported since 1999
Director:
Paul Withey
Professor:
Carol S. Chin, (D)
Kelly Knowlton, (D), Texas A&M, 1991, Gg

South Louisiana Community College
South Louisiana Community College (1999)
320 Devalcourt
Lafayette, LA 70506
p. (337) 521-8983
http://www.slcc.cc.la.us

Tulane University
Dept of Earth and Environmental Sciences (B,M,D) ● (2016)
6823 St. Charles Ave.
101 Blessey Hall
New Orleans, LA 70118
p. (504) 865-5198
mreine@tulane.edu
http://www.tulane.edu/sse/eens
Enrollment (2015): B: 6 (0) M: 0 (2) D: 0 (2)
Chair:
Torbjörn E. Törnqvist, (D), Utrecht (Neth), 1993, Gs
Professor:
Mead Allison, (D), SUNY (Stony Brook), 1993, Gs
Karen Haley Johannesson, (D), Nevada, 1993, HgCg
Associate Professor:
Nancye H. Dawers, (D), Columbia, 1997, Gc
George C. Flowers, (D), California (Berkeley), 1979, Hw
Stephen A. Nelson, (D), California (Berkeley), 1979, Gi
Assistant Professor:
Nicole Gasparini, (D), MIT, 2003, Ngg
Brent Goehring, (D), Columbia, 2010, CsGtv
Kyle Martin Straub, (D), MIT, 2007, GgCg
Visiting Professor:
Jeffrey G. Agnew, (D), Louisiana State, 2008, Poe
Reda Amer, (D), St. Louis, 2011, OirGe
Jeffrey M. Sigler, (D), Yale, 2006, GgOwa
Emeritus:
Ronald L. Parsely, (D), Cincinnati, 1969, Pg

University of Louisiana at Lafayette
School of Geosciences (B,M) ● (2014)
BOX 44530
Lafayette, LA 70504-4530
p. (337) 482-6468
geology@louisiana.edu
http://geology.louisiana.edu
Administrative Assistant: Nadean S.. Bienvenu
Administrative Assistant: Pauline R. Greene
Enrollment (2012): B: 135 (33) M: 49 (17)
Director:
David M. Borrok, (D), Notre Dame, 2005, Cg
Assistant Director:
Durga Poudel, (D), Georgia (Athens), 1998, Ge
Carl Richter, (D), Tubingen, 1990, Ym
Professor:
Gary L. Kinsland, (D), Rochester, 1974, Yg
Brian E. Lock, (D), Cambridge, 1969, Gs
Herman H. Rieke, (D), S California, 1970, Np
Senior Scientist:
James E. Martin, (D), Washington, 1979, PvGg
Resource Facilitator:
Jim Foret, (M), Iowa State, 1971, Ge
Associate Professor:
Timothy W. Duex, (D), Texas, 1983, Hg
Jenneke Visser, (D), Amsterdam, 1983, Ge
Assistant Professor:
E. Griff Blakewood, (D), Louisiana State, 1990, Ge
Brian Schubert, (D), Binghamton, 2008, Cg

Instructor:
    Cathy Bishop, (M), Louisiana, Gg
    Kristie Cornell, (M), Louisiana (Lafayette), 2003, Gg
    William H. Schramm, (M), SW Louisiana, 1984, GeHwYg
Adjunct Professor:
    F. Clayton Breland, Jr., (D)
Emeritus:
    Walter P. Kessinger, (D), Louisiana State, 1974, Pm

University of Louisiana, Monroe
School of Science, Atmospheric Science Program (B) (2015)
700 University Avenue
Monroe, LA 71209-0550
    p. (318) 342-1822
    casehanks@ulm.edu
    http://www.ulm.edu/atmos/
    Enrollment (2012): B: 43 (9)
Associate Dean of Arts and Sciences:
    Michael A. Camille, (D), Texas A&M, 1991, Oy
Professor:
    Eric A. Pani, (D), Texas Tech, 1987, Oa
Associate Professor:
    Sean Chenoweth, (D), Wisconsin (Milwaukee), 2003, GmOir
Department Head:
    Anne T. Case Hanks, (D), Georgia Tech, 2008, Oae
Station Archeologist/Poverty Point:
    Diana M. Greenlee, (D), Washington, 2002, GaCo

University of New Orleans
Dept of Earth and Environmental Sciences (B,M,D) (2014)
2000 Lakeshore Drive
New Orleans, LA 70148
    p. (504) 280-6325
    djreed@uno.edu
    http://www.uno.edu/geology/
    Enrollment (2005): B: 106 (11) M: 35 (6) D: 4 (0)
Professor:
    William H. Busch, (D), Oregon State, 1981, Ou
    Terry L. Pavlis, (D), Utah, 1982, Gt
    Denise J. Reed, (D), Cambridge, 1986, Gm
    A. K. Mostofa Sarwar, (D), Indiana, 1983, Ye
    Laura F. Serpa, (D), Cornell, 1986, Ys
    William B. Simmons, (D), Michigan, 1973, Gz
    Ronald K. Stoessell, (D), California (Berkeley), 1977, Cl
Associate Professor:
    Kraig L. Derstler, (D), California (Davis), 1985, Pv
    Frank R. Hall, (D), Rhode Island, 1991, Ym
Assistant Professor:
    Mark A. Kulp, (D), Kentucky, 2000, Gr
    Christopher D. Parkinson, (D), London (UK), 1991, Gp
Adjunct Professor:
    Miles O. Hayes, (D), Texas, 1965, Gs
    Karen L. Webber, (D), Rice, 1988, Gv
    Michael A. Wise, (D), Manitoba, 1987, Gz
Emeritus:
    Gary C. Allen, (D), North Carolina, 1968, Gp
    Jacqueline Michel, (D), South Carolina, 1980, Cg

Maine

Bates College
Geology (B) (2016)
Carnegie Science Center
44 Campus Avenue
Lewiston, ME 04240-6084
    p. (207) 786-6490
    http://www.bates.edu/geology/
    f: https://www.facebook.com/groups/243958415633596/
    Administrative Assistant: Sylvia Deschaine
    Enrollment (2015): B: 27 (0)
Chair:
    Michael J. Retelle, (D), Massachusetts, 1985, Gl
Professor:
    J. Dykstra Eusden, Jr., (D), Dartmouth, 1988, Gc
    Beverly J. Johnson, (D), Colorado, 1998, Cl

Assistant Professor:
    Genevieve Robert, (D), Missouri, 2014, Cp
Assistant Instructor:
    Marita Bryant, (M), Free (Berlin), 1984, Gg
Lecturer:
    Gene A. Clough, (D), Caltech, 1978, Ym
Emeritus:
    John W. Creasy, (D), Harvard, 1974, Gx

Bowdoin College
Dept of Earth and Oceanographic Science (B) (2014)
6800 College Station
Brunswick, ME 04011
    p. (207) 725-3628
    mparker@bowdoin.edu
    http://www.bowdoin.edu/earth-oceanographic-science/
    Administrative Assistant: Marjorie Parker
    Enrollment (2014): B: 60 (27)
Rusack Professor of Environmental Studies:
    Philip Camill III, (D), Duke, 1999, PebSb
Professor:
    Rachel J. Beane, (D), Stanford, 1997, Gp
Chair:
    Collin Roesler, (D), Washington, 1992, OgpOr
Associate Professor:
    Peter D. Lea, (D), Colorado, 1989, Gl
Assistant Professor:
    Michéle LaVigne, (D), Rutgers, 2010, OcPe
    Emily M. Peterman, (D), California (Santa Barbara), 2009, Gtp
Service Learning Coord/Lab Instr:
    Cathryn K. Field, (M), Smith, 2000, Ge
Lab Instructor:
    Joanne Urquhart, (M), Dartmouth, 1987, Ge
Associate Professor:
    Edward P. Laine, (D), MIT, 1977, Gu

Colby College
Dept of Geology (B) (2015)
5800 Mayflower Hill
Waterville, ME 04901-8858
    p. (207) 859-5800
    amridky@colby.edu
    http://www.colby.edu/geologydept/
    Administrative Assistant: Alice M. Ridky
    Enrollment (2015): B: 29 (7)
Professor:
    Robert A. Gastaldo, (D), S Illinois, 1978, PbGs
    Robert E. Nelson, (D), Washington, 1982, Pe
Associate Professor:
    Walter A. Sullivan, (D), Wyoming, 2007, Gct
Assistant Professor:
    Tasha Dunn, (D), Vanderbilt, 2007, GpiGz
Visiting Professor:
    Bruce F. Rueger, (D), Colorado, 2002, Pl
Emeritus:
    Donald B. Allen, (D), Illinois, 1972, Eg
    Harold R. Pestana, (D), Iowa, 1965, Pi
Cooperating Faculty:
    S. Cole, (M), Illinois, 1975, On

University of Maine
School of Earth and Climate Sciences (B,M,D) (2016)
5790 Bryand Global Sciences Center
Orono, ME 04469-5790
    p. (207) 581-2152
    dianne.perro@umit.maine.edu
    http://www.umaine.edu/earthclimate/
    f: https://www.facebook.com/pages/UMaine-School-of-
    Earth-and-Climate-Sciences/238244500701
    Administrative Assistant: Dianne Perro
    Enrollment (2015): B: 42 (6) M: 13 (4) D: 14 (1)
Research Professor:
    Edward S. Grew, (D), Harvard, 1972, Gp
    Roger L. Hooke, (D), Caltech, 1965, Gm
Director:
    Scott E. Johnson, (D), James Cook, 1989, Gc

Professor:
Daniel F. Belknap, (D), Delaware, 1979, Gu
George H. Denton, (D), Yale, 1965, Gl
Brenda L. Hall, (D), Maine, 1997, Gl
Gordon S. Hamilton, (D), Cambridge, 1992, Ol
Joseph T. Kelley, (D), Lehigh, 1979, Gu
Peter O. Koons, (D), ETH (Switzerland), 1982, Gt
Karl J. Kreutz, (D), New Hampshire, 1998, Cs
Daniel R. Lux, (D), Ohio State, 1981, Gi
Kirk A. Maasch, (D), Yale, 1989, Oa
Paul A. Mayewski, (D), Ohio State, 1973, Pe
Aaron E. Putnam, (D), Maine, 2011, Gll
Andrew S. Reeve, (D), Syracuse, 1996, Hw
Associate Professor:
Christopher C. Gerbi, (D), Maine, 2005, Gt
Assistant Professor:
Katherine A. Allen, (D), Columbia, 2013, Gu
Alicia M. Cruz-Uribe, (D), Penn State, 2014, Gxx
Amanda A. Olsen, (D), Virginia Tech, 2007, Cl
Sean Smith, (D), Johns Hopkins, 2010, Hs
Research Assistant Professor:
Seth W. Campbell, (D), Maine, 2010, Gl
Researach Assistant Professor:
Gordon R. M. Bromley, (D), Maine, 2010, Gl
Instructor:
Alice R. Kelley, (M), Lehigh, 1981, Ga
Martin G. Yates, (D), Indiana, 1988, Eg
Emeritus:
Harold W. Borns, Jr., (D), Boston, 1959, Gl
Joseph V. Chernosky, Jr., (D), MIT, 1973, Gg
Terence J. Hughes, (D), Northwestern, 1968, Gl
Stephen A. Norton, (D), Harvard, 1967, Cl
Research Assistant Professor:
Sean Birkel, (D), Maine, 2010, Gl

School of Marine Sciences (B,M,D) O (2014)
5706 Aubert Hall, Rm 360
Orono, ME 04469-5706
p. (207) 581-4381
fchai@maine.edu
http://www.umaine.edu/marine/
Enrollment (2010): B: 145 (38) M: 56 (0) D: 9 (0)

University of Maine - Farmington
Dept of Geology (B) (2015)
173 High Street
Farmington, ME 04938
p. (207) 778-7402
dgibson@maine.edu
http://sciences.umf.maine.edu
Administrative Assistant: DeAnna Ridley
Enrollment (2015): B: 25 (7)
Chair:
Mariella Passarelli, (D), Emery, 1989, Co
Professor:
David Gibson, (D), Queens (Ireland), 1984, GigGz
Associate Professor:
Julia F. Daly, (D), Maine, 2002, GmlGu
Douglas N. Reusch, (D), Maine, 1998, GtCgOu
Emeritus:
Thomas E. Eastler, (D), Columbia, 1970, GeOrGg

University of Maine, Presque Isle
Div of Mathematics & Science (B) (2014)
181 Main Street
Presque Isle, ME 04769
p. (207) 768-9482
kevin.mccartney@umpi.edu
http://www.umpi.edu/
Department Secretary: Connie Leveque
Enrollment: No data reported since 1999
Chair:
Michael Knopp
Professor:
Kevin McCartney, (D), Florida State, 1988, Pm

College of Southern Maryland
Biological and Physical Sciences (A) (2010)
8730 Mitchell Rd
La Plata, MD 20646
p. (301) 934-7841
Billm@csmd.edu
http://www.csmd.edu/bio/index.html
Professor:
Tom Russ, (M), Kutztown, GgSo

Community College of Baltimore County, Catonsville
School of Mathematics & Science (A) (2015)
800 S. Rolling Road
Catonsville, MD 21228
p. (443) 840-5935
DLudwikoski@ccbcmd.edu
http://www.ccbcmd.edu/math_science/geology.html
Administrative Assistant: Annjeannette Black
Enrollment (2015): A: 3 (0)
Associate Professor:
David J. Ludwikoski, (M), Toledo, 1993, OegOn

Frederick Community College
Science Dept (A) (2014)
7932 Opossumtown Pike
Frederick, MD 21702
p. (301) 846-2510
shsmith@frederick.edu
http://www.frederick.edu/courses_and_programs/dept_science.aspx
Professor:
Richard Gottfried, (M), U of Penn, 1977, GgdGz
Associate Professor:
Natasha Cleveland, (M), Oge

Frostburg State University
Dept of Geography (B) (2010)
101 Braddock Rd.
Frostburg, MD 21532
p. (301) 687-4369
gyutzy@frostburg.edu
http://www.frostburg.edu/dept/geog/
Administrative Assistant: Gale Yutzy
Enrollment (2010): B: 65 (16)
Chair:
Craig L. Caupp, (D), Utah State, 1986, OnHs
Professor:
Henry W. Bullamore, (D), Iowa, 1978, On
Francis L. Precht, (D), Georgia, 1989, Oy
Associate Professor:
Fritz Kessler, (D), Kansas, 1999, Or
James C. Saku, (D), Saskatchewan, 1995, On
George W. White, (D), Oregon, 1994, On
Assistant Professor:
Phillip Allen, (D), Coventry (UK), 2005, GmePe
David L. Arnold, (D), Indiana, 1994, Oa
Matthew E. Ramspott, (D), Kansas, 2006, Or

Johns Hopkins University
Dept of Geography & Environmental Engineering (B,M,D) (2014)
313 Ames Hall
34th & Charles Streets
Baltimore, MD 21218-2681
p. (410) 516-7092
dogee@jhu.edu
http://www.jhu.edu/dogee
Enrollment: No data reported since 1999
Chair:
Edward John Bouwer, (D), Stanford, 1982, On
Professor:
William P. Ball, (D), Stanford, 1989, On

65

Grace S. Brush, (D), Harvard, 1956, Pl
Hugh Ellis, (D), Waterloo, 1984, On
Steve H. Hanke, (D), Colorado, 1969, On
Benjamin F. Hobbs, (D), Cornell, 1983, On
A. Lynn Roberts, (D), MIT, 1991, On
Erica J. Schoenberger, (D), California (Berkeley), 1984, On
Alan T. Stone, (D), Caltech, 1983, Cl
Peter W. Wilcock, (D), MIT, 1987, Gm
Associate Professor:
Markus Hilpert, (D), On
Assistant Professor:
Kai Loon Chen, (D), Yale, 2008, On
Seth Guikema, (D), Stanford, 2003, On
Catherine Norman, (D), California (Santa Barbara), 2005, On
Lecturer:
Hedy Alavi, (D), Ohio State, 1983, On
Emeritus:
John J. Boland, (D), Johns Hopkins, 1973, On
Charles R. O'Melia, (D), Michigan, 1963, On
Eugene D. Shchukin, (D), Moscow State, 1958, On
Senior Academic Program Coordinator:
Adena Rojas, (M), On

The Morton K. Blaustein Dept of Earth & Planetary Sciences
(B,M,D) (2015)
3400 N Charles Street
301 Olin Hall
Baltimore, MD 21218
p. (410) 516-7135
kgaines@jhu.edu
http://eps.jhu.edu/
Enrollment (2013): D: 33 (5)
Chair:
Thomas W.N. Haine, (D), Southampton, 1993, Op
Professor:
Peter L. Olson, (D), California (Berkeley), 1977, Yg
Darrell F. Strobel, (D), Harvard, 1969, Oa
Dimitri A. Sverjensky, (D), Yale, 1980, Cl
Darryn W. Waugh, (D), Cambridge, 1991, Oa
Associate Professor:
Anand Gnanadesikan, (D), MIT/WHOI, 1994, Op
Benjamin Passey, (D), Utah, 2007, Cs
Assistant Professor:
Sarah Horst, (D), Arizona, 2011
Naomi Levin, (D), Utah, 2008, Gs
Kevin Lewis, (D), Caltech, 2009
Benjamin Zaitchik, (D), Yale, 2006, Oa
Research Professor:
Katalin Szlavecz, (D), Eotvos (Hungary), 1981, Pi

Montgomery College
Dept of Physics, Engineering & Geosciences (A) (2011)
51 Mannakee Street
Rockville, MD 20850
p. (301) 279-5230
Muhammad.Kehnemouyi@montgomerycollege.edu
http://www.montgomerycollege.edu/Departments/phengrv/
Administrative Assistant: Mary (Deep) McGregor
Associate Professor:
Alan Cutler, (D), Geology
Instructional Laboratory Coordinator for Geosciences:
Kimberly Kelly, (B), Pittsburgh, On

St. Charles Community College
St. Charles Community College
4601 Mid Rivers Mall Drive
Cottleville, MO 63376
p. (636) 922-8000
nfo_desk@stchas.edu
http://www.stchas.edu/

Towson University
Dept of Physics, Astronomy & Geosciences (B) (2016)
8000 York Road
Towson, MD 21252-0001
p. (410) 704-3020

dschaefer@towson.edu
http://wwwnew.towson.edu/physics/geosciences/
Enrollment (2015): B: 28 (4)
Professor:
Rachel J. Burks, (D), Texas, 1985, Gc
David A. Vanko, (D), Northwestern, 1982, Gx
Assistant Professor:
Joel Moore, (D), Penn State, 2008, ClsGt
Wendy Nelson, (D), Penn State, 2009, Gi
Amy Williams, (D), California (Davis), 2014, Ca
Lecturer:
Tsigabu A. Gebrehiwet, (D), W Michigan, 2007, Hw
Gregory A. Shofner, (D), Maryland, 2011, Cg

United States Naval Academy
Dept of Oceanography (B) (2014)
572C Holloway Road
Annapolis, MD 21402-5026
p. (410) 293-6550
petrunci@usna.edu
http://www.nadn.navy.mil/Oceanography/
Administrative Assistant: Cynthia A.. Ervin
Enrollment (2014): B: 216 (117)
Professor:
Peter L. Guth, (D), MIT, 1980, GuOiy
Chair:
David R. Smith, (D), Texas A&M, 1979, Ow
Associate Professor:
Andrew C. Muller, (D), Old Dominion, 1998, Op
Cecily N. Steppe, (D), Delaware, 2001, Ob
Assistant Professor:
Bradford S. Barrett, (D), Oklahoma, 2007, Oa
Gina R. Henderson, (D), Delaware, 2010, Oa
Emil T. Petruncio, (D), Naval Postgrad Sch, 1996, Opr
Elizabeth R. Sanabia, (D), Naval Postgrad Sch, 2010, Ow
William J. Schulz, (D), Old Dominion, 1999, Opw
Joseph P. Smith, (D), Massachusetts (Boston), 2007, CmOg
Instructor:
Dwight E. Smith, (M), Naval Postgrad Sch, 2009, Owg
Megan D. Thomas, (M), Naval Postgrad Sch, 2005, Og
Oceanography Reference Librarian:
Barbara Yoakum, (M), South Carolina, 1985, On

University of Maryland
Dept of Geology (B,M,D) (2016)
Geology Building (#237), Room 1118
8000 Regents Drive
College Park, MD 20742-4211
p. (301) 405-4082
geology@umd.edu
http://www.geol.umd.edu
f: https://www.facebook.com/UMDGeology
Administrative Assistant: Dorothy Brown
Enrollment (2014): B: 48 (10) M: 4 (5) D: 24 (1)
Chair:
Richard J. Walker, (D), SUNY (Stony Brook), 1984, CcXcCg
Research Professor:
Robert Tucker, (D), Yale, 1985
Affiliate Professor:
Antonio Busalacchi, (D), Florida State, 1982, Og
Bruce James, (D), Vermont, 1981, Sc
Michael Kearney, (D), W Ontario, 1981, On
Raghuram G. Murtugudde, (D), Columbia, 1994, Obr
Jessica Sunshine, (D), Brown, 1993
Ning Zeng, (D), Arizona, 1994, Oa
Professor:
Michael Brown, (D), Keele, 1975, Gx
Philip A. Candela, (D), Harvard, 1982, CpgEg
James Farquhar, (D), Alberta, 1995, Cs
Alan J. Kaufman, (D), Indiana, 1990, Csg
Daniel Lathrop, (D), Texas, 1991, Yg
William F. McDonough, (D), Australian National, 1988, Cg
Senior Research Scientist:
Philip M. Piccoli, (D), Maryland, 1992, Cg
Igor Puchtel, (D), Russian Acad of Sci, 1992, CcgGi

Associate Professor:
    Michael N. Evans, (D), Columbia, 1999, CsOaGq
    Sujay Kaushal, (D), Colorado, 2003, OuGeHs
    Laurent G. Montesi, (D), MIT, 2002, YgsGt
    Sarah Penniston-Dorland, (D), Johns Hopkins, 2005, Gp
    Karen L. Prestegaard, (D), California (Berkeley), 1982, Hgw
    Wenlu Zhu, (D), SUNY (Stony Brook), 1996, YrNrHg
Associate Research Scientist:
    Richard Ash, (D), Open, 1990, Ca
Assistant Professor:
    Derrick Lampkin, (D)
    Vedran Lekic, (D), California (Berkeley), 2009, Ysg
    Nicholas Schmerr, (D), Arizona State, 2008, XyYs
Visiting Research Associate:
    Timothy Johnson, (D), Derby, 1999
    Zoltan Zajacz, (D), Swiss Fed Inst Tech, 2007
Research Associate:
    Jabrane Labidi, (D), Inst Physique du Globe de Paris, 2012, Cg
NSF Post-doc:
    Scott Burdick, (D), MIT, 2014, Ys
Research Associate:
    Katherine Bermingham, (D), Westfalische Wilhelms, 2011, XcCcg
    Shuiwang Duan, (D), Tulane, 2005, HsOu
    Melodie French, (D), Texas A&M, 2014, Ygx
    Joost Hoek, (D), Pennsylvania, 2004, CsgCa
    Tolulope M. Olugboji, (D), Yale, 2014, Ysg
Senior Lecturer:
    Thomas R. Holtz, Jr., (D), Yale, 1992, Pv
    John W. Merck, Jr., (D), Texas, 1997, Pv
Lecturer:
    Tracey Centorbi, (B), Maryland, 2003, Cg
Adjunct Associate Professor:
    Elizabeth Cottrell, (D), Columbia, 2004, CpgGx
Adjunct Assistant Professor:
    Anat Shahar, (D), California (Los Angeles), 2008, CspCa
Adjunct Professor:
    John Bohlke, (D), California (Berkeley), 1986, Cag
    Yingwei Fei, (D), CUNY, 1989, CpGxCg
    Roberta L. Rudnick, (D), Australian National, 1988, CgsCt
    Steven Shirey, (D), SUNY (Stony Brook), 1984, CgaCc
    Deborah Smith, (D), California (San Diego), 1985
    Sorena Sorensen, (D), California (Los Angeles), 1984, Gp
Visiting Professor:
    Saswata Hier-Majumder, (D), Minnesota, 2004, YgGq
Emeritus Professor:
    Ann G. Wylie, (D), Columbia, 1972, Gz
Emeritus Affiliate Research Professor:
    George Helz, (D), Penn State, 1970, HsGeCg
Associate Professor Emeritus:
    Peter B. Stifel, (D), Utah, 1964, Pg
Faculty Research Assistant:
    Todd Karwoski, (B), Maryland, 2005, Gg
    Rebecca Plummer, (M), Michigan, 2000, Csa
    Valentina Puchtel, (M), Moscow Geological Prospecting Acad, 1983

Dept of Plant Science & Landscape Architecture (B,M,D) (2014)
2102 Plant Sciences Building
College Park, MD 20742-4432
    p. (301) 405-4356
    asmurphy@umd.edu
    http://www.psla.umd.edu/
    Enrollment: No data reported since 1999
Professor:
    Christopher Walsh, (D), Cornell, 1980, On
Associate Professor:
    Gary D. Coleman, (D), Nebraska, 1989, On
    Jack B. Sullivan, (M), Virginia, 1980, Ou
Program Management Specialist:
    Kathy Hunt, On
Coordinator:
    Sue Burk, On

Marine-Estuarine-Environmental Sciences Graduate Program
(M,D) (2014)
1213 HJ Patterson Hall
University of Maryland
College Park, MD 20742

    p. (301) 405-6938
    mees@umd.edu
    http://www.mees.umd.edu
    Enrollment (2013): M: 6 (0) D: 12 (2)
Professor:
    Shenn-Yu Chao, (D), North Carolina State, 1979, Op
    Thomas R. Fisher, Jr., (D), Duke, 1975, Ob
    Patricia M. Gilbert, (D), Harvard, 1982, Ob
    Lawrence P. Sanford, (D), MIT, 1984, Op
    Diane Stoecker, (D), SUNY (Stony Brook), 1979, Ob
Associate Professor:
    William Boicourt, (D), Johns Hopkins, 1973, Op
    James Carton, (D), Princeton, 1983, Op
    Keith N. Eshleman, (D), MIT, 1985, Hg
    Micheal S. Kearney, (D), Ontario, 1981, Gu
    Karen L. Prestegaard, (D), California (Berkeley), 1982, Hw
Research Associate Professor:
    Jeffery C. Cornwell, (D), Alaska, 1983, Oc
Assistant Professor:
    Mark S. Castro, (D), Virginia, 1991, Oa
    Raleigh Hood, (D), California (San Diego), 1990, Ob
    Alba Torrents, (D), Johns Hopkins, 1992, Sb
Research Associate Professor:
    Todd M. Kana, (D), Harvard, 1982, Ob

Massachusetts

Amherst College
Dept of Geology (B) (2015)
P.O. Box 2238
Amherst, MA 01002-5000
    p. (413) 542-2233
    dbhutton@amherst.edu
    https://www.amherst.edu/academiclife/departments/geology
    Enrollment (2015): B: 22 (10)
Professor:
    John T. Cheney, (D), Wisconsin, 1975, Gi
    Peter D. Crowley, (D), MIT, 1985, Gc
    Tekla A. Harms, (D), Arizona, 1986, Gt
    Anna M. Martini, (D), Michigan, 1997, Cl
Assistant Professor:
    David S. Jones, (D), Harvard, 2009, Gs
Emeritus:
    Edward S. Belt, (D), Yale, 1963, Gs
    Margery C. Coombs, (D), Columbia, 1971, Pv

Bard College at Simon's Rock
Bard College at Simon's Rock (2014)
84 Alford Rd.
Great Barrington, MA 01230
    p. (413) 644-4400 .
    admin@simons-rock.edu
    http://www.simons-rock.edu/

Bentley University
Dept of Natural and Applied Sciences (B) (2015)
175 Forest Street
Waltham, MA 02452-4705
    p. (781) 891-2980
    pdavis@bentley.edu
    http://www.bentley.edu/sciences/
    Administrative Assistant: Martha E.. Keating
    Enrollment (2013): B: 60 (18)
Professor:
    P. Thompson Davis, (D), Colorado, 1980, Gl
    Rick Oches, (D), Massachusetts, 1994, GerGs
Associate Professor:
    David Szymanski, (D), Michigan State, 2007, GvfCg
Adjunct Professor:
    Robert P. Ackert, (D), MIT/WHOI, 2000, CcGlm
    Mark J. Benotti, (D), Stony Brook, 2006, OgGgOg
    Janette Gartner, (M), Massachusetts, 2000, Hy
Laboratory Director:
    Anna K. Tary, (M), Boston, 1999, Gl

Berkshire Community College
Environmental and Life Science Dept (A) (2014)
Pittsfield, MA 01201
  p. (413) 236-4601
  saleksa@berkshirecc.edu
  Enrollment: No data reported since 1999
Chair:
  Clifford D. Myers, (D), Maine, On
Professor:
  Thomas F. Tyning, (M), On
  Charles E. Weinstein, (M), Wisconsin, On
Instructor:
  Timothy Flanagan, (M), Antioch, 1983, Gg
Emeritus:
  Richard L. Ferren, (M), Louisiana State, On
  George Hamilton, (M), North Adams State Coll, On
  Mary R. Mercuri, (M), Catholic

Boston College
Dept of Earth & Environmental Sciences (B,M) (2014)
140 Commonwealth Avenue
213 Devlin Hall
Chestnut Hill, MA 02467-3809
  p. (617) 552-3640
  mccartfy@bc.edu
  http://www.bc.edu/geology
  Administrative Assistant: Margaret McCarthy
  Enrollment (2013): B: 23 (23) M: 14 (14)
Chair:
  John E. Ebel, (D), Caltech, 1981, Ys
Associate Professor:
  Rudolph Hon, (D), MIT, 1976, Gi
  Alan L. Kafka, (D), SUNY (Stony Brook), 1980, Yg
  Gail C. Kineke, (D), Washington, 1993, On
  Noah Snyder, (D), MIT, 2001, GgHg
Assistant Professor:
  Seth C. Kruckenberg, (D), Minnesota (Twin Cities), 2009, Gct
  Jeremy D. Shakun, (D), Oregon State, 2010, Gg
  Corinne I. Wong, (D), Texas (Austin), 2013, PeCsHw
Lab Coordinator:
  Kenneth G. Galli, (D), Massachusetts, 2003, Gg
Adjunct Professor:
  Paul K. Strother, (D), Harvard, 1980, Pb
Emeritus:
  J.Christopher Hepburn, (D), Harvard, 1972, Gg
  James W. Skehan, S.J., (D), Harvard, 1953, Gc

Weston Observatory (2015)
381 Concord Road
Weston, MA 02493
  p. (617) 552-8300
  weston.observatory@bc.edu
  http://www.bc.edu/westonobservatory
Director:
  Alan L. Kafka, (D), Stony Brook, 1980, Ys
Science Education:
  Michael Barnett, (D), Indiana, 2003, Oe
Senior Scientist:
  John E. Ebel, (D), Caltech, 1981, Yg
Seismology, Seismic Network Development:
  Michael Hagerty, (D), California (Santa Cruz), 1998, Ys
Seismic Analyst and Educational Seismologist:
  Anastasia Moulis, (M), Boston, 2003, Ys
Research Scientist:
  Seth Kruckenberg, (D), Minnesota (Twin Cities), 2009, Gc
Research Scientist:
  John J. Cipar, (D), Caltech, 1981, Ys
Research Associate:
  John H. Beck, (D), Boston, 1998, Pb
Adjunct Professor:
  Paul Strother, (D), Harvard, 1980, Pb
  Alfredo Urzua, (D), MIT, 1981, Ng
Visiting Professor:
  Vincent Murphy, (M), Boston, 1957, Yg
Emeritus:
  J. Christopher Hepburn, (D), Harvard, 1972, Gg

James W. Skehan, (D), Harvard, 1953, Gc

Boston University
Center for Remote Sensing (2014)
685 Commonwealth Avenue
Room 433
Boston, MA 02215
  p. (617) 353-9709
  crsadmin@bu.edu
  Administrative Assistant: Emily P. Johnson
  Enrollment: No data reported since 1999
Director:
  Farouk El-Baz, (D), Missouri (Rolla), 1964, Or
Professor:
  Sucharita Gopal, (D), California (Santa Barbara), 1988, Oi
  Alan Strahler, (D), Johns Hopkins, 1969, Or
  Curtis E. Woodcock, (D), California (Santa Barbara), 1986, Or
Associate Professor:
  Mark A. Friedl, (D), California (Santa Barbara), 1994, Or
  Kenneth L. Kvamme, (D), California (Santa Barbara), 1983, Ga
  Guido D. Salvucci, (D), MIT, 1994, Hq
Research Associate Professor:
  Magaly Koch, (D), Boston, 1993, Ga
  Cordula Robinson, (D), Univ Coll (UK), 1991, Gm
  Crystal Schaaf, (D), Boston, 1994, Or
Research Associate:
  Eman Ghoneim, (D), Southampton, 2002, Gm
Geology Librarian:
  Nasim Momen, On

Dept of Earth & Environment (B,M,D) (2015)
675 Commonwealth Avenue
Boston, MA 02215
  p. (617) 353-2525
  earth@bu.edu
  http://www.bu.edu/earth/
  Enrollment (2015): B: 70 (15) M: 15 (10) D: 50 (8)
Chair:
  David R. Marchant, (D), Edinburgh, 1994, Gm
Professor:
  Bruce Anderson, (D), Scripps, 1998, Oap
  James Lawford Anderson, (D), Gi
  Duncan M. FitzGerald, (D), South Carolina, 1977, On
  Mark Friedl, (D), California (Santa Barbara), 1993, Or
  Sucharita Gopal, California (Santa Barbara), 1988, Oi
  Tony Janetos, (D), 1980, On
  Richard Murray, (D), California (Berkeley), 1991, Cm
  Ranga Myneni, (D), Antwerp, 1985, Or
  Nathan Phillips, (D), Duke, 1997, Oy
  Guido D. Salvucci, (D), MIT, 1994, Hq
  Curtis Woodcock, (D), California (Santa Barbara), 1986, Or
Associate Professor:
  Rachel Abercrombie, (D), Reading, 1991, Gt
  Michael Dietze, (D), Duke, 2006, SfOr
  Sergio Fagherazzi, (D), Padua, 1999, Gm
  Robinson Fulweiler, (D), Rhode Island, 2007, Cm
  Lucy Hutyra, (D), Harvard, 2007, Oar
  Andrew Kurtz, (D), Cornell, 2000, Clg
Assistant Professor:
  Dan Li, (D), Princeton, 2013, HqOa
  Christine Regalla, (D), Penn State, 2013, Gt
  Diane Thompson, Arizona, 2013, ObPe
Research Associate:
  Farouk El-Baz, (D), Missouri, 1964, Or

Bridgewater State University
Dept of Geological Sciences (B) (2016)
Conant Science Building
Bridgewater, MA 02325
  p. (508) 531-1390
  Brenda.Flint@bridgew.edu
  http://www.bridgew.edu/EarthSciences/
  Administrative Assistant: Brenda Flint
  Enrollment (2010): B: 70 (0)
Chairperson:
  Robert Cicerone, (D), MIT, 1991, Ys

Professor:
Richard L. Enright, (D), Rutgers, 1969, Hg
Michael A. Krol, (D), Lehigh, 1996, GzxGt
Peter J. Saccocia, (D), Minnesota, 1991, Cm
Lecturer:
Joseph Doyle, (M), New Hampshire, Gg
Emeritus:
Robert F. Boutilier, (D), Boston, 1963, Gz
Ira E. Furlong, (D), Boston, 1960, Gm

Bristol Community College
Div of Mathematics, Science and Engineering (A) (2010)
777 Elsbree Street
Fall River, MA 02720
p. (508) 678-2811
John.Ahola@bristolcc.edu
Instructor:
John Ahola, Gg

Cape Cod Community College
Environmental Technology Program (2015)
2240 Iyannough Rd
West Barnstable, MA 02668
p. (508) 362-2131 x4468
junderwood@capecod.edu
http://www.capecod.edu/web/natsci/env

Fitchburg State University
Earth and Geographic Sciences (B) (2016)
160 Pearl Street
Fitchburg, MA 01420-2697
p. (978) 665-3246
egordon3@fitchburgstate.edu
http://www.fitchburgstate.edu/academics/academic-depart-
ments/earth-and-geographic-sciences-dept/
Administrative Assistant: Melissa Barrette
Enrollment (2015): B: 25 (2)
Associate Professor:
Elizabeth S. Gordon, (D), OcGeOe
Lawrence R. Guth, (D), Rice, 1991, Gc
Jane Huang, (D), Oi
Assistant Professor:
Reid A. Parsons, (D), XgHs

Hampshire College
Dept of Geology (B) (2010)
Amherst, MA 01002
p. (413) 582-5373
DOF@Hampshire.edu
Administrative Assistant: Joan Barrett
Associate Professor:
Steven Roof, (D), Massachusetts, 1995, OiPe
Assistant Professor:
Christina Cianfrani, (D), Vermont, Hw
Cooperating Faculty:
Helaine Selin, (M), SUNY (Albany), On

Harvard University
Dept of Earth and Planetary Sciences (B,D) ● (2015)
Hoffman Laboratory
20 Oxford Street
Cambridge, MA 02138-2902
p. (617) 495-2351
moffatt@eps.harvard.edu
http://www.eps.harvard.edu
Enrollment (2015): B: 25 (0) D: 54 (0)
Chair:
John Shaw, (D), Princeton, 1993, Gt
Research Professor:
Adam M. Dziewonski, (D), Polish Acad of Sci, 1965, Ys
Professor:
James G. Anderson, (D), Colorado, 1970, Oa
Jeremy Bloxham, (D), Cambridge, 1985, Yg
Brian F. Farrell, (D), Harvard, 1981, Ow
Peter Huybers, (D), MIT, 2004, Pe

Miaki Ishii, (D), Harvard, 2003, Yg
Daniel J. Jacob, (D), Caltech, 1985, Oa
Stein B. Jacobsen, (D), Caltech, 1980, Cc
Andrew H. Knoll, (D), Harvard, 1977, Pb
Zhiming Kuang, (D), CalTech, 2003, Oa
Charles H. Langmuir, (D), SUNY (Stony Brook), 1980, Cg
Scot T. Martin, (D), Caltech, 1995, Cg
James T. McCarthy, (D), Scripps, 1971, Ob
Michael B. McElroy, (D), Queen's, 1962, Oa
Brendan Meade, (D), MIT, 2004, Yg
Jerry X. Mitrovica, (D), Toronto, 1991, Yg
Ann Pearson, (D), MIT/WHOI, 2000, Cm
James R. Rice, (D), Lehigh, 1964, Yg
Daniel P. Schrag, (D), California (Berkeley), 1993, Cg
Eli Tziperman, (D), MIT/WHOI, 1987, Op
Steven C. Wofsy, (D), Harvard, 1971, Oa
Associate Professor:
David T. Johnston, (D), Maryland, 2007, CgPy
Francis Macdonald, (D), Harvard, 2009, Pe
Visiting Professor:
Sarah T. Stewart-Mukhopadhyay, (D), Caltech, 2002, Xg
Emeritus:
Charles W. Burnham, (D), MIT, 1961, Gz
Paul F. Hoffman, (D), Johns Hopkins, 1970, Gc
Ulrich Petersen, (D), Harvard, 1963, Eg
Visiting Associate Professor:
Sujoy Mukhopadhyay, (D), Caltech, 2002, Cg

Massachusetts Institute of Technology 🗋 ●
Dept of Earth, Atmospheric, & Planetary Sciences (B,M,D) ●
(2015)
77 Massachusetts Avenue, 54-918
Cambridge, MA 02139
p. (617) 253-2127
eapsinfo@mit.edu
http://eapsweb.mit.edu/
Enrollment (2015): B: 23 (7) M: 8 (10) D: 151 (25)
Head:
Robert van der Hilst, (D), Utrecht (Neth), 1990, Ys
Vice-President for Research:
Maria T. Zuber, (D), Brown, 1986, Xy
Professor:
Richard P. Binzel, (D), Texas, 1986, Xm
Samuel A. Bowring, (D), Kansas, 1985, Gg
Edward A. Boyle, (D), MIT, 1976, Oc
Kerry A. Emanuel, (D), MIT, 1978, Ow
Dara Entekhabi, (D), MIT, 1990, Hg
J. Brian Evans, (D), MIT, 1978, Yx
Raffaele Ferrari, (D), Scripps, 2001, Op
Glenn R. Flierl, (D), Harvard, 1975, Op
Timothy L. Grove, (D), Harvard, 1976, Gi
Bradford H. Hager, (D), Harvard, 1978, Ys
Thomas A. Herring, (D), MIT, 1983, Yd
Paola M. Malanotte-Rizzoli, (D), California (San Diego), 1978, Op
John C. Marshall, (D), Imperial Coll (UK), 1980, Op
F Dale Morgan, (D), MIT, 1981, Yg
Raymond A. Plumb, (D), Manchester, 1972, Ow
Ronald G. Prinn, (D), MIT, 1971, Oa
Daniel H. Rothman, (D), Stanford, 1986, Yg
Leigh H. Royden, (D), MIT, 1982, Gt
Sara Seager, (D), Harvard, 1999, Xy
Susan Solomon, (D), California (Berkeley), 1981, Oa
Roger Summons, (D), New South Wales, Py
Benjamin Weiss, (D), Caltech, 2003, Ym
Jack Wisdom, (D), Caltech, 1981, Og
Senior Research Scientist:
William Durham, (D), MIT, 1975, Cg
Michael Fehler, MIT, 1979, Yg
Chien Wang, (D), SUNY (Albany), 1992, Oa
Principal Research Scientist:
Nilanjan Chatterjee, (D), CUNY, 1989, Cg
Stephanie Dutkiewicz, (D), Rhode Island, 1997, Cg
Patrick Heimbach, Max Planck, 1998, Op
Robert W. King, (D), MIT, 1975, Yg
Eduardo Andrade Lima, (D), Catholic Univ. of Rio de Janeiro, Ym
Sai Ravela, (D), Massachusetts, 2002
Robert E. Reilinger, (D), Cornell, 1979, Yg

William Rodi, (D), 1989, Yg
C. Adam Schlosser, (D), Maryland, 1995, Oa
Associate Professor:
  Tanja Bosak, (D), Caltech, 2004, Py
  Dan Cziczo, (D), Chicago, 1999, Oa
  Michael Follows, (D), 1990, Op
  Colette Heald, (D), Harvard, 2005, Oa
  Oliver Jagoutz, (D), ETH (Switzerland), 2004, Gc
  Paul O'Gorman, (D), Caltech, 2004, Oa
  Shuhei Ono, (D), Penn State, 2001, PyCs
  Taylor Perron, (D), California (Berkeley), 2006, Gm
Assistant Professor:
  Kristin Bergmann, (D), Caltech, 2013, Gs
  Kerri Cahoy, (D), Stanford, 2008
  Timothy W. Cronin, (D), MIT, 2014, Oa
  Gregory Fournier, (D), Connecticut, 2009, Py
  David McGee, (D), Columbia, 2009, Cl
  Germán Prieto, (D), Calfornia (San Diego), 2007, Ys
  Hilke Schlichting, (D), Caltech, 2009, Xy
  Noelle Selin, (D), Harvard, 2007, Oa
Senior Lecturer:
  Lodovica Illari, (D), Imperial Coll (UK), 1982, Ow
Lecturer:
  Amanda Bosh, (D), MIT, 1994
Emeritus:
  B. Clark Burchfiel, (D), Yale, 1961, Gc
  Charles C. Counselman, III, (D)
  Frederick A. Frey, (D), Wisconsin, 1967, Ct
  Richard S. Lindzen, (D), Harvard, 1964, Ow
  Gordon H. Pettengill, (D), California (Berkeley), 1955, Og
  M. Gene Simmons, (D), Harvard, 1962, Yg
  John B. Southard, (D), Harvard, 1966, Gs
  Peter H. Stone, (D), Harvard, 1964, Oa
  M Nafi Toksoz, (D), Caltech, 1963, Ys
  Carl I. Wunsch, (D), MIT, 1967, Op
Principal Research Engineer:
  Christopher Hill, (D)

Mount Holyoke College
Dept of Geology (B) (2015)
50 College Street
Clapp Laboratory #304
South Hadley, MA 01075-6419
    p. (413) 538-2278
    cvasquez@mtholyoke.edu
    http://www.mtholyoke.edu/acad/geology
    f: https://www.facebook.com/groups/mhcgeoalums/
    Enrollment (2015): B: 21 (12)
Professor:
  Steven R. Dunn, (D), Wisconsin, 1989, Gp
  Girma Kebbede, (D), Syracuse, 1981, Oy
  Mark McMenamin, (D), California (Santa Barbara), 1984, PgGst
  Thomas L. Millette, (D), Clark, 1989, OriGm
  Alan Werner, (D), Colorado, 1988, GlOuGm
Associate Professor:
  Michelle J. Markley, (D), Minnesota, 1998, GcgGt
Assistant Professor:
  Serin D. Houston, (D), Syracuse, 2012, Oyn
Geoprocessing Lab Manager:
  Eugenio J. Marcano, (D), Cornell, 1994, OiSoOn
Emeritus:
  Martha M. Godchaux, (D), Oregon, 1969, Gv
Laboratory Director:
  Penny M. Taylor, (M), SUNY (Oneonta), 2000, Gg

Northeastern University
Dept of Marine and Environmental Sciences (B,M,D) O (2016)
14 Holmes Hall
360 Huntington Ave
Boston, MA 02115
    p. (617) 373-3176
    environment@neu.edu
    http://www.northeastern.edu/mes
    f: https://www.facebook.com/northeastern.mes
    Administrative Assistant: Danielle Walquist. Lynch
    Enrollment (2015): B: 811 (68) M: 13 (7) D: 31 (3)

Professor:
  Joseph Ayers, (D), California, On
  Richard H. Bailey, (D), North Carolina, 1973, Pi
  William Detrich, (D), Yale, On
  Brian Helmuth, (D), Washington, 1997, On
  Mark Patterson, (D), Harvard, On
Chair:
  Geoffrey Trussell, (D), William & Mary, On
Associate Chair:
  Rebeca Rosengaus, (D), Boston, On
Associate Professor:
  Jonathan Grabowski, (D), North Carolina, GuEg
  Malcolm Hill, (D), California (Santa Cruz), 1979, OiGz
  Justin Ries, (D), Johns Hopkins, Cm
  Martin E. Ross, (D), Idaho, 1978, Gi
Assistant Professor:
  Tarik Gouhier, (D), McGill, On
  Randall Hughes, (D), California, On
  David Kimbro, (D), California, On
  Steve Vollmer, (D), Harvard, On
Lecturer:
  Daniel Douglass, (D), Wisconsin (Madison), GlSdOa
  Tara Duffy, (D), Stony Brook, Ob
  Stephanie Eby, (D), Syracuse, On
Emeritus:
  Donald Cheney, (D), South Florida, On
  Gwilym Jones, (D), Indiana State, On
  Peter S. Rosen, (D), William & Mary, 1976, Onu
Business and Operations Manager:
  Heather Sears, (D), MIT, On
Co-op Coordinator:
  Sarah Klionsky

Salem State University
Geological Sciences Dept (B) (2013)
352 Lafayette Street
Salem, MA 01970
    p. (978) 542-6282
    dallen@salemstate.edu
    Enrollment (2009): B: 67 (13)
Chair:
  Douglas Allen, (D), Minnesota, 2003, CgHsCt
Professor:
  James L. Cullen, (D), Brown, 1984, GsPmOu
  Lindley S. Hanson, (D), Boston, 1988, GmlOn
  Jeanette M. Sablock, (D), Idaho, 1991, GzScOe
  Peter Sablock, (D), Idaho, 1991, GaYgGc
Associate Professor:
  J Bradford Hubeny, (D), Rhode Island, 2005, GeOnCs
Assistant Professor:
  Rory McFadden, (D), Minnesota, 2009, GpcGi
Lecturer:
  Michael Follis, (M), Ball State, 1978, GgEoGf

Smith College
Dept of Geosciences (B) (2015)
Clark Science Center
44 College Lane
Northampton, MA 01063
    p. (413) 585-3805
    dkortes@smith.edu
    http://www.science.smith.edu/departments/Geology/
    Administrative Assistant: Donna M.. Kortes
    Enrollment (2010): B: 27 (6)
Chair:
  Amy L. Rhodes, (D), Dartmouth, 1996, Cg
Professor:
  John B. Brady, (D), Harvard, 1975, Gx
  Bosiljka Glumac, (D), Tennessee, 1997, Gs
  Robert M. Newton, (D), Massachusetts, 1978, Gm
Associate Professor:
  Sara B. Pruss, (D), S California, 2004, Pg
Assistant Professor:
  Jack Loveless, (D), Cornell, 2007, Gtc
Lecturer:
  Mark E. Brandriss, (D), Stanford, 1994, Gx

Emeritus:
  H. Robert Burger, (D), Indiana, 1966, Gc
  H. Allen Curran, (D), North Carolina, 1968, Pg
Geoscience Technician:
  Michael Vollinger, (B), Massachusetts, 1993

Tufts University
Dept of Earth and Ocean Sciences (B) (2015)
Lane Hall
Medford, MA 02155
  p. (617) 627-3494
  jack.ridge@tufts.edu
  http://eos.tufts.edu/
  f: https://www.facebook.com/TuftsEOS
  Administrative Assistant: Janet Silvano
  Enrollment (2015): B: 22 (5)
Professor:
  John C. Ridge, (D), Syracuse, 1985, Gln
Professor:
  Grant Garven, (D), British Columbia, 1982, Hwy
Associate Professor:
  Anne F. Gardulski, (D), Syracuse, 1987, Grs
Assistant Professor:
  Andrew Kemp, (D), Pennsylvania, 2009, OnPmOg
  Molly McCanta, (D), Brown, 2004, Gi
Lecturer:
  Jacob Benner, (M), Utah, 2002, Pge
Emeritus:
  Robert L. Reuss, (D), Michigan, 1970, Gzi

University of Massachusetts Lowell
Dept of Environmental, Earth, & Atmospheric Sciences
(B,M) (2015)
1 University Avenue
University of Massachusetts
Lowell, MA 01854
  p. (978) 934-3900
  Erica_Gavin@uml.edu
  http://faculty.uml.edu/nelson_eby/EEAS.htm
  f: https://www.facebook.com/Earth.Sciences.UMass.
  Lowell?ref=hl
  Enrollment (2015): B: 102 (19) M: 17 (3)
Chair:
  G. Nelson Eby, (D), Boston, 1971, Cg
Professor:
  Frank P. Colby, (D), MIT, 1983, Ow
Associate Professor:
  Mathew Barlow, (D), Maryland, 1999, Oa
  Jian-Hua Chen, (D), North Carolina State, 1996, Oa
Assistant Professor:
  Kate Swanger, (D), Boston, 2009, Gl
Lecturer:
  Lori Weeden, (M), Boston, 2002, Gg
Emeritus:
  Arnold L. O'Brien, (D), Boston, 1973, Hw

University of Massachusetts, Amherst
Dept of Geosciences (B,M,D) (2015)
233 Morrill Science Center
611 North Pleasant St.
Amherst, MA 01003-9297
  p. (413) 545-2286
  head@geo.umass.edu
  http://www.geo.umass.edu/
  Enrollment (2015): B: 99 (35) M: 25 (10) D: 35 (3)
Distinguished University Professor:
  Raymond S. Bradley, (D), Colorado, 1974, Oa
Department Head:
  Julie Brigham-Grette, (D), Colorado, 1985, Gl
Professor:
  Stephen J. Burns, (D), Duke, 1987, Cs
  Michele L. Cooke-Andresen, (D), Stanford, 1996, Gc
  Robert DeConto, (D), Colorado, 1996, Oa
  Piper Gaubatz, (D), California (Berkeley), 1968, Oy
  R. Mark Leckie, (D), Colorado, 1984, Pm
  J. Michael Rhodes, (D), Australian National, 1970, Gv

Sheila J. Seaman, (D), New Mexico, 1988, Gi
  Michael L. Williams, (D), New Mexico, 1987, Gc
Associate Extension Professor:
  William Clement, (D), Wyoming, 1995, Yg
Associate Professor:
  David Boutt, (D), New Mexico Tech, 2004, Hw
  Steven Petsch, (D), Yale, 2000, Co
  Stan Stevens, (D), California (Berkeley), 1983, Oy
  Eve Vogel, (D), Oregon, 2007, Oy
  Jonathan D. Woodruff, (D), MIT, 2008, Gs
  Qian Yu, (D), California (Berkeley), 2005, Oi
Extension Assistant Professor:
  Christine Hatch, (D), California (Santa Cruz), 2007, Hw
  Michael Rawlins, (D), New Hampshire, 2006, Oa
Assistant Professor:
  Isla Castaneda, (D), Minnesota, 2007, Ca
  Haiying Gao, (D), Rhode Island, 2012, Ys
  Isaac J. Larsen, (D), Washington, 2013, Gm
Lecturer:
  Christopher D. Condit, (D), New Mexico, 1984, Gi
  Michael J. Jercinovic, (D), New Mexico, 1988, Gx
Adjunct Professor:
  Margery C. Coombs, (D), Columbia, 1973, On
  Douglas R. Hardy, (D), Massachusetts, 1995, Hy
  Casey D. Kennedy, (D), North Carolina State, 2008, Hg
  Douglas Kowaleski, (D), Boston, 2009, Gm
  Eileen McGowan, (D), Univ of Massachusetts, 2010, Xg
  Thomas L. Millette, (D), Clark, 1989, Oy
  Stephen Nathan, (D), Massachusetts, 2005, PmOg
  Liang Ning, (M), Nanjing, 2007, Ow
  Peter T. Panish, (D), Massachusetts, 1989, Gp
  Anthony Philpotts, (D), Cambridge, 1963, Gi
  Emily Riddle, (D), Cornell, 2011, Oa
  Nicholas Venti, (D), Delaware, 2012, Og
Emeritus:
  Laurie Brown, (D), Oregon State, 1974, Ym
  James A. Hafner, (D), Michigan, 1970, On
  John Hubert, (D), Penn State, 1958, Gs
  William D. McCoy, (D), Colorado, 1981, Oy
  George E. McGill, (D), Princeton, 1958, Gc
  Stearns A. Morse, (D), McGill, 1962, Gi
  Rutherford H. Platt, (D), Chicago, 1971, Ou
  Peter Robinson, (D), Harvard, 1963, Gc
  Richard W. Wilkie, (D), Washington, 1968, Oy
  Richard F. Yuretich, (D), Princeton, 1976, Cl
Massachusetts State Geologist:
  Stephen B. Mabee, (D), Massachusetts, 1992, GgHw

University of Massachusetts, Boston
School for the Environment (B,M,D) (2014)
100 Morrissey Boulevard
Boston, MA 02125
  p. (617) 287-7440
  sfe@umb.edu
  http://www.umb.edu/environment
  Enrollment (2010): B: 153 (27) M: 22 (12) D: 18 (4)
Director:
  Jack Wiggin, (M), Boston State Coll, 1981, Ou
Dean:
  Robyn Hannigan, (D), Rochester, ClmCt
Chair, Biology:
  Rick Kesseli, (D), California (Davis), 1985, Obn
Associate Dean, College of Management:
  David Levy, (D), Harvard, On
Professor:
  Bob Chen, (D), California (San Diego), 1992, CoOc
  Ron Etter, (D), Harvard, 1987, ObPoOn
  Zhongping Lee, (D), South Florida, Org
  William Robinson, (D), Northeastern, 1981, On
  Crystal Schaaf, (D), Boston, 1994, Orw
  Michael Shiaris, (D), Tennessee, 1979, On
  David Terkla, (D), California (Berkeley), On
  Roberta Wollons, (D), Chicago, On
  Wei Zhang, (D), Pittsburgh, On
  Meng Zhou, (D), SUNY (Stony Brook), Op
VP for Research, New England Aquarium:
  Scott Krauss, (D), New Hampshire, 2002, Ob

Director for Research, New England Aquarium:
  Michael Tlusty, (D), Syracuse, 1996, Ob
Senior Scientist:
  Moira Brown, (D), Guelph, 1995, Ob
  Julie Cavin, North Carolina, 2007, Ob
  Phillip Hamilton, (M), Massachusetts (Boston), 2002, Ob
  Kathleen Hunt, (D), Washington, 1997, Ob
  Charles Innis, (D), Penn, 1994, Ob
  Meghan Jeans, (D), Vermont Law School, 2002, On
  Amy Knowlton, (M), Rhode Island, 1997, Ob
  John Mandelman, (D), Northeastern, 2006, Ob
  Daniel Pendleton, (D), Cornell, 2010, Ob
  Rosalind Rolland, (D), Tufts, 1984, Ob
  Heather Tausig, (M), Boston, 1993, Og
  Timothy Werner, (M), Stanford, Ob
Director, Environmental Studies Program:
  Alan D. Christian, (D), Miami, 2002, OnGmCs
Co-Director, Center for Governance and Sustainability:
  Maria Ivanova, (D), Yale, On
Chair, English:
  Cheryl Nixon, (D), Harvard, On
Associate Professor:
  Conevery Bolton Valencius, (D), Harvard, 1998, Gh
  Robert Bowen, (D), S California, 1981, OnnOn
  Amy Den Ouden, (D), Connecticut, OnGa
  Ellen Douglas, (D), Tufts, 2002, HwqHy
  John Duff, (D), Washington, 1995, OnnOn
  Eugene Gallagher, (D), Washington, 1983, Ob
  Allen Gontz, (D), Maine, 2005, GmlYr
  Benyamin Lichtenstein, (D), Boston Coll, 1998, On
  Jose Martinez-Reyes, (D), Massachusetts, GaOn
  Deyang Qu, (D), Ottawa, Om
  Joshua Reid, (D), California (Davis), Ga
  Karen Ricciardi, (D), Vermont, Gq
  Juanita Urban-Rich, (D), Memorial, Ob
Associate Scientist:
  Andrew Rhyne, (D), Florida Inst of Tech, 2006, Ob
  Randi Rotjan, (D), Tufts, 2007, Ob
Assistant Professor:
  Jennifer Bowen, (D), Boston, 2005, ObPyOn
  Jarrett Byrnes, (D), California (Davis), 2008, ObnOn
  Steven Gray, (D), Rutgers, 2010, On
  Nardia Haigh, (D), Queensland, On
  Helen Poynton, (D), California (Berkeley), On
  David Timmons, (D), Massachusetts, On
Research Associate:
  Brooke Wikgren, (M), Miami, 2010, Oi
Lecturer:
  Deborah Metzel, (D), Maryland, 1998, EgOuy
  Michael Trust, Or
Director, Nantucket Field Station:
  Sarah Oktay, (D), Texas A&M, Oc
Research Engineer:
  Francesco Peri, (M), Massachusetts (Boston), On
Program Manager, Nantucket Semester Program:
  Elizabeth Boyle, (D), Massachusetts (Boston), Obn
Manager, GIS Lab:
  Helenmary Hotz, (M), Massachusetts (Boston), Oi
Director, Green Harbors Project:
  Anamarija Frankic, (D), VIMS, Oe

Wellesley College
Dept of Geosciences (B) (2011)
106 Central Street
Wellesley, MA 02481-8203
  p. (781) 283-3151
  dbraband@wellesley.edu
  http://www.wellesley.edu/Geosciences/
  Administrative Assistant: Rita Purcell
  Enrollment (2011): B: 25 (9)
Chair:
  Daniel J. Brabander, (D), Brown, 1997, Cl
Associate Professor:
  James Besancon, (D), MIT, 1976, GvHw
  David Hawkins, (D), MIT, 1996, Gzi
Emeritus:
  Margaret D. Thompson, (D), Harvard, 1976, Gc

Instructor:
  Kathleen W. Gilbert, (M), Miami, 1995, Cs

Williams College
Dept of Geosciences (B) (2015)
947 Main Street
Williamstown, MA 01267
  p. (413) 597-2221
  patricia.e.acosta@williams.edu
  http://www.williams.edu/Geoscience
  f: https://www.facebook.com/groups/
  williamsgeosciences/?fref=ts
  Administrative Assistant: Patricia E. Acosta
  Enrollment (2015): B: 36 (11)
Chair:
  Ronadh Cox, (D), Stanford, 1993, Gs
Professor:
  David P. Dethier, (D), Washington, 1977, Gm
  Paul Karabinos, (D), Johns Hopkins, 1981, Gc
  Reinhard A. Wobus, (D), Stanford, 1966, Gi
Associate Professor:
  Mea S. Cook, (D), MIT/WHOI, 2006, OuGe
Assistant Professor:
  Phoebe A. Cohen, (D), Harvard, 2010, Poy
Research Associate:
  Gudveig Baarli, (D), Oslo, 1989, Ps
  Mark E. Brandriss, (D), Stanford, 1993, Gi
Lecturer:
  Alex Apotsos, (D), MIT, 2007, Ge
Emeritus:
  William T. Fox, (D), Northwestern, 1962, Gs
  Markes E. Johnson, (D), Chicago, 1977, Ps
Cooperating Faculty:
  Helena F. Warburg, (M), Indiana Sch Lib Sci, 1987, On

Woods Hole Oceanographic Institution
Dept of Geology & Geophysics (D) (2015)
Woods Hole, MA 02543-1541
  p. (508) 289-2388
  etulka@whoi.edu
  http://www.whoi.edu/page.do?pid=7145
  Administrative Assistant: Maryanne F. Ferreira
  Enrollment (2014): D: 26 (0)
Chair:
  Daniel C. McCorkle, (D), Washington, 1987, Cm
Senior Scientist:
  Joan M. Bernhard, (D), California (San Diego), 1990, Cg
  Henry J B. Dick, (D), Yale, 1975, Gi
  Robert L. Evans, (D), Cambridge, 1991, Yr
  Daniel J. Fornari, (D), Columbia, 1978, Gu
  Chris German, (D), Cambridge, 1988, Gt
  Susan E. Humphris, (D), MIT/WHOI, 1977, Gu
  Lloyd D. Keigwin, (D), Rhode Island, 1979, Cs
  Jian Lin, (D), Brown, 1988, Gt
  Delia W. Oppo, (D), Columbia, 1989, Pm
  Deborah K. Smith, (D), California, 1985, Yr
  Ralph A. Stephen, (D), Cambridge, 1978, Ys
  Maurice A. Tivey, (D), Washington, 1988, Gt
Tenured Associate Scientist:
  Mark D. Behn, (D), MIT/WHOI, 2002, Yr
  Juan Pablo Canales Cisneros, (D), Barcelona, 1997, Yr
  Anne L. Cohen, (D), Cape Town, 1993, Pe
  Sarah B. Das, (D), Penn State, 2003, Pm
  Jeffrey Donnelly, (D), Brown, 2000, Gu
  Virginia Edgcomb, (D), Delaware, 1997, Cg
  Glenn A. Gaetani, (D), MIT, 1996, Gi
  Liviu Giosan, (D), SUNY (Stony Brook), 2001, Gu
  Daniel Lizarralde, (D), MIT/WHOI, 1997, Ys
  Olivier Marchal, (D), Paris, 1996, Pe
  Jeffrey J. McGuire, (D), MIT, 2000, Ys
  Robert A. Sohn, (D), California (San Diego), 1996, Yr
  S. Adam Soule, (D), Oregon, 2003, Gu
Associate Scientist:
  Andrew Ashton, (D), Duke, 2005, On
  Horst Marschall, (D), Heidelberg, 2005, Gp
  Sune G. Nielsen, (D), ETH (Switzerland), 2005, Cs

William Thompson, (D), Columbia, 2005, Pe
Assistant Scientist:
    Weifu Guo, (D), Caltech, 2008, Ca
    Veronique Le Roux, (D), Macquarie, 2008, Gi
Senior Research Specialist:
    James E. Broda, (B), Penn State, 1970, Gs
    John A. Collins, (D), MIT/WHOI, 1989, Ys
    Ann P. McNichol, (D), MIT, 1986, Oc
    Mark L. Roberts, (D), Duke, 1988, Yg
    Karl F. Von Reden, (D), Hamburg, 1983, Ct
Research Specialist:
    Jurek Blusztajn, (D), Polish Acad of Sci, 1985, Cc
    Alan R. Gagnon, (B), New Hampshire, 1983, Cs
    Steven J. Manganini, (B), Nasson, 1974, Ou
    Li Xu, (D), Xiamen, 1992, Yr
Information Systems Associate:
    S. Thompson Bolmer, (B), Colby, 1974, Yr
Engineer:
    Peter B. Landry, (B), NEIT, 1990, Ca
Research Associate:
    Kathryn L. Elder, (B), Massachusetts, 1985, Cs
    James R. Elsenbeck, (M), MIT/WHOI, 2007
    Kalina D. Gospodinova, (M), MIT/WHOI, 2012, Cm
    Joshua D. Hlavenka, (B), North Texas
    Peter C. Lemmond, (B), Lehigh, 1978, On
    Brett Longworth, (M), Massachusetts, 2005, Ou
    Brian D. Monteleone, (D), Syracuse, 2000, Cc
    Kathryn Rose, (M), California (Davis), 2007, Gu
Adjunct Scientist:
    Peter D. Bromirski, (D), Hawaii, 1993
    Johnson R. Cann, (D), Cambridge, 1963, Ys
    Colin Devey, (D), Oxford, 1986
    Javier Escartin, (D), MIT, 1996, Gg
    Andrea D. Hawkes, (D), Pennsylvania, 2008
    Gregory Hirth, (D), Brown, 1991, Gc
    Kuo-Fang (Denner) Huang, (D), National Cheng Kung, 2007
    Peter B. Kelemen, (D), Washington, 1987, Gi
    Yajing Liu, (D), Harvard, 2007
    John Maclennan, (D), Cambridge, 2000
    Larry Mayer, (D), Scripps, 1979, Gg
    Andrew M. McCaig, (D), Cambridge, 1983
    Jerry F. McManus, (D), Columbia, 1997, Pe
    Uri S. ten Brink, (D), Columbia, 1986, Yg
    David Thornalley, (D), Churchill, 2008
    Masako Tominaga, (D), Texas A&M, 2009
Emeritus:
    William A. Berggren, (D), Stockholm, 1962, Ps
    Carl O. Bowin, (D), Princeton, 1960, Yr
    William B. Curry, (D), Brown, 1980, Pm
    Graham S. Giese, (D), Chicago, 1966, On
    Stanley R. Hart, (D), MIT, 1960, Cg
    John M. Hayes, (D), MIT, 1966, Ct
    Susumu Honjo, (D), Hokkaido, 1961, Ou
    George P. Lohmann, (D), Brown, 1972, Pe
    David A. Ross, (D), California (San Diego), 1965, Gu
    Robert J. Schneider, (D), Oberlin, 1968, Yr
    Hans Schouten, (D), Utrecht (Neth), 1970, Yr
    Nobumichi Shimizu, (D), Tokyo, 1968, Ca
    Stephen A. Swift, (D), MIT/WHOI, 1986, Yr
    Brian E. Tucholke, (D), MIT/WHOI, 1973, Gu
    Elazar Uchupi, (D), S California, 1962, Ou
    Richard P. Von Herzen, (D), California (San Diego), 1960, Yh
    Frank B. Wooding, (B), Harvard, 1965, Yr

Dept of Marine Chemistry & Geochemistry (M,D) (2015)
360 Woods Hole Road
MS 25
Woods Hole, MA 02543-1541
    p. (508) 289-2328
    mcg@whoi.edu
    http://www.whoi.edu/page.do?pid=7146
    Administrative Assistant: Linda Cannata
    Administrative Assistant: Sheila A. Clifford
    Administrative Assistant: Donna Mortimer
    Administrative Assistant: Mary Zawoysky
    Enrollment (2015): D: 28 (5)

Chair:
    Scott C. Doney, (D), MIT, 1991, Cm
Associate Dean:
    Margaret K. Tivey, (D), Washington, 1989, Cm
Senior Scientist:
    Ken O. Buesseler, (D), MIT/WHOI, 1986, Oc
    Matthew A. Charette, (D), Rhode Island, 1998, Cm
    Konrad A. Hughen, (D), Colorado, 1997, Cc
    Mark D. Kurz, (D), MIT/WHOI, 1982, Cc
    Bernhard Peucker-Ehrenbrink, (D), Max Planck, 1994, Cm
    Christopher M. Reddy, (D), Rhode Island, 1997, Co
    Daniel J. Repeta, (D), MIT/WHOI, 1982, Co
    Jeffrey S. Seewald, (D), Minnesota, 1990, Cp
    James A. Yoder, (D), Rhode Island, 1979, Cm
Associate Scientist:
    Elizabeth B. Kujawinski, (D), MIT/WHOI, 2000, Oc
    Valier Galy, (D), Institut National Polytechnique de Lorrain, 2007, Cm
    Colleen Hansel, (D), Stanford, 2004, Cm
    Frieder Klein, (D), Bremen, 2009, Cm
    Tracy Mincer, (D), California (San Diego), 2004, Cm
    Mak A. Saito, (D), MIT/WHOI, 2001, Oc
    Amanda Spivak, (D), William and Mary, 2008, Cm
    Benjamin Van Mooy, (D), Washington, 2003, Oc
    Z. Aleck Wang, (D), Georgia, 2003, Cm
Assistant Scientist:
    Amy Apprill, (D), Hawaii, 2009, Oc
Research Associate:
    Joshua M. Curtice, (B), Massachusetts, 1992, Cc
    Helen Fredricks, (D), Plymouth (UK), 2000, Oc
    Matt McIlvin, (D), Massachusetts, 2004, Oc
    Steven M. Pike, (M), Rhode Island, 1998, Ca
    Sean Sylva, Oc
Information Systems Associate:
    Cyndy Chandler, (B), SUNY (Geneseo), 1975, Og
Information Systems Assoc:
    Ivan D. Lima, (D), Miami, 1999, Oc
Research Associate:
    Dawn Moran, Ob
    Jennie Rheuban, (M), Virginia, 2013, Oc
    Melissa Soule, Oc
    Gretchen Swarr, Oc
    Kristen Whalen, (D), MIT, 2008, Ob
Adjunct Professor:
    Minhan Dai, Cm
    Thomas Trull, Cm
Senior Research Specialist:
    Nelson M. Frew, (D), Washington, 1971, Ca
    Dempsey E. Lott, (M), Florida State, 1973, Oc
Scientist Emeritus:
    Michael P. Bacon, (D), MIT/WHOI, 1976, Oc
    Werner G. Deuser, (D), Penn State, 1963, Cs
    John W. Farrington, (D), Oc
    Frederick L. Sayles, (D), Manchester, 1968, Oc
    Geoffrey Thompson, (D), Manchester, 1965, Cm
    Oliver C. Zafiriou, (D), Johns Hopkins, 1966, Oc
Oceanographer Emeritus:
    Jean K. Whelan, (D), MIT, 1965, Co
Emeritus:
    William J. Jenkins, (D), McMaster, 1974, Oc
    William R. Martin, (D), MIT/WHOI, 1985, Oc
    Edward R. Sholkovitz, (D), California (San Diego), 1972, Oc
Senior Research Specialist:
    David M. Glover, (D), Alaska, 1985, Oc
Research Specialist:
    Carl G. Johnson, (M), Maine, 1983, Ca
    Robert K. Nelson, (B), C Connecticut State, 1980, Co
Senior Research Assistant:
    Justin Ossolinski, Oc
Research Specialist:
    Heather Benway, (D), Oregon State, 2005, Oc
    Krista Longnecker, (D), Oregon State U, 2004, Oc
Research Assistant:
    Jessica Drysdale, Oc
    Michaela Fendrock, Oc
    Kelsey Gosselin, Oc
    William Oestreich, Oc
    Zoe Sandwith, Oc

Postdoc:
  Tristan Horner, Oxford, 2012, Cm
Informations Systems Assoicate:
  Steven Gegg, Oc
Dept. Administrator:
  Mary Murphy
Assistant Scientist:
  David Nicholson, (D), Washington, 2009, Gu
  Scott Wankel, (D), Stanford, 2007, Cm
Senior Research Assistant (ret.):
  Margaret Sulanowska, Cm
Senior Research Assistant:
  Joanne Goudreau, Cm
Research Associate:
  Paul Henderson, Cm
Research Assistant:
  Kevin Cahill, Cm

Worcester State University
Earth, Environment and Physics (B) (2015)
486 Chandler Street
Worcester, MA 01602-2597
  p. (508) 929-8583
  whansen@worcester.edu
  http://www.worcester.edu/Earth-Environment-and-Physics/
  Enrollment (2015): B: 68 (9)
Chair:
  Patricia A. Benjamin, (D), Clark, 2002, Og
Associate Professor:
  Allison L. Dunn, (D), Harvard, 2006, OayHg
  William J. Hansen, (D), CUNY, 2002, OiyOr
Assistant Professor:
  Timothy L. Cook, (D), Massachusetts, 2009, GnsOg
  Douglas E. Kowalewski, (D), Boston, 2009, GmlOy
Instructor:
  Adam M. Davis, (D), Indiana, 2011, GgPyOy
  Mark O. Johnson, (D), Clark, 1993, Oy
  Ryan A. Portner, (D), Macquarie, 2010, GuvXg

Michigan

Adrian College
Geology Dept (A,B) (2015)
110 S. Madison St.
Adrian, MI 49221
  p. (517) 265-5161
  tmuntean@adrian.edu
  http://adrian.edu/academics/academic-departments/geology/
  f: https://www.facebook.com/groups/55153346895/
  Enrollment (2015): A: 1 (1) B: 14 (4)
Chair:
  Thomas Muntean, (D), Nevada, 2012, Gde
Professor:
  Sarah L. Hanson, (D), Utah, 1995, Giz

Albion College
Dept of Geological Sciences (B) O (2014)
611 E. Porter St.
Albion, MI 49224
  p. (517) 629-0759
  twilch@albion.edu
  http://www.albion.edu/geology/
  Enrollment (2014): B: 26 (11)
Chair:
  Thomas I. Wilch, (D), New Mexico Tech, 1997, GlvGm
Professor:
  William S. Bartels, (D), Michigan, 1986, Pv
  Beth Z. Lincoln, (D), California (Los Angeles), 1985, Gc
  Timothy N. Lincoln, (D), California (Los Angeles), 1978, EmCl
Associate Professor:
  Carrie A. Menold, (D), California (Los Angeles), 2006, Gpz
Assistant Professor:
  Michael McRivette, (D), California (Los Angeles), 2011, GtOir
Emeritus:
  Russell G. Clark, (D), Dartmouth, 1972, GiOi
  Lawrence D. Taylor, (D), Ohio State, 1962, Gl

Calvin College
Dept of Geology, Geography, & Environmental Studies (B) (2014)
3201 Burton SE
Grand Rapids, MI 49546
  p. (616) 526-8415
  jbascom@calvin.edu
  http://www.calvin.edu/academic/geology/
  Enrollment (2012): B: 60 (14)
Chair:
  Johnathan Bascom, (D), Iowa, 1989, Oy
Professor:
  Henry Aay, (D), Clark, 1978, Oyu
  Janel M. Curry, (D), Minnesota, 1985, Oy
  Ralph F. Stearley, (D), Michigan, 1990, PvOgGh
  Gerald K. Van Kooten, (D), California (Santa Barbara), 1980, EgCePi
Associate Professor:
  Deanna van Dijk, (D), Waterloo, 1998, GmOny
Assistant Professor:
  Kenneth A. Bergwerff, (M), Grand Valley State, 1988, Oe
  James Skillen, (D), Cornell, 2006, Ou
  Jason VanHorn, (D), Ohio State, 2007, Oi
Laboratory Manager/Instructor:
  Margene Brewer, (M), W Michigan, 1991, OnGgOn
Emeritus:
  Clarence Menninga, (D), Purdue, 1966, CcGg
  Davis A. Young, (D), Brown, 1969, Giz

Central Michigan University
Dept of Earth and Atmospheric Sciences (B) (2014)
314 Brooks Hall
Mount Pleasant, MI 48859
  p. (989) 774-3179
  sven.morgan@cmich.edu
  https://www.cmich.edu/colleges/cst/earth_atmos/Pages/
  Enrollment (2013): B: 49 (14)
Professor:
  Sven S. Morgan, (D), Virginia Tech, 1998, Gc
  Richard N. Mower, (D), Ow
  Mona Sirbescu, (D), Missouri, 2002, Gi
  Reed Wicander, (D), California (Los Angeles), 1973, Pl
Department Chair:
  Leigh Orf, (D), Wisconsin, 1997, Ow
Associate Professor:
  Martin Baxter, (D), St. Louis, 2006, Ow
  Patrick Kinnicutt, (D), MIT, 1995, Gq
Research Associate:
  James J. Student, (D), Virginia Tech, 2002, Gg
Lecturer:
  Maria Mercedes Gonzalez, (D), Nacional del Sur (Argentina), 1997, Em

Charles Stewart Mott Community College
Dept of Science and Mathematics (2011)
1401 East Court St.
Flint, MI 48503
  p. (810) 762-0279
  scimath@mcc.edu
  http://www.mcc.edu/3_academics/divisions/science_math.shtml
Professor:
  David Maguire, (M), E Michigan, 1981, Xg
Associate Professor:
  Sheila Swyrtek, (M), Minnesota (Duluth), 1996, Ga

Concordia University
Div of Natural Sciences (A,B,M) (2013)
4090 Geddes Road
Ann Arbor, MI 48105-2750
  p. (734) 995-7300
  nskov@cuaa.edu
  Enrollment: No data reported since 1999
Assistant Professor:
  James L. Refenes, (M), E Michigan, 2009, Oe

Delta College
Dept of Geology (A) (2014)
1961 Delta Road
University Center, MI 48710-0002
　　p. (989) 686-9252
　　tlclarey@delta.edu
　　Department Secretary: Barb Jurmanovich
　　Enrollment (2011): A: 8 (4)
Department Chair:
　　Timothy L. Clarey, (D), W Michigan, 1996, HwGcPv
Lecturer:
　　Mary C. Gorte, (M), Rensselaer, 1983, Gs
Emeritus:
　　Barry A. Carlson, (D), Michigan State, 1974, Yg
　　Paul A. Catacosinos, (D), Michigan State, 1972, Gr
Cooperating Faculty:
　　Kevin T. Dehne, (M), E Michigan, 1992, Oe

Eastern Michigan University
Dept of Geography & Geology (B) (2014)
Ypsilanti, MI 48197
　　p. (743) 487-8589
　　yulanda.woods@EMICH.EDU
　　Enrollment (2001): B: 135 (0)
Head:
　　Michael Kasenow, (D), W Michigan, 1994, Hg
　　Richard A. Sambrook, (D)
Professor:
　　Eugene Jaworski, (D), Louisiana State, 1971, Or
　　Carl F. Ojala, (D), Georgia, 1972, Oa
　　Constantine N. Raphael, (D), Louisiana State, 1967, Gu
Associate Professor:
　　Steven T. LoDuca, (D), Rochester, 1990, Pi
Assistant Professor:
　　Kevin Blake, (D), Wisconsin, 1998, Gl
　　Michael Bradley, (D), Utah, 1988, Gc
　　Maria-Serena Poli, (D), Padova, 1995, Pe

Ferris State University
Dept of Physical Sciences (2011)
ASC-3021
Big Rapids, MI 49307
　　p. (616) 592-2580
　　heckf@ferris.edu
　　http://www.ferris.edu/htmls/colleges/artsands/Physical-Sciences/HOME-Physical-Sciences.htm
Chair:
　　David Frank
Professor:
　　Frederick R. Heck, (D), Northwestern, 1987, Gg

Gogebic Community College
Math-Science Div (A) (2013)
E4946 Jackson Rd.
Ironwood, MI 49938
　　p. (906) 932-4231
　　admissions@gogebic.edu
　　http://www.gogebic.edu/academics/Math_Science/
Professor:
　　Bill Perkis, Gg

Grand Rapids Community College
Physical Sciences Dept (A) (2016)
143 Bostwick Avenue, NE
Grand Rapids, MI 49503
　　p. (616) 234-4248
　　jqualls@grcc.edu
　　http://www.grcc.edu/physci
　　Enrollment (2015): A: 2 (1)
Assistant Professor:
　　Tari Mattox, (M), N Illinois, 1984, GgvCg

Grand Valley State University
Dept of Geology (B) (2015)
1 Campus Drive

118 Padnos Hall
Allendale, MI 49401
　　p. (616) 331-3728
　　geodept@gvsu.edu
　　http://www.gvsu.edu/geology
　　Administrative Assistant: Janet H. Potgeter
　　Enrollment (2015): B: 148 (0)
Head:
　　Virginia L. Peterson, (D), Massachusetts, 1992, Gxc
Professor:
　　Patrick M. Colgan, (D), Wisconsin, 1996, GmlNg
　　Stephen R. Mattox, (D), N Illinois, 1992, OeGv
　　Figen A. Mekik, (D), N Illinois, 1999, Pem
　　Patricia E. Videtich, (D), Brown, 1982, Gd
　　John C. Weber, (D), Northwestern, 1995, Gc
Associate Professor:
　　Kevin C. Cole, (D), Arizona, 1990, Gz
　　Pablo A. Llerandi-Roman, (D), Purdue, 2007, Oe
　　Peter E. Riemersma, (D), Wisconsin, 1997, Hw
　　Peter J. Wampler, (D), Oregon State, 2004, HsOiGm
Assistant Professor:
　　Caitlin N. Callahan, (D), W Michigan, 2013, GgOg
　　Tara A. Kneeshaw, (D), Texas A&M, 2008, ClGe
Instructor:
　　Kelly L. Heid, (M), Mississippi State, 2011, Oe
　　Ryan G. Vannier, (D), Michigan State, 2014, CgGn
Visiting Professor:
　　Trisha A. Smrecak, (M), Cincinnatti, 2008, PieOe
　　Kevin G. Thaisen, (D), Tennessee, 2012, XgGxOi
Emeritus:
　　Thomas E. Hendrix, (D), Wisconsin, 1960, Gc
　　Richard H. Lefebvre, (D), Northwestern, 1966, Gx
　　William J. Neal, (D), Missouri, 1968, Gs
　　Norman W. Ten Brink, (D), Washington, 1971, Gm

Henry Ford Community College
Science Div (2004)
Dearborn, MI 48128
　　p. (313) 845-9632
　　cjacobs@hfcc.edu

Hope College
Dept of Geological & Environmental Sciences (B) (2015)
35 E 12th Street
P.O. Box 9000
Holland, MI 49422-9000
　　p. (616) 395-7540
　　bodenbender@hope.edu
　　http://www.hope.edu/academic/geology/
　　Enrollment (2015): B: 24 (8)
Chair:
　　Brian E. Bodenbender, (D), Michigan, 1994, Pi
Professor:
　　Edward C. Hansen, (D), Chicago, 1983, Gm
　　Graham F. Peaslee, (D), SUNY (Stony Brook), 1987, OnnGf
　　Jon W. Peterson, (D), Chicago, 1989, Ge
Adjunct Professor:
　　Suzanne DeVries-Zimmerman, (M), Princeton, 1989, Gge
Emeritus:
　　J. Cotter Tharin, (D), Illinois, 1960, Gs

Jackson Community College
Dept of Geology & Geography (A) (2012)
2111 Emmons Road
Jackson, MI 49201
　　p. (517) 787-0800 x157
　　AlbeeScSteven@jccmi.edu
　　http://www.jccmi.edu/academics/science/geo
　　Enrollment (2012): A: 200 (20)
Wilbur L. Dungy Endowed Chair in the Sciences:
　　Steven R. Albee-Scott, (D), Michigan, 2005, GePeSf

Lake Michigan College
Lake Michigan College (A) (2014)
Napier Avenue Campus

2755 E. Napier Avenue
Benton Harbor, MI 49022
    lovett@lakemichigancollege.edu
    http://www.lakemichigancollege.edu/index.
    php?option=com_content&task=view&id=509&Itemid=157
Instructor:
    Cole Lovett, Gg

Lake Superior State University
Geology and Physics (B) O (2015)
650 W. Easterday Avenue
Sault Ste. Marie, MI 49783
    p. (906) 635-2267
    pkelso@lssu.edu
    http://geology.lssu.edu/
    Administrative Assistant: Donna White
    Enrollment (2014): B: 37 (7)
Professor:
    Paul R. Kelso, (D), Minnesota, 1993, YmGct
Assistant Professor:
    Anna Lindquist, (D), Minnesota, 2013, YmGz
    Robin Mattheus, (D), North Carolina, 2009, GsOn
    Matt Spencer, (D), Penn State, 2005, Gl
Emeritus:
    Lewis M. Brown, (D), New Mexico, 1973, PiOe
Science Lab Manager:
    Benjamin Southwell, (M), Central Michigan, 2012, On

Macomb Community College, Center Campus
Dept of Science (Geology) (A) (2014)
44575 Garfield Road
Clinton Township, MI 48038-1139
    p. (586) 286-2154
    schaferc@macomb.edu
    Enrollment (2014): A: 9 (0)
Professor:
    Carl M. Schafer, (M), Montana, 1998, Gg

Michigan State University
Dept of Geological Sciences (B,M,D) (2015)
288 Farm Lane
East Lansing, MI 48824-1115
    p. (517) 355-4626
    geosci@msu.edu
    https://glg.natsci.msu.edu/
    f: Geological Sciences
    Enrollment (2014): M: 4 (0) D: 20 (0)
Chair:
    Ralph E. Taggart, (D), Michigan State, 1971, Pb
Professor:
    Kazuya Fujita, (D), Northwestern, 1979, Ys
    David T. Long, (D), Kansas, 1977, Cl
    Michael A. Velbel, (D), Yale, 1984, Gd
Associate Professor:
    Bruno Basso, (D), Michigan State, 2002, On
    Danita S. Brandt, (D), Yale, 1985, Pi
    Michael D. Gottfried, (D), Kansas, 1991, Pv
    David W. Hyndman, (D), Stanford, 1995, Hy
Assistant Professor:
    Julie C. Libarkin, (D), Arizona, 1999, Oe
    Tyrone Rooney, (D), Penn State, 2006, Gi
    Matt Schrenk, (D), Washington, 2005, Py
    Jay Zarnetske, (D), Oregon State, 2011, Hw

Michigan Technological University 🗇
A. E. Seaman Mineral Museum (2015)
1404 E. Sharon Avenue
Houghton, MI 49931
    p. (906) 487-2572
    tjb@mtu.edu
    http://www.museum.mtu.edu
Director:
    Theodore J. Bornhorst, (D), New Mexico, 1980, EgCgGx
Associate Curator:
    Christopher J. Stefano, (D), Michigan, 2010, GzxCg

Dept of Geological & Mining Engineering & Sciences (B,M,D) O
(2015)
1400 Townsend Drive
Dow Building, Room 630
Houghton, MI 49931-1295
    p. (906) 487-2531
    geo@mtu.edu
    http://www.mtu.edu/geo
    Administrative Assistant: Kelly M. McLean
    Enrollment (2015): B: 112 (12) M: 68 (10) D: 16 (1)
Chair & Professor:
    John S. Gierke, (D), Michigan Tech, 1990, Hy
Provost and Acting Dean, Graduate School:
    Jacqueline E. Huntoon, (D), Penn State, 1990, Gs
Professor:
    Theodore J. Bornhorst, (D), New Mexico, 1980, Eg
    Alex S. Mayer, (D), North Carolina, 1992, Hy
    James R. Wood, (D), Johns Hopkins, 1973, Cl
Associate Professor:
    Simon Carn, (D), Cambridge, 1999, OrGv
    Thomas Oommen, (D), Tufts, 2009, NeOi
    Aleksey K. Smirnov, (D), Rochester, 2002, Yv
    Gregory P. Waite, (D), Utah, 2004, Ys
    Shiliang Wu, (D), Harvard, 2007, OaCg
Assistant Professor:
    Roohollah Askari, (D), Calgary, 2013, Goo
    Snehamoy Chatterjee, (D), Indian Inst. of Technology, Nm
    Colleen B. Mouw, (D), Rhode Island, 2009, OurOu
    Ebrahim Tarshizi, (D), Nevada (Reno), 2014, Nm
Instructor:
    James M. Gillis, (B), Michigan Tech, 1983, Nmr
Adjunct Professor and Director, Great Lakes Research Ctr.:
    Guy A. Meadows, (D), Purdue, 1977, Gu
Adjunct Assistant Professor:
    Lizzette A. Rodriguez, (D), Michigan Tech, 2007, Gv
Department Facilities Manager:
    Robert Barron, (B), Michigan Tech, 1979, Og
Senior Lecturer:
    Jeremy Shannon, (D), Michigan Tech, 2006, Gg
Postdoctoral Research Fellow and Temporary Faculty:
    Rudiger Escobar-Wolf, (D), Michigan Tech, 2013, Gv
Postdoctoral Research Fellow:
    Jennifer Telling, (D), Georgia Tech, 2013, Yg
Research Scientist:
    Carol Asiala, (B), Michigan Tech, 1985
Cooperating Faculty:
    William I. Rose, (D), Dartmouth, 1970, Gv
    Roger M. Turpening, (D), Michigan, 1966, Ye

Mott Community College
Science and Mathematics (A) (2015)
1401 East Court St.
Flint, MI 48503
    p. (810) 232-9312
    sheila.swyrtek@mcc.edu
    http://www.mcc.edu
    Enrollment (2015): A: 4 (0)
Professor:
    David Maguire, (M), E Michigan, 1981, GgOg
    Sheila M. Swyrtek, (M), Minnesota (Duluth), 1997, GgOg

Muskegon Community College
Dept of Mathematics & Physical Sciences (A) (2013)
221 S. Quarterline Road
Muskegon, MI 49442
    p. (231) 777-0289
    amber.kumpf@muskegoncc.edu
    http://www.muskegoncc.edu/pages/652.asp
    Administrative Assistant: Tamera Owens
    Enrollment: No data reported since 1999
Instructor:
    Amber C. Kumpf, (M), Rhode Island, 2010, GgYrOu

Northwestern Michigan College
Northwestern Michigan College (2014)

1701 East Front Street
Traverse City, MI 49686
   p. (231) 995-1000
   information@nmc.edu
   http://www.nmc.edu

Oakland Community College
Natural Sciences Dept (A) (2015)
2900 Featherstone Road
Auburn Hills, MI 48326
   p. (248) 232-4538
   lgkodosk@oaklandcc.edu

Schoolcraft College
Dept of Geology (A) (2010)
18600 Haggerty Road
Livonia, MI 48151
   p. (734) 462-4400
   jrexius@schoolcraft.edu
   Enrollment: No data reported since 1999
Instructor:
   James E. Rexius, (M), E Michigan, 1978, Gl

University of Michigan
Dept of Climate and Space Sciences and Engineering
(B,M,D) (2015)
2455 Hayward
Ann Arbor, MI 48109-2143
   p. (734) 615-3583
   aoss-um@umich.edu
   http://aoss.engin.umich.edu/
   f: www.facebook.com/umclasp
   t: @umclasp
   Enrollment (2015): B: 31 (14) M: 44 (45) D: 53 (6)
Chair:
   James Slavin, (D), California (Los Angeles)
Professor:
   Sushil Atreya, (D), Michigan, Oa
   John Boyd, (D), Harvard
   R. Paul Drake, (D), California (San Diego)
   Lennard Fisk, (D), California (San Diego)
   Brian Gilchrist, (D), Stanford
   Tamas Gombosi, (D), Lóránd Eötvös
   Michael Liemohn, (D), Michigan
   Mark Moldwin, (D), Boston
   Joyce Penner, (D), Harvard
   Nilton Renno, (D), MIT
   Aaron Ridley, (D), Michigan
   Richard Rood, (D), Florida State
   Christopher Ruf, (D), Massachusetts (Amherst)
   Perry Samson, (D), Wisconsin (Madison)
   Thomas Zurbuchen, (D), Bern
Associate Professor:
   Xianglei Huang, (D), Caltech
   Christiane Jablonowski, (D), Michigan
   Xianzhe Jia, (D), California (Los Angeles)
   Justin C. Kasper, (D), MIT, 2003
   Susan Lepri, (D), Michigan
   Derek Posselt, (D), Colorado State
   Allison Steiner, (D), Georgia Tech
   Shasha Zou, (D), California (Los Angeles)
Assistant Professor:
   Jeremy Bassis, (D), Scripps
   Mark Flanner, (D), California (Irvine)
   Gretchen Keppel-Aleks, (D), Caltech
   Eric A. Kort, (D), Harvard
Assistant Research Scientist:
   Orenthal Tucker, (D)

Dept of Geological Sciences (B,M,D) (2014)
2534 C.C. Little Building
1100 North University Avenue
Ann Arbor, MI 48109-1005
   p. (734) 764-1435
   mukasa@umich.edu
   http://www.lsa.umich.edu/geo/

Administrative Assistant: Robert J. Patterer
   Enrollment (1999): B: 29 (8) M: 27 (5) D: 37 (12)
Chair:
   Rodney C. Ewing, (D), Stanford, 1974, Gz
Professor:
   Tomasz K. Baumiller, (D), Chicago, 1990, Pg
   Joel D. Blum, (D), Caltech, 1990, Cc
   Maria Clara Castro, (D), Paris, 1995, Hy
   Daniel C. Fisher, (D), Harvard, 1975, Pi
   Philip D. Gingerich, (D), Yale, 1974, Pv
   Stephen E. Kesler, (D), Stanford, 1966, Eg
   Rebecca A. Lange, (D), California (Berkeley), 1989, Gi
   Kyger C. Lohmann, (D), SUNY (Stony Brook), 1977, Cs
   Samuel B. Mukasa, (D), California (Santa Barbara), 1984, Cc
   Robert M. Owen, (D), Wisconsin, 1975, Oc
   Larry J. Ruff, (D), Caltech, 1981, Ys
   Gerald R. Smith, (D), Michigan, 1965, Ps
   Ben A. van der Pluijm, (D), New Brunswick, 1984, Gc
   Rob van der Voo, (D), Utrecht (Neth), 1969, Ym
   Lynn M. Walter, (D), Miami, 1983, Cl
   Youxue Zhang, (D), Columbia, 1989, Cp
Associate Professor:
   Udo Becker, (D), Virginia Tech, 1995, On
   Robyn J. Burnham, (D), Washington, 1987, Pb
   Todd A. Ehlers, (D), Utah, 2001, Yg
   Christopher J. Poulsen, (D), Penn State, 1999, Pe
   Jeroen Ritsema, (D), California (Santa Cruz), 1995, Ys
   Peter J. van Keken, (D), Utrecht (Neth), 1989, Yg
Assistant Professor:
   Marin Clark, (D), MIT, 2003, Gm
   Ingrid Hendy, (D), California (Santa Barbara), 2000, Py
   Nathan Niemi, (D), Caltech, 2001, Gc
   Jeffrey A. Wilson, (D), Chicago, 1999, Gg
Research Scientist:
   Jeffrey C. Alt, (D), Miami, 1984, Ou
   Catherine E. Badgley, (D), Yale, 1982, Pv
Associate Research Scientist:
   Chris Hall, (D), Toronto, 1982, Cc
   Shaopeng Huang, (D), Acad Sinica, 1990, Yh
   Josep M. Pares, (D), Barcelona, 1988, Ym
Assistant Research Scientist:
   James D. Gleason, (D), Arizona, 1994, Cg
   Jie Lian, (D), Michigan, 2003, Gz
   Mirjam Schaller, (D), Bern, 2001, Gm
Adjunct Assistant Research Scientist:
   Roland C. Rouse, (D), Michigan, 1972, Gz
Adjunct Assistant Professor:
   Karen L. Webber, (D), Rice, 1988, Gv
Adjunct Professor:
   John W. Geissman, (D), Michigan, 1980, Ym
   William B. Simmons, (D), Michigan, 1973, Gz
Emeritus:
   Charles Beck, (D), Cornell, 1955, Pg
   William Farrand, (D), Michigan, 1960, Ga
   William C. Kelly, (D), Columbia, 1954, Eg
   Philip A. Meyers, (D), Rhode Island, 1972, Co
   Theodore C. Moore, (D), California (San Diego), 1968, Ou
   James O'Neil, (D), Chicago, 1963, Cs
   Donald R. Peacor, (D), MIT, 1962, Gz
   Henry N. Pollack, (D), Michigan, 1963, Yh
   David K. Rea, (D), Oregon State, 1974, Gu
   Bruce H. Wilkinson, (D), Texas, 1973, Gs

University of Michigan, Dearborn
Dept of Natural Sciences (B,M) (2013)
4901 Evergreen Road
Dearborn, MI 48128
   p. (313) 593-5277
   kmurray@umd.umich.edu
   http://www.umd.umich.edu/?id=570101
   Enrollment (2013): B: 30 (4) M: 14 (3)
Acting Chair:
   Kent S. Murray, (D), California (Davis), 1981, Hw
Professor:
   Don Bord, (D), Dartmouth, 1976, Xy
Associate Professor:
   Jacob Napieralski, (D), Purdue, 2004, GmlOi

John Riebesell, (D), Chicago, 1975, Ou
Lecturer:
David Matzke, (M), Michigan, 1975, Xy
Adjunct Professor:
Michael Favor, (B), Michigan, 1985, On

Washtenaw Community College
Dept of Geology (A) (2010)
4800 E. Huron River Drive
Ann Arbor, MI 48105
    p. (734) 677-5111
    salbach@wccnet.edu
    Enrollment: No data reported since 1999
Head:
Suzanne M. Albach, (M), Mississippi State, 2005, OegGe

Wayne State University
Geology Dept (B,M) (2015)
0224 Old Main Building
4831 Cass Avenue
Detroit, MI 48201
    p. (313) 577-2506
    baskaran@wayne.edu
    http://sun2.science.wayne.edu/~geology/
    Enrollment (2011): B: 101 (15) M: 9 (1)
Acting Head:
David Njus
Professor:
Mark M. Baskaran, (D), Phy Res Lab (India), 1985, CcGg
Associate Professor:
Jeffrey L. Howard, (D), California (Santa Barbara), 1987, Gs
Lawrence D. Lemke, (D), Michigan, 2003, HwGse
Assistant Professor:
Edmond H. van Hees, (D), Michigan, 2000, GzxEg
Lecturer:
Charles F. Barker, (M), Boston, 1988, Gg
Ann Purdy, (D), Michigan State, 1995, Gg
Grazyna Sledzinski, (M), Wayne State, 1994, Gg
John M. Zawiskie, (M), Wayne State, 1979, Gg
Academic Services Officer:
David J. Lowrie, (B), Wayne State, 1964, Gg

Western Michigan University 🗋
Dept of Geosciences (B,M,D) O (2015)
1903 W Michigan Ave
Kalamazoo, MI 49008-5241
    p. (269) 387-5486
    breanne.e.lejeune@wmich.edu
    http://www.wmich.edu/geology/
    f: https://www.facebook.com/wmugeosciences/?fref=nf
    t: @WMUgeosciences
    Administrative Assistant: Breanne LeJeune
    Enrollment (2015): B: 108 (18) M: 51 (17) D: 12 (4)
Chair:
Mohamed Sultan, (D), Washington Univ, 1984, OriGe
Professor:
David Barnes, (D), California, 1982, GsOnn
Essam Heggy, (D), Paris VI (UPMC-Sorbonne Universites), 2002, Xg
Alan E. Kehew, (D), Idaho, 1977, GmlHw
Michelle A. Kominz, (D), Columbia, 1986, OuYgGu
R. V. Krishnamurthy, (D), Physical Research Lab-Dept of Space (India), 1984, Cs
Associate Professor:
Daniel P. Cassidy, (D), Notre Dame, 1995, Hw
Johnson R. Haas, (D), Washington Univ, 1993, Cl
Duane R. Hampton, (D), Colorado State, 1989, Hw
Heather L. Petcovic, (D), Oregon State, 2004, Oe
William A. Sauck, (D), Arizona, 1972, Yg
Assistant Professor:
Robb Gillespie, (D), SUNY, GsoGm
Stephen Kaczmarek, (D), Michigan State, 2005, Gd
Joyashish Thakurta, (D), Indiana, 2008, GiEg

Minnesota

Bemidji State University
Center for Environmental, Economic, Earth, & Space Studies
(A,B,M) (2015)
#27, 1500 Birchmont Drive NE
Bemidji, MN 56601
    p. (218) 755-2783
    tkroeger@bemidjistate.edu
    http://www.bemidjistate.edu/academics/departments/ceeess/
    Enrollment (2012): B: 109 (17) M: 23 (3)
Professor of Geology:
Timothy J. Kroeger, (D), North Dakota, 1995, PlGsHw
Professor:
Dragoljub D. Bilanovic, (D), Technion Israel Inst Tech, 1990, GePyCa
Assistant Professor:
Miriam Rios-Sanchez, (D), Michigan Tech, 2012, HwOr

Carleton College
Dept of Geology (B) (2015)
One North College Street
Northfield, MN 55057
    p. (507) 222-4407
    ehaberot@carleton.edu
    http://www.carleton.edu/departments/geol/
    Administrative Assistant: Ellen T. Haberoth
    Enrollment (2015): B: 38 (22)
Charles L. Denison Professor of Geology:
Mary E. Savina, (D), California (Berkeley), 1982, Gm
Professor:
Clinton A. Cowan, (D), Queen's, 1992, Gs
Cameron Davidson, (D), Princeton, 1991, Gx
Bereket Haileab, (D), Utah, 1994, Gx
Associate Professor:
Sarah J. Titus, (D), Wisconsin, 2006, Gc
Director, Science Ed Resource Center:
Cathryn A. Manduca, (D), Caltech, 1988, Gi
Emeritus:
Caryl E. Buchwald, (D), Kansas, 1966, Gg
Technical Director:
Jonathon L. Cooper, (B), W Washington, Gg

Century College
Earth Science Program (A) (2015)
3300 Century Avenue North
White Bear Lake, MN 55110
    p. (651) 779-3242
    joe.osborn@century.edu
    http://www.century.edu/futurestudents/programs/pnd.aspx?id=66
Acting Head:
Joe Osborn, (M), Og
Instructor:
Jill Bries-Korpik, (M), Og
John Oughton, Og

Fond du Lac Tribal and Community College
Fond du Lac Tribal and Community College (A) (2010)
2101 14th Street
Cloquet, MN 55720
    glang@fdltcc.edu
    http://www.fdltcc.edu/
Instructor:
Glenn Langhorst, (M), Minnesota (Duluth), Gg

Gustavus Adolphus College
Dept of Geology (B) (2015)
800 West College Avenue
St Peter, MN 56082
    p. (507) 933-7333
    jbartley@gustavus.edu
    http://www.gustavus.edu/geology
    Administrative Assistant: Jennifer Kruse
    Enrollment (2015): B: 23 (7)

Chair:
   Julie K. Bartley, (D), California (Los Angeles), 1994, GsPgGd
Associate Professor:
   Laura Triplett, (D), Minnesota, 2008, Gmn
   James L. Welsh, (D), Wisconsin, 1982, Gxc
Visiting Professor:
   Sadredin (Dean) Moosavi, (D), New Hampshire, Gm
Emeritus:
   Keith J. Carlson, (D), Chicago, 1966, Pv
Cooperating Faculty:
   Daniel Mollner, On

Inver Hills Community College
Geology Dept (A) (2015)
2500 East 80th Street
Inver Grove Heights, MN 55076
   jkorpik@inverhills.mnscu.edu
   http://www.inverhills.edu/Departments/Geology/
Instructor:
   Jill Bries Korpik, Gg

Itasca Community College
Geography/Geographic Info Systems (GIS) (2010)
Grand Rapids, MN 55744
   p. (218) 327-4227
   timothy.fox@itascacc.edu
   Administrative Assistant: Janice Padden
   Enrollment: No data reported since 1999
Related Staff:
   Robert J. Schwob, (M), Bemidji State, 1968, Oe

Lake Superior College
Liberal Arts & Sciences Dept (A) (2010)
2101 Trinity Rd.
Duluth, MN 55811
   m.whitehill@lsc.edu
   http://www.lsc.edu
Instructor:
   Matthew Whitehill, Gg

Macalester College
Geology Dept (B) (2015)
1600 Grand Avenue
St Paul, MN 55105
   p. (651) 696-6000
   macgregor@macalester.edu
   http://www.macalester.edu/geology/
   Enrollment (2015): B: 45 (11)
Chair:
   Kelly MacGregor, (D), California (Santa Cruz), 2002, GmOl
Professor:
   John P. Craddock, (D), Michigan, 1988, Gc
   Raymond R. Rogers, (D), Chicago, 1995, Gs
Associate Professor:
   Kristina A. Curry Rogers, (D), SUNY (Stony Brook), 2001, Pv
   Karl R. Wirth, (D), Cornell, 1991, Gi
Assistant Professor:
   Alan Chapman, (D), Caltech, 2011, Gct
Geology Lab Supervisor:
   Jeffrey T. Thole, (M), Washington State, 1991, Gg

Minneapolis Community and Technical College
Div of Arts and Sciences (1999)
1501 Hennepin Ave S
Minneapolis, MN 55403
   chuck.paulson@minneapolis.edu
   http://www.minneapolis.edu/academics/artsandsciences.cfm

Minnesota State University
Earth Science Program (B,M) (2015)
Department of Geography
206 Morris Hall
Mankato, MN 56001
   p. (507) 389-2617
   phillip.larson@mnsu.edu
   http://sbs.mnsu.edu/geography/
   Enrollment (2004): B: 50 (10)
Director:
   Phillip H. Larson, (D), Arizona State, 2013, GmOyHs
Professor:
   Donald A. Friend, (D), Arizona State, 1997, OyGm
   Bryce W. Hoppie, (D), California (Santa Cruz), 1996, GeHw
   Steven Losh, (D), Yale, 1985, GzxGo
   Martin D. Mitchell, (D), Illinois, 1993, Ou
   Ron Schirmer, (D), Minnesota, 2002, GaPb
   Fei Yuan, (D), Minnesota, 2003, Ori
Associate Professor:
   Ginger Schmid, (D), Texas State, 2004, SdGm
   Forrest Wilkerson, (D), Texas State, 2004, OawGm
   Chad Wittkop, (D), Minnesota, Gsr
Assistant Professor:
   Jonathan H. Anderson, (D), Penn State, 2009, Ga
   Rama Mohapatra, (D), Wisconsin (Milwaukee), 2012, Oi

Normandale Community College
Dept of Geography and Geology (A) (2015)
9700 France Avenue South
Bloomington, MN 55431
   p. (952) 358-7032
   paul.sabourin@normandale.edu
   http://www.normandale.edu/departments/stem-and-educa-
   tion/geography-and-geology
Instructor:
   David J. Berner, (M), Colorado
   Douglas J. Claycomb, (D), Texas A&M
   Richard P. Dunning, (D), Wisconsin
   Carolyn Dykoski, (M), Minnesota
   Annia Fayon, (D), Arizona State
   Lindsay Iredale, (M), Minnesota
   Paul D. Sabourin, (D), Minnesota
   Ronald D. Ward, (D), Georgia

North Hennepin Community College
Geology Dept (2014)
7411 85th Avenue N.
Brooklyn Park, MN 55445
   p. (763) 424-0863
   mjones@nhcc.edu
   http://www.nhcc.edu/academic-programs/academic-depart-
   ments/geology

Northland Community & Technical College
Liberal Arts Program (1999)
2022 Central Avenue NE
East Grand Forks, MN 56721
   p. (218) 683-8694
   http://www.northlandcollege.edu

Rochester Community & Technical College
Environmental Science (2011)
851 30th Ave SE
Rochester, MN 55904
   p. (507) 285-7220
   Cory.Rubin@roch.edu
   http://www.rctc.edu
Chair:
   John Tacinelli, (D), Minnesota, 2000, Gig

Saint Cloud State University
Dept of Atmospheric and Hydrologic Sciences (B) (2014)
720 4th Avenue South
St Cloud, MN 56301-4498
   p. (320) 308-3260
   arhansen@stcloudstate.edu
   http://www.stcloudstate.edu/eas/
   Administrative Assistant: Debbie Schlumpberger
   Enrollment (2012): B: 119 (31)
Professor:
   Anthony R. Hansen, (D), Iowa State, 1981, Ow

Minnesota

Professor:
    Kate S. Pound, (D), Otago (NZ), 1993, GeOe
    Robert A. Weisman, (D), SUNY (Albany), 1988, Ow
Associate Professor:
    Juan J. Fedele, (D), Illinois, 2003, Hg
    Jean L. Hoff, (D), North Dakota, 1989, HwOe
    Rodney Kubesh, (D), Illinois, 1991, Ow
Assistant Professor:
    Brian J. Billings, (D), Nevada (Reno), 2009, Ow

University of Minnesota, Duluth 🗗

Dept of Earth & Environmental Science (B,M,D) ● (2015)
229 Heller Hall
1114 Kirby Drive
Duluth, MN 55812
    p. (218) 726-8385
    dees@d.umn.edu
    http://www.d.umn.edu/dees/
    Administrative Assistant: Laura L. Chapin
    Administrative Assistant: Claudia J. Rock
    Enrollment (2015): B: 160 (28) M: 27 (9)
Professor:
    Erik T. Brown, (D), MIT, 1990, Og
    John W. Goodge, (D), California (Los Angeles), 1987, Gp
    Vicki L. Hansen, (D), California (Los Angeles), 1987, Gc
    Howard Mooers, (D), Minnesota, 1988, Gl
Associate Professor:
    Christina D. Gallup, (D), Minnesota, 1997, Cc
    Karen B. Gran, (D), Washington, 2005, Gms
    James D. Miller, (D), Minnesota, 1986, Gi
    John B. Swenson, (D), Minnesota, 2000, Gr
    Nigel J. Wattrus, (D), Minnesota, 1984, Yr
Assistant Professor:
    Latisha A. Brengman, (D), Tennessee, 2015, Gd
    Frederick A. Davis, (D), Minnesota (Twin Cities), 2012, Gi
    Christian Schardt, (D), Tasmania, EgCg
    Jacob A. Selander, (D), California (Davis), 2015, Gcm
    Byron A. Steinman, (D), Pittsburgh, 2011, Gn
Emeritus:
    James A. Grant, (D), Caltech, 1964, Gp
    John C. Green, (D), Harvard, 1960, Gi
    Thomas C. Johnson, (D), California (San Diego), 1975, Gn
    Ronald Morton, (D), Carleton, 1976, EgGv
    Richard W. Ojakangas, (D), Stanford, 1964, Gd
    George R. Rapp, (D), Penn State, 1960, Ga

University of Minnesota, Morris

Div of Science & Mathematics (B) (2014)
Geology Discipline
Science Building
600 East 4th Street
Morris, MN 56267
    p. (320) 589-6300
    geol@mrs.umn.edu
    http://www.mrs.umn.edu
    Enrollment (2002): B: 26 (9)
Coordinator:
    James F. Cotter, (D), Lehigh, 1984, Gl
Professor:
    James B. Van Alstine, (D), North Dakota, 1980, Pg
Associate Professor:
    Keith A. Brugger, (D), Minnesota, 1992, Gl
Emeritus:
    Peter M. Whelan, (D), California (Santa Cruz), 1988, Gx

University of Minnesota, Twin Cities

Dept of Civil, Environmental and Geo-Engineering (B,M,D) (2015)
500 Pillsbury Drive SE
Minneapolis, MN 55455
    p. (612) 625-5522
    cege@umn.edu
    http://www.ce.umn.edu/
    Enrollment (2010): B: 26 (8) M: 11 (4) D: 49 (2)
Head:
    John S. Gulliver, (D), Minnesota, 1980, Hs

Professor:
    Emmanuel M. Detournay, (D), Minnesota, 1983, Nr
    Andrew Drescher, (D), Inst of Fund Tech Res (Poland), 1968, So
    Efi Foufoula-Georgiou, (D), Florida, 1985, Hg
    Joseph F. Labuz, (D), Northwestern, 1985, Nr
    Otto D. Strack, (D), Delft (Neth), 1973, Hw
    Vaughan R. Voller, (D), Sunderland, 1980, Om
Associate Professor:
    Randal J. Barnes, (D), Colorado Mines, 1985, On
    Bojan B. Guzina, (D), Colorado, 1996, Nr
    Karl A. Smith, (D), Minnesota, 1980, Nx
Research Associate:
    Sonia Mogilevskaya, (D), Russian Acad of Sci, 1987, Ng
Adjunct Professor:
    Peter A. Cundall, (D), Nr

Dept of Earth Sciences (B,M,D) ○ (2015)
108 Pillsbury Hall
310 Pillsbury Drive SE
Minneapolis, MN 55455-0219
    p. (612) 624-1333
    esci@umn.edu
    http://www.esci.umn.edu
    Enrollment (2015): B: 52 (13) M: 8 (2) D: 35 (3)
Head:
    Donna L. Whitney, (D), Washington, 1991, Gp
Teaching Professor:
    Kent C. Kirkby, (D), Wisconsin, 1994, Gg
Distinguished Professor:
    R. Lawrence Edwards, (D), Caltech, 1988, Cc
Director, Minnesota Geological Survey:
    Harvey Thorleifson, (D), Colorado, 1989, Gg
Director of IRM:
    Bruce M. Moskowitz, (D), Minnesota, 1980, Ym
Professor:
    David L. Fox, (D), Michigan, 1999, Pg
    Marc M. Hirschmann, (D), Washington, 1992, Gi
    Peter J. Hudleston, (D), Imperial Coll (UK), 1969, Gc
    Emi Ito, (D), Chicago, 1979, Cs
    David L. Kohlstedt, (D), Illinois, 1970, Yx
    Sally G. Kohlstedt, (D), Illinois, 1972, On
    Katsumi Matsumoto, (D), Columbia, 2000, Oc
    Christopher Paola, (D), MIT/WHOI, 1983, Gs
    Justin Revenaugh, (D), MIT, 1989, Ys
    William E. Seyfried, Jr., (D), S California, 1977, Cm
    Christian P. Teyssier, (D), Monash, 1985, Gc
    David A. Yuen, (D), California (Los Angeles), 1978, Yg
Assoc Director of IRM:
    Joshua Feinberg, (D), California (Berkeley), 2005, Ym
Associate Professor:
    Karen L. Kleinspehn, (D), Princeton, 1982, Gt
Assistant Professor:
    Jake Bailey, (D), S California, 2008, Py
    Max Bezada, (D), Rice, 2010, Ys
    Crystal Ng, (D), MIT, 2008, Hy
    Cara M. Santelli, (D), MIT/WHOI, 2007, Py
    Ikuko Wada, (D), British Columbia, 2009, On
    Andrew Wickert, Colorado (Boulder), 2014, Gml
Microprobe Manager:
    Anette von der Handt, (D), GiCt
Research Associate:
    Dario Bilardello, (D), Ym
    Randy Calcote, (D), Minnesota, 2000, Py
    Hai Cheng, (D), Nanjing, 1988, Cc
    Kang Ding, (D), Acad Sinica, 1987, Cg
    Beverley Flood, (D), Py
    Nagasree Garapati, (D), Hq
    Côme Lefebvre, (D), Gp
    Yanbin Lu, (D), Pe
    Shenghua Mei, (D), Yx
    Mathilde Meijers, (D)
    Jed Mosenfelder, (D), Cp
    Amy Myrbo, (D), Minnesota, 2006, PeOe
    Nick Seaton, (D)
    Mark Shapley, Minnesota, 2005, Gn
    Ivanka Stefanova, (D), Sofia, 1991, Pl
    Chunyang Tan, (D), Zhejiang Univ, 2011, Cm

80

Mark Zimmerman, (D), Minnesota, 1999, Yx
Adjunct Professor:
James E. Almendinger, (D), Minnesota, 1988, Pe
Mike Berndt, (D), Minnesota, 1987, Cg
Val W. Chandler, (D), Purdue, 1977, Ye
Mark B. Edlund, (D), Michigan, 1998, Pe
Daniel R. Engstrom, (D), Minnesota, 1983, Pe
Annia K. Fayon, (D), Arizona State, 1997, Gc
Carrie E. Jennings, (D), Minnesota, 1996, Gl
Robert G. Johnson, (D), Iowa State, 1952, Pe
Thomas C. Johnson, (D), California (San Diego), 1975, Pe
James D. Miller, (D), Gx
Kristina Curry Rogers, (D), Pg
Raymond Rogers, (D), Pg
Anthony Runkel, (D), Texas, 1988, Gs
Emeritus:
E. Calvin Alexander, Jr., (D), Missouri (Rolla), 1970, Cc
Subir K. Banerjee, (D), Cambridge, 1963, Ym
Roger LeB Hooke, (D), Gl
Hans Olaf Pfannkuch, (D), Paris, 1962, Hw
James H. Stout, (D), Harvard, 1970, Gp
Paul W. Weiblen, (D), Minnesota, 1965, Gi
Herbert E. Wright, Jr., (D), Harvard, 1943, Gl
XRCT Lab Manager:
Brian Bagley, (D), Minnesota, 2011
Student Services:
Jennifer Petrie
Research Specialist:
Betty Wheeler, (M)
Postdoc:
Matej Pec, (D), Yx
PostDoc:
Alejandra Quintanilla Terminal, (D), Yx
Postdoc:
Jessica Rodysill, (D), Gn
Miki Tasaka, (D), Gy
Director, CSDCO:
Anders Noren, Gn
Dept Administrator:
Sharon J. Kressler, (B), On
Curator, LacCore:
Kristina Brady, (M), Minnesota, 2006, Gn
Agouron Institute Fellow:
Dan Jones, (D), Py
Geology Librarian:
Carolyn Bishoff, (M), On
Cooperating Faculty:
Martin O. Saar, (D), California (Berkeley), 2003, Hg

Dept of Soil, Water, & Climate (B,M,D) ● (2015)
1991 Upper Buford Circle
St. Paul, MN 55108-6028
p. (612) 625-8114
crosen@umn.edu
http://www.swac.umn.edu
Administrative Assistant: Marjorie J. Bonse
Enrollment (2015): B: 264 (43) M: 9 (3) D: 19 (3)
Head:
Carl J. Rosen, (D), California (Davis), 1983, Sc
Professor:
James C. Bell, (D), Penn State, 1990, Sd
Timothy J. Griffis, (D), McMaster, 2000, Oa
Satish C. Gupta, (D), Utah State, 1972, Sp
John A. Lamb, (D), Nebraska, 1984, Sc
David J. Mulla, (D), Purdue, 1983, Sp
Edward A. Nater, (D), California (Davis), 1987, Sd
Michael J. Sadowsky, (D), Hawaii, 1983, Sb
Michael A. Schmitt, (D), Illinois, 1985, Sc
Mark W. Seeley, (D), Nebraska, 1977, Oa
Jeffrey S. Strock, (D), North Carolina State, 1999, So
Associate Professor:
Daniel E. Kaiser, (D), Iowa State, 2007, Sc
Dylan B. Millet, (D), California (Berkeley), 2003, Oa
Albert L. Sims, (D), North Carolina State, 1992, Sc
Peter K. Snyder, (D), Wisconsin, 2003, Oa
Brandy M. Toner, (D), California (Berkeley), 2004, ScCmo
Tracy E. Twine, (D), Wisconsin, 2003, Oa

Kyungsoo Yoo, (D), California (Berkeley), 2003, Sd
Assistant Professor:
Fabian G. Fernandez, (D), Purdue, 2006, ScbSo
Jessica L. M. Gutknecht, (D), Wisconsin, 2007, Sb
Satoshi Ishii, (D), Minnesota, 2007, Sb
Nicolas Jelinski, (D), Minnesota, 2014, SdCs
Paulo H. Pagliari, (D), Wisconsin, 2012, Sc
Adjunct Professor:
John M. Baker, (D), Texas A&M, 1987, Sp
Gary Feyereisen, (D), Minnesota, 2005, Sp
Jane M F Johnson, (D), Minnesota, 1995, So
Randall K. Kolka, (D), Minnesota, 1996, So
Pamela J. Rice, (D), Iowa State, 1996, So
Kurt Spokas, (D), Minnesota, 2005, Spo
Rodney T. Venterea, (D), California (Davis), 2000, Sp
Emeritus:
Deborah L. Allan, (D), California (Riverside), 1987, Sb
James L. Anderson, (D), Wisconsin, 1976, Sd
Paul R. Bloom, (D), Cornell, 1978, Sc
H. H. Cheng, (D), Illinois, 1961, Sb
Terence H. Cooper, (D), Michigan State, 1975, Sd
Robert H. Dowdy, (D), Michigan State, 1966, Sc
William C. Koskinen, (D), Washington State, 1980, Sc
Gary L. Malzer, (D), Purdue, 1973, Sc
Jean A. Molina, (D), Cornell, 1967, Sb
John F. Moncrief, (D), Wisconsin, 1981, Sp
Gyles W. Randall, (D), Wisconsin, 1972, So
George W. Rehm, (D), Minnesota, 1969, Sc
Michael P. Russelle, (D), Nebraska, 1982, Sc
Executive Secretary:
Kari A. Jarcho, (B), On

University of Saint Thomas
Dept of Geology (B) (2010)
OWS 153
2115 Summit Avenue
St Paul, MN 55105
p. (651) 962-5241
khenriksen@stthomas.edu
http://www.stthomas.edu/geology/
Enrollment (2010): B: 16 (0)
Chair:
Melissa A. Lamb, (D), Stanford, 1998, GtcGs
Associate Professor:
Thomas A. Hickson, (D), Stanford, 1999, GsmGe
Kevin Theissen, (D), Stanford, GnOg
Assistant Professor:
Jennifer McGuire, (D), Michigan State, CgHsGb
Laboratory Director:
Erik Smith, (B), On

Vermilion Community College
Vermilion Community College (1999)
1900 East Camp Street
Ely, MN 55731
p. (218) 235-2173
http://www.vcc.edu/

Winona State University
Dept of Geoscience (B) (2014)
P.O. Box 5838
Winona, MN 55987
p. (507) 457-5260
geoscience@winona.edu
http://www.winona.edu/geology
Administrative Assistant: Abigail Kugel
Enrollment (2009): B: 61 (20)
Professor:
Jamie Ann Meyers, (D), Indiana, 1971, Gsd
Associate Professor & Director Southeastern Minnesota Water Resources Center:
Toby Dogwiler, (D), Missouri, 2002, GmHqOw
Associate Professor:
Stephen T. Allard, (D), Wyoming, 2003, GcpGz
Assistant Professor:
Jennifer LB Anderson, (D), Brown, 2004, XgYgOe

William L. Beatty, (D), Pittsburgh, 2003, Pg
Candace L. Kairies Beatty, (D), Pittsburgh, 2003, GeCl
Emeritus:
John F. Donovan, (D), Cornell, 1963, Eg
Dennis N. Nielsen, (D), North Dakota, 1973, Gm
Associate VP, Academic Affairs:
Nancy O. Jannik, (D), New Mexico Tech, 1989, Hw
College Laboratory Services Specialist:
Luke Zwiefelhofer, (B), Wyoming, 2004, On

Mississippi

Jackson State University
Physics, Atmospheric Sciences and Geoscience (B) (2014)
1400 J. R. Lynch St.
JSU Box 17660
Jackson, MS 39217
p. (601) 979-7012
mfadavi@jsums.edu
http://www.jsums.edu/cset/phyat.htm
Enrollment (2014): B: 9 (4)

Millsaps College
Dept of Geology (B) O (2016)
Box 150647
1701 North State Street
Jackson, MS 39210
p. (601) 974-1340
galics@millsaps.edu
http://www.millsaps.edu/geology/
Enrollment (2015): B: 15 (2)
Professor:
James B. Harris, (D), Kentucky, 1992, Ye
Chair:
Stan Galicki, (D), Mississippi, 2002, Ged
Assistant Professor:
Zachary A. Musselman, (D), Kentucky, 2006, Gm
Emeritus:
Delbert E. Gann, (D), Missouri Sch of Mines, 1976, Gz

Mississippi State University 🗂
Dept of Geosciences (B,M,D) (2015)
P. O. Box 5448
108 Hilbun Hall
East Lee Blvd.
Mississippi State, MS 39762
p. (662) 325-3915
whc5@geosci.msstate.edu
http://www.geosciences.msstate.edu/
f: https://www.facebook.com/pages/Department-of-Geosci-
ences-Mississippi-State-University/275657317621
Enrollment (2014): B: 505 (86) M: 224 (103) D: 24 (4)
Head:
William H. Cooke, III, (D), Mississippi State, 1997, OriOg
Professor:
Michael E. Brown, (D), North Carolina, 1999, Ow
Darrel W. Schmitz, (D), Texas A&M, 1991, Hw
Associate Professor:
Shrinidhi Ambinakudige, (D), Florida State, 2006, Oiy
Renee M. Clary, (D), Louisiana State, 2003, Oe
Jamie Dyer, (D), Georgia, 2005, Ow
Brenda L. Kirkland, (D), Louisiana State, 1992, Gd
John C. Rodgers, (D), Georgia, 1999, Oy
Kathleen M. Sherman-Morris, (D), Florida State, 2006, Ow
Assistant Professor:
Padmanava Dash, (D), Louisiana State, 2011, OrHg
Christopher Fuhrmann, (D), 2011, Oa
Rinat Gabitov, (D), Rensselaer Polytechnic Inst, 2005, Cas
Qingmin Meng, (D), Georgia, 2006, Oig
Andrew Mercer, (D), Oklahoma, 2008, Owa
Adam Skarke, (D), Delaware, 2013, GuYr
Kim Wood, (D), Arizona, 2012, OawOr
Research Associate:
Katarzynz Grala, (M), Iowa State, 2004, Oi
Instructor:
Christa M. Haney, (M), Mississippi State, 1999, Ow

Amy P. Moe-Hoffman, (M), Colorado, 2002, On
John A. Morris, (M), Mississippi State, 2007, OirOw
Lindsey Morschauser, (M), Mississippi State, Ow
Athena Nagel, (D), Mississippi State, 2014, OgiOr
Greg Nordstrom, (M), Mississippi State, 2007, Ow
Tim Wallace, (M), Mississippi State, 1994, Ow
Adjunct Professor:
Paul J. Croft, (D), Rutgers, 1991, Ow
Patrick J. Fitzpatrick, (D), Colorado State, 1995, Ow
James May, (D), Texas A&M, 1988, Hw
Jack C. Pashin, (D), Kentucky, 1990, GoEcGs
Janet E. Simms, (D), Texas A&M, 1991, Yg
Jayaram Veeramony, (D), Delaware, 1999, Og
Emeritus:
John M. Kaye, (D), Louisiana State, 1974, Gg
John E. Mylroie, (D), Rensselaer, 1977, Gm
Charles L. Wax, (D), Louisiana State, 1977, Oa
Distance Academic Coordinator:
Mary A. Dean
Business Manager:
Jerri Wright, (B), Mississippi Univ for Women, 1996
Academic Coordinator:
Tina Davis, (M), Mississippi Univ for Women
Related Staff:
Cynthia Bell

University of Mississippi
Dept of Geology & Geological Engineering (B,M,D) (2014)
School of Engineering
P.O. Box 1848
120A Carrier Hall
University, MS 38677-1848
p. (662) 915-7498
geology@olemiss.edu
http://www.engineering.olemiss.edu/gge/
Enrollment (2010): B: 121 (14) M: 10 (3) D: 7 (1)
Associate Professor:
Joel S. Kuszmaul, (D), California (Berkeley), 1993, Nr
Professor:
Gregg R. Davidson, (D), Arizona, 1995, Hw
Gregory L. Easson, (D), Missouri (Rolla), 1996, Or
R. P. Major, (D), Brown, 1984, Gd
Research Associate Professor:
Thomas M. McGee, (D), Utrecht (Neth), 1991, Ys
Associate Professor:
Adnan Aydin, (D), Memorial, 1994, Ng
Robert M. Holt, (D), New Mexico Tech, 2000, Hq
Research Assistant Professor:
Robin C. Buchannon, (D), Mississippi, 1995, Oo
Craig J. Hickey, (D), Alberta, 1994, Ys
Assistant Professor:
Terry L. Panhorst, (D), Nevada (Reno), 1996, Em
Brian F. Platt, (D), Kansas, 2009, Pg
Louis Zachos, (D), Texas (Austin), 2008, Ger
Instructor:
Cathy A. Grace, (M), Mississippi, 1996, Gg
Amanda Patterson
Emeritus:
Nolan B. Aughenbaugh, (D), Purdue, 1963, Nr
George D. Brunton, (D), Indiana, 1957, Ng

University of Southern Mississippi 🗂
Dept of Geography and Geology (B,M,D) (2015)
118 College Drive, Box 5051
Walker Science Building, Room 127
Hattiesburg, MS 39406
p. (601) 266-4729
franklin.heitmuller@usm.edu
http://www.usm.edu/geography-geology
Enrollment (2014): B: 114 (19) M: 30 (5) D: 4 (1)
Professor:
Andy Reese, (D), Louisiana State, 2003, Oy
Professor:
Clifton Dixon, (D), Texas A&M, 1988, On
Maurice A. Meylan, (D), Hawaii, 1978, Gu
Mark Miller, (D), Arizona, 1988, On

David M. Patrick, (D), Oklahoma, 1972, Ng
Associate Professor:
  Jerry Bass, (D), Texas, 2003, On
  Greg Carter, (D), Wyoming, 1985, Oyi
  David Cochran, (D), Kansas, 2005, On
  David Holt, (D), Arkansas, 2002, Oyi
  Bandana Kar, (D), South Carolina, 2008, Oi
  George Raber, (D), South Carolina, 2003, Oi
Assistant Professor:
  Grant Harley, (D), Tennessee, 2012, Oy
  Omar Harvey, (D), Texas A&M, 2010, GeHwg
  Frank Heitmuller, (D), Texas, 2009, Gms
Instructor:
  Lin F. Pope, (M), S Mississippi, 1983, Gz
  Vicki Tinnon, (D), Kansas State, 2010, On

Gulf Coast Research Laboratory (2006)
Department of Coastal Sciences
Geology Section
Ocean Springs, MS 39566-7000
  p. (601) 872-4200
  angelia.bone@usm.edu
  http://www.coms.usm.edu
  Administrative Assistant: Angelia Bone
Head:
  Ervin G. Otvos, (D), Massachusetts, 1964, On

Marine Science (B,M,D) (2016)
1020 Balch Boulevard
National Aeronautics and Space Administration
Stennis Space Center, MS 39529
  p. (228) 688-3177
  marine.science@usm.edu
  http://www.usm.edu/marine
  f: https://www.facebook.com/SouthernMissDepartmentOfMari-neScience
  t: @USMMarineSci
  Enrollment (2015): B: 17 (2) M: 30 (16) D: 13 (3)
Director of the Center for Gulf Studies:
  Denis A. Wiesenburg, (D), Oceanography, 1980, Oc
Department Chair:
  William Graham, (D), California (Santa Cruz), 1994, Ob
Professor:
  Vernon L. Asper, (D), MIT/WHOI, 1986, Ou
  Donald G. Redalje, (D), Hawaii, 1980, Ob
  Alan M. Shiller, (D), California (San Diego), 1982, Oc
Associate Professor:
  Stephan Howden, (D), Rhode Island, 1996, Op
  Scott Milroy, (D), South Florida, 2007, Ob
  Dmitri Nechaev, (D), Shirshov Inst, 1986, Op
  Jerry Wiggert, (D), S California, 1995, Op
Assistant Professor:
  Maarten Buijsman, (D), Utrecht, 2007, Op
  Ian Church, (D), New Brunswick, 2014, Hg
  Christopher T. Hayes, (D), 2013, Oc
  Jessica E. Pilarczyk, (D), Geology, 2011, Ou
  Davin Wallace, (D), Rice, 2010, Ou
Director, Hydrographic Science Academic Graduate Degree Program:
  Maxim F. van Norden, (M), Naval Postgrad Sch, 1979, Op
Instructor:
  Danielle Greenhow, (D), USF St. Petersburg, 2013, Og

Missouri

Metropolitan Community College-Blue River
Geology and Geography Program (A) (2015)
20301 E. 78 Highway
Independence, MO 64057-2053
  p. (816) 220-6622
  benjamin.wolfe@mcckc.edu
  http://www.mcckc.edu/progs/geol/geology/overview.asp

Metropolitan Community College-Kansas City
Geology Dept (A) (2013)
3200 Broadway
Kansas City, MO 64111

  p. (816) 604-3335
  melissa.renfrow@mcckc.edu
  http://mcckc.edu
Instructor:
  Alice Fuerst, Gg
  John Horn, (D), Nebraska, GgOy
  Carl Priesendorf, (M), Central Missouri, 1987, GgOy
  Laura Veverka, (M), Missouri (Kansas City), Oy
  Ben Wolfe, (M), Alaska (Fairbanks), 2001, GgOyg
Adjunct Professor:
  Janet Raymer, (M), Missouri S&T, GgEo

Mineral Area College
Science Dept (A) (2015)
5270 Flat River Road
P.O. Box 1000
Park Hills, MO 63601
  p. (573) 518-2314
  bscheidt@MineralArea.edu
  http://www.mineralarea.edu/faculty/academicDepartments/science.aspx
  Enrollment (2015): A: 4 (0)
Assistant Professor:
  Brian Scheidt, (M), S Illinois, Hw
Adjunct Professor:
  Jim Hrouda, (B), On
  Bill Mayberry, (B), On
  Katherine Perkins, (M)

Missouri State University
Dept of Geography, Geology & Planning (B,M) (2015)
901 S. National
Springfield, MO 65897
  p. (417) 836-5800
  Tdogwiler@missouristate.edu
  http://geosciences.missouristate.edu
  f: https://www.facebook.com/MSUGeographyGeologyand-Planning
  Administrative Assistant: Deana Gibson
  Enrollment (2015): B: 180 (43) M: 29 (11)
Department Head:
  Toby Dogwiler, (D), Missouri, 2002, HyGm
Professor:
  Kevin R. Evans, (D), Kansas, 1997, Gr
  Douglas R. Gouzie, (D), Kentucky, 1986, HwGe
  Melida Gutierrez, (D), Texas (El Paso), 1992, Cg
  Rajinder S. Jutla, (D), Virginia Tech, 1995, On
  Kevin L. Mickus, (D), Texas (El Paso), 1989, Yg
  Robert T. Pavlowsky, (D), Wisconsin, 1995, Gm
  Paul A. Rollinson, (D), Illinois, 1988, On
  Charles W. Rovey, (D), Wisconsin (Milwaukee), 1990, Hy
Associate Professor:
  Alice (Jill) Black, (D), Missouri, 2003, Oe
  Jun Luo, (D), Wisconsin (Milwaukee), Oi
  Judith Meyer, (D), Wisconsin, 1994, On
  Xin Miao, (D), California (Berkeley), 2005, Or
  Xiaomin Qiu, (D), Texas State, Oi
Assistant Professor:
  Timothy Brock, (D), Kentucky, 2014, On
  Mario Daoust, (D), McGill, Oa
  Ron Malega, (D), Georgia, On
  Diane M. May, (M), S Illinois (Edwardsville), 1974, On
  Gary Michelfelder, (D), Montana State, 2014, Gvi
Senior Instructor:
  Deborah Corcoran, (M), Michigan State, 1980, On
Associate Provost:
  John C. Catau, (D), Michigan State, 1973, On
Emeritus:
  David A. Castillon, (D), Michigan State, 1972, Gm
  William H. Cheek, (D), Michigan State, 1976, On
  William Corcoran, (D), Michigan State, 1981, Oa
  Stanley C. Fagerlin, (D), Missouri, 1980, Pg
  Russel L. Gerlach, (D), Nebraska, 1974, On
  Elias Johnson, (D), Oklahoma, 1977, Or
  Vincent E. Kurtz, (D), Oklahoma, 1960, Ps
  Erwin J. Mantei, (D), Missouri (Rolla), 1965, Ct

James F. Miller, (D), Wisconsin, 1970, Ps
Thomas D. Moeglin, (D), Nebraska, 1978, Ng
Thomas G. Plymate, (D), Minnesota, 1986, Gx
Milton D. Rafferty, (D), Nebraska, 1970, On
Senior Instructor:
    Damon Bassett, (M), Missouri, 2003, Pg
    Linnea Iantria, (M), George Washington, On

Missouri University of Science and Technology
Dept of Geology & Geophysics (B,M,D) (2004)
125 McNutt Hall
Rolla, MO 65409-0410
    p. (573) 341-4616
    rocks@umr.edu
    Administrative Assistant: Katherine W. Mattison
    Enrollment (2001): B: 76 (16) M: 18 (3) D: 11 (1)
Lecturer:
    Patrick S. Mulvany, (D), Missouri (Rolla), 1996, Gg
Adjunct Professor:
    John F. Burst, (D), Missouri, 1950, Eo
    Waldemar M. Dressel, (B), Missouri (Rolla), 1943, Gg
    Charles E. Robertson, (M), Maryland, 1960, Gc
    James E. Vandike, (M), SD Mines, 1979, Hg
    James H. Williams, (D), Missouri (Rolla), 1975, Gg
Emeritus:
    Shelton K. Grant, (D), Utah, 1966, Gz
    Richard D. Hagni, (D), Missouri, 1962, Em
    Geza K. Kisvarsanyi, (D), Missouri, 1966, Em
    Richard D. Rechtien, (D), Washington, 1964, Ye
    Gerald B. Rupert, (D), Missouri, 1964, Ye
    Alfred C. Spreng, (D), Wisconsin, 1950, Gr

Moberly Area Community College-Columbia Campus
Moberly Area Community College - Columbia Campus (1999)
601 Business Loop 70 West
Columbia, MO 65203
    p. (573) 234-1067
    SandyAnderson@macc.edu
    http://www.macc.edu/

Northwest Missouri State University
Dept of Geology-Geography (B,M) (2014)
800 University Drive
Maryville, MO 64468
    p. (660) 562-1723
    geosci@nwmissouri.edu
    Enrollment (2003): B: 176 (53)
Chair:
    C. Renee Rohs, (D), Kansas, 2000, Cg
Professor:
    Gregory D. Haddock, (D), Idaho, 1996, Oi
Associate Professor:
    Mark W. Corson, (D), South Carolina, 1997, Oy
    Theodore L. Goudge, (D), Oklahoma State, 1984, Oy
Assistant Professor:
    Patricia L. Drews, (D), South Carolina, 1999, Oi
    James Hickey, (D), Dartmouth, 2006, Ge
    Ming-Chih Hung, (D), Utah, 2003, Or
    Yanfen Le, (D), Georgia, 2005, Oi
    Leah D. Manos, (M), Tennessee, 1997, Oy
    John P. Pope, (D), Iowa, 2006, Ps
    Yi-Hwa Wu, (D), Utah, 2003, Oi
Instructor:
    Jeffrey Bradley, (M), Oklahoma State, 1991, Og
Emeritus:
    Richard M. Felton, (M), Missouri, 1979, Pg

Ozarks Technical Community College
Physical Sciences (1999)
1001 E. Chestnut Expressway
Springfield, MO 65802
    p. (417) 447-8238
    ehrichp@otc.edu

Saint Louis University
Earth & Atmospheric Sciences (B,M,D) (2014)
3642 Lindell Blvd
O'Neil Hall
Room 205
St. Louis, MO 63108
    p. (314) 977-3116
    dannevik@eas.slu.edu
    http://www.eas.slu.edu
    Administrative Assistant: Loretta Edwards
    Enrollment (2014): B: 60 (12) M: 13 (6) D: 7 (3)
Chair:
    William P. Dannevik, (D), St. Louis, 1984, Oa
Professor:
    David J. Crossley, (D), British Columbia, 1973, Yg
    Jack Fishman, (D), Oar
    Daniel Hanes, (D), Gus
    Robert B. Herrmann, (D), St. Louis, 1974, Ys
    Zaitao Pan, (D), Iowa State, 1996, Oa
    Lupei Zhu, (D), Caltech, 1998, Ys
Associate Professor:
    Karl Chauff, (D), Pg
    Benjamin de Foy, (D), Cambridge, 1998, Oa
    John Encarnacion, (D), Michigan, 1994, Gx
    Charles E. Graves, (D), Iowa State, 1988, Oa
    Robert W. Pasken, (D), St. Louis, 1981, Ow
Assistant Professor:
    Lisa Chambers, (D)
    Tim Eichler, (D), Oa
    Elizabeth Hasenmueller, (D)
    Ana Londono, (D), Gm
    Linda Warren, (D), Yg
Emeritus:
    Brian J. Mitchell, (D), S Methodist, 1970, Ys
    Albert J. Pallmann, (D), Cologne, 1958, Oa

University of Missouri
Dept of Geological Sciences (B,M,D) (2014)
101 Geology Building
Columbia, MO 65211
    p. (573) 882-6785
    HuckabeyM@missouri.edu
    http://geology.missouri.edu/
    Administrative Assistant: Marsha Huckabey
    Enrollment (2013): B: 60 (7) M: 13 (11) D: 21 (0)
Director of Geology Field Studies:
    Miriam Barquero-Molina, (D), Texas, 2009, Gt
Chair:
    Kevin L. Shelton, (D), Yale, 1982, EmCs
Professor:
    Cheryl A. Kelley, (D), North Carolina, 1993, Co
    Mian Liu, (D), Arizona, 1989, Yg
    Kenneth A. MacLeod, (D), Washington, 1992, Pg
    Peter I. Nabelek, (D), SUNY (Stony Brook), 1983, Ct
    Eric A. Sandvol, (D), New Mexico State, 1995, Ys
    Michael B. Underwood, (D), Cornell, 1982, Gs
    Alan Whittington, (D), Open, 1997, GvCp
Associate Professor:
    Martin Appold, (D), Johns Hopkins, 1998, Hw
    Robert L. Bauer, (D), Minnesota, 1981, Gc
    Francisco Gomez, (D), Cornell, 1999, Gt
Assistant Professor:
    John Huntley, (D), Virginia Tech, 2007, PqoPe
    James Schiffbauer, (D), Virginia Tech, 2009, Poi
Adjunct Professor:
    G. Randy Keller, (D), Texas Tech, 1973, Yg
    Timothy McHargue, (D)
    James Ni, (D), Cornell, 1984, Ygs
    Angela Speck, (D), Univ Coll (London), 1998, Xc
    Samson Tesfaye, (D), Colorado, 1999, GtcOr
Emeritus:
    Raymond L. Ethington, (D), Iowa, 1958, Pm
    Thomas J. Freeman, (D), Texas, 1962, Gd
    Glen R. Himmelberg, (D), Minnesota, 1965, Gp
Cooperating Faculty:
    Stephen Stanton, On

University of Missouri, Columbia 🗇

Dept of Soil, Environmental & Atmospheric Sciences (B,M,D)
(2014)
302 Anheuser-Busch Natural Resources Building
Columbia, MO 65211-7250
p. (573) 882-6301
MarketP@missouri.edu
http://www.snr.missouri.edu/seas/
Enrollment (2012): B: 165 (15) M: 24 (3) D: 13 (0)
Chair:
Patrick S. Market, (D), St. Louis, 1999, Oa
Professor:
Stephen H. Anderson, (D), North Carolina State, 1985, Sp
Clark J. Gantzer, (D), Minnesota, 1980, Os
Anthony R. Lupo, (D), Purdue, 1995, Oa
Peter P. Motavalli, (D), Cornell, 1989, Os
Extension:
Patrick E. Guinan, (D), Missouri, 2004, Oa
Associate Professor:
Neil I. Fox, (D), Salford (UK), 1998, Oa
Keith W. Goyne, (D), Penn State, 2003, Sc
Jason A. Hubbart, (D), Idaho, 2007, Hq
Randall J. Miles, (D), Texas A&M, 1981, Sd
Assistant Professor:
Bohumil Svoma, (D), Arizona State, 2013, Oa
Instructor:
Eric A. Aldrich, (M), Missouri, 2011, Oa
Adjunct Professor:
Robert J. Kremer, (D), Mississippi State, 1981, Os
Christopher K. Wikle, (D), Iowa State, Oa
Emeritus:
Robert W. Blanchar, (D), Minnesota, 1964, Sc
James R. Brown, (D), Iowa State, 1963, Os
Ernest C. Kung, (D), Wisconsin, 1963, Oa
Stephen E. Mudrick, (D), MIT, 1973, Oa
Other:
E Eugene Alberts, (D), Purdue, 1979, Hw
J Glenn Davis, (D), Iowa State, Os
Frieda Eivazi, (D), Iowa State, 1980, Sc
Newell R. Kitchen, (D), Colorado State, 1990, Sp
Robert N. Lerch, (D), Colorado State, 1990, Os
W. Gene Stevens, (D), Mississippi State, 1992, Os

University of Missouri-Kansas City

Dept of Geosciences (B,M,D) (2013)
5100 Rockhill Road
Room 420, Robert H. Flarsheim Hall
Kansas City, MO 64110-2499
p. (816) 235-1334
geosciences@umkc.edu
http://cas.umkc.edu/Geosciences/default.asp
Enrollment (2007): B: 85 (19) M: 13 (2) D: 11 (1)
Chair:
James B. Murowchick, (D), Penn State, 1984, CgGz
Waste Management Program:
Syed E. Hasan, (D), Purdue, 1978, Ng
Professor:
Steven L. Driever, (D), Georgia, 1977, On
Daniel P. Hopkins, (D), Louisiana State, 1987, On
Wei Ji, (D), Connecticut, 1991, Oy
Tina M. Niemi, (D), Stanford, 1992, Gt
Associate Professor:
Jimmy Adegoke, (D), Penn State, 2000, OagOa
Caroline P. Davies, (D), Arizona State, 2000, Pl
Jejung Lee, (D), Northwestern, 2001, GqHw
Julie Urbanik, (D), Clark, On
Emeritus:
Raymond M. Coveney, (D), Michigan, 1972, Em
Richard J. Gentile, (D), Missouri, 1965, Gr

Washington University

Environmental Studies Program (B) (2010)
Box 1169
One Brookings Drive
St. Louis, MO 63130-4899
p. (314) 935-7047
enstadmin@levee.wustl.edu
http://enst.wustl.edu
Administrative Assistant: Barbara Winston
Enrollment (2010): B: 161 (59)
Director:
Jan P. Amend, (D), California (Berkeley), 1995, Co
Professor:
Raymond E. Arvidson, (D), Brown, 1974, On
Richard Axelbaum, (D), California (Davis), 1988, Ng
Pratim Biswas, (D), Caltech, 1985, Ng
Robert Blankenship, (D), California (Berkeley), 1975, On
Robert E. Criss, (D), Caltech, 1981, Cs
Willem H. Dickhoff, (D), Free (Amsterdam), On
Mike Dudukovic, (D), Illinois Inst Tech, 1971, On
Robert F. Dymek, (D), Caltech, 2006, Gi
Claude Evans, (D), SUNY (Stony Brook), On
Bruce Fegley, (D), MIT, 1980, Xc
T.R. Kidder, (D), Harvard, 1988, On
Maxine I. Lipeles, (D), Harvard, 1979, On
William R. Lowry, (D), Stanford, 1988, On
Jill D. Pasteris, (D), Yale, 1980, On
Bruce Petersen, (D), Harvard, On
Robert Pollak, (D), MIT, 1964, On
Tab Rasmussen, (D), Duke, On
Barbara Schaal, (D), Yale, 1974, On
Glenn D. Stone, (D), Arizona, 1988, On
Robert W. Sussman, (D), Duke, 1972, On
Alan R. Templeton, (D), Michigan, 1972, On
Associate Professor:
Jon M. Chase, (D), Chicago, On
Clare Palmer, (D), On
Jen R. Smith, (D), Pennsylvania, 2001, Ga
Jay Turner, (D), Washington (St. Louis), 1993, On
Assistant Professor:
Jeff Catalano, (D), Stanford, 2004, Ca
Geoff Childs, (D), Indiana, On
Ellen Damschen, (D), North Carolina State, On
David A. Fike, (D), MIT, 2007, Cs
Daniel Giammar, (D), Caltech, 2001, On
Young-Shin Jun, Harvard, 2005, On
Tiffany Knight, (D), Pittsburgh, 2003, Pe
Ken Olsen, (D), Washington (St. Louis), 2000, On
John Orrock, (D), Iowa State, 2004, On
Engineering & Science Director:
Beth Martin, (M), Washington (St. Louis), 1996, Ng
Geology Librarian:
Clara McLeod, On

Washington University in St. Louis 🗇

Dept of Earth & Planetary Sciences (B,M,D) (2015)
Campus Box 1169
Rudolph Hall
1 Brookings Drive
St Louis, MO 63130-4899
p. (314) 935-5610
slava@wustl.edu
http://eps.wustl.edu
Administrative Assistant: Robert Gemignani
Enrollment (2010): B: 16 (3) M: 6 (7) D: 22 (8)
Chair:
Viatcheslav S. Solomatov, (D), Moscow Inst of Physics & Tech, 1990, Yg
Rudolph Professor of Earth & Planetary Sciences:
Bradley L. Jolliff, (D), SD Mines, 1987, Gx
James S. McDonnell Distinguished University Professor:
Raymond E. Arvidson, (D), Brown, 1974, Or
Professor:
Robert E. Criss, (D), Caltech, 1981, Cs
Robert F. Dymek, (D), Caltech, 1977, Gp
M. Bruce Fegley, (D), MIT, 1980, Xc
William B. McKinnon, (D), Caltech, 1981, Xg
Jill D. Pasteris, (D), Yale, 1980, Eg
William H. Smith, (D), Princeton, 1966, Xc
Douglas A. Wiens, (D), Northwestern, 1985, Ysg
Research Professor:
Anne M. Hofmeister, (D), Caltech, 1984, Gz

Randy L. Korotev, (D), Wisconsin, 1976, Ct
Katharina Lodders-Fegley, (D), Max Planck, 1991, Xc
Alian Wang, (D), Sci/Tech (France), 1987, Ca
Associate Professor:
Jeffrey G. Catalano, (D), Stanford, 2004, Cl
David Fike, (D), MIT, 2007, Cs
Jennifer R. Smith, (D), Pennsylvania, 2001, Ga
Michael E. Wysession, (D), Northwestern, 1991, Ys
Assistant Professor:
Alexander S. Bradley, (D), MIT, 2008, Py
Philip Skemer, (D), Yale, 2007, GcCp

William Jewell College
Dept of Biology (2011)
Liberty, MO 64068
 p. (816) 781-3806 x230
 allent@william.jewell.edu
 http://www.jewell.edu
Chair:
Tara Allen
Associate Professor:
Charles F. J. Newlon, (M), Missouri, 1962, Og

Montana

Flathead Valley Community College
Geology and Geography (A) (2015)
777 Grandview Drive
Kalispell, MT 59901
 p. (406) 756-3873
 aho@fvcc.edu
Instructor:
Anita Ho, (D), Oregon, Gg

Montana State University ◻
Dept of Earth Sciences (B,M,D) (2014)
P.O. Box 173480
226 Traphagen Hall
Bozeman, MT 59717-3480
 p. (406) 994-3331
 earth@montana.edu
 http://www.montana.edu/wwwes/
 Enrollment (2013): B: 219 (48) M: 37 (8) D: 17 (3)
Professor:
David R. Lageson, (D), Wyoming, 1980, Gc
David W. Mogk, (D), Washington, 1984, Gp
James G. Schmitt, (D), Wyoming, 1982, Gr
Cathy Whitlock, (D), Washington, 1983, Pey
William K. Wyckoff, (D), Syracuse, 1982, On
Associate Professor:
Todd C. Feeley, (D), California (Los Angeles), 1993, Gi
Michael Gardner, (D), Colorado Mines, 1993, Gsr
Jian-yi Liu, (D), Minnesota, 1992, On
Mark L. Skidmore, (D), Alberta, 2001, ClPyOy
David J. Varricchio, (D), Montana State, 1995, Pv
Assistant Professor:
Jean Dixon, (D), Dartmouth, 2009, Gm
Julia H. Haggerty, (D), Colorado, 2004, On
Jordy Hendrikx, (D), Canterbury (New Zealand), 2005, OnHsOa
Jamie McEvoy, (D), Arizona, 2013, Oe
Research Assistant Professor:
Dave Bowen, (M), Montana State, 1980, Gs
Frankie Jackson, (D), Montana State, 2007, Pv
David B. McWethy, (D), Montana State, 2007, PeSb
Colin Shaw, (D), New Mexico, 2001, GcEmGp
Kaj Williams, Colorado, Oa
Assistant Teaching Professor:
Stuart Challender, (M), Utah State, 1986, Oi
Regents Professor:
John R. Horner, Penn State, 2006, Pv

Dept of Land Resources & Environmental Sciences (B,M,D) (2014)
334 Leon Johnson Hall
P.O. Box 173120
Bozeman, MT 59717-3120

 p. (406) 994-7060
 jefj@montana.edu
 http://landresources.montana.edu/
 Department Secretary: Peggy Humphrey
 Enrollment (2000): B: 93 (13) M: 25 (2) D: 13 (0)
Chair:
Tracy M. Sterling, (D)
Professor:
James W. Bauder, (D), Utah State, 1974, Sf
Lisa J. Graumlich, (D), Washington, 1985, Ou
William P. Inskeep, (D), Minnesota, 1985, Sc
Jeffrey S. Jacobsen, (D), Oklahoma State, 1985, So
Gerald A. Nielsen, (D), Wisconsin, 1963, Sd
David M. Ward, (D), Wisconsin, 1975, On
Senior Scientist:
Dennis R. Neuman, (M), Montana State, 1972, On
Associate Professor:
Richard E. Engel, (D), Minnesota, 1983, Sc
Cliff Montagne, (D), Montana State, 1976, Sd
Jon M. Wraith, (D), Utah State, 1989, Sp
Assistant Professor:
Paul B. Hook, (D), Colorado State, 1992, Sf
Rick L. Lawrence, (D), Oregon State, 1998, Or
Adjunct Professor:
Douglas J. Dollhopf, (D), Montana State, 1975, On

Montana State University, Billings
Dept of Biological & Physical Sciences (2011)
1500 N. 30th Street
Billings, MT 59101
 p. (406) 657-2341 x2028
 nsuits@msubillings.edu
 Enrollment: No data reported since 1999
Head:
Stanley Wiatr
Dean:
Tasneem Khaleel, (D), Bangalore, 1970, Po
Professor:
Matt Benacquista, (D), Montana State, 1989, Xy
Thomas T. Zwick, (D), N Colorado, 1977, Oe

Montana Tech
Geophysical Engineering (B,M) O (2015)
1300 West Park Street
Butte, MT 59701
 p. (406) 496-4401
 mspeece@mtech.edu
 http://www.mtech.edu/academics/mines/geophysical/
 Enrollment (2015): B: 23 (3) M: 10 (3)
Head:
Marvin A. Speece, (D), Wyoming, 1992, Ye
Associate Professor:
Xiaobing Zhou, (D), Alaska (Fairbanks), 2002, Or
Assistant Professor:
Mohamed Khalil, (D), Giessen, 2002, YegGe
Khalid Miah, (D), Texas (Austin), 2008, YexYs
Emeritus:
Curtis A. Link, (D), Houston, 1993, Ye

Montana Tech of the University of Montana ◻
Dept of Chemistry & Geochemistry (B,M) (2014)
1300 West Park Street
Butte, MT 59701-8997
 p. (406) 496-4207
 dhobbs@mtech.edu
 Department Secretary: Wilma Immonen
 Enrollment: No data reported since 1999
Chair:
Douglas Cameron, (D), Purdue, 1979, Ca
Professor:
Douglas A. Coe, (D), Oregon State, 1974, Cg
Douglas A. Drew, (D), Wyoming, 1971, Cg
Donald Stierle, (D), California (Riverside), 1979, Co
Assistant Professor:
John D. Hobbs, (D), New Mexico, 1991, On

Research Associate:
  Wayne Olmsted, (B), Montana State, 1962, Ca
  Andrea Stierle, (D), Montana State, On
Instructor:
  Stephen R. Parker, (M), Indiana, 1972, On
Emeritus:
  Frank E. Diebold, (D), Colorado Mines, 1967, Cl
  Alexis Volborth, (D), Helsinki, 1954, Ca

Dept of Geological Engineering (B,M) (2015)
1300 West Park Street
Butte, MT 59701
  p. (406) 496-4262
  dconrad@mtech.edu
  http://www.mtech.edu/geo_eng
  Enrollment (2015): B: 34 (5) M: 24 (12)
Chair:
  Christopher H. Gammons, (D), Penn State, 1988, Cg
Professor:
  Mary M. MacLaughlin, (D), California (Berkeley), 1997, Nr
  Diane Wolfgram, (D), California (Berkeley), 1977, EgoNm
Associate Professor:
  Glenn D. Shaw, (D), California (Merced), 2009, HwCsHs
  Larry N. Smith, (D), New Mexico, 1999, GsoGm

Rocky Mountain College
Dept of Geology (B) (2016)
1511 Poly Drive
Billings, MT 59102
  p. (406) 657-1101
  kalakayt@rocky.edu
  http://www.rocky.edu/academics/academic-programs/
  undergraduate-majors/geology/
  Enrollment (2015): B: 22 (1)
Professor:
  Thomas J. Kalakay, (D), Wyoming, 2001, GcpGi
Associate Professor:
  Derek Sjostrom, (D), Dartmouth, 2002, ClGsHs
Assistant Professor:
  Emily Geraghty Ward, (D), Montana, 2007, Gc

Salish Kootenai College
Dept of Environmental Science (1999)
58138 US Hwy 93
Ronan, MT 59855
  bill_swaney@skc.edu
  http://www.skc.edu

University of Montana
Dept. of Geosciences (B,M,D) (2015)
32 Campus Drive #1296
Missoula, MT 59812-1296
  p. (406) 243-2341
  james.staub@umontana.edu
  http://www.umt.edu/geosciences
  Administrative Assistant: Christine Foster
  Administrative Assistant: Loreene Skeel
  Enrollment (2014): B: 100 (23) M: 12 (4) D: 16 (1)
Chair:
  James R. Staub, (D), South Carolina, 1985, Gs
Professor:
  Joel Harper, (D), Wyoming, 1997, Gl
  Marc S. Hendrix, (D), Stanford, 1992, Gs
  Nancy W. Hinman, (D), California (San Diego), 1987, Co
  James W. Sears, (D), Queens, 1979
  George D. Stanley, Jr., (D), Kansas, 1977, Pi
Associate Professor:
  Julia Baldwin, (D), MIT, 2003, Gp
  Rebecca Bendick, (D), Colorado, 2000, Yg
  Marco Maneta, (D), Extremadura (Spain), 2006
  Andrew Wilcox, (D), Colorado State, 2005, Gm
Assistant Professor:
  Payton Gardner, (D), Utah, 2009, Hw
Research Associate:
  Carrine E. Blank, (D), Berkley, 2002
  Michael Hofmann, (D), Montana, 2005

Lecturer:
  Kathleen Harper, (D), Wyoming, 1997
IT/GIS:
  Aaron M. Deskins, (B), Montana, 2005

University of Montana Western
Environmental Sciences Dept (B) O (2015)
710 South Atlantic Street
Dillon, MT 59725-3598
  p. (406) 683-7615
  rob.thomas@umwestern.edu
  http://www.facebook.com/UMWenvirosciences
  f: https://www.facebook.com/UMWenvirosciences/
  Administrative Assistant: Thomas G. Satterly
  Enrollment (2015): B: 95 (17)
Chair:
  Robert C. Thomas, (D), Washington, 1993, GsHsOe
Professor:
  Eric G. Dyreson, (D), Arizona, 1997, Gq
  Linda M. Lyon, (D), Washington State, 2003, Ou
  R. Stephen Mock, (D), Montana State, 1989, Ca
  Delena Norris-Tull, (D), Texas, 1990, Oe
  Sheila M. Roberts, (D), Calgary, 1996, Ge
  Eric S. Wright, (D), Colorado, 2002, Gq
  Craig E. Zaspel, (D), Montana State, 1975, On
Associate Professor:
  Michelle Anderson, (D), Montana, 2008, Hs
Assistant Professor:
  Rebekah Levine, (M), New Mexico, 2011, HgGmOa
Instructor:
  Nils Troedsson, (M), Montana, 1960, On
Adjunct Professor:
  Heidi Anderson-Folnagy, (D), Idaho, 2011, Gs
  Brenda J. Buck, (D), New Mexico State, 1996, Sdo
  Marvin E. Kauffman, (D), Princeton, 1960, Gr
Emeritus:
  Peter Bengeyfield, (M), West Virginia, 1969, Hg

Nebraska

Central Community College
Physical Science (A) (2015)
4500 63rd Street
PO Box 1027
Columbus, NE 68602
  p. (402) 562-1216
  dcondreay@cccneb.edu
  http://www.cccneb.edu/Science-and-Math/
Instructor:
  Denise Condreay, Og

Chadron State College
Dept of Geociences (B) O (2015)
1000 Main Street
Chadron, NE 69337
  p. (308) 432-6377
  mleite@csc.edu
  http://www.csc.edu/geoscience
  Administrative Assistant: Stacy Mittleider
  Enrollment (2013): B: 7 (4)
Chair:
  Wendy Jamison, (D)
Professor:
  Michael B. Leite, (D), Wyoming, 1992, Gg
Instructor:
  Jennifer Balmat, (M), Gg

Creighton University
Dept of Atmospheric Sciences (B,M) (2014)
2500 California Plaza
Omaha, NE 68178
  p. (402) 280-2641
  zehnder@creighton.edu
  Enrollment (2012): B: 10 (0) M: 3 (0)

Professor:
Joseph A. Zehnder, (D), Chicago, 1986, Oa
Associate Professor:
Jon M. Schrage, (D), Purdue, 1998, Ow
Assistant Professor:
Timothy J. Wagner, (D), Wisconsin, 2011, Oa
Adjunct Professor:
Richard Ritz, (M), Texas A&M, Ow
Emeritus:
Arthur V. Douglas, (D), Arizona, 1976, Og

University of Nebraska at Omaha
Dept of Geography and Geology (B,M) (2015)
6001 Dodge Street
DSC 260
Omaha, NE 68182-0199
p. (402) 554-2662
rshuster@unomaha.edu
http://www.unomaha.edu/college-of-arts-and-sciences/geology/
Administrative Assistant: Brenda Todd
Enrollment (2015): B: 82 (12)
Professor:
George F. Engelmann, (D), Columbia, 1978, PvGdr
Harmon D. Maher, Jr., (D), Wisconsin, 1984, GcsGt
Associate Professor:
Robert D. Shuster, (D), Kansas, 1985, GiaOe
Assistant Professor:
Bradley Bereitschaft, (D), North Carolina (Greensboro), 2012, Oyu
Ashlee LD Dere, (D), Penn State, 2014, SdGmCl
James J. Hayes, (D), Indiana, 2008, OruOi
Emeritus:
Jeffrey S. Peake, (D), Louisiana State, 1977, OyuOa
John F. Shroder, Jr., (D), Utah, 1967, GmlOy

University of Nebraska, Lincoln
Dept of Earth & Atmospheric Sciences (B,M,D) (2015)
214 Bessey Hall
Lincoln, NE 68588-0340
p. (402) 472-2663
tfrank2@unl.edu
http://eas.unl.edu/
f: https://www.facebook.com/UNLEarthAtmosSci
Administrative Assistant: Janelle Gerry
Administrative Assistant: Tina M. Gray
Enrollment (2015): B: 100 (21) M: 36 (17) D: 22 (10)
Chair:
Tracy D. Frank, (D), Michigan, 1996, GsCsm
Professor:
Christopher R. Fielding, (D), Durham (UK), 1982, Gs
Sherilyn C. Fritz, (D), Minnesota, 1985, Gn
David M. Harwood, (D), Ohio State, 1986, Pm
Qi S. Hu, (D), Colorado State, 1992, Oa
Robert M. Joeckel, (D), Iowa, 1993, GrSd
David B. Loope, (D), Wyoming, 1981, Gs
Robert J. Oglesby, (D), Yale, 1990, Oa
Clinton M. Rowe, (D), Delaware, 1988, Oa
David K. Watkins, (D), Florida State, 1984, Pm
Vitaly A. Zlotnik, (D), Moscow (USSR), 1979, Hwy
Associate Professor:
Mark R. Anderson, (D), Colorado, 1985, Oa
Adam L. Houston, (D), Illinois, 2004, Oa
Richard M. Kettler, (D), Michigan, 1990, Cl
Frank Rack, (D), Texas A&M, 1992, Ou
Ross Secord, (D), Michigan, 2004, PvCs
Jun Wang, (D), Alabama (Huntsville), 2006, Oa
Assistant Professor of Practice:
Deborah J. Bathke, (D), Ohio State, 2004, Oa
Assistant Professor:
Leilani A. Arthurs, (D), Notre Dame, 2007, OeCl
Caroline M. Burberry, (D), Imperial Coll, 2008, Gct
Lynne J. Elkins, (D), MIT/WHOI, 2009, GivCt
Matthew S. Van Den Broeke, (D), Oklahoma, 2011, Oa
Karrie A. Weber, (D), Alabama, 2002, Py
Research Assistant Professor:
Mindi L. Searls, (D), Washington, 2007, YgGg

Adjunct Professor:
John R. Griffin, (D), California, 1973, Eo
Professor of Practice:
Mary Anne Holmes, (D), Florida State, 1989, GsOu
Emeritus:
Ronald G. Goble, (D), Toronto, GxEg
Priscilla C. Grew, (D), California (Berkeley), 1967, Gg
Robert M. Hunt, (D), Columbia, 1971, Pv
Merlin P. Lawson, (D), Clark, 1973, Oy
Nancy Lindsley-Griffin, (D), California (Davis), 1982, Gt
Darryll T. Pederson, (D), North Dakota, 1971, Hw
Norman D. Smith, (D), Brown, 1967, Gs
Michael R. Voorhies, (D), Wyoming, 1966, Pv
William Wayne, (D), Indiana, 1943, Gm

School of Natural Resource Sciences (B,M,D) (2016)
Hardin Hall
3310 Holdrege Street
Lincoln, NE 68583-0961
p. (402) 472-3471
jcarroll2@unl.edu
http://snr.unl.edu/
Enrollment (2014): M: 4 (0) D: 9 (2)
Professor:
Ken F. Dewey, (D), Toronto, 1973, Ow
Michael J. Hayes, (D), Missouri, 1994, Oa
Qi (Steve) Hu, (D), Colorado State, 1992, Oa
Kenneth G. Hubbard, (D), Utah State, 1981, Oa
Robert Oglesby, (D), Yale, 1990, Oa
Elizabeth A. Walter-Shea, (D), Nebraska, 1987, Oa
Donald A. Wilhite, (D), Nebraska, 1975, Oa
Associate Professor:
Martha D. Shulski, (D), Minnesota, 2002, Oa
Andrew E. Suyker, (D), Nebraska, 2000, Oa
Assistant Professor:
Guillermo Baigorria, (D), Wageningen Univ, 2005, Ow
Climate Scientist:
Deborah J. Bathke, (D), Ohio State, 2004, Oa

University of Nebraska-Kearney
Dept of Geography (B) (2015)
203 Copeland Hall
Kearney, NE 68849
p. (308) 865-8355
combshj@unk.edu
Enrollment (2002): B: 165 (0)
Chair:
Jason Combs, (D), Nebraska, 2000
Professor:
Vijay Boken, (D), Manitoba, 1999
Paul Burger, (D), Oklahoma State, 1997
Jeremy Dillon, (D), Kansas, 2001
Associate Professor:
John Bauer, (D), Kansas, 2006
Instructor:
Nate Eidem, (D), Oregon State, 2011
Matt Engel, (D), Nebraska, 2007

Nevada
College of Southern Nevada - West Charleston Campus
Dept of Physical Sciences (A) (2015)
6375 W. Charleston Blvd.
Las Vegas, NV 89146
p. (702) 651-7475
physic@csn.edu
http://www.csn.edu/pages/2497.asp
Lead Faculty:
Barbara Graham, (M), Oyw
John E. Keller, (D), S Illinois, 2009, GeHw
Cynthia S. Shroba, (D), Illinois, Gg
Professor:
Patrick D. Clennan, (M), OyGe
Gale D. Martin, (M), Gg

Instructor:
Douglas Sims, (D), Kingston, 2011, GeSp

Desert Research Institute
Earth & Ecosystems Sciences (2015)
2215 Raggio Parkway
Reno, NV 89512-1095
  p. (775) 673-7300
  bj@dri.edu
Professor:
  John Arnone, (D), Yale, 1988, Py
  Colleen M. Beck, (D), California (Berkeley), 1979, Sa
  Christian H. Fritsen, (D), S California, 1996, Py
  Nicholas Lancaster, (D), Cambridge, 1977, Gm
  Eric McDonald, (D), New Mexico, 1994, Sd
  Alison E. Murray, (D), California (Santa Barbara), 1998, Py
  David E. Rhode, (D), Washington, 1987, Pe
Staff Geomorphologist:
  Sophie Baker, (M), Dalhousie, 2005, Gm
Associate Research Geomorphologist:
  Steven N. Bacon, (M), Humboldt State, 2003, Gm
Associate Professor:
  Kenneth D. Adams, (D), Nevada (Reno), 1997, Gm
  Thomas F. Bullard, (D), New Mexico, 1995, Gm
  Mary Cablk, (D), Oregon State, 1997, Or
  Lynn Fenstermaker, (D), Nevada, 2003, Or
  Giles Marion, (D), California (Berkeley), 1974, Sc
  Kenneth C. McGwire, (D), California (Santa Barbara), 1992, Oy
  David A. Mouat, (D), Oregon State, 1974, Ge
Assistant Professor:
  JoseLuis Antinao, (D), Dalhousie, 2009, Gm
  Amanda Keen-Zebert, (D), Texas State, 2007, Oy
  Donald E. Sabol, Jr, (D), Washington, 1991, Or
GIS/Remote Sensing Scientist:
  Timothy B. Minor, (M), California (Santa Barbara), 1982, Or
Assistant Research Ecologist:
  Richard Jasoni, (D), Texas A&M, 1998, So
Archaeological Technician:
  David Page, (M), Nevada (Reno), 2008, Ga

Great Basin College
Science Dept (A) (2014)
1500 College Parkway
Elko, NV 89801
  p. (775) 753-2120
  caroline.bruno@gbcnv.edu
  http://www2.gbcnv.edu/departments/SCI.html
Instructor:
  Carrie Bruno, OgSo
Adjunct Professor:
  Mira Kurka, Gg

Truckee Meadows Community College
Dept of Physical Sciences (2014)
7000 Dandini Boulevard
Reno, NV 89512
  p. (775) 673-7183
  loanderson@tmcc.edu
  http://www.tmcc.edu/physicalsci/

University of Nevada, Las Vegas ⛶
Geoscience Dept (B,M,D) (2014)
4505 S. Maryland Parkway
Box 454010
Las Vegas, NV 89154-4010
  p. (702) 895-3262
  geodept@unlv.edu
  http://geoscience.unlv.edu
  Administrative Assistant: Maria I. Figueroa
  Administrative Assistant: Elizabeth Y. Smith
  Enrollment (2011): B: 75 (13) M: 39 (11) D: 25 (5)
Department Chair:
  Michael L. Wells, (D), Cornell, 1991, Gc
Associate Chair:
  Eugene I. Smith, (D), New Mexico, 1970, Gi

Professor:
  Brenda J. Buck, (D), New Mexico State, 1996, Sd
  Jean S. Cline, (D), Virginia Tech, 1990, Em
  David K. Kreamer, (D), Arizona, 1982, Hw
  Margaret N. Rees, (D), Kansas, 1984, Gs
  Stephen Rowland, (D), California (Santa Cruz), 1978, Pi
  Wanda J. Taylor, (D), Utah, 1989, Gc
Water Resourse Director:
  Michael J. Nicholl, (D), Nevada (Reno), 1993
Associate Professor:
  Andrew D. Hanson, (D), Stanford, 1998, Co
  Matthew S. Lachniet, (D), Syracuse, 2001, PeCs
  Rodney V. Metcalf, (D), New Mexico, 1990, Gp
  Terry L. Spell, (D), SUNY (Albany), 1991, Cc
Associate Scientist:
  Ganqing Jiang, (D), Columbia, 2002, Gs
  Kathleen Zanetti, (M), Idaho, 1997, Gg
Assistant Professor:
  Elisabeth M. Hausrath, (D), Penn State, 2007, ScCl
Emeritus:
  Frederick W. Bachhuber, (D), New Mexico, 1971, Pl
Faculty in Residence:
  Scott A. Nowicki, (D), Arizona State, 2009, OreOi
Associate Reseach Professor:
  Pamela C. Burnley, (D), California (Davis), 1990, GpyGg

University of Nevada, Reno
Center for Neotectonic Studies (2010)
MS 0169
Reno, NV 89557-0169
  p. (775) 784-6067
  wesnousky@unr.edu
  http://neotectonics.seismo.unr.edu/CNSHome.html
Director:
  Steven Wesnousky, (D), Columbia, 1982, Ys

Center for Research in Economic Geology (M,D) (2015)
Mail Stop 1169
Reno, NV 89557-1169
  p. (775) 784-1382
  dawnsnell@unr.edu
  Administrative Assistant: Dawn Lee Snell
  Enrollment (2015): M: 3 (3)
Director:
  John Muntean, (D), Stanford, Eg

Dept of Geography (B,M,D) (2014)
Mail Stop 0154
Reno, NV 89557-0154
  p. (775) 784-6995
  kberry@unr.edu
  http://www.unr.edu/geography/
  Administrative Assistant: Shari Baughman
  Enrollment: No data reported since 1999
Chair:
  Kate Berry, (D), Colorado, 1993, Oy
Professor:
  Scott A. Mensing, (D), California (Berkeley), 1993, Oy
  Paul F. Starrs, (D), California (Berkeley), 1989, Oy
Associate Professor:
  Franco Biondi, (D), Arizona, 1994, Sf
Assistant Professor:
  Scott Bassett, (D), Harvard, 2001, Ou
  P. Anthony Brinkman, (D), California (Berkeley), 2003, Ou
  Jill Heaton, (D), Oregon State, 2001, Oi
Research Associate:
  Abbey Grimmer, (B), Nevada (Reno), 2009, Oi
  Scotty Strachan, (M), Nevada (Reno), 2001, Pe
Instructor:
  Mella Harmon, (M), Ou
Adjunct Professor:
  Douglas Boyle, (D), Arizona, Hg
  Jake Haughland, (D), Colorado (Boulder), 2003, Gm
  Kenneth McGwire, (D), California (Santa Barbara), 1992, Or
  Ken Nussear, (D), Nevada (Reno), 2004, On
  Victoria Randlett, (D), California (Berkeley), 1999, Ou
  Christopher Ryan, (M), Nevada (Reno), 1998, Oy

Peter Wigand, (D), Washington State, 1985, Pe

Dept of Geological Sciences and Engineering (B,M,D) (2015)
1664 N. Virginia St., MS 0172
Reno, NV 89557-0172
    p. (775) 784-6050
    geology@mines.unr.edu
    http://www.unr.edu/geology
    Enrollment: No data reported since 1999
Research Professor:
    Patricia H. Cashman, (D), S California, 1979, Gc
    Simon R. Poulson, (D), Penn State, 1990, Cs
Director, Great Basin Center for Geothermal Energy:
    Wendy M. Calvin, (D), Colorado, 1991, YeOr
Professor:
    John Anderson, (D), Columbia, 1976, Ys
    Greg B. Arehart, (D), Michigan, 1992, Eg
    James R. Carr, (D), Arizona, 1983, NgOuGg
    Robert Karlin, (D), Oregon State, 1984, Ou
    John N. Louie, (D), Caltech, 1987, Ye
    Paula J. Noble, (D), Texas, 1993, PmGnPs
    Tommy B. Thompson, (D), New Mexico, 1966, Eg
    James H. Trexler, (D), Washington, 1984, Gs
    Scott W. Tyler, (D), Nevada (Reno), 1990, Hw
    Robert J. Watters, (D), Imperial Coll (UK), 1972, Nrg
    Steven G. Wesnousky, (D), Columbia, 1982, Ys
Associate Dean, College of Science:
    Regina Tempel, (D), Colorado Mines, 1993, Cl
Assistant Professor:
    Ronald J. Breitmeyer, (D), Wisconsin, 2011, GeHwSp
    Stacia Gordon, (D), Minnesota, 2009, Gi
    Scott W. McCoy, (D), Colorado, 2012, GmNg
Lecturer:
    John K. McCormack, (D), Nevada (Reno), 1997, Gz
Cooperating Faculty:
    John W. Bell, (M), Arizona State, 1974, Ng
    Geoffrey Blewitt, (D), Caltech, 1986, Yd
    Tom Bullard, (D), New Mexico, 1995, Gm
    James E. Faulds, (D), New Mexico, 1989, Gc
    Nick Lancaster, (D), Chamberlain, 1977, Gm
    Greg Pohll, (D), Nevada (Reno), 1996, Hq
    Lisa A. Shevenell, (D), Nevada (Reno), 1990, Hw
    Lisa Stillings, (D), Penn State, 1994, Hw

Dept of Mining Engineering (B,M,D) (2014)
Mail Stop 0173
Reno, NV 89557-0173
    p. (775) 784-6961
    cscott@unr.edu
    http://www.unr.edu/cos/mining/
    Administrative Assistant: Carla Scott
    Enrollment (2011): B: 66 (5) M: 8 (0) D: 5 (0)
Chair:
    Danny L. Taylor, (D), Colorado Mines, 1980, Nm
Professor:
    Jaak Daemen, (D), Minnesota, 1975, Nr
    George Danko, (D), Budapest, 1985, Nm
    Pierre Mousset-Jones, (D), London, 1988, Nm
Associate Professor:
    Carl Nesbitt, (D), Nevada, 1990, Nx
    Thom Seal, (D), Idaho, 2004, Nx
Emeritus:
    Maurice Feunstenau, (D), Nx
Development Technician:
    John D. Leland, (M), Stanford, 1983, On

Graduate Program of Hydrologic Sciences (M,D) (2015)
1664 N. Virginia Street
MS 0175
Reno, NV 89557-0175
    p. (775) 784-1921
    hydro@unr.edu
    http://www.hydro.unr.edu
    Enrollment (2015): M: 32 (10) D: 8 (1)
Associate Professor:
    Laurel Saito, (D), Colorado State, 1999, HsgHq

Research Professor:
    Kumud Acharya, (D), Saitama, On
    Kenneth Adams, (D), Nevada (Reno), 1997, Gam
    Braimah Apambire, (D)
    John J. Arnone, (D), Yale, 1988, Sp
    Gayle L. Dana, (D), Nevada (Reno), 1997, Or
    Joseph Grzymski, (D)
    Roger Jacobson, (D), Penn State, 1973, Cg
    Nick Lancaster, (D), Cambridge, 1977, Gm
    Joseph McConnell, (D), Arizona, 1997, On
    Eric McDonald, (D), New Mexico, 1994, Sp
    Alison Murray, (D)
    Daniel Obrist, (D), Nevada (Reno), 2002
    Simon Poulson, (D), Penn State, 1990, Cls
    Ken Taylor, (D)
Research Professor:
    Christian H. Fritsen, (D), S California, 1995, Og
Professor:
    Franco Biondi, (D), Arizona, 1994
    Wendy Calvin, (D), Colorado (Boulder), 1991, YgOr
    George Danko, (D), Hungarian Acad of Sci, 1985, Hq
    Mae Gustin, (D), Arizona, 1988, Cg
    David Kreamer, (D), Arizona, 1982, HwGn
    John Louie, (D), Caltech, 1987, Yg
    Maureen McCarthy, (D)
    Glenn C. Miller, (D), California (Davis), 1977, Hg
    Paula Noble, (D), Texas (Austin), 1993, Gn
    Anna Panorska, (D), California (Santa Barbara), 1992
    Mark Pinsky, (D)
    Greg Pohll, (D), Nevada (Reno), 1996, Hwq
    Loretta Singletary, (D)
    Scott Tyler, (D), Nevada (Reno), 1990, Hg
    Mark Walker, (D), Cornell, 1998, On
Research Hydrologist:
    Brian Andraski, (D), Nevada (Reno)
Senior Scientist:
    Richard Niswonger, (D)
Research Hydrogeologist and Civil Engineer:
    Dave Decker, (D), Nevada (Reno), Hw
Associate Research Professor:
    Marcus Berli, (D), Swiss Fed Inst Tech, Sp
    Li Chen, (D), Chinese Acad of Sci
    Clay Cooper, (D), Nevada (Reno), Hy
    Ronald Hershey, (D), Nevada (Reno), HwCgs
    Alan Heyvaert, (D), California (Davis), 1998, GnHs
    Justin Huntington, (D), Nevada (Reno), 2011, HgOr
    Richard Jasoni, (D), Texas A&M
    Alexandra Lutz, (D), Nevada (Reno), Hw
    Kenneth McGwire, (D), California (Santa Barbara), 1992, Or
    Don Sada, (D)
    Rick Susfalk, (D)
    Julian Zhu, (D), Dalhousie
Associate Director:
    Rina Schumer, (D), Nevada (Reno), 2002, HqwHg
Associate Professor:
    Sudeep Chandra, (D), California (Davis), 2003, Hs
    Keith E. Dennett, (D), Georgia Tech, 1995, Hs
    Eric Marchand, (D), Colorado (Boulder), 2000
    Robert G. Qualls, (D), Georgia, 1989, On
    Sherman Swanson, (D), Oregon State, 1983, Hs
    Aleksey Telyakovskiy, (D), Wyoming, 2002, Hq
    Gina Tempel, (D), Colorado Mines, 1993, Cl
Associate Scientist:
    Lisa Shevenell, (D), Nevada (Reno), 1990, Hw
Assistant Research Professor:
    Rishi Parashar, (D), Purdue, 2008, Hq
    Seshadri Rajagopal, (D)
    Casey Schmidt, (D)
Assistant Research Hydrogeologist:
    Rosemary Carroll, (D), Nevada (Reno), 2010, Hq
Assistant Professor:
    Ronald Breitmeyer, (D), Wisconsin, 2011, HwGe
    Adrian Harpold, (D)
    Sage Hiibel, (D)
    Scott McCoy, (D)
    Ben Sullivan, (D)
    Paul Verburg, (D), Wageningen Ag Univ, 1998, Sp

Steve G. Wells, (D), Cincinnati, 1976, On
Yu (Frank) Yang, (D)
Research Associate:
Ramon Naranjo, (D), Nevada (Reno), 2012, CgHw
Lisa Stillings, (D), Penn State, 1994, Cm
Assistant Research Professor:
Tom Bullard, (D), New Mexico, 1995, Gm
Adjunct Professor:
Jonathan Price, (D)
Jim Thomas, (D), Nevada (Reno), 1996, Cg
Emeritus:
Dale Johnson, (D)
Wally Miller, (D)
Steve Wheatcraft, (D), Hawaii, 1979, Hw
Cooperating Faculty:
Chris Benedict
Jeanne Chambers, (D), Sf
David Prudic, (D), Nevada (Reno)
Michael Rosen, (D), Texas (Austin)
Keirith Snyder, (D)
Mark Weltz, (D)

Great Basin Center for Geothermal Energy (2015)
Mail Stop 0172
1664 N. Virginia St
Reno, NV 89557-0172
  p. (775) 784-7018
  geothermal@unr.edu
  www.gbcge.org
Director:
Wendy Calvin, (D), Colorado, 1991, OrYgXg
Professor:
John Louie, (D), Caltech, 1987, Yse
Research Professor:
James Faulds, (D), New Mexico, 1989, Gc
Research Associate:
Nick Hinz, (M), Nevada (Reno), 2004, Gcg
Staff Research Associate:
Chris Sladek, (B), Colorado State, 1994, Gg

Mackay School of Earth Sciences and Engineering (Director's Office) (2015)
Mail Stop 0168
Reno, NV 89557-0168
  p. (775) 784-6987
  juliehill@unr.edu
  http://www.mines.unr.edu/Mackay/
  Administrative Assistant: Julie Hill
Director:
Russell Fields, (M), Nevada (Reno), 1985
Thom Seal, (D), Idaho, 2004, Nx

Nevada Seismological Lab (2014)
Mail Stop 0174
Reno, NV 89557-0174
  p. (775) 784-4975
  mainofc@seismo.unr.edu
  http://www.seismo.unr.edu
  Administrative Assistant: Lori McClelland
  Administrative Assistant: Erik Williams
Director:
Graham Kent, (D), California (San Diego), 1992, Ys
Professor:
John G. Anderson, (D), Columbia, 1976, Ys
John N. Louie, (D), Caltech, 1987, Ye
Steve Wesnousky, (D), Columbia, 1982, Ys
Research Associate Professor:
Glenn P. Biasi, (D), Oregon, 1994, Ys
Ileana Tibuleac, (D), S Methodist, 1999, Ys
Assistant Director, Seismic Network Manager & Development Director:
Ken D. Smith, (D), Nevada (Reno), 1991, Ys
Adjunct Research Assistant Professor:
Satish Pullammanappallil, (D), Nevada (Reno), 1994, Ys
Adjunct Research Associate:
Bill Honjas, (M), Nevada (Reno), Ys
Emeritus Seismic Network Manager:
David von Seggern, (D), Penn State, 1982, Ys

Emeritus:
James N. Brune, (D), Columbia, 1961, Ys
Development Technician:
Ryan Presser, (A)
Volunteer Adjunct Faculty:
Aasha Pancha, (D), Nevada (Reno), 2007, Ys
Seismic Systems Analyst:
David Slater, (B), Calgary, 1990, Ys
Seismic Records Technician:
Tom Rennie, (D), Nevada (Reno), 2007, Ys
Programmer/Analyst, Seismic Network:
Gabriel Plank, (B), Cornell, 1994, Ys
Network Seismologist:
Diane dePolo, (M), Nevada (Reno), 1989, Ys
Development Technician:
Kent Straley
Associate Engineer:
John Torrisi, (A)

Wassuk College
Dept of Natural History (B) (2015)
Box 236
East Ely, NV 89315
  p. (702) 289-2168
Associate Professor:
Patrick J. Landon, (M), Montana, 1980, Oy
Adjunct Professor:
Jacob Rajala, (M), E Washington, 1976, On

Western Nevada College
Western Nevada College (2014)
2201 West College Parkway
Carson City, NV 89703
  p. (775) 445-4442
  Winnie.Kortemeier@wnc.edu
  http://www.wnc.edu/academics/division/sme/

New Hampshire

Dartmouth College
Dept of Earth Sciences (B,M,D) (2016)
228 Fairchild Hall, HB 6105
Hanover, NH 03755
  p. (603) 646-2373
  earth.sciences@dartmouth.edu
  http://www.dartmouth.edu/~earthsci
  f: www.facebook.com/DartmouthEarthSciences
  Enrollment (2015): B: 35 (9) M: 0 (5) D: 0 (3)
Chair:
William Brian Dade, (D), Washington, GsHgEo
Professor:
Xiahong Feng, (D), Case Western, 1991, Cs
Carl E. Renshaw, (D), Stanford, 1993, Hg
Associate Professor:
Robert L. Hawley, (D), Washington, 2005, Gl
Meredith Kelly, (D), Bern, 2003, Gl
Mukul Sharma, (D), Rochester, Ge
Leslie J. Sonder, (D), Harvard, 1986, Gq
Assistant Professor:
Erich C. Osterberg, (D), Maine, 2007, Oa
Devon Renock, (D), Michigan, GzCa
Justin V. Strauss, (D), Harvard, 2015, GsCg
Emeritus:
Gary D. Johnson, (D), Iowa State, 1971, Gr
Research Professor:
Brian P. Jackson, (D), Georgia, 1998, Ca

Keene State College
Dept of Geology (B) (2015)
Mail Stop 2001
229 Main Street
Keene, NH 03435-2001
  p. (603) 358-2553
  pnielsen@keene.edu
  http://www.keene.edu/academics/programs/geol/

Enrollment (2014): B: 17 (4)
Chair:
 Peter A. Nielsen, (D), Alberta, 1977, GxzGc
Associate Professor:
 Steven D. Bill, (D), Case Western, 1982, Pg
Adjunct:
 Carol Leger, (B), Keene State Coll, 2005, Og
 Dave Obolewicz, (M), Montana Tech, 1978, GgEmOw
Adjunct Professor:
 Charles M. Kerwin, (D), New Hampshire, 2006, Gg
 Edward M. Pokras, (D), Columbia, 1985, GgPmOb
Cooperating Faculty:
 Timothy T. Allen, (D), Dartmouth, 1992, Hw
 Jerry P. Jasinski, (D), Wyoming, 1977, Gz

Plymouth State University
Environmental Science and Policy Dept (B,M,D) (2014)
17 High Street
Plymouth, NH 03264
 p. (603) 536-2573
 warrent@plymouth.edu
 http://oz.plymouth.edu/esp
 Enrollment: No data reported since 1999
Chair:
 Warren Tomkiewicz, (D), Boston, 1987, OggOe
Professor:
 James P. Koermer, (D), Utah, 1980, Ow
 Larry T. Spencer, (D), Colorado State, 1968, Gg
Associate Professor:
 Mark P. Turski, (D), Texas, 1994, Og
Assistant Professor:
 Eric Hoffman, (D), SUNY (Albany), 2000, Ow

University of New Hampshire
Dept of Earth Sciences (B,M,D) (2015)
214 James Hall
56 College Road
Durham, NH 03824
 p. (603) 862-1718
 earth.sciences@unh.edu
 http://www.unh.edu/esci/
 Administrative Assistant: Susan E. Clark
 Enrollment (2015): B: 58 (19) M: 34 (8) D: 17 (2)
Chair:
 Julia G. Bryce, (D), California (Santa Barbara), 1998, Cg
Research Professor:
 Stephen E. Frolking, (D), New Hampshire, 1993, Oa
 Cameron P. Wake, (D), New Hampshire, 1993, Gl
Professor and Dean of CEPS:
 Samuel B. Mukasa, (D), California (Santa Barbara), 1984, CgGx
Affiliate Professor:
 Christopher E. Parrish, (D), Wisconsin (Madison), Or
Professor:
 William C. Clyde, (D), Michigan, 1997, Pg
 Matthew Huber, (D), California (Santa Cruz), 2001, Og
 John E. Hughes-Clarke, (D), Dalhousie, 1988, Og
 Larry A. Mayer, (D), California (San Diego), 1979, Gu
 David C. Mosher, (D), Dalhousie, 1993, Og
Research Associate Professor:
 Jack E. Dibb, (D), SUNY (Binghamton), 1988, Oa
 Larry G. Ward, (D), South Carolina, 1978, Gu
Associate Professor:
 Michael W. Palace, (D), New Hampshire, On
Affiliate Research Associate Professor:
 Mark A. Fahnestock, (D), Caltech, 1991, Ol
 Erik A. Hobbie, (D), Virginia, 1997, Cs
Affiliate Associate Professor:
 Mary D. Stampone, (D), Delaware, 2009, On
Associate Professor:
 Margaret S. Boettcher, (D), MIT/WHOI, 2005, Ygs
 Julia G. Bryce, (D), California (Santa Barbara), 1998, Cg
 J. Matthew Davis, (D), New Mexico Tech, 1994, Hw
 Joel E. Johnson, (D), Oregon State, 2004, Gus
 Jo Laird, (D), Caltech, 1977, Gp
 Joseph M. Licciardi, (D), Oregon State, 2000, Gl
 Thomas C. Lippmann, (M), Oregon State, 1992, On

 James M. Pringle, (D), MIT/WHOI, 1998, Op
 Ruth K. Varner, (D), New Hampshire, 2000, Oa
Affiliate Assistant Professor:
 Joseph Salisbury, On
Assistant Professor:
 Rosemarie E. Came, (D), MIT/WHOI, 2005, PeOnn
 Linda Kalnejais, (D), MIT/WHOI, 2005, Oc
 Anne F. Lightbody, (D), MIT, 2007, HgsOn
Affiliate Professor:
 Andrew Armstrong, (M), Johns Hopkins, 1991, On
Affiliate Professor:
 Douglas C. Vandemark, (M), New Hampshire, 2005, Or
Emeritus:
 Franz E. Anderson, (D), Washington, 1967, Yr
 Francis S. Birch, (D), Princeton, 1969, Yg
 Wallace A. Bothner, (D), Wyoming, 1967, Gc
 Janet W. Campbell, (D), Virginia Tech, 1973, Oa
 S. Lawrence Dingman, (D), Harvard, 1970, Hq
 Henri E. Gaudette, (D), Illinois, 1963, Cc
 Francis R. Hall, (D), Stanford, 1961, Hw
 Theodore C. Loder, (D), Alaska, 1971, Oc
 Cecil J. Schneer, (D), Cornell, 1954, Gz
 Herbert Tischler, (D), Michigan, 1961, Ps
Affiliate Faculty:
 Rochelle Wigley, (D), Cape Town (South Africa), 2005, CgGu

Dept of Natural Resources and the Environment (B,M,D) (2015)
215 James Hall
56 College Rd
Durham, NH 03824-3589
 p. (603) 862-1020
 john.halstead@unh.edu
 Administrative Assistant: Linda Scogin
 Enrollment: No data reported since 1999
Chair:
 Theodore E. Howard, (D), Oregon State, 1982, On
Professor:
 Robert D. Harter, (D), Purdue, 1966, Sc
Assistant Professor:
 Elizabeth A. Rochette, (D), Washington State, 1994, Sc

New Jersey

College of New Jersey
Physics Dept (2010)
North American Geological Alliance
Trenton, NJ 08650-4700
 p. (609) 771-1855 x2569
 wiitap@tcnj.edu

Director:
 Fredric R. Goldstein, (D), Rutgers, 1974, Oe
Adjunct Professor:
 Thomas Gillespie, (M), Rutgers, 1986, Gc
 John M. O'Brien, (D), California (Santa Barbara), 1973, Gs

Kean University
School of Environmental and Sustainability Sciences (B) (2014)
1000 Morris Avenue
Union, NJ 07083-0411
 p. (908) 737-3737
 bteasdal@kean.edu
 http://www.kean.edu/KU/College-of-Natural-Applied-Health-Sciences
 Enrollment (2006): B: 160 (0)
Professor:
 Robert Metz, (D), Rensselaer, 1967, Gr
 Shing Yoh, (D), Drexel, 1989, Ow
 Constantine S. Zois, (D), Rutgers, 1980, Ow
Executive Director:
 Paul J. Croft, (D), Rutgers, 1991, OwaOe
Associate Professor:
 Carrie M. Manfrino, (D), Miami, 1995, GuOb
Assistant Professor:
 Kikombo Ngoy, (D), Oregon, 1996, Oy
 Feng Qi, (D), Wisconsin, 2001, OiyOu

Secretary:
   Christina Pacia, On
Related Staff:
   William C. Heyniger, (B), Kean, 1995, On

Montclair State University
Dept of Earth & Environmental Studies (B,M) (2014)
1 Normal Avenue
Upper Montclair, NJ 07043
   p. (973) 655-4448
   ophorid@mail.montclair.edu
   http://www.csam.montclair.edu/earth/eesweb
   Enrollment (2002): B: 48 (12) M: 40 (19)
Chair:
   Jonathan M. Lincoln, (D), Northwestern, 1990, Gr
Associate Dean, Science & Mathematics:
   Michael A. Kruge, (D), California (Berkeley), 1985, Co
Professor:
   Harbans Singh, (D), Rutgers, 1973, On
   William Solecki, (D), Rutgers, 1990, Ou
   Rolf Sternberg, (D), Syracuse, 1971, On
   Robert W. Taylor, (D), St. Louis, 1971, On
   John V. Thiruvathukal, (D), Oregon State, 1968, Yg
Associate Dean:
   Duke U. Ophori, (D), Alberta, 1986, Hw
Associate Professor:
   Matthew L. Gorring, (D), Cornell, 1997, Gi
   Gregory A. Pope, (D), Arizona State, 1994, Gm
Assistant Professor:
   Mark J. Chopping, (D), Nottingham, 1998, Or
   Huan E. Feng, (D), SUNY (Stony Brook), 1997, Cm
Adjunct Professor:
   Kathryn Black, (M), Oklahoma, 1966, Oy
   Matthew S. Tomaso, (M), Texas, 1995, Ga
   Christine Valenti, (M), Montclair State, 1997, Gg
Emeritus:
   Barbara De Beus, On
Laboratory Director:
   Yoko Sato, (M), Montclair State, 2000, Gg

New Jersey City University
Dept of Geoscience/Geography (B) (2014)
Rossey Hall - Room 608
2039 Kennedy Boulevard
Jersey City, NJ 07305-1597
   p. (201) 200-3161
   lengland@njcu.edu
   http://www.njcu.edu/dept/geoscience%5Fgeography/
   Enrollment (2006): B: 37 (19)
Professor:
   Martin Abend, (D), Syracuse, 1955, Oy
Associate Professor:
   Deborah Freile, (D), Boston, 1992, Ge
Research Associate:
   John M. O'Brien, (D), California (Santa Barbara), 1973, Gs
Lecturer:
   William W. Montgomery, (D), W Michigan, 1998, Hw
Adjunct Professor:
   George Papcun, (M), Oe
   Howard Zlotkin, (M), Oe
Emeritus:
   John Marchisin, (M), Montclair State, 1965, Gg

Princeton University 🗇
Dept of Civil and Environmental Engineering (B,M,D) (2014)
E-Quad, Olden Street
Princeton, NJ 08544
   p. (609) 258-3598
   jsmith@Princeton.EDU
   http://cee.princeton.edu/
   Enrollment: No data reported since 1999
Professor:
   Michael A. Celia, (D), Princeton, 1983, Hw
   Francois M.M. Morel, (D), Caltech, 1971, Cm
   Jean-Herve Prevost, (D), Stanford, 1974, Ng
   James A. Smith, (D), Johns Hopkins, Hg

Associate Professor:
   Peter R. Jaffe, (D), Vanderbilt, 1981, Hg

Dept of Geosciences (B,D) (2016)
113 Guyot Hall
Princeton, NJ 08544-1003
   p. (609) 258-4101
   mrusso@Princeton.EDU
   http://www.geoweb.princeton.edu
   Administrative Assistant: Mary Rose Russo
   Enrollment (2015): B: 34 (8) D: 43 (5)
Chair:
   Bess B. Ward, (D), Washington, 1982, Ob
Associate Chair:
   Thomas S. Duffy, (D), Caltech, 1992, Gy
Professor:
   Gerta Keller, (D), Stanford, 1978, Pm
   Francois M M. Morel, (D), Caltech, 1971, Cl
   Tullis C. Onstott, (D), Princeton, 1980, Py
   Michael Oppenheimer, (D), Chicago, 1970, OaGe
   S. George H. Philander, (D), Harvard, 1970, Op
   Allan M. Rubin, (D), Stanford, 1988, Yg
   Jorge L. Sarmiento, (D), Columbia, 1978, Oc
   Daniel M. Sigman, (D), MIT, 1997, Cg
   Jeroen Tromp, (D), Princeton, 1992, Yss
Professional Specialist:
   Amal Jayakumar, (D), Goa, 1999, Cm
Associate Professor:
   Stephan A. Fueglistaler, (D), ETH (Switzerland), 2002, Oa
   Adam C. Maloof, (D), Harvard, 2004, Ym
   Satish C B. Myneni, (D), Ohio State, 1995, Sc
   R Blair Schoene, (D), MIT, 2006, Cc
   Frederik J. Simons, (D), MIT, 2002, Ys
Research Scholar:
   Anne Morel-Kraepiel, (D), Princeton, 2001, Em
   Xinning Zhang, (D), CalTech, 2010, Ou
Assistant Professor:
   John A. Higgins, (D), Harvard, 2009, Ob
   Jessica Irving, (D), Trinity Coll (Cambridge), 2009, Yg
   David Medvigy, (D), Harvard, 2006, Oa
Research Associate:
   Oliver Baars, (D), IFM-GEOMAR, 2011, Co
   Dmitry Borisov, (D), IPGP, 2014, Ysg
   Tra Dinh, (D), Washington, 2012, Oa
   Blake Dyer, (D), Princeton, 2015, Pe
   Hom Nath Gharti, (D), Oslo, 2011, Yg
   Christopher Harig, (D), Colorado, 2010, Yg
   Alya Pamukcu, (D), Vanderbilt, 2014, NgGe
   Youyi Ruan, (D), Virginia Tech, 2012, Ysg
   Herurisa Rusmanugroho, (D), Texas, 2011, Yg
   Daniel Stolper, (D), Caltech, 2014, Pe
   Sally June Tracy, (D), Caltech, 2015, Gy
   Annette Trierweiler, (D), Princeton, 2016, Og
   Nicolas Van Oostende, (D), Ghent, 2011, Ob
   Umair Waheed, (D), King Abdullah Univ of Sci & Tech, 2015, Ys
   June Wicks, (D), Caltech, 2013, Cg
Emeritus:
   Michael L. Bender, (D), Columbia, 1970, Cg
   William E. Bonini, (D), Wisconsin, 1957, Yg
   Lincoln S. Hollister, (D), Caltech, 1966, Gp
   Robert A. Phinney, (D), Caltech, 1961, Ys
Post Doctoral Research Fellow:
   Clara Blattler, (D), Oxford, 2012, Gg
   Sebastian Kopf, (D), Caltech, 2014, Py
Associate Research Scholar:
   Paul Gauthier, (D), Paris, 2010, Sb
   Bror F. Jonsson, (D), Stockholm, 2005, Op
   Chui Yim Maggie Lau, (D), Hong Kong, 2007, Og
   Sarah Jane White, (D), MIT, 2012, Ge
Associate Professional Specialist:
   Sergey Oleynik, (D), Moscow State, 1999, Cs
Undergraduate/Graduate Coordinator:
   Sheryl A. Robas, (A), 1975, On
Academic Lab Manager:
   Laurel P. Goodell, (M), Princeton, 1983, Oe
   Danielle M. Schmitt, (M), W Michigan, 1999, Oe

Environmental Engineering & Water Resources Program
(B,M,D) (2014)
E-220 Engineering Quad
Princeton, NJ 08544
  p. (609) 258-4655
  celia@Princeton.EDU
  Department Secretary: Maryann Rothberg
  Enrollment: No data reported since 1999
Director:
  Michael A. Celia, (D), Princeton, 1983, Hw
Professor:
  Peter R. Jaffe, (D), Vanderbilt, 1981, Hw
  Ignacio Rodriguez-Iturbe, (D), Colorado State, 1967, Hg
  James A. Smith, (D), Johns Hopkins, 1981, Hg
  Eric F. Wood, (D), MIT, 1974, Hg
Assistant Professor:
  Catherine A. Peters, (D), Carnegie Mellon, 1992, Hw

Program in Atmospheric & Oceanic Sciences (D) (2015)
300 Forrestal Road, Sayre Hall
Princeton, NJ 08540-6654
  p. (609) 258-6677
  stf@princeton.edu
  http://www.princeton.edu/aos/
  Enrollment (2012): D: 28 (6)
Professor:
  Michael Bender, (D), Columbia
  Michael Oppenheimer, (D), Chicago
  Stephen Pacala, (D), Stanford
  George Philander, (D), Harvard
  Jorge Sarmiento, (D), Columbia
  James Smith, (D), Johns Hopkins
Senior Scientist:
  Kirk Bryan, (D), MIT
  Syukuro Manabe, (D), Toyko
  Isidoro Orlanski, (D), MIT
Associate Professor:
  Denise Mauzerall, (D), Harvard
Assistant Professor:
  Stephan Fueglistaler, (D), ETH (Switzerland)
  David Medvigy, (D), Harvard
  Mark Zondlo, (D), Colorado
Lecturer:
  Thomas Delworth, (D), Wisconsin
  Leo Donner, (D), Chicago
  Stephen Garner, (D), MIT
  Stephen Griffies, (D), Pennsylvania
  Robert Hallberg, (D), Washington
  Isaac Held, (D), Princeton
  Larry Horowitz, (D), Harvard
  Sonya Legg, (D), Imperial Coll (UK)
  Yi Ming, (D), Princeton
  V. Ramaswamy, (D), SUNY (Albany)
  Gabriel Vecchi, (D), Washington
  Rong Zhang, (D), MIT
Emeritus:
  George Mellor, (D), MIT

Raritan Valley Community College
Dept of Biology (1999)
118 Lamington Road
Branchburg, NJ 08878
  p. (908) 526-1200
  dtrybuls@raritanval.edu

Richard Stockton College of New Jersey
Dept of Environmental Sciences (B,M) (2013)
Division of Natural Science and Mathematics
101 Vera King Farris Drive
Galloway, NJ 08205
  p. (609) 652-4620
  george.zimmermann@stockton.edu
  http://intraweb.stockton.edu/eyos/page.
  cfm?siteID=183&pageID=23
  Enrollment (2005): B: 122 (31)

Director, Coastal Research Center:
  Stewart Farrell, (D), Massachusetts, 1972, On
Professor:
  Raymond G. Mueller, (D), Kansas, 1981, So
  Lynn F. Stiles, (D), Cornell, 1970, On
  George Zimmermann, (D), Rutgers, 1982, On
Program Coordinator:
  Michael D. Geller, (D), SUNY (Binghamton), 1979, On
  Michael J. Hozik, (D), Massachusetts, 1981, Ym
Associate Professor:
  Tait Chirenje, (D), Florida, Sc
  William J. Cromartie, (D), Cornell, 1974, On
  Weihong Fan, (D), Colorado State, 1993, Oi
  Margaret Lewis, (D), SUNY (Stony Brook), 1995, Gg
Assistant Professor:
  Tracy Baker, (D), Wyoming, HgOr
  Judith Turk, (D), 2012, Sfo

Rider University
Geological, Environmental, & Marine Sciences (GEMS) (B) (2015)
2083 Lawrenceville Road
Lawrenceville, NJ 08648-3099
  p. (609) 896-5092
  husch@rider.edu
  Enrollment (2015): B: 9 (4)
Chair:
  Jonathan M. Husch, (D), Princeton, 1982, GieXg
Professor:
  Hongbing Sun, (D), Florida State, 1995, HwCgSc
Associate Professor:
  Kathleen M. Browne, (D), Miami, 1993, GuOe
  Daniel L. Druckebrod, (D), Virginia, 2003, Onn
  Reed A. Schwimmer, (D), Delaware, 1999, GsOgn
  Gabriela W. Smalley, (D), Maryland, 2002, ObcOp
Adjunct Professor:
  William B. Gallagher, (D), Pennsylvania, 1990, PvoGr
Emeritus:
  Mary Jo Hall, (D), Lehigh, 1981, Gs

Rutgers, State University of New Jersey
Earth and Planetary Sciences (B,M,D) (2016)
Wright Lab
610 Taylor Road
Piscataway, NJ 08854-8066
  p. (848) 445-2044
  cswish@eps.rutgers.edu
  http://geology.rutgers.edu/
  Enrollment (2010): B: 22 (0) M: 8 (3) D: 24 (3)
Chair:
  Carl C. Swisher III, (D), California (Berkeley), 1992, Cc
Graduate Program Director:
  James D. Wright, (D), Columbia, 1991, CsOuPm
Professor:
  Gail M. Ashley, (D), British Columbia, 1977, GsmSa
  Michael J. Carr, (D), Dartmouth, 1974, Gv
  Paul G. Falkowski, (D), British Columbia, 1975, ObCmPe
  Mark D. Feigenson, (D), Princeton, 1982, CgGiv
  Claude T. Herzberg, (D), Edinburgh, 1975, CpGi
  Dennis V. Kent, (D), Columbia, 1974, Ym
  George R. McGhee, Jr., (D), Rochester, 1978, PoqPi
  Kenneth G. Miller, (D), MIT/WHOI, 1982, GuPsm
  Gregory S. Mountain, (D), Columbia, 1981, GuYrGr
  Yair Rosenthal, (D), WHOI, CmlOc
  Roy W. Schlische, (D), Columbia, 1990, Gct
  Robert M. Sherrell, (D), MIT/WHOI, 1991, CmOu
  Martha O. Withjack, (D), Brown, 1977, Gct
Undergraduate Program Director:
  Vadim Levin, (D), Columbia, 1996, Ysg
Associate Professor:
  Craig S. Feibel, (D), Utah, 1988, GarGs
  Benjamin P. Horton, (D), Durham (UK), 1997, On
  Ying Fan Reinfelder, (D), Utah State, 1992, HwyOw
  Nathan Yee, (D), Notre Dame, 2001, PyCo
Assistant Professor:
  Robert E. Kopp, (D), Caltech, 2007, CoPye
  Jill Van Tongeren, (D), Columbia, 2010, GpcGt

Research Associate:
    James V. Browning, (D), Rutgers, 1996, GgsGr
    Jeremy S. Delaney, (D), Belfast, 1978, XgmGx
    Brent D. Turrin, (D), California (Berkeley), 1996, CcGvYm
Adjunct Professor:
    Peter P. Sugarman, (D), Rutgers, 1995, Gr
Distinguished Visiting Profesor:
    William A. Berggren, (D), Stockholm, 1962, PmsPe
Emeritus:
    Richard K. Olsson, (D), Princeton, 1958, PmGr
    Robert E. Sheridan, (D), Columbia, 1968, YrGu
Cooperating Faculty:
    John R. Reinfelder, (D), SUNY (Stony Brook), 1993, Cl
    Silke Severman, (D), Southampton, Cl

Rutgers, State University of New Jersey, Newark
Dept of Earth & Environmental Sciences (B,M,D) (2015)
101 Warren Street
Smith Hall, room 135
Newark, NJ 07102
    p. (973) 353-5100
    morrin@andromeda.rutgers.edu
    http://www.ncas.rutgers.edu/ees
    Administrative Assistant: M. Elizabeth Morrin
    Enrollment (2014): B: 25 (6) M: 12 (3) D: 19 (1)
Chair:
    Lee S. Slater, (D), Lancaster (UK), 1997, Yg
Professor:
    Yuan Gao, (D), Rhode Island, 1994, Oa
    Alexander E. Gates, (D), Virginia Tech, 1986, Gc
Associate Professor:
    Evert J. Elzinga, (D), Delaware, 2000, Sc
    Andrew E. Kasper, (D), Connecticut, 1970, Pb
    Adam B. Kustka, (D), Stony Brook, 2002, OgCmHs
Assistant Professor:
    Mihaela Glamoclija, (D), 2005, Py
    Kristina M. Keating, (D), Stanford, 2009, Yg
    Ashaki Rouff, (D), Stony Brook, 2004, Cl
Research Associate:
    Dimitrios Ntarlagiannis, (D), Rutgers, 2006, Yg
    Judith Robinson, (D), Rutgers, 2015, Yg
Emeritus:
    Warren Manspeizer, (D), Rutgers, 1964, Gr
    John H. Puffer, (D), Stanford, 1969, Gi
    Andreas H. Vassiliou, (D), Columbia, 1969, Gz

Stockton University
Geology Dept (B) ● (2015)
101 Vera King Farris Dr
Galloway, NJ 08205
    p. 609-626-6857
    matthew.severs@stockton.edu
    http://intraweb.stockton.edu/eyos/page.
    cfm?siteID=183&pageID=33
    Enrollment (2015): B: 38 (6)
Professor:
    Michael J. Hozik, (D), Massachusetts, 1976, GcYmg
    Yitzhak Y. Sharon, (D), Princeton, 1966, Yr
Associate Professor:
    Matthew Rocky Severs, (D), Virginia Tech, 2007, GxCgEg
Assistant Professor:
    Gordan Grguric, (D), Florida Inst of Tech, 1993, Oc
    Susanne Moskalski, (D), Delaware, GsOn
    Judy Turk, (D), SpGmSo
    Emma Witt, (D), Hgs
Other:
    Stewart C. Farrell, (D), Massachusetts, 1972, On

Union County College
Dept of Biology (A) (2014)
1033 Springfield Ave.
Cranford, NJ 07016
    p. (201) 709-7196
    daly@ucc.edu
    Administrative Assistant: Helen Gmitro
    Enrollment: No data reported since 1999

Associate Professor:
    Raymond J. Daly, (M), Rutgers, 1975, Pv

William Paterson University
Dept of Environmental Science (B) (2013)
Science Hall
Wayne, NJ 07470
    p. (201) 595-2721
    beckerm2@wpunj.edu
    http://www.wpunj.edu/cosh/departments/environmental-science/
    Enrollment (2011): B: 90 (3)
Chairman:
    Martin A. Becker, (D), Brooklyn Coll, 1997, PgOw
Professor:
    Richard R. Pardi, (D), Pennsylvania, 1983, Cc
Assistant Professor:
    Jennifer R. Callanan, (D), Montclair State, 2009, Gmz
    Karen Swanson, (D), Penn State, 1989, Cc

New Mexico

Eastern New Mexico University
Dept of Physical Sciences (B) (2015)
1500 S Ave K
STA 33
Portales, NM 88130
    p. (575) 562-2174
    jim.constantopoulos@enmu.edu
    http://liberal-arts.enmu.edu/sciences/
    Enrollment (2015): B: 16 (1)
Professor:
    James T. Constantopoulos, (D), Idaho, 1989, GezGx

Mesalands Community College
Mesalands Community College (A) (2010)
911 South Tenth Street
Pikes Peak community College

Tucumcari, NM 88401
    p. (575) 461-4413
    axelh@mesalands.edu
    http://www.mesalands.edu/
Instructor:
    Axel Hungerbuehler, (D), Bristol, Gg

New Mexico Community College
New Mexico Community College (2014)
525 Buena Vista Dr. SE
Albuquerque, NM 87106
    p. (505) 224-3000
    contactcenter@cnm.edu
    http://www.cnm.edu

New Mexico Highlands University
Natural Resources Management Dept (B,M) (2013)
P.O. Box 9000
Las Vegas, NM 87701
    p. (505) 454-3000
    lindlinej@nmhu.edu
    http://www.nmhu.edu/academics/undergraduate/arts_science/natural_resources/
    Enrollment (2012): B: 16 (4) M: 6 (1)
Professor:
    Jennifer Lindline, (D), Bryn Mawr, 1997, GizOe
Associate Professor:
    Michael S. Petronis, (D), New Mexico, 2005, YmGcv

New Mexico Institute of Mining and Technology
Dept of Earth & Environmental Science (B,M,D) ○ (2015)
801 Leroy Place
Socorro, NM 87801
    p. (575) 835-5634
    geos@nmt.edu
    http://www.ees.nmt.edu/

Enrollment (2014): B: 54 (9) M: 36 (18) D: 19 (2)
Chair:
  Penelope Boston, (D), Colorado (Boulder), 1985, On
Professor:
  Susan L. Bilek, (D), California (Santa Cruz), 2001, Ys
  Jan M. H. Hendrickx, (D), New Mexico State, 1984, Hw
  Philip R. Kyle, (D), Victoria Univ of Wellington (NZ), 1976, Giv
  Peter S. Mozley, (D), California (Santa Barbara), 1988, Gs
  Mark A. Person, (D), Johns Hopkins, 1990, HyYhg
  Fred M. Phillips, (D), Arizona, 1981, Hw
Senior Volcanologist, NMBG:
  William C. McIntosh, (D), New Mexico Tech, 1990, Cc
Associate Professor:
  Gary Axen, (D), Harvard, 1991, Gct
  Bruce I. Harrison, (D), New Mexico, 1992, Gm
  Glenn Spinelli, (D), California (Santa Cruz), 2002, Hw
Assistant Professor:
  Daniel Cadol, (D), Colorado State, 2010, HsGe
  Ronni Grapenthin, (D), Alaska (Fairbanks), 2012, Gv
  Kierran Maher, Washington State, Eg
  Jolante Van Wijk, (D), Vrije Universiteit (Amsterdam), 2002
Associate Research Professor:
  Mark Murray, (D), MIT, Yds
  David B. Reusch, (D), Penn State, 2003, On
  Dana S. Ulmer-Scholle, (D), S Methodist, 1992, Gs
Map Production Coordinator, NMBG:
  Phillip Miller
Technical Staff Member, Seimologist:
  Charlotte A. Rowe, (D), New Mexico Tech, 2000, Ys
Sr. Geochronologist/Co-Director NM Geochronology Research:
  Matthew T. Heizler, (D), California (Los Angeles), 1993, Cc
Senior Scientist:
  Robert S. Balch, (D), New Mexico Tech, 1997, Yse
Senior Mineralogist/Economic Geologist/ Director XRD Lab/Curator Mineral Museum:
  Virgil L. Lueth, (D), Texas (El Paso), 1988, GzEg
Senior Field Geologist:
  Steven M. Cather, (D), Texas (Austin), 1986, Gc
  Knning Daniel
  Daniel Koning, (M), New Mexico, 1999
Senior Economic Geologist:
  Virginia T. McLemore, (D), Texas (El Paso), 1993, Eg
Senior Associate Hydrogeologist/Water Resources Engineer :
  James T. McCord, (D), New Mexico Tech, 1989, Hq
Research Scientist:
  Thomas Dewers, (D), Indiana, 1990, Yx
Research Associate, NMBG:
  Matthew Zimmerer, New Mexico Tech
Professor of Biology:
  Thomas L. Kieft, (D), New Mexico, 1983
Principal Senior Petroleum Geologist:
  Ronald F. Broadhead, (M), Cincinnati, 1979, Eo
Principal Senior Environmental Geologist:
  David W. Love, (D), New Mexico, 1980, Ge
Principal Hydrologist:
  Daniel B. Stephens, (D), Arizona, 1979, Hw
Principal Geologist:
  Paul W. Bauer, (D), New Mexico Tech, 1988, Gc
Postdoc Fellow, USGS:
  Jesus Gomez, New Mexico Tech, 2014
Planetary Protection Officer, NASA:
  Catharine A. Conley, (D), Cornell, 1994, Py
Geophysicist/Field Geologist/Web Information Specialist:
  Shari A. Kelley, (D), S Methodist, 1984, Gt
Geologic Mapping Program Manager:
  J Michael Timmons, (D), New Mexico, 2004, GctGs
Geochemist & Deputy Director Manger of Electron Microprobe Lab:
  Nelia W. Dunbar, (D), New Mexico Tech, 1989, Cg
Emeritus Senior Principal Geophysicist:
  Marshall A. Reiter, (D), Virginia Tech, 1969, Yh
Emeritus Senior Field Geologist:
  Richard Chamberlin, (D), Colorado Mines, 1980, Gr
Emeritus Senior Environmental Geologist:
  John W. Hawley, (D), Illinois (Urbana Champaign), 1962, Ge
Emeritus Director and State Geologist:
  Charles E. Chapin, (D), Colorado Mines, 1965, Gv

Distinguished Member of Technical Staff:
  Vincent C. Tidwell, (D), New Mexico Tech, 1999, Hw
Chair/Associate Professor:
  Michelle Creech-Eakman, (D), Denver, 1997, XgPy
Cave & Karst Hydrologist:
  Lewis Land, (D), North Carolina (Chapel Hill), 1999, Hy
Associate Dean of Science and Wellness at Broward College:
  Michael J. Pullin, (D), Kent State, 1999
Assistant Professor, Boise State:
  Jeff Johnson, (D), Washington, 2000
Assistant Professor of Hydrogeology and Applied Geology, Purdue:
  Marty Frisbee, New Mexico Tech, 2010
Assistant Professor:
  Nigel J.F. Blamey, (D), New Mexico Tech, 2000, CaeCl
Adjunct Professor:
  Rhicard Aster, (D), California (San Diego), 1991
  Denis Cohen
  Derek Ford
  Charles (Jack) Oviatt
  Michael Underwood
  Patrizia Walder
Emeritus:
  Antonius J. Budding, (D), Amsterdam
  Andrew R. Campbell, (D), Harvard, 1984, Cs
  Kent C. Condie, (D), California (San Diego), 1965, Ct
  Gerardo W. Gross, (D), Penn State, 1959, Yx
  David B. Johnson, (D), Iowa, 1978, Ps
  Lawrence H. Lattman, (D), Cincinnati, 1953, Gm
  Allan R. Sanford, (D), Caltech, 1958, Ys
  John W. Schlue, (D), California (Los Angeles), 1975, Ys
  John L. Wilson, (D), MIT, 1974, Hw
Visiting Professor of Geochemistry:
  Ingar Walder, (D), New Mexico Tech
Seismic Lab Associate:
  Shane Ingate

Dept of Mineral Engineering (B,M,D) (2010)
Campus Station
Socorro, NM 87801-9990
  p. (505) 835-5345
  mojtabai@nmt.edu
  Department Secretary: Lucero Joanna
  Enrollment: No data reported since 1999
Chair:
  Navid Mojtabai, (D), Arizona, 1990, Nr
Professor:
  William X. Chavez, Jr., (D), California (Berkeley), 1984, Em
Associate Professor:
  Cathrine T. Aimone-Martin, (D), Northwestern, 1982, Ng
Assistant Professor:
  Baolin Deng, (D), Johns Hopkins, 1995, Cg
  Randal S. Martin, (D), Washington State, 1992, Oa
Adjunct Professor:
  William Haneberg, (D), Cincinnati, 1989, Ng
  Per-Anders Persson, (D), Cambridge, 1960, Nr
  Ingar F. Walder, (D), New Mexico Tech, 1991, Cl
Emeritus:
  George B. Griswold, (D), Arizona, Nx
  Kalman I. Oravecz, (D), Witwatersrand, 1967, Nr

New Mexico State University, Alamogordo
New Mexico State University, Alamogordo (2014)
2400 N. Scenic Drive
Alamogordo, NM 88310
  hrnmsua@nmsu.edu
  http://www.nmsua.edu

New Mexico State University, Grants
New Mexico State University - Grants (2014)
1500 N Third St
Grants, NM 87020
  p. (505) 287-6678
  ssgrants@nmsu.edu
  http://www.grants.nmsu.edu

New Mexico State University, Las Cruces

Dept of Geological Sciences (B,M) ● (2015)
MSC 3AB, Box 30001
1255 N. Horseshoe
Gardiner Hall, Room 171
Las Cruces, NM 88003
  p. (575) 646-2708
  geology@nmsu.edu
  http://www.nmsu.edu/~geology/
  Administrative Assistant: Lee Hubbard
  Enrollment (2015): B: 58 (4) M: 17 (4)
Head:
  Nancy J. McMillan, (D), S Methodist, 1986, Gi
Professor:
  Jeffrey M. Amato, (D), Stanford, 1995, Gc
Assistant Professor:
  Reed J. Burgette, (D), Oregon, 2008, Gtc
  Brian A. Hampton, (D), Purdue, 2006, Gst
  Frank C. Ramos, (D), California (Los Angeles), 2000, CgGg
Adjunct Professor:
  Emily R. Johnson, (D), Oregon, 2008, Gvi

Dept of Physics (M,D) (2014)
Graduate Program in Geophysics
Las Cruces, NM 88003
  p. (505) 646-3831
  jni@nmsu.edu
  http://geophysics.nmsu.edu
  Enrollment (2010): M: 1 (1) D: 1 (1)
Director:
  James F. Ni, (D), Cornell, 1984, Ys
Head:
  Stefan Zoner, (D), Arizona State, 1978, Yg
Professor:
  George H. Goedecke, (D), Rensselaer, 1961, Oa
Associate Professor:
  Thomas M. Hearn, (D), Caltech, 1985, Ys
  Boris Kiefer, (D), Michigan, GyYgOm

Dept of Plant & Environmental Sciences (A,B,M,D) (2011)
Box 30003
Dept. 3Q
Las Cruces, NM 88003-0003
  p. (505) 646-3405
  lmeyer@nmsu.edu
  http://aces.nmsu.edu/academics/pes/
  Department Secretary: Paula Ross
  Enrollment: No data reported since 1999
Head:
  LeRoy A. Daugherty, (D), Cornell, 1975, Sd
  Richard Pratt, (D)
Professor:
  William C. Lindemann, (D), Minnesota, 1978, Sb
  Bobby D. McCaslin, (D), Minnesota, 1974, Sc
  Theodore W. Sammis, (D), Arizona, 1974, Sp
Assistant Professor:
  Dean Heil, (D), California (Berkeley), 1991, Sc
  Tim L. Jones, (D), Washington State, 1989, Sp
  H. C. Monger, (D), New Mexico State, 1990, Sa

San Juan College

San Juan College (A) (2015)
4601 College Blvd.
Farmington, NM 87402
  p. (505) 566-3325
  burrisj@sanjuancollege.edu
  http://www.sanjuancollege.edu/geology
  Enrollment (2015): A: 16 (1)
Professor:
  John H. Burris, (D), Michigan State, 2004, GghGz

University of New Mexico

Dept of Earth & Planetary Sciences (B,M,D) ○ (2015)
221 Yale Blvd NE
Northrop Hall, Room 141
MSC03 2040
Albuquerque, NM 87131-0001
  p. (505) 277-4204
  epsdept@unm.edu
  http://epswww.unm.edu/
  Enrollment (2009): B: 184 (36) M: 34 (9) D: 27 (4)
Chair:
  Laura J. Crossey, (D), Wyoming, 1985, Cl
Professor:
  Carl A. Agee, (D), Columbia, 1988, Cp
  Yemane Asmerom, (D), Arizona, 1988, Cc
  Adrian J. Brearley, (D), Manchester (UK), 1984, Gz
  Maya Elrick, (D), Virginia Tech, 1990, Gs
  Peter J. Fawcett, (D), Penn State, 1994, Pe
  Tobias Fischer, (D), Arizona State, 1999, Gv
  David J. Gutzler, (D), MIT, 1986, Oa
  Karl E. Karlstrom, (D), Wyoming, 1980, Gt
  Leslie M. McFadden, (D), Arizona, 1982, Sd
  Grant A. Meyer, (D), New Mexico, 1993, Gm
  James J. Papike, (D), Minnesota, 1964, Ca
  Louis Scuderi, (D), California (Los Angeles), Pe
  Zachary D. Sharp, (D), Michigan, 1987, Cs
  Gary Weissmann, (D), California (Davis), Hw
Senior Scientist:
  Nieu-Viorel Atudorei, (D), Lausanne, 1998, Cs
  Victor J. Polyak, (D), Texas Tech, 1998, Cg
  Jane E. Selverstone, (D), MIT, 1985, Gp
Associate Professor:
  Joseph Galewsky, (D), California (Santa Cruz), 1996, Ow
Assistant Professor:
  Corinne E. Myers, (D), Kansas, 2013, Po
  Brandon Schmandt, (D), Oregon, 2011, Yg
  Lindsay Lowe Worthington, (D), Texas (Austin), 2010, Yg
Research Associate:
  Frans J.M. Rietmeijer, (D), Utrecht (Neth), 1979, Gp
Lecturer:
  Aurora Pun, (D), New Mexico, 1996, Ca
Adjunct Professor:
  Fraser Goff, (D), California (Santa Cruz), 1977, Cg
  Sean McKenna, (D), Colorado Mines
  Duane M. Moore, (D), Illinois (Urbana), 1963, Sc
  Thomas E. Williamson, (D), New Mexico, 1993, Pv
  Kenneth H. Wohletz, (D), Arizona State, 1980, Gv
Emeritus:
  Roger Y. Anderson, (D), Stanford, 1960, Gn
  Wolfgang E. Elston, (D), Columbia, 1953, Eg
  Rodney E. Ewing, (D), Stanford, 1974, Gz
  John W. Geissman, (D), Michigan, 1980, Ym
  Rhian Jones, (D), Manchester (UK), 1986, Gz
  Cornelis Klein, (D), Harvard, 1965, Gz
  Barry S. Kues, (D), Indiana, 1974, Pi
  Lee A. Woodward, (D), Washington, 1962, Gc

Inst of Meteoritics (2010)
MSC03 2050
1 University of New Mexico
Albuquerque, NM 87131
  p. (505) 277-1644
  agee@unm.edu
  Administrative Assistant: Shannon Clark
Professor:
  Carl B. Agee, (D), Columbia, 1988, XcGyCp
Research Professor:
  V. Rama Murthy, (D), Yale, 1957, XcCc
  James J. Papike, (D), Minnesota, 1964, Gz
  Robert C. Reedy, (D), Columbia, 1969, Xcy
  David C. Rubie, (D), Leicester, 1972, Xg
Senior Scientist III:
  David S. Draper, (D), Oregon, 1991, GiCpXc
  Penelope L. King, (D), Arizona State, 1999, GiXcCp
  David T. Lescinsky, (D), Arizona State, 1999, Gvi
  Horton E. Newsom, (D), Arizona, 1981, Xc
  Charles K. Shearer, Jr., (D), Massachusetts, 1983, Gi
Senior Scientist I:
  James M. Karner, (D), New Mexico, 2003, Gz
Research Specialist:
  Paul V. Burger, (M), New Mexico, 2005, Gz

Research Scientist III:
Michael N. Spilde, (M), SD Mines, 1987, Gz

Water Resources Program (2004)
1915 Roma NE, Room 1044
Albuquerque, NM 87131-1217
p. (505) 277-5249
lmcfadnm@unm.edu
http://www.unm.edu/~wrp/
Director:
Michael E. Campana, On

University of New Mexico - Taos
University of New Mexico - Taos (A,B) ● (2014)
1157 County Road 110
Ranchos de Taos, NM 87557
colnic@unm.edu
http://www.taos.unm.edu
Adjunct Professor:
Deborah Ragland, (D), Gg

University of New Mexico, Gallup
Div of Arts and Sciences (2015)
200 College Road
Gallup, NM 87301
p. (505) 863-7500
pwatt@unm.edu
http://www.gallup.unm.edu/

Western New Mexico University
Dept of Natural Sciences (2016)
P.O. Box 680
1000 West College Avenue
Silver City, NM 88062
p. (575) 538-6227
dowsem@wnmu.edu
http://natsci.wnmu.edu/
Enrollment: No data reported since 1999
Professor:
Mary E. Dowse, (D), West Virginia, 1980, Og

New York

Adelphi University
Environmental Studies Program (B,M) (2015)
South Avenue
Garden City, NY 11530
p. (516) 877-4170
schlosse@adelphi.edu
http://environmental-studies.adelphi.edu
Enrollment (2010): B: 35 (6) M: 22 (8)
Professor:
Anthony E. Cok, (D), Dalhousie, 1970, OuGeu
Assistant Professor:
Beth A. Christensen, (D), South Carolina, 1997, PmeGs

Adirondack Community College
Science Div (A) (2014)
640 Bay Road
Queensbury, NY 12804
p. (518) 743-2325
minkeld@sunyacc.edu
http://www.sunyacc.edu
Enrollment: No data reported since 1999

Alfred University
Dept of Geology (B) (2013)
Saxon Drive
Alfred, NY 14802
p. (607) 871-2208
fmuller@alfred.edu
http://ottohmuller.com/ENSweb2008/
Enrollment (2012): B: 15 (10)
Professor:
Michele M. Hluchy, (D), Dartmouth, 1988, Cl

Otto H. Muller, (D), Rochester, 1974, Gc

American Museum of Natural History
Dept of Earth & Planetary Sciences (2015)
Central Park West at 79th Street
New York, NY 10024-5192
p. (212)769-5390
norell@amnh.org
http://www.amnh.org/our-research/physical-sciences/earth-and-planetary-sciences
Administrative Assistant: Nanette Nicholson
Chair and Curator:
Denton Ebel, (D), Purdue, 1993, Xm
Curator:
George E. Harlow, (D), Princeton, 1977, Ga
Edmond A. Mathez, (D), Washington, 1981, Gx
James D. Webster, (D), Arizona State, 1987, Eg
Senior Scientific Assistant:
Beth A. Goldoff, (B), Wesleyan, 2002, Gi
Jamie Newman, (M), Brooklyn Coll, Gg
Scientific Assistant:
Saebuyl Choe, (B), Bates, 2014
Specialist:
Amanda White, (B), Drexel, 2011
Postdoctoral Fellow:
Celine Martin, (D), CRPG-CNRS, 2009
Patricia Nadeau, (D), Michigan Tech, 2011
Gokce Ustunisik, (D), Cincinnati, 2009
N. Alex Zirakparvar, (D), Syracuse, 2012
Graduate Student:
Ellen J. Crapster-Pregont, (B), Colby, 2010, Xm

Div of Paleontology (D) (2010)
Central Park West at 79th Street
New York, NY 10024
p. (212) 769-5815
norell@amnh.org
http://paleo.amnh.org/
Administrative Assistant: Judy Galkin
Enrollment (2009): D: 8 (0)
Chair, Professor and Curator:
Mark A. Norell, (D), Yale, 1989, Pv
Provost, Professor and Curator:
Michael J. Novacek, (D), California (Berkeley), 1978, Pv
Professor and Curator:
Niles Eldredge, (D), Columbia, 1969, Pi
Neil H. Landman, (D), Yale, 1982, Pi
John G. Maisey, (D), London, 1974, Pv
Jin Meng, (D), Columbia, 1991, Pv
Dean of the Richard Gilder Graduate School, Professor, and Frick Curator:
John J. Flynn, (D), Columbia, 1983, Pv
Frick Curator Emeritus:
Richard H. Tedford, (D), California (Berkeley), 1960, Pv
Curator Emeritus:
Roger L. Batten, (D), Columbia, 1956, Pi
Eugene S. Gaffney, (D), Columbia, 1969, Pv

Binghamton University
Dept of Geological Sciences and Environmental Studies
(B,M,D) (2013)
PO Box 6000
Binghamton, NY 13902-6000
p. (607) 777-2264
demicco@binghamton.edu
http://geology.binghamton.edu
Administrative Assistant: Carol Slavetskas
Enrollment (2012): B: 30 (0) M: 4 (0) D: 12 (0)
Chair:
Joseph R. Graney, (D), Michigan, 1994, Cl
Professor:
Robert V. Demicco, (D), Johns Hopkins, 1981, Gs
Steven R. Dickman, (D), California (Berkeley), 1977, Yg
David M. Jenkins, (D), Chicago, 1980, Cp
Tim K. Lowenstein, (D), Johns Hopkins, 1982, Cl
H. Richard Naslund, (D), Oregon, 1980, Gi

Associate Professor:
  Richard E. Andrus, (D), SUNY (Syracuse), 1974, Py
  Jeffrey S. Barker, (D), Penn State, 1984, Ys
  Peter L. K. Knuepfer, (D), Arizona, 1984, Gt
  Karen M. Salvage, (D), Penn State, 1998, Hw
Assistant Professor:
  Thomas Kulp, (D), Indiana, 2002, Py
Research Associate:
  Michael Hubenthal, (B), Slippery Rock, 1996, Oe
  Alan Jones, (D), Purdue, 1964, Ys
  Michael N. Timofeeff, (D), Binghamton, 2001, Cl
Emeritus:
  Donald R. Coates, (D), Columbia, 1956, Gm
  Thomas W. Donnelly, (D), Princeton, 1959, Gg
  William D. MacDonald, (D), Princeton, 1965, Gc
  James E. Sorauf, (D), Kansas, 1962, Pi
  Francis T. Wu, (D), Caltech, 1966, Ys

Brooklyn College (CUNY)
Dept of Geology (B,M,D) (2013)
2900 Bedford Avenue
Brooklyn, NY 11210
  p. (718) 951-5416
  wpowell@brooklyn.cuny.edu
  http://depthome.brooklyn.cuny.edu/geology/
  Administrative Assistant: Joseph DeStefano
  Enrollment (2009): B: 24 (5) M: 10 (4) D: 3 (1)
Chair:
  Wayne G. Powell, (D), Queen's, 1994, Gp
Professor:
  John A. Chamberlain, (D), Rochester, 1971, Po
  Constantin Cranganu, (D), Oklahoma, 1997, Go
  John Marra, (D), Dalhousie, 1977, Ob
  David E. Seidemann, (D), Yale, 1975, Cc
Associate Professor:
  Stephen U. Aja, (D), Washington State, 1989, Cl
Assistant Professor:
  Rebecca Boger, (D), William & Mary, 2002, OiHs
  Brett Branco, (D), Connecticut, 2007, GsOg
  Zhongqi Cheng, (D), Ohio State, 2001, Ca
Lecturer:
  Matt Garb, (M), Brooklyn Coll, Pg
Laboratory Director:
  Guillermo Rocha, (M), CUNY, 1994, Gg

Broome Community College
Dept of Physical Sciences (A) (2015)
Upper Front Street
Box 1017
Binghamton, NY 13902
  p. (607) 778-5000
  smithjj@sunybroome.edu
Professor:
  Bruce K. Oldfield, (M), SUNY (Binghamton), 1988, Gg
Assistant Professor:
  Jason J. Smith, (M), Binghamton, 2009, Ggs

Buffalo State College
Dept of Earth Sciences (B) (2015)
1300 Elmwood Avenue
Buffalo, NY 14222
  p. (716) 878-6731
  solargs@buffalostate.edu
  http://www.buffalostate.edu/earthsciences
  Administrative Assistant: Cindy Wong
  Enrollment (2015): B: 90 (35)
Chair:
  Gary S. Solar, (D), Maryland, 1999, GcpGt
Professor:
  Jill K. Singer, (D), Rice, 1986, GsOp
Planetarium Director:
  Kevin K. Williams, (D), Johns Hopkins, 2002, Xg
Associate Professor:
  Elisa T. Bergslien, (D), SUNY (Buffalo), 2002, ClHw
  Kevin K. Williams, (D), Johns Hopkins, 2002, GmXg

Assistant Professor:
  Bettina Martinez-Hackert, (D), SUNY (Buffalo), 2006, Gvm
Emeritus:
  John E. Mack, (D), Fordham, 1971, Xg
  Irving Tesmer, (D), Syracuse, Pg

Cayuga Community College
Math and Science (A) (2013)
197 Franklin Street
Auburn, NY 13021
  p. (315) 255-1743
  waters@cayuga-cc.edu
  http://www.cayuga-cc.edu/academics/programs_of_study/
  math_and_science.php
Professor:
  Abu Z. Badruddin, (D), SUNY Coll Env Sci, Oi
  Raymond F. Leszczynski, (M), SUNY (Albany), 1965, GglGm

City College (CUNY)
Dept of Earth & Atmospheric Sciences (B,M) (2010)
New York, NY 10031
  p. (212) 650-6984
  sbarnes@sci.ccny.cuny.edu
  Enrollment: No data reported since 1999
Chair:
  Jeffrey Steiner, (D), Stanford, 1970, Cp
Professor:
  Stanley Gedzelman, (D), MIT, 1970, Oa
  Edward E. Hindman, (D), Washington, 1975, Oa
  Margaret A. Winslow, (D), Columbia, 1979, Gc
Associate Professor:
  Patricia M. Kenyon, (D), Cornell, 1986, Yg
  Federica Raia, (D), Naples, 1997, Giv
  Pengfei Zhang, (D), Utah, 2000, Hw

Colgate University
Dept of Geology (B) (2015)
13 Oak Drive
Hamilton, NY 13346
  p. (315) 228-7201
  jmcnamara@colgate.edu
  http://www.colgate.edu/academics/departments-and-
  programs/geology
  Administrative Assistant: Jodi McNamara
  Enrollment (2015): B: 34 (17)
Associate Professor:
  Martin Wong, (D), California (Santa Barbara), 2005, Gtc
Professor:
  Richard April, (D), Massachusetts, 1978, Cg
  Amy Leventer, (D), Rice, 1988, Ou
  William H. Peck, (D), Wisconsin, 2000, GpiCs
  Paul Pinet, (D), Rhode Island, 1972, Ou
  Bruce Selleck, (D), Rochester, 1975, Gs
  Constance M. Soja, (D), Oregon, 1985, Pi
Associate Professor:
  Karen Harpp, (D), Cornell, 1994, GvCgGi
Assistant Professor:
  Aubreya Adams, (D), Penn State, 2010, Yg
Senior Lecturer:
  Dianne M. Keller, (M), Colgate, 1988, Gz
Emeritus:
  James McLelland, (D), Chicago, 1961, Gp

College of Staten Island
Engineering Science & Physics (2015)
2800 Victory Boulevard
Staten Island, NY 10314
  p. (718) 982-2827
  alan.benimoff@csi.cuny.edu
  http://www.library.csi.cuny.edu/dept/as/geo/geo.html
Associate Professor:
  Athanasios Koutavas, (D), Columbia, 2003, PeOg
Assistant Professor:
  David Lindo Atichati, (D), the Canary Islands, 2012, Gue
  Anderson A. Ohan, (M), New York, 1965, Gc

New York

99

Lecturer:
  Jane L. Alexander, (D), Univ Coll (London), 1998, Gse
  Alan I. Benimoff, (D), Lehigh, 1984, GizGp
Adjunct Lecturer:
  Imad Harone, (M), CUNY (Staten Island), Gg
  Edward Johnson, (M), CUNY (Staten Island), Gg
  Vladimir Jovanovic, (M), CUNY (Staten Island), Ge
Adjunct Associate Professor:
  Mosbah Kolkas, (D), CUNY, Gg
Adjunct Assistant Professor:
  Noureddin Amaach, (D), CUNY, Gg
  Rosemary McCall, (D), Gg
  Caitlyn Nichols, (D), CUNY, Ge

Columbia University

Dept of Earth & Environmental Engineering (2010)
Henry Krumb School of Mines
500 West 120 Street
918 Mudd Bldg
New York, NY 10027
  p. (212) 894-2905
  eee-coord@columbia.edu
  http://www.eee.columbia.edu/
  Administrative Assistant: Co'Quesie Gilbert
  Department Administrator: Barbara Algin
  Enrollment (1999): B: 6 (0) M: 13 (2) D: 3 (3)
Acting Chair:
  Nickolas J. Themelis, (D), McGill, 1961, Nx
Professor:
  Paul F. Duby, (D), Columbia, 1962, Nx
  Peter Schlosser, (D), Heidelberg, 1985, Cg
  Ponisseril Somasundaran, (D), California (Berkeley), 1964, Nx
  Tuncel M. Yegulalp, (D), Columbia, 1968, Nm
Associate Professor:
  Ross Bagtzoglou, (D), California (Berkeley), 1990, Hw
Senior Research Scientist:
  Roelof Versteeg, (D), Paris VII, 1991, Yg
Adjunct Professor:
  Vasilis M. Fthenakis, (D), New York, 1991, Oa
Emeritus:
  Stefan H. Boshkov, (M), Columbia, 1942, Nm
  John T. Kuo, (D), Stanford, 1958, Yg
  Malcolm T. Wane, (M), Columbia, 1954, Nm

Dept of Earth & Environmental Sciences (B,M,D) (2014)
P.O. Box 1000
61 Route 9W
Palisades, NY 10964
  p. (845) 365-8550
  carolm@ldeo.columbia.edu
  http://eesc.columbia.edu
  Enrollment (1999): B: 77 (13) M: 16 (10) D: 71 (9)
Vice Chair:
  Peter B. de Menocal, (D), Columbia, 1991, PeOuCg
Director, Lamont Doherty Earth Observatory:
  Sean Solomon, (D), MIT, 1971, Xy
Dir. Graduate Studies:
  Goran Ekstrom, (D), Harvard, 1987, Ys
Chair:
  Peter B. Kelemen, (D), Washington, 1988, GiCg
Professor:
  Wallace S. Broecker, (D), Columbia, 1958, CmOcPe
  Mark A. Cane, (D), MIT, 1975, OapPe
  Nicholas Christie-Blick, (D), California (Santa Barbara), 1979, Gs
  Joel E. Cohen, (D), Harvard, 1970, On
  Hugh Ducklow, (D), Harvard, 1977, Ob
  Peter M. Eisenberger, (D), Harvard, 1967, On
  Steven L. Goldstein, (D), Columbia, 1986, Csg
  Arnold L. Gordon, (D), Columbia, 1965, Op
  Kevin L. Griffin, (D), Duke, 1994, PbeOn
  Sidney R. Hemming, (D), SUNY (Stony Brook), 1994, CscPe
  Jerry F. McManus, (D), Columbia, 1989, PeOu
  William H. Menke, (D), Columbia, 1981, YsGvq
  John C. Mutter, (D), Columbia, 1982, Yr
  Paul E. Olsen, (D), Yale, 1983, PvoGr
  Stephanie L. Pfirman, (D), MIT, 1985, OpGe
  Terry A. Plank, (D), Columbia, 1993, GxCg

Lorenzo M. Polvani, (D), MIT, 1988, OwaGq
  G. Michael Purdy, (D), Cambridge, 1974, Yr
  Peter Schlosser, (D), Heidelberg, 1985, Hw
  Christopher H. Scholz, (D), MIT, 1967, YxNr
  Adam H. Sobel, (D), MIT, 1998, Oa
  Marc W. Spiegelman, (D), Cambridge, 1989, GqxCg
  Martin Stute, (D), Heidelberg, 1989, CsHgGe
  David Walker, (D), Harvard, 1972, CpGzCg
Associate Professor:
  Sonya Dyhrman, Scripps, 1999, Ob
  Arlene M. Fiore, (D), Harvard, 2003, Oa
  Baerbel Hoenisch, (D), Bremen, 2002, PeObCm
  Meredith Nettles, (D), Harvard, 2005, YsGl
  Maria Tolstoy, (D), California (San Diego), 1994, Yr
Assistant Professor:
  Ryan P. Abernathey, (D), MIT, 2012, Op
  Tiffany A. Shaw, (D), Toronto, 2009, Oa
Lecturer:
  Roger N. Anderson, (D), California (San Diego), 1973, Yh
  Anthony G. Barnston, (M), Illinois (Urbana), 1976, On
  Alberto Malinverno, (D), Columbia, 1989, Gug
  Benjamin S. Orlove, (D), California (Berkeley), 1975, Oa
  Andreas M. Thurnherr, (D), Southampton, 2000, Op
  Christopher J. Zappa, (D), Washington, 1999, Op
Adjunct Assistant Professor:
  Natalie T. Boelman, (D), Columbia, 2004, PbeOr
Adjunct Professor:
  Robert F. Anderson, (D), MIT, 1981, OcCmPe
  W. Roger Buck, IV, (D), MIT, 1984, YgGt
  John J. Flynn, (D), Columbia, 1983, PvyYm
  Alessandra M. Giannini, (D), Columbia, 2001, Oa
  Lisa M. Goddard, (D), Princeton, 1995, Oa
  Andrew Juhl, (D), California (San Diego), 2000, Ob
  Arthur L. Lerner-Lam, (D), California (San Diego), 1982, Ys
  Douglas G. Martinson, (D), Columbia, 1982, OpGq
  Ronald L. Miller, (D), MIT, 1990, Oa
  Mark A. Norell, (D), Yale, 1988, Pv
  Dorothy M. Peteet, (D), NYU, 1983, PleOn
  Andrew W. Robertson, (D), Reading (UK), 1984, Oa
  Joerg Schaefer, (D), ETH Zurich, 2000, Cg
  Christopher Small, (D), California (San Diego), 1993, OrYr
  Taro Takahashi, (D), Columbia, 1957, OcCg
  Mingfang Ting, (D), Princeton, 1990, Oa
  Felix Waldhauser, ETH Zurich, 1996, Ys
  Spahr C. Webb, (D), California (San Diego), 1984, Yrg
  Gisela Winckler, (D), Heidelberg, 1998, Cm
Emeritus:
  Dennis E. Hayes, (D), Columbia, 1966, Yr
  James D. Hays, (D), Columbia, 1964, PemOu
  Paul G. Richards, (D), Caltech, 1970, YsOn
  David H. Rind, (D), Columbia, 1976, Oar
  H. James Simpson, Jr., (D), Columbia, 1970, Cm
  Lynn R. Sykes, (D), Columbia, 1965, YsGt
Senior Administrative Manager:
  Carol S. Mountain, (B), Columbia, 1974, On
Business Manager:
  Sarah K. Odland, (M), Colorado, 1981, On
Asst. Director Climate and Society Program:
  Cynthia Thomson, (M), Columbia, 2009, On

Lamont-Doherty Earth Observatory (M,D) (2016)
P.O. Box 1000
61 Route 9W
Palisades, NY 10964
  p. (845) 359-2900
  director@ldeo.columbia.edu
  http://www.ldeo.columbia.edu
  Enrollment (2006): M: 40 (0) D: 83 (6)
Professor:
  Sean C. Solomon, (D), MIT, 1971, Xgy
Chair of DEES:
  Peter Kelemen, (D), Washington, 1987, Gi
Professor:
  Wallace S. Broecker, (D), Columbia, 1957, Cg
  Mark A. Cane, (D), MIT, 1975, Op
  Nicholas Christie-Blick, (D), California (Santa Barbara), 1979, Gs
  Peter B. deMenocal, (D), Columbia, 1991, Pe

Hugh W. Ducklow, (D), Harvard, 1977
Peter Eisenberger, (D), Harvard, 1967, On
Goran Ekstrom, (D), Harvard, 1987, Yg
Steven Goldstein, (D), Columbia, 1986, Cg
Arnold L. Gordon, (D), Columbia, 1965, Op
Kevin Griffin, (D), Duke, 1994, On
Sidney Hemming, (D), SUNY (Stony Brook), 1994, Cg
Jerry McManus, (D), Cm
William H. Menke, (D), Columbia, 1981, Ys
John C. Mutter, (D), Columbia, 1982, Yr
Paul E. Olsen, (D), Yale, 1983, Gm
Terry Plank, (D), Columbia, 1993, Cg
G. Michael Purdy, (D), Cambridge, 1974, Yr
Peter Schlosser, (D), Heidelberg, 1985, Hw
Christopher H. Scholz, (D), MIT, 1967, Ys
Adam Sobel, (D), MIT, 1998, Oa
Marc Spiegelman, (D), Cambridge, 1989, Ys
David Walker, (D), Harvard, 1972, Gx
Sr. PGI Research Scientist:
    Robin E. Bell, (D), Columbia, 1989, Yr
    Richard Seager, (D), Columbia, 1990, Ow
Senior Research Scientist:
    Sean M. Higgins, (D), Columbia, 2002, Gs
    Kerstin Lehnert, (D), Albert-Ludwigs Freiburg, 1989, Gi
Paros Sr. Research Scientist:
    Spahr Webb, (D), California (San Diego), 1984, Yr
Lamont Research Professor:
    Roger W. Buck, (D), MIT, 1984, Yr
    Brendon Buckley, (D), Tasmania, 1997, Pe
    Steven Chillrud, (D), Columbia, 1995, Cg
    Rosanne D'Arrigo, (D), Columbia, 1989, On
    James Davis, (D), MIT, 1986, Yd
    Suzana de Camargo, (D), Tech (Munich), 1992, Oa
    James Gaherty, (D), MIT, 1995, Ys
    Joaquim Goes, (D), Nagoya, 1996, Gu
    David S. Goldberg, (D), Columbia, 1985, Yr
    Won-Young Kim, (D), Uppsala, 1986, Ys
    Yochanan Kushnir, (D), Oregon State, 1985, Oa
    Braddock Linsley, (D), New Mexico, 1990, Pe
    Alberto Malinverno, (D), Columbia, 1989, Go
    Douglas G. Martinson, (D), Columbia, 1982, Op
    Joerg Schaefer, (D), Swiss Fed Inst, 2000, Pe
    Leonardo Seeber, (B), Columbia, 1964, Ys
    Bruce Shaw, (D), Chicago, 1989, Ys
    Christopher Small, (D), California (San Diego), 1993, Or
    William Smethie, (D), Washington, 1979, Cg
    Michael Steckler, (D), Columbia, 1980, Yv
    Ajit Subramaniam, (D), SUNY-Stony Brook, 1995, Obr
    Marco Tedasco, (D), Italian National Research Council, 2003, Olr
    Andreas Thurnherr, (D), Southampton, 1999, Op
    Mingfang Ting, (D), Princeton, 1990, Oa
    Alexander Van Geen, (D), MIT/WHOI, 1989, Cg
    Felix Waldhauser, (D), ETH (Switzerland), 1996, Ys
    Gisela Winckler, (D), Heidelberg, 1998, Cg
    Xiaojun Yuan, (D), California (San Diego), 1994, Op
Heezen Senior Research Scientist:
    Suzanne Carbotte, (D), California (Santa Barbara), 1992, Yr
Ewing LDEO Rsrch Professor:
    Robert F. Anderson, (D), MIT, 1981, Cg
    Edward R. Cook, (D), Arizona, 1985, Hw
    Taro Takahashi, (D), Columbia, 1957, Cm
Dir.Core Repository:
    Maureen Raymo, (D), Columbia, 1989, Pe
Deputy Director:
    Arthur L. Lerner-Lam, (D), California (San Diego), 1982, Ys
Associate Professor:
    Baerbel Hoenisch, (D), Alfred Wegener Inst (Germany), 2002, Cm
    Arlene Fiore, (D), Harvard, 2003, Oa
    Meredith Nettles, (D), Harvard, 2005, YsOl
    Maria Tolstoy, (D), California (San Diego), 1994, Yr
Lamont Associate Research Professor:
    Michela Biasutti, (D), Washington, 2003, Yr
    Benjamin C. Bostick, (D), Stanford, 2002, Sc
    Connie Class, (D), Karlsruhe, 1994, Cg
    Benjamin Holtzman, (D), Minnesota, 2003, Ys
    Andrew Juhl, (D), Scripps, 2000, Ob
    Alexey Kaplan, (D), Gubkin Inst of Tech (Moscow), 1990, Op

Michael Kaplan, (D), Colorado, 1999, Gl
Mikhail Kogan, (D), Inst of Physics (Moscow), 1977, Yd
Wade McGillis, (D), California (Berkeley), 1993, Cm
Raymond N. Sambrotto, (D), Alaska, 1983, Ob
David Schaff, (D), Stanford, 2001, Ys
Donna Shillington, (D), Wyoming, 2004, Yr
Jason Smerdon, (D), Michigan, 2004, Pe
Colin Stark, (D), Leeds (UK), 1991, Gg
Susanne Straub, (D), Kiel, 1991, Gv
Christopher Zappa, (D), Washington, 1999, Op
Assistant Professor:
    Ryan Abernathy, (D), MIT, 2012, Og
Special Research Scientist:
    Pierre E. Biscaye, (D), Yale, 1964, Cm
    Enrico Bonatti, (D), Pisa, 1967, Yr
    Dake Chen, (D), SUNY (Stony Brook), 1989, Op
    James R. Cochran, (D), Columbia, 1977, Yr
    Klaus H. Jacob, (D), Goethe (Frankfurt), 1968, Ys
    Stanley Jacobs, (B), MIT, 1962, Op
    Walter Pitman, (D), Columbia, 1967, Yr
    Paul G. Richards, (D), Caltech, 1970, Ys
    William B. F. Ryan, (D), Columbia, 1961, Yr
Research Scientist:
    Andrew Barclay, (D), Oregon, 1998, Ys
    Victoria Ferrini, (D), Stony Brook, 2004, Ou
    Helga Gomes, (D), Bombay, 1985, Ob
    Gilles Guerin, (D), Columbia, 2000, Gu
    Naomi Henderson, (D), Wisconsin, 1987, Yr
    Timothy Kenna, (D), MIT/WHOI, 2002, Cg
    Robert Newton, (D), Columbia, 2001, Ct
    Frank Nitsche, (D), Alfred Wegener Inst (Germany), 1997, Gu
Lamont Associate Jr. Rsrch Professor:
    Timothy Crone, Washington, 2007, Gu
    William Joseph D'Andrea, (D), Brown, 2008, Pe
    Pratigya J. Polissar, (D), Massachusetts, 2005, Gg
    Heather M. Savage, (D), Penn State, 2007, Ys
    Beizhan Yan, (D), Rensselaer, 2004, Cg
Lamont Assist. Rsrch Professor:
    Liala Andru-Hayles, (D), Barcelona, 2007, Pe
    Anne Becel, (D), Institut de Physique du Globe de Paris, 2006, Gu
    Natalie Boelman, (D), Columbia, 2004, Or
    Timothy T. Creyts, (D), British Columbia, 2007, Ol
    Solange Duhamel, (D), Aix-Maraseille II, Pe
    Einat Lev, (D), MIT, 2009, Gv
    Jonathan E. Nichols, (D), Brown, 2009, Pe
    Michael Previdi, (M), Rutgers, 2006, Oa
    Philipp Ruprecht, (D), Washington, 2009, Gv

Cornell University
Dept of Earth & Atmospheric Sciences (B,M,D) O (2015)
2122 Snee Hall
Ithaca, NY 14853-1504
    p. (607) 255-3474
    easinfo@cornell.edu
    http://www.eas.cornell.edu/
    Enrollment (2015): B: 37 (21) M: 6 (2) D: 29 (6)
Professor:
    Geoffrey A. Abers, (D), MIT, 1989, YsGt
    Richard W. Allmendinger, (D), Stanford, 1979, Gc
    Warren D. Allmon, (D), Harvard, 1988, PoePi
    Larry D. Brown, (D), Cornell, 1976, Ye
    Lawrence M. Cathles, (D), Princeton, 1968, Hy
    John L. Cisne, (D), Chicago, 1973, Pg
    Steven Colucci, (D), SUNY (Albany), 1982, Oa
    Arthur DeGaetano, (D), Rutgers, 1989, Oa
    Louis A. Derry, (D), Harvard, 1989, Cl
    Charles H. Greene, (D), Washington, 1985, Ob
    David Hysell, (D), Cornell, 1992, Onr
    Teresa A. Jordan, (D), Stanford, 1979, Gr
    Suzanne M. Kay, (D), Brown, 1975, GiCg
    Natalie M. Mahowald, (D), MIT, 1996, Oa
    Sara C. Pryor, (D), East Anglia, 1992, Oan
    Susan Riha, (D), Washington, 1980, Sf
    John F. H. Thompson, (D), Toronto, 1982, EgNx
    William M. White, (D), Rhode Island, 1977, Cc
    Daniel Wilks, (D), Oregon, 1986, Oa

Associate Professor:
  Rowena B. Lohman, (D), Caltech, 2004, YsOrGt
  Matthew E. Pritchard, (D), Caltech, 2003, Gv
Assistant Professor:
  Toby R. Ault, (D), Arizona, 2011, Ow
Sr. Lecturer:
  Bruce Monger, (D), Hawaii (Manoa), 1993, Ob
Senior Lecturer:
  Mark Wysocki, (M), Cornell, 1988, Oa
Adjunct Asst. Professor:
  Gregory P. Dietl, (D), North Carolina State, 2002, Peo
  Robert M. Ross, Harvard, 1990, PoGgs
Adjunct Professor:
  Martin J. Evans, (D), Wales, 1985, Eo
  Paula Mikkelsen, (D), Florida Inst of Technology, 1994, Pi
  Jason Phipps Morgan, (D), Brown, 1985, GvCmPe
  Manfred Strecker, (D), Cornell, 1987, Gt
  Martyn Unsworth, (D), Cambridge, 1991, Ye
Emeritus:
  Muawia Barazangi, (D), Columbia, 1971, Ys
  William A. Bassett, (D), Columbia, 1959, Gz
  John M. Bird, (D), Rensselaer, 1962, Gt
  Arthur L. Bloom, (D), Yale, 1959, Gm
  Bryan L. Isacks, (D), Columbia, 1965, Ys
  Daniel E. Karig, (D), California (San Diego), 1970, Yr
  Robert W. Kay, (D), Columbia, 1970, Giz
  Warren Knapp, (D), Wisconsin, 1968, Oa
  Frank H. T. Rhodes, (D), Birmingham, 1950, Pi
Cooperating Faculty:
  J. Thomas Brenna, (D), Cornell, 1985, Cg
  Oliver H. Gao, (D), California (Davis), 2004, On
  Alexander Hayes, (D), Xg
  Greg C. McLaskey, (D), California (Berkeley), 2011, Ys
  Thomas D. O'Rourke, (D), Illinois, 1975, Ng
  Andy L. Ruina, (D), Brown, 1981, Yx
  Steven W. Squyres, (D), Cornell, 1981, Xg
  Tammo S. Steenhuis, (D), Wisconsin, 1977, So
  Jefferson W. Tester, (D), MIT, 1971, On
  Zellman Warhaft, (D), London, 1975, On
  Max Zhang, (D), California (Davis), 2004, On

Institute for the Study of the Continents (2015)
2122 Snee Hall
Ithaca, NY 14853-1504
  p. (607) 255-3474
  easinfo@cornell.edu
  http://www.eas.cornell.edu/
  Enrollment (2010): M: 9 (0) D: 29 (4)
Wold Family Professor in Environmental Balance for Human Sustainability:
  John F.H. Thompson, (D), Toronto, 1982, Em
Professor:
  Geoffrey A. Abers, (D), MIT, 1989, Ys
  Richard W. Allmendinger, (D), Stanford, 1979, Gct
  Larry D. Brown, (D), Cornell, 1976, Ye
  Lawrence M. Cathles, (D), Princeton, 1968, EgYgGe
  Louis A. Derry, (D), Harvard, 1989, Cg
  David L. Hysell, (D), Cornell, 1992, Onr
  Teresa A. Jordan, (D), Stanford, 1979, Gr
  Suzanne M. Kay, (D), Brown, 1975, Gp
  William M. White, (D), Rhode Island, 1977, Ce
Associate Professor:
  Rowena B. Lohman, (D), Caltech, 2004, Yg
  Matthew E. Pritchard, (D), Caltech, 2003, YdGv
Assistant Professor:
  Katie M. Keranen, (D), Stanford, 2008, Ys
Visiting Professor:
  Franklin G. Horowitz, (D), Cornell, 1989, Nr
Emeritus:
  Muawia Barazangi, (D), Columbia, 1971, Ys
  Bryan L. Isacks, (D), Gmt
  Robert W. Kay, (D), Columbia, 1970, Gi

Dowling College
Dept of Earth & Marine Sciences (2006)
Oakdale, NY
  tanacrej@dowling.edu

Dutchess Community College
Dept of Mathematics, Physical, and Computer Sciences (A) (2014)
53 Pendell Road
Poughkeepsie, NY 12601
  p. (845) 431-8550
  rambo@sunydutchess.edu
  http://www.sunydutchess.edu/academics/departments/
  mathematicsphysicalandcomputersciences/
  Enrollment (2011): A: 20 (0)
Professor:
  Mark McConnaughhay, OgwEo
Associate Professor:
  Susan H. Conrad, GsmGg
  Tim Welling, GeOn

Graduate School of the City University of New York
PhD Program in Earth & Environmental Sciences (D) (2015)
365 Fifth Avenue
New York, NY 10016
  p. (212) 817-8240
  ees@gc.cuny.edu
  http://www.gc.cuny.edu/Page-Elements/Academics-
  Research-Centers-Initiatives/Doctoral-Programs/Earth-and-
  Environmental-Sciences
  Administrative Assistant: Lina C. McClain
  Enrollment (2004): D: 40 (4)
Distinguished Professor:
  Gerald M. Friedman, (D), Columbia, 1952, Gs
Executive Officer:
  Yehuda Klein
Professor:
  Hannes K. Brueckner, (D), Yale, 1968, Cc
  John A. Chamberlain, (D), Rochester, 1971, Po
  Nicholas K. Coch, (D), Yale, 1965, Gs
  Kathleen Crane, (D), California (San Diego), 1977, Yh
  Eric Delson, (D), Columbia, 1973, Pv
  Robert M. Finks, (D), Columbia, 1959, Pi
  Stanley D. Gedzelman, (D), MIT, 1970, Ow
  Victor Goldsmith, (D), Massachusetts, 1972, On
  Daniel Habib, (D), Penn State, 1965, Pl
  Charles A. Heatwole, (D), Michigan State, 1974, On
  Edward E. Hindman, (D), Washington, 1975, Ow
  Reza M. Khanbilvardi, (D), Penn State, 1983, Hy
  Arthur M. Langer, (D), Columbia, 1965, Gz
  Irene S. Leung, (D), California (Berkeley), 1969, Gz
  David J. Leveson, (D), Columbia, 1960, On
  David C. Locke, (D), Kansas State, 1965, Ca
  Allan Ludman, (D), Pennsylvania, 1969, Gg
  Cherukupalli E. Nehru, (D), Madras (India), 1963, Gi
  Robert S. Prezant, (D), Delaware (Lewes), 1981, Py
  David E. Seidemann, (D), Yale, 1976, Cc
  David H. Speidel, (D), Penn State, 1964, Cg
  Dennis Weiss, (D), New York, 1971, Pg
  Margaret S. Winslow, (D), Columbia, 1979, Gc
Associate Professor:
  Sean C. Ahearn, (D), Wisconsin, 1986, Or
  Stephen U. Aja, (D), Washington State, 1989, Cl
  Patrick W. G. Brock, (D), Leeds, 1963, Gg
  Lin A. Ferrand, (D), Princeton, 1988, Hq
  Patricia M. Kenyon, (D), Cornell, 1986, Yg
  Cecilia M. McHugh, (D), Columbia, 1993, Ou
  Inez Miyares, (D), Arizona State, 1994, On
  Jeffrey Steiner, (D), Stanford, 1970, Gx
Assistant Professor:
  Charles R. Ehlschlaeger, (D), California (Santa Barbara), 1998, On
  Mohamed B. Ibrahim, (D), Alberta, 1985, Oy
  Robert P. Nolan, (D), CUNY, 1986, Co
  Wayne G. Powell, (D), Queen's, 1994, Gp
  William G. Wallace, (D), SUNY (Stony Brook), 1996, Og
  Yan Zheng, (D), Columbia, 1999, Cm
Adjunct Professor:
  Niles Eldredge, (D), Columbia, 1969, Pg
  George E. Harlow, (D), Princeton, 1977, Gz
  Neil H. Landman, (D), Yale, 1982, Ps
  Edmond A. Mathez, (D), Washington, 1981, Gi

Jin Meng, (D), Columbia, 1991, Pv
Martin Prinz, (D), Columbia, 1961, Gi
Karl H. Szekielda, (D), Aix (France), 1967, Or
Emeritus:
Somdev Bhattacharji, (D), Chicago, 1959, Gt
Saul B. Cohen, (D), Harvard, 1955, Oy
Otto L. Franke, (D), Karlsruhe, 1962, Gc
William H. Harris, (D), Brown, 1971, Hw
Richard S. Liebling, (D), Columbia, 1963, Gz
Peter H. Mattson, (D), Princeton, 1957, Gc
Andrew McIntyre, (D), Columbia, 1967, Pe
Sara L. McLafferty, (D), Iowa, 1979, On
Joaquin Rodriguez, (D), Indiana, 1960, Pi
Surenda K. Saxena, (D), Uppsala, 1964, Cg
B. Charlotte Schrieber, (D), Rensselaer, 1974, Gd
Frederick C. Shaw, (D), Harvard, 1965, Pi
David L. Thurber, (D), Columbia, 1964, Cl

Hamilton College
Geosciences Dept (B) (2015)
198 College Hill Road
Clinton, NY 13323
    p. (315) 859-4142
    dbailey@hamilton.edu
    https://my.hamilton.edu/academics/
    departments?dept=Geosciences
    Enrollment (2015): B: 31 (13)
Chair:
David G. Bailey, (D), Washington State, 1990, GizGa
Professor:
Cynthia R. Domack, (D), Rice, 1985, Pg
Todd W. Rayne, (D), Wisconsin, 1993, Hy
Barbara J. Tewksbury, (D), Colorado, 1981, Gc
Associate Professor:
Michael L. McCormick, (D), Michigan, 2002, Py
Assistant Professor:
Catherine C. Beck, (D), Rutgers, 2015, GsnGr

Hartwick College
Dept of Geological and Environmental Sciences (B) (2011)
Johnstone Science Center
1 Hartwick Drive
Oneonta, NY 13820
    p. (607) 431-4658
    griffingd@hartwick.edu
    http://www.hartwick.edu/geology.xml
    Administrative Assistant: Nancy Heffernan
    Enrollment (2011): B: 28 (9)
Chair:
David H. Griffing, (D), Binghamton, 1994, GduGm
Professor Emeritus:
David Hutchison, (D), West Virginia, 1968, GxgGi
Professor:
Eric L. Johnson, (D), SUNY (Binghamton), 1990, GpcGi
Robert C. Titus, (D), Boston, 1974, Ps
Assistant Professor:
Zsuzsanna Balogh-Brunstad, (D), Washington State, 2006, Ge

Hobart & William Smith Colleges
Dept of Geoscience (B) ● (2016)
300 Pulteney Street
Geneva, NY 14456
    p. (315) 781-3586
    geoscience@hws.edu
    http://www.hws.edu/academics/geoscience/
    Enrollment (2015): B: 42 (14)
Professor:
Nan Crystal Arens, (D), Harvard, 1993, Po
John D. Halfman, (D), Duke, 1987, Gn
Neil Laird, (D), Illinois, 2001, Oa
D. Brooks McKinney, (D), Johns Hopkins, 1985, Gx
Associate Professor:
Tara M. Curtin, (D), Arizona, 2001, PeGs
David C. Kendrick, (D), Harvard, 1997, Po
Assistant Professor:
David Finkelstein, (D), Cgs

Nicholas Metz, (D), SUNY (Albany), 2011, Oa
Technician:
Barbara Halfman, On

Hofstra University
Dept of Geology, Environment, and Sustainability (B,M) (2015)
114 Hofstra University
Hempstead, NY 11549
    p. (516) 463-5564
    j.b.bennington@hofstra.edu
    http://www.hofstra.edu/Academics/Colleges/HCLAS/GEOL/
    f: https://www.facebook.com/GESatHU/
    Administrative Assistant: Lena Hiller
    Enrollment (2015): B: 19 (7)
Professor:
J Bret Bennington, (D), Virginia Tech, 1994, PeGs
Director of Sustainability Studies:
Robert Brinkmann, (D), Wisconsin, 1989, Os
Professor:
Dennis Radcliffe, (D), Queen's, 1966, Gz
Associate Professor:
Emma Christa Farmer, (D), Columbia, 2005, Ou
Assistant Professor:
Sandra J. Garren, (D), South Florida, 2014, Oi
Antonios E. Marcellos, (D), SUNY Albany, 2008, GxcGt
Adjunct Professor:
Nehru Cherukupalli, (D), Madras, 1963, Gg
Lillian Hess Tanguay, (D), CUNY, 1993, Gg
Richard Liebling, (D), Columbia, 1963, Gg
Steven C. Okulewicz, (M), CUNY (Brooklyn), 1979, Gg
Emeritus:
Charles M. Merguerian, (D), Columbia, 1985, Gc

Hudson Valley Community College
Biology, Chemistry, Physics Dept (2010)
80 Vandenburgh Ave.
Troy, NY 12180
    p. (518) 629-7453
    p.schaefer@hvcc.edu
Assistant Professor:
Ruth H. Major, (M), Syracuse, 1989, Ggh

Hunter College (CUNY)
Dept of Geography (B,M) (2014)
695 Park Avenue
Room 1006 North Building
New York, NY 10021
    p. (212) 772-5265
    imiyares@hunter.cuny.edu
    http://www.geo.hunter.cuny.edu
    Administrative Assistant: Dana G.. Reimer
    Enrollment (2006): B: 135 (30) M: 40 (8)
Chair:
Ines Miyares, (D), Arizona State, 1994, On
Professor:
Sean C. Ahearn, (D), Wisconsin, 1986, Oi
Philip Gersmehl, (D), Georgia, 1970, Oy
Charles A. Heatwole, (D), Michigan State, 1974, On
William Solecki, (D), Rutgers, 1990, Ou
Senior Scientist:
Karl H. Szekielda, (D), Marseille, 1967, Or
Associate Professor:
Jochen Albrecht, (D), Vechta (Germany), 1995, Oi
Allan Frei, (D), Rutgers, 1997, Hs
Rupal Oza, (D), Rutgers, 1999, On
Marianna Pavlovskaya, (D), Clark, 1998, Oi
Haydee Salmun, (D), Johns Hopkins, 1989, Yg
Assistant Professor:
Frank Buonaiuto, (D), SUNY (Stony Brook), 2003, On
Hongmian Gong, (D), Georgia, 1997, On
Mohamed Ibrahim, (D), Alberta, 1985, On
Wenge Ni-Meister, (D), Boston, 1997, Or
Randye L. Rutberg, (D), Columbia, 2000, Cc
Director, SPARs Lab:
Thomas Walter, (M), Miami (Ohio), 1984, On

Research Associate:
  Carol Gersmehl, (M), Georgia, 1970, Oe
Adjunct Professor:
  Jack Eichenbaum, (D), Michigan, 1972, Oy
  Anthony Grande, (M), CUNY (Baruch), 1999, On
  Edward Linky, (D), Duquesne Law, 1973, On
  Teodosia Manecan, (D), Bucharest, 1985, Gp
  Faye Melas, (D), CUNY, 1989, Gs
  Douglas Williamson, (D), CUNY, 2003, Oi
GeoScience Lab Tech:
  Amy Jeu, (M), Minnesota, 2002, Or

Lehman College (CUNY)
Earth, Environmental and Geospatial Sciences (B) (2015)
250 Bedford Park Boulevard West
Bronx, NY 10468-1589
  p. (718) 960-8660
  heather.sloan@lehman.cuny.edu
  http://www.lehman.edu/academics/eggs/
  Enrollment (2014): B: 24 (5)
Professor:
  Eric Delson, (D), Pv
  Irene S. Leung, (D), California (Berkeley), 1969, Gz
Associate Professor:
  Juliana Maantay, (D), Rutgers, Oi
Assistant Professor:
  Hari Pant, (D), Dalhousie, Cg
  Heather Sloan, (D), Paris VI, 1993, Yr
Emeritus:
  Frederick C. Shaw, (D), Harvard, 1965, Ps

Long Island University, Brooklyn Campus
Dept of Physics (2014)
1 University Plaza
Brooklyn, NY 11201-8423
  p. (718) 488-1011
  bkln-admissions@liu.edu
  http://www.liu.edu/Home/Brooklyn
Professor:
  Richard Macomber, (D), Iowa, 1963, Pg
Adjunct Professor:
  Richard A. Jackson, (D), Massachusetts, 1980, Gc
  Alan Siegelberg, (M), Brooklyn, 1977, Gg
Emeritus:
  Samuel R. Kamhi, (D), Columbia, 1963, Gz

Long Island University, C.W. Post Campus
Dept of Earth & Environmental Sciences (B,M) (2013)
720 Northern Boulevard
Brookville, NY 11548-1300
  p. (516) 299-2318
  maboorst@liu.edu
  Administrative Assistant: Beth Rondot
  Enrollment (1999): B: 1 (0)
Chair:
  Margaret F. Boorstein, (D), Columbia, 1977, Og
Associate Professor:
  Victor DiVenere, (D), Columbia, 1995, Ym
  Lillian Hess-Tanguay, (D), CUNY, 1993, Gs
  E Mark Pires, (D), Michigan State, 1998, Og
Emeritus:
  Robert S. Harrison, (D), Cambridge, 1965, Oy
  Heinrich Toots, (D), Wyoming, 1965, Pg

Monroe Community College
Geoscience Dept (A) (2016)
1000 E. Henrietta Road
Rochester, NY 14623
  p. (716) 292-2425
  drobertson@monroecc.edu
  Administrative Assistant: Judy Miller
  Enrollment (2013): A: 7 (0)
Associate Professor:
  Jessica Barone, (M), Ball State, Ge
  Michael Boester, (M), Oy

  Daniel E. Robertson, (M), Arizona State, 1986, Eg
Assistant Professor:
  Amanda Colosimo, (M), North Carolina, Gg
  Jonathan Little, (M), OylOi
  Jason Szymanski, (M), GlPe
Instructor:
  Heather Pierce, (M), Gg

Orange County Community College
Dept of Science, Engineering, and Architecture (A) (2015)
115 South Street
Middletown, NY 10940
  p. (845) 341-4570
  lawrenceobrien@sunyorange.edu
  Enrollment (2015): A: 3 (1)
Professor:
  Lawrence E. O'Brien, (M), Michigan, 1972, Gg

Pace University, New York Campus
Dept of Chemistry & Physical Sciences (2011)
1 Pace Plaza
New York, NY 10038
  p. (212) 346-1502
  mshirigarakani@pace.edu
  http://www.pace.edu/dyson/academic-departments-and-
  programs/chemistry-and-physical-sciences---nyc
  Department Secretary: Pat Calegari
Chair:
  Nigel Yartlett, (D)
Assistant Professor:
  Stephen T. Lofthouse, (M), Hunter (CUNY), 1974, Og
Adjunct Professor:
  Anatole Dolgoff, (M), Miami (Ohio), 1960, Og
  William Hansen, (M), Hunter, 1991, Oa
  John Marchisin, (M), Rutgers, 1965, Og
  Nathan Reiss, (D), New York, 1973, Oa

Paleontological Research Institution
Paleontological Research Instituion (2014)
1259 Trumansburg Road
Ithaca, NY 14850
  p. (607) 273-6623
  allmon@museumoftheearth.org
  http://www.priweb.org
Director:
  Warren D. Allmon, (D), Harvard, 1988, Po
Education Director:
  Robert M. Ross, (D), Harvard, 1990, Po

Plattsburgh State University (SUNY)
Center for Earth & Environmental Science (B) (2011)
101 Broad Street
102 Hudson Hall
Plattsburgh, NY 12901
  p. (518) 564-2028
  cees@plattsburgh.edu
  http://www.plattsburgh.edu/cees
  Enrollment (2006): B: 58 (0)
Chair:
  Robert Fuller
Distinguished Service Professor:
  James C. Dawson, (D), Wisconsin, 1970, Ge
Professor:
  Donald D. Adams, (D), Dalhousie, 1973, Cl
  Donald J. Bogucki, (D), Tennessee, 1970, Or
  David A. Franzi, (D), Syracuse, 1984, Gl
  Thomas H. Wolosz, (D), SUNY (Stony Brook), 1984, Pe
Assistant Professor:
  Edwin A. Romanowicz, (D), Syracuse, 1993, Hw
Adjunct Professor:
  Carol Treadwell-Steitz, (D), New Mexico, 1996, Gg

Queens College (CUNY)
School of Earth & Environmental Sciences (B,M,D) (2014)
65-30 Kissena Boulevard

Flushing, NY 11367
    p. (718) 997-3300
    george.hendrey@qc.cuny.edu
    http://www.qc.edu/EES
    Administrative Assistant: Gladys Sapigao
    Enrollment (2012): B: 150 (19) M: 19 (6) D: 11 (2)
Distinguished Professor, Director & Chair:
    George Hendrey, (D), Washington, 1973, Og
Professor:
    Nicholas K. Coch, (D), Yale, 1965, Gs
    N. Gary Hemming, (D), Stony Brook, 1993, CaOcGg
    Allan Ludman, (D), Pennsylvania, 1969, Gg
    Steven Markowitz, (D), Columbia Coll, 1981, GbOn
    Cecilia McHugh, (D), Columbia, 1993, Ou
    Alfredo Morabia, (D), Johns Hopkins, 1989, GbOn
    Yan Zheng, (D), Columbia, 1998, CgHwCm
Associate Professor:
    Jeffrey Bird, (D), California (Davis), 2001, Sbc
    Stephen Pekar, (D), Rutgers, 1999, PeGrOu
    Gillian Stewart, (D), Stony Brook, 2005, OgcCm
Assistant Professor:
    Timothy Eaton, (D), Wisconsin, 2002, HgwGg
    Gregory O'Mullan, (D), Princeton, 2005, PyOb
    Ashaki Rouff, (D), Stony Brook, 2004, Cac
    Chuixiang Yi, (D), Nanjing, 1991, Oaw
Emeritus:
    Eugene A. Alexandrov, (D), Columbia, 1959, Eg
    Patrick W. G. Brock, (D), Leeds, 1963, Gg
    Hannes K. Brueckner, (D), Yale, 1968, Cg
    Robert M. Finks, (D), Columbia, 1959, Pi
    Daniel Habib, (D), Penn State, 1965, Pl
    Peter H. Mattson, (D), Princeton, 1957, Gc
    Andrew McIntyre, (D), Columbia, 1967, Pe
    B. Charlotte Schreiber, (D), Rensselaer, 1974, Gd
    David H. Speidel, (D), Penn State, 1964, Cg
    David L. Thurber, (D), Columbia, 1964, Cl

Queensborough Community College
Dept of Biological Sciences and Geology (1999)
222-05 56th Avenue
Bayside, NY 11364
    p. (718) 631-6335
    MGorelick@qcc.cuny.edu
    http://www.qcc.cuny.edu/biologicalsciences/advisors.asp

Rensselaer Polytechnic Institute 🗇
Dept of Earth & Environmental Sciences (B,M,D) (2015)
Science Center 1W19
110 8th Street
Troy, NY 12180-3590
    p. (518) 276-6474
    ees@rpi.edu
    http://www.rpi.edu/dept/ees/
    Enrollment (2015): B: 30 (8) M: 2 (4) D: 13 (3)
Head:
    Frank S. Spear, (D), California (Los Angeles), 1976, GpCpGc
Professor:
    Peter A. Fox, (D), Monash, 1985, Oni
    Steven W. Roecker, (D), MIT, 1981, Yg
    E. Bruce Watson, (D), MIT, 1976, Cp
Associate Professor:
    Richard F. Bopp, (D), Columbia, 1979, Co
    Miriam E. Katz, (D), Rutgers, 2001, Pme
Assistant Professor:
    Karyn L. Rogers, (D), Washington Univ, 2006, PyCl
    Morgan F. Schaller, (D), Rutgers, 2011, CsPe
Research Associate Professor:
    Daniele J. Cherniak, (D), SUNY (Albany), 1990, Gx
Research Associate:
    Nichlos D. Tailby, (D), Australian National, 2010, Cpt
Emeritus:
    M. Brian Bayly, (D), Chicago, 1962, Gc
    Samuel Katz, (D), Columbia, 1955, Yg
    Robert G. La Fleur, (D), Rensselaer, 1961, Hw
    Donald S. Miller, (D), Columbia, 1960, Cc

Laboratory Director:
    Jared W. Singer, (D), Alfred, 2013, Ca

Skidmore College
Dept of Geosciences (B) (2015)
815 North Broadway
Saratoga Springs, NY 12866
    p. (518) 580-5190
    knichols@skidmore.edu
    http://www.skidmore.edu/academics/geo/
    Enrollment (2015): B: 15 (11)
Associate Professor:
    Amy Frappier, (D), New Hampshire, 2006, GePe
    Richard H. Lindemann, (D), Rensselaer, 1980, Pi
    Kyle K. Nichols, (D), Vermont, 2002, Gm
Assistant Professor:
    Greg Gerbi, (D), MIT/WHOI, OgYg
Instructor:
    Jennifer Cholnoky, (M), Rensselaer, 2013, Gg
Visiting Assistant Professor:
    Margaret Estapa, (D), Maine, 2011, Oc

St. Lawrence University
Dept of Geology (B) (2014)
Brown Hall
Canton, NY 13617-1475
    p. (315) 229-5851
    skelly@stlawu.edu
    http://www.stlawu.edu/academics/programs/geology
    f: https://www.facebook.com/SLUGeology
    Administrative Assistant: Sherrie Kelly
    Enrollment (2014): B: 46 (50)
Professor:
    Jeffrey R. Chiarenzelli, (D), Kansas, 1989, GzCg
Chair:
    Antun Husinec, (D), Zagreb, 2002, GsCsGo
Assistant Professor:
    Judith Nagel-Myers, (D), Muenster, 2006, PisPe
    Alexander K. Stewart, (D), Cincinnati, 2007, GlmHw
Research Associate:
    George W. Robinson, (D), Queens, 1978, Gz
Visiting Professor:
    Jennifer N. Gifford, (D), Florida, 2013, GtCcGp
Emeritus:
    J. Mark Erickson, (D), North Dakota, 1971, Poi
Technician:
    Matt VanBrocklin, (M), On

State University of New York at Oswego
Dept of Atmospheric and Geological Sciences (B) O (2015)
394 Shineman Science Center
Oswego, NY 13126
    p. (315) 312-3065
    christine.dallas@oswego.edu
    http://www.oswego.edu/ags
    Enrollment (2015): B: 160 (25)
Professor:
    Alfred J. Stamm, (D), Wisconsin, 1976, Ow
    Paul B. Tomascak, (D), Maryland, 1995, CgGzi
    David W. Valentino, (D), Virginia Tech, 1993, GtcGp
Associate Professor:
    Diana Boyer, (D), California (Riverside), 2007, Pi
    Scott Steiger, (D), Texas A&M, 2005, Ow
Assistant Professor:
    J Graham Bradley, (D), College (London), 2012, GeHwNg
    Rachel J. Lee, (D), Pittsburgh, 2013, GvOr
    Steven T. Skubis, (D), SUNY (Albany), 1994, Ow
    Michael Veres, (D), Nebraska Lincoln, 2014, Oa
Cooperating Faculty:
    Chris Hebblethwaite, On

Suffolk County Community College, Ammerman Campus
Dept of Physical Science (A) (2015)
533 College Road

Selden, NY 11784
p. (631) 451-4338
butkosd@sunysuffolk.edu
http://depthome.sunysuffolk.edu/Selden/PhysicalScience/
Enrollment (2015): A: 12 (8)

Professor:
Darryl J. Butkos, (M), Gg
Michael Inglis, (D), Og
Scott Mandia, (M), Penn State, 1990, Ow
Associate Professor:
Matthew Pappas, Og
Assistant Professor:
Sean Tvelia, (M), SUNY (Stony Brook), Gg
Adjunct Professor:
Jessica Dutton, Og
Michael Flanagan, Og
Philip Harrington, Og
Margaret Lomaga, Og
Brian Vorwald, Og

Sullivan County Community College
Mathematics and Natural Sciences (1999)
112 College Road
Lock Sheldrake, NY 12759
dlewkiewicz@sunysullivan.edu

SUNY Potsdam
Dept of Geology (B) (2015)
220 Timerman Hall
44 Pierrepont Avenue
Potsdam, NY 13676
p. (315) 267-2286
rygelmc@potsdam.edu
http://www.potsdam.edu/academics/AAS/Geology/
Administrative Assistant: Roberta Greene
Enrollment (2015): B: 72 (9)

Chair:
Michael C. Rygel, (D), Dalhousie, 2005, GsrGo
Associate Professor:
Christopher R. Kelson, (D), Georgia, 2006, EmGz
Assistant Professor:
Dylan J. Blumentritt, (D), Minnesota, 2013, HsGml
Emeritus:
Robert L. Badger, (D), Virginia Tech, 1989, Gip
James D. Carl, (D), Illinois, 1962, Gz
William T. Kirchgasser, (D), Cornell, 1967, Ps
Neal R. O'Brien, (D), Illinois, 1963, Gs
Frank A. Revetta, (D), Rochester, 1970, Yg

SUNY, Albany
Dept of Atmospheric and Environmental Sciences (B,M,D)
(2014)
1400 Washington Avenue
Albany, NY 12222
p. (518) 442-4466
chair@atmos.albany.edu
http://www.atmos.albany.edu
Enrollment (2004): B: 81 (27) M: 8 (5) D: 6 (4)

Chair:
Vincent P. Idone, (D), SUNY (Albany), 1982, Oa
Professor:
Lance F. Bosart, (D), MIT, 1969, Oa
Daniel Keyser, (D), Penn State, 1981, Oa
John E. Molinari, (D), Florida State, 1979, Oa
Senior Research Professor:
David R. Fitzjarrald, (D), Virginia, 1980, Oa
Richard R. Perez, (D), SUNY (Albany), 1983, Oa
James J. Schwab, (D), Harvard, 1983, Oa
Christopher J. Walcek, (D), California (Los Angeles), 1983, Oa
Wei-Chyung Wang, (D), Columbia, 1973, Oa
Associate Professor:
Robert G. Keesee, (D), Colorado, 1979, Oa
Christopher D. Thorncroft, (D), Reading, 1988, Oa
Research Associate:
Stephen S. Howe, (M), Penn State, 1981, Cs
David Knight, (D), Washington, 1987, Oa

SUNY, Buffalo
Dept of Geology (B,M,D) O (2015)
126 Cooke Hall
Buffalo, NY 14260
p. (716) 645-3489
geology@buffalo.edu
http://www.geology.buffalo.edu
t: @UBGeology
Administrative Assistant: Alison A. Lagowski
Enrollment (2014): B: 76 (38) M: 39 (13) D: 14 (4)

Chair:
Marcus I. Bursik, (D), Caltech, 1988, Gv
SUNY Distinguished Teaching Professor:
Charles E. Mitchell, (D), Harvard, 1983, Po
Director of Graduate Studies:
Gregory Valentine, (D), Santa Barbara, 1988, Gv
Professor:
Richelle Allen-King, (D), Waterloo, 1991, Cg
Mary Alice Coffroth, (D), Miami, 1988, Gu
Rossman F. Giese, (D), Columbia, 1962, Gz
Robert D. Jacobi, (D), Columbia, 1979, Gr
Howard R. Lasker, (D), Chicago, 1978, Gu
Associate Professor:
Jason P. Briner, (D), Colorado, 2003, Gl
Beata Csatho, (D), Miskolc (Hungary), 1993, YgOr
Tracy K. P. Gregg, (D), Arizona State, 1995, Gv
Research Assistant Professor:
Gerald J. Smith, (D), SUNY (Buffalo), 1997, Gs
Assistant Professor:
Estelle Chaussard, (D), Miami, 2013, GvOr
Christopher S. Lowry, (D), Wisconsin, 2008, Hw
Erasmus K. Oware, (D), Clemson, 2014, YgHq
Elizabeth K. Thomas, (D), Brown, 2014, Cos
Research Associate:
Anton Schenk, (D), Switzerland, 1972, Or
Adjunct Professor:
Gordon C. Baird, (D), Rochester, 1975, Pg
Gary S. Lash, (D), Lehigh, 1980, Gc
Carel J. van Oss, (D), Paris, 1955, Gy
Emeritus:
Parker Calkin, (D), Ohio, 1963, Gl
Michael F. Sheridan, (D), Stanford, 1965, Gv

SUNY, Cortland
Geology Dept (B,M) (2011)
342 Bowers Hall
PO Box 2000
Cortland, NY 13045
p. (607) 753-2815
GeologyDept@cortland.edu
http://www.cortland.edu/geology/
Administrative Assistant: Susan K. Nevins
Enrollment (2007): B: 48 (15) M: 8 (6)

Chair:
Robert S. Darling, (D), Syracuse, 1992, Gx
Professor:
Christopher P. Cirmo, (D), Syracuse, 1994, Hg
Associate Professor:
David J. Barclay, (D), SUNY (Buffalo), 1998, Gl
Christopher A. McRoberts, (D), Syracuse, 1994, Pg
Assistant Professor:
Gayle C. Gleason, (D), Brown, 1993, Gc
Lecturer:
Julie L. Barclay, (M), SUNY (Buffalo), 1998, Gg
Laboratory Director:
John R. Driscoll, (A), Northwest Electronic, 1974, On

SUNY, Fredonia
Dept of Geosciences (B) (2015)
280 Central Avenue
Fredonia, NY 14063-1020
p. (716) 673-3303
baird@fredonia.edu
http://www.fredonia.edu/department/geosciences
Enrollment (2015): B: 51 (4)

Chair:
  Gordon C. Baird, (D), Rochester, 1975, Ps
Professor:
  Gary G. Lash, (D), Lehigh, 1980, Gr
Associate Professor:
  Ann K. Deakin, (D), SUNY (Buffalo), 1996, OyiGg
Instructor:
  Kimberly Weborg-Benson, (M), Illinois, 1991, GgOaPy
Visiting lecturer:
  Xu Chu, (D), Yale, 2015, Giz
Adjunct Instrustor:
  Randy J. Woodbury, (M), SUNY (Fredonia), 1992, GeOuGl
Adjunct Professor:
  Randall H. Perry, (M), Maine, 2009, Gme

SUNY, Geneseo
Dept of Geological Sciences (B) (2015)
1 College Circle
ISC 235
Geneseo, NY 14454
  p. (585) 245-5291
  lounsbur@geneseo.edu
  http://www.geneseo.edu/geology
  Administrative Assistant: Diane E. Lounsbury
  Enrollment (2015): B: 130 (27)

Professor:
  Scott D. Giorgis, (D), Wisconsin, 2003, Gc
  D. Jeffrey Over, (D), Texas Tech, 1990, Ps
Chair:
  Benjamin J.C. Laabs, (D), Wisconsin, 2004, GmlGe
Associate Professor:
  Dori J. Farthing, (D), Johns Hopkins, 2001, Gz
  Amy L. Sheldon, (D), Utah, 2002, Hw
Assistant Professor:
  Nicholas H. Warner, (D), Arizona State, 2008, XgGrHg
Emeritus:
  Phillip D. Boger, (D), Ohio State, 1976, Cg
  William J. Brennan, (D), Colorado, 1968, Gc
  Richard B. Hatheway, (D), Cornell, 1969, Gx
  James W. Scatterday, (D), Ohio State, 1963, Po
  Richard A. Young, (D), Washington (St. Louis), 1966, Gm

SUNY, Maritime College
Science Dept (B) (2010)
6 Pennyfield Avenue
Bronx, NY 10465
  p. (718) 409-7380
  mdeangelis@sunymaritime.edu
  Enrollment (2009): B: 68 (22)

Chair:
  Kathy Olszewski, (D), SUNY (Stony Brook), 1994, Cg
Associate Professor:
  Marie deAngelis, (D), Washington, 1989, Oc
Assistant Professor:
  Anthony Manzi, (M), Montclair State, Ow

SUNY, New Paltz
Geology (B) (2016)
1 Hawk Drive
New Paltz, NY 12561
  p. (845) 257-3760
  vollmerf@newpaltz.edu
  http://www.newpaltz.edu/geology/
  Enrollment (2010): B: 98 (12)

Chair:
  Frederick W. Vollmer, (D), Minnesota, 1985, GctGx
Associate Professor:
  Alexander J. Bartholomew, (D), Cincinnati, 2006, GrPi
  Shafiul H. Chowdhury, (D), W Michigan, 1999, Hw
  Alvin S. Konigsberg, (D), Syracuse, 1969, Oa
  John A. Rayburn, (D), Binghamton, 2004, Gml
Assistant Professor:
  Gordana Garapić, (D), Boston, 2013, Gz
Lecturer:
  Kaustubh Patwardhan, (D), Johns Hopkins, 2009, Ggi

Adjunct Professor:
  Laurel Mutti, (M), Johns Hopkins, 2004, Gg
Emeritus:
  Gilbert J. Brenner, (D), Penn State, 1962, Pl
  Constantine Manos, (D), Illinois, 1963, Gs
  Martin S. Rutstein, (D), Brown, 1969, Gz
Related Staff:
  Donald R. Hodder, (B), SUNY (Geneseo), 1985, Gg

SUNY, Oneonta
Dept of Earth and Atmospheric Sciences (B,M) (2013)
Ravine Parkway
209 Sci. #1
Oneonta, NY 13820-4015
  p. (607) 436-3707
  James.Ebert@oneonta.edu
  http://www.oneonta.edu/academics/earths
  Enrollment (2012): B: 114 (39) M: 1 (1)
Distinguished Teaching Professor:
  James R. Ebert, (D), SUNY (Binghamton), 1984, GrsGd
Professor:
  Jerome B. Blechman, (D), Wisconsin, 1979, Oa
Associate Professor:
  Devin Castendyk, (D), Auckland, 2004, HwCl
Assistant Professor:
  Keith Brunstad, (M), GizEg
  Todd D. Ellis, (D), Colorate State, 2008, Oag
  Leigh M. Fall, (D), Texas A&M, 2010, Pgq
  Melissa Godek, (D), OwaOg
  Martha L. Growdon, (D), Indiana, 2010, Gcp
  Leslie E. Hasbargen, (D), Minnesota, 2003, GmSp
Emeritus:
  P. Jay Fleisher, (D), Washington State, 1967, Gl
  Arthur N. Palmer, (D), Indiana, 1969, Hg

SUNY, Purchase
Environmental Studies Program (B) (2015)
735 Anderson Hill Road
Purchase, NY 10577
  p. (914) 251-6646
  naturalsciences@purchase.edu
  http://www.purchase.edu/Departments/AcademicPrograms/
  las/sciences/EnvStudies/
  Enrollment (2014): B: 70 (0)
Professor:
  George P. Kraemer, (D), California (Los Angeles), 1989, Ob
Board of Study Coordinator:
  Ryan W. Taylor, (D), Oregon State, 2006, OiyOg
Emeritus:
  James M. Utter, (D), Rutgers, 1971, On

SUNY, Stony Brook
Dept of Geosciences (B,M,D) (2014)
Nicolls Road
Stony Brook, NY 11794-2100
  p. (631) 632-8200
  daniel.davis@stonybrook.edu
  http://www.geosciences.stonybrook.edu
  Enrollment (2005): B: 70 (15) M: 3 (4) D: 41 (3)
Professor:
  Daniel M. Davis, (D), MIT, 1983, Yg
  Gilbert N. Hanson, (D), Minnesota, 1964, Cc
  William E. Holt, (D), Arizona, 1989, Ys
  Robert C. Lieberman, (D), Columbia, 1969, Gy
  Scott M. McLennan, (D), Australian National, 1981, Cg
  Hanna Nekvasil, (D), Penn State, 1986, Cp
  Artem Oganov, (D), Univ Coll (London), 2002, Gz
  John B. Parise, (D), James Cook, 1980, Gz
  Richard J. Reeder, (D), California (Berkeley), 1980, ClGz
  Martin A. Schoonen, (D), Penn State, 1989, Cl
  Donald J. Weidner, (D), MIT, 1972, Gy
  Lianxing Wen, (D), Caltech, 1998, Ys
  Teng-fong Wong, (D), MIT, 1981, Yx
Associate Professor:
  Brian L. Phillips, (D), Illinois, 1990, Gz
  E. Troy Rasbury, (D), SUNY (Stony Brook), 1998, Cc

107

Assistant Professor:
  Timothy Glotch, (D), Arizona State, 2004, XgGz
  Michael Sperazza, (D), Montana, 2006, On
Curator:
  Stephen C. Englebright, (M), SUNY (Stony Brook), 1975, Oe
Lecturer:
  Christiane W. Stidham, (D), California (Berkeley), 1999, Yg
Adjunct Professor:
  Robert C. Aller, (D), Yale, 1977, Cm
  Henry J. Bokuniewicz, (D), Yale, 1976, Yr
  J. Kirk Cochran, (D), Yale, 1979, Oc
  Roger D. Flood, (D), MIT, 1978, Gu
  David W. Krause, (D), Michigan, 1982, Pv
  Baosheng Li, (D), SUNY (Stony Brook), 1996, Gy
  Maureen O'Leary, (D), Johns Hopkins, 1997, Pv
  Michael T. Vaughan, (D), SUNY (Stony Brook), 1979, Yx
Emeritus:
  Garman Harbottle, (D), Columbia, 1949, Cc
  Donald H. Lindsley, (D), Johns Hopkins, 1961, Cp
Laboratory Director:
  Owen C. Evans, (D), SUNY (Stony Brook), 1994, Cg

School of Marine and Atmospheric Sciences (B,M,D) (2015)
145 Endeavour Hall
Stony Brook, NY 11794-5000
  p. (516) 632-8700
  minghua.zhang@stonybrook.edu
  http://www.somas.stonybrook.edu
  Enrollment: No data reported since 1999
Professor:
  Josephine Y. Aller, (D), S California, 1975, Ob
  Edmund K. M. Chang, (D), Princeton, 1993, Oa
  J. Kirk Cochran, (D), Yale, 1979, Oc
  Brian Colle, (D), Washington, 1997, Oa
  David O. Conover, (D), Massachusetts, 1981, Ob
  Roger D. Flood, (D), MIT/WHOI, 1978, Ou
  Marvin A. Geller, (D), MIT, 1969, Oa
  Christopher Gobler, (D), SUNY (Stony Brook), 1999, Ob
  Sultan Hameed, (D), Manchester, 1968, Oa
  Darcy J. Lonsdale, (D), Maryland, 1979, Ob
  Glenn R. Lopez, (D), SUNY (Stony Brook), 1976, Ob
  Anne McElroy, (D), MIT/WHOI, 1985, Oc
  Ellen K. Pikitch, Indiana, 1983, Ob
  Mary I. Scranton, (D), MIT/WHOI, 1977, Oc
  R. Lawrence Swanson, (D), Oregon State, 1971, Og
  Gordon T. Taylor, (D), S California, 1983, Ob
  Minghua Zhang, (D), Inst of Atm Physics, 1987, Oa
Associate Professor:
  Bassem Allam, (D), W Brittany (France), 1998, Ob
  Robert A. Armstrong, (D), Minnesota, 1975, Ocb
  David Black, (D), Ou
  Bruce J. Brownawell, (D), MIT/WHOI, 1986, Oc
  Robert M. Cerrato, (D), Yale, 1980, Ob
  Jackie Collier, (D), Stanford, 1994, Ob
  Michael Frisk, (D), Maryland, 2004
  Marat Khairoutdinov, (D), Oklahoma, 1997, Oa
  Daniel A. Knopf, (D), Swiss Fed Inst Tech, 2003, Oa
  Kamazima M. Lwiza, (D), Wales, 1991, Oc
  John E. Mak, (D), California (San Diego), 1992, Oa
  Bradley Peterson, (D), S Alabama, 1998, Ob
  Joseph Warren, (D), MIT, 2001, Ob
  Robert E. Wilson, (D), Johns Hopkins, 1973, Op
Assistant Science Director, IOCS:
  Demian Chapman, (D), Nova Southeastern, 2007
Assistant Professor:
  Anthony Dvarskas, (D), Maryland (College Park), 2007
  Hyemi Kim, (D), Seoul Nat, 2008
  Janet Nye, (D), Maryland, 2008
  Christopher Wolfe, (D), Oregon State, 2006, Op
  Qingzhi Zhu, (D), Xiamen, 1997, Oc
Faculty Director Semester By The Sea:
  Kurt Bretsch, (D), South Carolina, 2005
Lecturer:
  Lesley Thorne, (D), Duke, 2010
Research Scientist:
  Wuyin Lin, (D), Stony Brook, 2002, Oa

Research Professor:
  Charles Flagg, (D), MIT, 1977, Op
Engineer:
  Douglas Hill, (D), Columbia, 1977
Ecologist, Author:
  Carl Safina, (D), Rutgers, 1987
Director Riverhead Foundation:
  Robert A. DiGiovanni, Jr., (M), Stony Brook, 2002
Adjunct Professor:
  James Ammerman, (D), Scripps, 1983
  Hannes Baumann, (D), Hamburg, 2006
  Howard Bluestein, MIT, 1976, Oa
  Paul Bowser, (D), Auburn, 1978
  Carl Brenninkmeijer, (D), Groningen, 1983
  Michael J. Cahill, (D), DePaul, 1978
  Andre Y. Chistoserdov, (D), Inst of Genetics & Selection (USSR), 1985
  Alistair Dove, Queensland, 1999
  Anga Engel, Oc
  Emmanuelle pales Espinosa, (D), Nante (France), 1999
  Mark Fast, (D), Dalhousie, 2005, Ob
  Scott Ferson, (D), Stony Brook, 1988
  Scott Fowler, (D), 1969
  Roxanne Karimi, (D), Dartmouth, 2007
  Kathryn Kavanagh, (D), James Cook, 1998
  Yangang Liu, (D), Nevada (Reno), 1998
  Stephan Munch, (D), Stony Brook, 2002, Ob
  John Rapaglia, (D), Stony Brook, 2007
  Frank J. Roethel, (D), SUNY (Stony Brook), 1981, Oc
  Jeffrey Tongue, Oa
  Andrew Vogelmann, (D), Penn State, 1994, Oa
  Duane E. Waliser, (D), Oa
  Douglas W. R. Wallace, (D), Dalhousie, 1985, Oc
  Jian Wang, (D), Caltech, 2002, Oa
Emeritus:
  Dong-Ping Wang, (D), Miami, 1975
Affiliated and Joint Faculty:
  Heather L. Lynch, (D), Harvard, 2006
Cooperating Faculty:
  Resit Akcakaya, (D), Stony Brook, 1989
  Stephen Baines, (D), Yale, 1993
  Lee K. Koppelman, (D), New York, 1968, On
  Jeffrey Levinton, (D), Yale, 1971, Ob
  Diana Padilla, (D), Alberta, 1987
  Sheldon Reaven, (D), California (Berkeley), 1975, On

SUNY, The College at Brockport
Dept of the Earth Sciences (B) (2014)
350 New Campus Drive
Brockport, NY 14420-2936
  p. (585) 395-2636
  earthsci@esc.brockport.edu
  http://www.brockport.edu/esc
  Enrollment (2012): B: 117 (16)
Associate Professor:
  James A. Zollweg, (D), Cornell, 1994, Hs
Professor:
  Whitney J. Autin, (D), Louisiana State, 1989, Gs
  Judy A. Massare, (D), Johns Hopkins, 1983, Pv
  Mark R. Noll, (D), Delaware, 1989, Cl
Associate Professor:
  Paul L. Richards, (D), Penn State, 1999, Hg
  Scott M. Rochette, (D), St. Louis, 1998, Ow
Adjunct Professor:
  David A. Boehm, (M), SUNY (Buffalo), 2003, Gg
  Christine Crafts, (B), SUNY (Brockport), 2000, Ow
  Jutta S. Dudley, (D), SUNY (Buffalo), 1998, Gg
  William G. Glynn, (M), Texas A&M, 1984, Gg
  Linda J. Schaffer, (M), SUNY (Brockport), 1988, Oe
Department Secretary:
  Lauri A. Kifer, (A), Monroe Comm Coll, 1997, On
Emeritus:
  Robert W. Adams, (D), Johns Hopkins, 1964, Gs
  John E. Hubbard, (D), Colorado State, 1968, Hg
  Richard M. Liebe, (D), Iowa, 1962, Ps
  John M. Williams, (B), Goshen, Oa

On Leave:
    Robert S. Weinbeck, (D), Iowa State, 1980, Oa
Systems Administrator:
    Thomas M. McDermott, On

SUNY, Ulster County Community College
STEM (A) (2015)
Burroughs 105
491 Cottekill Road
Stone Ridge, NY 12484
    p. (845) 687-5230
    schimmrs@sunyulster.edu
    http://people.sunyulster.edu/esc
    Enrollment: No data reported since 1999
Professor:
    Steven Schimmrich, (M), SUNY (Albany), 1991, Og
Assistant Professor:
    Karen Helgers, (M), SUNY (New Paltz), 1983, Og

Syracuse University
Dept of Earth Sciences (B,M,D) (2015)
204 Heroy Geology Laboratory
Syracuse, NY 13244-1070
    p. (315) 443-2672
    jofitch@syr.edu
    http://earthsciences.syr.edu
    Enrollment (2014): B: 54 (11) M: 13 (4) D: 16 (4)
Chair:
    Donald I. Siegel, (D), Minnesota, 1981, Hw
Professor:
    Suzanne L. Baldwin, (D), SUNY (Albany), 1988, Cc
    Paul G. Fitzgerald, (D), Melbourne, 1988, Gt
    Linda C. Ivany, (D), Harvard, 1997, Pe
    Jeffrey Karson, (D), SUNY (Albany), 1977, GtcGv
    Cathryn R. Newton, (D), California (Santa Cruz), 1983, Po
    Scott D. Samson, (D), Arizona, 1990, Cc
    Christopher A. Scholz, (D), Duke, 1989, Gs
Associate Professor:
    Laura Lautz, (D), Syracuse, 2005, Hg
Assistant Professor:
    Gregory Hoke, (D), Cornell, 2006
    Christopher Junium, (D), Penn State, 2010, CsPeCo
    Zunli Lu, (D), Rochester, 2008, Cg
    Robert Moucha, (D), Toronto, 2003, GtYeg
    Jay Thomas, (D), Virginia Tech, 2003, Gi
Instructor:
    Daniel Curewitz, (D), Duke, 1999, OgGct
Emeritus:
    M. E. Bickford, (D), Illinois, 1960, Cc
    James C. Brower, (D), Wisconsin, 1964, Po
Other:
    Bruce Wilkinson, (D), Texas, 1974, Gs

Union College
Geology Dept (B) (2015)
807 Union Street
Schenectady, NY 12308-3107
    p. (518) 388-6770
    geology@union.edu
    http://www.union.edu/academic_depts/geology/
    Administrative Assistant: Deborah A. Klein
    Enrollment (2015): B: 40 (15)
Chair:
    Donald T. Rodbell, (D), Colorado, 1991, GlmGe
Professor:
    John I. Garver, (D), Washington, 1989, GtCcGr
    Kurt T. Hollocher, (D), Massachusetts, 1985, GxCga
Associate Professor:
    Holli M. Frey, (D), Michigan, 2005, GvCag
    David P. Gillikin, (D), Vrije Univ (Brussel), 2005, Csm
Lecturer:
    Matthew R. Manon, (D), Michigan, 2008, Gp
    Anouk Verheyden-Gillikin, (D), Vrije Univ (Brussel), 2004
Emeritus:
    George H. Shaw, (D), Washington, 1971, Yx

Related Staff:
    William S. Neubeck, (M), SUNY (Binghamton), 1980, Gm

United States Military Academy
Dept of Geography & Environmental Engineering (B) (2014)
West Point, NY 10996
    p. (914) 938-2300
    Wiley.Thompson@usma.edu
    http://www.usma.edu/gene/SitePages/Home.aspx
    Department Secretary: Jean Keller
    Enrollment (2010): B: 342 (112)
Professor:
    John A. Brockhaus, (D), Idaho, 1987, Yd
    Marie C. Johnson, (D), Brown, 1990, Gi
    Jon C. Malinowski, (D), North Carolina, 1995, On
Department Chair:
    Wiley C. Thompson, (D), Oregon State, 2008, Oy

University of Rochester
Dept of Earth & Environmental Sciences (B,M,D) (2010)
227 Hutchison Hall
RC Box 270221
Rochester, NY 14627-0221
    p. (585) 275-5713
    ees@earth.rochester.edu
    http://www.earth.rochester.edu
    Administrative Assistant: Marjorie Goodison
    Enrollment: No data reported since 1999
Chair:
    Udo Fehn, (D), Munich, 1973, Eg
Professor:
    Asish R. Basu, (D), California (Davis), 1975, Gx
    Cynthia J. Ebinger, (D), MIT/WHOI, 1988, Gt
    Gautam Mitra, (D), Johns Hopkins, 1977, Gc
    Robert J. Poreda, (D), California (San Diego), 1983, Cg
    John A. Tarduno, (D), Stanford, 1987, Ym
Associate Professor:
    Carmala N. Garzione, (D), Arizona, 2000, Gs
Associate Scientist:
    Rory D. Cottrell, (D), Rochester, 2000, Ym
    Pennilyn Higgins, (D), Wyoming, 2000, Cs
Emeritus:
    Lawrence W. Lundgren, (D), Yale, 1958, Ge

Utica College
Dept of Geology (B) (2015)
Gordon Science Center
1600 Burrstone Road
Utica, NY 13502
    p. (315) 792-3134
    skanfoush@utica.edu
    https://www.utica.edu/academic/as/geoscience/new/bachelors.
    cfm
    Enrollment (2015): B: 10 (6)
Chair:
    Adam Schoonmaker, (D), SUNY (Albany), 2005, GczGx
Associate Professor:
    Sharon L. Kanfoush, (D), Florida, 2002, GsOuGn
Adjunct Professor:
    Lindsey Geary, (M), Florida State, 2008, Geg
    Tiffany McGivern, (M), Utica College, 2014, Geg
Emeritus:
    Herman Muskatt, (D), Syracuse, 1963, GgrPg

Vassar College
Dept of Earth Science & Geography (B) (2015)
Box 735
124 Raymond Avenue
Poughkeepsie, NY 12604-0735
    p. (845) 437-5540
    geo@vassar.edu
    http://earthscienceandgeography.vassar.edu/
    Administrative Assistant: Lois Horst
    Enrollment (2015): B: 12 (3)

Chair:
   Mary A. Cunningham, (D), Minnesota, 2001, OiyOu
Professor:
   Brian J. Godfrey, (D), California (Berkeley), 1984, Ou
   Kirsten M. Menking, (D), California (Santa Cruz), 1995, GmPeGc
   Joseph Nevins, (D), California (Los Angeles), Ou
   Jill S. Schneiderman, (D), Harvard, 1987, Gs
   Jeffrey R. Walker, (D), Dartmouth, 1987, GzvGp
   Yu Zhou, (D), Minnesota, 1995, Oun
Lab Technician and Collections Manager:
   Richard Jones, (M), California (Santa Cruz), 1996
GIS specialist:
   Neil Curri, (B), Oi

York College (CUNY)

Dept of Earth and Physical Sciences (B) ○ (2015)
94-20 Guy R. Brewer Blvd
Jamaica, NY 11451
   p. (718)262- 2654
   nkhandaker@york.cuny.edu
   http://www.york.cuny.edu/academics/departments/earth-and-physical-sciences/
   Enrollment (2015): B: 21 (5)
Geology Discipline Coordinator & CUNY Doctoral Faculty in Earth and Environmental Sciences:
   Nazrul I. Khandaker, (D), Iowa State, 1991, GdeOe
Chair:
   Timothy Paglione, (D), Boston, Xm
Professor:
   Stanley Schleifer, (D), CUNY, 1996, Ge
Associate Professor:
   Ratan K. Dhar, (D), CUNY Graduate Center, 2006, Hw
Emeritus:
   Stephen Lakatos, (D), Rensselaer, 1971, Cc
   Arthur P. Loring, (D), New York, 1966, Gm

North Carolina

Appalachian State University

Dept of Geography & Planning (B,M) (2014)
323 Rankin Science West
ASU Box 32066
Boone, NC 28608-2066
   p. (828) 262-3000
   youngje@appstate.edu
   http://www.geo.appstate.edu
   Enrollment (2001): B: 82 (46) M: 15 (7)
Chair:
   James E. Young, (D), Minnesota, 1994, Oe
Professor:
   Michael W. Mayfield, (D), Tennessee, 1984, Hs
   Peter T. Soule, (D), Georgia, 1989, Oa
   Roger A. Winsor, (D), Illinois, 1975, On
Associate Professor:
   Jeff Colby, (D), Colorado, 1995, Oi
   Richard J. Crepeau, (D), California (Irvine), 1995, On
   Kathleen Schroeder, (D), Minnesota, 1995, On
Assistant Professor:
   Chris Badurek, (D), Buffalo, 2005, Oi
   Rob Brown, (D), Louisiana State, 2001, On
   Jana Carp, (D), Illinois (Chicago), 1999, On
   Gabrielle Katz, (D), Colorado, 2001, Hg
   Baker Perry, (D), North Carolina, 2006, Og
Instructor:
   Arthur B. Rex, (M), Appalachian State, 1980, Oi
Lecturer:
   Terence Milstead, (D), Florida State, 2008, On
   Saskia van de Gevel, (D), Tennessee, 2008, Og
Emeritus:
   Neal G. Lineback, (D), Tennessee, 1970, Oy

Dept of Geology (B) (2014)
PO Box 32067
033 Rankin Science West
Boone, NC 28608-2067
   p. (828) 262-3049

   millerlj@appstate.edu
   http://www.geology.appstate.edu/
   Enrollment (2010): B: 59 (12)
Chair:
   Johnny A. Waters, (D), Indiana, 1976, Pi
Professor:
   Richard N. Abbott, (D), Harvard, 1977, Gzi
   Ellen A. Cowan, (D), N Illinois, 1988, Gma
   Roy Sidle, (D), Penn State, 1973, Hy
Associate Professor:
   Steven J. Hageman, (D), Illinois, 1992, Pie
Assistant Professor:
   William P. Anderson, (D), North Carolina State, 1999, Hw
   Sarah Carmichael, (D), Johns Hopkins, 2006, GxCg
   Chuanhui Gu, (D), Virginia, 2007, Cl
   Andrew Heckert, (D), New Mexico, Pv
   Cynthia Liutkus, (D), Rutgers, 2005, Gd
   Scott Marshall, (D), Massachusetts, 2008, YxGc
   Katherine Scharer, (D), Oregon, 2005, Gc
Lecturer:
   Laura Mallard, (M), Vermont, 2000, GtOe
   Christyanne Melendez, (M), N Arizona, Ggv
   Crystal Wilson, (M), Tennesse, 2006, Gt
   Brian Zimmer, (M), N Arizona, Gg
Adjunct Professor:
   Mark G. Adams, (D), North Carolina, 1995, Gp
   Keith C. Seramur, (M), N Illinois, 1988, Hw
Adjunct Faculty:
   Marg J. McKinney, (M), North Carolina, 1968, Pg
Emeritus:
   John E. Callahan, (D), Queen's, 1973, Eg
   Frank K. McKinney, (D), North Carolina, 1970, Pi
   Loren A. Raymond, (D), California (Davis), 1973, Gx
   Fred Webb, (D), Virginia Tech, 1965, Gr

Asheville-Buncombe Technical Community College

Dept of Chemistry and Physics (A) (2013)
340 Victoria Road
Asheville, NC 28801
   p. (828) 254-1921
   mfender@abtech.edu
   http://www1.abtech.edu/content/arts-and-sciences/chemistryphysics/chemistry-and-physics-overview
Instructor:
   John Bultman, Gg
Adjunct Professor:
   Dan Murphy, Gg

Brevard College

Geology Program (B) ○ (2015)
1 Brevard College Drive
Brevard, NC 28712
   p. (828) 884-8377
   reynoljh@brevard.edu
   http://www.brevard.edu/reynoljh/
   Administrative Assistant: Beth Banks
Geology Minor Coordinator:
   James H. Reynolds, (D), Dartmouth, 1987, GrvGe

Cape Fear Community College

Dept of Science (2011)
411 N. Front Street
Wilmington, NC 28401
   akolb@cfcc.edu
   http://cfcc.edu/programs/science/
Chair:
   Joy Smoots, (D)

Science Dept (A) (2014)
411 N Front St
Wilmington, NC 28401
   p. (910) 362-7674
   jsmoots@cfcc.edu
   http://cfcc.edu/programs/science/
   Enrollment (2013): A: 8 (5)

Instructor:
  Alvin L. Coleman, (M), Tennessee, Gg
  Phil Garwood, (D), Edith Cowans (Australia), 1978, Gg

Central Piedmont Community College
Sciences Div (A) (2013)
PO Box 35009
Charlotte, NC 28235
  p. (704) 330-6750
  David.Privette@cpcc.edu
  http://www.cpcc.edu/
Division Director:
  David Privette, (M), Georgia, 1978, Oy
Instructor:
  Alisa Hylton, (M), Wichita State, Gg
  Steppen Murphy, (M), S Illinois, Gue

Coastal Carolina University
Dept of Marine Science (2004)
Conway, NC 29528

Duke University
Div of Earth & Ocean Sciences (B,M,D) (2014)
Nicholas School of the Environment and Earth Sciences
Box 90227
Durham, NC 27708-0227
  p. (919) 684-5847
  bill.chameides@duke.edu
  http://www.nicholas.duke.edu/eos
  Enrollment (2010): B: 37 (15) D: 21 (0)
Chair:
  M. Susan Lozier, (D), Washington, 1989, Op
Professor:
  Paul A. Baker, (D), California (San Diego), 1981, Cl
  Alan E. Boudreau, (D), Washington, 1986, Gi
  Bruce H. Corliss, (D), Rhode Island, 1978, Pm
  Peter K. Haff, (D), Virginia, 1970, On
  Robert B. Jackson, (D), Utah State, 1992, On
  Emily M. Klein, (D), Columbia, 1988, Gi
  Lincoln F. Pratson, (D), Columbia, 1993, Gs
  Avner Vengosh, (D), Australian National, 1990, Hw
Associate Professor:
  A. Bradshaw Murray, (D), Minnesota, 1995, Ou
Associate Scientist:
  Gary S. Dwyer, (D), Duke, 1996, Gs
Assistant Professor:
  Nicolas Cassar, (D), Hawaii, 2003, Ob
  Wenhong Li, (D), Georgia Tech, On
Instructor:
  Alex Glass, (D), Illinois, 2006, Ggu
Adjunct Professor:
  David J. Erickson, (D), Rhode Island, 1987
  Peter E. Malin, (D), Princeton, 1978, Ys
  Bruce F. Molnia, (D), South Carolina, 1972, Or
  Daniel D. Richter, (D), Duke, 1980, Os
  William H. Schlesinger, (D), Cornell, 1976, On
Emeritus:
  Richard T. Barber, (D), Stanford, 1967, Ob
  Duncan Heron, (D), North Carolina, 1958, Gr
  Daniel A. Livingstone, (D), Yale, 1953, Pe
  Ronald D. Perkins, (D), Indiana, 1962, Gd
  Orrin H. Pilkey, Jr., (D), Florida State, 1962, Ou
Other:
  Fred K. Boadu, (D), Georgia Tech, 1994, Yg
  James S. Clark, (D), Minnesota, 1988, On
  Mark N. Feinglos, (D), McGill, 1973, Gz
  Richard F. Kay, (D), Yale, 1973, On

East Carolina University 🗐
Dept of Geological Sciences (B,M) ◯ (2015)
101 Graham Building
Greenville, NC 27858-4353
  p. (252) 328-6360
  culvers@ecu.edu
  http://www.geology.ecu.edu

Administrative Assistant: Dare Merritt
  Enrollment (2015): B: 78 (12) M: 31 (16)
Chair:
  Stephen J. Culver, (D), Wales, 1976, Pm
Distinguished Research Professor:
  Stanley R. Riggs, (D), Montana, 1967, Gu
Professor:
  David Reide Corbett, (D), Florida State, 1999, Oc
  David Mallinson, (D), S Florida, 1995, Gu
  Richard Miller, (D), North Carolina State, 1984, Or
  Catherine A. Rigsby, (D), California (Santa Cruz), 1989, Gs
Associate Professor:
  Eduardo Leorri, (D), Univ of Basque Country (Spain), 2003, GsPm
  Alex Manda, (D), Massachusetts, 2009, Hqw
  Siddhartha Mitra, (D), William & Mary, 1997, Co
  Donald W. Neal, (D), West Virginia, 1979, Gr
  Richard K. Spruill, (D), North Carolina, 1981, Hw
  Terri L. Woods, (D), S Florida, 1988, Cl
Assistant Professor:
  Adriana Heimann, (D), Iowa, 2006, GzpGi
  Eric Horsman, (D), Wisconsin, 2006, Gc
Teaching Associate Professor:
  Stephen B. Harper, (D), Georgia, 1996, Gm

Guilford College
Dept of Geology & Earth Science (B) (2015)
5800 West Friendly Avenue
Greensboro, NC 27410-4173
  p. (336) 316-2263
  ddobson@guilford.edu
  http://www.guilford.edu/academics/departments-and-
  programs/geology/
  f: Guilford College Department of Geology and Earth Sci-
  ences
  Enrollment (2015): B: 27 (8)
Professor:
  David M. Dobson, (D), Michigan, 1997, Gu
  Marlene McCauley, (D), California (Los Angeles), 1986, Cp
Assistant Professor:
  Holly Peterson, (D), British Columbia, 2014, HwGe
Emeritus:
  Cyril H. Harvey, (D), Nebraska, 1960, Gr

North Carolina Agricultural & Tech State University
Dept of Natural Resources and Environmental Design (B,M) (2010)
E. Market St
Carver Hall
Greensboro, NC 27411
  p. (919) 334-7543
  reddyg@ncat.edu
  Enrollment (2005): B: 14 (55)
Chair:
  Gudigopuram B. Reddy, (D), Georgia, 1974, So
Professor:
  M. R. Reddy, (D), Georgia, 1973, So
  Godfrey A. Uzochukwu, (D), Nebraska, 1983, Gz
Associate Professor:
  Charles Raczkowski, (D), North Carolina State, So
  Manuel Reyes, (D), Louisiana State, 1992, Hw

North Carolina Central University
Dept of Geography (B) (2010)
Box 19765
Durham, NC 27707-19765
  p. (919) 560-6233
  jguess@nccu.edu
  Department Office Assistant: Margaret B. Guy
  Enrollment: No data reported since 1999
Chair:
  Albert P. Barnett, (D), Arizona, 1980, Or
Professor:
  Woodrow W. Nichols, Jr., (D), California (Los Angeles), 1973, Oy
Associate Professor:
  Vinston Burton, Jr., (D), California (Los Angeles), 1974, Gm
  Jasper L. Harris, (D), North Carolina, 1983, Oy
  Harris Williams, (D), Arizona, 1979, Oy

North Carolina State University

Dept of Marine, Earth & Atmospheric Sciences (B,M,D) ○ (2015)
P.O. Box 8208
Raleigh, NC 27695-8208
  p. (919) 515-3711
  webmaster_meas@ncsu.edu
  http://www.meas.ncsu.edu
  f: https://www.facebook.com/measncsu
  t: @ncsumeas
  Enrollment (2015): B: 49 (7) M: 13 (3) D: 13 (3)
Head:
  Walter Robinson, (D), Columbia, 1985, Oa
Director of Graduate Programs:
  Gary M. Lackmann, (D), SUNY (Albany), 1995, Oa
  Elana L. Leithold, (D), Washington, 1987, Gs
Professor:
  Viney P. Aneja, (D), North Carolina State, 1977, Oa
  David J. DeMaster, (D), Yale, 1979, Oc
  David B. Eggleston, (D), William & Mary, 1991, Ob
  Ronald V. Fodor, (D), New Mexico, 1972, Gi
  Ruoying He, (D), S Florida, 2002, Op
  David McConnell, (D), Texas A&M, 1987, GgOe
  Helena Mitasova, (D), Slovak Tech, 1987, Oi
  Fred H. M. Semazzi, (D), Nairobi, 1983, Oa
  William J. Showers, (D), Hawaii, 1982, Cs
  Lian Xie, (D), Miami, 1992, Oa
  Sandra Yuter, (D), Washington, 1996, Oa
  Yang Zhang, (D), Iowa, 1994, Oa
State Climatologist:
  Ryan Boyles, (D), North Carolina State, 2002, Oa
Associate Professor:
  Anantha Aiyyer, (D), SUNY (Albany), 2003, Oa
  Sukanta Basu, (D), Minnesota, 2004, Oa
  DelWayne Bohnenstiehl, (D), Columbia, 2002, Yr
  Jingpu P. Liu, (D), William & Mary, 2001, Gu
  Karen McNeal, (D), Texas A&M, 2007, Oec
  Nicholas Meskhidze, (D), Georgia Tech, 2003, Oa
  Chris Osburn, (D), Lehigh, 2000, Cms
  Matthew Parker, (D), Colorado State, 2002, Ow
  Astrid Schnetzer, (D), Vienna, 2001, Ob
  Ping-Tung Shaw, (D), MIT/WHOI, 1982, Op
Assistant Professor:
  Stuart P. Bishop, (D), Rhode Island, 2012, OpGq
  Paul K. Byrne, (D), Dublin Trinity College, 2010, XgGcOr
  Markus Petters, (D), Wyoming, 2004, Oa
  Karl Wegmann, (D), Lehigh, 2008, Gm
Senior Research Professor:
  S. T. Rao, (D), SUNY (Albany), 1973, Oa
Emeritus:
  Satyapal S. Arya, (D), Colorado State, 1968, Oa
  John C. Fountain, (D), California (Santa Barbara), 1975, Hw
  James P. Hibbard, (D), Cornell, 1988, Gc
  Gerald S. Janowitz, (D), Johns Hopkins, 1967, Op
  Daniel Kamykowski, (D), California (San Diego), 1973, Ob
  Charles E. Knowles, (D), Texas A&M, 1970, Op
  Leonard J. Pietrafesa, (D), Washington, 1973, Op
  Sethu S. Raman, (D), Colorado, 1972, Oa
  Allen J. Riordan, (D), Wisconsin, 1977, Oa
  Dale A. Russell, (D), Columbia, 1964, Pv
  Edward F. Stoddard, (D), California (Los Angeles), 1976, Gp
  Gerald F. Watson, (D), Florida State, 1971, Oa
  Charles W. Welby, (D), MIT, 1952, Hw
  Donna L. Wolcott, (D), California (Berkeley), 1972, Ob
  Thomas G. Wolcott, (D), California (Berkeley), 1971, Ob

Dept of Soil Science (B,M,D) (2010)
Box 7619
Raleigh, NC 27695-7619
  p. (919) 515-2655
  deanna_osmond@ncsu.edu
  Administrative Assistant: Ashru Shah
  Enrollment (1997): B: 74 (12) M: 32 (2) D: 38 (1)
Professor:
  Aziz Amoozegar, (D), Arizona, 1977, Sp
  Stephen W. Broome, (D), North Carolina, 1973, Sf
  Donald K. Cassel, (D), California (Davis), 1968, Sp

John L. Havlin, (D), Colorado State, 1983, Sc
Dean L. Hesterberg, (D), California (Riverside), 1988, Sc
Michael T. Hoover, (D), Penn State, 1983, Sd
Greg D. Hoyt, (D), Georgia, 1981, Sb
Daniel W. Israel, (D), Oregon State, 1973, Sb
Harold J. Kleiss, Illinois, 1972, Sd
Deanna L. Osmond, (D), Cornell, 1991, Sb
Wayne P. Robarge, (D), Wisconsin, 1975, Sc
Thomas J. Smyth, (D), North Carolina State, 1981, Sc
Michael J. Vepraskas, (D), Texas A&M, 1980, Sd
Michael G. Wagger, (D), Kansas State, 1983, Sb
Associate Professor:
  David A. Crouse, (D), North Carolina State, 1996, Sc
  Carl Crozier, (D), North Carolina State, 1992, Sb
  David Lindbo, (D), Massachusetts, 1990, Sd
  Richard A. McLaughlin, (D), Purdue, 1985, Sc
Assistant Professor:
  Alexandria Graves, (D), Virginia Tech, 2003, Sb
  Wei Shi, (D), Purdue, Sb
  Jeffrey G. White, (D), Cornell, 1988, Or
Emeritus:
  James W. Gilliam, (D), Mississippi State, 1965, Sb

University of North Carolina Wilmington 🗐

Dept of Geography and Geology (B,M) (2014)
601 South College Road
Wilmington, NC 28403-5944
  p. (910) 962-3490
  lynnl@uncw.edu
  http://www.uncw.edu/earsci/
  Administrative Assistant: Catherine Morris
  Administrative Assistant: Anne Sutter
  Enrollment (2007): B: 78 (21) M: 32 (5)
Chair:
  Lynn A. Leonard, (D), S Florida, 1993, Gu
Professor:
  James A. Dockal, (D), Iowa, 1980, Gd
  Nancy R. Grindlay, (D), Rhode Island, 1991, Yg
  W. Burleigh Harris, (D), North Carolina, 1975, Gs
  Patricia H. Kelley, (D), Harvard, 1979, Pg
  Richard A. Laws, (D), California (Berkeley), 1983, Pm
  Paul A. Thayer, (D), North Carolina, 1967, Gd
Associate Professor:
  Lewis J. Abrams, (D), Rhode Island, 1992, Gu
  Michael M. Benedetti, (D), Wisconsin, 2000, Gm
  David E. Blake, (D), Washington State, 1991, Gp
  Douglas W. Gamble, (D), Georgia, 2000, Oy
  Joanne N. Halls, (D), South Carolina, 1996, Oi
  Eric J. Henry, (D), Arizona, 2001, Hw
  Mary E. Hines, (D), Louisiana State, 1992, Ou
  John R. Huntsman, (D), Bryn Mawr, 1978, Gc
  Michael S. Smith, (D), Washington (St. Louis), 1990, Gz
Assistant Professor:
  Craig R. Tobias, (D), William & Mary, 1999, Cs
Lecturer:
  Roger D. Shew, (M), North Carolina, 1979, Eo
Emeritus:
  Robert T. Argenbright, (D), California (Berkeley), 1990, On
  William J. Cleary, (D), South Carolina, 1972, Gu
Laboratory Director:
  Yvonne Marsan, (B), North Carolina (Wilmington), Oi

University of North Carolina, Asheville

Dept of Atmospheric Sciences (B) ○ (2015)
CPO 2450
One University Heights
Asheville, NC 28804-3299
  p. (828) 251-6149
  chennon@unca.edu
  http://www.atms.unca.edu
  f: https://www.facebook.com/uncaweather/
  Enrollment (2014): B: 35 (7)
Professor:
  Alex Huang, (D), Purdue, 1984, Oa
  Doug Miller, (D), Purdue, 1996, OanOn

Chair:
  Chris Hennon, (D), Ohio State, 2003, OanOn
Associate Professor:
  Chris Godfrey, (D), Oklahoma, 2007, OanOn

Dept of Environmental Studies (B) (2014)
CPO 2330
Asheville, NC 28804-8511
> p. (828) 251-6441
> irossell@unca.edu
> http://envr.unca.edu
> Administrative Assistant: Debra C. Robbins
> *Enrollment (2013): B: 144 (44)*

Professor:
  Delores M. Eggers, (D), North Carolina, 1999, On
  Kevin K. Moorhead, (D), Florida, 1986, Sb
  Barbara C. Reynolds, (D), Georgia, 2000, On
  Irene M. Rossell, (D), SUNY (Syracuse), 1995, On
Associate Professor:
  David P. Gillette, (D), Oklahoma, 2008, On
  Jeffrey D. Wilcox, (D), Wisconsin, 2007, HyGg
Assistant Professor:
  Jackie M. Langille, Tennessee, 2012, GctGe
  Brittani D. MdNamee, (D), Utah, 2013, Gzx

University of North Carolina, Chapel Hill
Dept of Geological Sciences (B,M,D) (2015)
CB 3315, Mitchell Hall
Chapel Hill, NC 27599-3315
> p. (919) 966-4516
> jonathan.lees@unc.edu
> http://www.geosci.unc.edu
> *Enrollment (2013): B: 55 (20) M: 9 (8) D: 13 (3)*

Chair:
  Jonathan M. Lees, (D), Washington, 1989, YsGv
Professor:
  Larry K. Benninger, (D), Yale, 1976, Cl
  Joseph G. Carter, (D), Yale, 1976, Po
  Drew S. Coleman, (D), Kansas, 1991, CcGit
  Allen F. Glazner, (D), California (Los Angeles), 1981, Git
  Jose A. Rial, (D), Caltech, 1979, Ys
Associate Professor:
  Louis R. Bartek, III, (D), Rice, 1989, Gu
  Laura J. Moore, (D), California (Santa Cruz), 1998, Gme
  Tamlin M. Pavelsky, (D), California (Los Angeles), 2008, Hg
  Kevin G. Stewart, (D), California (Berkeley), 1987, Gc
  Donna M. Surge, (D), Michigan, 2001, Pe
Assistant Professor:
  Xiaoming Liu, (D), Maryland, 2013, Cgl
Emeritus:
  Paul D. Fullagar, (D), Illinois, 1963, Cc
  A. Conrad Neumann, (D), Lehigh, 1963, Gu
  Joseph St. Jean, (D), Indiana, 1956, Pm
  Daniel A. Textoris, (D), Illinois, 1963, Gd

University of North Carolina, Charlotte
Dept of Geography & Earth Sciences (B,M,D) (2014)
9201 University City Boulevard
Charlotte, NC 28223-0001
> p. (704) 687-5973
> ges@uncc.edu.
> http://www.geoearth.uncc.edu/
> *Enrollment (2010): B: 280 (70) M: 86 (16) D: 32 (8)*

Professor:
  John F. Bender, (D), SUNY (Stony Brook), 1980, GiCtOu
  John A. Diemer, (D), SUNY (Binghamton), 1985, Gs
Associate Professor:
  Craig J. Allan, (D), York, 1992, Hg
  Andy R. Bobyarchick, (D), SUNY (Albany), 1983, Gc
  Scott P. Hippensteel, (D), Delaware, 2000, Gr
  Walter Martin, (D), Tennessee, 1984, Oa
  Ross Meentemeyer, (D), North Carolina, 2000, Oi
Assistant Professor:
  Manda S. Adams, (D), Wisconsin, 2005, Ow
  Matt Eastin, (D), Colorado State, 2003, Ow
  Martha Cary Eppes, (D), New Mexico, 2002, Os

Lecturer:
  Jake Armour, (M), New Mexico, 2002, Gg
  Terry Shirley, (M), Penn State, 2003, Oaw
Emeritus:
  Anne Jefferson, (D), Oregon State, 2006, HgGm
Laboratory Director:
  William Garcia, (M), Cincinnati, Pv

University of North Carolina, Pembroke
Geology & Geography Dept (B) (2015)
PO Box 1510
Pembroke, NC 28372-1510
> p. (910) 775-4024
> geo@uncp.edu
> http://www.uncp.edu/geo/
> *Enrollment (2015): B: 11 (3)*

Chair:
  Martin B. Farley, (D), Penn State, 1987, PlOe
Associate Professor:
  Dennis J. Edgell, (D), Kent State, 1992, Oa
Assistant Professor:
  Jefferson B. Chaumba, (D), Georgia, 2009, Gx
  Daren T. Nelson, (D), Utah, 2012, GmHwOi
Instructor:
  Jesse Rouse, (M), West Virginia, 2000, Oni
Lecturer:
  Amy Gross, (M), North Carolina (Wilmington), 2006, Gg
  Nathan E. Phillippi, (M), South Dakota State, 2004, Oni
Emeritus:
  Suellen Cabe, (D), North Carolina, 1984, Gg
  Thomas E. Ross, (D), Tennessee, 1977, Oy

Western Carolina University
Dept of Geosciences & Natural Resources (B) (2015)
Stillwell Building Room 331
Cullowhee, NC 28723-9047
> p. (828) 227-7367
> mlord@wcu.edu
> http://geology.wcu.edu
> *Enrollment (2015): B: 52 (12)*

Whitmire Prof Env Sci:
  Jerry R. Miller, (D), S Illinois, 1990, Gm
Director Prog Study Dev Shorelines:
  Robert S. Young, (D), Duke, 1995, GsOn
Dept. Head:
  Mark L. Lord, (D), North Dakota, 1988, HwGmOe
Associate Provost:
  Brandon Schwab, (D), Oregon, 2000, Gv
Assoc. Dean, Arts & Sciences:
  David A. Kinner, (D), Colorado, 2003, HgOe
Associate Professor:
  Benjamin R. Tanner, (D), Tennessee, 2005, Cos
  Cheryl Waters-Tormey, (D), Wisconsin, 2004, Gc
Assistant Professor:
  Amy Fagan, (D), Notre Dame, 2013, GiXg
  Frank Forcino, (D), Alberta, 2013, PgOeGr
  John P. Gannon, (D), Virginia Tech, 2014, HgSo
Instructor:
  Emily Stafford, (D), Alberta, 2014, PgGg
Emeritus:
  Steven P. Yurkovich, (D), Brown, 1972, Gx

North Dakota

Dickinson State University
Dept of Natural Science (B) (2011)
Dickinson, ND 58601
> p. (701) 227-2114
> Michael.Hastings@dickinsonstate.edu
> http://www.dsu.nodak.edu/
> *Enrollment: No data reported since 1999*

Chair:
  Michael Hastings
Associate Professor:
  Larry D. League, (M), Kansas, 1971, Oy

Minot State University
Dept of Geoscience (B) (2014)
500 University Avenue West
Minot, ND 58707
　　p. (701) 858-3873
　　john.webster@minotstateu.edu
　　Enrollment (2014): B: 37 (9)
Chair:
　　John R. Webster, (D), Indiana, 1992, Gi
Assistant Professor:
　　Joseph Collette, (D), California (Riverside), 2014, PgGsr
　　Kathyrn Kilroy, (D), Nevada (Reno), 1992, Hg
　　Joseph Krieg, (D), Iowa, 2007, GmOs

North Dakota State University
Dept of Geosciences (B,M,D) (2015)
NDSU Dept. 2745
P.O. Box 6050
Fargo, ND 58108-6050
　　p. (701) 231-8455
　　peter.oduor@ndsu.edu
　　http://www.ndsu.edu/geosci
　　Enrollment (2014): B: 50 (12) M: 2 (0)
Professor:
　　Kenneth E. Lepper, (D), Oklahoma State, 2001, Cc
Chair:
　　Peter Oduor, (D), Missouri (Rolla), 2004, Oi
Associate Professor:
　　Bernhardt Saini-Eidukat, (D), Minnesota, 1991, GiCg
Assistant Professor:
　　Stephanie S. Day, (D), Minnesota, 2012, GmOiu
　　Adam R. Lewis, (D), Boston, 2005, Gle
　　Lydia S. Tackett, (D), S California, 2014, PiGsPo
Instructor:
　　Jessie Rock, (M), North Dakota State, 2009, Og
Emeritus:
　　Allan C. Ashworth, (D), Birmingham, 1969, Pe
　　Donald P. Schwert, (D), Waterloo, 1978, PeGe

Dept of Soil Science (B,M,D) (2014)
Walster Hall
Fargo, ND 58105
　　p. (701) 231-8690
　　Thomas.Desutter@ndsu.edu
　　Administrative Assistant: Jacinda Wollan
　　Enrollment (2014): B: 18 (0) M: 10 (0) D: 4 (0)
Professor:
　　Francis Casey, (D), Iowa State, 2000, SpHq
　　Dave Franzen
　　Robert J. Goos, (D), Colorado, 1980, Sc
Associate Professor:
　　Larry J. Cihacek, (D), Iowa State, 1976, Og
Assistant Professor:
　　Amitava Chatterjee, Wyoming
　　Aaron Daigh, (D), Iowa State
　　Tom DeSutter, (D), Kansas State, Os
　　Ann-Marie Fortuna
　　David G. Hopkins, (D), North Dakota State, 1997, Sd
　　Abbey Wick, Wyoming

University of North Dakota 🗂
Dept of Geography (B,M) (2014)
221 Centennial Drive
Stop 9020
Grand Forks, ND 58202
　　p. (701) 777-4246
　　cindy.purpur@und.edu
　　http://arts-sciences.und.edu/geography/
　　Enrollment (2014): B: 35 (5) M: 9 (6)
Chair:
　　Bradley C. Rundquist, (D), Kansas State, 2000, OriOy
Professor:
　　Douglas C. Munski, (D), Illinois, 1978, Oe
　　Paul Todhunter, (D), California (Los Angeles), 1986, Oy
Associate Professor:
　　Devon A. Hansen, (D), Utah, 1999, Og

　　Gregory S. Vandeberg, (D), Kansas State, 2005, GmOi
　　Enru Wang, (D), Washington, 2005, Ogi
Assistant Professor:
　　Christopher Atkinson, (D), Kansas, 2010, Oai
　　Michael A. Niedzielski, (D), Ohio State, 2009, Oi

Harold Hamm School of Geology & Geological Engineering
(B,M,D) (2014)
81 Cornell Street
Stop 8358
Grand Forks, ND 58202
　　p. (701) 777-2248
　　joseph.hartman@engr.und.edu
　　http://engineering.und.edu/geology-and-geological-engineering/
　　Enrollment (2014): B: 78 (0) M: 17 (0) D: 10 (0)
Director:
　　Joseph H. Hartman, (D), Minnesota, 1984, Pi
Professor:
　　William D. Gosnold, (D), S Methodist, 1976, Yh
　　Richard D. LeFever, (D), California (Los Angeles), 1979, Gs
　　Stephan Nordeng, (D), Michigan, Go
　　Dexter Perkins, III, (D), Michigan, 1979, Gp
Associate Professor:
　　Philip J. Gerla, (D), Arizona, 1983, Hw
　　Ronald K. Matheney, (D), Arizona State, 1989, Cs
　　Jaakko Putkonen, (D), Washington, 1997, Gl
Assistant Professor:
　　Nels F. Forsman, (D), North Dakota, 1985, Eg
　　I-Hsuan Ho, (D), Iowa, Ng
　　Dongmei Wang, (D), China, Ng

Ohio

Ashland University
Dept of Chemistry/Geology/Physics (B) O (2015)
401 College Avenue
Ashland, OH 44805
　　p. (419) 289-5261
　　mhudson@ashland.edu
　　http://www.ashland.edu/departments/geology
　　Enrollment (2015): B: 11 (2)
Associate Professor:
　　Nigel Brush, (D), California (Los Angeles), 1992, GmdGa
　　Michael R. Hudson, (D), Miami (Ohio), 1994, GpzCa

Bowling Green State University 🗂
Dept of Geology (B,M) (2013)
190 Overman Hall
Bowling Green, OH 43403
　　p. (419) 372-2886
　　geology@bgsu.edu
　　http://www.bgsu.edu/departments/geology/
　　Administrative Assistant: Pat A. Wilhelm
　　Enrollment (2010): B: 29 (13) M: 23 (2)
Chair:
　　Sheila J. Roberts, (D), Arizona, 1992, CgHw
Professor:
　　James E. Evans, (D), Washington, 1988, Gs
　　Charles M. Onasch, (D), Penn State, 1977, Gc
　　Robert K. Vincent, (D), Michigan, 1973, Yg
Associate Professor:
　　John R. Farver, (D), Brown, 1988, Gy
　　Joseph P. Frizado, (D), Northwestern, 1980, Oi
　　Enrique Gomezdelcampo, (D), Tennessee, 2003, Ge
　　Kurt S. Panter, (D), New Mexico Tech, 1995, Gv
　　Jeffrey A. Snyder, (D), Ohio State, 1996, Gm
　　Peg M. Yacobucci, (D), Harvard, 1999, Po
Assistant Professor:
　　Peter Gorsevski, (D), Idaho, 2002, OirGm
Lecturer:
　　Nichole Elkins, (M), Georgia, 2002, GaOe
　　Christopher Pepple, (M), Oe
　　Paula J. Steinker, (D), Bowling Green, 1982, Pg
Emeritus:
　　Don C. Steinker, (D), California (Berkeley), 1969, Po

Department IT:
    William Butcher, (B), Rochester, 1972, Gg

Case Western Reserve University
Dept of Earth, Environmental and Planetary Sciences (B,M,D)
(2015)
10900 Euclid Avenue
A.W. Smith #112
Cleveland, OH 44106-7216
    p. (216) 368-3690
    lmd3@case.edu
    http://geology.case.edu
    Enrollment (2014): B: 12 (0) M: 2 (0) D: 8 (0)
Chair:
    James Van Orman, (D), MIT, 2000, Cg
Professor:
    Gerald Matisoff, (D), Johns Hopkins, 1978, Cl
    Peter L. McCall, (D), Yale, 1975, Po
    Peter J. Whiting, (D), California (Berkeley), 1990, Gm
Associate Professor:
    Ralph P. Harvey, (D), Pittsburgh, 1990, Xm
    Steven A. Hauck, II, (D), Washington (St. Louis), 2001, Yg
    Beverly Z. Saylor, (D), MIT, 1996, Gs
Adjunct Professor:
    Andrew Dombard, (D), Washington, 2000, Xy
    Joseph T. Hannibal, (D), Kent State, 1990, Pi
    Michael Ketterer, (D), Colorado, 1985, Ca
    David Saja, (D), Pennsylvania, 1999, Gc
Emeritus:
    Samuel M. Savin, (D), Caltech, 1967, Cs

Cedarville University
Dept of Science and Mathematics (B) (2015)
251 North Main Street
Cedarville, OH 45314
    p. (937) 766-7940
    trice@cedarville.edu
    http://www.cedarville.edu/Academics/Science-and-Mathe-
    matics/Geology.aspx
    f: https://www.facebook.com/cedarvillegeology
    Enrollment (2015): B: 28 (6)
Professor:
    Steven Gollmer, (D), Purdue, GzOwg
    John H. Whitmore, (D), Loma Linda, 2003, PgGsg
Associate Professor:
    Mark Gathany, (D), Colorado State, OiuSb
Assistant Professor:
    Thomas L. Rice, (M), Colorado Mines, 1987, GemEo
Adjunct Professor:
    Steve A. Austin, (D), Penn State, 1979, GsEcGd

Central State University
Intl Center for Water Resources Management (B) (2016)
C.J. McLin Bldg
Wilberforce, OH 45384
    p. (937) 376-6212
    knedunuri@centralstate.edu
    Enrollment (2015): B: 45 (3)
Professor and Chair:
    Krishna Kumar Nedunuri, (D), Purdue, 1999, HwCaSo
Dean of College of Science and Engineering:
    Subramania I. Sritharan, (D), Colorado State, 1984, Hg
Professor:
    Sam Laki, (D), Michigan State, 1992, EgSoHs
Associate Professor:
    Ramanitharan Kandiah, (D), Tulane, 2004, HqSoOi
    Xiaofang Wei, (D), Indiana State, 2008, OrgOe
    De Bonne N. Wishart, (D), YxCt
Assistant Professor:
    Ning Zhang, (D), West Virginia, 2012, Emo
Emeritus:
    Samuel Okunade, (D), Kent State, 1986, Gm

Cincinnati Museum Center
Geier Collections and Research Center (2015)

1301 Western Avenue
Cincinnati, OH 45203
    p. (513) 287-7000
    information@cincymuseum.org
    http://www.cincymuseum.org
Associate Vice President:
    Glenn W. Storrs, (D), Yale, 1986, Pv
Curator:
    Brenda Hunda, (D), California (Riverside), 2004, Pi
Research Associate:
    Carlton E. Brett, (D), Michigan, 1978, Po
    Brooke E. Crowley, (D), California (Santa Cruz), 2009, Pe
    Nigel C. Hughes, (D), Bristol, 1990, Pi
    David L. Meyer, (D), Yale, 1971, Pi
    Arnold I. Miller, (D), Chicago, 1986, Pq
    Joshua H. Miller, (D), Chicago, 2009, Pe
    Andrew Webber, (D), Cincinnati, 2007, Pi

Cleveland Museum of Natural History
Dept of Mineralogy (2015)
1 Wade Oval Drive
University Circle
Cleveland, OH 44106-1767
    p. (216) 231-4600 (Ext. 3229)
    dsaja@cmnh.org
    http://www.cmnh.org

Dept of Paleobotany (2010)
1 Wade Oval Drive
University Circle
Cleveland, OH 44106-1767
    p. (216) 231-4600
    schitale@cmnh.org
    http://www.cmnh.org/site/ResearchandCollections/Paleo-
    botany.aspx
Head:
    Shyamala Chitaley, (D), Reading (UK), 1955, Pb

Dept of Paleobotany & Paleecology (2015)
1 Wade Oval Drive
Cleveland, OH 44106-1767
    p. (216) 231-4600 (Ext. 3240)
    dsu@cmnh.org
    http://www.cmnh.org/site/ResearchandCollections/Inverte-
    bratePaleontology.aspx
Head:
    Joseph T. Hannibal, (D), Kent State, 1990, Pi
Assistant:
    Douglas Dunn, (A), Lakeland Comm Coll, 1974, Pg

Dept of Vertebrate Paleontology (2014)
1 Wade Oval Drive
University Circle
Cleveland, OH 44106-1767
    p. (216) 231-4600
    mryan@cmnh.org
    http://www.cmnh.org/site/ResearchandCollections/Verte-
    bratePaleontology.aspx
Head:
    Michael J. Ryan, (D)
Casting Technician:
    David Chapman
VP Tech:
    Gary Jackson

College of Wooster
Dept of Geology (B) (2015)
Scovel Hall
944 College Mall
Wooster, OH 44691-2363
    p. (330) 263-2380
    preeder@wooster.edu
    http://www.wooster.edu/academics/areas/geology
    f: https://www.facebook.com/pages/College-of-Wooster-
    Geology-Department/143144126437
    Enrollment (2015): B: 40 (10)

Chair:
Gregory C. Wiles, (D), SUNY (Buffalo), 1992, Gl
Professor:
Mark A. Wilson, (D), California (Berkeley), 1982, Pi
Associate Professor:
Shelley Judge, (D), Ohio State, 2007, Gt
Associate Scientist:
Meagen Pollock, (D), Duke, 2007, Gi

Cuyahoga Community College-Western Campus
Earth Science (A) (2011)
11000 Pleasant Valley Road
Parma, OH 44130
  p. (216) 987-5278
  Robert.Zaleha@tri-c.edu
Assistant Professor:
Robert Zaleha, Og
Instructor:
John L. Ezerskis, Og
Carol Fondran, Og
Joseph M. Lane, Og
Abby N. Norton-Krane, Og
Kathryn Sasowsky, Og
Adjunct Professor:
Gloria Britton, Og
Jennifer Deka, Og

Denison University
Dept of Geosciences (B) (2014)
F.W. Olin Science Hall
100 W. College Street
Granville, OH 43023
  p. (740) 587-6217
  hall@denison.edu
  http://www.denison.edu/academics/departments/geosciences/
  Administrative Assistant: Jude Hall
  Enrollment (2013): B: 9 (9)
Professor:
Tod A. Frolking, (D), Wisconsin, 1985, Oy
Associate Professor:
David H. Goodwin, (D), Arizona, 2002, Pi
David C. Greene, (D), Nevada (Reno), 1995, Gc
Assistant Professor:
Erik Klemetti, (D), Oregon State, 2005, GvxGg
Kate E. Tierney, (D), Ohio State, 2010, CgGrOg
Emeritus:
Kennard B. Bork, (D), Indiana, 1967, Pi
Robert J. Malcuit, (D), Michigan State, 1973, Gx

Hocking College
GeoEnvironmental Science Program (2015)
3301 Hocking Parkway
Nelsonville, OH 45764-9704
  p. (740) 753-6277
  caudillm@hocking.edu
  http://www.hocking.edu/programs/geoenvironmental
Professor:
Michael R. Caudill, (D), Tennessee, 1996, SdHwNg
Instructor:
Kimberly S. Caudill, (B), Ohio Univ, 1984, GeOuHw

Kent State University 🗐
Dept of Geology (B,M,D) O (2015)
221 McGilvrey Hall
Kent, OH 44242
  p. (330) 672-2680
  geology@kent.edu
  http://www.kent.edu/geology/
  Enrollment (2015): B: 154 (23) M: 22 (10) D: 9 (3)
Chair:
Daniel K. Holm, (D), Harvard, 1992, Gc
Professor:
Joseph D. Ortiz, (D), Oregon State, 1995, Gs
Carrie E. Schweitzer, (D), Kent State, 2000, Pi
Alison J. Smith, (D), Brown, 1991, Gn

Neil A. Wells, (D), Michigan, 1984, Gs
Associate Professor:
David B. Hacker, (D), Kent State, 1998, GcHw
Assistant Professor:
Tathagata Dasgupta, (D), Syracuse, 2010, Cg
Elizabeth M. Herndon, (D), Penn State, 2012, Cl
Anne J. Jefferson, (D), Oregon State, 2006, Hg
Christopher J. Rowan, (D), Southhampton, 2006, Gt
David M. Singer, (D), Stanford, 2008, Gze
Jeremy C. Williams, (D), Massachusetts (Boston), 2014, Cg
Emeritus:
Rodney M. Feldmann, (D), North Dakota, 1967, Pi
Donald F. Palmer, (D), Princeton, 1968, Yg
Abdul Shakoor, (D), Purdue, 1982, Ng
Related Staff:
Merida Keatts, (M), Kent State, 2000, On

Kent State University at Stark
Dept of Geology (B) O (2015)
6000 Frank Avenue NW
North Canton, OH 44720
  p. 330-244-3303
  cschweit@kent.edu
  http://www.personal.kent.edu/~cschweit/Stark/
  Administrative Assistant: Debra Stimer
  Enrollment (2015): B: 10 (0)
Chair:
Carrie E. Schweitzer, (D), Kent State, 2000, PiGg

Lakeland Community College
Geoscience Dept (A) (2015)
7700 Clocktower Drive
Kirtland, OH 44094
  p. (440) 525-7341
  dpierce@lakelandcc.edu
  http://www.lakelandcc.edu/academic/sh/geol/index.asp
Dr.:
David Pierce, (D), GgHsOw

Marietta College
Dept of Petroleum Engineering & Geology (B) (2016)
215 Fifth Street
Marietta, OH 45750
  p. (740) 376-4775
  pytlikl@marietta.edu
  http://w3.marietta.edu/departments/Petroleum_Engineering/
  Enrollment (2012): B: 360 (46)
Associate Professor:
Frederick R. Voner, (D), Miami, 1985, Gx
Assistant Professor:
Tej Gautam, (D), Kent State, 2012, Ge
David L. Jeffery, (D), Texas A&M, 2003, Go
Instructor:
Wendy Bartlett, (M), Texas A&M, Geo
Veronica Freeman, (M), Texas, 1993, Pg
Administrative Coordinator:
Laura Pytlik, (A), Marietta College, On

Miami University 🗐
Dept of Geology and Environmental Earth Sciences (B,M,D) O (2015)
250 S,. Patterson Avenue
118 Shideler Hall
Oxford, OH 45056
  p. (513) 529-3216
  edwardca@MiamiOh.edu
  http://www.units.muohio.edu/geology/
  Administrative Assistant: Cathy Edwards
  Enrollment (2015): B: 183 (27) M: 10 (9) D: 15 (3)
Janet & Elliot Baines Bicentenntial Professor & Chair:
Elisabeth Widom, (D), California (Santa Cruz), 1991, Cc
Professor:
Michael Brudzinski, (D), Illinois, 2002, Ys
Yildirm Dilek, (D), California (Davis), 1989, Gt
Hailiang Dong, (D), Michigan, 1997, Cg

John F. Rakovan, (D), SUNY (Stony Brook), 1996, Cl
Jason Rech, (D), Arizona, 2001, Gm
Associate Professor (Hamilton Campus:
Mark Krekeler, (D), Illinois (Chicago), 2003, Ge
Associate Professor & Director of IES:
Jonathan Levy, (D), Wisconsin, 1993, Hw
Associate Professor:
Brian S. Currie, (D), Arizona, 1998, Gs
Assistant Professor:
Claire McLeod, (D), Durham, 2012, Gx
Carrie Tyler, (D), Virginia Tech, 2012, Pb
Instructor:
Kenneth Brown, (D), Miami, 2015, Gx
Jill Mignery, (M), Miami, 2004
Lecturer (Middletown Campus:
Tammie Gerke, (D), Cincinnati, 1995
Lecturer:
Todd Dupont, (D), Penn State, 2004, Gl
Visiting Professor:
Hassan Mirnejad, (M), Carleton, 2001, GxCg
Emeritus:
A. Dwight Baldwin, Jr., (D), Stanford, 1966, Hw
Mark R. Boardman, (D), North Carolina, 1978, On
William K. Hart, (D), Case Western, 1982, Gi
John M. Hughes, (D), Dartmouth, 1981, Gz
Robert G. McWilliams, (D), Washington, 1968, Ps
John K. Pope, (D), Cincinnati, 1966, Pi
David M. Scotford, (D), Johns Hopkins, 1950, Gp
Laboratory Director:
David C. Kuentz, (M), Texas (Arlington), 1986, Ca
John P. Morton, (D), Texas, 1983
Postdoctoral Research Scholar:
Patri Larrea, (D), Zaragoza, 2014
Fara Rasoazanamparany, (D), Miami, 2015
Accounting Technician:
Gail Burger
Director Limper Geology Museum:
Kendall Hauer, (D), Miami, 1995, Gg
Cooperating Faculty:
R. Hays Cummins, (D), Texas A&M, 1984, Ge
William Renwick, (D), Clark, 1979, Gm

Mount Union College

Dept of Geology (B) (2014)
Alliance, OH 44601
p. (330) 823-3672
graylm@mountunion.edu
http://www.mountunion.edu/gy
Enrollment (2010): B: 8 (2)
Professor:
Lee M. Gray, (D), Rochester, 1985, PoGg
Department Chair:
Mark A. McNaught, (D), Rochester, 1991, Gcg
Adjunct Professor:
Leonard G. Epp, (D), Penn State, 1970, Ob

Muskingum University

Dept of Geology (B) (2015)
163 Stormont Street
New Concord, OH 43762
p. (740) 826-8306
svanhorn@muskingum.edu
http://muskingum.edu/dept/geology/
Enrollment (2014): B: 34 (5)
Chair:
Stephen R. Van Horn, (D), Connecticut, 1996, GeOiEo
Associate Professor:
Eric W. Law, (D), Case Western, 1982, Gp
David Rodland, (D), Virginia Tech, 2003, PgiPe

Northwest State Community College

Div of Arts and Sciences (1999)
22600 State Route 34
Archbold, OH 43502
levans@northweststate.edu
http://www.northweststate.edu

Oberlin College

Dept of Geology (B) (2015)
52 West Lorain Street
Oberlin, OH 44074-1044
p. (440) 775-8350
geology@oberlin.edu
http://new.oberlin.edu/arts-and-sciences/departments/geology/
Enrollment (2015): B: 60 (19)
Chair:
Dennis K. Hubbard, (D), South Carolina, 1977, Gsu
Professor:
Karla M. Parsons-Hubbard, (D), Rochester, 1993, Po
Bruce M. Simonson, (D), Johns Hopkins, 1982, GsXm
Steven F. Wojtal, (D), Johns Hopkins, 1982, Gc
Associate Professor:
F Zeb Page, (D), Michigan, 2005, GpCs
Assistant Professor:
Amanda H. Schmidt, (D), Washington, 2010, Gm
Cooperating Faculty:
Alison Ricker, (M), Rhode Island, 1977, On

Ohio State University ⌑

Atmospheric Sciences Program (B,M,D) (2011)
103 Bricker Hall
190 North Oval Mall
Columbus, OH 43210-1361
p. (614) 292-2514
mark.9@osu.edu
http://www.geography.ohio-state.edu/atmospheric-and-climatic-studies
Director:
Jeffery C. Rogers, (D), Colorado, 1979, Oa
Professor:
John N. Rayner, (D), Canterbury (NZ), 1965, Oa

Dept of Civil, Environmental & Geodetic Engineering (B,M,D) (2015)
470 Hitchcock Hall
2070 Neil Avenue
Columbus, OH 43210
p. (612) 292-2771
Grejner-Brzezinska.1@osu.edu
http://ceg.osu.edu
Enrollment (2014): B: 18 (11) M: 11 (6) D: 20 (5)
Professor and Chair:
Dorota A. Grejner-Brzezinska, (D), Ohio State, 1995, Yd
Research Professor:
Charles K. Toth, (D), OrYd
Professor:
Harvey J. Miller, (D), Ohio State, 1991, Oi
Associate Professor:
Alper Yilmaz, (D), Central Florida, 2004, Or

Dept of Geography (B,M,D) (2015)
1036 Derby Hall
154 North Oval Mall
Columbus, OH 43210-1361
p. (614) 292-2514
sui.10@osu.edu
http://www.geography.osu.edu/
Chair:
Daniel Sui
Professor:
David H. Bromwich, (D), Wisconsin, 1979, Oa
Ellen E. Mosley-Thompson, (D), Ohio State, 1979, Oa
Jeffrey C. Rogers, (D), Colorado, 1979, Oa
Associate Professor:
Jay S. Holgood, (D), Ohio State, 1984, Oa
Jialin Lin, (D), SUNY (Stony Brook), 2001, Oa
Bryan G. Mark, (D), Syracuse, 2001, Oa
Assistant Professor:
Alvaro Montenegro, (D), Florida State, 2003, Oa
Emeritus:
A. John Arnfield, (D), McMaster, 1973, Oa
John N. Rayner, (D), Canterbury (NZ), 1965, Oa

School of Earth Sciences (B,M,D) (2015)
275 Mendenhall Lab
125 South Oval Mall
Columbus, OH 43210-1398
 p. (614) 292-2721
 earthsciences@osu.edu
 http://www.earthsciences.osu.edu
 Administrative Assistant: Theresa Colson
 Administrative Assistant: Jacqueline Hartzell
 Administrative Assistant: Angie Rogers
 Enrollment (2011): M: 36 (16) D: 40 (2)
Director, Byrd Polar Research Center:
 William B. Lyons, (D), Connecticut, 1979, Cl
Ohio Research Scholar:
 David R. Cole, (D), Pennsylvania, 1980, Cg
Ohio Eminent Scholar:
 Michael G. Bevis, (D), Cornell, 1982, Yx
 Frank W. Schwartz, (D), Illinois, 1972, Hg
Associate Director, Administration:
 Lawrence A. Krissek, (D), Oregon State, 1982, Gs
Associate Dean:
 Anne E. Carey, (D), Nevada (Reno), 1995, Hq
Professor:
 Loren E. Babcock, (D), Kansas, 1990, Po
 Edwin S. Bair, (D), Penn State, 1980, Hw
 Michael Barton, (D), Manchester, 1975, Gx
 Yu-Ping Chin, (D), Michigan, 1988, Hg
 Jeffrey J. Daniels, (D), Colorado Mines, 1974, Yg
 Christopher Jekeli, (D), Ohio State, 1981, Yd
 Mark A. Kleffner, (M), Ohio State, 1988, Gr
 Matthew R. Saltzman, (D), California (Los Angeles), 1996, Gs
 CK Shum, (D), Texas, 1982, Yd
 Lonnie G. Thompson, (D), Ohio State, 1976, Gl
 Ralph R. B. von Frese, (D), Purdue, 1980, Ye
 Terry J. Wilson, (D), Columbia, 1983, Gc
Design Engineer:
 Dana Caccamise, (M)
Senior Scientist:
 John W. Olesik, (D), Wisconsin, 1982, Ca
 Yuchan Yi, (D), Ohio State, 1995, Ydv
Associate Professor:
 Douglas E. Alsdorf, (D), Cornell, 1996, Hg
 Ozeas Costa, (D), Plymouth, 2002, Ob
 Andrea G. Grottoli, (D), Houston, 1998, OcPe
 Ian M. Howat, (D), California (Santa Cruz), 2006, OlYd
 Motomu Ibaraki, (D), Waterloo, 1994, Hg
 Daniel N. Leavell, (D), Massachusetts, 1983, Ge
 Steven K. Lower, (D), Virginia Tech, 2001, Py
 Wendy R. Panero, (D), California (Berkeley), 2001, Yg
 Leonid Polyak, (D), Leningrad Gornyi Inst (Russia), 1985, OgGr
 Alan J. Saalfeld, (D), Maryland, 1993, Yd
 Burkhard A. Schaffrin, (D), Bonn, 1983, Yd
Senior Research Associate:
 Christopher Gardner, (M)
Research Scientist:
 Paolo Gabrielli, (D), LGGE Grenoble, 2004, CtPeOl
 Susan A. Welch, (D), Delaware, 1997, ClGeCs
Assistant Professor:
 Joel D. Barker, (D), Alberta, 2007, OlHg
 Ann Cook, (D), Columbia, 2010, Gu
 Thomas Darrah, (D), Rochester, 2009, Ge
 Michael T. Durand, (D), California, 2007, HgYd
 Joachim Moortgat, (D), Radboud, 2006
 Michael Wilkins, (D), Manchester, 2006
Research Associate:
 Junyi Guo
 Eric Kendrick
 How-wai (Peter) Luk
 Anthony Lutton, (D)
 Yohei Matsui
 Julie Sheets
 Stefanie Sherman, (D), Ohio State
 Utku Solpuker
 Victor Zagorodnov
Lecturer:
 Christena Cox, (D), Ohio State, 1994, GgoGc

 Deborah Leslie, (D)
 Christina Millan, (D), Ggc
Museum Curator :
 Dale Gnidovec, (M)
Adjunct Professor:
 Thomas G. Naymik, (D), Ohio State, 1978, Hw
Emeritus:
 William I. Ausich, (D), Indiana, 1978, Po
 Stig M. Bergstrom, (D), Lund (Sweden), 1961, Ps
 James Bradley
 James W. Collinson, (D), Stanford, 1966, Ps
 Charles E. Corbato, (D), California (Los Angeles), 1960, Ye
 James W. Downs, (D), Virginia Tech, 1983, Gz
 David H. Elliot, (D), Birmingham, 1965, Gi
 Gunter Faure, (D), MIT, 1961, Cc
 Kenneth A. Foland, (D), Brown, 1972, Cc
 Clyde Goad
 Charles Herdendorf
 Garry D. McKenzie, (D), Ohio State, 1968, Gl
 George E. Moore, (D), Harvard, 1947, Gc
 Ivan Mueller
 David Nickey
 Hallan C. Noltimier, (D), Newcastle upon Tyne, 1965, Ym
 Douglas E. Pride, (D), Illinois, 1969, Em
 Richard Rapp
 Walter C. Sweet, (D), Iowa, 1954, Ps
 Thomas N. Taylor, (D), Illinois, 1964, Pb
 Rodney T. Tettenhorst, (D), Illinois, 1960, Gz
 Russell O. Utgard, (D), Indiana, 1969, Ge
 Peter N. Webb, (D), Utrecht (Neth), 1966, Pm
Courtesy Appt.:
 Bryan Mark
Undergraduate Advisor:
 Karen Royce, (D), Ohio State
Systems Manager:
 Brent Curtiss
Systems Developer:
 Michael Seufer

School of Environment and Natural Resources (B,M,D) (2014)
2021 Coffey Road
Room 210 Koffman Hall
Columbus, OH 43210
 p. (614) 292-2265
 hendrick.15@osu.edu
 http://senr.osu.edu/
 Administrative Assistant: Mary Capoccia
 Enrollment: No data reported since 1999
Eminent Scholar:
 Richard P. Dick, (D), Iowa State, 1986, Sb
Associate Director:
 Donald J. Eckert, (D), Ohio State, 1978, Sc
Professor:
 Jerry M. Bigham, (D), North Carolina State, 1977, Sd
 Frank G. Calhoun, (D), Florida, 1971, Sd
 Warren A. Dick, (D), Iowa State, Sb
 Rattan Lal, (D), Ohio State, 1968, Sp
Associate Professor:
 Nicholas T. Basta, (D), Iowa State, 1989, Sc
 Edward L. McCoy, (D), Oregon State, 1984, Sp
Assistant Professor:
 Dawn Ferris, (D), Minnesota, 1997, Sf
 Brian K. Slater, (D), Wisconsin, 1994, Sd

Ohio University
Geological Sciences (B,M) ● (2015)
316 Clippinger Lab
Athens, OH 45701
 p. (740) 593-1101
 geological_sciences@ohio.edu
 http://www.ohio.edu/geology/
 Enrollment (2015): B: 90 (14) M: 24 (10)
Chair:
 Dina L. Lopez, (D), Louisiana State, 1992, CgGeq
Professor:
 Elizabeth H. Gierlowski-Kordesch, (D), Case Western, 1985, Gn
 R. Damian Nance, (D), Cambridge, 1978, Gtc

Alycia L. Stigall, (D), Kansas, 2004, Po
Associate Professor:
  Douglas H. Green, (D), Wisconsin, 1989, Yg
  Daniel Hembree, (D), Kansas, 2005, Pi
  David L. Kidder, (D), California (Santa Barbara), 1987, Gs
  Eung Seok Lee, (D), Indiana, 1999, Hw
  Keith A. Milam, (D), Tennessee, 2006, Xg
  Gregory C. Nadon, (D), Toronto, 1991, Gs
  Gregory S. Springer, (D), Colorado State, 2002, Gm
Emeritus:
  Gene W. Heien, (M), Indiana, 1962, Gz
  Royal H. Mapes, (D), Iowa, 1977, Pi
  Thomas R. Worsley, (D), Illinois, 1970, Og
Technician & Information Tech:
  Timothy A. Grubb, (A), Washington State Comm Coll, 2002
Administrative Associate:
  Cheri Sheets, (B), Ohio

Ohio Wesleyan University
Dept of Geology & Geography (B) (2015)
61 S. Sandusky Street
Delaware, OH 43015
  p. (740) 368-3615
  bsmartin@owu.edu
  http://geo.owu.edu
  Administrative Assistant: Kathryn M. Boger
  Administrative Assistant: Barbara Williams
  Enrollment (2014): B: 19 (11)
Director, Environmental Studies Program:
  John B. Krygier, (D), Penn State, 1995, Oi
Chair:
  Barton S. Martin, (D), Massachusetts, 1991, GxvCg
Professor:
  Karen H. Fryer, (D), Illinois, 1986, GcpGt
  Keith O. Mann, (D), Iowa, 1987, Pi
Assistant Professor:
  Nathanael S. Amador, (D), Penn State, 2015, OylOr
Visiting Professor:
  Nicholas J. Crane, (D), Ohio State, 2014, Ou
Emeritus:
  Richard D. Fusch, (D), Oregon, 1972, Ou
  David H. Hickcox, (D), Oregon, 1979, Oyw

Shawnee State University
Dept of Natural Sciences (A,B) ● (2015)
940 Second Street
Portsmouth, OH 45662
  p. (740) 351-3456
  kshoemaker@shawnee.edu
  http://www.shawnee.edu
  Administrative Assistant: Sharon Messer
  Enrollment (2015): A: 0 (1) B: 19 (6)
Associate Professor:
  Kurt A. Shoemaker, (D), Miami (Ohio), 2004, GxzGm
Assistant Professor:
  Erik B. Larson, (D), Mississippi State, 2014, GsmHg
Other:
  Jeffrey A. Bauer, (D), Ohio State, 1987, Ps

University of Akron
Dept of Geology & Environmental Science (B,M) ○ (2015)
Akron, OH 44325-4101
  p. (330) 972-7630
  butch@uakron.edu
  http://www.uakron.edu/geology/
  Administrative Assistant: Elaine Butcher
  Enrollment (2014): B: 150 (21) M: 41 (12)
Chair:
  James McManus, (D), CmOg
Professor:
  John A. Peck, (D), Rhode Island, 1995, Gs
  Ira D. Sasowsky, (D), Penn State, 1992, Hw
  David N. Steer, (D), Cornell, 1996, Ys
Associate Professor:
  Linda R. Barrett, (D), Michigan State, 1995, Sd
  La Verne M. Friberg, (D), Indiana, 1976, Gzx

Assistant Professor:
  Meera Chatterjee, (D), Oy
  Shanon P. Donnelly, (D), Indiana, 2009, Oi
  John M. Senko, (D), Oklahoma, 2004, Cg
Research Associate:
  Thomas J. Quick, (M), Akron, 1983, Ca
Lecturer:
  John F. Beltz, (M), Akron, 1992, Ggh
  Jeremy Spencer, (M), Oya
Adjunct Professor:
  Hazel Barton, (D), Colorado, 1997, Py
  Timothy Matney, (D), Pennsylvania, 1993, Ga

University of Akron - Wayne College
University of Akron - Wayne College (2014)
1901 Smucker Road
Orrville, OH 44667
  p. (330) 972-8934
  WayneCommunityRelations@uakron.edu
  http://www.wayne.uakron.edu/

University of Cincinnati
Dept of Geology (B,M,D) (2013)
500 Geology/Physics Building
P. O. Box 210013
Cincinnati, OH 45221-0013
  p. (513) 556-3732
  krista.smilek@uc.edu
  http://www.artsci.uc.edu/departments/geology.html
  Enrollment (2013): B: 86 (0) M: 10 (0) D: 11 (0)
Head:
  Lewis Owen, (D), Leicester (UK), 1988, GmlGt
Professor:
  Thomas J. Algeo, (D), Michigan, 1989, Gs
  Carlton E. Brett, (D), Michigan, 1978, Pe
  Warren D. Huff, (D), Cincinnati, 1963, Gz
  Attila I. Kilinc, (D), Penn State, 1969, Cp
  Thomas V. Lowell, (D), SUNY (Buffalo), 1986, Gl
  J. Barry Maynard, (D), Harvard, 1972, Cl
  David L. Meyer, (D), Yale, 1971, Pi
  Arnold I. Miller, (D), Chicago, 1986, Pi
  David Nash, (D), Michigan, 1977, Gm
Associate Professor:
  Craig Dietsch, (D), Yale, 1985, Gp
Assistant Professor:
  Andrew D. Czaja, (D), California (Los Angeles), 2006, PoCg
  Aaron Diefendorf, (D), Penn State, 2010, Co
  Eva Enkelmann, (D), CcGmt
  Amy Townsend-Small, (D), Texas, 2006, Co
  Dylan Ward, (D), Colorado, 2010, GmqOi
Adjunct Professor:
  Brenda R. Hanke, (D), California (Riverside), 2004, Pi
  Glenn W. Storrs, (D), Yale, 1986, Pv
Emeritus:
  Madeleine Briskin, (D), Brown, 1973, Pe
  John E. Grover, (D), Yale, 1972, Gz
  Paul E. Potter, (D), Chicago, 1952, Gs
Research Professor:
  Joshua H. Miller, (D), Chicago, 2009, PgvPe
  Yurena Yanes, PgeCs

University of Dayton
Dept of Geology (B) ● (2015)
300 College Park
SC 179
Dayton, OH 45469-2364
  p. (937) 229-3432
  dgoldman1@udayton.edu
  http://www.udayton.edu/artssciences/geology/
  Administrative Assistant: Darla Titus
  Enrollment (2015): B: 39 (6)
Chair:
  Daniel Goldman, (D), SUNY (Buffalo), 1993, PoqGr
Professor:
  Donald Pair, (D), Syracuse, 1991, Gl
  Michael R. Sandy, (D), London, 1984, Pi

Associate Professor:
Umesh Haritashya, (D), Indian Inst of Tech, 2005, OrGm
Andrea M. Koziol, (D), Chicago, 1988, Cp
Allen J. McGrew, (D), Wyoming, 1992, Gc
Shuang-Ye Wu, (D), Cambridge, 2000, Oy
Lecturer:
Zelalem Bedaso, (D), South Florida, Csl
Adjunct Professor:
Sue Klosterman, (M), Wright State, 2005, Gg
Andrew Rettig, (D), Cincinnati, 2014, Oy
Emeritus:
Charles J. Ritter, (D), Michigan, 1971, Ct

University of Toledo 🗗
Dept of Environmental Sciences (B,M,D) (2014)
2801 W. Bancroft Street
Toledo, OH 43606-3390
  p. (419) 530-2009
  eccarson@wisc.edu
  http://www.utoledo.edu/nsm/envsciences/
  Administrative Assistant: Patricia Hacker
  Enrollment (2011): B: 13 (3) M: 10 (5)
Director of the Lake Erie Research Center:
Carol A. Stepien, (D), S California, 1985, On
Chair:
Timothy G. Fisher, (D), Calgary, 1993, Gl
Professor:
Jiquan Chen, (D), Washington, 1991, On
Associate Professor:
Mark J. Camp, (D), Ohio State, 1974, Pi
Daryl F. Dwyer, (D), Michigan State, 1986, On
Johan F. Gottgens, (D), Florida, 1992, On
Scott Heckathorn, (D), Illinois, 1995, On
David E. Krantz, (D), South Carolina, 1988, Gs
James Martin-Hayden, (D), Connecticut, 1994, Hq
Daryl L. Moorhead, (D), Tennessee, 1985, On
Alison L. Spongberg, (D), Texas A&M, 1994, Co
Donald J. Stierman, (D), Stanford, 1977, Yg
Assistant Professor:
Richard H. Becker, (D), W Michigan, 2008, On
Jonathon Bossenbroek, (D), Colorado State (Ft. Collins), 2004, On
Thomas Bridgeman, (D), Michigan, 2001, On
Christine M. Mayer, (D), Illinois, 1998, On
William V. Sigler, (D), Purdue, 1999, On
Michael N. Weintraub, California, 2004, On

Wittenberg University
Dept of Geology (B) (2015)
P.O. Box 720
Springfield, OH 45501-0720
  p. (937) 327-7335
  jritter@wittenberg.edu
  http://www4.wittenberg.edu/academics/geol/
  f: https://www.facebook.com/WittenbergGeology
  Enrollment (2015): B: 14 (11)
Professor:
Kenneth W. Bladh, (D), Arizona, 1978, Gz
John B. Ritter, (D), Penn State, 1990, Gm
Associate Professor:
Michael J. Zaleha, (D), SUNY (Binghamton), 1994, Gs
Assistant Professor:
Sarah K. Fortner, (D), Ohio State, 2008, PyOaCl
Emeritus:
Katherine L. Bladh, (D), Arizona, 1976, Gi
Robert W. Morris, (D), Columbia, 1969, Pi

Wright State University
Dept of Earth and Environmental Science (B,M) (2014)
3640 Colonel Glenn Highway
260 Brehm Lab
Dayton, OH 45435
  p. (937) 775-2201
  david.schmidt@wright.edu
  http://www.wright.edu/ees/
  Enrollment (2010): B: 66 (8) M: 48 (15)

Director of Undergraduate Programs:
David Schmidt, (D), Ohio State, PiGd
Acting Chair:
David F. Dominic, (D), West Virginia, 1988, Gsr
Professor:
Christopher Barton, (D), Yale, Gqc
C. B. Gregor, (D), Utrecht (Neth), 1967, Gs
Allen Hunt, (D), California (Riverside), 1983, GqSp
Robert W. Ritzi, Jr., (D), Arizona, 1989, Hw
Associate Professor:
Abinash Agrawal, (D), North Carolina, 1990, ClHwPy
Songlin Cheng, (D), Arizona, 1984, Hw
Ernest C. Hauser, (D), Wisconsin, 1982, Ye
William Slattery, (D), CUNY, 1994, OeGr
Doyle Watts, (D), Michigan, 1979, YeOr
Assistant Professor:
Chad Hammerschmidt, (D), Connecticut, 2005, CmOc
Rebecca Teed, (D), Minnesota, 1999, OePe
Director of Sustainability:
Huntting (Hunt) Brown, (D), Ge
Emeritus:
Byron Kulander, (D), West Virginia, 1966, Gc
Benjamin H. Richard, (D), Indiana, 1966, Ye
Paul J. Wolfe, (D), Case Western, 1966, Ye

Youngstown State University
Dept of Geological & Environmental Sciences (B,M) (2014)
One University Plaza
2120 Moser Hall
Youngstown, OH 44555
  p. (330) 941-3612
  amjacobs@ysu.edu
  http://www.as.ysu.edu/~geology/
  Enrollment (2007): B: 48 (4) M: 21 (1)
Chair:
Jeffrey C. Dick, (D), Kent State, 1992, Ng
Professor:
Raymond E. Beiersdorfer, (D), California (Davis), 1992, Cg
Alan M. Jacobs, (D), Indiana, 1967, Ge
Director, Env Studies Program:
Isam E. Amin, (D), Nevada (Reno), 1987, Hw
Assistant Professor:
Joseph E. Andrew, (D), Kansas, 2002, Gc
Felicia P. Armstrong, (D), Oklahoma State, 2003, Sb
Shane V. Smith, (D), Washington State, 2005, Gs
Instructor:
Harry Bircher, (M), Youngstown State, 1995, Ge
Brian M. Greene, (D), Kent State, 2001, Ng
Lawrence P. Gurlea, (M), Pennsylvania, 1971, Cg
Engineering Adjunct:
Scott C. Martin, (D), Clarkson, 1984, Ge
Douglas M. Price, (D), Notre Dame, 1988, Cg
Emeritus:
Ann G. Harris, (M), Miami (Ohio), 1958, Ge
Ikram U. Khawaja, (D), Indiana, 1969, Ec
Charles R. Singler, (D), Nebraska, 1969, Gs
Cooperating Faculty:
Thomas P. Diggins, (D), SUNY, 1997, Py
Carl G. Johnston, (D), Cincinnati, 1992, Py

Zane State College
Oil and Gas Engineering Technology (A) (2015)
1555 Newark Rd
Zanesville, OH 43701
  p. (740) 588-1282
  nwelch@zanestate.edu
  http://www.zanestate.edu
  f: https://www.facebook.com/ZaneStateCollege
  t: @ZaneStateC

Oklahoma

Oklahoma City Community College
Physical Sciences (1999)
7777 South May Avenue
Oklahoma City, OK 73159

120

p. (405) 682-1611
dgregory@occc.edu
http://www.occc.edu

Oklahoma State University
Boone Pickens School of Geology (B,M,D) O (2015)
105 Noble Research Center
Stillwater, OK 74078-3031
p. (405) 744-6358
sandy.earls@okstate.edu
http://geology.okstate.edu
Administrative Assistant: Sandy Earls
Enrollment (2015): B: 157 (23) M: 64 (13) D: 24 (0)
Endowed Sun Chair:
Estella Atekwana, (D), Dalhousie, 1990, YgGt
Professor:
Mohamed Abdelsalam, (D), Gct
Michael Grammer, (D), GsEo
Jay M. Gregg, (D), Michigan State, 1982, Gs
Todd Halihan, (D), Texas, 2000, Hw
Jack Pashin, (D)
Associate Professor:
James Puckette, (D), Oklahoma State, 1996, Go
Assistant Professor:
Eliot Atekwana, (D), W Michigan, 1996, Cg
Jeffrey Byrnes, (D), Pittsburgh, 2002, GgvOn
Priyank Jaiswal, (D), Yg
Daniel Lao Davila, (D), Gc
Tracy Quan, (D), MIT/WHOI, 2005, Og
Natascha Riedinger, (D), Bremen, 2005, CgGu
Javier Vilcaez, (D), Tohoku Univ, 2009, Hw
Adjunct Professor:
Mary Hileman, (D), Michigan, 1973, Go
Emeritus:
Arthur Hounslow, (D), Carleton, 1968, Cl
Douglas Kent, (D), Iowa State, 1969, Hw
Wayne Pettyjohn, (D), Boston, 1964, Hw
Vernon Scott, (D), Utah, 1975, Oe
Gary Stewart, (D), Kansas, 1973, Go
John D. Vitek, (D), Iowa, 1973, Gm

Rogers State University
Dept of Mathematics and Physical Sciences (1999)
1701 W. Will Rogers Blvd.
Claremore, OK 74107
p. (918) 343-6812
vwood@rsu.edu
http://www.rsu.edu

Tulsa Community College
Science and Math (A) (2015)
909 S. Boston Avenue
Tulsa, OK 74119
p. (918) 595-7246
claude.bolze@tulsacc.edu
http://www.tulsacc.edu
Enrollment (2015): A: 38 (5)
Professor:
Claude E. Bolze, (M), Wright State, 1974, GgoPg
Adjunct Professor:
Martin Bregman, (D), New Mexico, 1971, YgGcg

University of Oklahoma ⬚
ConocoPhillips School of Geology & Geophysics (B,M,D) O
(2015)
100 East Boyd
710 Energy Center
Norman, OK 73019-0628
p. (405) 325-3253
geology@ou.edu
http://geology.ou.edu
Enrollment (2006): B: 87 (0) M: 40 (0) D: 24 (0)
Director:
R. Douglas Elmore, (D), Michigan, 1981, Ym

Professor:
Younane N. Abousleiman, (D), Delaware, 1991, Gg
Michael H. Engel, (D), Arizona, 1980, Co
G. Randy Keller, (D), Texas Tech, 1973, Yg
David London, (D), Arizona State, 1981, Cp
Kurt J. Marfurt, (D), Columbia, 1978, Ys
Shankar Mitra, (D), Johns Hopkins, 1977, Gc
R. Paul Philp, (D), Sydney, 1972, Co
Matthew J. Pranter, (D), Colorado Mines, Go
Matthew J. Pranter, Gos
Roger M. Slatt, (D), Alaska, 1970, Go
Gerilyn S. Soreghan, (D), Arizona, 1992, Gs
Stephen R. Westrop, (D), Toronto, 1984, Pi
Associate Professor:
Richard Lupia, (D), Chicago, 1997, Pm
John D. Pigott, (D), Northwestern, 1981, Ye
Barry L. Weaver, (D), Birmingham (UK), 1980, Ct
Assistant Professor:
Xiaowei Chen, (D), California (San Diego), 2013, YsGt
Shannon Dulin, (D), Oklahoma, 2014, Ym
Megan E. Elwood Madden, (D), Virginia Tech, 2005, Yg
Andrew S. Madden, (D), Virginia Tech, 2005, Gez
Michael J. Soreghan, (D), Arizona, 1994, Gs
Adjunct Professor:
Richard L. Cifelli, (D), Columbia, 1983, Pv
Emeritus:
Judson L. Ahern, (D), Cornell, 1980, Yg
James M. Forgotson, Jr., (D), Northwestern, 1956, Go
M. Charles Gilbert, (D), California (Los Angeles), 1965, Cp
Charles W. Harper, Jr., (D), Caltech, 1964, Pi
David W. Stearns, (D), Texas A&M, 1969, Gc
Cooperating Faculty:
Neil Suneson, (D), California (Santa Barbara), 1980, Gr
Electron Microprobe Operator:
George B. Morgan, (D), Oklahoma, 1988, Gi

Mewbourne School of Petroleum & Geological Engineering
(B,M,D) (2015)
100 East Boyd Street
Sarkeys Energy Center 1210
Norman, OK 73019-1001
p. (405) 325-2921
mpge@ou.edu
http://mpge.ou.edu/
f: https://www.facebook.com/OUMPGE
t: @ou_mpge
Enrollment (2015): B: 975 (133) M: 101 (25) D: 37 (4)
Director:
Chandra S. Rai, (D), Hawaii, 1977, Np
Graduate Liaison:
Deepak Devegowda, (D), Texas A&M, 2008, Np
Director Natural Gas Engineering & Management:
Suresh Sharma, (D), Oklahoma, 1968, Np
Professor:
Younane Abousleiman, (D), Delaware, 1991, Nr
Ramadan Ahmed, (D), Norwegian Univ of Sci & Tech, 2001, Np
Jeff Callard, (D), Louisiana State, 1994, Np
Ahmed Ghassemi, (D), Oklahoma, 1996, Nr
Ben Shiau, (D), Oklahoma, 1995
Carl H. Sondergeld, (D), Cornell, 1977, Np
Musharraf Zaman, (D), Bangladesh Univ of Eng and Tech, 1975, Np
Associate Professor:
Mashhad Fahes, (D), Imperial Coll (London), 2006, Np
Ahmad Jamili, (D), Kansas, 2004, Np
Rouzbeh Moghanloo, (D), Texas, 2012, Np
Maysam Pournik, (D), Texas A&M, 2008, Np
Catalin Teodoriu, (D), Ploiesti, Np
Xingru Wu, (D), Texas, 2006, Np
Assistant Professor:
Siddharth Misra, (D), Texas (Austin), 2015, Np
Ahmad Sakhaee-Pour, (D), Texas (Austin), 2012, Np
Instructor:
Ilham El-Monier, (D), Texas A&M, 2012, Np
Emeritus:
Faruk Civan, (D), Oklahoma, 1978, Np
Roy M. Knapp, (D), Kansas, 1973, Np
Jean-Claude Roegiers, (D), Minnesota, 1974, Nr

Subhash N. Shah, (D), New Mexico, 1974, Np

University of Tulsa ⬚
Dept of Geosciences (B,M,D) (2015)
800 S. Tucker Drive
Tulsa, OK 74104-9700
  p. (918) 631-2517
  pjm@utulsa.edu
  http://www.utulsa.edu/academics/colleges/college-of-engineering-and-natural-sciences/departments-and-schools/Department-of-Geosc
  Administrative Assistant: Beverly A. Phelps
  Enrollment (2015): B: 8 (8) M: 10 (10) D: 2 (2)
Professor:
  Peter J. Michael, (D), Columbia, 1983, Gi
Vice President for Research & Dean of Graduate School:
  Janet Haggerty, (D), Hawaii, 1982, Gu
Professor:
  Kerry Sublette, (D), Tulsa, 1985, Ge
Decker Dawson Associate Professor of Applied Geophysics:
  Jingyi Chen, (D), Chinese Acad of Sci, 2005, Yes
Associate Professor:
  Dennis R. Kerr, (D), Wisconsin, 1989, Gs
  Kumar Ramachandran, (D), Victoria, 2001, Ye
  J. Bryan Tapp, (D), Oklahoma, 1983, Gc
Assistant Professor:
  Junran Li, (D), Virginia, 2008, Gme
Research Associate:
  Robert W. Scott, (D), Kansas, 1967, Gs
Applied Associate Professor:
  Winton Cornell, (D), Rhode Island, 1987, GivCa
Emeritus:
  Colin Barker, (D), Oxford, 1965, Cg

Oregon

Central Oregon Community College
Dept of Science (A) (2014)
2600 NW College Way
Bend, OR 97701
  p. (541) 383-7557
  breynolds@cocc.edu
  http://science.cocc.edu/Programs_Classes/Geology/default.aspx
  Enrollment: No data reported since 1999
Associate Professor:
  Robert W. Reynolds, (D), Idaho, 1994, Gv

Oregon State University ⬚
College of Earth, Ocean, and Atmospheric Sciences (B,M,D)
● (2016)
104 CEOAS Administration Building
Corvallis, OR 97331-5503
  p. (541) 737-1201
  contact@coas.oregonstate.edu
  http://ceoas.oregonstate.edu
  Administrative Assistant: Melinda Jensen
  Enrollment (2010): B: 68 (9) M: 18 (5) D: 18 (1)
Interim Dean:
  Roy D. Haggerty, (D), Stanford, 1995, Hw
Director-Budget & Fiscal Planning:
  Sherman H. Bloomer, (D), California (San Diego), 1982, Gi
Director of Ocean Science Program:
  Rob Wheatcroft, (D), Washington, 1990, OgGg
Director of OCCRI:
  Phillip Mote, (D), Washington, 1994, Oa
Director of Marine Resource Management Program:
  Flaxen D. Conway, (M), Oregon State, 1986, Gu
Director of Geology Program:
  Edward J. Brook, (D), MIT, 1993, Ou
Director of Geography Program:
  Julia A. Jones, (D), Johns Hopkins, 1983, So
Director of Environmental Science Program:
  Laurence Becker, (D), California (Berkeley), 1989, On
Associate Dean for Research:
  Jack A. Barth, (D), MIT, 1987, On

Associate Dean for Academic Programs:
  Anita L. Grunder, (D), Stanford, 1986, Gi
Professor:
  Jeffrey R. Barnes, (D), Washington, 1983, Oa
  Hal Batchelder, (D), Oregon State, 1986, Op
  Kelly Benoit-Bird, (D), Hawaii, 2003, Gu
  Michael E. Campana, (D), Arizona, 1975, Hg
  Lorenzo Ciannelli, (D), Washington, 2002, Og
  Peter U. Clark, (D), Colorado, 1984, Gl
  Frederick (Rick) Colwell, (D), Virginia Tech, 1986, On
  Shanika de Silva, (D), Open (UK), 1987, Gv
  John H. Dilles, (D), Stanford, 1984, Em
  Gary D. Egbert, (D), Washington, 1987, Yr
  Martin R. Fisk, (D), Rhode Island, 1978, Yr
  Michael H. Freilich, (D), Scripps, 1981, On
  Chris Goldfinger, (D), Oregon State, 1994, Yr
  Miguel A. Goni, (D), Washington, 1992, Gu
  David W. Graham, (D), MIT, 1987, Cm
  Burke R. Hales, Washington, 1995, Oc
  Robert N. Harris, (D), Utah, 1996, Yhr
  Michael Harte, (D), Victoria, 1994, Gu
  Adam J. R Kent, (D), Australian National, 1995, Ca
  Michael P. Kosro, (D), Scripps, 1985, Onr
  Ricardo Letelier, (D), Hawaii, 1994, Obr
  Ricardo Matano, (D), Princeton, 1991, Oap
  Andrew J. Meigs, (D), S California, 1995, Gc
  Robert N. Miller, (D), California (Berkeley), 1976, Op
  Alan C. Mix, (D), Columbia, 1986, Cs
  James N. Moum, (D), British Columbia, 1984, Op
  Roger L. Nielsen, (D), S Methodist, 1983, Gi
  Anne Nolin, (D), California (Santa Barbara), 1993, Or
  Tuba Ozkan-Haller, (D), Delaware, 1998, On
  Clare Reimers, (D), Oregon State, 1982, Oc
  Roger Samelson, (D), Oregon State, 1987, Op
  Adam Schultz, (D), Washington, 1986, Yg
  Eric Skyllingstad, (D), Wisconsin, 1986, Ow
  William D. Smyth, (D), Toronto, 1990, Yr
  Yvette H. Spitz, (D), Old Dominion, 1995, Yr
  Marta E. Torres, (D), Oregon State, 1988, Cm
  Anne M. Trehu, (D), MIT/WHOI, 1982, Yr
  Aaron T. Wolf, (D), Wisconsin, 1992, Hg
Senior Research:
  Brian Haley, (D), Oregon State, 2004, Cs
Director, Water Resources Graduate Program:
  Mary V. Santelmann, (D), Minnesota, 1988, Oy
Associate Professor:
  Kim S. Bernard, (D), Rhodes, 2007
  Anders Carlson, (D), Oregon State, 2006, GlCt
  Byron Crump, (D), Washington, 1999
  Simon P. de Szoeke, (D), Washington, 2004, Opa
  Edward P. Dever, (D), MIT/WHOI, 1995, Op
  Theodore Durland, (D), Hawaii, 2006, Yg
  Hannah Gosnell, (D), Colorado, 2000, Ou
  Merrick Haller, (D), Delaware, 1999, Onr
  Randall A. Keller, (D), Oregon State, 1996, Gu
  Eric Kirby, (D)
  Anthony Koppers, (D), Free (Amsterdam), 1988, CgGv
  Alexander Kurapov, (D), St Petersburg, 1994, Yr
  Stephen Lancaster, (D), MIT, 1999, Hs
  Jim Lerczak, (D), Scripps, 2000, Op
  John L. Nabelek, (D), MIT/WHOI, 1984, GtYs
  Jonathan Nash, (D), Oregon State, 2000, Op
  David Noone, (D), Melbourne, 2001, Owg
  Peter Ruggiero, (D), Oregon State, 1997, On
  Andreas Schmittner, (D), Bern (Switzerland), 1999, OaYr
  Kipp Shearman, (D), Oregon State, 1999, Opn
  Joseph Stoner, (D), Québec (Montréal), 1995, Gsr
  Frank J. Tepley, III, (D), California (Los Angeles), 1999, GiCs
  Christoph Thomas, (D), Bayreuth, 2005, Owa
  Paul Vincent, (D), Colorado, 1998, Yd
  Richard J. Vong, (D), Washington, 1985, Oa
  Angelicque White, (D), Oregon State, 2006, Ob
Director of Atmospheric Science Program:
  Karen M. Shell, (D), Scripps, 2004, Oa
Associate Director of the Institute for Water and Watersheds :
  W. Todd Jarvis, (D), Oregon State, 2006, Hw

Assistant Professor:
  Jessica Creveling, (D), Harvard, 2012, GgsGr
  Jonathan Fram, (D), California (Berkeley), 2005, Op
  Jennifer Hutchings, Ol
  Lauren W. Juranek, Washington, 2007, Cm
  Robert Kennedy, (D), Oregon State, 2004, Ori
  Heather E. Lintz, (D), Oregon State, 2010, On
  Jennifer L. McKay, (D), British Columbia, 2004, Cm
  Larry O'Neill, (D), Oregon State, 2007, Owg
  Alyssa Shiel, (D), British Columbia, 2010, Cgs
  Emily L. Shroyer, (D), Oregon State, 2009, On
  Jamon Van Den Hoek, (D), Wisconsin (Madison), 2012, Our
  George Waldbusser, (D), Maryland (Baltimore), 2008, Ob
  Justin Wettstein, (D), Washington, 2007, Oa
Senior Instructor/Program Coordinator:
  Kaplan Yalcin, (D), New Hampshire, 2005, Og
Senior Instructor:
  Steve Cook, (D), Florida, 1995, On
Instructor:
  Lorene Yokoyama Becker, (M), Wisconsin, 1999, Oi
  Demian Hommel, (D), Oregon, 2009, On
  Rebecca Yalcin, (M), Maine, 2001, Gg
Distinguished Emeritus Professor:
  Dudley B. Chelton, (D), California (San Diego), 1980, Op
  Patricia Wheeler, (D), California (Irvine), 1976, Cm
Emeritus:
  John S. Allen, Jr., (D), Princeton, 1968, Op
  Andrew Bennett, (D), Harvard, 1971, Op
  John V. Byrne, (D), S California, 1957, Gu
  Douglas Caldwell, (D)
  Robert W. Collier, (D), MIT, 1981, Cm
  Timothy J. Cowles, (D), Duke, 1977, Ob
  Robert A. Duncan, (D), Yr
  Robert Holman, (D), Dalhousie, 1979, On
  Philip L. Jackson, (D), Kansas, 1977, Oy
  George Keller, (D), Yg
  A. Jon Kimerling, (D), Wisconsin, 1976, Or
  Gary Klinkhammer, (D), Rhode Island, 1979, Yr
  Robert J. Lillie, (D), Cornell, 1984, Ye
  Gordon E. Matzke, (D), Syracuse, 1975, Og
  Alan R. Niem, (D), Wisconsin, 1971, Gd
  Nicklas Pisias, (D), Rhode Island, 1978, Gu
  Fredrick G. Prahl, (D), Washington, 1982, Oc
  Barry Sherr, (D), Georgia, 1977, Ob
  Evelyn Sherr, (D), Duke, 1977, Ob
  Bernd Simoneit, (D), CgXc
  Lawrence Small, (D), Ob
  Robert Lloyd Smith, (D), Yr
  Ted P. Strub, (D), California (Davis), 1983, Oa
  Robert S. Yeats, (D), Washington, 1958, Gt
  J. Ronald Zaneveld, (D), Oregon State, 1971, Yr

Portland Community College-Sylvania Campus

Physical Science Dept (A) O (2015)
12000 SW 49th Ave.
Portland, OR 97219
  p. 971-722-8209
  patty.maazouz@pcc.edu
  http://www.pcc.edu/programs/geology/
Instructor:
  Talal Abdulkareem, (D)
  Gretchen Gebhardt, (M)
  Melinda Hutson, (D)
  Hollie Oakes-Miller, (M)
  Kristy Schepker, (M)

Portland State University

Dept of Geology (B,M,D) (2016)
P.O. Box 751
Portland, OR 97207
  p. (503) 725-3022
  streckm@pdx.edu
  http://www.pdx.edu/geology/
  Enrollment (2015): B: 156 (9) M: 20 (12) D: 1 (0)
Professor:
  Andrew G. Fountain, (D), Washington, 1992, Gl

Martin J. Streck, (D), Oregon State, 1994, Giv
Associate Professor:
  Kenneth M. Cruikshank, (D), Purdue, 1991, Gc
  Robert Benjamin Perkins, (D), Portland State, 2000, Hq
  Alexander (Alex) M. Ruzicka, (D), Arizona, 1996, Xm
Assistant Professor:
  John T. Bershaw, (D), Rochester, 2011, GsCs
  Adam M. Booth, (D), Oregon, 2012, GmOr
  Nancy A. Price, (D), Maine, 2012, GcOeGt
  Maxwell L. Rudolph, (D), California (Berkeley), 2012, Gq
  Ashley Streig, (D), Oregon, 2014, YsGt
Research Associate:
  Richard Hugo, (D), Washington State, 1998, Gy
Adjunct Professor:
  Sheila Alfsen
  Matthew Brunengo, (D), Portland State, 2012, GgNgGm
  Elizabeth Carter, (D), Lausanne, 1993, Pm
  Frank Granshaw
  Melinda Hutson, (D), Arizona, 1996, Xmc
  William Orr, (D), Michigan State, 1968, GgOg
  Carl Palmer
  Dick Pugh
  Arron Steiner
  Michelle Stoklosa, (D), Wisconsin (Madison), 2003, GdPiOg
  Barry Walker, (D), Oregon State, 2011, GiCgGv
Emeritus:
  Scott F. Burns, (D), Colorado, 1980, Ng
  Michael L. Cummings, (D), Wisconsin, 1978, Gg
  Paul E. Hammond, (D), Washington, 1963, Gi
  Ansel G. Johnson, (D), Stanford, 1973, Ye
  Richard E. Thoms, (D), California, 1965, Ps
Research Assistant:
  David Percy, (B), Portland State, 1999, Oi
Cooperating Faculty:
  Christina L. Hulbe, (D), Chicago, 1998, Gl

Rogue Community College
Science Dept-Physical Sciences-Geology (1999)
3345 Redwood Highway
Grants Pass, OR 97527
  p. (541) 245-7527
  jvanbrunt@roguecc.edu
  http://learn.roguecc.edu/science/physical.htm

Southern Oregon University
Dept of Geology (B) (2014)
1250 Siskiyou Boulevard
Ashland, OR 97520
  p. (541) 552-6479
  lane@sou.edu
  Administrative Assistant: Susan Koralek
  Enrollment (2006): B: 45 (5)
Chair:
  Charles L. Lane, (D), California (Los Angeles), 1987, Hg
Dean, Science:
  Joseph L. Graf, Jr., (D), Yale, 1975, Em
Professor:
  Jad A. D'Allura, (D), California (Davis), 1977, Gc
Associate Professor:
  Eric Dittmer, (M), San Jose State, 1972, Gg
Adjunct Professor:
  Vernon J. Crawford, (M), Oregon, 1970, Gg
  Harry W. Smedes, (D), Washington, 1959, Gi
  Richard Ugland, (M), Utah, 1974, Gg
Emeritus:
  Monty A. Elliott, (D), Oregon State, 1971, Gr
  William B. Purdom, (D), Arizona, 1960, Gx

Southwestern Oregon Community College
Dept of Geology (A) (2015)
1988 Newmark
Coos Bay, OR 97420-2912
  p. (541) 888-7216
  rmetzger@socc.edu
  Enrollment (2013): A: 2 (0)

Professor:
Ronald A. Metzger, (D), Iowa, 1991, Pms

Tillamook Bay Community College
Associate of Science (1999)
2510 First Street
Tillamook, OR 97141
    bannan@tillamookbay.cc

Treasure Valley Community College
Career and Technical Education ● (2015)
650 College Blvd.
Ontario, OR 97914
    p. (541) 881-8866
    dtinkler@tvcc.cc
    http://www.tvcc.cc.or.us/science/Index.htm
    f: https://www.facebook.com/profile.
    php?id=100005312898088
Dr.:
    Dorothy Tinkler, (D), Texas Tech, 2003, Oi

Umpqua Community College
Dept of Geology Transfer Program (1999)
P.O. Box 967
1140 Umpqua College Rd.
Roseburg, OR 97470
    p. (541) 440-4654
    Jason.Aase@umpqua.edu
    http://www.umpqua.edu/degree-programs/55

University of Oregon 🗂
Dept of Geography (B,M,D) (2015)
107 Condon Hall
Eugene, OR 97403-1251
    p. (541) 346-4555
    uogeog@uoregon.edu
    http://geography.uoregon.edu
    Enrollment (2009): B: 167 (55) M: 22 (9) D: 19 (5)
Head:
    Amy Lobben, (D), Michigan State, 1999, OinOn
Interim Dean:
    W. Andrew Marcus, (D), Colorado, 1987
Professor:
    Patrick J. Bartlein, (D), Wisconsin, 1978, Pe
    Patricia F. McDowell, (D), Wisconsin, 1980, Gm
    Alexander B. Murphy, (D), Chicago, 1987, On
    Peter A. Walker, (M), Oregon, 1966, On
Associate Professor:
    Daniel Buck, (D), California (Berkeley), 2002, On
    Shaul E. Cohen, (D), Chicago, 1991, On
    Mark Fonstad, (D), Arizona State, 2000, Oy
    Dan Gavin, (D), Washington, 2000, Oy
    Derrick Hindery, (D), California (Los Angeles), 2003, On
    Xiaobo Su, (D), Singapore, 2007, On
Assistant Professor:
    Christopher Bone, (D), Simon Fraser, 2009, Oi
    Katharine Meehan, (D), Arizona, 2010, On
    Hedda R. Schmidtke, (D), Hamburg, 2004
Instructor:
    Nicholas Kohler, (D), Oregon, 2004, Oi
Emeritus:
    Stanton A. Cook, (D), California (Berkeley), 1960, On
    Susan W. Hardwick, (D), California (Davis), 2000, On
    Carl L. Johannessen, (D), California (Berkeley), 1959, On
    Alvin W. Urquhart, California (Berkeley), 1962, On
    Ronald Wixman, (D), Columbia, 1978, On

Dept of Geological Sciences (B,M,D) ○ (2015)
1272 University of Oregon
Eugene, OR 97403-1272
    p. (541) 346-4573
    sthoms@uoregon.edu
    http://www.uoregon.edu/~dogsci/
    Enrollment (2015): B: 122 (23) M: 8 (7) D: 23 (4)

Department Head:
    Rebecca J. Dorsey, (D), Princeton, 1989, Gr
Professor:
    Eugene D. Humphreys, (D), Caltech, 1982, YsGt
    Mark H. Reed, (D), California (Berkeley), 1977, Em
    Gregory J. Retallack, (D), New England, 1978, Pb
    Joshua J. Roering, (D), California (Berkeley), 2000, Gm
    Douglas R. Toomey, (D), MIT/WHOI, 1987, YsGt
    Paul Wallace, (D), California (Berkeley), 1991, GviCg
    Ray J. Weldon, (D), Caltech, 1986, Gc
Associate Professor:
    Ilya N. Bindeman, (D), Chicago, 1998, Cs
    Emilie E. Hooft, (D), MIT, 1996, Yr
    Samantha Hopkins, (D)
    Qusheng Jin, (D)
    Alan W. Rempel, (D), Cambridge, 2001, Nr
Assistant Professor:
    Edward Davis, (D)
    Dave Sutherland, (D)
    James Watkins, (D)
Instructor:
    Marli G. Miller, (D), Washington, 1997, Gc
Assoc Dean Natural Science:
    A. Dana Johnston, (D), Minnesota, 1983, Cp
Emeritus:
    Sam Boggs, Jr., (D), Colorado, 1964, Gd
    M. Allan Kays, (D), Washington (St. Louis), 1960, Gp
    Alexander R. McBirney, (D), California (Berkeley), 1961, Gv
    William N. Orr, (D), Michigan State, 1967, Pm
    Norman M. Savage, (D), Sydney, 1968, Pi
    Harve S. Waff, (D), Oregon, 1970, Yg
Office & Business Manager:
    Sandy K. Thoms, (B)
Cooperating Faculty:
    John M. Logan, (D), Oklahoma, 1965, Nr
    Elise Mezger Weldon, (M), S California, 1986, Gl

Western Oregon University
Earth and Physical Science Dept. (B) (2015)
345 N. Monmouth Ave.
Monmouth, OR 97361
    p. (503) 838-8398
    taylors@wou.edu
    http://www.wou.edu/earthscience
    Enrollment (2015): B: 40 (10)
Professor:
    Jeffrey A. Myers, (D), Santa Barbara, 1998, Gs
    Stephen B. Taylor, (D), West Virginia, 1999, Gm
    Jeffrey H. Templeton, (D), Oregon State, 1998, Gv
Assistant Professor:
    Melinda Shimizu, (D), Arizona State, 2014, OirOg
Instructor:
    Don Ellingson, (M), W Oregon, 1988, OwgXg
    Jeremiah Oxford, (M), Oregon State, 2006, Og
    Grant Smith, (D), Oregon State, 2012, Og
    Phillip Wade, (M), San Diego State, 1991, Oge

Willamette University
Environmental and Earth Sciences Dept (2014)
900 State Street
Salem, OR 97301
    p. (503) 370-6587
    spike@willamette.edu
    http://www.willamette.edu/cla/ees/
Chair:
    Scott Pike, (D), Georgia, 2000, Gg
Professor:
    Karen Arabas, (D), Penn State, 1997, On
    H. Peter Eilers, (D), Oregon State, 1974, On
Endowed Dempsey Chair:
    Joe Bowersox, (D), Wisconsin, 1995, On

Pennsylvania

Allegheny College
Dept of Geology (B) (2015)

520 North Main Street
Meadville, PA 16335
    p. (814) 332-2350
    robrien@allegheny.edu
    http://www.allegheny.edu/academics/geo/
    Enrollment (2015): B: 20 (0)
Associate Professor:
    Rachel O'Brien, (D), Washington State, 2000, Hw
Assistant Professor:
    Theresa M. Schwartz, (D), Stanford, 2015, Gs
Visiting Professor:
    Erin Birsic, (M), Wisconsin (Madison), 2015, Gi
Currently Provost and Dean of the College:
    Ron B. Cole, (D), Rochester, 1993, Gt

Bloomsburg University
Dept of Geography and Geosciences (B) (2014)
400 East Second Street
Bloomsburg, PA 17815-1301
    p. (570) 389-4108
    dspringe@bloomu.edu
    http://departments.bloomu.edu/geo/
    Enrollment (2007): B: 45 (12)
Professor:
    Shahalam M.N. Amin, (D), Kent State, 1991, GeScOn
    John E. Bodenman, (D), Penn State, 1995, Ou
    Sandra J. Kehoe-Forutan, (D), Queensland, 1991, Onu
    Michael K. Shepard, (D), Washington (St. Louis), 1994, XgYgOr
    Dale A. Springer, (D), Virginia Tech, 1982, PivOe
    Karen M. Trifonoff, (D), Kansas, 1994, Oi
Associate Professor:
    Patricia J. Beyer, (D), Arizona State, 1997, HsOyGm
    Cynthia Venn, (D), Pittsburgh, 1996, OgClOc
Assistant Professor:
    Jeffrey C. Brunskill, (D), SUNY (Buffalo), 2005, OiwOy
    John G. Hintz, (D), Kentucky, 2005, Oin
    Brett T. McLaurin, (D), Wyoming, 2000, GrsGd
    Jennifer B. Whisner, (D), Tennesse, 2010, GmHw
    S. Christopher Whisner, (D), Tennesse, 2005, GciGz
Department Secretary:
    Jade L. Swartwood, On

Bryn Mawr College
Dept of Geology (B) (2016)
101 North Merion Avenue
Bryn Mawr, PA 19010-2899
    p. (610) 526-5115
    aweil@brynmawr.edu
    http://www.brynmawr.edu/geology/
    Enrollment (2015): B: 32 (14)
Professor:
    Arlo B. Weil, (D), Michigan, 2001, Gc
Associate Professor:
    Donald C. Barber, (D), Colorado, 2001, Gs
    Pedro Marenco, (D), S California, 2008, PgCsPo
Assistant Professor:
    Selby Cull, (D), Washington, 2011, XgGzx
Research Associate:
    Katherine Marenco, (D), S California, 2009, PgoPe
    Frank S. Welsh
Emeritus:
    Maria Luisa B. Crawford, (D), California (Berkeley), 1965, Gx
    William A. Crawford, (D), California (Berkeley), 1965, Cg
    Lucian B. Platt, (D), Yale, 1960, Gc
    W. Bruce Saunders, (D), Iowa, 1970, Pi

Bucknell University
Geology and Environmental Geosciences (B) (2015)
231 O'Leary Center
Lewisburg, PA 17837
    p. (570) 577-1382
    cdaniel@bucknell.edu
    http://www.bucknell.edu/Geology
    f: http://www.facebook.com/BucknellGeology
    Administrative Assistant: Carilee Dill
    Enrollment (2015): B: 37 (10)

Chair:
    Christopher G. Daniel, (D), Rensselaer, 1998, Gp
Professor:
    Mary Beth Gray, (D), Rochester, 1991, Gc
    Carl S. Kirby, (D), Virginia Tech, 1993, Cl
    R. Craig Kochel, (D), Texas, 1980, Gm
    Jeffrey M. Trop, (D), Purdue, 2000, Gs
Associate Professor:
    Ellen K. Herman, (D), Penn State, 2006, Hw
    Robert W. Jacob, (D), Brown, 2006, Yg
Emeritus:
    Jack C. Allen, (D), Princeton, 1962, GizGe
    Edward Cotter, (D), Princeton, 1963, GmPg
Laboratory Director:
    Brad C. Jordan, (M), Rhode Island, 1983, Gi

California University of Pennsylvania
Dept of Earth Sciences (B) (2015)
250 University Avenue
California, PA 15419
    p. (724) 938-4180
    wickham@calu.edu
    http://www.cup.edu/eberly/earthscience
    Administrative Assistant: Pamela Higinbotham
    Enrollment (2015): B: 195 (25)
Chair:
    Thomas Wickham, (D), Penn State, 2000, Oy
Associate Professor:
    Thomas Mueller, (D), Illinois, 1999, Oi
Assistant Professor:
    John Confer, (D), Penn State, 1997, On
    Kyle Fredrick, (D), SUNY (Buffalo), 2008, GgHg
    Swarndeep S. Gill, (D), Wyoming, 2002, Oa
    Chad Kauffman, (D), Nebraska, 2000, Oa
    Susan Ryan, (D), Calgary, 2005, Og

Carnegie Museum of Natural History
Section of Vertebrate Paleontology (2014)
4400 Forbes Avenue
Pittsburgh, PA 15213
    p. (412) 622-5782
    beardc@CarnegieMNH.org
    http://www.carnegiemnh.org/vp/
    Enrollment: No data reported since 1999
Curator:
    K. Christopher Beard, (D), Johns Hopkins, 1989, Pv
Curator:
    Mary R. Dawson, (D), Kansas, 1957, Pv
Preparator:
    Dan Pickering, (B), Carnegie Mellon, 1983, On
    Alan R. Tabrum, (M), SD Mines, 1981, Pv
    Norman Wuerthele, (B), Pittsburgh, 1966, Pv
Curator & Associate Director:
    Zhexi Luo, (D), California (Berkeley), 1987, Pv
Curator:
    David S. Berman, (D), California (Los Angeles), 1969, Pv
Collections Manager:
    Amy C. Henrici, (M), Pittsburgh, 1990, Pv
Assistant Curator:
    Matthew C. Lamanna, (D), Pennsylvania, 2004, Pv

Clarion University
Dept of Biology and Geosciences (B) O (2016)
840 Wood Street
Clarion, PA 16214
    p. (814) 393-2317
    cking@clarion.edu
    http://www.clarion.edu/BIGS
    Enrollment (2015): B: 97 (24)
Professor:
    Yasser M. Ayad, (D), Montreal, 2000, Oi
    Valentine U. James, (D), Texas A&M, Ou
    Anthony J. Vega, (D), Louisiana State, 1994, OapOw
    Craig E. Zamzow, (D), Texas, 1983, Gi

Delaware County Community College
STEM (A) (2013)
901 Media Line Road
Media, PA 19063
p. (610) 359-5082
jsnyder2@dccc.edu
http://www.dccc.edu/
Professor:
Daniel Childers, Og
Associate Professor:
Jennifer L. Snyder, (D), W Michigan, 1998, Og

Dickinson College
Dept of Earth Sciences (B) (2015)
P.O. Box 1773
Carlisle, PA 17013-2896
p. (717) 245-1355
key@dickinson.edu
http://www.dickinson.edu/academics/programs/earth-
sciences/
Administrative Assistant: Debra Peters
Enrollment (2015): B: 23 (3)
Associate Professor:
Peter B. Sak, (D), Penn State, 2002, Gcm
Professor:
Marcus M. Key, Jr., (D), Yale, 1988, Pi
Associate Professor:
Benjamin R. Edwards, (D), British Columbia, 1997, GivCg
Emeritus:
Jeffery W. Niemitz, (D), S California, 1978, ClOuGn
Noel Potter, Jr., (D), Minnesota, 1969, Gm
William W. Vernon, (D), Lehigh, 1964, Gz
Technician:
Robert Dean, (M), Texas (El Paso), 2004, Gi

Environmental Studies & Environmental Science (2004)
P.O. Box 1773
Carlisle, PA 17013-2896
p. (717) 245-1355
heiman@dickinson.edu
Administrative Assistant: Patricia Braught
Enrollment (1997): B: 54 (13)
Chair:
Michael Heiman, (D), California (Berkeley), 1983, Ou
Associate Professor:
Candie Wilderman, (D), Johns Hopkins, 1984, Hs
Visiting Professor:
Kirsten Hural, (D), Cornell, 1997, Gg

Drexel University
Dept of Biodiversity, Earth & Environmental Science (B,M,D)
(2015)
3201 Arch St
Suite 240
Philadelphia, PA 19104
p. (215) 571-4639
loyc@drexel.edu
http://drexel.edu/bees/
f: https://www.facebook.com/groups/DrexelBEES/
Enrollment (2015): B: 21 (0) D: 8 (1)
Pilsbry Chair of Malacology:
Gary Rosenberg, (D), Harvard, 1989, Pi
Professor:
David Velinsky, (D), Old Dominion, 1987, OcCms
Associate Professor:
Ted Daeschler, (D), Pennsylvania, 1998, PvGgPy
Assistant Professor:
Loyc Vanderkluysen, (D), Hawaii, 2008, GviGz
Adjunct Professor:
Mitch Cron, (M), Pennsylvania, 2013, Gge
Peter D. Muller, (D), Binghamton, 1980, Gce
Assistant Research Professor:
Jerry V. Mead, (D), SUNY-Syracuse, 2007, OiHgGm

Edinboro University of Pennsylvania
Dept of Geosciences (B) (2015)
126 Cooper Hall
230 Scotland Road
Edinboro, PA 16444-0001
p. (814) 732-2529
geosciences@edinboro.edu
http://www.edinboro.edu/academics/schools-and-depart-
ments/cshp/departments/geosciences/
f: https://www.facebook.com/pages/Edinboro-University-
Geosciences-Department/426407214146067
Enrollment (2015): B: 141 (24)
Chair:
Laurie A. Parendes, (D), Oregon State, 1997, On
Brian S. Zimmerman, (D), Washington State, 1991, Em
Professor:
Baher A. Ghosheh, (D), SUNY (Buffalo), 1988, On
David Hurd, (D), Cleveland State, 1997, Og
Henry Lawrence, (D), Oregon, 1985, Ou
Kerry A. Moyer, (D), Penn State, 1993, Oa
Joseph F. Reese, (D), Texas, 1995, Gc
Eric Straffin, (D), Nebraska, 2000, Gm
Dale Tshudy, (D), Kent State, 1993, Pi
Associate Professor:
Karen Eisenhart, (D), Colorado, 2004, Oy
Wook Lee, (D), Ohio State, Oi
Assistant Professor:
Richard Deal, (D), South Carolina, 2000, Oi
Tadesse Kidane-Mariam, (D), Iowa, 2001, On
Tamara Misner, (D), Pittsburgh, 2013, GmHs

Elizabethtown College
Dept of Physics & Engineering (B) (2014)
One Alpha Drive
Esbenshade Room 160
Elizabethtown, PA 17022-2298
p. (717) 361-1392
mcfaddenj@etown.edu
http://www.etown.edu/PhysicsEngineering.aspx
Administrative Assistant: Jennifer McFadden
Associate Professor:
Michael A. Scanlin, (D), Penn State, Ye
Emeritus:
David Ferruzza, (M), MIT, 1967, Oa

Franklin and Marshall College
Dept of Earth and Environment (B) (2015)
PO Box 3003
Lancaster, PA 17604-3003
p. (717) 291-4133
diane.kadyk@fandm.edu
http://www.fandm.edu/earthandenvironment.xml
f: https://www.facebook.com/pages/FM-Department-of-
Earth-Environment/153052838071694
t: @FandMENE
Administrative Assistant: Diane L. Kadyk
Enrollment (2014): B: 99 (28)
Chair:
Dorothy J. Merritts, (D), Arizona, 1987, Gm
Professor:
Carol B. de Wet, (D), Cambridge, 1989, Gs
Stanley A. Mertzman, (D), Case Western, 1971, Gi
Robert S. Sternberg, (D), Arizona, 1982, Ym
Roger D. K. Thomas, (D), Harvard, 1970, PoGh
Associate Professor:
Andrew P. deWet, (D), Cambridge, 1989, Ge
Zeshan Ismat, (D), Rochester, 2002, Gc
James E. Strick, (D), Princeton, 1997, Ghe
Robert C. Walter, (D), Case Western, 1981, Cc
Christopher J. Williams, (D), Pennsylvania, 2002, Pe
Assistant Professor:
Eilzabeth De Santo, (D), Univ Coll (London), On
Paul Harnik, (D), Chicago, 2009, Pg
Director of Public Policy:
Richard V. Pepino, (M), Villanova, 1970, Ou

Adjunct Professor:
  Suzanna L. Richter, (D), Pennsylvania, 2006, Ge
Visiting Professor:
  Timothy D. Bechtel, (D), Brown, 1989, GeYg
Laboratory Director:
  Steven Sylvester, (M), Franklin & Marshall, 1971, Ca

Gannon University
Earth Science Program (B) (2011)
109 University Square
PMB 3183
Erie, PA 16541
  p. (814) 871-7453
  olanrewa001@gannon.edu
  http://www.gannon.edu/
  Enrollment: No data reported since 1999
Assistant Professor:
  Johnson Olanrewaju, (D), Penn State, 2002, Cg

Harrisburg Area Community College
Science (A) (2015)
One HACC Drive
Harrisburg, PA 17110
  p. 800-222-4222
  http://www.hacc.edu/AboutHACC/ContactUs/index.cfm
  http://www.hacc.edu/index.cfm
  f: https://www.facebook.com/HACC64
  t: @hacc_info
  Enrollment (2014): A: 6 (2)
Professor:
  James E. Baxter, P.G., (M), Penn State, 1983, GgHwGm

Indiana University of Pennsylvania
Dept of Geoscience (B) (2015)
111 Walsh Hall
Indiana, PA 15705
  p. (724) 357-2379
  geoscience-info@iup.edu
  http://www.iup.edu/geoscience
  Enrollment (2015): B: 115 (19)
Chair:
  Steven A. Hovan, (D), Michigan, 1993, Ou
Professor:
  Karen Rose Cercone, (D), Michigan, 1984, Cl
  John F. Taylor, (D), Missouri, 1984, Ps
Associate Professor:
  Kenneth S. Coles, (D), Columbia, YgOe
  Katie Farnsworth, (D), Virginia Inst Marine Sci, Ong
  Jon C. Lewis, (D), Connecticut, Gc
Assistant Professor:
  Yvonne K. Branan, (D), Michigan Tech, Gv
  Nicholas Deardorff, (D), Oregon, Gv
  Gregory Mount, (D), Florida Atlantic, 2014, Hy
  Jonathan P. Warnock, (D), N. Illinois, 2013, GsPe
Instructor:
  Cinda Brode, (M)
  Thomas R. Moore, Eo
Emeritus:
  Joseph C. Clark, (D), Stanford, 1966, Gr
  Frank W. Hall, (D), Montana, 1969, Gc
  Darlene S. Richardson, (D), Columbia, 1974, Gd
  Connie J. Sutton, (M), Indiana (Penn), 1968, Oe

Juniata College
Dept of Environmental Science & Studies (2004)
1700 Moore Street
Huntingdon, PA 16652
  johnson@juniata.edu
  http://www.juniata.edu/departments/environmental/

Dept of Geology (B) ● (2014)
1700 Moore St
Huntingdon, PA 16652
  p. (814) 641-3601
  mutti@juniata.edu

http://departments.juniata.edu/geology
  Enrollment (2014): B: 35 (10)
Professor:
  Laurence J. Mutti, (D), Harvard, 1978, GxzSc
Dept. Chair:
  Ryan Mathur, (D), Arizona, 2000, CeGcHw
Assistant Professor:
  Matthew Powell, (D), Johns Hopkins, 2005, PieGs
Emeritus:
  J. Peter Trexler, (D), Michigan, 1964, Ps
  Robert H. Washburn, (D), Columbia, 1966, Gs

Kutztown University of Pennsylvania
Dept of Physical Science (B) (2015)
Boehm Science Building Room 135
Kutztown, PA 19530
  p. (610) 683-4447
  simpson@kutztown.edu
  http://www.kutztown.edu/acad/geology
  Department Secretary: Donna Moore
  Enrollment (2015): B: 51 (14)
Chair:
  Edward L. Simpson, (D), Virginia Tech, 1987, Gs
Professor:
  Kurt Friehauf, (D), Stanford, 1998, EmCgGx
  Sarah E. Tindall, (D), Arizona, 2000, Gc
Assistant Professor:
  Erin Kraal, (D), California (Santa Cruz), XgGm
  Adrienne Oakley, (D), Hawaii, 2009, YrOun
  Jacob Sewall, (D), California (Santa Cruz), 2004, GeOa
  Laura Sherrod, (D), W Michigan, 2007, YgHw

La Salle University
Dept of Geology & Environmental Science (B) (2015)
20th and Olney Avenue
Philadelphia, PA 19141
  p. (215) 951-1268
  bart@lasalle.edu
  http://www.lasalle.edu/geology
  Enrollment (2015): B: 30 (9)
Chair:
  Henry A. Bart, (D), Nebraska, 1974, Gs
Professor:
  Alice L. Hoersch, (D), Johns Hopkins, 1977, Gp
Adjunct Professor:
  Natalie Flynn, (D), Temple, 1999, Gz

Lafayette College
Dept of Geology & Environmental Geosciences (B) (2014)
116 Van Wickle Hall
4 South College Drive
Easton, PA 18042
  p. (610) 330-5193
  geology@lafayette.edu
  http://geology.lafayette.edu
  Department Secretary: Rohana Meyerson
  Enrollment (2013): B: 57 (13)
Professor:
  Dru Germanoski, (D), Colorado State, 1989, Gm
  Guy L. Hovis, (D), Harvard, 1971, Gy
Associate Professor:
  Kira Lawrence, (D), Brown, 2005, Gg
  Lawrence L. Malinconico, (D), Dartmouth, 1982, Yg
  David Sunderlin, (D), Chicago, 2004, Gg
Research Associate:
  Mary Ann Malinconico, (D), Columbia, 2002, Eo
Emeritus:
  Richard W. Faas, (D), Iowa State, 1964, Gs
Laboratory Director:
  John R. Wilson, (M), Virginia Tech, 2001, Oi

Lehigh University
Dept of Earth & Environmental Sciences (B,M,D) (2014)
1 W. Packer Ave.
Bethlehem, PA 18015-3001

p. (610) 758-3660
ljc0@lehigh.edu
http://www.ees.lehigh.edu
Administrative Assistant: Laura J. Cambiotti
Enrollment (2007): M: 15 (0) D: 12 (0)

Chair:
Frank J. Pazzaglia, (D), Penn State, 1993, Gm
Professor:
David J. Anastasio, (D), Johns Hopkins, 1988, Gc
Gray E. Bebout, (D), California (Los Angeles), 1989, Gp
Edward B. Evenson, (D), Michigan, 1972, Gl
Kenneth P. Kodama, (D), Stanford, 1978, Ym
Anne S. Meltzer, (D), Rice, 1988, Ys
Dork Sahagian, (D), Chicago, 1987, PeGvr
Peter K. Zeitler, (D), Dartmouth, 1983, Cc
Associate Professor:
Robert K. Booth, (D), Wyoming, 2003, On
Bruce R. Hargreaves, (D), California (Berkeley), 1977, Ob
Donald P. Morris, (D), Colorado, 1990, On
Stephen C. Peters, (D), Michigan, 2001, Cl
Joan Ramage, (D), Cornell, 2001, Or
Zicheng Yu, (D), Toronto, 1997, Pe
Assistant Professor:
Benjamin S. Felzer, (D), Brown, 1995, Oa
Research Associate:
Claudio Berti, (D), Chieti, 2009, Gt
Bruce D. Idleman, (D), SUNY (Albany), 1990, Cc
Joshua Stachnik, (D), Wyoming, 2010, Ys
Emeritus:
Bobb Carson, (D), Washington, 1971, Gu
Paul B. Myers, (D), Lehigh, 1960, Hw

Lock Haven University
Dept of Geology & Physics (B) (2013)
301 West Church Street
Lock Haven, PA 17745-2390
p. (570) 484-2048
mkhalequ@lhup.edu
Administrative Assistant: Barbara Greene
Enrollment (2007): B: 30 (5)

Professor:
Md. Khalequzzaman, (D), 1998, HwOni
Associate Scientist:
Loretta D. Dickson, (D), Connecticut, 2006, GicGe
Thomas C. Wynn, (D), Virginia Tech, 2004, GsPiEo

Mansfield University
Dept of Geosciences (A,B) O (2016)
Belknap Hall
Mansfield, PA 16933
p. (570) 662-4613
jdemchak@mansfield.edu
http://geoggeol.mansfield.edu/
Enrollment (2015): A: 9 (5) B: 140 (38)

Chair:
Jennifer Demchak, (D), West Virginia, 2005, Hs
Professor:
Russell L. Dodson, (D), Michigan State, 1984, Gm
Associate Professor:
Christopher Kopf, (D), Massachusetts, 1999, Gcp
Assistant Professor:
Linda Kennedy, (D), UNC Greensboro, 2012, Oy
Andy Shears, (D), Kent State, 2011, Oi
Ledrew Stocks, (D), Kent State, 2010, OyGgm

Mercyhurst University
Dept of Geology (B,M,D) (2012)
501 East 38th Street
Erie, PA 16546
p. (814) 824-2581
adovasio@mercyhurst.edu
http://mai.mercyhurst.edu
Enrollment (2012): B: 16 (3)

Director:
James M. Adovasio, (D), Utah, 1970, GafGs

Professor:
M. Raymond Buyce, (D), Rensselaer, 1975, GsaOn
Assistant Professor:
Nicholas Lang, (D), Minnesota, 2006, GvXgGc
Lyman Perscio, (D), New Mexico, 2012, GsSpHg
Instructor:
Scott McKenzie, (B), Edinboro, 1976, PgXmOe
Adjunct Professor:
Frank Vento, (D), Pittsburgh, 1985, GaOsGm

Millersville University
Dept of Earth Sciences (B,M) (2013)
PO Box 1002
Millersville, PA 17551
p. (717) 872-3289
esci@millersville.edu
http://www.millersville.edu/esci
Enrollment (2010): B: 23 (4)

Chair:
Richard D. Clark, (D), Wyoming, 1987, Oa
Professor:
L. Lynn Marquez, (D), Northwestern, 1998, Cg
Sepideh Yalda, (D), St. Louis, 1997, Oa
Associate Professor:
Alex J. DeCaria, (D), Maryland, 2000, Oa
Jason R. Price, (D), Michigan State, 2003, Gs
Todd D. Sikora, (D), Penn State, 1996, Oa
Assistant Professor:
Sam Earman, (D), New Mexico Tech, 2004, Hw
Ajoy Kumar, (D), Old Dominion, 1996, Op
Robert Vaillancourt, (D), Rhode Island, 1996, Obc
Instructor:
Joseph Calhoun, (B), Penn State, Oa
Mary Ann Schlegel, (M), MIT/WHOI, 1998, Og
Professor:
Robert S. Ross, (D), Florida State, 1977, Oa
Emeritus:
William M. Jordan, (D), Wisconsin, 1965, Gs
Bernard L. Oostdam, (D), Delaware, 1971, Ou
Charles K. Scharnberger, (D), Washington (St. Louis), 1971, Gc

Montgomery County Community College
Dept of Science, Technology, Engineering, and Math (A) (2010)
Blue Bell, PA 19422
p. (215) 641-6446
rkuhlman@mc3.edu
Professor:
Robert Kuhlman, (M), Bryn Mawr, 1975, Gg
Instructor:
George Buchanan, (M), Drexel, 1992, Ng
Adjunct Professor:
Laurie Martin-Vermilyea, (D), South Carolina, 1992, Oe
Frank Roberts, (D), Bryn Mawr, 1969, Gp
Kelly C. Spangler, (M), Drexel, 2003
Anthony Stevens, (M), Florida, 1981, Ge

Moravian College
Dept of Physics & Earth Science (B) (2015)
1200 Main Street
Bethlehem, PA 18018-6650
p. (610) 861-1437
krieblek@moravian.edu
http://www.physics.moravian.edu
Department Secretary: Lou Ann Vlahovic
Enrollment (2010): B: 4 (0)

Chair:
Kelly Krieble, (D), Lehigh, 1993, OnnOn

Pennsylvania State University, Erie
Geoscience Dept (2011)
Erie, PA 16510
p. (814) 898-6277
amf11@psu.edu
http://www.personal.psu.edu/faculty/a/m/amf11/

Chair:
    Anthony M. Foyle
Assistant Professor:
    Eva Tucker, (M), Cincinnati, 1962, Gg

Pennsylvania State University, Hazleton
Bachelor of Arts in Letters, Arts, and Sciences (A,B) (2016)
76 University Drive
Hazleton, PA 18202
    p. (570) 450-3000
    dhv1@psu.edu
    http://www.hn.psu.edu
    Enrollment (2012): B: 2 (0)
Senior Instructor:
    Daniel H. Vice, (D), Penn State, 1996, EgGgEm

Pennsylvania State University, Monaca
Dept of Geosciences (B) (2011)
100 University Drive
Monaca, PA 15061
    p. (412) 773-3867
    jac7@psu.edu
    http://www.br.psu.edu/default.htm
    Enrollment: No data reported since 1999
Assistant Professor:
    John A. Ciciarelli, (D), Penn State, 1971, Gg

Pennsylvania State University, University Park
Dept of Geosciences (B,M,D) (2015)
503 Deike Building
University Park, PA 16802-2714
    p. (814) 865-6711
    lkump@psu.edu
    http://www.geosc.psu.edu/
    Administrative Assistant: Tina Vancas
    Enrollment (2015): B: 122 (45) M: 45 (15) D: 95 (7)
Head:
    Lee R. Kump, (D), S Florida, 1986, Cl
Evan Pugh Professor:
    Richard B. Alley, (D), Wisconsin, 1987, Gl
    James F. Kasting, (D), Michigan, 1979, Oa
Distinguished Professor:
    Katherine H. Freeman, (D), Indiana, 1991, Co
Director, Earth & Mineral Science Museum:
    Russell W. Graham, (D), Texas, 1976, Pv
Director, Earth & Env Systems Inst:
    Susan L. Brantley, (D), Princeton, 1987, Cg
Director, Astrobiology Research Center:
    Christopher H. House, (D), California (Los Angeles), 1999, Py
Associate Head, Undergraduate Program:
    Peter Heaney, (D), Johns Hopkins, 1989, Gz
Associate Head, Graduate Programs:
    Demian M. Saffer, (D), California (Santa Cruz), 1999, Hw
Professor:
    Charles J. Ammon, (D), Penn State, 1991, Ys
    Sridhar Anandakrishnan, (D), Wisconsin, 1990, Ys
    Michael A. Arthur, (D), Princeton, 1979, Ou
    David M. Bice, (D), California (Berkeley), 1989, Gg
    Timothy J. Bralower, (D), California (San Diego), 1986, Pe
    Terry Engelder, (D), Texas A&M, 1973, Nr
    Donald M. Fisher, (D), Brown, 1988, Gc
    Kevin P. Furlong, (D), Utah, 1981, Gt
    Tanya Furman, (D), MIT, 1989, Cg
    Klaus Keller, (D), Princeton, 2000, Og
    Michael E. Mann, (D), Yale, 1998, Oa
    Chris Marone, (D), Columbia, 1988, Yx
    Andrew A. Nyblade, (D), Michigan, 1992, Yg
    Mark E. Patzkowsky, (D), Chicago, 1992, Po
    Rudy L. Slingerland, (D), Penn State, 1977, Gs
    Peter D. Wilf, (D), Penn, 1998, Py
Senior Scientist:
    Todd Sowers, (D), Rhode Island, 1991, Cs
Associate Professor:
    Matthew S. Fantle, (D), California (Berkeley), 2005, Cs
    Peter C. LaFemina, (D), Miami, 2005, Yd
    Jennifer L. Macalady, (D), California (Davis), 2000, Py

Assistant Professor:
    Roman DiBiase, (D), Arizona State, 2011, Gmt
    Maureen D. Feineman, (D), California (Berkeley), 2004, Cp
    Elizabeth Hajek, (D), Wyoming, 2009, Gs
    Eliza Richardson, (D), MIT, 2002, Ys
    Tess A. Russo, (D), California (Santa Cruz), 2012, Hw
    Christelle Wauthier, (D), Leige, 2011, On
Emeritus:
    Shelton S. Alexander, (D), Caltech, 1963, Ys
    Hubert L. Barnes, (D), Columbia, 1958, Cp
    Roger J. Cuffey, (D), Indiana, 1966, Pg
    David H. Eggler, (D), Colorado, 1967, Cp
    David P. Gold, (D), McGill, 1963, Gc
    Earl K. Graham, Jr., (D), Penn State, 1969, Yx
    Roy J. Greenfield, (D), MIT, 1965, Yg
    Albert L. Guber, (D), Illinois, 1962, Pe
    Benjamin F. Howell, Jr., (D), Caltech, 1949, Ys
    Derrill M. Kerrick, (D), California (Berkeley), 1968, Gp
    Hiroshi Ohmoto, (D), Princeton, 1969, Cs
    Richard R. Parizek, (D), Illinois, 1961, Hw
    Arthur W. Rose, (D), Caltech, 1958, Ce
    Robert F. Schmalz, (D), Harvard, 1959, Gu
    Alfred Traverse, (D), Harvard, 1951, Pl
    Barry Voight, (D), Columbia, 1964, Gv
    William B. White, (D), Penn State, 1962, Cg

Dept of Meteorology (B,M,D) (2015)
503 Walker Building
University Park, PA 16802-5013
    p. (814) 865-0478
    meteodept@meteo.psu.edu
    http://www.met.psu.edu
Professor and Head:
    David J. Stensrud, (D), Ow
Professor:
    Peter R. Bannon, (D), Colorado, 1979, Ow
    William H. Brune, (D), Johns Hopkins, 1978, Ow
    Eugene E. Clothiaux, (D), Brown, Ow
    Kenneth J. Davis, (D), Colorado, 1992, Ow
    Jenni L. Evans, (D), Monash, 1990, Ow
    Jerry Y. Harrington, (D), Colorado State, 1997, Ow
    Gregory S. Jenkins, (D), Ow
    James F. Kasting, (D), Michigan, 1979, Ow
    Johannes Verlinde, (D), Colorado State, 1992, Ow
    George S. Young, (D), Colorado State, Ow
Associate Head:
    Hampton N. Shirer, (D), Penn State, 1978, Ow
Associate Professor:
    Raymond G. Najjar, (D), Princeton, 1990, Ow
Assistant Professor:
    Steven J. Greybush, Maryland, Ow
    Matthew Kumjian, (D), Ow
    Sukyoung Lee, (D), Princeton, 1991, Ow
Research Assistant:
    William F. Ryan, (M), Maryland, 1990, Ow
Director, Meteorology Computing:
    Charles Pavloski, (D), Penn State, 2004, Ow
Research Associate:
    Aijun Deng, (D), Penn State, 1999, Ow
    Arthur Person, (M), Penn State, 1983, Ow
    William Syrett, (M), Penn State, 1987, Ow
Instructor:
    Frederick J. Gadomski, (M), Penn State, 1983, Ow
    Paul Knight, (M), Penn State, 1977, Ow
Distinguished Professor:
    J. Michael Fritsch, (D), Colorado State, 1978, Ow
Associate Research Professor:
    David R. Stauffer, (D), Penn State, 1990, Ow
Emeritus:
    Craig F. Bohren, (D), Arizona, 1975, Ow
    John J. Cahir, (D), Penn State, 1971, Ow
    Toby N. Carlson, (D), Imperial Coll (UK), 1965, Ow
    John H. E. Clark, (D), Florida State, 1969, Ow
    John A. Dutton, (D), Wisconsin, Ow
    William M. Frank, (D), Colorado State, 1976, Ow
    Alistair B. Fraser, (D), Imperial Coll (UK), 1968, Ow
    Charles L. Hosler, (D), Penn State, 1951, Ow

Dennis Lamb, (D), Washington, 1970, Ow
Nelson L. Seaman, (D), Penn State, 1977, Ow
Dennis W. Thomson, (D), Wisconsin, 1968, Ow
John C. Wyngaard, (D), Penn State, 1967, Ow

Dept of Plant Science (A,B,M,D) (2014)
119 Tyson Building
University Park, PA 16802
    p. (814) 865-6541
    rpm12@psu.edu
    http://plantscience.psu.edu/
    Enrollment: No data reported since 1999
Professor:
    Douglas B. Beegle, (D), Penn State, 1983, Sc
    Jean-Marc Bollag, (D), Basel, 1959, Sb
    Edward J. Ciolkosz, (D), Wisconsin, 1967, Sd
    Daniel D. Fritton, (D), Iowa State, 1968, Sp
    Sridhar Komarneni, (D), Wisconsin, 1973, Sc
    Gary W. Petersen, (D), Wisconsin, 1965, Sd
Associate Professor:
    Peter J. Landschoot, (D), Rhode Island, 1988, So
    Gregory W. Roth, (D), Penn State, 1987, So
Assistant Professor:
    Rick L. Day, (D), Penn State, 1991, Ou
Research Associate:
    Barry M. Evans, (M), Penn State, 1977, Sd
    Douglas A. Miller, (M), Penn State, 1987, Sd
Adjunct Professor:
    Andrew S. Rogowski, (D), Iowa State, 1964, Sp
    Lawrence A. Schardt, (M), Penn State, 1996, Sd

Earth and Mineral Sciences Museum & Art Gallery (2015)
116 Deike Building
University Park, PA 16802
    p. (814) 865-6336
    museum@ems.psu.edu
    http://www.ems.psu.edu/outreach/museum
    Enrollment: No data reported since 1999
Director:
    Russell W. Graham, (D), Texas, 1976, Pve

John and Willie Leone Family Dept of Energy and Mineral Engineering (B,M,D) (2014)
110 Hosler Building
University Park, PA 16802
    p. (814) 865-3437
    eme@ems.psu.edu
    http://www.eme.psu.edu/mnge
    Enrollment (2000): B: 16 (6) M: 6 (2)
Program Chair, and Deike Endowed Chair in Mining Engineering:
    Jeffery L. Kohler, (D), Penn State, 1982, Nm
Associate Professor:
    Antonio Nieto, (D), Colorado Mines, 2002, Nm
    Jamal Rostami, (D), Colorado Mines, 1997, Nm
Assistant Professor:
    Shimin Liu, (D), S Illinois, 2013, Nm

Point Park University
Dept of Environmental Studies (A,B) (2015)
201 Wood Street
Pittsburgh, PA 15222-1994
    p. (412) 392-3900
    jkudlac@pointpark.edu
    http://www.pointpark.edu/Academics/Schools/SchoolofArtsandSciences/Departments/NaturalSciencesandEngineeringTechnology
    Administrative Assistant: Roberta T. Gallick
    Enrollment: No data reported since 1999
Head:
    Mark O. Farrell, (D), Carnegie Mellon, 1978, On
Professor:
    John J. Kudlac, (D), Pittsburgh, Ng

Shippensburg University
Geography-Earth Science Dept (B,M) (2015)
1871 Old Main Drive

Shippensburg, PA 17257
    p. (717) 477-1685
    tlmyers@ship.edu
    http://www.ship.edu/~geog/
    Administrative Assistant: Tammy Myers
Chair:
    William L. Blewett, (D), Michigan State, 1991, Oy
Professor:
    Thomas P. Feeney, (D), Georgia, 1997, Gm
    Kurtis G. Fuellhart, (D), Penn State, 1998, On
    Timothy W. Hawkins, (D), Arizona State, 2004, Oa
    Paul G. Marr, (D), Denver, 1996, Oi
    George M. Pomeroy, (D), Akron, 1999, Ou
    Janet S. Smith, (D), Georgia, 1999, Oi
    Christopher J. Woltemade, (D), Wisconsin, 1993, Hg
Associate Professor:
    Michael T. Applegarth, (D), Arizona State, 2001, Or
    Sean Cornell, (D), Cincinnati, 2008, Gg
    Scott A. Drzyzga, (D), Michigan State, 2007, Oi
    Alison E. Feeney, (D), Michigan State, 1998, On
    Claire A. Jantz, (D), Maryland, 2005, Ou
    Kay R. Williams, (D), Georgia, 1995, Oa
    Joseph T. Zume, (D), Oklahoma, 2007, Hg

Slippery Rock University
Dept of Geography, Geology, and the Environment (B) (2011)
Slippery Rock, PA 16057
    p. (724) 738-2048
    jack.livingston@sru.edu
    http://academics.sru.edu/gge
    Administrative Assistant: Bonita L. Vinton
    Enrollment (2006): B: 50 (9)
Chair:
    Jack Livingston
Associate Professor:
    Patrick A. Burkhart, (D), Lehigh, 1994, Hg
Assistant Professor:
    Patricia A. Campbell, (D), Pittsburgh, 1994, Gc
    Xianfeng Chen, (D), West Virginia, 2005, Or
    Tamra A. Schiappa, (D), Boise State, 1999, Pi
    Julie A. Snow, (D), Rhode Island, 2002, Oa
    Michael G. Stapleton, (D), Delaware, 1995, So
    Michael J. Zieg, (D), Johns Hopkins, 2001, Gi

State Museum of Pennsylvania
Section of Paleontology & Geology (2014)
300 North Street
Harrisburg, PA 17120-0024
    p. (717) 783-9897
    c-sjasinsk@pa.gov
    http://www.statemuseumpa.org/geologyc.html
    f: https://www.facebook.com/StateMuseumofPA
Acting Curator:
    Steven E. Jasinski, (D), Pennsylvania, pend, PvgPy

Susquehanna University
Dept of Earth & Environmental Sciences (B) (2010)
514 University Ave
Selinsgrove, PA 17870
    p. (570) 372-4216
    straubk@susqu.edu
    http://www.susqu.edu/ees
    Enrollment (2009): B: 29 (7)
Chair:
    Jennifer M. Elick, (D), Tennessee, 1999, Pe
Associate Professor:
    Daniel E. Ressler, (D), Iowa State, 1998, Sp
    Derek J. Straub, (D), Oa
    Katherine H. Straub, (D), Colorado State, 2002, Ow
Assistant Professor:
    Ahmed Lachhab, (D), Iowa, 2006, Hw

Temple University
Earth & Environmental Science (B,M,D) (2014)
1901 N. 13th Street

Beury Hall, Rm. 326
Philadelphia, PA 19122-6081
    p. (215) 204-8227
    scox@temple.edu
    http://www.temple.edu/geology
    Administrative Assistant: Shelah Cox
    Enrollment (2005): M: 11 (0)
Chair:
    David E. Grandstaff, (D), Princeton, 1974, Cl
(Emeritus 2014):
    George H. Myer; (D), Yale, 1965, Gz
Professor:
    Jonathan Nyquist, (D), Wisconsin, 1986, Yg
    Laura Toran, (D), Wisconsin, 1986, Hw
Associate Professor:
    Ilya Buynevich, (D), Boston, 2001, GsrOg
    Dennis O. Terry, (D), Nebraska, 1998, Gr
Assistant Professor:
    Alexandra Davatzes, (D), Stanford, 2003, Gs
    Nicholas Davatzes, (D), Stanford, 2003, GcNr
    Bojeong Kim, (D)
    Sujith Ravi, (D)
Emeritus:
    Gene C. Ulmer, (D), Penn State, 1964, Cp
Asst. Lab Manager/Bldg. Coordinator:
    Donald Deigh-Kai, (M), Temple, 2008

Thiel College
Dept of Environmental Science (B) (2010)
Greenville, PA 16125
    p. (412) 589-2821
    areinsel@thiel.edu
    Enrollment (2004): B: 23 (3)
Professor:
    James H. Barton, (D), N Colorado, 1977, Oy

University of Pennsylvania
Dept of Earth & Environmental Science (B,M,D) (2015)
240 S. 33rd Street
Philadelphia, PA 19104-6316
    p. (215) 898-5724
    earth@sas.upenn.edu
    http://www.sas.upenn.edu/earth/
    Enrollment: No data reported since 1999
Chair:
    Reto Giere, (D)
Professor:
    Peter Dodson, (D), Yale, 1974, Pv
    Hermann W. Pfefferkorn, (D), Muenster, 1968, Pb
Associate Professor:
    David Goldsby, (D)
    Douglas Jerolmack, (D), MIT, 2006, GmYxHq
    Stephen P. Phipps, (D), Princeton, 1984, Gc
    Alain Plante, (D), Alberta, 2001, SbCoOs
Assistant Professor:
    Irina Marinov
    Lauren Sallan, (D)
    Jane Willenbring, (D), Dalhousie, 2006, GmCcOl
Labratory Manager:
    David R. Vann, (D), Pennsylvania, 1993, Py
Lecturer:
    Edward L. Doheny, (D), Indiana, 1967, Ng
    Stanley L. Laskowski, (M), Drexel, 1973, Ge
    Willig B. Sarah, (D), Pennsylvania, 1988, Ge
Emeritus:
    Robert F. Giegengack, Jr., (D), Yale, 1968, Gg
    Arthur H. Johnson, (D), Cornell, 1975, So
Teaching Faculty:
    Jane Dmochowski, (D), Caltech, 2004, Yg
    Gomaa I. Omar, (D), Pennsylvania, 1985, Cc
Graduate Group Coordinator:
    Joan Buccilli
Director, Professional Masters Programs:
    Yvette Bordeaux, (D), Pennsylvania, 2000, Po
Department Administrator:
    Arlene Mand, (B), 1971, On

Associate Director:
    Maria Andrews, (M)

University of Pittsburgh
Dept of Geology & Environmental Science (B,M,D) ● (2016)
200 SRCC Building
4107 O'Hara Street
Pittsburgh, PA 15260-3332
    p. (412) 624-8780
    gpsgrad@pitt.edu
    http://www.geology.pitt.edu
    Enrollment (2015): M: 15 (0) D: 24 (0)
Chair:
    Mark B. Abbott, (D), Minnesota, 1995, Gs
Associate Professor:
    Rosemary C. Capo, (D), California (Los Angeles), 1990, Cl
    William P. Harbert, (D), Stanford, 1987, Ym
    Michael S. Ramsey, (D), Arizona State, 1996, Or
    Brian W. Stewart, (D), California (Los Angeles), 1990, Cc
    Josef Werne, (D), Northwestern, 2000, Co
Assistant Professor:
    Daniel J. Bain, (D), Johns Hopkins, 2004, Hg
    Emily M. Elliott, (D), Johns Hopkins, 2003, Hg
    Nadine McQuarrie, (D), Arizona, 2001, Gct
Environmental Reporter, Pittsburgh Post-Gazette:
    S. Don Hopey
Instructor:
    Lindsay Baxter
    Emily Collins
    Marion Divers, (D), Pittsburgh, 2013
Lecturer:
    R. Ward Allebach
    Mark Collins, (M), Pittsburgh, 1985, On
    Charles E. Jones, (D), Oxford, 1992, Gg
Adjunct Professor:
    Robert S. Hedin, (D), Rutgers, 1987, Ge
    Matthew C. Lamanna, (D), Pennsylvania, 2004, Pv
Visiting Professor:
    J. Brian Balta
Emeritus:
    Thomas Anderson
    William Cassidy, (D), 1969, Xg
    Jack Donahue
    Bruce W. Hapke, (D), Cornell, 1962, Xy
    Edward G. Lidiak, (D), Rice, 1963, Gi
    Harold B. Rollins, (D), Columbia, 1967, Pe
Professor - Catholic University of Santisima Concepcion:
    Sergio Contreras
Lecturer:
    Steven C. Latta
Other:
    John S. Pallister
    Matthew Watson

University of Pittsburgh, Bradford
Dept of Petroleum Technology (A) (2012)
300 Campus Drive
Bradford, PA 16701-2898
    p. (814) 362-7569
    aap@pitt.edu
    http://www.upb.pitt.edu/academics/petroleumtechnology.
    aspx
    Administrative Assistant: Janet Shade
    Enrollment (2010): A: 28 (8)
Program Director:
    Assad I. Panah, (D), Oklahoma, 1966, GorGc

West Chester University
Dept of Geology & Astronomy (B,M) (2014)
750 South Church Street
Merion Science Center
West Chester, PA 19383
    p. (610) 436-2727
    mhelmke@wcupa.edu
    http://geology.wcupa.edu
    Enrollment (2014): B: 106 (23) M: 29 (9)

131

Professor:
 Richard M. Busch, (D), Pittsburgh, 1984, Oe
 Marc R. Gagne, (D), Georgia, 1994, On
 Steven C. Good, (D), Colorado, 1993, Pe
 Timothy M. Lutz, (D), Pennsylvania, 1979, Gq
 LeeAnn Srogi, (D), Pennsylvania, 1988, Gp
Chair:
 Martin F. Helmke, (D), Iowa State, 2003, HwSdOg
Associate Professor:
 Cynthia G. Fisher, (D), Colorado, 1991, Ou
 Joby Hilliker, (D), Penn State, 2001, Ow
 Arthur Smith, (D), Pennsylvania, 1975, Oe
 Karen M. Vanlandingham, (D), Arizona State, 1999, On
Assistant Professor:
 Howell Bosbyshell, (D), Bryn Mawr, 2000, Gc
 Cynthia V. Hall, (D), Georgia Tech, 2008, Cg
 Daria L. Nikitina, (D), Delaware, 2000, Gm

Wilkes University
Dept of Environmental Engineering & Earth Sciences (B) (2015)
84 West South Street
Wilkes-Barre, PA 18766
 p. (570) 408-4610
 brian.whitman@wilkes.edu
 http://wilkes.edu/academics/colleges/science-and-engi-
 neering/environmental-engineering-earth-sciences/
 Enrollment (2010): B: 27 (5)
Chair:
 Sid P. Halsor, (D), Michigan Tech, 1989, Giv
Professor:
 Dale A. Bruns, (D), Idaho State, 1981, OirSf
 Kenneth M. Klemow, (D), SUNY (Syracuse), 1982, Py
 Prahlad N. Murthy, (D), Texas A&M, 1993, OanOn
 Brian T. Redmond, (D), Rensselaer, 1982, Gs
 Michael A. Steele, (D), Wake Forest, 1988, Py
Associate Professor:
 Marleen Troy, (D), Drexel, 1989, Hw
 Brian E. Whitman, (D), Michigan Tech, 1998, HqwSb
Assistant Professor:
 Holly Frederick, (D), Penn State, 1999, Sdb
Lecturer:
 Mark A. Kaster, (M), Saint Louis, 1993, Ow
 Julie McMonagle, (M), Lehigh, 1991, Gg
Emeritus:
 James M. Case, (D), Dalhousie, 1979, Ob

York College of Pennsylvania
Dept of Physical Science (2010)
York, PA 17405
 p. (717) 846-7788 x333
 jforesma@ycp.edu
Assistant Professor:
 William Kreiger, (D), Penn State, 1976, Gi
Adjunct Professor:
 Ralph Eisenhart, (M), Penn State, 1994, Gg
 Jeri L. Jones, (B), Catawba, 1977, Ga

Puerto Rico

University of Puerto Rico
Dept of Geology (B,M) (2014)
Box 9017
Mayaguez, PR 00681-9017
 p. (787) 265-3845
 thomase.miller@upr.edu
 http://geology.uprm.edu/
 Enrollment (2004): B: 19 (19) M: 2 (2)
Professor:
 James Joyce, (D), Northwestern, 1985, Ng
Assistant Professor:
 Eugenio Asencio, (D), South Carolina, 2002, Ys
 Fernando Gilbes, (D), S Florida, 1996, Or
 Thomas E. Miller, (D), McMaster, 1986, Gm
 Wilson R. Ramirez, (D), Tulane, 2000, Gd
 Hernan Santos, (D), Colorado, 1999, Pi

Rhode Island

Brown University
Dept of Earth, Environmental and Planetary Sciences (B,M,D)
(2015)
Box 1846, 324 Brook Street
Providence, RI 02912
 p. (401) 863-3339
 Patricia_Davey@brown.edu
 http://www.brown.edu/academics/earth-environmental-
 planetary-sciences/
 f: https://www.facebook.com/BrownGeologicalSciences
 t: @BrownGeoSci
 Enrollment (2015): B: 44 (23) M: 0 (6) D: 51 (12)
Chair:
 Greg Hirth, (D), Brown, 1991, GcyYg
Professor:
 Reid F. Cooper, (D), Cornell, 1983, Gy
 Karen M. Fischer, (D), MIT, 1988, Ys
 Donald W. Forsyth, (D), MIT/WHOI, 1974, Yr
 James W. Head, III, (D), Brown, 1969, Xg
 Timothy D. Herbert, (D), Princeton, 1987, Pe
 Yongsong Huang, (D), Bristol (UK), 1997, Co
 Yan Liang, (D), Chicago, 1994, Cp
 Amanda H. Lynch, (D), Melbourne, 1993, OaGe
 John F. Mustard, (D), Brown, 1990, Or
 E. Marc Parmentier, (D), Cornell, 1975, Yg
Associate Professor of Research:
 Steven C. Clemens, (D), Brown, 1990, Ou
Associate Professor:
 Meredith Hastings, (D), Princeton, 2004, Oa
 Stephen Parman, (D), MIT, 2001, CpgCt
 James M. Russell, (D), Minnesota, 2004, Gn
 Alberto E. Saal, (D), MIT/WHOI, 2000, Cg
Assistant Professor:
 Colleen Dalton, (D), Harvard, 2007, Ys
 Baylor Fox-Kemper, (D), MIT, 2003, Op
 Brandon C. Johnson, (D), Purdue, 2013, Xg
 Jung-Eun Lee, (D), California (Berkeley), 2005
 Ralph E. Milliken, (D), Brown, 2006
Research Associate:
 David Murray, (D), Oregon State, 1987, Ou
Adjunct Professor:
 Mark Altabet, (D), Oc
 Maureen Conte, (D), Columbia, 1989, CgPe
Emeritus:
 L. Peter Gromet, (D), Caltech, 1979, Cc
 John F. Hermance, (D), Toronto, 1967, Yg
 Paul C. Hess, (D), Harvard, 1968, Gi
 Carle M. Pieters, (D), MIT, 1977, Or
 Warren L. Prell, (D), Columbia, 1974, Ou
 Malcolm J. Rutherford, (D), Johns Hopkins, 1968, Cp
 Peter H. Schultz, (D), Texas, 1972, Xg
 Jan A. Tullis, (D), California (Los Angeles), 1971, Gc
 Terry E. Tullis, (D), California (Los Angeles), 1971, Yx
 Thompson Webb, III, (D), Wisconsin, 1971, Pe
Department Manager:
 Nancy Fjeldheim, (B), Ohio State, 1972, On
Academic Program Manager:
 Patricia M. Davey, (B), Rhode Island Coll, 1986, On

Community College of Rhode Island
Dept of Physics (Geology & Oceanography Div) (A) (2015)
400 East Avenue
Warwick, RI 02886
 p. (401) 333-7443
 kkortz@ccri.edu
 http://www.ccri.edu/physics/
Professor:
 Karen Kortz, (D), Rhode Island, 2009, OeGg
Associate Professor:
 Emily Burns, (D), Gg
 Paul White, (D), Gg
Assistant Professor:
 Duayne Rieger, (D), Ys

Providence College

Biology Dept (A) (2004)
Providence, RI 02918
    p. (401) 865-2250
    chwood@providence.edu
    Enrollment: No data reported since 1999
Professor:
    Craig B. Wood, (D), Harvard, 1992, Pv
Associate Professor:
    Michael S. Zavada, (D), Connecticut, 1982, On

Roger Williams University

College of Arts & Sciences (B) (2011)
Bristol, RI 02809
    p. (401) 254-3087
    jborden@rwu.edu
    Department Secretary: Valerie Catalano
    Enrollment: No data reported since 1999
Head:
    Mark D. Gould, (D), Rhode Island, 1973, Ob
Chair:
    Paul Webb
Professor:
    Thomas Doty, (D), Rhode Island, 1977, Ob
    Richard Heavers, (D), Rhode Island, 1977, Op
    Thomas J. Holstein, (D), Brown, 1969, On
    Martine Villalard-Bohnsack, (D), Rhode Island, 1971, Ob
Assistant Professor:
    Tim Scott, (D), SUNY (Stony Brook), 1993, Ob

University of Rhode Island 🗋

Dept of Geosciences (B,M,D) (2015)
9 East Alumni Ave.,
Kingston, RI 02881
    p. (401) 874-2265
    http://www.uri.edu/cels/geo/
    Administrative Assistant: Lorraine Bailey
    Enrollment (2015): B: 75 (10) M: 14 (9) D: 1 (2)
Professor & Chair:
    David E. Fastovsky, (D), Wisconsin, 1986, PvGsPs
Associate Dean:
    Anne I. Veeger, (D), Arizona, 1991, HwCl
Professor:
    Thomas B. Boving, (D), Arizona, 1999, Hw
Associate Professor:
    Brian K. Savage, (D), Caltech, 2004, Ys
Assistant Professor:
    Dawn Cardace, (D), Washington Univ, GpPy
    Simon E. Engelhart, (D), Pennsylvania, OnGmYs
    Soni M. Pradhanang, (D), Hw
Emeritus:
    J. Allan Cain, (D), Northwestern, 1962, Gx
    O Don Hermes, (D), North Carolina, 1967, Gi
    Daniel P. Murray, (D), Brown, 1976, GpOe

Graduate School of Oceanography (M,D) (2014)
215 South Ferry Road
Narragansett, RI 02882
    p. (401) 874-6222
    TheDean@gso.uri.edu
    http://www.gso.uri.edu
    Enrollment (2010): M: 41 (12) D: 31 (8)
Research Professor:
    Theodore J. Smayda, (D), Oslo, 1967, Ob
Associate Dean:
    Mark Wimbush, (D), California (San Diego), 1969, Op
Professor:
    Robert D. Ballard, (D), Rhode Island, 1974, Ga
    Steven N. Carey, (D), Rhode Island, 1982, Ou
    Jeremy S. Collie, (D), MIT/WHOI, 1985, Ob
    Peter Cornillon, (D), Cornell, 1973, Op
    Steven L. D'Hondt, (D), Princeton, 1989, Ou
    Edward G. Durbin, (D), Rhode Island, 1976, Ob
    Isaac Ginis, (D), Inst Exp Meteor, 1986, Op
    Tetsu Hara, (D), MIT, 1990, Op

Paul E. Hargraves, (D), William & Mary, 1968, Ob
David L. Hebert, (D), Dalhousie, 1988, Op
Christopher Kincaid, (D), Johns Hopkins, 1990, Ou
John King, (D), Minnesota, 1983, Ou
Roger Larson, (D), California (San Diego), 1970, Ou
Margaret Leinen, (D), Rhode Island, 1980, Ou
John T. Merrill, (D), Colorado, 1976, Oc
S. Bradley Moran, (D), Dalhousie, 1991, Oc
Scott W. Nixon, (D), North Carolina, 1970, Ob
Candace Oviatt, (D), Rhode Island, 1967, Ob
Hans Thomas Rossby, (D), MIT, 1966, Op
Lewis Rothstein, (D), Hawaii, 1983, Op
Haraldur Sigurdsson, (D), Durham (UK), 1970, Ou
Jennifer Specker, (D), Oregon State, 1980, Ob
Robert Tyce, (D), California (San Diego), 1976, Ou
D. Randolph Watts, (D), Cornell, 1973, Op
Karen Wishner, (D), California (San Diego), 1979, Ob
Associate Professor:
    Brian G. Heikes, (D), Michigan, 1984, Oa
    Yang Shen, (D), Brown, 1994, Ou
    David C. Smith, (D), California (San Diego), 1994, Ob
Marine Research Scientist:
    Percy Donaghay, (D), Oregon State, 1980, Ob
    Kathleen Donohue, (D), Rhode Island, 1996, Op
    Dian J. Gifford, (D), Dalhousie, 1986, Ob
    Alfred K. Hanson, Jr., (D), Rhode Island, 1981, Oc
    Robert D. Kenney, (D), Rhode Island, 1984, Ob
    Barbara K. Sullivan-Watts, (D), Oregon State, 1977, Og
Associate Dean:
    John Farrell, (D), Brown, 1991, Ou
Adjunct Professor:
    Lawrence J. Buckley, (D), New Hampshire, 1975, Oc
    Richard J. Pruell, (D), Rhode Island, 1984, Co
    Charles T. Roman, (D), Delaware, 1981, Ob
Emeritus:
    H. Perry Jeffries, (D), Rutgers, 1959, Ob
    John A. Knauss, (D), California, 1959, Op
    Theodore A. Napora, (D), Yale, 1964, Ob
    Michael E. Pilson, (D), California (San Diego), 1964, Oc
    James G. Quinn, (D), Connecticut, 1967, Oc
    Kenneth A. Rahn, (D), Michigan, 1971, Oc
    Saul B. Saila, (D), Cornell, 1952, Ob
    Jean-Guy Schilling, (D), MIT, 1966, Ou
    John M. Sieburth, (D), Minnesota, 1954, Ob
    Elijah V. Swift, (D), Johns Hopkins, 1967, Ob

South Carolina

Clemson University

Bob Campbell Geology Museum (A,B,M,D) (2014)
140 Discovery Lane
Clemson, SC 29634-0130
    p. (864) 656-4602
    tsteadm@clemson.edu
    http://www.clemson.edu/geomuseum
Director:
    Todd A. Steadman, (M), Louisiana State, 1987, OnnOn
Curator:
    David J. Cicimurri, (M), SD Mines, 1998, Pv
Curator:
    Christian M. Cicimurri, (M), SD Mines, 1999, Pv

Environmental Engineering and Earth Sciences (B,M) (2014)
321 Calhoun Drive
Room 445 Brackett Hall
Clemson, SC 29634-0919
    p. (864) 656-3438
    bcowans@clemson.edu
    http://www.clemson.edu/ces/departments/eees/
    Administrative Assistant: Cynthia Rae Gravely
    Enrollment (2013): B: 40 (9) M: 8 (6)
Chair:
    Tanju Karanfil, (D), Michigan, 1995, NgOnn
Professor:
    James W. Castle, (D), Illinois, 1978, Gd
    Ronald W. Falta, (D), California (Berkeley), 1990, Hq
    Cindy M. Lee, (D), Colorado Mines, 1990, Cg

Lawrence C. Murdoch, (D), Cincinnati, 1991, Hw
Mark Schlautman, (D), Caltech, 1992, Cg
Assistant Professor:
Stephen M.J Moysey, (D), Stanford, 2005, Hw
Brian A. Powell, (D), Clemson, 2004, Cg
Lindsay C. Shuller-Nickles, (D), Michigan, 2010, Gz
Research Associate:
Scott E. Brame, (M), Clemson, 1993, Hw
Lecturer:
Alan B. Coulson, (D), South Carolina, 2009, PoGgCs
Adjunct Professor:
C. Brannon Andersen, (D), Syracuse, 1994, Cl
Christian M. Cicimurri, (M), South Dakota, 1999, Pv
Brian Looney, (D), Minnesota, 1984, Hq
Vaneaton Price, (D), North Carolina, 1969, Ce
Tommy Temples, (D), South Carolina, 1996, GoYg
Emeritus:
Lois B. Krause, (D), Clemson, 1996, Oe
Fred Molz, (D), Stanford, 1970, Sp
John R. Wagner, (D), South Carolina, 1993, Oe
Richard D. Warner, (D), Stanford, 1971, Gz

College of Charleston
Dept of Geology & Environmental Geosciences (B,M) (2015)
66 George Street
Charleston, SC 29424
   p. (843) 953-5589
   colganm@cofc.edu
   http://geology.cofc.edu/
   f: https://www.facebook.com/Geology.CofC/
   Administrative Assistant: Stacey K. Hassard
   Enrollment (2015): B: 121 (29)
Professor:
Timothy J. Callahan, (D), New Mexico Tech, 2001, Hw
Chair:
Mitchell W. Colgan, (D), California (Santa Cruz), 1990, PeGe
Associate Professor:
Erin K. Beutel, (D), Northwestern, 2000, Gct
Scott Harris, (D), Delaware, 1990, GaOn
Steven C. Jaumé, (D), Columbia, 1994, Ys
Norman S. Levine, (D), Purdue, 1995, OiGeOu
Cassandra R. Runyon, (D), Hawaii, 1988, XgOse
Leslie R. Sautter, (D), South Carolina, 1990, Ob
Vijay M. Vulava, (D), Swiss Fed Inst Tech, 1998, CgHwSc
Assistant Professor:
K. Adem Ali, (D), Kent State, 2011, Ge
Barbara Beckingham, (D), Maryland, 2011, Cl
John Chadwick, (D), Florida, 2002, Gig
Emeritus:
James L. Carew, (D), Texas, 1978, Po
Michael P. Katuna, (D), North Carolina, 1974, Gus
Robert L. Nusbaum, (D), Missouri (Rolla), 1984, Gz
Alexander W. Ritchie, (D), Texas, 1975, Gc
Laboratory Director:
Robin Humphreys, (M), Charleston (South Carolina), 2000, Ge

Furman University
Earth and Environmental Sciences (B) (2015)
3300 Poinsett Highway
Greenville, SC 29613
   p. (864) 294-2052
   weston.dripps@furman.edu
   http://ees.furman.edu
   Administrative Assistant: Nina Anthony
   Enrollment (2015): B: 63 (22)
Professor:
C. Brannon Andersen, (D), Syracuse, 1994, ClGe
John M. Garihan, (D), Penn State, 1973, Gc
William A. Ranson, (D), Massachusetts, 1979, GxzGp
Chair:
Weston R. Dripps, (D), Wisconsin, 2003, HwsGe
Associate Professor:
Suresh Muthukrishnan, (D), Purdue, 2002, OiGm
Assistant Professor:
Matt Cohen, (D), Arizona State, 2015, On

Emeritus:
Kenneth A. Sargent, (D), Oklahoma, 1973, Hy

University of South Carolina
Dept of Earth and Ocean Sciences (B,M,D) ● (2015)
Earth and Water Science Building
701 Sumter Street
EWS 617
Columbia, SC 29208
   p. (803) 777-4535
   chair@geol.sc.edu
   http://www.geol.sc.edu/
   Enrollment (2014): B: 88 (14) M: 14 (11) D: 26 (1)
Senior Associate Dean:
Robert C. Thunell, (D), Rhode Island, 1978, Pe
Chair:
George Voulgaris, (D), Southampton (U.K.), 1992, On
Professor:
Claudia Benitez-Nelson, (D), MIT/WHOI, 1999, Oc
Subrahmanyam Bulusu, (D), Southampton (U.K.), 1998, Op
James N. Kellogg, (D), Princeton, 1981, Yg
Camelia Knapp, (D), Cornell, 2000, YeGt
James H. Knapp, (D), MIT, 1989, Ye
Venkataraman Lakshmi, (D), Princeton, 1995, Hg
Thomas J. Owens, (D), Utah, 1984, Ys
Associate Professor:
David Barbeau, Jr., (D), Arizona, 2003, Gs
Michael Bizimis, (D), Florida State, 2001, GiCg
Howie Scher, (D), Florida, 2005, GuCl
Raymond Torres, (D), California (Berkeley), 1997, Hy
Scott M. White, (D), California (Santa Barbara), 2001, Yr
Alicia M. Wilson, (D), Johns Hopkins, 1999, Hw
Sasha Yankovsky, (D), Marine Hydrophysical (Ukraine), 1991, OpnOw
Gene M. Yogodzinkski, (D), Cornell, 1993, Gi
Assistant Professor:
Susan Q. Lang, (D), Washington, 2006, Oc
Andrew L. Leier, (D), Arizona, 2005, Gs
Lori A. Ziolkowski, (D), California (Irvine), 2009, CoOcCs
Research Professor, Director of Undergraduate Studies:
Gwendelyn Geidel, (D), South Carolina, 1982, Hw
Emeritus:
John R. Carpenter, (D), Florida State, 1964, Oe
Arthur D. Cohen, (D), Penn State, 1968, Ec
Robert Ehrlich, (D), Louisiana State, 1965, Gs
Christopher G. Kendall, (D), Imperial Coll (UK), 1966, Gs
Ian Lerche, (D), Manchester, 1965, Yg
Willard S. Moore, (D), SUNY (Stony Brook), 1969, Cc
Donald Secor, (D), Stanford, 1962, Gc
W. Edwin Sharp, (D), California (Los Angeles), 1964, Gz
Pradeep Talwani, (D), Stanford, 1973, Ys
Douglas F. Williams, (D), Rhode Island, 1976, Cs

Marine Science Program (B,M,D) (2015)
701 Sumter Street, EWSC 617
Columbia, SC 29208
   p. (803) 777-2692
   khamilton@geol.sc.edu
   http://www.msci.sc.edu
   Enrollment (2015): B: 285 (50) M: 10 (7) D: 14 (1)
Director:
Ronald Benner, (D), Georgia, 1984, ObCo
Professor:
Claudia R. Benitez-Nelson, (D), MIT/WHOI, 1999, OcCm
James T. Morris, (D), Yale, 1979, Ob
Joseph M. Quattro, (D), Rutgers, 1991, Ob
Timothy J. Shaw, (D), California (San Diego), 1988, OcCt
Robert C. Thunell, (D), Rhode Island, 1978, PmsCs
George Voulgaris, (D), Southampton, 1992, OpnOo
Associate Professor:
Subrahmanyam Bulusu, (D), Southampton, 1998, OrpOa
James Pinckney, (D), South Carolina, 1992, Obn
Tammi Richardson, (D), Dalhousie, 1996, Ob
Richard M. Showman, (D), Washington, 1979, Ob
Scott M. White, (D), California (Santa Barbara), 2001, YrOu
Alexander Yankovsky, (D), Marine Hydrophysical (Ukraine), 1991, Opn

Assistant Professor:
 Michael Bizimis, (D), Florida State, 2001, GiCg
 Jean Ellis, (D), Texas A&M, 2006, GmOna
 Blaine Griffen, (D), New Hampshire, 2007, Ob
 Susan Q. Lang, (D), Washington, 2006, OcCo
 Ryan Rykaczewski, (D), Scripps, 2009, Obp
 Howard Scher, (D), Florida, 2005, OuCcPe
 Lori A. Ziolkowski, (D), California (Irvine), 2009, CoOcCs
Research Associate:
 Dennis M. Allen, (D), Lehigh, 1978, ObGe
 Dianne I. Greenfield, (D), Stony Brook, 2002, Ob
 W. Joe Jones, (D), California (Santa Cruz), 2001, Ob
 Matthew E. Kimball, (D), Rutgers, 2008, Obn
 Erik M. Smith, (D), Maryland, 2000, Obn
Emeritus:
 Bruce C. Coull, (D), Lehigh, 1968, Obn
 John M. Dean, (D), Purdue, 1962, Obn
 Robert J. Feller, (D), Washington, 1977, Obn
 Madilyn M. Fletcher, (D), Univ Coll (North Wales), 1975, Obn
 Sarah A. Woodin, (D), Washington, 1972, Ob

University of South Carolina - Lancaster
University of South Carolina - Lancaster (A) (2015)
P.O. Box 889
Lancaster, SC 29721
 p. (803) 313-7129
 martek@mailbox.sc.edu
 http://usclancaster.sc.edu

Winthrop University
Dept of Chemistry, Physics, & Geology (2015)
Sims Science Building
Winthrop University
Rock Hill, SC 29733
 p. (803) 323-4949
 bolandi@winthrop.edu
 http://chem.winthrop.edu
Chair, Environmental Sciences and Studies Program:
 Marsha S. Bollinger, (D), South Carolina, 1986, CmOgCc
Professor:
 Irene B. Boland, (D), South Carolina, 1996, GtgOe
Associate Professor:
 Gwen M. Daley, (D), Virginia Tech, 1999, PqgGs
 Scott P. Werts, (D), Johns Hopkins, 2006, ScbPy

Wofford College
Dept of Geology (2011)
Wofford College
429 North Church Street
Spartanburg, SC 29303-3663
 p. (864) 597-4527
 fergusonta@wofford.edu
 http://www.wofford.edu/geology/
Director:
 Terry A. Ferguson, (D), Tennessee, 1988, Ga

South Dakota

Black Hills State University
School of Natural Sciences (B) (2015)
1200 University Street, Unit 9008
Spearfish, SD 57799-9008
 p. (605) 642-6506
 Abigail.Domagall@bhsu.edu
 http://www.bhsu.edu/Academics/ProgramsMajors/Natu-
 ralSciences/EnvironmentalPhysicalScience/tabid/888/
 f: https://www.facebook.com/EnvPhysSciBHSU/?ref=hl
 Enrollment (2015): B: 29 (6)
Professor:
 Mark Gabel, (D), Iowa State, 1982, Pb
Assistant Professor:
 Abigail M S Domagall, (D), Univ at Buffalo, 2008, GveOe

Oglala Lakota College
Dept of Math, Science, & Technology (1999)

P.O. Box 490
Kyle, SD 57755
 p. (605) 455-6124
 hlagarry@olc.edu
 http://www.olc.edu/local_links/smet/

South Dakota School of Mines & Technology
Dept of Atmospheric and Environmental Sciences (B,M,D) (2014)
501 E. St. Joseph Street
Rapid City, SD 57701-3995
 p. (605) 394-2291
 Pamela.Cox@sdsmt.edu
 http://www.ias.sdsmt.edu/
 Enrollment (2011): B: 15 (0) M: 14 (3)
Professor:
 Andrew G. Detwiler, (D), SUNY (Albany), 1980, Oa
Associate Professor:
 William J. Capehart, (D), Penn State, 1997, Oa
 Donna V. Kliche, (D), SD Mines, 2007, OaaOa
 P. V. Sundareshwar, (D), South Carolina, 2002, OeCgSb
Assistant Professor:
 Adam French, (D), North Carolina State, 2011, Oaw
 Lisa Kunza, (D), Wyoming, 2012, HsOe
Instructor:
 Darren R. Clabo, (M), SD Mines, 2009, OaaOa
Emeritus:
 John H. Helsdon, (D), SUNY (Albany), 1979, Oa
 Mark R. Hjelmfelt, (D), Chicago, 1980, Oa
 Paul L. Smith, (D), Carnegie Inst, 1960, Oa

Dept of Geology & Geological Engineering (B,M,D) O (2015)
501 E. Saint Joseph St.
Rapid City, SD 57701-3901
 p. (605) 394-2461
 geologyinfo@sdsmt.edu
 http://geology.sdsmt.edu
 f: https://www.facebook.com/SDSMTGeologyGeologicalEn-
 gineering
 Administrative Assistant: Cleo J. Heenan
 Enrollment (2015): B: 190 (25) M: 35 (6) D: 12 (0)
Field Station Director:
 Nuri Uzunlar, (D), SD Mines, 1993, Gg
Department Head; Director Museum of Geology:
 Laurie C. Anderson, (D), Wisconsin, 1991, Pio
Professor:
 Edward F. Duke, (D), Dartmouth, 1984, Gi
 Timothy L. Masterlark, (D), Wisconsin, 2000, Yg
 Maribeth H. Price, (D), Princeton, 1995, Oir
 Larry D. Stetler, (D), Washington State, 1993, Ng
Senior Scientist:
 William M. Roggenthen, (D), Princeton, 1980, NgYg
Associate Professor:
 J. Foster Sawyer, (D), SD Mines, 2006, NgGo
Assistant Professor:
 Zeynep O. Baran, (D), Miami, 2012, Gco
 Christina L. Belanger, (D), Chicago, 2011, PimPe
 Kurt W. Katzenstein, (D), Nevada (Reno), 2008, NgrOr
 Liangping Li, (D), Polytechnic Univ of Valencia (Spain), 2011, Hqw
 Darrin C. Pagnac, (D), California (Riverside), 2005, Pv
Coordinator and Instructor:
 Christopher J. Pellowski, (D), SD Mines, 2012, Gg
Associate Director Museum of Geology:
 Sally Y. Shelton, (M), Texas Tech, 1984, Pg
Emeritus:
 Arden D. Davis, (D), SD Mines, 1983, Hw
 James E. Fox, (D), Wyoming, 1972, Gs
 Alvis L. Lisenbee, (D), Penn State, 1972, Gc
 James E. Martin, (D), Washington, 1979, Ps
 Colin J. Paterson, (D), Otago (NZ), 1978, Eg
 Perry H. Rahn, (D), Penn State, 1965, Ng
 Jack A. Redden, (D), Harvard, 1956, Gp

South Dakota State University
Plant Science Dept (A,B,M,D) (2014)
Soil Science Program
SAG 244 Box 2207-A

Brookings, SD 57007-1096
p. (605) 688-5123
howard.woodard@sdstate.edu
http://plantsci.sdstate.edu/
Enrollment (2011): M: 10 (4) D: 6 (1)
Distinguished Professor:
Douglas D. Malo, (D), North Dakota State, 1975, Sd
Dean:
Gary D. Lemme, (D), Nebraska, 1979, Sd
Professor:
Dwayne L. Beck, (D), South Dakota State, 1983, Ou
Bruce H. Bleakley, (D), Florida, 1986, Sb
Charles G. Carlson, (D), South Dakota State, 1978, Hw
David E. Clay, (D), Minnesota, 1988, Sb
James J. Doolittle, (D), Texas A&M, 1991, Sc
Ronald H. Gelderman, (D), North Dakota State, 1987, Sc
Thomas E. Schumacher, (D), Michigan State, 1982, Sp
Howard J. Woodard, (D), Rutgers, 1985, ScoGg
Associate Professor:
Robert K. Berg, Jr., (D), Iowa State, 1987, Sb
Research Associate:
Anthony G. Bly, (M), South Dakota State, 1992, Sc
Joseph Schumacher, (M), South Dakota State, 1990, Sp
Adjunct Professor:
Paul E. Fixen, (D), Colorado State, 1979, Sc
Dianne H. Rickerl, (D), Auburn, 1986, Sf
Emeritus:
James R. Gerwing, (M), Minnesota, 1978, Sc
Robert Kohl, (D), Utah State, 1962, So

University of South Dakota
Dept of Earth Sciences & Physics (B) (2011)
414 East Clark Street
Vermillion, SD 57069-2390
p. (605) 677-5649
esci@usd.edu
http://www.usd.edu/earthsciences/
Enrollment (2011): B: 25 (9)
Chair:
Timothy H. Heaton, (D), Harvard, 1988, PvOg
Associate Professor:
Brennan T. Jordan, (D), Oregon State, 2002, GiOw
Assistant Professor:
Mark R. Sweeney, (D), Washington State, 2004, Gs
Instructor:
Jeanne M. Fromm, (M), Idaho State, 1995, GgHs

Tennessee

Austin Peay State University
Geosciences Dept (B) (2010)
601 College St
Clarksville, TN 37044
p. (931) 221-7454
sirkr@apsu.edu
http://www.apsu.edu/geosciences
Enrollment (2009): B: 72 (9)
Interim Director:
Robert A. Sirk, (D), Kent State, 1991, GeOyu
Professor:
Phyllis A. Camilleri, (D), Wyoming, 1994, Gct
Daniel L. Frederick, (D), Tennessee, 1994, Gsr
Phillip R. Kemmerly, (D), Oklahoma State, 1973, GmeHg
Gregory D. Ridenour, (D), Texas A&M, 1993, OiaOn
Associate Professor:
Jack Deibert, (D), Wyoming, Gsr
Assistant Professor:
Christopher Gentry, (D), Indiana State, 2008, Oyi
Christine Mathenge, (D), Indiana, 2008, Oy
Emeritus:
D. M. S. Bhatia, (D), Missouri (Rolla), 1976, Ca
James X. Corgan, (D), Louisiana State, 1967, Pg
Byron J. Webb, (M), Memphis, Oy
R. Kenton Wibking, (D), Nebraska, Oy
Laboratory Director:
Richard Wheeler, (M), Brigham Young, Gg

Middle Tennessee State University
Dept of Geosciences (B,M) (2015)
Box 9
Kirksey Old Main, Room 325B
Murfreesboro, TN 37132
p. (615) 898-2726
karen.wolfe@mtsu.edu
http://mtsu.edu/geosciences
f: MTSU Geosciences
t: @MTSUGeosciences
Administrative Assistant: Karen M. Wolfe
Enrollment (2015): B: 103 (28) M: 15 (3)
Chair:
Warner Cribb, (D), Ohio State, 1993, GipGz
Professor:
Mark J. Abolins, (D), Caltech, 1999, Gc
James A. Henry, (D), Kansas, 1978, Oa
Ronald L. Zawislak, (D), Wyoming, 1980, Ye
Associate Professor:
Clay D. Harris, (D), Indiana, 1992, Gs
Melissa Lobegeier, (D), James Cook, 2001, Pmg
Assistant Professor:
Jeremy Aber, (D), Kansas State, 2011, Oyi
Patricia Boda, (D), Minnesota, 2007, OinOn
Henrique G. Momm, (D), Mississippi, 2008, OiHsOr
Research Associate:
Zada Law, (M), Wisconsin, 1980, Oi
Lecturer:
Alan Brown, (M), Illinois State, 2005, Gg
Laura Collins, (M), Mississippi State, 2005, Gg
Michael W. Hiett, (M), Kentucky, 1995, Gg

Motlow State Community College
Dept of Natural Sciences (A) (2014)
PO Box 8500
Lynchburg, TN 37352-8500
p. (931) 393-1810
lmayo@mscc.edu
http://www.mscc.edu/natural_science/
Instructor:
Lisa L Herring Mayo, (M), Mississippi State, 2000, GgOge

Pellissippi State Community College
Natural and Behavioral Sciences (1999)
10915 Hardin Valley Road
P.O. Box 22990
Knoxville, TN 37801
p. (865) 694-6685
jkelley@pstcc.edu
http://www.pstcc.edu

Roane State Community College - Oak Ridge
Mathematics and Sciences (Geology) (A) (2011)
276 Patton Lane
Harriman , TN 37748
p. (865) 481-2000
leea@roanestate.edu
http://aclee1234.fortunecity.com
Professor:
Arthur C. Lee, (D), S California, 1994

Sewanee: University of the South
Dept of Forestry & Geology (B) (2010)
735 University Avenue
Sewanee, TN 37383-1000
p. (931) 598-1271
pete.pekins@unh.edu
http://www.sewanee.edu/EnvStudies
Enrollment: No data reported since 1999
Chair:
Scott Torreano, (D), Georgia, 1991, Sf
Professor:
Martin A. Knoll, (D), Texas (El Paso), 1988, Hw

Donald B. Potter, Jr., (D), Massachusetts, 1985, Gc
Stephen A. Shaver, (D), Stanford, 1984, Eg
Associate Professor:
C. Ken Smith, (D), Florida, 1996, Sf
Adjunct Professor:
Glendon W. Smalley, (D), Tennessee, 1975, Sf

Tennessee Tech University
Dept of Earth Sciences (B) (2015)
PO Box 5062
Cookeville, TN 38505
p. (931) 372-3121
MHarrison@tntech.edu
http://www.tntech.edu/earth/home/
Administrative Assistant: Peggy Medlin
Enrollment (2015): B: 56 (19)
Chair:
Michael J. Harrison, (D), Illinois (Urbana-Champaign), 2002, Gc
Professor:
Evan A. Hart, (D), Tennessee, 2000, Oy
H. Wayne Leimer, (D), Missouri, 1969, Gz
Ping-Chi Li, (D), Iowa, 1992, Oi
Assistant Professor:
Joseph Asante, (D), Nevada (Las Vegas), 2012, HwOr
Jeannette Wolak, (D), Montana State, 2011, Gsr
Adjunct Professor:
Jason E. Duke, (M), Tennessee Tech, 1995, Oi
Emeritus:
Larry W. Knox, (D), Indiana, 1974, Pm

University of Memphis
Center for Earthquake Research & Information (CERI) (M,D)
(2014)
3876 Central Avenue, Suite 1
Memphis, TN 38152-3050
p. (901) 678-2007
jbrthlm@memphis.edu
http://www.ceri.memphis.edu/
Enrollment (2011): M: 7 (3) D: 16 (1)
Chair, Department of Earth Sciences:
Mervin J. Bartholomew, (D), Virginia Tech, 1971, Gt
CERI Founding Director:
Archibald C. Johnston, (D), Colorado, 1979, Ys
CERI Director of Academic Programs:
Christine A. Powell, (D), Princeton, 1976, Ys
CERI Director:
Charles A. Langston, (D), Caltech, 1976, Ys
Professor:
Jer-Ming Chiu, (D), Cornell, 1982, Ys
Roy B. Van Arsdale, (D), Utah, 1979, Gc
Associate Professor:
Randel Tom Cox, (D), Missouri, 1995, GtcGm
Jose M. Pujol, (D), Wyoming, 1985, Ye
DES Graduate Coordinator:
Arleen Alice Hill, (D), Og
USGS:
Oliver Boyd, (D), Colorado, 2004, YgGtg
Research Scientist:
Stephen P. Horton, (D), Nevada (Reno), 1992, Ys
Assoc. Research Professor :
Chris Cramer, (D), Stanford, 1976, Ys
Assoc. Research Professor:
Maria Beatrice Magnani, (D), Studi di Perugia, 2000, YesYg
Assoc. Research Professor :
Robert Smalley, Jr., (D), Cornell, 1988, Yd
Assoc. Research Professor:
Mitchell M. Withers, (D), New Mexico Tech, 1997, Ys
Assistant Research Professor:
Heather DeShon, (D), California (Santa Cruz), 2004, Ysg
Research Scientist:
Shu-Choiung Chiu, (D), Memphis, 2010, Ys

Dept of Earth Sciences (B,M,D) O (2015)
111 Johnson Hall
488 Patterson Street
Memphis, TN 38152-3550

p. (901) 678-4571 or 678-4358
dlarsen@memphis.edu
http://memphis.edu/earthsciences/
Enrollment (2015): B: 61 (16) M: 30 (3) D: 40 (3)
Chair:
Daniel Larsen, (D), New Mexico, 1994, Cl
Director, Confucius Institute:
Hsiang-Te Kung, (D), Tennessee, 1980, Oy
Director, Center for Earthquake Research and Information:
Charles A. Langston, (D), Caltech, 1976, Ys
Professor:
Mervin J. Bartholomew, (D), Virginia Tech, 1971, Gtc
Jer-Ming Chiu, (D), Cornell, 1982, Ys
Randel T. Cox, (D), Missouri, 1995, Gm
David H. Dye, (D), Washington, 1980, Ga
Christine A. Powell, (D), Princeton, 1976, Ys
Jose Pujol, (D), Wyoming, 1985, Ye
Roy B. Van Arsdale, (D), Utah, 1979, Gc
Associate Professor:
Arleen A. Hill, (D), South Carolina, 2002, On
Andrew M. Mickelson, (D), Ohio State, 2002, Ga
Esra Ozdenerol, (D), Louisiana State, 2000, Oi
Director, Chucalissa Museum:
Robert P. Connolly, (D), Illinois (Urbana-Champaign), 1996,
GaOnn
Associate Scientist:
Stephen Horton, (D), Nevada (Reno), 1992, Yg
Assistant Professor:
Anzhelika Antipova, (D), Louisiana State, 2010, On
Eunseo Choi, (D), Caltech, 2008, Gt
Eric Daub, (D), Yx
Youngsang Kwon, (D), SUNY (Buffalo), 2012, Oi
Ryan M. Parish, (D), Memphis, 2013, Ga
Research Associate:
Chris H. Cramer, (D), Stanford, 1976, Ys
Robert Smalley, Jr., (D), Cornell, 1988, Ys
Mitchell M. Withers, (D), New Mexico Tech, 1997, Ys
Instructor:
Julie Johnson, (D), Florida International, 2012, Gx
Pamela M. Riddick, (M), Memphis, 1990, On
Adjunct Professor:
Ryan Csontos, (D), Memphis, 2007, GcOiHw
Emeritus:
Phili B. Deboo, (D), Louisiana State, 1963, Pg
Robert W. Deininger, (D), Rice, 1964, Gx
James Dorman, (D), Columbia, 1961, Ys
Archibald C. Johnston, (D), Colorado, 1979, Ys
David N. Lumsden, (D), Illinois (Urbana), 1965, Gd
George H. Swihart, (D), Chicago, 1987, Gx

University of Tennessee at Chattanooga
Biology, Geology, and Environmental Science (B) (2016)
615 McCallie Ave., Dept. 2653
Chattanooga, TN 37403
p. (423) 425-4341
http://www.utc.edu/biology-geology-environmental-science/
division-geology/
f: https://www.facebook.com/GeologyatUTC
Enrollment (2015): B: 53 (23)
Professor:
Habte G. Churnet, (D), Tennessee, 1979, GxgOg
Jonathan W. Mies, (D), North Carolina, 1990, GctHg
Associate Professor:
Amy Brock-Hon, (D), Nevada, 2007, Os
Assistant Professor:
Ann E. Holmes, (D), Columbia, 1997, Gs
Adjunct Professor:
Gregory Brodie, (M), Purdue, 1979, Ge
Geology Laboratory Coordinator:
Wayne K. Williams, (M), Memphis State, 1980, Gg

University of Tennessee, Knoxville
Dept of Earth & Planetary Sciences (B,M,D) (2015)
306 Earth & Planetary Sciences Building
Knoxville, TN 37996-1410
p. (865) 974-2366

eps@utk.edu
http://web.eps.utk.edu/
f: https://www.facebook.com/UTEPS
Enrollment (2015): B: 140 (38) M: 21 (7) D: 27 (7)
Head:
  Larry D. McKay, (D), Waterloo, 1991, HyGe
Distinguished Scientist:
  Robert D. Hatcher, Jr., (D), Tennessee, 1965, Gc
Professor:
  Thomas W. Broadhead, (D), Iowa, 1978, Pi
  William M. Dunne, (D), Bristol (UK), 1980, Gc
  Christopher Fedo, (D), Virginia Tech, 1994, GsXg
  Linda Kah, (D), Harvard, 1997, Gs
  Michael L. McKinney, (D), Yale, 1985, GePo
  Harry Y. McSween, Jr., (D), Harvard, 1977, XcGi
  Jeffery E. Moersch, (D), Cornell, 1997, Xg
  Edmund Perfect, (D), Cornell, 1986, Sp
  Lawrence A. Taylor, (D), Lehigh, 1968, Cp
Associate Professor:
  Devon Burr, (D), Arizona, 2003, XgGm
  Annette S. Engel, (D), Texas, 2004, Cl
  Micah Jessup, (D), Virginia Tech, 2007, Gc
Assistant Professor:
  Joshua Emery, (D), Arizona, 2003, Xg
  Andrew Steen, (D), UNC Chapel Hill, 2009, CoOb
  Colin Sumrall, (D), Texas, 1997, Pi
  Anna Szynkiewicz, (D), Wroclaw, Poland, 2004, Cs
Lecturer:
  William Deane, (M), Tennessee, 1998, Gg
Research Associate Professor:
  Lawrence A. Anovitz, (D), Michigan, 1987, Cp
Adjunct Professor:
  Julie Bartley, (D), Gs
  Hassina Bilheux, (D), On
  Burt Carter, (D), Pe
  David R. Cole, (D), Penn State, 1980, Ca
  Steven Driese, (D), Wisconsin, SaPeGs
  Alice Layton, (D), Purdue, 1987, On
  Peter Lemiszki, (D), Tennessee, Gc
  Timothy McCoy, (D), Xm
  David Mittlefehldt, (D), Xm
  Scott Murchie, (D), Xg
  Ryan Otter, (D), On
  Tommy Phelps, (D), On
  Johnny Waters, (D), Pg
  Richard T. Williams, II, (D), Virginia Tech, 1979, Yg
Emeritus:
  Don W. Byerly, (D), Tennessee, 1966, Ge
  G. Michael Clark, (D), Penn State, 1966, Gm
  Theodore C. Labotka, (D), Caltech, 1978, Gp
  Kula C. Misra, (D), W Ontario, 1973, Eg
  Kenneth R. Walker, (D), Yale, 1969, Pe
Other:
  Melanie A. Mayes, (D), Tennessee, 2006, ClGeHw
Cooperating Faculty:
  Janet L. Hopson, (D), Tennessee, 1994, On
  Robert Riding, (D), UK, Gs

University of Tennessee, Martin
Dept of Agriculture, Geosciences, and Natural Resources (B) (2014)
256 Brehm Hall
Martin, TN 38238
  p. (731) 881-7260
  mehlhorn@utm.edu
  http://www.utm.edu/departments/caas/agnr/geosciences/
  Enrollment (2013): B: 29 (13)
Professor:
  Paula M. Gale, (D), Arkansas, 1988, OsSdc
  Michael A. Gibson, (D), Tennessee, 1988, PgiOe
  Jefferson S. Rogers, (D), Illinois, 1995, On
  Robert M. Simpson, (D), Indiana State, 2000, OawOi
Associate Professor:
  Stan P. Dunagan, (D), Tennessee, 1998, GsSa
Assistant Professor:
  Thomas A. DePriest, (D), Union (Jackson), 2009, Oe
  Benjamin P. Hooks, (D), Maine, 2009, GciNr

Instructor:
  Eleanor E. Gardner, (M), Georgia, GgPg
Emeritus:
  William T. McCutchen, (M), Berea, 1967, Gg
  Robert P. Self, (D), Rice, 1971, Gs
  Helmut C. Wenz, (M), W Michigan, 1968, On

Vanderbilt University
Earth and Environmental Sciences (B,M,D) (2015)
SC Science & Engineering Bldg
2301 Vanderbilt Place, SC5726
VU Station B 351805
Nashville, TN 37235
  p. (615) 322-2976
  jewell.beasleystanley@vanderbilt.edu
  http://www.vanderbilt.edu/ees/
  f: https://www.facebook.com/groups/393646734010753/
  Enrollment (2015): B: 25 (9) M: 11 (5) D: 10 (2)
Chair:
  Steven L. Goodbred, Jr., (D), William & Mary, 1999, GsOg
Professor:
  John C. Ayers, (D), Rensselaer, 1991, Cg
  Ralf Bennartz, (D), Free Univ of Berlin, 1997, Oar
  David J. Furbish, (D), Colorado, 1985, GmHg
  George Hornberger, (D), Stanford, 1970, Hg
  Calvin F. Miller, (D), California (Los Angeles), 1977, Gi
Director of Graduate Studies:
  Guilherme Gualda, (D), Chicago, 2010, GivGz
Associate Professor:
  Jonathan M. Gilligan, (D), Yale, 1991, GeOa
Assistant Professor:
  Simon Darroch, (D), Yale, 2014, Poi
  Larisa R.G DeSantis, (D), Florida, 2009, Pve
  Maria Luisa Jorge, (D), Illinois (Chicago), 2007, Py
  Jessica L. Oster, (D), California (Davis), 2010, Cls
Senior Lecturer:
  Lily L. Claiborne, (D), Vanderbilt, 2011, GiCg
  Neil P. Kelley, (D), California (Davis), 2012, GgOgPg
  Daniel J. Morgan, (D), Washington, 2009, GmCc
Emeritus:
  Leonard P. Alberstadt, (D), Oklahoma, 1967, Gd
  Molly F. Miller, (D), California (Los Angeles), 1977, Pe
  Authur L. Reesman, (D), Missouri, 1966, Gg
  William G. Siesser, (D), Cape Town, 1971, Pm
  Richard G. Stearns, (D), Northwestern, 1953, Yg
Related Staff:
  Aaron K. Covey, (M), Vanderbilt, 2008, Ge

Volunteer State Community College
Volunteer State Community College (2014)
1800 Nashville Pike
Gallatin, TN 37006
  p. (615) 230-3294
  Clark.Cropper@volstate.edu
  http://www.volstate.edu

Walters State Community College
Walters State Community College (1999)
500 South Davy Crockett Parkway
Morristown, TN 37813
  p. (423) 585-6764
  http://www.ws.edu

Texas

Alamo Colleges-San Antonio College
Natural Sciences (2015)
1819 N Main Ave
San Antonio, TX 78212
  p. (210) 486-0045
  gstanley@alamo.edu
  http://alamo.edu/sac/earthsci/
Professor:
  Dean Lambert, (D), UT-Austin, Oy

Associate Professor:
Anne D. Dietz, (M), Tx A&M - Kingsville, OgGg
Full-Time Adjunct:
Dwight Jurena, (M), RPI, GgOg
Adjunct Professor:
Thomas S. Girhard, (M), Texas State, Oyw
Robert Janusz, (M), UT-San Antonio, Og
Ryan E. Rudnicki, (D), Penn State, Oy
Charles K. Smith, (M), Texas State, Oy

Alamo Colleges-Palo Alto College
Dept of Geology (A) (2015)
1400 W. Villaret Blvd
San Antonio, TX 78224
    p. (210) 486-3000
    ghagen@alamo.edu
    http://alamo.edu/pac/geology/

Alvin Community College
Dept of Geology (A) (2013)
3110 Mustang Rd
Alvin, TX 77511
    p. (281) 756-5670
    ddevery@alvincollege.edu
    Enrollment (2012): A: 2 (1)
Dept. Chair of Physical Sciences:
Dora Devery, (M), Texas Christian, 1979, Gg

Amarillo College
Dept of Physical Science (2015)
P.O. Box 447
Amarillo, TX 79178
    p. (806) 371-5333
    rdhobbs@actx.edu
    https://www.actx.edu/pscience/
    Enrollment (2009): A: 3 (0)
Professor:
Richard D. Hobbs, (D), Wyoming, 1998, OrGc
Adjunct Professor:
David Pertl, (M), West Texas A&M, 1984, Go

Angelo State University
Dept of Physics and Geosciences (B) O (2015)
ASU Station #10904
San Angelo, TX 76909
    p. (325) 942-2242
    joseph.satterfield@angelo.edu
    http://www.angelo.edu/dept/physics/Geosciences/geoscience.
    php
    Enrollment (2015): B: 63 (14)
Planetarium Director:
Mark S. Sonntag, (D), Indiana, 1971, Xg
Professor:
Joseph I. Satterfield, (D), Rice, 1995, Gc
Visiting Assistant Professor:
Fred L. Wilson, (D), Kansas, 1964, Gm
Assistant Professor:
Fawn M. Last, (D), Manitoba, 2013, Gsn
Heather Lehto, (D), USF, 2012, GvYs
James W. Ward, (D), Kentucky, 2008, HwClOn
Adjunct Professor:
Cary D. Carman, (B), Angelo State, 1999, Hg
Steven Lyons, (D), Hawaii, 1981, Ow
Robert Purkiss, (M), Texas Tech, 1991, Gg

Austin Community College District
Dept of Earth and Environmental Sciences (A) (2016)
11928 Stonehollow Drive
Austin, TX 78758-3190
    p. (512) 223-4875
    gstaff@austincc.edu
    http: //austincc.edu/ees/
    Administrative Assistant: Oralia Guerra
    Enrollment (2015): A: 478 (0)

Chair:
George M. Staff, (D), Texas A&M, 1983, Pe
Professor:
Robert H. Blodgett, (D), Texas (Austin), 1990, GseOe
Ronald A. Johns, (D), Texas (Austin), 1993, Pi
Assistant Professor:
Peter J. Wehner, (M), Vanderbilt, 1992, Gv
Adjunct Professor:
Heather L. Beatty, (M), Texas Tech, 1992, Ge
Peter A. Boone, (D), Texas A&M, 1972, Gro
Thomas W. Brown, (M), Indiana, 1987, Ges
M. Jennifer Cooke, (D), Texas (Austin), 2005, GmCl
Amy J. Cunningham, (M), Cincinnati, 1992, OeGg
Leslie S. Davis, (M), Florida State, 1986, Op
Meredith Y. Denton-Hedrick, (M), Texas A&M, 1992, Ye
Dennis P. Dunn, (D), Texas (Austin), 2002, EgGt
Kusali R. Gamage, (D), Florida, 2005, HyOuPm
Khaled Hasan, (D), Texas A&M, 1995, Or
Ian C. Jones, (D), Texas (Austin), 2002, Hw
Richard V. McGehee, (D), Texas (Austin), 1963, GgOn
Glynda L. Mercier, (M), Texas A&M, 2013, On
Frank M. Mikan, (M), Ohio State, 1973, CgOe
Ata U. Rahman, (D), Texas Tech, 1983, Ge
Fabienne M. Rambaud, (M), Texas (Austin), 2005, Eg
Carolyn M. Riess, (M), Texas at El Paso, 1984, Goe
Raymond M. Slade, Jr., (B), Southwest Texas, 1971, HgsHq
Jason H. Stephens, (D), Texas (Austin), 2014, YrGuYe
Wenxian Tan, (D), Texas (Austin), 2013, Obg
Anne Turner, (M), Texas (Austin), 1986, Hg
Science Laboratory Technician:
John S. Conners, Oe
Shannon M. Grace, (B), Texas State, 2010, On
Deanna M. Sharp, (B), Angelo State, 2002, One
Cooperating Faculty:
Daniel R. Dewberry, (M), Texas (Austin), 1992, On
David J. Froehlich, (D), Texas (Austin), 1996, Pv

Baylor University 📖
Dept of Geosciences (B,M,D) ● (2016)
One Bear Place #97354
101 Bagby Ave.
BSB, 4th Floor, Rm. D409
Waco, TX 76798-7354
    p. (254) 710-2361
    paulette_penney@baylor.edu
    http://www.baylor.edu/geology/
    Administrative Assistant: Janelle Atchley
    Administrative Assistant: Jamie J.. Ruth
    Enrollment (2015): B: 87 (15) M: 15 (4) D: 22 (3)
Chair:
Stacy C. Atchley, (D), Nebraska, 1990, GroGo
W.M. Keck Foundation Professor of Geophysics:
Robert Jay Pulliam, (D), California (Berkeley), 1991, YsrYg
Graduate Program Director:
Steven G. Driese, (D), Wisconsin, 1982, SaGe
Professor:
Peter M. Allen, (D), S Methodist, 1977, HgNg
Rena M. Bonem, (D), Oklahoma, 1975, Pei
Vincent S. Cronin, (D), Texas A&M, 1988, Gc
Stephen I. Dworkin, (D), Texas, 1991, ClGd
Stephen Forman, (D), Colorado, Cc
Don M. Greene, (D), Oklahoma, 1980, Oyw
Lee C. Nordt, (D), Texas A&M, 1996, SdGa
Kenneth Wilkins, (D), Florida, 1982, Pv
Joe C. Yelderman, Jr., (D), Wisconsin, 1983, Hw
Associate Professor:
John A. Dunbar, (D), Texas, 1989, YgHg
Daniel J. Peppe, (D), Yale, 2009, PbYmPe
Joseph D. White, (D), Montana, 1998, Or
Assistant Professor:
Kenneth S. Befus, (D), Texas (Austin), 2014, GviGv
William C. Hockaday, (D), Ohio State, 2006, CoaSb
Scott C. James, (D), California (Irvine), 2001, HwGeHw
Emeritus:
Harold H. Beaver, (D), Wisconsin, 1954, Go
William G. Brown, (D), Alaska, 1987, Gc
Thomas T. Goforth, (D), S Methodist, 1973, Yg

Don F. Parker, (D), Texas, 1976, Giv
Instrumentation Specialist:
  Timothy Meredith
  Ren Zhang, (D), McMaster, 2007, Cs
Laboratory Director:
  Sharon Browning, Gg
Office Manager:
  Paulette Penney, On

Blinn College
Agricultural and Natural Science Programs (A) (2013)
902 College Avenue
Brenham, TX 77833
  p. (979) 830-4200
  cl.metz@blinn.edu
  http://www.blinn.edu/natscience/index.htm
Instructor:
  Michael Dalman, Gg
  Cynthia Lawry, (D), Gg

Brookhaven College
Science/Math Div - Geology Dept (2010)
3939 Valley View Lane
Farmers Branch, TX 75244
  p. (972) 860-4758
  EvonneC@dcccd.edu
  http://www.brookhavencollege.edu/instruction/math-sci-ence/science/geology/
Head:
  Susan M. Maxey, (M), Texas (Dallas), 1976, OgGoPl

Coastal Bend College
Science Div (A) (2013)
3800 Charco Road
Beeville, TX 78102
  p. (361) 354-2423
  amgarza@coastalbend.edu
  http://www.coastalbend.edu/acdem/science/
  Administrative Assistant:
  Enrollment (2011): A: 3 (0)
Instructor:
  Danny Burns, (M), Ball State, 1984, Ogn
  Richard Cowart, (M), Texas A&M (Corpus Christi), 1997, Og

Collin College - Central Park Campus
Dept of Geology (A) (2015)
2200 W. University Drive
McKinney, TX 75071
  p. (972) 548-6790
  bburkett@collin.edu
  http://www.collin.edu/geology/
  Enrollment (2015): A: 30 (0)
Professor:
  Brett Burkett, (M), SUNY (Buffalo), 2008, Gvg

Collin College - Preston Ridge Campus
Dept of Geology and Environmental Science (A) (2014)
9700 Wade Boulevard
Frisco, TX 75035
  p. (972) 377-1635
  smay@collin.edu
Chair:
  Amira Shaham-Albalancy, (D), On
Professor:
  Heinrich Goetz, (M), Texas A&M, 1997, Ge
  Paul Manganelli, (M), Boston Coll, 1998
  S Judson May, (D), New Mexico, 1980, GgoGc
Lab Instructor:
  Mike Winslow, (M), Texas (Arlington), 1983

Collin College - Spring Creek Campus
Dept of Geology and Environmental Science (A) (2015)
2800 E. Spring Creek Parkway
Plano, TX 75074
  p. (972) 578-5518

dbabcock@collin.edu
http://www.collin.edu/academics/programs/geology.html
Enrollment (2012): A: 10 (0)
Chair:
  Daphne H. Babcock, (M), Memphis, 1989, Geg
Professor:
  Shannon Burkett
Geology Lab Instructor:
  Mark Turner, Gg

Del Mar College
Dept of Natural Sciences (A) (2013)
Corpus Christi, TX 78404
  p. (512) 886-1240
  jhalcomb@delmar.edu
  Enrollment: No data reported since 1999
Instructor:
  Walter V. Kramer, (M), Texas (El Paso), 1970, Gg
  Roger T. Steinberg, (M), Tennessee, 1981, Gr
Emeritus:
  Mary S. Thorpe, (M), Baylor, 1966, Ge

El Centro College-
Dallas Community College District
Geology Program (A) (2010)
801 Main Street
Dallas, TX 75202
75202
  p. (214) 860-2734
  MKadjar@dcccd.edu
  http://www.elcentrocollege.edu/Program/ArtSci/Geology/
Coordinator:
  Mickey Kadjar, (M), Paris, Gg
Adjunct Professor:
  Nancy Fields, (M), Baylor, Gg
  Alice Ruffel, (M), Oklahoma, Gg
  Bethan Salle, Gg

El Paso Community College
Dept of Geological Sciences (A) (2015)
P.O. Box 20500
El Paso, TX 79998
  p. (915) 831-5161
  kdevaney@epcc.edu
  http://epcc.edu/InstructionalPrograms/geologicalsciences
Coordinator - Valle Verde:
  Russell Smith, (M), Florida, Gg
Coordinator - Transmountain Campus:
  Kathleen Devaney, (D), California (Los Angeles), 1992, Gg
Coordinator - Northwest Campus:
  Deborah Caskey, (M), Texas, Gg
Professor:
  Sulaiman Abushagur, (D), Texas (El Paso), Gg
Associate Professor:
  Joshua Villalobos, (M), Texas (El Paso), Gg
Instructor:
  Robert Rohbaugh, (M), UTEP
Adjunct Professor:
  Brenda Barnes, (D), Texas (El Paso), Gg
  Lawrence Bothern, (M), New Mexico State, Gg
  Sabrina Canalda, (M), Texas (El Paso), Gg
  Tina Carrick, (M), Texas (El Paso), Gg
  Emile Couroux, Gg
  Alexandra Falcon, Gg
  Musa Hussein, (D), Texas (El Paso), Gg
  Adriana Perez, (M), Texas (El Paso), Gg
  Kirk Rothemund, Gg

Hardin-Simmons University
Dept of Geology & Environmental Science (B) (2015)
Box 16164
2200 Hickory Street
Abilene, TX 79698-6164
  p. (325) 670-1383
  ouimette@hsutx.edu

http://www.hsutx.edu/academics/undergraduate/holland/geology
Enrollment (2015): B: 20 (5)
Head:
    Mark A. Ouimette, (D), Texas (El Paso), 1994, GieGt
Associate Professor:
    Steven Rosscoe, (D), Texas Tech, 2008, PmGsPs
Assistant Professor:
    Marla Potess, (D), Texas Tech, 2010, Ge

Hill College
Div of Mathematics and Sciences (1999)
112 Lamar
Hillsboro, TX 76645
    p. 254-659-7500
    rroberts@hillcollege.edu
    http://www.hillcollege.edu/academics/Traditional/Math_Science_EdServices/Geology.html

Houston Community College System
Geology Dept (A) (2010)
22 Waugh Drive
Houston, TX 77077
    p. (713) 718-5641
    dwight.kranz@hccs.edu
    http://learningwebsys.hccs.edu/discipline/geology/
    Enrollment: No data reported since 1999
Chair:
    Dwight S. Krantz, (M), Texas A&M, 1980, Gg
Professor:
    Alta S. Cate, (D), Houston, Gg
    Jeffrey Lewis, (M), San Diego State, Gg
    Carolyn Rindosh Miller, (M), S California, Gg
    Al O'Neill, (M), Rutgers, Gg

Kilgore College
Dept of Chemistry and Geology (A) O (2015)
1100 Broadway
Kilgore, TX 75662
    p. (903) 983-8253
    pbuchanan@kilgore.edu
    Enrollment (2015): A: 6 (2)
Dr.:
    Paul Buchanan, (D), Houston, 1995, GgiXm

Lamar University
Dept of Earth and Space Sciences (B) (2010)
P.O. Box 10031
Beaumont, TX 77710
    p. (409) 880-8236
    jim.jordan@lamar.edu
    http://ess.lamar.edu
    Enrollment (1999): B: 35 (2)
Professor:
    Jim L. Jordan, (D), Rice, 1975, Cc
University Professor:
    James W. Westgate, (D), Texas, 1988, Pe
Professor:
    Roger W. Cooper, (D), Minnesota, 1978, Gi
    Donald E. Owen, (D), Kansas, 1963, Gr
Associate Professor:
    Joseph M. Kruger, (D), Arizona, Yg
Instructor:
    Bennetta Schmidt, (D), Gg
Captain:
    Mark Adams, (M), Houston (Clear Lake), Xg
Adjunct Professor:
    Cynthia L. Parish, (M), Lamar, 2004, Gg
    Carla M. Tucker, (M), Texas, Hg
Laboratory Coordinator:
    Karen M. Woods, (B), Lamar, On

Laredo Community College
Dept of Natural Sciences & Kinesiology (2014)
Cigarroa Science Building Room 217
West End Washington Street

Laredo, TX 78040
    p. (956) 721-5195
    glenn.blaylock@laredo.edu
    http://www.laredo.edu/cms/LCC/Instruction/Divisions/Sciences/Natural_Sciences/Science/
    Enrollment: No data reported since 1999
Professor:
    Glenn W. Blaylock, (M), Brigham Young, 1998, Gg
Instructor:
    Mark T. Childre, (M), Texas (San Antonio)

Lee College
Dept of Physical Sciences (A) (2016)
P. O.Box 818
Baytown, TX 77522
    p. (281) 425-6552
    jdobberstine@lee.edu
    Enrollment (2015): A: 7 (0)
Professor:
    Sharon Gabel, (D), SUNY, 1991, GseGg

Lonestar College - CyFair
Geology Dept (2013)
9191 Barker Cypress Road
Cypress, TX 77433
    p. (281) 290-3919
    michael.r.konvicka@lonestar.edu
    http://www.lonestar.edu/geology-dept-cyfair.htm

Lonestar College - Kingwood
Geology Dept (1999)
20000 Kingwood Drive
Kingwood, TX 77339
    p. (281) 312-1629
    Jean.Whileyman@lonestar.edu
    http://www.lonestar.edu/geology-dept-kingwood.htm

Lonestar College - Montgomery
Geology Dept (2013)
3200 College Park Drive
Conroe, TX 77384
    p. (936) 273-7077
    Michael.J.Sundermann@lonestar.edu
    http://www.lonestar.edu/geology-dept-montgomery.htm
Professor:
    Nathalie N. Brandes, (M), New Mexico Tech
    John R. Kleist, (D), Texas

Lonestar College - North Harris
Geology Dept (2014)
2700 W.W. Thorne Drive
Houston, TX 77073-3499
    p. (281) 618-5685
    tom.hobbs@lonestar.edu
    Enrollment (2007): A: 20 (0)
Head:
    Thomas M. C. Hobbs, (M), Texas (El Paso), 1979, Gg
Professor:
    Peter E. Price, (M), Kentucky, 1979, Oi
Adjunct Professor:
    Penni Major, (M), Gg
    Michelle Mc Mahon, (D), Aberdeen, 1993, Go
    Victor S. Resnic, (D), Nat Pet Inst (Russia), 1971, Go
    Linda C. Tran, (B), Texas A&M, 1999, Oi

Lonestar College - Tomball
Geology Dept (1999)
30555 Tomball Parkway
Tomball, TX 77375
    p. (281) 351-3324
    David.O.Bary@lonestar.edu
    http://www.lonestar.edu/geology-dept-tomball.htm

Texas

McLennan Community College
Geology Dept (A) (2010)
1400 College Drive
Waco, TX 76708
    p. (254) 299-8442
    efagner@mclennan.edu
    http://www.mclennan.edu/departments/geol/
Instructor:
    Elaine Alexander, Gg

Midland College
Math and Science Div (A) (2015)
3600 N. Garfield
Midland, TX 79705
    p. (432) 685-4612
    kwaggoner@midland.edu
    http://www.midland.edu/~msd/
    Enrollment (2011): A: 14 (6)
Associate Professor:
    Joan Gawloski, (M), Baylor, GgzGe
    Antony Giles, (M), GgvGi
Assistant Professor:
    Keonho Kim, (D), GgOwPi
Adjunct Professor:
    Karen Waggoner, (D), Texas Tech, GghGc

Midwestern State University
Kimbell School of Geosciences (B,M) (2015)
3410 Taft
Wichita Falls, TX 76308
    p. (940) 397-4250
    geology.program@mwsu.edu
    http://www.mwsu.edu/academics/scienceandmath/geosciences
    f: https://www.facebook.com/MSUGeosProgram/
    Enrollment (2015): B: 85 (15) M: 9 (0)
Chair & Prothro Distinguished Associate Professor of Geological
Science:
    Jonathan D. Price, (D), Oklahoma, 1998, GiCgGz
Robert L. Bolin Distinguished Professor of Petroleum Geology:
    W. Scott Meddaugh, (D), Harvard, 1982, GoCe
Associate Professor and Graduate Advisor:
    Rebecca L. Dodge, (D), Colorado Mines, 1982, Ore
Assistant Professor:
    Jesse R. Carlucci, (D), Oklahoma, 2012, PisGs
Adjunct Professor:
    Black L. Lisa, (M), Texas Christian, 2008, EoGg
    Jay D. Murray, (D), Califiornia Inst of Technology, 1978, Gi
Emeritus:
    John Kocurko, (D), Texas Tech, 1972, Gs

North Lake College-
Dallas Community College District
Math and Natural Sciences (A) (2010)
5001 North MacArthur Boulevard
Irving, TX 75038
    p. (972) 273-3500
    memays@dcccd.edu
    http://www.northlakecollege.edu/academics/mathscience/
    index.html
Instructor:
    Leonard Kubicek, Gg

Odessa College
Dept of Geology, Anthropology & Geography (A) (2013)
201 W. University
Odessa, TX 79762
    p. (915) 335-6558
    dedwards@odessa.edu
    Enrollment (2010): A: 1 (1)
Associate Professor:
    Gerald B. McAfee, (M), Sul Ross State, 1966, Pi

Paris Junior College
Dept of Science (2014)
2400 Clarksville Street
Paris, TX 75460
    p. 903-782-0481
    mbarnett@parisjc.edu
    http://www.parisjc.edu/index.php/pjc2/directory-index/C208

Rice University
Center for Computational Geophysics (M,D) (2016)
MS-126
PO Box 1892
Houston, TX 77251-1892
    p. (713) 348-3574
    dmberry@rice.edu
    http://earthscience.rice.edu/centers/ccg/
    Enrollment (2014): M: 57 (12) D: 46 (6)
Associate Director:
    Alan Levander, (D), Stanford, 1984, Ys
    William S. Symes, (D), Harvard, 1975, On
Professor:
    Richard G. Gordon, (D), Stanford, 1979, Gt
    Adrian Lenardic, (D), California (Los Angeles), 1995, Gc
    Julia K. Morgan, (D), Cornell, 1993, Gc
    Fenglin Niu, (D), Tokyo, 1997, Ysg
    Dale S. Sawyer, (D), MIT, 1982, Ys
    Colin A. Zelt, (D), British Columbia, 1989, Ys
Assistant Professor:
    Brandon Dugan, (D), Penn State, 2003, Gu
    Helge Gonnermann, (D), California (Berkeley), 2004, Gv

Dept of Civil and Environmental Engineering (M,D) (2014)
P.O. Box 1892
MS 317
Houston, TX 77251-1892
    p. (713) 348-4951
    alvarez@rice.edu
    http://ceve.rice.edu/
    Enrollment: No data reported since 1999
Chair:
    Joseph B. Hughes, (D), Iowa, 1992, On
Professor:
    Philip B. Bedient, (D), Florida, 1975, Hw
    Arthur A. Few, Jr., (D), Rice, 1969, Oa
    Mason B. Tomson, (D), Oklahoma State, 1972, Cg
    Calvin H. Ward, (D), Cornell, 1960, Og
    Mark R. Wiesner, (D), Johns Hopkins, 1985, Og
Lecturer:
    James B. Blackburn, (D), Texas, 1972, Ou
Adjunct Associate Professor:
    Stanley M. Pier, (D), Purdue, 1952, Co
Adjunct Assistant Professor:
    Charles J. Newell, (D), Rice, 1989, Hw
Adjunct Professor:
    Jean-Yves Bottero, (D), Nancy, 1979, On
Cooperating Faculty:
    John Hunter, (M), Indiana Sch Lib Sci, 1974, On

Dept of Earth Science (B,M,D) (2015)
MS 126
PO Box 1892
Houston, TX 77251-1892
    p. (713) 348-4880
    geol@rice.edu
    http://earthscience.rice.edu/
    Enrollment (2015): B: 28 (8) M: 45 (18) D: 40 (5)
Chair:
    Richard G. Gordon, (D), Stanford, 1979, Ym
Professor:
    John B. Anderson, (D), Florida State, 1972, Gu
    Rajdeep Dasgupta, (D), Minnesota, 2006, GxCg
    Gerald R. Dickens, (D), Michigan, 1996, Yr
    Andre W. Droxler, (D), Miami, 1984, Gs
    Cin-Ty A. Lee, (D), Harvard, 2001, Cg
    Adrian Lenardic, (D), California, 1995, Yg
    Alan R. Levander, (D), Stanford, 1984, Ye

Caroline A. Masiello, (D), California (Irvine), 1999, On
Julia K. Morgan, (D), Cornell, 1993, Gt
Fenglin Niu, (D), Tokyo, 1997, Ys
Dale S. Sawyer, (D), MIT, 1982, Yr
Colin A. Zelt, (D), British Columbia, 1989, Yg
Associate Professor:
Brandon Dugan, (D), Penn State, 2003, Hg
Helge Gonnermann, (D), California (Berkeley), 2004, Gv
Assistant Professor:
Jeffrey A. Nittrouer, (D), Texas, 2010, Gms
Laurence Yeung, (D), CsOa
Adjunct Professor:
Vitor Abreu, (D), Rice, 1998, Gg
K. K. Bissada, (D), Washington (St. Louis), 1967, Cg
Stephen H. Danbom, (D), Connecticut, 1975, Gg
Jeffrey J. Dravis, (D), Rice, 1980, Gs
Paul M. Harris, (D), Miami, 1977, Yr
N Ross Hill, (D), Virginia, 1978
Thomas A. Jones, (D), Northwestern, 1969, Gq
Stephen J. Mackwell, (D), Australian National, 1985, Yg
Patrick J. McGovern, (D), MIT, 1996, Xy
David L. Olgaard, (D), MIT, 1985, Yg
W C. Riese, (D), New Mexico, 1980, Eg
Stephanie S. Shipp, (D), Rice, 1999, Oe
Emeritus:
Hans G. Ave Lallemant, (D), Leiden (Neth), 1967, Gc
Albert W. Bally, (D), Zurich, 1953, Gg
H. C. Clark, (D), Stanford, 1966, Ng
Jean-Claude DeBremaecker, (D), California (Berkeley), 1952, Yg
Gerald H. F. Gardner, (D), Princeton, 1953, Yg
Dieter Heymann, (D), Amsterdam, 1958, Xm
William P. Leeman, (D), Oregon, 1974, Gi
Andreas Luttge, (D), Tubingen, 1990, Cg
John C. Stormer, Jr., (D), California (Berkeley), 1971, Gi
Manik Talwani, (D), Columbia, 1959, Yr
Peter R. Vail, (D), Northwestern, 1959, Gr
Department Coordinator:
Sandra Flechsig, On
Department Administrator:
Lee Willson, On

Saint Mary's University
Dept of Physics and Earth Sciences (2011)
One Camino Santa Maria
San Antonio, TX 78228-8569
p. (210) 436-3235
dfitzgerald@stmarytx.edu
http://www.stmarytx.edu/acad/physicsandearthscience
Enrollment: No data reported since 1999
Chair:
Paul Nienaber
Professor:
David Fitzgerald, (M), Iowa, 1977, Gd
Associate Professor:
Gene W. Lene, (D), Texas, 1981, Ge

Sam Houston State University
Geology Program (B) (2011)
Box 2148
Huntsville, TX 77341
p. (409) 294-1566
bio_bjc@shsu.edu
Enrollment (2009): B: 53 (7)
Chair:
Brian J. Cooper, (D), Virginia Tech, 1988, Gz
Professor:
Christopher T. Baldwin, (D), Liverpool, 1976, Gs
Dennis I. Netoff, (D), Colorado, 1977, Gm
Assistant Professor:
Joseph C. Hill, (D), Missouri, 2006, Gc

San Antonio Community College
Dept of Chemistry/Earth Sciences/Astronomy (A) (2013)
1300 San Pedro Avenue
CG Rm 207
San Antonio, TX 78212

p. (210) 486-0045
tstaggs@alamo.edu
http://www.alamo.edu/sac/earthsci
Enrollment (1999): A: 2 (0)
Professor:
Dean P. Lambert, (D), Texas, 1992, Oyi
Associate Professor:
Anne D. Dietz, (M), Texas A&M (Kingsville), 1989, PgOg
George R. Stanley, (M), Texas (San Antonio), 2006, OigGe
David A. Wood, (D), Arizona, 2000, Onn
Adjunct Professor:
Thomas Adams, (D), 2011, PvGg
T Scott Girhard, (M), SW Texas State, Oyw
Robert Janusz, (M), Texas (San Antonio), Gg
Dwight Jurena, (M), Rensselaer, GgOg
Ryan E. Rudnicki, (D), Penn State, 1979, Oyr
C. Keith Smith, (M), Texas State, 2005, Oy
Cooperating Faculty:
Steve Dingman, On

San Jacinto Community College-Central
Geology Dept (1999)
8060 Spencer Hwy.
Pasadena, TX 77089
p. (281) 998-6150 x1882
Karen.Purpera@sjcd.edu
http://www.sanjac.edu/

San Jacinto Community College-North
Geology Dept (2013)
5800 Uvalde
Houston, TX 77049
p. (281) 998-6150 x7210
Kevin.Davis@sjcd.edu
http://www.sanjac.edu/

San Jacinto Community College-South
Geology Dept (1999)
13735 Beamer Rd.
Houston, TX 77089
p. (281) 998-6150 x4662
Joe.Granata@sjcd.edu
http://www.sanjac.edu/

Southern Methodist University
Roy M. Huffington Dept of Earth Sciences (B,M,D) (2013)
Post Office Box 750395
Dallas, TX 75275-0395
p. (214) 768-2750
geol@smu.edu
http://www.smu.edu/earthsciences
Administrative Assistant: Stephanie L. Schwob
Enrollment (2013): B: 60 (15) M: 13 (3) D: 17 (3)
Chair:
Robert T. Gregory, (D), Caltech, 1981, Cs
Professor:
Bonnie F. Jacobs, (D), Arizona, 1983, Pl
Louis L. Jacobs, (D), Arizona, 1977, Pv
Zhong Lu, (D), Alaska (Fairbanks), 1996, Or
Brian W. Stump, (D), California (Berkeley), 1979, Ys
John V. Walther, (D), California (Berkeley), 1978, Cg
Crayton J. Yapp, (D), Caltech, 1980, Csl
Associate Professor:
Heather R. DeShon, (D), California (Santa Cruz), 2004, Ysr
Matthew J. Hornbach, (D), Wyoming, 2005, YrhYe
M. Beatrice Magnani, (D), Perugia, 2000, YsGtYe
Neil J. Tabor, (D), California (Davis), 2002, Sd
Associate Scientist:
Kurt M. Ferguson, (D), S Methodist, 1990, Cs
Christopher T. Hayward, (D), S Methodist, 1997, Ys
Ian J. Richards, (D), Tennessee, 1994, Cs
Adjunct Professor:
Anthony R. Fiorillo, (D), Pennsylvania, 1989, Pv
John B. Wagner, (D), Texas (Dallas), 2000, Gs
Alisa Winkler, (D), S Methodist, 1990, Pv

Dale A. Winkler, (D), Texas, 1985, Pv

Emeritus:

David D. Blackwell, (D), Harvard, 1968, Yh
James E. Brooks, (D), Washington, 1954, Gr
Michael J. Holdaway, (D), California (Berkeley), 1963, Gp
Robert L. Laury, (D), Wisconsin, 1966, Gd
A. Lee McAlester, (D), Yale, 1960, Pe

Stephen F. Austin State University

Dept of Geology (B,M) ○ (2015)
PO Box 13011 SFA Station
Nacogdoches, TX 75962
p. (936) 468-3701
geology@sfasu.edu
http://www.geology.sfasu.edu/
Administrative Assistant: Shana R. Scott
Enrollment (2010): B: 71 (13) M: 14 (3)

Chair:

Wesley A. Brown, (D), Texas (El Paso)

Professor:

Volker W. Gobel, (D), Colorado Mines, 1972, Gi
Russell L. Nielson, (D), Utah, 1981, Gr

Associate Professor:

Chris A. Barker, (D), South Carolina, 1998, Gc
Kevin W. Stafford, (D), New Mexico Tech

Instructor:

Patricia S. Sharp, (M), Stephen F. Austin, 1978, Gg

Lecturer/Lab Coordinator:

Melinda Shaw Faulkner, (M), Stephen F. Austin

Emeritus:

Ernest B. Ledger, (D), Texas A&M, 1981, Ca

Sul Ross State University

Dept of Biology, Geology and Physical Sciences (B,M) ○ (2015)
Box C-64
Alpine, TX 79832
p. (432) 837-8112
measures@sulross.edu
http://www.sulross.edu/section/366/geology
Enrollment (2015): B: 24 (0) M: 17 (0)

Professor:

Elizabeth A. Measures, (D), Idaho, 1992, Gdq
David Rohr, (D), Oregon State, 1978, PiGd
Kevin Urbanczyk, (D), Washington State, 1993, GiOi

Lecturer:

Jesse Kelsch, (M), New Mexico, Gct

Tarleton State University

Dept of Chemistry, Geosciences, and Environmental Science
(B) (2014)
Box T-540
Stephenville, TX 76402
p. (254) 968-9143
rinard@tarleton.edu
http://www.tarleton.edu/~physci
Administrative Assistant: Kate Caballero
Enrollment (2010): B: 42 (7)

Professor:

Phillip A. Murry, (D), S Methodist, 1982, Pv

Associate Professor:

Stephen W. Field, (D), Massachusetts, 1988, Gz
Carol A. Thompson, (D), Iowa, 1993, Hy

Assistant Professor:

Bethany D. Rinard, (D), S Methodist, 2004, Gv

Tarrant County College- Northeast Campus

Natural Science Dept (A) (2015)
828 Harwood Road
Hurst, TX 76054
p. (817) 515-6565
hayden.chasteen@tccd.edu
Enrollment (2011): A: 650 (30)

Associate Professor:

Meena Balakrishnan, (D), GggGg
Kevin M. Barrett, (D), Texas State, 2012, OagOr

Professor:

Hayden R. Chasteen, (M), Northeast Louisiana, 1981, GgeGg

Temple College

Temple College (2014)
2600 South First Street
Temple, TX 76504
p. (254) 298-8472
john.mcclain@templejc.edu
http://www.templejc.edu/

Texas A&M University

Center For Tectonophysics (M,D) (2014)
3115 TAMU
Department Geology & Geophysics
College of Geosciences
College Station, TX 77843-3115
p. (979) 845-3296
chesterf@tamu.edu
http://tectono.tamu.edu/
Enrollment (2014): M: 8 (3) D: 11 (3)

Director:

Frederick Chester, (D), Texas A&M, 1988, GcNrYx

Assistant Director:

Andreas Kronenberg, (D), Brown, 1983, GtyGc

Professor:

Judith Chester, (D), Texas A&M, 1992, GcNrGo

Associate Professor:

Benchuan Duan, (D), California (Riverside), 2006, YgsGq
Julie Newman, (D), Rochester, 1982, Gct
Marcelo Sanchez, (D), Univ Politecnica de Catalunya, 2004, SpNr
David Sparks, (D), Brown, 1992, YdGq

Assistant Professor:

Hiroko Kitajima, (D), Texas A&M, 2010, YxSpGc
Julia S. Reece, (D), Texas (Austin), 2011, SpGso

Dept of Atmospheric Sciences (B,M,D) (2016)
3150 TAMU
College Station, TX 77843-3150
p. (979) 845-7671
brady-dennis@tamu.edu
http://atmo.tamu.edu/
Enrollment (2014): B: 117 (36) M: 48 (5) D: 20 (4)

Instructional Professor:

Don T. Conlee, (D), Texas A&M, 1994

Distinguished Professor:

Gerald North, (D), 1966, Oa

Distinguished Professor :

Renyi Zhang, (D), MIT, 1993, Oa

Department Head:

Ping Yang, (D), Utah, 1995, Oa

Professor:

Kenneth P. Bowman, (D), Princeton, 1984, Ow
Ping Chang, (D), Princeton, 1988, Op
Donald R. Collins, (D), Caltech, 1999, Oa
Andrew Dessler, (D), Harvard, 1994, On
John Nielsen-Gammon, (D), MIT, 1990, Oa
Richard L. Panetta, (D), Wisconsin, 1978, Ow
R. Saravanan, (D), Princeton, 1990, Oa
Courtney Schumacher, (D), Washington, 2002, Oa
Istvan Szunyogh, (D), Hungarian Academy of Sciences, 1994, Oa

Associate Professor:

Sarah D. Brooks, (D), Colorado, 2002, Oa
Craig Epifanio, (D), Washington, Oa
Robert Korty, (D), MIT, 2005, Oa
Mark Lemmon, (D), Arizona, 1994, Oa
Gunnar Schade, (D), Johannes-Gutenberg (Germany), 1997, Oa

Instructional Assistant Professor:

Tim Logan

Assistant Professor:

Christopher J. Nowotarski, (D), Penn State, 2013, Owa
Anita Rapp, (D), Colorado State, 2008, Or
Yuxuan Wang, (D), Harvard, 2005, Oa

Adjunct Professor:

Larry Carey, (D), Colorado State, 1999, Oa

Christopher A. Davis, (D), MIT, 1990, Ow
Alex Dessler, (D), Duke, 1956, Oa
Hung-Lung Allen Huang, (D), Wisconsin, 1989, Or
Christian D. Kummerow, (D), Minnesota, 1987, Oa
Steve Lyons, (D), Hawaii, 1981, Ow
Chris Snyder, (D), MIT, 1989, Oa
Wei-Kuo Tao, (D), Illinois, 1982, Oa
Emeritus:
Richard E. Orville, (D), Arizona, 1966, Oa

Dept of Geography (B,M,D) (2014)
810 Eller O&M Building
3147 TAMU
College Station, TX 77843-3147
 p. (979) 845-7141
 cbruton@geog.tamu.edu
 http://geog.tamu.edu/
 Enrollment (2009): B: 156 (40) M: 16 (8) D: 18 (3)
Professor:
Robert S. Bednarz, (D), Chicago, 1975, Oe
Sarah W. Bednarz, (D), Texas A&M, 1992, Oe
John R. Giardino, (D), Nebraska, 1979, Gm
Michael R. Waters, (D), Arizona, 1983, Ga
Associate Professor:
David M. Cairns, (D), Iowa, 1995, Oy
Andrew Klein, (D), Cornell, 1997, Or
Daniel Z. Sui, (D), Goergia, 1993, Or
Vatche P. Tchakerian, (D), California (Los Angeles), 1989, Gm
Assistant Professor:
Anne Chin, (D), Arizona State, 1994, Gm
Research Associate:
Jean A. Bowman, (M), Rutgers, 1984, Hg
Emeritus:
Clarissa T. Kimber, (D), Wisconsin, 1969, Oy

Dept of Geology & Geophysics (B,M,D) (2015)
3115 TAMU
College Station, TX 77843-3115
 p. (979) 845-2451
 bruton@geo.tamu.edu
 http://geoweb.tamu.edu
 Enrollment (2012): B: 278 (41) M: 81 (21) D: 66 (5)
Head:
John R. Giardino, (D), Nebraska, 1979, GmNg
Regents Professor:
Mary J. Richardson, (D), MIT, 1980, Op
Professor:
Tom Blasingame, (D), Texas A&M, 1989, Np
Richard L. Carlson, (D), Washington, 1976, GtYd
Frederick M. Chester, (D), Texas A&M, 1988, GcNr
Judith Chester, (D), Texas A&M, 1992, GcNr
Mark Everett, (D), Toronto, 1991, Ym
Ethan Grossman, (D), S California, 1982, Cs
Andrew Hajash, (D), Texas A&M, 1975, Cp
Bruce Herbert, (D), California (Riverside), 1992, Ge
Andreas Kronenberg, (D), Brown, 1983, GyNr
Franco Marcantonio, (D), Columbia, 1994, Ct
Anne Raymond, (D), Chicago, 1983, Pb
William W. Sager, (D), Hawaii, 1979, Ou
Yuefeng Sun, (D), Columbia, 1994, Go
Thomas E. Yancey, (D), California (Berkeley), 1971, Pg
Associate Research Professor:
Renald Guillemette, (D), Stanford, 1983, Gz
Associate Professor:
Richard L. Gibson, Jr., (D), MIT, 1991, Yse
Will Lamb, (D), Wisconsin, 1987, Gp
Brent Miller, (D), Dalhousie, 1997, Cc
Julie Newman, (D), Rochester, 1993, Gc
Thomas Olszewski, (D), Penn State, 2000, Pe
Michael Pope, (D), Virginia Tech, 1995, GrCc
David Sparks, (D), Brown, 1992, Yg
Debbie Thomas, (D), North Carolina, 2002, Ou
Hongbin Zhan, (D), Nevada (Reno), 1996, Hw
Assistant Professor:
Benchun Duan, (D), California (Riverside), 2006, Yg
Mike Tice, (D), Stanford, 2006, Py

Assistant Dean :
Eric Riggs, (D), California (Riverside), 2000, Gy
Lecturer:
Alfonso Benavides-Iglesias, (D), Texas A&M, 2007, Ys
Emeritus:
Christopher Mathewson, (D), Arizona, 1971
Jack Vitek, (D), Iowa, 1973, Gm
Technical Laboratory Director:
Michael Heaney, (D), Texas A&M, 1998, Pg
Dean of College of Geosciences:
Kate Miller, (D), Stanford, 1991, Ys

Dept of Oceanography (M,D) (2015)
1204 Eller O&M Blg
MS 3146
College Station, TX 77843-3146
 p. (979) 845-7211
 dthomas@ocean.tamu.edu
 http://ocean.tamu.edu
 Enrollment (2015): M: 28 (7) D: 40 (8)
Director, Texas Sea Grant:
Pamela Plotkin, (D), Texas A&M, 1994, Ob
Head:
Debbie Thomas, (D), North Carolina, 2002, Ou
Executive Associate Dean for Research:
Jack G. Baldauf, (D), California (Berkeley), 1984, Ou
Director, Geochemical and Environmental Research Group:
Anthony Knap, (D), Southampton, Oc
Professor:
Douglas C. Biggs, (D), MIT/WHOI, 1976, Ob
David A. Brooks, (D), Miami, 1975, Op
Lisa Campbell, (D), SUNY (Stony Brook), 1985, Ob
Ping Chang, (D), Princeton, 1988, Op
Piers Chapman, (D), North Wales, 1982, Oc
Wilford D. Gardner, (D), MIT/WHOI, 1978, Ou
Benjamin S. Giese, (D), Washington, 1989, Op
Gerardo Gold-Bouchot, (D), Center for Research & Advan Studies (Mexico), 1991, Oc
Robert D. Hetland, (D), Florida State, 1999, Op
Patrick Louchouarn, (D), Quebec (Montreal), 1997, Oc
Alejandro H. Orsi, (D), Texas A&M, 1993, Op
Antonietta Quigg, (D), Monash, 2000, Ob
Mary Jo Richardson, (D), MIT/WHOI, 1980, Gu
Gilbert T. Rowe, (D), Duke, 1968, Ob
Peter H. Santschi, (D), Switzerland (Berne), 1975, Oc
Niall C. Slowey, (D), MIT, 1991, Ou
Shari A. Yvon-Lewis, (D), Miami, 1994, Oc
Senior Scientist:
Norman Guinasso, (D), Texas A&M, 1975, Op
Troy Holcombe, (D), Columbia, Ou
Matthew K. Howard, (D), Texas A&M, 1992, Op
Ann E. Jochens, (D), Texas A&M, 1977, Op
Adam Klaus, (D), Hawaii, 1991, Gu
Terry L. Wade, (D), Rhode Island, 1978, Oc
Associate Professor:
Rainier Amon, (D), Texas, 1995, Ob
Ayal Anis, (D), Oregon State, 1993, Op
Timothy M. Dellapenna, (D), William & Mary, 1999, Ou
Steven F. DiMarco, (D), Texas (Dallas), 1991, Op
Anja Schulze, (D), Victoria, 2001, Ob
Achim Stoessel, (D), Max Planck, 1990, Op
Daniel C.O Thornton, (D), Queen Mary (London), 1995, Ob
Associate Scientist:
Steven K. Baum, (D), Texas A&M, 1996, Op
Jose L. Sericano, (D), Texas A&M, 1993, Cm
Assistant Professor:
Jessica Fitzsimmons, (D), MIT/WHOI, 2013, Oc
Kathryn Shamberger, (D), Washington, 2011, Oc
Jason Sylvan, (D), Rutgers, 2008, Ob
Yige Zhang, (D), Yale, 2014, Co
Research Associate:
Shinichi Kobara, (D), Texas A&M, Oi
Marion Stoessel, (M), Hamburg, 1984, Op
Zhankun Wang, (D), Massachusetts (Dartmouth), 2009, Op
Instructor:
Chrissy Wiederwohl, (D), Texas A&M, 2012, Op

Distinguished Professor Emeritus:
  Robert A. Duce, (D), MIT, 1964, Oc
  Worth D. Nowlin, Jr., (D), Texas A&M, 1966, Op
Distinguished Professor:
  Gerald R. North, (D), Wisconsin, 1966, Ow
Director, Texas Sea Grant College Program:
  Robert R. Stickney, (D), Florida State, 1971, Ob
Emeritus:
  George A. Jackson, (D), Caltech, 1976, Op
  Bobby J. Presley, (D), California, 1969, Oc
  Robert H. Stewart, (D), California (San Diego), 1969, Op

Dept of Soil & Crop Sciences (B,M,D) (2015)
TAMU 2474
College Station, TX 77843-2474
  p. (979) 845-4678
  cmorgan@tamu.edu
  http://soilcrop.tamu.edu
  Administrative Assistant: Carol J. Rhodes
  Enrollment (2014): M: 12 (2) D: 12 (3)
State Soil Env Specialist:
  Sam E. Feagley, (D), Missouri, 1979, Sc
Resident Director:
  Jaroy Moore, (D), Texas A&M, 1973, Sc
Professor:
  Frank M. Hons, (D), Texas A&M, 1978, Sc
  Mark L. McFarland, (D), Texas A&M, 1988, Sc
  Kevin J. McInnes, (D), Kansas State, 1985, Sp
  Cristine L. S. Morgan, (D), Wisconsin, 2003, Spd
  Tony L. Provin, (D), Purdue, 1995, Sc
  Edward C. A. Runge, (D), Iowa State, 1963, Sd
  Paul Schwab, (D), Colorado State, 1981, Sc
Associate Professor:
  Jacqueline A. Aitkenhead-Peterson, (D), New Hampshire, 2000, Hs
  Youjun Deng, (D), Texas A&M, 2001, GzSc
  Fugen Dou, (D), Texas A&M, 2005, Os
  Terry Gentry, (D), Arizona, Sb
Assistant Professor:
  Paul DeLaune, (D), Univ of Arkansas, 2002, Os
  Haly L. Neely, (D), Texas A&M, 2014, Spd
  Anil Somenhally, (D), Texas A&M, 2010, Sb
Emeritus:
  Joe B. Dixon, (D), Wisconsin, 1958, Sc
  Charles T. Hallmark, (D), Ohio State, 1977, Sd

Texas A&M University, Commerce
Dept of Biological & Environmental Sciences (B,M) (2011)
Commerce, TX 75429
  p. (903) 886-5378
  Haydn_Fox@tamu-commerce.edu
  http://www.tamu-commerce.edu/biology/
  Enrollment: No data reported since 1999
Assistant Professor:
  Haydn A "Chip" Fox, (D), South Carolina, 1994, HgGe

Texas A&M University, Corpus Christi
Environmental Science Program (B,M) (2015)
6300 Ocean Drive
Corpus Christi, TX 78412
  p. (361) 825-2814
  jennifer.smith-engle@tamucc.edu
  http://pens.tamucc.edu/
  Enrollment (2015): B: 169 (25) M: 32 (12)
Director of National Spill Control School:
  Howard Wood, (M), American Military, On
Regents Professor:
  Suzette Chopin, (D), Louisiana State Univ Med Center, On
Program Coordinator:
  Jennifer M. Smith-Engle, (D), Georgia, 1983, Gs
Endowed Chair for Fisheries and Ocean Health:
  Greg Stunz, (D), Texas A&M, 1999, On
Chair, Physical and Environmental Sciences Dept.:
  Richard Coffin, (D), Delaware, 1986, Oc
Professor:
  Joe Fox, (D), Texas A&M, On
  James Gibeaut, (D), South Florida, On

Richard McLaughlin, (D), California (Berkeley), On
David Yoskowitz, (D), Texas Tech, On
Director of Center for Coastal Studies:
  Paul Zimba, (D), Mississippi State, 1990, On
Associate Professor:
  Fereshteh Billiot, (D), Louisiana State
  Kirk Cammerata, (D), Kentucky, 1987, On
  Patrick Larkin, (D), Texas A&M, 1999, On
  Cherie McCollough, (D), Texas (Austin), 2005, On
  Riccardo Moxzzachiodi, (D), Pisa, 1999, On
  Thomas Naehr, (D), Christian-Albrechts (Germany), 1996, Gu
  Toshiaki Shinoda, (D), Oa
  James Silliman, (D), Michigan, 1998, Co
Assistant Professor:
  Mark Besonen, (D), Massachusetts (Amherst), Gma
  Darek Bogucki, (D), S California, Op
  Jeremy Conkle, (D), Louisiana State, 2010, On
  Andreas Fahlman, (D), Carleton, 2000, On
  Joseph David Felix, (D)
  Xinping Hu, (D), Old Dominion, 2007, Oc
  Chuntao Liu, (D), Wyoming, 2003, Oa
  Dorina Murgulet, (D), Alabama, 2009, Hw
  Jennifer Pollack, (D), South Carolina, 2006, Ob
  Michael Wetz, (D), Oregon State, 2006, Ob
  Kim Withers, (D), Texas A&M, 1994, On
  Feiqin Xie, (D), Arizona, 2006, Oa

Physical and Environmental Sciences (B,M,D) (2015)
6300 Ocean Drive
Corpus Christi, TX 78412
  p. (361) 825-6000
  tania.anders@tamucc.edu
  http://geology.tamucc.edu/
  Enrollment (2013): B: 76 (13)
Professor:
  Jennifer M. Smith-Engle, (D), Georgia, 1983, Gs
Associate Professor:
  Thomas H. Naehr, (D), GEOMAR (Kiel), 1996, GuCm
Assistant Professor:
  Mark Besonen, (D), Massachusetts, 2008, GaPeGm
  Dorina Murgulet, (D), Alabama, 2009, Hw
Professional Assistant Professor:
  Tania-Maria Anders, (D), Kiel, 1997, GugPi

Texas A&M University, Kingsville
Dept of Geosciences (B) (2014)
Campus Box 164
Kingsville, TX 78363
  p. (512) 595-3310
  kftlm00@tamuk.edu
  Enrollment (2012): B: 55 (10)
Professor:
  Jim R. Norwine, (D), Indiana State, 1971, Oa
Associate Professor:
  Thomas L. McGehee, (D), Texas (Dallas), 1987, Cl
Assistant Professor:
  Jaehyung Yu, (D), Texas A&M, 2005, Oi
Lecturer:
  John S. Buckley, (D), Texas, 1983, Pv
Visiting Professor:
  Aiguo Bian, (D), Texas A&M, 2006, Hq

Texas Christian University 🗗
School of Geology, Energy, and the Environment (B,M) (2015)
TCU Box 298830
2950 West Bowie
Fort Worth, TX 76129
  p. (817) 257-7270
  a.busbey@tcu.edu
  http://www.geo.tcu.edu/
  Administrative Assistant: Terri Mabe
  Enrollment (2014): B: 78 (11) M: 28 (5)
Director:
  Ken M. Morgan, (D), Wisconsin, 1978, OrGeOi
TCU Provost and Academic Vice Chancellor:
  R. Nowell Donovan, (D), Newcastle upon Tyne, 1972, GdcGt

Director of the Institute for Environmental Studies:
   Michael C. Slattery, (D), Oxford, 1994, HgSpOy
Professor:
   Richard E. Hanson, (D), Columbia, 1983, GxvGt
   John M. Holbrook, (D), Indiana, 1992, Gsr
Geology Program Coordinator:
   Arthur B. Busbey, (D), Chicago, 1982, PgvGr
Assistant Director:
   Helge Alsleben, (D), S California, 2005, GctGg
Assistant Professor:
   Victoria J. Bennett, (D), Leeds, 2004, On
   Rhiannon G. Mayne, (D), Tennessee, 2008, XmgXc
   Xiangyang Xie, (D), Wyoming, 2007, GoEog
Lecturer:
   Kristi Argenbright, (M), Texas Christian, GgOn
Adjunct Professor:
   Floyd Henk, Jr., (M), Texas Christian, 1981, Go
   Timothy J. McCoy, (D), Hawaii, 1994, Xm
Emeritus:
   John Breyer, (D), Nebraska, 1977, GsdEo
   Arthur J. Ehlmann, (D), Utah, 1953, GzXm
Professor of Professional Practice:
   Milton Enderlin, (M), Texas Christian, 2010, Nr
   Becky Johnson, (M), Texas Christian, 1995, GeHwOu
   Tamie Morgan, (M), Texas Christian, 1984, Oi

Texas Tech University
Dept of Geosciences (B,M,D) O (2016)
Box 41053
2500 Broadway
Science 125
Lubbock, TX 79409-1053
   p. (806) 834-0497
   alison.winton@ttu.edu
   www.geosciences.ttu.edu
   Enrollment (2015): B: 390 (33) M: 48 (21) D: 23 (0)
Chair:
   Jeffrey A. Lee, (D), Arizona State, 1990, Oy
Horn Professor:
   Sankar Chatterjee, (D), Calcutta, 1970, Pv
Professor:
   George B. Asquith, (D), Wisconsin, 1966, Go
   Calvin G. Barnes, (D), Oregon, 1982, Gi
   James E. Barrick, (D), Iowa, 1978, Ps
   Gary S. Elbow, (D), Pittsburgh, 1972
   Juske Horita, (D), Texas A&M, 1997
   Thomas M. Lehman, (D), Texas, 1985, Gs
   Moira K. Ridley, (D), Nebraska, 1997, Cl
   John L. Schroeder, (D), Texas Tech, 1999, Oa
   Paul J. Sylvester, (D)
   Aaron S. Yoshinobu, (D), S California, 1999, Gct
Associate Professor:
   Perry L. Carter, (D), Ohio State, 1998
   Harold Gurrola, (D), California (San Diego), 1995, Ys
   Callum J. Hetherington, (D), Basel (Switzerland), 2001
   Haraldur R. Karlsson, (D), Chicago, 1988, Cl
   David W. Leverington, (D), Manitoba, 2001, Oiy
   Kevin R. Mulligan, (D), Texas A&M, 1997, OiGmSo
   Seiichi Nagihara, (D), Texas, 1992, Oi
   Christopher C. Weiss, (D), Oklahoma, 2004, OaaOa
Assistant Professor:
   Brian C. Ancell, (D), Washington, 2006, Oa
   Eric C. Bruning, (D), Oklahoma, 2008, Oa
   Guofeng Cao, (D), California (Santa Barbara), 2011, Oi
   Johannes M L Dahl, (D), Ludwig-Maximilians (Germany), 2010, Owa
   Song-Lak Kang, (D), Penn State, 2007, Oa
   Dustin E. Sweet, (D), Oklahoma, 2009, Gs
   Jennifer K. Vanos, (D), Guelph, 2012, Oa
Research Associate:
   Melanie A. Barnes, (D), Texas Tech, 2001, Cg
Instructor:
   Steven R. Cobb, Oa
   Linda L. Jones, (M), California (Los Angeles), 1986
   Justin E. Weaver, (M), Texas Tech, 1992, Oa
Professor:
   Richard E. Peterson, (D), Missouri, 1971, Oa

Unit Coordinator:
   Alisan C. Sweet, (M), Oklahoma, 2011, Gs
   Debra J. Walker
Senior Technician:
   James M. Browning
Senior Business Assistant:
   Mary A. Winton, (B), Texas Tech, 1992, OnnOn
Computer Technician:
   Darren W. Hedrick
Academic Advisor:
   Celeste N. Yoshinobu, (M), San Diego State, 1994

Trinity University
Dept of Geosciences (B) (2015)
One Trinity Place, #45
San Antonio, TX 78212-7200
   p. (210) 999-7092
   dsmith@trinity.edu
   f: https://new.trinity.edu/academics/departments/geosciences/majors-minors
   Enrollment (2015): B: 30 (14)
Chair:
   Diane R. Smith, (D), Rice, 1984, Gi
Professor:
   Thomas W. Gardner, (D), Cincinnati, 1978, Gm
   Daniel J. Lehrmann, (D), Kansas, 1993, PiGs
Associate Professor:
   Glenn C. Kroeger, (D), Stanford, 1987, Yg
   Benjamin E. Surpless, (D), Stanford, 1999, Gcx
   Kathleen D. Surpless, (D), Stanford, 2001, Gs
Adjunct Professor:
   Leslie F. Bleamaster III, (D), S Methodist, 2003, Xg
Emeritus:
   Walter Coppinger, (D), Miami (Ohio), 1974, Gc
   Robert L. Freed, (D), Michigan, 1966, Gz

Tyler Junior College
Dept of Geology (1999)
1327 South Baxter Avenue
Tyler, TX 75701
   p. (903) 510-2232
   gbra@tjc.edu
   http://www.tjc.edu/

University of Houston
Allied Geophysical Lab (2014)
Houston, TX 77204-4231
   p. (713) 743-9150
   rrstewart@uh.edu
   http://www.agl.uh.edu
Director:
   Robert R. Stewart, (D), MIT, 1983, Ye

Dept of Earth and Atmospheric Sciences (B,M,D) O (2015)
312 Science and Research Building 1
4800 Calhoun Rd.
Houston, TX 77204-5007
   p. (713) 743-3399
   hzhou@uh.edu
   http://www.eas.uh.edu
   Administrative Assistant: Jim Parker
   Administrative Assistant: Hannah Walker
   Administrative Assistant: Anja Wells
   Enrollment (2015): B: 421 (100) M: 144 (66) D: 117 (12)
Department Chair:
   Hua-Wei Zhou, (D), Caltech, 1989, YseYg
Professor:
   Alan Brandon, (D), Alberta, 1992, GiCac
   Kevin Burke, (D), London, 1953, Gt
   John F. Casey, (D), SUNY (Albany), 1980, GtiGu
   John P. Castagna, (D), Texas, 1983, Ye
   Henry S. Chafetz, (D), Texas, 1970, Gd
   Evgeny Chesnokov, (D), Russian Acad of Sci, 1987, YseYx
   Stuart A. Hall, (D), Newcastle, 1976, Ym
   Shuhab Khan, (D), Texas (Dallas), 2001, Or
   Aibing Li, (D), Brown, 2000, Ys

Rosalie F. Maddocks, (D), Kansas, 1965, Pm
Paul Mann, (D), SUNY (Albany), 1983
Arch M. Reid, (D), Pittsburgh, 1964, Gi
William Sager, (D), Hawaii, 1983
Jonathan Snow, (D), MIT/WHOI, 1992, Ca
Robert Stewart, (D), MIT, 1983, Ye
Robert Talbot, (D), Wisconsin (Madison), 1981
Arthur Weglein, (D), CUNY, 1980, Ye
University Distinguished Research Professor:
Fred Hilterman, (D), Colorado Mines, 1970, Ye
Research Professor:
Adry Bissada, (D), Washington, 1967, Co
Gennady Goloshubin, (D), Inst Physics of Earth (Moscow), 1991, Ye
De-hua Han, (D), Stanford, 1987, Ye
Leon Thomsen, (D), Columbia, 1969, Ye
Adjunct faculty:
Janok Bhattacharya, (D), McMaster, 1989
Barry Lefer, (D), New Hampshire, 1997, Oa
Associate Professor:
Regina M. Capuano, (D), Arizona, 1988, Hw
Peter Copeland, (D), SUNY (Albany), 1990, CcGt
William R. Dupre, (D), Stanford, 1975, On
Ian Evans, (D), Texas A&M, 1971, Gr
Xun Jiang, (D), Caltech, 2006
Thomas Lapen, (D), Wisconsin, 2005, Gz
Michael Murphy, (D), California (Los Angeles), 2000, Gc
Bernhard Rappenglueck, (D), Munich, 1996, Oa
Alexander Robinson, (D), California (Los Angeles), 2005, Gc
Guoquan Wang, (D), Inst of Geology (China), 2001
Visiting Associate Professor:
Virginia Sisson, (D), Princeton, 1985, Gi
Research Associate Professor:
Yongjun Gao, (D), Georg-August, 2004, CstCa
Donald Van Niewenhuise, (D), South Carolina, 1978, Ps
Instructional Assistant Professor:
Daniel Hauptvogel, (D), City Univ of New York, 2015
Jennifer N. Lytwyn, (D), Houston, 1993, Gi
Assistant Professor:
Yunsoo Choi, (D), Georgia Tech, 2007
Qi Fu, (D), Minnesota, 2006
Margarete Jadamec, (D), California (Davis), 2009
Joel Saylor, (D), Arizona, 2008
Juan Carlos Silva-Tamayo, (D), Univ Bern, 2009
Julia Wellner, (D), Rice, 2001, Gs
Yingcai Zheng, (D), California (Santa Cruz), 2007
Research Scientist:
Tom Bjorklund, (D), Houston, 2002, Gco
Martin Cassidy, (D), Houston, 2005, GoCo
Nikolay Dyaur, (D), Russian Acad of Sci, 1986, Yxs
Xiangshan Li, (D), Tulane, 2000, Oaw
Research Professor:
James Lawrence, (D), Caltech, 1970, Cl
Peter Percell, (D), California (Berkeley), 1973, Oa
Research Associate Professor:
Dale Bird, (D), Houston, 2004
Robert Wiley, (D), Colorado Mines, 1980
Research Assistant Professor:
James Flynn, (M), Houston, 1991
Charlotte Sjunneskog, (D), Uppsala, 2002
Lecturer:
Peter Bartok, (M), SUNY (Buffalo), 1972, Go
Edip Baysal, (D), Houston, 1982
Colin Sayers, (M), Arizona State, 1984
Senior Researcher:
Mike Darnell, (B), Texas A&M, 1974
Postdoctoral Fellow:
Hao Hu, (D), CAS Inst of Geology and Geophysics, 2015, Ye
Wonbae Jeon, (D), Pusan National Univ, 2014
Adjunct Professor:
Mosab Nasser, (D), Tromso, 2001
Adjunct:
Joe Curiale, (D), Oklahoma
Amy Kelly, (D), MIT, 2009
Gary Morris, (D), Rice, 1995
Researcher:
Min Sun
Ewa Szymczyk

Fuyong Yan
Laboratory Supervisor:
Minako Righter, (D), Graduate Univ for Advanced Studies, 2006
IT Staff:
Jay Krishnan, (B), Houston, 2001, On

University of Houston Downtown
Dept of Natural Sciences (2014)
1 Main Street
Houston, TX 77002
   p. (713) 221-8015
   merrillg@uhd.edu
Professor:
Glen K. Merrill, (D), Louisiana State, 1968, Pi
Penny A. Morris-Smith, (D), California (Berkeley), 1975
Associate Professor:
Kenneth S. Johnson, (D), Texas Tech, 1995, Gi
Lecturer:
Donald S. Musselwhite, (D), 1995

University of North Texas
Dept of Geography (B,M) (2015)
1155 Union Circle #305279
Denton, TX 76203
   p. (940) 565-2091
   geog@unt.edu
   http://www.geography.unt.edu
   Administrative Assistant: Tami Deaton
   Enrollment: No data reported since 1999
Professor:
Paul F. Hudak, (D), California (Santa Barbara), 1991, Hw
Professor:
C. Reid Ferring, (D), Texas (Dallas), 1993, Ga
Joseph R. Oppong, (D), Alberta, 1992, On
Harry F. L. Williams, (D), Simon Fraser, 1989, Gm
Associate Professor:
Pinliang Dong, (D), New Brunswick, 2003, Oi
Kent M. McGregor, (D), Kansas, 1982, Oag
Lisa A. Nagaoka, (D), Washington, 2000, Ga
Feifei Pan, (D), Georgia Tech, 2002, Hw
Murray Rice, (D), Saskatchewan, 1995, On
Chetan Tiwari, (D), Iowa, 2008, Oi
Steve Wolverton, (D), North Texas, 2001, Ga
Assistant Professor:
Waquar Ahmed, (D), Clark, 2007, On
Ipsita Chatterjee, (D), Clark, 2007, On
Matthew Fry, (D), Texas (Austin), 2008, On
Alexandra Ponette-Gonzalez, (D), Yale, 2011, On

University of Texas at Austin ⌐
Dept of Marine Science (M,D) ● (2015)
750 Channel View Drive
Port Aransas, TX 78373-5015
   p. (361) 749-6730
   facsearch@utlists.utexas.edu
   http://www.utmsi.utexas.edu
   f: www.facebook.com/utmsi
   Enrollment (2015): M: 16 (6) D: 16 (1)
Associate Chair:
Edward J. Buskey, (D), Rhode Island, 1983, Ob
Professor:
Kenneth H. Dunton, (D), Alaska, 1985, Ob
Lee A. Fuiman, (D), Michigan, 1983, Ob
Peter Thomas, (D), Leicester (UK), 1977, Ob
Tracy A. Villareal, (D), Rhode Island, 1989, Ob
Associate Professor:
Bryan A. Black, (D), Penn State, 2003, Sf
Deana L. Erdner, (D), MIT/WHOI, 1997, Ob
Zhanfei Liu, (D), Stony Brook, 2006, Og
James W. McClelland, (D), Boston, 1998, Ob
Assistant Professor:
Brett Baker, (D), Michigan, 2014, Oe
Brad Erisman, (D), California (San Diego), 2008, Ob
Andrew J. Esbaugh, (D), Queens, 2005, Ob
Amber K. Hardison, (D), William & Mary, 2010, Cm

Lecturer:
  Gerard C. Shank, (D), North Carolina, 2003, Ob
Emeritus:
  Wayne S. Gardner, (D), Wisconsin, 1971, Ob
  Gloria J. Holt, (D), Texas A&M, 1976, Ob

Inst for Geophysics (2014)
JJ Pickle Research Campus
10100 Burnet Road, Bldg. 196 (ROC)
Austin, TX 78758
  p. (512) 471-6156
  utig@ig.utexas.edu
  http://www.ig.utexas.edu/
Associate Director:
  Ian W. D. Dalziel, (D), Edinburgh, 1963, Gt
  Cliff Frohlich, (D), Cornell, 1976, Ys
Research Professor:
  William E. Galloway, (D), Texas, 1971, Gs
  Stephen P. Grand, (D), Caltech, 1986, Ys
  Yosio Nakamura, (D), Penn State, 1963, Ys
  Mrinal K. Sen, (D), Hawaii, 1987, Ye
Professor:
  Paul L. Stoffa, (D), Columbia, 1974, Ye
Senior Scientist:
  James A. Austin, Jr., (D), MIT/WHOI, 1978, Gu
  Nathan L. Bangs, (D), Columbia, 1990, Gu
  John A. Goff, (D), MIT/WHOI, 1990, Yr
  Lawrence A. Lawver, (D), California (San Diego), 1976, Yr
  Paul Mann, (D), SUNY (Albany), 1983, Gt
  Thomas H. Shipley, (D), Rice, 1975, Yr
  Frederick W. Talyor, (D), Cornell, 1979, Pe
Research Scientist:
  Donald D. Blankenship, (D), Wisconsin, 1989, Yg
  Gail L. Christeson, (D), MIT/WHOI, 1994, Yr
  Craig S. Fulthorpe, (D), Northwestern, 1988, Gs
  Kirk D. McIntosh, (D), California (Santa Cruz), 1992, Yr
  Robert J. Pulliam, (D), California (Berkeley), 1991, Ys
Research Associate:
  Sean S. Gulick, (D), Lehigh, 1999, Yr
  John W. Holt, (D), Caltech, 1997, Ye
  Charles Jackson, (D), Chicago, 1998, Pe
  Luc L. Lavier, (D), Columbia, 1999, Yg
  David L. Morse, (D), Washington, 1997, Yg
  Hillary C. Olson, (D), Stanford, 1988, Ps
  Robert B. Scott, (D), McGill, 1999, Og
  Roustam K. Seifoullaev, (D), Baku State, 1979, Ye
  Harm Van Avendonk, (D), Scripps, 1998, Yg
Emeritus:
  Milo M. Backus, (D), MIT, 1956, Ye
  Arthur E. Maxwell, (D), Scripps, 1959, Og
Postdoc:
  Christina Holland, (D), S Florida, 2003, Og
  Matthew Hornbach, (D), Wyoming, 2004, Yg
  Timothy Whiteaker, (D), Texas, 2004, Gs
Project Coordinator:
  Patricia E. Ganey-Curry, (B), Texas A&M, 1978, On
Program Manager:
  Katherine K. Ellins, (D), Columbia, 1988, On
Related Staff:
  Mark Wiederspahn, (B), Bucknell, 1975, On

Jackson School of Geosciences (B,M,D) (2016)
Jackson School of Geosciences
2225 Speedway, Stop C1160
Austin, TX 78712-1692
  p. (512) 471-5172
  communications@jsg.utexas.edu
  http://www.jsg.utexas.edu
  Enrollment (2012): B: 315 (66) M: 142 (56) D: 157 (12)
Dean, Jackson School of Geosciences:
  Sharon Mosher, (D), Illinois, 1978, Gc
Chair, Department of Geological Sciences:
  Ronald J. Steel, (D), Glasgow (UK), 1970, Gs
Director, Institute for Geophysics:
  Terry Quinn, (D), Brown, 1989, Pe
Director, Bureau of Economic Geology:
  Scott W. Tinker, (D), Colorado, 1996, Go

Acting Director, Energy & Earth Resources Graduate Program:
  William L. Fisher, (D), Kansas, 1961, Gr
Professor:
  Jay L. Banner, (D), SUNY (Stony Brook), 1986, Cl
  Christopher J. Bell, (D), California (Berkeley), 1997, Pv
  Philip Bennett, (D), Syracuse, 1988, Hg
  William D. Carlson, (D), California (Los Angeles), 1980, Gp
  Mark P. Cloos, (D), California (Los Angeles), 1981, Gc
  Kerry H. Cook, (D), North Carolina State, 1984, OaPe
  Ian W. D. Dalziel, (D), Edinburgh, 1963, Gt
  Robert E. Dickinson, (D), MIT, 1966, Oa
  Peter B. Flemings, (D), Cornell, 1990, Gr
  Sergey B. Fomel, (D), Stanford, 1991, Ye
  Rong Fu, (D), Columbia, 1991, Oa
  James E. Gardner, (D), Rhode Island, 1993, Gv
  Omar Ghattas, (D), Duke, 1988, Gq
  Stephen P. Grand, (D), McGill, 1986, Yg
  Brian Horton, (D), Arizona, 1998, Gs
  Charles Kerans, (D), Carleton, 1982, Gsr
  Gary A. Kocurek, (D), Wisconsin, 1980, Gs
  J. Richard Kyle, (D), W Ontario, 1977, Em
  Leon E. Long, (D), Columbia, 1959, Cc
  David Mohrig, (D), HsGs
  Timothy B. Rowe, (D), California (Berkeley), 1987, Pv
  Mrinal K. Sen, (D), Hawaii, 1987, Ye
  John M. Sharp, Jr., (D), Illinois, 1974, Hq
  James T. Sprinkle, (D), Harvard, 1971, Pi
  Daniel Stockli, (D), Stanford, 1999, Gc
  Paul L. Stoffa, (D), Columbia, 1974, Ye
  Robert H. Tatham, (D), Columbia, 1975, Yg
  Clark R. Wilson, (D), California (San Diego), 1975, Yg
  Zong-Liang Yang, (D), Macquarie, 1992, Ow
Senior Research Scientist:
  James A. Austin, Jr., (D), MIT, 1979, Pi
  Nathan L. Bangs, (D), Columbia, 1990, Gc
  Donald D. Blankenship, (D), Wisconsin, 1989, Gl
  Gail S. Christeson, (D), MIT, 1994, Yr
  Shirley P. Dutton, (D), Texas, 1986, Gs
  Clifford A. Frohlich, (D), Cornell, 1976, YsGt
  Craig S. Fulthorpe, (D), Northwestern, 1988, GusGr
  John A. Goff, (D), MIT, 1990, Gu
  Bob A. Hardage, (D), Oklahoma State, 1967, Yes
  Susan D. Hovorka, (D), Texas, 1990, Gs
  Michael R. Hudec, (D), Wyoming, 1990, Gc
  Martin P. A. Jackson, (D), Cape Town, 1976, Gtc
  Stephen E. Laubach, (D), Illinois, 1986, Gs
  Lawrence A. Lawver, (D), Scripps, 1976, Yr
  Robert G. Loucks, Texas, 1976, Gs
  F. Jerry Lucia, (M), Minnesota, 1954, Eo
  Kitty L. Milliken, (D), Texas, 1985, Gd
  Jeffrey G. Paine, (D), Texas, 1991, On
  Stephen C. Ruppel, (D), Tennessee, 1979, Gs
  Bridget R. Scanlon, Kentucky, Hg
  Thomas H. Shipley, (D), Rice, 1975, Ys
  Frederick W. Taylor, (D), Cornell, 1978, Pe
  Lesli J. Wood, (D), Colorado State, 1992, Eo
  Michael H. Young, (D), Arizona, 1995, GeHw
  Hongliu Zeng, (D), Texas, 1994, YsGs
Associate Professor:
  Bayani Cardenas, (D), New Mexico Tech, 2006, Hw
  Elizabeth J. Catlos, (D), California (Los Angeles), 2000, GzCg
  Julia A. Clarke, (D), Yale, 2002, Pv
  Richard A. Ketcham, (D), Texas, 1995, Gzq
  John Lassiter, (D), California (Berkeley), 1995, Cc
  Randall A. Marrett, (D), Cornell, 1990, Gc
Assistant Professor:
  Jaime D. Barnes, (D), New Mexico, 2006, CgsCc
  Whitney Behr, (D), S California, 2011, Gc
  Daniel O. Breecker, (D), New Mexico, 2008, ScCs
  Ginny A. Catania, (D), Washington, 1994, Ol
  Marc A. Hesse, (D), Stanford, 2008, Gqo
  Joel P. Johnson, (D), MIT, 2007, Gs
  Wonsuck Kim, (D), Minnesota, 2007, Gsr
  Luc L. Lavier, (D), Columbia, 1999, Gt
  Jung-Fu Lin, (D), Chicago, 2002, GyYm
  Kevan Moffett, (D), Stanford, 2010, HwGe
  Timothy M. Shanahan, (D), Arizona, 2007, PeGsCg

149

Kyle T. Spikes, (D), Stanford, 2008, Ye
Energy Economist:
Svetlana Ikonnikova, (D), Humboldt (Berlin), 2007, Ego
Research Associate:
Todd Caldwell, (D), Nevada (Reno), 2011, Sp
Sigrid Clift, (B), Texas, 1989, Og
Brent Elliott, (D), Helsinki, 2001, GzcGt
Andras Fall, (D), Virginia Tech, 2008, Goc
Peter P. Flaig, (D), Wisconsin, 2002, Gs
Qilong Fu, (D), Regina, 2005, Gsr
Ursula Hammes, Colorado, 1992, Gr
Nicholas W. Hayman, (D), Washington, 2003, Ou
Seyyed Abolfazi Hosseini, (D), Tulsa, 2008, Eo
Farzam Javadpour, (D), Calgary, 2006, Eo
Carey King, (D), Texas, 2004, Eog
Gang Luo, (D), Missouri, Gtc
Lorena G. Moscardelli, (D), Texas, 2007, GmYs
Hardie S. Nance, (M), Texas, 1978, Grc
Maria-Aikaterini Nikolinakou, (D), MIT, 2008, Np
Yuko Okumura, (D), Hawaii, 2005, OaPe
Cornel Olariu, (D), Texas (Dallas), 2005, Gr
Mariana Olariu, (D), Texas (Dallas), 2007, Gr
Christopher Omelon, Cg
Katherine D. Romanak, (D), Texas, 1997, Cg
Diana C. Sava, (D), Stanford, 2004, Yg
Timothy L. Whiteaker, (D), Texas, 2004, Oi
Brad Wolaver, (D), Texas, 2008, HwGe
Changbing Yang, Hw
Christopher K. Zahm, (D), Colorado Mines, 2002, Yg
Mehdi Zeidouni, (D), Calgary, 2011, Eo
Tongwei Zhang, (D), Chinese Acad of Sci, 1999, Cgs
Senior Lecturer:
Mark A. Helper, (D), Texas, 1985, Gc
Lecturer:
Mary F. Poteet, (D), California (Berkeley), 2001, Pg
Adjunct Professor:
Laurie S. Duncan, (D), Texas
Marcus Gary, (D), Texas, 2009, Hgs
Emeritus:
Daniel Barker, (D), Princeton, 1961, Gi
Robert E. Boyer, (D), Michigan, 1959, Gt
Richard T. Buffler, (D), California (Berkeley), 1967, Gu
Peter T. Flawn, (D), Yale, 1951, Eg
Robert L. Folk, (D), Penn State, 1952, Gd
William E. Galloway, (D), Texas, 1971, Gs
Edward C. Jonas, (D), Illinois, 1954, Gz
Lynton S. Land, (D), Lehigh, 1966, Cl
Wann Langston, Jr., (D), California (Berkeley), 1952, Pv
Ernest L. Lundelius, (D), Chicago, 1954, Pv
Earle F. McBride, (D), Johns Hopkins, 1960, Gd
Yosio Nakamura, (D), Penn State, 1963, Ys
Douglas Smith, (D), Caltech, 1969, Gi
Senior Energy Economist:
Gurcan Gulen, (D), Boston Coll, 1996, Eg
Research Associate Professor:
Sean S. Gulick, (M), Lehigh, 1999, Gc
John W. Holt, (D), Caltech, 1997, OlXyg
Research Assistant Professor:
Suzanne A. Pierce, (D), Texas, HwOn
Research Affiliate:
James N. Connelly, (D), Memorial, 1991, Cc

University of Texas, Arlington
Dept of Earth & Environmental Sciences (B,M,D) O (2015)
Box 19049
500 Yates Street
Arlington, TX 76019
    p. (817) 272-2987
    geology@uta.edu
    http://www.uta.edu/ees/
    Enrollment (2014): B: 189 (29) M: 70 (21) D: 28 (3)
Professor:
Asish Basu, (D), California (Davis), 1975, GxCcs
Glen Mattioli, (D), Northwestern, 1987, GitYd
Merlynd K. Nestell, (D), Oregon State, 1966, Pm
John S. Wickham, (D), Johns Hopkins, 1969, Gc

Associate Professor:
Qinhong (Max) Hu, (D), Arizona, 1995, HwCa
Andrew Hunt, (D), Liverpool, 1988, GbCg
Arne M. Winguth, (D), Hamburg, 1997, Opa
Assistant Professor:
Majie Fan, (D), Arizona, 2009, GstCs
Ashley Griffith, (D), Stanford, 2008, Gct
Liz Griffith, (D), Stanford, 2008, CslCm
Ashanti Johnson, (D), OgGe
Adjunct Professor:
John Damuth, (D), Columbia, GsuYr
Galena P. Nestell, (D), Vsegi (Russia), 1990, Pm
Cornelia Winguth, (D), Hamburg, 1998, GugOm
Emeritus:
Brooks Ellwood, (D), Rhode Island, 1977, Yg
Christopher R. Scotese, (D), Chicago, 1985, Gt

University of Texas, Dallas ⬚
Dept of Geosciences (B,M,D) (2015)
Mail Stop ROC21
800 W Campbell Rd
Richardson, TX 75083-3021
    p. (972) 883-2401
    geosciences@utdallas.edu
    Administrative Assistant: Gloria J. Eby
    Enrollment (2006): B: 40 (2) M: 18 (6) D: 30 (7)
Professor and Program :
John Dr. Geissman, (D), Gt
Professor :
John S. Oldow, (D), Northwestern, 1978, Gc
Director, Center for Lithospheric Studies:
George A. McMechan, (M), Toronto, 1972, Ys
Professor:
Carlos L. V. Aiken, (D), Arizona, 1976, Yv
William I. Manton, (D), Witwatersrand, 1968, Cc
Robert J. Stern, (D), California (San Diego), 1979, Gt
Research Professor:
Robert B. Finkelman, (D), Maryland, 1980, Gb
Associate Professor:
Tom H. Brikowski, (D), Arizona, 1987, Hw
John F. Ferguson, (D), S Methodist, 1981, Yg
Sr. Lecturer :
Prabin . Shilpakar, (D), Texas (Dallas), 2014, GcYdGc
Senior Lecturer:
William R. Griffin, (D), Texas (Dallas), 2008, Gg
Ignacio Pujana, (D), Texas (Dallas), 1997, Pm
Retired Professor:
Richard M. Mitterer, (D), Florida State, 1966, Co
Emile A. Pessagno, Jr., (D), Princeton, 1960, Pm
Dean C. Presnall, (D), Penn State, 1963, Cp
Retired President and Professor:
Robert H. Rutford, (D), Minnesota, 1969, Gl
Retired Associate Professor:
James L. Carter, (D), Rice, 1965, Eg

Science/Mathematics Education Program (M) (2011)
P. O. Box 830688 FN33
Richardson, TX 75080-9688
    p. (972) 883-2496
    mont@utdallas.edu
    http://www.utdallas.edu/dept/SciMathEd
Professor:
Thomas R. Butts, (D), Michigan State, 1973, On
Fred L. Fifer, (D), Vanderbilt, 1973, On
Associate Professor:
Cynthia E. Ledbetter, (D), Texas A&M, 1987, On
Assistant Professor:
Homer A. Montgomery, (D), Texas (Dallas), 1988, Pg
Mary Urquhart, (D), Colorado, 1999, Xy
Instructor:
Barbara Curry, (M), Texas (Dallas), 1998, On

University of Texas, El Paso
Dept of Geological Sciences (B,M,D) O (2015)
500 W. University Avenue
El Paso, TX 79968-0555

p. (915) 747-5501
jdkubicki@utep.edu
http://science.utep.edu/geology/
Enrollment (2014): B: 178 (32) M: 55 (15) D: 29 (5)
Professor:
  James D. Kubicki, (D), Yale, 1989, ClGe
Chair:
  Laura F. Serpa, (D), Cornell, 1986, Ye
Professor:
  Elizabeth Y. Anthony, (D), Arizona, 1986, Gi
  Diane I. Doser, (D), Utah, 1984, Ys
  Katherine A. Giles, (D), Go
  Richard S. Jarvis, (D), Oy
  Richard P. Langford, (D), Utah, 1989, Gs
  Terry L. Pavlis, (D), Utah, 1982, Gc
  Nicholas E. Pingitore, Jr., (D), Brown, 1973, Cl
  Aaron A. Velasco, (D), California (Santa Cruz), 1993, Yx
Senior Scientist:
  Steven H. Harder, (D), Texas (El Paso), 1986, Yg
Associate Professor:
  Thomas E. Gill, (D), California (Davis), 1995, Ge
  Philip C. Goodell, (D), Harvard, 1970, Ce
  Jose M. Hurtado, (D), MIT, 2002, Gt
  Deana Pennington, (D), Oregon State, 2002, Oi
Assistant Professor:
  Benjamin Brunner, (D), ETH, 2003, Cs
  Lixin Jin, (D), Ge
  Marianne Karplus, (D), Stanford, 2012, Ysg
  Lin Ma, (D), Hg
Research Associate:
  Gail Arnold, (D), Rochester, 2004, Cs
  Hector Gonzalez-Huizar, (D), Texas (El Paso), Ys
Emeritus:
  Kenneth F. Clark, (D), New Mexico, 1966, Eg
  David V. Le Mone, (D), Michigan State, 1964, Ps
  Robert H. Schmidt, Jr., (D), California (Los Angeles), 1968, Oy
Science/Eng Research Tech:
  Galen M. Kaip, (M), Texas (El Paso), 1998, Yx
Network Manager:
  Carlos J. Montana, (M), Texas (El Paso), 1992, Yg

University of Texas, Pan American
Dept of Physics & Geology (B) (2011)
1201 W. University Drive
Edinburg, TX 78539
  p. (512) 381-3523
  bhatti@panam.edu
  http://www.utpa.edu/dept/physci/
  Enrollment: No data reported since 1999
Chair:
  Steven Tidrow
Assistant Professor:
  Ruben A. Mazariegos, (D), Texas A&M, 1993, Ye
  Eric R. Rieken, (D), Washington State, 1993, Gt

University of Texas, Permian Basin
Dept of Geology (B,M) (2011)
4901 E. University Boulevard
Odessa, TX 79762-0001
  p. (432) 552-2243
  mutis_e@utpb.edu
  Enrollment (2005): B: 18 (4) M: 12 (0)
Chair:
  Emilio Mutis-Duplat, (D), Texas, 1972, Gp
Assistant Professor:
  Emily L. Stoudt, (D), Ohio State, 1975, GdPsi
Lecturer:
  William L. Basham, (D), Oklahoma, 1978, Ye
  Lori L. Manship, (D), Texas Tech, 2008, PioOi
  Robert C. Trentham, (D), Texas (El Paso), 1981, Go

University of Texas, San Antonio
Dept of Geological Sciences (B,M) (2015)
One UTSA Circle
San Antonio, TX 78249-0663
  p. (210) 458-4455

geosciences@utsa.edu
http://www.utsa.edu/geosci
Enrollment (2015): B: 188 (0) M: 52 (5)
Professor:
  Lance L. Lambert, (D), Iowa, 1992, Pg

Victoria College
Victoria College (A) (2015)
2200 E. Red River
Victoria, TX 77901
  p. (361)573-3291 (Ext.3432)
  matthew.weiler@VictoriaCollege.edu
  http://www.victoriacollege.edu

Wayland Baptist University
Dept.of Geology (B) (2015)
1900 W. 7th Street
Plainview, TX 79072
  p. (806) 291-1115
  walsht@wbu.edu
  http://www.wbu.edu/academics/schools/math_and_science/
  geology/
  Enrollment (2015): B: 7 (1)
Professor:
  Don Parker, (D), GivCg
  Tim R. Walsh, (D), Texas Tech, 2002, GsPmGo
Assistant Professor:
  Mark Bryan, (M), Oklahoma State, 2001, GeoPs

Weatherford College
Weatherford College (1999)
225 College Park Drive
Weatherford, TX 76086
  p. (817) 598-6277
  http://www.wc.edu

West Texas A&M University
Dept of Life, Earth & Environmental Sciences (B,M) (2015)
P. O. Box 60808, WT Station
Canyon, TX 79016-0001
  p. (806) 651-2570
  dsissom@wtamu.edu
  http://www.wtamu.edu/academics/life-earth-environmental-
  sciences.aspx
  Administrative Assistant: Debi Adams
  Enrollment (2013): B: 13 (2)
Chair:
  David Sissom, (D), On
Professor:
  Joseph C. Cepeda, (D), Texas, 1977, GiHw
  David B. Parker, (D), Nebraska, 1996, Sbf
  William J. Rogers, (D), Texas A&M, 1999, On
  Gerald E. Schultz, (D), Michigan, 1966, PvGzOg
Associate Professor:
  Gary C. Barbee, (D), 2004, OisHq
Instructor:
  Cindy D. Meador, (M), West Texas A&M, 1989, Og
  Joe D. Rogers, (M), WTSU (WTAMU), 1987, Ga
  William C. Rogers, (M), WTAMU, 2005, Ge
  Lynn C. Rosa, (M), Oklahoma, 1984, Og

Western Texas College
Math and Science Dept (2011)
6200 College Avenue
Snyder, TX 79549
  p. (325) 573-8511
  http://wtc.edu/science/index.html
Assistant Professor:
  Troy Lilly, (M)

Wharton County Junior College-Sugarland Campus
Wharton County Junior College - Sugarland Campus (2014)
14004 University Blvd.
Sugarland, TX 77479
  p. (281) 239-1559

dannyg@wcjc.edu
http://www.wcjc.edu

Wharton County Junior College-Wharton Campus
Wharton County Junior College - Wharton Campus (2014)
911 Boling Highway
Wharton, TX 77488
   p. (979) 532-6506
   dannyg@wcjc.edu
   http://www.wcjc.edu

Utah

Brigham Young University
Dept of Geography (B) (2015)
690 SWKT
Provo, UT 84602
   p. (801) 378-3851
   geography@byu.edu
   http://www.geography.byu.edu/
   Department Secretary: Karen R. Bryce
Chair:
   Matthew J. Shumway, (D), Indiana, 1991, On
Professor:
   Richard H. Jackson, (D), Clark, 1970, Ou
Associate Professor:
   James A. Davis, (D), Arizona State, 1992, On
   Chad Emmett, (D), Chicago, 1991, On
   Perry J. Hardin, (D), Utah, 1989, Or
Assistant Professor:
   Matthew F. Bekker, (D), Iowa, 2002, Oy
   Jeffrey O. Durrant, (D), Hawaii, 2001, Ge
   Mark W. Jackson, (D), South Carolina, 2001, Or
   Samuel M. Otterstrom, (D), Louisiana State, 1997, Ou
   Brandon Plewe, (D), Buffalo, 1997, Oi
Instructor:
   Jeffry S. Bird, (M), Brigham Young, 1990, Oy
Emeritus:
   Lloyd E. Hudman, (D), Kansas, 1968, On

Dept of Geological Sciences (B,M) (2013)
S 389 ESC
Provo, UT 84602
   p. (801) 422-3918
   geology.office@byu.edu
   http://www.geology.byu.edu
   Administrative Assistant: Kristine B.. Mortenson
   Enrollment (2013): B: 152 (30) M: 38 (7)
Professor:
   Barry R. Bickmore, (D), Virginia Tech, 2000, Cg
   Eric H. Christiansen, (D), Arizona State, 1981, GiXgEm
   Michael J. Dorais, (D), Georgia, 1987, Gi
   Ron Harris, (D), London (UK), 1989, Gc
   Jeffrey D. Keith, (D), Wisconsin, 1982, Eg
   Bart J. Kowallis, (D), Wisconsin, 1981, Gg
   John H. McBride, (D), Cornell, 1987, Ye
   Thomas H. Morris, (D), Wisconsin, 1986, Gr
   Stephen T. Nelson, (D), California (Los Angeles), 1991, Cs
   Scott M. Ritter, (D), Wisconsin, 1986, Ps
   David G. Tingey, (M), Brigham Young, 1989, On
Associate Professor:
   Brooks B. Britt, (D), Calgary, 1993, Pg
   Jani Radebaugh, (D), Arizona, 2005, Xg
   Summer Rupper, (D), Washington, 2004, OlPe
   Randall Skinner, (M), Brigham Young, 1996, Gg
Assistant Professor:
   Gregory T. Carling, (D), Utah, 2012, HwCst
Adjunct Professor:
   Thomas C. Anderson, Gg
   Aase Arvid, Gg
Visiting Professor:
   R. William Keach II, (M), Cornell, 1986, YeEoGg
Emeritus:
   James L. Baer, (D), Brigham Young, 1968, Go
   Myron G. Best, (D), California (Berkeley), Gg
   Dana T. Griffen, (D), Virginia Tech, 1976, Gz

   Lehi F. Hintze, (D), Columbia, 1951, Pg
   Alan L. Mayo, (D), Idaho, 1982, Hw
   Wade E. Miller, (D), California (Berkeley), 1968, Pv
   R. Paul Nixon, (D), Brigham Young, 1972, Go
   Morris S. Petersen, (D), Iowa, 1962, Gso
   William R. Phillips, (D), Utah, 1954, Gz

Salt Lake City Community College-Jordan Campus
Dept of Geosciences (1999)
4600 South Redwood Road
Salt Lake City, UT 84123
   p. (801)957-4150
   adam.dastrup@slcc.edu
   http://www.slcc.edu

Snow College
Dept of Geology (A) (2015)
Ephraim, UT 84627
   p. (435) 283-7519
   geology@snow.edu
   http://www.snow.edu/geology
   f: Snow College Geology
   Enrollment (2015): A: 4 (3)
Chair:
   Renee M. Faatz, (M), Ohio State, 1985, Gg
Assistant Professor:
   Ted L. Olson, (M), Utah, 1976, Ys
   Charles Yeager, (D), Indiana State, 2013, Oyi

Southern Utah University
Dept of Physical Science (B) O (2015)
351 West University Blvd.
Cedar City, UT 84720
   p. (435) 586-7900
   jenniferhargrave@suu.edu
   http://www.suu.edu/geology
   f: https://www.facebook.com/SUUGeologyClub
   Administrative Assistant: Rhonda Riley
   Enrollment (2015): B: 30 (8)
Professor:
   Robert L. Eves, (D), Washington State, 1991, GrOeCl
Assistant Professor:
   Jennifer E. Hargrave, (D), Oklahoma, 2009, PvGrs
   Jason Kaiser, (D), Oregon State, 2014, GzvCg
   John S. MacLean, (D), Montana, 2009, GctOe
Emeritus:
   C. Frederick Lohrengel, II, (D), Brigham Young, 1968, GsrPs

University of Utah 🗇
Dept of Atmospheric Sciences (B,M,D) (2015)
135 S 1460 E, Rm 819
Salt Lake City, UT 84112-0110
   p. (801) 581-6136
   atmos-advising@lists.utah.edu
   http://www.atmos.utah.edu
   Enrollment (2015): B: 54 (6) M: 24 (7) D: 20 (1)
Professor:
   Timothy J. Garrett, (D), Washington, 2000, Oa
   John Horel, (D), Washington, 1982, Oa
   Steven Krueger, (D), California (Los Angeles), 1985, Oa
   Gerald Mace, (D), Penn State, 1994, Oa
   Zhaoxia Pu, (D), Lanzhou, 1997, Oa
   Jim Steenburgh, (D), Washington, 1995, Oa
   Edward Zipser, (D), Florida State, 1965, Oa
Chair:
   Kevin D. Perry, (D), Washington, 1995, Oa
Associate Professor:
   Anna Gannet Hallar, (D), Colorado (Boulder), 2003, Oa
   John Chun-Han Lin, (D), Harvard, 2003, Oa
   Thomas Reichler, (D), Calfornia (San Diego), 2003, Oa
   Courtenay Strong, (D), Virginia, 2005, Oa

Dept of Geography (B,M,D) (2014)
260 S. Central Campus Drive
Rm 270

Salt Lake City, UT 84112-9155
    p. (801) 581-8218
    thomas.kontuly@geog.utah.edu
    http://www.geog.utah.edu
    Administrative Assistant: Susan Van Roosendaal
    Enrollment: No data reported since 1999
Chair:
    George F. Hepner, (D), Arizona State, 1979, Oy
Professor:
    Donald R. Currey, (D), Kansas, 1969, Gm
    Thomas M. Kontuly, (D), Pennsylvania, 1978, On
    Chung M. Lee, (D), Michigan, 1961, Ou
Assistant Professor:
    Thomas J. Cova, (D), California (Santa Barbara), 1999, Oi
    Richard R. Forster, (D), Cornell, 1997, Or
Adjunct Professor:
    Jeffrey R. Keaton, (D), Texas A&M, 1988, On
    Elliott W. Lips, (M), Colorado State, 1990, Gm
Emeritus:
    Philip C. Emmi, (D), North Carolina, 1979, Ou
    Roger M. Mccoy, (D), Kansas, 1967, Or
    Merrill K. Ridd, (D), Northwestern, 1963, Or
Professor-Lecturer:
    Arthur Hampson, (D), Hawaii, 1980, Oy
Assistant Professor:
    Trevor J. Davis, (D), British Columbia, 1999, Oi
Other:
    Fred E. May, (D), Virginia Tech, 1976, On

Dept of Geology & Geophysics (B,M,D) ● (2015)
Frederick Albert Sutton Building, Rm 383
115 South 1460 East
Salt Lake City, UT 84112-0102
    p. (801) 581-7062
    gg@utah.edu
    http://www.earth.utah.edu/
    Administrative Assistant: Judy Martinez
    Administrative Assistant: Dustin Porlas
    Enrollment (2014): B: 55 (0) M: 50 (0) D: 25 (0)
Research Professor:
    Walter J. Arabasz, (D), Caltech, 1971, Ys
Departmental Chair:
    John M. Bartley, (D), MIT, 1981, Oi
Dean, College of Mines & Earth Sciences:
    Francis H. Brown, (D), California (Berkeley), 1971, Gg
Professor:
    John R. Bowman, (D), Michigan, 1976, Cs
    Paul Brooks, (D)
    Thure E. Cerling, (D), California (Berkeley), 1977, Cl
    Marjorie A. Chan, (D), Wisconsin, 1982, Gs
    Allan A. Ekdale, (D), Rice, 1974, Pe
    William P. Johnson, (D), Colorado, 1993, Ng
    Barbara P. Nash, (D), California (Berkeley), 1971, Gi
    Erich U. Petersen, (D), Michigan, 1983, Em
    Peter H. Roth, (D), ETH (Switzerland), 1970, Pm
    Douglas K. Solomon, (D), Waterloo, 1992, Hw
    Michael S. Zhdanov, (D), Moscow State, 1968, Ye
Research Associate Professor:
    Kristine L. Pankow, (D), California, 1999, Ys
Director, Seismograph Stations:
    Keith Koper, (D), Washington, 1998
Associate Director, Global Change and Sustainability Center:
    Brenda Bowen, (D), Gse
Associate Professor:
    Gabriel Bowen, (D), California (Santa Cruz), 2003, Cs
    Paul W. Jewell, (D), Princeton, 1989, Hg
    Cari Johnson, (D), Stanford, 2003, Gs
    David L. Naftz, (D), Colorado Mines, 1993, Cg
    Michael Thorne, (D), Arizona State, 2005, YgGc
Research Associate Professor:
    James C. Pechmann, (D), Caltech, 1983, Ys
Research Assistant Professor:
    Diego Fernandez, (D), Buenos Aires, 1991, Cg
Research:
    Alex Gribenko, (D), Yg
Lecturer:
    Holly Godsey, (D), Oe

Assistant Professor:
    Lauren Birgenheier, (D), Nebraska (Lincoln), 2007, Gso
    David A. Dinter, (D), MIT, 1994, Gt
    Randall B. Irmis, (D), California (Berkeley), 2008, Sa
    Fan-Chi Lin, (D), Colorado (Boulder), 2009
    Peter Lippert, (D), California (Santa Cruz), 2010
    Lowell Miyagi, (D), California (Berkeley), 2009, Gz
    Jeffrey Moore, (D), California (Berkeley), 2007, Ngr
    Lisa Stright, (D), Stanford, 2011, Ggo
Research Assistant Professor:
    Desmond E. Moser, (D), Queen's, 1993, Cc
Adjunct Associate Professor:
    Robert N. Harris, (D), Utah, 1996, Gu
    Victor Heilweil, (D), Utah, 2003, Hw
    James Kirkland, (D), Colorado
    Virginia B. Sisson, (D), Princeton, 1985, Gp
Adjunct Assistant Professor:
    Kathleen Nicoll, (D), Arizona, 1998, Gs
Adjunct Professor:
    Richard Allis, (N)
    David Applegate, (D), MIT, 1994, Cg
    Lukas Baumgartner, (N)
    Harley M. Benz, (D), Utah, 1986, Ys
    Anke Friedrich, (D), MIT, 1998
    John M. Harris, (D), Texas, Pv
    William G. Pariseau, (D), Minnesota, 1966, Nr
    Gerard T. Schuster, (D), Columbia, 1984, Ye
    Aurel Trandafir, (D), Kyoto, 2004, Nr
    Phillip E. Wannamaker, (D), Utah, 1983, Ye
Emeritus:
    Ronald L. Bruhn, (D), Columbia, 1976, Gc
    David S. Chapman, (D), Michigan, 1976, Yh
    Susan L. Halgedahl, (D), California (Santa Barbara), 1981, Ym
    Richard D. Jarrard, (D), California (San Diego), 1975, Gu
    William T. Parry, (D), Utah, 1961, Cg
    M. Dane Picard, (D), Princeton, 1963, Gd
    Robert B. Smith, (D), Utah, 1967, Ys

Dept of Mining Engineering (B,M,D) (2011)
135 South 1460 East
Room 313
Salt Lake City, UT 84112-0113
    p. (801) 581-7198
    mineeng@mines.utah.edu
    http://www.mines.utah.edu/mining
    Enrollment (2009): B: 48 (11) M: 6 (3) D: 1 (0)
Chair:
    Michael G. Nelson, (D), West Virginia, 1989, Nm
Professor:
    Michael K. McCarter, (D), Utah, 1972, Nm
    William G. Pariseau, (D), Minnesota, 1966, Nr
Adjunct Associate Professor:
    Stephen Bessinger, (D), Nm
Associate Professor:
    Felipe Calizaya, (D), Colorado Mines, 1985, Nm
Assistant Professor:
    James Donovan, (D), Virginia Tech, 2003, Nmr
Adjunct Associate Professor:
    Helmut H. Doelling, (D), Utah, 1964, Gg
    Duane L. Whiting, (B), Utah, 1959, Hw
Adjunct Professor:
    Krishna P. Sinha, (D), Minnesota, 1979, Nr
    Jeffrey Whyatt, (D), Nm
    Zavis Zavodni, (D), Nm

Energy & Geoscience Institute (M) ● (2016)
423 Wakara Way
Suite 300
Salt Lake City, UT 84108
    p. (801) 581-5126
    egidirector@egi.utah.edu
    http://www.egi.utah.edu
Director:
    Raymond A. Levey, (D), South Carolina, 1981, Eo
Professor:
    Richardson B. Allen, (D), Columbia, 1983, GctOi
    Alastair Fraser, (D), Edinburgh, Gco

John McLennan, (D), Toronto, 1980, Nrp
Brian McPherson, (D), Utah, 1996, Ye
Joseph N. Moore, (D), Penn State, 1975, Gv
Michal Nemcok, (D), Comenius (Czech), 1991, Gc
Peter E. Rose, (D), Utah, 1993, Np
Rasoul Sorkhabi, (D), Japan, 1991, GctGc
Phillip E. Wannamaker, (D), Utah, 1983, Ye
Scientific Staff :
Julia Kotulova, (D), Komenius Univ Bratislava (Slovakia), CoGo
Senior Scientist:
Bryony Richards-McClung, (D), Go
Stuart Simmons, (D), Minnesota, 1986, Gz
Lansing Taylor, (D), Stanford, 1999, Gc
David Thul, (D), Colorado Mines, 2014, Gg
Associate Professor:
Glenn W. Johnson, (D), South Carolina, 1997, Gq
Greg Nash, (D), Utah, Gt
Marylin Segall, (D), 1991, GeOu
Assistant Professor:
Shu Jiang , (D), China Univ of Geosciences (Wuhan), GoYsNp
Sudeep Kanungo, (D), Univ Coll (London), Pms
Research Associate:
Kenneth L. Shaw, (B), British Columbia, 1965, Ye
Instructor:
William Keach, (M), Cornell, 1986, GoYes
Adjunct Professor:
Ian Walton, (D), Manchester (UK), 1972, Gq

Utah State University 📖
Dept of Geology (B,M,D) (2015)
4505 Old Main Hill
Logan, UT 84322-4505
p. (435) 797-1273
geology@usu.edu
http://geology.usu.edu/
Enrollment (2012): M: 27 (5) D: 11 (1)
Curator of Paleontology, CEU Prehistoric Museum:
Kenneth Carpenter, (D), Colorado, PviPo
Head:
W. David Liddell, (D), Michigan, 1979, GsPo
Professor:
James P. Evans, (D), Texas A&M, 1987, Gc
Mary S. Hubbard, (D), MIT, Gc
Susanne U. Janecke, (D), Utah, 1991, Gt
John W. Shervais, (D), California (Santa Barbara), 1979, Gi
Undergraduate Advisor:
Thomas E. Lachmar, (D), Idaho, 1989, Hw
Graduate Director:
Joel L. Pederson, (D), New Mexico, 1999, Gm
Associate Professor:
Carol M. Dehler, (D), New Mexico, 2001, Gs
Michelle Fleck, (D), Wyoming, Oe
Anthony R. Lowry, (D), Utah, 1994, Yd
Assistant Professor:
Alexis K. Ault, (D), Colorado, 2012, GtCc
Benjamin J. Burger, (D), Colorado, 2009, PgGs
Dennis L. Newell, (D), New Mexico, 2007, Cl
Tammy M. Rittenour, (D), Nebraska, 2004, Gm
Emeritus:
Donald W. Fiesinger, (D), Calgary, 1975, Gi
Peter T. Kolesar, (D), California (Riverside), 1973, Cg
Robert Q. Oaks, Jr., (D), Yale, 1965, Gs

Utah State University Eastern
Dept of Geology (A) (2015)
451 East 400 North
Price, UT 84501
p. (435) 613-5232
michelle.fleck@usu.edu
Enrollment (2015): A: 6 (0)
Associate Professor:
Michelle Cooper Fleck, (D), Wyoming, GgOy

Utah Valley University
Dept. of Earth Science (B) (2015)
800 West University Parkway

Orem, UT 84058
p. (801) 863-8582
HORNSDA@uvu.edu
http://www.uvu.edu/
Enrollment (2015): B: 179 (14)
Professor:
Daniel Horns, (D), NgGet
Paul Tayler, (D), OaGg
Associate Professor:
Joel Bradford, (M), Utah, Gae
Michael Bunds, (D), GctGe
Eddy Cadet, (D), Ge
James Callison, (D), GeSfOs
Steven Emerman, (D), HgYgGe
Daniel Stephen, (D), PiGsPe
Assistant Professor:
Hilary Hungerford, (D), Ou
Nathan Toke', (D), NgGtOi
Weihong Wang, (D), CmGeOi
Alessandro Zanazzi, (D), CgsPe

Weber State University
Dept of Geosciences (B) O (2015)
1415 Edvalson St. Dept 2507
Ogden, UT 84408-2507
p. (801) 626-7139
rford@weber.edu
http://weber.edu/geosciences/
f: https://www.facebook.com/WSUGeosciences?ref=hl
Administrative Assistant: Marianne Bischoff
Enrollment (2015): B: 155 (14)
Dean, College of Science:
David J. Matty, (D), Rice, 1984, Gi
Chair:
Richard L. Ford, (D), California (Los Angeles), 1997, Gm
Professor:
Michael W. Hernandez, (D), Utah, 2004, Ori
Marek Matyjasik, (D), Kent State, 1997, Hw
W. Adolph Yonkee, (D), Utah, 1990, Gc
Assistant Professor:
Elizabeth A. Balgord, (D), Arizona, 2015, Grs
Instructor:
Helen K. Barker, (M), Brigham Young, 1975, Gg
Stephen C. Hallin, (M), Colorado State, 1991, Ow
David Larsen, (M), Brigham Young, 1987, Ge
Gregory B. Nielsen, (D), Utah, 2010, Gg
Visiting Professor:
Sara Summers, (M), Notre Dame, 2012, Gz
Emeritus:
Sydney R. Ash, (D), Reading (UK), 1966, Pb
Jeffrey G. Eaton, (D), Colorado, 1987, Ps
Richard W Moyle, (D), Iowa, 1963, Ps
E. Fred Pashley, (D), Arizona, 1966, Gg
James R. Wilson, (D), Utah, 1976, Gz

Vermont

Castleton University
Dept of Natural Sciences (Geology) (B) (2016)
Castleton University
233 South Street
Castleton, VT 05735
p. (802) 468-1238
tim.grover@castleton.edu
http://www.castleton.edu/academics/undergraduate-pro-
grams/geology/
Enrollment (2015): B: 12 (3)
Professor:
Timothy W. Grover, (D), Oregon, 1988, Gp
Helen N. Mango, (D), Dartmouth, 1992, Cg

Johnson State College
Dept of Environmental & Health Sciences (A,B) (2013)
337 College Hill
Johnson, VT 05656-9464
p. (802) 635-1325

Tania.Bacchus@jsc.edu
Enrollment (2010): B: 37 (11)
Professor:
Tania S. Bacchus, (D), Maine, 1993, GuOw
Leslie H. Kanat, (D), Cambridge, 1986, Gc

Lyndon State College
Dept of Atmospheric Sciences (B) (2010)
PO Box 919
Lyndonville, VT 05851
p. (802) 626-6254
nolan.atkins@lyndonstate.edu
http://meteorology.lyndonstate.edu
Department Secretary: Brenda Sweet
Enrollment (2012): B: 96 (9)
Professor:
Nolan T. Atkins, (D), California (Los Angeles), 1995, Oa
Bruce F. Berryman, (D), Wisconsin, 1974, Oa
Assistant Professor:
Shafer Jason, (D), Utah, 2005, Oa
System Administrator:
Tucker Mark, (B), Lyndon State, Oa

Middlebury College
Geology Dept (B) (2014)
276 Bicentennial Hall
Middlebury, VT 05753
p. (802) 443-5029
geology_chair@middlebury.edu
http://www.middlebury.edu/academics/geol
Administrative Assistant: Eileen Brunetto
Enrollment (2014): B: 28 (8)
Chair:
Jeffrey S. Munroe, (D), Wisconsin, 2001, Gl
Professor:
Raymond A. Coish, (D), W Ontario, 1977, Gi
Patricia L. Manley, (D), Columbia, 1989, Yr
Peter C. Ryan, (D), Dartmouth, 1994, Cl
David P. West, (D), Maine (Orono), 1993, Gc
Assistant Professor:
Will Amidon, (D), Caltech, 2010, Gm
Visiting Professor:
Thomas O. Manley, (D), Columbia, 1981, Op

Norwich University
Dept of Earth and Environmental Sciences (B) (2015)
158 Harmon Drive
Northfield, VT 05663
p. (802) 485-2304
rdunn@norwich.edu
http://scimath.norwich.edu/geology-environmental-science/
Enrollment (2015): B: 16 (9)
Professor:
Richard K. Dunn, (D), Delaware, 1998, GslGa
Professor:
David S. Westerman, (D), Lehigh, 1972, Gxi
Assistant Professor:
G. Christopher Koteas, (D), Massachusetts, 2010, GitYh
Research Associate:
George E. Springston, (M), Massachusetts, 1990, GmNgYg
Lecturer:
Laurie Grigg, (D), Oregon, 2000, PeOiGe

University of Vermont 🔲
Dept of Geology (B,M) (2015)
Delehanty Hall
Burlington, VT 05405-0122
p. (802) 656-3396
geology@uvm.edu
Administrative Assistant: Robin Hopps
Administrative Assistant: Srebrenka Mrsic
Enrollment (2015): B: 48 (0) M: 13 (0)
Professor:
Paul R. Bierman, (D), Washington, 1993, Gm
John M. Hughes, (D), Dartmouth, 1981, Gz

Keith A. Klepeis, (D), Texas, 1993, Gc
Charlotte J. Mehrtens, (D), Chicago, 1979, Gs
Chair:
Andrea Lini, (D), ETH (Switzerland), 1994, CsGn
Associate Professor:
Laura E. Webb, (D), Stanford, 1999, Gtx
Research Assistant Professor:
Nicolas Perdrial, (D), Strasbourg (France), 2007, GezCl
Andrew W. Schroth, (D), Dartmouth, 2007, ClGz
Assistant Professor:
Julia Perdrial, (D), Strasbourg, 2008, ClSc
Lecturer:
Stephen F. Wright, (D), Minnesota, 1988, Gc
Emeritus:
David P. Bucke, (D), Oklahoma, 1969, Gg
Barry L. Doolan, (D), SUNY (Binghamton), 1970, Gx
John C. Drake, (D), Harvard, 1967, Cl
Senior Research Technician:
Gabriela Mora-Klepeis, (M), Texas (Austin), 1992, CacGi

Dept of Plant & Soil Science (B,M,D) (2014)
Jeffords Hall
63 Carrigan Drive
Burlington, VT 05405-1737
p. (802) 656-2630
pss@uvm.edu
http://www.uvm.edu/~pss/
Enrollment: No data reported since 1999

Virginia

Central Virginia Community College
Science, Math, and Engineering (A) (2013)
3506 Wards Road
Lynchburg, VA 24502
p. (434) 832-7707
laubj@cvcc.vccs.edu
http://www.cvcc.vccs.edu/Academics/SME/default.asp
Instructor:
Mark Tinsley, Og

College of William & Mary
Dept of Geology (B) (2015)
PO Box 8795
McGlothlin-Street Hall
Williamsburg, VA 23187-8795
p. (757) 221-2440
crroex@wm.edu
http://www.wm.edu/geology
Administrative Assistant: Carol Roe
Enrollment (2015): B: 70 (20)
Chair:
Christopher M. Bailey, (D), Johns Hopkins, 1994, Gc
Professor:
Gregory S. Hancock, (D), California (Santa Cruz), 1998, Gm
Rowan Lockwood, (D), Chicago, 2001, Po
R. Heather Macdonald, (D), Wisconsin, 1984, GsOe
Brent E. Owens, (D), Washington (St. Louis), 1992, Gz
Associate Professor:
James Kaste, (D), Dartmouth, 2003, ClcSc
Assistant Professor:
Nicholas Balascio, (D), Massachusetts (Amherst), 2011, OyGnl
Research Associate:
Carl R. Berquist, Jr., (D), William & Mary, 1986, Ou
Lecturer:
Rebecca Jiron, (D), California (Santa Barbara), 2015, GmtOg
Emeritus:
Stephen C. Clement, (D), Cornell, 1964, Gz
P. Geoffrey Feiss, (D), Harvard
Gerald H. Johnson, (D), Indiana, 1965, Pg
Director of Laboratories & Technical Support:
Linda D. Morse, (B), Virginia Tech, 1983, Ge

School of Marine Science (M,D) (2015)
Virginia Institute of Marine Science
P. O. Box 1346

Gloucester Point, VA 23062-1246
p. (804) 684-7105
ad-as@vims.edu
http://www.vims.edu
Enrollment (2015): M: 6 (1) D: 11 (1)
Research Professor:
Jian Shen, (D), William & Mary, 1996, Op
Department Chair:
Carl T. Friedrichs, (D), MIT/WHOI, 1993, On
Professor:
Deborah A. Bronk, (D), Maryland, 1992, Oc
Elizabeth A. Canuel, (D), North Carolina, 1992, Oc
Courtney K. Harris, (D), Virginia, 1999, On
Steven A. Kuehl, (D), North Carolina State, 1985, Ou
Jerome P-Y. Maa, (D), Florida, 1986, On
Harry Wang, (D), Johns Hopkins, 1983, Op
Research Associate Professor:
William G. Reay, (D), Virginia Tech, 1992, Hg
Y. Joseph Zhang, (D), Wollongong (Australia), 1996, Op
Associate Professor:
John M. Brubaker, (D), Oregon State, 1979, Op
Assistant Professor:
Donglai Gong, (D), Rutgers, 2010, Op
Christopher J. Hein, (D), Boston, 2012, Ou
Matthew L. Kirwan, (D), Duke, 2007, Gm
Elizabeth H. Shadwick, (D), Dalhousie, 2010, Oc

George Mason University
Dept of Atmospheric, Oceanic, and Earth Sciences (B,M,D) (2015)
Research Hall 206
4400 University Drive
Fairfax, VA 22030-4444
p. (703) 993-9587
eschnei1@gmu.edu
http://aoes.gmu.edu/
Administrative Assistant: Stephanie O'Neill
Administrative Assistant: Natalie Vu
Enrollment (2015): B: 72 (25) M: 4 (0) D: 21 (2)
University Professor:
Edwin K. Schneider, (D), Harvard, 1976, Oa
University Professor:
Jagadish Shukla, (D), MIT, 1976, Oa
Professor:
Timothy DelSole, (D), Harvard, 1993, Oa
Richard J. Diecchio, (D), North Carolina, 1980, Gr
Paul A. Dirmeyer, (D), Maryland, 1992, Oa
Robert M. Hazen, (D), Harvard, 1975, Om
Linda Hinnov, (D), Johns Hopkins, 1994, GrYg
Bohua Huang, (D), Maryland, 1992, Op
Jim Kinter, (D), Princeton, 1984, Oa
Paul Schopf, (D), Princeton, 1978, Opa
David M. Straus, (D), Cornell, 1977, Oa
Associate Professor:
Zafer Boybeyi, (D), North Carolina State, 1993, Oa
Long S. Chiu, (D), MIT, 1980, Oa
Barry Klinger, (D), MIT/WHOI, 1992, Op
Randolph McBride, (D), Louisiana State, 1997, On
Cristiana Stan, (D), Colorado State, 2005, Oa
Term Assistant Professor:
Amelinda Webb, (D), Yale, 2013, Gg
Assistant Professor:
Natalie Burls, (D), Cape Town, 2010, Oap
Kathy Pegion, (D), George Mason, 2007, Oap
Mark Uhen, (D), Michigan, 1996, Pv
Term Associate Professor:
Stacey Verardo, (D), CUNY, 1995, Pe
Term Assistant Professor:
Giuseppina Kysar Mattietti, (D), George Washington, 2001, Gi
Term Associate Professor:
Julia Nord, (D), CUNY (Brooklyn), 1989, Gzg

Hampton University
Center for Marine & Coastal Environmental Studies (B) (2014)
100 Queen Street
Hampton, VA 23668

p. (757) 727-5783
george.burbanck@hamptonu.edu
Enrollment (2010): B: 32 (9)
Chair:
George P. Burbanck, (D), Delaware, 1981, On
Professor:
Benjamin E. Cuker, (D), North Carolina State, 1981, Ob
Associate Professor:
Robert A. Jordan, (D), Michigan, 1970, Ob
Assistant Professor:
Deidre M. Gibson, (D), Georgia, 2000, Ob
Adjunct Faculty:
Emory Morgan, (M), Oe
Related Staff:
Gary Morgan, (B), North Carolina State, 2007, OnnOn

James Madison University
Dept of Geology & Environmental Science (B) (2014)
MSC 6903
Memorial Hall
Harrisonburg, VA 22807
p. (703) 568-6130
ulansksl@jmu.edu
http://www.jmu.edu/geology/
Department Secretary: Sandra Delawder
Enrollment: No data reported since 1999
Head:
Stanley L. Ulanski, (D), Virginia, 1977, Og
Professor:
Roddy V. Amenta, (D), Bryn Mawr, 1971, Gc
Lynn S. Fichter, (D), Michigan, 1972, Gr
Lance E. Kearns, (D), Delaware, 1977, Gz
William C. Sherwood, (D), Lehigh, 1961, So
Associate Professor:
Steven J. Baedke, (D), Indiana, 1998, Hy
Lewis S. Eaton, (D), Virginia, 1999, Gm
Eric J. Pyle, (D), Georgia, 1995, Oe
Kristen E. St. John, (D), Ohio State, 1998, Ou
Assistant Professor:
Steven J. Whitmeyer, (D), Boston, Gc

Lynchburg College
Environmental Science (B) O (2015)
1501 Lakeside Dr.
Lynchburg, VA 24501
p. (434) 544-8415
haiar@lynchburg.edu
http://www.lynchburg.edu/envsci.xml
Enrollment (2013): B: 40 (10)
Professor:
David R. Perault, (D), Oklahoma, 1998, Ge
Associate Professor:
Brooke Haiar, (D), Oklahoma, 2008, PoGeg

Mary Washington College
Dept of Geography (B) (2014)
1301 College Avenue
Fredericksburg, VA 22401-5358
p. (540) 654-1470
shanna@umw.edu
http://www.mwc.edu/geog
Enrollment (2006): B: 80 (0)
Chair:
Joseph W. Nicholas, (D), Georgia, 1991, Oy
Associate Professor:
Donald N. Rallis, (D), Penn State, 1992, On
Assistant Professor:
Dawn S. Bowen, (D), Queen's, 1998, On
Stephen P. Hanna, (D), Kentucky, 1997, Or
Farhang Rouhani, (D), Arizona, 2001, On

Mountain Empire Community College
Mountain Empire Community College (1999)
3441 Mountain Empire Road
Big Stone Gap, VA 24219

p. (276) 523-7460
creynolds@mecc.edu
http://www.me.vccs.edu/

Northern Virginia Community College-Alexandria
Geology Program (A) (2010)
3001 North Beauregard Street
Alexandria, VA 22311
cknights@nvcc.edu
http://www.nvcc.edu/campuses-and-centers/alexandria/
academic-divisions/science/geology.html
Assistant Dean of Geology:
Victor Zabielski, (D), Gg
Adjunct Professor:
Joe Marx, (M), CalTech, Gg

Northern Virginia Community College-Annandale
Geology Program (A) (2015)
8333 Little River Turnpike
Annandale, VA 22003
p. (703) 323-3276
cbentley@nvcc.edu
http://www.nvcc.edu/campuses-and-centers/annandale/
academic-divisions/math-science--engineering/gol.html
Enrollment (2011): A: 10 (10)
Professor:
Kenneth Rasmussen, (D), North Carolina, 1989, Gus
Assistant Professor:
Callan Bentley, (M), Maryland, 2004, Gg
Instructor:
Shelley Jaye, (M), Wayne State, 1984, Giy

Northern Virginia Community College-Loudoun Campus
Natural and Applied Science Div - Dept of Geology (2015)
1000 Harry Flood Byrd Highway
Sterling, VA 20164
p. (703) 450-2612
wbour@nvcc.edu
http://www.nvcc.edu/campuses-and-centers/loudoun/
academic-divisions/natural/geo.html
Associate Professor:
William Bour, (M), George Washington, 1993, Gge
William Straight, (D), North Carolina State, GgPv
Assistant Professor:
Okia Ikwuazorm, (M), Gg

Northern Virginia Community College-Woodbridge
Geology Program (A) (2015)
2645 College Drive
Woodbridge, VA 22191
p. (703) 878-5614
eburtis@nvcc.edu
http://www.nvcc.edu/woodbridge/divisions/natural.html
Enrollment (2014): A: 6 (1)
Instructor:
Erik Burtis, (M), Montana, GgcGi

Old Dominion University
Dept of Ocean, Earth & Atmospheric Sciences (B,M,D) (2015)
4600 Elkhorn Avenue
Norfolk, VA 23529-0496
p. (757) 683-4285
rharvey@odu.edu
http://www.ocean.odu.edu
Enrollment (2015): B: 113 (13) M: 22 (14) D: 16 (1)
Professor and Chair:
H. Rodger Harvey, (D), 1985, CoOc
Professor:
Larry P. Atkinson, (D), Dalhousie, 1972, Op
David J. Burdige, (D), California (San Diego), 1983, Oc
Gregory A. Cutter, (D), California (Santa Cruz), 1982, Oc
Dennis A. Darby, (D), Wisconsin, 1971, Ou
Frederdick C. Dobbs, (D), Florida State, 1987, Ob

Chester E. Grosch, (D), Stevens Inst of Tech, 1967, Op
Eileen E. Hofmann, (D), North Carolina State, 1980, Op
John M. Klinck, (D), Iowa, 1980, Op
Margaret Mulholland, (D), Maryland, 1998, Ob
Donald J. P. Swift, (D), North Carolina, 1964, Ou
Associate Professor:
Alexander Bochdansky, (D), Memorial, 1997, Ob
Jennifer Georgen, (D), MIT/WHOI, 2001, Gu
John R. McConaugha, (D), S California, 1977, Ob
Nora Noffke, (D), Oldenburg, 1997, Ge
Matthew Schmidt, (D), California, 2005, Ou
G. Richard Whittecar, Jr., (D), Wisconsin, 1979, Ou
Assistant Professor:
P. Dreux Chappell, (D), MIT/WHOI, 2009, Oc
Emeritus:
Ann Gargett, (D), British Columbia, 1970, Op
Ronald E. Johnson, (D), Oregon State, 1971, Op
George Oertel, (D), Iowa, 1971, Ou
Thomas Royer, (D), Texas A&M, 1969, Op
Joseph H. Rule, (D), Missouri, 1972, Ou
George T. F. Wong, (D), MIT/WHOI, 1976, Oc

Patrick Henry Community College
Art, Science, Business, and Technology Dept (A) (2011)
645 Patriot Avenue
Martinsville, VA 24112
bdooley@ph.vccs.edu
http://www.ph.vccs.edu/
Assistant Professor:
Brett Dooley, (M), Virginia Tech, 2005, Gg

Piedmont Virginia Community College
Associate of Science (1999)
501 College Drive
Charlottesville, VA 22902
p. (434) 961-5446
khudson@pvcc.edu
http://www.pvcc.edu/

Radford University
Dept of Geology (B) (2014)
Box 6939
Radford University
Radford, VA 24142
p. (540) 831-5652
geology@radford.edu
http://www.radford.edu/~geol-web
Administrative Assistant: Theresa Gawthrop
Enrollment (2013): B: 62 (12)
Associate Professor:
Jonathan L. Tso, (D), Virginia Tech, 1987, Gcp
Professor:
Rhett B. Herman, (D), Montana State, 1996, Yg
Parvinder S. Sethi, (D), North Carolina State, 1994, Gz
Chester F. Watts, (D), Purdue, 1983, NgrHw
Director, Museum of the Earth Sciences:
Stephen W. Lenhart, (D), Kentucky, 1985, Pi
Associate Professor:
Elizabeth McClellan, (D), Tennessee, GipGd
Research Associate:
Judy Ehlen, (D), Birmingham, 1990, Gm
Emeritus:
Robert C. Whisonant, (D), Florida State, 1967, Gsa

Randolph-Macon College
Environmental Studies Program (B) (2015)
P.O. Box 5005
Ashland, VA 23005
p. (804) 752-3745
mfenster@rmc.edu
http://www.rmc.edu/academics/environmental-studies.aspx
Enrollment (2015): B: 4 (7)
Watts Professor of Science:
Michael S. Fenster, (D), Boston, 1995, OnGue

Adjunct Professor:
  Leonard N. Ford, Jr., (D), California (Los Angeles), 1981, CgGrPs
  Charles Saunders, (M), East Carolina, 1990, Ghx

Rappa Hannock Community College
Rappa Hannock Community College (2014)
12745 College Drive
Glenns, VA 23149
  p. (804) 435-8970
  babdul-malik@rappahannock.edu
  http://www.rappahannock.edu

Tidewater Community College
Geophysical Sciences Dept (A) (2010)
Virginia Beach, VA 23456
  p. (757) 822-7264
  tcclayr@tcc.edu
  Enrollment: No data reported since 1999
Instructor:
  Rodney Clayton, Gg
  Jim Coble, Gg
  Mike Lyle, Gg
  Azam Tabrizi, (M), London, 1978, Pm
  John Waugh, Gg

University of Mary Washington
Dept of Earth and Environmental Sciences (B) (2014)
1301 College Avenue
Fredericksburg, VA 22401-5358
  p. (540) 654-1016
  cwhipkey@umw.edu
  http://cas.umw.edu/ees/
  Enrollment (2013): B: 90 (28)
Chair:
  Charles Whipkey, (D), Pittsburgh, 1999, Cg
Professor:
  Michael L. Bass, (D), Virginia Tech, 1976, On
  Grant R. Woodwell, (D), Yale, 1985, Gc
Associate Professor:
  Ben O. Kisila, (D), Arkansas, 2002, Hs
  Neil E. Tibert, (D), Massachusetts, 2002, Pm
Assistant Professor:
  Melanie Szulczewski, (D), Wisconsin, 1999, Osg
Instructor:
  Sarah A. Morealli, (M), Pittsburgh, 2010, Gg
Emeritus:
  Robert L. McConnell, (D), California (Santa Barbara), 1972, Ge

University of Virginia
Blandy Experimental Farm (2014)
400 Blandy Farm Lane
Boyce, VA 22620
  p. (540) 837-1758
  Blandy@virginia.edu
  http://blandy.virginia.edu/
Director:
  David E. Carr, (D), Maryland, 1990, On
Associate Director:
  Kyle J. Haynes, (D), Louisiana State, 2004, On

Dept of Environmental Sciences (B,M,D) (2016)
Clark Hall
291 McCormick Road
Box 400123
Charlottesville, VA 22904
  p. (804) 924-7761
  cba4a@virginia.edu
  http://www.evsc.virginia.edu
  Enrollment: No data reported since 1999
Research Full Professor:
  Peter Berg, (D), Tech (Denmark), 1988, So
  Jack Cosby, (D), Virginia, 1982, Hs
  William Keene, (M), Virginia, 1981, Oa
  G. Carleton Ray, (D), Columbia, 1960, Ob
  Robert J. Swap, (D), Virginia, 1996, On

Chair:
  Michael L. Pace, (D), Georgia, 1981, On
Professor:
  Paolo D'Odorico, (D), Padova, 1998, Hg
  Robert Davis, (D), Delaware, 1988, Oa
  Howard E. Epstein, (D), Colorado State, 1997, On
  James N. Galloway, (D), California (San Diego), 1972, Oa
  Janet S. Herman, (D), Penn State, 1982, Cl
  Alan D. Howard, (D), Johns Hopkins, 1970, Gm
  Deborah Lawrence, (D), Duke, 1998, On
  Manuel Lerdau, (D), Stanford, 1994, On
  Stephen A. Macko, (D), Texas, 1981, Co
  Karen McGlathery, (D), Cornell, 1992, Ob
  Aaron L. Mills, (D), Cornell, 1975, So
  Herman H. Shugart, Jr., (D), Georgia, 1971, Og
  David E. Smith, (D), Texas A&M, 1982, Ob
  Vivian E. Thomson, (D), Virginia, 1997, On
  Patricia L. Wiberg, (D), Washington, 1987, Og
Research Associate Professor:
  Linda K. Blum, (D), Cornell, 1980, Sb
  David E. Carr, (D), Maryland, 1990, On
  Kyle J. Haynes, (D), Louisiana State, 2004, On
  Jennie L. Moody, (D), Michigan, 1986, Oa
  John H. Porter, (D), Virginia, 1988, Or
Associate Professor:
  Stephan F. J DeWekker, (D), British Columbia, 2002, Oa
  Matthew A. Reidenbach, (D), Stanford, 2004, Hg
  Todd M. Scanlon, (D), Virginia, 2002, Hg
  Thomas M. Smith, (D), Tennessee, 1982, Og
Research Assistant Professor:
  Karen C. Rice, (D), Virginia, 2001, HgCg
  Arthur C. Schwarzschild, (D), Virginia, 2004, On
Assistant Professor:
  Kevin M. Grise, (D), Colorado State, 2011, Oa
  Sally Pusede, (D), Oa
Lecturer:
  Thomas H. Biggs, (D), Arizona, 1997, OyGxe
Emeritus:
  Robert Dolan, (D), Louisiana State, 1965, Gm
  Bruce P. Hayden, (D), Chicago, 1968, Oa
  Bruce W. Nelson, (D), Illinois, 1955, Gs
  Wallace E. Reed, (D), Chicago, 1967, Or
  William F. Ruddiman, (D), Columbia, 1969, Gu

Shenandoah Watershed Study (B,M,D) (2015)
Department of Environmental Sciences
Clark Hall
Charlottesville, VA 22904
  p. (434) 924-3382
  tms2v@virginia.edu
  http://people.virginia.edu/~swas/POST/scripts/overview.php
Associate Professor:
  Todd M. Scanlon, (D), Virginia, 2002, Hgs
Research Scientist:
  Ami L. Riscassi, (D), Virginia, 2009

Virginia Coast Reserve Long Term Ecological Research
(2015)
291 McCormick Road
P.O. Box 400123
Charlottesville, VA 22904-4123
  p. 434-924-0558
  kjm4k@virginia.edu
  http://www.vcrlter.virginia.edu
Professor:
  Karen J. McGlathery, (D), Cornell, 1992, Obn

University of Virginia College, Wise
Dept of Natural Science (B) (2015)
1 College Avenue
Wise, VA 24293
  p. (276) 328-0203
  blw@uvawise.edu
  Administrative Assistant: Brenda Whitaker
  Enrollment: No data reported since 1999
Instructor:
  Robert D. VanGundy, (M), North Carolina, 1983, GeHgOg

Virginia Highlands Community College

Virginia Highlands Community College (2014)
100 VHCC Drive
Abingdon, VA 24212
p. (276)739-2433
jsurber@vhcc.edu
http://www.vhcc.edu

Virginia Polytechnic Institute & State University

Dept of Civil & Environmental Engineering (B,M,D) (2015)
750 Drillfield Drive
200 Patton Hall
Blacksburg, VA 24061-0105
p. (703) 231-6635
mwiddows@vt.edu
http://www.cee.vt.edu/
Administrative Assistant: Beth Lucus
Enrollment: No data reported since 1999
Graduate Chair:
   Mark A. Widdowson, (D), Auburn, HwSpHq
Professor:
   Glenn Moglen, (D), MIT, HqgOi
Associate Professor:
   Randel Dymond, (D), Penn State, HqsOi
   Jennifer Irish, (D), Delaware, Oog
   Kyle Strom, (D), Iowa, HsGs
Assistant Professor:
   Erich Hester, (D), North Carolina, Hsw

Dept of Crop & Soil Environmental Sciences (B,M,D) (2010)
240 Smyth Hall
Blacksburg, VA 24061-0404
p. (540) 231-6305
tlthomps@vt.edu
http://www.cses.vt.edu
Department Secretary: Nancy Shields
Enrollment (2001): B: 98 (0) M: 14 (0) D: 7 (0)
Head:
   John R. Hall, III, (D), Ohio State, 1971, So
Professor:
   Marcus M. Alley, (D), Virginia Tech, 1975, Sc
   James C. Baker, (D), Virginia Tech, 1978, Sd
   Walter L. Daniels, (D), Virginia Tech, 1985, Sd
   Stephen J. Donohue, (D), Purdue, 1974, Sc
   Gregory K. Evanylo, (D), Georgia, 1982, Sc
   Charles Hagedorn, (D), Iowa, 1974, Sb
   Gregory L. Mullins, (D), Purdue, 1985, Sc
   Raymond B. Reneau, (D), Florida, 1969, Sc
   Lucian W. Zelazny, (D), Virginia Tech, 1970, Sc
Associate Professor:
   Duane F. Berry, (D), Michigan State, 1984, Sb
   Matthew J. Eick, (D), Delaware, 1995, Sc
   Naraine Persaud, (D), Florida, 1978, Sp
Assistant Professor:
   John M. Galbraith, (D), Cornell, 1997, Sp
   Carl E. Zipper, (D), Virginia Tech, 1986, Oe
Adjunct Professor:
   Domy C. Adriano, (D), Kansas State, 1970, Sc
   V. C. Baligar, (D), Mississippi State, 1975, Sc
   Pamela J. Thomas, (D), Virginia Tech, 1998, Sd

Dept of Geography (B,M,D) (2010)
115 Major Williams Hall
Blacksburg, VA 24061-0115
p. (540) 231-7557
carstens@vt.edu
Enrollment (2010): B: 170 (49) M: 17 (9) D: 8 (0)
Head:
   Laurence W. Carstensen, (D), North Carolina, 1981, Oi
Professor:
   James B. Campbell, (D), Kansas, 1976, Or
Associate Professor:
   Lawrence S. Grossman, (D), Australian National, 1979, On
   Lisa M. Kennedy, (D), Tennessee, Pe
   Resler M. Lynn, (D), Texas State, Oy

Instructor:
   David Carroll, (M), Mississippi State, Ow

Dept of Geosciences (B,M,D) (2014)
4044 Derring Hall
Blacksburg, VA 24061
p. (540) 231-6521
wilcar@vt.edu
http://www.geos.vt.edu
Administrative Assistant: Carolyn S. Williams
Enrollment (2010): B: 92 (16) M: 14 (10) D: 42 (6)
Chair:
   Kenneth A. Eriksson, (D), Witwatersrand, 1977, Gs
Research Professor:
   Ross J. Angel, (D), Cambridge, 1986, Gz
   Robert P. Lowell, (D), Oregon State, 1972, Yr
Professor:
   Robert J. Bodnar, (D), Penn State, 1985, Cg
   Patricia M. Dove, (D), Princeton, 1991, Cl
   Michael F. Hochella, Jr., (D), Stanford, 1981, Cl
   Scott D. King, (D), Caltech, 1990, Yg
   Michal J. Kowalewski, (D), Arizona, 1995, Py
   Richard D. Law, (D), London, 1981, Gc
   J. Fred Read, (D), W Australia, 1971, Gs
   J. Donald Rimstidt, (D), Penn State, 1979, Cl
   Nancy L. Ross, (D), Arizona State, 1985, Gz
   Robert J. Tracy, (D), Massachusetts, 1975, Gp
   Shuhai Xiao, (D), Harvard, 1998, Pi
Research Associate Professor:
   Martin C. Chapman, (D), Virginia Tech, 1998, Ys
Associate Professor:
   Thomas J. Burbey, (D), Nevada (Reno), 1994, Hw
   John A. Hole, (D), British Columbia, 1993, Ye
   Madeline E. Schreiber, (D), Wisconsin, 1999, Hw
   James A. Spotila, (D), Caltech, 1998, Gt
   Chester J. Weiss, (D), Texas A&M, 1998, Ye
Assistant Professor:
   Barbara M. Bekken, (D), Stanford, 1990, Eg
   Ying Zhou, (D), Princeton, 2004, Ys
Sr. Research Associate:
   Jing Zhao, (D), Chinese Acad of Sci, 1997
Research Associate:
   Nizhou Han, (D), Iowa State, 1996, Sc
Instructor:
   Neil E. Johnson, (D), Virginia Tech, 1986, GzEg
Adjunct Professor:
   James S. Beard, (D), California (Davis), 1985, Gi
   John A. Chermak, (D), Virginia Tech, 1989, Cg
   Benedetto DeVivo, (D)
   Alton C. Dooley, (D), Louisiana State, 1998
   Nicholas C. Fraser, (D), Aberdeen, 1984, Pv
   William S. Henika, (M), Virginia, 1969, Ng
   David W. Houseknecht, (D), Penn State, 1978, Gd
   Jerry L. Hunter, (D), North Carolina, 1991, Ca
   Matthew J. Mikulich, (D), Utah, 1971, Ye
   Csaba Szabo, (D), Virginia Tech, 1994, Gi
   Chester F. Watts, (D), Purdue, 1983, Ngg
Emeritus:
   Richard K. Bambach, (D), Yale, 1969, Po
   F. Donald Bloss, (D), Chicago, 1951, Gz
   G. A. Bollinger, (D), St. Louis, 1967, Ys
   Cahit Coruh, (D), Istanbul, 1970, Ye
   James R. Craig, (D), Lehigh, 1965, Eg
   Gordon C. Grender, (D), Penn State, 1960, Go
   David A. Hewitt, (D), Yale, 1970, Cp
   Wallace D. Lowry, (D), Rochester, 1943, Gc
   Dewey M. McLean, (D), Stanford, 1969, Pe
   Paul H. Ribbe, (D), Cambridge, 1963, Gz
   Edwin S. Robinson, (D), Wisconsin, 1964, Yg
   A. Krishna Sinha, (D), California (Santa Barbara), 1969, Gt
   J. Arthur Snoke, (D), Yale, 1969, Ys
Educational Administrator for Outreach:
   S. Llyn Sharp, (M), Virginia Tech, 1990, Oe
Cooperating Faculty:
   Edward Lener, (M), Virginia Tech, 1997, On

Virginia Wesleyan College
Dept of Earth and Environmental Sciences (B) (2015)
1584 Wesleyan Dr
Norfolk, VA 23502
  p. 757.455.3200
  jchaley@vwc.edu
  http://www.vwc.edu/earth-and-envirmental-sciences/
  f: https://www.facebook.com/vwc.ees?fref=ts
  Enrollment (2015): B: 22 (0)
Professor:
  John C. Haley, (D), Johns Hopkins, 1986, GgeOi
Associate Professor:
  Elizabeth Malcolm, (D), Michigan, 2002, OaCgOg
  Garry Noe, (D), California (Riverside), 1982, HsOin

Virginia Western Community College
Geology Dept (A) (2010)
3095 Colonial Avenue
Roanoke, VA 24038
  p. (540) 857-7273
  abalog-szabo@virginiawestern.edu
  Enrollment: No data reported since 1999
Professor:
  Anna Balog-Szabo, (D), Virginia Tech, 1996, Gs

Washington & Lee University
Dept of Geology (B) (2015)
204 West Washington Street
Lexington, VA 24450
  p. (540) 458-8800
  geology@wlu.edu
  http://geology.wlu.edu
  Administrative Assistant: Sarah Wilson
  Enrollment (2015): B: 40 (17)
Professor:
  Lisa Greer, (D), Miami, 2001, GsPe
  David J. Harbor, (D), Colorado State, 1990, Gm
Associate Professor:
  Elizabeth P. Knapp, (D), Virginia, 1997, Cl
  Jeffrey Rahl, (D), Yale, 2005, Gt
Emeritus:
  Frederick Schwab, (D), Harvard, 1967, Gd
  Edgar W. Spencer, (D), Columbia, 1957, Gc
Laboratory Supervisor:
  Emily Flowers Falls, (M), Eastern Kentucky, 2009, Gg

Washington

Bellevue College
Earth and Space Sciences Program (A) (2014)
3000 Landerholm Circle SE
Bellevue, WA 98007
  p. (425) 564-3158
  kshort@bellevuecollege.edu
  http://scidiv.bellevuecollege.edu/
Instructor:
  Cary Easterday, (M), GgPg
  Gwyn Jones, (M), Gg
  Deborah Minium, (M), Gg
  Rob Viens, (D), Washington, GgOg

Central Washington University
Dept of Geological Sciences (B,M) (2013)
400 East University Way
MS 7418
Ellensburg, WA 98926-7418
  p. (509) 963-2701
  chair@geology.cwu.edu
  http://www.geology.cwu.edu
  Enrollment (2010): B: 97 (17) M: 20 (8)
Chair:
  Carey A. Gazis, (D), Caltech, 1994, Cs
Director, PANGA Laboratory:
  Timothy I. Melbourne, (D), Caltech, 1998, Yd
Professor:
  Wendy A. Bohrson, (D), California (Los Angeles), 1993, Gvi
  Lisa L. Ely, (D), Arizona, 1992, Gm
  Jeffrey Lee, (D), Stanford, 1990, Gct
GPS Data Analyst:
  Marcelo Santillan, (M), Memphis, 2003, Yd
Associate Scientist:
  Marie A. Ferland, (D), Sydney, 1991, Gu
Assistant Professor:
  Susan Kaspari, (D), Maine, 2007, Pe
  Audrey Huerta, (D), MIT, 1998, Ygd
  Breanyn MacInnes, (D), Washington, 2010, GseGu
  Chris Mattinson, (D), Stanford, 2006, Gzp
  Walter Szeliga, (D), Colorado, 2010, YgsYd
Research Associate:
  Paul Winberry, Penn State, 2008, Yg
Scientific Instructional Tech Supervisor:
  Nick Zentner, (M), Idaho State, 1989, Gg
Lecturer:
  Keegan Fengler, (M), C Washington, Gg
  Winston Norrish, (D), Cincinnati, 1990, GgeGo
Emeritus:
  Robert Bentley, (D), Columbia, 1969, Gi
  Steven Farkas, (D), New Mexico, 1965, Gs
  James R. Hinthorne, (D), California (Santa Barbara), 1974, Ca
  M. Meghan Miller, (D), Stanford, 1987, Yd
  L. Don Ringe, (D), Washington State, 1968, Gml
  Charles M. Rubin, (D), Caltech, 1990, Gt
Systems Administrator:
  Craig Scrivner, (D), Caltech, 1998
PANGA Network Engineer:
  Andy Miner, (M), C Washington, Yd

Centralia College
Earth Sciences Program (A) (2016)
600 Centralia College Blvd
Centralia, WA 98531
  p. (360) 736-9391
  ppringle@centralia.edu
  http://www.centralia.edu/academics/earthscience/
  Enrollment (2015): A: 3 (1)
Professor:
  Patrick Pringle, (M), Akron, 1982, OgGvOn

Eastern Washington University
Dept of Geology (B) (2009)
130 Science Building
Cheney, WA 99004-2439
  p. (509) 359-2286
  charbolt@ewu.edu
  http://cshe.cslabs.ewu.edu/deptGEO/x55894.html
  Administrative Assistant: Carolyn Harbolt
  Enrollment (2009): B: 52 (12)
Professor:
  John P. Buchanan, (D), Colorado State, 1985, Hw
  Ernest H. Gilmour, (D), Montana, 1967, Pi
  Linda B. McCollum, (D), SUNY (Binghamton), 1980, Po
  Jennifer A. Thomson, (D), Massachusetts, 1992, Gp
Associate Professor:
  Richard L. Orndorff, (D), Kent State, 1994, Ge
Assistant Professor:
  Carmen Nezat, (D), Michigan, 2006, CgGeg
Emeritus:
  James I. Hoffman, (D), Michigan State, 1969, Em
  Mohammed Ikramuddin, (D), Miami, 1974, Ca
  Eugene P. Kiver, (D), Wyoming, 1968, Gl
  James R. Snook, (D), Washington, 1962, Gc
  William K. Steele, (D), Case Western, 1970, Yg
Scientific Instructional Tech:
  Charles R. Strout, (B), Montana Min Sci & Tech, 1978, Gg

Edmonds Community College
Geology (A) (2013)
20000 68th Ave W
Lynnwood, WA 98036
  p. (425) 640-1918

mkelly@edcc.edu
http://www.edcc.edu/stem/geology/
Enrollment (2013): A: 4 (0)
Instructor:
  Maria Kelly, Og
Adjunct Professor:
  Dylan Ahearn, (D), California (Davis)
  Thomas Hamilton, Og

Everett Community College
Dept of Physical Sciences (A) (2014)
2000 Tower Street
Everett, WA 98201
  p. (425) 388-9429
  sdamp@everettcc.edu
  http://www.everettcc.edu/programs/mathsci/physical/
Instructor:
  Steve Grupp, (M), Colorado Mines, GgOg
Adjunct Professor:
  Alecia Spooner, Og

Grays Harbor College
Dept of Geology & Oceanography (A) (2010)
Aberdeen, WA 98520
  p. (206) 538-4299
  jhillier@ghc.edu
  Enrollment: No data reported since 1999
Professor:
  John Hillier, (D), Cornell, OgCa
Emeritus:
  James B. Phipps, (D), Oregon State, 1974, Gu

Green River Community College
Dept of Geology (A) (2015)
12401 S.E. 320th
Auburn, WA 98092-3699
  p. (253) 833-9111 (Ext. 4248)
  http://www.greenriver.edu/academics/areas-of-study/details/earth-science.htm
Instructor:
  Kathryn A. Hoppe, (D), Princeton, 1999, OggPg
  Katie Shaw, (M), Washington, OggGg

Highline College
Physical Sciences Dept/Geology Program (A) (2015)
MS 29-3
 PO Box 98000
2400 S. 240th St.
Des Moines, WA 98198-9800
  p. (206) 878-3710
  ebaer@highline.edu
  http://geology.highline.edu/
  Enrollment (2015): A: 5 (0)
Instructor:
  Eric M. Baer, (D), California (Santa Barbara), 1995, GgvOg
  Caroline Pew, (M), Washington, 2013, Oe
  Stephaney Puchalski, (D), Indiana, 2011, PgGg
  Michael Valentine, (D), Massachusetts (Amherst), 1990, Gt
  Carla Whittington, (M), Indiana, GgvOg

Lower Columbia College
Earth Sciences (Natural Sciences Dept.) (A) (2010)
P.O. Box 3010
Longview, WA 98632
  p. (360) 442-2883
  dcordero@lowercolumbia.edu
  http://lowercolumbia.edu/nr/exeres/394D4C4D-1A8A-4F33-AAA9-F85C71386644
  Enrollment (2001): A: 8 (4)
Professor:
  David I. Cordero, (M), Portland State, 1997, Og

North Seattle Community College, North Campus
Earth Science (1999)
9600 College Way North

Seattle, WA 98103
  p. (206) 934-4509
  tfurutani@sccd.ctc.edu
  http://www.northseattle.edu/

Northwest Indian College
Native Environmental Studies (2014)
2522 Kwina Road
Bellingham, WA 98226
  p. (360) 392-4256
  toreiro@nwic.edu
  http://www.nwic.edu/degrees-and-certificates/bsnes-bachelors-degree

Olympic College
Mathematics, Engineering, Sciences, and Health Div (A) (2014)
Bremerton, WA 98310
  p. (360) 475-7777
  SMacias@olympic.edu
  http://www.olympic.edu/Students/AcadDivDept/MESH/Sciences/Geology/
  Enrollment: No data reported since 1999
Instructor:
  Steve E. Macias, (M), Washington, 1996, Gg
Adjunct Professor:
  Katie Howard, Gg

Pacific Lutheran University
Dept of Geosciences (B) (2013)
12180 S. Park
Tacoma, WA 98447
  p. (253) 535-7378
  geos@plu.edu
  http://www.plu.edu/geosciences/
  Enrollment (2013): B: 52 (11)
Chair:
  Jill M. Whitman, (D), California (San Diego), 1989, Ou
Professor:
  Steven R. Benham, (D), Indiana, 1979, Gd
  Duncan Foley, (D), Ohio State, 1978, Hy
Associate Professor:
  Rosemary McKenney, (D), Penn State, 1997, Gm
Assistant Professor:
  Peter B. Davis, (D), Minnesota, 2008, GcpGz
  Claire E. Todd, (D), Washington, 2007, Glm

Peninsula College
Environmental Science (1999)
1502 East Lauridsen Boulevard
Port Angeles, WA 98362
  p. (360) 452-9277
  jganzhorn@pencol.edu
  http://www.pc.ctc.edu

Pierce College
Pierce College (2014)
9401 Farwest Drive SW
Lakewood, WA 98498
  p. (253) 964-6676
  zayacjm@piercecollege.edu
  http://www.piercecollege.edu/departments/physics_planetary_sciences/geology.asp

Seattle Central Community College
Div of Science & Mathematics (2010)
1701 Broadway
Seattle, WA 98122
  p. (206) 587-3858
  jhull@sccd.ctc.edu
  http://seattlecentral.edu/sci-math/
Instructor:
  Katie Gagnon, (D), California (San Diego), 2007, Oug
  Joseph M. Hull, (D), Rochester, 1988, Gc

Adjunct Professor:
   Michael Harrell, Gg

Shoreline Community College
Geology & Earth Sciences (A) (2010)
16101 Greenwood Avenue North
Seattle, WA 98133
   p. (206) 546-4659
   eagosta@shoreline.edu
   http://www.shoreline.edu/science/geology.htm
   Enrollment: No data reported since 1999

Spokane Community College
Dept of Earth Science (1999)
1810 N. Greene Street
Spokane, WA 99217
   virginia.tomlinson@scc.spokane.edu
   http://www.scc.spokane.edu

Tacoma Community College
Dept of Earth Sciences (A) (2015)
6501 South 19th Street
Tacoma, WA 98466
   p. (253) 566-5060
   rhitz@tacomacc.edu
   http://www.tacomacc.edu/academics/mathematicsscienc-
   esandengineeringdivision/science/programs/earthscience/
   Enrollment (2015): A: 8 (2)
Professor:
   Ralph B. Hitz, (D), California (Santa Barbara), 1997, Og
Adjunct Professor:
   Jim McDougall, (D), Og
   James Peet, (D), Washington
   Michael Valentine, (D), Og

University of Puget Sound
Geology Dept (B) (2016)
1500 N. Warner Street
Tacoma, WA 98416-1048
   p. (253) 879-3814
   mvalentine@pugetsound.edu
   http://www.pugetsound.edu/academics/departments-and-
   programs/undergraduate/geology/
   f: https://www.facebook.com/upsgeology
   Administrative Assistant: Leslie Levenson
   Enrollment (2015): B: 27 (10)
Chair:
   Michael J. Valentine, (D), Massachusetts, 1990, YmGc
Professor:
   Barry Goldstein, (D), Minnesota, 1985, Gl
   Tepper H. Jeffrey, (D), Washington, 1991, GiCgGv
Associate Professor:
   Kena L. Fox-Dobbs, (D), California (Santa Cruz), 2006, PgCsGe
Instructor:
   Ken Clark, (M), W Washington, 1989, GgcGi
Emeritus:
   Z. Frank Danes, (D), Charles (Prague), 1949, Yv
   Albert A. Eggers, (D), Dartmouth, 1972, Gv

University of Washington
Dept of Atmospheric Sciences (B,M,D) (2014)
Box 351640
Seattle, WA 98195-1640
   p. (206) 543-4250
   chair@atmos.washington.edu
   http://www.atmos.washington.edu
   Enrollment (2012): B: 60 (17) M: 30 (9) D: 35 (9)
Professor and Chair:
   Gregory J. Hakim, (D), SUNY (Albany), 1997, Oa
Research Associate Professor:
   Roger T. Marchand, (D), Virginia Tech, 1997, Oa
Professor:
   Thomas P. Ackerman, (D), Washington, 1976, Oa
   David S. Battisti, (D), Washington, 1988, Oa
   Christopher S. Bretherton, (D), MIT, 1984, Oa

Dale R. Durran, (D), MIT, 1981, Oa
Qiang Fu, (D), Utah, 1991, Oa
Dennis L. Hartmann, (D), Princeton, 1975, Oa
Robert A. Houze, (D), MIT, 1972, Oa
Lyatt Jaegle, (D), Caltech, 1996, Oa
Daniel A. Jaffe, (D), Washington, 1987, Oa
Clifford F. Mass, (D), Washington, 1978, Oa
Peter B. Rhines, (D), Trinity Coll (Cambridge), 1967, Op
Stephen G. Warren, (D), Harvard, 1973, Yg
Associate Professor:
   Cecilia M. Bitz, (D), Washington, 1997, Oa
   Dargan M. Frierson, (D), Princeton, 2005, Oa
   Joel A. Thornton, (D), California (Berkeley), 2002, Oa
   Robert Wood, (D), Manchester, 1997, Oa
Research Assistant Professor:
   Jerome Patoux, (D), Washington, 2003, Oa
Assistant Professor:
   Becky Alexander, (D), California (San Diego), 2002, Oa
   Abigail L. S. Swann, (D), California (Berkeley), 2010, Oan
Sr. Lecturer PT:
   Lynn A. McMurdie, (D), Washington, 1989, Oa
Adjunct Associate Professor:
   Jessica D. Lundquist, (D), Scripps, 2004, Oa
   Nathan J. Mantua, (D), Washington, 1994, Oa
Adjunct Assistant Professor:
   Eric P. Salathe Jr., (D), Yale, 1994, Oa
Adjunct Professor:
   David C. Catling, (D), Oxford, 1994, Oa
   Gerard H. Roe, (D), MIT, 1999, Oa
   Eric J. Steig, (D), Washington, 1996, GlCg
   LuAnne Thompson, (D), MIT, 1990, Og
   Ka-Kit Tung, (D), Harvard, 1977, Oa
Research Professor Emeritus:
   James E. Tillman, (M), MIT, Oa
Emeritus:
   Marcia B. Baker, (D), Washington, Oa
   Robert A. Brown, (D), Washington, 1969, Oa
   Joost A. Businger, (D), State (Utrecht), Oa
   Robert J. Charlson, (D), Washington, Oa
   David S. Covert, (D), Washington, 1974, Oa
   Robert G. Fleagle, (D), New York, Oa
   Thomas C. Grenfell, (D), Washington, 1972, Oa
   Halstead Harrison, (D), Stanford, 1960, Oa
   Dean A. Hegg, (D), Washington, 1979, Oa
   Gary A. Maykut, (D), Washington, Oa
   Edward S. Sarachik, (D), Brandeis, Oa
   John M. Wallace, (D), MIT, 1966, Oa
Affiliate Professor:
   Shuyi S. Chen, (D), Penn State, 1990, Oa
   D. Edmunds Harrison, (D), Harvard, 1977, Oa
   James E. Overland, (D), New York, 1973, Oa
   Lawrence F. Radke, (D), Washington, 1968, Oa
   Philip J. Rasch, (D), Florida State, 1984, Oa
Affiliate Associate Professor:
   Timothy S. Bates, (D), Washington, 1992, Oa
   Nicholas A. Bond, (D), Washington, 1986, Oa
   Bradley R. Colman, (D), MIT, 1984, Oa
   F. Anthony Eckel, (D), Washington, 2003, Oa
   Philip W. Mote, (D), Washington, 1994, Oa
   Mark T. Stoelinga, (D), Washington, 1993, Oa
   Sandra E. Yuter, (D), Washington, 1996, Oa
Affiliate Assistant Professor:
   Bonnie Light, (D), Washington, 2000, Oa

Dept of Earth & Space Sciences (B,M,D) (2015)
070 Johnson Hall
Box 351310
Seattle, WA 98195-1310
   p. (206) 543-1190
   essadv@uw.edu
   http://www.ess.washington.edu
   Enrollment (2014): B: 158 (60) M: 30 (19) D: 63 (13)
Chair:
   Robert M. Winglee, (D), Sydney, 1984, XyYx
Research Professor:
   Howard B. Conway, (D), Canterbury (NZ), 1986, Ol
   Alan R. Gillespie, (D), Caltech, 1982, GmOlr

James A. Mercer, (D), Washington, 1983, GuYr
Dale P. Winebrenner, (D), Washington, 1985, Olr
Affiliate Professor:
Brian Atwater, (D), Ys
Arthur Frankel, (D), Ys
Joan Gomberg, (D), YsGt
Frank Gonzalez, (D), Or
Tony Irving, (D), CgXmGi
Richard Sack, (D), CgOn
Affiliate Assistant Professor:
Ralph Haugerud, (D), Oi
Brian L. Sherrod, (D), YsGt
Professor:
George W. Bergantz, (D), Johns Hopkins, 1988, Gi
Joanne (Jody) Bourgeois, (D), Wisconsin, 1980, GsrGh
J. Michael Brown, (D), Minnesota, 1980, Gy
Roger Buick, (D), W Australia, 1986, PeoPm
David C. Catling, (D), Oxford, 1994, On
Darrel S. Cowan, (D), Stanford, 1972, Gct
Kenneth C. Creager, (D), California (San Diego), 1984, Ys
Bernard Hallet, (D), California (Los Angeles), 1975, GmOl
Robert H. Holzworth, (D), California (Berkeley), 1977, YxXy
Heidi B. Houston, (D), Caltech, 1987, YsGt
David R. Montgomery, (D), California (Berkeley), 1991, Gm
Bruce K. Nelson, (D), California (Los Angeles), 1985, CcGi
Charles A. Nittrouer, (D), Washington, 1978, GuYr
Eric J. Steig, (D), Washington, 1996, CsOl
John E. Vidale, (D), Caltech, 1986, YsGt
Edwin D. Waddington, (D), British Columbia, 1981, Ol
Peter D. Ward, (D), McMaster, 1976, Po
Stephen G. Warren, (D), Harvard, 1973, Oal
Research Associate Professor:
Evan H. Abramson, (D), MIT, 1985, Gy
Paul A. Bodin, (D), Colorado, 1992, Ys
Michael P. McCarthy, (D), Washington, 1988, XyYx
Robert I. Odom, (D), Washington, 1980, YrGu
Ronald S. Sletten, (D), Washington, 1995, OsSb
Affiliate Associate Professor:
Olivier Bachmann, (D), Geneva, 2000, Giv
Gary Bust, (D)
Amit Mushkin, (D), OrCcGm
Adjunct Associate Professor:
Katherine Sian Davies-Vollum, (D), Oxford (UK), 1994, GsrPe
Associate Professor:
Elizabeth (Liz) Nesbitt, (D), California (Berkeley), 1982, Pim
Gerard H. Roe, (D), MIT, 1999, OaGmOl
John O.H Stone, (D), Cambridge, 1986, Cca
Fangzhen Teng, (D), Maryland, 2005, Cg
Research Assistant Professor:
Erika M. Harnett, (D), Washington, 2003, XyGev
Stephen E. Wood, (D), California (Los Angeles), 1999, On
Adjunct Assistant Professor:
Christian A. Sidor, (D), Chicago, 2000, Pv
Assistant Professor:
Juliet Crider, (D), Stanford, 1998, Gc
Alison Duvall, (D), Michigan, 2011, GmcGt
Drew J. Gorman-Lewis, (D), Notre Dame, 2006, PyCl
Katharine W. Huntington, (D), MIT, 2006, Gt
Senior Lecturer:
Terry W. Swanson, (D), Washington, 1994, CcGe
Kathy G. Troost, (D), Oun
Lecturer:
Brian Collins, Gm
Adjunct Professor:
David S. Battisti, (D), Washington, 1988, Oa
Donald E. Brownlee, (D), Washington, 1971, Xgy
John R. Delaney, (D), Arizona, 1977, GuYr
Harlan Paul Johnson, (D), Washington, 1972, Gu
John D. Sahr, (D), Cornell, 1990, YgXy
William S.D Wilcock, (D), MIT, 1992, Gu
Research Professor Emeritus:
Stephen D. Malone, (D), Nevada (Reno), 1972, YsGt
Gary A. Maykut, (D), Washington, 1969, OalYr
Emeritus:
John B. Adams, (D), Washington, 1961, GcXgOr
Patricia M. Anderson, (D), Brown, 1982, Ple
Marcia B. Baker, (D), Washington, 1971, OaYg

John R. Booker, (D), California (San Diego), 1968, YmGt
Eric S. Cheney, (D), Yale, 1964, Eg
Robert S. Crosson, (D), Stanford, 1966, YsGct
Bernard W. Evans, (D), Oxford (UK), 1959, Gp
I. Stewart (Stu) McCallum, (D), Chicago, 1968, Gi
Ronald T. Merrill, (D), California (Berkeley), 1967, Ygm
George K. Parks, (D), California (Berkeley), 1966, YxXy
Stephen C. Porter, (D), Yale, 1962, Gl
Charles F. Raymond, (D), Caltech, 1969, Ol
John M. Rensberger, (D), California (Berkeley), 1967, Pv
Stewart W. Smith, (D), Caltech, 1961, Ys
Minze Stuiver, (D), Groningen (Neth), 1958, Cc
Joseph A. Vance, (D), Washington, 1957, Gi
Senior Computer Specialist:
Harvey Greenberg, (M), Cal State (Chico), 1977
QRC Curator - Special Collections:
Bax Barton
Postdoctoral Researcher:
Kate Allstadt, (D), Washington, 2013, Ys
Qinghua Ding, (D)
Jon Toner, (D)

School of Oceanography (B,M,D) (2014)
Box 357940
Seattle, WA 98195-7940
    p. (206) 543-5060
    admin@ocean.washington.edu
    http://www.ocean.washington.edu/
    Enrollment (2003): B: 62 (13) M: 45 (14) D: 47 (10)
Director:
Russell E. McDuff, (D), California (San Diego), 1978, Oc
Research Professor:
Mark L. Holmes, (D), Washington, 1975, Ou
Ronald L. Shreve, (D), Caltech, 1959, Yr
Professor:
Knut Aagaard, (D), Washington, 1966, Op
John A. Baross, (D), Washington, 1972, Ob
Roy Carpenter, (D), California (San Diego), 1968, Oo
William O. Criminale, Jr., (D), Johns Hopkins, 1960, Op
Eric A. D'Asaro, (D), MIT/WHOI, 1980, Oc
John R. Delaney, (D), Arizona, 1977, Yr
Jody W. Deming, (D), Maryland, 1981, Ob
Allan H. Devol, (D), Washington, 1975, Oc
Steven R. Emerson, (D), Columbia, 1974, Oc
Charles C. Eriksen, (D), MIT, 1977, Op
Bruce W. Frost, (D), California (San Diego), 1969, Ob
Michael C. Gregg, (D), California (San Diego), 1971, Op
G. Ross Heath, (D), Scripps, 1968, Cm
Barbara M. Hickey, (D), California (San Diego), 1975, Op
H. Paul Johnson, (D), Washington, 1972, Yr
Marvin D. Lilley, (D), Oregon State, 1983, Ob
Seelye Martin, (D), Johns Hopkins, 1967, Op
James W. Murray, (D), MIT/WHOI, 1973, Oc
Charles A. Nittrouer, (D), Washington, 1978, Ou
Arthur R. M. Nowell, (D), British Columbia, 1975, Ou
Paul D. Quay, (D), Columbia, 1977, Oc
Peter B. Rhines, (D), Cambridge, 1967, Op
Jeffrey E. Richey, (D), California (Davis), 1973, Oc
Thomas B. Sanford, (D), MIT, 1967, Op
Associate Professor:
Virginia E. Armbrust, (D), MIT/WHOI, 1990, Ob
Susan L. Hautala, (D), Washington, 1992, Op
Bruce M. Howe, (D), California (San Diego), 1986, Op
Mitsuhiro Kawase, (D), Princeton, 1986, Op
Richard G. Keil, (D), Delaware, 1991, Oc
Deborah S. Kelley, (D), Dalhousie, 1990, Ou
Evelyn J. Lessard, (D), Rhode Island, 1984, Ob
Parker MacCready, (D), Washington, Op
Stephen C. Riser, (D), Rhode Island, 1980, Op
LuAnne Thompson, (D), MIT/WHOI, 1990, Op
Mark J. Warner, (D), California (San Diego), 1988, Op
William S. D. Wilcock, (D), MIT/WHOI, 1992, Ou
Kevin L. Williams, (D), Washington State, 1985, Op
Research Assistant Professor:
Miles G. Logsdon, (D), Washington, 1997, Oi
Andrea S. Ogston, (D), Washington, 1997, Ou

Andrew Barclay, (D), Oregon, 1998, Gu
Daniel Grunbaum, (D), Cornell, 1992, Ob
Anitra E. Ingalls, (D), SUNY (Stony Brook), 2002, Oc
Jeffrey D. Parsons, (D), Illinois, 1998, Ou
Gabrielle L. Rocap, (D), MIT/WHOI, 2000, Ob
Senior Lecturer:
Christina M. Emerick, (D), Oregon State, 1985, Ou
Lecturer:
Richard M. Strickland, (M), Washington, 1975, Ob
Adjunct Professor:
Rose Ann Cattolico, (D), SUNY (Stony Brook), 1973, On
Robert Francis, (D), Washington, 1970, Ob
Barbara B. Krieger-Brockett, (D), Wayne State, 1976, Ob
Ronald T. Merrill, (D), California (Berkeley), 1967, Ym
Bruce K. Nelson, (D), California (Los Angeles), 1985, Cc
Edward Sarachik, (D), Brandeis, 1966, Oa
Robert C. Spindel, (D), Yale, 1971, Op
Emeritus:
George C. Anderson, (D), Washington, 1954, Ob
Karl Banse, (D), Kiel, 1955, Ob
Joe S. Creager, (D), Texas A&M, 1958, Ou
Alyn C. Duxbury, (D), Texas A&M, 1963, On
Terry E. Ewart, (D), Washington, 1965, Op
Richard H. Gammon, (D), Harvard, 1970, Oc
Eric L. Kunze, (D), Washington, 1985, Op
Joyce C. Lewin, (D), Yale, 1953, Ob
Brian T. R. Lewis, (D), Wisconsin, 1970, Yr
Dean A. McManus, (D), Kansas, 1959, Ou
Gunnar I. Roden, (M), California (Los Angeles), 1956, Op
David A. Rothrock, (D), Cambridge, 1968, Op
Richard W. Sternberg, (D), Washington, 1965, Ou
Cooperating Faculty:
Matthew H. Alford, (D), California (San Diego), 1998, Op
Edward T. Baker, (D), Washington, 1973, Ou
Laurie Balistrieri, (M), Washington, 1977, Oc
John Bullister, (D), California (San Diego), 1984, Oc
David A. Butterfield, (D), Washington, 1990, Yr
Glenn A. Cannon, (D), Johns Hopkins, 1969, Op
Meghan F. Cronin, (D), Rhode Island, 1993, Op
Brian D. Dushaw, (D), California (San Diego), 1992, Op
Richard A. Feely, (D), Texas A&M, 1974, Oc
Don E. Harrison, (D), Harvard, 1977, Op
Albert Hermann, (N), Op
Robin T. Holcomb, (D), Stanford, 1981, Ou
Gregory C. Johnson, (D), MIT/WHOI, 1990, Op
Peter A. Jumars, (D), California (San Diego), 1974, Ob
Kathryn A. Kelly, (D), California (San Diego), 1983, Op
William S. Kessler, (D), Washington, 1989, Op
Craig M. Lee, (D), Washington, 1995, Op
Michael J. McPhaden, (D), California (San Diego), 1980, Og
Curtis D. Mobley, (D), Maryland, 1977, Ob
Harold O. Mofjeld, (D), Washington, 1970, Op
Dennis W. Moore, (D), Harvard, 1968, Op
James H. Morison, (D), Washington, 1980, Op
Jeffrey Napp, (D), California (San Diego), 1986, Ob
Jan Newton, (D), Washington, 1989, Ob
Jeffrey A. Nystuen, (D), California (San Diego), 1985, Op
Joan M. Oltman-Shay, (D), California, 1986, Op
Mary Jane Perry, (D), California (San Diego), 1974, Ob
Thomas Pratt, (N), Gu
Joseph A. Resing, (D), Hawaii, 1997, Oc
Christopher L. Sabine, (D), Hawaii, 1992, Oc
Randy Shuman, (D), Washington, 1978, Op
Laurenz A. Thomsen, (D), Kiel, 1992, Ob
Cynthia T. Tynan, (D), California (San Diego), 1993, Ob
Rebecca A. Woodgate, (D), Oxford, 1994, Op

Walla Walla Community College
Walla Walla Community College (2014)
500 Tausick Way
Walla Walla, WA 99362
p. (509) 527-4278
steven.may@wwcc.edu
http://www.wwcc.edu

Washington State University
Dept of Crop & Soil Sciences (B,M,D) (2014)
201 Johnson Hall
P.O. Box 646420
Pullman, WA 99164-6420
p. (509) 335-3475
alexande@mail.wsu.edu
http://css.wsu.edu/
Enrollment (2000): B: 8 (1) M: 13 (4) D: 11 (2)
Chair:
Richard Koenig, (D)
Professor:
David F. Bezdicek, (D), Minnesota, 1967, Sb
James B. Harsh, (D), California (Berkeley), 1983, Sc
Shiou Kuo, (D), Maine, 1973, Sc
Thomas A. Lumpkin, (D), Hawaii, 1978, On
William L. Pan, (D), North Carolina, 1983, Sb
John P. Reganold, (D), California (Davis), 1980, Ou
Senior Scientist:
Robert G. Stevens, (D), Colorado State, 1971, Sb
Associate Professor:
Craig G. Cogger, (D), Cornell, 1979, Ou
Joan R. Davenport, (D), Guelph, 1985, Sb
Bruce E. Frazier, (D), Wisconsin, 1975, Or
Frank J. Peryea, (D), California, 1983, Sc
Assistant Professor:
Markus Flury, (D), Swiss Fed Inst Tech, 1994, Sp
Adjunct Professor:
Alan J. Busacca, (D), California (Davis), 1982, Sa
Ann C. Kennedy, (D), North Carolina State, 1985, Sb
Robert I. Papendick, (D), South Dakota State, 1962, Sp
Jeffery L. Smith, (D), Washington State, 1983, Sb

Dept of Environmental and Ecosystem Sciences (B,M,D) (2014)
PO Box 644430
Troy Hall 305
Pullman, WA 99164-4430
p. (509) 335-8538
ckkeller@wsu.edu
http://esrp.wsu.edu
Administrative Assistant: Elaine O'Fallon
Enrollment: No data reported since 1999
Chair:
William W. Budd, (D), Pennsylvania, 1983, On
Professor:
Gerald L. Young, (D), Indiana, 1968, On
Senior Scientist:
Antone L. Brooks, (D), Cornell, 1967, On
Associate Professor:
F. Andrew Ford, (D), Dartmouth, 1975, On
Eldon H. Franz, (D), Illinois, 1971, Sf
R. Gene Schreckhise, (D), Colorado State, 1974, On
Assistant Professor:
Edward J. Brook, (D), MIT/WHOI, 1993, Gl
Theodora A. Tsongas, (D), Colorado, 1976, On
Adjunct Professor:
James L. Conca, (D), Caltech, 1985, On
John R. Johnson, (D), British Columbia, 1973, On
Emmett B. Moore, (D), Minnesota, 1956, On
C. David Whiteman, (D), Colorado State, 1980, On
James A. Wise, (D), Washington, 1970, On
Judith V. Wright, (D), Oregon, 1985, On
Emeritus:
George W. Hinman, (D), Carnegie Mellon, 1952, On
Cooperating Faculty:
Cindy Kaag, (D), Washington State, 2008, On

Peter Hooper GeoAnalytical Lab (B,M,D) (2016)
School of the Environment
1228 Webster Physical Sciences Building
Washington State University
Pullman, WA 99164-2812
p. (509) 335-1626
geolab@mail.wsu.edu
http://environment.wsu.edu/facilities/geolab/
Professor:
John A. Wolff, (D), London (UK), 1983, Gi

164

Research Associate:
  Owen K. Neill, (D), Alaska (Fairbanks), 2012, Ca
Emeritus:
  Franklin F. Foit, Jr., (D), Michigan, 1968, Gz
Laboratory Manager:
  Scott Boroughs, (D), Washington State, 2010, GiCa
Research Technologist:
  Charles Knaack, (M), Washington State, 1991, Ca

School of the Environment (B,M,D) ● (2015)
Webster 1228
P.O. Box 642812
Pullman, WA 99164-2812
  p. (509) 335-3009
  soe@wsu.edu
  http://environment.wsu.edu/
  Enrollment (2009): B: 34 (11) M: 30 (9) D: 11 (5)
Professor:
  Stephen Bollens, (D), Washington, 1990, Ob
  David R. Gaylord, (D), Wyoming, 1983, Gs
  C. Kent Keller, (D), Waterloo, 1987, Hw
  Peter B. Larson, (D), Caltech, 1983, Cs
  Dirk Schulze-Makuch, (D), Wisconsin (Milwaukee), 1996, Hw
  John A. Wolff, (D), Imperial Coll (UK), 1983, Giv
Associate Professor:
  Long P. Long , (D), Princeton, 2010, Gc
  Jeffrey D. Vervoort, (D), Cornell, 1994, Ca
Clinical Assistant Professor:
  Allyson Beall, (D)
Assistant Professor:
  Catherine Cooper, (D), Rice, 2005, Yg
Research Associate:
  Scott Boroughs, (D), Washington State, 2010, Gv
  Zhenqing Shi, (D)
  Victor Valencia, (D), Arizona, Og
Instructor:
  Kurt Wilkie, (D)
Adjunct Professor:
  Cailin Huyck Orr
  Regan L. Patton, (D), Washington State, 1997, Gc
  Stephen P. Reidel, (D), Washington State, 1978, Gi
Emeritus:
  Franklin F. Foit, Jr., (D), Michigan, 1968, Gz
  Andrew Ford, (D), Dartmouth, 1975, Ou
  George Hinman
  Philip E. Rosenberg, (D), Penn State, 1960, GzCg
  A. John Watkinson, (D), Imperial Coll (UK), 1972, Gc
  Gary D. Webster, (D), California, 1966, Pis

Wenatchee Valley College
Earth Sciences (A) (2012)
1300 Fifth Street
Wenatchee, WA 98801
  p. (509) 682-6754
  rdawes@wvc.edu
  http://www.wvc.edu
Professor:
  Ralph Dawes, (D), Washington, 1993, GgeOw
Adjunct Professor:
  Kelsay Stanton, (M), W Washington, 2005, GgOe

Western Washington University 🗇
Dept of Geology (B,M) ○ (2015)
516 High Street
Bellingham, WA 98225-9080
  p. (360) 650-3582
  chris.sutton@wwu.edu
  http://geology.wwu.edu/
  Administrative Assistant: Chris Sutton
  Enrollment (2010): B: 127 (35) M: 17 (6)
Chair:
  Bernard A. Housen, (D), Michigan, 1994, Ym
Professor:
  Susan M. DeBari, (D), Stanford, 1991, GxOe
  Thor A. Hansen, (D), Yale, 1978, Pg
  Scott R. Linneman, (D), Wyoming, 1990, GmOe

Robert J. Mitchell, (D), Michigan Tech, 1996, Hw
  Elizabeth R. Schermer, (D), MIT, 1989, Gt
Associate Professor:
  Jackie Caplan-Auerbach, (D), Hawaii, Ys
  Douglas H. Clark, (D), Washington, 1995, Gl
Assistant Professor:
  Colin B. Amos, (D), California (Santa Barbara), 2007, Gc
  Brady Z. Foreman, (D), Wyoming, 2012, Grs
  Sean R. Mulcahy, (D), California (Davis), 2009, GpzGp
  Melissa S. Rice, (D), Cornell, 2012, XgGs
  Pete Stelling, (D), Alaska (Fairbanks), 2003, GxEgGv
Research Associate:
  M. Clark Blake, (D), Stanford, 1965, Gt
  Russell F. Burmester, (D), Princeton, 1974, Ym
  Charles A. Ross, (D), Yale, 1964, Pm
Emeritus:
  R. Scott Babcock, (D), Washington, 1970, Cg
  Edwin H. Brown, (D), California (Berkeley), 1966, Gp
  Don J. Easterbrook, (D), Washington, 1962, Gm
  David C. Engebretson, (D), Stanford, 1983, Gt
  James L. Talbot, (D), Adelaide, 1962, Gc

Whatcom Community College
Science Dept (A) (2015)
237 W. Kellogg Road
Bellingham, WA 98226
  p. (360) 383-3539
  nlangstraat@whatcom.ctc.edu
  http://www.whatcom.ctc.edu
Assistant Professor:
  Kaatje Kraft, (D), Arizona State, 2014, Gg
Adjunct Professor:
  Bernie Dougan, (M), W Washington, 1990, Gg

Whitman College
Dept of Geology (B) (2015)
345 Boyer
Walla Walla, WA 99362
  p. (509) 527-5225
  nicolakp@whitman.edu
  http://www.whitman.edu/geology
  Administrative Assistant: Patti Moss
  Enrollment (2015): B: 67 (19)
Chair, Associate Professor:
  Kirsten P. Nicolaysen, (D), MIT, 2001, GiCgGa
Professor:
  Kevin R. Pogue, (D), Oregon State, 1993, Gc
  Patrick K. Spencer, (D), Washington, 1984, Pg
Assistant Professor:
  Nicholas Bader, (D), California (Santa Cruz), 2006, SpGeOi
  Lyman P. Persico, New Mexico, 2012, Gm
Visiting Assistant Professor:
  Bryn Kimball, (D), Penn State, 2009, ClEgGz
  Grant T. Shimer, (D), Alaska (Fairbanks), 2013, Gsr
Emeritus:
  Robert J. Carson, (D), Washington, 1970, Gm
Geology Technologist:
  Angela McGuire, (M), W Washington, 2014, Gi

Yakima Valley College
Dept of Geology (A) (2010)
P. O. Box 22520
16th Ave. & Nob Hill Blvd.
Yakima, WA 98907
  p. (509) 575-2350 x2366
  dhuycke@yvcc.edu
  http://www.yvcc.edu/FutureStudents/AcademicOptions/
  Programs/PhysicalSciences/Geology/Pages/
  Enrollment (2005): A: 4 (0)
Instructor:
  David Huycke, (M), Wyoming, 1979, Gg

West Virginia

Concord University

Dept of Physical Sciences (B) O (2015)
1000 Vermillion St.
Athens, WV 24712-1000
p. (304) 384-5327
allenj@concord.edu
http://hub.concord.edu/physci
t: @CUGeology
Enrollment (2015): B: 33 (7)
Chair:
Joseph L. Allen, (D), Kentucky, 1994, Gc
Associate Professor:
Stephen C. Kuehn, (D), Washington State, 2002, CaGv
Research Associate:
Lewis Cook, (D), West Virginia, 2010, GbPg
Robert Peck, (D), Pennsylvania, 1969, Pg
Lecturer:
Eva Lyon, (M), Utah State, 2012, Gg
Adjunct Professor:
Alyce Lee, (D), Texas A&M, 2009, Og

Fairmont State University

College of Science and Technology (B) (2015)
1201 Locust Avenue
Fairmont, WV 26554
p. (304) 367-4393
dhemler@fairmontstate.edu
Coordinator of Geoscience Program:
Deb Hemler, (D), West Virginia, 1997, Oe
Instructor:
Pamela Casto, (M), Oe
Todd Ensign, (M), N Arizona, Oe
Jaime L. Ford, (M), Fairmont State, 2014, Oe
Visiting Professor:
Marcie Raol, (M), West Virginia, Oe

Marshall University

Dept of Geology (B,M) (2015)
One John Marshall Drive
Huntington, WV 25755
p. (304) 696-6720/(304) 696-6756
geology@marshall.edu
http://marshall.edu/geology
Enrollment (2015): B: 28 (5) M: 3 (0)
Professor:
Ronald L. Martino, (D), Rutgers, 1981, Gs
Chair:
William L. Niemann, (D), Missouri (Rolla), 1999, Ng
Associate Professor:
Aley El Shazly, (D), Stanford, 1991, GpiCg
Assistant Professor:
Mitchell Scharman, (D), Texas (El Paso), 2011, GctYg

Potomac State College

Dept of Geology & Geography (A) (2010)
101 Fort Avenue
Keyser, WV 26726
p. (304) 788-6956
JJNinesteel@mail.wvu.edu
Enrollment: No data reported since 1999
Professor:
Judy J. Ninesteel, (M), West Virginia, 1995, Hg

West Virginia University

Dept of Geology & Geography (B,M,D) (2015)
330 Brooks Hall
P.O. Box 6300
98 Beechurst Ave.
Morgantown, WV 26506-6300
p. (304) 293-5603
steve.kite@mail.wvu.edu
http://www.geo.wvu.edu

Enrollment (2011): B: 165 (21) M: 45 (10) D: 13 (1)
Professor:
Robert E. Behling, (D), Ohio State, 1971, Gm
Timothy R. Carr, (D), Wisconsin, 1981, GoYe
Joseph J. Donovan, (D), Penn State, 1992, Hq
Thomas W. Kammer, (D), Indiana, 1982, Pi
Henry W. Rauch, (D), Penn State, 1972, Hw
John J. Renton, (D), West Virginia, 1965, Ec
Timothy A. Warner, (D), Purdue, 1992, Or
Thomas H. Wilson, (D), West Virginia, 1980, Ye
Chair:
J. Steven Kite, (D), Wisconsin, 1983, Gm
Associate Chair:
Helen M. Lang, (D), Oregon, 1983, Gpz
Associate Professor:
Kathleen Benison, (D), GrsCm
Dengliang Gao, (D), Duke, 1997, Ye
Jaime Toro, (D), Stanford, 1998, Gc
Dorothy Vesper, (D), Penn State, 2002, Hw
Teaching Assistant Professor:
Joe Lebold, (D), West Virginia, 2005, OePs
Assistant Professor:
Shikha Sharma, (D), Lucknow Univ (India), 1998, Csa
Amy L. Weislogel, (D), Stanford, 2006, Gs
Adjunct Professor:
Katherine Lee Avary, (M), North Carolina, 1978, Go
Bascom (Mitch) Blake, (D), West Virginia, 2009, Gs
Alan Brown, (D), Louisiana State, 2002, EoYe
Katherine R. Bruner, (D), West Virginia, 1991, Gd
David Campagna, (D), Purdue, 1990, Gc
Blaine Cecil, (D), West Virginia, 1965, Ec
Phillip Dinterman
Harry Edenborn, (D), Rutgers, 1982, Scb
Evan J. Fedorko, (M), West Virginia, Oi
Nick Fedorko, (M), West Virginia, 1998, Ec
William Grady, (M), West Virginia, 1978, Ec
Michael Ed Hohn, (D), Indiana, 1976, Gq
Paula J. Hunt, (M), Purdue, 1988, Gg
Ronald McDowell, (D), Colorado Mines, 1987, Gg
Douglas Patchen, (D), Syracuse, 1971, Go
Zhihong Zheng
Paul F. Ziemkiewicz,
Emeritus:
Alan C. Donaldson, (D), Penn State, 1959, Gs
Robert C. Shumaker, (D), Cornell, 1960, Go
Richard A. Smosna, (D), Illinois, 1973, GrEo

Wisconsin

Beloit College

R.D. Salisbury Dept of Geology (B) (2016)
700 College Street
Beloit, WI 53511
p. (608) 363-2223
rougviej@beloit.edu
http://www.beloit.edu/geology/
f: https://www.facebook.com/groups/47867916990/
Enrollment (2015): B: 20 (11)
Chair:
James R. Rougvie, (D), Texas, 1999, GxpGz
Professor:
Carl V. Mendelson, (D), California (Los Angeles), 1981, Pm
Susan K. Swanson, (D), Wisconsin, 2001, Hw
Tech & Safety Officer:
Stephen M. Ballou, (B), Beloit, 1998, Gg
Cooperating Faculty:
Carol Mankiewicz, (D), Wisconsin, 1987, Gs

Lawrence University

Dept of Geology (B) (2016)
711 E Boldt Way
Appleton, WI 54912
p. (920) 832-6731
knudsena@lawrence.edu
http://www.lawrence.edu/dept/geology/
Administrative Assistant: Ellen c. Walsh

Enrollment (2015): B: 20 (5)
Professor:
  Marcia Bjornerud, (D), Wisconsin, 1987, Gc
Associate Professor:
  Jeffrey J. Clark, (D), Johns Hopkins, 1997, Gm
Assistant Professor:
  Andrew Knudsen, (D), Idaho, 2002, Cg
Visiting Professor:
  Ellen K. Schaal, (D), Stanford, 2014, Pg
Emeritus:
  John C. Palmquist, (D), Iowa, 1961, Gc
  Theodore W. Ross, (D), Washington State, 1969, Gg
  Ronald W. Tank, (D), Indiana, 1962, Ge

Milwaukee Public Museum
Dept of Geology (2011)
800 W. Wells Street
Milwaukee, WI 53233
  p. (414) 278-2741
  sheehan@mpm.edu
  http://www.mpm.edu/collect/geology/geosec-noframes.html
Chair:
  Peter M. Sheehan, (D), California (Berkeley), 1971, Pi

Northland College
Dept of Geosciences (B) ● (2015)
1411 Ellis Avenue
Ashland, WI 54806
  p. (715) 682-1852
  tfitz@northland.edu
  Enrollment (2015): B: 23 (7)
Professor:
  Bruce A. Goetz, (M), S Illinois, 1969, GgmHg
Associate Professor:
  Thomas J. Fitz, (D), Delaware, 1999, GgxGc
Instructor:
  Cynthia May, (M), Penn State, 2007, Oiy

Saint Norbert College
Geology Dept (B) (2015)
100 Grant Street
De Pere, WI 54115
  p. (920) 403-3987
  tim.flood@snc.edu
  http://www.snc.edu
  Enrollment (2015): B: 23 (7)
Professor:
  Tim P. Flood, (D), Michigan State, 1987, Gv
  Nelson R. Ham, (D), Wisconsin, 1994, Gl
Assistant Professor:
  Rebecca McKean , (D), Nebraska, 2009, GdPgGh

University of Wisconsin Colleges
Dept of Geography & Geology (A) (2016)
UW Sheboygan
1 University Dr
Sheboygan , WI 53081
  p. (920) 459-6619
  jim.mccluskey@uwc.edu
  http://www.uwc.edu/depts/geography-geology
Chair:
  Karl Byrand, (D), Maryland, 1999, Ony
Chair/CEO UW Marathon County:
  Keith Montgomery, (D), Waterloo, 1986, OyGg
Professor:
  Diann Kiesel, (D), Wisconsin, 1998, GgOyGg
  Robert McCallister, (D), Wisconsin, 1996, OyGgOn
Dean/CEO UW Washington County:
  Alan Paul Price, (D), California (Los Angeles), 1998, OyGgOn
Associate Professor:
  Iddrisu Adam, (D), Wilfrid Laurier, 2001, OynOn
  Norlene Emerson, (D), Wisconsin, 2002, GgOy
  Michael Jurmu, (D), Indiana State, 1999, OyGgOn
Assistant Professor:
  Beth Johnson, (D), N Illinois, 2009, Glh

James McCluskey, (D), Rutgers, 1987, OinOn
Miclelle Palma, (D), Georgia, 2012, OnnOn
Andrew Shears, (D), Kent State, 2011, Oin
Keith West, (D), Wisconsin (Milwaukee), 2007, OynOn
Instructor:
  Sanborn Robert, (M), 1991, GgOyn
  Mengist Teklay Berhe
Lecturer:
  Jane Fairchild, (M), Wisconsin, 2003, Ow
  Seth Rankin, (M), Wisconsin (Milwaukee), 1974, OnnOn
Emeritus:
  Thomas Bitner, (M), OynOn
  James Brey, (D), Wisconsin, OywOn
  Richard Cleek, (M), OnyOn
  Garret Deckert, (M), OynOn
  Edwin Dommissee, (M), OyGgOn
  James Heidt, (M), On
  Cary Komoto, (D), Minnesota, 1994, OnnOn
  Kenneth Korb, (D)
  Gene E. Musolf, (D), Wisconsin, 1970, Oy
  Shamim Naim, (D)
  Randall Rohe, (D), Colorado, 1978, OyGgOn
  Leonard Weis, (D)
  Barbara Williams, (D)

University of Wisconsin, Eau Claire
Dept of Geology (B) (2015)
157 Phillips Hall
Eau Claire, WI 54702-4004
  p. (715) 836-3732
  steinklm@uwec.edu
  http://www.uwec.edu/academic/geology
  Administrative Assistant: Lorilie M. Steinke
  Enrollment (2011): B: 88 (0)
Chair:
  Kent M. Syverson, (D), Wisconsin, 1992, Gl
Professor:
  Karen G. Havholm, (D), Texas, 1991, Oe
  Robert L. Hooper, (D), Washington State, 1983, Gz
  Phillip D. Ihinger, (D), Caltech, 1991, Gx
  J. Brian Mahoney, (D), British Columbia, 1994, Gs
Assistant Professor:
  Scott K. Clark, (D), Illinois (Urbana-Champaign), 2007, Oe
  Geoffrey S. Pignotta, (D), S California, 2006, Gcg
Senior Lecturer:
  Lori D. Snyder, (M), British Columbia, 1994, Gx

University of Wisconsin, Extension
Dept of Environmental Sciences (2009)
3817 Mineral Point Road
Madison, WI 53705-5100
  p. (608) 262-1705
  kmzwettl@wisc.edu
Professor:
  John W. Attig, (D), Wisconsin, 1984, Gl
  Kenneth R. Bradbury, (D), Wisconsin, 1982, Hw
  Thomas J. Evans, (D), Wisconsin, 1994, Gg
  James M. Robertson, (D), Michigan, 1972, Eg
Associate Professor:
  Madeline B. Gotkowitz, (M), New Mexico, 1993, Hw
  David J. Hart, (D), Wisconsin, 2000, Hw
Assistant Professor:
  Eric C. Carson, (D), Wisconsin, 2003, Gl
  Patrick I. McLaughlin, (D), Cincinnati, 2006, Gr
Emeritus:
  Lee Clayton, (D), Illinois, 1965, Gl

University of Wisconsin, Green Bay ☐
Dept of Natural and Applied Science-Geoscience Program (B,M)
(2015)
LS-465
2420 Nicolet Drive
Green Bay, WI 54311
  p. (920) 465-2371
  luczajj@uwgb.edu
  http://www.uwgb.edu/geoscience/

Enrollment (2015): B: 16 (3) M: 6 (0)
Interim Chair:
 Kevin J. Fermanich, (D), Wisconsin, 1995, SpHwOu
Professor:
 John A. Luczaj, (D), Johns Hopkins, 2000, GsgHw
Associate Professor:
 Steven J. Meyer, (D), Nebraska, 1990, OawOg
Assistant Professor:
 Ryan Currier, (D), Johns Hopkins, 2011, GizGg
Emeritus:
 Steven I. Dutch, (D), Columbia, 1976, GcgGe
 Ronald D. Stieglitz, (D), Illinois, 1972, Gr

University of Wisconsin, Madison ⬁
Center for Limnology (M,D) (2016)
680 North Park Street
Madison, WI 53706
 p. (608)262-3014
 steve.carpenter@wisc.edu
 http://limnology.wisc.edu/
 Enrollment: No data reported since 1999
Chair:
 Kenneth Potter, (D), Johns Hopkins, Ng
Professor:
 Michael S. Adams, (D), California (Riverside), 1968, Ob
 Anders W. Andren, (D), Florida State, 1972, Oc
 David E. Armstrong, (D), Wisconsin, 1966, Oc
 Steve Carpenter, (D), Wisconsin, 1979, Ob
 Calvin B. DeWitt, (D), Michigan, 1963, Ob
 Stanley I. Dodson, (D), Washington, 1970, Ob
 Linda K. Graham, (D), Michigan, 1975, Ob
 John A. Hoopes, (D), MIT, 1965, Oo
 James F. Kitchell, (D), Colorado, 1970, Ob
 John E. Kutzbach, (D), Wisconsin, 1966, Pe
 William C. Sonzogni, (D), Wisconsin, 1974, Oc
 Joy Zedler, (D), Wisconsin, 1968, Ob
Associate Professor:
 Emily Stanley, (D), Arizona State, 1993, Ob
Assistant Professor:
 Sarah Hotchkiss, (D), Minnesota, 1998, Ob
 Carol Lee, (D), Washington, 1998, Ob
 Zheng-yu Liu, (D), MIT, 1991, Op
 Katherine McMahon, (D), California (Berkeley), 2002, Ng
 Jake Vander Zanden, (D), McGill, 1999, On
 Chin Wu, (D), MIT, Ng

Dept of Atmospheric & Oceanic Sciences (B,M,D) (2015)
1225 W. Dayton Street
Atmospheric, Oceanic & Space Science Building
Madison, WI 53706-1695
 p. (608)262-2828
 aos@aos.wisc.edu
 http://www.aos.wisc.edu
 Enrollment (2011): B: 24 (14) M: 32 (9) D: 34 (5)
Chair:
 Grant W. Petty, (D), Washington, 1990, Or
Professor:
 Steven A. Ackerman, (D), Colorado State, 1987, Or
 Matthew H. Hitchman, (D), Washington, 1985, Oa
 Zhengyu Liu, (D), MIT, 1991, Op
 Jonathan E. Martin, (D), Washington, 1992, Ow
 Michael C. Morgan, (D), MIT, 1994, Ow
 Gregory J. Tripoli, (D), Colorado State, 1986, Ow
 Pao-Kuan Wang, (D), California (Los Angeles), 1978, Oa
Senior Scientist:
 Edwin W. Eloranta, (D), Wisconsin, 1972, Yr
Affiliate:
 Tracey Holloway, (D), Princeton, 2001, Oa
Affiliate :
 Chris Kucharik, (D), Wisconsin, 1997, Oa
 John W. Williams, (D), Brown, 1999, Pe
Associate Professor:
 Ankur R. Desai, (D), Penn State, 2006, Oa
 Galen McKinley, (D), MIT, 2002, Ob
 Daniel J. Vimont, (D), Washington, 2001, Oa
Affiliate:
 Samuel Stechmann, (D), Courant Inst, 2008, Ona

Assistant Professor:
 Larissa E. Back, (D), Washington, 2007, Oa
 Tristan S. L'Ecuyer, (D), Colorado State, 2001, Oa
Adjunct Associate Professor:
 Jeffrey R. Key, (D), Colorado, 1988, Or
Adjunct :
 Andrew Heidinger, (D), Colorado State, 1998, Or
Adjunct Professor:
 Larry K. Berg, (D), British Columbia, Oa
 James Kossin, (D), Colorado State, 2000, Oa
 Steven Platnick, (D), Arizona, Or
Emeritus:
 Francis P. Bretherton, (D), Cambridge, 1961, Og
 Stefan L. Hastenrath, (D), Bonn, 1959, Oa
 David D. Houghton, (D), Washington, 1963, Oa
 Donald R. Johnson, (D), Wisconsin, 1965, Oa
 John E. Kutzbach, (D), Wisconsin, 1966, Oa
 John M. Norman, (D), Wisconsin, 1971, So
 Robert A. Ragotzkie, (D), Wisconsin, 1953, Ob
 John A. Young, (D), MIT, 1966, Oa
Research Specialist:
 Dierk T. Polzin, (B), Wisconsin, Oa
Emeritus:
 Linda M. Keller, (M), Wisconsin, Oa

Dept of Geography (B,M,D) (2014)
550 N. Park St.
Madison, WI 53706
 p. (608) 262-2138
 smkahn@geography.wisc.edu
 http://www.geography.wisc.edu
 Enrollment (2010): B: 157 (30) M: 59 (4) D: 0 (1)

Dept of Geoscience (B,M,D) ● (2015)
1215 West Dayton Street
Madison, WI 53706
 p. (608) 262-8960
 geodept@geology.wisc.edu
 http://geoscience.wisc.edu/geoscience/
 Enrollment (2009): B: 58 (17) M: 20 (6) D: 42 (4)
Chair:
 Harold Tobin, (D), California (Santa Cruz), 1995, Yg
Professor:
 Jean M. Bahr, (D), Stanford, 1986, Hw
 Philip E. Brown, (D), Michigan, 1980, Em
 Alan R. Carroll, (D), Stanford, 1991, Gs
 D. Charles DeMets, (D), Northwestern, 1988, Ym
 Kurt Feigl, (D), MIT, 1991, Yd
 Dana H. Geary, (D), Harvard, 1986, Po
 Laurel Goodwin, (D), California (Berkeley), 1988, Gc
 Clark M. Johnson, (D), Stanford, 1986, Cc
 D. Clay Kelly, (D), North Carolina, 1999, Pm
 Eric E. Roden, (D), Maryland, 1990, Py
 Bradley S. Singer, (D), Wyoming, 1990, Cc
 Clifford H. Thurber, (D), MIT, 1981, Ys
 Basil Tikoff, (D), Minnesota, 1994, Gc
 John W. Valley, (D), Michigan, 1980, Gp
 Herbert F. Wang, (D), MIT, 1971, Yg
Senior Scientist:
 Brian L. Beard, (D), Wisconsin, 1992, Cc
 John Fournelle, (D), Johns Hopkins, 1989, Gi
Associate Professor:
 Shanan Peters, (D), Chicago, 2003, Gs
Assistant Professor:
 Shaun Marcott, (D), Oregon State, 2011, GlPe
 Huifang Xu, (D), Johns Hopkins, 1993, Gz
 Lucas Zoet, (D), Penn State, 2012, Gl
Adjunct Professor:
 Randy J. Hunt, (D), Wisconsin, 1993, Hw
Emeritus:
 Mary P. Anderson, (D), Stanford, 1973, Hw
 Charles R. Bentley, (D), Columbia, 1959, Yg
 Carl J. Bowser, (D), California (Los Angeles), 1965, Cl
 Charles W. Byers, (D), Yale, 1973, Pe
 Nikolas I. Christensen, (D), Wisconsin, 1963, Yx
 David L. Clark, (D), Iowa, 1957, Pm
 Robert H. Dott, Jr., (D), Columbia, 1955, Gs

Louis J. Maher, Jr., (D), Minnesota, 1961, Pl
Gordon L. Medaris, (D), California, 1966, Gi
David M. Mickelson, (D), Ohio State, 1971, Gl
Lloyd C. Pray, (D), Caltech, 1952, Gs
Museum Director:
Richard Slaughter, (D), Iowa, 2001, Pg
Geology Librarian:
Marie Dvorzak, (M), On
Related Staff:
Kenneth R. Bradbury, (D), Wisconsin, 1982, Hw
Dante Fratta, (D), Georgia Tech, 1999, Ng
Madeline B. Gotkowitz, (M), New Mexico Tech, 1993, Hw
David J. Hart, (D), Wisconsin, 2000, Hg
Thomas S. Hooyer, (D), Iowa State, 1999, Hg
David Krabbenhoft, (D), Wisconsin, 1988, Hg
James M. Robertson, (D), Michigan, 1972, Eg

Dept of Soil Science (B,M,D) (2011)
1525 Observatory Drive
Madison, WI 53706-1299
p. (608) 262-2633
slspeth@wisc.edu
http://www.soils.wisc.edu
Enrollment (2011): B: 34 (4) M: 16 (2) D: 8 (2)
Chair:
William L. Bland, (D), Wisconsin, 1984, Sp
Professor:
Phillip W. Barak, (D), Hebrew (Israel), 1988, Sc
William F. Bleam, (D), Cornell, 1984, Sc
James G. Bockheim, (D), Washington, 1972, Sf
William J. Hickey, (D), California (Riverside), 1990, Sb
King-Jau S. Kung, (D), Cornell, 1984, Sp
Birl Lowery, (D), Oregon, 1980, Sp
Frederick W. Madison, (D), Wisconsin, 1972, Sd
Kevin McSweeney, (D), Illinois, 1984, Sd
J. Mark Powell, (D), Texas A&M, 1989, So
Stephen J. Ventura, (D), Wisconsin, 1989, Or
Associate Professor:
Teri C. Balser, (D), California (Berkeley), 2000, Sb
Nick J. Balster, (D), Idaho, 1999, Sf
Carrie A.M Laboski, (D), Minnesota, 2001, So
Joel A. Pedersen, (D), California (Los Angeles), 2001, So
Assistant Professor:
Matthew D. Ruark, (D), Purdue, 2006, So
Douglas J. Soldat, (D), Cornell, 2007, So
Emeritus:
Larry G. Bundy, (D), Iowa, 1973, So
Robin F. Harris, (D), Wisconsin, 1972, Sb
Philip A. Helmke, (D), Wisconsin, 1971, Sc
Keith A. Kelling, (D), Wisconsin, 1974, So
Wayne R. Kusssow, (D), Wisconsin, 1966, So
John M. Norman, (D), Wisconsin, 1971, Sp
E. Jerry Tyler, (D), North Carolina, 1975, Sd

Geological Engineering (B,M,D) ● (2015)
1415 Engineering Drive
2205 Engineering Hall
Madison, WI 53706-1691
p. (608) 890-2662
likos@wisc.edu
http://www.gle.wisc.edu
Enrollment (2014): B: 140 (27) M: 13 (8) D: 15 (3)
Chair:
William J. Likos, (D), Colorado Mines, 2000, NgSp
Professor:
Jean M. Bahr, (D), Stanford, 1987, Hw
Kurt L. Feigl, (D), Gt
Laurel Goodwin, (D), California (Berkeley), 1998, Gt
Kenneth W. Potter, (D), Johns Hopkins, 1976, Hg
Clifford Thurber, (D), MIT, 1981, Ysx
Basil Tikoff, (D), Minnesota, 1997, Gc
Harold J. Tobin, Yr
Herbert F. Wang, (D), MIT, 1971, Yx
Chin Wu, (D), MIT, Hs
Associate Professor:
Dante Fratta, (D), Georgia Tech, 1999, Yx
Steven P. Loheide, (D), Stanford, 2006, Hw

James M. Tinjum, (D), Wisconsin, 2003, Ng
Assistant Professor:
Michael Cardiff, (D), Stanford, 2010, Hw
Matt Ginder-Vogel, (D), Stanford, 2006, Sc
Hiroki Sone, (D), Stanford, 2012, Yx
Emeritus:
Mary P. Anderson, NAE, (D), Stanford, 1973, Hw
Tuncer B. Edil, (D), Northwestern, 1973, Ng
Bezalel C. Haimson, (D), Minnesota, 1968, Nr

University of Wisconsin, Milwaukee 🗐
Dept of Geosciences (B,M,D) (2015)
P.O. Box 413
Milwaukee, WI 53201-0413
p. (414) 229-4561
geosci-office@uwm.edu
http://www4.uwm.edu/letsci/geosciences/
f: https://www.facebook.com/UWMgeosci
Enrollment (2014): B: 75 (17) M: 19 (8) D: 10 (1)
Professor:
Timothy J. Grundl, (D), Colorado, 1988, HwCl
Mark T. Harris, (D), Johns Hopkins, 1988, Gs
John L. Isbell, (D), Ohio State, 1990, Gs
Keith A. Sverdrup, (D), Scripps, 1981, Ys
Associate Professor:
Barry I. Cameron, (D), N Illinois, 1998, Gvi
Dyanna M. Czeck, (D), Minnesota, 2001, Gc
Stephen Q. Dornbos, (D), S California, 2003, Pve
Margaret L. Fraiser, (D), S California, 2005, Pi
Thomas S. Hooyer, (D), Iowa State, 1999, Gl
Lindsay J. McHenry, (D), Rutgers, 2004, Gz
Shangping Xu, (D), Princeton, 2005, Hg
Assistant Professor:
Julie Bowles, (D), Calfornia (San Diego), 2005, Ym
Erik L. Gulbranson, (D), California (Davis), 2011, CgPe
Weon Shik Han, (D), New Mexico Tech, 2008, Hw
Adjunct Professor:
Daniel T. Feinstein, (M), Wisconsin, 1986, Hw
Peter M. Sheehan, (D), California (Berkeley), 1971, Pi
Emeritus:
Douglas S. Cherkauer, (D), Princeton, 1972, Hw
William F. Kean, Jr., (D), Pittsburgh, 1972, Ym
Norman Lasca, (D), Michigan, 1965, Gm

University of Wisconsin, Oshkosh
Geography Dept (B) (2016)
800 Algoma Avenue
Oshkosh, WI 54901
p. (414) 424-4105
longco@uwosh.edu
http://www.uwosh.edu/geography/
Enrollment (2015): B: 45 (21)

Geology Dept (B) O (2015)
645 Dempsey Trail
Oshkosh, WI 54901-8649
p. (920) 424-4460
mode@uwosh.edu
http://www.uwosh.edu/departments/geology/
Administrative Assistant: Courtney Maron
Enrollment (2015): B: 62 (8)
Chair:
William N. Mode, (D), Colorado, 1980, Gl
Professor:
Eric E. Hiatt, (D), Colorado, 1997, Gs
Maureen A. Muldoon, (D), Wisconsin, 1999, Hw
Timothy S. Paulsen, (D), Illinois, 1997, Gc
Jennifer M. Wenner, (D), Boston, 2001, Gi
Assistant Professor:
Benjamin W. Hallett, (D), Rensselaer Polytechnic Inst, 2012, Gpx
Joseph E. Peterson, (D), N Illinois, 2010, PgGr
Lecturer:
Christie M. Demosthenous, (M), Illinois, 1996, Gz
Emeritus:
Norris W. Jones, (D), Virginia Tech, 1968, Gi
Gene L. La Berge, (D), Wisconsin, 1963, Eg

Thomas S. Laudon, (D), Wisconsin, 1963, Yg
James W. McKee, (D), Louisiana State, 1967, Gr
Brian K. McKnight, (D), Oregon State, 1970, Gd
Instrumentation Specialist:
Thomas J. Suszek, (M), Minnesota (Duluth), 1991, Gg

University of Wisconsin, Parkside
Dept of Geosciences (B) (2015)
Box 2000
900 Wood Road
Kenosha, WI 53141
    p. (262) 595-2744
    li@uwp.edu
    Enrollment (2015): B: 35 (14)
Chair:
Li Zhaohui, (D), SUNY (Buffalo), 1994, ClGzHw
Professor:
John D. Skalbeck, (D), Nevada (Reno), HwYgGg
Assistant Professor:
Rachel Headley, (D)
Research Associate:
Julie Kindelman, (D), Hs
Emeritus:
Gerald A. Fowler, PgGg
Allan F. Schneider, (D), Gl
James H. Shea, (D), Gs

University of Wisconsin, Platteville
Dept of Geography & Geology (B) (2011)
Platteville, WI 53818
    p. (608) 342-1791
    rawlingj@uwplatt.edu
    http://www.uwplatt.edu/geography/
    Enrollment: No data reported since 1999
Professor:
Charles W. Collins, (D), Nova, 1985, Gm
Associate Professor:
Richard A. Waugh, (D), Wisconsin, 1995, Gc
Assistant Professor:
Todd Stradford, (D), Oklahoma, 1994, Or
Mari A. Vice, (D), S Illinois, 1993, Gd
Emeritus:
William A. Broughton, (B), Wisconsin, 1938, Em
Kenneth A. Shubak, (M), Michigan, 1966, Pi

University of Wisconsin, River Falls
Dept of Plant & Earth Science (B) (2011)
410 S. Third Street
River Falls, WI 54022
    p. (715) 425-3345
    michael.d.middleton@uwrf.edu
    http://www.uwrf.edu/pes/geol/
    Program Assistant: Sue Freiermuth
    Enrollment (2006): B: 42 (19)
Chair:
Donavon H. Taylor
Professor:
Robert W. Baker, (D), Minnesota, 1976, Gl
William S. Cordua, (D), Indiana, 1973, Gx
Michael D. Middleton, (D), Colorado, 1983, Pv
Eric M. Sanden, (D), Texas Tech, 1993, Or
Donavon Taylor, (D), Minnesota, 1981, Sp
Ian S. Williams, (D), California (Santa Barbara), 1981, Yg
Associate Professor:
Kerry L. Keen, (D), Minnesota, 1992, Hw
Assistant Professor:
Laine C. Vignona, (D), Rice, 1999, Cl

University of Wisconsin, Stevens Point
Dept of Geography and Geology (B) (2015)
2001 Fourth Avenue
Stevens Point, WI 54481
    p. (715) 346-2629
    Dozsvath@uwsp.edu
    http://www.uwsp.edu/geo/

Administrative Assistant: Mary Clare Sorenson
    Enrollment (2010): B: 49 (8)
Professor:
Kevin P. Hefferan, (D), Duke, 1992, GcxGt
Neil C. Heywood, (D), Colorado, 1988, Oy
Eric J. Larson, Oregon State, 2001, Or
Karen A. Lemke, (D), Iowa, 1988, Gm
David L. Ozsvath, (D), SUNY (Binghamton), 1985, Hw
Keith W. Rice, (D), Kansas, 1989, Oir
Michael E. Ritter, (D), Indiana, 1986, Ow
Associate Professor:
Samantha W. Kaplan, (D), Wisconsin, 2003, GnPlGd
Ismaila Odogba, (D), Louisville, 2009, Oui
Instructor:
Timothy T. Kennedy, (M), Wisconsin, 2009, Oir

University of Wisconsin, Superior
Dept of Natural Sciences (B,M) (2014)
PO Box 2000
Belknap & Catlin
Superior, WI 54880
    p. (715) 394-8322
    natsci@uwsuper.edu
    Enrollment: No data reported since 1999
Professor:
William Bajjali, (D), Ottawa, 1994, HwCsGm
Assistant Professor:
Kristin E. Riker-Coleman, (D), Minnesota, 2008, Gg

University of Wisconsin, Whitewater
Geography, Geology, and Environmental Science (B) (2016)
800 W Main Street
Whitewater, WI 53190
    p. (262) 472-1071
    olsons@uww.edu
    Enrollment (2015): B: 59 (30)
Professor:
Peter Jacobs, (D), UW-Madison, 1994, SdaGm
Associate Professor:
Juk Bhattacharyya, (D), Minnesota, 2000, Gce
Rex Hanger, (D), California (Berkeley), 1992, PigGs
Science Outreach Director:
Anna Courtier, (D), Minnesota, 2009, Ysg

Wyoming

Casper College
Geology Dept (A) (2013)
Division of Physical Sciences
125 College Drive
Casper, WY 82601
    p. (307) 268-2513
    ksundell@caspercollege.edu
    http://www.caspercollege.edu/physcience/geology/
    Administrative Assistant: Shereen Mosier
    Enrollment (2012): A: 16 (4)
Head:
Kent A. Sundell, (D), California (Santa Barbara), 1985, Gg
Instructor:
Melissa Connely, (M), Utah State, 2000, Gs
Kenneth Kreckel, (B), Michigan Tech, 1970, EoYeGg
Gerald E. Nelson, (D), Kansas, 1983, Gm
Dana P. Van Burgh, (M), N Colorado, 1962, Oe

Central Wyoming College
Earth, Energy, Environment (A) (2015)
2660 Peck Avenue
Riverton, WY 82501
    p. (307) 855-2000
    ssmaglik@cwc.edu
    http://www.cwc.edu/academics/programs/earthenviron
    f: https://www.facebook.com/cwc.edu/
    Enrollment (2015): A: 5 (0)
Professor:
Suzanne M. Smaglik, (M), Colorado Mines, 1987, GgOeCg

Assistant Professor:
    Jacki Klancher, (M), Oi

Eastern Wyoming College
Eastern Wyoming College (A) (2010)
3200 West C. Street
Torrington, WY 82240
    p. (307) 532-8330
    stuart.nelson@ewc.wy.edu
    http://www.ewc.wy.edu/
Instructor:
    Chris Wenzel, GgOn

Northwest College
Northwest College (2014)
231 West 6th Street
Powell, WY 82435
    p. 307.754.6405
    Mark.Kitchen@northwestcollege.edu
    http://www.nwc.cc.wy.us/

University of Wyoming 🗇
Dept of Geology and Geophysics (B,M,D) ● (2015)
Dept. 3006
1000 E. University Ave.
Laramie, WY 82071
    p. (307) 766-3386
    geol-geophys@uwyo.edu
    http://www.uwyo.edu/geolgeophys/
    Enrollment (2015): B: 157 (26) M: 28 (7) D: 31 (2)
Head:
    Paul L. Heller, (D), Arizona, 1983, GrsGt
Professor:
    Carrick M. Eggleston, (D), Stanford, 1991, Cl
    B. Ronald Frost, (D), Washington, 1973, Gp
    Carol D. Frost, (D), Cambridge, 1984, Cc
    W. Steven Holbrook, (D), Stanford, 1989, Ys
    Neil F. Humphrey, (D), Washington, 1987, Gm
    Barbara E. John, (D), California (Santa Barbara), 1987, Gc
    Subhashis Mallick, (D), Hawaii, 1987, YseYg
    James D. Myers, (D), Johns Hopkins, 1979, Gi
    Kenneth W.W Sims, (D), California (Berkeley), 1995, CgGvCa
Senior Scientist:
    Susan M. Swapp, (D), Yale, 1982, Gp
Associate Professor:
    Michael J. Cheadle, (D), Cambridge, 1989, Yg
    Po Chen, (D), S California, 2005, YseYg
    Mark T. Clementz, (D), California (Santa Cruz), 2002, Py
    Kenneth G. Dueker, (D), Oregon, 1994, Ys
    Robert R. Howell, (D), Arizona, 1980, XgOr
    John P. Kaszuba, (D), Colorado Mines, 1997, CgGze
    Clifford S. Riebe, (D), California (Berkeley), 2000, ClGme
    Bryan N. Shuman, (D), Brown, 2001, PeGne
    Ye Zhang, (D), Indiana, 2005, Hy
Associate Scientist:
    Janet Dewey, (M), Auburn, 1993, Ca
    Laura Vietti, (D), Minnesota, 2014, Pv
Assistant Professor:
    Ellen Currano, (D), Penn State, 2008, Pb
    Dario Grana, (D), Stanford, 2013, Ye
    Brandon McElroy, (D), Texas, 2009, Gsm
    Andrew D. Parsekian, (D), Rutgers, 2011, Yg
Research Associate:
    Kevin R. Chamberlain, (D), Washington (St. Louis), 1990, Cc
Lecturer:
    Erin A. Campbell-Stone, (D), Wyoming, 1997, GcEo
Adjunct Professor:
    Vladimir Alvarado, (D), Minnesota, 1996, Np
    Eric A. Erslev, (D), Harvard, 1981, GctGg
    Warren B. Hamilton, (D), California (Los Angeles), 1951, Gt
    Peter H. Hennings, (D), Texas, 1991, Gc
    Ranie Lynds, (D), Wyoming, 2005, Gsr
Department Secretary:
    Deborah Prusia
Academic Coordinator:
    Lexi N. Edwards

Western Wyoming Community College
Western Wyoming Community College (2014)
2500 College Drive
Rock Springs, WY 82901
    p. (307) 382-1662
    webmaster@wwcc.wy.edu
    http://www.wwcc.wy.edu/academics/geology/default.htm

Algeria

Algerian Petroleum Institute
Algerian Petroleum Institute (B) (2010)
Avenue 1er Novembre
Boumerdes, Skikda, Oran 35000
    p. +213 (0) 24 81 90 56
    iap@iap.dz
    http://www.iap.dz/

Centre Universitaire de Khemis Miliana
Institut de Sciences de la Nature et de la Terre (B) (2010)
Route de Theniet El-Had
Khemis Miliana, Khemis Miliana 44225
    p. +213-27-66-42-32
    amoukabli@univ-km.dz
    http://www.cukm.org/

Universite Abou Bekr Belkaid de Tlemcen
Faculté des sciences de la nature et de la vie et sciences de la terre et de l'univers (B) (2014)
BP 119
Tlemcen 13000
    p. (+213) 040.91.59.09
    webcri@mail.univ-tlemcen.dz
    http://snv.univ-tlemcen.dz/

Universite Badji Mokhtar
Faculte des Sciences de la Terre: Amenagement du territoire, Geologie, Hydraulique, Mines (B) (2010)
BP 12
Annaba 23000
    d.fst@univ-annaba.dz
    http://www.univ-annaba.org/

Universite d' Oran
Faculté des Sciences de la Terre, de Géographie et de l'Aménagement du Territoire (B) (2010)
Es-Senia, El-Mnouar, Oran 31000
    p. +213 (41) 416939
    contact@univ-oran.dz
    http://www.univ-oran.dz/dep_geographie.htm

Universite D'Oran
Faculté des Sciences de la Terre, de la Géographie et de l'Amenagement du Territoire (B) (2015)
Rue du Colonel Lofti
Es-Senia, El-Mnouar, Oran 31000
    p. +213 (0) 41 58 19 47
    contact@univ-oran.dz
    http://www.univ-oran.dz/facultes/F_Terre/index.html

Universite de Annaba
Inst of Natural Sciences (2013)
BP 12
El Hadjar
Annaba
    http://www.univ-annaba.org/

Universite de Batna
Dept de Sciences de la Terre (B) (2014)
1, Rue Chahid Boukhlouf Mohamed
El Hadi, Batna 5000
    p. (+213) 033.86.06.02

recteur@univ-batna.dz
http://www.univ-batna.dz/

Universite de Jijel
Dept de Geologie (B,M,D) (2012)
Ouled Aissa, Jijel
    p. +213 (34) 498016
    webmaster@univ-jijel.dz
    http://www.univ-jijel.dz/

Universite de Mentouri
Dept des Sciences de la Terre/Geologie (B) (2011)
Campus Ahmed Zouaghi
B.P. 325 Route d Ain El Bey
, Constantine 25000
    p. 213 031 90 38 52
    univ-constantine@fr.fm
    http://www.umc.edu.dz/fst/

Dept de l'Amenagement du territoire (B) (2014)
Campus Ahmed Zouaghi
B.P. 325 Route d Ain El Bey
, Constantine 25000
    p. (+213) 31.90.02.07
    univ-constantine@fr.fm
    http://www.umc.edu.dz/vf/index.php/recherche-scientifique/
    annuaire-des-laboratoires/110-faculte-des-sciences-de-la-
    terre-/398-de

Universite des Sciences et de la Technologie
Inst of Earth Sciences (2011)
Houari Boumediene
B.P. 139 Dar El Beida
Eldjazair

Universite des Sciences et de la Technologie d'Oran
Dept de Geologie (B) (2011)
 Oran
    http://www.univ-usto.dz/

Universite des Sciences et de la Technologie Houari Boumediene
Faculte de Sciences de la Tere, Geographie et Amenagement du Territoire (B) (2014)
USTHB-IST BP 32 El Alia
Bab-Ezzouar Alger 16123
    p. (+213) 21247904
    aouabadi@usthb.dz
    http://www.usthb.dz/fst/

Universite Djillali Liabes Sidi Bel Abbes
Faculte des Sciences de la Nature et de la vie (B) (2010)
BP 89
Sidi Bel Abbes 22000
    p. +213 (48) 543018
    mbouziani@univ-sba.dz
    http://www.univ-sba.dz/

Universite Kasdi Merbah Ouargla
Dept des Hydrocarbures (B) (2010)
Route de Ghardaia
Ouargia
    p. +213 (29) 712468
    info@ouargla-univ.dz
    http://www.ouargla-univ.dz/index-FR.htm

Dept de Geologie (B) (2010)
Route de Ghardaia
Ouargla
    p. +213 (29) 712468
    info@ouargla-univ.dz
    http://193.194.92.30/spip/dept/filiere-hydrocarbures-chimie.
    htm

Universite M'hamed Bouguerra de Boumerdes
Faculte des Hydrocarbures et de la chimie (B) (2010)
Avenue de Ildependance
Boumerdes 35000
    p. +213 (24) 816420
    mhattab@umbb.dz
    http://www.umbb.dz/

Universite Saad Dahlab, Blida
Dept des Sciences de l'Eau et de l'Environnement (B) (2010)
BP 270
Blida 9000
    p. +213 (25) 433625
    contact@univ-blida.dz
    http://www.univ-blida.dz/fac_ingenieur/index.html

Angola

Universidade Agostinho Neto
Faculdade de Geologia (B) (2014)
Av. 4 de Fevereiro
No. 7
2 andar
Luanda C. P. 815
    p. +244-222-333-816
    info@geologia-uan.com
    http://www.geologia-uan.com/

Universidade Independente de Angola
Engenharia dos Recursos Naturais e Ambiente (B) (2013)
Rua da Missao
Bairro Morro Bento II - Corimba
Luanda
    p. (+244) 222 33 89 70
    unia@unia.ao
    http://www.unia.ao/curso.php?cr=6
Vice-Rector:
    Nuno Nascimento Gomes, (M), Lisbon, 1992, GesGu

Universite de Angola
Dept of Geology (2004)
Avenida 4 de Fevereiro 7
Caixa postal 815-C
Luanda

Argentina

Servicio Geologico Minero Argentino
Servicio Geologico Minero Argentino (2011)
Av. Julio Argentino Roca 651. P.B
Capital Federal
    mjanit@mecon.gov.ar
    http://www.segemar.gov.ar/

Universidad Nacional de Buenos Aires
Dept Ciencias Geologicas (2011)
University City Pavilion II
 Mayor Braque 2160 - CP: C1428EHA
Buenos Aires 1653
    p. (011) 4576-3329
    graciela@gl.fcen.uba.ar
    http://www.gl.fcen.uba.ar/

Universidad Nacional de Catamarca
Facultad de Tecnologia Y Ciencias Aplicadas (2011)
Maximio Victoria No. 55
San Fernando del Valle de Catamarca (470, Catamarca CP 4700
    p. (54) 0383-4435 112 int. 112
    daa@tecno.unca.edu.ar
    http://tecno.unca.edu.ar

Universidad Nacional de Cordoba
Facultad de Ciencias Exactas, Fisicas Y Naturales (2015)

Apartado 35-2060 UCR
San Pedro de Montes de Oca
San Jose, Cordoba
  p. +03514332098
  geologia@ucr.ac.cr
  http://www.geologia.ucr.ac.cr/

Universidad Nacional de Jujuy
Instituto de Geologia y Mineria (2011)
San Salvador de Jujuy , Jujuy
  narce@idgym.unju.edu.ar
  http://www.idgym.unju.edu.ar/

Universidad Nacional de la Pampa
Dept of Geologia (2011)
Uruguay 151, 6300 Santa Rosa
La Pampa
  susanapaccapelo@exactas.unlpam.edu.ar
  http://www.exactas.unlpam.edu.ar/

Universidad Nacional de la Patagonia San Juan Bosco
Facultad de Ciencias Naturales (2011)
Comodoro Rivadavia , Chubut
  secacademica@unp.edu.ar
  http://www.unp.edu.ar/

Universidad Nacional de La Plata
School of Astronomy and Geophysics (2015)
Paseo del Bosque s/n
 B1900FWA
  p. (0221)-423-6593
  academic@fcaglp.unlp.edu.ar
  http://www.fcaglp.unlp.edu.ar/

Universidad Nacional de Rio Cuarto
Dept. of Geology (B,D) O (2014)
ocampanella@gmail.com
mvillegas@exa.unrc.edu.ar
Rio Cuarto , Cordoba C.P. X5804BYA
  p. (0358) 467-6198
  webgeo@exa.unrc.edu.ar
  http://geo.exa.unrc.edu.ar/
Associate Professor:
  Monica B. Villegas, (M), UNRC, 1995, Gsc
Adjunct Professor:
  Hector Daniel Origlia, (M), Arizona State, 1999, NgOn

Universidad Nacional de Rio Negro
Dept. of Geology (2011)
Building Perito Moreno - Pacheco 460
General Roca , Rio Negro
  sedevallemedio@unrn.edu.ar
  http://www.unrn.edu.ar

Universidad Nacional de Salta
Facultad de Ciencias Naturales (2014)
Salta
  p. (0387) 425-5413
  decnat@unsa.edu.ar
  http://naturales.unsa.edu.ar/

Universidad Nacional de San Juan
Facultad de Ciencias Exactas, Físicas y Naturales (2015)
Parque de Mayo
5400 San Juan
  comunicacionfcefyn1@gmail.com
  http://exactas.unsj.edu.ar/

Universidad Nacional de San Luis
Facultad de Ciencias Exactas, Fisico, Matematicas Y Naturales (2011)
Ejército de los Andes 950

San Luis D5700HHW
  p. +54 (2652) 424027
  sacadfmn@unsl.edu.ar
  http://webfmn.unsl.edu.ar/index.php

Universidad Nacional de Tucuman
Facultad de Ciencias Naturales E Instituto Miguel Lillo (D) (2013)
Miguel Lillo 205
S.M. de Tucuman
San Miguel de Tucuman, Tucuman CP4000
  p. 0381-4239456
  info@csnat.unt.edu.ar
  http://www.csnat.unt.edu.ar/

Universidad Nacional del Comahue
Dept of Geology and Petroleum (2015)
School of Engineering
Buenos Aires 1400
Neuquen 18300 , Patagonia
  p. +54-299-4490300
  sacadfi@uncoma.edu.ar
  http://www.uncoma.edu.ar/

Universidad Nacional del Sur
Departamento de Geologia (2011)
San Juan 670
Primer Piso
Bahia Blanca
Buenos Aires 8000
  p. 54-(0291)-4595147
  secgeo@uns.edu.ar
  http://www.uns.edu.ar/

Australia

New South Wales Resources & Energy
New South Wales Resources & Energy (2014)
NSW Resource & Energy, PO Box 344
Hunter Regional Mail Centre
, NSW 2310
  p. 1300 736 122
  geologicalsurvey.info@trade.nsw.gov.au
  http://www.resourcesandenergy.nsw.gov.au/

Australian National University
Dept of Earth & Marine Sciences (B,M,D) (2005)
47 Daley Road
Canberra, ACT 0200
  p. 02 6125 2056
  ems@anu.edu.au
  http://ems.anu.edu.au/
Reader:
  D C "Bear" McPhail, (D), Princeton, 1991, Cl
Professor:
  Patrick De Deckker, (D), 1981, Gu

Research School of Earth Sciences (M,D) (2015)
Mills Rd.
Canberra, ACT 0200
  p. +61 2 6125 3406
  Director.rses@anu.edu.au
  http://rses.anu.edu.au/

Curtin University
Dept of Mining Engineering (B,M,D) (2012)
P. O. Box 597
Kalgoorlie
  e.topal@curtin.edu.au

Dept of Applied Geology (B,M,D) (2012)
GPO Box U1987
Perth, WA 6845
  p. +618 92667968
  P.Kinny@curtin.edu.au

Dept of Exploration Geophysics (B,M,D) (2015)
GPO Box U1987
Perth, WA 6845
  p. +61 8 9266-3565
  Geophysics-GeneralEnquiries@curtin.edu.au
  http://www.geophysics.curtin.edu.au/
  f: https://www.facebook.com/ExplorationGeophysicsCurtin-nUniversity
  t: @CurtinGeophys
  Enrollment (2014): B: 27 (13) M: 26 (4) D: 28 (6)
Professor:
  Boris Gurevich, (D), Moscow, 1988, Ye
Senior Lecturer:
  Vassily Mikhaltsevitch, (D), Kaliningrad State, 1997, Ye
  Andrew Peter Squelch, (D), Nottingham, 1998, NmYe
Research Fellow:
  Michael Carson, (D), Univ Coll (Dublin), 2000, Yx
  Aleksandar Dzunic, (M), Belgrade, 1989, YgsYe
Head of Department:
  Andrej Bona, (D), Calgary, 2002, Yx
Associate Professor:
  Brett D. Harris, (D), Curtin, 2002, HwYve
  Anton W. Kepic, (D), British Columbia, 1990, YexYg
  Maxim Lebedev, (D), Mowcow Inst Phys & Tech, 1990, Yx
  Roman Pevzner, (D), Moscow State, 2004, Yxx
  Milovan Urosevic, (D), Curtin, 1998, YerYx
Lecturer:
  Robert Galvin, (D), Curtin, 2006, Ye
  Stanislav Glubokovskikh, (D), Lomonosov Moscow State, 2012, Yxe
  Mahyar Madadi, (D), Inst Adv Studies Basic Sci (Zanjan), 1997, Ye
  Andrew Pethick, (D), Curtin, 2013, YevYg
  Konstantin Tertyshnikov, (D), Curtin, 2014, Ye
  Stephanie Vialle, (D), Paris 7 Univ, 2008, Yx
  Sasha Ziramov, (M), Belgrade, 2005, Ye
Lecturer:
  Eric Takam, (D), Simon Fraser, 2011, Ye
Senior Technical Officer:
  Dominic J. Howman, (B), Curtin, 1994, Ye

Federation University Australia

Dept of Geology (B,M,D) ● (2016)
Federation University
P. O. Box 663
Ballarat, VIC 3353
  p. 613 53279354
  k.dowling@federation.edu.au

Flinders University

School of Environment (B,M,D) (2014)
GPO Box 2100
Adelaide, SA 5001
  p. +61 8 8201 7577
  dean.sote@flinders.edu.au
  http://www.ssn.flinders.edu.au/geog/
  Enrollment (2012): B: 44 (14) M: 15 (5) D: 37 (4)
Professor:
  Andrew Millington, (D), Sussex (UK), OuyOr
Professor:
  Okke Batelaan, (D), Hw
  Peter Cook, (D), Hw
  Nancy Cromar, (D), Napier (UK), On
  Howard Fallowfield, (D), Leeds (UK), On
  Iain Hay, (D), Washington, 1989, Oyy
  Patrick Hesp, (D), Sydney, GmOy
  Craig Simmons, (D), Adelaide (Australia), Hw
Associate Professor:
  Richard Bentham, (D), Central Lancashire (UK), On
  Erick Bestland, (D), Wisconsin, GsSa
  Gour Dasvarma, On
  John Edwards, (D), Adelaide (Australia), On
  Jorg Hacker, (D), Ora
  Jochen Kaempf, (D), Hamburg, Op

Andew Love, (D), Hw
  Adrian Werner, (D), Queensland (Australia), Hw
Senior Lecturer:
  David Bass, (D), New England, Oy
  Simon Benger, (D), Oiy
  Beverley Clarke, (D), Adelaide (Australia), On
  Huade Guan, (D), New Mexico Tech, Hgw
  John Hutson, (D), Natal, Spc
  Andrew McGrath, (D), Ora
  Udoy Saikia, (D), On
Lecturer:
  Samantha de Ritter, (M), Flinders (Australia), Oe
  Caecilia Ewenz, (D), Bonn, Ow
  Stephen Fildes, (M), Adelaide (Australia), Ori
  Mark Lethbridge, (D), South Australia, Oiy
  Graziela Miot da Silva, (D), Fed Rio Grande do Sul (Brazil), Gug
  Vincent Post, (D), Amsterdam, Hw
  Kirstin Ross, (D), South Australia, On
Adjunct Professor:
  Sebastian Lamontangne, (D), Hw
  Jim Smith, On
  Ben van den Akker, (D), Flinders (Australia), On
  Maria Zotti, On
Visiting Professor:
  Geoffrey Codd, (D), On
Laboratory Director:
  Raj Indela, Cg
  Rob Keane, (B), Flinders (Australia), Oi

Geoscience Australia

Geoscience Australia (2015)
GPO Box 378
Canberra, ACT 2601
  p. +61 2 6249 9111
  ref.library@ga.gov.au
  http://www.ga.gov.au/

Government of South Australia - Department for State Development

Geological Survey of South Australia (2015)
GPO Box 320
Adelaide, SA 5001
  p. +61 8 8463 3000
  DSD.minerals@sa.gov.au
  http://www.minerals.statedevelopment.sa.gov.au
  t: @pace2020

James Cook University

College of Science Technology & Engineering (B,M,D) ○ (2015)
Building 015
College Science Technolgy & Engineering
James Cook University
Townsville, QLD 4811
  p. 07 4781 5047
  paul.dirks@jcu.edu.au
  https://www.jcu.edu.au/college-of-science-technology-and-engineering
  Enrollment (2015): B: 407 (67) M: 7 (1) D: 20 (1)

School of Earth & Environmental Sciences (B,M,D) (2013)
Building 34 Room 212
JAMES COOK UNIVERSITY, QLD 4811
  p. 07 47815047
  ees@jcu.edu.au
  http://www.jcu.edu.au/ees/

James Cook University of North Queensland

Economic Geology Research Centre (A,B,M,D) ○ (2014)
EGRU
James Cook University
Townsville, QLD 4811
  p. +61 7 4781 4726
  egru@jcu.edu.au
  http://www.jcu.edu.au/egru

La Trobe University
Environmental Geoscience (B,M,D) (2013)
Environmental Geoscience
La Trobe University
Victoria 3086
Melbourne, VIC 3086
    p. +61 3 9479 1273
    john.webb@latrobe.edu.au
    http://www.latrobe.edu.au/envsci/
    Enrollment (2012): B: 2 (2) D: 10 (0)
Associate Professor:
    John A. Webb, (D), Queensland, 1982, Ge
Lecturer:
    Vincent J. Morand, (D), Sydney, 1987, GgcGt
    Susan Q. White, (D), La Trobe, 2005, GmgGe

Macquarie University
Graduate School of the Environment (2004)
North Ryde, NSW 2109
    robyn.dowling@mq.edu.au
    http://www.gse.mq.edu.au/

Dept of Earth and Planetary Sciences (B,M,D) O (2015)
North Ryde
Sydney, NSW 2109
    p. 61-2-98508426
    eps-admin@mq.edu.au
    http://www.eps.mq.edu.au/
    f: https://www.facebook.com/MQeps/?fref=ts

Monash University
School of Earth, Atmosphere and Environment (B,M,D)
(2015)
PO Box 28E
Clayton, VIC 3800
    p. +61 3 99054884
    earth-atmosphere-environment@monash.edu
    http://www.earth.monash.edu.au/

Queensland University of Technology
School of Earth, Environmental & Biological Sciences
(B,M,D) O (2015)
GPO Box 2434
2 George Street
Brisbane, QLD 4001
    p. 61 7 3138 2324
    nm.davis@qut.edu.au
    https://www.qut.edu.au/science-engineering/our-schools/
    school-of-earth-environmental-and-biological-sciences/
    earth-sciences
    f: https://www.facebook.com/QUTEarthScienceUnder-
    graduatePage/
    Administrative Assistant: Noelene Davis
    Enrollment (2015): B: 25 (35) M: 15 (2) D: 9 (1)
Professor:
    Peter R. Grace, (D), Queensland, 1989, Sb
    David A. Gust, (D), Australian National, 1982, GiCpGt
Senior Research Fellow :
    Charlotte M. Allen, (D), Virginia Tech, CcaGi
Research Fellow:
    Henrietta Cathey, (D), Utah, 2006, Gip
Associate Professor:
    Scott E. Bryan, (D), Monash, 1999, GitGs
Senior Lecturer:
    Craig Sloss, (D), Wollongong (Australia), 2005, GsrGm
    Jessica Trofimovs, (D), Monash, 2003, GsrGu
Research Associate:
    Coralie Siegel, (D), QUT, 2015, GiCc
Lecturer:
    Oliver M. Gaede, (D), W Australia, YeNrYs
    Patrick Hayman, (D), Monash, 2009, EgGvp
    David T. Murphy, (D), Queensland, 2002, CgEgCc
    Luke Nothdurft, (D), Queensland Tech, 2009, GdCmGg
    Clemens Scheer, (D), Bonn, 2008, SbGe

    Christoph Schrank, (D), Toronto, 2009, GcqGt
Adjunct Professor:
    Christopher Fielding, (D), Durham, Gsr
Emeritus:
    Malcolm E. Cox, (D), Auckland, 1986, Hw
    John Rigby, Pb
Analytical Laboratory Coordinator :
    Wan-Ping (Sunny) Hu, (D), Canterbury, Ca
Other:
    Shane Russell, (B), Queensland Tech, Ca
Technician - Geology:
    Alex Hepple, (M), QUT, 2012, GpiGg
Senior Technician - Geology :
    Will Stearman, (B), Queensland Tech, 2011, Geg

Southern Cross University
School of Environment, Science & Engineering (2010)
P. O. Box 157
Lismore, NSW
    dgartsid@scu.edu.au
    http://www.scu.edu.au/schools/esm
Professor:
    Donald Gartside, (D), Melbourne
    Peter Saenger, (D), Melbourne
Associate Professor:
    Bill Boyd, (D), Glasgow, 1982, Pe
    Bradley Eyre, (D), Queensland Tech, Gs
    Peter Harrison, (D), James Cook
    Graham Jones, (D), James Cook, Ca
    Alison Specht, (D), Queensland, Sf
    Leigh Sullivan, (D), Sydney, 1988, Sc
Research Associate:
    Malcolm William Clark, (D), Ca
Lecturer:
    Danny Bucher, (D), S Cross, 2001
    Murray Cullen, (M), Griffith, Sc
    Leigh Davison, (D), New South Wales, 1974, Hs
    Simon Hartley, (B), New England
    John Doland Nichols, (D), N Arizona
    Graeme Palmer, (B), Australian National
    Sumith Pathirana, (D), Kent State, Or
    Amanda Reichelt-Brushett, (D), S Cross
    Kathryn Taffs, (D), Adelaide, Pe
    Michael Whelan

University of Adelaide
School of Earth and Environmental Sciences (2013)
Adelaide, SA 5000
    p. +61 8 8303 3999
    graham.heinson@adelaide.edu.au
    http://www.ees.adelaide.edu.au/

Australian School of Petroleum (M,D) (2014)
ASP
Santos Bldg
Adelaide, SA 5005
    p. 61-8-8313-4311
    admin@asp.adelaide.edu.au
    http://www.asp.adelaide.edu.au/

University of Canberra
Institute for Applied Ecology (2011)
    sarre@aerg.canberra.edu.au
    http://enterprise.canberra.edu.au/WWW/www-crcfe.nsf

School of Education, Science, Tecnology and Maths (2004)
P. O. Box 1
Belconnen, ACT
    ken.mcqueen@canberra.edu.au
    http://scides.canberra.edu.au/rehs/

University of Melbourne
School of Earth Sciences (B,M,D) (2014)
Melbourne, VIC 3010
    p. +61 3 8344 9866

head@earthsci.unimelb.edu.au
http://www.earthsci.unimelb.edu.au

University of New England
Earth Sciences (A,B,M,D) O (2015)
Armidale
NSW
2351
Armidale, NSW 2351
    p. +61-2-67732101
    geology@une.edu.au
    http://www.une.edu.au/about-une/academic-schools/
    school-of-environmental-and-rural-science/research/life-
    earth-and-environment/e
Associate Professor:
    John R. Paterson, (D), Macquarie, 2005, PioPs
Lecturer:
    Phil R. Bell, (D), Alberta, 2011, PgvPo
    Luke Milan, (D), GgcGp
    Nancy Vickery, (D), New England, GgeYg
Emeritus:
    Paul Ashley, (D), Macquarie, EgGeEm
    Peter Flood, (D), EcGt
    Ian Metcalfe, (D), PigGt

University of New South Wales
School of Biological, Earth & Environmental Sciences
(B,M,D) (2015)
UNSW
Sydney, NSW 2052
    p. 61 2 93852961
    bees@unsw.edu.au
    http://www.bees.unsw.edu.au/index.html
    Enrollment (2013): B: 80 (24) M: 5 (0) D: 14 (4)
Associate Professor:
    David R. Cohen, (D), New South Wales, 1990, Cet
Professor:
    Michael Archer, (D), Pv
    Andy Baker, (D), HwCs
    James Goff, (D), Gsm
    Martin van Kranendonk, (D), Queens (Canada), GxPeGd
Associate Professor:
    Suzanne Hand, (D), Pv
    Bryce Kelly, (D), New South Wales, HwYg
    Shawn Laffan, (D), OiSf
Dr:
    Ian Graham, (D), UTS Sydney, 1995, GxEg
    Paul Lennox, (D), Monash, 1985, Gc
Lecturer:
    Catherine Chague-Goff, (D), CgGs
Adjunct Professor:
    Derecke Palmer, (D), New South Wales, 2001, Ye
Visiting Professor:
    Colin R. Ward, (D), New South Wales, 1971, Gs

University of Newcastle
Discipline of Earth Sciences (B,M,D) O (2014)
School of Environmental & Life Sciences
University Drive
Callaghan, NSW 2308
    p. +61 2 4921 8976
    name.surname@newcastle.edu.au
    http://www.newcastle.edu.au/school/environ-life-science/
    Enrollment (2014): B: 132 (121) D: 5 (3)
Associate Professor:
    Silvia Frisia, (D), Milan, Italy, 1991, ClPeGd
    Phil Geary, (D), UWS, HwOsHw
    Gregory Hancock, (D), OiGmm
Lecturer:
    Judy Bailey, (D), Newcastle, 1993, Ec
    David Boutelier, (D), Gtc
    Alistair Hack, (D), GcCgEm
    Anthony Kiem, (D), HqOai
    Bill Landenberger, (D), Newcastle, Gi
    Danielle Verdon-Kidd, (D), HqOai

University of Queensland
School of Earth Sciences (B,M,D) O (2015)
Faculty of Science
Steele Building
Brisbane, QLD 4072
    p. +61 7 3365 1180
    enquiries@earth.uq.edu.au
    http://www.earth.uq.edu.au/
    Enrollment (2015): B: 106 (57) M: 38 (5) D: 60 (6)

University of South Australia
Dept of Geosciences (2004)
GPO Box 2471
Adelaide, SA 5001
    study@unisa.edu.au

University of Sydney
School of Geosciences (A,B,M,D) (2014)
Madsen Building F09
Sydney, NSW 2006
    p. +61 2 9351 2912
    sue.taylor@sydney.edu.au
    http://www.geosci.usyd.edu.au/index.shtml
Professor:
    Jonathan Aitchison, (D), UNE, 1989, GrtPm
Professor:
    Geoffrey L. Clarke, (D), Melbourne, 1987, Gp
    Dietmar Muller, (D), Scripps, 1989, Yrg

University of Tasmania
ARC Center of Excellence in Ore Deposits (M,D) O (2015)
Private Bag 79
Hobart, TAS 7001
    steve.calladine@utas.edu.au
    www.utas.edu.au/codes

School of Earth Sciences / ARC Centre for Excellence in Ore
Deposits (CODES) (B,M,D) (2013)
Private Bag 79
Hobart, TAS 7001
    p. 61 3 6226 2476
    Rose.Pongratz@utas.edu.au
    http://www.utas.edu.au/earth-sciences/home
Director:
    Ross R. Large, (D), New England, Eg
Head:
    J Bruce Gemmell, (D), Dartmouth, 1987, Eg
Professor:
    David R. Cooke, (D), Monash, Eg
    Anthony J. Crawford, (D), Melbourne, Gi
    Jocelyn McPhie, (D), New England, Gv
Associate Professor:
    Ron F. Berry, (D), Flinders (Australia), Gc
Lecturer:
    Garry J. Davidson, (D), Tasmania, Cs
    Peter J. McGoldrick, (D), Melbourne, Ce
    Anya Reading, (D), Ysg
    Michael Roach, (N), Tasmania, Yg

University of Western Australia
School of Earth & Environment (B,M,D) (2013)
M004
35 Stirling Highway
Crawley, WA 6009
    p. 6488 1921
    enquiry-see@uwa.edu.au
    http://www.see.uwa.edu.au/

University of Wollongong
School of Earth & Environmental Sciences (B,M,D) (2010)
Northfields Avenue
Wollongong, NSW 2522
    p. 61 2 4221 4419
    zenobia@uow.edu.au
    http://www.uow.edu.au/science/eesc/

Australia

Austria

Geological Survey of Austria
Geologische Bundesanstalt von Osterreich (2011)
Neulinggasse 38, A 1030
Vienna
  p. 43-1-712 56 74
  office@geologie.ac.at
  http://www.geolba.ac.at/

Karl-Franzens-Universitaet Graz
Inst for Earth Science (2014)
Heinrichstraße 26
8010 Graz
  p. +43 316 380-5587
  walter.kurz@uni-graz.at
  http://erdwissenschaften.uni-graz.at/index_en.php

Leopold-Franzens-Universitaet Innsbruck
Inst fuer Geologie (2016)
Innrain 52-f
6020 Innsbruck
  p. +43 (0) 512 / 507 - 96125
  dekanat-geowiss@uibk.ac.at
  http://www.uibk.ac.at/fakultaeten/geo_und_atmosphaeren-wissenschaften/

Montan Universitaet
Dept of Applied Geological Sciences and Geophysics (2011)
Inst. for Prospecting
A-8700 Leoben
  geologie@mu-leoben.at

Technische Universitaet Graz
Earth Sciences (2011)
Rechbauerstrasse 12
A-8010 Graz
  p. +43(0)316 873 6360
  martin.dietzel@tugraz.at

University Leoben
Dept of Geology (2005)
Montanuniversitat Leoben
Kaiser Franz Josef-Strasse 18
Leoben A-8700
  geologie@unileoben.ac.at
  http://www.unileoben.ac.at/~buero62/geologie/geologie.html

University of Innsbruck
Institute of Geology (A,B,M,D) (2015)
Innrain 52f
A-6020
Innsbruck, Austria 6020
  p. +43 512 507-54300
  regina.gratzl@uibk.ac.at
  http://www.uibk.ac.at/geologie

University of Salzburg
Inst fuer Geowissenschaften (2011)
Hellbrunner Strasse 34
A-5020 Salzburg
  p. +43-662-8044-5200 oder 5400
  geo@sbg.ac.at
  http://www.uni-salzburg.at/geo

University of Vienna
Dept of Meteorology and Geophysics (B,M,D) ● (2015)
Althanstrasse 14
A-1090 Vienna
  p. 0043 1 4277 53701
  img-wien@univie.ac.at
  http://imgw.univie.ac.at/en/imgw/
  Enrollment (2015): B: 182 (5) M: 19 (1) D: 8 (2)
Univ.-Prof.:
  Goetz Bokelmann, (D), Princeton, 1992, Ygs
Univ.-Prof.:
  Vanda Grubisic, (D), Yale, 1995, Oaw
o.Univ.-Prof.:
  Reinhold Steinacker, (D), Innsbruck, 1975, Owa

Dept of Geography (2005)
Althanstrasse 14
Vienna A-1090
  p. 00431427753401
  geographie.spl@univie.ac.at
  http://www.univie.ac.at/Geologie/
Head:
  Thilo Hofmann, (D)

Azerbaijan

Baku State University
The Faculty of Geology (2005)
23 Z. Khalilov Street
370145 Baku
  geology@bsu.az
  http://www.ceebd.co.uk/ceeed/un/az/az003.htm

Bangladesh

Jahangirnagar University
Dept of Geological Sciences (2011)
University Campus, Savar, Dhaka
Dhaka
  p. 0088 2 7791045-51 (Ext. 1402)
  rabiulju@gmail.com
  http://www.juniv.edu/home.php?pg=faculty_science

Rajshahi University
Dept of Geology & Mining (2015)
Motihar, Rajshahi
Rajshahi
  p. +880 721-750041
  chair.geology@ru.ac.bd
  http://www.ru.ac.bd/geol/index.htm

University of Dhaka
Dept of Geology (2011)
Nilkhet, Dhaka 1000
  p. 0088 2 9661900-ext (7300/7310)
  duregstr@bangla.net
  http://www.univdhaka.edu/department/common/home.php?bodyid=GLG

Belgium

Faculte Polytechnique de Mons
Dept of Geology (2004)
Fue de Houdain 9
7000 Mons
  gfa@fpms.ac.be

Faculte Univ Catholique de Mons
Dept of Geology (2004)
Chaussee de Binche 151
B-7000 Mons

Facultes Univ Notre Dame de la Paix
Dept Geologie (2004)
Rue de Bruxelles 61
B-5000 Namur
  vincent.hallet@fundp.ac.be

Geological Survey of Belgium
Service geologique de Belgique (2011)
Department VII
of the Royal Belgian Institute of Natural Sciences (RBINS)
13, Rue Jenner
1000 Brussels
    p. +32 (0)2.788.76.61
    bgd@natuurwetenschappen.be
    http://www.naturalsciences.be/geology/

Ghent University
Dept of Geology and Soil Science (B,M,D) ● (2015)
Krijgslaan 281-S8
Gent B-9000
    p. +32 9 331 01 01
    we13@ugent.be
    http://www.earthweb.ugent.be/index.php/
    f: https://www.facebook.com/GeologieUGent
Head:
    Marc De Batist, (D), GnuGs
Professor:
    Stephen Louwye, (D)
Associate Professor:
    Veerle Cnudde, (D)
    Luc Lebbe, (D)
    David Van Rooij, (D)
    Kristine Walraevens, (D)
Assistant Professor:
    Sebastien Bertrand, (D)
    Johan De Grave, (D)
    Thijs Vandenbroucke, (D)

Katholieke Universiteit Leuven
Dept of Earth and Environmental Science (B,M,D) (2014)
Department of Earth & Environmental Sciences
Redingenstraat 16
B-3000 Leuven-Heverlee
    p. (+32) 016 321450
    erik.mathjis@ees.kuleaven.be
    http://ees.kuleuven.be/
Professor:
    Patrick Degryse, (D), GaCeGf
    Jan Elsen, (D), Gz
    Philippe Muchez, (D), EmCe
    Manuel Sintubin, (D), GtcGa
    Robert Speijer, (D), Pym
    Rudy Swennen, Gso
Associate Professor:
    Okke Batelaan, (D), Hw
    Sarah Fowler, (D), Gip
Assistant Professor:
    Marijke Huysmans, (D), Hw

Dept of Geology - Geography (2004)
Redingenstraat 16
B-3000 Leuven
    Patrick.Degryse@ees.kuleuven.be

Universite Catholique de Louvain
Dept of Geology (2014)
Bâtiment Mercator
place Louis Pasteur 3
B-1348 Louvain-la-Neuve
    p. (32) 10 47 32 97
    monique.descampsl@uclouvain.be
    http://www.uclouvain.be/geo.html

Universite de Gembloux
Les ressources vivantes et l'environnement (2004)
B-5800 Gembloux

Universite de Liege
Dept of Geology (B,M,D) (2007)
Batiment B18 (secretariat)
Sart Tilman

Liege B-4000
    p. 32 4 366 22 51
    TH.Billen@ulg.ac.be
    http://www.ulg.ac.be/geolsed/geologie
chargé de cours:
    Nathalie Fagel, (D), GsuGe
    Hans-Balder Havenith, (D), Liège, Ge
Professor:
    Frederic P. Boulvain, (D), Brussels, 1990, Gs
    Andre-Mathieu Fransolet, (D), Liege, Gz
    Emmanuelle Javaux, (D), Dalhousie, 1999, Pl
    Edouard Poty, (D), Liege, Pi
    Jacqueline Vander Auwera, (D), Louvain-la-Neuve, Gx

Universite de Mons
Dept of Geology (2004)
Place du Pare 20
B-7000 Mons

Universite Libre de Bruxelles (ULB)
Département des Sciences de la Terre et de l'Environnement
(2004)
50, Ave. F. Roosevelt
Brussels 1050
    Pierre.Regnier@ulb.ac.be

University of Mons
Dept of Geology and Applied Geology (M,D) ○ (2016)
rue de Houdain, 9
Mons
    gfa@umons.ac.be

Vrije University Brussel
Earth System Sciences (D) (2015)
ESSC-WE-VUB
Faculty of Sciences
Pleinlaan 2
Brussels 1050
    p. 0113226293394
    phclaeys@vub.ac.be
    http://we.vub.ac.be/~essc
    Enrollment (2015): D: 2 (0)
Head:
    Philippe Claeys, (D), California, 1993, CgPyXc
Professor:
    Edward Keppens, (D), Vrije (Brussel), 1983, CsGeg

Bolivia
Universidad Mayor de San Andres
Dept of Geology (2014)
P. O. Box 12198
Campus Universitario Cota Cota, Calle 27
La Paz
    p. (591-2) 2441983
    webmaster@umsa.bo
    http://www.geologia.umsa.bo/

Botswana
Geological Survey of Botswana
Geological Survey of Botswana (2014)
Khama One Avenue
Plot 1734
Lobatse
    p. +267 5330327
    http://www.gov.bw/en/Ministries--Authorities/Ministries/Min-
    istry-of-Minerals-Energy-and-Water-Resources-MMWER/
    Departments1/Depar

University of Botswana
Dept of Geology (B) (2014)
4775 Notwane Rd.
Private Bag UB00704

Gaborone
  p. (267)355 2529
  geology@mopipi.ub.bw
  http://www.ub.bw/home/ac/1/fac/1/dep/79/Geology/

Dept of Environmental Science (B) (2010)
4775 Notwane Road
Private Bag UB 0022
Gaborone
  p. (267) 355-0000
  admissions@mopipi.ub.bw
  http://www.ub.bw/learning_faculties.cfm?pid=588

Brazil

Federal University of Bahia Geophysics
CPGG (2004)
Salvador
BA
  yeda@cpgg.ufba.br
  http://www/pppg.ufba.br/

Geological Survey of Brazil
Servico Geologico do Brasil (2011)
Av. SGAN- Quadra 603 - conjunto J
Parte A - 1º andar
, Brasilia - DF 70830-030
  cprmsede@df.cprm.gov.br
  http://www.cprm.gov.br/

Universidad Federal de Rio Grande do Sul
Institute de Geociencia (2004)
Avenida Bento Gonçalves, 9500
Porto Alegre, RS - 91.501-970
  p. +55 51 3308-6337
  igeo@ufrgs.br
  http://www.ufrgs.br/english/the-university/institutes-facul-
  ties-and-schools/institute-of-geoscience

Universidade de Brasília
Instituto de Geociências (2011)
Campus Universitário Darcy Ribeiro ICC - Ala Central
CEP 70.910-900 - Brasilia DF
Caixa Postal 04465.
 CEP 70919-970
  p. +61 3307-2433
  igd@unb.br
  http://www.igd.unb.br/

Universidade de Sao Paulo
Inst de Geociencias (2014)
Rua do Lago
562 Cidade Universitaria
05508-080 São Paulo
  p. 63.025.530/0007-08
  gmgigc@usp.br
  http://www.igc.usp.br/

Inst Oceanografico (2004)
Cidade Universitaria, Av.
Travessa 3 no 380
05508-900 Sao Paulo - SP

Universidade do Vale do Rio Dos Sinos
Inst de Geociencias (2004)
Av. Unisinos
950 - Cristo Rei
93 000 Sao Leopoldo - RS

Universidade Federal da Bahia
Inst de Geociencias (2004)
Rua Augusto Viana s/n - Canela, 40 410 Salvador - BA
  geologia@ufba.br

Universidade Federal de Minas Gerais
Inst de Geociencias (2014)
Av. Antonio Carlos 6.627
 Pampulha, , 31 270 Belo Horizont
  p. 55(31) 3409-5420
  dir@igc.ufmg.br
  http://www.igc.ufmg.br/

Universidade Federal de Ouro Preto
Dept de Geologia (2014)
Campus Morro do Cruzeiro
35 400 Ouro Preto
  p. (31) 3559-1600
  web@degeo.ufop.br
  http://www.degeo.ufop.br/

Universidade Federal de Pernambuco
Centro de Tecnologia - Geociencias (2014)
Av. Agamenon Magalhaes s/n - Santo Amaro, 50 000 Recife - PE
  p. (81) 2126.8105
  secretaria.proacad@ufpe.br
  http://www.ufpe.br/proacad/index.php?option=com_content
  &view=article&id=150&Itemid=138

Universidade Federal do Ceara
Inst de Geociencias (2004)
Av. Da Universidade
2853 - Benfica
60 000 Fortaleza - CE

Universidade Federal do Para
Inst. de Geociencias (2014)
Campus Guama
Caixa postal 1611
Belem
  p. (91) 3201-7107
  dirig@ufpa.br
  http://www.ig.ufpa.br/site/

Universidade Federal Fluminense
Dept de Geociencias (2014)
Av. Gal. Milton Tavares de Souza
  p. +55 (21) 2629-5951
  gge@vm.uff.br
  http://www.uff.br/degeografia/

Universidade Federal Rural do Rio de Janeiro
Inst de Geociencias (2004)
Km 47 da Antigua Rodovia Rio/Sao Paulo - Seropedico
23 460 Itaguai - RJ

University of Campinas Geoscience Institute
Inst de Geociencias (2004)
Caixa Postal: 6152
13083-970
Campinas
  secretaria.prpg@reitoria.unicamp.br
  http://www.ige.unicamp.br/

Bulgaria

Bulgarian Academy of Sciences
Geological Institute (D) (2013)
Acad.G.Bonchev st. bl.24
Sofia 1113
  p. +0359 2 8723 563
  geolinst@geology.bas.bg
  http://www.geology.bas.bg/
Professor Dr, DSc:
  Kristalina Christova Stoykova, (D), Bulgaria Acad Sci, 2008, PsmPe
Associate Professor:
  Iliana Boncheva, (D)
  Thomas Noubar Kerestedjian, (D), Bulgaria Acad Sci, 1990, GzeEg

Mining and Geology University
Geology Dept (2013)
Studentski Grad
Sofia 1756
  p. 8060221
  dekangpf@mgu.bg

Ministry of Environment and Water
Ministry of Environment and Water (2011)
22 Maria Louiza Blvd.
Sofia, 1000
  minister@moew.government.bg
  http://www.moew.government.bg/

Sofia University St. Kliment Ohridski
Dept of Geology and Paleontology (2005)
1504 Sofia
15 Tsar Osvobodtel Blvd.
Geology of Fossil, Fuel, Organic Petrology, Organic Geochemistry
room 276
  mivanov@gea.uni-sofia.bg
  http://www.uni-sofia.bg/newweb/faculties/geo/departments/geo

Dept of Cartography & GIS (B,M,D) (2012)
1504 Sofia
15 Tsar Osvobodtel Blvd.
GIS, General Physical Geography, Landscape Ecology, Agroecology
Sofia, Sofia 1504
  p. 9308261
  popov@gea.uni-sofia.bg
  http://www.gis.gea.uni-sofia.bg/

University of Mining and Geology, St. Ivan Rilski
Faculty of Geology (2004)
Studentski grad
1100 Sofia
  dekangpf@mgu.bg
  http://www.mgu.bg/frame/html

Burkina Faso

Universite de Ouagadougou
L'Unité de Formation et de Recherche en Sciences de la Vie et de la Terre (UFR/SVT) (B) (2014)
03 BP 7021, Ougadougou 03
  p. +226 50-30-70-64/65
  webmaster@univ-ouaga.bf
  http://www.univ-ouaga.bf.html/formations/ufr_SVT/frFor-mtnsSVTdip1.html

Burundi

Universite du Burundi
Dept of Earth Sciences (B) O (2015)
B.P. 2700
Bujumbura, Burundi
  p. 00257 22 22 55 56
  webmaster@ub.edu.bi
  http://www.ub.edu.bi/

Faculté des Sciences (2014)
B.P. 2700
Bjumbura
  p. 0025722222059
  http://www.ub.edu.bi/ub-fac6.php

Cameroon

Bamenda University of Science and Technology
Dept of Geology (B) (2014)
PO Box 277
Bamenda, NW Province
  p. +237 7726 1789
  http://www.bamendauniversity.com/

Universite de Buea
Dept of Geology and Environmental Science (B) (2014)
PO Box 63
Buea, South West Province
  p. 237-332-2134
  vpktitanji@yahoo.co.uk
  http://ubuea.cm/

Universite de Douala
FACULTY OF SCIENCES (B,M,D) (2014)
BP 2701
Douala, Cameroun
  p. (237) 33 40 75 69
  infos.fs@univ-douala.com
  http://www.facsciences-univ-douala.cm/index.php/contact

Universite de Dschang
FACULTE D'AGRONOMIE ET DES SCIENCES AGRICOLES (B,M) (2014)
POB 96
Dschang
  p. (237) 33 45 15 66
  agro.50tenair@gmail.com

Universite de Ngaoundere
School of Geology and Mining (B) (2014)
BP 454
Ngaoundere
  p. +(237) 225 2767
  http://www.univ-ndere.cm/index.php?LANG=EN&ETS=043
  3A030F35FE61&RUB=E2C0BE24560D78C

Universite de Yaounde 1
Dept des Sciences de la Terre (B) (2014)
BP 812
Yanounde
  p. (237) 222 56 60
  facsciences@uy1.uninet.cm
  http://www.facsciences.uninet.cm/act_aca_dst.html

Canada

Aboriginal Affairs & Northern Development Canada
Aboriginal Affairs and Northern Development Canada (2016)
Mineral Resources Division
PO Box 100
Iqaluit, NU X0A 0H0
  p. (867) 975-4293
  nunavutarchives@aandc.gc.ca
  http://nunavutgeoscience.ca/

Acadia University
Dept of Earth and Environmental Science (B,M) ● (2015)
Huggins Science Hall
12 University Avenue
Wolfville, NS B4P 2R6
  p. (902) 585-1208
  ees@acadiau.ca
  http://ees.acadiau.ca/
  Enrollment (2015): B: 83 (16) M: 6 (1)
Head:
  Ian S. Spooner, (D), Calgary, 1994, Ge
Professor:
  Sandra M. Barr, (D), British Columbia, 1973, Gi
  Peir K. Pufahl, (D), British Columbia, 2001, Gs
  Robert P. Raeside, (D), Calgary, 1982, Gp
  Clifford R. Stanley, (D), British Columbia, 1988, Cg
Assistant Professor:
  Nelson O'Driscoll, (D), Ottawa, 2003, CgGgOn
Instructor:
  David McMullin, (D), British Columbia, 1991, Oe
Geology Tech:
  Pam Frail, Gg

Brandon University

Dept of Geology (B,M) ● (2015)
270 18th Street
Brandon, MB R7A 6A9
   p. (204) 727-9677
   somarina@brandonu.ca
   http://www.brandonu.ca/geology
   Enrollment (2015): B: 60 (9) M: 1 (0)
Professor:
   Rong-Yu Li, (D), Alberta, 2002, PgmGg
   A. Hamid Mumin, (D), W Ontario, 1994, EgGzt
   Simon A. J Pattison, (D), McMaster, 1992, GsoGd
   Alireza Somarin, (D), New England, 1999, Gig
Emeritus:
   Robert K. Springer, (D), California (Davis), 1971, Gi
   Harvey R. Young, (D), Queen's, 1973, Gd
Instructional Associate:
   Peter J. Adamo, (B), Brandon, 2000, Gg
Laboratory Director:
   Michelle Huminicki, (D), Memorial, 2005, EgGz

Brock University

Dept of Earth Sciences (B,M) ● (2015)
500 Glenridge Avenue
St. Catharines, ON L2S 3A1
   p. 905 688-5550
   dgadoury@brocku.ca
   http://www.brocku.ca/mathematics-science/departments-
   and-centres/earth-sciences
   Enrollment (2014): B: 89 (33) M: 12 (7)
Professor:
   Uwe Brand, (D), Ottawa, 1979, Cl
   Richard J. Cheel, (D), McMaster, 1984, Gs
   Frank Fueten, (D), Toronto, 1989, Gc
   Martin J. Head, (D), Aberdeen, 1990, Pl
   Francine G. McCarthy, (D), Dalhousie, 1992, Pm
   John Menzies, (D), Edinburgh, 1976, Gl
Associate Professor:
   Gregory C. Finn, (D), Memorial, 1989, Gx
   Daniel P. McCarthy, (D), Saskatchewan, 1993, Gl
   Mariek Schmidt, (D), Oregon State, 2005, GivXg
Assistant Professor:
   Nigel Blamey, (D), New Mexico Tech, 2000, EgCg
Adjunct Professor:
   Paul Budkewitsch, (M), Toronto, 1990, GeOrHq
   Andrew W. Panko, (D), McMaster, 1985, Ge

Cape Breton University

Math, Physics, Geology (B) (2013)
P.O. Box 5300
Sydney, NS B1P 6L2
   p. (902) 539-5300
   fenton_isenor@cbu.ca
   Enrollment: No data reported since 1999
Instructor:
   Fenton M. Isenor, (M), Acadia, 2000, GgNgGm
Emeritus:
   Erwin L. Zodrow, (D), Pi

Capilano University

Geology Dept (A,B) (2010)
2055 Purcell Way
North Vancouver, BC V7J 3H5
   p. (604) 986-1911
   sciences@capilanou.ca
   http://www.capilanou.ca/programs/geology.html
   Enrollment (1999): B: 33 (0)
Head:
   Dileep J A Athaide, (M), British Columbia, 1974, GgOge
Professor:
   Jennifer Getsinger, (D), British Columbia

Carleton University 🗋

Dept of Earth Sciences (B,M,D) ● (2015)
1125 Colonel By Drive
Ottawa, ON K1S 5B6
   p. (613) 520-5633
   earth.sciences@carleton.ca
   http://earthsci.carleton.ca/
   f: https://www.facebook.com/pages/Department-of-Earth-
   Sciences-Carleton-University/510369329037382
   t: @ErthSciCarleton
Chair:
   George R. Dix, (D), Syracuse, 1988, Gs
Professor:
   Keith Bell, (D), Oxford, 1964, Cc
   R. Timothy Patterson, (D), California (Los Angeles), 1986, Pm
   Giorgio Ranalli, (D), Illinois, 1970, Yg
   Claudia Schroder-Adams, (D), Dalhousie, 1986, Pm
   George B. Skippen, (D), Johns Hopkins, 1966, Cg
   Richard P. Taylor, (D), Leicester, 1980, Cg
   David H. Watkinson, (D), Penn State, 1965, Em
Associate Professor:
   Gail M. Atkinson, (D), W Ontario, 1993, Ne
   John Blenkinsop, (D), British Columbia, 1972, Cc
   Sharon D. Carr, (D), Carleton, 1990, Gt
   Fred A. Michel, (D), Waterloo, 1982, Hw
Lecturer:
   Ildi Munro, (M), Waterloo, 1975, Pg
Adjunct Professor:
   Robert Berman, (D), British Columbia, 1983, Gp
   Brian L. Cousens, (D), California (Santa Barbara), 1990, Cc
   Steve L. Cumbaa, (D), Florida, 1975, Pv
   J. Allan Donaldson, (D), Johns Hopkins, 1960, Gs
   T. Scott Ercit, (D), Manitoba, 1986, Gz
   Harold Gibson, (D), Carleton, 1990, Em
   Simon Hanmer, (D), Chelsea (UK), 1977, Gc
   Mark D. Hannington, (D), Toronto, 1989, Em
   Jarmila Kukalova-Peck, (D), Charles (Prague), 1962, Pi
   Dale A. Leckie, (D), McMaster, 1983, Gs
   R. R. Rainbird, (D), Western, 1991, Gs
Emeritus:
   F. K. North, (D), Oxford, 1951, Go

Dalhousie University 🗋

Dept of Oceanography (B,M,D) (2015)
Life Sciences Centre
1355 Oxford Street
PO Box 15000
Halifax, NS B3H 4R2
   p. (902) 494-3557
   oceanography@dal.ca
   http://oceanography.dal.ca/
   Enrollment (2015): M: 22 (6) D: 31 (2)
Chair:
   Paul S. Hill, (D), Washington, 1992, Gs
Professor:
   Christopher Beaumont, (D), Dalhousie, 1973, Yg
   Bernard P. Boudreau, (D), Yale, 1985, Cl
   Katja Fennel, (D), Rostock, 1998, Ob
   Jonathan Grant, (D), South Carolina, 1981, Ob
   Alex E. Hay, (D), British Columbia, 1981, Op
   Dan Kelley, (D), Dalhousie, 1986, Op
   Markus Kienast, (D), British Columbia, 2002, Cs
   Marlon R. Lewis, (D), Dalhousie, 1984, Ob
   Anna Metaxas, (D), Dalhousie, 1994, Ob
   Jinyu Sheng, (D), Memorial, 1991, Op
   Christopher T. Taggart, (D), McGill, 1986, Ob
   Helmuth Thomas, (D), Rostock, 1997, Oc
   Keith R. Thompson, (D), Liverpool, 1979, Op
   Douglas Wallace, (D), Dalhousie, 1985, Oc
Associate Professor:
   Tetjana Ross, (D), Manitoba, 2003, Op
Assistant Professor:
   Christopher Algar, (D), Dalhousie, 2009, Obc
   David Barclay, (D), California (San Diego), 2011, Op
   Stephanie Kienast, (D), British Columbia, 2002, Gu
Adjunct Professor:
   Kumiko Azetsu-Scott, (D), Dalhousie, 1992, Oc
   Mark Baumgartner, (D), Oregon, 2002, Ob
   Susanne Craig, (D), Strathclyde, 2000, Op

Peter Cranford, (D), Dalhousie, 1998, Ob
Claudio DiBacco, (D), California (San Diego), 1999, Ob
Dale Ellis, (D), McMaster, 1976, Op
Kenneth Frank, (D), Toledo, 1978, Ob
Richard Greatbatch, (D), Cambridge, 1981, Op
David Greenberg, (D), Liverpool, 1975, Op
David Hebert, (D), Dalhousie, 1988, Op
Paul Hines, (D), Bath, 1989, Op
Bruce D. Johnson, (D), Dalhousie, 1979, Oc
Arne Kortzinger, (D), Kiel, 1995, Oc
Sebastian Krastel, (D), Kiel, 1999, Yr
William K. W. Li, (D), Dalhousie, 1978, Ob
Keith E. Louden, (D), MIT, 1976, Yr
Youyu Lu, (D), Victoria, 1997, Op
Hugh MacIntyre, (D), Deleware, 1996, Ob
Timothy Milligan, (M), Dalhousie, 1997, Gs
David C. Mosher, (D), Dalhousie, 1993, Ou
Andreas Oschlies, (D), Kiel, 1994, Ob
William Perrie, (D), MIT, 1979, Opw
David J.W. Piper, (D), Cambridge, 1969, Gu
Harold C. Ritchie, (D), McGill, 1982, Ow
Barry R. Ruddick, (D), MIT, 1977, Op
Peter C. Smith, (D), MIT/WHOI, 1973, Op
Ulrich Sommer, (D), Vienna, 1977, Ob
Toste Tanhua, (D), Goteborg, 1997, Oc
Emeritus:
Anthony J. Bowen, (D), California (San Diego), 1967, On
John J. Cullen, (D), California (San Diego), 1980, Ob
Robert O. Fournier, (D), Rhode Island, 1967, Ob
Eric L. Mills, (D), Yale, 1964, Ob
Robert M. Moore, (D), Southampton, 1977, Oc

Dept of Earth Sciences (B,M,D) (2014)
Halifax, NS B3H 3J5
p. (902) 494-2358
earth.sciences@dal.ca
http://earthsciences.dal.ca/index2.html
Enrollment (1999): B: 69 (27) M: 14 (5) D: 20 (6)
Chair:
Martin R. Gibling, (D), Ottawa, 1978, Gs
Professor:
D. Barrie Clarke, (D), Edinburgh, 1969, Gi
Rebecca A. Jamieson, (D), Memorial, 1979, Gx
Peter H. Reynolds, (D), British Columbia, 1967, Cc
David B. Scott, (D), Dalhousie, 1977, Pm
Grant D. Wach, (D), Oxford, 1993, Go
Associate Research Professor:
Gunter K. Muecke, (D), Oxford, 1969, Cg
Associate Professor:
Nicholas Culshaw, (D), Ottawa, 1983, Gc
John C. Gosse, (D), Lehigh, 1994, Cg
Djordje Grujic, (D), ETH (Switzerland), 1992, Gt
Patrick J.C. Ryall, (D), Dalhousie, 1974, Yg
Assistant Professor:
Lawrence Plug, (D), Alaska (Fairbanks), 2000, Gm
Research Associate:
Isabelle Coutand, (D), Rennes, Gg
Lubomir F. Jansa, (D), Charles (Prague), 1967, Gr
Robert Raeside, (D), Calgary, 1982, Gx
Alan Ruffman, (M), Dalhousie, 1966, Ys
John Waldron, (D), Edinburgh, 1981, Gc
Senior Instructor:
Peter I. Wallace, (M), McMaster, 1975, Gg
Instructor:
Charles C. Walls, (M), Dalhousie, 1996, Oi
Honorary Research Associate:
Prasanta Mukhopadhyay, (D), Jadavpur, 1971, Ec
Graham Williams, (D), Sheffield, 1964, Pl
Adjunct Professor:
Juergen Adam, (D), Tech (Berlin)
Alan J. Anderson, (D), Queen's, Cg
Sandra Barr, (D), British Columbia, 1973, Gx
Hugo Beltrami, (D), Quebec (Montreal), Gg
John Calder, (D), Dalhousie, 1991, Ec
Sonya Dehler, (D), British Columbia, Gg
Jarda Dostal, (D), McMaster, 1974, Cg
Don Fox, (D), Dalhousie, Gg

Paul T. Gayes, (D), SUNY (Stony Brook), 1986, Gs
Peter E. Jones, (D), British Columbia, 1963, Op
Lisa M. Kellman, (D), Quebec (Montreal), 1998, Cg
Daniel Kontak, (D), Queen's, Gg
Joel Kronfeld, (D), Rice, 1972, Cg
Michael Melchin, (D), Western, 1987, Pg
Peta J. Mudie, (D), Dalhousie, 1980, Pl
J. Brendan Murphy, (D), McGill, 1982, Gx
Michael Parsons, (D), Stanford, Gg
Georgia Pe-Piper, (D), Cambridge, 1971, Gv
David Piper, (D), Cantab, 1969, Gs
Paul T. Robinson, (D), California (Berkeley), 1964, Gv
Andre Rochon, (D), Quebec, Gg
Matthew Salisbury, (D), Washington, 1974, Yr
Ralph Stea, (D), Dalhousie, 1995, Gu
Hans J. Wielens, (D), Utrecht (Neth), 1979, Go
Emeritus:
H.B. S. Cooke, (D), Witwatersrand, 1947, Pv
Franco Medioli, (D), Parma, 1959, Pm
G. Clinton Milligan, (D), Harvard, 1961, Gc
Marcos Zentilli, (D), Queen's, 1974, Eg
On Leave:
Dorothy I. Godfrey-Smith, (D), Simon Fraser, 1991, Cc
Administrator:
Ann Bannon, (B), Dalhousie, 2001, On
Cooperating Faculty:
Christopher Beaumont, (D), Dalhousie, 1973, Ys

Douglas College
Dept of Earth and Environmental Sciences, Faculty of Science and Technology (A) (2014)
P.O. Box 2503
New Westminster, BC V3L 5B2
p. (604) 527-5400
waddingtond@douglascollege.ca
http://www.douglascollege.ca/programs-courses/faculties/science-technology/earth-and-environmental-sciences
Enrollment: No data reported since 1999
Chair:
David C. Waddington, (M), Queens (Kingston), 1991, OgGuc
Instructor:
Randal Mindell, (D), Alberta, 2008, PbGsg
Nathalie Vigouroux-Caillibot, (D), Simon Fraser, 2013, GvzGg
Other:
Michael C. Wilson, (D), Calgary, 1981, GaPgGs
Related Staff:
Denis Beausoleil, (M), Victoria, 2010, Og
Tiffany Johnson, (M), Carleton, 2011, Og

Lakehead University 📄
Geology (B,M) ● (2015)
955 Oliver Road
Thunder Bay, ON P7B 5E1
p. (807) 343-8461
kristine.carey@lakeheadu.ca
https://www.lakeheadu.ca/academics/departments/geology
Administrative Assistant: Kristine M. Carey
Enrollment (2015): B: 101 (24) M: 12 (5)
Chair:
Peter N. Hollings, (D), Saskatchewan, 1998, Eg
Professor:
Philip W. Fralick, (D), Toronto, 1985, Gs
Mary Louise Hill, (D), Princeton, 1985, Gc
Associate Professor:
Andrew G. Conly, (D), Toronto, 2003, Eg
Assistant Professor:
Amanda Diochon, (D), Dalhousie, 2009, Ge
Shannon Zurevinski, (D), Alberta, 2009, Gz
Emeritus:
Graham J. Borradaile, (D), Liverpool, 1971, Ym
Manfred M. Kehlenbeck, (D), Queen's, 1971, Gc
Stephen A. Kissin, (D), Toronto, 1974, Em
Edward L. Mercy, (D), Imperial Coll (UK), 1955, Cg
Roger H. Mitchell, (D), McMaster, 1969, Gi
Geology Technician:
Kristi Tavener, On

Geology Technician:
    Anne Hammond, (B), Lakehead, 1999, On

Laurentian University, Sudbury
Dept of Earth Sciences (B,M,D) (2007)
Ramsey Lake Road
Sudbury, ON P3E 2C6
    p. (705) 675-1151 x6575
    rmehes@laurentian.ca
    Administrative Assistant: Roxane J. Bourgouin-Mehes
    Enrollment (2007): B: 48 (14) M: 32 (4) D: 6 (0)
Chair:
    Andrew M. McDonald, (D), Carleton, 1992, Gz
Canada Research Chair, Precambrian Geology:
    Balz Kamber, (D), Bern, 1995, Cs
Professor:
    Michael Lesher, (D), W Australia, 1984, Em
    Darrel Long, (D), W Ontario, 1976, Gs
    David A. Pearson, (D), London, 1967, Oe
Associate Professor:
    Ann Gallie, (D), British Columbia, 1990, Or
    Harold L. Gibson, (D), Carleton, 1990, Em
    Daniel J. Kontak, (D), Queens, 1985, Eg
    Bruno Lafrance, (D), New Brunswick, 1990, Gc
    Stephen Piercey, (D), British Columbia, 2001, Ce
Assistant Professor:
    Pedro J. Jugo, (D), Alberta, 2003, Gi
    Doug Tinkham, (D), Alabama, 2002, Gp
    Elizabeth Turner, (D), Queens, 1999, Pg
Emeritus:
    Anthony E. Beswick, (D), London, 1965, Gi
    Paul Copper, (D), London, 1965, Pi
    James F. Davies, (D), Toronto, 1963, Em
    Richard James, (D), Manchester, 1967, Gp
    Reid R. Keays, (D), McMaster, 1968, Em
    Don H. Rousell, (D), Manitoba, 1965, Gc
    Robert E. Whitehead, (D), New Brunswick, 1973, Ce

McGill University
Dept of Mining & Materials Engineering (B,M,D) (2013)
Rm 125 FDA Building
3450 University Street
Montreal, QC H3A 2A7
    p. (514) 398-4986
    roussos.dimitrakopoulos@mcgill.ca
    http://www.mcgill.ca/minmat/mining
    Enrollment (2000): B: 6 (0)
Chair:
    Stephen Yue, (D), Leeds, 1979, Nx
Professor:
    George Demopoulos, (D), McGill, 1982, Nx
    Roussos Dimitrakopoulos, (D), Ecole Polytechnique, 1989, Nm
    James A. Finch, (D), McGill, 1973, Nx
    Raynald Gauvin, (D)
    Roderick I. Guthrie, (D), London, 1967, Nx
    Ferri Hassani, (D), Nottingham, 1981, Nm
    Hani Mitri, (D), Nottingham, 1981, Nm
    Hani Mitri, (D), Nottingham
    Frank Mucciardi, (D), McGill, 1980, Nx
Post-Retirement:
    Michel L. Bilodeau, (D), McGill, 1975, Nm
Associate Professor:
    Mathieu Brochu, (D), McGill
    Mainul Hasan, (D), McGill, 1987, Nx
    Showan Nazhat, (D)
    Mihriban Pekguleryuz, (D), McGill
Assistant Professor:
    Kirk Bevan, (D), Purdue
    Marta Cerruti, (D)
    Richard Chromik, (D), SUNY
    In-Ho Jung, (D), Ecole Poly (Montreal)
    Nathaniel Quitoriano, (D), MIT
    Jun Song, (D), Princeton
    Kristian Waters, (D)
Lecturer:
    John W. Mossop, (B), McGill, 1955, Nm

Forence Paray, (D), McGill
Adjunct Professor:
    Robin A.L. Drew, (D), Newcastle, 1980, Nx
    Ahmad Hemani, (D), Salford (UK), Nm
Emeritus:
    John E. Gruzleski, (D), Toronto, 1967, Nx
    John J. Jonas, (D), Cambridge, 1960, Nx
    Gordon W. Smith, (D), McGill, 1967, Nx

Dept of Earth & Planetary Sciences (B,M,D) ● (2015)
3450 University Street
Room 238
Montreal, QC H3A 0E8
    p. (514) 398-6767
    kristy.thornton@mcgill.ca
    http://www.mcgill.ca/eps
    Enrollment (2015): B: 42 (17) M: 15 (10) D: 33 (7)
Chair:
    Alfonso Mucci, (D), Miami, 1981, Cm
Retired:
    Reinhard Hesse, (D), Tech (Munich), 1964, Gs
Professor:
    Don Baker, (D), Penn State, 1985, Cp
    Olivia G. Jensen, (D), British Columbia, 1971, Yg
    John Stix, (D), Toronto, 1989, Gv
    Anthony E. Williams-Jones, (D), Queen's, 1973, Ce
Associate Professor:
    Galen Halverson, (D), Harvard, 2003, GsCs
    Jeffrey M. McKenzie, (D), Syracuse, 2005, Hw
    Jeanne Paquette, (D), SUNY (Stony Brook), 1991, Gz
    Boswell Wing, (D), Johns Hopkins, 2004, Cs
Assistant Professor:
    Kim Berlo, (D), Bristol, 2006, Gv
    Natalya Gomez, (D), Harvard, 2013, Og
    Rebecca Harrington, (D), California (Los Angeles), 2008, Ys
    James Kirkpatrick, (D), Glasgow, 2008, Gc
    Yajing Liu, (D), Harvard, 2007, Ygs
    Christie Rowe, (D), California (Santa Cruz), 2007, Gc
    Vincent van Hinsberg, (D), Bristol, 2006, EgCg
Earth System Science Faculty Lecturer:
    William G. Minarik, (D), Rensselaer, 1993, Cp
Adjunct Professor:
    Eric Galbraith, (D), British Columbia, 2006, OgPe
    Heather Short, (D), Maine, 2006, Gc
    Bjorn Sundby, (D), Bergen (Norway), 1966, Cm
Emeritus:
    Jafar Arkani-Hamed, (D), MIT, 1969, Xy
    Don Francis, (D), MIT, 1974, Gi
    Andrew J. Hynes, (D), Cambridge, 1972, Gc
    Wallace H. MacLean, (D), McGill, 1968, Em
    Robert F. Martin, (D), Stanford, 1969, Gi
    Colin Stearn, (D), Yale, Ps

Dept of Atmospheric & Oceanic Sciences (B,M,D) (2016)
805 Sherbrooke Street West
Room 945
Montreal, QC H3A 0B9
    p. (514) 398-3764
    john.gyakum@mcgill.ca
    http://www.mcgill.ca/meteo
    Administrative Assistant: Karen Moore
    Enrollment (2015): B: 22 (7) M: 18 (12) D: 33 (4)
Professor:
    Parisa A. Ariya, (D), York, 1996, Oa
    John R. Gyakum, (D), MIT, 1981, Ow
    Man Kong Yau, (D), MIT, 1977, Oa
Associate Professor:
    Peter Bartello, (D), McGill, 1988, Oa
    Frederic Fabry, (D), McGill, 1994, Oa
    Pavlos Kollias, (D), Miami, 2000, Ora
    David Straub, (D), Washington, 1990, Op
    Bruno Tremblay, (D), McGill, Op
Assistant Professor:
    Yi Huang, (D), Princeton, 2007, OrYgOa
    Daniel Kirshbaum, (D), Washington, 2005, Oaw
    Timothy Merlis, (D), Caltech, 2011, Oaw
    Thomas Colin Preston, (D), Duke, 2011, OanOn

Andreas Zuend, (D), ETH, 2007, Oaw
Adjunct Professor:
  Gilbert Brunet, (D), McGill, 1989
  Ashu Dastoor, (D), IIT
  Luc Fillion, (D), McGill, 1991, Owa
  Pierre Gauthier, (D), McGill, 1988, Oa
  Hai Lin, (D), McGill, 1995, Oa
  Damon H. Matthews, (D), Victoria, 2004
  Jaime Palter, (D), Duke, 2007, OagOe
  Seok-Woo Son, (D), Penn State, 2006
Emeritus:
  Jacques F. Derome, (D), Michigan, 1968, Oa
  Henry G. Leighton, (D), Alberta, 1968, Oa
  Lawrence A. Mysak, (D), Harvard, 1966, Op
  Isztar I. Zawadzki, (D), McGill, 1972, Oa

McMaster University

School of Geography & Earth Sciences (B,M,D) (2015)
1280 Main Street West
General Science Building
Room 206
Hamilton, ON L8S 4K1
  p. (905) 525-9140 (Ext. 24535)
  geograd@mcmaster.ca
  http://www.science.mcmaster.ca/geo/geomain.html
  Enrollment (2015): B: 276 (90) M: 49 (14) D: 46 (9)
Director:
  K. Bruce Newbold, (D), McMaster, 1994, Ge
Professor:
  M. Altaf Arain, (D), Arizona, 1997, Hg
  Janok Bhattacharya, (D), McMaster, 1989, Gr
  Sean Carey, (D), McMaster, 2000, Hg
  Vera Chouinard, (D), McMaster, 1986, On
  Paulin Coulibaly, (D), Laval, 2000, Hg
  Alan P. Dickin, (D), Oxford, 1981, Cc
  Carolyn H. Eyles, (D), Toronto, 1986, Gs
  Richard S. Harris, (D), Queen's, 1981, Ou
  H. Antonio Paez, (D), Tohoku, 2000, Eg
  Edward G. Reinhardt, (D), Carleton, 1996, Pm
  W. Jack Rink, (D), Florida State, 1990, Cc
  Darren M. Scott, (D), McMaster, 2000, Oi
  Gregory F. Slater, (D), Toronto, 2001, Cg
  James E. Smith, (D), Waterloo, 1995, Hw
  J. Michael Waddington, (D), York, 1995, Pe
  Lesley A. Warren, (D), Toronto, 1994, CgHg
  Allison M. Williams, (D), York, 1997, On
  Robert D. Wilton, (D), S California, 1999, On
Associate Professor:
  Joseph I. Boyce, (D), Toronto, 1997, Og
  Maureen Padden, (D), Zurich, 2001, Cg
  Niko Yiannakoulias, (D), Alberta, 2006, Ge
Adjunct:
  Matthias Peichl, (D), McMaster, 2009
Assistant Professor:
  Luc Bernier, (D), McMaster, 2007, Cg
  Sang-Tae Kim, (D), McGill, 2006, Cg
  Michael Mercier, (D), McMaster, 2004, Ou
  Suzanne Mills, (D), Saskatchewan, 2007, On
  Matthias Sweet, (D), Pennsylvania, 2012
Adjunct:
  Stacey Mater, (M), McMaster, 2011
Lecturer:
  John MacLachlan, (D), McMaster, 2011, Gs
Adjunct Professor:
  Howard Barker, (D), McMaster, 1991
  Jing Chen, (D), Reading (UK), 1986
  Allan S. Crowe, (D), Alberta, 1987
  Ian G. Droppo, (D), Exeter (UK), 2000
  Susan J. Elliott, (D), McMaster, 1992, Ge
  Tim Lotimer, (M), Waterloo, 1977
  Hanna Maoh, (D), McMaster, 2005
  Dan McKenny, (D), Australian National
  Michael Pisaric, (D), Queens
  Ulrich Riller, (D), Toronto, 1996, Og
  Dominique Rissolo, (D), California (Riverside), 2001
  Corinne Schuster-Wallace, (D), Wilfred Laurier, 2001
  Amanjot Singh, (D), Braunschweig (Germany), 2001

Spencer Snowling, (D), McMaster, 2000
S Martin Taylor, (D), Victoria (Canada), 1974
Ross Upshur, (D), McMaster, 1986
Christopher Werner, (D), Florida State, 2007
University Professor:
  John D. Eyles, (D), London, 1983, Ge
  Henry P. Schwarcz, (D), Caltech, 1960, Cs
Emeritus:
  Brian T. Bunting, (D), London, 1970
  Andrew F. Burghardt, (D), Wisconsin, 1958
  Paul Clifford, (D), London, 1956
  James H. Crocket, (D), MIT
  John J. Drake, (D), McMaster, 1973
  Derek C. Ford, (D), Oxford, 1963, Gm
  Doug Grundy, (D), Manchester (UK), 1966
  Fred L. Hall, (D), MIT, 1975
  Pavlos S. Kanaroglou, (D), McMaster, 1987, Og
  Leslie J. King, (D), Iowa, 1960
  James R. Kramer, (D), Michigan, 1958, Cl
  Kao Lee Liaw, (D), Clark, 1972
  Robert McNutt, (D), MIT, 1965
  Gerry V. Middleton, (D), London (UK), 1954
  William A. Morris, (D), Open, 1974, Yg
  Yorgos Papageorgiou, (D), Ohio State, 1970
  Walter G. Peace, (D), McMaster, 1996, Ou
  Michael J. Risk, (D), S California, 1971, Po
  Wayne R. Rouse, (D), McGill, 1968
  Roger G. Walker, (D), Oxford, 1964
  Ming-Ko Woo, (D), British Columbia, 1972, Hg

Memorial University of Newfoundland

Dept of Earth Sciences (B,M,D) (2015)
Centre for Earth Resources Research, Room ER 4063
Alexander Murray Building
St. John's, NL A1B 3X5
  p. (709) 864-8142
  earthsci@mun.ca
  http://www.mun.ca/earthsciences
  Enrollment: No data reported since 1999
Professor:
  Ali E. Aksu, (D), Dalhousie, 1980, Gu
  Elliott T. Burden, (D), Calgary, 1982, Pl
  Gregory R. Dunning, (D), Memorial, 1984, Cc
  Joseph P. Hodych, (D), Toronto, 1971, Ym
  George A. Jenner, (D), Tasmania, 1982, Gi
  Toby C. J. S. Rivers, (D), Ottawa, 1976, Gp
  Derek H.C. Wilton, (D), Memorial, 1984, Eg
Associate Professor:
  Tomas J. Calon, (D), Leiden (Neth), 1978, Gc
  Charles A. Hurich, (D), Wyoming, 1988, Ys
  Aphrodite D. Indares, (D), Montreal, 1989, Gp
  Roger A. Mason, (D), Aberdeen, 1978, Gz
  Michael A. Slawinski, (D), Calgary, 1996, Ys
  Paul J. Sylvester, (D), Washington (St. Louis), 1984, Ca
Assistant Professor:
  Alison Leitch, (D), Australian National, 1986, Yg
First Year Lab Instructor:
  Roberta (Robbie) Hicks, (M), Yr
Emeritus:
  Jeremy Hall, (D), Glasgow, 1971, Ys
  Richard N. Hiscott, (D), McMaster, 1977, Gs
  Henry Longerich, (D), Indiana, 1967, Cg
  Michael G. Rochester, (D), Utah, 1959, Yg

Mount Allison University

Dept of Geography (B,M) (2004)
144 Main Street
Sackville, NB E4L 1A7
  p. (506) 364-2326
  dmossman@mta.ca
  http://www.mta.ca/departments/geography
  Enrollment: No data reported since 1999
Research Professor:
  David J. Mossman, (D), Otago (NZ), 1970, Em
Associate Professor:
  Jeffery W. Ollerhead, (D), Guelph, 1994, Yr

Assistant Professor:
    James Xinxia Jiang, (D), Southampton, Gg
Research Associate:
    Thomas A. Clair, (D), McMaster, 1991, Hy
Emeritus:
    Laing Ferguson, (D), Edinburgh, 1960, Pi

Mount Royal University
Dept of Earth Sciences (A,B) (2013)
4825 Mount Royal Gate SW
Calgary, AB T3E 6K6
    p. (403) 440-6165
    lstadnyk@mtroyal.ca
    http://www.mtroyal.ab.ca/scitech/earth.shtml
    Administrative Assistant: Leona Stadnyk
    Enrollment: No data reported since 1999
Chair:
    Paul Johnston, (D), W Australia, 1986, Pi
Professor:
    John Cox, (D), Aberdeen, 1994, Eo
Associate Professor:
    Katherine Boggs, (D), Calgary, 2004, Gt
    Pamela MacQuarrie, (M), Calgary, 1988, Oy
    Barbara McNicol, (D), Calgary, 1997, Og
Related Staff:
    Michael Clark, (B), Adams, 1976, Og

Natural Resources Canada
Ressources Naturelles Canada (2011)
580 Booth Street , 21st Floor
Ottawa, ON K1A 0E4
    debra.tompkinscaron@canada.ca
    http://www.nrcan.gc.ca/

Queen's University
Dept of Geological Sciences and Geological Engineering
(B,M,D) ● (2015)
#240, Bruce Wing, Miller Hall
36 Union St.
Kingston, ON K7L 3N6
    p. (613) 533-2597
    geolundergradassistant@queensu.ca
    www.queensu.ca/geol
    Enrollment (2011): B: 232 (47) M: 46 (20) D: 18 (5)
Head:
    Jean Hutchinson, (D), Toronto, 1992
Professor:
    Alexander Braun, (D), Johann Wolfgang Goethe, 1999, Yg
    Mark Diederichs, (D), Toronto, Nr
    John M. Dixon, (D), Connecticut, 1974, Gc
    Georgia Fotopoulos, (D), Calgary, 2003, Yd
    Noel P. James, (D), McGill, 1972, Gd
    Kurt Kyser, (D), California (Berkeley), EgGsYg
    Guy M. Narbonne, (D), Ottawa, 1981, Pi
    Gema Olivo, (D), Québec (Montréal), 1995, Eg
    Ronald C. Peterson, (D), Virginia Tech, 1980, Gz
    Victoria H. Remenda, (D), Waterloo, 1993, Hw
Associate Professor:
    Laurent Godin, (D), Carleton, Goc
    John A. Hanes, (D), Toronto, 1979, Cc
    Heather E. Jamieson, (D), Queen's, 1982, Ge
    Daniel Layton-Matthews, (D), Toronto, EgGx
Research Associate:
    Doug A. Archibald, (D), Queen's, 1982, Cc
Adjunct Professor:
    Rob Harrap, (M), Carleton, 1990, Gc
Emeritus:
    Alan H. Clark, (D), Manchester, 1964, Em
    Robert W. Dalrymple, (D), McMaster, 1977, Gs
    Herwart Helmstaedt, (D), New Brunswick, 1968, Gc
    Raymond A. Price, (D), Princeton, 1958, Gt

Royal Ontario Museum
Dept of Palaeobiology (2013)
100 Queen's Park

Toronto, ON M5S 2C6
    p. (416) 586-5591
    davidru@rom.on.ca
Curator Of Vertebrate Palaeontology:
    David C. Evans, (D), Toronto, 2007, PvoPq
Assistant Curator:
    David M. Rudkin, (B), Toronto, 1975, Pi
Assistant Curator:
    Kevin L. Seymour, (D), Toronto, 1999, PvoPg

Dept of Mineralogy (2015)
100 Queen's Park
Toronto, ON M5S 2C6
    p. (416) 586-5820
    naturalhistory@rom.on.ca
    t: @ROMEarthSci
Emeritus:
    Robert I. Gait, (D), Manitoba, 1967, Gz
    Frederick J. Wicks, (D), Oxford, 1969, Gz
Curator:
    Kimberly T. Tait, (D), Arizona, 2007, GzyXm

Dept of Earth Sciences (2010)
100 Queen's Park
Toronto, ON M5S 2C6
    p. (416) 856-5811
    annetteb@rom.on.ca
    Enrollment: No data reported since 1999
Curatorial Assistant:
    Vincent Vertolli, (M), Toronto, 1974, Gx

Royal Tyrrell Museum of Palaeontology
Royal Tyrrell Museum of Palaeontology (2013)
P.O. Box 7500
Drumheller, AB T0J 0Y0
    p. (403) 823-7707
    tyrrell.info@gov.ab.ca
    http://www.tyrrellmuseum.com/
    Enrollment: No data reported since 1999
Executive Director:
    Andrew G. Neuman, (M), Alberta, 1986, Pv
Director, Preservation and Research:
    Donald B. Brinkman, (D), McGill, 1979, Pv
Curator:
    Dennis R. Braman, (D), Calgary, 1981, Pl
    David A. Eberth, (D), Toronto, 1987, Gs
    James D. Gardner, (D), Alberta, 2000, Pv
    Donald Henderson, (D), Bristol, 2000, Pv
    Craig Scott, (D), Alberta, 2008, Pv
Curator:
    Francois Therrien, (D), Johns Hopkins, 2004, Pv
Post-doctoral fellow:
    Caleb Brown, (D), Toronto, 2013, Pv

Saint Francis Xavier University
Dept of Earth Sciences (B,M) (2015)
P.O Box 5000
Antigonish, NS B2G 2W5
    p. (902) 867-5109
    igreen@stfx.ca
    http://sites.stfx.ca/earth_sciences/
    Enrollment (2015): B: 11 (15) M: 13 (3)
Professor:
    Alan J. Anderson, (D), Queen's, 1990, Gx
    Hugo Beltrami, (D), UQAM, 1993, YhOa
    Lisa M. Kellman, (D), Quebec (Montreal), 1997, CsOs
    Michael J. Melchin, (D), Western, 1987, Pi
    J. Brendan Murphy, (D), McGill, 1982, Gt
Associate Professor:
    Dave A. Risk, (D), Dalhousie, 2006, Osr
Instructor:
    Cindy Murphy, (M), McGill, 1984, Gg
    Colette Rennie, (M), Queen's, 1987, Gg
    Matthew Schumacher, (M), Waterloo, 2006, Og
    Sid Taylor, (M), Memorial, 1977, Gg

Simon Fraser University
Dept of Earth Sciences (B,M) (2010)
8888 University Drive
Burnaby, BC V5A 1S6
    p. (604) 291-5387
    bcward@sfu.ca
    http://www.sfu.ca/earth-sciences
    Enrollment (2003): B: 546 (0) M: 25 (0)
Chair:
    Diana M. Allen, (D), Carleton, 1996, Hy
Professor:
    John J. Clague, (D), British Columbia, 1973, Gl
    Douglas Stead, (D), Nottingham, 1984, Ng
Associate Professor:
    Andrew J. Calvert, (D), Cambridge, 1985, Ys
    James A. Mac Eachern, (D), Alberta, 1994, Gs
    Dan D. Marshall, (D), Lausanne, 1995, Ca
    Peter S. Mustard, (D), Carleton, 1990, Gs
    Derek J. Thorkelson, (D), Carleton, 1992, Gt
    Brent C. Ward, (D), Alberta, 1992, Ge
Assistant Professor:
    Gwenn Flowers, (D), British Columbia, 2000, Gl
    H. Daniel (Dan) Gibson, (D), Carleton, 2003, Gc
    Dirk Kirste, (D), Calgary, 2001, Cg
    Glyn Williams-Jones, (D), Open, 2001, Gv
Lecturer:
    Kevin Cameron, (M), Memorial, 1986, Gg
    Roberta Dunlop, (M), British Columbia, 1984, Gx

Sir Wilfred Grenfell College
Environmental Science Unit (B) (2010)
Division of Science
University Drive
Corner Brook, NF A2H 6P9
    p. (709) 637-6289
    dparkins@grenfell.mun.ca

    http://www.swgc.mun.ca
    Department Secretary: Phyllis Langdon
    Enrollment: No data reported since 1999
Chair:
    William J. Iams, (D), Memorial, 1977, Og
Assistant Professor:
    Pierre M. Rouleau, (D), Alberta, 1994, Yg
    Michael P. Rutherford, (D), Alberta, 1991, Sb
Adjunct Professor:
    Antony R. Berger, (D), Liverpool (UK), 1967, Ge

The Manitoba Museum
Dept. of Geology & Paleontology (2015)
190 Rupert Avenue
Winnipeg, MB R3B 0N2
    p. (204) 956-2830
    gyoung@manitobamuseum.ca
    http://www.manitobamuseum.ca
    Administrative Assistant: Claire Zimmerman
Museum Librarian:
    Cindi Steffan, (N), On
Curator:
    Graham A. Young, (D), New Brunswick, 1988, Pie

Universite du Quebec
INRS centre Eau Terre Environnement (Quebec Geoscience Center) (M,D) (2015)
490 de la Couronne
Quebec, QC G1K 9A9
    p. + (418) 654-4677
    info@ete.inrs.ca
    http://www.ete.inrs.ca
    Administrative Assistant: Pascale Cote
Professor:
    Mario Bergeron, (D), McMaster, 1985, Ca
    Normand Bergeron, (D), SUNY (Buffalo), 1994, Gm
    Monique Bernier, (D), Or
    Fateh Chebana, Hq
    Karem Chokmani, Oi

Pierre Francus, PeGs
Jannette B. Frandsen, On
Bernard Giroux, Yeg
Erwan Gloaguen, Ye
Yves Gratton, Op
Lyal B. Harris, GcYg
Marc R. LaFleche, (D), Montpellier II, 1991, Ct
Rene Lefebvre, (D), Laval, 1994, Hw
Michel Malo, Gc
Richard Martel, (D), Laval, 1996, Hw
Claudio Paniconi, Hw
Pierre-Simon Ross, GvEg
Senior Scientist:
    Jean H. Bedard, (D), Montreal, 1985, Gi
    Christian Begin, (D), Laval, 1991, Pe
    Louise Corriveau, (D), McGill, 1989, Gp
    Benoit Dube, (D), Quebec (Chicoutimi), 1990, Em
    Denis Lavoie, (D), Laval, 1988, Gs
    Yves Michaud, (D), Laval, 1991, Gm
    Leopold Nadeau, (D), Carleton, 1990, Gt
    Michel Parent, (D), W Ontario, 1987, Gl
    Didier Perret, (D), Laval, 1995, Ng
Research Associate:
    Esther Asselin, (M), Laval, 1986, Pl
    Eric Boisvert, (M), Quebec (Montreal), 1994, On
    Pierre Brouillette, (B), Laval, 1982, Gg
    Kathleen Lauziere, (M), Quebec (Chicoutimi), 1989, Gg
    Marc R. Luzincourt, (B), Quebec (Montreal), 1982, Cs
    Anna Smirnov, (M), Memorial, 1997, Cs

Universite du Quebec a Chicoutimi
Sciences de la Terre (B,M,D) ● (2016)
555, Boulevard de l'Universite
Chicoutimi, QC G7H 2B1
    p. (418) -545- 5011 (Ext. 5202)
    ue_sc-terre@uqac.ca
    Enrollment (2015): B: 69 (7) M: 27 (8) D: 13 (0)
Director:
    Michael D. Higgins, (D), McGill, 1980, Gi
Professor:
    Sarah- Jane Barnes, (D), Toronto, 1983, EgGiCt
    Paul Bedard, (D), UQAC, 1992, CaGzEg
    Romain Chesnaux, (D), École Polytechnique de Montréal, Québec, Canada, 2005, Hw
    Pierre Cousineau, (D), Laval, 1986, Gd
    Real Daigneault, (D), Laval, 1991, GcEgOi
    Damien Gaboury, (D), UQAC, 1999, EmCe
    Alain Rouleau, (D), Waterloo, 1984, Hw
    Ali Saeidi, (D), Institut National Polytechnique de Lorraine, France, 2010, Nr
    Edward W. Sawyer, (D), Toronto, 1983, Gp
Instructor:
    Denis Cote, (M), Quebec (Chicoutimi), 1986, Gi
Lecturer:
    Philippe Page, (D), INRS-ETE, 2006, Gi
Adjunct Professor:
    Sylvain Raffini, (D), UQAM, 2008, GcHw
Emeritus:
    Guy Archambault, (D), Nr
    Edward H. Chown, (D), Johns Hopkins, 1963, Gx
    Jayanta Guha, (D), Jadavpur, 1967, Eg
    Denis W. Roy, (D), Princeton, 1976, Gc
Laboratory Director:
    Dany Savard, (M), UQAC, 2010, Ca

Universite du Quebec a Montreal
Département des sciences de la Terre et de l'atmosphere (B,M,D) (2015)
C.P. 8888, succursale Centre-ville
Montreal, QC H3C 3P8
    p. +1 514-987-3000
    dept.sct@uqam.ca
    http://scta.uqam.ca
    Administrative Assistant: France Beauchemin
    Enrollment: No data reported since 1999

Professor:
    Florent Barbecot, (D), Hw
    Jean-Pierre Blanchet, (D), Toronto, 1984, Pe
    Gilles Couture, (D), British Columbia, 1987, Yg
    Fiona Ann Darbyshire, (D), Cambridge, 2000, Ys
    Anne de Vernal, (D), UdeM, Montreal, 1986, Pm
    Alessandro Marco Forte, (D), Toronto, 1989, Yg
    Pierre Gauthier, (D), McGill, 1988, Ow
    Eric Girard, (D), McGill, 1999, Ow
    Normand Goulet, (D), Queen's, 1976, Gc
    Cherif Hamzaoui, (D), Alziers, 1980, Yg
    Alfred Jaouich, (D), Minnesota, 1975, Sc
    Michel Jebrak, (D), Orleans, 1984, Eg
    Michel Lamothe, (D), W Ontario, 1985, Gl
    Rene Laprise, (D), Toronto, 1988, Oa
    Marie Larocque, (D), de Poitiers, France, 1998, Hw
    Marc Michel Lucotte, (D), McGill, 1987, Oc
    Daniele Luigi Pinti, (D), France, 1993, Cs
    Martin Roy, (D), Oregon, 1998, Gl
    Ross Stevenson, (D), Arizona, 1989, Cg
    Laxmi Sushama, (D), Melbourne, 1999, Hy
    Julie Mireille Thériault, (D), McGill, 2009, On
    Enrico Torlaschi, (D), Ecole Polytechnique (Milan), 1976, Ow
    Alain Tremblay, (D), Laval, 1989, Gct
    David Widory, (D), IPGP-Université, 1999, Cs
Associate Professor:
    Sanda Balescu, (D), Libre de Bruxelles, 1988, Pe
    Jean Côté, Oa
    Bernard Dugas, Oa
    Stephane Faure, (D), INRS-Georessources, 1995, Gc
    Philippe Gachon, (D), UQAM, 1999, Oa
    Michel Gauthier, (D), Polytechnique (Montreal), 1982, Eg
    Jean-François Helie, (D), UQAC, 2004, Cs
    Claude Hillaire-Marcel, (D), Paris VI, 1979, Cs
    Jean-Claude Mareschal, (D), Texas A&M, 1975, Yg
    Andre Poirier, (D), UQAM, 2005, Cs
    Gilbert P. Prichonnet, (D), Bordeaux, 1967, Pi
    William W. Shilts
    Gabriel-Constantin Voicu, (D), UQAM, 1995, GcCg

Universite du Quebec a Rimouski
Inst des sciences de la mer de Rimouski (M,D) (2014)
310, Allee des Ursulines
Rimouski, QC G5L 3A1
    p. (418) 723- 8617
    andre_rochon@qc.ca
    http://www.ismer.ca
    Enrollment: No data reported since 1999
Director:
    Serge Demers, (D), Laval, 1981, Ob
Professor:
    Celine Audet, (D), Laval, 1985, Ob
    Jean-Claude Brethes, (D), Aix-Marseille, 1978, Ob
    Jean-Pierre Gagne, (D), Montreal, 1993, Oc
    Michel Gosselin, (D), Laval, 1990, Ob
    Vladimir G. Koutitonsky, (D), SUNY (Stony Brook), 1985, Op
    Jocelyne Pellerin, (D), Laval, 1982, Ob
    Emilien Pelletier, (D), McGill, 1983, Oc
    Suzanne Roy, (D), Dalhousie, 1986, Ob
    Bjorn Sundby, (D), Bergen (Norway), 1966, Oc
    Bruno Zakardjian, (D), Paris, 1994, Ob

Universite Laval 🗇
Dept de geologie (B,M,D) (2010)
Pavillon Pouliot
Faculte des Sciences et de genie
Ste-Foy, QC G1K 7P4
    p. (418) 656-2193
    ggl@ggl.ulaval.ca
    http://www.ggl.ulaval.ca
    Enrollment (2002): B: 127 (27) M: 30 (6) D: 20 (3)
Head:
    Josee Duchesne, (D), Laval, 1993, Gz
Professor:
    Georges Beaudoin, (D), Ottawa, 1991, Em
    Richard Fortier, (D), Montreal, 1994, Yg

Paul W. Glover, (D), East Anglia (UK), 1989, Yx
    Rejean J. Hebert, (D), Brest, 1985, Gi
    Jacques E. Locat, (D), Sherbrooke, 1982, Ng
    Fritz Neuweiler, (D), Berlin, 1995, GsdPo
    Rene Therrien, (D), Waterloo, 1993, Hw
Eletron Microprobe Specialist:
    Marc Choquette, (D), Laval, 1988, On
Associate Scientist:
    Pauline Dansereau, (M), Laval, 1988, Gs
    Andre Levesque, (B), Laval, 1979, Gz
    Pierre Therrien, (M), Laval, 1986, Gq
Research Associate:
    Danielle Cloutier, (D), Laval, GeOg
Adjunct Professor:
    Marc Constantin, (D), Brest, 1995, Gi
    Benoit Fournier, (D), Laval, 1993, NgOmGg
Technician:
    Eric David, (B), Laval, On
    Jean Frenette, (B), Laval, 1985, Gz
    Martin Plante, Cg

University of Alberta
Dept of Earth & Atmospheric Sciences (B,M,D) ● (2015)
126 Earth Sciences Building
Edmonton, AB T6G 2E3
    p. (780) 492-3265
    eas@ualberta.ca
    http://www.ualberta.ca/EAS/
    f: https://www.facebook.com/UofAEarthandAtmospheric-
    SciencesDepartment
    t: @UofA_EAS
    Enrollment (2014): B: 180 (0) M: 55 (0) D: 88 (0)
Acting Chair:
    Robert A. Creaser, (D), La Trobe, 1990, Cc
Professor & Inaugural Director, Planning Program:
    Sandeep Agrawal, (D), Ou
Professor:
    Robert W. Luth, (D), California (Los Angeles), 1985, Gi
    Martin J. Sharp, (D), Aberdeen, 1982, Ol
Distinguished University Professor:
    S. George Pemberton, (D), McMaster, 1979, Gr
Canada Research Chair:
    Thomas Stachel, (D), Wurzburg, 1991, Gi
Associate Dean (Research):
    Larry M. Heaman, (D), McMaster, 1986, Cc
Associate Chair:
    Thomas Chacko, (D), North Carolina, 1987, Gp
    Murray Gingras, (D), North Carolina, 1987, Go
Professor:
    Andrew B.G Bush, (D), Toronto, 1995, Oa
    Michael W. Caldwell, (D), McGill, 1995, Pv
    Octavian Catuneanu, (D), Toronto, 1996, Gs
    Philippe Erdmer, (D), Queen's, 1982, Gc
    John Gamon, (D), California (Davis), 1989, Or
    Christopher Herd, (D), New Mexico, 2001, Gi
    Brian Jones, (D), Ottawa, 1974, Ps
    Kurt Konhauser, (D), W Ontario, 1993, Py
    Lindsey Leighton, (D), Michigan, 1999, Pi
    Hans G. Machel, (D), McGill, 1985, Go
    Karlis Muehlenbachs, (D), Chicago, 1971, Cs
    Graham Pearson, (D), Leeds, Cec
    David Potter, (D), Newcastle upon Tyne, Ye
    Gerhard Reuter, (D), McGill, 1985, Ow
    Jeremy P. Richards, (D), Australian National, 1990, Em
    Benoit Rivard, (D), Washington (St. Louis), 1990, Or
    Benjamin J. Rostron, (D), Alberta, 1995, Hw
    G. Arturo Sanchez-Azofeifa, (D), New Hampshire, 1996, Oi
    Bruce Sutherland, (D), Toronto, 1994, Cm
    Martyn Unsworth, (D), Cambridge, GtvYe
    John W.F Waldron, (D), Edinburgh, 1981, Gc
    John D. Wilson, (D), Guelph, 1980, Ow
    John-Paul Zonneveld, (D), Alberta, 1999, Go
Associate Professor:
    Duane Froese, (D), Calgary, 2001, Gm
    Theresa D. Garvin, (D), McMaster, 1999, On
    Sarah Gleeson, (D), Imperial Coll (UK), 1996, Eg
    Nicholas Harris, (D), Stanford, Gso

Jeffrey Kavanaugh, (D), British Columbia, 2001, Ng
G. Peter Kershaw, (D), Alberta, 1983, Gm
Tara McGee, (D), Australian National, 1996, On
Carl A. Mendoza, (D), Waterloo, 1993, Hw
Paul Myers, (D), Victoria, 1996, Og
Assistant Professor:
Daniel Alessi, (D), Notre Dame, Cl
Damian Collins, (D), Simon Fraser, 2004, On
Leith Deacon, (D), Ou
Long Li, (D), Lehigh, 2006, CsGpv
Manish Shirgaokar, (D), Ou
Robert Summers, (D), Guelph, 2005, On
Distinguished University Professor:
Nathaniel W. Rutter, (D), Alberta, 1966, Ge
Emeritus:
Halfdan Baadsgaard, (D), ETH (Switzerland), 1955, Cc
Ronald A. Burwash, (D), Minnesota, 1955, Gp
Ian A. Campbell, (D), Colorado, 1968, Gm
Brian D. Chatterton, (D), Australian National, 1970, Pi
David M. Cruden, (D), London, 1969, Nr
John England, (D), Colorado, 1974, Gm
Kenneth J. Fairbairn, (D), Melbourne, 1968, On
Richard C. Fox, (D), Kansas, 1965, Pv
Keith D. Hage, (D), Chicago, 1957, Ow
M. John Hodgson, (D), Toronto, 1973, On
R. Geoffrey Ironside, (D), Durham, 1965, On
Edgar L. Jackson, (D), Toronto, 1974, On
Leszek A. Kosinski, (D), Warsaw, 1958, On
Jiri Krupicka, (D), Prague, 1947, Gp
Arleigh H. Laycock, (D), Minnesota, 1957, Hg
Edward P. Lozowski, (D), Toronto, 1970, Oa
Harry J. McPherson, (D), McGill, 1967, Gm
Roger D. Morton, (D), Nottingham, 1959, Em
O.F. George Sitwell, (D), Toronto, 1968, On
Peter J. Smith, (D), Edinburgh, 1964, On
Charles R. Stelck, (D), Stanford, 1951, Ps
József Tóth, (D), Utrecht (Neth), 1965, Hw

Inst of Geophysical Research (B,M,D) (2010)
Mailstop #615
CEB/Physics
Edmonton, AB T6G 2G7
p. (780) 492-3521
bruce.sutherland@ualberta.ca
http://www-geo.phys.ualberta.ca/institute/
Administrative Assistant: Lee Grimard
Enrollment: No data reported since 1999
Director:
Douglas R. Schmitt, (D), Caltech, 1987, Yx
Professor:
Robert A. Creaser, (D), La Trobe, 1992, Cc
T. Bryant Moodie, (D), Toronto, 1972, On
Robert Rankin, (D), North Wales, 1984, Xy
Gerhard W. Reuter, (D), McGill, 1985, Oa
Wojciech Rozmus, (D), Inst Nuc Res (Poland), On
John C. Samson, (D), Alberta, 1971, Xy
Martin J. Sharp, (D), Aberdeen, Gl
John Shaw, (D), Reading, 1969, Gl
Samuel S. Shen, (D), Wisconsin, Oa
Bruce R. Sutherland, (D), Toronto, 1994, On
Gordon E. Swaters, (D), British Columbia, 1985, Op
Richard D. Sydora, (D), Texas, 1985, Xy
Martyn Unsworth, (D), Cambridge, On
John D. Wilson, (D), Guelph, 1980, Oa
Associate Professor:
Andrew B. G. Bush, (D), Toronto, Oa
Carl Mendoza, (D), Waterloo, 1993, Hw
Benoit Rivard, (D), Washington, 1990, Or
Ben Rostron, (D), Alberta, On
Mauricio D. Sacchi, (D), British Columbia, Ys
Assistant Professor:
Francis Fenrich, (D), Alberta, 1997, Xy
Jeff Gu, (D), Harvard, 2001, Ys
Moritz Heimpel, (D), Johns Hopkins, 1995, On
Vadim Kravchinsky, (D), Irkutsk, 1996, Ym
Paul Myers, (D), Victoria, 1992, Op

Emeritus:
Michael E. Evans, (D), Australian National, 1969, Ym
Keith D. Hage, (D), Chicago, 1957, Oa
F. Walter Jones, (D), McGill, 1968, Ym
Edward P. Lozowski, (D), Toronto, 1970, Oa
Roger D. Morton, (D), Nottingham, 1959, Em
Edo Nyland, (D), California (Los Angeles), 1967, Ys
David Rankin, (D), Alberta, 1960, Ym
Gordon Rostoker, (D), British Columbia, 1966, Xy
J. Timothy Spanos, (D), Alberta, 1977, Ys

University of British Columbia 🗐
Dept of Earth, Ocean, and Atmospheric Sciences (B,M,D) O (2015)
2020-2207 Main Mall
Vancouver, BC V6T 1Z4
p. (604) 827-5284
acairns@eos.ubc.ca
http://www.eoas.ubc.ca
Enrollment (2010): B: 361 (105) M: 111 (20) D: 93 (15)
Director, Geological Engineering Program:
Roger D. Beckie, (D), Princeton, 1992, Hg
Honorary Professor:
Mati Raudsepp, (D), Manitoba, 1984, Gz
Dean, Science:
Simon M. Peacock, (D), California (Los Angeles), 1985, Gg
Canada Research Chair:
Roger Francois, (D), British Columbia, 1987, Cm
Dominique Weis, (D), Libre de Bruxelles, 1982, Cc
Professor:
Susan E. Allen, (D), Cambridge, 1988, Op
Raymond J. Andersen, (D), California (San Diego), 1975, Oc
Neil Balmforth, (D), Cambridge, 1990, Oa
Michael G. Bostock, (D), Australian National, 1991, Ys
R. Marc Bustin, (D), British Columbia, 1979, Ec
Gregory M. Dipple, (D), Johns Hopkins, 1991, Gp
Erik Eberhardt, (D), Saskatchewan, 1998, Ng
Lee A. Groat, (D), Manitoba, 1988, Gz
Felix J. Herrmann, (D), Delft (Neth), 1997, Yx
Oldrich Hungr, (D), Alberta, 1981, Gm
Mark Jellinek, (D), Australian National, 1999, Gg
Catherine L. Johnson, (D), San Diego, 1994
Ulrich Mayer, (D), Waterloo, 1999, Nm
James K. Mortensen, (D), California (Santa Barbara), 1983, Cc
Douglas W. Oldenburg, (D), California (Santa Barbara), 1974, Yg
Evgeny Pakhomov, (D), Russian Acad of Sci, 1992, Ob
James Kelly Russell, (D), Calgary, 1984, Gi
James S. Scoates, (D), Wyoming, 1994, Gi
J. Leslie Smith, (D), British Columbia, 1978, Hw
Paul L. Smith, (D), McMaster, 1981, Pg
Douw G. Steyn, (D), British Columbia, 1980, Oa
Roland B. Stull, (D), Washington, 1975, Oa
Curtis Suttle, (D), British Columbia, 1987, Ob
NSERC Industrial Research Chair in Computational Geoscience:
Eldad Haber, (D), British Columbia, 1997, YgOn
Director, MDRU:
Craig Hart, (D), W Australia, 2004, Eg
Canada Research Chair:
Maria Maldonado, (D), McGill, 1999, Ob
Christian Schoof, (D), Oxford, 2002, Ol
Associate Professor:
Philip Austin, (D), Washington, 1987, Oa
Kurt A. Grimm, (D), California (Santa Cruz), 1992, Gs
Mark Johnson, (D), Cornell, 2005, SpNg
Lori Kennedy, (D), Texas A&M, 1996, Gc
Maya G. Kopylova, (D), Moscow, 1990, Gi
Kristin J. Orians, (D), California (Santa Cruz), 1992, Cm
Richard A. Pawlowicz, (D), MIT/WHOI, 1994, Op
Philippe Tortell, (D), Princeton, 2001, Ob
Assistant Professor:
Kenneth Hickey, (D), James Cook, 1995, Gz
Valentina Radic, (D), Alaska (Fairbanks), 2008, OlaOg
Honorary Research Associate:
Kevin Kingdon, (M), British Columbia, 1998, Yg
Michael Maxwell, (D), British Columbia, 1986, Yg
Research Associate:
Thomas Bissig, (D), Queens, 2001, EmCg
Farhad Bouzari, (D), Queens, 2003, Eg

Amanda Bustin, (D), Victoria, 2006, YgNg
Philip T. Hammer, (D), California (San Diego), 1991, Ys
Brian Hunt, (D), Tasmania, 2005, Ob
Bruno Kieffer, (D), Grenoble, 2002, Cs
Henryk Modzelewski, (D), British Columbia, 2004, Oa
Roger Pieters, (D), California (Santa Barbara), Op
Lin-Ping Song, (D), Sichuan (China), 1996, Ng
Dave E. Williams, (D), British Columbia, 1987, Oc
Instructor:
Mary Lou Bevier, (D), California (Santa Barbara), 1982, Cc
Sara Harris, (D), Oregon State, 1998, Ou
Tara Ivanochko, (D), British Columbia, 2004, Ou
Stuart Sutherland, (D), Leicester (UK), 1992, Pg
Lecturer:
Brett Gilley, (M), Simon Fraser, 2003, Gg
Francis H. M. Jones, (M), British Columbia, 1987, Ye
Honorary Lecturer:
Dileep Athaide, (M), British Columbia, 1975, Gg
Adjunct Professor:
Robert G. Anderson, (D), Carleton, 1983, Gt
Stephen Billings, (D), Sydney, 1998, Yg
Alex Cannon, (D), British Columbia, 2009, Oa
Edward Carmack, (D), Washington, 1972, Op
Michael G. G. Foreman, (D), British Columbia, 1984, Op
James Haggart, (D), California (Davis), 1984, Pg
Catherine J. Hickson, (D), British Columbia, 1987, Gv
Mark Holzer, (D), Simon Fraser, 1990, Oa
R. Lynn Kirlin, (D), Utah State, 1968, Oa
Doug McCollor, (D), British Columbia, 2008, Oaw
Barry Narod, (D), British Columbia, 1979, Yx
Michael Orchard, (D), Hull, 1975, PgGg
Thomas F. Pedersen, (D), Edinburgh, 1979, Ou
K. Wayne Savigny, (D), Alberta, 1980, Ng
Barbara H. Scott Smith, (D), Edinburgh, 1977, Gz
John F. H. Thompson, (D), Toronto, 1984, Em
Richard E. Thomson, (D), British Columbia, 1971, Op
Richard Tosdal, (D), California (Santa Barbara), 1988, Em
Knut von Salzen, (D), Hamburg, 1997, Oa
Chi S. Wong, (D), California (San Diego), 1968, Cm
Emeritus:
Peter M. Bradshaw, (D), Durham (UK), 1965, Ce
Stephen E. Calvert, (D), California (San Diego), 1964, Cm
Richard L. Chase, (D), Princeton, 1963, Gu
Garry K. C. Clarke, (D), Toronto, 1967, Yg
Ronald M. Clowes, (D), Alberta, 1969, Ys
Robert M. Ellis, (D), Alberta, 1964, Ys
William K. Fletcher, (D), Imperial Coll (UK), 1968, Ce
Michael Healey, (D), Aberdeen, 1969, Ob
William Hsieh, (D), British Columbia, 1981, Op
Alan G. Lewis, (D), Hawaii, 1961, Ob
Stephen G. Pond, (D), British Columbia, 1965, Op
R. Doncaster Russell, (D), Toronto, 1954, Yg
Alastair J. Sinclair, (D), British Columbia, 1964, Em
Frank J. R. Taylor, (D), Cape Town, 1965, Ob
Undergraduate Program Coordinator:
Teresa Woodley, On
Secretary to the Head:
Selene Chan, (B), British Columbia, 1995, On
Office Support:
Alicia Cairns, On
Human Resources Manager:
Cary Thomson, On
Graduate Coordinator:
Audrey Van Slyck
Finance Clerk:
Anita Lam, On
Kathy Scott, On
Director of Resources and Operations:
Renee Haggart, On
Computer Department Manager:
John Amor, On

Soil Science (B,M,D) (2015)
2357 Main Mall
Vancouver, BC V6T 1Z4
p. (604) 822-1219
maja.krzic@ubc.ca

http://www.landfood.ubc.ca/academics/graduate/soil-science-msc-phd/
Enrollment (2015): B: 4 (4) M: 8 (6) D: 11 (3)
Professor:
T. Andrew Black, (D), Wisconsin, 1969, Sp
Christopher Chanway, (D), British Columbia, 1987, Sb
Sue Grayston, (D), Sheffield, 1988, Sb
Cindy Prescott, (D), Calgary, 1988, Sb
Suzanne Simard, (D), Oregon State, 1995, Sb
Associate Professor:
Maja Krzic, (D), British Columbia, 1997, Sf
Assistant Professor:
Sean Smukler, (D), California (Davis), 2008, Os
Lecturer:
Sandra Brown, (D), British Columbia, 1997, Sp
Emeritus:
Arthur A. Bomke, (D), Illinois, 1972, Sc
Sietan Chieng, (D), McGill, 1980, Sp
Leslie M. Lavkulich, (D), Cornell, 1969, Sd
Michael D. Novak, (D), British Columbia, 1981, Sp
Hans D. Schreier, (D), British Columbia, 1976, Og

University of Calgary
Dept of Geology & Geophysics (B,M,D) (2014)
2500 University Drive NW
Calgary, AB T2N 1N4
p. (403) 220-5841
lrlines@ucalgary.ca
http://www.geo.ucalgary.ca/
Enrollment (2003): B: 268 (73) M: 61 (19) D: 27 (4)
Head:
Larry R. Lines, (D), British Columbia, 1976, Ye
Professor:
Laurence R. Bentley, (D), Princeton, 1990, Hw
James R. Brown, (D), Uppsala, 1972, Ys
Frederick A. Cook, (D), Cornell, 1980, Ys
Kenneth Duckworth, (D), Leeds, 1964, Ye
Edward D. Ghent, (D), California, 1964, Gp
Terence M. Gordon, (D), Princeton, 1969, Gq
Charles M. Henderson, (D), Calgary, 1988, Pm
Ian E. Hutcheon, (D), Carleton, 1977, Cl
Federico F. Krause, (D), Calgary, 1979, Gs
Edward S. Krebes, (D), Alberta, 1980, Ys
Donald C. Lawton, (D), Auckland, 1979, Ye
James W. Nicholls, (D), California, 1969, Gi
Gerald D. Osborn, (D), California, 1972, Gm
David R. Pattison, (D), Edinburgh, 1985, Gp
Ronald J. Spencer, (D), Johns Hopkins, 1981, Cg
Deborah A. Spratt, (D), Johns Hopkins, 1980, Gc
Robert R. Stewart, (D), MIT, 1983, Ye
Patrick Wu, (D), Toronto, 1982, Ys
Associate Professor:
Russell L. Hall, (D), McMaster, 1976, Pi
Masaki Hayashi, (D), Waterloo, 1996, Hw
Alan R. Hildebrand, (D), Arizona, 1992, Xm
John C. Hopkins, (D), McGill, 1972, Gs
Gary F. Margrave, (D), Alberta, 1981, Ye
Bernhard Mayer, (D), Ludwig-Maximilians, 1993, Cs
Brian J. Moorman, (D), Carlton, 1997, Gm
Cynthia L. Riediger, (D), Waterloo, 1991, Co
Cathy Ryan, (D), Waterloo, 1994, Hw
Assistant Professor:
Jean-Michel Maillol, (D), Alberta, 1992, Ym
Senior Instructor:
Jon W. Jones, (D), Calgary, 1972, Gp
Honorary Professor:
Brian Norford, (D), Yale, 1959, Gr
Adjunct Professor:
John C. Bancroft, (D), Brigham Young, 1975, Ng
Benoit Beauchamp, (D), Calgary, 1987, Pm
Philip J. Currie, (D), McGill, 1981, Pv
Susan L. Gordon, (D), Waterloo, 1999, Hw
Stephen E. Grasby, (D), Calgary, 1997, Hw
William D. Gunter, (D), Johns Hopkins, 1974, Cl
J. Bruce Jamieson, (D), Calgary, 1996, Ne
Apostolos Kantzas, (D), Waterloo, 1988, Ng
Thomas F. Moslow, (D), South Carolina, 1980, Co

Peter E. Putnam, (D), Calgary, 1985, Gs
Gerald M. Ross, (D), Carleton, 1983, Gt
Selim Sayegh, (D), McGill, 1980, Gs
John-Paul Zonneveld, (D), Alberta, 1999, Pm
Emeritus:
Peter Bayliss, (D), New South Wales, 1967, Gz
Finley A. Campbell, (D), Princeton, 1958, Em
Peter E. Gretener, (D), ETH (Switzerland), 1953, Ng
Leonard V. Hills, (D), Alberta, 1965, Pl
Alfred A. Levinson, (D), Michigan, 1952, Eg
Alan E. Oldershaw, (D), Liverpool, 1967, Gs
Philip S. Simony, (D), London, 1963, Gc
Norman C. Wardlaw, (D), Glasgow, 1960, Go

University of Guelph
School of Environmental Sciences (B,M,D) (2015)
Guelph, ON N1G 2W1
  p. (519) 824-2052
  earnaud@uoguelph.ca
  http://www.ses.uoguelph.ca
  Enrollment (2005): B: 89 (31) M: 48 (11) D: 20 (3)
Director:
Jonathan Newman, (D), Albany, 1990, On
Director, Controlled Environment Systems Research Facility:
Michael Dixon, (D), Edinburgh, On
Canada Research Chair in Recombinant Antibody Technology:
Christopher C. Hall, (D), Alberta, On
Associate Dean, Research, OAC:
Beverley A. Hale, (D), Guelph, 1989, Ct
Associate Dean, Academics, OAC:
Jonathan Schmidt, (D), Toronto, On
Professor:
Paul Goodwin, (D), California (Davis), On
Ernesto Guzman, (D), California (Davis), On
Tom Hsiang, (D), Washington, On
Hung Lee, (D), McGill, On
Stephen Marshall, (D), Guelph, On
Gard Otis, (D), Kansas, On
Cynthia Scott-Dupree, (D), Simon Fraser, On
Jack Trevors, (D), Waterloo, On
R. Paul Voroney, (D), Saskatchewan, 1983, Sb
Claudia Wagner Riddle, (D), Guelph, 1992, Ow
Director of the Arboretum:
Shelley Hunt, (D), Guelph, On
Dean, OAC:
Rob J. Gordon, (D), Guelph, Oa
Canada Research Chair in Microbial Ecology:
Kari Dunfield, (D), Saskatchewan, Sb
Associate Professor:
Madhur Anand, (D), W Ontario, On
Emmanuelle Arnaud, (D), McMaster, 2002, Gls
Susan Glasauer, (D), Tech (Munich), 1995, Py
Marc Habash, (D), Guelph, On
Rebecca Hallett, (D), Simon Fraser, On
Richard Heck, (D), Saskatchewan, Sd
John Lauzon, (D), Guelph, So
Ivan O'Halloran, (D), Saskatchewan, 1986, So
Gary Parkin, (D), Guelph, 1994, Hw
Paul Sibley, (D), Waterloo, On
Jon Warland, (D), Guelph, 1999, Oa
Assistant Professor:
Tim Rennie, On
Laura Van Eerd, (D), Guelph, On
Alan Watson, (M), Guelph, On
Instructor:
Neil Rooney, (D), McGill, On
Emeritus:
George Barron, (D), Iowa State, On
Greg J. Boland, (D), Guelph, On
Michael E. Brookfield, (D), Reading (UK), 1973, PgGrt
Ward Chesworth, (D), McMaster, 1967, Cl
Les J. Evans, (D), Wales, 1974, Cl
Austin Fletcher, (D), Alberta, On
Terry J. Gillespie, (D), Guelph, 1968, Ow
Michael J. Goss, (D), Reading, So
Pieter H. Groenevelt, (D), Wageningen (Neth), 1969, Sp
Robert Hall, (D), Melbourne, On

Stewart G. Hilts, (D), Toronto, 1981, On
Peter Kevan, (D), Alberta, On
Kenneth M. King, (D), Wisconsin, 1956, Oa
I. Peter Martini, (D), McMaster, 1966, Gsl
Raymond G. McBride, (D), Guelph, 1982, Os
Murray H. Miller, (D), Purdue, 1957, So
Kaushik Narinder, On
Leonard Ritter, On
Keith Solomon, (D), Illinois, On
Gerry Stephenson, On
George W. Thurtell, (D), Wisconsin, 1965, Oa
H. Peter Van Straaten, (D), Goettingen, 1974, En

University of Lethbridge
Dept of Geography (B,M) (2004)
4401 University Drive
Lethbridge, AB T1K 3M4
  p. (403) 329-2225
  geography.chair@uleth.ca
  http://home.uleth.ca/geo
  Administrative Assistant: Margaret Cook
  Enrollment (2002): B: 94 (24) M: 9 (1)
Chair:
Ian E. MacLachlan, (D), Toronto, 1990, Oe
Professor:
Walter E. Aufrecht, (D), Toronto, On
Rene W. Barendregt, (D), Queen's (Kingston), 1977, Gm
Robert J. Rogerson, (D), Macquarie, 1979, Gm
Associate Professor:
James M. Byrne, (D), Alberta, 1990, Hg
Thomas Johnston, (D), Waterloo, 1988, Oe
Derek R. Peddle, (D), Waterloo, 1997, Or
Assistant Professor:
Craig Coburn, (D), Simon Fraser, 2002, Oy
Susan Dakin, (D), Waterloo, 2000, Oe
Hester Jiskoot, (D), Leeds, 2000, Gl
Stefan Kienzle, (D), Heidelberg, 1993, Oi
Ivan Townshend, (D), Calgary, 1997, On
Wei Xu, (D), Guelph, 1998, Oi
Adjunct Professor:
John Dormaar, (D), Alberta, 1961, So
Ron Hall, On
Larry Herr, (D), On
Daniel L. Johnson, (D), British Columbia, 1983, On
Pano George Karkanis, (D), Uppsala, 1966, So
Ross McKenzie, (D), On
Anne Smith, (D)
Derald Smith, (D), On
Emeritus:
Roy J. Fletcher, (D), Clark, 1968, Oa

University of Manitoba 📑
Geological Sciences (B,M,D) (2014)
240 Wallace Building
125 Dysart Road
Winnipeg, MB R3T 2N2
  p. (204) 474-9371
  Mostafa.Fayek@ad.umanitoba.ca
  http://www.umanitoba.ca/geoscience
  Administrative Assistant: Brenda Miller
  Enrollment (2014): M: 12 (3) D: 8 (2)
Head:
Ian J. Ferguson, (D), Australian National, 1988, Ye
Professor:
Anton Chakhmouridian, (D), St. Petersburg, 1997, Gz
Nancy Chow, (D), Memorial, 1986, Gs
Robert J. Elias, (D), Cincinnati, 1979, Pi
Mostafa Fayek, (D), Saskatchewan, 1996, Cs
Norman M. Halden, (D), Glasgow, 1983, Cg
Frank C. Hawthorne, (D), McMaster, 1973, Gz
William M. Last, (D), Manitoba, 1980, GsnGo
Soren Rysgaard, (D), Aarhus (Denmark), 1995, Gl
Elena Sokolova, (D), Moscow, 1980, Gz
Senior Scholar:
George S. Clark, (D), Columbia, 1967, Cc
Barbara L. Sherriff, (D), McMaster, 1988, Gz

Allan C. Turnock, (D), Johns Hopkins, 1960, Gp
Associate Professor:
   Alfredo Camacho, (D), Australian National, 1998, Gt
   Andrew Frederiksen, (D), British Columbia, 2000, Ys
Assistant Professor:
   Genevieve Ali, (D), Montreal, 2010, Hw
   Zou Zou Kuzyk, (D), Manitoba, 2009, Cg
Research Associate:
   Yassir Abdu, (D), Uppsala, 2004, Gz
Instructor:
   Karen Ferreira, (M), Manitoba, 1984, Gg
   William Mandziuk, (M), Manitoba, 1989, Gg
   Jeffrey Young, (M), Manitoba, 1992, Gg
Adjunct Professor:
   Scott Anderson, (D), Dalhousie, 1998
   Christian Bohm, (D), ETH (Switzerland), 1996, Cg
   William Buhay
   David Corrigan, (D), Carleton, Gt
   Jody Deming, (D), Maryland, 1981, On
   Michel Houle, (D), Laurentian, 2008, Gv
   Brooke Milne, (D), Ga
   Vince Palace, (D), Manitoba, 1996
   James Reist, (D), Toronto, 1983
   Graham A. Young, (D), New Brunswick, 1988, Pi
Emeritus:
   William C. Brisbin, (D), California (Los Angeles), 1970, Gc
   Robert B. Ferguson, (D), Toronto, 1948, Gz
   Wooil Moon, (D), British Columbia, 1976, Ys
   James T. Teller, (D), Cincinnati, 1970, Gs
Laboratory Director:
   Panseok Yang, (D), Memorial, 2002, Ca
Related Staff:
   Neil Ball, (B), Manitoba, 1982, Gz
   Laura Bergen, (M), Manitoba, 2013
   Mark Cooper, (M), Manitoba, 1997, Gz
   Mulu Serzu, (D), Manitoba, 1990, Yg
   Ryan Sharpe, (M), Manitoba, 2012
   Ravinder Sidhu
   Misuk Yun, (M), Manitoba, 1986, Cs

University of New Brunswick

Dept of Geology (B,M,D) (2014)
Fredericton, NB E3B 5A3
   p. (506) 453-4803
   geology@unb.ca
   Administrative Secretary: Merrill Ann Beatty
   Enrollment: No data reported since 1999
Chair:
   Joseph C. White, (D), W Ontario, 1979, Gc
Professor:
   Bruce E. Broster, (D), W Ontario, 1982, Gl
   John Todd Dunn, (D), Alberta, 1983, Gi
   Ronald K. Pickerill, (D), Liverpool, 1974, Pg
   John G. Spray, (D), Cambridge, 1980, Gp
   Paul F. Williams, (D), Sydney, 1969, Gc
Associate Professor:
   Nicholas J. Susak, (D), Princeton, 1981, Cg
Assistant Professor:
   Karl Butler, (D), British Columbia, 1996, Yg
   Cliff S.J. Shaw, (D), W Ontario, 1994, Gi
Research Associate:
   James Whitehead, (D), New Brunswick, 1998, Gg
Honorary Research Professor:
   Henk W. Van De Poll, (D), Swansea, 1970, Gs
Adjunct Professor:
   Richard A. F. Grieve, (D), Toronto, 1970, Xg
   David R. Lentz, (D), Ottawa, 1992, Cg
   Randall F. Miller, (D), Waterloo, 1984, Pg
Emeritus:
   Arnold L. McAllister, (D), McGill, 1950, Em
Geology Librarian:
   Eszter Schwenke, On

University of New Brunswick Saint John

Dept of Biological Sciences (B,M,D) (2015)
PO Box 5050

100 Tucker Park Road
Saint John, NB E2L 4L5
   p. (506) 648-5607
   lwilson@unbsj.ca
   http://www.unbsj.ca/sase/biology/
   Enrollment (2007): B: 2 (0) M: 1 (0)
Professor:
   Lucy A. Wilson, (D), Paris VI, 1986, Ga
Emeritus:
   Alan Logan, (D), Durham (UK), 1962, Ob

University of Ottawa

Dept of Earth and Environmental Sciences (B,M,D) (2015)
15025, 120 University
PO Box 450, Station A
Ottawa, ON K1N 6N5
   p. (613) -56-2-58 x x 6870)
   hdegouf@uottawa.ca
   http://www.science.uottawa.ca/est/eng/welcome.html
   Enrollment (2012): B: 78 (18) M: 29 (11) D: 12 (2)
Chair:
   Andre Desrochers, (D), Memorial, 1986, Gs
Professor:
   R. William C. Arnott, (D), Alberta, 1987, GsSo
   Ian D. Clark, (D), Paris - Sud, 1988, Hw
   Jack Robert Cornett, (D), McGill, 1982, GgOgn
   Danielle Fortin, (D), Quebec, 1992, Py
   Mark Hannington, (D), Toronto, 1989, Eg
   Keiko Hattori, (D), Tokyo, 1977, Cg
   Michel R. Robin, (D), Waterloo, 1991, Hw
Associate Professor:
   Glenn A. Milne, (D), Toronto, 1998, YgOag
   David Schneider, (D), Lehigh, 2000, GtxGg
Replacement Professor:
   Olivier Nadeau, (D), McGill, 2011, Gx
Assistant Professor:
   Tom A. Al, (D), Waterloo, 1996, HwCgOg
   Pascal Audet, (D), British Columbia, 2008, YgGc
   Sarah Dare, (D), Cardiff, 2007, Gz
   Jonathan O'Neil, (D), McGill, 2009, Cgc
Lecturer:
   Simone Dumas, (D), Ottawa, 2004, GsOg
Adjunct Professor:
   Frits P. Agterberg, (D), Utrecht (Neth), 1961, Gq
   Eric De Kemp, (D), Québec (Chicoutimi), 2000, OirOg
   David Andrew Fisher, (D), Copenhagen, 1978, Ol
   William K. Fyson, (D), Reading (UK), 1960, Gc
   Quentin Gall, (D), Carleton, 1994, Gs
   Richard Goulet, (D), Ottawa, 2001, CgPyGe
   Jeffrey Wayne Hedenquist, (D), Auckland, 1983, Eg
   Donald D. Hogarth, (D), McGill, 1959, Gz
   Dogan Paktunc, (D), Ottawa, 1983, Gz
   Patricia Rasmussen, (D), Waterloo, 1993, Ge
Emeritus:
   Jan Veizer, (D), Australian National, 1971, Cl

University of Regina

Dept of Geology (B,M,D) ● (2015)
3737 Wascana Parkway
Regina, SK S4S 0A2
   p. 306- 585-4147
   geology.office@uregina.ca
   http://www.uregina.ca/science/geology/
   Administrative Assistant: Van Tran
   Enrollment: No data reported since 1999
Professor:
   Stephen L. Bend, (D), Newcastle, Gox
   Kathryn Bethune, (D), Queens, GcpGt
   Guoxiang Chi, (D), Queens, Eg
   Ian Coulson, (D), Birmingham (UK), 1996, Gvi
   Hairuo Qing, (D), McGill, 1991, GsCg
Associate Professor:
   Janis Dale, (D), Queens, Gml
   Osman Salad Hersi
Assistant Professor:
   Maria Velez, (D), Amsterdam, Pg

Lecturer:
Tsilavo Fahrimahefa
Adjunct Professor:
Kenneth E. Ashton, (D), Gp
Pier L. Binda, (D), Alberta, 1970, Ge
Donald M. Kent, (D), Alberta, 1968, Gs
Emeritus:
Laurence W. Vigrass, (D), Stanford, 1961, Eo

University of Saskatchewan
Dept of Geological Sciences (B,M,D) O (2015)
114 Science Place
Saskatoon, SK S7N 5E2
p. (306) 966-5683
sam.butler@usask.ca
artsandscience.usask.ca/geology/
Enrollment (2014): B: 218 (59) M: 41 (4) D: 23 (3)
Head:
James B. Merriam, (D), York, 1976, Yg
Professor:
Kevin M. Ansdell, (D), Saskatchewan, 1992, EgCgGt
James F. Basinger, (D), Alberta, 1979, Pb
Luis Buatois, (D), Buenos Aires, 1992, Ps
Sam Butler, (D), Toronto, 2000, Yg
Graham George, (D), Sussex, 1983, Cg
Jim Hendry, (D), Waterloo, 1984, Hw
Chris Holmden, (D), Alberta, 1995, Csc
Robert W. Kerrich, (D), Imperial Coll (UK), 1975, Cg
Gabriela Mangano, (D), Buenos Aires, 1992, PsGs
Igor Morozov, (D), Moscow State, 1985, Ys
Yuanming Pan, (D), W Ontario, 1990, Gx
William P. Patterson, (D), Michigan, 1995, CsPe
Brian R. Pratt, (D), Toronto, 1989, Pg
Robin W. Renaut, (D), London, 1982, Gs
Associate Professor:
Ingrid Pickering, (D), Imperial (UK), 1990, Cg
Assistant Professor:
Matthew B. Lindsay, (D), Waterloo, 2009, ClGg
Camille Partin, (D), Gtc
Research Associate:
Bhaskar I. Pandit, (D), Toronto, 1971, Ys
Adjunct Professor:
Irvine Annesley, (D), Ottawa, 1989, Gi
Ning Chen, (D), Saskatchewan, 2001, Gz
David Greenwood, (D), Pg
Tom Kotzer, (D), Saskatchewan, 1993, CgEg
Kyle Larson, (D)
Joyce McBeth, (D), Ge
Brett Moldovan, (D), Cg
Len Wassenaar, (D), Waterloo, 1990, Hw
Derek A. Wyman, (D), Saskatchewan, 1990, Cg
Emeritus:
Willi K. Braun, (D), Tubingen, 1958, Ps
William G. E. Caldwell, (D), Glasgow, 1957, Ps
Leslie C. Coleman, (D), Princeton, 1955, Gz
Donald J. Gendzwill, (D), Saskatchewan, 1969, Ye
Zoltan Hajnal, (D), Manitoba, 1970, Ys
Mel R. Stauffer, (D), Australian National, 1964, Gc
Cooperating Faculty:
De De Dawson, On
Ernest G. Walker, (D), Texas, 1980, Pv

University of Toronto
Dept of Physics, Geophysics Div (B,M,D) (2013)
60 St. George Street
Toronto, ON M5S 1A7
p. (416) 978-5175
cliao@physics.utoronto.ca
http://www.physics.utoronto.ca
Enrollment (2004): M: 4 (3) D: 10 (0)
Professor:
Bernd Milkereit, (B), Kiel, 1984, Ye
Emeritus:
Richard C. Bailey, (D), Cambridge, 1970, Yg
Richard N. Edwards, (D), Cambridge, 1970, Yr

Dept of Geology (B,M,D) (2014)
Earth Sciences Centre
22 Russell Street
Toronto, ON M5S 3B1
p. (416) 978-3022
welcome@geology.utoronto.ca
http://www.geology.utoronto.ca
Business Officer: Silvanna Papaleo
Enrollment: No data reported since 1999
Chair:
Alexander Cruden, (D), Uppsala, 1989, Gt
Professor:
Richard C. Bailey, (D), Cambridge, 1970, Yg
Nicholas Eyles, (D), Leicester (UK), 1978, Gl
Grant F. Ferris, (D), Guelph, 1985, Gn
Henry C. Halls, (D), Toronto, 1970, Ym
Kenneth W.F. Howard, (D), Birmingham, 1979, Hw
Andrew D. Miall, (D), Ottawa, 1969, Gs
Barbara Sherwood Lollar, (D), Waterloo, 1990, Cs
Edward T. C. Spooner, (D), Manchester (UK), 1976, En
Peter H. von Bitter, (D), Kansas, 1971, Pm
Director, Jack Satterly Geochronology Lab:
Michael Andrew Hamilton, (D), Massachusetts, 1993, Cc
Associate Professor:
James Brenan, (D), Rensselaer, 1990, Gi
Donald W. Davis, (D), Alberta, 1978, Cc
Grant S. Henderson, (D), W Ontario, 1983, Gz
James E. Mungall, (D), McGill, 1993, Ec
Russell N. Pysklywec, (D), Toronto, 1998, Yg
Daniel J. Schulze, (D), Texas, 1982, Gi
Assistant Professor:
Jörg Bollmann, (D), Swiss Fed Inst Tech, 1995, Pm
Rebecca Ghent, (D), S Methodist, 2002, Or
Jochen Halfar, (D), Stanford, 1999, Pe
Gopalan Srinivasan, (D), Maharaja SayajiRao, 1995, Ow
Ulrich B. Wortmann, (D), Tech (Munich), Gg
Research Associate:
Colin Bray, (D), Oxford, 1980, Cs
Lecturer:
Carl-Georg Bank, (D), British Columbia, 2002, Og
Adjunct Professor:
Jean-Bernard Caron, (D), Toronto, 2005, Pi
Marianne Douglas, (D), Queens, 1993, Gn
Martin J. Head, (D), Aberdeen, 1991, Pi
John H. McAndrews, (D), Minnesota, 1964, Pl
Myrna Joyce S. Simpson, (D), Alberta, 1999, Ge
Emeritus:
G M. Anderson, (D), Toronto, 1961, Cp
J. J. Fawcett, (D), Manchester, 1961, Gp
John Gittins, (D), Cambridge, 1959, Gi
Alan M. Goodwin, (D), Wisconsin, 1953, Gg
Thomas E. Krogh, (D), MIT, 1964, Cc
Anthony J. Naldrett, (D), Queen's, 1964, Ec
Geoffrey Norris, (D), Cambridge, 1964, Pl
Pierre-Yves F. Robin, (D), MIT, 1974, Gc
John C. Rucklidge, (D), Manchester, 1962, Ge
W. M. Schwerdtner, (D), Free (Berlin), 1961, Gc
Steven D. Scott, (D), Penn State, 1968, Cp
John A. Westgate, (D), Alberta, 1964, Gl
Frederick J. Wicks, (D), Oxford, 1969, Gz
Chief Librarian:
Bruce Garrod, On

University of Victoria
School of Earth & Ocean Sciences (B,M,D) O (2015)
P.O. Box 1700
3800 Finnerty Road
Victoria, BC V8W 2Y2
p. (250) 721-6120
seos@uvic.ca
http://www.uvic.ca/science/seos/
Enrollment: No data reported since 1999
Director:
Stephen T. Johnston, (D), Alberta, 1993, Gc
Associate Director (SCIENCE) NEPTUNE Canada:
Kim Juniper, (D), Canterbury, 1982, Ob

Associate Dean of Science:
  Kathryn Gillis, (D), Dalhousie, 1987, Gp
Professor:
  Dante Canil, (D), Alberta, 1989, Gi
  Laurence Coogan, (D), Leicester, UK, Gi
  Stanley E. Dosso, (D), British Columbia, 1990, Op
  Adam Monahan, (D), British Columbia, 2000, On
  George D. Spence, (D), British Columbia, 1984, Ys
  Verena Tunnicliffe, (D), Yale, 1980, Ob
  Michael J. Whiticar, (D), Kiel, 1978, Co
Associate Professor:
  Jay Cullen, (D), Rutgers, 2001, Oc
  John Dower, (D), Victoria, 1994, Ob
  Roberta Hamme, Washington, 2003, Oc
  Jody Klymak, (D), Washington, 2001, Op
  Vera Pospelova, (D), McGill, 2003, Pe
  Eileen Van Der Flier-Keller, (D), W Ontario, 1985, Cl
  Diana Varela, (D), British Columbia, 1998, Ob
Assistant Professor:
  Colin Goldblatt, (D), East Anglia, 2008, Oa
  Lucinda Leonard, (D), Victoria, Yg
  Kristin Morell, (D), Penn State, Gc
Adjunct Professor:
  Vivek Arora, (D), Melbourne, Oa
  Vaughn Barrie, (D), Wales, 1986, Gu
  Melvyn E. Best, (D), MIT, 1970, Ye
  John Cassidy, (D), UBC, Ys
  James Christian, (D), Hawaii
  Kenneth L. Denman, (D), British Columbia, 1972, Op
  Gregory M. Flato, (D), , 1991, Oa
  John C. Fyfe, (D), McGill, 1987, Oa
  Richard J. Hebda, (D), British Columbia, 1977, Pl
  Roy D. Hyndman, (D), Australian National, 1967, Ys
  Dave Lefebure, (D), Carleton, 1986, Eg
  Victor M. Levson, (D), Alberta, 1995, Gl
  Robie W. Macdonald, (D), Dalhousie, 1972, Oc
  David L. Mackas, (D), Dalhousie, 1977, Ob
  Norman McFarlane, (D), Michigan, 1974, Oa
  Garry C. Rogers, (D), British Columbia, 1983, Ys
  George J. Simandl, (D), Ecole Polytechnique, 1992, En
  Richard Thomson, (D), British Columbia, 1971, Og
  Kelin Wang, (D), W Ontario, 1989, Yg
  Michael Wilmut, (D), Queen's, 1971, On
Emeritus:
  Christopher R. Barnes, (D), Ottawa, 1964, Pm
  Ross N. Chapman, (D), British Columbia, 1975, Op
  Christopher J. R. Garrett, (D), Cambridge, 1968, Op
  John T. Weaver, (D), Saskatchewan, 1959, Ym
On Leave:
  Andrew J. Weaver, (D), British Columbia, 1987, Op
Administrative Officer:
  Terry P. Russell, (B), Victoria, 2000, On

University of Waterloo
Dept of Earth and Environmental Sciences (B,M,D) (2015)
Waterloo, ON N2L 3G1
    p. (519) 888-4567 x32069
    klalbrec@uwaterloo.ca
    https://uwaterloo.ca/earth-environmental-sciences/
    Administrative Assistant: Lorraine Albrecht
    Enrollment: No data reported since 1999
Chair:
  Barry G. Warner, (D)
Professor:
  David W. Blowes, (D), Waterloo, 1990, Cg
  Mario Coniglio, (D), Memorial, 1985, Gr
  Maurice B. Dusseault, (D), Alberta, 1977, Ng
  Thomas W. D. Edwards, (D), Waterloo, 1987, Cs
  Stephen George Evans, (D), Alberta, 1983, Ng
  Shaun K. Frape, (D), Queen's, 1979, Cl
  Shoufa Lin, (D), New Brunswick, 1992, On
  Carol J. Ptacek, (D), Waterloo, 1992, Cg
  David L. Rudolph, (D), Waterloo, 1989, Hq
  Sherry L. Schiff, (D), Columbia, 1986, Ng
  Edward A. Sudicky, (D), Waterloo, 1983, Hw
  Philippe Van Cappellen, (D)

Associate Professor:
  Anthony E. Endres, (D), British Columbia, 1991, Pe
  Walter Illman, (D)
  Martin Ross, (D)
  Andre Unger, (D), Waterloo, 1995, Hw
Assistant Professor:
  Nandita Basu, (D)
  Carl Guilmette, (D)
  Brian Kendall, (D)
  Lingling Wu, (D)
Lecturer:
  Eric C. Grunsky, (D)
  John Johnson, (D)
  Isabelle McMartin, (D)
  Brent Wolfe, (D)
Adjunct Professor:
  Edward C. Appleyard, (D), Cambridge, 1963, Gp
  Gail Atkinson, (D)
  James F. Barker, (D), Waterloo, 1979, Co
  Steven Berg, (D)
  Alec Blyth, (D)
  Thomas Bullen, (D)
  Lauren Charlet, (D)
  John A. Cherry, (D), Illinois, 1966, Hw
  Peter Condon, (D)
  Rick Devlin
  Michael English, (D)
  Nicholas Eyles, (D)
  John F. Gartner, On
  John J. Gibson, (D), Waterloo, 1996, Cs
  Susan Glasuer, (D)
  David Good, (D)
  John Gosse, (D)
  Douglas Gould, (D)
  Norman Halden, (D)
  Daniel Hammarlund, (D)
  Jens Hartman, (D)
  Lin Huang, (D)
  Daniel Hunkeler, (D)
  Hyoun-Tae Hwang, (D)
  Richard Jackson, (D)
  Sun-Wook Jeen, (D)
  Michael Krom, (D)
  David R. Lee, (D), Virginia Tech, 1976, Hw
  Yuri Leonenko, (D)
  John Lin, (D)
  Robert Linnen, (D), McGill, 1992, Eg
  Benoit Made, (D)
  Uli Mayer, (D)
  Hossein Memarian, (D)
  John Molson
  Alan V. Morgan, (D), Birmingham, 1970, Gl
  Christopher Neville, (D)
  Dogan Paktunc, (D)
  Sorab Panday, (D)
  Young-Jin Park, (D), Hq
  Gary Parkin, (N)
  Peter Pehme, (D)
  Jennifer Pell, (D)
  Richard Peltier, (D)
  Terry D. Prowse, (D), Canterbury, 1981, Cg
  William Quinton, (D)
  Eric J. Reardon, (D), Penn State, 1974, Cl
  Rashid Rehan, (D)
  Iain Samson, (D)
  Houston C. Saunderson, (N)
  James Sloan, (D)
  James Smith
  John Spoelstra, (D)
  Andrew Stumpf, (D)
  William Taylor, (D)
  Rene Therrien, (D)
  Harvey Thorleifson, (D)
  Martin Thullner, (D)
  Benoit Valley, (D)
  Garth Van der Kamp, (D), Amsterdam, 1973, Hw
  Jan van der Kruk, (D)

Cees van Staal
Andrea Vander Woude, (D)
Owen L. White, (D), Illinois, 1970, Ng
C. Wolkersdorfer, (D)
Wenjiao Xiao, (D)
Leiming Zhang, (D)
Emeritus:
Emil O. Frind, (D), Toronto, 1971, Hq
Robert W. Gillham, (D), Illinois, 1973, Hq
Paul Karrow, (D), Illinois, 1957, Gl
Research Professor:
Ramon Aravena, (D), Waterloo, 1993, Co
Research Associate Professor:
Will Robertson, (D), Waterloo, 1992, Hw
Other:
Brewster Conant, Hw

University of Windsor

Dept of Earth and Environmental Sciences (B,M,D) (2011)
401 Sunset Avenue
Windsor, ON N9B 3P4
  p. (519) 253-3000 x2486
  earth@uwindsor.ca
  http://www.uwindsor.ca/ees
  Administrative Assistant: Sharon Horne
  Enrollment (2001): B: 52 (0) M: 8 (0)
Head:
Iain M. Samson, (D), Strathclyde, 1983, EgCg
Professor:
Aaron Fisk, (D), Manitoba, 1998, ObCs
V. Chris Lakhan, (D), Toronto, 1982, Ori
Ali Polat, (D), Saskatchewan, 1998, GixCc
Frank Simpson, (D), Jagellonian (Krakow), 1968, Gs
Alan S. Trenhaile, (D), Wales, 1969, Gm
Associate Professor:
Maria T. Cioppa, (D), Lehigh, 1997, Ym
Joel Gagnon, (D), McGill, 2006, CalEg
Phil A. Graniero, (D), Toronto, 2001, OiHg
Cyril G. Rodrigues, (D), Carleton, 1980, Pm
Christopher Weisener, (D), South Australia, 2003, ClGe
Jianwen Yang, (D), Toronto, 1997, HwYg
Instructor:
Denis Tetrault, (D), Western, 2002, Gg
Emeritus:
Brian J. Fryer, (D), MIT, 1971, Cla
Peter P. Hudec, (D), Rensselaer, 1965, Ng
Terence E. Smith, (D), Wales, 1963, Gi
David T. A. Symons, (D), Toronto, 1965, Ym
Andrew Turek, (D), Australian National, 1966, Cc
On Leave:
Ihsan S. Al-Aasm, (D), Ottawa, 1985, Gd

Western University

Dept of Earth Sciences (B,M,D) O (2015)
Biology & Geology Building
Room 1026
1151 Richmond Street North
London, ON N6A 5B7
  p. (519) 661-3187
  earth-sc@uwo.ca
  http://www.uwo.ca/earth/
  f: Earth Sciences at Western University
  t: @westernuEarth
  Enrollment (2015): M: 62 (25) D: 56 (8)
Robert Hodder Chair:
Robert Linnen, (D), McGill, 1992, EmCe
NSERC Industrial Research Chair:
Gail M. Atkinson, (D), W Ontario, 1993, YssYs
Cross-Appt.-Home Dept: Physics & Astronomy, UWO:
Peter Brown, (D), W Ontario, 1999, OnXm
Chair, Dept. Earth Sciences (P.Eng.):
R. Gerhard Pratt, (D), Imperial Coll (UK), 1989, Yeg
Canada Research Chair:
Frederick J. Longstaffe, (D), McMaster, 1978, Cs
Professor:
Stephen R. Hicock, (D), W Ontario, 1980, Gl

Jisuo Jin, (D), Saskatchewan, 1988, Pi
A Guy Plint, (D), Oxford, 1980, Gs
Richard A. Secco, (D), W Ontario, 1988, Gy
Kristy F. Tiampo, (D), Colorado, 2000, Yd
Industrial Research Chair, Joint Appt Physics & Astronomy, U.W.O:
Gordon R. Osinski, (D), New Brunswick, 2004, XgcGp
Industrial Research Chair:
Neil Banerjee, (D), Victoria, 2001, EgCgGx
Cross-Appt.UWO: Physics&Astronomy:
Robert Shcherbakov, (D), Cornell, 2002, YgsYd
Sean Shieh, (D), Hawaii, 1998, Yg
Canada Research Chair, Cross Appt. Biology&Geography, UWO:
Brian Branfireun, (D), McGill U, On
(P.Eng.,P.Geo.):
Robert A. Schincariol, (D), Ohio State, 1993, HwGg
Associate Professor:
Burns A. Cheadle, (D), W Ontario, 1986, Go
Patricia Corcoran, (D), Dalhousie, 2001, Gd
Roberta L. Flemming, (D), Queen's, 1997, Gz
Dazhi Jiang, (D), New Brunswick, 1996, GcgGg
Elizabeth Webb, (D), W Ontario, 2001, Cs
Research Adjunct Professor:
Natalie Pietrzak-Renaud, (D), W Ontario, 2011, Eg
Joint appointment with Geography, U.W.O.:
Desmond Moser, (D), Queens, 1993, GtCcXg
Canada Research Chair:
Audrey Bouvier, (D), École Normale Supérieure de Lyon, 2005, Xc
Assistant Professor:
Rob Carpenter, (D), W Ontario, 2004
Phil JA McCausland, (D), Western, 2002, YmXm
Sheri Molnar, (D), U Victoria, 2011, Ys
Catherine Neish, (D), U Arizona, 2008, On
Cameron J. Tsujita, (D), McMaster, 1995, Pi
Tony Withers, (D), Bristol, 1997, Cp
Research Scientist:
Li Huang, (M), Concordia, 1992, Yr
Research Associate:
Po-Yu (Paul) Shen, (D), W Ontario, 1975, Yh
W.S. Fyfe Visiting Scientist- in- Residence:
David Good, (D), McMaster, 1992
Research Professor:
Lalu Mansinha, (D), British Columbia, 1962, Ys
Research Associate:
Brian R. Hart, (D), W Ontario, 1995, Ca
Brandon University:
Rong-Yu Li, (D), U Alberta, 2002, On
Associate Professor of Biology-Cross appointment with Earth Sciences:
Irena F. Creed, (D), Toronto, 1998, OnSfPy
Associate Curator of Mineralogy, Royal Ontario Museum/Professor,
University of Toronto:
Kim Tait, (D), U Arizona, 2007
Adjunct Professor:
Ed Cloutis, (D), U Alberta, 1989
Claudia Cochrane, (M), W Ontario, Go
Richard Grieve, (D), U Toronto, 1970
Matt Izawa, (D), W Ontario, 2012, Gz
Sobhi Nasir, (D), Wuerzburg, 1989
Sergey Samsonov, (D), W Ontario, 2007
Gordon Southam, (D), Guelph, 1990, Py
Yves Thibault, (D), W Ontario, 1990
Livio Tornabene, (D), U Tennessee, 2007, On
Lisa Van Loon, (D), Ohio State, 2007
Emeritus:
Alan Beck, (D), Australian National, 1964, On
W. Glen E. Caldwell, (D), Glasgow, 1957, Pm
William R. Church, (D), Wales, 1961, Gt
Norman A. Duke, (D), Manitoba, 1983, Eg
Michael E. Fleet, (D), Manchester, 1963, Gz
Akio Hayatsu, (D), U Toronto, 1965, Cc
Robert W. Hodder, (D), California (Berkeley), 1959, Eg
Alfred C. Lenz, (D), Princeton, 1959, Pi
Robert F. Mereu, (D), W Ontario, 1962, Ys
H Wayne Nesbitt, (D), Johns Hopkins, 1975, Cl
H. Currie Palmer, (D), Princeton, 1963, Ym
Grant M. Young, (D), Glasgow, 1967, Gc
Research Scientist:
Charles T. Wu, (D), W Ontario, 1984, On

York University
Earth and Space Science and Engineering (B,M,D) ● (2015)
4700 Keele Street
Toronto, ON M3J 1P3
  p. (416) 736-5245
  esse@yorku.ca
  http://www.yorku.ca/esse
  Administrative Assistant: Paola Panaro
  Enrollment (2010): B: 100 (38)
Professor:
  Qiuming Cheng, (D), Ottawa, 1994, Oi
  Christian Haas, (D), Bremen, 1996, Yg
  Gary T. Jarvis, (D), Cambridge, 1978, Yg
  Ian C. McDade, (D), Belfast, 1979, Or
  Tom McElroy, (D), Oa
  Spiros Pagiatakis, (D), New Brunswick, 1988, Yd
  Peter A. Taylor, (D), Bristol, 1967, Oa
Chair:
  Regina Lee, (D), Toronto, 2000
Associate Professor:
  Costas Armenakis, (D), New Brunswick, 1988, Or
  Sunil Bisnath, (D), New Brunswick, 2004
  Yongsheng Chen, Oa
  Michael Daly, (D)
  Baoxin Hu, (D), Boston, 1998, Or
  Mary Ann Jenkins, (D), Toronto, 1986, Oa
  Gary P. Klaassen, (D), Toronto, 1983, Oa
  Brendan Quine, (D)
  Jinjun Shan, (D)
  Gunho Sohn, (D)
  George Vukovich, (D), Oa
  James Whiteway, (D), York, 1994, Oa
  Zheng Hong (George) Zhu, (D)
Assistant Professor:
  William Colgan, (D), Yg
  Mark Gordon, (D), Oa
  John E. Moores, (D), Arizona, 2008
Lecturer:
  Hugh Chesser, (M), Toronto, 1987
  Franz Newjland, (D)
  Jian-Guo Wang, (D)
Emeritus:
  Keith D. Aldridge, (D), MIT, 1967, Yg
  John Miller, (D), Saskatchewan, 1969, Or
  Gordon G. Shepherd, (D), Toronto, 1956
  Douglas E. Smylie, (D), Toronto, 1963, Yg
  Anthony M. K. Szeto, (D), Australian National, 1982, Yg

Cape Verde

Universidade de Cabo Verde
Dept de Ciencia e Tecnologia (M,D) (2015)
Campus de Palmarejo - CP 279
Palmarejo, Praia - Cabo Verde
Praia
Praca Antonio Lereno, Praia CP 379C
  p. +238 261 99 01
  joao.semedo@docente.unicv.edu.cv
  http://www.unicv.edu.cv/dct

Departamento de Engenharias e Ciencias do Mar (B,M) (2013)
Ribeira de Julião
CP 163
Mindelo, São Vicente CP 163
  p. +238 2326561/62
  alexandra.delgado@docente.unicv.edu.cv
  http://www.unicv.edu.cv

Universidade Jean Piaget de Cabo Verde
Ecologia e Desenvolvimento (B) (2014)
Campus Universitario da Cidade da Praia
Praia
  p. +238 629085
  info@unipiaget.cv
  http://www.unipiaget.cv/pdf/cursos/ecdm.pdf

Central African Republic

Universite de Bangui
Dept de Chimie-Biologie-Geologie (B) (2014)
BP 1450
Avenue des Martyrs
Bangui
  p. (236) 61 20 05
  info@univ-bangui.info
  http://www.univ-bangui.org/

Chad

Universite de N'Djamena
Dept de Geologie (B) (2010)
BP 1117
Avenue Mobutu
N'Djamena
  sg@undt.info
  http://www.undt.info/

Chile

Servicio National de Geologia y Mineria de Chile
Servicio National de Geologia y Mineria de Chile (2013)
Avda Sta Maria N° 0104
Providence
  p. 56-2-7375050
  oirs@sernageomin.cl
  http://www.sernageomin.cl/

Universidad Austral de Chile
Inst de Geociencias (2004)
Campus "Isla Teja", Casilla 567, Valdivia
  p. +56 63 2293861
  egeologia@uach.cl

Universidad Catolica del Norte
Dept de Ciencias Geologicas (2014)
Avenida Angamos 610, ,
Casilla 1280, Antofagasta
  p. (55) 2355968
  mbembow@ucn.cl
  http://www.ucn.cl/facultades/SitioDeInteres/?cod=2&codIte
  m=110&codPrincipal=1124

Universidad de Chile
Dept de Geologia (2004)
Plaza Ercilla 803
Casilla 13148
Correo 21
Santiago
  acastruc@cec.uchile.cl

Dept de Geofisica (2005)
Blanco Encalada 2002
Casilla 2777
Santiago
  p. (56 2)696 6563
  ekausel@dgf.uchile.cl
  http://www.dgf.uchile.cl/index.html

Universidad de Concepcion
Inst de Geologia Economica Aplicada (2014)
Barrio Universitario - Victor Lamas 1290
 Casilla 4107
Concepcion, Region del Bio-Bio
  p. (56) 41 220 44 88
  maravenah@udec.cl
  http://www.udec.cl/postgrado/?q=node/39&codigo=4161

Dept de Geociencia (2004)
Cabina 13 - Barrio Universitario

Casilla 3-C
4250-1 Concepcion
Region del Bio-Bio

China

Capital Normal University
College of Resources, Environment and Tourism (2011)
West 3rd Ring Road North 105#
Beijing 100048
  p. 86 10 68903321
  info@mail.cnu.edu.cn
  http://www.cnu.edu.cn

China Geological Survey
China Geological Survey (2014)
24 Huangsi Dajie,
Xicheng District
Beijing 100011
  p. +86 10 51632963 51632906
  enwebmaster@mail.cgs.gov.cn
  http://www.cgs.gov.cn/

China University of Geosciences, Beijing
Geosciences (2011)
No.29, Xueyuan Road,
Haidian District
Beijing 100083
  http://www.cugb.edu.cn/EnglishWeb/index.html

China University of Geosciences, Wuhan
Faculty of Geosciences (2011)
No. 388, Lumo Road, Hongshan District
Wuhan 430074
  p. 86-27-87481030
  cugxb@cug.edu.cn
  http://en.cug.edu.cn/cug/index.asp

China University of Mining and Technology, Beijing
College of Geoscience and Surveying Engineering (2011)
Beijing
  dcxy@cumtb.edu.cn
  http://dcxy.cumtb.edu.cn/

Nanjing University
Dept of Earth Sciences (2011)
22 Hankou Road
Nanjing , Jiangsu
  wsj@nju.edu.cn
  http://www.nju.edu.cn/cps/site/njueweb/fg/index.php

University of Hong Kong
Dept of Earth Sciences (B,M,D) (2015)
James Lee Building
Pokfulam Road
Hong Kong
  p. (852) 2859 1084
  earthsci@hku.hk
  http://www.earthsciences.hku.hk

Colombia

EAFIT University
Dept of Geology (2014)
Carrera 49 No. 7 Sur - 50
Medellin
  p. 01 8000515 900
  contacto@eafit.edu.co

Escuela de Ingenieria de Antioquia
Dept of Geologic Engineering (2004)
Calle 25 Sur
#42-63 Envigado

Medellin
  http://www.eia.edu.co/site/index.php/pregrados/programas/
  ing-geologica.html

Universidad de Santander
Environmental Engineering (B,M) (2014)
Facultad Ingenierias
Cll 70 No. 55-210 Campus Universitario Lagos del Cacique
Bucaramanga, Santander
  p. +57 7 6516500
  nmantilla@udes.edu.co
  http://www.udes.edu.co/programas-profesionales/facultad-
  ingenierias/ingenieria-ambiental.html

Universidad Industrial de Santander
School of Geology (B,M) O (2015)
Cra 27 Calle 9 Ciudad Universitaria
Bucaramanga, Santander 1
  p. 57-7-6343457
  escgeo@uis.edu.co
  http://geologia.uis.edu.co/eisi/
Director:
  Juan Diego Colegial Gutierrez, (D), 2004, GeNgOr
Professor:
  Luis Carlos Mantilla Figueroa, (D), EgCec

Universidad Nacional de Colombia
Dept de Geociencias (2004)
Carrera 30 No. 45-03, Edificio 224
Calle 45, Cr. 30
Bogota
  gpsepulvedac@unal.edu.co

Costa Rica

Universidad de Costa Rica
Escuela Centroamericana de Geologia (2004)
Apartado 35-2060 UCR
San Pedro de Montes de Oca
San Jose
  geologia@ucr.ac.cr

Croatia

Croatian Institute of Geology
Croatian Geological Survey (2011)
Sachsova 2
P.O.Box 268
Zagreb HR-10000
  p. +38516160888
  ured@hgi-cgs.hr
  http://www.hgi-cgs.hr/

University of Zagreb
Dept of Geology, Faculty of Science (B,M,D) (2010)
Horvatovac 102a
Zagreb HR-10000
  p. +38514605960
  godsjek@geol.pmf.hr
  http://www.geol.pmf.hr
  Enrollment (2010): B: 121 (27) M: 28 (11) D: 30 (6)
full professor:
  Mladen Juraèiæ, (D), Zagreb, 1987, GueCm
associate professor:
  Dražen Balen, (D), Zagreb, 1999, GxpGi
full professor:
  Darko Tibljaš, (D), Zagreb, 1996, GzScGx
  Vlasta Æosoviæ, (D), Zagreb, 1996, PemPs
emeritus:
  Ivan Gušiæ, (D), Zagreb, 1974, GgPsm

Cyprus

Cyprus Geological Survey
Cyprus Geological Survey (2015)
1 Lefkonos Street
2064 Lefkosia
p. +357 22409213
director@gsd.moa.gov.cy
http://www.moa.gov.cy/gsd

Czech Republic

Charles University
Inst of Hydrogeology, Engineering Geology and Applied Geophysics (2005)
Albertov 6
128 43 Praha 2
uhigug@natur.cuni.cz
http://prfdec.natur.cuni.cz/~geophys/ustav/katedra.htm

Institute of Petrology and Structural Geology (B,M,D) (2014)
Albertov 6
Praha 2 128 43
p. 00420-221951524
petrol@natur.cuni.cz
http://petrol.natur.cuni.cz
Enrollment (2012): B: 3 (5) M: 15 (4) D: 15 (0)
Assoc. Prof.:
David Dolejs, (D), 2004, GiCpg
Professor:
Shah Wali Faryad, (D), 1990, GpzGi

Dept of Geophysics (B,M,D) (2013)
KG MFF UK
V Holesovickach 2
180 00 Prague 8, Czech Republic
Prague, Czech Republic 180 00
geo@mff.cuni.cz
http://geo.mff.cuni.cz

Czech Geological Survey
Cesky Geologicky Ustav (2013)
Klarov 3
118 21 Praha 1
p. +420 257 089 500
secretar@geology.cz
http://www.geology.cz

Geofond (2011)
Kostelni 26
Prague PSC 170 06
p. +420 234 742 111
vstrupl@geofond.cz
http://www.geofond.cz/cz/domu

Masaryk University
Dept of Geological Sciences (B,M,D) O (2016)
Faculty of Science
Kotlarska 2
Brno 611 37
p. +420 549 49 4322
geologie@sci.muni.cz
http://ugv.cz/
f: https://www.facebook.com/chci.byt.geolog/?fref=ts
Enrollment (2014): B: 155 (68) M: 88 (46) D: 70 (8)
Head:
Josef Zeman, (A), CgpCe
Professor:
Jiri Kalvoda, (A), PsePm
Milan Novak, (A), GzpGi
Antonín Prichystal, (A), GgaGv
Associate Professor:
Ondrej Babek, (D), Gds
Martin Ivanov, (A), PgiPe
Jaromir Leichmann, (A), GxpGi
Zdenek Losos, Gz

Rostislav Melichar, (A), GtcGr
Slavomír Nehyba, (A), GsdGg
Marek Slobodnik, (A), GeEg
Assistant Professor:
Martin Knizek, (D), NgmNr
Tomas Kuchovsky, (D), Hgy
Adam Ricka, (D), Hgy
Research Associate:
Renata Copjakova, (D), Gz
Radek Skoda, (D), Gz
Lecturer:
Nela Dolakova, (A), Plg
Emeritus:
Rostislav Brzobohaty, (A), PgsPe
Rudolf Musil, (A), Pgv

Dept of Mineralogy, Petrology and Geochemistry (2004)
Kotlarska 2
611 37 Brno
losos@sci.muni.cz
http://www.muni.cz/sci/structure/315020.html

Dept of Geography (2004)
Kotlarska 2
611 37 Brno
dobro@sci.muni.cz
http://www.muni.cz/sci/structure/315030.html

Technical University of Ostrava
Faculty of Mining & Geology (2004)
Vysoka Skola Banska v Ostrava
17.listopadu 15/2172
708-33 Ostrava
p. +420 597 325 456
fwk@aqua.dtu.dk
http://www.hgf.vsb.cz/cs

D.R. of Congo

Marien Ngouabi University
Faculty of Science and Technology (B,M,D) O (2014)
Face Square Général Charles De Gaulle
Bacongo
BP:69
Brazzaville, Congo
p. (+242) 06 623 61 22
jm_ouamba@yahoo.fr
http://www.univ-mngb.net/fs/

Universite de Kinshasa
Dept des Sciences de la Terre (B) (2014)
PO Box 190
Kinshasa XI
p. (+243) 82 333 96 93
rectorat@unikin.cd
www.unikin.cd

Départements et filières Sciences Agronomiques (B) (2010)
PO Box 190
Kinshas XI
p. +243 89 89 20 507
fbkapuku@hotmail.com
http://www.unikin.cd/ogec/

Universite de Lubumbashi
Dept de Geologie (B) (2011)
B.P. 1825
Lubumbashi, Katanga
http://www.unilu.ac.cd/En/Pages/default.aspx

Universite de Lumumbashi
Faculté des sciences (B) (2014)
BP 1825
Lubumbashi

p. +243 263-22-5403
unilu@unilu.net
http://www.unilu.ac.cd/En/Pages/default.aspx

Denmark

Aarhus University
Dept of Earth Sciences (2005)
C. F. Mollers Alle
DK-800 Arhus C
bo@geo.au.dk
http://www.geo.aau.dk.english/index_f.html

Danmarks og Gonlands Geologiske Undersogelse (GEUS)
Danish Geological Survey (2011)
O. Voldgade 10,
1350 Kbh. K
geus@geus.dk
http://www.geus.dk/

Roskilde University
QuadLab, ENSPAC (2014)
Universitetsvej 1
Roskilde DK-4000
p. 45 46743097
storey@ruc.dk
http://www.quadlab.dk/bcms-ui-base/

Technical University of Denmark
Dept of Earth Sciences (2004)
Anker Engelunsved
DK-2800 Lyngby
fwk@aqua.dtu.dk
http://www.igg.dtu.dk/index_z.htm

University of Copenhagen
Inst for Geography and Geology (2011)
Oster Voldgage 5-7
DK-1350 Copenhagen K
p. +4535322400
geo@geo.ku.dk
http://geo.ku.dk/

Dept of Geophysics (2015)
Juliane Maries Vej 30
Copenhagen 2100 Copenhagen
p. +45 353 20605
losos@sci.muni.cz
http://www.nbi.ku.dk/theinstitute/page52794.htm

Geological Museum (2011)
Oster Voldgade 5-7
Copenhagen K DK-1350
p. +45 35322345
rcp@snm.ku.dk
http://geologi.snm.ku.dk/english/

Djibouti

Insitut de Physique du Globe de Paris, (IPGP)
Dept of Volcanic Systems
(B) (2010)
Observatoire Géophysique d'Arta, BP 1888
p. (253) 42 21 92
obsarta@bow.intnet.dj
http://volcano.ipgp.jussieu.fr/djibouti/stationdj.html

Universite de Djibouti
Dept de Geologie/Biologie (B) (2010)
BP 1904
p. +253-250459
webmaster@univ.edu.dj
http://www.univ.edu.dj/facultes.fsti.bg.html

Dominican Republic

Mineterio de Energie y Minas Republica Dominica
Servicio Geologico Nacional Republica Dominica (2015)
Ave Winston Churchill No 75
Edificio J.F. Martinez 3er Piso
Santa Domingo
p. (809) 732 0363
smunoz@sgn.gov.do
http://www.sgn.gov.do

Ecuador

Escuela Politecnica Nacional
Facultad de Geologia, Minas y Petroleos (2014)
Ladron de Guevara E11
253 Quito
p. (593-02) 2-507 - 126
deparamento.geologia@epn.edu.ec
http://www.epn.edu.ec/index.php?option=com_content
&view=article&id=1202%3Adepartamento-de-geologia-
dg&catid=163&Itemid=342

Escuela Superior Politecnica Del Litoral
Facultad de Ciencias de la Tierra (2014)
Km 30.5, Via Perimentral
Guayaquil EC090150

Universidad de Guayaquil
Facultad de Ciencias Naturales (2004)
Av Raul Gomez Lynx s / n Av Juan Tanca Marengo
Guayaquil
p. 3080777 to 3080758
carmenbonifaz@hotmail.com
http://fccnnugye.com/

Egypt

Ain Shams University
Dept of Geology (B) (2010)
Abbassia 11566
Cairo 11566
p. +20(2)6830963
deans@asunet.shams.edu.eg
http://sci.shams.edu.eg/Departments_Geology_Index.ASP

Dept of Geophysics (B) (2010)
Abbassia 11566
Cairo 11566
p. +20(2)6830963
deans@asunet.shams.edu.eg
http://sci.shams.edu.eg/Departments_Geophysics_Index.
ASP

Al Azhar University
Dept of Geology (B) (2010)
Yosief Abbas Street
Cairo 11787
p. +20 (2) 262 3274
esam150860@yahoo.com
http://www.uazhar.edu.eg/bfac/sci/jiolojy.htm

Alexandria University
Dept of Geology (A,B,M,D) O (2015)
Baghdad Street
Qism Moharram Bek
Alexandria 21511
p. (+203) 3921595
sc-dean@alexu.edu.eg
http://www.sci.alexu.edu.eg/en/Departments/Default.
aspx?Dept=4
f: https://www.facebook.com/groups/GSAU.alex/
Enrollment (2014): B: 26 (0)

Professor:
  Galal Mohamed I Galal, (D), Germany, 1994, GgPe
  Khalil I. Khalil Ebeid, (D), Germany, 1995, GgEg
  Kadry Nasser Sediek, (D), USSR, 1991, GgsGd
  Mohamad Nasser Shaaban, (D), U.S.A., 1992, GgsGd
Assistant Lecturer:
  Ahmed Ibrahim Dyab, (M), Egypt, 2013, Gg
Assistant Professor:
  Hossam EL-Din Ahmed EL-S Helba, (D), Germany, 1994, GgOm
  Ahmed Sadek Mansour, (D), Egypt, 1999, Ggs
Instructor:
  Sara Akram M. Mahmoud, (B), Egypt, 2006, Gg
Emeritus Professor:
  Mohamed Waguih El Dakkak, (D), Egypt, 1971, GgsGd
  Galal Abd EL-Ham Ewas, (D), Norway, 1969, GgNr
  Hanafy M. Holail, (D), 1988, Ggs
  Rousine Tanios Toni, (D), Egypt, 1967, GgPg
Emeritus Lecturer:
  Mohamed M. Tamish, (D), West Germany, 1988, GgsCg
Emeritus Professor:
  Mohamed Ahmed Rashed, (D), Moscow - USSR, 1984, GgOs

Dept of Environmental Sciences (B) (2010)
22 Al-Guish Avenue
Alexandria
  p. +20 (3) 591 1152
  alexandria_university@yahoo.com
  http://www.alex.edu.eg/dept.jsp?FC=4&CODE=09

Oceanography Dept (B) (2010)
22 Al-Guish Avenue
Alexandria
  p. +20 (3) 591 1152
  alexandria_university@yahoo.com
  http://www.alex.edu.eg/dept.jsp?FC=4&CODE=07

American University of Cairo
Dept of Petroleum and Energy Engineering (B) (2010)
New Cairo Campus: AUC Avenue
PO Box 74
New Cairo 11835
  p. +20.2.2615.1000
  maretta@aucegypt.edu
  http://www.aucegypt.edu/academics/dept/peng/Pages/
  default.aspx

Assiut University
Mining & Metallurgical Engineering Dept (B) (2010)
Assiut Governorate
Assiut City
PO Box 71515
Assiut 71515
  p. +20 (88) 235 7007
  webmastr@aun.edu.eg
  http://www.aun.edu.eg/fac_eng?Dpart/Mining/Mining.htm

Dept of Geology (B) (2010)
Assiut Governorate
Assiut City
PO Box 71515
Assiut 71515
  p. +20 (88) 235 7007
  sci@aun.edu.eg
  http://www.aun.edu.eg/fac_sci/depart/ge1.htm

Beni Suef University
Geology Dept (B) (2015)
Salah Salem Street
Beni Suef 62511
  p. +(20) 822324879, +(20) 2082232
  elsherif_zakaria@yahoo.com

  http://193.227.1.224/sci/

British University in Egypt
Petroleum Engineering (B) (2010)
Misr Ismalia Road
El Sherouk City 11837

  enas.sabry@bue.edu.eg

  http://www.bue.edu.eg/

Cairo University
Dept of Geophysics (B) (2010)
University Avenue - Univeristy Square
Giza
  p. +20 (2) 572 9584
  http://www.freewebtown.com/geophysics2/

Mining, Petroleum, and Metallurgical Engineering (B) (2014)
University Avenue - University Square
Giza
  p. +20 (2) 572 9584
  nahed_ecae2003@yahoo.com
  http://www.eng.cu.edu.eg/dept/en/mpm/index.htm

Dept of Geology (B) (2010)
University Avenue - University Square
Giza, Cairo
  p. +20 (2) 572 9584
  portal@cu.edu.eg
  http://www.cu.edu.eg/english/

El Mansoura University
Dept of Geology (B,M,D) (2014)
Faculty of Science
at Mansoura
Department of Geology
Mansoura, Dakahliya governorat 35516
  p. +20 050 2242388 Ext. 582
  ghazala@mans.edu.eg
  http://www.mans.edu.eg/facscim/english/GeologyHome/
  default.htm
  Enrollment (2012): B: 250 (230) M: 25 (13) D: 15 (7)
Head:
  Hosni H. Ghazala, (D), Mansoura, 1990, Ygx

El Zagazig University
Dept of Geology (B) (2010)
Zagazig
  p. +20 (55) 324 577
  info@zu.edu.eg
  http://www.zu.edu.eg/

Fayoum University
Geology Dept (B,D) (2015)
fayoum-Egypt University Zone
Fayoum 63514
  p. +20 01005858505
  ags00@fayoum.edu.eg
  http://www.fayoum.edu.eg/English/Science/Geology/About-
  Board.aspx
Professor:
  ahmad gaber shedied, (D), Cairo, 1995, GgHww

Mansoura University
Geology Dept (B,M,D) (2014)
60, El Gomhoria Street
El Mansoura 35516
  p. 002-050-2242388
  syelbeialy@mans.edu.eg
  http://scifac.mans.edu.eg/en/scientific-dept/geology-
  department

Minia University
Geology & Chemistry Dept (B) (2010)

Minia
p. +(208-6) 324 420 #321 443
minia@frcu.eun.rg
http://www.minia.edu.eg

Sohag University
Geology Dept (B) (2010)
EL Kawaser
PO Box 82524
Sohag 82524
p. +(20) 93 4605745
conf11icca@sohag-univ.edu.eg
http://www.sohag-univ.edu.eg/

South Valley University
Dept of Geology (Aswan Campus) (B) (2010)
Qena 83523
p. +20 (96) 339 756
mohammedsm2003@yahoo.com
http://www.svu.edu.eg/arabic/aswan/sci/en/depart/Geology/
Geology.htm

Tanta University
Dept of Geology (B) (2014)
El-Geish Street
Tanta 31527
p. +20 (40) 337 7929
president@tainta.edu.eg
http://www.tanta.edu.eg/ar/Tanta/3elom/geology.html

The Egyptian Geological Survey and Mining Authority
(2011)
egov@ad.gov.eg
http://www.egsma.gov.eg/

Zagazig University
Dept of Geology (B,M,D) (2011)
Sharkia Governorate
Zagazig City
geology@zu.edu.eg
http://www.zu.edu.eg/

Eritrea

University of Asmara
Dept of Marine Sciences (B) (2011)
PO Box 1220
Asmara
p. 291 1 161926 (Ext. 259)
Zekeria@marine.uoa.edu.er
http://www.uoa.edu.er/academics/dmarine/index.html

Estonia

Geological Survey of Estonia
Eesti Geoloogiakeskus OU (2011)
Juniper tee 82
Tallinn 12618
p. 672 0094
egk@egk.ee
http://www.egk.ee/

University of Tartu
Inst of Geology (B,M,D) ● (2015)
Ravila 14a
Tartu 50411
p. +372 7 375 891
geol@ut.ee
http://www.lote.ut.ee/geoloogia
Enrollment (2015): B: 4 (0) M: 7 (0) D: 3 (0)

Ethiopia

Addis Ababa University
Dept of Planetary and Earth Sciences (2011)
PO Box 1176
Addis Ababa
p. 251-111239462
balem@geo.aau.edu.at
http://www.aau.edu.et/index.php/earth-sciences

School of Civil & Environmental Engineering (B) (2010)
PO Box 1176
Addis Ababa
seyoum@sc.aau.edu.et
http://www.aau.edu.et/index.php/earth-sciences

Arba Minch University
Dept of Geology (B) (2011)
PO Box 21
, Arba Minch
p. 251-468814972
yoditayalew@fastmail.fm
http://www.arbaminch-univ.com/

College of Natural Sciences (B) (2010)
PO Box 21
Arba Minch
p. +251-46-8810070
alemayehu.hailemicael@amu.edu.et
http://www.arbamich-univ.com/WTIMeteorlogy.html#

Water & Environmental Engineering (B) (2011)
PO Box 21
Arba Minch
p. +251-46-8810070
nigussie_tg@yahoo.com
http://www.arbaminch-univ.com/WTIWEE.html

Mekelle University
Dept of Earth Science (B) (2014)
P.O.Box: 231
Management Building, Main Campus
Mekelle
p. (+251) 344 40 40 05
cciad.mu@gmail.com
http://www.mu.edu.et/index.php/department-of-earth-
science

Institute of Geo-information and Earth Observation Sciences
(B) (2014)
P.O.Box: 231
Management Building, Main Campus
Makelle
p. +251 914 720398
meseleagw@yahoo.com
http://www.mu.edu.et/index.php/programs/ethiopia-institute-
of-technology-mekelle/institute-of-geo-information-and-
earth-observat

Semera University
Dept of Geology (B) (2011)
PO Box 132
Semera
p. 251-336660603
semerauniversity@ethionet.et

Wollega University
Dept of Geology (B) (2011)
PO Box 395 Nekemte
Nekemte
p. 251-576615038
wu@ethionet.et
http://www.wuni.edu.et/

Fiji

Ministry of Lands and Mineral Resources
Mineral Resources Dept of Fiji (2011)
Private Mail Bag, GPO
Suva
   p. (679) 338 1611
   director@mrd.gov.fj
   http://www.mrd.gov.fj/

University of the South Pacific
Div of Earth and Environment Science (2007)
Private Mail Bag
GPO Suva
Suva, Fiji Islands
   kahsai_k@usp.ac.fj
   http://www.sidsnet.org/pacific/usp/earth/

Finland

Abo Akademi University
Geology and Mineralogy (B,M,D) O (2016)
Domkyrkotorget 1
Turku Fi-20500
   p. (+)358442956429
   geologi@abo.fi
   http://www.abo.fi/fakultet/geologi
   Enrollment (2015): B: 26 (8) M: 50 (4) D: 9 (2)
Professor:
   Olav Eklund, (D), Abo Akademi Univ, 1993, GxeGz

Geological Survey of Finland
Geologian tutkimuskeskus (2015)
P.O.Box 96
Espoo FI-02151
   p. +358 29 503 0000
   gtk@gtk.fi
   www.gtk.fi
   f: https://www.facebook.com/GTK.FI
   t: @GTK_FI
Director, Strategy and Planning:
   Jarmo Kohonen, (D)
Director, Projects and Customers:
   Petri Lintinen, (D)
Director, Operative Units:
   Olli Breilin, (M)
Director, Human Resources, Talent Management and Working Environments:
   Helena Tammi, (M)
Director, Communications and Marketing:
   Marie-Louise Wiklund, (M)
Director General:
   Mika Nykänen, (M)
Digital Innovations and Corporate data:
   Mikko Eklund, (M)
Director, Science and Innovation:
   Pekka Nurmi, (D)

Helsinki University of Technology
Dept of geoengineering (2004)
Otakaari 1
SF-02150 Espoo
   leena.korkiala-tanttu@aalto.fi
   http://www.hut.fi/Units/Departments/MK/

University of Helsinki
Dept of Geosciences and Geography (B,M,D) (2015)
Gustaf Hällströmink 2
P.O. BOX 68
Helsinki 00014
   p. 358-294150827
   Mia.Kotilainen@helsinki.fi
   http://www.helsinki.fi/geology/
   Enrollment (2007): B: 0 (6) M: 26 (15) D: 6 (0)

Head:
   Juha A. Karhu, (D), Helsinki, 1993, Csg

University of Oulu
Dept of Geology (B,M,D) O (2014)
Linnanmaa
FIN-90014
Oulu
   vesa.peuraniemi@oulu.fi
   http://cc.oulu.fi/~geolwww/Geology.htm

Dept of Geophysics (2007)
   sofianos@metal.ntua.gr
   http://www.gh.oulu.fi/

France

Institut de Physique du Globe de Paris (2015)
1 rue Jussieu
75238 Paris Cedex 05
   p. (018) 395-7400
   secretdir@ipgp.fr
   http://www.ipgp.fr

Bates University
Quaternary Geology and Sedimentology Laboratory (2004)
70, avenue Leon Lachamp - Case 907
13288 Marseille Cedex 09
   sdescha2@bates.edu

Bureau de Recherches Geologiques et Minieres
BRGM-Orleans (2011)
3 avenue Claude-Guillemin
BP 36009
, Orleans 45060 Cedex 2
   p. +33 (0)2 38 64 34 34
   http://www.brgm.fr/

Catholic University of the West
Environmental Management (2004)
3, place Andre Leroy
BP 808
49008 Anger

Centre de Recheches Petrographiques et geochimiques
Center of Petrographic and Geochemical Research (CRPG du CNRS) (2004)
15, rue Notre Dame des Pauvres
BP 20
54501 Vandoeuvre Les Nancy Cedex
   p. + 33 (0)3 83 59 42 02
   dir@crpg.cnrs-nancy.fr
   http://www.crpg.cnrs-nancy.fr

Ecole des Mines de Paris
Ecole des Mines de Paris (2014)
60-62, Boulevard Saint Michel
75272 PARIS cedex 06
Paris, France 75272
   isabelle.olzenski@mines-paristech.fr
   http://www.ensmp.fr/Eng/ENSMP/aboutENSMP.html

Ecole Nationale Supérieure de Géologie (ENSG)
ENSGéologie (M,D) (2015)
2 Rue du Doyen Marcel Roubault
TSA 70605
VANDOEUVRE-LES-NANCY, Lorraine F-54518
   p. 33 (0)3 83 59 64 15
   ensg-contact@univ-lorraine.fr
   http://www.ensg.univ-lorraine.fr/

Director:
    MONTEL Jean-Marc, (D), Eg

Ecole Nationale Superieure des Mines de Nancy
Ecole des Mines de Nancy (M,D) ● (2016)
Campus ARTEM
92 rue du Sergent Blandan
NANCY 54042
    judith.sausse@mines-nancy.univ-lorraine.fr
    http://www.mines-nancy.univ-lorraine.fr/content/
    g%C3%A9oing%C3%A9nierie/
    f: https://www.facebook.com/groups/geoingenierie/

Ecole Nationale Superieure des Mines de Saint Etiene
    (2014)
158 Cours Fauriel
CS 62362
Saint Etienne 42023
    p. (+33) (0)4 77 420 278
    accueil@ccsti-larotonde.com
    http://www.mines-stetienne.fr/fr

Ecole Normale Superieure de Paris
Dept of Geosciences (M,D) ● (2015)
24 rue Lhomond
Paris 75005
    p. (+33) (0)1 44 32 22 11
    delescluse@geologie.ens.fr
    http://www.geosciences.ens.fr
    Enrollment (2015): M: 20 (10) D: 29 (6)

ENSPM - Institut Francais du Petrole
Centre Exploration (2004)
1-4 avenue de Bois Preau
BP 311
92506 Rueil Malmaison

French Institute for Research Exploitation of the Sea (IFREMER)
Dept of Marine Geosciences (2004)
BP 70
29263 Plouzane

Higher Natl School of Mines at Saint-Etienne (ENSME)
Departement Geosciences et environnement (A,B,M,D) (2013)
158, cours Fauriel
42023 Saint-Etienne Cedex 02
    guy@emse.fr

Higher Natl School of Mines in Paris (ENSMP)
Deparment of Earth Sciences and environment (2004)
35, rue Saint-Honore
77305 Fontainebleau Cedex

Inst of Interdisciplinary Research de Geologie et de Mecanique (IRIGM)
Dept of Geosciences and Environment (2004)
Domaine Univ de Grenoble - BP 53 X
35041 Grenoble Cedex
    infos@iribhm.org

Inst of Physics of the Globe-Paris VII
Lab de Geochimie, Geomateriaux, Geomag, Sismo, Tech, Obser Volcanologiques (2004)
Tour 14/24 - 2e etage, 4, place Jussieu
75252 Paris Cedex 05

Institut de Physique Du Globe De Paris
    (M,D) (2013)
1 rue Jussieu
Building Cuvier
Paris 75005
    p. 01 83 95 7400
    webmaster@ipgp.fr
    http://www.ipgp.fr/

Institut Polytechnique LaSalle Beauvais (ex-IGAL)
Dept of Geosciences (B,M,D) (2014)
19 Rue Pierre WAGUET - BP 30313
Beauvais 60026 cedex
    p. +33 (0) 3 44 06 89 91
    yannick.vautier@lasalle-beauvais.fr
    http://www.lasalle-beauvais.fr/
    Administrative Assistant: Nathalie Lermurier
Director of the Geosciences Department:
    Yannick Vautier, Inst Géologique Albert-de-Laparent, 1999, GodCo
Director of the Education Program in Geosciences:
    Hervé Leyrit, (D), Gv
Director of School/Companies relations:
    Pascal Barrier, (D), Inst Géologique Albert-de-Laparent, PmGsPs
Professor:
    Olivier Pourret, (D), Rennes I (France), 2006, CgaGe
    Lahcen Zouhri, (D), Lille (France), 2000, HwgGe
Geotechnics:
    Bassam Barakat, (D), Ecole Centrale Paris (France), 1991, NrgGq
Engineer in Mining & Quarry:
    Lucien Corbineau, Inst Géologique Albert-de-Laparent, 2007, EgGgNm
Engineer in Marine Geology:
    Olivier Bain, Inst Géologique Albert-de-Laparent, 2000, OuGgOi
Engineer in Geotechnics:
    Jean-David Vernhes, Engineer of Polytech Paris UPMC (France), 1998, YgNgr
Engineer in Geology:
    Benoit Proudhon, Inst Géologique Albert-de-Laparent, 1997, GgcGt
Associate Professor:
    Jessica Bonhoure, (D), CREGU-Nancy, 2007, GziCc
    Sadek Brahmi, (D), UPMC Paris VI (France), 1991, Nr
    Claudia Cherubini, (D), Bari (Italia), 2007, HwgGe
    Cyril Gagnaison, (D), Sorbonne (France), 2006, PgGsa
    Sébastien Laurent-Charvet, (D), Orléans (France), 2001, GctOe
    Pascale Lutz, (D), Pau (France), 2002, YgxYd
    Mohamed Nasraoui, (D), ENSMP, 1996, EgGzEm
    Elsa Ottavi-Pupier, (D), CRPG-CNRS Nancy, 1996, GvzGi
    Sébastien Potel, (D), Bâle, 2001, GpzGi
    Elodie Saillet, (D), Glasgow (UK), 2009, GctGo
    Renaud Toullec, (D), Bordeaux (France), 2006, GsoEo
    Ghislain Trullenque, (D), Basel (Switzerland), 2005, GcNrGg

Laboratoire d'Hydrologie et de Geochimie de Strasbourg
    (2014)
1, rue Blessing
67084 Strasbourg Cedex
    p. (+33) (0)3 68 85 04 02
    marie-claie.pierret@unistra.fr
    http://lhyges.unistra.fr/PIERRET-Marie-Claire,250?lang=fr

National Institute of Applied Science
Lab de Mineralogie et Geotechnique (2014)
20, avenue des Buttes de Coesmes
35043 Rennes Cedex 7
    p. (+33) (0)2 23 23 82 00
    olivier.guillou@insa-rennes.fr
    http://www.insa-rennes.fr/insa-rennes.html

National Polytechnic Inst. of Grenoble
Ecole Doctorale Terre, Univers, Environnement (2004)
Domaine Univ de Grnoble - BP 95
46 avenue Félix Viallet
Cedex 1
Grenoble 38031

Pytheas Institute-Earth Sciences and Astronomy Observatory (PYTHEAS)
Faculte des Sciences de Luminy (2004)
Laboratoires de Geologie Marine et Sedimentologie
70 avenue Leon Lachamp
13288 Marseille

Toulouse University
Satellite Geophysics and Oceanography Laboratory (M,D) (2014)
14, Avenue Edouard Belin
31400 Toulouse
p. (+33) (0)5 61 33 29 02
directeur@legos.obs-mip.fr
http://www.legos.obs-mip.fr/Presentation-generale?set_language=en&cl=en

Universite Blaise Pascal (Clermont Ferrand II)
Dept des Sciences de la Terra (2014)
34 Avenue Carnot
63038 Clermont Ferrand Cedex
p. (+33) 04 73 34 67 22
cecile.sergere@univ-bpclermont.fr
http://wwwobs.univ-bpclermont.fr/lmv/cursus/

Université Claude Bernard Lyon 1
Laboratoire de Géologie de Lyon: Terre, Planètes, Environnement (B,M,D) (2015)
Bd du 11 Novembre
Campus de La Doua
Bâtiment Géode
Villeurbanne 69622
p. 0033 (0)472445800
emanuela.mattioli@univ-lyon1.fr
http://lgltpe.ens-lyon.fr/
Administrative Assistant: Marie-Jeanne Barrière
Enrollment (2012): B: 36 (30) M: 16 (16) D: 10 (10)
Professor:
  Pascal Allemand
  Fabrice Cordey
  Gilles Cuny
  Isabelle Daniel
  Gilles Dromart
  philippe Gillet
  Stephane Labrosse
  Christophe Lécuyer
  Emanuela Mattioli
  Guillemette Ménot
  Cathy Quantin
  Pierre Thomas
Senior Scientist:
  Thierry Alboussiere
  janne Blichert toft
  Bernard Bourdon
  Eric Debayle
  Vincent Grossi
  Serge Légendre
  Bruno Reynard
  yanick Ricard
  Jean Vannier
  Ricard Yanick
Associate Professor:
  Muriel Andréani
  Frederic Chambat
  Claude Colombié
  Nicolas Coltice
  Véronique Daviéro-Gomez
  Renaud Deguen
  Véronique Gardien
  Bernard Gomez
  Vincent Langlois
  Gweltaz Maheo
  Gweltaz Mahéo
  Matthew Makou

  Jean-Emmanuel Martelat
  Davide Olivero
  Jean-Philippe Perrillat
  Sylvain Pichat
  Bernard Pittet
  Frédéric Quillévéré
  Stéphane Reboulet
  Philippe Sorrel
  Guillaume Suan
  Benoît Tauzin
Associate Scientist:
  Romain Amiot
  Vincent Balter
  Razvan Caracas
  Fabien Dubuffet
  Philippe Herve Leloup
  Laurence Lemelle
  Jan Matas
Assistant Professor:
  Muriel Andreani
  Anne-Marie Aucourt
  Regis Chirat
  Claude Colombie
  Veronique Daviero
Research Associate:
  Thomas Bodin
  caroline Fitoussi
  Bertrand Lefebvre
Emeritus:
  francis Albarede
On Leave:
  Gilles Escarguel
  philippe Oger
Related Staff:
  Emmanuelle Albalat
  Florent Arnaud-Godet
  Herve Cardon

Universite d'Orleans
Dept des Sciences de la Terre (2004)
BP. 6759
45067 Orleans
scolarite-osuc@univ-orleans.fr

Universite de Bordeaux I
Dept des Sciences de la Terra et de la Mer (2014)
341 Cours de la Liberation
Talence 33400
p. (+33) 05 40 00 88 79
termer@adm.u-bordeaux1.fr
http://www.u-bordeaux1.fr/universite/organisation/composantes-ufr-instituts/ufr-des-sciences-de-la-terre-et-de-la-mer.html

Universite de Bourgogne
UFR Sciences Vie, Terre & Environnement (B,M,D) (2015)
6 boulevard Gabriel
21100 Dijon
direction-ufrsvte@u-bourgogne.fr
http://ufr-svte.u-bourgogne.fr/

Universite de Bretagne Occidentale
Departement des Sciences de la Terre (2014)
3 Rue des Archives
Brest 29287
p. (+33) 02 98 01 61 88
alain.cottignies@univ-brest.fr
http://www.univ-brest.fr/ufr-sciences/menu/Les_departements/Sciences_de_la_Terre

Universite de Caen
Dept des Sciences de la Terre (2014)
Esplanade de la Paix
Caen 14000
p. (+33) 02 31 56 55 87

isabelle.villette@unicagen.fr
http://ufrsciences.unicaen.fr/departements/departement-
des-sciences-de-la-terre/

Universite de Lorraine-Faculte des Sciences et Technologies

Dept Geosciences (B,M) ● (2014)
Boulevard des Aiguillettes
BP 239
54506 Vandoeuvre Les Nancy
    p. (+33) (0)3 83 68 47 18
    bernard.lathuiliere@univ-lorraine.fr
    http://www.geologie.uhp-nancy.fr/Php/index.php
    Enrollment (2014): B: 31 (0) M: 51 (0)

Universite de Montpellier

Geosciences Montpellier (M,D) (2015)
2 place Eugene Bataillon
CC 060
Montpellier cedex 5 34095
    p. (+33) (0)4 67 14 36 43
    dirgm@gm.univ-montp2.fr
    http://www.gm.univ-montp2.fr/?lang=fr

Universite de Nice - Faculte des Sciences

Departement sciences de la terre (2004)
28 avenue Valrose
06034 Nice
    hassani@geoazur.unice.fr

Universite de Paris Sud (Orsay)

Dept Sciences de la Terre (B,M,D) ● (2015)
15 Rue Georges Clemenceau
Orsay 91400
    p. (+33) (0)1 69 15 49 09
    hermann.zeyen@u-psud.fr
    http://geosciences.geol.u-psud.fr/
    Enrollment (2015): B: 91 (36) M: 156 (43) D: 28 (17)

Universite de Paris VI

Center of Geosynamics Research (2014)
4 Place Jussieu
Paris 75005
    p. (+33) 01 44 27 46 98
    licence.sciterre@upmc.fr
    http://www.upmc.fr/en/education/diplomas/sciences_and_
    technologies/bachelor_s_degrees/department_of_earth_
    sciences.html

Lab of Sub-Marine Geodynamics (CEROV) (2004)
Port de la Darse - BP 48
06230 Villefranche-Sur-Mer

Universite de Paris VII

Dept des Sciences Physiques de la Terre (2014)
4 place Jussieu
75251 Paris
    p. (+33) (0)1 57 27 57 27
    zarie.rouas@univ-paris-diderot.fr

Universite de Pau

Dept of Geology (A,B,M,D) (2014)
I.P.R.A. - Geologie
Avenue de L'Universite
Pau 64230
    joelle.arriulou@univ-pau.fr
    http://www.univ-pau.fr/RECHERCHE/GEOPHY/

Universite de Pau et des Pays de l'Adour

Faculte des Sciences (2014)
Avenue de l'Universite
64000 Pau

Universite de Rennes I

Dept. de Geosciences (2015)
2 Rue du Thabot
35065 Rennes Cedex
    p. (+33) (0)2 23 23 60 76
    florentin.paris@orange.fr
    http://www.geosciences.univ-rennes1.fr/?lang=en

Universite de Strasbourg

Ecole et Observatoire des Sciences de la Terre (B,M,D) ● (2014)
5 rue Descartes
67084 Strasbourg cedex F
    p. (+33) (0)3 68 85 03 53
    eost-contact@unistra.fr
    http://eost.unistra.fr/nouveautes-du-site/
Director:
    Frederic Masson, (D)
Laboratory Director:
    Ulrich Achauer, (D), Karlsruhe, 1990, Ysg

Université Jean Monnet, Saint-Etienne

Département de Géologie - Faculté des Sciences et Te-chiques (B,M,D) ● (2015)
23 rue du Dr. Paul Michelon
Saint-Etienne Cedex F-42023
    p. (+33) (0)4 77 48 15 85
    veronique.lavastre@univ-st-etienne.fr
    http://portail.univ-st-etienne.fr/bienvenue/presentation/ufr-
    des-sciences-dpt-geologie-327810.kjsp
Head:
    Bertrand N. MOINE, (D), Macquarie Uni., Sydney, & Uni. J. Monnet St-Etienne, 2000, CgtGx
Professor:
    Jean-Yves COTTIN, (D), Muséum d Histoires Naturelles, Paris, 1978
    Damien GUILLAUME, (D)
    Jean-François MOYEN, (D), 2000, GiCtGp
Assistant Professor:
    Marie-Christine GERBE, (D), GisOe

Universite Paul Sabatier (Toulouse III)

Dept Sciences de la Terre (2015)
118 Route de Narbonne
31062 Toulouse
    p. (+33) (0)5 82 52 57 21
    fsi.sec@univ-tlse3.fr
    http://www.univ-tlse3.fr/04628859/0/fiche___pagelibre/&RH
    =ACCUEIL&RF=1237305837890

Université de Franche-Comté

Sciences environnementales (2011)
Sciences et techniques
Service Scolarité
16, route de Gray
25030 Besançon cedex
    p. 03 81 66 62 09 / 62 11
    Scolarite.UFR-ST@univ-fcomte.fr
    http://sciences.univ-fcomte.fr/formations/listedesformations.
    htm

Faculte des Sciences et Techniques (2014)
16, route de Gray
25030 Besancon Cedex
    p. (+33) (0)3 81 66 62 09
    scolarite.ufr-2t@univ-fcomte.fr
    http://sciences.univ-fcomte.fr/pages/fr/menu3795/forma-
    tions/licence--sciences-de-la-vie-16862-15340.html

University of Caen

Dept des Sciences de la Terre (2004)
Lab de Geologie structurals
Esplanadde de la Paix
14032 Caen Cedex

University of Franche - Comte
Lab de Geol Strucurale et appliquee (2004)
Faculte des Sci et Techniques
Place Leclerc
25030 Besancon

University of Francois Rabelais
Laboratoire de Geologie (2014)
Parc de Grandmot
37200 Tours

University of Lille
Dept of Geology (B,M,D) ● (2015)
Cite Scientifique
Batiment SN-5
Villeneuve D'Ascq 59655
    bruno.vendeville@univ-lille1.fr
    http://www.univ-lille1.fr/geosciences/

University of Louis Pasteur (Strasbourg 1)
School and Observatory of Earth Sciences
  (2004)
1, rue Blessing
67084 Strasbourg Cedex

University of Maine
Faculte des Sci - Lab de Geologie (2014)
Avenue Olivier Messiasen
72085 Le Mans
    p. (+33) (0)2 43 83 30 00
    biogel@univ-lemans.fr
    http://sciences.univ-lemans.fr/Biologie-Geosciences

University of Montpellier II
Observatoire des sciences de l'univers OREME
  (2004)
2, place Eugene Bataillon
34095 Montpellier Cedex 05
    contact@oreme.org

University of Nantes
Departement des Sci de la Terre (2004)
2, rue de la Houssiniere
44072 Nantes Cedex 03

University of Nice
Dept of Earth Science
  (2004)
Faculte des Sciences
28, avenue Valrose
06034 Nice Cedex
    hassani@geoazur.unice.fr

University of Nice-Sopia Antipollis-1
Laboratoire des Sciences de la Terre (2004)
Rue A. Einstein
06560 Valbonne
    Sylvie.DELLA-VITTORIA@unice.fr
    http://www-geoazur.unice.fr/

University of Orleans
Dept des Sciences de la Terre (2004)
Domaine de la Source
BP 6759
45067 Orleans Cedex 02

University of Perpignan
Centre de Sed et Geochimie marines (2014)
52 Avenue Paul Alduy
66100 Perpignan
    p. (+33) (0)4 68 66 21 39
    facscien@univ-perp.fr

University of Picardy
Dept de Geologie (2014)
Chemin du Thil
80000 Amiens
    p. (+33) (0)4 22 82 76 65
    mohamed.benlahsen@u-picardie.fr
    http://www.u-picardie.fr/jsp/fiche_structure.jsp?STNAV=US
    &RUBNAV=&CODE=US&LANGUE=0

University of Pierre & Marie Curie
Lab de Paleobotanique et Palnologue evol (2004)
12, rue Cuvier
75005 Paris

University of Pierre & Marie Curie (Paris VI)
Dept de Geotectonique (2011)
Tour 26 - ler etage (Boite 219)
4, place Jussieu
75252 Paris Cedex 05

Dept of Living Earth and Environment (2010)
Tour 15 - 4e etage
4, place Jussieu
75252 Paris Cedex 05
    chrystele.sanloup@upmc.fr

    http://www.ipgp.jussieu.fr/

University of Poitiers
Dept des Sciences de la Terre (2014)
40, ave du Recteur Pineau
86022 Poitiers Cedex

University of Provence (Aix-Marseille I)
Lab de Geol Structurale et appliquee (2004)
Centre Saint Charles
3, place Victor Hugo - Case 28
13331 Marseille Cedex 3

University of Reims-Champagne
Dept des Sciences de la Terre (2014)
Moulin de la Housse - BP 1039
51687 Reims Cedex
    p. (+33) (0)3 26 91 34 19
    scolarite.sceiences@univ-reims.fr
    http://www.univ-reims.fr/formation/ufr-instituts-et-ecoles/ufr-
    sciences-exactes-et-naturelles/presentation,8370.html?

University of Rouen-Upper Normandy
Dept de Geologie (2015)
1 Rue Thomas Becket
76821 Mont-Saint-Aignan
    p. (+33) (0)2 35 14 68 26
    francoise.baillot@univ-rouen.fr

University of Savoy
Laborotoire de Geologie (2004)
Faculte des Sci et Techniques
Campus de Technolac, BP 1104
73011 Chambery Cedex

University of Science & Technology of Lille
Inst Des Sciences De La Terre (2004)
Flandres - Artois, Cite Scientifique
Bat SN5, BP 36
59655 Villeneuve D'Ascq Cedex

University of West Brittany
Earth Sciences (2004)
Groupement de Recherche: GEDO
6, avenue Le Gorgeu
29287 Brest

Gabon

Universite des Sciences et Techniques de Masuku
Dept de Geologie (B) (2014)
BP 901
Franceville
    p. (+241) 01 67 75 78
    http://www.labogabon.net/ustm/facscience/index.html

Universite Omar Bongo
Dept de Geologie (B) (2010)
BP 13 131
Boulevard Leon Mba
Libreville
    p. +241 73 20 45, (241-72) 69 10
    uob@internetgabon.com
    http://www.uob.ga/

Germany

State Survey for Geology and Mining of Sachsen-Anhalt
State Survey for Geology and Mining of Sachsen-Anhalt (2016)
Halle, Saxony-Anhalt D-06035
    p. +49 345 52 12 0
    poststelle@lagb.mw.sachsen-anhalt.de
    http://www.lagb.sachsen-anhalt.de

Aachen University of Technology
Inst of Structural Geology, Tectonics and Geomechanics (2005)
Lochnerstr 4-20
D-52056
    ged@ged.rwth-aachen.de

    http://www.ged.rwth-aachen.de

Baden-Wuerttemberg - Landesamt fuer Geologie, Rohstoffe und Bergbau (LGRB)
Regional Government of Freiburg State Office of Geology, Raw Materials and Mining (2015)
Albertstrasse 5
Freiburg, Baden-Wuerttemberg 79104
    p. ++49 9761 208 3000
    abteilung9@rpf.bwl.de
    http://www.lgrb-bw.de/

Brandenburg - Landesamt fuer Geowissenschaften und Rohstoffe (LGRB)
State Office for Mining , Geology and Minerals of Brandenburg (2011)
Inselstrabe 26
03046 Cottbus
    info@lbgr.brandenburg.de
    http://www.lbgr.brandenburg.de

Bundesanstalt fur Geowissenschaften und Rohstoffe (BGR)
Federal Institute for Geosciences and Natural Resources (2015)
Stilleweg 2
Hannover 30655
    poststelle@bgr.de
    http://www.bgr.bund.de

Christian-Albrechts-Universitaet
Geology Dept (2011)
Olshausenstrasse 40/60
2300 Kiel 1

Ernst-Moritz-Arndt Universitaet
Institut fur Geographie und Geologie (2014)
Domstrabe 11
17489 Griesswald
    p. (+49) (0) 3834 86-4502
    geogra@uni-greifswald.de
    http://www.mnf.uni-greifswald.de/institute/geo.html

Freiberg City College
Sektion Geowissenschaften (2014)
Bertoldstrabe 17
79085 Freiberg
    p. (+49) 761 203-67342
    studyinfo@ucf.uni-freiburg.de
    http://www.ucf.uni-freiburg.de/

Freie Universitaet Berlin
Inst fur Geologie (2013)
Malteserstr. 74-100
12249 Berlin
    p. (030) 838-70 575
    plansec@zedat.fu-berlin.de
    http://www.geo.fu-berlin.de/geol/index.html

Inst fuer Palaontologie (2011)
Maltese-Strasse
74-100, Haus D
D-12249 Berlin
    palaeont@zedat.fu-berlin.de
    http://userpage.fu-berlin.de/~palaeont/WELCOME.HTM

Friedrich-Schiller-University Jena
Institute for Geosciences (B,M,D) ● (2014)
Burgweg 11
Jena 07749
    p. 0049(0)3641/948600
    geowissenschaften@uni-jena.de
    http://www.geo.uni-jena.de
    Enrollment (2014): B: 17 (43) M: 16 (22) D: 69 (12)
Univ.-Prof. Dr.:
    Sabine Attinger, (D), Hy
    Florian Bleibinhaus, (D), Yx
    Georg Büchel, (D), Gg
    Christoph Heubeck, (D), Gh
    Nina Kukowski, (D), Ygx
    Falko H. Langenhorst, (D), Gz
    Juraj Majzlan, (D), Gz
    Kai U. Totsche, (D), Bayreuth, 1994, HwClOs
    Kamil Ustaszewski, (D), Gc
    Lothar Viereck, (D)
Jun.-Prof. Dr.:
    Anke Kleidon-Hildebrandt, (D)

Garching Technical University
Inst fur Geologie und Mineralogie (2004)
Lichtenbergergstrasse 4
0-8046 Garching
    rieder@tum.de

Geologischer Dienst
Bavarian Environment Agency (2013)
Buergermeister-Ulrich-Strasse 160
Augsburg 86179
    poststelle@lfu.bayern.de
    http://www.lfu.bayern.de/geologie/

Geologischer Dienst Nordrhein-Westfalen
NRW Geological Survey (2013)
Postfach 10 07 63
De-Greiff-Strasse 195
Krefeld D-47707
    p. +49-2151-897-0
    geoinfo@gd.nrw.de
    http://www.gd.nrw.de/home.php

Geologisches Institut der Universitaet
Dept of Geology (2011)

Plelcherwael 1
87 Wuerzburg

Georg-August University of Goettingen
Dept of Geobiology (B,M,D) (2015)
Goldschmidstr. 3
Goettingen, Lower Saxony 37077
p. +49 551 397951
jreitne@gwdg.de
http://www.geobiologie.uni-goettingen.de/
Enrollment (2014): B: 8 (8) M: 2 (2) D: 4 (4)
Prof.Dr.:
Joachim Reitner, (D), PyyPy
Professor:
Volker Thiel, Dr., (D), CooCo
Dr.:
Gernot Arp, Dr., (D), PyyPy
Andreas Reimer, (D), OcCmm
Dr.:
Jan-Peter Duda, (D), 2014

Goethe Universitaet
Fachbereich Geowissenschaften (2014)
Altenhoferallee 1
60438 Frankfurt
p. (+49) (0)69 798 40208
dekanat-geowiss@em.uni-frankfurt.de
http://www.uni-frankfurt.de/fb/fb11/index.html

Hamburg - Geological Survey
Ministry of Urban Development and Environmental Protection Agency for the Environment (2014)
Neuenfelder Straße 19
21109 Hamburg
gla@bsu.hamburg.de
http://www.geologie.hamburg.de

Helmholtz-Zentrum Potsdam Deutsches GeoForschungsZentrum
GeoForschungs Zentrum GFZ (2014)
Telegrafenberg 14473
14473 Potsdam
p. (+49) 331 288-1045
presse@gfz-potsdam.de
http://www.gfz-potsdam.de/startseite/

Hessen - Landesamt fuer Umwelt und Geologie
(2011)
65203 Wiesbaden, Rheingaustraße 186
p. 0611-6939-0
http://www.hlug.de/

Humboldt Universitaet zu Berlin
Palaontologisches Museum (2011)
Invaliden Strasse 43
0-4010 Berlin

Institut fur Palaontologie
Dept of Geology (2004)
O. Weidlich, Fohrenweg 19
W-8504 Stein
palsek@univie.ac.at

Karlsruhe Institute of Technology
Geophysical Institut (B,M,D) (2010)
Hertzstr. 16
Karlsruhe 76187
p. +49-721-6084431
Friedemann.Wenzel@kit.edu
http://www-gpi.physik.uni-karlsruhe.de/
Enrollment (2010): B: 15 (0) D: 10 (0)

Professor:
Thomas Bohlen, (D), Yx
Senior Scientist:
Thomas Forbriger, (D), Ys
Joachim J.R. Ritter, (D), Ys
Research Associate:
Rebecca Harrington, (D), Ys

Institute for Applied Geosciences (2011)
Hertzstr. 16
Karlsruhe
susanne.winter@kit.edu
http://www.agw.kit.edu/

Institute for Mineralogy and Geochemistry (2011)
Adenauerring 20b
Karlsruhe D-76131
p. +49 721 608- 43323
img@img.uka.de
http://www.img.kit.edu/

Dept of Geology (2014)
Kaiserstrasse 12
76131 Karlsruhe
p. (+49) 721 608 4219 2/43651
geophysik@gpi.kit.edu
http://www.bgu.kit.edu/index.php

Ludwig-Maximilians-Universitaet Muenchen
Dept of Earth & Enviromental Sciences (B,M,D) (2009)
Theresienstr. 41/III
Munich 80333
p. 0049/89/21804250
dekanat20@lmu.de
http://min.geo.uni-muenchen.de/
Enrollment (2007): B: 173 (28) M: 12 (0) D: 24 (0)
Director:
Donald Bruce Dingwell, Giv
Professor:
Alexander Altenbach, Pg
Wladyslaw Altermann, Gg
Michael Amler, Pg
Valerian Bachtadse, Yg
Hans-Peter Bunge, Yg
Christina De Campos, Gz
Karl Thomas Fehr, Gz
Friedrich Frey, Gz
Anke Friedrich, (D)
Stuart Gilder, Yg
Wolfgang Heckel, Gz
Ernst Hegner, Gz
Soraya Heuss-Aßbichler, Gz
Heiner Igel, Yg
Harald Immel, Pg
Bernd Lammerer, Gg
Reinhold Leinfelder, Pg
Rocco Malservisi, Yg
Robert Marschik, Gg
Ludwig Masch, Gz
Wolfgang Moritz, Gz
Bettina Reichenbacher, Pg
Wolfgang Schmahl, Gz
Klaus Weber-Diefenbach, Gg
Christian Wolkersdorfer, Gg
Other:
Kirill Aldushin, Gz
Greta Barbi, Yg
Robert Barsch, Yg
Johannes Birner, Gg
Florian Bleibinhaus, Yg
Hans Boysen, Gz
Gilbert Britzke, Yg
Benoit Cordonnier, Gz
Alexander Dorfman, Gz
Thomas Dorfner, Gz
Barbara Emmer, Yg
Werner Ertel-Ingrisch, Gz

Andreas Fichtner, Yg
Michaela Frei, Gg
Frantisek Gallovic, Yg
Helmut Gebrande, Yg
Alexander Gigler, Yg
Peter Gille, Gz
Stefan Grießl, Gz
Hagen Göttlich, Gz
Marc Hennemeyer, Gz
Katja Henßel, Pg
Kai-Uwe Hess, Gz
Maria Linda Iaccheri, Gg
Giampiero Iaffaldano, Yg
Guntram Jordan, Gz
Ines Kaiser-Bischoff, Gz
Thorsten Kowalke, Pg
Thomas Kunzmann, Gz
Martin Käser, Yg
Markus Lackinger, Gz
Yan Lavallee, Yg
Maike Lübbe, Gz
Götz Meisterernst, Gz
Timo Casjen Merkel, Gz
Marcus Mohr, Yg
Lena Müller, Gz
Dieter Müller-Sohnius, Gz
Malik Naumann, Pg
Jens Oser, Yg
Sohyun Park, Gz
Karin Paschert, Gg
Rossitza Pentcheva, Gz
Nikolai Petersen, Yg
Helen Pfuhl, Yg
Antonio Sebastian Piazzoni, Yg
Christina Plattner, Yg
Josep Puente Alvarez de la
Oliver Riedel, Gz
Alexander Rocholl, Gz
Javier Rubio-Sierra, Gz
Gertrud Rößner, Pg
Dieter Schmid, Pg
Julius Schneider, Gz
Bernhard Schuberth, Yg
Oliver Spieler, Gz
Robert Stark, Gz
Katja Steffens, Gg
Stefan Strasser, Gz
Marco Stupazzini, Yg
Frank Söllner, Gg
Frank Trixler, Gz
Ferdinand Walther, Gz
Joachim Wassermann, Yg
Laura Wehrmann, Pg
Michael Winklhofer, Yg
Ayhan Yurtsever, Gz
Matthias Zeitlhöfler, Gg
Albert Zink, Gz

**Div of Palaeontology & Geobiology, Dept of Earth and Env
Sci** (B,M,D) O (2015)
Richard-Wagner-Strasse 10
Muenchen, Bavaria 80333
geobiologie@geo.lmu.de
http://www.palmuc.de
Prof. Dr.:
Gert Woerheide, (D), Pyo
Prof. Dr.:
William Orsi, (D), PyOn
Bettina Reichenbacher, (D), PogPv

Marburg Chome University
Geology Dept (2014)
Deutschhausstrabe 10
35032 Marburg
p. (+49) 06421/28-24257
edda.walz@geo.uni-marburg.de
https://www.uni-marburg.de/fb19_alt

208

Martin-Luther-Universitaet Halle-Wittenberg
Inst for Geosciences and Geography (B,M,D) (2015)
Von-Seckendorff-Platz 3
D-06120 Halle
p. ++49-045-55 26010
direktor@geo.uni-halle.de
http://www.geo.uni-halle.de
Director:
Herbert Pöllmann, (D), 1984, Gz

Mecklenburg-Vorpommern - Landesamt fuer Umwelt, Naturschutz und Geologie
State office for the Environment, Nature Conservation and Geology (2015)
Goldberger Strasse 12
18273 Gustrow
p. ++49-3843-777 0
poststelle@lung.mv-regierung.de
http://www.lung.mv-regierung.de/

Niedersachsen - Landesamt fuer Bodenforschung
(2014)
p. +49 (0)511-643-0
poststelle-hannover@lbeg.niedersachsen.de
http://www.lbeg.niedersachsen.de

Rheinisch-Westfaelische Technische Hochschule Aachen
Fachgruppe fuer Geowissenschaften und Geographie (2011)
Lochnerstr. 4-20 (Haus B)
Aachen 52056
p. 0241 80 96219
geowiss@rwth-aachen.de
http://www.fgeo.rwth-aachen.de/

Rheinland-Pfalz-Landesamt fuer Geologie und Bergbau
State Office for Geology and Mining (2011)
Emy-Roeder-Strabe 5
PO Box 100 255
Mainz-Hechtsheim D-55129
office@lgb-rlp.de
http://www.lgb-rlp.de/

RWTH Aachen University
Institute of Geology and Palaeontology (2004)
Facultat fur Bergbau
Huttenwesen und Geowissenschaften/Wulwestr 2
D-5100 Aacen
geo.sek@emr.rwth-aachen.de

Sachsen-Landesamt fuer Umwelt und Geologie (LfUG)
Saxon State Agency for Environment, Agriculture and Geology (2011)
Postfach 54 01 37
Dresden 01 311
lfulg@smul.sachsen.de
http://www.smul.sachsen.de/

Technische Hochschule
Institute of Applied Geoscience (2014)
Karolinenplatz 5
64289 Darmstadt
p. (+49) 6151 16-2171
herrmann@geo.tu-darmstadt.de
http://www.geo.tu-darmstadt.de/iag/index.de.jsp

Technische Universitaet Bergakademie Freiberg
Faculty for Geosciences, Geoengineering and Mining (2011)
Bergakademis Freiberg

Postfach 47/Bernhard-Cotta Strasse
Freiberg
    p. +49 (0)3731 / 39 - 3249
    Andrea.Thuemmel@geort.tu-freiberg.de
    http://tu-freiberg.de/fakult3/index.en.html

Technische Universitaet Berlin
Applied Geosciences (2011)
Str. Des 17 Juni 135
W-1000 Berlin 12
    p. +49 30314-7260 5
    http://www.geo.tu-berlin.de/

Technische Universitaet C.W. Braunschweig
Inst fuer Geologie und Palaontologie (2013)
Fachbereich fur Physik und Geowissenschaften
Pockelstrasse 14
D-3300 Braunschweig DEN

Institute of Environmental Geology (2011)
Postfach 3329
Braunschweig D-38023
    geosecret@tu-bs.de
    http://www.tu-braunschweig.de/iug

Inst fuer Geophysik und Meteorologie (2011)
Mendelssohnstr 2-3
D-3300 Braunschweig

Technische Universitaet Clausthal
Institut fuer Geologie und Palaeontologie (2013)
LeibnizstraBe 10
D-38678
Clausthal-Zellerfeld 38678
    Office@geologie.tu-clausthal.de
    http://www.geologie.tu-clausthal.de/

Inst for Petroleum Engineering (2015)
Agricolastrasse 10
38678 Clausthal-Zellerfeld
    p. +49-5323-72-2239
    marion.bischof@tu-clausthal.de
    http://www.ite.tu-clausthal.de/

Technische Universitaet Darmstadt
Institute of Applied Geosciences (B,M,D) (2011)
Schnittspahnstr. 9
Darmstadt D-64287
    p. +49 6151 16 2171
    iag@geo.tu-darmstadt.de
    http://www.geo.tu-darmstadt.de/
    Enrollment (2011): B: 280 (3) M: 54 (0) D: 29 (2)
Acting head:
    Hans-Joachim Kleebe, GzOm
Professor:
    Rafael Ferreiro Maehlmann, Gxp
    Matthias Hinderer, Gs
    Andreas Hoppe, GgOui
    Stephan Kempe, GgCgHs
    Ingo Sass, Ng
    Christoph Schueth, Hw
    Stephan Weinbruch, GzOwm

Technische Universitaet Muenchen
Engineering Geology (B,M,D) ● (2014)
Arcisstr. 21
Munich, Bavaria 80333
    p. +498928925851
    geologie@tum.de
    http://www.eng.geo.tum.de/
    Administrative Assistant: Katja Lokau
    Enrollment (2014): B: 55 (0) M: 66 (0) D: 19 (4)
Chair-Prof.:
    Kurosch Thuro, (D), Technische Univ Muenchen, 1995, NgrGg

Professor:
    Hans Albert Gilg, (D), ETH (Switzerland), EgnEg
    Michael Krautblatter, (D), Erlangen, GmNrOi
Senior Scientist:
    Gerhard Lehrberger, (D), TUM, EgGxg
    Bernhard Lempe, (D), TUM, 2012, GlgNg
    Michael Rieder, (D), Technische Univ Muenchen, GgxGs
Associate Professor:
    Inga Moeck, (D), GcgOn
Research Associate:
    Peter Ellecosta, (M), TUM, Ngr
    Sibylle Knapp, (M), ETH Zurich, GsgGm
    Mathias Köster, (M), TU Dresden, CgGzEg
    Philipp Mamot, (M), Bonn, GmOg
    Florian Menschik, (M), Technische Univ Muenchen, GqOiNr
    Lukas Paysen-Petersen, (M), Technische Univ Muenchen, 2013,
    NgrGq
    Bettina Sellmeier, (M), Technische Univ Muenchen, Ngr
    Carola Wieser, (M), Technische Univ Muenchen, Ngr
    Lisa Wilfing, (M), Technische Univ Muenchen, Ngr
Lecturer:
    Kerry Leith, (D), ETH Zurich, 2012, GmNrOi
    Marion Nickmann, (D), Technische Univ Muenchen, 2006, Ng
Laboratory Director:
    Heiko Käsling, (D), TUM, 2009, NrmNg

Technische Universitat Dresden
Dept of Geosciences (2015)
Mommsenstr 13
0-8027 Dresden
    p. +49 351 463-32863
    doris.salomon@tu-dresden.de
    http://tu-dresden.de/die_tu_dresden/fakultaeten/fakultaet_
    forst_geo_und_hydrowissenschaften/fachrichtung_geowis-
    senschaften

Thuringen-Landesanstalt fuer Umwelt und Geologie
Thuringen State Institute for Environment and Geology (2011)
Goeschwitzer Str forty-one
07745 Jena
    Poststelle@tlug.thueringen.de
    http://www.tlug-jena.de/de/tlug/

Universitaet Bochum
Institut fuer Geologie, Mineralogie und Geophysik (B,M,D) (2013)
Universitaetsstr. 150
Bochum 44780
    p. +49 234 32 23233
    sabine.sitter@ruhr-uni-bochum.de
    http://www.ruhr-uni-bochum.de/gmg/

Universitaet Bonn
**Steinmann-Institut für Geologie, Mineralogie und Paläontolo-
gie** (B,M,D) ● (2014)
Nussallee 8
Bonn 53115
    p. +49 228 73 4803
    tmartin@uni-bonn.de
    http://www.steinmann.uni-bonn.de/

Universitaet Bremen
Fachbereich 5 Geowissenschaften (A,B,M,D) ● (2015)
Postfach 330440
Bremen, Bremen 28359
    info@geo.uni-bremen.de
    http://www.geo.uni-bremen.de
    *Enrollment (2015): A: 249 (0) B: 274 (52) M: 249 (62) D:
    111 (29)*

Universitaet Erlangen-Nuernberg
Institut fur Geographie (2011)
Kochstr. 4/4
91054 Erlangen
    p. 09131/85-22633

common@geographie.uni-erlangen.de
http://www.geographie.uni-erlangen.de/

anke.allner@uni-hamburg.de
http://www.cen.uni-hamburg.de/

Universitaet Erlangen-Nürnberg
Geozentrum Nordbayern (2011)
Schlossgarten 5
91054 Erlangen
 p. 09131/85-22615
 geologie@geol.uni-erlangen.de
 http://www.geol.uni-erlangen.de

Universitaet Frankfurt
Institut fur Geowissenschaften (2011)
Fachbereisch 17
Senckenberganlage 32-34
6000 Frankfurt
 geowissenschaften@em.uni-frankfurt.de
 http://www.geo.uni-frankfurt.de/ifg/

Universitaet Freiburg
Institut fur Geo- und Umweltnaturwissenschaften - Geologie
(B,M,D) (2015)
Albertstr. 23-B
Freiburg i. Br., Baden-Wuerttemberg 79104
 ulmer@uni-freiburg.de
 https://portal.uni-freiburg.de/geologie

Universitaet Giessen
Inst fuer Geowissenschaften und LithosphSrenforshung (2014)
Senckenbergstrasse 3
35390 Giessen
 p. (+49) 641 990
 brigitte.becker-lins@geolo.uni-giessen.de
 http://www.uni-giessen.de/fbr08/geolith/

Universitaet Goettingen
Geowissenschaftliches Zentrum (2011)
Goldschmidstr. 3
Lower Saxony
Gottingen D-37077
 p. +49 551 397951
 bhinz@gwdg.de
 http://www.uni-goettingen.de/de/125309.html

Universitaet Greifswald
Institute for Geography and Geology (2011)
F.L. Jahn Strasse 17
Greifswald
 p. +49 (0)3834 86-4570
 geologie@uni-greifswald.de
 http://www.mnf.uni-greifswald.de/institute/geo.html

Universitaet Halle-Wittenberg
Institute for Geosciences and Geographie (A,B,M,D) ● (2015)
Von-Seckendorff-Platz 3/4
Halle D-06120
 p. +49-0345-55 26055
 direktor@geo.uni-halle.de
 http://www.geo.uni-halle.de/

Universitaet Hamburg
Institute of Geophysics (B,M,D) ● (2015)
Bundesstrasse 55
Hamburg 20146
 p. +4940428382973
 dirk.gajewski@uni-hamburg.de
 www.geo.uni-hamburg.de/de/geophysik.html
 Enrollment (2013): B: 76 (46) M: 38 (13) D: 32 (3)
Professor:
 Dirk J. Gajewski, (D), Karlsruhe, 1987, YesYg

Center for Earth System Research and Sustainability (M,D) (2015)
Bundesstrasse 53
Hamburg 20146
210

Universitaet Hannover
Institut fur Geologie (2011)
Fachbeleich Erdwissenschaften
Callinstrasse 30
D-30167 Hannover
 p. +49-(0)511-762 2343
 sekretariat@geowi.uni-hannover.de
 http://www.geologie.uni-hannover.de

Universitaet Heidelberg
Facultat fur Chemie und Geowissenschaften (2014)
Im Neuenheimer Feld 234
69120 Heidelberg
 p. (+49) 06221/544 844
 dcg@urz.uni-heidelberd.de
 http://www.chemgeo.uni-hd.de/

Insitut fuer Geowissenschaften (2011)
Im Neuenheimer Feld 236
Heidelberg D-69120
 p. 06221-54-8291
 Elfriede.Hofmann@geow.uni-heidelberg.de
 http://www.geow.uni-heidelberg.de/

Universitaet Leipzig
Institut fur Geophysik und Geologie (2011)
Talstrasse 35
04103 Leipzig
 geologie@rz.uni-leipzig.de
 http://www.uni-leipzig.de/~geo/

Universitaet Mainz
Institut fur Geowissenschaften (B,M,D) ● (2015)
J.-J.-Becher-Weg 21
D-55128 Mainz
 p. +49 6131 39 22857
 mertz@uni-mainz.de
 http://www.geowiss.uni-mainz.de/
Head:
 Bernd R. Schöne, (D), PegPi
Professor:
 Jonathan M. Castro, (D), Gv
 Boris PJ Kaus, (D), Yg
 Michael Kersten, (D), Ca
 Cees W. Passchier, (D), Gt
 Denis Scholz, (D), Cl
 Frank Sirocko, (D), Gs
 Richard W. White, (D), Gp
Adjunct Professor:
 Dieter Mertz, (D), Cc

Universitaet Marburg
Inst fuer Geologie und Palaontologie (2011)
Biergenstrasse 12
Lahnberge
D-3550 Marburg-Lahn

Universitaet Muenster
Institut fur Geologie und Palaeontologie (B,M,D) ● (2015)
Corrensstr. 24
D-48149 Münster
 p. +49 251-83 33974
 sklaus@uni-muenster.de
 http://www.uni-muenster.de/GeoPalaeontologie/
 Enrollment (2015): B: 183 (0) M: 60 (0) D: 9 (0)
Professor:
 Christine Achten, (D), Frankfurt, 2002, CloEg
 Heinrich Bahlburg, (D), Tech (Berlin), 1986, Gsg
 Ralf Thomas Becker, (D), Bochum, 1990, Pg
 Ralf Hetzel, (D), Gcm
 Hans Kerp, (D), Utrecht, 1986, Pb

Harald Strauss, (D), Göttingen, 1985, CsGg

Institut fuer Mineralogie (2011)
Corrensstrabe 24
Muenster 48149
    p. +49 251 83-33464
    minsek@uni-muenster.de
    http://www.uni-muenster.de/Mineralogie/

Universitaet of Kiel
Institute of Geoscience (2014)
Christian-Albrechts-Platz 4
24118 Kiel
    p. (+49) 431 880 3900
    wussow@geophysik.uni-kiel.de
    http://www.ifg.uni-kiel.de/6+M52087573ab0.html

Universitaet Oldenburg
Institute for Chemistry and Biology of the Marine Environment
(2014)
Carl-von-Ossietzky-Str. 9-11
Box 2503
Oldenburg 26111
    p. +49-0441-798-5342
    director@icbm.de
    http://www.icbm.uni-oldenburg.de/

Universitaet Potsdam
Institute for Earth and Environmental Sciences (B,M,D) (2013)
Karl-Liebknecht-Str. 24-25
Potsdam 14476
    p. +49 331 977 2116
    sekretariat@geo.uni-potsdam.de
    http://www.geo.uni-potsdam.de/
    Enrollment (2013): B: 319 (14) M: 79 (11) D: 122 (16)

Universitaet Stuttgart
Inst fuer Geol und Palaontogisch (2011)
Fakultaet-7-Geo. und Biowissenschaften
Boblinger Str. 72
D-7000 Stuttgart 10

Universitaet Trier
Lehrstuhl fuer Geologie (B,M,D) (2016)
Geowissenschaften (FB VI)
Trier 54286
    p. 0651 201 4647
    ensch@uni-trier.de
    http://www.uni-trier.de/index.php?id=2632
    Enrollment (2015): B: 67 (12) M: 41 (9) D: 5 (4)

Regional and Environmental Science (2014)
Behringstrabe 21
D-54296 Trier
    p. (+49) (0) 651-201-4528
    dekanatfb6@uni-trier.de
    http://www.uni-trier.de/index.php?id=2220

Universitaet Tuebingen
Institute for Geoscience (2011)
72076 Tuebingen
Sigwartstr. 10
    Christophe.Pascal@rub.de
    http://www.ifg.uni-tuebingen.de/

Universitaet Würzburg
Institut für Geographie und Geologie (2011)
Am Hubland
97074 Würzburg
    p. +49 (0) 931 / 31-85555
    http://www.geographie.uni-wuerzburg.de

Institut für Paläontologie (2011)
Pleicherwall 1

D-97070 Würzburg
    p. 49 0931- 31 25 97
    i-palaeontologie@mail.uni-wuerzburg.de
    http://www.palaeontologie.uni-wuerzburg.de

Universitaet zu Koeln
Institute for Geology and Mineralogy (2011)
Cologne
    p. +49 221 470-5619
    ellen.stefan@uni-koeln.de
    http://www.geologie.uni-koeln.de/

University of Bayreuth
Bayerisches Geoinstitut (M,D) (2015)
Bayreuth 95440
    p. +49(0)921 55-3700
    bayerisches.geoinstitut@uni-bayreuth.de
    http://www.bgi.uni-bayreuth.de/

University of Cologne
Institute of Geophysics and Meteorology (B,M,D) (2014)
Pohligstraße 3
D-50969 Köln
    p. +49 (0)221 470 2552
    sekretar@geo.uni-koeln.de
    http://www.geomet.uni-koeln.de/en/general/home/

Dept of Geology and Mineralogy (B,M,D) ● (2014)
Zuelpicherstr. 49a
50674 Koeln
    p. +49-221-470-5619
    ellen.stefan@uni-koeln.de
    http://www.uni-koeln.de/math-nat-fak/geologie/index.html

West Wilhelms Universitat
Dept of Applied Geology (2004)
Schlossplatz 2
4400 Muenster

Westfälische Wilhelms-Universität Münster
Fachbereich Geowissenschaften (B,M,D) (2012)
Robert-Koch-Straße 29
D-48149 Münster
    p. +49 251 83-33906
    dekangeo@uni-muenster.de
    http://www.uni-muenster.de/Geowissenschaften/

Ghana

Kwame Nkrumah University of Science and Technology
Petroleum Engineering (B) (2010)
    http://www.knust.edu.gh/ceng/faculties.php

Dept of Geomatic Engineering (B,M,D) ○ (2015)
geomaticeng@knust.edu.gh
Kumasi PMB KNUST
    p. +233 (0)3220 60227
    geomaticeng@knust.edu.gh
    http://www.knust.edu.gh/ceng/faculties.php

Geological Engineering (B,M,D) ● (2015)
Geological Engineering Department
College of Engineering
KNUST
Kumasi PMB
    geologicaleng@knust.edu.gh
    http://archive.knust.edu.gh/pages/index.php?siteid=geoleng
Lecturer:
    Bukari Ali, (D), Birmingham (England), 1996, HwNgYg
    Godfrey C. Amedjoe, (M), Ghana, 2005, GidGc
    Emmanuel K. Appiah-Adjei, (D), Hohai (China), 2013, HwgGg
    Samuel Banash, (M)
    Gordon Foli, (M), 2004

Ghana

Solomon S. Gidigasu, (M), Sci & Tech (Ghana), 2013, GeOrNr
Emmanuel Mensah, Sci & Tech (China), 1998, Eg

University of Development Studies
Earth and Environmental Science (B) (2010)
PO Box 1350
Tamale
    p. +233 (71) 22422
    moconnel@uno.edu
    http://www.uds.edu.gh/

University of Ghana
Dept of Earth Science (B,M,D) ● (2014)
PO Box LG 58
Legon
Accra
    p. +233-244-116-879
    pmnude@ug.edu.gh
    http://www.ug.edu.gh/index1.php?linkid=185&sublinkid=40
    &subsublinkid=36
    Enrollment (2013): B: 336 (104) M: 105 (33) D: 2 (1)
Dean of Science:
    Daniel K. Asiedu, (D), GsCgGd
Professor:
    Bruce K. Banoeng-Yakubo, (D), Ghana, GcHw
Senior Scientist:
    Thomas K. Armah, (D), YgeYe
    Jacob M. Kutu, (D), GctGc
    Patrick Asamoah Sakyi, (D), Cg
Head of Department:
    Prosper M. NUDE, (D), Ghana, GipGx
Associate Professor:
    Thomas M. Akabzaa, (D), Ghana, 2004, EgGeNm
    David Atta-Peters, (D), Ghana, Pl
    Johnson Manu, (D), GzEgGz
    Frank K. Nyame, (D), Cg
    Sandow M. Yidana, (D), Hwq
Lecturer:
    Francis Achampong, (D), Ngr
    Chris Y. Anani, (D), Gsd
    Larry-Pax CHEGBELEH, (D), Ng
    Yvonne A.S Loh, (M), Hw
    Issac A. Oppong, (D), Np

University of Mines and Technology
Dept of Geological Engineering (B) (2014)
PO Box 237
Tarkwa
    p. +233 3123 20935
    sps@umat.edu.gh
    http://www.umat.edu/gh/UndergraduatePrograms/geology.
    html

Dept of Geomatic Engineering (B) (2014)
PO Box 237
Tarkwa
    p. +233(0)362 20324
    gm@umat.edu.gh
    http://www.umat.edu.gh/UndergraduatePrograms/geomatic.
    html

Dept of Mineral Engineering (B) (2014)
PO Box 237
Tarkwa
    p. +233(0)362 21136
    mr@umat.edu.gh
    http://www.umat.edu.gh/UndergraduatePrograms/mineral.
    html

Dept of Mining Engineering (B) (2014)
PO Box 237
Tarkwa
    p. +233 3123 20935
    mn@umat.edu.gh
    http://www.umat.edu.gh/UndergraduatePrograms/Mining.
    html

Greece

Aristotle University of Thessaloniki
School of Geology (2014)
GR-541 24
Thessaloniki 54124
    p. (+30) 2310 99.8450
    info@geo.auth.gr
    http://www.geo.auth.gr/index_en.htm

Greek Institute of Geology & Mineral Exploration
Greek Institute of Geology & Mineral Exploration (2014)
1, Spirou Louis St.,
Olympic Village
Acharnae P.C. 13677
    dirgen@igme.gr
    http://www.igme.gr

National Technical University of Athens
Dept of Mining Engineering and Metallurgy (2011)
Zographou Campus
15 780 Athens
    secretary@metal.ntua.gr
    http://www.metal.ntua.gr/div-geology/index.html

University of Athens
Faculty of Geology and Geoenvironment (2004)
National & Capodistran Univ. of Athens
Panepistimioupolis, Ilistra
Athens
    secr@geol.uoa.gr
    http://www.geol.uoa.gr/engindex.htm

University of Patras
Dept of Geology (2004)
26110 Patras

Guatemala

Universidad sde San Carlos de Guatemala
Centro de Estudios Superiores de Energia y Minas (2014)
Ciudad Universitaria Zona 12, Guatemala City 01012
    p. (502) 2418-9139 ex. 86211
    usacesem@ing.usac.edu.gt
    http://cesem.ingenieria.usac.edu.gt/

Guinea

Univerité Gamal Abdel Nasser de Conakry
Faculty of Geology and Mining (M) ● (2014)
BP 1147
Conakry, Guinée
    p. +224 631 54 48 38
    sekoumoussa@gmail.com
    http://www.uganc.org/index.php/2013-01-12-06-22-44/cere

Guyana

Guyana Geology and Mines Commission
Guyana Geology and Mines Commission (2011)
Upper Brickdam
Georgetown
    p. 226-5591, 225-2862
    http://www.ggmc.gov.gy/

Haiti

Ecole Nacionale de Geologie Appliquee
Ecole Nacionale de Geologie Appliquee (2004)
B.P. 1560-Varreux, Port-au-Prince

Hungary

Eotvos Lorand University
Insitute of Geography and Earth Sciences (B,M,D) ● (2014)
Pazmany Peter setany 1/C
Budapest H-1117
   p. (+36 1) 381 2191
   ffi@ffi.elte.hu
   http://geosci.elte.hu/en_index.htm
   Enrollment (2014): B: 900 (360) M: 300 (120) D: 40 (18)
Professor:
   Judit Bartholy, (D), Eotvos Lorand, 1978, Ow
Professor:
   Kristof Petrovay, (D), Eotvos Lorand, 1992, Xy
Associate Professor:
   Gábor Timár, (D), Eotvos Lorand, 2003, YgdOi
Research Professor:
   János Lichtenberger, (D), Hungarian Academy of Sciences, 1996, OarXy
Professor:
   Miklos Kazmer, (D), Eotvos Lorand, 1982, PgoGh
Associate Professor:
   Agnes Gorog, (D), Eotvos Lorand, Pmi
   László Lenkey, (D), VU Amsterdam, 1999, YhHwGa
   Balázs Székely, (D), Uni Tuebingen, 2001, GmOri
Associate Scientist:
   Orsolya Ferencz, (D), Budapest, 2001, XyOr
   Anikó Kern, (D), Eotvos Lorand, 2012, OrwOa
   Gábor Molnár, (D), Eotvos Lorand, 2004, OrYgOi
Assistant Professor:
   László Balázs, (D), Eotvos Lorand, 2009, EoYeg
   Attila Galsa, (D), Eotvos Lorand, 2004, YehYg
   Attila Osi, (D), Eotvos Lorand, PviPe
   Emoke Toth, (D), Eotvos Lorand, PmsPb
Research Associate:
   Istvan Szente, (D), Eotvos Lorand, Pig
Professor:
   Ferenc Horváth, (D), Eotvos Lorand, 1971, YgGhc
   Péter Márton, (D), Eotvos Lorand, 1971, YmgYs

Hungarian Geological Survey
Hungarian Geological Institute (1999)
Stefánia út 14
Budapest HU-1143
   p. 36 1267 1433
   hamort@mgsz.hu

Hungarian Office for Mining and Geology
Hungarian Office for Mining and Geology (2014)
PO Box 95
1590 Budapest 1145
   p. (+36-1) 301-2900
   hivatal@mbfh.hu
   http://www.mbfh.hu

Jozsef Attila University
Dept of Mineralogy, Geochem & Petrology (2004)
P O Box 651
H-6701 Szeged

Dept of Geology & Paleontology (2004)
Egyetum u. 2-6
H-6722 Szeged

Univesity of Szeged
Dept of Physical Geography and Geoinformatics (B,M,D) (2015)
SZTE Termeszeti Foldrajzi Tanszek
Szeged, 6722 Egyetem utca 2. PF:653
Szeged
   p. 0036 62544158
   mezosi@geo.u-szeged.hu
   http://www.geo.u-szeged.hu/ANG/HPfirst.html
   Enrollment (2012): D: 20 (0)

Professor:
   Janos Rakonczai, (D), 1978, Oe

Iceland

Landmælingar Íslands
National Land Survey of Iceland (2015)
Stillholt 16-18 300 Akranes
Akranes 300
   p. 4309000
   lmi@lmi.is
   http://www.lmi.is/

University of Iceland
Faculty of Earth Science (2014)
Öskju, Sturlugötu 7
101 Reykjavik
   p. (+354) 5254600
   dagrun@hi.is
   http://english.hi.is/sens/faculty_of_earth_sciences/about_faculty

India

Aligarh Muslim University
Dept of Geology (B,M,D) ● (2014)
Aligarh - U.P.
Aligarh, Uttar Pradesh 202002
   p. 0571-2700615
   lakrao@yahoo.com
   http://www.amu.ac.in/fsc/no4.html

Andhra University
Dept of Geology (2011)
Vishakha-patnam-530 003
College of Science and Technology
, Andhra Pradesh
   p. 91-891-2844888
   principal_science@andhrauniversity.info
   http://www.andhrauniversity.info/

Anna University
Dept of Geology (2011)
Guindy, Chennai-600 025,
Tamil Nadu
   p. 044-22358442 / 8444 / 8452
   geonag@gmail.com
   http://www.annauniv.edu/index.php

Annamalai University
Faculty of Marine Sciences (2011)
Annamalainagar-608 025
Tamil Nadu
   p. 91 - 4144 - 238248
   info@annamalaiuniversity.ac.in
   http://annamalaiuniversity.ac.in/marinesciences.htm

Banaras Hindu University
Dept of Geology (B,M,D) (2015)
Varanasi
U.P. 221005
   hbsrivastava@gmail.com
   http://www.bhu.ac.in/Geology/index.html
Professor:
   HARI BAHADUR SRIVASTAVA, (D), BHU, 1980, GctGp

Bharathidasan University
Dept of Geology (2011)
School of Geosciences
Tiruchirapalli 620 024
   p. +91 431 2407034
   drmm_bdu@yahoo.co.uk
   http://www.bdu.ac.in/schools/geo_sciences/geology/

Candigarh University
Dept of Geology (2016)
National Highway 95
Chandigarh, Punjab 140413
    p. (+91) 2724481
    chairperson_geology@pu.ac.in
    http://geology.puchd.ac.in/

Cochin University of Science & Technology
Dept of Geology (2014)
Kochi
    p. +91(484)2577550
    akv@cusat.ac.in
    http://www.cusat.ac.in/

Geological Survey of India
Geological Survey of India (2011)
27, J.L.Nehru Road
West Bengal Kolkata-700016
    dg@gsi.gov.in
    http://www.portal.gsi.gov.in

Goa University
Dept of Earth Science (B,M,D) ● (2015)
Taleigao Plateau
Goa University P.O.
Taleigao Plateau
Panaji, Goa 403 206
    p. +91-0832-6519329
    mkotha@unigoa.ac.in
    http://www.unigoa.ac.in/department.
    php?adepid=11&mdepid=3
    Enrollment (2015): M: 15 (15) D: 5 (1)
Head:
    Adiveppa G. Chachadi, (D), IIT, Roorkee, 1989, HwYeHs
Professor:
    Mahender Kotha, (D), IIT Bombay, 1987, GsoOi
Associate Professor:
    Vishwanath T. A., (D), IIT, Kharagpur, 1986, GpzGg
    Anthony V. Viegas, (D), Goa, 1997, Gig

Guru Nanak Dev University
Dept of Geology (2011)
Amritsar
    http://www.gndu.ac.in/

Indian Institute of Science Education and Research, Kolkata
Dept of Earth Science (B,M,D) (2013)
Mohanpur Campus
Nadia
Mohanpur (Kolkata) , West Bengal 741252
    des.chair@iiserkol.ac.in
    http://earth.iiserkol.ac.in/

Indian Institute of Technology
Dept of Applied Geology (2011)
Bombay, Powai
Bombay
    ayaz@iitb.ac.in
    http://www.geos.iitb.ac.in/

Indian Institute of Technology, Kharagpur
Dept of Geology & Geophysics (B,M,D) (2011)
Kharagpur, Kharagpur
West Bengal 721302
Kharagpur, West Bengal 721302
    p. +91-3222-282268
    head@gg.iitkgp.ernet.in
    http://www.iitkgp.ac.in/departments/home.
    php?deptcode=MG

Indian Institute of Technology, Roorkee
Dept of Earth Sciences (M,D) (2010)
Department of Earth Sciences
IITRoorkee
Roorkee, Uttrakhand 247667
    p. +911332285532
    des.iitr@gmail.com
    http://members.tripod.com/rurkiu/acd-earth/index.html

Indian School of Mines
Dept of Applied Geology (2011)
Dhanbad
West Bengal 826 004
    p. +91-326-2296616
    agl@ismdhanbad.ac.in
    http://www.ismdhanbad.ac.in/depart/geology/index.htm

Institute of Science
Dept of Geology (2011)
Aurangabad 431004
Aurangabad , Maharashtra
    p. +91 (0240) 2400586
    director@inosca.org
    http://www.inosca.org

Jadavpur University
Dept of Applied Geology (B,M,D) (2013)
Jadavpur
Calcutta
    p. +913324572268
    hod@geology.jdvu.ac.in
    http://www.jaduniv.edu.in/view_department.php?deptid=76

Jmia Millia Islamia
Dept of Geography (2011)
Jamia Nagar
New Delhi-25
    rocketibrahim@yahoo.com
    http://jmi.ac.in/aboutjamia/departments/geography/introduction

Kurukshetra University
Dept of Geology (1999)

Lucknow University
Dept of Geology (2011)
Lucknow 226007 U.P.
    info@lkouniv.ac.in
    http://www.lkouniv.ac.in/dept_geology.htm

Maharaja Sayajirao University of Baroda
Dept of Geology (2011)
Baroda - Gujarat
    p. (919) 426721547
    ischamyal@yahoo.com
    http://www.msubaroda.ac.in/science/index.php

Nagpur University
Dept of Geology (2011)
Rao Bahadur D. Laxminarayan Educational Campus
Law College Square
Amravati Road
Nagpur 440 001
    p. +91-712-253241
    geodeptplacecell@gmail.com
    http://www.nagpuruniversity.org/links/FacultyofScience.htm

Osmania University
Dept of Geology (2011)
Hyderabad 500007 A.P.
    http://www.osmania.ac.in/

Panjab University
Centre for Petroleum and Applied Geology (U.I.E.A.S.T.) (2011)
Chandigarh 160014
>rpatnaik@pu.ac.in
>http://pu.ac.in/

Pondicherry University
Dept of Earth Science (B,M,D) (2013)
The Head
Department of Earth Sciences
Pondicherry University
Pondicherry 605 014
>p. +914132656741
>head.esc@pondiuni.edu.in
>http://www.pondiuni.edu.in/department/department-earth-sciences

Professor:
>Balakrishnan Srinivasan, (D), Jawaharlal Nehru (India), 1986, CcGiz

Presidency College
Dept of Geology (2011)
College Street
Calcutta
>hnb.geol@presidencycollegekolkata.ac.in
>http://www.concentric.net/~slahiri/pc/Department/Geology/geo

Pt. Ravishankar Shukla University
School of Studies in Geology and Water Resource Management (M,D) (2014)
SOS Geology
Pt. Ravishankar Shukla UNiversity
Raipur, Chhattisgarh 492010
>geology@prsu.com
>http://www.prsu.ac.in/
>*Enrollment (2013): M: 15 (0) D: 4 (1)*

Professor:
>Srikant k. Pande, (D), Nagoya, 1986, GgHyg
Professor:
>Ninad Bodhankar, (D), Raipur, 1992, GcNm
>Kosiyath Rghavan Na Hari, (D), Vikram Univ Ujjain, 1992, GiiCp
>Mohammad Wahdat Yar Khan, (D), AMU, Aligarh, 1979, GdEgCl

University College of Science, Osmania University
Centre of Exploration Geophysics (M,D) O (2015)
Osmania University Main Rd.
Osmania University Campus
Hyderabad, Telengana 500007
>p. (+91) 40-27097116
>hod.geophysics@gmail.com
>http://www.osmania.ac.in/
>*Enrollment (2015): M: 60 (0) D: 12 (0)*

Head:
>Dr. Veeraiah B, (D), Osmania, 2005, YexYg
Assistant Professor:
>Dr Udaya Laxm Gakka, (D), Osmania, 2009, HwYge
>Dr Ram Raj Mathur, (D), Osmania, YemYx

University of Baroda
Dept of Geology (2011)
Baroda , Vadodara 390 002
>swanikhil@yahoo.co.in
>http://www.msubaroda.ac.in/deptindex.php?ffac_code=2&fdept_code=6

University of Delhi
Dept of Geology (B,M,D) ● (2014)
Department of Geology
University of Delhi
Delhi
New Delhi 110 007
>p. 27667073
>csdubey@gmail.com
>http://www.du.ac.in/

Enrollment (2014): B: 105 (1200) M: 60 (600) D: 30 (130)

University of Madras
Dept of Geology (2011)
Maraimalai Adigalar Campus
Chennai 600 005
>p. 044 - 22202790
>spmohan50@hotmail.com
>http://www.unom.ac.in/departments/geology/geology.html

Dept of Geology (2011)
Madras, 600 025
Maraimalai Adigalar Campus
>spmohan50@hotmail.com
>http://www.unom.ac.in/departments/geology/geology.html

University of Mysore
Dept of Geology (2011)
Mysore 570 005
>p. +91 821 2419724
>bb@geology.uni-mysore.ac.in
>http://www.uni-mysore.ac.in/geology/#A

University of Pune
Dept of Geology (2011)
Ganeshkhind Road
Pune, Maharashtra 411 007
>p. +91-020-25601360
>geology@unipune.ac.in
>http://www.unipune.ac.in/dept/science/geology/default.htm

Vijayanagara SriKrishnaDevaraya University
Dept of Applied Geology (M,D) (2012)
Dr.C.Venkataiah
Professor of Geology
Vijayanagara SriKrishnaDevaraya University
Bellary, Karnataka 583 104
>p. (937) 909-0588
>venkataiah.c@gmail.com
>http://www.vskub.ac.in

Indonesia

Direktorat Vulkanologi
Volcanological Survey of Indonesia (2011)
Jl. Diponegoro 57
Bandung , West Java
>http://portal.vsi.esdm.go.id/

Gadjah Mada University
Dept of Geology (2014)
Jalan Bulaksmur
Yogzakarta 55281
>p. (+62) 274 6492340
>geografi@geo.ugm.ac.id
>http://geo.ugm.ac.id/main/

Indonesian Directorate General of Geology and Mineral Resources
Ministry of Mines and Energy (2011)
>pengaduan@esdm.go.id
>http://www.esdm.go.id

Institut Teknologi Bandung
Dept of Geology (2014)
Jalan Ganesa, No. 10
Bandung 40132, Jawa Barat
>p. 022 2514990
>sisfo@fitb.ac.id
>http://www.fitb.itb.ac.id/en/

Dept of Geological Engineering (2004)
Jl. Ganesha 10
Bandung, 40135
    geologi@gc.itb.ac.id

Trisakti University
Faculty of Earth and Energy Technologies (2004)
Jl. Kiai Tapa, Grogel
Jakarta 11440
    p. 5663232 Ext. 8510

Universitas Hasanudin
Dept of Geological Engineering (2004)
Jl. Perintis Kemerdekaan
Ujung Pandang 90245

Universitas Padjadjaran
Dept of Geological Engineering
   (2004)
Jl. Raya Bandung-Sumedang km.21,
Jatinangor

Universitas Pakuan
Dept of Geological Engineering (2014)
Jl. Pakuan, PO Box 452
Bogor 16143, Jawa Barat
    p. 0251-8312206
    rektorat@unpak.ac.id
    http://www.unpak.ac.id/

Iran

Bu-Ali University
Dept of Geology (A,D) O (2015)
Barati@basu.ac.ir
Hamedan , Hamedan 65174
    p. 0098-0811-38381460
    Barati@basu.ac.ir
    http://www.basu.ac.ir
    Administrative Assistant: Meisam Gholipoor

University of Tabriz
Dept of Earth Sciences (B,M,D) ● (2014)
29 Bahman Blvd.
University of Tabriz
Tabriz , East Azerbaijan 51664
    p. +98 (411) 3335 9894
    moazzen@tabrizu.ac.ir
    http://www.tabrizu.ac.ir
    Enrollment (2014): B: 22 (33) M: 35 (28) D: 12 (7)
Dean of Faculty:
    Asghar Asghari Moghadam, (D), UK, 1992, HwqHy
Professor:
    Ali Asghar Calagari, (D), UK, 1997, EgmCg
    Ahmad Jahangiri, (D), India, 2000, GivGg
    Mohsen -. Moayyed, (D), Iran, 2000, Gig
    Mohssen -. Moazzen, (D), UK, 1999, GpCgGz
Associate Professor:
    Robab Hajialioghli, (D), Iran, 2007, Gpt
    Hosseinzadeh Mohammad Reza, (D), Iran, 2005, Egm
Head of the Department:
    Ali Kadkhodai Ilkhchi, (D), Iran, 2008, NpEo
Assistant Professor:
    Ebrahim Asghari Ka, (D), Iran, 2001, Ngr
    Ghafour Alavi, (D), Eg
    Nasir Amel, Iran, 2004, GivGg
    Ghodrat Barzegari, (D), Iran, Nr
    Mohammad Hassanpour Sedghi, Iran, 2011, YsNeYg
    Fatemeh Mesbahi, (D), Iran, Gt
    Ata Nadiri, (D), Iran, 2012, Hgw
    Kamal Siahcheshm, (D), Iran, 2011, Egm
    Reza Vaezi, (D), Iran, 2010, GeHgs
    Behzad Zamani, (D), Iran, 2004, GtYs

Instructor:
    Rahim Jomeiri, (M), Iran, 1992, Yg
    Maqsood Orouji, (M), Ca
    Naser Samimi, (B), Iran, Gg
Lecturer:
    Siavosh Sartipzadeh, (M), Iran, Pm

Ireland

Ulster University, Coleraine
School of Geography and Environmental Sciences (B,M,D) ●
(2015)
Cromore Road
Coleraine BT521SA
    p. 0044(0)2870124401
    a.moore@ulster.ac.uk
    http://www.ulster.ac.uk/es

Geological Survey of Ireland
Geological Survey of Ireland (2011)
Beggars Bush
Haddington Road
Dublin 4
    john.butler@gsi.ie
    http://www.gsi.ie/

Geological Survey of Northern Ireland
Geological Survey of Northern Ireland (2011)
Colby House
Stranmillis Court
Belfast BT9 5BF
    gsni@detini.gov.uk
    http://www.bgs.ac.uk/GSNI/

National University of Ireland Galway
Earth and Ocean Sciences (B,D) (2014)
Earth & Ocean Sciences
National University of Ireland
University Road
Galway
    p. + 353 (0)91 492 126
    lorna.larkin@nuigalway.ie
    http://www.nuigalway.ie/eos/
Head:
    Martin Feely, (D), National Univ of Ireland, Goz
Professor:
    Peter Croot, (D), Otago, Ct
Lecturer:
    Rachel R. Cave, (D), South Hampton, Cm
    Eve Daly, (D), National Univ of Ireland, Yg
    Tiernan Henry, (M), Wisconsin (Madison), Hg
    John Murray, (D), Trinity College, PgGs
    Robin Raine, (D), National Univ of Ireland, Yg
    Tyrrell Shane, (D), Univ Coll (Dublin), Gs
    Martin White, (D), Southampton, Hg

Trinity College
Dept of Geology (2015)
Department of Geology
Museum Building
Trinity College-Dublin
Dublin 2
    p. +353 01 896 1074
    earth@tcd.ie
    http://www.tcd.ie/Geology/
Chair:
    Balz Kamber, Ge
Associate Professor:
    Catherine Coxon, GeOu
    Robin Edwards, Ge
    Patrick N. Wyse Jackson, Ob
Assistant Professor:
    David Chew, Cc
    Quentin G. Crowley, Cc
    Seán h. mcClenaghan, Eg

Chris Nicholas, Eo
Catherine V. Rose, Cg
Emma L. Tomlinson, Cc

University College Cork
Dept of Geology (B,M,D) (2005)
Donovans Road
Cork
    p. +353 21 4902657
    bees@ucc.ie

    http://www.ucc.ie/ucc/depts/geology/
    Administrative Assistant: Patricia Hegarty
Head:
    John Gamble, Gi
Professor:
    Ken Higgs, Pl
Research Associate:
    Tara Davis, Yg
    Jim Smith, Pl
Lecturer:
    Alistair Allen, Gp
    Bettie Higgs, Yg
    Ed Jarvis, Pl
    Ivor MacCarthy, (D), 1974, Gs
    Pat Meere, (D), NUI (Ireland), 1992, Gc
    John Reavy, Gi
    Andy J. Wheeler, (D), Cambridge, 1994, Gu
Other:
    Mary Lehane, On
    Mick O'Callaghan, On
    Dan Rose, On

University College Dublin
UCD School of Geological Sciences (2014)
Science Centre West
University College Dublin
Belfield, Dublin 4
    p. +353 1 716 2331
    geology@ucd.ie
    http://www.ucd.ie/geology/
Head:
    J. Stephen Daly
Professor:
    Peter D. W. Haughton
    Frank McDermott
    Patrick M. Shannon
    John J. Walsh
Associate Professor:
    Christopher J. Bean
    Ian D. Somerville
Lecturer:
    Conrad Childs
    Aggeliki Georgiopopoulou
    Ivan Lokmer
    Tom Manzocchi
    Julian F. Menuge
    Patrick J. Orr

Israel

Ben Gurion University of the Negev
Dept of Geological and Env Sciences (2009)
P.O. Box 653
84105 Beer Sheva
    edav@bgumail.bgu.ac.il
    http://www.bgu.ac.il/geol/

Geological Survey of Israel
Geological Survey of Israel (2011)
30 Malkhe Israel St.
Jerusalem, 95501
    ask_gsi@gsi.gov.il
    http://www.gsi.gov.il/

Hebrew University of Jerusalem
Faculty of Advanced Environmental Studies (2004)
Givat Ram
Jerusalem 91904
    envstudies@savion.huji.ac.il

Inst of Earth Sciences (2004)
Jerusalem 91904
    kerenbe@savion.huji.ac.il
    http://earth.es.huji.ac.il/machon/

Tel Aviv University
Dept of Geophysical, Atmospheric and Planetary Sciences
(B,M,D) (2013)
Ramat Aviv
P O Box 30940
Tel Aviv 69978 69978
    p. 972-3-6408633
    batshevc@tauex.tau.ac.il
    http://geophysics.tau.ac.il/
Full Professor:
    Shmuel Marco, (D), Gg

Geosciences (B,M,D) ● (2014)
Levanon Road
Ramat Aviv
Tel Aviv 6997801
    p. 972-3-6408633
    shmulikm@tau.ac.il
    http://geophysics.tau.ac.il/
Emeritus:
    Akiva Bar-Nun, Hebrew, 1968, Xc
Professor:
    Pinhas Alpert, (D), Hebrew, 1980, OarOw
    Zvi Ben-Avraham, (D), WHOI-MIT, 1973, YrGt
    Shmulik Marco, (D), Hebrew U, Jerusalem, 1997, Ggc
    Morris Podolak, (D), Yeshiva Univ, 1974, OnnOn
    Colin G. Price, (D), Columbia, 1993, Oa
    Moshe Reshef, (D), Tel-Aviv Univ, 1985, Yeg
Principal Research Assoc. (Assoc. Professor):
    Lev Eppelbaum, (D), Inst. of Geophysics of Georgia, 1989, YvmGt
Senior Scientist:
    Pavel Kishcha, (D), Russian Academy of Sciences, 1985, Oa
Dr:
    Nili Harnik, (D), MIT, 2000, Oa
Assistant Professor:
    Ravit Helled, (M), Tel-Aviv Univ, 2008, Xy
Lecturer:
    Gilles Hillel Wust-Bloch, (D), 1990, Ys
    Alon Ziv, (D), Ys

Italy

Alma Mater Studiorum Università di Bologna
Dipartimento di Scienze Biologiche, Geologiche e Ambientali
(B,M,D) O (2016)
Piazza di Porta San Donato 1
Bologna 40126
    p. ++39 - 051 - 2094238
    alessandro.gargini@unibo.it
    http://www.bigea.unibo.it/it
    Enrollment (2015): B: 8 (50) M: 9 (40) D: 3 (10)

Servizio Geologico d'Italia
Servizio Geologico d'Italia (2011)
Via Vitaliano Brancati
Roma 48-00144
    p. (+39) 0650071
    emergenzeambientali@isprambiente.it
    http://www.isprambiente.gov.it/it/servizi-per-lambiente/il-servizio-geologico-ditalia

Università degli Studi di Padova
Dept of Geosciences (B,M,D) (2015)
Via G. Gradenigo 6

Padova 35131
> p. +390498279110
> geoscienze.direzione@unipd.it
> http://www.geoscienze.unipd.it/

Full Professor:
> Gilberto Artioli, (D), Chicago, 1985, GzyOm
> Giuliano Bellieni, (M), Gv
> Alessandro Caporali, (D), Ludwig Maximilian (Germany), 1979, YdsOr
> Alberto Carton, (M), Gm
> Giorgio Cassiani, (D), YgHs
> Bernardo Cesare, (D), Gp
> Silvana Martin, Gc
> Fabrizio Nestola, (D), Modena and Reggio Emilia, 2003, Gz
> Giorgio Pennacchioni, Gc
> Cristina Stefani, Gd
> Massimiliano Zattin, (D), Gs

Associate Professor:
> Claudia Agnini, (D), Padova, 2007, PmeGu
> Andrea D'Alpaos, (D), Hs
> Giulio Di Toro, (D), Gc
> Paolo Fabbri, Hw
> Elena Fornaciari, (D), Pgm
> Massimiliano Ghinassi, (D), Gs
> Andrea Marzoli, (D), Cg
> Matteo Massironi, (D), XgOr
> Claudio Mazzoli, Gx
> Stefano Monari, Pg
> Paolo Nimis, Eg
> Nereo Preto, (D), Gs
> Gabriella Salviulo, Gz
> Raffaele Sassi, Ggx
> Paolo Scotton, Hg
> Luciano Secco, Gz
> Richard Spiess, Gp
> Nicola Surian, Gm
> Dario Visona', Gi
> Annalisa Zaja, Yg
> Dario Zampieri, Gc

Assistant Professor:
> Jacopo Boaga, (D), Yg
> Aldino Bondesan, (M), Padova, 1986, GmlOi
> Anna Breda, (D), Padova, 2003, GsrGg
> Luca Capraro, (D), Padova, 2002, PelGg
> Maria Chiara Dalconi, (D), Gz
> Manuele Faccenda, (D), Gq
> Mario Floris, (D), NgOr
> Alessandro Fontana, (D), Gm
> Antonio Galgaro, Ng
> Roberto Gatto, Pg
> Luca Giusberti, (D), Pm
> Lara Maritan, (D), Gx
> Christine Marie Meyzen, (D), Cg
> Paolo Mozzi, (D), Gm
> Leonardo Piccinini, (D), Hg
> Manuel Rigo, (D), Gs
> Alberta Silvestri, (D), Gz

Università degli Studi di Pavia
Dept of Earth and Environmental Sciences (A,B,M,D) O (2014)
via Ferrata, 1
Pavia 27100
> p. +30 0382 985754
> dvagnini@unipv.it
> http://sciter.unipv.eu/site/home.html
> *Enrollment (2014): B: 45 (25) M: 25 (14) D: 15 (5)*

Universita Degli Studi di Siena
Centro di GeoTecnologie (2011)
Via Vetri Vecchi 34
San Giovanni Valdarno 52027
> p. +390559119400
> bottacchi@unisi.it
> http://www.geotecnologie.unisi.it

Universita di Bari
Dept Geomineralogico (2013)
Via E. Orabona
4-70125 Bari
> scandale@geomin.uniba.it
> http://www.geomin.uniba.it/frame.htm

Universita di Cagliari
Dept di Geoingegneria e Tecnologie Ambientali (2006)
Via Marengo,3
09124 Cagliari
> p. +39 70 675 52/29
> mazzella@unica.it

> http://geoing.unica.it/digita.htm

Professor:
> Prof. Antonio AM MAZZELLA, Gq

Universita di Calabria
Dept of Biology Ecology and Earth Science (DIBEST) (D) (2013)
87036 Arcavacata di Rende
Calabria
> crisci@unical.it
> http://www.unical.it

Universita di Camerino
Dept Scienze della Terra (2014)
via E. Betti 1/A
62032 Camerino
> p. (+39) 737402126
> sst@pec.unicam.it
> http://www.sst.unicam.it/SST/en/course-of-degree

Universita di Catania
Inst Scienze della Terra (2014)
Corso Italia 57
95129 Catania
> p. (+39) 095-7195730
> giovali@unict.it
> http://www3.unict.it/idgeg/

Universita di Firenze
Dept Scienze della Terra (B,M,D) ● (2014)
via La Pira 4
50121 Firenze
> direttore@geo.unifi.it
> http://www.dst.unifi.it/

Universita di Genova
Dept Scienze della Terra Ambiente e Vita - DISTAV (B,D) (2015)
Corso Europa 26
16132 Genoa
> p. +39 010 353 8311
> direttore@dipteris.unige.it
> http://www.distav.unige.it/drupalint/index.php

Professor:
> Egidio Armadillo, (D), Ye

Research Associate:
> Donato Belmonte, (D), Cg

Università di Modena e Reggio Emilia
Dept di Scienze Chimiche e Geologiche (B,M,D) (2013)
Largo S. Eufemia, 19
Modena, Italy 41121
> p. 390592055885
> direttore.chimgeo@unimore.it
> http://www.dscg.unimore.it/
> *Enrollment (2013): B: 23 (13) M: 14 (4) D: 10 (9)*

Universita di Napoli FEDERICO II
Dipartimento di Scienze della Terra, dell'Ambiente e delle Risorse (B,M,D) ● (2015)
L.go S. Marcellino, 10

Naples 80138
p. +390812538112
piergiulio.cappelletti@unina.it
http://www.distar.unina.it

Universita di Perrugia
Dept Scienze della Terra (2014)
Piazza Università, 1
06100 Perugia
cclgeol@unipg.it
http://cclgeol.unipg.it/cclgeol/

Università di Torino
Dept Scienze della Terra (B,M,D) ● (2016)
via Valperga Caluso 35
10125 Torino
p. 011.6705144
segreteria.dst@unito.it
http://www.dst.unito.it/do/home.pl
Enrollment (2015): B: 201 (20) M: 77 (6) D: 31 (6)
Professor:
Fernando Camara Artigas, (D), Gz
Rodolfo Carosi, (D), Gc
Daniele Castelli, (D), Gx
Associate Professor:
Rossella Arletti, (D), Gz
Elena Belluso, (D), Gz
Piera Benna, (M), Gz
Alessandro Borghi, (D), Gx
Marco Bruno, (D), Gz
Paola Cadoppi, (D), Gc
Giorgio Carnevale, (D), Pg
Cesare Comina, (D), Yx
Domenico Antonio De Luca, (D), Hy
Francesco dela Pierre, (D), Gd
Massimo Delfino, (D), Pg
Anna Maria Ferrero, (D), Nr
Andrea Festa, (D), Gc
Maria Gabriella Forno, (M), Gg
Giandomenico Fubelli, (D), Gm
Marco Gattiglio, (D), Gc
Marco Giardino, (D), Gm
Roberto Giustetto, (D), Gz
Giuseppe Mandrone, (D), Ng
Luca Martire, (D), Gd
Michele Motta, (M), Oy
Mauro Prencipe, (D), Gz
Franco Rolfo, (D), Gx
Piergiorgio Rossetti, (M), Eg
Marco Rubbo, (M), Gz
Assistant Professor:
Roberto Ajassa, (M), Oy
Gianni Balestro, (D), Gc
Carlo Bertok, (D), Gd
Sabrina Maria Rita Bonetto, (D), Ng
Silvana Capella, (D), Gz
Corrdao Cigolini, (M), Gv
Emanuele Costa, (D), Gz
Anna d'Atri, (D), Gr
Simona Ferrando, (D), Gx
Simona Fratianni, (D), Oy
Franco Gianotti, (D), Gg
Daniele Giordano, (D), Gv
Chiara Teresa Groppo, (D), Gx
Francesca Lozar, (D), Pg
Edoardo Martinetto, (D), Pb
Luciano Masciocco, (M), Ge
Luigi Motta, (M), Oy
Marco Davide Tonon, (M), Oe
Sergio Carmelo Vinciguerra, (D), Nr
Elena Zanella, (D), Ym
Emeritus:
Emiliano Bruno, (M), Gz
Ezio Callegari, (M), Gx
Roberto Compagnoni, (M), Gx
Giovanni Ferraris, (M), Gz

Giulio Pavia, (M), Pg
Germano Rigault de la Longrais, (M), Gz

Universita di Trieste
Inst Geologia e Paleontologia (2004)
P. le Europa 1
34127 Trieste

Inst Geografia e Geologia (2014)
via Valerio 12/1
34127 Trieste
p. +39 040 5582045
dmg@pec.units.it
http://www.geoscienze.units.it/

Università di Udine
Dipartimento di Georisorse e Territorio (2010)
Dipartimento di Georisorse e Territorio
Via Cotonificio 114
33100 Udine
beinat@dgt.uniud.it
http://udgtls.dgt.uniud.it/

Universita di Urbino
Inst di Geologia Applicata (2014)
Via Muzio Oddi 14
61029 Urbino

Universita Pisa
Dept of Geosciences (D) (2004)
via S. Maria 53
56126 Pisa
p. +39050847260
martinelli@dst.unipi.it
http://www.dst.unipi.it/

University of Ferrara
Dept of Geology (2014)
Via Savonarola, 9
44121 Ferrara
p. (+39) 0532 293493
mob_int@unife.it
http://www.unife.it/international/education/double-de-
grees-1/geological-sciences-ferrara-cadiz

University of Milano
Dept of Geology (2014)
Via Festa Del Perdono 7
20126 Milano
p. (+39) 02 6448 1
foreign.office@unimib.it
http://www.unimib.it/go/46204/Home/English/Academic-
Programs/Mathematics-Physics-and-Natural-Sciences/
Geological-Sciences-and-Te

University of Naples
Dipartimento di Scienze della Terra, dell'Ambiente e delle Risorse (2004)
80138
Napoli
piergiulio.cappelletti@unina.it
http://www.dgv.unina.it/dgv_eng.html

University of Parma
Dept of Physics and Earth Sciences (B,M,D) (2014)
Parco Area delle Scienze 157/A
Parma 43100
p. +39 0521 905326
dipterr@unipr.it
http://www.difest.unipr.it
Professor:
Fulvio Celico, (D), Hgw
Research Associate:
Andrea Artoni, (D), Gtr

Tiziano Boschetti, (D), Cgs

University of Siena
Dept of Physical Science, Earth, and Environment (B,M,D) ●
(2014)
Strada Laterina, 8
Siena 53100
   p. (+39) 0577 233938
   pec.dsfta@pec.unisipec.it
   http://www.dsfta.unisi.it/it
   f: https://www.facebook.com/dsfta.siena?ref=hl
Professor:
   Mauro Coltorti, (M), GmYg

Jamaica

University of the West Indies Mona Campus
Dept of Geography and Geology (B,M,D) (2014)
University of the West Indies
Mona
Kingston KGN7
   p. 876-927-2728
   geoggeol@uwimona.edu.jm
   http://myspot.mona.uwi.edu/dogg/
Head:
   Simon F. Mitchell, (D), Liverpool, 1993, GsgGs

Japan

Akita University
Deparment of Earth Science and Technology (2004)
1-1 Tagata Gakuen-cho, Akita-shi
Akita

Ehime University
Dept of Earth Sciences (2004)
   yinouchi@sci.ehime-u.ac.jp
   http://www.ehime-u.ac.jp/~cutie

Geological Survey of Japan
Geological Survey of Japan (2011)
   http://www.gsj.jp/

Hirosaki University
Dept of Earth Science (2004)
   wata@cc.hirosaki-u.ac.jp
   http://sci.hirosaki-u.ac.jp/~earth/

Hiroshima University
Dept of Earth and Planetary Systems Science (2005)
Kagami-yama 1-3-1
Higashi-Hiroshima
Hiroshima 739
   chikako@sci.hiroshima-u.ac.jp
   http://www.geol.sci.hiroshima-u.ac.jp/

Kagoshima University
Faculty of Science (2004)
   koko@sci.kagoshima-u.ac.jp
   http://earth.sci.kagoshima-u.ac.jp/

Kanazawa University
Dept of Earth Sciences (2004)
Kakuma-machi
Kanazawa 920-1192
   fsci-pla-director@edu.kobe-u.ac.jp
   http://earth.s.kanazawa-u.ac.jp/

Kobe University
Earth & Planetary Sciences (2004)
   fsci-pla-director@edu.kobe-u.ac.jp
   http://shidahara1.earth.s.kobe-u.ac.jp/

Kumamoto University
Dept of Earth and Environment (B,M,D) (2011)
2-39-1, Kurokami
Kumamoto City 860-8555
   p. 81-96-342-3411
   tadao@sci.kumamoto-u.ac.jp
   http://www.sci.kumamoto-u.ac.jp/earthsci
Professor:
   Shiro Hasegawa, (D), Pm
   Toshiaki Hasenaka, (D), Gv
   Hiroki Matsuda, (D), Gs
   Tadao Nishiyama, (D), Gp
   Hidetoshi Shibuya, (D), Ymg
   Jun Shimada, (D), Hw
   Akira Yoshiasa, (D), Gz

Nagoya University
Dept of Earth and Planetary Sciences (2006)
   env@post.jimu.nagoya-u.ac.jp
   http://www.eps.nagoya-u.ac.jp/

Shizuoka University
Inst of Geosciences (2005)
Shizuoka 422-8529
   setmasu@ipc.shizuoka.ac.jp
   http://www.sci.shizuoka.ac.jp/~geo/Welcome.html

Tohoku University
Dept of Mineralogy, Petrology and Economic Geology (2015)
Sendai 980-8578
   kaiho@m.tohoku.ac.jp
   http://www.ganko.tohoku.ac.jp/

Tsukuba University
College of Geoscience (2004)
   kankyojoho@ynu.ac.jp
   http://www.geo.tsukuba.ac.jp/

University of Tokyo
Deparment of Earth and Planetary Science (2004)
3-1, Hongo 7chome, Bunkyo-ku
Tokyo
   ilo@adm.s.u-tokyo.ac.jp
   http://www.eri.u-tokyo.ac.jp/

University of Toyama
Deptt of Earth Sciences (B,M,D) (2015)
3190 Gofuku
Toyama City, Toyama Prefecture 930-8555
   p. 81-76-445-6654
   takeuchi@sci.u-toyama.ac.jp
   http:/www.sci.u-toyama.ac.jp/earth/
   Enrollment (2015): B: 208 (0) M: 36 (0) D: 7 (0)
Professor:
   Akira Takeuchi, (D), Osaka City, 1979, GtcYe
   Tohru Watanabe, (D), Tokyo, 1991, YxsGv
Associate Professor:
   Shigekazu Kusumoto, (D), Kyoto, 1999, YvdGt

Yokohama National University
Dept of Environment and Natural Sciences (2004)
   kankyojoho@ynu.ac.jp
   http://chigaku.ed.ynu.ac.jp/geology-e.html

Kenya

Jomo Kenyatta University of Agriculture & Technology
Geomatic Engineering and Geospatial Information Systems
(B,M,D) (2014)
PO Box 62000
-00200 Nairobi
Nairobi

p. +254-67-5352391
gegis@eng.jkuat.ac.ke
http://www.jkuat.ac.ke/departments/gegis/
Enrollment (2014): B: 175 (35) M: 45 (19) D: 8 (0)
Chair:
Thomas G. Ngigi, (D), Chiba Univ (Japan), 2007, OriOr
Lecturer:
Nathan O. Agutu, Jomo Kenyatta Univ of Ag and Tech, OgiOr
Mark Boitt, (M), Stuttgart Univ of Applied Sci, 2010, OgrOi
George W. Chege, (M), Jomo Kenyatta Univ of Ag and Tech, 2014, OgrOi
Charles Gaya, (M), Stuttgart Univ of Applied Sci, 2002, OrgOi
Andrew Imwati, (D), Nairobi, OggOi
Benson K. Kenduiywo, (M), Twente, 2012, OrgOi
Fridah K. Kirimi, (M), Jomo Kenyatta Univ of Ag and Tech, 2010, OiiOr
Moffat G. Magondu, (M), Jomo Kenyatta Univ of Ag and Tech, 2014, OirOg
Felix N. Mutua, (D), Tokyo, 2012, OigOr
Nancy Mwangi, (M), Jomo Kenyatta Univ of Ag and Tech, 2008, OiiOr
Mercy W. Mwaniki, (M), Jomo Kenyatta Univ of Ag and Tech, 2010, OiiOr
Eunice W. Nduati, (M), Jomo Kenyatta Univ of Ag and Tech, 2014, OrrOi
Patroba A. Odera, (D), Kyoto, 2012, YdOge
Hunja Waithaka, (D), Hokkaido, YdOgi
Charles B. Wasomi, (M), Stuttgart Univ of Applied Sci, OrrOi

Dept of Environmental Studies (B) (2011)
P.O. Box 62000 00200
Nairobi
pro@jkuat.ac.ke
http://www.jkuat.ac.ke/

Kenyatta University
School of Environmental Sciences (B,M,D) (2010)
Maseno
p. +254-057-351620/2
chairman-envscience@ku.ac.ke
http://www.maseno.ac.ke/index3.
php?section=schools&page=school-encironment

University of Nairobi
Dept of Geology (B) (2015)
PO Box 30197
Nairobi
p. +254 20 4449856
geology@uonbi.ac.ke
http://geology.uonbi.ac.ke/

Dept of Geography (B) (2010)
PO Box 30917
Nairobi
p. +254 (020) 318262 (28400)
murimi.shadrack@ku.ac.ke
http://uonbi.ac.ke/departments/?dept_code=HF&&face_code=32

Dept of Meteorology (B,M,D) (2011)
PO Box 30197
Nairobi 00100
p. 254 020-4449004 (2070)
dept-meteo@uonbi.ac.ke
http://www.uonbi.ac.ke

Korea, South

Korea University
Earth and Environmental Sciences (B,M,D) (2015)
Anam-dong, Seongbuk-Gu
Seoul 136-713
p. 82-2-3290-3170
sjchoh@korea.ac.kr
http://ees.korea.ac.kr/
Enrollment (2015): B: 100 (27) M: 30 (13) D: 8 (4)

Head:
Meehye Lee, (D), Rhode Island, 1999, OagCm
Vice President for Research Affairs:
Seong-Taek Yun, (D), Korea, 1991, ClsHy
Vice Dean of Office of Planning and Budget:
Young Jae Lee, (D), SUNY Stony Brook, 2005, ScGze
Vice Dean of College of Science:
Ho Young Jo, (D), Wisconsin, 2003, NgCaGe
Professor:
Seon-Gyu Choi, (D), Waseda, 1983, GzEmg
Seong-Jae Doh, (D), Rhode Island, 1987, YmgYe
Jin-Han Ree, (D), SUNY Albany, Gct
Associate Professor:
Suk-Joo Choh, (D), Texas (Austin), 2004, GdsPg
Scott A. Whattam, (D), Hong Kong, 2002, GiCtg

Latvia

Latvija Valst Geologijas Dienests
Latvia State Geological Survey (2011)
Moscow street 165
Riga, LV-1019
lvgma@lvgma.gov.lv
http://mapx.map.vgd.gov.lv/geo3/

University of Latvia
Faculty of Geographical and Earth Sciences (2004)
10 Alberta Str.
202-203 Room
Riga
zeme@lu.lv
http://www.lu.lv/e_strukt/fakult/geog/info/

Lebanon

American University of Beirut
Dept of Geology (2004)
Faculty of Arts and Sciences
P.O.Box 11-0236
Riad El-Solh
Beirut 1107 2020
p. (961)-1-340460/ext. 4160
arahman@aub.edu.lb

Lesotho

National University of Lesotho
Dept of Geology & Mines (B) (2010)
P.O. Box 750, Maseru
p. (266) 34 0601
registrar@nul.ls
http://www.nul.ls/

Dept of Geography and Environmental Science (B) (2014)
P.O. Roma 180
Maseru 100
p. +266 2234 0601
registrar@nul.ls
http://www.nul.ls/faculties/fost/geography/index.html

Liberia

University of Liberia
Dept of Geology (B) (2014)
Capitol Hill
PO Box 9020
Monrovia 9020
p. 231-6-422-304
weekso@fiu.edu
http://www.universityliberia.org/ul_course_master_list_biology.htm

Dept of Mining Engineering (B) (2010)
Captiol Hill
PO Box 9020

Monrovia 9020
p. +231 6422304
weekso@fiu.edu
http://www.universityliberia.org/ul_course_master_list_min-
ing.htm

Libya

Oil Companies School
Oil Companies School (B) (2010)
info@ocslibya.com
http://www.geocites.com/chatalaine/OCS.html

Petroleum Training and Qualifying Institute (PTQI)
(B) (2014)
Gergarish Road 9KM - Asiahia
Tripoli
p. +218 21 4833771-5
info@ptqi.edu.ly
http://www.ptqi.edu.ly/online/en_home.php#

University of Garyounis
Dept of Geology (B) (2014)
PO Box 1308
Benghazi
p. +218-61-86304
uni.office@uob.edu.ly
http://www.garyounis.edu/

Lithuania

Lithuania Geological Survey, Ministry of Environment
Lithuanian Geological Survey (2015)
S. Konarskio St. 35
LT-03123 Vilnius
indre.virbickiene@lgt.lt
http://www.lgt.lt/

Vilniaus Pedagoginis Universitetas
Dept of Geology (2014)
Studentu 39, 2034 Vilnius
p. (8 5) 275 89 35
gmtf.dekanatas@leu.lt
http://www.leu.lt/lt/gmtf/gmtf_apie_mus/all.html

Vilniaus Universitetas
Dept of Hydrogeology & Engin Geol (2014)
Giurlionio 21/27, 2009, Vilnius
p. 239 8278
robert.mokrik@gf.vu.lt
http://www.vu.lt/en/scientific-report-2012/faculties-and-
institutes/faculty-of-natural-sciences

Dept of Geology and Mineralogy (B,M,D) ● (2015)
Ciurlionio str. 21/27
LT03101
Vilnius LT03101
p. +370 5 2398272
eugenija.rudnickaite@gf.vu.lt
http://www.geol.gf.vu.lt/lt
Enrollment (2015): B: 8 (8) M: 11 (11) D: 10 (3)

Luxembourg

Service Geologique du Luxembourg
Service Geologique du Luxembourg (2011)
23, rue du Chemin de Fer
L-8057 Bertrange
geologie@pch.etat.lu
http://www.pch.public.lu/administration/organigramme/geo/

Madagascar

Universite d' Antananarivo
Dept of Chemistry (B) (2010)
BP 566
Antananarivo 101
p. +261 20 22 326 39
presidence@univ-antananarivo.mg
http://www.univ-antananarivo.mg/

Dept of Biology (B) (2010)
BP 566
Antananarivo 101
p. +261 20 22 329 39
doyen-sciences@univ-antananarivo.mg
http://www.univ-antananarivo.mg/

Dept des Sciences de la Terre (A,B,M,D) (2014)
BP 566
Antananarivo 101
p. 00261331152423
ratrimovoahangy@yahoo.fr
http://www.univ-antananarivo.mg/
Enrollment (2014): M: 14 (0)

Universite de Mahajanga
Dept de Sciences de la Terre et Sciences de l'Environnement
(B) (2014)
p. +261 32 05 579 44

Malawi

Mzuzu University
Faculty of Environmental Sciences (B) (2014)
Private Bag 201
Mzuzu
p. +(265) 1 320 722/ 320 575
registrar@mzuni.ac.mw
http://www.mzuni.ac.mw/index.php?option=com_content&vi
ew=article&id=21&Itemid=15

University of Malawi
Dept of Natural Resources Management (B) (2010)
PO Box 219
Lilongwe
p. (265) 01 277 260
david.mkwambisi@bunda.luanar.mw

http://www.bunda.unima.mw/nrm.thm

Chancellor College, Natural Resources and Environment
Centre (B) (2014)
PO Box 280
Zomba
p. +(265) 1 524 685
geo@chanco.unima.mw
http://www.chanco.unima.mw/department/department.php
?DepartmentID=4&Source=Department_of_Geography_
and_Earth_Sciences

Malaysia

Minerals and Geoscience Department Malaysia
Minerals and Geoscience Dept Malaysia (2011)
20th Floor, Bangunan Tabung Haji
Jalan Tun Razak
50658 Kuala Lumpur
jmgkll@jmg.gov.my
http://www.jmg.gov.my/

National University of Malaysia
Geology Dept (2004)
43600 Bangi
Selangor
dftsm@ftsm.ukm.my

Universiti Putra Malaysia
Dept of Environmental Sciences (2004)
43400 UPM Serdang
    admin@env.upm.edu.my
    http://fsas.upm.edu.my/~sas/envpage/Dept.html

University of Malaya
Dept of Geology (B,M,D) (2007)
Dept. of Geology
University of Malaya
50603 Kuala Lumpur, Malaysia.
Kuala Lumpur, Selangor 50603
    p. 03-79674203
    science@um.edu.my
    http://www.um.edu.my
Head:
  Wan Hasiah Abdullah, (D), Newcastle upon Tyne, 1994, Ec
Professor:
  Teh Guan Hoe, (D), Heidelberg, Ca
  Lee Chai Peng, (D), Liverpool, Pg
  John Kuna Raj, (D), Malaya, 1983, Ng
  Denis N.K Tan, (M), Malaya, Go
Associate Professor:
  Abd Rashid Ahmad, (D), Oxford, Sc
  Azman Abdul Ghani, (D), Liverpool, Gi
  Mohamed Ali Hasan, (M), Ulster, Hg
  Azhar Hj Hussin, (D), London, Gs
  Tajul Anuar Jamaluddin, (D), Wales, 1997, Ng
  Mustaffa Kamal Shuib, (M), London, 1986, Gc
  Samsudin Hj. Taib, (D), Durham, Yg
Lecturer:
  Nuraiteng Tee Abdullah, (D), London, Gr
  Ahmad Tajuddin Hj Ibrahim, (D), Newcastle upon Tyne, Ng
  Che Noorliza Lat, (M), Nevada (Reno), 1989, Yg
  Mat Ruzlin Maulud, (B), Malaya, On
  Nur Iskandar Taib, (D), Indiana, Gi
  Ismail Yusoff, (D), Norwich, Hg

Mali

Universite de Bamako
Sciences de la Terre (B) (2010)
BP 3206
Bamako
    p. (223) 222 32 44
    phine.romagnoli@unige.ch
    http://www.ml.refer.org/u-bamako/spip.php?article.137

Malta

University of Malta
Dept of Geosciences (M,D) O (2015)
Department of Geosciences
University of Malta
Msida Campus
Msida MSD2080
    p. (+356) 2340 2362
    geo.sci@um.edu.mt
    http://www.um.edu.mt/science/geosciences
    Enrollment (2015): M: 5 (0) D: 4 (0)
Dr:
  Pauline Galea, (D), Victoria Univ of Wellington (NZ), 1993, YsgOg
Associate Professor:
  Aldo Drago, (D), Southampton, Opg
  Raymond Ellul, (D), Oa
Dr:
  Sebastiano D'Amico, (D), YsgOg
  Anthony Galea, (D), Trieste, Opg
  Aaron Micallef, (D), Southampton, Gug
Lecturer:
  Noel Aquilina, (D), Birmingham, Oaw
  Adam Gauci, (M), Op

Mauritania

Universite de Nouakchott
Dept de Geologie (B) (2014)
BP 5026
Nouakchott
    p. (222) 25 13 82
    awa@univ-nkc.mr
    http://www.univ-nkc.mr/spip.php?rubrique34

Mauritius

University of Mauritius
Mauritius Radio Telescope (B) (2014)
Reduit
    p. (230) 454 1041
    nalini@uom.ac.mu
    http://www.uom.ac.mu/mrt/mrt2.html

Dept of Chemical and Environmental Engineering (B) (2010)
Reduit
    p. (230) 454 1041
    deanfeng@uom.ac.mu

    http://www.uom.ac.mu/Faculties/FOE/CEE/index.asp

Mexico

Centro de Estudios Superiores del Estado Sonora
Escuela Superior de Geociencias (B) (2004)
Col. Las Quintas
Hermosillo, SO 83240
    p. 621/5-37-78
    manuel.valenzuela@ues.mx
    Department Secretary: Manuel Valenzuela-Renteria
Director:
  Marco A. Gonzalez-Juarez, (B), Sonora, 1977, Gg
Associate Professor:
  Jesus E. Cruz-Teran, (B), Sonora, 1979, On
  Leopoldo Diaz-Encinas, (B), Chihuahua, 1988, Em
  Gustavo E. Durazo-Tapia, (B), Sonora, 1981, Em
  Francisco A. Esparza-Yanez, (B), Sonora, 1983, Gg
  Raul A. Gongora-Jurado, (B), Autonoma de Chihuahua, 1977, Nm
  Maria B. Hurtado-De La Ree, (B), Sonora, 1987, Nx
  Leobardo Lopez-Pineda, (B), Nacional Auton, 1980, Yg
  Jesus F. Maytorena-Silva, (B), Sonora, 1981, Gr
  Rogelio Monreal-Saavedra, (D), Texas (Dallas), 1989, Gr
  Gerardo Monteverde-Gutierrez, (B), Sonora, 1980, Nm
  Arnulfo Salazar-Avila, (B), Sonora, 1981, Nx
  Angel Slistan-Grijalva, (B), Sonora, 1981, Nm
Instructor:
  Luis G. Vite-Picazo, (B), Nacional Auton, 1946, Nm

Centro de Investigación Científica y de Educación Superior de Ensenada
Earth Sciences Div (M,D) (2015)
Carretera Tijuana-Ensenada # 3918
Zona Playitas
Ensenada, Baja California 22860
    p. (01152-664)1750500
    dir-ct@cicese.mx
    http://www.cicese.mx
    Enrollment (2010): M: 44 (8) D: 20 (2)
Titular researcher:
  Edgardo Canon-Tapia, (D), Hawaii, 1996, GvYmGt
Research Associate:
  Jose G. Acosta, (M), CICESE (Ensenada), 1980, Ne
  Jesus M. Brassea, (M), Cinvestav, 1986, Ye
  Juan M. Espinosa, (M), CICESE (Ensenada), 1983, Ye
  Jose J. Gonzalez, (M), CICESE (Ensenada), 1986, Yd
  Alejandro Hinojosa, (M), CICESE (Ensenada), 1988, Or
  Luis H. Mendoza, (M), CICESE (Ensenada), 1982, Ne
  Alfonso Reyes, (B), UNAM, Ne
Titular researcher:
  Raul Castro, (D), Nevada (Reno), 1991, Ys

Juan Contreras, (D), Columbus, 1999, Gt
Luis A. Delgado-Argote, (D), UNAM, 2000, GitGu
Francisco Esparza, (D), CICESE (Ensenada), 1991, Ye
John Fletcher, (D), Utah, 1994, Gpt
Carlos Flores, (D), Toronto, 1986, Ye
Jose Frez, (M), California (Los Angeles), 1980, Ys
Juan Garcia, (D), Oregon State, 1990, Yv
Ewa Glowacka, (D), Polish Acad of Sci, 1991, Ys
Enrique Gomez, (D), Toronto, 1981, Ye
Titular Researcher:
Mario Gonzalez-Escobar, (D), CICESE, 2002, YesYs
Titular researcher:
Antonio Gonzalez-Fernandez, (D), Complutense, 1996, Gu
Javier Helenes, (D), Stanford, 1980, Gr
Thomas Kretzschmar, (D), Tubingen, 1995, Ge
Margarita Lopez, (D), Toronto, 1985, Cc
Juan Madrid, (M), Toronto, 1972, Ys
Arturo Martin, (D), Paris XI Orsay, 1988, Gd
Luis Munguia, (D), California (San Diego), 1982, Ys
Alejandro Nava, (D), California (San Diego), 1980, Ys
Marco A. Perez, (D), CICESE, 1995, Ye
Jose M. Romo, (D), CICESE (Ensenada), 2002, Ye
Pratap Sahay, (D), Alberta, 1986, Ys
Rogelio Vazquez, (D), CICESE (Ensenada), 2002, Ye
Antonio Vidal, (D), CICESE (Ensenada), 2001, Ys
Bodo Weber, (D), Gp

Ciudad Universitaria
Facultad de Ingenieria (2014)
C.P. 04510
p. 56 22 08 66
fainge@servidor.unam.mx
http://www.ingenieria.unam.mx/

Consejo de Recursos Minerales
Consejo de Recursos Minerales (2014)
Blvd. F. Angeles 93.5 km.
Centro Minero Nacional Pachuca
Hidalgo 42080
gciadoctec@sgm.gob.mx
http://www.coremisgm.gob.mx/

Universidad Autonoma de Baja California Sur
Departamento Académico de Geología Marina (2004)
Carretera Sur Km 5-1/2
Cd. Universitaria
La Paz

Dept of Marine Geology (B) (2004)
Carretera al Sur km 5.5, Box 19-B
La Paz, BS 23000
p. 682/2-47-55/2-01-40/2-45-69
gemarina@uabcs.mx
Chair:
Alejandro Alvarez-Arellano, (M), Nacional Auton, 1984, Gs
Professor:
Rodolfo Cruz-Orozco, (D), Louisiana State, 1974, Gu
Javier Gaitan-Moran, (M), Intl Inst-Aerospace Sur & Earth Sci, 1986, Or
Carlos A. Galli-Olivier, (D), Utah, 1968, Gd
Jose I. Peredo-Jaime, (B), Auto de Baja California, 1978, Og
Luis R. Segura-Vernis, (D), Nacional Autonoma, 1977, Pi
Associate Professor:
Alejandro J. Carillo-Chavez, (M), Cincinnati, 1981, Gp
Efrain Cornejo-Luna, (B), Nacional Auton, 1969, Gq
Genaro Martinez-Gutierrez, (B), Inst Politecnico Nac, 1982, Gr
Cesar Martinez-Noriega, (B), Nacional Auton, Ou
Jaime I. Monroy-Sanchez, (M), 1987, Ge
Miriam Nunez-Velazco, (B), Tech (Madero), 1980, Go
Jose A. Perez-Venzor, (B), Autonoma (SLP), 1978, Gi
Ramon Pimentel-Hernandez, (B), Inst Politecnico Nac, 1980, Yg
Humberto Rojas-Soriano, (B), Nacional Auton, 1983, Gz
Paulino Rojo-Garcia, (B), Inst Politecnico Nac, 1983, Gc
Assistant Professor:
Luis A. Herrera-Gil, (B), Nacional Auton, 1980, Pg

Lecturer:
Cesar A. Lopez-Ferreira, (B), Nacional Auton, 1979, Hw
Cooperating Faculty:
Oscar Rodriguez-Plasencia, (B), Escuela Militar de Met, 1959, Ow

Universidad Autonoma de Chihuahua
Facultad de Ingenieria (B,M) (2004)
Circuito Universitario Campus 2
Chihuahua, CH 31170
p. (614) 442-9500
mvazquez@uach.mx
Director:
Arturo Leal-Bejarano, (B), Autonoma de Chihuahua, 1976, On
Head:
Arturo Lujan-Lopez, (M), Essex, 1975, On
Chair:
Socorro I. Aguirre-Moriel, (B), ITR (Switzerland), 1979, Nx
Hector M. Mendoza-Aguilar, (B), Autonoma de Chihuahua, 1980, Nx
Professor:
Rafael Chavez-Aguirre, (M), Autonoma de Chihuahua, 1993, Hw
Adolfo Chavez-Rodriguez, (D), Arizona, 1987, Hy
Miguel Franco-Rubio, (M), Nacional Autonoma, 1978, Eg
Rafael Madrigal-Rubio, (B), Nacional Auton, 1969, Ng
Teodulo Mena-Zambrano, (B), Inst Politecnico Nac, 1964, Ng
Hector Minor-Velazquez, (B), Autonoma de Chihuahua, 1978, Nx
Ignacio A. Reyes-Cortes, (B), Texas (El Paso), 1997, Gx
Manuel Reyes-Cortes, (B), Nacional Auton, 1970, Gi
Miguel Royo-Ochoa, (M), Autonoma de Chihuahua, 1997, Hw
David H. Ruiz-Cisneros, (B), Autonoma de Chihuahua, 1974, Nx
Luis M. Trevizo-Cano, (B), Autonoma de Chihuahua, 1978, Nx

Universidad Autonoma de Nuevo Leon
Facultad de Ciencias de la Tiera (2004)
Hacienda Guadalupe Km. 8 Camino a Cerro Prieto. - Linares, N 67700
p. (81) 8329 4170 Ext. 4170
fmedina@fct.uanl.mx
http://www.fct.uanl.mx/portal/index.php

Universidad Autonoma de San Luis Potosi
Area de Ciencias de la Terra (B,M) (2004)
Facultad de Ingenieri#2.a
Av. Dr. Manuel Nava No. 8
San Luis Potosi#2., SL 78290
p. (48) 13-82-22
mlr@fciencias.uaslp.mx
mlr@fciencias.uaslp.mx
Department Secretary: Juan Manuel Torres Aguilera
Director:
Hector David Atisha-Castillo, (M), Texas, 1978, On
Head:
Joel Milan-Navarro, (M), Nancy (France), 1979, Or
Professor:
Jose Refugio Acevedo-Arroyo, (B), Nacional Auton, 1957, Ng
Luis Garcia-Gutierrez, (M), Stanford, 1951, Eg
Panfilo R. Martinez-Macias, (M), Nacional Auton, 1995, Gc
Francisco Javier Orozco-Villasenor, (M), Colorado State, 1983, Eg
Ramon Ortiz-Aguirre, (M), Madrid, 1979, Hg
Carlos Francisco Puente-Muniz, (B), Autonoma (SLP), 1979, Hw
Delfino C. Ruvalcaba-Ruiz, (D), Colorado State, 1982, Em
Juan Manuel Torres-Agulera, (B), Autonoma (SLP), 1980, Gx
Librarian:
Panfilo R. Martinez-Macias, On

Universidad Autonoma de Sonora
Ejecutivo de la Unidad Regional Norte (2004)
Av. Universidad e Irigoyen
Col. Ortiz
Hermosillo

Universidad de Guanajuato
Departamento de Ingeniería en Minas, Metalurgia y Geología (B) O (2016)
Sede San Matias

Ex Hda. de San Matías s/n
Col. San Javier
Guanajuato, Guanajuato C.P. 36025
   p. ((+473) 73 2 2291 (Ext. 5304)
   juancho@ugto.mx
   http://www.di.ugto.mx/minas/index.php/antecedentes
   Enrollment (2015): B: 7 (7)

Universidad Nacional Autonoma de Mexico
Facultad de Ingeniería (B) (2014)
Av. Universidad 3000, Ciudad Universitaria
Coyoacán, CP 4510
   p. 56 22 08 66
   fainge@servidor.unam.mx
   http://www.ingenieria.unam.mx/paginas/Carreras/ing-
   enieriaMinas/ingMinas_Desc.php
Director:
   Antonio Nieto Antunez, (M), Stanford, 1970, Nm
Professor:
   Angelica Casillas, (B), Inst Politecnico Nac, 1976, Hw
   Esteban Cedillo, (D), Heidelberg, 1988, Em
   Juventino Martinez, (D), Paris VI, 1980, Gt
   Edgardo Meave, (B), Guanajuato, 1947, Gg
   Francisco Medina, (B), Guanajuato, 1982, Og
   Ricardo Navarro, (B), Inst Politecnico Nac, 1973, Nm
   Salvador Ulloa, (B), Guanajuato, 1947, Eg
   Fernando Vasallo, (D), Lomonosov (USSR), 1982, Em
   Carlos Yanez, (B), Inst Politecnico Nac, 1976, Ce

Div de Estudios de Posgrado-Campus Morelos (2004)
C.P. 62550
Facultad de Ingeneria
Jiutepec, MR
   p. (73) 19 39 57 (x. 135)
Director:
   Alvaro Munoz Mendoza, (D), Strathclyde, 1989, On
Acting Head:
   Hugo Acosta Borbon, (M), Nacional Auton, 1992, On
   Esperanza Ramirez Camperos, (M), Nacional Auton, 1989, On

Inst de Geofisica (2004)
   losos@sci.muni.cz
   http://tlacaelel.igeofcu.unam.mx/index.eng.html

Inst de Geologia (M,D) (2010)
Apdo. postal 70-296
Ciudad Universitaria
Delegacion Coyoacan, DF 04510
   p. (52) 5622 4314
   jatkins@illinois.edu
   http://132.248.20.1/geol.htm
   Administrative Assistant: Ana María Rodriguez Simental
Director:
   Dante J. Moran-Zenteno, (D), Nacional Auton, 1992, Cc
Head:
   Susana A. Alaniz Alvarez, (D), Nacional Auton, 1995, Gc
   Luca Ferrari Pedraglio, (D), Milan, 1992, Gt
   Sergio Cevallos Ferriz, (D), Alberta, 1990, Po
   Carlos M. Gonzalez Leon, (D), Arizona, 1992, Gr
   Klavdia Oleschko Loutkova, (D), Lomosov (Moscow), 1984, So
   Maria S. Lozano Garcia, (D), d'Aix (Marseilles), 1979, Pe
   Francisco J. Vega Vera, (D), Nacional Auton, 1988, Py
Chair:
   Gustavo Tolson Jones, (D), Nacional Auton, 1998, Gc
Senior Scientist:
   Shelton Applegate-Pleasants, (D), Chicago, 1961, Pv
   Jorge Aranda, (D), Oregon, 1982, Gi
   Blanca E. Buitron-Sanchez, (D), Nacional Auton, 1974, Pi
   Oscar Carranza-Castaneda, (D), Nacional Auton, 1989, Pv
   Gerardo Carrasco-Nunez, (D), Michigan Tech, 1993, Gv
   Ana L. Carreno, (D), d'Orsay (Paris), 1979, Pm
   Miguel Carrillo Martinez, (D), Paris VI, 1976, Pb
   Liberto De Pablo, (D), Ohio State, 1958, Gz
   Rodolfo Del Arenal-Capetillo, (B), Nacional Auton, 1960, Hw
   Ismael Ferrusquia, (D), Houston, 1971, Gr
   David Flores-Roman, (D), Nacional Auton, 1981, So
   Celestina Gonzalez-Arreola, (D), Nacional Auton, 1989, Pi

Jose C. Guerrero-Garcia, (D), Texas (Dallas), 1975, Ym
John D. Keppie, (D), Glasgow, 1964, Gt
Victor M. Malpica-Cruz, (D), Bordeaux, 1980, Gs
Enrique Martinez Hernandez, (D), Michigan State, 1979, Pl
Juventino Martinez-Reyes, (D), Paris VI, 1980, Gt
Luis M. Mitre-Salazar, (D), Paris IV, 1978, Ge
Adrian Ortega, (D), Waterloo, 1993, Hw
Fernando Ortega-Gutierrez, (D), Leeds (UK), 1975, Gp
Sergio Palacios-Mayorga, (M), Nacional Auton, 1972, So
Jerjes Pantoja-Alor, (M), Arizona, 1963, Gg
Maria del Carmen Perrilliat-Montoya, (D), Nacional Auton, 1969, Pi
Angel Nieto Samaniego, (D), Nacional Auton, 1994, Gc
Christina D. Siebe Grabach, (D), Hohenheim (Germany), 1993, Sc
Alicia Silva-Pineda, (D), Nacional Auton, 1980, Po
Max Suter-Cargnelutti, (D), Basel, 1978, Gt
Jordi Tritlla, (D), Barcelona, 1994, Eg
Ana B. Villasenor-Martinez, (D), Nacional Auton, 1991, Pi
Reinhard Weber-Gobel, (D), Tubingen, 1967, Po
Associate Scientist:
   Gerardo J. Aguirre Diaz, (D), Texas, 1993, Gv
   Thierry Calmus, (D), Paris VI, 1983, Gu
   Antoni Camprubi, (D), Barcelona, 1998, Eg
   Alejandro J. Carillo Chavez, (D), Wyoming, 1996, Hg
   Elena Centeno Garcia, (D), Arizona, 1994, Gt
   Rodolfo Corona-Esquivel, (M), Nacional Auton, 1985, Em
   Mariano Elias-Herrera, (M), Nacional Auton, 1982, Gp
   Maria L. Flores-Delgadillo, (M), Nacional Auton, 1987, So
   Gilberto Hernandez-Silva, (D), Nacional Auton, 1983, So
   Rafael Huizar-Alvarez, (D), Franche Comte, 1989, Hw
   Cesar Jacques Ayala, (D), Cincinnati, 1983, Gr
   Marisol Montellano-Ballesteros, (D), California (Berkeley), 1986, Pv
   Amabel M. Oretega Rivera, (D), Queens, 1997, Cc
   Odranoel Quintero, (D), Sorbonne, 1995, Gc
   Jose L. Rodriguez-Castaneda, (M), Pittsburgh, 1984, Gg
   Jaime Roldan Quintana, (M), Iowa, 1976, Gv
   Gerardo Sanchez-Rubio, (M), Imperial Coll (UK), 1984, Gv
   Jesu Sole, (D), Barcelona, 1996, Cc
   Luis F. Vassallo-Morales, (D), Lomonosov, 1981, Em
   Maria G. Villasenor-Cabral, (M), Leeds (UK), 1974, Ca
Research Associate:
   Irma Aguilera-Ortiz, (B), Iberoameric, 1971, Ca
   Victor M. Davila-Alcocer, (M), Texas (Dallas), 1986, Ps
   Jose G. Solorio-Munguia, (B), Nacional Auton, 1958, Gz
Adjunct Professor:
   J. Duncan Keppie, (D), Glasgow (Scotland), 1967, Gt
   Luis Silva-Mora, (D), d'Aix (Marseilles), 1979, Gi
Emeritus:
   Gloria Alencaster-Ybarra, (D), Nacional Auton, 1969, Pi
   Zoltan De Cserna, (D), Columbia, 1955, Gt
Geology Librarian:
   Teresa Soledad Medina Malagon, (B), On

Mongolia

Gazarchin Institute
Gazarchin Institute (2011)
Bayanzurkh District
Ulaanbaatar 46
   gazarchin_institute@gazarchin.edu.mn
   http://www.gazarchin.edu.mn/

Mineral Resources Authority of Mongolia
Mineral Resources Authority of Mongolia (2013)
   info@mram.gov.mn
   http://www.mram.gov.mn/

Mongolian University of Science and Technology
School of Geology and Petroleum Engineering (2011)
Bagatoiruu-46, P. O. Box-520
Ulaanbaatar 46
   p. 976-11-312291
   jepces@must.edu.mn
   http://www.gs.edu.mn

National University of Mongolia
Geology and Geography Faculty (2011)
Ikh Surguuliin gudamj - 1, Baga Toiruu,
Sukhbaatar district,
Ulaanbaatar
 p. 976-11-311890
 geo@num.edu.mn
 http://geo.num.edu.mn

Morocco

Ecole Nationale de l' Industrie Minerale
Dept de Mines (B) (2010)
Avenue Hadj Ahmed Cherkaoui
BP 753
Adgal, Rabat
 p. (+212) 037 68 02 30
 zaydi@enim.ac.ma
 http://www.enim.ac.ma/formation/mines

Dept de Sciences des Materiaux (B) (2010)
Avenue Hadj Ahmed Cherkaoui
BP 753
Agdal, Rabat
 p. (+212) 037 68 02 30
 zaydi@enim.ac.ma
 http://www.enim.ac.ma/formation/materiaux/

Dept de Sciences de la Terre (B) (2010)
Avenue Hadj Ahmed Cherkaoui
BP 753
Agdal, Rabat
 p. (+212) 037 68 02 30
 zaydi@enim.ac.ma
 http://www.enim.ac.ma/formation/sciences_de_la_terre/

ONAREP-Naional Office of Petroleum Research
ONAREP - Naional Office of Petroleum Research (B) (1999)
PO Box 8030
Rabat 10050
 p. +212 37 28-1616

ONHYM
National Office of Hydrocarbons and Mines (2011)
 rh@onhym.com
 http://www.onhym.com/Default.aspx?alias=www.onhym.
 com/EN

School of Mines of Marrakech
School of Mines (B,M,D) (2011)
Rue Machaar, El Harm Quartier Issil-B.P. 38
Marrakech
 p. 212-30-97-79

Universite Abdelmalek Essaadi
Faculte de Sciences de Tetouen (B) (2010)
BP 2121
Tetouan 93002
 p. +212 (0) 39 97 24 23
 presidence@uae.ma
 http://www.fst.ac.ma/stu.html

Dept de Sciences de la Terre (B) (2014)
 p. +212 539 97 93 16
 presidence@uae.ma
 http://www.uae.ma/portail/FR/

Universite Cadi Ayyad
Dept of Geology (2014)
Prince Moulay Abdellah
BP 515
Marakech
 p. +212 (0)5 24 43 46 49
 http://www.fssm.ucam.ac.ma/pages/geologie.php

Universite Hassan 1er - Settat
Dept de Geologie Apliquee (B) (2014)
BP 577
Settat 26000
 p. 05.23.40.07.36
 http://www.fsts.ac.ma/fsts/index/php?option=com_content&
 task=view&id=37&Itemid=12

Universite Hassan II
Dept of Geology (B) (2014)
9, Rue Tarik Bnou Zia
Anfa Casablanca
 p. 0522 23 06 80
 z.hilmi@fsac.ac.ma
 http://www.fsac.ac.ma/depart/geo/index.html

Universite Hassan II - Mohammedia
Dept de Sciences de la Terre (B) (2013)
279 Cite Yassmina
Mohammedia, Casablanca
 p. +212(33)314635
 presidence@univh2m.ac.ma

Universite Ibn Tofail
Dept de Geologie (B,M,D) ● (2014)
Abdelhakboua@Yahoo.com
Kenitra 14 000
 p. +212 061984449
 abdelhakboua@yahoo.com
 http://www.univ-ibntofail.ac.ma/fre/departments.php?esp=4
 &rub=14&srub=36&srub_=96
 Enrollment (2014): B: 14 (0) M: 23 (0) D: 7 (0)

Universite Ibn Zohr, Agadir
Dept de Sciences de la Terre (B) (2010)
BP 32/S
Agadir 80000
 p. +212 (28) 22 71 25
 acma2008@esta.ac.ma
 http://www.esta.ac.ma/

Universite Mohammed 1er (Oujda)
Ecole Nationale des Sciences Appliquees d'Al Hoceima
(ENSAH) (B) (2010)
BP 724
Oujda 60000
 p. +212(56)500612
 presidence@ump.ma
 http://webserver1.ump.ma/ecoles_facultes/ensah

Dept des Sciences de la Terre (B,M,D) (2011)
BP 717
, 60000 Oujda
 p. (212)536500601/02
 fso@fso.ump.ma
 http://sciences1.univ-oujda.ac.ma/index.htm

Universite Mohammed V
Dept of Geology (2014)
BP 554
Rue Michlifen Agdal
Rbat-Chellah
 p. +212 05 37 77 54 71
 http://www.fsr.ac.ma/ancien/index.php/departement/giolo-
 gie.html

Dept of Geology (B) (2010)
4 Avenue Ibn Battouta
BP 1014 RP
Rabat-Chellah
 p. +212 (0) 37 77 18 34/35/38
 belbijou@um5a.ac.ma
 http://www.fsr.ac.ma/

Universite Mohammed V (Agdal)
Dept de Genie Minerale (B) (2010)
Avenue Ibnsina
BP 765
Adgal Raba
    p. (212 - 537) 77.26.47 - 77.19.0
    contact@um5a.ac.ma
    http://www.emi.ac.ma

Universite Moulay Ismail, Meknes
Dept de Sciences de la Terre (B) (2014)
Marjane II BP 298
Meknes 5003
    p. +212 5 35 53 78 96
    doyen@fs-umi.ac.ma
    http://ww.umi.ac.ma/

Universite Sidi Mohammed Ben Abdallah
Dept of Geology (2014)
Dhar El Mahraz
BP 42
Atlas-Fes
    p. 06 61 35 04 81
    dept_geo@fsdmfes.ac.ma
    http://www.fsdmfes.ac.ma/Presentation/Departements/
    Geologie.php

University Mohammed I
Dept of Geology (B,M,D) (2013)
Faculté des Sciences Bd. Mohammed VI
BP 717
Oujda, Oujda-Angad 60000
    p. (212)667772215
    mbouabdellah2002@yahoo.fr
    http://webserver1.ump.ma/

Mozambique

Universidade Eduardo Mondlane
Escola Superior de Ciencias Marinhas e Costeiras (B) (2014)
CP 128
Avenida 1 de Julho
Bairro Chuabo Dembe
Didad de Quelimane, Zambezia
    p. +258 24900500/1
    valera.dias@uem.mz
    http://www.marine.uem.mz/

Laboratorio de Gemologia (B,M) (2014)
Av. Julius Nyerere 3453, Departamento de Física
Campus Universitário
Maputo
    p. (+258) 21 497003
    uthui@zebra.uem.mz
    http://www.fisica.uem.mz/index.php?option=com_content&
    view=article&id=51&Itemid=57

Universidade Lurio
Faculdade de Engenharia e Ciencias Naturais (B) (2014)
Av. 25 de Setembro
N. 958
Pemba, Cabo Delgado
    p. (+258) 27 221238
    fecn@unilurio.ac.mz
    http://www.unilurio.ac.mz/faculdades_pmb_pt.htm

Namibia

The Geological Survey of Namibia in Windhoek
The Geological Survey of Namibia in Windhoek (2015)
Private Bag 13297
Windhoek
    p. +264-61-2848111

gschneider@mme.gov.na
http://www.mme.gov.na/gsn/

University of Namibia
Dept of Geology (B,M,D) ● (2015)
Private Bag 13301
Windhoek 9000
    p. (+264 61) 206 3712
    ttjipura@unam.na
    http://www.unam.na/faculties/science/departments.html
    Enrollment (2015): B: 16 (12) M: 6 (1)
Chair:
    Ansgar Wanke, Germany, GsCl
Associate Professor:
    Frederick Akalemwa Kamona, (D), Germany, 1991, EgGzCe
    Benjamin S. Mapani, (D), Melbourne, 1994, GtcGp
Lecturer:
    Martin Harris, (M), Geosciences (Beijing), 2013
    Regmi Kamal, (D), Australian National, 2013
    Albertina Nakwafila, (M), Stellenbosch, 2014
    Ester Shalimba, (M), Beijing, 2014, Gpg
    Collen Uahengo, (M), Geosciences (Beijing), 2013
    Shoopala Uugulu, (M), France, 2012
    Heike Wanke, Germany, Hw

Nepal

Tribhuvan University
Central Dept of Geology (2004)
Gandhi Bhavan, Kirtipur, Kathmandu
    info@geology.edu.np
    http://www.geology.edu.np/

Netherlands

Delft University of Technology
Dept of Geology (2004)
Julianlaan 163
2628 Delft
    M.A.Hicks@tudelft.nl

National Geological Survey of the Netherlands
National Geological Survey of the Netherlands (2011)
Princetonlaan 6
3584 CB Utrecht
    p. (+31)30-2564256
    http://www.en.geologicalsurvey.nl/

Royal NIOZ
Marine Organic Biogeochemistry (2013)
Landsdiep 4
't Horntje 1797 SZ
    Jaap.Damste@nioz.nl
    http://www.nioz.nl

State University of Groningen
Faculty of Spatial Sciences (B,M) (2015)
P.O. Box 800
Groningen, Netherlands 9700 AV
    p. +31 50 363 8891
    i.l.veen@rug.nl
    http://www.rug.nl/frw
    f: http://www.facebook.com/FRWRUG
    t: @FRW_RUG
    Enrollment (2014): B: 190 (0) M: 60 (0)

State University of Utrecht
Faculty of Geoscience (B,M,D) (2014)
P.O. Box 80.115
Utrecht 3508 TA
    p. (+31) (0)30 253 2044
    info@geo.uu.nl
    http://www.uu.nl/faculty/geosciences/EN/Contact/Pages/

Technical Univ. of Delft
Dept of Applied Geology (A,B,M,D) ● (2014)
P. O. Box 5048
Stevinweg 1
2600-GA Delft
　　p. +31 15 27 86019
　　h.h.m.zwiers@tudelft.nl
　　http://www.citg.tudelft.nl/over-faculteit/afdelingen/geosci-ence-engineering/

Universiteit Utrecht
Faculty of Geosciences (B,M) (2015)
Budapestlaan 4b
Utrecht 3584 CD
　　p. +31 30 253 7890
　　mscinfo.geo@uu.nl
　　http://www.geo.uu.nl/

University of Amsterdam
Dept of Geology (2014)
Science Park 904
1098 XH Amsterdam
　　p. +31 (0)20525 8626
　　info-science@uva.nl

University of Twente
Faculty of Geo-Information Sciences and Earth Observation (M,D) (2016)
P.O. Box 217
7500 AA Enschede
　　p. +31 (0)53 487 44 44
　　info-itc@utwente.nl
　　http://www.itc.nl

University of Utrecht
Dept of Earth Sciences (2013)
Heidelberglaan 2
P.O. Box 80115
Utrecht
　　C.Marcelis@geo.uu.nl

VU University Amsterdam
Faculty of Earth and Life Sciences, Dep. of Earth Sciences (B,M,D) ● (2015)
De Boelelaan 1085-1087
1081 HV Amsterdam 1081 HV
　　p. +31 (0)20 59 87000
　　f.bosse@vu.nl
　　http://www.falw.vu.nl/en/index.asp#
　　Enrollment (2015): B: 248 (56) M: 67 (45)
Professor:
　　Gareth Davies, (D), GivGf
　　John Reijmer, (D), Gsu
　　Wim van Westrenen, (D), CpGz
　　Jan Wijbrans, (D), Cc
Assistant Professor:
　　Fraukje Brouwer, (D), Gxc
　　Klaudia Kuiper, (D), Cc
　　Frank Peeters, (D), GuPs
　　Pieter Vroon, (D), GvCg
Research Associate:
　　Janne Koornneef, (D), GvCa
Dr:
　　Bernd Andeweg, (D), 2002, GtcGg
　　Ron Kaandorp, (D), Gg
　　Anco Lankreijer, (D), GctGg
　　Els Ufkes, (D), Pm

Netherlands Antilles

Royal NIOZ
Marine Geology (2011)
Landsdiep 4
Den Burg 1797 SZ

　　p. +31(0)222 369 300
　　Jens.Greinert@nioz.nl
　　http://www.nioz.nl

Physical Oceanography (2011)
Landsdiep 4
Den Burg 1797 SZ
　　Hendrik.van.Aken@nioz.nl
　　http://www.nioz.nl

New Zealand

Institute of Geological and Nuclear Sciences Ltd (New Zealand)
Institute of Geological and Nuclear Sciences Ltd (New Zealand) (2015)
1 Fairway Drive, Avalon 5010. PO Box 30-368, 5040.
Lower Hutt
　　p. +64-4-570-1444
　　G.Alderwick@gns.cri.nz
　　http://www.gns.cri.nz/
　　f: https://www.facebook.com/gnsscience

Massey University
Soil and Earth Sciences Group (2004)
Private Bag
Palmerston North
　　p. 0800 MASSEY (0800 627 739)
　　contact@massey.ac.nz
　　http://www.massey.ac.nz/massey/learning/programme-course-paper/programme.cfm?major_code=2044&prog_id=92431

University of Auckland
School of Environment (2009)
Private Bag 92019
Auckland Mail Center
Auckland 1142
　　p. 64 9 3737599
　　geology@auckland.ac.nz

　　http://www.auckland.ac.nz/glg/geology.htm

University of Canterbury
Dept of Geological Sciences (B,M,D) ● (2016)
Private Bag 4800
Christchurch 8140
　　p. (643) 364-2700
　　geology@canterbury.ac.nz
　　http://www.geol.canterbury.ac.nz/title.html
　　Enrollment (2014): B: 28 (0) M: 0 (35) D: 0 (20)
Professor Hazard & Disaster Management:
　　Timothy R H Davies, (D)
Professor:
　　James Cole, (D), Wellington, Gv
　　Jarg Pettinga, (D), Auckland, Gt
Senior Lecturer:
　　Kari N. Bassett, (D), Minnesota, 1995, Gs
　　Catherine Reid, (D), Po
Lecturer:
　　Darren Gravley, (D), Gv
　　Samuel Hampton, (D), Canterbury, Gq
　　Ben Kennedy, (D), Gv
　　Valerie Zimmer, (D), Ng

University of Otago
Dept of Geology (B,M,D) (2015)
P. O. Box 56
360 Leith Walk
Dunedin 9054
　　p. +64 3 479-7519
　　geology@otago.ac.nz
　　http://www.otago.ac.nz/geology/
　　Enrollment (2005): M: 20 (0) D: 22 (0)

Professor:
    Alan F. Cooper, (D), Otago, 1970, GpiGt
    Dave Craw, (D), Otago, 1981, Eg
    Richard J. Norris, (D), Oxford, 1969, Gct
Head of Department:
    R. Ewan Fordyce, (D), Canterbury (NZ), 1981, Pv
Associate Professor:
    Daphne E. Lee, (D), Otago, 1980, Pib
    James D. L. White, (D), California (Santa Barbara), 1989, Gvs
Senior Lecturer:
    J. Michael Palin, (D), Yale, 1992, CcGi
Senior Lecturer:
    Andrew R. Gorman, (D), British Columbia, 2001, YrgYe
    Candace E. Martin, (D), Yale, 1990, ClcGz
Lecturer:
    Virginia G. Toy, (D), Otago, 2008, Gct
Dr:
    Christopher M. Moy, (D), Gus
Adjunct Professor:
    Gary S. Wilson, (D), Victoria (NZ), 1993, GuYmGs
Emeritus:
    Douglas S. Coombs, (D), Gi
    Rick H. Sibson, (D), Imperial Coll (UK), 1977, Gc

University of Waikato
Dept of Earth Sciences (2014)
Private Bag 3105
Hamilton 3240
    p. +64 7 838 4625
    science@waikato.ac.nz
    http://sci.waikato.ac.nz/study/subjects/earth-sciences

Victoria University of Wellington
School of Geography, Environment and Earth Sciences
(A,B,M,D) O (2014)
P. O. Box 600
Wellington 6040
    p. +6444636108
    geo-enquiries@vuw.ac.nz
    http://www.geo.vuw.ac.nz/
    Enrollment (2012): B: 153 (107) M: 51 (22)
Professor:
    Tim Little, (D), Stanford, 1988, Gct

Dept of Geology (2015)
P. O. Box 600
Wellington
    p. +64 4 463 5337
    geo-enquiries@vuw.ac.nz
    http://www.victoria.ac.nz/sgees/study/postgraduate-study/
    geology/

Nicaragua
University of Managua
Centro de Investigaciones Geocientificas (2004)
Colonia Miguel Bonilla No. 165, P.O. Box A-131 Cc. Managua,
Managua

Niger
Institut de Recherche pour le Developpement au Niger
Institut de Recherche pour le Developpement au Niger (B)
(2010)
Avenue de Maradi
Niamey BP 11 416
    p. (227) 20 75 38 27
    irdniger@ird.ne
    http://www.ird.ne/

Universite Abdou Moumouni de Niamey
Dept de Geologie (2014)
B.P. 10662
Niamey
    p. (227) 20 31 50 72
    http://www.secheresse.info/article.php3?id_article=1664
Doyen:
    Abdoulaye M. Alassane

Nigeria

Adekunle Ajasin University
Dept of Earth Sciences (B) (2010)
Akungba Akoko, Ikare Akoko 23401
    p. +234 (34) 246444
    iosazuwa@yahoo.com
    http://www.ajasin.edu.ng/academics/index.php

African University of Science & Technology
Petroleum Engineering (B,M) (2010)
PMB 681
Abuja F.C.T.
Km 10 Airport Road
Garki
    p. +234 9 7800680
    http://aust.edu.ng/

Ahmadu Bello University
Dept of Geology (2014)
Sokoto Road
Samaru-Zaria
Zaria 2222, Kaduna
    p. +234 (69) 50 691
    ybijimi@yahoo.com
    http://www.abu.edu.ng/

American University of Nigeria
School of Arts and Sciences (B) (2010)
Lamido Zubairu Way
PMB 2250, Yola 23455
    p. +234 (805) 5485 702
    dsas@aun.edu.ng

    http://www.abti-american.edu.ng

Caleb University
Dept of Environmental Protection and Management (B) (2010)
PMB 21238
Ikeja GPO, Lagos
    p. +234-1-764-7312
    info@calebuniversity.edu.ng
    http://calebuniversity.edu.ng/courses.php?coll_id=4

Dept of Surveying and Geoinformatics (B) (2010)
PMB 21238
Ikeja GPO, Lagos
    p. +234-1-764-7312
    info@calebuniversity.edu.ng
    http://calebuniversity.edu.ng/courses.php?collUid=4

Crawford University
Dept of Mathematics and Physical Sciences (B) (2010)
PMB 2001
Faith City
    p. +234 (1) 8134785
    ccrawford@rsu.edu

    http://www.crawforduniversity.edu.ng

Delta State University
Dept of Geology (B) (2014)
PMB 1
Abraka
    p. +234 (54) 66009
    delsu03@yahoo.com
    htttp://www.delsunigeria.net/
Director:
    S. H. O. Egboh, (D)

Chair:
    E. Adaikpoh, (D)

Enugu State University of Science and Technology
Dept of Geology and Mining (B) (2010)
MB 01660, Enugu
    p. +234 (42) 451319
    esut@compuserve.com
    http://www.esut.edu.ng/

Dept of Geography and Meteorology (B) (2010)
MB 01660, Enugu
    p. +234 (42) 451319
    esut@compuserve.com
    http://www.esut.edu.ng/

Federal Polytechnic, Bida
Dept of Survey and Geoinformatics (B) (2010)
    http://www.fedpolybidaportal.com/

Dept of Quantitative Surveying (B) (2010)
    http://www.fedpolybidaportal.com/

Federal Polytechnic, Offa
School of Environmental Studies (B) (2010)
    http://www.fedpoffa.edu.ng/

Federal University of Technology
Dept of Applied Geophysics (B,M,D) (2014)
PMB 704
Akure, Ondo
    p. +234 803-595-9029
    joamigun@futa.edu.ng
    http://agp.futa.edu.ng/page.php?pageid=179

Federal University of Technology, Akure
Earth & Mineral Sciences (B) (2010)
PMB 704
Akure
    p. +234 (34) 243744
    sems@futa.edu.ng
    http://www.futa.edu.ng/sems/

Applied Geology (B) ● (2016)
PMB 704
Akure, Ondo
    p. +234 (0) 803 667 2708
    agy@futa.edu.ng
    http://www.futa.edu.ng/agy/
    Enrollment (2015): B: 85 (70)
Professor:
    Yinusa A. Asiwaju-Bello, (D), Leeds, GgHgNg
    Idowu O. Odeyemi, (D), Ibadan, 1976, GgxOr
Doctor:
    O A.G Jegede, (D), Akure, GgNgg
    C T. Okonkwo, (D), Keele, GgxGc
    S A. Opeloye, (D), Bauchi, GgoGs
Mrs:
    Oluwaseyi A. Bamisaye, (M), Akure, 2007, GgOr
Mr:
    Mohammed O. Adepoju, (M), Akure, 2004, GgEg
    Adeshina L. Adisa, (M), Akure, 2012, GgCe
    Isaac O. Ajigo, (M), Jos, 2013, GgNm
    Timothy I. Asowata, (M), Ibadan, 2010, Gge
    Sunday O. Daramola, (M), Akure, 2012, GgNg
    Oladimeji Rilwan Egbeyemi, (M), Ibadan, 2004, GgCg
    Emmanuel Eghietseme Igonor, (M), Ibadan, 2007, GgCe
    Osazuwa A. Ogbahon, (M), Akure, 2011, Ggo
    Joshua O. Owoseni, (M), Ibadan, GgHw
Doctor:
    P S. Ola, (D), Akure, GgoGs
    Solomon O. Olabode, (D), Akure, GgoGs

Federal University of Technology, Yola
Dept of Surveying & Geoinformatics (B) (2010)
PMB 2076
Yola
    p. +234 (803) 6065646
    survey@futy.edu.ng
    http://www.futy.edu.ng/academic/dsurvey.htm

Dept of Geography (B) (2010)
PMB 2076
Yola
    p. +234 (803) 6065646
    geography@futy.edu.ng
    http://www.futy.edu.ng/academic/dgeography.htm

Dept of Soil Science (B) (2010)
PMB 2076
Yola
    p. +234 805 3372 784
    soilscience@futy.edu.ng
    http://www.futy.edu.ng/academic/dsoil.htm

Dept of Geology (B) (2010)
PMB 2076
Yola
    p. +234 (803) 6065646
    geology@futy.edu.ng
    http://www.futy.edu.ng/academic/dgeology.htm

Gombe State University
Dept of Geology (B) (2010)
    abdullahimahadi@gomsu.org
    http://www.gomsu.org/

Dept of Geography (B) (2010)
    abdullahimahadi@gomsu.org
    http://www.gomsu.org/

Ladoke Akintola University of Technology
Dept of Earth Sciences (B) (2016)
PMB 4000
Ogbomoso, Oyo 4000
    p. +234 8033539911
    contact@lautech.edu.ng
    http://www.lautech.edu.ng/Academics/undergraduates/
    FPAS/index.html
    Enrollment (2015): B: 13 (13)
Dr:
    Oyelowo Gabriel Bayowa, (D), Obafemi Awolowo, 2013, GggGg
Dr:
    Olufunmi Abosede Adewoye, (D), Ladoke Akintola, 2014, GeeGe
Dr:
    Moruffdeen Adedapo Adabanija, (D), Ibadan, 2009, GggGg
Mr:
    Olukayode Adegoke Afolabi, (M), Ibadan, 2000, GxxGx
    Ismaila Abiodun Akinlabi, (M), Ibadan, 2011, GggGg
    Mustapha Taiwo Jimoh, (M), Ibadan, 2006, GxxGx
    Lanre Lateef Kolawole, (M), Newcastle, 1985, GeeGe
    Olusola Christophe Oduneye, (M), Ibadan, 2009, GooGo
    Gbenga Olakunle Ogungbesan, (M), Ibadan, 2006, GooGo

Lagos State Polytechnic
School of Environmental Studies (Quantity Surveying) (B) (2010)
    fadebanjo@nou.edu.ng
    http://mylaspotech.net/

National Open University of Nigeria
School of Science & Technology (B) (2010)
PO Box 1866
Bauchi
    p. +234 1-8188849, +234 1-4820720
    registrar@nou.edu.ng
    http://www.nou.edu.ng/noun/indexs.jsp

Nnamdi Azikiwe University

Dept of Geology/Meteorology and Env Management (B) (2010)
PMB 5025
Awka, Nnewi 5025
    p. +234 (46) 550018
    emmaojukwu@unizik.edu.ng
    http://www.unizikeduportal.org/

Dept of Geological Sciences (B) (2010)
Awka Campas
PMB 5025
Awka, Nnewi 5025
    p. +234 (46) 550018
    info@unizik.edu.ng
    http:wwwww.unizikeduportal.org/

Obafemi Awolowo University

Dept of Geology (B,M,D) ● (2015)
Ile-Ife, Osun State 220002
    p. 08128181062
    geoife@oauife.edu.ng
    http://gly.oauife.edu.ng/
    Enrollment (2014): B: 213 (0) M: 24 (0) D: 12 (0)
Head:
  A. A. Adepelumi, (D), YgsNe
Professor:
  S. A. Adekola, (D), GdoCg
  O. Afolabi, Yg
  J. O. Ajayi, Oo
  T. R. Ajayi, CgEgGe
  O. A. Alao, (D), Yg
  U. K. Benjamin, GoCg
  S. L. Fadiya, (D), God
  D. E. Falebita, (D), Yg
  A. O. Ige, Cg
  A. O. Ige, Cg
  E. James-Aworeni, Hg
  J. I. Nwachukwu, GoCg
  O. O. Ocan, GtzGp
  S. B. Ojo, Yg
  V. O. Olarewaju, GozCg
  A. O. Olorunfemi, Go
  M. O. Olorunfemi, Yg
  A. A. Oyawale, GeoCg
  M. A. Rahaman, GpcGi
  B. M. Salami, Hg
  I. A. Tubosun
Associate Professor:
  A Adetunji, (D), EgGi
Research Associate:
  M. A. Olayiwola, GugPi
  O. M. Oyebanjo

Dept of Soil Science (B) (2010)
Ile-Ife
    p. +234 (36) 230 290
    ifepsy@yahoo.com
    http://www.oauife.edu.ng/faculties/agric/soil_sci.html

Dept of Geography (B,M,D) ○ (2014)
Ile-Ife
    p. +234 (70) 37772355
    sinaayanlade@yahoo.co.uk
    http://www.oauife.edu.ng/faculties/soc_sciences/depart-
    ments/geo/home.htm

Rivers State University of Science & Technology

Inst of Geoscience & Space Technology (IGST) (2011)
P.M.B. 5080
Nkpolu - Oroworukwo
Port Harcourt, Rivers State
    info@ust.edu.ng
    http://www.ust.edu.ng/

Universite de Niamey

Dept de Geologie (2004)
BP 10662, Niamey

University Ibadan

Dept of Geology (B) (2010)
Ibadan
    p. +234-2-810-3168
    alexodaibo@yahoo.com
    http://www.ui.edu.ng/?q=departmentofgeology

University of Ado - Ekiti

Geology Dept (B) (2010)
PMB 5363
Ado-Ekiti
    p. +234 (30) 250026
    info@eksu.edu.ng

    http://www.unadportal.com/

Dept of Agricultural Sciences (B) (2010)
PMB 5363
Ado-Ekiti
    p. +234 (30) 250026
    http://www.unadportal.com/

University of Benin

Dept of Geology (B,M,D) ● (2015)
P. M. B. 1155
Benin City, Edo State
    p. 234 0802 345 5681
    registrar@uniben.edu
    http://www.uniben.edu/physicalscielcdfaculty.html
Professor:
  Godwin Osarenkhoe Asuen, (D), EcGsg
Professor:
  Christopher Nnaemeka Akujieze, (D), HwGeHg
  Williams Ogbevire Emofurieta, (D), GzCeGe
  Tony Uzozili Onyeobi, (D), NrgGq
Associate Professor:
  Isaac Okpeseyi Imasuen, (D), CpGeCg
Senior Lecturer:
  Ben Obelenwa Ezenabor, (M), HgOrGe
  Franklin A. Lucas, (D), PmlGr
Lecturer II:
  Aitalokhai Joel Edegbai, (M), GosPi
  Efetobore Gladys Maju-Oyovwikowhe, (M), GszGo
  Sikiru Adeoye Salami, (D), YgeGg
Lecturer I:
  Ovie Odokuma-Alonge, (M), CgGip
Graduate Assistant:
  Tomilola Andre-Obayanju, (B), NgHgGe
Assistant Lecturer:
  Aiyevbekpen Helen Akenzua-Adamcyzk, (M), GeHgGg
  Nosa Samuel Igbinigie, (M), GorGg
  Alexander Ogbamikhumi, (M), YsgGg
  Sunday Erapkpower Okunuwadje, (M), GsoGd
  Edoseghe Edwin Osagiede, (M), GctGx

Dept of Petroleum Engineering (B) (2010)
PMB 115
Benin City, Edo State
    p. 234 0802 345 5681
    deanengineering@uniben.edu

    http://www.uniben.edu/UniversityOfBenin-PetroleumEngi-
    neering.html

University of Calabar

Dept of Geology (B) (2014)
PMB 1115 Eta Agbo Road,
Calabar Municipal, Cross River State
    p. (+234) 8173740083
    general@unical.edu.ng
    http://www.unical.edu.ng/pages/programs_courses/sci-

ences.php?nav=departments

Nse U. Essien

University of Ibadan
Dept of Petroleum Engineering (B) (2010)
Ibadan
p. +234-2-810-3168
oe.owaba@mail.ui.edu.ng
http://www.ui.edu.ng/?q=petengine

Dept of Geology (B,M,D) (2014)
Ibadan, Oyo State
p. 02-8101100-8101104
uigeology@yahoo.com
http://sci.ui.edu.ng/geowelcome
Head:
M. N. Tijani, HgNg
Professor:
I. M. Akaegbobi, Cg
A. A. Elueze, Eg
A. I. Olayinka, Yg
Lecturer:
A. E. Abimbola, Cg
O. C. Adeigbe, Go
G. O. Adeyemi, NgHg
O. A. Boboye, Go
A. T. Bolarinwa, EgGz
O. A. Ehinola, Goe
M. E. Nton, Go
O. A. Okunlola, Eg
M. A. Oladunjoye, Yg
A. S. Olatunji, Cg
O. O. Osinowo, Yg
I. A. Oyediran, Ng

University of Ilorin
Dept of Geology and Mineral Sciences (B) (2014)
PMB 1515
p. +234 (31) 221691
deanfacsci@unilorin.edu.ng
http://www.unilorin.edu.ng/unilorin/index.php/sciences-dept/
geology-mineral-sciences
Head:
J.I. D. Adekeye, (D), GoCg
Professor:
S. O. Akande, (D), EgCg
O. Ogunsanwo, Ng
Lecturer:
A. Abdurrahman, (M), CeEg
A. D. Adedcyin, (M), Eg
O. A. Adekeye, (D), Pm
S.M. A. Adelana, (M), HgYgGe
D. A. Alao, NgGz
O. O. Ige, (M), Ng
O. J. Ojo, GoPm
A. K. Olawuyi, Yg
O. A. Omotoso, (M), Ge
W. O. Raji, (M), Ye

University of Jos
Dept of Geosciences and Mining (B) (2014)
PMB 2084
Jos 930001
p. +234 (73) 559 52
vc@unijos.edu.ng
http://www.unijos.edu.ng/

University of Lagos
Dept of Civil and Environmental Engineering (B) (2010)
Akoka
Yaba, Lagos
p. +234 (1) 493 2660 3
informationunit@unilag.edu.ng
http://www.unilag.edu.ng/index.php?page=about_

departmentdetail&sno=11

Dept Surveying and Geoinformatics (B) (2010)
Akoka
Yaba, Lagos
p. +234 (1) 493 2660 3
informationunit@unilag.edu.ng
http://www.unilag.edu.ng/index.php?page=about_
departmentdetail&sno=16

Dept of Petroleum and Gas Engineering (B) (2010)
Akoka
Yaba, Lagos
p. +234 (1) 493 2660 3
informationunit@unilag.edu.ng
http://www.unilag.edu.ng/index.php?page=home

Dept of Metalurgical and Materials Engineering (B) (2010)
Akoka
Yaba, Lagos
p. +234 (1) 493 2600 3
informationunit@unilag.edu.ng
http://www.unilag.edu.ng/index.php?page=home

University of Maiduguri
Dept of Geology (2014)
PMB 1069 FEA
Maiduguri
info@unimaid.edu.ng
http://www.unimaid.edu.ng/root/faculty_of_sciences/
dept_geology.html

University of Maiduguri, Borno State
Dept of Geology (B,M,D) (2014)
Bama Road
PMB 1069
Maiduguri
p. +234 (76) 231730
info@unimaid.edu.ng
http://www.unimaid.edu.ng/home.php
Professor:
I. B. Goni
Assistant Professor:
Saidu Baba
Lecturer:
Sani Adamu
Kyari M. Ajar
Musa Malana Aji
Fati Bukar
Shettima Bukar
Jalo M. El-Nafaty
Millitus V. Joseph
Samaila C. Kali
Yakubu B. Mohd
Mohammed Poukar
Aishatu Sani
Manaja Mijinyawa Uba
Sidi M. Waru
Asabe Kuku Yahaya
Soloman N. Yusuf
A. Adam Zarma

University of Nigeria
Dept of Geology (B) (2010)
Nsukka
micah.osilike@unn.edu.ng
http://www.unn.edu.ng/physicalsciences/content/
view/700/601/

University of Nigeria Nsukka
Dept of Geoinformatics and Surveying (B) (2010)
batho.okolo@unn.edu.ng
http://www.unn.edu.ng/environmentalstudies/content/
view/27/44/

Dept of Geology (B) (2014)
anthony.okonta@unn.edu.ng
http://unn.edu.ng/department/geology
Lecturer:
Alloysuis Okwudili Anyiam
Luke I. Manah
Smart Chicka Obiora

University of Port Harcourt
Dept of Geography & Environmental Management (B) (2010)
East/ West Road
PMB 5323
Choba, Port Harcourt 500001
p. +234 (84) 230890-99
uniport@uniport.edu.ng
http://uniport.edu.ng/

Dept of Geology (B) (2014)
East/ West Road
P.M.B. 5323
Choba, Port Harcourt 500001
p. +234 (0)84 817 941
uniport@uniport.edu.ng
http://www.uniport.edu.ng/faculties/science.html

Dept of Petroleum and Gas Engineering (B) (2010)
East/ West Road
PMB 5323
Choba, Port Harcourt 500001
p. +234 (84) 230890-99
dean@eng.uniport.edu.ng
http://uniport.edu.ng/

University of Uyo
Faculty of Agriculture (B,M,D) (2015)
PMB 1017
Uyo, Akwa Ibom State 520001
p. +234 (85) 200303
vc@uniuyo.edu.ng
http://www.uniuyo.edu.ng/index.htm

Faculty of Engineering (B,M,D) (2010)
PMB 1017
Uyo
p. +234 (85) 200303
vc@uniuyo.edu.ng
http://www.uniuyo.edu.ng/index.htm

Faculty of Science Education (B,M,D) (2010)
PMB 1017
Uyo
p. +234 (85) 200303
vc@uniuyo.edu.ng
http://www.uniuyo.edu.ng/index.htm

Faculty of Social Science (B,M,D) (2010)
PMB 1017
Uyo
p. +234 (85) 200303
vc@uniuyo.edu.ng
http://www.uniuyo.edu.ng/index.htm

Faculty of Environmental Studies (B,M,D) (2010)
PMB 1017
Uyo
p. +234 (85) 200303
vc@uniuyo.edu.ng
http://www.uniuyo.edu.ng/index.htm

Western Delta University
Geology and Petroleum Studies (B) (2010)
PMB 10
Oghara
p. +234 (70) 35400531
info@wdu.edu.ngg
http://www.wduniversity.org/

Wukari Jubilee University
Dept of Geography and Environmental Conservation (B)
(2010)
PMB 1019
Wukari, Taraba State
p. +234 (080) 80329138
wukari_jubilee@yahoo.com
http://wukarijubileeuniversity.org/

Norway

NLH
Dept of Soil Sciences (2015)
P.O. Box 28
1432 AS
p. +47 67 23 00 00
post@nmbu.no
http://www.umb.no/noragric/

Norges Geologiske Undersokelse
Geological Survey of Norway (2015)
Postboks 6315 Sluppen
7491 Trondheim
ngu@ngu.no
http://www.ngu.no/no/

Norwegian Institute of Science and Technology
Dept of Geology and Mineral Resources Engineering (2004)
N-7034 Trondheim
postmottak@ivt.ntnu.no

Norwegian Institute of Technology
Faculty of Engineering Science and Technology (2004)
S. P. Andersens vei 15A
N7034 Trondheim
p. 73594779
ingvald.strommen@ntnu.no

NTNU Norwegian University of Science and Technology
Dept of Geology and Mineral Resources Engineering
(B,M,D) (2014)
Sem Sælands vei 1
7491 Trondheim
Trondheim
p. (+47) 73 59 48 00
iigb-info@ivt.ntnu.no
http://www.ntnu.no/igb
f: https://www.facebook.com/geologibergNTNU

University of Bergen
Dept of Earth Science (2008)
Allegaten 41
N-5007 Bergen
post@geo.uib.no
http://www.geo.uib.no/

University of Oslo
Deptartment of Geosciences (B,M,D) (2015)
Post Box 1047, Blindern
N-0316 Oslo
p. +47 22856656
geosciences@geo.uio.no
http://www.mn.uio.no/geo/
f: https://www.facebook.com/uiogeo/

Mineralogical-Geological Museum (2014)
Sars gate 1
P.O. Box 1172
Blindern, Oslo 0318
p. +47 228 55050
postmottak@nhm.uio.no

http://www.nhm.uio.no/english/

University of Tromso
Geology Dept (2004)
N-9037 Tromso
kai.mortensen@uit.no
http://www.ibg.uit.no/geologi/geo_eng_end.html

Oman

Sultan Qaboos University
Dept of Earth Science (B,M,D) ● (2014)
123 Al-Khod
P.O. Box 36
Muscat
 p. +968 2414 6832
 khirbash@squ.edu.om
 http://www.squ.edu.om/earth-sci/tabid/11718/language/en-US/
 Enrollment (2013): B: 85 (60) M: 5 (25) D: 2 (1)
Head:
 Salah Al-Khirbash, (D)

Pakistan

COMSATS
Institute of Information Technology (2011)
Park Road, Chak Shahzad
Islamabad
 p. +92-51-9247000-2
 info@ciit.edu.pk
 http://www.comsats.edu.pk/

Geological Survey of Pakistan
(2014)
 p. (+958) 9211032
 qta@gsp.gov.pk
 http://www.gsp.gov.pk/

Institute of Space Technology
Institute of Space Technology (B,M,D) (2013)
P.O. Box 2750
Islamabad 44000
 p. 92.51.9075100
 info@ist.edu.pk
 http://www.ist.edu.pk/

National University of Sciences and Technology
Institute of Geographic Information System (2011)
RIMMS building, NUST H-12 Campus
Islamabad
 p. +92-51-90854400
 info@igis.nust.edu.pk
 http://igis.nust.edu.pk/

Sind University Pakistan
Dept of Geology (2004)
University of Sindh, Allama I.I. Kazi Campus
Jamshoro
Sindh 76080
 p. 92-22-9213172-9213181-90 Ext:
 dean.science@usindh.edu.pk

University of Engineering and Technology
Geological Engineering (2011)
 stgillani@uet.edu.pk
 http://www.uet.edu.pk/faculties/facultiesinfo/geological/
 index.html?RID=introduction

University of Karachi
Dept of Geology (2014)
KARACHI-75270
 p. 99261300-06 Ext: 2295
 vc@uok.edu.pk

---

http://uok.edu.pk/faculties/geology/

University of Sargodha
Dept of Earth Science (B,M,D) ● (2014)
Sargodha
 earthscience@uos.edu.pk
 http://www.uos.edu.pk

College of Agriculture (2011)
Sargodha
 agri@uos.edu.pk
 http://www.uos.edu.pk

University of the Punjab
Dept of Geography (2011)
New Campus
Lahore 54590
 chairman@geog.pu.edu.pk
 http://pu.edu.pk/home/department/46/Department-of-
 Geography

Panama

Universidad de Panama
Facultad de Ciencias Naturales, Exactas y Technologia (2004)
Urbanizacion El Cangrejo, Estafeta Universitaria
 ciencias@ancon.up.ac.pa

Paraguay

Universidad Nacional se Asuncion
Dept de Geologia (2004)
University Campus Km. 11, Asuncion
 facen@facen.una.py

Peru

Geological Survey of Peru
Instituto Geologico Minero y Metalurgico - INGEMMET (2013)
Av. Canada 1470 San Borja
Lima
 p. 051-1-6189800
 webmaster@ingemmet.gob.pe
 http://www.ingemmet.gob.pe/

San Agustin's Natl University
Escuela Academico Profesional de Ingenieria Geologica y Geofisica (2011)
Av. Indraendencia #1015
Arequipa
 p. (054) 244498
 geologia@unsa.edu.pe
 http://www.unsa.edu.pe

Univ Nacional de Ingeneiria
Escuela Academico Profesional de Ingenieria Geologica (2011)
Av. Tupac Amaru S/N
Rimac, Lima
 esanchez@uingemmet.gob.pe
 http://www.uni.edu.pe/sitio/academico/facultades/geo-
 logica/

Univ Nacional Mayor San Marcos
Escuela Academico Profesional de Ingenieria Geologica (2011)
Av. Venezuela S/N
Lima
 j_jacay@yahoo.com
 http://www.unmsm.edu.pe

science@unr.edu

Philippines

University of the Philippines
National Institute of Geological Sciences (B,M,D) ● (2014)
C.P. Garcia corner Velasquez Street
Diliman, Quezon City 1101
p. (+632) 9296046
inquire@nigs.org
http://nigs.org

Poland

AGH University of Science and Technology
Faculty of Geology, Geophysics, and Environmental Protection (2014)
A. Mickiewicza 30 Ave.
30-059 Krakow
p. +48 12 633 29 36
aglown@geol.agh.edu.pl
http://www.wggios.agh.edu.pl/

Faculty of Mining and Geoengineering (2014)
Al. Mickiewicza 30
PL-30059 Krakow
p. +48 12 617 21 15
gorn@agh.edu.pl

Jagiellonian University
Institute of Geological Sciences (2010)
Oleandry 2a Str.
30-063 Krakow
sekretariat.ing@uj.edu.pl
http://www.ing.uj.edu.pl

Ministry of Environmental Protection, Natural Resources and Forestry
Dept of Geology (2011)
st. Wawelska 52/54
00-922 Warsaw
Departament.Geologii.i.Koncesji.Geologicznych@mos.gov.pl
http://www.mos.gov.pl/dg/dga1.htm

Panstwowy Instytut Geologiczny
Polish Geological Institute (2011)
Ul. Rakowiecka 4 ,
PL-00-975 Warszawa
sekretariat@pgi.gov.pl
http://www.pgi.gov.pl/

Polish Academy of Sciences
Institute of Geological Sciences (2004)
Al Zwirki i Wigury 93
02-089 Warsaw
p. (+48 22) 620 33 46, 656 60 63
wydzial_3@pan.pl

Silesian University of Technology
Faculty of Mining and Geology (B,M,D) ● (2015)
Wydzial Gornictwa i Geologii
Politechnika Slaska
ul.Akademicka 2
Gliwice 44-100
p. +48 32 2371283
rg@polsl.pl
http://www.polsl.pl/Wydzialy/RG/Strony/Witamy.aspx
Enrollment (2014): B: 2556 (615) M: 327 (283) D: 98 (5)

Univ of Mining & Metallurgy
Dept of Mining and Metallurgical Engineering (2004)
Inst. of Drilling & Oil Exploration
Krakow

University of Wroclaw
Inst of Geological Sciences (B,M,D) (2015)
Pl. Maksa Borna 9
50-205 Wroclaw
p. (+4871) 321-10-76
sekretariat@ing.uni.wroc.pl
http://www.ing.uni.wroc.pl/ang/

Portugal

Istituto Geologico e Mineiro (IGM)
Geological and Mining Institute of Portugal (2011)
Estrada da Portela
Zambujal
atendimento@ineti.pt
http://www.ineti.pt/

Oporto University
Dept of Geology (2004)
Faculdade de Ciencias do Porto
Praca de Gomes Teixeira
4099-002 PORTO
lic.geo.diretor@fc.up.pt
http://www.fc.up.pt/depts/geo/indexi.html

Universidade da Madeira
Dept de Biologia (B) (2010)
Campus Universitario da Penteada
9000-390 Funchal
p. +251 291 705 380
thd@uma.pt
http://www.uma.pt/Unidades/Biologia/

Universidade de Aveiro
Dept de Geociencias (B,M,D) (2014)
Campo Universitario Santiago
Aveiro 3810-193
p. +351 234 370 357
tavares.rocha@ua.pt
www.ua.pt/geo
Professor:
Eduardo Ferreira da Silva, (D), CeGbCl

Universidade de Coimbra
Dept de Ciencias da Terra (2007)
Largo Marques de Pombal
Coimbra 3000-272 Coimbra
p. +351-239 860 500
luisneves@ci.uc.pt
http://www.dct.uc.pt
Associate Professor:
Alcides Castilho Pereira, (D), 1992, GebOr

Universidade de Lisboa
Dept of Geology (A,B,M,D) ● (2015)
Ed. C6, Campo Grande
Campo Grande
Lisboa 1749-016
p. +35121 750 00 66 / + 351 21 75
dgeologia@fc.ul.pt
http://www.fc.ul.pt/en/dg?refer=1
f: https://www.facebook.com/Departamento-de-Geologia-FCUL-192772970763173/?ref=ts
Professor:
Maria da Conceição Pombo Freitas, (D), Lisbon, 1996, GusGe

Universidade de Trás-os-Montes e Alto Douro
Departamento de Geologia (B,M,D) (2013)
Apartado 1013
Vila Real 5001-801
p. +351259350224
geologia@utad.pt

http://www.geologia.utad.pt

Professor:
Maria E.P. Gomes, (D), UTAD, 1996, GiCgGz
Associate Professor:
Ana M.P. Alencoão, (D), UTAD, 1998, HgGgm
Artur A.A. Sá, (D), UTAD, 2005, PgiPs
Assistant Professor:
Maria E.P.S. Abreu, (D), UTAD, 2012, GaaGa
João C.C.V. Baptista, (D), UTAD, 1998, GmmGa
Maria R.M. Costa, (D), UTAD, 2000, Hw
Paulo J.C. Favas, (D), UTAD, 2008, GeCtGg
José M.M. Lourenço, (D), UTAD, 2006, YeOin
Alcino S. Oliveira, (D), uTAD, 2002, Hww
Anabela R.R.C. Oliveira, (D), UTAD, 2011, Gss
Fernando A.L. Pacheco, (D), UTAD, 2001, Hq
Luís M.O. Sousa, (D), 2001, EnGgNg
Rui J.S. Teixeira, (D), UTAD, 2008
Nuno M.O.C.M. Vaz, (D), UTAD, 2010, PmlYg

Universidade do Minho
Dept de Ciencias da Terra (B,M,D) (2004)
Campus de Gualtar
Braga 4710-057
  p. 351 253 604 300
  paula@dct.uminho.pt
  http://www.dct.uminho.pt/index/index.html

Universidade Nova de Lisboa
Dept de Ciencias da Terra (2014)
Qta. da Torre
 2829-516 Caparica
  p. (351) 212 948 573
  dct.secretariado@fct.unl.pt
  http://www.dct.fct.unl.pt/

Qatar

University of Qatar
Dept of Geology (B) (2015)
PO Box 2713
Doha
Doha
  hamadsaad@qu.edu.qa
  http://www.angelfire.com/ms/GeoQU/
Professor:
Sobhi J. Nasir, (D), Germany, 1986, Gx
Associate Professor:
Hamad A. Al-Saad, (D), Egypt, 1996, PsGsu
Abdulali A. Sadiq, (D), Southampton (UK), 1995, Or
Assistant Professor:
Latifa B. AL-Nouimy, (D), Egypt, 1994, Hgw
Sief A. Alhajari, (D), North Carolina, 1992, Hgw

Reunion

Universite de la Reunion
Faculte de Sciences et Technologie - Sciences de la Terre
(B) (2014)
15, avenue Rene Cassin
CS 92003
Saint-Denis, Cedex 9 97744
  p. (262) 0262 938697
  jean-lambert.join@univ-reunion.fr
  http://sciences.univ-reunion.fr/rubrique.php3?id_ru-
  brique=72

Laboratoire GeoSciences Reunion (B,M,D) (2013)
15 avenue Rene Cassin
BP 7151
Saint Denis, Messag Cedex 9 97744
  vfamin@univ-reunion.fr
  http://www.geosciencesreunion.fr/
Professor:
Laurent Michon, (D), GtvGg
Professor:
Jean-Lambert Join, HwGsHg

236

Associate Professor:
Vincent Famin, (D), GcCgGg
Fabrice R. Fontaine, (D), Ysg
Claude Smutek, NrOrg

Romania

Al. I. Cuza University of Iasi
Dept of Geology (B,M,D) (2016)
geology@uaic.ro
B-dul Carol I nr. 20A
Iasi, Iasi 700505-RO, Ia
  geology@uaic.ro
  geology.uaic.ro
  Enrollment (2015): B: 59 (26) M: 40 (18) D: 11 (5)
Head:
Nicolae Buzgar, (D), Al. I. Cuza Iasi, 1998, GziGd
Conferentiar/ Reader:
Crina Miclaus, (D), Al. I. Cuza Iasii, 2001, Gsr
Professor:
Ovidiu Gabriel Iancu, (D), Al. I. Cuza Iasii, 1998, GpXgCg
Dan Stumbea, (D), Univ Babes-Bolya, 1998, Gez
Assistant Professor:
Traian Gavriloaiei, (D), Al. I. Cuza Iasi, 1999, CaOa
Lecturer:
Andrei Ionut Apopei, (D), Al. I. Cuza Iasi, 2014, GziGg
Andrei Buzatu, (D), Al. I. Cuza Iasi, 2014, GziGg
Mitica Pintilei, (D), Al. I. Cuza Iasi, 2010, CgeCt
Oana Stan, (D), Al. I. Cuza Iasii, 2009, Ge

Babes-Bolyai University
Faculty of Biology and Geology, Dept of Geology (B,M,D)
(2013)
Str. M. Kogalniceanu nr.1
RO - 400084 Cluj-Napoca
Cluj-Napoca 400084
  p. +40-264-405371
  ibucur@bioge.ubbcluj.ro
  http://www.ubbcluj.ro/faculties/biolgeol.html
Chair:
Sorin Filipescu, (D), Babes-Bolyai, 1996, GrPm
Professor:
Ioan Bucur, (D), Babes-Bolyai, 1991, PgmGs
Vlad Codrea, (D), Babes-Bolyai, 1995, PvGo

Institul Geologic al Romaniei
Geological Institute of Romania (2011)
Caransebes, 1 Sector 1
Bucuresti
  office@igr.ro
  http://www.igr.ro/

Universitatea din Bucuresti
Faculty of Geology and Geophysics (2004)
 Sector 5, 36-46 Mihail Kogalniceanu Blvd
Bucharest 50107
  p. +40-21-307 73 00
  secretariatgg@gmail.com
  http://www.unibuc.ro/e/facultati/geologie-geofizica

Rwanda

Universite Nationale du Rwanda
Dept of Geology (B) (2014)
Faculty of Science
PO Box 56
Butare
  p. +250 (0) 252 530 122
  info@nur.ac.rw
  http://www.nur.ac.rw/

Dept of Geography (B) (2010)
PO Box 56
Butare
  p. +250 (0) 252 530 122

info@nur.ac.rw
http://ww.nur.ac.rw/

Saudi Arabia

King Abdulaziz University
Dept of Geology (2015)
P. O. Box 1744
Building No 55
Jeddah 21441
jha25@hotmail.com
http://earthscience.kau.edu.sa/Default.aspx?Site_
ID=145&Lng=EN

King Fahd University of Petroleum and Minerals
Geosciences Dept (B,M,D) ● (2015)
P. O. Box 5070
KFUPM
Dhahran 31261
p. +96638602620
c-es@kfupm.edu.sa
http://www.kfupm.edu.sa/departments/es/default.aspx
Enrollment (2015): B: 52 (8) M: 77 (17) D: 6 (0)
Professor:
Gabor Korvin, (D), Heavy Industry (Hungary), 1979, Yx
Associate Professor:
Osman Abdullatif, (D), Khartoum, 1993, Gso
Abdulwahab Abokhodair, (D), California (Santa Cruz), 1978, Ym
Khalid Al-Ramadan, (D), Uppsala, Go
Abdulaziz Al-Shaibani, (D), Texas A&M, 1999, HwGeg
Abdullatif Al-Shuhail, (D), Texas A&M, 1998, Ygs
Mustafa Hariri, (D), SD Mines, 1995, GcOr
Michael Kaminski, (D), GuPm
Mohammad Makkawi, (D), Colarado Mines, 1998, Hw
Bassam Tawabini, (D), King Fahd, 2002, Ge
Assistant Professor:
Waleed Abdulghani, (D), Go
Abdullah Al-Shuhail, (D), Calgary, 2011, Ye
Ismail Kaka, (D), Carleton (Ottawa), 2006, Ys
Mohammed Qurban, (D)
Lecturer:
Ayman Al-Lehyani, (M), King Fahd, Yg
Mutasim Sami Osman, (M), KFUPM, 2014

Saudi Geological Survey
Saudi Geological Survey (2011)
P.O. Box: 54141
21514
p. 966-2-619-5000
sgs@sgs.org.sa
http://www.sgs.org.sa/Arabic/Pages/default.aspx

Senegal

Universite Cheikh Anta Diop
Dept de Geologie (B) (2011)
Faculte Des Sciences
BP 5005
Dakar-Fann
p. +221 869.27.66
fst@ucad.edu.sn
http://fst.ucad.sn/index.php?option=com_content&task=vie
w&id=19&Itemid=35

Institut des Sciences de l' Environneum (ISE) (B) (2010)
BP 5005
Dakar-Fann
p. +221 869.27.66
diengdiomaye@yahoo.fr
http://196.1.95.4/ise/index_ISE.htm

Sierra Leone

Njala University
Dept of Mining and Metallurgy (B) (2010)
Freetown
p. +232-22-228788, +232-22-226851
nuc@sierratel.sl
http://www.nu-online.com/

Dept of Soil Science (A,B,M,D) (2015)
Freetown
p. +232-22-228788, +232-22-226851
nuc@sierratel.sl
http://ww.nu-online.com/

Dept of Geography & Rural Development (B) (2010)
Freetown
p. +232-22-228788, +232-22-226851
nuc@sierratel.sl
http://www.nu-online.com/

Institute of Environmental Management and Quality Control (B)
(2010)
Freetown
p. +232-22-228788, +232-22-226851
nuc@sierratel.sl
http://www.nu-online.com/

University of Sierra Leone
Dept of Geology (2014)
PO Box 87
Freetown
aiah_gbakima2000@yahoo.com
http://www.tusol.org/programmes

Slovakia

Comenius University
Dept of Geology and Paleontology (A,B,M,D) O (2015)
Faculty of Science
Mlynska dolina G
Ilkovičova 6
Bratislava, Slovakia 842 15
p. 00421260296529
kgp@fns.uniba.sk
http://geopaleo.fns.uniba.sk/
Enrollment (2015): B: 7 (4) M: 4 (4) D: 11 (5)
Professor:
Michal Kováč,, (D), GsPeGg
Professor:
Dusan Plasienka, (D), Gt
Daniela Reháková, (D), PgmPe

Dionyz Stur Institute of Geology
Geology Dept (2015)
Mlynska Dolina 1
81704 Bratislava 11
p. 02 / 59375111
secretary@geology.sk
http://www.geology.sk/new/en

Geologicka Sluzba Slovenskej Republiky
Geological Survey of Slovak Republic (2011)
Mill Valley 1
817 04 Bratislava 11
secretary@geology.sk
http://www.sguds.sk

Kosice Technical University
**Faculty of Mining, Ecology, Process Control and Geotech-
nology** (2014)
Fakulta BERG
Park Komenskeho 12
040 01 Kosice
p. +421-55-602 1111

sekrd.fberg@tuke.sk
http://www.fberg.tuke.sk/bergweb/index.
php?IdLang=0&Selection=4

Slovenia

Geoloski zavod Slovenije
Geological Survey of Slovenia (M,D) (2014)
Dimiceva ulica 14
Ljubljana SI - 1000
p. +386 1 2809702
www@geo-zs.si
http://www.geo-zs.si

University of Ljubljaa
Oddelek za Geologijo (2011)
Askerceva 12
Ljubljana
spela.turic@ntf.uni-lj.si
http://www.ntf.uni-lj.si/og

University of Ljubljana
Faculty of natural science and engineering (2014)
Aškerčeva c. 12
Ljubljana 1000
p. 01/470-45-00
tanja.kocevar@ntf.uni-lj.si
http://www.uni-lj.si/academies_and_faculties/facul-
ties/2013071111502957/

Somalia

Burao University
Dept of Community Development (B) (2010)
p. +252 7126481
Universityburao@hotmail.com
http://www.buraouniversity.com/rural_and_environmen-
tal_studies.htm

Mogadishu University
Somali Centre for Water and Environment (B) (2014)
p. (252)-5-932454/ 223433/ 658479
info@mogadishuuniversity.com
http://www.mogadishuuniversity.com/index.html

Nugaal University
Institute of Geology (B) (2015)
Lasanod
p. +252 275 4063 / 7412619
nugaaluniversity@gmail.com
http://www.nugaaluniversity.com/index.html

South Africa

Cape Peninsula University of Technology
Dept of Environmental and Occupational Studies (B) (2010)
Cape Town
p. (+27) 021 959 6230
ntapanev@cput.ac.za
http://www.cput.ac.za/

Geological Survey of South Africa
Council for Geoscience ● (2015)
Private Bag X112
Pretoria 0001
p. 0027128411911
info@geoscience.org.za
http://www.geoscience.org.za/
Executive Manager:
  Fhatuwani L. Ramagwede, (M), 2011, EgGzEg

Nelson Mandela Metropolitan University
Centre for African Conservation Ecology (M,D) O (2015)
Summerstand Campus (South)
PO Box 77000
Port Elizabeth 6031
p. +27 41 504 2308
Graham.Kerley@nmmu.ac.za
http://ace.nmmu.ac.za/

Coastal and Marine Research Institute (B) (2010)
Summerstand Campus (South)
PO Box 77000
Port Elizabeth 6031
p. +27 41 5042877
cmr@nmmu.ac.za
http://www.nmmu.ac.za/default.asp?id=380&bhcp=1

Dept of Geoscience (B,M,D) (2014)
PO Box 77000
Summerstrand, Port Elizabeth 6031
p. 041 504 2325
sheila.entress@nmmu.ac.za
http://geosci.nmmu.ac.za/
Administrative Assistant: Sheila Entress
Enrollment (2002): B: 65 (22) M: 7 (0) D: 1 (0)
Head:
  Nigel Webb, (D)
Professor:
  Maarten De Wit
  Vincent Kakembo, Sp
Associate Professor:
  Moctar Doucoure, (D)
  Daniel Mikes, (D)
Lecturer:
  Callum Anderson, (M)
  Wilma Britz, (D)
  Gideon Brunsdon, (M)
  Anton de Wit, (D)
  Pakama Syongwana, (D)
  Nicolas Tonnelier, (D)
  Leizel Williams-Bruinders, (M)
Emeritus:
  Peter Booth, (D)
  Anthony Christopher
Post-Doctoral Fellowship:
  Bastien Linol, (D)
Related Staff:
  Paul Baldwin
  Willie Deysel

North-West University
School of Environmental and Health Sciences (B) (2010)
Private Bag x 1290
Potchefstroom 2520
p. (27) 18 299 2528
plbmsc@puk.ac.za
http://www.puk.ac.za/opencms/export/PUK/html/fakulteite/
natur/geol/index_e.html

Rhodes University
Institute for Water Research (M,D) (2014)
PO Box 94
Grahamstown 6140
p. +27 46 62224014 / 6222428 / 62
registrar@ru.ac.za
http://www.ru.ac.za/static/institutes/iwr//?request=institutes/
iwr/
Professor:
  Denis Hughes, (D), Wales, 1978, Hqs

Dept of Geology (B,M,D) (2014)
PO Box 94
Grahamstown , Eastern Cape Provinc 6140
p. +27 (0)46 603 8309
geolsec@ru.ac.za
http://www.ru.ac.za/geology/
Administrative Assistant: Ashley Goddard
Administrative Assistant: Vuyokazi Nkayi

Head:
    Steve Prevec, Cg
Professor:
    Steffen Butner, Gc
    Annette Gotz, Gs
    Peter Horvath, (D), Gp
    Bantubonke Izwe Ntsaluba, Gi
    Briony Proctor
    Hari Tsikos, CgEg
    Yon Yao, Eg
Associate Scientist:
    Billy De Klerk, Pg
    Robert Gess, Pg
    Rose Prevec
    Mike Skinner
Emeritus:
    Roger Jacobs
    J.S. "Goonie" Marsh, Gi
Laboratory Director:
    Gelu Costin, Gp
Cooperating Faculty:
    John Hepple

Dept of Geography (B) (2010)
PO Box 94
Grahamstwon 6140
    p. +27 (0)46 603 8111
    registrar@ru.ac.za
    http://oldwww.ru.ac.za/academic/departments/geography/

Stellenbosch University
Dept of Earth Sciences (B,M,D) (2015)
Private Bag X1
Matieland, Western Cape 7602
    p. +27 (0)21 808 3219
    lcon@sun.ac.za
    http://www.sun.ac.za/earthSci/
Professor:
    Alakendra N. Roychoudhury, (D), Georgia Tech, 1999, ClmOc

Dept of Process Engineering (Chemical and Mineral Processing) (B,M,D) (2015)
Private Bag X1
Matieland 7602
    p. +27 21 808-4485
    chemeng@sun.ac.za
    http://www.chemeng.sun.ac.za/

Tshwane University of Technology
Dept of Environmental Health (B) (2010)
Private Bag X680
Staatsartillerie Road
Pretoria West 0001
    p. +27 (0)12 382 5911
    general@tut.ac.za
    http://www.tut.ac.za/Pages/default.aspx

Dept of Environmental, Water & Earth Sciences (B,M,D) (2015)
Private Bag x680
Pretoria 0001
    p. 012 382 6232
    gerberme@tut.ac.za
    http://www.tut.ac.za/Students/facultiesdepartments/science/
    departments/environscience/Pages/default.aspx
    Administrative Assistant: Sarah Galebies
    Administrative Assistant: Retha Gerber
    Enrollment (2015): B: 59 (37) M: 1 (0)
Lecturer:
    Chamunorwa Kambewa, (M), MSc Mineral Exploration, 1998,
    CgeOe
    Thando Majodina, (M), GgzGe
    Skhumbuzo Sibeko, (B), GggGg
Other:
    Mlindelwa Lupankwa, (D), HywGg

University of Cape Town
Dept of Oceanography (B) (2010)
Private Bag X3
Rhondebosch 7701
    p. +27 (0) 21 650-3277
    cashifa.karriem@uct.ac.za
    http://www.sea.uct.ac.za/index.php

Dept of Environmental and Geographical Science (B) (2010)
Shell Environmental & Geographical Science Building
South Lane, Upper Campus
Private Bad X3
Rondebosch 7701
    p. (27) 21 - 6502873 / 4
    sci-science@uct.ac.za
    http://www.egs.uct.ac.za/

Dept of Geological Sciences (B,M,D) ● (2016)
Private Bag X3
Rondebosch 7701, Western Cape
    p. +27 (0)21-650-2931 
    head.geologicalsciences@uct.ac.za
    http://www.geology.uct.ac.za/
    Administrative Assistant: Lynn Evon
    Administrative Assistant: Denise Lesch
    Enrollment (2014): B: 30 (30) M: 30 (8) D: 10 (0)
Head:
    Chris Harris, GiCsGg
Professor:
    Steve Richardson, Cg
Senior Scientist:
    Nicholas Laidler
    Petrus Le Roux
    Christel Tinguely
Associate Professor:
    John Compton, Cm
Associate Scientist:
    Fayrooza Rawoot
Lecturer:
    Emese Bordy, Gs
    Johann Diener, Gp
    Lynnette Greyling, Eg
    Phillip Janney
    Beth Kahle, YgEoYg
Laboratory Director:
    Kerryn Gray

University of Fort Hare
Dept of Geography, Land Use, and Environmental Sciences
(B) (2014)
Private Bag X1314
Alice 5700
    p. +27 (0)40 602 2011
    wkoll@ufh.ac.za
    http://www.ufh.ac.za/

Dept of Geology (2014)
Sobukwe Walk 8
Livingstone Hall
Alice, Eastern Cape 5700
    p. +27 (0)40 602 2011
    wkoll@ufh.ac.za
    http://wvw.ufh.ac.za/departments/geology/
Head:
    Oswald Gwavava
Lecturer:
    CJ Gunter
    Vuyokazi Mazomba
Related Staff:
    Luzuko Sigabi

Dept of Geographic Information Systems (B) (2014)
Private Bag X1314
Alice 5700
    p. +27 (0)40 602 2011
    wkoll@ufh.ac.za

http://www.ufh.ac.za/departments/gis/gishome.html

University of Johannesburg
Dept of Geography, Environmental Management & Energy Studies (B,M,D) (2014)
PO Box 524
Auckland Park, Gauteng 2006
p. +27 (0)11 559 2433
science@uj.ac.za
http://www.uj.ac.za/Default.aspx?alias=www.uj.ac.za/geography
Dr:
Isaac T. Rampedi, (D), South Africa, 2010, PySdHg

Dept of Geology (B) (2010)
PO Box 524
Kingsway & University (APK Campus)
Auckland Park 2006
p. +27 (11) 559-4701
brucec@uj.ac.za
http://www.uj.ac.za/Default.aspx?alias=www.uj.ac.za/geology

Dept of Mine Surveying (B) (2010)
p. +27 (0)11 559-6186
engineeringbe@uj.ac.za
http://www.uj.ac.za/Default.aspx?alias=www.uj.ac.za/minesurv

Dept of Mining Engineering (B) (2010)
PO Box 17011
Doornfontein 2028
p. +27 (0)11 559-6628
pearln@uj.ac.za
http://www.uj.ac.za/Default.aspx?alias=www.uj.ac.za/mining

University of KwaZulu-Natal
School of Civil Engineering Surveying & Construction (B) (2014)
Centenary Building
King George V Avenue
Durban 4041
p. (+27) 2603065
troisc@ukzn.ac.za
http://geomatics.ukzn.ac.za/HomePage2247.aspx

Centre for Water Resources Research (B,M,D) (2015)
Room 203
Rabie Saunders Building
Pietermaritzburg, KwaZulu-Natal 3201
p. +27-(0)33-260 5490
smithers@ukzn.ac.za
http://cwrr.ukzn.ac.za/

School of Environmental Sciences (B,M) (2014)
Howard College Campus
King George V Avenue
Durban
p. + 27 031 260 2416
sheriffs@ukzn.ac.za
http://ses.ukzn.ac.za/homepage.aspx

School of Geological Sciences (A,B,M,D) (2012)
Private Bag X 54001
University Road ; Westville
Durban 4000
, KwaZulu-Natal
p. +27 (0)31 260 2516
mackroryd@ukzn.ac.za
http://www.geology.ukzn.ac.za/

University of Limpopo
School of Physical and Mineral Science (B) (2015)
Turfloop Campus
Private Bag X1106
Sovenga 0727

p. +27(0) 15 268 3492
SPMS@ul.ac.za
http://www.ul.ac.za/index.php?Entity=School%20Main%20Menu&school_id=9
Administrative Assistant: M. D.. Ramusi
Head:
K. E. Rammutia
Professor:
J. Dunlevey
M. Khanyi
M. A. Letsoalo
M. A. Mahladisa
R. M. Makwela
T, Mobakazi
T. E. Mosuang
J. M. T. Mphahlele
T. T. Netshisaulu
M. Netsianda
P. Ntoahee
O. O. Nubi
M. Phala
M. J. Ramusi
L. Wilsenach
Related Staff:
J. P. T. Crafford

Dept of Soil Sciences (B) (2014)
Turfloop Campus
Private Bag X1106
Sovenga 0727
p. +27 (0)15 268 9111
Funso.Kutu@ul.ac.za
http://www.ul.ac.za/index.php?Entity=agri_soil_scie

Geography & Environmental Studies Dept (B) (2014)
Turfloop Campus
Private Bag X1106
Sovenga 0727
p. (+27) (0)15 268 3756
salphy.ramokolo@ul.ac.za
http://www.ul.ac.za/index.php?Entity=agri_geo_environ

University of Pretoria
Centre of Environmental Studies (M,D) (2010)
Pretora 0002
p. +27 (0)12 420-3111
mdobson@zoology.up.ac.za
http://www.up.ac.za/centre-environmental-studies/index.php

University of Pretoria Natural Hazards Centre (M,D) (2015)
Department of Geology
University of Pretoria, Private Bag X20, Hatfield,
PRETORIA, 0028
Pretoria 0028
p. +27 (0)12 420 3613
andrzej.kijko@up.ac.za
http://www.up.ac.za/university-of-pretoria-natural-hazard-centre-africa
Professor:
Andrzej Kijko, (D), Ysg
Research Associate:
Ansie Smit, (M)

Dept of Mining Engineering (B,M,D) (2014)
Pretoria 0002
p. +27 0 12 420-3111
csc@up.ac.za
http://web.up.ac.za/default.asp?ipkCategoryID=2520

Dept of Geography, Geoinformatics and Meteorology (B,M,D) (2015)
Room 3-7
Geography Building
Cnr Lynnwood and University Roads
Hatfield, Pretoria 0083
p. +27 (0)12 420 3536

240

lunga.ngcongo@up.ac.za
http://web.up.ac.za/ggm
Administrative Assistant: M. C.. van Aardt
Head:
C.J. deW. Rautenbach
Associate Professor:
Serena M. Coetzee, (D)
P. D. Sumner
Lecturer:
Daniel Darkey
Nerhene Davis
Liesl Dyson
Joos Esterhuizen
Natalie S. Haussmann
Michael Loubser
P. L. Philemon Tsela
Barend van der Merwe
Fritz van der Merwe
Related Staff:
Ingrid Booysen
Popi Mahlangu
Tebogo Moremi
Erika Pretorius

Dept of Geology (B) (2010)
Pretoria 0002
   p. +27 (0)12 420 2454
   pat.eriksson@up.ac.za
   http://web.up.ac.za/default.asp?ipkCategoryID=2048

University of Stellenbosch
Centre for Geographical Analysis (B) (2010)
Private Bag X1
Matieland 7602
   p. (27) 21 808 3218
   avn@sun.ac.za
   http://academic.sun.ac.za/cga/expertise/user.
   asp?UserID=11

University of the Free State
Dept of Geology (B,M,D) ● (2014)
PO Box 339
Bloemfontein, Free State Province 9300
   p. +27 (0)51 401 2515
   roelofsef@ufs.ac.za
   http://natagri.ufs.ac.za/content.aspx?DCode=108
   Enrollment (2014): B: 237 (98) M: 13 (9) D: 4 (0)
Dr:
Frederick Roelofse, (D), the Witwatersrand, Gip
Prof:
Willem van der Westhuizen, (D), the Free State, CgGgv
Prof:
Wayne Colliston, (D), the Free State, GcNr
Chris Gauert, (D), Pretoria, EgGi
Marian Tredoux, (D), the Witwatersrand, Cga
Ms:
Justine Magson, (B), the Free State, CgGi
Thendo Mapholi, (B), the Free State, Ggp
Makhadi Rinae, (B), the Free State, Gge
Mr:
Adriaan Odendaal, (B), the Free State, Ggs
Rentel Raimund, (M), Stellenbosch, Gz
Dr:
Johann Claassen, (D), Pretoria, Nx
Hermann Praekelt, (D), the Free State, Gcs
Ms:
Megan Purchase, (M), the Free State, On

Centre for Environmental Management (B) (2010)
Po Box 338
Bloemfontein 9300
   p. +27(0)51-4019111
   avenantMF@ufs.ac.za
   http://www.ufs.ac.za/faculties/index.
   php?FCode=04&DCode=106

Institute for Groundwater Studies (B,M,D) (2016)
PO Box 339
Internal Bus 56
Bloemfontein 9300
   p. +27(0)51-4019111
   vermeulend@ufs.ac.za
   http://www.ufs.ac.za/igs

University of the Western Cape
International Ocean Institute of Southern Africa (B) (2010)
Private Bag X17
Bellville 7535
   p. +27 21 959 3088
   info@uwc.ac.za
   http://www.ioisa.org.za/

Dept of Earth Science (B) (2014)
Modderdam Road
Private Bag X17
Bellville, Cape Town 7530
   p. +27 (0)21 959 2223
   wdavids@uwc.ac.za
   http://www.uwc.ac.za/Faculties/NS/EarthScience/Pages/
   default.aspx
   Administrative Assistant: Caroline Barnard
   Administrative Assistant: Wasielah Davids
   Administrative Assistant: Chantal Johannes
   Administrative Assistant: Mandy Naidoo
Head:
Charles Okujeni, (D), Berlin, Germany
Chair:
Jacqueline Goldin, (D), UCT
Yongxin Xu
Professor:
Jan van Bever Donkey, (D)
Dominic Mazvimavi, (D), Wageningen Univ, 2003
Associate Professor:
Ebernard Braune
Lecturer:
Marcelene Andrews
James Ayuk Ayuk, (M), UWC
Lewis Jonkey, (M)
Thokozani Kanyerere
Mimonitu Opuwari, (D), UWC
Henok Solomon, (M), UWC
VLIR Coordinator:
Shauib Dustay
HIVE Manager:
Yafah Hoosain, (M), UWC
Deputy Head:
Theo Scheepers, (M), Stellenbosch
Related Staff:
Janine Becorney
Shamiel Davids
Peter Meyer

University of the Witwatersrand
School of Geography, Archaeology and Environmental Studies (B) (2014)
Private Bag 32050
Wits, Johannesburg
   p. +27 11 717 6503
   donna.koch@wits.ac.za
   http://web.wits.ac.za/Academic/Science/Geography/Home.htm

School of Mining Engineering (B,M,D) ● (2015)
Private Bag 3
WITS, Johannesburg 2050
   p. +27 11-717-7003
   bekir.genc@wits.ac.za
   http://web.wits.ac.za/Academic/EBE/MiningEng/

School of Geosciences (B,M,D) ● (2016)
Faculty of Science
Private Bag 3
Wits, Johannesburg 2050

p. 27 11 717 6547
sharon.ellis@wits.ac.za
http://web.wits.ac.za/Academic/Science/GeoSciences/Home.htm
Professor:
 Lewis D. Ashwal, (D), Princeton, 1979, GxCgGz
 Roger L. Gibson, (D), Cambridge, 1990, GcpGg
 Kim AA Hein, (D), Tasmania, 1995, GgEmGc
 Judith A. Kinnaird, (D), St. Andrews, 1987, EmGi
Associate Professor:
 Paul A.M. Nex, (D), Univ Coll (Cork), 1997, Eg
Dr:
 Michael QW Jones, (D), the Witwatersrand, 1981, YhGtYg
Electron Microprobe Scientist:
 Peter Horvath, (D), Eotvos Lorand, 2002, GpCpGz
Dr:
 Grant M. Bybee, (D), the Witwatersrand, 2013, Gi
 Katie A. Smart, (D), Alberta, 2011, CsGx
Doctor:
 Zubair A. Jinnah, (D), the Witwatersrand, 2011, GsPg
Emeritus:
 Carl R. Anhaeusser, (D), the Witwatersrand, 1983, GgEgOg

University of Venda
Mining and Environmental Geology (A,B,M,D) (2013)
School of Environmental Science
Private Bag X5050
Thohoyandou , Limpopo Province 0950
 p. +27 159628580
 ogolaj@univen.ac.za
 http://www.univen.ac.za/environmental_sciences/dep_min-ing_environmental.html
Dr.:
 Milton Kataka, (D), Witwatersrand, 2003

University of Venda for Science & Technology
GIS Resource Centre (B,M,D) (2015)
GIS Resource Centre
Private Bag x5050
Thohoyandou, Limpopo 0950
 p. +27 15 962 8044
 farai.dondofema@univen.ac.za
 http://www.univen.ac.za/environmental_sciences/gis_cen-tre.html
 t: @chinomukutu3
 Enrollment (2015): B: 90 (0) M: 8 (0) D: 1 (0)
Chief Technician:
 Farai Dondofema, (M), Zimbabwe, 2007, OrHgOi

Institute of Semi-Arid Environment and Disaster Management (B) (2014)
 p. (+27) 015 962 8513
 ndidzum@univen.ac.za
 http://www.univen.ac.za/index.php?Entity=Institute%20of%20Semi-Arid%20Environment&Sch=3

Dept of Geography and Geo-Information Sciences (B) (2014)
University of Venda
Private Bag X5050
Thohoyandou, Limpopo 0950
 p. +27 15 962 8593
 nthaduleni.nethengwe@univen.ac.za
 http://www.univen.ac.za/enviornmental_sciences/dep_ge-ography_geo_sciences.html
Head:
 N. S. Nethengwe, (D), West Virginia
Lecturer:
 T. M. Helwamondo, (D), UP
 E. Kori, (M), Univen
 M. J. Mokgoebo, (M), Univen
 N. V. Mudau, (M), Univen
 A. Muyoki, (D), Howard
 M. Nembudani, (M), Stellenbosch
Related Staff:
 K. H. Mathivha, (M), Univen

Dept of Hydrology and Water Resources (B) (2014)
University of Venda
Private Bag X5050
Thohoyandou, Limpopo 0950
 p. +27 015 962 8513
 environmental@univen.ac.za
 http://www.univen.ac.za/environmental_sciences/dep_hy-drology_water.html
Head:
 J. O. Odiyo, (D)
Lecturer:
 J. R. Gumbo, (D)
 P. M. Kundu, (D)
 R. Makungo, (M)
Related Staff:
 T. R. Nkuna, (M)

University of Zululand
Dept of Geography and Environmental Studies (B) (2010)
Private Bag X1001
KwaDlangezwa 3886
 p. +27 (035) 902 6282
 lshandu@pan.uzulu.ac.za
 http://www.uzulu.ac.za/scie_geo_env.php

Dept of Hydrology (B,M,D) O (2015)
Private Bag X1001
KwaDlangezwa 3886
 p. +27 (035) 902 6282
 SimonisJ@unizulu.ac.za
 http://www.uzulu.ac.za/scie_hydro.php
 Enrollment (2014): B: 60 (30)

Spain

Coruna University
University Institute of Geology (D) (2016)
Edificio Servicios Centrales de Investigación
Campus de Elviña s/n
La Coruna 15071
 p. 0034 981167000
 xeoloxia@udc.es
 http://www.udc.es/iux
 Enrollment (2015): D: 8 (80)
Director:
 Juan Ramon Vidal Romaní, (D), Complutense (Madrid), 1983, GmIGc
Professor:
 Antonio Paz Gonzalez, (D), Santiago de Compostela, 1982, Sd
Paleontologist:
 Aurora Grandal d'Anglade, (D), Coruña, 1993, Pv
Associate Professor:
 Elena Pilar de Uña Alvarez, (D), Santiago de Compostela, 1986, Oy
 Cruz Iglesias, (D), Corunna, 2001, GaOmNr
 María Teresa Taboada Castro, (D), Santiago de Compostela, 1990, Sd
Associate Scientist:
 Marcos Vaqueiro Rodriguez, (M), Vigo (Spain), GcmYd
Research Associate:
 Jorge Sanjurjo, (D), Corunna, 2005, GaCcPy

Instituto De Ciencias Del Mar
Consejo Superior de Investigaciones (2014)
Promenade de la Barcelona
08003 Barcelona
 p. (+34) 63 230 95 00
 secredir@icm.csic.es
 http://www.icm.csic.es/

Instituto Geologico y Minero de Espana
Instituto Geologico y Minero de Espana (2011)
Rios Rosas, 23
28003 Madrid
 igme@igme.es
 http://www.igme.es

Univ Complutense de Madrid
Facultad de Ciencias Geologicas (B,M) (2010)
C/ Jose Antonio Novais 12
Cuidad Universitaria
Madrid E-28040
    p. 34 91394 4819
    infoweb@geo.ucm.es
    http://www.ucm.es/centros/webs/fgeo
    Enrollment (2010): M: 89 (0)
Dean:
    Eumenio Ancochea, (D), Fac CC Geologicas (Madrid), 1972, Gvv
International Relations Vicedean:
    Agustin P. Pieren, (D), Fac CC Geologicas, 1982, GrEgg

Universidad Autonoma de Madrid
Departamento de Geologia y Geoquimica (M,D) O (2016)
Facultad de ciencias
Campus de Cantoblanco, C/ Francisco Tomás y Valiente, 7
Módulo 06, 6ª planta
Madrid 28049
    p. 91 497 48 00
    directora.geologia@uam.es
    http://www.uam.es/GyG
    Enrollment (2014): M: 15 (5) D: 11 (7)

Universidad de Alicante
Environment and Earth Sciences Dept (B,M,D) (2013)
Facultad de Ciencia
San Vicente de Raspeig
Alicante E-03080
    p. (+34) 96 590 3552
    dctma@ua.es
    http://dctma.ua.es/en/environment-and-earth-sciences-department.html

Universidad de Granada
Dept de Geologia (2004)
Andalusian Institute of Geophysics
Campus Universitario de la Cartuja
18071 Granada
    jaguirre@ugr.es
    http://www.ugr.es/iag/iagpds.html

Universidad de Huelva
Geologia (B,M,D) (2011)
Huelva
    p. 959219809
    secgeo@uhu.es
    http://www.uhu.es/dgeo/

Universidad de Jaen
Departamento de Geologia (B,M,D) O (2015)
Edificio B-3
Campus Universitario
Jaen 23071
    p. +34-953-212295
    jmmolina@ujaen.es
    http://geologia.ujaen.es/

Universidad de Las Palmas de Gran Canaria
Dept de Fisica (B) (2011)
C/Juan de Quesada, nº 30
, Las Palmas de Gran C 35001
    p. (+34) 928 451 000/023
    universidad@ulpgc.es
    http://www.dfis.ulpgc.es/

Facultad de Ciencias del Mar (B,M,D) (2014)
Edificio de Ciencias Básicas
Campus Universitario de Tafira
Las Palmas de Gran Canaria, Las Palmas 35017
    p. +34 928 452 900
    sec_dec_fcm@ulpgc.es

    www.fcm.ulpgc.es
    f: https://www.facebook.com/groups/www.fcm.ulpgc.es/?fref=ts

Universidad de Murcia
Dept of Geography and Regional Planning (2004)
Facultad de Sciencia
Calle Santo Cristo 1
Murcia 30100
    p. (868) 88-7446
    jagb@um.es

Universidad de Oviedo
Dept de Geologia (2005)
Campus de Llamaquique
Jesus Arias de Velasco, s/n
33005 Oviedo E-33005
    geodir@geol.uniovi.es
    http://www.geol.uniovi.es/

Universidad de Pais Vascu
Dept de Geologia (2004)
Facultad de Sciencia
37008 Salamanca
    p. 946015491
    sec-centro.fct@ehu.es

Universidad de Palma de Mallorca
Dept de Geologia/Geofisica (2004)
Facultad de Sciencia
07012 Palma

Universidad de Sevilla
Applied Geology to Civil Engineering (D) O (2014)
Departamento de Cristalografía y Mineralogía
calle Profesor García González 1
Seville 410012
    p. +34954556318
    igonza@us.es
    http://www.departamento.us.es/dcmqa/
Professor:
    Isabel González, (D), GzeSc

Universidad de Valencia
Dept de Geologia (M,D) (2015)
Faculty of Biological Sciences
Building A (2nd and 3rd floor)
C/ Dr. Moliner, 50
Burjassot- (Valencia) 46100
    p. (+34) 96 354 46 02
    dep.geologia@uv.es
    http://www.uv.es/geologia

Universidad de Valladolid
Dept of Geography (2004)
Facultad de Faculty of Philosophy and Arts
Palacio Santa Cruz/Plaza Santa Cruz B
Valladolid
    p. +34 983 423 005
    belart@fyl.uva.es

Universidad de Zaragoza
Facultad de Ciencias (2004)
50.009 Zaragoza
    anperez@posta.unizar.es
    http://wzar.unizar.es/acad/fac/geolo/adepo.html

Museo Paleontologico de la Universidad (2004)
    mpznavas@unizar.es
    http://ebro.unizar.es/uz/museo/

Universitat Autonoma de Barcelona
Geologia (B,M,D) (2013)

Facultat de Ciencies, Edifici C
Campus UAB
Bellaterra
08193
 p. +34 93 581 3022
 d.geologia@uab.es
 http://departaments.uab.cat/geologia/
Professor:
 David Gómez Gras, (D), Gd
Professor:
 María Luísa Arboleya Cimadevilla, (D), Gc
 Joan Bach Plaza, (D), Gg
 Esteve Cardellach López, (D), GzeCs
 Jordi Carreras Planells, (D), Gc
 Esmeralda Caus Gracia, (D), Pm
 Eugènia Estop Graells, (D), Gz
 Francisco Martínez Fernández, (D), GpCp
 Juan Francesc Piniella Febrer, (D), Gz
 Antoni Teixell Cácharo, GtcYx
Associate Professor:
 Lluís Casas Duocastella, (D), GzaYm
 Mercè Corbella Cordomí, (D), GzCl
 Elena Druguet Tantiña, (D), Gc
 Joan Estalrich López, (D), HgGe
 Rita Estrada Oliveras, (D), Grs
 Gúmer García Galán, (D), GiCg
 Eulàlia Gili Folch, Pge
 Ricard Martínez Ribas, (D), Pi
 Oriol Oms Llobet, (D), GrsYm
 Josep Maria Pons Muñoz, Pv
 Joan Reche Estrada, (D), GpCp
 Eduard Remacha Grau, (D), Gro
 Mario Zarroca Hernández, (D), YgNg
Assistant Professor:
 Rogelio Linares, (D), NgYx
 Valentí Oliveras Castro, (D), Gvi
 Joan Poch Serra, (D), Gr
Lecturer:
 Julien Babault, (D), OiGm
 Albert Griera Artigas, (D), GcCl
 Enric Vicens Batet, (D), Pg

Universitat de Barcelona
Estratigrafia, Paleontologia i Geociencies marines (2006)
c/Marti Franques, s/n
08028
Barcelona
 p. +33 934021384
 secretaria-geologia@ub.edu
 http://www.ub.es/dpep/1welcom3.htm

Dept de Geoquimica, Petrologia I Prospeccio Geologica (2004)
Marti Franques, s/n
Barcelona
8028
 dept-geoquimica@ub.edu
 http://www.ub.es/geoquimi/index.html

Facultat de Geologia (B,M,D) O (2016)
Martí Franqués s/n
Catalanes 585
Barcelona 08028
 p. +34 934 021 337
 deganat-geologia@ub.edu
 http://www.ub.edu/geologia/en/

Universitat de les Illes Balears
Dept de Ciencies de la Terra (B,M,D) (2013)
Carretera de Valldemossa, km 7.5
Palma, Balearic Islands 07122
 p. +34 971172362
 dct@uib.es
 http://www.uib.es/depart/dctweb/home.htm

University of the Basque Country
Departamento de Geodinamica (B,M,D) (2014)
244

Facultad de Ciencia y Tecnología
Barrio Sarriena, s/n
48080 Bilbao, Vizcaya 48940 Leioa
 p. + 34. 94 601 2563
 julia.cuevas@ehu.es
 http://www.geodinamica.ehu.es/s0001-home1/es/

Univesidad de Malaga
Dept de Geography (2004)
El Ejido
29071 Malaga
 rlarrubia@uma.es

Sri Lanka
Sabaragamuwa University of Sri Lanka
Dept of Natural Resources (2011)
P.O Box 02
Belihuloya , Sabaragamuwa Provinc
 p. 0094-45-2280293
 head_nr@sab.ac.lk
 http://www.sab.ac.lk

Sri Lanka Geological Survey & Mines Bureau
Sri Lanka Geological Survey & Mines Bureau (2011)
Senanayake Building, No 4, Galle Road,
Dehiwala
 gsmb@slt.lk
 http://www.gsmb.gov.lk/

University of Moratuwa
Dept of Earth Resources Engineering (2011)
Katubedda, Moratuwa
Western Province
Moratuwa
 p. 0094-11-2650353
 shiromi@earth.mrt.ac.lk
 http://www.ere.mrt.ac.lk/

University of Peradeniya
Dept of Geology (2011)
Central Province
Peradeniya 22000
 p. 0094-81 2394 200/201
 geology@pdn.ac.lk
 http://www.pdn.ac.lk/sci/geology/

Uwa Wellassa University of Sri Lanka
Dept Mineral Resources & Technology (2011)
2nd Mile Post Passara Road
Badulla , Uwa province
 p. 0094-55-2226400
 info@uwu.ac.lk
 http://www.uwu.ac.lk/

Sudan
Cairo University
Dept of Geology (2004)
Khartoum Branch
PO Box 1055
Khartoum

El-Neelain University
Dept of Geology (B) (2010)
Gamhuria Street
Khartoum
 p. +249 (183) 77-441
 http://www.neelain.edu/sd/english.index.htm

Gama'at El Khartoum
Dept of Geology (2014)
PO Box 321

Khartoum
> geology@uofk.edu
> http://science.uofk.edu/index.php?option=com_content&vie
> w=article&id=101&Itemid=128&lang=en

International University of Africa
Dept of Geology (B) (2010)
PO Box 2469
Khartoum
> p. (+249) 183 223211
> minerals@iua.edu.sd
> http://www.iua.edu.sd/upldep.htm

Sudan University of Science and Technology
Surveying Engineering Dept (B) (2010)
Southern and Northern Campus
Khartoum
> p. +249183468622
> ceng@sustech.edu
> http://www.sustech.edu/faculty_en/department.php?coll_no
> =9&chk=a7b751cd18a66f8cd84b301f24267aab

College of Water & Environmental Engineering (B) (2010)
> p. +24985200512 / 985200511 / 918
> cwst@sustech.edu
> http://www.sustech.edu/faculty_en/index.php?coll_no=13&c
> hk=cdf8953eb5124fa6f08f046043be8bf

College of Petroleum Engineering and Technology (B) (2010)
Southern Campus
Khartoum
> cpeng@sustech.edu
> http://www.sustech.edu/faculty_en/index.php?coll_no=23&c
> hk=1d4f14cee52598202e0fc32a12b2dfc2

University of Dongola
Dept of Geology (B) (2014)
PO Box 47
Northern Province, Dongola
> p. +249-241-821-516, +249-241-821
> http://www.uofd.edu.sd/index.php/ar/

University of Gezira
Dept of Geology (2014)
Faculty of Science and Technology
PO Box 20
Wad Medani
> p. (002) 49511825724
> webinfo@uofg.edu.sd
> http://uofg.edu.sd/ENV/

University of Juba
Dept of Geology and Mining (B) (2010)
PO Box 321/1
Khartoum Center, Juba
> p. +249 (83) 222125
> info@juba.edu.sd
> http://www.juba.edu.sd/

Dept of Environmental Studies (B) (2010)
PO Box 321/1
Khartoum Center, Juba
> p. +249 (83) 222125
> info@juba.edu.sd
> http://www.juba.edu.sd/

University of Khartoum
Dept of Geology (B,M,D) (2014)
PO Box 321
Khartoum 11115
> geology@uofk.edu
> http://www.uofk.edu/
Head:
> Ibahim Abdu Mohamed

Professor:
> Saad Eldin Hamad Moha Ali
> Abdelhalim Hassan Elnadi, Goz
Associate Professor:
> Abdelwahab Yousif Abbas
> Salah Bashir Abdalla, Ng
> Osman Mahmoud Abdelatif
> Samia Abdelrahman
> Badr Eldin Khal Agmed
> Fath Elrahman ali Birair
> Omar Elbadri ali Elmaki
> Abdelhafiz Gad Almula
> Mohamed Zaid Awad
> Insaf Sanhoory Babiker
> Almed Sulaiman Daood
> Abdalla Guma Farwa
Instructor:
> Eltayeb Elasha Abdalia
> Sami Osman Ibrahim
> Amro Shaikh Idris Ahmed
> Waleed Elmahdi Siddig
> Saif Eldin Sir Elkhatim
Lecturer:
> Amany Ali Badi
Related Staff:
> Walaa Elnasir Ibrahim

Marine Research Laboratory in Suakin (B) (2010)
PO Box 321
Khartoum 11115
> science@uofk.edu
> https://www.fkm.utm.my/marine/mtl/?Album:Visitor

University of Kordofan
Dept of Soil and Water Sciences (B) (2014)
> p. 860008-611-00249
> hadiaabdelatif@kordofan.edu.sd
> http://science.kordofan.edu.sd/

University of Neelain
Dept of Geology (B) (2011)
> science_dean@neelain.edu.sd
> http://www.neelain.edu.sd/

University of the Red Sea
Dept of Geology (B) (2014)
PO Box 24
Red Sea, Port Sudan
> p. +249-311-219-28
> redseauniv44@hotmail.com

Suriname

Anton de Kom Universiteit van Suriname
Environmental Sciences Dept (B) O (2016)
Universiteitscomplex Leysweg
P.O.B. 9212
Gebouw 17
Paramaribo, n.a. n.a.
> p. 597465558 (Ext. 308)
> s.carilho@uvs.edu
> http://adekus.uvs.edu/section/sectSection.
> php?secID=5304&lb=Onderwijs%20.%20Technologie%20
> .%20Milieu
> f: Anton de Kom University of Suriname

Anton de Kom University of Suriname
Dept of Geology & Mining (2004)
Leysweg, P.O. Box 9212, Universiteits Complex, Gebouw VI

Swaziland

University of Swaziland
Dept of Geography, Environmental Science and Planning
(B,M,D) (2014)

Private Bag 4
Kwaluseni M201
   p. (+268) 2517-0000
   kwaluseni@uniswa.sz
   http://www.uniswa.sz/academics/science/gep

Sweden

Sweden

Chalmers University of Technology
Dept of Geology (2005)
S-412 96 Goteborg
Gothenburg
   lars.o.ericsson@chalmers.se
   http://geo.chalmers.se/index.htm

Karlstad University
Risk Management (B,M,D) ● (2014)
Karlstad University
Karlstad 65188
   Magnus.Johansson@kau.se
   http://www.kau.se/riskhantering

Lund University
Dept of Geology, Historical Geology & Paleontology (2014)
Soluegatan 12
223 62 Lund
   p. (+46) 462221424
   mikael.calner@geol.lu.se
   http://www.science.lu.se/

Stockholm University
Dept of Geological Sciences (B,M,D) (2013)
Svante Arrheniusväg 8
106 91 Stockholm
   office@geo.su.se
   http://www.geo.su.se

Sveriges geologiska Undersokning
Geological Survey of Sweden (2013)
 Box 670
751 28 Uppsala
   sgu@sgu.se
   http://www.sgu.se/

Umea Universitet
Dept of Ecology and Environmental Science (2013)
Natural Sciences, Johan Bures Road 14, Umeå
S-901 87 Umea
   p. +46 90 786 50 00
   jolina.orrell@emg.umu.se
   http://www.emg.umu.se

University of Gothenberg
Master of Earth Science (2004)
Box 100
S-405 30 Gothenburg
   p. +46 31-786 0000

University of Stockholm
Dept of Geology and Geochemistry (2006)
106 91 Stockholm
   Barbara@geo.su.se
   http://www.geo.su.se/

Uppsala Universitet
Dept of Earth Sciences (B,M,D) ● (2014)
Villavagen 16
UPPSALA SE-752 36
   p. +46-18-4710000
   PREFEKT@geo.uu.se
   http://www.geo.uu.se/default.asp?pageid=1&lan=1

Switzerland

Basel University
Dept of Earth Sciences (2012)
Bernoullistr.32
CH-4056 Basel
   Joelle.Glanzmann@unibas.ch
   http://duw.unibas.ch/

Inst of Earth Sciences (2004)
Bernoullistrasse 30
Basel 4056
   joelle.glanzmann@unibas.ch
   http://therion.minpet.unibas.ch/minpet/index.html

ETH Hoenggerberg
Geophysical Inst ETH (2014)
Sonneggstrasse 5
8092 Zurich
   p. +41 44 633 26 05
   christoph.baerlocher@erdw.ethz.ch
   http://www.geophysics.ethz.ch/

ETH Zurich
Dept of Earth Sciences (2012)
ETH-Zenrum
CH-8092 Zurich
   info@erdw.ethz.ch
   http://www.erdw.ethz.ch/

Federal Office for the Environment (FOEN)
Federal Office for the Environment (FOEN) (2015)
info@bafu.admin.ch
Bern 3003
   p. 0041313229311
   info@bafu.admin.ch
   http://www.bafu.admin.ch/
   t: @bafuCH

University of Basel
Geol & Palaeontological Inst (2012)
Bernouillistrasse 32
CH-4056 Basale
   joelle.glanzmann@unibas.ch
   http://www.unibas.ch/earth/GPI/paleo/index.htm

University of Fribourg
Div of Earth Sciences (2004)
Chemin du Musee 6
Perolles
CH-1700 Fribourg
   nicole.bruegger@unifr.ch
   http://www.unifr.ch/geology/

University of Geneva
Section of Earth Sciences and Environment (2009)
13, rue des Maraichers
 Geneva CH-1205
   p. 0041223796628
   christine.lovis@unige.ch
   http://www.unige.ch/sciences/terre/

University of Lausanne
Faculty of Geosciences and Environment (B,M,D) ● (2015)
Geopolis
Lausanne CH-1015
   p. +41 21 692 43 00
   francois.bussy@unil.ch
   www.unil.ch/gse/home.html
   Enrollment (2015): B: 384 (112) M: 299 (102) D: 143 (11)

University of Neuchatel
Centre for Hydrogeology and Geothermics (B,M,D) (2013)
Rue Emile-Argand 11

CH-2000 Neuchatel
secretariat.chyn@unine.ch
http://www.unine.ch/chyn

Universität Bern
Institut für Geologie (B,M,D) (2015)
Baltzerstrasse 1+3
Bern CH-3012
p. +41 (0) 31 631 87 61
info@geo.unibe.ch
http://www.geo.unibe.ch

Syria

Damascus University
Dept of Geology (2004)
Jammah Dimasq
Damscus

Taiwan

Academia Sinica
Institute of Earth Sciences (D) (2015)
128, Section 2, Academia Road, Nangang
Taipei 11529
p. 886-2-2783-9910
jhwang@earth.sinica.edu.tw
http://www.earth.sinica.edu.tw/index_e.php
Distinguished Researcg Fellow:
Jeen-Hwa Wang, (D), SUNY, 1982, Ys
Research Fellow:
Li Zhao, (D), Princeton, 1995, YsgGt
Associate Research Fellow:
Wu-Cheng Chi, (D), California (Berkeley), GtuGo
Assistant Research Fellow:
Wen-che Yu, (D), Stony Brook, 2007, Ys

Central Geological Survey (MOEA) of Taiwan
Central Geological Survey (MOEA) of Taiwan (2013)
District No. 2, Lane 109
Taipei 235
cgs@moeacgs.gov.tw
http://www.moeacgs.gov.tw/main.jsp

Chinese Culture University
Dept of Geology (2004)
Hanaoka Yangmingshan
Taipei 1111455
p. (02) 2861-0511 rpm 26105
crssge@staff.pccu.edu.tw

National Cheng-Kung University
Dept Earth Sciences (2004)
Tainan
wong56@mail.ncku.edu.tw

National Chung Cheng University
Inst of Seismology (2004)
168 University Rd
Min-Hsiung Chia-Yi
p. (886) -5--2720 x 9 ext: 61201?61209)
seismo@ccu.edu.tw
http://www.eq.ccu.edu.tw

National Taiwan University
Inst of Geology (2004)
245 Choushan Road, Taipei 106-17

Tanzania

ARDHI University
School of Geospatial Sciences and Technolgy (B,M,D) (2012)

P.O.Box 35176
Dar es Salaam
hagai@aru.ac.tz
http://www.aru.ac.tz/page.php?id=63
Enrollment (2012): B: 120 (112) M: 10 (2) D: 6 (0)

Geological Survey of Tanzania
Geological Survey of Tanzania (2011)
P .O Box 903
Dodoma
madini-do@gst.go.tz
http://www.gst.go.tz/

University of Dar es Salaam
Dept of Geology (B,M,D) ● (2015)
PO Box 35052
Dar es Salaam
p. +255 22 2410013
geology@udsm.ac.tz
http://www.conas.udsm.ac.tz/geology/
Enrollment (2015): B: 65 (53) M: 17 (0)
Head:
Nelson Boniface, (D), Kiel, GcpGz
Professor:
Justian R. Ikingura, (D), Carleton, 1989, EgCgGi
Makenya A. Maboko, (D), Australian National, 1991, GpCgGx
Senior Lecturer:
Charles Z. Kaaya, (D), Cologne, 1993, GrsGu
Isaac Muneji Marobhe, (D), Helsinki Univ of Tech (Finland), 1990, YegYx
Associate Professor:
Shukrani Manya, (D), Dar Es Salaam, 2008, CgGzg
Hudson H. Nkotagu, (D), TU Berlin, 1994, HwgGe
Lecturer:
Kasanzu Charles, (D), 2014, Ggh
Emmanuel Kazimoto, (D), Kiel, 2014, EgGi
Elisante E. Mshiu, (D), Martin Luther Germany, 2014, OrGg
Gabriel D. Mulibo, (D), Penn State, 2013, Ysg
Ferdinand W. Richard, (D), Uppsala, Sweden, 1999, YsGt

Institute of Marine Sciences (B) (2011)
Mizingani Road
PO Box 35091
Zanzibar
p. 255-24-2232128/2230741
director@ims.udsm.ac.tz
http://www.ims.udsm.ac.tz

University of Dodoma
Dept of Geology and Petroleum Studies (2011)
P.O Box 259
Dodoma
p. +255 26 2310000
vc@udom.ac.tz
http://www.udom.ac.tz/

School of Mines and Petroleum Engineering (2011)
PO Box 259
Dodoma
p. +255 22 2410013
vc@udom.ac.tz
http://www.udom.ac.tz

Thailand

Asian Institute of Technology
Dept of Geology (2014)
P.O. Box 4
Klong Luang
Pathumthani 12120, Bangkok 10501
p. +66 (0) 2524 6057
supamas@ait.ac.th
http://www.set.ait.ac.th/page.php?fol=gte&page=gte

Thailand

247

Dept of Mineral Resources
(2011)
75/10 Rama 6 Road, Phayathai
Bangkok 10400
pornthip@dmr.go.th
http://www.dmr.go.th/

Togo

Universite de Lome
Dept de Geologie (B) (2014)
BP 1515
Lomé , TOGO
p. (+228) 22-25-50-93

Tunisia

Birzeit University
Dept of Geology (2011)
Faculty of Science
P. O. Box 14
7021 Jarzouna Tunis
Bizerte
p. 216590717
fsb@fsb.rnu.tn
http://www.fsb.rnu.tn/index_fr/contact.html

Universite de Carthage
Dept de Geologie (B) (2010)
Jarzouna 7021
p. +21671841353
fsb@fsb.rnu.tn
http://www.fsb.rnu.tn/fsbindex.htm

Universite de Gabes
Dept de Sciences de la Terre (B) (2014)
Cite Riadh
Zerig, Gabes 6072
p. +216 75 394 800
mail@fsg.rnu.tn
http:www/fsg.rnu.tn/PRESENTATION.htm

**Inst Superieur des Sciences et Techniques des Eaux de
Gabes** (B) (2010)
Cite Riadh
Zerig, Gabes 6072
p. +216 75 394 800
isstegb@isstegb.rnu.tn
http://www.isstegb.rnu.tn/francais/index.htm

Universite de Sfax
Dept de Sciences de la Terre (B) (2010)
Route de l Aeroport km 0.5
Sfax 3029
p. 216 74 276 400
fss@www.fss.rnu.tn
http://www.fss.rnu.tn

Dept de Genie Materiaux (B) (2010)
B.P:w.3038
Sfax
p. (216) 74 274 088
enis@enis.rnu.tn
http://www.enis.rnu.tn/content/enis00003.htm

Dept de Genie Georessources et Environnement (B) (2010)
B.P:w.3038
Sfax
p. (216) 74 274 088
enis@enis.rnu.tn
http://www.enis.rnu.tn/content/enis00003.htm

Universite de Tunis
Dept of Geology (2011)
Faculty of Science
248

1 Rue de Beja
Tunis 2092
p. 21671872600
http://www.fst.rnu.tn/fr/index.php

Turkey

Canakkale Onsekiz Mart University
Jeoloji Bolumu (2011)
Terzioglu Campus
Canakkale 17020
sztutkun@comu.edu.tr
http://jeoloji.comu.edu.tr/

Cukurova Universitesi
Jeoloji Muhendisligi Bolumu (B,M,D) ● (2014)
Faculty of Engineering and Architecture, Department of Geological Engineering
01330 Adana
Balcali
p. (+ 90 322) 338 67 15
parlak@cu.edu.tr
http://jeoloji.cu.edu.tr
Professor:
    Osman Parlak, (D), Geneva, 1996, GipCc

Eskisehir Universitesi
Maden Muhendisligi Bolumu (2004)
Muhendislik Fakultesi
Yunus Emre Kampusu
Eskisehir

Firat University
Dept of Geological Engineering (A,B,M,D) ○ (2015)
Department of Geological Engineering
23119 Elazig Turkey
Elazig 23100
p. 424-2370000-5979
asasmaz@firat.edu.tr
http://jeo.muh.firat.edu.tr/tr/node/104
f: https://www.facebook.com/groups/firatjeoloji/
Chair:
    Ahmet Sasmaz, EgGeCe
Professor:
    Ercan Aksoy, (A), Ggt
    Ahmet Feyzi Bingol, (A), GipGv
    Bahattin Cetindag, (A), NgYv
    Ahmet Sagiroglu, (A), Egm
Associate Professor:
    Dicle Bal Akkoca, (D), EnCo
    Melahat Beyarslan, (D), GipGx
    Hasan Celik, (A), GscOu
    Zulfu Gurocak, (A), Nrg
    Leyla Kalender, (A), CgcCs
    Calibe Koc Tasgin, (A), GsdGg
    Sevcan Kurum, (A), GivGx
Assistant Professor:
    Bünyamin Akgul, (D), GzyGi
    Muharrem Akgul, (D), Ecg
    Murat Inceoz, (D), GctGm
    Ayse Didem Kılıç, (D), GxpGy
    Esra Ozel Yıldırım, (D), Gxi
    Ozlem Oztekin Okan, (D), HgwHs
    Melek Ural, (D), GivCc
Research Assistant:
    Hatice Kara, Cg
    Mehmet Kokum, (M), Indiana, 2012, GttGg
    Nevin Ozturk, Cg
Research Asistant:
    Elif Akgun, GgcGt
    Onur Alkaç, GgsGu
    Gizem Arslan, GxiGp
    Yasemin Aslan, Nr
    Serap Colak Erol, (D), GgcGt
    Mehmet Ali Erturk, GiCc

Mustafa Kanik, (D), NrSo
Sibel Kaygili, GgPgs
Mahmut Palutoglu, (D), YgsGc
Mustafa Eren Rizeli, Gxi
Abdullah Sar, GviGp
İsmail Yıldırım, ScGix

Hacettepe University
Geological Engineering Dept (2005)
Muhendislik Fakultesi
Beytepe Kampusu
tunay@hacettepe.edu.tr
http://www.jeo.hun.edu.tr/800x600.htm

Hydrogeological Engineering Programme (B,M,D) ● (2015)
Beytepe Campus
Ankara 06800
p. +90 (312) 297730
ekmekci@hacettepe.edu.tr
http://www.hacettepe.edu.tr/
Enrollment (2015): B: 235 (42) M: 12 (0) D: 11 (3)
Professor:
Sakir Simsek, (D), Istanbul, 1982, Hw
Serdar Bayari, (D), Hacettepe, 1991, Hw
Mehmet Ekmekci, (D), HwyCs
Galip Yüce, (D), Hw
Nur Naciye Özyurt, (D), Hacettepe, Hw
Assistant Professor:
Turker Kurttas, (D), Hacettepe, 1997, HwgOr
Levent Tezcan, (D), Hacettepe, 1993, Hw

Istanbul Universitesi
Jeoloji Bolumu (2014)
Muhendislik Fakultesi
Beyazit
p. 0 (212) 473 70 70 ex. 17600
koral@istanbul.edu.tr
http://muhendislik.istanbul.edu.tr/jeoloji/?p=6909

ITU
Jeoloji Bolumu (2014)
Maden Fakultesi
80394, Macka
Istanbul

Middle East Technical University
Inst of Marine Science (2014)
Div. of Marine Geology & Geophysics
P.O. Box 28
33731 Erdemli-Mersin
p. +90-324 521 3434
adminims@metu.edu.tr
http://www.ims.metu.edu.tr/

Dept of Geological Engineering (B,M,D) (2010)
Inonu Bulvari
ODTU
Ankara TR-06531
p. +90-312-2102682
gesin@metu.edu.tr
http://www.geoe.metu.edu.tr/

Mineral Research and Exploration General Directorate of Turkey
(2014)
p. +90 312 201 11 51
mta@mta.gov.tr
http://www.mta.gov.tr/

Selcuk Universitesi
Faculty of Sciences (2004)
Muhendislik Fakultesi
42040 Konya

p. (+)903322412484
fen@selcuk.edu.tr

Uganda

Gulu University
Faculty of Agriculture and Environment (B,M,D) (2016)
P.O. Box 166
Gulu
p. +256782673491
d.ongeng@gu.ac.ug
http://www.gu.ac.ug

Dept of Geography (B) ● (2015)
P.O. Box 166
Gulu
p. +256772517488
charles.okumu52@gmail.com
http://www.gu.ac.ug/index.php?option=com_content&view=
category&layout=blog&id=48&Itemid=66
Lecturer:
Expedito Nuwategeka, (D), Gulu, 2015, OyyGv

Kabale University
Dept of Environmental Science and Natural Resources (B) (2010)
PO Box 317
Kabale
p. 256-4864-22803
akampabf@gmail.com
http://www.kabaleuniversity.ac.ag/

Makerere University
Dept of Geology and Petroleum Studies (2014)
P. O. Box 7062
Kampala 041
p. +256 41 532631-4
http://mak.ac.ug/
Instructor:
Kevin Aanyu, (M), Mak
Wycliff Kawule, (M), ITC
Robert Mamgbi, (M), CT-Prague
Lecturer:
Erasmus Barifajio, (D), Mak
John Mary Kiberu, (D), TUB
Agnes Alaba Kuterama, (M), ITC
Andrew Muwanga, (D), Brausnschweig
Immaculate Nakimera Ssemanda, (D), Mak

Dept of Geography, Geoinformatics & Climatic Sciences (B) (2010)
PO Box 7062
Kampala
p. +256-41-53126 1
geog@caes.mak.ac.ug
http://www.geography.mak.ac.ug/

Institute of Environment and Natural Resources (B) (2014)
PO Box 7062
Kampala 041
p. 256 414 530134
fkansiime@muienr.mak.ac.ug
http://muienr.mak.ac.ug/

Ndejje University
Faculty of Forest Science & Environmental Management (B) (2014)
PO Box 7088
Kampala, Ndejje Hill
p. +256-0392-730326
forest@ndejjeuniversity.ac.ug
http://www.ndejjeuniversity.ac.ug/academics.htm

Ukraine

National Mining University (in Ukraine)
State Mining University of Ukraine (2005)

19 Karl Marx Avenue
Dnepropetrovsk
320600
dfr@nmuu.dp.ua
http://www.apex.dp.ua/english/uageo/ukraine.html

United Arab Emirates

United Arab Emirates University
Dept of Geology (B,M,D) ● (2014)
P.O. Box 15551
College of Science, UAE University
Jamma Street
Al-Ain, Abu Dhabi 9713
p. +971-3-7136380
Ahmed.murad@uaeu.ac.ae

United Kingdom

Aberystwyth University
Dept of Geography & Earth Sciences (B,M,D) (2015)
Llandinam Building
Penglais
Aberystwyth SY23 3DB
p. 01970 622606
gesstaff@aber.ac.uk
http://www.aber.ac.uk/en/iges

Anglia Ruskin University
Dept of Life Sciences (2014)
Cambridge Campus
East Road
Cambridge CB1 1PT
p. +44 845 271 3333
michael.cole@anglia.ac.uk
http://www.anglia-ruskin.ac.uk/ruskin/en/home/faculties/fst/
departments/lifesciences.html

Bangor University
School of Ocean Sciences (B,M,D) (2013)
Menai Bridge,
Isle of Anglesey
LL59 5AB
p. +44-1248-382854
oss011@bangor.ac.uk
http://www.sos.bangor.ac.uk/

Birkbeck College
Dept of Earth and Planetary Sciences (2014)
Department of Earth and Planetary Sciences
University of London - Birkbeck
Malet Street
Bloomsbury, London WC1E 7HX
p. +44 (0)20 7631 6665
p.gaunt@bbk.ac.uk
http://www.bbk.ac.uk/geology/
Administrative Assistant: Peter Gaunt
Head:
    Gerald Roberts, Ne
Professor:
    Charlie Bristow, Gs
    Andy Carter, Og
    Ian Crawford, On
    Hilary Downes, Cg
Instructor:
    Karen Hudson-Edwards, Gez
Lecturer:
    Andy Beard
    Simon Drake, Gv
    Dominic Fortes, Og
    Peter Grinford, Xg
    Steve Hirons, Cl
    Philip Hopley, Pe
    Vincent C. H. Tong, Yg
    Charlie Underwood, c.un, Pg

Phillip Pogge von Strandmann, Cs

British Antarctic Survey
British Antarctic Survey (2015)
High Cross, Madingley Road
Cambridge CB3 0ET
p. +44 (0)1223 221400
trr@bas.ac.uk
http://www.antarctica.ac.uk/

British Geological Survey
British Geological Survey (2012)
Environmental Science Centre
Nicker Hill
Keyworth
Nottingham NG12 5GG
p. 0115 936 3100
enquiries@bgs.ac.uk
http://www.bgs.ac.uk/

Cardiff University
School of Earth and Ocean Sciences (B,M,D) (2014)
Main Building
Park Place
Cardiff, Wales CF10 3YE
p. +44 (0)29 2087 4830
earth-ug@cf.ac.uk
http://www.cardiff.ac.uk/earth/
Enrollment (2002): B: 174 (0) M: 18 (0) D: 28 (0)
Head:
    R J. Parkes
Professor:
    J A. Cartwright, (D), Ys
    Dianne Edwards, (D), Pb
    I Hall, On
    A Harris
    C Harris, Ge
    B Leake
    R J. Lisle, Gc
    C MacLeod, Gu
    J A. Pearce, Cg
    P N. Pearson, Pe
    D Rickard, Cg
    V P. Wright, Gs
Commander:
    N Rodgers, (D), Ow
Lecturer:
    Tiago Alves
    Rhoda Ballinger, (D), On
    Stephen Barker, Pe
    C M. Berry, (D), Pb
    P J. Brabham, (D), Ye
    L C. Cherns, Pg
    Jose Constantine, (D), Hy
    J H. Davies, Yg
    I Fryett, On
    TC Hales, (D), Gm
    A Hemsley, Pl
    T Jones, Ge
    A C. Kerr, Gx
    C Lear, Ou
    Johan Lissenberg
    Sergio Lourenco, (D), Sp
    R Perkins, On
    J Pike, On
    H M. Prichard, Gx
    H Sass
    H D. Smith, On
    S J. Wakefield, Cm
    C F. Wooldridge, On
    Y Yang, Hg

Durham University
Dept of Earth Sciences (B,M,D) (2015)
Science Laboratories

South Road
Durham DH1 3LE
>   p. +44 0191 3342300
>   earth.sciences@durham.ac.uk
>   http://www.dur.ac.uk/earthsciences/

Director:
Richard Davies, Eo
Ed Llewellin, Gv
Head:
Jon Gluyas, Eo
Professor:
Andrew Aplin, Go
Kevin Burton, Cc
Jon Davidson, Cm
Neil R. Goulty, (D), Cambridge, Yg
David Harper, Pg
Jim McElwaine, Yg
Yaoling Niu, On
Instructor:
Mark Allen, Gs
Darren Grocke, Pe
Simon Mathias, Oi
Dave Selby, Cc
Jeroen van Hunen, Gv
Lecturer:
James Baldini, Hs
Richard James Brown, Gv
Pablo Cubillas, Cg
Chris Dale, Oa
Nicola De Paola, Gc
Chris Greenwell, GzEo
Richard Hobbs, Ys
Claie Horwell, Gz
Stuart Jones, Gs
Lara Kalnins
Colin G. Macpherson, (D), London, 1994, Cg
Kenneth J. McCaffrey, (D), Durham, Gc
Christine Peirce, (D), Cambridge, Yg
Helen Williams, Cs
Fred Worrall, (D), Cambridge, Cg
Senior Lecturer:
Howard A. Armstrong, (D), Nottingham, 1983, Pg
Research Assistant:
Jonathan Imber, (D), Durham, Gc
Reader:
Gillian R. Foulger, (D), Durham, Yg
Robert E. Holdsworth, (D), Leeds, Gc

Edinburgh University
School of Geosciences (B,M,D) ● (2015)
Kings Buildings
West Mains Road
Edinburgh EH9 3JW
>   p. +44 (0) 131 651 7068
>   sarah.mcallister@ed.ac.uk
>   http://www.geos.ed.ac.uk/
>   f: https://www.facebook.com/geosciences/
>   t: @geoscienceesed

Director:
Bruce M. Gittings, (M), Edinburgh, Oi
Paul R. van Gardingen, (D), On
Head:
Alexander W. Tudhope, (D), Cs
Chair:
Chris Dibben, On
Mark D. A. Rounsevell, (D), Ou
Charles W. J. Withers, (D)
Professor:
Emily S. Brady, (D), Glas, Ge
Andrew Curtis, Ys
Andrew J. Dugmore, Gae
J. Godfrey Fitton, Gi
Simon L. Harley, Gt
R. Stuart Haszeldine, (D), Strath, Oa
Gabriele C. Hegerl, (D), Oa
Dick Kroon, Gg

Ian G. Main, (D), Ys
Patrick Meir, (D), Edinburgh
Maurizio Mencuccini, (D), Florence
John B. Moncrieff, Oa
Peter W. Neinow, (D), Cantab, Ol
Paul Palmer, Oa
Jamie R. Pearce, (D), Ge
Alastair H. F. Robertson, (D), Leics, Gt
Hugh D. Sinclair, (D), Os
David Stevenson, (D), Oa
Michael A. Summerfield, (D), Oxcon, Gm
Simon F. B. Tett, Ow
Kathryn A. Whaler, Ym
Mathew Williams, Oa
Wyn Williams, Ym
Iain H. Woodhouse, (D), H-W, Oi
Rachel A. Woods, (D), Open, Gs
Anton M. Ziolkowski, (D), Cantabury, Go
Senior Scientist:
Nicola Cayzer, (D), Edinburgh, Yg
Richard Hinton, Cg
Research Associate:
Andrew Bell, Gt
Ian B. Butler, (D), Cg
John Craven, Yg
Jan C. de Hogg, Ge
Walter Geibert, Cc
Chris L. Hayward, Ga
Sian Henley, (D)
Mark Naylor, (D), Edinburgh, Gt
Anthony J. Newton, (D), Edinburgh, On
Laetitia Pichevin, (D), Bordeaux, Cg
John A. Stevenson, Gv
David Wright
Instructor:
Richard L. H. Essery, Oa
Raja Ganeshram, Pg
Heather Lovell, On
Andrew T. Mcleod, Og
Bryne T. Ngwenya, (D), Reed, Co
Hugh C. Pumphrey, (D), Mississippi, Oa
David Reay, (D), Oa
Tom Slater, (D), London, On
Samantha Staddon
Lecturer:
Simon J. Allen
Mikael Attal
Massimo Bollasina, Oa
Geoffrey Bromily, (D), Ge
Eliza Calder, Gv
Mark Chapman, (D), Yg
Gregory L. Cowie, Co
Julie Cupples, On
Kyle Dexter
Ruth Doherty, (D), Edinburgh, Oa
Rowan Ellis, On
Florian Fusseis, Gc
Daniel Goldberg
Noel Gourmelen
Margaret C. Graham, Ge
Kate V. Heal, Co
Nicholas R. J. Hulton, Ol
Antonio Ioris, Ge
Gail D. Jackson, PbGe
Caleb Johnston
Simon Jung, Og
Linda Kirstein, Gt
Eric Laurier, On
Caroline Lehmann, (D)
Fraser MacDonal
William A. Mackaness, Oi
Ondrej Masek, (D), Ng
Christopher I. McDermott, Hg
Marc J. Metzger, (D), Wageningen, Ge
Nina J. Morris
Simon N. Mudd, (D), Hg
Caroline Nichol

Eva Panagiotakopulu, Pe
Genevieve Patenaude, (D), Ge
Jan Penrose, (D), Toronto
Kanchana Ruwanpura
Casey Ryan
Kate Saunders, Gv
Simon J. Shackley, Eg
Niamh K. Shortt, Eg
Sran P. Sohi, (D), London, Os
Neil Stuart, Oi
Daniel Swanton, (D), Durham
Jenny A. Tait
Alexander Thomas
Dan van der Horst, (D), Eg
Mark Wilkinson, (D)
Merwether Wilson, Ob
Ronald M. Wilson, (D)
Emeritus:
John Grace, Oa
Teaching Fellow:
Thomas Challads, Hg
Other:
Stuart M. V. Gilfillan, (D), Manchester, Oa
Andrew S. Hein, (D), Edinburgh
Tetsuya Komabayashi, (D), Gz
Isla Myers-Smith
Jeremy Turk
Marisa Wilson, (D), Oxcon
Related Staff:
Susan Rigby

Exeter University
Camborne School of Mines (2014)
College of Engineering, Mathematics and Physical Sciences
University of Exeter
Penryn Campus
Penryn, Cornwall TR10 9FE
p. (+44) 1392 661000
cornwall@exeter.ac.uk
http://emps.exeter.ac.uk/geology/contact/
Director:
John Coggan, (D), Newcastle, Nx
Charlie Moon, (D), Imperial Coll, Nx
Neill Wood, (B), Imperial Coll (London), 1983, Oo
Acting Head:
Hylke J. Glass, Gz
Professor:
Stephen Hasselbo, Gs
Kip Jeffrey, Nx
Bernd Lottermoser, Ca
Lecturer:
Jens Andersen, Gi
Ian Bailey, Ol
Robert Barley
Christopher Bryan, Nx
Patrick Foster, Nm
Sam Hughes, Gt
Gareth Kennedy, Nm
Kate Littler, (D), Univ Coll (London), Pe
John Macadam, Ge
Lewis Meyer, (D), Exeter, Nm
Kathryn Moore, (D), Bristol, 1999, Ge
Kim Moreton, On
Richard Pascoe, (D), Gz
Duncan Pirrie
Robin Shail, (D), Keele, 1992, Gtc
Ross Stickland
David Watkins, Hg
Andrew Wetherelt, Nm
Paul Wheeler, Nx
Ben Williamson, (D), London, 1991, EmGv

Heriot-Watt University
Institute of Petroleum Engineering (2014)
Research Park, Riccarton

Heriot-Watt University
Edinburgh Campus
Edinburgh
p. +44 (0) 131 451 3543
enquiries@pet.hw.ac.uk
http://www.pet.hw.ac.uk/
Director:
John Ford
Andy Gardiner
Helen Lever, Go
Eric Mackay
James M. Somerville, Np
Dominic Tatum, Ec
Rink van Dijke
Head:
Dorrik Stow
Chair:
Sebastian Geigor
John Underhill
Professor:
Patrick Corbett, Np
Gary Couples, Np
David Davies, Ng
Mahmoud Jamiolahmady
Colin MacBeth
Mercedes Maroto-Valer, Ge
Ken Sorbie
Adrian C. Todd, Np
Assistant Professor:
Jalal Foroozesh, Hs
Research Associate:
Ross Anderson, Eo
Lorraine Boak
Rod Burgass
Antonin Chapoy
Romain Chassagne
Alexader Graham
Sally Hamilton, Gs
Oleg Ishkov
Rachel Jamieson
Maria-Daphne Mangriotis, Ys
Peter Olden
Laurence Ormerod
Scott Shaw
Robin Shield, Cg
Mike Singleton
Oscar Vazquez
Michael Watson, Gb
Jinhai Yang
Instructor:
Erkal Ersoy
Saleh Goodarzian
Samantha Llott, Go
Steve McDougall
Lecturer:
Vasily Demyanov, Oi
Florian Doster, Hg
Ahmed H. Elsheikh
Julian Fennema, Eg
Zeyun Jian
Helen Lewis
Jingsheng Ma, Yg
Khafiz Muradov, (D)
Gillian E. Pickup, Hw
Asghar Shams, Yg
Karl D. Stephen
Visiting Professor:
Ian Collins, Cm
Luiz Carlos M. Palemo
Qing Wang
Laboratory Director:
Jim Buckman
Mike Christie
Other:
Bahman Tohidi
Related Staff:
Jamie Kerr

252

Imperial College
Earth Science and Engineering (2015)
Imperial College London
South Kensington Campus
London SW7 2AZ
    p. +44 (0)20 7589 5111
    philip.allen@imperial.ac.uk
    http://www3.imperial.ac.uk/earthscienceandengineering
Director:
    Nigel Brandon, Ge
Professor:
    Martin J. Blunt, (D), Cambridge, 1988, NpHw
Head:
    Johannes Cilliers, (D), Cape Town, 1994, Gz
Chair:
    Philip Allen, Gs
    Alastair Fraser, (D), Glasgow, 1995, Go
    Alain Gringarten, (D), Stanford, 1971, Np
    Matthew Jackson, (D), Liverpool, 1997
    Howard Johnson, Go
    Peter King, (D), Cambridge, 1982, Np
    Ann Muggeridge, (D), Oxford, 1986, Np
    Yanghua Wang, (D), Imperial Coll, 1997, Yg
Professor:
    John Cosgrove, (D), Imperial Coll (London), 1972, Gc
    Sevket Durucan, Ng
    Sanjeev Gupta, Gs
    Joanna Morgan, (D), Cambridge, 1988, Yg
    Jane Plant, Ge
    Mark Rehkamper, (D), Mainz, 1995, Cs
    Mark Sephton, (D), Open, 1996, Xm
    Velisa Vesovic, (D), Imperial Coll, 1998, Np
    Michael Warner, (D), York, 1979, Ys
    R. W. Zimmerman, (D), California (Berkeley), Nr
Research Associate:
    Rebecca Bell, (D), Southampton, 2008, Gt
    Branko Bijeljic, (D), Imperial Coll, 2000, Np
    Raphael Blumenfeld, (D), Cambridge, On
    Rhordri Davies, (D), Cardiff, 2007, Yg
    David Ham, (D), TU Delft, 2005, Yg
    Zita Martins, (D), Leiden, 2007, Xm
    Christopher Pain, Yg
    Randall Perry, Og
Instructor:
    Jenny Collier, (D), Cambridge, 1989, Yr
    Saskia Goes, (D), California (Santa Cruz), 1995, Yg
    Gary Hampson, (D), Liverpool, 1995, Gd
    Christopher Jackson, (D), Manchester, 2002, Gt
    Anna Korre, Ng
    Jian Guo Liu, (D), Imperial Coll, 2002, Or
    Lidia Lonergan, (D), Oxford, 1991, Gt
    Stephen Neethling, (D), UMIST, 1999, Gz
    Emma Passmore
    Matthew Piggot, Bath, 2001, Hg
    Dominik Weiss, (D), Berne, Ge
    Jamie Wilkinson, (D), Southampton, 1989, Em
Lecturer:
    Ian Bastow, (D), Leeds, 2005, Yg
    Gareth Collins, (D), Imperial Coll (London), 2002, Xm
    Matthew Genge, (D), Univ Coll (London), 1993, Xm
    Gerard Gorman, (D), Imperial Coll (London), 2005, Yg
    Kathryn Hadler, (D), Manchester, 2006, Gz
    Cedric John, (D), Potsdam, 2003, Gs
    Samuel Krevor, Eo
    John-Paul Latham, (D), Imperial Coll, 2003
    Philippa J. Mason, Or
    Adrian Muxworthy, (D), Oxford, 1998, Ym
    Julie Prytulak, (D), Bristol, 2008, Gg
    Mark Sutton, (D), Wales-Cardiff, 1996, Pg
    Tina van de Flierdt, (D), ETH Zuerich, 2003, Cs
    Alex Whittaker, (D), Edinburgh, 2007, Gt
Visiting Professor:
    Rosalind Coogon, Cs
Emeritus:
    John Woods, (D), Imperial Coll, 1964

Keele University
Geography, Geology and the Environment (B,M,D) (2016)
William Smith Building,
Keele University
Keele, Staffordshire ST5 5BG
    p. (+44) 01782 733615
    gge@keele.ac.uk
    http://www.keele.ac.uk/gge/
    f: https://www.facebook.com/KeeleGeologyGeoscience
    t: @KeeleGeology
    Enrollment (2014): B: 149 (45) M: 29 (15) D: 10 (2)
Professor:
    Annette Götz , GsPmGg
Associate Professor:
    Nigel Cassidy, Ygx
    Stuart Egan, Ggc
    Ralf Gertisser, Giv
    Jamie Pringle, Yg
    Ian Stimpson, YesYg
Research Associate:
    Sam Toon, Ys
    Rachel Westwood, Yx
Instructor:
    Steven Rogers, Gg
Lecturer:
    Stu Clarke, Gdo
    Ralf Halama, GpiCa
    Michael Montenari, PmgPs
Emeritus:
    Peter Styles, YgvYs

Kingston University
School of Geography, Geology and Environment (2014)
Penrhyn Road Centre
Penrhyn Road
Kingston upon Thames
Surrey KT1 2EE
    p. +44 (0)20 8417 9000
    G.Gillmore@kingston.ac.uk
    http://www.kingston.ac.uk/geolsci/
Director:
    Stuart Downward
Head:
    Gavin Gillmore, (D), Univ Coll (London), Gb
Professor:
    Ian Jarvis, (D), Oxon, 1979, Cg
    Peter Treloar, (D), Glasgow, 1978, Gc
    Nigel Walford, (D), London, 1981, Oi
    Martyn Waller, (D), CNAA
Instructor:
    Peter Hooda, (D), London, 1992, Em
    Annie Hughes, (D), Bristol, 1997, Oi
    Mike Smith, (D), Sheffield, 1999, Or
Lecturer:
    Andy Adam-Bredford
    Alistair Baird
    Douglas Brown, Oi
    Kerry Brown, (D), Stony Brook, 2004, Ge
    Norman Cheun, Ge
    Tracey Coates
    Hadrian Cook, (D), East Anglia, 1986, Ge
    Peter Garside, (D), Liverpool
    Paul Grant
    Ian Greatbatch, (D), 2008, Oi
    Frances Harris, (D), Kingston, 1995
    Mary Kelly
    David Kidd, (D), St. Andrews, 2005, Oi
    James Lambert-Smith, (D), Kingston, 2014, Gg
    Andrew Miles, (D), Edinburgh, 2012, Gz
    Stephanie Mills, (D), Witwatersrand, 2006, Ol
    Pamela Murphy
    Colin Ryall
    Christopher Satow, (D), London, 2012, Ge
    Neil Thomas
Visiting Professor:
    Rosalind Taylor

Emeritus:
  Richard Moody
  Andy Rankin
Other:
  Andrew Swan

Leicester University
Geology Dept (B,M) (2014)
University Road
Leicester LE1 7RH
  p. +44 (0)116 252 3933
  geology@le.ac.uk
  http://www2.le.ac.uk/departments/geology
Head:
  Richard England, Yg
Professor:
  Sarah Davies, Gs
  Mike Lovell, Yg
  Randy Parrish, Cs
  Mark Purnell, Po
  Andy Saunders
  Mark Williams, Po
Lecturer:
  Stewart Fishwick, Yg
  Sarah Gabbott, Po
  Tom Harvey, Po
  Gawen Jenkin
  Max Moorkamp, Yg
  Mike Norry, Pe
  Dan Smith, Ge
  Richard Walker, Gs
  Jan Zalasiewicz, Po

Liverpool John Moores University
School of Natural Sciences and Psychology (B,M,D) (2014)
Byrom Street
Liverpool L3 3AF
  p. (+44) 0151 904 6300
  j.r.kirby@ljmu.ac.uk
  http://www.ljmu.ac.uk/NSP/index.htm
  t: @ljmugeog
  Enrollment (2014): B: 230 (0)
Professor:
  Andy Tattersall
Dr:
  Jason Kirby

Newcastle University
Dept of Civil Engineering (2015)
Drummond Building
Newcastle upon Tyne, NE1 7RU
  C.M.Earle-Storey@newcastle.ac.uk
  http://www.ncl.ac.uk/~ncivil/index.htm

Nottingham Trent University
Dept of animal, rural, and environmental sciences (2004)
Burton Street
Nottingham NG1 4BU
  p. +44 (0)115 941 8418
  anne.coules@ntu.ac.uk
  http://www.ntu.ac.uk

Polytechnic Southwest
Dept of Earth Sciences (2014)
Drake Circus
Plymouth, Devon PL4 8AA
  p. (+44) (0)1752 584584
  science.environment@plymouth.ac.uk
  http://www5.plymouth.ac.uk/schools/school-of-geography-earth-and-environmental-sciences/earth-sciences

Queens University Belfast
School of Geography, Archaeology & Palaeoecology (B,M,D) (2010)
University Road
254

Belfast BT7 1NN
  k.rice@qub.ac.uk
  http://www.qub.ac.uk/gap

Staffordshire Polytechnic
Dept of Applied Sciences (2014)
College Road, Stroke-on-Trent
Staffordshire ST4 2DE
  p. (+44) 1782 294000
  r.boast@staffs.ac.uk
  http://www.staffs.ac.uk/academic_depts/sciences/subjects/environment/index.jsp

Geography and the Environment (2004)
  j.w.wheeler@staffs.ac.uk
  http://www.staffs.ac.uk/sands/scis/geology/geology.html#

Swansea University Prifysgol Abertawe
Dept of Earth Sciences (2014)
Wallace Building
Swansea University
Singleton Park
Swansea, Wales SA2 8PP
  p. +44 (0) 1792 205678 ext 8112
  geography@swansea.ac.uk
  http://www.swansea.ac.uk/geography/

Teesside Polytechnic
School of Science and Engineering (2004)
Tees Valley
Middlesborough TS1 3BA
  p. 01642 738800
  sse-admissions@tees.ac.uk
  http://www.tees.ac.uk/schools/sse/index.cfm

The Open University
Dept of Environment, Earth & Ecosystems (B,M,D) (2015)
Faculty of Science
The Open University
Walton Hall
Milton Keynes MK7 6AA
  p. +44 (0) 1908 652886
  Env-Earth-Ecosystems-Enquiries@open.ac.uk
  http://www.open.ac.uk/science/environment-earth-ecosystems/
  f: https://www.facebook.com/pages/OU-Environment-Earth-Ecosystems/234968859948707
  t: @OU_EEE
Professor:
  Fabrizio Ferrucci, Yg
  David Gowing, (D), Lancaster, 1991, Pb
  Nigel Harris, (D), Cambridge, 1973, Gt
  Simon Kelley, (D), London, 1985, Cs
  Walter Oechel, Oa
Associate Scientist:
  Peter Sheldon
Research Associate:
  Marie-Laure Bagard
  Gareth Davies, (D), Cranfield, Oe
Reader:
  Neil Edwards, (D)
Instructor:
  Stephen Blake, (D), Lancaster, 1982, Gv
  Mark Brandon, (D), Cambridge, 1995, Og
Lecturer:
  Pallavi Anand, (D), Cambridge, Og
  Tom Argles, (D), Oxon, Oi
  Angela L. Coe, (D), Oxford, Gs
  Anthony Cohen, (D), Cambridge, 1988, Cs
  Sarah Davies, (D), Sheffield, Oe
  Miranda Dyson, (D), Witwatersrand, 1989, Py
  Tamsin Edwards, (D)
  Richard Holliman, (D), Open, Oe
  Dave McGarvie, (D), Lancaster, 1985, Gv
  Philip Sexton, (D), Southampton, 2000, Ge
  Mike Widdowson, (D), Oxford-Wolfson College, 1990, Gv

Carlton Wood
Visiting Professor:
Stephen Self
Edward Youngs
Emeritus:
Phil Potts
Robert Spicer, (D), Imperial, 1975

The University of Sunderland
Faculty of Applied Science (2014)
Edinburgh Building
City Campus
Chester Rd.
Sunderland SR1 3SD
p. (+44) 191 515 2000
john.macintyre@sunderland.ac.uk
http://www.sunderland.ac.uk/faculties/apsc/ourdepartments/cet/

University College London
Dept of Earth Sciences (B,M,D) (2015)
Gower Street
, London WC1E 6BT
p. +44 (0)20 7679 2363
earthsci@ucl.ac.uk
http://www.ucl.ac.uk/es
f: EarthSciences UcL
Professor:
Dario Alfe, (D), Scuola Internazionale Superiore di Studi Avanzati di Trieste, 1997, Gz
Tim Atkinson, (D), Bristol, 1971, Hg
Paul Brown, (D), Univ Coll (London), 1986, Pm
David Dobson, (D), Univ Coll (London), 1995, Gz
Carolina Lithgow-Bertelloni, (D), California (Berkeley), 1994, Yg
John McArthur, (D), Imperial Coll, 1974, Cl
Jacqueline McGlade, (D), Guelph, 1980, Ge
Philip Meredith, (D), Imperial Coll, 1983, Nr
Eric Oelkers, (D), California (Berkeley), Cm
Kevin Pickering, (D), Oxford, 1979, Gs
David Price, Cambridge, 1981, Gz
Chris Rapley, Og
Peter Sammonds, (D), Univ Coll (London), 1988, Nr
Graham Shields-Zhou, (D), Eidgenössische Technische Hochschule Zürich, 1997, Cg
Lars Stixrude, (D), California (Berkeley), 1991, Yg
Julienne Stroeve, Ol
Juergen Thurow, (D), Eberhard-Karls-Universität Tübingen, 1987, Gs
Paul Upchurch, (D), Cambridge, 1993, Po
Lidunka Vocadlo, (D), Univ Coll (London), 1993, Gz
Bridget Wade, Pm
Ian Wood, (D), Univ Coll (London), 1977, Gz
Lecturer:
Willy Burgess, (D), Birmingham, 1987, Hg
Anna Ferreira, (D), Oxford, 1005, Ys
Andrew Fortes, (D), Univ Coll (London), 2004, Xy
Anjali Goswani, (D), Chicago, 2005, Po
Adrian Jones, (D), Durham, 1980, Gi
Chris Kilburn, (D), Univ Coll (London), 1984, Yx
Wendy Kirk, Gp
Tom Mitchell, Gc
Dominic Papineau, Cg
Alex Song, (D), Caltech, Ys
Pieter Vermeesch, (D), Stanford, 2005, Cc
Phillip Pogge von Strandmann, (D), Open, 2006, Cs
Emeritus:
Bill McGuire, (D), Univ Coll (London), 1980, Gv

University College of Swansea
Dept of Geography (2004)
Singleton Park
Swansea SA2 8PP

University of Aberdeen
Dept of Geology and Petroleum Geology (B,M) (2014)

Meston Building
King's College
Aberdeen AB24 3UE
geology@abdn.ac.uk
http://www.abdn.ac.uk/geology/
Head:
David Jolley, (D)
Chair:
Ian Alsop, (D)
Rob Butler
Adrian Hartley
John Howell
Andrew Hurst
Ben Kneller
David MacDonald
Ron Steel
Randell Stephenson
Research Associate:
Steven Andrews
Robert Daly
Jyldz Tabyldy Kyzy
Sam Spinks
Christian Vallejo
Instructor:
David Muirhead
Lecturer:
Clare Bond
Stephen Bowden
Dave Healy
Malcolm J. Hole
David Iacopini
Joyce Neilson
Colin North
Nick Schofield

University of Bedfordshire
Dept of Life Sciences (2014)
Park Square
Luton, Bedfordshire LU1 3JU
p. +44 1234 400400
international@beds.ac.uk
http://www.beds.ac.uk/howtoapply/departments/science

University of Birmingham
School of Geography, Earth & Environmental Sciences (2014)
School of Geography, Earth and Environmental Sciences
University of Birmingham
Edgbaston, Birmingham B15 2TT
p. +44 (0)121 414 5531
m.p.smith@bham.ac.uk
http://www.birmingham.ac.uk/schools/gees/index.aspx
Director:
Rob MacKenzie
Head:
David Hannah, Hg
Chair:
Eugenia Valsami-Jones
Professor:
Ian Fairchild
Stuart Harrad
Roy Harrison
Jamie Lead
Alexander Milner
Tim Reston
Jon Sadler
John Tellam
Associate Professor:
Paul Anderson
Bridin Carroll
Arshad Isakjee
Lloyd Jenkins
Research Associate:
Mohamed A. Abdallah
Salim Alam
Mohammed Baalousha

David Beddows
Ian Boomer
Leigh Crilley
Mark Cuthbert
Simon Dixon
Jonathan Eden
Sophie Hadfield-Hill
James Hale
Stephanie Handley-Sidhu
Marie Hutton
Kieran Khamis
Megan Klaar
Marcus Kohler
James Levine
Yuning Ma
Paul Martin
Sara Martinez-Loriente
Mauro Masiol
Heiko Moossen
Catherine L. Muller
Martin Müller
Irina Nikolova
Irina Nikolova
Matt O'Callaghan
Isabella Romer Roche
Zongbo Shi
Shei Sia Su
Rick Thomas
Amey S. Tilak
Sarah Jane Veevers
Saskia Warren
Sebastian Watt
Jianxin Yin
Deputy Head of School:
    William Bloss
Instructor:
    James Bendle
    Lee Chapman
    Jason Hilton
    Dominique Moran
    Jonathan Oldfield
    Ian Phillips
    Jo Southworth
Lecturer:
    Lauren Andres
    Daniel Arribas-Bel
    Austin Barber
    Nicholas Barrand
    Rebecca Bartlett
    Lesley Batty
    Mike Beazley
    Chris Bradley
    Xioaming Cai
    Andy Chambers
    Julian Clark
    Rosie Day
    Juana Maria Delgado-Saborit
    Warren Eastwood
    Steven Emery
    Sara Fregonese
    Guy Harrington
    Alan Hastie
    Alan Herbert
    Phil Jones
    Stephen Jones
    Nick Kettridge
    Stephen Krause
    Mark Ledger
    Peter Lee
    Agnieszka Leszczynski
    Iseult Lynch
    Zena Lynch
    Vlad Mykhnenko
    Patricia Noxolo
    Francis Pope
    Jessica Pykett
    Adam Ramadan

Joanna Renshaw
Michael Riley
Michael Rivett
John Round
Ivan Sansom
Greg Sambrook Smith
Carl Stevenson
Emmanouil Tranos
James Wheeley
Martin Widman
Birmingham Fellow & Academic Keeper, Lapworth Museum of Geology:
    Richard Butler
Other:
    Tom Dunkley Jones
Related Staff:
    Melanie Bickerton

University of Bristol
School of Earth Sciences (B,M,D) (2016)
Wills Memorial Building
Queens Road
Bristol BS8 1RJ
    p. +44 117 954 5400
    m.j.walter@bristol.ac.uk
    http://www.bristol.ac.uk/earthsciences/
    f: https://www.facebook.com/School-of-Earth-Sciences-
    Bristol-University-146277648746662/
    t: @UOBEarthscience
    Enrollment (2013): B: 25 (9) M: 44 (5)
Professor:
    Michael Walter , (D), 1991, GiCpg

University of Cambridge
Dept of Earth Sciences (B,D) (2015)
Downing Street
Cambridge , Cambridgeshire CB2 3EQ
    p. +44 (0)1223 333400
    jaj2@cam.ac.uk
    http://www.esc.cam.ac.uk
Head:
    James Jackson, YgGt
Professor:
    Michael Bickle, GtYgGo
    Nicholas J. Butterfield, Po
    Michael Carpenter, Gy
    Harry Elderfield, Ge
    David Hodell, Ge
    Marian Holness, Gi
    Dan McKenzie, YgGt
    Simon Conway Morris, Po
    Keith Priestley, YgGt
    Simon Redfern, Gz
    Ekhard Salje, Gy
    Nicky White, YgGt
    Robert White, YgGt
    Eric Wolff, Ge
    Andy Woods, YgGt
Lecturer:
    David Al-Attar, YdGt
    Alex Copley, YgGt
    Sanne Cottaar, Ys
    Neil Davies, Gs
    Marie Edmonds, Gv
    Ian Farnan, Gz
    Sally Gibson, Gi
    Richard Harrison, Gz
    Tim Holland, Gp
    John Maclennan, Gi
    Kenneth McNamara, Po
    Jerome Anthony Neufeld, GoYgGt
    David Norman, Po
    John Rudge, YgGt
    Luke Skinner, Ge
    Ed Tipper, Cl
    Alexandra Turchyn, Ge
    Nigel Woodcock, Gtt

University of Derby

Geographical, Earth and Environmental Sciences (B,M)
(2014)
Kedleston Road
Derby DE22 1GAB
p. +44 (0) 1332 591703
fehs@derby.ac.uk
http://www.derby.ac.uk/science/gees/
Enrollment (2013): B: 120 (30) M: 9 (10)
Head:
Hugh Rollinson, Cg
Professor:
Aradhana Mehra, Co
Instructor:
Jacob Adentunji, Ge
Andrew Johnson, Ob
Lecturer:
Martin Whiteley, Go

University of East Anglia

School of Env Sciences (2015)
Norwich Research Park
Norwich NR4 7TJ
p. +44 (0)1603 592542
env.enquiries@uea.ac.uk
http://www.uea.ac.uk/environmental-sciences
Director:
Corinne Le Quere, Ge
Head:
Julian Andrews, (D), Leicester, 1984, Cs
Professor:
Jan Alexander, (D), Leeds, Gt
Ian Bateman, Ge
Simon Clegg, (D), 1986, Op
Brett Day, (D), UEA, 2004, Ge
Alastair Grant, (D), Wales, Ge
Karen Heywood, Op
Kevin Hiscock, (D), Birmingham, Hg
Tim Jickells, (D), Southampton, Ob
Phillip Jones, Oa
Andy Jordan, Ge
Andrew Lovett, Oi
Coling Murrell, Oa
Carlos Peres, Sf
Ian Renfrew, Ow
Ian Renfrew, Ow
Bill Sturges, Oa
Roland von Glasow, (D), Max-Planck-Inst in Mainz, Yg
Andrew Watkinson, Ge
Sir Robert Watson
Research Associate:
Amy Binner
Instructor:
Alex Baker, (D), Plymouth Marine Lab, On
Jenni Barclay, (D), Bristol, Gv
Paul Burton, (D), Cambridge, Ys
Mark Chapman, (D), East Anglia, Pm
Paul Dolman, Ou
Jan Kaiser, Cs
Gill Malin, Ob
Adrian Matthews, (D), Reading, Ow
Timothy Osborn, Oa
Claire Reeves, (D), UEA, Cg
Carol Robinson, Ob
Parvadha Suntharalingam, Oc
Cock von Oosterhout, (D), Leiden
Rachel Warren, Eg
Lecturer:
Annela Anger-Kraavi, EgGe
Annela Anger-Kraavi, Eg
Victor Bense, Hg
Alan Bond, (D), Lancaster, Ge
Jason Chilvers, (D), Univ Coll (London), Ge
Pietro Cosentino, Yg
Stephen Dorling, Ow

Aldina Franco, (D), UEA, Ge
Robert Hall, (D), Proudman Oceanographic Laboratory, On
Tom Hargreaves, Ge
Richard Herd, (D), Lancaster, Gv
Martin Johnson, Cm
Manoj Joshi, (D), Oxford, Oi
Iain Lake, Ge
Irene Lorenzoni, Eg
Nikolai Pedentchouk, (D), Penn State, 2004, Cs
Jane Powell, Ge
Brian Reid, GeCg
Gill Seyfang, Og
Congxiao Shang, (D), Queen Mary, Hw
Peter Simmons, Eg
Trevor Tolhurst, Sb
Jenni Turner, (D), 2008, Gt
Naomi Vaughan, (D), UEA, Ow
Charlie Wilson, (D), British Columbia, Ge
Xiaoming Zhai, (D), Dalhousie, Og
Professorial Fellow:
Kerry Turner, GeEg

University of Exeter

Camborne School of Mines (2004)
Redruth, Cornwall
TR15 3SE
C.Jeffrey@exeter.ac.uk
http://www.ex.ac.uk/CSM/

University of Glasgow

School of Geographical and Earth Sciences (2015)
The Gregory Building
East Quadrangle
University Avenue
Glasgow G12 8QQ
p. +44 (0) 141 330 5436
GES-General@glasgow.ac.uk
http://www.gla.ac.uk/schools/ges/
Head:
Maggie Cusack, Gz
Professor:
Paul Bishop
John Briggs, Ou
Roderick Brown, Cc
Deborah Dixon
Trevor Hoey, Gs
Martin Lee, Gz
Christopher Philo
Senior Scientist:
Nicolas Beaudoin
Research Associate:
Enateri Alakpa
Susan Fitzer, Ob
Michael Gallagher
Lydia Hallis
Ulrich Kelka
Angela Last
Paula Lindgren, Oa
Alistair Mcgowan, Pg
Larissa Naylor
Instructor:
Gorden Curry, Ge
Anne Dunlop
David Forrest, Oi
Jim Hansom, On
Mhairi Harvey
Hayden Lorimer
Hannah Mathers
Rhian Meara
Alan Owen, Pg
Hester Parr
Vernon Phoenix
Daisy Rood
Lecturer:
Brian Bell, So
David Brown, Gvs

Seamus Coveney, Oi
Tim Dempster, Gz
Jane Drummond, Oi
Derek Fabel, Xg
David Featherstone
Nick Kamenos
Ozan Karaman
Daniel Koehn, Gt
Cheryl Mcgeachan
Simon Naylor
Cristina Persano

University of Leeds
School of Earth and Environment (B,M,D) (2014)
Maths/Earth and Environment Building
The University of Leeds
Leeds LS2 9JT
    p. +44 113 343 2846
    enquiries@see.leeds.ac.uk
    http://earth.leeds.ac.uk/
Head:
    Robert Mortimer, Ge
Chair:
    Christopher Collier
    Simon Poulton, Co
    Peter Taylor, Ge
Professor:
    John Barrett, Ge
    Liane G. Benning, Ce
    Alan Blyth, Oa
    Ian Brooks, (D), UMIST, On
    Ken Carslaw, (D), East Anglia, 1994, Oa
    Andy Challinor, (D), Leds, 1999, Ow
    Martyn Chipperfield, (D), Cambridge, Oa
    Surage Dessai, (D), East Anglia
    Andy Dougil, (D), Sheffield, Os
    Paul Field
    Quentin Fishe, Np
    Piers Forster, (D), Reading, 1994, Ow
    Paul Glover, Gd
    Andy Gouldson, Ge
    Alan Haywood, Pe
    Steve Hencher, Ng
    Andy Hooper, Ydg
    Greg Houseman, (D), Cambridge, Yg
    Michael Krom, Cm
    Bill McCaffrey, Gs
    Stephen Mobbs, Oa
    Jurgen Neuberg, (D), Colorado, Gv
    Jouni Paavola, Ge
    Doug Parker, (D), Reading, Ow
    Jeff Peakall, Gs
    Andrew Shepherd
    Lindsay C. Stinger, Ge
    Graham Stuart, Ys
    Paul Wignall, PgGs
    Tim Wright, Yd
    Bruce Yardley, Cg
    William Young, (D), Ge
Associate Professor:
    Doug Angus, Ys
    Stephen Arnold, (D), Leeds, Oa
    Wolfgang Buermann, (D), Boston, 2012, Ou
    Ian Burke, (D), Southampton, Ge
    Steven Dobbie, (D), Dalhousie, Oa
    Luuk Flesken, (D), Wageningen Univ, Ge
    Phil Livermore, Ym
    Daniel Morgan, (D), Open Univ, 2003, Giv
    Jon Mound, (D), Toronto, 2001, Gt
    Noelle Odling, (D), Queens, Hg
    Caroline Peacock, (D), Bristol, Sb
    Sally Russell, (D), Queensland, Ge
    Dominick Spracklen, (D), Leeds, 1999, On
    Julia Steinberger, Ou
    Jared West, Hg
Research Associate:
    David Banks, Cg

Simon Bottrell
Fiona Gill
Lauren Gregoire, (D), Bristol
Ruza Ivanovic, (D), Bristol
John Marsham, (D), Edinburgh, 2003, Oa
Instructor:
    Nick Dixon, (D), Leeds, 2002, Ou
    Tim Foxon, Ge
    Clare Gordon, Oi
    Chris Green
    Dave Hodgson
    Jacqueline Houghton
    Damian Howells
    Geoff Lloyd, (D), Birmingham, 1984
    Sebastian Rost, Ys
Lecturer:
    Ralf Barkemeyer
    Emma Bramham, Ym
    Robert Chapman
    Roger Clark, (D), Leeds, Ys
    Martin Dallimer, (D), Edinburgh, 2001, Ge
    Monica Di Gregorio, (D), London School of Economics, Eg
    Jen Dyer, (D), Leeds, Ge
    Alan Gadian
    Dabo Guan, Eg
    Jason Harvey, (D), 2005, Cg
    Mark Hildyard
    George Holmes, Ge
    Andrea Jackson, (D), Lancaster, Oa
    Julia Leventon, (D), Cent, Ge
    Crispin Little, (D), Bristol, 1995, Pg
    Piroska Lorinczi, (D), Leeds, 2002, Ng
    Vernon Manville
    Andrew McCair, (D), Cambridge, 1983, Gc
    Jim McQuaid, (D), Leeds, Oa
    Lucie Middlemiss, (D), Leeds, 2009, Ge
    Nigel Mountney, Gs
    Rob Newton, (D), Leeds, Ge
    Alice OWen, (D), Leeds
    Douglas Paton, Gc
    Richard Phillips, (D), Oxford, Gt
    Claire Quinn, (D), Kings College, Ge
    Andrew Ross, (D), Cambridge, Ow
    Susannah Sallu, Ga
    Ivan Savov, (D), South Florida, 2004, Cg
    Anne Tallontire
    Mark Thomas, (D), Ng
    Taija Torvela, (D), Akademi, 2007, Gc
    James van Alstine, Ge
    Xianyun Wen, (D), Hg
Visiting Professor:
    Jane Francis, Pe
    Tim Needham, Gc
Emeritus:
    Rob Knipe, Gt
Related Staff:
    Samantha Haynes, Go

University of Liverpool
School of Environmental Sciences (B,M,D) (2014)
Jane Herdman Building
4 Brownlow Street
Liverpool, Merseyside L69 3GP
    p. +44 151 794 5146
    envsci@liv.ac.uk
    http://www.liv.ac.uk/environmental-sciences/index.html

Dept of Earth, Ocean, and Ecological Sciences (2014)
Jane Herdman Building
4 Brownlow Street
Liverpool L69 3GP
    p. +44 (0)151 795 4642
    nataly.jones@liverpool.ac.uk
    http://www.liv.ac.uk/earth-ocean-and-ecological-sciences/
Head:
    Andreas Rietbrock, YsGv

Professor:
  Daniel Faulkner, Ys
  Chris Frid, Ob
  Richard Holme, Ym
  Peter Kokelaar, GstGv
  Nick Kusznir, Yd
  Yan Lavallee, Gv
  Rob Marrs, Os
  Jim Marshall, Cs
  Jonathan Sharples, Ocp
  Stan van der Berg, Em
  John Wheeler, Em
  Richard Worden, Gs
Research Associate:
  Katherine Allen, Oi
  James Ball
  Helen Bloomfield, Ob
  Stephen Crowley, Gs
  Jonathan Lauderdale, Og
  Claire Melet
  Andreas Nilsson, Ym
  Vassil Roussenov, Og
  Anu Thompson, Oc
  Xiao Wang
  Tsuyuko Yamanaka, Ob
Lecturer:
  Charlotte Jeffrey Abt, On
  Andy Biggin, Ym
  Alan Boyle, Gt
  Bryony Caswell, Ob
  Silvio De Angelis, Ys
  Rob Duller, Gvs
  Liz Fisher, Co
  Jonathan Green, Ob
  Mimi Hill, Ym
  Janine Kavanagh, Gv
  Helen Kinvig, Gs
  Claire Mahaffey, Oc
  Elisabeth Mariani, Nr
  Kate Parr, Pe
  John Piper, YmGt
  Leonie Robinson, Ob
  Isabelle Ryder, Gt
  Matthew Spencer, Og
  Neil Suttie
  Alessandro Tagliabue, Oc
  Jack Thomson, Ob
Other:
  Sara Henton De Angelis
  Jackie Kendrick
  Rachel Salaun, Oc
  Felix von Aulock

University of London, Royal Holloway & Bedford New College
Dept of Earth Sciences (B,M,D) (2015)
Department of Earth Sciences
Royal Holloway University of London
Egham Hill
Egham , Surrey TW20 0EX
    p. +44 (0) 1784 443 581
    info@es.rhul.ac.uk
    https://www.royalholloway.ac.uk/earthsciences/home.aspx
    t: @RHULEarthSci
Head:
  Peter Burgess, Gs
Professor:
  Margaret Collinson, Po
  Agust Gudmundsson, Gc
  Robert Hall, Gt
  Martin King, Oa
  Dave Mattey, Cs
  Ken McClay, Gc
  Jason Morgan, Yg
  Wolfgang Muller, Cs
  Euan Nisbet, Og

Matthew Thirlwall, Cs
Dave Waltham, Yg
Lecturer:
  Jurgen Adam, Gc
  Dave Alderton, Gz
  Kevin Clemitshaw, Ge
  Howard Falcon-Lang, Pg
  Francisco J. Hernandez-Molina, Gs
  Saswata Hier-Majumder, Yg
  Daniel Le Heron, Og
  Christina Manning, Cg
  Steve Smith, Ge
  Paola Vannucchi, Gu
  Ian Watkinson, Gt
Emeritus:
  Andrew Cunningham Scott, Pb
Laboratory Director:
  Nathalie Grassineau, Cs
  David Lowry, Cs

University of Manchester
School of Earth, Atmospheric and Environmental Science
(2015)
Williamson Building
Oxford Road
, Manchester M13 9PL
    p. +44 (0) 161 306 9360
    earth.support@manchester.ac.uk
    Administrative Assistant: Steven Olivier
Director:
  Stephen Boult, Hg
Chair:
  Jonathan Redfern, (D), Bristol, 1990, Gso
Professor:
  Mike Bowman, (D), Wales, Go
  Gregg Butler
  Andrew Chamberlain, Ga
  Thomas Choularton, (D), Manchester, 1987, Oa
  Hue Coe, (D), UMIST, 1993, Oa
  Stephen Flint, Go
  Martin Gallagher, (D), UMIDST, 1986, Oa
  Jamie Gilmour, (D), Sheffield
  Colin Hughes, (D), Open, 1992, Go
  Francis Livens, Cg
  Jonathan Lloyd, (D), Canterbury, 1993, Ge
  Ian Lyon, (D), 1993, Xc
  Gordon McFiggans, (D), UEA, 2000, Oa
  Richard Pattrick, (D), 1980, Gz
  Carl Percival, (D), Oxford, 1995, Oa
  David Poyla, (D), Manchester, 1987, Cm
  Ernest Rutter, (D), Imperial Coll, Gc
  David Schultz, Ow
  Kevin Taylor, Go
  David Vaughan, (D), Oxford, 1971, Gz
  Geraint Vaughan, (D), Oxford, 1982, Oa
  Roy Wogelius, (D), Northwestern, 1990, Cg
Research Associate:
  Karl Beswick, Oa
  Alastair Booth, Oa
  Pieter Bots, Ge
  Gerard Capes, Oa
  Deborah Chavrit, (D), Nantes (France), 2010, Gi
  Patricia Clay, (D), Open, 2010, Cs
  Filipa Cox
  Ian Crawford, Oa
  Sarah Crowther, (D), Oxford, 2003, Oa
  Christopher Dearden, Oa
  Patrick Dowey
  Helen Downie, Ge
  Nicholas Edwards, Pg
  Christopher Emersic, (D)
  Torsten Henkel, Cs
  Hazel Jones, Oa
  Nimisha Joshi
  Richard Kift, Oa
  Kimberly Leather, Oa
  Dantong Liu, Oa

Douglas Lowe, Oa
William Morgan, Oa
Miquel Poyatos-More
Laura Richards, Ge
Hugo Ricketts, Oa
Athanasios Rizoulis, Ge
Andrew Smedley, Oa
Robert Sparkes, (D), Cambridge, 2012
Jonathan Taylor, (D), Manchester
Karen Theis, (D), Manchester, 2008, On
James Whitehead, Oa
Paul Williams, Oa
Instructor:
Neil Mitchell, (D), Oxford 1989, Gu
Lecturer:
Grant Allen, (D), Leicester, 2005, Oa
Simon Brocklehurst, (D), MIT, 2002, Gm
Kate Brodie, (D), Imperial Coll, 1979, Gc
Rufus Brunt, (D), Leeds, Gs
Michael Buckley, (D), York, 2008, Ga
Ray Burgess, (D), Open, Cs
Victoria Coker, (D), Manchester, 2007, Gz
Paul Connolly, (D), Manchester, 2006, Oa
Stephen Covery-Crump, (D), Univ Coll (London), 1992
Giles Droop, (D), Oxford, 1979, Gp
Victoria Egerton, Pg
David Hodgetts, (D), Keele, 1995, Gsc
Cathy Hollis, (D), Aberdeen, 1995, Gs
Merren Jones, (D), Whyoming, 1997, Gst
Julian Mecklenburgh, Gc
John Nudds, (D), Dunhelm, 1975, Pg
Clare Robinson, (D), Lancaster, 1990, Co
Stefan Schroeder, (D), Bern, 2000, Go
Bart van Dongen, Utrecht, 2003, Co
Emeritus:
Christopher Henderson
Peter Jonas
Grenville Turner, (D), Oxford, 1962, Xc

University of Newcastle Upon Tyne
School of Civil Engineering and Geosciences (2014)
Newcastle University
Newcastle upon Tyne
NE1 7RU
p. +44 (0)191 208 6323
ceg@ncl.ac.uk
http://www.ncl.ac.uk/ceg/
Head:
Bryn Jones
Jon Mills, Ng
Professor:
Margaret Carol Bell, Ge
Andras Bordossy, Og
Peter Clarke, Yd
Chris Kilsby, Hg
Stephen Larter, Gg
Zhenhong Li, Yd
Phillip Moore, Yd
Research Associate:
David Alderson, Oi
Joana Baptista, Ng
Stephen Blenkinson, On
Bernard Bowler, Go
Aidan Burton
Allistair Ford, Gq
Ian Martin, Yd
Kirill Palamartchouk, Yd
Liz Petrie, Yd
Instructor:
James Barhurst, Gs
Neil Gray, Py
Helen Talbot, Co
Lecturer:
Geoffrey Abbott, Co
Carolyn Aitkens
Jamie Amezaga, Ge
Stuart Barr, Oi

Colin Davie, Ng
Stuart Edwards, Gq
Gaetano Elia, gaet, Ng
David Fairbairn, Gq
Rachel Gaulton, Or
Jean Hall, Ng
Christina Maerz, Gg
Geoffrey Parkin, Hg
Nigel Penna, Gq
Paul Quinn, Hg
Crees van der Land, Go
Visiting Professor:
Tina Abreau
Xuwen An
Rick Brassington, Hg
Related Staff:
Peter Cunningham, Hg

University of Nottingham
Dept of Mineral Resources (2004)
University Park
Nottingham HG7 2RD
wpadmin@nottingham.ac.uk

University of Oxford
Dept of Earth Sciences (2014)
Department of Earth Sciences
South Parks Road
Oxford, Oxfordshire OX1 3AN
p. +44 1865 272000
reception@earth.ox.ac.uk
http://www.earth.ox.ac.uk/
Head:
Alex Halliday, Cs
Chair:
Christopher Ballentine, Xg
Phillip England, Gt
Professor:
Martin Brasier, Po
Joe Cartwright, Gs
Shamita Das, Gtv
Donalf G. Fraser, Cg
Gideon Henderson, Cg
Samar Khatiwala
Barry Parsons, Yd
David Pyle, Gtv
Ros Rickaby, Gz
Mike Searle, Gt
Tony Watts, Gu
Bernard Wood, Gz
John Woodhouse, Yg
Lecturer:
Roger Benson, Po
Heather Bouman, Cg
Matt Friedman, Po
Lars Hansen, Gz
Hugh Jenkyns, Gr
Helen Johnson, Og
Richard Katz, Cg
Graeme Lloyd, Gs
Tamsin Mather, Gv
Conall Mac Niocaill, Gt
Don Porcelli, Cg
Stuart Robinson, Gdr
Karin Sigloch, Yg
Richard Walker, Or
Dave Waters, Gp

University of Plymouth
Dept of Earth Sciences (2015)
Drake Circus
Plymouth, Devon PL4 8AA
p. +44 (0)1752 584584
science.technology@plymouth.ac.uk
http://www.plymouth.ac.uk/schools/sogees

Head:
  Mark Anderson, (D), Wales Cardiff, Gct
Professor:
  Terry Morris, (D), Edinburgh, Gt
  Greogry Price, (D), Reading, 1994, Gsr
  Iain Stewart, (D), Bristol, 1990
Associate Professor:
  Stephen Grimes, (D), Cardiff, 1998, Cs
  Martin Stokes, (D), Plymouth, 1997, Gm
  Graeme Taylor, Yg
  Matthew Watkinson, (D), Open, 1989, Gs
Lecturer:
  Sarah Boulton, (D), Edinburgh, 2005, Or
  Paul Cole, (D), 1990, Gv
  Arjan Dijkstra, (D), Utrecht, 2001, Gi
  Meriel FitzPatrick, (D), Plymouth, 1992, Oe
  Luca Menegon, (D), Padua, 2006, Gct
  Andrew Merritt, (D), Leeds, 2010, Ng
  Kevin Page, (D), Univ Coll (London), 1988, Gr
  Christopher Smart, (D), Southampton, 1993, Pg
  Colin Wilkins, (D), James Cook (North Queensland), 1991, Eg
Emeritus:
  Malcolm Hart, (D), London, Pm

University of Portsmouth
School of Earth and Environmental Sciences (2014)
Burnaby Road
Portsmouth, Hampshire PO1 3QL
  p. +44 (0)23 9284 2257
  sees.enquiries@port.ac.uk
  http://www.sci.port.ac.uk/departments/academic/sees
Head:
  Rob Strachan, (D), Keele, 1982, Cc
Professor:
  Andrew Gale, (D), Ggr
  Jim Smith, (D), Ge
Research Associate:
  Emilie Braund, (D), Graz, 2011, Gz
  Fay Couceiro, (D), On
  Penny Lancaster, (D), Bristol, 2011, Gz
  Robert Loveridge
  Darren Naish
  David Ray, (D)
  Alan Raybould, (D)
  Steve Sweetman, (D), Pg
  Mark Whitton, (D), Portsmouth, 2008, Pg
Instructor:
  Chris Dewdney, (D), Birkbeck, 1983, Yg
  Gary Fones, (D), Central Lancashire, Cm
  David Loydell, (D), Gr
  David Martill, (D), Po
  Craig Storey, (D), Leicester, 2002, Gp
Lecturer:
  John Allen, (D), Southampton, 1996, Og
  Hooshyar Assadullahi
  Philip Benson, (D)
  Michelle Bloor, (D), Hg
  Dean Bullen, (D), Gt
  Anthony Butcher, (D), Pg
  James Darling, (D), Bristol, 2009, Cs
  Mike Fowler, (D), Imperial, Gi
  David Franklin, (D), Ym
  Martyn Gardiner, (D)
  Andy Gibson, (D), Eg
  David Giles, Gm
  Michelle Hale, (D), Flinders, Og
  Nick Koor
  Nicholas Minter, (D), Bristol, 2007, Gs
  Derek Rust, (D), Gt
  Camen Solana, (D), Gv
  Richard Teeuw, (D), Oi
  Melvin M. Vopson, (D), Central Lancashire, 2002, Yg
  Nick Walton, Hw
  John Whalley, (D), Gc
  Malcolm Whitworth, (D)

University of Reading
Soil Research Centre (B,M,D) (2012)
Department of Geography and Environmental Science
School of Human and Environmental Sciences
Whiteknights
Reading RG6 6AB
  p. +44 (0)118 378 8911
  shes@reading.ac.uk
  http://www.reading.ac.uk/soil-research-centre
Professor:
  Chris Collins, (D), Sb
Associate Professor:
  Stuart Black, (D), Lancaster, Cc
  Chris Collins, (D), Sc
  McGoff Hazel, (D), Liverpool, Pg
  Steve Robinson, (D), Sf
  Liz Shaw, (D), Sb
  Anne Verhoef, (D), Sp
Dr:
  Joanna Clark, (D), Leeds, Sc

University of South Wales
Geology Section (2004)
Department of Science
Pontypridd

University of Southampton
Ocean and Earth Science (B,M,D) ● (2015)
University of Southampton Waterfront Campus
National Oceanography Centre Southampton
European Way
Southampton, Hampshire SO14 3ZH
  p. +44 (0)23 8059 2011
  soes@soton.ac.uk
  http://www.southampton.ac.uk/oes
  f: https://www.facebook.com/UoSOceanography?fref=ts
  https://www.facebook.com/UoSGeoscience?fref=ts
  t: @OceanEarthUoS
Royal Society Wolfson Reserch Merit Award holder:
  Eelco J. Rohling, (D), Utrecht, 1991, Op
Professorial Research Fellow:
  Ian S. Robinson, (D), Warwick, 1973, Or
  John G. Shepherd, (D), Cambridge, 1970, Oa
MBA Senior Resarch Fellow:
  David Sims, (D), Plymouth, 1994, Ob
Head of Physical Oceanography Research Group:
  Sybren Drijfhout, (D), Utrecht, 1992, Op
Head of Palaeoceanography and Palaeoclimate Research Group:
  Paul A. Wilson, (D), Cambridge, 1995, GsCg
Head of Marine Biogeochemistry Research Group:
  Toby Tyrrell, (D), Edinburgh, 1993, Oc
Head of Graduate School of the NOCS:
  Stephen Roberts, (D), Open, 1986, Cg
Head of Geochemistry Research Group:
  Rachael James, (D), Cambridge, 1995, Oc
Head of Department:
  Rachel A. Mills, (D), Cambridge, 1992, Cm
Director of Research:
  Martin R. Palmer, (D), Leeds, 1984, Cg
Director of Education:
  Lisa McNeill, (D), Oregon State, 1998, GtYr
Professor:
  Eric P. Achterberg, (D), Liverpool, 1994, Oc
  Carl L. Amos, (D), Imperial Coll, 1974, Gs
  Nicholas R. Bates, (D), Southampton, 1995, Oc
  Colin Brownlee, (D), Newcastle upon Tyne, Ob
  Harry Bryden, (D), MIT/WHOI, 1975, Op
  Jonathan M. Bull, (D), Edinburgh, 1990, Yr
  Ian Croudace, (D), Birmingham, 1980, Ge
  Gavin Foster, (D), Open, 2000, Csg
  Tim Henstock, (D), Cambridge, 1994, Yg
  Alan Kemp, (D), Edinburgh, 1985, Pe
  Robert Marsh, (D), Southampton, 2000, Op
  John Marshall, (D), Bristol, 1981, PlGo
  Timothy A. Minshull, (D), Cambridge, 1990, Yr
  Christopher Mark Moore, (D), Southampton, 2002, Ob

Alberto Naveira Garabato, (D), Liverpool, 1999, Op
Duncan A. Purdie, (D), Wales, 1982, Ob
Martin Solan, (D), National Univ of Ireland (Galway), 2000, Ob
Peter Statham, (D), Southampton, 1983, Ob
Damon Teagle, (D), Cambridge, 1993, Cg
Jorg Wiedenmann, Ulm (Germany), 2000, Ob
Head of Marine Biology and Ecoplogy Research Group:
Chris Hauton, (D), Southampton, 1995, Ob
Head of Geology and Geophysics Research Group[:
Justin Dix, (D), St. Andrews, 1994, GaYs
Associate Professor:
Jonathan Copley, (D), Southampton, 1998, Ob
Gareth Dyke, (D), Bristol, 2000, Pv
Lawrence Hawkins, (D), Southampton, 1985, Pi
Antony Jensen, (D), Southampton, 1982, Ob
Derek Keir, (D), Royal Holloway (London), 2006, Gtv
Cathy Lucas, (D), Southampton, 1993, Ob
Juerg M. Matter, (D), Swiss Fed Inst Tech, 2001, Ng
Catherine A. Rychert, (D), Brown, 2007, Yg
Sven Thatje, (D), Bremen, 2003, Ob
Clive Trueman, (D), Bristol, 1997, Cg
Neil Wells, (D), Reading, 1974, Opw
Assistant Professor:
Maeve Lohan, Southampton, 2003, Ob
Teaching Fellow:
Judith Coggon, (D), Durham, 2010, Cg
Laura Grange, (D), Southampton, 2005, Ob
Senior Tutor:
Andy J. Barker, (D), Univ of Wales (Cardiff), 1983, Gg
Senior Lecturer:
Rex N. Taylor, (D), Southampton, 1987, GvCa
(SMMI Lecturer):
Steven Bohaty, (D), California (Santa Cruz), 2006, Og
Lecturer:
Amanda E. Bates, Victoria, 2006, Ob
Claudie Beaulieu, (D), Quebec, 2009, Op
Simon R. Boxall, (D), Liverpool, 1985, Op
Tom Ezard, Imperial Coll (London), 2007
Phillip Fenberg, (D), California (San Diego), 2008, Ob
Eleanor Frajka-Williams, (D), Washington, 2009, Op
Thomas Gernon, (D), Bristol, 2007, Og
Jasmin A. Godbold, Aberdeen, 2009, Ob
Phillip A. Goodwin, Liverpool, 2007, Pe
Ivan D. Haigh, (D), Southampton, 2009, On
Nicholas Harmon, (D), Brown, 2007, Yr
Kevin Oliver, (D), East Anglia, 2003, Op
Marc Rius, (D), Barcelona, 2008, Ob
Florian Sevellec, (D), UBO, 2007, Op
Esther Sumner, (D), Bristol, 2009, Gs
Jessica H. Whiteside, (D), Columbia, 2006, Pe
Chuang Xuan, (D), Florida, 2010, Pe
Emeritus Professor:
Robert B. Whitmarsh, (D), Cambridge, 1967, Yr
Senior Lecturer:
Thomas Bibby, (D), Imperial Coll (London), 2003, Ob
Ian Harding, (D), Cambridge, 1986, Pml

University of St. Andrews
School of Geography & Geosciences (2004)
Division of Geology
St. Andrews
Fife KY16 9ST

Dept of Earth and Environmental Science (B,M,D) (2015)
Irvine Building
North St.
Fife, Scotland KY16 9AL
    p. (+44) (0)1334 463940
    earthsci@st-andrews.ac.uk
    http://earthsci.st-andrews.ac.uk/
    f: https://www.facebook.com/EarthSciStA/
    t: @EarthSciStA
Director:
Richard Bates, (D), Wales, Yx
Tony Prave, Pg
Ruth Robinson, (D), Penn State, 1997, Gs

Head:
Peter Cawood, (D), Sydney, 1980, Gt
Professor:
Colin Ballantyne, (D)
Research Associate:
Nicky Allison, (D), Edinburgh, 1994, Oc
Mark Claire, (D), Washington, Oa
Catherine Cole, (D), Southampton, 2013, Cm
Ruth Hindshaw, (D), ETH Zürich, 2011, Cs
Gareth Izon, (D), Cg
Coralie Mills
James Rae, (D), Bristol, Cg
Lecturer:
Andrea Burke, Cs
Adriam Finch, Gz
Timothy Hill, (D), Edinburgh, 2003, Ge
Tim Raub, (D), Yale, 2008, Py
Vincent Rinterknecht, Ol
Michael Singer, (D), California (Santa Barbara), 2003, Hg
John Walden, (D), Wolverhampton Polytechnic, 1990, Ym
Robert Wilson, (D), W Ontario, 2003, On
Aubrey Zerkle, (D), Penn State, 2006, Co

University of Wales
Dept of Earth and Ocean Sciences (2014)
College of Cardiff
Main Building
Park Place
, Cardiff CF1 3YE
    p. +44 (0)29 208 74830
    earth-ug@cf.ac.uk
    http://www.cardiff.ac.uk/earth/
Head:
R. John PArkes, Cg
Professor:
Thomas Blenkinspo
Dianne Edwards, Pb
Ian R. Hall
Richard Lisle
Chris MacLeod, Og
Wolfgang Maier
Paul Pearson, PmCg
Instructor:
Stephen Barker
Huw Davies
Andrew Kerr, Og
Jenny Pike, Og
Hazel Prichard, EgGz
Lecturer:
Tiego Alves, Og
Liz Bagshaw
Rhoda Ballinger, On
Chris Berry
Peter Brabham, Ng
David Buchs
Alan Channing, Gd
Lesley Cherns
Jose Constantine
Ake Fagereng
T. C. Hales, Gt
Alan Hemsley, Pl
Tim Jones
Eli Lazarus, On
C. Johan Lissenberg
Iain MacDonald, Ca
Rupert Perkins
Phil Renforth
David Reynolds
Henrik Sass, Co
Simon Wakefield
Laboratory Director:
Caroline Lear, Og
Tutorial Fellow:
Ian Fryett
Nick Rodgers, Xm

Geography and Earth Sciences (2014)
Llandinam Building
Penglais Campus
Aberystwyth SY23 3DB
  p. +44(0) 1970 622 606
  dges@aber.ac.uk
  http://www.aber.ac.uk/en/iges/
Director:
  Neil Glasser
Head:
  Rhys Jones
Professor:
  John Grattan
  Michael Hambrey
  Matthew Hannah
  Alun Hubbard
  Bryn Hubbard
  David Kay
  Henry Lamb
  Richard Lucas
  Mark Macklin
  Alex Maltman
  Nick Pearce
  Mark Whitehead
  Michael Woods
Research Associate:
  Ron Fuge
Instructor:
  Peter Abrahams
  Peter Merriman
  Andrew Mitchell
  Helen Roberts
  Andrew Thomas
  Stephen Tooth
Lecturer:
  Charlie Bendall
  Paul Brewer
  Peter Bunting
  Rachel Carr
  Rhys Dafydd Jones
  Sarah Davies
  Carina Fearnley
  Elizabeth Gagen
  Hywel Griffiths
  Kevin Grove
  Andrew Hardy
  Jesse Heley
  Tom Holt
  Gareth Hoskins
  Tristram Irvine-Fynn
  Cerys Jones
  Bill Perkings
  Kimberly Peters
  George Petropoulos
  Mitch Rose
  Joe Williams
  Richard Williams
  Sophie Wynne-Jones
Teaching Fellow:
  Stefania Amici

School of Ocean Sciences (2014)
Bangor University
Menai Bridge
Anglesey, Bangor LL59 5AB
  p. (01248) 382851
  oss011@bangor.ac.uk
  http://www.bangor.ac.uk/oceansciences/
Director:
  Colin Jago
Professor:
  David Bowers
  Alan Davies
  Michel Kaiser
  Hilary Kennedy
  Chris Richardson
  Tom Rippeth

  James Scourse
  John Simpson
  David Thomas
Instructor:
  Jan Geert Hiddink
  Stuart Jenkins
Lecturer:
  Martin Austin
  Jaco H. Baas
  Paul Butler
  Andrew Davies
  Lui Gimenez
  Mattias Green
  Cara Hughes
  Dei Huws
  Suzanna Jackson
  Lewis LeVay
  Shelagh Malham
  Irene Martins
  Ian McCarthy
  Gay Mitchelson-Jacob
  Simon P. Neill
  Anna Pienkowski
  Martin Skov
  John Russel Turner
  Katrien van Landeghem
  Stephanie Wilson
Related Staff:
  Timothy Whitton

Uruguay

Direccion Nacional de Mineria y Geologia de Uruguay
Direccion Nacional de Mineria y Geologia de Uruguay (2015)
Hervidero 2861
Montevideo, Montevideo 11800
  p. + 5982 2001951
  infomiem@miem.gub.uy
  http://www.dinamige.gub.uy/

Universidad de la Republica Montevideo
Dept de Geologia (2004)
Avenida 18 de Julio 1968, Montevideo

Universidad de la Republica Oriental del Uruguay (UDELAR)
Instituto de Geología y Paleontología (2011)
Avenida 18 de Julio 1968, Montevideo
CP11 400
Montevideo 10773
  http://www.fcien.edu.uy/menu2/estructura2/ingepa2.html

Universidad de la Republica Oriental del Uruguay (UDELAR)
Deptartamento de Geografia (B) (2015)
Iguá 4225 Piso 14 Sur C.P: 11400
Montevideo, Montevideo 11400
  p. (598-2) 525 15 52
  geotecno@fcien.edu.uy
  http://geografia.fcien.edu.uy/
Professor:
  Virginia Fernández, (M), Girona, 2001, OirOn
Assistant Professor:
  Yuri Resnichenko, (M), la República, 2010, OirOn

Dept de Suelos y Aguas (2011)
  p. (598 2) 359 82 72
  suelosyaguas@fagro.edu.uy
  http://suelosyaguas.fagro.edu.uy/

263

Uzbekistan

Institute of Geology and Geophysics
(2011)
http://www.ingeo.uz/

Institute of Mineral Resources
(2013)
gpniimr@evo.uz
http://www.gpniimr.uz/

National University of Uzbekistan
Faculty of Geology (2011)
Tashkent
University City 100095
   p. +998712460224
   geology@nuu.uz
   http://nuu.uz/geolog

Tashkent State Technical University
Faculty of Geology (2011)
Uzbekistan, Tashkent, 10095 Universitetskaya street, 2
   p. +998712464600
   TFTU_info@mail.ru

The State Committee for Nature Protection
(2011)
100 159, Tashkent, pl. Independence, 5
   info@uznature.uz
   http://www.uznature.uz

The State Committee of the Republic of Uzbekistan on Geology and Mineral Resources
(2011)
11, T.Shevchenko str., Tashkent, Republic of Uzbekistan 100060
   p. +998 (71) 256-8653
   geolcom@bcc.com.uz
   http://www.uzgeolcom.uz

Uzbekistan National Oil and Gas Company - Uzbekneftegaz (UNG)
(2014)
100047, city Street, Tashkent.
Istiqbol, 21
   p. +998 (71) 233-5757
   kans@uzneftegaz.uz
   http://www.uzneftegaz.uz

Venezuela

Universidad Central de Venezuela
Inst de Ciencias de la Tierra (2014)
Los Chaguaramos, Apdo. 3895, 1010-A Caracas
   p. 0212 6366236
   coordinv@ciens.ucv.ve
   http://www.coordinv.ciens.ucv.ve/investigacion/genci/sitios/35/index.html

Escuela de Geologia, Minas y Geofisica (2004)
Ciudad Universitaria, 47028 Caracas 1041 A

Universidad de la Este, Cumana
Dept de Geologia y Minas (2004)
Apartado Postal 245, Cumana (Estado Sucre)

Universidad de Los Andes
Dept de Geologia y Minas (2014)
Avenida 3, Independencia, La Hechlcera, Merida
   ocamacho@ula.ve
   http://llama.adm.ula.ve/pingenieria/index.php?option=com_content&view=article&id=313&Itemid=215

Escuela de Ingenieria Geologica (2004)
Av. Tulio Febres C., Merida 5101

Universidad de Oriente, Nucleo Bolivar
Escuela de Ciencias de la Tierra (2004)
Av. Universidad, Campus Universitario La Sabanita, Ciudad Bolivar

Universidad Simon Bolivar
Coordinacion de Ingenieria Geofisica (2015)
Valle de Sarteneja, Baruta, Edo. Miranda 80659, Caracas 1080
   p. 9063545
   coord-geo@usb.ve
   http://www.gc.usb.ve/geocoordweb/index.html

Vietnam

Hanoi University of Mining & Geology
Faculty of Geology (A,B,M,D) O (2015)
Duc Thang Ward - North Tu Liem Distr.
Hanoi
   p. +84-4-38387567
   diachat@humg.edu.vn
   khoadiachat.edu.vn
   Enrollment (2015): B: 2800 (420) M: 205 (50) D: 24 (6)
Dean of Faculty:
   Lam Van Nguyen, (D), Hanoi Univ of Mining and Geology, 2002, HwGeHg
Deputy Dean of Faculty:
   Thanh Xuan Ngo, (D), Okayama Uni of Science (Japan), 2009, GtcGi

Zambia

Copperbelt University
Mining Dept (B) (2010)
Kitwe
   deansot@cbu.ac.zm
   http://www.cbu.edu.zm/technology

University of Zambia
Dept of Metallurgy and Mineral Processing (B) (2010)
PO Box 32379
, Lusaka
   p. +360-21-1-250871
   registrar@unza.zm
   http://www.unza.zm/index.php?option=com_content&task=view&id=479&Itemid=574

Zimbabwe

Africa University
Faculty of Agriculture and Natural Sciences (B) (2014)
Fairview Rd (Off- Nyanga Rd)
PO Box 1320
Old Mutare, Mutare
   p. +2632060075
   info@africau.edu
   http://www.africau.edu/academic/default.htm

University of Zimbabwe
Dept of Geology (B,M,D) (2014)
Building B047
University of Zimbabwe
P.O. Box MP167
Mount Pleasant, Harare
   p. 303211 Ext. 15032
   gchipari@science.uz.ac.zw
   http://www.uz.ac.zw/index.php/2013-07-09-08-51-40/the-department-of-geology/226-sci/dept-sci/geology-dpt/826-dr-lrm-nhamo
   Enrollment (2012): B: 27 (17) M: 1 (0) D: 3 (1)
Chair:
   LRM Nhamo

Lecturer:
  Trendai Jnila, (D)
  Isidro Rafael Vit Manuel, (D)
  Maideyi Lydia Meck, (D)

Dept of Geography & Environmental Science (B,M,D) (2013)
PO Box MP167
Mount Pleasant, Harare
      p. +263-04-303211
      geography@arts.uz.ac.zw
      http://www.uz.ac.zw/science/geography/

Institute of Mining Research (B) (2010)
PO Box MP167
Mount Pleasant, Harare
      p. +263-4-336418
      imr@science.uz.ac.zw
      http://www.uz.ac.zw/

Dept of Mining Engineering (B) (2014)
PO Box MP167
Mount Pleasant, Harare
      p. (263) 4 -3335 x ext: 17089)
      kudzie@eng.uz.ac.zw
      http://www.uz.ac.zw/index.php/mining-about

Dept of Geoinformatics and Surveying (B) (2014)
PO Box MP167
Mount Pleasant, Harare
      p. +263 772 318 473
      bukalt@eng.uz.ac.zw
      http://www.uz.ac.zw/index.php/fac-of-eng/department-of-
      geoinformatics-and-surveying

Theses and Dissertations, 2013

The following section documents all of the 2013 geoscience dissertations and theses from U.S. and Canadian institutions that were reported to GeoRef Information Services. If you have questions about the data or to make sure your institution's data is included in the future, please contact Monika Long at ml@agiweb.org.

sedimentary rocks on Mars; insight from Rover and orbital observations and terrestrial field analogs

Hamecher, Emily A., *Studies of the equation of state and elasticity of mantle minerals*

Levine, Xavier Josselin, *Dynamics of Earth's Hadley circulation*

Li, King-Fai, *Atmospheric trace gases as probes of chemistry and dynamics*

Lin, Yunung Nina, *Using space geodesy to constrain variations in seismogenic behavior on subduction megathrusts*

Line, Michael Robert, *Characterization of exoplanet atmospheres; spectral retrieval and chemistry*

Meng, Lingsen, *Navigating earthquake physics with high-resolution array back-projection*

Ortega Culaciati, Francisco Hernan, *Aseismic deformation in subduction megathrusts; central Andes and north-east Japan*

Osburn, Magdalena Rose, *Isotopic proxies for microbial and environmental change; insights hydrogen isotopes and the Ediacaran Khufai Formation*

Philibosian, Belle, *Characterization of diverse megathrust fault behavior related to seismic supercycles, Mentawai Islands, Sumatra*

Phillips-Alonge, Kristin Eileen, *Structure of the subduction system in southern Peru from seismic array data*

Skinner, Steven Michael, *Plate tectonic constraints on flat subduction and paleomagnetic constraints on rifting*

Thomas, Claire Waller, *Liquid silicate equation of state; using shock waves to understand the properties of the deep Earth*

Thompson, Jeffrey Muir, *The short-timescale behavior of glacial ice*

Wang, Yu, *Earthquake geology of Myanmar*

Wicks, June Ki, *Sound velocities and equation of state of iron-rich (Mg,Fe)O*

Williams, Nneka Njeri Akosua, *Defining the relationship between seismicity and deformation at regional and local scales*

Wolf, Aaron Samuel, *Probing the thermodynamic properties of mantle rocks in solid and liquid states*

Zhang, Xi, *Aerosols and chemistry in the planetary atmospheres*

California State University at Bakersfield
Masters

Blunt, Ashleigh B., *Latest Pleistocene through Holocene lake levels from the TL05-4 cores, Tulare Lake, CA*

Goodell, Jonathan Andrew, *Carbon capture and sequestration and CO2 enhanced oil recovery in the Monterey Stevens sandstone at North Coles Levee, San Joaquin Valley, California*

California State University at Fresno
Masters

Lessel, Jerrod Glenn, *New thermobarometers for Martian igneous rocks*

Masutsubo, Nobuaki, *Diverse metamorphic trajectories, imbricated ocean plate stratigraphy, and fault rocks, Yuba River area, Feather River ultramafic belt, California*

California State University at Long Beach
Masters

AlShammary, Nawaf S., *Hetergeneous oil saturation in submarine channel and adjacent facies, Monterey Formation, Point Fermin, Palos Verdes, California*

De Masi, Conni L., *Ancient sedimentary fill of the Waucobi Lake Beds as an archive for Owens Valley, California; tectonics and climate*

Guillaume, Jonathan K., *Testing the structural role of the Santa Maria Basin in the rotation of the western Transverse Ranges and the magnetostratigraphy of the McDonald Shale, Temblor Range, California*

Strickland, Heather M., *Fracture networks and mechanical stratigraphy in the Monterey-equivalent Pismo Formation and its relationship to primary sedimentology and stratigraphy at Montana de Oro State Park, California*

California State University at Northridge
Masters

Ahlstrom, Martha M., *Post-fire debris flow erosion in the San Gabriel Mountains, California : evidence from the Station Fire, 2009*

Bender-Whitaker, Carrie, *Holocene-Pleistocene sand provenance in the Canterbury Basin, eastern South Island, New Zealand*

Doran, Linda M., *Characterizing modern stream sand to better understand reservoir sandstone provenance in the Taranaki Basin, New Zealand*

Escobar, Lennin de Jesus, *Rayleigh wave phase velocities beneath the oceanic and continental margin of the North American and Pacific plate boundary*

Graham, Joshua Tate, *Late Holocene glacial advances in the Klamath Mountains, Northern California, determined from 10Be cosmogenic exposure dating and dendrochronology*

Mohammadebrahim, Ehsan, *Seismic strong motion array project (SSMAP) and September 5, 2012 (M[W]=7.6) earthquake in the Nicoya Peninsula, Costa Rica*

Nunley, Melissa, *Seismic anisotropy beneath the African plate*

Sotirov, Teodor, *Rayleigh wave phase velocities and anisotropy of old oceanic lithosphere in the Pacific*

Carleton University
Doctorate

Courtney Mustaphi, Colin John, *A landscape-scale assessment of Holocene fire regime controls in south-eastern British Columbia, Canada*

Mumford, Thomas, *Petrology of the Blatchford Lake intrusive suite, Northwest Territories, Canada*

van Rooyen, Deanne, *Structural, geochronological, and thermochronological constraints on the evolution of orogenic infrastructure in the Thor-Odin-Pinnacles area of southeastern British Columbia*

Masters

Cran, Carley Angela, *Spatial and temporal variability of lake accumulation rates in subarctic Northwest Territories, Canada*

Fry, Christopher A., *3D laser imaging and modeling of iron meteorites and tektites*

Magnus, Seamus Johannes, *Geology and geochemistry of the Raglan Hills Metagabbro*

McCarron, Travis, *Unravelling the P-T-t history of Grenvillian metamorphism in the Mazinaw Domain, southeastern Ontario; insights from phase equilibria modeling and geospeedometry*

Olson, Laura Christina, *The 3-D imaging of drill core for fracture mapping*

Stevens, Christopher, *Petrography, geochemistry and isotopic analysis of Paleogene volcanism in the Fish Creek Mountains, Great Basin, north-central Nevada*

Varve, Susan Agatha, *Stratigraphy, geochemistry, and origin of the Fish Creek Mountains Tuff, Battle Mountain area, north-central Nevada, U.S.A.*

Williamson, Nicole, *Volcano-stratigraphy and major element geochemistry of the southern Natkusiak Formation flood basalts of Victoria Island; insights into the initiation of the Neoproterozoic Franklin magmatic event*

Columbia University
Doctorate

Allen, Katherine Ann, *Boron in Foraminiferal Calcite as an Indicator of Seawater Carbonate Chemistry*

Brusatte, Stephen, *The Phylogeny of Basal Coelurosaurian Theropods (Archosauria : Dinosauria) and Patterns of Morphological Evolution during the Dinosaur-Bird Transition*

Feighery, John E., *A Combined Field And Laboratory Investigation Into The Transport Of Fecal Indicator Microorganisms Through A Shallow Drinking Water Aquifer In Bangladesh*

Homburg, Janelle, *Field and theoretical investigations of strain localization : Effects of mineralogy, shear heating and grain size evolution on deformation in the Earth*

Marjanovic, Milena, *Signatures of present and past melt distribution along fast and intermediate spreading centers*

Ruiz Carrascal, Carlos Daniel, *Adaptation strategies to climate change in the Tropics : analysis of two multifactorial systems (high-altitude Andean ecosystems and Plasmodium falciparum malaria infections)*

Sritrairat, Sanpisa, *Multiproxy Analyses of Past Vegetation, Climate, and Sediment Dynamics in Hudson River Wetlands*

Dalhousie University
Doctorate

Butler, Jared P., *Crustal subduction and the exhumation of (ultra) high-pressure terranes; contrasting modes with examples from the Alps and Caledonides*

Gerlings, Joanna, *A deep seismic analysis of the Flemish Cap continental margin off Newfoundland, Canada*

Hidy, Alan J., *Cosmogenic nuclide quantification of paleo-fluvial sedimentation rates in response to climate change*

Theses & Dissertations

267

Masters

O'Brien, Kelsey Elizabeth, *Radon-222 potential in tills of Halifax, Nova Scotia*

Bachelor

Braden, Zoe M., *Paleoproterozoic pressure-temperature-deformation path in the Newton Fiord region, eastern Baffin Island, Nunavut*

Broughm, Shannon, *Petrogenesis of REE-mineralized granite dykes in the northeastern Cobequid Highlands, Nova Scotia*

Burg, James S., *Microbially induced sedimentary structures in the Carboniferous Horton Bluff Formation near Hantsport, Nova Scotia*

Dickson, Carla, *Structural geology of the Bear River Formation (Halifax Group) and White Rock Formation (Rockville Notch Group) contact in the Cape St. Marys area, southwest Nova Scotia*

Forstner, Tara, *Bedrock incision and relief generation of western Hangay Mountains, Mongolia*

Gaudet, Matthew A., *Mineralogical study of uranium and niobium mineralization at the main intrusion of the Lofdal carbonatite complex, Namibia, Africa*

Manoukian, Lori, *Flow unit characterization of the Early Cretaceous Missisauga Formation using Venture B-13 Well*

Marshall, Nicole R., *Late Quaternary variations of the Labrador Current in Flemish Pass*

Morrison, Natasha, *An investigatin into UV fluorescence in feldspar group minerals*

Pfeiffer, Daniel G., *Monazite (U-Th-Pb) dating the polyphase tectonometamorphism in the Government Point and Cunard Formations, SW Nova Scotia*

Slater, Evan, *Geochemical and fluid inclusion study of hydrothermal mineralization in the Busang southeast zone, Kalimantan, Indonesia; unique insight into the Bre-X scandal*

Tobey, Dawn, *Sequence stratigraphy of the Banquereau Formation, offshore Nova Scotia*

Tyler, Samuel R. L., *Structures and southern boundary zone of the Nepewassi Domain, Central Gneiss Belt, Grenville Province, ON*

Walsh, Michael, *Low-temperature cooling history of the Olympus-Ossa Massif; new insights from zircon and apatite (U-Th)/He thermochronology and thermal modelling*

Wongus, Derek, *The crystallization of K-feldspar megacrysts in granitoids from southwestern Nova Scotia*

Dartmouth College
Masters

Andersen, Jenica J., *Mobilization of mercury-contaminated sediment in a regulated river, Androscoggin River, northern New Hampshire*

Baber, Margaret B., *Surface-exposure (10Be) dating of the Omurubaho moraines in the Rwenzori Mountains of Uganda*

Bigl, Matthew F., *Late stage lowering and drainage of glacial Lake Hitchcock in the upper valley region of Vermont and New Hampshire*

Hallock, Hannah R., *Variations in Os/Ir and 187Os/188Os ratios across the K-Pg boundary from Stevns Klint and Hell Creek; implications for the global iridium distribution*

Jiang, Hehe, *Chronology, sources and dispersal of Middle Jurassic-early Late Cretaceous tephra in an evolving foreland basin, north central Wyoming*

Landau, Kelly S., *Insights into the behavior of osmium in the ocean*

Lauder, Alex, *Evaporation and transport of water isotopologues from Greenland lakes*

Michalak, Samuel, *A record of Bajocian and early Bathonian restricted marine sedimentation along the cratonic margin of the Sundance Sea, Bighorn Basin, WY*

Morriss, Blaine F., *On the detection and evolution of supraglacial lakes and catastrophic drainage events on the Greenland ice sheet*

Putnam, Annie L., *Tracking the moisture sources of storms at Borrow, Alaska : seasonal variations and isotopic characteristics*

Underwood, John Wentworth, III, *Source and fate of suspended sediment during stormflow*

Yang, Jie, *Physical and photochemical controls on Hg partitioning*

East Carolina University
Masters

Nixon, Justin E., *The influence of fracture characteristics on groundwater flow systems in fractured igneous and metamorphic rocks of North Carolina (USA)*

Florida State University
Doctorate

Mitchell-Tapping, Aleta M., *High-resolution calcareous nannofossil biostratigraphic applications; examples from the Upper Cretaceous Southern Ocean (ODP Leg 183) and Paleocene Equatorial Atlantic (ODP Leg 207)*

Fort Hays State University
Masters

Deering, Elizabeth K., *Identification and paleoecology of mammoth teeth from the vertebrate paleontology collection at the Sternberg Museum of Natural History, Hays, Kansas*

Luna, Anthony, *3D seismic analysis and characterization of a stacked turbidite channel; Niger Delta Complex*

Neeley, Christopher, *Utilizing a magnetometer to locate abandoned oil wells in Butler County, Kansas*

Staab, Adam, *An evaluation of the source area for the former Norges Cleaners tetrachloroethylene plume near Centennial Boulevard and Vine Street, Hays, KS, over a 20-year span using past data to estimate the plume concentration reduction*

Georgia State University
Masters

Barrett, Stephen R., *Investigating The Local Food System: A Mixed Methods Study Of Sustainability in Southwest Atlanta*

Breytenbach, Elvira, *Following the Rains: Evidence and Perceptions Relating to Rainfall Variability in Western Uganda*

Chiang, Andrew, *Evaluating The Performance Of A Filtered Area Weighting Method In Population Estimation For Public Health Studies*

Cosentino, Giovanni R., *Comparing Vegetation Cover in the Santee Experimental Forest, South Carolina (USA), Before and After Hurricane Hugo: 1989-2011*

Ilic, Karla A., *Evaluating Disparities in Quality of Life in the City of Atlanta Using an Urban Health Index*

McCartha, Daniel, *A Hurricane Record of Jekyll Island, Georgia*

Rinaldi, Parisa N, *Relationships Between Landscape Features and Nutrient Concentrations in an Agricultural Watershed in Southwestern Georgia: An Integrated Geographic Information Systems Approach*

Srymanske, Roy H, *When Does A Stream Gain The Ability To Create Its Own Channel? A Field Study In Northwest Georgia On The Conasauga River*

Illinois State University
Masters

Flaherty, Stephen T., *Three-dimensional modeling and hydrogeologic insights into glacial outwash deposits near Woodstock, IL*

Iowa State University of Science and Technology
Masters

Morrison, Alexander Kevin, *Limitations on the study of tile drainage using a distributed parameter hydrologic model and stable isotopes*

Kent State University
Masters

Atallah, Nidal Walid, *An investigation of the origin of Rock City and cause of piping problems at Mountain Lake, Giles County, Virginia*

Lakehead University
Masters

Kerkermeier, Leah, *Growth and arsenic adsorption of recent ferromanganese lacustrine precipitates in Nova Scotia and northern Ontario*

Bachelor

Belshaw, Patrick, *A Textural and Geochemical Study of a Granophyric Sill in the Jarvis Area, Thunder Bay*

D'Angelo, Michael, *Igneous Textures and Mineralogy of the Steepledge Intrusion, Northern Ontario*

Daniel, Lafreniere, *A Regional Geochemical Study of the Gunflint Formation*

Fry, Kyle, *A Geochemical and Petrogenetic Study of Three Granitic Dike Swarms within the Southern North Caribou Terrane*

Koroscil, Jesse P.J., *Deformation of the Animikie Group North of Lake Superior*

Seaby, Jordan, *A Geochemical Study of Diabase Sills Related to the Midcontinent Rift*

Smyk, Emily, *Geochemistry and Petrography Study of a Mesoarchean Felsic Metavolcanic Unit Near Musselwhite Mine, North Caribou Greenstone Belt*

Massachusetts Institute of Technology
Doctorate

Meredith, Laura Kelsey, *Field measurement of the fate of atmospheric H in a forest environment : from canopy to soil*

Owens, Stephanie Anne, *Advances in measurements of particle cycling and fluxes in the ocean*

Masters

Sahin, Sedar Cihan, *Surface deformation analysis over a hydrocarbon reservoir using InSAR with ALOS-PALSAR data*

Slim, Mirna I., *Influence of topographic stress on rock fracture : a two-dimensional numerical model for arbitrary surface topography and comparisons with borehole observations*

McMaster University

Doctorate

Banting, Bennett, *Seismic performance quantification of concrete block masonry structural walls with confined boundary elements and development of the normal strain-adjusted shear strength expression (NSSSE)*

Masters

Fitzgerald, Alexander, *Calculating the groundwater contribution of phosphorus and nitrogen to a small urban stream, Barrie, Ontario*

Miami University (Ohio)

Doctorate

Holtkamp, Stephen Gregg, *New methods for detecting earthquake swarms and transient motion to characterize how faults slip*

Sit, Stefany, *New methods in geophysics and science education to analyze slow fault slip and promote active e-learning*

Masters

Barrett, Heather Ann, *A comparative transmission electron microscopy investigation of defects and textures in cryptomelane*

Crifo, Camilla, *Variations in angiosperm leaf vein density have implications for interpreting life form in the fossil record*

Engin, Can, *Structural architecture and tectonic evolution of the Ulukisla sedimentary basin in south-central Turkey*

Lehmann, Sophie Butler, *Climatic and tectonic implications of a mid-Miocene landscape; examination of the Tarapaca Pediplain, Atacama Desert, Chile*

Schroeder, Melissa Light, *Palynological reconstructions of early Eocene flora of the Wind River basin, Wyoming*

Tully, Jennifer L., *An electron microscopy and inductively coupled plasma-mass spectroscopy investigation of Great Miami River sediment pollution in the industrialized landscape of Hamilton, Ohio*

Walkup, Laura Casey, *Tephrostratigraphic and geochemical investigation of compositionally heterogeneous silicic tephra in the middle Awash region, Afar, Ethiopia*

Michigan Technological University

Doctorate

Escobar-Wolf, Rudiger P., *Volcanic processes and human exposure as elements to build a risk model for Volcan de Fuego, Guatemala*

Guth, Alexandria L., *Spatial and temporal evolution of the volcanics and sediments of the Kenya Rift*

Ibrahim, Mohamed S., *Amplitude-versus-angle analysis and wide-angle-inversion of crosswell seismic dta in a carbonate reservoir*

Richardson, Joshua P., *Differentiating path and source processes in complex geologic structure through passive seismic studies; Bering Glacier, Alaska and Villarrica Volcano, Chile*

Masters

Alami, Daniele, *Relationship between static stress change and volcanism; how and if tectonic earthquake could influence volcanic activity; example of El Reventador Volcano, Ecuador*

Bonny, Estelle, *Ground-based and satellite remote sensing of paroxysmal eruptions at Etna Volcano, 2011-2012*

Cigala, Valeria, *Fossil bubbles in porphyritic basaltic pyroclasts produced by small and large strombolian eruptions at Pacaya, Guatemala*

Cobin, Patrice F., *Probabilistic modeling of rainfall induced landslide hazard assessment in San Juan La Laguna, Solola#2., Guatemala*

Jiang, Changyi, *Computational prediction of the sporulation network in clostridium thermocellum*

Keyport, Ren N., *A comparison of pixel-based versus object oriented analysis of landslides using historical remote sensing data*

Krewcun, Lucie G., *A study of $SO<2$` emissions and ground surface displacements at Lastarria Volcano, Antofagasta region, northern Chile*

Menassian, Sarah, *Validation of a "displacement tomography"*

inversion method for modeling sheet intrusions

Michels, Alexander C. *Paleomagnetic study of the Portage Lake volcanics exposed in the Quincy Mine*

Sealing, Christine R. *Characterizing the first historic eruption of Nabro, Eritrea; insights from thermal and UV remote sensing*

Tubman, Stephanie C. *Spring discharge monitoring in low-resource settings; a case study of Concepcio#2.n Chiquirichapa, Guatemala*

Wooten, Kelly M. *TanDEM-X high resolution DEMs and their applications to flow modeling*

Mississippi State University

Masters

Calhoun, Kayla J., *Investigation of parent source material in Smith County, Mississippi*

Cooper, Max P., *Verification of post-glacial speleogenesis and the origins of epigene maze caves in New York*

Montana State University

Doctorate

Melick, Jesse J., *Subsurface description and modeling of geologic heterogeneity in large subsurface datasets; using temporal and scalar hierarchies, Powder River Basin, WY and MT, U.S.A.*

Montana Tech of the University of Montana

Masters

Beecher, Michael E. *Predicting brittle zone sin the Bakken Formation using well logs and seismic data*

Carlson, Luke *Managed recharge and base-flow enhancement in an unconsolidated aquifer in the Boulder River valley, Montana*

Griffith, Amanda *Paragenesis and fluid inclusion study of epithermal Au-Ag veins at the Drumlummon Mine, Marysville, Montana*

Larson, Eric D., *Evaluating the performance of natural fibers impregnated with metallic nanoparticles to remove copper form aqueous media*

Overland, Brandon *Alterations to unconfined compressive strength in limestone cores due to injection of $CO<2$` at supercritical conditions*

Northern Arizona University

Masters

Lindner, Philip J. *Provenance study of latest Paleozoic to Mesozoic El Antimonio Group, Sonora, Mexico*

Schaller, Elizabeth M. *Isotopic flow determination and geochemical and geomorphic impacts on vegetation cover for western North American springs ecosystems*

Northern Illinois University

Masters

Adams, Ryan F., *Geophysical identification of subsurface cavities and fractures near a Superfund site south of Rockford, Illinois*

Bailey, Clinton R., *Determining the sources of water for conduit "sandboil" springs at the Nature Conservancy's Nachusa Grasslands Preserve, Franklin Grove, Illinois*

Kenroy, Philip R., *Fracture-controlled paleohydrologic systems in the vicinity of salt diapirs*

Todd, Kasey A., *The effects of shear deformation on planetesimal core segregation; results from in-situ X-ray microtomography*

Northwestern University

Doctorate

Joo, Young J., *Late Cretaceous Carbon Isotope Chemostratigraphy and Analysis of Perturbations in Global Carbon and Sulfur Biogeochemical Cycles*

Lou, Xiaoting *Inferred and Predicted Seismic Velocities of the North American Mantle*

Ohio State University

Doctorate

Cai, Shanshan, *Advancing the methodologies for mapping land cover trajectories using MODIS time series data*

D'Ambrosio, Jessica L., *Perspectives on the geomorphic evolution and ecology of modified channels and two-stage ditches in the agriculturally-dominated Midwestern United States*

Enderlin, Ellyn M., *Observations and modeling of Greenland outlet glacier dynamics*

Goodwin, Bradley P., *Recent environmental changes on the Antarctic Peninsula as recorded in an ice core from the Bruce Plateau*

Leslie, Deborah L., *The application of stable isotopes, delta11B, delta18O, and deltaD, in geochemical and hydrological investigations*

269

Theses & Dissertations

Maurer, Kyle D., *Effects of climate, forest structure, soil water, & scale on biosphere-atmosphere gas exchange in a Great Lakes mixed- deciduous forest*

Millan, Cristina, *Syntectonic fluid flux in a glaciated rift basin; record from vein arrays in the AND-1B and AND-2A sedimentary rock cores, Victoria Land Basin, Antarctica*

Pejcha, Ondrej, *The neutrino mechanism of core-collapse super-novae*

Reinemann, Scott Alan, *Holocene climate and environmental change in the Great Basin of the Western United States : a paleolimnological approach*

Schoepf, Verena, *Physiology and biogeochemistry of corals subjected to repeat bleaching and combined ocean acidification and warming*

Sedlacek, Alexa Ruth Clements, *Strontium isotope stratigraphy and carbonate sedimentology of the Latest Permian to Early Triassic in the Western United States, northern Iran and southern China*

Shalek, Kyle James, *Geophysical numerical modeling approach for characterizing and monitoring potential carbon sequestration injection sites*

Sulistioadi, Yohanes Budi, *Satellite altimetry and hydrologic modeling of poorly-gauged tropical watershed*

Wilson, Aaron Benjamin, *Using the NCAR CAM 4 to confirm SAM's modulation of the ENSO teleconnection to Antarctica and access changes to this interaction during various ENSO flavor events*

Yoon, Yeosang, *Evaluation of the potential to estimate river discharge using measurements from the upcoming SWOT mission*

Zhang, Li, *Remote sensing of water quality in Lake Erie using MODIS imagery data*

Masters

Baumann, Justin H., *The effects of elevated temperature stress on the acquisition and allocation of carbon to lipids in Hawaiian corals*

Hawrylak, Matthew R., *Geomechanical assessment of the Cincinnati Group as a caprock*

Liu, Shuai, *Laboratory investigations on the geochemical response of groundwater-sediment environment to hydraulic fracturing fluids*

Matheny, Ashley Michelle, *Quantifying the sensitivity of land-surface models to hydrodynamic stress limitations on transpiration*

Peteya, Jennifer Anita, *Resolving details of the nonbiomineralized anatomy of trilobites using computed tomographic imaging techniques*

Shaffer, Jared M., *The effects of spatial resolution on digital soil attribute mapping*

Stanich, Nicholas A., *Soil physical property characteristics and chronosequence analysis about a glacial fore-field in Skaftafellsjkull, Iceland*

Stucker, James Douglas, *The effects of urban land use type on low order stream geochemistry, Columbus, Ohio*

Tost, Brian Christopher, *Low porosity mistaken for natural gas hydrate at Alaminos Canyon, Gulf of Mexico; implications for gas hydrate exploration in marine sediment reservoirs*

Voyles, Joseph Stephen, *Geochemical microelectrodes for the in situ monitoring of metals concentration and mobility in contaminated sediments*

Xi, Zhouxin, *Estimating and mapping the LAI and mean crown radius of forest from airborne images : a case study in the Zaleski State Forest*

Zhang, Fang, *Flood damage and vulnerability assessment for Hurricane Sandy in New York City*

Bachelor

Bisson, Kelsey, *Spatial distribution of visible desert salts in the McMurdo region, Antarctica*

Blocher, Will, *Determining the architecture of the Terror Rift from stratal dips in reflection seismology profiles*

Clendenin, Chad L., *Biogenic silica and phosphate pools in soils of the North Appalachian Experimental Watershed, Ohio; evaluation of the effects of different agricultural practices*

Crock, Abigail R., *Analysis of potential methane hydrate accumulations in a Block 857 Alaminos Canyon well site, Gulf of Mexico*

Dailey, Kelsey, *Evaluating anthropogenic impact on water quality of Ohio rivers over time*

Diamond, Charles W., *Ocean oxygenation during the Middle Ordovician; links to biodiversification?*

Gress, Nathan M., *Crust-magma interactions of the Hengill volcanic complex in Iceland*

Martin, Nicholas, *Remote sensing of river widths and discharge estimation for the mainstem Congo River*

Michalak, John C., *Nutrient geochemistry in north central Ohio lakes*

Myers, Jeremy R., *Crinoids from the Silurian of western Ohio and Indiana*

Nadler, Cara, *Climate-driven dynamics of lakes and wetlands in the Rainwater Basin, Nebraska and its ecological implications*

O'Connor, Ethan, *How accurately can river height, width, slope and discharge be estimated from ideal SWOT outputs?*

Perez, Victor J., *Characterization & isolation of organic molecules from Mississippian-age crinoids*

Rine, Matthew J., *An exploratory study of ephemeral snow cover in the Midwest and the potential hydrologic impacts on the Great Lakes with a warming climate*

Rosenbeck, Loren Andrew, *A morphometric and alignment analysis of volcanic seamounts to determine stress directions, northwestern Ross Sea, Antarctica*

Tenison, Andrew J., *Pressure of partial crystallization of Katla magmas : implications for magma chamber depth and for the magma plumbing system*

Thompson, Jeffrey R., *Microevolutionary response in Lower Mississippian camerate crinoids to predation pressure*

Trigg, Cody R., *Carbon isotope variations on ancient carbonate platforms; the roles of organic carbon burial and sea level*

Oregon State University

Doctorate

Bauska, Thomas K., *Carbon cycle variability during the last millennium and last deglaciation*

Haxel, Joseph H., *Submarine earthquakes, volcanic eruptions and ambient noise in the Northeast Pacific*

Lange, Amy E., *Magmatic processes beneath mid-ocean ridges; insights from mineral and glass chemistry in plagioclase ultraphyric basalts*

Loewen, Matthew W., *Volatile mobility of trace metals in volcanic systems*

Masters

Drinnan, Megan R., *Biotic alteration of oceanic basalt glass*

Erhardt, Morgan William, *A Bayesian approach to marine spatial planning*

Legg, Nicholas T., *Debris flows in glaciated catchments; a case study on Mount Rainier, Washington*

Mitchell, Logan E., *The late Holocene atmospheric methane budget reconstructed from ice cores*

Serafin, Katherine A., *Simulating extreme total water levels using a time-dependent, extreme value approach*

Wafforn, Stephanie R., *Structural geology of the Mount Polley Cu-Au district, south-central British Columbia*

Pennsylvania State University at University Park

Doctorate

Cleveland, Kenneth Michael, *Fault rupture segmentation*

Graham, Heather, *Molecular and isotopic indicators of canopy closure in ancient forests and the effects of environmental gradients on leaf alkane expression*

Kaproth-Gerecht, Bryan, *The evolution of fault strength, permeability, and acoustic properties in experimental studies from fault initiation through the seismic cycle*

Lauer, Rachel M., *Subduction zone hydrogeology : quantifying fluid sources, pathways, and pressure*

Magill, Clayton R., *Molecular and isotopic perspectives on early human habitats at Olduvai Gorge, Tanzania*

Olson, Roman, *How well can historical temperature observations constrain climate sensitivity?*

Regalla, Christine A., *Cenozoic forearc tectonics in northeastern Japan : relationships between outer forearc subsidence and plate boundary kinematics*

Masters

Alpern, Jennifer S., *The influence of fluid properties on geometric complexity and breakdown pressure of hydraulic fracture*

Baumann, Beth A., *The effect of Archean oceans on cyanobacteria, green sulfur bacteria and the rise of oxygen*

Carter, Megan R., *Exploring a 60-year record of manganese deposition in Marietta, Ohio using soil chemistry and atmospheric dispersion modeling*

Deane, James A., *The effect of oxygen fugacity on the equilibrium partitioning of lithium between olivine and clinopyroxene*

Donovan, Michael P., *Novel insect leaf-mining at Mexican Hat,*

Montana (early Paleocene) and the demise of cretaceous leaf miners

Harman, Chester E., *Atmospheric production of glycolaldehyde under hazy prebiotic conditions*

Millard, Craig L., *Evaluating controls on crevasse-splay growth in modern and ancient fluvial systems*

Mondro, Claire A., *Strain history of the Taiwan orogenic belt, measured from syntectonic pressure shadows*

Murray, Timothy T, *A monogenetic alkali basalt field east of the Andean arc between 34 and 35 S : implications for mantle composition*

Olson, Stephanie L., *Quantifying the areal extent and dissolved oxygen concentrations of Archean oxygen oases*

Puls, Brendan, *Electron transfer and the roles of flavins during iron(III) reduction by Shewanella oneidensis*

Rosenberg, Russell H., *Late Miocene erosion and evolution of topography along the western slope of the Colorado Rockies*

Bachelor

Bingham, Nina, *Carbon, nitrogen and manganese in shale soil profiles along a climate gradient*

Gorski, Irena, *The use of water sensors to examine water chemistry related to Marcellus Shale natural gas development*

Gould, Timothy, *An investigation of groundwater communication in the Lake Perez Basin and the applicability of distributed temperature sensing technology to ecological problems*

Stevens, Nathan T., *Impurity influence on normal grain growth and conductance in the WAIS Divide 06A ice core, Antarctica*

Princeton University
Doctorate

Huang, Kuan, *Studies of the oxygen and carbon cycles in the surface ocean*

Bachelor

Burton, Nicholas M., *Temperature-dependent methanotrophy in High Arctic permafrost; implications for global warming*

Chen, Christine Y., *Lake Bonneville's tilted paleoshorelines revisited; implications for late Pleistocene climate*

Eggers, Gabriel Logan, *A regionalized maximum-likelihood estimation of the spatial structure of Venusian topography*

Gronewold, Jeffrey D., *The implications of mafic enclaves on magmatic differentiation and pluton emplacement; geochronological and geochemical insights from the Bergell Intrusion, N. Italy*

Kanno, Cynthia Mai, *A novel apatite-based sorbent for defluoridation; synthesis and sorption characteristics of nano-micro crystalline apatite on limestone*

Shoenfelt, Elizabeth Marie, *The nature of reactive thiols on bacterial cell envelopes and their reactivity with aqueous Hg>2+`*

Trost, Emily Victoria, *High-stress conditions in early Paleocene benthic Foraminifera; evidence from NW Atlantic ODP Site 1050C*

Rensselaer Polytechnic Institute
Doctorate

Baker, Benjamin Ian, *2.5d teleseismic waveform tomography with application to the Tien Shan*

Xing, Lingbo, *An experimental study of Th and U of partitioning and diffusion in hydrous rhyolitic melts*

Southern Illinois University at Carbondale
Masters

Cox, Ryan W., *Model of contaminant transport, Saline Valley Aquifer, Gallatin County Illinois*

Dande, Suresh, *Estimation of down-dip limit of the Tonga seismogenic zone from ocean bottom seismograph data*

Matulaitis, Ilona I., *Benthic foraminiferal analysis from Barilari Bay, western Antarctic Peninsula margin*

Moorehead, Anthony J., *Igneous intrusions at Hicks Dome, southern Illinois, and their relationship to fluorine-base metal-rare earth element mineralization*

Ocubalidet, Seare G., *Controls on organic carbon accumulation in the Late Devonian New Albany Shale, west-central Kentucky, Illinois Basin*

Verbanaz, Ryan, *Benthic foraminiferal assemblage analysis as part of the LARISSA project for Barilari Bay, western Antarctic Peninsula*

Walters, Evan Robert, *Sulfate reducing bioreactor dependence on organic substrates for long-term remediation of acid mine drainage : field experiments*

Southern Methodist University

Doctorate

Araujo, Ricardo, *Aspects of plesiosaur locomotion; insights from Angolan specimens, eusauropterygian heritage, myology and osteology*

Fisher, Aileen, *West Texas array experiment; noise and source characterization of short-range infrasound and acoustic signals, along with lab and field evaluation of InterMountain Laboratories infrasound microphones*

Kimura, Yuri, *Evolutionary patterns of tooth shape in relation to diet inferred by stable carbon isotope of tooth enamel in murine rodents from the Miocene of northern Pakistan*

Park, Junghyun, *Infrasound signal processing from regional arrays and seismic characteristics of North Korean nuclear explosions*

Rosenau, Nicholas A., *Paleoclimate reconstruction of Pennsylvanian paleoequatorial environments; coupling terrestrial and marine proxies*

Masters

Collins, Elizabeth M., *Calcite-filled veins of the Austin Chalk Formation; using a combination of geochemistry and structural geology to constrain the post-depositional history*

Dingwall, Ryan Kenneth, *Thermal modeling of step-out targets at the Soda Lake geothermal field, Churchill County, Nevada*

Stanford University
Doctorate

Dralus, Danica, *Chemical interactions between silicates and their pore fluids; how they affect rock physics properties from atomic to reservoir scales*

Masters

Aljamaan, Hamza M., *Experimental investigation of shale physical and transport properties*

Ibarra, Daniel Enrique, *Applying uranium-series isotope geochemistry and geochronology to Great Basin Pleistocene paleohydrology*

Itthisawatpan, Kasama, *Upscaling of two-phase flow with capillary pressure heterogeneity effects*

Kouba, Claire Marie, *Contemporary weathering fluxes and the importance of solute reservoirs along an erosional gradient, Feather River, CA*

Lagasca, John Reuben, *Fines migration and compaction in diatomites and a micromodel investigation of oil sand reservoirs*

Lund Snee, Jens-Erik, *Geology and geochronology of Cenozoic units in the Pinon Range and Huntington Valley, Nevada*

Mayer, Kristin A., *Reactive transport simulations in variably-saturated porous media; phosphorus depletion for a pygmy forest-like ecosystem*

Narakornpijit, Kumnoon, *Process modeling and optimization of post-combustion carbon capture using a N<2`-selective membrane*

Pettit, Mollie M., *Long-term bluff retreat in Pacifica, California*

Rui, Jiang, *Pressure preconditioning using proper orthogonal decomposition*

Sriyanong, Pasawich, *Element-based formulations for coupled flow, transport, and chemical reactions*

Thirawarapan, Chanya, *Simplified one-dimensional model for alkali surfactant polymer floods*

Valverde, Lawrence R., *Fracture characterization via electrical impedance and resistance*

Bachelor

Rosen, Valerie B., *A reactive transport model of hillslopes along an erosional gradient, Feather River, California*

Stephen F. Austin State University
Masters

Byrd, Bryan F., *Carbonate diagenesis and secondry mineralization of cavernous porosity in Amazing Maze Cave, Pecos County, Texas*

Heyt, Kelly E., *Quantitative differences between 2D and 3D seismic data in the High Island east addition, Gulf of Mexico*

SUNY, University of Buffalo
Doctorate

Ball, Jessica L., *Field and numerical investigations of lava dome hydrothermal systems and their effects on dome stability*

Paul Nesaraja, Pauline, *Nature of surface interactions regulating the growth of E coli K-12 MG1655 on glass, muscovite and hematite*

Masters

Amin, Jamal, *Lateral variations in strata competence and alternating eruption styles in time and space as morphological controls on*

a maar crater in the Lunar Crater Volcanic Field, Nevada, USA

Feiner, Kathleen, *The Effects of Beaver Damming on Groundwater Flow Through a Wetland, Beaver Meadow, NY*

Johnson, Peter J., *The 38 ka Marcath Eruption at Lunar Crater Volcanic Field, Nevada : Characteristics of a Monogenetic Basaltic Tephra Fall Deposit*

Mamer, Ethan, *Quantifying fine scale discharge to surface water using the amplitude-shift method with distributed temperature measurements*

O'Brien, Timothy M., *Correlation of lava flows on Cascade volcanoes : Tool development and example from Burney Spring Mountain, California*

Pendleton, Simon L., *10Be chronology of late Pleistocene and holocene glaciation of the Alapah Mountain and Arrigetch Peaks Areas, Central Brooks Range, Alaska*

Rezvanbehbahani, Soroush, *Temporal history of ice dynamics contribution to volume changes of the southeast Greenland Ice sheet*

Smolen, Mickael, *Pit crater formation laboratory simulations and applications to Mars*

Texas A&M University
Doctorate

Al-Ghamdi, Nasser Mohammad S. *Integrated core-based sequence stratigraphy, chemostratigraphy and diagenesis of the Lower Cretaceous (Barremian-Aptian), Biyadh and Shu'aiba Formations, a giant oil field, Saudi Arabia*

Heo, Joong Hyeok, *Assessment of water resources in a humid watershed and a semi-arid watershed; Neches River basin, TX and Canadian River basin, NM*

Mohamed, Ahmed Mohamed Anwar Sayed, *Semi-analytical solution for multiphase fluid flow applied to CO2 sequestration in geologic porous media*

Xie, Ruifang, *Tracing paleoclimate over the past 25,000 years using evidence from radiogenic isotopes*

You, Kehua, *Influence of atmospheric pressure and water table fluctuations on gas phase flow and transport of volatile organic compounds (VOCs) in unsaturated zones*

Texas Christian University
Masters

Blair, Charles Grant, *Microfacies sedimentology of the lower-middle Kindblade Formation, Slick Hills, southwestern Oklahoma*

Garcia, Sarah Lynn, *An analysis of anomalous meteorite, Enon; classification and thermal history*

Kiesel, Meredith Ann, *Chemostratigraphy and elemental analysis of the Mississippian Barnett Shale Formation using energy-dispersive X-ray fluorescence spectrometry, Fort Worth Basin, Johnson County, Texas*

Lisenby, Peyton Everett, *Distinguishing reaches in a tropical headwater stream, Costa Rica; utilizing morphology, instream wood, and terrestrial laser scanning in hydraulic characterization*

Tulane University
Doctorate

Gonzalez-Caver, Erika Lewis, *Geochemistry of Quaternary basic volcanic rocks from the Mexican volcanic belt*

Masters

Pendergraft, Matthew Allen, *Investigating oil degradation and mixing in coastal environments using ramped pyrolysis*

Ramatchandirane, Cyndhia, *Coastal marsh formation and its relation to sediment exchange along the Chenier Plain in southwest Louisiana*

Universite Laval
Doctorate

Leblanc, Anne-Marie, *Modelisation tridimensionnelle du regime thermique du pergelisol de la valle de Salluit au Quebec nordique en fonction de differents scenarios de rechauffement climatique*

Masters

Brun Kone, Mathy Yasmina, *Developpement d'un modele numerique d'ecoulement 3D des eaux souterraines du bassin versant de la riviere Chaudiere, Quebec*

Ntiharirizwa, Seconde, *Le potentiel en ressources minerales du Burundi, nord-est de la ceinture orogenique Kibarienne, Afrique centre-orientale*

Sterckx, Arnaud, *Etude des facteurs influencant le rendement des puits d'alimentation de particuliers qui exploitent le roc fracture en Outaouais, Quebec, Canada*

Tremblay, Joniel, *Optimisation de la carbonatation minerale de divers residus miniers ultramafiques*

University of Alabama at Tuscaloosa
Doctorate

Compton, Sarah Katherine, *Using linear inverse methods and finite element models to explore sensitivity to homogeneous elastic half-space assumptions in deformation models of the 2000 eruption of Hekla Volcano, Iceland*

Gatewood, Matthew Patrick, *Utilizing high-precision geochronology to evaluate the rates of geologic processes*

Masters

Anderson, Bryan Scott, *Magmatism, metamorphism, and deformation in the Mountain Home metamorphic complex, Blue Mountains Province, Oregon, and its role in Late Jurassic deformation in the western North American Cordillera*

Ellis, John H., *Evaluation of submarine groundwater discharge and groundwater quality using a novel coupled approach; isotopic tracer techniques and numerical modeling*

Fields, Daniel, *Laboratory incubations of Macondo oil-derived hydrocarbons in Alabama salt marsh sediments and water*

Holler, Robert Andrew, *Metamorphism of the Wenatchee Ridge orthogneiss; a combined application of geochronology and phase equilibrium modeling*

Hunt, Bryan Wallace, *Regional Norphlet facies correlation, analysis and implications for paleostructure and provenance, eastern Gulf of Mexico*

Lovell, Thomas Rudolph, *Detrital zircon U-Pb age constraints on the provenance of the Late Jurassic Norphlet Formation, eastern Gulf of Mexico; implications for paleogeography*

Lutz, Brandon, *Kinematic analysis of the southern Funeral Mountains; implications for Cenozoic extensional tectonics*

Mulayim, Oguz, *Microfacies analysis, depositional environments and sequence stratigraphy of the Late Cretaceous Karababa and Derdere Formations in the Cemberlitas oil field, Adiyaman, southeastern Turkey*

Nwafor, Emeka, *Crustal structure of the eastern Gulf of Mexico*

Rentschler, Erika Kristine, *Deepwater Horizon oil spill; using microcosms to study effects of crude oil in coastal sediments*

Spry, Jacob Micah, *Investigating the presence and distribution of organic components in bacterial magnetite*

Yezerski, Donald Jordan, *Structural geometry of the frontal Ouachitas-Arkoma Basin transition zone in western Arkansas*

University of Alaska at Fairbanks
Doctorate

Bartholomaus, Timothy Chester, *Seismicity, seawater and seasonality; new insights into iceberg calving from Yahtse Glacier, Alaska*

Buurman, Helena, *Volcano seismicity in Alaska*

Habermann, Marijke, *Basal shear strength inversions for ice sheets with an application to Jakobshavn Isbrae, Greenland*

Henton, Sarah Massey, *Experiment vs. nature; using amphiboles to test models of magma storage and pre-eruptive magma dynamics preceding the 2006 eruption of Augustine Volcano, Alaska*

Jafarov, Elchin, *The effects of changes in climate and other environmental factors on permafrost evolution*

Jones, Benjamin M., *Remote sensing of Arctic landscape dynamics*

McNabb, Robert Whitfield, *On the frontal ablation of Alaska tidewater glaciers*

Neill, Owen Kelly, *Petrologic and geochemical tracers of magmatic movement in volcanic arc systems; case studies from the Aleutian Islands and Kamchatka, Russia*

Podrasky, David Bryan, *Jakobshavn Isbrae; velocity variations from hourly to decadal time scales at Greenland's fastest tidewater glacier*

Shimer, Grant, *Sedimentology and stratigraphy of the Nanushuk Formation and related foreland basin deposits, central Brooks Range foothills, Alaska*

Steensen, Torge S., *Satellite to model comparisons of volcanic ash emissions in the North Pacific*

Trussel, Barbara Lea, *Rapid thinning and collapse of lake calving Yakutat Glacier, southeast Alaska*

Masters

Billings, Matthew E., *Lime treatment of interior and south-central Alaskan soils*

Chittambakkam, Arvind A., *Development of a reservoir stimulation model at Pilgrim Hot Springs, Alaska using TOUGH2*

Jones, Joshua M., *Landfast sea ice formation and deformation near*

Barrow, Alaska; variability and implications for ice stability

Kentner, Adrienne, *Petrological constraints on the origin of enclaves from Kasatochi Volcano, Aleutian Islands, Alaska*

Kienholz, Christian, *New algorithms for the compilation of glacier inventories*

Miller, Joshua K., *A conceptual model of the Pilgrim Hot Springs geothermal system, Seward Peninsula, Alaska*

Perttu, Brian, *Igneous rocks and structures of the Nixon Fork Mine, Alaska, and their relations to ores*

Rowell, Colin, *Three dimensional volcano-acoustic source localization at Karymsky Volcano, Kamchatka, Russia*

Vance, Gabrielle T., *The influence of climate and tectonics on topography in the Hayes Range and its foothills*

Yang, Kun, *Observation and analysis on the characteristics of strain induced by frost heave for a full-scale buried, chilled gas pipeline*

Young, Joanna C., *Temperature index modeling of the Kahiltna Glacier; comparison to multiple field and geodetic mass balance datasets*

University of Arizona
Doctorate

Bigio, Erica Renee, *Late Holocene fire and climate history of the western San Juan Mountains, Colorado; results from alluvial stratigraphy and tree-ring methods*

Bloch, Elias Morgan, *Diffusion kinetics of lutetium and hafnium in garnet and clinopyroxene; experimental determination and consequences for >176`Lu->176`Hf geochronometry*

Guenthner, William Rexford, *Zircon (U-Th)/He dates from radiation damaged crystals; a new damage-He diffusivity model for the zircon (U-Th)/He thermochronometer*

Ivory, Sarah Jean, *Vegetation and climate of the African tropics for the last 500,000 years*

Painter, Clayton S., *Sequence stratigraphy, geodynamics, and detrital geo-thermochronology of Cretaceous foreland basin deposits, Western Interior U.S.A.*

Thompson, Diane Marie, *Variability and trends in the tropical Pacific and the El Nino-Southern Oscillation inferred from coral and lake archives*

Masters

Dettinger, Matthew P., *Calibrating and testing the volcanic glass paleoaltimeter in South America*

Evenson, Nathan Samuel, *Hematite and Mn oxide (U-Th)/He dates from the Buckskin-Rawhide detachment system, western Arizona; constraining the timing of mineralization and gaining insights into hematite (U-Th)/He systematics*

Kortyna, Cullen D., *Structural and thermochronologic constraints on kinematics, timing and shortening during inversion of the Salta Rift into the Andean fold-thrust belt, northwest Argentina*

McDougall, Noah, *Post-rift volcanism and extension in the Guinea Plateau, West Africa interpreted from 3-D seismic data; potential link to Grimaldi seamount-chain magmatism*

Mizer, Jason D., *Uranium-lead geochronology of magmatism in the Central Mining District, New Mexico*

Morrison, Shaunna, *Crystal structures of rare earth element minerals and crystal-chemistry of Martian soil from Rocknest, Gale Crater, Mars*

Pecha, Mark E., *Detrital zircon U-Pb geochronology and Hf isotope geochemistry of the Yukon-Tanana Terrane, Coast Mountains, southeast Alaska*

Runyon, Simone E., *Contrasting Fe oxide-rich mineralization in the Yerington District, Nevada*

White, Lara Y., *Orbital forcing of Asian monsoon rainfall based on 10Be in Chinese loess*

Zamora, Hector A., *Post-dam sediment dynamics and processes in the Colorado River estuary and its implications for habitat restoration*

University of Arkansas at Fayetteville
Masters

Adkins, Jennifer, *Assessment and conceptualization of groundwater flow in the Edwards Aquifer through the Knippa Gap in Uvalde County, Texas*

Boyer, Lane Markes, *Insights into the timing, origin, and deformation of the Highland Mountains gneiss dome in southwestern Montana, USA*

Buckland, Karen Nicole Mason, *A geomechanical study of the Mississippian Boone Formation*

Cains, William, *Sedimentary provenance of the Wedington Member, Fayetteville Shale, from age relations of detrital zircons*

Jones, Douglas Eben, *Bedrock geological map of the Rockhouse Quadrangle, Carroll and Madison Counties, Arkansas*

Minor, Paul Marchand, *Analysis of tripolitic chert in the Boone Formation (Lower Mississippian, Osagean), northwest Arkansas and southwestern Missouri*

Sherman, Janelle Renee, *Hydrogeology and chemical characterization of hydrocarbon in domestic water wells, Rancho Villa Subdivision, Rogers, Arkansas*

Wittman, Brett Robert, *Subsurface stratigraphy and characterization of Mississippian (Osagean to Meramecian) carbonate reservoirs of the northern Anadarko Shelf, north-central Oklahoma*

University of British Columbia
Doctorate

Caruthers, Andrew Harry, *Pliensbachian-Toarcian (Early Jurassic) extinction in western North America*

Chudy, Thomas Christof, *The petrogenesis of the Ta-bearing Fir carbonatite system, east-central British Columbia, Canada*

Dzikowski, Tashia Jayne, *A comparative study of the origin of carbonate-hosted gem corundum deposits in Canada*

Luo, Yiming, *Applications of U-decay series isotopes to studying the meridional overturning circulation and particle dynamics in the ocean*

Pandey, Bishnu Hari, *Investigation of variation of motions between free field and foundation in seismic soil-structure interaction of structures with rigid shallow foundation*

Rasmussen, Kirsten Louise, *The timing, composition, and petrogenesis of syn- to post-accretionary magmatism in the Northern Cordilleran Miogeocline, eastern Yukon and southwestern Northwest Territories*

Razique, Abdul, *Magmatic evolution and genesis of the giant Reko Diq H14-H15 porphyry copper-gold deposit, District Chagai, Balochistan-Pakistan*

Simmons, Adam Thomas, *Magmatic and hydrothermal stratigraphy of Paleocene and Eocene porphyry Cu-Mo deposits in southern Peru*

Smithyman, Brendan Robert, *Developments in waveform tomography of land seismic data with applications in south-central British Columbia*

Vaughan, Jeremy Reid, *Tracing hydrothermal fluid flow in the rock record; geochemical and isotopic constraints on fluid flow in carlin-type gold systems*

Xu, Wanjing, *Acid rock drainage remediation with Bear River clinoptilolite in a slurry bubble column*

Zangeneh, Neda, *Numerical simulation of hydraulic fracture, stress shadow effects and induced seismicity in jointed rock*

Masters

Bailey, Leif Anthony, *Late Jurassic fault-hosted gold mineralization of the Golden Saddle Deposit, White Gold District, Yukon Territory*

Blaskovich, Randy J., *Characterizing waste rock using automated quantitative electron microscopy*

Cox, David, *Surficial and geochemical evolution of periglacial soils; applications to mineral exploration in Yukon*

Dalsin, Mallory Linda, *The mineralogy, geochemistry and geochronology of the Wicheeda carbonatite complex, British Columbia*

Dick, Graham John, *Development of an early warning time-of-failure analysis methodology for open pit mine slopes utilizing the spatial distribution of ground-based radar monitoring data*

Dixon, Andrea, *Mineralogy and geochemistry of pegmatites on Mount Begbie, British Columbia*

Fretz, Nathan Mackenzie, *Multi-year hydrologic response of experimental waste-rock piles in a cold climate; active-zone development, net infiltration, and fluid flow*

Johnson, James, *Seismic wavefield reconstruction using reciprocity*

Le Souef, Kate Elizabeth, *Physical modelling of tidal resonance in a submarine canyon*

Lepore, William Adamas, *Petrophysical and physicochemical controlling parameters on stable isotope depletion patterns in carbonate rocks from auriferous hydrothermal fluid infiltration at the Long Canyon sediment-hosted gold deposit; NE Nevada*

McClenaghan, Lindsay, *Geology and genesis of the Newton bulk-tonnage gold-silver deposit central British Columbia*

Roworth, Megan Rose, *Understanding the effect of freezing on rock mass behaviour as applied to the Cigar Lake mining method*

Venturi, Chantal Margot, *Stratigraphy, petrography and major* element mineral chemistry of the Wadi Qutabah layered mafic complex, Yemen

von Flotow, Claudia, *Temporal adjustments of a streambed following an episodic sediment supply regime*

Wrighton, Timothy Michael, *Placer gold microchemical characterization and shape analysis applied as an exploration tool in western Yukon*

University of California at Davis
Doctorate

Bennett, Scott Edmund Kelsey, *The role of rift obliquity in formation of the Gulf of California*

Harwood, Cara Lynne, *Microbial and metazoan influences on microbialite growth structures; insights from recent lacustrine microbialites in Pavilion Lake, BC, and Cambrian thrombolites from the Great Basin, CA and NV*

Vetter, Lael, *Combined stable isotope and trace element analyses on single planktic foraminifer shells; insights from live culture experiments and paleoceanographic applications*

Masters

Colla, Christopher A., *Calcium-isotope fractionation in synthetic mineral aqueous systems, combining theory and experiment*

Moclock, Leslie Grace, *Timing and kinematics of deformation in the Bear Mountains fault zone, Sierra Nevada foothills, California*

Unangst, Nathan, *Estimation of aquatic locomotion strategies in fossil marine amniotes utilizing extant analogues*

Wildgoose, Maya Margaret, *Delineating a P-T-t path for the Ruby terrane blueschist (Alaska) using lutetium-hafnium and >40`Argon/>39`Argon dating techniques*

University of California at Santa Barbara
Doctorate

Moore, John, *Studies on Cambrian small shelly fossils*

Mosolf, Jesse, *Stratigraphy, structure, and geochronology of the Abanico Formation in the Principal Cordillera, central Chile; evidence of protracted volcanism and implications for Andean tectonics*

Masters

Norman, Bryan Wells, *Structural evolution of the central Schell Creek Range, White Pine County, Nevada*

Shusta, Stephani Setsuko, *Sulfur isotope fractionation accompanies dimethylsulfide disproportionation by Methanosarcina sp. strain MTP4*

Wampler, David, *Tectonic geomorphology of the Gaviota coast*

University of California at Santa Cruz
Doctorate

Chen, Erinna M., *Ocean tidal dissipation and its role in solar system satellite evolution*

Michalak, Melanie J., *Exhumation of the Peruvian Andes; insights from mineral chronometers*

Yan, Rui, *Acoustic and elastic reverse-time migration; novel angle-domain imaging conditions and applications*

Masters

Karr, Jered Andrew, *Taphonomic biases in the insect fossil record; inconsistent preservation over geologic time*

University of Colorado at Boulder
Doctorate

Aboktef, Adel, *Sequence-stratigraphic controls on sandstone diagenesis; an example from the Williams Fork Formation, Piceance Basin, Colorado*

Larsen, Darren Jon, *Holocene climate evolution and glacier fluctuations inferred from proglacial lake sediments at Hvitarvatn, central Iceland*

Marcucci, Emma Cordts, *A multi-faceted approach to characterize acid-sulfate alteration processes in volcanic hydrothermal systems on Earth and Mars*

Masters

Butcher, Lesley Ann, *Re-thinking the Laramide; investigating the role of fluids in producing surface uplift using xenolith mineralogy and geochronology*

Howard, Amanda Leigh, *Hafnium isotope evidence on the provenance of #DF1.1 Ga detrital zircons from western North America*

Huda, Shahen Ahmed, *Modeling the effects of bed topography on fluvial erosion by saltating bed load*

University of Delaware
Doctorate

Nebel, Stephanie Hope, *Reconstructing the origin and history of buried channel-fill sequences offshore of Cedar Island, Virginia*

Skarke, Adam D., *Coastal morphodynamics of the estuary-shelf interface*

University of Florida
Doctorate

Kurz, Marie Juliette, *Biogeochemical and hydrologic controls on solute sources and cycling in a biologically productive karst river*

Lovering, Jessica Loren, *The role of marsh platform morphology in the geomorphic response of tidal inlet systems to sea level rise*

University of Hawaii at Manoa
Doctorate

Anderson, Tiffany R., *Shoreline data analysis*

Aryal, Arjun, *Landslide deformation character inferred from terrestrial laser scanner data*

Parcheta, Carolyn, *Weak-intensity, basaltic, explosive volcanism; dynamics of Hawaiian fountains*

Romine, Bradley M., *Historical shoreline changes on beaches of the Hawaiian Islands with relation to human impacts, sea level, and other influences on beach dynamics*

Masters

Barnes, Jessica L., *Fluid flow, gas accumulations, and gas hydrate formation in Kumano forearc basin determined by seismic reflection interpretation and well data correlation*

Howell, Samuel M., *The origin of the asymmetry in the Iceland Hotspot along the Mid-Atlantic Ridge from continental breakup to present-day*

University of Houston
Doctorate

Echegu, Simon, *Geological and geochemical investigation of the petroleum systems of the Permian Basin of West Texas and southeast New Mexico*

Imrecke, Daniel, *Tectonic evolution of the southeast Pamir*

Jiang, Tao, *Connection of elastic and transport properties; effective medium study in anisotropic porous media*

Li, Lun, *Seismic velocity, radial anisotropy in the crust and upper mantle of northeastern Tibetan Plateau from surface wave tomography*

Mukherjee, Tania, *Time-lapse scenario modeling and VSP analysis for an EOR reservoir in Oman*

Roy, Soumya, *Near-surface characterization via seismic surface-wave inversion*

Shaulis, Barry, *Terrestrial and cosmochemical applications of U-Pb zircon baddeleyite and phosphate chronology*

Yao, Qiuliang, *Velocity dispersion and wave attenuation in reservoir rocks*

Yu, Hua, *Calibration of effective pressure coefficient for the Gulf of Mexico*

Masters

Adejuyigbe, Olawale, *Correlation between the volumes of slurry and the volume of fracture in Barnett Shale*

Akbas, Omer, *Microseismic monitoring; physical modeling and source characterization*

Arres, Nicole, *Flexural modeling of the Himalayan foreland basin; implications for the presence of a forebulge and formation of basement ridges*

Babalola, Ayodeji, *Resolution of sub-seismic reservoirs by the application of spectral decomposition and spectral inversion methods in Boonsville Field, north central Texas*

Bektas, Serdar, *Detrital zircon investigation in the late Proterozoic to early Paleozoic tectonic history of the Qing Shan region of the Nan Shan, northeast Tibet*

Buechmann, Daniel, *Provenance, detrital zircon U-Pb geochronology and tectonic significance of Middle Cretaceous sandstone from the Alberta foreland basin*

Burrough, Toby M., *Spatial and temporal variability in vertical deformation in Willowbend, TX derived from long-term GPS and extensometer observations*

Campbell, Christopher Eric, *Valley widening and the composite nature of valley margin sequence boundaries; evidence from the Neilson wash compound valley fill, Cretaceous Ferron Sandstone, Utah*

Chroback, Marcus, *Hydrocarbon potential of the Antrim Shale along the southern margin of the Michigan Basin*

Cook, Megan A., *Lateral and temporal facies variations in a Quaternary travertine deposit, Belen, New Mexico*

d'Souza, Danfix, *Facies architecture, and controls on channel-belt geometry; Cretaceous-Ferron Notom Delta, Utah, U.S.A.*

Dale, Alex, *Crustal type tectonic origin and petroleum potential of the Bahamas carbonate platform*

Dischington, Petter, *Likely counter point bars in course-grained meandering fluvial deposits in the Brushy Basin Member of the Jurassic Morrison Formation*

Griffin, Cameron, *Facies architecture paleo-hydraulics and fluvial style of a falling stage terrace deposit within a compound incised valley system, Ferron Notom Delta, Utah*

Grosshans, Therica, *Lu-Hf and Sm-Nd ages and source compositions of depleted shergottite Tissint*

Han, Xu, *Integrated remote sensing and geophysical study of the Hockley Fault in Harris County, Texas*

Herrera, Henry, *A petroleum system study of the cratonic Williston Basin in North Dakota, USA; the role of Laramide Orogeny*

Hilton, Benjamin David, *3D allostratigraphic mapping and facies heterogeneity of a compound tributary incised valley system, Turonian Ferron Sandstone, Notom Delta, south-central Utah*

Huang, Feifei, *Using pair correlation function as a tool to identify the location for the shale gas/oil reservoir based on the experimental well log data*

Huang, Long, *Fluid substitution and AVAZ analysis of fractured domains; an ultrasonic experimental study*

Ikediobi, Uchenna, *Crustal structure of Salton Trough; constraints from gravity modeling*

Juranovic, Alejandro E., *Diffraction imaging; a Stratton Field, TX case study*

Kabazi, Hana, *Microstructural and metamorphic analysis of the Malton gneiss dome, southern Canadian Cordillera*

Karacay, Ayca, *Subsidence study in northwest Harris County using GPS, LiDAR and InSAR remote sensing techniques*

Kent, Jeremy, *Geochemistry of lunar granulites and implications for the composition and history of the lunar crust*

Kocoglu, Sebnem, *Description of the Bakken Formation's rock properties of the Williston Basin, North Dakota*

Kose, Sukru Gokhan, *Crustal architecture, Cretaceous rise and igneous activity of Sabine, Monroe and Jackson uplifts, northern Gulf of Mexico basin*

Li, An, *Structural evolution of the Himalayan thrust belt*

Lin, Rongrong, *Extracting polar anisotropy parameters from seismic data and well logs*

Lin, Xinglu, *Optimal background model extraction and improvement of RTM illumination on basis of Born modeling*

Loocke, Matthew, *Arc foundations and subduction initiation in the Izu-Bonin Forearc*

Mason, Maria Virginia, *Multicomponent seismic imaging of sand reservoirs; middle Magdalena Valley, Colombia*

McConnell, Allison, *Geochemical investigation of the origin of hydrocarbon occurrences in up-dip Wilcox Group reservoirs at Raccoon Bend Field, southeast Texas Gulf Coast Basin*

McGarity, Heather Anne, *Facies and stratigraphic framework of the Eagle Ford Shale in south Texas*

Montes, Omar A., *Quantitative comparison of channel-belt dimensions, internal architecture and characteristics of two fluvial systems in Sequence 1, Ferron Notom Delta, south-central Utah, U.S.A.*

Nguyen, Nam Hien, *Tracing enriched mantle components along the Gakkel Ridge, Arctic Ocean*

Ortega, Jesse A., *Groundwater withdrawal and aquifer compaction; a case study in Addicks, Texas*

Osakwe, Emmanuel Olisejindu, *Estimation of the source mechanisms of microseismic events from a Barnett Shale play*

Oyepeju, Alli, *Origin of cratonic basins; testing the rifting model for their formation*

Pachon Parr, Luis, *Subsurface mapping and 3D flexural modeling of the Putumayo foreland basin, Colombia*

Porifi, Gisela, *Conventional vs high-resolution seismic simultaneous inversion and rock property characterization of the Olmos and Eagle Ford unconventional plays, McMullen County, south Texas*

Qi, Jie, *Faults and discontinuities analysis; application to Barnett Shale data*

Qin, Xuan, *VP-Vs relations of organic-rich shales*

Quintanar, Jessica, *Remote sensing, planform and sedimentological analysis of the Plain of Tineh, Egypt for the remains of the Pelusiac River, a defunct branch of the Nile River*

Raschilla, Robert, *Hydrocarbon potential of the upper Green River petroleum system in the Uinta Basin, Utah; a basin modeling approach*

Record, Colby, *A petroleum system analysis of the Espanda Basin of the Rio Grande Rift, New Mexico*

Sanchez, Gabriel, *Determining the trace and kinematics of the Wang Long Point Fault in Houston, Texas using LiDAR data and continuous GPS monitoring*

Sayers, Jordan E., *Enhancement of the geological features of the Scotian Basin by the application of spectral inversion, offshore Nova Scotia*

Schmidt, Kevin, *A geophysical study of active faulting in Fort Bend County, Texas*

Surek, Melahat Asli, *Cluster analysis of the Balakhany VIII reservoir unit with spectral gamma ray logs Azeri-Chirag-Gunashli Field, offshore Azerbaijan*

Turolski, Arkadiusz, *Near-surface geophysical imaging of complex structures; Meteor Crater, AZ and Jemez Pueblo, NM*

Wang, Xixi, *Imaging crustal structure beneath Texas from receiver functions*

Wang, Xu, *Love wave tomography of the central Tien Shan from ambient seismic noise*

Yao, Yao, *Rayleigh wave tomography of Texas from seismic ambient noise*

Yapar, Ozbil, *Investigation of the interaction between salt movement, faulting and deposition, using high-resolution 3-D seismic data; Eugene Island south addition, Gulf of Mexico*

Yuan, Duo, *Building 3-D crustal model with radial anisotropy in Iceland from ambient seismic noise tomography*

Zhang, Minyu, *S-wave velocity estimation using converted-wave VSP data*

Bachelor

Slotsve, Erik, *Geologic map of the Snowbird fluorite deposit, Mineral County, Montana; implications for its genesis*

University of Idaho
Doctorate

Bandli, Bryan R., *Application of electron backscatter diffraction to analytical challenges of asbestiform minerals*

Boggs, Kevin G., *Improved baseflow forecasting*

McNamee, Brittani D., *Characterization of minerals; from the classroom to soils to talc deposits*

Patthoff, D. Alex, *Tectonic history of the south polar terrain of Saturn's moon Enceladus and evidence for a global ocean*

Masters

Greth, Jeremy, *EPSCoR evapotranspiration and energy balance flux site in southern Idaho supports hydroclimate modeling*

McMillin, Amelia M., *Assessment of linkage likelihood in segmented normal fault systems in the Tharsis region, Mars*

Nuzum, Kirk A., *Numerical modeling to determine the rate of heat transfer from a geothermal hot spring*

Piersol, Mark W., *On a common mantle source for the western Snake River plain and Saddle Mountain basalts*

Weigner, Madeline, *Late Devonian shelly fossils from the Jefferson Formation, Grandview Canyon, east-central Idaho*

Wilson, Emily Lorraine, *The geochemical evolution of Santa Cruz Island, Galapagos Archipelago*

University of Illinois at Urbana-Champaign
Doctorate

Basu, Anirban, *Isotopic fractionation of chromium and uranium during abiotic and microbial Cr(VI) reduction and microbial U(VI) reduction*

Coopersmith, Evan, *Data-driven modeling of hydroclimatic trends and soil moisture; multi-scale data integration and decision support*

Funk, Jason, *Settlement of the Kansai International Airport islands*

Kim, Byungmin, *Seismic hazard analysis and seismic slope stability evaluation using discrete faults in northwestern Pakistan*

Kwack, Jaehyuk, *A variational multiscale framework for non-Newtonian fluid models*

Min, Dahhea, *Combined irregular roughness and favorable-pressure-gradient effects in a turbulent boundary layer*

Motta, Davide, *Meander migration with physically-based bank erosion*

Muhammad, Kashif, *Case history-based analysis of liquefaction in sloping ground*

Muszynski, Mark, *Evaluating soil pressures on a deep foundation element due to liquefaction-induced lateral spreading*

Perillo, Mauricio, *Flow, sediment transport and bedforms under combined flows*

Phillips, Camilo, *Dynamic soil modeling in site response and soil;*

large pile interaction analysis

Riley, James, *The fluvial dynamics of confluent meander bends*

Wang, Jihua, *Solving large-scale spatial optimization problems in groundwater management*

Wang, Ruiyu, *Effect of self-stratification of sediment suspensions in turbulent plane Couette flow*

Yeh, Tzu-Hao, *Numerical study on internal flow structures of subaqueous density underflows and stratified open-channel flows*

Masters

Brauer, Edward, *The effect of dikes on water surfaces in a mobile bed*

Czapiga, Matthew, *Systematic connectivity in single thread meandering alluvial rivers; statistical generalization of hydraulic geometry*

Domrois, Stefanie, *The Midcontinent exposed; Precambrian basement topography, and fault-and-fold zones, within the cratonic platform of the United States*

Eickhoff, Brooke Alane, *Relative timing of dolomitization and silica cementation in the Cambrian Potosi and Eminence Dolomites in the Illinois Basin, USA*

Feng, Ye, *Teleseismic tomography beneath Hi-CLIMB station array in western Tibetan Plateau*

Gemperline, Johanna, *Controls on the extent of the Laurentide ice sheet in southern Illinois*

Goodwell, Allison, *Landscape vulnerability to flood impacts in a human-dominated floodplain*

Moor, Johnathan, *Performance and microbial community structure of Midwestern groundwater pretreatment reactors*

Seid, Mary Jean, *Tectonics of the Wolf Creek fault zone, southern Illinois; a consequence of late Paleozoic transpression and transtension at the southeastern end of the Ste. Genevieve fault system*

Slaven, Samuel, *Monitoring tracer stones through the potholes of Fall Creek Gorge near Williamsport, Indiana*

Wang, Guoyin, *Design and application of flux corrected transport for reactive solute transport modeling*

Woo, Dong Kook, *Soil carbon and nitrogen cycle modeling for bioenergy crops*

Zhang, Guimiao, *The elastic properties of fine-grained polycrystalline and amorphous samples by Brillouin scattering*

University of Iowa
Doctorate

Kilgore, Susan Marlena, *The use of multi-channel ground penetrating radar and stream monitoring to investigate the seasonal evolution of englacial and subglacial drainage systems at the terminus of Exit Glacier, Alaska*

Spencer, Marc Richard, *Phylogenetic and biogeographic assessment of ornithischian diversity throughout the Mesozoic; a species-level analysis from origin to extinction*

Masters

Baratta, Vanessa Marrie, *The effects of freeze-thaw cycles on the infiltration rates of three bioretention cell soil mixtures*

Cukierski, Daniel Owen, *Textural and compositional analysis of Fe-Ni metallic spherules in impact melt from Monturaqui Crater, Chile*

Drehobi, Marissa Beth, *Paleoecological reconstruction of Mid-Cretaceous plant communities from the Dakota Formation of Iowa, USA*

Ferraro, Jaclyn Marie, *Relationships between deformation and mesothermal veins in the Sunshine Mine area, Coeur d'Alene District, Idaho*

Matzke, Jeffrey Alan, *Geophysical investigation of the stone zone and loamy mantle on the Iowan surface*

Monson, Jessica Laura Bruse, *A characterization of soil organic matter in Holocene paleosols from Kansas*

Schettler, Megan Elizabeth, *Characterization of water movement in a reconstructed slope in Keokuk, Iowa, using advanced geophysical techniques*

University of Kansas
Doctorate

Firdous, Rubina, *Factors affecting the reactivity of granular iron in contact with chlorinated solvents*

Li, Zhaoqi, *Diagenetic controls on porosity and permeability in Miocene carbonates, La Molata, Spain*

Miller, Brian, *3-D seismic methods for shallow imaging beneath pavement*

Myers, Corinne Emanuelle, *Paleobiogeography of the North*

American Late Cretaceous Western Interior Seaway; the impact of abiotic vs. biotic factors on macroevolutionary patterns of marine vertebrates and invertebrates

Szymanski, Eugene, *Timing, kinematics, and spatial distribution of Miocene extension in the central Arabian margin of the Red Sea rift system*

Masters

Anderson, Brendan M., *Viewing paleontology through a geochemical lens; 2 case studies*

Fairchild, Justin M., *Paleotopography and sea-level controls on facies distribution and stratal architecture in the Westerville Limestone Member (Upper Pennsylvanian) NE Kansas and NW Missouri*

Harlow, R. Hunter, *Depositional and paleoclimatic evolution of the Cenozoic High Plains Succession from core; Haskell Co., Kansas*

King, Bradley, *Fluid flow, thermal history, and diagenesis of the Cambrian-Ordovician Arbuckle Group and overlying units in south-central Kansas*

Perll, Christopher P., *Evaluating GPR polarization effects for imaging fracture channeling and estimating fracture properties*

Schwenk, Jacob Tyler, *Constrained parameterization of the multichannel analysis of surface waves approach with application at Yuma Proving Ground, Arizona*

Wasserman, Hannah Nicole, *Heterogeneity and depositional variability of reef sand aprons; integrated field and modeling of the dynamics of Holocene Aranuka Atoll, Republic of Kiribati, Equatorial Pacific*

University of Kentucky
Doctorate

Almayahi, Ali Z., *Shear-wave imaging and birefringence in a complex near-surface geological environment*

Tripathi, Ganesh N., *Spatio-temporal variability in groundwater discharge and contaminant fluxes along a channelized stream in western Kentucky*

Masters

Hatch, Rachel S., *Distribution and impacts of petroleum hydrocarbons in Louisiana tidal marsh sediments following the Deepwater Horizon oil spill*

Leib, Susan E., *Thermobarometry of metamorphosed pseudotachylyte and determination of seismic rupture depth during Devonian Caledonian extension, north Norway*

Schumacher, Anne M., *Modeling of CO_2 water-rock interactions in a Mississippian sandstone reservoir of Kentucky*

University of Louisiana at Lafayette
Masters

Bearb, Nicholas A., *Sedimentology of the Miocene Bigenerina humblei and Amphistegina "B" sandstones in Hog Bayou Field, offshore Block East Cameron 1 and Cameron Parish, Louisiana; a well log based study*

Etienne, Mark R., *Geoelectrical resistivity modeling of a hydrocarbon plume at Lookout Release site, St. Helena Parish, Louisiana*

Strong, Martell, *Investigation and characterization of features on a Cretaceous-Paleogene seismic horizon in northern Louisiana*

University of Maine
Doctorate

Buchanan Sneed, Sharon, *Ice core chemistry; enhanced sea ice proxy and a micrometer resolution analysis*

Fan, Zhiqiang, *Primary migration of hydrocarbons through microfracture propagation in petroleum source rocks*

Koffman, Bess, *Atmospheric dust deposition in West Antarctica over the past two millennia*

Slemmons, Krista E. H., *The influence of glacial meltwater on alpine and arctic lake phytoplankton throughout the Holocene*

Masters

Beckwith, Walter Isles, *Maya obsidian of the Three Rivers region, Belize*

Bon, Christiaan, *Using hydrologic measurements to investigate free phase gas in a Maine peatland, USA*

Buttersworth Koffman, Tobias Nicholas, *Glacial geology of Miers Valley, Antarctica; a record of the western margin of the Ross Sea ice sheet during the local last glacial maximum*

Jackson, Margaret S., *Glacial history of Salmon Valley, Royal Society Range, Antarctica*

Medford, Aaron, *Holocene glacial history of Renland, East Greenland reconstructed from lake sediments*

Morey, Timothy J., *Improving the performance of the Parallel Ice Sheet Model on a large-scale, distributed supercomputer*

Sorrell, Lee M., *Periodic episodes of catastrophic aeolian sand deposition, Shetland UK*

Wheeler, Lauren Bronwyn, *Modeling the influence of the last glacial maximum ice load on the tectonics of southeast Alaska and the South Island, New Zealand*

University of Manitoba
Masters

Gallagher, Shaun Vincent, *Geology, geochemistry and geochronology of the East Bay gold trend, Red Lake, Ontario, Canada*

University of Minnesota at Duluth
Masters

Cantarero, Sebastian, *Multiproxy paleoclimatic record from geochemical analyses of Lake Chalco sediments, a closed basin lake in central Mexico*

Goldner, Jennifer Noelle, *Structure and metamorphism along the Burntside Lake shear zone near Ely, Minnesota*

Graupner, Melanie, *Structural and geologic mapping of southern Tellus Regio, Venus; implications for crustal plateau formation*

Halbur, Julia, *Frequency and spatial distribution of avulsion nodes on river deltas as a function of wave energy*

Hougardy, Devin, *The Late-Quaternary geologic history of Lake of the Woods, Minnesota*

Neitzel, Grant, *Monitoring event-scale stream bluff erosion with repeat terrestrial*

Radakovich, Amy Laureen, *Metamorphic petrology of glacial clasts from the Byrd Glacier drainage; implications for the crustal history of East Antarctica*

Slonecker, Aaron, *Structural and geologic mapping of northern Tellus Regio, Venus*

Wick, Molly J., *Identifying erosional hotspots in streams along the North Shore of Lake Superior, Minnesota using high-resolution elevation and soils data*

University of Missouri at Columbia
Masters

Brito, John, *Strategies for defining chemical connectivity between streams and wetlands*

Grzovic, Mark L., *Composition of magmatic fluids in the Harney Peak Granite, Black Hills, South Dakota*

Hansen, Emma Grace, *Geochemical studies of gold mineralizing events in the Discovery-Ormsby and Clan Lake areas of the Yellowknife greenstone belt, Northwest Territories, Canada*

McKee, Tyler J., *Uncertainty propagation and parameter sensitivity analyses of relative permittivity models for use in soils*

Nicholson, Brooke, *Effect of increasing trimethylamine and organic matter concentration on stable carbon isotopes of methane produced in hypersaline, substrate limited environments*

Senefeld, Laura, *Organic matter remineralization in the sediment of two acid mine drainage lakes*

University of Nevada at Las Vegas
Masters

Giallorenzo, Michael A., *Application of (U-Th)/He and >40`Ar/>39`Ar thermochronology to the age of thrust faulting in the Sevier orogenic belt*

Russo, Angela G., *Pennsylvanian to Cretaceous folds and thrusts in south-central Nevada; evidence from the Timpahute Range*

Stoller, Heather Marie, *Ichnology and paleoecology of the Jurassic Aztec Sandstone*

Tu, Valerie M., *Dissolution rates of amorphous Al- and Fe-phosphates and their relevance to phosphate mobility on Mars*

University of New Hampshire
Masters

Dorich, Christopher D., *Comparison of greenhouse gas emissions on an organic and Conventional dairy farm in New Hampshire*

Fandel, Christina L., *Observations of pockmark flow structure in Belfast Bay, Maine*

Korkolis, Evangelos, *In situ observation of shear zone microstructures and strain localization using a transparent rotary shear apparatu*

Korkolis, Evangelos, *In situ observation of shear zone microstructures and strain localization using a transparent rotary shear apparatus*

Kurnianto, Sofyan, *Modeling long-term carbon accumulation in tropical peat swamp forest ecosystems*

McKenna, Lindsay A., *Patterns of bedform migration and mean tidal currents in Hampton Harbor Inlet, New Hampshire, USA*

Schweinsberg, Avriel D., *Clastic flux records of Holocene glacier and climate variability in sediment cores from the Cordillera Vilcabamba of southern Peru*

University of North Carolina at Wilmington
Masters

Mason, Patricia H., *Biostratigraphy and paleoecology of Late Cretaceous Foraminifera from the Dixon Core, southeastern North Carolina*

Reidhaar, Paula, *Spatial and temporal distribution of Pyrodinium bahamense cysts in sediments of Mangrove Lagoon, St. Croix, USVI*

Rhodes, Daniel Luke, *Lithologic and structural relationships of northeastern Carolina terrane rocks in the Lake Michie 1:24K quadrangle, North Carolina*

University of North Dakota
Doctorate

Burton-Kelly, Matthew Earl, *Examining the continuity of the long-lived (Triassic-Recent) freshwater mussel genus Diplodon (family Hyriidae)*

McDonald, Mark Richmond, *Geophysical investigation and assessment of the Rye Patch Known Geothermal Resource Area, Rye Patch, Nevada*

Masters

Buer, Nicolas Hans, *Characterization of phosphorus, nitrogen, and sulfur concentrations in a paired disturbed and natural wetland in northwest Minnesota*

He, Jun, *Research about low permeability measurement*

Njoku, Godswill Osinachi, *Correcting heat flow data in the United States to account for climate change*

Skitt, Troy (Troy JD), *Lithological and sequence stratigraphic examination of the Madison Group marker beds, eastern Williston Basin margin, North Dakota*

University of Oklahoma
Doctorate

Albaghdady, Alsharef A., *Organic geochemical characterization of source rocks (Sirt Shale) and crude oils form central Sirt Basin, Libya*

Altamar, Roderick Perz, *Brittleness estimation from seismic measurement in unconventional reservoirs; application to the Barnett Shale*

Davogustto Cataldo, Oswaldo Ernesto, *Quantitative geophysical investigations at the Diamond M Field, Scurry County, Texas*

Keiser, Leslie Jo, *Physical and chemical weathering in modern and Permian proximal fluvial systems*

Liao, Zonghu, *Dynamic shear rupture along faults; experiments and simulations*

Roy, Atish, *Latent space classification of seismic facies*

Swindle, Andrew, *Size-dependent reactivity of magnetite nanoparticles; a bridge between laboratory and field investigations*

Masters

Al-Masoodi, Mouin M., *Viscoelastic creep of Eagle Ford Shale*

Benton, Alexander Keith, *An integrated diagenetic and paleomagnetic study of the Haynesville Shale, Harrison County, Texas*

Bernal, Andrea Serna, *Geological characterization of the Woodford Shale, McAlister Cemetery Quarry, Criner Hills, Ardmore Basin, Oklahoma*

Buening, Jonathan D., *An integrated geophysical and geological study of the relationships between the Grenville Orogen and Mid-Continent rift system*

Castillo Morales, Luis Alejandro, *Integrated reservoir characterization of the Ordovician-Silurian Hunton Carbonate, north Cherokee Platform, Oklahoma*

da Silva Rodriguez, Melia Rebeca, *Production correlation to 3D seismic attributes in the Barnett Shale, Texas*

Dowdell, Benjamin Lewis, *Prestack seismic analysis of Mississippian lime resource play in the Midcontinent, U.S.A.*

Eccles, Thaddeus Maxwell, *Structure of the southwestern Uncompahgre Plateau (western Colorado) near äUnaweep Canyon*

Fernandez Abad, Alfredo, *3D seismic attribute expression of the Ellenburger Group karst-collapse features and their effects on the production of the Barnett Shale, Fort Worth Basin, Texas*

Foster, Tyler Matthew, *Environments and provenance of redbeds of the Dog Creek Shale (Midcontinent); implications for Middle Permian paleoclimate in western Pangaea*

Hawkins, Dalton Wayne, *3D marine seismic processing for interpretation of the Jeju Basin, South Korea*

Haynes, Justin, *Diagenesis within the Mississippian limestone;*

north central Oklahoma

Heard, Grant L., *The timing and origin of magnetization of the Madison and Chugwater Formations at Sheep Mountain Anticline, Wyoming*

Hogan, Cullen M., *Precise locations of central Oklahoma seismicity, 2010-2013*

Horne, Rebecca C., *Distribution of magmatism within the crust beneath the Main Ethiopian Rift and adjacent plateaus; melt bodies, intrusion, and underplating*

Kane, Molly Mae, *Detrital zircon geochronology of a core in western Kansas; implications for Permian paleogeography and paleoclimate*

Kerr, Edwin Pierce, IV, *Structural analysis of the Bremstein fault complex offshore mid-Norway*

Maner, James Lavada, IV, *Experimental syntheses of garnet, tourmaline, and cordierite from boron-bearing, peraluminous granitic melt; phase relations, elemental partitioning, and potential for geothermometry*

Molinares Blanco, Carlos Eduardo, *Stratigraphy and palynomorphs composition of the Woodford Shale in the Wyche Farm Shale Pit, Pontotoc County, Oklahoma*

Patel, Gaurangkumar, *An integrated study of the Castle Valley salt diapir, Paradox Basin, Utah*

Sevinc, Sezer, *Poroviscoelasticity of an Eagleford Mudstone under in-situ fluids and pressure*

Stuchly, Ellen, *Hydrocarbon sweet spots in the Eagle Ford Formation, south Texas; delineation through basin modeling*

Wang, Tang, *Improving lateral resolution on a legacy 3D survey; Central Basin Platform, Texas*

White, Henry George, III, *Fracturing of Mississippi lime, Oklahoma; experimental, seismic attributes and image logs' analyses*

Williams, Michael Thomas, *Evolution of the Delaware Basin, West Texas and southeast New Mexico*

University of Oregon
Doctorate

Metzger, Christine, *Paleosol Records of Middle Miocene Climate Change*

Verba, Circe, *Potential Impacts of Formation Waters on the Integrity of Class H Cement and Reservoir Rock in Carbon (Co-) Sequestration Settings*

Masters

Castonguay, Samuel, *Structural Evolution of the Virgin Spring Phase of the Amargosa Chaos, Death Valley, California, USA*

Famoso, Nicholas, *The Evolution of Occlusal Enamel Complexity in Middle Miocene to Recent Equids (Mammalia: Perissodactyla) of North America*

MacKenzie, Kristen, *The Geology and Paleontology of Coglan Buttes, Oregon*

Paulson, Kathryn, *Generation of Structural Relief by Fault Propagation Folding, Tien Shan, Kyrgzstan*

Rabjohns, Kelley, *Impact of Aquifer Heterogeneity on Geomicrobial Kinetics*

Walsh, Lucy, *Implications for Volcanic Hazards in the Central and Southern Cascades Based on Gas Emissions During Explosive Cinder Cone Activity*

University of Ottawa
Doctorate

Cousineau, Melanie L., *Tracing biogeochemical processes using sulfur stable isotopes; two novel applications*

Jamieson, John William, *Size, age, distribution and mass accumulation rates of seafloor hydrothermal sulfide deposits*

Zhang, Steven, *Formation mechanism and computational modelling of Isle of Rum plagioclase stellates*

Masters

Coffin, Lindsay, *Sedimentology, stratigraphy and petrography of the Permian-Triassic coal-bearing New Lenton Deposit, Bowen Basin, Australia*

Jatar, Muriel M., *Assessing the effect of selenium on the life-cycle of two aquatic invertebrates; "Cerio daphnia dubia" and "Chironomus dilutus"*

Stern, Fabio Gianotti, *Geochemistry of the ultramafic rocks from the Bay of Island ophiolitic complex, Newfoundland*

Tekin, Elif, *Anaerobic ammonium oxidation in groundwater contaminated by fertilizers*

Van Lankvelt, Amanda, *Protracted magmatism within the North Caribou Terrane, Superior Province; petrology, geochronology, and*

geochemistry of Meso- to Neoarchean TTG suites

Bachelor

Al-Mufti, Omar, *Dune or dune-like cross-stratification in deep-marine sandstones of the Neoproterozoic Windermere Supergroup, Cariboo Mountains, British Columbia, Canada*

Bibby, Claire L., *Sedimentology of the Upper Ordovician carbonate succession, Hudson Bay Platform, northern Ontario*

Boulerice, Alexandre, *Compositions of alteration minerals associated with uranium mineralization, Athabasca Basin, northern Saskatchewan*

Cossette, Elise, *Dating deformation with in-situ >40`Ar/>39`Ar methods in the West Cycladic detachment system; rheological implications of mica neocrystallization in quartz- and calcite-rich rocks*

Craig, Andrew, *Using >18`O and >2`H to investigate the water balance of a controlled and uncontrolled tile drained soy field in Casselman, Ontario*

Dube Bourgeois, Vincent, *Characterization of roadcut lithologies, including metasomatized marbles, from the Central Metasedimentary Belt, Grenville Province, Ontario*

English, Michelle, *Lateral facies changes in matrix-rich sandstones, upper Kaza Group, Windermere Supergroup, Cariboo Mountains, British Columbia, Canada*

Ferderber, Jessica Lee, *Exploring the Tehery region; correlating supracrustal sequences using detrital zircon geochronology, Rae Craton, Nunavut*

Leminski, Danika, *The stratigraphy and sedimentology of Middle-Upper Ordovician Mingan Formation in the subsurface of the Anticosti Basin, Gulf of St. Lawrence*

Pickering, Julia, *Characterization of carbon in Archean graphitic argillites of the Abitibi greenstone belt, Timmins-Kirkland Lake, ON*

University of Rhode Island
Doctorate

Lytle, Marion Lynn, *Geochemical constraints on mantle sources and melting conditions in Pacific back-arc basins*

Masters

Ashmankas, Cristin Elizabeth, *A history of sea ice in the Cenozoic Arctic Ocean*

Hartwell, Anne M., *A reconstruction of N-15/N-14 global of deep ocean nitrate in the past using pore fluid*

Kelly, Joshua, *1891 AD submarine eruptive processes and geochemical studies of floating scoria at Foerstner Volcano, Pantelleria*

Sauvage, Justine, *Determination of in-situ dissolved inorganic carbon and alkalinity in marine sedimentary interstitial water*

University of South Florida at Saint Petersburg
Doctorate

Paul, Shubhabrata, *Ecology of the late Neogene extinctions; perspectives from the Plio-Pleistocene of Florida*

University of South Florida at Tampa
Doctorate

Courtland, Leah M., *Deciphering deposits; using ground penetrating radar and numerical modeling to characterize the emplacement mechanisms and associated energetics of scoria cone eruption and construction*

Puscas, Cristina M., *Hypogene speleogenesis in the Cerna River basin, SW Romania; a sedimentological, mineralogical, and stable isotopic approach*

Masters

Brownell, Andrew T., *Morphological changes associated with tropical storm Debby in the vicinity of two tidal inlets, John's Pass and Blind Pass, west-central Florida*

Davis, Denise Marie, *Distinguishing processes that induce temporal beach profile changes using principal component analysis; a case study at Long Key, west-central Florida*

Kiflu, Henok Gidey, *Optimized correlation of geophysical and geotechnical methods in sinkhole investigations; emphasizing on spatial variations in west-central Florida*

Sampson, Jacqueline M., *The extent of phosphorus redox chemistry in west central Florida waters*

Szenay, Brian, *Modeling potential chemical environments; implications for astrobiology*

Wilson, Jessica Norman, *Stable isotopes and trace elements in tooth enamel bioapatite; effects of diagenesis and pretreatment on primary paleoecological information*

University of Southern Mississippi
Doctorate

Hopper, Nathan Lee, *A geographical approach for integrating belief networks and Geographic Information Sciences to probabilistically predict river depth*

Masters

Allen, John Edward, Jr., *Determining hydrocarbon distribution using resistivity, Tuscaloosa Marine Shale, southwestern Mississippi*

Ewing, Michael Edward, *The effects of snowmelt percolation on stratified pollen records : a cooler study / by Michael Edward Ewing*

Fahrenbruch, Matthew Lee, *Waves of change : tourism and vulnerability in San Juan del Sur, Nicaragua*

Fleming, John Andrew Sebastian, *Sedimentary characteristics of an estuarine marsh system and the roles of storm overwash, micro-tidal currents, and organic production : Big Branch Marsh, Louisiana*

Loeffler, Joel Kenneth, *Cretaceous and Paleogene stratigraphy of Forrest County, Mississippi*

Norville, Courtney Shea, *Drive-by geography : perceptions of urban growth and land use in Hattiesburg, Mississippi*

Rhoads, Joy Delaine, *Legislated landscape : a comparison of New Deal farm communities in Hattiesburg, McComb, and Tupelo, Mississippi*

Wissing, Thomas Paul, *Renewable ocean energy site selection using a GIS : Gulf Coast potential*

University of Texas at Austin

Doctorate

Alhussain, Mohammed Abdullah, *Fracture characterization of a carbonate reservoir in the Arabian Peninsula*

Betka, Paul Michael, *Structure of the Patagonian fold-thrust belt in the Magallanes region of Chile, 53-55 lat.*

Campbell, Terence A., *Correction for distortion in polarization of reflected shear-waves in isotropic and anisotropic media*

Chang, Kyung Won, *Carbon dioxide storage in geologically heterogeneous formations*

Dixon, Joshua Francis, *Shelf-edge deltas; stratigraphic complexity and relationship to deep-water deposition*

Huerta, Nicolas J., *Time dependent leakage of CO2 saturated water along a cement fracture*

Kordi, Masoumeh, *Characterization and prediction of reservoir quality in chlorite-coated sandstones; evidence from the Late Cretaceous lower Tuscaloosa Formation at Cranfield Field, Mississippi, U.S.A.*

Lake, Ethan Taliaferro, *Geochemical and thermal insights into caldera-forming "super-eruptions"*

Lester, Ryan, *From rifting to collision; the evolution of the Taiwan Mountain Belt*

Shaw, John Burnham, *The kinematics of distributary channels on the Wax Lake Delta, coastal Louisiana, USA*

Shi, Mingjie, *Simulating and quantifying land-surface biogeochemical, hydrological, and biogeophysical processes using the Community Land Model Version 4*

Smith, Isaac Blaine, *On the spiral troughs of Mars*

Stocker, Michelle Renae, *Contextualizing vertebrate faunal dynamics; new perspectives from the Triassic and Eocene of western North America*

Wong, Corinne, *Delineating controls on hydrologic variability and water geochemistry in central Texas*

Xue, Yang, *Novel stochastic inversion methods and workflow for reservoir characterization and monitoring*

You, Yao, *Dynamics of dilative slope failure*

Masters

Burroughs, Robert Wayne, *Fossils, phylogeny, and anatomical regions; insights exemplified through turtles*

Burrus, Joshua Bruce, *Structural and stratigraphic evolution of the Weepah Hills area, NV; transition from basin-and-range extension to Miocene core complex formation*

Dai, Yue, *Coal gasification in China : policies, innovation, and technology transfer*

Delbecq, Katherine Lynn, *Physical models of tsunami deposition; an investigation of morphodynamic controls*

Ditkof, Julie Nicole, *Time-lapse seismic monitoring for enhanced oil recovery and carbon capture and storage field site at the Cranfield Field, Mississippi*

Duncan, Mark Hamilton, *The northeastern Gulf of Mexico; volcanic or passive margin? Seismic implications of the Gulf of Mexico Basin opening project*

Dunlap, Dallas Brogdon, *Seismic geomorphology of the Safi Haute Mer exploration block, offshore Morocco's Atlantic margin*

Eckhart, Jeanne Lynn, *Water use by the oil and gas industry; an assessment of two Texas regions*

Gao, Baiyuan, *Pore pressure within dipping reservoirs in overpressure basins*

Gawey, Marlo Rose, *Experimental analysis and modeling of perfluorocarbon transport in the vadose zone; implications for monitoring CO<2` leakage at CCS sites*

Ghosh, Shaunak, *Multiple suppression in the t-x-p domain*

Goktas, Pinar, *Morphologies and controls on development of Pliocene-Pleistocene carbonate platforms; northern Carnarvon Basin, Northwest Shelf of Australia*

Gutowski, Gail Ruth, *Effect of modeled pre-industrial Greenland ice sheet surface mass balance bias on uncertainty in sea level rise projections in 2100*

Hiebert, Samuel Franz, *High-resolution correlation framework of the Grayburg Formation-Shattuck Escarpment and Plowman Ridge; testing models of shelf-to-basin*

Hingst, Mary Catherine, *Geochemical effects of elevated methane and carbon dioxide in near-surface sediments above an EOR/CCUS site*

Hudock, Jessica Wager, *Barrier island associated washover fan and flood tidal delta systems; a geomorphologic analysis and proposed classification scheme for modern washover fans and examination of a flood tidal delta complex in the Cretaceous upper McMurray Formation, Alberta*

Kahraman, Ibrahim, *Analysis of a LNAPL recovery system using LDRM in a South Texas facility*

Kanarek, Michael Richard, *Understanding the effects of wildfire on soil moisture dynamics*

Levina, Mariya, *Cenozoic sedimentation and exhumation of the foreland basin system in the Precordillera fold-thrust belt (31-32#DGS), southern Central Andes, Argentina*

Malin, Reed Ahti, *Geoscience and decision making for geothermal energy; a case study*

Markez, Damian, *Structural framework and seismic geomorphology of the Cretaceous beneath the Mad Dog area, deep to ultradeep waters of Gulf of Mexico*

Marsh, Adam Douglas, *The osteology of Sarahsaurus aurifontanalis and geochemical observations of the dinosaurs from the type quarry of Sarahsaurus (Kayenta Formation), Coconino County, Arizona*

Martinez, Alexandre Mathieu Pierre, *Laboratory study of calcium based sorbents impacts on mercury bioavailability in contaminated sediments*

McCann, Cody James, *Urbanization and its effects on channel morphology*

Morris, Zachary Stephen, *Skeletal ontogeny of Monodelphis domestica (Mammalia, Didelphidae); quantifying variation, variability, and technique bias in ossification sequence reconstruction*

Morshed, Sharif Munjur, *Seismic sensitivity to variations of rock properties in the productive zone of the Marcellus Shale, WV*

Ned, Allison Marie, *Dynamic stratigraphy and sediment partitioning of high-supply fluvial succession in Maastrichtian source-to-sink system*

Parker, John Alexandre, *Outcrop analysis of ooid grainstones in the Permian Grayburg Formation, Shattuck Escarpment, New Mexico*

Poci, Elisabeta, *Establishing a national water resources geodatabase system in Albania : a case study of challenges in a transitioning country*

Pommer, Laura Elizabeth, *Natural fracture cementation in the Marcellus Formation*

Porse, Sean Laurids, *Using analytical and numerical modeling to assess deep groundwater monitoring parameters at carbon capture, utilization, and storage sites*

Ramlal, Kristie Anuradha, *Controls on late Neogene deep-water slope channel architecture in a bathymetrically complex seafloor setting; a quantitative study along the southeastern Caribbean Plate margin, Columbus Basin, Trinidad*

Rhatigan, Caleb Hayes, *Thermochronometric investigation of Paleozoic stratigraphic and thermal evolution of the Western Desert, Egypt*

Roberts, Forrest Daniel, *Identifying and mapping clay-rich intervals in the Fayetteville Shale; influence of clay on natural gas production intervals*

Rodriguez Sanchez, Juan Camilo, *Challenges and opportunities for the development of shale resources in Colombia*

Sanguinito, Sean Michael, *Investigating the effect of high-angle normal faulting on unroofing histories of the Santa Catalina-Rincon and Harcuvar metamorphic core complexes, using apatite fission-track and apatite and zircon (U-Th)/He thermochronometry*

Smith, Gordon Allen, Jr., *Fault and fracture systems related to reactivation of pre-existing structural elements, Devils River Uplift and Maverick Basin, Texas*

Sullivan, John R., Jr, *Characterization of drought in Texas using NLDAS soil moisture data*

Sydow, Lindsey A., *Cinder Pool's sulfur chemistry; implications for the origin of life in hydrothermal environments*

Tomasek, Abigail A., *Hydrodynamic flow modeling of Barton Springs Pool*

Trautman, Marin Cherise, *Hidden intrusions and molybdenite mineralization beneath the Kucing Liar skarn, Ertsberg-Grasberg mining district, Papua, Indonesia*

Vann, Nataleigh Kristine, *Slope to basin-floor evolution of channels to Lobes, Jurassic Los Molles Formation, Neuquen Basin, Argentina*

Vitek, Natasha Slonim, *The eastern box turtle (Terrapene carolina) in space and time*

Waite, Elizabeth Leslie, *Decision support for project selection in Texas water planning*

Wallace, Kerstan Josef, *Use of 3-dimensional dynamic modeling of CO<2` injection for comparison to regional static capacity assessments of Miocene sandstone reservoirs in the Texas State Waters, Gulf of Mexico*

Wang, Kai, *Evaluation of a land surface solar radiation partitioning scheme using remote sensing and site level FPAR datasets*

Wicks, Travis Zhi-Rong, *The use of D>13`C values of leporid teeth as indicators of past vegetation*

Wood, Stephanie Grace, *Lithofacies, depositional environments, and sequence stratigraphy of the Pennsylvanian (Morrowan-Atokan) Marble Falls Formation, central Texas*

Xia, Yu, *Dynamics of the eastern edge of the Rio Grande Rift*

Yi, Hyukjoong, *Analysis of the potential impacts of shale gas development*

Zadrozny, Katherine Elaine, *Documenting, demonstrating and enhancing an offshore geotechnical database for reliability-based foundation design*

Bachelors

Barghouty, Lubna, *Surface-related multiple elimination and velocity-independent imaging of a 2D seismic line from the Viking Graben dataset*

Berney, Jesse, *Regional variability in mid-latitude glaciers on Mars from orbital data; implications for formation*

Camacho, Jason Neal, *The influence of the Permian syndepositional fracture network on the modern geomorphology at Slaughter Canyon, New Mexico*

Carlson, Brandee, *Basin depth control on the fluvial autogenic processes of deltaic systems*

DeSanto, John Boone, *Evaluating transience of a potential geothermal flux anomaly beneath a tributary ice stream of Thwaites Glacier, West Antarctica*

Eldam, Rania, *Petrogenesis of several serpentinites within the Franciscan Complex and Coast Range Ophiolite, western California*

Kim, Han Kyul, *The 2500 B.P. savanna expansion of west central Africa; humans or climate? Understanding the relationship between the Iron-Age Bantu migration, climate change, and abrupt vegetation disturbance in the African tropical forest zone during the late Holocene*

Prather, Timothy John, *Chlorine and hydrogen isotope geochemistry of obsidian glasses; behavior during volcanic degassing at Mono Craters, CA*

Speciale, Pamela Ann, *Geochemistry and geochronology of the Beypazari granitoid pluton (north central Turkey); tectonic implications*

Sripanich, Yanade, *An efficient algorithm for two-point seismic ray tracing in layered media*

University of Texas at Dallas
Doctorate

Xu, Kun, *Frequency-domain seismic-wave modeling, migration, and full-waveform inversion*

University of Toledo

Masters

Baca, Kira, *Environmental impacts on the development and dune activity of Oxbow Lake along the southwest coast of Lake Michigan at Saugatuck, Michigan, USA*

Blockland, Joseph, *The surficial geology of Fulton County, Ohio; insight into the late Pleistocene-early Holocene glaciated landscape of the Huron-Erie Lake Plain, Fulton County, Ohio, USA*

Siemer, Kyle, *You've got that sinking feeling; measuring subsidence above abandoned underground mines in Ohio, USA*

Zmijewski, Kirk, *Connecting the dots; using remote sensing to identify glossy and common buckthorn (Frangula alnus and Rhamnus cathartica) in the Oak Openings region of NW Ohio*

University of Tulsa
Masters

Abatan, Oluwasegun, *Meandering channel facies architecture using ground penetrating radar, Ferron Sandstone (Upper Cretaceous) Emery Co., Utah*

Altintas, Yalin, *Subsurface sequence stratigraphy of Boggy Formation (Middle Pennsylvanian), McIntosh County, OK*

Anderson, Sloan, *Facies architecture of meandering fluvial riffle elements, Ferron Sandstone of Utah*

Arabaci, Ercan, *Comparison of post-stack seismic inversion methods; reservoir characterization of the Boonsville 3-D seismic data set, Fort Worth Basin*

Arpaci, Taner, *Analysis of amplitude versus offset (AVO) variations and comparison with prestack and poststack inversion results for lithology and pore fluid discrimination in the Scotian Basin, Nova Scotia, Canada*

Astore, Claire E., *Geochemical characterization of produced water from an unconventional reservoir*

Ball, Aaron, *Structural cross sections of the Boktukola Syncline in the central Ouachita Mountains of southeastern Oklahoma*

Duggins, Will, *Facies architecture and sequence stratigraphy of part of the Desmoinesian Granite Wash, Texas Panhandle and western Oklahoma*

Dycus, Matt, *Structural characterization of the Wilzetta fault zone; Lincoln, Pottawatomie, and Creek Counties, Oklahoma*

Gargili, Damla, *Middle-upper Albian Comanche shelf sequence stratigraphy, Fredericksburg Group, Texas*

Kilic, Derya, *Structural analysis of the Eola-Robberson Field using balanced cross sections, Garvin County, Oklahoma*

Ozsoy, Serkan, *Petrological and petrophysical study of Oswego Limestone in west central Kay County, Oklahoma*

Postelwait, Bethany, *Chemoprovenance of deepwater Atoka mudrocks in part of the frontal belt Ouachita Mountains, Oklahoma*

Sagin, Firat, *Subsurface sequence stratigraphy of a part of Cherokee Group, Boggy and Senora Formations, northeastern Oklahoma*

Zhao, Tao, *Evaluation of RBF neural networks in reservoir characterization; applied to Boonsville 3-D seismic data*

University of Utah
Doctorate

Davis, Michel Gregory, *Ground temperature and climate change*

Farrell, Jamie Mark, *Seismicity and tomographic imaging of the Yellowstone crustal magmatic-tectonic system*

Masbruch, Melissa Dawn, *Groundwater temperature and flow studies in the Great Basin*

Porter, John Philip, *Source, emplacement, and evolution of the Morgan Creek Pluton, Sierra Nevada Batholith, California, USA*

Potter-McIntyre, Sally Latham, *Biogeochemical signatures in iron (oxyhydr)oxide diagenetic precipitates; chemical, mineralogical and textural markers*

Xu, Zhengwei, *Three-dimension Cole-Cole model inversion of induced polarization data based on regularized conjugate gradient method*

Masters

Black, Brooks M., *Methyl mercury hotspots and sources in the Great Salt Lake, Utah, adjacent freshwater bays and impounded wetlands*

Dooling, Patrick Ryan, *Tidal facies, stratigraphic architecture, and along-strike variability of a high energy, transgressive shoreline, Late Cretaceous, Kaiparowits Plateau, southern Utah*

Edwards, Mason Cole, *Geothermal resource assessment of the Basin and Range Province in western Utah*

Fu, Haiyan, *Interpretation of complex resistivity of rocks using GEMTIP analysis*

Gammans, Christine Naomi Louise, *Low-angle normal faulting in* the Basin and Range-Colorado Plateau transition zone during the January 3, 2011 Circleville, UT earthquake sequence

Gonzalez, Alexander Brian, *Geochemical and mineralogical evaluation of CO<2'-brine-rock experiments; characterizing porosity and permeability variations in the Cambrian Mt. Simon Sandstone*

Good, Kelly Ann, *The tectonic geomorphology and Quaternary geology of the Katalla River valley, Alaska*

Good, Thoms Roger, *Life in an ancient sea of sand; trace fossil associations and their paleoecological implications in the Upper Triassic/Lower Jurassic Nugget Sandstone, northeastern Utah*

Gwynn, Mark Leon, *Tectonic versus volcanic origin of the summit depression at Medicine Lake Volcano, California*

Hale, John Mark, *Infrasound signal characteristics of small earthquakes*

Hardwick, Christian Lynn, *Geothermal resources in southwestern Utah; gravity and magnetotelluric investigations*

Jehle, Glynis Elizabeth, *An ecological snapshot of the early Pleistocene at Kokiselei, Kenya*

Jensen, Kevin James, *SPdKS analysis of ultra-low velocity zones beneath the western Pacific*

Kwong, Kevin Brian, *Imaging the fault ruptures of the great 2012 Indian Ocean intraplate earthquakes form back-projection of teleseismic P-waves*

Levitt, Carolyn Gale, *Bone histology and growth of chasmosaurine ceratopsid dinosaurs from the late Campanian Kaiparowits Formation, southern Utah*

Lively, Joshua Ryan, *New baenid turtles from the Cretaceous Kaiparowits Formation of southern Utah; implications for Laramidian biogeography*

Maibauer, Bianca Jean, *Carbon isotope stratigraphy of early Eocene hyperthermals in the Bighorn Basin, Wyoming, USA; analogues for modern anthropogenic carbon emission*

Manangon, Lucia Eliana, *Mass recoveries in nano to microparticle analysis of enviornmental samples via flow field flow fractionation-inductively-coupled plasma mass spectrometry*

McCauley, Andrew Donald, *Sequence stratigraphy, depositional history, and hydrocarbon potential of the Mancos Shale, Uinta Basin, Utah*

Miller, Olivia Leigh, *Tracing dust provenance, cycling, and history in the Wastch Mountains using strontium isotopes and tree rings*

Moyes, Alexander Jay, *Clay mineralogy and chemical variation in uranium roll-front deposits in the Gas Hills uranium district, Wyoming*

Pettinga, Luke Andrew, *Tectonic controls on alluvial architecture in the Upper Cretaceous John Henry Member, Straight Cliffs Formation, southern Utah*

Rosenberg, Morgan Joshua, *Facies, stratigraphic architecture, and lake evolution of the oil shale bearing Green River Formation, eastern Uinta Basin, Utah*

Schloss, James William, *An interdisciplinary geological and geomorphic characterization and landslide investigation in Red Butte Canyon, Utah*

Yao, Yao, *Evaluation of one-dimensional seismic models of the lunar interior*

University of Vermont
Masters

Scott, Megan, *Stratigraphic evidence for tectonically driven subsidence during deposition of the Middlebury formation (Middle Ordovician), western Vermont*

University of Victoria
Masters

Heathfield, Derek Kenneth, *Erosive water levels and beach-dune morphodynamics, Wickaninnish Bay, Pacific Rim National Park Reserve, British Columbia, Canada*

Newton, Brandi, *Evaluating the Distribution of Water Resources in Western Canada using a Synoptic Climatological Approach*

Sanderson, Bruce Owen, *Damaging Earthquakes and Their Implications for the Transfusion Medicine Function of the Health care System on Vancouver Island, British Columbia*

Bachelors

Deschenes, Steeve, *Modeling Heavy Metals in Soil Using Spatial Regression Analysis*

University of Western Ontario
Doctorate

Alipour, Samira, *Application of differential and polarimetric synthetic aperture radar (SAR) interferometry for studying natural hazards*

Angiel, Piotr Jan, *Allostratigraphy, sedimentology and paleogeography of the Cretaceous upper Fort St. John Group (upper Albian-lower Cenomanian) in northeastern British Columbia*

Babaie Mahani, Alireza, *Variability in characteristics of ground motions across North America*

Battler, Melissa M., *Arctic cold spring mineralgy as an indicator of spring deposits, water, and habitable environments on Mars*

Chehreh Chelgani, Saeed, *Study on the surface chemistry behavior of pyrochlore during froth flotation*

Dehkordi, S. Emad, *Hydrogeological and thermal sustainability of geothermal borehole heat exchangers*

Kazemian, Javad, *Spatial heterogeneities in a simple earthquake fault model*

Kiarasi, Soushyant, *High pressure-temperature electrical resistivity experiments on Fe-Si alloys bearing on conductive heat flow at the top of the outer core*

Pontefract, Alexandra Janine, *Impact craters as habitats for life; endolithic colonization of shocked gneiss from the Haughton impact structure, Devon Island, Canada*

Shankar, Bhairavi, *A multispectral assessment of complex impact craters on the lunar farside*

Shuster, Jeremiah P., *The biogeochemical cycling of gold under surface and near-surface environmental conditions*

Sohrabi Hashjin, Akbar, *The Trentonian (Late Ordovician) brachiopod fauna of Ontario; evolution through a global warming event*

Masters

Bellissimo, Nicolle S., *Origins of stable isotopic variations in late Pleistocene horse enamel and bone from Alberta*

Freckelton, Candace N., *A physical and geochemical characterization of southwestern Ontario's breathing well region*

Ganderton, Nikolas B., *Mapping and zircon geochronology of the Lyon Inlet boundary zone, Nunavut; a crustal scale break in the Churchill Province*

Jiang, Peng, *Pore morphometrics and thermal evolution of organic-matter microporosity, Colorado Group, Western Canada foreland basin*

McCutcheon, Jenine, *Microbially induced magnesium carbonation reactions as a strategy for carbon sequestration in ultramafic mine tailings*

Mohammed, Aaron A., *Mitigating permafrost degradation due to linear disturbances in sub-arctic peatlands*

Robinson, Gregory B., *Potassium metasomatism at the polymetallic NICO Deposit, Northwest Territories, Canada*

Shivak, Jared N., *New mineralogical and geochemical characterization of Martian meteorites; implications for habitability and astrobiological exploration of Mars*

University of Wisconsin at Green Bay
Masters

Wauters, Gary, *Paleoecological perspectives; the Brussels Hill Pit Cave faunal assemblage, with a focus on short-tailed shrews and graphical explorations of Holocene paleomammalogy in Wisconsin*

University of Wisconsin at Madison
Doctorate

Doebbert, Amalia C., *Applications of detrital zircon geochronology and isotope geochemistry in provenance study*

Zhang, Fangfu, *Investigation of the role of anaerobic microorganisms in sedimentary dolomite formation*

Masters

Blum, Tyler B., *Oxygen isotope evolution of the Lake Owyhee volcanic field, Oregon, and implications for the evolution of the Snake River plain-Yellowstone low D>18'O large igneous province*

Braudy, Nicole, *Deformation history of West Mountian, west-central Idaho : implications for the western Idaho shear zone*

Du, Miao, *Comparing nonlinear climate responses to orbital-insolation during the early Miocene and Pleistocene; a bicoherence study*

Feenstra, Jessica P., *Microseismicity and 3D tomography of the central Alpine Fault, South Island, New Zealand*

Foltz, Timothy L., *Chemostratigraphy and petrology of the Sauk Sequence in northwestern Montana; deciphering the causes of stable carbon isotope variability in marine carbonates*

Fredericks, Kyle, *Petrophysical properties of a deformation band*

fault zone in the Entrada Sandstone, Utah

Meulemans, Ashley J., *Tomographic imaging of mine-induced stress changes in North Aurora, Illinois*

Ostrander, Ray J., *Effects of climate variability on evolutionary tempo and mode in Cretaceous and Neogene marine molluscs*

Potier, Chelsea E., *Subsurface tiltmeter observations of solid earth tides and rock excavation in northeastern Illinois*

Pruitt, Aaron H., *Potential impacts of climate change on groundwater/surface water interaction, Chequamegon-Nicolet National Forest, Wisconsin*

Walters, Andrew Philip, *Cyclostratigraphic evaluation of repetitive sedimentary microfacies from the Green River Formation, Utah*

University of Wisconsin at Milwaukee
Doctorate

Henry, Lindsey C., *Late Paleozoic glaciation and ice sheet collapse over western and eastern Gondwana; sedimentology and stratigraphy of glacial to post-glacial strata in western Argentina and Tasmania, Australia*

Masters

Johnson, Kimberly Rose, *Deformation and fluid interactions in the Mineral Fork diamictites, Antelope Island, Utah*

Kult, Jonathan Martin, *Regionalization of hydrologic response in the Great Lakes basin; considerations of temporal variability*

Sieger, Danielle, *Re-examination of changes in fluvial stacking pattern across the P-T boundary in the Central Transantarctic Mountains, Antarctica*

Stapleton, Elizabeth, *Development of green solvent modified zeolite (GSMZ) for the removal of chemical contaminants from water*

Thorp, Anna Maria, *Applying geochemistry to investigate the occurrence of riverbank inducement into a shallow aquifer in southeastern Wisconsin*

University of Wyoming
Doctorate

Hansen, Steven M., *A scattered view of the Earth's lithosphere; constraints from receiver function analyses of temporary array data in western North America*

Lee, En-Jui, *Full-3D waveform inversions and their applications in Southern California*

Padhi, Amit, *Robust pre-stack seismic waveform inversion for acoustic, elastic isotropic and anisotropic media parameters*

Wei, Chenji, *Formation evaluation and numerical modeling on hydraulic fracturing for an emerging marine shale gas reservoir*

Masters

Adhikari, Samar, *Amplitude-variation-with offset, prestack waveform, and neural network inversion; a comparative study using real data example from the Rock Springs Uplift, Wyoming*

Carnes, Jacob D., *A detailed study of mineral compositions and dihedral angles within the Hannah Peak section of the Dufek Intrusion Pensacola Mountains, Antarctica*

Colwell, Lauren E., *On the petrogenesis of titanite (sphene) in oceanic crust*

Foster, Katherine A., *The lithosphere-asthenosphere boundary and mid-lithospheric discontinuity beneath the USArray with Sp receiver functions*

Hahm, William Jesse, *Bedrock composition regulates ecosystems and landscape evolution in the Sierra Nevada Batholith, California*

Landis, Claire E., *Composition and spatial distribution of volatile deposits in Loki Patera, Io*

Marcon, Virginia M., *Carbon dioxide-water-rock interaction in a carbonate reservoir capped by a clay; an experimental investigation on the evolution of trace metals*

Nelson, Jeffrey D., *Assessment tools for assigning leakage risk to individual wells at a geologic sequestration site in Wyoming*

Shafer, Luke R., *Assessing injection zone fracture permeability through identification of critically stressed fracture orientations at the Rock Springs Uplift CO2 sequestration site, SW Wyoming*

Trampush, Sheila M., *An approach to paleoslope reconstruction with an application to the Jurassic Morrison Formation in southeast Utah*

Xu, Jing, *Full-wave tomography for crustal structure in California using ambient noise Green's function*

Utah State University
Masters

Allen, Eric B., *Dendrochronology in northern Utah; modeling sensitivity and reconstructing Logan River flows*

Washington University
Doctorate

Paniello, Randal Christopher, *Volatization of extraterrestrial materials as determined by zinc isotopic analysis*

Seddio, Stephen Michael, *The diversity, petrogenesis, and geochronology of granitic lunar lithologies*

Wesleyan University
Masters

Golder, Keenan B., *Geomorphology of Eridania Basin, Mars; a study of the evolution of chaotic terrain and a paleolake*

Harner, Patrick Lee, *Potential Martian evaporites and their spectral signatures*

Maxbauer, Daniel Paul, *Constraints on atmospheric CO2 obtained from fossil Metasequoia for the middle Eocene polar forests on Axel Heiberg Island, Nunavut, Canada*

Western Michigan University
Doctorate

Hayden, Travis Gary, *Examining Antarctica from a geodynamic perspective; backstripping, ice thickness, tectonics and erosion*

Masters

Barone, Steven, *Development and evaluation of an inquiry-based unit for teaching about paleoclimate and climate change*

Bouali, El Hachemi Yousef, *Utilizing persistent scatterer interferometry to investigate the nature and factors controlling Nile Delta subsidence*

Crane, Renee Elizabeth, *Activated carbon preconditioning to reduce contaminant leaching in cement-based stabilization of soils*

Gilchrist, Ann M., *Surface complexation modeling of CR(VI) absorption on mineral assemblages*

Lingle, Derrick, *Origin of high levels of ammonium in groundwater, Ottawa County, Michigan*

MacLeod, Andrew K., *Adsorption of hexavalent chromium on hydrous manganese oxide*

Pollard, Katherine A., *Analysis of depositional facies and geological controls on reservoir quality in Lower-Middle Devonian Sylvania Sandstone, Midland County, Michigan*

Sherwood, Mary K., *Using soil organic matter as an iron chelate to enhance the efficiency of modified Fenton oxidation of diesel fuel in Arctic soils*

Towne, Shannon M., *Late Mississippian (Chesterian) through Early Pennsylvanian (Atokan) strata, Michigan Basin, U.S.A.*

Workman, Seth Jordan, *Integrating depositional facies and sequence stratigraphy in characterizing unconventional reservoirs; Eagle Ford Shale, South Texas*

Yellich, John A., *The geology of the South Antelope Pass area of the southern Peloncillo Mountains, Hidalgo County, New Mexico*

Zdan, Stephen A., *Stratigraphic controls on diagenetic pathways in the St. Peter Sandstone, Michigan Basin*

Bachelors

Troy, Amy, *Co and Cr adsorption on maghemite, quartz, and maghemite-quartz mixtures*

Western Washington University
Masters

Beaulieu, Jezra, *Thermal and hydrological conditions of the Goethe rock glacier, central Sierra Nevada, California*

Bloom, Rose, *Determining garnet crystallizaiton kinetics form growth zoning and Mn-calibrated Sm-Nd ages*

Brayfield, Brandon M., *Modeling slope failure in the Jones Creek watershed, Acme, Washington*

Capuana, Erica M., *Assessment of riparian conditions in the Nooksack River Basin with the combination of LiDAR, multi-spectral imagery and GIS*

Christmas, Anna-Mai Florentine, *Effects of ocean acidification on dispersal behavior in the larval stage of the Dungeness crab and the Pacific Green Shore crab*

Gravon, Rachael Dawn, *Summer phytoplankton diversity in small lakes of Northwest Washington*

He, Bowei, *Relationship between Lake Whatcom algae density, water quality and filtration rate at the Bellingham Water Treatment Plant, WA*

Hines, Eleanor, *Regional risk assessment of the Puyallup River Watershed and the evaluation of low impact development in meeting management goals*

Weaver, Meghan E., *Characterization of coarse sediment transport on a mixed sand and gravel beach; Cherry Point Aquatic Reserve, Blaine, Washington*

Whelan, Paul W., *Incipient soil development in the recently degla-ciated Easton foreland, Mt. Baker, Washington*

Wong , Siana, *Phytoplankton ecology in four high-elevation lakes of the North Cascades, WA*

Woods Hole Oceanographic Institution
Doctorate

Bernstein, Whitney Nicole, *Variations in coral reef net community calcification and aragonite saturation state on local and global scales*

Fitzsimmons, Jessica Nicole, *The marine biogeochemistry of dis-solved and colloidal iron*

McGary, R. Shane, *The CAFE experiment; a joint seismic and MT investigation of the Cascadia subduction system*

Miller, Nathaniel, *Evolution of oceanic margins; rifting in the Gulf of California and sediment diapirism and mantle hydration during subduction*

Pontbriand, Claire Willis, *Deep explosive volcanism on the Gak-kel Ridge and seismological constraints on shallow recharge at TAG active mound*

Yale University
Doctorate

Mitchell, Ross Nelson, *Supercontinents, true polar wander, and paleogeography of the Slave Craton*

Vorhies, Sarah Hutchinson, *Pressure-temperature conditions, tim-ing, timescales, and mechanisms of metamorphism in the Barrovian zones, Scotland*

Geological Surveys of the United States

Alabama

Geological Survey of Alabama
Geological Survey of Alabama (2016)
420 Hackberry Lane
P.O. Box 869999
Tuscaloosa, AL 35486-6999
  p. (205) 349-2852
  ntew@gsa.state.al.us
  http://www.gsa.state.al.us/
State Geologist:
  Berry H (Nick) Tew , (D), Alabama, 1999, GroGs
Division Manager, Geologic Investigations Division:
  Sandy M. Ebersole, (D), Alabama, 2009, Og
Division Manager, Energy Investigations Program:
  Denise J. Hills, (M), Delaware, 1998, Gg
Division Manager, Ecosystems Investigations :
  Stuart W. McGregor, (M), Tennessee Tech, 1987, Hs
Deputy Director, GSA:
  Patrick E. O'Neil, (D), Alabama, 1993, Hs
Acting Director, Groundwater Assessment Program:
  Patrick E. O'Neil, (D), Alabama, 1993, Hw
Manager, Petroleum Systems & Technology:
  David C. Kopaska-Merkel, (D), Kansas, 1983, Gs
Manager, Geochemical Laboratory:
  Robert E. Meintzer, (D), Manitoba, 1987, Cg
Manager, Coastal Resources:
  Stephen C. Jones, (M), Alabama, 1996, Hg
Geologist:
  Gene Daniel Irvin, (M), Alabama, 1994, Gg
Visiting Professor:
  William A. Thomas, (D), Virginia Tech, 1959, Gg
Scientific Aid:
  Arthur McLin
Intern:
  Jamekia Dawson
GIS Specialist:
  Anthony Tavis, (B), Alabama, 2010, Gg
  Elizabeth Anne Wynn, (M), Alabama, 2008, Gm
Geologist:
  Mirza A. Beg, (M), Roorkee, 1964, Gz
  Richard E. Carroll, (D), Michigan State, 1992, EcPlGo
  William T. Jackson Jr, (M), Memphis, 2012, GcsGt
  Stephen P. Jennings, (M), Mississippi, 1987, Hg
  Guohai Jin, (M), Zhejiang, 1989, Np
  Matthew P. McKay, (D), West Virginia, 2015, GtoCc
  Mac McKinney, (B), Alabama, 2007, Gg
  Neil E. Moss, (M), Alabama, 1987, Hw
  Marcella Redden, (M), Alabama, 2004, Gg
  David Tidwell, (M), South Florida, 2005, Gm
Chemist:
  Rick Wagner, (B), Texas (San Antonio), 1982, Cg
Biologist:
  Rebecca A. Bearden, (B), Auburn, 2007, Hs

Alaska

Alaska Division of Geological & Geophysical Surveys
Dept of Natural Resources (2015)
3354 College Road
Fairbanks, AK 99709-3707
  p. (907) 451-5010
  dggspubs@alaska.gov
  http://www.dggs.alaska.gov
  f: http://www.facebook.com/pages/Fairbanks-AK/Alaska-DGGS/346699054500
  t: @akdggs
Director & State Geologist:
  Steven S. Masterman, (M), EgNg
Petroleum Geologist I:
  David Lepain, (D), Alaska (Fairbanks), 1993, EoGos

GeoScientist I:
  Laurel E. Burns, (D), Stanford, Ye
  James G. Clough, (M), Alaska (Fairbanks), 1981, GsEoGt
  Melanie B. Werdon, (D), Alaska (Fairbanks), Eg
Geologist V:
  Larry K. Freeman, (M), Oregon State, 1982, Eg
  Kenneth R. Papp, (M), Alaska (Fairbanks), Gg
  Janet R. G. Schaefer, (M), Alaska (Fairbanks), Gv
  De Anne S.P. Stevens, (M), Alaska (Fairbanks), Ng
Geologist IV:
  Nicole Kinsman, (D), On
  Rich D. Koehler, (D), Humboldt State, Gt
  Marwan A. Wartes, (D), Wisconsin, Gso
  Gabriel J. Wolken, (D), Gm
Geohydrologist-Geologist IV:
  Ronnie Daanen, (D), Minnesota (St. Paul), Hy

Alberta

Alberta Geological Survey
Alberta Geological Survey (2015)
402, Twin Atria Building
4999 - 98 Avenue
Edmonton, AB T6B 2X3
  p. (780) 638-4491
  AGS-Info@aer.ca
  http://www.ags.gov.ab.ca/

Arizona

Arizona Geological Survey
Arizona Geological Survey (2015)
416 West Congress Street
Suite 100
Tucson, AZ 85701-1381
  p. (520) 770-3500
  inquiries@azgs.az.gov
  http://www.azgs.az.gov
  f: https://www.facebook.com/AZ.Geological.Survey
  t: @AZGeology
Director & State Geologist:
  M. Lee Allison, (D), Massachusetts (Amherst), Gg
Chief, Mapping Program:
  Phil A Pearthree, (D), Arizona, 1990, GemGm
Chief, Geoinformatics:
  Stephen M. Richard, (D), California (Santa Barbara), 1988, GcOiGq
Chief, Environmental Geology:
  Philip A. Pearthree, (D), Arizona, 1990, GmeHg
Chief, Economic Geology:
  Nyal Niemuth, (B), GgEg
Research Geologist:
  Charles A. Ferguson, (D), Calgary, Gc
  Brian F. Gootee, (M), Arizona, Gm
  Brad Johnson, (D), Carleton, 1994, Gs
  Ann Youberg, (D), Arizona, Gm
  Jeri J. Young, (D), Arizona State, Gm
Oil & Gas Administrator:
  Steven L. Rauzi, (M), Utah State, 1980, Eo
Geologist II:
  Joseph P. Cook, (M), Arizona, So
Other:
  Jessica Good, Oi
Chief, Geologic Extension Service:
  Michael F. Conway, (D), Michigan Tech, 1993, OeGvg

Arkansas

Arkansas Geological Survey
Arkansas Geological Survey (2014)
Vardelle Parham Geology Center
3815 West Roosevelt Road
Little Rock, AR 72204

p. (501) 296-1877
ags@arkansas.gov
http://www.geology.ar.gov/home/
Administrative Assistant: Laure Hinze
Director & State Geologist:
  Bekki C. White, (M), Centenary, 1993, GoEoGg
Geologist Supervisor:
  William L. Prior, (M), Memphis State, 1979, GggEc
Information Systems Analyst:
  James K. Curry, (M), S Methodist, 1978, On
Geologist:
  Sandra Chandler, Oe
  Andrew Haner, Oi
  David Johnston, Gg
  Lea Nondorf, Cg
Senior Petroleum Geologist:
  Peng Li, (D), Alabama, 2007, Gog
  M. Ed Ratchford, (D), Idaho, 1994, GocEo
Professional Geologist:
  Richard Hutto, (B), Arkansas Tech, 1994, Gg
GIS Analyst:
  Nathan H. Taylor, (B), 2007, OiyGe
Geology Supervisor:
  Scott Ausbrooks, (B), Arkansas, 2001, YsGeg
  Angela Chandler, (M), Arkansas, 1996, GgaGg
  Doug Hanson, (M), Memphis State, 1991, Gg
Geologist:
  Ty Johnson, (M), Arkansas, 2008, GgOi
  Daniel S. Rains, (B), Arkansas, 2002, GgOi
Deputy Director & Asst State Geologist:
  Mac B. Woodward, (B), S State, 1957, Gog

British Columbia

British Columbia Geological Survey & Development
British Columbia Geological Survey & Development (2011)
PO Box 9333 Stn Prov Govt
Victoria, BC V8W 9N3
  Geological.Survey@gov.bc.ca
  http://www.empr.gov.bc.ca/MINING/GEOSCIENCE/
  Pages/default.aspx

California

California Geological Survey
California Geological Survey (2015)
801 K Street
MS 24-01
Sacramento, CA 95814
  p. (916) 322-1080
  cgshq@consrv.ca.gov
  http://www.consrv.ca.gov/CGS/Pages/Index.aspx
State Geologist:
  John G. Parrish, (D)
Supervising Engineering Geologist:
  John Clinkenbeared, (B), Eg
  Anthony F. Shakal, (D), MIT, 1980, Ys
  Christopher J. Wills, (M), Wisconsin, Ng
Supervising Engineering Geologist:
  Timothy P. McCrink, (M), New Mexico Tech, 1982, Ng
  William Short, (M), Ng
Senior Engineering Geologist (Supervisor):
  Jennifer Thornburg, (M), California (Santa Cruz), Ng
Senior Engineering Geologist:
  Rui Chen, (D), Edmonton, Nr
  Ron C. Churchill, (D), Minnesota, 1980, Cg
  Cliff Davenport, (B), Ng
  Tim Dawson, (M), Ng
  Marc Delattre, (M), Ng
  Jim Falls, (B), Ng
  Pamela J. Irvine, (M), California (Berkeley), 1977, Ng
  Pamela Irvine, (M), Ng
  Donald Lindsay, (M), Ng
  David Longstreth, (M), Ng
  Gerald Marshall, (B), Ng

Steven Reynolds, (M), Ng
  Anne Rosinski, (M), Ng
  Michael A. Silva, (B), California (Davis), 1978, Ng
  Jim Thompson, (B), Ng
  Rick I. Wilson, (B), Fresno State, 1987, Ge
Senior Engineer:
  Moh J. Huang, (D), Caltech, 1983, Ne
Geologist:
  Lawrence Busch, (A), Eg
  Chris T. Higgins, (M), California (Davis), 1977, Gg
Engineering Geologist:
  Patrick Brand, (M), Ng
  David Branum, (B), Ng
  John Church, (B), Eg
  Kevin Doherty, (M), Ng
  Michael Fuller, (B), Ng
  Carlos Guiterrez, (B), Sacramento State, Ng
  Will Harris, (B), Ng
  Wayne Haydon, (M), Ng
  Cheryl Hayhurst, (B), Ng
  Janis Hernandez, (M), Ng
  Peter Holland, (M), Ng
  Jeremy Lancaster, (M), Ng
  Mike Manson, (B), Ng
  Maxime Mareschal, (M), Ng
  Brian Olson, (M), Ng
  John Oswald, (B), Ng
  Florante Perez, Ng
  Cindy L. Pridmore, (M), San Diego State, 1983, Ng
  Pete Roffers, (M), Ng
  Ron Rubin, (M), Ng
  Gordon Seitz, (D), Ng
  Joshua Smith, (B), Eg
  Brian Swanson, (M), Ng
  Mark Weigers, (M), Ng
Civil Engineer:
  Badie Rowshandel, (D), Ne

Colorado

Colorado Geological Survey
Colorado Geological Survey (2015)
1801 19th Street
Golden, CO 80401
  p. 303-384-2655
  cgs_pubs@mines.edu
  http://www.coloradogeologicalsurvey.org/
  f: https://www.facebook.com/ColoradoGeologicalSurvey
State Geologist:
  Karen Berry, (B), Colorado Mines, NgOu
Senior Mapping Geologist:
  Matt Morgan, (M), Colorado Mines, 2006, GgmXm
Senior Hydrogeologist:
  Peter Barkmann, (M), Montana, 1984, HwGcg
Senior Geothermal Geologist:
  Paul Morgan, (D), Imperial Coll, 2003, YhGtYg
Senior Engineering Geologist:
  Jonathan Lovekin, (M), Colorado Mines, 2007, NgOuGs
Engineering Geologist:
  Jill Carlson, (B), Wesleyan, 1987, NgOu
Hydrogeologist:
  Lesley Sebol, (D), Waterloo, 2005, HwGeOg
GIS Hazard Analyst:
  Francis Scot Fitzgerald, (M), Denver, 2011, OirGg
GIS Analyst:
  Karen Morgan, OiyHw
Geologist:
  Kassandra Lindsey, (M), Portland State, 2015, NgGmOi
  Mike O'Keeffe, (M), New Mexico Inst of Mining and Technology,
    1994, GgeEg
Engineering Geologist:
  Kevin McCoy, (D), Colorado Mines, 2015, NgOiHw
Senior Engineering Geologist:
  Jonathan White, (B), Eastern Illinois, 1983, NgOuGg
Scientific & Technical Graphic Designer:
  Larry Scott, (B), the Arts, 1985, Oy

Connecticut

Dept of Energy and Environmental Protection
Connecticut Geological Survey (2016)
Office of Information Management
79 Elm Street, 6th floor
Hartford, CT 06106-5127
    p. (860) 424-3540
    deep.ctgeosurvey@ct.gov
    http://www.ct.gov/deep/geology
State Geologist:
    Margaret A. Thomas, (M), Connecticut, 1983, Gg
Senior Research Associate:
    Randolph P. Steinen, (D), Brown, 1973, Gs
Civil Engineer:
    Thomas E. Nosal, (M), C Connecticut State, 1992, On
Plant Ecologist:
    Nelson DeBarros, (M), Penn State, 2011, On
Research Associate:
    Lindsey Belliveau, (B), E Connecticut State, 2013, Gm
    Teresa K. Gagnon, (M), Boston Coll, 1992, Gg
Resource Assistant:
    James M. Bogart, (B), S Connecticut State, 2015

Delaware

University of Delaware
Delaware Geological Survey (2015)
Delaware Geological Survey
257 Academy Street, Room 205
Newark, DE 19716-7501
    p. (302) 831-2833
    delgeosurvey@udel.edu
    http://www.dgs.udel.edu
    Administrative Assistant: Karen L. D'Amato
    Administrative Assistant: Laura K. Wisk
State Geologist:
    David R. Wunsch, (D), Kentucky, 1992, CmNg
Hydrogeologist:
    A. Scott Andres, (M), Lehigh, 1984, Hg
Senior Scientist:
    Peter P. McLaughlin, (D), Louisiana State, 1989, HgPm
Hydrogeologist:
    Thomas E. McKenna, (D), Texas (Austin), 1997, Hg
Hydrogeologist:
    Changming He, (D), Nevada (Reno), 2004, GqHg
Associate Scientist:
    Stefanie J. Baxter, (M), Delaware, 1994, On
Research Associate:
    John A. Callahan, (M), Delaware, 2014, Ori
    Jaime L. Tomlinson, (M), Delaware, 2006, Hg
Emeritus:
    John H. Talley, (M), Franklin and Marshall, 1974, Oa
Scientist:
    Kevin W. Ramsey, (D), Delaware, 1988, Oa
    William Schenck, (M), Delaware, 1997, OiGi
GIS Specialist:
    Lillian T. Wang, (M), Delaware, 2005, Oi

Florida

Florida Geological Survey
Florida Dept of Environmental Protection (2015)
Commonwealth Building
3000 Commonwealth Blvd, Suite 1
Tallahassee, FL 32303
    p. (850) 617-0300
    jonathan.arthur@dep.state.fl.us
    http://www.dep.state.fl.us/geology/
State Geologist:
    Jonathan D. Arthur, (D), Florida State, 1994, HwCg
Assistant State Geologist:
    Guy H. Means, (M), Florida State, 2009, PgGe

Georgia

Georgia Dept of Natural Resources
Georgia Environmental Protection Div (2014)
Environmental Protection Division
2 Martin Luther King Jr. Dr., Suite 1152
East Tower
Atlanta, GA 30334-9004
    p. 404-657-5947
    askepd@gaepd.org
    http://epd.georgia.gov/

Hawaii

Dept of Land & Natural Resources
Commission on Water Resource Management (2015)
Kalanimoku Building
P.O. Box 621
1151 Punchbowl Street
Honolulu, HI 96809
    p. (808) 587-0214
    dlnr.cwrm@hawaii.gov
    http://dlnr.hawaii.gov/cwrm

Idaho

University of Idaho
Idaho Geological Survey (2015)
875 Perimeter Dr. MS 3014
University of Idaho
Moscow, ID 83844-3014
    p. (208) 885-7991
    igs@uidaho.edu
    http://www.idahogeology.org/
Director:
    Michael Ratchford, (D), Idaho, 1994, GcoEg
Acting Head:
    Reed S. Lewis, (D), Oregon State, 1990, Gg
Professor:
    John A. Welhan, (D), California (San Diego), 1981, Hw
Associate Professor:
    Virginia S. Gillerman, (D), California (Berkeley), 1982, Eg
Assistant Professor:
    William M. Phillips, (D), Arizona, 1997, Gm
Senior Petroleum Geologist:
    Renee L. Breedlovestrout, (D), Idaho, 2011, GoPbGr
Senior Geologist:
    Dennis M. Feeney, (M), W Washington, 2008, GsYgGg
Emeritus Director :
    Roy M. Breckenridge, (D), Wyoming, 1975, Gg
Emeritus Director:
    Kurt L. Othberg, (D), Idaho, 1991, Gg
Manager, Digital Geological Mapping:
    Loudon R. Stanford, (M), Idaho, 1982, GlmGg
Staff:
    Jane S. Freed, (B), Idaho, 1995, Oi
Research Assistant:
    Glenda K. Bull

Illinois

Illinois State Geological Survey
Energy & Earth Resource Center (2014)
615 E. Peabody Drive.
Champaign, IL 61820-6964
    p. (217) 244-2430
    finley@isgs.uiuc.edu
Center Director:
    Robert J. Finley, (D), South Carolina, 1975, Eo
Scientist:
    Latif A. Khan, (D), Tech, 1971, Nx
Senior Scientist:
    Richard A. Cahill, (D), Illinois, 1980, Ca
    Scott M. Frailey, (D), Missouri (Rolla), 1989, Ng
    David G. Morse, (D), Johns Hopkins, 1979, Eo
    Massoud Rostam-Abadi, (D), Wayne State, 1982, On
    William R. Roy, (D), Illinois, 1985, Sc

Scientist:
    Mei-In (Melissa) Chou, (D), Michigan State, 1977, Co
    Sheng-Fu Joseph Chou, (D), Michigan State, 1977, Co
    Joseph A. Devera, (M), S Illinois, 1985, Gr
    Ivan G. Krapac, (M), Illinois, 1987, Ca
    Zakaria Lasemi, (D), Miami, 1990, En
    Hannes E. Leetaru, (D), Illinois, 1997, Eo
    Donald G. Mikulic, (D), Oregon State, 1979, Ps
    Beverly Seyler, (M), SUNY, 1978, Eo
Associate Scientist:
    Cheri A. Chenoweth, (B), Illinois, 1979, Ec
    Joan E. Crockett, (B), Illinois, 1983, Eo
    John P. Grube, (M), Colorado Mines, 1984, Eo
    Bryan G. Huff, (M), Illinois, 1984, Eo
    Rex A. Knepp, (M), Go
Assistant Scientist:
    F. Brett Denny, (B), Missouri (Rolla), 1985, Gr
    Scott D. Elrick, (M), California (Riverside), 1998, Ec
    Christopher P. Korose, (B), Illinois, 1995, Ec
    Vinodkumar A. Patel, (B), Inst of Tech, 1973, On
Emeritus:
    Pam Cookus, On
Assistant Scientist:
    Kathleen M. Henry, (B), Illinois State, 1982, Gg

Geologic Mapping and Hydrogeology Center (2014)
615 East Peabody Drive
Champaign, IL 61820-6964
    p. (217) 244-2430
    keefer@isgs.illinois.edu
    Administrative Assistant: Bonnie Renfrew
Head:
    Donald Keefer, (M), Illinois (Urbana), 1992, Hw
Senior Scientist:
    Robert A. Bauer, (M), Illinois, 1983, Nr
    Leon R. Follmer, (D), Illinois, 1970, Sd
    Keith C. Hackley, (M), Illinois, 1984, Cs
    Ardith K. Hansel, (D), Illinois, 1980, Gl
    Samuel V. Panno, (M), S Illinois, 1978, Cg
Scientist:
    Michael L. Barnhardt, (D), Illinois, 1979, Gm
    Michael J. Chrzastowski, (D), Delaware, 1986, Ou
    Brandon B. Curry, (D), Illinois, 1995, Pe
    David R. Larson, (M), Nebraska, 1976, Hw
    Edward Mehnert, (D), Illinois, 1997, Hw
    Christopher J. Stohr, (D), Illinois, 1996, Ng
    C. Pius Weibel, (D), Illinois, 1987, Gr
Assistant Scientist:
    Edward C. Smith, (B), Illinois State, 1985, Hw
    Andrew J. Stumpf, (D), New Brunswick, 2001, Gl
Associate Scientist:
    William S. Dey, (M), Illinois, 1983, Hw
    David A. Grimley, (D), Illinois, 1996, Ym
    Hue-Hwa Hwang, (D), Illinois, 1985, Cs
    Richard J. Rice, (B), Illinois State, 1980, Hw
    Wen-June Su, (M), Illinois, 1985, Ng
    Robert C. Vaiden, (M), Illinois, 1985, Hw
    Hong Wang, (D), Illinois, 1996, Cc
Assistant Scientist:
    Sallie E. Greenberg, (M), Illinois, 1997, Cs
    Andrew C. Phillips, (D), Illinois (Chicago), 1993, Gm

Illinois State Water Survey
Analytical Chemistry and Technology (2004)
2204 Griffith Drive
Champaign, IL 61820
    p. (217) 333-9321
    smothers@sws.uiuc.edu
    http://www.sws.uiuc.edu
Head, Analytical Chemistry & Tech:
    Kent W. Smothers, (B), Blackburn, 1980, Cg
Senior Chemist:
    Gary R. Peyton, (M), North Texas, 1968, On
Senior Scientist:
    Michael E. Caughey, (D), Texas, 1988, Co
    Thomas R. Holm, (D), Caltech, 1978, Hw
    Shundar Lin, (D), Syracuse, 1967, Hs

Michael L. Machesky, (D), Wisconsin, 1986, Cg
    Donald P. Roseboom, (M), Bradley, 1976, Hy
Associate Chemist:
    Jane E. Rothert, (M), Washington State, 1977, Og
Lab Director:
    Daniel Webb, (M), Illinois, Hg
Laboratory Director:
    Loretta M. Skowron, (B), Illinois, 1976, Ca

Atmospheric Sciences Div (2004)
2204 Griffith Drive
Champaign, IL 61820
    p. (217) 333-2210
    jatkins@illinois.edu

Illinois State Water Survey (2004)
2204 Griffith Drive
Champaign, IL 61820
    p. (217) 333-2210
    debbie@illinois.edu
Principal Scientist:
    Nani G. Bhowmik, (D), Colorado State, 1968, Hs
Senior Professional Scientist:
    H. Vernon Knapp, (M), Kansas, 1980, Hs
Associate Hydrogeologist:
    Steven D. Wilson, (M), Illinois, 1988, Hw
Professional Scientist:
    William C. Bogner, (M), Illinois, 1983, Hs
Associate Professional Scientist:
    Walton R. Kelly, (D), Virginia, 1993, Hw
    George S. Roadcap, (M), Ohio State, 1990, Hw
    Renjie Xia, (D), Illinois, 1991, Hs
Assistant Professional Scientist:
    Deva K. Borah, (D), Mississippi, 1979, Hq
Assistant Hydrogeologist:
    Randall A. Locke, III, (M), Iowa, 1994, Hw
    Scott C. Meyer, (M), North Carolina, 1987, Hw
Office of the Director (2013)
2204 Griffith Drive
Champaign, IL 61820
    p. (217) 244-5459
    demissie@illinois.edu
    http://www.isws.illinois.edu

University of Illinois
Illinois State Geological Survey/Prairie Research Institute
(2015)
615 E. Peabody Dr.
Champaign, IL 61820-6964
    p. (217) 333-4747
    info@isgs.illinois.edu
    http://www.isgs.edu
State Geologist:
    Richard Berg, (D), Ggg
Head:
    Scott D. Elrick, (M), Ec
    Anne L. Erdmann, (M), Ge
    Zakaria Lasemi, (D), Gdr
    Randall A. Locke II, (M), Cg
    James J. Miner, (M), Sf
    Mark A. Yacucci, (M), Oi
Senior Scientist:
    Steven E. Brown, (M), Gl

University of Illinois, Urbana-Champaign
Illinois State Geological Survey (2015)
615 East Peabody Drive
Champaign, IL 61820-6964
    p. 217-333-4747
    info@isgs.illinois.edu
    https://www.isgs.illinois.edu/
    Administrative Assistant: Tamra S. Montgomery
Illinois State Geologist:
    E. Donald McKay III, (D), Illinois, 1977, GlrGs
Senior Geologist:
    A. L. Erdmann, (M), Ge

Geoscience Information Stewardship:
MArk Yacucci, (M), Illinois State
Associate Geologist:
Scott D. Elrick, (M), GoEc
Chief Scientist:
Richard C. Berg, (D), Illinois, 1979, Gem
Interim Chief Scientist, Head of Quaternary and Engineering Geology:
Steven E. Brown, (M), Wisconsin (Madison), GlNg
Head Hydrogeology and Geophysics:
Donald A. Keefer, (M), Illinois, Hw
Head Geochemistry:
Randall Locke, (M), Cl
Head Bedrock and Industrial Minerals:
Zakaria Lasemi, (D), Illinois, Eg
Director Advanced Energy Technology:
Robert J. Finley, (D), GoEo
Senior Scientist:
Donald E. Luman, (D), Or
Senior Bedrock Geologist:
C. Pius Weibel, (D), Gl
Wetlands Geology Specialist:
Colleen Long, (M), North Carolina (Chapel Hill), 2012, Gg
Jessica Monson, (M), Gg
Wetlands Geologist and Head:
James J. Miner, (M), Gg
Wetlands Geologist:
Jessica R. Ackerman, On
Team Leader/Associate Geologist:
Dale R. Schmidt, (M), Ge
Team Leader:
D. Adomaitis, Ge
Senior Petroleum Geologist:
Hannes E. Leetaru, (D), Gg
Senior Paleontologist:
Joseph A. Devera, (M), Pg
Senior Geophysicist:
Timothy H. Larson, (D)
Senior Geochemist:
Samuel V. Panno, (M), Hw
Principal Engineering Geologist:
R. A. Bauer, (M), Ng
Petroleum Geologist:
Bryan G. Huff, (M), EcGo
Hydrogeologist and Assistant Section Head:
Yu-Feng Forrest Lin, (D), Wisconsin (Madison), 2002, Hg
Hydrogeologist:
David R. Larson, (M), Hg
Geologic Specialist:
Zohreh Khorasgani Askari, (M), Go
Shane K. Butler, (M), Gz
Alan R. Myers, (B), EcGo
Jennifer M. Obrad, (M), EcGo
Mary J. Seid, (M), Gz
Engineering Geologist:
Christopher J. Stohr, (D), Illinois (Urbana-Champaign), Or
Associate Wetlands Geologist:
Steven Benton, Gg
Keith W. Carr, (M), Gg
Eric T. Plankell, (M), Hw
Geoff Pociask, (M), Hw
Associate Sedimentologist:
Xiaodong Miao, (D), Wisconsin (Madison), 2005, Gm
Associate Quaternary Geologist:
Olivier J. Caron, (D), Univ du Québec à Montréal, Ng
David A. Grimley, (D), Illinois, 1996, Ng
Andrew C. Phillips, (D), Ng
Andrew J. Stumpf, (D), Gl
Associate Petroleum Geologist:
Joan Crockett, (B), GoEc
Associate Isotope Geochemist:
Dana Labotka, (D), Tennessee, Cs
Associate Geologist:
Curtis C. Albert, (B), HgYg
Curt S. Blakley, (B), Cg
Cheri Chenoweth, GoEc
Christopher P. Korose, (M), EcGo
Edward C. Smith, (B), Hw

Tim Young, (B), Illinois (Urbana Champaign), 1989, Hw
Associate Geohydrologist:
William S. Dey, (M), HgYg
Jason F. Thomason, (D), Hw
Associate Geochemist:
Shari E. Fanta, (M), Cg
Hue-Hwa Ellen Hwang, (D), Cg
Associate Engineering Geologist:
Greg A. Kientop, (M), Ge
Associate Economic Geologist:
F. Brett Denny, (M), GzEg
Associate Director Advanced Energy Technology Initiative:
Sallie Greenberg, (D)
Assistant Wetlands Geologist:
Kathleen E. Bryant, (M), Gg
Melinda C. Higley
Assistant Section Head:
B. Brandon Curry, (D), Illinois (Urbana-Champaign), 1995, Gel
Assistant Petroleum Geologist:
Nathan D. Webb, (M), EcGo
Assistant Geologist:
James Damico, (M)
Craig R. Decker, (B)
Scott R. Ellis, (B), Ge
Bradley Ettlie, (B), Ge
Jared Freiburg, (M)
James W. Geiger, (B), Ge
Nathan P. Grigsby, (B)
Matthew P. Spaeth, (M), Ge
Assistant Geochemist:
Peter M. Berger, (M), Illinois (Urbana-Champaign), 2008, Cg
Assistant Director:
Mona M. Knight, (M), On
Other:
Randall A. Locke, (M), Iowa, 1994, Cg
Edwards Mehnert, (D), Illinois (Urbana-Champaign), 1998, Hg
Hong Wang, Illinois (Urbana-Champaign), 1996, Cg
Related Staff:
Torie L. Strole, (B), On

Indiana

indiana University
Indiana Geological Survey (2015)
611 North Walnut Grove Avenue
Bloomington, IN 47405
p. 812-855-7636
igsinfo@indiana.edu
http://igs.indiana.edu/
State Geologist & Director:
Todd A. Thompson, (D), Bloomington, 1987
Assistant Director, Technical Services:
Richard T. Hill, (B), Oi
State Geologist Emeritus/Senior Scientist:
John C. Steinmetz, (D), Miami, 1978, Pm
Research Geophysicist/Hydrologist:
Kevin M. Ellett, (M), California (Davis), 2002, YeHw
Head, Subsurface Geology:
Charles W. Zuppann, (M), Vanderbilt, 1974, Go
Head, Geologic Mapping:
Nancy R. Hasenmueller, (M), Ohio State, Ge
Senior Scientist:
Tracy Branam, (M), Indiana, Cg
Walter Hasenmueller, (M), Ohio State, 1970, Gr
Sally L. Letsinger, (M), Indiana, 2001, Hq
Maria Mastalerz, (D), Silesian Tech, 1988, Ec
John A. Rupp, (M), E Washington, 1980, Go
Reservoir Geologist:
Cristian R. Medina, (M), Indiana, 2007, Go
Head, Center for Geospatial Data Analysis:
Shawn Naylor, (M), Indiana, Hw
Associate Scientist:
Christopher Dintaman, (M), Indiana, Hw
Agnieszka Drobniak, (D), Ec
Rebecca A. Meyer, Ec
Research Scientist:
Patrick I. McLaughlin, (D), Cincinnati, 2006, GrClGs

Quaternary Geologist:
    Henry Loope, (D), Wisconsin, 2013, Gls

Iowa

Iowa Dept of Natural Resources
Iowa Geological and Water Survey (2014)
109 Trowbridge Hall
Iowa City, IA 52242-1319
    p. (319) 335-1575
    MaryPat.Heitman@dnr.iowa.gov
    http://www.igsb.uiowa.edu
    Administrative Assistant: Mary Pat. Heitman
Research Geologist:
    Richard A. Langel, (M), Iowa, 1996, Gg
State Geologist:
    Robert D. Libra, Gg
Section Supervisor, Geology and Groundwater Studies:
    J. Michael Gannon, (M), Arizona, Gg
Section Supervisor, Geographic Information:
    Chris Ensminger
Research Geologist:
    Mary R. Howes, Gg
    Lynette S. Seigley, (M), Iowa, Gg
Natural Resource Biologist:
    Jacklyn Gautsch, (B), Wisconsin, On
IOWATER Coordinator and Research Geologist:
    Mary P. Skopec, (D), Iowa, On
GIS Technician:
    Chris Kahle, (M), Kansas, Oi
Geologist 3, Research Geologist:
    Paul Hiaibao Liu, (D), Nebraska, Gg
    Robert M. McKay, (B), Tulane, Gg
    Deborah J. Quade, (M), Iowa, Gg
    Robert Rowden, (M), Iowa, Gg
    Keith Schilling, (M), Iowa State, Gg
    Stephanie Tassier-Surine, (M), Massachusetts, Gg
    Paul E. VanDorpe, (M), Wayne State, Gg
Geologist 3, Remote Sensing Analyst:
    James D. Giglierano, (M), Purdue, GgOri
    Pete Kollasch, (M), Iowa, GgOri
Geologist 3, GIS Analyst:
    Kathryne Clark, (M), New Mexico, GgOi
Geologist 3, Geographic Information System Analyst:
    Calvin Wolter, (B), Arizona, GgOi
Geologist 2, Research Geologist:
    Michael Bounk, (M), Iowa, Gg
    Chad Fields, (M), N Iowa, Gg
Geologist 3, NRGIS Library Manager and GIS Analyst:
    Casey Kohrt, (B), Iowa State, GgOi

Kansas

University of Kansas
Kansas Geological Survey (2015)
1930 Constant Avenue
West Campus
Lawrence, KS 66047-3724
    p. (785) 864-3965
    jbogle@kgs.ku.edu
    http://www.kgs.ku.edu/
    f: www.facebook.com/KansasGeologicalSurvey
    t: @ksgeology
Interim Director:
    Rex C. Buchanan, (M), Wisconsin, 1982, Oe
Section Chief, Senior Scientist:
    James J. Butler, Jr., (D), Stanford, 1987, Hw
    Richard D. Miller, (D), Leoben, 2007, Ye
Section Chief, Senior Research Associate:
    Robert S. Sawin, (M), Kansas State, 1977, Gg
Manager, Wichita Well Sample Library:
    Mike Dealy, (B), Fort Hays State, 1979, Gg
Manager, GIS Section/DASC:
    Kenneth A. Nelson, (B), Kansas, 1993, Oy
Manager, Geohydrology Support Services:
    Blake Wilson, (M), Kansas State, 1993, Oi

Senior Scientific Fellow:
    John H. Doveton, (D), Edinburgh, 1969, Go
    Evan K. Franseen, (D), Wisconsin, 1989, Gs
    Lynn W. Watney, (D), Kansas, 1985, Gr
    Donald O. Whittemore, (D), Penn State, 1973, Hw
Senior Scientist:
    Greg A. Ludvigson, (D), Iowa, 1988, Gr
    Rolfe D. Mandel, (D), Kansas, 1991, Ga
Assistant Scientist:
    Andrea Brookfield, (D), Waterloo, 2009, Hy
    Gaisheng Liu, (D), Alabama, 2004, Hy
    Kerry D. Newell, (D), Kansas, 1996, Go
    Jon J. Smith, (D), Kansas, 2007, Gg
Associate Scientist:
    Geoffrey C. Bohling, (D), Kansas, 1999, Hw
Senior Research Associate:
    Jason Rush, (M), Texas, 2001, Gg
Senior Research Assistant:
    Eileen Battles, (B), Kansas, 1993, Oy
    Edward Reboulet, (M), Boise State, 2003, Hy
Petroleum Engineer:
    Yehven I. Holubnyak, (M), North Dakota, 2008, On
Geologist, Data Resources Library:
    Daniel R. Suchy, (D), McGill, 1992, Gg
Assistant Research Professor:
    Julian Ivanov, (D), Kansas, 2002, Yg
Emeritus, Senior Scientist:
    Pieter Berendsen, (D), California (Riverside), 1971, Cg
    Robert W. Buddemeier, (D), Washington, 1969, Hy
    Tim R. Carr, (D), Wisconsin, 1981, Gg
    John C. Davis, (D), Kansas, 1967, Gq
    Lee C. Gerhard, (D), Kansas, 1964, Gr
    Daniel F. Merriam, (D), Kansas, 1961, Gg
    Ricardo Olea, (D), Kansas, 1982, Gq
Emeritus, Senior Scientific Fellow:
    Lawrence L. Brady, (D), Kansas, 1971, Gg
Emeritus, Associate Scientist:
    Truman Waugh, (B), Washburn, 1963, Ca
Emeritus, Assistant Director:
    Lawrence H. Skelton, (M), Wichita State, 1991, Gg
Senior Research Assistant:
    Brett Bennet, (B), Kansas, 1982, Ng
Hydrogeochemist:
    Jordi Batlle-Aguilar, (D), Liege, 2008, Hy
Geology Extension Coordinator:
    Susan G. Stover, (M), Kansas, 1993, Gg
Assistant Scientist:
    Tandis Bidgoli, (D), Kansas, 2014, Gc

Kentucky

University of Kentucky
Kentucky Geological Survey (2016)
228 Mining & Minerals Resources Building
504 Rose Street
Lexington, KY 40506-0107
    p. (859) 257-5500
    jerryw@uky.edu
    http://www.uky.edu/KGS
Interim State Geologist and Director:
    Gerald A. Weisenfluh, (D), South Carolina, 1982, Ec
Head, Western Kentucky Office:
    David A. Williams, (M), E Kentucky, 1979, Eg
Head, Water Resources Section:
    Chuck J. Taylor, (M), Kentucky, 1992, Gg
Head, Geoscience Information Management:
    Doug C. Curl, (M), Tennessee, 1998, Gc
Head, Geologic Hazards Section:
    Zhenming Wang, (D), Kentucky, 1998, Ys
Head, Energy & Minerals:
    David C. Harris, (M), Stony Brook, 1982, Go
Manager, Well Sample & Core Library:
    Patrick J. Gooding, (M), E Kentucky, 1983, Eo
Geologist:
    Rick Bowersox, (D), South Florida, 2006, Go
Technology Transfer Officer:
    Michael J. Lynch, (B), E Kentucky, 1975, On

Manager, Administration:
    Kathryn E. Ellis, (M), Kentucky, 2012
Hydrogeologist:
    E. Glynn Beck, (M), East Carolina, 1997, Hw
    James C. Currens, (M), E Kentucky, 1978, Hg
    Junfeng Zhu, (D), Arizona, 2005, Hw
Geologist:
    Matt Crawford, (M), Eastern Kentucky, 2001, On
    Bart Davidson, (M), E Kentucky, 1986, Hg
    Cortland F. Eble, (D), West Virginia, 1988, Pl
    Stephen F. Greb, (D), Kentucky, 1992, Gz
    John Hickman, (D), Kentucky, 2011, Eo
    Brandon C. Nuttall, (B), Eastern Kentucky, 1971, Eo
    Thomas M. Parris, (D), California (Santa Barbara), 1998, Eo
    Thomas N. Sparks, (M), Duke, 1979, Gg

Louisiana

Louisiana State University
Basin Research Energy Section (2004)
Louisiana Geological Survey/LSU
208 Howe Russell Geoscience Complex
Baton Rouge, LA 70803-4101
    p. (225) 578-8328
    mhorn@lsu.edu
    http://www.bri.lsu.edu
    Office Coordinator: Cherri B. Webre
Associate Professor:
    Ronald K. Zimmerman, (D), Louisiana State, 1966, Go
Assistant Professor:
    Clayton F. Breland, (D), Tennessee, 1980, Ye
    John B. Echols, (D), Louisiana State, 1966, Go
Research Associate:
    Brian J. Harder, (B), Louisiana State, 1981, Eo
    Bobby L. Jones, (B), Louisiana State, 1953, Go
    Phillip W. Lemay, (B), Centenary, 1999, Gg
    Michael B. Miller, (M), North Carolina, 1982, Go
    Lloyd R. Milner, (B), Louisiana State, 1985, Gg
    Patrick M. O'Neill, (B), Louisiana State, 1985, Sf
Computer Analyst:
    Reed J. Bourgeois, (B), Louisiana State, 1983, On
Accountant Technician:
    Carla Domingue, On

Louisiana Geological Survey (2014)
3079-Energy,
Coast and Environment Bldg.
Baton Rouge, LA 70803
    p. (225) 578-5320
    hammer@lsu.edu
    http://www.lgs.lsu.edu
State Geologist and Professor:
    Chacko J. John, (D), Delaware, 1977, GosGe
Assistant Professor:
    Douglas A. Carlson, (D), Wisconsin (Milwaukee), 2001, Hw
    Marty R. Horn, (D), Texas (Arlington), 1996, EoGgr
GIS Coordinator:
    Hampton Peele, (M), Louisiana State, 1997, Oi
Computer Analyst:
    Reed J. Bourgeois, (B), Nichols State, 1985, On
Research Associate:
    Brian J. Harder, (B), Louisiana State, 1981, Eo
    Paul V. Heinrich, (M), Illinois, 1982, Gs
    Bobby Jones
    Richard P. McCulloh, (M), Texas, 1977, Gg
    Lloyd R. Milner, (B), Louisiana State, 1985, Gg
    Patrick M. O'Neill, (B), Louisiana State, 1985, Sf
    Robert L. Paulsell, (B), Louisiana State, 1987, Oy
    Lisa G. Pond, (B), Louisiana State, 1987, Og
    Arren Schulingkamp, Gg
Cartographic Manager:
    John I. Snead, (B), Louisiana State, 1978, Gm
Assistant Director:
    John E. Johnston, III, (M), Texas, 1977, EoGe
Office Coordinator:
    Melissa H. Esnault, (B), On

Accountant Technician:
    Jeanne Johnson, On

Maine

Dept of Agriculture, Conservation, and Forestry
Maine Geological Survey (2015)
93 State House Station
Augusta, ME 04333-0093
    p. (207) 287-2801
    mgs@maine.gov
    http://www.maine.gov/dacf/mgs/
    Administrative Assistant: Aline Smith
State Geologist:
    Robert G. Marvinney, (D), Syracuse, 1986, Gg
State Soil Scientist:
    David Rocque, Sd
Senior Geologist:
    Robert A. Johnston, (B), Bridgewater State, 1973, Gg
Physical Geologist:
    Henry N. Berry IV, (D), Massachusetts, 1989, Gg
Marine Geologist:
    Stephen M. Dickson, (D), Maine, 1999, On
Hydrogeologist:
    Daniel B. Locke, (B), Maine, 1982, Hw
    Thomas K. Weddle, (D), Boston, 1991, GlHw
Director, Earth Resources Information:
    Christian Halsted, (B), Oi
Marine Geologist:
    Peter Slovinsky, (M), South Carolina, 2001, Gu
GIS Coordinator:
    Amber Whittaker, (M), New Mexico, 2006, OiGcCg

Manitoba

Manitoba Geological Survey
Manitoba Mineral Resources (2015)
360-1395 Ellice Avenue
Winnipeg, MB R3G 3P2
    christian.bohm@gov.mb.ca
    http://www.manitoba.ca/iem/index.html
Director:
    Christian Bohm, (D), ETH Zurich, 1996, GgCgEg
Head:
    Scott Anderson, EgGcCg
Chair:
    Michelle Nicolas, GrsGo

Maryland

Maryland Department of Natural Resources
Hydrogeology & Hydrology Program (2013)
2300 St. Paul Street
Baltimore, MD 21218-5210
    p. (410) 554-5500
    JHalka@dnr.state.md.us
    http://www.mgs.md.gov
    Administrative Assistant: Donajean M. Appel
Hydrogeologist-Sedimentary Geologist:
    Andrew W. Staley, (M), Wisconsin, 1992, Hy
Hydrogeologist:
    Grufon Achmad, (D), Missouri, 1973, Hw
    David W. Bolton, (M), W Michigan, 1988, Hw
    David D. Drummond, (M), George Washington, 1988, Hy
    Mark T. Duigon, (M), Indiana, 1977, Hy
    John M. Wilson, (B), Maryland, 1976, Hw
Environmental Geologist:
    Heather Quinn, (M), Florida, 1988, Ge

Maryland Geological Survey (2015)
2300 St. Paul Street
Baltimore, MD 21218-5210
    p. (410) 554-5500
    MGS.info@maryland.gov
    http://www.mgs.md.gov/
    Administrative Assistant: Jeanne Gary

Director:
   Richard A. Ortt, (B), Johns Hopkins, 1991, GeOrYr
Program Chief, Hydrology & Hydrogeology:
   David Bolton, (M), W Michigan, 1988, Hgw
Program Chief, Coastal and Environmental Geology:
   Stephen Van Ryswick, (B), Maryland, 2002, GeSoYr
Hydrogeologist:
   Grufon Achmad, (D), Missouri, 1973, Hw
   David Andreasen, (B), Maryland, 1985, Hw
   Andrew Staley, (M), Wisconsin, 1992, Hw
Geologist (Outreach Coordinator):
   Dale W. Shelton, (B), Towson, 1986, GgOe
Geologist:
   David K. Brezinski, (D), Pittsburgh, 1984, GrPgGg
   Johanna Gemperline, (M), Illinois, 2013, Hw
   Heather Quinn, (M), Florida, 1988, GrOi

Massachusetts

Massachusetts Geological Survey
Dept of Geosciences (2016)
Univ of Massachusetts (Amherst)
611 North Pleasant Street
Amherst, MA 01002
   p. (413) 545-2286
   sbmabee@geo.umass.edu
State Geologist:
   Stephen B. Mabee, (D), Massachusetts, 1992, Hw

Minnesota

University of Minnesota
Minnesota Geological Survey (2015)
2609 West Territorial Road
Saint Paul, MN 55114-1009
   p. 612-626-2969
   mgs@umn.edu
   http://www.mngs.umn.edu/
   f: https://www.facebook.com/MinnesotaGeologicalSurvey
Director:
   Harvey Thorleifson, (D), Colorado, 1989, Gl

Mississippi

Mississippi Office of Geology
Environmental Geology Div (2009)
P.O. Box 20307
2380 Highway 80 West
Jackson, MS 39289-1307
   p. (601) 961-5500
   john_marble@deq.state.ms.us
Division Director:
   John C. Marble, (B), Mississippi State, 1974, Ge

Geospatial Resources Div (2013)
P.O. Box 2279
700 N. State St
Jackson, MS 39225-2279
   p. (601) 961-5500
   barbara_yassin@deq.state.ms.us
   www.deq.state.ms.us
Geologist:
   Steven D. Champlin, (B), Alabama, 1976, Go
GIS Analyst:
   Barbara E. Yassin, (B), Illinois State, 1989, Oyi
Geologist:
   Peter S. Hutchins, (B), Millsaps, 1990, On
Mining & Reclamation Div (2004)
P.O. Box 20307
2380 Highway 80 West
Jackson, MS 39289-1307
   p. (601) 961-5500
   Ken_McCarley@deq.state.ms.us
   Secretary: Tamara Duckworth
   Secretary: Sandra Saik

Division Director:
   J.Kendrick McCarley, (M), Mississippi, 1996, Ng
Assistant Division Director:
   Stanley C. Thieling, (M), Iowa, 1973, Go
Geologist:
   Michael Akin, (B), Mississippi State, 1995, Ge
   James L. Matheny, (B), Delta State, 1994, On
   Jim F. McMullin, (B), Millsaps, 1959, Gg
   Thomas M. Ray, (M), S Mississippi, 1975, Gg
Biologist:
   David J. Wickens, (B), Mississippi, 1991, On
Related Staff:
   Robert J. Millette, (B), SW Louisiana, 1989, On
   James E. Starnes, (B), Millsaps, 1996, Gg

Mississippi Dept of Environmental Quality (2014)
P.O. Box 2279
Jackson, MS 39225-2279
   p. (601) 961-5500
   michael_bograd@deq.state.ms.us
   http://www.deq.state.ms.us/
State Geologist:
   Michael B. E. Bograd, (M), Mississippi, 2002, Gg

Surface Geology Div (2010)
P.O. Box 2279
700 North State Street
Jackson, MS 39225
   p. (601) 961-5500
   david_dockery@deq.state.ms.us
Division Director:
   David T. Dockery, (D), Tulane, 1991, PiGgPs
Geologist:
   James E. Starnes, (B), Millsaps, 1996, GgaPi
   David E. Thompson, (B), Mississippi State, 1986, GrEg
Environmental Scientist:
   Kenneth D. Davis, (B), Mississippi State, 1968, Gr
Cooperating Faculty:
   Daniel W. Morse, (B), Texas, 1982, On

Missouri

Missouri Department of Natural Resources
Missouri Geological Survey (2015)
PO Box 250
111 Fairgrounds Rd
Buehler Building
Rolla, MO 65402-0250
   p. 573-368-2100
   geology@dnr.mo.gov
   http://www.dnr.mo.gov/geology/
State Geologist:
   Joe Gillman, (B), Missouri State
Asst. State Geologist:
   Jerry Prewett, (B), Missouri State
Director:
   Carey Bridges
Technical Assistant III:
   Cecil Boswell
Section Chief:
   Larry Pierce
   Peter Price
Geologist III - Subsurface Investigations and Waste Management
Unit:
   Terry Hawkins
Geologist II - Subsurface Investigations and Waste Management
Unit:
   Peter Bachle
   Brenna MacDonald
   John Pate
Geologist II - Geologic Mapping:
   Kyle Ganz
   Mike Siemens
Geologist II - Geologic Investigations Unit:
   Molly Starkey
   Vicki Voigt

Geologist II - Environmental Assistance Unit:
  Fletcher Bone
  Neil Elfrink
  Jeremiah Jackson
Geologist II - Energy Resources Unit:
  Joey Baughman
  Jeff Crews
Geologist I - Geologic Mapping:
  Trevor Ellis
Executive I:
  Connie Edwards
Designated Principal Assistant:
  Summer Young
Chief of Subsurface Investigations and Waste Management Unit:
  Glen Young
Chief of Geologic Mapping:
  Edith Starbuck
Chief of Environmental Assistance Unit:
  Sherri Stoner
Chief of Energy Resources Unit:
  Chris Vierrether
Technical Assistant IV:
  Dan Norwald
Technical Assistant III:
  Fred Shaw
Chief of Geologic Investigations Unit:
  Cheryl Seeger

Missouri Dept of Agriculture
Land Survey Program (2013)
PO Box 937
Land Survey Building/1251A Gale Drive
Rolla, MO 65402-0937
  p. (573) 368-2300
  darrell.pratte@mda.mo.gov
  http://mda.mo.gov/weights/landsurvey/
State Land Surveyor:
  Darrell D. Pratte, On

Missouri Dept of Natural Resources
Dam & Reservoir Safety (2015)
PO Box 250
Buehler Bldg/111 Fairgrounds Rd
Rolla, MO 65402
  p. (573) 368-2175
  bob.clay@dnr.mo.gov
Professional Staff:
  Robert Clay, (M), Oklahoma State, 1977, On
Professional Staff:
  Glenn D. Lloyd, (B), On
Other:
  Paul Simon, (B), MST
  Ryan Stack, (B), MST

Div of Geology and Land Survey (2014)
PO Box 250
111 Fairgrounds Road
Rolla, MO 65402-0250
  p. (573) 368-2100
  joe.gillman@dnr.mo.gov
  http://www.dnr.state.mo.us/geology.htm
  Administrative Assistant: Tami L.. Allison
State Geologist & Division Director:
  Mimi R. Garstang, (B), Southwest Missouri State, Ge
Deputy Director & Assistant State Geologist:
  James W. Duley, (B), C Missouri, 1975, Hy

Geological Survey Program (2015)
PO Box 250
111 Fairgrounds Rd
Rolla, MO 65402-0250
  p. (573) 368-2143
  gspgeol@dnr.mo.gov
  http://www.dnr.mo.gov/geology
Professional Staff:
  Joe Gillman, (B), Missouri State, 1992, Gg

Senior Scientist:
  Pat Mulvany, (D), Missouri S&T, 1996
Unit Chief:
  Justin Davis, (M), Missouri S&T, 2012
  Cheryl M. Seeger, (D), Missouri S&T, 2003, Gig
  Edith Starbuck, (M), Missouri S&T, 1987, Gg
  Sherri Stoner, (B), Missouri State, 1991, Ge
  Chris Vierrether, (M), Missouri S&T, 1988, OnEc
  Glen Young, (M), SE Missouri State, 1994, Gg
Section Chief:
  Larry Pierce, (M), On
  Peter Price, (B), Missouri S&T, 1977, GeHy
  Kyle Rollins, (B), Missouri State, 1986, Oy
Program Director:
  Carey Bridges, (M), Missouri (Columbia), 1999, Gg
Geologist:
  Joey Baughman, (B), Missouri S&T, 2012, Gg
  Peter Bachle, (B), Missouri S&T, 1997, Gg
  Fletcher Bone, (B), Central Missouri, 2007, Gg
  David Bridges, (M), Missouri S&T, 2011
  John Corley, (M), Missouri, 2014, Gg
  Jeff Crews, (M), Missouri S&T, 2004, Hy
  Neil Elfrink, (M), Oregon State, 1987, Gg
  Trevor Ellis, (B), Missouri S&T, 2010, Gg
  Kyle Ganz, (M), Missouri S&T, 2013
  Airin Haselwander, (B), Missouri S&T, 2011, Gg
  Terry Hawkins, (B), Brigham, 1988, Gg
  Thomas Herbst, (M), Missouri Sci & Tech, 2014, Gg
  Jeremiah Jackson, (M), Missouri State, 2011, Gg
  Brenna McDonald, (B), SE Missouri State, 1997, Ge
  Brad Mitchell, (M), Missouri S&T, 2010
  Matt Parker, (B), Missouri S&T, 1993
  John Pate, (B), Tennessee, 2007, Ge
  Michael A. Siemens, (B), Wichita State, 1985, Ge
  Molly Starkey, (M), Missouri State, 2011
  Vicki Voigt, (B), Missouri S&T, 2010, Gg
Geological Tech:
  Cecil Boswell, On
  Eric Hohl, On
  Karen Loveland, On
  Dan Nordwald, On
  Patrick Scheel, On
  Fred Shaw, On
Environmental Specialist:
  Andrew Combs
Deputy Director:
  Jerry Prewett, (B), Missouri State, 1992, Gg

Water Resources Program (2015)
PO Box 250
111 Fairgrounds Rd
Rolla, MO 65401-0250
  p. (573) 368-2175
  mowaters@dnr.mo.gov
  http://www.dnr.state.mo.us/dgls/
Deputy Director:
  Andrea Collier
Geologist:
  Scott Kaden, On
Associate Scientist:
  Robert Bacon, Hs
Professional Staff:
  Cynthia Brookshire, (B), Hw
  Charles Du Charme, (B), Hs

Montana
Montana Tech of The University of Montana
Montana Bureau of Mines & Geology (A,B,M) (2015)
1300 West Park Street
Butte, MT 59701-8997
  p. (406) 496-4180
  jmetesh@mtech.edu
  http://www.mbmg.mtech.edu
  f: https://www.facebook.com/MontanaGeology/
  Administrative Assistant: Margaret Delaney
  Administrative Assistant: Charlotte McKenzie

Administrative Assistant: Bette Wasik
State Geologist:
John J. Metesh, (D), Montana, 2003, Hw
Assistant Director RET:
Marvin R. Miller, (M), Indiana, 1965, Hw
Director, Contracts & Grants:
Carleen Cassidy, (B), Montana Tech, On
Research Division Chief:
Thomas W. Patton, (M), Montana Tech, 1987, Hw
Senior Hydrogeologist:
Jon C. Reiten, (M), North Dakota, 1983, Hw
Senior Research Hydrogeologist:
John R. Wheaton, (M), Montana, 1987, Hw
Hydrogeologist:
Ginette ABDO, (M), Penn State, 1989, Gg
Groundwater Assessment Program Manager:
John I. La Fave, (M), Texas, 1987, Hw
Geologist:
Michael C. Stickney, (M), Montana, 1980, YsGt
Associate Research Geologist:
Catherine McDonald, (M)
Geologist:
Susan M. Vuke, (M), Montana, 1982, Gg
Hydrogeologist:
Gary Icopini, (D), Michigan State, 2000, Hw
Assistant Research Hydrogeologist:
Camela Carstarphen, (M), Oregon State, 1991, Hw
Assistant Research Geologist:
Phyllis Hargrave, (M), Montana Tech, 1990, Gg
Jeffrey Lonn, (M), Montana, 1985, Gg
Sr. Research Hydrogeologist:
Thomas E. Michalek, (M), Montana, 2001, HgwHs
Sr. Hydrogeologist:
Kirk B. Waren, (M), Wright State, 1988, HwsOe
Hydrogeologist:
Andrew L. Bobst, (B), Binghamton, 2000, HyCgEo
Terence E. Duaime, (B), Montana Tech, 1978, Hq
Research Associate:
Colleen Elliot, (D), Gc
Senior Research Geologist, Museum Curator:
Richard B. Berg, (D), Montana, 1964, En
Seismic Analyst:
Deborah Smith
Research Assistant III:
Jaqueline R. Timmer, (B), Montana Tech, 1990, Ca
Publications Editor:
Susan A. Barth, (M), Montana Tech, 2009, On
Professional Scientist/Hydro:
Nicholas Tucci
Hydrogeologist:
Daniel D. Blythe, (B), Montana State, 2006, Hws
GIS Specialist:
Ken L. Sandau, (A), Montana Tech, 1999, Oi
Paul R. Thale, (M), Montana State, 1994, Oi
Geologic Cartographer:
Susan M. Smith, (B), Montana State, 1970, On
Chemist:
Ashley Huft, (B), Montana Tech, 2008, Ca
Associate Research Professor:
Steve F. McGrath, (M), Montana Tech, 1992, CaEgCe
Assistant Hydrogeologist:
Mary K. Sutherland, (M), Montana, 2009, Hws
Accounting Associate:
Joanne Lee
Other:
Nancy Favero, Info Sys Tech
Computer Software Eng/Applications:
Luke Buckley, On

Nebraska

Unversity of Nebraska - Lincoln
Conservation & Survey Div (D) (2014)
Conservation & Survey Division
3310 Holdrege Street
616 Hardin Hall
Lincoln, NE 68583-0996

p. (402) 472-3471
mkuzila1@unl.edu
http://snr.unl.edu/csd/
Director:
Mark S. Kuzila, (D), Nebraska, 1988, Sd
Professor:
Xun-Hong Chen, (D), Wyoming, 1994, Hq
David C. Gosselin, (D), SD Mines, 1987, CgHw
James W. Merchant, (D), Kansas, 1984, Oru
Senior Scientist:
Susan Olafsen-Lackey, (B), SD Mines, 1982, Hw
Steven S. Sibray, (M), New Mexico, 1977, HwGg
Jozsef Szilagyi, (D), California (Davis), 1997, Hq
Associate Professor:
Matt Joeckel, (D), Iowa, 1993, GsrGg
Assistant Professor:
Paul Hanson, (D), Nebraska, 2005, Gm
Research Associate:
Leslie M. Howard, (M), Nebraska, 1989, Oyi
Emeritus:
Marvin P. Carlson, (D), Nebraska, 1969, Gt
Robert F. Diffendal, (D), Nebraska, 1971, Gr
Duane A. Eversoll, (M), Nebraska, 1977, Ng
Anatoly Gitelson, (D), Inst Radio Technology (Russia), 1972, On
James W. Goeke, (M), Colorado State, 1970, Hw
Donald C. Rundquist, (D), Nebraska, 1977, Ori
James Swinehart, (D), Gg

Nevada

University of Nevada
Nevada Bureau of Mines and Geology (2015)
Mail Stop 178
Reno, NV 89557-0088
p. (775) 682-8766
jfaulds@unr.edu
http://www.nbmg.unr.edu/
f: https://www.facebook.com/Nevada-Bureau-of-Mines-and-Geology-106397989390636/
Administrative Assistant: Alex Nesbitt
State Geologist:
James E. Faulds, (D), New Mexico, 1989, Gc
Professor:
Geoffrey Blewitt, (D), Caltech, 1996, Yd
Christopher D. Henry, (D), Texas, 1975, Gg
Geologic Mapping Specialist:
Seth Dee, (M), Oregon, 2006, Gg
Nicholas Hinz, (M), Nevada (Reno), 2007, Gg
Senior Scientist:
Alan R. Ramelli, (M), Nevada (Reno), 1988, Ng
Director, Center for Research in Economic Geology:
John Muntean, (D), Stanford, 1998, Eg
Associate Professor:
Craig M. dePolo, (D), Nevada (Reno), 1998, Ng
William Hammond, (D), Oregon, 2000, Yd
Corne Kreemer, (D), SUNY (Stony Brook), 2001, Yd
Assistant Professor:
Rich Koehler, (D), Nevada (Reno), Ne
Mike Ressel, (D), Nevada (Reno), 2005, Eg
Geologic Information Specialist:
David A. Davis, (M), Nevada (Reno), 1990, Gg
Emeritus:
John W. Bell, (M), Arizona State, 1974, Ng
Stephen B. Castor, (D), Nevada (Reno), 1972, Eg
Larry J. Garside, (M), Nevada (Reno), 1968, Gg
Liang-Chi Hsu, (D), California (Los Angeles), 1966, Cp
Daphne D. LaPointe, (M), Montana, 1977, Gg
Paul J. Lechler, (D), Nevada (Reno), 1995, Cg
Jonathan G. Price, (D), California (Berkeley), 1977, Gg
Joseph V. Tingley, (M), Nevada (Reno), 1963, Em
Susan L. Tingley, (B), California (Los Angeles), 1966, Oy

New Brunswick

New Brunswick Dept of Energy and Mines
New Brunswick Dept of Energy and Mines (2015)

Hugh John Flemming Forestry Centre
P. O. Box 6000
Fredericton, NB E3B 5H1
   p. (506) 453-3826
   geoscience@gnb.ca
   http://www.gnb.ca/energy

New Hampshire

New Hampshire Geological Survey
New Hampshire Dept of Environmental Services (2014)
29 Hazen Drive
P.O.Box 95
Concord, NH 03302-0095
   p. (603) 271-1975
   geology@des.nh.gov
   http://des.nh.gov/organization/commissioner/gsu/
State Geologist:
   Frederick H. Chormann, Jr., (M), New Hampshire, 1985, HyOiGm
Outreach Coordinator:
   Lee Wilder, (M), New Hampshire, 1964, GgOee
Hydrologist:
   Jeremy D. Nicoletti, (B), James Madison, 2009, GgHg
   Neil F. Olson, (M), Idaho State, 2010, GeHy
Geoscience Program Specialist:
   Gregory A. Barker, (B), Rhode Island, 1985, GgOin
Fluvial Geomorphology Specialist:
   Shane Csiki, (M), Kansas State, 2005, OyGm

New Jersey

New Jersey Geological Survey
New Jersey Geological and Water Survey (2015)
PO Box 420, Mail Code:29-01
Trenton, NJ 08625-0420
   p. (609) 292-1185
   njgsweb@dep.nj.gov
   http://www.state.nj.us/dep/njgs/
   Administrative Assistant: Tenika Jacobs
Bureau Chief:
   David L. Pasicznyk, (B), Temple, 1979, Yg
State Geologist:
   Jeffrey L. Hoffman, (M), Princeton, 1981, Hq
Section Chief:
   William P. Graff, (B), Clark, 1979, Oy
Research Scientist 1:
   Gregory C. Herman, (D), Rutgers, 1997, Gc
   Steven E. Spayd, (M), UMD New Jersey, 2004, HwGb
   Scott D. Stanford, (D), Rutgers, 2001, Gl
   Peter J. Sugarman, (D), Rutgers, 1995, Gr
Supervising Geologist:
   Stephen W. Johnson, (B), Richard Stockton, 1974, Hw
   Eric W. Roman, (M), Temple, 1999, Hw
   Jane Uptegrove, (M), Rutgers, 2003, Gr
Supervising Env Specialist:
   John Curran, (B), Kean, 1975, Hw
   Helen L. Rancan, (M), Stevens, 1995, Hs
Supervising Env Engineer:
   Richard Shim-Chim, (B), Toronto, 1973, Hw
Research Scientist 2:
   James T. Boyle, (M), New Mexico Tech, 1984, Hw
   John H. Dooley, (M), New Mexico Tech, 1983, CgGf
   Suhas L. Ghatge, (M), W Michigan, 1984, Yve
   Donald H. Monteverde, (D), Rutgers, 2008, Gr
   Ronald W. Witte, (M), Lehigh, 1988, Gl
GIS Specialist 1:
   Zehdreh Allen-Lafayette, (M), Syracuse, 1994, Oi
   Mark A. French, (B), Rutgers, 1989, Hq
   Ted J. Pallis, (M), Montclair State, 1994, Oi
   Ronald Pristas, (B), Penn State, 1990, Oi
Principal Environmental Specialist:
   Raymond T. Bousenberry, (M), New Jersey Inst Tech, 2007, Ge
   Steven D. Domber, (M), Wisconsin, 2000, Hw
   Gregg M. Steidl, (B), Rutgers, 1995, Ge
GIS Specialist 2:
   Michael W. Girard, (B), Bloomsberg, 1996, Oi

Investigator:
   Walter Marzulli, Oy

New Mexico

New Mexico Institute of Mining & Technology
New Mexico Bureau of Geology & Mineral Resources (2015)
801 Leroy Place
Socorro, NM 87801-4796
   p. (575) 835-5420
   greer@nmbg.nmt.edu
   http://geoinfo.nmt.edu/
Director and State Geologist:
   L Greer Price, (M), Washington, 1974, Gg
Senior Volcanologist:
   William C. McIntosh, (D), New Mexico Tech, 1990, Cc
Field Geologist:
   Bruce Allen, (D), New Mexico, 1993, Gm
Senior Field Geologist:
   Steven M. Cather, (D), Texas, 1986, Gs
Principal Senior Geologist:
   Paul W. Bauer, (D), New Mexico Tech, 1988, Gp
Adjunct Faculty:
   George S. Austin, (D), Iowa, 1971, En
   David W. Love, (D), New Mexico, 1980, Ge
Senior Mining Engineer:
   Robert W. Eveleth, (B), New Mexico Tech, 1969, Nm
Senior Field Geologist:
   Richard M. Chamberlin, (D), Colorado Mines, 1980, Gg
Senior Env Geologist Emeritus:
   John W. Hawley, (D), Illinois, 1962, Ge
Senior Chemist:
   Lynn A. Brandvold, (M), North Dakota State, 1964, Ca
Principal Senior Geophysicist:
   Marshall A. Reiter, (D), Virginia Tech, 1969, Yh
Geologist:
   James M. Barker, (M), California (Santa Barbara), 1972, En
Emeritus Director & State Geologist:
   Peter Scholle, (D)
Emeritus:
   Charles E. Chapin, (D), Colorado Mines, 1966, Gt
   Ibrahim H. Gundiler, (D), New Mexico Tech, 1975, Nx
Webmaster/Geologist:
   Adam S. Read, (M), New Mexico, 1997, Gg
Senior Lab Associate:
   Lisa Peters, (M), Texas (El Paso), 1987, Gg
Senior Geophysicist, Field Geologist:
   Shari Kelley, (D), S Methodist, 1984, Yg
Principal Senior Petroleum Geologist:
   Ronald F. Broadhead, (M), Cincinnati, 1979, Go
Principal Senior Hydrogeologist:
   Peggy Johnson, (M), New Mexico Tech, 1990, Hw
Minerals Outreach Liason:
   Virginia McLemore, (D), Texas (El Paso), 1994, Em
Mineralogist/Economic Geologist:
   Virgil W. Lueth, (D), Texas, 1988, Gg
Manager, Digital Cartography Lab:
   Glen Jones, (B), New Mexico Tech, 1989, On
Hydrologist; Hydrogeology Program Manager:
   Stacy Timmons, (M), Oregon State, 2002, Gg
Hydrogeologist:
   Lewis A. Land, (D), North Carolina, 1999, Hg
GIS Cartographer:
   David J. McCraw, (M), New Mexico, 1985, Oy
Geological Librarian:
   Maureen Wilks, (D), New Mexico Tech, 1991, Gp
Geochronologist:
   Matthew T. Heizler, (D), California (Los Angeles), 1993, Cc
Field Geologist:
   Geoffrey Rawling, (D), New Mexico Tech, 2002, Gg
Economic Geologist:
   Douglas Bland, (M), Wyoming, 1982, Eg
Deputy Director; Geochemist:
   Nelia W. Dunbar, (D), New Mexico Tech, 1989, Gi
Deputy Director & Manager, Geologic Mapping Program:
   Michael Timmons, (D), New Mexico, 2004, Gg

Chemistry Lab Manager:
    Bonnie A. Frey, (M), New Mexico Tech, 2002, Cg
Related Staff:
    Gretchen K. Hoffman, (M), Arizona, 1979, Ec

New York

New York State Geological Survey
New York State Geological Survey (2014)
3000 Cultural Education Center
Madison Avenue
Albany, NY 12230
    p. (518) 473-6262
    djornov@mail.nysed.gov
    http://www.nysm.nysed.gov/nysgs/
    Administrative Assistant: Donna Jornov
State Paleontologist and Paleontology Curator:
    Ed Landing, (D), Michigan, 1979, Ps
Curator of Sedimentary Geology:
    Charles Ver Straeten, (D), Rochester, 1996, Grs
Curator of Geology:
    Marian Lupulescu, (D), Jassy (Romania), 1987, Gz
Senior Scientist:
    Andrew Kozlowski, (D), W Michigan, 2002, Gl
    Langhorne Smith, (D), Virginia Tech, 1996, Go
Museum Scientist 1:
    Brian Bird, (D), GlOi
Project Geologist:
    James Leone, (B), SUNY (Albany), 2006, EoGoCg
    Brian Slater, (M), SUNY (Albany), 2007, GoEoGr
Education Specialist:
    Kathleen Bonk, (B), SUNY (Albany), 2009, GoCg
    Brandon L. Graham
Paleontology Collections Technician:
    Frank Mannolini
Geoarchaeologist, Quaternary Geologist:
    Julieann van Nest, (D), Iowa, 1997, Ga
Technician:
    Michael Pascussi, (A), Schenectady Comm Coll, 1999, Eo
Related Staff:
    Michael E. Hawkins, (B), USNY Regents, 1982, Gz
    Linda A. VanAller-Hernick, (B), St Rose, 1974, Pgb
Cooperating Faculty:
    Barry Floyd, (M), Rensselaer, 1987, On

North Carolina

North Carolina Geological Survey
Dept of Environmental Quality (2015)
1612 Mail Service Center
Raleigh, NC 27699-1612
    p. 919-707-9210
    kenneth.b.taylor@ncdenr.gov
    http://portal.ncdenr.org/lr/geological_home
    Administrative Assistant: Joyce Sanford
Division Director:
    Tracy E. Davis, (B), North Carolina State, 1987
State Geologist:
    Kenneth B. Taylor, (D), St Louis, 1991, Ys
Senior Geologist:
    Philip Bradley, (M), North Carolina State
Senior Geologist :
    Bart Cattanach, (M), North Carolina State
Senior Geologist:
    Kathleen M. Farrell, (D), Louisiana State, 1989, Gs
    Jeffrey C. Reid, (D), Georgia, 1981
Engineering Geologist:
    Richard M. Wooten, (M), Georgia, 1980
Project Geologist:
    Randy Bechtel, (M), Oe
Geologist I:
    Nick Bozdog, (B), Gg
    Kenny Gay, Gz
    Heather Hanna, (M), Duke, 2004, On

North Dakota

North Dakota Geological Survey
North Dakota Geological Survey (2015)
1016 E. Calgary Ave.
600 East Boulevard Avenue
Bismarck, ND 58505-0840
    p. (701) 328-8000
    emurphy@nd.gov
    https://www.dmr.nd.gov/ndgs/
State Geologist:
    Edward C. Murphy, (M), North Dakota, 1983, On
Paleontologist:
    Jeff Person, Pg
GIS Specialist:
    Elroy Kadrmas, Oi
Geologist:
    Ned Kruger, Gg
    Julie A. LeFever, Gg
    Lorraine Manz, (D), London, 1998, Gg
    Tim Nesheim, (M), Iowa, 2009, Gg

Northern Territory

Northern Territory Government Minerals and Energy
Northern Territory Government Minerals and Energy (2011)
48-50 Smith St
Paspalis Centrepoint Building
GPO Box 3000
Darwin, NT 0800
    p. +61 8 8999 5511
    minerals@nt.gov.au
    http://www.minerals.nt.gov.au

Northwest Territories

Northwest Territories Geological Survey
Industry Tourism and Investment - Government of the Northwest Territories (2015)
P.O. Box 1320
Yellowknife, NT X1A 2L9
    p. (867) 765-6622
    NTGS@gov.nt.ca
    http://www.nwtgeoscience.ca/

Nova Scotia

Geological Survey of Canada
Atlantic Div (2012)
Bedford Institute of Oceanography
1 Challenger Drive
P.O. Box 1006
Dartmouth, NS B2Y 4A2
    p. (902) 426-4386
    Pat.Dennis@NRCan-RNCan.gc.ca
    http://gsc.nrcan.gc.ca/org/atlantic/index_e.php

Nova Scotia Natural Resources
Nova Scotia Natural Resources (2014)
P.O. Box 698
Founders Square
Halifax, NS B3J 3M8
    p. (902) 424-5935
    http://www.gov.ns.ca/natr/

Ohio

Ohio Dept of Natural Resources
Div of Geological Survey (2015)
2045 Morse Road Bldg. C-1
Columbus, OH 43229
    p. (614) 265-6576
    geo.survey@dnr.state.oh.us
    http://www.ohiodnr.com/geosurvey/

Head:
Thomas J. Serenko, (D), Imperial Coll (London), Eg
Geologist:
Ronald A. Riley, (M), Bowling Green, 1980, Go
Senior Scientist:
Frank Fugitt, (B), Ohio Univ, GrHw
Geologic Assistant:
Madge R. Fitak, (B), Mt Union, 1972, Gg

Div of Geological Survey (2015)
2045 Morse Road
Bldg. C-2
Columbus, OH 43229-6693
p. (614) 265-6576
geo.survey@dnr.state.oh.us
http://geosurvey.ohiodnr.gov/

Oklahoma

University of Oklahoma
Oklahoma Geological Survey (2014)
100 East Boyd
Energy Center
Suite N-131
Norman, OK 73019-0628
p. (405) 325-3031
ogs@ou.edu
http://www.ogs.ou.edu/homepage.php
Director:
G. Randy Keller, (D), Texas Tech, 1973, YgGtEo
Seismologist:
Amberlee Darold, (M), Oregon, 2012, Ys
Geologist:
Julie M. Chang, (D), Texas (El Paso), 2006, GgOnn
Brittany Pritchett, Go
Thomas M. Stanley, Gr
Other:
Kyle E. Murray, (D), Colorado Mines, 2003, Hw

Ontario

Ontario Geological Survey
Ontario Geological Survey (2016)
933 Ramsey Lake Road
Sudbury, ON P3E6B5
p. (705) 670-5758
tracy.livingstone@ontario.ca
http://www.mndm.gov.on.ca/en/mines-and-minerals/geology
f: www.facebook.com/OGSgeology
t: @OGSgeology
Director:
Jack Parker
A/Senior Manager, Earth Resources & Geoscience Mapping Section:
James Schweyer
Senior Manager, Resident Geologist Program:
Rob Ferguson
Senior Manager, Geoservices Section:
Ed Debicki

Oregon

Oregon Dept of Geology & Mineral Industries
Baker City Field Office (2014)
1995 Third St, Suite D
Baker City, OR 97814
p. (541) 523-3133
mark.ferns@dogami.state.or.us
http://www.oregongeology.org
Field Geologist:
Jason D. McClaughry, (M), Washington State, 2003, GrvGs
Regional Geologist:
Mark L. Ferns, (M), Oregon, 1979, GrtGi

Coastal Field Office (2014)
PO Box 1033
Newport, OR 97365

p. (541) 574-6658
Jonathan.Allan@dogami.state.or.us
Regional Geologist:
Rob Witter, (D), Oregon, 1999, Og
Geologist:
George R. Priest, (D), Oregon State, 1980, Gg
Coastal Section Supervisor:
Jonathan C. Allan, (D), Canterbury (NZ), 1998, Gm

Grants Pass Field Office (2004)
5375 Monument Drive
Grants Pass, OR 97526-8513
p. (541) 476-2496
tom.wiley@dogami.state.or.us
http://www.oregongeology.org
Department Secretary: Kathleen McGee
Resident Geologist:
Frank Hladky, (M), Idaho State, 1986, Gg
Regional Geologist:
Tom Wiley, (M), Stanford, 1983, Gg

Oregon Dept of Geology & Mineral Industries (2007)
800 NE Oregon St
Suite 965
Portland, OR 97232
p. (971) 673-1555
james.roddey@dogami.state.or.us
http://www.oregongeology.org
State Geologist:
Vicki S. McConnell, (D)

Oregon Dept of Geology and Mineral Industries (2014)
800 NE Oregon Street
Suite 965
Portland, OR 97232-2162
p. (971) 673-1555
alyssa.pratt@dogami.state.or.us
http://www.oregongeology.org
State Geologist:
Vicki S. McConnell, (D), Alaska (Fairbanks), 1996, Gv
Regional Geologist:
Thomas J. Wiley, (M), Stanford, 1983, Gg
Chief Scientist:
Ian P. Madin, (M), Oregon State, Gg
Regional Geologist:
Jonathan C. Allan, (D), Canterbury (NZ), 1998, Gm
Jason McClaughry, (M), WSU, 2003, Gg
Reclamationist:
Robert Brinkmann, Ge
Ben Mundie, Ge
Industrial Minerals Geologist:
Clark Niewendorp, (M), Eg
Geotechnical Earthquake Engineer:
Yumei Wang, (M), California (Berkeley), 1988, Ne
Geologist:
Lina Ma, (M), Ge
Engineering Gelogist:
Bill Burns, (M), Portland State, 1999, Ng
Natural Resource Specialist, Oil and Gas Program:
Robert Houston, (M), Oregon, Ge
Assistant Director - MLRR:
Tom Ferrero, (M), Hw

Pennsylvania

Pennsylvania Bureau of Topographic & Geologic Survey
DCNR-Pennsylvania Geological Survey (2015)
3240 Schoolhouse Road
Middletown, PA 17057-3534
p. (717) 702-2017
ra-askdcnr@pa.gov
http://www.dcnr.state.pa.us/topogeo/
f: https://www.facebook.com/PennsylvaniaGeology
Administrative Assistant: Connie Cross
Administrative Assistant: Elizabeth C. Lyon

State Geologist and Bureau Director:
    Gale C. Blackmer, (D), Penn State, 1992, Gc
Geologist Manager:
    Michael E. Moore, (B), Penn State, 1975, HwOi
Assistant Bureau Director   :
    Kristin M. Carter, (M), Lehigh, 1993, GoHw
Senior Geologic Scientist:
    Rose-Anna Behr, (M), New Mexico Tech, 1999, GcEc
    Helen L. Delano, (M), SUNY (Binghamton), 1979, GgmNg
    Clifford H. Dodge, (M), Northwestern, 1976, GrEcGh
    Kristen Hand, (B), Nicholls State, HwGg
    William E. Kochanov, (M), West Virginia, 1983, GgPg
    Antonette K. Markowski, (M), S Illinois, 1990, Ec
    Victoria V. Neboga, (M), Kiev State, 1985, Hw
    Caron O'Neil, (M), Pittsburgh, 1986, GgOn
    Katie Schmid, (M), Pittsburgh, 2005, Go
    Stephen G. Shank, (D), Penn State, 1993, GziGp
    James R. Shaulis, (M), Penn State, 1985, EcOe
    Thomas G. Whitfield, (B), West Virginia, 1973, Oi
Geologist Supervisor:
    John H. Barnes, (M), SUNY (Buffalo), 1972, Gg
    Brian Dunst, (B), Indiana of Pennsylvania, 1982, EgoHw
    Gary M. Fleeger, (M), Illinois, 1980, HwGl
    Stuart O. Reese, (M), Tennessee, 1986, Hw
Geologic Scientist:
    Robin Anthony, (B), Case Western, Go
    Aaron D. Bierly, (B), Pitt-Johnstown, Gg
    Mark A. Brown, (M), Swinburne Univ of Tech, 2009, OiXm
    Leonard J. Lentz, (M), North Carolina State, 1983, Ec
    John C. Neubaum, (B), Kutztown, 1983, Ecn
Librarian:
    Jody L. Smale, (M), Clarion, 2010
IT Technician:
    Mark A Dornes
IT Generalist:
    David Fletcher
IT Adminstrator:
    Sandipkumar P. Patel, (B)
Clerk Typist:
    Lynn J. Levino, Go
    Jody L. Rebuck, (B), Messiah
    Renee Speicher

Puerto Rico

Puerto Rico Bureau of Geology
Dept of Natural & Environmental Resources (2004)
Apartado 9066600
Puerta de Tierra Station
San Juan, PR 00906-6600
    p. (787) 722-2526
Director:
    Vanessa del S. Rodriguez, On

Quebec

Quebec Ministere des Ressourses Naturelles
Quebec Ministere des Ressourses Naturelles (2014)
5700 4eme avenue ouest
local A-409
Quebec, QC G1H 6R1
    p. 1-866-248-6936
    services.clientele@mern.gouv.qc.ca
    http://www.mern.gouv.qc.ca/

Queensland

Queensland Environment and Resource Management
Queensland Environment and Resource Management
(2011)
GPO Box 2454
Brisbane, QLD 4001
    info@derm.qld.gov.au
    http://www.derm.qld.gov.au/

Rhode Island

University of Rhode Island 1
Rhode Island Geological Survey (D) (2015)
9 East Alumni Ave.
314 Woodward Hall
University of Rhode Island
Kingston, RI 02881
    p. 401.874.2191
    rigsurv@etal.uri.edu
    http://www.uri.edu/cels/geo/GEO_risurvey.html
    Administrative Assistant: Cheryl Grasso
Chair:
    David Fastovsky, (D), Wisconsin (Madison), 1986, Pv
State Geologist (Research Professor Emeritus):
    Jon C. Boothroyd, (D), South Carolina, 1974, GslOn
Professor:
    Thomas Boving, (D), Arizona (Tucson), 1999, Hg
Assistant Professor:
    Dawn Cardace, (D), Washington Univ (St. Louis), 2006, Py
    Simon Engelhard, (D), Pennsylvania, 2010, Gg
    Brian Savage, (D), Caltech, 2004, Ys
Lecturer:
    Elizabeth Laliberte, (D), Rhode Island, 1997, Og
Research Associate:
    Bryan A. Oakley, (D), Rhode Island, 2012, Gsl

Saskatchewan

Saskatchewan Energy and Resources
Saskatchewan Ministry of the Economy (2015)
1000 - 2103 - 11th Avenue
Regina, SK S4P 3Z8
    p. (306) 787-2528
    Elaine.Peake@gov.sk.ca
    http://www.er.gov.sk.ca/

South Carolina

Dept of Natural Resources
South Carolina Geological Survey (2014)
5 Geology Road
Columbia, SC 29212
    p. 803.896.7931
    scgs@dnr.sc.gov
    http://www.dnr.sc.gov/geology/
Director:
    Charles W. Clendenin, Jr., (D), Witwatersrand, 1989, Eg
Geologist III:
    William R. Doar, III, (D), South Carolina, 2014
    Kerry McCarney-Castle, (D), South Carolina, Gs
Chief Geologist:
    C. Scott Howard, (D), Delaware
Geologist II:
    Katherine E. Luciano, (M), College of Charleston, Gg
Program Manager-Drilling:
    Joe Koch, Og
Digitizer II:
    Matt Henderson, (B), South Carolina, Oi

South Dakota

South Dakota Dept of Environment and Natural Resources
Geological Survey Program (2015)
Akeley-Lawrence Science Center
University of South Dakota
414 East Clark Street
Vermillion, SD 57069-2390
    p. (605) 677-5227
    derric.iles@usd.edu
    http://www.sdgs.usd.edu/
State Geologist:
    Derric L. Iles, (M), Iowa State, 1977, HwGg

Tennessee

Tennessee Geological Survey
Dept of Environment & Conservation (2015)
William R. Snodgrass TN Tower
312 Rosa L. Parks Ave., 12th Floor
Nashville, TN 37243
p. (615) 532-1502
Ronald.Zurawski@tn.gov
http://www.tn.gov/environment/tdg
State Geologist:
Ronald P. Zurawski, (M), Vanderbilt, 1973, GgEog
Environmental Scientist:
Albert B. Horton, (M), Vanderbilt, 1981, GgOi
Environmental Consultant:
Michael L. Hoyal, (B), Tennessee, 1979, Gog
Peter J. Lemiszki, (D), Tennessee, 1992, GcOiGg
Environmental Scientist:
Vince Antonacci, (M), Ball State, 1987, GgOi
Barry W. Miller, (M), Tennessee, 1989, EcOiGg
Admin. Services Asst. 2 :
Carolyn A. Patton

Texas

University of Texas at Austin, Jackson School of Geosciences
Bureau of Economic Geology (2014)
University Station, Box X
Austin, TX 78713-8924
p. (512) 471-1534
begmail@beg.utexas.edu
http://www.beg.utexas.edu
Director:
Scott W. Tinker, (D), Colorado, 1996, Go
Associate Director:
Jay P. Kipper, (M), Trinity (San Antonio), 1983, On
Eric C. Potter, (M), Oregon State, 1975, Eo
Senior Research Scientist:
Shirley P. Dutton, (D), Texas, 1986, Gd
Bob A. Hardage, (D), Oklahoma State, 1967, Yg
Susan D. Hovorka, (D), Texas, 1990, Gd
Mike Hudec, (D), Wyoming, 1990, Gg
Martin P. A. Jackson, (D), Cape Town, 1976, Gc
Stephen E. Laubach, (D), Illinois, 1986, Gc
Bob Loucks, (D), Texas, 1976, Go
Bridget R. Scanlon, (D), Kentucky, 1985, Hw
Research Scientist:
William A. Ambrose, (M), Texas, 1983, Gs
Senior Scientist:
Ian Duncan, (D), British Columbia, 1982, Gg
F. Jerry Lucia, (M), Minnesota, 1954, Go
Stephen C. Ruppel, (D), Tennessee, 1979, Gd
Senior Research Scientist:
Kitty L. Milliken
Research Scientist:
Peter Eichhubl, (D)
Sergey Fomel, (D), Stanford, 2002, Yx
Jeffrey G. Paine, (D), Washington, 1991, Gr
Julia Stowell Gale, (D), Exeter (UK), 1987, Gc
Hongliu Zeng, (D), Texas, 1994, Gs
Associate Professor:
Charles Kerans, (D), Carleton, 1982, Gd
Research Scientist:
Tim Dooley, (D), London (UK), 1994, Gc
Research Scientist Associate:
John R. Andrews, (B), North Carolina, 1990, Oi
Research Scientist:
Jean-Philippe Nicot, (D), Texas, 1998, Ng
Research Associate:
Bruce Cutright
Qilong Fu, (D)
H, Scott Hamlin, (D), Texas, Gr
Ursula Hammes, (D), Colorado, 1992, Gg
Farzam Javadpour, (D)

Timothy A. Meckel, (D)
Osareni C. Ogiesoba, (D)
Katherine D. Romanak, (D)
Diana Sava, (D), Stanford, 2004, Yg
Changbing Yang, (D)
Christopher K. Zahm, (D)
Beverly Blakeney DeJarnett, (M), Penn State, 1986, Gg
Edward W. Collins, (M), Stephen F. Austin, 1978, Ge
Micheal V. DeAngelo, (M), Texas (El Paso), 1988, Ye
Xavier Janson, (D), Miami, 2002, Gr
Research Scientist Associate IV:
Robert Reed, (D), Texas, 1999, Gc
Research Scientist Associate:
Seay Nance, (D), Texas, 1988, Gg
Research Scientist Associate IV:
Robert C. Reedy, (M), New Mexico Tech, 1996, Hg
IT Manager:
Ron Russell, (M), Oklahoma, 1993, On
Associate Director:
Michael H. Young, Arizona, 1995, Ge
512-471-7135:
George Bush, (B), Texas Tech
Research Scientist Associate V:
Tucker F. Hentz, (M), Kansas, 1982, Go
Research Scientist Associate IV:
Thomas A. Tremblay, (M), Texas, 1992, Oy
Research Scientist Associate:
Caroline Breton, (B), Texas, 2001, Oi
Dallas B. Dunlap, (B), Texas, 1997, Ye
Tiffany Hepner, (M), S Florida, 2000, Og
Project Manager:
Rebecca C. Smyth, (M), Texas, 1995, Hg
Ramon H. Trevino, (M), Texas (Arlington), 1988, Go
Related Staff:
Joseph S. Yeh, (B), Fu-Jen Catholic, 1977, Gm

Utah

Utah Geological Survey
Dept of Natural Resources (2015)
1594 West North Temple, Ste 3110
Box 146100
Salt Lake City, UT 84114-6100
p. (801) 537-3300
rickallis@utah.gov
geology.utah.gov
f: www.facebook.com/pages/Utah-Geological-Survey/251490738585
t: @utahgeological
State Geologist:
Richard G. Allis, (D), Toronto, 1977, Go
Program Manager:
Steve D. Bowman, (D), Nevada (Reno), 2002, NgGe
Michael D. Hylland, (M), Oregon State, 1990, Gg
Mike Lowe, (M), Utah State, 1985, Hw
David E. Tabet, (M), Wisconsin, 1974, Ec
Grant C. Willis, (M), Brigham Young, 1983, Gg
Curator Core Research Center:
Peter J. Nielsen, (M), Brigham Young, 1992, Eo
Financial Manager II:
Jodi T. Patterson, (M), Weber State, 2002, On

Environmental Sciences Program (2004)
1594 West North Temple, Ste 3110
PO Box 146100
Salt Lake City, UT 84114-6100
p. (801) 537-3389
mikelowe@utah.gov
http://geology.utah.gov
Manager:
Mike Lowe, (M), Utah State, 1985, Hw
Geologist:
Charles E. Bishop, (B), Utah, 1986, Hw
Hugh A. Hurlow, (D), Washington, 1982, Hw
Janae Wallace, (M), N Arizona, 1993, Hw
Senior Geologist:
James I. Kirkland, (D), Colorado, 1990, Pg

Senior Scientist:
  David B. Madsen, (D), Missouri, 1973, Ga
Research Associate:
  Martha C. Hayden, (B), Utah, 1978, Pv
Geotechnician:
  Alison Corey, On

Geologic Hazards Program (2014)
1594 West North Temple
P O Box 146100
Salt Lake City, UT 84114-6100
  p. (801) 537-3300
  rickallis@utah.gov
  http://geology.utah.gov/ghp/
Program Manager:
  Steve D. Bowman, (D), Nevada (Reno), 2002, NgOn
Senior Scientist:
  William R. Lund, (B), Idaho, 1970, Ng
Paleoseismologist:
  Christopher B. DuRoss, (M), Utah, 2004, Ng
Landslide Geologist:
  Gregg Beukelman, (M), Boise State, Ng
Hazards Mapping Geologist:
  Jessica Castleton, (B), Weber State, 2005, Ng
  Adam McKean, (M), Brigham Young, 2011, Ng
Hazards Geologist:
  Tyler R. Knudsen, (M), Nevada (Las Vegas), 2005, Ng
  Gregory N. McDonald, (B), Utah, 1992, Ng
Hazard Mapping Geologist:
  Ben Erickson, (M), Utah, 2011, Ng
Debris Flow/Landslide Geologist:
  Richard E. Giraud, (M), Idaho, 1986, Ng
Geologist:
  Mike Hylland, (M), Oregon State, 1990, PgYs
GIS Analyst:
  Corey Unger, (B), Weber State, 2001, Oi

Geologic Information and Outreach Program (2010)
1594 West North Temple Ste 3110
PO Box 146100
Salt Lake City, UT 84114-6100
  p. (801) 537-3325
  rebeccamedina@utah.gov
  http://geology.utah.gov
Manager:
  Sandra N. Eldredge, (B), Skidmore, 1978, Oe
Geologist:
  William F. Case, (B), Westminster, 1967, Ng
  Mark R. Milligan, (M), Utah, 1995, Gg
  Christine M. Wilkerson, (B), Utah, 1985, Gg
Bookstore Manager:
  Patricia Stokes, On
Geology Librarian:
  Mage Yonetani, On

Geologic Mapping Program (2015)
1594 West North Temple, Ste 3110
PO Box 146100
Salt Lake City, UT 84114-6100
  p. (801) 537-3355
  grantwillis@utah.gov
  http://geology.utah.gov
Senior Scientist:
  Robert Biek, (M), N Illinois, 1988, Gg
Senior Geologist:
  Donald Clark, (M), N Illinois, 1987, Gg
  Jonathan K. King, (M), Wyoming, 1984, Gg
  Douglas Sprinkel, (M), Utah State, 1981, Gg
Manager:
  Grant C. Willis, (M), Brigham Young, 1983, Gg
GIS Analyst:
  J Buck Ehler, (B), Utah State, 2004, Gg
  Basia Matyjasik, (B), Warsaw, 1988, Gg
Senior GIS Analyst:
  Kent D. Brown, On

Utah Dept of Natural Resources (2014)

1594 West North Temple, Suite 3110
P.O. Box 146100
Salt Lake City, UT 84114-6100
  p. (801) 537-3300
  rickallis@utah.gov
  http://geology.utah.gov
  Administrative Assistant: Dianne Davis
Director:
  Richard G. Allis, (D), Toronto, 1977, Eg
Deputy Director:
  Kimm M. Harty, (M), Alberta, 1984, Gm
Program Manager:
  Steve Bowman, (D), U Nev Reno, 2000, Ng

Vermont

Agency of Natural Resources, Dept of Environmental Conservation
Vermont Geological Survey (2015)
1 National Life Drive
Main 2
Montpelier, VT 05620-3902
  p. (802) 522-5210
  marjorie.gale@vermont.gov
  http://www.anr.state.vt.us/dec/geo/vgs.htm
State Geologist:
  Marjorie H. Gale, (M), Vermont, 1980, GgcGe
Geologist -Environmental Scientist:
  Jonathan Kim, (D), Buffalo, 1995, GetCg

Victoria

Geological Survey of Victoria
Victoria - Dept of State Development, Business and Innovation
(2014)
GPO Box 4509
Melbourne, VIC 3001
  p. +61 3 1300366356
  customer.service@dsdbi.vic.gov.au
  http://www.energyandresources.vic.gov.au/

Victoria-Dept of Sustainability and Environment
Dept of Sustainability and Environment (2014)
8 Nicholson Street
East Melbourne, VIC 3002
  p. +61 3 5332 5000
  peter.walsh@parliament.vic.gov.au
  http://www.dse.vic.gov.au/

Virginia

Division of Geology and Mineral Resources
Southwestern Minerals & Geology Section (2004)
P.O. Box 144
453 West Main St
Abingdon, VA 24210
  p. (540) 676-5577
  steve.walz@dmme.virginia.gov
  http://www.dmme.virginia.gov/divisionmineralresources.
  shtml

Virginia Dept of Mines, Minerals & Energy (2015)
Fontaine Research Park
900 Natural Resources Drive
Suite 500
Charlottesville, VA 22903
  p. (434) 951-6341
  david.spears@dmme.virginia.gov
  http://dmme.virginia.gov/DGMR/divisiongeologymineral-
  resources.shtml
State Geologist:
  David B. Spears, (M), Virginia Tech, 1983
Manager, Geologic Mapping:
  Matthew J. Heller, (M), North Carolina State, 1996, Gg
Manager, Economic Geology:
  William L. Lassetter, (M), Nevada (Reno), 1996, Hw

Professional Staff:
 Carl R. Berquist, Jr., (D), William & Mary, 1986, Gr

University of Virginia
Virginia State Climatology Office (2014)
291 McCormick Road
P.O. Box 400123
Charlottesville, VA 22904-4123
 p. 434-924-0548
 climate@virginia.edu
 http://climate.virginia.edu/home.htm
Director:
 Patrick J. Michaels, (D), Wisconsin, 1979, Oa

Washington

Geological Survey of Western Australia
Geological Survey of Western Australia (2013)
Mineral House
100 Plain Street
East Perth , WA 6004
 p. +61 8 9222 3459
 Rick.Rogerson@dmp.wa.gov.au
 http://www.dmp.wa.gov.au/index.aspx

Washington Division of Geology & Earth Resources
Washington Dept of Natural Resources (2015)
1111 Washington Street, SE, MS 47007
Olympia, WA 98504-7007
 p. (360) 902-1450
 geology@dnr.wa.gov
 http://www.dnr.wa.gov/geology/
Geology Librarian:
 Stephanie Earls, (M), Washington, 2010, Gge
State Geologist:
 David K. Norman, (M), Utah, 1980, Gg

West Virginia

West Virginia Geological & Economic Survey
West Virginia Geological & Economic Survey (2015)
Mont Chateau Research Center
1 Mont Chateau Road
Morgantown, WV 26508-8079
 p. (304) 594-2331
 info@geosrv.wvnet.edu
 http://www.wvgs.wvnet.edu
 f: https://www.facebook.com/WVGeoSurvey
State Geologist:
 Michael Ed. Hohn, (D), Indiana, 1976, Eg

Wisconsin

University of Wisconsin, Extension
Wisconsin Geological and Natural History Survey (2015)
3817 Mineral Point Road
Madison, WI 53705-5100
 p. (608) 262-1705
 jill.pongetti@wgnhs.uwex.edu
 http://www.wisconsingeologicalsurvey.org
State Geologist and Director:
 James M. Robertson, (D), Michigan, 1972, Eg
Hydrogeologist:
 Madeline B. Gotkowitz, (M), New Mexico Tech, 1993, Hw
 David J. Hart, (D), Wisconsin, 2000, HwYg
Assistant Director; Hydrogeologist:
 Kenneth R. Bradbury, (D), Wisconsin, 1982, Hw
Geologist:
 Eric C. Carson, (D), Wisconsin, 2003, Gl
 Patrick I. McLaughlin, (D), Cincinnati, 2006, GrPe
Professor:
 Thomas J. Evans, (D), Wisconsin, 1994, Eg
Emeritus:
 John W. Attig, (D), Wisconsin, 1984, Gl

 Bruce A. Brown, (D), Manitoba, 1984, GcEg
Outreach Manager:
 M. Carol McCartney, (D), Wisconsin, 1979, OegOn
Geotechnician:
 Peter M. Chase, (B), Wisconsin (Milwaukee), 1985, Gg
Geologist:
 William G. Batten, (B), Wisconsin, 1973, GgHw
 Irene D. Lippelt, (B), Manitoba, 1978, Gg
 Esther K. Stewart, (M), Idaho State, 2008, Gg

Wyoming

Wyoming State Geological Survey
Wyoming State Geological Survey (2016)
P.O. Box 1347
Laramie, WY 82073
 p. (307) 766-2286
 wsgs-info@wyo.gov
 http://www.wsgs.wyo.gov/
State Geologist:
 Thomas A. Drean
Head:
 Seth Wittke, Ng
Geologist:
 Chris Carroll, Ec
 Robert Gregory, En
 Ranie Lynds, Eo
 Jim Rodgers, Gg
 Jim Stafford, Hg
 Wayne Sutherland, En
 Karl Taboga, Hw
 Rachel Toner, Eo
Other:
 Jacob Carnes, Gg
 Andrea Loveland, Gg

Yukon

Yukon Geological Survey
Yukon Geological Survey (2011)
, YT
 suzanne.roy@gov.yk.ca
 http://www.geology.gov.yk.ca/

U.S. Federal Agencies & International Organizations

Agencies and Intl Organizations

International Union of Geological Sciences
Executive Secretariat (2015)
Chinese Academy of Geologic Sciences
No26, Baiwanzhuang Road
Xicheng District
Beijing 100037
    p. 86-10-8833-3287
    iugs.beijing@gmail.com
    http://www.iugs.org
IUGS President:
  Roland Oberhansli
IUGS Vice President:
  Yildirim Dilek
  Marko Komac
IUGS Treasurer:
  Dong Shuwen
IUGS Secretary General:
  Ian Lambert
IUGS Past President:
  Alberto C. Riccardi
IUGS Councillor (2012-2016):
  Hassina Mouri
  Yujiro Ogawa
IUGS Councillor (2010-2014):
  Wesley Hill
  Sampat K. Tandon

United Nations Education, Scientific, and Cultural Organization
International Geoscience Programme (2014)
Division of Ecological and Earth Sciences
1 rue Miollis
Paris, Cedex 15 F-75732
    p. +33 (0)1 45 68 10 00
    m.alaawah@unesco.org
    http://www.unesco.org/new/en/natural-sciences/
    environment/earth-sciences/international-geoscience-
    programme/
IGCP Chairperson:
  Patricia Vickers-Rich, (D), Columbia, 1972
Team Leader, Hydrogeology:
  Gil Mahe
Team Leader, Global Change and Evolution of Life:
  Guy Narbonne
Team Leader, Geohazards:
  Andrej Gosar
Team Leader, Geodynamic:
  George Gibson
Team Leader, Earth Resources:
  Robert Moritz
IGCP/SIDA Representative:
  Vivi Vajda, (D), Lund, 1998

Argonne National Laboratory
Chemical Technology Div (2004)
9700 South Cass Avenue
Building 205
Argonne, IL 60439
    p. (630) 252-4383
    bertlinga@anl.gov
Senior Scientist:
  Milton Blander, (D), Yale, 1953, Xc
Associate Scientist:
  Allen J. Bakel, (D), Oklahoma, 1990, Co
  Ronald P. Chiarello, (D), Northeastern, 1990, Om
  Donald G. Graczyk, (D), Wisconsin, 1975, Cs
  Ben D. Holt, (D), Illinois Inst of Tech, 1969, Ca
  James J. Mazer, (D), Northwestern, 1987, Cl
  David J. Wronkiewicz, (D), New Mexico Tech, 1989, Cg
Adjunct Professor:
  Neil C. Sturchio, (D), Washington (St. Louis), 1983, Cg

Related Staff:
  Alice M. Essling, (B), St. Xavier, 1956, Ca
  Edmund A. Huff, (M), Chicago, 1957, Ca
  Francis J. Markun, (B), Lewis, 1961, Cc
  Florence P. Smith, (B), Southern, 1968, Ca

Geosciences & Information Technology Section (2014)
9700 South Cass Avenue
Argonne, IL 60439
    p. (630) 252-6034
    djmiller@anl.gov
    Department Secretary: Sue Baumann
Manager, Geosciences & Information Tech:
  Lisa A. Durham, (M), Purdue, 1989, Hw
Assistant System Engineer:
  Cheong-yip R. Yuen, (D), Wisconsin (Milwaukee), 1986, Ge
Associate Scientist:
  Robert L. Johnson, (D), Cornell, 1991, On
Research Associate:
  John Ditmars, (D), Caltech, 1971, On
  Jennifer Herbert, (B), N Illinois, 1997, Gg
  Zhenhua Jiang, (D), Duke, 1992, On
  David S. Miller, (D), Johns Hopkins, 1995, Ge
  Terri L. Patton, (M), NE Illinois, 1989, Cl
  John J. Quinn, (M), Minnesota, 1992, Hq
  Gus T. Williams, (D), Northwestern, 1994, Hq
Geology Librarian:
  Swati Wagh, On

Environmental Research Div (2014)
9700 South Cass Avenue
Argonne, IL 60439
    p. (630) 252-3879
    bmlesht@anl.gov
    http://www.anl.gov/ER/
Senior Scientist:
  Jeffrey S. Gaffney, (D), California (Riverside), 1975, Oa
  Raymond M. Miller, (D), Illinois State, 1975, Sb
  Marvin L. Wesely, (D), Wisconsin, 1970, Oa
Associate Scientist:
  Jacqueline C. Burton, (D), Tennessee, 1978, Cg
  Richard L. Coulter, (D), Penn State, 1976, Oa
  Paul V. Doskey, (D), Wisconsin, 1982, Oa
  Paul A. Fenter, (D), Pennsylvania, 1990, Gy
  Julie D. Jastrow, (D), Chicago, 1994, Sb
  Lorraine M. LaFreniere, (D), Wisconsin, 1980, On
  In Young Lee, (D), California (Los Angeles), 1975, Oa
  Barry M. Lesht, (D), Chicago, 1977, Op
  Nancy A. Marley, (D), Florida State, 1984, Oa
  William T. Meyer, (D), Imperial Coll (UK), 1973, Cg
  Robert A. Sedivy, (M), Georgia Tech, 1979, Hw
  Jack D. Shannon, (D), Oklahoma, 1975, Ow
  Douglas L. Sisterson, (M), Wyoming, 1975, Oa
  Mohamed Sultan, (D), Washington (St. Louis), 1984, Cg
  John L. Walker, (D), Imperial Coll (UK), 1964, Cg
  Y Eugene Yan, (D), Ohio State, 1998, Gg
Research Associate:
  Richard H. Becker, (M), Washington (St. Louis), Or
  David R. Cook, (M), Penn State, 1977, Ow
  Clyde B. Dennis, (M), Florida, 1979, On
  Richard L. Hart, (B), Illinois Inst of Tech, 1970, Oa
  Timothy J. Martin, (B), Beloit, 1974, Oa
  Barney W. Nashold, (M), Illinois (Chicago Circle), 1976, On
  Kent A. Orlandini, (B), Illinois, 1957, Cc
  Candace M. Rose, (B), Benedictine Coll, 1985, On

Environmental Science Div (2015)
9700 South Cass Avenue
Bldg 240
Argonne, IL 60439
    p. (630) 252-3107
    quinnj@anl.gov
    http://www.evs.anl.gov

Senior Scientist:
  Richard L. Coulter, (D), Penn State, 1976, Ow
  Randall Gentry, (D), Memphis, 1998, Hw
  Robert L. Johnson, (D), Cornell, 1991, Hg
  Rao Kotamarthi, (D), Iowa, 1991, Oa
  Lorraine LaFreniere, (D), Wisconsin, 1977, HwGgEg
  Karen Smith, (M), S Methodist, 1982, Hw
Associate Scientist:
  Edwin Campos, (D), McGill, 2007, Oa
  Young-Soo Chang, (D), Iowa, 1987, Oa
  Scott Collis, (D), Australian National, 2007, Oa
  David Cook, (M), Penn State, 1977, Oa
  Lisa Durham, (M), Purdue, 1989, Hw
  Yan Feng, (D), Michigan, 2005, Oa
  Virendra Ghate, (D), Miami, 2009, Oa
  Nicki Hickmon, (M), Oklahoma, 2004, Oa
  Umakant Mishra, (D), Ohio State, 2009, Os
  Terri Patton, (M), NE Illinois, 1989, Gg
  John Quinn, (D), Minnesota, 2009, Hw
  Michael Ritsche, (M), N Illinois, 2001, Oa
  Robert Sedivy, (M), Georgia Tech, 1979, Hw
  Doug Sisterson, (M), Wyoming, 1975, Oa
  Eugene Yan, (D), Ohio State, 1998, Hw

Energy Systems Div (2005)
9700 South Cass Avenue
Bldg 362 E-340
Argonne, IL 60439-4815
    p. (630) 252-3392
    fking@anl.gov
    Administrative Assistant: Barbara Sullivan
Head:
  Donald O. Johnson, (D), Illinois, 1972, Gr
Senior Scientist:
  Lyle D. McGinnis, (D), Illinois, 1965, Yg
Scientist:
  Kenneth L. Brubaker, (D), Wisconsin, 1972, Oa
  Dorland E. Edgar, (D), Purdue, 1976, Gm
  Steven F. Miller, (B), Knox, 1984, Gg
  R. Eric Zimmerman, (D), Northwestern, 1972, Ng
Research Associate:
  Paul C. Heigold, (D), Illinois, 1969, Yg
  Theresa C. Scholtz, (B), N Illinois, 1985, Ge
  Michael D. Thompson, (M), N Illinois, 1989, Yg
Related Staff:
  John F. Schneider, (M), N Illinois, 1977, Ca
  Linda M. Shem, (M), Northwestern, 1991, Ge
  Patrick L. Wilkey, (M), Illinois, 1976, Ng

Chemistry Div (2005)
9700 South Cass Avenue
Argonne, IL 60439
    p. (630) 972-3570
    sgiblin@anl.gov
Senior Scientist:
  Dieter M. Gruen, (D), Chicago, 1951, Om
  Michael J. Pellin, (D), Illinois, 1978, Om
Associate Scientist:
  Wallis F. Calaway, (D), Indiana, 1975, Om

Bureau of Land Management
California State Office (1999)
2800 Cottage Way
Suite W-1623
Sacramento, CA 95825
    p. (916) 978-4400
    mdipinto@blm.gov

Arizona State Office (1999)
One North Central Ave
Suite 800
Phoenix, AZ 85004
    p. (602) 417-9500
    egomez@blm.gov

Alaska State Office (1999)
222 West Seventh Ave

#13
Anchorage, AK 99513
    p. (907) 271-3212
    dlassuy@blm.gov

National Training Center (1999)
9828 North 31st Avenue
Phoenix, AZ 85051
    p. (602) 906-5500
    dwilkins@blm.gov

National Operations Center (1999)
PO Box 25047
Denver, CO 80225
    p. (303) 236-8857
    lgraham@blm.gov

Headquarters Directorate (1999)
1849 C Street NW
Rm 5665
Washington, DC 20240
    p. (202) 208-3801
    director@blm.gov

Idaho State Office (1999)
1387 South Vinnell Way
Boise, ID 83709
    p. (208) 373-4000
    sellis@blm.gov

Colorado State Office (1999)
2850 Youngfield Street
Lakewood, CO 80215
    p. (303) 239-3600
    hhankins@blm.gov

Wyoming State Office (1999)
PO Box 1828
Cheyenne, WY 82003
    p. (307) 775-6256
    jcamargo@blm.gov

Utah State Office (1999)
440 West 200 South
Suite 500
Salt Lake City, UT 84101
    p. (801) 539-4001
    utsomail@blm.gov

Oregon State Office (1999)
333 SW 1st Avenue
Portland, OR 97204
    p. (503) 808-6001
    b2jackso@blm.gov

New Mexico State Office (1999)
301 Dinosaur Trail
Santa Fe, NM 87502
    p. (505) 954-2098
    jjuen@blm.gov

Nevada State Office (1999)
1340 Financial Blvd
Reno, NV 89502
    p. (775) 861-6400
    jswickard@blm.gov

Eastern States Office (1999)
7450 Boston Boulevard
Springfield, VA 22153
    p. (703) 440-1600
    es_general_web@blm.gov

Montana State Office (1999)
5001 Southgate Drive
Billings, MT 59101
    p. (406) 896-5012

kiszler@blm.gov

Dept of Agriculture
Natural Resources Conservation Service (2004)
14th and Independence Ave., SW
Washington, DC 20250
  p. (202) 720-7246
  terri.gill@wdc.usda.gov
  http://www.nrcs.usda.gov

Agricultural Research Service (2014)
10300 Baltimore Blvd
Building 003, Rm 223
BARC-WEST
Beltsville, MD 20705
  p. (301) 504-6078
  terri.gill@wdc.usda.gov
  http://www.ars.usda.gov

Dept of Commerce
National Inst of Standards & Technology (2015)
100 Bureau Drive
Stop 1070
Gaithersburg, MD 20899-3460
  p. (301) 975-2758
  inquiries@nist.gov
  http://www.nist.gov/

National Oceanic & Atmospheric Administration (2004)
Silver Spring Metro Center 3
1315 East-West Highway
Silver Spring, MD 20910-3282
  p. (202) 482-3436
  kathryn.sullivan@noaa.govkathryn.sullivan@noaa.gov
  http://www.noaa.gov

Dept of Defense
Office of Naval Research (2004)
Ballston Towers #1
800 North Quincy Street
Arlington, VA 22203
  p. (703) 696-4767
  http://www.onr.navy.mil/

Naval Oceanography Command (2004)
U.S. Naval Observatory
34th Street & Massachusetts Avenue, NW
Washington, DC 20007
  p. (202) 762-1020
  http://www.oceanographer.navy.mil

Space & Naval Warfare Systems Command (2004)
4301 Pacific Highway
San Diego, CA 92110-3127
  p. (619) 524-7053
  http://www.spawar.navy.mil/

Naval Intelligence Command (2004)
4251 Suitland Road
Washington, DC 20395-5720
  p. (301) 669-4000
  http://www.nmic.navy.mil/

U.S. Special Operations Command (Air Force) (2004)
100 Bartley Street
Hurlburt Field, FL 32544-5273
  p. (850) 884-2323
  http://www.af.mil/sites/afsoc.html

U.S. Army Corps of Engineers (2004)
441 G Street, NW
Washington, DC 20314
  p. (202) 761-0001
  http://www.usace.army.mil/working.html

U.S. Army Chemical & Biological Defense Command

(2004)
The Pentagon
Washington, DC 20310
  p. (703) 695-0363
  http://www.army.mil/csa/

Air Force Center for Environmental Excellence (2004)
3207 North Road
Brooks Air Force Base, TX 78235-5363
  p. (210) 536-2162

Air Weather Service (2004)
106 Peacekeeper Drive
Offutt Air Force Base, NE 68113-4039
  p. (402) 294-5749

Space Command (2004)
150 Vandenberg Street
Peterson Air Force Base, CO 80914-4020
  p. (719) 554-3001
  http://www.af.mil/sites/afspc.shtml

U.S. Army Research Laboratory Command (2004)
The Pentagon
Washington, DC 20310
  p. (703) 695-0363
  http://www.army.mil/csa/

Defense Threat Reduction Agency (2004)
8725 John T. Kingman Road
MS 6201
Ft. Belvoir, VA 22060-6201
  p. (703) 767-4883
  dtra.publicaffairs@dtra.mil
  http://www.dtra.mil

Dept of Energy
Assistant Secretary for Environment, Safety & Health
(2004)
Forrestal Building
1000 Independence Avenue, SW
Washington, DC 20585-0119
  p. (202) 586-6151
  http://www.eh.doe.gov/

Office of Energy Projects (2004)
Federal Energy Regulatory Commission
888 First Street, NE
Washington, DC 20426
  p. (202) 219-2700

Office of Resource Management (2004)
Forrestal Building
1000 Independence Avenue, SW
Washington, DC 20585-0620
  p. (202) 586-3521

**Assistant Secretary for Energy Efficiency & Renewable
Energy** (2004)
Forrestal Building
1000 Independence Avenue, SW
Washington, DC 20585-0121
  p. (202) 586-9220
  http://www.eren.doe.gov/

Office of Nuclear Energy, Science & Technology (2004)
Forrestal Building
1000 Independence Avenue, SW
Washington, DC 20585-0117
  p. (202) 586-6630
  http://www.ne.doe.gov/

Assistant Secretary for Environmental Management
(2014)
Forrestal Building
1000 Independence Avenue, SW
Washington, DC 20585-0113

p. (202) 586-7709
EM.WebContentManager@em.doe.gov
http://www.em.doe.gov/

Office of Oil & Gas (2004)
Forrestal Building
1000 Independence Avenue, SW
Washington, DC 20585-0640
p. (202) 586-6012

Coal & Power Systems (2004)
Forrestal Building
1000 Independence Avenue, SW
Washington, DC 20585-0320
p. (202) 586-1650

Office of Coal, Nuclear, Electric & Alternate Fuels (2004)
COMSAT Building
950 L'Enfant Plaza, SW
Washington, DC 20024
p. (202) 287-7990

Energy Information Administration (2004)
Forrestal Building
1000 Independence Avenue, SW
Washington, DC 20585-0601
p. (202) 586-8800
howard.gruenspecht@eia.gov
http://www.eia.doe.gov/

Dept of Health & Human Services
Agency for Toxic Substances & Disease Registry (2004)
1600 Clifton Road
Atlanta, GA 30333
p. (404) 639-7000
http://www.atsdr.cdc.gov/atsdrhome.html

Centers for Disease Control & Prevention (2004)
1600 Clifton Rd.
Atlanta, GA 30333
p. (404) 639-3535
http://www.cdc.gov

Dept of Labor
Mine Safety & Health Administration (2004)
Balston Tower #3
4015 Wilson Boulevard
Arlington, VA 22203
p. (703) 235-1385
http://www.msha.gov

Dept of State
Intl Boundary & Water Commission, US & Mexico (2004)
The Commons
4171 North Mesa, Suite C-310
El Paso, TX 79902-1441
p. 1-800-262-8857
john.merino@ibwc.state.gov

Dept of the Interior
U.S. Fish & Wildlife Service (2004)
1849 C. Street N.W.
Washington, DC 20240
p. (202) 208-4545
http://www.fws.gov/

Bureau of Land Management (2014)
Office of Public Affairs
1849 C Street, Room 406-LS
Washington, DC 20240
p. (202) 208-3801
director@blm.gov
http://www.blm.gov

Office of the Secretary (2014)

1849 C. Street N.W.
Washington, DC 20240
p. (202) 208-3100
feedback@ios.doi.gov
http://www.doi.gov

Bureau of Indian Affairs (2004)
1849 C. Street N.W.
Washington, DC 20240
p. (202) 208-7163
http://www.doi.gov/bureau-indian-affairs.html

Bureau of Reclamation (2004)
1849 C. Street N.W.
Washington, DC 20240
p. (202) 513-0501
http://www.usbr.gov

National Park Service (2004)
1849 C. Street N.W.
Washington, DC 20240
p. (202) 208-4621
http://www.nps.gov

Office of Surface Mining, Reclamation & Enforcement
(2014)
1951 Constitution Ave. N.W.
Washington, DC 20240
p. (202) 208-2565
osm-getinfo@osmre.gov
http://www.osmre.gov/

Dept of the Treasury
Internal Revenue Service (2004)
1111 Constitution Avenue, NW
Washington, DC 20224
p. (202) 622-9511
http://www.irs.ustreas.gov

Dept of Transportation
U.S. Coast Guard (2004)
2100 Second Street, SW
Washington, DC 20593
p. (202) 366-4000
http://www.uscg.mil

Federal Aviation Administration (2004)
800 Independence Avenue, SW
Washington, DC 20591
p. (202) 267-3484
http://www.faa.gov

Environmental Protection Agency
**Office of Emergency & Remedial Response (Superfund/Oil
Programs)** (2004)
Crystal Gateway One
1235 Jefferson Davis Highway
Arlington, VA 22202
p. (703) 603-8960
oilinfo@epamail.epa.gov
http://www.epa.gov/superfund

Office of Underground Storage Tanks (2004)
Crystal Gateway One
1235 Jefferson Davis Highway
Arlington, VA 22202
p. (703) 603-9900
hoskinson.carolyn@epa.gov

Assistant Administrator for Water Programs (2004)
1200 Pennsylvania Avenue, NW
Washington, DC 20460
p. (202) 260-5700
kopocis.ken@epa.gov

Office of Wetlands, Oceans & Watersheds (2004)

Fairchild Building
499 South Capitol Street, SW
Washington, DC 20003
  p. (202) 260-7166
  ow-general@epa.gov

Office of Science & Technology (2004)
1200 Pennsylvania Avenue, NW
Washington, DC 20460
  p. (202) 260-5400
  klee@ostp.eop.gov

National Enforcement Investigations Center (2015)
P.O. Box 25277
Denver Federal Building 25
Denver, CO 80225
  p. (303) 462-9270
  middleton.carrie@epa.gov
Senior Scientist:
  Carrie A. Middleton, (M), Colorado Mines, 2008, OriGf

National Center for Environmental Research (2004)
Ronald Reagan Building
1300 Pennsylvania Avenue, NW
Washington, DC 20004
  p. (202) 564-6825
  johnson.jim@epa.gov

National Center for Environmental Assessment (2015)
USEPA-ORD-NCEA-8623P
1200 Pennsylvania Avenue, NW
Washington, DC 20460
  p. (703) 347-8623
  frithsen.jeff@epa.gov
  http://www.epa.gov/ncea

National Air & Radiation Environmental Laboratory (2004)
540 South Morris Avenue
Montgomery, AL 36115-2601
  p. (334) 270-3404
  clark.michael@epa.gov

Safety, Health & Environmental Management Div (2014)
1200 Pennsylvania Avenue, NW
Washington, DC 20460
  p. (202) 564-1640
  dfe@epa.gov

Office of Solid Waste (2014)
1301 Constitutiion Ave. NW
Arlington, VA 22202
  p. (202) 566-0200
  aastanislaus@epa.gov
  http://www2.epa.gov/aboutepa/about-office-solid-waste-
  and-emergency-response-oswer

Office of Science Policy (2013)
Ronald Reagan Building
1300 Pennsylvania Avenue, NW
Washington, DC 20004
  p. (202) 564-6705
  hauchman.fred@epa.gov

Office of Atmospheric Programs (2004)
501 Third Street, NW
Washington, DC 20001
  p. (202) 564-9140
  dunham.sarah@epa.gov

Office of Ground Water & Drinking Water (2004)
1200 Pennsylvania Avenue, NW
Washington, DC 20460
  p. (202) 260-5400
  Greenamyer.Janice@epamail.epa.gov

Assistant Administrator for Environmental Information
(2004)

1200 Pennsylvania Avenue, NW
Washington, DC 20460
  p. (202) 564-6665
  jackson.malcolm@epa.gov

Federal Emergency Management Agency
Office of the Director (2004)
500 C Street, SW
Washington, DC 20472
  p. (202) 646-4600
  http://www.fema.gov/

Jet Propulsion Laboratory
Earth & Space Sciences Div (2014)
Geology & Planetology Section
Pasadena, CA 91109
  p. (818) 354-3440
  daniel.j.mccleese@jpl.nasa.gov
  Department Administrative Manager: Murray Geller
Lead Scientist:
  Bruce E. Banerdt, (D), S California, 1983, Xy
Section Manager:
  Ronald G. Blom, (D), California (Santa Barbara), 1987, Or
Section Member:
  Michael J. Abrams, (M), Caltech, 1973, Or
  Ronald E. Alley, (M), Northwestern, 1972, Or
  Diana L. Blaney, (D), Hawaii, 1990, Xg
  Bonnie J. Buratti, (D), Cornell, 1983, Or
  Robert E. Crippen, (D), California (Santa Barbara), 1989, Or
  Joy A. Crisp, (D), Princeton, 1984, Gv
  Thomas C. Duxbury, (M), Purdue, 1966, On
  Diane L. Evans, (D), Washington, 1981, Gm
  Tom G. Farr, (D), Washington, 1981, Gm
  Matthew P. Golombek, (D), Massachusetts, 1981, Gc
  Ken E. Herkenhoff, (D), Caltech, 1989, Xg
  Simon J. Hook, (D), Durham (UK), 1989, Or
  Erik R. Ivins, (M), California (Los Angeles), 1976, Gt
  Anne B. Kahle, (D), California (Los Angeles), 1975, Or
  Harold R. Lang, (D), Calgary, 1983, Gr
  Kyle C. McDonald, (D), Michigan, 1991, On
  Robert M. Nelson, (D), Pittsburgh, 1978, Xg
  Eni G. Njoku, (D), MIT, 1976, Or
  Frank D. Palluconi, (M), Penn State, 1963, Or
  David C. Pieri, (D), Cornell, 1979, Gt
  Jeffrey J. Plant, (D), Washington (St. Louis), 1991, On
  Jeffrey Plescia, (D), S California, 1985, On
  Carol A. Raymond, (D), Columbia, 1989, Yr
  Suzanne E. Smrekar, (D), S Methodist, 1990, Xy
  Linda J. Spilker, (D), California (Los Angeles), 1992, Xy
  Ellen R. Stofan, (D), Brown, 1989, Xg
  Glenn J. Veeder, (D), Caltech, 1974, On
Senior Scientist:
  Ronald S. Sanders, (D), Brown, 1970, Gr

Lawrence Livermore National Laboratory
Atmospheric, Earth and Energy Div (2015)
7000 East Avenue
PO Box 808
Livermore, CA 94551
  p. (925) 423-4412
  pls-webmaster@mail.llnl.gov
  http://www-pls.llnl.gov

Atmospheric, Earth and Energy (2013)
7000 East Avenue
L-203
Livermore, CA 94550
  p. (925) 423-1848
  antoun1@llnl.gov
  https://www-pls.llnl.gov/?url=about_pls-atmospheric_
  earth_and_energy_division
  Administrative Assistant: Laura Long
Head:
  Kenneth J. Jackson, (D), California (Berkeley), 1983, Cl
Senior Scientist:
  Roger D. Aines, (D), Caltech, 1984, Cg

Bill L. Bourcier, (D), Oregon State, 1983, Cg
Thomas A. Buscheck, (D), California (Berkeley), 1984, Ng
Steven Carle, (D), California (Davis), 1996, Hw
Charles R. Carrigan, (D), California (Los Angeles), 1977, Yg
Susan A. Carroll, (D), Northwestern, 1988, Cl
M Lee Davisson, (M), California (Davis), 1992, Cg
Quingyun Duan, (D), Arizona, 1991, Hg
Robert C. Finkel, (D), California (San Diego), 1974, Cg
Samuel (Julio) J. Friedmann, (D), MIT, Gg
Richard B. Knapp, (D), Arizona, 1978, Ng
Gayle A. Pawloski, (B), Cal State (Hayward), 1979, Gg
Abelardo L. Ramirez, (M), Purdue, 1979, Ng
Sarah K. Roberts, (M), Arizona State, 1990, Cl
Andrew F. Tompson, (D), Princeton, 1985, Ng
Jeffrey L. Wagoner, (M), California (Riverside), 1977, Gs
Ananda M. Wijesinghe, (D), MIT, 1978, Nr
Sun Yunwei, (D), Israel Inst of Tech, 1995, Ng
Mavrik Zavarin, Yr

Los Alamos National Laboratory
Chemistry Div (B,M,D) (2004)
P.O. Box 1663
Los Alamos, NM 87545
   p. (505) 667-4457
   chemistry@lanl.gov
   http://pearl1.lanl.gov/external/default.htm
Division Leader:
   Alexander J. Gancarz, (D), Caltech, 1976, Cc
Staff:
   Kent D. Abney, (D), Colorado State, 1987, On
   Stephen F. Agnew, (D), Washington State, 1981, On
   Moses Attrep, (D), Arkansas, 1965, Oe
   Timothy M. Benjamin, (D), Caltech, 1979, Ca
   Scott M. Bowen, (D), New Mexico, 1983, Ca
   James R. Brainard, (D), Indiana, 1979, On
   Jeffrey C. Bryan, (D), Washington, 1988, On
   Carol J. Burns, (D), California (Berkeley), 1987, On
   Timothy P. Burns, (D), Nebraska, 1986, Co
   Gilbert W. Butler, (D), California (Berkeley), 1967, Cc
   Edwin P. Chamberlain, (D), Texas A&M, 1971, Cc
   David L. Clark, (D), Indiana, 1986, On
   Dean A. Cole, (D), Iowa, 1985, Co
   David B. Curtis, (D), Oregon State, 1974, Cc
   Paul R. Dixon, (D), Yale, 1989, On
   Robert J. Donahoe, (D), North Carolina State, 1985, On
   Stephen K. Doorn, (D), Northwestern, 1989, On
   Clarence J. Duffy, (D), British Columbia, 1977, Cg
   Deward W. Efurd, (D), Arkansas, 1975, Ct
   Phillip G. Eller, (D), Ohio State, 1971, On
   June T. Fabryka-Martin, (D), Arizona, 1988, Hg
   Bryan J. Fearey, (D), Iowa State, 1986, Cc
   David L. Finnegan, (D), Maryland, 1984, Oa
   John R. Fitzpatrick, (M), New Mexico, 1983, On
   Malcolm M. Fowler, (D), Washington (St. Louis), 1972, Oa
   Sammy R. Garcia, (B), New Mexico Highlands, 1972, Ca
   Russell E. Gritzo, (B), New Mexico State, 1983, On
   Richard C. Heaton, (D), Illinois, 1973, On
   Sara B. Helmick, (B), Southwestern, 1955, On
   David R. Janecky, (D), Minnesota, 1982, Cl
   Kung King-Hsi, (D), Cornell, 1989, On
   Scott Kinkead, (D), Idaho, 1983, On
   Gregory J. Kubas, (D), Northwestern, 1970, Oa
   Pat J. Langston-Unkefer, (D), Texas A&M, 1978, Co
   Patrick A. Longmire, (D), New Mexico, 1991, On
   Michael MacInnes, (M), Wisconsin, 1969, On
   Allen S. Mason, (D), Miami, 1974, Oa
   Charles M. Miller, (D), Stanford, 1980, Cc
   Geoffrey G. Miller, (D), Rensselaer, 1984, Cc
   Terrance L. Morgan, (M), Colorado State, 1984, Ng
   David Morris, (D), North Carolina State, 1984, Cc
   Eugene J. Mroz, (D), Maryland, 1976, Oa
   Michael T. Murrell, (D), California (San Diego), 1980, Cc
   Allen E. Ogard, (D), Chicago, 1957, Hw
   Jose A. Olivares, (D), Iowa State, 1985, Cs
   Hain Oona, (D), Arizona, 1979, On
   Kevin C. Ott, (D), Caltech, 1983, On
   Edward S. Patera, (D), Arizona State, 1982, Cg

Richard E. Perrin, (B), Denver, 1952, Cc
Eugene J. Peterson, (D), Arizona State, 1976, Ct
Dennis Phillips, (D), Hawaii, 1976, Co
Jane Poths, (D), Chicago, 1982, Cc
Pamela Z. Rogers, (D), California (Berkeley), 1981, Cl
Donald J. Rokop, (D), Lake Forest, 1985, Cc
Robert S. Rundberg, (D), CUNY, 1978, Gq
Nancy N. S. Sauer, (D), Iowa State, 1986, On
Norman C. Schroeder, (D), Iowa State, 1985, Cc
Louis A. Silks, (B), Suffolk, 1978, On
Paul H. Smith, (D), California (Berkeley), 1987, On
Zita V. Svitra, (B), Roosevelt, 1967, On
Basil I. Swanson, (D), Northwestern, 1969, On
C. Drew Tait, (D), North Carolina State, 1984, Cp
Wayne A. Taylor, (B), New Mexico, 1978, Cl
Kimberly W. Thomas, (D), California (Berkeley), 1978, Ct
Joseph L. Thompson, (D), Penn State, 1963, Ct
Ines Triay, (D), Miami, 1985, Hg
Clifford J. Unkefer, (D), Minnesota, 1981, On
David J. Vieira, (D), California (Berkeley), 1978, On
Jerry B. Wilhelmy, (D), California (Berkeley), 1969, On
Kurt Wolfsberg, (D), Washington (St. Louis), 1959, Cc
William H. Woodruff, (D), Purdue, 1972, On
Mary Anne Yates, (D), Carnegie Mellon, 1976, On
Emeritus:
   Ernest A. Bryant, (D), Washington (St. Louis), 1956, Cg
   Merle E. Bunker, (D), Indiana, 1950, On
   William R. Daniels, (D), New Mexico, 1965, Ct
   Donald L. Hull, (M), Iowa State, 1974, On

Earth & Environmental Sciences Div (2014)
P.O. Box 1663
Los Alamos, NM 87545
   p. (505) 667-3644
   wallacet@lanl.gov
Director:
   Terry C. Wallace, Jr., (D), Caltech, 1983, Ys
Technical Staff:
   Paul Aamodt, (M), Nevada, 1991, On
   Douglas Alde, (D), Illinois, 1979, On
   M. James Aldrich, (D), New Mexico, 1972, Gc
   W. Scott Baldridge, (D), Caltech, 1979, Gi
   Fairley J. Barnes, (D), New Mexico State, 1986, On
   Naomi M. Becker, (D), Wisconsin, 1991, Hg
   Kay H. Birdsell, (M), Colorado, 1985, Hq
   James D. Blacic, (D), California (Los Angeles), 1971, Nr
   Rainer Bleck, (D), Penn State, 1968, Ow
   James E. Bossert, (D), Colorado State, 1990, Oa
   Christopher R. Bradley, (D), MIT, 1993, Yg
   Thomas L. Brake, (M), New Mexico State, 1985, Nr
   David E. Broxton, (M), New Mexico, 1976, Gx
   Wendee M. Brunish, (D), Illinois, 1981, On
   Gilles Y. Bussod, (D), California (Los Angeles), 1988, Yx
   Katherine Campbell, (D), New Mexico, 1979, Gq
   James W. Carey, (D), Harvard, 1990, Ca
   Theodore C. Carney, (M), Colorado State, 1981, Ng
   Gregory L. Cole, (D), Arizona, 1990, Og
   Steffanie Coonley, (M), New Mexico, 1984, On
   Keeley R. Costigan, (D), Colorado State, 1992, Oa
   William Cottingame, (D), Texas, 1984, Oa
   James L. Craig, (B), Nevada, 1974, Gg
   Bruce M. Crowe, (D), California (Santa Barbara), 1974, Gv
   Zora V. Dash, (M), New Mexico, 1988, On
   Deborah J. Daymon, (M), Idaho, 1994, On
   Micheline Devaurs, (M), Utah State, 1983, Hg
   Kalpak Dighe, (D), Clemson, 1994, On
   John C. Dinsmoor, (B), Colorado Mines, 1989, Nm
   Alison M. Dorries, (D), Harvard, 1986, On
   Donald S. Dreesen, (B), New Mexico, 1968, Np
   David V. Duchane, (D), Michigan, 1978, On
   Michael H. Ebinger, (D), Purdue, 1988, So
   C L Edwards, (D), New Mexico Tech, 1975, Yg
   C. James Elliott, (D), Yale, On
   Scott M. Elliott, (D), California, 1983, Oa
   Perry D. Farley, (D), Oklahoma, 1981, On
   George T. Farmer, (D), Cincinnati, 1968, Hw
   David N. Fogel, (M), Cal State, 1997, On

Carl W. Gable, (D), Harvard, 1989, Gt
Edward S. Gaffney, (D), Caltech, 1973, Yg
Anthony F. Gallegos, (D), Colorado State, 1970, Py
Jamie N. Gardner, (D), California (Davis), 1985, Gg
Fraser Goff, (D), California (Santa Cruz), 1977, Cg
Carl R. Hagelberg, (D), Oregon State, 1992, On
Jeffrey C. Hansen, (B), Weber State, 1971, On
Charles D. Harrington, (D), Indiana, 1970, Gm
Hans E. Hartse, (D), New Mexico Tech, 1991, Ys
Ward L. Hawkins, (B), Nevada (Reno), 1977, Og
Grant Heiken, (D), California (Santa Barbara), 1972, Gv
Donald D. Hickmott, (D), MIT, 1988, Gp
Steve T. Hildebrand, (D), Texas (Dallas), 1993, Ys
Emil F. Homuth, (D), Washington, 1974, Ye
Leigh S. House, (D), Columbia, 1982, Ys
Lianjie Huang, (D), Paris, 1994, Yg
Paul A. Johnson, (M), Arizona, 1984, Yg
Eric M. Jones, (D), Wisconsin, 1970, Oa
Hemendra N. Kalia, (D), Missouri Sch of Mines, 1970, Nm
Jim C. Kao, (D), Illinois, 1985, Oa
Danny Katzman, (M), New Mexico, 1991, Gg
Elizabeth Keating, (D), Wisconsin, 1995, Gg
Sharad Kelkar, (M), Texas, 1979, Np
C. F. Keller, Jr., (D), Indiana, 1969, Oa
Richard G. Kovach, (M), Naval Postgrad Sch, 1979, Nm
Donathon J. Krier, (M), New Mexico, 1980, Gv
Thomas D. Kunkle, (D), Hawaii, 1978, Xy
Edward M. Kwicklis, (M), Colorado, 1987, Gg
Chung Chieng A. Lai, (D), Texas A&M, 1984, Ow
Schon S. Levy, (M), Texas, 1975, Gi
Peter C. Lichtner, (D), Mainz, 1974, On
Rodman Linn, (D), New Mexico State, 1997, Ng
Lynn McDonald, (M), Cal State, On
Maureen A. McGraw, (D), California (Berkeley), 1996, On
Laurie A. McNair, (D), Carnegie Mellon, 1995, On
Wayne R. Meadows, (B), Cal State (Bakersfield), 1974, Yg
Theodore Mockler, (M), Carnegie Mellon, 1986, On
Orrin B. Myers, (D), Colorado State, 1992, Py
Balu Nadiga, (D), Caltech, 1992, On
Brent D. Newman, (D), New Mexico Tech, 1996, Gg
John W. Nyhan, (D), Colorado State, 1972, So
Ronald D. Oliver, (B), Oregon Inst of Tech, 1972, Yg
Howard J. Patton, (D), MIT, 1978, Yg
Frank V. Perry, (D), California, 1988, Gv
William S. Phillips, (D), MIT, 1985, Yg
Eugene W. Pokorny, (B), Missouri, 1979, Nm
William M. Porch, (D), Washington, 1971, Yg
Allyn R. Pratt, (M), Boise State, 1977, Ge
George Randall, (D), SUNY (Binghamton), Yg
Steen Rasmussen, (D), Tech (Denmark), 1985, Yg
Jon M. Reisner, (D), Iowa State, Oa
Steven L. Reneau, (D), California (Berkeley), 1988, Gm
Douglas O. Revelle, (D), Michigan, 1974, Oa
Peter Roberts, (D), MIT, 1989, Ys
Bruce A. Robinson, (D), MIT, 1985, On
R. Roussel-Dupre, (D), Colorado, 1979, On
Thomas J. Shankland, (D), Harvard, 1966, Yx
Catherine H. Smith, (D), New Mexico State, 1995, Ca
Wendy E. Soll, (D), MIT, 1991, Hw
Everett P. Springer, (D), Utah State, 1983, Hq
Lee Steck, (D), California, Gg
Robert P. Swift, (D), Washington, 1969, Nr
E.M.D. Symbalisty, (D), Chicago, 1984, On
Steven R. Taylor, (D), MIT, 1980, Ys
James Tencate, (D), Texas, 1992, On
Bryan J. Travis, (D), Florida State, 1974, Hq
David T. Vaniman, (D), California (Santa Cruz), 1976, Gx
Richard G. Warren, (M), New Mexico, 1972, Gi
Douglas J. Weaver, (M), Nevada, 1995, On
Thomas A. Weaver, (D), Chicago, 1973, Yg
Rodney W. Whitaker, (D), Indiana, 1976, Oa
Earl M. Whitney, (D), Utah, On
Judith L. Winterkamp, (B), Texas, 1977, On
Kenneth H. Wohletz, (D), Arizona State, 1980, Gv
Giday WoldeGabriel, (D), Case Western, 1987, Gx
Andrew V. Wolfsberg, (D), Stanford, 1993, Hw
George A. Zyvoloski, (D), California (Santa Barbara), 1975, Ng

Project Leader:
    Mark T. Peters, (D), Chicago, 1992, Yg
Technical Staff:
    James N. Albright, (D), Chicago, 1969, Yg
    Donald W. Brown, (M), California (Los Angeles), 1961, Nr
    Larry Allan Jones, (B), Nebraska, 1972, Ng
Other:
    Christina "Tina" Behr-Andres, (D), Michigan Tech, 1992, On

National Aeronautics & Space Administration
Lyndon B. Johnson Space Center (2004)
Houston, TX 77058-3696
    p. (281) 483-5309
    jsc-techtran@mail.nasa.gov
    jsc-techtran@mail.nasa.gov

NASA Headquarters (2004)
Washington, DC 20546-0001
    p. (202) 358-2345
    info-center@hq.nasa.gov
    http://www.hq.nasa.gov/

George C. Marshall Space Flight Center (2004)
Marshall Space Flight Center, AL 35812-0001
    p. (256) 544-1910
    patrick.e.scheuermann@nasa.gov

Goddard Space Flight Center (2004)
Greenbelt Road
Greenbelt, MD 20771-0001
    p. (301) 286-5121
    catherine.maynard@nasa.gov

Langley Research Center Office of Communications (2015)
11 Langley Boulevard
Hampton, VA 23681-0001
    p. (757) 864-6120
    rob.wyman@nasa.gov
    http://www.nasa.gov/langley
    f: https://www.facebook.com/nasalarc
    t: @NASA_Langley

Ames Research Center (2004)
Building BN200
Moffett Field, CA 94035-1000
    p. (650) 604-5111
    michael.mewhinney@nasa.gov

National Oceanic and Atmospheric Administration
National Centers for Environmental Information (2015)
David Skaggs Research Center
325 Broadway
Boulder, CO 80303
    p. (303) 497-6826
    ngdc.info@noaa.gov
    http://www.ngdc.noaa.gov/
    f: http://www.facebook.com/NOAANCEIoceangeo
    t: @NOAANCEIocngeo

National Science Foundation
Office of the Director (2015)
4201 Wilson Boulevard
Arlington, VA 22230
    p. (703) 292-5111
    fcordova@nsf.gov
    http://www.nsf.gov
    f: https://www.facebook.com/US.NSF
    t: @NSF

Directorate for Geosciences (2015)
4201 Wilson Boulevard
Room 705
Arlington, VA 22230
    p. (703) 292-8500

mcavanau@nsf.gov
http://www.geo.nsf.gov/
f: https://www.facebook.com/US.NSF
t: @NSF_GEO
Assistant Director:
  Roger Wakimoto
Deputy Assistant Director:
  Margaret Cavanaugh
Senior Advisor:
  Craig R. Robinson
Program Director for International Activities:
  Maria Uhle

Div of Polar Programs (2014)
4201 Wilson Boulevard
Arlington, VA 22230
  p. (703) 292-8030
  kfalkner@nsf.gov
  http://www.nsf.gov/div/index.jsp?org=PLR
  f: https://www.facebook.com/pages/Division-of-Polar-Pro-
  grams-National-Science-Foundation/1392901317615113
Division of Polar Programs:
  Kelly K. Falkner, (D)
Section for Arctic Sciences:
  Eric Saltzman, (D)
Section for Antarctic Sciences:
  Scott G. Borg, (D)
Section for Antarctic Infrastructure and Logistics:
  Brian W. Stone, (M)
Specialized Support Manager, Antarctic Infrastructure & Logistics Section:
  Arthur J. Brown
Senior Advisor:
  Susanne M. LaFratta-Decker
Program Manager, Techology Development, Antarctic Infrastructure
& Logistics Section:
  Patrick D. Smith
Program Manager, System Operations & Logistics, Antarctic
Infrastructure & Logistics Section:
  Paul Sheppard
Polar Cyberinfrastructure Program Director:
  Marco Tedesco, (D)
Outreach and Education Program Manager:
  Peter West
Operations Manager, Antarctic Infrastructure & Logistics Section:
  Margaret A. Knuth
Ocean Project Manager, Antarctic Infrastructure & Logistics Section:
  Timothy M. McGovern
Facilities Engineering Projects Manager, Antarctic Infrastructure &
Logistics Section:
  Ben D. Roth
Facilities Construction & Maintenance Manager, Antarctic
Infrastructure & Logistics Section:
  Peter Ridilla
Environmental Policy Specialist:
  Li Ling Hamady, (D)
Environmental Officer:
  Polly A. Penhale, (D)
Chief Program Manager, Antarctic Infrastructure & Logistics Section:
  George Blaisdell
Aviation Program Manager, Antarctic Infrastructure & Logistics Section:
  Michael Scheuermann
Arctic System Science Program Director:
  Neil R. Swanberg, (D)
Arctic Social Sciences Program Director:
  Anna M. Kerttula de Echave, (D)
Arctic Research Support & Logistics Program Manager:
  Patrick R. Haggerty
Arctic Research Support & Logistics Associate Program Manager:
  Renee Crain
Arctic Observing Network Program Director:
  Erica L. Key, (D)
Arctic Natural Sciences Program Director:
  Henrietta Edmonds, (D)
  Ming-Yi Sun, (D)
  William J. Wiseman, (D)
Antarctic Research Support Manager:
  Jessie L. Crain

Antarctic Research & Logistics Integration Associate Program Director:
  Nature McGinn, (D)
Antarctic Organisms and Ecosystems Program Director:
  Charles Amsler, (D)
Antarctic Ocean and Atmospheric Sciences Program Director:
  Peter Milne, (D)
Antarctic Integrated System Science Program Director:
  Lisa M. Clough, (D)
Antarctic Glaciology Program Director:
  Julie M. Palais, (D)
Antarctic Earth Sciences Program Director:
  Mark Kurz, (D)
Antarctic Astrophysics and Geospace Science Program Director:
  Vladimir Papitashvili, (D)

Ocean Sciences Div (2015)
4201 Wilson Boulevard
Arlington, VA 22230
  p. (703) 292-8580
  rwmurray@nsf.gov
  http://www.nsf.gov/div/index.jsp?div=OCE
Division Director:
  Richard W. Murray
Section Head for Integrative Programs Section:
  Bauke Houtman
Program Director for Ship Operations Program:
  Rose Dufour
Program Director for Physical Oceanography Program:
  Eric C. Itsweire
  Alberto Mestas-Nunez
  Baris Mete Uz
Program Director for Oceanographic Instrumentation and Technical
Service Programs:
  James Holik
Program Director for Ocean Observatories Initiative:
  Jean M. McGovern
Program Director for Ocean Education Programs:
  Elizabeth L. Rom
Program Director for Ocean Drilling Programs:
  James F. Allan
Program Director for Marine Geology and Geophysics Program:
  Candace O. Major
  Barbara Ransom
Program Director for Chemical Oceanography Program:
  Donald Rice
Program Director for Biological Oceanography Program:
  David L. Garrison
Program Director:
  John Walter
Program Directof for Ocean Drilling Programs:
  Thomas Janacek
Associate Program Director for Oceanographic Technology and
Interdisciplinary Coordination Program:
  Kandace S. Binkley

Earth Sciences Div (2014)
4201 Wilson Boulevard
Arlington, VA 22230
  p. (703) 292-8550
  weharris@nsf.gov
  http://www.nsf.gov/div/index.jsp?div=EAR
  t: @NSF_EAR
Division Director:
  Wendy Harrison
Section Head for Deep Earth Processes Section:
  James H. Whitcomb
Section Head (Acting) for Surface Earth Processes Section:
  Thomas Torgersen
Program Director for Instrumentation and Facilities:
  David Lambert
Program Director for Sedimentary Geology and Paleobiology
Program:
  Yusheng "Christopher" Liu
Program Director for Tectonics Program:
  David M. Fountain
  Stephen S. Harlan
Program Director for Sedimentary Geology and Paleobiology

Program:
Paul E. Filmer
H. Richard Lane
Program Director for Petrology and Geochemistry Program:
Sonia Esperanca
Program Director for Instrumentation and Facilities:
Jonathan Wynn
Russell C. Kelz
Program Director for Hydrologic Sciences:
Ni-Bin Chang
Shemin Ge
Program Director for Geophysics Program:
Raffaella Montelli
Robin Reichlin
Zheng Kang Shen
Program Director for Geomorphology and Land Use Dynamics:
Paul Cutler
Jessica H. Robin
Program Director for Geobiology and Low Temp Geochemistry:
Deborah Aruguete
Enriqueta C. Barrera
Program Director for Education and Human Resources:
Lina Patino
Program Director for Earthscope:
Gregory J. Anderson
Margaret Benoit
Program Director for Deep Earth Processes Section:
Charles H. Estabrook
Program Director for Continental Dynamics:
Leonard E. Johnson
Associate Program Director for Petrology and Geochemistry Program:
Jennifer Wade

Atmospheric and Geospace Sciences Div (2015)
4201 Wilson Boulevard
Arlington, VA 22230
    p. (703) 292-8520
    pshepson@nsf.gov
    http://www.nsf.gov/div/index.jsp?div=AGS
Division Director:
Paul B. Shepson
Section Head for NCAR/Facilities Section:
Stephan P. Nelson
Section Head for Geospace Section:
Richard A. Behnke
Section Head for Atmosphere Section:
David J. Verardo
Program Director for Solar Terrestrial Research Program:
Therese M. Jorgensen
Program Director for Physical and Dynamic Meteorology Program:
A. Gannet Hallar
Chungu Lu
Bradley F. Smull
Program Director for Paleoclimate Program:
Candace O. Major
Program Director for Magnetospheric Physics Program:
Raymond J. Walker
Program Director for Geospace Facilities:
Robert M. Robinson
Program Director for Education and Cross Disciplinary Activities Program:
Linda George
Program Director for Climate and Large Scale Dynamics Program & Carbon and Water in Earth Systems Program:
Eric T. DeWeaver
Program Director for Climate and Large Scale Dynamics Program:
Anjuli Bamzai
Program Director for Atmospheric Chemistry Program:
Peter Milne
Anne-Marie Schmoltner
Program Director for Aeronomy Program:
Anja Stromme
Program Coodinator for NCAR/Facilities Section:
Sarah L. Ruth
Facilities Program Manager for NCAR/Facilities Section:
Linnea M. Avallone
Assistant Program Director for Atmosphere Section:
Nicholas F. Anderson

Nuclear Regulatory Commission
NRC Headquarters (2004)
One White Flint North Building
11555 Rockville Pike
Rockville, MD 20852
    p. (301) 415-8200
    http://www.nrc.gov/

Oak Ridge National Laboratory
Energy Div (2004)
P.O. Box 2008
Oak Ridge, TN 37831-6187
    p. (615) 574-5510
    milorasl@ornl.gov
    Administrative Assistant: Teresa D. Ferguson
Director:
Robert B. Shelton, (D), S Illinois, 1970, On
Chair:
Donald W. Lee, (D), Michigan, 1977, Hw
Senior Scientist:
Richard H. Ketelle, (M), Tennessee, 1977, Ge
Russell Lee, (D), McMaster, 1978, Oy
William P. Staub, (D), Iowa State, 1969, Ng
Research Associate:
Arthur C. Curtis, (M), Colorado State, 1993, Ge
Robert O. Johnson, (D), Tennessee, 1984, Hg
Richard R. Lee, (M), Temple, 1982, Gr
John D. Tauxe, (D), Texas, 1994, Hw

Environmental Sciences Div (2014)
P.O. Box 2008
Mail Stop 6035
Oak Ridge, TN 37831
    p. (865) 574-7374
    envsci@ornl.gov
    http://www.esd.ornl.gov
Director:
Stephen G. Hildebrand, (D), Michigan, 1973, On
Senior Scientist:
Marshall Adams, (D), North Carolina, 1974, Ob
Jeff Amthor, (D), Yale, 1987, Sf
Tom Ashwood, (M), Murray State, 1975, Ge
Mark Bevelhimer, (D), Tennessee, 1990, Hs
Terence J. Blasing, (D), Wisconsin, 1975, Oa
Thomas Boden, (M), Miami, 1985, Oa
Craig Brandt, (M), Tennessee, 1988, Ge
Scott C. Brooks, (D), Virginia, 1994, Cl
Robert S. Burlage, (D), Tennessee, 1990, Sb
Meng-Dawn Cheng, (D), Illinois, 1986, Oa
Robert B. Cook, (D), Columbia, 1981, Cg
William E. Doll, (D), Wisconsin, 1983, Yg
Thomas O. Early, (D), Washington (St. Louis), 1969, Cl
Baohua Gu, (D), California (Berkeley), 1991, Cl
Philip M. Jardine, (D), Virginia Tech, 1985, Sc
Liyuan Liang, (D), Caltech, 1988, Cl
Steven E. Lindberg, (D), Florida State, 1979, Cl
John F. McCarthy, (D), Rhode Island, 1975, Co
Gerilynn R. Moline, (D), Wisconsin, 1992, Hw
Tony V. Palumbo, (D), North Carolina State, 1980, Sb
Tommy J. Phelps, (D), Wisconsin, 1985, Sb
Ellen D. Smith, (M), Wisconsin, 1979, Hg
Brian P. Spalding, (D), Cornell, 1976, Sc
Robert S. Turner, (D), Pennsylvania, 1983, Cl
David B. Watson, (M), New Mexico Tech, 1983, Hw
Olivia M. West, (D), MIT, 1991, Ng
Associate Scientist:
Tammy Beaty, Oi
Mary Anna Bogle, (M), Miami, 1975, Ge
Norman D. Farrow, (B), Oregon State, 1974, Hg
Deputy Director:
Gary K. Jacobs, (D), Penn State, 1981, Cg

Pacific Northwest National Laboratory
Energy and Environmental Directorate (2014)
Environmental Technology Div

Agencies & Intl Organizations

309

PO Box 999 MSIN K6-96
Richland, WA 99352
  p. (509) 371-7171
  tyler.gilmore@pnnl.gov
Senior Scientist:
  Khris B. Olsen, (M), Wyoming, 1976, Cg
  Ronald M. Smith, (M), Washington State, 1977, Hg
  Frank A. Spane, (D), Nevada (Reno), 1977, Hg
  James E. Szecsody, (D), Arizona, 1988, So
  Christopher J. Thompson, (D), Washington, 1994, Ca
  Paul D. Thorne, (M), Arizona, 1983, Hg
  Mark D. Williams, (M), Indiana, 1993, Hw
Associate Scientist:
  Darrell R. Newcomer, (M), Montana Min Sci & Tech, 1988, Hw
  Vincent R. Vermeul, (M), Oregon State, 1990, Hg

Hydrology (2014)
Environmental Technology Div
PO Box 999 MSIN K9-36
Richland, WA 99352
  p. (509) 372-6045
  mike.fayer@pnnl.gov
Head:
  Mark D. Freshley, (M), Arizona, 1982, Hw
Senior Research Engineer:
  Mark D. White, (D), Colorado State, 1986, Hy
Senior Scientist:
  Diana H. Bacon, (D), Washington State, 1997, Hq
  Michael J. Fayer, (D), Massachusetts, 1984, Hq
  Randy R. Kirkham, (D), Washington, 1993, Hq
  Philip D. Meyer, (D), Illinois, 1992, Hw
  Martinus Oostrom, (B), Wageningen Ag, 1984, Hq
  Marshall C. Richmond, (D), Iowa, 1987, Hs
  Timothy D. Scheibe, (D), Stanford, 1993, Hw
  Lance W. Vail, (M), Montana State, 1982, Hg
  Mark S. Wigmosta, (D), Washington, 1991, Hs
  Steven B. Yabusaki, (M), Washington, 1986, Hg
Associate Scientist:
  Cynthia L. Rakowski, (M), Utah State, 1996, On
Research Associate:
  William A. Perkins, (B), Oregon State, 1985, Hg

Applied Geology & Geochemistry (2014)
Environmental Technology Div
Wayne J. Martin, Manager
PO Box 999 MSIN K6-81
Richland, WA 99352
  p. (509) 376-5952
  wayne.martin@pnl.gov
  http://www.pnl.gov/agg
  Administrative Assistant: Charissa J. Chou
Head:
  George R. Holdren, (D), Johns Hopkins, 1977, Cl
Staff Scientist:
  Christopher J. Murray, (D), Stanford, 1992, Gq
Lab Fellow:
  Bernard P. McGrail, (D), Columbia Southern, 1996, Cg
Senior Scientist:
  Douglas B. Barnett, (M), E Washington, 1985, Em
  Bruce N. Bjornstad, (M), E Washington, 1980, Gs
  Kirk J. Cantrell, (D), Georgia Tech, 1989, Cl
  Amy P. Gamerdinger, (D), Cornell, 1989, Cl
  Tyler J. Gilmore, (M), Idaho, 1987, Hg
  Floyd N. Hodges, (D), Texas, 1975, Cg
  Duane G. Horton, (D), Illinois, 1983, Gz
  Kenneth M. Krupka, (D), Penn State, 1984, Cl
  George V. Last, (M), Washington State, 1997, Ge
  Jonathan W. Lindberg, (M), Washington State, 1995, Ec
  Shas V. Mattigod, (D), Washington State, 1976, Cl
  Alan C. Rohay, (D), Washington, 1982, Ys
  Herbert T. Schaef, (M), Texas Tech, 1991, Cg
  R. Jeffrey Serne, (B), Washington, 1969, Cg
  Mark D. Sweeney, (B), C Washington, 1985, Yg
  Bruce A. Williams, (B), Colorado Mines, 1980, Ng
Associate Scientist:
  Yi-Ju Chien, (M), Stanford, 1998, Gq
  Jonathan P. Icenhower, (D), Oklahoma, 1995, Cl

David C. Lanigan, (B), Michigan Tech, 1980, Hg
Virginia L. Legore, (B), Oregon State, 1974, Cg
Clark W. Lindenmeier, (M), E Washington, 1995, Cg
Paul F. Martin, (B), Pacific Lutheran, 1982, Cg
Kent E. Parker, (M), Washington State, 1995, Cg
Research Associate:
  Alexandra B. Amonette, (M), CUNY, 1976, Cg
  Deborah S. Burke, (B), E Washington, 1992, Sc
  Elsa A. Camacho, (B), Heritage, 1996, Cg
  Matthew J. O'Hara, (B), Montana, 1996, Cg
  Robert D. Orr, (B), N State, 1994, Ca

Sandia National Laboratory
Geoscience and Environment (2014)
1515 Eubank SE
P.O. Box 5800
Albuquerque, NM 87185
  gobrela@sandia.gov
  http://www.sandia.gov/

Smithsonian Institution
Smithsonian Astrophysical Observatory (2015)
60 Garden Street
Cambridge, MA 02138
  p. (617) 495-7100
  calcock@cfa.harvard.edu
  https://www.cfa.harvard.edu/sao
  f: https://www.facebook.com/HarvardSmithsonianCenter-
  ForAstrophysics

Smithsonian Environmental Research Center (2014)
P.O. Box 28
Edgewater, MD 21037
  p. (443) 482-2205
  gallagherr@si.edu
  http://www.serc.si.edu

U.S. Geological Survey
Regional Director, Southeast (2014)
1770 Corporate Drive, Suite 500
Norcross, GA 30093
  p. (770) 409-7701
  jdweaver@usgs.gov
  http://www.usgs.gov

Regional Director, Northeast (2014)
12201 Sunrise Valley Drive, MS 953
Reston, VA 20192
  p. (703) 648-6660
  druss@usgs.gov
  http://www.usgs.gov

Regional Director, Midwest (2014)
1451 Green Road
Ann Arbor, MI 48105
  p. (737) 214-7207
  lcarl@usgs.gov
  http://www.usgs.gov

Regional Director, Northwest (2014)
909 1st Avenue
Seattle, WA 98104
  p. (206) 220-4600
  ddlynch@usgs.gov
  http://www.usgs.gov

Regional Director, Southwest Region (2014)
West 6th Ave & Kipling Street
P.O. Box 25045, Mail Stop 911
Denver Federal Center
Denver, CO 80225-0046
  p. (303) 236-5438
  methridge@usgs.gov
  http://www.usgs.gov

Regional Director, Pacific (2014)

Modoc Hall
3030 State University Drive East
Suite 3005
Sacramento, CA 95819
    p. (916) 278-9551
    mark_sogge@usgs.gov
    http://www.usgs.gov

Office of the Director (2014)
12201 Sunrise Valley Drive, MS 100
Reston, VA 20192
    p. (703) 648-7411
    abwade@usgs.gov
    www.usgs.gov

Director, Office of Science Quality & Integrity (2015)
12201 Sunrise Valley Drive, MS 911
Reston, VA 20192
    p. (703) 648-6601
    athornhill@usgs.gov
    http://www.usgs.gov

Associate Director, Climate and Land-Use Change (2014)
12201 Sunrise Valley Drive, MD 409
Reston, VA 20192
    p. (703) 648-5215
    sryker@usgs.gov
    http://www.usgs.gov

Northwest Regional Safety Manager (2015)
2130 SW 5th Ave
Portland, OR 97201
    p. (503) 251-3262
    wsimonds@usgs.gov
    http://www.usgs.gov

Associate Director, Office of Budget, Planning, & Integration (2014)
12201 Sunrise Valley Drive, MS 105
Reston, VA 20192
    p. (703) 648-4443
    cburzyk@usgs.gov
    http://www.usgs.gov

Associate Director, Water (2014)
12201 Sunrise Valley Drive, MD 150
Reston, VA 20192
    p. (703) 648-4557
    whwerkhe@usgs.gov
    http://www.usgs.gov

Associate Director, Ecosystems (2015)
12201 Sunrise Valley Drive, MS 300
Reston, VA 20192
    p. (703) 648-4050
    akinsinger@usgs.gov
    http://www.usgs.gov

Associate Director, Human Capital (2014)
12201 Sunrise Valley Drive, MS 201
Reston, VA 20192
    p. (703) 648-7261
    dwade@usgs.gov
    http://www.usgs.gov

Associate Director, Administration & Enterprise Information (2004)
12201 Sunrise Valley Drive, MS 201
Reston, VA 20192
    p. (703) 648-7261
    http://www.usgs.gov

Associate Director, Office of Communications & Publishing (2015)
12201 Sunrise Valley Drive, MS 119
Reston, VA 20192
    p. (703) 648-5750

bwainman@usgs.gov
http://www.usgs.gov

Associate Director, Core Science Systems (2014)
12201 Sunrise Valley Drive, MD 108
Reston, VA 20192
    p. (703) 648-5747
    kgallagher@usgs.gov
    http://www.usgs.gov

SPECIALTY CODES

Specialty codes are used to indicate the research or teaching specialities of faculty members listed in the directory. Bold numbers are totals for each major category. Numbers in parentheses are individual specialty totals.

Specialties (vertical side tab)

GEOLOGY   5932
Gg	General Geology (1216)
Ga	Archaeological Geology (106)
Ge	Environmental Geology (560)
Gm	Geomorphology (482)
Gl	Glacial Geology (206)
Gu	Marine Geology (195)
Gz	Mineralogy & Crystallography (481)
Gn	Paleolimnology (46)
Go	Petroleum Geology (241)
Gx	General Petrology (209)
Gi	Igneous Petrology (462)
Gp	Metamorphic Petrology (241)
Gd	Sedimentary Petrology (156)
Gs	Sedimentology (716)
Gr	Physical Stratigraphy (267)
Gc	Structural Geology (663)
Gt	Tectonics (467)
Gv	Volcanology (282)
Gq	Mathematical Geology (65)
Gy	Mineral Physics (60)
Gh	History of Geology (25)
Gb	Geomedicine (13)
Gf	Forensic Geology (11)

ECONOMIC GEOLOGY   532
Eg	General Economic Geology (256)
Ec	Coal (69)
Em	Metals (107)
En	Non-Metals (21)
Eo	Oil and Gas (99)

GEOCHEMISTRY   1832
Cg	General Geochemistry (560)
Ca	Analytical Geochemistry (142)
Cp	Experimental Petrology/Phase Equilibria (87)
Ce	Exploration Geochemistry (44)
Cc	Geochronology & Radioisotopes (266)
Cl	Low-temperature Geochemistry (274)
Cm	Marine Geochemistry (165)
Co	Organic Geochemistry (119)
Cs	Stable Isotopes (268)
Ct	Trace Element Distribution (59)

GEOPHYSICS   1613
Yg	General Geophysics (586)
Yx	Experimental Geophysics (89)
Ye	Exploration Geophysics (203)
Yd	Geodesy (71)
Ym	Geomagnetism & Paleomagnetism (125)
Yv	Gravity (18)
Yh	Heat Flow (24)
Ys	Seismology (496)
Yr	Marine Geophysics (171)

PALEONTOLOGY   1526
Pg	General Paleontology (259)
Ps	Paleostratigraphy (105)
Pm	Micropaleontology (160)
Pb	Paleobotany (70)
Pl	Palynology (60)
Pq	Quantitative Paleontology (12)
Pv	Vertebrate Paleontology (244)
Pi	Invertebrate Paleontology (219)
Po	Paleobiology (171)
Pe	Paleoecology & Paleoclimatology (293)
Py	Geobiology (115)

HYDROLOGY   1782
Hg	General Hydrology (294)
Hw	Ground Water/Hydrogeology (638)
Hq	Quantitative Hydrology (96)
Hs	Surface Waters (122)
Hy	Geohydrology (91)

SOIL SCIENCE   1217
Sp	Soil Physics/Hydrology (102)
Sc	Soil Chemistry/Mineralogy (166)
Sd	Pedology/Classification/Morphology (81)
Sf	Forest Soils/Rangelands/Wetlands (50)
Sb	Soil Biology/Biochemistry (93)
Sa	Paleopedology/Archeology (13)
So	Other Soil Science (157)

ENGINEERING GEOLOGY   579
Ng	General Engineering Geology (291)
Ne	Earthquake Engineering (19)
Nx	Mining Tech/Extractive Metallurgy (47)
Nm	Mining Engineering (89)
Np	Petroleum Engineering (57)
Nr	Rock Mechanics (106)

OCEANOGRAPHY   1496
Og	General Oceanography (199)
Ob	Biological Oceanography (454)
Oc	Chemical Oceanography (241)
Ou	Geological Oceanography (141)
Op	Physical Oceanography (386)
On	Shore and Nearshore Processes (112)

PLANETOLOGY   295
Xc	Cosmochemistry (57)
Xg	Extraterrestrial Geology (118)
Xy	Extraterrestrial Geophysics (81)
Xm	Meteorites & Tektites (61)

OTHER   4144
Og	General Earth Sciences (340)
Oa	Atmospheric Sciences (847)
Oe	Earth Science Education (240)
Oy	Physical Geography (303)
Oo	Ocean Engineering/Mining (27)
Or	Remote Sensing (358)
Os	Soil Science (62)
Ow	Meteorology (304)
Om	Material Science (37)
Ou	Land Use/Urban Geology (100)
Oi	Geographic Information Systems (427)
Ol	Glaciology (48)
On	Not Elsewhere Classified (1417)

TOTAL   20,948

Faculty Specialty Index

GEOLOGY

General Geology

Baughman, Joey, Missouri Dept of Natural Resources
Abbott, Lon, University of Colorado
ABDO, Ginette, Montana Tech of The University of Montana
Abousleiman, Younane N., University of Oklahoma
Abreu, Vitor, Rice University
Abushagur, Sulaiman, El Paso Community College
Adabanija, Moruffdeen A., Ladoke Akintola University of Technology
Adamo, Peter J., Brandon University
Adepoju, Mohammed O., Federal University of Technology, Akure
Adisa, Adeshina L., Federal University of Technology, Akure
Ahola, John, Bristol Community College
Ajigo, Isaac O., Federal University of Technology, Akure
Akgun, Elif, Firat University
Akinlabi, Ismaila A., Ladoke Akintola University of Technology
Aksoy, Ercan, Firat University
Alexander, Dane, Western Michigan University
Alexander, Elaine, McLennan Community College
Alkaç, Onur, Firat University
Allen, Jeffrey J., South Dakota Dept of Environment and Natural Resources
Allison, Alivia J., Emporia State University
Allison, M. L., Arizona Geological Survey
Altermann, Wladyslaw, Ludwig-Maximilians-Universitaet Muenchen
Amaach, Noureddin, College of Staten Island
Anderson, Paula, University of Arkansas, Fayetteville
Anderson, Thomas C., Brigham Young University
Andronicos, Chris, Purdue University
Anglen, Brandy, Fresno City College
Anhaeusser, Carl R., University of the Witwatersrand
Antonacci, Vince, Tennessee Geological Survey
Argenbright, Kristi, Texas Christian University
Armour, Jake, University of North Carolina, Charlotte
Arvid, Aase, Brigham Young University
Ashwell, Paul A., University of Canterbury
Asiwaju-Bello, Yinusa A., Federal University of Technology, Akure
Asowata, Timothy I., Federal University of Technology, Akure
Athaide, Dileep, University of British Columbia
Athaide, Dileep J., Capilano University
Athey, Jennifer E., Alaska Division of Geological & Geophysical Surveys
Bach Plaza, Joan, Universitat Autonoma de Barcelona
Bachle, Peter, Missouri Dept of Natural Resources
Baer, Eric M., Highline College
Baker, Cathy, Arkansas Tech University
Balakrishnan, Meena, Tarrant County College- Northeast Campus
Ballero, Deniz Z., Georgia Perimeter College - Online
Ballou, Stephen M., Beloit College
Bally, Albert W., Rice University
Balmat, Jennifer, Chadron State College
Balsley, Christopher, Southern Connecticut State University
Bamisaye, Oluwaseyi A., Federal University of Technology, Akure
Barclay, Julie L., SUNY, Cortland
Barker, Andy J., University of Southampton
Barker, Charles F., Wayne State University
Barker, Gregory A., New Hampshire Geological Survey
Barker, Helen K., Weber State University
Barminski, Robert, Hartnell College
Barnes, Brenda, El Paso Community College
Barnes, John H., Pennsylvania Bureau of Topographic & Geologic Survey
Batten, William G., University of Wisconsin, Extension
Baxter, P.G., James E., Harrisburg Area Community College
Bayowa, Oyelowo G., Ladoke Akintola University of Technology
Beatty, Lynne, Johnson County Community College
Beltrami, Hugo, Dalhousie University
Beltz, John F., University of Akron
Bender, Hallock J., Mt. San Antonio College
Bennett, Sara, Western Illinois University
Benson, Donna M., Mesa Community College
Benson, Robert G., Adams State University
Bentley, Callan, Northern Virginia Community College - Annandale
Benton, Steven, University of Illinois, Urbana-Champaign
Berg, Richard, University of Illinois
Berry IV, Henry N., Dept of Agriculture, Conservation, and Forestry
Best, Myron G., Brigham Young University
Beyer, Adam, Nicholls State University
Bice, David M., Pennsylvania State University, University Park
Biek, Robert, Utah Geological Survey
Bierly, Aaron D., Pennsylvania Bureau of Topographic & Geologic Survey
Birner, Johannes, Ludwig-Maximilians-Universitaet Muenchen
Bishop, Cathy, University of Louisiana at Lafayette
Blakeney DeJarnett, Beverly, University of Texas at Austin, Jackson School of Geosciences
Blattler, Clara, Princeton University
Blaylock, Glenn W., Laredo Community College
Boehm, David A., SUNY, The College at Brockport
Bograd, Michael B., Mississippi Office of Geology

Bohm, Christian, Manitoba Geological Survey
Bolze, Claude E., Tulsa Community College
Bone, Fletcher, Missouri Dept of Natural Resources
Boroughs, Terry J., American River College
Bothern, Lawrence, El Paso Community College
Bouker, Polly A., Georgia Perimeter College
Bounk, Michael, Iowa Dept of Natural Resources
Bour, William, Northern Virginia Community College - Loudoun Campus
Bouse, Robin, El Camino College
Bowles, Zack, Mesa Community College
Bowring, Samuel A., Massachusetts Institute of Technology
Bozdog, Nick, North Carolina Geological Survey
Brady, Lawrence L., University of Kansas
Branciforte, Chloe, Mesa Community College
Breckenridge, Roy M., University of Idaho
Bridges, Carey, Missouri Dept of Natural Resources
Bries Korpik, Jill, Inver Hills Community College
Brill, Jr., Richard C., Honolulu Community College
Brock, Patrick W. G., Queens College (CUNY)
Brock, Patrick W. G., Graduate School of the City University of New York
Brouillette, Pierre, Universite du Quebec
Brown, Alan, Middle Tennessee State University
Brown, Francis H., University of Utah
Browning, James V., Rutgers, The State University of New Jersey
Browning, Sharon, Baylor University
Brunengo, Matthew , Portland State University
Bruschke, Freddi Jo, California State University, Fullerton
Bryant, Kathleen E., University of Illinois, Urbana-Champaign
Bryant, Marita, Bates College
Buchanan, Paul, Kilgore College
Buchwald, Caryl E., Carleton College
Bucke, David P., University of Vermont
Bulger, Daniel E., Georgia Perimeter College - Decatur
Bultman, John, Asheville-Buncombe Technical Community College
Burns, Emily, Community College of Rhode Island
Burris, John H., San Juan College
Burtis, Erik, Northern Virginia Community College - Woodbridge
Butcher, William, Bowling Green State University
Butkos, Darryl J., Suffolk County Community College, Ammerman Campus
Büchel, Georg, Friedrich-Schiller-University Jena
Byrnes, Jeffrey, Oklahoma State University
Cabe, Suellen, University of North Carolina, Pembroke
Caldwell, Andy, Front Range Community College - Larimer
Callahan, Caitlin N., Grand Valley State University
Cameron, Kevin, Simon Fraser University
Canalda, Sabrina, El Paso Community College
Carnes, Jacob, Wyoming State Geological Survey
Carr, Keith W., University of Illinois, Urbana-Champaign
Carr, Tim R., University of Kansas
Carrick, Tina, El Paso Community College
Caskey, Deborah, El Paso Community College
Cate, Alta S., Houston Community College System
Cervato, Cinzia C., Iowa State University of Science & Technology
Chadima, Sarah A., South Dakota Dept of Environment and Natural Resources
Chamberlin, Richard M., New Mexico Institute of Mining & Technology
Chandler, Angela, Arkansas Geological Survey
Chang, Julie M., University of Oklahoma
Charles, Kasanzu, University of Dar es Salaam
Chase, Peter M., University of Wisconsin, Extension
Chasteen, Hayden R., Tarrant County College- Northeast Campus
Chernosky, Jr., Joseph V., University of Maine
Cherukupalli, Nehru, Hofstra University
Cholnoky, Jennifer, Skidmore College
Christensen, Wesley P., South Dakota Dept of Environment and Natural Resources
Ciciarelli, John A., Pennsylvania State University, Monaca
Clark, Donald, Utah Geological Survey
Clark, Kathryne, Iowa Dept of Natural Resources
Clark, Ken, University of Puget Sound
Clayton, Rodney, Tidewater Community College
Coble, Jim, Tidewater Community College
Colak Erol, Serap, Firat University
Coleman, Alvin L., Cape Fear Community College
Collins, Laura, Middle Tennessee State University
Colosimo, Amanda, Monroe Community College
Conquy, Xenia, Broward College
Cooper, Jennifer, Southern Connecticut State University
Cooper, Jonathon L., Carleton College
Corley, John, Missouri Dept of Natural Resources
Cornell, Kristie, University of Louisiana at Lafayette
Cornell, Sean, Shippensburg University
Cornett, Jack R., University of Ottawa
Cotera, Jr., Augustus S., Northern Arizona University
Couroux, Emile, El Paso Community College
Coutand, Isabelle, Dalhousie University
Cox, Christena, Ohio State University
Craig, James L., Los Alamos National Laboratory
Crain, John R., College of the Sequoias

Crawford, Vernon J., Southern Oregon University
Creveling, Jessica, Oregon State University
Criswell, James, Cape Fear Community College
Cron, Mitch, Drexel University
Cronoble, James M., Metropolitan State College of Denver
Cummings, Michael L., Portland State University
Curtis, Lynn A., Broward College, Central Campus
Cvetko Tešoviæ, Blanka, University of Zagreb
Dalman, Michael, Blinn College
Damir, Buckoviæ, University of Zagreb
Danbom, Stephen H., Rice University
Daramola, Sunday O., Federal University of Technology, Akure
Davis, Adam M., Worcester State University
Davis, David A., University of Nevada
Dawes, Ralph, Wenatchee Valley College
Day, Damon P., Mt. San Antonio College
Deakin, Joann, Cochise College
Dealy, Mike, University of Kansas
Deane, William, University of Tennessee, Knoxville
Dee, Seth, University of Nevada
deGroot, Robert, California State University, Fullerton
Dehler, Sonya, Dalhousie University
Delano, Helen L., Pennsylvania Bureau of Topographic & Geologic Survey
Devaney, Kathleen, El Paso Community College
Devery, Dora, Alvin Community College
Devlahovich, Vincent A., College of the Canyons
DeVries-Zimmerman, Suzanne, Hope College
Di Fiori, Sara, El Camino College
Dinklage, William, Santa Barbara City College
Dittmer, Eric, Southern Oregon University
Doelling, Helmut H., University of Utah
Donnelly, Thomas W., Binghamton University
Dooley, Brett, Patrick Henry Community College
Dougan, Bernie, Whatcom Community College
Doyle, Joseph, Bridgewater State University
Dressel, Waldemar M., Missouri University of Science and Technology
Drobny, Gerry, Cosumnes River College
Dudley, Jutta S., SUNY, The College at Brockport
Duncan, Ian, University of Texas at Austin, Jackson School of Geosciences
Dushman, Beth, American River College
Dyab, Ahmed I., Alexandria University
Earls, Stephanie, Washington Division of Geology & Earth Resources
Easterday, Cary, Bellevue College
Edson, Carol, Las Positas College
Egan, Stuart, Keele University
Egbeyemi, Oladimeji R., Federal University of Technology, Akure
Ehler, J B., Utah Geological Survey
Eisenhart, Ralph, York College of Pennsylvania
El Dakkak, Mohamed W., Alexandria University
Elfrink, Neil, Missouri Dept of Natural Resources
Ellis, Trevor, Missouri Dept of Natural Resources
Emerson, Norlene, University of Wisconsin Colleges
Engelhard, Simon, University of Rhode Island
Escartin, Javier, Woods Hole Oceanographic Institution
Esparza-Yanez, Francisco A., Centro de Estudios Superiores del Estado Sonora
Evans, Thomas J., University of Wisconsin, Extension
Ewas, Galal A., Alexandria University
Faatz, Renee M., Snow College
Fagnan, Brian A., South Dakota Dept of Environment and Natural Resources
Fahrenbach, Mark D., South Dakota Dept of Environment and Natural Resources
Falcon, Alexandra, El Paso Community College
Fantozzi, Joanna , California State University, Fullerton
Farquharson, Phil, MiraCosta College
Farrell, Michael, Cuyamaca College
Fengler, Keegan , Central Washington University
Ferney, Natasha, College of Western Idaho
Ferreira, Karen, University of Manitoba
Fields, Chad, Iowa Dept of Natural Resources
Fields, Nancy, El Centro College - Dallas Community College District
Figg, Sean, Palomar College
Filkorn, Harry, Los Angeles Pierce College
Finley, Mark, Heartland Community College
Fitak, Madge R., Ohio Dept of Natural Resources
Fitchett, Rebekah, Northeastern Illinois University
Fitz, Thomas J., Northland College
Flanagan, Timothy, Berkshire Community College
Fleck, Michelle C., Utah State University Eastern
Flower, Hjilary, Saint Petersburg College, Clearwater
Flowers Falls, Emily, Washington & Lee University
Follis, Michael, Salem State University
Forno, Maria Gabriella, Università di Torino
Fox, Don, Dalhousie University
Frail, Pam, Acadia University
Frank, Bob, College of Western Idaho
Fredrick, Kyle, California University of Pennsylvania
Freed, Andrew M., Purdue University
Frei, Michaela, Ludwig-Maximilians-Universitaet Muenchen
Friedmann, Samuel (Julio) J., Lawrence Livermore National Laboratory
Fromm, Jeanne M., University of South Dakota
Frost, Gina M., San Joaquin Delta College

Fuerst, Alice, Metropolitan Community College-Kansas City
Gagnon, Teresa K., Dept of Energy and Environmental Protection
Galal, Galal M., Alexandria University
Gale, Andrew, University of Portsmouth
Gale, Marjorie H., Agency of Natural Resources, Dept of Environmental Conservation
Galli, Kenneth G., Boston College
Gannon, J. Michael, Iowa Dept of Natural Resources
Garcia, Antonio, California Polytechnic State University
Gardner, Eleanor E., University of Tennessee, Martin
Gardner, Jamie N., Los Alamos National Laboratory
Garrett, Maureen, Arizona Western College
Garside, Larry J., University of Nevada
Garwood, Phil, Cape Fear Community College
Gawloski, Joan, Midland College
Gianotti, Franco, Università di Torino
Giegengack, Jr., Robert F., University of Pennsylvania
Giglierano, James D., Iowa Dept of Natural Resources
Gildner, Raynond F., Indiana University / Purdue University, Fort Wayne
Giles, Antony, Midland College
Gilley, Brett, University of British Columbia
Gillis, Robert J., Division of Geological & Geophysical Surveys
Gillman, Joe, Missouri Dept of Natural Resources
Glass, Alex, Duke University
Glynn, William G., SUNY, The College at Brockport
Goetz, Bruce A., Northland College
Gonzalez-Juarez, Marco A., Centro de Estudios Superiores del Estado Sonora
Goodwin, Alan M., University of Toronto
Gottfried, Richard, Frederick Community College
Gould, Alex, Alaska Division of Geological & Geophysical Surveys
Gould, Joseph C., Saint Petersburg College, Clearwater
Grace, Cathy A., University of Mississippi
Grew, Priscilla C., University of Nebraska, Lincoln
Griffin, William R., University of Texas, Dallas
Gross, Amy, University of North Carolina, Pembroke
Grover, Jeff, Cuesta College
Grupp, Steve, Everett Community College
Gušiæ, Ivan, University of Zagreb
Hagadorn, James W., Denver Museum of Nature & Science
Hale, Leslie, Smithsonian Institution / National Museum of Natural History
Haley, John C., Virginia Wesleyan College
Hall, Chad, Georgia Perimeter College - Decatur
Hall, Tracy, Georgia Highlands College
Hamdan, Abeer, Phoenix College
Hamecher, Emily, California State University, Fullerton
Hammes, Ursula, University of Texas at Austin, Jackson School of Geosciences
Hams, Jacquelyn E., Los Angeles Valley College
Hand, Linda M., College of San Mateo
Hanna, Ruth L., Las Positas College
Hanson, Doug, Arkansas Geological Survey
Hargrave, Phyllis, Montana Tech of The University of Montana
Harma, Roberta L., Moorpark College
Harone, Imad, College of Staten Island
Harrell, Michael, Seattle Central Community College
Harrison, Linda , Western Michigan University
Hart, George, Louisiana State University
Hartley, Susan, Lake Superior College
Harun, Nina T., Division of Geological & Geophysical Surveys
Haselwander, Airin, Missouri Dept of Natural Resources
Hauer, Kendall, Miami University
Hawkins, John, Auburn University
Hawkins, Terry, Missouri Dept of Natural Resources
Hayes, Garry F., Modesto Junior College
Hayes, Garry F., California State University, Stanislaus
Heck, Frederick R., Ferris State University
Heerschap, Lauren, Fort Lewis College
Hegner, Ernst, Ludwig-Maximilians-Universitaet Muenchen
Heidlauf, Lisa, Wheaton College
Hein, Kim A., University of the Witwatersrand
Helba, Hossam EL-Din A., Alexandria University
Heller, Matthew J., Division of Geology and Mineral Resources
Henley, Barbara D., Mercer University
Henry, Christopher D., University of Nevada
Henry, Kathleen M., Illinois State Geological Survey
Hepburn, J. Christopher, Boston College
Hepburn, J.Christopher, Boston College
Herbert, Jennifer, Argonne National Laboratory
Herbst, Thomas, Missouri Dept of Natural Resources
Hernandez, Larry, MiraCosta College
Herring Mayo, Lisa L., Motlow State Community College
Herriott, Trystan, Division of Geological & Geophysical Surveys
Herzig, Chuck, El Camino College
Hess Tanguay, Lillian, Hofstra University
Hetherington, Jean, Diablo Valley College
Hickcox, C W., Emory University
Hiett, Michael W., Middle Tennessee State University
Higgins, Chris T., California Geological Survey
Hill, Chris, Grossmont College
Hills, Denise J., Geological Survey of Alabama
Hinz, Nicholas, University of Nevada
Hirner, Sarah M., University of Northern Colorado

Ho, Anita, Flathead Valley Community College
Hobbs, Thomas M., Lonestar College - North Harris
Hochstaedter, Alfred, Monterey Peninsula College
Hodder, Donald R., SUNY, New Paltz
Holail, Hanafy M., Alexandria University
Holmes, Stevie L., South Dakota Dept of Environment and Natural Resources
Hood, Teresa A., University of Miami
Hood, William C., Colorado Mesa University
Hopkins, David M., University of Alaska, Fairbanks
Hoppe, Andreas, Technische Universitaet Darmstadt
Horn, John, Metropolitan Community College-Kansas City
Horton, Albert B., Tennessee Geological Survey
House, Martha, Pasadena City College
Howard, Katie, Olympic College
Howes, Mary R., Iowa Dept of Natural Resources
Hudec, Mike, University of Texas at Austin, Jackson School of Geosciences
Hungerbuehler, Axel, Mesalands Community College
Hunt, Paula J., West Virginia University
Hural, Kirsten, Dickinson College
Hussein, Musa, El Paso Community College
Hutto, Richard, Arkansas Geological Survey
Huycke, David, Yakima Valley Community College
Hylland, Michael D., Utah Geological Survey
Hylton, Alisa, Central Piedmont Community College
Iaccheri, Maria Linda, Ludwig-Maximilians-Universitaet Muenchen
Idstein, Peter J., University of Kentucky
Igonor, Emmanuel E., Federal University of Technology, Akure
Ikwuazorm, Okia, Northern Virginia Community College - Loudoun Campus
Irvin, Gene D., Geological Survey of Alabama
Isenor, Fenton M., Cape Breton University
Jackson, Hiram, Cosumnes River College
Jackson, Jeremiah, Missouri Dept of Natural Resources
Jaecks, Glenn, American River College
Janusz, Robert, San Antonio Community College
Jegede, O A., Federal University of Technology, Akure
Jellinek, Mark, University of British Columbia
Jensen, Ann R., South Dakota Dept of Environment and Natural Resources
Jiang, James Xinxia, Mount Allison University
Johnson, Darren J., South Dakota Dept of Environment and Natural Resources
Johnson, Edward, College of Staten Island
Johnson, Kurt, Alaska Division of Geological & Geophysical Surveys
Johnson, Kurt J., Division of Geological & Geophysical Surveys
Johnson, Ty, Arkansas Geological Survey
Johnston, David, Arkansas Geological Survey
Johnston, Paul J., Emporia State University
Johnston, Robert A., Dept of Agriculture, Conservation, and Forestry
Jones, Charles E., University of Pittsburgh
Jones, Gwyn, Bellevue College
Jurena, Dwight, Alamo Colleges - San Antonio College
Jurena, Dwight, San Antonio Community College
Kaandorp, Ron, VU University Amsterdam
Kadjar, Mickey, El Centro College - Dallas Community College District
Kaldor, Michael, Miami-Dade Community College (Wolfson Campus)
Kapp, Jessica, University of Arizona
Karwoski, Todd, University of Maryland
Katzman, Danny, Los Alamos National Laboratory
Kavage-Adams, Rebecca, Maryland Department of Natural Resources
Kaye, John M., Mississippi State University
Kaygili, Sibel, Firat University
Keating, Elizabeth, Los Alamos National Laboratory
Keene, Deborah A., University of Alabama
Kelley, Neil P., Vanderbilt University
Kempe, Stephan, Technische Universitaet Darmstadt
Kerwin, Charles M., Keene State College
Kerwin, Michael W., University of Denver
Khalil Ebeid, Khalil I., Alexandria University
Kiesel, Diann, University of Wisconsin Colleges
Kim, Keonho, Midland College
King, Jonathan K., Utah Geological Survey
Kirkby, Kent C., University of Minnesota, Twin Cities
Klaus, James S., University of Miami
Klee, Thomas M., Hillsborough Community College
Klosterman, Sue, University of Dayton
Knowlton, Kelly, Northwestern State University
Kochanov, William E., Pennsylvania Bureau of Topographic & Geologic Survey
Kodosky, Larry, Oakland Community College
Koenig, Brian, College of the Desert
Kohrt, Casey, Iowa Dept of Natural Resources
Kolkas, Mosbah, College of Staten Island
Kollasch, Pete, Iowa Dept of Natural Resources
Kontak, Daniel, Dalhousie University
Kowallis, Bart J., Brigham Young University
Kraft, Kaatje, Whatcom Community College
Kraft, Kaatje, Mesa Community College
Kramer, J. Curtis, University of the Pacific
Kramer, Kate, McHenry County College
Kramer, Walter V., Del Mar College
Krantz, Dwight S., Houston Community College System
Kroon, Dick, Edinburgh University
Kruger, Ned , North Dakota Geological Survey

Kubicek, Leonard, North Lake College - Dallas Community College District
Kuhlman, Robert, Montgomery County Community College
Kukoè, Duje, University of Zagreb
Kumpf, Amber C., Muskegon Community College
Kuntz, Mark R., Elgin Community College
Kurka, Mira, Great Basin College
Kutis, Michael, Ball State University
Kwicklis, Edward M., Los Alamos National Laboratory
Lacy, Tor, Cerritos College
Lambert-Smith, James, Kingston University
Lammerer, Bernd, Ludwig-Maximilians-Universitaet Muenchen
Langel, Richard A., Iowa Dept of Natural Resources
Langhorst, Glenn, Fond du Lac Tribal and Community College
LaPointe, Daphne D., University of Nevada
Larter, Stephen, University of Newcastle Upon Tyne
Lauziere, Kathleen, Universite du Quebec
Lawrence, Kira, Lafayette College
Lawry, Cynthia, Blinn College
Leetaru, Hannes E., University of Illinois, Urbana-Champaign
LeFever, Julie A., North Dakota Geological Survey
Leite, Michael B., Chadron State College
Lemay, Phillip W., Louisiana State University
LePain, David L., Division of Geological & Geophysical Surveys
Leszczynski, Raymond F., Cayuga Community College
Levy, Melissa H., American River College
Lewis, Chris, City College of San Francisco
Lewis, Jeffrey, Houston Community College System
Lewis, Margaret, Richard Stockton College of New Jersey
Lewis, Mary, Contra Costa College
Lewis, Reed S., University of Idaho
Liauw, Henri L., Broward College
Libra, Robert D., Iowa Dept of Natural Resources
Liebling, Richard, Hofstra University
Lippelt, Irene D., University of Wisconsin, Extension
Liu, Paul Hiaibao, Iowa Dept of Natural Resources
Lombard, Armand J., Mesa Community College
Long, Colleen, University of Illinois, Urbana-Champaign
Lonn, Jeffrey, Montana Tech of The University of Montana
Loveland, Andrea, Wyoming State Geological Survey
Lovett, Cole, Lake Michigan College
Lowrie, David J., Wayne State University
Lu, Yuehan, University of Alabama
Luciano, Katherine E., Dept of Natural Resources
Ludman, Allan, Queens College (CUNY)
Ludman, Allan, Graduate School of the City University of New York
Lueth, Virgil W., New Mexico Institute of Mining & Technology
Lužar-Oberiter, Borna, University of Zagreb
Lyle, Mike, Tidewater Community College
Lyman, John C., Bakersfield College
Lyon, Eva, Concord University
Mabee, Stephen B., University of Massachusetts, Amherst
Macias, Steve E., Olympic College
MacLachlan, James, Metropolitan State College of Denver
Madin, Ian P., Oregon Dept of Geology & Mineral Industries
Maerz, Christina, University of Newcastle Upon Tyne
Magee, Robert, Virginia Wesleyan College
Maguire, David, Mott Community College
Mahaffee, Tina, Middle Georgia College
Mahlen, Nancy J., SUNY, Geneseo
Mahmoud, Sara A., Alexandria University
Majodina, Thando, Tshwane University of Technology
Major, Penni, Lonestar College - North Harris
Major, Ruth H., Hudson Valley Community College
Mandziuk, William, University of Manitoba
Mansour, Ahmed S., Alexandria University
Manz, Lorraine, North Dakota Geological Survey
Mapholi, Thendo, University of the Free State
Marchisin, John, New Jersey City University
Marco, Shmuel, Tel Aviv University
Marco, Shmulik, Tel Aviv University
Mariant, Judy, San Jose City College
Marschik, Robert, Ludwig-Maximilians-Universitaet Muenchen
Marshall, Thomas R., South Dakota Dept of Environment and Natural Resources
Martin, Charles W., Earlham College
Martin, Gale D., College of Southern Nevada - West Charleston Campus
Martinez-Hackert, Bettina, SUNY, Buffalo
Martinuš, Maja, University of Zagreb
Marty, Kevin, Imperial Valley College
Martz, Todd, University of California, San Diego
Marvinney, Robert G., Dept of Agriculture, Conservation, and Forestry
Marx, Joe, Northern Virginia Community College - Alexandria
Mata, Scott, California State University, Fullerton
Mattox, Tari, Grand Rapids Community College
Matyjasik, Basia, Utah Geological Survey
May, S J., Collin College - Preston Ridge Campus
Mayer, Larry, Woods Hole Oceanographic Institution
McAdams, Alexis, Northwestern University
McArthur, Russell , City College of San Francisco
McCall, Rosemary, College of Staten Island
McClaughry, Jason, Oregon Dept of Geology & Mineral Industries

McConnell, David, North Carolina State University
McCoy, Floyd W., Windward Community College
McCraley, Tia, Arizona Western College
McCulloch, Debia F., Georgia Perimeter College
McCulloh, Richard P., Louisiana State University
McCutchen, William T., University of Tennessee, Martin
McDowell, Ronald, West Virginia University
McGehee, Richard V., Austin Community College District
McKay, Robert M., Iowa Dept of Natural Resources
McKinney, Mac, Geological Survey of Alabama
McMonagle, Julie, Wilkes University
McNeill, Donald F., University of Miami
Meave, Edgardo, Universidad Nacional Autonoma de Mexico
Meldahl, Keith H., MiraCosta College
Melendez, Christyanne, Appalachian State University
Merriam, Daniel F., University of Kansas
Metzler, Christopher V., MiraCosta College
Meyer, Jeffrey W., Santa Barbara City College
Mezger, Jochen, University of Alaska Fairbanks
Michel, Suzanne, Cuyamaca College
Milan, Luke, University of New England
Millan, Christina, Ohio State University
Millen, Timothy M., Elgin Community College
Miller, Carolyn R., Houston Community College System
Miller, David, California State University, Bakersfield
Miller, Steven F., Argonne National Laboratory
Miller-Hicks, Bryan, Cuyamaca College
Milligan, Mark R., Utah Geological Survey
Milner, Lloyd R., Louisiana State University
Milner, Lloyd R., Louisiana State University
Miner, James J., University of Illinois, Urbana-Champaign
Minium, Deborah, Bellevue College
Moll, Nancy E., College of the Desert
Monet, Julie, California State University, Chico
Monson, Jessica, University of Illinois, Urbana-Champaign
Montayne, Simone, Alaska Division of Geological & Geophysical Surveys
Montayne, Simone, Division of Geological & Geophysical Surveys
Montwill, Gail F., Santiago Canyon College
Morand, Vincent J., La Trobe University
Morealli, Sarah A., University of Mary Washington
Morgan, Matt, Colorado Geological Survey
Morris, Billy, Georgia Highlands College
Mulvany, Patrick S., Missouri University of Science and Technology
Munn, Barbara J., California State University, Sacramento
Murphy, Cindy, Saint Francis Xavier University
Murphy, Dan, Asheville-Buncombe Technical Community College
Muskatt, Herman, Utica College
Mustart, David A., San Francisco State University
Mutti, Laurel, SUNY, New Paltz
Nance, Seay, University of Texas at Austin, Jackson School of Geosciences
Nesheim, Tim, North Dakota Geological Survey
Newman, Brent D., Los Alamos National Laboratory
Newman, Jamie, American Museum of Natural History
Nicholl, Amy, University of Northern Colorado
Nicoletti, Jeremy D., New Hampshire Geological Survey
Nielsen, Gregory B., Weber State University
Niemuth, Nyal, Arizona Geological Survey
Norman, David K., Washington Division of Geology & Earth Resources
Norrish, Winston, Central Washington University
O'Brien, Lawrence E., Orange County Community College
O'Connor, Yuet-Ling, Pasadena City College
O'Keeffe, Mike, Colorado Geological Survey
O'Neil, Caron, Pennsylvania Bureau of Topographic & Geologic Survey
O'Neill, Al, Houston Community College System
Obolewicz, Dave, Keene State College
Odendaal, Adriaan, University of the Free State
Odeyemi, Idowu O., Federal University of Technology, Akure
Ogbahon, Osazuwa A., Federal University of Technology, Akure
Okonkwo, C T., Federal University of Technology, Akure
Okulewicz, Steven C., Hofstra University
Ola, P S., Federal University of Technology, Akure
Olabode, Solomon O., Federal University of Technology, Akure
Oldfield, Bruce K., Broome Community College
Oldham, Richard L., American River College
Opeloye, S A., Federal University of Technology, Akure
Opperman, William, Broward College
Orr, William , Portland State University
Oswald, Peter J., University of Alaska, Anchorage
Othberg, Kurt L., University of Idaho
Owoseni, Joshua O., Federal University of Technology, Akure
Pande, Srikant k., Pt. Ravishankar Shukla University
Pantoja-Alor, Jerjes, Universidad Nacional Autonoma de Mexico
Papp, Kenneth R., Division of Geological & Geophysical Surveys
Papp, Kenneth R., Alaska Division of Geological & Geophysical Surveys
Parish, Cynthia L., Lamar University
Parnella, Bill, University of Delaware
Parrick, Brittany, Ohio Dept of Natural Resources
Parsons, Michael, Dalhousie University
Paschert, Karin, Ludwig-Maximilians-Universitaet Muenchen
Pashley, E. F., Weber State University

Patton, Jason A., Arkansas Tech University
Patton, Terri, Argonne National Laboratory
Patwardhan, Kaustubh, SUNY, New Paltz
Pawloski, Gayle A., Lawrence Livermore National Laboratory
Peacock, Simon M., University of British Columbia
Pellowski, Christopher J., South Dakota School of Mines & Technology
Perez, Adriana, El Paso Community College
Perkis, Bill, Gogebic Community College
Pesavento, Jim, Palomar College
Peters, Lisa, New Mexico Institute of Mining & Technology
Peterson, Joseph E., Elgin Community College
Phelps, William, Riverside City College
Phillips, Michael, Illinois Valley Community College
Pierce, David, Lakeland Community College
Pierce, Heather, Monroe Community College
Pike, Scott, Willamette University
Pirie, Diane H., Florida International University
Pokras, Edward M., Keene State College
Polissar, Pratigya J., Columbia University
Poole, T. Craig, Fresno City College
Posloviæ, Hrvoje, University of Zagreb
Prewett, Jerry, Missouri Dept of Natural Resources
Price, Jonathan G., University of Nevada
Price, L G., New Mexico Institute of Mining & Technology
Prichystal, Antonin, Masaryk University
Priesendorf, Carl, Metropolitan Community College-Kansas City
Priest, George R., Oregon Dept of Geology & Mineral Industries
Prior, William L., Arkansas Geological Survey
Prothero, Donald, Los Angeles Pierce College
Proudhon, Benoit, Institut Polytechnique LaSalle Beauvais (ex-IGAL)
Prytulak, Julie, Imperial College
Purdy, Ann, Wayne State University
Purkiss, Robert, Angelo State University
Putnam, Roger, California State University, Stanislaus
Quade, Deborah J., Iowa Dept of Natural Resources
Quinn, Heather A., Maryland Department of Natural Resources
Ragland, Deborah, University of New Mexico - Taos
Rains, Daniel S., Arkansas Geological Survey
Rashed, Mohamed A., Alexandria University
Rath, Carolyn, California State University, Fullerton
Rathburn, Sara L., Colorado State University
Rawling, Geoffrey, New Mexico Institute of Mining & Technology
Ray, Waverly, Cuyamaca College
Raymer, Janet, Metropolitan Community College-Kansas City
Read, Adam S., New Mexico Institute of Mining & Technology
Redden, Marcella, Geological Survey of Alabama
Reesman, Authur L., Vanderbilt University
Reif, Samantha, Lincoln Land Community College
Reioux, David, Alaska Division of Geological & Geophysical Surveys
Rennie, Colette, Saint Francis Xavier University
Repka, James, Saddleback Community College
Rieder, Michael, Technische Universitaet Muenchen
Riker-Coleman, Kristin E., University of Wisconsin, Superior
Rinae, Makhadi, University of the Free State
Riordan, Jean A., Division of Geological & Geophysical Surveys
Riordan, Jean, Alaska Division of Geological & Geophysical Surveys
Rivera, Mark, University of Alaska, Anchorage
Robert, Sanborn, University of Wisconsin Colleges
Robinson, Francis J., Yale University
Robinson, Richard, Santa Monica College
Robinson, Sarah, United States Air Force Academy
Rocha, Guillermo, Brooklyn College (CUNY)
Roche, James E., Louisiana State University
Rochon, Andre, Dalhousie University
Rodgers, Jim, Wyoming State Geological Survey
Rodriguez-Castaneda, Jose L., Universidad Nacional Autonoma de Mexico
Rogers, Steven, Keele University
Ross, Theodore W., Lawrence University
Rothemund, Kirk, El Paso Community College
Rounds, Steven W., California State University, Sacramento
Rowden, Robert, Iowa Dept of Natural Resources
Ruetz, Joseph W., Stanford University
Ruffel, Alice, El Centro College - Dallas Community College District
Rumrill, Julie, Southern Connecticut State University
Ruppert, Kelly R., California State University, Fullerton
Rush, Jason, University of Kansas
Russ, Tom, College of Southern Maryland
Sacramentogrilo, Isabelle, San Diego State University
Salle, Bethan, El Centro College - Dallas Community College District
Samimi, Naser, University of Tabriz
Sassi, Raffaele, Università degli Studi di Padova
Sato, Yoko, Montclair State University
Sawin, Robert S., University of Kansas
Schafer, Carl M., Macomb Community College, Center Campus
Scheffler, Joanna, Mesa Community College
Schenck, William S., University of Delaware
Schilling, Keith, Iowa Dept of Natural Resources
Schmidt, Bennetta, Lamar University
Schulingkamp, Arren, Louisiana State University
Schultz, Jan, Santa Barbara City College

Sediek, Kadry N., Alexandria University
Seigley, Lynette S., Iowa Dept of Natural Resources
Semken, Steven, Arizona State University
Shaaban, Mohamad N., Alexandria University
Shade, Harry, West Valley College
Shakun, Jeremy D., Boston College
Shannon, Jeremy, Michigan Technological University
Sharp, Patricia S., Stephen F. Austin State University
shedied, ahmad g., Fayoum University
Sheets, H. David, SUNY, Buffalo
Shelton, Dale W., Maryland Department of Natural Resources
Shields, William, Illinois State University
Shimizu, Melinda, Mesa Community College
Shinn, Eugene, University of South Florida
Shorey, Christian V., Colorado School of Mines
Shroba, Cynthia S., College of Southern Nevada - West Charleston Campus
Sibeko, Skhumbuzo, Tshwane University of Technology
Sicard, Karri, Alaska Division of Geological & Geophysical Surveys
Siegelberg, Alan, Long Island University, Brooklyn Campus
Sigler, Jeffrey M., Tulane University
Sinha, Ashish, California State University, Dominguez Hills
Skelton, Lawrence H., University of Kansas
Skinner, Randall, Brigham Young University
Sladek, Chris, University of Nevada, Reno
Sledzinski, Grazyna, Wayne State University
Smaglik, Suzanne M., Central Wyoming College
Smith, Jason J., Broome Community College
Smith, Jon J., University of Kansas
Smith, Mike, Front Range Community College - Larimer
Smith, Russell, El Paso Community College
Smithson, Jayne, Contra Costa College
Snyder, Daniel, Middle Georgia College
Snyder, Noah, Boston College
Sparks, Thomas N., University of Kentucky
Speed, Don, Phoenix College
Spencer, Larry T., Plymouth State University
Sprinkel, Douglas, Utah Geological Survey
Stakes, Debra, Cuesta College
Stanton, Kathryn, Sacramento City College
Stanton, Kelsay, Wenatchee Valley College
Starbuck, Edith, Missouri Dept of Natural Resources
Stark, Colin, Columbia University
Steck, Lee, Los Alamos National Laboratory
Steffens, Katja, Ludwig-Maximilians-Universitaet Muenchen
Steinmann, Kim, Western Michigan University
Stewart, Dion C., Georgia Perimeter College at Alpharetta Center
Stewart, Esther K., University of Wisconsin, Extension
Stine, Alexander, San Francisco State University
Stover, Susan G., University of Kansas
Straight, William, Northern Virginia Community College - Loudoun Campus
Straub, Kyle M., Tulane University
Straw, Byron, University of Northern Colorado
Stright, Lisa, University of Utah
Strout, Charles R., Eastern Washington University
Student, James J., Central Michigan University
Stumpf, Andrew , Illinois State University
Suchy, Daniel R., University of Kansas
Sundell, Ander, College of Western Idaho
Sundell, Kent A., Casper College
Sunderlin, David, Lafayette College
Suszek, Thomas J., University of Wisconsin, Oshkosh
Swyrtek, Sheila M., Mott Community College
Söllner, Frank, Ludwig-Maximilians-Universitaet Muenchen
Tajik, Atieh, Georgia State University
Tamish, Mohamed M., Alexandria University
Tapanila, Lori, Idaho State University
Tassier-Surine, Stephanie, Iowa Dept of Natural Resources
Tavis, Anthony, Geological Survey of Alabama
Taylor, Carolyn, Mesa Community College
Taylor, Chuck J., University of Kentucky
Taylor, Penny M., Mount Holyoke College
Taylor, Sid, Saint Francis Xavier University
Tetrault, Denis, University of Windsor
Thole, Jeffrey T., Macalester College
Thomas, Margaret A., Dept of Energy and Environmental Protection
Thomas, William A., Geological Survey of Alabama
Thorleifson, Harvey, University of Minnesota, Twin Cities
Thornberry-Ehrlich, Trista L., Colorado State University
Thul, David, University of Utah
Timmons, Michael, New Mexico Institute of Mining & Technology
Timmons, Stacy, New Mexico Institute of Mining & Technology
Tolley, William, Southern Connecticut State University
Tomiæ, Vladimir, University of Zagreb
Toni, Rousine T., Alexandria University
Towery, Brooke L., Pensacola Junior College
Treadwell-Steitz, Carol, Plattsburgh State University (SUNY)
Trewogy, Janis D., Principia College
Tucker, Eva, Pennsylvania State University, Erie
Turbeville, John, MiraCosta College
Turner, Mark, Collin College - Spring Creek Campus

Turner, III, Henry , University of Arkansas, Fayetteville
Tvelia, Sean, Suffolk County Community College, Ammerman Campus
Ugland, Richard, Southern Oregon University
Uzunlar, Nuri, South Dakota School of Mines & Technology
Valenti, Christine, Montclair State University
Van Ry, Mike, California State University, Fullerton
VanDorpe, Paul E., Iowa Dept of Natural Resources
Vickery, Nancy, University of New England
Vidoviæ, Jelena, University of Zagreb
Viens, Rob, Bellevue College
Vig, Pradeep K., Kaskaskia College
Villalobos, Joshua, El Paso Community College
Vinton, Bonita L., Slippery Rock University
Vogel, Marilyn, California State University, Stanislaus
Voigt, Vicki, Missouri Dept of Natural Resources
Vuke, Susan M., Montana Tech of The University of Montana
Wacker, Michael, Florida International University
Wadleigh, Hank, Cypress College
Waggoner, Karen, Midland College
Wakefield, Kelli, Mesa Community College
Wallace, Peter I., Dalhousie University
Walsh, Emily O., University of Iowa
Warter, Marwan A., Division of Geological & Geophysical Surveys
Waugh, John, Tidewater Community College
Webb, Amelinda, George Mason University
Weber, Diane, Illinois Central College
Weber-Diefenbach, Klaus, Ludwig-Maximilians-Universitaet Muenchen
Weborg-Benson, Kimberly, SUNY, Fredonia
Weeden, Lori, University of Massachusetts Lowell
Wein, Agatha, Cuyamaca College
Wenzel, Chris, Eastern Wyoming College
Werhner, Matthew J., Hillsborough Community College
Whatley, Robin L., Columbia College Chicago
Wheeler, Richard, Austin Peay State University
White, Paul, Community College of Rhode Island
Whitehead, James, University of New Brunswick
Whitehill, Matthew, Lake Superior College
Whittier, Michael, California State University, Stanislaus
Whittington, Carla, Highline College
Wiese, Katryn, City College of San Francisco
Wilder, Lee, New Hampshire Geological Survey
Wiley, Thomas J., Oregon Dept of Geology & Mineral Industries
Wilkerson, Christine M., Utah Geological Survey
Willahan, Duane, Gavilan College
Williams, Curtis J., Cypress College
Williams, James H., Missouri University of Science and Technology
Williams, Wayne K., University of Tennessee at Chattanooga
Willis, Grant C., Utah Geological Survey
Willis, Marc, Fullerton College
Willsey, Shawn P., College of Southern Idaho
Wilson, Jeffrey A., University of Michigan
Wolfe, Ben, Metropolitan Community College-Kansas City
Wolkersdorfer, Christian, Ludwig-Maximilians-Universitaet Muenchen
Wolter, Calvin, Iowa Dept of Natural Resources
Wood, Jacqueline, Delgado Community College
Woodall, Debra W., Daytona State College
Woolsey, Jamie, University of Arkansas, Fayetteville
Wortmann, Ulrich B., University of Toronto
Wright, Clay, College of Western Idaho
Wypych, Alicja, Alaska Division of Geological & Geophysical Surveys
Yalcin, Rebecca, Oregon State University
Yan, Y E., Argonne National Laboratory
Yoshida, Glenn, Los Angeles Southwest College
Young, Glen, Missouri Dept of Natural Resources
Young, Jeffrey, University of Manitoba
Zabel, Garrett E., Colorado Mountain College
Zabielski, Victor, Northern Virginia Community College - Alexandria
Zanetti, Kathleen, University of Nevada, Las Vegas
Zawiskie, John M., Wayne State University
Zayac, John M., Los Angeles Pierce College
Zeithöfler, Matthias, Ludwig-Maximilians-Universitaet Muenchen
Zentner, Nick, Central Washington University
Zhang, Chunfu, Fort Hays State University
Zimmer, Brian, Appalachian State University
Zurawski, Ronald P., Tennessee Geological Survey

Archaeological Geology

Abreu, Maria E., Universidade de Trás-os-Montes e Alto Douro
Adams, Kenneth, University of Nevada, Reno
Adovasio, James M., Mercyhurst University
Anderson, Jonathan H., Minnesota State University
Ballard, Robert D., University of Rhode Island
Besonen, Mark, Texas A&M University, Corpus Christi
Bowers, Peter, University of Alaska, Fairbanks
Bradford, Joel, Utah Valley University
Buckley, Michael, University of Manchester
Chamberlain, Andrew, University of Manchester
Connolly, Robert P., University of Memphis
Degryse, Patrick, Katholieke Universiteit Leuven
Dix, Justin, University of Southampton

Dugmore, Andrew J., Edinburgh University
Dye, David H., University of Memphis
Elkins, Nichole, Bowling Green State University
Fadem, Cynthia, Earlham College
Farrand, William, University of Michigan
Feibel, Craig S., Rutgers, The State University of New Jersey
Ferguson, Terry A., Wofford College
Ferring, C. Reid, University of North Texas
Garrison, Ervan G., University of Georgia
Greenlee, Diana M., University of Louisiana, Monroe
Gundersen, James N., Wichita State University
Harlow, George E., American Museum of Natural History
Harris, Scott, College of Charleston
Haynes, Jr., C. Vance, University of Arizona
Hayward, Chris L., Edinburgh University
Heinzel, Chad E., University of Northern Iowa
Holliday, Vance, University of Arizona
Iglesias, Cruz, Coruna University
Jones, Jeri L., York College of Pennsylvania
Kelley, Alice R., University of Maine
Koch, Magaly, Boston University
Kvamme, Kenneth L., Boston University
Lee-Gorishti, Yolanda, Southern Connecticut State University
Madsen, David B., Utah Geological Survey
Mandel, Rolfe, University of Kansas
Mandel, Rolfe D., University of Kansas
Martinez-Reyes, Jose, University of Massachusetts, Boston
Mason, Owen, University of Alaska, Fairbanks
Matney, Timothy, University of Akron
Mickelson, Andrew M., University of Memphis
Milne, Brooke, University of Manitoba
Nagaoka, Lisa A., University of North Texas
Page, David, Desert Research Institute
Parish, Ryan M., University of Memphis
Pope, Richard, University of Derby
Rapp, George R., University of Minnesota, Duluth
Reid, Joshua, University of Massachusetts, Boston
Reitz, Elizabeth J., University of Georgia
Rogers, Joe D., West Texas A&M University
Sablock, Peter, Salem State University
Sallu, Susannah, University of Leeds
Sanjurjo, Jorge, Coruna University
Schiffman, Robert A., Bakersfield College
Schirmer, Ron, Minnesota State University
Smith, Jen R., Washington University
Smith, Jennifer R., Washington University in St. Louis
Stafford, C. Russell, Indiana State University
Swyrtek, Sheila, Charles Stewart Mott Community College
Thieme, Donald, Valdosta State University
Tomaso, Matthew S., Montclair State University
van Nest, Julieann, New York State Geological Survey
Vento, Frank, Mercyhurst University
Waters, Michael R., Texas A&M University
Whitney, Sandra, University of Georgia
Wilson, Lucy A., University of New Brunswick Saint John
Wilson, Michael C., Douglas College
Wolverton, Steve, University of North Texas

Environmental Geology

Aden, Douglas , Ohio Dept of Natural Resources
Adentunji, Jacob, University of Derby
Adewoye, Olufunmi A., Ladoke Akintola University of Technology
Adomaitis, D., University of Illinois, Urbana-Champaign
Aharon, Paul, University of Alabama
Akenzua-Adamcyzk, Aiyevbekpen H., University of Benin
Albee-Scott, Steven R., Jackson Community College
Ali, K. Adem, College of Charleston
Amezaga, Jamie, University of Newcastle Upon Tyne
Amin, Shahalam M., Bloomsburg University
Apotsos, Alex, Williams College
Argyilan, Erin, Indiana University Northwest
Ashwood, Tom, Oak Ridge National Laboratory
Babcock, Daphne H., Collin College - Spring Creek Campus
Balogh-Brunstad, Zsuzsanna, Hartwick College
Barone, Jessica, Monroe Community College
Barrett, John, University of Leeds
Bartholemew, Paul, University of New Haven
Bartlett, Wendy, Marietta College
Bartolucci, Valerio, Broward College, Central Campus
Bateman, Ian, University of East Anglia
Beatty, Heather L., Austin Community College District
Bechtel, Timothy D., Franklin and Marshall College
Beebe, Alex, University of South Alabama
Bell, Margaret C., University of Newcastle Upon Tyne
Berg, Richard C., University of Illinois, Urbana-Champaign
Berger, Antony R., Sir Wilfred Grenfell College
Bilanovic, Dragoljub D., Bemidji State University
Binda, Pier L., University of Regina
Bircher, Harry, Youngstown State University
Blakewood, E. G., University of Louisiana at Lafayette

Bogle, Mary Anna, Oak Ridge National Laboratory
Bond, Alan, University of East Anglia
Boss, Stephen K., University of Arkansas, Fayetteville
Bots, Pieter, University of Manchester
Bousenberry, Raymond T., New Jersey Geological Survey
Bradley, J G., State University of New York at Oswego
Brady, Emily S., Edinburgh University
Brake, Sandra S., Indiana State University
Brandon, Nigel, Imperial College
Brandt, Craig, Oak Ridge National Laboratory
Breitmeyer, Ronald J., University of Nevada, Reno
Brinkmann, Robert, Oregon Dept of Geology & Mineral Industries
Brodie, Gregory, University of Tennessee at Chattanooga
Bromily, Geoffrey, Edinburgh University
Brown, Huntting (Hunt), Wright State University
Brown, Kerry, Kingston University
Brown, Thomas W., Austin Community College District
Bryan, Mark, Wayland Baptist University
Budikova, Dagmar, Illinois State University
Budkewitsch, Paul, Brock University
Burke, Ian, University of Leeds
Byerly, Don V., University of Tennessee, Knoxville
Cadet, Eddy, Utah Valley University
Callison, James, Utah Valley University
Caudill, Kimberly S., Hocking College
Chappell, James R., Colorado State University
Chernoff, Barry, Wesleyan University
Cheun, Norman, Kingston University
Chilvers, Jason, University of East Anglia
Clemitshaw, Kevin, University of London, Royal Holloway & Bedford New College
Cloutier, Danielle, Universite Laval
Colegial Gutierrez, Juan D., Universidad Industrial de Santander
Collins, Edward W., University of Texas at Austin, Jackson School of Geosciences
Constantopoulos, James T., Eastern New Mexico University
Cook, Hadrian, Kingston University
Covey, Aaron K., Vanderbilt University
Coxon, Catherine, Trinity College
Croudace, Ian, University of Southampton
Cummins, R. Hays, Miami University
Curry, B. B., University of Illinois, Urbana-Champaign
Curry, B. B., Northern Illinois University
Curry, Gorden, University of Glasgow
Curtis, Arthur C., Oak Ridge National Laboratory
Dallimer, Martin, University of Leeds
Darrah, Thomas, Ohio State University
Davis, R. Laurence, University of New Haven
Davis, Steven J., University of California, Irvine
Dawson, James C., Plattsburgh State University (SUNY)
Day, Brett, University of East Anglia
de Hogg, Jan C., Edinburgh University
Denniston, Rhawn F., Cornell College
deWet, Andrew P., Franklin and Marshall College
Dimmick, Charles W., Central Connecticut State University
Diochon, Amanda, Lakehead University
Downie, Helen, University of Manchester
Duncan, Ian J., University of Texas at Austin
Durrant, Jeffrey O., Brigham Young University
Dyer, Jen, University of Leeds
Eastler, Thomas E., University of Maine - Farmington
Edwards, Robin, Trinity College
Elderfield, Harry, University of Cambridge
Elliott, Susan J., McMaster University
Ellis, Scott R., University of Illinois, Urbana-Champaign
Erdmann, A. L., University of Illinois, Urbana-Champaign
Erdmann, Anne L., University of Illinois
Ettlie, Bradley, University of Illinois, Urbana-Champaign
Eyles, John D., McMaster University
Favas, Paulo J., Universidade de Trás-os-Montes e Alto Douro
Field, Cathryn K., Bowdoin College
Flesken, Luuk, University of Leeds
Florea, Lee J., Ball State University
Foret, Jim, University of Louisiana at Lafayette
Foxon, Tim, University of Leeds
Franco, Aldina, University of East Anglia
Frappier, Amy, Skidmore College
Freile, Deborah, New Jersey City University
Galicki, Stan, Millsaps College
Garstang, Mimi R., Missouri Dept of Natural Resources
Gautam, Tej, Marietta College
Geary, Lindsey, Utica College
Geiger, James W., University of Illinois, Urbana-Champaign
Gidigasu, Solomon S., Kwame Nkrumah University of Science and Technology
Gill, Thomas E., University of Texas, El Paso
Gilligan, Jonathan M., Vanderbilt University
Goetz, Heinrich, Collin College - Preston Ridge Campus
Gomes, Nuno N., Universidade Independente de Angola
Gomezdelcampo, Enrique, Bowling Green State University
Gouldson, Andy, University of Leeds
Graham, Margaret C., Edinburgh University
Grant, Alastair, University of East Anglia

Hanson, Chris, Arizona Geological Survey
Hargreaves, Tom, University of East Anglia
Harris, Ann G., Youngstown State University
Harris, C, Cardiff University
Harris, Jr., Stanley E., Southern Illinois University Carbondale
Harvey, Omar, University of Southern Mississippi
Hasenmueller, Nancy R., indiana University
Havenith, Hans-Balder, Universite de Liege
Hawley, John W., New Mexico Institute of Mining & Technology
Hawley, John W., New Mexico Institute of Mining and Technology
Hedin, Robert S., University of Pittsburgh
Herbert, Bruce, Texas A&M University
Hickey, James, Northwest Missouri State University
Hill, Timothy, University of St. Andrews
Hodell, David, University of Cambridge
Holmes, George, University of Leeds
Hoppie, Bryce W., Minnesota State University
Houston, Robert, Oregon Dept of Geology & Mineral Industries
Howell, Dave, Leicester University
Hubeny, J B., Salem State University
Hudson-Edwards, Karen, Birkbeck College
Humphreys, Robin, College of Charleston
Ioris, Antonio, Edinburgh University
Jackman, Toni K., Wichita State University
Jacobs, Alan M., Youngstown State University
Jamieson, Heather E., Queen's University
Jin, Lixin, University of Texas, El Paso
Johnson, Becky, Texas Christian University
Jones, T, Cardiff University
Jordan, Andy, University of East Anglia
Jovanovic, Vladimir, College of Staten Island
Kairies Beatty, Candace L., Winona State University
Kamber, Balz, Trinity College
Keller, John E., College of Southern Nevada - West Charleston Campus
Ketelle, Richard H., Oak Ridge National Laboratory
Kientop, Greg A., University of Illinois, Urbana-Champaign
Kim, Jonathan, Agency of Natural Resources, Dept of Environmental Conservation
Kipphut, George W., Murray State University
Kirchner, James W., University of California, Berkeley
Kolawole, Lanre L., Ladoke Akintola University of Technology
Krekeler, Mark, Miami University
Kretzschmar, Thomas, Centro de Investigación Científica y de Ed Superior de Ensenada
Lake, Iain, University of East Anglia
Larsen, David, Weber State University
Laskowski, Stanley L., University of Pennsylvania
Last, George V., Pacific Northwest National Laboratory
Le Quere, Corinne, University of East Anglia
Leavell, Daniel N., Ohio State University
Lenczewski, Melissa E., Northern Illinois University
Lene, Gene W., Saint Mary's University
Leventon, Julia, University of Leeds
Lloyd, Jonathan, University of Manchester
Love, David W., New Mexico Institute of Mining and Technology
Love, David W., New Mexico Institute of Mining & Technology
Lundgren, Lawrence W., University of Rochester
Ma, Lina, Oregon Dept of Geology & Mineral Industries
Macadam, John, Exeter University
Madden, Andrew S., University of Oklahoma
Maroto-Valer, Mercedes, Heriot-Watt University
Martin, Scott C., Youngstown State University
Masciocco, Luciano, Università di Torino
Matthews, Robert A., University of California, Davis
May, Michael, Western Kentucky University
Mayer, Margaret, Dine' College
McBeth, Joyce, University of Saskatchewan
McConnell, Robert L., University of Mary Washington
McCullough, Jr., Edgar J., University of Arizona
McDonald, Brenna, Missouri Dept of Natural Resources
McDowell, Robin J., Georgia Perimeter College
McGivern, Tiffany, Utica College
McGlade, Jacqueline, University College London
McKinney, Michael L., University of Tennessee, Knoxville
Metzger, Marc J., Edinburgh University
Meyer, Brian, Georgia State University
Meyer, W. Craig, Los Angeles Pierce College
Middlemiss, Lucie, University of Leeds
Miller, David S., Argonne National Laboratory
Mitre-Salazar, Luis M., Universidad Nacional Autonoma de Mexico
Moloney, Marguerite M., Nicholls State University
Monroy-Sanchez, Jaime I., Universidad Autonoma de Baja California Sur
Moore, Kathryn, Exeter University
Morse, Linda D., College of William & Mary
Mortimer, Robert, University of Leeds
Mouat, David A., Desert Research Institute
Mundie, Ben, Oregon Dept of Geology & Mineral Industries
Newbold, K. B., McMaster University
Newton, Rob, University of Leeds
Nichols, Caitlyn, College of Staten Island
Noffke, Nora, Old Dominion University

Null, E. Jan, San Francisco State University
Oches, Rick, Bentley University
Olson, Neil F., New Hampshire Geological Survey
Omotoso, O. A., University of Ilorin
Orndorff, Richard L., Eastern Washington University
Ortt, Richard A., Maryland Department of Natural Resources
Oyawale, A. A., Obafemi Awolowo University
Paavola, Jouni, University of Leeds
Panko, Andrew W., Brock University
Pate, John, Missouri Dept of Natural Resources
Patenaude, Genevieve, Edinburgh University
Pearce, Jamie R., Edinburgh University
Pearthree, Phil A., Arizona Geological Survey
Perault, David R., Lynchburg College
Perdrial, Nicolas, University of Vermont
Pereira, Alcides C., Universidade de Coimbra
Peterson, Jon W., Hope College
Piotrowski, Alexander, University of Cambridge
Plant, Jane, Imperial College
Pohopien, Kazimierz M., Mt. San Antonio College
Pope, Jeanette K., DePauw University
Potess, Marla, Hardin-Simmons University
Poudel, Durga, University of Louisiana at Lafayette
Pound, Kate S., Saint Cloud State University
Powell, Jane, University of East Anglia
Pratt, Allyn R., Los Alamos National Laboratory
Price, Peter, Missouri Dept of Natural Resources
Punyasena, Surangi, University of Illinois, Urbana-Champaign
Quinn, Claire, University of Leeds
Rahman, Ata U., Austin Community College District
Rasmussen, Patricia, University of Ottawa
Reeves, Donald Matt, University of Alaska, Anchorage
Reid, Brian, University of East Anglia
Rezaie-Boroon, Mohammad H., California State University, Los Angeles
Rice, Thomas L., Cedarville University
Richards, Laura, University of Manchester
Richter, Suzanna L., Franklin and Marshall College
Rizoulis, Athanasios, University of Manchester
Roberts, Sheila M., University of Montana Western
Rogers, William C., West Texas A&M University
Rucklidge, John C., University of Toronto
Ruhl, Laura S., University of Arkansas at Little Rock
Russell, Sally, University of Leeds
Rutter, Nathaniel W., University of Alberta
Sarah, Willig B., University of Pennsylvania
Satow, Christopher, Kingston University
Schleifer, Stanley, York College (CUNY)
Schmidt, Dale R., University of Illinois, Urbana-Champaign
Schneider, Jim, Orange Coast College
Scholtz, Theresa C., Argonne National Laboratory
Schramm, William H., University of Louisiana at Lafayette
Schulte, Kimberly, Georgia Perimeter College
Scott, Robert B., University of Texas at Austin
Segall, Marylin, University of Utah
Sewall, Jacob, Kutztown University of Pennsylvania
Sexton, Philip, The Open University
Sharma, Mukul, Dartmouth College
Shem, Linda M., Argonne National Laboratory
Siemens, Michael A., Missouri Dept of Natural Resources
Simpson, Myrna Joyce S., University of Toronto
Sims, Douglas , College of Southern Nevada - West Charleston Campus
Sirk, Robert A., Austin Peay State University
Skinner, Luke, University of Cambridge
Sloan, Doris, University of California, Berkeley
Slobodnik, Marek, Masaryk University
Smith, Dan, Leicester University
Smith, Jim, University of Portsmouth
Smith, Steve, University of London, Royal Holloway & Bedford New College
Snider, Henry I., Eastern Connecticut State University
Spaeth, Matthew P., University of Illinois, Urbana-Champaign
Spahr, Paul, Ohio Dept of Natural Resources
Spooner, Ian S., Acadia University
Stahle, David W., University of Arkansas, Fayetteville
Stan, Oana, Al. I. Cuza University of Iasi
Stearman, Will, Queensland University of Technology
Steidl, Gregg M., New Jersey Geological Survey
Stevens, Anthony, Montgomery County Community College
Stinger, Lindsay C., University of Leeds
Stoner, Sherri, Missouri Dept of Natural Resources
Stumbea, Dan, Al. I. Cuza University of Iasi
Sturm, Diana, University of South Alabama
Sublette, Kerry, University of Tulsa
Sylvia, Elizabeth R., Maryland Department of Natural Resources
Tank, Ronald W., Lawrence University
Tawabini, Bassam, King Fahd University of Petroleum and Minerals
Taylor, Peter, University of Leeds
Thorpe, Mary S., Del Mar College
Turchyn, Alexandra, University of Cambridge
Turner, Kerry, University of East Anglia
Urquhart, Joanne, Bowdoin College

319

Utgard, Russell O., Ohio State University
Vaezi, Reza, University of Tabriz
van Alstine, James, University of Leeds
Van Horn, Stephen R., Muskingum University
Van Ryswick, Stephen, Maryland Department of Natural Resources
VanGundy, Robert D., University of Virginia College, Wise
Visser, Jenneke, University of Louisiana at Lafayette
Walsh, Maud, Louisiana State University
Wang, Zhi (Luke), California State University, Fresno
Ward, Brent C., Simon Fraser University
Watkinson, Andrew, University of East Anglia
Webb, John A., La Trobe University
Weiss, Dominik, Imperial College
Welling, Tim, Dutchess Community College
White, Sarah Jane, Princeton University
Wilson, Charlie, University of East Anglia
Wilson, Rick I., California Geological Survey
Wolff, Eric, University of Cambridge
Woodbury, Randy J., SUNY, Fredonia
Yiannakoulias, Niko, McMaster University
Young, Michael H., University of Texas at Austin, Jackson School of Geosciences
Young, William, University of Leeds
Yuen, Cheong-yip R., Argonne National Laboratory
Zachos, Louis, University of Mississippi

Geomorphology

, Ros Fatimah M., University of Malaya
Adams, Kenneth D., Desert Research Institute
Adams, Peter N., University of Florida
Allan, Jonathan C., Oregon Dept of Geology & Mineral Industries
Allen, Bruce, New Mexico Institute of Mining & Technology
Allen, Phillip, Frostburg State University
Amidon, Will, Middlebury College
Anders, Alison M., University of Illinois, Urbana-Champaign
Anderson, Robert, University of Colorado
Anderson, Robert S., University of California, Santa Cruz
Anderson, Suzanne, University of Colorado
Antinao, JoseLuis, Desert Research Institute
Aslan, Andres, Colorado Mesa University
Bacon, Steven N., Desert Research Institute
Baker, Sophie, Desert Research Institute
Baker, Victor R., University of Arizona
Baptista, João C., Universidade de Trás-os-Montes e Alto Douro
Barendregt, Rene W., University of Lethbridge
Barnhardt, Michael L., Illinois State Geological Survey
Beget, James E., University of Alaska Fairbanks
Behling, Robert E., West Virginia University
Belliveau, Lindsey, Dept of Energy and Environmental Protection
Benedetti, Michael M., University of North Carolina Wilmington
Bergeron, Normand, Universite du Quebec
Berta, Susan, Indiana State University
Besonen, Mark , Texas A&M University, Corpus Christi
Bierman, Paul R., University of Vermont
Blisniuk, Kim, San Jose State University
Bloom, Arthur L., Cornell University
Bondesan, Aldino, Università degli Studi di Padova
Bookhagen, Bodo, University of California, Santa Barbara
Booth, Adam M., Portland State University
Bradley, William C., University of Colorado
Brocklehurst, Simon, University of Manchester
Brush, Nigel, Ashland University
Bull, William B., University of Arizona
Bullard, Thomas F., Desert Research Institute
Bullard, Tom, University of Nevada, Reno
Burbank, Douglas W., University of California, Santa Barbara
Burke, Raymond M., Humboldt State University
Burton, Jr., Vinston, North Carolina Central University
Caine, T. Nelson, University of Colorado
Campbell, Ian A., University of Alberta
Carson, Robert J., Whitman College
Carton, Alberto, Università degli Studi di Padova
Carver, Gary A., Humboldt State University
Castillon, David A., Missouri State University
Chenoweth, Sean, University of Louisiana, Monroe
Chin, Anne, Texas A&M University
Clark, G. Michael, University of Tennessee, Knoxville
Clark, James A., Wheaton College
Clark, Jeffrey J., Lawrence University
Clark, Marin, University of Michigan
Coates, Donald R., Binghamton University
Colgan, Patrick M., Grand Valley State University
Collins, Brian, University of Washington
Collins, Charles W., University of Wisconsin, Platteville
Coltorti, Mauro, University of Siena
Cooke, M. J., Austin Community College District
Cornwell, Kevin J., California State University, Sacramento
Cotter, Edward, Bucknell University
Cowan, Ellen A., Appalachian State University
Cox, Randel T., University of Memphis
Crosby, Benjamin T., Idaho State University

Currey, Donald R., University of Utah
Dale, Janis, University of Regina
Daly, Julia F., University of Maine - Farmington
Day, Stephanie S., North Dakota State University
Dethier, David P., Williams College
DiBiase, Roman , Pennsylvania State University, University Park
Dietrich, William E., University of California, Berkeley
Dixon, Jean, Montana State University
Dixon, John C., University of Arkansas, Fayetteville
Dodson, Russell L., Mansfield University
Dogwiler, Toby, Winona State University
Dogwiler, Toby J., Illinois State University
Dolan, Robert, University of Virginia
Dort, Jr., Wakefield, University of Kansas
Durbin, James, University of Southern Indiana
Duvall, Alison, University of Washington
Easterbrook, Don J., Western Washington University
Eaton, Lewis S., James Madison University
Edgar, Dorland E., Argonne National Laboratory
Ehlen, Judy, Radford University
Ellis, Jean, University of South Carolina
Ely, Lisa L., Central Washington University
England, John, University of Alberta
Evans, Diane L., Jet Propulsion Laboratory
Fagherazzi, Sergio, Boston University
Farr, Tom G., Jet Propulsion Laboratory
Feeney, Thomas P., Shippensburg University
Finnegan, Noah J., University of California, Santa Cruz
Fontana, Alessandro, Università degli Studi di Padova
Ford, Derek C., McMaster University
Ford, Richard L., Weber State University
Froese, Duane, University of Alberta
Fubelli, Giandomenico, Università di Torino
Furbish, David J., Vanderbilt University
Furlong, Ira E., Bridgewater State University
Gabet, Emmanuel, San Jose State University
Garcia, Antonio F., California Polytechnic State University
Garcia, Marcelo, University of Illinois, Urbana-Champaign
Gardner, Thomas W., Trinity University
Germanoski, Dru, Lafayette College
Ghoneim, Eman, Boston University
Giardino, John R., Texas A&M University
Giardino, Marco, Università di Torino
Giles, David, University of Portsmouth
Gillam, Mary L., Fort Lewis College
Gillespie, Alan, Humboldt State University
Gillespie, Alan R., University of Washington
Gontz, Allen, University of Massachusetts, Boston
Gootee, Brian F., Arizona Geological Survey
Gordon, Steven J., United States Air Force Academy
Gosse, John, University of Kansas
Gran, Karen B., University of Minnesota, Duluth
Guccione, Margaret J., University of Arkansas, Fayetteville
Gutowski, Vincent P., Eastern Illinois University
Hales, TC, Cardiff University
Hallet, Bernard, University of Washington
Hancock, Gregory S., College of William & Mary
Hansen, Edward C., Hope College
Hanson, Lindley S., Salem State University
Hanson, Paul, Unversity of Nebraska - Lincoln
Harbor, David J., Washington & Lee University
Harper, Stephen B., East Carolina University
Harrington, Charles D., Los Alamos National Laboratory
Harrison, Bruce I., New Mexico Institute of Mining and Technology
Hasbargen, Leslie E., SUNY, Oneonta
Haughland, Jake, University of Nevada, Reno
Heitmuller, Frank, University of Southern Mississippi
Hesp, Patrick, Flinders University
Hesp, Patrick A., Louisiana State University
Higgins, Charles G., University of California, Davis
Hooke, Roger L., University of Maine
Hooks, W. Gary, University of Alabama
Hopkins, Kenneth D., University of Northern Colorado
Howard, Alan D., University of Virginia
Humphrey, Neil F., University of Wyoming
Hungr, Oldrich, University of British Columbia
Hyatt, James A., Eastern Connecticut State University
Isacks, Bryan L., Cornell University
Jerolmack, Douglas, University of Pennsylvania
Jiron, Rebecca, College of William & Mary
Kaufman, Darrell S., Northern Arizona University
Kehew, Alan E., Western Michigan University
Keller, Edward A., University of California, Santa Barbara
Kelsey, Harvey M., Humboldt State University
Kemmerly, Phillip R., Austin Peay State University
Kendrick, Katherine J., University of California, Riverside
Kenny, Ray, Fort Lewis College
Kershaw, G. Peter, University of Alberta
Kirwan, Matthew L., College of William & Mary
Kite, J. Steven, West Virginia University

Knott, Jeffrey R., California State University, Fullerton
Kochel, R. Craig, Bucknell University
Kowaleski, Douglas, University of Massachusetts, Amherst
Kowalewski, Douglas E., Worcester State University
Krautblatter, Michael, Technische Universitaet Muenchen
Krieg, Joseph, Minot State University
Laabs, Benjamin J., SUNY, Geneseo
Lamb, Michael P., California Institute of Technology
Lancaster, Nicholas, Desert Research Institute
Lancaster, Nick, University of Nevada, Reno
Larsen, Isaac J., University of Massachusetts, Amherst
Larson, Phillip H., Minnesota State University
Lasca, Norman, University of Wisconsin, Milwaukee
Lattman, Lawrence H., New Mexico Institute of Mining and Technology
Lehre, Andre K., Humboldt State University
Leith, Kerry, Technische Universitaet Muenchen
Lemke, Karen A., University of Wisconsin, Stevens Point
Li, Junran, University of Tulsa
Lifton, Nathaniel A., Purdue University
Linneman, Scott R., Western Washington University
Lips, Elliott W., University of Utah
Londono, Ana, Saint Louis University
Long, Ann D., University of Illinois, Urbana-Champaign
Loring, Arthur P., York College (CUNY)
MacGregor, Kelly, Macalester College
Madej, Mary Ann, Humboldt State University
Mamot, Philipp, Technische Universitaet Muenchen
Marchant, David R., Boston University
Marchetti, David W., Western State Colorado University
Marshall, Jeffrey S., California State Polytechnic University, Pomona
McCoy, Scott W., University of Nevada, Reno
McDowell, Patricia F., University of Oregon
McKenney, Rosemary, Pacific Lutheran University
McMillan, Margaret E., University of Arkansas at Little Rock
McPherson, Harry J., University of Alberta
Menking, Kirsten M., Vassar College
Merritts, Dorothy J., Franklin and Marshall College
Meyer, Grant A., University of New Mexico
Miao, Xiaodong, University of Illinois, Urbana-Champaign
Michaud, Yves, Universite du Quebec
Miller, Jerry R., Western Carolina University
Miller, Thomas E., University of Puerto Rico
Misner, Tamara, Edinboro University of Pennsylvania
Montgomery, David R., University of Washington
Moore, Andrew, Earlham College
Moore, Laura J., University of North Carolina, Chapel Hill
Moorman, Brian J., University of Calgary
Moosavi, Sadredin (Dean), Gustavus Adolphus College
Morgan, Daniel J., Vanderbilt University
Moscardelli, Lorena G., University of Texas at Austin
Mossa, Joann, University of Florida
Mount, Jeffrey F., University of California, Davis
Mozzi, Paolo, Università degli Studi di Padova
Musselman, Zachary A., Millsaps College
Mylroie, John E., Mississippi State University
Namikas, Steven, Louisiana State University
Napieralski, Jacob, University of Michigan, Dearborn
Nash, David, University of Cincinnati
Nelson, Daren T., University of North Carolina, Pembroke
Nelson, Gerald E., Casper College
Nelson, Robert S., Illinois State University
Netoff, Dennis I., Sam Houston State University
Neubeck, William S., Union College
Newton, Robert M., Smith College
Nichols, Kyle K., Skidmore College
Nielsen, Dennis N., Winona State University
Nikitina, Daria L., West Chester University
Nittrouer, Jeffrey A., Rice University
Okunade, Samuel, Central State University
Olsen, Paul E., Columbia University
ONeal, Michael, University of Delaware
Orme, Amalie, California State University, Northridge
Osborn, Gerald D., University of Calgary
Oskin, Michael, University of California, Davis
Ouimet, William, University of Connecticut
Oviatt, Charles G., Kansas State University
Owen, Lewis, University of Cincinnati
Parker, Gary, University of Illinois, Urbana-Champaign
Patton, Peter C., Wesleyan University
Pavlowsky, Robert T., Missouri State University
Pazzaglia, Frank J., Lehigh University
Pearthree, Philip A., Arizona Geological Survey
Pederson, Joel L., Utah State University
Pelletier, Jon D., University of Arizona
Perron, Taylor, Massachusetts Institute of Technology
Perry, Randall H., SUNY, Fredonia
Phillips, Andrew C., Illinois State Geological Survey
Phillips, William M., University of Idaho
Pierce, Jen, Boise State University

Pinter, Nicholas, University of California, Davis
Pitlick, John, University of Colorado
Pizzuto, James E., University of Delaware
Plug, Lawrence, Dalhousie University
Polk, Jason, Western Kentucky University
Pope, Gregory A., Montclair State University
Potter, Jr., Noel, Dickinson College
Rayburn, John A., SUNY, New Paltz
Rech, Jason, Miami University
Reed, Denise J., University of New Orleans
Refsnider, Kurt, Prescott College
Reid, Leslie, Humboldt State University
Reneau, Steven L., Los Alamos National Laboratory
Renwick, William, Miami University
Rhoads, Bruce, University of Illinois, Urbana-Champaign
Rhodes, Dallas D., Georgia Southern University
Rice-Snow, R. Scott, Ball State University
Ringe, L. Don, Central Washington University
Rittenour, Tammy M., Utah State University
Ritter, John B., Wittenberg University
Robinson, Cordula, Boston University
Rockwell, Thomas K., San Diego State University
Roering, Joshua J., University of Oregon
Rogerson, Robert J., University of Lethbridge
Rossi, Matthew, Northwestern University
Savina, Mary E., Carleton College
Sawyer, Carol F., University of South Alabama
Schaller, Mirjam, University of Michigan
Schiefer, Erik, Northern Arizona University
Schmidt, Amanda H., Oberlin College
Schmutz, Phillip P., University of West Florida
Shepherd, Stephanie , Auburn University
Shreve, Ronald L., University of California, Los Angeles
Shroder, Jr., John F., University of Nebraska at Omaha
Sklar, Leonard, San Francisco State University
Snead, John I., Louisiana State University
Snyder, Jeffrey A., Bowling Green State University
Souch, Catherine J., Indiana University, Indianapolis
Springer, Gregory S., Ohio University
Springston, George E., Norwich University
Stine, Scott W., California State University, East Bay
Stokes, Martin, University of Plymouth
Straffin, Eric, Edinboro University of Pennsylvania
Strasser, Jeffrey C., Augustana College
Summerfield, Michael A., Edinburgh University
Surian, Nicola, Università degli Studi di Padova
Székely, Balázs, Eotvos Lorand University
Taylor, Stephen B., Western Oregon University
Tchakerian, Vatche P., Texas A&M University
Ten Brink, Norman W., Grand Valley State University
Thorson, Robert M., University of Connecticut
Tidwell, David, Geological Survey of Alabama
Tomkin, Jonathan H., University of Illinois, Urbana-Champaign
Toy, Terrence J., University of Denver
Tranel, Lisa, Illinois State University
Trenhaile, Alan S., University of Windsor
Triplett, Laura, Gustavus Adolphus College
Tucker, Greg E., University of Colorado
van Dijk, Deanna, Calvin College
Vandeberg, Gregory S., University of North Dakota
Vidal Romani, Juan Ramon, Coruna University
Vitek, Jack, Texas A&M University
Vitek, John D., Oklahoma State University
Wakabayashi, John, California State University, Fresno
Walters, James C., University of Northern Iowa
Ward, Dylan, University of Cincinnati
Wayne, William, University of Nebraska, Lincoln
Webb, Robert H., University of Arizona
Wegmann, Karl, North Carolina State University
Weirich, Frank H., University of Iowa
Werner, Bradley T., University of California, San Diego
Whisner, Jennifer B., Bloomsburg University
White, Susan Q., La Trobe University
Whiting, Peter J., Case Western Reserve University
Wickert, Andrew, University of Minnesota, Twin Cities
Wilcock, Peter W., Johns Hopkins University
Wilcox, Andrew, University of Montana
Willenbring, Jane, University of Pennsylvania
Williams, Harry F. L., University of North Texas
Williams, Kevin K., Buffalo State College
Wilson, Fred L., Angelo State University
Wilson, Greg C., Grand Valley State University
Wilson, Monte D., Boise State University
Wohl, Ellen E., Colorado State University
Wolken, Gabriel J., Alaska Division of Geological & Geophysical Surveys
Wood, Spencer H., Boise State University
Wynn, Elizabeth Anne, Geological Survey of Alabama
Yanites, Brian J., University of Idaho
Yeh, Joseph S., University of Texas at Austin, Jackson School of Geosciences
Youberg, Ann, Arizona Geological Survey

Young, Jeri J., Arizona Geological Survey
Young, Richard A., SUNY, Geneseo

Glacial Geology

Aber, James S., Emporia State University
Alley, Richard B., Pennsylvania State University, University Park
Andrews, John T., University of Colorado
Angle, Michael , Ohio Dept of Natural Resources
Arnaud, Emmanuelle, University of Guelph
Attig, John W., University of Wisconsin, Extension
Baker, Robert W., University of Wisconsin, River Falls
Balogh, Richard S., Antelope Valley College
Barclay, David J., SUNY, Cortland
Berthold, Angela, University of Minnesota
Bevis, Kenneth A., Hanover College
Bird, Brian, New York State Geological Survey
Birkel, Sean, University of Maine
Blake, Kevin, Eastern Michigan University
Blankenship, Donald D., University of Texas at Austin
Borns, Jr., Harold W., University of Maine
Brigham-Grette, Julie, University of Massachusetts, Amherst
Briner, Jason P., SUNY, Buffalo
Bromley, Gordon R., University of Maine
Brook, Edward J., Washington State University
Broster, Bruce E., University of New Brunswick
Brown, Steven E., University of Illinois, Urbana-Champaign
Brugger, Keith A., University of Minnesota, Morris
Calkin, Parker, SUNY, Buffalo
Campbell, Seth W., University of Maine
Carlson, Anders, Oregon State University
Carson, Eric C., University of Wisconsin, Extension
Clague, John J., Simon Fraser University
Clark, Douglas H., Western Washington University
Clark, Peter U., Oregon State University
Clayton, Lee, University of Wisconsin, Extension
Clebnik, Sherman M., Eastern Connecticut State University
Cotter, James F., University of Minnesota, Morris
Crossen, Kristine J., University of Alaska, Anchorage
Davis, P. Thompson, Bentley University
Dengler, Elizabeth, University of Minnesota
Denton, George H., University of Maine
Douglass, Daniel, Northeastern University
Dupont, Todd, Miami University
Enderlin, Ellyn M., University of Maine
Evenson, Edward B., Lehigh University
Eyles, Nicholas, University of Toronto
Fisher, Timothy G., Indiana University / Purdue University, Indianapolis
Fisher, Timothy G., University of Toledo
Fleisher, P. Jay, SUNY, Oneonta
Flowers, Gwenn, Simon Fraser University
Fountain, Andrew G., Portland State University
Franzi, David A., Plattsburgh State University (SUNY)
Goldstein, Barry, University of Puget Sound
Gowan, Angela, University of Minnesota
Hall, Brenda L., University of Maine
Ham, Nelson R., Saint Norbert College
Hansel, Ardith K., Illinois State Geological Survey
Harper, Joel, University of Montana
Hawley, Robert L., Dartmouth College
Hicock, Stephen R., Western University
Hooke, Roger L., University of Minnesota, Twin Cities
Hooyer, Thomas S., University of Wisconsin, Milwaukee
Horton, Jennifer, University of Minnesota
Hughes, Terence J., University of Maine
Hughes III, Richard O., Crafton Hills College
Hulbe, Christina L., Portland State University
Iverson, Neal R., Iowa State University of Science & Technology
Jennings, Carrie E., University of Minnesota, Twin Cities
Jiskoot, Hester, University of Lethbridge
Johnson, Beth , University of Wisconsin Colleges
Johnson, James B., Colorado Mesa University
Kaplan, Michael, Columbia University
Karrow, Paul, University of Waterloo
Kelly, Meredith, Dartmouth College
Kiver, Eugene P., Eastern Washington University
Knaeble, Alan, University of Minnesota
Kozlowski, Andrew, New York State Geological Survey
Lamothe, Michel, Universite du Quebec a Montreal
Larour, Eric Y., SUNY, Buffalo
Lea, Peter D., Bowdoin College
Lempe, Bernhard, Technische Universitaet Muenchen
Leonard, Eric M., Colorado College
Levson, Victor M., University of Victoria
Lewis, Adam R., North Dakota State University
Licciardi, Joseph M., University of New Hampshire
Licht, Kathy J., Indiana University / Purdue University, Indianapolis
Loope, Henry, indiana University
Lowell, Thomas V., University of Cincinnati
Lusardi, Barb, University of Minnesota
Marcott, Shaun, University of Wisconsin, Madison

Marshall, Katherine, University of Minnesota
McCarthy, Daniel P., Brock University
McKay III, E. Donald, University of Illinois, Urbana-Champaign
McKenzie, Garry D., Ohio State University
Menzies, John, Brock University
Meyer, Gary, University of Minnesota
Mickelson, David M., University of Wisconsin, Madison
Mode, William N., University of Wisconsin, Oshkosh
Mooers, Howard, University of Minnesota, Duluth
Morgan, Alan V., University of Waterloo
Munroe, Jeffrey S., Middlebury College
Nguyen, Maurice, University of Minnesota
Pair, Donald, University of Dayton
Parent, Michel, Universite du Quebec
Porter, Stephen C., University of Washington
Putkonen, Jaakko, University of North Dakota
Putnam, Aaron E., University of Maine
Retelle, Michael J., Bates College
Rexius, James E., Schoolcraft College
Ridge, John C., Tufts University
Rodbell, Donald T., Union College
Roy, Martin, Universite du Quebec a Montreal
Rutford, Robert H., University of Texas, Dallas
Rysgaard, Soren, University of Manitoba
Schneider, Allan F., University of Wisconsin, Parkside
Schulz, Layne D., South Dakota Dept of Environment and Natural Resources
Sharp, Martin J., University of Alberta
Shaw, John, University of Alberta
Spencer, Matt, Lake Superior State University
Staley, Amie, University of Minnesota
Stanford, Loudon R., University of Idaho
Stanford, Scott D., New Jersey Geological Survey
Stansell, Nathan D., Northern Illinois University
Steig, Eric J., University of Washington
Stewart, Alexander K., St. Lawrence University
Stumpf, Andrew J., Illinois State Geological Survey
Stumpf, Andrew J., University of Illinois, Urbana-Champaign
Swanger, Kate, University of Massachusetts Lowell
Syverson, Kent M., University of Wisconsin, Eau Claire
Szymanski, Jason, Monroe Community College
Tary, Anna K., Bentley University
Taylor, Lawrence D., Albion College
Thackray, Glenn D., Idaho State University
Thompson, Lonnie G., Ohio State University
Thorleifson, Harvey, University of Minnesota
Todd, Claire E., Pacific Lutheran University
Totten, Stanley M., Hanover College
Tulaczyk, Slawek, University of California, Santa Cruz
Wagner, Kaleb, University of Minnesota
Wake, Cameron P., University of New Hampshire
Weddle, Thomas K., Dept of Agriculture, Conservation, and Forestry
Weibel, C. P., University of Illinois, Urbana-Champaign
Weldon, Elise M., University of Oregon
Werner, Alan, Mount Holyoke College
Westgate, John A., University of Toronto
Whorton, Erin, Alaska Division of Geological & Geophysical Surveys
Wilch, Thomas I., Albion College
Wiles, Gregory C., College of Wooster
Witte, Ronald W., New Jersey Geological Survey
Wright, Jr., Herbert E., University of Minnesota, Twin Cities
Zoet, Lucas, University of Wisconsin, Madison

Marine Geology

Abrams, Lewis J., University of North Carolina Wilmington
Aiello, Ivano, Moss Landing Marine Laboratories
Aksu, Ali E., Memorial University of Newfoundland
Allen, Katherine A., University of Maine
Aluwihare, Lihini I., University of California, San Diego
Anders, Tania-Maria, Texas A&M University, Corpus Christi
Anderson, John B., Rice University
Austin, Jr., James A., University of Texas at Austin
Bacchus, Tania S., Johnson State College
Bangs, Nathan L., University of Texas at Austin
Barclay, Andrew, University of Washington
Barrie, Vaughn, University of Victoria
Bartek, III, Louis R., University of North Carolina, Chapel Hill
Becel, Anne, Columbia University
Belknap, Daniel F., University of Maine
Benoit-Bird, Kelly, Oregon State University
Bentley, Samuel J., Louisiana State University
Brooks, Gregg R., Eckerd College
Brown, Kevin M., University of California, San Diego
Browne, Kathleen M., Rider University
Buffler, Richard T., University of Texas at Austin
Byrne, John V., Oregon State University
Calmus, Thierry, Universidad Nacional Autonoma de Mexico
Carson, Bobb, Lehigh University
Chase, Richard L., University of British Columbia
Cleary, William J., University of North Carolina Wilmington
Coffroth, Mary Alice, SUNY, Buffalo

Conway, Flaxen D., Oregon State University
Cook, Ann, Ohio State University
Crone, Timothy, Columbia University
Cruz-Orozco, Rodolfo, Universidad Autonoma de Baja California Sur
Curray, Joseph R., University of California, San Diego
De Deckker, Patrick, Australian National University
Delaney, John R., University of Washington
Dobson, David M., Guilford College
Donnelly, Jeffrey, Woods Hole Oceanographic Institution
Donoghue, Joseph F., Florida State University
Driscoll, Neal W., University of California, San Diego
Dugan, Brandon, Rice University
Edwards, Margo H., University of Hawai'i, Manoa
Ferland, Marie A., Central Washington University
Fialko, Yuri A., University of California, San Diego
Flood, Roger D., SUNY, Stony Brook
Fornari, Daniel J., Woods Hole Oceanographic Institution
Freeman-Lynde, Raymond, University of Georgia
Freitas, Maria da Conceição P., Universidade de Lisboa
Fryer, Patricia B., University of Hawai'i, Manoa
Fulthorpe, Craig S., University of Texas at Austin
Gee, Jeffrey S., University of California, San Diego
Georgen, Jennifer, Florida State University
Georgen, Jennifer, Old Dominion University
Giosan, Liviu, Woods Hole Oceanographic Institution
Goes, Joaquim, Columbia University
Goff, John A., University of Texas at Austin
Goni, Miguel A., Oregon State University
Gonzalez-Fernandez, Antonio, Centro de Investigación Científica y de Ed
    Superior de Ensenada
Grabowski, Jonathan, Northeastern University
Greene, H. Gary, Moss Landing Marine Laboratories
Greenstein, Benjamin J., Cornell College
Guerin, Gilles, Columbia University
Guth, Peter L., United States Naval Academy
Haggerty, Janet, University of Tulsa
Hanes, Daniel, Saint Louis University
Harris, Robert N., University of Utah
Harte, Michael, Oregon State University
Humphris, Susan E., Woods Hole Oceanographic Institution
Jacobson, Gary L., Grossmont College
Jarrard, Richard D., University of Utah
Johnson, Harlan P., University of Washington
Johnson, Joel E., University of New Hampshire
Juraèiæ, Mladen, University of Zagreb
Kaminski, Michael, King Fahd University of Petroleum and Minerals
Katuna, Michael P., College of Charleston
Kearney, Micheal S., University of Maryland
Keller, Randall A., Oregon State University
Kelley, Joseph T., University of Maine
Kienast, Stephanie, Dalhousie University
Klasik, John A., California State Polytechnic University, Pomona
Klaus, Adam, Texas A&M University
Kroenke, Loren W., University of Hawai'i, Manoa
Laine, Edward P., Bowdoin College
Lasker, Howard R., SUNY, Buffalo
Leonard, Lynn A., University of North Carolina Wilmington
Lindo Atichati, David, College of Staten Island
Liu, Jingpu P., North Carolina State University
Lonsdale, Peter F., University of California, San Diego
MacLeod, C, Cardiff University
Malinverno, Alberto , Columbia University
Mallinson, David, East Carolina University
Manfrino, Carrie M., Kean University
Mayer, Larry A., University of New Hampshire
McCoy, Jr., Floyd W., University of Hawai'i, Manoa
Meadows, Guy A., Michigan Technological University
Mercer, James A., University of Washington
Meylan, Maurice A., University of Southern Mississippi
Micallef, Aaron, University of Malta
Miller, Kenneth G., Rutgers, The State University of New Jersey
Miot da Silva, Graziela, Flinders University
Mitchell, Neil, University of Manchester
Moberly, Ralph, University of Hawai'i, Manoa
Mountain, Gregory S., Rutgers, The State University of New Jersey
Moy, Christopher M., University of Otago
Naehr, Thomas H., Texas A&M University, Corpus Christi
Neumann, A. Conrad, University of North Carolina, Chapel Hill
Nicholson, David, Woods Hole Oceanographic Institution
Nitsche, Frank, Columbia University
Nittrouer, Charles A., University of Washington
Norris, Richard D., University of California, San Diego
Offerman, Katherine, Maryland Department of Natural Resources
Olayiwola, M. A., Obafemi Awolowo University
Overbeck, Jaquelyn , Division of Geological & Geophysical Surveys
Patton, Jason R., Humboldt State University
Peeters, Frank, VU University Amsterdam
Peterson, Larry C., University of Miami
Phipps, James B., Grays Harbor College
Piper, David J., Dalhousie University

Pisias, Nicklas, Oregon State University
Portner, Ryan A., Worcester State University
Pratt, Thomas, University of Washington
Raphael, Constantine N., Eastern Michigan University
Rasmussen, Kenneth, Northern Virginia Community College - Annandale
Rea, David K., University of Michigan
Reed, Donald L., San Jose State University
Richardson, Mary Jo, Texas A&M University
Richaud, Mathieu, California State University, Fresno
Riggs, Stanley R., East Carolina University
Rodolfo, Kelvin S., University of Illinois at Chicago
Rose, Kathryn, Woods Hole Oceanographic Institution
Ross, David A., Woods Hole Oceanographic Institution
Ruddiman, William F., University of Virginia
Scher, Howie, University of South Carolina
Schmalz, Robert F., Pennsylvania State University, University Park
Schwartz, David, Cabrillo College
Simms, Alex, University of California, Santa Barbara
Skarke, Adam, Mississippi State University
Slovinsky, Peter, Dept of Agriculture, Conservation, and Forestry
Soule, S. Adam, Woods Hole Oceanographic Institution
Stea, Ralph, Dalhousie University
Treude, Tina, University of California, Los Angeles
Tucholke, Brian E., Woods Hole Oceanographic Institution
Van Andel, Tjeerd H., Stanford University
Vannucchi, Paola, University of London, Royal Holloway & Bedford New College
Ward, Larry G., University of New Hampshire
Watts, Tony, University of Oxford
Wehmiller, John F., University of Delaware
Wheeler, Andy J., University College Cork
Wilcock, William S., University of Washington
Wilson, Gary S., University of Otago
Winguth, Cornelia, University of Texas, Arlington

Mineralogy & Crystallography
Abbott, Richard N., Appalachian State University
Abdu, Yassir, University of Manitoba
Aber, Susan W., Emporia State University
Ague, Jay J., Yale University
Akgul, Bünyamin, Firat University
Alderton, Dave, University of London, Royal Holloway & Bedford New College
Aldushin, Kirill, Ludwig-Maximilians-Universitaet Muenchen
Alfe, Dario, University College London
Altaner, Stephen P., University of Illinois, Urbana-Champaign
Angel, Ross J., Virginia Polytechnic Institute & State University
Apopei, Andrei I., Al. I. Cuza University of Iasi
Arletti, Rossella, Università di Torino
Artioli, Gilberto, Università degli Studi di Padova
Ball, Neil, University of Manitoba
Bassett, William A., Cornell University
Bayliss, Peter, University of Calgary
Beg, Mirza A., Geological Survey of Alabama
Belluso, Elena, Università di Torino
Benna, Piera, Università di Torino
Bermanec, Vladimir, University of Zagreb
Bish, David L., Indiana University, Bloomington
Bladh, Kenneth W., Wittenberg University
Blanchard, Frank N., University of Florida
Bloss, F. Donald, Virginia Polytechnic Institute & State University
Bonhoure, Jessica, Institut Polytechnique LaSalle Beauvais (ex-IGAL)
Boutilier, Robert F., Bridgewater State University
Boysen, Hans, Ludwig-Maximilians-Universitaet Muenchen
Braund, Emilie, University of Portsmouth
Brearley, Adrian J., University of New Mexico
Brown, Cathe, Smithsonian Institution / National Museum of Natural History
Brown, Jr., Gordon E., Stanford University
Bruno, Emiliano, Università di Torino
Bruno, Marco, Università di Torino
Burger, Paul V., University of New Mexico
Burnham, Charles, Fort Lewis College
Burnham, Charles W., Harvard University
Burns, Peter C., University of Notre Dame
Butler, Shane K., University of Illinois, Urbana-Champaign
Buzatu, Andrei, Al. I. Cuza University of Iasi
Buzgar, Nicolae, Al. I. Cuza University of Iasi
Camara Artigas, Fernando, Università di Torino
Capella, Silvana, Università di Torino
Cardellach López, Esteve, Universitat Autonoma de Barcelona
Carl, James D., SUNY Potsdam
Carrigan, Charles W., Olivet Nazarene University
Casas Duocastella, Lluís, Universitat Autonoma de Barcelona
Catlos, Elizabeth J., University of Texas at Austin
Chakhmouridian, Anton, University of Manitoba
Chen, Ning, University of Saskatchewan
Chiarenzelli, Jeffrey R., St. Lawrence University
Choi, Seon-Gyu, Korea University
Cilliers, Johannes, Imperial College
Clement, Stephen C., College of William & Mary
Cody, Robert, Iowa State University of Science & Technology
Cofer, Harland E., Georgia Southwestern State University

Paquette, Jeanne, McGill University
Parise, John B., SUNY, Stony Brook
Park, Sohyun, Ludwig-Maximilians-Universitaet Muenchen
Pascoe, Richard, Exeter University
Pattrick, Richard, University of Manchester
Peacor, Donald R., University of Michigan
Pentcheva, Rossitza, Ludwig-Maximilians-Universitaet Muenchen
Peterson, Ronald C., Queen's University
Phillips, Brian L., SUNY, Stony Brook
Phillips, William R., Brigham Young University
Piniella Febrer, Juan Francesc, Universitat Autonoma de Barcelona
Pope, Lin F., University of Southern Mississippi
Post, Jeffrey E., Smithsonian Institution / National Museum of Natural History
Potter, Lee S., University of Northern Iowa
Prencipe, Mauro, Università di Torino
Price, David, University College London
Pöllmann, Herbert, Martin-Luther-Universitaet Halle-Wittenberg
Radcliffe, Dennis, Hofstra University
Raimund, Rentel, University of the Free State
Raudsepp, Mati, University of British Columbia
Redfern, Simon, University of Cambridge
Renock, Devon, Dartmouth College
Reuss, Robert L., Tufts University
Ribbe, Paul H., Virginia Polytechnic Institute & State University
Rickaby, Ros, University of Oxford
Riedel, Oliver, Ludwig-Maximilians-Universitaet Muenchen
Rigault de la Longrais, Germano, Università di Torino
Robinson, George W., St. Lawrence University
Robinson, Paul D., Southern Illinois University Carbondale
Rocholl, Alexander, Ludwig-Maximilians-Universitaet Muenchen
Rojas-Soriano, Humberto, Universidad Autonoma de Baja California Sur
Rosenberg, Philip E., Washington State University
Ross, Nancy L., Virginia Polytechnic Institute & State University
Rossman, George R., California Institute of Technology
Rouse, Roland C., University of Michigan
Rubbo, Marco, Università di Torino
Rubio-Sierra, Javier, Ludwig-Maximilians-Universitaet Muenchen
Rutstein, Martin S., SUNY, New Paltz
Sablock, Jeanette M., Salem State University
Salviulo, Gabriella, Università degli Studi di Padova
Schmahl, Wolfgang, Ludwig-Maximilians-Universitaet Muenchen
Schneer, Cecil J., University of New Hampshire
Schneider, Julius, Ludwig-Maximilians-Universitaet Muenchen
Schroeder, Paul A., University of Georgia
Scott Smith, Barbara H., University of British Columbia
Secco, Luciano, Università degli Studi di Padova
Seid, Mary J., University of Illinois, Urbana-Champaign
Sethi, Parvinder S., Radford University
Shank, Stephen G., Pennsylvania Bureau of Topographic & Geologic Survey
Sharp, Thomas G., Arizona State University
Sharp, W. Edwin, University of South Carolina
Shen, Guoyin, Carnegie Institution of Washington
Sherriff, Barbara L., University of Manitoba
Shuller-Nickles, Lindsay C., Clemson University
Sicard, Karri R., Division of Geological & Geophysical Surveys
Silvestri, Alberta, Università degli Studi di Padova
Simmons, Stuart, University of Utah
Simmons, William B., University of New Orleans
Simmons, William B., University of Michigan
Singer, David M., Kent State University
Skinner, H. Catherine W., Yale University
Skoda, Radek, Masaryk University
Smith, Michael S., University of North Carolina Wilmington
Smyth, Joseph R., University of Colorado
Snow, Eleanour, University of South Florida, Tampa
Sokolova, Elena, University of Manitoba
Solorio-Munguia, Jose G., Universidad Nacional Autonoma de Mexico
Spieler, Oliver, Ludwig-Maximilians-Universitaet Muenchen
Spilde, Michael N., University of New Mexico
Stark, Robert, Ludwig-Maximilians-Universitaet Muenchen
Stefano, Christopher J., Michigan Technological University
Strasser, Stefan, Ludwig-Maximilians-Universitaet Muenchen
Summers, Sara, Weber State University
Swope, R. J., Indiana University / Purdue University, Indianapolis
Tait, Kimberly T., Royal Ontario Museum
Tettenhorst, Rodney T., Ohio State University
Tibljaš, Darko, University of Zagreb
Tomašiæ, Nenad, University of Zagreb
Trixler, Frank, Ludwig-Maximilians-Universitaet Muenchen
Twelker, Evan I., Division of Geological & Geophysical Surveys
Uzochukwu, Godfrey A., North Carolina Agricultural & Tech State University
van Hees, Edmond H., Wayne State University
Vassiliou, Andreas H., Rutgers, The State University of New Jersey, Newark
Vaughan, David, University of Manchester
Vernon, William W., Dickinson College
Vocadlo, Lidunka, University College London
Walker, Jeffrey R., Vassar College
Walther, Ferdinand, Ludwig-Maximilians-Universitaet Muenchen
Warner, Richard D., Clemson University
Webb, Christine, Smithsonian Institution / National Museum of Natural History

Weinbruch, Stephan, Technische Universitaet Darmstadt
Wenk, Hans-Rudolf, University of California, Berkeley
Werdon, Melanie B., Division of Geological & Geophysical Surveys
Wicks, Frederick J., University of Toronto
Wicks, Frederick J., Royal Ontario Museum
Wilson, James R., Weber State University
Winchell, Robert E., California State University, Long Beach
Wise, Michael A., University of New Orleans
Wise, Michael A., Smithsonian Institution / National Museum of Natural History
Wood, Bernard, University of Oxford
Wood, Ian, University College London
Wylie, Ann G., University of Maryland
Wypych, Alicia, Division of Geological & Geophysical Surveys
Xu, Huifang, University of Wisconsin, Madison
Yoshiasa, Akira, Kumamoto University
Yurtsever, Ayhan, Ludwig-Maximilians-Universitaet Muenchen
Zink, Albert, Ludwig-Maximilians-Universitaet Muenchen
Zurevinski, Shannon, Lakehead University
Šæavnièar, Stjepan, University of Zagreb
Žigoveèki Gobac, Željka, University of Zagreb

Paleolimnology

Anderson, Roger Y., University of New Mexico
Axford, Yarrow, Northwestern University
Brady, Kristina, University of Minnesota, Twin Cities
Brant, Lynn A., University of Northern Iowa
Brenner, Mark, University of Florida
Buchheim, H. Paul, Loma Linda University
Cook, Timothy L., Worcester State University
De Batist, Marc, Ghent University
Douglas, Marianne, University of Toronto
Ferris, Grant F., University of Toronto
Fritz, Sherilyn C., University of Nebraska, Lincoln
Gierlowski-Kordesch, Elizabeth H., Ohio University
Glaser, Paul H., University of Minnesota, Twin Cities
Halfman, John D., Hobart & William Smith Colleges
Heyvaert, Alan, University of Nevada, Reno
Johnson, Thomas C., University of Minnesota, Duluth
Kaplan, Samantha W., University of Wisconsin, Stevens Point
Kirby, Matthew E., California State University, Fullerton
Lisiecki, Lorraine, University of California, Santa Barbara
Noren, Anders, University of Minnesota, Twin Cities
Porter, Susannah, University of California, Santa Barbara
Rodysill, Jessica, University of Minnesota, Twin Cities
Russell, James M., Brown University
Shapley, Mark, University of Minnesota, Twin Cities
Smith, Alison J., Kent State University
Steinman, Byron A., University of Minnesota, Duluth
Stevens (Landon), Lora R., California State University, Long Beach
Theissen, Kevin, University of Saint Thomas

Petroleum Geology

Abdulghani, Waleed, King Fahd University of Petroleum and Minerals
Adeigbe, O. C., University of Ibadan
Adekeye, J. I. D., University of Ilorin
Al-Ramadan, Khalid, King Fahd University of Petroleum and Minerals
Ali, Hendratta N., Fort Hays State University
Allis, Richard G., Utah Geological Survey
Andrews, Richard D., University of Oklahoma
Anthony, Robin, Pennsylvania Bureau of Topographic & Geologic Survey
Aplin, Andrew, Durham University
Arnold, Dan, Heriot-Watt University
Askari, Roohollah, Michigan Technological University
Askari, Zohreh K., University of Illinois, Urbana-Champaign
Asquith, George B., Texas Tech University
Avary, Katherine L., West Virginia University
Baer, James L., Brigham Young University
Bartok, Peter, University of Houston
Beaver, Harold H., Baylor University
Bend, Stephen L., University of Regina
Benjamin, U. K., Obafemi Awolowo University
Boboye, O. A., University of Ibadan
Bonk, Kathleen, New York State Geological Survey
Bowersox, J. Richard, University of Kentucky
Bowler, Bernard, University of Newcastle Upon Tyne
Bowman, Mike, University of Manchester
Breedlovestrout, Renee L., University of Idaho
Broadhead, Ronald F., New Mexico Institute of Mining & Technology
Burton, Bradford R., Western State Colorado University
Carr, Timothy R., West Virginia University
Carr, Timothy R., University of Kansas
Carter, Kristin M., Pennsylvania Bureau of Topographic & Geologic Survey
Cassidy, Martin, University of Houston
Champlin, Steven D., Mississippi Office of Geology
Cheadle, Burns A., Western University
Chenoweth, Cheri, University of Illinois, Urbana-Champaign
Cochrane, Claudia, Western University
Connors, Christopher, Washington & Lee University
Cranganu, Constantin, Brooklyn College (CUNY)
Crockett, Joan, University of Illinois, Urbana-Champaign
Curtis, John B., Colorado School of Mines

Dallegge, Todd A., University of Northern Colorado
Doveton, John H., University of Kansas
Echols, John B., Louisiana State University
Edegbai, Aitalokhai J., University of Benin
Ehinola, O. A., University of Ibadan
Eide, Elizabeth A., National Academy of Sciences/National Research Council
Elnadi, Abdelhalim H., University of Khartoum
Elrick, Scott D., University of Illinois, Urbana-Champaign
Fadiya, S. L., Obafemi Awolowo University
Fall, Andras, University of Texas at Austin
Feely, Martin, National University of Ireland Galway
Finley, Robert J., University of Illinois, Urbana-Champaign
Flint, Stephen, University of Manchester
Folorunso, I. O., University of Ilorin
Forgotson, Jr., James M., University of Oklahoma
Fraser, Alastair, Imperial College
Giles, Katherine A., University of Texas, El Paso
Gillespie, Janice, California State University, Bakersfield
Gingras, Murray, University of Alberta
Godin, Laurent, Queen's University
Graham, Stephan A., Stanford University
Grender, Gordon C., Virginia Polytechnic Institute & State University
Hanks, Catherine L., University of Alaska Fairbanks
Harris, David C., University of Kentucky
Harun, Nina, Alaska Division of Geological & Geophysical Surveys
Haun, John D., Colorado School of Mines
Haynes, Samantha, University of Leeds
Henk, Jr., Floyd, Texas Christian University
Hentz, Tucker F., University of Texas at Austin, Jackson School of Geosciences
Herrmann, Leo A., Louisiana Tech University
Hileman, Mary, Oklahoma State University
Hoyal, Michael L., Tennessee Geological Survey
Hughes, Colin, University of Manchester
Igbinigie, Nosa S., University of Benin
Jeffery, David L., Marietta College
Jiang , Shu, University of Utah
John, Chacko J., Louisiana State University
Johnson, Howard, Imperial College
Jones, Bobby L., Louisiana State University
Keach, William, University of Utah
Knepp, Rex A., Illinois State Geological Survey
Leech, Mary, San Francisco State University
Leetaru, Hannes E., University of Illinois, Urbana-Champaign
Lever, Helen, Heriot-Watt University
Levino, Lynn J., Pennsylvania Bureau of Topographic & Geologic Survey
Li, Peng, Arkansas Geological Survey
Llott, Samantha, Heriot-Watt University
Loucks, Bob, University of Texas at Austin, Jackson School of Geosciences
Lucia, F. Jerry, University of Texas at Austin, Jackson School of Geosciences
Machel, Hans G., University of Alberta
Malinverno, Alberto, Columbia University
Mazzullo, Salvatore J., Wichita State University
Mc Mahon, Michelle, Lonestar College - North Harris
Meddaugh, W. S., Midwestern State University
Medina, Cristian R., indiana University
Miller, Michael B., Louisiana State University
Neufeld, Jerome A., University of Cambridge
Newell, Kerry D., University of Kansas
Nixon, R. Paul, Brigham Young University
Nordeng, Stephan, University of North Dakota
North, F. K., Carleton University
Nton, M. E., University of Ibadan
Nunez-Velazco, Miriam, Universidad Autonoma de Baja California Sur
Nwachukwu, J. I., Obafemi Awolowo University
Oduneye, Olusola C., Ladoke Akintola University of Technology
Ogungbesan, Gbenga O., Ladoke Akintola University of Technology
Ojo, O. J., University of Ilorin
Olarewaju, V. O., Obafemi Awolowo University
Olorunfemi, A. O., Obafemi Awolowo University
Panah, Assad I., University of Pittsburgh, Bradford
Pashin, Jack C., Mississippi State University
Patchen, Douglas, West Virginia University
Pertl, David, Amarillo College
Pranter, Matthew J., University of Oklahoma
Pritchett, Brittany, University of Oklahoma
Puckette, James, Oklahoma State University
Ratchford, M. E., Arkansas Geological Survey
Resnic, Victor S., Lonestar College - North Harris
Richards-McClung, Bryony, University of Utah
Riess, Carolyn M., Austin Community College District
Riley, Ronald A., Ohio Dept of Natural Resources
Rupp, John A., indiana University
Schmid, Katie, Pennsylvania Bureau of Topographic & Geologic Survey
Schroeder, Stefan, University of Manchester
Shumaker, Robert C., West Virginia University
Simpson, Altus, Cypress College
Slater, Brian, New York State Geological Survey
Slatt, Roger M., University of Oklahoma
Smith, Langhorne, New York State Geological Survey
Sonnenberg, Stephen A., Colorado School of Mines

Stewart, Gary, Oklahoma State University
Stright, Lisa, Colorado State University
Sullivan, Raymond, San Francisco State University
Sun, Yuefeng, Texas A&M University
Tan, Denis N., University of Malaya
Taylor, Kevin, University of Manchester
Temples, Tommy, Clemson University
Tinker, Scott W., University of Texas at Austin, Jackson School of Geosciences
Trentham, Robert C., University of Texas, Permian Basin
Trevino, Ramon H., University of Texas at Austin, Jackson School of Geosciences
van der Land, Crees, University of Newcastle Upon Tyne
Vautier, Yannick, Institut Polytechnique LaSalle Beauvais (ex-IGAL)
Wach, Grant D., Dalhousie University
Wardlaw, Norman C., University of Calgary
Weimer, Paul, University of Colorado
White, Bekki C., Arkansas Geological Survey
Whiteley, Martin, University of Derby
Wielens, Hans J., Dalhousie University
Wood, Lesli, Colorado School of Mines
Woodward, Mac B., Arkansas Geological Survey
Xie, Xiangyang, Texas Christian University
Zimmerman, Ronald K., Louisiana State University
Ziolkowski, Anton M., Edinburgh University
Zonneveld, John-Paul, University of Alberta
Zuppann, Charles W., indiana University

General Petrology

Afolabi, Olukayode A., Ladoke Akintola University of Technology
Ague, Jay J., Yale University
Anderson, Alan J., Saint Francis Xavier University
Arslan, Gizem, Firat University
Ashwal, Lewis D., University of the Witwatersrand
Balen, Dražen, University of Zagreb
Barr, Sandra, Dalhousie University
Barton, Michael, Ohio State University
Basu, Asish, University of Texas, Arlington
Basu, Asish R., University of Rochester
Bickel, Charles E., San Francisco State University
Biševac, Vanja, University of Zagreb
Blackburn, William H., University of Kentucky
Borghi, Alessandro, Università di Torino
Brady, John B., Smith College
Brandriss, Mark E., Smith College
Brouwer, Fraukje , VU University Amsterdam
Brown, Kenneth, Miami University
Brown, Michael, University of Maryland
Broxton, David E., Los Alamos National Laboratory
Cain, J. Allan, University of Rhode Island
Callegari, Ezio, Università di Torino
Cameron, Kenneth L., University of California, Santa Cruz
Carmichael, Sarah, Appalachian State University
Castelli, Daniele, Università di Torino
Chaumba, Jefferson B., University of North Carolina, Pembroke
Cherniak, Daniele J., Rensselaer Polytechnic Institute
Chesner, Craig A., Eastern Illinois University
Chown, Edward H., Universite du Quebec a Chicoutimi
Churnet, Habte G., University of Tennessee at Chattanooga
Compagnoni, Roberto, Università di Torino
Compton, Robert R., Stanford University
Cordell, Ann S., University of Florida
Cordua, William S., University of Wisconsin, River Falls
Cortes, Joaquin A., SUNY, Buffalo
Crawford, Maria Luisa B., Bryn Mawr College
Creasy, John W., Bates College
Cruz-Uribe, Alicia M., University of Maine
Darling, Robert S., SUNY, Cortland
Dasgupta, Rajdeep, Rice University
Davidson, Cameron, Carleton College
DeBari, Susan M., Western Washington University
Deininger, Robert W., University of Memphis
Dobrzhinetskaya, Larissa F., University of California, Riverside
Doolan, Barry L., University of Vermont
Dunlop, Roberta, Simon Fraser University
Eklund, Olav, Abo Akademi University
Encarnacion, John, Saint Louis University
Erickson, Rolfe C., Sonoma State University
Ferrando, Simona, Università di Torino
Ferreiro Maehlmann, Rafael, Technische Universitaet Darmstadt
Finn, Gregory C., Brock University
Frank, Charles O., Southern Illinois University Carbondale
Ganguly, Jiba, University of Arizona
Goble, Ronald G., University of Nebraska, Lincoln
Gonzales, David A., Fort Lewis College
Graham, Ian, University of New South Wales
Gray, Norman H., University of Connecticut
Groppo, Chiara Teresa, Università di Torino
Hacker, Bradley R., University of California, Santa Barbara
Haileab, Bereket, Carleton College
Hanson, Richard E., Texas Christian University
Hatheway, Richard B., SUNY, Geneseo

Holden, Gregory S., Colorado School of Mines
Hollocher, Kurt T., Union College
Hughes, Scott S., Idaho State University
Hutchison, David, Hartwick College
Ihinger, Phillip D., University of Wisconsin, Eau Claire
Jamieson, Rebecca A., Dalhousie University
Jercinovic, Michael J., University of Massachusetts, Amherst
Jimoh, Mustapha T., Ladoke Akintola University of Technology
Johnson, Julie, University of Memphis
Jolliff, Bradley L., Washington University in St. Louis
Kılıc, Ayse Didem, Firat University
Kerr, A C., Cardiff University
Keskinen, Mary J., University of Alaska Fairbanks
Lefebvre, Richard H., Grand Valley State University
Leichmann, Jaromir, Masaryk University
Lewy, Robert, Bakersfield College
Malcuit, Robert J., Denison University
Manning, Craig E., University of California, Los Angeles
Marcellos, Antonios E., Hofstra University
Maritan, Lara, Università degli Studi di Padova
Martin, Barton S., Ohio Wesleyan University
Mathez, Edmond A., American Museum of Natural History
Mazzoli, Claudio, Università degli Studi di Padova
McKinney, D. Brooks, Hobart & William Smith Colleges
McLeod, Claire, Miami University
Miller, James D., University of Minnesota, Twin Cities
Mirnejad, Hassan , Miami University
Moecher, David P., University of Kentucky
Moore, Daniel K., Brigham Young University - Idaho
Murphy, J. Brendan, Dalhousie University
Mutti, Laurence J., Juniata College
Nadeau, Olivier, University of Ottawa
Nasir, Sobhi J., University of Qatar
Nesse, William D., University of Northern Colorado
Nielsen, Peter A., Keene State College
Noblett, Jeffrey B., Colorado College
Ozel Yıldırım, Esra , Firat University
Pan, Yuanming, University of Saskatchewan
Peterson, Virginia L., Grand Valley State University
Plank, Terry A., Columbia University
Plymate, Thomas G., Missouri State University
Prichard, H M., Cardiff University
Ptacek, Anton D., San Diego State University
Purdom, William B., Southern Oregon University
Raeside, Robert, Dalhousie University
Ranson, William A., Furman University
Raymond, Loren A., Appalachian State University
Reyes-Cortes, Ignacio A., Universidad Autonoma de Chihuahua
Rizeli, Mustafa Eren, Firat University
Roadifer, Jack E., Colorado Mesa University
Rolfo, Franco, Università di Torino
Rougvie, James R., Beloit College
Severs, Matthew R., Stockton University
Sharma, Shiv K., University of Hawai'i, Manoa
Shoemaker, Kurt A., Shawnee State University
Snyder, Lori D., University of Wisconsin, Eau Claire
Steiner, Jeffrey, Graduate School of the City University of New York
Stelling, Pete, Western Washington University
Swihart, George H., University of Memphis
Thompson, Allan M., University of Delaware
Thy, Peter, University of California, Davis
Torres-Agulera, Juan Manuel, Universidad Autonoma de San Luis Potosi
Van Buer, Nicholas J., California State Polytechnic University, Pomona
van Kranendonk, Martin, University of New South Wales
Vander Auwera, Jacqueline, Universite de Liege
Vaniman, David T., Los Alamos National Laboratory
Vanko, David A., Towson University
Vertolli, Vincent, Royal Ontario Museum
Voner, Frederick R., Marietta College
Walker, David, Columbia University
Warren, Jessica, University of Delaware
Weaver, Stephen G., Colorado College
Welsh, James L., Gustavus Adolphus College
Wendlandt, Richard F., Colorado School of Mines
Westerman, David S., Norwich University
Whelan, Peter M., University of Minnesota, Morris
WoldeGabriel, Giday, Los Alamos National Laboratory
Yurkovich, Steven P., Western Carolina University

Igneous Petrology

Adams, Gerald E., Columbia College Chicago
Albee, Arden L., California Institute of Technology
Allen, Jack C., Bucknell University
Amedjoe, Godfrey C., Kwame Nkrumah University of Science and Technology
Amel, Nasir, University of Tabriz
Andersen, Jens, Exeter University
Anderson, James Lawford, Boston University
Annesley, Irvine, University of Saskatchewan
Anthony, Elizabeth Y., University of Texas, El Paso
Aranda, Jorge, Universidad Nacional Autonoma de Mexico

Bachmann, Olivier, University of Washington
Badger, Robert L., SUNY Potsdam
Bailey, David G., Hamilton College
Baldridge, W. Scott, Los Alamos National Laboratory
Barker, Daniel, University of Texas at Austin
Barnes, Calvin G., Texas Tech University
Barr, Sandra M., Acadia University
Barth, Andrew P., Indiana University / Purdue University, Indianapolis
Beard, James S., Virginia Polytechnic Institute & State University
Bedard, Jean H., Universite du Quebec
Bender, E. E., Orange Coast College
Bender, John F., University of North Carolina, Charlotte
Benimoff, Alan I., College of Staten Island
Bentley, Robert, Central Washington University
Bergantz, George W., University of Washington
Beswick, Anthony E., Laurentian University, Sudbury
Beyarslan, Melahat, Firat University
Bingol, Ahmet Feyzi, Firat University
Birsic, Erin, Allegheny College
Bizimis, Michael, University of South Carolina
Blackerby, Bruce A., California State University, Fresno
Bladh, Katherine L., Wittenberg University
Bloomer, Sherman H., Oregon State University
Boerboom, Terry, University of Minnesota
Boroughs, Scott, Washington State University
Boudreau, Alan E., Duke University
Brandon, Alan, University of Houston
Brandriss, Mark E., Williams College
Brenan, James, University of Toronto
Brophy, James G., Indiana University, Bloomington
Browne, Brandon L., Humboldt State University
Brueseke, Matthew E., Kansas State University
Brunstad, Keith, SUNY, Oneonta
Bryan, Scott E., Queensland University of Technology
Bybee, Grant M., University of the Witwatersrand
Byerly, Gary R., Louisiana State University
Canil, Dante, University of Victoria
Carmichael, Ian S., University of California, Berkeley
Castillo, Paterno R., University of California, San Diego
Cathey, Henrietta, Queensland University of Technology
Cecil, M. R., California State University, Northridge
Cepeda, Joseph C., West Texas A&M University
Chadwick, John , College of Charleston
Chavrit, Deborah, University of Manchester
Cheney, John T., Amherst College
Christiansen, Eric H., Brigham Young University
Chu, Xu , SUNY, Fredonia
Clague, David A., University of Hawai'i, Manoa
Claiborne, Lily L., Vanderbilt University
Clark, Russell G., Albion College
Clarke, D. Barrie, Dalhousie University
Clemens-Knott, Diane, California State University, Fullerton
Coish, Raymond A., Middlebury College
Coleman, Robert G., Stanford University
Condit, Christopher D., University of Massachusetts, Amherst
Constantin, Marc, Universite Laval
Coogan, Laurence, University of Victoria
Coombs, Douglas S., University of Otago
Cooper, Kari M., University of California, Davis
Cooper, Roger W., Lamar University
Cornell, Winton, University of Tulsa
Cote, Denis, Universite du Quebec a Chicoutimi
Cottle, John, University of California, Santa Barbara
Crawford, Anthony J., University of Tasmania
Cribb, Warner, Middle Tennessee State University
Currier, Ryan, University of Wisconsin, Green Bay
Davies, Gareth, VU University Amsterdam
Davis, Frederick A., University of Minnesota, Duluth
Dean, Robert, Dickinson College
Delgado-Argote, Luis A., Centro de Investigación Científica y de Ed Superior de Ensenada
Dick, Henry J B., Woods Hole Oceanographic Institution
Dickson, Loretta D., Lock Haven University
Dijkstra, Arjan, University of Plymouth
Dingwell, Donald Bruce, Ludwig-Maximilians-Universitaet Muenchen
Dolejs, David, Charles University
Dorais, Michael J., Brigham Young University
Downs, Robert T., University of Arizona
Draper, David S., University of New Mexico
Duke, Edward F., South Dakota School of Mines & Technology
Dunbar, Nelia W., New Mexico Institute of Mining & Technology
Dunn, John Todd, University of New Brunswick
Dymek, Robert F., Washington University
Edwards, Benjamin R., Dickinson College
Elders, Wilfred A., University of California, Riverside
Elkins, Lynne J., University of Nebraska, Lincoln
Elliot, David H., Ohio State University
Erturk, Mehmet Ali, Firat University
Fagan, Amy, Western Carolina University
Feeley, Todd C., Montana State University

Fernandez, Louis A., California State University, San Bernardino
Fiesinger, Donald W., Utah State University
Filiberto, Justin, Southern Illinois University Carbondale
Fitton, J. G., Edinburgh University
Fleming, Thomas H., Southern Connecticut State University
Flower, Martin F. J., University of Illinois at Chicago
Fodor, Ronald V., North Carolina State University
Fournelle, John, University of Wisconsin, Madison
Fowler, Mike, University of Portsmouth
Fowler, Sarah, Katholieke Universiteit Leuven
Fox, Lydia K., University of the Pacific
Francis, Don, McGill University
Gaetani, Glenn A., Woods Hole Oceanographic Institution
Gamble, John, University College Cork
Garcia, Michael O., University of Hawai'i, Manoa
García Galán, Gúmer, Universitat Autonoma de Barcelona
Garrison, Jennifer, California State University, Los Angeles
Geist, Dennis J., University of Idaho
Gerbe, Marie-Christine, Université Jean Monnet, Saint-Etienne
Gertisser, Ralf, Keele University
Ghani, Azman Abdul, University of Malaya
Gibson, David, University of Maine - Farmington
Gibson, Sally, University of Cambridge
Gill, James B., University of California, Santa Cruz
Gittins, John, University of Toronto
Glazner, Allen F., University of North Carolina, Chapel Hill
Gobel, Volker W., Stephen F. Austin State University
Goldoff, Beth A., American Museum of Natural History
Gomes, Maria E., Universidade de Trás-os-Montes e Alto Douro
Gordon, Stacia , University of Nevada, Reno
Gorring, Matthew L., Montclair State University
Green, John C., University of Minnesota, Duluth
Grove, Timothy L., Massachusetts Institute of Technology
Grunder, Anita L., Oregon State University
Gualda, Guilherme, Vanderbilt University
Gust, David A., Queensland University of Technology
Haddock, Gerald H., Wheaton College
Halsor, Sid P., Wilkes University
Hammer, Julia E., University of Hawai'i, Manoa
Hammersley, Lisa, California State University, Sacramento
Hammond, Paul E., Portland State University
Hannah, Judith L., Colorado State University
Hanson, Sarah L., Adrian College
Hari, Kosiyath R., Pt. Ravishankar Shukla University
Harris, Chris, University of Cape Town
Hart, William K., Miami University
Hearn, Carter, Smithsonian Institution / National Museum of Natural History
Hebert, Rejean J., Universite Laval
Herd, Christopher, University of Alberta
Hermes, O D., University of Rhode Island
Herrstrom, Eileen A., University of Illinois, Urbana-Champaign
Hess, Paul C., Brown University
Hidalgo, Paulo, Georgia State University
Higgins, Michael D., Universite du Quebec a Chicoutimi
Hirschmann, Marc M., University of Minnesota, Twin Cities
Hirt, William H., College of the Siskiyous
Holness, Marian, University of Cambridge
Hon, Rudolph, Boston College
Husch, Jonathan M., Rider University
Huysken, Kristin, Indiana University Northwest
Irvine, T. Neil, Carnegie Institution of Washington
Jahangiri, Ahmad, University of Tabriz
Jaye, Shelley, Northern Virginia Community College - Annandale
Jeffrey, Tepper H., University of Puget Sound
Jenner, George A., Memorial University of Newfoundland
Johnson, Kenneth S., University of Houston Downtown
Johnson, Kevin T. M., University of Hawai'i, Manoa
Johnson, Marie C., United States Military Academy
Jones, Adrian, University College London
Jones, Norris W., University of Wisconsin, Oshkosh
Jordan, Brad C., Bucknell University
Jordan, Brennan T., University of South Dakota
Jugo, Pedro J., Laurentian University, Sudbury
Kay, Robert W., Cornell University
Kay, Suzanne M., Cornell University
Kelemen, Peter, Columbia University
Kelemen, Peter B., Woods Hole Oceanographic Institution
Kelemen, Peter B., Columbia University
Kempton, Pamela D., Kansas State University
King, Penelope L., University of New Mexico
Klein, Emily M., Duke University
Kopylova, Maya G., University of British Columbia
Koteas, G. Christopher, Norwich University
Kreiger, William, York College of Pennsylvania
Kurum, Sevcan, Firat University
Kyle, Philip R., New Mexico Institute of Mining and Technology
Kysar Mattietti, Giuseppina, George Mason University
Lackey, Jade Star, Pomona College
Landenberger, Bill, University of Newcastle
Lange, Rebecca A., University of Michigan

Le Roux, Veronique, Woods Hole Oceanographic Institution
Leeman, William P., Rice University
Lehnert, Kerstin, Columbia University
Lesher, Charles E., University of California, Davis
Levy, Schon S., Los Alamos National Laboratory
Lidiak, Edward G., University of Pittsburgh
Lindline, Jennifer, New Mexico Highlands University
Luth, Robert W., University of Alberta
Lux, Daniel R., University of Maine
Lytwyn, Jennifer N., University of Houston
Maclennan, John, University of Cambridge
Mahood, Gail A., Stanford University
Manduca, Cathryn A., Carleton College
Marsh, J.S., Rhodes University
Marta, Patino Douce, University of Georgia
Martin, Robert F., McGill University
Mathez, Edmond A., Graduate School of the City University of New York
Mattioli, Glen, University of Texas, Arlington
Matty, David J., Weber State University
McCallum, I. Stewart (Stu), University of Washington
McCanta, Molly, Tufts University
McClellan, Elizabeth, Radford University
McGuire, Angela, Whitman College
McMillan, Nancy J., New Mexico State University, Las Cruces
Medaris, Gordon L., University of Wisconsin, Madison
Mertzman, Stanley A., Franklin and Marshall College
Michael, Peter J., University of Tulsa
Miller, Calvin F., Vanderbilt University
Miller, James D., University of Minnesota, Duluth
Miller, Jonathan S., San Jose State University
Mills, James G., DePauw University
Mitchell, Roger H., Lakehead University
Moayyed, Mohsen -., University of Tabriz
Morgan, Daniel, University of Leeds
Morgan, George B., University of Oklahoma
Morse, Stearns A., University of Massachusetts, Amherst
Moyen, Jean-François, Université Jean Monnet, Saint-Etienne
Murray, Jay D., Midwestern State University
Myers, James D., University of Wyoming
Nash, Barbara P., University of Utah
Naslund, H. Richard, Binghamton University
Natland, James, University of Miami
Naumann, Terry R., University of Alaska, Anchorage
Neal, Clive R., University of Notre Dame
Nehru, Cherukupalli E., Graduate School of the City University of New York
Nelson, Stephen A., Tulane University
Nelson, Wendy, Towson University
Nicholls, James W., University of Calgary
Nicholson, Kirsten N., Ball State University
Nicolaysen, Kirsten P., Whitman College
Nielsen, Roger L., Oregon State University
Ntsaluba, Bantubonke I., Rhodes University
Nude, Prosper M., University of Ghana
Ouimette, Mark A., Hardin-Simmons University
Page, Philippe, Universite du Quebec a Chicoutimi
Parker, Don, Wayland Baptist University
Parker, Don F., Baylor University
Parlak, Osman, Cukurova Universitesi
Perez-Venzor, Jose A., Universidad Autonoma de Baja California Sur
Perfit, Michael R., University of Florida
Petrinec, Zorica, University of Zagreb
Philpotts, Anthony R., University of Connecticut
Philpotts, Anthony, University of Massachusetts, Amherst
Pickard, Megan, Brigham Young University - Idaho
Polat, Ali, University of Windsor
Pollock, Meagen, College of Wooster
Price, Jonathan D., Midwestern State University
Prinz, Martin, Graduate School of the City University of New York
Puffer, John H., Rutgers, The State University of New Jersey, Newark
Raia, Federica, City College (CUNY)
Ratajeski, Kent, University of Kentucky
Reagan, Mark K., University of Iowa
Reavy, John, University College Cork
Reid, Arch M., University of Houston
Reid, Mary R., Northern Arizona University
Reidel, Stephen P., Washington State University
Reyes-Cortes, Manuel, Universidad Autonoma de Chihuahua
Roden, Michael F., University of Georgia
Roelofse, Frederick, University of the Free State
Rooney, Tyrone, Michigan State University
Ross, Martin E., Northeastern University
Russell, James K., University of British Columbia
Saini-Eidukat, Bernhardt, North Dakota State University
Schmidt, Mariek, Brock University
Schmitt, Axel K., University of California, Los Angeles
Schulze, Daniel J., University of Toronto
Schwab, Brandon E., Humboldt State University
Schwartz, Joshua J., California State University, Northridge
Scoates, James S., University of British Columbia
Seaman, Sheila J., University of Massachusetts, Amherst

Seeger, Cheryl M., Missouri Dept of Natural Resources
Sen, Gautam, Florida International University
Shaw, Cliff S., University of New Brunswick
Shearer, Jr., Charles K., University of New Mexico
Shervais, John W., Utah State University
Shuster, Robert D., University of Nebraska at Omaha
Siegel, Coralie, Queensland University of Technology
Sigurdson, David, California State University, Dominguez Hills
Silva-Mora, Luis, Universidad Nacional Autonoma de Mexico
Sinton, John M., University of Hawai'i, Manoa
Sirbescu, Mona, Central Michigan University
Sisson, Virginia, University of Houston
Size, William B., Emory University
Smedes, Harry W., Southern Oregon University
Smith, Diane R., Trinity University
Smith, Douglas, University of Texas at Austin
Smith, Eugene I., University of Nevada, Las Vegas
Smith, Matthew C., University of Florida
Smith, Terence E., University of Windsor
Somarin, Alireza, Brandon University
Spera, Frank J., University of California, Santa Barbara
Springer, Robert K., Brandon University
Stachel, Thomas, University of Alberta
Stern, Charles R., University of Colorado
Stewart, Michael A., University of Illinois, Urbana-Champaign
Stork, Allen L., Western State Colorado University
Stormer, Jr., John C., Rice University
Streck, Martin J., Portland State University
Stull, Robert J., California State University, Los Angeles
Szabo, Csaba, Virginia Polytechnic Institute & State University
Tacinelli, John, Rochester Community & Technical College
Taib, Nur Iskandar, University of Malaya
Tepley, III, Frank J., Oregon State University
Thakurta, Joyashish, Western Michigan University
Thomas, Jay, Syracuse University
Ural, Melek, Firat University
Urbanczyk, Kevin, Sul Ross State University
Vance, Joseph A., University of Washington
Vennum, Walt, Sonoma State University
Vetter, Scott K., Centenary College of Louisiana
Viegas, Anthony V., Goa University
Visona', Dario, Università degli Studi di Padova
von der Handt, Anette, University of Minnesota, Twin Cities
Wadsworth, William B., Whittier College
Walker, Barry , Portland State University
Walker, James A., Northern Illinois University
Walter , Michael , University of Bristol
Warren, Richard G., Los Alamos National Laboratory
Webster, John R., Minot State University
Weiblen, Paul W., University of Minnesota, Twin Cities
Weiland, Thomas J., Georgia Southwestern State University
Weng, Yi-Hua, Ball State University
Wenner, Jennifer M., University of Wisconsin, Oshkosh
Whattam, Scott A., Korea University
White, Craig M., Boise State University
White, John C., Eastern Kentucky University
Whitney, James A., University of Georgia
Wirth, Karl R., Macalester College
Wittke, James, Northern Arizona University
Wobus, Reinhard A., Williams College
Wolf, Michael B., Augustana College
Wolff, John A., Washington State University
Worcester, Peter A., Hanover College
Woyski, Margaret S., California State University, Fullerton
Wulff, Andrew H., Whittier College
Yogodzinski, Gene M., University of South Carolina
Young, Davis A., Calvin College
Zamzow, Craig E., Clarion University
Zieg, Michael J., Slippery Rock University
Zou, Haibo, Auburn University

Metamorphic Petrology
Adams, Mark G., Appalachian State University
Allen, Alistair, University College Cork
Allen, Gary C., University of New Orleans
Appleyard, Edward C., University of Waterloo
Ashton, Kenneth E., University of Regina
Baldwin, Julia, University of Montana
Bauer, Paul W., New Mexico Institute of Mining & Technology
Beane, Rachel J., Bowdoin College
Bebout, Gray E., Lehigh University
Berg, Christopher A., University of West Georgia
Berg, Jonathan H., Northern Illinois University
Berman, Robert, Carleton University
Blake, David E., University of North Carolina Wilmington
Brown, Edwin H., Western Washington University
Burnley, Pamela C., University of Nevada, Las Vegas
Burwash, Ronald A., University of Alberta
Cardace, Dawn, University of Rhode Island
Carillo-Chavez, Alejandro J., Universidad Autonoma de Baja California Sur

Carlson, William D., University of Texas at Austin
Cesare, Bernardo, Università degli Studi di Padova
Chacko, Thomas, University of Alberta
Clarke, Geoffrey L., University of Sydney
Cooper, Alan F., University of Otago
Corriveau, Louise, Universite du Quebec
Costin, Gelu, Rhodes University
Daniel, Christopher G., Bucknell University
Dawson, Jane P., Iowa State University of Science & Technology
Day, Howard W., University of California, Davis
DeAngelis, Michael T., University of Arkansas at Little Rock
Devore, George W., Florida State University
Diener, Johann, University of Cape Town
Dietsch, Craig, University of Cincinnati
Dipple, Gregory M., University of British Columbia
Droop, Giles, University of Manchester
Dunn, Steven R., Mount Holyoke College
Dunn, Tasha, Colby College
Dymek, Robert F., Washington University in St. Louis
Eckert, James O., Yale University
El Shazly, Aley, Marshall University
Elias-Herrera, Mariano, Universidad Nacional Autonoma de Mexico
Evans, Bernard W., University of Washington
Farrar, Stewart S., Eastern Kentucky University
Faryad, Shah Wali, Charles University
Fawcett, J. J., University of Toronto
Fletcher, John, Centro de Investigación Cientifica y de Ed Superior de Ensenada
Foster Jr., Charles T., University of Iowa
Frost, B. Ronald, University of Wyoming
Ghent, Edward D., University of Calgary
Giaramita, Mario J., California State University, Stanislaus
Gillis, Kathryn, University of Victoria
Goodge, John W., University of Minnesota, Duluth
Grant, James A., University of Minnesota, Duluth
Grew, Edward S., University of Maine
Grover, Timothy W., Castleton University
Hacker, Bradley R., University of California, Santa Barbara
Hajialioghli, Robab, University of Tabriz
Halama, Ralf, Keele University
Hallett, Benjamin W., University of Wisconsin, Oshkosh
Hames, Willis E., Auburn University
Hawkins, James W., University of California, San Diego
Henry, Darrell J., Louisiana State University
Hepple, Alex, Queensland University of Technology
Hickmott, Donald D., Los Alamos National Laboratory
Himmelberg, Glen R., University of Missouri
Hoersch, Alice L., La Salle University
Hoisch, Thomas D., Northern Arizona University
Holdaway, Michael J., Southern Methodist University
Holland, Tim, University of Cambridge
Hollister, Lincoln S., Princeton University
Horvath, Peter, Rhodes University
Horvath, Peter, University of the Witwatersrand
Hudson, Michael R., Ashland University
Iancu, Ovidiu G., Al. I. Cuza University of Iasi
Indares, Aphrodite D., Memorial University of Newfoundland
James, Richard, Laurentian University, Sudbury
Joesten, Raymond, University of Connecticut
Johnson, Eric L., Hartwick College
Jones, Jon W., University of Calgary
Kay, Suzanne M., Cornell University
Kays, M. Allan, University of Oregon
Kerrick, Derrill M., Pennsylvania State University, University Park
Kirk, Wendy, University College London
Krupicka, Jiri, University of Alberta
La Tour, Timothy E., Georgia State University
Labotka, Theodore C., University of Tennessee, Knoxville
Laird, Jo, University of New Hampshire
Lamb, Will, Texas A&M University
Lang, Helen M., West Virginia University
Law, Eric W., Muskingum University
Lefebvre, Cóme, University of Minnesota, Twin Cities
Liou, Juhn G., Stanford University
Maboko, Makenya A., University of Dar es Salaam
Magloughlin, Jerry F., Colorado State University
Mahan, Kevin H., University of Colorado
Manecan, Teodosia, Hunter College (CUNY)
Manon, Matthew R., Union College
Marko, Wayne, Northwestern University
Marschall, Horst, Woods Hole Oceanographic Institution
Martínez Fernández, Francisco, Universitat Autonoma de Barcelona
Mayborn, Kyle R., Western Illinois University
McFadden, Rory, Salem State University
McLelland, James, Colgate University
Menold, Carrie A., Albion College
Metcalf, Rodney V., University of Nevada, Las Vegas
Metzger, Ellen P., San Jose State University
Moazzen, Mohssen -., University of Tabriz
Mogk, David W., Montana State University
Morton, Douglas M., University of California, Riverside

Mulcahy, Sean R., Western Washington University
Murray, Daniel P., University of Rhode Island
Mutis-Duplat, Emilio, University of Texas, Permian Basin
Nishiyama, Tadao, Kumamoto University
Ortega-Gutierrez, Fernando, Universidad Nacional Autonoma de Mexico
Page, F Zeb, Oberlin College
Panish, Peter T., University of Massachusetts, Amherst
Parkinson, Christopher D., University of New Orleans
Patino-Douce, Alberto E., University of Georgia
Pattison, David R., University of Calgary
Peck, William H., Colgate University
Penniston-Dorland, Sarah, University of Maryland
Perkins, III, Dexter, University of North Dakota
Pervunina, Aelita, Institute of Geology (Karelia, Russia)
Plummer, Charles C., California State University, Sacramento
Potel, Sébastien, Institut Polytechnique LaSalle Beauvais (ex-IGAL)
Powell, Wayne G., Graduate School of the City University of New York
Powell, Wayne G., Brooklyn College (CUNY)
Radakovich, Amy, University of Minnesota
Raeside, Robert P., Acadia University
Rahaman, M. A., Obafemi Awolowo University
Reche Estrada, Joan, Universitat Autonoma de Barcelona
Redden, Jack A., South Dakota School of Mines & Technology
Rietmeijer, Frans J., University of New Mexico
Rivers, Toby C. J. S., Memorial University of Newfoundland
Roberts, Frank, Montgomery County Community College
Roselle, Gregory T., Brigham Young University - Idaho
Rosenfeld, John L., University of California, Los Angeles
Rumble, III, Douglas, Carnegie Institution of Washington
Sawyer, Edward W., Universite du Quebec a Chicoutimi
Schiffman, Peter, University of California, Davis
Scotford, David M., Miami University
Selverstone, Jane E., University of New Mexico
Shalimba, Ester, University of Namibia
Sisson, Virginia B., University of Utah
Sorensen, Sorena S., Smithsonian Institution / National Museum of Natural History
Sorensen, Sorena, University of Maryland
Spear, Frank S., Rensselaer Polytechnic Institute
Spiess, Richard, Università degli Studi di Padova
Spray, John G., University of New Brunswick
Srogi, LeeAnn, West Chester University
Stoddard, Edward F., North Carolina State University
Storey, Craig, University of Portsmouth
Stout, James H., University of Minnesota, Twin Cities
Stowell, Harold H., University of Alabama
Swapp, Susan M., University of Wyoming
T. A., Vishwanath, Goa University
Thomson, Jennifer A., Eastern Washington University
Tinkham, Doug, Laurentian University, Sudbury
Tracy, Robert J., Virginia Polytechnic Institute & State University
Turnock, Allan C., University of Manitoba
Valley, John W., University of Wisconsin, Madison
Van Tongeren, Jill, Rutgers, The State University of New Jersey
Walsh, Emily O., Cornell College
Waters, Dave, University of Oxford
Weber, Bodo, Centro de Investigación Científica y de Ed Superior de Ensenada
White, Richard W., Universitaet Mainz
Whitney, Donna L., University of Minnesota, Twin Cities
Wilks, Maureen, New Mexico Institute of Mining & Technology
Wintsch, Robert P., Indiana University, Bloomington
Woodland, Bertram G., Field Museum of Natural History
Zhai, Xiaoming, College of Lake County

Sedimentary Petrology

Adekola, S. A., Obafemi Awolowo University
Al-Aasm, Ihsan S., University of Windsor
Alberstadt, Leonard P, Vanderbilt University
Argast, Anne S., Indiana University / Purdue University, Fort Wayne
Babek, Ondrej, Masaryk University
Basu, Abhijit, Indiana University, Bloomington
Benham, Steven R., Pacific Lutheran University
Benson, Donald J., University of Alabama
Bertog, Janet, Northern Kentucky University
Bertok, Carlo, Università di Torino
Boggs, Jr., Sam, University of Oregon
Brengman, Latisha A., University of Minnesota, Duluth
Bruner, Katherine R., West Virginia University
Budd, David A., University of Colorado
Bullard, Reuben G., Northern Kentucky University
Carozzi, Albert V., University of Illinois, Urbana-Champaign
Castle, James W., Clemson University
Chafetz, Henry S., University of Houston
Channing, Alan, University of Wales
Choh, Suk-Joo, Korea University
Clarke, Stu, Keele University
Corcoran, Patricia, Western University
Cousineau, Pierre, Universite du Quebec a Chicoutimi
DeCelles, Peter G., University of Arizona
dela Pierre, Francesco, Università di Torino
Dockal, James A., University of North Carolina Wilmington

Donovan, R. Nowell, Texas Christian University
Dutton, Shirley P., University of Texas at Austin, Jackson School of Geosciences
Fitzgerald, David, Saint Mary's University
Folk, Robert L., University of Texas at Austin
Franseen, Evan K., University of Kansas
Freeman, Thomas J., University of Missouri
Fritsche, A. E., California State University, Northridge
Galli-Olivier, Carlos A., Universidad Autonoma de Baja California Sur
Gelbaum, Carol, Georgia Perimeter College
Glover, Paul, University of Leeds
Gómez Gras, David, Universitat Autonoma de Barcelona
Griffing, David H., Hartwick College
Hampson, Gary , Imperial College
Heckel, Philip H., University of Iowa
Horton, Jr., Robert A., California State University, Bakersfield
Housekn echt, David W., Virginia Polytechnic Institute & State University
Hovorka, Susan D., University of Texas at Austin, Jackson School of Geosciences
James, Noel P., Queen's University
Kaczmarek, Stephen , Western Michigan University
Kerans, Charles, University of Texas at Austin, Jackson School of Geosciences
Khan, Mohammad Wahdat Y., Pt. Ravishankar Shukla University
Khandaker, Nazrul I., York College (CUNY)
Kirkland, Brenda L., Mississippi State University
Kuhnhenn, Gary L., Eastern Kentucky University
Lasemi, Zakaria, University of Illinois
Laury, Robert L., Southern Methodist University
Liutkus, Cynthia, Appalachian State University
Lowe, Donald R., Stanford University
Lumsden, David N., University of Memphis
Major, R. P., University of Mississippi
Martin, Arturo, Centro de Investigación Científica y de Ed Superior de Ensenada
Martire, Luca, Università di Torino
McBride, Earle F., University of Texas at Austin
McKean , Rebecca, Saint Norbert College
McKnight, Brian K., University of Wisconsin, Oshkosh
Measures, Elizabeth A., Sul Ross State University
Melim, Leslie A., Western Illinois University
Milliken, Kitty L., University of Texas at Austin
Montañez, Isabel P., University of California, Davis
Moore, Bruce R., University of Kentucky
Moshier, Stephen O., Wheaton College
Muntean, Thomas, Adrian College
Nick, Kevin, Loma Linda University
Niem, Alan R., Oregon State University
Nothdurft, Luke, Queensland University of Technology
Ojakangas, Richard W., University of Minnesota, Duluth
Pedone, Vicki A., California State University, Northridge
Perkins, Ronald D., Duke University
Picard, M. Dane, University of Utah
Railsback, L. Bruce, University of Georgia
Ramirez, Wilson R., University of Puerto Rico
Randazzo, Anthony F., University of Florida
Richardson, Darlene S., Indiana University of Pennsylvania
Robinson, Stuart, University of Oxford
Ruppel, Stephen C., University of Texas at Austin, Jackson School of Geosciences
Saja, David B., Cleveland Museum of Natural History
Sandberg, Philip A., University of Illinois, Urbana-Champaign
Savrda, Charles E., Auburn University
Schreiber, B. Charlotte, Queens College (CUNY)
Schreiber, B. Charlotte, Graduate School of the City University of New York
Schwab, Frederick, Washington & Lee University
Siegrist, jr Henry G., University of Guam
Stefani, Cristina, Università degli Studi di Padova
Stoklosa, Michelle , Portland State University
Stoudt, Emily L., University of Texas, Permian Basin
Sutterlin, Peter G., Wichita State University
Suttner, Lee J., Indiana University, Bloomington
Sutton, Sally J., Colorado State University
Textoris, Daniel A., University of North Carolina, Chapel Hill
Thayer, Paul A., University of North Carolina Wilmington
Uddin, Ashraf, Auburn University
Velbel, Michael A., Michigan State University
Vice, Mari A., University of Wisconsin, Platteville
Videtich, Patricia E., Grand Valley State University
Walker, Theodore R., University of Colorado
Winterer, Edward ., University of California, San Diego
Young, Harvey R., Brandon University
Zeigler, E. Lynn, Georgia Perimeter College

Sedimentology

Abbott, Mark B., University of Pittsburgh
Abbott, Patrick L., San Diego State University
Abdullatif, Osman, King Fahd University of Petroleum and Minerals
Adams, Robert W., SUNY, The College at Brockport
Alexander, Jane L., College of Staten Island
Algeo, Thomas J., University of Cincinnati
Allen, Mark, Durham University
Allen, Philip, Imperial College
Allison, Mead, Tulane University
Alvarez-Arellano, Alejandro, Universidad Autonoma de Baja California Sur

Ambrose, William A., University of Texas at Austin, Jackson School of Geosciences
Amos, Carl L., University of Southampton
Anani, Chris Y., University of Ghana
Andersen, David W., San Jose State University
Anderson, Thomas B., Sonoma State University
Anderson-Folnagy, Heidi, University of Montana Western
Anfinson, Owen, Sonoma State University
Anglen, Jeff, California State University, Fresno
Arnott, R. William C., University of Ottawa
Ashley, Gail M., Rutgers, The State University of New Jersey
Asiedu, Daniel K., University of Ghana
Austin, Steve A., Cedarville University
Autin, Whitney J., SUNY, The College at Brockport
Bahlburg, Heinrich, Universitaet Muenster
Baldwin, Christopher T., Sam Houston State University
Balog-Szabo, Anna, Virginia Western Community College
Barbeau, Jr., David, University of South Carolina
Barber, Donald C., Bryn Mawr College
Barhurst, James, University of Newcastle Upon Tyne
Barnes, David, Western Michigan University
Bart, Henry A., La Salle University
Bartley, Julie, University of Tennessee, Knoxville
Bartley, Julie K., Gustavus Adolphus College
Bassett, Kari N., University of Canterbury
Beck, Catherine C., Hamilton College
Behl, Richard J., California State University, Long Beach
Bekker, Andrey, University of California, Riverside
Belt, Edward S., Amherst College
Berger, Wolfgang H., University of California, San Diego
Bergmann, Kristin, Massachusetts Institute of Technology
Bershaw, John T., Portland State University
Best, James L., University of Illinois, Urbana-Champaign
Bestland, Erick, Flinders University
Birgenheier, Lauren, University of Utah
Bjornstad, Bruce N., Pacific Northwest National Laboratory
Blake, Bascom (Mitch) , West Virginia University
Blodgett, Robert H., Austin Community College District
Blum, Michael D., University of Kansas
Boothroyd, Jon C., University of Rhode Island
Bordy, Emese, University of Cape Town
Boulvain, Frederic P., Universite de Liege
Bourgeois, Joanne (Jody), University of Washington
Bowen, Brenda , University of Utah
Bowen, Dave , Montana State University
Branco, Brett, Brooklyn College (CUNY)
Brand, Brittany, Boise State University
Breda, Anna, Università degli Studi di Padova
Breyer, John, Texas Christian University
Bristow, Charlie, Birkbeck College
Broda, James E., Woods Hole Oceanographic Institution
Brunt, Rufus, University of Manchester
Burgess, Peter, University of London, Royal Holloway & Bedford New College
Burns, Diane M., Eastern Illinois University
Busby, Cathy J., University of California, Santa Barbara
Buyce, M. Raymond, Mercyhurst University
Buynevich, Ilya, Temple University
Caputo, Mario V., San Diego State University
Carrapa, Barbara, University of Arizona
Carroll, Alan R., University of Wisconsin, Madison
Cartwright, Joe, University of Oxford
Caruthers, Andrew, Western Michigan University
Cassel, Elizabeth J., University of Idaho
Cather, Steven M., New Mexico Institute of Mining & Technology
Catuneanu, Octavian, University of Alberta
Celik, Hasan, Firat University
Chan, Marjorie A., University of Utah
Cheel, Richard J., Brock University
Chow, Nancy, University of Manitoba
Chowns, Timothy M., University of West Georgia
Christie-Blick, Nicholas, Columbia University
Clift, Peter, Louisiana State University
Clough, James G., Alaska Division of Geological & Geophysical Surveys
Coch, Nicholas K., Queens College (CUNY)
Coch, Nicholas K., Graduate School of the City University of New York
Coe, Angela L., The Open University
Colburn, Ivan P., California State University, Los Angeles
Cole, Rex D., Colorado Mesa University
Connely, Melissa, Casper College
Conrad, Susan H., Dutchess Community College
Cope, Tim D., DePauw University
Corsetti, Frank A., University of Southern California
Cowan, Clinton A., Carleton College
Cox, Ronadh, Williams College
Crowley, Stephen, University of Liverpool
Cullen, James L., Salem State University
Currie, Brian S., Miami University
Dade, William B., Dartmouth College
Dalrymple, Robert W., Queen's University
Damuth, John, University of Texas, Arlington
Dansereau, Pauline, Universite Laval

Davatzes, Alexandra, Temple University
Davies, Neil, University of Cambridge
Davies, Sarah, Leicester University
Davies-Vollum, Katherine Sian, University of Washington
Davis, Jr., Richard A., University of South Florida, Tampa
de Wet, Carol B., Franklin and Marshall College
Dehler, Carol M., Utah State University
Deibert, Jack, Austin Peay State University
Demicco, Robert V., Binghamton University
Deocampo, Daniel M., Georgia State University
Desrochers, Andre, University of Ottawa
Diemer, John A., University of North Carolina, Charlotte
Dix, George R., Carleton University
Dominic, David F., Wright State University
Donaldson, Alan C., West Virginia University
Donaldson, J. Allan, Carleton University
Dott, Jr., Robert H., University of Wisconsin, Madison
Dravis, Jeffrey J., Rice University
Droste, John B., Indiana University, Bloomington
Droxler, Andre W., Rice University
Drummond, Carl N., Indiana University / Purdue University, Fort Wayne
Dumas, Simone, University of Ottawa
Dunagan, Stan P., University of Tennessee, Martin
Dunn, Richard K., Norwich University
Dutta, Prodip K., Indiana State University
Dutton, Shirley P., University of Texas at Austin
Dwyer, Gary S., Duke University
Eberth, David A., Royal Tyrrell Museum of Palaeontology
Edmonds, Douglas A., Indiana University, Bloomington
Egenhoff, Sven O., Colorado State University
Ehrlich, Robert, University of South Carolina
Elliott, Jr., William S., University of Southern Indiana
Elrick, Maya, University of New Mexico
Enos, Paul, University of Kansas
Eriksson, Kenneth A., Virginia Polytechnic Institute & State University
Ethridge, Frank G., Colorado State University
Evans, James E., Bowling Green State University
Eyles, Carolyn H., McMaster University
Eyre, Bradley, Southern Cross University
Faas, Richard W., Lafayette College
Fagel, Nathalie, Universite de Liege
Fan, Majie, University of Texas, Arlington
Farkas, Steven, Central Washington University
Farrell, Kathleen M., North Carolina Geological Survey
Fedo, Christopher, University of Tennessee, Knoxville
Feeney, Dennis M., University of Idaho
Fielding, Christopher, Queensland University of Technology
Fielding, Christopher R., University of Nebraska, Lincoln
Fillmore, Robert P., Western State Colorado University
Finzel, Emily S., University of Iowa
Fischer, Alfred G., University of Southern California
Flaig, Peter P., University of Texas at Austin
Fletcher, Charles H., University of Hawai'i, Manoa
Fouke, Bruce W., University of Illinois, Urbana-Champaign
Fox, James E., South Dakota School of Mines & Technology
Fox, William T., Williams College
Fralick, Philip W., Lakehead University
Frank, Tracy D., University of Nebraska, Lincoln
Franseen, Evan K., University of Kansas
Frazier, William J., Columbus State University
Friedman, Gerald M., Graduate School of the City University of New York
Fu, Qilong, University of Texas at Austin
Fulthorpe, Craig S., University of Texas at Austin
Gabel, Sharon, Lee College
Gaines, Robert R., Pomona College
Gall, Quentin, University of Ottawa
Galloway, William E., University of Texas at Austin
Gardner, Michael, Montana State University
Garrison, Robert E., University of California, Santa Cruz
Garzione, Carmala N., University of Rochester
Gayes, Paul T., Dalhousie University
Gaylord, David R., Washington State University
Gerhard, Lee C., University of Kansas
Ghinassi, Massimiliano, Università degli Studi di Padova
Gianniny, Gary, Fort Lewis College
Gibling, Martin R., Dalhousie University
Gillespie, Robb, Western Michigan University
Ginsburg, Robert N., University of Miami
Glenn, Craig R., University of Hawai'i, Manoa
Glumac, Bosiljka, Smith College
Goff, James, University of New South Wales
Goldstein, Robert H., University of Kansas
Goodbred, Jr., Steven L., Vanderbilt University
Gore, Pamela J. W., Emory University
Gore, Pamela J. W., Georgia Perimeter College
Gorte, Mary C., Delta College
Gotz, Annette, Rhodes University
Grammer, Michael, Oklahoma State University
Greene, Todd, California State University, Chico
Greer, Lisa, Washington & Lee University

Gregg, Jay M., Oklahoma State University
Gregor, C. B., Wright State University
Grigsby, Jeffry D., Ball State University
Grimm, Kurt A., University of British Columbia
Grippo, Alessandro, Santa Monica College
Grotzinger, John P., California Institute of Technology
Grove, Karen, San Francisco State University
Guo, Junhua "., California State University, Bakersfield
Gupta, Sanjeev, Imperial College
Götz, Annette, Keele University
Hajek, Elizabeth, Pennsylvania State University, University Park
Hall, Mary Jo, Rider University
Halverson, Galen, McGill University
Hamilton, Sally, Heriot-Watt University
Hampton, Brian A., New Mexico State University, Las Cruces
Harris, Clay D., Middle Tennessee State University
Harris, Mark T., University of Wisconsin, Milwaukee
Harris, Nicholas, University of Alberta
Harris, W. Burleigh, University of North Carolina Wilmington
Harrison, III, William B., Western Michigan University
Hasiuk, Franciszek J., Iowa State University of Science & Technology
Hasselbo, Stephen, Exeter University
Hayes, Miles O., University of New Orleans
Haywick, Douglas W., University of South Alabama
Hazel, Jr., Joseph E., Northern Arizona University
Heinrich, Paul V., Louisiana State University
Hendrix, Marc S., University of Montana
Hernandez-Molina, Francisco J., University of London, Royal Holloway & Bedford New College
Hess-Tanguay, Lillian, Long Island University, C.W. Post Campus
Hesse, Reinhard, McGill University
Hiatt, Eric E., University of Wisconsin, Oshkosh
Hickson, Thomas A., University of Saint Thomas
Higgins, Sean M., Columbia University
Hill, Paul S., Dalhousie University
Hinderer, Matthias, Technische Universitaet Darmstadt
Hine, Albert C., University of South Florida
Hiscott, Richard N., Memorial University of Newfoundland
Hodgetts, David, University of Manchester
Hoey, Trevor, University of Glasgow
Holbrook, John M., Texas Christian University
Hollis, Cathy, University of Manchester
Holmes, Ann E., University of Tennessee at Chattanooga
Holmes, Mary Anne, University of Nebraska, Lincoln
Hopkins, John C., University of Calgary
Horton, Brian, University of Texas at Austin
Hovorka, Susan D., University of Texas at Austin
Howard, Jeffrey L., Wayne State University
Hubbard, Dennis K., Oberlin College
Hubert, John, University of Massachusetts, Amherst
Huntoon, Jacqueline E., Michigan Technological University
Hurtgen, Matthew T., Northwestern University
Husinec, Antun, St. Lawrence University
Hussin, Azhar Hj, University of Malaya
Ingersoll, Raymond V., University of California, Los Angeles
Isbell, John L., University of Wisconsin, Milwaukee
Jackson, Chester W., Georgia Southern University
Jaeger, John M., University of Florida
Janson, Xavier, University of Texas at Austin
Jiang, Ganqing, University of Nevada, Las Vegas
Jinnah, Zubair A., University of the Witwatersrand
Joeckel, Matt, Unversity of Nebraska - Lincoln
John, Cedric, Imperial College
Johnson, Brad, Arizona Geological Survey
Johnson, Cari, University of Utah
Johnson, Joel P., University of Texas at Austin
Jones, D. M., Ohio Dept of Natural Resources
Jones, David S., Amherst College
Jones, Lawrence, Colorado Mesa University
Jones, Merren, University of Manchester
Jones, Stuart, Durham University
Jordan, William M., Millersville University
Kah, Linda, University of Tennessee, Knoxville
Kamola, Diane, University of Kansas
Kanfoush, Sharon L., Utica College
Keith, Brian D., Indiana University, Bloomington
Kendall, Christopher G., University of South Carolina
Kent, Donald M., University of Regina
Kerans, Charles, University of Texas at Austin
Kerr, Dennis R., University of Tulsa
Kidder, David L., Ohio University
Kidwell, Susan M., University of Chicago
Kilibarda, Zoran, Indiana University Northwest
Kim, Wonsuck, University of Texas at Austin
Kinvig, Helen, University of Liverpool
Knapp, Sibylle, Technische Universitaet Muenchen
Koc Tasgin, Calibe, Firat University
Kocurek, Gary A., University of Texas at Austin
Kocurko, John, Midwestern State University
Kokelaar, Peter, University of Liverpool

Kopaska-Merkel, David C., Geological Survey of Alabama
Kotha, Mahender, Goa University
Ková, Michal, Comenius University
Kovaêiæ, Marijan, University of Zagreb
Kraft, John C., University of Delaware
Krantz, David E., University of Toledo
Kraus, Mary J., University of Colorado
Krause, Federico F., University of Calgary
Krissek, Lawrence A., Ohio State University
Kurtanjek, Dražen, University of Zagreb
Langford, Richard P., University of Texas, El Paso
Larson, Erik B., Shawnee State University
Last, Fawn M., Angelo State University
Last, William M., University of Manitoba
Laubach, Stephen E., University of Texas at Austin
Lavoie, Denis, Universite du Quebec
Leckie, Dale A., Carleton University
LeFever, Richard D., University of North Dakota
Lehman, Thomas M., Texas Tech University
Leier, Andrew L., University of South Carolina
Leithold, Elana L., North Carolina State University
Leorri, Eduardo, East Carolina University
Levin, Naomi, Johns Hopkins University
Liddell, W. David, Utah State University
Lierman, Robert T., Eastern Kentucky University
Link, Paul K., Idaho State University
Linn, Anne M., National Academy of Sciences/National Research Council
Little, William W., Brigham Young University - Idaho
Lloyd, Graeme, University of Oxford
Lock, Brian E., University of Louisiana at Lafayette
Lohrengel, II, C. Frederick, Southern Utah University
Long, Darrel, Laurentian University, Sudbury
Loope, David B., University of Nebraska, Lincoln
Loucks, Robert G., University of Texas at Austin
Luczaj, John A., University of Wisconsin, Green Bay
Ludvigson, Gregory A., University of Kansas
Lynds, Ranie, University of Wyoming
Mac Eachern, James A., Simon Fraser University
MacCarthy, Ivor, University College Cork
Macdonald, R. Heather, College of William & Mary
MacInnes, Breanyn, Central Washington University
Macintyre, Ian G., Smithsonian Institution / National Museum of Natural History
MacLachlan, John, McMaster University
Mahoney, J. Brian, University of Wisconsin, Eau Claire
Maju-Oyovwikowhe, Efetobore G., University of Benin
Malpica-Cruz, Victor M., Universidad Nacional Autonoma de Mexico
Manker, John P., Georgia Southwestern State University
Mankiewicz, Carol, Beloit College
Manos, Constantine, SUNY, New Paltz
Marjanac, Tihomir, University of Zagreb
Marsaglia, Kathleen M., California State University, Northridge
Martini, I. Peter, University of Guelph
Martino, Ronald L., Marshall University
Marzolf, John E., Southern Illinois University Carbondale
Matsuda, Hiroki, Kumamoto University
Mattheus, Robin, Lake Superior State University
McCaffrey, Bill, University of Leeds
McCarney-Castle, Kerry, Dept of Natural Resources
McCarthy, Paul, University of Alaska Fairbanks
McCrone, Alistair W., Humboldt State University
McElroy, Brandon, University of Wyoming
McGlue, Michael M., University of Kentucky
McHargue, Timothy, University of Missouri
Mehrtens, Charlotte J., University of Vermont
Melas, Faye, Hunter College (CUNY)
Merrill, Robert D., California State University, Fresno
Meyers, Jamie A., Winona State University
Miall, Andrew D., University of Toronto
Miclaus, Crina, Al. I. Cuza University of Iasi
Middleton, Larry T., Northern Arizona University
Milligan, Timothy, Dalhousie University
Minter, Nicholas, University of Portsmouth
Mitchell, Simon F., University of the West Indies Mona Campus
Morton, Robert, University of South Florida, Tampa
Moskalski, Susanne, Stockton University
Mount, Jeffrey F., University of California, Davis
Mountney, Nigel, University of Leeds
Mozley, Peter S., New Mexico Institute of Mining and Technology
Mrinjek, Ervin, University of Zagreb
Mustard, Peter S., Simon Fraser University
Myers, Jeffrey A., Western Oregon University
Myrow, Paul M., Colorado College
Nadon, Gregory C., Ohio University
Nalin, Ronny, Loma Linda University
Neal, William J., Grand Valley State University
Nehyba, Slavomír, Masaryk University
Nelson, Bruce W., University of Virginia
Neuweiler, Fritz, Universite Laval
Nicoll, Kathleen, University of Utah
O'Brien, John M., New Jersey City University

O'Brien, John M., College of New Jersey
O'Brien, Neal R., SUNY Potsdam
O'Connell, Suzanne B., Wesleyan University
Oakley, Bryan A., University of Rhode Island
Oaks, Jr., Robert Q., Utah State University
Ogg, James G., Purdue University
Okunuwadje, Sunday E., University of Benin
Oldershaw, Alan E., University of Calgary
Oliveira, Anabela R., Universidade de Trás-os-Montes e Alto Douro
Ortiz, Joseph D., Kent State University
Paola, Christopher, University of Minnesota, Twin Cities
Pattison, Simon A., Brandon University
Peakall, Jeff, University of Leeds
Pearson, Eugene F., University of the Pacific
Peck, John A., University of Akron
Perscio, Lyman, Mercyhurst University
Peters, Shanan, University of Wisconsin, Madison
Petersen, Morris S., Brigham Young University
Pickering, Kevin, University College London
Pikelj, Kristina, University of Zagreb
Piper, David, Dalhousie University
Plink-Bjorklund, Piret, Colorado School of Mines
Plint, A G., Western University
Potter, Paul E., University of Cincinnati
Potter-McIntyre, Sally, Southern Illinois University Carbondale
Powell, Ross D., Northern Illinois University
Pratson, Lincoln F., Duke University
Pray, Lloyd C., University of Wisconsin, Madison
Preto, Nereo, Università degli Studi di Padova
Price, Greogry, University of Plymouth
Price, Jason R., Millersville University
Pufahl, Peir K., Acadia University
Putnam, Peter E., University of Calgary
Qing, Hairuo, University of Regina
Rainbird, R. R., Carleton University
Ramirez, Pedro C., California State University, Los Angeles
Ramsey, Kelvin W., University of Delaware
Rankey, Gene, University of Kansas
Read, J. Fred, Virginia Polytechnic Institute & State University
Reams, Max W., Olivet Nazarene University
Redfern, Jonathan, University of Manchester
Redmond, Brian T., Wilkes University
Rees, Margaret N., University of Nevada, Las Vegas
Reid, Ruth P., University of Miami
Reid, Steven K., Morehead State University
Reijmer, John, VU University Amsterdam
Renaut, Robin W., University of Saskatchewan
Retzler, Andrew, University of Minnesota
Ridgway, Kenneth D., Purdue University
Riding, Robert, University of Tennessee, Knoxville
Rigo, Manuel, Università degli Studi di Padova
Rigsby, Catherine A., East Carolina University
Roberts, Harry H., Louisiana State University
Robinson, Ruth, University of St. Andrews
Rogers, Raymond R., Macalester College
Runkel, Anthony, University of Minnesota
Ruppel, Stephen C., University of Texas at Austin
Rygel, Michael C., SUNY Potsdam
Saltzman, Matthew R., Ohio State University
Sayegh, Selim, University of Calgary
Saylor, Beverly Z., Case Western Reserve University
Schieber, Juergen, Indiana University, Bloomington
Schneiderman, Jill S., Vassar College
Scholz, Christopher A., Syracuse University
Schwartz, Theresa M., Allegheny College
Schwimmer, Reed A., Rider University
Scott, Robert W., University of Tulsa
Self, Robert P., University of Tennessee, Martin
Selleck, Bruce, Colgate University
Setterholm, Dale, University of Minnesota
Shane, Tyrrell, National University of Ireland Galway
Shaw, John B., University of Arkansas, Fayetteville
Shea, James H., University of Wisconsin, Parkside
Shilts, William W., University of Illinois, Urbana-Champaign
Shimer, Grant T., Whitman College
Simonson, Bruce M., Oberlin College
Simpson, Edward L., Kutztown University of Pennsylvania
Simpson, Frank, University of Windsor
Singer, Jill K., Buffalo State College
Singler, Charles R., Youngstown State University
Sirocko, Frank, Universitaet Mainz
Slingerland, Rudy L., Pennsylvania State University, University Park
Sloss, Craig, Queensland University of Technology
Smith, Gerald J., SUNY, Buffalo
Smith, Jon, University of Kansas
Smith, Larry N., Montana Tech of the University of Montana
Smith, Norman D., University of Nebraska, Lincoln
Smith, Shane V., Youngstown State University
Smith-Engle, Jennifer M., Texas A&M University, Corpus Christi
Sommerfield, Christopher K., University of Delaware

Soreghan, Gerilyn S., University of Oklahoma
Soreghan, Michael J., University of Oklahoma
Soster, Frederick M., DePauw University
Southard, John B., Massachusetts Institute of Technology
Staub, James R., University of Montana
Steel, Ronald J., University of Texas at Austin
Steenberg, Julia, University of Minnesota
Steinen, Randolph P., Dept of Energy and Environmental Protection
Stoner, Joseph, Oregon State University
Strauss, Justin V., Dartmouth College
Sumner, Dawn Y., University of California, Davis
Sumner, Esther, University of Southampton
Surpless, Kathleen D., Trinity University
Sweeney, Mark R., University of South Dakota
Sweet, Alisan C., Texas Tech University
Sweet, Dustin E., Texas Tech University
Swennen, Rudy, Katholieke Universiteit Leuven
Swett, Keene, University of Iowa
Syvitski, James P., University of Colorado
Tedesco, Lenore P., Indiana University / Purdue University, Indianapolis
Teller, James T., University of Manitoba
Tharin, J. Cotter, Hope College
Thomas, Robert C., University of Montana Western
Thurow, Juergen, University College London
Totten, Matthew W., Kansas State University
Toullec, Renaud, Institut Polytechnique LaSalle Beauvais (ex-IGAL)
Trexler, James H., University of Nevada, Reno
Triplehorn, Donald M., University of Alaska Fairbanks
Trofimovs, Jessica, Queensland University of Technology
Trop, Jeffrey M., Bucknell University
Törnqvist, Torbjörn E., Tulane University
Ulmer-Scholle, Dana S., New Mexico Institute of Mining and Technology
Underwood, Michael B., University of Missouri
Van De Poll, Henk W., University of New Brunswick
Villegas, Monica B., Universidad Nacional de Rio Cuarto
Voice, Peter , Western Michigan University
Wagner, John B., Southern Methodist University
Wagoner, Jeffrey L., Lawrence Livermore National Laboratory
Walker, Richard, Leicester University
Walsh, J.P., East Carolina University
Walsh, Tim R., Wayland Baptist University
Walton, Anthony W., University of Kansas
Wang, Ping, University of South Florida, Tampa
Wanke, Ansgar, University of Namibia
Wanless, Harold R., University of Miami
Ward, Colin R., University of New South Wales
Ward, Wesley, Northern Arizona University
Warner, Mont M., Boise State University
Warnock, Jonathan P., Indiana University of Pennsylvania
Wartes, Marwan A., Alaska Division of Geological & Geophysical Surveys
Washburn, Robert H., Juniata College
Watkinson, Matthew, University of Plymouth
Weislogel, Amy L., West Virginia University
Wellner, Julia, University of Houston
Wells, Neil A., Kent State University
Whalen, Michael T., University of Alaska Fairbanks
Whisonant, Robert C., Radford University
Whiteaker, Timothy, University of Texas at Austin
Wilkinson, Bruce, Syracuse University
Wilkinson, Bruce H., University of Michigan
Wilson, Carol A., Louisiana State University
Wilson, Paul A., University of Southampton
Wittkop, Chad, Minnesota State University
Wolak, Jeannette, Tennessee Tech University
Woodruff, Jonathan D., University of Massachusetts, Amherst
Woods, Adam D., California State University, Fullerton
Woods, Adam D., Santiago Canyon College
Woods, Rachel A., Edinburgh University
Worden, Richard, University of Liverpool
Wright, V P., Cardiff University
Wynn, Thomas C., Lock Haven University
Yang, Wan, Wichita State University
Yeager, Kevin, University of Kentucky
Young, Robert S., Western Carolina University
Zaleha, Michael J., Wittenberg University
Zambito, Jay, University of Wisconsin, Extension
Zattin, Massimiliano, Università degli Studi di Padova
Zeng, Hongliu, University of Texas at Austin, Jackson School of Geosciences

Physical Stratigraphy
Aalto, Kenneth R., Humboldt State University
Abdullah, Nuraiteng Tee, University of Malaya
Aitchison, Jonathan, University of Sydney
Alvarez, Walter, University of California, Berkeley
Anderson, Raymond R., University of Iowa
Anglès Vila, Marc, Universitat Autonoma de Barcelona
Archer, Allen W., Kansas State University
Aschoff, Jennifer, University of Alaska, Anchorage
Atchley, Stacy C., Baylor University
Balgord, Elizabeth A., Weber State University

Bart, Philip J., Louisiana State University
Bartholomew, Alexander J., SUNY, New Paltz
Benison, Kathleen , West Virginia University
Berquist, Jr., Carl R., Division of Geology and Mineral Resources
Bhattacharya, Janok, McMaster University
Blakey, Ronald C., Northern Arizona University
Boone, Peter A., Austin Community College District
Brezinski, David K., Maryland Department of Natural Resources
Brooks, James E., Southern Methodist University
Catacosinos, Paul A., Delta College
Chamberlin, Richard, New Mexico Institute of Mining and Technology
Chipping, David H., California Polytechnic State University
Clark, Joseph C., Indiana University of Pennsylvania
Coniglio, Mario, University of Waterloo
Cramer, Bradley D., University of Iowa
d'Atri, Anna, Università di Torino
Dalton, Richard F., New Jersey Geological Survey
Dattilo, Benjamin F., Indiana University / Purdue University, Fort Wayne
Denny, F. Brett, Illinois State Geological Survey
Devera, Joseph A., Illinois State Geological Survey
Diecchio, Richard J., George Mason University
Diffendal, Robert F., Unversity of Nebraska - Lincoln
Dodge, Clifford H., Pennsylvania Bureau of Topographic & Geologic Survey
Dorsey, Rebecca J., University of Oregon
Drzewiecki, Peter A., Eastern Connecticut State University
Eberli, Gregor P., University of Miami
Ebert, James R., SUNY, Oneonta
Elliott, Monty A., Southern Oregon University
Estrada Oliveras, Rita, Universitat Autonoma de Barcelona
Evanoff, Emmett, University of Northern Colorado
Evans, Ian, University of Houston
Evans, Kevin R., Missouri State University
Eves, Robert L., Southern Utah University
Farquhar, Winifred C., College of the Holy Cross
Ferns, Mark L., Oregon Dept of Geology & Mineral Industries
Ferrusquia, Ismael, Universidad Nacional Autonoma de Mexico
Fichter, Lynn S., James Madison University
Filipescu, Sorin, Babes-Bolyai University
Fisher, Victor A., California State University, Chico
Fisher, William L., University of Texas at Austin
Flemings, Peter B., University of Texas at Austin
Foreman, Brady Z., Western Washington University
Freeman, Rebecca, University of Kentucky
Fugitt, Frank, Ohio Dept of Natural Resources
Gardulski, Anne F., Tufts University
Gentile, Richard J., University of Missouri-Kansas City
Gerhard, Lee C., University of Kansas
Gonzalez Leon, Carlos M., Universidad Nacional Autonoma de Mexico
Hamlin, H, Scott, University of Texas at Austin, Jackson School of Geosciences
Hammes, Ursula, University of Texas at Austin
Harvey, Cyril H., Guilford College
Hasenmueller, Walter, indiana University
Hattin, Donald E., Indiana University, Bloomington
Heermance, Richard V., California State University, Northridge
Helenes, Javier, Centro de Investigación Científica y de Ed Superior de Ensenada
Heller, Paul L., University of Wyoming
Heron, Duncan, Duke University
Hinnov, Linda, George Mason University
Hippensteel, Scott P., University of North Carolina, Charlotte
Holland, Steven M., University of Georgia
Jacobi, Robert D., SUNY, Buffalo
Jacques Ayala, Cesar, Universidad Nacional Autonoma de Mexico
Jansa, Lubomir F., Dalhousie University
Janson, Xavier, University of Texas at Austin, Jackson School of Geosciences
Jenkyns, Hugh, University of Oxford
Joeckel, Robert M., University of Nebraska, Lincoln
Johnson, Donald O., Argonne National Laboratory
Johnson, Gary D., Dartmouth College
Johnson, William C., University of Kansas
Jordan, Robert R., University of Delaware
Jordan, Teresa A., Cornell University
Kaaya, Charles Z., University of Dar es Salaam
Kauffman, Marvin E., University of Montana Western
Kehler, Philip L., University of Arkansas at Little Rock
King, Norman R., University of Southern Indiana
King, Jr., David T., Auburn University
Kleffner, Mark A., Ohio State University
Kulp, Mark A., University of New Orleans
Lang, Harold R., Jet Propulsion Laboratory
Langenheim, Jr., Ralph L., University of Illinois, Urbana-Champaign
Lash, Gary G., SUNY, Fredonia
Lee, Richard R., Oak Ridge National Laboratory
Lincoln, Jonathan M., Montclair State University
Loydell, David, University of Portsmouth
Lozinsky, Richard P., Fullerton College
Ludvigson, Greg A., University of Kansas
Lundblad, Steven P., University of Hawai'i, Hilo
Manger, Walter, University of Arkansas, Fayetteville
Manspeizer, Warren, Rutgers, The State University of New Jersey, Newark
Martinez-Gutierrez, Genaro, Universidad Autonoma de Baja California Sur

Matson, Sam, Boise State University
Maytorena-Silva, Jesus F., Centro de Estudios Superiores del Estado Sonora
McClaughry, Jason D., Oregon Dept of Geology & Mineral Industries
McKee, James W., University of Wisconsin, Oshkosh
McLaughlin, Patrick I., Indiana University
McLaughlin, Patrick I., University of Wisconsin, Extension
McLaughlin, Jr., Peter P., University of Delaware
McLaurin, Brett T., Bloomsburg University
Meckel, Timothy A., University of Texas at Austin
Merriam, Daniel F., Wichita State University
Metz, Robert, Kean University
Monreal-Saavedra, Rogelio, Centro de Estudios Superiores del Estado Sonora
Monteverde, Donald H., New Jersey Geological Survey
Morris, Thomas H., Brigham Young University
Nance, Hardie S., University of Texas at Austin
Neal, Donald W., East Carolina University
Nicolas, Michelle, Manitoba Geological Survey
Nielson, Russell L., Stephen F. Austin State University
Norford, Brian, University of Calgary
Olariu, Cornel, University of Texas at Austin
Olariu, Mariana, University of Texas at Austin
Oms Llobet, Oriol, Universitat Autonoma de Barcelona
Osleger, David A., University of California, Davis
Owen, Donald E., Lamar University
Page, Kevin, University of Plymouth
Paine, Jeffrey G., University of Texas at Austin, Jackson School of Geosciences
Parcell, William C., Wichita State University
Pemberton, S. George, University of Alberta
Peterson, Gary L., San Diego State University
Peterson, Larry C., University of Miami
Pieren, Agustin P., Univ Complutense de Madrid
Poch Serra, Joan, Universitat Autonoma de Barcelona
Pope, Michael , Texas A&M University
Quinn, Heather, Maryland Department of Natural Resources
Remacha Grau, Eduard, Universitat Autonoma de Barcelona
Reynolds, James H., Brevard College
Sadler, Peter M., University of California, Riverside
Sanders, Ronald S., Jet Propulsion Laboratory
Schmitt, James G., Montana State University
Scott, Thomas M., University of South Florida, Tampa
Simmons, Lizanne V., Santiago Canyon College
Smosna, Richard A., West Virginia University
Snyder, Walter S., Boise State University
Spreng, Alfred C., Missouri University of Science and Technology
Stanley, Thomas M., University of Oklahoma
Steinberg, Roger T., Del Mar College
Stieglitz, Ronald D., University of Wisconsin, Green Bay
Sugarman, Peter J., New Jersey Geological Survey
Sugarman, Peter P., Rutgers, The State University of New Jersey
Suneson, Neil , University of Oklahoma
Swenson, John B., University of Minnesota, Duluth
Terry, Dennis O., Temple University
Tew , Berry H., Geological Survey of Alabama
Uptegrove, Jane, New Jersey Geological Survey
Vail, Peter R., Rice University
Valenzuela-Renteria, Manuel, Centro de Estudios Superiores del Estado Sonora
Van de Water, Peter, California State University, Fresno
Ver Straeten, Charles, New York State Geological Survey
Vondra, Carl F., Iowa State University of Science & Technology
Watney, Lynn W., University of Kansas
Watney, W. Lynn, University of Kansas
Webb, Fred, Appalachian State University
Weibel, C. Pius, Illinois State Geological Survey
Weimer, Robert J., Colorado School of Mines
Zachry, Doy L., University of Arkansas, Fayetteville
Zenger, Donald H., Pomona College

Structural Geology
 Bodhankar, Ninad, Pt. Ravishankar Shukla University
Abdelsalam, Mohamed, Oklahoma State University
Abolins, Mark J., Middle Tennessee State University
Adam, Jurgen, University of London, Royal Holloway & Bedford New College
Adams, John B., University of Washington
Alaniz Alvarez, Susana A., Universidad Nacional Autonoma de Mexico
Aldrich, M. James, Los Alamos National Laboratory
Allard, Stephen T., Winona State University
Allen, Joseph L., Concord University
Allen, Richardson B., University of Utah
Allison, David T., University of South Alabama
Allmendinger, Richard W., Cornell University
Alsleben, Helge, Texas Christian University
Amato, Jeffrey M., New Mexico State University, Las Cruces
Amenta, Roddy V., James Madison University
Amos, Colin B., Western Washington University
Anastasio, David J., Lehigh University
Anderson, James L., University of Hawai'i, Hilo
Anderson, Mark, University of Plymouth
Andrew, Joseph E., Youngstown State University
Arboleya Cimadevilla, María Luísa, Universitat Autonoma de Barcelona
Armstrong, Phillip A., California State University, Fullerton

Arrowsmith, Ramon, Arizona State University
Ave Lallemant, Hans G., Rice University
Axen, Gary, New Mexico Institute of Mining and Technology
Aydin, Atilla, Stanford University
Babaie, Hassan A., Georgia State University
Bailey, Christopher M., College of William & Mary
Baird, Graham, University of Northern Colorado
Balestro, Gianni, Università di Torino
Bangs, Nathan L., University of Texas at Austin
Banoeng-Yakubo, Bruce K., University of Ghana
Baran, Zeynep O., South Dakota School of Mines & Technology
Barineau, Clinton I., Columbus State University
Barker, Chris A., Stephen F. Austin State University
Barnes, Charles W., Northern Arizona University
Bauer, Paul W., New Mexico Institute of Mining and Technology
Bauer, Robert L., University of Missouri
Bayly, M. Brian, Rensselaer Polytechnic Institute
Behr, Rose-Anna, Pennsylvania Bureau of Topographic & Geologic Survey
Behr, Whitney, University of Texas at Austin
Bemis, Sean, University of Kentucky
Berry, Ron F., University of Tasmania
Bethune, Kathryn, University of Regina
Betka, Paul, Alaska Division of Geological & Geophysical Surveys
Beutel, Erin K., College of Charleston
Bhattacharyya, Juk, University of Wisconsin, Whitewater
Bidgoli, Tandis, University of Kansas
Bilodeau, William L., California Lutheran University
Bishop, Kim, California State University, Los Angeles
Bjorklund, Tom, University of Houston
Bjornerud, Marcia, Lawrence University
Blackmer, Gale C., Pennsylvania Bureau of Topographic & Geologic Survey
Bobyarchick, Andy R., University of North Carolina, Charlotte
Boniface, Nelson, University of Dar es Salaam
Bosbyshell, Howell, West Chester University
Bothner, Wallace A., University of New Hampshire
Bradley, Michael, Eastern Michigan University
Brandon, Mark T., Yale University
Brennan, William J., SUNY, Geneseo
Brisbin, William C., University of Manitoba
Brodie, Kate, University of Manchester
Brogan, George, Irvine Valley College
Brown, Bruce A., University of Wisconsin, Extension
Brown, William G., Baylor University
Bruhn, Ronald L., University of Utah
Bunds, Michael, Utah Valley University
Burberry, Caroline M., University of Nebraska, Lincoln
Burchfiel, B. C., Massachusetts Institute of Technology
Burger, H. Robert, Smith College
Burks, Rachel J., Towson University
Burmeister, Kurtis C., University of the Pacific
Butner, Steffen, Rhodes University
Bykerk-Kauffman, Ann, California State University, Chico
Byrne, Timothy, University of Connecticut
Cadoppi, Paola, Università di Torino
Calon, Tomas J., Memorial University of Newfoundland
Camilleri, Phyllis A., Austin Peay State University
Campagna, David, West Virginia University
Campbell, Patricia A., Slippery Rock University
Campbell-Stone, Erin A., University of Wyoming
Carlson, Diane H., California State University, Sacramento
Carosi, Rodolfo, Università di Torino
Carreras Planells, Jordi, Universitat Autonoma de Barcelona
Cashman, Patricia H., University of Nevada, Reno
Cashman, Susan M., Humboldt State University
Caskey, John, San Francisco State University
Cather, Steven M., New Mexico Institute of Mining and Technology
Çemen, Ibrahim, University of Alabama
Chapman, Alan, Macalester College
Chester, Frederick M., Texas A&M University
Chester, Judith, Texas A&M University
Clayton, Robert W., Brigham Young University - Idaho
Cloos, Mark P., University of Texas at Austin
Coleman, Jr., Paul J., University of California, Los Angeles
Colliston, Wayne, University of the Free State
Connelly, Jeffrey B., University of Arkansas at Little Rock
Coogan, James, Western State Colorado University
Cooke-Andresen, Michele L., University of Massachusetts, Amherst
Coppinger, Walter, Trinity University
Cosgrove, John, Imperial College
Cowan, Darrel S., University of Washington
Cowgill, Eric S., University of California, Davis
Craddock, John P., Macalester College
Crespi, Jean M., University of Connecticut
Crider, Juliet, University of Washington
Cronin, Vincent S., Baylor University
Crooke, Levi A., Geological Survey of Alabama
Crowley, Peter D., Amherst College
Cruikshank, Kenneth M., Portland State University
Csontos, Ryan, University of Memphis
Culshaw, Nicholas, Dalhousie University

Curl, Doug C., University of Kentucky
Czeck, Dyanna M., University of Wisconsin, Milwaukee
D'Allura, Jad A., Southern Oregon University
Daigneault, Real, Universite du Quebec a Chicoutimi
Davatzes, Nicholas, Temple University
Davis, George H., University of Arizona
Davis, Gregory A., University of Southern California
Davis, Peter B., Pacific Lutheran University
Dawers, Nancye H., Tulane University
De Paola, Nicola, Durham University
Di Toro, Giulio, Università degli Studi di Padova
DiPietro, Joseph A., University of Southern Indiana
Dixon, John M., Queen's University
Dooley, Tim, University of Texas at Austin, Jackson School of Geosciences
Douglas, Bruce, Indiana University, Bloomington
Draper, Grenville, Florida International University
Druguet Tantiña, Elena, Universitat Autonoma de Barcelona
Duebendorfer, Ernest M., Northern Arizona University
Dumitru, Trevor, Stanford University
Dunne, George C., California State University, Northridge
Dunne, William M., University of Tennessee, Knoxville
Dunning, Jeremy D., Indiana University, Bloomington
Dutch, Steven I., University of Wisconsin, Green Bay
Elliot, Colleen, Montana Tech of The University of Montana
Erdmer, Philippe, University of Alberta
Erslev, Eric A., Colorado State University
Erslev, Eric A., University of Wyoming
Eusden, Jr., J. Dykstra, Bates College
Evans, James P., Utah State University
Evans, Mark, Central Connecticut State University
Famin, Vincent, Universite de la Reunion
Faulds, James E., University of Nevada, Reno
Faure, Stephane, Universite du Quebec a Montreal
Fayon, Annia K., University of Minnesota, Twin Cities
Ferguson, Charles A., Arizona Geological Survey
Ferre, Eric C., Southern Illinois University Carbondale
Festa, Andrea, Università di Torino
Fischer, Mark P., Northern Illinois University
Fisher, Donald M., Pennsylvania State University, University Park
Franke, Otto L., Graduate School of the City University of New York
Fraser, Alastair, University of Utah
Fryer, Karen H., Ohio Wesleyan University
Fryxell, Joan E., California State University, San Bernardino
Fueten, Frank, Brock University
Fusseis, Florian, Edinburgh University
Fyson, William K., University of Ottawa
Gani, Nahid, Western Kentucky University
Garihan, John M., Furman University
Gates, Alexander E., Rutgers, The State University of New Jersey, Newark
Gattiglio, Marco, Università di Torino
Geraghty Ward, Emily, Rocky Mountain College
Gibson, H. Daniel (Dan), Simon Fraser University
Gibson, Roger L., University of the Witwatersrand
Gibson, Ronald C., Golden West College
Gillespie, Thomas, College of New Jersey
Gilotti, Jane A., University of Iowa
Giorgis, Scott D., SUNY, Geneseo
Girty, Gary H., San Diego State University
Gleason, Gayle C., SUNY, Cortland
Gold, David P., Pennsylvania State University, University Park
Golombek, Matthew P., Jet Propulsion Laboratory
Goodwin, Laurel, University of Wisconsin, Madison
Goulet, Normand, Universite du Quebec a Montreal
Gray, Mary Beth, Bucknell University
Greene, David C., Denison University
Griera Artigas, Albert, Universitat Autonoma de Barcelona
Griffith, Ashley, University of Texas, Arlington
Groshong, Jr., Richard H., University of Alabama
Gross, Michael, Florida International University
Groszos, Mark S., Valdosta State University
Growdon, Martha L., SUNY, Oneonta
Gudmundsson, Agust, University of London, Royal Holloway & Bedford New College
Guitierrez-Alonso, Gabriel, Florida International University
Gulick, Sean S., University of Texas at Austin
Guth, Lawrence R., Fitchburg State University
Hack, Alistair, University of Newcastle
Hacker, David B., Kent State University
Hall, Frank W., Indiana University of Pennsylvania
Hanley, Thomas B., Columbus State University
Hanmer, Simon, Carleton University
Hannula, Kimberly, Fort Lewis College
Hansen, Vicki L., University of Minnesota, Duluth
Hariri, Mustafa, King Fahd University of Petroleum and Minerals
Harrap, Rob, Queen's University
Harris, Lyal B., Universite du Quebec
Harris, Ron, Brigham Young University
Harrison, Michael J., Tennessee Tech University
Hatcher, Jr., Robert D., University of Tennessee, Knoxville
Hefferan, Kevin P., University of Wisconsin, Stevens Point
Heimsath, Arjun, Arizona State University

Helmstaedt, Herwart, Queen's University
Helper, Mark A., University of Texas at Austin
Hendrix, Thomas E., Grand Valley State University
Hennings, Peter H., University of Wyoming
Herman, Gregory C., New Jersey Geological Survey
Hetherington, Eric D., College of the Sequoias
Hetzel, Ralf, Universitaet Muenster
Hibbard, James P., North Carolina State University
Hill, Joseph C., Sam Houston State University
Hill, Mary Louise, Lakehead University
Hinz, Nick, University of Nevada, Reno
Hirth, Greg, Brown University
Hirth, Gregory, Woods Hole Oceanographic Institution
Hodges, Kip V., Arizona State University
Hoffman, Paul F., Harvard University
Holdsworth, Robert E., Durham University
Holm, Daniel K., Kent State University
Hooks, Benjamin P., University of Tennessee, Martin
Horsman, Eric, East Carolina University
Hozik, Michael J., Stockton University
Hubbard, Mary S., Utah State University
Hudec, Michael R., University of Texas at Austin
Hudleston, Peter J., University of Minnesota, Twin Cities
Hull, Joseph M., Seattle Central Community College
Huntsman, John R., University of North Carolina Wilmington
Hurst, Stephen D., University of Illinois, Urbana-Champaign
Hynes, Andrew J., McGill University
Imber, Jonathan, Durham University
Inceoz, Murat, Firat University
Ismat, Zeshan, Franklin and Marshall College
Jackson, Martin P. A., University of Texas at Austin, Jackson School of Geosciences
Jackson, Richard A., Long Island University, Brooklyn Campus
Jackson Jr, William T., Geological Survey of Alabama
Jacobson, Carl E., Iowa State University of Science & Technology
Jagoutz, Oliver, Massachusetts Institute of Technology
Jessup, Micah, University of Tennessee, Knoxville
Jiang, Dazhi, Western University
Jirsa, Mark, University of Minnesota
John, Barbara E., University of Wyoming
Johnson, Arvid M., Purdue University
Johnson, Scott E., University of Maine
Johnston, Scott, California Polytechnic State University
Johnston, Stephen T., University of Victoria
Jones, Gustavo Tolson, Universidad Nacional Autonoma de Mexico
Kalakay, Thomas J., Rocky Mountain College
Kanat, Leslie H., Johnson State College
Kapp, Paul, University of Arizona
Karabinos, Paul, Williams College
Kath, Randal L., University of West Georgia
Kehlenbeck, Manfred M., Lakehead University
Kelsch, Jesse, Sul Ross State University
Kelty, Thomas, California State University, Long Beach
Kennedy, Lori, University of British Columbia
Kirkpatrick, James, McGill University
Klepeis, Keith A., University of Vermont
Klimczak, Christian , University of Georgia
Kopf, Christopher, Mansfield University
Kruckenberg, Seth C., Boston College
Krugh, W C., California State University, Bakersfield
Kuiper, Yvette D., Colorado School of Mines
Kulander, Byron, Wright State University
Kutu, Jacob M., University of Ghana
Lafrance, Bruno, Laurentian University, Sudbury
Lageson, David R., Montana State University
Langille, Jackie M., University of North Carolina, Asheville
Lankreijer, Anco, VU University Amsterdam
Lao Davila, Daniel, Oklahoma State University
Lapusta, Nadia, California Institute of Technology
Lash, Gary S., SUNY, Buffalo
Laubach, Stephen E., University of Texas at Austin, Jackson School of Geosciences
Laurent-Charvet, Sébastien, Institut Polytechnique LaSalle Beauvais (ex-IGAL)
Law, Richard D., Virginia Polytechnic Institute & State University
Lee, Jeffrey, Central Washington University
Lemiszki, Peter, University of Tennessee, Knoxville
Lemiszki, Peter J., Tennessee Geological Survey
Lenardic, Adrian, Rice University
Lennox, Paul, University of New South Wales
Lewis, Jon C., Indiana University of Pennsylvania
Lincoln, Beth Z., Albion College
Lisenbee, Alvis L., South Dakota School of Mines & Technology
Lisle, R J., Cardiff University
Little, Tim, Victoria University of Wellington
Livaccari, Richard F., Colorado Mesa University
Long , Long P., Washington State University
Lowry, Wallace D., Virginia Polytechnic Institute & State University
Luther, Amy, Louisiana State University
MacDonald, William D., Binghamton University
MacLean, John S., Southern Utah University
Maher, Jr., Harmon D., University of Nebraska at Omaha
Malo, Michel, Universite du Quebec

Malone, David H., Illinois State University
Markley, Michelle J., Mount Holyoke College
Marrett, Randall A., University of Texas at Austin
Marshak, Stephen, University of Illinois, Urbana-Champaign
Martin, Silvana, Università degli Studi di Padova
Martinez-Macias, Panfilo R., Universidad Autonoma de San Luis Potosi
Marty, Kevin G., Imperial Valley College
Mattson, Peter H., Queens College (CUNY)
Mattson, Peter H., Graduate School of the City University of New York
McCaffrey, Kenneth J., Durham University
McCair, Andrew, University of Leeds
McClay, Ken, University of London, Royal Holloway & Bedford New College
McClelland, William C., University of Iowa
McGill, George E., University of Massachusetts, Amherst
McGrew, Allen J., University of Dayton
McIntosh, Kirk D., University of Texas at Austin
McNaught, Mark A., Mount Union College
McNulty, Brendan A., California State University, Dominguez Hills
McQuarrie, Nadine, University of Pittsburgh
Mecklenburgh, Julian, University of Manchester
Meere, Pat, University College Cork
Meigs, Andrew J., Oregon State University
Menegon, Luca, University of Plymouth
Merguerian, Charles M., Hofstra University
Mies, Jonathan W., University of Tennessee at Chattanooga
Miller, Elizabeth L., Stanford University
Miller, Marli G., University of Oregon
Miller, Robert B., San Jose State University
Milligan, G. Clinton, Dalhousie University
Miranda, Elena A., California State University, Northridge
Mitchell, Tom, University College London
Mitra, Gautam, University of Rochester
Mitra, Shankar, University of Oklahoma
Moeck, Inga, Technische Universitaet Muenchen
Mookerjee, Matty, Sonoma State University
Moore, George E., Ohio State University
Moore, J. Casey, University of California, Santa Cruz
Morell, Kristin, University of Victoria
Morgan, Julia K., Rice University
Morgan, Sven S., Central Michigan University
Mosher, Sharon, University of Texas at Austin
Mueller, Karl J., University of Colorado
Muller, Otto H., Alfred University
Muller, Peter D., Drexel University
Murphy, Michael, University of Houston
Needham, Tim, University of Leeds
Nemcok, Michal, University of Utah
Neuhauser, Kenneth R., Fort Hays State University
Newman, Julie, Texas A&M University
Niemi, Nathan, University of Michigan
Norris, Richard J., University of Otago
Northrup, Clyde J., Boise State University
Nourse, Jonathan A., California State Polytechnic University, Pomona
O'Hara, Kieran D., University of Kentucky
O'Meara, Stephanie, Colorado State University
Oertel, Gerhard, University of California, Los Angeles
Ohan, Anderson A., College of Staten Island
Oldow, John S., University of Texas, Dallas
Onasch, Charles M., Bowling Green State University
Osagiede, Edoseghe E., University of Benin
Palmquist, John C., Lawrence University
Paterson, Scott R., University of Southern California
Paton, Douglas, University of Leeds
Patton, Regan L., Washington State University
Paulsen, Timothy S., University of Wisconsin, Oshkosh
Pavlis, Terry L., University of Texas, El Paso
Pawley, Alison, University of Manchester
Pearson, David M., Idaho State University
Pennacchioni, Giorgio, Università degli Studi di Padova
Perry, Bruce, California State University, Long Beach
Petrie, Elizabeth S., Western State Colorado University
Phipps, Stephen P., University of Pennsylvania
Pignotta, Geoffrey S., University of Wisconsin, Eau Claire
Pinan-Llamas, Aranzazu, Indiana University / Purdue University, Fort Wayne
Platt, John, University of Southern California
Platt, Lucian B., Bryn Mawr College
Pogue, Kevin R., Whitman College
Pollard, David D., Stanford University
Potter, Jr., Donald B., Sewanee: University of the South
Praekelt, Hermann, University of the Free State
Price, Nancy A., Portland State University
Quintero, Odranoel, Universidad Nacional Autonoma de Mexico
Raffini, Sylvain, Universite du Quebec a Chicoutimi
Ratchford, Michael , University of Idaho
Reber, Jacqueline, Iowa State University of Science & Technology
Ree, Jin-Han, Korea University
Reed, Robert, University of Texas at Austin, Jackson School of Geosciences
Reese, Joseph F., Edinboro University of Pennsylvania
Reinen, Linda A., Pomona College
Resor, Phillip G., Wesleyan University

Rhodes, Brady P., California State University, Fullerton
Richard, Stephen M., Arizona Geological Survey
Ritchie, Alexander W., College of Charleston
Robertson, Charles E., Missouri University of Science and Technology
Robin, Pierre-Yves F., University of Toronto
Robinson, Alexander, University of Houston
Robinson, Delores, University of Alabama
Robinson, Kevin, San Diego State University
Robinson, Peter, University of Massachusetts, Amherst
Rodgers, David W., Idaho State University
Roeske, Sarah M., University of California, Davis
Rogers, Robert D., California State University, Stanislaus
Rojo-Garcia, Paulino, Universidad Autonoma de Baja California Sur
Rousell, Don H., Laurentian University, Sudbury
Rowe, Christie, McGill University
Rowley, David B., University of Chicago
Roy, Denis W., Universite du Quebec a Chicoutimi
Rusmore, Margaret E., Occidental College
Rutter, Ernest, University of Manchester
Saillet, Elodie, Institut Polytechnique LaSalle Beauvais (ex-IGAL)
Saja, David, Case Western Reserve University
Sak, Peter B., Dickinson College
Saleeby, Jason B., California Institute of Technology
Samaniego, Angel Nieto, Universidad Nacional Autonoma de Mexico
Satterfield, Joseph I., Angelo State University
Scharer, Katherine, Appalachian State University
Scharman, Mitchell, Marshall University
Scharnberger, Charles K., Millersville University
Schlische, Roy W., Rutgers, The State University of New Jersey
Schmidt, Keegan L., Lewis-Clark State College
Schoonmaker, Adam, Utica College
Schrank, Christoph, Queensland University of Technology
Schwerdtner, W. M., University of Toronto
Secor, Donald, University of South Carolina
Selander, Jacob A., University of Minnesota, Duluth
Shaw, Colin, Montana State University
Shilpakar, Prabin ., University of Texas, Dallas
Short, Heather, McGill University
Shuib, Mustaffa Kamal, University of Malaya
Sibson, Rick H., University of Otago
Siddoway, Christine S., Colorado College
Simony, Philip S., University of Calgary
Singleton, John, Colorado State University
Skehan, James W., Boston College
Skehan, S.J., James W., Boston College
Skemer, Philip, Washington University in St. Louis
Snook, James R., Eastern Washington University
Solar, Gary S., Buffalo State College
Sorkhabi, Rasoul, University of Utah
Spencer, Edgar W., Washington & Lee University
Spratt, Deborah A., University of Calgary
SRIVASTAVA, HARI B., Banaras Hindu University
Stauffer, Mel R., University of Saskatchewan
Stearns, David W., University of Oklahoma
Stewart, Kevin G., University of North Carolina, Chapel Hill
Stimac, John P., Eastern Illinois University
Stinson, Amy L., Santiago Canyon College
Stinson, Amy L., Irvine Valley College
Stockli, Daniel, University of Texas at Austin
Stockli, Daniel F., University of Kansas
Stowell Gale, Julia, University of Texas at Austin, Jackson School of Geosciences
Strayer, Luther M., California State University, East Bay
Sullivan, Walter A., Colby College
Suneson, Neil H., University of Oklahoma
Surpless, Benjamin E., Trinity University
Talbot, James L., Western Washington University
Tapp, J. B., University of Tulsa
Taylor, Lansing, University of Utah
Taylor, Wanda J., University of Nevada, Las Vegas
Tewksbury, Barbara J., Hamilton College
Teyssier, Christian P., University of Minnesota, Twin Cities
Thompson, Margaret D., Wellesley College
Tikoff, Basil, University of Wisconsin, Madison
Timmons, J M., New Mexico Institute of Mining and Technology
Tindall, Sarah E., Kutztown University of Pennsylvania
Titus, Sarah J., Carleton College
Tobisch, Othmar T., University of California, Santa Cruz
Toro, Jaime, West Virginia University
Torvela, Taija, University of Leeds
Toy, Virginia G., University of Otago
Treloar, Peter, Kingston University
Tremblay, Alain, Universite du Quebec a Montreal
Trudgill, Bruce D., Colorado School of Mines
Trullenque, Ghislain, Institut Polytechnique LaSalle Beauvais (ex-IGAL)
Trupe, Charles H., Georgia Southern University
Tso, Jonathan L., Radford University
Tull, James F., Florida State University
Tullis, Jan A., Brown University
Twiss, Robert J., University of California, Davis
Ustaszewski, Kamil, Friedrich-Schiller-University Jena

Van Arsdale, Roy B., University of Memphis
van der Pluijm, Ben A., University of Michigan
Vaqueiro Rodriguez, Marcos, Coruna University
Vogl, Jim, University of Florida
Voicu, Gabriel-Constantin, Universite du Quebec a Montreal
Vollmer, Frederick W., SUNY, New Paltz
Waag, Charles J., Boise State University
Waldron, John, Dalhousie University
Waldron, John W., University of Alberta
Walker, J. Douglas, University of Kansas
Waters-Tormey, Cheryl, Western Carolina University
Watkinson, A. John, Washington State University
Waugh, Richard A., University of Wisconsin, Platteville
Weber, John C., Grand Valley State University
Weil, Arlo B., Bryn Mawr College
Weldon, Ray J., University of Oregon
Wells, Michael L., University of Nevada, Las Vegas
Wernicke, Brian P., California Institute of Technology
West, David P., Middlebury College
Whalley, John, University of Portsmouth
Whisner, S. Christopher, Bloomsburg University
White, Joseph C., University of New Brunswick
Whitmeyer, Steven J., James Madison University
Wickham, John S., University of Texas, Arlington
Wilkerson, M. S., University of Illinois, Urbana-Champaign
Wilkerson, M. Scott, DePauw University
Williams, Michael L., University of Massachusetts, Amherst
Williams, Paul F., University of New Brunswick
Wilson, Terry J., Ohio State University
Winslow, Margaret A., City College (CUNY)
Winslow, Margaret S., Graduate School of the City University of New York
Withjack, Martha O., Rutgers, The State University of New Jersey
Wojtal, Steven F., Oberlin College
Woodward, Lee A., University of New Mexico
Woodwell, Grant R., University of Mary Washington
Workman-Ford, Kerry, California State University, Fresno
Wright, Stephen F., University of Vermont
Yikilmaz, Burak, University of California, Davis
Yonkee, W. A., Weber State University
Yoshinobu, Aaron S., Texas Tech University
Young, Grant M., Western University
Zampieri, Dario, Università degli Studi di Padova
Zimmerman, Jr., Jay, Southern Illinois University Carbondale

Tectonics

Abercrombie, Rachel, Boston University
Akciz, Sinan, University of California, Los Angeles
Alexander, Jan, University of East Anglia
Anderson, Robert G., University of British Columbia
Andeweg, Bernd , VU University Amsterdam
Andrews, Graham D., California State University, Bakersfield
Artoni, Andrea, University of Parma
Ault, Alexis K., Utah State University
Avouac, Jean-Philippe, California Institute of Technology
Barnhart, William, University of Iowa
Barquero-Molina, Miriam, University of Missouri
Barth, Nicolas, University of California, Riverside
Bartholomew, Mervin J., University of Memphis
Bell, Andrew, Edinburgh University
Bell, Rebecca, Imperial College
Berti, Claudio, Lehigh University
Bhattacharji, Somdev, Graduate School of the City University of New York
Bickle, Michael, University of Cambridge
Bieler, David B., Centenary College of Louisiana
Bird, John M., Cornell University
Blake, M. Clark, Western Washington University
Boggs, Katherine, Mount Royal University
Boland, Irene B., Winthrop University
Boutelier, David, University of Newcastle
Boyer, Robert E., University of Texas at Austin
Boyle, Alan, University of Liverpool
Bradshaw, John, University of Canterbury
Brown, Sarah, California State University, Bakersfield
Bullen, Dean, University of Portsmouth
Burgette, Reed J., New Mexico State University, Las Cruces
Burgmann, Roland, University of California, Berkeley
Burke, Kevin, University of Houston
Busby, Cathy J., University of California, Davis
Camacho, Alfredo, University of Manitoba
Carlson, Marvin P., Unversity of Nebraska - Lincoln
Carlson, Richard L., Texas A&M University
Carr, Sharon D., Carleton University
Casey, John F., University of Houston
Cawood, PEter, University of St. Andrews
Centeno Garcia, Elena, Universidad Nacional Autonoma de Mexico
Chapin, Charles E., New Mexico Institute of Mining & Technology
Chi, Wu-Cheng, Academia Sinica
Choi, Eunseo, University of Memphis
Church, William R., Western University
Cole, Ron B., Allegheny College

Conrad, Clint, University of Hawai'i, Manoa
Contreras, Juan, Centro de Investigación Científica y de Ed Superior de Ensenada
Corrigan, David, University of Manitoba
Cox, Randel T., University of Memphis
Cruden, Alexander, University of Toronto
Cunningham, William D., Eastern Connecticut State University
Dallmeyer, R. David, University of Georgia
Dalziel, Ian W. D., University of Texas at Austin
Das, Shamita, University of Oxford
De Cserna, Zoltan, Universidad Nacional Autonoma de Mexico
Dewey, John, University of California, Davis
Dickinson, William R., University of Arizona
Dilek, Yildirm, Miami University
Dinter, David A., University of Utah
Dolan, James F., University of Southern California
Dooley, Tim P., University of Texas at Austin
Driscoll, Peter E., Carnegie Institution of Washington
Ducea, Mihai N., University of Arizona
Dumond, Gregory, University of Arkansas, Fayetteville
Ebinger, Cynthia J., University of Rochester
Engebretson, David C., Western Washington University
England, Phillip, University of Oxford
Feigl, Kurt L., University of Wisconsin, Madison
Ferrari Pedraglio, Luca, Universidad Nacional Autonoma de Mexico
Fitzgerald, Paul G., Syracuse University
Fosdick, Julie C., Indiana University, Bloomington
Foster, David A., University of Florida
Furlong, Kevin P., Pennsylvania State University, University Park
Gable, Carl W., Los Alamos National Laboratory
Gale, Julia F., University of Texas at Austin
Gans, Phillip B., University of California, Santa Barbara
Garver, John I., Union College
Gehrels, George E., University of Arizona
Geissman, John D., University of Texas, Dallas
Gerbi, Christopher C., University of Maine
German, Chris, Woods Hole Oceanographic Institution
Gifford, Jennifer N., St. Lawrence University
Gomez, Francisco, University of Missouri
Goodwin, Laurel, University of Wisconsin, Madison
Gordon, Richard G., Rice University
Greenberg, Jeffrey K., Wheaton College
Gries, John C., Wichita State University
Grose, L. Trowbridge, Colorado School of Mines
Grujic, Djordje, Dalhousie University
Guenthner, Willy, University of Illinois, Urbana-Champaign
Hales, T. C., University of Wales
Hall, Clarence A., University of California, Los Angeles
Hall, Robert, University of London, Royal Holloway & Bedford New College
Hamilton, Warren B., University of Wyoming
Haq, Saad, Purdue University
Harley, Simon L., Edinburgh University
Harms, Tekla A., Amherst College
Harris, Nigel, The Open University
Hemphill-Haley, Mark, Humboldt State University
Hourigan, Jeremy K., University of California, Santa Cruz
Hughes, Sam, Exeter University
Huntington, Katharine W., University of Washington
Hurtado, Jose M., University of Texas, El Paso
Insel, Nadja, Northeastern Illinois University
Ivins, Erik R., Jet Propulsion Laboratory
Jackson, Christopher, Imperial College
Jackson, Martin P., University of Texas at Austin
Janecke, Susanne U., Utah State University
Jayko, Angela S., Humboldt State University
John, Hickman B., University of Kentucky
Judge, Shelley, College of Wooster
Karlstrom, Karl E., University of New Mexico
Karson, Jeffrey, Syracuse University
Kato, Terence T., California State University, Chico
Keir, Derek, University of Southampton
Keller, Edward A., University of California, Santa Barbara
Kelley, Shari A., New Mexico Institute of Mining and Technology
Keppie, J. Duncan, Universidad Nacional Autonoma de Mexico
Keppie, John D., Universidad Nacional Autonoma de Mexico
Kirstein, Linda, Edinburgh University
Kleinspehn, Karen L., University of Minnesota, Twin Cities
Klemperer, Simon L., Stanford University
Knipe, Rob, University of Leeds
Knuepfer, Peter L. K., Binghamton University
Koehler, Rich D., Alaska Division of Geological & Geophysical Surveys
Koehn, Daniel, University of Glasgow
Kokum, Mehmet, Firat University
Koons, Peter O., University of Maine
Kronenberg, Andreas, Texas A&M University
Lamb, Melissa A., University of Saint Thomas
Lavier, Luc L., University of Texas at Austin
Lin, Jian, Woods Hole Oceanographic Institution
Lindsley-Griffin, Nancy, University of Nebraska, Lincoln
Lonergan, Lidia, Imperial College

Loveless, Jack, Smith College
Luo, Gang, University of Texas at Austin
Mallard, Laura, Appalachian State University
Mann, Paul, University of Texas at Austin
Mapani, Benjamin S., University of Namibia
Martinez, Juventino, Universidad Nacional Autonoma de Mexico
Martinez-Reyes, Juventino, Universidad Nacional Autonoma de Mexico
May, Daniel J., University of New Haven
McDowell, Rob J., Georgia Perimeter College
McGill, Sally F., California State University, San Bernardino
McKay, Matthew P., Geological Survey of Alabama
McNeill, Lisa, University of Southampton
McPherson, Robert C., Humboldt State University
McRivette, Michael, Albion College
Melichar, Rostislav, Masaryk University
Melosh, Henry J., University of Arizona
Mesbahi, Fatemeh, University of Tabriz
Michon, Laurent, Universite de la Reunion
Miller, Meghan, University of Southern California
Molnar, Peter, University of Colorado
Moore, Gregory F., University of Hawai'i, Manoa
Moores, Eldridge M., University of California, Davis
Moores, Eldridge M., University of California, Davis
Morgan, Julia K., Rice University
Morris, Terry, University of Plymouth
Moser, Desmond, Western University
Moucha, Robert, Syracuse University
Mound, Jon, University of Leeds
Murphy, J. Brendan, Saint Francis Xavier University
Möller, Andreas, University of Kansas
Nabelek, John L., Oregon State University
Nadeau, Leopold, Universite du Quebec
Nadin, Elisabeth, University of Alaska Fairbanks
Nance, R. Damian, Ohio University
Nash, Greg, University of Utah
Naylor, Mark, Edinburgh University
Ngo, Thanh X., Hanoi University of Mining & Geology
Niemi, Tina M., University of Missouri-Kansas City
Niocaill, Conall M., University of Oxford
Ocan, O. O., Obafemi Awolowo University
Onderdonk, Nate, California State University, Long Beach
Onderdonk, Nathan, California State University, Los Angeles
Partin, Camille, University of Saskatchewan
Passchier, Cees W., Universitaet Mainz
Pavlis, Terry L., University of New Orleans
Peterman, Emily M., Bowdoin College
Pettinga, Jarg, University of Canterbury
Pezzopane, Silvio K., Humboldt State University
Phillips, Richard, University of Leeds
Pieri, David C., Jet Propulsion Laboratory
Plasienka, Dusan, Comenius University
Prentice, Carol S., Humboldt State University
Price, Raymond A., Queen's University
Pyle, David, University of Oxford
Rahl, Jeffrey, Washington & Lee University
Regalla, Christine, Boston University
Reusch, Douglas N., University of Maine - Farmington
Reynolds, Stephen J., Arizona State University
Richter, Frank M., University of Chicago
Rieken, Eric R., University of Texas, Pan American
Robertson, Alastair H., Edinburgh University
Ross, Gerald M., University of Calgary
Rowan, Christopher J., Kent State University
Royden, Leigh H., Massachusetts Institute of Technology
Rubin, Charles M., Central Washington University
Rust, Derek, University of Portsmouth
Ryder, Isabelle, University of Liverpool
Schermer, Elizabeth R., Western Washington University
Schneider, David, University of Ottawa
Scotese, Christopher R., University of Texas, Arlington
Searle, Mike, University of Oxford
Shail, Robin, Exeter University
Shaw, John, Harvard University
Sinha, A. Krishna, Virginia Polytechnic Institute & State University
Sintubin, Manuel, Katholieke Universiteit Leuven
Spotila, James A., Virginia Polytechnic Institute & State University
Srimal, Neptune, Florida International University
Steltenpohl, Mark G., Auburn University
Stern, Robert J., University of Texas, Dallas
Stock, Joann M., California Institute of Technology
Stoddard, Paul R., Northern Illinois University
Strecker, Manfred, Cornell University
Streepey Smith, Meg, Earlham College
Suter-Cargnelutti, Max, Universidad Nacional Autonoma de Mexico
Takeuchi, Akira, University of Toyama
Taylor, Brian, University of Hawai'i, Manoa
Taylor, Michael H., University of Kansas
Teixell Cácharo, Antoni, Universitat Autonoma de Barcelona
Tesfaye, Samson, University of Missouri
Thigpen, Ryan, University of Kentucky

Thomas, William A., University of Kentucky
Thorkelson, Derek J., Simon Fraser University
Tivey, Maurice A., Woods Hole Oceanographic Institution
Turner, Jenni, University of East Anglia
Umhoefer, Paul J., Northern Arizona University
Unsworth, Martyn, University of Alberta
Valentine, Michael , Highline College
Valentino, David W., State University of New York at Oswego
vanKeken, Peter E., Carnegie Institution of Washington
Wallace, Laura, University of Texas at Austin
Watkinson, Ian, University of London, Royal Holloway & Bedford New College
Webb, Laura E., University of Vermont
Whipple, Kelin, Arizona State University
Whittaker, Alex, Imperial College
Willis, Julie B., Brigham Young University - Idaho
Wilson, Crystal, Appalachian State University
Wong, Martin, Colgate University
Woodcock, Nigel, University of Cambridge
Wright, James (Jim) E., University of Georgia
Yeats, Robert S., Oregon State University
Yin, An, University of California, Los Angeles
Yule, J. Douglas, California State University, Northridge
Zamani, Behzad, University of Tabriz

Volcanology

Aguirre Diaz, Gerardo J., Universidad Nacional Autonoma de Mexico
Anderson, Steve, University of Northern Colorado
Anderson, Jr., Alfred T., University of Chicago
Andrews, Benjamin, Smithsonian Institution / National Museum of Natural History
Banik, Tenley, Illinois State University
Barclay, Jenni, University of East Anglia
Befus, Kenneth S., Baylor University
Bellieni, Giuliano, Università degli Studi di Padova
Berlo, Kim, McGill University
Besancon, James, Wellesley College
Blake, Stephen, The Open University
Bohrson, Wendy A., Central Washington University
Boroughs, Scott, Washington State University
Branan, Yvonne K., Indiana University of Pennsylvania
Branney, Mike, Leicester University
Brown, David, University of Glasgow
Brown, Richard J., Durham University
Burkett, Brett, Collin College - Central Park Campus
Bursik, Marcus I., SUNY, Buffalo
Calder, Eliza, Edinburgh University
Cameron, Barry I., University of Wisconsin, Milwaukee
Cameron, Cheryl E., Division of Geological & Geophysical Surveys
Cameron, Cheryl, Alaska Division of Geological & Geophysical Surveys
Camp, Victor E., San Diego State University
Canon-Tapia, Edgardo, Centro de Investigación Científica y de Ed Superior de Ensenada
Carr, Michael J., Rutgers, The State University of New Jersey
Carrasco-Nunez, Gerardo, Universidad Nacional Autonoma de Mexico
Castro, Jonathan M., Universitaet Mainz
Chapin, Charles E., New Mexico Institute of Mining and Technology
Chapman, Marshall, Morehead State University
Chaussard, Estelle, SUNY, Buffalo
Cigolini, Corrdao, Università di Torino
Clarke, Amanda, Arizona State University
Cole, James, University of Canterbury
Cole, Paul, University of Plymouth
Connor, Charles B., University of South Florida, Tampa
Coulson, Ian, University of Regina
Crisp, Joy A., Jet Propulsion Laboratory
Crowe, Bruce M., Los Alamos National Laboratory
Davis, Fred, Smithsonian Institution / National Museum of Natural History
de Silva, Shanika, Oregon State University
Deardorff, Nicholas, Indiana University of Pennsylvania
Dennen, Rob, Smithsonian Institution / National Museum of Natural History
Domagall, Abigail M., Black Hills State University
Drake, Simon, Birkbeck College
Dufek, Josef, Georgia Institute of Technology
Duffield, Wendell A., Northern Arizona University
Duller, Rob, University of Liverpool
Edmonds, Marie, University of Cambridge
Eggers, Albert A., University of Puget Sound
Escobar-Wolf, Rudiger, Michigan Technological University
Fagents, Sarah, University of Hawai'i, Manoa
Fischer, Tobias, University of New Mexico
Fiske, Richard S., Smithsonian Institution / National Museum of Natural History
Flood, Tim P., Saint Norbert College
Frey, Holli M., Union College
Gardner, James E., University of Texas at Austin
Genareau, Kimberly, University of Alabama
Giordano, Daniele, Università di Torino
Godchaux, Martha M., Mount Holyoke College
Gonnermann, Helge, Rice University
Graettinger, Alison H., SUNY, Buffalo
Grapenthin, Ronni, New Mexico Institute of Mining and Technology
Gravley, Darren, University of Canterbury
Green, Jack, California State University, Long Beach

Gregg, Tracy K. P., SUNY, Buffalo
Gutmann, James T., Wesleyan University
Harpp, Karen, Colgate University
Harwood, Richard D., Black Hawk College
Hasenaka, Toshiaki, Kumamoto University
Hausback, Brian, California State University, Sacramento
Hazlett, Richard W., Pomona College
Head, Elisabet M., Northeastern Illinois University
Heiken, Grant, Los Alamos National Laboratory
Heliker, Christina C., University of Hawai'i, Hilo
Herd, Richard, University of East Anglia
Herrick, Julie, Smithsonian Institution / National Museum of Natural History
Hickson, Catherine J., University of British Columbia
Holm, Richard F., Northern Arizona University
Hon, Ken, University of Hawai'i, Hilo
Houghton, Bruce F., University of Hawai'i, Manoa
Houle, Michel, University of Manitoba
Johnson, Emily R., New Mexico State University, Las Cruces
Kauahikaua, James P., University of Hawai'i, Manoa
Kavanagh, Janine, University of Liverpool
Kennedy, Ben, University of Canterbury
Kieffer, Susan W., University of Illinois, Urbana-Champaign
Klemetti, Erik, Denison University
Kobs-Nawotniak, Shannon E., Idaho State University
Kohut, Ed, University of Delaware
Koornneef, Janne, VU University Amsterdam
Krier, Donathon J., Los Alamos National Laboratory
Lang, Nicholas, Mercyhurst University
Larsen, Jessica F., University of Alaska Fairbanks
Lavallee, Yan, University of Liverpool
Lee, Rachel J., State University of New York at Oswego
Lehto, Heather, Angelo State University
LeMasurier, Wesley E., University of Colorado, Denver
Lescinsky, David T., University of New Mexico
Lev, Einat , Columbia University
Leyrit, Hervé, Institut Polytechnique LaSalle Beauvais (ex-IGAL)
Llewellin, Ed, Durham University
Lockwood, John P., University of Hawai'i, Hilo
Magsino, Sammantha L., Nat Academy of Sciences/National Research Council
Manga, Michael, University of California, Berkeley
Maria, Tony, University of Southern Indiana
Martinez-Hackert, Bettina, Buffalo State College
Mather, Tamsin, University of Oxford
McBirney, Alexander R., University of Oregon
McConnell, Vicki S., Oregon Dept of Geology & Mineral Industries
McGarvie, Dave, The Open University
McGuire, Bill, University College London
McPhie, Jocelyn, University of Tasmania
Melson, William G., Smithsonian Institution / Nat Museum of Natural History
Memeti, Valbone , California State University, Fullerton
Michelfelder, Gary, Missouri State University
Moore, Joseph N., University of Utah
Neuberg, Jurgen, University of Leeds
Oliveras Castro, Valentí, Universitat Autonoma de Barcelona
Ort, Michael H., Northern Arizona University
Ottavi-Pupier, Elsa, Institut Polytechnique LaSalle Beauvais (ex-IGAL)
Panter, Kurt S., Bowling Green State University
Pe-Piper, Georgia, Dalhousie University
Perry, Frank V., Los Alamos National Laboratory
Phipps Morgan, Jason, Cornell University
Popp, Christoph, Smithsonian Institution / National Museum of Natural History
Pritchard, Matthew E., Cornell University
Putirka, Keith D., California State University, Fresno
Reynolds, Robert W., Central Oregon Community College
Rhodes, J. Michael, University of Massachusetts, Amherst
Riggs, Nancy, Northern Arizona University
Rinard, Bethany D., Tarleton State University
Robinson, Paul T., Dalhousie University
Rodrigquez, Lizzette A., Michigan Technological University
Roldan Quintana, Jaime, Universidad Nacional Autonoma de Mexico
Roman, Diana C., Carnegie Institution of Washington
Rose, William I., Michigan Technological University
Ross, Pierre-Simon, Universite du Quebec
Ruprecht, Philipp, Columbia University
Sanchez-Rubio, Gerardo, Universidad Nacional Autonoma de Mexico
Sar, Abdullah, Firat University
Saunders, Kate, Edinburgh University
Schaefer, Janet R., Division of Geological & Geophysical Surveys
Schaefer, Janet R. G., Alaska Division of Geological & Geophysical Surveys
Schwab, Brandon , Western Carolina University
Sennert, Sally K., Smithsonian Institution / National Museum of Natural History
Shea, Thomas, University of Hawai'i, Manoa
Sheridan, Michael F., SUNY, Buffalo
Smith, Alan L., California State University, San Bernardino
Solana, Camen, University of Portsmouth
Stevenson, John A., Edinburgh University
Stix, John, McGill University
Straub, Susanne, Columbia University
Swanson, Donald A., University of Hawai'i, Manoa
Szymanski, David, Bentley University

Taylor, Rex N., University of Southampton
Teasdale, Rachel, California State University, Chico
Templeton, Jeffrey H., Western Oregon University
Ukstins Peate, Ingrid, University of Iowa
Valentine, Gregory, SUNY, Buffalo
van Hunen, Jeroen, Durham University
Van Ry, Michael, Orange Coast College
Vanderkluysen, Loyc, Drexel University
Venzke, Edward, Smithsonian Institution / National Museum of Natural History
Vigouroux-Caillibot, Nathalie, Douglas College
Voight, Barry, Pennsylvania State University, University Park
Vroon, Pieter, VU University Amsterdam
Wallace, Paul, University of Oregon
Webber, Karen L., University of New Orleans
Webber, Karen L., University of Michigan
Wehner, Peter J., Austin Community College District
White, James D., University of Otago
Whittington, Alan, University of Missouri
Widdowson, Mike, The Open University
Williams, Stanley N., Arizona State University
Williams-Jones, Glyn, Simon Fraser University
Wilson, Thomas, University of Canterbury
Wohletz, Kenneth H., Los Alamos National Laboratory
Wohletz, Kenneth H., University of New Mexico
Wulff, Andrew, Western Kentucky University
Wunderman, Richard, Smithsonian Institution / Nat Museum of Natural History

Mathematical Geology
Agterberg, Frits P., University of Ottawa
Barton, Christopher, Wright State University
Bolton, Edward W., Yale University
Campbell, Katherine, Los Alamos National Laboratory
Chien, Yi-Ju, Pacific Northwest National Laboratory
Chou, Charissa J., Pacific Northwest National Laboratory
Cornejo-Luna, Efrain, Universidad Autonoma de Baja California Sur
Davis, John C., University of Kansas
de Hoop, Maarten, Purdue University
Doveton, John H., University of Kansas
Dyreson, Eric G., University of Montana Western
Edwards, Stuart, University of Newcastle Upon Tyne
Faccenda, Manuele, Università degli Studi di Padova
Fairbairn, David, University of Newcastle Upon Tyne
Ford, Allistair, University of Newcastle Upon Tyne
Ghattas, Omar, University of Texas at Austin
Gordon, Terence M., University of Calgary
Hampton, Samuel, University of Canterbury
Harbaugh, John W., Stanford University
Harding, Chris, Iowa State University of Science & Technology
He, Changming, University of Delaware
Hesse, Marc A., University of Texas at Austin
Hohn, Michael E., West Virginia University
Hunt, Allen, Wright State University
Johnson, Glenn W., University of Utah
Jones, Thomas A., Rice University
Journel, Andre G., Stanford University
Kinnicutt, Patrick, Central Michigan University
Lee, Jejung, University of Missouri-Kansas City
Lutz, Timothy M., West Chester University
MAZZELLA, Prof. Antonio A., Universita di Cagliari
Menschik, Florian, Technische Universitaet Muenchen
Murray, Christopher J., Pacific Northwest National Laboratory
Olea, Ricardo, University of Kansas
Penna, Nigel, University of Newcastle Upon Tyne
Ricciardi, Karen, University of Massachusetts, Boston
Rogova, Galina L., SUNY, Buffalo
Rudolph, Maxwell L., Portland State University
Rundberg, Robert S., Los Alamos National Laboratory
Sonder, Leslie J., Dartmouth College
Spiegelman, Marc W., Columbia University
Sun, Alexander, University of Texas at Austin
Switzer, Paul, Stanford University
Therrien, Pierre, Universite Laval
Walton, Ian, University of Utah
Wright, Eric S., University of Montana Western

Mineral Physics
Abramson, Evan H., University of Washington
Anderson, Orson L., University of California, Los Angeles
Bass, Jay D., University of Illinois, Urbana-Champaign
Brown, J. Michael, University of Washington
Bukowinski, Mark S., University of California, Berkeley
Carpenter, Michael, University of Cambridge
Chen, Jiuhua, Florida International University
Cohen, Ronald E., Carnegie Institution of Washington
Cooper, Reid F., Brown University
Duffy, Thomas S., Princeton University
Farver, John R., Bowling Green State University
Fenter, Paul A., Argonne National Laboratory
Fenter, Paul, University of Illinois at Chicago
Goncharov, Alexander F., Carnegie Institution of Washington
Hovis, Guy L., Lafayette College

Hugo, Richard, Portland State University
Jackson, Jennifer M., California Institute of Technology
Jacobsen, Steven D., Northwestern University
Jeanloz, Raymond, University of California, Berkeley
Karato, Shun-ichiro, Yale University
Kavner, Abby, University of California, Los Angeles
Kiefer, Boris, New Mexico State University, Las Cruces
Knittle, Elise, University of California, Santa Cruz
Kronenberg, Andreas, Texas A&M University
Lee, Kanani K., Yale University
Li, Baosheng, SUNY, Stony Brook
Lieberman, Robert C., SUNY, Stony Brook
Lin, Jung-Fu, University of Texas at Austin
Liu, Zhenxian, Carnegie Institution of Washington
Militzer, Burkhard, University of California, Berkeley
Riggs, Eric, Texas A&M University
Salje, Ekhard, University of Cambridge
Saxena, Surendra K., Florida International University
Secco, Richard A., Western University
Stracher, Glenn B., East Georgia State College
Struzhkin, Viktor V., Carnegie Institution of Washington
Tasaka, Miki, University of Minnesota, Twin Cities
Tracy, Sally J., Princeton University
Tschauner, Oliver, University of Nevada, Las Vegas
van Oss, Carel J., SUNY, Buffalo
Weidner, Donald J., SUNY, Stony Brook
Williams, Quentin, University of California, Santa Cruz

History of Geology
Bolton Valencius, Conevery, University of Massachusetts, Boston
Case, Stephen, Olivet Nazarene University
Chyba, Christopher F., Stanford University
Drobnyk, John W., Southern Connecticut State University
Heubeck, Christoph, Friedrich-Schiller-University Jena
Saunders, Charles, Randolph-Macon College
Strick, James E., Franklin and Marshall College

Geomedicine
Cook, Lewis, Concord University
Finkelman, Robert B., University of Texas, Dallas
Gillmore, Gavin, Kingston University
Hunt, Andrew, University of Texas, Arlington
Markowitz, Steven, Queens College (CUNY)
Morabia, Alfredo, Queens College (CUNY)
Watson, Michael, Heriot-Watt University

ECONOMIC GEOLOGY
General Economic Geology
Adedcyin, A. D., University of Ilorin
Adetunji, A, Obafemi Awolowo University
Akabzaa, Thomas M., University of Ghana
Akande, S. O., University of Ilorin
Alavi, Ghafour, University of Tabriz
Alexandrov, Eugene A., Queens College (CUNY)
Allard, Gilles O., University of Georgia
Allen, Donald B., Colby College
Anderson, Scott, Manitoba Geological Survey
Anger-Kraavi, Annela, University of East Anglia
Ansdell, Kevin M., University of Saskatchewan
Arehart, Greg B., University of Nevada, Reno
Ashley, Paul, University of New England
Banerjee, Neil, Western University
Barnes, Sarah- J., Universite du Quebec a Chicoutimi
Barton, Mark D., University of Arizona
Bekken, Barbara M., Virginia Polytechnic Institute & State University
Blamey, Nigel, Brock University
Bland, Douglas, New Mexico Institute of Mining & Technology
Bolarinwa, A. T., University of Ibadan
Bornhorst, Theodore J., Michigan Technological University
Bouzari, Farhad, University of British Columbia
Brimhall, George H., University of California, Berkeley
Burt, Donald M., Arizona State University
Busch, Lawrence, California Geological Survey
Calagari, Ali Asghar, University of Tabriz
Callahan, John E., Appalachian State University
Camprubi, Antoni, Universidad Nacional Autonoma de Mexico
Carlisle, Donald, University of California, Los Angeles
Carter, James L., University of Texas, Dallas
Castor, Stephen B., University of Nevada
Cathles, Lawrence M., Cornell University
Cheney, Eric S., University of Washington
Chi, Guoxiang, University of Regina
Church, John, California Geological Survey
Clark, Kenneth F., University of Texas, El Paso
Clendenin, Jr., Charles W., Dept of Natural Resources
Clinkenbeared, John, California Geological Survey
Conly, Andrew G., Lakehead University
Cook, Robert B., Auburn University
Cooke, David R., University of Tasmania

Corbineau, Lucien, Institut Polytechnique LaSalle Beauvais (ex-IGAL)
Coron, Cynthia R., Southern Connecticut State University
Craig, James R., Virginia Polytechnic Institute & State University
Craw, Dave, University of Otago
Crawford, Thomas J., University of West Georgia
Di Gregorio, Monica, University of Leeds
Donovan, John F., Winona State University
Duke, Norman A., Western University
Dunn, Dennis P., Austin Community College District
Dunst, Brian, Pennsylvania Bureau of Topographic & Geologic Survey
Elston, Wolfgang E., University of New Mexico
Elueze, A. A., University of Ibadan
Evans, Thomas J., University of Wisconsin, Extension
Fehn, Udo, University of Rochester
Feltrin, Leo, Western University
Fennema, Julian, Heriot-Watt University
Flawn, Peter T., University of Texas at Austin
Forsman, Nels F., University of North Dakota
Franco-Rubio, Miguel, Universidad Autonoma de Chihuahua
Freeman, Larry K., Alaska Division of Geological & Geophysical Surveys
Garcia-Gutierrez, Luis, Universidad Autonoma de San Luis Potosi
Gauert, Chris, University of the Free State
Gauthier, Michel, Universite du Quebec a Montreal
Gemmell, J B., University of Tasmania
Gibson, Andy, University of Portsmouth
Gilg, Hans Albert, Technische Universitaet Muenchen
Gillerman, Virginia S., University of Idaho
Gillerman, Virginia S., Boise State University
Gleeson, Sarah, University of Alberta
Greyling, Lynnette, University of Cape Town
Guan, Dabo, University of Leeds
Guha, Jayanta, Universite du Quebec a Chicoutimi
Gulen, Gurcan, University of Texas at Austin
Hannington, Mark, University of Ottawa
Harris, DeVerle P., University of Arizona
Hart, Craig, University of British Columbia
Hayman, Patrick, Queensland University of Technology
Hedenquist, Jeffrey W., University of Ottawa
Hodder, Robert W., Western University
Hohn, Michael E., West Virginia Geological & Economic Survey
Hollenbaugh, Kenneth M., Boise State University
Holley, Elizabeth, Colorado School of Mines
Hollings, Peter N., Lakehead University
Huminicki, Michelle, Brandon University
Ikingura, Justian R., University of Dar es Salaam
Ikonnikova, Svetlana, University of Texas at Austin
Jean-Marc, MONTEL, Ecole Nationale Supérieure de Géologie (ENSG)
Jebrak, Michel, Universite du Quebec a Montreal
Jessey, David R., California State Polytechnic University, Pomona
Kamilli, Robert J., University of Arizona
Kamona, Frederick A., University of Namibia
Karginoglu, Yusuf, Firat University
Kazimoto, Emmanuel, University of Dar es Salaam
Keith, Jeffrey D., Brigham Young University
Kelly, William C., University of Michigan
Kesler, Stephen E., University of Michigan
Kish, Stephen A., Florida State University
Kontak, Daniel J., Laurentian University, Sudbury
Kyser, Kurt, Queen's University
La Berge, Gene L., University of Wisconsin, Oshkosh
Laki, Sam, Central State University
Large, Ross R., University of Tasmania
Lasemi, Zakaria, University of Illinois, Urbana-Champaign
Layton-Matthews, Daniel, Queen's University
Lefebure, Dave, University of Victoria
Lehrberger, Gerhard, Technische Universitaet Muenchen
Levinson, Alfred A., University of Calgary
Linnen, Robert, University of Waterloo
Lorenzoni, Irene, University of East Anglia
Maher, Kierran, New Mexico Institute of Mining and Technology
Mantilla Figueroa, Luis C., Universidad Industrial de Santander
Masterman, Steve S., Division of Geological & Geophysical Surveys
Masterman, Steven S., Alaska Division of Geological & Geophysical Surveys
mcClenaghan, Seán h., Trinity College
McLemore, Virginia T., New Mexico Institute of Mining and Technology
Mensah, Emmanuel, Kwame Nkrumah University of Science and Technology
Metzel, Deborah, University of Massachusetts, Boston
Misra, Kula C., University of Tennessee, Knoxville
Mohammad Reza, Hosseinzadeh, University of Tabriz
Morton, Ronald, University of Minnesota, Duluth
Mumin, A. Hamid, Brandon University
Muntean, John, University of Nevada, Reno
Nasraoui, Mohamed, Institut Polytechnique LaSalle Beauvais (ex-IGAL)
Nex, Paul A., University of the Witwatersrand
Niewendorp, Clark, Oregon Dept of Geology & Mineral Industries
Nimis, Paolo, Università degli Studi di Padova
Okunlola, O. A., University of Ibadan
Olivo, Gema, Queen's University
Orozco-Villasenor, Francisco Javier, Universidad Autonoma de San Luis Potosi
Paez, H. A., McMaster University

Pasteris, Jill D., Washington University in St. Louis
Paterson, Colin J., South Dakota School of Mines & Technology
Petersen, Ulrich, Harvard University
Pietrzak-Renaud, Natalie, Western University
Potra, Adriana, University of Arkansas, Fayetteville
Prichard, Hazel, University of Wales
Ramagwede, Fhatuwani L., Geological Survey of South Africa
Rambaud, Fabienne M., Austin Community College District
Ressel, Mike, University of Nevada
Ridley, John R., Colorado State University
Riese, W C., Rice University
Robertson, Daniel E., Monroe Community College
Robertson, James M., University of Wisconsin, Extension
Robertson, James M., University of Wisconsin, Madison
Rossetti, Piergiorgio, Università di Torino
Sagiroglu, Ahmet, Firat University
Samson, Iain M., University of Windsor
Sasmaz, Ahmet, Firat University
Schardt, Christian, University of Minnesota, Duluth
Seedorff, Eric, University of Arizona
Serenko, Thomas J., Ohio Dept of Natural Resources
Shackley, Simon J., Edinburgh University
Shaver, Stephen A., Sewanee: University of the South
Shortt, Niamh K., Edinburgh University
Siahcheshm, Kamal, University of Tabriz
Simmons, Peter, University of East Anglia
Smith, Joshua, California Geological Survey
Steele-MacInnes, Matthew, University of Arizona
Stucker, J D., Ohio Dept of Natural Resources
Talley, John H., University of Delaware
Thompson, John F., Cornell University
Thompson, Tommy B., University of Nevada, Reno
Titley, Spencer R., University of Arizona
Tritlla, Jordi, Universidad Nacional Autonoma de Mexico
Twelker, Evan, Alaska Division of Geological & Geophysical Surveys
Ulloa, Salvador, Universidad Nacional Autonoma de Mexico
van der Horst, Dan, Edinburgh University
van Hinsberg, Vincent, McGill University
Van Kooten, Gerald K., Calvin College
Vance, R. K., Georgia Southern University
Vice, Daniel H., Pennsylvania State University, Hazleton
Warren, Rachel, University of East Anglia
Webster, James D., American Museum of Natural History
Werdon, Melanie B., Alaska Division of Geological & Geophysical Surveys
Wilkins, Colin, University of Plymouth
Williams, David A., University of Kentucky
Wilton, Derek H., Memorial University of Newfoundland
Wolfgram, Diane, Montana Tech of the University of Montana
Yao, Yon, Rhodes University
Yates, Martin G., University of Maine
Yellich, John, Western Michigan University
Zentilli, Marcos, Dalhousie University

Coal

Abdullah, Wan Hasiah, University of Malaya
Akgul, Muharrem, Firat University
Asuen, Godwin O., University of Benin
Bailey, Judy, University of Newcastle
Blakeman, Audrey, Ohio Dept of Natural Resources
Bustin, R. Marc, University of British Columbia
Calder, John, Dalhousie University
Cardott, Brian J., University of Oklahoma
Carroll, Chris, Wyoming State Geological Survey
Carroll, Richard E., Geological Survey of Alabama
Cecil, Blaine, West Virginia University
Chenoweth, Cheri A., Illinois State Geological Survey
Cohen, Arthur D., University of South Carolina
Crelling, John C., Southern Illinois University Carbondale
Drobniak, Agnieszka, indiana University
Elrick, Scott D., University of Illinois
Elrick, Scott D., Illinois State Geological Survey
Fedorko, Nick, West Virginia University
Flood, Peter, University of New England
Grady, William, West Virginia University
Greb, Stephen F., University of Kentucky
Hoffman, Gretchen K., New Mexico Institute of Mining & Technology
Hower, James C., University of Kentucky
Huff, Bryan G., University of Illinois, Urbana-Champaign
Huggett, William, Southern Illinois University Carbondale
Khawaja, Ikram U., Youngstown State University
Korose, Christopher P., Illinois State Geological Survey
Korose, Christopher P., University of Illinois, Urbana-Champaign
Kuehn, Kenneth W., Western Kentucky University
Lentz, Leonard J., Pennsylvania Bureau of Topographic & Geologic Survey
Lindberg, Jonathan W., Pacific Northwest National Laboratory
Markowski, Antonette K., Pennsylvania Bureau of Topographic & Geologic Survey
Mastalerz, Maria, Indiana University
Mastalerz, Maria D., Indiana University, Bloomington
Meyer, Rebecca A., Indiana University
Miller, Barry W., Tennessee Geological Survey

Mukhopadhyay, Prasanta, Dalhousie University
Mungall, James E., University of Toronto
Myers, Alan R., University of Illinois, Urbana-Champaign
Naldrett, Anthony J., University of Toronto
Neubaum, John C., Pennsylvania Bureau of Topographic & Geologic Survey
Obrad, Jennifer M., University of Illinois, Urbana-Champaign
Pheifer, Raymond N., Eastern Illinois University
Renton, John J., West Virginia University
Rimmer, Susan M., Southern Illinois University Carbondale
Robl, Thomas , University of Kentucky
Shaulis, James R., Pennsylvania Bureau of Topographic & Geologic Survey
Sorrell, Lee, Ohio Dept of Natural Resources
Tabet, David E., Utah Geological Survey
Tatum, Dominic, Heriot-Watt University
Webb, Nathan D., University of Illinois, Urbana-Champaign
Weisenfluh, Gerald A., University of Kentucky

Metals

Atkinson, Jr., William W., University of Colorado
Barnett, Douglas B., Pacific Northwest National Laboratory
Beaudoin, Georges, Universite Laval
Bissig, Thomas, University of British Columbia
Broughton, William A., University of Wisconsin, Platteville
Brown, Philip E., University of Wisconsin, Madison
Campbell, Finley A., University of Calgary
Cedillo, Esteban, Universidad Nacional Autonoma de Mexico
Chavez, Jr., William X., New Mexico Institute of Mining and Technology
Clark, Alan H., Queen's University
Cline, Jean S., University of Nevada, Las Vegas
Corona-Esquivel, Rodolfo, Universidad Nacional Autonoma de Mexico
Coveney, Raymond M., University of Missouri-Kansas City
Crowe, Douglas E., University of Georgia
Davies, James F., Laurentian University, Sudbury
Diaz-Encinas, Leopoldo, Centro de Estudios Superiores del Estado Sonora
Dilles, John H., Oregon State University
Dube, Benoit, Universite du Quebec
Durazo-Tapia, Gustavo E., Centro de Estudios Superiores del Estado Sonora
Einaudi, Marco T., Stanford University
Fifarek, Richard, Southern Illinois University Carbondale
Friehauf, Kurt, Kutztown University of Pennsylvania
Gaboury, Damien, Universite du Quebec a Chicoutimi
Gibson, Harold L., Laurentian University, Sudbury
Gibson, Harold, Carleton University
Gonzalez, Maria M., Central Michigan University
Graf, Jr., Joseph L., Southern Oregon University
Guilbert, John M., University of Arizona
Hagni, Richard D., Missouri University of Science and Technology
Hannington, Mark D., Carleton University
Hase, Harold W., Colorado Mesa University
Hitzman, Murray W., Colorado School of Mines
Hoffman, James I., Eastern Washington University
Hooda, Peter, Kingston University
Hutchinson, Richard W., Colorado School of Mines
Keays, Reid R., Laurentian University, Sudbury
Kelson, Christopher R., SUNY Potsdam
Kinnaird, Judith A., University of the Witwatersrand
Kissin, Stephen A., Lakehead University
Kisvarsanyi, Geza K., Missouri University of Science and Technology
Koestel, Mark, Mt. San Antonio College
Kyle, J. Richard, University of Texas at Austin
Lesher, Michael, Laurentian University, Sudbury
Lincoln, Timothy N., Albion College
Linnen, Robert, Western University
Macfarlane, Andrew W., Florida International University
MacLean, Wallace H., McGill University
McAllister, Arnold L., University of New Brunswick
McLemore, Virginia, New Mexico Institute of Mining & Technology
Melchiorre, Erik, California State University, San Bernardino
Monecke, Thomas, Colorado School of Mines
Morel-Kraepiel, Anne, Princeton University
Morton, Roger D., University of Alberta
Mossman, David J., Mount Allison University
Muchez, Philippe, Katholieke Universiteit Leuven
Newberry, Rainer J., University of Alaska Fairbanks
Panhorst, Terry L., University of Mississippi
Petersen, Erich U., University of Utah
Pride, Douglas E., Ohio State University
Reed, Mark H., University of Oregon
Richards, Jeremy P., University of Alberta
Ripley, Edward M., Indiana University, Bloomington
Romberger, Samuel B., Colorado School of Mines
Ruvalcaba-Ruiz, Delfino C., Universidad Autonoma de San Luis Potosi
Salaun, Pascal, University of Liverpool
Shelton, Kevin L., University of Missouri
Sinclair, Alastair J., University of British Columbia
Spry, Paul G., Iowa State University of Science & Technology
Stein, Holly J., Colorado State University
Stensrud, Howard L., California State University, Chico
Thompson, John F., Cornell University
Thompson, John F. H., University of British Columbia

Tingley, Joseph V., University of Nevada
Tosdal, Richard, University of British Columbia
van der Berg, Stan, University of Liverpool
Vasallo, Fernando, Universidad Nacional Autonoma de Mexico
Vassallo-Morales, Luis F., Universidad Nacional Autonoma de Mexico
Watkinson, David H., Carleton University
Wheeler, Greg, California State University, Sacramento
Wheeler, John, University of Liverpool
Wilkinson, Jamie, Imperial College
Williamson, Ben, Exeter University
Zhang, Ning, Central State University
Zimmerman, Brian S., Edinboro University of Pennsylvania

Non-Metals

Austin, George S., New Mexico Institute of Mining & Technology
Bal Akkoca, Dicle, Firat University
Barker, James M., New Mexico Institute of Mining & Technology
Berg, Richard B., Montana Tech of The University of Montana
Calengas, Peter L., Western Illinois University
Gregory, Robert, Wyoming State Geological Survey
Krukowski, Stanley T., University of Oklahoma
Lasemi, Zakaria, Illinois State Geological Survey
McClellan, Guerry H., University of Florida
Power, W. Robert, Georgia State University
Simandl, George J., University of Victoria
Sousa, Luis M., Universidade de Trás-os-Montes e Alto Douro
Spooner, Edward T. C., University of Toronto
Sutherland, Wayne, Wyoming State Geological Survey
Van Straaten, H. Peter, University of Guelph

Oil and Gas

Anderson, Ross, Heriot-Watt University
Balázs, László, Eotvos Lorand University
Broadhead, Ronald F., New Mexico Institute of Mining and Technology
Brown, Alan, West Virginia University
Burst, John F., Missouri University of Science and Technology
Cox, John, Mount Royal University
Crockett, Joan E., Illinois State Geological Survey
Davies, Richard, Durham University
Deisher, Jeffrey , Ohio Dept of Natural Resources
Erenpreiss, Matt, Ohio Dept of Natural Resources
Evans, Martin J., Cornell University
Fakhari, Mohammad, Ohio Dept of Natural Resources
Finley, Robert J., Illinois State Geological Survey
Gillis, Robert, Alaska Division of Geological & Geophysical Surveys
Gluyas, Jon, Durham University
Gooding, Patrick J., University of Kentucky
Griffin, John R., University of Nebraska, Lincoln
Grube, John P., Illinois State Geological Survey
Haneberg-Diggs, Dominique , Ohio Dept of Natural Resources
Harder, Brian J., Louisiana State University
Herriott, Trystan, Alaska Division of Geological & Geophysical Surveys
Hickman, John, University of Kentucky
Hooks, Chris H., Geological Survey of Alabama
Horn, Marty R., Louisiana State University
Hosseini, Seyyed Abolfazi, University of Texas at Austin
Huff, Bryan G., Illinois State Geological Survey
Javadpour, Farzam, University of Texas at Austin
Johnston, III, John E., Louisiana State University
King, Carey, University of Texas at Austin
Kreckel, Kenneth, Casper College
Krevor, Samuel, Imperial College
Leetaru, Hannes E., Illinois State Geological Survey
Leighton, Morris W., University of Illinois, Urbana-Champaign
Leone, James, New York State Geological Survey
Lepain, David, Alaska Division of Geological & Geophysical Surveys
Levey, Raymond A., University of Utah
Lisa, Black L., Midwestern State University
Lucia, F. J., University of Texas at Austin
Lynds, Ranie, Wyoming State Geological Survey
Malinconico, Mary Ann, Lafayette College
Marder, Igor, Antelope Valley College
Moore, Thomas R., Indiana University of Pennsylvania
Morse, David G., Illinois State Geological Survey
Nicholas, Chris, Trinity College
Nielsen, Peter J., Utah Geological Survey
Nuttall, Brandon C., University of Kentucky
Oldershaw, Michael, Bakersfield College
Parris, Thomas M., University of Kentucky
Pascussi, Michael, New York State Geological Survey
Potter, Eric C., University of Texas at Austin, Jackson School of Geosciences
Rauzi, Steven L., Arizona Geological Survey
Seyler, Beverly, Illinois State Geological Survey
Shew, Roger D., University of North Carolina Wilmington
Solis, Michael, Ohio Dept of Natural Resources
Toner, Rachel, Wyoming State Geological Survey
Vigrass, Laurence W., University of Regina
Wood, Lesli J., University of Texas at Austin
Zeidouni, Mehdi, University of Texas at Austin

GEOCHEMISTRY
General Geochemistry

Abimbola, A. E., University of Ibadan
Affek, Hagit P., Yale University
Aines, Roger D., Lawrence Livermore National Laboratory
Ajayi, T. R., Obafemi Awolowo University
Akaegbobi, I. M., University of Ibadan
Allen, Douglas, Salem State University
Allen-King, Richelle, SUNY, Buffalo
Amonette, Alexandra B., Pacific Northwest National Laboratory
Anbar, Ariel, Arizona State University
Anderson, Alan J., Dalhousie University
Anderson, Robert F., Columbia University
Applegate, David, University of Utah
April, Richard, Colgate University
Arrhenius, Gustaf, University of California, San Diego
Atekwana, Eliot, Oklahoma State University
Ayers, John C., Vanderbilt University
Babcock, R. S., Western Washington University
Baharlou, Alan, Eastern Illinois University
Bales, Roger C., University of Arizona
Bank, Tracy L., SUNY, Buffalo
Banks, David, University of Leeds
Barker, Colin, University of Tulsa
Barnes, Jaime D., University of Texas at Austin
Barnes, Melanie A., Texas Tech University
Beiersdorfer, Raymond E., Youngstown State University
Belmonte, Donato, Universita di Genova
Bender, Michael L., Princeton University
Berendsen, Pieter, University of Kansas
Berger, Peter M., University of Illinois, Urbana-Champaign
Berkelhammer, Max, University of Illinois at Chicago
Berndt, Mike, University of Minnesota, Twin Cities
Bernhard, Joan M., Woods Hole Oceanographic Institution
Bernier, Luc, McMaster University
Bickmore, Barry R., Brigham Young University
Bird, Dennis K., Stanford University
Bissada, K. K., Rice University
Blake, Ruth E., Yale University
Blakley, Curt S., University of Illinois, Urbana-Champaign
Blowes, David W., University of Waterloo
Bodnar, Robert J., Virginia Polytechnic Institute & State University
Boger, Phillip D., SUNY, Geneseo
Bohm, Christian, University of Manitoba
Borowski, Walter S., Eastern Kentucky University
Borrok, David M., University of Louisiana at Lafayette
Boschetti, Tiziano, University of Parma
Bouman, Heather, University of Oxford
Bourcier, Bill L., Lawrence Livermore National Laboratory
Branam, Tracy, indiana University
Brantley, Susan L., Pennsylvania State University, University Park
Brenna, J. T., Cornell University
Broecker, Wallace S., Columbia University
Brooks, Paul D., University of Arizona
Brueckner, Hannes K., Queens College (CUNY)
Bryant, Ernest A., Los Alamos National Laboratory
Bryce, Julia G., University of New Hampshire
Burton, Jacqueline C., Argonne National Laboratory
Buseck, Peter R., Arizona State University
Butler, Ian B., Edinburgh University
Camacho, Elsa A., Pacific Northwest National Laboratory
Centorbi, Tracey, University of Maryland
Chague-Goff, Catherine, University of New South Wales
Chatterjee, Nilanjan, Massachusetts Institute of Technology
Chen, Chu-Yung, University of Illinois, Urbana-Champaign
Chermak, John A., Virginia Polytechnic Institute & State University
Chillrud, Steven, Columbia University
Chorover, Jonathan D., University of Arizona
Churchill, Ron C., California Geological Survey
Claeys, Philippe, Vrije University Brussel
Clark, Jordan, University of California, Santa Barbara
Class, Connie, Columbia University
Coe, Douglas A., Montana Tech of the University of Montana
Coggon, Judith, University of Southampton
Cole, David R., Ohio State University
Collier, James D., Fort Lewis College
Conte, Maureen, Brown University
Cook, Robert B., Oak Ridge National Laboratory
Cowman, Tim C., South Dakota Dept of Environment and Natural Resources
Crawford, William A., Bryn Mawr College
Cubillas, Pablo, Durham University
Dasgupta, Tathagata, Kent State University
Davisson, M L., Lawrence Livermore National Laboratory
Dawson, M. Robert, Iowa State University of Science & Technology
Deng, Baolin, New Mexico Institute of Mining and Technology
Derry, Louis A., Cornell University
Ding, Kang, University of Minnesota, Twin Cities
Dong, Hailiang, Miami University
Dooley, John H., New Jersey Geological Survey

Dostal, Jarda, Dalhousie University
Downes, Hilary, Birkbeck College
Drew, Douglas A., Montana Tech of the University of Montana
Duffy, Clarence J., Los Alamos National Laboratory
Dunbar, Nelia W., New Mexico Institute of Mining and Technology
Durham, William, Massachusetts Institute of Technology
Dutkiewicz, Stephanie, Massachusetts Institute of Technology
Dutton, Andrea, University of Florida
Eby, G. Nelson, University of Massachusetts Lowell
Edgcomb, Virginia, Woods Hole Oceanographic Institution
Eichhubl, Peter, University of Texas at Austin
Eiler, John M., California Institute of Technology
Evans, Owen C., SUNY, Stony Brook
Fajkoviæ, Hana, University of Zagreb
Fanta, Shari E., University of Illinois, Urbana-Champaign
Farley, Kenneth A., California Institute of Technology
Farmer, G. Lang, University of Colorado
Feigenson, Mark D., Rutgers, The State University of New Jersey
Fernandez, Diego, University of Utah
Finkel, Robert C., Lawrence Livermore National Laboratory
Finkelstein, David, Hobart & William Smith Colleges
Flegal, Russell, University of California, Santa Cruz
Flowers, Rebecca, University of Colorado
Ford, Jr., Leonard N., Randolph-Macon College
Foustoukos, Dionysis, Carnegie Institution of Washington
Fraser, Donalf G., University of Oxford
Frey, Bonnie A., New Mexico Institute of Mining & Technology
Furman, Tanya, Pennsylvania State University, University Park
Gambrell, Robert P., Louisiana State University
Gammons, Christopher H., Montana Tech of the University of Montana
Garbesi, Karina, California State University, East Bay
George, Graham, University of Saskatchewan
Gleason, James D., University of Michigan
Goff, Fraser, University of New Mexico
Goff, Fraser, Los Alamos National Laboratory
Goldstein, Steven, Columbia University
Gosse, John C., Dalhousie University
Gosselin, David C., Unversity of Nebraska - Lincoln
Goulet, Richard, University of Ottawa
Grant, Willard H., Emory University
Gulbranson, Erik L., University of Wisconsin, Milwaukee
Gurlea, Lawrence P., Youngstown State University
Gustin, Mae, University of Nevada, Reno
Gutierrez, Melida, Missouri State University
Gysi, Alex, Colorado School of Mines
Halden, Norman M., University of Manitoba
Hall, Cynthia V., West Chester University
Hart, Stanley R., Woods Hole Oceanographic Institution
Hartnett, Hilairy, Arizona State University
Harvey, Jason, University of Leeds
Hattori, Keiko, University of Ottawa
Hemming, Sidney, Columbia University
Henderson, Gideon, University of Oxford
Hervig, Richard, Arizona State University
Hickey-Vargas, Rosemary, Florida International University
Hinton, Richard, Edinburgh University
Hodges, Floyd N., Pacific Northwest National Laboratory
Hudson, Robert J. M., University of Illinois, Urbana-Champaign
Hwang, Hue-Hwa E., University of Illinois, Urbana-Champaign
Ige, A. O., Obafemi Awolowo University
Indela, Raj, Flinders University
Irving, Tony, University of Washington
Izon, Gareth, University of St. Andrews
Jacobs, Gary K., Oak Ridge National Laboratory
Jacobson, Roger, University of Nevada, Reno
Jarvis, Ian, Kingston University
Jerde, Eric, Morehead State University
Johnston, David T., Harvard University
Jull, A. J. Timothy, University of Arizona
Kalender, Leyla, Firat University
Kallemeyn, Gregory, University of California, Los Angeles
Kambewa, Chamunorwa , Tshwane University of Technology
Kamenov, George D., University of Florida
Kaplan, Isaac R., University of California, Los Angeles
Kara, Hatice, Firat University
Kaszuba, John P., University of Wyoming
Katz, Richard, University of Oxford
Kearney, Kenneth, University of Illinois at Chicago
Kellman, Lisa M., Dalhousie University
Kenna, Timothy, Columbia University
Kerrich, Robert W., University of Saskatchewan
Kim, Sang-Tae, McMaster University
Kirste, Dirk, Simon Fraser University
Knudsen, Andrew, Lawrence University
Kolesar, Peter T., Utah State University
Koppers, Anthony, Oregon State University
Koretsky, Carla, Western Michigan University
Kotzer, Tom, University of Saskatchewan
Kronfeld, Joel, Dalhousie University
Ku, Teh-Lung, University of Southern California

Kuzyk, Zou Zou, University of Manitoba
Köster, Mathias, Technische Universitaet Muenchen
Labidi, Jabrane, University of Maryland
Langmuir, Charles H., Harvard University
Le Roex, Anton, University of Cape Town
Lechler, Paul J., University of Nevada
Lee, Cin-Ty A., Rice University
Lee, Cindy M., Clemson University
Legore, Virginia L., Pacific Northwest National Laboratory
Lentz, David R., University of New Brunswick
Lerman, Abraham, Northwestern University
Lindenmeier, Clark W., Pacific Northwest National Laboratory
Liu, Xiaoming, University of North Carolina, Chapel Hill
Livens, Francis, University of Manchester
Locke, Randall A., University of Illinois, Urbana-Champaign
Locke II, Randall A., University of Illinois
Longerich, Henry, Memorial University of Newfoundland
Lopez, Dina L., Ohio University
Loyd, Sean, California State University, Fullerton
Lu, Zunli, Syracuse University
Luttge, Andreas, Rice University
Lyons, Timothy, University of California, Riverside
Macpherson, Colin G., Durham University
Magson, Justine, University of the Free State
Mango, Helen N., Castleton University
Manning, Christina, University of London, Royal Holloway & Bedford New College
Manya, Shukrani, University of Dar es Salaam
Marquez, L. Lynn, Millersville University
Martin, Paul F., Pacific Northwest National Laboratory
Martin, Scot T., Harvard University
Marzoli, Andrea, Università degli Studi di Padova
McDonough, William F., University of Maryland
McGrail, Bernard P., Pacific Northwest National Laboratory
McGuire, Jennifer, University of Saint Thomas
McIntosh, Jennifer C., University of Arizona
McKibben, Michael A., University of California, Riverside
McLennan, Scott M., SUNY, Stony Brook
Meduniæ, Gordana, University of Zagreb
Meintzer, Robert E., Geological Survey of Alabama
Meixner, Thomas, University of Arizona
Mercy, Edward L., Lakehead University
Meyer, William T., Argonne National Laboratory
Meyzen, Christine M., Università degli Studi di Padova
Michel, Jacqueline, University of New Orleans
Mikan, Frank M., Austin Community College District
MOINE, Bertrand N., Université Jean Monnet, Saint-Etienne
Moldovan, Brett, University of Saskatchewan
Muecke, Gunter K., Dalhousie University
Mukasa, Samuel B., University of New Hampshire
Mukhopadhyay, Sujoy, Harvard University
Mukhopadhyay, Sujoy, University of California, Davis
Murowchick, James B., University of Missouri-Kansas City
Murphy, David T., Queensland University of Technology
Naftz, David L., University of Utah
Nagy, Kathryn L., University of Illinois at Chicago
Naranjo, Ramon, University of Nevada, Reno
Nezat, Carmen, Eastern Washington University
Nondorf, Lea, Arkansas Geological Survey
Nyame, Frank K., University of Ghana
O'Driscoll, Nelson, Acadia University
O'Hara, Matthew J., Pacific Northwest National Laboratory
O'Neil, Jonathan, University of Ottawa
Odokuma-Alonge, Ovie, University of Benin
Odom, LeRoy A., Florida State University
Olanrewaju, Johnson, Gannon University
Olatunji, A. S., University of Ibadan
Olsen, Khris B., Pacific Northwest National Laboratory
Olszewski, Kathy, SUNY, Maritime College
Omelon, Christopher, University of Texas at Austin
Ozturk, Nevin, Firat University
Padden, Maureen, McMaster University
Palinkaš, Ladislav, University of Zagreb
Palmer, Martin R., University of Southampton
Panno, Samuel V., Illinois State Geological Survey
Pant, Hari, Lehman College (CUNY)
Papanastassiou, D.A. (Dimitri), California Institute of Technology
Papineau, Dominic, University College London
Parker, Kent E., Pacific Northwest National Laboratory
PArkes, R. J., University of Wales
Parris, Thomas M., University of Kentucky
Parry, William T., University of Utah
Patera, Edward S., Los Alamos National Laboratory
Pearce, J A., Cardiff University
Peate, David W., University of Iowa
Piccoli, Philip M., University of Maryland
Pichevin, Laetitia, Edinburgh University
Pickering, Ingrid, University of Saskatchewan
Pintilei, Mitica, Al. I. Cuza University of Iasi
Plank, Terry, Columbia University
Plante, Martin, Universite Laval

Polyak, Victor J., University of New Mexico
Porcelli, Don, University of Oxford
Poreda, Robert J., University of Rochester
Pourmand, Ali, University of Miami
Pourret, Olivier, Institut Polytechnique LaSalle Beauvais (ex-IGAL)
Powell, Brian A., Clemson University
Prevec, Steve, Rhodes University
Price, Douglas M., Youngstown State University
Prohiæ, Esad, University of Zagreb
Prowse, Terry D., University of Waterloo
Ptacek, Carol J., University of Waterloo
Rae, James, University of St. Andrews
Ramos, Frank C., New Mexico State University, Las Cruces
Reeves, Claire, University of East Anglia
Reiners, Peter, University of Arizona
Rhodes, Amy L., Smith College
Richardson, Steve, University of Cape Town
Rickard, D, Cardiff University
Riedinger, Natascha, Oklahoma State University
Roberts, Sheila J., Bowling Green State University
Roberts, Stephen, University of Southampton
Rohs, C. Renee, Northwest Missouri State University
Rollinson, Hugh, University of Derby
Romanak, Katherine D., University of Texas at Austin
Rose, Catherine V., Trinity College
Rudnick, Roberta L., University of Maryland
Ruiz, Joaquin, University of Arizona
Ruttenberg, Kathleen C., University of Hawai'i, Manoa
Saal, Alberto E., Brown University
Sack, Richard, University of Washington
Sakyi, Patrick A., University of Ghana
Salters, Vincent J., Florida State University
Savov, Ivan, University of Leeds
Saxena, Surenda K., Graduate School of the City University of New York
Schaef, Herbert T., Pacific Northwest National Laboratory
Schaefer, Joerg, Columbia University
Schauble, Edwin A., University of California, Los Angeles
Schlautman, Mark, Clemson University
Schlosser, Peter, Columbia University
Schrag, Daniel P., Harvard University
Schubert, Brian, University of Louisiana at Lafayette
Seitz, Jeffery C., California State University, East Bay
Senko, John M., University of Akron
Serne, R. Jeffrey, Pacific Northwest National Laboratory
Shahar, Anat, Carnegie Institution of Washington
Sheldon, Amy L., SUNY, Buffalo
Shiel, Alyssa, Oregon State University
Shield, Robin, Heriot-Watt University
Shields-Zhou, Graham, University College London
Shirey, Steven, University of Maryland
Shofner, Gregory A., Towson University
Sigman, Daniel M., Princeton University
Simoneit, Bernd, Oregon State University
Sims, Kenneth W., University of Wyoming
Skinner, Brian J., Yale University
Skippen, George B., Carleton University
Slater, Gregory F., McMaster University
Smethie, William, Columbia University
Speidel, David H., Queens College (CUNY)
Speidel, David H., Graduate School of the City University of New York
Spencer, Ronald J., University of Calgary
Stack, Andrew, Georgia Institute of Technology
Stanley, Clifford R., Acadia University
Stebbins, Jonathan F., Stanford University
Steele, Kenneth F., University of Arkansas, Fayetteville
Stevenson, Ross, Universite du Quebec a Montreal
Strmiæ Palinkaš, Sabina, University of Zagreb
Sturchio, Neil C., University of Illinois at Chicago
Sturchio, Neil C., Argonne National Laboratory
Sultan, Mohamed, Argonne National Laboratory
Susak, Nicholas J., University of New Brunswick
Taylor, Richard P., Carleton University
Teagle, Damon, University of Southampton
Tefend, Karen S., University of West Georgia
Teng, Fangzhen, University of Washington
Thomas, Jim, University of Nevada, Reno
Tierney, Kate E., Denison University
Tomascak, Paul B., State University of New York at Oswego
Tomson, Mason B., Rice University
Tredoux, Marian, University of the Free State
Trueman, Clive, University of Southampton
Tsikos, Hari, Rhodes University
van der Westhuizen, Willem, University of the Free State
Van Geen, Alexander, Columbia University
Van Orman, James, Case Western Reserve University
Vannier, Ryan G., Grand Valley State University
Varekamp, Johan C., Wesleyan University
Vulava, Vijay M., College of Charleston
Wagner, Rick, Geological Survey of Alabama
Walker, John L., Argonne National Laboratory

Walther, John V., Southern Methodist University
Wang, Hong, University of Illinois, Urbana-Champaign
Wang, Jianwei, Louisiana State University
Wang, Yang, Florida State University
Wang, Zhengrong, Yale University
Warburton, David L., Florida Atlantic University
Warren, Lesley A., McMaster University
West, Josh, University of Southern California
Whipkey, Charles, University of Mary Washington
White, William B., Pennsylvania State University, University Park
Wicks, June, Princeton University
Wigley, Rochelle, University of New Hampshire
Williams, Jeremy C., Kent State University
Winckler, Gisela, Columbia University
Wogelius, Roy, University of Manchester
Wooden, Joseph, Stanford University
Worrall, Fred, Durham University
Wronkiewicz, David J., Argonne National Laboratory
Wyman, Derek A., University of Saskatchewan
Yan, Beizhan, Columbia University
Yardley, Bruce, University of Leeds
Zanazzi, Alessandro, Utah Valley University
Zeman, Josef, Masaryk University
Zhang, Tongwei, University of Texas at Austin
Zheng, Yan, Queens College (CUNY)
Zolotov, Mikhail Y., Arizona State University

Analytical Geochemistry

Aguilera-Ortiz, Irma, Universidad Nacional Autonoma de Mexico
Ash, Richard, University of Maryland
Bedard, Paul, Universite du Quebec a Chicoutimi
Benjamin, Timothy M., Los Alamos National Laboratory
Bergeron, Mario, Universite du Quebec
Bhatia, D. M. S., Austin Peay State University
Bhattacharyya, Sidhartha, University of Alabama
Blamey, Nigel J., New Mexico Institute of Mining and Technology
Bohlke, John, University of Maryland
Bowen, Scott M., Los Alamos National Laboratory
Brandvold, Lynn A., New Mexico Institute of Mining & Technology
Cahill, Richard A., Illinois State Geological Survey
Cameron, Douglas, Montana Tech of the University of Montana
Carey, James W., Los Alamos National Laboratory
Castaneda, Isla, University of Massachusetts, Amherst
Catalano, Jeff, Washington University
Cheng, Zhongqi, Brooklyn College (CUNY)
Clark, Malcolm W., Southern Cross University
Cole, David R., University of Tennessee, Knoxville
De Carlo, Eric H., University of Hawai'i, Manoa
Dewey, Janet, University of Wyoming
Essling, Alice M., Argonne National Laboratory
Frew, Nelson M., Woods Hole Oceanographic Institution
Gabitov, Rinat, Mississippi State University
Gagnon, Joel, University of Windsor
Garcia, Sammy R., Los Alamos National Laboratory
Gavriloaiei, Traian, Al. I. Cuza University of Iasi
Guo, Weifu, Woods Hole Oceanographic Institution
Halbig, Joseph B., University of Hawai'i, Hilo
Hart, Brian R., Western University
Hemming, N. G., Queens College (CUNY)
Hinthorne, James R., Central Washington University
Hoe, Teh Guan, University of Malaya
Holt, Ben D., Argonne National Laboratory
Hu, Wan-Ping (Sunny), Queensland University of Technology
Huff, Edmund A., Argonne National Laboratory
Huft, Ashley, Montana Tech of The University of Montana
Hunter, Jerry L., Virginia Polytechnic Institute & State University
Ikramuddin, Mohammed, Eastern Washington University
Jackson, Brian P., Dartmouth College
Johnson, Carl G., Woods Hole Oceanographic Institution
Jones, Graham, Southern Cross University
Kent, Adam J., Oregon State University
Kersten, Michael, Universitaet Mainz
Ketterer, Michael, Case Western Reserve University
Knaack, Charles, Washington State University
Krapac, Ivan G., Illinois State Geological Survey
Kuehn, Stephen C., Concord University
Kuentz, David C., Miami University
Landry, Peter B., Woods Hole Oceanographic Institution
Ledger, Ernest B., Stephen F. Austin State University
Locke, David C., Graduate School of the City University of New York
Lottermoser, Bernd, Exeter University
MacDonald, Iain, University of Wales
Marshall, Dan D., Simon Fraser University
McGrath, Steve F., Montana Tech of The University of Montana
Messo, Charles W., University of Dar es Salaam
Mock, R. Stephen, University of Montana Western
Mora-Klepeis, Gabriela, University of Vermont
Mujumba, Jean K., University of Dar es Salaam
Navarre-Sitchler, Alexis, Colorado School of Mines
Neill, Owen K., Washington State University

Olesik, John W., Ohio State University
Olmsted, Wayne, Montana Tech of the University of Montana
Orouji, Maqsood, University of Tabriz
Orr, Robert D., Pacific Northwest National Laboratory
Papike, James J., University of New Mexico
Pike, Steven M., Woods Hole Oceanographic Institution
Pollack, Gerald, Georgia Perimeter College
Pun, Aurora, University of New Mexico
Quick, Thomas J., University of Akron
Ragland, Paul C., Florida State University
Ranville, James, Colorado School of Mines
Rose, Timothy, Smithsonian Institution / National Museum of Natural History
Rouff, Ashaki, Queens College (CUNY)
Russell, Shane, Queensland University of Technology
Savard, Dany, Universite du Quebec a Chicoutimi
Schneider, John F., Argonne National Laboratory
Shimizu, Nobumichi, Woods Hole Oceanographic Institution
Singer, Jared W., Rensselaer Polytechnic Institute
Smith, Catherine H., Los Alamos National Laboratory
Smith, Florence P., Argonne National Laboratory
Snow, Jonathan, University of Houston
Sylvester, Paul J., Memorial University of Newfoundland
Sylvester, Steven, Franklin and Marshall College
Thomas, Donald M., University of Hawai'i, Manoa
Thompson, Christopher J., Pacific Northwest National Laboratory
Timmer, Jaqueline R., Montana Tech of The University of Montana
Underwood, Ben, Indiana University, Bloomington
Vervoort, Jeffrey D., Washington State University
Villasenor-Cabral, Maria G., Universidad Nacional Autonoma de Mexico
Voelker, Bettina, Colorado School of Mines
Volborth, Alexis, Montana Tech of the University of Montana
Wang, Alian, Washington University in St. Louis
Waugh, Truman, University of Kansas
Williams, Amy, Towson University
Williams, Kim R., Colorado School of Mines
Yang, Panseok, University of Manitoba

Experimental Petrology/Phase Equilibria

Agee, Carl A., University of New Mexico
Anderson, G M., University of Toronto
Anovitz, Lawrence A., University of Tennessee, Knoxville
Asimow, Paul D., California Institute of Technology
Baker, Don, McGill University
Barnes, Hubert L., Pennsylvania State University, University Park
Candela, Philip A., University of Maryland
Cottrell, Elizabeth, Smithsonian Institution / National Museum of Natural History
Cottrell, Elizabeth, University of Maryland
Eggler, David H., Pennsylvania State University, University Park
Ernst, W. Gary, Stanford University
Fei, Yingwei, Carnegie Institution of Washington
Fei, Yingwei, University of Maryland
Feineman, Maureen D., Pennsylvania State University, University Park
Frank, Mark R., Northern Illinois University
Gilbert, M. Charles, University of Oklahoma
Hajash, Andrew, Texas A&M University
Herzberg, Claude T., Rutgers, The State University of New Jersey
Hewitt, David A., Virginia Polytechnic Institute & State University
Hsu, Liang-Chi, University of Nevada
Imasuen, Isaac O., University of Benin
Jenkins, David M., Binghamton University
Johnston, A. Dana, University of Oregon
Kilinc, Attila I., University of Cincinnati
Koster Van Groos, August F., University of Illinois at Chicago
Koziol, Andrea M., University of Dayton
Liang, Yan, Brown University
Lindsley, Donald H., SUNY, Stony Brook
London, David, University of Oklahoma
Lundstrom, Craig C., University of Illinois, Urbana-Champaign
McCauley, Marlene, Guilford College
Minarik, William G., McGill University
Montana, Art, University of California, Los Angeles
Mosenfelder, Jed, University of Minnesota, Twin Cities
Munoz, James L., University of Colorado
Mysen, Bjorn O., Carnegie Institution of Washington
Nekvasil, Hanna, SUNY, Stony Brook
Newton, Robert C., University of California, Los Angeles
Parman, Stephen, Brown University
Presnall, Dean C., University of Texas, Dallas
Robert, Genevieve, Bates College
Rutherford, Malcolm J., Brown University
Scott, Steven D., University of Toronto
Seewald, Jeffrey S., Woods Hole Oceanographic Institution
Simmons, Craig, Colorado School of Mines
Spera, Frank J., University of California, Santa Barbara
Steiner, Jeffrey, City College (CUNY)
Stolper, Edward M., California Institute of Technology
Tailby, Nichlos D., Rensselaer Polytechnic Institute
Tait, C. Drew, Los Alamos National Laboratory
Taylor, Lawrence A., University of Tennessee, Knoxville
Ulmer, Gene C., Temple University

van Westrenen, Wim, VU University Amsterdam
Walker, David, Columbia University
Watson, E. Bruce, Rensselaer Polytechnic Institute
Windom, Kenneth E., Iowa State University of Science & Technology
Withers, Tony, Western University
Wyllie, Peter J., California Institute of Technology
Zhang, Youxue, University of Michigan

Exploration Geochemistry
Abdurrahman, A., University of Ilorin
Benning, Liane G., University of Leeds
Borojeviæ Šoštariæ, Sibila, University of Zagreb
Bradshaw, Peter M., University of British Columbia
Closs, L. Graham, Colorado School of Mines
Cohen, David R., University of New South Wales
da Silva, Eduardo F., Universidade de Aveiro
Dreschoff, Gisela, University of Kansas
Fletcher, William K., University of British Columbia
Goodell, Philip C., University of Texas, El Paso
Li, Chusi, Indiana University, Bloomington
Mathur, Ryan, Juniata College
McGoldrick, Peter J., University of Tasmania
Pearson, Graham, University of Alberta
Piercey, Stephen, Laurentian University, Sudbury
Price, Vaneaton, Clemson University
Rose, Arthur W., Pennsylvania State University, University Park
White, William M., Cornell University
Whitehead, Robert E., Laurentian University, Sudbury
Williams-Jones, Anthony E., McGill University
Yanez, Carlos, Universidad Nacional Autonoma de Mexico

Geochronology & Radioisotopes
Ackert, Robert P., Bentley University
Alexander, Jr., E. Calvin, University of Minnesota, Twin Cities
Allen, Charlotte M., Queensland University of Technology
Archibald, Doug A., Queen's University
Asmerom, Yemane, University of New Mexico
Baadsgaard, Halfdan, University of Alberta
Baksi, Ajoy K., Louisiana State University
Baldwin, Suzanne L., Syracuse University
Baskaran, Mark M., Wayne State University
Beard, Brian L., University of Wisconsin, Madison
Bell, Keith, Carleton University
Bevier, Mary Lou, University of British Columbia
Bickford, M. E., Syracuse University
Black, Stuart, University of Reading
Blackburn, Terrence, University of California, Santa Cruz
Blenkinsop, John, Carleton University
Blum, Joel D., University of Michigan
Blusztajn, Jurek, Woods Hole Oceanographic Institution
Blythe, Ann, Occidental College
Brown, Roderick, University of Glasgow
Brueckner, Hannes K., Graduate School of the City University of New York
Burton, Kevin, Durham University
Butler, Gilbert W., Los Alamos National Laboratory
Carlson, Richard W., Carnegie Institution of Washington
Chamberlain, Edwin P., Los Alamos National Laboratory
Chamberlain, Kevin R., University of Wyoming
Chaudhuri, Sambhudas, Kansas State University
Cheng, Hai, University of Minnesota, Twin Cities
Chew, David, Trinity College
Clark, George S., University of Manitoba
Coleman, Drew S., University of North Carolina, Chapel Hill
Connelly, James N., University of Texas at Austin
Copeland, Peter, University of Houston
Cousens, Brian L., Carleton University
Cowart, James B., Florida State University
Creaser, Robert A., University of Alberta
Crowley, Jim, Boise State University
Crowley, Quentin G., Trinity College
Curtice, Joshua M., Woods Hole Oceanographic Institution
Curtis, David B., Los Alamos National Laboratory
Curtis, Garniss H., University of California, Berkeley
Davis, Donald W., University of Toronto
Davis, Terry E., California State University, Los Angeles
DePaolo, Donald J., University of California, Berkeley
Dickin, Alan P., McMaster University
Dulai, Henrietta, University of Hawai'i, Manoa
Dunning, Gregory R., Memorial University of Newfoundland
Edwards, R. Lawrence, University of Minnesota, Twin Cities
Enkelmann, Eva, University of Cincinnati
Faure, Gunter, Ohio State University
Fearey, Bryan L., Los Alamos National Laboratory
Foland, Kenneth A., Ohio State University
Forman, Stephen, Baylor University
Frost, Carol D., University of Wyoming
Fullagar, Paul D., University of North Carolina, Chapel Hill
Gallup, Christina D., University of Minnesota, Duluth
Gancarz, Alexander J., Los Alamos National Laboratory
Gansecki, Cheryl A., University of Hawai'i, Hilo
Gaudette, Henri E., University of New Hampshire

Geibert, Walter, Edinburgh University
Georgiev, Svetoslav, Colorado State University
Godfrey-Smith, Dorothy I., Dalhousie University
Gromet, L. P., Brown University
Hall, Chris, University of Michigan
Hamilton, Michael Andrew, University of Toronto
Hanan, Barry B., San Diego State University
Hanes, John A., Queen's University
Hanson, Gilbert N., SUNY, Stony Brook
Harbottle, Garman, SUNY, Stony Brook
Harrison, T. Mark, University of California, Los Angeles
Hauri, Erik H., Carnegie Institution of Washington
Hayatsu, Akio, Western University
Heaman, Larry M., University of Alberta
Heatherington, Ann L., University of Florida
Heizler, Matthew T., New Mexico Institute of Mining & Technology
Horan, Mary F., Carnegie Institution of Washington
Hourigan, Jeremy, University of California, Santa Cruz
Hughen, Konrad A., Woods Hole Oceanographic Institution
Hurst, Richard W., California State University, Los Angeles
Idleman, Bruce D., Lehigh University
Jacobsen, Stein B., Harvard University
Johnson, Clark M., University of Wisconsin, Madison
Jordan, Jim L., Lamar University
Karner, Daniel B., Sonoma State University
Kimbrough, David L., San Diego State University
Konter, Jasper G., University of Hawai'i, Manoa
Krogh, Thomas E., University of Toronto
Krummenacher, Daniel, San Diego State University
Kuiper, Klaudia, VU University Amsterdam
Kurz, Mark D., Woods Hole Oceanographic Institution
Lakatos, Stephen, York College (CUNY)
Lassiter, John, University of Texas at Austin
Lepper, Kenneth E., North Dakota State University
Lively, Rich, University of Minnesota
Long, Leon E., University of Texas at Austin
Lopez, Margarita, Centro de Investigación Cientifica y de Ed Superior de Ensenada
Manton, William I., University of Texas, Dallas
Markey, Richard, Colorado State University
Markun, Francis J., Argonne National Laboratory
McDowell, Fred W., University of Texas at Austin
McIntosh, William C., New Mexico Institute of Mining and Technology
McLean, Noah, University of Kansas
Menninga, Clarence, Calvin College
Mertz, Dieter, Universitaet Mainz
Miller, Brent, Texas A&M University
Miller, Charles M., Los Alamos National Laboratory
Miller, Donald S., Rensselaer Polytechnic Institute
Miller, Geoffrey G., Los Alamos National Laboratory
Miller, Gifford H., University of Colorado
Min, Kyoungwon, University of Florida
Mock, Timothy D., Carnegie Institution of Washington
Monteleone, Brian D., Woods Hole Oceanographic Institution
Montgomery, Carla W., Northern Illinois University
Moore, Willard S., University of South Carolina
Moran-Zenteno, Dante J., Universidad Nacional Autonoma de Mexico
Morris, David, Los Alamos National Laboratory
Mortensen, James K., University of British Columbia
Moser, Desmond E., University of Utah
Mueller, Paul A., University of Florida
Mukasa, Samuel B., University of Michigan
Murrell, Michael T., Los Alamos National Laboratory
Nelson, Bruce K., University of Washington
Noakes, John E., University of Georgia
O'Fallon, Elaine, Washington State University
Omar, Gomaa I., University of Pennsylvania
Oretega Rivera, Amabel M., Universidad Nacional Autonoma de Mexico
Orlandini, Kent A., Argonne National Laboratory
Osmond, John K., Florida State University
Palin, J. Michael, University of Otago
Pardi, Richard R., William Paterson University
Perrin, Richard E., Los Alamos National Laboratory
Poths, Jane, Los Alamos National Laboratory
Puchtel, Igor, University of Maryland
Rasbury, E. Troy, SUNY, Stony Brook
Renne, Paul, University of California, Berkeley
Reynolds, Peter H., Dalhousie University
Rhodes, Edward J., University of California, Los Angeles
Rink, W. J., McMaster University
Rokop, Donald J., Los Alamos National Laboratory
Rubin, Kenneth H., University of Hawai'i, Manoa
Rutberg, Randye L., Hunter College (CUNY)
Samson, Scott D., Syracuse University
Schmitz, Mark D., Boise State University
Schoene, R B., Princeton University
Schroeder, Norman C., Los Alamos National Laboratory
Seidemann, David E., Graduate School of the City University of New York
Seidemann, David E., Brooklyn College (CUNY)
Selby, Dave, Durham University
Shea, Erin, University of Alaska, Anchorage

Shirey, Steven B., Carnegie Institution of Washington
Silver, Leon T., California Institute of Technology
Singer, Bradley S., University of Wisconsin, Madison
Sole, Jesu, Universidad Nacional Autonoma de Mexico
Spell, Terry L., University of Nevada, Las Vegas
Spencer, Joel Q., Kansas State University
Srinivasan, Balakrishnan, Pondicherry University
Stewart, Brian W., University of Pittsburgh
Stone, John O., University of Washington
Strachan, Rob, University of Portsmouth
Stuiver, Minze, University of Washington
Swanson, Karen, William Paterson University
Swanson, Terry W., University of Washington
Swisher III, Carl C., Rutgers, The State University of New Jersey
Tera, Fouad, Carnegie Institution of Washington
Tomlinson, Emma L., Trinity College
Turek, Andrew, University of Windsor
Turrin, Brent D., Rutgers, The State University of New Jersey
Van Schmus, W. Randall, University of Kansas
Vermeesch, Pieter, University College London
Walker, Richard J., University of Maryland
Walter, Robert C., Franklin and Marshall College
Wampler, J. Marion, Georgia State University
Wang, Hong, Illinois State Geological Survey
Wasserburg, Gerald J., California Institute of Technology
Weis, Dominique, University of British Columbia
White, William M., Cornell University
Widom, Elisabeth, Miami University
Wijbrans, Jan, VU University Amsterdam
Wolfsberg, Kurt, Los Alamos National Laboratory
Yang, Gang, Colorado State University
Yin, Qing-zhu, University of California, Davis
Zeitler, Peter K., Lehigh University
Zhuang, Guangsheng, Louisiana State University
Zimmerman, Aaron, Colorado State University
Zreda, Marek, University of Arizona

Low-temperature Geochemistry
Achten, Christine, Universitaet Muenster
Adams, Donald D., Plattsburgh State University (SUNY)
Agrawal, Abinash, Wright State University
Aja, Stephen U., Graduate School of the City University of New York
Aja, Stephen U., Brooklyn College (CUNY)
Alessi, Daniel, University of Alberta
Alexander, Clark R., Georgia Institute of Technology
Andersen, C. B., Clemson University
Andersen, C. Brannon, Furman University
Angino, Ernest E., University of Kansas
Baker, Paul A., Duke University
Banner, Jay L., University of Texas at Austin
Baron, Dirk, California State University, Bakersfield
Beckingham, Barbara, College of Charleston
Benner, Shawn, Boise State University
Benninger, Larry K., University of North Carolina, Chapel Hill
Bergslien, Elisa T., Buffalo State College
Berner, Elizabeth K., Yale University
Berner, Robert A., Yale University
Bertine, Kathe K., San Diego State University
Bischoff, William D., Wichita State University
Blanton, Jackson O., Georgia Institute of Technology
Boudreau, Bernard P., Dalhousie University
Bowser, Carl J., University of Wisconsin, Madison
Brabander, Daniel J., Wellesley College
Brand, Uwe, Brock University
Brooks, Scott C., Oak Ridge National Laboratory
Burke, Roger A., University of Georgia
Cantrell, Kirk J., Pacific Northwest National Laboratory
Cao, Hongsheng, Wichita State University
Capo, Rosemary C., University of Pittsburgh
Carroll, Susan A., Lawrence Livermore National Laboratory
Casey, William H., University of California, Davis
Catalano, Jeffrey G., Washington University in St. Louis
Cercone, Karen Rose, Indiana University of Pennsylvania
Cerling, Thure E., University of Utah
Chesworth, Ward, University of Guelph
Christina, Thomas D., Georgia Institute of Technology
Cody, Anita M., Iowa State University of Science & Technology
Crossey, Laura J., University of New Mexico
Datta, Saugata, Kansas State University
Derry, Louis A., Cornell University
Diebold, Frank E., Montana Tech of the University of Montana
Donahoe, Rona J., University of Alabama
Dostie, Philip, Bates College
Dove, Patricia M., Virginia Polytechnic Institute & State University
Drake, John C., University of Vermont
Dworkin, Stephen I., Baylor University
Early, Thomas O., Oak Ridge National Laboratory
Eggleston, Carrick M., University of Wyoming
Elliott, W. Crawford, Georgia State University
Elswick, Erika R., Indiana University, Bloomington

Engel, Annette S., University of Tennessee, Knoxville
Evans, Les J., University of Guelph
Fein, Jeremy B., University of Notre Dame
Ferrell, Jr., Ray E., Louisiana State University
Frape, Shaun K., University of Waterloo
Frisia, Silvia, University of Newcastle
Fryer, Brian J., University of Windsor
Gamerdinger, Amy P., Pacific Northwest National Laboratory
Ghosh, Swapan K., Indiana University / Purdue University, Indianapolis
Graedel, Thomas E., Yale University
Graf, Donald L., University of Illinois, Urbana-Champaign
Grandstaff, David E., Temple University
Graney, Joseph R., Binghamton University
Graustein, William C., Yale University
Gu, Baohua, Oak Ridge National Laboratory
Gu, Chuanhui, Appalachian State University
Gunter, William D., University of Calgary
Haas, Johnson R., Western Michigan University
Hannigan, Robyn, University of Massachusetts, Boston
Hanor, Jeffrey S., Louisiana State University
Harrison, Wendy J., Colorado School of Mines
Heikoop, Jeffrey, University of South Florida, Tampa
Herman, Janet S., University of Virginia
Herndon, Elizabeth M., Kent State University
Hirons, Steve, Birkbeck College
Hixon, Amy, University of Notre Dame
Hluchy, Michele M., Alfred University
Hochella, Jr., Michael F., Virginia Polytechnic Institute & State University
Holdren, George R., Pacific Northwest National Laboratory
Hounslow, Arthur, Oklahoma State University
Hui, Alice, Indiana University, Bloomington
Hutcheon, Ian E., University of Calgary
Icenhower, Jonathan P., Pacific Northwest National Laboratory
Jacinthe, Pierre-Andre, Indiana University / Purdue University, Indianapolis
Jackson, Kenneth J., Lawrence Livermore National Laboratory
Jacobson, Andrew D., Northwestern University
Jahnke, Richard, Georgia Institute of Technology
Janecky, David R., Los Alamos National Laboratory
Johnson, Beverly J., Bates College
Karlsson, Haraldur R., Texas Tech University
Kaste, James, College of William & Mary
Kastner, Miriam, University of California, San Diego
Kelly, Jacque L., Georgia Southern University
Kettler, Richard M., University of Nebraska, Lincoln
Kimball, Bryn, Whitman College
Kirby, Carl S., Bucknell University
Knapp, Elizabeth P., Washington & Lee University
Kneeshaw, Tara A., Grand Valley State University
Kramer, James R., McMaster University
Krupka, Kenneth M., Pacific Northwest National Laboratory
Ku, Timothy C., Wesleyan University
Kubicki, James D., University of Texas, El Paso
Kump, Lee R., Pennsylvania State University, University Park
Kurtz, Andrew, Boston University
Land, Lynton S., University of Texas at Austin
Larsen, Daniel, University of Memphis
Lawrence, James, University of Houston
Leckie, James O., Stanford University
Liang, Liyuan, Oak Ridge National Laboratory
Lindberg, Steven E., Oak Ridge National Laboratory
Lindsay, Matthew B., University of Saskatchewan
Locke, Randall, University of Illinois, Urbana-Champaign
Long, Austin, University of Arizona
Long, David T., Michigan State University
Lowenstein, Tim K., Binghamton University
Lyons, William B., Ohio State University
Macalady, Donald L., Colorado School of Mines
Martin, Candace E., University of Otago
Martin, Ellen E., University of Florida
Martin, Jonathan E., University of Florida
Martini, Anna M., Amherst College
Matisoff, Gerald, Case Western Reserve University
Mattigod, Shas V., Pacific Northwest National Laboratory
Maurice, Patricia, University of Notre Dame
Mayes, Melanie A., University of Tennessee, Knoxville
Maynard, J. Barry, University of Cincinnati
Mazer, James J., Argonne National Laboratory
McArthur, John, University College London
McGee, David, Massachusetts Institute of Technology
McGehee, Thomas L., Texas A&M University, Kingsville
McPhail, D C "Bear", Australian National University
Merino, Enrique, Indiana University, Bloomington
Moore, Joel, Towson University
Morel, Francois M M., Princeton University
Munk, LeeAnn, University of Alaska, Anchorage
Murphy, William M., California State University, Chico
Nelson, Marc A., University of Arkansas, Fayetteville
Nesbitt, H W., Western University
Neumann, Klaus, Ball State University
Newell, Dennis L., Utah State University

Marine Geochemistry

Valentine, David, University of California, Santa Barbara
Wakefield, S J., Cardiff University
Wang, Weihong, Utah Valley University
Wang, Z. Aleck, Woods Hole Oceanographic Institution
Wankel, Scott, Woods Hole Oceanographic Institution
Weiss, Ray F., University of California, San Diego
Wheeler, Patricia, Oregon State University
Winckler, Gisela, Columbia University
Windom, Herbert L., Georgia Institute of Technology
Wong, Chi S., University of British Columbia
Wunsch, David R., University of Delaware
Yoder, James A., Woods Hole Oceanographic Institution
Zachos, James C., University of California, Santa Cruz
Zheng, Yan, Graduate School of the City University of New York

Organic Geochemistry

Abbott, Geoffrey, University of Newcastle Upon Tyne
Amend, Jan P., Washington University
Anderson, Ken B., Southern Illinois University Carbondale
Aravena, Ramon, University of Waterloo
Baars, Oliver, Princeton University
Bada, Jeffrey L., University of California, San Diego
Bakel, Allen J., Argonne National Laboratory
Banfield, Jillian, University of California, Berkeley
Barker, James F., University of Waterloo
Bianchi, Thomas S., University of Florida
Bissada, Adry, University of Houston
Blair, Neal E., Northwestern University
Bopp, Richard F., Rensselaer Polytechnic Institute
Brassell, Simon C., Indiana University, Bloomington
Burns, Timothy P., Los Alamos National Laboratory
Chen, Bob, University of Massachusetts, Boston
Chou, Mei-In (Melissa), Illinois State Geological Survey
Chou, Sheng-Fu Joseph, Illinois State Geological Survey
Cody, George D., Carnegie Institution of Washington
Cole, Dean A., Los Alamos National Laboratory
Cowie, Gregory L., Edinburgh University
Diefendorf, Aaron, University of Cincinnati
Engel, Michael H., University of Oklahoma
Filley, Timothy R., Purdue University
Fisher, Liz, University of Liverpool
Francis, Robert D., California State University, Long Beach
Freeman, Katherine H., Pennsylvania State University, University Park
Hanson, Andrew D., University of Nevada, Las Vegas
Harvey, H. Rodger, Old Dominion University
Hayes, John M., Indiana University, Bloomington
Heal, Kate V., Edinburgh University
Hinman, Nancy W., University of Montana
Hites, Ronald A., Indiana University, Bloomington
Hockaday, William C., Baylor University
Huang, Yongsong, Brown University
Kelley, Cheryl A., University of Missouri
Kenig, Fabien, University of Illinois at Chicago
Kopp, Robert E., Rutgers, The State University of New Jersey
Kotulova, Julia, University of Utah
Kruge, Michael A., Montclair State University
Langston-Unkefer, Pat J., Los Alamos National Laboratory
Lee, Cindy, SUNY, Stony Brook
Liss, Peter, University of East Anglia
Love, Gordon, University of California, Riverside
MacCarthy, Patrick, Colorado School of Mines
Macko, Stephen A., University of Virginia
McCarthy, John F., Oak Ridge National Laboratory
Mehra, Aradhana, University of Derby
Meyers, Philip A., University of Michigan
Mitra, Siddhartha, East Carolina University
Mitterer, Richard M., University of Texas, Dallas
Moldowan, J. Michael, Stanford University
Moslow, Thomas F., University of Calgary
Nelson, Robert K., Woods Hole Oceanographic Institution
Ngwenya, Bryne T., Edinburgh University
Nolan, Robert P., Graduate School of the City University of New York
Passarelli, Mariella, University of Maine - Farmington
Perdue, Edward Michael, Georgia Institute of Technology
Petsch, Steven, University of Massachusetts, Amherst
Phillips, Dennis, Los Alamos National Laboratory
Philp, R. Paul, University of Oklahoma
Pier, Stanley M., Rice University
Poulton, Simon, University of Leeds
Pratt, Lisa M., Indiana University, Bloomington
Pruell, Richard J., University of Rhode Island
Reddy, Christopher M., Woods Hole Oceanographic Institution
Repeta, Daniel J., Woods Hole Oceanographic Institution
Riediger, Cynthia L., University of Calgary
Robinson, Clare, University of Manchester
Sass, Henrik, University of Wales
Sepúlveda, Julio C., University of Colorado
Sessions, Alex L., California Institute of Technology
Silliman, James, Texas A&M University, Corpus Christi
Spongberg, Alison L., University of Toledo

Steen, Andrew, University of Tennessee, Knoxville
Stierle, Donald, Montana Tech of the University of Montana
Talbot, Helen, University of Newcastle Upon Tyne
Tanner, Benjamin R., Western Carolina University
Thiel, Dr., Volker, Georg-August University of Goettingen
Thomas, Elizabeth K., SUNY, Buffalo
Tierney, Jessica, University of Arizona
Townsend-Small, Amy, University of Cincinnati
van Dongen, Bart, University of Manchester
Van Vleet, Edward S., University of South Florida
Venkatesan, M I., University of California, Los Angeles
Visscher, Pieter T., University of Connecticut
Visscher, Pieter, University of Connecticut
Voorhees, Kent J., Colorado School of Mines
Wakeham, Stuart G., Georgia Institute of Technology
Werne, Josef, University of Pittsburgh
Whelan, Jean K., Woods Hole Oceanographic Institution
Whiticar, Michael J., University of Victoria
Zerkle, Aubrey, University of St. Andrews
Zhang, Yige, Texas A&M University
Zimmerman, Andrew, University of Florida
Ziolkowski, Lori A., University of South Carolina

Stable Isotopes

Anderson, Thomas F., University of Illinois, Urbana-Champaign
Anderson, William T., Florida International University
Andrews, Julian, University of East Anglia
Arnold, Gail, University of Texas, El Paso
Atudorei, Nieu-Viorel, University of New Mexico
Bao, Huiming, Louisiana State University
Bedaso, Zelalem, University of Dayton
Berke, Melissa, University of Notre Dame
Bindeman, Ilya N., University of Oregon
Bowen, Gabriel, University of Utah
Bowman, John R., University of Utah
Bray, Colin, University of Toronto
Brunner, Benjamin, University of Texas, El Paso
Burgess, Ray, University of Manchester
Burke, Andrea, University of St. Andrews
Burns, Stephen J., University of Massachusetts, Amherst
Campbell, Andrew R., New Mexico Institute of Mining and Technology
Clay, Patricia, University of Manchester
Clayton, Robert N., University of Chicago
Cohen, Anthony, The Open University
Conroy, Jessica, University of Illinois, Urbana-Champaign
Coogon, Rosalind, Imperial College
Criss, Robert E., Washington University in St. Louis
Darling, James, University of Portsmouth
Davidson, Garry J., University of Tasmania
Denniston, Rhawn F., University of Iowa
Dettman, David, University of Arizona
Deuser, Werner G., Woods Hole Oceanographic Institution
Dodd, Justin P., Northern Illinois University
Dorale, Jeffrey A., University of Iowa
Eastoe, Christopher J., University of Arizona
Edwards, Thomas W. D., University of Waterloo
Elder, Kathryn L., Woods Hole Oceanographic Institution
Evans, Michael N., University of Maryland
Evans, Samantha, Boise State University
Fantle, Matthew S., Pennsylvania State University, University Park
Farquhar, James, University of Maryland
Fayek, Mostafa, University of Manitoba
Feng, Xiahong, Dartmouth College
Ferguson, Kurt M., Southern Methodist University
Fike, David, Washington University in St. Louis
Fisher, David E., University of Miami
Foster, Gavin, University of Southampton
Fricke, Henry C., Colorado College
Gagnon, Alan R., Woods Hole Oceanographic Institution
Gao, Yongjun, University of Houston
Gazis, Carey A., Central Washington University
Gibson, John J., University of Waterloo
Gilbert, Kathleen W., Wellesley College
Gillikin, David P., Union College
Goehring, Brent, Tulane University
Goldstein, Steven L., Columbia University
Gonzalez, Luis A., University of Kansas
Graczyk, Donald G., Argonne National Laboratory
Grassineau, Nathalie, University of London, Royal Holloway & Bedford New College
Greenberg, Sallie E., Illinois State Geological Survey
Gregory, Robert T., Southern Methodist University
Griffith, Liz, University of Texas, Arlington
Grimes, Stephen, University of Plymouth
Grossman, Ethan, Texas A&M University
Hackley, Keith C., Illinois State Geological Survey
Haley, Brian, Oregon State University
Halliday, Alex, University of Oxford
Helie, Jean-François, Universite du Quebec a Montreal
Hemming, Sidney R., Columbia University
Henkel, Torsten, University of Manchester

Higgins, Pennilyn, University of Rochester
Hillaire-Marcel, Claude, Universite du Quebec a Montreal
Hilton, David R., University of California, San Diego
Hindshaw, Ruth, University of St. Andrews
Hobbie, Erik A., University of New Hampshire
Hoek, Joost, University of Maryland
Holk, Gregory J., California State University, Long Beach
Holmden, Chris, University of Saskatchewan
Horton, Travis, University of Canterbury
Howe, Stephen S., SUNY, Albany
Hren, Michael, University of Connecticut
Hwang, Hue-Hwa, Illinois State Geological Survey
Ingram, B. Lynn, University of California, Berkeley
Ito, Emi, University of Minnesota, Twin Cities
Jahren, A. Hope, University of Hawai'i, Manoa
Junium, Christopher, Syracuse University
Kaiser, Jan, University of East Anglia
Kamber, Balz, Laurentian University, Sudbury
Kaplan, Isaac R., University of California, Los Angeles
Karhu, Juha A., University of Helsinki
Kaufman, Alan J., University of Maryland
Keigwin, Lloyd D., Woods Hole Oceanographic Institution
Kelley, Simon, The Open University
Kellman, Lisa M., Saint Francis Xavier University
Keppens, Edward, Vrije University Brussel
Kieffer, Bruno, University of British Columbia
Kienast, Markus, Dalhousie University
Kirtland Turner, Sandra, University of California, Riverside
Knauth, L. Paul, Arizona State University
Kohn, Matthew, Boise State University
Krantz, David E., University of Delaware
Kreutz, Karl J., University of Maine
Krishnamurthy, R. V., Western Michigan University
Labotka, Dana, University of Illinois, Urbana-Champaign
Lambert, W. J., University of Alabama
Larson, Peter B., Washington State University
Leavitt, Steven W., University of Arizona
Lefticariu, Liliana, Southern Illinois University Carbondale
Li, Long, University of Alberta
Lini, Andrea, University of Vermont
Lohmann, Kyger C., University of Michigan
Longstaffe, Frederick J., Western University
Lowry, David, University of London, Royal Holloway & Bedford New College
Luzincourt, Marc R., Universite du Quebec
Marshall, Jim, University of Liverpool
Matheney, Ronald K., University of North Dakota
Mattey, Dave, University of London, Royal Holloway & Bedford New College
Mayer, Bernhard, University of Calgary
Michalski, Greg, Purdue University
Miller, Christian A., University of Hawai'i, Manoa
Mix, Alan C., Oregon State University
Muehlenbachs, Karlis, University of Alberta
Muller, Wolfgang, University of London, Royal Holloway & Bedford New College
Nelson, Stephen T., Brigham Young University
Nielsen, Sune G., Woods Hole Oceanographic Institution
O'Neil, James, University of Michigan
Ohmoto, Hiroshi, Pennsylvania State University, University Park
Oleynik, Sergey, Princeton University
Olivares, Jose A., Los Alamos National Laboratory
Parrish, Randy, Leicester University
Passey, Benjamin, Johns Hopkins University
Patterson, William P., University of Saskatchewan
Pedentchouk, Nikolai, University of East Anglia
Perry, Eugene C., Northern Illinois University
Pinti, Daniele Luigi, Universite du Quebec a Montreal
Plummer, Rebecca, University of Maryland
Poirier, Andre, Universite du Quebec a Montreal
Popp, Brian N., University of Hawai'i, Manoa
Poulson, Simon R., University of Nevada, Reno
Ravelo, Christina, University of California, Santa Cruz
Rehkamper, Mark, Imperial College
Richards, Ian J., Southern Methodist University
Rye, Danny M., Yale University
Savin, Samuel M., Case Western Reserve University
Schaller, Morgan F., Rensselaer Polytechnic Institute
Schimmelmann, Arndt, Indiana University, Bloomington
Schwarcz, Henry P., McMaster University
Sedlacek, Alexa, University of Northern Iowa
Shahar, Anat, University of Maryland
Sharma, Shikha, West Virginia University
Sharp, Zachary D., University of New Mexico
Sherwood Lollar, Barbara, University of Toronto
Shieh, Yuch-Ning, Purdue University
Showers, William J., North Carolina State University
Smart, Katie A., University of the Witwatersrand
Smirnov, Anna, Universite du Quebec
Sowers, Todd, Pennsylvania State University, University Park
St. Amour, Natalie , Western University
Steig, Eric J., University of Washington
Strauss, Harald, Universitaet Muenster

Stute, Martin, Columbia University
Syrup, Krista, Moraine Valley Community College
Szynkiewicz, Anna, University of Tennessee, Knoxville
Taylor, Hugh P., California Institute of Technology
Thirlwall, Matthew, University of London, Royal Holloway & Bedford New College
Tobias, Craig R., University of North Carolina Wilmington
Tudhope, Alexander W., Edinburgh University
van de Flierdt, Tina, Imperial College
von Strandmann, Phillip P., University College London
von Strandmann, Phillip P., Birkbeck College
Wahlen, Martin, University of California, San Diego
Wanamaker, Alan D., Iowa State University of Science & Technology
Wang, Jianhua, Carnegie Institution of Washington
Webb, Elizabeth, Western University
Welp, Lisa, Purdue University
Wenner, David B., University of Georgia
White, James W. C., University of Colorado
Widory, David, Universite du Quebec a Montreal
Williams, Douglas F., University of South Carolina
Williams, Helen, Durham University
Wing, Boswell, McGill University
Wright, James D., Rutgers, The State University of New Jersey
Yapp, Crayton J., Southern Methodist University
Yeung, Laurence, Rice University
Young, Edward D., University of California, Los Angeles
Yun, Misuk, University of Manitoba
Zhang, Ren, Baylor University
Zierenberg, Robert A., University of California, Davis

Trace Element Distribution
Clausen, Ben, Loma Linda University
Condie, Kent C., New Mexico Institute of Mining and Technology
Croot, Peter, National University of Ireland Galway
Cullers, Robert L., Kansas State University
Daniels, William R., Los Alamos National Laboratory
Efurd, Deward W., Los Alamos National Laboratory
Frey, Frederick A., Massachusetts Institute of Technology
Gabrielli, Paolo, Ohio State University
Hale, Beverley A., University of Guelph
Hayes, John M., Woods Hole Oceanographic Institution
Kar, Aditya, Fort Valley State University
Korotev, Randy L., Washington University in St. Louis
Kyte, Frank T., University of California, Los Angeles
LaFleche, Marc R., Universite du Quebec
Liese, Homer C., University of Connecticut
Mantei, Erwin J., Missouri State University
Marcantonio, Franco, Texas A&M University
Nabelek, Peter I., University of Missouri
Newton, Robert, Columbia University
Nicolescu, Stefan, Yale University
Peterson, Eugene J., Los Alamos National Laboratory
Ritter, Charles J., University of Dayton
Ryan, Jeffrey G., University of South Florida, Tampa
Seifert, Karl E., Iowa State University of Science & Technology
Simonetti, Tony, University of Notre Dame
Thomas, Kimberly W., Los Alamos National Laboratory
Thompson, Joseph L., Los Alamos National Laboratory
Von Reden, Karl F., Woods Hole Oceanographic Institution
Weaver, Barry L., University of Oklahoma
Wildeman, Thomas R., Colorado School of Mines
Yokochi, Reika, University of Illinois at Chicago

GEOPHYSICS
General Geophysics
Adams, Aubreya, Colgate University
Adepelumi, A. A., Obafemi Awolowo University
Afolabi, O., Obafemi Awolowo University
Ahern, Judson L., University of Oklahoma
Ahmed, Mohamed , Western Michigan University
Aihaiti, Muhetaer, Carnegie Institution of Washington
Al-Lehyani, Ayman, King Fahd University of Petroleum and Minerals
Al-Shuhail, Abdullatif, King Fahd University of Petroleum and Minerals
Alao, O. A., Obafemi Awolowo University
Albright, James N., Los Alamos National Laboratory
Aldridge, Keith D., York University
Anderson, Megan L., Colorado College
Angelopoulos, Vassilis, University of California, Los Angeles
Armah, Thomas K., University of Ghana
Armstrong, John, Carnegie Institution of Washington
Atekwana, Estella, Oklahoma State University
Audet, Pascal, University of Ottawa
Bachtadse, Valerian, Ludwig-Maximilians-Universitaet Muenchen
Backus, George E., University of California, San Diego
Bailey, Richard C., University of Toronto
Barbi, Greta, Ludwig-Maximilians-Universitaet Muenchen
Barsch, Robert, Ludwig-Maximilians-Universitaet Muenchen
Bastow, Ian, Imperial College
Batzle, Michael L., Colorado School of Mines
Beaumont, Christopher, Dalhousie University
Becker, Alex, University of California, Berkeley

Bendick, Rebecca, University of Montana
Bentley, Charles R., University of Wisconsin, Madison
Bercovici, David, Yale University
Beresnev, Igor A., Iowa State University of Science & Technology
Billen, Magali I., University of California, Davis
Billings, Stephen, University of British Columbia
Bina, Craig R., Northwestern University
Birch, Francis S., University of New Hampshire
Bird, G. Peter, University of California, Los Angeles
Blankenship, Donald D., University of Texas at Austin
Bleibinhaus, Florian, Ludwig-Maximilians-Universitaet Muenchen
Bleistein, Norman, Colorado School of Mines
Bloxham, Jeremy, Harvard University
Boadu, Fred K., Duke University
Boaga, Jacopo, Università degli Studi di Padova
Boehler, Reinhard, Carnegie Institution of Washington
Boettcher, Margaret S., University of New Hampshire
Bokelmann, Goetz, University of Vienna
Bonini, William E., Princeton University
Boyd, Oliver, University of Memphis
Bradley, Christopher R., Los Alamos National Laboratory
Braun, Alexander, Queen's University
Bregman, Martin, Tulsa Community College
Briggs, Derek E., Yale University
Britzke, Gilbert, Ludwig-Maximilians-Universitaet Muenchen
Brodholt, John, University College London
Brooks, Debra A., Santiago Canyon College
Buck, IV, W. R., Columbia University
Bunge, Hans-Peter, Ludwig-Maximilians-Universitaet Muenchen
Busse, Friedrich H., University of California, Los Angeles
Bustin, Amanda, University of British Columbia
Butler, Karl, University of New Brunswick
Butler, Robert, University of Arizona
Butler, Sam, University of Saskatchewan
Calvin, Wendy, University of Nevada, Reno
Campbell, David L., University of Iowa
Carlson, Barry A., Delta College
Carpenter, Phillip J., Northern Illinois University
Carrigan, Charles R., Lawrence Livermore National Laboratory
Cassiani, Giorgio, Università degli Studi di Padova
Cassidy, Nigel, Keele University
Cayzer, Nicola, Edinburgh University
Chapman, Mark, Edinburgh University
Chase, Clement G., University of Arizona
Cheadle, Michael J., University of Wyoming
Chow, Paul, Carnegie Institution of Washington
Clarke, Garry K. C., University of British Columbia
Clement, William, University of Massachusetts, Amherst
Coakley, Bernard, University of Alaska Fairbanks
Coles, Kenneth S., Indiana University of Pennsylvania
Colgan, William, York University
Comas, Xavier, Florida Atlantic University
Cooper, Catherine , Washington State University
Copley, Alex, University of Cambridge
Cosentino, Pietro, University of East Anglia
Couture, Gilles, Universite du Quebec a Montreal
Craig, Mitchell S., California State University, East Bay
Craven, John, Edinburgh University
Crossley, David J., Saint Louis University
Csatho, Beata, SUNY, Buffalo
Daly, Eve, National University of Ireland Galway
Daniels, Jeffrey J., Ohio State University
Davies, J H., Cardiff University
Davies, Rhordri, Imperial College
Davis, Daniel M., SUNY, Stony Brook
Davis, Tara, University College Cork
DeBremaecker, Jean-Claude, Rice University
Dengler, Lorinda, Humboldt State University
Dewdney, Chris, University of Portsmouth
Dickman, Steven R., Binghamton University
Dieterich, James H., University of California, Riverside
Dmochowski, Jane, University of Pennsylvania
Doll, William E., Oak Ridge National Laboratory
Dorman, Leroy M., University of California, San Diego
Duan, Benchuan, Texas A&M University
Dunbar, John A., Baylor University
Durland, Theodore, Oregon State University
Dzunic, Aleksandar, Curtin University
Ebel, John E., Boston College
Edwards, C L, Los Alamos National Laboratory
Ehlers, Todd A., University of Michigan
Ekstrom, Goran, Columbia University
Ellwood, Brooks, University of Texas, Arlington
Elwood Madden, Megan E., University of Oklahoma
Emmer, Barbara, Ludwig-Maximilians-Universitaet Muenchen
England, Richard, Leicester University
Falebita, D. E., Obafemi Awolowo University
Fehler, Michael, Massachusetts Institute of Technology
Ferguson, John F., University of Texas, Dallas
Ferrucci, Fabrizio, The Open University

Fichtner, Andreas, Ludwig-Maximilians-Universitaet Muenchen
Fishwick, Stewart, Leicester University
Flesch, Lucy M., Purdue University
Forte, Alessandro Marco, Universite du Quebec a Montreal
Fortier, Richard, Universite Laval
Foulger, Gillian R., Durham University
French, Melodie, University of Maryland
Gaffney, Edward S., Los Alamos National Laboratory
Gaidos, Eric J., University of Hawai'i, Manoa
Gallovic, Frantisek, Ludwig-Maximilians-Universitaet Muenchen
Gardner, Gerald H. F., Rice University
Gebrande, Helmut, Ludwig-Maximilians-Universitaet Muenchen
Gharti, Hom Nath, Princeton University
Ghazala, Hosni H., El Mansoura University
Gilder, Stuart, Ludwig-Maximilians-Universitaet Muenchen
Goes, Saskia, Imperial College
Goforth, Thomas T., Baylor University
Goodliffe, Andrew, University of Alabama
Gorman, Gerard, Imperial College
Goulty, Neil R., Durham University
Graham, Gina R., Alaska Division of Geological & Geophysical Surveys
Gramsch, Stephen, Carnegie Institution of Washington
Grand, Stephen P., University of Texas at Austin
Green, Douglas H., Ohio University
Greenfield, Roy J., Pennsylvania State University, University Park
Gregg, Patricia, University of Illinois, Urbana-Champaign
Gribenko, Alex, University of Utah
Grindlay, Nancy R., University of North Carolina Wilmington
Haas, Christian, York University
Haber, Eldad, University of British Columbia
Ham, David, Imperial College
Hamzaoui, Cherif, Universite du Quebec a Montreal
Hardage, Bob A., University of Texas at Austin, Jackson School of Geosciences
Harder, Steven H., University of Texas, El Paso
Harig, Christopher, Princeton University
Harry, Dennis L., Colorado State University
Hauck, II, Steven A., Case Western Reserve University
Heigold, Paul C., Argonne National Laboratory
Henson, Harvey, Southern Illinois University Carbondale
Henstock, Tim, University of Southampton
Henyey, Thomas L., University of Southern California
Herman, Rhett B., Radford University
Hermance, John F., Brown University
Hier-Majumder, Saswata, Univ of London, Royal Holloway & Bedford New College
Hier-Majumder, Saswata, University of Maryland
Higgs, Bettie, University College Cork
Hornbach, Matthew, University of Texas at Austin
Horton, Stephen, University of Memphis
Horváth, Ferenc, Eotvos Lorand University
Houseman, Greg, University of Leeds
Huang, Lianjie, Los Alamos National Laboratory
Huerta, Audrey, Central Washington University
Iaffaldano, Giampiero, Ludwig-Maximilians-Universitaet Muenchen
Igel, Heiner, Ludwig-Maximilians-Universitaet Muenchen
Irving, Jessica, Princeton University
Ishii, Miaki, Harvard University
Ivanov, Julian, University of Kansas
Jackson, James, University of Cambridge
Jacob, Robert W., Bucknell University
Jaiswal, Priyank, Oklahoma State University
Jarvis, Gary T., York University
Jensen, Olivia G., McGill University
Johnson, Kaj, Indiana University, Bloomington
Johnson, Paul A., Los Alamos National Laboratory
Johnson, Verner C., Colorado Mesa University
Jomeiri, Rahim, University of Tabriz
Jurdy, Donna M., Northwestern University
Kafka, Alan L., Boston College
Kahle, Beth, University of Cape Town
Kaplinski, Matthew A., Northern Arizona University
Katz, Samuel, Rensselaer Polytechnic Institute
Kaus, Boris P., Universitaet Mainz
Kavner, Abby, University of California, Los Angeles
Keating, Kristina M., Rutgers, The State University of New Jersey, Newark
Keller, G. Randy, University of Missouri
Keller, G. Randy, University of Oklahoma
Keller, George, Oregon State University
Kelley, Shari, New Mexico Institute of Mining & Technology
Kellogg, James N., University of South Carolina
Kellogg, Louise H., University of California, Davis
Kenyon, Patricia M., City College (CUNY)
Kenyon, Patricia M., Graduate School of the City University of New York
King, Robert W., Massachusetts Institute of Technology
King, Scott D., Virginia Polytechnic Institute & State University
Kingdon, Kevin, University of British Columbia
Kinsland, Gary L., University of Louisiana at Lafayette
Korenaga, Jun, Yale University
Kroeger, Glenn C., Trinity University
Kruger, Joseph M., Lamar University
Kruse, Sarah E., University of South Florida, Tampa

Kukowski, Nina, Friedrich-Schiller-University Jena
Kuo, John T., Columbia University
Käser, Martin, Ludwig-Maximilians-Universitaet Muenchen
Lat, Che Noorliza, University of Malaya
Lathrop, Daniel, University of Maryland
Laudon, Thomas S., University of Wisconsin, Oshkosh
Lavallee, Yan, Ludwig-Maximilians-Universitaet Muenchen
Lavier, Luc L., University of Texas at Austin
Leitch, Alison, Memorial University of Newfoundland
Lenardic, Adrian, Rice University
Leonard, Lucinda, University of Victoria
Lerche, Ian, University of South Carolina
Lewis, Stephen D., California State University, Fresno
Lin, Guochin, University of Miami
Lithgow-Bertelloni, Carolina, University College London
Liu, Lanbo, University of Connecticut
Liu, Lijun, University of Illinois, Urbana-Champaign
Liu, Mian, University of Missouri
Liu, Yajing, McGill University
Lohman, Rowena B., Cornell University
Lopez-Pineda, Leobardo, Centro de Estudios Superiores del Estado Sonora
Louie, John, University of Nevada, Reno
Lovell, Mike, Leicester University
Luttrell, Karen, Louisiana State University
Lutz, Pascale, Institut Polytechnique LaSalle Beauvais (ex-IGAL)
Ma, Jingsheng, Heriot-Watt University
Mackwell, Stephen J., Rice University
Mahatsente, Rezene, University of Alabama
Malinconico, Lawrence L., Lafayette College
Malservisi, Rocco, Ludwig-Maximilians-Universitaet Muenchen
Mao, Ho-kwang (David), University of Chicago
Mareschal, Jean-Claude, Universite du Quebec a Montreal
Masterlark, Timothy L., South Dakota School of Mines & Technology
Mavko, Gerald M., Stanford University
Maxwell, Michael, University of British Columbia
McElwaine, Jim, Durham University
McGeary, Susan, University of Delaware
McGinnis, Lyle D., Argonne National Laboratory
McKenzie, Dan, University of Cambridge
Meade, Brendan, Harvard University
Meadows, Wayne R., Los Alamos National Laboratory
Meert, Joseph G., University of Florida
Meng, Yue, Carnegie Institution of Washington
Merriam, James B., University of Saskatchewan
Merrill, Ronald T., University of Washington
Mickus, Kevin L., Missouri State University
Milne, Glenn A., University of Ottawa
Mitrovica, Jerry X., Harvard University
Mohr, Marcus, Ludwig-Maximilians-Universitaet Muenchen
Montana, Carlos J., University of Texas, El Paso
Montesi, Laurent G., University of Maryland
Moorkamp, Max, Leicester University
Morgan, F D., Massachusetts Institute of Technology
Morgan, Jason, University of London, Royal Holloway & Bedford New College
Morgan, Joanna, Imperial College
Morris, William A., McMaster University
Morrison, H. Frank, University of California, Berkeley
Morse, David L., University of Texas at Austin
Mukerji, Tapan, Stanford University
Murphy, Vincent, Boston College
Ni, James, University of Missouri
Ntarlagiannis, Dimitrios, Rutgers, The State University of New Jersey, Newark
Nunn, Jeffrey A., Louisiana State University
Nur, Amos M., Stanford University
Nyblade, Andrew A., Pennsylvania State University, University Park
Nyquist, Jonathan, Temple University
Ogiesoba, Osareni C., University of Texas at Austin
Ojo, S. B., Obafemi Awolowo University
Oladunjoye, M. A., University of Ibadan
Olawuyi, A. K., University of Ilorin
Olayinka, A. I., University of Ibadan
Oldenburg, Douglas W., University of British Columbia
Olgaard, David L., Rice University
Olhoeft, Gary R., Colorado School of Mines
Oliver, Ronald D., Los Alamos National Laboratory
Olorunfemi, M. O., Obafemi Awolowo University
Olson, Peter L., Johns Hopkins University
Oser, Jens, Ludwig-Maximilians-Universitaet Muenchen
Osinowo, O. O., University of Ibadan
Oware, Erasmus K., SUNY, Buffalo
Pain, Christopher, Imperial College
Palmer, Donald F., Kent State University
Palutoglu, Mahmut, Firat University
Panero, Wendy R., Ohio State University
Park, Changyong, Carnegie Institution of Washington
Parmentier, E. Marc, Brown University
Parsekian, Andrew D., University of Wyoming
Pasicznyk, David L., New Jersey Geological Survey
Patton, Howard J., Los Alamos National Laboratory
Peavy, Samuel T., Georgia Southwestern State University

Peirce, Christine, Durham University
Peters, Mark T., Los Alamos National Laboratory
Petersen, Nikolai, Ludwig-Maximilians-Universitaet Muenchen
Pfuhl, Helen, Ludwig-Maximilians-Universitaet Muenchen
Phillips, William S., Los Alamos National Laboratory
Piazzoni, Antonio Sebastian, Ludwig-Maximilians-Universitaet Muenchen
Pimentel-Hernandez, Ramon, Universidad Autonoma de Baja California Sur
Plattner, Christina, Ludwig-Maximilians-Universitaet Muenchen
Porch, William M., Los Alamos National Laboratory
Priestley, Keith, University of Cambridge
Pringle, Jamie, Keele University
Pulliam, Jay, University of Texas at Austin
Pysklywec, Russell N., University of Toronto
Raine, Robin, National University of Ireland Galway
Ranalli, Giorgio, Carleton University
Randall, George, Los Alamos National Laboratory
Rasmussen, Steen, Los Alamos National Laboratory
Ravat, Dhananjay, University of Kentucky
Reilinger, Robert E., Massachusetts Institute of Technology
Revetta, Frank A., SUNY Potsdam
Rice, James R., Harvard University
Richard, Robert, University of California, Los Angeles
Richards, Mark A., University of California, Berkeley
Richardson, Randall M., University of Arizona
Roach, Michael, University of Tasmania
Roberts, Mark L., Woods Hole Oceanographic Institution
Robinson, Edwin S., Virginia Polytechnic Institute & State University
Robinson, Judith, Rutgers, The State University of New Jersey, Newark
Rochester, Michael G., Memorial University of Newfoundland
Rodi, William, Massachusetts Institute of Technology
Roecker, Steven W., Rensselaer Polytechnic Institute
Romanovsky, Vladimir, University of Alaska Fairbanks
Rothman, Daniel H., Massachusetts Institute of Technology
Rouleau, Pierre M., Sir Wilfred Grenfell College
Rubin, Allan M., Princeton University
Rudge, John, University of Cambridge
Rusmanugroho, Herurisa, Princeton University
Russell, Christopher T., University of California, Los Angeles
Russell, R. Doncaster, University of British Columbia
Russo, Raymond, University of Florida
Ryall, Patrick J., Dalhousie University
Rychert, Catherine A., University of Southampton
Sabra, Karim, Georgia Institute of Technology
Sahr, John D., University of Washington
Salami, Sikiru A., University of Benin
Salmun, Haydee, Hunter College (CUNY)
Sammis, Charles G., University of Southern California
Sass, John H., Northern Arizona University
Sauck, William A., Western Michigan University
Sava, Diana, University of Texas at Austin, Jackson School of Geosciences
Schmandt, Brandon, University of New Mexico
Schriver, David, University of California, Los Angeles
Schubert, Gerald, University of California, Los Angeles
Schuberth, Bernhard, Ludwig-Maximilians-Universitaet Muenchen
Schultz, Adam, Oregon State University
Searls, Mindi L., University of Nebraska, Lincoln
Segall, Paul, Stanford University
Serzu, Mulu, University of Manitoba
Shams, Asghar, Heriot-Watt University
Shcherbakov, Robert, Western University
Sherrod, Laura, Kutztown University of Pennsylvania
Shieh, Sean, Western University
Sigloch, Karin, University of Oxford
Simila, Gerald W., California State University, Northridge
Simmons, M. G., Massachusetts Institute of Technology
Simms, Janet E., Mississippi State University
Sinogeikin, Stanislav, Carnegie Institution of Washington
Sit, Stefany, University of Illinois at Chicago
Slater, Lee S., Rutgers, The State University of New Jersey, Newark
Sleep, Norman H., Stanford University
Smylie, Douglas E., York University
Solomatov, Viatcheslav S., Washington University in St. Louis
Solomon, Sean C., Carnegie Institution of Washington
Sonett, Charles P., University of Arizona
Sparks, David, Texas A&M University
Stearns, Richard G., Vanderbilt University
Steele, William K., Eastern Washington University
Stein, Carol A., University of Illinois at Chicago
Stidham, Christiane W., SUNY, Stony Brook
Stierman, Donald J., University of Toledo
Stixrude, Lars, University College London
Stupazzini, Marco, Ludwig-Maximilians-Universitaet Muenchen
Styles, Peter, Keele University
Suckale, Jenny, Stanford University
Sweeney, Mark D., Pacific Northwest National Laboratory
Szeliga, Walter, Central Washington University
Szeto, Anthony M. K., York University
Taib, Samsudin Hj., University of Malaya
Tatham, Robert H., University of Texas at Austin
Taylor, Graeme, University of Plymouth

Telling, Jennifer, Michigan Technological University
ten Brink, Uri S., Woods Hole Oceanographic Institution
Thiruvathukal, John V., Montclair State University
Thompson, George A., Stanford University
Thompson, Michael D., Argonne National Laboratory
Thorne, Michael, University of Utah
Timár, Gábor, Eotvos Lorand University
Tobin, Harold, University of Wisconsin, Madison
Tong, Vincent C., Birkbeck College
Tsai, Victor, California Institute of Technology
Tsoflias, George P., University of Kansas
Turcotte, Donald L., University of California, Davis
Van Avendonk, Harm, University of Texas at Austin
van Keken, Peter J., University of Michigan
Velli, Marco, University of California, Los Angeles
Vernhes, Jean-David, Institut Polytechnique LaSalle Beauvais (ex-IGAL)
Versteeg, Roelof, Columbia University
Vincent, Robert K., Bowling Green State University
von Glasow, Roland, University of East Anglia
Vopson, Melvin M., University of Portsmouth
Waff, Harve S., University of Oregon
Waltham, Dave, University of London, Royal Holloway & Bedford New College
Wang, Chi-Yuen, University of California, Berkeley
Wang, Herbert F., University of Wisconsin, Madison
Wang, Kelin, University of Victoria
Wang, Yanghua, Imperial College
Warren, Linda, Saint Louis University
Warren, Stephen G., University of Washington
Wassermann, Joachim, Ludwig-Maximilians-Universitaet Muenchen
Weaver, Thomas A., Los Alamos National Laboratory
Weeraratne, Dayanthie, California State University, Northridge
Wettlaufer, John S., Yale University
White, Nicky, University of Cambridge
White, Robert, University of Cambridge
Whitman, Dean, Florida International University
Williams, Ian S., University of Wisconsin, River Falls
Williams, II, Richard T., University of Tennessee, Knoxville
Wilson, Clark R., University of Texas at Austin
Winberry, Paul, Central Washington University
Winklhofer, Michael, Ludwig-Maximilians-Universitaet Muenchen
Woodhouse, John, University of Oxford
Woods, Andy, University of Cambridge
Worthington, Lindsay L., University of New Mexico
Xiao, Yuming, Carnegie Institution of Washington
Yuen, David A., University of Minnesota, Twin Cities
Zahm, Christopher K., University of Texas at Austin
Zaja, Annalisa, Università degli Studi di Padova
Zarroca Hernández, Mario, Universitat Autonoma de Barcelona
Zelt, Colin A., Rice University
Zha, Changsheng, Carnegie Institution of Washington
Zhang, Chi, University of Kansas
Zoback, Mark D., Stanford University
Zoner, Stefan , New Mexico State University, Las Cruces

Experimental Geophysics
Anderson, Orson L., University of California, Los Angeles
Bates, Richard, University of St. Andrews
Bevis, Michael G., Ohio State University
Bleibinhaus, Florian, Friedrich-Schiller-University Jena
Bohlen, Thomas, Karlsruhe Institute of Technology
Bona, Andrej, Curtin University
Bridges, Frank, University of California, Santa Cruz
Bussod, Gilles Y., Los Alamos National Laboratory
Carson, Michael, Curtin University
Christensen, Nikolas I., University of Wisconsin, Madison
Comina, Cesare, Università di Torino
Daub, Eric, University of Memphis
Dewers, Thomas, New Mexico Institute of Mining and Technology
Dyaur, Nikolay, University of Houston
Evans, J. B., Massachusetts Institute of Technology
Fomel, Sergey, University of Texas at Austin, Jackson School of Geosciences
Fratta, Dante, University of Wisconsin, Madison
Glover, Paul W., Universite Laval
Glubokovskikh, Stanislav, Curtin University
Graham, Jr., Earl K., Pennsylvania State University, University Park
Green, II, Harry W., University of California, Riverside
Gross, Gerardo W., New Mexico Institute of Mining and Technology
Heinz, Dion L., University of Chicago
Hemley, Russell J., Carnegie Institution of Washington
Herrmann, Felix J., University of British Columbia
Holzworth, Robert H., University of Washington
Kaip, Galen M., University of Texas, El Paso
Kilburn, Chris, University College London
Kitajima, Hiroko, Texas A&M University
Kohlstedt, David L., University of Minnesota, Twin Cities
Korvin, Gabor, King Fahd University of Petroleum and Minerals
Lebedev, Maxim, Curtin University
Manghnani, Murli H., University of Hawai'i, Manoa
Mao, Ho-kwang, Carnegie Institution of Washington
Marone, Chris, Pennsylvania State University, University Park

Marshall, Hans-Peter, Boise State University
Marshall, Scott, Appalachian State University
McNamara, Allen, Arizona State University
Mei, Shenghua, University of Minnesota, Twin Cities
Narod, Barry, University of British Columbia
Parks, George K., University of Washington
Pec, Matej, University of Minnesota, Twin Cities
Pevzner, Roman, Curtin University
Quintanilla Terminal, Alejandra, University of Minnesota, Twin Cities
Ruina, Andy L., Cornell University
Schmitt, Douglas R., University of Alberta
Scholz, Christopher H., Columbia University
Shankland, Thomas J., Los Alamos National Laboratory
Shaw, George H., Union College
Shu, Jinfu, Carnegie Institution of Washington
Somayazulu, Maddury, Carnegie Institution of Washington
Sone, Hiroki, University of Wisconsin, Madison
Tullis, Terry E., Brown University
Tyburczy, James A., Arizona State University
Vanorio, Tiziana, Stanford University
Vaughan, Michael T., SUNY, Stony Brook
Velasco, Aaron A., University of Texas, El Paso
Vialle, Stephanie , Curtin University
Wang, Herbert F., University of Wisconsin, Madison
Watanabe, Tohru, University of Toyama
Westwood, Rachel, Keele University
Wishart, De Bonne N., Central State University
Wong, Teng-fong, SUNY, Stony Brook
Zebker, Howard A., Stanford University
Zimmerman, Mark, University of Minnesota, Twin Cities

Exploration Geophysics
Al-Shuhail, Abdullah, King Fahd University of Petroleum and Minerals
Alumbaugh, David L., University of California, Berkeley
Armadillo, Egidio, Universita di Genova
B, Dr. V., University College of Science, Osmania University
Backus, Milo M., University of Texas at Austin
Basham, William L., University of Texas, Permian Basin
Becker, Alex, University of California, Berkeley
Benson, Robert D., Colorado School of Mines
Best, Melvyn E., University of Victoria
Biondi, Biondo L., Stanford University
Black, Ross A., University of Kansas
Brabham, P J., Cardiff University
Bradford, John, Boise State University
Brassea, Jesus M., Centro de Investigación Científica y de Ed Superior de Ensenada
Breland, Clayton F., Louisiana State University
Brown, Larry D., Cornell University
Burns, Laurel E., Alaska Division of Geological & Geophysical Surveys
Calvin, Wendy M., University of Nevada, Reno
Carmichael, Robert S., University of Iowa
Castagna, John P., University of Houston
Chandler, Val W., University of Minnesota, Twin Cities
Chen, Jingyi, University of Tulsa
Claerbout, Jon F., Stanford University
Clayton, Robert W., California Institute of Technology
Corbato, Charles E., Ohio State University
Coruh, Cahit, Virginia Polytechnic Institute & State University
Davis, Thomas L., Colorado School of Mines
DeAngelo, Micheal V., University of Texas at Austin, Jackson School of Geosciences
Denton-Hedrick, Meredith Y., Austin Community College District
Donaldson, Paul R., Boise State University
Duckworth, Kenneth, University of Calgary
Dunlap, Dallas B., University of Texas at Austin, Jackson School of Geosciences
Ellett, Kevin M., Indiana University
Esparza, Francisco, Centro de Investigación Científica y de Ed Superior de Ensenada
Espinosa, Juan M., Centro de Investigación Científica y de Ed Superior de Ensenada
Ferguson, Ian J., University of Manitoba
Flores, Carlos, Centro de Investigación Científica y de Ed Superior de Ensenada
Fomel, Sergey B., University of Texas at Austin
Gaede, Oliver M., Queensland University of Technology
Gajewski, Dirk J., Universitaet Hamburg
Galsa, Attila, Eotvos Lorand University
Galvin, Robert, Curtin University
Gao, Dengliang, West Virginia University
Gendzwill, Donald J., University of Saskatchewan
Giroux, Bernard, Universite du Quebec
Gloaguen, Erwan, Universite du Quebec
Goloshubin, Gennady, University of Houston
Gomez, Enrique, Centro de Investigación Científica y de Ed Superior de Ensenada
Gonzalez-Escobar, Mario, Centro de Investigación Científica y de Ed Superior de Ensenada
Grana, Dario, University of Wyoming
Gurevich, Boris, Curtin University
Hale, Dave, Colorado School of Mines
Han, De-hua, University of Houston
Hardage, Bob A., University of Texas at Austin
Harris, James B., Millsaps College
Hauser, Ernest C., Wright State University
Hilterman, Fred, University of Houston

Hinze, William J., Purdue University
Hole, John A., Virginia Polytechnic Institute & State University
Holt, John W., University of Texas at Austin
Homuth, Emil F., Los Alamos National Laboratory
Howman, Dominic J., Curtin University
Hu, Hao, University of Houston
Jiracek, George R., San Diego State University
Johnson, Ansel G., Portland State University
Jones, Francis H., University of British Columbia
Keach II, R. William, Brigham Young University
Kepic, Anton W., Curtin University
Khalil, Mohamed, Montana Tech
Knapp, Camelia, University of South Carolina
Knapp, James H., University of South Carolina
Larner, Kenneth L., Colorado School of Mines
Lawton, Donald C., University of Calgary
Lee, Ki Ha, University of California, Berkeley
Levander, Alan R., Rice University
Lillie, Robert J., Oregon State University
Lines, Larry R., University of Calgary
Link, Curtis A., Montana Tech
Louie, John N., University of Nevada, Reno
Lourenço, José M., Universidade de Trás-os-Montes e Alto Douro
Madadi, Mahyar, Curtin University
Magnani, Maria B., University of Memphis
Margrave, Gary F., University of Calgary
Marobhe, Isaac M., University of Dar es Salaam
Mathur, Dr R., University College of Science, Osmania University
Mazariegos, Ruben A., University of Texas, Pan American
McBride, John H., Brigham Young University
McPherson, Brian, University of Utah
Miah, Khalid, Montana Tech
Mikhaltsevitch, Vassily, Curtin University
Mikulich, Matthew J., Virginia Polytechnic Institute & State University
Milkereit, Bernd, University of Toronto
Miller, Richard D., University of Kansas
Morrison, Huntly Frank, University of California, Berkeley
Olsen, Kim B., San Diego State University
Palmer, Derecke, University of New South Wales
Perez, Marco A., Centro de Investigación Científica y de Ed Superior de Ensenada
Pethick, Andrew, Curtin University
Pigott, John D., University of Oklahoma
Potter, David, University of Alberta
Pratt, R. Gerhard, Western University
Pujol, Jose M., University of Memphis
Pujol, Jose, University of Memphis
Raef, Abdelmoneam E., Kansas State University
Raji, W. O., University of Ilorin
Ramachandran, Kumar, University of Tulsa
Rechtien, Richard D., Missouri University of Science and Technology
Rector, James W., University of California, Berkeley
Reshef, Moshe, Tel Aviv University
Richard, Benjamin H., Wright State University
Romo, Jose M., Centro de Investigación Científica y de Ed Superior de Ensenada
Rupert, Gerald B., Missouri University of Science and Technology
Sarwar, A. K. Mostofa, University of New Orleans
Sava, Paul, Colorado School of Mines
Scanlin, Michael A., Elizabethtown College
Schuster, Gerard T., University of Utah
Seifoullaev, Roustam K., University of Texas at Austin
Sen, Mrinal K., University of Texas at Austin
Serpa, Laura F., University of Texas, El Paso
Sexton, John L., Southern Illinois University Carbondale
Shaw, Kenneth L., University of Utah
Snieder, Roel, Colorado School of Mines
Speece, Marvin A., Montana Tech
Spikes, Kyle T., University of Texas at Austin
Sprenke, Kenneth F., University of Idaho
Sternberg, Ben K., University of Arizona
Stewart, Robert R., University of Calgary
Stewart, Robert R., University of Houston
Stimpson, Ian, Keele University
Stoffa, Paul L., University of Texas at Austin
Takam, Eric, Curtin University
Tertyshnikov, Konstantin, Curtin University
Thomsen, Leon, University of Houston
Tsvankin, Ilya D., Colorado School of Mines
Turpening, Roger M., Michigan Technological University
Unsworth, Martyn, Cornell University
Urosevic, Milovan, Curtin University
Vazquez, Rogelio, Centro de Investigación Científica y de Ed Superior de Ensenada
von Frese, Ralph R., Ohio State University
Wannamaker, Phillip E., University of Utah
Watts, Doyle, Wright State University
Weglein, Arthur, University of Houston
Weiss, Chester J., Virginia Polytechnic Institute & State University
Wilson, Thomas H., West Virginia University
Wolfe, Paul J., Wright State University
Zawislak, Ronald L., Middle Tennessee State University
Zhang, Bo, University of Alabama

Zhdanov, Michael S., University of Utah
Ziramov, Sasha, Curtin University

Geodesy

Al-Attar, David, University of Cambridge
Bennett, Richard, University of Arizona
Blewitt, Geoffrey, University of Nevada, Reno
Brockhaus, John A., United States Military Academy
Caporali, Alessandro, Università degli Studi di Padova
Clarke, Peter, University of Newcastle Upon Tyne
Davis, James , Columbia University
Elliott, Julie, Purdue University
Feigl, Kurt, University of Wisconsin, Madison
Flake, Rex , Central Washington University
Fotopoulos, Georgia, Queen's University
Freymueller, Jeffrey T., University of Alaska Fairbanks
Funning, Gareth, University of California, Riverside
Gonzalez, Jose J., Centro de Investigación Científica y de Ed Superior de Ensenada
Grejner-Brzezinska, Dorota A., Ohio State University
Hammond, William, University of Nevada
Herring, Thomas A., Massachusetts Institute of Technology
Hooper, Andy, University of Leeds
Jekeli, Christopher, Ohio State University
Kogan, Mikhail, Columbia University
Kreemer, Corne, University of Nevada
Kusznir, Nick, University of Liverpool
LaFemina, Peter C., Pennsylvania State University, University Park
Li, Zhenhong, University of Newcastle Upon Tyne
Lowry, Anthony R., Utah State University
Martin, Ian, University of Newcastle Upon Tyne
Melbourne, Timothy I., Central Washington University
Miller, M. Meghan, Central Washington University
Miner, Andy, Central Washington University
Moore, Phillip, University of Newcastle Upon Tyne
Murray, Mark, New Mexico Institute of Mining and Technology
Odera, Patroba A., Jomo Kenyatta University of Agriculture & Technology
Pagiatakis, Spiros, York University
Palamartchouk, Kirill, University of Newcastle Upon Tyne
Parsons, Barry, University of Oxford
Petrie, Liz, University of Newcastle Upon Tyne
Pritchard, Matthew E., Cornell University
Rundle, John, University of California, Davis
Saalfeld, Alan J., Ohio State University
Santillan, Marcelo, Central Washington University
Schaffrin, Burkhard A., Ohio State University
Shum, CK, Ohio State University
Smalley, Jr., Robert, University of Memphis
Smith-Konter, Bridget R., University of Hawai'i, Manoa
Sparks, David, Texas A&M University
Spinler, Joshua C., University of Arkansas at Little Rock
Tiampo, Kristy F., Western University
Vincent, Paul, Oregon State University
Waithaka, Hunja, Jomo Kenyatta University of Agriculture & Technology
Wdowinski, Shimon, University of Miami
Wells, David E., University of Southern Mississippi
Wright, Tim, University of Leeds
Yi, Yuchan, Ohio State University

Geomagnetism & Paleomagnetism

Abokhodair, Abdulwahab, King Fahd University of Petroleum and Minerals
Banerjee, Subir K., University of Minnesota, Twin Cities
Biggin, Andy, University of Liverpool
Bilardello, Dario, University of Minnesota, Twin Cities
Bogue, Scott W., Occidental College
Booker, John R., University of Washington
Borradaile, Graham J., Lakehead University
Bowles, Julie, University of Wisconsin, Milwaukee
Braginsky, Stanislav I., University of California, Los Angeles
Bramham, Emma , University of Leeds
Brown, Laurie, University of Massachusetts, Amherst
Burmester, Russell F., Western Washington University
Channell, James E., University of Florida
Chen, Xiaojia, Carnegie Institution of Washington
Cioppa, Maria T., University of Windsor
Clough, Gene A., Bates College
Coe, Robert S., University of California, Santa Cruz
Constable, Catherine G., University of California, San Diego
Cottrell, Rory D., University of Rochester
De Boer, Jelle Z., Wesleyan University
DeMets, D. Charles, University of Wisconsin, Madison
DiVenere, Victor, Long Island University, C.W. Post Campus
Doh, Seong-Jae, Korea University
Douglass, David N., Pasadena City College
Dulin, Shannon, University of Oklahoma
Ellwood, Brooks B., Louisiana State University
Elmore, R. Douglas, University of Oklahoma
Evans, David A., Yale University
Evans, Michael E., University of Alberta
Everett, Mark, Texas A&M University
Feinberg, Joshua, University of Minnesota, Twin Cities
Franklin, David, University of Portsmouth

Fraser-Smith, Antony C., Stanford University
Geissman, John W., University of New Mexico
Geissman, John W., University of Michigan
Gordon, Richard G., Rice University
Grimley, David A., Illinois State Geological Survey
Guerrero-Garcia, Jose C., Universidad Nacional Autonoma de Mexico
Halgedahl, Susan L., University of Utah
Hall, Frank R., University of New Orleans
Hall, Stuart A., University of Houston
Halls, Henry C., University of Toronto
Harbert, William P., University of Pittsburgh
Herrero-Bervera, Emilio, University of Hawai'i, Manoa
Hill, Mimi, University of Liverpool
Hodych, Joseph P., Memorial University of Newfoundland
Holme, Richard, University of Liverpool
Housen, Bernard A., Western Washington University
Hozik, Michael J., Richard Stockton College of New Jersey
Huang, Kainian, University of Florida
Jackson, Michael, University of Minnesota, Twin Cities
Jones, F. Walter, University of Alberta
Kean, Jr., William F., University of Wisconsin, Milwaukee
Kelso, Paul R., Lake Superior State University
Kent, Dennis V., Rutgers, The State University of New Jersey
Kodama, Kenneth P., Lehigh University
Kravchinsky, Vadim, University of Alberta
Larson, Edwin E., University of Colorado
Layer, Paul, University of Alaska Fairbanks
Lima, Eduardo A., Massachusetts Institute of Technology
Lindquist, Anna, Lake Superior State University
Livermore, Phil, University of Leeds
Lund, Steven P., University of Southern California
Maillol, Jean-Michel, University of Calgary
Maloof, Adam C., Princeton University
Marshall, Claude Monte, San Diego State University
Márton, Péter, Eotvos Lorand University
McCausland, Phil J., Western University
McWilliams, Michael O., Stanford University
Merrill, Ronald T., University of Washington
Moskowitz, Bruce M., University of Minnesota, Twin Cities
Muxworthy, Adrian, Imperial College
Negrini, Robert M., California State University, Bakersfield
Nilsson, Andreas, University of Liverpool
Noltimier, Hallan C., Ohio State University
Opdyke, Neil D., University of Florida
Palmer, H. C., Western University
Pares, Josep M., University of Michigan
Park, Stephen K., University of California, Riverside
Parker, Robert L., University of California, San Diego
Paty, Carol M., Georgia Institute of Technology
Petronis, Michael S., New Mexico Highlands University
Piper, John, University of Liverpool
Rankin, David, University of Alberta
Richter, Carl, University of Louisiana at Lafayette
Roberts, Paul H., University of California, Los Angeles
Shibuya, Hidetoshi, Kumamoto University
Sternberg, Robert S., Franklin and Marshall College
Stone, David B., University of Alaska Fairbanks
Symons, David T., University of Windsor
Tarduno, John A., University of Rochester
Tauxe, Lisa, University of California, San Diego
Valentine, Michael J., University of Puget Sound
van der Voo, Rob, University of Michigan
Verosub, Kenneth L., University of California, Davis
Walden, John, University of St. Andrews
Weaver, John T., University of Victoria
Weiss, Benjamin, Massachusetts Institute of Technology
Whaler, Kathryn A., Edinburgh University
Williams, Wyn, Edinburgh University
Zanella, Elena, Università di Torino
Zhao, Xixi, University of California, Santa Cruz

Gravity
Aiken, Carlos L., University of Texas, Dallas
Danes, Z. Frank, University of Puget Sound
Eppelbaum, Lev, Tel Aviv University
Ervin, C. Patrick, Northern Illinois University
Garcia, Juan, Centro de Investigación Científica y de Ed Superior de Ensenada
Ghatge, Suhas L., New Jersey Geological Survey
Grannell, Roswitha B., California State University, Long Beach
Kusumoto, Shigekazu, University of Toyama
Li, Yaoguo, Colorado School of Mines
Smirnov, Aleksey K., Michigan Technological University
Steckler, Michael, Columbia University

Heat Flow
Anderson, Roger N., Columbia University
Beltrami, Hugo, Saint Francis Xavier University
Blackwell, David D., Southern Methodist University
Chapman, David S., University of Utah
Crane, Kathleen, Graduate School of the City University of New York
Gosnold, William D., University of North Dakota

Harris, Robert N., Oregon State University
Hsieh, Wen-Pin, Academia Sinica
Huang, Shaopeng, University of Michigan
Jones, Michael Q., University of the Witwatersrand
Lenkey, László, Eotvos Lorand University
Morgan, Paul, Northern Arizona University
Morgan, Paul, Colorado Geological Survey
Pollack, Henry N., University of Michigan
Reiter, Marshall A., New Mexico Institute of Mining and Technology
Sclater, John G., University of California, San Diego
Shen, Po-Yu (Paul), Western University
Smith, Douglas L., University of Florida
Von Herzen, Richard P., Woods Hole Oceanographic Institution

Seismology
Abers, Geoffrey A., Cornell University
Achauer, Ulrich, Universite de Strasbourg
Agnew, Duncan C., University of California, San Diego
Alexander, Shelton S., Pennsylvania State University, University Park
Allen, Clarence R., California Institute of Technology
Allen, Richard M., University of California, Berkeley
Allstadt, Kate, University of Washington
Ammon, Charles J., Pennsylvania State University, University Park
Ampuero, Jean-Paul, California Institute of Technology
Anandakrishnan, Sridhar, Pennsylvania State University, University Park
Anderson, John, University of Nevada, Reno
Anderson, John G., University of Nevada, Reno
Angus, Doug, University of Leeds
Arabasz, Walter J., University of Utah
Archuleta, Ralph J., University of California, Santa Barbara
Asencio, Eugenio, University of Puerto Rico
Assatourians, Karen, Western University
Aster, Richard, Colorado State University
Atkinson, Gail M., Western University
Atwater, Brian, University of Washington
Ausbrooks, Scott, Arkansas Geological Survey
Balch, Robert S., New Mexico Institute of Mining and Technology
Barazangi, Muawia, Cornell University
Barclay, Andrew, Columbia University
Barker, Jeffrey S., Binghamton University
Beaumont, Christopher, Dalhousie University
Beck, Susan L., University of Arizona
Becker, Thorsten W., University of Southern California
Beghein, Caroline, University of California, Los Angeles
Ben-Zion, Yehuda, University of Southern California
Benavides-Iglesias, Alfonso, Texas A&M University
Benz, Harley M., University of Utah
Beroza, Gregory C., Stanford University
Bezada, Max, University of Minnesota, Twin Cities
Biasi, Glenn P., University of Nevada, Reno
Bilek, Susan L., New Mexico Institute of Mining and Technology
Bilham, Roger, University of Colorado
Blake, Daniel, Ohio Dept of Natural Resources
Blakely, Robert F., Indiana University, Bloomington
Bodin, Paul A., University of Washington
Bollinger, G. A., Virginia Polytechnic Institute & State University
Borisov, Dmitry, Princeton University
Bostock, Michael G., University of British Columbia
Bowman, David D., California State University, Fullerton
Braile, Lawrence W., Purdue University
Brodsky, Emily, University of California, Santa Cruz
Brown, James R., University of Calgary
Brudzinski, Michael, Miami University
Brumbaugh, David S., Northern Arizona University
Brune, James N., University of Nevada, Reno
Burdick, Scott, University of Maryland
Burton, Paul, University of East Anglia
Calvert, Andrew J., Simon Fraser University
Cann, Johnson R., Woods Hole Oceanographic Institution
Caplan-Auerbach, Jackie, Western Washington University
Cardimona, Steve, Mendocino College
Cartwright, J A., Cardiff University
Cassidy, John, University of Victoria
Castro, Raul, Centro de Investigación Científica y de Ed Superior de Ensenada
Chapman, Martin C., Virginia Polytechnic Institute & State University
Chen, Po, University of Wyoming
Chen, Wang-Ping, University of Illinois, Urbana-Champaign
Chen, Xiaowei, University of Oklahoma
Chesnokov, Evgeny, University of Houston
Chiu, Jer-Ming, University of Memphis
Chiu, Shu-Choiung, University of Memphis
Chowdhury, Dipak K., Indiana University / Purdue University, Fort Wayne
Christensen, Douglas, University of Alaska Fairbanks
Cicerone, Robert, Bridgewater State University
Cipar, John J., Boston College
Clark, Roger, University of Leeds
Clowes, Ronald M., University of British Columbia
Cochran, Elizabeth, University of California, Riverside
Collins, John A., Woods Hole Oceanographic Institution
Conder, James, Southern Illinois University Carbondale

Cook, Frederick A., University of Calgary
Cormier, Vernon F., University of Connecticut
Cottaar, Sanne , University of Cambridge
Courtier, Anna, University of Wisconsin, Whitewater
Cramer, Chris H., University of Memphis
Creager, Kenneth C., University of Washington
Crosson, Robert S., University of Washington
Curtis, Andrew, Edinburgh University
D'Amico, Sebastiano, University of Malta
Dalton, Colleen, Brown University
Darbyshire, Fiona Ann, Universite du Quebec a Montreal
Darold, Amberlee, University of Oklahoma
Davis, Paul M., University of California, Los Angeles
Day, Steven M., San Diego State University
De Angelis, Silvio, University of Liverpool
dePolo, Diane, University of Nevada, Reno
DeShon, Heather, University of Memphis
DeShon, Heather R., Southern Methodist University
Dorman, James, University of Memphis
Doser, Diane I., University of Texas, El Paso
Dreger, Douglas S., University of California, Berkeley
Dueker, Kenneth G., University of Wyoming
Dunham, Eric M., Stanford University
Dziewonski, Adam M., Harvard University
Ebel, John E., Boston College
Ekstrom, Goran, Columbia University
Ellis, Robert M., University of British Columbia
Faulkner, Daniel, University of Liverpool
Ferreira, Anna, University College London
Fischer, Karen M., Brown University
Fontaine, Fabrice R., Universite de la Reunion
Forbriger, Thomas, Karlsruhe Institute of Technology
Ford, Heather, University of California, Riverside
Fox, Jeff, Ohio Dept of Natural Resources
Frankel, Arthur, University of Washington
Frazer, L. N., University of Hawai'i, Manoa
Frederiksen, Andrew, University of Manitoba
Frez, Jose, Centro de Investigación Científica y de Ed Superior de Ensenada
Frohlich, Clifford A., University of Texas at Austin
Fujita, Kazuya, Michigan State University
Gabrielov, Andrei, Purdue University
Gaherty, James, Columbia University
Galea, Pauline, University of Malta
Gao, Haiying, University of Massachusetts, Amherst
Garces, Milton A., University of Hawai'i, Manoa
Garnero, Edward, Arizona State University
Ghosh, Abhijit, University of California, Riverside
Gibson, Jr., Richard L., Texas A&M University
Gilbert, Hersh, Purdue University
Gilbert, J. Freeman, University of California, San Diego
Gilpin, Bernard J., Golden West College
Glowacka, Ewa, Centro de Investigación Científica y de Ed Superior de Ensenada
Gomberg, Joan, University of Washington
Gonzalez-Huizar, Hector, University of Texas, El Paso
Grand, Stephen P., University of Texas at Austin
Gu, Jeff, University of Alberta
Gurnis, Michael C., California Institute of Technology
Gurrola, Harold, Texas Tech University
Hager, Bradford H., Massachusetts Institute of Technology
Hagerty, Michael, Boston College
Hajnal, Zoltan, University of Saskatchewan
Hall, Jeremy, Memorial University of Newfoundland
Hamburger, Michael W., Indiana University, Bloomington
Hamilton, Warren, Colorado School of Mines
Hammer, Philip T., University of British Columbia
Hansen, Samantha E., University of Alabama
Harkrider, David G., California Institute of Technology
Harrington, Rebecca, McGill University
Harrington, Rebecca, Karlsruhe Institute of Technology
Harris, Jerry M., Stanford University
Hartse, Hans E., Los Alamos National Laboratory
Hassanpour Sedghi, Mohammad, University of Tabriz
Hauksson, Egill, California Institute of Technology
Hawman, Robert B., University of Georgia
Hayward, Christopher T., Southern Methodist University
Hearn, Thomas M., New Mexico State University, Las Cruces
Helmberger, Donald V., California Institute of Technology
Herrmann, Robert B., Saint Louis University
Hickey, Craig J., University of Mississippi
Hildebrand, Steve T., Los Alamos National Laboratory
Hobbs, Richard, Durham University
Holbrook, W. S., University of Wyoming
Holland, Austin A., University of Oklahoma
Holt, William E., SUNY, Stony Brook
Holtzman, Benjamin, Columbia University
Honjas, Bill, University of Nevada, Reno
Horton, Stephen P., University of Memphis
House, Leigh S., Los Alamos National Laboratory
Houston, Heidi B., University of Washington

Howell, Jr., Benjamin F., Pennsylvania State University, University Park
Humphreys, Eugene D., University of Oregon
Hurich, Charles A., Memorial University of Newfoundland
Hyndman, Roy D., University of Victoria
Isacks, Bryan L., Cornell University
Jackson, David D., University of California, Los Angeles
Jacob, Klaus H., Columbia University
James, David E., Carnegie Institution of Washington
Jasbinsek, John J., California Polytechnic State University
Jaumé, Steven C., College of Charleston
Ji, Chen, University of California, Santa Barbara
Johnson, Jeffrey , Boise State University
Johnson, Lane R., University of California, Berkeley
Johnson, Roy A., University of Arizona
Johnston, Archibald C., University of Memphis
Jones, Alan, Binghamton University
Jones, Craig H., University of Colorado
Jordan, Thomas H., University of Southern California
Kafka, Alan L., Boston College
Kaka, Ismail, King Fahd University of Petroleum and Minerals
Kanamori, Hiroo, California Institute of Technology
Karplus, Marianne, University of Texas, El Paso
Kent, Graham, University of Nevada, Reno
Keranen, Katie M., Cornell University
Kijko, Andrzej, University of Pretoria
Kim, Won-Young, Columbia University
Knopoff, Leon, University of California, Los Angeles
Kovach, Robert L., Stanford University
Krebes, Edward S., University of Calgary
Langston, Charles A., University of Memphis
Lay, Thorne, University of California, Santa Cruz
Lees, Jonathan M., University of North Carolina, Chapel Hill
Lekic, Vedran, University of Maryland
Lerner-Lam, Arthur L., Columbia University
Levander, Alan, Rice University
Levin, Vadim, Rutgers, The State University of New Jersey
Li, Aibing, University of Houston
Li, Yong-Gang, University of Southern California
Liberty, Lee M., Boise State University
Linde, Alan T., Carnegie Institution of Washington
Liner, Christopher , University of Arkansas, Fayetteville
Lizarralde, Daniel, Woods Hole Oceanographic Institution
Lohman, Rowena B., Cornell University
Long, Maureen D., Yale University
Lorenzo, Juan M., Louisiana State University
Louie, John, University of Nevada, Reno
Ma, Shuo, San Diego State University
Madrid, Juan, Centro de Investigación Científica y de Ed Superior de Ensenada
Magnani, M. Beatrice, Southern Methodist University
Main, Ian G., Edinburgh University
Malin, Peter E., Duke University
Mallick, Subhashis, University of Wyoming
Malone, Stephen D., University of Washington
Mangriotis, Maria-Daphne , Heriot-Watt University
Mansinha, Lalu, Western University
Marfurt, Kurt J., University of Oklahoma
Masters, T. Guy, University of California, San Diego
McClelland, Lori, University of Nevada, Reno
McGee, Thomas M., University of Mississippi
McGuire, Jeffrey J., Woods Hole Oceanographic Institution
McLaskey, Greg C., Cornell University
McMechan, George A., University of Texas, Dallas
McNally, Karen C., University of California, Santa Cruz
Meltzer, Anne S., Lehigh University
Meng, Lingsen, University of California, Los Angeles
Menke, William H., Columbia University
Mereu, Robert F., Western University
Miller, Kate, Texas A&M University
Minster, J. Bernard H., University of California, San Diego
Mitchell, Brian J., Saint Louis University
Molnar, Sheri, Western University
Moon, Wooil, University of Manitoba
Morozov, Igor, University of Saskatchewan
Moulis, Anastasia, Boston College
Mulibo, Gabriel D., University of Dar es Salaam
Munguia, Luis, Centro de Investigación Científica y de Ed Superior de Ensenada
Nakamura, Yosio, University of Texas at Austin
Nava, Alejandro, Centro de Investigación Científica y de Ed Superior de Ensenada
Nettles, Meredith, Columbia University
Newman, Andrew V., Georgia Institute of Technology
Ni, James F., New Mexico State University, Las Cruces
Nissen-Meyer, Targe, University of Oxford
Niu, Fenglin, Rice University
Nowack, Robert L., Purdue University
Nyland, Edo, University of Alberta
Ogbamikhumi, Alexander, University of Benin
Oglesby, David D., University of California, Riverside
Okal, Emile A., Northwestern University
Okaya, David A., University of Southern California
Oliver, Adolph A., Chabot College

Olson, Ted L., Snow College
Olugboji, Tolulope M., University of Maryland
Owens, Thomas J., University of South Carolina
Pancha, Aasha, University of Nevada, Reno
Pandit, Bhaskar I., University of Saskatchewan
Pankow, Kristine L., University of Utah
Panning, Mark, University of Florida
Park, Jeffrey J., Yale University
Pavlis, Gary L., Indiana University, Bloomington
Pechmann, James C., University of Utah
Pelton, John R., Boise State University
Peng, Zhigang, Georgia Institute of Technology
Pennington, Wayne D., Michigan Technological University
Phinney, Robert A., Princeton University
Plank, Gabriel, University of Nevada, Reno
Polet, Jascha, California State Polytechnic University, Pomona
Powell, Christine A., University of Memphis
Pride, Steven, University of California, Berkeley
Prieto, Germán, Massachusetts Institute of Technology
Pullammanappallil, Satish, University of Nevada, Reno
Pulliam, Robert J., University of Texas at Austin
Pulliam, Robert J., Baylor University
Reading, Anya, University of Tasmania
Rector, III, James W., University of California, Berkeley
Rennie, Tom, University of Nevada, Reno
Revenaugh, Justin, University of Minnesota, Twin Cities
Rial, Jose A., University of North Carolina, Chapel Hill
Richard, Ferdinand W., University of Dar es Salaam
Richards, Paul G., Columbia University
Richardson, Eliza, Pennsylvania State University, University Park
Rieger, Duayne, Community College of Rhode Island
Rietbrock, Andreas, University of Liverpool
Ritsema, Jeroen, University of Michigan
Ritter, Joachim J., Karlsruhe Institute of Technology
Roberts, Peter, Los Alamos National Laboratory
Rogers, Garry C., University of Victoria
Rohay, Alan C., Pacific Northwest National Laboratory
Romanowicz, Barbara A., University of California, Berkeley
Rost, Sebastian, University of Leeds
Rowe, Charlotte A., New Mexico Institute of Mining and Technology
Ruan, Youyi, Princeton University
Ruff, Larry J., University of Michigan
Ruffman, Alan, Dalhousie University
Sacchi, Mauricio D., University of Alberta
Sacks, I. Selwyn, Carnegie Institution of Washington
Sahay, Pratap, Centro de Investigación Científica y de Ed Superior de Ensenada
Salyards, Stephen L., University of California, Los Angeles
Sandvol, Eric A., University of Missouri
Sanford, Allan R., New Mexico Institute of Mining and Technology
Savage, Brian K., University of Rhode Island
Savage, Heather M., Columbia University
Sawyer, Dale S., Rice University
Schaff, David, Columbia University
Schlue, John W., New Mexico Institute of Mining and Technology
Scholz, Christopher H., Columbia University
Schutt, Derek L., Colorado State University
Schwab, Fred, University of California, Los Angeles
Schwartz, Susan Y., University of California, Santa Cruz
Seeber, Leonardo, Columbia University
Serpa, Laura F., University of New Orleans
Shakal, Anthony F., California Geological Survey
Shaw, Bruce, Columbia University
Shearer, Peter M., University of California, San Diego
Sheehan, Anne F., University of Colorado
Sherrod, Brian L., University of Washington
Shipley, Thomas H., University of Texas at Austin
Simons, Frederik J., Princeton University
Simons, Mark, California Institute of Technology
Slater, David, University of Nevada, Reno
Slawinski, Michael A., Memorial University of Newfoundland
Smalley, Jr., Robert, University of Memphis
Smith, Ken D., University of Nevada, Reno
Smith, Robert B., University of Utah
Smith, Stewart W., University of Washington
Smythe, William, University of California, Los Angeles
Snoke, J. Arthur, Virginia Polytechnic Institute & State University
Song, Alex, University College London
Song, Xiaodong, University of Illinois, Urbana-Champaign
Spanos, J. Timothy, University of Alberta
Spence, George D., University of Victoria
Spetzler, Hartmut A., University of Colorado
Spiegelman, Marc, Columbia University
Stachnik, Joshua, Lehigh University
Steeples, Donald W., University of Kansas
Steer, David N., University of Akron
Steidl, Jamison H., University of California, Santa Barbara
Stein, Seth, Northwestern University
Stephen, Ralph A., Woods Hole Oceanographic Institution
Stickney, Michael C., Montana Tech of The University of Montana
Street, Ronald L., University of Kentucky

Streig, Ashley, Portland State University
Stuart, Graham, University of Leeds
Stump, Brian W., Southern Methodist University
Sverdrup, Keith A., University of Wisconsin, Milwaukee
Sykes, Lynn R., Columbia University
Talwani, Pradeep, University of South Carolina
Tanimoto, Toshiro, University of California, Santa Barbara
Tape, Carl, University of Alaska Fairbanks
Taylor, Kenneth B., North Carolina Geological Survey
Taylor, Steven R., Los Alamos National Laboratory
Teng, Ta-liang, University of Southern California
Thurber, Clifford H., University of Wisconsin, Madison
Tibuleac, Ileana, University of Nevada, Reno
Toksoz, M N., Massachusetts Institute of Technology
Toomey, Douglas R., University of Oregon
Toon, Sam, Keele University
Tromp, Jeroen, Princeton University
Van Avendonk, Harm J., University of Texas at Austin
van der Hilst, Robert, Massachusetts Institute of Technology
van der Lee, Suzan, Northwestern University
Vidal, Antonio, Centro de Investigación Científica y de Ed Superior de Ensenada
Vidale, John E., University of Washington
Von Hillebrandt, Christa, University of Puerto Rico
von Seggern, David, University of Nevada, Reno
Wagner, Lara S., Carnegie Institution of Washington
Waheed, Umair, Princeton University
Waite, Gregory P., Michigan Technological University
Waldhauser, Felix, Columbia University
Wallace, Jr., Terry C., Los Alamos National Laboratory
Wang, Jeen-Hwa, Academia Sinica
Wang, Zhenming, University of Kentucky
Ward, Steven N., University of California, Santa Cruz
Warner, Michael, Imperial College
Wen, Lianxing, SUNY, Stony Brook
Wesnousky, Steve, University of Nevada, Reno
Wesnousky, Steven G., University of Nevada, Reno
Wiens, Douglas A., Washington University in St. Louis
Williams, Erik, University of Nevada, Reno
Withers, Mitchell M., University of Memphis
Wolf, Lorraine W., Auburn University
Wolny, Dave, Colorado Mesa University
Woolery, Edward W., University of Kentucky
Wu, Francis T., Binghamton University
Wu, Patrick, University of Calgary
Wu, Ru-shan, University of California, Santa Cruz
Wust-Bloch, Gilles H., Tel Aviv University
Wysession, Michael E., Washington University in St. Louis
Xie, Xiao-bi, University of California, Santa Cruz
Yu, Wen-che, Academia Sinica
Zandt, George, University of Arizona
Zelt, Colin A., Rice University
Zeng, Hongliu, University of Texas at Austin
Zhan, Zhongwen, California Institute of Technology
Zhao, Li, Academia Sinica
Zhou, Hua-Wei, University of Houston
Zhou, Ying, Virginia Polytechnic Institute & State University
Zhu, Lupei, Saint Louis University
Ziv, Alon, Tel Aviv University

Marine Geophysics
Anderson, Franz E., University of New Hampshire
Antonellini, Marco, Stanford University
Archer, David, University of Chicago
Barry, James P., Stanford University
Becker, Keir, University of Miami
Behn, Mark D., Woods Hole Oceanographic Institution
Bell, Robin E., Columbia University
Ben-Avraham, Zvi, Tel Aviv University
Biasutti, Michela, Columbia University
Bohnenstiehl, DelWayne, North Carolina State University
Bokuniewicz, Henry J., SUNY, Stony Brook
Bolmer, S. Thompson, Woods Hole Oceanographic Institution
Bonatti, Enrico, Columbia University
Borja, Ronaldo I., Stanford University
Bowin, Carl O., Woods Hole Oceanographic Institution
Buck, Roger W., Columbia University
Bull, Jonathan M., University of Southampton
Butterfield, David A., University of Washington
Canales Cisneros, Juan Pablo, Woods Hole Oceanographic Institution
Cande, Steven C., University of California, San Diego
Carbotte, Suzanne, Columbia University
Chamberlain, C. Page, Stanford University
Christeson, Gail L., University of Texas at Austin
Cochran, James R., Columbia University
Collier, Jenny, Imperial College
Constable, Steven C., University of California, San Diego
Cooper, Alan K., Stanford University
Delaney, John R., University of Washington
Dickens, Gerald R., Rice University
Duennebier, Frederick K., University of Hawai'i, Manoa

Duncan, Robert A., Oregon State University
Dunn, Robert A., University of Hawai'i, Manoa
Edwards, Richard N., University of Toronto
Egbert, Gary D., Oregon State University
Eloranta, Edwin W., University of Wisconsin, Madison
Evans, Robert L., Woods Hole Oceanographic Institution
Farges, Francois, Stanford University
Fisk, Martin R., Oregon State University
Forsyth, Donald W., Brown University
Freyberg, David L., Stanford University
Fricker, Helen A., University of California, San Diego
Goff, John A., University of Texas at Austin
Goldberg, David S., Columbia University
Goldfinger, Chris, Oregon State University
Gorelick, Steven, Stanford University
Gorman, Andrew R., University of Otago
Grasmueck, Mark, University of Miami
Gulick, Sean S., University of Texas at Austin
Harmon, Nicholas, University of Southampton
Harris, Paul M., Rice University
Harrison, Christopher G., University of Miami
Hayes, Dennis E., Columbia University
Henderson, Naomi, Columbia University
Hey, Richard N., University of Hawai'i, Manoa
Hicks, Roberta (Robbie), Memorial University of Newfoundland
Hildebrand, John A., University of California, San Diego
Hooft, Emilie E., University of Oregon
Hornbach, Matthew J., Southern Methodist University
Huang, Li, Western University
Ito, Garrett T., University of Hawai'i, Manoa
Johnson, H. Paul, University of Washington
Karig, Daniel E., Cornell University
Kitanidis, Peter K., Stanford University
Klemperer, Simon L., Stanford University
Klinkhammer, Gary, Oregon State University
Krastel, Sebastian , Dalhousie University
Kummerow, Christian D., Colorado State University
Kurapov, Alexander, Oregon State University
Lawver, Lawrence A., University of Texas at Austin
Lewis, Brian T. R., University of Washington
Louden, Keith E., Dalhousie University
Lowell, Robert P., Virginia Polytechnic Institute & State University
Luyendyk, Bruce P., University of California, Santa Barbara
MacAyeal, Douglas R., University of Chicago
Mack, Seymour, California State University, Fresno
Madsen, John A., University of Delaware
Manley, Patricia L., Middlebury College
Martinez, Fernando, University of Hawai'i, Manoa
McClain, James S., University of California, Davis
McIntosh, Kirk D., University of Texas at Austin
Minshull, Timothy A., University of Southampton
Mittelstaedt, Eric L., University of Idaho
Monismith, Stephen G., Stanford University
Muller, Dietmar, University of Sydney
Mutter, John C., Columbia University
Nilsson, Anders, Stanford University
Oakley, Adrienne, Kutztown University of Pennsylvania
Odom, Robert I., University of Washington
Ollerhead, Jeffery W., Mount Allison University
Orcutt, John A., University of California, San Diego
Pitman, Walter, Columbia University
Purdy, G. Michael, Columbia University
Raymond, Carol A., Jet Propulsion Laboratory
Rodriguez Simental, Ana Maria, Universidad Nacional Autonoma de Mexico
Ryan, William B. F., Columbia University
Salisbury, Matthew, Dalhousie University
Sandwell, David T., University of California, San Diego
Sawyer, Dale S., Rice University
Schneider, Robert J., Woods Hole Oceanographic Institution
Schouten, Hans, Woods Hole Oceanographic Institution
Sharon, Yitzhak Y., Stockton University
Sheridan, Robert E., Rutgers, The State University of New Jersey
Shillington, Donna, Columbia University
Shipley, Thomas H., University of Texas at Austin
Shreve, Ronald L., University of Washington
Silver, Eli A., University of California, Santa Cruz
Sloan, Heather, Lehman College (CUNY)
Smith, Deborah K., Woods Hole Oceanographic Institution
Smith, Robert L., Oregon State University
Smyth, William D., Oregon State University
Sohn, Robert A., Woods Hole Oceanographic Institution
Sorlien, Christopher C., University of California, Santa Barbara
Spitz, Yvette H., Oregon State University
Spormann, Alfred, Stanford University
Stephens, Jason H., Austin Community College District
Swift, Stephen A., Woods Hole Oceanographic Institution
Talwani, Manik, Rice University
Thompson, David W. J., Colorado State University
Tobin, Harold J., University of Wisconsin, Madison
Tolstoy, Maria, Columbia University

Trehu, Anne M., Oregon State University
Wattrus, Nigel J., University of Minnesota, Duluth
Webb, Spahr C., Columbia University
Wessel, Paul, University of Hawai'i, Manoa
Wetzel, Laura R., Eckerd College
White, Scott M., University of South Carolina
Whitmarsh, Robert B., University of Southampton
Wooding, Frank B., Woods Hole Oceanographic Institution
Xu, Li, Woods Hole Oceanographic Institution
Zaneveld, J. R., Oregon State University
Zavarin, Mavrik, Lawrence Livermore National Laboratory
Zhu, Wenlu, University of Maryland

PALEONTOLOGY
General Paleontology
Altenbach, Alexander, Ludwig-Maximilians-Universitaet Muenchen
Amler, Michael, Ludwig-Maximilians-Universitaet Muenchen
Anderson, Wayne I., University of Northern Iowa
Armstrong, Howard A., Durham University
Bailey, Jack B., Western Illinois University
Baird, Gordon C., SUNY, Buffalo
Bajraktareviæ, Zlatan, University of Zagreb
Bassett, Damon, Missouri State University
Baumiller, Tomasz K., University of Michigan
Beatty, William L., Winona State University
Beck, Charles, University of Michigan
Becker, Ralf Thomas, Universitaet Muenster
Behlke, Adam, Denver Museum of Nature & Science
Bell, Phil R., University of New England
Benner, Jacob, Tufts University
Berry, David R., California State Polytechnic University, Pomona
Bill, Steven D., Keene State College
Boyer, Diana L., SUNY, Buffalo
Branstrator, Jon W., Earlham College
Bray, Emily, University of Colorado
Britt, Brooks B., Brigham Young University
Brookfield, Michael E., University of Guelph
Brzobohaty, Rostislav, Masaryk University
Bucur, Ioan, Babes-Bolyai University
Burger, Benjamin J., Utah State University
Busbey, Arthur B., Texas Christian University
Bush, Andrew M., University of Connecticut
Butcher, Anthony, University of Portsmouth
Carnevale, Giorgio, Università di Torino
Chauff, Karl, Saint Louis University
Cherns, L C., Cardiff University
Cisne, John L., Cornell University
Clyde, William C., University of New Hampshire
Collette, Joseph, Minot State University
Coorough, Patricia J., Milwaukee Public Museum
Corgan, James X., Austin Peay State University
Cramer, Howard R., Emory University
Cuffey, Roger J., Pennsylvania State University, University Park
Curran, H. Allen, Smith College
Davydov, Vladimir I., Boise State University
De Klerk, Billy, Rhodes University
Deboo, Phili B., University of Memphis
Delfino, Massimo, Università di Torino
Devera, Joseph A., University of Illinois, Urbana-Champaign
Dietz, Anne D., San Antonio Community College
Domack, Cynthia R., Hamilton College
Dunn, Douglas, Cleveland Museum of Natural History
Edwards, Nicholas, University of Manchester
Egerton, Victoria, University of Manchester
Eldredge, Niles, Graduate School of the City University of New York
Fagerlin, Stanley C., Missouri State University
Falcon-Lang, Howard, Univ of London, Royal Holloway & Bedford New College
Fall, Leigh M., SUNY, Oneonta
Felton, Richard M., Northwest Missouri State University
Fio, Karmen, University of Zagreb
Fisher, Frank, University of Colorado
Foote, Michael J., University of Chicago
Forcino, Frank, Western Carolina University
Fornaciari, Elena, Università degli Studi di Padova
Fowler, Gerald A., University of Wisconsin, Parkside
Fox, David L., University of Minnesota, Twin Cities
Fox-Dobbs, Kena L., University of Puget Sound
Freeman, Veronica, Marietta College
Gagnaison, Cyril, Institut Polytechnique LaSalle Beauvais (ex-IGAL)
Ganeshram, Raja, Edinburgh University
Garb, Matt, Brooklyn College (CUNY)
Gatto, Roberto, Università degli Studi di Padova
Gess, Robert, Rhodes University
Gibson, Michael A., University of Tennessee, Martin
Gili Folch, Eulàlia, Universitat Autonoma de Barcelona
Green, Keith E., Cypress College
Greenwood, David , University of Saskatchewan
Haggart, James, University of British Columbia
Hansen, Thor A., Western Washington University
Harnik, Paul, Franklin and Marshall College

Harper, David, Durham University
Harries, Peter J., University of South Florida, Tampa
Hazel, McGoff, University of Reading
Heaney, Michael , Texas A&M University
Henderson, Wayne G., California State University, Fullerton
Henßel, Katja, Ludwig-Maximilians-Universitaet Muenchen
Herrera-Gil, Luis A., Universidad Autonoma de Baja California Sur
Hintze, Lehi F., Brigham Young University
Hylland, Mike, Utah Geological Survey
Immel, Harald, Ludwig-Maximilians-Universitaet Muenchen
Ivanov, Martin, Masaryk University
Johnson, Gerald H., College of William & Mary
Jones, Douglas S., University of Florida
Kazmer, Miklos, Eotvos Lorand University
Kelley, Patricia H., University of North Carolina Wilmington
Kern, J. Philip, San Diego State University
Kirkland, James I., Utah Geological Survey
Kirschvink, Joseph L., California Institute of Technology
Klapper, Gilbert , Northwestern University
Kowalke, Thorsten, Ludwig-Maximilians-Universitaet Muenchen
Lambert, Lance L., University of Texas, San Antonio
Laporte, Leo F., University of California, Santa Cruz
Leinfelder, Reinhold, Ludwig-Maximilians-Universitaet Muenchen
Li, Rong-Yu, Brandon University
Linsley, David, Colgate University
Little, Crispin, University of Leeds
Lozar, Francesca, Università di Torino
Lucas-Clark, Joyce, City College of San Francisco
MacLeod, Kenneth A., University of Missouri
Macomber, Richard, Long Island University, Brooklyn Campus
Mandra, York T., San Francisco State University
Marenco, Katherine, Bryn Mawr College
Marenco, Pedro, Bryn Mawr College
Mata, Scott, Orange Coast College
Mcgowan, Alistair, University of Glasgow
McHugh, Julia, Colorado Mesa University
McKenzie, Scott, Mercyhurst University
McKinney, Marg J., Appalachian State University
McMenamin, Mark, Mount Holyoke College
McRoberts, Christopher A., SUNY, Cortland
Means, Guy H., Florida Geological Survey
Melchin, Michael, Dalhousie University
Mezga, Aleksandar, University of Zagreb
Miller, Joshua H., University of Cincinnati
Miller, Randall F., University of New Brunswick
Moe-Hoffman, Amy P., University of Colorado
Monaco, Pat, University of Colorado
Monari, Stefano, Università degli Studi di Padova
Montgomery, Homer A., University of Texas, Dallas
Moro, Alan, University of Zagreb
Munro, Ildi, Carleton University
Murray, John, National University of Ireland Galway
Musil, Rudolf, Masaryk University
Naumann, Malik, Ludwig-Maximilians-Universitaet Muenchen
Nudds, John, University of Manchester
Orchard, Michael, University of British Columbia
Owen, Alan, University of Glasgow
Parsely, Ronald L., Tulane University
Peck, Robert, Concord University
Peng, Lee Chai, University of Malaya
Perez-Huerta, Alberto, University of Alabama
Person, Jeff, North Dakota Geological Survey
Peterson, Joseph E., University of Wisconsin, Oshkosh
Petuch, Edward J., Florida Atlantic University
Pezelj, Đurðica, University of Zagreb
Pickerill, Ronald K., University of New Brunswick
Platt, Brian F., University of Mississippi
Poteet, Mary F., University of Texas at Austin
Pratt, Brian R., University of Saskatchewan
Prave, Tony, University of St. Andrews
Pruss, Sara B., Smith College
Puchalski, Stephaney, Highline College
Reháková, Daniela, Comenius University
Reichenbacher, Bettina, Ludwig-Maximilians-Universitaet Muenchen
Robinson, Richard A., University of Kansas
Rodland, David, Muskingum University
Rogers, Kristina C., University of Minnesota, Twin Cities
Rogers, Raymond, University of Minnesota, Twin Cities
Rößner, Gertrud, Ludwig-Maximilians-Universitaet Muenchen
Sá, Artur A., Universidade de Trás-os-Montes e Alto Douro
Schaal, Ellen K., Lawrence University
Schmid, Dieter, Ludwig-Maximilians-Universitaet Muenchen
Scotchmoor, Judith, University of California, Berkeley
Scudder, Sylvia J., University of Florida
Shelton, Sally Y., South Dakota School of Mines & Technology
Shropshire, K. Lee, University of Northern Colorado
Siewers, Fredrick D., Western Kentucky University
Slaughter, Richard, University of Wisconsin, Madison
Smart, Christopher, University of Plymouth

Smith, Dena M., University of Colorado
Smith, Paul L., University of British Columbia
Sorauf, James E., University of South Florida, Tampa
Spencer, Patrick K., Whitman College
Squires, Richard L., California State University, Northridge
Stafford, Emily, Western Carolina University
Steinker, Paula J., Bowling Green State University
Stifel, Peter B., University of Maryland
Stratton, James F., Eastern Illinois University
Superchi-Culver, Tonia, University of Colorado
Sutherland, Stuart, University of British Columbia
Sutton, Mark, Imperial College
Sweetman, Steve, University of Portsmouth
Tesmer, Irving, Buffalo State College
Thompson, Jann W. M., Smithsonian Institution / National Museum of Natural
History
Toots, Heinrich, Long Island University, C.W. Post Campus
Turner, Elizabeth, Laurentian University, Sudbury
Underwood, Charlie, Birkbeck College
Van Alstine, James B., University of Minnesota, Morris
Van Iten, Heyo, Hanover College
VanAller-Hernick, Linda A., New York State Geological Survey
Velez, Maria, University of Regina
Vicens Batet, Enric, Universitat Autonoma de Barcelona
Wallace, Steve, University of Colorado
Waters, Johnny, University of Tennessee, Knoxville
Wehrmann, Laura, Ludwig-Maximilians-Universitaet Muenchen
Weiss, Dennis, Graduate School of the City University of New York
White, Lisa D., San Francisco State University
Whitmore, John H., Cedarville University
Whitton, Mark, University of Portsmouth
Wignall, Paul, University of Leeds
Wilson, Laura E., Fort Hays State University
Yancey, Thomas E., Texas A&M University
Yanes, Yurena, University of Cincinnati

Paleostratigraphy

Al-Saad, Hamad A., University of Qatar
Arden, Daniel D., Georgia Southwestern State University
Baarli, Gudveig, Williams College
Baird, Gordon C., SUNY, Fredonia
Barrick, James E., Texas Tech University
Bauer, Jeffrey A., Shawnee State University
Berggren, William A., Woods Hole Oceanographic Institution
Bergstrom, Stig M., Ohio State University
Braun, Willi K., University of Saskatchewan
Buatois, Luis, University of Saskatchewan
Caldwell, William G. E., University of Saskatchewan
Carter, Burchard D., Georgia Southwestern State University
Cohen, Andrew S., University of Arizona
Collinson, James W., Ohio State University
Davila-Alcocer, Victor M., Universidad Nacional Autonoma de Mexico
Eaton, Jeffrey G., Weber State University
Ettensohn, Frank R., University of Kentucky
Finney, Stanley C., California State University, Long Beach
Flory, Richard A., California State University, Chico
Grubb, Barbara, Mt. San Antonio College
Johnson, David B., New Mexico Institute of Mining and Technology
Johnson, Markes E., Williams College
Jones, Brian, University of Alberta
Kalvoda, Jiri, Masaryk University
Kirchgasser, William T., SUNY Potsdam
Kurtz, Vincent E., Missouri State University
Landing, Ed, New York State Geological Survey
Landman, Neil H., Graduate School of the City University of New York
Le Mone, David V., University of Texas, El Paso
Leatham, W. Britt, California State University, San Bernardino
Lewis, Gerald L., Pasadena City College
Liebe, Richard M., SUNY, The College at Brockport
Longoria, Jose F., Florida International University
Mangano, Gabriela, University of Saskatchewan
Martin, James E., South Dakota School of Mines & Technology
Maurrasse, Florentin J-M. R., Florida International University
McWilliams, Robert G., Miami University
Mikulic, Donald G., Illinois State Geological Survey
Miller, James F., Missouri State University
Miller, Richard H., San Diego State University
Moyle, Richard W., Weber State University
Murphy, Michael A., University of California, Riverside
Olson, Hillary C., University of Texas at Austin
Over, D. Jeffrey, SUNY, Geneseo
Pope, John P., Northwest Missouri State University
Ritter, Scott M., Brigham Young University
Sageman, Bradley B., Northwestern University
Shapiro, Russell, California State University, Chico
Shaw, Frederick C., Lehman College (CUNY)
Smith, Gerald R., University of Michigan
Stearn, Colin, McGill University
Stelck, Charles R., University of Alberta
Stevens, Calvin H., San Jose State University

Stoykova, Kristalina C., Bulgarian Academy of Sciences
Sweet, Walter C., Ohio State University
Taylor, John F., Indiana University of Pennsylvania
Thoms, Richard E., Portland State University
Tischler, Herbert, University of New Hampshire
Titus, Robert C., Hartwick College
Tobin, Tom S., University of Alabama
Trexler, J. Peter, Juniata College
Van Niewenhuise, Donald, University of Houston
Witzke, Brian J., University of Iowa
Zinsmeister, William J., Purdue University

Micropaleontology

Adekeye, O. A., University of Ilorin
Agnini, Claudia, Università degli Studi di Padova
Arnold, Anthony J., Florida State University
Barnes, Christopher R., University of Victoria
Barrier, Pascal, Institut Polytechnique LaSalle Beauvais (ex-IGAL)
Beauchamp, Benoit, University of Calgary
Berggren, William A., Rutgers, The State University of New Jersey
Bollmann, Jörg, University of Toronto
Brown, Paul, University College London
Burke, Collette D., Wichita State University
Buzas, Martin A., Smithsonian Institution / National Museum of Natural History
Caldwell, W. Glen E., Western University
Carreno, Ana L., Universidad Nacional Autonoma de Mexico
Carter, Elizabeth, Portland State University
Caus Gracia, Esmeralda, Universitat Autonoma de Barcelona
Chapman, Mark, University of East Anglia
Christensen, Beth A., Adelphi University
Ciesielski, Paul F., University of Florida
Clark, David L., University of Wisconsin, Madison
Corliss, Bruce H., Duke University
Culver, Stephen J., East Carolina University
Curry, William B., Woods Hole Oceanographic Institution
Das, Sarah B., Woods Hole Oceanographic Institution
de Vernal, Anne, Universite du Quebec a Montreal
Eicher, Donald, University of Colorado
Ethington, Raymond L., University of Missouri
Finger, Ken, University of California, Berkeley
Fluegeman, Richard H., Ball State University
Frankel, Larry, University of Connecticut
Fritts, Paul J., California State University, Long Beach
Giusberti, Luca, Università degli Studi di Padova
Goldstein, Susan T., University of Georgia
Gorog, Agnes, Eotvos Lorand University
Hallock-Muller, Pamela, University of South Florida
Harding, Ian, University of Southampton
Hart, Malcolm, University of Plymouth
Harwood, David M., University of Nebraska, Lincoln
Hasegawa, Shiro, Kumamoto University
Hemphill-Haley, Eileen, Humboldt State University
Henderson, Charles M., University of Calgary
Huber, Brian T., Smithsonian Institution / National Museum of Natural History
Hunt, Gene, Smithsonian Institution / National Museum of Natural History
Ingle, Jr., James C., Stanford University
Johnson, Katherine, Eastern Illinois University
Kanungo, Sudeep, University of Utah
Kariminia, Seyed, Georgia Perimeter College
Katz, Miriam E., Rensselaer Polytechnic Institute
Keller, Gerta, Princeton University
Kelly, D. Clay, University of Wisconsin, Madison
Kessinger, Walter P., University of Louisiana at Lafayette
Klapper, Gilbert, University of Iowa
Knox, Larry W., Tennessee Tech University
Laws, Richard A., University of North Carolina Wilmington
Leadbetter, Jared R., California Institute of Technology
Leckie, R. Mark, University of Massachusetts, Amherst
Licari, Gerald R., East Los Angeles College
Ling, Hsin-Yi, Northern Illinois University
Lobegeier, Melissa, Middle Tennessee State University
Lucas, Franklin A., University of Benin
Lundin, Robert F., Arizona State University
Lupia, Richard, University of Oklahoma
Maddocks, Rosalie F., University of Houston
Martin, Ronald E., University of Delaware
McCarthy, Francine G., Brock University
McCartney, Kevin, University of Maine, Presque Isle
Medioli, Franco, Dalhousie University
Mendelson, Carl V., Beloit College
Metzger, Ronald A., Southwestern Oregon Community College
Montenari, Michael, Keele University
Nathan, Stephen, University of Massachusetts, Amherst
Nathan , Stephen, Eastern Connecticut State University
Nations, Jack D., Northern Arizona University
Nestell, Galena P., University of Texas, Arlington
Nestell, Merlynd K., University of Texas, Arlington
Noble, Paula J., University of Nevada, Reno
Olsson, Richard K., Rutgers, The State University of New Jersey
Oppo, Delia W., Woods Hole Oceanographic Institution

Orr, William N., University of Oregon
Patterson, R. Timothy, Carleton University
Pearson, Paul, University of Wales
Pessagno, Jr., Emile A., University of Texas, Dallas
Pujana, Ignacio, University of Texas, Dallas
Reinhardt, Edward G., McMaster University
Roberts, Charles, Mt. San Antonio College
Robinson, Edward, Florida International University
Rodrigues, Cyril G., University of Windsor
Ross, Charles A., Western Washington University
Rosscoe, Steven, Hardin-Simmons University
Roth, Peter H., University of Utah
Sartipzadeh, Siavosh, University of Tabriz
Scherer, Reed P, Northern Illinois University
Schroder-Adams, Claudia, Carleton University
Scott, David B., Dalhousie University
Sen Gupta, Barun K., Louisiana State University
Siesser, William G., Vanderbilt University
Sloan, Jon R., California State University, Northridge
St. Jean, Joseph, University of North Carolina, Chapel Hill
Steinmetz, John C., indiana University
Stott, Lowell D., University of Southern California
Tabrizi, Azam, Tidewater Community College
Thomas, Ellen, Yale University
Thomas, Ellen, Wesleyan University
Thunell, Robert C., University of South Carolina
Tibert, Neil E., University of Mary Washington
Toth, Emoke, Eotvos Lorand University
Ufkes, Els , VU University Amsterdam
Vaz, Nuno M., Universidade de Trás-os-Montes e Alto Douro
von Bitter, Peter H., University of Toronto
Wade, Bridget, University College London
Walker, Sally E., University of Georgia
Watkins, David K., University of Nebraska, Lincoln
Webb, Peter N., Ohio State University
Wise, Jr, Sherwood W., Florida State University
Zonneveld, John-Paul, University of Calgary

Paleobotany

Arens, Nan, University of California, Berkeley
Ash, Sydney R., Weber State University
Basinger, James F., University of Saskatchewan
Beck, John H., Boston College
Berry, C M., Cardiff University
Boelman, Natalie T., Columbia University
Boyce, Charles K., University of Chicago
Burnham, Robyn J., University of Michigan
Carrillo Martinez, Miguel, Universidad Nacional Autonoma de Mexico
Chitaley, Shyamala, Cleveland Museum of Natural History
Crane, Peter, Yale University
Currano, Ellen, University of Wyoming
Dilcher, David L., University of Florida
DiMichele, William A., Smithsonian Institution / National Museum of Natural History
Donoghue, Michael J., Yale University
Doyle, James A., University of California, Davis
Duncan, Thomas, University of California, Berkeley
Edwards, Dianne, Cardiff University
Edwards, Dianne, University of Wales
Erwin, Diane, University of California, Berkeley
Gabel, Mark, Black Hills State University
Gastaldo, Robert A., Colby College
Gowing, David, The Open University
Griffin, Kevin L., Columbia University
Heath, Kathleen M., Indiana State University
Hu, Shusheng, Yale University
Jackson, Gail D., Edinburgh University
Jarzen, David M., University of Florida
Kasper, Andrew E., Rutgers, The State University of New Jersey, Newark
Kerp, Hans, Universitaet Muenster
Knoll, Andrew H., Harvard University
Manchester, Steven R., University of Florida
Martinetto, Edoardo, Università di Torino
McElwain, Jenny, Field Museum of Natural History
Miller, Ian, Denver Museum of Nature & Science
Mindell, Randal, Douglas College
Ornduff, Robert, University of California, Berkeley
Peppe, Daniel J., Baylor University
Pfefferkorn, Hermann W., University of Pennsylvania
Raymond, Anne, Texas A&M University
Retallack, Gregory J., University of Oregon
Rigby, John, Queensland University of Technology
Scott, Andrew C., University of London, Royal Holloway & Bedford New College
Strother, Paul K., Boston College
Strother, Paul, Boston College
Taggart, Ralph E., Michigan State University
Taylor, Edith, University of Kansas
Taylor, Thomas N., University of Kansas
Taylor, Thomas N., Ohio State University
Thomasson, Joseph R., Fort Hays State University
Tiffney, Bruce H., University of California, Santa Barbara

Tyler, Carrie, Miami University
Wing, Scott L., Smithsonian Institution / National Museum of Natural History

Palynology

Anderson, Patricia M., University of Washington
Asselin, Esther, Universite du Quebec
Atta-Peters, David, University of Ghana
Bachhuber, Frederick W., University of Nevada, Las Vegas
Baker, Richard G., University of Iowa
Braman, Dennis R., Royal Tyrrell Museum of Palaeontology
Brenner, Gilbert J., SUNY, New Paltz
Brush, Grace S., Johns Hopkins University
Burden, Elliott T., Memorial University of Newfoundland
Darrell, James H., Georgia Southern University
Davies, Caroline P., University of Missouri-Kansas City
Davis, Owen K., University of Arizona
Delusina, Irina, University of California, Davis
Dolakova, Nela, Masaryk University
Eble, Cortland F., University of Kentucky
Farley, Martin B., University of North Carolina, Pembroke
Fowell, Sarah, University of Alaska Fairbanks
Habib, Daniel, Graduate School of the City University of New York
Habib, Daniel, Queens College (CUNY)
Head, Martin J., Brock University
Hebda, Richard J., University of Victoria
Hemsley, A, Cardiff University
Hemsley, Alan, University of Wales
Higgs, Ken, University College Cork
Hills, Leonard V., University of Calgary
Jacobs, Bonnie F., Southern Methodist University
Jarvis, Ed, University College Cork
Javaux, Emmanuelle, Universite de Liege
Kroeger, Timothy J., Bemidji State University
Leyden, Barbara W., University of South Florida, Tampa
Maher, Jr., Louis J., University of Wisconsin, Madison
Marshall, John, University of Southampton
Martinez Hernandez, Enrique, Universidad Nacional Autonoma de Mexico
McAndrews, John H., University of Toronto
Mudie, Peta J., Dalhousie University
Norris, Geoffrey, University of Toronto
O'Keefe, Jennifer, Morehead State University
Peteet, Dorothy M., Columbia University
Rich, Fredrick J., Georgia Southern University
Rueger, Bruce F., Colby College
Smith, Jim, University College Cork
Stefanova, Ivanka, University of Minnesota, Twin Cities
Traverse, Alfred, Pennsylvania State University, University Park
Warny, Sophie, Louisiana State University
Wicander, Reed, Central Michigan University
Williams, Graham, Dalhousie University

Quantitative Paleontology

Belasky, Paul, Ohlone College
Daley, Gwen M., Winthrop University
Huntley, John, University of Missouri
Miller, Arnold I., Cincinnati Museum Center
Steadman, David W., University of Florida

Vertebrate Paleontology

Adams, Thomas, San Antonio Community College
Applegate-Pleasants, Shelton, Universidad Nacional Autonoma de Mexico
Archer, Michael, University of New South Wales
Badgley, Catherine E., University of Michigan
Barnes, Lawrence G., Los Angeles County Museum of Natural History
Barnosky, Anthony D., University of California, Berkeley
Bartels, William S., Albion College
Beard, K. Christopher, Carnegie Museum of Natural History
Behrensmeyer, Anna K., Smithsonian Institution / National Museum of Natural History
Bell, Christopher J., University of Texas at Austin
Berman, David S., Carnegie Museum of Natural History
Bloch, Jonathan, University of Florida
Bolt, John R., Field Museum of Natural History
Brand, Leonard R., Loma Linda University
Brinkman, Donald B., Royal Tyrrell Museum of Palaeontology
Brochu, Christopher A., University of Iowa
Brown, Caleb, Royal Tyrrell Museum of Palaeontology
Buckley, John S., Texas A&M University, Kingsville
Caldwell, Michael W., University of Alberta
Campbell, Kenneth E., Los Angeles County Museum of Natural History
Carlson, Keith J., Gustavus Adolphus College
Carpenter, Kenneth, Utah State University
Carpenter, Kenneth, University of Colorado
Carrano, Matthew T., Smithsonian Institution / National Museum of Natural History
Carranza-Castaneda, Oscar, Universidad Nacional Autonoma de Mexico
Chatterjee, Sankar, Texas Tech University
Chiappe, Luis M., Los Angeles County Museum of Natural History
Cicimurri, Christian M., Clemson University
Cicimurri, David J., Clemson University
Cifelli, Richard L., University of Oklahoma
Clarke, Julia A., University of Texas at Austin

Clemens, William A., University of California, Berkeley
Clemens, William A., University of Alaska, Fairbanks
Codrea, Vlad, Babes-Bolyai University
Congleton, John D., University of West Georgia
Cooke, H.B. S., Dalhousie University
Coombs, Margery C., Amherst College
Covert, Herbert, University of Colorado
Cox, Shelley M., Los Angeles County Museum of Natural History
Cumbaa, Steve L., Carleton University
Currie, Philip J., University of Calgary
Curry Rogers, Kristina A., Macalester College
Daeschler, Ted, Drexel University
Daly, Raymond J., Union County College
Dawson, Mary, University of Colorado
Dawson, Mary R., Carnegie Museum of Natural History
Delson, Eric, Lehman College (CUNY)
Delson, Eric, Graduate School of the City University of New York
Derstler, Kraig L., University of New Orleans
DeSantis, Larisa R., Vanderbilt University
Dodson, Peter, University of Pennsylvania
Dornbos, Stephen Q., University of Wisconsin, Milwaukee
Druckenmiller, Patrick S., University of Alaska Fairbanks
Dundas, Robert G., California State University, Fresno
Dyke, Gareth, University of Southampton
Dzanh, Trihn, University of Colorado
Eberle, Jaelyn J., University of Colorado
Elliott, David K., Northern Arizona University
Emry, Robert, Smithsonian Institution / National Museum of Natural History
Engelmann, George F., University of Nebraska at Omaha
Esperante, Raul, Loma Linda University
Evans, David C., Royal Ontario Museum
Farlow, James O., Indiana University / Purdue University, Fort Wayne
Fastovsky, David E., University of Rhode Island
Fearon, Jamie L., Wheaton College
Fiorillo, Anthony R., Southern Methodist University
Flynn, John J., American Museum of Natural History
Flynn, John J., Columbia University
Fordyce, R. Ewan, University of Otago
Fox, Richard C., University of Alberta
Fraser, Nicholas C., Virginia Polytechnic Institute & State University
Froehlich, David J., Austin Community College District
Gaffney, Eugene S., American Museum of Natural History
Gallagher, William B., Rider University
Garcia, William, University of North Carolina, Charlotte
Gardner, James D., Royal Tyrrell Museum of Palaeontology
Gauthier, Jacques A., Yale University
Getty, Mike, Denver Museum of Nature & Science
Gillette, David D., Northern Arizona University
Gingerich, Philip D., University of Michigan
Goodwin, Mark B., University of California, Berkeley
Gottfried, Michael D., Michigan State University
Graham, Russell W., Pennsylvania State University, University Park
Grandal d'Anglade, Aurora, Coruna University
Grande, Lance, Field Museum of Natural History
Gray, Robert S., Santa Barbara City College
Green, Harry W., University of California, Berkeley
Guthrie, Dale, University of Alaska, Fairbanks
Hammer, William R., Augustana College
Hand, Suzanne, University of New South Wales
Hargrave, Jennifer E., Southern Utah University
Harris, John M., Los Angeles County Museum of Natural History
Harris, John M., University of Utah
Harris, Judith A., University of Colorado
Hayden, Martha C., Utah Geological Survey
Heaton, Timothy H., University of South Dakota
Heckert, Andrew, Appalachian State University
Henderson, Donald, Royal Tyrrell Museum of Palaeontology
Henrici, Amy C., Carnegie Museum of Natural History
Hill, Andrew, Yale University
Holroyd, Pat, University of California, Berkeley
Holtz, Jr., Thomas R., University of Maryland
Horner, John R., Montana State University
Hunt, Robert M., University of Nebraska, Lincoln
Indeck, Jeff, University of Colorado
Ivy, Logan D., Denver Museum of Nature & Science
Jackson, Frankie, Montana State University
Jacobs, Louis L., Southern Methodist University
Jasinski, Steven E., State Museum of Pennsylvania
Johnson, Ned K., University of California, Berkeley
Knell, Michael, Southern Connecticut State University
Koch, Paul L., University of California, Santa Cruz
Krause, David W., SUNY, Stony Brook
Krishtalka, Leonard, University of Kansas
Lamanna, Matthew C., Carnegie Museum of Natural History
Lamanna, Matthew C., University of Pittsburgh
Lamb, James P., University of West Alabama
Langston, Jr., Wann, University of Texas at Austin
Lidicker, Jr., William Z., University of California, Berkeley
Lindsay, Everett H., University of Arizona
Lundelius, Ernest L., University of Texas at Austin

Luo, Zhexi, Carnegie Museum of Natural History
Lyson, Tyler, Denver Museum of Nature & Science
MacFadden, Bruce J., University of Florida
Maisey, John G., American Museum of Natural History
Makovicky, Peter J., Field Museum of Natural History
Marcot, Jonathan, University of Colorado
Martin, James E., University of Louisiana at Lafayette
Massare, Judy A., SUNY, The College at Brockport
McDonald, Greg, University of Colorado
McFadden, Bruce J., University of Florida
McLeod, Samuel A., Los Angeles County Museum of Natural History
McNassor, Cathy, Los Angeles County Museum of Natural History
Meng, Jin, Graduate School of the City University of New York
Meng, Jin, American Museum of Natural History
Merck, Jr., John W., University of Maryland
Middleton, Michael D., University of Wisconsin, River Falls
Miller, Wade E., Brigham Young University
Montellano-Ballesteros, Marisol, Universidad Nacional Autonoma de Mexico
Morales, Michael, Emporia State University
Motani, Ryosuke, University of California, Davis
Murry, Phillip A., Tarleton State University
Naples, Virginia, Northern Illinois University
Neuman, Andrew G., Royal Tyrrell Museum of Palaeontology
Njau, Jackson K., Indiana University, Bloomington
Norell, Mark A., American Museum of Natural History
Norell, Mark A., Columbia University
Norris, Christopher A., Yale University
Novacek, Michael J., American Museum of Natural History
O'Leary, Maureen, SUNY, Stony Brook
Olsen, Paul E., Columbia University
Osi, Attila, Eotvos Lorand University
Padian, Kevin, University of California, Berkeley
Pagnac, Darrin C., South Dakota School of Mines & Technology
Parham, James, California State University, Fullerton
Patton, James L., University of California, Berkeley
Polly, P D., Indiana University, Bloomington
Pomeroy, Diana, Orange Coast College
Pons Muñoz, Josep Maria, Universitat Autonoma de Barcelona
Ray, Clayton E., Smithsonian Institution / National Museum of Natural History
Rensberger, John M., University of Washington
Rieppel, Olivier C., Field Museum of Natural History
Robinson, Peter, University of Colorado
Rowe, Timothy B., University of Texas at Austin
Rowell, Thelma, University of California, Berkeley
Russell, Dale A., North Carolina State University
Sagebiel, J. C., San Bernardino County Museum
Samonds, Karen, Northern Illinois University
Sankey, Julia, California State University, Stanislaus
Schiebout, Judith A., Louisiana State University
Schultz, Gerald E., West Texas A&M University
Schwartz, Hilde, University of California, Santa Cruz
Schwimmer, David R., Columbus State University
Scott, Craig, Royal Tyrrell Museum of Palaeontology
Sears, Karen, University of Colorado
Secord, Ross, University of Nebraska, Lincoln
Semken, Jr., Holmes A., University of Iowa
Sertich, Joseph, Denver Museum of Nature & Science
Seymour, Kevin L., Royal Ontario Museum
Shaw, Christopher A., Los Angeles County Museum of Natural History
Sidor, Christian A., University of Washington
Smith, Kathlyn M., Georgia Southern University
Stearley, Ralph F., Calvin College
Stewart, Joe D., Los Angeles County Museum of Natural History
Storrs, Glenn W., Cincinnati Museum Center
Storrs, Glenn W., University of Cincinnati
Sumida, Stuart S., California State University, San Bernardino
Tabrum, Alan R., Carnegie Museum of Natural History
Tedford, Richard H., American Museum of Natural History
Therrien, Francois, Royal Tyrrell Museum of Palaeontology
Turnbull, William D., Field Museum of Natural History
Uhen, Mark, George Mason University
Varricchio, David J., Montana State University
Vietti, Laura, University of Wyoming
Voorhies, Michael R., University of Nebraska, Lincoln
Vrba, Elisabeth S., Yale University
Walker, Ernest G., University of Saskatchewan
Whistler, David P., Los Angeles County Museum of Natural History
White, Tim, University of California, Berkeley
Wilkins, Kenneth, Baylor University
Williamson, Thomas E., University of New Mexico
Winkler, Alisa, Southern Methodist University
Winkler, Dale A., Southern Methodist University
Wood, Craig B., Providence College
Woodburne, Michael O., University of California, Riverside
Wuerthele, Norman, Carnegie Museum of Natural History
Wyss, Andre R., University of California, Santa Barbara
Zakrzewski, Richard J., Fort Hays State University

Invertebrate Paleontology

Adrain, Jonathan M., University of Iowa

Alencaster-Ybarra, Gloria, Universidad Nacional Autonoma de Mexico
Anderson, John R., Georgia Perimeter College
Anderson, Laurie C., South Dakota School of Mines & Technology
Austin, Jr., James A., University of Texas at Austin
Bailey, Richard H., Northeastern University
Batten, Roger L., American Museum of Natural History
Belanger, Christina L., South Dakota School of Mines & Technology
Beus, Stanley S., Northern Arizona University
Bishop, Gale A., Georgia Southern University
Blake, Daniel B., University of Illinois, Urbana-Champaign
Bodenbender, Brian E., Hope College
Bonuso, Nicole, California State University, Fullerton
Bork, Kennard B., Denison University
Boyer, Diana, State University of New York at Oswego
Brandt, Danita S., Michigan State University
Briggs, Derek E., Yale University
Broadhead, Thomas W., University of Tennessee, Knoxville
Brown, Lewis M., Lake Superior State University
Buitron-Sanchez, Blanca E., Universidad Nacional Autonoma de Mexico
Buss, Leo W., Yale University
Butts, Susan H., Yale University
Cairns, Stephen, Smithsonian Institution / National Museum of Natural History
Caldwell, Roy L., University of California, Berkeley
Camp, Mark J., University of Toledo
Carlucci, Jesse R., Midwestern State University
Caron, Jean-Bernard, University of Toronto
Chatelain, Edward E., Valdosta State University
Chatterton, Brian D., University of Alberta
Clark, Murlene W., University of South Alabama
Copper, Paul, Laurentian University, Sudbury
Day, James E., Illinois State University
Deline, Brad, University of West Georgia
Dutro, Thomas, Smithsonian Institution / National Museum of Natural History
Eldredge, Niles, American Museum of Natural History
Elias, Robert J., University of Manitoba
Erwin, Douglas H., Smithsonian Institution / National Museum of Natural History
Evanoff, Emmett, University of Colorado
Feldmann, Rodney M., Kent State University
Ferguson, Laing, Mount Allison University
Finks, Robert M., Queens College (CUNY)
Finks, Robert M., Graduate School of the City University of New York
Fisher, Daniel C., University of Michigan
Fraiser, Margaret L., University of Wisconsin, Milwaukee
Full, Robert J., University of California, Berkeley
Gangloff, Roland A., University of Alaska, Fairbanks
Gilmour, Ernest H., Eastern Washington University
Gonzalez-Arreola, Celestina, Universidad Nacional Autonoma de Mexico
Goodwin, David H., Denison University
Hageman, Steven J., Appalachian State University
Hall, Russell L., University of Calgary
Hanger, Rex, University of Wisconsin, Whitewater
Hanke, Brenda R., University of Cincinnati
Hannibal, Joseph T., Case Western Reserve University
Hannibal, Joseph T., Cleveland Museum of Natural History
Harper, Jr., Charles W., University of Oklahoma
Hartman, Joseph H., University of North Dakota
Hawkins, Lawrence, University of Southampton
Head, Martin J., University of Toronto
Hegna, Thomas A., Western Illinois University
Hembree, Daniel, Ohio University
Hendricks, Jonathan, San Jose State University
Hughes, Nigel C., Cincinnati Museum Center
Hunda, Brenda, Cincinnati Museum Center
Isaacson, Peter E., University of Idaho
Jablonski, David, University of Chicago
James, Matthew J., Sonoma State University
Jin, Jisuo, Western University
Johns, Ronald A., Austin Community College District
Johnston, Paul, Mount Royal University
Kammer, Thomas W., West Virginia University
Key, Jr., Marcus M., Dickinson College
Kues, Barry S., University of New Mexico
Kukalova-Peck, Jarmila, Carleton University
Labandeira, Conrad C., Smithsonian Institution / National Museum of Natural History
Landman, Neil H., American Museum of Natural History
Lee, Daphne E., University of Otago
Leggitt, Leroy, Loma Linda University
Lehrmann, Daniel J., Trinity University
Leighton, Lindsey, University of Alberta
Lenhart, Stephen W., Radford University
Lenz, Alfred C., Western University
Lewis, Ronald D., Auburn University
Lidgard, Scott H., Field Museum of Natural History
Lindberg, David R., University of California, Berkeley
Lindemann, Richard H., Skidmore College
Lockley, Martin G., University of Colorado, Denver
LoDuca, Steven T., Eastern Michigan University
Mann, Keith O., Ohio Wesleyan University
Manship, Lori L., University of Texas, Permian Basin
Mapes, Royal H., Ohio University

Martinez Ribas, Ricard, Universitat Autonoma de Barcelona
Mason, Charles E., Morehead State University
McAfee, Gerald B., Odessa College
McKinney, Frank K., Appalachian State University
Melchin, Michael J., Saint Francis Xavier University
Merrill, Glen K., University of Houston Downtown
Metcalfe, Ian, University of New England
Meyer, David L., University of Cincinnati
Meyer, David L., Cincinnati Museum Center
Mikkelsen, Paula, Cornell University
Mikkelsen, Paula, Paleontological Research Institution
Miller, Arnold I., University of Cincinnati
Miller, William C., Humboldt State University
Morris, Robert W., Wittenberg University
Nagel-Myers, Judith, St. Lawrence University
Narbonne, Guy M., Queen's University
Nesbitt, Elizabeth (Liz), University of Washington
Nitecki, Matthew H., Field Museum of Natural History
Parker, William C., Florida State University
Paterson, John R., University of New England
Perrilliat-Montoya, Maria del Carmen, Universidad Nacional Autonoma de Mexico
Pestana, Harold R., Colby College
Plotnick, Roy E., University of Illinois at Chicago
Pojeta, John, Smithsonian Institution / National Museum of Natural History
Pope, John K., Miami University
Portell, Roger W., University of Florida
Poty, Edouard, Universite de Liege
Powell, Matthew, Juniata College
Prichonnet, Gilbert P., Universite du Quebec a Montreal
Rhodes, Frank H. T., Cornell University
Ritterbush, Linda A., California Lutheran University
Rodriguez, Joaquin, Graduate School of the City University of New York
Rohr, David, Sul Ross State University
Rosenberg, Gary, Drexel University
Rowell, Albert J., University of Kansas
Rowland, Stephen, University of Nevada, Las Vegas
Rudkin, David M., Royal Ontario Museum
Sandy, Michael R., University of Dayton
Santos, Hernan, University of Puerto Rico
Saul, Lou Ella R., Los Angeles County Museum of Natural History
Saunders, W. Bruce, Bryn Mawr College
Savage, Norman M., University of Oregon
Schiappa, Tamra A., Slippery Rock University
Schmidt, David, Wright State University
Schweitzer, Carrie E., Kent State University
Segura-Vernis, Luis R., Universidad Autonoma de Baja California Sur
Shaw, Frederick C., Graduate School of the City University of New York
Sheehan, Peter M., Milwaukee Public Museum
Sheehan, Peter M., University of Wisconsin, Milwaukee
Shubak, Kenneth A., University of Wisconsin, Platteville
Smrecak, Trisha A., Grand Valley State University
Soja, Constance M., Colgate University
Sorauf, James E., Binghamton University
Spinosa, Claude, Boise State University
Springer, Dale A., Bloomsburg University
Sprinkle, James T., University of Texas at Austin
Stanley, Jr., George D., University of Montana
Stephen, Daniel, Utah Valley University
Stock, Carl W., University of Alabama
Sumrall, Colin, University of Tennessee, Knoxville
Szente, Istvan, Eotvos Lorand University
Szlavecz, Katalin, Johns Hopkins University
Tackett, Lydia S., North Dakota State University
Tapanila, Leif, Idaho State University
Tshudy, Dale, Edinboro University of Pennsylvania
Tsujita, Cameron J., Western University
Villasenor-Martinez, Ana B., Universidad Nacional Autonoma de Mexico
Visaggi, Christy, Georgia State University
Votaw, Robert, Indiana University Northwest
Wagner, Peter J., Field Museum of Natural History
Waller, Thomas R., Smithsonian Institution / National Museum of Natural History
Warme, John E., Colorado School of Mines
Waters, Johnny A., Appalachian State University
Webber, Andrew, Cincinnati Museum Center
Webster, Gary D., Washington State University
Webster, Mark, University of Chicago
Westrop, Stephen R., University of Oklahoma
Wilson, Mark A., College of Wooster
Xiao, Shuhai, Virginia Polytechnic Institute & State University
Young, Graham A., The Manitoba Museum
Young, Graham A., University of Manitoba
Zodrow, Erwin L., Cape Breton University
Zumwalt, Gary S., Louisiana Tech University

Paleobiology

Allmon, Warren D., Paleontological Research Institution
Allmon, Warren D., Cornell University
Arens, Nan Crystal, Hobart & William Smith Colleges
Ausich, William I., Ohio State University
Awramik, Stanley M., University of California, Santa Barbara

Babcock, Loren E., Ohio State University
Bambach, Richard K., Virginia Polytechnic Institute & State University
Benson, Roger, University of Oxford
Blackwelder, Patricia L., University of Miami
Bordeaux, Yvette, University of Pennsylvania
Brasier, Martin, University of Oxford
Brehman, Thomas R., Oakton Community College
Brett, Carlton E., Cincinnati Museum Center
Brower, James C., Syracuse University
Budd, Ann F., University of Iowa
Buss, Leo W., Yale University
Butterfield, Nicholas J., University of Cambridge
Caldwell, Roy, University of California, Berkeley
Carew, James L., College of Charleston
Carlson, Sandra J., University of California, Davis
Caron, Jean-Bernard, Royal Ontario Museum
Carter, Joseph G., University of North Carolina, Chapel Hill
Chamberlain, John A., Brooklyn College (CUNY)
Chamberlain, John A., Graduate School of the City University of New York
Cheetham, Alan H., Smithsonian Institution / National Museum of Natural History
Chin, Karen, University of Colorado
Clark, II, George R., Kansas State University
Cohen, Phoebe A., Williams College
Collins, Laurel S., Florida International University
Collinson, Margaret, University of London, Royal Holloway & Bedford New College
Coulson, Alan B., Clemson University
Cowen, Richard, University of California, Davis
Crane, Peter R., University of Chicago
Czaja, Andrew D., University of Cincinnati
Darroch, Simon, Vanderbilt University
Dietl, Gregory, Paleontological Research Institution
Dodd, J. Robert, Indiana University, Bloomington
Droser, Mary L., University of California, Riverside
Erickson, J. Mark, St. Lawrence University
Ferriz, Sergio Cevallos, Universidad Nacional Autonoma de Mexico
Flessa, Karl W., University of Arizona
Friedman, Matt, University of Oxford
Gabbott, Sarah, Leicester University
Gahn, Forest J., Brigham Young University - Idaho
Gaidos, Eric J., University of Hawai'i, Manoa
Geary, Dana H., University of Wisconsin, Madison
Goldman, Daniel, University of Dayton
Goswani, Anjali, University College London
Gray, Lee M., Mount Union College
Haiar, Brooke, Lynchburg College
Harvey, Tom, Leicester University
Hickman, Carole S., University of California, Berkeley
Hughes, Nigel C., University of California, Riverside
Jackson, Jeremy B. C., University of California, San Diego
Kauffman, Erle G., Indiana University, Bloomington
Kendrick, David C., Hobart & William Smith Colleges
Khaleel, Tasneem, Montana State University, Billings
Koehl, Mimi A. R., University of California, Berkeley
LaBarbera, Michael C., University of Chicago
Lieberman, Bruce S., University of Kansas
Lindberg, David R., University of California, Berkeley
Lipps, Jere H., University of California, Berkeley
Lockwood, Rowan, College of William & Mary
Martill, David, University of Portsmouth
Mattheus, Paul E., University of Alaska, Fairbanks
McCall, Peter L., Case Western Reserve University
McCollum, Linda B., Eastern Washington University
McGhee, Jr., George R., Rutgers, The State University of New Jersey
McNamara, Kenneth, University of Cambridge
Mead, James I., Northern Arizona University
Mitchell, Charles E., SUNY, Buffalo
Morris, Simon C., University of Cambridge
Myers, Corinne E., University of New Mexico
Newton, Cathryn R., Syracuse University
Norman, David, University of Cambridge
Pachut, Jr., Joseph F., Indiana University / Purdue University, Indianapolis
Parsons-Hubbard, Karla M., Oberlin College
Patzkowsky, Mark E., Pennsylvania State University, University Park
Purnell, Mark, Leicester University
Raup, David M., University of Chicago
Reichenbacher, Bettina, Ludwig-Maximilians-Universitaet Muenchen
Reid, Catherine, University of Canterbury
Risk, Michael J., McMaster University
Rosenberg, Gary D., Indiana University / Purdue University, Indianapolis
Ross, Robert M., Paleontological Research Institution
Ross, Robert M., Cornell University
Runnegar, Bruce, University of California, Los Angeles
Scatterday, James W., SUNY, Geneseo
Schiffbauer, James, University of Missouri
Schopf, J. William, University of California, Los Angeles
Silva-Pineda, Alicia, Universidad Nacional Autonoma de Mexico
Slatkin, Montgomery, University of California, Berkeley
Smith, Dena M., University of Colorado
Steinker, Don C., Bowling Green State University
Stetter, Karl O., University of California, Los Angeles

Stigall, Alycia L., Ohio University
Thomas, Roger D. K., Franklin and Marshall College
Upchurch, Paul, University College London
Valentine, James W., University of California, Berkeley
Wake, David B., University of California, Berkeley
Wake, Marvalee H., University of California, Berkeley
Ward, Peter D., University of Washington
Weber-Gobel, Reinhard, Universidad Nacional Autonoma de Mexico
West, Ronald R., Kansas State University
Williams, Mark, Leicester University
Wood, Aaron R., Iowa State University of Science & Technology
Yacobucci, Peg M., Bowling Green State University
Zalasiewicz, Jan, Leicester University

Paleoecology & Paleoclimatology

Susan K., Central Washington University
Almendinger, James E., University of Minnesota, Twin Cities
Andru-Hayles, Liala , Columbia University
Andrus, C. Fred T., University of Alabama
Ashworth, Allan C., North Dakota State University
Balescu, Sanda, Universite du Quebec a Montreal
Barker, Stephen, Cardiff University
Bartlein, Patrick J., University of Oregon
Begin, Christian, Universite du Quebec
Bennington, J Bret, Hofstra University
Billups, Katharina, University of Delaware
Blanchet, Jean-Pierre, Universite du Quebec a Montreal
Bonem, Rena M., Baylor University
Bottjer, David J., University of Southern California
Boyd, Bill, Southern Cross University
Bralower, Timothy J., Pennsylvania State University, University Park
Brett, Carlton E., University of Cincinnati
Briskin, Madeleine, University of Cincinnati
Buckley, Brendon, Columbia University
Buick, Roger, University of Washington
Byers, Charles W., University of Wisconsin, Madison
Caissie, Beth E., Iowa State University of Science & Technology
Came, Rosemarie E., University of New Hampshire
Camill III, Philip, Bowdoin College
Capraro, Luca, Università degli Studi di Padova
Carter, Burt, University of Tennessee, Knoxville
Chapin, F. Stuart, University of California, Berkeley
Charles, Christopher D., University of California, San Diego
Clapham, Matthew E., University of California, Santa Cruz
Cobb, Kim M., Georgia Institute of Technology
Cohen, Anne L., Woods Hole Oceanographic Institution
Cole, Julia E., University of Arizona
Colgan, Mitchell W., College of Charleston
Crowley, Brooke E., Cincinnati Museum Center
Curry, Brandon B., Illinois State Geological Survey
Curtin, Tara M., Hobart & William Smith Colleges
Curtis, Jason H., University of Florida
D'Andrea, William J., Columbia University
D'Antonio, Carla, University of California, Berkeley
de Menocal, Peter B., Columbia University
Dekens, Petra, San Francisco State University
deMenocal, Peter B., Columbia University
Dietl, Gregory P., Cornell University
Douglas, Robert G., University of Southern California
Duhamel, Solange, Columbia University
Dyer, Blake, Princeton University
Edlund, Mark B., University of Minnesota, Twin Cities
Ekdale, Allan A., University of Utah
Elick, Jennifer M., Susquehanna University
Endres, Anthony E., University of Waterloo
Engstrom, Daniel R., University of Minnesota, Twin Cities
Fariduddin, Mohammad, Northeastern Illinois University
Fawcett, Peter J., University of New Mexico
Francis, Jane, University of Leeds
Francus, Pierre, Universite du Quebec
Fritts, Harold C., University of Arizona
Good, Steven C., West Chester University
Goodwin, Phillip A., University of Southampton
Grigg, Laurie, Norwich University
Grocke, Darren, Durham University
Guber, Albert L., Pennsylvania State University, University Park
Halfar, Jochen, University of Toronto
Hasiotis, Stephen T., University of Kansas
Hays, James D., Columbia University
Haywood, Alan, University of Leeds
He, Helen, University of East Anglia
Herbert, Timothy D., Brown University
Herrmann, Achim, Louisiana State University
Hill, Tessa M., University of California, Davis
Hirschboeck, Katherine A., University of Arizona
Hoenisch, Baerbel, Columbia University
Hopley, Philip, Birkbeck College
Hu, Feng-Sheng, University of Illinois, Urbana-Champaign
Hughes, Malcolm K., University of Arizona
Huybers, Peter, Harvard University

Ishman, Scott E., Southern Illinois University Carbondale
Ivany, Linda C., Syracuse University
Jackson, Charles S., University of Texas at Austin
Johnson, Claudia C., Indiana University, Bloomington
Johnson, Robert G., University of Minnesota, Twin Cities
Johnson, Thomas C., University of Minnesota, Twin Cities
Kemp, Alan, University of Southampton
Kennedy, Lisa M., Virginia Polytechnic Institute & State University
Knight, Tiffany, Washington University
Koutavas, Athanasios, College of Staten Island
Kutzbach, John E., University of Wisconsin, Madison
Lachniet, Matthew S., University of Nevada, Las Vegas
Linsley, Braddock, Columbia University
Littler, Kate, Exeter University
Livingstone, Daniel A., Duke University
Lohmann, George P., Woods Hole Oceanographic Institution
Lozano Garcia, Maria S., Universidad Nacional Autonoma de Mexico
Lu, Yanbin, University of Minnesota, Twin Cities
Lynch-Stieglitz, Jean, Georgia Institute of Technology
Macdonald, Francis, Harvard University
Mancini, Ernest A., University of Alabama
Mann, Daniel H., University of Alaska, Fairbanks
Marchal, Olivier, Woods Hole Oceanographic Institution
Martin, Anthony J., Emory University
Martin, Pamela, University of Chicago
Mayewski, Paul A., University of Maine
McAlester, A. Lee, Southern Methodist University
McIntyre, Andrew, Graduate School of the City University of New York
McIntyre, Andrew, Queens College (CUNY)
McLean, Dewey M., Virginia Polytechnic Institute & State University
McManus, Jerry F., Columbia University
McManus, Jerry F., Woods Hole Oceanographic Institution
McWethy, David B., Montana State University
Mekik, Figen A., Grand Valley State University
Miller, Joshua H., Cincinnati Museum Center
Miller, Keith B., Kansas State University
Miller, Molly F., Vanderbilt University
Mishler, Brent, University of California, Berkeley
Myrbo, Amy, University of Minnesota, Twin Cities
Nelson, Robert E., Colby College
Nichols, Jonathan E., Columbia University
Norry, Mike, Leicester University
Oleinik, Anton, Florida Atlantic University
Olszewski, Thomas, Texas A&M University
Ortegren, Jason, University of West Florida
Pagani, Mark, Yale University
Panagiotakopulu, Eva, Edinburgh University
Parr, Kate, University of Liverpool
Pearson, P N., Cardiff University
Pekar, Stephen, Queens College (CUNY)
Poli, Maria-Serena, Eastern Michigan University
Pospelova, Vera, University of Victoria
Poulsen, Christopher J., University of Michigan
Power, Mary E., University of California, Berkeley
Powers, Elizabeth, California State University, Bakersfield
Quinn, Terry, University of Texas at Austin
Raymo, Maureen, Columbia University
Rhode, David E., Desert Research Institute
Rindsberg, Andrew K., University of West Alabama
Rollins, Harold B., University of Pittsburgh
Royer, Dana, Wesleyan University
Sahagian, Dork, Lehigh University
Sauer, Peter, Indiana University, Bloomington
Schaefer, Joerg, Columbia University
Schellenberg, Stephen A., San Diego State University
Schelske, Claire L., University of Florida
Schneider, Tapio, California Institute of Technology
Schwert, Donald P., North Dakota State University
Schöne, Bernd R., Universitaet Mainz
Scuderi, Louis, University of New Mexico
Severinghaus, Jeffrey P., University of California, San Diego
Shaak, Graig D., University of Florida
Shanahan, Timothy M., University of Texas at Austin
Shroat-Lewis, Rene A., University of Arkansas at Little Rock
Shuman, Bryan N., University of Wyoming
Sims, Hallie J., University of Iowa
Sloan, Lisa C., University of California, Santa Cruz
Smerdon, Jason, Columbia University
Speer, James, Indiana State University
Spero, Howard J., University of California, Davis
Sremac, Jasenka, University of Zagreb
Staff, George M., Austin Community College District
Stolper, Daniel, Princeton University
Strachan, Scotty, University of Nevada, Reno
Surge, Donna M., University of North Carolina, Chapel Hill
Swetnam, Thomas W., University of Arizona
Taffs, Kathryn, Southern Cross University
Talyor, Frederick W., University of Texas at Austin
Taylor, Frederick W., University of Texas at Austin
Thompson, William, Woods Hole Oceanographic Institution

Thunell, Robert C., University of South Carolina
Verardo, Stacey, George Mason University
Vermeij, Geerat J., University of California, Davis
Waddington, J. M., McMaster University
Walker, Kenneth R., University of Tennessee, Knoxville
Webb, III, Thompson, Brown University
Weldeab, Syee, University of California, Santa Barbara
Westgate, James W., Lamar University
Whiteside, Jessica H., University of Southampton
Whitlock, Cathy, Montana State University
Wigand, Peter, University of Nevada, Reno
Williams, Christopher J., Franklin and Marshall College
Williams, John W., University of Wisconsin, Madison
Wolosz, Thomas H., Plattsburgh State University (SUNY)
Wong, Corinne I., Boston College
Woodhouse, Connie, University of Arizona
Xuan, Chuang, University of Southampton
Yu, Zicheng, Lehigh University
Æosoviæ, Vlasta, University of Zagreb

Geobiology

Andrus, Richard E., Binghamton University
Arnone, John, Desert Research Institute
Arp, Dr., Gernot, Georg-August University of Goettingen
Bailey, Jake, University of Minnesota, Twin Cities
Barton, Hazel, University of Akron
Bosak, Tanja, Massachusetts Institute of Technology
Bradley, Alexander S., Washington University in St. Louis
Calcote, Randy, University of Minnesota, Twin Cities
Cardace, Dawn, University of Rhode Island
Chan, Clara, University of Delaware
Chaput, Dominique, Smithsonian Institution / National Museum of Natural History
Clementz, Mark T., University of Wyoming
Colman, Albert, University of Chicago
Conley, Catharine A., New Mexico Institute of Mining and Technology
Diggins, Thomas P., Youngstown State University
Dupraz, Christophe, University of Connecticut
Dyson, Miranda, The Open University
Farmer, Jack D., Arizona State University
Flood, Beverley, University of Minnesota, Twin Cities
Fortin, Danielle, University of Ottawa
Fortner, Sarah K., Wittenberg University
Fournier, Gregory, Massachusetts Institute of Technology
Fowle, David A., University of Kansas
Fritsen, Christian H., Desert Research Institute
Gallegos, Anthony F., Los Alamos National Laboratory
Glamoclija, Mihaela , Rutgers, The State University of New Jersey, Newark
Glasauer, Susan, University of Guelph
Gorman-Lewis, Drew J., University of Washington
Gray, Neil, University of Newcastle Upon Tyne
Hendy, Ingrid, University of Michigan
House, Christopher H., Pennsylvania State University, University Park
Johnston, Carl G., Youngstown State University
Jones, Dan, University of Minnesota, Twin Cities
Jorge, Maria Luisa, Vanderbilt University
Klemow, Kenneth M., Wilkes University
Konhauser, Kurt, University of Alberta
Kopf, Sebastian, Princeton University
Kowalewski, Michal J., Virginia Polytechnic Institute & State University
Kulp, Thomas, Binghamton University
Lower, Steven K., Ohio State University
Macalady, Jennifer L., Pennsylvania State University, University Park
Marshall, Craig, University of Kansas
McCormick, Michael L., Hamilton College
Meyer Dombard, DArcy, University of Illinois at Chicago
Mock, Thomas, University of East Anglia
Murray, Alison E., Desert Research Institute
Myers, Orrin B., Los Alamos National Laboratory
Nealson, Kenneth, University of Southern California
Newman, Dianne K., California Institute of Technology
O'Mullan, Gregory, Queens College (CUNY)
Olcott Marshall, Alison, University of Kansas
Ono, Shuhei, Massachusetts Institute of Technology
Onstott, Tullis C., Princeton University
Orphan, Victoria, California Institute of Technology
Orsi, William, Ludwig-Maximilians-Universitaet Muenchen
Osburn, Magdalena , Northwestern University
Prezant, Robert S., Graduate School of the City University of New York
Rampedi, Isaac T., University of Johannesburg
Rathburn, Anthony, Indiana State University
Raub, Tim, University of St. Andrews
Reitner, Joachim, Georg-August University of Goettingen
Robbins, Lisa, University of South Florida, Tampa
Roberts, Jennifer A., University of Kansas
Roden, Eric E., University of Wisconsin, Madison
Rogers, Karyn L., Rensselaer Polytechnic Institute
Sanford, Robert A., University of Illinois, Urbana-Champaign
Santelli, Cara M., University of Minnesota, Twin Cities
Santelli, Cara, Smithsonian Institution / National Museum of Natural History
Sanudo, Sergio, University of Southern California

Schrenk, Matt, Michigan State University
Seibt, Ulrike, University of California, Los Angeles
Southam, Gordon, Western University
Speijer, Robert, Katholieke Universiteit Leuven
Steele, Michael A., Wilkes University
Summons, Roger, Massachusetts Institute of Technology
Thompson, Joel B., Eckerd College
Tice, Mike, Texas A&M University
Vann, David R., University of Pennsylvania
Vega Vera, Francisco J., Universidad Nacional Autonoma de Mexico
Weber, Karrie A., University of Nebraska, Lincoln
Wilf, Peter D., Pennsylvania State University, University Park
Woerheide, Gert, Ludwig-Maximilians-Universitaet Muenchen
Yee, Nathan, Rutgers, The State University of New Jersey

HYDROLOGY
General Hydrology
Adelana, S.M. A., University of Ilorin
AL-Nouimy, Latifa B., University of Qatar
Albert, Curtis C., University of Illinois, Urbana-Champaign
Alencoão, Ana M., Universidade de Trás-os-Montes e Alto Douro
Alhajari, Sief A., University of Qatar
Allan, Craig J., University of North Carolina, Charlotte
Allen, Peter M., Baylor University
Alsdorf, Douglas E., Ohio State University
Andres, A. S., University of Delaware
Arain, M. A., McMaster University
Atkinson, Tim, University College London
Bain, Daniel J., University of Pittsburgh
Baker, Tracy, Richard Stockton College of New Jersey
Becker, Naomi M., Los Alamos National Laboratory
Beckie, Roger D., University of British Columbia
Bengeyfield, Peter, University of Montana Western
Bennett, Philip, University of Texas at Austin
Bense, Victor, University of East Anglia
Bloor, Michelle, University of Portsmouth
Bolton, David, Maryland Department of Natural Resources
Boult, Stephen, University of Manchester
Boving, Thomas, University of Rhode Island
Bowman, Jean A., Texas A&M University
Boyle, Douglas, University of Nevada, Reno
Brassington, Rick, University of Newcastle Upon Tyne
Brown, David L., California State University, Chico
Burgess, Willy, University College London
Burkhart, Patrick A., Slippery Rock University
Byrne, James M., University of Lethbridge
Campana, Michael E., Oregon State University
Carey, Sean, McMaster University
Carillo Chavez, Alejandro J., Universidad Nacional Autonoma de Mexico
Carman, Cary D., Angelo State University
Celico, Fulvio, University of Parma
Challads, Thomas, Edinburgh University
Chaubey, Indrajeet, Purdue University
Chin, Yu-Ping, Ohio State University
Church, Ian, University of Southern Mississippi
Cirmo, Christopher P., SUNY, Cortland
Clark, Jordan, University of California, Santa Barbara
Coulibaly, Paulin, McMaster University
Crawford, Nicholas, Western Kentucky University
Cunningham, Peter, University of Newcastle Upon Tyne
Currens, James C., University of Kentucky
D'Odorico, Paolo, University of Virginia
Dahlke, Helen E., University of California, Davis
Darby, Jeannie, University of California, Davis
Davidson, Bart, University of Kentucky
Devaurs, Micheline, Los Alamos National Laboratory
Dey, William S., University of Illinois, Urbana-Champaign
Doran, Peter, Louisiana State University
Doster, Florian, Heriot-Watt University
Duan, Quingyun, Lawrence Livermore National Laboratory
Duex, Timothy W., University of Louisiana at Lafayette
Dugan, Brandon, Rice University
Durand, Michael T., Ohio State University
Eaton, Timothy, Queens College (CUNY)
Elliott, Emily M., University of Pittsburgh
Emerman, Steven, Utah Valley University
Enright, Richard L., Bridgewater State University
Entekhabi, Dara, Massachusetts Institute of Technology
Eshleman, Keith N., University of Maryland
Estalrich López, Joan, Universitat Autonoma de Barcelona
Ezenabor, Ben O., University of Benin
Fabryka-Martin, June T., Los Alamos National Laboratory
Farrow, Norman D., Oak Ridge National Laboratory
Fedele, Juan J., Saint Cloud State University
Foufoula-Georgiou, Efi, University of Minnesota, Twin Cities
Fox, Haydn A., Texas A&M University, Commerce
Gannon, John P., Western Carolina University
Gary, Marcus, University of Texas at Austin
Gilmore, Tyler J., Pacific Northwest National Laboratory
Grieneisen, Michael L., University of California, Davis

Groves, Christopher, University of Kentucky
Groves, Christopher, Western Kentucky University
Guan, Huade, Flinders University
Hagan, Robert M., University of California, Davis
Hannah, David, University of Birmingham
Hanson, Blaine R., University of California, Davis
Hart, David J., University of Wisconsin, Madison
Harter, Thomas, University of California, Davis
Hasan, Mohamed Ali, University of Malaya
Heffer, Kes, Heriot-Watt University
Heimann, William H., Fort Hays State University
Heitz, Leroy F., University of Guam
Henry, Tiernan, National University of Ireland Galway
Hernes, Peter J., University of California, Davis
Hill, Mary C., University of Kansas
Hiscock, Kevin, University of East Anglia
Hooyer, Thomas S., University of Wisconsin, Madison
Hornberger, George, Vanderbilt University
Hubbard, John E., SUNY, The College at Brockport
Huntington, Justin, University of Nevada, Reno
Ibaraki, Motomu, Ohio State University
Inamdar, Shreeram, University of Delaware
Jacobs, Katharine L., University of Arizona
Jaffe, Peter R., Princeton University
James-Aworeni, E., Obafemi Awolowo University
Jefferson, Anne, University of North Carolina, Charlotte
Jefferson, Anne J., Kent State University
Jennings, Stephen P., Geological Survey of Alabama
Jewell, Paul W., University of Utah
Johannesson, Karen H., Tulane University
Johnson, Robert L., Argonne National Laboratory
Johnson, Robert O., Oak Ridge National Laboratory
Jones, Stephen C., Geological Survey of Alabama
Kasenow, Michael, Eastern Michigan University
Katz, Gabrielle, Appalachian State University
Kelly, Walton R., Illinois State University
Kennedy, Casey D., University of Massachusetts, Amherst
Kesel, Richard H., Louisiana State University
Keyantash, John, California State University, Dominguez Hills
Kilroy, Kathyrn, Minot State University
Kilsby, Chris, University of Newcastle Upon Tyne
Kinner, David A., Western Carolina University
Krabbenhoft, David, University of Wisconsin, Madison
Kuchovsky, Tomas, Masaryk University
Lakshmi, Venkataraman, University of South Carolina
Land, Lewis A., New Mexico Institute of Mining & Technology
Lane, Charles L., Southern Oregon University
Lanigan, David C., Pacific Northwest National Laboratory
Larson, David R., University of Illinois, Urbana-Champaign
Lautz, Laura, Syracuse University
Laycock, Arleigh H., University of Alberta
Lee, Michael D., California State University, East Bay
Levine, Rebekah, University of Montana Western
Lightbody, Anne F., University of New Hampshire
Lin, Yu-Feng F., University of Illinois, Urbana-Champaign
Liu, Gaisheng, University of Kansas
Ma, Lin, University of Texas, El Paso
McDermott, Christopher I., Edinburgh University
McElwee, Carl D., University of Kansas
McKenna, Thomas E., University of Delaware
McLaughlin, Peter P., University of Delaware
McNamara, James P., Boise State University
Megdal, Sharon B., University of Arizona
Mehnert, Edward, Illinois State University
Mehnert, Edwards, University of Illinois, Urbana-Champaign
Michalek, Thomas E., Montana Tech of The University of Montana
Miller, Glenn C., University of Nevada, Reno
Mudd, Simon N., Edinburgh University
Nadiri, Ata, University of Tabriz
Ninesteel, Judy J., Potomac State College
O'Driscoll, Michael A., East Carolina University
O'Reilly, Catherine M., Illinois State University
Odling, Noelle, University of Leeds
Ortiz-Aguirre, Ramon, Universidad Autonoma de San Luis Potosi
Oztekin Okan, Ozlem, Firat University
Palmer, Arthur N., SUNY, Oneonta
Parkin, Geoffrey, University of Newcastle Upon Tyne
Pavelsky, Tamlin M., University of North Carolina, Chapel Hill
Perkins, William A., Pacific Northwest National Laboratory
Pettijohn, J. C., University of Illinois, Urbana-Champaign
Piccinini, Leonardo, Università degli Studi di Padova
Piggot, Matthew, Imperial College
Potter, Kenneth W., University of Wisconsin, Madison
Prestegaard, Karen L., University of Maryland
Puente, Carlos E., University of California, Davis
Quinn, Paul, University of Newcastle Upon Tyne
Reay, William G., College of William & Mary
Reedy, Robert C., University of Texas at Austin, Jackson School of Geosciences
Reidenbach, Matthew A., University of Virginia
Renshaw, Carl E., Dartmouth College

Rice, Karen C., University of Virginia
Richards, Paul L., SUNY, The College at Brockport
Ricka, Adam, Masaryk University
Rodriguez-Iturbe, Ignacio, Princeton University
Root, Tara L., Florida Atlantic University
Rouse, Joseph D., University of Guam
Saar, Martin O., University of Minnesota, Twin Cities
Salami, B. M., Obafemi Awolowo University
Sandoval, Samuel, University of California, Davis
Sandoval Solis, Samuel, University of California, Davis
Scanlon, Bridget R., University of Texas at Austin
Scanlon, Todd M., University of Virginia
Schnoebelen, Douglas J., University of Iowa
Schwartz, Frank W., Ohio State University
Scotton, Paolo, Università degli Studi di Padova
Screaton, Elizabeth J., University of Florida
Singer, Michael, University of St. Andrews
Slade, Jr., Raymond M., Austin Community College District
Slattery, Michael C., Texas Christian University
Smith, Ellen D., Oak Ridge National Laboratory
Smith, James A., Princeton University
Smith, Michael, Geological Survey of Alabama
Smith, Ronald M., Pacific Northwest National Laboratory
Smyth, Rebecca C., University of Texas at Austin, Jackson School of Geosciences
Soroushian, Soroosh, University of California, Irvine
Spane, Frank A., Pacific Northwest National Laboratory
Sritharan, Subramania I., Central State University
Stafford, Jim, Wyoming State Geological Survey
Steele, Ken, University of Arkansas, Fayetteville
Thorne, Paul D., Pacific Northwest National Laboratory
Tijani, M. N., University of Ibadan
Tomlinson, Jaime L., University of Delaware
Triay, Ines, Los Alamos National Laboratory
Tucker, Carla M., Lamar University
Turner, Anne, Austin Community College District
Tyler, Scott, University of Nevada, Reno
Vail, Lance W., Pacific Northwest National Laboratory
Vandike, James E., Missouri University of Science and Technology
Vermeul, Vincent R., Pacific Northwest National Laboratory
Wallender, Wesley W., University of California, Davis
Watkins, David, Exeter University
Wen, Xianyun, University of Leeds
West, Jared, University of Leeds
White, Jeffrey R., Indiana University, Bloomington
White, Martin, National University of Ireland Galway
Witt, Emma, Stockton University
Wolf, Aaron T., Oregon State University
Woltemade, Christopher J., Shippensburg University
Woo, Ming-Ko, McMaster University
Wood, Eric F., Princeton University
Xu, Shangping, University of Wisconsin, Milwaukee
Yabusaki, Steven B., Pacific Northwest National Laboratory
Yan, Eugene, University of Illinois at Chicago
Yang, Y, Cardiff University
Ye, Ming, Florida State University
You, Jinsheng, University of Nebraska, Lincoln
Yusoff, Ismail, University of Malaya
Zaccaria, Daniele, University of California, Davis
Zhang, Minghua , University of California, Davis
Ziemer, Robert, Humboldt State University
Zume, Joseph T., Shippensburg University

Ground Water/Hydrogeology
Simsek, Sakir, Hacettepe University
Achmad, Grufon, Maryland Department of Natural Resources
Akujieze, Christopher N., University of Benin
Al, Tom A., University of Ottawa
Al-Shaibani, Abdulaziz, King Fahd University of Petroleum and Minerals
Alberts, E E., University of Missouri, Columbia
Ali, Bukari, Kwame Nkrumah University of Science and Technology
Ali, Genevieve, University of Manitoba
Allen, Timothy T., Keene State College
Amin, Isam E., Youngstown State University
Anderson, Mary P., University of Wisconsin, Madison
Anderson, William P., Appalachian State University
Anderson, NAE, Mary P., University of Wisconsin, Madison
Andreasen, David C., Maryland Department of Natural Resources
Appiah-Adjei, Emmanuel K., Kwame Nkrumah University of Science and Technology
Appold, Martin, University of Missouri
Arthur, Jonathan D., Florida Geological Survey
Asante, Joseph, Tennessee Tech University
Asghari Moghadam, Asghar, University of Tabriz
Bagtzoglou, Ross, Columbia University
Bahr, Jean M., University of Wisconsin, Madison
Bair, Edwin S., Ohio State University
Bajjali, William, University of Wisconsin, Superior
Baker, Andy, University of New South Wales
Baldwin, Jr., A. Dwight, Miami University
Barbecot, Florent, Universite du Quebec a Montreal
Barkmann, Peter, Colorado Geological Survey

Barrash, Warren, Boise State University
Batelaan, Okke, Katholieke Universiteit Leuven
Batelaan, Okke, Flinders University
Bayari, Serdar, Hacettepe University
Beck, E. G., University of Kentucky
Becker, Matthew, California State University, Long Beach
Bedient, Philip B., Rice University
Behnke, Jerold J., California State University, Chico
Belanger, Thomas V., Florida Institute of Technology
Bennett, Steven W., Western Illinois University
Bentley, Laurence R., University of Calgary
Bergamaschi, Brian, California State University, Sacramento
Bethke, Craig M., University of Illinois, Urbana-Champaign
Bishop, Charles E., Utah Geological Survey
Blythe, Daniel D., Montana Tech of The University of Montana
Boateng, Samuel, Northern Kentucky University
Bogner, Jean, University of Illinois at Chicago
Bohling, Geoffrey C., University of Kansas
Bolster, Diogo, University of Notre Dame
Bolton, David W., Maryland Department of Natural Resources
Booth, Colin J., Northern Illinois University
Boutt, David, University of Massachusetts, Amherst
Boving, Thomas B., University of Rhode Island
Boyle, James T., New Jersey Geological Survey
Bradbury, Kenneth R., University of Wisconsin, Madison
Bradbury, Kenneth R., University of Wisconsin, Extension
Brame, Scott E., Clemson University
Bratcher, Susan, California State University, Fresno
Breitmeyer, Ronald, University of Nevada, Reno
Brewer, Kevin E., Olivet Nazarene University
Brikowski, Tom H., University of Texas, Dallas
Brookfield, Andrea, University of Kansas
Brookshire, Cynthia, Missouri Dept of Natural Resources
Brusseau, Mark L., University of Arizona
Buchanan, John P., Eastern Washington University
Burbey, Thomas J., Virginia Polytechnic Institute & State University
Burnett, Earl E., Arizona Western College
Butler, James M., University of Kansas
Butler, Jr., James J., University of Kansas
Callahan, Timothy J., College of Charleston
Capuano, Regina M., University of Houston
Cardenas, Bayani, University of Texas at Austin
Cardiff, Michael, University of Wisconsin, Madison
Carle, Steven, Lawrence Livermore National Laboratory
Carling, Gregory T., Brigham Young University
Carlson, Catherine A., Eastern Connecticut State University
Carlson, Charles G., South Dakota State University
Carlson, Douglas A., Louisiana State University
Carstarphen, Camela, Montana Tech of The University of Montana
Casillas, Angelica, Universidad Nacional Autonoma de Mexico
Cassidy, Daniel P., Western Michigan University
Castendyk, Devin, SUNY, Oneonta
Celia, Michael A., Princeton University
Chachadi, Adiveppa G., Goa University
Chavez-Aguirre, Rafael, Universidad Autonoma de Chihuahua
Cheng, Songlin, Wright State University
Cherkauer, Douglas S., University of Wisconsin, Milwaukee
Cherry, John A., University of Waterloo
Cherubini, Claudia, Institut Polytechnique LaSalle Beauvais (ex-IGAL)
Chesnaux, Romain, Universite du Quebec a Chicoutimi
Chowdhury, Shafiul H., SUNY, New Paltz
Cianfrani, Christina, Hampshire College
Clarey, Timothy L., Delta College
Clark, Ian D., University of Ottawa
Conant, Brewster, University of Waterloo
Cook, Edward R., Columbia University
Cook, Peter, Flinders University
Costa, Maria R., Universidade de Trás-os-Montes e Alto Douro
Cox, Malcolm E., Queensland University of Technology
Croxen III, Fred W., Arizona Western College
Curran, John, New Jersey Geological Survey
Davidson, Gregg R., University of Mississippi
Davis, Arden D., South Dakota School of Mines & Technology
Davis, J. Matthew, University of New Hampshire
Davis, Ralph K., University of Arkansas, Fayetteville
Decker, Dave, University of Nevada, Reno
Del Arenal-Capetillo, Rodolfo, Universidad Nacional Autonoma de Mexico
Denizman, Can, Valdosta State University
Devlin, J. R., University of Kansas
Dey, William S., Illinois State Geological Survey
Dhar, Ratan K., York College (CUNY)
Dimova, Natasha T., University of Alabama
Dintaman, Christopher, indiana University
Domber, Steven E., New Jersey Geological Survey
Doran, Peter T., University of Illinois at Chicago
Doss, Paul K., University of Southern Indiana
Douglas, Ellen, University of Massachusetts, Boston
Dripps, Weston R., Furman University
Druhan, Jennifer, University of Illinois, Urbana-Champaign
Durham, Lisa A., Argonne National Laboratory

Earman, Sam, Millersville University
Ekmekci, Mehmet, Hacettepe University
El-Kadi, Aly I., University of Hawai'i, Manoa
Ellis, Andre, California State University, Los Angeles
Esling, Steven P., Southern Illinois University Carbondale
Evans, David G., California State University, Sacramento
Fabbri, Paolo, Università degli Studi di Padova
Fairley, Jerry P., University of Idaho
Famiglietti, James, University of California, Irvine
Farmer, George T., Los Alamos National Laboratory
Feinstein, Daniel T., University of Wisconsin, Milwaukee
Ferre, Paul A., University of Arizona
Ferrero, Tom, Oregon Dept of Geology & Mineral Industries
Filipovic, Dragan, South Dakota Dept of Environment and Natural Resources
Fisher, Andrew T., University of California, Santa Cruz
Fitzpatrick, Stephan, Georgia Perimeter College
Fleeger, Gary M., Pennsylvania Bureau of Topographic & Geologic Survey
Flowers, George C., Tulane University
Fogg, Graham E., University of California, Davis
Fountain, John C., North Carolina State University
Freshley, Mark D., Pacific Northwest National Laboratory
Frisbee, Marty, Purdue University
Fryar, Alan E., University of Kentucky
Gakka, Dr U., University College of Science, Osmania University
Gardner, Payton, University of Montana
Garven, Grant, Tufts University
Ge, Shemin, University of Colorado
Geary, Phil, University of Newcastle
Gebrehiwet, Tsigabu A., Towson University
Geidel, Gwendelyn, University of South Carolina
Gemperline, Johanna M., Maryland Department of Natural Resources
Gentry, Randall, Argonne National Laboratory
Gerla, Philip J., University of North Dakota
Godsey, Sarah E., Idaho State University
Goeke, James W., Unversity of Nebraska - Lincoln
Gordon, Ryan, Dept of Agriculture, Conservation, and Forestry
Gordon, Susan L., University of Calgary
Gorelick, Steven M., Stanford University
Gotkowitz, Madeline B., University of Wisconsin, Extension
Gotkowitz, Madeline B., University of Wisconsin, Madison
Gouzie, Douglas R., Missouri State University
Grasby, Stephen E., University of Calgary
Grismer, Mark E., University of California, Davis
Grundl, Timothy J., University of Wisconsin, Milwaukee
Gurdak, Jason, San Francisco State University
Habana, Nathan C., University of Guam
Haggerty, Roy D., Oregon State University
Halihan, Todd, Oklahoma State University
Hall, Francis R., University of New Hampshire
Hampton, Duane R., Western Michigan University
Han, Weon Shik, University of Wisconsin, Milwaukee
Hand, Kristen, Pennsylvania Bureau of Topographic & Geologic Survey
Harbor, Jon M., Purdue University
Hargis, David, University of Arizona
Harris, Brett D., Curtin University
Harris, William H., Graduate School of the City University of New York
Hart, David J., University of Wisconsin, Extension
Harter, Thomas L., University of California, Davis
Hatch, Christine, University of Massachusetts, Amherst
Hayashi, Masaki, University of Calgary
Hays, Phillip D., University of Arkansas, Fayetteville
Heilweil, Victor, University of Utah
Helmke, Martin F., West Chester University
Hendrickx, Jan M., New Mexico Institute of Mining and Technology
Hendry, Jim, University of Saskatchewan
Henry, Eric J., University of North Carolina Wilmington
Herman, Ellen K., Bucknell University
Hershey, Ronald, University of Nevada, Reno
Hibbs, Barry, California State University, Los Angeles
Hindle, Tobin, Florida Atlantic University
Hinson, Amye, Geological Survey of Alabama
Hoff, Jean L., Saint Cloud State University
Hoover, Karin A., California State University, Chico
Horner, Tim C., California State University, Sacramento
Howard, Kenneth W., University of Toronto
Howe, Thomas, Western Michigan University
Hu, Bill X., Florida State University
Hu, Qinhong (Max), University of Texas, Arlington
Hudak, Paul F., University of North Texas
Huizar-Alvarez, Rafael, Universidad Nacional Autonoma de Mexico
Hunt, Randy J., University of Wisconsin, Madison
Hurlow, Hugh A., Utah Geological Survey
Huysmans, Marijke, Katholieke Universiteit Leuven
Icopini, Gary, Montana Tech of The University of Montana
Iles, Derric L., South Dakota Dept of Environment and Natural Resources
Iqbal, Mohammad Z., University of Northern Iowa
Isiorho, Solomon A., Indiana University / Purdue University, Fort Wayne
Jaffe, Peter R., Princeton University
James, Scott C., Baylor University
Jannik, Nancy O., Winona State University

Jarvis, W. T., Oregon State University
Jenson, John W., University of Guam
Johnson, Peggy, New Mexico Institute of Mining & Technology
Johnson, Stephen W., New Jersey Geological Survey
Johnson, Thomas M., University of Illinois, Urbana-Champaign
Join, Jean-Lambert, Universite de la Reunion
Jones, Ian C., Austin Community College District
Juster, Thomas C., University of South Florida, Tampa
Keefer, Donald A., University of Illinois, Urbana-Champaign
Keefer, Donald, Illinois State Geological Survey
Keen, Kerry L., University of Wisconsin, River Falls
Keller, C. Kent, Washington State University
Kelly, Bryce, University of New South Wales
Kelly, Walton R., Illinois State Water Survey
Kent, Douglas, Oklahoma State University
Khalequzzaman, Md., Lock Haven University
Knoll, Martin A., Sewanee: University of the South
Kreamer, David, University of Nevada, Reno
Kreamer, David K., University of Nevada, Las Vegas
Kurttas, Turker, Hacettepe University
La Fave, John I., Montana Tech of The University of Montana
La Fleur, Robert G., Rensselaer Polytechnic Institute
Lachhab, Ahmed, Susquehanna University
Lachmar, Thomas E., Utah State University
LaFreniere, Lorraine, Argonne National Laboratory
Lambert, Carolyn D., University of Northern Colorado
Lamontangne, Sebastian, Flinders University
Langman, Jeffrey, University of Idaho
Larocque, Marie, Universite du Quebec a Montreal
Larson, David R., Illinois State Geological Survey
Lassetter, William L., Division of Geology and Mineral Resources
Laton, W. R., California State University, Fullerton
Lee, David R., University of Waterloo
Lee, Donald W., Oak Ridge National Laboratory
Lee, Eung Seok, Ohio University
Lee, Ming-Kuo, Auburn University
Lefebvre, Rene, Universite du Quebec
Lemke, Lawrence D., Wayne State University
Leonhart, Leo S., University of Arizona
Levy, Jonathan, Miami University
Locke, Daniel B., Dept of Agriculture, Conservation, and Forestry
Locke, III, Randall A., Illinois State Water Survey
Loh, Yvonne A., University of Ghana
Loheide, Steven P., University of Wisconsin, Madison
Lopez-Ferreira, Cesar A., Universidad Autonoma de Baja California Sur
Lord, Mark L., Western Carolina University
Love, Andew, Flinders University
Lowe, Mike, Utah Geological Survey
Lowry, Christopher S., SUNY, Buffalo
Lutz, Alexandra, University of Nevada, Reno
Mabee, Stephen B., Massachusetts Geological Survey
MacNish, Robert, University of Arizona
Macpherson, Gwen L., University of Kansas
Makkawi, Mohammad, King Fahd University of Petroleum and Minerals
Marino, M. A., University of California, Davis
Marino, Miguel A., University of California, Davis
Martel, Richard, Universite du Quebec
Matyjasik, Marek, Weber State University
May, James, Mississippi State University
Mayer, James R., University of West Georgia
Mayo, Alan L., Brigham Young University
McCurdy, Maureen, Louisiana Tech University
McKenzie, Jeffrey M., McGill University
McMurtry, John L., California State University, Chico
Mehnert, Edward, Illinois State Geological Survey
Mendoza, Carl A., University of Alberta
Metesh, John J., Montana Tech of The University of Montana
Meyer, Philip D., Pacific Northwest National Laboratory
Meyer, Scott C., Illinois State Water Survey
Michael, Holly, University of Delaware
Michel, Fred A., Carleton University
Milewski, Adam, University of Georgia
Miller, Marvin R., Montana Tech of The University of Montana
Mitchell, Robert J., Western Washington University
Moffett, Kevan, University of Texas at Austin
Moline, Gerilynn R., Oak Ridge National Laboratory
Montgomery, William W., New Jersey City University
Moore, Michael E., Pennsylvania Bureau of Topographic & Geologic Survey
Moran, Jean, California State University, East Bay
Moss, Neil E., Geological Survey of Alabama
Moysey, Stephen M., Clemson University
Muldoon, Maureen A., University of Wisconsin, Oshkosh
Murdoch, Lawrence C., Clemson University
Murgulet, Dorina, Texas A&M University, Corpus Christi
Murray, Kent S., University of Michigan, Dearborn
Murray, Kyle E., University of Oklahoma
Myers, Paul B., Lehigh University
Narasimhan, T. N., University of California, Berkeley
Naylor, Shawn, indiana University
Naymik, Thomas G., Ohio State University

Neboga, Victoria V., Pennsylvania Bureau of Topographic & Geologic Survey
Nedunuri, Krishna K., Central State University
Newcomer, Darrell R., Pacific Northwest National Laboratory
Newell, Charles J., Rice University
Nguyen, Lam V., Hanoi University of Mining & Geology
Nicot, Jean-Philippe, University of Texas at Austin
Nkotagu, Hudson H., University of Dar es Salaam
Noonan, Mathew T., South Dakota Dept of Environment and Natural Resources
Norman, Ralph R., Geological Survey of Alabama
Noyes, Joanne M., South Dakota Dept of Environment and Natural Resources
O'Brien, Arnold L., University of Massachusetts Lowell
O'Brien, Rachel, Allegheny College
O'Neil, Patrick E., Geological Survey of Alabama
Oberdorfer, June A., San Jose State University
Ogard, Allen E., Los Alamos National Laboratory
Olafsen-Lackey, Susan, Unversity of Nebraska - Lincoln
Oliveira, Alcino S., Universidade de Trás-os-Montes e Alto Douro
Olyphant, Greg A., Indiana University, Bloomington
Ophori, Duke U., Montclair State University
Opper, Carl, Saint Petersburg College, Clearwater
Ortega, Adrian, Universidad Nacional Autonoma de Mexico
Osborn, Stephen G., California State Polytechnic University, Pomona
Ozsvath, David L., University of Wisconsin, Stevens Point
Pan, Feifei, University of North Texas
Paniconi, Claudio, Universite du Quebec
Panno, Samuel V., University of Illinois, Urbana-Champaign
Parizek, Richard R., Pennsylvania State University, University Park
Parkin, Gary, University of Guelph
Patton, Thomas W., Montana Tech of The University of Montana
Pederson, Darryll T., University of Nebraska, Lincoln
Peters, Catherine A., Princeton University
Peterson, Eric W., Illinois State University
Peterson, Holly, Guilford College
Pettyjohn, Wayne, Oklahoma State University
Pfannkuch, Hans O., University of Minnesota, Twin Cities
Phillips, Fred M., New Mexico Institute of Mining and Technology
Pickup, Gillian E., Heriot-Watt University
Pierce, Suzanne A., University of Texas at Austin
Plankell, Eric T., University of Illinois, Urbana-Champaign
Pociask, Geoff, University of Illinois, Urbana-Champaign
Pohll, Greg, University of Nevada, Reno
Post, Vincent , Flinders University
Pradhanang, Soni M., University of Rhode Island
Prestegaard, Karen L., University of Maryland
Price, Rene, Florida International University
Puente-Muniz, Carlos Francisco, Universidad Autonoma de San Luis Potosi
Quinn, John, Argonne National Laboratory
Rains, Mark C., University of South Florida, Tampa
Rauch, Henry W., West Virginia University
Reese, Stuart O., Pennsylvania Bureau of Topographic & Geologic Survey
Reeve, Andrew S., University of Maine
Reichard, James S., Georgia Southern University
Reinfelder, Ying Fan, Rutgers, The State University of New Jersey
Reiten, Jon C., Montana Tech of The University of Montana
Remenda, Victoria H., Queen's University
Remson, Irwin, Stanford University
Reyes, Manuel, North Carolina Agricultural & Tech State University
Rice, Richard J., Illinois State Geological Survey
Rich, Thomas B., South Dakota Dept of Environment and Natural Resources
Riemersma, Peter E., Grand Valley State University
Rios-Sanchez, Miriam, Bemidji State University
Ritzi, Jr., Robert W., Wright State University
Roadcap, George S., Illinois State Water Survey
Robbins, Gary A., University of Connecticut
Robertson, Will, University of Waterloo
Robin, Michel R., University of Ottawa
Roman, Eric W., New Jersey Geological Survey
Romanowicz, Edwin A., Plattsburgh State University (SUNY)
Ronayne, Michael J., Colorado State University
Rose, Seth E., Georgia State University
Rostron, Benjamin J., University of Alberta
Rouleau, Alain, Universite du Quebec a Chicoutimi
Royo-Ochoa, Miguel, Universidad Autonoma de Chihuahua
Russo, Tess A., Pennsylvania State University, University Park
Ryan, Cathy, University of Calgary
Saffer, Demian M., Pennsylvania State University, University Park
Saint, Prem K., California State University, Fullerton
Salvage, Karen M., Binghamton University
Samuelson, Alan C., Ball State University
Sanders, Laura L., Northeastern Illinois University
Sanford, William E., Colorado State University
Sasowsky, Ira D., University of Akron
Scanlon, Bridget R., University of Texas at Austin, Jackson School of Geosciences
Scheibe, Timothy D., Pacific Northwest National Laboratory
Scheidt, Brian, Mineral Area College
Schincariol, Robert A., Western University
Schlosser, Peter, Columbia University
Schmitz, Darrel W., Mississippi State University
Schreiber, Madeline E., Virginia Polytechnic Institute & State University
Schueth, Christoph, Technische Universitaet Darmstadt

Schulmeister, Marcia K., Emporia State University
Schulze-Makuch, Dirk, Washington State University
Scott, Christopher A., University of Arizona
Sebol, Lesley, Colorado Geological Survey
Sedivy, Robert A., Argonne National Laboratory
Sendlein, Lyle V. A., University of Kentucky
Seramur, Keith C., Appalachian State University
Shang, Congxiao, University of East Anglia
Shaw, Glenn D., Montana Tech of the University of Montana
Sheldon, Amy L., SUNY, Geneseo
Shevenell, Lisa A., University of Nevada, Reno
Shim-Chim, Richard, New Jersey Geological Survey
Shimada, Jun, Kumamoto University
Sibray, Steven S., Unversity of Nebraska - Lincoln
Siegel, Donald I., Syracuse University
Simmons, Craig, Flinders University
Simpkins, William W., Iowa State University of Science & Technology
Singha, Kamini, Colorado School of Mines
Skalbeck, John D., University of Wisconsin, Parkside
Smith, Edward C., University of Illinois, Urbana-Champaign
Smith, Edward C., Illinois State Geological Survey
Smith, J. Leslie, University of British Columbia
Smith, James E., McMaster University
Smith, James E., University of Arizona
Smith, Karen, Argonne National Laboratory
Soll, Wendy E., Los Alamos National Laboratory
Solomon, Douglas K., University of Utah
Spangler, Daniel P., University of Florida
Spayd, Steven E., New Jersey Geological Survey
Spinelli, Glenn, New Mexico Institute of Mining and Technology
Springer, Abraham E., Northern Arizona University
Spruill, Richard K., East Carolina University
Staley, Andrew, Maryland Department of Natural Resources
Stephens, Daniel B., New Mexico Institute of Mining and Technology
Stewart, Mark T., University of South Florida, Tampa
Stillings, Lisa, University of Nevada, Reno
Stotler, Randy, University of Kansas
Strack, Otto D., University of Minnesota, Twin Cities
Sudicky, Edward A., University of Waterloo
Suen, C. J., California State University, Fresno
Sun, Hongbing, Rider University
Sutherland, Mary K., Montana Tech of The University of Montana
Swanson, Susan K., Beloit College
Tabidian, M. Ali, California State University, Northridge
Taboga, Karl, Wyoming State Geological Survey
Tauxe, John D., Oak Ridge National Laboratory
Tezcan, Levent, Hacettepe University
Therrien, Rene, Universite Laval
Thomason, Jason F., University of Illinois, Urbana-Champaign
Tick, Geoffrey, University of Alabama
Tidwell, Vincent C., New Mexico Institute of Mining and Technology
Tilton, Eric E., University of Colorado
Tipping, Robert, University of Minnesota
Toran, Laura, Temple University
Tóth, József, University of Alberta
Totsche, Kai U., Friedrich-Schiller-University Jena
Troy, Marleen, Wilkes University
Tyler, Scott W., University of Nevada, Reno
Unger, Andre, University of Waterloo
Upchurch, Sam B., University of South Florida, Tampa
Vacher, H. Leonard, University of South Florida, Tampa
Vaiden, Robert C., Illinois State Geological Survey
Van Der Hoven, Steve, Illinois State University
Van der Kamp, Garth, University of Waterloo
Veeger, Anne, University of Rhode Island
Veeger, Anne I., University of Rhode Island
Vengosh, Avner, Duke University
Vesper, Dorothy, West Virginia University
Vilcaez, Javier, Oklahoma State University
Wallace, Janae, Utah Geological Survey
Walton, Nick, University of Portsmouth
Wang, Dong, California State University, Fresno
Wanke, Heike, University of Namibia
Ward, James W., Angelo State University
Waren, Kirk B., Montana Tech of The University of Montana
Wassenaar, Len, University of Saskatchewan
Watson, David B., Oak Ridge National Laboratory
Weissmann, Gary, University of New Mexico
Welby, Charles W., North Carolina State University
Welhan, John A., University of Idaho
Welhan, John A., Idaho State University
Werner, Adrian , Flinders University
Wheatcraft, Steve, University of Nevada, Reno
Wheaton, John R., Montana Tech of the University of Montana
Whiting, Duane L., University of Utah
Whittemore, Donald O., University of Kansas
Wicks, Carol M., Louisiana State University
Widdowson, Mark A., Virginia Tech
Williams, Mark D., Pacific Northwest National Laboratory
Wilson, Alicia M., University of South Carolina

Wilson, John L., New Mexico Institute of Mining and Technology
Wilson, Lorne G., University of Arizona
Wilson, Steven D., Illinois State Water Survey
Wolaver, Brad, University of Texas at Austin
Wolfsberg, Andrew V., Los Alamos National Laboratory
Wood, Thomas R., University of Idaho
Yan, Eugene, Argonne National Laboratory
Yang, Changbing, University of Texas at Austin
Yang, Jianwen, University of Windsor
Yelderman, Jr., Joe C., Baylor University
Yidana, Sandow M., University of Ghana
Young, Tim, University of Illinois, Urbana-Champaign
Yüce, Galip, Hacettepe University
Zarnetske, Jay, Michigan State University
Zhan, Hongbin, Texas A&M University
Zhang, Pengfei, City College (CUNY)
Zhang, You-Kuan, University of Iowa
Zheng, Chunmiao, University of Alabama
Zhu, Junfeng, University of Kentucky
Zlotnik, Vitaly A., University of Nebraska, Lincoln
Zouhri, Lahcen, Institut Polytechnique LaSalle Beauvais (ex-IGAL)
Zreda, Marek G., University of Arizona
Özyurt, Nur N., Hacettepe University

Quantitative Hydrology
Bacon, Diana H., Pacific Northwest National Laboratory
Benson, David A., Colorado School of Mines
Bian, Aiguo, Texas A&M University, Kingsville
Birdsell, Kay H., Los Alamos National Laboratory
Borah, Deva K., Illinois State Water Survey
Carey, Anne E., Ohio State University
Carroll, Rosemary, University of Nevada, Reno
Chebana, Fateh, Universite du Quebec
Chen, Xun-Hong, Unversity of Nebraska - Lincoln
Covington, Matthew, University of Arkansas, Fayetteville
Danko, George, University of Nevada, Reno
Dingman, S. Lawrence, University of New Hampshire
Donovan, Joseph J., West Virginia University
Duaime, Terence E., Montana Tech of The University of Montana
Duckstein, Lucien, University of Arizona
Dymond, Randel, Virginia Tech
Falta, Ronald W., Clemson University
Fayer, Michael J., Pacific Northwest National Laboratory
Ferrand, Lin A., Graduate School of the City University of New York
Flores, Alejandro N., Boise State University
French, Mark A., New Jersey Geological Survey
Frind, Emil O., University of Waterloo
Garapati, Nagasree, University of Minnesota, Twin Cities
Gillham, Robert W., University of Waterloo
Hoffman, Jeffrey L., New Jersey Geological Survey
Holt, Robert M., University of Mississippi
Hubbart, Jason A., University of Missouri, Columbia
Hughes, Denis, Rhodes University
Kandiah, Ramanitharan, Central State University
Kiem, Anthony, University of Newcastle
Kirkham, Randy R., Pacific Northwest National Laboratory
Letsinger, Sally L., indiana University
Li, Dan, Boston University
Li, Liangping, South Dakota School of Mines & Technology
Loague, Keith, Stanford University
Looney, Brian, Clemson University
Maddock, III, Thomas, University of Arizona
Manda, Alex, East Carolina University
Martin-Hayden, James, University of Toledo
McCord, James T., New Mexico Institute of Mining and Technology
Meko, David M., University of Arizona
Michaud, Jene D., University of Hawai'i, Hilo
Moglen, Glenn, Virginia Tech
Neuman, Shlomo P., University of Arizona
Oostrom, Martinus, Pacific Northwest National Laboratory
Pacheco, Fernando A., Universidade de Trás-os-Montes e Alto Douro
Pangle, Luke, Georgia State University
Parashar, Rishi, University of Nevada, Reno
Park, Young-Jin, University of Waterloo
Perkins, Robert B., Portland State University
Pohll, Greg, University of Nevada, Reno
Puente, Carlos E., University of California, Davis
Quinn, John J., Argonne National Laboratory
Restrepo, Jorge I., Florida Atlantic University
Rudolph, David L., University of Waterloo
Salvucci, Guido D., Boston University
Schumer, Rina, University of Nevada, Reno
Sharp, Jr., John M., University of Texas at Austin
Sorooshian, Soroosh, University of Arizona
Springer, Everett P., Los Alamos National Laboratory
Stockton, Charles W., University of Arizona
Sukop, Michael, Florida International University
Szidarovszky, Ferenc, University of Arizona
Szilagyi, Jozsef, Unversity of Nebraska - Lincoln
Telyakovskiy, Aleksey, University of Nevada, Reno

Thorbjarnarson, Kathryn W., San Diego State University
Travis, Bryan J., Los Alamos National Laboratory
Verdon-Kidd, Danielle, University of Newcastle
Whitman, Brian E., Wilkes University
Williams, Gus T., Argonne National Laboratory
Yeh, Tian-Chyi J., University of Arizona
Zhang, Yong, University of Alabama

Surface Waters
Aitkenhead-Peterson, Jacqueline A., Texas A&M University
Anderson, Michelle, University of Montana Western
Bacon, Robert, Missouri Dept of Natural Resources
Baldini, James, Durham University
Bauer, Carl J., University of Arizona
Bearden, Rebecca A., Geological Survey of Alabama
Bevelhimer, Mark, Oak Ridge National Laboratory
Beyer, Patricia J., Bloomsburg University
Bhowmik, Nani G., Illinois State Water Survey
Blumentritt, Dylan J., SUNY Potsdam
Bogner, William C., Illinois State Water Survey
Cadol, Daniel, New Mexico Institute of Mining and Technology
Chandra, Sudeep, University of Nevada, Reno
Clark, Robert A., University of Arizona
Cosby, Jack, University of Virginia
D'Alpaos, Andrea, Università degli Studi di Padova
Davison, Leigh, Southern Cross University
Demchak, Jennifer, Mansfield University
Dennett, Keith E., University of Nevada, Reno
Du Charme, Charles, Missouri Dept of Natural Resources
Duan, Shuiwang, University of Maryland
Foroozesi, Jalal, Heriot-Watt University
Franz, Kristie, Iowa State University of Science & Technology
Frei, Allan, Hunter College (CUNY)
Goodrich, David C., University of Arizona
Grable, Judy, Valdosta State University
Gulliver, John S., University of Minnesota, Twin Cities
Gupta, Hoshin V., University of Arizona
Hamlet, Alan, University of Notre Dame
Harris, Randa R., University of West Georgia
Hawkins, R. B., University of Arizona
Helz, George, University of Maryland
Hester, Erich, Virginia Tech
Ince, Simon, University of Arizona
Johnston, K. R. Gina, California State University, Chico
Khosrowpanah, Shahram, University of Guam
Kindelman, Julie, University of Wisconsin, Parkside
Kisila, Ben O., University of Mary Washington
Knapp, H. Vernon, Illinois State Water Survey
Knight, Allen W., University of California, Davis
Kunza, Lisa, South Dakota School of Mines & Technology
Lancaster, Stephen, Oregon State University
Lansey, Kevin E., University of Arizona
Lisle, Thomas, Humboldt State University
Lund, Jay R., University of California, Davis
Maxwell, Reed M., Colorado School of Mines
Mayfield, Michael W., Appalachian State University
McGregor, Stuart W., Geological Survey of Alabama
McIsaac, Gregory F., University of Illinois, Urbana-Champaign
Mohrig, David, University of Texas at Austin
Noe, Garry, Virginia Wesleyan College
O'Neil, Patrick E., Geological Survey of Alabama
Price, Katie, Georgia State University
Rancan, Helen L., New Jersey Geological Survey
Richard, Gigi, Colorado Mesa University
Richmond, Marshall C., Pacific Northwest National Laboratory
Royer, Todd, Indiana University, Bloomington
Saito, Laurel, University of Nevada, Reno
Scott, Verne H., University of California, Davis
Shuttleworth, W. James, University of Arizona
Smerdon, Ernest T., University of Arizona
Smith, Laurence C., University of California, Los Angeles
Smith, Sean, University of Maine
Stieglitz, Marc, Georgia Institute of Technology
Strom, Kyle, Virginia Tech
Swanson, Sherman, University of Nevada, Reno
Troch, Peter A., University of Arizona
Valdes, Juan B., University of Arizona
Wampler, Peter J., Grand Valley State University
Washburne, James C., University of Arizona
White, Jeffrey, Indiana University, Bloomington
Wigmosta, Mark S., Pacific Northwest National Laboratory
Wilderman, Candie, Dickinson College
Wu, Chin, University of Wisconsin, Madison
Xia, Renjie, Illinois State Water Survey
Zollweg, James A., SUNY, The College at Brockport

Geohydrology
Allen, Diana M., Simon Fraser University
Andres, A. S., University of Delaware
Attinger, Sabine, Friedrich-Schiller-University Jena
Baedke, Steven J., James Madison University

Batlle-Aguilar, Jordi, University of Kansas
Beddows, Patricia A., Northwestern University
Bobst, Andrew L., Montana Tech of The University of Montana
Brookfield, Andrea, University of Kansas
Buddemeier, Robert W., University of Kansas
Burkart, Michael R., Iowa State University of Science & Technology
Castro, Maria Clara, University of Michigan
Cathles, Lawrence M., Cornell University
Chavez-Rodriguez, Adolfo, Universidad Autonoma de Chihuahua
Chormann, Jr., Frederick H., New Hampshire Geological Survey
Clair, Thomas A., Mount Allison University
Constantine, Jose, Cardiff University
Cooper, Clay, University of Nevada, Reno
Crews, Jeff, Missouri Dept of Natural Resources
Daanen, Ronnie, Alaska Division of Geological & Geophysical Surveys
De Luca, Domenico Antonio, Università di Torino
Dogwiler, Toby, Missouri State University
Dowd, John F., University of Georgia
Drake, Lon D., University of Iowa
Duley, James W., Missouri Dept of Natural Resources
Fogg, Graham E., University of California, Davis
Foley, Duncan, Pacific Lutheran University
Gamage, Kusali R., Austin Community College District
Gartner, Janette, Bentley University
Gierke, John S., Michigan Technological University
Haitjema, Hendrik M., Indiana University / Purdue University, Indianapolis
Hardy, Douglas R., University of Massachusetts, Amherst
Hong, Sung-ho, Murray State University
Hyndman, David W., Michigan State University
Khanbilvardi, Reza M., Graduate School of the City University of New York
Knight, Rosemary J., Stanford University
Land, Lewis, New Mexico Institute of Mining and Technology
Leap, Darrell I., Purdue University
Liu, Gaisheng, University of Kansas
Lovell, Mark D., Brigham Young University - Idaho
Lupankwa, Mlindelwa , Tshwane University of Technology
Mayer, Alex S., Michigan Technological University
McIntosh, Jennifer, University of Arizona
McKay, Larry D., University of Tennessee, Knoxville
McKenna, Thomas E., University of Delaware
Mount, Gregory, Indiana University of Pennsylvania
Ng, Crystal, University of Minnesota, Twin Cities
Nobes, David, University of Canterbury
Oshun, Jasper, Humboldt State University
Person, Mark A., New Mexico Institute of Mining and Technology
Rayne, Todd W., Hamilton College
Reboulet, Edward, University of Kansas
Rovey, Charles W., Missouri State University
Sargent, Kenneth A., Furman University
Sidle, Roy, Appalachian State University
Sushama, Laxmi, Universite du Quebec a Montreal
Thompson, Carol A., Tarleton State University
Torres, Raymond, University of South Carolina
White, Mark D., Pacific Northwest National Laboratory
Wilcox, Jeffrey D., University of North Carolina, Asheville
Zhang, Ye, University of Wyoming

SOIL SCIENCE
Soil Physics/Hydrology
Amoozegar, Aziz, North Carolina State University
Anderson, Stephen H., University of Missouri, Columbia
Arnone, John J., University of Nevada, Reno
Bader, Nicholas, Whitman College
Baker, John M., University of Minnesota, Twin Cities
Berli, Marcus, University of Nevada, Reno
Black, T. Andrew, University of British Columbia
Bland, William L., University of Wisconsin, Madison
Boast, Charles W., University of Illinois, Urbana-Champaign
Brown, Sandra, University of British Columbia
Burger, Martin, University of California, Davis
Caldwell, Todd, University of Texas at Austin
Casey, Francis, North Dakota State University
Cassel, Donald K., North Carolina State University
Chieng, Sietan, University of British Columbia
Cushman, John, Purdue University
Ellsworth, Timothy R., University of Illinois, Urbana-Champaign
Fermanich, Kevin J., University of Wisconsin, Green Bay
Feyereisen, Gary, University of Minnesota, Twin Cities
Flury, Markus, Washington State University
Fritton, Daniel D., Pennsylvania State University, University Park
Galbraith, John M., Virginia Polytechnic Institute & State University
Grattan, Stephen R., University of California, Davis
Grismer, Mark E., University of California, Davis
Groenevelt, Pieter H., University of Guelph
Gupta, Satish C., University of Minnesota, Twin Cities
Hook, James E., University of Georgia
Hopmans, Jan W., University of California, Davis
Horton, Robert, Iowa State University of Science & Technology
Hutson, John , Flinders University
Jawitz, James W., University of Florida

Johnson, Mark, University of British Columbia
Jones, Tim L., New Mexico State University, Las Cruces
Kakembo, Vincent, Nelson Mandela Metropolitan University
Kanemasu, Edward T., University of Georgia
Kirkham, Mary Beth, Kansas State University
Kitchen, Newell R., University of Missouri, Columbia
Kluitenberg, Gerard J., Kansas State University
Kung, King-Jau S., University of Wisconsin, Madison
Lal, Rattan, Ohio State University
Lourenco, Sergio, Cardiff University
Lowery, Birl, University of Wisconsin, Madison
McCoy, Edward L., Ohio State University
McDonald, Eric, University of Nevada, Reno
McInnes, Kevin J., Texas A&M University
Molz, Fred, Clemson University
Moncrief, John F., University of Minnesota, Twin Cities
Morgan, Cristine L., Texas A&M University
Mulla, David J., University of Minnesota, Twin Cities
Neely, Haly L., Texas A&M University
Nielsen, Donald R., University of California, Davis
Niu, Guo-Yue, University of Texas at Austin
Nkedi-Kizza, Peter, University of Florida
Norman, John M., University of Wisconsin, Madison
Novak, Michael D., University of British Columbia
Papendick, Robert I., Washington State University
Pasternack, Gregory B., University of California, Davis
Perfect, Edmund, University of Tennessee, Knoxville
Persaud, Naraine, Virginia Polytechnic Institute & State University
Radcliffe, David E., University of Georgia
Radke, Jerry K., Iowa State University of Science & Technology
Reece, Julia S., Texas A&M University
Ressler, Daniel E., Susquehanna University
Rogowski, Andrew S., Pennsylvania State University, University Park
Sammis, Theodore W., New Mexico State University, Las Cruces
Sanchez, Marcelo, Texas A&M University
Schumacher, Joseph, South Dakota State University
Schumacher, Thomas E., South Dakota State University
Selim, Hussein M., Louisiana State University
Simmons, F. William, University of Illinois, Urbana-Champaign
Spokas, Kurt, University of Minnesota, Twin Cities
Stone, Loyd, Kansas State University
Taylor, Donavon, University of Wisconsin, River Falls
Thomas, John, University of Florida
Turk, Judy, Stockton University
Venterea, Rodney T., University of Minnesota, Twin Cities
Verburg, Paul, University of Nevada, Reno
Verhoef, Anne, University of Reading
Warrick, Arthur W., University of Arizona
Welch, Steve M., Kansas State University
Wierenga, Peter J., University of Arizona
Wierenga, Peter J., University of Arizona
Wraith, Jon M., Montana State University
Yeh, Jim, University of Arizona

Soil Chemistry/Mineralogy
Adriano, Domy C., Virginia Polytechnic Institute & State University
Adriano, Domy C., University of Georgia
Ahmad, Abd Rashid, University of Malaya
Alley, Marcus M., Virginia Polytechnic Institute & State University
Appel, Christopher (Chip) S., California Polytechnic State University
Artiola, Janick F., University of Arizona
Baligar, V. C., Virginia Polytechnic Institute & State University
Barak, Phillip W., University of Wisconsin, Madison
Basta, Nicholas T., Ohio State University
Beegle, Douglas B., Pennsylvania State University, University Park
Bertsch, Paul M., University of Georgia
Blanchar, Robert W., University of Missouri, Columbia
Bleam, William F., University of Wisconsin, Madison
Bloom, Paul R., University of Minnesota, Twin Cities
Bly, Anthony G., South Dakota State University
Bomke, Arthur A., University of British Columbia
Bostick, Benjamin C., Columbia University
Breecker, Daniel O., University of Texas at Austin
Burke, Deborah S., Pacific Northwest National Laboratory
Casey, William H., University of California, Davis
Chirenje, Tait, Richard Stockton College of New Jersey
Chorover, Jon, University of Arizona
Clark, Joanna, University of Reading
Collins, Chris, University of Reading
Crouse, David A., North Carolina State University
Cullen, Murray, Southern Cross University
Curry, Joan E., University of Arizona
Dahlgran, Randy, University of California, Davis
Dixon, Joe B., Texas A&M University
Donohue, Stephen J., Virginia Polytechnic Institute & State University
Doolittle, James J., South Dakota State University
Dowdy, Robert H., University of Minnesota, Twin Cities
Dudley, Lynn M., Florida State University
Eckert, Donald J., Ohio State University
Edenborn, Harry, West Virginia University

Eick, Matthew J., Virginia Polytechnic Institute & State University
Eivazi, Frieda, University of Missouri, Columbia
Elzinga, Evert J., Rutgers, The State University of New Jersey, Newark
Engel, Richard E., Montana State University
Evangelou, V. P., Iowa State University of Science & Technology
Evanylo, Gregory K., Virginia Polytechnic Institute & State University
Feagley, Sam E., Texas A&M University
Fendorf, Scott E., Stanford University
Fernandez, Fabian G., University of Minnesota, Twin Cities
Fixen, Paul E., South Dakota State University
Gascho, Gary J., University of Georgia
Gaston, Lewis A., Louisiana State University
Gelderman, Ronald H., South Dakota State University
Gerwing, James R., South Dakota State University
Ginder-Vogel, Matt, University of Wisconsin, Madison
Goos, Robert J., North Dakota State University
Goyne, Keith W., University of Missouri, Columbia
Guertal, Elizabeth A., Auburn University
Han, Nizhou, Virginia Polytechnic Institute & State University
Harris, Jr., Willie G., University of Florida
Harsh, James B., Washington State University
Harter, Robert D., University of New Hampshire
Hassett, John J., University of Illinois, Urbana-Champaign
Havlin, John L., North Carolina State University
He, Zhenli, University of Florida
Heil, Dean, New Mexico State University, Las Cruces
Helmke, Philip A., University of Wisconsin, Madison
Hemzacek Laukant, Jean M., Northeastern Illinois University
Hesterberg, Dean L., North Carolina State University
Hettiarachchi, Ganga, Kansas State University
Hons, Frank M., Texas A&M University
Howe, Julie, Auburn University
Inskeep, William P., Montana State University
James, Bruce, University of Maryland
Jaouich, Alfred, Universite du Quebec a Montreal
Jardine, Philip M., Oak Ridge National Laboratory
Jones, Robert L., University of Illinois, Urbana-Champaign
Kabengi, Nadine, Georgia State University
Kaiser, Daniel E., University of Minnesota, Twin Cities
Kissel, David E., University of Georgia
Komarneni, Sridhar, Pennsylvania State University, University Park
Koskinen, William C., University of Minnesota, Twin Cities
Kuo, Shiou, Washington State University
Laird, David A., Iowa State University of Science & Technology
Lamb, John A., University of Minnesota, Twin Cities
Lee, Young Jae, Korea University
Li, Yuncong, University of Florida
Ma, Lena Q., University of Florida
Malzer, Gary L., University of Minnesota, Twin Cities
Marion, Giles, Desert Research Institute
McCaslin, Bobby D., New Mexico State University, Las Cruces
McFarland, Mark L., Texas A&M University
McLaughlin, Richard A., North Carolina State University
Miller, William P., University of Georgia
Mitchell, Charles C., Auburn University
Moore, Duane M., University of New Mexico
Moore, Jaroy, Texas A&M University
Mullins, Gregory L., Virginia Polytechnic Institute & State University
Mulvaney, Richard L., University of Illinois, Urbana-Champaign
Mylavarapu, S R., University of Florida
Myneni, Satish C B., Princeton University
Nair, Vimala D., University of Florida
O'Connor, George A., University of Florida
Odom, John W., Auburn University
Olson, Kenneth R., University of Illinois, Urbana-Champaign
Pagliari, Paulo H., University of Minnesota, Twin Cities
Peck, Theodore R., University of Illinois, Urbana-Champaign
Peryea, Frank J., Washington State University
Pierzynski, Gary M., Kansas State University
Plank, Owen C., University of Georgia
Provin, Tony L., Texas A&M University
Quade, Jay, University of Arizona
Rehm, George W., University of Minnesota, Twin Cities
Reneau, Raymond B., Virginia Polytechnic Institute & State University
Robarge, Wayne P., North Carolina State University
Rochette, Elizabeth A., University of New Hampshire
Rosen, Carl J., University of Minnesota, Twin Cities
Roy, William R., Illinois State Geological Survey
Russelle, Michael P., University of Minnesota, Twin Cities
Schmitt, Michael A., University of Minnesota, Twin Cities
Schwab, Paul, Texas A&M University
Segars, William P., University of Georgia
Shuman, Larry M., University of Georgia
Siebe Grabach, Christina D., Universidad Nacional Autonoma de Mexico
Silveira, Maria, University of Florida
Sims, Albert L., University of Minnesota, Twin Cities
Smyth, Thomas J., North Carolina State University
Spalding, Brian P., Oak Ridge National Laboratory
Strawn, Daniel G., University of Idaho
Stucki, Joseph W., University of Illinois, Urbana-Champaign

Sullivan, Leigh, Southern Cross University
Tatabatai, M. A., Iowa State University of Science & Technology
Thien, Steve J., Kansas State University
Toner, Brandy M., University of Minnesota, Twin Cities
Toor, Gurpal, University of Florida
Touchton, Joseph T., Auburn University
Trumbore, Susan E., University of California, Irvine
Wang, Jim, Louisiana State University
Werts, Scott P., Winthrop University
Wood, Charles W., Auburn University
Woodard, Howard J., South Dakota State University
Wright, Alan, University of Florida
Zelazny, Lucian W., Virginia Polytechnic Institute & State University

Pedology/Classification/Morphology

Anderson, James L., University of Minnesota, Twin Cities
Baker, James C., Virginia Polytechnic Institute & State University
Barrett, Linda R., University of Akron
Bell, James C., University of Minnesota, Twin Cities
Bigham, Jerry M., Ohio State University
Birkeland, Peter W., University of Colorado
Buck, Brenda J., University of Montana Western
Buck, Brenda J., University of Nevada, Las Vegas
Burras, Lee, Iowa State University of Science & Technology
Calhoun, Frank G., Ohio State University
Caudill, Michael R., Hocking College
Ciolkosz, Edward J., Pennsylvania State University, University Park
Collins, Mary E., University of Florida
Cooper, Terence H., University of Minnesota, Twin Cities
Darmody, Robert G., University of Illinois, Urbana-Champaign
Daugherty, LeRoy A., New Mexico State University, Las Cruces
Dere, Ashlee L., University of Nebraska at Omaha
Evans, Barry M., Pennsylvania State University, University Park
Follmer, Leon R., Illinois State Geological Survey
Frederick, Holly, Wilkes University
Hallmark, Charles T., Texas A&M University
Heck, Richard, University of Guelph
Hoover, Michael T., North Carolina State University
Hopkins, David G., North Dakota State University
Jacobs, Peter, University of Wisconsin, Whitewater
Jelinski, Nicolas, University of Minnesota, Twin Cities
Johnson-Maynard, Jodi, University of Idaho
Kleiss, Harold J., North Carolina State University
Kuzila, Mark S., Unversity of Nebraska - Lincoln
Lavkulich, Leslie M., University of British Columbia
Lemme, Gary D., South Dakota State University
Lindbo, David, North Carolina State University
Madison, Frederick W., University of Wisconsin, Madison
Malo, Douglas D., South Dakota State University
Mbila, Monday O., Alabama A&M University
McDaniel, Paul A., University of Idaho
McDonald, Eric, Desert Research Institute
McFadden, Leslie M., University of New Mexico
McSweeney, Kevin, University of Wisconsin, Madison
Miles, Randall J., University of Missouri, Columbia
Miller, Douglas A., Pennsylvania State University, University Park
Montagne, Cliff, Montana State University
Nater, Edward A., University of Minnesota, Twin Cities
Nielsen, Gerald A., Montana State University
Nordt, Lee C., Baylor University
Paz Gonzalez, Antonio, Coruna University
Petersen, Gary W., Pennsylvania State University, University Park
Post, Donald F., University of Arizona
Ransom, Mickey D., Kansas State University
Rice, Thomas J., California Polytechnic State University
Rocque, David, Dept of Agriculture, Conservation, and Forestry
Runge, Edward C. A., Texas A&M University
Ryder, Roy, University of South Alabama
Sandor, Jonathan A., Iowa State University of Science & Technology
Schardt, Lawrence A., Pennsylvania State University, University Park
Schmid, Ginger, Minnesota State University
Shaw, Joey N., Auburn University
Slater, Brian K., Ohio State University
Taboada Castro, Maria T., Coruna University
Tabor, Neil J., Southern Methodist University
Thomas, Pamela J., Virginia Polytechnic Institute & State University
Thompson, Michael L., Iowa State University of Science & Technology
Tyler, E. Jerry, University of Wisconsin, Madison
Vepraskas, Michael J., North Carolina State University
West, Larry T., University of Georgia
Yoo, Kyungsoo, University of Minnesota, Twin Cities

Forest Soils/Rangelands/Wetlands

Amthor, Jeff, Oak Ridge National Laboratory
Balster, Nick J., University of Wisconsin, Madison
Bauder, James W., Montana State University
Biondi, Franco, University of Nevada, Reno
Black, Bryan A., University of Texas at Austin
Bockheim, James G., University of Wisconsin, Madison
Broome, Stephen W., North Carolina State University

Chambers, Jeanne, University of Nevada, Reno
Clark, Mark W., University of Florida
Clark, Melissa, Indiana University, Bloomington
Comerford, Nicholas B., University of Florida
David, Mark B., University of Illinois, Urbana-Champaign
Dietze, Michael, Boston University
Ferris, Dawn, Ohio State University
Fick, Walter H., Kansas State University
Franz, Eldon H., Washington State University
Gunderson, Lance, Emory University
Hallock, Brent G., California Polytechnic State University
Hook, Paul B., Montana State University
Inglett, Patrick, University of Florida
Krzic, Maja, University of British Columbia
Laingen, Christopher R., Eastern Illinois University
Meretsky, Vicky J., Indiana University, Bloomington
Miner, James J., University of Illinois
O'Neill, Patrick M., Louisiana State University
Osborne, Todd, University of Florida
Owensby, Clenton E., Kansas State University
Peres, Carlos, University of East Anglia
Posler, Gerry L., Kansas State University
Reddy, K R., University of Florida
Rickerl, Dianne H., South Dakota State University
Riha, Susan, Cornell University
Robinson, Steve, University of Reading
Senock, Randy S., California State University, Chico
Smalley, Glendon W., Sewanee: University of the South
Smith, C. Ken, Sewanee: University of the South
Specht, Alison, Southern Cross University
Taskey, Ronald D., California Polytechnic State University
Torreano, Scott, Sewanee: University of the South
Turk, Judith , Richard Stockton College of New Jersey
Wegner, John, Emory University

Soil Biology/Biochemistry

Allan, Deborah L., University of Minnesota, Twin Cities
Armstrong, Felicia P., Youngstown State University
Balser, Teri C., University of Wisconsin, Madison
Berg, Jr., Robert K., South Dakota State University
Berry, Duane F., Virginia Polytechnic Institute & State University
Bezdicek, David F., Washington State University
Bird, Jeffrey, Queens College (CUNY)
Bleakley, Bruce H., South Dakota State University
Blum, Linda K., University of Virginia
Bollag, Jean-Marc, Pennsylvania State University, University Park
Breitenbeck, Gary A., Louisiana State University
Burlage, Robert S., Oak Ridge National Laboratory
Chanway, Christopher, University of British Columbia
Cheng, H. H., University of Minnesota, Twin Cities
Chorover, Jonathan, University of Arizona
Clay, David E., South Dakota State University
Collins, Chris, University of Reading
Crozier, Carl, North Carolina State University
Davenport, Joan R., Washington State University
Dick, Richard P., Ohio State University
Dick, Warren A., Ohio State University
Dunfield, Kari, University of Guelph
Feng, Yucheng, Auburn University
Gauthier, Paul, Princeton University
Gentry, Terry, Texas A&M University
Gerba, Charles P., University of Arizona
Gilliam, James W., North Carolina State University
Grace, Peter R., Queensland University of Technology
Graham, Jr., James H., University of Florida
Graves, Alexandria, North Carolina State University
Grayston, Sue, University of British Columbia
Gutknecht, Jessica L., University of Minnesota, Twin Cities
Hagedorn, Charles, Virginia Polytechnic Institute & State University
Harris, Glendon H., University of Georgia
Harris, Robin F., University of Wisconsin, Madison
Hartel, Peter G., University of Georgia
Hickey, William J., University of Wisconsin, Madison
Hoyt, Greg D., North Carolina State University
Hsiao, Theodore C., University of California, Davis
Ishii, Satoshi, University of Minnesota, Twin Cities
Israel, Daniel W., North Carolina State University
Jastrow, Julie D., Argonne National Laboratory
Kennedy, Ann C., Washington State University
Knudsen, Guy, University of Idaho
Lindemann, William C., New Mexico State University, Las Cruces
Matson, Pamela A., Stanford University
Miller, Raymond M., Argonne National Laboratory
Molina, Jean A., University of Minnesota, Twin Cities
Moorhead, Kevin K., University of North Carolina, Asheville
Morra, Matthew J., University of Idaho
Ogram, Andrew V., University of Florida
Osmond, Deanna L., North Carolina State University
Palumbo, Tony V., Oak Ridge National Laboratory
Pan, William L., Washington State University

Parker, David B., West Texas A&M University
Peacock, Caroline, University of Leeds
Phelps, Tommy J., Oak Ridge National Laboratory
Plante, Alain, University of Pennsylvania
Prescott, Cindy, University of British Columbia
Rice, Chuck W., Kansas State University
Ruehr, Thomas A., California Polytechnic State University
Rutherford, Michael P., Sir Wilfred Grenfell College
Sadowsky, Michael J., University of Minnesota, Twin Cities
Scheer, Clemens, Queensland University of Technology
Shaw, Liz, University of Reading
Shi, Wei, North Carolina State University
Silva, Lucas C., University of California, Davis
Simard, Suzanne, University of British Columbia
Smith, Jeffery L., Washington State University
Somenhally, Anil, Texas A&M University
Stevens, Robert G., Washington State University
Tolhurst, Trevor, University of East Anglia
Torrents, Alba, University of Maryland
Voroney, R. Paul, University of Guelph
Wagger, Michael G., North Carolina State University
Wilkie, Ann C., University of Florida

Paleopedology/Archeology
Beck, Colleen M., Desert Research Institute
Busacca, Alan J., Washington State University
Driese, Steven G., Baylor University
Driese, Steven, University of Tennessee, Knoxville
Follmer, Leon R., University of Illinois, Urbana-Champaign
Herrmann, Edward W., Indiana University, Bloomington
Irmis, Randall B., University of Utah
Monger, H. C., New Mexico State University, Las Cruces

Other Soil Science
Adamsen, Floyd, University of Arizona
Adee, Eric, Kansas State University
Aiken, Robert, Kansas State University
Beatty, Susan W., University of Colorado
Bell, Brian, University of Glasgow
Berg, Peter, University of Virginia
Bundy, Larry G., University of Wisconsin, Madison
Cabrera, Miguel L., University of Georgia
Cambardella, Cynthia, Iowa State University of Science & Technology
Ciampitti, Ignacio, Kansas State University
Claassen, Mark, Kansas State University
Coleman, Tommy L., Alabama A&M University
Cook, Joseph P., Arizona Geological Survey
Cramer, Gary, Kansas State University
Cruse, Richard M., Iowa State University of Science & Technology
Daroub, Samira H., University of Florida
Dingus, Delmar D., California Polytechnic State University
Dormaar, John, University of Lethbridge
Drescher, Andrew, University of Minnesota, Twin Cities
Duncan, Stewart, Kansas State University
Eberle, Bill, Kansas State University
Ebinger, Michael H., Los Alamos National Laboratory
Ehler, Stan, Kansas State University
Ferre, Paul (Ty), University of Arizona
Fjell, Dale, Kansas State University
Flores-Delgadillo, Maria L., Universidad Nacional Autonoma de Mexico
Flores-Roman, David, Universidad Nacional Autonoma de Mexico
Fritz, Allan, Kansas State University
Gordon, Barney, Kansas State University
Goss, Michael J., University of Guelph
Haag, Lucas, Kansas State University
Hall, III, John R., Virginia Polytechnic Institute & State University
Halverson, Larry, Iowa State University of Science & Technology
Henning, Stanley J., Iowa State University of Science & Technology
Hernandez-Silva, Gilberto, Universidad Nacional Autonoma de Mexico
Hochmuth, George J., University of Florida
Holman, John, Kansas State University
Hopmans, Jan W., University of California, Davis
Houlton, Ben, University of California, Davis
Jacobsen, Jeffrey S., Montana State University
Janssen, Keith, Kansas State University
Jasoni, Richard, Desert Research Institute
Johnson, Arthur H., University of Pennsylvania
Johnson, Jane M., University of Minnesota, Twin Cities
Jones, Julia A., Oregon State University
Jugulam, Mithila, Kansas State University
Karkanis, Pano G., University of Lethbridge
Karlen, Douglas L., Iowa State University of Science & Technology
Kaspar, Thomas A., Iowa State University of Science & Technology
Keeney, Dennis R., Iowa State University of Science & Technology
Kelling, Keith A., University of Wisconsin, Madison
Killorn, Randy J., Iowa State University of Science & Technology
Kohl, Robert, South Dakota State University
Kolka, Randall K., University of Minnesota, Twin Cities
Kusssow, Wayne R., University of Wisconsin, Madison
Laboski, Carrie A., University of Wisconsin, Madison
Landschoot, Peter J., Pennsylvania State University, University Park

Lauzon, John, University of Guelph
Liang, George, Kansas State University
Liebens, Johan, University of West Florida
Lindsey, Michal, Louisiana State University
Loutkova, Klavdia Oleschko, Universidad Nacional Autonoma de Mexico
Loynachan, Thomas E., Iowa State University of Science & Technology
Mackowiak, Cheryl, University of Florida
Mallarino, Antonio W., Iowa State University of Science & Technology
Mengel, David, Kansas State University
Miller, Gerald A., Iowa State University of Science & Technology
Miller, Murray H., University of Guelph
Mills, Aaron L., University of Virginia
Min, Doo-Hong, Kansas State University
Moorberg, Colby, Kansas State University
Mooreman, Thomas B., Iowa State University of Science & Technology
Moran, Susan, University of Arizona
Morgan, Kelly, University of Florida
Morris, Geoffrey, Kansas State University
Mueller, Raymond G., Richard Stockton College of New Jersey
Nelson, Nathan, Kansas State University
Norman, John M., University of Wisconsin, Madison
Nyhan, John W., Los Alamos National Laboratory
O'Halloran, Ivan, University of Guelph
Obour, Augustine, Kansas State University
Obreza, Thomas A., University of Florida
Palacios-Mayorga, Sergio, Universidad Nacional Autonoma de Mexico
Pedersen, Joel A., University of Wisconsin, Madison
Perumal, Ram, Kansas State University
Peterson, Dallas, Kansas State University
Picardal, Flynn W., Indiana University, Bloomington
Polito, Thomas A., Iowa State University of Science & Technology
Powell, J. Mark, University of Wisconsin, Madison
Prasad, Vara , Kansas State University
Presley, DeAnn, Kansas State University
Raczkowski, Charles, North Carolina Agricultural & Tech State University
Randall, Gyles W., University of Minnesota, Twin Cities
Rasmussen, Craig, University of Arizona
Rechcigl, John E., University of Florida
Reddy, Gudigopuram B., North Carolina Agricultural & Tech State University
Reddy, M. R., North Carolina Agricultural & Tech State University
Regehr, David, Kansas State University
Rice, Pamela J., University of Minnesota, Twin Cities
Rolston, Dennis E., University of California, Davis
Roozeboom, Kraig, Kansas State University
Roth, Gregory W., Pennsylvania State University, University Park
Ruark, Matthew D., University of Wisconsin, Madison
Ruiz-Diaz, Dorivar, Kansas State University
Santos, Eduardo, Kansas State University
Sartain, Jerry B., University of Florida
Sassenrath, Gretchen, Kansas State University
Schaap, Marcel, University of Arizona
Schafer, Jr., John W., Iowa State University of Science & Technology
Schapaugh, Bill T., Kansas State University
Schlegel, Alan, Kansas State University
Schumann, Arnold W., University of Florida
Sherwood, William C., James Madison University
Shoup, Doug, Kansas State University
Shroyer, Jim, Kansas State University
Shuford, James W., Alabama A&M University
Silvertooth, Jeffrey C., University of Arizona
Smith, Terry L., California Polytechnic State University
Soldat, Douglas J., University of Wisconsin, Madison
Stahlman, Phillip, Kansas State University
Stapleton, Michael G., Slippery Rock University
Steenhuis, Tammo S., Cornell University
Strock, Jeffrey S., University of Minnesota, Twin Cities
Stubler, Craig, California Polytechnic State University
Sweeny, Daniel, Kansas State University
Szecsody, James E., Pacific Northwest National Laboratory
Tesso, Tesfaye, Kansas State University
Thompson, Curtis, Kansas State University
Tomlinson, Peter, Kansas State University
Vanderlip, Richard, Kansas State University
Voss, Regis D., Iowa State University of Science & Technology
Walworth, James, University of Arizona
Whitney, D.A., Kansas State University
Wilson, P. Christopher, University of Florida
Zhang, Guorong, Kansas State University

ENGINEERING GEOLOGY
General Engineering Geology
Ebrahim A., University of Tabriz
Abdalla, Salah B., University of Khartoum
Acevedo-Arroyo, Jose Refugio, Universidad Autonoma de San Luis Potosi
Achampong, Francis, University of Ghana
Adams, Herbert G., California State University, Northridge
Adeyemi, G. O., University of Ibadan
Aimone-Martin, Cathrine T., New Mexico Institute of Mining and Technology
Alao, D. A., University of Ilorin
Andre-Obayanju, Tomilola, University of Benin

Axelbaum, Richard, Washington University
Aydin, Adnan, University of Mississippi
Bancroft, John C., University of Calgary
Baptista, Joana, University of Newcastle Upon Tyne
Bauer, R. A., University of Illinois, Urbana-Champaign
Bell, David, University of Canterbury
Bell, John W., University of Nevada, Reno
Bennet, Brett, University of Kansas
Berry, Karen, Colorado Geological Survey
Beukelman, Gregg, Utah Geological Survey
Biswas, Pratim, Washington University
Bonetto, Sabrina Maria Rita, Università di Torino
Bower, Kathleen M., Eastern Illinois University
Bowman, Steve D., Utah Geological Survey
Brabham, Peter, University of Wales
Brady, Roland H., California State University, Fresno
Brand, Patrick, California Geological Survey
Branum, David, California Geological Survey
Brunkal, Holly, Western State Colorado University
Brunton, George D., University of Mississippi
Buchanan, George, Montgomery County Community College
Burns, Bill, Oregon Dept of Geology & Mineral Industries
Burns, Scott F., Portland State University
Buscheck, Thomas A., Lawrence Livermore National Laboratory
Carlson, Jill, Colorado Geological Survey
Carney, Theodore C., Los Alamos National Laboratory
Caron, Olivier J., University of Illinois, Urbana-Champaign
Carr, James R., University of Nevada, Reno
Case, William F., Utah Geological Survey
Castleton, Jessica, Utah Geological Survey
Cetindag, Bahattin, Firat University
CHEGBELEH, Larry-Pax, University of Ghana
Clark, H. C., Rice University
Daanen, Ronald P., Division of Geological & Geophysical Surveys
Davenport, Cliff, California Geological Survey
Davie, Colin, University of Newcastle Upon Tyne
Davies, David, Heriot-Watt University
Dawson, Tim, California Geological Survey
Delattre, Marc, California Geological Survey
dePolo, Craig M., University of Nevada
Dick, Jeffrey C., Youngstown State University
Doheny, Edward L., University of Pennsylvania
Doherty, Kevin, California Geological Survey
DuRoss, Christopher B., Utah Geological Survey
Durucan, Sevket, Imperial College
Dusseault, Maurice B., University of Waterloo
Eberhardt, Erik, University of British Columbia
Edil, Tuncer B., University of Wisconsin, Madison
Elia, Gaetano, University of Newcastle Upon Tyne
Ellecosta, Peter , Technische Universitaet Muenchen
Erickson, Ben, Utah Geological Survey
Evans, Stephen G., University of Waterloo
Eversoll, Duane A., Unversity of Nebraska - Lincoln
Falls, Jim, California Geological Survey
Ferriz, Horacio, California State University, Stanislaus
Floris, Mario, Università degli Studi di Padova
Fournier, Benoit, Universite Laval
Frailey, Scott M., Illinois State Geological Survey
Fratta, Dante, University of Wisconsin, Madison
Fuller, Michael, California Geological Survey
Galgaro, Antonio, Università degli Studi di Padova
Gasparini, Nicole, Tulane University
Giraud, Richard E., Utah Geological Survey
Gould, Alexander I., Division of Geological & Geophysical Surveys
Greene, Brian M., Youngstown State University
Gretener, Peter E., University of Calgary
Grimley, David A., University of Illinois, Urbana-Champaign
Guiterrez, Carlos, California Geological Survey
Hall, Jean, University of Newcastle Upon Tyne
Haneberg, William, New Mexico Institute of Mining and Technology
Harris, Will, California Geological Survey
Hasan, Syed E., University of Missouri-Kansas City
Haydon, Wayne, California Geological Survey
Hayhurst, Cheryl, California Geological Survey
Hencher, Steve, University of Leeds
Henika, William S., Virginia Polytechnic Institute & State University
Hernandez, Janis, California Geological Survey
Higgins, Jerry D., Colorado School of Mines
Ho, I-Hsuan, University of North Dakota
Holland, Peter, California Geological Survey
Holzer, Thomas, Stanford University
Horns, Daniel, Utah Valley University
Hubbard, Trent, Alaska Division of Geological & Geophysical Surveys
Hudec, Peter P., University of Windsor
Ibrahim, Ahmad Tajuddin Hj, University of Malaya
Ige, O. O., University of Ilorin
Irvine, Pamela J., California Geological Survey
Jamaluddin, Tajul Anuar, University of Malaya
Jo, Ho Young, Korea University
Johnpeer, Gary D., Cerritos College

Johnson, Sarah E., Northern Kentucky University
Johnson, William P., University of Utah
Jones, Larry Allan, Los Alamos National Laboratory
Joyce, James, University of Puerto Rico
Kantzas, Apostolos, University of Calgary
Karanfil, Tanju, Clemson University
Katzenstein, Kurt W., South Dakota School of Mines & Technology
Kavanaugh, Jeffrey, University of Alberta
Knapp, Richard B., Lawrence Livermore National Laboratory
Knizek, Martin, Masaryk University
Knudsen, Tyler R., Utah Geological Survey
Korre, Anna, Imperial College
Kreylos, Oliver, University of California, Davis
Krohn, James, Los Angeles Pierce College
Kudlac, John J., Point Park University
Lancaster, Jeremy, California Geological Survey
Likos, William J., University of Wisconsin, Madison
Linares, Rogelio, Universitat Autonoma de Barcelona
Lindsay, Donald, California Geological Survey
Lindsey, Kassandra, Colorado Geological Survey
Linn, Rodman, Los Alamos National Laboratory
Locat, Jacques E., Universite Laval
Lokau, Katja, Technische Universitaet Muenchen
Longstreth, David, California Geological Survey
Lorinczi, Piroska, University of Leeds
Lovekin, Jonathan, Colorado Geological Survey
Lund, William R., Utah Geological Survey
Lupogo, Keneth, University of Dar es Salaam
Madrigal-Rubio, Rafael, Universidad Autonoma de Chihuahua
Mandrone, Giuseppe, Università di Torino
Manson, Mike, California Geological Survey
Mareschal, Maxime, California Geological Survey
Marshall, Gerald, California Geological Survey
Martel, Stephen J., University of Hawai'i, Manoa
Martin, Beth, Washington University
Masek, Ondrej, Edinburgh University
Matter, Juerg M., University of Southampton
McCoy, Kevin, Colorado Geological Survey
McCrink, Timothy P., California Geological Survey
McDonald, Gregory N., Utah Geological Survey
McKean, Adam, Utah Geological Survey
McMahon, Katherine, University of Wisconsin, Madison
Mena-Zambrano, Teodulo, Universidad Autonoma de Chihuahua
Merifield, Paul M., University of California, Los Angeles
Merritt, Andrew, University of Plymouth
Mills, Jon, University of Newcastle Upon Tyne
Moeglin, Thomas D., Missouri State University
Mogilevskaya, Sonia, University of Minnesota, Twin Cities
Moore, Jeffrey, University of Utah
Morgan, Terrance L., Los Alamos National Laboratory
Nickmann, Marion, Technische Universitaet Muenchen
Nicot, Jean-Philippe, University of Texas at Austin, Jackson School of Geosciences
Niemann, William L., Marshall University
Nieto, Alberto S., University of Illinois, Urbana-Champaign
O'Rourke, Thomas D., Cornell University
Ogunsanwo, O., University of Ilorin
Olson, Brian , California Geological Survey
Origlia, Hector D., Universidad Nacional de Rio Cuarto
Oswald, John, California Geological Survey
Oyediran, I. A., University of Ibadan
Pamukcu, Alya, Princeton University
Patrick, David M., University of Southern Mississippi
Paysen-Petersen, Lukas, Technische Universitaet Muenchen
Pennuto, Christopher, SUNY, Buffalo
Perez, Florante, California Geological Survey
Perret, Didier, Universite du Quebec
Pestrong, Raymond, San Francisco State University
Phillips, Andrew C., University of Illinois, Urbana-Champaign
Pipkin, Bernard W., University of Southern California
Pluhar, Chris, California State University, Fresno
Poeter, Eileen P., Colorado School of Mines
Potter, Kenneth, University of Wisconsin, Madison
Poulton, Mary M., University of Arizona
Poulton, Mary, University of Arizona
Prevost, Jean-Herve, Princeton University
Pridmore, Cindy L., California Geological Survey
Rahn, Perry H., South Dakota School of Mines & Technology
Raj, John K., University of Malaya
Ramelli, Alan R., University of Nevada
Ramirez, Abelardo L., Lawrence Livermore National Laboratory
Reynolds, Steven, California Geological Survey
Rockaway, John D., Northern Kentucky University
Roffers, Pete, California Geological Survey
Roggenthen, William M., South Dakota School of Mines & Technology
Rosinski, Anne, California Geological Survey
Rubin, Ron, California Geological Survey
Santi, Paul M., Colorado School of Mines
Sass, Ingo, Technische Universitaet Darmstadt
Savigny, K. Wayne, University of British Columbia
Sawyer, J. F., South Dakota School of Mines & Technology

Schiff, Sherry L., University of Waterloo
Seitz, Gordon, California Geological Survey
Sellmeier, Bettina, Technische Universitaet Muenchen
Shakoor, Abdul, Kent State University
Short, William, California Geological Survey
Silva, Michael A., California Geological Survey
Song, Lin-Ping, University of British Columbia
Staub, William P., Oak Ridge National Laboratory
Stead, Douglas, Simon Fraser University
Stetler, Larry D., South Dakota School of Mines & Technology
Stevens, De Anne S., Alaska Division of Geological & Geophysical Surveys
Stohr, Christopher J., Illinois State Geological Survey
Su, Wen-June, Illinois State Geological Survey
Swanson, Brian, California Geological Survey
Thomas, Mark, University of Leeds
Thompson, Jim, California Geological Survey
Thornburg, Jennifer, California Geological Survey
Thuro, Kurosch, Technische Universitaet Muenchen
Tinjum, James M., University of Wisconsin, Madison
Toke', Nathan, Utah Valley University
Tompson, Andrew F., Lawrence Livermore National Laboratory
Turner, A. Keith, Colorado School of Mines
Urzua, Alfredo, Boston College
Villeneuve, Marlene C., University of Canterbury
Walton, Gabriel, Colorado School of Mines
Wang, Dongmei, University of North Dakota
Watts, Chester F., Radford University
Watts, Chester F., Virginia Polytechnic Institute & State University
Weber, Gerald E., University of California, Santa Cruz
Weigers, Mark, California Geological Survey
West, Olivia M., Oak Ridge National Laboratory
West, Terry R., Purdue University
White, Jonathan, Colorado Geological Survey
White, Owen L., University of Waterloo
Whorton, Erin N., Division of Geological & Geophysical Surveys
Wieser, Carola, Technische Universitaet Muenchen
Wilfing, Lisa, Technische Universitaet Muenchen
Wilkey, Patrick L., Argonne National Laboratory
Williams, Bruce A., Pacific Northwest National Laboratory
Williams, John W., San Jose State University
Wills, Christopher J., California Geological Survey
Wittke, Seth, Wyoming State Geological Survey
Wolken, Gabriel J., Division of Geological & Geophysical Surveys
Wu, Chin, University of Wisconsin, Madison
Yunwei, Sun, Lawrence Livermore National Laboratory
Zimmer, Valerie, University of Canterbury
Zimmerman, R. Eric, Argonne National Laboratory
Zyvoloski, George A., Los Alamos National Laboratory

Earthquake Engineering
Acosta, Jose G., Centro de Investigación Científica y de Ed Superior de Ensenada
Atkinson, Gail M., Carleton University
Heaton, Thomas H., California Institute of Technology
Huang, Moh J., California Geological Survey
Jamieson, J. Bruce, University of Calgary
Koehler, Rich, University of Nevada
Kutter, Bruce, University of California, Davis
Mendoza, Luis H., Centro de Investigación Científica y de Ed Superior de Ensenada
Michaels, Paul, Boise State University
Oommen, Thomas, Michigan Technological University
Reyes, Alfonso, Centro de Investigación Científica y de Ed Superior de Ensenada
Roberts, Gerald, Birkbeck College
Rowshandel, Badie, California Geological Survey
Wang, Yumei, Oregon Dept of Geology & Mineral Industries

Mining Tech/Extractive Metallurgy
Aguirre-Moriel, Socorro I., Universidad Autonoma de Chihuahua
Bryan, Christopher, Exeter University
Claassen, Johann, University of the Free State
Coggan, John, Exeter University
Demopoulos, George, McGill University
Dessureault, Sean, University of Arizona
Doyle, Fiona M., University of California, Berkeley
Drew, Robin A., McGill University
Duby, Paul F., Columbia University
Evans, James W., University of California, Berkeley
Feunstenau, Maurice, University of Nevada, Reno
Finch, James A., McGill University
Fuerstenau, Douglas W., University of California, Berkeley
Griswold, George B., New Mexico Institute of Mining and Technology
Gruzleski, John E., McGill University
Gundiler, Ibrahim H., New Mexico Institute of Mining & Technology
Guthrie, Roderick I., McGill University
Hasan, Mainul, McGill University
Hiskey, J. Brent, University of Arizona
Hurtado-De La Ree, Maria B., Centro de Estudios Superiores del Estado Sonora
Jeffrey, Kip, Exeter University
Jonas, John J., McGill University
Khan, Latif A., Illinois State Geological Survey
Kinabo, Crispin P., University of Dar es Salaam
Lee, Jaeheon, University of Arizona

Mendoza-Aguilar, Hector M., Universidad Autonoma de Chihuahua
Minor-Velazquez, Hector, Universidad Autonoma de Chihuahua
Moon, Charlie, Exeter University
Mucciardi, Frank, McGill University
Nesbitt, Carl, University of Nevada, Reno
Ruiz-Cisneros, David H., Universidad Autonoma de Chihuahua
Salazar-Avila, Arnulfo, Centro de Estudios Superiores del Estado Sonora
Sastry, Kalanadh V. S., University of California, Berkeley
Seal, Thom, University of Nevada, Reno
Smith, Gordon W., McGill University
Smith, Karl A., University of Minnesota, Twin Cities
Somasundaran, Ponisseril, Columbia University
Themelis, Nickolas J., Columbia University
Trevizo-Cano, Luis M., Universidad Autonoma de Chihuahua
Wheeler, Paul, Exeter University
Yue, Stephen, McGill University

Mining Engineering
MASSACCI, Prof. Giorgio, Universita di Cagliari
Bandopadhyay, Sukumar, University of Alaska, Fairbanks
Bessinger, Stephen, University of Utah
Bilodeau, Michel L., McGill University
Boshkov, Stefan H., Columbia University
Brune, Jürgen, Colorado School of Mines
Calizaya, Felipe, University of Utah
Chatterjee, Snehamoy, Michigan Technological University
Chen, Gang, University of Alaska, Fairbanks
Dagdelen, Kadri, Colorado School of Mines
Danko, George, University of Nevada, Reno
Dimitrakopoulos, Roussos, McGill University
Dinsmoor, John C., Los Alamos National Laboratory
Donovan, James, University of Utah
Eveleth, Robert W., New Mexico Institute of Mining & Technology
Foster, Patrick, Exeter University
Ganguli, Rajive, University of Alaska, Fairbanks
Gillis, James M., Michigan Technological University
Gongora-Jurado, Raul A., Centro de Estudios Superiores del Estado Sonora
Hafez, Sabry ., University of Alaska, Fairbanks
Hassani, Ferri, McGill University
Hemani, Ahmad, McGill University
Honkaer, Rick, University of Kentucky
Kalia, Hemendra N., Los Alamos National Laboratory
Kaunda, Rennie, Colorado School of Mines
Kennedy, Gareth, Exeter University
Kim, Eunhye, Colorado School of Mines
Kim, Kwangmin, University of Arizona
Kohler, Jeffery L., Pennsylvania State University, University Park
Kovach, Richard G., Los Alamos National Laboratory
Kuchta, Mark, Colorado School of Mines
Liu, Shimin, Pennsylvania State University, University Park
Lusk, Braden , University of Kentucky
MANCA, Prof. Pierpaolo P., Universita di Cagliari
Mayer, Ulrich, University of British Columbia
McCarter, Michael K., University of Utah
Meyer, Lewis, Exeter University
Miller, Hugh, Colorado School of Mines
Mitri, Hani, McGill University
Momayez, Moe, University of Arizona
Monteverde-Gutierrez, Gerardo, Centro de Estudios Superiores del Estado Sonora
Mossop, John W., McGill University
Mousset-Jones, Pierre, University of Nevada, Reno
Nabighian, Misac, Colorado School of Mines
Navarro, Ricardo, Universidad Nacional Autonoma de Mexico
Nelson, Michael G., University of Utah
Nelson, Priscilla, Colorado School of Mines
Nieto, Antonio, Pennsylvania State University, University Park
Nieto Antunez, Antonio, Universidad Nacional Autonoma de Mexico
Novak, Thomas, University of Kentucky
Petr, Vilem, Colorado School of Mines
Pokorny, Eugene W., Los Alamos National Laboratory
Rostami, Jamal, Pennsylvania State University, University Park
Silva-Castro, Jhon, University of Kentucky
Slistan-Grijalva, Angel, Centro de Estudios Superiores del Estado Sonora
Sottile, Jr., Joseph, University of Kentucky
Spangler, Eleanor, Alaska Division of Geological & Geophysical Surveys
Squelch, Andrew P., Curtin University
Tarshizi, Ebrahim, Michigan Technological University
Taylor, Danny L., University of Nevada, Reno
Tenorio, Victor, University of Arizona
Tharp, Thomas M., Purdue University
Vite-Picazo, Luis G., Centro de Estudios Superiores del Estado Sonora
Wala, Andrew M., University of Kentucky
Wane, Malcolm T., Columbia University
Wedding, William C., University of Kentucky
Wetherelt, Andrew, Exeter University
Whyatt, Jeffrey, University of Utah
Yegulalp, Tuncel M., Columbia University
Zavodni, Zavis, University of Utah
Zhang, Jinhong, University of Arizona
Zipf, Karl, Colorado School of Mines

Petroleum Engineering

Ahmed, Ramadan, University of Oklahoma
Alvarado, Vladimir, University of Wyoming
Bijeljic, Branko, Imperial College
Blasingame, Tom, Texas A&M University
Blunt, Martin J., Imperial College
Callard, Jeff, University of Oklahoma
Civan, Faruk, University of Oklahoma
Cooper, George A., University of California, Berkeley
Corbett, Patrick, Heriot-Watt University
Couples, Gary, Heriot-Watt University
Devegowda, Deepak, University of Oklahoma
Dreesen, Donald S., Los Alamos National Laboratory
El-Monier, Ilham, University of Oklahoma
Fahes, Mashhad, University of Oklahoma
Fishe, Quentin , University of Leeds
Gringarten, Alain, Imperial College
Jamili, Ahmad, University of Oklahoma
Jin, Guohai, Geological Survey of Alabama
Kadkhodai Ilkhchi, Ali, University of Tabriz
Kelkar, Sharad, Los Alamos National Laboratory
King, Peter, Imperial College
Knapp, Roy M., University of Oklahoma
Misra, Siddharth, University of Oklahoma
Moghanloo, Rouzbeh, University of Oklahoma
Muggeridge, Ann, Imperial College
Nikolinakou, Maria-Aikaterini, University of Texas at Austin
Oppong, Issac A., University of Ghana
Patzek, Tad W., University of California, Berkeley
Pournik, Maysam, University of Oklahoma
Rai, Chandra S., University of Oklahoma
Rieke, Herman H., University of Louisiana at Lafayette
Rose, Peter E., University of Utah
Sakhaee-Pour, Ahmad, University of Oklahoma
Shah, Subhash N., University of Oklahoma
Sharma, Suresh, University of Oklahoma
Somerville, James M., Heriot-Watt University
Sondergeld, Carl H., University of Oklahoma
Teodoriu, Catalin, University of Oklahoma
Todd, Adrian C., Heriot-Watt University
Vesovic, Velisa, Imperial College
Wang, Fred P., University of Texas at Austin
Wu, Xingru, University of Oklahoma
Zaman, Musharraf, University of Oklahoma

Rock Mechanics

Abousleiman, Younane, University of Oklahoma
Agioutantis, Zach , University of Kentucky
Archambault, Guy, Universite du Quebec a Chicoutimi
Asbury, Brian, Colorado School of Mines
Aslan, Yasemin, Firat University
Aughenbaugh, Nolan B., University of Mississippi
Barakat, Bassam, Institut Polytechnique LaSalle Beauvais (ex-IGAL)
Barzegari, Ghodrat, University of Tabriz
Bauer, Robert A., Illinois State Geological Survey
Blacic, James D., Los Alamos National Laboratory
Brahmi, Sadek, Institut Polytechnique LaSalle Beauvais (ex-IGAL)
Brake, Thomas L., Los Alamos National Laboratory
Brown, Donald W., Los Alamos National Laboratory
Chen, Rui, California Geological Survey
Cruden, David M., University of Alberta
Cundall, Peter A., University of Minnesota, Twin Cities
Daemen, Jaak, University of Nevada, Reno
Detournay, Emmanuel M., University of Minnesota, Twin Cities
Diederichs, Mark, Queen's University
Enderlin, Milton, Texas Christian University
Engelder, Terry, Pennsylvania State University, University Park
Ferrero, Anna Maria, Università di Torino
Germanovich, Leonid, Georgia Institute of Technology
Ghassemi, Ahmed, University of Oklahoma
Gordon, Robert B., Yale University
Gurocak, Zulfu, Firat University
Guzina, Bojan B., University of Minnesota, Twin Cities
Haimson, Bezalel C., University of Wisconsin, Madison
Hawkins, Stephen J., University of Southampton
Horowitz, Franklin G., Cornell University
Kanik, Mustafa, Firat University
Kemeny, John M., University of Arizona
Kulatilake, Pinnaduwa H. S. W., University of Arizona
Kuszmaul, Joel S., University of Mississippi
Käsling, Heiko, Technische Universitaet Muenchen
Labuz, Joseph F., University of Minnesota, Twin Cities
Logan, John M., University of Oregon
MacLaughlin, Mary M., Montana Tech of the University of Montana
Mariani, Elisabeth, University of Liverpool
McLennan, John, University of Utah
Meredith, Philip, University College London
Mojtabai, Navid, New Mexico Institute of Mining and Technology
Onyeobi, Tony U., University of Benin
Oravecz, Kalman I., New Mexico Institute of Mining and Technology

Ozbay, M. Ugur, Colorado School of Mines
Pariseau, William G., University of Utah
Perry , Kyle, University of Kentucky
Persson, Per-Anders, New Mexico Institute of Mining and Technology
Rempel, Alan W., University of Oregon
Roegiers, Jean-Claude, University of Oklahoma
Saeidi, Ali, Universite du Quebec a Chicoutimi
Sammonds, Peter, University College London
Sinha, Krishna P., University of Utah
Smutek, Claude, Universite de la Reunion
Swift, Robert P., Los Alamos National Laboratory
Trandafir, Aurel, University of Utah
Unrug, Kot F., University of Kentucky
Vinciguerra, Sergio, Leicester University
Vinciguerra, Sergio Carmelo, Università di Torino
Watters, Robert J., University of Nevada, Reno
Wijesinghe, Ananda M., Lawrence Livermore National Laboratory
Zimmerman, R. W., Imperial College

OCEANOGRAPHY

General Oceanography

Abernathy, Ryan, Columbia University
Allen, John, University of Portsmouth
Allen, Ted T., Jacksonville University
Alves, Tiego, University of Wales
Anand, Pallavi, The Open University
Arrigo, Kevin, Stanford University
Barros, Tony, Miami-Dade Community College (Wolfson Campus)
Becker, Janet M., University of Hawai'i, Manoa
Benotti, Mark J., Bentley University
Bidigare, Robert R., University of Hawai'i, Manoa
Bohaty, Steven, University of Southampton
Brandes, Jay, Georgia Institute of Technology
Brandon, Mark, The Open University
Brown, Erik T., University of Minnesota, Duluth
Buchanan, Donald G., San Bernardino Valley College
Busalacchi, Antonio, University of Maryland
Carlin, Joe, California State University, Fullerton
Chamberlin, Sean, Fullerton College
Chandler, Cyndy, Woods Hole Oceanographic Institution
Ciannelli, Lorenzo, Oregon State University
Cooney, Michael, University of Hawai'i, Manoa
Curewitz, Daniel, Syracuse University
Deen, Patricia A., Palomar College
Denton, George, University of South Florida
Dong, Charles, El Camino College
Eicken, Hajo, University of Alaska Fairbanks
Falkowski, Paul G., University of Hawai'i, Manoa
Field, Richard T., University of Delaware
Fritsen, Christian H., University of Nevada, Reno
Froelich, Philip, Florida State University
Galbraith, Eric, McGill University
Gerbi, Greg, Skidmore College
Gomez, Natalya, McGill University
Greenhow, Danielle, University of Southern Mississippi
Grossman, Walter, San Bernardino Valley College
Hale, Michelle, University of Portsmouth
Hepner, Tiffany, University of Texas at Austin, Jackson School of Geosciences
Hernes, Peter, University of California, Davis
Holland, Christina, University of Texas at Austin
Holliday, Joseph W., El Camino College
Hoover, Kenneth D., Jacksonville University
Hoyt, William H., University of Northern Colorado
Hughes-Clarke, John E., University of New Hampshire
Iams, William J., Sir Wilfred Grenfell College
Jackson, Karen E., Jacksonville University
Johnson, Ashanti, University of Texas, Arlington
Johnson, Helen, University of Oxford
Judkins, Heather L., Saint Petersburg College, Clearwater
Jung, Simon, Edinburgh University
Keller, Klaus, Pennsylvania State University, University Park
Kerr, Andrew, University of Wales
Kustka, Adam B., Rutgers, The State University of New Jersey, Newark
Kuwabara, James, City College of San Francisco
Laliberte, Elizabeth, University of Rhode Island
Lauderdale, Jonathan, University of Liverpool
Leach, Harry, University of Liverpool
Lear, Caroline, University of Wales
Ledbetter, Michael T., University of Arkansas at Little Rock
Lee, Alyce, Concord University
Lee, Stephen C., Los Angeles Pierce College
Leinen, Margaret, University of California, San Diego
Lenz, Petra H., University of Hawai'i, Manoa
Liu, Zhanfei, University of Texas at Austin
Ma, Yanxia, Louisiana State University
MacLeod, Chris, University of Wales
Maxwell, Arthur E., University of Texas at Austin
McCarthy, Daniel, Jacksonville University
McPhaden, Michael J., University of Washington
Moore, Dennis, University of Hawai'i, Manoa

Morris, Kalon, Saddleback Community College
Mosher, David C., University of New Hampshire
Muir, William, San Bernardino Valley College
Myers, Paul, University of Alberta
Noyes, Jim, El Camino College
Pellenbarg, Robert, College of the Desert
Peredo-Jaime, Jose I., Universidad Autonoma de Baja California Sur
Pike, Jenny, University of Wales
Polyak, Leonid, Ohio State University
Quan, Tracy, Oklahoma State University
Radulski, Robert, Southern Connecticut State University
Rappe, Michael S., University of Hawai'i, Manoa
Roesler, Collin, Bowdoin College
Roussenov, Vassil, University of Liverpool
Schlegel, Mary A., Millersville University
Schneider, Niklas, University of Hawai'i, Manoa
Schroeder, William W., Dauphin Island Sea Lab
Scott, Robert B., University of Texas at Austin
Seyfang, Gill, University of East Anglia
Small, Curtis, Jacksonville University
Spencer, Matthew, University of Liverpool
Steger, John M., Miami Dade College (Kendall Campus)
Stewart, Gillian, Queens College (CUNY)
Sullivan-Watts, Barbara K., University of Rhode Island
Swanson, R. L., SUNY, Stony Brook
Tausig, Heather, University of Massachusetts, Boston
Thomas, Megan D., United States Naval Academy
Thompson, LuAnne, University of Washington
Thomson, Richard, University of Victoria
Thurman, Harold V., Mt. San Antonio College
Tomkiewicz, Warren, Plymouth State University
Trujillo, Alan P., Palomar College
Tucker, Stevens P., Naval Postgraduate School
Ulanski, Stanley L., James Madison University
Veeramony, Jayaram, Mississippi State University
Venn, Cynthia, Bloomsburg University
Venti, Nicholas, University of Massachusetts, Amherst
Walker, Nan D., Louisiana State University
Wallace, William G., Graduate School of the City University of New York
Wheatcroft, Rob, Oregon State University
Wiberg, Patricia L., University of Virginia
Williams, Ric, University of Liverpool
Wiltshire, John C., University of Hawai'i, Manoa
Wolcott, Ray, Cuyamaca College
Wolff, George, University of Liverpool
Yin, Jianjun, University of Arizona
Yon, Lisa, Palomar College
Zhai, Xiaoming, University of East Anglia

Biological Oceanography

Adams, Marshall, Oak Ridge National Laboratory
Adams, Michael S., University of Wisconsin, Madison
Algar, Christopher, Dalhousie University
Allam, Bassem, SUNY, Stony Brook
Allen, Dennis M., University of South Carolina
Allen, Eric E., University of California, San Diego
Aller, Josephine Y., SUNY, Stony Brook
Amon, Rainier, Texas A&M University
Anderson, George C., University of Washington
Armbrust, Virginia E., University of Washington
Atkinson, Marlin J., University of Hawai'i, Manoa
Audet, Celine, Universite du Quebec a Rimouski
Auster, Peter, University of Connecticut
Azam, Farooq, University of California, San Diego
Baltz, Donald M., Louisiana State University
Banse, Karl, University of Washington
Barber, Bruce, University of South Florida
Barber, Richard T., Duke University
Barlow, Jay P., University of California, San Diego
Baross, John A., University of Washington
Bartlett, Douglas H., University of California, San Diego
Bates, Amanda E., University of Southampton
Baumann, Hannes, University of Connecticut
Baumgartner, Mark, Dalhousie University
Benfield, Mark C., Louisiana State University
Benner, Ronald, University of South Carolina
Bibby, Thomas, University of Southampton
Bienfang, Paul K., University of Hawai'i, Manoa
Biggs, Douglas C., Texas A&M University
Blake, Norman J., University of South Florida
Bloomfield, Helen, University of Liverpool
Boar, Rosalind, University of East Anglia
Bochdansky, Alexander, Old Dominion University
Bollens, Stephen, Washington State University
Boudrias, Michel A., University of San Diego
Bowen, Jennifer, University of Massachusetts, Boston
Boyle, Elizabeth , University of Massachusetts, Boston
Breitbart, Mya, University of South Florida
Brethes, Jean-Claude, Universite du Quebec a Rimouski
Briggs, John C., University of South Florida

Brown, Moira, University of Massachusetts, Boston
Brownlee, Colin, University of Southampton
Bruno, Barbara, University of Hawai'i, Manoa
Bucklin, Ann, University of Connecticut
Burton, Ronald S., University of California, San Diego
Buskey, Edward J., University of Texas at Austin
Byrnes, Jarrett, University of Massachusetts, Boston
Campbell, Lisa, Texas A&M University
Carlile, Amy L., University of New Haven
Carney, Robert S., Louisiana State University
Carpenter, Steve, University of Wisconsin, Madison
Carr, Mark, University of California, Santa Cruz
Case, James M., Wilkes University
Cassar, Nicolas, Duke University
Caswell, Bryony, University of Liverpool
Cavin, Julie, University of Massachusetts, Boston
Cerrato, Robert M., SUNY, Stony Brook
Checkley, David M., University of California, San Diego
Church, Matthew, University of Hawai'i, Manoa
Clague, David A., Stanford University
Clements, Lee Ann J., Jacksonville University
Collie, Jeremy S., University of Rhode Island
Collier, Jackie, SUNY, Stony Brook
Conover, David O., SUNY, Stony Brook
Copley, Jonathan, University of Southampton
Costa, Daniel P., University of California, Santa Cruz
Costa, Ozeas, Ohio State University
Coull, Bruce C., University of South Carolina
Cowles, Timothy J., Oregon State University
Cranford, Peter, Dalhousie University
Croll, Don, University of California, Santa Cruz
Cuba, Thomas, University of South Florida
Cuker, Benjamin E., Hampton University
Cullen, John J., Dalhousie University
D'Elia, Christopher, University of South Florida
Daly, Kendra L., University of South Florida
Dam, Hans G., University of Connecticut
Dayton, Paul K., University of California, San Diego
Dean, John M., University of South Carolina
Demers, Serge, Universite du Quebec a Rimouski
Deming, Jody W., University of Washington
Denton, Gary R. W., University of Guam
DeWitt, Calvin B., University of Wisconsin, Madison
DiBacco, Claudio, Dalhousie University
Dieterle, Dwight A., University of South Florida
Dobbs, Frederick C., Old Dominion University
Dodson, Stanley I., University of Wisconsin, Madison
Donaghay, Percy, University of Rhode Island
Doty, Thomas, Roger Williams University
Dower, John, University of Victoria
Drazen, Jeffrey C., University of Hawai'i, Manoa
Ducklow, Hugh, Columbia University
Duffy, Tara , Northeastern University
Dunton, Kenneth H., University of Texas at Austin
Durbin, Edward G., University of Rhode Island
Dyhrman, Sonya, Columbia University
Eggleston, David B., North Carolina State University
Ellis, Hugh I., University of San Diego
Epp, Leonard G., Mount Union College
Erdner, Deana L., University of Texas at Austin
Erisman, Brad, University of Texas at Austin
Esbaugh, Andrew J., University of Texas at Austin
Etter, Ron , University of Massachusetts, Boston
Falkowski, Paul G., Rutgers, The State University of New Jersey
Fast, Mark, SUNY, Stony Brook
Felbeck, Horst, University of California, San Diego
Feller, Robert J., University of South Carolina
Fenberg, Phillip, University of Southampton
Fennel, Katja, Dalhousie University
Fisher, Jr., Thomas R., University of Maryland
Fisk, Aaron, University of Windsor
Fitzer, Susan, University of Glasgow
Fletcher, Madilyn M., University of South Carolina
Fournier, Robert O., Dalhousie University
Francis, Robert, University of Washington
Frank, Kenneth, Dalhousie University
Franks, Peter J. S., University of California, San Diego
Frid, Chris, University of Liverpool
Frost, Bruce W., University of Washington
Fuiman, Lee A., University of Texas at Austin
Gaasterland, Terry, University of California, San Diego
Gallagher, Eugene, University of Massachusetts, Boston
Gardner, Wayne S., University of Texas at Austin
Gates, Ruth D., University of Hawai'i, Manoa
Gibson, Deidre M., Hampton University
Gifford, Dian J., University of Rhode Island
Gilbert, Patricia M., University of Maryland
Gobler, Christopher, SUNY, Stony Brook
Godbold, Jasmin A., University of Southampton
Goetze, Erica, University of Hawai'i, Manoa

Gomes, Helga, Columbia University
Gosselin, Michel, Universite du Quebec a Rimouski
Gould, Mark D., Roger Williams University
Graham, Linda K., University of Wisconsin, Madison
Graham, Michael, Moss Landing Marine Laboratories
Graham, William, University of Southern Mississippi
Grange, Laura J., University of Southampton
Grant, Jonathan, Dalhousie University
Green, Jonathan, University of Liverpool
Greene, Charles H., Cornell University
Greenfield, Dianne I., University of South Carolina
Griffen, Blaine, University of South Carolina
Grigg, Richard W., University of Hawai'i, Manoa
Grunbaum, Daniel, University of Washington
Haderlie, Eugene C., Naval Postgraduate School
Hamilton, Phillip, University of Massachusetts, Boston
Hargraves, Paul E., University of Rhode Island
Hargreaves, Bruce R., Lehigh University
Harvey, James T., Moss Landing Marine Laboratories
Hastings, Philip A., University of California, San Diego
Hauton, Chris, University of Southampton
Healey, Michael, University of British Columbia
Heath, Carolyn, Fullerton College
Heil, Cynthia, University of South Florida
Hessler, Robert R., University of California, San Diego
Higgins, John A., Princeton University
Holland, Nicholas D., University of California, San Diego
Holt, Gloria J., University of Texas at Austin
Hood, Raleigh, University of Maryland
Hopkins, Thomas L., University of South Florida
Hopkins, Thomas S., Dauphin Island Sea Lab
Hotchkiss, Sarah, University of Wisconsin, Madison
Humm, Harold J., University of South Florida
Hunt, Brian, University of British Columbia
Hunt, Kathleen, University of Massachusetts, Boston
Innis, Charles, University of Massachusetts, Boston
Irlandi, Elizabeth A., Florida Institute of Technology
Jeffries, H. Perry, University of Rhode Island
Jehl, Joseph R., University of San Diego
Jensen, Antony, University of Southampton
Jickells, Tim, University of East Anglia
Johnson, Andrew, University of Derby
Jones, W. J., University of South Carolina
Jordan, Robert A., Hampton University
Juhl, Andrew, Columbia University
Jumars, Peter A., University of Washington
Juniper, Kim, University of Victoria
Kamykowski, Daniel, North Carolina State University
Kana, Todd M., University of Maryland
Karl, David M., University of Hawai'i, Manoa
Kaufmann, Ronald S., University of San Diego
Kelley, Christopher, University of Hawai'i, Manoa
Kelly, John, University of New Haven
Kemp, Paul, University of Hawai'i, Manoa
Kenney, Robert D., University of Rhode Island
Kent, Donald B., University of San Diego
Kesseli, Rick, University of Massachusetts, Boston
Kimball, Matthew E., University of South Carolina
Kirschenfeld, Taylor, University of West Florida
Kitchell, James F., University of Wisconsin, Madison
Knowlton, Amy , University of Massachusetts, Boston
Knowlton, Nancy, University of California, San Diego
Kooyman, Gerald L., University of California, San Diego
Kraemer, George P., SUNY, Purchase
Krauss, Scott , University of Massachusetts, Boston
Krieger-Brockett, Barbara B., University of Washington
Landry, Michael R., University of California, San Diego
LaRock, Paul A., Louisiana State University
Lee, Carol, University of Wisconsin, Madison
Leichter, James J., University of California, San Diego
Lessard, Evelyn J., University of Washington
Letelier, Ricardo, Oregon State University
Levin, Lisa A., University of California, San Diego
Levinton, Jeffrey, SUNY, Stony Brook
Lewin, Joyce C., University of Washington
Lewis, Alan G., University of British Columbia
Lewis, Marlon R., Dalhousie University
Li, William K., Dalhousie University
Lilley, Marvin D., University of Washington
Lin, Senjie, University of Connecticut
Logan, Alan, University of New Brunswick Saint John
Lohan, Maeve, University of Southampton
Lonsdale, Darcy J., SUNY, Stony Brook
Lopez, Glenn R., SUNY, Stony Brook
Lowery, Mary Sue, University of San Diego
Lucas, Cathy, University of Southampton
MacIntyre, Hugh, Dalhousie University
Mackas, David L., University of Victoria
Maldonado, Maria, University of British Columbia
Malin, Gill, University of East Anglia

Mandelman, John, University of Massachusetts, Boston
Marra, John, Brooklyn College (CUNY)
Martiny, Adam, University of California, Irvine
McCarthy, James T., Harvard University
McClelland, James W., University of Texas at Austin
McConaugha, John R., Old Dominion University
McGlathery, Karen J., University of Virginia
McGowan, John A., University of California, San Diego
McKinley, Galen, University of Wisconsin, Madison
McManus, George B., University of Connecticut
Mendelssohn, Irving A., Louisiana State University
Metaxas, Anna, Dalhousie University
Meylan, Anne, University of South Florida
Miller, Douglas C., University of Delaware
Mills, Eric L., Dalhousie University
Milroy, Scott, University of Southern Mississippi
Mobley, Curtis D., University of Washington
Monger, Bruce, Cornell University
Moore, Christopher M., University of Southampton
Moran, Dawn, Woods Hole Oceanographic Institution
Morris, James T., University of South Carolina
Mueller, Erich M., University of South Alabama
Mulholland, Margaret, Old Dominion University
Munch, Stephan, SUNY, Stony Brook
Murtugudde, Raghuram G., University of Maryland
Napora, Theodore A., University of Rhode Island
Napp, Jeffrey, University of Washington
Newman, William A., University of California, San Diego
Newton, Jan, University of Washington
Nixon, Scott W., University of Rhode Island
Norris, Dean R., Florida Institute of Technology
Ohman, Mark D., University of California, San Diego
Oliver, John S., Moss Landing Marine Laboratories
Oliver, Matthew J., University of Delaware
Oschlies, Andreas, Dalhousie University
Oviatt, Candace, University of Rhode Island
Pakhomov, Evgeny, University of British Columbia
Palenik, Brian, University of California, San Diego
Paul, John H., University of South Florida
Peebles, Ernst B., University of South Florida
Pellerin, Jocelyne, Universite du Quebec a Rimouski
Pendleton, Daniel, University of Massachusetts, Boston
Penry, Deborah L., University of California, Berkeley
Perrin, William F., University of California, San Diego
Perry, Mary Jane, University of Washington
Peterson, Bradley, SUNY, Stony Brook
Pikitch, Ellen K., SUNY, Stony Brook
Pinckney, James, University of South Carolina
Plotkin, Pamela, Texas A&M University
Pollack, Jennifer, Texas A&M University, Corpus Christi
Potts, Donald C., University of California, Santa Cruz
Powers, Sean, University of South Alabama
Purdie, Duncan A., University of Southampton
Quattro, Joseph M., University of South Carolina
Quigg, Antonietta, Texas A&M University
Rabalais, Nancy N., Louisiana State University
Ragotzkie, Robert A., University of Wisconsin, Madison
Ray, G. Carleton, University of Virginia
Redalje, Donald G., University of Southern Mississippi
Rhyne, Andrew, University of Massachusetts, Boston
Richardson, Tammi, University of South Carolina
Rius, Marc, University of Southampton
Robinson, Carol, University of East Anglia
Robinson, Leonie, University of Liverpool
Rocap, Gabrielle L., University of Washington
Rolland, Rosalind, University of Massachusetts, Boston
Roman, Charles T., University of Rhode Island
Rosenblatt, Richard H., University of California, San Diego
Rotjan, Randi, University of Massachusetts, Boston
Roughgarden, Joan, Stanford University
Rouse, Gregory W., University of California, San Diego
Rowe, Gilbert T., Texas A&M University
Roy, Suzanne, Universite du Quebec a Rimouski
Ruttan, Lore, Emory University
Rykaczewski, Ryan, University of South Carolina
Saila, Saul B., University of Rhode Island
Sambrotto, Raymond N., Columbia University
Sautter, Leslie R., College of Charleston
Schnetzer, Astrid, North Carolina State University
Schulze, Anja, Texas A&M University
Scott, Tim, Roger Williams University
Selph, Karen E., University of Hawai'i, Manoa
Shank, Gerard C., University of Texas at Austin
Shaw, Richard F., Louisiana State University
Sherr, Barry, Oregon State University
Sherr, Evelyn, Oregon State University
Showman, Richard M., University of South Carolina
Shuman, Randy, University of Washington
Shumway, Sandra, University of Connecticut
Sibert, John R., University of Hawai'i, Manoa

Sieburth, John M., University of Rhode Island
Silver, Mary W., University of California, Santa Cruz
Sims, David, University of Southampton
Small, Lawrence, Oregon State University
Smalley, Gabriela W., Rider University
Smayda, Theodore J., University of Rhode Island
Smith, Craig R., University of Hawai'i, Manoa
Smith, David C., University of Rhode Island
Smith, David E., University of Virginia
Smith, Erik M., University of South Carolina
Smith, Jennifer E., University of California, San Diego
Smith, Paul E., University of California, San Diego
Solan, Martin, University of Southampton
Sommer, Ulrich , Dalhousie University
Sousa, Wayne P., University of California, Berkeley
Specker, Jennifer, University of Rhode Island
Stakes, Debra S., Stanford University
Stanley, Emily, University of Wisconsin, Madison
Statham, Peter, University of Southampton
Steppe, Cecily N., United States Naval Academy
Steward, Grieg F., University of Hawai'i, Manoa
Stewart, Brent S., University of San Diego
Stickney, Robert R., Texas A&M University
Stoecker, Diane, University of Maryland
Strickland, Richard M., University of Washington
Subramaniam, Ajit, Columbia University
Sugihara, George, University of California, San Diego
Suttle, Curtis, University of British Columbia
Swain, Geoffrey W., Florida Institute of Technology
Swift, Elijah V., University of Rhode Island
Sylvan, Jason, Texas A&M University
Taggart, Christopher T., Dalhousie University
Tan, Wenxian, Austin Community College District
Taylor, Frank J. R., University of British Columbia
Taylor, Gordon T., SUNY, Stony Brook
Thatje, Sven, University of Southampton
Thomas, Florence, University of Hawai'i, Manoa
Thomas, Peter, University of Texas at Austin
Thompson, Diane, Boston University
Thomsen, Laurenz A., University of Washington
Thomson, Jack, University of Liverpool
Thornton, Daniel C., Texas A&M University
Tlusty, Michael, University of Massachusetts, Boston
Toonen, Robert, University of Hawai'i, Manoa
Torres, Joseph J., University of South Florida
Tortell, Philippe, University of British Columbia
Tunnicliffe, Verena, University of Victoria
Turner, Robert E., Louisiana State University
Tynan, Cynthia T., University of Washington
Urban-Rich, Juanita, University of Massachusetts, Boston
Vacquier, Victor D., University of California, San Diego
Vaillancourt, Robert, Millersville University
Van Oostende, Nicolas, Princeton University
Varela, Diana, University of Victoria
Vargo, Gabriel A., University of South Florida
Vaudrey, Jamie, University of Connecticut
Villalard-Bohnsack, Martine, Roger Williams University
Villareal, Tracy A., University of Texas at Austin
Waldbusser, George, Oregon State University
Walsh, John J., University of South Florida
Ward, Bess B., Princeton University
Ward, J. Evan, University of Connecticut
Warren, Joseph, SUNY, Stony Brook
Wells, Randy, University of South Florida
Welschmeyer, Nicholas A., Moss Landing Marine Laboratories
Weng, Kevin, University of Hawai'i, Manoa
Werner, Timothy, University of Massachusetts, Boston
Weston, Donald, University of California, Berkeley
Wetz, Michael, Texas A&M University, Corpus Christi
Whalen, Kristen, Woods Hole Oceanographic Institution
White, Angelicque, Oregon State University
Wiedenmann, Jorg, University of Southampton
Wilson, Merwether, Edinburgh University
Wishner, Karen, University of Rhode Island
Wolcott, Donna L., North Carolina State University
Wolcott, Thomas G., North Carolina State University
Woodin, Sarah A., University of South Carolina
Wyse Jackson, Patrick N., Trinity College
Yamanaka, Tsuyuko, University of Liverpool
Yandle, Tracy, Emory University
Young, Richard E., University of Hawai'i, Manoa
Zakardjian, Bruno, Universite du Quebec a Rimouski
Zedler, Joy, University of Wisconsin, Madison
Zehr, Jonathan P., University of California, Santa Cruz
Zhang, Huan, University of Connecticut

Chemical Oceanography
Achterberg, Eric P., University of Southampton
Allison, Nicky, University of St. Andrews
Altabet, Mark, Brown University

Andersen, Raymond J., University of British Columbia
Anderson, Robert F., Columbia University
Andren, Anders W., University of Wisconsin, Madison
Apprill, Amy, Woods Hole Oceanographic Institution
Armstrong, David E., University of Wisconsin, Madison
Armstrong, Robert A., SUNY, Stony Brook
Azetsu-Scott, Kumiko, Dalhousie University
Bacon, Michael P., Woods Hole Oceanographic Institution
Balistrieri, Laurie, University of Washington
Barbeau, Katherine A., University of California, San Diego
Bates, Nicholas R., University of Southampton
Baumann, Zofia, University of Connecticut
Benitez-Nelson, Claudia R., University of South Carolina
Benway, Heather, Woods Hole Oceanographic Institution
Bishop, James K., University of California, Berkeley
Boyle, Edward A., Massachusetts Institute of Technology
Brewer, Peter G., Stanford University
Bronk, Deborah A., College of William & Mary
Brownawell, Bruce J., SUNY, Stony Brook
Bruland, Kenneth W., University of California, Santa Cruz
Buckley, Lawrence J., University of Rhode Island
Buesseler, Ken O., Woods Hole Oceanographic Institution
Bullister, John, University of Washington
Burdige, David J., Old Dominion University
Canuel, Elizabeth A., College of William & Mary
Chan, Kwan M., California State University, Long Beach
Chapman, Piers, Texas A&M University
Chappell, P. D., Old Dominion University
Clarke, Antony D., University of Hawai'i, Manoa
Cochran, J. Kirk, SUNY, Stony Brook
Coffin, Richard, Texas A&M University, Corpus Christi
Corbett, David R., East Carolina University
Cornwell, Jeffery C., University of Maryland
Culberson, Charles H., University of Delaware
Cullen, Jay, University of Victoria
Cutter, Gregory A., Old Dominion University
deAngelis, Marie, SUNY, Maritime College
Delaney, Margaret L., University of California, Santa Cruz
DeMaster, David J., North Carolina State University
Devol, Allan H., University of Washington
Druffel, Ellen R. M., University of California, Irvine
Drysdale, Jessica, Woods Hole Oceanographic Institution
Duce, Robert A., Texas A&M University
Duedall, Iver W., Florida Institute of Technology
Emerson, Steven R., University of Washington
Emile-Geay, Julien, University of Southern California
Engel, Anga, SUNY, Stony Brook
Estapa, Margaret, Skidmore College
Fanning, Kent A., University of South Florida
Farrington, John W., Woods Hole Oceanographic Institution
Feakins, Sarah, University of Southern California
Feely, Richard A., University of Washington
Fendrock, Michaela, Woods Hole Oceanographic Institution
Fenical, William H., University of California, San Diego
Fisher, Nicholas S., SUNY, Stony Brook
Fitzgerald, William F., University of Connecticut
Fitzsimmons, Jessica, Texas A&M University
Fogel, Marilyn L., University of Delaware
Fox, Lewis, Broward College, Central Campus
Fredricks, Helen, Woods Hole Oceanographic Institution
Gagne, Jean-Pierre, Universite du Quebec a Rimouski
Gammon, Richard H., University of Washington
Garcia-Rubio, Luis H., University of South Florida
Gegg, Steven, Woods Hole Oceanographic Institution
Gieskes, Joris M., University of California, San Diego
Glover, David M., Woods Hole Oceanographic Institution
Gold-Bouchot, Gerardo, Texas A&M University
Gordon, Elizabeth S., Fitchburg State University
Gosselin, Kelsey, Woods Hole Oceanographic Institution
Granger, Julie, University of Connecticut
Grguric, Gordan, Stockton University
Grottoli, Andrea G., Ohio State University
Hales, Burke R., Oregon State University
Hamme, Roberta, University of Victoria
Hanson, Jr., Alfred K., University of Rhode Island
Hayes, Christopher T., University of Southern Mississippi
Helmstetter, Michael F., Florida Institute of Technology
Hollander, David J., University of South Florida
Hu, Xinping , Texas A&M University, Corpus Christi
Huebert, Barry J., University of Hawai'i, Manoa
Ingalls, Anitra E., University of Washington
James, Rachael, University of Southampton
Jenkins, William J., Woods Hole Oceanographic Institution
Johnson, Bruce D., Dalhousie University
Kalnejais, Linda, University of New Hampshire
Keaffaber, J. J., Florida Institute of Technology
Keil, Richard G., University of Washington
Kiene, Ronald P., University of South Alabama
Knap, Anthony, Texas A&M University
Kortzinger, Arne, Dalhousie University

Kujawinski, Elizabeth B., Woods Hole Oceanographic Institution
Lang, Susan Q., University of South Carolina
LaVigne, Michéle, Bowdoin College
Lea, David W., University of California, Santa Barbara
Lima, Ivan D., Woods Hole Oceanographic Institution
Loder, Theodore C., University of New Hampshire
Longnecker, Krista, Woods Hole Oceanographic Institution
Lott, Dempsey E., Woods Hole Oceanographic Institution
Louchouarn, Patrick, Texas A&M University
Lucotte, Marc Michel, Universite du Quebec a Montreal
Lund, David, University of Connecticut
Lwiza, Kamazima M., SUNY, Stony Brook
Macdonald, Robie W., University of Victoria
Mahaffey, Claire, University of Liverpool
Marchitto, Thomas M., University of Colorado
Martin, William R., Woods Hole Oceanographic Institution
Mason, Robert, University of Connecticut
Matsumoto, Katsumi, University of Minnesota, Twin Cities
McDuff, Russell E., University of Washington
McElroy, Anne, SUNY, Stony Brook
McIlvin, Matt, Woods Hole Oceanographic Institution
McNichol, Ann P., Woods Hole Oceanographic Institution
Measures, Christopher, University of Hawai'i, Manoa
Merrill, John T., University of Rhode Island
Moffett, James, University of Southern California
Moore, Robert M., Dalhousie University
Moran, S. Bradley, University of Rhode Island
Murray, James W., University of Washington
Nuzzio, Donald B., University of Delaware
Oestreich, William, Woods Hole Oceanographic Institution
Oktay, Sarah, University of Massachusetts, Boston
Ossolinski, Justin, Woods Hole Oceanographic Institution
Owen, Robert M., University of Michigan
Paytan, Adina, Stanford University
Pelletier, Emilien, Universite du Quebec a Rimouski
Pennock, Jonathan R., Dauphin Island Sea Lab
Pilson, Michael E., University of Rhode Island
Prahl, Fredrick G., Oregon State University
Precedo, Laura, Broward College, Central Campus
Presley, Bobby J., Texas A&M University
Pyrtle, Ashanti J., University of South Florida
Quay, Paul D., University of Washington
Quinn, James G., University of Rhode Island
Rahn, Kenneth A., University of Rhode Island
Ravelo, Ana C., University of California, Santa Cruz
Reimer, Andreas, Georg-August University of Goettingen
Reimers, Clare, Oregon State University
Resing, Joseph A., University of Washington
Rheuban, Jennie, Woods Hole Oceanographic Institution
Richey, Jeffrey E., University of Washington
Roethel, Frank J., SUNY, Stony Brook
Russell, Joellen, University of Arizona
Sabine, Christopher L., University of Washington
Saito, Mak A., Woods Hole Oceanographic Institution
Salaun, Rachel, University of Liverpool
Sandwith, Zoe, Woods Hole Oceanographic Institution
Santschi, Peter H., Texas A&M University
Sarmiento, Jorge L., Princeton University
Sayles, Frederick L., Woods Hole Oceanographic Institution
Schwartz, Matthew C., University of West Florida
Scranton, Mary I., SUNY, Stony Brook
Shadwick, Elizabeth H., College of William & Mary
Shamberger, Kathryn, Texas A&M University
Sharp, Jonathan H., University of Delaware
Sharples, Jonathan, University of Liverpool
Shaw, Timothy J., University of South Carolina
Shieh, Chih-Shin, Florida Institute of Technology
Shiller, Alan M., University of Southern Mississippi
Sholkovitz, Edward R., Woods Hole Oceanographic Institution
Simjouw, Jean-Paul, University of New Haven
Skoog, Annelie, University of Connecticut
Sonzogni, William C., University of Wisconsin, Madison
Soule, Melissa, Woods Hole Oceanographic Institution
Sundby, Bjorn, Universite du Quebec a Rimouski
Suntharalingam, Parvadha, University of East Anglia
Swarr, Gretchen, Woods Hole Oceanographic Institution
Sylva, Sean, Woods Hole Oceanographic Institution
Tagliabue, Alessandro, University of Liverpool
Takahashi, Taro, Columbia University
Tanhua, Toste , Dalhousie University
Thomas, Helmuth, Dalhousie University
Thompson, Anu, University of Liverpool
Timmermans, Mary-Louise, Yale University
Tobias, Craig, University of Connecticut
Traganza, Eugene D., Naval Postgraduate School
Tyrrell, Toby, University of Southampton
Ullman, William J., University of Delaware
Van Mooy, Benjamin, Woods Hole Oceanographic Institution
Velinsky, David, Drexel University
Veron, Alain J., University of Delaware

Vlahos, Penny, University of Connecticut
Wade, Terry L., Texas A&M University
Wallace, Douglas, Dalhousie University
Wallace, Douglas W. R., SUNY, Stony Brook
Wiesenburg, Denis A., University of Southern Mississippi
Williams, Dave E., University of British Columbia
Windsor, Jr., John G., Florida Institute of Technology
Wong, George T. F., Old Dominion University
Yao, Wensheng, University of South Florida
Yvon-Lewis, Shari A., Texas A&M University
Zafiriou, Oliver C., Woods Hole Oceanographic Institution
Zhu, Qingzhi, SUNY, Stony Brook

Geological Oceanography

Alexander, Clark R., Georgia Southern University
Alt, Jeffrey C., University of Michigan
Arthur, Michael A., Pennsylvania State University, University Park
Asper, Vernon L., University of Southern Mississippi
Bain, Olivier, Institut Polytechnique LaSalle Beauvais (ex-IGAL)
Baker, Edward T., University of Washington
Baldauf, Jack G., Texas A&M University
Berquist, Jr., Carl R., College of William & Mary
Billups, Katharina, University of Delaware
Black, David, SUNY, Stony Brook
Brook, Edward J., Oregon State University
Busch, William H., University of New Orleans
Bush, David M., University of West Georgia
Byrne, Timothy, University of Connecticut
Carey, Steven N., University of Rhode Island
Chrzastowski, Michael J., Illinois State Geological Survey
Clemens, Steven C., Brown University
Cok, Anthony E., Adelphi University
Cook, Mea S., Williams College
Creager, Joe S., University of Washington
D'Hondt, Steven L., University of Rhode Island
Darby, Dennis A., Old Dominion University
Dellapenna, Timothy M., Texas A&M University
Dudley, Walter, University of Hawai'i, Manoa
Emerick, Christina M., University of Washington
Farmer, Emma C., Hofstra University
Farrell, John, University of Rhode Island
Ferrini, Victoria, Columbia University
Finney, Bruce P., University of Alaska, Fairbanks
Fisher, Cynthia G., West Chester University
Flood, Roger D., SUNY, Stony Brook
Gagnon, Katie, Seattle Central Community College
Gardner, Wilford D., Texas A&M University
Harris, Sara, University of British Columbia
Hayman, Nicholas W., University of Texas at Austin
Hein, Christopher J., College of William & Mary
Ho, David, University of Hawai'i, Manoa
Holcomb, Robin T., University of Washington
Holcombe, Troy, Texas A&M University
Holmes, Mark L., University of Washington
Honjo, Susumu, Woods Hole Oceanographic Institution
Hovan, Steven A., Indiana University of Pennsylvania
Ivanochko, Tara, University of British Columbia
Karlin, Robert, University of Nevada, Reno
Kelley, Deborah S., University of Washington
Kincaid, Christopher, University of Rhode Island
King, John, University of Rhode Island
Kominz, Michelle A., Western Michigan University
Kuehl, Steven A., College of William & Mary
Larson, Roger, University of Rhode Island
Lear, C, Cardiff University
Leinen, Margaret, University of Rhode Island
Leventer, Amy, Colgate University
Locker, Stanley D., University of South Florida
Longworth, Brett, Woods Hole Oceanographic Institution
Manganini, Steven J., Woods Hole Oceanographic Institution
Martinez-Noriega, Cesar, Universidad Autonoma de Baja California Sur
McHugh, Cecilia M., Graduate School of the City University of New York
McHugh, Cecilia, Queens College (CUNY)
McManus, Dean A., University of Washington
Moore, Theodore C., University of Michigan
Mosher, David C., Dalhousie University
Mottl, Michael J., University of Hawai'i, Manoa
Mouw, Colleen B., Michigan Technological University
Murray, A. Bradshaw, Duke University
Murray, David, Brown University
Muza, Jay P., Broward College, Central Campus
Naar, David F., University of South Florida
Nittrouer, Charles A., University of Washington
Nowell, Arthur R. M., University of Washington
Oertel, George, Old Dominion University
Ogston, Andrea S., University of Washington
Oostdam, Bernard L., Millersville University
Parsons, Jeffrey D., University of Washington
Pedersen, Thomas F., University of British Columbia
Pilarczyk, Jessica E., University of Southern Mississippi

Pilkey, Jr., Orrin H., Duke University
Pinet, Paul, Colgate University
Prell, Warren L., Brown University
Quinn, Terrence, University of South Florida
Rack, Frank, University of Nebraska, Lincoln
Rule, Joseph H., Old Dominion University
Sager, William W., Texas A&M University
Scher, Howard, University of South Carolina
Schilling, Jean-Guy, University of Rhode Island
Schmidt, Matthew, Old Dominion University
Shen, Yang, University of Rhode Island
Sigurdsson, Haraldur, University of Rhode Island
Slowey, Niall C., Texas A&M University
Smith, Stephen V., University of Hawai'i, Manoa
Snoeckx, Hilde, University of West Florida
St. John, Kristen E., James Madison University
Stanley, Daniel J., Smithsonian Institution / National Museum of Natural History
Sternberg, Richard W., University of Washington
Swift, Donald J. P., Old Dominion University
Thomas, Debbie, Texas A&M University
Tyce, Robert, University of Rhode Island
Uchupi, Elazar, Woods Hole Oceanographic Institution
Wallace, Davin, University of Southern Mississippi
Whitman, Jill M., Pacific Lutheran University
Whittecar, Jr., G. Richard, Old Dominion University
Wilcock, William S., University of Washington
Zarillo, Gary A., Florida Institute of Technology
Zeebe, Richard E., University of Hawai'i, Manoa
Zhang, Xinning, Princeton University

Physical Oceanography

Aagaard, Knut, University of Washington
Abernathey, Ryan P., Columbia University
Alford, Matthew H., University of Washington
Allen, Susan E., University of British Columbia
Allen, Jr., John S., Oregon State University
Andrefouet, Serge, University of South Florida
Anis, Ayal, Texas A&M University
Armi, Laurence, University of California, San Diego
Atkinson, Larry P., Old Dominion University
Barclay, David, Dalhousie University
Batchelder, Hal, Oregon State University
Baum, Steven K., Texas A&M University
Beaulieu, Claudie, University of Southampton
Bennett, Andrew, Oregon State University
Bishop, Stuart P., North Carolina State University
Bogucki, Darek, Texas A&M University, Corpus Christi
Bohlen, Walter F., University of Connecticut
Boicourt, William, University of Maryland
Bordoni, Simona, California Institute of Technology
Bostater, Charles R., Florida Institute of Technology
Bourke, Robert H., Naval Postgraduate School
Bowman, Malcolm J., SUNY, Stony Brook
Boxall, Simon R., University of Southampton
Bracco, Annalisa, Georgia Institute of Technology
Breaker, Laurence, Moss Landing Marine Laboratories
Brooks, David A., Texas A&M University
Brubaker, John M., College of William & Mary
Bryden, Harry, University of Southampton
Buckingham, Michael J., University of California, San Diego
Buijsman, Maarten, University of Southern Mississippi
Bulusu, Subrahmanyam, University of South Carolina
Cane, Mark A., Columbia University
Cannon, Glenn A., University of Washington
Carder, Kendall L., University of South Florida
Carmack, Edward, University of British Columbia
Carter, Glenn, University of Hawai'i, Manoa
Carton, James, University of Maryland
Cessi, Paola, University of California, San Diego
Chang, Ping, Texas A&M University
Chao, Shenn-Yu, University of Maryland
Chapman, Ross N., University of Victoria
Chelton, Dudley B., Oregon State University
Chen, Dake, Columbia University
Chiu, Ching-Sang, Naval Postgraduate School
Chu, Peter C., Naval Postgraduate School
Clegg, Simon, University of East Anglia
Cole, Rick, University of South Florida
Collins, Curtis A., Naval Postgraduate School
Cornillon, Peter, University of Rhode Island
Cox, Charles S., University of California, San Diego
Craig, Susanne , Dalhousie University
Crease, James, University of Delaware
Criminale, Jr., William O., University of Washington
Cronin, Meghan F., University of Washington
D'Asaro, Eric A., University of Washington
Davis, Leslie S., Austin Community College District
de Szoeke, Simon P., Oregon State University
Denman, Kenneth L., University of Victoria
Dever, Edward P., Oregon State University

Di Lorenzo, Emanuele, Georgia Institute of Technology
Dierssen, Heidi, University of Connecticut
DiMarco, Steven F., Texas A&M University
Donohue, Kathleen, University of Rhode Island
Donovan, Jeff C., University of South Florida
Dorman, Clive E., San Diego State University
Dosso, Stanley E., University of Victoria
Drago, Aldo, University of Malta
Drijfhout, Sybren, University of Southampton
Dushaw, Brian D., University of Washington
Edson, James, University of Connecticut
Ellis, Dale, Dalhousie University
English, David C., University of South Florida
Eriksen, Charles C., University of Washington
Ewart, Terry E., University of Washington
Fedorov, Alexey V., Yale University
Ferrari, Raffaele, Massachusetts Institute of Technology
Fewings, Melanie, University of Connecticut
Firing, Eric, University of Hawai'i, Manoa
Flagg, Charles, SUNY, Stony Brook
Flament, Pierre J., University of Hawai'i, Manoa
Flierl, Glenn R., Massachusetts Institute of Technology
Flynn, Russell L., Cypress College
Follows, Michael, Massachusetts Institute of Technology
Foreman, Michael G. G., University of British Columbia
Fox-Kemper, Baylor, Brown University
Frajka-Williams, Eleanor, University of Southampton
Fram, Jonathan, Oregon State University
Galea, Anthony, University of Malta
Galperin, Boris, University of South Florida
Garfield, Newell (Toby), San Francisco State University
Gargett, Ann, Old Dominion University
Garrett, Christopher J. R., University of Victoria
Garwood, Roland W., Naval Postgraduate School
Gauci, Adam, University of Malta
Giese, Benjamin S., Texas A&M University
Gille, Sarah T., University of California, San Diego
Ginis, Isaac, University of Rhode Island
Gnanadesikan, Anand, Johns Hopkins University
Gong, Donglai, College of William & Mary
Gordon, Arnold L., Columbia University
Gratton, Yves, Universite du Quebec
Greatbatch, Richard , Dalhousie University
Greenberg, David, Dalhousie University
Gregg, Michael C., University of Washington
Grosch, Chester E., Old Dominion University
Guinasso, Norman, Texas A&M University
Haine, Thomas W., Johns Hopkins University
Hara, Tetsu, University of Rhode Island
Harrison, Don E., University of Washington
Hautala, Susan L., University of Washington
Hay, Alex E., Dalhousie University
He, Ruoying, North Carolina State University
Heavers, Richard, Roger Williams University
Hebert, David L., University of Rhode Island
Hebert, David, Dalhousie University
Heimbach, Patrick, Massachusetts Institute of Technology
Hendershott, Myrl C., University of California, San Diego
Herbers, Thomas H., Naval Postgraduate School
Hermann, Albert, University of Washington
Hetland, Robert D., Texas A&M University
Heywood, Karen, University of East Anglia
Hickey, Barbara M., University of Washington
Hines, Paul, Dalhousie University
Hofmann, Eileen E., Old Dominion University
Howard, Matthew K., Texas A&M University
Howden, Stephan, University of Southern Mississippi
Howe, Bruce M., University of Washington
Hsieh, William, University of British Columbia
Huang, Bohua, George Mason University
Ierley, Glenn R., University of California, San Diego
Jackson, George A., Texas A&M University
Jacobs, Stanley, Columbia University
Janowitz, Gerald S., North Carolina State University
Jochens, Ann E., Texas A&M University
Johnson, Gregory C., University of Washington
Johnson, Ronald E., Old Dominion University
Jones, Peter E., Dalhousie University
Jonsson, Bror F., Princeton University
Justic, Dubravko, Louisiana State University
Kaempf, Jochen, Flinders University
Kaplan, Alexey, Columbia University
Kawase, Mitsuhiro, University of Washington
Kelley, Dan, Dalhousie University
Kelly, Kathryn A., University of Washington
Kessler, William S., University of Washington
Klinck, John M., Old Dominion University
Klinger, Barry, George Mason University
Kloosterziel, Rudolf C., University of Hawai'i, Manoa
Klymak, Jody, University of Victoria

Knauss, John A., University of Rhode Island
Knowles, Charles E., North Carolina State University
Koutitonsky, Vladimir G., Universite du Quebec a Rimouski
Kumar, Ajoy, Millersville University
Kunze, Eric L., University of Washington
Kuperman, William A., University of California, San Diego
Lebow, Ruth Y., Los Angeles Pierce College
Lee, Craig M., University of Washington
Lerczak, Jim, Oregon State University
Lesht, Barry M., Argonne National Laboratory
Lesht, Barry, University of Illinois at Chicago
Liu, Zheng-yu, University of Wisconsin, Madison
Lombardo, Kelly, University of Connecticut
Lozier, M. Susan, Duke University
Lu, Youyu, Dalhousie University
Lukas, Roger, University of Hawai'i, Manoa
Luther, Douglas S., University of Hawai'i, Manoa
Luther, Mark E., University of South Florida
MacCready, Parker, University of Washington
Magaard, Lorenz, University of Hawai'i, Manoa
Malanotte-Rizzoli, Paola M., Massachusetts Institute of Technology
Manley, Thomas O., Middlebury College
Marsh, Robert, University of Southampton
Marshall, John C., Massachusetts Institute of Technology
Martin, Seelye, University of Washington
Martinson, Douglas G., Columbia University
Maslowski, Wieslaw, Naval Postgraduate School
Maul, George A., Florida Institute of Technology
McCreary, Julian P., University of Hawai'i, Manoa
McManus, Margaret Anne, University of Hawai'i, Manoa
Melville, W. Kendall, University of California, San Diego
Merrifield, Mark A., University of Hawai'i, Manoa
Miller, Robert N., Oregon State University
Mitchum, Gary T., University of South Florida
Mofjeld, Harold O., University of Washington
Moore, Dennis W., University of Washington
Moore, Jefferson K., University of California, Irvine
Morison, James H., University of Washington
Moum, James N., Oregon State University
Muller, Andrew C., United States Naval Academy
Muller, Peter, University of Hawai'i, Manoa
Munk, Walter H., University of California, San Diego
Myers, Paul, University of Alberta
Mysak, Lawrence A., McGill University
Nash, Jonathan, Oregon State University
Naveira Garabato, Alberto, University of Southampton
Nechaev, Dmitri, University of Southern Mississippi
Niiler, Pearn P., University of California, San Diego
Nowlin, Jr., Worth D., Texas A&M University
Nystuen, Jeffrey A., University of Washington
O'Donnell, James, University of Connecticut
Oliver, Kevin, University of Southampton
Oltman-Shay, Joan M., University of Washington
Orsi, Alejandro H., Texas A&M University
Ortt, Jr., Richard A., Maryland Department of Natural Resources
Paduan, Jeffrey D., Naval Postgraduate School
Pawlowicz, Richard A., University of British Columbia
Perrie, William, Dalhousie University
Perry, David J., Chabot College
Petruncio, Emil T., United States Naval Academy
Pfirman, Stephanie L., Columbia University
Philander, S. George H., Princeton University
Pieters, Roger, University of British Columbia
Pietrafesa, Leonard J., North Carolina State University
Pinkel, Robert, University of California, San Diego
Pond, Stephen G., University of British Columbia
Powell, Brian, University of Hawai'i, Manoa
Powell, Thomas M., University of California, Berkeley
Primeau, Francois, University of California, Irvine
Pringle, James M., University of New Hampshire
Qiu, Bo, University of Hawai'i, Manoa
Radko, Timour, Naval Postgraduate School
Reid, Joseph L., University of California, San Diego
Resio, D. R., Florida Institute of Technology
Rhines, Peter B., University of Washington
Richards, Kelvin J., University of Hawai'i, Manoa
Richardson, Mary J., Texas A&M University
Riser, Stephen C., University of Washington
Roden, Gunnar I., University of Washington
Roemmich, Dean H., University of California, San Diego
Rohling, Eelco J., University of Southampton
Ross, Tetjana, Dalhousie University
Rossby, Hans T., University of Rhode Island
Rothrock, David A., University of Washington
Rothstein, Lewis, University of Rhode Island
Rouse, Jr., Lawrence J., Louisiana State University
Royer, Thomas, Old Dominion University
Ruddick, Barry R., Dalhousie University
Rudnick, Daniel L., University of California, San Diego
Salmon, Richard L., University of California, San Diego

Samelson, Roger, Oregon State University
Sanford, Lawrence P., University of Maryland
Sanford, Thomas B., University of Washington
Schopf, Paul, George Mason University
Schulz, William J., United States Naval Academy
Semtner, Albert J., Naval Postgraduate School
Send, Uwe, University of California, San Diego
Sevellec, Florian, University of Southampton
Shaw, Ping-Tung, North Carolina State University
Shearman, Kipp, Oregon State University
Shen, Jian, College of William & Mary
Sheng, Jinyu, Dalhousie University
Smith, Ned P., Florida Institute of Technology
Smith, Peter C., Dalhousie University
Southam, John R., University of Miami
Spindel, Robert C., University of Washington
Stanton, Timothy P., Naval Postgraduate School
Stewart, Robert H., Texas A&M University
Stoessel, Achim, Texas A&M University
Stoessel, Marion, Texas A&M University
Stramski, Dariusz, University of California, San Diego
Straub, David, McGill University
Swaters, Gordon E., University of Alberta
Talley, Lynne D., University of California, San Diego
Thompson, Andrew F., California Institute of Technology
Thompson, Keith R., Dalhousie University
Thompson, LuAnne, University of Washington
Thomson, Richard E., University of British Columbia
Thurnherr, Andreas, Columbia University
Thurnherr, Andreas M., Columbia University
Timmermann, Axel, University of Hawai'i, Manoa
Tokmakian, Robin T., Naval Postgraduate School
Tremblay, Bruno, McGill University
Tziperman, Eli, Harvard University
van Norden, Maxim F., University of Southern Mississippi
Veronis, George, Yale University
Von Schwind, Joseph J., Naval Postgraduate School
Voulgaris, George, University of South Carolina
Wang, Harry, College of William & Mary
Wang, Zhankun, Texas A&M University
Warner, Mark J., University of Washington
Watts, D. Randolph, University of Rhode Island
Weaver, Andrew J., University of Victoria
Webster, Ferris, University of Delaware
Weisberg, Robert H., University of South Florida
Wells, Neil, University of Southampton
Whitney, Michael, University of Connecticut
Wickham, Jacob B., Naval Postgraduate School
Wiederwohl, Chrissy, Texas A&M University
Wiggert, Jerry, University of Southern Mississippi
Williams, Kevin L., University of Washington
Wilson, Robert E., SUNY, Stony Brook
Wimbush, Mark, University of Rhode Island
Winguth, Arne M., University of Texas, Arlington
Wolfe, Christopher, SUNY, Stony Brook
Woodgate, Rebecca A., University of Washington
Wu, Jin, University of Delaware
Wunsch, Carl I., Massachusetts Institute of Technology
Yankovsky, Alexander, University of South Carolina
Yankovsky, Sasha, University of South Carolina
Young, William R., University of California, San Diego
Yuan, Xiaojun, Columbia University
Zappa, Christopher J., Columbia University
Zhang, Y. J., College of William & Mary
Zhou, Meng, University of Massachusetts, Boston

Shore and Nearshore Processes

Ashton, Andrew, Woods Hole Oceanographic Institution
Baker, Alex, University of East Anglia
Ballinger, Rhoda, University of Wales
Barth, Jack A., Oregon State University
Baxter, Stefanie J., University of Delaware
Boardman, Mark R., Miami University
Bowen, Anthony J., Dalhousie University
Buonaiuto, Frank, Hunter College (CUNY)
Burbanck, George P., Hampton University
Camann, Eleanor J., Red Rocks Community College
Couceiro, Fay, University of Portsmouth
Dickson, Stephen M., Dept of Agriculture, Conservation, and Forestry
Dunbar, Robert B., Stanford University
Dupre, William R., University of Houston
Duxbury, Alyn C., University of Washington
Eilers, H. Peter, Willamette University
Engelhart, Simon E., University of Rhode Island
Farnsworth, Katie, Indiana University of Pennsylvania
Farrell, Stewart, Richard Stockton College of New Jersey
Fenster, Michael S., Randolph-Macon College
FitzGerald, Duncan M., Boston University
Frandsen, Jannette B., Universite du Quebec
Freilich, Michael H., Oregon State University

Friedrichs, Carl T., College of William & Mary
Gibeaut, James, Texas A&M University, Corpus Christi
Giese, Graham S., Woods Hole Oceanographic Institution
Goldsmith, Victor, Graduate School of the City University of New York
Griggs, Gary B., University of California, Santa Cruz
Guza, Robert T., University of California, San Diego
Haigh, Ivan D., University of Southampton
Hall, Robert, University of East Anglia
Haller, Merrick, Oregon State University
Hansom, Jim, University of Glasgow
Harris, Courtney K., College of William & Mary
Harris, Lee E., Florida Institute of Technology
Holman, Robert, Oregon State University
Horton, Benjamin P., Rutgers, The State University of New Jersey
Inman, Douglas L., University of California, San Diego
Jackson, Chester M., Georgia Southern University
Kearney, Michael, University of Maryland
Kemp, Andrew, Tufts University
Kennedy, Andrew, University of Notre Dame
Kineke, Gail C., Boston College
Kinsman, Nicole, Alaska Division of Geological & Geophysical Surveys
Koppelman, Lee K., SUNY, Stony Brook
Kosro, Michael P., Oregon State University
Lazarus, Eli, University of Wales
Lippmann, Thomas C., University of New Hampshire
Maa, Jerome P-Y., College of William & Mary
MacMahan, Jamie, Naval Postgraduate School
McBride, Randolph, George Mason University
McManus, Margaret A., University of California, Santa Cruz
Meyer-Arendt, Klaus J., University of West Florida
Niu, Yaoling, Durham University
Oakley, Bryan, Eastern Connecticut State University
Otvos, Ervin G., University of Southern Mississippi
Ozkan-Haller, Tuba, Oregon State University
Paine, Jeffrey G., University of Texas at Austin
Roberts Briggs, Tiffany M., Florida Atlantic University
Robinson, William, University of Massachusetts, Boston
Rosen, Peter S., Northeastern University
Ruggiero, Peter, Oregon State University
Seibel, Erwin, San Francisco State University
Shroyer, Emily L., Oregon State University
Sommerfield, Christopher K., University of Delaware
Thornton, Edward B., Naval Postgraduate School
Thosteson, Eric D., Florida Institute of Technology
Trembanis, Arthur C., University of Delaware
Vander Zanden, Jake, University of Wisconsin, Madison
Voulgaris, George, University of South Carolina
Westerink, Joannes J., University of Notre Dame
Winant, Clinton D., University of California, San Diego

PLANETOLOGY

Cosmochemistry

Agee, Carl B., University of New Mexico
Alexander, Conel M., Carnegie Institution of Washington
Bar-Nun, Akiva, Tel Aviv University
Bermingham, Katherine, University of Maryland
Blake, Geoffrey A., California Institute of Technology
Blander, Milton, Argonne National Laboratory
Bodenheimer, Peter, University of California, Santa Cruz
Bouvier, Audrey, Western University
Boynton, William V., University of Arizona
Brown, Robert H., University of Arizona
Burnett, Donald S., California Institute of Technology
Ciesla, Fred, University of Chicago
Dauphas, Nicolas, University of Chicago
Davis, Andrew, University of Chicago
Drake, Michael J., University of Arizona
Fegley, M. Bruce, Washington University in St. Louis
Greenwood, James P., Wesleyan University
Grossman, Lawrence, University of Chicago
Humayan, Munir, Florida State University
Huntress, Jr., Wesley T., Carnegie Institution of Washington
Korycansky, Don, University of California, Santa Cruz
Kring, David, University of Arizona
Lal, Devendra, University of California, San Diego
Lewis, John S., University of Arizona
Lin, Douglas, University of California, Santa Cruz
Lodders-Fegley, Katharina, Washington University in St. Louis
Lunine, Jonathan I., University of Arizona
Lyon, Ian, University of Manchester
MacPherson, Glenn J., Smithsonian Institution / National Museum of Natural History
McKeegan, Kevin D., University of California, Los Angeles
McSween, Jr., Harry Y., University of Tennessee, Knoxville
Mojzsis, Stephen J., University of Colorado
Murthy, V. Rama, University of New Mexico
Newsom, Horton E., University of New Mexico
Nittler, Larry R., Carnegie Institution of Washington
Reedy, Robert C., University of New Mexico
Smith, William H., Washington University in St. Louis
Speck, Angela, University of Missouri

Swindle, Timothy, University of Arizona
Turner, Grenville, University of Manchester
Vogt, Steven, University of California, Santa Cruz

Extraterrestrial Geology

Adams, Mark, Lamar University
Anderson, Jennifer L., Winona State University
Asphaug, Erik, University of California, Santa Cruz
Baker, Victor R., University of Arizona
Ballentine, Christopher, University of Oxford
Batygin, Konstantin, California Institute of Technology
Blaney, Diana L., Jet Propulsion Laboratory
Bleamaster III, Leslie F., Trinity University
Brownlee, Donald E., University of Washington
Burr, Devon, University of Tennessee, Knoxville
Byrne, Paul K., North Carolina State University
Cahill, Karen R., Smithsonian Institution / National Museum of Natural History
Cassidy, William, University of Pittsburgh
Christensen, Philip R., Arizona State University
Craddock, Robert A., Smithsonian Institution / National Air & Space Museum
Creech-Eakman, Michelle, New Mexico Institute of Mining and Technology
Cull, Selby, Bryn Mawr College
Delaney, Jeremy S., Rutgers, The State University of New Jersey
Dietz, Richard D., University of Northern Colorado
Ehlmann, Bethany, California Institute of Technology
Elachi, Charles, California Institute of Technology
Emery, Joshua, University of Tennessee, Knoxville
Fabel, Derek, University of Glasgow
Gilmore, Martha S., Wesleyan University
Glotch, Timothy, SUNY, Stony Brook
Grant, John A., Smithsonian Institution / National Air & Space Museum
Grieve, Richard A. F., University of New Brunswick
Grinford, Peter, Birkbeck College
Grosfils, Eric B., Pomona College
Hayes, Alexander, Cornell University
Head, III, James W., Brown University
Heggy, Essam, Western Michigan University
Herkenhoff, Ken E., Jet Propulsion Laboratory
Horgan, Briony, Purdue University
Howell, Robert R., University of Wyoming
Hynek, Brian M., University of Colorado
Jakosky, Bruce M., University of Colorado
Johnson, Brandon C., Brown University
Karuntillake, Suniti, Louisiana State University
Kleinhans, Frederick W., Indiana University / Purdue University, Indianapolis
Knutson, Heather, California Institute of Technology
Kraal, Erin, Kutztown University of Pennsylvania
Leake, Martha A., Valdosta State University
Li, Lin, Indiana University / Purdue University, Indianapolis
Lorenz, Ralph, University of Arizona
Mack, John E., Buffalo State College
Maguire, David, Charles Stewart Mott Community College
Massironi, Matteo, Università degli Studi di Padova
Maxwell, Ted A., Smithsonian Institution / National Air & Space Museum
McEwen, Alfred S., University of Arizona
McGowan, Eileen, University of Massachusetts, Amherst
McKinnon, William B., Washington University in St. Louis
Milam, Keith A., Ohio University
Minton, David, Purdue University
Moersch, Jeffery E., University of Tennessee, Knoxville
Mouginis-Mark, Peter J., University of Hawai'i, Manoa
Murchie, Scott, University of Tennessee, Knoxville
Nelson, Robert M., Jet Propulsion Laboratory
Osinski, Gordon R., Western University
Parsons, Reid A., Fitchburg State University
Piatex, Jennifer L., Central Connecticut State University
Radebaugh, Jani, Brigham Young University
Regas, James L., California State University, Chico
Rice, Melissa S., Western Washington University
Rubie, David C., University of New Mexico
Runyon, Cassandra R., College of Charleston
Schultz, Peter H., Brown University
Shepard, Michael K., Bloomsburg University
Sheppard, Scott S., Carnegie Institution of Washington
Solomon, Sean C., Columbia University
Sonntag, Mark S., Angelo State University
Squyres, Steven W., Cornell University
Stewart-Mukhopadhyay, Sarah T., Harvard University
Stofan, Ellen R., Jet Propulsion Laboratory
Strom, Robert G., University of Arizona
Thaisen, Kevin G., Grand Valley State University
Turtle, Elizabeth, University of Arizona
Warner, Nicholas H., SUNY, Geneseo
Watters, Thomas R., Smithsonian Institution / National Air & Space Museum
Weinberger, Alycia J., Carnegie Institution of Washington
Williams, Kevin K., Buffalo State College
Zimbelman, James R., Smithsonian Institution / National Air & Space Museum

Extraterrestrial Geophysics

Angelopoulos, Vassilis, University of California, Los Angeles
Arkani-Hamed, Jafar, McGill University

Asphaug, Erik, University of California, Santa Cruz
Aurnou, Jonathan M., University of California, Los Angeles
Banerdt, Bruce E., Jet Propulsion Laboratory
Benacquista, Matt, Montana State University, Billings
Bord, Don, University of Michigan, Dearborn
Brown, Michael E., California Institute of Technology
Coleman, Paul J., University of California, Los Angeles
Dombard, Andrew, Case Western Reserve University
Dombard, Andrew J., University of Illinois at Chicago
Fenrich, Francis, University of Alberta
Ferencz, Orsolya, Eotvos Lorand University
Fortes, Andrew, University College London
Garrick-Bethell, Ian, University of California, Santa Cruz
Giacalone, Joe, University of Arizona
Glatzmaier, Gary A., University of California, Santa Cruz
Goldreich, Peter M., California Institute of Technology
Greenberg, Richard J., University of Arizona
Hapke, Bruce W., University of Pittsburgh
Harnett, Erika M., University of Washington
Helled, Ravit , Tel Aviv University
Hood, Lonnie L., University of Arizona
Hubbard, William B., University of Arizona
Jewitt, David, University of California, Los Angeles
Jokipii, Jack R., University of Arizona
Kivelson, Margaret G., University of California, Los Angeles
Kulkarni, Shrinivas R., California Institute of Technology
Kunkle, Thomas D., Los Alamos National Laboratory
Larsen, Kristine, Central Connecticut State University
Lucey, Paul G., University of Hawai'i, Manoa
Margot, Jean-Luc, University of California, Los Angeles
Matzke, David, University of Michigan, Dearborn
McCarthy, Michael P., University of Washington
McGovern, Patrick J., Rice University
McPherron, Robert L., University of California, Los Angeles
Muhleman, Duane O., California Institute of Technology
Newman, William I., University of California, Los Angeles
Paige, David A., University of California, Los Angeles
Petrovay, Kristof, Eotvos Lorand University
Rankin, Robert, University of Alberta
Robinson, R. Craig, Central Connecticut State University
Rostoker, Gordon, University of Alberta
Russell, Christopher T., University of California, Los Angeles
Samson, John C., University of Alberta
Schlichting, Hilke, Massachusetts Institute of Technology
Schmerr, Nicholas, University of Maryland
Seager, Sara, Massachusetts Institute of Technology
Smrekar, Suzanne E., Jet Propulsion Laboratory
Solomon, Sean , Columbia University
Spilker, Linda J., Jet Propulsion Laboratory
Steele, Andrew, Carnegie Institution of Washington
Stevenson, David J., California Institute of Technology
Sydora, Richard D., University of Alberta
Urquhart, Mary, University of Texas, Dallas
Walker, Raymond J., University of California, Los Angeles
Winglee, Robert M., University of Washington
Zuber, Maria T., Massachusetts Institute of Technology

Meteorites & Tektites

Albin, Edward, Georgia Perimeter College - Online
Beck, Andrew, Smithsonian Institution / National Museum of Natural History
Binzel, Richard P., Massachusetts Institute of Technology
Bullock, Emma, Smithsonian Institution / National Museum of Natural History
Clarke, Jr., Roy S., Smithsonian Institution / National Museum of Natural History
Collins, Gareth, Imperial College
Corrigan, Catherine, Smithsonian Institution / National Museum of Natural History
Crapster-Pregont, Ellen J., American Museum of Natural History
Ebel, Denton, American Museum of Natural History
French, Bevan, Smithsonian Institution / National Museum of Natural History
Gardner-Vandy, Kathryn, Smithsonian Institution / Nat Museum of Natural History
Genge, Matthew, Imperial College
Glass, Billy P., University of Delaware
Goreva, Yulia, Smithsonian Institution / National Museum of Natural History
Grocholski, Brent, Smithsonian Institution / National Museum of Natural History
Hartman, Ron N., Mt. San Antonio College
Harvey, Ralph P., Case Western Reserve University
Heymann, Dieter, Rice University
Hildebrand, Alan R., University of Calgary
Hutson, Melinda, Portland State University
Keil, Klaus, University of Hawai'i, Manoa
Krot, Alexander N., University of Hawai'i, Manoa
Martins, Zita, Imperial College
Mayne, Rhiannon G., Texas Christian University
McCoy, Timothy J., Smithsonian Institution / National Museum of Natural History
McCoy, Timothy J., Texas Christian University
McCoy, Timothy, University of Tennessee, Knoxville
Melosh, H. J., Purdue University
Mittlefehldt, David, University of Tennessee, Knoxville
Paglione, Timothy, York College (CUNY)
Rodgers, Nick, University of Wales
Rubin, Alan E., University of California, Los Angeles

Ruzicka, Alexander (Alex) M., Portland State University
Scott, Edward R., University of Hawai'i, Manoa
Sephton, Mark, Imperial College
Singerling, Sheryl, Smithsonian Institution / National Museum of Natural History
Sipiera, Paul P., Mercer University
Swindle, Timothy D., University of Arizona
Taylor, G. Jeffrey, University of Hawai'i, Manoa
Wadhwa, Meenakshi, Field Museum of Natural History
Warren, Paul, University of California, Los Angeles
Wasson, John T., University of California, Los Angeles
Welzenbach, Linda, Smithsonian Institution / National Museum of Natural History

OTHER

General Earth Sciences

Agutu, Nathan O., Jomo Kenyatta University of Agriculture & Technology
Admire, Amanda R., Humboldt State University
Ahrens, Donald C., Modesto Junior College
Angelo, Joseph A., Florida Institute of Technology
Bank, Carl-Georg, University of Toronto
Barron, Robert, Michigan Technological University
Beach Davis, Janet, Heartland Community College
Beausoleil, Denis, Douglas College
Benjamin, Patricia A., Worcester State University
Berry, Leonard, Florida Atlantic University
Boitt, Mark , Jomo Kenyatta University of Agriculture & Technology
Booher, Gary, El Camino College
Boorstein, Margaret F., Long Island University, C.W. Post Campus
Bordossy, Andras, University of Newcastle Upon Tyne
Boyce, Joseph I., McMaster University
Bradley, Jeffrey, Northwest Missouri State University
Branlund, Joy, Southwestern Illinois College - Sam Wolf Granite City Campus
Bretherton, Francis P., University of Wisconsin, Madison
Bries-Korpik, Jill, Century College
Britton, Gloria, Cuyahoga Community College - Western Campus
Brod, Joseph D., Hillsborough Community College
Bruening, Susan, Eastern Connecticut State University
Bruno, Carrie, Great Basin College
Burlakova, Lyubov, SUNY, Buffalo
Burns, Danny, Coastal Bend College
Busa, Mark, Middlesex Community College
Caldwell, Marianne O., Hillsborough Community College
Carlson, Galen R., California State University, Fullerton
Carlson, Heath, Eastern Connecticut State University
Carter, Andy, Birkbeck College
Champion, Kyle M., Hillsborough Community College
Chege, George W., Jomo Kenyatta University of Agriculture & Technology
Childers, Daniel, Delaware County Community College
Cihacek, Larry J., North Dakota State University
Clark, Michael, Mount Royal University
Cleaveland, Malcolm, University of Arkansas, Fayetteville
Cleveland, Natasha, Frederick Community College
Clift, Sigrid, University of Texas at Austin
Cole, Gregory L., Los Alamos National Laboratory
Condreay, Denise, Central Community College
Cordero, David I., Lower Columbia College
Cornebise, Michael W., Eastern Illinois University
Cowart, Richard, Coastal Bend College
Cumpston, Jennifer, Oakton Community College
Davis, James A., Eastern Illinois University
de Wit, Cary, University of Alaska Fairbanks
Deka, Jennifer, Cuyahoga Community College - Western Campus
DeLima, Lynn-Ann, Eastern Connecticut State University
Dennison, Robert, Heartland Community College
Dietz, Anne D., Alamo Colleges - San Antonio College
Dod, Bruce D., Mercer University
Dolgoff, Anatole, Pace University, New York Campus
Douglas, Arthur V., Creighton University
Douthat, Jr., James R., Hillsborough Community College
Dowse, Mary E., Western New Mexico University
Dutton, Jessica, Suffolk County Community College, Ammerman Campus
Ebersole, Sandy M., Geological Survey of Alabama
Erski, Theodore, McHenry County College
Ezerskis, John L., Cuyahoga Community College - Western Campus
Fatherree, James W., Hillsborough Community College
Fielding, Lynn, El Camino College
Flanagan, Michael, Suffolk County Community College, Ammerman Campus
Fondran, Carol, Cuyahoga Community College - Western Campus
Fortes, Dominic, Birkbeck College
Foss, Donald J., College of Marin
Gernon, Thomas, University of Southampton
Gibbs, Samantha J., University of Southampton
Goetz, Andrew R., University of Denver
Goulden, Michael L., University of California, Irvine
Hall, John C., University of West Alabama
Hamilton, Thomas, Edmonds Community College
Hansen, Devon A., University of North Dakota
Harrington, Philip, Suffolk County Community College, Ammerman Campus
Haverluk, Terry W., United States Air Force Academy
Hawkins, Ward L., Los Alamos National Laboratory
Hayes, Van E., Hillsborough Community College

Helgers, Karen, SUNY, Ulster County Community College
Hendrey, George, Queens College (CUNY)
Hill, Arleen A., University of Memphis
Hillier, John, Grays Harbor College
Hitz, Ralph B., Tacoma Community College
Hoppe, Kathryn A., Green River Community College
Huber, Matthew, University of New Hampshire
Hurd, David, Edinboro University of Pennsylvania
Ide, Kayo, University of California, Los Angeles
Imwati, Andrew, Jomo Kenyatta University of Agriculture & Technology
Inglis, Michael, Suffolk County Community College, Ammerman Campus
Janusz, Robert, Alamo Colleges - San Antonio College
Johnson, Jean M., Dalton State Community College
Johnson, Kathleen, University of California, Irvine
Johnson, Tiffany, Douglas College
Kanaroglou, Pavlos S., McMaster University
Kane, Mustapha, Florida Gateway College
Keeling, David, Western Kentucky University
Kellner, Patricia, Los Angeles Harbor College
Kelly, Maria, Edmonds Community College
Khade, Vishnu R., Eastern Connecticut State University
Koch, Joe, Dept of Natural Resources
Lane, Joseph M., Cuyahoga Community College - Western Campus
Lau, Chui Yim Maggie, Princeton University
Le Heron, Daniel, University of London, Royal Holloway & Bedford New College
Lebofsky, Larry A., University of Arizona
Leger, Carol, Keene State College
Leighty, Robert S., Mesa Community College
Lerch, Derek, Feather River College
Levasseur, Emile , Eastern Connecticut State University
Locke, James L., College of Marin
Lofthouse, Stephen T., Pace University, New York Campus
Lomaga, Margaret, Suffolk County Community College, Ammerman Campus
Lowe, John C., George Washington University
Mack, John, Los Angeles Harbor College
MacNeil, James E., Hillsborough Community College
Marchisin, John, Pace University, New York Campus
Marlowe, Brian W., Hillsborough Community College
Martin, John W., San Jose City College
Matzke, Gordon E., Oregon State University
Maxey, Susan M., Brookhaven College
McConnaughhay, Mark, Dutchess Community College
McDougall, Jim, Tacoma Community College
Mcleod, Andrew T., Edinburgh University
McNicol, Barbara, Mount Royal University
Meador, Cindy D., West Texas A&M University
Medina, Francisco, Universidad Nacional Autonoma de Mexico
Moreno, Rafael, Metropolitan State College of Denver
Morton, Bruce, Eastern Connecticut State University
Motyka, James, Eastern Connecticut State University
Munasinghe, Tissa, Los Angeles Harbor College
Nagel, Athena, Mississippi State University
Narey, Martha A., University of Denver
Neumann, Patricia, El Camino College
Neves, Douglas, El Camino College
Newlon, Charles F. J., William Jewell College
Nisbet, Euan, University of London, Royal Holloway & Bedford New College
North, Leslie, Western Kentucky University
Norton-Krane, Abby N., Cuyahoga Community College - Western Campus
Olney, Jessica L., Hillsborough Community College
Olney, Matthew P., Hillsborough Community College
Osborn, Joe, Century College
Oughton, John, Century College
Oxford, Jeremiah, Western Oregon University
Oymayan, Avo, Florida Gateway College
Pappas, Matthew, Suffolk County Community College, Ammerman Campus
Paradise, Thomas R., University of Arkansas, Fayetteville
Pedley, Kate, University of Canterbury
Peprah, Ebenezer, El Camino College
Perry, Baker, Appalachian State University
Perry, Randall, Imperial College
Pettengill, Gordon H., Massachusetts Institute of Technology
Pires, E M., Long Island University, C.W. Post Campus
Pittman, Jason, Folsom Lake College
Pond, Lisa G., Louisiana State University
Pringle, Patrick, Centralia College
Rapley, Chris, University College London
Renfrew, Melanie, Los Angeles Harbor College
Riller, Ulrich, McMaster University
Ritter, Paul, Heartland Community College
Rock, Jessie, North Dakota State University
Rosa, Lynn C., West Texas A&M University
Roth, Leonard T., Hillsborough Community College
Ryan, Susan, California University of Pennsylvania
Sasowsky, Kathryn, Cuyahoga Community College - Western Campus
Schimmrich, Steven, SUNY, Ulster County Community College
Schreier, Hans D., University of British Columbia
Schulze, Karl, Waubonsee Community College
Schumacher, Matthew, Saint Francis Xavier University
Shaw, Katie, Green River Community College

Shugart, Jr., Herman H., University of Virginia
Smilnak, Roberta A., Metropolitan State College of Denver
Smith, Grant, Western Oregon University
Smith, H. Dixon, Metropolitan State College of Denver
Smith, Steven J., University of Northern Iowa
Smith, Thomas M., University of Virginia
Snyder, Jennifer L., Delaware County Community College
Soash, Norman E., Hillsborough Community College
Southon, John, University of California, Irvine
Spooner, Alecia, Everett Community College
Springer, Kathleen B., San Bernardino County Museum
Stermer, Ed, Illinois Central College
Stone, Jim, Aims Community College
Sullivan, Donald G., University of Denver
Taylor, Matthew, University of Denver
Thomas, Ray G., University of Florida
Tidwell, Allan, Chipola College
Tinsley, Mark, Central Virginia Community College
Tongdee, Poetchanaporn, Hillsborough Community College
Travers, Steven, Heartland Community College
Trierweiler, Annette, Princeton University
Turski, Mark P., Plymouth State University
Valencia, Victor, Washington State University
Valentine, Michael, Tacoma Community College
Van Cleave, Kevan A., Hillsborough Community College
van de Gevel, Saskia, Appalachian State University
Veblen, Thomas T., University of Colorado
Voorhees, David H., Waubonsee Community College
Vorwald, Brian, Suffolk County Community College, Ammerman Campus
Waddington, David C., Douglas College
Wade, Phillip, Western Oregon University
Walter, Nathan A., University of West Georgia
Wang, Enru, University of North Dakota
Ward, Calvin H., Rice University
Warger, Jane, Chaffey College
Webb, Craig A., Mt. San Antonio College
White, Susan, Los Angeles Harbor College
Wiesner, Mark R., Rice University
Williams, Mark W., University of Colorado
Wills, William V., Hillsborough Community College
Winterbottom, Wesley, Eastern Connecticut State University
Wisdom, Jack, Massachusetts Institute of Technology
Witkowski, Christine, Middlesex Community College
Witter, Rob, Oregon Dept of Geology & Mineral Industries
Worsley, Thomas R., Ohio University
Yacucci, Mark, Heartland Community College
Yalcin, Kaplan, Oregon State University
Yu, Jin-Yi, University of California, Irvine
Zaleha, Robert, Cuyahoga Community College - Western Campus

Atmospheric Sciences
Ackerman, Thomas P., University of Washington
Adegoke, Jimmy, University of Missouri-Kansas City
Agee, Ernest M., Purdue University
Aiyyer, Anantha, North Carolina State University
Aldrich, Eric A., University of Missouri, Columbia
Alexander, Becky, University of Washington
Allard, Jason, Valdosta State University
Allen, Grant, University of Manchester
Allen, Robert J., University of California, Riverside
Alpert, Pinhas, Tel Aviv University
Anastasio, Cort, University of California, Davis
Ancell, Brian C., Texas Tech University
Anderson, Bruce, Boston University
Anderson, James G., Harvard University
Anderson, Mark R., University of Nebraska, Lincoln
Aneja, Viney P., North Carolina State University
Antonescu, Adrian, University of Manchester
Aquilina, Noel , University of Malta
Arakawa, Akio, University of California, Los Angeles
Ariya, Parisa A., McGill University
Arnfield, A. John, Ohio State University
Arnold, David L., Frostburg State University
Arnold, Stephen, University of Leeds
Arora, Vivek, University of Victoria
Arya, Satyapal S., North Carolina State University
Atkins, Nolan T., Lyndon State College
Atkinson, Christopher, University of North Dakota
Atreya, Sushil, University of Michigan
Austin, Philip, University of British Columbia
Back, Larissa E., University of Wisconsin, Madison
Baker, Marcia B., University of Washington
Baldwin, Michael, Purdue University
Balmforth, Neil, University of British Columbia
Barlow, Mathew, University of Massachusetts Lowell
Barnes, Jeffrey R., Oregon State University
Barrett, Bradford S., United States Naval Academy
Barrett, Kevin M., Tarrant County College- Northeast Campus
Barry, Roger G., University of Colorado
Bartello, Peter, McGill University

Basu, Sukanta, North Carolina State University
Bates, Timothy S., University of Washington
Bathke, Deborah J., University of Nebraska, Lincoln
Battisti, David S., University of Washington
Beard, Kenneth V., University of Illinois, Urbana-Champaign
Bennartz, Ralf, Vanderbilt University
Berg, Larry K., University of Wisconsin, Madison
Bergin, Michael H., Georgia Institute of Technology
Berryman, Bruce F., Lyndon State College
Beswick, Karl, University of Manchester
Bierly, Gregory, Indiana State University
Birner, Thomas, Colorado State University
Bitz, Cecilia M., University of Washington
Black, Robert X., Georgia Institute of Technology
Blasing, Terence J., Oak Ridge National Laboratory
Blechman, Jerome B., SUNY, Oneonta
Bluestein, Howard, SUNY, Stony Brook
Blyth, Alan, University of Leeds
Boden, Thomas, Oak Ridge National Laboratory
Boering, Kristie, University of California, Berkeley
Bollasina, Massimo, Edinburgh University
Bond, Nicholas A., University of Washington
Bonneau, Laurent, Yale University
Booth, Alastair, University of Manchester
Bosart, Lance F., SUNY, Albany
Bossert, James E., Los Alamos National Laboratory
Boybeyi, Zafer, George Mason University
Boyles, Ryan, North Carolina State University
Bradley, Raymond S., University of Massachusetts, Amherst
Bretherton, Christopher S., University of Washington
Bromwich, David H., Ohio State University
Brooks, Sarah D., Texas A&M University
Brown, Robert A., University of Washington
Brubaker, Kenneth L., Argonne National Laboratory
Bruning, Eric C., Texas Tech University
Burls, Natalie, George Mason University
Bush, Andrew B., University of Alberta
Businger, Joost A., University of Washington
Calhoun, Joseph, Millersville University
Campbell, Janet W., University of New Hampshire
Campos, Edwin, Argonne National Laboratory
Cane, Mark A., Columbia University
Cannon, Alex, University of British Columbia
Capehart, William J., South Dakota School of Mines & Technology
Capes, Gerard, University of Manchester
Carey, Larry, Texas A&M University
Carslaw, Ken, University of Leeds
Case Hanks, Anne T., University of Louisiana, Monroe
Castro, Mark S., University of Maryland
Cataneo, Robert, Eastern Illinois University
Catling, David C., University of Washington
Cess, Robert D., SUNY, Stony Brook
Chameides, William L., Duke University
Chang, Edmund K., SUNY, Stony Brook
Chang, Hai-ru, Georgia Institute of Technology
Chang, Young-Soo, Argonne National Laboratory
Charlevoix, Donna J., University of Illinois, Urbana-Champaign
Charlson, Robert J., University of Washington
Chen, Jian-Hua, University of Massachusetts Lowell
Chen, Shuyi S., University of Washington
Chen, Tsing-Chang, Iowa State University of Science & Technology
Chen, Yongsheng, York University
Cheng, Meng-Dawn, Oak Ridge National Laboratory
Chipperfield, Martyn, University of Leeds
Chiu, Long S., George Mason University
Choularton, Thomas , University of Manchester
Chu, Pao-Shin, University of Hawai'i, Manoa
Chuang, Patrick Y., University of California, Santa Cruz
Clabo, Darren R., South Dakota School of Mines & Technology
Claire, Mark, University of St. Andrews
Clark, Richard D., Millersville University
Clarke, Antony D., University of Hawai'i, Manoa
Cobb, Steven R., Texas Tech University
Coe, Hue, University of Manchester
Colle, Brian, SUNY, Stony Brook
Collett, Jr., Jeffrey L., Colorado State University
Collins, Donald R., Texas A&M University
Collins, William D., University of California, Berkeley
Collis, Scott, Argonne National Laboratory
Colman, Bradley R., University of Washington
Colucci, Steven, Cornell University
Connolly, Paul, University of Manchester
Cook, David , Argonne National Laboratory
Cook, Kerry H., University of Texas at Austin
Corcoran, William, Missouri State University
Costigan, Keeley R., Los Alamos National Laboratory
Côté, Jean, Universite du Quebec a Montreal
Cottingame, William, Los Alamos National Laboratory
Coulter, Richard L., Argonne National Laboratory
Covert, David S., University of Washington

Crawford, Ian, University of Manchester
Crawford, James, Georgia Institute of Technology
Cronin, Timothy W., Massachusetts Institute of Technology
Crowther, Sarah, University of Manchester
Curry, Judith A., Georgia Institute of Technology
Cziczo, Dan, Massachusetts Institute of Technology
Dale, Chris, Durham University
Dannevik, William P., Saint Louis University
Daoust, Mario, Missouri State University
Davis, Robert, University of Virginia
de Camargo, Suzana, Columbia University
de Foy, Benjamin, Saint Louis University
Dearden, Christopher, University of Manchester
DeCaria, Alex J., Millersville University
DeConto, Robert, University of Massachusetts, Amherst
DeGaetano, Arthur, Cornell University
DelSole, Timothy, George Mason University
Dempsey, David P., San Francisco State University
Deng, Yi, Georgia Institute of Technology
Denning, A.Scott, Colorado State University
Derome, Jacques F., McGill University
Desai, Ankur R., University of Wisconsin, Madison
Dessler, Alex, Texas A&M University
Detwiler, Andrew G., South Dakota School of Mines & Technology
DeWekker, Stephan F., University of Virginia
Dibb, Jack E., University of New Hampshire
Dickinson, Robert E., University of Texas at Austin
Diem, Jeremy E., Georgia State University
Dinh, Tra, Princeton University
Dirmeyer, Paul A., George Mason University
Dobbie, Steven, University of Leeds
Dobler, Scott, Western Kentucky University
Doherty, Ruth, Edinburgh University
Dominguez, Francina, University of Illinois, Urbana-Champaign
Doskey, Paul V., Argonne National Laboratory
Dugas, Bernard, Universite du Quebec a Montreal
Dunn, Allison L., Worcester State University
Durkee, Josh, Western Kentucky University
Durran, Dale R., University of Washington
Dutcher, Allen, University of Nebraska, Lincoln
Dwyer, Joseph R., Florida Institute of Technology
Eckel, F. Anthony, University of Washington
Edgell, Dennis J., University of North Carolina, Pembroke
Eichler, Tim, Saint Louis University
Elliott, Scott M., Los Alamos National Laboratory
Ellis, Todd D., SUNY, Oneonta
Ellul, Raymond , University of Malta
Epifanio, Craig, Texas A&M University
Essery, Richard L., Edinburgh University
Esslinger, Kelly L., Arizona Western College
Fabry, Frederic, McGill University
Fan, Xingang, Western Kentucky University
Felzer, Benjamin S., Lehigh University
Feng, Song, University of Arkansas, Fayetteville
Feng, Yan, Argonne National Laboratory
Fernando, Joe, University of Notre Dame
Ferruzza, David, Elizabethtown College
Few, Jr., Arthur A., Rice University
Fink, Uwe, University of Arizona
Finnegan, David L., Los Alamos National Laboratory
Fiore, Arlene, Columbia University
Fiore, Arlene M., Columbia University
Fishman, Jack, Saint Louis University
Fitzjarrald, David R., SUNY, Albany
Flato, Gregory M., University of Victoria
Fleagle, Robert G., University of Washington
Fletcher, Roy J., University of Lethbridge
Foster, Stuart, Western Kentucky University
Fovell, Robert, University of California, Los Angeles
Fowler, Malcolm M., Los Alamos National Laboratory
Fox, Neil I., University of Missouri, Columbia
Frame, Jeffrey, University of Illinois, Urbana-Champaign
Frederick, John E., University of Chicago
French, Adam, South Dakota School of Mines & Technology
Frierson, Dargan M., University of Washington
Frolking, Stephen E., University of New Hampshire
Fthenakis, Vasilis M., Columbia University
Fu, Qiang, University of Washington
Fu, Rong, University of Texas at Austin
Fueglistaler, Stephan A., Princeton University
Fuhrmann, Christopher, Mississippi State University
Fultz, Dave, University of Chicago
Fung, Inez, University of California, Berkeley
Fyfe, John C., University of Victoria
Gachon, Philippe, Universite du Quebec a Montreal
Gaffney, Jeffrey S., Argonne National Laboratory
Gallagher, Martin, University of Manchester
Galloway, James N., University of Virginia
Gallus, William A., Iowa State University of Science & Technology
Gao, Yuan, Rutgers, The State University of New Jersey, Newark

Garcia, Oswaldo, San Francisco State University
Garrett, Timothy J., University of Utah
Gauthier, Pierre, McGill University
Gedzelman, Stanley, City College (CUNY)
Geller, Marvin A., SUNY, Stony Brook
Ghate, Virendra, Argonne National Laboratory
Ghil, Michael, University of California, Los Angeles
Giannini, Alessandra M., Columbia University
Gilfillan, Stuart M., Edinburgh University
Gill, Swarndeep S., California University of Pennsylvania
Gimmestad, Gary, Georgia Institute of Technology
Gluhovsky, Alexander, Purdue University
Goddard, Lisa M., Columbia University
Godfrey, Chris, University of North Carolina, Asheville
Goedecke, George H., New Mexico State University, Las Cruces
Goldblatt, Colin, University of Victoria
Goodman, Paul, University of Arizona
Goodrich, Greg, Western Kentucky University
Gordon, Mark, York University
Gordon, Rob J., University of Guelph
Grace, John, Edinburgh University
Granger, Darryl E., Purdue University
Graves, Charles E., Saint Louis University
Grenfell, Thomas C., University of Washington
Griffis, Timothy J., University of Minnesota, Twin Cities
Grise, Kevin M., University of Virginia
Grotjahn, Richard , University of California, Davis
Grubisic, Vanda, University of Vienna
Guinan, Patrick E., University of Missouri, Columbia
Gutowski, William J., Iowa State University of Science & Technology
Gutzler, David J., University of New Mexico
Hage, Keith D., University of Alberta
Hakim, Gregory J., University of Washington
Hallar, Anna G., University of Utah
Hameed, Sultan, SUNY, Stony Brook
Hansen, William, Pace University, New York Campus
Hanson, Howard, Florida Atlantic University
Harnik, Nili, Tel Aviv University
Harrison, D. Edmunds, University of Washington
Harrison, Halstead, University of Washington
Harshvardhan, Purdue University
Hart, Richard L., Argonne National Laboratory
Hartmann, Dennis L., University of Washington
Hastenrath, Stefan L., University of Wisconsin, Madison
Hastings, Meredith, Brown University
Haszeldine, R. S., Edinburgh University
Hauser, Rolland K., California State University, Chico
Hawkins, Timothy W., Shippensburg University
Hayden, Bruce P., University of Virginia
Hayes, Michael J., University of Nebraska, Lincoln
Heald, Colette, Colorado State University
Heald, Colette, Massachusetts Institute of Technology
Hegerl, Gabriele C., Edinburgh University
Hegg, Dean A., University of Washington
Heikes, Brian G., University of Rhode Island
Helsdon, John H., South Dakota School of Mines & Technology
Hence, Deanna, University of Illinois, Urbana-Champaign
Henderson, Gina R., United States Naval Academy
Hennon, Chris, University of North Carolina, Asheville
Henry, James A., Middle Tennessee State University
Hickmon, Nicki, Argonne National Laboratory
Hindman, Edward E., City College (CUNY)
Hirschboeck, Katherine K., University of Arizona
Hitchman, Matthew H., University of Wisconsin, Madison
Hjelmfelt, Mark R., South Dakota School of Mines & Technology
Holberg, Jay B., University of Arizona
Holgood, Jay S., Ohio State University
Holloway, Tracey, University of Wisconsin, Madison
Holzer, Mark, University of British Columbia
Horel, John, University of Utah
Horton, Daniel, Northwestern University
Houghton, David D., University of Wisconsin, Madison
Houston, Adam L., University of Nebraska, Lincoln
Houze, Robert A., University of Washington
Hoyos, Carlos, Georgia Institute of Technology
Hu, Qi (Steve), University of Nebraska, Lincoln
Huang, Alex, University of North Carolina, Asheville
Hubbard, Kenneth G., University of Nebraska, Lincoln
Huey, Gregory L., Georgia Institute of Technology
Hugli, Wilbur G., University of West Florida
Hunten, Donald M., University of Arizona
Hutyra, Lucy, Boston University
Idone, Vincent P., SUNY, Albany
Ingersoll, Andrew P., California Institute of Technology
Ito, Takamitsu, Colorado State University
Jackson, Andrea, University of Leeds
Jacob, Daniel J., Harvard University
Jaegle, Lyatt, University of Washington
Jaffe, Daniel A., University of Washington
Jain, Atul K., University of Illinois, Urbana-Champaign

Jason, Shafer, Lyndon State College
Jenkins, Mary Ann, York University
Jewett, Brian, University of Illinois, Urbana-Champaign
Johnson, Donald R., University of Wisconsin, Madison
Johnson, Richard H., Colorado State University
Jones, Eric M., Los Alamos National Laboratory
Jones, Hazel, University of Manchester
Jones, Phillip, University of East Anglia
Kang, Song-Lak, Texas Tech University
Kao, Jim C., Los Alamos National Laboratory
Kasting, James F., Pennsylvania State University, University Park
Kauffman, Chad, California University of Pennsylvania
Keables, Michael J., University of Denver
Keeling, Ralph F., University of California, San Diego
Keene, William, University of Virginia
Keesee, Robert G., SUNY, Albany
Keller, Linda M., University of Wisconsin, Madison
Keller, Jr., C. F., Los Alamos National Laboratory
Kennel, Charles F., University of California, San Diego
Keyser, Daniel, SUNY, Albany
Khairoutdinov, Marat, SUNY, Stony Brook
Kieu, Chanh Q., Indiana University, Bloomington
Kift, Richard, University of Manchester
Kim, Hyemi, Georgia Institute of Technology
Kim, Saewung, University of California, Irvine
King, Kenneth M., University of Guelph
King, Martin, University of London, Royal Holloway & Bedford New College
Kinter, Jim, George Mason University
Kirkpatrick, Cody, Indiana University, Bloomington
Kirlin, R. Lynn, University of British Columbia
Kirshbaum, Daniel, McGill University
Kishcha, Pavel, Tel Aviv University
Klaassen, Gary P., York University
Kliche, Donna V., South Dakota School of Mines & Technology
Knapp, Warren, Cornell University
Knight, David, SUNY, Albany
Knopf, Daniel A., SUNY, Stony Brook
Koehler, Thomas , United States Air Force Academy
Konigsberg, Alvin S., SUNY, New Paltz
Korty, Robert, Texas A&M University
Kossin, James, University of Wisconsin, Madison
Kota, Jozsef, University of Arizona
Kotamarthi, Rao, Argonne National Laboratory
Kreidenweis, Sonia M., Colorado State University
Krueger, Steven, University of Utah
Kuang, Zhiming, Harvard University
Kubas, Gregory J., Los Alamos National Laboratory
Kucharik, Chris, University of Wisconsin, Madison
Kummerow, Christian D., Texas A&M University
Kung, Ernest C., University of Missouri, Columbia
Kursinski, Robert, University of Arizona
Kushnir, Yochanan, Columbia University
Kutzbach, John E., University of Wisconsin, Madison
L'Ecuyer, Tristan S., University of Wisconsin, Madison
Lackmann, Gary M., North Carolina State University
Laird, Neil, Hobart & William Smith Colleges
Laprise, Rene, Universite du Quebec a Montreal
Lasher-Trapp, Sonia, University of Illinois, Urbana-Champaign
Lazarus, Steven M., Florida Institute of Technology
Leather, Kimberly, University of Manchester
Lee, In Young, Argonne National Laboratory
Lee, Meehye, Korea University
Lefer, Barry, University of Houston
Leighton, Henry G., McGill University
Lemmon, Mark, Texas A&M University
Lew, Jeffrey, University of California, Los Angeles
Li, Tim, University of Hawai'i, Manoa
Li, Xiangshan, University of Houston
Lichtenberger, János, Eotvos Lorand University
Light, Bonnie, University of Washington
Lin, Gong-yuh, California State University, Northridge
Lin, Hai, McGill University
Lin, Jialin, Ohio State University
Lin, John C., University of Utah
Lin, Wuyin, SUNY, Stony Brook
Lindgren, Paula, University of Glasgow
Liou, Kuo Nan, University of California, Los Angeles
Liu, Chuntao, Texas A&M University, Corpus Christi
Liu, Dantong, University of Manchester
Liu, Jiping, Georgia Institute of Technology
Liu, Ping, SUNY, Stony Brook
Lowe, Douglas, University of Manchester
Lozowski, Edward P., University of Alberta
Lundquist, Jessica D., University of Washington
Luo, Chao, Georgia Institute of Technology
Lupo, Anthony R., University of Missouri, Columbia
Lynch, Amanda H., Brown University
Lyons, Lawrence, University of California, Los Angeles
Lyons, Walter A., University of Northern Colorado
Maasch, Kirk A., University of Maine

Mace, Gerald, University of Utah
Magnusdottir, Gudrun, University of California, Irvine
Mahmood, Rezaul, Western Kentucky University
Mahowald, Natalie M., Cornell University
Mak, John E., SUNY, Stony Brook
Mak, Mankin, University of Illinois, Urbana-Champaign
Malcolm, Elizabeth, Virginia Wesleyan College
Maloney, Eric, Colorado State University
Mann, Michael E., Pennsylvania State University, University Park
Manning, Andrew, University of East Anglia
Mantua, Nathan J., University of Washington
Marchand, Roger T., University of Washington
Mark, Bryan G., Ohio State University
Mark, Tucker, Lyndon State College
Market, Patrick S., University of Missouri, Columbia
Marley, Nancy A., Argonne National Laboratory
Marsham, John, University of Leeds
Martin, Randal S., New Mexico Institute of Mining and Technology
Martin, Timothy J., Argonne National Laboratory
Martin, Walter, University of North Carolina, Charlotte
Mason, Allen S., Los Alamos National Laboratory
Mass, Clifford F., University of Washington
Matano, Ricardo, Oregon State University
Maykut, Gary A., University of Washington
Mayor, Shane D., California State University, Chico
McCollor, Doug, University of British Columbia
McElroy, Michael B., Harvard University
McElroy, Tom, York University
McFarlane, Norman, University of Victoria
McFiggans, Gordon, University of Manchester
McGregor, Kent M., University of North Texas
McMurdie, Lynn A., University of Washington
McQuaid, Jim, University of Leeds
McWilliams, James C., University of California, Los Angeles
Mechoso, Carlos R., University of California, Los Angeles
Medvigy, David, Princeton University
Merlis, Timothy, McGill University
Meskhidze, Nicholas, North Carolina State University
Metz, Nicholas, Hobart & William Smith Colleges
Meyer, Steven J., University of Wisconsin, Green Bay
Michaels, Patrick J., University of Virginia
Miller, Doug, University of North Carolina, Asheville
Miller, Ronald L., Columbia University
Millet, Dylan B., University of Minnesota, Twin Cities
Mitchell, Jonathan, University of California, Los Angeles
Mobbs, Stephen, University of Leeds
Modzelewski, Henryk, University of British Columbia
Molina, Mario J., University of California, San Diego
Molinari, John E., SUNY, Albany
Monahan, Edward C., University of Connecticut
Moncrieff, John B., Edinburgh University
Montenegro, Alvaro, Ohio State University
Monteverdi, John P., San Francisco State University
Moody, Jennie L., University of Virginia
Morgan, William, University of Manchester
Mosley-Thompson, Ellen E., Ohio State University
Mote, Philip W., University of Washington
Mote, Phillip, Oregon State University
Moyer, Elisabeth, University of Chicago
Moyer, Kerry A., Edinboro University of Pennsylvania
Mroz, Eugene J., Los Alamos National Laboratory
Mudrick, Stephen E., University of Missouri, Columbia
Mullen, Steven L., University of Arizona
Murrell, Coling, University of East Anglia
Murthy, Prahlad N., Wilkes University
Nakamura, Noboru, University of Chicago
Nappo, Carmen, Georgia Institute of Technology
Nathan, Terrence R., University of California, Davis
Neelin, J. David, University of California, Los Angeles
Nenes, Athanasios, Georgia Institute of Technology
Nesbitt, Stephen W., University of Illinois, Urbana-Champaign
Newman, Steven B., Central Connecticut State University
Nielsen-Gammon, John, Texas A&M University
Niyogi, Dev, Purdue University
Nogueira, Ricardo, Georgia State University
Norris, Joel R., University of California, San Diego
North, Gerald, Texas A&M University
Norwine, Jim R., Texas A&M University, Kingsville
O'Gorman, Paul, Massachusetts Institute of Technology
Oechel, Walter, The Open University
Oglesby, Robert, University of Nebraska, Lincoln
Oglesby, Robert J., University of Nebraska, Lincoln
Ojala, Carl F., Eastern Michigan University
Okalebo, Jane, University of Nebraska, Lincoln
Okumura, Yuko, University of Texas at Austin
Oppenheimer, Michael, Princeton University
Orlove, Benjamin S., Columbia University
Orville, Richard E., Texas A&M University
Osborn, Timothy, University of East Anglia
Osterberg, Erich C., Dartmouth College

Overland, James E., University of Washington
Overpeck, Jonathan T., University of Arizona
Pallmann, Albert J., Saint Louis University
Palmer, Paul, Edinburgh University
Palter, Jaime, McGill University
Pan, Zaitao, Saint Louis University
Pani, Eric A., University of Louisiana, Monroe
Patoux, Jerome, University of Washington
Paulson, Suzanne, University of California, Los Angeles
Pegion, Kathy, George Mason University
Percell, Peter, University of Houston
Percival, Carl, University of Manchester
Perez, Richard R., SUNY, Albany
Perry, Kevin D., University of Utah
Peterson, Richard E., Texas Tech University
Petters, Markus, North Carolina State University
Pierrehumbert, Raymond T., University of Chicago
Polzin, Dierk T., University of Wisconsin, Madison
Powell, Mark L., Los Angeles Pierce College
Prather, Kimberly A., University of California, San Diego
Prather, Michael J., University of California, Irvine
Preston, Thomas C., McGill University
Previdi, Michael, Columbia University
Price, Colin G., Tel Aviv University
Prinn, Ronald G., Massachusetts Institute of Technology
Pryor, Sara C., Cornell University
Pu, Zhaoxia, University of Utah
Pumphrey, Hugh C., Edinburgh University
Pusede, Sally, University of Virginia
Radke, Lawrence F., University of Washington
Raman, Sethu S., North Carolina State University
Ramanathan, V., University of California, San Diego
Ramsey, Kevin W., University of Delaware
Randall, David A., Colorado State University
Rao, S. T., North Carolina State University
Rappenglueck, Bernhard, University of Houston
Rasch, Philip J., University of Washington
Rauber, Robert M., University of Illinois, Urbana-Champaign
Rawlins, Michael, University of Massachusetts, Amherst
Ray, Pallav, Florida Institute of Technology
Rayner, John N., Ohio State University
Reay, David, Edinburgh University
Reichler, Thomas, University of Utah
Reisner, Jon M., Los Alamos National Laboratory
Reiss, Nathan, Pace University, New York Campus
Reuter, Gerhard W., University of Alberta
Revelle, Douglas O., Los Alamos National Laboratory
Richter, David, University of Notre Dame
Ricketts, Hugo, University of Manchester
Riddle, Emily, University of Massachusetts, Amherst
Riemer, Nicole, University of Illinois, Urbana-Champaign
Rind, David H., Columbia University
Riordan, Allen J., North Carolina State University
Ritsche, Michael, Argonne National Laboratory
Robertson, Andrew W., Columbia University
Robinson, Walter A., University of Illinois, Urbana-Champaign
Robinson, Walter, North Carolina State University
Roe, Gerard H., University of Washington
Rogers, Jeffery C., Ohio State University
Ross, Robert S., Millersville University
Rowe, Clinton M., University of Nebraska, Lincoln
Russell, Armistead G., Georgia Institute of Technology
Russell, Lynn M., University of California, San Diego
Rutledge, Steven A., Colorado State University
Salathe Jr., Eric P., University of Washington
Saltzman, Eric S., University of California, Irvine
Sandel, Bill R., University of Arizona
Sarachik, Edward S., University of Washington
Saravanan, R., Texas A&M University
Schade, Gunnar, Texas A&M University
Schlesinger, Michael E., University of Illinois, Urbana-Champaign
Schlosser, C. Adam, Massachusetts Institute of Technology
Schmittner, Andreas, Oregon State University
Schneider, Edwin K., George Mason University
Schroeder, John L., Texas Tech University
Schubert, Wayne H., Colorado State University
Schumacher, Courtney, Texas A&M University
Schwab, James J., SUNY, Albany
Seeley, Mark W., University of Minnesota, Twin Cities
Selin, Noelle, Massachusetts Institute of Technology
Semazzi, Fred H. M., North Carolina State University
Shaw, Tiffany A., Columbia University
Shell, Karen M., Oregon State University
Shellito, Lucinda, University of Northern Colorado
Shen, Samuel S., University of Alberta
Shen, Xinhua, University of Northern Iowa
Shepherd, John G., University of Southampton
Shepson, Paul B., Purdue University
Shinoda, Toshiaki, Texas A&M University, Corpus Christi
Shirley, Terry, University of North Carolina, Charlotte

Shukla, Jagadish, George Mason University
Shulski, Martha D., University of Nebraska, Lincoln
Sikora, Todd D., Millersville University
Simpson, Robert M., University of Tennessee, Martin
Sisterson, Doug, Argonne National Laboratory
Sisterson, Douglas L., Argonne National Laboratory
Smedley, Andrew, University of Manchester
Smith, Paul L., South Dakota School of Mines & Technology
Smith, Phillip J., Purdue University
Smith, Ronald B., Yale University
Snodgrass, Eric R., University of Illinois, Urbana-Champaign
Snow, Julie A., Slippery Rock University
Snyder, Chris, Texas A&M University
Snyder, Peter K., University of Minnesota, Twin Cities
Snyder, Richard L., University of California, Davis
Sobel, Adam H., Columbia University
Sokolik, Irina, Georgia Institute of Technology
Solomon, Susan, Massachusetts Institute of Technology
Somerville, Richard C., University of California, San Diego
Soule, Peter T., Appalachian State University
Srivastava, Ramesh C., University of Chicago
Sriver, Ryan, University of Illinois, Urbana-Champaign
St. John, James C., Georgia Institute of Technology
Stan, Cristiana, George Mason University
Staten, Paul W., Indiana University, Bloomington
Steenburgh, Jim, University of Utah
Stevens, Philip S., Indiana University, Bloomington
Stevenson, David, Edinburgh University
Steyn, Douw G., University of British Columbia
Stickel, Robert, Georgia Institute of Technology
Stoelinga, Mark T., University of Washington
Stone, Peter H., Massachusetts Institute of Technology
Stramler, Kirstie L., City College of San Francisco
Straub, Derek J., Susquehanna University
Straus, David M., George Mason University
Strobel, Darrell F., Johns Hopkins University
Strong, Courtenay, University of Utah
Strub, Ted P., Oregon State University
Stull, Roland B., University of British Columbia
Sturges, Bill, University of East Anglia
Stutz, Jochen P., University of California, Los Angeles
Sun, Wen-Yih, Purdue University
Suyker, Andrew E., University of Nebraska, Lincoln
Svoma, Bohumil, University of Missouri, Columbia
Swann, Abigail L., University of Washington
Szunyogh, Istvan, Texas A&M University
Tadesse, Tsegaye, University of Nebraska, Lincoln
Takle, Eugene S., Iowa State University of Science & Technology
Talley, John H., University of Delaware
Tao, Wei-Kuo, Texas A&M University
Tatarskii, Viatcheslav, Georgia Institute of Technology
Tayler, Paul, Utah Valley University
Taylor, Elwynn, Iowa State University of Science & Technology
Taylor, Gregory R., California State University, Chico
Taylor, Peter A., York University
Thorncroft, Christopher D., SUNY, Albany
Thorne, Richard M., University of California, Los Angeles
Thornton, Joel A., University of Washington
Thurtell, George W., University of Guelph
Tillman, James E., University of Washington
Ting, Mingfang, Columbia University
Tomasko, Martin G., University of Arizona
Tongue, Jeffrey, SUNY, Stony Brook
Trapasso, Louis M., Western Kentucky University
Trapp, Robert J., University of Illinois, Urbana-Champaign
Tung, Ka-Kit, University of Washington
Tung, Wen-wen, Purdue University
Turco, Richard, University of California, Los Angeles
Twine, Tracy E., University of Minnesota, Twin Cities
Van Den Broeke, Matthew S., University of Nebraska, Lincoln
van den Heever, Sue, Colorado State University
Vanos, Jennifer K., Texas Tech University
Varner, Ruth K., University of New Hampshire
Vaughan, Geraint, University of Manchester
Vega, Anthony J., Clarion University
Veres, Michael, State University of New York at Oswego
Vimont, Daniel J., University of Wisconsin, Madison
Vincent, Dayton G., Purdue University
Vogelmann, Andrew, SUNY, Stony Brook
von Salzen, Knut, University of British Columbia
Vonder Haar, Thomas H., Colorado State University
Vong, Richard J., Oregon State University
Vukovich, George, York University
Wagner, Timothy J., Creighton University
Walcek, Christopher J., SUNY, Albany
Waliser, Duane E., SUNY, Stony Brook
Wallace, John M., University of Washington
Walsh, John E., University of Illinois, Urbana-Champaign
Walter-Shea, Elizabeth A., University of Nebraska, Lincoln
Wang, Chien, Massachusetts Institute of Technology

Wang, Hsiang-Jui, Georgia Institute of Technology
Wang, Jian, SUNY, Stony Brook
Wang, Jun, University of Nebraska, Lincoln
Wang, Pao-Kuan, University of Wisconsin, Madison
Wang, Wei-Chyung, SUNY, Albany
Wang, Yuhang, Georgia Institute of Technology
Wang, Yuqing, University of Hawai'i, Manoa
Wang, Yuxuan, Texas A&M University
Wang, Zhuo, University of Illinois, Urbana-Champaign
Warland, Jon, University of Guelph
Warren, Stephen G., University of Washington
Watson, Gerald F., North Carolina State University
Waugh, Darryn W., Johns Hopkins University
Wax, Charles L., Mississippi State University
Weare, B. C., University of California, Davis
Weaver, Justin E., Texas Tech University
Weber, Rodney J., Georgia Institute of Technology
Webster, Peter J., Georgia Institute of Technology
Weinbeck, Robert S., SUNY, The College at Brockport
Weiss, Christopher C., Texas Tech University
Wennberg, Paul O., California Institute of Technology
Wesely, Marvin L., Argonne National Laboratory
Wettstein, Justin, Oregon State University
Whitaker, Rodney W., Los Alamos National Laboratory
Whitehead, James, University of Manchester
Whiteway, James, York University
Wikle, Christopher K., University of Missouri, Columbia
Wilhelmson, Robert B., University of Illinois, Urbana-Champaign
Wilhite, Donald A., University of Nebraska, Lincoln
Wilkerson, Forrest, Minnesota State University
Wilks, Daniel, Cornell University
Williams, John M., SUNY, The College at Brockport
Williams, Kaj, Montana State University
Williams, Kay R., Shippensburg University
Williams, Mathew, Edinburgh University
Williams, Paul, University of Manchester
Willoughby, Hugh E., Florida International University
Wilson, John D., University of Alberta
Wine, Paul H., Georgia Institute of Technology
Wofsy, Steven C., Harvard University
Wood, Kim, Mississippi State University
Wood, Robert, University of Washington
Wu, Shiliang, Michigan Technological University
Wu, Xiaoqing, Iowa State University of Science & Technology
Wu, Yutian, Purdue University
Wuebbles, Donald J., University of Illinois, Urbana-Champaign
Wysocki, Mark, Cornell University
Xie, Feiqin, Texas A&M University, Corpus Christi
Xie, Lian, North Carolina State University
Yalda, Sepideh, Millersville University
Yang, Ping, Texas A&M University
Yarger, Douglas N., Iowa State University of Science & Technology
Yau, Man Kong, McGill University
Yi, Chuixiang, Queens College (CUNY)
Young, John A., University of Wisconsin, Madison
Yung, Yuk L., California Institute of Technology
Yuter, Sandra, North Carolina State University
Yuter, Sandra E., University of Washington
Zaitchik, Benjamin, Johns Hopkins University
Zawadzki, Isztar I., McGill University
Zehnder, Joseph A., Creighton University
Zender, Charles, University of California, Irvine
Zeng, Ning, University of Maryland
Zhang, Henian, Georgia Institute of Technology
Zhang, Minghua, SUNY, Stony Brook
Zhang, Renyi, Texas A&M University
Zhang, Xi, University of California, Santa Cruz
Zhang, Yang, North Carolina State University
Zhu, Ping, Florida International University
Zipser, Edward, University of Utah
Zuend, Andreas, McGill University

Earth Science Education
Albach, Suzanne M., Washtenaw Community College
Arthurs, Leilani A., University of Nebraska, Lincoln
Attrep, Moses, Los Alamos National Laboratory
Aylward, Linda, Illinois Central College
Baker, Brett, University of Texas at Austin
Barnett, Michael, Boston College
Bechtel, Randy, North Carolina Geological Survey
Bednarski, Marsha, Central Connecticut State University
Bednarz, Robert S., Texas A&M University
Bednarz, Sarah W., Texas A&M University
Bergwerff, Kenneth A., Calvin College
Bitting, Kelsey S., University of Kansas
Black, Alice (Jill), Missouri State University
Blankenbicker, Adam, Smithsonian Institution / National Museum of Natural History
Buchanan, Rex C., University of Kansas
Burns, Sandra, Central Connecticut State University
Busch, Richard M., West Chester University

Butcher, Patricia M., California State University, Fullerton
Carpenter, John R., University of South Carolina
Casto, Pamela, Fairmont State University
Chandler, Sandra, Arkansas Geological Survey
Clark, Scott K., University of Wisconsin, Eau Claire
Clary, Renee M., Mississippi State University
Coburn, Daniel, Southern Connecticut State University
Conners, John S., Austin Community College District
Conway, Michael F., Arizona Geological Survey
Cooney, Timothy M., University of Northern Iowa
Crowder, Margaret, Western Kentucky University
Cunningham, Amy J., Austin Community College District
d'Alessio, Matthew, California State University, Northridge
Dakin, Susan, University of Lethbridge
Davies, Gareth, The Open University
Davies, Sarah, The Open University
De Kock, Walter E., University of Northern Iowa
de Ritter, Samantha, Flinders University
Dehne, Kevin T., Delta College
DeKraker, Dan, Cerritos College
DePriest, Thomas A., University of Tennessee, Martin
Dieckmann, Melissa S., Eastern Kentucky University
Eldredge, Sandra N., Utah Geological Survey
Elkins, Joe T., University of Northern Colorado
Emerson, Cheryl R., Illinois Central College
Engels, Jennifer, University of Hawai'i, Manoa
Englebright, Stephen C., SUNY, Stony Brook
Ensign, Todd, Fairmont State University
Ferguson, Julie , University of California, Irvine
FitzPatrick, Meriel, University of Plymouth
Fleck, Michelle, Utah State University
Ford, Jaime L., Fairmont State University
Frankic, Anamarija, University of Massachusetts, Boston
Gersmehl, Carol, Hunter College (CUNY)
Godsey, Holly, University of Utah
Goldstein, Fredric R., College of New Jersey
Goodell, Laurel P., Princeton University
Gray, Kyle R., University of Northern Iowa
Havholm, Karen G., University of Wisconsin, Eau Claire
Heid, Kelly L., Grand Valley State University
Heine, Sallie, Augustana College
Hemler, Deb, Fairmont State University
Herman, Theodore C., West Valley College
Holliman, Richard, The Open University
Hubenthal, Michael, Binghamton University
Hunter, Arlene , The Open University
Jahanyar, Alireza, University of Tabriz
Johnston, Thomas, University of Lethbridge
King-Rundel, Judith A., California State University, Dominguez Hills
Kornreich Wolf, Susan, Augustana College
Kortz, Karen, Community College of Rhode Island
Krause, Lois B., Clemson University
Krockover, Gerald H., Purdue University
Kusnick, Judith E., California State University, Sacramento
LaDue, Nicole D., Northern Illinois University
Lebold, Joe, West Virginia University
Libarkin, Julie C., Michigan State University
Llerandi-Roman, Pablo A., Grand Valley State University
Ludwikoski, David J., Community College of Baltimore County, Catonsville
MacLachlan, Ian E., University of Lethbridge
Martin-Vermilyea, Laurie, Montgomery County Community College
Mathison, Mark E., Iowa State University of Science & Technology
Mattox, Stephen R., Grand Valley State University
McCartney, M. C., University of Wisconsin, Extension
McEvoy, Jamie , Montana State University
McMullin, David, Acadia University
McNeal, Karen, North Carolina State University
Messina, Paula, San Jose State University
Morgan, Emory, Hampton University
Morton, Allan E., Central Arizona College
Mulkey, Sean, Illinois Central College
Munski, Douglas C., University of North Dakota
Nakagawa, Masami, Colorado School of Mines
Norris-Tull, Delena, University of Montana Western
Papcun, George, New Jersey City University
Pearson, David A., Laurentian University, Sudbury
Pepple, Christopher, Bowling Green State University
Petcovic, Heather L., Western Michigan University
Petit, Martin A., Illinois Central College
Pew, Caroline, Highline College
Phillips, Paul, Fort Hays State University
Preston, William L., California Polytechnic State University
Pyle, Eric J., James Madison University
Rakonczai, Janos, Univesity of Szeged
Raol, Marcie, Fairmont State University
Refenes, James L., Concordia University
Schaffer, Linda J., SUNY, The College at Brockport
Schmitt, Danielle M., Princeton University
Schwob, Robert J., Itasca Community College
Scott, Vernon, Oklahoma State University

Sharp, S. L., Virginia Polytechnic Institute & State University
Shelton, Dale W., Maryland Department of Natural Resources
Shepardson, Daniel, Purdue University
Shipp, Stephanie S., Rice University
Skalac, Priscilla, Olivet Nazarene University
Slattery, William, Wright State University
Smith, Arthur, West Chester University
Spurr, Aaron, University of Northern Iowa
Stevens, Michael, University of Northern Iowa
Sundareshwar, P. V., South Dakota School of Mines & Technology
Sutton, Connie J., Indiana University of Pennsylvania
Teed, Rebecca, Wright State University
Thompson, Kenneth W., Emporia State University
Tonon, Marco Davide, Università di Torino
Van Burgh, Dana P., Casper College
Viskupic, Karen, Boise State University
Wagner, John R., Clemson University
Weaver Bowman, Kristin, California State University, Fullerton
Wright, Carrie L., University of Southern Indiana
Young, James E., Appalachian State University
Zipper, Carl E., Virginia Polytechnic Institute & State University
Zlotkin, Howard, New Jersey City University
Zwick, Thomas T., Montana State University, Billings

Physical Geography

Aay, Henry, Calvin College
Abend, Martin, New Jersey City University
Aber, Jeremy, Middle Tennessee State University
Adam, Iddrisu, University of Wisconsin Colleges
Adams, Steven, Antelope Valley College
Ajassa, Roberto, Università di Torino
All, John, Western Kentucky University
Amador, Nathanael S., Ohio Wesleyan University
Aubert, John E., American River College
Balascio, Nicholas, College of William & Mary
Barnett, Roger T., University of the Pacific
Barton, James H., Thiel College
Bascom, Johnathan, Calvin College
Bass, David, Flinders University
Bates, Mary, College of the Canyons
Battles, Eileen, University of Kansas
Beeton, Jared M., Adams State University
Bein, F. L., Indiana University, Indianapolis
Bekker, Matthew F., Brigham Young University
Bereitschaft, Bradley, University of Nebraska at Omaha
Berry, Kate, University of Nevada, Reno
Biggs, Thomas H., University of Virginia
Bird, Jeffry S., Brigham Young University
Bitner, Thomas, University of Wisconsin Colleges
Black, Kathryn, Montclair State University
Blackburn, William, Western Kentucky University
Blewett, William L., Shippensburg University
Boester, Michael, Monroe Community College
Brey, James, University of Wisconsin Colleges
Brothen, Jerry, El Camino College
Brothers, Timothy S., Indiana University / Purdue University, Indianapolis
Brothers, Timothy S., Indiana University, Indianapolis
Butzow, Dean G., Lincoln Land Community College
Cairns, David M., Texas A&M University
Camille, Michael A., University of Louisiana, Monroe
Campbell, Glenn A., Eastern Kentucky University
Carter, Greg, University of Southern Mississippi
Chacko, Elizabeth, George Washington University
Chaddock, Lisa, Cuyamaca College
Chaney, Phil L., Auburn University
Chatterjee, Meera, University of Akron
Cheung, Wing, Palomar College
Clennan, Patrick D., College of Southern Nevada - West Charleston Campus
Coburn, Craig, University of Lethbridge
Cohen, Saul B., Graduate School of the City University of New York
Comrie, Andrew, University of Arizona
Corson, Mark W., Northwest Missouri State University
Coveney, Eamonn, Fort Hays State University
Croft, Gary M., San Bernardino Valley College
Csiki, Shane, New Hampshire Geological Survey
Curry, Janel M., Calvin College
Dawsey, Cyrus B., Auburn University
de Uña Alvarez, Elena P., Coruna University
Deakin, Ann K., SUNY, Fredonia
Deckert, Garret, University of Wisconsin Colleges
DeWeese, Georgina G., University of West Georgia
Dexter, Leland R., Northern Arizona University
Dommissee, Edwin, University of Wisconsin Colleges
Dubsky, Scott , United States Air Force Academy
Duncan, Ian, City College of San Francisco
Ebiner, Matt, El Camino College
Eichenbaum, Jack, Hunter College (CUNY)
Eisenhart, Karen, Edinboro University of Pennsylvania
Engstrom, Vanessa, San Bernardino Valley College
Foltltin, Thomas, George Washington University

Fonstad, Mark, University of Oregon
Fratianni, Simona, Università di Torino
Friend, Donald A., Minnesota State University
Frolking, Tod A., Denison University
Fuller, Doult O., George Washington University
Gamble, Douglas W., University of North Carolina Wilmington
Gaubatz, Piper, University of Massachusetts, Amherst
Gavin, Dan, University of Oregon
Gentry, Christopher, Austin Peay State University
Gersmehl, Philip, Hunter College (CUNY)
Girhard, T S., San Antonio Community College
Girhard, Thomas S., Alamo Colleges - San Antonio College
Goudge, Theodore L., Northwest Missouri State University
Graff, William P., New Jersey Geological Survey
Graham, Barbara, College of Southern Nevada - West Charleston Campus
Greene, Don M., Baylor University
Hall, Luke D., Ventura College
Hampson, Arthur, University of Utah
Harley, Grant, University of Southern Mississippi
Harris, Jasper L., North Carolina Central University
Harrison, Robert S., Long Island University, C.W. Post Campus
Hart, Evan A., Tennessee Tech University
Harty, John P., Johnson County Community College
Hay, Iain, Flinders University
Heibel, Todd, San Bernardino Valley College
Hepner, George F., University of Utah
Hess, Darrel E., City College of San Francisco
Heywood, Neil C., University of Wisconsin, Stevens Point
Hickcox, David H., Ohio Wesleyan University
Hobbs, Chasidy, University of West Florida
Holt, David, University of Southern Mississippi
Houston, Serin D., Mount Holyoke College
Howard, Leslie M., University of Nebraska - Lincoln
Ibrahim, Mohamed B., Graduate School of the City University of New York
Jackson, Philip L., Oregon State University
Jain, Cathy, Palomar College
Jarvis, Richard S., University of Texas, El Paso
Ji, Wei, University of Missouri-Kansas City
Johnson, Mark O., Worcester State University
Johnston, Andrew K., Smithsonian Institution / National Air & Space Museum
Jordan, Karen J., University of South Alabama
Jurmu, Michael, University of Wisconsin Colleges
Karpilo, Jr, Ronald J., Colorado State University
Kebbede, Girma, Mount Holyoke College
Keen-Zebert, Amanda, Desert Research Institute
Kennedy, Linda, Mansfield University
Key, Doug, Palomar College
Khan, Belayet H., Eastern Illinois University
Kiage, Lawrence M., Georgia State University
Kilcoyne, John R., Metropolitan State College of Denver
Kimber, Clarissa T., Texas A&M University
Kung, Hsiang-Te, University of Memphis
Laity, Julie E., California State University, Northridge
Lambert, Dean P., San Antonio Community College
Lambert, Dean, Alamo Colleges - San Antonio College
Landon, Patrick J., Wassuk College
Lawson, Merlin P., University of Nebraska, Lincoln
League, Larry D., Dickinson State University
Lee, Jeffrey A., Texas Tech University
Lee, Russell, Oak Ridge National Laboratory
Lew, Alan A., Northern Arizona University
Lineback, Neal G., Appalachian State University
Little, Jonathan, Monroe Community College
LoVetere, Crystal, Cerritos College
Lynn, Resler M., Virginia Polytechnic Institute & State University
MacQuarrie, Pamela, Mount Royal University
Maher, John, Johnson County Community College
Maio, Chris, University of Alaska Fairbanks
Mann, Dan, University of Alaska Fairbanks
Manos, Leah D., Northwest Missouri State University
Markwith, Scott H., Florida Atlantic University
Martinson, Tom L., Auburn University
Marzulli, Walter, New Jersey Geological Survey
Mathenge, Christine, Austin Peay State University
McCallister, Robert, University of Wisconsin Colleges
McCoy, William D., University of Massachusetts, Amherst
McCraw, David J., New Mexico Institute of Mining & Technology
McGrath, Jr., Dorn C., George Washington University
McGwire, Kenneth C., Desert Research Institute
Mensing, Scott A., University of Nevada, Reno
Millette, Thomas L., University of Massachusetts, Amherst
Minnich, Richard A., University of California, Riverside
Miretti, Domenick, East Los Angeles College
Montgomery, Keith, University of Wisconsin Colleges
Montoya, Judith, Northern Arizona University
Motta, Luigi, Università di Torino
Motta, Michele, Università di Torino
Musolf, Gene E., University of Wisconsin Colleges
Nelson, Kenneth A., University of Kansas
Ngoy, Kikombo, Kean University

Nicholas, Joseph W., Mary Washington College
Nichols, Jr., Woodrow W., North Carolina Central University
Norwood, James, Auburn University
Nuwategeka, Expedito, Gulu University
Ogbuchiekwe, Edmund Jekwu, San Bernardino Valley College
Olson, Kimberly, American River College
Paulsell, Robert L., Louisiana State University
Peake, Jeffrey S., University of Nebraska at Omaha
Pesses, Michael, Antelope Valley College
Phillips, Nathan, Boston University
Pinnt, Todd, Arizona Western College
Precht, Francis L., Frostburg State University
Price, Alan P., University of Wisconsin Colleges
Price, Marie D., George Washington University
Privette, David, Central Piedmont Community College
Rahman, Abu, Antelope Valley College
Reese, Andy, University of Southern Mississippi
Rettig, Andrew, University of Dayton
Robinson, Michael A., Santa Barbara City College
Rodgers, John C., Mississippi State University
Rohe, Randall, University of Wisconsin Colleges
Rollins, Kyle, Missouri Dept of Natural Resources
Rose, I. S., University of West Georgia
Ross, Thomas E., University of North Carolina, Pembroke
Rudnicki, Ryan E., Alamo Colleges - San Antonio College
Rudnicki, Ryan E., San Antonio Community College
Ryan, Christopher, University of Nevada, Reno
Sandlin, Stephen H., San Bernardino Valley College
Santelmann, Mary V., Oregon State University
Saunders, Ralph, California State University, Dominguez Hills
Schafer, Tom, Fort Hays State University
Schmidt, Lisa, San Bernardino Valley College
Schmidt, Jr., Robert H., University of Texas, El Paso
Scott, Larry, Colorado Geological Survey
Scott, Thomas A., University of California, Riverside
Sharkey, Debra, Cosumnes River College
Smith, C. K., San Antonio Community College
Smith, Charles K., Alamo Colleges - San Antonio College
Smith, Steven C., American River College
Spencer, Jeremy, University of Akron
Stahmann, Paul, McHenry County College
Starrs, Paul F., University of Nevada, Reno
Stern, Herschel I., MiraCosta College
Stevens, Stan, University of Massachusetts, Amherst
Stocks, Ledrew, Mansfield University
Sullivan, James D., East Los Angeles College
Swarts, Stanley W., Northern Arizona University
Thompson, Wiley C., United States Military Academy
Thomsen, Charles E., American River College
Tingley, Susan L., University of Nevada
Todhunter, Paul, University of North Dakota
Tremblay, Thomas A., University of Texas at Austin, Jackson School of Geosciences
van Leeuwen, Willem, University of Arizona
Van Stan, John, Georgia Southern University
Veverka, Laura, Metropolitan Community College-Kansas City
Vogel, Eve, University of Massachusetts, Amherst
Webb, Byron J., Austin Peay State University
Welford, Mark R., Georgia Southern University
West, Keith, University of Wisconsin Colleges
White, Scott, Fort Lewis College
Wibking, R. Kenton, Austin Peay State University
Wickham, Thomas, California University of Pennsylvania
Wilkie, Richard W., University of Massachusetts, Amherst
Wilkins, David E., Boise State University
Williams, Harris, North Carolina Central University
Wilson, Jeffey S., Indiana University, Indianapolis
Wu, Shuang-Ye, University of Dayton
Wyckoff, John W., University of Colorado, Denver
Yassin, Barbara E., Mississippi Office of Geology
Yeager, Charles, Snow College
Zhou, Yuyu, Iowa State University of Science & Technology
Zorba, Molly, Antelope Valley College

Ocean Engineering/Mining
Ajayi, J. O., Obafemi Awolowo University
Becker, Janet M., University of Hawai'i, Manoa
Buchannon, Robin C., University of Mississippi
Carpenter, Roy, University of Washington
Fries, David P., University of South Florida, Saint Petersburg
Gibson, Carl H., University of California, San Diego
Hall, Michael, University of South Florida, Saint Petersburg
Hodgkiss, Jr., William S., University of California, San Diego
Hoopes, John A., University of Wisconsin, Madison
Irish, Jennifer, Virginia Tech
Kaltenbacher, Eric A., University of South Florida, Saint Petersburg
Langebrake, Larry C., University of South Florida, Saint Petersburg
Lembke, Chad E., University of South Florida, Saint Petersburg
Patten, James T., University of South Florida, Saint Petersburg
Reichard, Ronnal, Florida Institute of Technology
Russell, D. R., University of South Florida, Saint Petersburg

Sahoo, Prasanta, Florida Institute of Technology
Samson, Scott A., University of South Florida, Saint Petersburg
Short, R. T., University of South Florida, Saint Petersburg
Swain, Geoffry, Florida Institute of Technology
Tilbury, Graham, University of South Florida, Saint Petersburg
Weaver, Robert, Florida Institute of Technology
Wood, Neill, Exeter University
Wood, Stephen L., Florida Institute of Technology

Remote Sensing

Aanstoos, James V., Iowa State University of Science & Technology
Abrams, Michael J., Jet Propulsion Laboratory
Ackerman, Steven A., University of Wisconsin, Madison
Ahearn, Sean C., Graduate School of the City University of New York
Alley, Ronald E., Jet Propulsion Laboratory
Aly, Mohamed H., University of Arkansas, Fayetteville
Applegarth, Michael T., Shippensburg University
Arvidson, Raymond E., Washington University in St. Louis
Barnett, Albert P., North Carolina Central University
Barros, Jose Antonio, Florida International University
Becker, Richard H., Argonne National Laboratory
Berlin, Graydon L., Northern Arizona University
Bernier, Monique, Universite du Quebec
Binford, Micheal W., University of Florida
Blom, Ronald G., Jet Propulsion Laboratory
Boelman, Natalie, Columbia University
Bogucki, Donald J., Plattsburgh State University (SUNY)
Boulton, Sarah, University of Plymouth
Brewer, Micheal, George Washington University
Broadfoot, Lyle A., University of Arizona
Bulusu, Subrahmanyam, University of South Carolina
Buratti, Bonnie J., Jet Propulsion Laboratory
Cablk, Mary, Desert Research Institute
Callahan, John A., University of Delaware
Calvin, Wendy, University of Nevada, Reno
Campbell, Bruce A., Smithsonian Institution / National Air & Space Museum
Campbell, James B., Virginia Polytechnic Institute & State University
Carn, Simon, Michigan Technological University
Chen, Shu-Hua, University of California, Davis
Chen, Xianfeng, Slippery Rock University
Chopping, Mark J., Montclair State University
Cooke, III, William H., Mississippi State University
Crippen, Robert E., Jet Propulsion Laboratory
Dana, Gayle L., University of Nevada, Reno
Dash, Padmanava, Mississippi State University
Di Girolamo, Larry, University of Illinois, Urbana-Champaign
Dixon, Tim, University of Miami
Dodge, Rebecca L., Midwestern State University
Dondofema, Farai, University of Venda for Science & Technology
Easson, Gregory L., University of Mississippi
El-Baz, Farouk, Boston University
Fenstermaker, Lynn, Desert Research Institute
Ferris, Michael H., California State University, Dominguez Hills
Fildes, Stephen , Flinders University
Flynn, Luke P., University of Hawai'i, Manoa
Forster, Richard R., University of Utah
Fox, Amelia A., Fort Hays State University
Frankenberg, Christian, California Institute of Technology
Frazier, Bruce E., Washington State University
Friedl, Mark A., Boston University
Frost, Eric G., San Diego State University
Gaitan-Moran, Javier, Universidad Autonoma de Baja California Sur
Gallie, Ann, Laurentian University, Sudbury
Gammack-Clark, James, Florida Atlantic University
Gamon, John, University of Alberta
Gaulton, Rachel, University of Newcastle Upon Tyne
Gaya, Charles , Jomo Kenyatta University of Agriculture & Technology
Ghent, Rebecca, University of Toronto
Gibson, Glen, United States Air Force Academy
Gilbes, Fernando, University of Puerto Rico
Giraldo, Mario A., California State University, Northridge
Glenn, Nancy, Boise State University
Goetz, Alexander, University of Colorado
Gonzalez, Frank, University of Washington
Hacker, Jorg, Flinders University
Hanna, Stephen P., Mary Washington College
Hardin, Perry J., Brigham Young University
Haritashya, Umesh, University of Dayton
Hasan, Khaled, Austin Community College District
Hay, Rodrick, California State University, Dominguez Hills
Hayes, James J., University of Nebraska at Omaha
Heidinger, Andrew, University of Wisconsin, Madison
Hernandez, Michael W., Weber State University
Hinojosa, Alejandro, Centro de Investigación Científica y de Ed Superior de Ensenada
Hobbs, Richard D., Amarillo College
Hook, Simon J., Jet Propulsion Laboratory
Hu, Baoxin, York University
Hu, Zhiyong, University of West Florida
Huang, Hung-Lung Allen, Texas A&M University

Huang, Yi, McGill University
Hung, Ming-Chih, Northwest Missouri State University
Hutchinson, Charles F., University of Arizona
Jackson, Mark W., Brigham Young University
Jaworski, Eugene, Eastern Michigan University
Jeu, Amy, Hunter College (CUNY)
Jin, Yufang, University of California, Davis
Johnson, Elias, Missouri State University
Kahle, Anne B., Jet Propulsion Laboratory
Kenduiywo, Benson K., Jomo Kenyatta University of Agriculture & Technology
Kennedy, Robert, Oregon State University
Kern, Anikó, Eotvos Lorand University
Kessler, Fritz, Frostburg State University
Key, Jeffrey R., University of Wisconsin, Madison
Khan, Shuhab, University of Houston
Kimerling, A. Jon, Oregon State University
Klein, Andrew, Texas A&M University
Klemas, Victor, University of Delaware
Kollias, Pavlos, McGill University
Kudela, Raphael M., University of California, Santa Cruz
Lakhan, V. Chris, University of Windsor
Larson, Eric J., University of Wisconsin, Stevens Point
Lawrence, Rick L., Montana State University
Lee, Keenan, Colorado School of Mines
Lee, Zhongping , University of Massachusetts, Boston
Liu, Jian G., Imperial College
Lu, Zhong, Southern Methodist University
Lulla, Kamlesh, University of Delaware
Luman, Donald E., University of Illinois, Urbana-Champaign
Lyon, Ronald J. P., Stanford University
Marsh, Stuart E., University of Arizona
Mason, Philippa J., Imperial College
Mccoy, Roger M., University of Utah
McDade, Ian C., York University
McFarquhar, Greg M., University of Illinois, Urbana-Champaign
McGrath, Andrew, Flinders University
McGwire, Kenneth, University of Nevada, Reno
Merchant, James W., Unversity of Nebraska - Lincoln
Meyer, Franz J., University of Alaska Fairbanks
Miao, Xin, Missouri State University
Middleton, Carrie A., Environmental Protection Agency
Milan-Navarro, Joel, Universidad Autonoma de San Luis Potosi
Miller, John, York University
Miller, Richard, East Carolina University
Millette, Thomas L., Mount Holyoke College
Minor, Timothy B., Desert Research Institute
Molnár, Gábor, Eotvos Lorand University
Molnia, Bruce F., Duke University
Morgan, Ken M., Texas Christian University
Mshiu, Elisante E., University of Dar es Salaam
Muller-Karger, Frank E., University of South Florida
Mushkin, Amit, University of Washington
Mustard, John F., Brown University
Myneni, Ranga , Boston University
Nduati, Eunice W., Jomo Kenyatta University of Agriculture & Technology
Ngigi, Thomas G., Jomo Kenyatta University of Agriculture & Technology
Ni-Meister, Wenge, Hunter College (CUNY)
Njoku, Eni G., Jet Propulsion Laboratory
Nolin, Anne, Oregon State University
Nowicki, Scott A., University of Nevada, Las Vegas
Palluconi, Frank D., Jet Propulsion Laboratory
Parrish, Christopher E., University of New Hampshire
Pathirana, Sumith, Southern Cross University
Peddle, Derek R., University of Lethbridge
Peltzer, Gilles, University of California, Los Angeles
Petty, Grant W., University of Wisconsin, Madison
Pieters, Carle M., Brown University
Platnick, Steven, University of Wisconsin, Madison
Porter, John H., University of Virginia
Prakash, Anupma, University of Alaska Fairbanks
Price, Kevin, Kansas State University
Quisenberry, Dan R., Mercer University
Ramage, Joan, Lehigh University
Ramsey, Michael S., University of Pittsburgh
Ramspott, Matthew E., Frostburg State University
Rapp, Anita, Texas A&M University
Reed, Wallace E., University of Virginia
Ridd, Merrill K., University of Utah
Rivard, Benoit, University of Alberta
Roberts, Charles E., Florida Atlantic University
Robinson, Ian S., University of Southampton
Rundquist, Bradley C., University of North Dakota
Rundquist, Donald C., Unversity of Nebraska - Lincoln
Sadiq, Abdulali A., University of Qatar
Sanden, Eric M., University of Wisconsin, River Falls
Schaaf, Crystal, Boston University
Schaaf, Crystal, University of Massachusetts, Boston
Schenk, Anton, SUNY, Buffalo
Shi, Xuan, University of Arkansas, Fayetteville
Small, Christopher, Columbia University

Smith, Mike, Kingston University
Smith, Peter, University of Arizona
Steffen, Konrad, University of Colorado
Stohr, Christopher J., University of Illinois, Urbana-Champaign
Stradford, Todd, University of Wisconsin, Platteville
Strahler, Alan, Boston University
Strain, Priscilla L., Smithsonian Institution / National Air & Space Museum
Sui, Daniel Z., Texas A&M University
Sultan, Mohamed, Western Michigan University
Szekielda, Karl H., Graduate School of the City University of New York
Szekielda, Karl H., Hunter College (CUNY)
Toth, Charles K., Ohio State University
Trust, Michael, University of Massachusetts, Boston
Tullis, Jason A., University of Arkansas, Fayetteville
Turner, Eugene, California State University, Northridge
Ustin, Susan L., University of California, Davis
Ustin, Susan L., University of California, Davis
Vandemark, Douglas C., University of New Hampshire
Velicogna, Isabella, University of California, Irvine
Ventura, Stephen J., University of Wisconsin, Madison
Viertel, Dave, Eastern Illinois University
Walker, Richard, University of Oxford
Warner, Timothy A., West Virginia University
Wasomi, Charles B., Jomo Kenyatta University of Agriculture & Technology
Watson, Kelly, Eastern Kentucky University
Wei, Xiaofang, Central State University
Weng, Qihao, Indiana State University
White, Jeffrey G., North Carolina State University
White, Joseph D., Baylor University
Woo, David, California State University, East Bay
Woodcock, Curtis E., Boston University
Yan, Xiao-Hai, University of Delaware
Yilmaz, Alper, Ohio State University
Yool, Stephen R., University of Arizona
Yuan, Fei, Minnesota State University
Zhang, Caiyun, Florida Atlantic University
Zhou, Wei (Wendy), Colorado School of Mines
Zhou, Xiaobing, Montana Tech

Soil Science

Balser, Teri , University of Florida
Bonczek, James, University of Florida
Brinkmann, Robert, Hofstra University
Brock-Hon, Amy, University of Tennessee at Chattanooga
Brown, James R., University of Missouri, Columbia
Budke, William, Ventura College
Curry, Susan, University of Florida
Dahlgren, Randy A., University of California, Davis
Davis, J G., University of Missouri, Columbia
DeLaune, Paul, Texas A&M University
DeSutter, Tom, North Dakota State University
Dou, Fugen, Texas A&M University
Dougil, Andy, University of Leeds
Eppes, Martha C., University of North Carolina, Charlotte
Gale, Paula M., University of Tennessee, Martin
Gantzer, Clark J., University of Missouri, Columbia
Geisseler, Daniel, University of California, Davis
Gerber, Stefan, University of Florida
Golabi, Mohammad H., University of Guam
Hopmans, Jan W., University of California, Davis
Horwath, William R., University of California, Davis
Inglett, Kanika Sharma, University of Florida
Jackson, Louise E., University of California, Davis
Kramer, Marc, University of Florida
Kremer, Robert J., University of Missouri, Columbia
Lerch, Robert N., University of Missouri, Columbia
Marrs, Rob, University of Liverpool
McBride, Raymond G., University of Guelph
Mishra, Umakant, Argonne National Laboratory
Motavalli, Peter P., University of Missouri, Columbia
O'Geen, Toby, University of California, Davis
Parikh, Sanjai, University of California, Davis
Richards, James H., University of California, Davis
Richter, Daniel D., Duke University
Risk, Dave A., Saint Francis Xavier University
Scow, Kate, University of California, Davis
Sinclair, Hugh D., Edinburgh University
Sleezer, Richard O., Emporia State University
Sletten, Ronald S., University of Washington
Smukler, Sean, University of British Columbia
Sohi, Sran P., Edinburgh University
Southard, Randal J., University of California, Davis
Stevens, W. G., University of Missouri, Columbia
Szulczewski, Melanie, University of Mary Washington
Wesley Wood, Charley, University of Florida

Meteorology

Adams, Manda S., University of North Carolina, Charlotte
Arritt, Raymond W., Iowa State University of Science & Technology
Ault, Toby R., Cornell University
Babb, David M., Pennsylvania State University, University Park

Bahrmann, Chad, Pennsylvania State University, University Park
Baigorria, Guillermo, University of Nebraska, Lincoln
Bannon, Peter R., Pennsylvania State University, University Park
Barbor, RADM Ken E., University of Southern Mississippi
Barnes, Gary M., University of Hawai'i, Manoa
Bartholy, Judit, Eotvos Lorand University
Baxter, Martin, Central Michigan University
Bell, Michael, University of Hawai'i, Manoa
Billings, Brian J., Saint Cloud State University
Blackwell, Keith G., University of South Alabama
Bleck, Rainer, Los Alamos National Laboratory
Bohren, Craig F., Pennsylvania State University, University Park
Bowman, Kenneth P., Texas A&M University
Brown, Michael E., Mississippi State University
Brown, Paul W., University of Arizona
Brune, William H., Pennsylvania State University, University Park
Businger, Steven, University of Hawai'i, Manoa
Cahir, John J., Pennsylvania State University, University Park
Carlson, Richard E., Iowa State University of Science & Technology
Carlson, Toby N., Pennsylvania State University, University Park
Carroll, David, Virginia Polytechnic Institute & State University
Challinor, Andy, University of Leeds
Chang, Chih-Pei, Naval Postgraduate School
Chen, Hway-Jen, Naval Postgraduate School
Chen, Yi-Leng, University of Hawai'i, Manoa
Clark, John H., Pennsylvania State University, University Park
Clothiaux, Eugene E., Pennsylvania State University, University Park
Colby, Frank P., University of Massachusetts Lowell
Cook, David R., Argonne National Laboratory
Corona, Thomas J., Metropolitan State College of Denver
Coulter, Richard L., Argonne National Laboratory
Cox, Helen M., California State University, Northridge
Crafts, Christine, SUNY, The College at Brockport
Creasey, Robert L., Naval Postgraduate School
Croft, Paul J., Kean University
Croft, Paul J., Mississippi State University
Cullen, Heidi, Georgia Institute of Technology
Czarnetzki, Alan C., University of Northern Iowa
Dahl, Johannes M., Texas Tech University
Davidson, Kenneth L., Naval Postgraduate School
Davis, Christopher A., Texas A&M University
Davis, Kenneth J., Pennsylvania State University, University Park
Deng, Aijun, Pennsylvania State University, University Park
Dewey, Ken F., University of Nebraska, Lincoln
Dixon, P. Grady, Fort Hays State University
Dorling, Stephen, University of East Anglia
Duncan Tabb, Neva, Saint Petersburg College, Clearwater
Durkee, Philip A., Naval Postgraduate School
Dutton, John A., Pennsylvania State University, University Park
Dyer, Jamie, Mississippi State University
Eastin, Matt, University of North Carolina, Charlotte
Ellingson, Don, Western Oregon University
Elsberry, Russell L., Naval Postgraduate School
Emanuel, Kerry A., Massachusetts Institute of Technology
Estberg, Gerald N., University of San Diego
Evans, Jenni L., Pennsylvania State University, University Park
Ewenz, Caecilia, Flinders University
Fairchild, Jane, University of Wisconsin Colleges
Farrell, Brian F., Harvard University
Ferger, Marisa, Pennsylvania State University, University Park
Fillion, Luc, McGill University
Finley, Jason P., Los Angeles Pierce College
Fitzpatrick, Patrick J., Mississippi State University
Flory, David M., Iowa State University of Science & Technology
Flynn, Wendilyn, University of Northern Colorado
Forster, Piers, University of Leeds
Frank, William M., Pennsylvania State University, University Park
Fraser, Alistair B., Pennsylvania State University, University Park
Frederickson, Paul A., Naval Postgraduate School
Fritsch, J. Michael, Pennsylvania State University, University Park
Fullmer, James W., Southern Connecticut State University
Gadomski, Frederick J., Pennsylvania State University, University Park
Galewsky, Joseph, University of New Mexico
Gauthier, Pierre, Universite du Quebec a Montreal
Gedzelman, Stanley D., Graduate School of the City University of New York
Gillespie, Terry J., University of Guelph
Girard, Eric, Universite du Quebec a Montreal
Godek, Melissa, SUNY, Oneonta
Greybush, Steven J., Pennsylvania State University, University Park
Griswold, Jennifer, University of Hawai'i, Manoa
Guest, Peter S., Naval Postgraduate School
Gutowski, William J., Iowa State University of Science & Technology
Gyakum, John R., McGill University
Hacker, Joshua P., Naval Postgraduate School
Hage, Keith D., University of Alberta
Hallin, Stephen C., Weber State University
Hamill, Paul, McHenry County College
Haney, Christa M., Mississippi State University
Haney, Robert, Naval Postgraduate School
Hansen, Anthony R., Saint Cloud State University

Harr, Patrick A., Naval Postgraduate School
Harrington, Jerry Y., Pennsylvania State University, University Park
Hehr, John G., University of Arkansas, Fayetteville
Hilliker, Joby, West Chester University
Hindman, Edward E., Graduate School of the City University of New York
Hoffman, Eric, Plymouth State University
Hosler, Charles L., Pennsylvania State University, University Park
Illari, Lodovica, Massachusetts Institute of Technology
Jenkins, Gregory S., Pennsylvania State University, University Park
Jordan, Mary S., Naval Postgraduate School
Kaster, Mark A., Wilkes University
Kasting, James F., Pennsylvania State University, University Park
Kimball, Sytske K., University of South Alabama
Knight, Paul, Pennsylvania State University, University Park
Koermer, James P., Plymouth State University
Kubesh, Rodney, Saint Cloud State University
Kumjian, Matthew, Pennsylvania State University, University Park
Lai, Chung Chieng A., Los Alamos National Laboratory
Lamb, Dennis, Pennsylvania State University, University Park
Lander, Mark A., University of Guam
Lee, Sukyoung, Pennsylvania State University, University Park
Leonard, Meredith L., Los Angeles Valley College
Lerach, David G., University of Northern Colorado
Lindzen, Richard S., Massachusetts Institute of Technology
Liu, Yongqiang, Georgia Institute of Technology
Lyons, Steve, Texas A&M University
Lyons, Steven, Angelo State University
Mandia, Scott, Suffolk County Community College, Ammerman Campus
Manzi, Anthony, SUNY, Maritime College
Martin, Jonathan E., University of Wisconsin, Madison
Matthews, Adrian, University of East Anglia
McGauley, Michael G., Miami Dade College (Kendall Campus)
Mendenhall, Larry, Mt. San Antonio College
Mercer, Andrew, Mississippi State University
Montgomery, Michael T., Naval Postgraduate School
Moore, Richard W., Naval Postgraduate School
Morgan, Michael C., University of Wisconsin, Madison
Morschauser, Lindsey, Mississippi State University
Mower, Richard N., Central Michigan University
Murphree, James Thomas, Naval Postgraduate School
Murray, Andrew, University of South Alabama
Najjar, Raymond G., Pennsylvania State University, University Park
Nielsen, Kurt E., Naval Postgraduate School
Nietfeld, Daniel, Creighton University
Ning, Liang, University of Massachusetts, Amherst
Noone, David, Oregon State University
Nordstrom, Greg, Mississippi State University
North, Gerald R., Texas A&M University
Nowotarski, Christopher J., Texas A&M University
Nuss, Wendell A., Naval Postgraduate School
O'Neill, Larry, Oregon State University
Orf, Leigh, Central Michigan University
Panetta, Richard L., Texas A&M University
Park, Myung-Sook, Naval Postgraduate School
Parker, Doug, University of Leeds
Parker, Matthew, North Carolina State University
Parks, Carlton R., Florida Institute of Technology
Pasken, Robert W., Saint Louis University
Pavloski, Charles, Pennsylvania State University, University Park
Penny, Andrew, Naval Postgraduate School
Person, Arthur, Pennsylvania State University, University Park
Plumb, Raymond A., Massachusetts Institute of Technology
Polvani, Lorenzo M., Columbia University
Priest, Eric, College of Lake County
Renard, Robert J., Naval Postgraduate School
Renfrew, Ian, University of East Anglia
Reuter, Gerhard, University of Alberta
Ritchie, Harold C., Dalhousie University
Ritter, Michael E., University of Wisconsin, Stevens Point
Ritz, Richard, Creighton University
Rochette, Scott M., SUNY, The College at Brockport
Rockwood, Anthony A., Metropolitan State College of Denver
Rodgers, N, Cardiff University
Rodriguez-Plasencia, Oscar, Universidad Autonoma de Baja California Sur
Ross, Andrew, University of Leeds
Russell, William H., Los Angeles Pierce College
Ryan, William F., Pennsylvania State University, University Park
Sanabia, Elizabeth R., United States Naval Academy
Scarnato, Barbara V., Naval Postgraduate School
Schaffer, David L., Wichita State University
Schrage, Jon M., Creighton University
Schultz, David, University of Manchester
Seager, Richard, Columbia University
Seaman, Nelson L., Pennsylvania State University, University Park
Shannon, Jack D., Argonne National Laboratory
Sherman-Morris, Kathleen M., Mississippi State University
Shirer, Hampton N., Pennsylvania State University, University Park
Skubis, Steven T., State University of New York at Oswego
Skyllingstad, Eric, Oregon State University
Smith, Andrea, University of Northern Colorado

Smith, David R., United States Naval Academy
Smith, Dwight E., United States Naval Academy
Srinivasan, Gopalan, University of Toronto
Stamm, Alfred J., State University of New York at Oswego
Stammer, Detlef B., University of California, San Diego
Stauffer, David R., Pennsylvania State University, University Park
Steiger, Scott, State University of New York at Oswego
Steinacker, Reinhold, University of Vienna
Stensrud, David J., Pennsylvania State University, University Park
Stevens, Duane E., University of Hawai'i, Manoa
Straub, Katherine H., Susquehanna University
Syrett, William, Pennsylvania State University, University Park
Terwey, Wes, University of South Alabama
Tett, Simon F., Edinburgh University
Thomas, Christoph, Oregon State University
Thomson, Dennis W., Pennsylvania State University, University Park
Torlaschi, Enrico, Universite du Quebec a Montreal
Tripoli, Gregory J., University of Wisconsin, Madison
Underwood, Stephen J., Georgia Southern University
Utley, Tom, Florida Institute of Technology
Vaughan, Naomi, University of East Anglia
Verlinde, Johannes, Pennsylvania State University, University Park
Vernon, James Y., Los Angeles Pierce College
Wagner Riddle, Claudia, University of Guelph
Wallace, Tim, Mississippi State University
Wang, Bin, University of Hawai'i, Manoa
Wang, Qing, Naval Postgraduate School
Wash, Carlyle H., Naval Postgraduate School
Weisman, Robert A., Saint Cloud State University
Williams, Aaron, University of South Alabama
Williams, Forrest, Naval Postgraduate School
Williams, Roger T., Naval Postgraduate School
Wilson, John D., University of Alberta
Wyngaard, John C., Pennsylvania State University, University Park
Wysong, Jr., James F., Hillsborough Community College
Yang, Zong-Liang, University of Texas at Austin
Yoh, Shing, Kean University
Young, George S., Pennsylvania State University, University Park
Yow, Donald M., Eastern Kentucky University
Zois, Constantine S., Kean University

Material Science
Calaway, Wallis F., Argonne National Laboratory
Chiarello, Ronald P., Argonne National Laboratory
Chrzan, Daryl, University of California, Berkeley
deFontaine, Didier, University of California, Berkeley
DeJonghe, Lutgard, University of California, Berkeley
Devine, Thomas M., University of California, Berkeley
Eberhart, Mark E., Colorado School of Mines
Ferrari, Mauro, University of California, Berkeley
Glaeser, Andreas, University of California, Berkeley
Gronsky, Ronald, University of California, Berkeley
Gruen, Dieter M., Argonne National Laboratory
Haller, Eugene, University of California, Berkeley
Hayden, Geoffrey W., Mercer University
Hazen, Robert M., George Mason University
Hojjatie, Barry, Valdosta State University
Morris, Jr., J. W., University of California, Berkeley
Navrotsky, Alexandra, University of California, Davis
Pellin, Michael J., Argonne National Laboratory
Qu, Deyang, University of Massachusetts, Boston
Ritchie, Robert O., University of California, Berkeley
Sands, Timothy, University of California, Berkeley
Strobel, Timothy A., Carnegie Institution of Washington
Voller, Vaughan R., University of Minnesota, Twin Cities
Weber, Eicke, University of California, Berkeley
Weertman, Johannes, Northwestern University

Land Use/Urban Geology
Agrawal, Sandeep , University of Alberta
Barile, Diane D., Florida Institute of Technology
Barile, Diane, Florida Institute of Technology
Bassett, Scott, University of Nevada, Reno
Beck, Dwayne L., South Dakota State University
Blackburn, James B., Rice University
Bodenman, John E., Bloomsburg University
Bonine, Michael E., University of Arizona
Bremer, Keith, Fort Hays State University
Briggs, John, University of Glasgow
Brinkman, P. Anthony, University of Nevada, Reno
Buermann, Wolfgang, University of Leeds
Cogger, Craig G., Washington State University
Crane, Nicholas J., Ohio Wesleyan University
Davidson, Fiona M., University of Arkansas, Fayetteville
Day, Rick L., Pennsylvania State University, University Park
Deacon, Leith, University of Alberta
Dixon, Nick, University of Leeds
Dolman, Paul, University of East Anglia
Emmi, Philip C., University of Utah
Ford, Andrew, Washington State University
Fusch, Richard D., Ohio Wesleyan University

Godfrey, Brian J., Vassar College
Gosnell, Hannah, Oregon State University
Graff, Thomas O., University of Arkansas, Fayetteville
Graumlich, Lisa J., Montana State University
Harmon, Mella, University of Nevada, Reno
Harris, Richard S., McMaster University
Heiman, Michael, Dickinson College
Hines, Mary E., University of North Carolina Wilmington
Hintz, Rashauna, University of Arkansas, Fayetteville
Holl, Karen D., University of California, Santa Cruz
Hungerford, Hilary, Utah Valley University
Jackson, Richard H., Brigham Young University
James, Valentine U., Clarion University
Jantz, Claire A., Shippensburg University
Kaushal, Sujay, University of Maryland
Larson, David J., California State University, East Bay
Lawrence, Henry, Edinboro University of Pennsylvania
Lee, Chung M., University of Utah
Lyon, Linda M., University of Montana Western
Marston, Sallie A., University of Arizona
Mercier, Michael , McMaster University
Millington, Andrew, Flinders University
Mitchell, Martin D., Minnesota State University
Nevins, Joseph, Vassar College
Odogba, Ismaila, University of Wisconsin, Stevens Point
Otterstrom, Samuel M., Brigham Young University
Peace, Walter G., McMaster University
Pepino, Richard V., Franklin and Marshall College
Platt, Rutherford H., University of Massachusetts, Amherst
Pomeroy, George M., Shippensburg University
Randlett, Victoria, University of Nevada, Reno
Reganold, John P., Washington State University
Riebesell, John, University of Michigan, Dearborn
Rounsevell, Mark D., Edinburgh University
Shirgaokar, Manish, University of Alberta
Skillen, James, Calvin College
Solecki, William, Montclair State University
Solecki, William, Hunter College (CUNY)
Steinberger, Julia, University of Leeds
Sullivan, Jack B., University of Maryland
Thomas, Valerie, Georgia Institute of Technology
Troost, Kathy G., University of Washington
Van Den Hoek, Jamon, Oregon State University
Wiggin, Jack, University of Massachusetts, Boston
Zhou, Yu, Vassar College

Geographic Information Systems

Adhikari, Sanchayeeta, California State University, Northridge
Ahearn, Sean C., Hunter College (CUNY)
Albrecht, Jochen, Hunter College (CUNY)
Alderson, David, University of Newcastle Upon Tyne
Algeo, Catherine, Western Kentucky University
Allen, Katherine, University of Liverpool
Allen-Lafayette, Zehdreh, New Jersey Geological Survey
Ambinakudige, Shrinidhi, Mississippi State University
Amer, Reda, Tulane University
Andrews, John R., University of Texas at Austin, Jackson School of Geosciences
Anthony-Zajanc, Kate, Idaho State University
Argles, Tom, The Open University
Athey, Jennifer E., Division of Geological & Geophysical Surveys
Ayad, Yasser M., Clarion University
Babault, Julien, Universitat Autonoma de Barcelona
Badruddin, Abu Z., Cayuga Community College
Badurek, Chris, Appalachian State University
Bailey, Keiron D., University of Arizona
Barbee, Gary C., West Texas A&M University
Barr, Stuart, University of Newcastle Upon Tyne
Bartley, John M., University of Utah
Bauer, Emily, University of Minnesota
Beaty, Tammy, Oak Ridge National Laboratory
Becker, Lorene Y., Oregon State University
Benger, Simon, Flinders University
Benson, Jane L., Murray State University
Betchwars, Corey, University of Minnesota
Bloechle, Amber, University of West Florida
Bloomgren, Bruce, University of Minnesota
Boda, Patricia, Middle Tennessee State University
Boger, Rebecca, Brooklyn College (CUNY)
Bone, Christopher, University of Oregon
Boroushaki, Soheil, California State University, Northridge
Bottenberg, H. Carrie, Idaho State University
Boyack, Diana L., Idaho State University
Breton, Caroline, University of Texas at Austin, Jackson School of Geosciences
Brown, Douglas, Kingston University
Brown, Mark A., Pennsylvania Bureau of Topographic & Geologic Survey
Bruns, Dale A., Wilkes University
Brunskill, Jeffrey C., Bloomsburg University
Busby, Michael R., Murray State University
Cao, Guofeng, Texas Tech University
Carstensen, Laurence W., Virginia Polytechnic Institute & State University

Cary, Kevin, Western Kentucky University
Cetin, Haluk, Murray State University
Challender, Stuart, Montana State University
Cheng, Qiuming, York University
Chokmani, Karem, Universite du Quebec
Chopra, Prame N., Australian National University
Christopherson, Gary, University of Arizona
Colby, Jeff, Appalachian State University
Cothren, Jackson D., University of Arkansas, Fayetteville
Cova, Thomas J., University of Utah
Coveney, Seamus, University of Glasgow
Cseri, Mick, Indiana University / Purdue University, Fort Wayne
Cunningham, Mary A., Vassar College
Curri, Neil, Vassar College
Dai, Dajun, Georgia State University
Dark, Shawna J., California State University, Northridge
Davis, Trevor J., University of Utah
De Kemp, Eric, University of Ottawa
Deal, Richard, Edinboro University of Pennsylvania
Delparte, Donna M., Idaho State University
Demyanov, Vasily, Heriot-Watt University
DiNaso, Steven, Eastern Illinois University
Diver, Kim, Wesleyan University
Dong, Pinliang, University of North Texas
Donnelly, Shanon P., University of Akron
Drews, Patricia L., Northwest Missouri State University
Drummond, Jane, University of Glasgow
Drzyzga, Scott A., Shippensburg University
Duke, Jason E., Tennessee Tech University
Earle, Robert, American River College
Fan, Weihong, Richard Stockton College of New Jersey
Fedorko, Evan J., West Virginia University
Fernández, Virginia, Universidad de la Republica Oriental del Uruguay (UDELAR)
Fitzgerald, Francis S., Colorado Geological Survey
Forrest, David, University of Glasgow
Freed, Jane S., University of Idaho
Frizado, Joseph P., Bowling Green State University
Gallagher, Patricia E., Division of Geological & Geophysical Surveys
Garren, Sandra J., Hofstra University
Gathany, Mark, Cedarville University
Gauthier, Donald J., Los Angeles Valley College
Girard, Michael W., New Jersey Geological Survey
Gittings, Bruce M., Edinburgh University
Good, Jessica, Arizona Geological Survey
Gopal, Sucharita, Boston University
Gordon, Clare, University of Leeds
Gorsevski, Peter, Bowling Green State University
Grala, Katarzynz, Mississippi State University
Graniero, Phil A., University of Windsor
Greatbatch, Ian, Kingston University
Grimmer, Abbey, University of Nevada, Reno
Grunwald, Sabine, University of Florida
Haddock, Gregory D., Northwest Missouri State University
Halls, Joanne N., University of North Carolina Wilmington
Halsted, Christian, Dept of Agriculture, Conservation, and Forestry
Hamilton, Jacqueline, University of Minnesota
Hancock, Gregory, University of Newcastle
Haner, Andrew, Arkansas Geological Survey
Hansen, William J., Worcester State University
Haugerud, Ralph, University of Washington
Hawthorne, Timothy, Georgia State University
Heaton, Jill, University of Nevada, Reno
Henderson, Matt, Dept of Natural Resources
Hendricks, Mike, Division of Geological & Geophysical Surveys
Herried, Brad, University of Minnesota, Twin Cities
Hick, Steven, University of Denver
Hill, Malcolm, Northeastern University
Hill, Richard T., indiana University
Hintz, John G., Bloomsburg University
Hong, Jessie, University of West Georgia
Hotz, Helenmary, University of Massachusetts, Boston
Howard, Hugh H., American River College
Huang, Jane, Fitchburg State University
Huffman, French T., Eastern Kentucky University
Hughes, Annie, Kingston University
Jennings, Nathan, American River College
Joshi, Manoj, University of East Anglia
Juntunen, Thomas, University of Minnesota, Twin Cities
Kadrmas, Elroy, North Dakota Geological Survey
Kahle, Chris, Iowa Dept of Natural Resources
Kambesis, Patricia, Western Kentucky University
Kar, Bandana, University of Southern Mississippi
Keane, Rob, Flinders University
Kelleher, Cole, University of Minnesota, Twin Cities
Kennedy, Timothy T., University of Wisconsin, Stevens Point
Kidd, David, Kingston University
Kienzle, Stefan, University of Lethbridge
Kirimi, Fridah K., Jomo Kenyatta University of Agriculture & Technology
Klancher, Jacki, Central Wyoming College
Kobara, Shinichi, Texas A&M University

Kohler, Nicholas, University of Oregon
Kostelnick, John, Illinois State University
Krizek, Jeffrey, San Bernardino Valley College
Kronenfeld, Barry J., Eastern Illinois University
Krygier, John B., Ohio Wesleyan University
Kwon, Youngsang, University of Memphis
Laffan, Shawn, University of New South Wales
Law, Zada, Middle Tennessee State University
Le, Yanfen, Northwest Missouri State University
Lee, Wook, Edinboro University of Pennsylvania
Lethbridge, Mark, Flinders University
Leverington, David W., Texas Tech University
Levine, Norman S., College of Charleston
Li, Gary, California State University, East Bay
Li, Ping-Chi, Tennessee Tech University
Limp, W. F., University of Arkansas, Fayetteville
Lisichenko, Richard, Fort Hays State University
Lobben, Amy, University of Oregon
Logsdon, Miles G., University of Washington
Lovett, Andrew, University of East Anglia
Lukinbeal, Christopher, University of Arizona
Luo, Jun, Missouri State University
Lupo, Tom, American River College
Maantay, Juliana, Lehman College (CUNY)
Maas, Regan, California State University, Northridge
Machovina, Brett , United States Air Force Academy
Mackaness, William A., Edinburgh University
Magondu, Moffat G., Jomo Kenyatta University of Agriculture & Technology
Marcano, Eugenio J., Mount Holyoke College
Marr, Paul G., Shippensburg University
Marsan, Yvonne, University of North Carolina Wilmington
Marzen, Luke J., Auburn University
Mathias, Simon, Durham University
May, Cynthia, Northland College
McCluskey, James, University of Wisconsin Colleges
McKinney, Nathan, University of West Florida
Mead, Jerry V., Drexel University
Meentemeyer, Ross, University of North Carolina, Charlotte
Meng, Qingmin, Mississippi State University
Metcalf, Meredith, Eastern Connecticut State University
Miller, Harvey J., Ohio State University
Miller, Max, Front Range Community College - Westminster
Mitasova, Helena, North Carolina State University
Mohapatra, Rama, Minnesota State University
Momm, Henrique G., Middle Tennessee State University
Morgan, John D., University of West Florida
Morgan, Karen, Colorado Geological Survey
Morgan, Tamie, Texas Christian University
Morris, John A., Mississippi State University
Mueller, Thomas, California University of Pennsylvania
Mulligan, Kevin R., Texas Tech University
Muthukrishnan, Suresh, Furman University
Mutua, Felix N., Jomo Kenyatta University of Agriculture & Technology
Mwangi, Nancy , Jomo Kenyatta University of Agriculture & Technology
Mwaniki, Mercy W., Jomo Kenyatta University of Agriculture & Technology
Nagihara, Seiichi, Texas Tech University
Nemon, Amy, Western Kentucky University
Niedzielski, Michael A., University of North Dakota
Nimako, Solomon Nana Kwaku, San Bernardino Valley College
Obermeyer, Nancy J., Indiana State University
Oduor, Peter, North Dakota State University
Ozdenerol, Esra, University of Memphis
Palladino, Steve D., Ventura College
Pallis, Ted J., New Jersey Geological Survey
Palmer, Evan, United States Air Force Academy
Pavlovskaya, Marianna, Hunter College (CUNY)
Peele, Hampton, Louisiana State University
Pennington, Deana, University of Texas, El Paso
Percy, David, Portland State University
Plewe, Brandon, Brigham Young University
Porter, Claire, University of Minnesota, Twin Cities
Portillo, Danny, United States Air Force Academy
Price, Maribeth H., South Dakota School of Mines & Technology
Price, Peter E., Lonestar College - North Harris
Pristas, Ronald, New Jersey Geological Survey
Proctor, Elizabeth, City College of San Francisco
Qi, Feng, Kean University
Qiu, Xiaomin, Missouri State University
Raber, George, University of Southern Mississippi
Resnichenko, Yuri, Universidad de la Republica Oriental del Uruguay (UDELAR)
Rex, Arthur B., Appalachian State University
Rice, Keith W., University of Wisconsin, Stevens Point
Ridenour, Gregory D., Austin Peay State University
Robinson, Lori, University of Minnesota
Robinson, Michael, Georgia Southern University
Roof, Steven, Hampshire College
Rowley, Rex J., Illinois State University
Sadd, James L., Occidental College
Sanchez-Azofeifa, G. Arturo, University of Alberta
Sandau, Ken L., Montana Tech of The University of Montana

Schenck, William, University of Delaware
Scott, Darren M., McMaster University
Seong, Jeong C., University of West Georgia
Shears, Andrew, University of Wisconsin Colleges
Shears, Andy, Mansfield University
Shimizu, Melinda, Western Oregon University
Smith, Betty E., Eastern Illinois University
Smith, Janet S., Shippensburg University
Stanley, George R., San Antonio Community College
Stuart, Neil, Edinburgh University
Stutsman, Sam, University of South Alabama
Sun, Yifei, California State University, Northridge
Sutton, Paul C., University of Denver
Taylor, Nathan H., Arkansas Geological Survey
Taylor, Ryan W., SUNY, Purchase
Teeuw, Richard, University of Portsmouth
Thale, Paul R., Montana Tech of The University of Montana
Thayn, Jonathan B., Illinois State University
Tinkler, Dorothy, Treasure Valley Community College
Tiwari, Chetan, University of North Texas
Tong, Daoqin, University of Arizona
Tran, Linda C., Lonestar College - North Harris
Trifonoff, Karen M., Bloomsburg University
Tu, Wei, Georgia Southern University
Unger, Corey, Utah Geological Survey
VanHorn, Jason, Calvin College
Veisze, Paul M., American River College
Vincent, Paul, Valdosta State University
Wahl, Tim, University of Minnesota
Walford, Nigel, Kingston University
Walls, Charles C., Dalhousie University
Wang, Lillian T., University of Delaware
Weber, Keith, Idaho State University
Weiss, Alfred W., Waubonsee Community College
Wen, Yuming, University of Guam
Whiteaker, Timothy L., University of Texas at Austin
Whitfield, Thomas G., Pennsylvania Bureau of Topographic & Geologic Survey
Whittaker, Amber, Dept of Agriculture, Conservation, and Forestry
Wikgren, Brooke, University of Massachusetts, Boston
Williamson, Douglas, Hunter College (CUNY)
Wilson, Blake, University of Kansas
Wilson, John R., Lafayette College
Wilson, Roy R., Eastern Connecticut State University
Woodhouse, Iain H., Edinburgh University
Wu, Yi-Hwa, Northwest Missouri State University
Xie, Zhixiao, Florida Atlantic University
Xu, Wei, University of Lethbridge
Yacucci, Mark A., University of Illinois
Yan, Jun, Western Kentucky University
Ye, Gordon, City College of San Francisco
Yu, Jaehyung, Texas A&M University, Kingsville
Yu, Qian, University of Massachusetts, Amherst
Zhang, Qiaofeng (Robin), Murray State University

Glaciology
Bailey, Ian, Exeter University
Barker, Joel D., Ohio State University
Booth, Adam, Imperial College
Catania, Ginny A., University of Texas at Austin
Conway, Howard B., University of Washington
Creyts, Timothy T., Columbia University
Dupont, Todd, University of California, Irvine
Fahnestock, Mark A., University of New Hampshire
Fisher, David A., University of Ottawa
Hamilton, Gordon S., University of Maine
Hock, Regine M., University of Alaska Fairbanks
Holt, John W., University of Texas at Austin
Howat, Ian M., Ohio State University
Hulton, Nicholas R., Edinburgh University
Hutchings, Jennifer, Oregon State University
Mills, Stephanie, Kingston University
Neinow, Peter W., Edinburgh University
Pettit, Erin C., University of Alaska Fairbanks
Radic, Valentina, University of British Columbia
Raymond, Charles F., University of Washington
Rignot, Eric, University of California, Irvine
Rinterknecht, Vincent, University of St. Andrews
Rupper, Summer, Brigham Young University
Schoof, Christian, University of British Columbia
Sharp, Martin J., University of Alberta
Stearns, Leigh, University of Kansas
Stroeve, Julienne, University College London
Tedasco, Marco, Columbia University
Waddington, Edwin D., University of Washington
Winebrenner, Dale P., University of Washington
Winkler, Stefan, University of Canterbury

Not Elsewhere Classified
(Deep) McGregor, Mary, Montgomery College
Aamodt, Paul, Los Alamos National Laboratory
Abney, Kent D., Los Alamos National Laboratory

Abt, Charlotte J., University of Liverpool
Acharya, Kumud, University of Nevada, Reno
Ackerman, Jessica R., University of Illinois, Urbana-Champaign
Acosta, Patricia E., Williams College
Acosta Borbon, Hugo, Universidad Nacional Autonoma de Mexico
Adams, Debi, West Texas A&M University
Adrain, Tiffany S., University of Iowa
Agnew, Stephen F., Los Alamos National Laboratory
Aguilera, Juan Manuel Torres, Universidad Autonoma de San Luis Potosi
Ahmed, Waquar, University of North Texas
Alavi, Hedy, Johns Hopkins University
Albrecht, Lorraine, University of Waterloo
Albright, Katia, University of Nevada, Reno
Alde, Douglas, Los Alamos National Laboratory
Algin, Barbara, Columbia University
Ali-Bray, Julie, Mt. San Antonio College
Allison, Tami L., Missouri Dept of Natural Resources
Ambruster, W. Scott, University of Alaska, Fairbanks
Amelung, Falk, University of Miami
Amor, John, University of British Columbia
Anand, Madhur, University of Guelph
Andersen, Elaine, Stanford University
Antar, Ali A., Central Connecticut State University
Anthony, Leona M., University of Hawai'i, Manoa
Anthony, Nina, Furman University
Antipova, Anzhelika, University of Memphis
Arabas, Karen, Willamette University
Argenbright, Robert T., University of North Carolina Wilmington
Armstrong, Andrew, University of New Hampshire
Arnold, Jayne H., Earlham College
Arundale, Wendy H., University of Alaska, Fairbanks
Arvidson, Raymond E., Washington University
Ashour-Abdalla, Maha, University of California, Los Angeles
Atisha-Castillo, Hector David, Universidad Autonoma de San Luis Potosi
Au, Whitlow W L., University of Hawai'i, Manoa
Aufrecht, Walter E., University of Lethbridge
Ayers, Joseph , Northeastern University
Bailey, Lorraine, University of Rhode Island
Baldizon, Ileana, Miami-Dade Community College (Wolfson Campus)
Ball, Elizabeth, University of Nevada, Reno
Ball, William P., Johns Hopkins University
Ballinger, Rhoda, Cardiff University
Banks, Beth, Brevard College
Bannister, Bryant, University of Arizona
Bannon, Ann, Dalhousie University
Barmore, Garrett, University of Nevada, Reno
Barnbaum, Cecilia S., Valdosta State University
Barnes, Fairley J., Los Alamos National Laboratory
Barnes, Randal J., University of Minnesota, Twin Cities
Barnston, Anthony G., Columbia University
Barrett, Joan, Hampshire College
Barron, George, University of Guelph
Barth, Susan A., Montana Tech of The University of Montana
Bartl, Simona, Moss Landing Marine Laboratories
Baskin, Perry A., Valdosta State University
Bass, Jerry, University of Southern Mississippi
Bass, Michael L., University of Mary Washington
Basso, Bruno, Michigan State University
Baumann, Sue, Argonne National Laboratory
Beasley-Stanley, Jewell D., Vanderbilt University
Beatty, Merrill Ann, University of New Brunswick
Beck, Alan, Western University
Becker, Laurence, Oregon State University
Becker, Richard H., University of Toledo
Becker, Udo, University of Michigan
Bederman, Sanford H., Georgia State University
Behr-Andres, Christina "Tina", Los Alamos National Laboratory
Belanger, Thomas V., Florida Institute of Technology
Bellew, Angela, University of Iowa
Bennett, Victoria J., Texas Christian University
Bentham, Richard, Flinders University
Berchem, Jean, University of California, Los Angeles
Bernknopf, Richard, Stanford University
Betancourt, Julio, University of Arizona
Bettis III, E. A., University of Iowa
Bienvenu, Nadean S., University of Louisiana at Lafayette
Bilheux, Hassina, University of Tennessee, Knoxville
Bischoff, Marianne, Weber State University
Bischoff, Carolyn, University of Minnesota, Twin Cities
Black, Annjeannette , Community College of Baltimore County, Catonsville
Black, Richard A., Southern Illinois University Carbondale
Blankenship, Robert, Washington University
Blenkinson, Stephen, University of Newcastle Upon Tyne
Blumenfeld, Raphael, Imperial College
Boger, Kathryn M., Ohio Wesleyan University
Boisvert, Eric, Universite du Quebec
Boland, Greg J., University of Guelph
Boland, John J., Johns Hopkins University
Booth, Robert K., Lehigh University
Boss, Alan P., Carnegie Institution of Washington

Bossenbroek, Jonathon , University of Toledo
Boston, Penelope, New Mexico Institute of Mining and Technology
Boswell, Cecil, Missouri Dept of Natural Resources
Bottero, Jean-Yves, Rice University
Bourgeois, Reed J., Louisiana State University
Bourgouin-Mehes, Roxane J., Laurentian University, Sudbury
Bouwer, Edward John, Johns Hopkins University
Bowen, Dawn S., Mary Washington College
Bowen, Robert, University of Massachusetts, Boston
Bowersox, Joe, Willamette University
Bowles, Ann B., University of San Diego
Bozzato, Edda, Laurentian University, Sudbury
Bradley, Michael D., University of Arizona
Brainard, James R., Los Alamos National Laboratory
Branfireun, Brian, Western University
Braught, Patricia, Dickinson College
Brewer, Margene, Calvin College
Bridgeman, Thomas, University of Toledo
Brock, Timothy, Missouri State University
Brooks, Antone L., Washington State University
Brooks, Ian, University of Leeds
Brown, Bradford D., University of Idaho
Brown, Kent D., Utah Geological Survey
Brown, Peter, Western University
Brown, Rob, Appalachian State University
Brunetto, Eileen, Middlebury College
Brunish, Wendee M., Los Alamos National Laboratory
Bryan, Jeffrey C., Los Alamos National Laboratory
Bryant, Anita M., University of West Georgia
Bryce, Karen R., Brigham Young University
Buck, Daniel, University of Oregon
Buckley, Luke, Montana Tech of The University of Montana
Budd, William W., Washington State University
Bullamore, Henry W., Frostburg State University
Bunker, Merle E., Los Alamos National Laboratory
Burk, Sue, University of Maryland
Burns, Carol J., Los Alamos National Laboratory
Burns, John W., Mt. San Antonio College
Busse, Friedrich H., University of California, Los Angeles
Butler, R. Paul, Carnegie Institution of Washington
Butts, Thomas R., University of Texas, Dallas
Byrand, Karl, University of Wisconsin Colleges
Caballero, Kate, Tarleton State University
Cailliet, Gregor M., Moss Landing Marine Laboratories
Cairns, Alicia, University of British Columbia
Calegari, Pat, Pace University, New York Campus
Cambiotti, Laura J., Lehigh University
Cammerata, Kirk , Texas A&M University, Corpus Christi
Campana, Michael E., University of New Mexico
Cantarero, Debra A., Pasadena City College
Capoccia, Mary, Ohio State University
Carey, Kristine M., Lakehead University
Carey, Tara, Black Hawk College
Carp, Jana, Appalachian State University
Carr, David E., University of Virginia
Carzoli, John, Oakton Community College
Cassidy, Carleen, Montana Tech of The University of Montana
Catalano, Valerie, Roger Williams University
Catau, John C., Missouri State University
Catling, David C., University of Washington
Cattolico, Rose Ann, University of Washington
Caupp, Craig L., Frostburg State University
Chambers, John E., Carnegie Institution of Washington
Chan, Selene, University of British Columbia
Chandler, Kristopher, Georgia Perimeter College
Chase, Anne, University of Arizona
Chase, Jon M., Washington University
Chatterjee, Ipsita, University of North Texas
Cheek, William H., Missouri State University
Chen, Jiquan, University of Toledo
Chen, Kai Loon, Johns Hopkins University
Cheney, Donald, Northeastern University
Chief, Karletta, University of Arizona
Childs, Geoff, Washington University
Chopin, Suzzette, Texas A&M University, Corpus Christi
Choquette, Marc, Universite Laval
Chouinard, Kyle, Western Michigan University
Chouinard, Vera, McMaster University
Christian, Alan D., University of Massachusetts, Boston
Christopher, Micol, Mt. San Antonio College
Clark, David L., Los Alamos National Laboratory
Clark, James S., Duke University
Clark, Robert O., Northern Arizona University
Clark, Shannon, University of New Mexico
Clay, Robert, Missouri Dept of Natural Resources
Cleek, Richard, University of Wisconsin Colleges
Cochran, David, University of Southern Mississippi
Codd, Geoffrey, Flinders University
Coffin, Richard B., University of Delaware
Cohen, Joel E., Columbia University

Cohen, Matt, Furman University
Cohen, Shaul E., University of Oregon
Colby, Bonnie C., University of Arizona
Cole, S., Colby College
Coleman, Gary D., University of Maryland
Collins, Damian, University of Alberta
Collins, Lisa, Northwestern University
Collins, Mark, University of Pittsburgh
Colwell, Frederick (Rick), Oregon State University
Conca, James L., Washington State University
Confer, John, California University of Pennsylvania
Conkle, Jeremy, Texas A&M University, Corpus Christi
Cook, Stanton A., University of Oregon
Cook, Steve, Oregon State University
Cookus, Pam, Illinois State Geological Survey
Coombs, Margery C., University of Massachusetts, Amherst
Coonley, Steffanie, Los Alamos National Laboratory
Corcoran, Deborah, Missouri State University
Corey, Alison, Utah Geological Survey
Costello, Margaret, California State University, Long Beach
Cote, Pascale, Universite du Quebec
Cox, Shelah, Temple University
Crawford, Ian, Birkbeck College
Crawford, Matt, University of Kentucky
Creed, Irena F., Western University
Crepeau, Richard J., Appalachian State University
Crimmins, Michael, University of Arizona
Cromar, Nancy, Flinders University
Cromartie, William J., Richard Stockton College of New Jersey
Crozier, George F., Dauphin Island Sea Lab
Crumbly, Isaac J., Fort Valley State University
Cruz-Teran, Jesus E., Centro de Estudios Superiores del Estado Sonora
Csaplar, Csilla, Stanford University
Cupples, Julie, Edinburgh University
Curry, Barbara, University of Texas, Dallas
Curry, James K., Arkansas Geological Survey
D'Arrigo, Rosanne, Columbia University
Damschen, Ellen, Washington University
Dash, Zora V., Los Alamos National Laboratory
Dasvarma, Gour, Flinders University
Daugherty, Carolyn M., Northern Arizona University
Davey, Patricia M., Brown University
David, Eric, Universite Laval
Davis, James A., Brigham Young University
Dawson, De De, University of Saskatchewan
Daymon, Deborah J., Los Alamos National Laboratory
De Beus, Barbara, Montclair State University
De Santo, Eilzabeth, Franklin and Marshall College
Dean, Jeffrey S., University of Arizona
Deaton, Tami, University of North Texas
DeBarros, Nelson, Dept of Energy and Environmental Protection
DeGraff, Jerry, California State University, Fresno
Delawder, Sandra, James Madison University
Deming, Jody, University of Manitoba
Den Ouden, Amy, University of Massachusetts, Boston
Dennis, Clyde B., Argonne National Laboratory
Dennis, Pam, University of Florida
Desch, Steven, Arizona State University
Deschaine, Sylvia, Bates College
Dessler, Alexander, University of Arizona
Dessler, Andrew, Texas A&M University
Detrich, William, Northeastern University
Dewberry, Daniel R., Austin Community College District
Dibben, Chris, Edinburgh University
Dickerson, Richard E., University of California, Los Angeles
Dickhoff, Willem H., Washington University
Dighe, Kalpak, Los Alamos National Laboratory
Dill, Carilee, Bucknell University
Dingman, Steve, San Antonio Community College
Ditmars, John, Argonne National Laboratory
Divine, Aaron, Northern Arizona University
Dixon, Clifton, University of Southern Mississippi
Dixon, Michael, University of Guelph
Dixon, Paul R., Los Alamos National Laboratory
Doherty, Cheryl, University of Delaware
Dollhopf, Douglas J., Montana State University
Domingue, Carla, Louisiana State University
Donahoe, Robert J., Los Alamos National Laboratory
Donohue, Mary M., DePauw University
Doorn, Stephen K., Los Alamos National Laboratory
Dorries, Alison M., Los Alamos National Laboratory
Driever, Steven L., University of Missouri-Kansas City
Driscoll, John R., SUNY, Cortland
Druckebrod, Daniel L., Rider University
Duchane, David V., Los Alamos National Laboratory
Dudukovic, Mike, Washington University
Duff, John, University of Massachusetts, Boston
Duffey, Patricia, Fort Hays State University
Duxbury, Thomas C., Jet Propulsion Laboratory
Dvorzak, Marie, University of Wisconsin, Madison

Dwyer, Daryl F., University of Toledo
Earls, Sandy, Oklahoma State University
Ebert, David, Moss Landing Marine Laboratories
Eby, Gloria J., University of Texas, Dallas
Eby, Stephanie, Northeastern University
Edwards, John , Flinders University
Eggers, Delores M., University of North Carolina, Asheville
Ehlschlaeger, Charles R., Graduate School of the City University of New York
Eisenberger, Peter M., Columbia University
Eller, Phillip G., Los Alamos National Laboratory
Ellins, Katherine K., University of Texas at Austin
Elliott, C. James, Los Alamos National Laboratory
Ellis, Hugh, Johns Hopkins University
Ellis, Rowan, Edinburgh University
Emmett, Chad, Brigham Young University
Epstein, Howard E., University of Virginia
Esnault, Melissa H., Louisiana State University
Esser, Corinne, University of California, Davis
Evans, Claude, Washington University
Even, Paula, University of Northern Iowa
Eyrich, Terry L., Merced College
Fadiman, Maria, Florida Atlantic University
Fahlman, Andreas, Texas A&M University, Corpus Christi
Fairbairn, Kenneth J., University of Alberta
Fallowfield, Howard, Flinders University
Fares, Mary A., Valdosta State University
Farley, Perry D., Los Alamos National Laboratory
Farrell, Mark O., Point Park University
Favor, Michael, University of Michigan, Dearborn
Feeney, Alison E., Shippensburg University
Ferguson, Teresa D., Oak Ridge National Laboratory
Ferreira, Maryanne F., Woods Hole Oceanographic Institution
Ferren, Richard L., Berkshire Community College
Fifer, Fred L., University of Texas, Dallas
Fish, Jennifer M., University of California, Santa Cruz
Fitzpatrick, John R., Los Alamos National Laboratory
Fitzsimmons, Kevin, University of Arizona
Fjeldheim, Nancy, Brown University
Flaherty, Frank A., Valdosta State University
Flechsig, Sandra, Rice University
Fletcher, Austin, University of Guelph
Flores-Garcia, Mari C., California State University, Northridge
Floyd, Barry, New York State Geological Survey
Fogel, David N., Los Alamos National Laboratory
Foley, John P., Montana Tech of The University of Montana
Ford, F. Andrew, Washington State University
Foster, Christine, University of Montana
Foster, Michael, Moss Landing Marine Laboratories
Foti, Pamela, Northern Arizona University
Fox, Joe, Texas A&M University, Corpus Christi
Fox, Laurel R., University of California, Santa Cruz
Fox, Peter A., Rensselaer Polytechnic Institute
Freiermuth, Sue, University of Wisconsin, River Falls
Frieman, Edward A., University of California, San Diego
Frisk, DeAnn, Iowa State University of Science & Technology
Fry, Matthew, University of North Texas
Fryett, I, Cardiff University
Fuellhart, Kurtis G., Shippensburg University
Gagne, Marc R., West Chester University
Gallick, Roberta T., Point Park University
Ganey-Curry, Patricia E., University of Texas at Austin
Gao, Mengsheng, University of Florida
Gao, Oliver H., Cornell University
Garcia, Jan, Occidental College
Garrod, Bruce, University of Toronto
Gartner, John F., University of Waterloo
Garvin, Theresa D., University of Alberta
Gautsch, Jacklyn, Iowa Dept of Natural Resources
Gehrels, Tom, University of Arizona
Geller, Jonathan, Moss Landing Marine Laboratories
Geller, Michael D., Richard Stockton College of New Jersey
Geller, Murray, Jet Propulsion Laboratory
Gemignani, Robert, Washington University in St. Louis
Gerhardt, Hannes, University of West Georgia
Gerlach, Russel L., Missouri State University
Gerry, Janelle, University of Nebraska, Lincoln
Ghosheh, Baher A., Edinboro University of Pennsylvania
Giammar, Daniel, Washington University
Gibbs, Gaynell, Louisiana State University
Gibson, Deana, Missouri State University
Gifford-Gonzalez, Dianne, University of California, Santa Cruz
Gilbert, Co'Quesie, Columbia University
Gillespie, Thomas, Emory University
Gillette, David P., University of North Carolina, Asheville
Gitelson, Anatoly, Unversity of Nebraska - Lincoln
Glaser, Brian, Black Hawk College
Glenn, Ed, University of Arizona
Gmitro, Helen, Union County College
Goldhamer, David A., University of California, Davis
Gong, Hongmian, Hunter College (CUNY)

Gonzalez, Richard, University of San Diego
Good, Daniel B., Georgia Southern University
Goodin, Ruth, University of Miami
Goodison, Marjorie, University of Rochester
Goodwin, Paul, University of Guelph
Gordon, Andrew, University of Guelph
Gottgens, Johan F., University of Toledo
Gouhier, Tarik, Northeastern University
Grace, Shannon M., Austin Community College District
Grande, Anthony, Hunter College (CUNY)
Grant, John, East Los Angeles College
Grasso, Cheryl, University of Rhode Island
Grattan, Stephen R., University of California, Davis
Gravely, Cynthia Rae, Clemson University
Gray, Sarah, University of San Diego
Gray, Steven, University of Massachusetts, Boston
Green, Brittany, Kansas State University
Greene, Barbara, Lock Haven University
Greene, Pauline R., University of Louisiana at Lafayette
Greene, Roberta, SUNY Potsdam
Griffin, Kevin, Columbia University
Griffith, Caitlin, University of Arizona
Gripshover, Margaret "Peggy", Western Kentucky University
Gritzo, Russell E., Los Alamos National Laboratory
Groppi, Christopher, Arizona State University
Grossman, Lawrence S., Virginia Polytechnic Institute & State University
Guerra, Oralia, Austin Community College District
Guikema, Seth, Johns Hopkins University
Guy, Margaret B., North Carolina Central University
Guzman, Ernesto, University of Guelph
Habash, Marc, University of Guelph
Hacker, Patricia, University of Toledo
Haddad, Brent, University of California, Santa Cruz
Haff, Peter K., Duke University
Hafner, James A., University of Massachusetts, Amherst
Hagelberg, Carl R., Los Alamos National Laboratory
Haggart, Renee, University of British Columbia
Haggerty, Julia H., Montana State University
Haigh, Nardia, University of Massachusetts, Boston
Halfman, Barbara, Hobart & William Smith Colleges
Hall, Christopher C., University of Guelph
Hall, I, Cardiff University
Hall, Jude, Denison University
Hall, Robert, University of Guelph
Hall, Ron, University of Lethbridge
Hallett, Rebecca, University of Guelph
Hamilton, George, Berkshire Community College
Hammersley, Charles, Northern Arizona University
Hammond, Anne, Lakehead University
Haney, Mary, University of South Florida, Tampa
Hanke, Steve H., Johns Hopkins University
Hankins, Katherine B., Georgia State University
Hanna, Heather, North Carolina Geological Survey
Hansen, Jeffrey C., Los Alamos National Laboratory
Hardwick, Susan W., University of Oregon
Hardy, Shaun J., Carnegie Institution of Washington
Harris, Virginia M., Wesleyan University
Hassard, Stacey K., College of Charleston
Hawley, Rebecca D., Northern Arizona University
Haymet, Anthony D., University of California, San Diego
Haynes, Kyle J., University of Virginia
Heaton, Richard C., Los Alamos National Laboratory
Heatwole, Charles A., Hunter College (CUNY)
Heatwole, Charles A., Graduate School of the City University of New York
Hebblethwaite, Chris, State University of New York at Oswego
Heckathorn, Scott, University of Toledo
Heenan, Cleo J., South Dakota School of Mines & Technology
Hegarty, Patricia, University College Cork
Heidt, James, University of Wisconsin Colleges
Heimpel, Moritz, University of Alberta
Heitman, Mary P., Iowa Dept of Natural Resources
Helmick, Sara B., Los Alamos National Laboratory
Helmuth, Brian, Northeastern University
Hendrikx, Jordy, Montana State University
Henshel, Diane S., Indiana University, Bloomington
Herr, Larry, University of Lethbridge
Heyniger, William C., Kean University
Higinbotham, Pamela, California University of Pennsylvania
Hildebrand, Stephen G., Oak Ridge National Laboratory
Hill, Arleen A., University of Memphis
Hill, Julie, University of Nevada, Reno
Hiller, Lena, Hofstra University
Hilpert, Markus, Johns Hopkins University
Hilts, Stewart G., University of Guelph
Hinderaker, Pam, Iowa State University of Science & Technology
Hindery, Derrick, University of Oregon
Hinman, George W., Washington State University
Hobbs, Benjamin F., Johns Hopkins University
Hobbs, John D., Montana Tech of the University of Montana
Hockey, Thomas A., University of Northern Iowa

Hodges, Jackie, Fort Valley State University
Hodgson, M. John, University of Alberta
Hohl, Eric, Missouri Dept of Natural Resources
Holbrook, Amanda, Morehead State University
Hollenbeck, Diane, Metropolitan State College of Denver
Holstein, Thomas J., Roger Williams University
Holubnyak, Yehven I., University of Kansas
Hommel, Demian, Oregon State University
Hopkins, Daniel P., University of Missouri-Kansas City
Hopson, Janet L., University of Tennessee, Knoxville
Horne, Sharon, University of Windsor
Howard, Theodore E., University of New Hampshire
Hrouda, Jim, Mineral Area College
Hsiang, Tom, University of Guelph
Hsiao, Theodore C., University of California, Davis
Huang, Norden E., University of Delaware
Huckabey, Marsha, University of Missouri
Hudman, Lloyd E., Brigham Young University
Huffman, Debra E., University of South Florida
Huffman, Robert L., Mercer University
Hughes, Joseph B., Rice University
Hughes, Randall, Northeastern University
Hull, Donald'L., Los Alamos National Laboratory
Humphrey, Peggy, Montana State University
Hunt, Kathy, University of Maryland
Hunt, Shelley, University of Guelph
Hunter, John, Rice University
Huntoon, Laura, University of Arizona
Hutchins, Peter S., Mississippi Office of Geology
Hysell, David L., Cornell University
Iantria, Linnea, Missouri State University
Ibrahim, Mohamed, Hunter College (CUNY)
Immonen, Wilma, Montana Tech of the University of Montana
Ironside, R. Geoffrey, University of Alberta
Ivanova, Maria, University of Massachusetts, Boston
Ivy, Russell L., Florida Atlantic University
Jackson, Edgar L., University of Alberta
Jackson, Robert B., Duke University
Jacobs, Tenika, New Jersey Geological Survey
Janetos, Tony, Boston University
Jarcho, Kari A., University of Minnesota, Twin Cities
Jeans, Meghan, University of Massachusetts, Boston
Jensen, Melinda, Oregon State University
Jensen, Scott W., South Dakota Dept of Environment and Natural Resources
Jiang, Zhenhua, Argonne National Laboratory
Joanna, Lucero, New Mexico Institute of Mining and Technology
Johannesen, Carl L., University of Oregon
Johnson, Daniel L., University of Lethbridge
Johnson, Emily P., Boston University
Johnson, Jeanne, Louisiana State University
Johnson, John R., Washington State University
Johnson, Judy L., University of Alaska, Fairbanks
Johnson, Robert E., Western Illinois University
Johnson, Robert L., Argonne National Laboratory
Johnston, Karin, George Washington University
Jones, Glen, New Mexico Institute of Mining & Technology
Jones, Gwilym, Northeastern University
Jones, Minnie O., University of Illinois at Chicago
Jones, III, John P., University of Arizona
Jornov, Donna, New York State Geological Survey
Joseph, Miranda, University of Arizona
Jun, Young-Shin, Washington University
Jurmanovich, Barb, Delta College
Juszczyk, Carmen, University of Colorado
Jutla, Rajinder S., Missouri State University
Kaag, Cindy, Washington State University
Kaden, Scott, Missouri Dept of Natural Resources
Karl, Tami S., Florida State University
Kay, Richard F., Duke University
Keala, Lori, Pomona College
Keating, Martha E., Bentley University
Keaton, Jeffrey R., University of Utah
Keatts, Merida, Kent State University
Kehoe-Forutan, Sandra J., Bloomsburg University
Keil, Charles, Wheaton College
Keller, Jean, United States Military Academy
Kelly, Kimberly, Montgomery College
Kelly, Sherrie, St. Lawrence University
Kennedy, Christina B., Northern Arizona University
Kennel, Charles F., University of California, Los Angeles
Kettmann, Elizabeth, Sonoma State University
Kevan, Peter, University of Guelph
Keyser, Jan, University of South Alabama
Khurana, Krishan, University of California, Los Angeles
Kidane-Mariam, Tadesse, Edinboro University of Pennsylvania
Kidder, T.R., Washington University
Kifer, Lauri A., SUNY, The College at Brockport
Kile, Susan, Eastern Illinois University
Kim, Stacy, Moss Landing Marine Laboratories
Kimbro, David, Northeastern University

King-Hsi, Kung, Los Alamos National Laboratory
Kinkead, Scott, Los Alamos National Laboratory
Kipper, Jay P., University of Texas at Austin, Jackson School of Geosciences
Knauss, Virginia L., California State University, Dominguez Hills
Knight, Mona M., University of Illinois, Urbana-Champaign
Kohlstedt, Sally G., University of Minnesota, Twin Cities
Komoto, Cary, University of Wisconsin Colleges
Kontuly, Thomas M., University of Utah
Koralek, Susan, Southern Oregon University
Kosinski, Leszek A., University of Alberta
Kostov, Svilen, Georgia Southwestern State University
Krauss, Lawrence, Arizona State University
Kressler, Sharon J., University of Minnesota, Twin Cities
Krieble, Kelly, Moravian College
Krishnan, Jay, University of Houston
Kruse, Jennifer, Gustavus Adolphus College
Kugel, Abigail, Winona State University
Kuntz, Kara, Fort Hays State University
LaBella, Joel, Wesleyan University
LaFreniere, Lorraine M., Argonne National Laboratory
Lagowski, Alison A., SUNY, Buffalo
Lam, Anita, University of British Columbia
Lane, Mark, Palomar College
Langdon, Phyllis, Sir Wilfred Grenfell College
Lanoue, Christopher A., South Dakota Dept of Environment and Natural Resources
Larkin, Patrick, Texas A&M University, Corpus Christi
Larock, B. E., University of California, Davis
Larsen, Suzanne, University of Colorado
Larson, Harold P., University of Arizona
Lauretta, Dante, University of Arizona
Laurier, Eric, Edinburgh University
Lavallee, Daniel, University of California, Santa Barbara
Lawrence, Deborah, University of Virginia
Layton, Alice, University of Tennessee, Knoxville
Leal-Bejarano, Arturo, Universidad Autonoma de Chihuahua
Ledbetter, Cynthia E., University of Texas, Dallas
Lee, Hung, University of Guelph
Lehane, Mary, University College Cork
LeJeune, Breanne, Western Michigan University
Leland, John D., University of Nevada, Reno
Leland, John, University of Nevada, Reno
Lemmond, Peter C., Woods Hole Oceanographic Institution
Lener, Edward, Virginia Polytechnic Institute & State University
Lerdau, Manuel, University of Virginia
Lermurier, Nathalie, Institut Polytechnique LaSalle Beauvais (ex-IGAL)
Leveque, Connie, University of Maine, Presque Isle
Leveson, David J., Graduate School of the City University of New York
Levy, David, University of Massachusetts, Boston
Li, Rong-Yu, Western University
Li, Wenhong, Duke University
Lichtenstein, Benyamin, University of Massachusetts, Boston
Lichtner, Peter C., Los Alamos National Laboratory
Lin, Hsing K., University of Alaska, Fairbanks
Lin, Shoufa, University of Waterloo
Lin, Xiaomao, Kansas State University
Linky, Edward, Hunter College (CUNY)
Lintz, Heather E., Oregon State University
Lipeles, Maxine I., Washington University
Liu, Jian-yi, Montana State University
Lloyd, Glenn D., Missouri Dept of Natural Resources
Loeb, Valerie, Moss Landing Marine Laboratories
Long, Laura, Lawrence Livermore National Laboratory
Longmire, Patrick A., Los Alamos National Laboratory
Lounsbury, Diane E., SUNY, Geneseo
Loveland, Karen, Missouri Dept of Natural Resources
Lovell, Heather, Edinburgh University
Lowry, William R., Washington University
Loxsom, Fred, Eastern Connecticut State University
Lucus, Beth, Virginia Tech
Lujan-Lopez, Arturo, Universidad Autonoma de Chihuahua
Lumpkin, Thomas A., Washington State University
Lynch, Michael J., University of Kentucky
Lyon, Elizabeth C., Pennsylvania Bureau of Topographic & Geologic Survey
Mabe, Terri, Texas Christian University
Maciha, Mark J., Northern Arizona University
MacInnes, Michael, Los Alamos National Laboratory
Mahler, Robert L., University of Idaho
Maier, Raina M., University of Arizona
Malagon, Teresa Soledad Medina, Universidad Nacional Autonoma de Mexico
Malega, Ron, Missouri State University
Malhotra, Renu, University of Arizona
Malinowski, Jon C., United States Military Academy
Mand, Arlene, University of Pennsylvania
Mangel, Mark S., University of California, Santa Cruz
Manz, Lorraine, North Dakota Geological Survey
Marks, Dennis W., Valdosta State University
Marshall, Stephen, University of Guelph
Martin, Freddie A., Louisiana State University
Martin, Mona, Southern Illinois University Carbondale
Martinez, Judy, University of Utah

Martinez-Macias, Panfilo R., Universidad Autonoma de San Luis Potosi
Masiello, Caroline A., Rice University
Maskell, Derek, University of California, Berkeley
Massey, Michael, California State University, East Bay
Mattison, Katherine W., Missouri University of Science and Technology
Maulud, Mat Ruzlin, University of Malaya
May, Diane M., Missouri State University
May, Fred E., University of Utah
Mayberry, Bill, Mineral Area College
Mayer, Christine M., University of Toledo
McArthur, Russell, San Francisco State University
McAtee, Mike, California State Polytechnic University, Pomona
McClain, Lina C., Graduate School of the City University of New York
McCollough, Cherie, Texas A&M University, Corpus Christi
McConnell, Joseph, University of Nevada, Reno
McCoy, Sue, Cosumnes River College
McCulley, Dawn, California State University, Stanislaus
McDermott, Thomas M., SUNY, The College at Brockport
McDonald, Kyle C., Jet Propulsion Laboratory
McDonald, Lynn, Los Alamos National Laboratory
McFadden, Jennifer, Elizabethtown College
McGee, Tara, University of Alberta
McGraw, Maureen A., Los Alamos National Laboratory
McKenzie, Charlotte, Montana Tech of The University of Montana
McKenzie, Connie, Louisiana Tech University
McKenzie, Phyllis, Smithsonian Institution / Nat Museum of Natural History
McKenzie, Ross, University of Lethbridge
McLafferty, Sara L., Graduate School of the City University of New York
McLaughlin, Richard, Texas A&M University, Corpus Christi
McLeod, Clara, Washington University
McMillan, Robert S., University of Arizona
McNair, Laurie A., Los Alamos National Laboratory
McNamara, Jodi, Colgate University
Medlin, Peggy, Tennessee Tech University
Meehan, Katharine, University of Oregon
Mercier, Glynda L., Austin Community College District
Merritt, Dare, East Carolina University
Messer, Sharon, Shawnee State University
Meyer, Judith, Missouri State University
Meyerson, Rohana, Lafayette College
Miller, Judy, Monroe Community College
Miller, Mark, University of Southern Mississippi
Miller, Ted R., South Dakota Dept of Environment and Natural Resources
Mills, Suzanne, McMaster University
Milstead, Terence, Appalachian State University
Mitchneck, Beth A., University of Arizona
Mittleider, Stacy, Chadron State College
Miyares, Ines, Hunter College (CUNY)
Miyares, Inez, Graduate School of the City University of New York
Mockler, Theodore, Los Alamos National Laboratory
Moe-Hoffman, Amy P., Mississippi State University
Mollner, Daniel, Gustavus Adolphus College
Momen, Nasim, Boston University
Momohara, Kristin, University of Hawai'i, Manoa
Monahan, Adam, University of Victoria
Montgomery, Tamra S., University of Illinois, Urbana-Champaign
Moodie, T. Bryant, University of Alberta
Mooney, Phillip, Sonoma State University
Moore, Clyde, Louisiana State University
Moore, Donna, Kutztown University of Pennsylvania
Moore, Emmett B., Washington State University
Moorhead, Daryl L., University of Toledo
Morehouse, Barbara, University of Arizona
Moreton, Kim, Exeter University
Morgan, Gary, Hampton University
Morgan, Siobahn M., University of Northern Iowa
Morin, Paul, University of Minnesota, Twin Cities
Morrin, M. Elizabeth, Rutgers, The State University of New Jersey, Newark
Morris, Brenda, Palomar College
Morris, Catherine, University of North Carolina Wilmington
Morris, Donald P., Lehigh University
Mortenson, Kristine B., Brigham Young University
Moss, Patti, Whitman College
Mountain, Carol S., Columbia University
Moxzzachiodi, Riccardo, Texas A&M University, Corpus Christi
Munoz Mendoza, Alvaro, Universidad Nacional Autonoma de Mexico
Murphy, Alexander B., University of Oregon
Murphy, Edward C., North Dakota Geological Survey
Myers, Clifford D., Berkshire Community College
Myers, Tammy, Shippensburg University
Nadiga, Balu, Los Alamos National Laboratory
Nakatsuka, James, University of California, Los Angeles
Narinder, Kaushik, University of Guelph
Nashold, Barney W., Argonne National Laboratory
Neish, Catherine, Western University
Nesbitt, Alex, University of Nevada
Neuman, Dennis R., Montana State University
Nevins, Susan K., SUNY, Cortland
Newman, Jonathan, University of Guelph
Newton, Anthony J., Edinburgh University

Newton, Seth A., Geological Survey of Alabama
Nichols, Liz, Irvine Valley College
Nichols, Terry E., University of Arkansas, Fayetteville
Nicholson, Nanette, American Museum of Natural History
Nielsen, Mary, University of South Dakota
Nixon, Cheryl, University of Massachusetts, Boston
Noll, Michael G., Valdosta State University
Nordwald, Dan, Missouri Dept of Natural Resources
Norman, Catherine, Johns Hopkins University
Nosal, Thomas E., Dept of Energy and Environmental Protection
Nussear, Ken, University of Nevada, Reno
O'Callaghan, Mick, University College Cork
O'Day, Sandra, Central Connecticut State University
O'Melia, Charles R., Johns Hopkins University
O'Neil, Jennifer, University of Nevada, Reno
Obia, Godson C., Eastern Illinois University
Occhiuzzi, Tony, Mesa Community College
Odland, Sarah K., Columbia University
Offerman, Katherine A., Maryland Department of Natural Resources
Oglesby, Elizabeth, University of Arizona
Okafor, Florence A., Alabama A&M University
Olsen, Ken, Washington University
Olson, James R., South Dakota Dept of Environment and Natural Resources
Oona, Hain, Los Alamos National Laboratory
Oppong, Joseph R., University of North Texas
Orrock, John, Washington University
Ortmann, Anthony L., Murray State University
Oswalt, Ginny L., University of Arkansas at Little Rock
Otis, Gard, University of Guelph
Ott, Kevin C., Los Alamos National Laboratory
Otter, Ryan, University of Tennessee, Knoxville
Otto, LeeAnn, University of San Diego
Ouellette, Vicki, University of Northern Colorado
Owens, Tamera, Muskegon Community College
Oza, Rupal, Hunter College (CUNY)
Pace, Michael L., University of Virginia
Pacia, Christina, Kean University
Padden, Janice, Itasca Community College
Palace, Michael W., University of New Hampshire
Palm, Risa I., Georgia State University
Palma, Miclelle, University of Wisconsin Colleges
Palmer, Christina, California State University, San Bernardino
Palmer, Clare, Washington University
Papaleo, Silvanna, University of Toronto
Parendes, Laurie A., Edinboro University of Pennsylvania
Parker, Jim, University of Houston
Parker, Joan, Moss Landing Marine Laboratories
Parker, Marjorie, Bowdoin College
Parker, Stephen R., Montana Tech of the University of Montana
Parrish, Pia, San Diego State University
Parsons, Gail, Augustana College
Pasteris, Jill D., Washington University
Patel, Vinodkumar A., Illinois State Geological Survey
Patronas, Dennis, Dauphin Island Sea Lab
Patterson, Jodi T., Utah Geological Survey
Patterson, Mark, Northeastern University
Peaslee, Graham F., Hope College
Penney, Paulette, Baylor University
Pepper, Ian L., University of Arizona
Peri, Francesco, University of Massachusetts, Boston
Perkins, R, Cardiff University
Perro, Dianne, University of Maine
Petersen, Bruce, Washington University
Peterson, Peter A., Iowa State University of Science & Technology
Phelps, Tommy, University of Tennessee, Knoxville
Phillippi, Nathan E., University of North Carolina, Pembroke
Pickering, Dan, Carnegie Museum of Natural History
Pickett, Nicki, Broward College, Central Campus
Pierce, Larry, Missouri Dept of Natural Resources
Pike, J, Cardiff University
Plane, David A., University of Arizona
Plant, Jeffrey J., Jet Propulsion Laboratory
Plescia, Jeffrey, Jet Propulsion Laboratory
Podolak, Morris, Tel Aviv University
Pollak, Robert, Washington University
Polovina, Jeffrey J., University of Hawai'i, Manoa
Ponette-Gonzalez, Alexandra, University of North Texas
Porlas, Dustin, University of Utah
Powers, Roger W., University of Alaska, Fairbanks
Poynton, Helen, University of Massachusetts, Boston
Pratte, Darrell D., Missouri Dept of Agriculture
Prewitt, Charles, University of Arizona
Prichard, Terry L., University of California, Davis
Pugh, Teresa, Vanderbilt University
Pundsack, Jonathan, University of Minnesota, Twin Cities
Purcell, Rita, Wellesley College
Purchase, Megan, University of the Free State
Purtle, Jennifer M., University of Arkansas, Fayetteville
Pytlik, Laura, Marietta College
Qualls, Robert G., University of Nevada, Reno

Quintero, Sylvia, University of Arizona
Radice, Mona, University of California, Berkeley
Rafferty, Milton D., Missouri State University
Rajala, Jacob, Wassuk College
Rakowski, Cynthia L., Pacific Northwest National Laboratory
Rallis, Donald N., Mary Washington College
Ramirez Camperos, Esperanza, Universidad Nacional Autonoma de Mexico
Rankin, Seth, University of Wisconsin Colleges
Rasmussen, Tab, Washington University
Reaven, Sheldon, SUNY, Stony Brook
Renfrew, Bonnie, Illinois State Geological Survey
Rennie, Tim, University of Guelph
Reusch, David B., New Mexico Institute of Mining and Technology
Reynolds, Barbara C., University of North Carolina, Asheville
Rhoads, James, Arizona State University
Rhodes, Carol J., Texas A&M University
Rice, Benjamin, Northwestern University
Rice, Murray, University of North Texas
Ricker, Alison, Oberlin College
Riddick, Pamela M., University of Memphis
Ridgwell, Andy, University of California, Riverside
Ridky, Alice M., Colby College
Ridley, DeAnna, University of Maine - Farmington
Rieke, George H., University of Arizona
Riley, James, University of Arizona
Riley, Rhonda, Southern Utah University
Ritter, Leonard, University of Guelph
Rivera, Edna L., University of Illinois at Chicago
Robas, Sheryl A., Princeton University
Robbins, Debra C., University of North Carolina, Asheville
Roberts, A. Lynn, Johns Hopkins University
Robinson, Bruce A., Los Alamos National Laboratory
Robinson, David, The Open University
Robinson, Mark, Arizona State University
Rodriguez, Vanessa del S., Puerto Rico Bureau of Geology
Roe, Carol, College of William & Mary
Roemer, Elizabeth, University of Arizona
Rogers, Jefferson S., University of Tennessee, Martin
Rogers, William J., West Texas A&M University
Roinstad, Lori L., South Dakota Dept of Environment and Natural Resources
Rojas, Adena, Johns Hopkins University
Rollinson, Paul A., Missouri State University
Rondot, Beth, Long Island University, C.W. Post Campus
Rooney, Neil, University of Guelph
Rose, Candace M., Argonne National Laboratory
Rose, Dan, University College Cork
Rosengaus, Rebeca , Northeastern University
Ross, Kirstin, Flinders University
Ross, Paula, New Mexico State University, Las Cruces
Rossell, Irene M., University of North Carolina, Asheville
Rostam-Abadi, Massoud, Illinois State Geological Survey
Rostron, Ben, University of Alberta
Rothberg, Maryann, Princeton University
Rouhani, Farhang, Mary Washington College
Rouse, Jesse, University of North Carolina, Pembroke
Roussel-Dupre, R., Los Alamos National Laboratory
Rowland, Scott K., University of Hawai'i, Manoa
Rozmus, Wojciech, University of Alberta
Rumstay, Kenneth S., Valdosta State University
Russell, Ron, University of Texas at Austin, Jackson School of Geosciences
Russell, Terry P., University of Victoria
Russell, Theresa J., University of Arkansas, Fayetteville
Russo, Mary Rose, Princeton University
Ruzicka, Jaromir, University of Hawai'i, Manoa
Sabala-Foreman, Susan M., Northern Arizona University
Saikia, Udoy, Flinders University
Saku, James C., Frostburg State University
Salisbury, Joseph, University of New Hampshire
Sammarco, Paul W., Louisiana State University
Samuelson, D. James, San Jose City College
Sanchez, Charles, University of Arizona
Santander, Erma, University of Arizona
Sapigao, Gladys, Queens College (CUNY)
Sarin, Manmohan, University of Delaware
Saripalli, Srikanth, Arizona State University
Satterly, Thomas G., University of Montana Western
Sauer, Nancy N. S., Los Alamos National Laboratory
Scannapieco, Evan, Arizona State University
Schaal, Barbara, Washington University
Schauss, Kim E., University of Southern Indiana
Scheel, Patrick, Missouri Dept of Natural Resources
Scheidemen, Kathy J., University of California, Santa Barbara
Schell, Marie, Western University
Schlesinger, William H., Duke University
Schlumpberger, Debbie, Saint Cloud State University
Schmidt, Jonathan, University of Guelph
Schoenberger, Erica J., Johns Hopkins University
Schreckhise, R. Gene, Washington State University
Schroeder, Kathleen, Appalachian State University
Schwankl, Larry J., University of California, Davis

Schwarzschild, Arthur C., University of Virginia
Schwenke, Eszter, University of New Brunswick
Schwob, Stephanie L., Southern Methodist University
Scogin, Linda, University of New Hampshire
Scott, Kathy, University of British Columbia
Scott, Shana R., Stephen F. Austin State University
Scott-Dupree, Cynthia, University of Guelph
Sears, Heather, Northeastern University
Selin, Helaine, Hampshire College
Serrano, Carmen, Florida Institute of Technology
Shade, Janet, University of Pittsburgh, Bradford
Shah, Ashru, North Carolina State University
Shaham-Albalancy, Amira, Collin College - Preston Ridge Campus
Sharma, Govind, Alabama A&M University
Sharp, Deanna M., Austin Community College District
Shaw, Fred, Missouri Dept of Natural Resources
Shchukin, Eugene D., Johns Hopkins University
Sheley, Christina, Indiana University, Bloomington
Shelton, Robert B., Oak Ridge National Laboratory
Shiaris, Michael, University of Massachusetts, Boston
Shields, Nancy, Virginia Polytechnic Institute & State University
Shock, Everett, Arizona State University
Showman, Adam, University of Arizona
Shumway, Matthew J., Brigham Young University
Sibley, Paul, University of Guelph
Sigler, William V., University of Toledo
Signer, Marcia, University of Colorado
Silks, Louis A., Los Alamos National Laboratory
Silvano, Janet, Tufts University
Simon, Kathy, California Polytechnic State University
Simonetti, Stephanie, University of Notre Dame
Simovich, Marie, University of San Diego
Singh, Harbans, Montclair State University
Sinz, Stacy, California State University, Sacramento
Sissom, David , West Texas A&M University
Sitwell, O.F. George, University of Alberta
Skeel, Loreene, University of Montana
Skopec, Mary P., Iowa Dept of Natural Resources
Slater, Tom, Edinburgh University
Slavetskas, Carol, Binghamton University
Smith, Derald, University of Lethbridge
Smith, Donald R., University of California, Santa Cruz
Smith, Elizabeth Y., University of Nevada, Las Vegas
Smith, Erik, University of Saint Thomas
Smith, H D., Cardiff University
Smith, Jim, Flinders University
Smith, K. L., Wichita State University
Smith, Paul H., Los Alamos National Laboratory
Smith, Peter J., University of Alberta
Smith, Susan M., Montana Tech of The University of Montana
Solomon, Keith, University of Guelph
Somers, Jr., Arnold E., Valdosta State University
Sorenson, Mary Clare, University of Wisconsin, Stevens Point
Southwell, Benjamin, Lake Superior State University
Spears, Ellen, Emory University
Spencer, Mary R., University of Kentucky
Sperazza, Michael, SUNY, Stony Brook
Spracklen, Dominick, University of Leeds
Stadnyk, Leona, Mount Royal University
Stahl, Terry L., Carnegie Institution of Washington
Stampone, Mary D., University of New Hampshire
Standridge, Debbie, Georgia Southwestern State University
Stanton, Stephen, University of Missouri
Starr, Richard, Moss Landing Marine Laboratories
Starrfield, Sumner, Arizona State University
Steadman, Todd A., Clemson University
Stechmann, Samuel, University of Wisconsin, Madison
Steele, Carol S., University of South Florida, Saint Petersburg
Steffan, Cindi, The Manitoba Museum
Steller, Diana, Moss Landing Marine Laboratories
Stephenson, Gerry, University of Guelph
Stepien, Carol A., University of Toledo
Sternberg, Rolf, Montclair State University
Stevens, Joan M., California Polytechnic State University
Stierle, Andrea, Montana Tech of the University of Montana
Stiles, Lynn F., Richard Stockton College of New Jersey
Stimer, Debra, Kent State University at Stark
Stokes, Patricia, Utah Geological Survey
Stone, Glenn D., Washington University
Strangeway, Robert J., University of California, Los Angeles
Streett, Pamela S., University of Arizona
Strole, Torie L., University of Illinois, Urbana-Champaign
Stunz, Greg, Texas A&M University, Corpus Christi
Su, Xiaobo, University of Oregon
Sullivan, Barbara, Argonne National Laboratory
Summers, Robert, University of Alberta
Sussman, Robert W., Washington University
Sutherland, Bruce R., University of Alberta
Sutton, Chris, Western Washington University
Svitra, Zita V., Los Alamos National Laboratory

Swanson, Basil I., Los Alamos National Laboratory
Swap, Robert J., University of Virginia
Swartwood, Jade L., Bloomsburg University
Sweet, Brenda, Lyndon State College
Swetnam, Thomas W., University of Arizona
Swindall, Diane, University of California, Davis
Symbalisty, E.M.D., Los Alamos National Laboratory
Symes, William S., Rice University
Taney, R. Marieke, Northern Arizona University
Tanji, K. K., University of California, Davis
Tavener, Kristi, Lakehead University
Taylor, David J., University of Chicago
Taylor, Robert W., Montclair State University
Templeton, Alan R., Washington University
Tencate, James, Los Alamos National Laboratory
Teplitski, Max, University of Florida
Ter-Simonian, Vardui, University of Southern California
Terkla, David, University of Massachusetts, Boston
Tester, Jefferson W., Cornell University
Theis, Karen, University of Manchester
Thériault, Julie Mireille, Universite du Quebec a Montreal
Thompson, Glennis, University of California, Berkeley
Thomson, Cary, University of British Columbia
Thomson, Cynthia, Columbia University
Thomson, Vivian E., University of Virginia
Timmons, David, University of Massachusetts, Boston
Tingey, David G., Brigham Young University
Tinnon, Vicki, University of Southern Mississippi
Tissot, Philippe , Texas A&M University, Corpus Christi
Todd, Brenda, University of Nebraska at Omaha
Torcellini, Paul, Eastern Connecticut State University
Tornabene, Livio, Western University
Townshend, Ivan, University of Lethbridge
Tracy, Matthew, United States Air Force Academy
Trevors, Jack, University of Guelph
Triplehorn, Judy, University of Alaska, Fairbanks
Troedsson, Nils, University of Montana Western
Trost, G K., University of Arkansas, Fayetteville
Trout, Jennifer, Western Michigan University
Trussell, Geoffrey, Northeastern University
Tsongas, Theodora A., Washington State University
Tuller, Markus, University of Arizona
Turner, Jay, Washington University
Tyning, Thomas F., Berkshire Community College
Underwood, Marlene, San Jose City College
Unkefer, Clifford J., Los Alamos National Laboratory
Unsworth, Martyn, University of Alberta
Urbanik, Julie, University of Missouri-Kansas City
Urquhart, Alvin W., University of Oregon
Utter, James M., SUNY, Purchase
van den Akker, Ben, Flinders University
Van Eerd, Laura, University of Guelph
van Gardingen, Paul R., Edinburgh University
Van Leuven, Judy, University of California, Santa Cruz
Van Otten, George A., Northern Arizona University
Van Roosendaal, Susan, University of Utah
VanBrocklin, Matt, St. Lawrence University
Vancas, Tina, Pennsylvania State University, University Park
Vanlandingham, Karen M., West Chester University
Varadi, Ferenc D., University of California, Los Angeles
Varady, Robert G., University of Arizona
Vasquez, Cecile I., Mount Holyoke College
Veeder, Glenn J., Jet Propulsion Laboratory
Vieira, David J., Los Alamos National Laboratory
Vierrether, Chris, Missouri Dept of Natural Resources
Vlahovic, Lou Ann, Moravian College
Vollmer, Steve, Northeastern University
Wada, Ikuko, University of Minnesota, Twin Cities
Wadhwa, Meenakshi, Arizona State University
Wagh, Swati, Argonne National Laboratory
Waite, Cynthia, University of Southern California
Walker, Mark, University of Nevada, Reno
Walker, Peter A., University of Oregon
Walker, Raymond J., University of California, Los Angeles
Walraven, Brenda, Mercer University
Walrod, Amanda G., University of Arkansas, Fayetteville
Walsh, Christopher, University of Maryland
Walsh, Daniel E., University of Alaska, Fairbanks
Walsh, Ellen c., Lawrence University
Walter, Thomas, Hunter College (CUNY)
Warburg, Helena F., Williams College
Ward, David M., Montana State University
Ward, Marie D., University of Alaska, Fairbanks
Warhaft, Zellman, Cornell University
Warren, Richard L., University of Arizona
Waterstone, Marvin, University of Arizona
Watson, Alan, University of Guelph
Wauthier, Christelle, Pennsylvania State University, University Park
Weaver, Douglas J., Los Alamos National Laboratory
Webre, Cherri B., Louisiana State University

Weinberg, Joan M., University of Arizona
Weinstein, Charles E., Berkshire Community College
Weintraub, Michael N., University of Toledo
Wells, Steve G., University of Nevada, Reno
Welton, Leicha, University of Alaska, Fairbanks
Wenz, Helmut C., University of Tennessee, Martin
Wesler, Kit W., Murray State University
Wetzel, Dan L., University of Alaska, Fairbanks
Whitaker, Brenda, University of Virginia College, Wise
White, George W., Frostburg State University
Whiteman, C. David, Washington State University
Whitney, Earl M., Los Alamos National Laboratory
Wiederspahn, Mark, University of Texas at Austin
Wilder, Margaret, University of Arizona
Wilhelmy, Jerry B., Los Alamos National Laboratory
Williams, Allison M., McMaster University
Williams, Barbara, Ohio Wesleyan University
Williams, Carolyn S., Virginia Polytechnic Institute & State University
Williams, Nancy, Kansas State University
Willson, Lee, Rice University
Wilmut, Michael, University of Victoria
Wilson, Robert, University of St. Andrews
Wilson, Sarah, Washington & Lee University
Wilson, Thomas B., University of Arizona
Wilton, Robert D., McMaster University
Winsor, Roger A., Appalachian State University
Winston, Barbara, Washington University
Winterkamp, Judith L., Los Alamos National Laboratory
Winton, Mary A., Texas Tech University
Wise, James A., Washington State University
Withers, Kim, Texas A&M University, Corpus Christi
Wixman, Ronald, University of Oregon
Wolfe, Karen M., Middle Tennessee State University
Wollan, Jacinda, North Dakota State University
Wollons, Roberta, University of Massachusetts, Boston
Wong, Cindy, Buffalo State College
Wood, Carolyn F., Dauphin Island Sea Lab
Wood, Howard , Texas A&M University, Corpus Christi
Wood, Stephen E., University of Washington
Woodard, Gary C., University of Arizona
Woodley, Teresa, University of British Columbia
Woodruff, William H., Los Alamos National Laboratory
Woods, Karen M., Lamar University
Wooldridge, C F., Cardiff University
Wortel, Matthew J., University of Iowa
Wright, Judith V., Washington State University
Wright, Kathyrn, Western Michigan University
Wu, Charles T., Western University
Wu, David T., Colorado School of Mines
Wyckoff, William K., Montana State University
Yarbrough, Robert A., Georgia Southern University
Yates, Mary Anne, Los Alamos National Laboratory
Yelle, Roger, University of Arizona
Yoakum, Barbara, United States Naval Academy
Yochem, Pam, University of San Diego
Yonetani, Mage, Utah Geological Survey
Yoskowitz, David , Texas A&M University, Corpus Christi
Young, Donald W., University of Arizona
Young, Gerald L., Washington State University
Young, Patrick, Arizona State University
Young, Priscilla E., South Dakota Dept of Environment and Natural Resources
Yow, Sonja H., Eastern Kentucky University
Yutzy, Gale, Frostburg State University
Zajac, Roman N., University of New Haven
Zaspel, Craig E., University of Montana Western
Zavada, Michael S., Providence College
Zeiger, Elaine, Field Museum of Natural History
Zelizer, Nora, Princeton University
Zhang, Max, Cornell University
Zhang, Wei, University of Massachusetts, Boston
Zhu, Chen, Indiana University, Bloomington
Zhuang, Qianlai, Purdue University
Zimba, Paul, Texas A&M University, Corpus Christi
Zimmerman, Claire, The Manitoba Museum
Zimmermann, George, Richard Stockton College of New Jersey
Zotti, Maria, Flinders University
Zurick, David, Eastern Kentucky University
Zwiefelhofer, Luke, Winona State University

Faculty Index

Agee, Carl A., (505) 277-1644 agee@unm.edu,
University of New Mexico – Cp
Agee, Ernest M., (765) 494-3282 eagee@purdue.edu,
Purdue University – Oa
Agioutantis, Zach , 859-257-953 zach.agioutantis@uky.edu,
University of Kentucky – Nr
Agnew, Duncan C., (858) 534-2590 dagnew@ucsd.edu,
University of California, San Diego – Ys
Agnew, Stephen F., (505) 665-1764 Los Alamos National Laboratory – On
Agnini, Claudia, 39-049-827918 claudia.agnini@unipd.it,
Università degli Studi di Padova – PmeGu
Agrawal, Abinash, 937 775-3455 abinash.agrawal@wright.edu,
Wright State University – ClHwPy
Agrawal, Sandeep , 780-492-1230 sagrawal@ualberta.ca,
University of Alberta – Ou
Agterberg, Frits P., 613-996-2374 Frits.Agterberg@nrcan-rncan.gc.ca,
University of Ottawa – Gq
Ague, Jay J., 203-432-3171 jay.ague@yale.edu, Yale University – Gzx
Aharon, Paul, 205-348-2528 paharon@ua.edu, University of Alabama – Ge
Ahearn, Sean C., (212) 772-5327, Graduate School of the City University of New
York – Or
Ahern, Judson L., (405) 325-4480 jahern@ou.edu,
University of Oklahoma – Yg
Ahmad, Abd Rashid, 03-79674156 abrashid@um.edu.my,
University of Malaya – Sc
Ahmed, Mohamed , (269) 387-4980 mohamed.ahmed@wmich.edu,
Western Michigan University – YgOrHw
Ahmed, Ramadan, r.ahmed@ou.edu, University of Oklahoma – Np
Ahmed, Waquar, 940-565-2721 waquar.ahmed@unt.edu,
University of North Texas – On
Ahola, John, John.Ahola@bristolcc.edu, Bristol Community College – Gg
Ahrens, Donald C., (209) 575-6300, Modesto Junior College – Og
Aiello, Ivano, (831) 771-4400 iaiello@mlml.calstate.edu,
Moss Landing Marine Laboratories – Gu
Aiken, Carlos L., (972) 883-2450 aiken@utdallas.edu,
University of Texas, Dallas – Yv
Aiken, Robert, (785) 462-6281 raiken@ksu.edu,
Kansas State University – So
Aines, Roger D., (925) 423-7184 aines1@llnl.gov,
Lawrence Livermore National Laboratory – Cg
Aitchison, Jonathan, geoscience.headofschool@sydney.edu.au,
University of Sydney – GrtPm
Aitkenhead-Peterson, Jacqueline A., 979-845-3682 JPeterson@ag.tamu.edu,
Texas A&M University – Hs
Aiyyer, Anantha, 919-515-7973 aaiyyer@ncsu.edu,
North Carolina State University – Oa
Aja, Stephen U., (718) 951-5405 Graduate School of the City University of New
York – Cl
Aja, Stephen U., 7189515000 x2881 suaja@brooklyn.cuny.edu,
Brooklyn College (CUNY) – Cl
Ajassa, Roberto, roberto.ajassa@unito.it, Università di Torino – Oy
Ajayi, J. O., 234-803-401-4357 owoajayi@oauife.edu.ng,
Obafemi Awolowo University – Oo
Ajayi, T. R., 234-803-725-8924 traajayi@oauife.edu.ng,
Obafemi Awolowo University – CgEgGe
Ajigo, Isaac O., 08032107038 ioajigo@futa.edu.ng,
Federal University of Technology, Akure – GgNm
Akabzaa, Thomas M., 233-246325685 akabzaa@ug.edu.gh,
University of Ghana – EgGeNm
Akaegbobi, I. M., izumike2002@yahoo.com,
University of Ibadan – Cg
Akciz, Sinan, 310-825-3463 sakciz@ucla.edu,
University of California, Los Angeles – Gt
Akenzua-Adamcyzk, Aiyevbekpen H., aiyevbekpen.akenzua@uniben.edu,
University of Benin – GeHgGg
Akgul, Bünyamin, 00904242370000-5988 bakgul@firat.edu.tr,
Firat University – GzyGi
Akgul, Muharrem, 00904242370000-5993 makgul@firat.edu.tr,
Firat University – Ecg
Akgun, Elif , 00904242370000-5972 efiratligil@firat.edu.tr,
Firat University – GgcGt
Akinlabi, Ismaila A., +2348050225113 iaakinlabi@lautech.edu.ng,
Ladoke Akintola University of Technology – GggGg
Aksoy, Ercan, 00904242370000-5974 Firat University – Ggt
Aksu, Ali E., (709) 737-8385 aaksu@sparky2.esd.mun.ca,
Memorial University of Newfoundland – Gu
Akujieze, Christopher N., krisjiaku@yahoo.com,
University of Benin – HwGeHg
Al, Tom A., 613-562-5800 6966 tom.al@uottawa.ca,
University of Ottawa – HwCgOg
Al-Aasm, Ihsan S., (519) 253-3000, ext. 2494 alaasm@uwindsor.ca,
University of Windsor – Gd
Al-Attar, David, +44 (0) 1223 348935 da380@cam.ac.uk,
University of Cambridge – YdGt
Al-Lehyani, Ayman, +96638601661 allehyani@kfupm.edu.sa,
King Fahd University of Petroleum and Minerals – Yg
Al-Ramadan, Khalid, +96638607175 ramadank@kfupm.edu.sa,
King Fahd University of Petroleum and Minerals – Go
Al-Saad, Hamad A., hamadsaad@qu.edu.qa,
University of Qatar – PsGsu

Al-Shaibani, Abdulaziz, +96638604002 shaibani@kfupm.edu.sa,
King Fahd University of Petroleum and Minerals – HwGeg
Al-Shuhail, Abdullah, +966138602538 shuhail@kfupm.edu.sa,
King Fahd University of Petroleum and Minerals – Ye
Al-Shuhail, Abdullatif, +96638603584 ashuhail@kfupm.edu.sa,
King Fahd University of Petroleum and Minerals – Ygs
Alao, O. A., 234-805-466-7314 olade77@yahoo.com,
Obafemi Awolowo University – Yg
Alavi, Hedy, (410) 516-7091 alavi@jhu.edu,
Johns Hopkins University – On
Albach, Suzanne M., 734-677-5111 salbach@wccnet.edu,
Washtenaw Community College – OegGe
Albee, Arden L., 626.395.6260 aalbee@caltech.edu,
California Institute of Technology – GizXg
Albee-Scott, Steven R., (517) 796-8526 albeescsteven@jccmi.edu,
Jackson Community College – GePeSf
Alberstadt, Leonard P., 615-322-2160 leonard.p.alberstadt@vanderbilt.edu,
Vanderbilt University – Gd
Albert, Curtis C., 217-244-2188 abert@illinois.edu,
University of Illinois, Urbana-Champaign – HgYg
Alberts, E E., 573-882-1144 University of Missouri, Columbia – Hw
Albin, Edward, Edward.Albin@gpc.edu,
Georgia Perimeter College - Online – Xm
Albrecht, Jochen, 212-772-5221 jochen@hunter.cuny.edu,
Hunter College (CUNY) – Oi
Albrecht, Lorraine, klalbrec@uwaterloo.ca,
University of Waterloo – On
Albright, James N., (505) 667-4318 j_albright@lanl.gov,
Los Alamos National Laboratory – Yg
Albright, Katia, (775) 682-8370 kalbright@unr.edu,
University of Nevada, Reno – On
Alde, Douglas, (505) 667-0488 dxa@lanl.gov,
Los Alamos National Laboratory – On
Alderson, David, +44 (0) 191 208 7121 david.alderson@ncl.ac.uk,
University of Newcastle Upon Tyne – Oi
Alderton, Dave, +44 1784 443585 D.Alderton@rhul.ac.uk,
University of London, Royal Holloway & Bedford New College – Gz
Aldrich, Eric A., 573-882-6301 aldriche@missouri.edu,
University of Missouri, Columbia – Oa
Aldrich, M. James, (505) 667-1495 jaldrich@lanl.gov,
Los Alamos National Laboratory – Gc
Aldridge, Keith D., (416)736-5245 keith@yorku.ca,
York University – Yg
Aldushin, Kirill, 089/2180 4337 kirill.aldushin@lrz.uni-muenchen.de,
Ludwig-Maximilians-Universitaet Muenchen – Gz
Alessi, Daniel, 780-492-3265 alessi@ualberta.ca,
University of Alberta – Cl
Alexander, Becky, 206-543-0164 beckya@atmos.washington.edu,
University of Washington – Oa
Alexander, Clark R., 912-598-2329 clark.alexander@skio.usg.edu,
Georgia Southern University – OuGsOn
Alexander, Conel M., (202) 478-8478 alexander@dtm.ciw.edu,
Carnegie Institution of Washington – Xc
Alexander, Dane, (269) 387-5486 dane.alexander@wmich.edu,
Western Michigan University – GgOnn
Alexander, Elaine, (254) 299-8442 ealexander@mclennan.edu,
McLennan Community College – Gg
Alexander, Jan, +44 (0)1603 59 3759 j.alexander@uea.ac.uk,
University of East Anglia – Gt
Alexander, Jane L., 718-982-3013 jane.alexander@csi.cuny.edu,
College of Staten Island – Gse
Alexander, Shelton S., (814) 863-7246 shel@geosc.psu.edu,
Pennsylvania State University, University Park – Ys
Alexander, Jr., E. Calvin, 612-624-3517 alexa001@umn.edu,
University of Minnesota, Twin Cities – Cc
Alfe, Dario, +44 202 7679 32361 d.alfe@ucl.ac.uk,
University College London – Gz
Alford, Matthew H., 206-221-3257 malford@apl.washington.edu,
University of Washington – Op
Algar, Christopher, (902) 494-7192 calgar@dal.ca,
Dalhousie University – Obc
Algeo, Catherine, (270) 745-5922 katie.algeo@wku.edu,
Western Kentucky University – Oi
Algeo, Thomas J., (513) 556-4195 thomas.algeo@uc.edu,
University of Cincinnati – Gs
Algin, Barbara, (212) 854-2905 ba110@columbia.edu,
Columbia University – On
Ali, Bukari, +233 20 330 7976 bukariali@yahoo.co.uk,
Kwame Nkrumah University of Science and Technology – HwNgYg
Ali, Genevieve, 204-474-7266 Genevieve.Ali@umanitoba.ca,
University of Manitoba – Hw
Ali, Hendratta N., (785) 628-4608 hnali@fhsu.edu,
Fort Hays State University – GogYs
Ali, K. Adem, (843) 953-0877 alika@cofc.edu,
College of Charleston – Ge
Alkaç, Onur, 00904242370000-5970 oalkac@firat.edu.tr,
Firat University – GgsGu
All, John, (270) 745-5975 john.all@wku.edu,
Western Kentucky University – Oyr
Allam, Bassem, (632) 632-8745 bassem.allam@stonybrook.edu,

Anandakrishnan, Sridhar, (814) 863-6742 sak@essc.psu.edu,
Pennsylvania State University, University Park – Ys
Anastasio, Cort, 530-754-6095 canastasio@ucdavis.edu,
University of California, Davis – Oa
Anastasio, David J., (610) 758-5117 dja2@lehigh.edu,
Lehigh University – Gc
Anbar, Ariel, 480-965-0767 anbar@asu.edu,
Arizona State University – Cg
Ancell, Brian C., 806-834-3143 brian.ancell@ttu.edu,
Texas Tech University – Oa
Anders, Alison M., 217-244-3917 amanders@illinois.edu,
University of Illinois, Urbana-Champaign – Gm
Anders, Tania-Maria, (361) 825-3755 tania.anders@tamucc.edu,
Texas A&M University, Corpus Christi – GugPi
Andersen, C. B., brannon.andersen@furman.edu,
Clemson University – Cl
Andersen, C. Brannon, (864) 294-3366 brannon.andersen@furman.edu,
Furman University – ClGe
Andersen, David W., (408) 924-5014 david.andersen@sjsu.edu,
San Jose State University – GsCl
Andersen, Jens, +44 01326 371836 J.C.Andersen@exeter.ac.uk,
Exeter University – Gi
Andersen, Raymond J., (604) 822-4511 randersn@eos.ubc.ca,
University of British Columbia – Oc
Anderson, Alan J., (902) 867-2309 aanderso@stfx.ca,
Saint Francis Xavier University – Gx
Anderson, Alan J., 902-863-5413 aanderso@stfx.ca,
Dalhousie University – Cg
Anderson, Bruce, brucea@bu.edu, Boston University – Oap
Anderson, G M., (416) 978-2062 University of Toronto – Cp
Anderson, James G., (617) 495-5922 anderson@huarp.harvard.edu,
Harvard University – Oa
Anderson, James L., 808-974-7640 jamesa@hawaii.edu,
University of Hawai'i, Hilo – GctYd
Anderson, James L., (612) 625-0279 jandersn@soils.umn.edu,
University of Minnesota, Twin Cities – Sd
Anderson, James Lawford, lawford@bu.edu,
Boston University – Gi
Anderson, Jennifer L., 507-457-2457 jlanderson@winona.edu,
Winona State University – XgYgOe
Anderson, John, (775) 784-4265 jga@seismo.unr.edu,
University of Nevada, Reno – Ys
Anderson, John B., (713) 348-4652 johna@rice.edu,
Rice University – Gu
Anderson, John G., (775) 784-4265 jga@seismo.unr.edu,
University of Nevada, Reno – Ys
Anderson, John R., 770-274-5077 john.anderson@gpc.edu,
Georgia Perimeter College – PiGsOi
Anderson, Jonathan H., (507) 389-1301 jonathan.anderson@mnsu.edu,
Minnesota State University – Ga
Anderson, Ken B., 618-453-7389 kanderson@geo.siu.edu,
Southern Illinois University Carbondale – Co
Anderson, Laurie C., (605) 394-1290 Laurie.Anderson@sdsmt.edu,
South Dakota School of Mines & Technology – Pio
Anderson, Mark, +44 1752 584768 M.Anderson@plymouth.ac.uk,
University of Plymouth – Gct
Anderson, Mark R., (402) 472-6656 manderson4@unl.edu,
University of Nebraska, Lincoln – Oa
Anderson, Mary P., (914) 365-8335 andy@geology.wisc.edu,
University of Wisconsin, Madison – Hw
Anderson, Megan L., 719-389-6512 mlanderson@coloradocollege.edu,
Colorado College – YgGt
Anderson, Michelle, (406) 683-7076 michelle.anderson@umwestern.edu,
University of Montana Western – Hs
Anderson, Orson L., (310) 825-2386 University of California, Los Angeles – Yx
Anderson, Patricia M., pata@uw.edu, University of Washington – Ple
Anderson, Paula, 479-575-3355 pea001@uark.edu,
University of Arkansas, Fayetteville – Gg
Anderson, Raymond R., (319) 335-1589 Raymond.Anderson@dnr.iowa.gov,
University of Iowa – Gr
Anderson, Robert, 303-735-4684 Robert.S.Anderson@Colorado.EDU,
University of Colorado – Gm
Anderson, Robert F., 845-365-8508 Columbia University – Cg
Anderson, Robert G., (604) 822-2449 University of British Columbia – Gt
Anderson, Robert S., (831) 459-3342 randerson@es.ucsc.edu,
University of California, Santa Cruz – Gm
Anderson, Roger N., (845) 365-8335 anderson@ldeo.columbia.edu,
Columbia University – Yh
Anderson, Ross, +44 (0) 131 451 3798 ross.anderson@pet.hw.ac.uk,
Heriot-Watt University – Eo
Anderson, Scott, scott.anderson@gov.mb.ca,
Manitoba Geological Survey – EgGcCg
Anderson, Stephen H., 573-882-6303 andersons@missouri.edu,
University of Missouri, Columbia – Sp
Anderson, Steve, 970-381-0448 Steven.Anderson@unco.edu,
University of Northern Colorado – GvgOe
Anderson, Suzanne, 303-765-0951 suzanne.anderson@colorado.edu,
University of Colorado – Gm
Anderson, Thomas B., anderset@sonoma.edu,
Sonoma State University – GsrGd

Anderson, Wayne I., (319) 273-3125 wayne.anderson@uni.edu,
University of Northern Iowa – Pg
Anderson, William P., andersonwp@appstate.edu,
Appalachian State University – Hw
Anderson, William T., (305) 348-2693 andersow@fiu.edu,
Florida International University – Cs
Anderson, Jr., Alfred T., (773) 702-8138 University of Chicago – Gv
Anderson, NAE, Mary P., (608) 262-2396 andy@geology.wisc.edu,
University of Wisconsin, Madison – Hw
Anderson-Folnagy, Heidi, (406) 683-7134 heidi.anderson@umwestern.edu,
University of Montana Western – Gs
Andeweg, Bernd , 31 20 5987339 bernd.andeweg@vu.nl,
VU University Amsterdam – GtcGg
Andre-Obayanju, Tomilola, tomilola.obayanju@uniben.edu,
University of Benin – NgHgGe
Andreasen, David, 410-260-8814 david.andreasen@maryland.gov,
Maryland Department of Natural Resources – Hw
Andren, Anders W., (608) 262-2470 University of Wisconsin, Madison – Oc
Andres, A. S., 302-831-2833 asandres@udel.edu, University of Delaware – Hy
Andrews, Benjamin, (202) 633-1818 andrewsb@si.edu,
Smithsonian Institution / National Museum of Natural History – Gv
Andrews, Graham D., 661-654-3281 gdma1977@gmail.com,
California State University, Bakersfield – GtvGx
Andrews, John R., 512-471-1534 john.andrews@beg.utexas.edu,
University of Texas at Austin, Jackson School of Geosciences – Oi
Andrews, John T., 303-492-5183 john.t.andrews@colorado.edu,
University of Colorado – Gl
Andrews, Julian, +44 (0)1603 59 2536 j.andrews@uea.ac.uk,
University of East Anglia – Cs
Andrews, Richard D., 405-325-3991 rdandrews@ou.edu,
University of Oklahoma – Go
Andronicos, Chris, (765) 494-5982 candroni@purdue.edu,
Purdue University – Gg
Andrus, C. Fred T., 205-348-5177 fandrus@geo.ua.edu,
University of Alabama – PeGaCs
Andrus, Richard E., (607) 777-2453 Binghamton University – Py
Aneja, Viney P., 91951557808 viney_aneja@ncsu.edu,
North Carolina State University – Oa
Anfinson, Owen, anfinson@sonoma.edu, Sonoma State University – GsdGg
Angel, Ross J., (540) 231-7974 rangel@vt.edu,
Virginia Polytechnic Institute & State University – Gz
Angelo, Joseph A., (407) 768-8000 Florida Institute of Technology – Og
Angelopoulos, Vassilis, (310) 794-7090 vassilis@ucla.edu,
University of California, Los Angeles – XyOa
Anger-Kraavi, Annela, +44 (0)1603 59 2633 a.anger-kraavi@uea.ac.uk,
University of East Anglia – Eg
Angino, Ernest E., (785) 843-7503 University of Kansas – Cl
Angle, Michael , 614 265 6602 mike.angle@dnr.state.oh.us,
Ohio Dept of Natural Resources – GlgHw
Anglen, Brandy, (559) 442-4600 brandy.anglen@fresnocitycollege.edu,
Fresno City College – Gg
Anglès Vila, Marc, ++34935811085 marc.angles@uab.cat,
Universitat Autonoma de Barcelona – Gr
Angus, Doug, +4401133431326 d.angus@leeds.ac.uk,
University of Leeds – Ys
Anhaeusser, Carl R., 011-7176581 Carl.anhaeusser@wits.ac.za,
University of the Witwatersrand – GgEgOg
Anis, Ayal, (409) 740-4987 anisa@tamug.tamu.edu,
Texas A&M University – Op
Ansdell, Kevin M., (306) 966-5698 kevin.ansdell@usask.ca,
University of Saskatchewan – EgCgGt
Antar, Ali A., (860) 832-2931 antar@ccsu.edu,
Central Connecticut State University – On
Anthony, Elizabeth Y., (915) 747-5483 eanthony@geo.utep.edu,
University of Texas, El Paso – Gi
Anthony, Leona M., (808) 956-8763 leonaa@hawaii.edu,
University of Hawai'i, Manoa – On
Anthony, Nina, 864-294-2052 nina.anthony@furman.edu,
Furman University – On
Anthony, Robin, 412-442-4295 robanthony@pa.gov,
Pennsylvania Bureau of Topographic & Geologic Survey – Go
Anthony-Zajanc, Kate, anthcath@isu.edu, Idaho State University – Oi
Antinao, JoseLuis, 775-673-7450 JoseLuis.antinao@dri.edu,
Desert Research Institute – Gm
Antonacci, Vince, (615) 532-1507 Vince.Antonacci@tn.gov,
Tennessee Geological Survey – GgOi
Antonellini, Marco, marcoa@pangea.stanford.edu, Stanford University – Yr
Antonescu, Adrian, +44 0161 306-3911 bogdan.antonescu@manchester.ac.uk,
University of Manchester – Oa
Aplin, Andrew, +44 191 33 42332 Durham University – Go
Apopei, Andrei I., +40232201463 andrei.apopei@uaic.ro,
Al. I. Cuza University of Iasi – GziGg
Apotsos, Alex, 413-597-5082 alex.apotsos@williams.edu,
Williams College – Ge
Appel, Christopher (Chip) S., (805) 756-1691 cappel@calpoly.edu,
California Polytechnic State University – Sc
Appiah-Adjei, Emmanuel K., +233 20 7934 556 ekappiah-adjei.soe@knust.edu.gh,
Kwame Nkrumah University of Science and Technology – HwgGg
Applegarth, Michael T., (717) 477-1712 mtappl@ship.edu,
Shippensburg University – Or

Lyndon State College – Oa

Atkinson, Christopher, christopher.atkinson@und.edu,
University of North Dakota – Oai

Atkinson, Gail M., 519-661-2111 x.84207 gatkins6@uwo.ca,
Western University – YssYs

Atkinson, Gail M., gma@ccs.carleton.ca, Carleton University – Ne

Atkinson, Larry P., (757) 683-4926 atkinson@ccpo.odu.edu,
Old Dominion University – Op

Atkinson, Marlin J., 235-2224 mja@hawaii.edu,
University of Hawai'i, Manoa – Ob

Atkinson, Tim, +44 020 7679 37711 t.atkinson@ucl.ac.uk,
University College London – Hg

Atkinson, Jr., William W., 303-492-6103 william.atkinson@colorado.edu,
University of Colorado – Em

Atreya, Sushil, (734) 936-0489 atreya@umich.edu,
University of Michigan – Oa

Attig, John W., (608) 262-6131 jwattig@wisc.edu,
University of Wisconsin, Extension – Gl

Attinger, Sabine, 0049(0)3641/948651 sabine.attinger@ufz.de,
Friedrich-Schiller-University Jena – Hy

Attrep, Moses, (505) 667-0088 Los Alamos National Laboratory – Oe

Atudorei, Nieu-Viorel, atudorei@unm.edu,
University of New Mexico – Cs

Atwater, Brian, 206-553-2927 atwater@ess.washington.edu,
University of Washington – Ys

Au, Whitlow W L., 808-247-5026 wau@hawaii.edu,
University of Hawai'i, Manoa – On

Aubert, John E., (916) 484-8637 aubertj@arc.losrios.edu,
American River College – Oy

Audet, Celine, (418) 723-1986 (Ext. 1744) celine_audet@uqar.qc.ca,
Universite du Quebec a Rimouski – Ob

Audet, Pascal, (613)562-5800 2344 pascal.audet@uottawa.ca,
University of Ottawa – YgGc

Aufrecht, Walter E., (403) 329-2485 aufrecht@uleth.ca,
University of Lethbridge – On

Aughenbaugh, Nolan B., (662) 915-5819 naughenb@olemiss.edu,
University of Mississippi – Nr

Ault, Alexis K., aault@email.arizona.edu, Utah State University – GtCc

Ault, Toby R., 607-255-1509 tra38@cornell.edu,
Cornell University – Ow

Aurnou, Jonathan M., (310) 825-2054 aurnou@epss.ucla.edu,
University of California, Los Angeles – XyYmg

Ausbrooks, Scott, 501 683-0119 scott.ausbrooks@arkansas.gov,
Arkansas Geological Survey – YsGeg

Ausich, William I., (614) 292-3353 ausich.1@osu.edu,
Ohio State University – Po

Auster, Peter, 860-405-9118 peter.auster@uconn.edu,
University of Connecticut – Ob

Austin, George S., (505) 835-5230 george@gis.nmt.edu,
New Mexico Institute of Mining & Technology – En

Austin, Philip, (604) 822-2175 paustin@eos.ubc.ca,
University of British Columbia – Oa

Austin, Jr., James A., (512) 471-0450 jamie@ig.utexas.edu,
University of Texas at Austin – Gu

Austin, Jr., James A., jamie@utig.ig.utexas.edu, University of Texas at Austin – Pi

Autin, Whitney J., 585-395-5738 dirtguy@esc.brockport.edu,
SUNY, The College at Brockport – Gs

Avary, Katherine L., 304 594 2331 avary@geosrv.wvnet.edu,
West Virginia University – Go

Ave Lallemant, Hans G., (713) 348-4889 ave@rice.edu,
Rice University – Gc

Avouac, Jean-Philippe, 626.395.2350 avouac@gps.caltech.edu,
California Institute of Technology – GtYs

Awramik, Stanley M., (805) 893-3830 Awramik@geol.ucsb.edu,
University of California, Santa Barbara – Po

Axelbaum, Richard, rla@me.wustl.edu, Washington University – Ng

Axen, Gary, 575.835.5178 gaxen@ees.nmt.edu,
New Mexico Institute of Mining and Technology – Gct

Axford, Yarrow, 847.467.2268 yarrow@earth.northwestern.edu,
Northwestern University – GnPmi

Ayad, Yasser M., yayad@clarion.edu, Clarion University – Oi

Aydin, Adnan, (662) 915-1342 aaydin@olemiss.edu,
University of Mississippi – Ng

Aydin, Atilla, (650) 725-8708 aydin@pangea.stanford.edu,
Stanford University – Gc

Ayers, John C., 615-322-2158 john.c.ayers@vanderbilt.edu,
Vanderbilt University – Cg

Ayers, Joseph , 7815817370 x309 lobster@neu.edu,
Northeastern University – On

Aylward, Linda, (309) 694-5256 Illinois Central College – Oe

Azam, Farooq, (858) 534-6850 fazam@ucsd.edu,
University of California, San Diego – Ob

Azetsu-Scott, Kumiko, (902) 426-8572 azetsu-scottk@mar.dfo-mpo.gc.ca,
Dalhousie University – Oc

B

Baadsgaard, Halfdan, budb@powersurfr.com, University of Alberta – Cc

Baarli, Gudveig, 413-597-2329 gudveig.baarli@williams.edu,
Williams College – Ps

Baars, Oliver, 609-258-2489 obaars@princeton.edu,

Princeton University – Co

Babaie, Hassan A., (404) 413-5766 hbabaie@gsu.edu,
Georgia State University – Gc

Babault, Julien, ++935812556 julien.babault@uab.cat,
Universitat Autonoma de Barcelona – OiGm

Babb, David M., (814) 863-3918 dbabb@essc.psu.edu,
Pennsylvania State University, University Park – Ow

Babcock, Daphne H., (972) 578-5518 dbabcock@collin.edu,
Collin College - Spring Creek Campus – Gg

Babcock, Loren E., (614) 292-0358 babcock.5@osu.edu,
Ohio State University – Po

Babcock, R. S., (360) 650-3592 babcock@wwu.edu,
Western Washington University – Cg

Babek, Ondrej, +420 549 49 3163 Masaryk University – Gds

Bacchus, Tania S., (802) 635-1329 Tania.Bacchus@jsc.edu,
Johnson State College – GuOw

Bach Plaza, Joan, ++935811272 joan.bach@uab.cat,
Universitat Autonoma de Barcelona – Gg

Bachhuber, Frederick W., bachhubf@nevada.edu,
University of Nevada, Las Vegas – Pl

Bachle, Peter, (573) 368-2472 peter.bachle@dnr.mo.gov,
Missouri Dept of Natural Resources – Gg

Bachmann, Olivier, baolivie@ethz.ch, University of Washington – Giv

Bachtadse, Valerian, 089/2180 4237 valerian@geophysik.uni-muenchen.de,
Ludwig-Maximilians-Universitaet Muenchen – Yg

Back, Larissa E., 608-262-0776 lback@wisc.edu,
University of Wisconsin, Madison – Oa

Backus, George E., (858) 534-2468 gebackus@ucsd.edu,
University of California, San Diego – Yg

Bacon, Diana H., (509) 372-6132 diana.bacon@pnl.gov,
Pacific Northwest National Laboratory – Hq

Bacon, Michael P., (508) 289-2559 mbacon@whoi.edu,
Woods Hole Oceanographic Institution – Oc

Bacon, Robert, (573) 526-0807 Missouri Dept of Natural Resources – Hs

Bacon, Steven N., 775-673-7473 Steve.Bacon@dri.edu,
Desert Research Institute – Gm

Bada, Jeffrey L., (858) 534-4258 jbada@ucsd.edu,
University of California, San Diego – Co

Bader, Nicholas, 509-527-5113 baderne@whitman.edu,
Whitman College – SpGeOi

Badger, Robert L., (315) 267-2624 badgerrl@potsdam.edu,
SUNY Potsdam – Gip

Badgley, Catherine E., (734) 763-6448 cbadgley@umich.edu,
University of Michigan – Pv

Badruddin, Abu Z., 315 2948610 ext.231 badruddin@cayuga-cc.edu,
Cayuga Community College – Oi

Badurek, Chris, (828) 262-7054 badurekca@appstate.edu,
Appalachian State University – Oi

Baedke, Steven J., (540) 568-6156 baedkesj@jmu.edu,
James Madison University – Hy

Baer, Eric M., 206-878-3710 ebaer@highline.edu,
Highline College – GgvOg

Baer, James L., james_baer@byu.edu, Brigham Young University – Go

Bagtzoglou, Ross, (212) 854-3154 Columbia University – Hw

Baharlou, Alan, 217-581-2626 abaharlou@eiu.edu,
Eastern Illinois University – Cg

Bahlburg, Heinrich, +49-251-83-33935 bahlbur@uni-muenster.de,
Universitaet Muenster – Gsg

Bahr, Jean M., (608) 262-5513 jmbahr@geology.wisc.edu,
University of Wisconsin, Madison – Hw

Bahrmann, Chad, 814-865-9500 cbahrmann@psu.edu,
Pennsylvania State University, University Park – Ow

Baigorria, Guillermo, gbaigorria@unl.edu,
University of Nebraska, Lincoln – Ow

Bailey, Christopher M., (757) 221-2445 cmbail@wm.edu,
College of William & Mary – Gc

Bailey, David G., (315) 859-4142 dbailey@hamilton.edu,
Hamilton College – GizGa

Bailey, Ian, +4401326 259322 I.Bailey@exeter.ac.uk,
Exeter University – Ol

Bailey, Jack B., (309) 298-1481 JB-Bailey@wiu.edu,
Western Illinois University – Pg

Bailey, Jake, 612-624-1603 baileyj@umn.edu,
University of Minnesota, Twin Cities – Py

Bailey, Judy, 61 02 4921 5415 Judy.Bailey@newcastle.edu.au,
University of Newcastle – Ec

Bailey, Keiron D., kbailey@email.arizona.edu, University of Arizona – Oi

Bailey, Lorraine, (401) 874-2265 lbailey@mail.uri.edu,
University of Rhode Island – On

Bailey, Richard C., (416) 978-3231 bailey@physics.utoronto.ca,
University of Toronto – Yg

Bailey, Richard H., (617) 373-3181 r.bailey@neu.edu,
Northeastern University – Pi

Bain, Daniel J., (412) 624-8780 dbain@pitt.edu,
University of Pittsburgh – Hg

Bain, Olivier, +33(0)3 44069304 olivier.bain@lasalle-beauvais.fr,
Institut Polytechnique LaSalle Beauvais (ex-IGAL) – OuGgOi

Bair, Edwin S., (614) 292-6197 bair.1@osu.edu,
Ohio State University – Hw

Baird, Gordon C., baird@fredonia.edu,

Barclay, Andrew, 206-543-8956 barclay@ldeo.columbia.edu,
   University of Washington – Gu
Barclay, David, (902) 494-4164 dbarclay@dal.ca,
   Dalhousie University – Op
Barclay, David J., (607) 753-2921 barclayd@cortland.edu,
   SUNY, Cortland – Gl
Barclay, Jenni, +44 (0)1603 59 3887 j.barclay@uea.ac.uk,
   University of East Anglia – Gv
Barclay, Julie L., barclayj@cortland.edu, SUNY, Cortland – Gg
Barendregt, Rene W., (403) 329-2530 barendregt@uleth.ca,
   University of Lethbridge – Gm
Barhurst, James, +44 (0) 191 208 5431 james.bathurst@ncl.ac.uk,
   University of Newcastle Upon Tyne – Gs
Barile, Diane, (321) 674-8096 dmes@fit.edu,
   Florida Institute of Technology – Ou
Barineau, Clinton I., 706 569-3026 barineau_clinton@columbusstate.edu,
   Columbus State University – GctGx
Barker, Andy J., +44 (0)23 80593641 A.J.Barker@soton.ac.uk,
   University of Southampton – Gg
Barker, Charles F., (313) 831-7279 cfbarker@earthlink.net,
   Wayne State University – Gg
Barker, Chris A., (936) 468-2340 cbarker@sfasu.edu,
   Stephen F. Austin State University – Gc
Barker, Colin, (918) 631-3014 colin-barker@utulsa.edu,
   University of Tulsa – Cg
Barker, Daniel, (512) 471-5502 danbarker@mail.utexas.edu,
   University of Texas at Austin – Gi
Barker, Gregory A., (603) 271-7332 gbarker@des.state.nh.us,
   New Hampshire Geological Survey – GgOin
Barker, James M., (505) 825-5114 jbark@nmt.edu,
   New Mexico Institute of Mining & Technology – En
Barker, Jeffrey S., (607) 777-2522 jbarker@binghamton.edu,
   Binghamton University – Ys
Barker, Joel D., (614) 292-0138 barker.246@osu.edu,
   Ohio State University – OlHg
Barker, Stephen, barkers3@cardiff.ac.uk, Cardiff University – Pe
Barkmann, Peter, 303-384-2642 barkmann@mines.edu,
   Colorado Geological Survey – HwGcg
Barlow, Jay P., (858) 546-7178 jbarlow@ucsd.edu,
   University of California, San Diego – Ob
Barlow, Mathew, (978) 934-3908 mathew_barlow@uml.edu,
   University of Massachusetts Lowell – Oa
Barminski, Robert, 831-770-7056 rbarminski@aol.com,
   Hartnell College – GgOg
Barmore, Garrett, 775-784-4528 gbarmore@unr.edu,
   University of Nevada, Reno – On
Barnbaum, Cecilia S., (229) 249-2645 cbarnbau@valdosta.edu,
   Valdosta State University – On
Barnes, Calvin G., 806-834-7389 cal.barnes@ttu.edu,
   Texas Tech University – Gi
Barnes, Charles W., chuck.barnes@nau.edu, Northern Arizona University – Gc
Barnes, Christopher R., (250) 721-8847 crbarnes@uvic.ca,
   University of Victoria – Pm
Barnes, David, (269) 387-8617 dave.barnes@wmich.edu,
   Western Michigan University – GsOnn
Barnes, Fairley J., (505) 667-4933 fyb@lanl.gov,
   Los Alamos National Laboratory – On
Barnes, Gary M., gbarnes@hawaii.edu, University of Hawai'i, Manoa – Ow
Barnes, Hubert L., (814) 865-7573 barnes@geosc.psu.edu,
   Pennsylvania State University, University Park – Cp
Barnes, Jaime D., jdbarnes@jsg.utexas.edu,
   University of Texas at Austin – CgsCc
Barnes, Jeffrey R., (541) 737-5685 barnes@coas.oregonstate.edu,
   Oregon State University – Oa
Barnes, John H., 717.702.2025 jbarnes@pa.gov,
   Pennsylvania Bureau of Topographic & Geologic Survey – Gg
Barnes, Lawrence G., (213) 763-3329 lbarnes@nhm.org,
   Los Angeles County Museum of Natural History – Pv
Barnes, Melanie A., 806-834-7965 melanie.barnes@ttu.edu,
   Texas Tech University – Cg
Barnes, Randal J., (612) 625-5828 University of Minnesota, Twin Cities – On
Barnes, Sarah- J., 418 545 5011 sjbarnes@uqac.ca,
   Universite du Quebec a Chicoutimi – EgGiCt
Barnett, Albert P., (919) 560-3324 North Carolina Central University – Or
Barnett, Douglas B., (509) 376-3416 brent.barnett@pnl.gov,
   Pacific Northwest National Laboratory – Em
Barnett, Michael, 617-552-8300 barnetge@bc.edu, Boston College – Oe
Barnett, Roger T., rbarnett@pacific.edu, University of the Pacific – Oy
Barnhardt, Michael L., (217) 244-2766 barnhart@isgs.uiuc.edu,
   Illinois State Geological Survey – Gm
Barnhart, William, (319) 384-4732 william-barnhart-1@uiowa.edu,
   University of Iowa – Gt
Barnosky, Anthony D., (510) 642-9487 University of California, Berkeley – Pv
Barnston, Anthony G., (845) 680-4447 tonyb@iri.columbia.edu,
   Columbia University – On
Baron, Dirk, (661) 654-3044 dbaron@csub.edu,
   California State University, Bakersfield – Cl
Barone, Jessica, 585-292-2448 jbarone@monroecc.edu,
   Monroe Community College – Ge
Baross, John A., (206) 543-0833 University of Washington – Ob

Barquero-Molina, Miriam, (573) 882-9557 barqueromolinam@missouri.edu,
   University of Missouri – Gt
Barr, Sandra M., (902) 585-1340 sandra.barr@acadiau.ca,
   Acadia University – Gi
Barr, Stuart, +44 (0) 191 208 6449 stuart.barr@ncl.ac.uk,
   University of Newcastle Upon Tyne – Oi
Barrash, Warren, (208) 426-1229 wb@cgiss.boisestate.edu,
   Boise State University – HwYx
Barrett, Bradford S., 410-293-6567 bbarrett@usna.edu,
   United States Naval Academy – Oa
Barrett, John, +44(0) 113 34 32394 j.r.barrett@leeds.ac.uk,
   University of Leeds – Ge
Barrett, Kevin M., (817) 515-6352 kevin.barrett@tccd.edu,
   Tarrant County College- Northeast Campus – OagOr
Barrett, Linda R., (330) 972-7620 barrett@uakron.edu,
   University of Akron – Sd
Barrick, James E., 806-834-2717 jim.barrick@ttu.edu,
   Texas Tech University – Ps
Barrie, Vaughn, (250) 363-6424 University of Victoria – Gu
Barrier, Pascal, +33(0)3 44068975 pascal.barrier@lasalle-beauvais.fr,
   Institut Polytechnique LaSalle Beauvais (ex-IGAL) – PmGsPs
Barron, George, gbarron@uoguelph.ca,
   University of Guelph – On
Barron, Robert, (906) 487-2096 rjbarron@mtu.edu,
   Michigan Technological University – Og
Barros, Tony, (305) 237-3754 tbarros@mdc.edu,
   Miami-Dade Community College (Wolfson Campus) – Og
Barry, Roger G., (303) 492-5488 University of Colorado – Oa
Barsch, Robert, 089/2180 4201 barsch@geophysik.uni-muenchen.de,
   Ludwig-Maximilians-Universitaet Muenchen – Yg
Bart, Henry A., (215) 951-1268 bart@lasalle.edu,
   La Salle University – Gs
Bart, Philip J., (225) 388-3109 pbart@geol.lsu.edu,
   Louisiana State University – Gr
Bartek, III, Louis R., (919) 962-0687 bartek@email.unc.edu,
   University of North Carolina, Chapel Hill – Gu
Bartello, Peter, (514) 398-8075 peter.bartello@mcgill.ca,
   McGill University – Oa
Bartels, William S., (517) 629-0313 wbartels@albion.edu,
   Albion College – Pv
Barth, Andrew P., (317) 274-1243 ibsz100@iupui.edu,
   Indiana University / Purdue University, Indianapolis – Gi
Barth, Jack A., (541) 737-1607 barth@coas.oregonstate.edu,
   Oregon State University – On
Barth, Nicolas, (951) 827-3138 nic.barth@ucr.edu,
   University of California, Riverside – Gt
Barth, Susan A., 406-496-4687 sbarth@mtech.edu,
   Montana Tech of The University of Montana – On
Bartholemew, Paul, Pbartholomew@newhaven.edu
   University of New Haven – GeOiGz
Bartholomew, Alexander J., 845-257-3765 barthola@newpaltz.edu,
   SUNY, New Paltz – GrPi
Bartholomew, Mervin J., (901) 678-1613 jbrthlm1@memphis.edu,
   University of Memphis – Gt
Bartholy, Judit, +36 20 3722945 bartholy@caesar.elte.hu,
   Eotvos Lorand University – Ow
Bartl, Simona, 831-771-4400 sbartl@mlml.calstate.edu,
   Moss Landing Marine Laboratories – On
Bartlein, Patrick J., (541) 346-4967 bartlein@uoregon.edu,
   University of Oregon – Pe
Bartlett, Douglas H., (858) 534-5233 dbartlett@ucsd.edu,
   University of California, San Diego – Ob
Bartlett, Wendy, 740-376-4775 bartletw@marietta.edu,
   Marietta College – Geo
Bartley, John M., (801) 58--7162 john.bartley@utah.edu,
   University of Utah – Oi
Bartley, Julie, 507-933-7307 jbartley@gustavus.edu,
   University of Tennessee, Knoxville – Gs
Bartok, Peter, peter@bartokinc.com,
   University of Houston – Go
Bartolucci, Valerio, (954) 201-6678 vbartolu@broward.edu,
   Broward College, Central Campus – Ge
Barton, Christopher, 937 775-3444 chris.barton@wright.edu,
   Wright State University – Gqc
Barton, Hazel, 330-972-7155 bartonh@uakron.edu,
   University of Akron – Py
Barton, James H., (412) 589-2821 Thiel College – Oy
Barton, Mark D., (520) 621-8529 mdbarton@email.arizona.edu,
   University of Arizona – Eg
Barton, Michael, (614) 292-3132 barton.2@osu.edu,
   Ohio State University – Gx
Barzegari, Ghodrat, Gbarzegari@gmail.com, University of Tabriz – Nr
Bascom, Johnathan, (616) 526-7053 jbascom@calvin.edu,
   Calvin College – Oy
Basham, William L., 432 552-2057 basham_w@utpb.edu,
   University of Texas, Permian Basin – Ye
Basinger, James F., (306) 966-5684 jim.basinger@usask.ca,
   University of Saskatchewan – Pb
Baskaran, Mark M., (313) 577-3262 Baskaran@wayne.edu,
   Wayne State University – CcGg

Faculty Index -B

411

Baskin, Perry A., (229) 259-5052 pbaskin@valdosta.edu,
Valdosta State University – On
Bass, David, david.bass@flinders.edu.au, Flinders University – Oy
Bass, Jay D., (217) 333-1018 jaybass@illinois.edu,
University of Illinois, Urbana-Champaign – Gy
Bass, Jerry, 601 266-4732 joby@usm.edu,
University of Southern Mississippi – On
Bass, Michael L., (540) 654-1424 mbass@umw.edu,
University of Mary Washington – On
Bassett, Damon, (417) 836-4897 dbassett@missouristate.edu,
Missouri State University – Pg
Bassett, Kari N., (03) 366-7001 ext 7732 kari.bassett@canterbury.ac.nz,
University of Canterbury – Gs
Bassett, Scott, (775) 784-1434 sbassett@unr.edu,
University of Nevada, Reno – Oa
Bassett, William A., wab7@cornell.edu, Cornell University – Gz
Basta, Nicholas T., 614-292-6282 basta.4@osu.edu,
Ohio State University – Sc
Bastow, Ian, +44 20 759 42974 i.bastow@imperial.ac.uk,
Imperial College – Yg
Basu, Abhijit, 8128556654/5581 basu@indiana.edu,
Indiana University, Bloomington – Gd
Basu, Asish, (817) 272-2987 abasu@uta.edu,
University of Texas, Arlington – GxCcs
Basu, Asish R., (585) 275-2413 abasu@earth.rochester.edu,
University of Rochester – Gx
Basu, Sukanta, (919) 513-7776 sbasu5@ncsu.edu,
North Carolina State University – Oa
Batchelder, Hal, (541) 737-4500 hbatch@pices.int,
Oregon State University – Op
Bateman, Ian, +44 (0)1603 59 3125 i.bateman@uea.ac.uk,
University of East Anglia – Ge
Bates, Amanda E., +44(0)23 8059 8046 A.E.Bates@soton.ac.uk,
University of Southampton – Ob
Bates, Mary, (661) 362-5054 Mary.Bates@canyons.edu,
College of the Canyons – Oyg
Bates, Nicholas R., N.R.Bates@soton.ac.uk, University of Southampton – Oc
Bates, Richard, +44 01334 463997 crb@st-andrews.ac.uk,
University of St. Andrews – Yx
Bates, Timothy S., 206-526-6248 Tim.Bates@noaa.gov,
University of Washington – On
Bathke, Deborah J., 402-472-6199 dbathke2@unl.edu,
University of Nebraska, Lincoln – Oa
Bathke, Deborah J., dbathke2@unl.edu, University of Nebraska, Lincoln – Oa
Batlle-Aguilar, Jordi, 785-864-2113 jba@kgs.ku.edu,
University of Kansas – Hy
Batten, William G., (608) 262-9903 wgbatten@wisc.edu,
University of Wisconsin, Extension – GghHw
Battisti, David S., (206) 543-2019 battisti@uw.edu,
University of Washington – Oa
Battles, Eileen, (785) 864-2129 battles@kgs.ku.edu,
University of Kansas – Oy
Batygin, Konstantin, 626-395-2920 kbatygin@gps.caltech.edu,
California Institute of Technology – Xg
Batzle, Michael L., (303) 384-2067 mbatzle@mines.edu,
Colorado School of Mines – Yg
Bauder, James W., (406) 994-5685 jbauder@montana.edu,
Montana State University – Sf
Bauer, Carl J., cjbauer@email.arizona.edu,
University of Arizona – Hs
Bauer, Emily, (612) 626-0909 bauer010@umn.edu,
University of Minnesota – Oi
Bauer, Jeffrey A., (740) 351-3421 jbauer@shawnee.edu,
Shawnee State University – Ps
Bauer, Paul W., (505) 835-5106 bauer@nmbg.nmt.edu,
New Mexico Institute of Mining & Technology – Gp
Bauer, R. A., 217-244-2394 rabauer@illinois.edu,
University of Illinois, Urbana-Champaign – Ng
Bauer, Robert L., (573) 882-3759 BauerR@missouri.edu,
University of Missouri – Gc
Baum, Steven K., (979) 845-0793 sbaum@ocean.tamu.edu,
Texas A&M University – Op
Baumann, Hannes, 860-405-9297 hannes.baumann@uconn.edu,
University of Connecticut – Ob
Baumann, Zofia, 860-405-9281 zofia.baumann@uconn.edu,
University of Connecticut – Oc
Baumgartner, Mark, mbaumgartner@whoi.edu, Dalhousie University – Ob
Baumiller, Tomasz K., (734) 764-7543 tomaszb@umich.edu,
University of Michigan – Pg
Baxter, Martin, 989-774-2055 baxte1ma@cmich.edu,
Central Michigan University – Ow
Baxter, Stefanie J., 302-831-1576 steff@udel.edu,
University of Delaware – On
Baxter, P.G., James E., 717-780-2377 jebaxter@hacc.edu,
Harrisburg Area Community College – GgHwGm
Bayari, Serdar, +90 (312) 2977740 serdar@hacettepe.edu.tr,
Hacettepe University – Hw
Bayliss, Peter, (403) 220-5026 University of Calgary – Gz
Bayly, M. Brian, baylym@rpi.edu, Rensselaer Polytechnic Institute – Gc
Bayowa, Oyelowo G., +2348030820291 obayowa@lautech.edu.ng,

Ladoke Akintola University of Technology – GggGg
Beach Davis, Janet, (309) 268-8513 janet.beach-davis@heartland.edu,
Heartland Community College – Og
Beane, Rachel J., (207) 725-3160 rbeane@bowdoin.edu,
Bowdoin College – Gp
Beard, Brian L., 608-262-1806 beardb@geology.wisc.edu,
University of Wisconsin, Madison – Cc
Beard, James S., (540) 666-8611 jim.beard@vmnh.virginia.gov,
Virginia Polytechnic Institute & State University – Gi
Beard, K. Christopher, (412) 622-5782 beardc@CarnegieMNH.org,
Carnegie Museum of Natural History – Pv
Beard, Kenneth V., (217) 333-1676 k-beard@uiuc.edu,
University of Illinois, Urbana-Champaign – Oa
Bearden, Rebecca A., 205-247-3623 rbearden@gsa.state.al.us,
Geological Survey of Alabama – Hs
Beasley-Stanley, Jewell D., 615-322-2976 jewell.beasleystanley@vanderbilt.edu,
Vanderbilt University – On
Beatty, Heather L., heather.beatty@austincc.edu,
Austin Community College District – Ge
Beatty, Lynne, 9134698500 x3785 lbeatty@jccc.edu,
Johnson County Community College – GgOy
Beatty, Merrill Ann, (506) 453-4803 mbeatty@unb.ca,
University of New Brunswick – On
Beatty, Susan W., (303) 492-8310 susan.beatty@colorado.edu,
University of Colorado – So
Beatty, William L., 507-474-5789 wbeatty@winona.edu,
Winona State University – Pg
Beaty, Tammy, (865) 574-0119 taw@ornl.gov,
Oak Ridge National Laboratory – Oi
Beaudoin, Georges, (418) 656-3141 beaudoin@ggl.ulaval.ca,
Universite Laval – Em
Beaulieu, Claudie, +44 (0)23 8059 6412 C.Beaulieu@soton.ac.uk,
University of Southampton – Op
Beaumont, Christopher, (902) 494-3779 chris.beaumont@dal.ca,
Dalhousie University – Yg
Beausoleil, Denis, 604-777-6117 beausoleild@douglascollege.ca,
Douglas College – Og
Beaver, Harold H., (254) 710-2184 harold_beaver@baylor.edu,
Baylor University – Go
Bebout, Gray E., (610) 758-5831 geb0@lehigh.edu,
Lehigh University – Gp
Bechtel, Randy, 919-707-9204 randy.bechtel@ncdenr.gov ,
North Carolina Geological Survey – Oe
Bechtel, Timothy D., 717 291-4133 timothy.bechtel@fandm.edu,
Franklin and Marshall College – GeYg
Beck, Catherine C., 315-859-4847 ccbeck@hamilton.edu,
Hamilton College – GsnGr
Beck, Charles, (734) 763-5089 chbeck@umich.edu,
University of Michigan – Pg
Beck, Colleen M., (702) 795-8077 colleen@dri.edu,
Desert Research Institute – Sa
Beck, Dwayne L., (605) 224-6357 Dwayne.Beck@sdstate.edu,
South Dakota State University – Ou
Beck, E. G., 270.827.3414 x23 ebeck@uky.edu,
University of Kentucky – Hw
Beck, John H., 617-552-8300 john.beck@bc.edu,
Boston College – Pb
Beck, Susan L., (520) 621-8628 slbeck@email.arizona.edu,
University of Arizona – Ys
Becker, Alex, (510) 643-9181 University of California, Berkeley – Yg
Becker, Janet M., (808) 956-6514 jbecker@soest.hawaii.edu,
University of Hawai'i, Manoa – Oo
Becker, Keir, 305 421-4661 kbecker@rsmas.miami.edu,
University of Miami – Yr
Becker, Laurence, (541) 737-9504 beckerla@geo.oregonstate.edu,
Oregon State University – On
Becker, Lorene Y., 541-737-6993 beckelo@geo.oregonstate.edu,
Oregon State University – Oi
Becker, Matthew, 562-985-8983 mbecker3@csulb.edu,
California State University, Long Beach – Hwg
Becker, Naomi M., (505) 667-2165 nmb@lanl.gov,
Los Alamos National Laboratory – Hg
Becker, Ralf Thomas, +49-251-83-33951 rbecker@uni-muenster.de,
Universitaet Muenster – Pg
Becker, Richard H., (630) 252-7595 Argonne National Laboratory – Or
Becker, Richard H., 419-530-4571 richard.becker@utoledo.edu,
University of Toledo – On
Becker, Thorsten W., 213-740-8365 twb@usc.edu,
University of Southern California – Ys
Becker, Udo, (734) 615-6894 ubecker@umich.edu,
University of Michigan – On
Beckie, Roger D., (604) 822-6462 rbeckie@eos.ubc.ca,
University of British Columbia – Hg
Beckingham, Barbara, (843) 953-0483 beckinghamba@cofc.edu,
College of Charleston – Cl
Bedard, Jean H., (418) 654-2671 jbedard@nrcan.gc.ca,
Universite du Quebec – Gi
Bedard, Paul, 4185455011, 2276 pbedard@uqac.ca,
Universite du Quebec a Chicoutimi – CaGzEg
Bedaso, Zelalem, 937-229-2393 zbedaso1@udayton.edu,

University of Dayton – Csl

Beddows, Patricia A., 847-491-7460 patricia@earth.northwestern.edu,
Northwestern University – HyGma

Bedient, Philip B., (713) 348-4953 bedient@rice.edu,
Rice University – Hw

Bednarski, Marsha, (860) 832-2943 bednarskim@ccsu.edu,
Central Connecticut State University – Oe

Bednarz, Robert S., (979) 845-7187 r-bednarz@tamu.edu,
Texas A&M University – Oe

Bednarz, Sarah W., (979) 845-1579 s-bednarz@tamu.edu,
Texas A&M University – Oe

Beebe, Alex, dbeebe@southalabama.edu, University of South Alabama – Ge

Beegle, Douglas B., (814) 863-1016 dbb@psu.edu,
Pennsylvania State University, University Park – Sc

Beeton, Jared M., (719) 587-7357 jmbeeton@adams.edu,
Adams State University – OySd

Befus, Kenneth S., Kenneth_Befus@baylor.edu, Baylor University – GviGv

Beg, Mirza A., 205-247-3624 mbeg@gsa.state.al.us,
Geological Survey of Alabama – Gz

Beget, James E., ffjeb1@uaf.edu, University of Alaska Fairbanks – Gm

Beghein, Caroline, (310) 825-0742 cbeghein@ucla.edu,
University of California, Los Angeles – Ysg

Begin, Christian, (418) 654-2675 cbegin@nrcan.gc.ca,
Universite du Quebec – Pe

Behl, Richard J., (562) 985-5850 behl@csulb.edu,
California State University, Long Beach – Gs

Behling, Robert E., (304) 293-5603 rbehling@wvu.edu,
West Virginia University – Gm

Behlke, Adam, 303-370-8328 Adam.Behlke@dmns.org,
Denver Museum of Nature & Science – Pg

Behn, Mark D., 508-289-3637 mbehn@whoi.edu,
Woods Hole Oceanographic Institution – Yr

Behr, Rose-Anna, 717-702-2035 rosbehr@pa.gov,
Pennsylvania Bureau of Topographic & Geologic Survey – GcEc

Behr, Whitney, 512-232-1941 behr@utexas.edu,
University of Texas at Austin – Gc

Behr-Andres, Christina "Tina", (505) 667-3644 behr-andres@lanl.gov,
Los Alamos National Laboratory – On

Behrensmeyer, Anna K., (202) 633-1307 Smithsonian Institution / National
Museum of Natural History – Pv

Beiersdorfer, Raymond E., (330) 941-1753 rebeiersdorfer@ysu.edu,
Youngstown State University – Cg

Bein, F. L., (317) 274-1100 Indiana University, Indianapolis – Oy

Bekken, Barbara M., (540) 231-4466 bekken@vt.edu,
Virginia Polytechnic Institute & State University – Eg

Bekker, Andrey, (951) 827-4611 andrey.bekker@ucr.edu,
University of California, Riverside – GsrCg

Bekker, Matthew F., (801) 422-1961 matthew_bekker@byu.edu,
Brigham Young University – Oy

Belanger, Christina L., (605) 394-2461 Christina.Belanger@sdsmt.edu,
South Dakota School of Mines & Technology – PimPe

Belanger, Thomas V., 321-674-7463 belanger@fit.edu,
Florida Institute of Technology – Hw

Belasky, Paul, 510-979-7938 pbelasky@ohlone.edu,
Ohlone College – PqiGs

Belknap, Daniel F., (207) 581-2159 belknap@maine.edu,
University of Maine – Gu

Bell, Andrew, +44 (0) 131 650 4918 a.bell@ed.ac.uk,
Edinburgh University – Gt

Bell, Brian, +44 01413306898 Brian.Bell@glasgow.ac.uk,
University of Glasgow – So

Bell, Christopher J., (512) 471-7301 cjbell@mail.utexas.edu,
University of Texas at Austin – Pv

Bell, David, (03) 3642-717 david.bell@canterbury.ac.nz,
University of Canterbury – Ng

Bell, James C., (612) 625-6703 jbell@soils.umn.edu,
University of Minnesota, Twin Cities – Sd

Bell, John W., (775) 784-1939 jbell@unr.edu,
University of Nevada – Ng

Bell, Keith, keith_bell@carleton.ca, Carleton University – Cc

Bell, Margaret C., +44 (0) 191 208 7936 margaret.bell@ncl.ac.uk,
University of Newcastle Upon Tyne – Ge

Bell, Michael, mmbell@hawaii.edu, University of Hawai'i, Manoa – Owr

Bell, Rebecca, +44 20 759 40903 rebecca.bell@imperial.ac.uk,
Imperial College – Gt

Bell, Robin E., 845-365-8827 Columbia University – Yr

Bellew, Angela, (319) 335-1819 angela-bellew@uiowa.edu,
University of Iowa – On

Bellieni, Giuliano, +390498279155 giuliano.bellieni@unipd.it,
Università degli Studi di Padova – Gv

Belliveau, Lindsey, 860-424-3581 lindsey.belliveau@ct.gov,
Dept of Energy and Environmental Protection – Gm

Belluso, Elena, elena.belluso@unito.it,
Università di Torino – Gz

Belmonte, Donato, +39 010 353 8136 Universita di Genova – Cg

Belt, Edward S., (413) 542-2712 esbelt@amherst.edu,
Amherst College – Gs

Beltrami, Hugo, 902-867-2326 hbeltram@stfx.ca,
Saint Francis Xavier University – YhOa

Beltz, John F., (330) 972-6687 jfb4@uakron.edu,

University of Akron – Ggh

Bemis, Sean, sean.bemis@uky.edu, University of Kentucky – GctYs

Ben-Zion, Yehuda, (213) 740-6734 ybz@earth.usc.edu,
University of Southern California – Ys

Benacquista, Matt, (406) 657-2341 Montana State University, Billings – Xy

Benavides-Iglesias, Alfonso, a.benavides@geos.tamu.edu,
Texas A&M University – Ys

Bend, Stephen L., (306) 585-4021 University of Regina – Gox

Bender, E. E., (714) 432-5681 ebender@occ.cccd.edu,
Orange Coast College – Giz

Bender, John F., 704-687- 5956 jfbender@email.uncc.edu,
University of North Carolina, Charlotte – GiCtOu

Bender, Michael L., (609) 258-5807 bender@princeton.edu,
Princeton University – Cg

Bendick, Rebecca, 406-243-5774 bendick@mso.umt.edu,
University of Montana – Yg

Benedetti, Michael M., (910) 962-7650 benedettim@uncw.edu,
University of North Carolina Wilmington – Gm

Benfield, Mark C., (225) 388-6372 mbenfie@lsu.edu,
Louisiana State University – Ob

Benger, Simon, simon.benger@flinders.edu.au, Flinders University – Oiy

Bengeyfield, Peter, 406-683-5538 apbengey@msn.com,
University of Montana Western – Hg

Benham, Steven R., (253) 535-7378 benhamsr@plu.edu,
Pacific Lutheran University – Gd

Benimoff, Alan I., 718-982-2835 alan.benimoff@csi.cuny.edu,
College of Staten Island – GizGp

Benison, Kathleen , 304-293-5603 West Virginia University – GrsCm

Benitez-Nelson, Claudia, 777-0018 cbnelson@geol.sc.edu,
University of South Carolina – Oc

Benjamin, Patricia A., 508-929-8606 pbenjamin@worcester.edu,
Worcester State University – Yr

Benjamin, Timothy M., (505) 667-5154 Los Alamos National Laboratory – Ca

Benjamin, U. K., 234-8038312732 uzochukwu.benjamin@oauife.edu.ng,
Obafemi Awolowo University – GoCg

Benna, Piera, piera.benna@unito.it, Università di Torino – Gz

Benner, Jacob, 617-627-2207 jacob.benner@tufts.edu,
Tufts University – Pge

Benner, Ronald, (803) 777-9561 benner@mailbox.sc.edu,
University of South Carolina – ObCo

Benner, Shawn, shawnbenner@gmail.com,
Boise State University – Clt

Bennet, Brett, 785-864-2117 bb@kgs.ku.edu,
University of Kansas – Ng

Bennett, Philip, (512) 471-3587 pbennett@mail.utexas.edu,
University of Texas at Austin – Hg

Bennett, Richard, 520-621-2324 rab@geo.arizona.edu,
University of Arizona – Yd

Bennett, Sara, 309/298-1905 SC-Bennett@wiu.edu,
Western Illinois University – Gg

Bennett, Steven W., (309) 298-1256 Sc-Bennett@wiu.edu,
Western Illinois University – Hw

Bennett, Victoria J., (817) 257-6603 v.bennett@tcu.edu,
Texas Christian University – On

Benning, Liane G., +44(0) 113 34 35220 l.g.benning@leeds.ac.uk,
University of Leeds – Ce

Benninger, Larry K., (919) 962-0699 lbenning@email.unc.edu,
University of North Carolina, Chapel Hill – Cl

Bennington, J Bret, 516 463-5568 geojbb@hofstra.edu,
Hofstra University – PeGs

Benoit-Bird, Kelly, 541-737-2063 kbenoit@coas.oregonstate.edu,
Oregon State University – Gu

Benotti, Mark J., 781.891.2980 mbenotti@bentley.edu,
Bentley University – OgGgOg

Bense, Victor, +44 (0)1603 59 1297 v.bense@uea.ac.uk,
University of East Anglia – Hg

Benson, David A., 303-273-3806 dbenson@mines.edu,
Colorado School of Mines – Hq

Benson, Donna M., (480) 461-7247 donnabenson@mesacc.edu,
Mesa Community College – Gg

Benson, Jane L., (270) 809-3106 jane.benson@murraystate.edu,
Murray State University – Oi

Benson, Robert D., (303) 273-3455 Colorado School of Mines – Ye

Benson, Robert G., (719) 587-7921 rgbenson@adams.edu,
Adams State University – Gg

Benson, Roger, +44 (1865) 272000 roger.benson@earth.ox.ac.uk,
University of Oxford – Po

Bentley, Callan, (703) 323-3276 cbentley@nvcc.edu,
Northern Virginia Community College - Annandale – Gg

Bentley, Charles R., (608) 238-8873 bentley@geology.wisc.edu,
University of Wisconsin, Madison – Yg

Bentley, Laurence R., (403) 220-4512 University of Calgary – Hw

Bentley, Samuel J., 225-578-5735 sjb@lsu.edu,
Louisiana State University – Gu

Benton, Steven, 217-244-0082 s-benton@illinois.edu,
University of Illinois, Urbana-Champaign – Gg

Benway, Heather, (508) 289-2838 hbenway@whoi.edu,
Woods Hole Oceanographic Institution – Oc

Benz, Harley M., benz@gldfs.cr.usgs.gov, University of Utah – Ys

Berchem, Jean, (310) 206-6484 jberchem@igpp.ucla.edu,

Boicourt, William, (410) 221-8426 boicourt@hpl.umces.edu,
    University of Maryland – Op
Boisvert, Eric, (418) 654-3705 eboisvert@nrcan.gc.ca,
    Universite du Quebec – On
Boitt, Mark , mboitt@jkuat.ac.ke ,
    Jomo Kenyatta University of Agriculture & Technology – OgrOi
Bokuniewicz, Henry J., (631) 632-8674 henry.bokuniewicz@stonybrook.edu,
    SUNY, Stony Brook – Yr
Boland, Greg J., (519) 824-4120 Ext.52755 gboland@uoguelph.ca,
    University of Guelph – On
Boland, Irene B., 803-323-4949 bolandi@winthrop.edu,
    Winthrop University – GtgOe
Boland, John J., (410) 516-7103 jboland@jhu.edu,
    Johns Hopkins University – On
Bolarinwa, A. T., at.bolarinwa@mail.ui.edu.ng, University of Ibadan – EgGz
Bollag, Jean-Marc, (814) 863-0843 jmbollag@psu.edu,
    Pennsylvania State University, University Park – Sb
Bollasina, Massimo, +44 (0) 131 650 4915 mbollasi@staffmail.ed.ac.uk,
    Edinburgh University – Oa
Bollens, Stephen, 509-335-3009 sbollens@vancouver.wsu.edu,
    Washington State University – Ob
Bollinger, G. A., (540) 231-6521 Virginia Polytechnic Institute & State University – Ys
Bollinger, Marsha S., 803-323-4944 bollingerm@winthrop.edu,
    Winthrop University – CmOgCc
Bollmann, Jörg, (416) 978-2061 bollmann@geology.utoronto.ca,
    University of Toronto – Pm
Bolmer, S. Thompson, (508) 289-2628 tbolmer@whoi.edu,
    Woods Hole Oceanographic Institution – Yr
Bolster, Diogo, Diogo.Bolster.5@nd.edu, University of Notre Dame – Hw
Bolt, John R., (312) 665-7629 jbolt@fieldmuseum.org,
    Field Museum of Natural History – Pv
Bolton, David, 410-554-5561 david.bolton@maryland.gov,
    Maryland Department of Natural Resources – Hgw
Bolton, Edward W., (203) 432-3149 edward.bolton@yale.edu,
    Yale University – Gq
Bolton Valencius, Conevery, conevery.valencius@umb.edu,
    University of Massachusetts, Boston – Gh
Bolze, Claude E., 918-595-7246 claude.bolze@tulsacc.edu,
    Tulsa Community College – GgoPg
Bomke, Arthur A., (604) 822-6534 University of British Columbia – Sc
Bona, Andrej, +61 8 9266 7194 A.Bona@curtin.edu.au,
    Curtin University – Yx
Bonatti, Enrico, 845-365-8699 Columbia University – Yr
Bonczek, James, 352-294-3112 bonczek@ufl.edu,
    University of Florida – OsHsg
Bond, Alan, +44 (0)1603 59 3402 alan.bond@uea.ac.uk,
    University of East Anglia – Ge
Bond, Nicholas A., Nicholas.Bond@noaa.gov,
    University of Washington – Oa
Bondesan, Aldino, 39-335-5473369 aldino.bondesan@gmail.com,
    Università degli Studi di Padova – GmlOi
Bone, Fletcher, 573-368-2183 fletcher.bone@dnr.mo.gov,
    Missouri Dept of Natural Resources – Gg
Bonem, Rena M., (254) 710-2187 rena_bonem@baylor.edu,
    Baylor University – Pei
Bonetto, Sabrina Maria Rita, sabrina.bonetto@unito.it,
    Università di Torino – Ng
Bonhoure, Jessica, +33(0)3 44068994 jessica.bonhoure@lasalle-beauvais.fr,
    Institut Polytechnique LaSalle Beauvais (ex-IGAL) – GziCc
Boniface, Nelson, +255222410013 nelson.boniface@udsm.ac.tz,
    University of Dar es Salaam – GcpCa
Bonine, Michael E., kebonine@u.arizona.edu, University of Arizona – Ou
Bonini, William E., (609) 258-3598 mrusso@princeton.edu,
    Princeton University – Yg
Bonk, Kathleen, 518-473-9988 kbonk@mail.nysed.gov,
    New York State Geological Survey – GoCg
Bonneau, Laurent, (203) 432-3142 laurent.bonneau@yale.edu,
    Yale University – Oa
Bonuso, Nicole, 657 278-8451 nbonuso@fullerton.edu,
    California State University, Fullerton – Pie
Booher, Gary, (310) 660-3593 gbooher@elcamino.edu,
    El Camino College – Og
Booker, John R., 206-543-1190 booker@ess.washington.edu,
    University of Washington – YmGt
Bookhagen, Bodo, (805) 893-3568 bodo@geog.ucsb.edu,
    University of California, Santa Barbara – Gm
Boone, Peter A., pboone@austincc.edu, Austin Community College District – Gro
Boorstein, Margaret F., (516) 299-2318 maboorst@liu.edu,
    Long Island University, C.W. Post Campus – Og
Booth, Adam, +44 20 759 46528 a.booth@imperial.ac.uk,
    Imperial College – Ol
Booth, Adam M., 503-725-3320 boothad@pdx.edu,
    Portland State University – GmOr
Booth, Alastair, murray.booth@manchester.ac.uk, University of Manchester – Oa
Booth, Colin J., (815) 753-1943 cjbooth@niu.edu,
    Northern Illinois University – Hw
Booth, Robert K., rkb205@lehigh.edu, Lehigh University – On
Boothroyd, Jon C., (401) 874-2265 jon_boothroyd@uri.edu,
    University of Rhode Island – GslOn
Bopp, Richard F., (518) 276-3075 boppr@rpi.edu,

Rensselaer Polytechnic Institute – Co
Borah, Deva K., (217) 244-8856 Illinois State Water Survey – Hq
Bord, Don, (313) 593-5483 dbord@umich.edu,
    University of Michigan, Dearborn – Xy
Bordeaux, Yvette, (215) 898-9191 bordeaux@sas.upenn.edu,
    University of Pennsylvania – Po
Bordoni, Simona, 626.395.2672 bordoni@gps.caltech.edu,
    California Institute of Technology – Op
Bordossy, Andras, +44 (0) 191 208 6319 andras.bardossy@ncl.ac.uk,
    University of Newcastle Upon Tyne – Og
Bordy, Emese, 021-650-2901 emese.bordy@uct.ac.za,
    University of Cape Town – Gs
Borghi, Alessandro, alessandro.borghi@unito.it, Università di Torino – Gx
Borisov, Dmitry, 609-258-4101 dborisov@princeton.edu,
    Princeton University – Ysg
Bork, Kennard B., (740) 587-6486 bork@denison.edu,
    Denison University – Pi
Bornhorst, Theodore J., 906-487-2721 tjb@mtu.edu,
    Michigan Technological University – EgCgGx
Borns, Jr., Harold W., (207) 581-2196 Borns@maine.edu,
    University of Maine – Gl
Borojeviæ Šoštariæ, Sibila, +38514605961 sborojsost@geol.pmf.hr,
    University of Zagreb – CegCc
Boroughs, Scott, 509-335-1626 scott.boroughs@wsu.edu,
    Washington State University – GiCa
Boroughs, Terry J., (916) 331-8596 BorougT@arc.losrios.edu,
    American River College – GgXgCg
Boroushaki, Soheil, 818-677-4715 soheil.boroushaki@csun.edu,
    California State University, Northridge – Oi
Borowski, Walter S., (859) 622-1277 w.borowski@eku.edu,
    Eastern Kentucky University – CgGo
Borradaile, Graham J., gjborrad@lakeheadu.ca, Lakehead University – Ym
Borrok, David M., 337-482-2888 dmb5953@louisiana.edu,
    University of Louisiana at Lafayette – Cg
Bosak, Tanja, 617-324-3959 tbosak@mit.edu,
    Massachusetts Institute of Technology – Py
Bosart, Lance F., (518) 442-4564 bosart@atmos.albany.edu,
    SUNY, Albany – Oa
Bosbyshell, Howell, (610) 436-2805 hbosbyshell@wcupa.edu,
    West Chester University – Gc
Boss, Alan P., (202) 478-8858 aboss@carnegiescience.edu,
    Carnegie Institution of Washington – On
Boss, Stephen K., (479) 575-7134 sboss@uark.edu,
    University of Arkansas, Fayetteville – GeYgGg
Bossenbroek, Jonathon , 419-530-8376 jonathon.bossenbroek@utoledo.edu,
    University of Toledo – On
Bossert, James E., (505) 667-6268 bossert@lanl.gov,
    Los Alamos National Laboratory – Oa
Bostater, Charles R., (321) 674-8096 bostater@fit.edu,
    Florida Institute of Technology – Op
Bostock, Michael G., (604) 822-2082 bostock@eos.ubc.ca,
    University of British Columbia – Ys
Boston, Penelope, 575.835.5657 pboston@nmt.edu,
    New Mexico Institute of Mining and Technology – On
Boswell, Cecil, 573-368-2146 cecil.boswell@dnr.mo.gov,
    Missouri Dept of Natural Resources – On
Bothern, Lawrence, 915-831-5088 lbothern@epcc.edu,
    El Paso Community College – Gg
Bothner, Wallace A., (603) 862-1718 wally.bothner@unh.edu,
    University of New Hampshire – Gc
Bots, Pieter, pieter.bots@manchester.ac.uk, University of Manchester – Ge
Bottenberg, H. Carrie, 208-282-3538 bottcarr@isu.edu,
    Idaho State University – OiGtc
Bottero, Jean-Yves, bottero@arbois.cerege.fr,
    Rice University – On
Bottjer, David J., (213) 740-6100 dbottjer@usc.edu,
    University of Southern California – Pe
Boudreau, Alan E., (919) 684-5646 boudreau@duke.edu,
    Duke University – Gi
Boudreau, Bernard P., (902) 494-8895 bernie.boudreau@dal.ca,
    Dalhousie University – Cl
Boudrias, Michel A., (619) 260-4600 boum@sandiego.edu,
    University of San Diego – Ob
Bouker, Polly A., 770-278-1320 polly.bouker@gpc.edu,
    Georgia Perimeter College – Gg
Boult, Stephen, +44 0161 275-3867 s.boult@manchester.ac.uk,
    University of Manchester – Hg
Boulton, Sarah, +44 1752 584762 sarah.boulton@plymouth.ac.uk,
    University of Plymouth – Or
Boulvain, Frederic P., 32 4 366 22 52 fboulvain@ulg.ac.be,
    Universite de Liege – Gs
Bouman, Heather, +44 (1865) 272019 Heather.Bouman@earth.ox.ac.uk,
    University of Oxford – Cg
Bounk, Michael, Michael.Bounk@dnr.iowa.gov,
    Iowa Dept of Natural Resources – Gg
Bour, William, (703) 450-2612 wbour@nvcc.edu,
    Northern Virginia Community College - Loudoun Campus – Gge
Bourcier, Bill L., (925) 423-3745 bourcier1@llnl.gov,
    Lawrence Livermore National Laboratory – Cg
Bourgeois, Joanne (Jody), 206-685-2443 jbourgeo@uw.edu,

Faculty Index -B

Brandt, Craig, (865) 574-1921 fcb@ornl.gov,
   Oak Ridge National Laboratory – Ge
Brandt, Danita S., 517-355-6595 brandt@msu.edu,
   Michigan State University – Pi
Brandvold, Lynn A., (505) 835-5517 lynnb@nmt.edu,
   New Mexico Institute of Mining & Technology – Ca
Branfireun, Brian, bbranfir@uwo.ca,
   Western University – On
Branlund, Joy, (618) 797-7451 joy.branlund@swic.edu,
   Southwestern Illinois College - Sam Wolf Granite City Campus – Og
Branney, Mike, +440116 252 3647 mjb26@le.ac.uk,
   Leicester University – Gv
Branstrator, Jon W., (765) 983-1339 jonb@earlham.edu,
   Earlham College – Pg
Brant, Lynn A., (319) 273-6160 lynn.brant@uni.edu,
   University of Northern Iowa – Gn
Brantley, Susan L., (814) 863-1739 brantley@geosc.psu.edu,
   Pennsylvania State University, University Park – Cg
Brasier, Martin, +44 (1865) 272074 martin.brasier@earth.ox.ac.uk,
   University of Oxford – Po
Brassea, Jesus M., jbrassea@cicese.mx,
   Centro de Investigación Científica y de Educación Superior de Ensenada – Ye
Brassell, Simon C., (812) 855-3786 simon@indiana.edu,
   Indiana University, Bloomington – Co
Brassington, Rick, +44 (0) 192 576 6754 rick.brassington@ncl.ac.uk,
   University of Newcastle Upon Tyne – Hg
Braught, Patricia, (717) 245-1355 braught@dickinson.edu,
   Dickinson College – On
Braun, Alexander, 613-533-6621 braun@queensu.ca,
   Queen's University – Yg
Braund, Emilie, +44 023 9284 2257 emilie.bruand@port.ac.uk,
   University of Portsmouth – Gz
Bray, Colin, (416) 978-6516 cjbray@quartz.geology.utoronto.ca,
   University of Toronto – Cs
Breaker, Laurence, 831-771-4400 lbreaker@mlml.calstate.edu,
   Moss Landing Marine Laboratories – Op
Brearley, Adrian J., (505) 277-4163 brearley@unm.edu,
   University of New Mexico – Gz
Breckenridge, Roy M., roybreck@uidaho.edu, University of Idaho – Gg
Breecker, Daniel O., 512-471-6166 breecker@jsg.utexas.edu,
   University of Texas at Austin – ScCs
Breedlovestrout, Renee L., 208-885-7560 reneeb@uidaho.edu,
   University of Idaho – GoPbGr
Brehman, Thomas R., (847) 376-7036 granite@oakton.edu,
   Oakton Community College – Po
Breitbart, Mya, (727) 553-3520 mya@marine.usf.edu,
   University of South Florida – Ob
Breitenbeck, Gary A., (504) 388-2110 Louisiana State University – Sb
Breitmeyer, Ronald, 775.682.6049 rbreitmeyer@unr.edu,
   University of Nevada, Reno – HwGe
Breland, Clayton F., (225) 388-8300 clayton@lgs.bri.lsu.edu,
   Louisiana State University – Ye
Bremer, Keith, (785) 628-4644 kabremer@fhsu.edu,
   Fort Hays State University – Oun
Brenan, James, (416) 978-0281 brenan@geology.utoronto.ca,
   University of Toronto – Gi
Brengman, Latisha A., 218-726-7586 lbrengma@d.umn.edu,
   University of Minnesota, Duluth – Gd
Brenna, J. T., (607) 255-9182 jtb4@cornell.edu,
   Cornell University – Cg
Brenner, Mark, (352) 392-9617 brenner@ufl.edu,
   University of Florida – Gn
Bretherton, Christopher S., 206-685-7414 breth@washington.edu,
   University of Washington – Oa
Bretherton, Francis P., (608)262-7497 fbretherton@charter.net,
   University of Wisconsin, Madison – Oa
Brethes, Jean-Claude, (418) 724-1779 cjmichau@globetrotter.net,
   Universite du Quebec a Rimouski – Ob
Breton, Caroline, 512-471-0322 cari.breton@beg.utexas.edu,
   University of Texas at Austin, Jackson School of Geosciences – Oi
Brett, Carlton E., (513) 556-4556 carlton.brett@uc.edu,
   Cincinnati Museum Center – Po
Brewer, Kevin E., 815-928-5632 kbrewer@olivet.edu,
   Olivet Nazarene University – HwOiNg
Brewer, Margene, (616) 526-8415 mkb25@calvin.edu,
   Calvin College – OnGgOn
Brewer, Micheal, (202) 994-6185 mbrewer@gwu.edu,
   George Washington University – Or
Brezinski, David K., 410-554-5526 david.brezinski@maryland.gov,
   Maryland Department of Natural Resources – GrPgGg
Bridgeman, Thomas, 419-530-8373 Thomas.Bridgeman@utoledo.edu,
   University of Toledo – On
Bridges, Carey, 573-368-2143 carey.bridges@dnr.mo.gov,
   Missouri Dept of Natural Resources – Gg
Bridges, Frank, (831) 459-2893 bridges@cats.ucsc.edu,
   University of California, Santa Cruz – Yx
Bries Korpik, Jill, (651) 450-3726 jkorpik@inverhills.mnscu.edu,
   Inver Hills Community College – Gg
Bries-Korpik, Jill, 651-779-3434 jill.brieskorpik@century.edu,
   Century College – Og

Briggs, Derek E., (203) 432-8590 derek.briggs@yale.edu,
   Yale University – Yg
Briggs, John, +44 0141 330 8744 John.Briggs@glasgow.ac.uk,
   University of Glasgow – Ou
Brigham-Grette, Julie, (413) 545-4840 brigham-grette@geo.umass.edu,
   University of Massachusetts, Amherst – Gl
Brikowski, Tom H., (972) 883-6242 brikowi@utdallas.edu,
   University of Texas, Dallas – Hw
Brill, Jr., Richard C., 808-845-9488 brill@hawaii.edu,
   Honolulu Community College – Gg
Brimhall, George H., 510.642.5868 brimhall@eps.berkeley.edu,
   University of California, Berkeley – Eg
Briner, Jason P., 716-645-4326 jbriner@buffalo.edu,
   SUNY, Buffalo – Gl
Brinkman, Donald B., (403) 823-7707 Royal Tyrrell Museum of Palaeontol-
   ogy – Pv
Brinkman, P. Anthony, 775-784-6995 brinkman@unr.edu,
   University of Nevada, Reno – Ou
Brinkmann, Robert, 516-463-7348 robert.brinkmann@hofstra.edu,
   Hofstra University – Os
Brinkmann, Robert, (541) 967-2039 Robert.D.Brinkmann@mlrr.oregongeology.com,
   Oregon Dept of Geology & Mineral Industries – Ge
Brisbin, William C., (204) 474-9454 w_brisbin@umanitoba.ca,
   University of Manitoba – Gc
Briskin, Madeleine, (513) 556-3009 madeleine.briskin@uc.edu,
   University of Cincinnati – Pe
Bristow, Charlie, +44 020 3073 8025 c.bristow@ucl.ac.uk,
   Birkbeck College – Gs
Britt, Brooks B., 801-422-7316 brooks_britt@byu.edu,
   Brigham Young University – Pg
Britton, Gloria, (216) 987-5228 Gloria.Britton@tri-c.edu,
   Cuyahoga Community College - Western Campus – Og
Britzke, Gilbert, 089/2180 4209 gilbert.brietzke@geophysik.uni-muenchen.de,
   Ludwig-Maximilians-Universitaet Muenchen – Yg
Broadfoot, Lyle A., (520) 621-4303 broadfoot@vega.lpl.arizona.edu,
   University of Arizona – Or
Broadhead, Ronald F., (505) 835-5202 ron@gis.nmt.edu,
   New Mexico Institute of Mining & Technology – Go
Broadhead, Thomas W., (865) 974-6002 twbroadhead@utk.edu,
   University of Tennessee, Knoxville – Pi
Brochu, Christopher A., (319) 353-1808 chris-brochu@uiowa.edu,
   University of Iowa – Pv
Brock, Patrick W. G., (718) 997-3328 Graduate School of the City University of
   New York – Gg
Brock, Timothy, (417)-836-5318 timothybrock@missouristate.edu,
   Missouri State University – On
Brock-Hon, Amy, (423) 425-4409 amy-brock-hon@utc.edu,
   University of Tennessee at Chattanooga – Os
Brockhaus, John A., (845) 938-2063 United States Military Academy – Yd
Brocklehurst, Simon, +44 0161 275-3037 Simon.H.Brocklehurst@manchester.ac.uk,
   University of Manchester – Gm
Brod, Joseph D., 813-744-8018 jbrod@hccfl.edu,
   Hillsborough Community College – Og
Broda, James E., (508) 289-2466 jbroda@whoi.edu,
   Woods Hole Oceanographic Institution – Gs
Brodholt, John, +44 020 7679 32622 j.brodholt@ucl.ac.uk,
   University College London – Yg
Brodie, Gregory, (423) 425-5915 gregory-brodie@utc.edu,
   University of Tennessee at Chattanooga – Ge
Brodie, Kate, +44 0161 275-3948 Kate.Brodie@manchester.ac.uk,
   University of Manchester – Gc
Brodsky, Emily, 831-459-1854 ebrodsky@pmc.ucsc.edu,
   University of California, Santa Cruz – Ys
Broecker, Wallace S., (845) 365-8413 broecker@ldeo.columbia.edu,
   Columbia University – CmOcPe
Brogan, George, 949-451-5687 gbrogan@ivc.edu,
   Irvine Valley College – Gc
Bromily, Geoffrey, +44 (0) 131 650 8519 geoffrey.bromiley@ed.ac.uk,
   Edinburgh University – Ge
Bromley, Gordon R., gordon.bromley@maine.edu,
   University of Maine – Gl
Bromwich, David H., (614) 688-5314 bromwich.1@osu.edu,
   Ohio State University – Oa
Bronk, Deborah A., (804) 684-7779 bronk@vims.edu,
   College of William & Mary – Oc
Brook, Edward J., (509) 546-9762 Washington State University – Gl
Brook, Edward J., (541) 737-8197 brooke@geo.oregonstate.edu,
   Oregon State University – Ou
Brookfield, Andrea, 785-864-2199 andrea@kgs.ku.edu,
   University of Kansas – Hy
Brookfield, Michael E., mbrookfi@hotmail.com, University of Guelph – PgGrt
Brooks, Antone L., (509) 372-7335 tbrooks@tricity.wsu.edu,
   Washington State University – On
Brooks, David A., (979) 845-5527 dbrooks@ocean.tamu.edu,
   Texas A&M University – Op
Brooks, Debra A., (714) 564-4788 Santiago Canyon College – Yg
Brooks, Gregg R., (727) 864-8992 brooksgr@eckerd.edu,
   Eckerd College – Gu
Brooks, Ian, +44(0) 113 34 36743 i.m.brooks@leeds.ac.uk,
   University of Leeds – On

Faculty Index -B

Brooks, Paul D., (520) 621-3424 brooks@hwr.arizona.edu,
University of Arizona – Cg
Brooks, Sarah D., (979) 845-5632 sbrooks@tamu.edu,
Texas A&M University – Oa
Brooks, Scott C., (865) 574-6398 3sb@ornl.gov,
Oak Ridge National Laboratory – Cl
Broome, Stephen W., (919) 515-2643 North Carolina State University – Sf
Brophy, James G., (812) 855-6417 brophy@indiana.edu,
Indiana University, Bloomington – Gi
Broster, Bruce E., (506) 453-4804 broster@unb.ca,
University of New Brunswick – Gl
Brothen, Jerry, (310) 660-3593 jbrothen@elcamino.edu,
El Camino College – Oy
Brothers, Timothy S., (317) 274-1101 Indiana University / Purdue University,
Indianapolis – Oy
Brouillette, Pierre, (418) 654-2567 pbrouill@nrcan.gc.ca,
Universite du Quebec – Gg
Brouwer, Fraukje , fraukje.brouwer@vu.nl, VU University Amsterdam – Gxc
Brower, James C., (315) 443-2672 Syracuse University – Po
Brown, Alan, abrown11@houston.oilfield.slb.com,
West Virginia University – EoYe
Brown, Bradford D., (208) 722-6701 University of Idaho – On
Brown, Bruce A., (608) 263-3201 babrown1@wisc.edu,
University of Wisconsin, Extension – GcEg
Brown, Caleb, (403) 823-7707 Royal Tyrrell Museum of Palaeontology – Pv
Brown, Cathe, (202) 633-1788 brownc@si.edu,
Smithsonian Institution / National Museum of Natural History – Gz
Brown, David, +44 01413307410 David.Brown@glasgow.ac.uk,
University of Glasgow – Gvs
Brown, David L., 530-898-4035 DLBrown@csuchico.edu,
California State University, Chico – Hg
Brown, Donald W., (505) 667-1926 dwb@lanl.gov,
Los Alamos National Laboratory – Nr
Brown, Douglas, +44 208 417 2245 Doug.Brown@kingston.ac.uk,
Kingston University – Oi
Brown, Edwin H., (360) 650-3645 ehbrown@cc.wwu.edu,
Western Washington University – Gp
Brown, Erik T., (218) 726-8891 etbrown@d.umn.edu,
University of Minnesota, Duluth – Og
Brown, Francis H., (801) 581-8767 frank.brown@utah.edu,
University of Utah – Gg
Brown, Huntting (Hunt), 937 775-4996 hunt.brown@wright.edu,
Wright State University – Ge
Brown, J. Michael, 206-616-6058 brown@ess.washington.edu,
University of Washington – Gy
Brown, James R., (403) 220-7484 jbrown@geo.ucalgary.ca,
University of Calgary – Ys
Brown, Kenneth, 513-5299-3225 brownkl3@miamioh.edu,
Miami University – Gx
Brown, Kent D., 801-537-3350 kentbrown@utah.gov,
Utah Geological Survey – On
Brown, Kerry, K.Brown@kingston.ac.uk,
Kingston University – Ge
Brown, Kevin M., (858) 534-5368 kmbrown@ucsd.edu,
University of California, San Diego – Gu
Brown, Larry D., (607) 255-6346 ldb7@cornell.edu,
Cornell University – Ye
Brown, Laurie, (413) 545-0245 lbrown@geo.umass.edu,
University of Massachusetts, Amherst – Ym
Brown, Lewis M., (906) 635-2155 lbrown@lssu.edu,
Lake Superior State University – PiOe
Brown, Mark A., 717-702-2077 markb@pa.gov,
Pennsylvania Bureau of Topographic & Geologic Survey – OiXm
Brown, Michael, (301) 405-4080 mbrown@geol.umd.edu,
University of Maryland – Gx
Brown, Michael E., (626) 395-8423 mbrown@gps.caltech.edu,
California Institute of Technology – Xy
Brown, Michael E., (662) 325-2906 mebrown@ra.msstate.edu,
Mississippi State University – Ow
Brown, Moira, mwbrown@neaq.org, University of Massachusetts, Boston – Ob
Brown, Paul, +44 020 7679 32431 p.bown@ucl.ac.uk,
University College London – Pm
Brown, Paul W., (520) 621-1319 pbrown@ag.arizona.edu,
University of Arizona – Ow
Brown, Peter, 5196612111 ext.86458 pbrown@uwo.ca,
Western University – OnXm
Brown, Philip E., (206) 543-9419 pbrown@geology.wisc.edu,
University of Wisconsin, Madison – Em
Brown, Richard J., +44 (0) 191 33 42303 richard.brown3@durham.ac.uk,
Durham University – Gv
Brown, Rob, (828) 262-7222 brownrn@appstate.edu,
Appalachian State University – On
Brown, Robert A., rabrown@atmos.washington.edu,
University of Washington – Oa
Brown, Robert H., (520) 626-9045 rhb@lpl.arizona.edu,
University of Arizona – Xc
Brown, Roderick, +44 01413305460 Roderick.Brown@glasgow.ac.uk,
University of Glasgow – Cc
Brown, Sandra, 604-822-5965 University of British Columbia – Sp
Brown, Steven E., 217-333-5143 steebrow@illinois.edu,

University of Illinois – Gl
Brown, Thomas W., tbrown1@austincc.edu,
Austin Community College District – Ges
Brown, William G., (254) 710-2075 william_brown@baylor.edu,
Baylor University – Gc
Brown, Jr., Gordon E., (650) 723-9168 gordon@pangea.stanford.edu,
Stanford University – Gz
Brownawell, Bruce J., (631) 632-8658 bruce.brownawell@stonybrook.edu,
SUNY, Stony Brook – Oc
Browne, Brandon L., 707-826-3950 blb519@humboldt.edu,
Humboldt State University – Gi
Browne, Kathleen M., (609) 896-5408 browne@rider.edu,
Rider University – GuOe
Browning, James V., 848-445-3368 jvb@rci.rutgers.edu,
Rutgers, The State University of New Jersey – GgsGr
Brownlee, Colin, +44 (0)1752 633347 University of Southampton – Ob
Brownlee, Donald E., 206-543-2888 brownlee@ess.washington.edu,
University of Washington – Xgy
Broxton, David E., 505-667-2492 broxton@lanl.gov,
Los Alamos National Laboratory – Gx
Brubaker, John M., (804) 684-7222 brubaker@vims.edu,
College of William & Mary – Op
Brubaker, Kenneth L., (630) 252-7630 Argonne National Laboratory – Oa
Brudzinski, Michael, 513-529-9758 brudzimr@MiamiOh.edu,
Miami University – Ys
Brueckner, Hannes K., (718) 997-3300 Graduate School of the City University of
New York – Cc
Brueckner, Hannes K., hannes@ldeo.columbia.edu,
Queens College (CUNY) – Cg
Brueseke, Matthew E., (785) 532-1908 brueseke@ksu.edu,
Kansas State University – GivGt
Brugger, Keith A., (320) 589-6310 bruggeka@mrs.umn.edu,
University of Minnesota, Morris – Gl
Bruhn, Ronald L., (801) 581-7162 ron.bruhn@utah.edu,
University of Utah – Gc
Bruland, Kenneth W., (831) 459-4587 bruland@cats.ucsc.edu,
University of California, Santa Cruz – Oc
Brumbaugh, David S., (928) 523-7191 david.brumbaugh@nau.edu,
Northern Arizona University – Ys
Brune, James N., (775) 784-4974 brune@seismo.unr.edu,
University of Nevada, Reno – Ys
Brune, Jürgen, 303.273.3704 jbrune@mines.edu,
Colorado School of Mines – Nm
Brune, William H., (814) 865-3286 whb2@psu.edu,
Pennsylvania State University, University Park – Ow
Brunengo, Matthew , 503-725-3391 mbruneng@pdx.edu,
Portland State University – GgNgGm
Bruner, Katherine R., (304) 293-5603 bruner@geo.wvu.edu,
West Virginia University – Gd
Brunetto, Eileen, (802) 443-5970 efahey@middlebury.edu,
Middlebury College – On
Bruning, Eric C., 806-834-3120 eric.bruning@ttu.edu,
Texas Tech University – Oa
Brunish, Wendee M., (505) 667-5724 wb@lanl.gov,
Los Alamos National Laboratory – On
Brunkal, Holly, 970.943.2180 hbrunkal@western.edu,
Western State Colorado University – NgGm
Brunner, Benjamin, 915-747-5501 benobru@gmail.com,
University of Texas, El Paso – Cs
Bruno, Barbara, (808) 956-0901 barb@hawaii.edu,
University of Hawai'i, Manoa – Ob
Bruno, Carrie, 775.753.2204 caroline.bruno@gbcnv.edu,
Great Basin College – OgSo
Bruno, Emiliano, emiliano.bruno@unito.it,
Università di Torino – Gz
Bruns, Dale A., 570-408-4603 dale.bruns@wilkes.edu,
Wilkes University – OirSf
Brunskill, Jeffrey C., 570-389-4355 jbrunski@bloomu.edu,
Bloomsburg University – OiwOy
Brunstad, Keith, 607 436-3066 Keith.Brunstad@oneonta.edu,
SUNY, Oneonta – GizEg
Brunt, Rufus, +44 0161 306-6816 rufus.brunt@manchester.ac.uk,
University of Manchester – Gs
Brunton, George D., (662) 236-4267 gebruntn@olemiss.edu,
University of Mississippi – Ng
Bruschke, Freddi Jo, 657-278-3551 fbruschke@fullerton.edu,
California State University, Fullerton – Gg
Brush, Grace S., (410) 516-7107 gbrush@jhu.edu,
Johns Hopkins University – Pl
Brush, Nigel, (419) 289-5271 nbrush@ashland.edu,
Ashland University – GmdGa
Brusseau, Mark L., (520) 621-3244 brusseau@ag.arizona.edu,
University of Arizona – Hw
Bryan, Christopher, +44 01326 259482 C.G.Bryan@exeter.ac.uk,
Exeter University – Nx
Bryan, Scott E., +61 7 3138 4827 scott.bryan@qut.edu.au,
Queensland University of Technology – GitGs
Bryant, Anita M., (678) 839-4051 abryant@westga.edu,
University of West Georgia – On
Bryant, Ernest A., (505) 667-2422 Los Alamos National Laboratory – Cg

Bryant, Kathleen E., 217-244-9045 kebryant@illinois.edu,
    University of Illinois, Urbana-Champaign – Gg
Bryant, Marita, (207) 786-6452 mbryant@bates.edu,
    Bates College – Gg
Bryce, Julia G., 603-862-3139 julie.bryce@unh.edu,
    University of New Hampshire – Cg
Bryce, Karen R., (801) 378-5470 karen_bryce@byu.edu,
    Brigham Young University – On
Bryden, Harry, +44 (023) 8059 6437 H.Bryden@noc.soton.ac.uk,
    University of Southampton – Op
Brzobohaty, Rostislav, +420 549 49 3326 rosta@sci.muni.cz,
    Masaryk University – PgsPe
Buatois, Luis, luis.buatois@usask.ca,
    University of Saskatchewan – Ps
Buchanan, Donald G., 9093844399 ext. 5467 dbuchanan@sbccd.cc.ca.us,
    San Bernardino Valley College – Og
Buchanan, George, gbuchana@mc3.edu,
    Montgomery County Community College – Ng
Buchanan, John P., (509) 359-7493 jbuchanan@ewu.edu,
    Eastern Washington University – Hw
Buchanan, Paul, (903) 983-8253 pbuchanan@kilgore.edu,
    Kilgore College – GgiXm
Buchanan, Rex C., (785) 864-2106 rex@kgs.ku.edu,
    University of Kansas – Oe
Buchannon, Robin C., (662) 915-7482 rcb@olemiss.edu,
    University of Mississippi – Oo
Buchheim, H. Paul, (909) 824-4300 Loma Linda University – GnsGr
Buck, Brenda J., (702) 895-3583 buckb@unlv.nevada.edu,
    University of Montana Western – Sdo
Buck, Brenda J., (702) 895-1694 buckb@unlv.nevada.edu,
    University of Nevada, Las Vegas – Sd
Buck, Daniel, (541) 346-2353 danielb@uoregon.edu,
    University of Oregon – On
Buck, Roger W., 845-365-8592 Columbia University – Yr
Bucke, David P., (802) 899-3584 david.bucke@uvm.edu,
    University of Vermont – Gg
Buckingham, Michael J., (858) 534-7977 mbuckingham@ucsd.edu,
    University of California, San Diego – Op
Buckley, Brendon, 845-365-8782 Columbia University – Pe
Buckley, John S., kfjsb00@tamuk.edu,
    Texas A&M University, Kingsville – Pv
Buckley, Lawrence J., (401) 874-6671 lbuckley@gso.uri.edu,
    University of Rhode Island – Oc
Buckley, Luke, 406-496-4677 lbuckley@mtech.edu,
    Montana Tech of The University of Montana – On
Buckley, Michael, +44(0)161 306 5175 M.Buckley@manchester.ac.uk,
    University of Manchester – Ga
Bucklin, Ann, 860-405-9260 ann.bucklin@uconn.edu,
    University of Connecticut – Ob
Bucur, Ioan, +40-264-405371 ibucur@bioge.ubbcluj.ro,
    Babes-Bolyai University – PgmGs
Budd, Ann F., (319) 335-1817 ann-budd@uiowa.edu,
    University of Iowa – Po
Budd, David A., (303) 492-3988 david.budd@colorado.edu,
    University of Colorado – Gd
Budd, William W., (509) 335-8536 budd@wsu.edu,
    Washington State University – On
Buddemeier, Robert W., (785) 864-2112 buddrw@kgs.ku.edu,
    University of Kansas – Hy
Budikova, Dagmar, (309)438-7643 dbudiko@ilstu.edu,
    Illinois State University – Ge
Buermann, Wolfgang, +44(0) 113 34 34958 w.buermann@leeds.ac.uk,
    University of Leeds – Ou
Buesseler, Ken O., (508) 289-2309 kbuesseler@whoi.edu,
    Woods Hole Oceanographic Institution – Oc
Buick, Roger, 206-543-1913 buick@ess.washington.edu,
    University of Washington – PeoPm
Buijsman, Maarten, (228) 688-2385 maarten.buijsman@usm.edu,
    University of Southern Mississippi – Op
Bukowinski, Mark S., (510) 642-0977 University of California, Berkeley – Gy
Bulger, Daniel E., 678-891-2415 Dan.Bulger@gpc.edu,
    Georgia Perimeter College - Decatur – GgOn
Bull, Jonathan M., +44 (0)23 8059 3078 bull@noc.soton.ac.uk,
    University of Southampton – Yr
Bull, William B., (520) 621-6024 University of Arizona – Gm
Bullamore, Henry W., (301) 687-4413 hbullamore@frostburg.edu,
    Frostburg State University – On
Bullard, Reuben G., 859-572-6907 bullardr@nku.edu,
    Northern Kentucky University – Gd
Bullard, Thomas F., (775) 673-7420 tbullard@dri.edu,
    Desert Research Institute – Gm
Bullen, Dean, +44 023 92 842289 dean.bullen@port.ac.uk,
    University of Portsmouth – Gt
Bullister, John, (206) 526-6741 bullister@pmel.noaa.gov,
    University of Washington – Oc
Bullock, Emma, bullocke@si.edu,
    Smithsonian Institution / National Museum of Natural History – Xm
Bultman, John, (828) 254-1921 ext 319 jbultman@abtech.edu,
    Asheville-Buncombe Technical Community College – Gg
Bulusu, Subrahmanyam, 803-777-2572 sbulusu@geol.sc.edu,

University of South Carolina – OrpOa
Bunds, Michael, (801) 863-6306 Michael.Bunds@uvu.edu,
    Utah Valley University – GctGe
Bundy, Larry G., (608) 263-2889 lgbundy@wisc.edu,
    University of Wisconsin, Madison – So
Bunge, Hans-Peter, 089/2180 4225 bunge@lmu.de,
    Ludwig-Maximilians-Universitaet Muenchen – Yg
Buonaiuto, Frank, 212-650-3092 frank.buonaiuto@hunter.cuny.edu,
    Hunter College (CUNY) – On
Buratti, Bonnie J., (818) 354-7427 Jet Propulsion Laboratory – Or
Burbanck, George P., (757) 727-5783 george.burbanck@hamptonu.edu,
    Hampton University – On
Burbank, Doug, (805) 893-7858 burbank@geol.ucsb.edu,
    University of California, Santa Barbara – Gmt
Burberry, Caroline M., 402-472-7157 cburberry2@unl.edu,
    University of Nebraska, Lincoln – Gct
Burbey, Thomas J., (540) 231-6696 tjburbey@vt.edu,
    Virginia Polytechnic Institute & State University – Hw
Burchfiel, B. C., (617) 253-7919 bcburch@mit.edu,
    Massachusetts Institute of Technology – Gc
Burden, Elliott T., (709) 737-8388 etburden@mun.ca,
    Memorial University of Newfoundland – Pl
Burdick, Scott, sburdick@umd.edu, University of Maryland – Ys
Burdige, David J., (757) 683-4930 dburdige@odu.edu,
    Old Dominion University – Oc
Burger, Benjamin J., 435-722-1778 benjamin.burger@usu.edu,
    Utah State University – PgGs
Burger, H. Robert, rburger@smith.edu,
    Smith College – Gc
Burger, Martin, 530-754-6497 mburger@ucdavis.edu,
    University of California, Davis – Spb
Burger, Paul V., (505) 277-3827 pvburger@unm.edu,
    University of New Mexico – Gz
Burgess, Peter, +44 1784 414083 Peter.Burgess@rhul.ac.uk,
    University of London, Royal Holloway & Bedford New College – Gs
Burgess, Ray, +44 0161 275-3958 ray.burgess@manchester.ac.uk,
    University of Manchester – Cs
Burgess, Willy, +44 020 7679 37820 william.burgess@ucl.ac.uk,
    University College London – Hg
Burgette, Reed J., 575-646-3782 burgette@nmsu.edu,
    New Mexico State University, Las Cruces – Gtc
Burgmann, Roland, (510) 643-9545 burgmann@seismo.berkeley.edu,
    University of California, Berkeley – Gt
Burk, Sue, 301-405-6244 University of Maryland – On
Burkart, Michael R., mburkart@iastate.edu,
    Iowa State University of Science & Technology – Hy
Burke, Andrea, +44 01334 463910 ab276@st-andrews.ac.uk,
    University of St. Andrews – Cs
Burke, Collette D., (316) 978-3140 Wichita State University – Pm
Burke, Deborah S., (509) 372-2483 deborah.burke@pnl.gov,
    Pacific Northwest National Laboratory – Sc
Burke, Ian, +44(0) 113 34 37532 lab 33965 i.t.burke@leeds.ac.uk,
    University of Leeds – Ge
Burke, Kevin, 713-743-3399 kburke@uh.edu,
    University of Houston – Gt
Burke, Raymond M., (707) 826-4292 rmb2@humboldt.edu,
    Humboldt State University – Gm
Burke, Roger A., (706) 542-2652 University of Georgia – Cl
Burkett, Brett, (976) 548-6510 bburkett@collin.edu,
    Collin College - Central Park Campus – Gvg
Burkhart, Patrick A., (724) 738-2502 patrick.burkhart@sru.edu,
    Slippery Rock University – Hg
Burks, Rachel J., (410) 704-3005 rburks@towson.edu,
    Towson University – Gc
Burlage, Robert S., (865) 574-7321 Oak Ridge National Laboratory – Sb
Burlakova, Lyubov, burlakle@buffalostate.edu, SUNY, Buffalo – Og
Burls, Natalie, 703-993-5756 nburls@gmu.edu,
    George Mason University – Oap
Burmeister, Kurtis C., (209) 946-2398 kburmeister@pacific.edu,
    University of the Pacific – GctEg
Burmester, Russell F., (360) 650-3654 russ.burmester@wwu.edu,
    Western Washington University – Ym
Burnett, Donald S., (626) 395-6117 burnett@gps.caltech.edu,
    California Institute of Technology – Xc
Burnett, Earl E., (928) 329-1030 Arizona Western College – HwGc
Burnham, Charles, burnham_c@fortlewis.edu, Fort Lewis College – Gz
Burnham, Robyn J., (734) 764-0489 rburnham@umich.edu,
    University of Michigan – Pb
Burnley, Pamela C., 702-895-2536 pamela.burnley@unlv.edu,
    University of Nevada, Las Vegas – GpyGg
Burns, Bill, (971) 673-1555 Oregon Dept of Geology & Mineral Industries – Ng
Burns, Carol J., (505) 665-1765 Los Alamos National Laboratory – On
Burns, Danny, 361-354-2405 deburns@coastalbend.edu,
    Coastal Bend College – Ogn
Burns, Diane M., (217) 581-2827 dmburns@eiu.edu,
    Eastern Illinois University – Gs
Burns, Emily, eburns@ccri.edu, Community College of Rhode Island – Gg
Burns, Laurel E., (907) 451-5021 laurel.burns@Alaska.gov,
    Alaska Division of Geological & Geophysical Surveys – Ye
Burns, Peter C., (574) 631-5380 peter.burns.50@nd.edu,

University of Notre Dame – Gz

Burns, Sandra, (860) 832-2934 burns@ccsu.edu,
Central Connecticut State University – Oe

Burns, Scott F., (503) 725-3389 burnss@pdx.edu,
Portland State University – Ng

Burns, Stephen J., (413) 545-0142 sburns@geo.umass.edu,
University of Massachusetts, Amherst – Cs

Burns, Timothy P., (505) 667-4600 Los Alamos National Laboratory – Co

Burr, Devon, (865) 974-2366 dburr1@utk.edu,
University of Tennessee, Knoxville – XgGm

Burras, Lee, (515) 294-0559 lburras@iastate.edu,
Iowa State University of Science & Technology – Sd

Burris, John H., (505) 566-3325 burrisj@sanjuancollege.edu,
San Juan College – GghGz

Bursik, Marcus I., (716) 645-4265 mib@geology.buffalo.edu,
SUNY, Buffalo – Gv

Burst, John F., (573) 341-4616 Missouri University of Science and Technology – Eo

Burt, Donald M., (480) 965-6180 donald.burt@asu.edu,
Arizona State University – Eg

Burtis, Erik, (703) 878-5614 eburtis@nvcc.edu,
Northern Virginia Community College - Woodbridge – GgcGi

Burton, Bradford R., 970.943.2252 bburton@western.edu,
Western State Colorado University – GocGt

Burton, Jacqueline C., (630) 252-8795 jcburton@anl.gov,
Argonne National Laboratory – Cg

Burton, Kevin, +44 (0) 191 33 44298 kevin.burton@durham.ac.uk,
Durham University – Cc

Burton, Paul, +44 (0)1603 59 2982 p.burton@uea.ac.uk,
University of East Anglia – Ys

Burton, Ronald S., (858) 534-7827 rburton@ucsd.edu,
University of California, San Diego – Ob

Burton, Jr., Vinston, (919) 560-6269 North Carolina Central University – Gm

Burwash, Ronald A., (780) 492-3085 ronald.burwash@telus.net,
University of Alberta – Gp

Busa, Mark, 860-343-5779 MBusa@mxcc.commnet.edu,
Middlesex Community College – OgEgYg

Busacca, Alan J., (509) 335-1859 busacca@wsu.edu,
Washington State University – Sa

Busalacchi, Antonio, (301) 405-5599 tonyb@essic.umd.edu,
University of Maryland – Og

Busbey, Arthur B., (817) 257-7301 a.busbey@tcu.edu,
Texas Christian University – PgvGr

Busby, Cathy J., cjbusby@ucdavis.edu, University of California, Davis – Gt

Busby, Michael R., (270) 809-3370 michael.busby@murraystate.edu,
Murray State University – Oi

Busch, Richard M., (610) 436-2716 rbusch@wcupa.edu,
West Chester University – Oe

Busch, William H., 504-280-7230 wbusch@uno.edu,
University of New Orleans – Ou

Buscheck, Thomas A., (925) 423-9390 buscheck1@llnl.gov,
Lawrence Livermore National Laboratory – Ng

Buseck, Peter R., (480) 965-3945 pbuseck@asu.edu,
Arizona State University – Cg

Bush, Andrew B., (780) 492-0351 andrew.bush@ualberta.ca,
University of Alberta – Oa

Bush, Andrew M., (860) 486-9358 andrew.bush@uconn.edu,
University of Connecticut – Pg

Bush, Andrew B. G., (780) 492-0351 andrew.bush@ualberta.ca,
University of Alberta – Oa

Bush, David M., (678) 839-4057 dbush@westga.edu,
University of West Georgia – Ou

Buskey, Edward J., (361) 749-3102 ed.buskey@utexas.edu,
University of Texas at Austin – Ob

Buss, Leo W., (203) 432-3869 Yale University – Po

Busse, Friedrich H., fbusse@igpp.ucla.edu,
University of California, Los Angeles – Yg

Bussod, Gilles Y., (505) 667-7220 gbussod@lanl.gov,
Los Alamos National Laboratory – Yx

Bustin, Amanda, abustin@eos.ubc.ca, University of British Columbia – YgNg

Bustin, R. Marc, (604) 822-6179 mbustin@eos.ubc.ca,
University of British Columbia – Ec

Butcher, Anthony, +44 023 92 842486 anthony.butcher@port.ac.uk,
University of Portsmouth – Pg

Butcher, Patricia M., (657) 278-3561 pbutcher@fullerton.edu,
California State University, Fullerton – Oeg

Butkos, Darryl J., 631-451-4354 butkosd@sunysuffolk.edu,
Suffolk County Community College, Ammerman Campus – Gg

Butler, Gilbert W., (505) 667-6005 Los Alamos National Laboratory – Cc

Butler, Ian B., +44 (0) 131 650 5885 ian.butler@ed.ac.uk,
Edinburgh University – Cg

Butler, James M., (785) 864-3965 jbutler@ku.edu,
University of Kansas – Hw

Butler, Karl, (506) 453-4804 University of New Brunswick – Yg

Butler, R. Paul, (202) 478-8866 pbutler@carnegiescience.edu,
Carnegie Institution of Washington – On

Butler, Robert, 503-943-7780 butler@up.edu,
University of Arizona – Yg

Butler, Sam, (306) 966-5702 sam.butler@usask.ca,
University of Saskatchewan – Yg

Butler, Shane K., 217-244-0800 sbutler4@illinois.edu,

University of Illinois, Urbana-Champaign – Gz

Butler, Jr., James J., (785) 864-2116 jbutler@kgs.ku.edu,
University of Kansas – Hw

Butner, Steffen, +27 (0)46-603-8775 s.buettner@ru.ac.za,
Rhodes University – Gc

Butterfield, David A., (206) 526-6722 dab3@u.washington.edu,
University of Washington – Yr

Butterfield, Nicholas J., +44 (0) 1223 333379 njb1005@esc.cam.ac.uk,
University of Cambridge – Po

Butts, Susan H., 203-432-3037 susan.butts@yale.edu,
Yale University – PiGsPe

Butzow, Dean G., 217-786-4923 dean.butzow@llcc.edu,
Lincoln Land Community College – Oy

Buyce, M. Raymond, rbuyce@mercyhurst.edu,
Mercyhurst University – GsaOn

Buynevich, Ilya, (215) 204-3661 coast@temple.edu,
Temple University – GsrOg

Buzas, Martin A., (202) 633-1313 Smithsonian Institution / National Museum of
Natural History – Pm

Buzatu, Andrei, +40232201463 andrei.buzatu@uaic.ro,
Al. I. Cuza University of Iasi – GziGg

Buzgar, Nicolae, +40232201462 nicolae.buzgar@uaic.ro,
Al. I. Cuza University of Iasi – GziGd

Bybee, Grant M., 011 717 6633 grant.bybee@wits.ac.za,
University of the Witwatersrand – Gi

Büchel, Georg, +49(0)3641 948640 georg.buechel@uni-jena.de,
Friedrich-Schiller-University Jena – Gg

Byerly, Don W., dbyerly@utk.edu, University of Tennessee, Knoxville – Ge

Byerly, Gary R., (225) 578-5318 glbyer@lsu.edu,
Louisiana State University – Gi

Byers, Charles W., (608) 262-2361 cwbyers@geology.wisc.edu,
University of Wisconsin, Madison – Pe

Bykerk-Kauffman, Ann, 530-898-6305 abykerk-kauffman@csuchico.edu,
California State University, Chico – GcOe

Byrand, Karl, (920) 459-6619 karl.byrand@uwc.edu,
University of Wisconsin Colleges – Ony

Byrne, James M., (403) 329-2002 byrne@uleth.ca,
University of Lethbridge – Hg

Byrne, John V., john.byrne@coas.oregonstate.edu,
Oregon State University – Gu

Byrne, Paul K., 919-513-2578 paul.byrne@ncsu.edu,
North Carolina State University – XgGcOr

Byrne, Robert H., (727) 553-1508 byrne@marine.usf.edu,
University of South Florida – Cm

Byrne, Timothy, (860) 486-3142 tim.byrne@uconn.edu,
University of Connecticut – Gc

Byrnes, Jarrett, jarrett.byrnes@umb.edu,
University of Massachusetts, Boston – ObnOn

Byrnes, Jeffrey, 405-744-6358 jeffrey.byrnes@okstate.edu,
Oklahoma State University – GgvOn

C

Caballero, Kate, (254) 968-9143 caballero@tarleton.edu,
Tarleton State University – On

Cablk, Mary, (775) 673-7371 mcablk@dri.edu,
Desert Research Institute – Or

Cabrera, Miguel L., (706) 542-1242 University of Georgia – So

Cadet, Eddy, (801) 863-8881 cadeted@uvu.edu,
Utah Valley University – Ge

Cadol, Daniel, 575-835-5645 dcadol@ees.nmt.edu,
New Mexico Institute of Mining and Technology – HsGe

Cadoppi, Paola, paola.cadoppi@unito.it, Università di Torino – Gc

Cahill, Kevin, (508) 289-2925 kcahill@whoi.edu,
Woods Hole Oceanographic Institution – Cm

Cahill, Richard A., 217-244-2532 cahill@isgs.uiuc.edu,
Illinois State Geological Survey – Ca

Cahir, John J., (814) 863-8358 cahir@ems.psu.edu,
Pennsylvania State University, University Park – Ow

Caine, T. Nelson, (303) 492-5053 University of Colorado – Gm

Cairns, Alicia, 604-827-5284 acairns@eos.ubc.ca,
University of British Columbia – On

Cairns, David M., (979) 845-2783 cairns@geog.tamu.edu,
Texas A&M University – Oy

Cairns, Stephen, cairnss@si.edu,
Smithsonian Institution / National Museum of Natural History – Pi

Caissie, Beth E., 515-294-7528 bethc@iastate.edu,
Iowa State University of Science & Technology – Pe

Calagari, Ali Asghar, +98 (411) 339 2699 calagari@tabrizu.ac.ir,
University of Tabriz – EgmCg

Calaway, Wallis F., (630) 972-3586 Argonne National Laboratory – Om

Calcote, Randy, 612-624-8526 calco001@umn.edu,
University of Minnesota, Twin Cities – Py

Calder, Eliza, +44 (0) 131 650 4910 ecalder@staffmail.ed.ac.uk,
Edinburgh University – Gv

Calder, John, (902) 424-2778 Dalhousie University – Ec

Caldwell, Andy, 970-204-8228 andrew.caldwell@frontrange.edu,
Front Range Community College - Larimer – Ge

Caldwell, Marianne O., mcaldwell@hccfl.edu,
Hillsborough Community College – Og

Caldwell, Michael W., 780-492-3458 mw.caldwell@ualberta.ca,

University of Alberta – Pv

Caldwell, Roy, (510) 642-1391 rlcaldwell@berkeley.edu,
University of California, Berkeley – Po

Caldwell, Todd, 512-471-2003 todd.caldwell@beg.utexas.edu,
University of Texas at Austin – Sp

Caldwell, W. Glen E., 519-661-3187 gcaldwel@uwo.ca,
Western University – Pm

Caldwell, William G. E., (519) 661-3857 University of Saskatchewan – Ps

Calegari, Pat, (212) 346-1502 Pace University, New York Campus – On

Calengas, Peter L., (309) 298-1151 PL-Calengas@wiu.edu,
Western Illinois University – En

Calhoun, Frank G., (330) 263-3722 scalhoun@coas.oregonstate.edu,
Ohio State University – Sd

Calhoun, Joseph, 717-872-3289 jcalhoun@hearst.com,
Millersville University – Oa

Calizaya, Felipe, (801) 581-5422 felipe.calizaya@utah.edu,
University of Utah – Nm

Callahan, Caitlin N., 616-331-3601 callahac@gvsu.edu,
Grand Valley State University – GgOg

Callahan, John A., 302-831-3584 diodata@udel.edu,
University of Delaware – Ori

Callahan, John E., (828) 262-2746 callahnje@appstate.edu,
Appalachian State University – Eg

Callahan, Timothy J., (843) 953-8278 callahant@cofc.edu,
College of Charleston – Hw

Callard, Jeff, callard@ou.edu, University of Oklahoma – Np

Callison, James, (801) 863-8679 JCallison@uvu.edu,
Utah Valley University – GeSfOs

Calon, Tomas J., (709) 737-8398 tcalon@sparky2.esd.mun.ca,
Memorial University of Newfoundland – Gc

Calvert, Andrew J., (604) 291-5387 acalvert@sfu.ca,
Simon Fraser University – Ys

Calvert, Stephen E., (604) 822-5210 calvert@eos.ubc.ca,
University of British Columbia – Cm

Calvin, Wendy, 775.784.1785 wcalvin@unr.edu,
University of Nevada, Reno – YgOr

Camacho, Alfredo, (204) 474-7413 camacho@cc.umanitoba.ca,
University of Manitoba – Gt

Camacho, Elsa A., (509) 376-5473 elsa.camacho@pnl.gov,
Pacific Northwest National Laboratory – Cg

Camann, Eleanor J., 303-914-6290 eleanor.camann@rrcc.edu,
Red Rocks Community College – OneGs

Camara Artigas, Fernando, fernando.camaraartigas@unito.it,
Università di Torino – Gz

Cambardella, Cynthia, (515) 294-2921 cindy.cambardella@ars.usda.gov,
Iowa State University of Science & Technology – So

Cambiotti, Laura J., ljc0@lehigh.edu, Lehigh University – On

Came, Rosemarie E., 603-862-1720 rosemarie.came@unh.edu,
University of New Hampshire – PeOnn

Cameron, Barry I., 414-229-3136 bcameron@uwm.edu,
University of Wisconsin, Milwaukee – Gvi

Cameron, Cheryl, (907) 451-5012 cheryl.cameron@alaska.gov,
Alaska Division of Geological & Geophysical Surveys – Gv

Cameron, Douglas, (406) 496-4247 dcameron@mtech.edu,
Montana Tech of the University of Montana – Ca

Cameron, Kevin, (604) 291-4703 kjc@sfu.ca,
Simon Fraser University – Gg

Camill III, Philip, 207-721-5149 pcamill@bowdoin.edu,
Bowdoin College – PebSb

Camille, Michael A., (318) 342-1750 University of Louisiana, Monroe – Oy

Camilleri, Phyllis A., 931-221-7317 camillerip@apsu.edu,
Austin Peay State University – Gct

Cammerata, Kirk , 361-825-2468 Kirk.Cammerata@tamucc.edu,
Texas A&M University, Corpus Christi – On

Camp, Mark J., (419) 530-2398 mark.camp@utoledo.edu,
University of Toledo – Pi

Camp, Victor E., (619) 594-7170 vcamp@mail.sdsu.edu,
San Diego State University – Gv

Campagna, David, 757 229 1661 david@campagna-associates.com,
West Virginia University – Gc

Campana, Michael E., (541) 737-2413 michael.campana@oregonstate.edu,
Oregon State University – Hg

Campbell, Andrew R., (575) 835-5327 campbell@nmt.edu,
New Mexico Institute of Mining and Technology – Cs

Campbell, Bruce A., 202-633-2472 Smithsonian Institution / National Air &
Space Museum – Or

Campbell, David L., (319) 335-1314 david-l-campbell@uiowa.edu,
University of Iowa – Yg

Campbell, Finley A., (403) 220-6801 University of Calgary – Em

Campbell, Glenn A., (859) 622-6474 glenn.campbell@eku.edu,
Eastern Kentucky University – Oy

Campbell, Ian A., ian.campbell@ualberta.ca, University of Alberta – Gm

Campbell, James B., (540) 231-5841 Virginia Polytechnic Institute & State
University – Or

Campbell, Katherine, (505) 667-2799 ksc@lanl.gov,
Los Alamos National Laboratory – Gq

Campbell, Kenneth E., (213) 763-3425 kcampbel@nhm.org,
Los Angeles County Museum of Natural History – Pv

Campbell, Lisa, (979) 845-5706 lcampbell@ocean.tamu.edu,
Texas A&M University – Ob

Campbell, Patricia A., (724) 738-4405 patricia.campbell@sru.edu,
Slippery Rock University – Gc

Campbell, Seth W., seth.campbell@maine.edu,
University of Maine – Gl

Campbell-Stone, Erin A., (307) 766-2053 erincs@uwyo.edu,
University of Wyoming – GcEo

Campos, Edwin, 630-252-0093 ecampos@anl.gov,
Argonne National Laboratory – Oa

Canalda, Sabrina, 915-831- 2617 mren@epcc.edu,
El Paso Community College – Gg

Canales Cisneros, Juan Pablo, (508) 289-2893 jpcanales@whoi.edu,
Woods Hole Oceanographic Institution – Yr

Cande, Steven C., (858) 534-1552 scande@ucsd.edu,
University of California, San Diego – Yr

Candela, Philip A., (301) 405-2783 candela@geol.umd.edu,
University of Maryland – CpgEg

Cane, Mark A., 845-365-8344 Columbia University – Op

Canil, Dante, (250) 472-4180 dcanil@uvic.ca,
University of Victoria – Gi

Cannon, Alex, (604) 325-7830 acannon@eos.ubc.ca,
University of British Columbia – Oa

Cantarero, Debra A., (626) 585-7138 dacantarero@paccd.cc.ca.us,
Pasadena City College – On

Cantrell, Kirk J., (509) 376-2136 kirk.cantrell@pnl.gov,
Pacific Northwest National Laboratory – Cl

Canuel, Elizabeth A., (804) 684-7134 ecanuel@vims.edu,
College of William & Mary – Oc

Cao, Guofeng, 806-834-8920 guofeng.cao@ttu.edu,
Texas Tech University – Oi

Cao, Hongsheng, 316-978-3140 Wichita State University – Cl

Capehart, William J., (605) 394-2291 William.Capehart@sdsmt.edu,
South Dakota School of Mines & Technology – Oa

Capella, Silvana, silvana.capella@unito.it, Università di Torino – Gz

Caplan-Auerbach, Jackie, 360-650-4153 jackie@geol.wwu.edu,
Western Washington University – Ys

Capo, Rosemary C., (412) 624-8873 rcapo@pitt.edu,
University of Pittsburgh – Cl

Capoccia, Mary, (614) 292-8522 capoccia.6@osu.edu,
Ohio State University – On

Caporali, Alessandro, 39-049-8279122 alessandro.caporali@unipd.it,
Università degli Studi di Padova – YdsOr

Capraro, Luca, 39-049-8279182 luca.capraro@unipd.it,
Università degli Studi di Padova – PelGg

Capuano, Regina M., 713-743-2957 capuano@uh.edu,
University of Houston – Hw

Caputo, Mario V., (909) 214-7742 mvcaputo@earthlink.net,
San Diego State University – GsdOn

Carbotte, Suzanne, 845-365-8895 Columbia University – Yr

Cardace, Dawn, (401) 874-9384 cardace@uri.edu,
University of Rhode Island – Py

Cardellach López, Esteve, ++34935813091 esteve.cardellach@uab.cat,
Universitat Autonoma de Barcelona – GzeCs

Cardenas, Bayani, 512-471-9425 cardenas@mail.utexas.edu,
University of Texas at Austin – Hw

Cardiff, Michael, 608-262-8960 cardiff@wisc.edu,
University of Wisconsin, Madison – Hw

Cardimona, Steve, (707) 468-3219 scardimo@mendocino.edu,
Mendocino College – Ys

Cardott, Brian J., 405-325-8065 bcardott@ou.edu,
University of Oklahoma – Ec

Carew, James L., (843) 953-5592 carewj@cofc.edu,
College of Charleston – Po

Carey, Anne E., (614) 292-2375 carey@geology.ohio-state.edu,
Ohio State University – Hq

Carey, James W., (505) 667-5540 bcarey@lanl.gov,
Los Alamos National Laboratory – Ca

Carey, Kristine M., (807) 343-8461 kristine.carey@lakeheadu.ca,
Lakehead University – On

Carey, Larry, 256-961-7909 larry.carey@nsstc.uah.edu,
Texas A&M University – Oa

Carey, Sean, 905-525-9140 (Ext. 20134) careysk@mcmaster.ca,
McMaster University – Hg

Carey, Steven N., (401) 874-6209 scarey@gso.uri.edu,
University of Rhode Island – Ou

Carey, Tara, 309-796-5274 careyt@bhc.edu,
Black Hawk College – On

Carle, Steven, (925) 423-5039 carle1@llnl.gov,
Lawrence Livermore National Laboratory – Hw

Carlile, Amy L., 203-479-4257 acarlile@newhaven.edu,
University of New Haven – Obn

Carlin, Joe, 657-278-3054 jcarlin@fullerton.edu,
California State University, Fullerton – Og

Carling, Gregory T., 801-422-2622 greg.carling@byu.edu,
Brigham Young University – HwCst

Carlisle, Donald, (310) 825-1934 carlisle@epss.ucla.edu,
University of California, Los Angeles – Eg

Carlson, Anders, 541-737-3625 acarlson@coas.oregonstate.edu,
Oregon State University – GlCt

Carlson, Barry A., bacarlso@delta.edu,
Delta College – Yg

Cassidy, Nigel, (+44) 01782 733180 n.j.cassidy@keele.ac.uk,
Keele University – Ygx
Cassidy, William, (412) 624-8886 University of Pittsburgh – Xg
Castagna, John P., 713-743-8699 jpcastagna@uh.edu,
University of Houston – Ye
Castaneda, Isla, 413 577-1124 isla@geo.umass.edu,
University of Massachusetts, Amherst – Ca
Castelli, Daniele, daniele.castelli@unito.it, Università di Torino – Gx
Castendyk, Devin, (607) 436-3064 Devin.Castendyk@oneonta.edu,
SUNY, Oneonta – HwCl
Castillo, Paterno R., (858) 534-0383 pcastillo@ucsd.edu,
University of California, San Diego – Gi
Castillon, David A., (417) 836-5800 Missouri State University – Gm
Castle, James W., (864) 656-5015 jcastle@clemson.edu,
Clemson University – Gd
Castleton, Jessica, (801) 537-3381 jessicacastleton@utah.gov,
Utah Geological Survey – Ng
Casto, Pamela, 304-367-8436 Pamela.M.Casto@ivv.nasa.gov,
Fairmont State University – Oe
Castor, Stephen B., 775-682-8766 scastor@unr.edu,
University of Nevada – Eg
Castro, Maria Clara, 734-615-3812 mccastro@umich.edu,
University of Michigan – Hy
Castro, Mark S., (301) 689-3115 castro@al.umces.edu,
University of Maryland – Oa
Castro, Raul, raul@cicese.mx,
Centro de Investigación Científica y de Educación Superior de Ensenada – Ys
Caswell, Bryony, +440151 795 4390 B.A.Caswell@liverpool.ac.uk,
University of Liverpool – Ob
Catalano, Jeff, 314-935-6015 catalano@levee.wustl.edu,
Washington University – Ca
Cataneo, Robert, 217-581-2626 rcataneo@eiu.edu,
Eastern Illinois University – Oa
Catania, Ginny A., 512-471-0403 gcatania@utig.ig.utexas.edu,
University of Texas at Austin – Ol
Catau, John C., (417) 836-4589 johncatau@missouristate.edu,
Missouri State University – On
Cate, Alta S., (713) 718-6052 alta.cate@hccs.edu,
Houston Community College System – Gg
Cather, Steven M., (505) 835-5153 steve@gis.nmt.edu,
New Mexico Institute of Mining & Technology – Gs
Cathey, Henrietta, +61 7 3138 0416 henrietta.cathey@qut.edu.au,
Queensland University of Technology – Gip
Cathles, Lawrence M., (607) 255-2844 lmc19@cornell.edu,
Cornell University – Hy
Catling, David C., 206-543-8653 dcatling@uw.edu,
University of Washington – On
Catlos, Elizabeth J., 512-471-4762 ejcatlos@gmail.com,
University of Texas at Austin – GzCg
Cattolico, Rose Ann, (206) 543-9363 racat@u.washington.edu,
University of Washington – Ob
Catuneanu, Octavian, (780) 492-6569 octavian.catuneanu@ualberta.ca,
University of Alberta – Gs
Caudill, Kimberly S., 740-753-6289 caudillk7007@hocking.edu,
Hocking College – GeOuHw
Caudill, Michael R., 740-753-6277 caudillm@hocking.edu,
Hocking College – SdHwNg
Caupp, Craig L., (301) 687-4755 ccaupp@frostburg.edu,
Frostburg State University – OnHs
Caus Gracia, Esmeralda, ++935812031 esmeralda.caus@uab.cat,
Universitat Autonoma de Barcelona – Pm
Cave, Rachel R., +353 (0)91 492 351 rachel.cave@nuigalway.ie,
National University of Ireland Galway – Cm
Cavin, Julie, j.cavin@hotmail.com, University of Massachusetts, Boston – Ob
Cawood, Peter, (+44) (0)1334 463911 pac20@st-andrews.ac.uk,
University of St. Andrews – Gt
Cayzer, Nicola, +44 (0) 131 650 8527 Nicola.Cayzer@ed.ac.uk,
Edinburgh University – Yg
Cecil, Blaine, 703 648 6415 bcecil@usgs.gov,
West Virginia University – Ec
Cecil, M. R., (818) 677-7009 robinson.cecil@csun.edu,
California State University, Northridge – GiCcGz
Celia, Michael A., (609) 258-5425 Princeton University – Hw
Celik, Hasan, 00904242370000-5980 hasancelik@firat.edu.tr,
Firat University – GscOu
Çemen, Ibrahim, 205-348-8019 icemen@ua.edu,
University of Alabama – Gct
Centorbi, Tracey, (301) 405-6965 tlcento@umd.edu,
University of Maryland – Cg
Cepeda, Joseph C., 806-651-2584 jcepeda@wtamu.edu,
West Texas A&M University – GiHw
Cercone, Karen Rose, (724) 357-5623 kcercone@iup.edu,
Indiana University of Pennsylvania – Cl
Cerling, Thure E., (801) 581-5558 thure.cerling@utah.edu,
University of Utah – Cl
Cerrato, Robert M., (631) 632-8666 robert.cerrato@stonybrook.edu,
SUNY, Stony Brook – Ob
Cervato, Cinzia C., (515) 294-7583 cinzia@iastate.edu,
Iowa State University of Science & Technology – Gg
Cesare, Bernardo, +390498279148 bernardo.cesare@unipd.it,

Università degli Studi di Padova – Gp
Cessi, Paola, (858) 534-0622 pcessi@ucsd.edu,
University of California, San Diego – Op
Cetin, Haluk, (270) 809-2085 hcetin@murraystate.edu,
Murray State University – OiGe
Cetindag, Bahattin, 00904242370000-5957 bcetindag@firat.edu.tr,
Firat University – NgYv
Chachadi, Adiveppa G., +91-832-6519330 chachadi@unigoa.ac.in,
Goa University – HwYeHs
Chacko, Elizabeth, (202) 994-6185 echack@gwu.edu,
George Washington University – Oy
Chacko, Thomas, (780) 492-5395 tom.chacko@ualberta.ca,
University of Alberta – Gp
Chaddock, Lisa, 6196604000 x3033 Lisa.Chaddock@gcccd.edu,
Cuyamaca College – Oy
Chadima, Sarah A., 605-677-6166 sarah.chadima@usd.edu,
South Dakota Dept of Environment and Natural Resources – Gg
Chadwick, John , (843) 953-5950 chadwickj@cofc.edu,
College of Charleston – Gig
Chafetz, Henry S., 713-743-3227 hchafetz@uh.edu,
University of Houston – Gd
Chague-Goff, Catherine, c.chague-goff@unsw.edu.au,
University of New South Wales – CgGs
Chakhmouridian, Anton, (204) 474-7278 chakhmou@ms.umanitoba.ca,
University of Manitoba – Gz
Challads, Thomas, +44 (0) 131 650 8543 tchallan@staffmail.ed.ac.uk,
Edinburgh University – Hg
Challender, Stuart, (406) 994-7566 schallender@montana.edu,
Montana State University – Oi
Challinor, Andy, +44(0) 113 34 33194 a.j.challinor@leeds.ac.uk,
University of Leeds – Ow
Chamberlain, Andrew, +44 (0)161 306 4176 andrew.chamberlain@manchester.ac.uk,
University of Manchester – Ga
Chamberlain, Edwin P., (718) 951-5416 Los Alamos National Laboratory – Cc
Chamberlain, John A., (718) 951-5926 Graduate School of the City University of
New York – Po
Chamberlain, John A., 7189515000 x2885 johnc@brooklyn.cuny.edu,
Brooklyn College (CUNY) – Po
Chamberlain, Kevin R., (307) 766-2914 kchamber@uwyo.edu,
University of Wyoming – Cc
Chamberlin, Richard, 575.835.5310 richard@nmbg.nmt.edu,
New Mexico Institute of Mining and Technology – Gr
Chamberlin, Sean, 714-992-7443 schamberlin@fullcoll.edu,
Fullerton College – OgcOb
Chambers, Jeanne, 775-784-5329 chambers@unr.edu,
University of Nevada, Reno – SfHg
Chambers, John E., (202) 478-8855 jchambers@carnegiescience.edu,
Carnegie Institution of Washington – On
Chameides, William L., 613-8004 bill.chameides@duke.edu,
Duke University – OaGe
Champion, Kyle M., 813-253-7326 Hillsborough Community College – Og
Champlin, Steven D., (601) 961-5506 stephen_champlin@deq.state.ms.us,
Mississippi Office of Geology – Go
Chan, Clara, 302-831-1819 cschan@udel.edu,
University of Delaware – PyCmGz
Chan, Kwan M., (562) 985-4817 kmchan@csulb.edu,
California State University, Long Beach – Oc
Chan, Marjorie A., (801) 581-6551 marjorie.chan@utah.edu,
University of Utah – Gs
Chan, Selene, (604) 822-2034 schan@eos.ubc.ca,
University of British Columbia – On
Chandler, Angela, (501) 683-0111 angela.chandler@arkansas.gov,
Arkansas Geological Survey – GgaGg
Chandler, Cyndy, (508) 289-2765 cchandler@whoi.edu,
Woods Hole Oceanographic Institution – Og
Chandler, Kristopher, 770-274-5050 kristopher.chandler@gpc.edu,
Georgia Perimeter College – OnnOn
Chandler, Sandra, (501) 683-0125 sandra.chandler@arkansas.gov,
Arkansas Geological Survey – Oe
Chandler, Val W., 612-627-4780 (Ext. 203) chand004@umn.edu,
University of Minnesota, Twin Cities – Ye
Chandra, Sudeep, 775.784.6221 sudeep@unr.edu,
University of Nevada, Reno – Hs
Chaney, Phil L., (334) 844-3420 chanepl@auburn.edu,
Auburn University – OynOn
Chang, Chih-Pei, 831-656-2840 cpchang@nps.edu,
Naval Postgraduate School – Ow
Chang, Edmund K., (631) 632-6170 kar.chang@stonybrook.edu,
SUNY, Stony Brook – Oa
Chang, Hai-ru, hrc@eas.gatech.edu, Georgia Institute of Technology – Oa
Chang, Julie M., 405-325-7055 jmchang@ou.edu,
University of Oklahoma – GgOnn
Chang, Ping, (979) 845-8196 pchang@ocean.tamu.edu,
Texas A&M University – Op
Chang, Young-Soo, (630) 252-4076 changy@anl.gov,
Argonne National Laboratory – Oa
Channell, James E., 352-392-3658 jetc@ufl.edu,
University of Florida – YmGt
Channing, Alan, +44(0)29 208 76213 ChanningA@cardiff.ac.uk,
University of Wales – Gd

Chanway, Christopher, christopher.chanway@ubc.ca,
University of British Columbia – Sb
Chao, Shenn-Yu, (410) 221-8427 chao@hpl.umces.edu,
University of Maryland – Op
Chapin, Charles E., (505) 835-5613 chapin@gis.nmt.edu,
New Mexico Institute of Mining & Technology – Gt
Chapin, Charles E., 505-344-5817 chapin@gis.nmt.edu,
New Mexico Institute of Mining and Technology – Gv
Chapin, F. Stuart, (510) 642-1003 University of California, Berkeley – Pe
Chapman, Alan, chapman@macalester.edu,
Macalester College – Gct
Chapman, David S., (801) 581-7642 david.chapman@utah.edu,
University of Utah – Yh
Chapman, Mark, +44 (0)1603 59 3114 mark.chapman@uea.ac.uk,
University of East Anglia – Pm
Chapman, Mark, +44 (0) 131 650 8521 mchapman@staffmail.ed.ac.uk,
Edinburgh University – Yg
Chapman, Marshall, (606) 783-5397 m.chapman@moreheadstate.edu,
Morehead State University – Gv
Chapman, Martin C., (540) 231-5036 mcc@vt.edu,
Virginia Polytechnic Institute & State University – Ys
Chapman, Piers, 979 845 7211 piers.chapman@tamu.edu,
Texas A&M University – Oc
Chapman, Ross N., (250) 472-4340 chapman@uvic.ca,
University of Victoria – Op
Chappell, James R., (970) 491-5147 Jim_Chappell@partner.nps.gov,
Colorado State University – Ge
Chappell, P. D., 757-683-4937 pdchappe@odu.edu,
Old Dominion University – Oc
Chaput, Dominique, chaputdl@si.edu,
Smithsonian Institution / National Museum of Natural History – Py
Charette, Matthew A., (508) 289-3205 mcharette@whoi.edu,
Woods Hole Oceanographic Institution – Cm
Charles, Christopher D., (858) 534-5911 ccharles@ucsd.edu,
University of California, San Diego – Pe
Charles, Kasanzu, Kcharls16@yahoo.com,
University of Dar es Salaam – Ggh
Charlevoix, Donna J., (217) 244-9575 charlevo@atmos.uiuc.edu,
University of Illinois, Urbana-Champaign – Oa
Charlson, Robert J., charlson@chem.washington.edu,
University of Washington – Oa
Chase, Anne, (520) 621-6004 achase@email.arizona.edu,
University of Arizona – On
Chase, Clement G., (520) 621-2417 cgchase@email.arizona.edu,
University of Arizona – Yg
Chase, Jon M., jchase@biology2.wustl.edu,
Washington University – On
Chase, Peter M., (608) 265.6003 pmchase@wisc.edu,
University of Wisconsin, Extension – Gg
Chase, Richard L., (604) 822-3086 rchase@eos.ubc.ca,
University of British Columbia – Gu
Chasteen, Hayden R., 817-515-6694 hayden.chasteen@tccd.edu,
Tarrant County College- Northeast Campus – GgeGg
Chatelain, Edward E., (229) 333-5758 echatela@valdosta.edu,
Valdosta State University – Pi
Chatterjee, Ipsita, 940-565-2372 Ipsita.Chatterjee@unt.edu,
University of North Texas – On
Chatterjee, Meera, (330) 972-2394 meera@uakron.edu,
University of Akron – Oy
Chatterjee, Nilanjan, (617) 253-1995 nchat@mit.edu,
Massachusetts Institute of Technology – Cg
Chatterjee, Sankar, 806-834-4590 sankar.chatterjee@ttu.edu,
Texas Tech University – Pv
Chatterjee, Snehamoy, 906/487-2516 schatte1@mtu.edu,
Michigan Technological University – Nm
Chatterton, Brian D., (780) 492-3085 brian.chatterton@ualberta.ca,
University of Alberta – Pi
Chaubey, Indrajeet, (765) 494-5013 ichaubey@purdue.edu,
Purdue University – Hg
Chaudhuri, Sambhudas, (785) 532-2246 ksuncsc@ksu.edu,
Kansas State University – Cc
Chauff, Karl, (314) 977-3143 chauff@eas.slu.edu,
Saint Louis University – Pg
Chaumba, Jefferson B., (910) 522-5787 jefferson.chaumba@uncp.edu,
University of North Carolina, Pembroke – Gx
Chaussard, Estelle, estellec@buffalo.edu,
SUNY, Buffalo – GvOr
Chavrit, Deborah, +44 0161 275-0760 deborah.chavrit@manchester.ac.uk,
University of Manchester – Gi
Cheadle, Burns A., 519-661-2111 x.89009 bcheadle@uwo.ca,
Western University – Go
Cheadle, Michael J., (307) 766-3206 cheadle@uwyo.edu,
University of Wyoming – Yg
Chebana, Fateh, fateh.chebana@ete.inrs.ca, Universite du Quebec – Hq
Checkley, David M., (858) 534-4228 dcheckley@ucsd.edu,
University of California, San Diego – Ob
Cheek, William H., (417) 836-4589 billcheek@missouristate.edu,
Missouri State University – On
Cheel, Richard J., (905) 688-5550 (Ext. 3512) RCheel@brocku.ca,
Brock University – Gs

Chelton, Dudley B., (541) 737-4017 chelton@coas.oregonstate.edu,
Oregon State University – Op
Chen, Bob, bob.chen@umb.edu, University of Massachusetts, Boston – CoOc
Chen, Dake, (845) 365-8496 Columbia University – Op
Chen, Gang, (907)474-6875 gchen@alaska.edu,
University of Alaska, Fairbanks – Nm
Chen, Hway-Jen, 831-656-3788 hjchen@nps.edu,
Naval Postgraduate School – Ow
Chen, Jian-Hua, (978) 934-4861 jianhua_chen@uml.edu,
University of Massachusetts Lowell – Oa
Chen, Jingyi, 918-631-2517 jingyi-chen@utulsa.edu,
University of Tulsa – Yes
Chen, Jiquan, (419) 530-2664 jiquan.chen@utoledo.edu,
University of Toledo – On
Chen, Jiuhua, 305-348-3030 chenj@fiu.edu,
Florida International University – Gyz
Chen, Po, 307-766-3086 pchen@uwyo.edu,
University of Wyoming – YseYg
Chen, Shu-Hua, 530-752-1822 shachen@ucdavis.edu,
University of California, Davis – OraOw
Chen, Shuyi S., schen@rsmas.miami.edu, University of Washington – Oa
Chen, Tsing-Chang, (515) 294-9874 tmchen@iastate.edu,
Iowa State University of Science & Technology – Oa
Chen, Wang-Ping, wpchen@illinois.edu,
University of Illinois, Urbana-Champaign – Ys
Chen, Xianfeng, (724) 738-2385 xianfeng.chen@sru.edu,
Slippery Rock University – Or
Chen, Xiaowei, 508-289-3820 xiaowei.fengr@gmail.com,
University of Oklahoma – YsGt
Chen, Xun-Hong, (402) 472-0772 xchen2@unl.edu,
Unversity of Nebraska - Lincoln – Hq
Chen, Yi-Leng, yileng@hawaii.edu, University of Hawai'i, Manoa – Ow
Chen, Yongsheng, (416)736-2100 #40124 yochen@yorku.ca,
York University – Oa
Cheney, Donald, d.cheney@neu.edu, Northeastern University – On
Cheney, Eric S., 206-543-1163 vaalbara@uw.edu,
University of Washington – Eg
Cheney, John T., (413) 542-2311 Amherst College – Gi
Cheng, H. H., (612) 625-1793 hcheng@soils.umn.edu,
University of Minnesota, Twin Cities – Sb
Cheng, Hai, 612-624-9598 cheng021@umn.edu,
University of Minnesota, Twin Cities – Cc
Cheng, Meng-Dawn, (423) 241-5918 ucn@ornl.gov,
Oak Ridge National Laboratory – Oa
Cheng, Qiuming, (416)736-2100 #22842 qiuming@yorku.ca,
York University – Oi
Cheng, Songlin, 937 775-3455 songlin.cheng@wright.edu,
Wright State University – Hw
Cheng, Zhongqi, 7189515000 x2647 zcheng@brooklyn.cuny.edu,
Brooklyn College (CUNY) – Ca
Chenoweth, Cheri, 217-244-4610 cchenowe@illinois.edu,
University of Illinois, Urbana-Champaign – GoEc
Chenoweth, Sean, (318) 342-1887 chenoweth@ulm.edu,
University of Louisiana, Monroe – GmOir
Cherkauer, Douglas S., 414-229-4563 aquadoc@uwm.edu,
University of Wisconsin, Milwaukee – Hw
Chermak, John A., 540-231-1785 jchermak@vt.edu,
Virginia Polytechnic Institute & State University – Cg
Cherniak, Daniele J., (518) 276-3358 chernd@rpi.edu,
Rensselaer Polytechnic Institute – Gx
Chernoff, Barry, 860 6852452 bchernoff@wesleyan.edu,
Wesleyan University – Ge
Cherubini, Claudia, +33(0)3 44068977 claudia.cherubini@lasalle-beauvais.fr,
Institut Polytechnique LaSalle Beauvais (ex-IGAL) – HwGe
Cherukupalli, Nehru, 516 463-6545 geonec@hofstra.edu,
Hofstra University – Gg
Chesnaux, Romain, 418-545-5011 ext: 5426 rchesnaux@uqac.ca,
Universite du Quebec a Chicoutimi – Hw
Chesner, Craig A., 217-581-6323 cachesner@eiu.edu,
Eastern Illinois University – Gx
Chesnokov, Evgeny, 713-743-2579 emchesnokov@uh.edu,
University of Houston – YseYx
Chester, Frederick, (979) 845-3296 chesterf@tamu.edu,
Texas A&M University – GcNrYx
Chester, Judith, (979) 845-1380 chesterj@geo.tamu.edu,
Texas A&M University – GcNr
Chesworth, Ward, (519) 824-4120 (Ext. 52457) wcheswor@uoguelph.ca,
University of Guelph – Cl
Cheun, Norman, +44 020 8417 2811 K.W.Cheung@kingston.ac.uk,
Kingston University – Ge
Cheung, Wing, 7607441150 ext. 3652 wcheung@palomar.edu,
Palomar College – Oyi
Chew, David, + 353 1 8963481 chewd@tcd.ie, Trinity College – Cc
Chi, Wu-Cheng, 886-2-2783-9910 ext 510 wchi@sinica.edu.tw,
Academia Sinica – GtuGa
Chiappe, Luis M., (213) 863-3323 lchiappe@nhm.org,
Los Angeles County Museum of Natural History – Pv
Chiarello, Ronald P., (630) 252-9327 Argonne National Laboratory – Om
Chiarenzelli, Jeffrey R., 315-229-5202 jchiarenzelli@stlawu.edu,
St. Lawrence University – GzCg

Chief, Karletta, (520) 626-5598 kchief@email.arizona.edu,
University of Arizona – On
Chien, Yi-Ju, (509) 373-4822 Yi-Hu.chien@pnl.gov,
Pacific Northwest National Laboratory – Gq
Chieng, Sietan, 604-822-4426 chieng@mail.ubc.ca,
University of British Columbia – Sp
Childers, Daniel, (610) 359-5242 dchilder@dccc.edu,
Delaware County Community College – Og
Childs, Geoff, gchilds@wustl.edu, Washington University – On
Chillrud, Steven, (845) 365-8893 Columbia University – Cg
Chilvers, Jason, +44 (0)1603 59 3130 jason.chilvers@uea.ac.uk,
University of East Anglia – Ge
Chin, Anne, (409) 845-7141 Texas A&M University – Gm
Chin, Karen, 303-735-3074 karen.chin@colorado.edu,
University of Colorado – Po
Chin, Yu-Ping, (614) 292-6953 yo@geology.ohio-state.edu,
Ohio State University – Hg
Chipperfield, Martyn, +44(0) 113 34 36459 m.chipperfield@leeds.ac.uk,
University of Leeds – Oa
Chipping, David H., (805) 756-1695 dchippin@calpoly.edu,
California Polytechnic State University – Grt
Chirenje, Tait, 609-652-4588 tait.chirenje@stockton.edu,
Richard Stockton College of New Jersey – Sc
Chiu, Ching-Sang, (831) 656-3239 chiu@nps.edu,
Naval Postgraduate School – Op
Chiu, Jer-Ming, (901) 678-2007 jerchiu@memphis.edu,
University of Memphis – Ys
Chiu, Long S., (703) 993-1984 lchiu@gmu.edu,
George Mason University – Oa
Chiu, Shu-Choiung, (901) 678-2007 sachi@memphis.edu,
University of Memphis – Ys
Choh, Suk-Joo, 82-2-3290-3180 sjchoh@korea.ac.kr,
Korea University – GdsPg
Choi, Eunseo, (901) 678-4923 echoi2@memphis.edu,
University of Memphis – Gt
Choi, Seon-Gyu, 82-2-3290-3174 seongyu@korea.ac.kr,
Korea University – GzEmg
Chokmani, Karem, karem.chokmani@ete.inrs.ca, Universite du Quebec – Oi
Cholnoky, Jennifer, 518-580-8127 jcholnok@skidmore.edu,
Skidmore College – Gg
Chopin, Suzzette, 361-825-6022 Suzzette.Chopin@tamucc.edu,
Texas A&M University, Corpus Christi – On
Chopping, Mark J., 973-655-4448 choppingm@mail.montclair.edu,
Montclair State University – Or
Chormann, Jr., Frederick H., (603) 2711975 Frederick.Chormann@des.nh.gov,
New Hampshire Geological Survey – HyOiGm
Chorover, Jonathan D., (520) 626-5635 chorover@cals.arizona.edu,
University of Arizona – Cg
Chou, Charissa J., (509) 372-3804 Charissa.chou@pnl.gov,
Pacific Northwest National Laboratory – Gq
Chou, Mei-In (Melissa), 217-244-0312 chou@isgs.uiuc.edu,
Illinois State Geological Survey – Co
Chou, Sheng-Fu Joseph, 217-244-2744 jchou@isgs.uiuc.edu,
Illinois State Geological Survey – Co
Chouinard, Kyle, (269) 387-5486 kyle.chouinard@wmich.edu,
Western Michigan University – OnnOn
Chouinard, Vera, (905) 525-9140 (Ext. 23518) chouinar@mcmaster.ca,
McMaster University – On
Choularton, Thomas , +44 0161 306-3950 choularton@manchester.ac.uk,
University of Manchester – Oa
Chow, Nancy, (204) 474-6451 n_chow@umanitoba.ca,
University of Manitoba – Gs
Chowdhury, Dipak K , (260) 481-6249 chowdhur@ipfw.edu,
Indiana University / Purdue University, Fort Wayne – Ys
Chowdhury, Shafiul H., chowdhus@newpaltz.edu, SUNY, New Paltz – Hw
Chown, Edward H., (418) 545-5011 Universite du Quebec a Chicoutimi – Gx
Chowns, Timothy M., (678) 839-4052 tchowns@westga.edu,
University of West Georgia – Gs
Christensen, Beth A., 516-877-4174 christensen@adelphi.edu,
Adelphi University – PmeGs
Christensen, Douglas, doug@giseis.alaska.edu,
University of Alaska Fairbanks – Ys
Christensen, Nikolas I., (608) 265-4469 chris@geology.wisc.edu,
University of Wisconsin, Madison – Yx
Christensen, Philip R., (480) 965-7105 phil.christensen@asu.edu,
Arizona State University – Xg
Christensen, Wesley P., 605-677-6149 wes.christensen@usd.edu,
South Dakota Dept of Environment and Natural Resources – Gg
Christeson, Gail L., (512) 471-6156 gail@ig.utexas.edu,
University of Texas at Austin – Yr
Christian, Alan D., alan.christian@umb.edu,
University of Massachusetts, Boston – OnGmCs
Christiansen, Eric H., 801422 2113 eric_christiansen@byu.edu,
Brigham Young University – GiXgEm
Christie-Blick, Nicholas, (845) 365-8821 Columbia University – Gs
Chrzan, Daryl, (510) 643-1624 dcchrzan@berkeley.edu ,
University of California, Berkeley – Om
Chrzastowski, Michael J., (217) 284-2194 chrzasto@isgs.uiuc.edu,
Illinois State Geological Survey – Ou
Chu, Pao-Shin, chu@hawaii.edu,

University of Hawai'i, Manoa – Oa
Chu, Peter C., (831) 656-3688 pcchu@nps.edu,
Naval Postgraduate School – Op
Chu, Xu , 716 673 3817 xu.chu@fredonia.edu,
SUNY, Fredonia – Giz
Chuang, Patrick Y., (831) 459-1501 pchuang@pmc.ucsc.edu,
University of California, Santa Cruz – Oa
Church, Ian, (228) 688-1510 ian.church@usm.edu,
University of Southern Mississippi – Hg
Church, Matthew, (808) 956-8779 mjchurch@hawaii.edu,
University of Hawai'i, Manoa – Ob
Church, Thomas M., (302) 831-2558 tchurch@udel.edu,
University of Delaware – Cm
Church, William R., (519) 661-3192 wrchurch@uwo.ca,
Western University – Gt
Churchill, Ron C., (916) 327-0745 California Geological Survey – Cg
Churnet, Habte G., (423) 425-4407 habte-churnet@utc.edu,
University of Tennessee at Chattanooga – GxgOg
Chyba, Christopher F., (650) 725-6468 cchyba@princeton.edu,
Stanford University – Gh
Ciampitti, Ignacio, (785) 532-6940 ciampitti@ksu.edu,
Kansas State University – So
Cianfrani, Christina, ccNS@hampshire.edu, Hampshire College – Hw
Ciannelli, Lorenzo, 541-737-3142 lciannelli@coas.oregonstate.edu,
Oregon State University – Ob
Cicerone, Robert, rcicerone@bridgew.edu, Bridgewater State University – Ys
Ciciarelli, John A., (412) 773-3867 jac7@psu.edu,
Pennsylvania State University, Monaca – Gg
Cicimurri, Christian M., (864) 650-8456 cmcici@clemson.edu,
Clemson University – Pv
Cicimurri, David J., (864) 656-4601 dcheech@clemson.edu,
Clemson University – Pv
Ciesielski, Paul F., (352) 392-2231 pciesiel@ufl.edu,
University of Florida – Pm
Ciesla, Fred, (773) 702-8169 University of Chicago – Xcg
Cifelli, Richard L., (405) 325-4712 rlc@ou.edu,
University of Oklahoma – Pv
Cigolini, Corrdao, corrado.cigolini@unito.it, Università di Torino – Gv
Cihacek, Larry J., (701) 231-8572 North Dakota State University – Og
Cilliers, Johannes, +44 20 759 47360 j.j.cilliers@imperial.ac.uk,
Imperial College – Gz
Ciolkosz, Edward J., (814) 865-1530 f8i@psu.edu,
Pennsylvania State University, University Park – Sd
Cioppa, Maria T., 519-253-3000 ext. 2502 mcioppa@uwindsor.ca,
University of Windsor – Ym
Cipar, John J., 617-552-8300 cipar@bc.edu, Boston College – Ys
Cirmo, Christopher P., (607) 753-2924 cirmoc@cortland.edu,
SUNY, Cortland – Hg
Cisne, John L., john.cisne@cornell.edu, Cornell University – Pg
Civan, Faruk, (405) 325-6778 fcivan@ou.edu,
University of Oklahoma – Np
Claassen, Johann, +27 (0)51 401 2593 claassenjo@ufs.ac.za,
University of the Free State – Nx
Claassen, Mark, (785) 532-6101 mclaasse@ksu.edu,
Kansas State University – So
Clabo, Darren R., 605-394-1996 Darren.Clabo@sdsmt.edu,
South Dakota School of Mines & Technology – OaaOa
Claerbout, Jon F., (650) 723-3717 Stanford University – Ye
Claeys, Philippe, 322 629-3391 phclaeys@vub.ac.be,
Vrije University Brussel – CgPyXc
Clague, David A., (808) 967-8819 clague@mbari.org,
University of Hawai'i, Manoa – Giv
Clague, David A., clague@mbari.org, Stanford University – Ob
Clague, John J., (604) 291-5387 Simon Fraser University – Gl
Claiborne, Lily L., 615-343-4515 lily.claiborne@vanderbilt.edu,
Vanderbilt University – GiCg
Claire, Mark, +44 01334 463688 mc229@st-andrews.ac.uk,
University of St. Andrews – Oa
Clapham, Matthew E., 831-459-1276 mclapham@pmc.ucsc.edu,
University of California, Santa Cruz – Pe
Clarey, Timothy L., (989) 686-9252 tlclarey@delta.edu,
Delta College – HwGcPv
Clark, Alan H., (613) 533-6187 Queen's University – Em
Clark, David L., (505) 665-0005 Los Alamos National Laboratory – On
Clark, David L., (608) 262-4972 dlc@geology.wisc.edu,
University of Wisconsin, Madison – Pm
Clark, Donald, (801) 537-3344 donclark@utah.gov,
Utah Geological Survey – Gg
Clark, Douglas H., (360) 650-7939 doug.clark@wwu.edu,
Western Washington University – Gl
Clark, G. Michael, (865) 974-6006 clarkgmorph@utk.edu,
University of Tennessee, Knoxville – Gm
Clark, George S., (204) 474-7343 gs_clark@umanitoba.ca,
University of Manitoba – Cc
Clark, H. C., (713) 527-4887 hcclark@owlnet.rice.edu,
Rice University – Ng
Clark, Ian D., 613 562-5800 Ext 6834 idclark@uottawa.ca,
University of Ottawa – Hw
Clark, James A., (630) 752-5163 james.clark@wheaton.edu,
Wheaton College – GmHy

Los Alamos National Laboratory – Oa

Costin, Gelu, +27 (0)46-603-8316 g.costin@ru.ac.za,
Rhodes University – Gp

Cote, Denis, (418) 545-5011 dcote@uqac.ca,
Universite du Quebec a Chicoutimi – Gi

Côté, Jean, 514 987-3000 #2351 cote.jean@uqam.ca,
Universite du Quebec a Montreal – Oa

Cote, Pascale, (418) 654-2601 pacote@nrcan.gc.ca,
Universite du Quebec – On

Cothren, Jackson D., (479) 575-6790 jcothre@uark.edu,
University of Arkansas, Fayetteville – Oi

Cottaar, Sanne , sc845@cam.ac.uk,
University of Cambridge – Ys

Cotter, James F., (320) 589-6312 cotterjf@mrs.umn.edu,
University of Minnesota, Morris – Gl

Cottingame, William, (505) 667-8339 wcottingame@lanl.gov,
Los Alamos National Laboratory – Oa

Cottle, John, (805) 893-3471 cottle@geol.ucsb.edu,
University of California, Santa Barbara – Gi

Cottrell, Elizabeth, (202) 633-1859 cottrelle@si.edu,
Smithsonian Institution / National Museum of Natural History – Cp

Cottrell, Rory D., rory@earth.rochester.edu, University of Rochester – Ym

Couceiro, Fay, +44 023 92 842294 fay.couceiro@port.ac.uk,
University of Portsmouth – On

Coulibaly, Paulin, (905) 525-9140 (Ext. 23354) couliba@mcmaster.ca,
McMaster University – Hg

Coull, Bruce C., 803-777-8997 bccoull@sc.edu,
University of South Carolina – Obn

Coulson, Alan B., (864) 656-1897 acoulso@clemson.edu,
Clemson University – PoGgCs

Coulter, Richard L., (631) 252-5833 rcoulter@anl.gov,
Argonne National Laboratory – Ow

Couples, Gary, +44 (0) 131 451 3123 gary.couples@pet.hw.ac.uk,
Heriot-Watt University – Np

Cousineau, Pierre, (418) 545-5011 pcousine@uqac.ca,
Universite du Quebec a Chicoutimi – Gd

Couture, Gilles, 514-987-3000 #8905 couture.gilles@uqam.ca,
Universite du Quebec a Montreal – Yg

Cova, Thomas J., (801) 581-7930 tom.cova@geog.utah.edu,
University of Utah – Oi

Coveney, Raymond M., (816) 235-2980 coveneyr@umkc.edu,
University of Missouri-Kansas City – Em

Coveney, Seamus, +44 0141 330 7750 Seamus.Coveney@glasgow.ac.uk,
University of Glasgow – Oi

Covert, David S., 206-685-7461 dcovert@atmos.washington.edu,
University of Washington – Oa

Covey, Aaron K., 615-322-2976 aaron.k.covey@vanderbilt.edu,
Vanderbilt University – Ge

Covington, Matthew, 479-575-3876 mcoving@uark.edu,
University of Arkansas, Fayetteville – HqGmg

Cowan, Clinton A., 507-222-7021 ccowan@carleton.edu,
Carleton College – Gs

Cowan, Darrel S., 206-543-4033 darrel@uw.edu,
University of Washington – Gct

Cowan, Ellen A., (828) 262-2260 cowanea@appstate.edu,
Appalachian State University – Gma

Cowart, James B., (850) 644-5784 jcowart@mailer.fsu.edu,
Florida State University – Cc

Cowart, Richard, (361) 644-3049Å recowart@coastalbend.edu,
Coastal Bend College – Og

Cowen, Richard, richard@blueaokfarm.com,
University of California, Davis – Po

Cowgill, Eric S., 530-754-6574 escowgill@ucdavis.edu,
University of California, Davis – Gc

Cowie, Gregory L., +44 (0) 131 650 8502 Dr.Greg.Cowie@ed.ac.uk,
Edinburgh University – Co

Cowles, Timothy J., tjc@coas.oregonstate.edu, Oregon State University – Ob

Cowman, Tim C., 605-677-6151 tim.cowman@usd.edu,
South Dakota Dept of Environment and Natural Resources – CgGg

Cox, Charles S., (858) 534-3235 cscox@ucsd.edu,
University of California, San Diego – Op

Cox, Christena, (614) 292-0138 cox.1@osu.edu,
Ohio State University – GgoGc

Cox, Helen M., 818-677-3512 helen.m.cox@csun.edu,
California State University, Northridge – OwgOr

Cox, John, (403) 440-6160 jcox@mtroyal.ca,
Mount Royal University – Eo

Cox, Malcolm E., 61 7 3138 1649 m.cox@qut.edu.au,
Queensland University of Technology – Hw

Cox, Randel T., (901) 678-4870 randycox@memphis.edu,
University of Memphis – GtcGm

Cox, Ronadh, (413) 597-2297 ronadh.cox@williams.edu,
Williams College – Gs

Cox, Shelah, 215 204-8227 scox@temple.edu,
Temple University – On

Cox, Shelley M., (323) 857-6318 scox@bcf.usc.edu,
Los Angeles County Museum of Natural History – Pv

Coxon, Catherine, + 353 1 8962235 cecoxon@tcd.ie,
Trinity College – GeOu

Craddock, John P., (651) 696-6620 craddock@macalester.edu,

Macalester College – Gc

Craddock, Robert A., 202-633-2473 Smithsonian Institution / National Air & Space Museum – Xg

Craig, James L., (505) 665-7996 jlcraig@lanl.gov,
Los Alamos National Laboratory – Gg

Craig, James R., (540) 231-5222 jrcraig@vt.edu,
Virginia Polytechnic Institute & State University – Eg

Craig, Mitchell S., (510) 885-3425 mitchell.craig@csueastbay.edu,
California State University, East Bay – Yg

Craig, Susanne , (902) 494-4381 susanne.craig@dal.ca,
Dalhousie University – Op

Crain, John R., (209) 730-3812 College of the Sequoias – Gg

Cramer, Bradley D., 785-842-1956 bradley-cramer@uiowa.edu,
University of Iowa – GrPsGs

Cramer, Chris, (901) 678-2007 ccramer@memphis.edu,
University of Memphis – Ys

Cramer, Gary, (620) 662-9021 gcramer@ksu.edu,
Kansas State University – So

Crane, Kathleen, (212) 772-5265 Graduate School of the City University of New York – Yh

Crane, Nicholas J., 740-368-3624 njcrane@owu.edu,
Ohio Wesleyan University – Ou

Crane, Peter, 203-432-5109 peter.crane@yale.edu,
Yale University – Pbo

Crane, Peter R., (773) 922-9410 University of Chicago – Po

Cranford, Peter, (902) 426-3277 cranfordp@mar.dfo-mpo.gc.ca,
Dalhousie University – Ob

Cranganu, Constantin, 7189515000 x2878 cranganu@brooklyn.cuny.edu,
Brooklyn College (CUNY) – Go

Crapster-Pregont, Ellen J., 212-769-5083 ellencp@ldeo.columbia.edu,
American Museum of Natural History – Xm

Craven, John, +44 (0) 131 650 7887 John.Craven@ed.ac.uk,
Edinburgh University – Yg

Craw, Dave, +64 3 479-7529 dave.craw@otago.ac.nz,
University of Otago – Eg

Crawford, Anthony J., 61 3 6226 2490 Tony.Crawford@utas.edu.au,
University of Tasmania – Gi

Crawford, Ian, +44 020 3073 8026 i.crawford@bbk.ac.uk,
Birkbeck College – On

Crawford, Ian, +44 0161 306-6850 I.Crawford@manchester.ac.uk,
University of Manchester – Oa

Crawford, James, 757-864-7231 j.h.crawford@larc.nasa.gov,
Georgia Institute of Technology – Oa

Crawford, Maria Luisa B., (610) 526-5111 mcrawfor@brynmawr.edu,
Bryn Mawr College – Gx

Crawford, Matt, 859.323.0510 mcrawford@uky.edu,
University of Kentucky – On

Crawford, Nicholas, (270) 745-5889 nicholas.crawford@wku.edu,
Western Kentucky University – Hg

Crawford, Thomas J., (678) 839-4062 University of West Georgia – Eg

Crawford, Vernon J., (541) 552-6479 crawford@sou.edu,
Southern Oregon University – Gg

Crawford, William A., (610) 526-5112 Bryn Mawr College – Cg

Creager, Kenneth C., 206-685-2803 kcc@ess.washington.edu,
University of Washington – Ys

Crease, James, (302) 645-4240 University of Delaware – Op

Creaser, Robert A., (780) 492-2942 robert.creaser@ualberta.ca,
University of Alberta – Cc

Creasey, Robert L., 831-656-3178 creasey@nps.edu,
Naval Postgraduate School – Ow

Creasy, John W., (207) 786-6153 jcreasy@bates.edu,
Bates College – Gx

Creech-Eakman, Michelle, 575-835-6756 mce@kestrel.nmt.edu,
New Mexico Institute of Mining and Technology – XgPy

Creed, Irena F., 519-661-2111 ext.84265 icreed@uwo.ca,
Western University – OnSfPy

Crelling, John C., (618) 453-7361 jcrelling@geo.siu.edu,
Southern Illinois University Carbondale – Ec

Crepeau, Richard J., (828) 262-7052 crepeaurj@appstate.edu,
Appalachian State University – Cc

Crespi, Jean M., (860) 486-0601 crespi@geol.uconn.edu,
University of Connecticut – Gc

Creveling, Jessica, 541-737-2112 crevelij@oregonstate.edu,
Oregon State University – GgsGr

Crews, Jeff, (573) 368-2356 jeff.crews@dnr.mo.gov,
Missouri Dept of Natural Resources – Hy

Cribb, Warner, (615) 898-2379 warner.cribb@mtsu.edu,
Middle Tennessee State University – GipGz

Crider, Juliet, 206-543-8715 juliet.crider@ess.washington.edu,
University of Washington – Gc

Criminale, Jr., William O., (206) 543-9506 lascala@amath.washington.edu,
University of Washington – Op

Crimmins, Michael, (520) 626-4244 crimmins@u.arizona.edu,
University of Arizona – On

Crippen, Robert E., (818) 354-2475 robert.e.crippen@jpl.nasa.gov,
Jet Propulsion Laboratory – Or

Crisp, Joy A., (818) 354-9036 Jet Propulsion Laboratory – Gv

Criss, Robert E., (314) 935-7441 criss@levee.wustl.edu,
Washington University in St. Louis – Cs

Criswell, James, (910) 392-7536 jcriswell@cfcc.edu,

D

Southern Oregon University – Gc

D'Alpaos, Andrea, +390498279117 andrea.dalpaos@unipd.it, Università degli Studi di Padova – Hs

D'Amico, Sebastiano, +356 2340 3101 sebdamico@gmail.com, University of Malta – YsgOg

D'Antonio, Carla, (510) 643-6341 University of California, Berkeley – Pe

D'Asaro, Eric A., (206) 545-2982 dasaro@apl.washington.edu, University of Washington – Op

d'Atri, Anna, anna.datri@unito.it, Università di Torino – Gr

D'Hondt, Steven L., (401) 792-6808 dhondt@gso.uri.edu, University of Rhode Island – Ou

D'Odorico, Paolo, (434) 924-7241 pd6v@virginia.edu, University of Virginia – Hg

da Silva, Eduardo F., eafsilva@ua.pt, Universidade de Aveiro – CeGbCl

Daanen, Ronald P., (907)451-5965 ronald.daanen@alaska.gov, Division of Geological & Geophysical Surveys – Ng

Dade, William B., 603-646-0286 William.B.Dade@Dartmouth.edu, Dartmouth College – GsHgEo

Daemen, Jaak, (775) 7844309 daemen@mines.unr.edu, University of Nevada, Reno – Nr

Daeschler, Ted, 215 299 1133 ebd29@drexel.edu, Drexel University – PvGgPy

Dagdelen, Kadri, (303) 273-3711 kdagdele@mines.edu, Colorado School of Mines – Nm

Dahl, Johannes M., 806-834-6197 johannes.dahl@ttu.edu, Texas Tech University – Owa

Dahlgran, Randy, 530-752-2814 radahlgren@ucdavis.edu, University of California, Davis – Sc

Dahlke, Helen E., hdahlke@ucdavis.edu, University of California, Davis – Hg

Dai, Dajun, 404 413 5750 geoddd@langate.gsu.edu, Georgia State University – Oi

Daigneault, Real, (418) 545-5011 rdaignea@uqac.ca, Universite du Quebec a Chicoutimi – GcEgOi

Dakin, Susan, (403) 329-2279 susan.dakin@uleth.ca, University of Lethbridge – Oe

Dalconi, Maria C., +390498279163 mariachiara.dalconi@unipd.it, Università degli Studi di Padova – Gz

Dale, Chris, +44 (0) 191 33 42342 christopher.dale@durham.ac.uk, Durham University – Oa

Dale, Janis, (306) 585-4840 University of Regina – Gml

Daley, Gwen M., 803-323-4973 daleyg@winthrop.edu, Winthrop University – PqgGs

Dallegge, Todd A., 970-351-1086 Todd.Dallegge@unco.edu, University of Northern Colorado – GosGr

Dallimer, Martin, +44(0) 113 34 35279 M.Dallimer@leeds.ac.uk, University of Leeds – Ge

Dallmeyer, R. David, (706) 542-7448 dallmeyr@uga.edu, University of Georgia – Gt

Dalman, Michael, (979) 830-4206 mdalman@blinn.edu, Blinn College – Gg

Dalrymple, Robert W., (613) 533-6186 dalrympl@queensu.ca, Queen's University – Gs

Dalton, Colleen, 401-863-5875 Colleen_Dalton@brown.edu, Brown University – Ys

Dalton, Richard F., (609) 292-2576 richard.dalton@dep.nj.gov, New Jersey Geological Survey – Gr

Daly, Eve, +353 (0)91 492 183 eve.daly@nuigalway.ie, National University of Ireland Galway – Yg

Daly, Julia F., 207-778-7403 dalyj@maine.edu, University of Maine - Farmington – GmlGu

Daly, Kendra L., (727) 553-1041 kdaly@marine.usf.edu, University of South Florida – Ob

Daly, Raymond J., daly@ucc.edu, Union County College – Pv

Dalziel, Ian W. D., (512) 471-0431 ian@ig.utexas.edu, University of Texas at Austin – Gt

Dam, Hans G., 860-405-9098 hans.dam@uconn.edu, University of Connecticut – Ob

Damir, Buckoviæ, +38514606106 buckovic@geol.pmf.hr, University of Zagreb – GgPms

Damschen, Ellen, damschen@wustl.edu, Washington University – On

Damuth, John, (817) 272-2987 damuth@uta.edu, University of Texas, Arlington – GsuYr

Dana, Gayle L., (775) 674-7538 gdana@dri.edu, University of Nevada, Reno – Or

Daniel, Christopher G., (570) 577-1133 cdaniel@bucknell.edu, Bucknell University – Gp

Daniels, Jeffrey J., (614) 292-1039 daniels.9@osu.edu, Ohio State University – Yg

Daniels, Walter L., (540) 231-7175 wdaniels@vt.edu, Virginia Polytechnic Institute & State University – Sd

Daniels, William R., (505) 667-4546 Los Alamos National Laboratory – Ct

Danko, George, (775) 784-4284 danko@mines.unr.edu, University of Nevada, Reno – Hq

Dannevik, William P., (314) 977-3115 dannevik@eas.slu.edu, Saint Louis University – Oa

Dansereau, Pauline, dansero@ggl.ulaval.ca, Universite Laval – Gs

Daoust, Mario, 417-836-5301 mariodaoust@missouristate.edu, Missouri State University – Oa

Daramola, Sunday O., 08060256588 sunday.daramola@gmail.com,

Federal University of Technology, Akure – GgNg

Darby, Dennis A., (757) 683-4701 ddarby@odu.edu, Old Dominion University – Ou

Darby, Jeannie, (916) 752-5670 University of California, Davis – Hg

Darbyshire, Fiona Ann, 514-987-3000 #5054 darbyshire.fiona_ann@uqam.ca, Universite du Quebec a Montreal – Ys

Dare, Sarah, 613-562-5800 6859 sdare@uottawa.ca, University of Ottawa – Gz

Dark, Shawna J., 818-677-6937 shawna.dark@csun.edu, California State University, Northridge – Oi

Darling, James, +44 023 92 842247 james.darling@port.ac.uk, University of Portsmouth – Cs

Darling, Robert S., (607) 753-2923 darlingr@cortland.edu, SUNY, Cortland – Gx

Darmody, Robert G., (217) 333-9489 University of Illinois, Urbana-Champaign – Sd

Darold, Amberlee, 405/325-8611 Amberlee.P.Darold-1@ou.edu, University of Oklahoma – Ys

Daroub, Samira H., (561) 993-1500 sdaroub@ufl.edu, University of Florida – So

Darrah, Thomas, (614) 688-2132 darrah.24@osu.edu, Ohio State University – Ge

Darrell, James H., (912) 478-5361 JDarrell@GeorgiaSouthern.edu, Georgia Southern University – Pl

Darroch, Simon, simon.a.darroch@vanderbilt.edu, Vanderbilt University – Poi

Das, Sarah B., 508-289-2464 sdas@whoi.edu, Woods Hole Oceanographic Institution – Pm

Dasgupta, Rajdeep, 713.348.2664 Rajdeep.Dasgupta@rice.edu, Rice University – GxCg

Dasgupta, Tathagata, 330-672-4104 tdasgupt@kent.edu, Kent State University – Cg

Dash, Padmanava, 662-325-3915 pd175@msstate.edu, Mississippi State University – OrHg

Dash, Zora V., (505) 667-1923 zvd@lanl.gov, Los Alamos National Laboratory – On

Datta, Saugata, (785) 532-2241 sdatta@ksu.edu, Kansas State University – ClHwGe

Dattilo, Benjamin F., 260-481-6250 dattilob@ipfw.edu, Indiana University / Purdue University, Fort Wayne – GrPiGs

Daugherty, LeRoy A., (505) 646-3406 New Mexico State University, Las Cruces – Sd

Dauphas, Nicolas, (773) 702-2930 University of Chicago – Xc

Davatzes, Alexandra, (215) 204-3907 alix@temple.edu, Temple University – Gs

Davatzes, Nicholas, (215) 204-2837 davatzes@temple.edu, Temple University – GcNr

Davenport, Joan R., (509) 786-9384 jdavenp@tricity.wsu.edu, Washington State University – Sb

Davey, Patricia M., 863-2449 patricia_davey@brown.edu, Brown University – On

David, Eric, (418) 656-8116 eric.david@ggl.ulaval.ca, Universite Laval – On

David, Mark B., (217) 333-4308 dmnicol@illinois.edu, University of Illinois, Urbana-Champaign – Sf

Davidson, Bart, 859-323-0524 bdavidson@uky.edu, University of Kentucky – Hg

Davidson, Cameron, 507-222-7144 cdavidso@carleton.edu, Carleton College – Gx

Davidson, Fiona M., (479) 575-3879 fdavidso@comp.uark.edu, University of Arkansas, Fayetteville – Ou

Davidson, Garry J., 61 3 6226 2815 Garry.Davidson@utas.edu.au, University of Tasmania – Ys

Davidson, Gregg R., (662) 915-5824 davidson@olemiss.edu, University of Mississippi – Hw

Davidson, Jon, +44 (0) 191 33 42328 j.p.davidson@durham.ac.uk, Durham University – Cm

Davidson, Kenneth L., 831-656-2309 kldavids@nps.edu, Naval Postgraduate School – Ow

Davie, Colin, +44 (0) 191 208 6458 colin.davie@ncl.ac.uk, University of Newcastle Upon Tyne – Ng

Davies, Caroline P., daviesc@umkc.edu, University of Missouri-Kansas City – Pl

Davies, David, +44 (0) 131 451 3569 david.davies@pet.hw.ac.uk, Heriot-Watt University – Ng

Davies, Gareth, g.r.davies@vu.nl, VU University Amsterdam – GivGf

Davies, Gareth, +44(0)7780864555 gareth.davies@open.ac.uk , The Open University – Ge

Davies, J H., huw@earth.cf.ac.uk, Cardiff University – Yg

Davies, James F., 7056751151, ext. 2298 Laurentian University, Sudbury – Em

Davies, Neil, +44 (0) 1223 333453 nsd27@cam.ac.uk, University of Cambridge – Gs

Davies, Rhodri, +44 20 759 45722 rhodri.davies@imperial.ac.uk, Imperial College – Yg

Davies, Richard, +44 (0) 191 33 49308 richard.davies@durham.ac.uk, Durham University – Eo

Davies, Sarah, sarah.davies@open.ac.uk, The Open University – Oe

Davies, Sarah, +440116 252 3624 sjd27@le.ac.uk, Leicester University – Gs

Davies-Vollum, Katherine Sian, 206-692-4626 ksdavies@u.washington.edu, University of Washington – GsrPe

Davis, Andrew, (773) 702-8164 University of Chicago – Xc

DeGaetano, Arthur, (607) 255-0385 atd2@cornell.edu,
Cornell University – Oa
deGroot, Robert, 657-278-8275 rdegroot@fullerton.edu,
California State University, Fullerton – Gg
Degryse, Patrick, patrick.degryse@ees.kuleuven.be,
Katholieke Universiteit Leuven – GaCeGf
Dehler, Carol M., (435) 797-0764 carol.dehler@usu.edu,
Utah State University – Gs
Dehne, Kevin T., (989) 686-9326 ktdehne@delta.edu,
Delta College – Oe
Deibert, Jack, (931) 221-6318 deibertj@apsu.edu,
Austin Peay State University – Gsr
Deininger, Robert W., (901) 678-2177 University of Memphis – Gx
Deisher, Jeffrey , 740 548 7348 Ohio Dept of Natural Resources – Eo
Deka, Jennifer, (216) 987-5827 Jennifer.Deka@tri-c.edu,
Cuyahoga Community College - Western Campus – Og
Dekens, Petra, (415) 338-6015 dekens@sfsu.edu,
San Francisco State University – Pe
DeKraker, Dan, 562-860-2451 ext.2668 ddekraker@cerritos.edu,
Cerritos College – Oe
Delaney, Jeremy S., (848) 445-3616 jsd@rci.rutgers.edu,
Rutgers, The State University of New Jersey – XgmGx
Delaney, John R., (206) 543-4830 jdelaney@u.washington.edu,
University of Washington – Yr
Delaney, Margaret L., (831) 459-4736 delaney@cats.ucsc.edu,
University of California, Santa Cruz – Oc
Delano, Helen L., 717.702.2031 hdelano@pa.gov,
Pennsylvania Bureau of Topographic & Geologic Survey – GgmNg
DeLaune, Paul, 940-552-9941x207 pbdelaune@ag.tamu.edu,
Texas A&M University – Os
Delawder, Sandra, delawdsa@jmu.edu,
James Madison University – On
Deline, Brad, (678) 839-4061 bdeline@westga.edu,
University of West Georgia – Pi
Dellapenna, Timothy M., (409) 740-4952 dellapet@tamug.tamu.edu,
Texas A&M University – Ou
Delparte, Donna M., 208-282-4419 delparte@isu.edu,
Idaho State University – Oi
DelSole, Timothy, 703-993-5715 tdelsole@gmu.edu,
George Mason University – Oa
Delson, Eric, (718) 960-8405 delson@amnh.org,
Graduate School of the City University of New York – Pv
Delusina, Irina, (530) 752-1861 idelusina@ucdavis.edu,
University of California, Davis – Pl
DeMaster, David J., (919) 515-7026 david_demaster@ncsu.edu,
North Carolina State University – Oc
Demchak, Jennifer, 570-662-4613 jdemchak@mansfield.edu,
Mansfield University – Hs
Demers, Serge, (418) 723-1986 (Ext. 1483) Universite du Quebec a Rimouski – Ob
DeMets, D. Charles, (608) 262-8598 chuck@geology.wisc.edu,
University of Wisconsin, Madison – Ym
Demicco, Robert V., (607) 777-2604 demicco@binghamton.edu,
Binghamton University – Gs
Deming, Jody, jdeming@u.washington.edu, University of Manitoba – On
Deming, Jody W., (206) 543-0845 jdeming@u.washington.edu,
University of Washington – Ob
Demopoulos, George, (514) 398-4755 McGill University – Nx
Demosthenous, Christie M., (920) 424-7167 demosthe@uwosh.edu,
University of Wisconsin, Oshkosh – Gz
Dempsey, David P., (415) 338-7716 ddempsey@norte.sfsu.edu,
San Francisco State University – Oa
Dempster, Tim, +4401413305445 Tim.Dempster@glasgow.ac.uk,
University of Glasgow – Gz
Demyanov, Vasily, +44 (0) 131 451 8298 vasily.demyanov@pet.hw.ac.uk,
Heriot-Watt University – Oi
Den Ouden, Amy, amy.denouden@umb.edu,
University of Massachusetts, Boston – OnGa
Deng, Aijun, (814) 863-8253 axd157@psu.edu,
Pennsylvania State University, University Park – Ow
Deng, Baolin, (505) 835-5505 New Mexico Institute of Mining and Technology – Cg
Deng, Yi, 404-385-1821 yi.deng@eas.gatech.edu,
Georgia Institute of Technology – OanOn
Deng, Youjun, 979-862-8476 YDeng@ag.tamu.edu,
Texas A&M University – GzSc
Dengler, Elizabeth, (612) 626-3379 edengler@umn.edu,
University of Minnesota – Gl
Dengler, Lorinda, (707) 826-3115 lad1@humboldt.edu,
Humboldt State University – Yg
Denicourt, Raymond, (813) 974-2236 University of South Florida, Tampa – Gz
Denizman, Can, (229) 333-5752 Valdosta State University – Hw
Denman, Kenneth L., (250) 363-8230 denmank@ec.gc.ca,
University of Victoria – Op
Dennen, Rob, dennenr@si.edu,
Smithsonian Institution / National Museum of Natural History – Gv
Dennett, Keith E., (775) 784-4056 kdennett@unr.edu,
University of Nevada, Reno – Hs
Denning, A.Scott, (970) 491-8359 denning@atmos.colostate.edu,
Colorado State University – Oa
Dennis, Clyde B., (630) 252-5999 cbdennis@anl.gov,
Argonne National Laboratory – On

Dennison, Robert, (309) 268-8646 robert.dennison@heartland.edu,
Heartland Community College – Og
Denniston, Rhawn F., (319) 895-4306 RDenniston@cornellcollege.edu,
University of Iowa – Cs
Denny, F. B., 618-985-3394 x240 fdenny@illinois.edu,
University of Illinois, Urbana-Champaign – GzEg
Denny, F. Brett, 618-985-3394 denny@isgs.uiuc.edu,
Illinois State Geological Survey – Gr
Denton, Gary R. W., (671) 735-2690 gdenton@uguam.uog.edu,
University of Guam – Ob
Denton, George H., (207) 581-2193 debbies@maine.edu,
University of Maine – Gl
Denton-Hedrick, Meredith Y., mdentonh@austincc.edu,
Austin Community College District – Ye
Deocampo, Daniel M., 404413-5750 deocampo@gsu.edu,
Georgia State University – Gsn
DePaolo, Donald J., (510) 642-7686 DJDePaolo@lbl.gov,
University of California, Berkeley – Cc
dePolo, Craig M., (775) 682-8770 eq_dude@sbcglobal.net,
University of Nevada – Ng
dePolo, Diane, (775) 784-4976 diane@seismo.unr.edu,
University of Nevada, Reno – Ys
DePriest, Thomas A., (731) 881-7441 tdepriest@utm.edu,
University of Tennessee, Martin – Oe
Dere, Ashlee L., 402 554 3317 adere@unomaha.edu,
University of Nebraska at Omaha – SdGmCl
Derome, Jacques F., (514) 398-5350 jacques.derome@mcgill.ca,
McGill University – Oa
Derry, Louis A., lad9@cornell.edu, Cornell University – Cg
Derstler, Kraig L., (504) 280-6799 kderstle@uno.edu,
University of New Orleans – Pv
Desai, Ankur R., (608) 265-9201 desai@aos.wisc.edu,
University of Wisconsin, Madison – Oa
DeSantis, Larisa R., 615-343-7831 larisa.desantis@vanderbilt.edu,
Vanderbilt University – Pve
Desch, Steven, (480) 965-7742 steve.desch@asu.edu,
Arizona State University – On
Deschaine, Sylvia, (207) 786-6490 sdescha2@bates.edu, Bates College – On
DeShon, Heather, 901-678-2007 hdeshon@memphis.edu,
University of Memphis – Ysg
DeShon, Heather R., 214-768-2916 Southern Methodist University – Ysr
Desrochers, Andre, 613-562-5838 adesro@uottawa.ca,
University of Ottawa – Gs
Dessler, Alexander, (520) 621-4589 dessler@vega.lpl.arizona.edu,
University of Arizona – On
Dessler, Andrew, 979-862-1427 adessler@tamu.edu,
Texas A&M University – On
Dessureault, Sean, (520) 621-2359 sdessure@email.arizona.edu,
University of Arizona – Nx
DeSutter, Tom, 701-231-8690 Thomas.Desutter@ndsu.edu,
North Dakota State University – Os
Dethier, David P., (413) 597-2078 david.p.dethier@williams.edu,
Williams College – Gm
Detournay, Emmanuel M., (612) 625-5522 detou001@tc.umn.edu,
University of Minnesota, Twin Cities – Nr
Detrich, William, (617) 373-4495 iceman@neu.edu,
Northeastern University – On
Dettman, David, (520) 621-4618 dettman@email.arizona.edu,
University of Arizona – Cs
Detwiler, Andrew G., (605) 394-1995 Andrew.Detwiler@sdsmt.edu,
South Dakota School of Mines & Technology – Oa
Deuser, Werner G., (508) 289-2551 wdeuser@whoi.edu,
Woods Hole Oceanographic Institution – Cs
Devaney, Kathleen, 915-831-5161 kdevaney@epcc.edu,
El Paso Community College – Gg
Devaurs, Micheline, (505) 667-1519 devaurs_micheline@lanl.gov,
Los Alamos National Laboratory – Hg
Devegowda, Deepak, deepak.devegowda@ou.edu,
University of Oklahoma – Np
Dever, Edward P., 541-737-2749 edever@coas.oregonstate.edu,
Oregon State University – Op
Devera, Joseph A., 618-985-3394 devera@isgs.uiuc.edu,
Illinois State Geological Survey – Gr
Devera, Joseph A., 618-985-3394 x241 j-devera@illinois.edu,
University of Illinois, Urbana-Champaign – Pg
Devery, Dora, 281-756-5670 ddevery@alvincollege.edu,
Alvin Community College – Gg
Devlahovich, Vincent A., (661) 362-3658 Vincent.Devlahovich@canyons.edu,
College of the Canyons – GgOye
Devlin, J. R., 785-864-4994 jfrickdevlin@gmail.com,
University of Kansas – Hw
Devol, Allan H., (206) 543-1292 devol@u.washington.edu,
University of Washington – Oc
DeVries-Zimmerman, Suzanne, (616) 395-7297 zimmerman@hope.edu,
Hope College – Gge
Dewberry, Daniel R., dandew@austincc.edu,
Austin Community College District – On
Dewdney, Chris, +44 023 92 842417 chris.dewdney@port.ac.uk,
University of Portsmouth – Yg
DeWeese, Georgina G., (678) 839-4065 gdeweese@westga.edu,

Old Dominion University – Ob

Dobler, Scott, (270) 745-7078 scott.dobler@wku.edu,
Western Kentucky University – Oa

Dobrzhinetskaya, Larissa F., (951) 827-2028 larissa@ucrac1.ucr.edu,
University of California, Riverside – Gx

Dobson, David, +44 020 7679 32398 d.dobson@ucl.ac.uk,
University College London – Gz

Dobson, David M., (336) 316-2278 ddobson@guilford.edu,
Guilford College – Gu

Dockal, James A., (910) 962-3494 dockal@uncw.edu,
University of North Carolina Wilmington – Gd

Dodd, J. Robert, (516) 632-8204 dodd@indiana.edu,
Indiana University, Bloomington – Po

Dodd, Justin P., 815-753-7949 jdodd@niu.edu,
Northern Illinois University – Cs

Dodge, Clifford H., 717.702.2036 cdodge@pa.gov,
Pennsylvania Bureau of Topographic & Geologic Survey – GrEcGh

Dodge, Rebecca L., 940-397-4475 rebecca.dodge@mwsu.edu,
Midwestern State University – Ore

Dodson, Peter, (215) 898-8784 dodsonp@vet.upenn.edu,
University of Pennsylvania – Pv

Dodson, Russell L., (570) 662-4614 rdodson@mansfield.edu,
Mansfield University – Gm

Dodson, Stanley I., (608) 262-6395 University of Wisconsin, Madison – Ob

Dogwiler, Toby, 507-457-5267 tdogwiler@winona.edu,
Winona State University – GmHqOw

Doh, Seong-Jae, 82-2-3290-3173 sjdoh@korea.ac.kr,
Korea University – YmgYe

Doheny, Edward L., (215) 898-6085 University of Pennsylvania – Ng

Doherty, Cheryl, (302) 831-2569 sparrow@udel.edu,
University of Delaware – On

Doherty, Ruth, +44 (0) 131 650 6759 ruth.doherty@ed.ac.uk,
Edinburgh University – Oa

Dolakova, Nela, +420 549 49 3542 nela@sci.muni.cz ,
Masaryk University – Plg

Dolan, James F., (213) 740-8599 dolan@usc.edu,
University of Southern California – Gt

Dolan, Robert, rd5q@virginia.edu, University of Virginia – Gm

Dolejs, David, +420-221951525 Charles University – GiCpg

Dolgoff, Anatole, (212) 346-1502 Pace University, New York Campus – Og

Doll, William E., d8e@ornl.gov, Oak Ridge National Laboratory – Yg

Dollase, Wayne A., (310) 825-3823 dollase@ucla.edu,
University of California, Los Angeles – Gz

Dollhopf, Douglas J., (406) 944-5594 dollhopf@montana.edu,
Montana State University – On

Dolman, Paul, +44 (0)1603 59 3175 p.dolman@uea.ac.uk,
University of East Anglia – Ou

Domack, Cynthia R., (315) 859-4710 cdomack@hamilton.edu,
Hamilton College – Pg

Domagall, Abigail M., 605-642-6506 Abigail.Domagall@bhsu.edu,
Black Hills State University – GveOe

Dombard, Andrew J., (312) 996-9206 adombard@uic.edu,
University of Illinois at Chicago – Xy

Domber, Steven E., (609) 984-6587 steven.domber@dep.nj.gov,
New Jersey Geological Survey – Hw

Domingue, Carla, (225) 388-8407 carla@lgs.bri.lsu.edu,
Louisiana State University – On

Dominguez, Francina, 217-265-5483 francina@illinois.edu,
University of Illinois, Urbana-Champaign – Oa

Dominic, David F., 937 775-3455 david.dominic@wright.edu,
Wright State University – Gsr

Donaghay, Percy, (401) 874-6944 donaghay@gso.uri.edu,
University of Rhode Island – Cl

Donahoe, Robert J., (505) 667-7603 Los Alamos National Laboratory – On

Donahoe, Rona J., 205-348-1879 rdonahoe@geo.ua.edu,
University of Alabama – Cl

Donaldson, Alan C., (304) 293-5603 adonalds@wvu.edu,
West Virginia University – Gs

Donaldson, Paul R., (208) 426-3639 pdonalds@boisestate.edu,
Boise State University – Ye

Dondofema, Farai, +27 15 962 80044 farai.dondofema@univen.ac.za,
University of Venda for Science & Technology – OrHgOi

Doney, Scott C., 508-289-3776 sdoney@whoi.edu,
Woods Hole Oceanographic Institution – Cm

Dong, Charles, (310) 660-3593 El Camino College – Og

Dong, Hailiang, (513) 529-2517 dongh@MiamiOh.edu,
Miami University – Cg

Dong, Pinliang, 940-565-2377 pinliang.dong@unt.edu,
University of North Texas – Oi

Donnelly, Jeffrey, 508-289-2994 jdonnelly@whoi.edu,
Woods Hole Oceanographic Institution – Gu

Donnelly, Shanon P., 330-972-7630 sd51@uakron.edu,
University of Akron – Oi

Donoghue, Joseph F., (850) 644-2703 jdonoghu@mailer.fsu.edu,
Florida State University – Gu

Donoghue, Michael J., 203-432-1935 michael.donoghue@yale.edu,
Yale University – Pbo

Donohue, Kathleen, (401) 874-6615 kdonohue@gso.uri.edu,
University of Rhode Island – Op

Donohue, Mary M., 765-658-4654 marydonohue@depauw.edu,

DePauw University – On

Donohue, Stephen J., (540) 231-9740 donohue@vt.edu,
Virginia Polytechnic Institute & State University – Sc

Donovan, James, 801.585.3029 james.donovan@utah.edu,
University of Utah – Nmr

Donovan, Jeff C., (727) 553-1116 jdonovan@marine.usf.edu,
University of South Florida – Op

Donovan, Joseph J., (304) 293-5603 donovan@geo.wvu.edu,
West Virginia University – Hq

Donovan, R. Nowell, (817) 257-7214 r.donovan@tcu.edu,
Texas Christian University – GdcGt

Doolan, Barry L., (802) 656-0248 bdoolan@uvm.edu,
University of Vermont – Gx

Dooley, Alton C., 276-634-4173 alton.dooley@vmnh.virginia.gov,
Virginia Polytechnic Institute & State University –

Dooley, Brett, bdooley@ph.vccs.edu,
Patrick Henry Community College – Gg

Dooley, John H., (609) 292-2576 john.dooley@dep.state.nj.us,
New Jersey Geological Survey – CgGf

Dooley, Tim, 512-471-8261 tim.dooley@beg.utexas.edu,
University of Texas at Austin, Jackson School of Geosciences – Gc

Doolittle, James J., (605) 688-4750 James.Doolittle@sdstate.edu,
South Dakota State University – Sc

Dorais, Michael J., (801) 422-1347 dorais@byu.edu,
Brigham Young University – Gi

Dorale, Jeffrey A., (319) 335-0822 jeffrey-dorale@uiowa.edu,
University of Iowa – Cs

Doran, Peter, pdoran@lsu.edu, Louisiana State University – Hgs

Doran, Peter T., (312) 413-7275 pdoran@lsu.edu,
University of Illinois at Chicago – Hw

Dorfman, Alexander, 089/2180 4275 Ludwig-Maximilians-Universitaet
Muenchen – Gz

Dorfner, Thomas, 089/2180 4278 dorfner@min.uni-muenchen.de,
Ludwig-Maximilians-Universitaet Muenchen – Gz

Dorling, Stephen, +44 (0)1603 59 2533 s.dorling@uea.ac.uk,
University of East Anglia – Ow

Dormaar, John, (403) 327-4561 University of Lethbridge – So

Dorman, Clive E., (619) 594-5707 cdorman@mail.sdsu.edu,
San Diego State University – Op

Dorman, James, (901) 678-4753 dorman@comcast.net,
University of Memphis – Ys

Dorman, Leroy M., (858) 534-2406 ldorman@ucsd.edu,
University of California, San Diego – Yg

Dornbos, Stephen Q., 414-229-6630 sdornbos@uwm.edu,
University of Wisconsin, Milwaukee – Pve

Dorries, Alison M., (505) 665-6952 adorries@lanl.gov,
Los Alamos National Laboratory – On

Dorsey, Rebecca J., (541) 346-4431 rdorsey@uoregon.edu,
University of Oregon – Gr

Dort, Jr., Wakefield, (785) 864-4974 University of Kansas – Gm

Doser, Diane I., (915) 747-5851 doser@geo.utep.edu,
University of Texas, El Paso – Ys

Doskey, Paul V., (630) 252-7662 pvdoskey@anl.gov,
Argonne National Laboratory – Oa

Doss, Paul K., (812) 465-7132 pdoss@usi.edu,
University of Southern Indiana – Hw

Dosso, Stanley E., (250) 472-4341 sdosso@uvic.ca,
University of Victoria – Op

Dostal, Jarda, (902) 420-5747 Dalhousie University – Cg

Doster, Florian, +44 (0)131 451 3171 florian.doster@pet.hw.ac.uk,
Heriot-Watt University – Hg

Dostie, Philip, (207) 786-6485 pdostie@bates.edu,
Bates College – Ol

Dott, Jr., Robert H., (608) 262-1856 rdott@geology.wisc.edu,
University of Wisconsin, Madison – Gs

Doty, Thomas, (401) 254-3066 Roger Williams University – Ob

Dou, Fugen, (409) 752-2741 ext. 2223 f-dou@aesrg.tamu.edu,
Texas A&M University – Os

Dougan, Bernie, (360) 383-3877 bdougan@whatcom.ctc.edu,
Whatcom Community College – Gg

Dougil, Andy, +44(0) 113 34 36782 a.j.dougill@leeds.ac.uk,
University of Leeds – Os

Douglas, Arthur V., (402) 280-2464 sonora@creighton.edu,
Creighton University – Og

Douglas, Bruce, (812) 855-3848 douglasb@indiana.edu,
Indiana University, Bloomington – Gc

Douglas, Ellen, ellen.douglas@umb.edu,
University of Massachusetts, Boston – HwqHy

Douglas, Marianne, (780) 492-0055 marianne.douglas@ualberta.ca,
University of Toronto – Gn

Douglas, Robert G., (213) 740-8275 rdouglas@usc.edu,
University of Southern California – Pe

Douglass, Daniel, (617) 373-4684 d.douglass@neu.edu,
Northeastern University – GlSdOa

Douglass, David N., (626) 585-7036 dndouglass@paccd.cc.ca.us,
Pasadena City College – Ym

Dove, Patricia M., (540) 231-2444 pdove@vt.edu,
Virginia Polytechnic Institute & State University – Cl

Doveton, John H., 785-864-3965 doveton@kgs.ku.edu,
University of Kansas – Gq

437

Kansas State University – So

Duncan, Thomas, (541) 737-5206 University of California, Berkeley – Pb

Duncan Tabb, Neva, 721-791-2758 Duncantabb.Neva@spcollege.edu,
Saint Petersburg College, Clearwater – Ow

Dundas, Robert G., (559) 278-6984 rdundas@csufresno.edu,
California State University, Fresno – PvGr

Dunfield, Kari, (519) 824-4120 xt 58088 dunfield@uoguelph.ca,
University of Guelph – Sb

Dunlap, Dallas B., (512) 471-4858 dallas.dunlap@beg.utexas.edu,
University of Texas at Austin, Jackson School of Geosciences – Ye

Dunlop, Roberta, (604) 291-4995 rdunlop@sfu.ca,
Simon Fraser University – Gx

Dunn, Allison L., 508-929-8641 adunn@worcester.edu,
Worcester State University – OayHg

Dunn, Dennis P., ddunn2@austincc.edu,
Austin Community College District – EgGt

Dunn, Douglas, 216-231-4600 ddunn@cmnh.org,
Cleveland Museum of Natural History – Pg

Dunn, John Todd, (506) 453-4804 University of New Brunswick – Gi

Dunn, Richard K., 802 485 2304 rdunn@norwich.edu,
Norwich University – GslGa

Dunn, Robert A., 808-956-3728 dunnr@hawaii.edu,
University of Hawai'i, Manoa – Yr

Dunn, Steven R., 413-538-2531 sdunn@mtholyoke.edu,
Mount Holyoke College – Gp

Dunn, Tasha, 207-859-5800 tldunn@colby.edu, Colby College – GpiGz

Dunne, George C., (818) 677-2511 george.dunne@csun.edu,
California State University, Northridge – Gc

Dunne, William M., (423) 974-4161 wdunne@utk.edu,
University of Tennessee, Knoxville – Gc

Dunning, Gregory R., (709) 737-8481 dunning@esd.mun.ca,
Memorial University of Newfoundland – Cc

Dunning, Jeremy D., (812) 856-4448 dunning@indiana.edu,
Indiana University, Bloomington – Gc

Dunst, Brian, 412-442-4230 bdunst@pa.gov,
Pennsylvania Bureau of Topographic & Geologic Survey – EgoHw

Dunton, Kenneth H., (361) 749-6744 ken.dunton@utexas.edu,
University of Texas at Austin – Ob

Dupont, Todd, 513-529-9734 dupontt@miamioh.edu,
Miami University – Gl

Dupont, Todd, 949-824-1133 tdupont@uci.edu,
University of California, Irvine – Ol

Dupraz, Christophe, 860-486-1394 christophe.dupraz@uconn.edu,
University of Connecticut – Py

Dupre, William R., 713-743-4987 wdupre@uh.edu,
University of Houston – On

Durand, Michael T., (614)247-4835 durand.8@osu.edu,
Ohio State University – HgYd

Durbin, Edward G., (401) 874-6850 edurbin@gso.uri.edu,
University of Rhode Island – Ob

Durbin, James, 812-465-1208 jdurbin@usi.edu,
University of Southern Indiana – Gm

Durham, Lisa, 630-252-3170 ladurham@anl.gov,
Argonne National Laboratory – Hw

Durham, William, wbdurham@mit.edu,
Massachusetts Institute of Technology – Cg

Durkee, Philip A., 831-656-2517 durkee@nps.edu,
Naval Postgraduate School – Owr

Durland, Theodore, 541-737-5058 tdurland@coas.oregonstate.edu,
Oregon State University – Yg

DuRoss, Christopher B., (801) 537-3348 christopherduross@utah.gov,
Utah Geological Survey – Ng

Durran, Dale R., 206-543-7440 durrand@atmos.washington.edu,
University of Washington – Oa

Durrant, Jeffrey O., (801) 422-4116 jodurrant@byu.edu,
Brigham Young University – Ge

Durucan, Sevket, +44 20 759 47354 s.durucan@imperial.ac.uk,
Imperial College – Ng

Dushaw, Brian D., (206) 685-4198 dushaw@apl.washington.edu,
University of Washington – Op

Dutch, Steven I., (920) 465-2371 dutchs@uwgb.edu,
University of Wisconsin, Green Bay – GcgGe

Dutcher, Allen, adutcher1@unl.edu, University of Nebraska, Lincoln – Oa

Dutkiewicz, Stephanie, 617-253-2454 stephd@ocean.mit.edu,
Massachusetts Institute of Technology – Cg

Dutro, Thomas, (202) 633-1322 Smithsonian Institution / National Museum of Natural History – Pi

Dutrow, Barbara L., (225) 388-2525 dutrow@geol.lsu.edu,
Louisiana State University – Gz

Dutta, Prodip K., (812) 237-2268 Prodip.Dutta@indstate.edu,
Indiana State University – Gs

Dutton, Andrea, 352-846-2413 adutton@ufl.edu, University of Florida – CgGsPe

Dutton, Jessica, duttonj@sunysuffolk.edu,
Suffolk County Community College, Ammerman Campus – Og

Dutton, John A., 814-865-1534 dutton@ems.psu.edu,
Pennsylvania State University, University Park – Ow

Dutton, Shirley P., (512) 471-0329 shirley.dutton@beg.utexas.edu,
University of Texas at Austin, Jackson School of Geosciences – Gd

Duvall, Alison, 206-211-8311 aduvall@uw.edu,
University of Washington – GmcGt

Duxbury, Thomas C., (818) 354-4301 Jet Propulsion Laboratory – On

Dvorzak, Marie, (608) 262-8956 mdvorzak@geology.wisc.edu,
University of Wisconsin, Madison – On

Dworkin, Stephen I., (254) 710-2186 steve_dworkin@baylor.edu,
Baylor University – ClGd

Dwyer, Daryl F., 419-5302661 daryl.dwyer@utoledo.edu,
University of Toledo – On

Dwyer, Gary S., (919) 681-8164 gsd3@duke.edu,
Duke University – Gs

Dwyer, Joseph R., 321-674-7208 jdwyer@fit.edu,
Florida Institute of Technology – Oa

Dyab, Ahmed I., 002-03-3921595 seawolf_5000@yahoo.com,
Alexandria University – Gg

Dyaur, Nikolay, 713-743-6539 ndyaur@uh.edu, University of Houston – Yxs

Dye, David H., 901-678-3330 daviddye@memphis.edu,
University of Memphis – Ga

Dyer, Blake, (609) 258-0836 bdyer@princeton.edu,
Princeton University – Pe

Dyer, Jamie, (662) 268-1032 Ext 220 jamie.dyer@msstate.edu,
Mississippi State University – Ow

Dyer, Jen, +44(0) 113 34 39086 j.dyer@leeds.ac.uk,
University of Leeds – Ge

Dyhrman, Sonya, 845-365-8165 sdyhrman@ldeo.columbia.edu,
Columbia University – Ob

Dyke, Gareth, +44 (0)23 8059 3110 gareth.dyke@soton.ac.uk,
University of Southampton – Pv

Dymek, Robert F., (314) 935-5344 bob_d@levee.wustl.edu,
Washington University in St. Louis – Gp

Dymond, Randel, (540) 231-9962 dymond@vt.edu,
Virginia Tech – HqsOi

Dyreson, Eric G., (406) 683-7275 eric.dyreson@umwestern.edu,
University of Montana Western – Gq

Dyson, Miranda, +44 (0)1908 653398 x 53398 miranda.dyson@open.ac.uk ,
The Open University – Py

Dziewonski, Adam M., (617) 495-2510 dziewons@eps.harvard.edu,
Harvard University – Ys

Dzunic, Aleksandar, +61 8 9266 2297 A.Dzunic@curtin.edu.au,
Curtin University – YgsYe

E

Earls, Sandy, 405-744-6358 sandy.earls@okstate.edu,
Oklahoma State University – On

Earls, Stephanie, 360 902-1473 stephanie.earls@dnr.wa.gov,
Washington Division of Geology & Earth Resources – Gge

Early, Thomas O., eot@ornl.gov, Oak Ridge National Laboratory – Cl

Earman, Sam, 717-871-2086 sam.earman@millersville.edu,
Millersville University – Hw

Easson, Gregory L., (662) 915-5995 geasson@olemiss.edu,
University of Mississippi – Or

Easterbrook, Don J., (360) 650-3583 don.easterbrook@wwu.edu,
Western Washington University – Gm

Easterday, Cary, cary.easterday@bellevuecollege.edu,
Bellevue College – GgPg

Eastin, Matt, 704-687-5914 mdeastin@uncc.edu,
University of North Carolina, Charlotte – Ow

Eastler, Thomas E., 207-778-7401 eastler@maine.edu,
University of Maine - Farmington – GeOrGg

Eastoe, Christopher J., (520) 621-1638 eastoe@email.arizona.edu,
University of Arizona – Cs

Eaton, Jeffrey G., jeaton@weber.edu, Weber State University – Ps

Eaton, Lewis S., (540) 568-3339 eatonls@jmu.edu,
James Madison University – Gm

Eaton, Timothy, 718-997-3327 timothy.eaton@qc.cuny.edu,
Queens College (CUNY) – HgwGg

Ebel, Denton, 212-769-5381 debel@amnh.org,
American Museum of Natural History – Xm

Ebel, John E., (617) 552-3399 ebel@bc.edu, Boston College – Ys

Eberhardt, Erik, (604) 827-5573 eeberhardt@eos.ubc.ca,
University of British Columbia – Ng

Eberhart, Mark E., (303) 273-3726 meberhar@mines.edu,
Colorado School of Mines – Om

Eberle, Bill, (785) 532-6101 weberle@ksu.edu,
Kansas State University – So

Eberle, Jaelyn J., 303-492-8069 jaelyn.eberle@colorado.edu,
University of Colorado – Pv

Eberli, Gregor P., 305 421-4678 geberli@rsmas.miami.edu,
University of Miami – Gr

Ebersole, Sandy M., 205-247-3613 sebersole@gsa.state.al.us,
Geological Survey of Alabama – Og

Ebert, David, 831-771-4400 debert@mlml.calstate.edu,
Moss Landing Marine Laboratories – On

Ebert, James R., (607) 436-3065 James.Ebert@oneonta.edu,
SUNY, Oneonta – GrsGd

Eberth, David A., 403-823-7707 Royal Tyrrell Museum of Palaeontology – Gs

Ebiner, Matt, (310) 660-3593 mebiner@elcamino.edu,
El Camino College – Oy

Ebinger, Cynthia J., 585-276-3364 ebinger@earth.rochester.edu,
University of Rochester – Gt

Ebinger, Michael H., (505) 667-3147 mhe@lanl.gov,
Los Alamos National Laboratory – So

439

University of South Carolina – GmOna
Ellis, Robert M., (604) 822-6574 rellis@eos.ubc.ca,
    University of British Columbia – Ys
Ellis, Rowan, +44 (0) 131 651 4447 Rowan.Ellis@ed.ac.uk.,
    Edinburgh University – On
Ellis, Scott R., 217-265-5105 ellis3@illinois.edu,
    University of Illinois, Urbana-Champaign – Ge
Ellis, Todd D., 607 436-2309 Todd.Ellis@oneonta.edu,
    SUNY, Oneonta – Oag
Ellis, Trevor, 573-368-2153 Trevor.Ellis@dnr.mo.gov,
    Missouri Dept of Natural Resources – Gg
Ellsworth, Timothy R., (217) 333-2055 University of Illinois, Urbana-Champaign – Sp
Ellwood, Brooks B., (225) 578-3416 ellwood@lsu.edu,
    Louisiana State University – Ym
Elmore, R. Douglas, (405) 325-4493 delmore@ou.edu,
    University of Oklahoma – Ym
Elnadi, Abdelhalim H., geology@uofk.edu, University of Khartoum – Goz
Eloranta, Edwin W., (608)262-7327 eloranta@lidar.ssec.wisc.edu,
    University of Wisconsin, Madison – Yr
Elrick, Maya, (505) 277-5077 dolomite@unm.edu,
    University of New Mexico – Gs
Elrick, Scott D., 217-333-3222 elrick@isgs.uiuc.edu,
    Illinois State Geological Survey – Ec
Elsberry, Russell L., 831-656-2373 elsberry@nps.edu,
    Naval Postgraduate School – Ow
Elsen, Jan, jan.elsen@ees.kuleuven.be, Katholieke Universiteit Leuven – Gz
Elswick, Erika R., (812) 855-2493 eelswick@indiana.edu,
    Indiana University, Bloomington – Cl
Elueze, A. A., aa.elueze@mail.ui.edu.ng, University of Ibadan – Eg
Elwood Madden, Megan E., (405) 325-1563 melwood@ou.edu,
    University of Oklahoma – Yg
Ely, Lisa L., (509) 963-2177 ely@cwu.edu, Central Washington University – Gm
Elzinga, Evert J., 973-353-5238 elzinga@andromeda.rutgers.edu,
    Rutgers, The State University of New Jersey, Newark – Sc
Emanuel, Kerry A., (617) 253-2462 emanuel@mit.edu,
    Massachusetts Institute of Technology – Ow
Emerick, Christina M., (206) 543-2491 tina@ocean.washington.edu,
    University of Washington – Ou
Emerman, Steven, (801) 863-6864 StevenE@uvu.edu,
    Utah Valley University – HgYgGe
Emerson, Cheryl R., (309) 694-5373 Illinois Central College – Oe
Emerson, Norlene, (608) 647-6186 x109 norlene.emerson@uwc.edu,
    University of Wisconsin Colleges – GgOy
Emerson, Steven R., (206) 543-0428 emerson@u.washington.edu,
    University of Washington – Oc
Emery, Joshua, (865) 974-2366 jemery2@utk.edu,
    University of Tennessee, Knoxville – Xg
Emile-Geay, Julien, 213-740-2945 julieneg@usc.edu,
    University of Southern California – Oc
Emmer, Barbara, 089/2180 4231 Ludwig-Maximilians-Universitaet Muenchen – Yg
Emmett, Chad, (801) 422-7886 chad_emmett@byu.edu,
    Brigham Young University – On
Emmi, Philip C., (801) 581-5562 pcemmi@geog.utah.edu,
    University of Utah – Ou
Emofurieta, Williams O., wemofu@uniben.edu,
    University of Benin – GzCeGe
Emry, Robert, (202) 633-1323 Smithsonian Institution / National Museum of
    Natural History – Pv
Encarnacion, John, (314) 977-3119 encarnjp@eas.slu.edu,
    Saint Louis University – Gx
Enderlin, Ellyn M., ellyn.enderlin@maine.edu, University of Maine – Gl
Enderlin, Milton, 817 257 5318 m.enderlin@tcu.edu,
    Texas Christian University – Nr
Endres, Anthony E., (519) 888-4567 (Ext. 3552) University of Waterloo – Pe
Engebretson, David C., (360) 650-3595 david.engebretson@wwu.edu,
    Western Washington University – Gt
Engel, Anga, mpeschke@geomar.de, SUNY, Stony Brook – Oc
Engel, Annette S., 865-974-2366 aengel1@utk.edu,
    University of Tennessee, Knoxville – Cl
Engel, Michael H., (405) 325-4435 ab1635@ou.edu,
    University of Oklahoma – Co
Engel, Richard E., (406) 994-5295 rengel@montana.edu,
    Montana State University – Sc
Engelder, Terry, (814) 865-3620 engelder@geosc.psu.edu,
    Pennsylvania State University, University Park – Nr
Engelhard, Simon, (401) 874-2187 engelhart@uri.edu,
    University of Rhode Island – Gg
Engelmann, George F., 402-554-4804 gengelmann@unomaha.edu,
    University of Nebraska at Omaha – PvGdr
Engels, Jennifer, 808-956-2562 engels@hawaii.edu,
    University of Hawai'i, Manoa – Oe
England, John, (780) 492-5673 john.england@ualberta.ca,
    University of Alberta – Gm
England, Phillip, +44 (1865) 272000 philip@earth.ox.ac.uk,
    University of Oxford – Gt
England, Richard, +440116 252 3522 hodgeology@le.ac.uk,
    Leicester University – Yg
Englebright, Stephen C., (631) 632-8230 SUNY, Stony Brook – Oe
English, David C., (727) 553-1503 denglish@marine.usf.edu,
    University of South Florida – Op

Engstrom, Daniel R., (612) 433-5953 (Ext. 18) dre@umn.edu,
    University of Minnesota, Twin Cities – Pe
Engstrom, Vanessa, vengstrom@valleycollege.edu,
    San Bernardino Valley College – Oy
Enos, Paul, (785) 864-2744 enos@KU.edu, University of Kansas – Gs
Enright, Richard L., (508) 531-1390 enright@bridgew.edu,
    Bridgewater State University – Hg
Ensign, Todd, 304-367-8438 tensign@fairmontstate.edu,
    Fairmont State University – Oe
Entekhabi, Dara, (617) 253-9698 darae@mit.edu,
    Massachusetts Institute of Technology – Hg
Epifanio, Craig, cepi@tamu.edu, Texas A&M University – Oa
Eppelbaum, Lev, +97236405086 levap@post.tau.ac.il,
    Tel Aviv University – YvmGt
Eppes, Martha C., 704-687-5993 meppes@uncc.edu,
    University of North Carolina, Charlotte – Os
Epstein, Howard E., (434) 924-4308 hee2b@virginia.edu,
    University of Virginia – On
Erdmann, A. L., 217-244-2502 aerdmann@illinois.edu,
    University of Illinois, Urbana-Champaign – Ge
Erdmer, Philippe, (403) 492-2676 philippe.erdmer@ualberta.ca,
    University of Alberta – Gc
Erdner, Deana L., (361) 749-6719 derdner@utexas.edu,
    University of Texas at Austin – Ob
Erenpreiss, Matt, 614 265 6627 matt.erenpreiss@dnr.state.oh.us,
    Ohio Dept of Natural Resources – Eo
Erickson, Ben, (801) 537-3388 benerickson@utah.gov,
    Utah Geological Survey – Ng
Erickson, J. Mark, (315) 379-5198 St. Lawrence University – Poi
Erickson, Rolfe C., (707) 664-2334 rolfe.erickson@sonoma.edu,
    Sonoma State University – Gx
Eriksen, Charles C., (206) 543-6528 eriksen@u.washington.edu,
    University of Washington – Op
Eriksson, Kenneth A., (540) 231-4680 kaeson@vt.edu,
    Virginia Polytechnic Institute & State University – Gs
Erisman, Brad, 361-749-6833 berisman@utexas.edu,
    University of Texas at Austin – Ob
Ernst, W. Gary, (650) 723-2750 ernst@pangea.stanford.edu,
    Stanford University – Cp
Erski, Theodore, (815) 455-8992 terski@mchenry.edu,
    McHenry County College – Og
Erslev, Eric A., (970) 491-6375 erslev@cnr.colostate.edu,
    Colorado State University – Gc
Erslev, Eric A., 307-766-3386 erslev@warnercnr.colostate.edu,
    University of Wyoming – GctGg
Ertel-Ingrisch, Werner, 089/2180 4275 ertel@min.uni-muenchen.de,
    Ludwig-Maximilians-Universitaet Muenchen – Gz
Erturk, Mehmet Ali, 00904242370000-5981 maerturk@firat.edu.tr,
    Firat University – GiCc
Ervin, C. Patrick, (815) 753-1943 pervin@niu.edu,
    Northern Illinois University – Yv
Erwin, Diane, (510) 642-3921 dmerwin@berkeley.edu,
    University of California, Berkeley – Pb
Erwin, Douglas H., (202) 633-1324 Smithsonian Institution / National Museum of
    Natural History – Pi
Esbaugh, Andrew J., (361) 749-6835 a.esbaugh@austin.utexas.edu,
    University of Texas at Austin – Ob
Escobar-Wolf, Rudiger, 906/487-3155 rpescoba@mtu.edu,
    Michigan Technological University – Gv
Eshleman, Keith N., (301) 689-3155 eshleman@al.umces.edu,
    University of Maryland – Hg
Esling, Steven P., (618) 453-7376 esling@siu.edu,
    Southern Illinois University Carbondale – HwGl
Esnault, Melissa H., (225) 578-5320 mesnau1@lsu.edu,
    Louisiana State University – On
Esparza, Francisco, fesparz@cicese.mx,
    Centro de Investigación Científica y de Educación Superior de Ensenada – Ye
Esser, Corinne, (530) 752-3668 caesser@ucdavis.edu,
    University of California, Davis – On
Essery, Richard L., +44 (0) 131 651 9093 Richard.Essery@ed.ac.uk,
    Edinburgh University – Oa
Essling, Alice M., (630) 252-3493 Argonne National Laboratory – Ca
Esslinger, Kelly L., kelly.esslinger@azwestern.edu,
    Arizona Western College – OapGg
Estalrich López, Joan, ++935811270 joan.estalrich@uab.cat,
    Universitat Autonoma de Barcelona – HgGe
Estapa, Margaret, 518-589-5477 mestapa@skidmore.edu,
    Skidmore College – Oc
Estop Graells, Eugènia, ++34935813089 eugenia.estop@uab.cat,
    Universitat Autonoma de Barcelona – Gz
Estrada Oliveras, Rita, ++34935811706 rita.estrada@uab.cat,
    Universitat Autonoma de Barcelona – Grs
Ethington, Raymond L., (573) 882-6470 EthingtonR@missouri.edu,
    University of Missouri – Pm
Ethridge, Frank G., (970) 491-6195 fredpet@cnr.colostate.edu,
    Colorado State University – Gs
Ettensohn, Dorothy, (213) 763-3327 dettenso@nhm.org,
    Los Angeles County Museum of Natural History – Gz
Ettensohn, Frank R., (859) 257-1401 f.ettensohn@uky.edu,
    University of Kentucky – Ps

Farrar, Stewart S., (859) 622-1279 Stewart.Farrar@eku.edu,
Eastern Kentucky University – Gp
Farrell, Brian F., (617) 495-2998 farrell@seas.harvard.edu,
Harvard University – Ow
Farrell, John, (401) 874-6561 jfarrell@gso.uri.edu,
University of Rhode Island – Ou
Farrell, Kathleen M., (919) 733-7353 kathleen.farrell@ncdenr.gov,
North Carolina Geological Survey – Gs
Farrell, Mark O., (412) 392-3879 Point Park University – On
Farrell, Michael, michaelfarrell.myefolio.com, Cuyamaca College – Gg
Farrell, Stewart, (609) 652-4245 farrells@stockton.edu,
Richard Stockton College of New Jersey – On
Farrington, John W., 508-289-3911 jfarrington@whoi.edu,
Woods Hole Oceanographic Institution – Oc
Farrow, Norman D., ndf@ornl.gov, Oak Ridge National Laboratory – Hg
Farthing, Dori J., 585-245-5298 farthing@geneseo.edu,
SUNY, Geneseo – Gz
Farver, John R., (419) 372-7203 jfarver@bgnet.bgsu.edu,
Bowling Green State University – Gy
Faryad, Shah Wali, +420221951521 faryad@natur.cuni.cz,
Charles University – GpzGi
Fastovsky, David, (401) 874-2185 defastov@uri.edu,
University of Rhode Island – Pv
Fatherree, James W., 813-253-7906 jfatherree@hccfl.edu,
Hillsborough Community College – Og
Faulds, James, (775) 682-8751 jfaulds@unr.edu,
University of Nevada, Reno – Gc
Faulkner, Daniel, +440151 794 5169 Faulkner@liverpool.ac.uk,
University of Liverpool – Ys
Faure, Gunter, (614) 292-3454 faure.1@osu.edu,
Ohio State University – Cc
Faure, Stephane, 514-987-3000 #2369 faure.stephane@uqam.ca,
Universite du Quebec a Montreal – Gc
Favas, Paulo J., 351259350220 pjcf@utad.pt,
Universidade de Trás-os-Montes e Alto Douro – GeCtGg
Favor, Michael, (313) 593-5235 University of Michigan, Dearborn – On
Fawcett, J. J., (416) 978-3027 fawcett@quartz.geology.utoronto.ca,
University of Toronto – Gp
Fawcett, Peter J., (505) 277-3867 fawcett@unm.edu,
University of New Mexico – Pe
Fayek, Mostafa, (204) 474-7982 fayek@cc.umanitoba.ca,
University of Manitoba – Cs
Fayer, Michael J., (509) 372-6045 mike.fayer@pnl.gov,
Pacific Northwest National Laboratory – Hq
Fayon, Annia K., 612-626-9805 fayon001@umn.edu,
University of Minnesota, Twin Cities – Gc
Feagley, Sam E., (979) 845-1460 s-feagley@tamu.edu,
Texas A&M University – Sc
Feakins, Sarah, 213-740-7168 feakins@usc.edu,
University of Southern California – Oc
Fearey, Bryan L., (505) 665-2423 Los Alamos National Laboratory – Cc
Fearon, Jamie L., (630) 752-5063 jamie.fearon@wheaton.edu,
Wheaton College – Pv
Feather, Russell, (202) 633-1793 featherr@si.edu,
Smithsonian Institution / National Museum of Natural History – Gz
Fedele, Juan J., 320-308-1049 jjfedele@stcloudstate.edu,
Saint Cloud State University – Hg
Fedo, Christopher, (865) 974-2366 cfedo@utk.edu,
University of Tennessee, Knoxville – GsXg
Fedorov, Alexey V., (203) 432-3153 alexey.fedorov@yale.edu,
Yale University – Op
Feeley, Todd C., (406) 994-6917 tfeely@umontana.edu,
Montana State University – Gi
Feely, Martin, +353 (0)91 492 129 martin.feely@nuigalway.ie,
National University of Ireland Galway – Goz
Feely, Richard A., (206) 526-6214 feely@pmel.noaa.gov,
University of Washington – Oc
Feeney, Alison E., (717) 477-1319 aefeen@ark.ship.edu,
Shippensburg University – On
Feeney, Dennis M., 208-885-5203 dmfeeney@uidaho.edu,
University of Idaho – GsYgGg
Feeney, Thomas P., (717) 477-1297 tpfeen@ark.ship.edu,
Shippensburg University – Gm
Fegley, Bruce, (314) 935-4852 bfegley@levee.wustl.edu,
Washington University – Xc
Fehler, Michael, 617-253-3589 fehler@mit.edu,
Massachusetts Institute of Technology – Yg
Fehn, Udo, (585) 275-7884 udo.fehn@rochester.edu,
University of Rochester – Eg
Fehr, Karl Thomas, 089/2180 4256 fehr@min.uni-muenchen.de,
Ludwig-Maximilians-Universitaet Muenchen – Gz
Fei, Yingwei, fei@gl.ciw.edu,
University of Maryland – CpGxCg
Fei, Yingwei, 202-478-8936 yfel@carnegiescience.edu,
Carnegie Institution of Washington – Cp
Feibel, Craig S., (848) 932-8853 feibel@rci.rutgers.edu,
Rutgers, The State University of New Jersey – GarGs
Feigenson, Mark D., (848) 445-3149 feigy@rci.rutgers.edu,
Rutgers, The State University of New Jersey – CgGiv
Feigl, Kurt, 608-262-0176 feigl@wisc.edu,

University of Wisconsin, Madison – Yd
Feigl, Kurt L., (608) 262-0176 feigl@wisc.edu,
University of Wisconsin, Madison – Gt
Fein, Jeremy B., (574) 631-6101 fein.1@nd.edu,
University of Notre Dame – Cl
Feinberg, Joshua, 612-624-8429 feinberg@umn.edu,
University of Minnesota, Twin Cities – Ym
Feineman, Maureen D., 814) 863-6649 mdf12@psu.edu,
Pennsylvania State University, University Park – Cp
Feinglos, Mark N., (919) 684-4005 feing002@mc.duke.edu,
Duke University – Gz
Feinstein, Daniel T., 414-962-2582 dtfeinst@usgs.gov,
University of Wisconsin, Milwaukee – Hw
Felbeck, Horst, (858) 534-6647 hfelbeck@ucsd.edu,
University of California, San Diego – Ob
Feldmann, Rodney M., (330) 672-2506 rfeldman@kent.edu,
Kent State University – Pi
Feller, Robert J., 803-777-3937 feller@biol.sc.edu,
University of South Carolina – Obn
Felton, Richard M., (660) 562-1569 rfelton@nwmissouri.edu,
Northwest Missouri State University – Pg
Feltrin, Leo, lfeltrin@uwo.ca, Western University – Eg
Felzer, Benjamin S., 610-758-3536 bsf208@lehigh.edu,
Lehigh University – Oa
Fenberg, Phillip, +44 (0)23 80592729 P.B.Fenberg@soton.ac.uk,
University of Southampton – Ob
Fendorf, Scott E., (650) 723-5238 fendorf@pangea.stanford.edu,
Stanford University – Sc
Fendrock, Michaela, (508) 289-2209 mfendrock@whoi.edu,
Woods Hole Oceanographic Institution – Oc
Feng, Huan E., (973) 655-7549 fengh@mail.montclair.edu,
Montclair State University – Cm
Feng, Song, 479-575-4748 songfeng@uark.edu,
University of Arkansas, Fayetteville – OaGgg
Feng, Xiahong, 603-646-1712 xiahong.feng@dartmouth.edu,
Dartmouth College – Cs
Feng, Yan, 630-252-2550 yfeng@anl.gov,
Argonne National Laboratory – Oa
Feng, Yucheng, (334) 844-3967 yfeng@acesag.auburn.edu,
Auburn University – Sb
Fengler, Keegan , 509.963.2719 keegan@geology.cwu.edu,
Central Washington University – Gg
Fenical, William H., (858) 534-2133 wfenical@ucsd.edu,
University of California, San Diego – Ob
Fennel, Katja, (902) 494-4526 katja.fennel@dal.ca,
Dalhousie University – Ob
Fennema, Julian, julian.fennema@pet.hw.ac.uk, Heriot-Watt University – Eg
Fenrich, Francis, (780) 492-2149 frances@space.ualberta.ca,
University of Alberta – Xy
Fenster, Michael S., (804)752-3745 mfenster@rmc.edu,
Randolph-Macon College – OnGue
Fenstermaker, Lynn, (702) 862-5412 lynn@dri.edu,
Desert Research Institute – Or
Fenter, Paul, (630) 252-7053 fenter@anl.gov,
University of Illinois at Chicago – Gy
Ferencz, Orsolya, orsi@sas.elte.hu, Eotvos Lorand University – XyOr
Ferger, Marisa, (814) 863-4229 mferger@psu.edu,
Pennsylvania State University, University Park – Ow
Ferguson, Charles A., 520-770-3500 Fergusongeo@arizona.edu,
Arizona Geological Survey – Gc
Ferguson, Ian J., (204) 474-9154 ij_ferguson@umanitoba.ca,
University of Manitoba – Ye
Ferguson, John F., (972) 883-2410 ferguson@utdallas.edu,
University of Texas, Dallas – Yg
Ferguson, Julie , (949)824-9411 julie.ferguson@uci.edu,
University of California, Irvine – Oe
Fergušon, Terry A., (864) 597-4527 fergusonta@wofford.edu,
Wofford College – Ga
Ferland, Marie A., 509-963-2829 ferlandm@cwu.edu,
Central Washington University – Gu
Fermanich, Kevin J., (920) 465-2240 fermanik@uwgb.edu,
University of Wisconsin, Green Bay – SpHwOu
Fernandez, Diego, (801) 587-9366 diego.fernandez@utah.edu,
University of Utah – Cg
Fernandez, Fabian G., 612-625-7460 fabiangf@umn.edu,
University of Minnesota, Twin Cities – ScbSo
Fernandez, Louis A., (909) 537-5024 California State University, San Bernardino – Gi
Fernández, Virginia, (598) 2525 1552 vivi@fcien.edu.uy,
Universidad de la Republica Oriental del Uruguay (UDELAR) – OirOn
Fernando, Joe, Harindra.J.Fernando.10@nd.edu,
University of Notre Dame – Oa
Ferns, Mark L., (541) 523-3133 mark.ferns@state.or.us,
Oregon Dept of Geology & Mineral Industries – GrtGi
Ferrand, Lin A., (212) 650-8017 Graduate School of the City University of New York – Hq
Ferrando, Simona, simona.ferrando@unito.it, Università di Torino – Gx
Ferrari, Raffaele, (617) 253-1291 raffaele@mit.edu,
Massachusetts Institute of Technology – Op
Ferre, Eric C., 618-453-7368 eferre@geo.siu.edu,
Southern Illinois University Carbondale – Gc

443

G

Gardulski, Anne F., 617-627-2891 anne.gardulski@tufts.edu,
Tufts University – Grs
Garfield, Newell (Toby), (415) 338-3713 garfield@sfsu.edu,
San Francisco State University – Op
Gargett, Ann, (757) 683-6009 gargett@ccpo.odu.edu,
Old Dominion University – Op
Garihan, John M., (864) 294-3363 jack.garihan@furman.edu,
Furman University – Gc
Garnero, Edward, (480) 965-7653 garnero@asu.edu,
Arizona State University – Ys
Garren, Sandra J., 516-463-5565 sandra.j.garren@hofstra.edu,
Hofstra University – Oi
Garrett, Christopher J. R., (250) 721-7702 garrett@uvphys.phys.uvic.ca,
University of Victoria – Op
Garrett, Timothy J., 801-581-5768 tim.garrett@utah.edu,
University of Utah – Oa
Garrick-Bethell, Ian, 831-459-1277 igarrick@ucsc.edu,
University of California, Santa Cruz – Xy
Garrison, Ervan G., (706) 542-1097 egarriso@uga.edu,
University of Georgia – Ga
Garrison, Jennifer, 323-343-2412 jgarris@calstatela.edu,
California State University, Los Angeles – Giv
Garrison, Robert E., (831) 459-5563 University of California, Santa Cruz – Gs
Garrod, Bruce, (416) 978-3538 bruce.garrod@utoronto.ca,
University of Toronto – On
Garside, Larry J., 775-784-6693 lgarside@unr.edu,
University of Nevada – Gg
Garstang, Mimi R., 573-368-2101 mimi.garstang@dnr.mo.gov,
Missouri Dept of Natural Resources – Ge
Gartner, Janette, (781) 891-2901 jgartner@bentley.edu,
Bentley University – Hy
Garven, Grant, 617-627-3795 Grant.Garven@tufts.edu,
Tufts University – Hwy
Garver, John I., (518) 388-6770 garverj@union.edu,
Union College – GtCcGr
Garvin, Theresa D., (780) 492-4593 theresa.garvin@ualberta.ca,
University of Alberta – On
Garwood, Phil, 910 392 7111 pgarwood@cfcc.edu,
Cape Fear Community College – Gg
Garwood, Roland W., garwood@nps.edu, Naval Postgraduate School – Op
Garzione, Carmala N., (585) 273-4572 garzione@earth.rochester.edu,
University of Rochester – Gs
Gascho, Gary J., (912) 386-3329 University of Georgia – Sc
Gasparini, Nicole, 504-862-3197 ngaspari@tulane.edu,
Tulane University – Ngg
Gastaldo, Robert A., (207) 859-5807 ragastal@colby.edu,
Colby College – PbGs
Gaston, Lewis A., (504) 388-1323 lagaston@agcenter.lsu.edu,
Louisiana State University – Sc
Gates, Alexander E., 973-353-5034 agates@andromeda.rutgers.edu,
Rutgers, The State University of New Jersey, Newark – Gc
Gates, Ruth D., (808) 236-7420 rgates@hawaii.edu,
University of Hawai'i, Manoa – Ob
Gathany, Mark, 937-766-3823 mgathany@cedarville.edu,
Cedarville University – OiuSb
Gattiglio, Marco, marco.gattiglio@unito.it, Università di Torino – Gc
Gatto, Roberto, +390498279172 roberto.gatto@unipd.it,
Università degli Studi di Padova – Pg
Gaubatz, Piper, (413) 545-0768 gaubatz@geo.umass.edu,
University of Massachusetts, Amherst – Oy
Gauci, Adam, adam.gauci@um.edu.mt, University of Malta – Op
Gaudette, Henri E., (603) 862-1718 University of New Hampshire – Cc
Gauert, Chris, +27 (0)51 401 2372 gauertcdk@ufs.ac.za,
University of the Free State – EgGi
Gaulton, Rachel, +44 (0) 191 208 6577 rachel.gaulton@ncl.ac.uk,
University of Newcastle Upon Tyne – Or
Gautam, Tej, 740-376-4371 tej.gautam@marietta.edu,
Marietta College – Ge
Gauthier, Donald J., (818) 778-5514 gauthidj@lavc.edu,
Los Angeles Valley College – OiyOw
Gauthier, Jacques, (203) 432-3150 jacques.gauthier@yale.edu,
Yale University – Pv
Gauthier, Michel, 514-987-3000 #4560 gauthier.michel@uqam.ca,
Universite du Quebec a Montreal – Eg
Gauthier, Paul, (609) 258-7442 ppg@princeton.edu,
Princeton University – Sb
Gauthier, Pierre, 514-987-3000 #3304 gauthier.pierre@uqam.ca,
Universite du Quebec a Montreal – Ow
Gauthier, Pierre, pierre.gauthier@ec.gc.ca,
McGill University – Oa
Gautsch, Jacklyn, 319-335-1761 jackie.gautsch@dnr.iowa.gov,
Iowa Dept of Natural Resources – On
Gavin, Dan, (541) 346-5787 dgavin@uoregon.edu,
University of Oregon – Oy
Gavriloaiei, Traian, +40-232-201462 tgavrilo@uaic.ro,
Al. I. Cuza University of Iasi – CaOa
Gawloski, Joan, 432-685-4630 jgawloski@midland.edu,
Midland College – GgzGe
Gay, Kenny, 9197337353 x28 kenny.gay@ncdenr.gov   ,
North Carolina Geological Survey – Gz

Gaya, Charles , cogaya@jkuat.ac.ke,
Jomo Kenyatta University of Agriculture & Technology – OrgOi
Gayes, Paul T., (803) 349-2213 Dalhousie University – Gs
Gaylord, David R., (509) 335-8127 gaylordd@wsu.edu,
Washington State University – Gs
Gazis, Carey A., 509.963-2820 cgazis@geology.cwu.edu,
Central Washington University – Cs
Ge, Shemin, 303-492-8323 ges@colorado.edu,
University of Colorado – Hw
Geary, Dana H., (608) 263-7754 dana@geology.wisc.edu,
University of Wisconsin, Madison – Po
Geary, Lindsey, (315)792-3134 Utica College – Geg
Geary, Phil, 61 02 4921 6726 Phil.Geary@newcastle.edu.au,
University of Newcastle – HwOsHw
Gebrande, Helmut, 089/2180 4235 gebrande@geophysik.uni-muenchen.de,
Ludwig-Maximilians-Universitaet Muenchen – Yg
Gebrehiwet, Tsigabu A., 410-704-2220 Tsigab@gmail.com,
Towson University – Hw
Gedzelman, Stanley, (212) 650-6470 City College (CUNY) – Oa
Gee, Jeffrey S., (858) 534-4707 jsgee@ucsd.edu,
University of California, San Diego – Gu
Gegg, Steven, (508) 289-3233 sgegg@whoi.edu,
Woods Hole Oceanographic Institution – Oc
Gehrels, George E., (520) 621-6026 ggehrels@email.arizona.edu,
University of Arizona – Gt
Gehrels, Tom, (520) 621-6970 tgehrels@lpl.arizona.edu,
University of Arizona – On
Geibert, Walter, +44 (0) 131 651 7704 Walter.Geibert@ed.ac.uk,
Edinburgh University – Cc
Geidel, Gwendelyn, (803) 777-7171 geidel@geol.sc.edu,
University of South Carolina – Hw
Geiger, James W., 217-265-8989 jgeiger@illinois.edu,
University of Illinois, Urbana-Champaign – Ge
Geissman, John D., 972-883-2403 geissman@utdallas.edu,
University of Texas, Dallas – Yt
Geissman, John W., (505) 277-3433 jgeiss@unm.edu,
University of New Mexico – Ym
Geist, Dennis J., (208) 885-6491 dgeist@uidaho.edu,
University of Idaho – Gi
Gelbaum, Carol, 770-274-5050 carol.gelbaum@gpc.edu,
Georgia Perimeter College – Gdg
Gelderman, Ronald H., (605) 688-4770 Ronald.Gelderman@sdstate.edu,
South Dakota State University – Sc
Geller, Jonathan, 831-771-4400 geller@mlml.calstate.edu,
Moss Landing Marine Laboratories – On
Geller, Marvin A., (631) 632-8701 marvin.geller@stonybrook.edu,
SUNY, Stony Brook – Oa
Geller, Michael D., (609) 652-4620 Richard Stockton College of New Jersey – On
Gemignani, Robert, (314) 935-4614 rgemigna@levee.wustl.edu,
Washington University in St. Louis – On
Gemmell, J B., 61 3 6226 2893 Bruce.Gemmell@utas.edu.au,
University of Tasmania – Eg
Gemperline, Johanna, 410-554-5552 johanna.gemperline@maryland.gov,
Maryland Department of Natural Resources – Hw
Genareau, Kimberly, 205-348-1878 kdg@ua.edu,
University of Alabama – Gvi
Gendzwill, Donald J., don.gendzwill@usask.ca,
University of Saskatchewan – Ye
Genge, Matthew, +44 20 759 46499 m.genge@imperial.ac.uk,
Imperial College – Xm
Gentile, Richard J., (816) 235-2974 gentiler@umkc.edu,
University of Missouri-Kansas City – Gr
Gentry, Christopher, 931-221-7478 gentryc@apsu.edu,
Austin Peay State University – Oyi
Gentry, Randall, 630-252-4440 rgentry@anl.gov,
Argonne National Laboratory – Hw
Gentry, Terry, 979-845-3041 tgentry@ag.tamu.edu,
Texas A&M University – Sb
George, Graham, 306-966-5722 g.george@usask.ca,
University of Saskatchewan – Cg
Georgen, Jennifer, 850-645-4987 georgen@gly.fsu.edu,
Florida State University – Gu
Georgen, Jennifer, 757-683-5198 jgeorgen@odu.edu,
Old Dominion University – Gu
Georgiev, Svetoslav, (970)-491-3789 svetoslav.georgiev@colostate.edu,
Colorado State University – CcGo
Geraghty Ward, Emily, wardem@msu.edu, Rocky Mountain College – Gc
Gerba, Charles P., (520) 621-6906 gerba@ag.arizona.edu,
University of Arizona – Sb
GERBE, Marie-Christine, 33-477485123 gerbe@univ-st-etienne.fr,
Université Jean Monnet, Saint-Etienne – GisOe
Gerber, Stefan, 352294-3174 sgerber@ufl.edu,
University of Florida – Os
Gerbi, Christopher C., 207 581-2153 University of Maine – Gt
Gerbi, Greg, 518-580-5127 ggerbi@skidmore.edu,
Skidmore College – OgYg
Gerhard, Lee C., 78538643965 leeg@sunflower.com,
University of Kansas – Gs
Gerhardt, Hannes, (678) 839-4064 hgerhard@westga.edu,
University of West Georgia – On

Vanderbilt University – GeOa

Gillikin, David P., 518 388-6679 gillikid@union.edu, Union College – Csm

Gillis, James M., (906) 487-1820 jmgillis@mtu.edu,
Michigan Technological University – Nmr

Gillis, Kathryn, 250-721-6120 kgillis@uvic.ca, University of Victoria – Gp

Gillis, Robert, (907) 451-5024 robert.gillis@alaska.gov,
Alaska Division of Geological & Geophysical Surveys – Eo

Gillman, Joe, (573) 368-2101 joe.gillman@dnr.mo.gov,
Missouri Dept of Natural Resources – Gg

Gillmore, Gavin, +44 020 8417 2518 G.Gillmore@kingston.ac.uk,
Kingston University – Gb

Gilmore, Martha S., (860) 685-3129 mgilmore@wesleyan.edu,
Wesleyan University – XgGmOr

Gilmore, Tyler J., (509) 376-2370 tyler.gilmore@pnl.gov,
Pacific Northwest National Laboratory – Hg

Gilmour, Ernest H., (509) 359-7480 egilmour@ewu.edu,
Eastern Washington University – Pi

Gilotti, Jane A., (319) 335-1097 jane-gilotti@uiowa.edu,
University of Iowa – Gc

Gilpin, Bernard J., (714) 895-8233 bgilpin@gwc.cccd.edu,
Golden West College – Ys

Gimmestad, Gary, (404) 407-6029 gary.gimmestad@gtri.gatech.edu,
Georgia Institute of Technology – Oa

Ginder-Vogel, Matt, 608-262-0768 mgindervogel@wisc.edu,
University of Wisconsin, Madison – Sc

Gingerich, Philip D., (734) 764-0490 gingeric@umich.edu,
University of Michigan – Pv

Gingras, Murray, 780-492-1963 mgringras@ualberta.ca,
University of Alberta – Go

Ginis, Isaac, (401) 874-6484 iginis@gso.uri.edu,
University of Rhode Island – Op

Ginsburg, Robert N., 305 421-4875 rginsburg@rsmas.miami.edu,
University of Miami – Gs

Giordano, Daniele, daniele.giordano@unito.it,
Università di Torino – Gv

Giorgis, Scott D., 585-245-5293 giorgis@geneseo.edu,
SUNY, Geneseo – Gc

Giosan, Liviu, 508-289-2257 lgiosan@whoi.edu,
Woods Hole Oceanographic Institution – Gu

Giraldo, Mario A., (818) 677-4431 mario.giraldo@csun.edu,
California State University, Northridge – OrHgOg

Girard, Eric, 514-987-3000 #3325 girard.eric@uqam.ca,
Universite du Quebec a Montreal – Ow

Girard, Michael W., (609) 292-2576 mike.girard@dep.state.nj.us,
New Jersey Geological Survey – Oi

Giraud, Richard E., (801) 537-3351 richardgiraud@utah.gov,
Utah Geological Survey – Ng

Girhard, T S., 486-0045 tgirhard@alamo.edu,
San Antonio Community College – Oyw

Girhard, Thomas S., tgirhard@alamo.edu,
Alamo Colleges - San Antonio College – Oyw

Girty, Gary H., (619) 594-2552 ggirty@mail.sdsu.edu,
San Diego State University – Gc

Gitelson, Anatoly, gitelson@calmit.unl.edu,
Unversity of Nebraska - Lincoln – On

Gittings, Bruce M., +44 (0) 131 650 2558 bruce@ed.ac.uk,
Edinburgh University – Oi

Gittins, John, 416 445 6096 j.gittins@utoronto.ca,
University of Toronto – Gi

Giusberti, Luca, +390498279183 luca.giusberti,
Università degli Studi di Padova – Pm

Giustetto, Roberto, roberto.giustetto@unito.it,
Università di Torino – Gz

Glamoclija, Mihaela , 973-353-2509 m.glamoclija@rutgers.edu,
Rutgers, The State University of New Jersey, Newark – Py

Glasauer, Susan, (519) 824-4120 xt52453 glasauer@uoguelph.ca,
University of Guelph – Py

Glaser, Brian, 309-796-5238 glaserb@bhc.edu,
Black Hawk College – On

Glaser, Paul H., 612-624-8395 glase001@umn.edu,
University of Minnesota, Twin Cities – Gn

Glass, Alex, 919 684 5847 alex.glass@duke.edu,
Duke University – Ggu

Glass, Billy P., (302) 831-8229 bglass@udel.edu,
University of Delaware – Xm

Glass, Hylke J., +44 01326 371823 H.J.Glass@exeter.ac.uk,
Exeter University – Gz

Glatzmaier, Gary A., (831) 459-5504 glatz@pmc.ucsc.edu,
University of California, Santa Cruz – Xy

Glazer, Brian, 808-956-6658 glazer@hawaii.edu,
University of Hawai'i, Manoa – Cm

Glazner, Allen F., 919-962-0689 afg@unc.edu,
University of North Carolina, Chapel Hill – Git

Gleason, Gayle C., (607) 753-2816 gleasong@cortland.edu,
SUNY, Cortland – Gc

Gleason, James D., 734-764-9523 jdgleaso@umich.edu,
University of Michigan – Cg

Gleeson, Sarah, 780-492-5071 sgleeson@ualberta.ca,
University of Alberta – Eg

Glenn, Craig R., (808) 956-2200 glenn@soest.hawaii.edu,

University of Hawai'i, Manoa – Gs

Glenn, Ed, (520) 626-2664 eglenn@ag.arizona.edu,
University of Arizona – On

Glenn, Nancy, 208.221.1245 nancyglenn@boisestate.edu,
Boise State University – OrNgOi

Gloaguen, Erwan, erwan.gloaguen@ete.inrs.ca,
Universite du Quebec – Ye

Glotch, Timothy, 631-632-1168 tglotch@notes.cc.sunysb.edu,
SUNY, Stony Brook – Eo

Glover, David M., (508) 289-2656 dglover@whoi.edu,
Woods Hole Oceanographic Institution – Oc

Glover, Paul, +44(0) 113 34 35213 P.W.J.Glover@Leeds.ac.uk,
University of Leeds – Gd

Glover, Paul W., 418-656-5180 paul.glover@ggl.ulaval.ca,
Universite Laval – Yx

Glowacka, Ewa, glowacka@cicese.mx,
Centro de Investigación Científica y de Educación Superior de Ensenada – Ys

Glubokovskikh, Stanislav, +618 9266-7190 stanislav.glubokovskikh@curtin.edu.au,
Curtin University – Yxe

Gluhovsky, Alexander, (765) 494-0670 aglu@purdue.edu,
Purdue University – Oa

Glumac, Bosiljka, (413) 585-3680 bglumac@smith.edu,
Smith College – Gs

Gluyas, Jon, +44 (0) 191 33 42302 j.g.gluyas@durham.ac.uk,
Durham University – Eo

Glynn, William G., wglynn@brockport.edu,
SUNY, The College at Brockport – Gg

Gnanadesikan, Anand, 410-516-0722 gnanades@jhu.edu,
Johns Hopkins University – Op

Gobel, Volker W., (936) 468-2493 vgobel@sfasu.edu,
Stephen F. Austin State University – Gi

Gobler, Christopher, (631) 632-5043 Christopher.Gobler@stonybrook.edu,
SUNY, Stony Brook – Ob

Godbold, Jasmin A., +44 (0)23 80593639 J.A.Goldbold@soton.ac.uk,
University of Southampton – Ob

Godchaux, Martha M., (208) 882-9062 Mount Holyoke College – Gv

Goddard, Lisa M., (845) 680-4430 goddard@iri.columbia.edu,
Columbia University – Oa

Godek, Melissa, 607 436-3069 Melissa.Godek@oneonta.edu,
SUNY, Oneonta – OwaOg

Godfrey, Brian J., 845-437-5544 godfrey@vassar.edu,
Vassar College – Ou

Godfrey, Chris, 828-232-5160 cgodfrey@unca.edu,
University of North Carolina, Asheville – OanOn

Godfrey-Smith, Dorothy I., (902) 494-1451 Dalhousie University – Cc

Godin, Laurent, 613-533-3223 godinl@queensu.ca,
Queen's University – Goc

Godsey, Holly, (801) 587-7865 University of Utah – Oe

Godsey, Sarah E., 208-282-3170 godsey@isu.edu,
Idaho State University – HwGm

Goedecke, George H., ggoedeck@nmsu.edu,
New Mexico State University, Las Cruces – Oa

Goehring, Brent, 504-862-3196 bgoehrin@tulane.edu,
Tulane University – CsGtv

Goeke, James W., (402) 472-3471 jgoeke@unl.edu,
Unversity of Nebraska - Lincoln – Hw

Goes, Saskia, +44 20 759 46434 s.goes@imperial.ac.uk,
Imperial College – Yg

Goetz, Alexander, 303-492-5086 goetz@cses.colorado.edu,
University of Colorado – Or

Goetz, Andrew R., 303-871-2866 agoetz@du.edu,
University of Denver – Og

Goetz, Bruce A., 715.682.1312 bgoetz@northland.edu,
Northland College – GgmHg

Goetz, Heinrich, (972) 377-1079 hgoetz@collin.edu,
Collin College - Preston Ridge Campus – Ge

Goetze, Erica, (808) 956-7156 egoetze@hawaii.edu,
University of Hawai'i, Manoa – Ob

Goff, Fraser, (505) 667-8060 fraser@lanl.gov,
Los Alamos National Laboratory – Cg

Goff, James, j.goff@unsw.edu.au,
University of New South Wales – Gsm

Goff, John A., (512) 471-0476 goff@ig.utexas.edu,
University of Texas at Austin – Yr

Goforth, Thomas T., (254) 710-2183 tom_goforth@baylor.edu,
Baylor University – Yg

Golabi, Mohammad H., 671-735-2143 mgolabi@uguam.uog.edu,
University of Guam – OsSpc

Gold, David P., (814) 865-7261 gold@ems.psu.edu,
Pennsylvania State University, University Park – Gc

Gold-Bouchot, Gerardo, 979-845-9826 ggold@tamu.edu,
Texas A&M University – Oc

Goldberg, David S., (845) 365-8674 Columbia University – Yr

Goldblatt, Colin, 250-721-6120 czg@uvic.ca,
University of Victoria – Oa

Goldfinger, Chris, (541) 737-9622 gold@coas.oregonstate.edu,
Oregon State University – Yr

Goldhamer, David A., (559) 646-6500 dagoldhamer@ucdavis.edu,
University of California, Davis – On

Goldman, Daniel, (937) 229-5637 dan.goldman@notes.udayton.edu,

451

University of California, Irvine – Og

Gouldson, Andy, +44(0) 113 34 36417 a.gouldson@leeds.ac.uk,
University of Leeds – Ge

Goulet, Normand, (514) 987-3375 r27254@er.uqam.ca,
Universite du Quebec a Montreal – Gc

Goulet, Richard, 613-943-9922 Richard.Goulet@cnsc-ccsn.gc.ca,
University of Ottawa – CgPyGe

Goulty, Neil R., 0191 3742513 n.r.goulty@durham.ac.uk,
Durham University – Yg

Gouzie, Douglas R., (417) 836-5228 douglasgouzie@missouristate.edu,
Missouri State University – HwGe

Gowan, Angela, (612) 626-6451 gowa0001@umn.edu,
University of Minnesota – Gl

Gowing, David, +44 (0)1908 659468 x 59468 david.gowing@open.ac.uk ,
The Open University – Pb

Goyne, Keith W., 573-882-0090 University of Missouri, Columbia – Sc

Grable, Judy, (229) 333-5752 Valdosta State University – Hs

Grabowski, Jonathan, 7815817370 x337 j.grabowski@neu.edu,
Northeastern University – GuEg

Grace, Cathy A., (662)915-1799 cag@olemiss.edu,
University of Mississippi – Gg

Grace, John, +44 (0) 131 650 5400 jgrace@ed.ac.uk,
Edinburgh University – Oa

Grace, Peter R., 61 7 3138 2610 pr.grace@qut.edu.au,
Queensland University of Technology – Sb

Grace, Shannon M., (512) 223-4891 sgrace@austincc.edu,
Austin Community College District – On

Graczyk, Donald G., (630) 252-3489 Argonne National Laboratory – Cs

Grady, William, 304 594 2331 grady@geosrv.wvnet.edu,
West Virginia University – Ec

Graedel, Thomas E., (203) 432-9733 thomas.graedel@yale.edu,
Yale University – Cl

Graf, Jr., Joseph L., (541) 552-6861 graf@sou.edu,
Southern Oregon University – Em

Graff, Thomas O., (479) 575-3878 tgraff@comp.uark.edu,
University of Arkansas, Fayetteville – Ou

Graff, William P., (609) 292-2576 bill.graff@dep.state.nj.us,
New Jersey Geological Survey – Oy

Graham, Barbara, 702-651-4173 barbara.graham@csn.edu,
College of Southern Nevada - West Charleston Campus – Oyw

Graham, David W., (541) 737-4140 dgraham@coas.oregonstate.edu,
Oregon State University – Cm

Graham, Gina, (907)451-5031 gina.graham@alaska.gov,
Division of Geological & Geophysical Surveys – Gz

Graham, Ian, i.graham@unsw.edu.au, University of New South Wales – GxEg

Graham, Linda K., (608) 262-2640 University of Wisconsin, Madison – Ob

Graham, Margaret C., +44 (0) 131 650 4767 Margaret.Graham@ed.ac.uk,
Edinburgh University – Ge

Graham, Michael, (831) 771-4400 mgraham@mlml.calstate.edu,
Moss Landing Marine Laboratories – Ob

Graham, Russell W., (814) 865-6336 graham@ems.psu.edu,
Pennsylvania State University, University Park – Pv

Graham, Stephan A., (650) 723-0507 graham@pangea.stanford.edu,
Stanford University – Go

Graham, William, (228) 688-3177 monty.graham@usm.edu,
University of Southern Mississippi – Ob

Graham, Jr., Earl K., (814) 865-2273 graham@ems.psu.edu,
Pennsylvania State University, University Park – Yx

Graham, Jr., James H., (863) 956-1151 jhgraham@ufl.edu,
University of Florida – Sb

Grala, Katarzynz, (662) 268-1032 Ext 222 kg160@msstate.edu,
Mississippi State University – Oi

Grammer, Michael, 405-744-6358 michael.grammer@okstate.edu,
Oklahoma State University – GsEo

Gran, Karen B., 218-726-7406 kgran@d.umn.edu,
University of Minnesota, Duluth – Gms

Grana, Dario, 307-766-3449 dgrana@uwyo.edu,
University of Wyoming – Ye

Grand, Stephen P., (512) 471-3005 steveg@maestro.geo.utexas.edu,
University of Texas at Austin – Yg

Grandal d'Anglade, Aurora, 00 34 981 167000 xeaurora@udc.es,
Coruna University – Pv

Grande, Anthony, 212-772-5265 tony.grande@hunter.cuny.edu,
Hunter College (CUNY) – On

Grande, Lance, (312) 665-7632 lgrande@fieldmuseum.org,
Field Museum of Natural History – Pv

Grandstaff, David E., (215) 204-8228 grand@temple.edu,
Temple University – Cl

Graney, Joseph R., (607) 777-6347 jgraney@binghamton.edu,
Binghamton University – Cl

Grange, Laura, +44 (0)23 80592786 L.J.Grange@noc.soton.a.cuk,
University of Southampton – Ob

Granger, Darryl E., (765) 494-0043 dgranger@purdue.edu,
Purdue University – Oa

Granger, Julie, 860-405-9094 julie.granger@uconn.edu,
University of Connecticut – Oc

Graniero, Phil A., (519) 253-3000 (Ext. 2485) graniero@uwindsor.ca,
University of Windsor – OiHg

Grannell, Roswitha B., (562) 985-4927 grannell@csulb.edu,
California State University, Long Beach – Yv

Grant, Alastair, +44 (0)1603 59 2537 a.grant@uea.ac.uk,
University of East Anglia – Ge

Grant, James A., (218) 726-7237 jgrant@d.umn.edu,
University of Minnesota, Duluth – Gp

Grant, John, (213) 265-8838 East Los Angeles College – On

Grant, John A., 202-633-2474 Smithsonian Institution / National Air & Space
Museum – Xg

Grant, Jonathan, (902) 494-2021 jon.grant@dal.ca,
Dalhousie University – Ob

Grant, Shelton K., (573) 341-4616 Missouri University of Science and Technology – Gz

Grapenthin, Ronni, 575-835-5924 rg@nmt.edu,
New Mexico Institute of Mining and Technology – Gv

Grasmueck, Mark, 305 421-4858 mgrasmueck@rsmas.miami.edu,
University of Miami – Yr

Grassineau, Nathalie, +44 1784 443810 Nathalie.Grassineau@rhul.ac.uk,
University of London, Royal Holloway & Bedford New College – Cs

Grasso, Cheryl, 401-874-2265 cgrasso@uri.edu,
University of Rhode Island – On

Grattan, Stephen R., (530) 752-1130 srgrattan@ucdavis.edu,
University of California, Davis – On

Grattan, Stephen R., 530-752-4618 srgrattan@ucdavis.edu,
University of California, Davis – Spp

Gratton, Yves, yves.gratton@ete.inrs.ca, Universite du Quebec – Op

Graumlich, Lisa J., (406) 994-5320 dalylisa@montana.edu,
Montana State University – Ou

Graustein, William C., (203) 287-2853 william.graustein@yale.edu,
Yale University – Cl

Gravely, Cynthia Rae, (864) 656-3438 gravelc@clemson.edu,
Clemson University – On

Graves, Alexandria, 919-513-0635 alexandria_graves@ncsu.edu,
North Carolina State University – Sb

Graves, Charles E., (314) 977-3121 gravesce@slu.edu,
Saint Louis University – Oa

Gravley, Darren, +64 3 3667001 Ext 45683 darren.gravley@canterbury.ac.nz,
University of Canterbury – Gv

Gray, Kyle R., 319-273-2809 kyle.gray@uni.edu,
University of Northern Iowa – OeGg

Gray, Lee M., (330) 823-3605 graylm@mountunion.edu,
Mount Union College – PoGg

Gray, Mary Beth, (570) 577-1146 mbgray@bucknell.edu,
Bucknell University – Gc

Gray, Neil, +44 (0) 191 208 4887 neil.gray@ncl.ac.uk,
University of Newcastle Upon Tyne – Py

Gray, Norman H., dlfox@umn.edu,
University of Connecticut – Gx

Gray, Robert S., (805) 965-0581 gray@sbcc.net,
Santa Barbara City College – PvGzx

Gray, Sarah, (860) 486-1386 sgray@sandiego.edu,
University of San Diego – On

Gray, Steven, steven.gray@umb.edu,
University of Massachusetts, Boston – On

Greatbatch, Ian, +44 020 8417 2879 I.Greatbatch@kingston.ac.uk,
Kingston University – Oi

Greatbatch, Richard , rgreatbatch@geomar.de, Dalhousie University – Op

Greb, Stephen F., 859-323-0542 greb@uky.edu, University of Kentucky – Gz

Green, Brittany, 785-532-6101 bdgreen@ksu.edu,
Kansas State University – On

Green, Douglas H., (740) 593-1843 green@ohio.edu,
Ohio University – Yg

Green, Harry W., (510) 642-3059 University of California, Berkeley – Pv

Green, Jack, (562) 985-4198 jgreen3@csulb.edu,
California State University, Long Beach – Gv

Green, John C., (218) 726-7208 jgreen@d.umn.edu,
University of Minnesota, Duluth – Gi

Green, Jonathan, +44 0151 795 4385 Jonathan.Green@liverpool.ac.uk,
University of Liverpool – Ob

Green, II, Harry W., (951) 827-4505 harry.green@ucr.edu,
University of California, Riverside – Yx

Greenberg, David, (902) 426-2431 greenbergd@mar.dfo-mpo.gc.ca,
Dalhousie University – Op

Greenberg, Jeffrey K., (630) 752-5866 jeffrey.greenberg@wheaton.edu,
Wheaton College – Gt

Greenberg, Richard J., (520) 621-6940 greenberg@lpl.arizona.edu,
University of Arizona – Xy

Greenberg, Sallie E., 217-244-4068 greenberg@isgs.uiuc.edu,
Illinois State Geological Survey – Cs

Greene, Barbara, (570) 484-2048 bgreene@lhup.edu,
Lock Haven University – On

Greene, Brian M., 412-395-7323 Brian.Greene@usace.army.mil,
Youngstown State University – Ng

Greene, Charles H., chg2@cornell.edu, Cornell University – Ob

Greene, David C., (740) 587-6476 greened@denison.edu,
Denison University – Gc

Greene, Don M., (254) 710-2193 don_greene@baylor.edu,
Baylor University – Oyw

Greene, Pauline R., (337) 482-6468 geology@louisiana.edu,
University of Louisiana at Lafayette – On

Greene, Roberta, 315-267-2286 greenera@potsdam.edu,
SUNY Potsdam – On

Gu, Jeff, (780) 492-2292 jgu@phys.ualberta.ca, University of Alberta – Ys
Gualda, Guilherme, 615-322-2976 g.gualda@vanderbilt.edu,
    Vanderbilt University – GivGz
Guan, Dabo, +44(0) 113 34 37432 d.guan@leeds.ac.uk,
    University of Leeds – Eg
Guan, Huade, huade.guan@flinders.edu.au, Flinders University – Hgw
Guccione, Margaret J., (479) 575-3354 guccione@comp.uark.edu,
    University of Arkansas, Fayetteville – GmaGg
Gudmundsson, Agust, +44 1784 276345 Agust.Gudmundsson@rhul.ac.uk,
    University of London, Royal Holloway & Bedford New College – Gc
Guenthner, Willy, wrg@illinois.edu,
    University of Illinois, Urbana-Champaign – GtzCg
Guerin, Gilles, (845)-365-8671 Columbia University – Gu
Guerra, Oralia, (512) 223-6052 oguerra1@austincc.edu,
    Austin Community College District – On
Guest, Peter S., 831-656-2451 pguest@nps.edu,
    Naval Postgraduate School – Ow
Guggenheim, Stephen J., (312) 996-3263 xtal@uic.edu,
    University of Illinois at Chicago – Gz
Guha, Jayanta, 418 545 5222 jguha@uqac.c,
    Universite du Quebec a Chicoutimi – Eg
Guilbert, John M., (520) 621-6024 j.guilbert@comcast.net,
    University of Arizona – Em
Guillemette, Renald, (979) 845-6301 guillemette@geo.tamu.edu,
    Texas A&M University – Gz
Guinan, Patrick E., 573-882-5909 guinanp@missouri.edu,
    University of Missouri, Columbia – Oa
Guinasso, Norman, (979) 862-2323 norman@geos.tamu.edu,
    Texas A&M University – Op
Gulbranson, Erik L., 414-229-1153 gulbrans@uwm.edu,
    University of Wisconsin, Milwaukee – CgPe
Gulen, Gurcan, 713-654-5404 gurcan.gulen@beg.utexas.edu,
    University of Texas at Austin – Eg
Gulick, Sean S., (512) 471-3262 sean@ig.utexas.edu,
    University of Texas at Austin – Yr
Gulliver, John S., (612) 625-4080 gulli003@tc.umn.edu,
    University of Minnesota, Twin Cities – Hs
Gundersen, James N., (316) 978-3140 Wichita State University – Ga
Gunderson, Lance, 404 727 8108 lgunder@emory.edu,
    Emory University – Sf
Gundiler, Ibrahim H., (505) 835-5730 gundiler@gis.nmt.edu,
    New Mexico Institute of Mining & Technology – Nx
Gunter, Mickey E., (208) 885-6015 mgunter@uidaho.edu,
    University of Idaho – Gz
Gunter, William D., (403) 472-4406 University of Calgary – Cl
Guo, Weifu, (508) 289-3380 wguo@whoi.edu,
    Woods Hole Oceanographic Institution – Ca
Gupta, Hoshin V., (520) 626-6974 hoshin.gupta@hwr.arizona.edu,
    University of Arizona – Hs
Gupta, Sanjeev, +44 20 759 46527 s.gupta@imperial.ac.uk,
    Imperial College – Gs
Gupta, Satish C., (612) 625-1241 sgupta@soils.umn.edu,
    University of Minnesota, Twin Cities – Sp
Gurdak, Jason, (415) 338-6869 jgurdak@sfsu.edu,
    San Francisco State University – Hw
Gurevich, Boris, +61 8 9266-7359 B.Gurevich@curtin.edu.au,
    Curtin University – Ye
Gurlea, Lawrence P., lisobar@aol.com, Youngstown State University – Cg
Gurnis, Michael C., (626) 395-6979 gurnis@gps.caltech.edu,
    California Institute of Technology – Ys
Gurocak, Zulfu, 00904242370000-5991 zgurocak@firat.edu.tr,
    Firat University – Nrg
Gurrola, Harold, 806-834-8625 harold.gurrola@ttu.edu,
    Texas Tech University – Ys
Gust, David A., 61 7 3138 2217 d.gust@qut.edu.au,
    Queensland University of Technology – GiCpGt
Gustin, Mae, 775.784.4203 mgustin@cabnr.unr.edu,
    University of Nevada, Reno – Cg
Guth, Lawrence R., 978-665-3082 lguth@fitchburgstate.edu,
    Fitchburg State University – Gc
Guth, Peter L., 410-293-6560 pguth@usna.edu,
    United States Naval Academy – GuOiy
Guthrie, Roderick I., (514) 398-4755 McGill University – Nx
Gutierrez, Melida, (417) 836-5967 mgutierrez@missouristate.edu,
    Missouri State University – Cg
Gutknecht, Jessica L., 612-626-8435 jgutknec@umn.edu,
    University of Minnesota, Twin Cities – Sb
Gutmann, James T., (860) 685-2258 jgutmann@wesleyan.edu,
    Wesleyan University – Gv
Gutowski, Vincent P., 217-581-3825 vpgutowski@eiu.edu,
    Eastern Illinois University – GmOy
Gutowski, William J., (515) 294-5632 gutowski@iastate.edu,
    Iowa State University of Science & Technology – Oa
Gutzler, David J., (505) 277-3328 gutzler@unm.edu,
    University of New Mexico – Oa
Guza, Robert T., (858) 534-0585 rguza@ucsd.edu,
    University of California, San Diego – On
Guzina, Bojan B., (612) 626-0789 guzina@wave.ce.umn.edu,
    University of Minnesota, Twin Cities – Nr
Guzman, Ernesto,   (519) 824-4120 Ext.53609 eguzman@uoguelph.ca,

University of Guelph – On
Gušiæ, Ivan, +38514606102 ivangusic@yahoo.com,
    University of Zagreb – GgPsm
Gyakum, John R., (514) 398-6076 john.gyakum@mcgill.ca,
    McGill University – Ow
Gysi, Alex, (303) 273-3828 agysi@mines.edu, Colorado School of Mines – Cg
Göttlich, Hagen, 089/2180 5615 goettlich@ennab.de,
    Ludwig-Maximilians-Universitaet Muenchen – Gz
Götz , Annette, +44 (0) 1782 733734 a.e.goetz@keele.ac.uk,
    Keele University – GsPmGg

H

Haag, Lucas, (785) 462-6281 lhaag@ksu.edu,
    Kansas State University – So
Haas, Christian, (416)736-2100 #77705 haasc@yorku.ca,
    York University – Yg
Haas, Johnson R., (269) 387-2878 johnson.haas@wmich.edu,
    Western Michigan University – Cl
Habana, Nathan C., (671) 735-2693 nhabana@uguam.uog.edu,
    University of Guam – Hw
Habash, Marc, (519) 824-4120 Ext.52748 mhabash@uoguelph.ca,
    University of Guelph – On
Haber, Eldad, (604) 822-4525 haber@eos.ubc.ca,
    University of British Columbia – YgOn
Habib, Daniel, (718) 997-3333 Graduate School of the City University of New
    York – Pl
Hacker, Bradley R., (805) 893-7952 hacker@geol.ucsb.edu,
    University of California, Santa Barbara – Gp
Hacker, David B., 330-672-8831 dhacker@kent.edu,
    Kent State University – GcHw
Hacker, Joshua P., 831-656-2722 jphacker@nps.edu,
    Naval Postgraduate School – Ow
Hacker, Patricia, 419-530-5058 patricia.hacker@utoledo.edu,
    University of Toledo – On
Hackley, Keith C., 217-244-2396 hackley@isgs.uiuc.edu,
    Illinois State Geological Survey – Cs
Haddad, Brent, (831) 459-4149 bhaddad@cats.ucsc.edu,
    University of California, Santa Cruz – On
Haddock, Gerald H., (630) 752-5063 Wheaton College – Gi
Haddock, Gregory D., (660) 562-1719 haddock@nwmissouri.edu,
    Northwest Missouri State University – Oi
Hadler, Kathryn, +44 20 759 47198 k.hadler@imperial.ac.uk,
    Imperial College – Gz
Hafez, Sabry, (907) 474- 6917 ssabour@alaska.edu,
    University of Alaska, Fairbanks – Nm
Haff, Peter K., (919) 684-5902 haff@duke.edu, Duke University – On
Hafner, James A., (413) 545-0778 hafner@geo.umass.edu,
    University of Massachusetts, Amherst – On
Hagadorn, James W., 303-370-6058 James.Hagadorn@dmns.org,
    Denver Museum of Nature & Science – GgsPg
Hagan, Robert M., (530) 752-0453 University of California, Davis – Hg
Hagedorn, Charles, (540) 231-4895 chagedor@vt.edu,
    Virginia Polytechnic Institute & State University – Sb
Hagelberg, Carl R., (505) 667-3596 drch@lanl.gov,
    Los Alamos National Laboratory – On
Hageman, Steven J., (828) 262-6609 hagemansj@appstate.edu,
    Appalachian State University – Pie
Hager, Bradford H., (617) 253-0126 bhhager@mit.edu,
    Massachusetts Institute of Technology – Ys
Hagerty, Michael, 617-552-8300 hagertmb@bc.edu, Boston College – Ys
Haggart, James, JHaggart@nrcan.gc.ca, University of British Columbia – Pg
Haggart, Renee, (604) 822-2789 rhaggart@eos.ubc.ca,
    University of British Columbia – On
Haggerty, Janet, 918-631-2304 janet-haggerty@utulsa.edu,
    University of Tulsa – Gu
Haggerty, Julia H., (406) 994-6904 julia.haggerty@montana.edu,
    Montana State University – On
Haggerty, Roy D., (541) 737-5195 haggertr@geo.oregonstate.edu,
    Oregon State University – Hw
Haggerty, Stephen E., 305-348-2617 haggerty@fiu.edu,
    Florida International University – Gz
Hagni, Richard D., (573) 341-4657 rhagni@umr.edu,
    Missouri University of Science and Technology – Em
Haiar, Brooke, haiar@lynchburg.edu, Lynchburg College – PoGeg
Haigh, Ivan D., +44 (023) 80596501 I.D.Haigh@soton.ac.uk,
    University of Southampton – On
Haigh, Nardia, nardia.haigh@umb.edu,
    University of Massachusetts, Boston – On
Haileab, Bereket, 507-222-5746 bhaileab@carleton.edu,
    Carleton College – Gx
Haimson, Bezalel C., 608/262-2563 bhaimson@wisc.edu,
    University of Wisconsin, Madison – Nr
Haine, Thomas W., (410) 516-7048 thomas.haine@jhu.edu,
    Johns Hopkins University – Op
Hajash, Andrew, (979) 845-0642 hajash@geo.tamu.edu,
    Texas A&M University – Cp
Hajek, Elizabeth, hajek@psu.edu,
    Pennsylvania State University, University Park – Gs
Hajnal, Zoltan, (306) 966-5694 zoltan.hajnal@usask.ca,
    University of Saskatchewan – Ys

Hakim, Gregory J., 206-685-2439 hakim@atmos.washington.edu,
University of Washington – Oa

Halama, Ralf, +44 (0) 1782 7 34960 r.halama@keele.ac.uk,
Keele University – GpiCa

Halbig, Joseph B., halbig@wazoo.com, University of Hawai'i, Hilo – Ca

Halden, Norman M., (204) 474-6910 nm_halden@umanitoba.ca,
University of Manitoba – Cg

Hale, Beverley A., (519) 824-4120 (Ext. 53434) bhale@uoguelph.ca,
University of Guelph – Ct

Hale, Dave, 303-273-3461 dhale@mines.edu, Colorado School of Mines – Ye

Hale, Leslie, (202) 633-1796 halel@si.edu,
Smithsonian Institution / National Museum of Natural History – Gg

Hale, Michelle, +44 023 92 842290 michelle.hale@port.ac.uk,
University of Portsmouth – Og

Hales, Burke R., (541) 737-8121 bhales@coas.oregonstate.edu,
Oregon State University – Oc

Hales, T. C., +44(0)29 208 74329 HalesT@cardiff.ac.uk,
University of Wales – Gt

Hales, TC, halest@cf.ac.uk, Cardiff University – Gm

Haley, Brian, 541-737-2649 bhaley@coas.oregonstate.edu,
Oregon State University – Cs

Haley, John C., 757-455-3407 jchaley@vwc.edu,
Virginia Wesleyan College – GgeOi

Halfar, Jochen, (905) 828-5419 jochen.halfar@utoronto.ca,
University of Toronto – Pe

Halfman, John D., (315) 781-3918 halfman@hws.edu,
Hobart & William Smith Colleges – Gn

Halgedahl, Susan L., (801) 581-7062 s.halgedahl@utah.edu,
University of Utah – Ym

Halihan, Todd, 405-744-6358 todd.halihan@okstate.edu,
Oklahoma State University – Hw

Hall, Anne M., (404) 727-2863 ahall04@emory.edu,
Emory University – Gz

Hall, Brenda L., (207) 581-2191 brendah@maine.edu,
University of Maine – Gl

Hall, Chad, Chad.Hall@gpc.edu, Georgia Perimeter College - Decatur – Gg

Hall, Chris, (734) 764-6391 cmhall@umich.edu,
University of Michigan – Cc

Hall, Christopher C., (519) 824-4120 Ext.52740 jchall@uoguelph.ca,
University of Guelph – On

Hall, Clarence A., (310) 825-1010 hall@epss.ucla.edu,
University of California, Los Angeles – Gt

Hall, Cynthia V., (610) 436-1003 chall@wcupa.edu,
West Chester University – Cg

Hall, Frank R., (504) 280-1105 frhall@mac.com,
University of New Orleans – Ym

Hall, Jean, +44 (0) 191 208 8783 jean.hall@ncl.ac.uk,
University of Newcastle Upon Tyne – Ng

Hall, Jeremy, (709) 737-7569 jeremyh@mun.ca,
Memorial University of Newfoundland – Ys

Hall, John C., 205 652 5468 jhall@uwa.edu,
University of West Alabama – Og

Hall, Jude, (740) 587-6217 hall@denison.edu, Denison University – On

Hall, Luke D., (805) 642-3211 lhall@vcccd.net, Ventura College – Oy

Hall, Michael, (727) 553-3916 mhall@seas.marine.usf.edu,
University of South Florida, Saint Petersburg – Oo

Hall, Robert, rhall@uoguelph.ca, University of Guelph – On

Hall, Robert, +44 1784 443897 Robert.Hall@rhul.ac.uk,
University of London, Royal Holloway & Bedford New College – Gt

Hall, Robert, +44 (0)1603 59 2550 robert.hall@uea.ac.uk,
University of East Anglia – On

Hall, Russell L., (403) 220-6678 University of Calgary – Pi

Hall, Stuart A., 713-743-3416 sahgeo@uh.edu,
University of Houston – Ym

Hall, Tracy, 678-872-8415 thall@highlands.edu,
Georgia Highlands College – Gg

Hall, III, John R., (504) 231-6305 jrhall3@vt.edu,
Virginia Polytechnic Institute & State University – So

Hallar, Anna G., 801-581-6136 gannet.hallar@utah.edu,
University of Utah – Oa

Haller, Merrick, 541-737-9141 hallerm@coas.oregonstate.edu,
Oregon State University – Onr

Hallet, Bernard, 206-685-2409 hallet@uw.edu,
University of Washington – GmOl

Hallett, Benjamin W., 920-424-0868 hallettb@uwosh.edu,
University of Wisconsin, Oshkosh – Gpx

Hallett, Rebecca, (519) 824-4120 Ext.54488 rhallett@uoguelph.ca,
University of Guelph – On

Halliday, Alex, +44 (1865) 272969 alex.halliday@earth.ox.ac.uk,
University of Oxford – Cs

Hallin, Stephen C., stephenhallin@weber.edu,
Weber State University – Ow

Hallmark, Charles T., (979) 845-4678 hallmark@tamu.edu,
Texas A&M University – Sd

Hallock, Brent G., (805)756-2436 bhallock@calpoly.edu,
California Polytechnic State University – Sf

Hallock-Muller, Pamela, (727) 553-1567 pmuller@marine.usf.edu,
University of South Florida – Pm

Halls, Henry C., 905-828-5363 hlhalls@utm.utoronto.ca,
University of Toronto – Ym

Halls, Joanne N., (910) 962-7614 hallsj@uncw.edu,
University of North Carolina Wilmington – Oi

Halsor, Sid P., (570) 408-4611 sid.halsor@wilkes.edu,
Wilkes University – Giv

Halsted, Christian, 207-287-7175 christian.h.halsted@maine.gov,
Dept of Agriculture, Conservation, and Forestry – Oi

Halverson, Galen, 514-398-4894 galen.halverson@mcgill.ca,
McGill University – GsCs

Halverson, Larry, (515) 294-0495 larryh@iastate.edu,
Iowa State University of Science & Technology – So

Ham, David, +44 20 759 46439 d.ham@imperial.ac.uk, Imperial College – Yg

Ham, Nelson R., (920) 403-3977 nelson.ham@snc.edu,
Saint Norbert College – Gl

Hamburger, Michael W., (812) 855-2934 hamburg@indiana.edu,
Indiana University, Bloomington – Ys

Hamdan, Abeer, abeer.hamdan@phoenixcollege.edu, Phoenix College – Gg

Hamecher, Emily, (657) 278-7096 ehamecher@fullerton.edu,
California State University, Fullerton – Gg

Hameed, Sultan, (631) 632-8319 sultan.hameed@stonybrook.edu,
SUNY, Stony Brook – Oa

Hames, Willis E., (334) 844-4881 hameswe@auburn.edu,
Auburn University – GpCc

Hamill, Paul, (815) 455-8698 phamill@mchenry.edu,
McHenry County College – Owg

Hamilton, George, (413) 499-4660 bhamilton@berkshirecc.edu,
Berkshire Community College – On

Hamilton, Gordon S., (207) 581-3446 gordon.hamilton@maine.edu,
University of Maine – Ol

Hamilton, Jacqueline, (612) 626-8292 stub0035@umn.edu,
University of Minnesota – Oi

Hamilton, Michael Andrew, (416) 946-7424 mahamilton@geology.utoronto.ca,
University of Toronto – Cc

Hamilton, Phillip, phamiltn@neaq.org, University of Massachusetts, Boston – Ob

Hamilton, Sally, +44 (0)131 451 3198 sally.hamilton@pet.hw.ac.uk,
Heriot-Watt University – Os

Hamilton, Thomas, 4256401339x7067 thomas.hamilton@edcc.edu,
Edmonds Community College – Og

Hamilton, Warren, 303-384-2047 whamilto@mines.edu,
Colorado School of Mines – Ys

Hamlin, H, Scott, 512-4759527 scott.hamlin@beg.utexas.edu,
University of Texas at Austin, Jackson School of Geosciences – Gr

Hamme, Roberta, 250-721-6120 rhamme@uvic.ca,
University of Victoria – Oc

Hammer, Julia E., 808-956-5996 jhammer@hawaii.edu,
University of Hawai'i, Manoa – GiCpGv

Hammer, Philip T., (604) 822-5703 phammer@eos.ubc.ca,
University of British Columbia – Ys

Hammer, William R., (309) 794-7487 williamhammer@augustana.edu,
Augustana College – Pv

Hammerschmidt, Chad, 937 775-3457 chad.hammerschmidt@wright.edu,
Wright State University – CmOc

Hammersley, Charles, (928) 523-6655 charles.hammersley@nau.edu,
Northern Arizona University – On

Hammersley, Lisa, 916-278-7200 hammersley@csus.edu,
California State University, Sacramento – Gig

Hammes, Ursula, 512-471-1891 ursula.hammes@beg.utexas.edu,
University of Texas at Austin – Gr

Hammond, Anne, (807) 343-8677 anne.hammond@lakeheadu.ca,
Lakehead University – On

Hammond, Douglas E., (213) 740-5837 dhammond@usc.edu,
University of Southern California – Cm

Hammond, Paul E., (503) 725-3387 hammondp@pdx.edu,
Portland State University – Gi

Hammond, William, 775 784-6436 whammond@unr.edu,
University of Nevada – Yd

Hampson, Arthur, (801) 585-5698 spike.hampson@geog.utah.edu,
University of Utah – Oy

Hampson, Gary , +44 20 759 46475 g.j.hampson@imperial.ac.uk,
Imperial College – Gd

Hampton, Brian A., 575-646-2997 bhampton@nmsu.edu,
New Mexico State University, Las Cruces – Gst

Hampton, Duane R., (269) 387-5496 duane.hampton@wmich.edu,
Western Michigan University – Hw

Hampton, Samuel, +64 3 3667001 Ext 6770 samuel.hampton@canterbury.ac.nz,
University of Canterbury – Gq

Hams, Jacquelyn E., (818) 778-5566 hamsje@lavc.edu,
Los Angeles Valley College – GgOue

Hamzaoui, Cherif, 514-987-3000 #6837 hamzaoui.cherif@uqam.ca,
Universite du Quebec a Montreal – Yg

Han, De-hua, 713-743-9293 dhan@uh.edu, University of Houston – Ye

Han, Nizhou, (540) 231-2403 nhan@vt.edu,
Virginia Polytechnic Institute & State University – Sc

Han, Weon Shik, 414-229-2493 hanw@uwm.edu,
University of Wisconsin, Milwaukee – Hw

Hanan, Barry B., (619) 594-6710 bhanan@mail.sdsu.edu,
San Diego State University – Cc

Hancock, Gregory, 61 02 4921 5090 Greg.Hancock@newcastle.edu.au,
University of Newcastle – OiGmm

Hancock, Gregory S., (757) 221-2446 gshanc@wm.edu,
College of William & Mary – Gm

Hauck, II, Steven A., (216) 368-3675 hauck@case.edu,
Case Western Reserve University – Yg
Hauer, Kendall, (513) 529-3220 hauerkl@MiamiOh.edu,
Miami University – Gg
Haugerud, Ralph, 206-713-7453 rah@ess.washington.edu,
University of Washington – Oi
Haughland, Jake, 775-784-6995 University of Nevada, Reno – Gm
Hauksson, Egill, (626) 395-6954 hauksson@gps.caltech.edu,
California Institute of Technology – Ys
Hauri, Erik H., (202) 478-8471 ehauri@carnegiescience.edu,
Carnegie Institution of Washington – Cc
Hausback, Brian, (916) 278-6521 hausback@csus.edu,
California State University, Sacramento – Gv
Hauser, Ernest C., 937 775-3455 ernest.hauser@wright.edu,
Wright State University – Ye
Hausrath, Elisabeth M., 702-895-1134 elisabeth.hausrath@unlv.edu,
University of Nevada, Las Vegas – ScCl
Hautala, Susan L., (206) 543-0596 susanh@ocean.washington.edu,
University of Washington – Op
Hauton, Chris, +44 (0)23 80595784 ch10@noc.soton.ac.uk,
University of Southampton – Ob
Havenith, Hans-Balder, 32 4 3662035 HB.Havenith@ulg.ac.be,
Universite de Liege – Ge
Haverluk, Terry W., (719) 333-8746 usafa.dfeg@usafa.edu,
United States Air Force Academy – Og
Havholm, Karen D., (715) 836-2945 havholkg@uwec.edu,
University of Wisconsin, Eau Claire – Oe
Havlin, John L., (919) 515-2655 havlin@ncsu.edu,
North Carolina State University – Sc
Hawkins, David, 781-283-3554 dhawkins@wellesley.edu,
Wellesley College – Gzi
Hawkins, James W., (858) 534-2161 jhawkins@ucsd.edu,
University of California, San Diego – Gp
Hawkins, John, 334-844-4894 jfh0005@auburn.edu,
Auburn University – Gg
Hawkins, Lawrence, +44 (0)23 80593426 leh@noc.soton.ac.uk,
University of Southampton – Pi
Hawkins, Michael E., (518) 486-2011 mhawkins@mail.nysed.gov,
New York State Geological Survey – Gz
Hawkins, R. B., (520) 621-7273 rhawkins@ag.arizona.edu,
University of Arizona – Hs
Hawkins, Stephen J., +44 (0)23 8059 3596 S.J.Hawkins@soton.ac.uk,
University of Southampton – Nr
Hawkins, Terry, (573) 368-2164 terry.hawkins@dnr.mo.gov,
Missouri Dept of Natural Resources – Gg
Hawkins, Timothy W., (717) 477-1662 twhawk@ship.edu,
Shippensburg University – Oa
Hawkins, Ward L., (505) 667-5835 whawkins@lanl.gov,
Los Alamos National Laboratory – Og
Hawley, John W., (505) 255-4847 hgeomatters@qwest.net,
New Mexico Institute of Mining & Technology – Ge
Hawley, Rebecca D., (928) 523-1251 d.hawley@nau.edu,
Northern Arizona University – On
Hawley, Robert L., 603-646-2373 Robert.Hawley@dartmouth.edu,
Dartmouth College – Gl
Hawman, Robert B., (706) 542-2398 rob@seismo.gly.uga.edu,
University of Georgia – Ys
Hawthorne, Frank C., (204) 474-8861 frank_hawthorne@umanitoba.ca,
University of Manitoba – Gz
Hawthorne, Timothy, 404-413-5771 thawthorne@gsu.edu,
Georgia State University – Oi
Hay, Alex E., (902) 494-6657 alex.hay@dal.ca, Dalhousie University – Op
Hay, Iain, iain.hay@flinders.edu.au, Flinders University – Oyy
Hay, Rodrick, (310) 243-2547 rhay@csudh.edu,
California State University, Dominguez Hills – Or
Hayashi, Masaki, (403) 220-2794 hayashi@ucalgary.ca,
University of Calgary – Hw
Hayden, Bruce P., (804) 924-0545 bph@virginia.edu,
University of Virginia – Oa
Hayden, Geoffrey W., (912) 752-2597 Mercer University – Om
Hayden, Martha C., (801) 537-3311 nrugs.mhayden@state.ut.us,
Utah Geological Survey – Pv
Hayes, Alexander, 607-255-1712 agh4@cornell.edu, Cornell University – Xg
Hayes, Christopher T., (228) 688-3469 christopher.t.hayes@usm.edu,
University of Southern Mississippi – Oc
Hayes, Dennis E., (845) 365-8470 deph@ldeo.columbia.edu,
Columbia University – Yr
Hayes, Garry F., (209) 575-6294 Modesto Junior College – Gg
Hayes, Garry F., GHayes@csustan.edu,
California State University, Stanislaus – Gg
Hayes, James J., 402-554-3862 jjhayes@unomaha.edu,
University of Nebraska at Omaha – OruOi
Hayes, John M., (914) 365-8470 jhayes@whoi.edu,
Indiana University, Bloomington – Co
Hayes, Michael J., (402) 472-4271 mhayes2@unl.edu,
University of Nebraska, Lincoln – Oa
Hayes, Miles O., 504-280-6325 mhayes@uno.edu,
University of New Orleans – Gs
Hayes, Van E., 813-253-7685 vhayes@hccfl.edu,
Hillsborough Community College – Og

Hayman, Nicholas W., 512-471-7721 hayman@ig.utexas.edu,
University of Texas at Austin – Ou
Hayman, Patrick, patrick.hayman@qut.edu.au,
Queensland University of Technology – EgGvp
Haymet, Anthony D., (858) 534-2827 thaymet@ucsd.edu,
University of California, San Diego – On
Haynes, Kyle J., (540) 837-1758 kjh8w@virginia.edu,
University of Virginia – On
Haynes, Samantha, +44(0) 113 34 34938 S.E.Haynes.ac.uk,
University of Leeds – Go
Haynes, Jr., C. Vance, (520) 621-6307 University of Arizona – Ga
Hays, James D., (845) 365-8403 jimhays@ldeo.columbia.edu,
Columbia University – PemOu
Hays, Phillip D., (479) 575-7343 pdhays@uark.edu,
University of Arkansas, Fayetteville – HwCsGg
Hayward, Chris L., +44 (0) 131 650 5827 chris.hayward@ed.ac.uk,
Edinburgh University – Ga
Haywick, Douglas W., (334) 460-6381 dhaywick@jaguar1.usouthal.edu,
University of South Alabama – Gs
Haywood, Alan, +44(0) 113 34 38657 earamh@leeds.ac.uk,
University of Leeds – Pe
Hazel, McGoff, H.J.McGoff@rdg.ac.uk, University of Reading – Pg
Hazel, Jr., Joseph E., (928) 523-9145 joseph.hazel@nau.edu,
Northern Arizona University – Gs
Hazen, Robert M., (703) 993-2163 rhazen@gmu.edu,
George Mason University – Om
Hazen, Robert M., 202-478-8962 rhazen@carnegiescience.edu,
Carnegie Institution of Washington – Gz
Hazlett, Richard W., (909) 621-8675 rhazlett@pomona.edu,
Pomona College – Gv
He, Changming, 302-831-4917 hchm@udel.edu,
University of Delaware – GqHg
He, Helen, +44 (0)1603 59 2091 yi.he@uea.ac.uk,
University of East Anglia – Pe
He, Ruoying, 919-513-0943 ruoying_he@ncsu.edu,
North Carolina State University – Op
He, Zhenli, 772-468-3922 zhe@ufl.edu, University of Florida – Sc
Head, Elisabet M., 773-442-6055 E-Head@neiu.edu,
Northeastern Illinois University – GvOrCg
Head, Martin J., (905) 688-5550 (Ext. 5216) mjhead@brocku.ca,
Brock University – Pl
Head, Martin J., 905 688 5550 x5216 mjhead@brocku.ca,
University of Toronto – Pi
Head, III, James W., (401) 863-2526 James_Head_III@Brown.edu,
Brown University – Xg
Heal, Kate V., +44 (0) 131 650 5420 K.Heal@ed.ac.uk,
Edinburgh University – Co
Heald, Colette, 970-491-8034 heald@atmos.colostate.edu,
Colorado State University – Oa
Heald, Colette, (617) 324-5666 heald@mit.edu,
Massachusetts Institute of Technology – Oa
Healey, Michael, (604) 822-4705 mhealey@eos.ubc.ca,
University of British Columbia – Ob
Heaman, Larry M., (780) 492-2778 larry.heaman@ualberta.ca,
University of Alberta – Cc
Heaney, Michael , (979) 845-7841 heaney@geo.tamu.edu,
Texas A&M University – Pg
Heaney, Peter, (814) 865-6821 heaney@geosc.psu.edu,
Pennsylvania State University, University Park – Gz
Hearn, Carter, (202) 633-1756 hearnc@si.edu,
Smithsonian Institution / National Museum of Natural History – Gi
Hearn, Thomas M., (505) 646-5076 thearn@nmsu.edu,
New Mexico State University, Las Cruces – Ys
Heath, Carolyn, 714-992-7444 cheath@fullcoll.edu,
Fullerton College – Ob
Heath, G. Ross, (206) 543-3153 rheath@u.washington.edu,
University of Washington – Cm
Heath, Kathleen M., (812) 237-3004 kheath@indstate.edu,
Indiana State University – Pb
Heatherington, Ann L., (352) 392-6220 aheath@ufl.edu,
University of Florida – Cc
Heaton, Jill, (775) 784-8056 jheaton@unr.edu, University of Nevada, Reno – Oi
Heaton, Richard C., (505) 667-1141 Los Alamos National Laboratory – On
Heaton, Thomas H., (626) 395-6897 heaton@gps.caltech.edu,
California Institute of Technology – Ne
Heaton, Timothy H., (605) 677-6122 Timothy.Heaton@usd.edu,
University of South Dakota – PvOg
Heatwole, Charles A., (212) 772-5323 Graduate School of the City University of
New York – On
Heavers, Richard, (401) 254-3095 Roger Williams University – Op
Hebblethwaite, Chris, chris.hebblethwaite@oswego.edu,
State University of New York at Oswego – On
Hebda, Richard J., (250) 387-5493 University of Victoria – Pl
Hebert, David, (902) 426-1216 david.hebert@dfo-mpo.gc.ca,
Dalhousie University – Op
Hebert, David L., (401) 874-6610 herbert@gso.uri.edu,
University of Rhode Island – Op
Hebert, Rejean J., 418-656-3137 herbert@ggl.ulaval.ca, Universite Laval – Gi
Heck, Frederick R., (616) 592-2588 heckf@ferris.edu,
Ferris State University – Gg

Henry, Darrell J., (225) 388-2693 dhenry@geol.lsu.edu,
Louisiana State University – Gp
Henry, Eric J., 910-962-7622 henrye@uncw.edu,
University of North Carolina Wilmington – Hw
Henry, James A., (615)904-8452 Jim.Henry@mtsu.edu,
Middle Tennessee State University – Oa
Henry, Kathleen M., 217-244-4990 henry@isgs.uiuc.edu,
Illinois State Geological Survey – Gg
Henry, Tiernan, +353 (0)91 495 096 tiernan.henry@nuigalway.ie,
National University of Ireland Galway – Hg
Henshel, Diane S., (812) 855-4556 dhenshel@indiana.edu,
Indiana University, Bloomington – On
Henson, Harvey, 618-536-6666 henson@geo.siu.edu,
Southern Illinois University Carbondale – Yg
Henstock, Tim, +44 (0)23 80596491 then@noc.soton.ac.uk,
University of Southampton – Yg
Hentz, Tucker F., (512) 471-7281 tucker.hentz@beg.utexas.edu,
University of Texas at Austin, Jackson School of Geosciences – Go
Henyey, Thomas L., (213) 740-5832 henyey@usc.edu,
University of Southern California – Yg
Henßel, Katja, 089/2180 6624 k.henssel@lrz.uni-muenchen.de,
Ludwig-Maximilians-Universitaet Muenchen – Pg
Hepburn, J. Christopher, 617-552-3642 john.hepburn@bc.edu,
Boston College – Gg
Hepner, George F., (801) 581-6021 george.hepner@geog.utah.edu,
University of Utah – Oy
Hepner, Tiffany, (512) 475-9572 tiffany.hepner@beg.utexas.edu,
University of Texas at Austin, Jackson School of Geosciences – Og
Hepple, Alex, 3138 5051 a.hepple@qut.edu.au,
Queensland University of Technology – GpiGg
Herbers, Thomas H., (831) 656-2917 herbers@nps.edu,
Naval Postgraduate School – Op
Herbert, Bruce, (979) 845-2405 herbert@geo.tamu.edu,
Texas A&M University – Ge
Herbert, Jennifer, (630) 252-0493 Argonne National Laboratory – Gg
Herbert, Timothy D., (401) 863-1207 Timothy_Herbert@Brown.edu,
Brown University – Pe
Herbst, Thomas, 573-368-2143 thomas.herbst@dnr.mo.gov,
Missouri Dept of Natural Resources – Gg
Herd, Christopher, 780-492-5798 herd@ualberta.ca,
University of Alberta – Gi
Herd, Richard, +44 (0)1603 59 3667 r.herd@uea.ac.uk,
University of East Anglia – Gv
Herkenhoff, Ken E., (818) 354-3539 ken.e.herkenhoff@jpl.nasa.gov,
Jet Propulsion Laboratory – Xg
Herman, Ellen K., (570) 577-3088 ekh008@bucknell.edu,
Bucknell University – Hw
Herman, Gregory C., (609) 984-6587 greg.herman@dep.state.nj.us,
New Jersey Geological Survey – Gc
Herman, Janet S., (804) 924-0553 jsh5w@virginia.edu,
University of Virginia – Cl
Herman, Rhett B., 540 831-5441 rherman@radford.edu,
Radford University – Yg
Hermance, John F., (401) 863-3830 John_Hermance@Brown.edu,
Brown University – Yg
Hermann, Albert, 206-526-6495 Albert.J.Hermann@noaa.gov,
University of Washington – Op
Hermes, O D., dhermes@uri.edu, University of Rhode Island – Gi
Hernandez, Larry, (760) 757-2121, x6329 lhernandez@miracosta.edu,
MiraCosta College – Gg
Hernandez, Michael W., 801-626-8186 mhernandez@weber.edu,
Weber State University – Ori
Hernandez-Molina, Francisco J., Javier.Hernandez-Molina@rhul.ac.uk,
University of London, Royal Holloway & Bedford New College – Gs
Herndon, Elizabeth M., 330-672-2680 eherndo1@kent.edu,
Kent State University – Cl
Hernes, Peter, 530-752-7827 pjhernes@ucdavis.edu,
University of California, Davis – Og
Hernes, Peter J., 530-754-4327 pjhernes@ucdavis.edu,
University of California, Davis – Hg
Heron, Duncan, (919) 684-5321 duncan.heron@duke.edu,
Duke University – Gr
Herrero-Bervera, Emilio, (808) 956-6192 herrero@soest.hawaii.edu,
University of Hawai'i, Manoa – Ym
Herrick, Julie, herrickj@si.edu,
Smithsonian Institution / National Museum of Natural History – Gv
Herried, Brad, 612-626-0505 herri147@umn.edu,
University of Minnesota, Twin Cities – Oi
Herring, Thomas A., (617) 253-5941 tah@mit.edu,
Massachusetts Institute of Technology – Yd
Herring Mayo, Lisa L., 931-393-2136 lmayo@mscc.edu,
Motlow State Community College – GgOge
Herriott, Trystan, (907)451-5011 trystan.herriott@alaska.gov,
Division of Geological & Geophysical Surveys – Gg
Herrmann, Achim, 225-578-3016 aherrmann@lsu.edu,
Louisiana State University – PeGd
Herrmann, Edward W., (812) 856-0587 edherrma@indiana.edu,
Indiana University, Bloomington – Sa
Herrmann, Felix J., (604) 822-8628 fherrmann@eos.ubc.ca,
University of British Columbia – Yx

Herrmann, Robert B., (314) 977-3120 rbh@eas.slu.edu,
Saint Louis University – Ys
Herrstrom, Eileen A., (217) 333-7732 herrstro@illinois.edu,
University of Illinois, Urbana-Champaign – Gi
Hershey, Ronald, 775.673.7393 ron.hershey@dri.edu,
University of Nevada, Reno – HwCgs
Hervig, Richard, (480) 965-8427 hervig@asu.edu,
Arizona State University – Cg
Herzberg, Claude T., (848) 445-3154 herzberg@rci.rutgers.edu,
Rutgers, The State University of New Jersey – CpGi
Herzig, Chuck, (310) 660-3593 cherzig@elcamino.edu,
El Camino College – GgOg
Hesp, Patrick A., (225) 578-6244 pahesp@lsu.edu,
Louisiana State University – Gm
Hess, Darrel E., (415) 239-3104 dhess@ccsf.edu,
City College of San Francisco – Oy
Hess, Kai-Uwe, 089/2180 4275 hess@min.uni-muenchen.de,
Ludwig-Maximilians-Universitaet Muenchen – Gz
Hess, Paul C., (401) 863-1929 Paul_Hess@Brown.edu, Brown University – Gi
Hess Tanguay, Lillian, 516 463-6545 geolht@hofstra.edu,
Hofstra University – Gg
Hess-Tanguay, Lillian, (516) 299-2318 lhess@liu.edu,
Long Island University, C.W. Post Campus – Gs
Hesse, Marc A., 512-471-0768 mhesse@jsg.utexas.edu,
University of Texas at Austin – Gqo
Hesse, Reinhard, 514-398-3627 reinhard.hesse@mcgill.ca,
McGill University – Gs
Hessler, Robert R., (858) 534-2665 rhessler@ucsd.edu,
University of California, San Diego – Ob
Hester, Erich, (540) 231-9758 ehester@vt.edu, Virginia Tech – Hsw
Hesterberg, Dean L., (919) 515-2636 North Carolina State University – Sc
Hetherington, Eric D., (209) 730-3812 College of the Sequoias – Gc
Hetherington, Jean, (925) 685-1230 (Ext. 462) jhetheri@dvc.edu,
Diablo Valley College – Gg
Hetland, Robert D., (979) 458-0096 rhetland@ocean.tamu.edu,
Texas A&M University – Op
Hettiarachchi, Ganga, (785) 532-7209 ganga@ksu.edu,
Kansas State University – Sc
Hetzel, Ralf, +49-251-83-33908 rahetzel@uni-muenster.de,
Universitaet Muenster – Gcm
Heubeck, Christoph, 0049(0)3641/948620 christoph.heubeck@uni-jena.de,
Friedrich-Schiller-University Jena – Gh
Heuss-Aßbichler, Soraya, 089/21804252 soraya@min.uni-muenchen.de,
Ludwig-Maximilians-Universitaet Muenchen – Gz
Hewitt, David A., (540) 231-6521 dhewitt@vt.edu,
Virginia Polytechnic Institute & State University – Cp
Hey, Richard N., (808) 956-8972 hey@soest.hawaii.edu,
University of Hawai'i, Manoa – Yr
Heymann, Dieter, (713) 348-4890 dieter@owlnet.rice.edu,
Rice University – Xm
Heyniger, William C., (908) 737-3628 wheynige@kean.edu,
Kean University – On
Heyvaert, Alan, 775.673.7322 alan.heyvaert@dri.edu,
University of Nevada, Reno – GnHs
Heywood, Karen, +44 (0)1603 59 2555 k.heywood@uea.ac.uk,
University of East Anglia – Op
Heywood, Neil C., (715) 346-4452 nheywood@uwsp.edu,
University of Wisconsin, Stevens Point – Oy
Hiatt, Eric E., (920) 424-7001 hiatt@uwosh.edu,
University of Wisconsin, Oshkosh – Gs
Hibbard, James P., (919) 515-7242 jim_hibbard@ncsu.edu,
North Carolina State University – Gc
Hibbs, Barry, (323) 343-2414 bhibbs@calstatela.edu,
California State University, Los Angeles – Hw
Hick, Steven, 303-871-2535 shick@du.edu,
University of Denver – Oi
Hickcox, C W., (404) 727-0118 geocwh@emory.edu,
Emory University – Gg
Hickey, Barbara M., (206) 543-4737 bhickey@u.washington.edu,
University of Washington – Op
Hickey, Craig J., (662) 915-5963 chickey@olemiss.edu,
University of Mississippi – Ys
Hickey, James, (660) 562-1817 jhickey@nwmissouri.edu,
Northwest Missouri State University – Ge
Hickey, Kenneth, (604) 822-3765 khickey@eos.ubc.ca,
University of British Columbia – Gz
Hickey, William J., (608) 262-9018 wjhickey@wisc.edu,
University of Wisconsin, Madison – Sb
Hickey-Vargas, Rosemary, (305) 348-3471 hickey@fiu.edu,
Florida International University – Cg
Hickman, Carole S., (510) 642-3429 University of California, Berkeley – Po
Hickman, John, (859) 323-0541 jhickman@uky.edu,
University of Kentucky – Eo
Hickmon, Nicki, 630-252-7662 nhickmon@anl.gov,
Argonne National Laboratory – Oa
Hickmott, Donald D., (505) 667-8753 dhickmott@lanl.gov,
Los Alamos National Laboratory – Gp
Hicks, Roberta (Robbie), (709) 737-8349 rhicks@mun.ca,
Memorial University of Newfoundland – Yr
Hickson, Catherine J., (604) 666-9772 chickson@telus.net,

University of British Columbia – Gv

Hickson, Thomas A., (651) 962-5241 tahickson@stthomas.edu,
University of Saint Thomas – GsmGe

Hicock, Stephen R., (519) 661-3189 shicock@uwo.ca,
Western University – Gl

Hidalgo, Paulo, phidalgoodio@gsu.edu, Georgia State University – GiCg

Hier-Majumder, Saswata, (301) 405-6979 saswata@umd.edu,
University of Maryland – YgGq

Hiett, Michael W., (615)898-5075 Michael.Hiett@mtsu.edu,
Middle Tennessee State University – Gg

Higgins, Charles G., paulaH88@hotmail.com ,
University of California, Davis – Gm

Higgins, Chris T., (916) 322-9997 California Geological Survey – Gg

Higgins, Jerry D., (303) 273-3817 jhiggins@mines.edu,
Colorado School of Mines – Ng

Higgins, John A., (609) 258-2756 jahiggin@princeton.edu,
Princeton University – Ob

Higgins, Michael D., 4185455011 x 5052 mhiggins@uqac.ca,
Universite du Quebec a Chicoutimi – Gi

Higgins, Pennilyn, pennilyn.higgins@rochester.edu,
University of Rochester – Cs

Higgs, Bettie, +353 21 4902117 b.higgs@ucc.ie, University College Cork – Yg

Higgs, Ken, +353 21 4902290 k.higgs@ucc.ie,
University College Cork – Pl

Higinbotham, Pamela, 724-938-4180 higinbotham@calu.edu,
California University of Pennsylvania – On

Hildebrand, Alan R., 403-220-2291 ahildebr@ucalgary.ca,
University of Calgary – Xm

Hildebrand, John A., (858) 534-4069 jhildebrand@ucsd.edu,
University of California, San Diego – Yr

Hildebrand, Stephen G., hildebrandsg@ornl.gov,
Oak Ridge National Laboratory – On

Hildebrand, Steve T., (505) 667-4318 hildebrand@lanl.gov,
Los Alamos National Laboratory – Ys

Hileman, Mary, 405-744-6358 mary.hileman@okstate.edu,
Oklahoma State University – Go

Hill, Andrew, 203-432-3813 andrew.hill@yale.edu, Yale University – Pve

Hill, Arleen A., 901-678-2589 aahill@memphis.edu,
University of Memphis – On

Hill, Chris, 619 644 7342 chris.hill@gcccd.net, Grossmont College – Gg

Hill, Joseph C., 936 294-1560 GEOJOE@shsu.edu,
Sam Houston State University – Gc

Hill, Julie, (775) 784-6987 juliehill@unr.edu, University of Nevada, Reno – On

Hill, Malcolm, (617) 373-4377 m.hill@neu.edu,
Northeastern University – OiGz

Hill, Mary C., 785-864-2728 mchill@ku.edu, University of Kansas – Hgq

Hill, Mary Louise, (807) 343-8319 mary.louise.hill@lakeheadu.ca,
Lakehead University – Gc

Hill, Mimi, +44 0151 794 3462 M.Hill@liverpool.ac.uk,
University of Liverpool – Ym

Hill, Paul S., (902) 494-2266 paul.hill@dal.ca, Dalhousie University – Gs

Hill, Richard T., (812) 855-9583 hill2@indiana.edu,
indiana University – Oi

Hill, Tessa M., (530) 752-0179 tmhill@ucdavis.edu,
University of California, Davis – Pe

Hill, Timothy, +44 01334 464013 tch2@st-andrews.ac.uk,
University of St. Andrews – Ge

Hillaire-Marcel, Claude, 514-987-3000 #3376 hillaire-marcel.claude@uqam.ca,
Universite du Quebec a Montreal – Cs

Hiller, Lena, 516 463-5564 geolzh@hofstra.edu, Hofstra University – On

Hillier, John, jhillier@ghc.edu, Grays Harbor College – OgCa

Hilliker, Joby, (610) 436-2213 jhilliker@wcupa.edu,
West Chester University – Ow

Hills, Denise J., 205-247-3694 dhills@gsa.state.al.us,
Geological Survey of Alabama – Gg

Hills, Leonard V., (403) 220-5848 University of Calgary – Pl

Hilterman, Fred, 713-850-7600 x3318 fhilterman@uh.edu,
University of Houston – Ye

Hilton, David R., (858) 822-0639 drhilton@ucsd.edu,
University of California, San Diego – Ye

Hilts, Stewart G., (519) 824-4120 (Ext. 52448) shilts@uoguelph.ca,
University of Guelph – On

Himmelberg, Glen R., himmelbergg@missouri.edu,
University of Missouri – Gp

Hindery, Derrick, (541) 346-6106 dhindery@uoregon.edu,
University of Oregon – On

Hindle, Tobin, 561 297-2846 thindle@fau.edu,
Florida Atlantic University – HwOi

Hindman, Edward E., (212) 650-6469 Graduate School of the City University of New York – Ow

Hindshaw, Ruth, +44 01334 463936 rh71@st-andrews.ac.uk,
University of St. Andrews – Cs

Hine, Albert C., (727) 553-1161 hine@usf.edu,
University of South Florida – Gs

Hines, Mary E., (910) 962-3012 hinese@uncw.edu,
University of North Carolina Wilmington – Ou

Hines, Paul, phines50@gmail.com, Dalhousie University – Op

Hinman, George W., (509) 335-8689 ghinman@wsu.edu,
Washington State University – On

Hinman, Nancy W., 406-243-5277 nancy.hinman@umontana.edu,

University of Montana – Co

Hinnov, Linda, 703-993-3082 lhinnov@gmu.edu,
George Mason University – GrYg

Hinojosa, Alejandro, alhinc@cicese.mx,
Centro de Investigación Científica y de Educación Superior de Ensenada – Or

Hinson, Amye, 205-247-3577 ahinson@gsa.state.al.us,
Geological Survey of Alabama – Hw

Hinton, Richard, +44 (0) 131 650 8548 Richard.Hinton@ed.ac.uk,
Edinburgh University – Cg

Hintz, John G., (570)389-4140 jhintz@bloomu.edu,
Bloomsburg University – Oin

Hintz, Rashauna, 479-575-3355 rmicken@uark.edu,
University of Arkansas, Fayetteville – Ou

Hintze, Lehi F., 801 422-6361 lehi.hintze@gmail.com,
Brigham Young University – Pg

Hinz, Nicholas, (775)784-1446 nhinz@unr.edu, University of Nevada – Gg

Hinze, William J., wjh730@comcast.net, Purdue University – Ye

Hippensteel, Scott P., 704-687-5992 shippens@email.uncc.edu,
University of North Carolina, Charlotte – Gr

Hirner, Sarah M., 970-351-2398 Sarah.Hirner@unco.edu,
University of Northern Colorado – Gg

Hirons, Steve, +44 020 3073 8028 s.hirons@ucl.ac.uk, Birkbeck College – Cl

Hirschboeck, Katherine K., (520) 621-6466 hirschbo@ltrr.arizona.edu,
University of Arizona – Oa

Hirschmann, Marc M., 612-625-6698 hirsc022@umn.edu,
University of Minnesota, Twin Cities – Gi

Hirt, William H., (530) 938-5255 hirt@siskiyous.edu,
College of the Siskiyous – Gi

Hirth, Greg, (401) 863-7063 Greg_Hirth@Brown.edu,
Brown University – GcyYg

Hirth, Gregory, 508-289-2776 Greg_Hirth@brown.edu,
Woods Hole Oceanographic Institution – Gc

Hiscock, Kevin, +44 (0)1603 59 3104 k.hiscock@uea.ac.uk,
University of East Anglia – Hg

Hiscott, Richard N., (709) 737-8394 rhiscott@sparky2.esd.mun.ca,
Memorial University of Newfoundland – Gs

Hiskey, J. Brent, (520) 621-6185 jbh@engr.arizona.edu,
University of Arizona – Nx

Hitchman, Matthew H., (608)262-4653 matt@aos.wisc.edu,
University of Wisconsin, Madison – Oa

Hites, Ronald A., (812) 855-0193 hitesr@indiana.edu,
Indiana University, Bloomington – Co

Hitz, Ralph B., (253) 566-5299 rhitz@tacomacc.edu,
Tacoma Community College – Og

Hitzman, Murray W., (303) 384-2127 mhitzman@mines.edu,
Colorado School of Mines – Em

Hixon, Amy, Amy.Hixon.2@nd.edu, University of Notre Dame – Cl

Hjelmfelt, Mark R., (605) 394-2291 Mark.Hjelmfelt@sdsmt.edu,
South Dakota School of Mines & Technology – Oa

Hluchy, Michele M., (607) 871-2838 Alfred University – Cl

Hlusko, Leslea, (510) 643-8838 hlusko@berkeley.edu,
University of California, Berkeley – Onn

Ho, Anita, (406) 756-3873 aho@fvcc.edu,
Flathead Valley Community College – Gg

Ho, David, (808) 956-3311 ho@hawaii.edu,
University of Hawai'i, Manoa – Ou

Ho, I-Hsuan, (701) 777-6156 ihsuan.ho@engr.und.edu,
University of North Dakota – Ng

Hobbie, Erik A., 603-862-3581 erik.hobbie@unh.edu,
University of New Hampshire – Cs

Hobbs, Benjamin F., (410) 516-4681 bhobbs@jhu.edu,
Johns Hopkins University – On

Hobbs, Chasidy, 850-474-2735 chobbs@uwf.edu,
University of West Florida – Oy

Hobbs, John D., dhobbs@mtech.edu,
Montana Tech of the University of Montana – On

Hobbs, Richard, +44 (0) 191 33 44295 r.w.hobbs@durham.ac.uk,
Durham University – Ys

Hobbs, Richard D., (806) 371-5333 rdhobbs@actx.edu,
Amarillo College – OrGc

Hobbs, Thomas M., 281-618-5796 Tom.Hobbs@nhmccd.edu,
Lonestar College - North Harris – Gg

Hochella, Jr., Michael F., (540) 231-6227 hochella@vt.edu,
Virginia Polytechnic Institute & State University – Cl

Hochmuth, George J., 352-392-1803 318 hoch@ufl.edu,
University of Florida – So

Hochstaedter, Alfred, (831) 646-4149 ahochstaedter@mpc.edu,
Monterey Peninsula College – GgOgg

Hock, Regine M., 907-474-7691 regine.hock@gi.alaska.edu,
University of Alaska Fairbanks – Ol

Hockaday, William C., (254)7102639 William_Hockaday@baylor.edu,
Baylor University – CoaSb

Hockey, Thomas A., (319) 273-2065 thomas.hockey@uni.edu,
University of Northern Iowa – On

Hodder, Donald R., (914) 257-3757 SUNY, New Paltz – Gg

Hodder, Robert W., (519) 433-9550 rhodder@uwo.ca,
Western University – Eg

Hodell, David, +44 (0) 1223 330270 dhod07@esc.cam.ac.uk,
University of Cambridge – Ge

Hodges, Floyd N., (509) 376-4627 floyd.hodges@pnl.gov,

Pacific Northwest National Laboratory – Cg

Hodges, Kip V., 480-965-5331 kvhodges@asu.edu, Arizona State University – Gc

Hodgetts, David, David.Hodgetts@manchester.ac.uk,
University of Manchester – Gsc

Hodgkiss, Jr., William S., (858) 534-1798 whodgkiss@ucsd.edu,
University of California, San Diego – Oo

Hodgson, M. John, john.hodgson@ualberta.ca, University of Alberta – On

Hodych, Joseph P., (709) 737-7567 jhodych@mun.ca,
Memorial University of Newfoundland – Ym

Hoe, Teh Guan, 03-79674231 tehgh@um.edu.my, University of Malaya – Ca

Hoek, Joost, (301) 405-2407 hoekj@umd.edu, University of Maryland – CsgCa

Hoenisch, Baerbel, (845) 365-8828 hoenisch@ldeo.columbia.edu,
Columbia University – PeObCm

Hoersch, Alice L., (215) 951-1269 hoersch@lasalle.edu,
La Salle University – Gp

Hoey, Trevor, +4401413307736 Trevor.Hoey@glasgow.ac.uk,
University of Glasgow – Gs

Hoff, Jean L., 320-308-5914 jhoff@stcloudstate.edu,
Saint Cloud State University – HwOe

Hoffman, Gretchen K., (505) 835-5640 gretchen@gis.nmt.edu,
New Mexico Institute of Mining & Technology – Ec

Hoffman, James I., (509) 359-4255 Eastern Washington University – Em

Hoffman, Jeffrey L., 609-984-6587 jeffrey.l.hoffman@dep.nj.gov,
New Jersey Geological Survey – Hq

Hoffman, Paul F., (617) 496-6380 paulfhoffman@gmail.com,
Harvard University – Gc

Hofmann, Eileen E., (757) 683-5334 Old Dominion University – Op

Hofmeister, Anne M., (314) 935-7440 hofmeist@levee.wustl.edu,
Washington University in St. Louis – Gz

Hogarth, Donald D., 613-731-8090 dhogarth@uottawa.ca,
University of Ottawa – Gz

Hohl, Eric, 573-368-2168 eric.hohl@dnr.mo.gov,
Missouri Dept of Natural Resources – On

Hoisch, Thomas J., (928) 523-1904 thomas.hoisch@nau.edu,
Northern Arizona University – Gp

Hojjatie, Barry, (229) 333-5753 bhojjati@valdosta.edu,
Valdosta State University – Om

Holail, Hanafy M., 002-03-3921595 hanafyholail@hotmail.com,
Alexandria University – Ggs

Holberg, Jay B., (520) 621-4571 holberg@vega.lpl.arizona.edu,
University of Arizona – Oa

Holbrook, Amanda, (606) 783-2381 a.holbrook@moreheadstate.edu,
Morehead State University – On

Holbrook, John M., 817-257-6275 john.holbrook@tcu.edu,
Texas Christian University – Gsr

Holbrook, W. S., (307) 766-2427 steveh@uwyo.edu,
University of Wyoming – Ys

Holcomb, Robin T., (206) 543-5274 rholcomb@ocean.washington.edu,
University of Washington – Ou

Holcombe, Troy, 979 845 3528 tholcombe@ocean.tamu.edu,
Texas A&M University – Ou

Holdaway, Michael J., (214) 692-2750 Southern Methodist University – Gp

Holden, Gregory S., (303) 273-3855 gholden@mines.edu,
Colorado School of Mines – Gx

Holdren, George R., (509) 376-2242 rich.holdren@pnl.gov,
Pacific Northwest National Laboratory – Cl

Holdsworth, Robert E., 0191 3742529 r.e.holdsworth@durham.ac.uk,
Durham University – Gc

Hole, John A., (540) 231-3858 hole@vt.edu,
Virginia Polytechnic Institute & State University – Ye

Holgood, Jay S., (614) 292-3999 hobgood.1@osu.edu,
Ohio State University – Oa

Holk, Gregory J., 562-985-5006 gholk@csulb.edu,
California State University, Long Beach – CsGxEm

Holl, Karen D., (831) 459-3668 kholl@cats.ucsc.edu,
University of California, Santa Cruz – Ou

Hollabaugh, Curtis L., (678) 839-4050 chollaba@westga.edu,
University of West Georgia – GzCg

Holland, Austin A., 405-325-8497 austin.holland@ou.edu,
University of Oklahoma – YsOnn

Holland, Nicholas D., (858) 534-2085 nholland@ucsd.edu,
University of California, San Diego – Ob

Holland, Steven M., (706) 542-0424 stratum@gly.uga.edu,
University of Georgia – Gr

Holland, Tim, +44 (0) 1223 333466 tjbh@esc.cam.ac.uk,
University of Cambridge – Gp

Hollander, David J., (727) 553-1019 davidh@usf.edu,
University of South Florida – Oc

Hollenbaugh, Kenneth M., (208) 426-3700 khollenb@boisestate.edu,
Boise State University – Eg

Holley, Elizabeth, 303-273-3409 eholley@mines.edu,
Colorado School of Mines – Eg

Holliday, Joseph W., 3106603593 xt. 3371 jholliday@elcamino.edu,
El Camino College – Og

Holliday, Vance, vthollid@email.arizona.edu, University of Arizona – Ga

Holliday, Vance, (520) 621-4734 vthollid@email.arizona.edu,
University of Arizona – Ga

Holliman, Richard, +44(0) 1908 654 646 x 54646 richard.holliman@open.ac.uk ,
The Open University – Oe

Hollings, Peter N., (807) 343-8329 peter.hollings@lakeheadu.ca,

Lakehead University – Eg

Hollis, Cathy, +44 0161 306-6583 Cathy.Hollis@manchester.ac.uk,
University of Manchester – Gs

Hollister, Lincoln S., (609) 258-4106 linc@princeton.edu,
Princeton University – Gp

Hollocher, Kurt T., (518) 388-6518 hollochk@union.edu,
Union College – GxCga

Holloway, Tracey, 608-262-5356 taholloway@wisc.edu,
University of Wisconsin, Madison – Oa

Holm, Daniel K., (330) 672-4094 dholm@kent.edu,
Kent State University – Gc

Holm, Richard F., richard.holm@nau.edu, Northern Arizona University – Gv

Holman, John, (620) 276-8286 jholman@ksu.edu,
Kansas State University – So

Holman, Robert, (541) 737-2914 holman@coas.oregonstate.edu,
Oregon State University – On

Holmden, Chris, (306) 966-5697 University of Saskatchewan – Csc

Holme, Richard, +44 0151 794 5254 R.T.Holme@liverpool.ac.uk,
University of Liverpool – Ym

Holmes, Ann E., (423) 425-1704 ann-holmes@utc.edu,
University of Tennessee at Chattanooga – Gs

Holmes, George, +44(0) 113 34 31163 G.Holmes@leeds.ac.uk,
University of Leeds – Ge

Holmes, Mark L., (206) 543-7313 mholmes@ocean.washington.edu,
University of Washington – Ou

Holmes, Mary Anne, 402-472-5211 mholmes2@unl.edu,
University of Nebraska, Lincoln – GsOu

Holmes, Stevie L., 605-677-6147 stevie.holmes@usd.edu,
South Dakota Dept of Environment and Natural Resources – Gg

Holness, Marian, +44 (0) 1223 333434 marian@esc.cam.ac.uk,
University of Cambridge – Gi

Holroyd, Pat, (510) 642-3733 pholroyd@berkeley.edu,
University of California, Berkeley – Pv

Holstein, Thomas J., (401) 254-3097 Roger Williams University – On

Holt, Ben D., (630) 252-4347 Argonne National Laboratory – Ca

Holt, David, 228-214-3255 david.h.holt@usm.edu,
University of Southern Mississippi – Oyi

Holt, Gloria J., (361) 749-6716 joanholt@utexas.edu,
University of Texas at Austin – Ob

Holt, John W., 512-471-0487 jack@ig.utexas.edu,
University of Texas at Austin – OlXyg

Holt, Robert M., (662) 915-6687 rmholt@olemiss.edu,
University of Mississippi – Hq

Holt, William E., 631-632-8215 william.holt@sunysb.edu,
SUNY, Stony Brook – Ys

Holtz, Jr., Thomas R., (301) 405-4084 tholtz@geol.umd.edu,
University of Maryland – Pv

Holubnyak, Yehven I., (785) 864-2070 eugene@kgs.ku.edu,
University of Kansas – On

Holzer, Mark, (604) 822-0531 mholzer@langara.bc.ca,
University of British Columbia – Oa

Holzworth, Robert H., 206-685-7410 bobholz@uw.edu,
University of Washington – YxXy

Hommel, Demian, 541-737-5070 hommeld@geo.oregonstate.edu,
Oregon State University – On

Homuth, Emil F., (702) 794-7351 fred_homuth@notes.ymp.gov,
Los Alamos National Laboratory – Ye

Hon, Ken, (808) 974-7302 kenhon@hawaii.edu,
University of Hawai'i, Hilo – Gvi

Hon, Rudolph, (617) 552-3656 hon@bc.edu, Boston College – Gi

Hong, Jessie, (678) 839-5466 jhong@westga.edu,
University of West Georgia – OieOy

Hong, Sung-ho, 270-809-2591 shong4@murraystate.edu,
Murray State University – HyGe

Honjas, Bill, (775) 784-6613 bhonjas@optimsoftware.com ,
University of Nevada, Reno – Ys

Honjo, Susumu, (508) 289-2589 shonjo@whoi.edu,
Woods Hole Oceanographic Institution – Ou

Honkaer, Rick, 859-257-1108 rick.honaker@uky.edu,
University of Kentucky – Nm

Hons, Frank M., (979) 845-3477 f-hons@tamu.edu,
Texas A&M University – Sc

Hood, Lonnie L., (520) 621-6936 lon@lpl.arizona.edu,
University of Arizona – Xy

Hood, Raleigh, (305) 361-4668 rhood@umces.edu,
University of Maryland – Ob

Hood, Teresa A., 305-284-8647 t.hood@miami.edu,
University of Miami – Gg

Hood, William C., (970) 241-8020 Colorado Mesa University – Gg

Hooda, Peter, +44 020 8417 2155 P.Hooda@kingston.ac.uk,
Kingston University – Em

Hooft, Emilie E., (541) 346-4762 emilie@uoregon.edu,
University of Oregon – Yr

Hook, James E., (912) 386-3182 University of Georgia – Sp

Hook, Paul B., (406) 944-3724 paul@intermountainaquatics.com,
Montana State University – Sf

Hook, Simon J., (818) 354-0974 simon@lithos.jpl.nasa.gov,
Jet Propulsion Laboratory – Or

Hooke, Roger L., (207) 581-2203 rhooke@acadia.net,
University of Maine – Gm

Hooks, Benjamin P., (731) 881-7430 bhooks@utm.edu,
University of Tennessee, Martin – GciNr
Hooks, Chris H., 205-247-3721 chooks@gsa.state.al.us,
Geological Survey of Alabama – EoGx
Hooks, W. Gary, (205) 348-1877 University of Alabama – Gm
Hooper, Andy, +44(0) 113 34 37723 a.hooper@leeds.ac.uk,
University of Leeds – Ydg
Hooper, Robert L., (715) 836-4932 hooperrl@uwec.edu,
University of Wisconsin, Eau Claire – Gz
Hoopes, John A., (608) 262-2977 University of Wisconsin, Madison – Oo
Hoover, Karin A., 530-898-6269 khoover@csuchico.edu,
California State University, Chico – Hw
Hoover, Kenneth D., (904) 745-7300 khoover@ju.edu,
Jacksonville University – Og
Hoover, Michael T., (919) 515-7305 North Carolina State University – Sd
Hooyer, Thomas S., 414-229-5594 hooyer@uwm.edu,
University of Wisconsin, Milwaukee – Gl
Hooyer, Thomas S., 608-263-4175 hooyer@uwm.edu,
University of Wisconsin, Madison – Hg
Hopkins, Daniel P., (816) 235-2973 hopkinsd@umkc.edu,
University of Missouri-Kansas City – On
Hopkins, David G., (701) 231-8948 North Dakota State University – Sd
Hopkins, David M., (907) 474-7565 University of Alaska, Fairbanks – Gg
Hopkins, John C., (403) 220-5842 hopkins@geo.ucalgary.ca,
University of Calgary – Gs
Hopkins, Kenneth D., (970) 351-2853 kenneth.hopkins@unco.edu,
University of Northern Colorado – Gm
Hopkins, Thomas S., (205) 348-1791 Dauphin Island Sea Lab – Ob
Hopley, Philip, +44 020 3073 8029 p.hopley@ucl.ac.uk,
Birkbeck College – Pe
Hopmans, Jan W., (916) 752-3060 University of California, Davis – So
Hoppe, Kathryn A., 253-833-9111 ext. 4323 khoppe@greenriver.edu,
Green River Community College – OggPg
Hoppie, Bryce W., (507) 389-2315 bryce.hoppie@mnsu.edu,
Minnesota State University – GeHw
Hopson, Janet L., 865-946-1460 hopsonj@ornl.gov,
University of Tennessee, Knoxville – On
Horan, Mary F., 202-478-8481 mhoran@carnegiescience.edu,
Carnegie Institution of Washington – Cc
Horel, John, 801-581-7091 john.horel@utah.edu,
University of Utah – Oa
Horgan, Briony, (765) 496-2290 briony@purdue.edu,
Purdue University – Xg
Horn, John, (816) 604-3132 John.Horn@mcckc.edu,
Metropolitan Community College-Kansas City – GgOy
Horn, Marty R., 225-578-2681 mhorn@lsu.edu,
Louisiana State University – GgGcr
Hornbach, Matthew J., 214-768-2389 Southern Methodist University – YrhYe
Hornberger, George, 615-322-2976 george.m.hornberger@vanderbilt.edu,
Vanderbilt University – Hg
Horne, Sharon, (519) 253-3000 ext, 2528 shorne@uwindsor.ca,
University of Windsor – On
Horner, John R., (406) 994-3982 jhorner@montana.edu,
Montana State University – Pv
Horner, Tim C., (916) 278-5635 hornertc@csus.edu,
California State University, Sacramento – HwGs
Horner, Tristan, (508) 289-3825 thorner@whoi.edu,
Woods Hole Oceanographic Institution – Cm
Horns, Daniel, (801) 863-8582 hornsda@uvu.edu,
Utah Valley University – NgGet
Horowitz, Franklin G., frank.horowitz@cornell.edu,
Cornell University – Nr
Horsman, Eric, 252 3285265 horsmane@ecu.edu,
East Carolina University – Gc
Horton, Albert B., (615) 532-1509 Albert.Horton@tn.gov,
Tennessee Geological Survey – GgOi
Horton, Benjamin P., (215) 573-5388 bphorton@marine.rutgers.edu,
Rutgers, The State University of New Jersey – On
Horton, Brian, 512-471-5172 horton@mail.utexas.edu,
University of Texas at Austin – Gs
Horton, Daniel, 847-467-6185 danethan@earth.northwestern.edu,
Northwestern University – OaPeOn
Horton, Duane G., (509) 376-6868 duane.horton@pnl.gov,
Pacific Northwest National Laboratory – Gz
Horton, Jennifer, (612) 626-4067 jmhorton@umn.edu,
University of Minnesota – Gl
Horton, Robert, (515) 294-7843 rhorton@iastate.edu,
Iowa State University of Science & Technology – Sp
Horton, Stephen P., (901) 678-2007 shorton@memphis.edu,
University of Memphis – Ys
Horton, Travis, +64 3 3667001 Ext 7734 travis.horton@canterbury.ac.nz,
University of Canterbury – Cs
Horton, Jr., Robert A., 661-654-3059 rhorton@csub.edu,
California State University, Bakersfield – GdsGo
Horváth, Ferenc, frankh@ludens.elte.hu, Eotvos Lorand University – YgGhc
Horvath, Peter, +27 (0)46-603-8312 p.horvath@ru.ac.za,
Rhodes University – Gp
Horvath, Peter, 011 717 6539 peter.horvath@wits.ac.za,
University of the Witwatersrand – GpCpGz
Horwath, William R., (530) 754-6029 wrhorwath@ucdavis.edu,
University of California, Davis – Os
Horwell, Claie, +44 (0) 191 33 42253 claire.horwell@durham.ac.uk,
Durham University – Gz
Hosler, Charles L., (814) 863-8358 hosler@ems.psu.edu,
Pennsylvania State University, University Park – Ow
Hosseini, Seyyed Abolfazi, 512-471-1534 seyyed.hosseini@beg.utexas.edu,
University of Texas at Austin – Eo
Houghton, Bruce F., (808) 956-2561 bhought@soest.hawaii.edu,
University of Hawai'i, Manoa – Gv
Houghton, David D., (608)262-0776 ddhought@wisc.edu,
University of Wisconsin, Madison – Oa
Hounslow, Arthur, 405-372-2328 Oklahoma State University – Cl
Hourigan, Jeremy, 831-459-2879 hourigan@ucsc.edu,
University of California, Santa Cruz – Cc
House, Christopher H., (814) 865-8802 chouse@geosc.psu.edu,
Pennsylvania State University, University Park – Py
House, Leigh S., (505) 667-1912 house@lanl.gov,
Los Alamos National Laboratory – Ys
Houseknecht, David W., 703-648-6466 dhouse@usgs.gov,
Virginia Polytechnic Institute & State University – Gd
Houseman, Greg, +44(0) 113 34 35206 g.a.houseman@leeds.ac.uk,
University of Leeds – Yg
Housen, Bernard A., (360) 650-3588 bernieh@wwu.edu,
Western Washington University – Ym
Houston, Adam L., ahouston2@unl.edu, University of Nebraska, Lincoln – Oa
Houston, Heidi B., 206-616-7092 hhouston@uw.edu,
University of Washington – YsGt
Houston, Robert, (541) 967-2039 Robert.A.Houston@mlrr.oregongeology.com,
Oregon Dept of Geology & Mineral Industries – Ge
Houston, Serin D., 413-538-2055 shouston@mtholyoke.edu,
Mount Holyoke College – Oyn
Houze, Robert A., 206-543-6922 houze@atmos.washington.edu,
University of Washington – Oa
Hovan, Steven A., (724) 357-5625 hovan@iup.edu,
Indiana University of Pennsylvania – Ou
Hovis, Guy L., (610) 330-5192 hovisguy@lafayette.edu,
Lafayette College – Gy
Hovorka, Susan D., 512-471-4863 susan.hovorka@beg.utexas.edu,
University of Texas at Austin – Gs
Howard, Alan D., (804) 924-0563 ah6p@virginia.edu,
University of Virginia – Gm
Howard, Hugh H., 916 484-8805 howardh@arc.losrios.edu,
American River College – Oi
Howard, Jeffrey L., (313) 577-3258 aa2675@wayne.edu,
Wayne State University – Gs
Howard, Katie, 360-475-7700 khoward@llion.org, Olympic College – Gg
Howard, Kenneth W., 416-287-7233 University of Toronto – Hw
Howard, Leslie M., (402) 472-9192 thoward@unl.edu,
Unversity of Nebraska - Lincoln – Oyi
Howard, Matthew K., (979) 862-4169 mkhoward@tamu.edu,
Texas A&M University – Op
Howard, Theodore E., (603) 862-1020 University of New Hampshire – On
Howat, Ian M., (614) 247-8944 howat.4@osu.edu,
Ohio State University – OlYd
Howden, Stephan, (228) 688-5284 stephan.howden@usm.edu,
University of Southern Mississippi – Op
Howe, Bruce M., (206) 543-9141 billhowe@cs.washington.edu,
University of Washington – Op
Howe, Julie, (334) 844-3972 jah0020@auburn.edu, Auburn University – Sc
Howe, Stephen S., (518) 442-5053 showe@albany.edu, SUNY, Albany – Cs
Howe, Thomas, (269) 387-5492 thomas.r.howe@wmich.edu,
Western Michigan University – Hw
Howell, Dave, +440116 252 3804 dah29@le.ac.uk,
Leicester University – Ge
Howell, Robert R., (307) 766-6296 rhowell@uwyo.edu,
University of Wyoming – XgOr
Howell, Jr., Benjamin F., (814) 863-0886 howellbf@aol.com,
Pennsylvania State University, University Park – Ys
Hower, James C., (859) 257-0261 james.hower@uky.edu,
University of Kentucky – Ec
Howes, Mary R., mary.howes@dnr.iowa.gov,
Iowa Dept of Natural Resources – Gg
Howman, Dominic J., +61 8 9266-2329 D.Howman@curtin.edu.au,
Curtin University – Ye
Hoyal, Michael L., (615) 532-1504 Mike.Hoyal@tn.gov,
Tennessee Geological Survey – Gog
Hoyos, Carlos, carlos.hoyos@eas.gatech.edu,
Georgia Institute of Technology – Oa
Hoyt, Greg D., (919) 684-3562 North Carolina State University – Sb
Hoyt, William H., (970) 351-2487 william.hoyt@unco.edu,
University of Northern Colorado – OgGsOe
Hozik, Michael J., (609) 652-4277 hozikm@stockton.edu,
Richard Stockton College of New Jersey – Ym
Hren, Michael, 860-486-9511 michael.hren@uconn.edu,
University of Connecticut – CslCo
Hrouda, Jim, (573) 518-2350 jimh@MineralArea.edu,
Mineral Area College – On
Hsiang, Tom, (519) 824-4120 Ext.52753 thsiang@uoguelph.ca,
University of Guelph – On
Hsiao, Theodore C., (530) 752-0691 tchsiao@ucdavis.edu,

University of California, Davis – Sb

Hsieh, Wen-Pin, 886-227839910-509 wphsieh@earth.sinica.edu.tw,
    Academia Sinica – YhGy

Hsieh, William, (604) 822-2821 whsieh@eos.ubc.ca,
    University of British Columbia – Op

Hsu, Liang-Chi, (775) 682-8746 lihsu@unr.edu, University of Nevada – Cp

Hu, Baoxin, (416)736-2100 #20557 baoxin@yorku.ca, York University – Or

Hu, Bill X., 850-644-3943 hu@gly.fsu.edu,
    Florida State University – Hw

Hu, Feng-Sheng, (217) 244-2982 fhu@illinois.edu,
    University of Illinois, Urbana-Champaign – Pe

Hu, Hao, hhu5@central.uh.edu, University of Houston – Ye

Hu, Qi S., 402-472-6642 QHU2@unl.edu, University of Nebraska, Lincoln – Oa

Hu, Qinhong (Max), 817 272 5398 maxhu@uta.edu,
    University of Texas, Arlington – HwCa

Hu, Shusheng, 203-432-3790 shusheng.hu@yale.edu,
    Yale University – PblGs

Hu, Wan-Ping (Sunny), +61 7 3138 7314 sunny.hu@qut.edu.au,
    Queensland University of Technology – Ca

Hu, Xinping , 361-825-3395 Xinping.Hu@tamucc.edu,
    Texas A&M University, Corpus Christi – Oc

Hu, Zhiyong, 850-474-3494 zhu@uwf.edu,
    University of West Florida – Or

Huang, Alex, (828) 232-5157 University of North Carolina, Asheville – Oa

Huang, Bohua, (703) 993-6084 bhuang@gmu.edu,
    George Mason University – Op

Huang, Kainian, (352) 392-2231 knhuang@ufl.edu, University of Florida – Ym

Huang, Li, (519) 661-3188 LHuang3@uwo.ca, Western University – Yr

Huang, Lianjie, (505) 665-1108 ljh@lanl.gov,
    Los Alamos National Laboratory – Yg

Huang, Moh J., (916) 322-9304 California Geological Survey – Ne

Huang, Norden E., (301) 286-8879 University of Delaware – On

Huang, Shaopeng, (734) 763-3169 shaopeng@umich.edu,
    University of Michigan – Yh

Huang, Yi, 514-398-8217 yi.huang@mcgill.ca,
    McGill University – OrYgOa

Huang, Yongsong, Yongsong_Huang@Brown.edu, Brown University – Co

Hubbard, Dennis K., 440-775-8346 dennis.hubbard@oberlin.edu,
    Oberlin College – Gsu

Hubbard, Kenneth G., (402) 472-8294 University of Nebraska, Lincoln – Oa

Hubbard, Mary S., 435.797.3686 Mary.hubbard@montana.edu,
    Utah State University – Gc

Hubbard, Trent, (907) 451-5009 trent.hubbard@alaska.gov,
    Alaska Division of Geological & Geophysical Surveys – Ng

Hubbard, William B., (520) 621-6942 hubbard@lpl.arizona.edu,
    University of Arizona – Xy

Hubbart, Jason A., 573-884-7732 hubbartj@missouri.edu,
    University of Missouri, Columbia – Hq

Hubenthal, Michael, 607-777-4612 hubenth@iris.edu,
    Binghamton University – Oe

Hubeny, J B., bhubeny@salemstate.edu, Salem State University – GeOnCs

Huber, Brian T., (202) 633-1328 Smithsonian Institution / National Museum of
    Natural History – Pm

Huber, Matthew, 603-862-1929 matthew.huber@unh.edu,
    University of New Hampshire – Og

Hubert, John, jhubert@geo.umass.edu,
    University of Massachusetts, Amherst – Gs

Huckabey, Marsha, (573) 882-2040 HuckabeyM@missouri.edu,
    University of Missouri – On

Hudak, Paul F., (940) 565-4312 paul.hudak@unt.edu,
    University of North Texas – Hw

Hudec, Michael R., 512-471-1428 michael.hudec@beg.utexas.edu,
    University of Texas at Austin – Gc

Hudec, Peter P., (519) 253-3000 ext. 2491 hudec@uwindsor.ca,
    University of Windsor – Ng

Hudleston, Peter J., 612-625-0046 hudle001@umn.edu,
    University of Minnesota, Twin Cities – Gc

Hudman, Lloyd E., (801) 378-4346 lloyd_hudman@byu.edu,
    Brigham Young University – On

Hudson, Michael R., (419) 289-5270 mhudson@ashland.edu,
    Ashland University – GpzCa

Hudson, Robert J. M., (217) 333-7641 rjhudson@uiuc.edu,
    University of Illinois, Urbana-Champaign – Cg

Hudson-Edwards, Karen, +44 0203 073 8030 k.hudson-edwards@bbk.ac.uk,
    Birkbeck College – Gez

Huebert, Barry J., (808) 956-6896 huebert@soest.hawaii.edu,
    University of Hawai'i, Manoa – Oc

Huerta, Audrey, 509.963.2718 huerta@geology.cwu.edu,
    Central Washington University – Ygd

Huey, Gregory L., (404) 894-5541 greg.huey@eas.gatech.edu,
    Georgia Institute of Technology – Oa

Huff, Bryan G., 217-244-2509 huff@isgs.uiuc.edu,
    Illinois State Geological Survey – Ca

Huff, Edmund A., (630) 252-3633 Argonne National Laboratory – Ca

Huff, Warren D., (513) 556-3731 warren.huff@uc.edu,
    University of Cincinnati – Gz

Huffman, Debra E., (727) 553-3930 debrah@usf.edu,
    University of South Florida – On

Huffman, French T., (859) 622-6968 tyler.huffman@eku.edu,
    Eastern Kentucky University – Oi

Huffman, Robert L., (912) 752-2704 Mercer University – On

Huft, Ashley, 406-496-4789 ahuft@mtech.edu,
    Montana Tech of The University of Montana – Ca

Huggett, William, 618-453-7392 huggett@geo.siu.edu,
    Southern Illinois University Carbondale – Ec

Hughen, Konrad A., (508) 289-3353 khughen@whoi.edu,
    Woods Hole Oceanographic Institution – Cc

Hughes, Annie, +44 020 8417 2603 Ku08925@kingston.ac.uk,
    Kingston University – Oi

Hughes, Colin, colin.hughes@manchester.ac.uk,
    University of Manchester – Go

Hughes, Denis, +27 46 6224014 d.hughes@ru.ac.za,
    Rhodes University – Hqs

Hughes, John M., (802) 656-9443 jmhughes@uvm.edu,
    University of Vermont – Gz

Hughes, John M., John.M.Hughes@uvm.edu, Miami University – Gz

Hughes, Joseph B., (713)348-5603 david.v.hughes@rice.edu,
    Rice University – On

Hughes, Malcolm K., (520) 621-6470 mhughes@ltrr.arizona.edu,
    University of Arizona – Pe

Hughes, Nigel C., nigel.hughes@ucr.edu, Cincinnati Museum Center – Pi

Hughes, Nigel C., (951) 827-3098 nigel.hughes@ucr.edu,
    University of California, Riverside – Po

Hughes, Randall, 7815817370 x314 rhughes@neu.edu,
    Northeastern University – On

Hughes, Sam, +44 07727 096492 S.P.Hughes@exeter.ac.uk,
    Exeter University – Gt

Hughes, Scott S., hughscot@isu.edu, Idaho State University – Gx

Hughes III, Richard O., 909-389-3237 rihughes@craftonhills.edu,
    Crafton Hills College – GlOe

Hughes-Clarke, John E., 603-862-5505 jhc@ccom.unh.edu,
    University of New Hampshire – Og

Hugli, Wilbur G., 850-474-3470 whugli@uwf.edu,
    University of West Florida – Oa

Hugo, Richard, 503-725-3356 hugo@pdx.edu, Portland State University – Gy

Hui, Alice, akhui@umail.iu.edu, Indiana University, Bloomington – Cl

Hull, Donald L., (505) 667-4151 Los Alamos National Laboratory – On

Hull, Joseph M., jhull@sccd.ctc.edu, Seattle Central Community College – Gc

Hulton, Nicholas R., +44 (0) 131 650 7543 Nick.Hulton@ed.ac.uk,
    Edinburgh University – Ol

Humayan, Munir, 850-644-5860 humayun@magnet.fsu.edu,
    Florida State University – XcCg

Huminicki, Michelle, huminickim@brandonu.ca,
    Brandon University – EgGz

Humphrey, Neil F., (307) 766-2728 neil@uwyo.edu,
    University of Wyoming – Gm

Humphrey, Peggy, (406) 994-5718 peggyh@montana.edu,
    Montana State University – On

Humphreys, Eugene D., (541) 346-5575 genehumphreys@gmail.com,
    University of Oregon – YsGt

Humphreys, Robin, (843) 953-7424 humphreysr@cofc.edu,
    College of Charleston – Ge

Humphris, Susan E., (508) 289-3451 shumphris@whoi.edu,
    Woods Hole Oceanographic Institution – Gu

Hunda, Brenda, (513) 455-7160 bhunda@cincymuseum.org,
    Cincinnati Museum Center – Pi

Hung, Ming-Chih, (660) 562-1797 mhung@nwmissouri.edu,
    Northwest Missouri State University – Or

Hungerbuehler, Axel, (575) 461-3466 axelh@mesalands.edu,
    Mesalands Community College – Gg

Hungerford, Hilary, (801) 863-7160 hilary.hungerford@uvu.edu,
    Utah Valley University – Ou

Hungr, Oldrich, (604) 822-8471 ohungr@eos.ubc.ca,
    University of British Columbia – Gm

Hunt, Allen, 937 775-3116 allen.hunt@wright.edu,
    Wright State University – GqSp

Hunt, Andrew, 817 272 2987 hunt@uta.edu,
    University of Texas, Arlington – GbCg

Hunt, Brian, (604) 822-9135 bhunt@eos.ubc.ca,
    University of British Columbia – Ob

Hunt, Gene, (202) 633-1331 Smithsonian Institution / National Museum of
    Natural History – Pm

Hunt, Kathleen, huntk@neaq.org, University of Massachusetts, Boston – Ob

Hunt, Paula J., 304-594-2331 phunt@geosrv.wvnet.edu,
    West Virginia University – Gg

Hunt, Randy J., rjhunt@usgs.gov, University of Wisconsin, Madison – Hw

Hunt, Robert M., (402) 472-4604 rhunt2@unl.edu,
    University of Nebraska, Lincoln – Pv

Hunt, Shelley, (519) 824-420 Ext.53065 shunt@uoguelph.ca,
    University of Guelph – On

Hunten, Donald M., (520) 621-4002 dhunten@lpl.arizona.edu,
    University of Arizona – On

Hunter, Arlene , +44 (0) 1908 655400 x55400 a.g.hunter@open.ac.uk ,
    The Open University – Oe

Hunter, Jerry L., 540-392-0540 hunterje@vt.edu,
    Virginia Polytechnic Institute & State University – Ca

Huntington, Justin, 775.673.7670 justin.huntington@dri.edu,
    University of Nevada, Reno – HgOr

Huntington, Katharine W., 206-543-1750 kate1@uw.edu,
    University of Washington – Gt

Franklin and Marshall College – Gc

Israel, Daniel W., (919) 515-2388 North Carolina State University – Sb

Ito, Emi, 612-624-7881 eito@umn.edu, University of Minnesota, Twin Cities – Cs

Ito, Garrett T., 808-956-9717 gito@hawaii.edu,
University of Hawai'i, Manoa – Yr

Ito, Takamitsu, 970-491-8206 ito@atmos.colostate.edu,
Colorado State University – Oa

Ivanochko, Tara, (604) 827-3179 tivanochko@eos.ubc.ca,
University of British Columbia – Og

Ivanov, Julian, (785) 864-2089 jivanov@kgs.ku.edu, University of Kansas – Yg

Ivanov, Martin, +420 549 49 4600 mivanov@sci.muni.cz ,
Masaryk University – PgiPe

Ivanova, Maria, maria.ivanova@umb.edu,
University of Massachusetts, Boston – On

Ivany, Linda C., 315-443-2672 lcivany@syr.edu, Syracuse University – Pe

Iverson, Neal R., (515) 294-8048 niverson@iastate.edu,
Iowa State University of Science & Technology – Gl

Ivins, Erik R., (818) 354-4785 Jet Propulsion Laboratory – Gt

Ivy, Logan D., (303) 370-6474 Logan.Ivy@dmns.org,
Denver Museum of Nature & Science – Pv

Ivy, Russell L., (561) 297-3295 ivy@fau.edu, Florida Atlantic University – On

Izawa, Matt, mizawa2@uwo.ca, Western University – Gz

Izon, Gareth, +44 01334 463936 gji3@st-andrews.ac.uk,
University of St. Andrews – Cg

J

Jablonski, David, (773) 702-8163 djablons@midway.uchicago.edu,
University of Chicago – Pi

Jacinthe, Pierre-Andre, pjacinth@iupui.edu,
Indiana University / Purdue University, Indianapolis – Cl

Jackson, Andrea, +44(0) 113 34 36728 a.v.jackson@leeds.ac.uk,
University of Leeds – Oa

Jackson, Brian P., 603-646-1272 Brian.Jackson@dartmouth.edu,
Dartmouth College – Ca

Jackson, Charles, (512) 471-0401 charles@ig.utexas.edu,
University of Texas at Austin – Pe

Jackson, Chester M., (912) 598-2328 cjackson@georgiasouthern.edu,
Georgia Southern University – OnGs

Jackson, Chester W., (912) 478-0174 cjackson@georgiasouthern.edu,
Georgia Southern University – GsmGu

Jackson, Christopher, +44 20 759 47450v c.jackson@imperial.ac.uk,
Imperial College – Gt

Jackson, David D., (310) 825-0421 djackson@ucla.edu,
University of California, Los Angeles – YsdYg

Jackson, Edgar L., ed.jackson@ualberta.ca, University of Alberta – On

Jackson, Frankie, (406) 994-6642 frankiej@montana.edu,
Montana State University – Pv

Jackson, Gail D., +44 (0) 131 650 5436 G.Jackson@ed.ac.uk,
Edinburgh University – PbGe

Jackson, George A., (979) 845-0405 gjackson@ocean.tamu.edu,
Texas A&M University – Op

Jackson, Hiram, (916) 691-7605 Cosumnes River College – Gg

Jackson, James, +44 (0) 1223 333481 jaj2@cam.ac.uk,
University of Cambridge – YgGt

Jackson, Jennifer M., (626) 395-6780 jackson@gps.caltech.edu,
California Institute of Technology – Gy

Jackson, Jeremiah, 573-368-2182 jeremiah.jackson@dnr.mo.gov,
Missouri Dept of Natural Resources – Gg

Jackson, Jeremy B. C., (858) 822-2432 jbjackson@ucsd.edu,
University of California, San Diego – Po

Jackson, Karen E., (904) 745-7300 Jacksonville University – Og

Jackson, Kenneth J., (925) 422-6053 jackson8@llnl.gov,
Lawrence Livermore National Laboratory – Cl

Jackson, Louise E., 530-754-9116 lejackson@ucdavis.edu,
University of California, Davis – Os

Jackson, Mark W., (801) 378-9753 mark_jackson@byu.edu,
Brigham Young University – Or

Jackson, Martin P., 512-475-9548 martin.jackson@beg.utexas.edu,
University of Texas at Austin – Gtc

Jackson, Michael, 612-624-5274 jacks057@umn.edu,
University of Minnesota, Twin Cities – Ym

Jackson, Philip L., jacksonp@geo.oregonstate.edu,
Oregon State University – Oy

Jackson, Richard A., (718) 460-1476 Long Island University, Brooklyn Campus – Gc

Jackson, Richard H., (801) 378-6063 richard_jackson@byu.edu,
Brigham Young University – Ou

Jackson, Robert B., 919 660 7408 jackson@duke.edu,
Duke University – On

Jackson Jr, William T., 205-247-3548 wjackson@gsa.state.al.us,
Geological Survey of Alabama – GcsGt

Jacob, Daniel J., (617) 495-1794 djj@io.harvard.edu, Harvard University – Oa

Jacob, Klaus H., (845) 365-8440 Columbia University – Ys

Jacob, Robert W., (570) 577-1791 rwj003@bucknell.edu,
Bucknell University – Yg

Jacobi, Robert D., (716) 645-4294 rdjacobi@acsu.buffalo.edu,
SUNY, Buffalo – Gr

Jacobs, Alan M., 330-941-2933 amjacobs@ysu.edu,
Youngstown State University – Ge

Jacobs, Katharine L., (520) 626-3054 jacobsk@email.arizona.edu,
University of Arizona – Hg

Jacobs, Louis L., (214) 768-2773 Southern Methodist University – Pv

Jacobs, Peter, jacobsp@uww.edu, University of Wisconsin, Whitewater – SdaGm

Jacobs, Stanley, (845) 365-8326 Columbia University – Op

Jacobs, Tenika, (609) 984-6587 tenika.jacobs@dep.state.nj.us,
New Jersey Geological Survey – On

Jacobsen, Jeffrey S., (406) 994-4605 jefj@montana.edu,
Montana State University – So

Jacobsen, Stein B., (617) 495-5233 jacobsen@neodymium.harvard.edu,
Harvard University – Cc

Jacobsen, Steven D., 847-467-1825 steven@earth.northwestern.edu,
Northwestern University – GyzOm

Jacobson, Andrew D., (847) 491-3132 adj@earth.northwestern.edu,
Northwestern University – ClPeCa

Jacobson, Carl E., cejac@iastate.edu,
Iowa State University of Science & Technology – Gc

Jacobson, Roger, (775) 673-7364 roger@dri.edu,
University of Nevada, Reno – Cg

Jaeger, John M., (352) 846-1381 jmjaeger@ufl.edu,
University of Florida – Gs

Jaegle, Lyatt, 206-685-2679 jaegle@atmos.washington.edu,
University of Washington – Oa

Jaffe, Daniel A., djaffe@u.washington.edu,
University of Washington – Oa

Jaffe, Peter R., (609) 258-4653 Princeton University – Hg

Jagoutz, Oliver, (617) 324-5514 jagoutz@mit.edu,
Massachusetts Institute of Technology – Gc

Jahangiri, Ahmad, +98 (411) 339 2695 jahangiri@tabriu.ac.ir,
University of Tabriz – GivGg

Jahren, A. Hope, 808-956-2363 jahren@hawaii.edu,
University of Hawai'i, Manoa – CsOs

Jain, Atul K., (217) 333-2128 jain1@illinois.edu,
University of Illinois, Urbana-Champaign – Oa

Jain, Cathy, 7607441150 xt. 2952 cjain@palomar.edu,
Palomar College – Oy

Jaiswal, Priyank, 405-744-6358 priyank.jaiswal@okstate.edu,
Oklahoma State University – Yg

Jakosky, Bruce M., 303-492-8004 bruce.jakosky@colorado.edu,
University of Colorado – Xg

Jamaluddin, Tajul Anuar, 03-79674152 taj@um.edu.my,
University of Malaya – Ng

James, Bruce, (301) 405-8573 brjames@umd.edu,
University of Maryland – Sc

James, David E., djames@carnegiescience.edu,
Carnegie Institution of Washington – YsGtYg

James, Matthew J., (707) 664-2301 james@sonoma.edu,
Sonoma State University – PiGhPo

James, Noel P., (613) 533-6170 jamesn@queensu.ca,
Queen's University – Gd

James, Rachael, +44 (0)23 80599005 R.H.James@soton.ac.uk,
University of Southampton – Oc

James, Richard, 7056751151, ext. 2271 rjames@laurentian.ca,
Laurentian University, Sudbury – Gp

James, Scott C., (254)710-2534 SC_James@baylor.edu,
Baylor University – HwGeHw

James, Valentine U., 814-393-1938 vjames@clarion.edu,
Clarion University – Ou

James-Aworeni, E., 234-705-326-6216 dawnjames@gmail.com,
Obafemi Awolowo University – Hg

Jamieson, Heather E., (613) 545-6181 Queen's University – Ge

Jamieson, J. Bruce, (403) 288-0803 University of Calgary – Ne

Jamieson, Rebecca A., (902) 494-3771 Dalhousie University – Gx

Jamili, Ahmad, ahmad.jamili@ou.edu, University of Oklahoma – Np

Janecke, Susanne U., (435) 797-3877 susanne.janecke@usu.edu,
Utah State University – Gt

Janecky, David R., (505) 667-7603 Los Alamos National Laboratory – Cl

Janetos, Tony, ajanetos@bu.edu, Boston University – On

Janowitz, Gerald S., (919) 515-7837 jerry_janowitz@ncsu.edu,
North Carolina State University – Op

Janson, Xavier, 512-475-9524 xavier.janson@beg.utexas.edu,
University of Texas at Austin – Gs

Janssen, Keith, (785) 532-6101 kjanssen@ksu.edu,
Kansas State University – So

Jantz, Claire A., 717-477-1399 cajant@ship.edu, Shippensburg University – Ou

Janusz, Robert, 210-486-0045 San Antonio Community College – Gg

Janusz, Robert, rjanusz@alamo.edu, Alamo Colleges - San Antonio College – Og

Jaouich, Alfred, 514-987-3000 #3378 jaouich.alfred@uqam.ca,
Universite du Quebec a Montreal – Sc

Jarcho, Kari A., (612) 625-5251 kjarcho@umn.edu,
University of Minnesota, Twin Cities – On

Jardine, Philip M., ipj@ornl.gov, Oak Ridge National Laboratory – Sc

Jarrard, Richard D., (801) 581-7062 r.jarrard@utah.edu,
University of Utah – Gu

Jarvis, Ed, +353 21 4902698 e.jarvis@ucc.ie, University College Cork – Pl

Jarvis, Gary T., (416)736-2100 #77710 jarvis@yorku.ca,
York University – Yg

Jarvis, Ian, +44 020 8417 2526 I.Jarvis@kingston.ac.uk,
Kingston University – Cg

Jarvis, Richard S., 915-747-5263 rsjarvis@utep.edu,
University of Texas, El Paso – Oy

Jarvis, W. T., 541-737-8052 Todd.Jarvis@oregonstate.edu,

Johnson, David B., (575) 835-5771 djohnson@nmt.edu,
New Mexico Institute of Mining and Technology – Ps
Johnson, Donald O., (630) 252-3392 Argonne National Laboratory – Gr
Johnson, Donald R., (608)262-2538 donj@ssec.wisc.edu,
University of Wisconsin, Madison – Oa
Johnson, Elias, (417) 836-5800 Missouri State University – Or
Johnson, Emily P., (617) 353-9709 Boston University – On
Johnson, Emily R., 575-646-3795 erj@nsmu.edu,
New Mexico State University, Las Cruces – Gvi
Johnson, Eric L., 1-607-4314658 johnsone@hartwick.edu,
Hartwick College – GpcGi
Johnson, Gary D., 603-636-2371 Gary.D.Johnson@dartmouth.edu,
Dartmouth College – Gr
Johnson, Glenn W., (801) 581-6151 gjohnson@egi.utah.edu,
University of Utah – Gq
Johnson, Gregory C., (206) 526-6806 University of Washington – Op
Johnson, H. Paul, (206) 543-8474 johnson@ocean.washington.edu,
University of Washington – Yr
Johnson, Helen, +44 01865 272142 Helen.Johnson@earth.ox.ac.uk,
University of Oxford – Og
Johnson, Howard, +44 20 759 46461 h.d.johnson@imperial.ac.uk,
Imperial College – Go
Johnson, Jane M., (320) 589-3411 University of Minnesota, Twin Cities – So
Johnson, Jean M., 706.272.2666 jmjohnson@daltonstate.edu,
Dalton State Community College – Og
Johnson, Jeanne, (225) 578-8407 jeannej@lsu.edu,
Louisiana State University – On
Johnson, Jeffrey , 208-426-2959 jeffrey.b.johnson@gmail.com,
Boise State University – YsGv
Johnson, Joel E., 603-862-1718 joel.johnson@unh.edu,
University of New Hampshire – Gus
Johnson, Joel P., 512-232-5288 joelj@jsg.utexas.edu,
University of Texas at Austin – Gs
Johnson, John R., (503) 725-3381 Washington State University – On
Johnson, Judy L., (907) 474-7388 jljohnson21@alaska.edu,
University of Alaska, Fairbanks – OnnOn
Johnson, Julie, 901-678-4217 jjhnsn79@memphis.edu,
University of Memphis – Gx
Johnson, Kaj, 812-855-3612 kajjohns@indiana.edu,
Indiana University, Bloomington – Yg
Johnson, Katherine, (217) 581-7270 kjohnson4@eiu.edu,
Eastern Illinois University – Pmi
Johnson, Kathleen, 949-824-6174 kathleen.johnson@uci.edu,
University of California, Irvine – Og
Johnson, Kenneth S., johnsonk@uhd.edu,
University of Houston Downtown – Gi
Johnson, Kevin T. M., 808-956-3444 kjohnso2@hawaii.edu,
University of Hawai'i, Manoa – Gi
Johnson, Kurt, (907) 696-0079 kurt.johnson@alaska.gov,
Alaska Division of Geological & Geophysical Surveys – Gg
Johnson, Lane R., LRJohnson@lbl.gov,
University of California, Berkeley – Ys
Johnson, Marie C., (845) 938-4855 marie-johnson@usma.edu,
United States Military Academy – Gi
Johnson, Mark, (604) 822-6919 mark.johnson@ubc.ca,
University of British Columbia – SpNg
Johnson, Mark O., mjohnson15@worcester.edu, Worcester State University – Oy
Johnson, Markes E., 413-597-2329 markes.e.johnson@williams.edu,
Williams College – Ps
Johnson, Martin, +44 (0)1603 59 1299 martin.johnson@uea.ac.uk,
University of East Anglia – Cm
Johnson, Ned K., (510) 642-3059 University of California, Berkeley – Pv
Johnson, Neil E., 540-231-1785 johnsonne@vt.edu,
Virginia Polytechnic Institute & State University – GzEg
Johnson, Paul A., (507) 933-7442 Los Alamos National Laboratory – Yg
Johnson, Peggy, (575) 835-5819 peggy@nmbg.nmt.edu,
New Mexico Institute of Mining & Technology – Hw
Johnson, Richard H., (970) 248-1672 johnson@atmos.colostate.edu,
Colorado State University – Oa
Johnson, Robert E., (309) 298-1368 RE-Johnson2@wiu.edu,
Western Illinois University – On
Johnson, Robert G., 612-626-0853 johns088@umn.edu,
University of Minnesota, Twin Cities – Pe
Johnson, Robert L., (630) 252-7004 rljohnson@anl.gov,
Argonne National Laboratory – On
Johnson, Robert O., (507) 933-7442 Oak Ridge National Laboratory – Hg
Johnson, Ronald E., (757) 683-4936 rejohnso@odu.edu,
Old Dominion University – Op
Johnson, Roy A., (520) 621-4890 johnson6@email.arizona.edu,
University of Arizona – Ys
Johnson, Sarah E., 859-572-6907 johnsonsa@nku.edu,
Northern Kentucky University – Ng
Johnson, Scott E., (207) 581-2142 johnsons@maine.edu,
University of Maine – Gc
Johnson, Stephen W., (609) 984-6587 steve.johnson@dep.state.nj.us,
New Jersey Geological Survey – Hw
Johnson, Thomas C., (218) 726-8128 tcj@d.umn.edu,
University of Minnesota, Duluth – Gn
Johnson, Thomas M., (217) 244-2002 tmjohnsn@illinois.edu,
University of Illinois, Urbana-Champaign – Hw

Johnson, Tiffany, 604-777-6117 johnsont@douglascollege.ca,
Douglas College – Og
Johnson, Ty, (501) 683-0153 ty.johnson@arkansas.gov,
Arkansas Geological Survey – GgOi
Johnson, Verner C., (970) 248-1672 vjohnson@coloradomesa.edu,
Colorado Mesa University – Yg
Johnson, William C., 785-864-5548 wcj@ku.edu,
University of Kansas – Grm
Johnson, William P., (801) 581-5033 william.johnson@utah.edu,
University of Utah – Ng
Johnston, A. Dana, (541) 346-5588 adjohn@uoregon.edu,
University of Oregon – Cp
Johnston, Andrew K., 202-633-2477 Smithsonian Institution / National Air &
Space Museum – Oy
Johnston, Archibald C., (901) 678-2007 ajohnstn@memphis.edu,
University of Memphis – Ys
Johnston, Carl G., 330-941-7151 cgjohnston@ysu.edu,
Youngstown State University – Py
Johnston, David, (501) 683-0126 david.johnston@arkansas.gov,
Arkansas Geological Survey – Gg
Johnston, David T., 617-496-5024 johnston@eps.harvard.edu,
Harvard University – CgPy
Johnston, K. R. Gina, gjohnston@csuchico.edu,
California State University, Chico – Hs
Johnston, Karin, (541) 346-5588 George Washington University – On
Johnston, Paul, (403) 440-6174 pajohnston@mtroyal.ca,
Mount Royal University – Pi
Johnston, Paul J., 620-341-5330 jillpaulj@hotmail.com,
Emporia State University – Gg
Johnston, Robert A., (207) 287-7177 robert.a.johnston@maine.gov,
Dept of Agriculture, Conservation, and Forestry – Gg
Johnston, Scott, 805-756-1650 scjohnst@calpoly.edu,
California Polytechnic State University – GcpCc
Johnston, Stephen T., 250 721-6120 stj@uvic.ca,
University of Victoria – Gc
Johnston, Thomas, (403) 329-2534 johnston@uleth.ca,
University of Lethbridge – Oe
Johnston, III, John E., (225) 578-8657 hammer@lsu.edu,
Louisiana State University – EoGe
Jokipii, Jack R., (520) 621-4256 jokipii@lpl.arizona.edu,
University of Arizona – Xy
Jolliff, Bradley L., (314) 935-5622 blj@levee.wustl.edu,
Washington University in St. Louis – Gx
Jomeiri, Rahim, +98 (411) 339 2704 University of Tabriz – Yg
Jonas, John J., (514) 398-4755 McGill University – Nx
Jones, Adrian, +44 020 7679 32415 adrian.jones@ucl.ac.uk,
University College London – Gi
Jones, Alan, (607) 777-2518 Binghamton University – Ys
Jones, Bobby L., (225) 388-8328 Louisiana State University – Go
Jones, Brian, (780) 492-3074 brian.jones@ualberta.ca,
University of Alberta – Ps
Jones, Charles E., (412) 624-6347 cejones@pitt.edu,
University of Pittsburgh – Gg
Jones, Craig H., 303-492-6994 craig.jones@colorado.edu,
University of Colorado – Ys
Jones, D. M., 740 548 7348 Dalton.Jones@dnr.state.oh.us,
Ohio Dept of Natural Resources – Gse
Jones, Dan, dsjones@umn.edu,
University of Minnesota, Twin Cities – Py
Jones, David S., (413) 542-2714 djones@amherst.edu, Amherst College – Gs
Jones, Douglas S., (352) 392-1721 dsjones@flmnh.ufl.edu,
University of Florida – Pg
Jones, Douglas S., 3523921721 x485 dsjones@flmnh.ufl.edu,
University of Florida – Pg
Jones, Eric M., (505) 667-6386 honais@lanl.gov,
Los Alamos National Laboratory – Oa
Jones, F. Walter, (780) 492-0667 wjones@phys.ualberta.ca,
University of Alberta – Ym
Jones, Francis H., (604) 822-2138 fjones@eos.ubc.ca,
University of British Columbia – Ye
Jones, Glen, (505) 835-5627 glen@gis.nmt.edu,
New Mexico Institute of Mining & Technology – On
Jones, Jon W., (403) 220-5024 University of Calgary – Gp
Jones, Julia A., (541) 737-1224 jonesj@geo.oregonstate.edu,
Oregon State University – So
Jones, Larry Allan, (505) 667-0142 ljones@lanl.gov,
Los Alamos National Laboratory – Ng
Jones, Lawrence, 970-248-1708 lajones@coloradomesa.edu,
Colorado Mesa University – Gs
Jones, Merren, Merren.A.Jones@manchester.ac.uk,
University of Manchester – Gst
Jones, Michael Q., (011) 717-6628 michael.jones@wits.ac.za,
University of the Witwatersrand – YhGtYg
Jones, Minnie O., (312) 996-3154 mojones@uic.edu,
University of Illinois at Chicago – On
Jones, Norris W., (920) 424-4460 jonesnw@uwosh.edu,
University of Wisconsin, Oshkosh – Gi
Jones, Peter E., 902-426-3869 Dalhousie University – Op
Jones, Phillip, +44 (0)1603 59 2090 p.jones@uea.ac.uk,
University of East Anglia – Oa

Jones, Rhian, 505-277-4204 rjones@unm.edu, University of New Mexico – Gz
Jones, Robert L., (217) 333-9490 University of Illinois, Urbana-Champaign – Sc
Jones, Stephen C., 205/247-3601 sjones@gsa.state.al.us,
    Geological Survey of Alabama – Hg
Jones, Stuart, +44 (0) 191 33 42319 stuart.jones@durham.ac.uk,
    Durham University – s
Jones, T, jonesTP@cf.ac.uk, Cardiff University – Ge
Jones, Tim L., (505) 646-3405 New Mexico State University, Las Cruces – Sp
Jones, W. J., (803) 777-4338 w.joe.jones@gmail.com,
    University of South Carolina – Ob
Jones, III, John P., jpjones@email.arizona.edu, University of Arizona – On
Jonsson, Bror F., (609) 258-2612 bjonsson@princeton.edu,
    Princeton University – Op
Jordan, Andy, +44 (0)1603 59 2552 a.jordan@uea.ac.uk,
    University of East Anglia – Ge
Jordan, Brad C., (570) 577-3024 jordan@bucknell.edu,
    Bucknell University – Gi
Jordan, Brennan T., (605) 677-6143 Brennan.Jordan@usd.edu,
    University of South Dakota – GiOw
Jordan, Guntram, 089/2180 4353 guntram.jodan@lrz.uni-muenchen.de,
    Ludwig-Maximilians-Universitaet Muenchen – Gz
Jordan, Jim L., (409) 880-8211 jim.jordan@lamar.edu,
    Lamar University – Cc
Jordan, Karen J., 251-460-6381 kjordan@southalabama.edu,
    University of South Alabama – Oyr
Jordan, Mary S., 831-656-7571 jordan@nps.edu,
    Naval Postgraduate School – Ow
Jordan, Robert A., (757) 727-5783 robert.jordan@hamptonu.edu,
    Hampton University – Ob
Jordan, Robert R., (302) 831-6415 rrjordan@udel.edu,
    University of Delaware – Gr
Jordan, Teresa A., (607) 255-3596 tej1@cornell.edu,
    Cornell University – Gr
Jordan, Thomas H., (213) 821-1237 tjordan@usc.edu,
    University of Southern California – Ys
Jorge, Maria Luisa, (615) 322-2160 malu.jorge@vanderbilt.edu,
    Vanderbilt University – Py
Jornov, Donna, djornov@mail.nysed.gov,
    New York State Geological Survey – On
Joshi, Manoj, +44 (0)1603 59 3647 m.joshi@uea.ac.uk,
    University of East Anglia – Oi
Journel, Andre G., (650) 723-1594 journel@pangea.stanford.edu,
    Stanford University – Gq
Judge, Shelley, (330) 263-2297 sjudge@wooster.edu,
    College of Wooster – Gt
Judkins, Heather L., Judkins.Heather@spcollege.edu,
    Saint Petersburg College, Clearwater – Og
Jugo, Pedro J., 7056751151, ext. 2106 pjugo@laurentian.ca,
    Laurentian University, Sudbury – Gi
Jugulam, Mithila, (785) 532-2755 mithila@ksu.edu,
    Kansas State University – So
Juhl, Andrew, 845-365-8837 andyjuhl@ldeo.columbia.edu,
    Columbia University – Ob
Jull, A. J. Timothy, (520) 621-6816 jull@u.arizona.edu,
    University of Arizona – Cg
Jung, Simon, +44 (0) 131 650 4837 Simon.Jung@ed.ac.uk,
    Edinburgh University – Og
Juniper, Kim, 250-721-6120 kjuniper@uvic.ca,
    University of Victoria – Ob
Junium, Christopher, 315-443-8969 ckjunium@syr.edu,
    Syracuse University – CsPeCo
Juntunen, Thomas, 612-626-0505 junt0015@umn.edu,
    University of Minnesota, Twin Cities – Oi
Juraèiæ, Mladen, +38514606099 mjuracic@geol.pmf.hr,
    University of Zagreb – GueCm
Juranek, Lauren W., 541-737-2368 ljuranek@coas.oregonstate.edu,
    Oregon State University – Cm
Jurdy, Donna M., (847) 491-7163 donna@earth.northwestern.edu,
    Northwestern University – YgXyg
Jurena, Dwight, djurena@alamo.edu,
    Alamo Colleges - San Antonio College – GgOg
Jurena, Dwight, 210-486-0062 djurena@alamo.edu,
    San Antonio Community College – GgOg
Jurmanovich, Barb, 989-686-9445 Delta College – On
Jurmu, Michael, (920) 929-1163 michael.jurmu@uwc.edu,
    University of Wisconsin Colleges – OyGgOn
Juster, Thomas C., (813) 974-9691 University of South Florida, Tampa – Hw
Juszczyk , Carmen , (303) 492-2330 CarmenJ@Colorado.EDU,
    University of Colorado – On
Jutla, Rajinder S., (417) 836-5298 rajinderjutla@missouristate.edu,
    Missouri State University – On

K

K, Ayse Didem, 00904242370000-5969 adkilic@firat.edu.tr,
    Firat University – GxpGy
Kabengi, Nadine, 404-413-5207 kabengi@gsu.edu,
    Georgia State University – ScClGe
Kaczmarek, Stephen , (269) 387-5479 stephen.kaczmarek@wmich.edu,
    Western Michigan University – Gd
Kaden, Scott, 573-368-2356 nrkades@mail.dnr.state.mo.us,

Missouri Dept of Natural Resources – On
Kadjar, Mickey, (214) 860-2734 MKadjar@dcccd.edu,
    El Centro College - Dallas Community College District – Gg
Kadkhodai Ilkhchi, Ali, +98 (411) 339 2724 University of Tabriz – NpEo
Kadrmas, Elroy, ekadrmas@nd.gov, North Dakota Geological Survey – Oi
Kafka, Alan L., (617) 552-3650 kafka@bc.edu, Boston College – Yg
Kah, Linda, (865) 974-2366 lckah@utk.edu,
    University of Tennessee, Knoxville – Gs
Kahle, Anne B., (818) 354-7265 anne@aster.jpl.nasa.gov,
    Jet Propulsion Laboratory – Or
Kahle, Beth, 021-650-2900 beth.kahle@uct.ac.za,
    University of Cape Town – YgEoYg
Kahle, Chris, Chris.Kahle@dnr.iowa.gov, Iowa Dept of Natural Resources – Oi
Kaip, Galen M., (915) 747-6817 kaip@geo.utep.edu,
    University of Texas, El Paso – Yx
Kairies Beatty, Candace L., 507-474-5789 ckairiesBeatty@winona.edu,
    Winona State University – GeCl
Kaiser, Daniel E., 612-624-3482 dekaiser@umn.edu,
    University of Minnesota, Twin Cities – Cg
Kaiser, Jan, +44 (0)1603 59 3393 j.kaiser@uea.ac.uk,
    University of East Anglia – Cs
Kaiser, Jason, 435-865-8275 jasonkaiser@suu.edu,
    Southern Utah University – GzvCg
Kaiser-Bischoff, Ines, 089/2180 4314 kaiser-bischoff@lmu.de,
    Ludwig-Maximilians-Universitaet Muenchen – Gz
Kaka, Ismail, +96638603879 skaka@kfupm.edu.sa,
    King Fahd University of Petroleum and Minerals – Ys
Kakembo, Vincent, 27 41 504 4516 Vincent.Kakembo@nmmu.ac.za,
    Nelson Mandela Metropolitan University – Sp
Kalakay, Thomas J., 406-657-1101 kalakayt@rocky.edu,
    Rocky Mountain College – GcpGi
Kaldor, Michael, (305) 237-3025 michael.kaldor@mdc.edu,
    Miami-Dade Community College (Wolfson Campus) – Gg
Kalender, Leyla, 00904242370000-5984 leylakalender@firat.edu.tr ,
    Firat University – CgcCs
Kalia, Hemendra N., (702) 295-5767 hemendra_kalia@notes.ymp.gov,
    Los Alamos National Laboratory – Nm
Kallemeyn, Gregory, (310) 825-3202 University of California, Los Angeles – Cg
Kalnejais, Linda, 603-862-1008 linda.kalnejais@unh.edu,
    University of New Hampshire – Oc
Kaltenbacher, Eric A., (727) 553-3959 eak@marine.usf.edu,
    University of South Florida, Saint Petersburg – Oo
Kalvoda, Jiri, +420 549 49 4756 dino@sci.muni.cz ,
    Masaryk University – PsePm
Kamber, Balz, 7056751151, ext. 2249 bkamber@laurentian.ca,
    Laurentian University, Sudbury – Cs
Kamber, Balz, + 353 1 8962957 kamberbs@tcd.ie,
    Trinity College – Ge
Kambesis, Patricia, (270) 745-5984 pat.kambesis@wku.edu,
    Western Kentucky University – OigHw
Kambewa, Chamunorwa , 078 321 6710 kambewac@tut.ac.za,
    Tshwane University of Technology – CgeOe
Kamenov, George D., 352-846-3599 kamenov@ufl.edu,
    University of Florida – Cg
Kamhi, Samuel R., (718) 460-1476 Long Island University, Brooklyn Campus
    – Gz
Kamilli, Robert J., (520) 670-5576 bkamilli@usgs.gov,
    University of Arizona – Eg
Kaminski, Michael, +966386025620 kaminski@kfupm.edu.sa,
    King Fahd University of Petroleum and Minerals – GuPm
Kammer, Thomas W., (304) 293-5603 tkammer@wvu.edu,
    West Virginia University – Pi
Kamola, Diane, (785) 864-2724 dlkamola@ku.edu,
    University of Kansas – Gs
Kamona, Frederick A., afkamona@unam.na,
    University of Namibia – EgGzCe
Kampf, Anthony R., (213) 763-3328 akampf@nhm.org,
    Los Angeles County Museum of Natural History – Gz
Kamykowski, Daniel, (919) 515-7894 dan_kamykowski@ncsu.edu,
    North Carolina State University – Ob
Kana, Todd M., (410) 221-8481 kana@hpl.umces.edu,
    University of Maryland – Ob
Kanamori, Hiroo, (626) 395-6914 hiroo@gps.caltech.edu,
    California Institute of Technology – Ys
Kanaroglou, Pavlos S., 905-525-9140 (Ext. 23525) pavlos@mcmaster.ca,
    McMaster University – Og
Kanat, Leslie H., (802) 635-1327 kanatl@jsc.vsc.edu,
    Johnson State College – Gc
Kandiah, Ramanitharan, 937 376 6260 rkandiah@centralstate.edu,
    Central State University – HqSoOi
Kane, Mustapha, 386.754. 4452 mustapha.kane@fgc.edu,
    Florida Gateway College – Og
Kanemasu, Edward T., (706) 542-2151 University of Georgia – Sp
Kanfoush, Sharon L., (315) 792-3134 skanfoush@utica.edu,
    Utica College – GsOuGn
Kang, Song-Lak, 806-834-1139 song-lak.kang@ttu.edu,
    Texas Tech University – Oa
Kanik, Mustafa, 00904242370000-5964 Firat University – NrSo
Kantzas, Apostolos, (403) 220-8907 akantzas@ucalgary.ca,
    University of Calgary – Ng

Kanungo, Sudeep, 801-585-7852 skanungo@egi.utah.edu,
University of Utah – Pms
Kao, Jim C., (505) 667-9226 Los Alamos National Laboratory – Oa
Kaplan, Alexey, (845) 365-8689 Columbia University – Op
Kaplan, Isaac R., (310) 825-5076 University of California, Los Angeles – Cg
Kaplan, Isaac R., (310) 825-5706 irkaplan@ucla.edu,
University of California, Los Angeles – Csg
Kaplan, Samantha W., 715-346-4149 skaplan@uwsp.edu,
University of Wisconsin, Stevens Point – GnPlGd
Kaplinski, Matthew A., (928) 523-9145 Northern Arizona University – Yg
Kapp, Jessica, 520-626-5701 jkapp@email.arizona.edu,
University of Arizona – Gg
Kapp, Paul, (520) 626-8763 pkapp@email.arizona.edu,
University of Arizona – Gc
Kar, Aditya, (912) 825-6844 Fort Valley State University – Ct
Kar, Bandana, 601-266-5786 bandana.kar@usm.edu,
University of Southern Mississippi – Oi
Kara, Hatice, 00904242370000-5965 haticekara@firat.edu.tr,
Firat University – Cg
Karabinos, Paul, (413) 597-2079 paul.m.karabinos@williams.edu,
Williams College – Gc
Karanfil, Tanju, (864) 656-1005 tkaranf@clemson.edu,
Clemson University – NgOnn
Karato, Shun-ichiro, (203) 432-3147 shun-ichiro.karato@yale.edu,
Yale University – Gy
Karginoglu, Yusuf , 00904242370000-5989 Firat University – Eg
Karhu, Juha A., 358-294150834 Juha.Karhu@helsinki.fi,
University of Helsinki – Csg
Karig, Daniel E., dek9@cornell.edu, Cornell University – Yr
Kariminia, Seyed, 770-274-5050 seyed.kariminia@gpc.edu,
Georgia Perimeter College – PmNgOe
Karkanis, Pano G., (403) 317-0156 Cel. karkanis@telusplanet.net,
University of Lethbridge – So
Karl, David M., (808) 956-8964 dkarl@soest.hawaii.edu,
University of Hawai'i, Manoa – Ob
Karl, Tami S., (850) 644-5861 karl@gly.fsu.edu,
Florida State University – On
Karlen, Douglas L., (515) 294-3336 Doug.Karlen@ars.usda.gov,
Iowa State University of Science & Technology – So
Karlin, Robert, (775) 784-1770 karlin@mines.unr.edu,
University of Nevada, Reno – Ou
Karlsson, Haraldur R., 806-834-7978 hal.karlsson@ttu.edu,
Texas Tech University – Cl
Karlstrom, Karl E., (505) 277-4346 kek1@unm.edu,
University of New Mexico – Gt
Karner, Daniel B., (707) 664-2854 karner@sonoma.edu,
Sonoma State University – Cc
Karner, James M., (505) 277-8327 University of New Mexico – Gz
Karpilo, Jr, Ronald J., (970) 225-3500 ron_karpilo@partner.nps.gov,
Colorado State University – Oy
Karplus, Marianne, (915) 747-5413 mkarplus@utep.edu,
University of Texas, El Paso – Ysg
Karson, Jeffrey, 315-443-7976 jakarson@syr.edu, Syracuse University – GtcGv
Karuntillake, Suniti, sunitiw@lsu.edu, Louisiana State University – Xg
Karwoski, Todd, (301) 405-0084 karwoski@geol.umd.edu,
University of Maryland – Gg
Kaspar, Thomas A., (515) 294-8873 Tom.Kaspar@ars.usda.gov,
Iowa State University of Science & Technology – So
Kaste, James, 757-221-2591 jmkaste@wm.edu,
College of William & Mary – ClcSc
Kaster, Mark A., 570-408-5046 mark.kaster@wilkes.edu,
Wilkes University – Ow
Kasting, James F., (814) 865-3207 kasting@essc.psu.edu,
Pennsylvania State University, University Park – Oa
Kastner, Miriam, (858) 534-2065 mkastner@ucsd.edu,
University of California, San Diego – Cl
Kaszuba, John P., 307-766-3392 jkaszub1@uwyo.edu,
University of Wyoming – CgGze
Kath, Randal L., (678) 839-4063 rkath@westga.edu,
University of West Georgia – Gc
Kato, Terence T., 530-898-5262 tkato@csuchico.edu,
California State University, Chico – Gt
Katuna, Michael P., katunam@cofc.edu, College of Charleston – Gus
Katz, Gabrielle, (828) 262-3000 katzgl@appstate.edu,
Appalachian State University – Hg
Katz, Miriam E., 518-276-8521 katzm@rpi.edu,
Rensselaer Polytechnic Institute – Pme
Katz, Richard, +44-1865-282122 richard.katz@earth.ox.ac.uk,
University of Oxford – Og
Katzenstein, Kurt W., (605) 394-2461 Kurt.Katzenstein@sdsmt.edu,
South Dakota School of Mines & Technology – NgrOr
Katzman, Danny, (505) 667-0599 katzman@lanl.gov,
Los Alamos National Laboratory – Gg
Kauahikaua, James P., (808) 967-7320 University of Hawai'i, Manoa – Gv
Kauffman, Chad, 724 938-5760 kauffman@cup.edu,
California University of Pennsylvania – Oa
Kauffman, Erle G., (812) 855-5154 Indiana University, Bloomington – Po
Kauffman, Marvin E., (406) 683-7615 marvsuekauffman@hotmail.com,
University of Montana Western – Gr
Kaufman, Alan J., (301) 405-0395 kaufman@geol.umd.edu,

University of Maryland – Csg
Kaufman, Darrell S., (928) 523-7192 darrell.kaufman@nau.edu,
Northern Arizona University – Gm
Kaufmann, Ronald S., (619) 260-5904 kaufmann@sandiego.edu,
University of San Diego – Ob
Kaunda, Rennie, 303-273-3772 rkaunda@mines.edu,
Colorado School of Mines – Nm
Kaushal, Sujay, (301) 405-0454 skaushal@umd.edu,
University of Maryland – OuGeHs
Kavage-Adams, Rebecca, 410-554-5553 rebecca.adams@maryland.gov,
Maryland Department of Natural Resources – Ggm
Kavanagh, Janine, +44-151-794-5150 Janine.Kavanagh@liverpool.ac.uk,
University of Liverpool – Gv
Kavanaugh, Jeffrey, 780-492-1740 jeff.kavanaugh@ualberta.ca,
University of Alberta – Ng
Kavner, Abby, (310) 206-3675 akavner@ucla.edu,
University of California, Los Angeles – GyYg
Kawase, Mitsuhiro, (206) 543-0766 kawase@ocean.washington.edu,
University of Washington – Op
Kay, Richard F., (919) 684-2143 richard.kay@duke.edu,
Duke University – On
Kay, Robert W., (607) 255-3461 rwk6@cornell.edu,
Cornell University – Giz
Kay, Suzanne M., (607) 255-4701 smk16@cornell.edu,
Cornell University – GiCg
Kaye, John M., (662) 325-3915 Mississippi State University – Gg
Kaygili, Sibel, 00904242370000-5962 skaygili@firat.edu.tr,
Firat University – GgPgs
Kays, M. Allan, (541) 346-4578 makays@oregon.uoregon.edu,
University of Oregon – Gp
Kazimoto, Emmanuel, ekazimoto@udsm.ac.tz,
University of Dar es Salaam – EgGi
Kazmer, Miklos, +36-1-372-2500 ext. 8627 mkazmer@gmail.com,
Eotvos Lorand University – PgoGh
Keables, Michael J., 303-871-2621 michael.keables@du.edu,
University of Denver – Oa
Keach, William, 801-585-1717 bkeach@egi.utah.edu,
University of Utah – GoYes
Keach II, R. William, 801-857-7728 bkeach@byu.edu,
Brigham Young University – YeEoGg
Keaffaber, J. J., (407) 768-8000 Florida Institute of Technology – Oc
Keala, Lori, (909) 621-8675 lkeala@pomona.edu, Pomona College – On
Kean, Jr., William F., 414-229-5231 wkean@uwm.edu,
University of Wisconsin, Milwaukee – Ym
Kearney, Kenneth, 312-413-3655 kkearn3@uic.edu,
University of Illinois at Chicago – Cg
Kearney, Micheal S., (301) 405-4057 kearneym@umd.edu,
University of Maryland – Gu
Kearns, Lance E., 540-568-6421 kearnsle@jmu.edu,
James Madison University – Gz
Keating, Elizabeth, (505) 665-6714 ekeating@lanl.gov,
Los Alamos National Laboratory – Gg
Keating, Kristina M., 973-353-1263 kmkeat@andromeda.rutgers.edu,
Rutgers, The State University of New Jersey, Newark – Yg
Keating, Martha E., (781) 891-2980 mkeating@bentley.edu,
Bentley University – On
Keaton, Jeffrey R., (801) 581-8218 University of Utah – On
Keatts, Merida, 330-672-2897 mkeatts@kent.edu,
Kent State University – On
Keays, Reid R., (705) 675-1151 Laurentian University, Sudbury – Em
Kebbede, Girma, 413-538-2004 gkebbede@mtholyoke.edu,
Mount Holyoke College – Oy
Keefer, Donald, 217 244-2786 keefer@isgs.uiuc.edu,
Illinois State Geological Survey – Hw
Keeling, David, (270) 745-4555 david.keeling@wku.edu,
Western Kentucky University – Og
Keeling, Ralph F., (858) 534-7582 rkeeling@ucsd.edu,
University of California, San Diego – Oa
Keen, Kerry L., (715) 425-3729 kerry.l.keen@uwrf.edu,
University of Wisconsin, River Falls – Hw
Keen-Zebert, Amanda, 775-673-7434 akz@dri.edu,
Desert Research Institute – Oy
Keene, Deborah A., 205-348-3334 dakeene@ua.edu,
University of Alabama – Gga
Keene, William, (804) 924-0586 wck@virginia.edu,
University of Virginia – Oa
Keeney, Dennis R., (515) 294-8066 drkeeney@iastate.edu,
Iowa State University of Science & Technology – So
Keesee, Robert G., (518) 442-4566 rgk@atmos.albany.edu,
SUNY, Albany – Oa
Kehew, Alan E., (269) 387-5495 alan.kehew@wmich.edu,
Western Michigan University – GmlHw
Kehoe-Forutan, Sandra J., (570) 389-4106 kehoe@bloomu.edu,
Bloomsburg University – Onu
Keigwin, Lloyd D., (508) 289-2784 lkeigwin@whoi.edu,
Woods Hole Oceanographic Institution – Cs
Keil, Charles, (630) 752-7271 chris.keil@wheaton.edu,
Wheaton College – On
Keil, Klaus, (808) 956-3898 University of Hawai'i, Manoa – Xm
Keil, Richard G., (206) 616-1947 rickkeil@ocean.washington.edu,

Louisiana State University – Hg

Keskinen, Mary J., 907-474-7769 ffmjk@uaf.edu,
University of Alaska Fairbanks – Gx

Kesler, Stephen E., (734) 763-5057 skesler@umich.edu,
University of Michigan – Eg

Kesseli, Rick, rick.kesseli@umb.edu,
University of Massachusetts, Boston – Obn

Kessinger, Walter P., (337) 984-3554 University of Louisiana at Lafayette – Pm

Kessler, Fritz, (301) 687-4266 fkessler@frostburg.edu,
Frostburg State University – Or

Kessler, William S., (206) 526-6221 kessler@pmel.noaa.gov,
University of Washington – Op

Ketcham, Richard A., (512) 471-6942 ketcham@mail.utexas.edu,
University of Texas at Austin – Gzq

Ketterer, Michael, (520) 523-7055 Case Western Reserve University – Ca

Kettler, Richard M., (402) 472-0882 rkettler1@unl.edu,
University of Nebraska, Lincoln – Cl

Kettmann, Elizabeth, (707) 664-2334 meyerel@sonoma.edu,
Sonoma State University – On

Kevan, Peter, pkevan@uoguelph.ca, University of Guelph – On

Key, Doug, 7607441150 ext.2515 dkey@palomar.edu, Palomar College – Oy

Key, Jeffrey R., (608)263-2605 jkey@ssec.wisc.edu,
University of Wisconsin, Madison – Or

Key, Jr., Marcus M., 717-245-1448 key@dickinson.edu, Dickinson College – Pi

Keyantash, John, (310) 243-2363 jkeyantash@csudh.edu,
California State University, Dominguez Hills – Hg

Keyser, Daniel, (518) 442-4559 keyser@atmos.albany.edu, SUNY, Albany – Oa

Khairoutdinov, Marat, (631) 632-6339 marat.khairoutdinov@stonybrook.edu,
SUNY, Stony Brook – Oa

Khalequzzaman, Md., (570) 484-2075 mkhalequ@lhup.edu,
Lock Haven University – HwOni

Khalil, Mohamed, 406-496-4716 mkhalil@mtech.edu,
Montana Tech – YegGe

Khalil Ebeid, Khalil I., 002-03-3921595 kebeid@yahoo.com,
Alexandria University – GgEg

Khan, Belayet H., 217-581-6246 bhkhan@eiu.edu,
Eastern Illinois University – Oyw

Khan, Latif A., 217-244-2383 info@isgs.illinois.edu,
Illinois State Geological Survey – Nx

Khan, Mohammad Wahdat Y., (982) 719-7331 mwykhan@rediffmail.com,
Pt. Ravishankar Shukla University – GdEgCl

Khan, Shuhab, 713-743-5404 sdkhan@uh.edu, University of Houston – Or

Khanbilvardi, Reza M., (215) 650-8009 Graduate School of the City University
of New York – Hy

Khandaker, Nazrul I., (718) 262-2079 nkhandaker@york.cuny.edu,
York College (CUNY) – GdeOe

Khawaja, Ikram U., john@cis.ysu.edu, Youngstown State University – Ec

Khosrowpanah, Shahram, (671) 735-2694 khosrow@uog.edu,
University of Guam – Hs

Khurana, Krishan, (310) 825-8240 University of California, Los Angeles – On

Kiage, Lawrence M., (404) 413-5777 geolkk@langate.gsu.edu,
Georgia State University – OyPlOr

Kidane-Mariam, Tadesse, (814) 732-1576 tadesse@edinboro.edu,
Edinboro University of Pennsylvania – On

Kidd, David, +44 020 8417 62541 David.Kidd@kingston.ac.uk,
Kingston University – Oi

Kidder, David L., (740) 593-1108 kidder@ohio.edu,
Ohio University – Gs

Kidder, T.R., trkidder@wustl.edu, Washington University – On

Kidwell, Susan M., (773) 702-3008 skidwell@midway.uchicago.edu,
University of Chicago – Gs

Kiefer, Boris, 575 646 1932 bkiefer@nmsu.edu,
New Mexico State University, Las Cruces – GyYgOm

Kieffer, Bruno, bkieffer@eos.ubc.ca,
University of British Columbia – Cs

Kieffer, Susan W., (217) 244-6206 skieffer@illinois.edu,
University of Illinois, Urbana-Champaign – Gv

Kienast, Markus, (902) 494-8338 markus.kienast@dal.ca,
Dalhousie University – Cs

Kienast, Stephanie, (902) 494-2203 stephanie.kienast@dal.ca,
Dalhousie University – Gu

Kiene, Ronald P., (251) 861-7526 rkiene@jaguar1.usouthal.edu,
University of South Alabama – Oc

Kientop, Greg A., 217-265-6581 gkientop@illinois.edu,
University of Illinois, Urbana-Champaign – Ge

Kienzle, Stefan, stefan.kienzle@uleth.ca,
University of Lethbridge – Oi

Kiesel, Diann, (608) 355-5223 diann.kiesel@uwc.edu,
University of Wisconsin Colleges – GgOyGg

Kieu, Chanh Q., (812) 856-5704 ckieu@indiana.edu,
Indiana University, Bloomington – Oa

Kifer, Lauri A., (585) 395-2636 lmulley@brockport.edu,
SUNY, The College at Brockport – On

Kift, Richard, +44 0161 306-8770 Richard.Kift@manchester.ac.uk,
University of Manchester – Oa

Kijko, Andrzej, +27 12 420 3613 andrzej.kijko@up.ac.za,
University of Pretoria – Ysg

Kilburn, Chris, +44 020 7679 37194 c.kilburn@ucl.ac.uk,
University College London – Yx

Kilcoyne, John R., (303) 556-4258 Metropolitan State College of Denver – Oy

Kile, Susan, 217-581-2626 skkile@eiu.edu,
Eastern Illinois University – On

Kilibarda, Zoran, 219-980-6753 zkilibar@iun.edu,
Indiana University Northwest – GsmGd

Kilinc, Attila I., (513) 556-5967 attila.kilinc@uc.edu,
University of Cincinnati – Cp

Killorn, Randy J., (515) 294-1923 rkillorn@iastate.edu,
Iowa State University of Science & Technology – So

Kilroy, Kathyrn, 701-858-3114 kathryn.kilroy@minotstateu.edu,
Minot State University – Hg

Kilsby, Chris, +44 (0) 191 208 5614 chris.kilsby@ncl.ac.uk,
University of Newcastle Upon Tyne – Hg

Kim, Eunhye, 303-273-3428 ekim1@mines.edu, Colorado School of Mines – Nm

Kim, Hyemi, (404) 894-1738 hyemi.kim@eas.gatech.edu,
Georgia Institute of Technology – Oa

Kim, Jonathan, (802) 522-5401 jon.kim@vermont.gov,
Agency of Natural Resources, Dept of Environmental Conservation – GetCg

Kim, Keonho, 432-685-4739 kkim@midland.edu, Midland College – GgOwPi

Kim, Kwangmin, kimkm@email.arizona.edu, University of Arizona – NmrNx

Kim, Saewung, (949)824-4531 saewungk@uci.edu,
University of California, Irvine – Oa

Kim, Sang-Tae, (905) 525-9140 (Ext. 26494) sangtae@mcmaster.ca,
McMaster University – Cg

Kim, Stacy, 831-771-4400 skim@mlml.calstate.edu,
Moss Landing Marine Laboratories – On

Kim, Won-Young, (845) 365-8387 Columbia University – Ys

Kim, Wonsuck, 512-471-4203 delta@jsg.utexas.edu,
University of Texas at Austin – Gsr

Kimball, Bryn, 509-527-4951 kimballb@whitman.edu,
Whitman College – ClEgGz

Kimball, Matthew E., 843-904-9030 matt@belle.baruch.sc.edu,
University of South Carolina – Obn

Kimball, Sytske K., skimball@southalabama.edu,
University of South Alabama – Ow

Kimber, Clarissa T., (409) 845-7141 Texas A&M University – Oy

Kimbro, David, 7815817370 x310 d.kimbro@neu.edu,
Northeastern University – On

Kimbrough, David L., (619) 594-1385 dkimbrough@mail.sdsu.edu,
San Diego State University – Cc

Kimerling, A. Jon, kimerlia@geo.oregonstate.edu,
Oregon State University – Or

Kincaid, Christopher, (401) 874-6571 kincaid@gso.uri.edu,
University of Rhode Island – Ou

Kineke, Gail C., (617) 552-3655 gail.kineke.1@bc.edu, Boston College – On

King, Carey, 512-471-5468 cking@jsg.utexas.edu,
University of Texas at Austin – Eog

King, John, (401) 874-6594 jking@gso.uri.edu,
University of Rhode Island – Ou

King, Jonathan K., (801) 537-3354 jonking@utah.gov,
Utah Geological Survey – Gg

King, Kenneth M., (519) 824-4120 (Ext. 52453) kenmking@rogers.com,
University of Guelph – Oa

King, Martin, +44 1784 414038 M.King@rhul.ac.uk,
University of London, Royal Holloway & Bedford New College – Oa

King, Norman R., (812) 464-1794 nking@usi.edu,
University of Southern Indiana – Gr

King, Penelope L., (505) 277-1643 penking@unm.edu,
University of New Mexico – GiXcCp

King, Peter, +44 0 759 47362 peter.king@imperial.ac.uk,
Imperial College – Np

King, Robert W., (617) 253-7064 rwk@chandler.mit.edu,
Massachusetts Institute of Technology – Yg

King, Scott D., 540-231-6521 Virginia Polytechnic Institute & State University – Yg

King, Jr., David T., (334) 844-4882 kingdat@auburn.edu,
Auburn University – GrOn

King-Rundel, Judith A., 310 243-3205 dendrochick@aol.com,
California State University, Dominguez Hills – Oe

Kingdon, Kevin, kevin.kingdon@skyresearch.com,
University of British Columbia – Yg

Kinkead, Scott, (505) 665-1760 Los Alamos National Laboratory – On

Kinnaird, Judith A., 27117176583 judith.kinnaird@wits.ac.za,
University of the Witwatersrand – EmGi

Kinner, David A., (828) 227-3821 dkinner@wcu.edu,
Western Carolina University – HgOe

Kinnicutt, Patrick, 989-774-2294 kinni1p@cmich.edu,
Central Michigan University – Gq

Kinsland, Gary L., (337) 482-6824 glkinsland@louisiana.edu,
University of Louisiana at Lafayette – Yg

Kinsman, Nicole, 907-451-5026 nicole.kinsman@alaska.gov,
Alaska Division of Geological & Geophysical Surveys – On

Kinter, Jim, (703) 993-5700 ikinter@gmu.edu,
George Mason University – Oa

Kinvig, Helen, +440151 795 4657 H.Kinvig@liverpool.ac.uk,
University of Liverpool – Gs

Kipper, Jay P., (512) 475-9505 jay.kipper@beg.utexas.edu,
University of Texas at Austin, Jackson School of Geosciences – On

Kipphut, George W., (270) 809-2847 gkipphut@murraystate.edu,
Murray State University – GeOg

Kirby, Carl S., (570) 577-1385 kirby@bucknell.edu,
Bucknell University – Cl

Kirby, Matthew E., (657) 278-2158 mkirby@fullerton.edu,
California State University, Fullerton – GnPeGg
Kirchgasser, William T., (315) 267-2296 kirchgwt@potsdam.edu,
SUNY Potsdam – Ps
Kirchner, James W., (510) 643-8559 kirchner@seismo.berkeley.edu,
University of California, Berkeley – Ge
Kirimi, Fridah K., fkirimi@jkuat.ac.ke,
Jomo Kenyatta University of Agriculture & Technology – OiiOr
Kirk, Wendy, +44 020 7679 37900 w.kirk@ucl.ac.uk,
University College London – Gp
Kirkby, Kent C., (612) 624-1392 kirkby@tc.umn.edu,
University of Minnesota, Twin Cities – Gg
Kirkham, Mary Beth, (785) 532-0422 mbk@ksu.edu,
Kansas State University – Sp
Kirkham, Randy R., (509) 372-6038 rr_kirkham@pnl.gov,
Pacific Northwest National Laboratory – Hq
Kirkland, Brenda L., 662-268-1032 Ext 228 kirkland@geosci.msstate.edu,
Mississippi State University – Gd
Kirkland, James I., (801) 537-3307 nrugs.jkirklan@state.ut.us,
Utah Geological Survey – Pg
Kirkpatrick, Cody, (812) 855-3481 codykirk@indiana.edu,
Indiana University, Bloomington – Oa
Kirkpatrick, James, 514-398-7442 james.kirkpatrick@mcgill.ca,
McGill University – Gc
Kirlin, R. Lynn, (250) 721-8681 lkirlin@comcast.net,
University of British Columbia – Oa
Kirschenfeld, Taylor, 850-474-2746 University of West Florida – Ob
Kirschvink, Joseph L., (626) 395-6136 kirschvink@caltech.edu,
California Institute of Technology – Pg
Kirshbaum, Daniel, 514-398-3347 daniel.kirshbaum@mcgill.ca,
McGill University – Oaw
Kirste, Dirk, 604-291-5365 dkirste@sfu.ca, Simon Fraser University – Cg
Kirstein, Linda, +44 (0) 131 650 4838 Linda.Kirstein@ed.ac.uk,
Edinburgh University – Gt
Kirtland Turner, Sandra, (951) 827-3191 sandra.kirtlandturner@ucr.edu,
University of California, Riverside – Cs
Kirwan, Matthew L., 804-684-7054 kirwan@vims.edu,
College of William & Mary – Gm
Kish, Stephen A., (850) 644-2064 kish@gly.fsu.edu,
Florida State University – Eg
Kishcha, Pavel, 972-3-6407411 pavelk@post.tau.ac.il,
Tel Aviv University – Oa
Kisila, Ben O., (540) 654-1107 bkisila@umw.edu,
University of Mary Washington – Hs
Kissel, David E., (706) 542-0900 University of Georgia – Sc
Kissin, Stephen A., (807) 343-8220 stephen.kissin@lakeheadu.ca,
Lakehead University – Em
Kisvarsanyi, Geza K., (573) 341-4616 Missouri University of Science and
Technology – Em
Kitajima, Hiroko, 979.458.2717 kitaji@tamu.edu,
Texas A&M University – YxSpGc
Kitchell, James F., (608) 262-9512 University of Wisconsin, Madison – Ob
Kitchen, Newell R., 573-882-1138 kitchenn@missouri.edu,
University of Missouri, Columbia – Sp
Kite, J. Steven, (304) 293-5603 Steve.Kite@mail.wvu.edu,
West Virginia University – Gm
Kivelson, Margaret G., (310) 825-3435 mkivelson@igpp.ucla.edu,
University of California, Los Angeles – Xy
Kiver, Eugene P., (509) 359-7959 eugene.kiver@ewu.edu,
Eastern Washington University – Gl
Klaassen, Gary P., (416)736-2100 #77727 gklaass@yorku.ca,
York University – Oa
Klancher, Jacki, 307-855-2205 jklanche@cwc.edu,
Central Wyoming College – Oi
Klapper, Gilbert, g-klapper@northwestern.edu, Northwestern University – PgiPo
Klasik, John A., 909-869-3453 jaklasik@csupomona.edu,
California State Polytechnic University, Pomona – Gu
Klaus, Adam, (979) 845-3055 aklaus@odpemail.tamu.edu,
Texas A&M University – Gu
Klaus, James S., 305-284-3426 j.klaus@miami.edu, University of Miami – Gg
Klee, Thomas M., (813) 253-7259 tklee@hccfl.edu,
Hillsborough Community College – Gg
Kleffner, Mark A., (614) 295-8208 kleffner.1@osu.edu,
Ohio State University – Gr
Klein, Andrew, (979) 845-7179 klein@geog.tamu.edu,
Texas A&M University – Or
Klein, Cornelis, (505) 277-2023 cklein@unm.edu,
University of New Mexico – Gz
Klein, Emily M., (919) 684-5965 ek4@duke.edu, Duke University – Gi
Klein, Frieder, fklein@whoi.edu,
Woods Hole Oceanographic Institution – Cm
Kleinhans, Frederick W., (317) 274-6904 fkleinha@iupui.edu,
Indiana University / Purdue University, Indianapolis – Xg
Kleinspehn, Karen L., 612-624-0537 klein004@umn.edu,
University of Minnesota, Twin Cities – Gt
Kleiss, Harold J., (919) 515-2643 North Carolina State University – Sd
Klemas, Victor, (302) 831-8256 klemas@udel.edu,
University of Delaware – Or
Klemetti, Erik, 740-587-5788 klemettie@denison.edu,
Denison University – GvxGg

Klemow, Kenneth M., (570) 408-4758 kenneth.klemow@wilkes.edu,
Wilkes University – Py
Klemperer, Simon L., (650) 723-8214 Stanford University – Gt
Klepeis, Keith A., (802) 656-0247 kklepeis@uvm.edu,
University of Vermont – Gc
Kliche, Donna V, 605-394-1957 Donna.Kliche@sdsmt.edu,
South Dakota School of Mines & Technology – OaaOa
Klimczak, Christian, klimczak@uga.edu, University of Georgia – Gc
Klinck, John M., (757) 683-6005 Klinck@ccpo.odu.edu,
Old Dominion University – Op
Klinger, Barry, (703) 993-9227 bklinger@gmu.edu,
George Mason University – Op
Klinkhammer, Gary, (541) 737-5209 gklinkhammer@coas.oregonstate.edu,
Oregon State University – Yr
Kloosterziel, Rudolf C., 808-956-7668 rudolf@soest.hawaii.edu,
University of Hawai'i, Manoa – Op
Klosterman, Sue, (937) 229-2661 Sue.Klosterman@notes.udayton.edu,
University of Dayton – Gg
Kluitenberg, Gerard J., (785) 532-7215 gjk@ksu.edu,
Kansas State University – Sp
Klymak, Jody, 250-721-6120 jklymak@uvic.ca, University of Victoria – Op
Knaack, Charles, (509) 335-6742 knaack@wsu.edu,
Washington State University – Ca
Knaeble, Alan, (612) 626-2495 knaeb001@umn.edu,
University of Minnesota – Gl
Knap, Anthony, 979-862-2323 ext 111 tknap@tamu.edu,
Texas A&M University – Oc
Knapp, Camelia, 777-8491 camelia@geol.sc.edu,
University of South Carolina – YeGt
Knapp, Elizabeth P., (540) 458-8867 knappe@wlu.edu,
Washington & Lee University – Cl
Knapp, H. Vernon, (217) 333-4423 vknapp@uiuc.edu,
Illinois State Water Survey – Hs
Knapp, James H., (803) 777-6886 knapp@geol.sc.edu,
University of South Carolina – Ye
Knapp, Richard B., (925) 423-3328 knapp4@llnl.gov,
Lawrence Livermore National Laboratory – Ng
Knapp, Roy M., 405-325-6829 knapp@ou.edu,
University of Oklahoma – Np
Knapp, Sibylle, +49 (89) 289 25895 sibylle.knap@)tum.de,
Technische Universitaet Muenchen – GsgGm
Knapp, Warren, (607) 255-3034 wwk2@cornell.edu, Cornell University – Oa
Knauss, John A., (401) 874-6141 jknauss@gso.uri.edu,
University of Rhode Island – Op
Knauss, Virginia L., (310) 243-3377 vknauss@csudh.edu,
California State University, Dominguez Hills – On
Knauth, L. Paul, (480) 965-2867 knauth@asu.edu,
Arizona State University – Cs
Kneeshaw, Tara A., 616-331-8996 kneeshta@gvsu.edu,
Grand Valley State University – ClGe
Knell, Michael, 203-392-5836 knellm1@southernct.edu,
Southern Connecticut State University – PvGg
Knepp, Rex A., 217-244-2422 knepp@isgs.uiuc.edu,
Illinois State Geological Survey – Go
Knight, Allen W., (530) 752-0453 aknight557@aol.com,
University of California, Davis – Hs
Knight, David, (518) 442-4204 knight@atmos.albany.edu,
SUNY, Albany – Oa
Knight, Mona M., 217-244-2390 mmknight@illinois.edu,
University of Illinois, Urbana-Champaign – On
Knight, Paul, (814) 863-4229 knight@mail.meteo.psu.edu,
Pennsylvania State University, University Park – Ow
Knight, Rosemary J., (650) 723-4746 Stanford University – Hy
Knight, Tiffany, tknight@biology2.wustl.edu,
Washington University – Pe
Knipe, Rob, +44(0) 113 34 35208 knipe@rdr.leeds.ac.uk,
University of Leeds – Gt
Knittle, Elise, (831) 459-4949 eknittle@pmc.ucsc.edu,
University of California, Santa Cruz – Gy
Knizek, Martin, +420 549 49 6298 kniza@sci.muni.cz,
Masaryk University – NgmNr
Knoll, Andrew H., (617) 495-9306 aknoll@harvard.edu,
Harvard University – Pb
Knoll, Martin A., (931) 598-1713 mknoll@sewanee.edu,
Sewanee: University of the South – Hw
Knopf, Daniel A., (631) 632-3092 Daniel.Knopf@stonybrook.edu,
SUNY, Stony Brook – Oa
Knopoff, Leon, (310) 825-1885 knopoff@physics.ucla.edu,
University of California, Los Angeles – Gy
Knott, Jeffrey R., (657) 278-5547 jknott@fullerton.edu,
California State University, Fullerton – Gmg
Knowles, Charles E., (919) 515-7943 ernie_knowles@ncsu.edu,
North Carolina State University – Op
Knowlton, Amy, aknowlton@neaq.org,
University of Massachusetts, Boston – Ob
Knowlton, Nancy, (858) 822-2486 nknowlton@ucsd.edu,
University of California, San Diego – Ob
Knox, Larry W., (931) 372-3523 lknox@tntech.edu,
Tennessee Tech University – Pm
Knudsen, Andrew, (920) 832-6731 knudsena@lawrence.edu,

Lawrence University – Cg
Knudsen, Guy, gknudsen@uidaho.edu, University of Idaho – Sb
Knudsen, Tyler R., (435) 865-9036 tylerknudsen@utah.gov,
    Utah Geological Survey – Ng
Knuepfer, Peter L. K., (607) 777-2389 Binghamton University – Gt
Knutson, Heather, 626.395.4268 hknutson@caltech.edu,
    California Institute of Technology – Xg
Kobara, Shinichi, 979 845 4089 shinichi@tamu.edu,
    Texas A&M University – Oi
Kobs-Nawotniak, Shannon E., (208) 282-3365 kobsshan@isu.edu,
    Idaho State University – Gv
Koc Tasgin, Calibe, 00904242370000-5976 calibekoc@firat.edu.tr,
    Firat University – GsdGg
Koch, Joe, (803) 896-4167 kochj@dnr.sc.gov, Dept of Natural Resources – Og
Koch, Magaly, mkoch@bu.edu, Boston University – Ga
Koch, Paul L., (831) 459-5861 pkoch@pmc.ucsc.edu,
    University of California, Santa Cruz – Pv
Kochanov, William E., 717.702.2033 wkochanov@pa.gov,
    Pennsylvania Bureau of Topographic & Geologic Survey – GgPg
Kochel, R. Craig, (570) 577-3032 kochel@bucknell.edu,
    Bucknell University – Gm
Kocurek, Gary A., (512) 471-5855 garyk@mail.utexas.edu,
    University of Texas at Austin – Gs
Kocurko, John, 940-397-4250 Midwestern State University – Gs
Kodama, Kenneth P., (610) 758-3663 kpk0@lehigh.edu,
    Lehigh University – Ym
Kodosky, Larry, 248-232-4538 lgkodosk@oaklandcc.edu,
    Oakland Community College – GgvEg
Koehl, Mimi A. R., (510) 642-8103 University of California, Berkeley – Po
Koehler, Rich, rkoehler@unr.edu, University of Nevada – Ne
Koehler, Rich D., (907) 451-5006 richard.koehler@alaska.gov,
    Alaska Division of Geological & Geophysical Surveys – Gt
Koehler, Thomas , (719) 333-8712 thomas.koehler@usafa.edu,
    United States Air Force Academy – Oa
Koehn, Daniel, Daniel.Koehn@glasgow.ac.uk, University of Glasgow – Gt
Kogan, Mikhail, (845) 365-8882 Columbia University – Yd
Kohl, Robert, 605-688-4747 South Dakota State University – So
Kohler, Jeffery L., 814-865-9834 JK9@psu.edu,
    Pennsylvania State University, University Park – Nm
Kohler, Nicholas, (541) 346-4160 nicholas@uoregon.edu,
    University of Oregon – Oi
Kohlstedt, David L., 612-626-1544 dlkohl@umn.edu,
    University of Minnesota, Twin Cities – Yx
Kohlstedt, Sally G., 612-624-9368 sgk@umn.edu,
    University of Minnesota, Twin Cities – On
Kohn, Matthew, mattkohn@boisestate.edu, Boise State University – CsGpPv
Kohut, Ed, 302-831-2569 ekoh@udel.edu,
    University of Delaware – GvxGg
Kokelaar, Peter, +440151 794 5188 P.Kokelaar@liverpool.ac.uk,
    University of Liverpool – GstGv
Kokum, Mehmet, 00904242370000-5963 mkokum@firat.edu.tr,
    Firat University – GttGg
Kolawole, Lanre L., +2348032277598 llkolawole@lautech.edu.ng,
    Ladoke Akintola University of Technology – GeeGe
Kolesar, Peter T., peter.t.kolesar@gmail.com, Utah State University – Cg
Kolka, Randall K., (218) 326-7100 University of Minnesota, Twin Cities – So
Kollias, Pavlos, 514-398-1500 pavlos.kollias@mcgill.ca,
    McGill University – Ora
Komabayashi, Tetsuya, +44 (0) 131 650 8518 tetsuya.komabayashi@ed.ac.uk,
    Edinburgh University – Gz
Komarneni, Sridhar, (814) 865-1542 komarneni@psu.edu,
    Pennsylvania State University, University Park – Sc
Kominz, Michelle A., (269) 387-5340 michelle.kominz@wmich.edu,
    Western Michigan University – OuYgGu
Komoto, Cary, cary.komoto@normandale.edu,
    University of Wisconsin Colleges – OnnOn
Konhauser, Kurt, 780-492-2571 kurtk@ualberta.ca,
    University of Alberta – Py
Konigsberg, Alvin S., (914) 257-3758 SUNY, New Paltz – Oa
Kontak, Daniel J., 7056751151, ext. 2352 dkontak@laurentian.ca,
    Laurentian University, Sudbury – Eg
Konter, Jasper G., 808-956-8705 jkonter@hawaii.edu,
    University of Hawai'i, Manoa – CcGiCt
Kontuly, Thomas M., (801) 581-8218 thomas.kontuly@geog.utah.edu,
    University of Utah – On
Koons, Peter O., (207)-581-2158 peter.koons@maine.edu,
    University of Maine – Gt
Kooyman, Gerald L., (858) 534-2091 gkooyman@ucsd.edu,
    University of California, San Diego – Ob
Kopaska-Merkel, David C., 205-247-3695 davidkm@gsa.state.al.us,
    Geological Survey of Alabama – Gs
Kopf, Christopher, 570-662-4615 ckopf@mansfield.edu,
    Mansfield University – Gcp
Kopf, Sebastian, 609-258-4101 skopf@princeton.edu,
    Princeton University – Py
Kopp, Robert E., (848) 445-3412 robert.kopp@rutgers.edu,
    Rutgers, The State University of New Jersey – CoPye
Koppers, Anthony, 541-737-5425 akoppers@coas.oregonstate.edu,
    Oregon State University – CgGv
Kopylova, Maya G., (604) 822-0865 mkopylova@eos.ubc.ca,

University of British Columbia – Gi
Koralek, Susan, koralek@sou.edu, Southern Oregon University – On
Korenaga, Jun, (203) 432-7381 jun.korenaga@yale.edu,
    Yale University – Yg
Koretsky, Carla, (269) 387-3230 carla.koretsky@wmich.edu,
    Western Michigan University – CglOn
Kornreich Wolf, Susan, (309) 794-7369 susanwolf@augustana.edu,
    Augustana College – Oe
Korose, Christopher P., 217-333-7256 korose@illinois.edu,
    Illinois State Geological Survey – Ec
Korotev, Randy L., (314) 935-5637 korotev@wustl.edu,
    Washington University in St. Louis – Ct
Korre, Anna, +44 20 759 47372 a.korre@imperial.ac.uk,
    Imperial College – Ng
Korty, Robert, 979-847-9090 korty@tamu.edu, Texas A&M University – Oa
Kortz, Karen, kkortz@ccri.edu, Community College of Rhode Island – OeGg
Korvin, Gabor, +96638603265 gabor@kfupm.edu.sa,
    King Fahd University of Petroleum and Minerals – Yx
Korycansky, Don, (831) 459-5843 University of California, Santa Cruz – Xc
Koskinen, William C., (612) 625-4276 koskinen@soils.umn.edu,
    University of Minnesota, Twin Cities – Sc
Kosro, Michael P., (541) 737-3079 kosro@coas.oregonstate.edu,
    Oregon State University – Onr
Kossin, James, 608-265-5356 kossin@ssec.wisc.edu,
    University of Wisconsin, Madison – Oa
Kostelnick, John, 309-438-7679 jckoste@ilstu.edu,
    Illinois State University – Oi
Koster Van Groos, August F., (312) 996-8678 kvg@uic.edu,
    University of Illinois at Chicago – Cp
Kostov, Svilen, 229-931-2321 skostov@gsw.edu,
    Georgia Southwestern State University – On
Kota, Jozsef, (520) 621-4396 kota@lpl.arizona.edu,
    University of Arizona – Oa
Kotamarthi, Rao, 630-252-7164 vrkotamarthi@anl.gov,
    Argonne National Laboratory – Oa
Koteas, G. Christopher, 802 485 3321 gkoteas@norwich.edu,
    Norwich University – GitYh
Kotha, Mahender, +91-832-6519329 mkotha@unigoa.ac.in,
    Goa University – GsoOi
Kotulova, Julia, jkotulova@egi.utah.edu, University of Utah – CoGo
Koutavas, Athanasios, 718-982-2972 tom.koutavas@csi.cuny.edu,
    College of Staten Island – PeOg
Koutitonsky, Vladimir G., (418) 724-1986 (Ext. 1763) vgk@uqar.qc.ca,
    Universite du Quebec a Rimouski – Op
Ková, Michal, +421260296555 kovacm@fns.uniba.sk,
    Comenius University – GsPeGg
Kovach, Richard G., (702) 295-6180 rkovach@lanl.gov,
    Los Alamos National Laboratory – Nm
Kovach, Robert L., (650) 723-4827 Stanford University – Ys
Kovaèiæ, Marijan, +38514605963 mkovacic@geol.pmf.hr,
    University of Zagreb – GsdGx
Kowaleski, Douglas, 857-234-9339 dkowal@geo.umass.edu,
    University of Massachusetts, Amherst – Gm
Kowalewski, Douglas E., 508-929-8646 douglas.kowalewski@worcester.edu,
    Worcester State University – GmlOy
Kowalewski, Michal J., (540) 231-5951 michalk@vt.edu,
    Virginia Polytechnic Institute & State University – Py
Kowalke, Thorsten, 089/2180 6733 t.kowalke@lrz.uni-muenchen.de,
    Ludwig-Maximilians-Universitaet Muenchen – Pg
Kowallis, Bart J., 801-422-2467 bart_kowallis@byu.edu,
    Brigham Young University – Gg
Koziol, Andrea M., (937) 229-2954 Andrea.Koziol@notes.udayton.edu,
    University of Dayton – Cp
Kozlowski, Andrew, 518 486-2012 akozlows@mail.nysed.gov,
    New York State Geological Survey – Gl
Kraal, Erin, 484-646-5859 kraal@kutztown.edu,
    Kutztown University of Pennsylvania – XgGm
Krabbenhoft, David, 608-821-3843 dpkrabbe@usgs.gov,
    University of Wisconsin, Madison – Hg
Kraemer, George P., 914-251-6640 george.kraemer@purchase.edu,
    SUNY, Purchase – Ob
Kraft, Kaatje, (360) 383-3539 kkraft@whatcom.ctc.edu,
    Whatcom Community College –
Kramer, J. Curtis, (209) 946-2482 ckramer@pacific.edu,
    University of the Pacific – Gg
Kramer, James R., (905) 525-9140 kramer@mcmaster.ca,
    McMaster University – Cl
Kramer, Kate, (815) 479-7877 kkramer@mchenry.edu,
    McHenry County College – GgOg
Kramer, Marc, 352-294-3165 mgkramer@ufl.edu, University of Florida – Os
Kramer, Walter V., 361.698.1385 wkramer@delmar.edu, Del Mar College – Gg
Krantz, David E., (419) 530-2662 david.krantz@utoledo.edu,
    University of Toledo – Gs
Krantz, Dwight S., (713) 718-5641 dwight.kranz@hccs.edu,
    Houston Community College System – Gg
Krapac, George A., 217-333-6442 krapac@isgs.uiuc.edu,
    Illinois State Geological Survey – Ca
Krastel, Sebastian , skrastel@geophysik.uni-kiel.de, Dalhousie University – Yr
Kraus, Mary J., 303-492-7251 mary.kraus@colorado.edu,
    University of Colorado – GsSa

475

Krause, David W., (631) 444-3117 david.krause@sunysb.edu,
 SUNY, Stony Brook – Pv
Krause, Federico F., (403) 220-5845 fkrause@ucalgary.ca,
 University of Calgary – Gs
Krause, Lois B., (864) 656-7653 Clemson University – Oe
Krauss, Lawrence, (480) 965-6378 krauss@asu.edu,
 Arizona State University – On
Krauss, Scott , skrauss@neaq.org, University of Massachusetts, Boston – Ob
Krautblatter, Michael, +49 89 28925866 m.krautblatter@tum.de,
 Technische Universitaet Muenchen – GmNrOi
Kravchinsky, Vadim, (780) 492-5591 vkrav@phys.ualberta.ca,
 University of Alberta – Ym
Kreamer, David, 702.895.3553 dave.kreamer@unlv.edu,
 University of Nevada, Reno – HwGn
Krebes, Edward S., (403) 220-5028 University of Calgary – Ys
Kreckel, Kenneth, 307-268-3457 kkreckel@caspercollege.edu,
 Casper College – EoYeGg
Kreemer, Corne, 775 682-8780 kreemer@unr.edu, University of Nevada – Yd
Kreidenweis, Sonia M., (970) 491-8350 sonia@atmos.colostate.edu,
 Colorado State University – Oa
Kreiger, William, wkreiger@ycp.edu, York College of Pennsylvania – Gi
Krekeler, Mark, 513-785-3106 krekelmp@miamioh.edu,
 Miami University – Ge
Kremer, Robert J., 573-882-6408 University of Missouri, Columbia – Os
Kressler, Sharon J., 612-625-5068 kress004@umn.edu,
 University of Minnesota, Twin Cities – On
Kretzschmar, Thomas, tkretzsc@cicese.mx,
 Centro de Investigación Científica y de Educación Superior de Ensenada – Ge
Kreutz, Karl J., (207)-581-3011 karl.kreutz@maine.edu,
 University of Maine – Cs
Krevor, Samuel, s.krevor@imperial.ac.uk, Imperial College – Eo
Krieble, Kelly, (610) 861-1437 krieblek@moravian.edu,
 Moravian College – OnnOn
Krieg, Joseph, 701-858-4205 joseph.krieg@minotstateu.edu,
 Minot State University – GmOs
Krieger-Brockett, Barbara B., (206) 543-2216 krieger@cheme.washington.edu,
 University of Washington – Ob
Krier, Donathon J., (505) 665-7834 krier@lanl.gov,
 Los Alamos National Laboratory – Gv
Kring, David, (520) 621-2024 kring@lpl.arizona.edu,
 University of Arizona – Xc
Krishnamurthy, R. V., (269) 387-5501 r.v.krishnamurthy@wmich.edu,
 Western Michigan University – Cs
Krishnan, Jay, 713-743-1385 jkrishnan@uh.edu, University of Houston – On
Krishtalka, Leonard, (785) 864-4540 krishtalka@ku.edu,
 University of Kansas – Pv
Krissek, Lawrence A., (614) 292-1924 krissek.1@osu.edu,
 Ohio State University – Gs
Krockover, Gerald H., (765) 494-5795 hawk1@purdue.edu,
 Purdue University – Oe
Kroeger, Glenn C., (210) 999-7607 gkroeger@trinity.edu,
 Trinity University – Yg
Kroeger, Timothy J., 218-755-2783 tkroeger@bemidjistate.edu,
 Bemidji State University – PlGsHw
Kroenke, Loren W., (808) 956-7845 kroenke@soest.hawaii.edu,
 University of Hawai'i, Manoa – Gu
Krogh, Thomas E., (416) 586-5811 tomk@rom.on.ca,
 University of Toronto – Cc
Krohn, James, krohnjp@piercecollege.edu, Los Angeles Pierce College – Ng
Krom, Michael, +44(0) 113 34 30477 M.D.Krom@leeds.ac.uk,
 University of Leeds – Cm
Kronenberg, Andreas, (979) 845-0132 a-kronenberg@geos.tamu.edu,
 Texas A&M University – GtyGc
Kronenfeld, Barry J., 217-581-7014 bjkronenfeld@eiu.edu,
 Eastern Illinois University – Oig
Kroon, Dick, +44 (0) 131 651 7089 D.Kroon@ed.ac.uk,
 Edinburgh University – Gg
Krot, Alexander N., 808-956-3900 sasha@higp.hawaii.edu,
 University of Hawai'i, Manoa – Xm
Kruckenberg, Seth, 617-552-8300 seth.kruckenberg@bc.edu,
 Boston College – Gc
Kruckenberg, Seth C., 617-552-3647 seth.kruckenberg@bc.edu,
 Boston College – Gct
Krueger, Steven, 801-581-3903 steve.krueger@utah.edu,
 University of Utah – Oa
Kruge, Michael A., 973-655-7668 krugem@mail.montclair.edu,
 Montclair State University – Co
Kruger, Joseph M., (409) 880-8233 joseph.kruger@lamar.edu,
 Lamar University – Yg
Kruger, Ned , ekadrmas@nd.gov, North Dakota Geological Survey – Gg
Krugh, W C., 661-654-3126 wkrugh@csub.edu,
 California State University, Bakersfield – GcmCc
Krukowski, Stanley T., 405-325-3031 skrukowski@ou.edu,
 University of Oklahoma – En
Krupka, Kenneth M., (509) 376-4412 ken.krupka@pnl.gov,
 Pacific Northwest National Laboratory – Cl
Kruse, Jennifer, (507) 933-7333 jkruse@gustavus.edu,
 Gustavus Adolphus College – On
Kruse, Sarah E., (813) 974-7341 University of South Florida, Tampa – Yg
Krygier, John B., (740) 368-3622 jbkrygie@owu.edu,

Ohio Wesleyan University – Oi
Krzic, Maja, 604-822-0252 maja.krzic@ubc.ca,
 University of British Columbia – Sf
Ku, Teh-Lung, (213) 740-5826 rku@usc.edu,
 University of Southern California – Cg
Ku, Timothy C., (860)685-2265 tcku@wesleyan.edu, Wesleyan University – Cl
Kuang, Zhiming, 617-495-2354 kuang@eps.harvard.edu,
 Harvard University – Oa
Kubas, Gregory J., (505) 667-5846 Los Alamos National Laboratory – Oa
Kubesh, Rodney, 320-308-4217 rjkubesh@stcloudstate.edu,
 Saint Cloud State University – Ow
Kubicek, Leonard, (972) 273-3508 lenkubicek@dcccd.edu,
 North Lake College - Dallas Community College District – Gg
Kubicki, James D., 915-747-5501 jdkubicki, University of Texas, El Paso – ClGe
Kucharik, Chris, 608-890-3021 kucharik@wisc.edu,
 University of Wisconsin, Madison – Oa
Kuchovsky, Tomas, +420 549 49 5452 tomas@sci.muni.cz ,
 Masaryk University – Hgy
Kuchta, Mark, (303) 273-3308 mkuchta@mines.edu,
 Colorado School of Mines – Nm
Kudela, Raphael M., (831) 459-3290 kudela@cats.ucsc.edu,
 University of California, Santa Cruz – Or
Kudlac, John J., (412) 392-3423 Point Park University – Ng
Kuehl, Steven A., (804) 684-7118 kuehl@vims.edu,
 College of William & Mary – Ou
Kuehn, Kenneth W., (270) 745-3082 kenneth.kuehn@wku.edu,
 Western Kentucky University – Ec
Kuehn, Stephen C., 304-384-6322 sckuehn@concord.edu,
 Concord University – CaGv
Kuentz, David C., (513) 529-5992 kuentzdc@MiamiOh.edu,
 Miami University – Ca
Kues, Barry S., (505) 277-3626 bkues@unm.edu,
 University of New Mexico – Pi
Kugel, Abigail, 507-457-5260 akugel@winona.edu,
 Winona State University – On
Kuhlman, Robert, rkuhlman@mc3.edu,
 Montgomery County Community College – Gg
Kuhnhenn, Gary L., (859) 622-8140 gary.kuhnhenn@eku.edu,
 Eastern Kentucky University – Gd
Kuiper, Klaudia, k.f.kuiper@vu.nl, VU University Amsterdam – Cc
Kuiper, Yvette D., 303-273-3105 ykuiper@mines.edu,
 Colorado School of Mines – Gc
Kujawinski, Elizabeth B., (508) 289-3696 ekujawinski@whoi.edu,
 Woods Hole Oceanographic Institution – Oc
Kukoè, Duje, +38514606111 duje.kukoc@geol.pmf.hr,
 University of Zagreb – Gg
Kukowski, Nina, 0049(0)3641/948680 nina.kukowski@uni-jena.de,
 Friedrich-Schiller-University Jena – Ygx
Kulander, Byron, byron.kulander@wright.edu, Wright State University – Gc
Kulatilake, Pinnaduwa H. S. W., (520) 621-6064 kulatila@u.arizona.edu,
 University of Arizona – Nr
Kulkarni, Shrinivas R., (626) 395-4010 srk@astro.caltech.edu,
 California Institute of Technology – Xy
Kulp, Mark A., (504) 280-1170 mkulp@uno.edu,
 University of New Orleans – Gr
Kulp, Thomas, tkulp@binghamton.edu, Binghamton University – Py
Kumar, Ajoy, 717-871-2432 Ajoy.Kumar@millersville.edu,
 Millersville University – Op
Kumjian, Matthew, 814-863-1581 kumjian@psu.edu,
 Pennsylvania State University, University Park – Ow
Kummerow, Christian D., (970) 491-7473 kummerow@atmos.colostate.edu,
 Colorado State University – Yr
Kump, Lee R., (814) 863-1274 lkump@psu.edu,
 Pennsylvania State University, University Park – Cl
Kumpf, Amber C., (231) 777-0289 amber.kumpf@muskegoncc.edu,
 Muskegon Community College – GgYrOu
Kung, Ernest C., 573-882-5909 University of Missouri, Columbia – Oa
Kung, Hsiang-Te, (901) 678-4538 hkung@memphis.edu,
 University of Memphis – Oy
Kung, King-Jau S., (608) 262-6530 kskung@wisc.edu,
 University of Wisconsin, Madison – Sp
Kunkle, Thomas D., (505) 667-1259 Los Alamos National Laboratory – Xy
Kuntz, Kara, (785) 628-5804 kkuntz@fhsu.edu,
 Fort Hays State University – On
Kuntz, Mark R., (847) 697-1000 mkuntz@elgin.edu,
 Elgin Community College – Og
Kunza, Lisa, (605) 394-2449 lisa.kunza@sdsmt.edu,
 South Dakota School of Mines & Technology – HsOe
Kunze, Eric L., (206) 543-8467 kunze@uvic.ca,
 University of Washington – Op
Kunzmann, Thomas, 089/2180 4292 kunzmann@min.uni-muenchen.de,
 Ludwig-Maximilians-Universitaet Muenchen – Gz
Kuo, Shiou, (206) 840-4573 skuo@wsu.edu,
 Washington State University – Sc
Kuperman, William A., (858) 534-1803 wak@mpl.ucsd.edu,
 University of California, San Diego – Op
Kurapov, Alexander, 541-737-2865 kurapov@coas.oregonstate.edu,
 Oregon State University – Yr
Kurka, Mira, 775-777-1054 mira.kurka@gbcnv.edu,
 Great Basin College – Gg

Kursinski, Robert, (520) 626-3338 kursinsk@atmo.arizona.edu,
University of Arizona – Oa
Kurtanjek, Dražen, +38514605965 dkurtan@inet.hr,
University of Zagreb – GsdGg
Kurttas, Turker, +90-312-2977760 kurttast@gmail.com,
Hacettepe University – HwgOr
Kurtz, Andrew, kurtz@bu.edu, Boston University – Clg
Kurtz, Vincent E., (417) 836-5800 Missouri State University – Ps
Kurum, Sevcan, 00904242370000-5992 skurum@firat.edu.tr,
Firat University – GivGx
Kurz, Mark D., (508) 289-2328 mkurz@whoi.edu,
Woods Hole Oceanographic Institution – Cc
Kushnir, Yochanan, (845) 365-8669 Columbia University – Oa
Kusnick, Judith E., (916) 278-4692 California State University, Sacramento – Oe
Kusssow, Wayne R., (608) 263-3631 wrkussow@wisc.edu,
University of Wisconsin, Madison – So
Kustka, Adam B., 973-353-5509 kustka@andromeda.rutgers.edu,
Rutgers, The State University of New Jersey, Newark – OgCmHs
Kusumoto, Shigekazu, 81-76-445-6653 kusu@sci.u-toyama.ac.jp,
University of Toyama – YvdGt
Kuszmaul, Joel S., (662) 915-7499 kuszmaul@olemiss.edu,
University of Mississippi – Nr
Kusznir, Nick, +44-151-794-5182 N.Kusznir@liverpool.ac.uk,
University of Liverpool – Yd
Kutis, Michael, 765-285-2487 mkutis@bsu.edu,
Ball State University – Gg
Kutzbach, John E., (608)262-0392 jek@facstaff.wisc.edu,
University of Wisconsin, Madison – Oa
Kuwabara, James, 415-452-7776 kuwabara@usgs.gov,
City College of San Francisco – Og
Kuzila, Mark S., (402) 472-7537 mkuzila@unl.edu,
Unversity of Nebraska - Lincoln – Sd
Kuzyk, Zou Zou, 204-272-1535 umkuzyk@cc.umanitoba.ca,
University of Manitoba – Cg
Kvamme, Kenneth L., (617) 353-3415 Boston University – Ga
Kwicklis, Edward M., (505) 665-7408 kwicklis@lanl.gov,
Los Alamos National Laboratory – Gg
Kyle, J. Richard, (512) 471-4351 rkyle@mail.utexas.edu,
University of Texas at Austin – Em
Kyle, Philip R., (575) 835-5995 kyle@nmt.edu,
New Mexico Institute of Mining and Technology – Giv
Kysar Mattietti, Giuseppina, (703) 993-9269 gkysar@gmu.edu,
George Mason University – Gi
Kyser, Kurt, 613-533-6179 kyserk@queensu.ca,
Queen's University – EgGsYg
Kyte, Frank T., (310) 825-2015 kyte@igpp.ucla.edu,
University of California, Los Angeles – Ct
Käser, Martin, 089/2180 4138 martin.kaeser@geophysik.uni-muenchen.de,
Ludwig-Maximilians-Universitaet Muenchen – Yg
Käsling, Heiko, +49 89 289 25831 heiko.kaesling@tum.de,
Technische Universitaet Muenchen – NrmNg
Köster, Mathias, +49 (89) 289 25893 mathias.koester@tum.de,
Technische Universitaet Muenchen – CgGzEg

L

L'Ecuyer, Tristan S., 608-262-2828 University of Wisconsin, Madison – Oa
La Berge, Gene L., (920) 424-4460 laberge@uwosh.edu,
University of Wisconsin, Oshkosh – Eg
La Fave, John I., 406-496-4306 jlafave@mtech.edu,
Montana Tech of The University of Montana – Hw
La Tour, Timothy E., 404413-5767 tlatour@gsu.edu,
Georgia State University – Gp
Laabs, Benjamin J., 585-245-5305 laabs@geneseo.edu,
SUNY, Geneseo – GmlGe
Labandeira, Conrad C., (202) 633-1336 Smithsonian Institution / National Museum of Natural History – Pi
LaBarbera, Michael C., (773) 702-8092 mlabarbe@uchicago.edu,
University of Chicago – Po
LaBella, Joel, (860)685-2242 jlabella@wesleyan.edu,
Wesleyan University – On
Laboski, Carrie A., (608) 263-2795 laboski@wisc.edu,
University of Wisconsin, Madison – So
Labotka, Dana, 217-244-7972 dlabotka@illinois.edu,
University of Illinois, Urbana-Champaign – Cs
Labotka, Theodore C., (865) 974-4805 tlabotka@utk.edu,
University of Tennessee, Knoxville – Gp
Labuz, Joseph F., (612) 625-9060 jlabuz@umn.edu,
University of Minnesota, Twin Cities – Nr
Lachhab, Ahmed, 570-374-4215 lachhab@susqu.edu,
Susquehanna University – Hw
Lachmar, Thomas E., (435) 797-1247 tom.lachmar@gmail.com,
Utah State University – Hw
Lachniet, Matthew S., 702-895-4388 matthew.lachniet@unlv.edu,
University of Nevada, Las Vegas – PeCs
Lackey, Jade Star, 909-621-8677 jadestar.lackey@pomona.edu,
Pomona College – GipCs
Lackinger, Markus, 089/2180 Ludwig-Maximilians-Universitaet Muenchen – Gz
Lackmann, Gary M., 919-515-1439 gary@ncsu.edu,
North Carolina State University – Oa
Lacy, Tor, tlacy@cerritos.edu,

Cerritos College – Gg
LaDue, Nicole D., 815-753-7935 nladue@niu.edu,
Northern Illinois University – Oe
LaFemina, Peter C., 814-865-7326 pfemina@geosc.psu.edu,
Pennsylvania State University, University Park – Yd
Laffan, Shawn, shawn.laffan@unsw.edu.au,
University of New South Wales – OiSf
LaFleche, Marc R., (418) 654-2670 marc.richer-lafleche@ete.inrs.ca,
Universite du Quebec – Ct
Lafrance, Bruno, (705) 675-1151 (Ext. 2264) blafrance@nickel.laurentian.ca,
Laurentian University, Sudbury – Gc
LaFreniere, Lorraine, (630) 252-7969 lafreniere@anl.gov,
Argonne National Laboratory – HwGgEg
Lageson, David R., (406) 994-6913 lageson@montana.edu,
Montana State University – Ge
Lagowski, Alison A., (716) 645-4856 aal@buffalo.edu, SUNY, Buffalo – On
Lai, Chung Chieng A., (505) 665-6635 cal@lanl.gov,
Los Alamos National Laboratory – Ow
Laine, Edward P., edlaine@bowdoin.edu, Bowdoin College – Gu
Laingen, Christopher R., (217) 581-2999 crlaingen@eiu.edu,
Eastern Illinois University – SfOn
Laird, David A., (515) 294-1581 dalaird@iastate.edu,
Iowa State University of Science & Technology – Sc
Laird, Jo, (603) 862-1718 jl@cisunix.unh.edu,
University of New Hampshire – Gp
Laird, Neil, 315-781-3603 laird@hws.edu,
Hobart & William Smith Colleges – Oa
Laity, Julie E., (818) 677-3532 julie.laity@csun.edu,
California State University, Northridge – Oy
Lakatos, Stephen, (718) 262-2589 York College (CUNY) – Cc
Lake, Iain, +44 (0)1603 59 3744 i.lake@uea.ac.uk,
University of East Anglia – Ge
Lakhan, V. Chris, 519-253-3000 ext. 2183 lakan@uwindsor.ca,
University of Windsor – Ori
Laki, Sam, (937) 376-6272 slaki@centralstate.edu,
Central State University – EgSoHs
Lakshmi, Venkataraman, (803) 777-3552 vlakshmi@geol.sc.edu,
University of South Carolina – Hg
Lal, Devendra, (858) 534-2134 laluwihare@ucsd.edu,
University of California, San Diego – Xc
Lal, Rattan, 614-292-9069 lal.1@osu.edu, Ohio State University – Sp
Laliberte, Elizabeth, (401) 874-5512 elalib@mail.uri.edu,
University of Rhode Island – Og
Lam, Anita, 604-822-2736 alam@eos.ubc.ca,
University of British Columbia – On
Lamanna, Matthew C., (412) 624-8780 University of Pittsburgh – Pv
Lamanna, Matthew C., (412) 578-2696 lamannam@carnegiemnh.org,
Carnegie Museum of Natural History – Pv
Lamb, Dennis, (814) 865-0174 lno@psu.edu,
Pennsylvania State University, University Park – Ow
Lamb, James P., 205-652-3725 jlamb@uwa.edu,
University of West Alabama – PvePg
Lamb, John A., (612) 625-1772 jlamb@soils.umn.edu,
University of Minnesota, Twin Cities – Sc
Lamb, Melissa A., (651) 962-5242 malamb@stthomas.edu,
University of Saint Thomas – GtcGs
Lamb, Michael P., 626.395.3612 mpl@gps.caltch.edu,
California Institute of Technology – Gm
Lamb, Will, (979) 845-3075 lamb@geo.tamu.edu,
Texas A&M University – Gp
Lambert, Carolyn D., 970-351-2647 Carolyn.Lambert@unco.edu,
University of Northern Colorado – Hw
Lambert, Dean, dlambert@alamo.edu,
Alamo Colleges - San Antonio College – Oy
Lambert, Dean P., 210-486-0471 dlambert@alamo.edu,
San Antonio Community College – Oyi
Lambert, Lance L., (210) 458-4455 Lance.Lambert@utsa.edu,
University of Texas, San Antonio – Pg
Lambert, W. J., 205-348-4404 jlambert@ua.edu,
University of Alabama – CsPeCg
Lambert-Smith, James, J.S.Lambert-Smith@kingston.ac.uk,
Kingston University – Gg
Lammerer, Bernd, 089/2180 6517 lammerer@iaag.geo.uni-muenchen.de,
Ludwig-Maximilians-Universitaet Muenchen – Gg
Lamothe, Michel, 514-987-3000 #3361 lamothe.michel@uqam.ca,
Universite du Quebec a Montreal – Gl
Lancaster, Nicholas, (775) 673-7304 nick@dri.edu,
Desert Research Institute – Gm
Lancaster, Penny, +44 023 9284 2272 penny.lancaster@port.ac.uk,
University of Portsmouth – Gz
Lancaster, Stephen, 541-737-9258 lancasts@geo.oregonstate.edu,
Oregon State University – Hs
Land, Lewis, 575-887-5508 lland@nmbg.nmt.edu,
New Mexico Institute of Mining and Technology – Hy
Land, Lewis A., 505-887-5505 lland@gis.nmt.edu,
New Mexico Institute of Mining & Technology – Hg
Land, Lynton S., (804) 453-6605 JandL@rivnet.net,
University of Texas at Austin – Cl
Landenberger, Bill, 61 02 4921 6366 Bill.Landenberger@newcastle.edu.au,
University of Newcastle – Gi

Lander, Mark A., (671) 735-2685 mlander@uguam.uog.edu,
University of Guam – Ow

Landing, Ed, 518-473-8071 elanding@mail.nysed.gov,
New York State Geological Survey – Ps

Landman, Neil H., (212) 769-5712 American Museum of Natural History – Pi

Landman, Neil H., (212) 769-5723 Graduate School of the City University of
New York – Ps

Landry, Michael R., (858) 534-4702 mlandry@ucsd.edu,
University of California, San Diego – Ob

Landry, Peter B., (508) 289-3443 plandry@whoi.edu,
Woods Hole Oceanographic Institution – Ca

Landschoot, Peter J., (814) 863-1017 pcl11@psu.edu,
Pennsylvania State University, University Park – So

Lane, Charles L., (541) 552-6114 lane@sou.edu,
Southern Oregon University – Hg

Lane, Joseph M., (216) 987-5227 Joseph.Lane@tri-c.edu,
Cuyahoga Community College - Western Campus – Og

Lane, Mark, 7607441150 xt. 2951 mlane@palomar.edu, Palomar College – On

Lang, Harold R., (304) 293-5603 harold@lithos.jpl.nasa.gov,
Jet Propulsion Laboratory – Gr

Lang, Helen M., 304-293-5469 hlang@wvu.edu,
West Virginia University – Gpz

Lang, Nicholas, 814-824-3646 nlang@mercyhurst.edu,
Mercyhurst University – GvXgGc

Lang, Susan Q., 803-777-8832 slang@geol.sc.edu,
University of South Carolina – OcCo

Lange, Rebecca A., (734) 764-7421 becky@umich.edu,
University of Michigan – Gi

Langebrake, Larry C., (727) 553-1008 Larry.langebrake@sri.com,
University of South Florida, Saint Petersburg – Oo

Langel, Richard A., 319-335-4102 richard.langel@dnr.iowa.gov,
Iowa Dept of Natural Resources – Gg

Langenheim, Jr., Ralph L., rlangenh@illinois.edu,
University of Illinois, Urbana-Champaign – Gr

Langenhorst, Falko H., 0049(0)3641/948730 falko.langenhorst@uni-jena.de,
Friedrich-Schiller-University Jena – Gz

Langer, Arthur M., (718) 951-4793 Graduate School of the City University of
New York – Gz

Langford, Richard P., (915) 747-5968 langford@geo.utep.edu,
University of Texas, El Paso – Gs

Langhorst, Glenn, 218-879-0719 glang@fdltcc.edu,
Fond du Lac Tribal and Community College – Gg

Langille, Jackie M., (828) 251-6453 jlangill@unca.edu,
University of North Carolina, Asheville – GctGe

Langman, Jeffrey, 208-885-0310 jlangman@uidaho.edu,
University of Idaho – Hwy

Langmuir, Charles H., (617) 384-9948 langmuir@eps.harvard.edu,
Harvard University – Cg

Langston, Charles A., (901) 678-2007 clangstn@memphis.edu,
University of Memphis – Ys

Langston, Jr., Wann, (512) 471-7736 wannl@mail.utexas.edu,
University of Texas at Austin – Pv

Langston-Unkefer, Pat J., (505) 665-2556 Los Alamos National Laboratory – Co

Lanigan, David C., (509) 376-9308 david.lanigan@pnl.gov,
Pacific Northwest National Laboratory – Hg

Lankreijer, Anco, a.lankreijer@vu.nl, VU University Amsterdam – GctGg

Lanoue, Christopher A., 605-677-6153 chris.lanoue@usd.edu,
South Dakota Dept of Environment and Natural Resources – On

Lansey, Kevin E., (520) 621-2512 lansey@engr.arizona.edu,
University of Arizona – Hs

Lao Davila, Daniel, 405-744-6358 daniel.lao_davila@okstate.edu,
Oklahoma State University – Gc

Lapen, Thomas, 713-743-6122 tjlapen@uh.edu,
University of Houston – Gz

LaPointe, Daphne D., (775) 682-8772 dlapoint@unr.edu,
University of Nevada – Gg

Laporte, Leo F., laporte@ucsc.edu, University of California, Santa Cruz – Pg

Laprise, Rene, 514-987-3000 #3302 laprise.rene@uqam.ca,
Universite du Quebec a Montreal – Oa

Lapusta, Nadia, (626) 395-2277 lapusta@caltech.edu,
California Institute of Technology – GcYs

Large, Ross R., 61 3 6226 2819 Ross.Large@utas.edu.au,
University of Tasmania – Eg

Larkin, Patrick, 361-825-3258 Patrick.Larkin@tamucc.edu,
Texas A&M University, Corpus Christi – On

Larner, Kenneth L., klarner@mines.edu, Colorado School of Mines – Ye

LaRock, Paul A., (225) 388-6307 Louisiana State University – Ob

Larocque, Marie, 514-987-3000 #1515 larocque.marie@uqam.ca,
Universite du Quebec a Montreal – Hw

Larsen, Daniel, (901) 678-4358 dlarsen@memphis.edu,
University of Memphis – Cl

Larsen, Isaac J., 413-545-0538 ilarsen@geo.umass.edu,
University of Massachusetts, Amherst – Gm

Larsen, Jessica F., 907-474-7992 jflarsen@alaska.edu,
University of Alaska Fairbanks – Gv

Larsen, Kristine, (860) 832-2938 larsen@ccsu.edu,
Central Connecticut State University – Xy

Larson, David J., 510-885-3132 david.larson@csueastbay.edu,
California State University, East Bay – Ou

Larson, David R., 217-244-2770 dlarson@isgs.uiuc.edu,

Illinois State Geological Survey – Hw

Larson, Edwin E., 303-492-6172 University of Colorado – Ym

Larson, Eric J., 715-346-4098 Eric.Larsen@uwsp.edu,
University of Wisconsin, Stevens Point – Or

Larson, Erik B., 740-351-3144 elarson@shawnee.edu,
Shawnee State University – GsmHg

Larson, Harold P., (520) 621-6943 hplarson@u.arizona.edu,
University of Arizona – On

Larson, Peter B., (509) 335-3095 plarson@wsu.edu,
Washington State University – Cs

Larson, Phillip H., (507) 389-2617 phillip.larson@mnsu.edu,
Minnesota State University – GmOyHs

Larson, Roger, (401) 874-6165 rlar@uri.edu, University of Rhode Island – Ou

Larter, Stephen, +44 (0) 191 208 5956 alex.leathard@ncl.ac.uk,
University of Newcastle Upon Tyne – Gg

Lasca, Norman, 414-229-4602 nplasca@uwm.edu,
University of Wisconsin, Milwaukee – Gm

Lasemi, Zakaria, 217-244-6944 lasemi@isgs.uiuc.edu,
Illinois State Geological Survey – En

Lash, Gary G., (716) 673-3842 lash@fredonia.edu, SUNY, Fredonia – Gr

Lash, Gary S., lash@fredonia.edu, SUNY, Buffalo – Gc

Lasher-Trapp, Sonia, 217-244-4250 slasher@illinois.edu,
University of Illinois, Urbana-Champaign – Oa

Lasker, Howard R., 716-645-4870 hlasker@buffalo.edu, SUNY, Buffalo – Gu

Laskowski, Stanley L., (215) 573-3164 slaskows@sas.upenn.edu,
University of Pennsylvania – Ge

Lassetter, William L., 434-9516361 william.lassetter@dmme.virginia.gov,
Division of Geology and Mineral Resources – Hw

Lassiter, John, (512) 471-4002 lassiter1@mail.utexas.edu,
University of Texas at Austin – Cc

Last, Fawn M., Fawn.last@angelo.edu, Angelo State University – Gsn

Last, George V., (509) 376-3961 george.last@pnl.gov,
Pacific Northwest National Laboratory – Ge

Last, William M., (204) 474-8361 wm_last@umanitoba.ca,
University of Manitoba – GsnGo

Lat, Che Noorliza, 03-79674157 noorliza@um.edu.my,
University of Malaya – Yg

Lathrop, Daniel, (301) 405-1594 lathrop@umd.edu,
University of Maryland – Yg

Latimer, Jennifer, 812-237-2254 jlatimer@indstate.edu,
Indiana State University – CmGe

Laton, W. R., (657) 278-7514 wlaton@fullerton.edu,
California State University, Fullerton – HwGg

Lattman, Lawrence H., (575) 266-9606 lhlattman@comcast.net,
New Mexico Institute of Mining and Technology – Gm

Lau, Chui Yim Maggie, 609-258-6899 maglau@princeton.edu,
Princeton University – Og

Laubach, Stephen E., 512-471-6303 steve.laubach@beg.utexas.edu,
University of Texas at Austin – Gs

Lauderdale, Jonathan, J.Lauderdale@liverpool.ac.uk ,
University of Liverpool – Og

Laudon, Thomas S., (414) 424-4464 ectoproct@sbcglobal.net,
University of Wisconsin, Oshkosh – Yg

Laurent-Charvet, Sébastien, +33(0)3 44068995 sébastien.laurent-charvet@lasalle-
beauvais.fr, Institut Polytechnique LaSalle Beauvais (ex-IGAL) – GctOe

Lauretta, Dante, (520) 626-1138 lauretta@lpl.arizona.edu,
University of Arizona – On

Laurier, Eric, +44 (0) 131 651 4303 Eric.Laurier@ed.ac.uk,
Edinburgh University – On

Lautz, Laura, 315-443-1196 lklautz@syr.edu, Syracuse University – Hg

Lauziere, Kathleen, (418) 654-2658 klauzier@nrcan.gc.ca,
Universite du Quebec – Gg

Lauzon, John, (519) 824-4120 (Ext. 52459) lauzonj@uoguelph.ca,
University of Guelph – So

Lavallee, Daniel, (805) 893-8446 daniel@crustal.ucsb.edu,
University of California, Santa Barbara – On

Lavallee, Yan, +440151 794 5183 Yan.Lavallee@liverpool.ac.uk,
University of Liverpool – Gv

Lavallee, Yan, 089/2180 4221 yanlavallee@hotmail.com,
Ludwig-Maximilians-Universitaet Muenchen – Yg

Lavier, Luc L., 512-471-0455 luc@ig.utexas.edu,
University of Texas at Austin – Gt

LaVigne, Michéle, 207-798-4283 mlavign@bowdoin.edu ,
Bowdoin College – OcPe

Lavkulich, Leslie M., (604) 822-3477 University of British Columbia – Sd

Lavoie, Denis, (418) 654-2571 delavoie@nrcan.gc.ca,
Universite du Quebec – Gs

Law, Eric W., (740) 826-8242 ericlaw@muskingum.edu,
Muskingum University – Gp

Law, Richard D., (540) 231-6685 rdlaw@vt.edu,
Virginia Polytechnic Institute & State University – Gc

Law, Zada, 615-494-7641 Zada.Law@mtsu.edu,
Middle Tennessee State University – Oi

Lawrence, Deborah, (434) 924-0581 dl3c@virginia.edu,
University of Virginia – On

Lawrence, Henry, (814) 732-1572 hlawrence@edinboro.edu,
Edinboro University of Pennsylvania – Ou

Lawrence, James, jimrslawrence@gmail.com, University of Houston – Cl

Lawrence, Kira, 610-330-5194 lawrenck@lafayette.edu,
Lafayette College – Gg

478

Lawrence, Rick L., (406) 994-5409 Montana State University – Or
Lawry, Cynthia, (979) 830-4406 Cynthia.Lawry@blinn.edu,
 Blinn College – Gg
Laws, Richard A., (910) 962-4125 laws@uncw.edu,
 University of North Carolina Wilmington – Pm
Lawson, Merlin P., (402) 472-5358 mlawson1@unl.edu,
 University of Nebraska, Lincoln – Oy
Lawton, Donald C., (403) 220-5718 University of Calgary – Ye
Lawver, Lawrence A., (512) 471-0433 lawver@ig.utexas.edu,
 University of Texas at Austin – Yr
Lay, Thorne, (831) 459-3164 tlay@pmc.ucsc.edu,
 University of California, Santa Cruz – Ys
Layer, Paul, 907-474-5514 pwlayer@alaska.edu,
 University of Alaska Fairbanks – Ym
Layton, Alice, 865-974-8072 alayton@utk.edu,
 University of Tennessee, Knoxville – On
Layton-Matthews, Daniel, 613-533-6338 dlayton@queensu.ca,
 Queen's University – EgGx
Lazarus, Eli, +44(0)29 208 75563 LazarusED@cardiff.ac.uk,
 University of Wales – On
Lazarus, Steven, (321) 674-8096 Florida Institute of Technology – Oa
Lazarus, Steven M., 321-674-2160 slazarus@fit.edu,
 Florida Institute of Technology – Oa
Le, Yanfen, 660-562-1525 le@nwmissouri.edu,
 Northwest Missouri State University – Oi
Le Heron, Daniel, +44 1784 443615 Daniel.le-Heron@rhul.ac.uk,
 University of London, Royal Holloway & Bedford New College – Og
Le Mone, David V., (915) 747-5275 lemone@geo.utep.edu,
 University of Texas, El Paso – Ps
Le Quere, Corinne, +44 (0)1603 59 2840 c.lequere@uea.ac.uk,
 University of East Anglia – Ge
Le Roex, Anton, 021-650-2902 anton.leroex@uct.ac.za,
 University of Cape Town – Cg
Le Roux, Veronique, (508) 289-3549 vleroux@whoi.edu,
 Woods Hole Oceanographic Institution – Gi
Le Voyer, Marion, (202) 633-1817 levoyerm@si.edu,
 Smithsonian Institution / National Museum of Natural History – Gz
Lea, David W., (805) 893-8665 lea@geol.ucsb.edu,
 University of California, Santa Barbara – Oc
Lea, Peter D., (207) 725-3439 plea@bowdoin.edu, Bowdoin College – Gl
Leach, Harry, +44 0151 794 4097 Leach@liverpool.ac.uk ,
 University of Liverpool – Og
Leadbetter, Jared R., 626.395.4182 jleadbetter@caltech.edu,
 California Institute of Technology – Pm
Leake, Martha A., (229) 333-5756 mleake@valdosta.edu,
 Valdosta State University – Xg
Leap, Darrell I., (765) 494-3699 mountains2oceans@comcast.net,
 Purdue University – Hy
Lear, C, carrie@earth.cf.ac.uk, Cardiff University – Ou
Lear, Caroline, +44(0)29 208 79004 LearC@cardiff.ac.uk,
 University of Wales – Og
Leatham, W. Britt, (909) 537-5322 bleatham@csusb.edu,
 California State University, San Bernardino – Ps
Leather, Kimberly, Kimberley.Leather@manchester.ac.uk,
 University of Manchester – Oa
Leavell, Daniel N., (740) 366-9342 leavell.6@osu.edu,
 Ohio State University – Ge
Leavens, Peter B., 302-831-8106 pbl@udel.edu,
 University of Delaware – Gz
Leavitt, Steven W., (520) 621-6468 sleavitt@ltrr.arizona.edu,
 University of Arizona – Cs
Lebedev, Maxim, +61 8 9266 3519 M.Lebedev@curtin.edu.au,
 Curtin University – Yx
Lebofsky, Larry A., (520) 621-6947 lebofsky@lpl.arizona.edu,
 University of Arizona – Og
Lebold, Joe, 304-293-0749 Joe.Lebold@mail.wvu.edu,
 West Virginia University – OePs
Lechler, Paul J., (775) 682-8773 plechler@unr.edu,
 University of Nevada – Cg
Leckie, R. Mark, (413) 545-1948 mleckie@geo.umass.edu,
 University of Massachusetts, Amherst – Pm
Lee, Alyce, 304-256-0270 alee@concord.edu, Concord University – Og
Lee, Chung M., (801) 581-8218 chunglee@geog.utah.edu,
 University of Utah – Ou
Lee, Cin-Ty A., 713.348.5084 ctlee@rice.edu, Rice University – Cg
Lee, Cindy, (632) 632-8741 cindy.lee@stonybrook.edu,
 SUNY, Stony Brook – Co
Lee, Cindy M., 864656-0672 lc@clemson.edu, Clemson University – Cg
Lee, Craig M., (206) 685-7656 craig@apl.washington.edu,
 University of Washington – Op
Lee, Daphne E., +64 3 479-7525 daphne.lee@otago.ac.nz,
 University of Otago – Pib
Lee, Eung Seok, (740) 593-1101 leee1@ohio.edu, Ohio University – Hw
Lee, Hung, (519) 824-4120 Ext.53828 hlee@uoguelph.ca,
 University of Guelph – On
Lee, In Young, (630) 252-8724 Argonne National Laboratory – Oa
Lee, Jaeheon, 520-626-4967 jaeheon@email.arizona.edu,
 University of Arizona – Nx
Lee, Jeffrey, (509) 963-2801 jeff@geology.cwu.edu,
 Central Washington University – Gct

Lee, Jeffrey A., 806-834-8228 jeff.lee@ttu.edu, Texas Tech University – Oy
Lee, Jejung, leej@umkc.edu, University of Missouri-Kansas City – GqHw
Lee, Kanani K., (203) 432-4354 kanani.lee@yale.edu, Yale University – Gy
Lee, Keenan, (303) 273-3808 klee@mines.edu, Colorado School of Mines – Or
Lee, Martin, +4401413302634 Martin.Lee@glasgow.ac.uk,
 University of Glasgow – Gz
Lee, Meehye, 82-2-3290-3178 meehye@korea.ac.kr,
 Korea University – OagCm
Lee, Michael D., 510-885-3155 michael.lee@csueastbay.edu,
 California State University, East Bay – Hg
Lee, Ming-Kuo, (334) 844-4898 leeming@auburn.edu, Auburn University – Hw
Lee, Rachel J., (315) 312-5506 rachel.lee@oswego.edu,
 State University of New York at Oswego – GvOr
Lee, Sukyoung, (814) 863-1587 slg9@psu.edu,
 Pennsylvania State University, University Park – Ow
Lee, Wook, (814) 732-2291 wlee@edinboro.edu,
 Edinboro University of Pennsylvania – Oi
Lee, Young Jae, 82-2-3290-3181 youngjlee@korea.ac.kr,
 Korea University – ScGze
Lee, Zhongping , zhongping.lee@umb.edu,
 University of Massachusetts, Boston – Org
Lee-Gorishti, Yolanda, 203-392-6647 yolanda.lee-gorishti@uconn.edu,
 Southern Connecticut State University – GaOe
Leech, Mary, (415) 338-1144 leech@sfsu.edu,
 San Francisco State University – Go
Leeman, William P., (713) 348-4892 leeman@rice.edu, Rice University – Gi
Lees, Jonathan M., (919) 962-0695 jonathan.lees@unc.edu,
 University of North Carolina, Chapel Hill – YsGv
Leetaru, Hannes E., (217) 333-5058 leetaru@isgs.uiuc.edu,
 University of Illinois, Urbana-Champaign – Go
Lefebvre, Rene, (418) 654-2651 rene.lefebvre@ete.inrs.ca,
 Universite du Quebec – Hw
LeFever, Richard D., (701) 777-3014 richard.lefever@engr.und.edu,
 University of North Dakota – Gs
Lefticariu, Liliana, (618) 453-7373 lefticariu@geo.siu.edu,
 Southern Illinois University Carbondale – CsgGe
Leger, Carol, 603.358.2570 cleger@keene.edu, Keene State College – Og
Leggitt, Leroy, lleggitt@llu.edu, Loma Linda University – Pi
Legore, Virginia L., (509) 376-5019 virginia.legore@pnl.gov,
 Pacific Northwest National Laboratory – Cg
Lehane, Mary, +353 21 4902764 m.lehane@ucc.ie, University College Cork – On
Lehman, Thomas M., 806-834-3148 tom.lehman@ttu.edu,
 Texas Tech University – Gs
Lehrberger, Gerhard, +49 89 289 25832 lehrberger@tum.de,
 Technische Universitaet Muenchen – EgGxg
Lehre, Andre K., (707) 826-3165 akl1@humboldt.edu,
 Humboldt State University – Gm
Lehrmann, Daniel J., 210-999-7654 dlehrmann@trinity.edu,
 Trinity University – PiGs
Lehto, Heather, heather.lehto@angelo.edu, Angelo State University – GvYs
Leichmann, Jaromir, +420 549 49 5559 leichman@sci.muni.cz ,
 Masaryk University – GxpGi
Leichter, James J., (858) 822-5330 jleichter@ucsd.edu,
 University of California, San Diego – Ob
Leier, Andrew L., 803-777-9941 aleier@geol.sc.edu,
 University of South Carolina – Gs
Leighton, Henry G., (514) 398-3766 henry.leighton@mcgill.ca,
 McGill University – Oa
Leighton, Lindsey, 780-492-3983 lleighto@ualberta.ca,
 University of Alberta – Pi
Leighty, Robert S., (480) 461-7021 rleighty@mesacc.edu,
 Mesa Community College – Og
Leimer, H. Wayne, (931) 372-3522 hwleimer@tntech.edu,
 Tennessee Tech University – Gs
Leinen, Margaret, 858-534-2827 University of California, San Diego – OgPe
Leinen, Margaret, (401) 874-6222 mleinen@nsf.gov,
 University of Rhode Island – Ou
Leinfelder, Reinhold, 089/2180 6629 r.leinfelder@lrz.uni-muenchen.de,
 Ludwig-Maximilians-Universitaet Muenchen – Pg
Leitch, Alison, (709) 737-3306 aleitch@mun.ca,
 Memorial University of Newfoundland – Yg
Leite, Michael B., (308) 432-6377 mleite@csc.edu,
 Chadron State College – Gg
Leith, Kerry, +49 (89) 289 - 25867 kerry.leith@tum.de,
 Technische Universitaet Muenchen – GmNrOi
Leithold, Elana L., (919) 515-7282 lonnie_leithold@ncsu.edu,
 North Carolina State University – Gs
Leitz, Robert E., (303) 556-3072 Metropolitan State College of Denver – Gz
LeJeune, Breanne, (269) 387-5485 breanne.e.lejeune@wmich.edu,
 Western Michigan University – On
Lekic, Vedran, (301) 405-4086 ved@umd.edu, University of Maryland – Ysg
Leland, John, 775-784-6670 jleland@unr.edu, University of Nevada, Reno – On
Lemay, Phillip W., (225) 388-6922 philip@lgs.bri.lsu.edu,
 Louisiana State University – Gg
Lembke, Chad E., (727) 553-3976 clembke@marine.usf.edu,
 University of South Florida, Saint Petersburg – Oo
Lemiszki, Peter, 865-594-6200 Peter.Lemiszki@tn.gov,
 University of Tennessee, Knoxville – Gc
Lemiszki, Peter J., (865) 594-5596 Peter.Lemiszki@tn.gov,
 Tennessee Geological Survey – GcOiGg

University of Florida – ScOs

Li, Zhenhong, +44 (0) 191 208 5704 zhenhong.li@ncl.ac.uk,
University of Newcastle Upon Tyne – Yd

Liang, George, (785) 532-6101 gliang@ksu.edu,
Kansas State University – So

Liang, Liyuan, 865-241-3933 2ll@ornl.gov,
Oak Ridge National Laboratory – Cl

Liang, Yan, (401) 863-9477 Yan_Liang@Brown.edu,
Brown University – Cp

Liauw, Henri L., hliauwap@broward.edu, Broward College – Gg

Libarkin, Julie C., 517-355-8369 libarkin@msu.edu,
Michigan State University – Oe

Liberty, Lee M., (208) 426-1166 lml@cgiss.boisestate.edu,
Boise State University – Ys

Libra, Robert D., Robert.Libra@dnr.iowa.gov,
Iowa Dept of Natural Resources – Gg

Licari, Gerald R., (213) 265-8838 East Los Angeles College – Pm

Licciardi, Joseph M., 603-862-1718 joe.licciardi@unh.edu,
University of New Hampshire – Gl

Licht, Kathy J., (317) 278-1343 Indiana University / Purdue University, Indianapolis – Gl

Lichtenberger, János, lityi@sas.elte.hu, Eotvos Lorand University – OarXy

Lichtner, Peter C., (505) 667-3420 lichtner@lanl.gov,
Los Alamos National Laboratory – On

Liddell, W. David, (435) 797-1261 dave.liddell@usu.edu,
Utah State University – GsPo

Lidgard, Scott H., (312) 665-7625 slidgard@fieldmuseum.org,
Field Museum of Natural History – Pi

Lidiak, Edward G., (412) 624-8871 egl@pitt.edu, University of Pittsburgh – Gi

Lidicker, Jr., William Z., (510) 642-3059 University of California, Berkeley – Pv

Liebe, Richard M., (585) 395-5100 (Ext. 7524) rliebe@weather.brockport.edu,
SUNY, The College at Brockport – Ps

Liebens, Johan, 850-474-2065 liebens@uwf.edu, University of West Florida – So

Lieberman, Bruce S., (785) 864-2741 blieber@ku.edu,
University of Kansas – Po

Lieberman, Robert C., (631) 632-8214 robert.liebermann@sunysb.edu,
SUNY, Stony Brook – Gy

Liebling, Richard, 516 463-6545 georsl@hofstra.edu, Hofstra University – Gg

Liebling, Richard S., (212) 772-5412 Graduate School of the City University of New York – Gz

Lierman, Robert T., (859) 622-1278 tom.lierman@eku.edu,
Eastern Kentucky University – Gsr

Lifton, Nathaniel A., (765) 494-0754 nlifton@purdue.edu,
Purdue University – GmCc

Light, Bonnie, 206-543-9824 bonnie@apl.washington.edu,
University of Washington – Oa

Lightbody, Anne F., 603-862--0711 anne.lightbody@unh.edu,
University of New Hampshire – HgsOn

Likos, William J., 608-890-2662 likos@wisc.edu,
University of Wisconsin, Madison – NgSp

Lilley, Marvin D., (206) 543-0859 lilley@ocean.washington.edu,
University of Washington – Ob

Lillie, Robert J., lillier@geo.oregonstate.edu, Oregon State University – Ye

Lima, Eduardo A., 617-324-2829 limaea@mit.edu,
Massachusetts Institute of Technology – Ym

Lima, Ivan D., ilima@whoi.edu, Woods Hole Oceanographic Institution – Oc

Limp, W. F., 479-575-7909 flimp@uark.edu,
University of Arkansas, Fayetteville – Oi

Lin, Douglas, (831) 459-2732 lin@lick.ucsc.edu,
University of California, Santa Cruz – Xc

Lin, Gong-yuh, gongyuh.lin@csun.edu,
California State University, Northridge – Oa

Lin, Hsing K., (907) 474-6347 hklin@alaska.edu,
University of Alaska, Fairbanks – On

Lin, Jialin, (614) 292-6634 lin.789@osu.edu, Ohio State University – Oa

Lin, Jian, (508) 289-2576 jlin@whoi.edu,
Woods Hole Oceanographic Institution – Gt

Lin, John C., 801-581-7530 john.lin@utah.edu, University of Utah – Oa

Lin, Jung-Fu, 512-471-8054 afu@jsg.utexas.edu,
University of Texas at Austin – GyYm

Lin, Senjie, 860-405-9168 senjie.lin@uconn.edu, University of Connecticut – Ob

Lin, Shoufa, (519) 888-4567 (Ext. 6557) shoufa@uwaterloo.ca,
University of Waterloo – On

Lin, Wuyin, (631) 632-3141 Wuyin.Lin@stonybrook.edu,
SUNY, Stony Brook – Oa

Lin, Xiaomao, (785) 532-6166 xlin@ksu.edu, Kansas State University – On

Lin, Yu-Feng F., 217-333-0235 yflin@illinois.edu,
University of Illinois, Urbana-Champaign – Hg

Linares, Rogelio, ++935811259 rogelio.linares@uab.cat,
Universitat Autonoma de Barcelona – NgYx

Lincoln, Beth Z., (517) 629-0331 Albion College – Gc

Lincoln, Jonathan M., (973) 655-7273 lincolnj@mail.montclair.edu,
Montclair State University – Gr

Lincoln, Timothy N., 517-629-0486 tlincoln@albion.edu,
Albion College – EmCl

Lindberg, David R., (510) 642-3926 University of California, Berkeley – Pi

Lindberg, Jonathan W., (509) 376-5005 jon.lindberg@pnl.gov,
Pacific Northwest National Laboratory – Ec

Lindberg, Steven E., partnerships@ornl.gov,
Oak Ridge National Laboratory – Cl

Lindbo, David, (919) 793-4428 North Carolina State University – Sd

Linde, Alan T., (202) 478-8835 alinde@carnegiescience.edu,
Carnegie Institution of Washington – Ys

Lindemann, Richard H., (518) 580-5196 rlindemann@skidmore.edu,
Skidmore College – Pi

Lindemann, William C., (505) 646-3405 New Mexico State University, Las Cruces – Sb

Lindenmeier, Clark W., (509) 376-8419 clark.lindenmeier@pnl.gov,
Pacific Northwest National Laboratory – Cg

Lindgren, Paula, 441413305442 Paula.Lindgren@glasgow.ac.uk,
University of Glasgow – Oa

Lindline, Jennifer, (505) 426-2046 lindlinej@nmhu.edu,
New Mexico Highlands University – GizOe

Lindo Atichati, David, (718) 982-2919 david.Lindo@csi.cuny.edu,
College of Staten Island – Gue

Lindquist, Anna, 906-635-2140 alindquist1@lssu.edu,
Lake Superior State University – YmGz

Lindsay, Everett H., (520) 621-6024 ehlind@geo.arizona.edu,
University of Arizona – Pv

Lindsay, Matthew B., (306) 966-5693 matt.lindsay@usask.ca,
University of Saskatchewan – ClGg

Lindsey, Kassandra, 303-384-2660 kolindsey@mines.edu,
Colorado Geological Survey – NgGmOi

Lindsey, Michal, (504) 388-2110 mlindsey@agctr.lsu.edu,
Louisiana State University – So

Lindsley, Donald H., (631) 632-8195 donald.lindsley@sunysb.edu,
SUNY, Stony Brook – Cp

Lindsley-Griffin, Nancy, (402) 472-2629 nlg@unl.edu,
University of Nebraska, Lincoln – Gt

Lindzen, Richard S., (617) 253-2432 rlindzen@mit.edu,
Massachusetts Institute of Technology – Ow

Lineback, Neal G., (828) 262-3000 linebackng@appstate.edu,
Appalachian State University – Oy

Liner, Christopher , 479-575-4835 liner@uark.edu,
University of Arkansas, Fayetteville – YseGg

Lines, Larry R., (403) 220-5841 University of Calgary – Ye

Lini, Andrea, (802) 656-0245 andrea.lini@uvm.edu,
University of Vermont – CsGn

Link, Curtis A., (406) 496-4165 clink@mtech.edu, Montana Tech – Ye

Link, Paul K., (208) 282-3365 linkpaul@isu.edu,
Idaho State University – Gs

Linky, Edward, 212-772-5265 linky.edward@epamail.epa.gov,
Hunter College (CUNY) – On

Linn, Anne M., (202) 334-2744 alinn@nas.edu,
National Academy of Sciences/National Research Council – Gs

Linn, Rodman, (505) 665-6254 rrl@lanl.gov,
Los Alamos National Laboratory – Ng

Linneman, Scott R., (360) 650-7207 Scott.Linneman@wwu.edu,
Western Washington University – GmOe

Linnen, Robert, 519-661-2111 x89207 rlinnen@uwo.ca,
Western University – EmCe

Lintz, Heather E., 541-737-2996 hlintz@coas.oregonstate.edu,
Oregon State University – On

Liou, Juhn G., (650) 723-2716 liou@pangea.stanford.edu,
Stanford University – Gp

Lipeles, Maxine I., (314) 935-5482 milipeles@seas.wustl.edu,
Washington University – On

Lippelt, Irene D., (608) 262-7430 ilippelt@wisc.edu,
University of Wisconsin, Extension – Gg

Lippmann, Thomas C., 603-862-4450 lippmann@ccom.unh.edu,
University of New Hampshire – On

Lipps, Jere H., (510) 642-9006 University of California, Berkeley – Po

Lips, Elliott W., (801) 581-8218 elliott.lips@geog.utah.edu,
University of Utah – Gm

Lisenbee, Alvis L., (605) 394-2461 Alvis.Lisenbee@sdsmt.edu,
South Dakota School of Mines & Technology – Gc

Lisichenko, Richard, 785-628-4159 rlisiche@fhsu.edu,
Fort Hays State University – Oi

Lisiecki, Lorraine, (805) 893-4437 lisiecki@geol.ucsb.edu,
University of California, Santa Barbara – Gn

Lisle, R J., lisle@cf.ac.uk, Cardiff University – Gc

Lisle, Thomas, (707) 825-2930 tel7001@humboldt.edu,
Humboldt State University – Hs

Liss, Peter, +44 (0)1603 59 2563 p.liss@uea.ac.uk,
University of East Anglia – Co

Lithgow-Bertelloni, Carolina, +44 020 7679 37220 c.lithgow-bertelloni@ucl.ac.uk,
University College London – Yg

Little, Crispin, +44(0) 113 34 36621 earctsl@leeds.ac.uk,
University of Leeds – Pg

Little, Jonathan, jlittle@monroecc.edu, Monroe Community College – OylOi

Little, Tim, +64 4 463 6198 Tim.Little@vuw.ac.nz,
Victoria University of Wellington – Gct

Little, William W., (208) 496-2427 littlew@byui.edu,
Brigham Young University - Idaho – GsdGm

Littler, Kate, +44 01326255725 K.Littler@exeter.ac.uk, Exeter University – Pe

Liu, Chuntao, 361-825-3845 Chuntao.Liu@tamucc.edu,
Texas A&M University, Corpus Christi – Oa

Liu, Dantong, dantong.liu@manchester.ac.uk, University of Manchester – Oa

Liu, Gaisheng, 785-864-2115 gliu@kgs.ku.edu, University of Kansas – Hy

Liu, Jian G., +44 20 759 46418 j.g.liu@imperial.ac.uk,

481

M

University of Alabama – YgmYv

Maher, John, 9134698500 x5953 jmaher1@jccc.edu,
    Johnson County Community College – Oy

Maher, Kierran, 575-835-6354 kmaher@nmt.edu,
    New Mexico Institute of Mining and Technology – Eg

Maher, Jr., Harmon D., 402-554-4807 harmon_maher@unomaha.edu,
    University of Nebraska at Omaha – GcsGt

Maher, Jr., Louis J., (608) 262-9595 maher@geology.wisc.edu,
    University of Wisconsin, Madison – Pl

Mahlen, Nancy J., (585) 245-5016 mahlen@geneseo.edu,
    SUNY, Geneseo – GgpCc

Mahler, Robert L., (208) 885-7025 University of Idaho – On

Mahmood, Rezaul, (270) 745-5979 rezaul.mahmood@wku.edu,
    Western Kentucky University – Oa

Mahmoud, Sara A., 002-03-3921595 geo_soso2006@yahoo.com,
    Alexandria University – Gg

Mahoney, J. Brian, (715) 836-4952 mahonej@uwec.edu,
    University of Wisconsin, Eau Claire – Gs

Mahood, Gail A., (650) 723-1429 gail@pangea.stanford.edu,
    Stanford University – Gi

Mahowald, Natalie M., nmm63@cornell.edu, Cornell University – Oa

Maier, Raina M., (520) 621-7231 rmaier@ag.arizona.edu,
    University of Arizona – On

Maillol, Jean-Michel, (403) 220-8393 maillol@ucalgary.ca,
    University of Calgary – Ym

Main, Ian G., +44 (0) 131 650 4911 Ian.Main@ed.ac.uk,
    Edinburgh University – Ys

Maio, Chris, (907) 474-5651 cvmaio@alaska.edu,
    University of Alaska Fairbanks – Oy

Maisey, John G., (212) 769-5811 American Museum of Natural History – Pv

Majodina, Thando, (012) 382-6283 majodinato@tut.ac.za,
    Tshwane University of Technology – GgzGe

Major, Penni, 281-765-7865 penny.westerfeld@nhmccd.edu,
    Lonestar College - North Harris – Gg

Major, R. P., (662) 915-5440 rpm@cedar.olemiss.edu,
    University of Mississippi – Gd

Major, Ruth H., 518-629-7131 Hudson Valley Community College – Ggh

Maju-Oyovwikowhe, Efetobore G., efetobore.maju-oyovwikowhe@uniben.edu,
    University of Benin – GszGo

Majzlan, Juraj, +49(0)3641 948700 juraj.majzlan@uni-jena.de,
    Friedrich-Schiller-University Jena – Gz

Mak, John E., (631) 632-8673 john.mak@stonybrook.edu,
    SUNY, Stony Brook – Oa

Mak, Mankin, (217) 333-8071 mak@atmos.uiuc.edu,
    University of Illinois, Urbana-Champaign – Oa

Makkawi, Mohammad, +96638602621 makkawi@kfupm.edu.sa,
    King Fahd University of Petroleum and Minerals – Hw

Makovicky, Peter J., (312) 665-7633 pmakovicky@fieldmuseum.org,
    Field Museum of Natural History – Pv

Malahoff, Alexander, (808) 956-6802 malahoff@hawaii.edu,
    University of Hawai'i, Manoa – Cm

Malanotte-Rizzoli, Paola M., (617) 253-2451 rizzoli@mit.edu,
    Massachusetts Institute of Technology – Op

Malcolm, Elizabeth, 757-233-8751 emalcolm@vwc.edu,
    Virginia Wesleyan College – OaCgOg

Malcuit, Robert J., malcuit@denison.edu, Denison University – Gx

Malega, Ron, 417-836-4556 rmalega@missouristate.edu,
    Missouri State University – On

Malhotra, Renu, (520) 626-5899 renu@lpl.arizona.edu,
    University of Arizona – On

Malin, Gill, +44 (0)1603 59 2531 g.malin@uea.ac.uk,
    University of East Anglia – Ob

Malin, Peter E., (919) 681-8889 p.malin@auckland.ac.nz,
    Duke University – Ys

Malinconico, Lawrence L., (610) 330-5195 malincol@lafayette.edu,
    Lafayette College – Yg

Malinowski, Jon C., (845) 938-4673 mal@usma.edu,
    United States Military Academy – On

Malinverno, Alberto , (845) 365-8577 alberto@ldeo.columbia.edu,
    Columbia University – Gug

Mallard, Laura, mallardl@appstate.edu, Appalachian State University – GtOe

Mallarino, Antonio W., (515) 294-6200 apmallar@iastate.edu,
    Iowa State University of Science & Technology – So

Mallick, Subhashis, 307-766-2884 smallick@uwyo.edu,
    University of Wyoming – YseYg

Mallinson, David, (252) 328-1344 mallinsond@ecu.edu,
    East Carolina University – Gu

Malo, Douglas D., (605) 688-4586 Douglas.Malo@sdstate.edu,
    South Dakota State University – Sd

Malo, Michel, michel.malo@ete.inrs.ca, Universite du Quebec – Gc

Malone, David H., (309) 4387649 dhmalon@ilstu.edu,
    Illinois State University – Gc

Malone, Stephen D., 206-685-3811 steve@ess.washington.edu,
    University of Washington – YsGt

Maloney, Eric, 970-491-3368 emaloney@atmos.colostate.edu,
    Colorado State University – Oa

Maloof, Adam C., (609) 258-4101 maloof@princeton.edu,
    Princeton University – Ym

Malservisi, Rocco, 089/2180 4202 malservisi@rsmas.miami.edu,
    Ludwig-Maximilians-Universitaet Muenchen – Yg

Malzer, Gary L., (612) 625-6728 gmalzer@soils.umn.edu,
    University of Minnesota, Twin Cities – Sc

Mamot, Philipp, +49 (89) 289 25895 philipp.mamot@tum.de,
    Technische Universitaet Muenchen – GmOg

MANCA, Prof. Pierpaolo P., 070-675-5529 ppmanca@unica.it,
    Universita di Cagliari – Nm

Manchester, Steven R., 3523921721 x495 steven@flmnh.ufl.edu,
    University of Florida – Pb

Manchester, Steven R., (352) 392-1721 steven@flmnh.ufl.edu,
    University of Florida – Pb

Mancini, Ernest A., 205-348-4319 emancini@geo.ua.edu,
    University of Alabama – Pe

Mand, Arlene, (215) 573-3164 amand@sas.upenn.edu,
    University of Pennsylvania – On

Manda, Alex, 252 328 9403 Mandaa@ecu.edu,
    East Carolina University – Hqw

Mandel, Rolfe, 785-864-2171 mandel@ku.edu, University of Kansas – Ga

Mandelman, John, jmandelman@neaq.org,
    University of Massachusetts, Boston – Ob

Mandia, Scott, 631-451-4104 mandias@sunysuffolk.edu,
    Suffolk County Community College, Ammerman Campus – Ow

Mandra, York T., (415) 338-2061 ytmandra@sfsu.edu,
    San Francisco State University – Pg

Mandrone, Giuseppe, giuseppe.mandrone@unito.it,
    Università di Torino – Ng

Manduca, Cathryn A., 507-222-7096 cmanduca@carleton.edu,
    Carleton College – Gi

Mandziuk, William, (204) 474-7826 mandziu0@cc.umanitoba.ca,
    University of Manitoba – Gg

Manecan, Teodosia, (212) 772-5265 tmanecan@hunter.cuny.edu,
    Hunter College (CUNY) – Gp

Manfrino, Carrie M., (908) 737-3697 cmanfrin@kean.edu,
    Kean University – GuOb

Manga, Michael, (510) 643-8532 manga@seismo.berkeley.edu,
    University of California, Berkeley – GvXy

Manganini, Steven J., (508) 289-2778 smanganini@whoi.edu,
    Woods Hole Oceanographic Institution – Ou

Mangano, Gabriela, 306-966-5730 gabriela.mangano@usask.ca,
    University of Saskatchewan – PsGs

Mangel, Mark S., (831) 459-5785 msmangel@cats.ucsc.edu,
    University of California, Santa Cruz – On

Manger, Walter, 479-575-3355 wmanger@uark.edu,
    University of Arkansas, Fayetteville – Gr

Manghnani, Murli H., (808) 956-7825 murli@soest.hawaii.edu,
    University of Hawai'i, Manoa – Yx

Mango, Helen N., (802) 468-1478 helen.mango@castleton.edu,
    Castleton University – Cg

Mangriotis, Maria-Daphne , +44 (0) 131 451 3565 maria.mangriotis@pet.hw.ac.uk,
    Heriot-Watt University – Ys

Mankiewicz, Carol, (608) 363-2371 mankiewi@beloit.edu, Beloit College – Gs

Manley, Patricia L., (802) 443-5430 patmanley@middlebury.edu,
    Middlebury College – Yr

Manley, Thomas O., (802) 443-3114 tmanley@middlebury.edu,
    Middlebury College – Op

Mann, Dan, dhmann@alaska.edu, University of Alaska Fairbanks – Oy

Mann, Daniel H., (907) 474-5872 University of Alaska, Fairbanks – Pe

Mann, Keith O., (740) 368-3620 komann@owu.edu,
    Ohio Wesleyan University – Pi

Mann, Michael E., (814) 863-4075 mann@meteo.psu.edu,
    Pennsylvania State University, University Park – Oa

Mann, Paul, (512) 471-0452 paulm@ig.utexas.edu,
    University of Texas at Austin – Gt

Manning, Andrew, a.manning@uea.ac.uk, University of East Anglia – Oa

Manning, Christina, +44 1784 443835 c.manning@es.rhul.ac.uk,
    University of London, Royal Holloway & Bedford New College – Cg

Manning, Craig E., (310) 206-3290 manning@epss.ucla.edu,
    University of California, Los Angeles – GxCp

Manon, Matthew R., (518) 388-8015 manonm@union.edu, Union College – Gp

Manos, Leah D., (660) 562-1385 lmanos@nwmissouri.edu,
    Northwest Missouri State University – Oy

Manship, Lori L., 432 552 2245 manship_l@utpb.edu,
    University of Texas, Permian Basin – PioOi

Mansinha, Lalu, (519) 661-3145 mansinha@uwo.ca, Western University – Ys

Mansour, Ahmed S., 002-03-3921595 ah_sadek@hotmail.com,
    Alexandria University – Ggs

Manspeizer, Warren, (973) 353-5100 mansp@andromeda.rutgers.edu,
    Rutgers, The State University of New Jersey, Newark – Gr

Mantei, Erwin J., (417) 836-5446 emantei@missouristate.edu,
    Missouri State University – Ct

Mantilla Figueroa, Luis C., lcmantil@uis.edu.co,
    Universidad Industrial de Santander – EgCec

Manton, William I., (972) 883-2441 manton@utdallas.edu,
    University of Texas, Dallas – Cc

Mantua, Nathan J., nmantua@u.washington.edu,
    University of Washington – Oa

Manz, Lorraine, (701) 328-8005 lmanz@nd.gov,
    North Dakota Geological Survey – On

Manzi, Anthony, 718-409-7371 amanzi@sunymaritime.edu,
    SUNY, Maritime College – Ow

Mao, Ho-kwang, 202-478-8960 hmao@carnegiescience.edu,

Louisiana State University – Gg

McCullough, Jr., Edgar J., (520) 621-6024 University of Arizona – Ge

McCurdy, Maureen, (318) 257-3165 mm@coes.latech.edu,
Louisiana Tech University – Hw

McCurry, Michael O., (208) 282-3960 mccumich@isu.edu,
Idaho State University – Gz

McDade, Ian C., (416)736-2100 #22859 mcdade@yorku.ca,
York University – Or

McDaniel, Paul A., (208) 885-7012 University of Idaho – Sd

McDermott, Christopher I., +44 (0) 131 650 5931 cmcdermo@staffmail.ed.ac.uk,
Edinburgh University – Hg

McDermott, Thomas M., (585) 395-5718 SUNY, The College at Brockport – On

McDonald, Andrew M., 7056751151, ext. 2266 amcdonald@laurentian.ca,
Laurentian University, Sudbury – Gz

McDonald, Brenna, (573) 368-2163 brenna.mcdonald@dnr.mo.gov,
Missouri Dept of Natural Resources – Ge

McDonald, Eric, (775) 673-7302 emcdonald@dri.edu,
University of Nevada, Reno – Sp

McDonald, Gregory N., (801) 537-3383 gregmcdonald@utah.gov,
Utah Geological Survey – Ng

McDonald, Kyle C., (818) 354-3440 kyle.mcdonald@jpl.nasa.gov,
Jet Propulsion Laboratory – On

McDonald, Lynn, (505) 667-1582 lmcdonald@lanl.gov,
Los Alamos National Laboratory – On

McDonough, William F., (301) 405-5561 mcdonoug@geol.umd.edu,
University of Maryland – Cg

McDougall, Jim, 253-566-5060 JMcDougall@tacomacc.edu,
Tacoma Community College – Og

McDowell, Fred W., (512) 471-1672 mcdowell@mail.utexas.edu,
University of Texas at Austin – Cc

McDowell, Patricia F., (541) 346-4567 pmcd@uoregon.edu,
University of Oregon – Gm

McDowell, Rob J., 770-274-5466 Robin.McDowell@gpc.edu,
Georgia Perimeter College – Gts

McDowell, Robin J., Robin.McDowell@gpc.edu,
Georgia Perimeter College – Geg

McDowell, Ronald, 304 594 2331 mcdowell@geosrv.wvnet.edu,
West Virginia University – Gg

McDuff, Russell E., (206) 545-1947 mcduff@ocean.washington.edu,
University of Washington – Oc

McElroy, Anne, (631) 632-8488 anne.mcelroy@stonybrook.edu,
SUNY, Stony Brook – Oc

McElroy, Brandon, 307-766-3601 bmcelroy@uwyo.edu,
University of Wyoming – Gsm

McElroy, Michael B., (617) 495-9261 mbm@io.harvard.edu,
Harvard University – Oa

McElroy, Tom, (416)736-2100 #22113 tmcelroy@yorku.ca,
York University – Oa

McElwain, Jenny, (312) 665-7635 jennifer.mcelwain@gmail.com,
Field Museum of Natural History – Pb

McElwaine, Jim, +44 (0) 191 33 42286 Durham University – Yg

McElwee, Carl D., (785) 864-3965 cmcelwee@ku.edu,
University of Kansas – Hg

McEvoy, Jamie, (406) 994-4069 jamie.mcevoy@montana.edu,
Montana State University – Oe

McEwen, Alfred, (520) 621-4573 mcewen@lpl.arizona.edu,
University of Arizona – Xg

McFadden, Bruce J., (352) 846-2000 bmacfadd@flmnh.ufl.edu,
University of Florida – Pv

McFadden, Jennifer, 717-361-1392 mcfaddenj@etown.edu,
Elizabethtown College – OnnOn

McFadden, Leslie M., (505) 277-6121 lmcfadnm@unm.edu,
University of New Mexico – Sd

McFadden, Rory, rmcfadden@salemstate.edu, Salem State University – GpcGi

McFarland, Mark L., (979) 845-5366 ml-mcfarland@tamu.edu,
Texas A&M University – Sc

McFarlane, Norman, (250) 363-8227 norm.mcfarlane@ec.gc.ca,
University of Victoria – Oa

McFarquhar, Greg M., (217) 265-5458 mcfarq@illinois.edu,
University of Illinois, Urbana-Champaign – Or

McFiggans, Gordon, +44 0161 306-3954 Gordon.B.Mcfiggans@manchester.ac.uk,
University of Manchester – Oa

McGarvie, Dave, +44 (0) 131 549 7140 x 71140 dave.mcgarvie@open.ac.uk ,
The Open University – Gv

McGauley, Michael G., 305-237-2687 mmcgaule@mdc.edu,
Miami Dade College (Kendall Campus) – Owp

McGeary, Susan, (302) 831-8174 smcgeary@udel.edu,
University of Delaware – Yg

McGee, David, (617) 324-3545 davidmcg@mit.edu,
Massachusetts Institute of Technology – Cl

McGee, Tara, 780-492-3042 tmcgee@ualberta.ca, University of Alberta – On

McGee, Thomas M., (662) 915-7320 mmcgee@mmri.olemiss.edu,
University of Mississippi – Ys

McGehee, Richard V., rmcgehee@austincc.edu,
Austin Community College District – GgOn

McGehee, Thomas L., (512) 595-3590 kftlm00@tamuk.edu,
Texas A&M University, Kingsville – Cl

McGhee, Jr., George R., (848) 445-3832 mcghee@rci.rutgers.edu,
Rutgers, The State University of New Jersey – PoqPi

McGill, George E., (413) 545-0140 University of Massachusetts, Amherst – Gc

McGill, Sally F., (909) 537-5347 smcgill@csusb.edu,
California State University, San Bernardino – Gt

McGinnis, Lyle D., (630) 252-8722 Argonne National Laboratory – Yg

McGivern, Tiffany, (315)792-3134 Utica College – Geg

McGlade, Jacqueline, +44 020 7679 32839 jacquie.mcglade@ucl.ac.uk,
University College London – Ge

McGlathery, Karen, (804) 924-0558 kjm4k@virginia.edu,
University of Virginia – Ob

McGlue, Michael M., 859-257-3758 michael.mcglue@uky.edu,
University of Kentucky – Gso

McGoldrick, Peter J., 61 3 6226 7209 University of Tasmania – Ce

Mcgowan, Alistair, +4401413305449 Alistair.McGowan@glasgow.ac.uk,
University of Glasgow – Pg

McGowan, Eileen, 413-586-8305 emcgowan@geo.umass.edu,
University of Massachusetts, Amherst – Xg

McGowan, John A., (858) 534-2074 jmcgowan@ucsd.edu,
University of California, San Diego – Ob

McGrail, Bernard P., (509) 376-9193 pete.mcgrail@pnl.gov,
Pacific Northwest National Laboratory – Cg

McGrath, Steve F., 406-496-4767 smcgrath@mtech.edu,
Montana Tech of The University of Montana – CaEgCe

McGrath, Jr., Dorn C., (202) 994-6185 dornmcg@gwu.edu,
George Washington University – Oy

McGraw, Maureen A., (505) 665-8128 mcgraw@lanl.gov,
Los Alamos National Laboratory – On

McGregor, Kent M., (940) 565-2380 kent.mcgregor@unt.edu,
University of North Texas – Oag

McGregor, Stuart W., 205-247-3629 smcgregor@gsa.state.al.us,
Geological Survey of Alabama – Hs

McGrew, Allen J., (937) 229-3455 Allen.McGrew@notes.udayton.edu,
University of Dayton – Gc

McGuire, Angela, 509-527-5696 cotaac@whitman.edu, Whitman College – Gi

McGuire, Bill, +44 020 7679 33449 w.mcguire@ucl.ac.uk,
University College London – Gv

McGuire, Jeffrey J., (508) 289-3290 jmcguire@whoi.edu,
Woods Hole Oceanographic Institution – Ys

McGuire, Jennifer, 651-962-5254 jtmcguire@stthomas.edu,
University of Saint Thomas – CgHsGb

McGwire, Kenneth, 775.673.7324 ken.mcgwire@dri.edu,
University of Nevada, Reno – Or

McHargue, Timothy, timmchar@stanford.edu,
University of Missouri – Gs

McHenry, Lindsay J., 414-229-3951 lmchenry@uwm.edu,
University of Wisconsin, Milwaukee – Gz

McHugh, Cecilia, (718) 997-3330 cecilia.mchugh@qc.cuny.edu,
Queens College (CUNY) – Ou

McHugh, Cecilia M., (718) 997-3322 Graduate School of the City University of
New York – Ou

McHugh, Julia, 970-248-1993 jumchugh@coloradomesa.edu,
Colorado Mesa University – Pgv

McIlvin, Matt, 508-289-2884 mmcilvin@whoi.edu,
Woods Hole Oceanographic Institution – Oc

McInnes, Kevin J., (979) 845-5986 k-mcinnes@tamu.edu,
Texas A&M University – Sp

McIntosh, Jennifer, 520-626-2282 mcintosh@hwr.arizona.edu,
University of Arizona – Hy

McIntosh, Kirk D., 512-471-0480 kirk@ig.utexas.edu,
University of Texas at Austin – Gc

McIntosh, William C., (575) 835-5324 mcintosh@nmt.edu,
New Mexico Institute of Mining and Technology – Cc

McIntyre, Andrew, (718) 997-3329 Graduate School of the City University of
New York – Pe

McIsaac, Gregory F., (217) 333-9411 University of Illinois, Urbana-Champaign – Hs

McKay, Jennifer L., 541-737-4054 mckay@coas.oregonstate.edu,
Oregon State University – Cm

McKay, Larry D., (865) 974-5498 lmckay@utk.edu,
University of Tennessee, Knoxville – HyGe

McKay, Matthew P., 205-247-3669 mmckay@gsa.state.al.us,
Geological Survey of Alabama – GtoCc

McKay, Robert M., Robert.McKay@dnr.iowa.gov,
Iowa Dept of Natural Resources – Gg

McKay III, E. Donald, (217) 333-0044 emckay@illinois.edu,
University of Illinois, Urbana-Champaign – GlrGs

McKean, Adam, (801) 537-3386 adammckean@utah.gov,
Utah Geological Survey – Ng

McKean , Rebecca, 920-403-3227 rebecca.mckean@snc.edu,
Saint Norbert College – GdPgGh

McKee, James W., (414) 424-4460 mckee@athenet.net,
University of Wisconsin, Oshkosh – Gr

McKeegan, Kevin D., (310) 825-3580 mckeegan@epss.ucla.edu,
University of California, Los Angeles – XcCsc

McKenna, Thomas E., 302-831-2833 mckennat@udel.edu,
University of Delaware – Hy

McKenna, Thomas E., 302-831-8257 mckennat@udel.edu,
University of Delaware – Hg

McKenney, Rosemary, 253-535-8726 mckennra@plu.edu,
Pacific Lutheran University – Gm

McKenzie, Charlotte, 406-496-4180 cmckenzie@mtech.edu,
Montana Tech of The University of Montana – On

McKenzie, Connie, mckenzie@coes.latech.edu,

489

Louisiana Tech University – On

McKenzie, Garry D., (614) 292-0655 mckenzie.4@osu.edu,
Ohio State University – Gl

McKenzie, Jeffrey M., 514-398-3833 jeffrey.mckenzie@mcgill.ca,
McGill University – Hw

McKenzie, Phyllis, (202) 633-1860 mckenzie@si.edu,
Smithsonian Institution / National Museum of Natural History – On

McKenzie, Ross, ross.mckenzie@agric.gov.ab.ca,
University of Lethbridge – On

McKenzie, Scott, 814-824-2382 smckenzie@mercyhurst.edu,
Mercyhurst University – PgXmOe

McKibben, Michael A., (951) 827-3444 michael.mckibben@ucr.edu,
University of California, Riverside – Cg

McKinley, Galen, 608-262-4817 galen@aos.wisc.edu,
University of Wisconsin, Madison – Ob

McKinney, D. Brooks, (315) 781-3304 dbmck@hws.edu,
Hobart & William Smith Colleges – Gx

McKinney, Frank K., (828) 262-2748 mckinneyfk@appstate.edu,
Appalachian State University – Pi

McKinney, Mac, 205-247-3549 mmckinney@gsa.state.al.us,
Geological Survey of Alabama – Gg

McKinney, Marg J., (828) 262-2747 mckinnymj@appstate.edu,
Appalachian State University – Pg

McKinney, Michael L., (865) 974-6359 mmckinne@utk.edu,
University of Tennessee, Knoxville – GePo

McKinney, Nathan, 850-474-3207 nmckinney@uwf.edu,
University of West Florida – Oi

McKinnon, William B., (314) 935-5604 mckinnon@wustl.edu,
Washington University in St. Louis – Xg

McKnight, Brian K., (414) 424-4460 briankmcknight@yahoo.com,
University of Wisconsin, Oshkosh – Gd

McLafferty, Sara L., (212) 772-5224 slm@everest.hunter.cuny.edu,
Graduate School of the City University of New York – On

McLaskey, Greg C., gcm8@cornell.edu, Cornell University – YsGc

McLaughlin, Patrick I., 812-855-1350 pimclaug@iu.edu,
indiana University – GrClGs

McLaughlin, Patrick I., (608) 262-8658 pimclaughlin@wisc.edu,
University of Wisconsin, Extension – Gr

McLaughlin, Peter P., 302-831-8263 ppmclau@udel.edu,
University of Delaware – HgPm

McLaughlin, Richard, 361-825-2010 richard.mclaughlin@tamucc.edu,
Texas A&M University, Corpus Christi – On

McLaughlin, Richard A., (919) 515-7306 North Carolina State University – Sc

McLaurin, Brett T., 570-389-4142 bmclauri@bloomu.edu,
Bloomsburg University – GrsGd

McLean, Dewey M., (540) 231-6521 dmclean@vt.edu,
Virginia Polytechnic Institute & State University – Pe

McLean, Noah, noahmc@ku.edu,
University of Kansas – Cc

McLemore, Virginia, (505) 835-5521 ginger@gis.nmt.edu,
New Mexico Institute of Mining & Technology – Em

McLennan, John, 801-587-7925 jmclennan@egi.utah.edu,
University of Utah – Nrp

McLennan, Scott M., (631) 632-8194 scott.mclennan@sunysb.edu,
SUNY, Stony Brook – Cg

Mcleod, Andrew T., +44 (0) 131 650 5434 Andy.McLeod@ed.ac.uk,
Edinburgh University – Og

McLeod, Claire, 513-529-9662 mcleodcl@miamioh.edu,
Miami University – Gx

McLeod, Clara, cpmcleod@wustl.edu,
Washington University – On

McLeod, Samuel A., (213) 763-3325 smcleod@ref.usc.edu,
Los Angeles County Museum of Natural History – Pv

McManus, Dean A., (206) 543-0587 mcmanus@u.washington.edu,
University of Washington – Ou

McManus, George B., 860-405-9164 george.mcmanus@uconn.edu,
University of Connecticut – Ob

McManus, James, (330) 972-7991 jmcmanus@uakron.edu,
University of Akron – CmOg

McManus, Jerry F., (508) 289-3328 jmcmanus@whoi.edu,
Woods Hole Oceanographic Institution – Pe

McManus, Jerry F., (845) 365-8722 jmcmanus@ldeo.columbia.edu,
Columbia University – PeOu

McManus, Margaret A., (831) 459-4736 University of California, Santa Cruz – On

McManus, Margaret Anne, (808) 956-8623 mamc@hawaii.edu,
University of Hawai'i, Manoa – Op

McMechan, George A., (972) 883-2419 mcmec@utdallas.edu,
University of Texas, Dallas – Ys

McMenamin, Mark, 413-538-2280 mmcmenam@mtholyoke.edu,
Mount Holyoke College – PgGst

McMillan, Margaret E., (501) 569-3024 memcmillan@ualr.edu,
University of Arkansas at Little Rock – Gm

McMillan, Nancy J., 575-646-5000 nmcmilla@nmsu.edu,
New Mexico State University, Las Cruces – Gi

McMillan, Robert S., (520) 621-6968 bob@lpl.arizona.edu,
University of Arizona – On

McMonagle, Julie, 570-408-4604 julie.mcmonagle@wilkes.edu,
Wilkes University – Gg

McMullin, David, (902) 585-1276 david.mcmullin@acadiau.ca,
Acadia University – Oe

McMurdie, Lynn A., 206-685-9405 mcmurdie@atmos.washington.edu,
University of Washington – Oa

McMurtry, Gary M., (808) 956-6858 garym@soest.hawaii.edu,
University of Hawai'i, Manoa – Cm

McMurtry, John L., jmcmurtry@csuchico.edu,
California State University, Chico – Hw

McNair, Laurie A., (505) 665-3328 mcnair@lanl.gov,
Los Alamos National Laboratory – On

McNally, Karen C., kmcnally@pmc.ucsc.edu,
University of California, Santa Cruz – Ys

McNamara, Allen, 480-965-1733 allen.mcnamara@asu.edu,
Arizona State University – Yx

McNamara, James P., (208) 426-1354 jmcnamar@boisestate.edu,
Boise State University – Hg

McNamara, Jodi, (315) 228-7201 jmcnamara@colgate.edu,
Colgate University – On

McNamara, Kenneth, +44 (0) 1223 333410 kmcn07@esc.cam.ac.uk,
University of Cambridge – Po

McNassor, Cathy, (213) 763-3389 mcnassor@bcf.usc.edu,
Los Angeles County Museum of Natural History – Pv

McNaught, Mark A., (330) 829-8226 mcnaugma@mountunion.edu,
Mount Union College – Gcg

McNeal, Karen, (919) 515-0383 ksmcneal@ncsu.edu,
North Carolina State University – Oec

McNeill, Donald F., 305-284-3360 d.mcneill@miami.edu,
University of Miami – Gg

McNeill, Lisa, +44 (0)23 80593640 lcmn@noc.soton.ac.uk,
University of Southampton – GtYr

McNichol, Ann P., (508) 289-3394 amcnichol@whoi.edu,
Woods Hole Oceanographic Institution – Oc

McNicol, Barbara, (403) 440-6175 bmcnicol@mtroyal.ca,
Mount Royal University – Og

McNulty, Brendan A., (310) 243-3412 bmcnulty@csudh.edu,
California State University, Dominguez Hills – Gc

McPhaden, Michael J., (206) 526-6783 mcphaden@pmel.noaa.gov,
University of Washington – Og

McPhail, D C "Bear", +61 2 6125 2776 bear@ems.anu.edu.au,
Australian National University – Cl

McPherron, Robert L., (310) 825-1882 rmcpherr@igpp.ucla.edu,
University of California, Los Angeles – Xy

McPherson, Brian, 801-581-5634 bmcpherson@egi.utah.edu,
University of Utah – Ye

McPherson, Robert C., (707) 826-5828 rm4@humboldt.edu,
Humboldt State University – Gt

McPhie, Jocelyn, 61 3 6226 2892 Jocelyn.McPhie@utas.edu.au,
University of Tasmania – Gv

McQuaid, Jim, +44(0) 113 34 36724 J.B.McQuaid@leeds.ac.uk,
University of Leeds – Oa

McQuarrie, Nadine, (412) 624-8870 nmcq@pitt.edu,
University of Pittsburgh – Gct

McRivette, Michael, 517-629-0276 mmcrivette@albion.edu,
Albion College – GtOir

McRoberts, Christopher A., (607) 753-2925 mcroberts@cortland.edu,
SUNY, Cortland – Pg

McSween, Jr., Harry Y., (865) 974-6359 mcsween@utk.edu,
University of Tennessee, Knoxville – XcGi

McSweeney, Kevin, (608) 262-0331 kmcsween@wisc.edu,
University of Wisconsin, Madison – Sd

McWethy, David B., (406) 994-6915 dmcwethy@montana.edu,
Montana State University – PeSb

McWilliams, James, (310) 206-2829 jcm@atmos.ucla.edu,
University of California, Los Angeles – Oa

McWilliams, Michael O., (650) 723-3718 mcwilliams@stanford.edu,
Stanford University – Ym

McWilliams, Robert G., mcwillrg@MiamiOh.edu, Miami University – Ps

MdNamee, Brittani D., 828-350-4554 bmcnamee@unca.edu,
University of North Carolina, Asheville – Gzx

Mead, James I., mead@etsu.edu, Northern Arizona University – Po

Mead, Jerry V., 215.405.5091 jerry.v.mead@drexel.edu,
Drexel University – OiHgGm

Meade, Brendan, 617-495-8921 meade@fas.harvard.edu,
Harvard University – Yg

Meador, Cindy D., 806-651-2582 cmeador@wtamu.edu,
West Texas A&M University – Og

Meadows, Guy A., 906/487-1106 gmeadows@mtu.edu,
Michigan Technological University – Gu

Meadows, Wayne R., (505) 665-0291 wmeadows@lanl.gov,
Los Alamos National Laboratory – Yg

Means, Guy H., (850) 617-0312 Florida Geological Survey – PgGe

Measures, Christopher, (808) 956-8693 chrism@soest.hawaii.edu,
University of Hawai'i, Manoa – Oc

Measures, Elizabeth A., (432) 837-8117 measures@sulross.edu,
Sul Ross State University – Gdq

Mechoso, Carlos R., (310) 825-3057 mechoso@atmos.ucla.edu,
University of California, Los Angeles – Oa

Meckel, Timothy A., 512-471-4306 tip.meckel@beg.utexas.edu,
University of Texas at Austin – Gr

Mecklenburgh, Julian, +440161 275-3821 Julian.Mecklenburgh@manchester.ac.uk,
University of Manchester – Gc

Medaris, Gordon L., (608) 262-2708 medaris@geology.wisc.edu,

490

Santa Barbara City College – GgzGx

Meyer, Judith, (417) 836-5604 judithmeyer@missouristate.edu,
Missouri State University – On

Meyer, Lewis, +44 01326 253766 L.H.I.Meyer@exeter.ac.uk,
Exeter University – Nm

Meyer, Philip D., (503) 417-7552 philip.meyer@pnl.gov,
Pacific Northwest National Laboratory – Hw

Meyer, Rebecca A., (812) 855-2687 reameyer@indiana.edu,
Indiana University – Ec

Meyer, Scott C., (217) 333-5382 Illinois State Water Survey – Hw

Meyer, Steven J., (920) 465-5022 meyers@uwgb.edu,
University of Wisconsin, Green Bay – OawOg

Meyer, W. Craig, (818) 710-4241 meyerwc@piercecollege.edu,
Los Angeles Pierce College – GePm

Meyer, William T., (630) 969-6586 meyer@iastate.edu,
Argonne National Laboratory – Cg

Meyer Dombard, DArcy, 312-996-2423 drmd@uic.edu,
University of Illinois at Chicago – Py

Meyer-Arendt, Klaus J., 850-474-2792 kjma@uwf.edu,
University of West Florida – On

Meyers, Jamie A., 507-457-5266 jmeyers@winona.edu,
Winona State University – Gsd

Meyers, Philip A., (734) 764-0597 pameyers@umich.edu,
University of Michigan – Co

Meylan, Anne, (727) 896-8626 University of South Florida – Ob

Meylan, Maurice A., (601) 266-4527 mmeylan@otr.usm.edu,
University of Southern Mississippi – Gu

Meyzen, Christine M., +390498279153 christine.meyzen@unipd.it,
Università degli Studi di Padova – Cg

Mezga, Aleksandar, +38514606116 amezga@geol.pmf.hr,
University of Zagreb – Pg

Mezger, Jochen, (907) 474-7809 jemezger@alaska.edu,
University of Alaska Fairbanks – Gg

Miah, Khalid, (406) 496-4888 kmiah@mtech.edu,
Montana Tech – YexYs

Miall, Andrew D., (416) 978-8841 miall@quartz.geology.utoronto.ca,
University of Toronto – Gs

Miao, Xiaodong, 217-244-2516 miao@illinois.edu,
University of Illinois, Urbana-Champaign – Gm

Miao, Xin, (417) 836-5173 xinmiao@missouristate.edu,
Missouri State University – Or

Micallef, Aaron, aaron.micallef@um.edu.mt, University of Malta – Gug

Michael, Holly, 302-831-4197 hmichael@udel.edu, University of Delaware – Hw

Michael, Peter J., 918 631 3017 pjm@utulsa.edu, University of Tulsa – Gi

Michaels, Patrick J., (804) 924-0549 pmichaels@cato.org,
University of Virginia – Oa

Michaels, Paul, (208) 426-1929 pm@cgiss.boisestate.edu,
Boise State University – Ne

Michalek, Thomas E., 406-496-4405 tmichalek@mtech.edu,
Montana Tech of The University of Montana – HgwHs

Michalski, Greg, (765) 494-3704 gmichals@purdue.edu, Purdue University – Cs

Michaud, Jene D., 808-974-7411 jene@hawaii.edu,
University of Hawai'i, Hilo – HqwGm

Michaud, Yves, (418) 654-2647 Universite du Quebec – Gm

Michel, Fred A., fmichel@ccs.carleton.ca, Carleton University – Hw

Michel, Jacqueline, 504-280-6325 jmichel@uno.edu,
University of New Orleans – Cg

Michel, Suzanne, 6196447454 x3028 Suzanne.Michel@gcccd.edu,
Cuyamaca College – Ug

Michelfelder, Gary, 417-836-3171 garymichelfelder@missouristate.edu,
Missouri State University – Gvi

Mickelson, Andrew M., 901-678-4505 amicklsn@memphis.edu,
University of Memphis – Ga

Mickelson, David M., (608) 262-7863 mickelson@geology.wisc.edu,
University of Wisconsin, Madison – Gl

Mickus, Kevin L., (417) 836-6375 kevinmickus@missouristate.edu,
Missouri State University – Yg

Miclaus, Crina, 00402324095 miclaus@uaic.ro,
Al. I. Cuza University of Iasi – Gsr

Middlemiss, Lucie, +44(0) 113 34 35246 L.K.Middlemiss@leeds.ac.uk,
University of Leeds – Ge

Middleton, Carrie A., 303-462-9270 middleton.carrie@epa.gov,
Environmental Protection Agency – OriGf

Middleton, Larry T., (928) 523-2429 larry.middleton@nau.edu,
Northern Arizona University – Gs

Middleton, Michael D., (715) 425-3139 michael.d.middleton@uwrf.edu,
University of Wisconsin, River Falls – Pv

Mies, Jonathan W., (423) 425-4606 Jonathan-Mies@utc.edu,
University of Tennessee at Chattanooga – GctHg

Mikan, Frank M., (512) 327-1213 fmikan@austincc.edu,
Austin Community College District – CgOe

Mikhaltsevitch, Vassily, +61 8 9266-4976 V.Mikhaltsevitch@curtin.edu.au,
Curtin University – Ye

Mikkelsen, Paula, mikkelsen@museumoftheearth.org, Cornell University – Pi

Mikkelsen, Paula, 607-273-6623 x 20 pmm37@cornell.edu,
Paleontological Research Institution – Pi

Mikulic, Donald G., 217-244-2518 mikulic@isgs.uiuc.edu,
Illinois State Geological Survey – Ps

Mikulich, Matthew J., 719-395-6794 mjmikulich@msn.com,
Virginia Polytechnic Institute & State University – Ye

Milam, Keith A., (740) 593-1106 milamk@ohio.edu, Ohio University – Xg

Milan, Luke, lmilan@une.edu.au, University of New England – GgcGp

Miles, Randall J., 573-882-6607 University of Missouri, Columbia – Sd

Milewski, Adam, (706) 542-2652 University of Georgia – Hw

Militzer, Burkhard, militzer@seismo.berkeley.edu,
University of California, Berkeley – Gy

Milkereit, Bernd, (416) 978-2466 bm@physics.utoronto.ca,
University of Toronto – Ye

Millan, Christina, (614) 292-0865 millan.2@osu.edu,
Ohio State University – Ggc

Millen, Timothy M., 847-697-1000 tmillen@elgin.edu,
Elgin Community College – Gg

Miller, Arnold I., (513) 556-4022 arnold.miller@uc.edu,
Cincinnati Museum Center – Pq

Miller, Barry W., (865) 594-5599 Barry.Miller@tn.gov,
Tennessee Geological Survey – EcOiGg

Miller, Brent, (979) 458-3671 bvmiller@geo.tamu.edu,
Texas A&M University – Cc

Miller, Calvin F., 615-322-2232 calvin.miller@vanderbilt.edu,
Vanderbilt University – Gi

Miller, Carolyn R., (713) 718-5744 carolyn.miller@hccs.edu,
Houston Community College System – Gg

Miller, Charles M., (505) 667-8415 Los Alamos National Laboratory – Cc

Miller, Christian A., 808-956-9607 cmiller3@hawaii.edu,
University of Hawai'i, Manoa – CslCm

Miller, David, dmiller37@csub.edu,
California State University, Bakersfield – GgzGs

Miller, David S., (630) 252-7191 Argonne National Laboratory – Ge

Miller, Donald S., 518 478 0758 milled2@rpi.edu,
Rensselaer Polytechnic Institute – Cc

Miller, Doug, 828-232-5158 dmiller@unca.edu,
University of North Carolina, Asheville – OanOn

Miller, Douglas A., (814) 863-7207 dam8@psu.edu,
Pennsylvania State University, University Park – Sd

Miller, Douglas C., (302) 645-4277 dmiller@udel.edu,
University of Delaware – Ob

Miller, Elizabeth L., (650) 723-1149 miller@pangea.stanford.edu,
Stanford University – Gc

Miller, Geoffrey G., (506) 643-2361 Los Alamos National Laboratory – Cc

Miller, Gerald A., (515) 294-1923 soil@iastate.edu,
Iowa State University of Science & Technology – So

Miller, Gifford H., 303-492-6962 gmiller@colorado.edu,
University of Colorado – Cc

Miller, Glenn C., (775) 784-4108 gcmiller@unr.edu,
University of Nevada, Reno – Hg

Miller, Harvey J., (801) 585-3972 miller.81@osu.edu,
Ohio State University – Oi

Miller, Hugh, 303-273-3558 hbmiller@mines.edu,
Colorado School of Mines – Nm

Miller, Ian, 303-370-8351 Ian.Miller@dmns.org,
Denver Museum of Nature & Science – PbGg

Miller, James D., 218-726-6582 mille066@tc.umn.edu,
University of Minnesota, Duluth – Gi

Miller, James D., 218-726-8385 mille066@d.umn.edu,
University of Minnesota, Twin Cities – Gx

Miller, James F., (417) 836-5800 Missouri State University – Ps

Miller, Jerry R., (828) 227-7367 jmiller@wcu.edu,
Western Carolina University – Gm

Miller, John, (416)736-5245 jrmiller@yorku.ca,
York University – Or

Miller, Jonathan S., (408) 924-5015 jonathan.miller@sjsu.edu,
San Jose State University – GiCc

Miller, Joshua H., josh.miller@uc.edu,
Cincinnati Museum Center – Pe

Miller, Kate, (979) 845-3651 kcmiller@tamu.edu, Texas A&M University – Ys

Miller, Keith S., (785) 532-2250 kbmill@ksu.edu, Kansas State University – Pe

Miller, Kenneth G., (848) 445-3622 kgm@rci.rutgers.edu,
Rutgers, The State University of New Jersey – GuPsm

Miller, M. Meghan, (509) 963-2825 meghan@cwu.edu,
Central Washington University – Yd

Miller, Mark, 601-266-4729 m.m.miller@usm.edu,
University of Southern Mississippi – On

Miller, Marli G., (541) 346-4410 millerm@uoregon.edu,
University of Oregon – Gc

Miller, Marvin R., 406-496-4155 mmiller@mtech.edu,
Montana Tech of The University of Montana – Hw

Miller, Max, 303-404-5415 max.miller@frontrange.edu,
Front Range Community College - Westminster – OiyOe

Miller, Meghan, 213-740-6106 meghan@unavco.org,
University of Southern California – Gt

Miller, Michael B., (225) 388-3412 byron@lgs.bri.lsu.edu,
Louisiana State University – Go

Miller, Molly F., 615-322-3528 molly.miller@vanderbilt.edu,
Vanderbilt University – Pe

Miller, Murray H., (519) 824-4120 (Ext. 53758) jmmiller7@sympatico.ca,
University of Guelph – So

Miller, Randall F., (506) 643-2361 University of New Brunswick – Pg

Miller, Raymond M., (630) 252-3395 rmmiller@anl.gov,
Argonne National Laboratory – Sb

Miller, Richard, 252 328 9372 millerri@ecu.edu,

492

N

University of Arkansas, Fayetteville – On
Nichols, Jr., Woodrow W., (919) 560-5171 North Carolina Central University – Oy
Nicholson, David, (508) 289-3547 dnicholson@whoi.edu,
  Woods Hole Oceanographic Institution – Gu
Nicholson, Kirsten N., 765-285-8268 knichols@bsu.edu,
  Ball State University – Gi
Nicholson, Nanette, 212-769-5390 nnicholson@amnh.org,
  American Museum of Natural History – On
Nick, Kevin, knick@llu.edu, Loma Linda University – Gdb
Nickmann, Marion, +49 89 289 25853 nickmann@tum.de,
  Technische Universitaet Muenchen – Ng
Nicolas, Michelle, michelle.nicolas@gov.mb.ca,
  Manitoba Geological Survey – GrsGo
Nicolaysen, Kirsten P., 509-527-4934 nicolakp@whitman.edu,
  Whitman College – GiCgGa
Nicolescu, Stefan, 203-432-3141 stefan.nicolescu@yale.edu,
  Yale University – CtGpz
Nicoletti, Jeremy D., (603) 271-5762 jeremy.nicoletti@des.nh.gov,
  New Hampshire Geological Survey – GgHg
Nicoll, Kathleen, (801) 581-8218 kathleen.nicoll@geog.utah.edu,
  University of Utah – Gs
Nicot, Jean-Philippe, 512-471-6246 jp.nicot@beg.utexas.edu,
  University of Texas at Austin – Hw
Niedzielski, Michael A., michael.niedzielski@und.edu,
  University of North Dakota – Oi
Nielsen, Donald R., (530) 753-5760 drnielsen@ucdavis.edu,
  University of California, Davis – Sp
Nielsen, Gerald A., (406) 994-5075 nielsenmontana@aol.com,
  Montana State University – Sd
Nielsen, Kurt E., 831-656-2295 nielsen@nps.edu,
  Naval Postgraduate School – Ow
Nielsen, Mary, 605-677-5649 Mary.Nielsen@usd.edu,
  University of South Dakota – On
Nielsen, Peter A., (603) 358-2553 pnielsen@keene.edu,
  Keene State College – GxzGc
Nielsen, Peter J., (801) 537-3359 peternielsen@utah.gov,
  Utah Geological Survey – Eo
Nielsen, Roger L., (541) 737-1235 nielsenr@geo.oregonstate.edu,
  Oregon State University – Gi
Nielsen, Sune G., (508) 289-2837 snielsen@whoi.edu,
  Woods Hole Oceanographic Institution – Cs
Nielsen-Gammon, John, n-g@tamu.edu, Texas A&M University – Oa
Nielson, Russell L., (936) 468-2248 rnielson@sfasu.edu,
  Stephen F. Austin State University – Gr
Niem, Alan R., niema@geo.oregonstate.edu, Oregon State University – Gd
Niemann, William L., (304) 696-6721 niemann@marshall.edu,
  Marshall University – Ng
Niemi, Nathan, 734-764-6377 naniemi@umich.edu, University of Michigan – Gc
Niemi, Tina M., (816) 235-5342 niemit@umkc.edu,
  University of Missouri-Kansas City – Gt
Niemitz, Jeffery W., niemitz@dickinson.edu,
  Dickinson College – ClOuGn
Niemuth, Nyal, 602-771-1604 nyal.niemuth@azgs.az.gov,
  Arizona Geological Survey – GgEg
Nieto, Antonio, 814-863-1620 anieto@psu.edu,
  Pennsylvania State University, University Park – Nm
Niewendorp, Clark, (971) 673-1555 clark.niewendorp@dogami.state.or.us,
  Oregon Dept of Geology & Mineral Industries – Eg
Niiler, Pearn P., (858) 534-4100 pniiler@ucsd.edu,
  University of California, San Diego – Op
Nikitina, Daria L., (610) 436-3103 dnikitina@wcupa.edu,
  West Chester University – Gm
Nikolinakou, Maria-Aikaterini, 512-475-6613 mariakat@austin.utexas.edu,
  University of Texas at Austin – N
Nimis, Paolo, +390498279161 paolo.nimis@unipd.it,
  Università degli Studi di Padova – Eg
Ninesteel, Judy J., (304) 788-6956 JJNinesteel@mail.wvu.edu,
  Potomac State College – Hg
Ning, Liang, 814-8760987 lun115@psu.edu,
  University of Massachusetts, Amherst – Ow
Niocaill, Conall M., +44 (0)1865 282135 conallm@earth.ox.ac.uk,
  University of Oxford – Gt
Nisbet, Euan, +44 1784 443809 E.Nisbet@rhul.ac.uk,
  University of London, Royal Holloway & Bedford New College – Og
Nissen-Meyer, Targe, +44 (1865) 282149 tarje.nissen-meyer@earth.ox.ac.uk,
  University of Oxford – Ys
Nitecki, Matthew H., (312) 665-7093 mnitecki@fmnh.org,
  Field Museum of Natural History – Pi
Nittler, Larry R., (202) 478-8460 lnittler@carnegiescience.edu,
  Carnegie Institution of Washington – Xc
Nittrouer, Charles A., 206-543-5099 nittroue@ocean.washington.edu,
  University of Washington – GuYr
Nittrouer, Jeffrey A., 713.348.4886 nittrouer@rice.edu,
  Rice University – Gms
Niu, Fenglin, 713.348.4122 niu@rice.edu, Rice University – Ys
Niu, Guo-Yue, niu@geo.utexas.edu, University of Texas at Austin – SpOa
Niu, Yaoling, +44 (0) 191 33 42311 yaoling.niu@durham.ac.uk,
  Durham University – On
Nixon, Cheryl, cheryl.nixon@umb.edu, University of Massachusetts, Boston – On
Nixon, R. Paul, 801-422-4657 paul_nixon@byu.edu,

Brigham Young University – Go
Nixon, Scott W., (401) 874-6803 University of Rhode Island – Ob
Niyogi, Dev, (765) 494-9531 climate@purdue.edu, Purdue University – Oa
Njau, Jackson K., (812) 856-3170 jknjau@indiana.edu,
  Indiana University, Bloomington – Pv
Njoku, Eni G., (818) 354-3693 eni.g.njoku@jpl.nasa.gov,
  Jet Propulsion Laboratory – Or
Nkedi-Kizza, Peter, (352) 392-1951 kizza@ufl.edu, University of Florida – Sp
Nkotagu, Hudson H., nkotaguh@yahoo.com,
  University of Dar es Salaam – HwgGe
Noakes, John E., (706) 542-1395 University of Georgia – Cc
Nobes, David, +64 3 3667001 Ext7733 david.nobes@canterbury.ac.nz,
  University of Canterbury – Hy
Noble, Paula J., 775-784-6211 noblepj@unr.edu,
  University of Nevada, Reno – PmGnPs
Noblett, Jeffrey B., (719) 389-6516 jnoblett@coloradocollege.edu,
  Colorado College – Gx
Noe, Garry, 757-455-3284 gnoe@vwc.edu, Virginia Wesleyan College – HsOin
Noffke, Nora, nnoffke@odu.edu, Old Dominion University – Ge
Nogueira, Ricardo, 404-413-5791 rnogueira@gsu.edu,
  Georgia State University – Oaw
Nolan, Robert P., (718) 951-4242 Graduate School of the City University of New
  York – Co
Nolin, Anne, (541) 737-8051 nolina@geo.oregonstate.edu,
  Oregon State University – Or
Noll, Mark R., (585) 395-5717 mnoll@esc.brockport.edu,
  SUNY, The College at Brockport – Cl
Noll, Michael G., (229) 333-7143 mgnoll@valdosta.edu,
  Valdosta State University – On
Noltimier, Hallan C., (614) 292-9796 noltimier.2@osu.edu,
  Ohio State University – Ym
Nondorf, Lea, (501) 683-0110 lea.nondorf@arkansas.gov,
  Arkansas Geological Survey – Cg
Noonan, Mathew T., 605-677-6152 matthew.noonan@usd.edu,
  South Dakota Dept of Environment and Natural Resources – Hw
Noone, David, (541) 737-3629 dcn@coas.oregonstate.edu,
  Oregon State University – Owg
Nord, Julia, (703) 993-3395 jnord@gmu.edu,
  George Mason University – Gzg
Nordeng, Stephan, (701) 777-3455 stephan.nordeng@engr.und.edu,
  University of North Dakota – Go
Nordstrom, Greg, 662-268-1032 Ext 248 gjn2@msstate.edu,
  Mississippi State University – Ow
Nordt, Lee C., (254) 710-4288 lee_nordt@baylor.edu,
  Baylor University – SdGa
Nordwald, Dan, 573-368-2451 dan.nordwald@dnr.mo.gov,
  Missouri Dept of Natural Resources – On
Norell, Mark A., (212) 769-5804 American Museum of Natural History – Pv
Noren, Anders, 612-626-3298 noren021@umn.edu,
  University of Minnesota, Twin Cities – Gn
Norford, Brian, (403) 292-7000 University of Calgary – Gr
Norman, David, +44 (0) 1223 333426 dn102@esc.cam.ac.uk,
  University of Cambridge – Po
Norman, David K., 360-902-1439 dave.norman@dnr.wa.gov,
  Washington Division of Geology & Earth Resources – Gg
Norman, John M., (608)262-4576 jmnorman@wisc.edu,
  University of Wisconsin, Madison – So
Norman, Ralph R., (205) 247-3587 rnorman@gsa.state.al.us ,
  Geological Survey of Alabama – Hwg
Norris, Christopher A., 203-432-3748 christopher.norris@yale.edu,
  Yale University – Pv
Norris, Dean R., (321) 674-8096 norris@fit.edu,
  Florida Institute of Technology – Ob
Norris, Geoffrey, (416) 978-4851 norris@quartz.geology.utoronto.ca,
  University of Toronto – Pl
Norris, Joel R., (858) 822-4420 jnorris@ucsd.edu,
  University of California, San Diego – Oa
Norris, Richard D., (858) 822-1868 rnorris@ucsd.edu,
  University of California, San Diego – Gu
Norris, Richard J., +64 3 479-7520 richard.norris@otago.ac.nz,
  University of Otago – Gct
Norris-Tull, Delena, 406-683-7043 delena.norris@umwestern.edu,
  University of Montana Western – Oe
Norrish, Winston, 509.963.2192 norrishw@geology.cwu.edu,
  Central Washington University – GgeGo
Norry, Mike, +440116 252 3803 nah@le.ac.uk, Leicester University – Pe
North, Gerald R., (979) 845-8083 g-north@tamu.edu,
  Texas A&M University – Ow
North, Leslie, leslie.north@wku.edu, Western Kentucky University – Og
Northrup, Clyde J., (208) 426-1581 cjnorth@boisestate.edu,
  Boise State University – Gc
Norton, Stephen A., (207) 581-2156 norton@maine.edu,
  University of Maine – Cl
Norton-Krane, Abby N., (216) 987-5227 Abby.Norton-Krane@tri-c.edu,
  Cuyahoga Community College - Western Campus – Og
Norwine, Jim R., (512) 595-3589 kfjrn00@tamuk.edu,
  Texas A&M University, Kingsville – On
Norwood, James, 334-844-3414 jan0003@auburn.edu,
  Auburn University – Oy
Nosal, Thomas E., 86004243590 thomas.nosal@ct.gov,

Offerman, Katherine, 410-554-5543 Katherine.offerman@maryland.gov,
  Maryland Department of Natural Resources – GuYrOi
Oganov, Artem, 631-632-1429 artem.oganov@sunysb.edu,
  SUNY, Stony Brook – Gz
Ogard, Allen E., (505) 667-6344 Los Alamos National Laboratory – Hw
Ogbahon, Osazuwa A., 08064253825 oaogbahon@futa.edu.ng,
  Federal University of Technology, Akure – Ggo
Ogbamikhumi, Alexander, alexander.ogbamikhumi@uniben.edu,
  University of Benin – YsgGg
Ogg, James G., (765) 494-8681 jogg@purdue.edu, Purdue University – Gs
Ogiesoba, Osareni C., 512-471-6250 osareni.ogiesoba@beg.utexas.edu,
  University of Texas at Austin – Ygs
Oglesby, David D., (951) 827-2036 david.oglesby@ucr.edu,
  University of California, Riverside – Ys
Oglesby, Elizabeth, eoglesby@email.arizona.edu, University of Arizona – On
Oglesby, Robert J., (402) 472-1507 roglesby2@unl.edu,
  University of Nebraska, Lincoln – Oa
Ogram, Andrew V., 3523921951 (Ext 211) aogram@ufl.edu,
  University of Florida – Sb
Ogston, Andrea S., (206) 543-0768 ogston@ocean.washington.edu,
  University of Washington – Ou
Ogungbesan, Gbenga O., +2348005432408 googungbesan@lautech.edu.ng,
  Ladoke Akintola University of Technology – GooGo
Ogunsanwo, O., femiogunsanwo2003@yahoo.com,
  University of Ilorin – Ng
Ohan, Anderson A., 718-982-2829 anderson.ohan@csi.cuny.edu,
  College of Staten Island – Gc
Ohman, Mark D., (858) 534-2754 mohman@ucsd.edu,
  University of California, San Diego – Ob
Ohmoto, Hiroshi, (814) 865-4074 ohmoto@geosc.psu.edu,
  Pennsylvania State University, University Park – Cs
Ojakangas, Richard W., (218) 726-7923 rojakang@d.umn.edu,
  University of Minnesota, Duluth – Gd
Ojala, Carl F., (313) 487-0218 Eastern Michigan University – Oa
Ojo, O. J., solafoluk@yahoo.com, University of Ilorin – GoPm
Ojo, S. B., 234-803-703-7226 sbojo@oauife.edu.ng,
  Obafemi Awolowo University – Yg
Okafor, Florence A., (256) 372-4926 florence.okafor@aamu.edu,
  Alabama A&M University – OnEn
Okal, Emile A., (847) 491-3238 emile@earth.northwestern.edu,
  Northwestern University – YsgYr
Okalebo, Jane, jane.akalebo@gmail.com, University of Nebraska, Lincoln – Oa
Okaya, David A., (213) 740-7452 okaya@earth.usc.edu,
  University of Southern California – Ys
Okulewicz, Steven C., 516 463-6545 geosco@hofstra.edu,
  Hofstra University – Gg
Okumura, Yuko, 512-471-0383 yukoo@ig.utexas.edu,
  University of Texas at Austin – OaPe
Okunade, Samuel, (937) 376-6455 Central State University – Gm
Okunlola, O. A., o.okunlola@mail.ui.edu.ng, University of Ibadan – Eg
Ola, P S., 08035927594 psola@futa.edu.ng,
  Federal University of Technology, Akure – GgoGs
Olabode, Solomon O., 08033783498
  Federal University of Technology, Akure – GgoGs
Oladunjoye, M. A., ma.oladunjoye@mail.ui.edu.ng,
  University of Ibadan – Yg
Olafsen-Lackey, Susan, (402) 371-6512 slackey@unl.edu,
  Unversity of Nebraska - Lincoln – Hw
Olanrewaju, Johnson, 814-871-7453 olanrewa001@gannon.edu,
  Gannon University – Cg
Olarewaju, V. O., 234-803-403-2030 volarewa@oauife.edu.ng,
  Obafemi Awolowo University – GozCg
Olariu, Cornel, 512-471-1519 cornelo@jsg.utexas.edu,
  University of Texas at Austin – Gr
Olariu, Mariana, iulialet@yahoo.com, University of Texas at Austin – Gr
Olayiwola, M. A., 234-806-448-7416 mayiwola@oauife.edu.ng,
  Obafemi Awolowo University – GugPi
Olcott Marshall, Alison, (785) 864-1917 olcott@ku.edu,
  University of Kansas – Py
Oldenburg, Douglas W., (604) 822-5406 doldenburg@eos.ubc.ca,
  University of British Columbia – Yg
Oldershaw, Alan E., (403) 220-3258 oldersha@geo.ucalgary.ca,
  University of Calgary – Gs
Oldham, Richard L., 568-3100 (12147) OldhamR@arc.losrios.edu,
  American River College – Gg
Oldow, John S., (972) 883-2403 oldow@utdallas.edu,
  University of Texas, Dallas – Gc
Olea, Ricardo, rolea@usgs.gov, University of Kansas – Gq
Oleinik, Anton, (561) 297-3297 aoleinik@fau.edu,
  Florida Atlantic University – Pe
Olesik, John W., (614) 292-6954 olesik.2@osu.edu,
  Ohio State University – Ca
Oleynik, Sergey, 609 258-2390 soleynik@princeton.edu,
  Princeton University – Cs
Olhoeft, Gary R., (303) 273-3458 golhoeft@mines.edu,
  Colorado School of Mines – Yg
Olivares, Jose A., (505) 665-2643 Los Alamos National Laboratory – Cs
Oliveira, Alcino S., soliveir@utad.pt,
  Universidade de Trás-os-Montes e Alto Douro – Hww
Oliver, Adolph A., (415) 786-6865 Chabot College – Ys

Oliver, Kevin, +44 (0)23 80596490 K.Oliver@noc.soton.ac.uk,
  University of Southampton – Op
Oliver, Matthew J., 302-645-4079 moliver@udel.edu,
  University of Delaware – ObrOg
Oliver, Ronald D., (702) 794-7095 ron_oliver@lanl.gov,
  Los Alamos National Laboratory – Yg
Oliveras Castro, Valentí, ++935813092 valenti.oliveras@uab.cat,
  Universitat Autonoma de Barcelona – Gvi
Olivo, Gema, 613 533-6998 olivo@queensu.ca, Queen's University – Eg
Ollerhead, Jeffery W., (506) 364-2428 jollerhead@mta.ca,
  Mount Allison University – Yr
Olmsted, Wayne, (406) 496-4151 Montana Tech of the University of Montana – Ca
Olney, Jessica L., 813-253-7647 jolney2@hccfl.edu,
  Hillsborough Community College – OgGg
Olney, Matthew P., molney@hccfl.edu,
  Hillsborough Community College – OgGg
Olorunfemi, A. O., 234-803-392-1712 akinrewa@oauife.edu.ng,
  Obafemi Awolowo University – Go
Olorunfemi, M. O., 234-903-719-2169 mlorunfe@oauife.edu.ng,
  Obafemi Awolowo University – Yg
Olsen, Amanda A., 207 581-2194 amanda.olsen@umit.maine.edu,
  University of Maine – Cl
Olsen, Ken, kolsen@wustl.edu, Washington University – On
Olsen, Khris B., (509) 376-4114 kb.olsen@pnl.gov,
  Pacific Northwest National Laboratory – Cg
Olsen, Kim B., 619-594-2649 kbolsen@mail.sdsu.edu,
  San Diego State University – Ye
Olsen, Paul E., (845) 365-8491 Columbia University – Gm
Olson, Hillary C., (512) 471-0455 olson@utig.ig.utexas.edu,
  University of Texas at Austin – Ps
Olson, James R., 605-677-6866 jim.olson@usd.edu,
  South Dakota Dept of Environment and Natural Resources – On
Olson, Kenneth R., (217) 333-9639 University of Illinois, Urbana-Champaign – Sc
Olson, Kimberly, olsonk@arc.losrios.edu, American River College – Oye
Olson, Neil F., (603) 271-2875 neil.olson@des.nh.gov,
  New Hampshire Geological Survey – GeHy
Olson, Peter L., (410) 516-7707 olson@jhu.edu,
  Johns Hopkins University – Yg
Olson, Ted L., 435 283-7533 ted.olson@snow.edu, Snow College – Ys
Olsson, Richard K., (848) 445-3043 olsson@rci.rutgers.edu,
  Rutgers, The State University of New Jersey – PmGr
Olszewski, Kathy, 718-409-7366 jhoffman@sunymaritime.edu,
  SUNY, Maritime College – Cg
Olszewski, Thomas, 979-845-2465 tomo@geo.tamu.edu,
  Texas A&M University – Pe
Oltman-Shay, Joan M., (425) 644-9660 University of Washington – Op
Olugboji, Tolulope M., olugboji@umd.edu, University of Maryland – Ysg
Olyphant, Greg A., (812) 855-5154 olyphant@indiana.edu,
  Indiana University, Bloomington – Hw
Omar, Gomaa I., (215) 898-6908 gomar@sas.upenn.edu,
  University of Pennsylvania – Cc
Omelon, Christopher, 512-471-5440 omelon@jsg.utexas.edu,
  University of Texas at Austin – Cg
Omotoso, O. A., deletoso2002@yahoo.com, University of Ilorin – Ge
Oms Llobet, Oriol, ++34935811218 joseporiol.oms@uab.cat,
  Universitat Autonoma de Barcelona – GrsYm
Onasch, Charles M., (419) 372-7197 conasch@bgnet.bgsu.edu,
  Bowling Green State University – Yg
Onderdonk, Nate, (562) 985-2654 nonderdo@csulb.edu,
  California State University, Long Beach – Gt
Onderdonk, Nathan, 323 343 2412 nonderdo@csulb.edu,
  California State University, Los Angeles – Gt
ONeal, Michael, 302-831-8273 michael@udel.edu,
  University of Delaware – Gm
Ono, Shuhei, (617) 253-0474 sono@mit.edu,
  Massachusetts Institute of Technology – PyCs
Onstott, Tullis C., (609) 258-6898 tullis@princeton.edu,
  Princeton University – Py
Onyeobi, Tony U., tony.onyeobi@uniben.edu, University of Benin – NrgGq
Oommen, Thomas, (906) 487-2045 toommen@mtu.edu,
  Michigan Technological University – NeOi
Oona, Hain, (505) 667-5685 Los Alamos National Laboratory – On
Oostdam, Bernard L., 717-871-9928 boostdam@hotmail.com,
  Millersville University – Ou
Oostrom, Martinus, (509) 372-6044 mart.oostrom@pnl.gov,
  Pacific Northwest National Laboratory – Hq
Opdyke, Neil D., (352) 392-6127 drno@ufl.edu, University of Florida – Ym
Opeloye, S A., 08060981972 Federal University of Technology, Akure – GgoGs
Ophori, Duke U., (973) 655-7558 ophorid@mail.montclair.edu,
  Montclair State University – Hw
Oppenheimer, Michael, (609) 258-2338 omichael@princeton.edu,
  Princeton University – OaGe
Opper, Carl, 727-791-2536 opper.carl@spcollege.edu,
  Saint Petersburg College, Clearwater – Hw
Opperman, William, wopperma@broward.edu, Broward College – Gg
Oppo, Delia W., 508-289-2681 doppo@whoi.edu,
  Woods Hole Oceanographic Institution – Pm
Oppong, Joseph R., (940) 565-2181 oppong@unt.edu,
  University of North Texas – On
Orchard, Michael, 604-669-0909 morchard@nrcan.gc.ca,

P

Pierzynski, Gary M., 785-532-6101 gmp@ksu.edu,
  Kansas State University – Sc
Pieters, Carle M., (401) 863-2417 Carle_Pieters@Brown.edu,
  Brown University – Or
Pieters, Roger, (604) 822-4297 rpieters@eos.ubc.ca,
  University of British Columbia – Op
Pietrafesa, Leonard J., (919) 515-3717 leonard_pietrafesa@ncsu.edu,
  North Carolina State University – Op
Pietrzak-Renaud, Natalie, 519-473-3766 npietrz@uwo.ca,
  Western University – Eg
Pignotta, Geoffrey S., 715-836-4982 pignotgs@uwec.edu,
  University of Wisconsin, Eau Claire – Gcg
Pigott, John D., (405) 325-4498 jpigott@ou.edu,
  University of Oklahoma – Ye
Pike, J, PikeJ@cf.ac.uk, Cardiff University – On
Pike, Jenny, +44(0)29 208 75181 PikeJ@cardiff.ac.uk,
  University of Wales – Og
Pike, Scott, 503-370-6587 spike@willamette.edu,
  Willamette University – Gg
Pike, Steven M., (508) 289-2350 spike@whoi.edu,
  Woods Hole Oceanographic Institution – Ca
Pikelj, Kristina, +38514606113 kpikelj@geol.pmf.hr,
  University of Zagreb – Gs
Pikitch, Ellen K., (631) 632-9599 ellen.pikitch@stonybrook.edu,
  SUNY, Stony Brook – Ob
Pilarczyk, Jessica E., (228) 688-3177 jessica.pilarczyk,
  University of Southern Mississippi – Ou
Pilkey, Jr., Orrin H., (919) 684-4238 opilkey@geo.duke.edu,
  Duke University – Ou
Pilson, Michael E., (401) 874-6104 pilson@gso.uri.edu,
  University of Rhode Island – Oc
Pinan-Llamas, Aranzazu, 260-481-6253 pinana@ipfw.edu,
  Indiana University / Purdue University, Fort Wayne – GcdGp
Pinckney, James, 803-777-7133 pinckney@sc.edu,
  University of South Carolina – Obn
Pinet, Paul, (315) 228-7656 ppinet@colgate.edu,
  Colgate University – Ou
Pingitore, Jr., Nicholas E., (915) 747-5754 nick@geo.utep.edu,
  University of Texas, El Paso – Cl
Piniella Febrer, Juan Francesc, ++34935813088 juan.piniella@uab.cat,
  Universitat Autonoma de Barcelona – Gz
Pinkel, Robert, (858) 534-2056 rpinkel@ucsd.edu,
  University of California, San Diego – Op
Pinnt, Todd, todd.pinnt@azwestern.edu, Arizona Western College – Oyi
Pinter, Nicholas, (530) 754-1041 npinter@ucdavis.edu,
  University of California, Davis – Gm
Pinti, Daniele Luigi, 514-987-3000 #2572 pinti.daniele@uqam.ca,
  Universite du Quebec a Montreal – Cs
Pintilei, Mitica, 0040232401494 mpintilei@gmail.com,
  Al. I. Cuza University of Iasi – CgeCt
Piotrowski, Alexander, +44 (0) 1223 333473 apio04@esc.cam.ac.uk,
  University of Cambridge – Ge
Piper, David J., (902) 426-6580 dpiper@nrcan.gc.ca,
  Dalhousie University – Gu
Piper, John, +44 0151 794 3461 Sg04@liverpool.ac.uk,
  University of Liverpool – YmGt
Pipkin, Bernard W., (213) 740-6106 pipkin@usc.edu,
  University of Southern California – Ng
Pires, E M., (516) 299-2318 mark.pires@liu.edu,
  Long Island University, C.W. Post Campus – Og
Pirie, Diane H., (305) 348-2876 Florida International University – Gg
Pisias, Nicklas, npisias@coas.oregonstate.edu, Oregon State University – Gu
Pitlick, John, (303) 492-5906 pitlick@colorado.edu,
  University of Colorado – Gm
Pittman, Jason, (916) 608-6668 PittmaJ@flc.losrios.edu,
  Folsom Lake College – OgiOi
Pizzuto, James E., (302) 831-2710 pizzuto@udel.edu,
  University of Delaware – Gm
Plane, David A., plane@email.arizona.edu, University of Arizona – On
Plank, Gabriel, (775) 784-7039 gabe@seismo.unr.edu,
  University of Nevada, Reno – Ys
Plank, Owen C., (706) 542-9072 University of Georgia – Sc
Plank, Terry A., (845) 365-8410 tplank@ldeo.columbia.edu,
  Columbia University – GxCg
Plankell, Eric T., 217-265-8029 eplankel@illinois.edu,
  University of Illinois, Urbana-Champaign – Hw
Plant, Jane, +44 20 759 47416 jane.plant@imperial.ac.uk, Imperial College – Ge
Plant, Jeffrey J., (818) 393-3799 plant@jpl.nasa.gov,
  Jet Propulsion Laboratory – On
Plante, Alain, 215-898-9269 aplante@sas.upenn.edu,
  University of Pennsylvania – SbCoOs
Plante, Martin, (418) 656-8121 martin.plante@ggl.ulaval.ca,
  Universite Laval – Cg
Plasienka, Dusan, 0042160296529 plasienka@fns.uniba.sk,
  Comenius University – Gt
Platnick, Steven, steven.platnick@nasa.gov,
  University of Wisconsin, Madison – Or
Platt, Brian F., 662-915-5440 bfplatt@olemiss.edu,
  University of Mississippi – Pg
Platt, John, 213-821-1194 jplatt@usc.edu,
  University of Southern California – Gc
Platt, Rutherford H., (413) 545-2499 rplatt@geo.umass.edu,
  University of Massachusetts, Amherst – Ou
Plattner, Christina, 089/21804220 christina.plattner@geophysik.uni-muenchen.de,
  Ludwig-Maximilians-Universitaet Muenchen – Yg
Plescia, Jeffrey, (202) 358-0295 Jet Propulsion Laboratory – On
Plewe, Brandon, (801) 378-4161 brandon_plewe@byu.edu,
  Brigham Young University – Oi
Plink-Bjorklund, Piret, (303) 384-2042 pplink@mines.edu,
  Colorado School of Mines – Gs
Plint, A G., (519) 661-3179 gplint@uwo.ca, Western University – Gs
Plotkin, Pamela, 979-845-3902 plotkin@tamu.edu,
  Texas A&M University – Ob
Plotnick, Roy E., (312) 996-2111 plotnick@uic.edu,
  University of Illinois at Chicago – Pi
Plug, Lawrence, 902-494-1200 lplug@is.dal.ca, Dalhousie University – Gm
Pluhar, Chris, 559-278-1128 cpluhar@csufresno.edu,
  California State University, Fresno – NgGe
Plumb, Raymond A., (617) 253-6281 rap@rossby.mit.edu,
  Massachusetts Institute of Technology – Ow
Plummer, Charles C., plummercc@csus.edu,
  California State University, Sacramento – Gp
Plummer, Rebecca, (301) 405-6980 rplummer@umd.edu,
  University of Maryland – Csa
Plymate, Thomas G., (417) 836-4419 tomplymate@missouristate.edu,
  Missouri State University – Gx
Poch Serra, Joan, ++935811085 joan.poch@uab.cat,
  Universitat Autonoma de Barcelona – Gr
Pociask, Geoff, 217-265-8212 pociask@illinois.edu,
  University of Illinois, Urbana-Champaign – Hw
Podolak, Morris, (052) 838-0976 morris@post.tau.ac.il,
  Tel Aviv University – OnnOn
Poeter, Eileen P., (303) 273-3829 epoeter@mines.edu,
  Colorado School of Mines – Ng
Pogue, Kevin R., (509) 527-5955 pogue@whitman.edu, Whitman College – Gc
Pohll, Greg, 775-682-6349 greg.pohll@dri.edu,
  University of Nevada, Reno – Hwq
Poirier, Andre, 514-987-3000 #1718 Universite du Quebec a Montreal – Cs
Pojeta, John, (202) 633-1347 Smithsonian Institution / National Museum of
  Natural History – Pi
Pokorny, Eugene W., (702) 295-7496 eugene_pokorny@lanl.gov,
  Los Alamos National Laboratory – Nm
Pokras, Edward M., epokras@keene.edu, Keene State College – GgPmOb
Polat, Ali, 519-253-3000 x2495 polat@uwindsor.ca,
  University of Windsor – GixCc
Polet, Jascha, 909-869-3459 jjpolet@csupomona.edu,
  California State Polytechnic University, Pomona – Ysg
Polito, Thomas A., (515) 294-0513 tpolito@iastate.edu,
  Iowa State University of Science & Technology – So
Polk, Jason, jason.polk@wku.edu, Western Kentucky University – Gm
Pollack, Gerald, 770-274-5566 gerald.pollack@gpc.edu,
  Georgia Perimeter College – CaGiOe
Pollack, Henry N., (734) 763-0084 hpollack@umich.edu,
  University of Michigan – Yh
Pollack, Jennifer, 361-825-2041 Jennifer.Pollack@tamucc.edu,
  Texas A&M University, Corpus Christi – Ob
Pollak, Robert, pollak@wustl.edu, Washington University – On
Pollard, David D., (650) 723-4679 dpollard@pangea.stanford.edu,
  Stanford University – Gc
Pollock, Meagen, (330) 263-2202 mpollock@wooster.edu,
  College of Wooster – Gi
Polly, P D., (812) 855-7994 pdpolly@indiana.edu,
  Indiana University, Bloomington – PvgPq
Polovina, Jeffrey J., (808) 983-5390 jeffrey.polovina@noaa.gov,
  University of Hawai'i, Manoa – On
Polvani, Lorenzo M., (212) 854-7331 lmp3@columbia.edu,
  Columbia University – OwaGq
Polyak, Leonid, (614) 292-2602 polyak.1@osu.edu,
  Ohio State University – OgGr
Polyak, Victor J., 505-277-4204 polyak@unm.edu,
  University of New Mexico – Cg
Polzin, Dierk T., dtpolzin@wisc.edu, University of Wisconsin, Madison – Oa
Pomeroy, George M., (717) 477-1776 gmpome@ship.edu,
  Shippensburg University – Ou
Pond, Lisa G., (225) 578-0401 lgpond@lsu.edu,
  Louisiana State University – Gp
Pond, Stephen G., (604) 822-2205 spond@eos.ubc.ca,
  University of British Columbia – Op
Ponette-Gonzalez, Alexandra, 940-565-4012 alexandra.ponette@unt.edu,
  University of North Texas – On
Pons Muñoz, Josep Maria, ++935811054 josepmaria.pons@uab.cat,
  Universitat Autonoma de Barcelona – Pv
Poole, T. Craig, (559) 442-4600 craig.poole@fresnocitycollege.edu,
  Fresno City College – Gg
Pope, Gregory A., (973) 655-7385 popeg@mail.montclair.edu,
  Montclair State University – Gm
Pope, Jeanette K., 765-658-4105 jpope@depauw.edu,
  DePauw University – Ge
Pope, John P., (660) 562-1211 jppope@nwmissouri.edu,
  Northwest Missouri State University – Ps

University of Nevada – Gg
Price, Katie, 404-413-5780 kprice@gsu.edu,
 Georgia State University – HsGm
Price, Kevin, (785) 532-6101 kpprice@ksu.edu, Kansas State University – Or
Price, L G., (575) 835-5752 greer@nmbg.nmt.edu,
 New Mexico Institute of Mining & Technology – Gg
Price, Maribeth H., (605) 394-2468 Maribeth.Price@sdsmt.edu,
 South Dakota School of Mines & Technology – Oir
Price, Marie D., (202) 994-6187 George Washington University – Oy
Price, Nancy A., 503-725-3398 naprice@pdx.edu,
 Portland State University – GcOeGt
Price, Peter, (573) 368-2131 peter.price@dnr.mo.gov,
 Missouri Dept of Natural Resources – GeHy
Price, Peter E., 281-765-7764 Peter.E.Price@nhmccd.edu,
 Lonestar College - North Harris – Oi
Price, Raymond A., (613) 533-6542 pricera@queensu.ca, Queen's University – Gt
Price, Rene, (305) 348-3119 pricer@fiu.edu,
 Florida International University – Hw
Prichard, Hazel, +44(0)29 208 74323 Prichard@cardiff.ac.uk,
 University of Wales – EgGz
Prichard, Terry L., (559) 468-2086 tlprichard@ucdavis.edu,
 University of California, Davis – On
Prichonnet, Gilbert P., 514-987-3000 #3383 prichonnet.gilbert@uqam.ca,
 Universite du Quebec a Montreal – Pi
Prichystal, Antonín, +420 549 49 6699 prichy@sci.muni.cz ,
 Masaryk University – GgaGv
Pride, Douglas E., (614) 292-9523 pride.1@osu.edu,
 Ohio State University – Em
Pride, Steven, (510) 495-2823 SRPride@lbl.gov,
 University of California, Berkeley – Ys
Pridmore, Cindy L., (916) 925-6902 California Geological Survey – Ng
Priesendorf, Carl, (816) 604-2549 carl.priesendorf@mcckc.edu,
 Metropolitan Community College-Kansas City – GgOy
Priest, Eric, 847-543-6539 epriest@clcillinois.edu,
 College of Lake County – Owe
Priest, George R., (541) 574-6642 george.priest@dogami.state.or.us,
 Oregon Dept of Geology & Mineral Industries – Gg
Priestley, Keith, +44 (0) 1223 337195 University of Cambridge – YgGt
Prieto, Germán, 617-324-7279 gprieto@mit.edu,
 Massachusetts Institute of Technology – Ys
Primeau, Francois, 949-824-9435 fprimeau@uci.edu,
 University of California, Irvine – Op
Pringle, James M., (603) 862-5000 jpringle@cisunix.unh.edu,
 University of New Hampshire – Op
Pringle, Jamie, (+44) 01782 733163 j.k.pringle@keele.ac.uk,
 Keele University – Yg
Pringle, Patrick, 360-736-9361 ppringle@centralia.edu,
 Centralia College – OgGvOn
Prinn, Ronald G., 617-253-2452 rprinn@mit.edu,
 Massachusetts Institute of Technology – Oa
Prinz, Martin, (212) 769-5381 Graduate School of the City University of New
 York – Gi
Prior, William L., 501 683-0117 bill.prior@arkansas.gov,
 Arkansas Geological Survey – Oi
Pristas, Ronald, (609) 984-6587 ron.pristas@dep.state.nj.us,
 New Jersey Geological Survey – Oi
Pritchard, Matthew E., (607) 255-4870 mp337@cornell.edu,
 Cornell University – Gv
Pritchett, Brittany, 405-325-7331 brittanyp@ou.edu ,
 University of Oklahoma – Go
Privette, David, (704)330-6750 David.Privette@cpcc.edu,
 Central Piedmont Community College – Oy
Prohiæ, Esad, +38514605963 eprohic@geol.pmf.hr,
 University of Zagreb – CglGe
Proudhon, Benoit, +33(0)3 44068996 benoit.proudhon@lasalle-beauvais.fr,
 Institut Polytechnique LaSalle Beauvais (ex-IGAL) – GgcGt
Provin, Tony L., (979) 862-4955 t-provin@tamu.edu,
 Texas A&M University – Sc
Pruell, Richard J., (401) 782-3000 University of Rhode Island – Co
Pruss, Sara B., (413) 585-3948 spruss@smith.edu, Smith College – Pg
Pryor, Sara C., 607-255-3376 sp2279@cornell.edu, Cornell University – Oan
Prytulak, Julie, +44 20 759 46474 j.prytulak@imperial.ac.uk,
 Imperial College – Gg
Ptacek, Anton D., ptacek2@juno.com, San Diego State University – Gx
Pu, Zhaoxia, 801-585-3864 zhaoxia.pu@utah.edu, University of Utah – Oa
Puchtel, Igor, (301) 405-4054 ipuchtel@umd.edu,
 University of Maryland – CcgGi
Puckette, James, 405-744-6358 jim.puckette@okstate.edu,
 Oklahoma State University – Go
Puente, Carlos E., (916) 752-0689 University of California, Davis – Hg
Pufahl, Peir K., 902-585-1858 peir.pufahl@acadiau.ca,
 Acadia University – Gs
Puffer, John H., 973-353-5100 jpuffer@andromeda.rutgers.edu,
 Rutgers, The State University of New Jersey, Newark – Gi
Pugh, Teresa, 615 322 2975 teri.pugh@vanderbilt.edu,
 Vanderbilt University – On
Pujana, Ignacio, (972) 883-2461 pujana@utdallas.edu,
 University of Texas, Dallas – Pm
Pujol, Jose, (901) 678-4827 jpujol@memphis.edu,
 University of Memphis – Ye

Pullammanappallil, Satish, (775) 784-613 satish@seismo.unr.edu,
 University of Nevada, Reno – Ys
Pulliam, Jay, 512-471-0376 jay@ig.utexas.edu,
 University of Texas at Austin – Yg
Pulliam, Robert J., (512) 471-6156 jay@ig.utexas.edu,
 University of Texas at Austin – Ys
Pulliam, Robert J., (254)710-2183 jay_pulliam@baylor.edu,
 Baylor University – YsrYg
Pumphrey, Hugh C., +44 (0) 131 650 6026 Hugh.Pumphrey@ed.ac.uk,
 Edinburgh University – Oa
Pun, Aurora, (505) 277-5629 apun@unm.edu, University of New Mexico – Ca
Pundsack, Jonathan, 612-626-0505 pundsack@umn.edu,
 University of Minnesota, Twin Cities – On
Punyasena, Surangi, punyasena@life.illinois.edu,
 University of Illinois, Urbana-Champaign – Ge
Purcell, Rita, 781-283-3151 rpurcell@wellesley.edu, Wellesley College – On
Purdie, Duncan A., +44 (0)23 80592263 duncan.purdie@noc.soton.ac.uk,
 University of Southampton – Ob
Purdom, William B., (541) 552-6494 purdom@sou.edu,
 Southern Oregon University – Gx
Purdy, Ann, (248) 628-1562 Wayne State University – Gg
Purdy, G. Michael, (845) 365-8348 mpurdy@ldeo.columbia.edu,
 Columbia University – Yr
Purkiss, Robert, 325-486-6987 robert.purkiss@angelo.edu,
 Angelo State University – Gg
Purnell, Mark, +440116 252 3645 map2@le.ac.uk, Leicester University – Po
Purtle, Jennifer M., (501) 575-7317 jms14@comp.uark.edu,
 University of Arkansas, Fayetteville – On
Pusede, Sally, (434) 924-4544 sep6a@virginia.edu,
 University of Virginia – Oa
Putirka, Keith D., (559) 278-4524 kputirka@csufresno.edu,
 California State University, Fresno – GviGp
Putkonen, Jaakko, (701) 777-3213 jaakko.putkonen@engr.und.edu,
 University of North Dakota – Gl
Putnam, Aaron E., 207-581-2186 aaron.putnam@maine.edu,
 University of Maine – Gll
Putnam, Peter E., (403) 215-7850 University of Calgary – Gs
Putnam, Roger, RPutnam1@csustan.edu,
 California State University, Stanislaus – Ggi
Pyle, Eric J., 540-568-7115 pyleej@jmu.edu, James Madison University – Oe
Pyrtle, Ashanti J., apyrtle@seas.marine.usf.edu, University of South Florida – Oc
Pysklywec, Russell N., (416) 978-4852 russ@geology.utoronto.ca,
 University of Toronto – Yg
Pytlik, Laura, 740-376-4775 pytlikl@marietta.edu, Marietta College – On
Pöllmann, Herbert, +345 5526110 herbert.poellman@geo.uni-halle.de,
 Martin-Luther-Universitaet Halle-Wittenberg – Gz

Q

Qi, Feng, (908) 737-3702 fqi@kean.edu, Kean University – OiyOu
Qiu, Bo, (808) 956-4098 bo@soest.hawaii.edu,
 University of Hawai'i, Manoa – Op
Qiu, Xiaomin, (417) 836-3129 qiu@missouristate.edu,
 Missouri State University – Oi
Qu, Deyang, deyang.qu@umb.edu, University of Massachusetts, Boston – Om
Quade, Jay, 520-626-3223 quadej@email.arizona.edu,
 University of Arizona – Sc
Qualls, Robert G., (775) 327-5014 qualls@unr.edu,
 University of Nevada, Reno – On
Quan, Tracy, 405-744-6358 tracy.quan@okstate.edu,
 Oklahoma State University – Og
Quattro, Joseph M., 803-777-3240 josephq@mailbox.sc.edu,
 University of South Carolina – Ob
Quay, Paul D., (206) 545-8061 pdquay@u.washington.edu,
 University of Washington – Oc
Quick, Thomas J., (330) 972-6935 tquick@uakron.edu,
 University of Akron – Ca
Quigg, Antonietta, 409 740 4990 quigga@tamu.edu,
 Texas A&M University – Ob
Quinn, Claire, +44(0) 113 34 38700 c.h.quinn@leeds.ac.uk,
 University of Leeds – Ge
Quinn, Heather, 410-554-5522 heather.quinn@maryland.gov,
 Maryland Department of Natural Resources – GrOi
Quinn, James G., (401) 874-6219 jgquinn@gso.uri.edu,
 University of Rhode Island – Oc
Quinn, John, (630) 252-5357 quinnj@anl.gov, Argonne National Laboratory – Hw
Quinn, Paul, +44 (0) 191 208 5773 p.f.quinn@ncl.ac.uk,
 University of Newcastle Upon Tyne – Hg
Quinn, Terry, 512-471-0377 quinn@ig.utexas.edu,
 University of Texas at Austin – Pe
Quintanilla Terminal, Alejandra, aquintan@umn.edu,
 University of Minnesota, Twin Cities – Yx
Quintero, Sylvia, (520) 621-6025 squinter@email.arizona.edu,
 University of Arizona – On

R

Rabalais, Nancy N., (225) 851-2800 Louisiana State University – Ob
Raber, George, 601-266-5807 george.raber@usm.edu,
 University of Southern Mississippi – Oi
Rack, Frank, frack2@unl.edu, University of Nebraska, Lincoln – Ou

Rayne, Todd W., (315) 859-4698 trayne@hamilton.edu,
    Hamilton College – Hy
Rayner, John N., (614) 292-2514 Ohio State University – Oa
Rea, David K., (734) 936-0521 davidrea@umich.edu,
    University of Michigan – Gu
Read, Adam S., (505) 366-2533 adamread@gis.nmt.edu,
    New Mexico Institute of Mining & Technology – Gg
Read, J. Fred, (540) 231-5124 jread@vt.edu,
    Virginia Polytechnic Institute & State University – Gs
Reading, Anya, 61 3 6226 2477 anya.reading@utas.edu.au,
    University of Tasmania – Ysg
Reagan, Mark K., (319) 335-1802 mark-reagan@uiowa.edu,
    University of Iowa – Gi
Reams, Max W., (815) 939-5394 mreams@olivet.edu,
    Olivet Nazarene University – GsmPg
Reaven, Sheldon, (631) 632-8765 sheldon.reaven@stonybrook.edu,
    SUNY, Stony Brook – On
Reavy, John, +353 21 4902886 j.reavy@ucc.ie, University College Cork – Gi
Reay, David, +44 (0) 131 650 7723 david.reay@ed.ac.uk,
    Edinburgh University – Oa
Reay, William G., 804-684-7119 wreay@vims.edu,
    College of William & Mary – Hg
Reber, Jacqueline, (515) 294-7513 jreber@iastate.edu,
    Iowa State University of Science & Technology – Gct
Reboulet, Edward, 785-864-2173 reboulet@kgs.ku.edu,
    University of Kansas – Hy
Rech, Jason, 513-529-1935 rechja@MiamiOh.edu, Miami University – Gm
Rechcigl, John E., 813-633-4111 rechcigl@ufl.edu,
    University of Florida – So
Reche Estrada, Joan, ++935811781 joan.reche@uab.cat,
    Universitat Autonoma de Barcelona – GpCp
Rechtien, Richard D., (573) 341-4616 Missouri University of Science and
    Technology – Ye
Rector, James W., (510) 643-7820 University of California, Berkeley – Ye
Redalje, Donald G., (228) 688-1174 donald.redalje@usm.edu,
    University of Southern Mississippi – Ob
Redden, Jack A., (605) 394-2461 South Dakota School of Mines & Technology – Gp
Redden, Marcella, 205-247-3654 mmcintyre@gsa.state.al.us,
    Geological Survey of Alabama – Gg
Reddy, Christopher M., (508) 289-2316 creddy@whoi.edu,
    Woods Hole Oceanographic Institution – Co
Reddy, Gudigopuram B., 336-334-7543 reddyg@ncat.edu,
    North Carolina Agricultural & Tech State University – So
Reddy, K R., (352) 392-1803 krr@ufl.edu, University of Florida – Sf
Redfern, Jonathan, +440161 275-3773 Jonathan.Redfern@manchester.ac.uk,
    University of Manchester – Gso
Redfern, Simon, +44 (0) 1223 333475 satr@cam.ac.uk,
    University of Cambridge – Gz
Redmond, Brian T., (570) 408-4803 brian.redmond@wilkes.edu,
    Wilkes University – Gs
Ree, Jin-Han, 82-2-3290-3175 reejh@korea.ac.kr,
    Korea University – Gct
Reece, Julia S., 979-458-2728 jreece@geos.tamu.edu,
    Texas A&M University – SpGso
Reed, Denise J., (504) 280-7395 djreed@uno.edu,
    University of New Orleans – Gm
Reed, Donald L., (408) 924-5036 donald.reed@sjsu.edu,
    San Jose State University – GuYg
Reed, Mark H., (541) 346-5587 mhreed@uoregon.edu,
    University of Oregon – Em
Reed, Robert, (512) 475-8786 rob.reed@beg.utexas.edu,
    University of Texas at Austin, Jackson School of Geosciences – Gc
Reed, Wallace E., wer@virginia.edu, University of Virginia – Or
Reeder, Richard J., 631-632-8208 rjreeder@stonybrook.edu,
    SUNY, Stony Brook – ClGz
Reedy, Robert C., (512) 471-7244 bob.reedy@beg.utexas.edu,
    University of Texas at Austin, Jackson School of Geosciences – Hg
Reedy, Robert C., (505) 277-0300 rreedy@unm.edu,
    University of New Mexico – Xcy
Rees, Margaret N., (702) 895-3890 peg.rees@unlv.edu,
    University of Nevada, Las Vegas – Gs
Reese, Andy, 601-266-4729 andy.reese@usm.edu,
    University of Southern Mississippi – Oy
Reese, Joseph F., (814) 732-2529 jreese@edinboro.edu,
    Edinboro University of Pennsylvania – Gc
Reese, Stuart O., 717.702.2028 sreese@pa.gov,
    Pennsylvania Bureau of Topographic & Geologic Survey – Hw
Reesman, Authur L., 615-322-2976 Vanderbilt University – Gg
Reeve, Andrew S., (207) 581-2353 asreeve@maine.edu,
    University of Maine – Hw
Reeves, Claire, +44 (0)1603 59 3625 c.reeves@uea.ac.uk,
    University of East Anglia – Cg
Reeves, Donald Matt, (907) 786-1372 dmreeves2@uaa.alaska.edu,
    University of Alaska, Anchorage – GeHgOn
Refenes, James L., (734) 995-7594 james.refenes@cuaa.edu,
    Concordia University – Oe
Refsnider, Kurt, (928) 350-2256 kurt.refsnider@prescott.edu,
    Prescott College – GmlPe
Regalla, Christine, cregalla@bu.edu, Boston University – Gt
Reganold, John P., (509) 335-8856 reganold@wsu.edu,
    Washington State University – Ou
Regehr, David, (785) 532-6101 dregehr@ksu.edu,
    Kansas State University – So
Reháková, Daniela, +421260296700 rehakova@fns.uniba.sk,
    Comenius University – PgmPe
Rehkamper, Mark, +44 20 759 46391 markrehk@imperial.ac.uk,
    Imperial College – Cs
Rehm, George W., (612) 625-6210 grehm@soils.umn.edu,
    University of Minnesota, Twin Cities – Sc
Reichard, James S., (912) 478-1153 JReich@GeorgiaSouthern.edu,
    Georgia Southern University – Hw
Reichard, Ronnal, (321) 674-7522 Florida Institute of Technology – Oo
Reichenbacher, Bettina, 089/2180 6603 b.reichenbacher@lrz.uni-muenchen.de,
    Ludwig-Maximilians-Universitaet Muenchen – Pg
Reichler, Thomas, 801-585-0040 thomas.reichler@utah.edu,
    University of Utah – Oa
Reid, Arch M., 713-893-1327 areid@uh.edu, University of Houston – Gi
Reid, Brian, +44 (0)1603 59 2357 b.reid@uea.ac.uk,
    University of East Anglia – GeCg
Reid, Catherine, 3667001 Ext 7764 catherine.reid@canterbury.ac.nz,
    University of Canterbury – Po
Reid, Jeffrey C., (919) 707-9205 Jeff.Reid@ncdenr.gov,
    North Carolina Geological Survey
Reid, Joseph L., (858) 534-2055 jreid@ucsd.edu,
    University of California, San Diego – Op
Reid, Joshua, josh.reid@umb.edu, University of Massachusetts, Boston – Ga
Reid, Leslie, (707) 825-2933 lreid@fs.fed.us,
    Humboldt State University – Gm
Reid, Mary R., (928) 523-7200 mary.reid@nau.edu,
    Northern Arizona University – Gi
Reid, Ruth P., 305 421-4606 preid@rsmas.miami.edu,
    University of Miami – Gs
Reid, Steven K., 606-783-5293 s.reid@morehead-st.edu,
    Morehead State University – Gs
Reidel, Stephen P., (509) 376-9932 sreidel@wsu.edu,
    Washington State University – Gi
Reidenbach, Matthew A., (434) 243-4937 mar5jj@virginia.edu,
    University of Virginia – Hg
Reif, Samantha, 217-786-2764 Samantha.Reif@llcc.edu,
    Lincoln Land Community College – Gg
Reijmer, John, j.j.g.reijmer@vu.nl,
    VU University Amsterdam – Gsu
Reilinger, Robert E., (617) 253-7860 reilinge@erl.mit.edu,
    Massachusetts Institute of Technology – Yg
Reimer, Andreas, +49 (0)551 392164 areimer@gwdg.de,
    Georg-August University of Goettingen – OcCmm
Reimers, Clare, 541-737-0220 creimers@coas.oregonstate.edu,
    Oregon State University – Oc
Reinen, Linda A., (909) 621-8672 lreinen@pomona.edu,
    Pomona College – Gct
Reiners, Peter, 520-626-2236 reiners@email.arizona.edu,
    University of Arizona – Cg
Reinfelder, John R., 848-932-8013 reinfelder@envsci.rutgers.edu,
    Rutgers, The State University of New Jersey – Cl
Reinfelder, Ying Fan, (848) 445-2044 yingfan@rci.rutgers.edu,
    Rutgers, The State University of New Jersey – HwyOw
Reinhardt, Edward G., (905) 525-9140 (Ext. 27594) ereinhar@mcmaster.ca,
    McMaster University – Pm
Reioux, David, 907-451-5968 david.reioux@alaska.gov,
    Alaska Division of Geological & Geophysical Surveys – Gg
Reisner, Jon M., (505) 665-1889 reisner@lanl.gov,
    Los Alamos National Laboratory – Oa
Reiss, Nathan, (212) 346-1502 Pace University, New York Campus – Oa
Reiten, Jon C., 406-657-2630 jreiten@mtech.edu,
    Montana Tech of The University of Montana – Hw
Reiter, Marshall A., (505) 835-5306 mreiter@nmt.edu,
    New Mexico Institute of Mining & Technology – Yh
Reitner, Joachim, +49 (0)551 397950 jreitne@gwdg.de,
    Georg-August University of Goettingen – PyyPy
Reitz, Elizabeth J., (706) 542-1464 ereitz@arches.uga.edu,
    University of Georgia – Ga
Remacha Grau, Eduard, ++935811603 eduard.remacha@uab.cat,
    Universitat Autonoma de Barcelona – Gro
Remenda, Victoria H., (613) 533-6594 remendav@queensu.ca,
    Queen's University – Hw
Rempel, Alan W., 541-346-6316 rempel@uoregon.edu,
    University of Oregon – Nr
Remson, Irwin, (650) 723-9191 Stanford University – Hw
Renard, Robert J., 831-375-2354 bobandotty@aol.com,
    Naval Postgraduate School – Ow
Renaut, Robin W., (306) 966-5705 robin.renaut@usask.ca,
    University of Saskatchewan – Gs
Reneau, Raymond B., (540) 231-9779 reneau@vt.edu,
    Virginia Polytechnic Institute & State University – Sc
Reneau, Steven L., (505) 665-3151 sreneau@lanl.gov,
    Los Alamos National Laboratory – Gm
Renfrew, Bonnie, 217-244-2430 renfrew@isgs.uiuc.edu,
    Illinois State Geological Survey – On
Renfrew, Ian, +44 (0)1603 59 2557 i.renfrew@uea.ac.uk,
    University of East Anglia – Ow

Richter, Frank M., (773) 702-8118 richter@geosci.uchicago.edu,
  University of Chicago – Gt
Richter, Suzanna L., (717) 358-5843 suzanna.richter@fandm.edu,
  Franklin and Marshall College – Ge
Ricka, Adam, +420 549 49 6605 ricka@sci.muni.cz ,
  Masaryk University – Hgy
Rickaby, Ros, +44 (1865) 272034 rosalind.rickaby@earth.ox.ac.uk,
  University of Oxford – Gz
Rickard, D, rickard@cf.ac.uk, Cardiff University – Cg
Rickerl, Dianne H., (605) 688-5541 Timothy.Nichols@sdstate.edu,
  South Dakota State University – Sf
Ricketts, Hugo, +44 0161 306-3911 h.ricketts@manchester.ac.uk,
  University of Manchester – Oa
Ridd, Merrill K., (801) 581-7939 merrill.ridd@geog.utah.edu,
  University of Utah – Or
Riddick, Pamela M., priddick@memphis.edu, University of Memphis – On
Riddle, Emily, 607-242-4579 emily.riddle@noaa.gov,
  University of Massachusetts, Amherst – Oa
Ridenour, Gregory D., (931) 221-7454 ridenourg@apsu.edu,
  Austin Peay State University – OiaOn
Ridge, John C., 617-627-3494 jack.ridge@tufts.edu, Tufts University – Gln
Ridgway, Kenneth D., (765) 494-3269 ridge@purdue.edu,
  Purdue University – Gs
Ridgwell, Andy, (951) 827-3186 andy@seao2.org,
  University of California, Riverside – On
Riding, Robert, 865-974-2366 rriding@utk.edu,
  University of Tennessee, Knoxville – Gs
Ridky, Alice M., (207) 859-5800 amridky@colby.edu,
  Colby College – On
Ridley, DeAnna, 207-778-7363 DRIDLEY@maine.edu,
  University of Maine - Farmington – On
Ridley, John R., (970) 491-5943 jridley@cnr.colostate.edu,
  Colorado State University – Eg
Ridley, Moira K., 806-834-0627 moira.ridley@ttu.edu,
  Texas Tech University – Cl
Riebe, Clifford S., 307-766-3965 criebe@uwyo.edu,
  University of Wyoming – ClGme
Riebesell, John, (313) 593-5132 jriebese@umich.edu,
  University of Michigan, Dearborn – Ou
Riedel, Oliver, 089/2180 4335 oliver.riedl@lrz.uni-muenchen.de,
  Ludwig-Maximilians-Universitaet Muenchen – Gz
Rieder, Michael, +49 89 28925864 rieder@tum.de,
  Technische Universitaet Muenchen – GgxGs
Riediger, Cynthia L., (403) 220-8783 riediger@geo.ucalgary.ca,
  University of Calgary – Co
Riedinger, Natascha, 405-744-6358 natascha.riedinger@okstate.edu,
  Oklahoma State University – CgGu
Rieger, Duayne, 814-341-1674 drieger@ccri.edu,
  Community College of Rhode Island – Ys
Rieke, George H., (520) 621-2832 grieke@as.arizona.edu,
  University of Arizona – On
Rieke, Herman H., 337-482-6556 hhr8668@louisiana.edu,
  University of Louisiana at Lafayette – Np
Rieken, Eric R., (210) 381-3526 University of Texas, Pan American – Gt
Riemer, Nicole, 217-244-2844 nriemer@illinois.edu,
  University of Illinois, Urbana-Champaign – Oa
Riemersma, Peter E., 616-331-3553 riemersp@gvsu.edu,
  Grand Valley State University – Hw
Rieppel, Olivier C., (312) 665-7630 orieppel@fieldmuseum.org,
  Field Museum of Natural History – Pv
Ries, Justin, 7815817370 x342 j.ries@neu.edu,
  Northeastern University – Cm
Rietbrock, Andreas, +44-151-794-5181 A.Rietbrock@liverpool.ac.uk,
  University of Liverpool – YsGv
Rietmeijer, Frans J., (505) 277-5733 fransjmr@unm.edu,
  University of New Mexico – Gp
Rigby, John, 61 7 3138 1638 j.rigby@qut.edu.au,
  Queensland University of Technology – Pb
Riggs, Eric, 9798453651 emriggs@geos.tamu.edu, Texas A&M University – Gy
Riggs, Nancy, (928) 523-9362 nancy.riggs@nau.edu,
  Northern Arizona University – Gv
Riggs, Stanley R., (252) 328-6015 riggss@ecu.edu, East Carolina University – Gu
Rignot, Eric, 949-824-3739 erignot@uci.edu,
  University of California, Irvine – Ol
Rigo, Manuel, +390498279175 manuel.rigo@unipd.it,
  Università degli Studi di Padova – Gs
Rigsby, Catherine A., (252) 328-4297 rigsbyc@ecu.edu,
  East Carolina University – Gs
Riha, Susan, (607) 255-1729 sjr4@cornell.edu, Cornell University – Sf
Riker-Coleman, Kristin E., 715-394-8410 krikerco@uwsuper.edu,
  University of Wisconsin, Superior – Gg
Riley, James, (520) 626-6681 jjriley@ag.arizona.edu,
  University of Arizona – On
Riley, Rhonda, riley@suu.edu, Southern Utah University – On
Riley, Ronald A., (614) 265-6573 ron.riley@dnr.state.oh.us,
  Ohio Dept of Natural Resources – Go
Riller, Ulrich, rilleru@mcmaster.ca, McMaster University – Og
Rimmer, Susan M., (618) 453-7369 srimmer@geo.siu.edu,
  Southern Illinois University Carbondale – EcCgGo
Rimstidt, J. Donald, (540) 231-6894 jdr02@vt.edu,

Virginia Polytechnic Institute & State University – Cl
Rinard, Bethany D., (254) 968-9894 hingabd@unk.edu,
  Tarleton State University – Gv
Rind, David H., (212) 678-5593 drind@giss.nasa.gov,
  Columbia University – Oar
Rindsberg, Andrew K., 205 652 3416 arindsberg@uwa.edu,
  University of West Alabama – PeGePi
Rink, W. J., (905) 525-9140 (Ext. 24178) rinkwj@mcmaster.ca,
  McMaster University – Cc
Rinterknecht, Vincent, +44 01334 462382 vr10@st-andrews.ac.uk,
  University of St. Andrews – Ol
Riordan, Allen J., (919) 515-7973 al_riordan@ncsu.edu,
  North Carolina State University – Oa
Riordan, Jean, (907) 696-0079 jean.riordan@alaska.gov,
  Alaska Division of Geological & Geophysical Surveys – Gg
Rios-Sanchez, Miriam, 218-755-2595 mriossanchez@bemidjistate.edu,
  Bemidji State University – HwOr
Ripley, Edward M., (812) 855-1196 ripley@indiana.edu,
  Indiana University, Bloomington – Em
Riser, Stephen C., (206) 543-1187 riser@ocean.washington.edu,
  University of Washington – Op
Risk, Dave A., drisk@stfx.ca, Saint Francis Xavier University – Osr
Risk, Michael J., (905) 525-9140 riskmj@mcmaster.ca,
  McMaster University – Po
Ritchie, Alexander W., (843) 953-5591 ritchiea@cofc.edu,
  College of Charleston – Gc
Ritchie, Harold C., (902) 494-5192 hritchie@phys.ocean.dal.ca,
  Dalhousie University – Ow
Ritsche, Michael, 630-252-1554 mtritsche@anl.gov,
  Argonne National Laboratory – Oa
Ritsema, Jeroen, 734-615-6405 jritsema@umich.edu,
  University of Michigan – Ys
Rittenour, Tammy M., 435-797-3282 tammy.rittenour@usu.edu,
  Utah State University – Gm
Ritter, Charles J., (937) 229-2953 University of Dayton – Ct
Ritter, Joachim J., +49-721-6084539 joachim.ritter@kit.edu,
  Karlsruhe Institute of Technology – Ys
Ritter, John B., (937) 327-7332 jritter@wittenberg.edu,
  Wittenberg University – Gm
Ritter, Leonard, (519) 824-4120 Ext.52980 lritter@uoguelph.ca,
  University of Guelph – On
Ritter, Michael E., 715-346-4449 mritter@uwsp.edu,
  University of Wisconsin, Stevens Point – Ow
Ritter, Paul, (309) 268-8640 paul.ritter@heartland.edu,
  Heartland Community College – Og
Ritter, Scott M., 801-4224239 scott_ritter@byu.edu,
  Brigham Young University – Ps
Ritterbush, Linda A., (805) 493-3265 ritterbu@clunet.edu,
  California Lutheran University – Pi
Ritz, Richard, (402) 280-2461 richard.ritz@afwa.af.mil,
  Creighton University – Ow
Ritzi, Jr., Robert W., 937 775-3455 robert.ritzi@wright.edu,
  Wright State University – Hw
Rius, Marc, +44 (0)23 8059 3275 M.Rius@soton.ac.uk,
  University of Southampton – Ob
Rivard, Benoit, (780) 492-0345 benoit.rivard@ualberta.ca,
  University of Alberta – Or
Rivera, Edna L., 312-996-6123 eriver15@uic.edu,
  University of Illinois at Chicago – On
Rivera, Mark, 907-786-1235 marivera@uaa.alaska.edu,
  University of Alaska, Anchorage – Gg
Rivers, Toby C. J. S., (709) 737-8392 trivers@sparky2.esd.mun.ca,
  Memorial University of Newfoundland – Gp
Rizeli, Mustafa Eren, 00904242370000-5961 merizeli@firat.edu.tr,
  Firat University – Gxi
Rizoulis, Athanasios, +44 0161 275-0311 A.Rizoulis@manchester.ac.uk,
  University of Manchester – Ge
Roach, Michael, 61 3 6226 2474 University of Tasmania – Yg
Roadcap, George S., (217) 333-7951 Illinois State Water Survey – Hw
Robarge, Wayne P., (919) 515-1454 North Carolina State University – Sc
Robas, Sheryl A., (609) 258-6144 srobas@princeton.edu,
  Princeton University – On
Robbins, Debra C., (828) 251-6441 drobbins@unca.edu,
  University of North Carolina, Asheville – On
Robbins, Gary A., (860) 486-2448 gary.robbins@uconn.edu,
  University of Connecticut – Hw
Robert, Genevieve, (207) 786-6105 grobert@bates.edu,
  Bates College – Cp
Robert, Sanborn, (262) 335-5263 robert.sanborn@uwc.edu,
  University of Wisconsin Colleges – GgOyn
Roberts, A. Lynn, (410) 516-4387 lroberts@jhu.edu,
  Johns Hopkins University – On
Roberts, Charles E., (561) 297-3254 croberts@fau.edu,
  Florida Atlantic University – Or
Roberts, Frank, (504) 388-2964 Montgomery County Community College – Gp
Roberts, Gerald, +44 020 3073 8033 gerald.roberts@ucl.ac.uk,
  Birkbeck College – Ne
Roberts, Harry H., (225) 388-2964 harry@antares.esl.lsu.edu,
  Louisiana State University – Gs
Roberts, Jennifer A., (785) 864-4997 jenrob@ku.edu,

University of Kansas – Py

Roberts, Mark L., (508) 289-3654 mroberts@whoi.edu,
Woods Hole Oceanographic Institution – Yg

Roberts, Paul H., (310) 206-2707 roberts@math.ucla.edu,
University of California, Los Angeles – Ym

Roberts, Peter, (505) 667-1199 proberts@lanl.gov,
Los Alamos National Laboratory – Ys

Roberts, Sarah K., (925) 423-4112 roberts28@llnl.gov,
Lawrence Livermore National Laboratory – Cl

Roberts, Sheila J., (419) 372-0354 sjrober@bgnet.bgsu.edu,
Bowling Green State University – CgHw

Roberts, Sheila M., (406) 683-7017 sheila.roberts@umwestern.edu,
University of Montana Western – Ge

Roberts, Stephen, +44 ()023 80593246 steve.roberts@noc.soton.ac.uk,
University of Southampton – Cg

Roberts Briggs, Tiffany M., 561-297-4669 briggst@fau.edu,
Florida Atlantic University – On

Robertson, Alastair H., +44 (0) 131 650 8546 Alastair.Robertson@ed.ac.uk,
Edinburgh University – Gt

Robertson, Andrew W., 845-680-4491 awr@iri.columbia.edu,
Columbia University – Oa

Robertson, Charles E., (573) 341-4616 Missouri University of Science and
Technology – Gc

Robertson, Daniel E., 585-292-2422 drobertson@monroecc.edu,
Monroe Community College – Eg

Robertson, James M., (608) 263-7384 jmrober1@facstaff.wisc.edu,
University of Wisconsin, Madison – Eg

Robin, Michel R., 613-562-5800 Ext 6852 mrobin@uottawa.ca,
University of Ottawa – Hw

Robin, Pierre-Yves F., 905 828-5419 University of Toronto – Gc

Robinson, Alexander, 713-743-2547 acrobinson@uh.edu,
University of Houston – Gc

Robinson, Bruce A., (505) 667-1910 robinson@lanl.gov,
Los Alamos National Laboratory – On

Robinson, Carol, +44 (0)1603 59 3174 carol.robinson@uea.ac.uk,
University of East Anglia – Ob

Robinson, Clare, +44 0161 275-3296 A.Rizoulis@manchester.ac.uk,
University of Manchester – Co

Robinson, Cordula, cordula@crsa.bu.edu, Boston University – Gm

Robinson, David, +44 (0)1908 653493 x 53493 david.robinson@open.ac.uk ,
The Open University – On

Robinson, Delores, dmr@ua.edu, University of Alabama – Gc

Robinson, Edward, (305) 348-3572 draper@fiu.edu,
Florida International University – Pm

Robinson, Edwin S., (540) 231-6521 esrobinson@vt.edu,
Virginia Polytechnic Institute & State University – Yg

Robinson, Francis J., (203) 432-2033 francis.robinson@yale.edu,
Yale University – Gg

Robinson, George W., grobinson@stlawu.edu, St. Lawrence University – Gz

Robinson, Ian S., +44 (0)23 80593438 isr@noc.soton.ac.uk,
University of Southampton – Or

Robinson, Judith, 973-353-1976 judy.robinson@rutgers.edu,
Rutgers, The State University of New Jersey, Newark – Yg

Robinson, Kevin, (619) 594-1386 rockrobinson@gmail.com,
San Diego State University – Gc

Robinson, Leonie, +44 0151 795 4387 Leonie.Robinson@liverpool.ac.uk,
University of Liverpool – Ob

Robinson, Lori, (612) 626-7429 robin126@umn.edu,
University of Minnesota – Oi

Robinson, Mark, (480) 727-9691 mark.s.robinson@asu.edu,
Arizona State University – On

Robinson, Michael, (912) 598-3310 mike.robinson@skio.usg.edu,
Georgia Southern University – Oin

Robinson, Michael A., marobinson3@sbcc.edu,
Santa Barbara City College – OyiOw

Robinson, Paul D., (618) 453-7373 robinson@geo.siu.edu,
Southern Illinois University Carbondale – Gz

Robinson, Paul T., (902) 494-2361 Dalhousie University – Gv

Robinson, Peter, (413) 545-2286 University of Massachusetts, Amherst – Gc

Robinson, Peter, 303-492-5211 peter.robinson@colorado.edu,
University of Colorado – Pv

Robinson, R. Craig, (860) 832-2950 Central Connecticut State University – Xy

Robinson, Richard, robinson_richard@smc.edu,
Santa Monica College – Gg

Robinson, Richard A., (785) 864-2739 rrobin@ku.edu,
University of Kansas – Pg

Robinson, Ruth, +44 01334 463996 rajr@st-andrews.ac.uk,
University of St. Andrews – Gs

Robinson, Sarah, (719) 333-9287 sarah.robinson@usafa.edu,
United States Air Force Academy – GgOi

Robinson, Steve, j.s.robinson@reading.ac.uk, University of Reading – Sf

Robinson, Stuart, +44 (1865) 272058 stuartr@earth.ox.ac.uk,
University of Oxford – Gdr

Robinson, Walter, 919-515-7002 walter_robinson@ncsu.edu,
North Carolina State University – Oa

Robinson, Walter A., (217) 333-2292 robinson@atmos.uiuc.edu,
University of Illinois, Urbana-Champaign – Oa

Robinson, William, william.robinson@umb.edu,
University of Massachusetts, Boston – On

Rocha, Guillermo, 7189515000 x2887 grocha@brooklyn.cuny.edu,

Brooklyn College (CUNY) – Gg

Roche, James E., (225) 388-2707 jroche@geol.lsu.edu,
Louisiana State University – Gg

Rochester, Michael G., (709) 737-7565 mrochest@morgan.ucs.mun.ca,
Memorial University of Newfoundland – Yg

Rochette, Elizabeth A., (603) 862-0713 University of New Hampshire – Sc

Rochette, Scott M., (585) 395-2603 srochett@brockport.edu,
SUNY, The College at Brockport – Ow

Rocholl, Alexander, 089/2180 4293 rocholl@min.uni-muenchen.de,
Ludwig-Maximilians-Universitaet Muenchen – Gz

Rock, Jessie, 701-231-7951 jessie.rock@ndsu.edu,
North Dakota State University – Og

Rockaway, John D., 859-572-5412 rockawayj@nku.edu,
Northern Kentucky University – Ng

Rockwell, Thomas K., (619) 594-4441 trockwell@mail.sdsu.edu,
San Diego State University – Gm

Rockwood, Anthony A., (303) 556-8399 Metropolitan State College of Denver – Ow

Rocque, David, 207-287-2666 david.rocque@maine.gov,
Dept of Agriculture, Conservation, and Forestry – Sd

Rodbell, Donald T., (518) 388-6034 rodbelld@union.edu,
Union College – GlmGe

Roden, Eric E., (608) 260-0724 eroden@geology.wisc.edu,
University of Wisconsin, Madison – Py

Roden, Gunnar I., (206) 543-5627 giroden@u.washington.edu,
University of Washington – Op

Roden, Michael F., (706) 542-2416 mroden@uga.edu,
University of Georgia – Gi

Rodgers, David W., 208-282-4634 rodgdavi@isu.edu,
Idaho State University – Gc

Rodgers, Jim, (307) 766-2286 Ext. 255 james.rodgers@wyo.gov ,
Wyoming State Geological Survey – Gg

Rodgers, John C., (662) 325-0732 jcr100@msstate.edu,
Mississippi State University – Oy

Rodgers, N, RodgersN@cf.ac.uk, Cardiff University – Ow

Rodgers, Nick, +44(0)29 208 79064 RodgersN@cardiff.ac.uk,
University of Wales – Xm

Rodi, William, (617) 253-7855 rodi@mit.edu,
Massachusetts Institute of Technology – Yg

Rodland, David, (740) 826-8425 drodland@muskingum.edu,
Muskingum University – PgiPe

Rodolfo, Kelvin S., krodolfo@uic.edu, University of Illinois at Chicago – Gu

Rodrigues, Cyril G., 519-253-3000 ext. 2499 cgr@uwindsor.ca,
University of Windsor – Pm

Rodriguez, Joaquin, (212) 772-5321 Graduate School of the City University of
New York – Pi

Rodriguez, Vanessa del S., (787) 722-2526 Puerto Rico Bureau of Geology – On

Rodriguez-Iturbe, Ignacio, (609) 258-2287 irodrigu@princeton.edu,
Princeton University – Hg

Roe, Carol, 757-221-2440 crroex@wm.edu, College of William & Mary – On

Roe, Gerard H., 206-697-3298 gerard@ess.washington.edu,
University of Washington – OaGmOl

Roecker, Steven W., (518) 276-6773 roecks@rpi.edu,
Rensselaer Polytechnic Institute – Yg

Roegiers, Jean-Claude, (405) 325-6787 jroegiers@ou.edu,
University of Oklahoma – Nr

Roelofse, Frederick, +27 (0)51 401 9001 roelofsef@ufs.ac.za,
University of the Free State – Gip

Roemer, Elizabeth, (520) 621-2897 eroemer@pirlmail.lpl.arizona.edu,
University of Arizona – On

Roemmich, Dean H., (858) 534-2307 droemmich@ucsd.edu,
University of California, San Diego – Op

Roering, Joshua J., (541) 346-5574 jroering@uoregon.edu,
University of Oregon – Gm

Roeske, Sarah M., (530) 752-4933 smroeske@ucdavis.edu,
University of California, Davis – Gc

Roesler, Collin, 207-725-3842 croesler@bowdoin.edu,
Bowdoin College – OgpOr

Roethel, Frank J., (631) 632-8732 frank.roethel@stonybrook.edu,
SUNY, Stony Brook – Oc

Rogers, Garry C., (250) 363-6450 University of Victoria – Ys

Rogers, Jefferson S., (731) 881-7442 jrogers@utm.edu,
University of Tennessee, Martin – On

Rogers, Jeffery C., (614) 292-0148 rogers.21@osu.edu,
Ohio State University – Oa

Rogers, Joe D., 806-651-2570 West Texas A&M University – Ga

Rogers, Karyn L., (518) 276-2372 rogerk5@rpi.edu,
Rensselaer Polytechnic Institute – PyCl

Rogers, Pamela Z., (505) 667-1765 Los Alamos National Laboratory – Cl

Rogers, Raymond R., (651) 696-6434 rogersk@macalester.edu,
Macalester College – Gs

Rogers, Robert D., (209) 667-3466 rrogers1@csustan.edu,
California State University, Stanislaus – GcmGt

Rogers, Steven, (+44) 01782 733752 s.l.rogers@keele.ac.uk,
Keele University – Gg

Rogers, William J., 806-651-2581 West Texas A&M University – On

Rogerson, Robert J., (403) 329-5117 rogerson@uleth.ca,
University of Lethbridge – Gm

Roggenthen, William M., (605) 394-2461 William.Roggenthen@sdsmt.edu,
South Dakota School of Mines & Technology – NgYg

Rogowski, Andrew S., (814) 863-8758 asr@psu.edu,

Rutter, Nathaniel W., (780) 492-3085 nat.rutter@ualberta.ca,
University of Alberta – Ge
Ruzicka, Alexander (Alex) M., (503) 725-3372 ruzickaa@pdx.edu,
Portland State University – Xm
Ruzicka, Jaromir, jaromirr@hawaii.edu,
University of Hawai'i, Manoa – On
Ryall, Patrick J., (902) 494-3465 pryall@is.dal.ca,
Dalhousie University – Yg
Ryan, Cathy, (403) 220-2793 ryan@geo.ucalgary.ca,
University of Calgary – Hw
Ryan, Jeffrey G., (813) 974-1598 ryan@shell.cas.usf.edu ,
University of South Florida, Tampa – Ct
Ryan, Peter C., (802) 443-2557 pryan@middlebury.edu,
Middlebury College – Cl
Ryan, Susan, (724) 938-4531 ryan@calu.edu,
California University of Pennsylvania – Og
Ryan, William F., (814) 865-0478 Pennsylvania State University, University
Park – Ow
Ryan, William B. F., (845) 365-8312 Columbia University – Yr
Rychert, Catherine A., +44 (0)23 80598663 C.Rychert@soton.ac.uk,
University of Southampton – Yg
Ryder, Isabelle, +44-151-794-5143 I.Ryder@liverpool.ac.uk,
University of Liverpool – Gt
Ryder, Roy, rryder@southalabama.edu,
University of South Alabama – SdOry
Rye, Danny M., (203) 432-3174 danny.rye@yale.edu, Yale University – Cs
Rygel, Michael C., (315) 267-3401 rygelmc@potsdam.edu,
SUNY Potsdam – GsrGo
Rykaczewski, Ryan, 803-777-8159 rykaczer@mailbox.sc.edu,
University of South Carolina – Obp
Rysgaard, Soren, 204-272-1611 rysgaard@umanitoba.ca,
University of Manitoba – Gl
Rößner, Gertrud, 089/2180 6612 g.roessner@lrz.uni-muenchen.de,
Ludwig-Maximilians-Universitaet Muenchen – Pg

S

Sá, Artur A., asa@utad.pt, Universidade de Trás-os-Montes e Alto Douro – PgiPs
Saal, Alberto E., (401) 863-7238 Alberto_Saal@Brown.edu,
Brown University – Cg
Saalfeld, Alan J., 614 292 6665 saalfeld.1@osu.edu,
Ohio State University – Yd
Saar, Martin O., 612-625-7332 saar@umn.edu,
University of Minnesota, Twin Cities – Hg
Sabala-Foreman, Susan M., (928) 523-4561 Northern Arizona University – On
Sabine, Christopher L., (206) 526-4809 chris.sabine@noaa.gov,
University of Washington – Oc
Sablock, Jeanette M., jsablock@salemstate.edu, Salem State University – GzScOe
Sabra, Karim, (404) 385-6193 Georgia Institute of Technology – Yg
Sacchi, Mauricio D., (780) 492-1060 sacchi@phys.ualberta.ca,
University of Alberta – Ys
Saccocia, Peter J., psaccocia@bridgew.edu, Bridgewater State University – Cm
Sack, Richard, 425-880-4418 rosack@uw.edu, University of Washington – CgOn
Sacks, I. Selwyn, (202) 478-8839 ssacks@carnegiescience.edu,
Carnegie Institution of Washington – Ys
Sacramentogrilo, Isabelle, 619-594-5607 isacramentogrilo@mail.sdsu.edu,
San Diego State University – Gg
Sadd, James L., 323 259 2518 jsadd@oxy.edu, Occidental College – Oi
Sadiq, Abdulali A., sadiqa@qu.edu.qa, University of Qatar – Or
Sadler, Peter M., (951) 827-5616 peter.sadler@ucr.edu,
University of California, Riverside – GrPs
Sadowsky, Michael J., (612) 624-2706 sadowsky@soils.umn.edu,
University of Minnesota, Twin Cities – Sb
Saeidi, Ali, 418-545-5011, ext: 2561 asaeidi@uqac.ca,
Universite du Quebec a Chicoutimi – Nr
Saffer, Demian M., 814-865-7965 dsaffer@geosc.psu.edu,
Pennsylvania State University, University Park – Hw
Sagebiel, J. C., 909 307-2669 237 jsagebiel@sbcm.sbcounty.gov,
San Bernardino County Museum – Pv
Sageman, Bradley B., (847) 467-2257 brad@earth.northwestern.edu,
Northwestern University – PsGsPe
Sager, William W., (979) 845-9828 wsager@ocean.tamu.edu,
Texas A&M University – Ou
Sagiroglu, Ahmet, 00904242370000-5990 sagiroglu@firat.edu.tr,
Firat University – Egm
Sahagian, Dork, 610-758-6379 dork.sahagian@lehigh.edu,
Lehigh University – PeGvr
Sahay, Pratap, pratap@cicese.mx,
Centro de Investigación Científica y de Educación Superior de Ensenada – Ys
Sahoo, Prasanta, (321) 674-8147 Florida Institute of Technology – Oo
Sahr, John D., 206-616-7175 jdsahr@ee.washington.edu,
University of Washington – YgXy
Saila, Saul B., (401) 874-6485 saila@gso.uri.edu,
University of Rhode Island – Ob
Saillet, Elodie, +33(0)3 44067563 elodie.saillet@lasalle-beauvais.fr,
Institut Polytechnique LaSalle Beauvais (ex-IGAL) – GctGo
Saini-Eidukat, Bernhardt, (701) 231-8785 bernhardt.saini-eidukat@ndsu.edu,
North Dakota State University – GiCg
Saint, Prem K., psaint@fullerton.edu, California State University, Fullerton – Hw
Saito, Laurel, 775-784-1921 lsaito@cabnr.unr.edu,
University of Nevada, Reno – HsgHq

Saito, Mak A., 508-289-3696 msaito@whoi.edu,
Woods Hole Oceanographic Institution – Oc
Saja, David B., 2162314600 x3229 dsaja@cmnh.org,
Cleveland Museum of Natural History – Gdc
Sak, Peter B., 717-245-1423 sakp@dickinson.edu, Dickinson College – Gcm
Sakhaee-Pour, Ahmad, 405-325-3306 sakhaee@ou.edu,
University of Oklahoma – Np
Saku, James C., (301) 687-4724 jsaku@frostburg.edu,
Frostburg State University – On
Salami, B. M., 234-803-321-9685 salamibm@oauife.edu.ng,
Obafemi Awolowo University – Hg
Salami, Sikiru A., sikiru.salami@uniben.edu, University of Benin – YgeGg
Salathe Jr., Eric P., 206-616-5351 salathe@washington.edu,
University of Washington – Oa
Salaun, Pascal, +44-151-794-4101 Pascal.Salaun@liverpool.ac.uk,
University of Liverpool – Em
Salaun, Rachel, +440151 795 4649 Rachel.Jeffreys@liverpool.ac.uk ,
University of Liverpool – Oc
Saleeby, Jason B., (626) 395-6141 jason@gps.caltech.edu,
California Institute of Technology – Gc
Salisbury, Joseph, 603-862-0849 joe.salisbury@unh.edu,
University of New Hampshire – On
Salje, Ekhard, +44 (0) 1223 768321 ekhard@esc.cam.ac.uk,
University of Cambridge – Gy
Sallu, Susannah, +44(0) 113 34 31641 s.sallu@leeds.ac.uk,
University of Leeds – Ga
Salmon, Richard L., (858) 534-2090 rsalmon@ucsd.edu,
University of California, San Diego – Op
Salmun, Haydee, (212) 772-5224 hsalmun@hunter.cuny.edu,
Hunter College (CUNY) – Yg
Salters, Vincent J., (850) 644-1934 salters@magnet.fsu.edu,
Florida State University – Cg
Saltzman, Eric S., 949-824-3936 esaltzma@uci.edu,
University of California, Irvine – Oa
Saltzman, Matthew R., 614 292-0481 saltzman.11@osu.edu,
Ohio State University – Gs
Salviulo, Gabriella, +390498279157 gabriella.salviulo@unipd.it,
Università degli Studi di Padova – Gz
Salvucci, Guido D., (617) 353-8344 gdsalvuc@bu.edu,
Boston University – Hq
Salyards, Stephen L., (310) 825-3043 salyards@epss.ucla.edu,
University of California, Los Angeles – Ys
Sambrotto, Raymond N., (845) 365-8402 Columbia University – Ob
Samelson, Roger, 541-737-4752 rsamelson@coas.oregonstate.edu,
Oregon State University – Op
Sammarco, Paul W., (225) 851-2800 Louisiana State University – On
Sammis, Charles G., (213) 740-5836 sammis@usc.edu,
University of Southern California – Yg
Sammis, Theodore W., (505) 646-3405 New Mexico State University, Las Cruces – Sp
Sammonds, Peter, +44 020 7679 32422 p.sammonds@ucl.ac.uk,
University College London – Nr
Samonds, Karen, 815-753-3201 ksamonds@niu.edu,
Northern Illinois University – Pv
Sample, James C., (928) 523-0881 james.sample@nau.edu,
Northern Arizona University – Cl
Samson, Iain M., 519-253-3000 ext. 2489 ims@uwindsor.ca,
University of Windsor – EgCg
Samson, John C., (780) 492-3616 samson@space.ualberta.ca,
University of Alberta – Xy
Samson, Scott A., (727) 553-3915 samson@seas.marine.usf.edu,
University of South Florida, Saint Petersburg – Oo
Samson, Scott D., 315-443-2672 sdsamson@syr.edu, Syracuse University – Cc
Samuelson, Alan C., (765) 285-8270 Ball State University – Hw
Samuelson, D. James, (408) 288-3716 San Jose City College – Yg
Sanabia, Elizabeth R., 410-293-6556 sanabia@usna.edu,
United States Naval Academy – Ow
Sanchez, Charles, (520) 782-3836 sanchez@ag.arizona.edu,
University of Arizona – On
Sanchez, Marcelo, 979.862.6604 msanchez@civil.tamu.edu,
Texas A&M University – SpNr
Sanchez-Azofeifa, G. Arturo, (780) 492-1822 arturo.sanchez@ualberta.ca,
University of Alberta – Oi
Sandau, Ken L., 406-496-4151 ksandau@mtech.edu,
Montana Tech of The University of Montana – Oi
Sandel, Bill R., (520) 621-4305 sandel@vega.lpl.arizona.edu,
University of Arizona – Oa
Sanden, Eric M., (715) 425-3729 eric.m.sanden@uwrf.edu,
University of Wisconsin, River Falls – Or
Sanders, Laura L., (773) 442-6051 L-Sanders@neiu.edu,
Northeastern Illinois University – HwGe
Sanders, Ronald S., (818) 354-2867 sanders@jpl.nasa.gov,
Jet Propulsion Laboratory – Gr
Sandlin, Stephen H., 909-389-8644 ssandlin@sbccd.cc.ca.us,
San Bernardino Valley College – Oy
Sandor, Jonathan A., (515) 294-2209 jasandor@iastate.edu,
Iowa State University of Science & Technology – Sd
Sandoval Solis, Samuel, 530-750-9722 samsandoval@ucdavis.edu,
University of California, Davis – Hg
Sandvol, Eric A., (573) 884-9616 sandvole@missouri.edu,
University of Missouri – Ys

517

Schauble, Edwin A., (310) 825-3880 schauble@ucla.edu,
University of California, Los Angeles – Cgs
Schauss, Kim E., 812 464-1701 keschauss@usi.edu,
University of Southern Indiana – On
Scheel, Patrick, 573-368-2243 patrick.scheel@dnr.mo.gov,
Missouri Dept of Natural Resources – On
Scheer, Clemens, clemens.scheer@qut.edu.au,
Queensland University of Technology – SbGe
Scheibe, Timothy D., (509) 372-6065 tim.scheibe@pnl.gov,
Pacific Northwest National Laboratory – Hw
Scheidemen, Kathy J., (805) 893-7615 kathys@icess.ucsb.edu,
University of California, Santa Barbara – On
Scheidt, Brian, 573-518-2314 bscheidt@MineralArea.edu,
Mineral Area College – Hw
Schell, Marie, (519) 661-3191 mschell@uwo.ca, Western University – On
Schellenberg, Stephen A., 61959421039 saschellenberg@mail.sdsu.edu,
San Diego State University – Pe
Schelske, Claire L., (352) 392-9617 University of Florida – Pe
Schenck, William, 302-831-8262 rockman@udel.edu,
University of Delaware – OiGi
Scher, Howard, 803-777-2410 hscher@geol.sc.edu,
University of South Carolina – OuCcPe
Scherer, Reed P., (815) 753-7951 reed@niu.edu,
Northern Illinois University – Pm
Schermer, Elizabeth R., (360) 650-3658 schermer@geol.wwu.edu,
Western Washington University – Gt
Schiappa, Tamra A., (724) 738-2829 tamra.schiappa@sru.edu,
Slippery Rock University – Pi
Schieber, Juergen, (812) 856-4740 jschiebe@indiana.edu,
Indiana University, Bloomington – Gs
Schiebout, Judith A., (225) 578-2717 schiebout@geol.lsu.edu,
Louisiana State University – Pv
Schiefer, Erik, (928) 523-6535 Erik.Schiefer@nau.edu,
Northern Arizona University – GmOyi
Schiffbauer, James, (573) 882-9501 schiffbauerj@missouri.edu,
University of Missouri – Poi
Schiffman, Peter, (530) 752-3669 pschiffman@ucdavis.edu,
University of California, Davis – Gp
Schilling, Jean-Guy, (401) 874-6628 jgs@gso.uri.edu,
University of Rhode Island – Ou
Schilling, Keith, Keith.Schilling@dnr.iowa.gov,
Iowa Dept of Natural Resources – Gg
Schimmelmann, Arndt, (812) 855-7645 aschimme@indiana.edu,
Indiana University, Bloomington – Cs
Schimmrich, Steven, (845) 687-7683 schimmrs@sunyulster.edu,
SUNY, Ulster County Community College – Og
Schincariol, Robert A., (519) 661-3732 schincar@uwo.ca,
Western University – HwGg
Schirmer, Ron, (507) 389-6929 ronald.schirmer@mnsu.edu,
Minnesota State University – GaPb
Schlautman, Mark, 864656-4059 mschlau@clemson.edu,
Clemson University – Cg
Schlegel, Alan, (620) 376-4761 schlegel@ksu.edu,
Kansas State University – So
Schleifer, Stanley, 718-262-2726 sschleifer@york.cuny.edu,
York College (CUNY) – Ge
Schlesinger, Michael E., (217) 333-2192 schlesin@illinois.edu,
University of Illinois, Urbana-Champaign – Oa
Schlesinger, William H., (919) 613-8004 schlesin@duke.edu,
Duke University – On
Schlichting, Hilke, (617) 324-7278 hilke@mit.edu,
Massachusetts Institute of Technology – Xy
Schlische, Roy W., (848) 445-3142 schlisch@rci.rutgers.edu,
Rutgers, The State University of New Jersey – Gct
Schlosser, C. Adam, 617-253-3983 casch@mit.edu,
Massachusetts Institute of Technology – Oa
Schlosser, Peter, (845) 365-8707 Columbia University – Hw
Schlue, John W., jwschlue@yahoo.com,
New Mexico Institute of Mining and Technology – Ys
Schlumpberger, Debbie, 320-308-3260 dmschlumpberger@stcloudstate.edu,
Saint Cloud State University – On
Schmahl, Wolfgang, 089/2180 4311 Wolfgang.Schmahl@lrz.uni-muenchen.de,
Ludwig-Maximilians-Universitaet Muenchen – Gz
Schmalz, Robert F., (814) 865-3836 rfs3@psu.edu,
Pennsylvania State University, University Park – Gu
Schmandt, Brandon, 505.277.4204 bschmandt@unm.edu,
University of New Mexico – Yg
Schmerr, Nicholas, 301-405-4385 nschmerr@umd.edu,
University of Maryland – XyYs
Schmid, Dieter, 089/2180 6635 d.schmid@lrz.uni-muenchen.de,
Ludwig-Maximilians-Universitaet Muenchen – Pg
Schmid, Ginger, (507) 389-2617 ginger.schmid@mnsu.edu,
Minnesota State University – SdGm
Schmid, Katie, 412-442-4232 kschmid@pa.gov,
Pennsylvania Bureau of Topographic & Geologic Survey – Go
Schmidt, Amanda H., 440-775-8351 amanda.schmidt@oberlin.edu,
Oberlin College – Gm
Schmidt, Bennetta, bennetta.schmidt@lamar.edu, Lamar University – Gg
Schmidt, Dale R., 217-300-1169 schmidt2@illinois.edu,
University of Illinois, Urbana-Champaign – Ge

Schmidt, David, 937 775-3539 david.schmidt@wright.edu,
Wright State University – PiGd
Schmidt, Jonathan, (519) 824-4120 Ext.53966 jonschm@uoguelph.ca,
University of Guelph – On
Schmidt, Keegan L., 208 790-2283 klschmidt@lcsc.edu,
Lewis-Clark State College – Gc
Schmidt, Lisa, lschmidt@sbccd.cc.ca.us, San Bernardino Valley College – Oy
Schmidt, Matthew, 757-683-4285 mwschmid@odu.edu,
Old Dominion University – Ou
Schmidt, Jr., Robert H., (915) 544-9736 schmidt@geo.utep.edu,
University of Texas, El Paso – Oy
Schmitt, Axel K., (310) 206-5760 axel@argon.ess.ucla.edu,
University of California, Los Angeles – GiCc
Schmitt, Danielle M., (609) 258-7015 dschmitt@princeton.edu,
Princeton University – Oe
Schmitt, Douglas R., (780) 492-3985 doug@phys.ualberta.ca,
University of Alberta – Yx
Schmitt, James G., (406) 994-6903 jschmitt@montana.edu,
Montana State University – Gr
Schmitt, Michael A., (612) 625-7017 mschmitt@soils.umn.edu,
University of Minnesota, Twin Cities – Sc
Schmittner, Andreas, 541-737-9952 aschmittner@coas.oregonstate.edu,
Oregon State University – OaYr
Schmitz, Darrel W., 662-268-1032 Ext 241 schmitz@geosci.msstate.edu,
Mississippi State University – Hw
Schmitz, Mark D., 208-426-5907 markschmitz@boisestate.edu,
Boise State University – CcaCg
Schmutz, Phillip P., 850-474-3418 pschmutz@uwf.edu,
University of West Florida – Gm
Schneider, David, 613-562-5800-6155 David.Schneider@uottawa.ca,
University of Ottawa – GtxGg
Schneider, Edwin K., (703) 993-5364 eschnei1@gmu.edu,
George Mason University – Oa
Schneider, Jim, 7144320202 x21317 jschneider@occ.cccd.edu,
Orange Coast College – Geu
Schneider, John F., (630) 252-8923 Argonne National Laboratory – Ca
Schneider, Julius, 089/2180 4354 julius.schneider@lrz.uni-muenchen.de,
Ludwig-Maximilians-Universitaet Muenchen – Gz
Schneider, Niklas, (808) 956-8383 nschneid@hawaii.edu,
University of Hawai'i, Manoa – Og
Schneider, Robert J., 508-289-2756 rschneider@whoi.edu,
Woods Hole Oceanographic Institution – Yr
Schneider, Tapio, (626) 395-6143 tapio@gps.caltech.edu,
California Institute of Technology – PeOg
Schneiderman, Jill S., 845-437-5542 schneiderman@vassar.edu,
Vassar College – Gs
Schnetzer, Astrid, (919) 515-7837 aschnet@ncsu.edu,
North Carolina State University – Ob
Schnoebelen, Douglas J., (319) 358-3617 douglas-schnoebelen@uiowa.edu,
University of Iowa – Hg
Schoenberger, Erica J., (410) 516-6158 ericas@jhu.edu,
Johns Hopkins University – On
Schoene, R B., (609) 258-5747 bschoene@princeton.edu,
Princeton University – Cc
Scholtz, Theresa C., (630) 252-6499 Argonne National Laboratory – Ge
Scholz, Christopher A., 315-443-2672 cascholz@syr.edu,
Syracuse University – Gs
Scholz, Christopher H., (845) 365-8360 Columbia University – Ys
Schoof, Christian, (604) 822-3063 cschoof@eos.ubc.ca,
University of British Columbia – Ol
Schoonen, Martin A., (631) 632-8007 martin.schoonen@sunysb.edu,
SUNY, Stony Brook – Cl
Schoonmaker, Adam, 792-2577 adschoonmaker@utica.edu,
Utica College – GczGx
Schoonmaker, Jane E., (808) 956-9935 jane@soest.hawaii.edu,
University of Hawai'i, Manoa – Cl
Schopf, J. William, (310) 825-1170 schopf@epss.ucla.edu,
University of California, Los Angeles – Po
Schopf, Paul, (703) 993-3609 pschopf@gmu.edu,
George Mason University – Opa
Schouten, Hans, (508) 289-2574 hschouten@whoi.edu,
Woods Hole Oceanographic Institution – Yr
Schrag, Daniel P., (617) 495-7676 schrag@eps.harvard.edu,
Harvard University – Cg
Schrage, Jon M., (402) 280-5759 schragej@gmail.com,
Creighton University – Ow
Schramm, William H., 225-978-6786 bill.schramm@la.gov,
University of Louisiana at Lafayette – GeHwYg
Schrank, Christoph, +61 7 3138 1583 christoph.schrank@qut.edu.au,
Queensland University of Technology – GcqGt
Schreckhise, R. Gene, (509) 375-9323 Washington State University – On
Schreiber, B. Charlotte, (718) 997-3300 Queens College (CUNY) – Gd
Schreiber, Madeline E., (540) 231-3377 Virginia Polytechnic Institute & State
University – Hw
Schreier, Hans D., (604) 822-4401 University of British Columbia – Og
Schrenk, Matt, (517) 884-7966 schrenkm@msu.edu,
Michigan State University – Py
Schreiber, B. Charlotte, (718) 997-3300 Graduate School of the City University
of New York – Gd
Schriver, David, (310) 825-6663 dave@igpp.ucla.edu,

519

Western University – Gy

Secord, Ross, 402-472-2663 rsecord2@unl.edu,
University of Nebraska, Lincoln – PvCs

Sediek, Kadry N., 002-03-3921595 kknsed@yahoo.com,
Alexandria University – GgsGd

Sedivy, Robert, 402-465-9021 rasedivy@anl.gov,
Argonne National Laboratory – Hw

Sedivy, Robert A., (630) 252-1897 rasedivy@anl.gov,
Argonne National Laboratory – Hw

Sedlacek, Alexa, 319-273-3072 alexa.sedlacek@uni.edu,
University of Northern Iowa – Cs

Seeber, Leonardo, (845) 365-8385 Columbia University – Ys

Seedorff, Eric, (520) 626-3921 seedorff@email.arizona.edu,
University of Arizona – Eg

Seeger, Cheryl M., (573) 368-2184 cheryl.seeger@dnr.mo.gov,
Missouri Dept of Natural Resources – Gig

Seeley, Mark W., (612) 625-4724 mseeley@umn.edu,
University of Minnesota, Twin Cities – Oa

Seewald, Jeffrey S., (508) 289-2966 jseewald@whoi.edu,
Woods Hole Oceanographic Institution – Cp

Segall, Marylin, 801-585-5730 mpsegall@egi.utah.edu,
University of Utah – GeOu

Segall, Paul, (650) 725-7241 Stanford University – Yg

Segars, William P., (706) 542-9072 University of Georgia – Sc

Seibel, Erwin, (415) 338-2061 San Francisco State University – On

Seibt, Ulrike, (310) 206-4442 useibt@ucla.edu,
University of California, Los Angeles – PyCg

Seid, Mary J., 217-244-8171 maryseid@illinois.edu,
University of Illinois, Urbana-Champaign – Gz

Seidemann, David E., (718) 951-5761 Graduate School of the City University of
New York – Cc

Seidemann, David E., 7189515000 x2882 dseidemann@earthlink.net,
Brooklyn College (CUNY) – Cc

Seifert, Karl E., (515) 294-5265 kseifert@iastate.edu,
Iowa State University of Science & Technology – Ct

Seifoullaev, Roustam K., (512) 232-3223 roustam@utig.ig.utexas.edu,
University of Texas at Austin – Ye

Seigley, Lynette S., 319-335-1598 lynette.seigley@dnr.iowa.gov,
Iowa Dept of Natural Resources – Gg

Seitz, Jeffery C., (510) 885-3438 jeff.seitz@csueastbay.edu,
California State University, East Bay – CgOeGx

Selander, Jacob A., 218-726-6211 jselande@d.umn.edu,
University of Minnesota, Duluth – Gcm

Selby, Dave, +44 (0) 191 33 42294 david.selby@durham.ac.uk,
Durham University – Cc

Selim, Hussein M., (504) 388-2110 Louisiana State University – Sp

Selin, Noelle, (617) 324-2592 selin@mit.edu,
Massachusetts Institute of Technology – Oa

Selleck, Bruce, (315) 228-7949 bselleck@colgate.edu,
Colgate University – Gs

Sellmeier, Bettina, +49 (89) 289 25822 sellmeier@tum.de,
Technische Universitaet Muenchen – Ngr

Selph, Karen E., (808) 956-7941 selph@hawaii.edu,
University of Hawai'i, Manoa – Ob

Selverstone, Jane E., (505) 277-6528 selver@unm.edu,
University of New Mexico – Gp

Semazzi, Fred H. M., (919) 515-1434 fred_semazzi@ncsu.edu,
North Carolina State University – Oa

Semken, Steven, (480) 965-7965 ssemken@asu.edu,
Arizona State University – Gg

Semken, Jr., Holmes A., (319) 335-1830 holmes-semken@uiowa.edu,
University of Iowa – Pv

Semtner, Albert J., sbert@nps.edu, Naval Postgraduate School – Op

Sen, Gautam, (305) 348-2299 seng@fiu.edu,
Florida International University – Gi

Sen, Mrinal K., (512) 471-0466 University of Texas at Austin – Ye

Sen Gupta, Barun K., (225) 388-5984 barun@geol.lsu.edu,
Louisiana State University – Pm

Send, Uwe, (858) 822-6710 usend@ucsd.edu,
University of California, San Diego – Op

Senko, John M., (330) 972-8047 senko@uakron.edu, University of Akron – Cg

Sennert, Sally K., (202) 633-1805 kuhns@si.edu,
Smithsonian Institution / National Museum of Natural History – GvOr

Senock, Randy S., 530-898-5603 rsenock@csuchico.edu,
California State University, Chico – Sf

Seong, Jeong C., 678839069 jseong@westga.edu,
University of West Georgia – Oi

Sephton, Mark, +44 20 759 46542 m.a.sephton@imperial.ac.uk,
Imperial College – Xm

Sepúlveda, Julio C., jsepulveda@Colorado.edu, University of Colorado – Co

Seramur, Keith C., (828) 262-3049 Appalachian State University – Hw

Serenko, Thomas J., 614 265 6598 Thomas.Serenko@dnr.state.oh.us,
Ohio Dept of Natural Resources – Eg

Sericano, Jose L., (979) 862-2323 jose@gerg.tamu.edu,
Texas A&M University – Cm

Serne, R. Jeffrey, (509) 376-8429 jeff.serne@pnl.gov,
Pacific Northwest National Laboratory – Cg

Serpa, Laura F., (504) 280-6801 lserpa@uno.edu,
University of New Orleans – Ys

Serpa, Laura F., 915-747-6058 serpa@geo.utep.edu,

University of Texas, El Paso – Ye

Serrano, Carmen, (321) 674-8096 serrano@fit.edu,
Florida Institute of Technology – On

Serrano, Carmen, (207) 872-3244 serrano@fit.edu,
Florida Institute of Technology – On

Sertich, Joseph, 303-370-6331 Joe.Sertich@dmns.org,
Denver Museum of Nature & Science – Pv

Sessions, Alex L., 626.395.6445 als@gps.caltech.edu,
California Institute of Technology – Co

Sethi, Parvinder S., (540) 831-5619 psethi@radford.edu,
Radford University – Gz

Setterholm, Dale, (612) 626-5119 sette001@umn.edu,
University of Minnesota – Gs

Sevellec, Florian, +44 (0)23 80594850 Florian.Sevellec@noc.soton.ac.uk,
University of Southampton – Op

Severinghaus, Jeffrey P., (858) 822-2483 jseveringhaus@ucsd.edu,
University of California, San Diego – Pe

Severman, Silke, 848-932-6555X236 silke@marine.rutgers.edu,
Rutgers, The State University of New Jersey – ClmOc

Severs, Matthew R., 609-626-6857 matthew.severs@stockton.edu,
Stockton University – GxCgEg

Sewall, Jacob, 484-646-5864 sewall@kutztown.edu,
Kutztown University of Pennsylvania – GeOa

Sexton, John L., (618) 453-7374 sexton@geo.siu.edu,
Southern Illinois University Carbondale – Ye

Sexton, Philip, philip.sexton@open.ac.uk, The Open University – Ge

Seyfang, Gill, +44 (0)1603 59 2956 g.seyfang@uea.ac.uk,
University of East Anglia – Og

Seyfried, Jr., William E., 612-624-1333 wes@umn.edu,
University of Minnesota, Twin Cities – Cm

Seyler, Beverly, 217-244-2389 seyler@isgs.uiuc.edu,
Illinois State Geological Survey – Eo

Seymour, Kevin L., kevins@rom.on.ca, Royal Ontario Museum – PvoPg

Shaaban, Mohamad N., 002-03-3921595 Moshaaban@yahoo.com,
Alexandria University – GgsGd

Shaak, Graig D., 3523921721 x257 gdshaak@flmnh.ufl.edu,
University of Florida – Pe

Shackley, Simon J., +44 (0) 131 650 7862 Simon.Shackley@ed.ac.uk,
Edinburgh University – Eg

Shade, Harry, 4087412045 x 3678 geology1@earthlink.net,
West Valley College – Gg

Shade, Janet, 814-362-7560 jas144@pitt.edu,
University of Pittsburgh, Bradford – On

Shadwick, Elizabeth H., 804-684-7247 shadwick@vims.edu,
College of William & Mary – Oc

Shah, Subhash N., (405) 325-6871 subhash@ou.edu,
University of Oklahoma – Np

Shaham-Albalancy, Amira, (972) 377-1563 Aalbalancy@collin.edu,
Collin College - Preston Ridge Campus – On

Shahar, Anat, 202-478-8929 ashahar@carnegiescience.edu,
Carnegie Institution of Washington – Cg

Shail, Robin, +44 01326 371826 R.K.Shail@exeter.ac.uk,
Exeter University – Gtc

Shakal, Anthony F., (916) 322-7481 California Geological Survey – Ys

Shakoor, Abdul, (330) 672-2968 ashakoor@kent.edu,
Kent State University – Ng

Shakun, Jeremy D., 617-552-1625 jeremy.shakun@bc.edu,
Boston College – Gg

Shalimba, Ester, +264-61-2063745 eshalimba@unam.na,
University of Namibia – Gpg

Shamberger, Kathryn, 979-845-5752 katie.shamberger@tamu.edu,
Texas A&M University – Oc

Shams, Asghar, +44 (0)131 451 3904 asghar.shams@pet.hw.ac.uk,
Heriot-Watt University – Yg

Shanahan, Timothy M., 512-232-7051 tshanahan@jsg.utexas.edu,
University of Texas at Austin – PeGsCg

Shane, Tyrrell, +353 (0)91 494387 shane.tyrrell@nuigalway.ie,
National University of Ireland Galway – Gs

Shang, Congxiao, +44 (0)1603 59 3123 c.shang@uea.ac.uk,
University of East Anglia – Hw

Shank, Gerard C., 512-550-7139 cshank@utexas.edu,
University of Texas at Austin – Ob

Shank, Stephen G., 717-702-2021 stshank@pa.gov,
Pennsylvania Bureau of Topographic & Geologic Survey – GziGp

Shankland, Thomas J., (505) 667-4907 shanklan@lanl.gov,
Los Alamos National Laboratory – Yx

Shannon, Jack D., (630) 252-5807 jack_shannon@anl.gov,
Argonne National Laboratory – Ow

Shannon, Jeremy, (906) 487-3573 jmshanno@mtu.edu,
Michigan Technological University – Gg

Shapiro, Russell, 530-898-4300 rsshapiro@csuchico.edu,
California State University, Chico – Ps

Shapley, Mark, shap0029@umn.edu, University of Minnesota, Twin Cities – Gn

Sharkey, Debra, (916) 691-7210 Cosumnes River College – Oy

Sharma, Govind, (205) 851-5462 aamaxs01@aamu.edu,
Alabama A&M University – On

Sharma, Mukul, 603-646-0024 Mukul.Sharma@dartmouth.edu,
Dartmouth College – Ge

Sharma, Shikha, 304-293-5603 Shikha.Sharma@mail.wvu.edu,
West Virginia University – Csa

Spencer, Joel Q., (785) 532-2249 joelspen@ksu.edu,
Kansas State University – CcGs
Spencer, Larry T., (804) 683-5189 lts@oz.plymouth.edu,
Plymouth State University – Gg
Spencer, Mary R., 859-257-8359 mary.spencer@uky.edu,
University of Kentucky – On
Spencer, Matt, (906) 635-2085 mspencer@lssu.edu,
Lake Superior State University – Gl
Spencer, Matthew, +44 0151 795 4399 M.Spencer@liverpool.ac.uk,
University of Liverpool – Og
Spencer, Patrick K., (509) 527-5222 spencerp@whitman.edu,
Whitman College – Pg
Spencer, Ronald J., (403) 220-6447 spencer@geo.ucalgary.ca,
University of Calgary – Cg
Spera, Frank J., (805) 893-4880 University of California, Santa Barbara – Cp
Sperazza, Michael, 631-632-1687 michael.sperazza@sunysb.edu,
SUNY, Stony Brook – On
Spero, Howard J., (530) 752-3307 hjspero@ucdavis.edu,
University of California, Davis – PeCs
Spetzler, Hartmut A., 303-492-6715 spetzler@colorado.edu,
University of Colorado – Ys
Spiegelman, Marc, (845) 365-8425 Columbia University – Ys
Spieler, Oliver, 089/2180 4221 spieler@min.uni-muenchen.de,
Ludwig-Maximilians-Universitaet Muenchen – Gz
Spiess, Richard, +390498279150 richard.spiess@unipd.it,
Università degli Studi di Padova – Gp
Spikes, Kyle T., 512-471-7674 kyle.spikes@jsg.utexas.edu,
University of Texas at Austin – Ye
Spilde, Michael N., (505) 277-5430 mspilde@unm.edu,
University of New Mexico – Gz
Spilker, Linda J., (818) 354-1647 linda.j.spilker@jpl.nasa.gov,
Jet Propulsion Laboratory – Xy
Spindel, Robert C., (206) 543-1310 spindel@apl.washington.edu,
University of Washington – Op
Spinelli, Glenn, 575.835.6512 spinelli@nmt.edu,
New Mexico Institute of Mining and Technology – Hw
Spinler, Joshua C., 501-569-3544 jxspinler@ualr.edu,
University of Arkansas at Little Rock – YdGt
Spinosa, Claude, (208) 426-5905 cspinosa@boisestate.edu,
Boise State University – Pi
Spitz, Yvette H., 541-737-3227 yspitz@coas.oregonstate.edu,
Oregon State University – Yr
Spivak, Amanda, (508) 289-4847 aspivak@whoi.edu,
Woods Hole Oceanographic Institution – Cm
Spokas, Kurt, 612-626-2834 kurt.spokas@ars.usda.gov,
University of Minnesota, Twin Cities – Spo
Spongberg, Alison L., (419) 530-4091 alison.spongberg@utoledo.edu,
University of Toledo – Co
Spooner, Alecia, 425-388-9003 aspooner@everettcc.edu,
Everett Community College – Og
Spooner, Edward T. C., (416) 978-3280 etcs@geology.utoronto.ca,
University of Toronto – En
Spooner, Ian S., (902) 585-1312 ian.spooner@acadiau.ca,
Acadia University – Ge
Spotila, James A., (540) 231-2109 spotila@vt.edu,
Virginia Polytechnic Institute & State University – Gt
Spracklen, Dominick, +44(0) 113 34 37488 d.v.spracklen@leeds.ac.uk,
University of Leeds – On
Spratt, Deborah A., (403) 220-6446 spratt@geo.ucalgary.ca,
University of Calgary – Gc
Spray, John G., (506) 453-3550 jgs@unb.ca, University of New Brunswick – Gp
Spreng, Alfred C., (573) 341-4669 aspreng@umr.edu,
Missouri University of Science and Technology – Gr
Sprenke, Kenneth F., (208) 885-5791 ksprenke@uidaho.edu,
University of Idaho – Ye
Springer, Abraham E., (928) 523-7198 abe.springer@nau.edu,
Northern Arizona University – Hw
Springer, Dale A., (570) 389-4747 dspringe@bloomu.edu,
Bloomsburg University – PivOe
Springer, Everett P., (505) 667-0569 everetts@lanl.gov,
Los Alamos National Laboratory – Hq
Springer, Gregory S., (740) 593-9436 springeg@ohio.edu,
Ohio University – Gm
Springer, Kathleen B., (909) 307-2669 242 kspringer@sbcm.sbcounty.gov,
San Bernardino County Museum – Og
Springer, Robert K., springer@brandonu.ca, Brandon University – Gi
Springston, George E., 802 485 2734 gsprings@norwich.edu,
Norwich University – GmNgYg
Sprinkel, Douglas, (801) 537-3316 douglassprinkel@utah.gov,
Utah Geological Survey – Gg
Sprinkle, James T., (512) 471-4264 echino@mail.utexas.edu,
University of Texas at Austin – Pi
Spruill, Richard K., (252) 328-4399 spruillr@ecu.edu,
East Carolina University – Hw
Spry, Paul G., (515) 294-9637 pgspry@iastate.edu,
Iowa State University of Science & Technology – Em
Spurr, Aaron, 319-273-3789 aaron.spurr@uni.edu,
University of Northern Iowa – Oe
Squelch, Andrew P., +61 8 6436 8725 A.Squelch@curtin.edu.au,
Curtin University – NmYe

Squires, Richard L., (818) 677-2514 richard.squires@csun.edu,
California State University, Northridge – Pg
Squyres, Steven W., (607) 255-3508 sws6@cornell.edu,
Cornell University – Xg
Sremac, Jasenka, +38514606108 jsremac@yahoo.com,
University of Zagreb – PesPb
Srimal, Neptune, (305) 919-5969 srimal@fiu.edu,
Florida International University – Gt
Srinivasan, Balakrishnan, +914132655008 sbala.esc@pondiuni.edu.in,
Pondicherry University – CcGiz
Srinivasan, Gopalan, (416) 946-0278 srini@geology.utoronto.ca,
University of Toronto – Ow
Sritharan, Subramania I., (937) 376-6275 sri@centralstate.edu,
Central State University – Hg
SRIVASTAVA, HARI B., +919415353606 hbsrivastava@gmail.com,
Banaras Hindu University – GctGp
Srivastava, Ramesh C., (773) 702-8125 srivast@geosci.uchicago.edu,
University of Chicago – Oa
Sriver, Ryan, 217-300-0364 rsriver@illinois.edu,
University of Illinois, Urbana-Champaign – Oa
Srogi, LeeAnn, (610) 436-2721 esrogi@wcupa.edu,
West Chester University – Gp
St. Amour, Natalie , nstamour@uwo.ca, Western University – Cs
St. Jean, Joseph, (919) 966-4516 jstjean@email.unc.edu,
University of North Carolina, Chapel Hill – Pm
St. John, James C., (404) 894-1754 jim.stjohn@eas.gatech.edu,
Georgia Institute of Technology – Oa
St. John, Kristen E., 540-568-6675 stjohnke@jmu.edu,
James Madison University – Ou
Stachel, Thomas, 780-492-0865 thomas.stachel@ualberta.ca,
University of Alberta – Gi
Stachnik, Joshua, 610-758-2581 jcs612@lehigh.edu,
Lehigh University – Ys
Stack, Andrew, (404) 894-3895 stackag@ornl.gov ,
Georgia Institute of Technology – Cg
Stadnyk, Leona, (403) 440-6165 lstadnyk@mtroyal.ca,
Mount Royal University – On
Staff, George M., (512) 223-4875 gstaff@austincc.edu,
Austin Community College District – Pe
Stafford, C. Russell, (812) 237-3989 Russell.Stafford@indstate.edu,
Indiana State University – Gam
Stafford, Emily, (828) 227-7367 esstafford@wcu.edu,
Western Carolina University – PgGg
Stafford, Jim, (307) 766-2286 Ext. 252 james.stafford@wyo.gov,
Wyoming State Geological Survey – Hg
Stahl, Terry L., (202) 478-8870 stahl@dtm.ciw.edu,
Carnegie Institution of Washington – On
Stahle, David W., (479) 575-3703 dstahle@uark.edu,
University of Arkansas, Fayetteville – GegGg
Stahlman, Phillip, (785) 625-3425 stahlman@ksu.edu,
Kansas State University – So
Stahmann, Paul, (815) 479-7593 pstahmann@mchenry.edu,
McHenry County College – Oyg
Stakes, Debra, (805) 546-3100 dstakes@cuesta.edu, Cuesta College – Gg
Staley, Amie, (612) 626-4819 astaley@umn.edu,
University of Minnesota – Gl
Staley, Andrew, 410-260-8818 andrew.staley@maryland.gov,
Maryland Department of Natural Resources – Hw
Staley, Andrew, (410) 260-8818 andrewstaley@maryland.gov,
Maryland Department of Natural Resources – Hw
Stamm, Alfred J., (315) 312-2806 stamm@oswego.edu,
State University of New York at Oswego – Ow
Stammer, Detlef B., (858) 822-3376 dstammer@ucsd.edu,
University of California, San Diego – Ow
Stampone, Mary D., 603-862-3136 mary.stampone@unh.edu,
University of New Hampshire – On
Stan, Cristiana, (703) 993-5391 cstan@gmu.edu,
George Mason University – Oa
Stan, Oana, 0040232201467 cristina.stan@uaic.ro,
Al. I. Cuza University of Iasi – Ge
Standridge, Debbie, Deborah.Standridge@gsw.edu,
Georgia Southwestern State University – On
Stanford, Loudon R., 208-885-7479 stanford@uidaho.edu,
University of Idaho – GlmGg
Stanford, Scott D., 609-292-2576 scott.stanford@dep.state.nj.us,
New Jersey Geological Survey – Gl
Stanley, Clifford R., (902) 585-1344 cliff.stanley@acadiau.ca,
Acadia University – Cg
Stanley, Daniel J., (202) 633-1354 Smithsonian Institution / National Museum of
Natural History – Ou
Stanley, George R., 210-486-0045 gstanley@alamo.edu,
San Antonio Community College – OigGe
Stanley, Thomas M., 405-325-7281 tmstanley@ou.edu,
University of Oklahoma – Gr
Stanley, Jr., George D., (406) 243-5693 george.stanley@umontana.edu,
University of Montana – Pi
Stansell, Nathan D., 815-753-1943 nstansell@niu.edu,
Northern Illinois University – Gl
Stanton, Kathryn, 916-558-2343 stantok@scc.losrios.edu,
Sacramento City College – GgPg

527

University of Hawai'i, Manoa – Ob

Stewart, Alexander K., 315-229-5087 astewart@stlawu.edu,
St. Lawrence University – GlmHw

Stewart, Brian W., (412) 624-8883 bstewart@pitt.edu,
University of Pittsburgh – Cc

Stewart, Dion C., 678-240-6227 Dion.Stewart@gpc.edu,
Georgia Perimeter College at Alpharetta Center – Gg

Stewart, Esther K., (608) 263-3201 esther.stewart@wgnhs.uwex.edu,
University of Wisconsin, Extension – Gg

Stewart, Gary, 405-372-6063 Oklahoma State University – Go

Stewart, Gillian, 718-997-3104 gillian.stewart@qc.cuny.edu,
Queens College (CUNY) – OgCm

Stewart, Joe D., (213) 763-3318 jdstewar@nhm.org,
Los Angeles County Museum of Natural History – Pv

Stewart, Kevin G., (919) 962-0683 kgstewar@email.unc.edu,
University of North Carolina, Chapel Hill – Gc

Stewart, Mark T., (813) 974-8749 mark@usf.edu,
University of South Florida, Tampa – Hw

Stewart, Michael A., 217-244-5025 stewart1@illinois.edu,
University of Illinois, Urbana-Champaign – Gi

Stewart, Robert, 713-743-3081 rrstewart@uh.edu,
University of Houston – Ye

Stewart, Robert H., rstewart@ocean.tamu.edu, Texas A&M University – Op

Stewart, Robert R., 713-743-3399 rrstewart@uh.edu, University of Houston – Ye

Stewart, Robert R., (403) 220-3265 stewart@ucalgary.ca,
University of Calgary – Ye

Stewart-Mukhopadhyay, Sarah T., (617) 496-6462 sstewart@eps.harvard.edu,
Harvard University – Xg

Steyn, Douw G., (604) 822-8995 dsteyn@eos.ubc.ca,
University of British Columbia – Oa

Stickel, Robert, (404) 385-4413 robert.stickel@eas.gatech.edu,
Georgia Institute of Technology – Oa

Stickney, Michael C., 406-496-4332 mstickney@mtech.edu,
Montana Tech of The University of Montana – YsGt

Stickney, Robert R., (979) 845-3854 stickney@tamu.edu,
Texas A&M University – Ob

Stidham, Christiane W., 631 632-8059 christiane.stidham@sunysb.edu,
SUNY, Stony Brook – Yg

Stieglitz, Marc, (404) 385-6530 marc.stieglitz@ce.gatech.edu,
Georgia Institute of Technology – Hsg

Stieglitz, Ronald D., (920) 465-2371 stieglir@uwgb.edu,
University of Wisconsin, Green Bay – Gr

Stierle, Andrea, (406) 496-4117 andrea.stierle@umontana.edu,
Montana Tech of the University of Montana – On

Stierman, Donald J., (419) 530-2860 donald.stierman@utoledo.edu,
University of Toledo – Yg

Stigall, Alycia L., (740) 593-0393 stigall@ohio.edu,
Ohio University – Po

Stiles, Lynn F., (609) 652-4677 stilesl@pollux.stockton.edu,
Richard Stockton College of New Jersey – On

Stillings, Lisa, (775) 784-5803 University of Nevada, Reno – Cm

Stimac, John P., 217-581-6245 jpstimac@eiu.edu,
Eastern Illinois University – Gct

Stimer, Debra, 330-244-3511 Kent State University at Stark – On

Stimpson, Ian, (+44) 01782 733182 i.g.stimpson@keele.ac.uk,
Keele University – YesYg

Stine, Alexander, 415-338-1209 stine@sfsu.edu,
San Francisco State University – Gg

Stine, Scott W., 510-885-3159 scott.stine@csueastbay.edu,
California State University, East Bay – Gm

Stinger, Lindsay C., +44(0) 113 34 37530 l.stringer@leeds.ac.uk,
University of Leeds – Ge

Stinson, Amy L., 949-451-5622 astinson@ivc.edu,
Irvine Valley College – Gc

Stinson, Amy L., (949) 361-1260 mesiem@aol.com,
Santiago Canyon College – Gc

Stix, John, 514-398-5391 john.stix@mcgill.ca, McGill University – Gv

Stixrude, Lars, +44 020 7679 37929 l.stixrude@ucl.ac.uk,
University College London – Yg

Stock, Carl W., 205-348-1883 cstock@geo.ua.edu,
University of Alabama – Pi

Stock, Joann M., (626) 395-6938 jstock@gps.caltech.edu,
California Institute of Technology – Gf

Stockli, Daniel, 512-475-6037 stockli@jsg.utexas.edu,
University of Texas at Austin – Gc

Stocks, Ledrew, 570-662-4612 lstocks@mansfield.edu,
Mansfield University – OyGgm

Stockton, Charles W., (520) 621-7680 stockton@ltrr.arizona.edu,
University of Arizona – Hq

Stoddard, Edward F., (919) 515-7939 skip_stoddard@ncsu.edu,
North Carolina State University – Gp

Stoddard, Paul R., (815) 753-7929 pstoddard@niu.edu,
Northern Illinois University – Gt

Stoecker, Diane, (410) 221-8407 stoecker@hpl.umces.edu,
University of Maryland – Ob

Stoelinga, Mark T., 206-708-8588 mstoelinga@3tier.com,
University of Washington – Oa

Stoessel, Achim, (979) 862-4170 astoessel@ocean.tamu.edu,
Texas A&M University – Op

Stoessel, Marion, 979 845 7662 mstoessel@ocean.tamu.edu,

Texas A&M University – Op

Stoessell, Ronald K., (504) 280-6795 rstoesse@uno.edu,
University of New Orleans – Cl

Stofan, Ellen R., (818) 354-2076 ellen.r.stofan@jpl.nasa.gov,
Jet Propulsion Laboratory – Xg

Stoffa, Paul L., (512) 471-6405 pauls@ig.utexas.edu,
University of Texas at Austin – Ye

Stohr, Christopher J., 217-244-2186 stohr@isgs.uiuc.edu,
Illinois State Geological Survey – Ng

Stokes, Martin, +44 1752 584772 M.Stokes@plymouth.ac.uk,
University of Plymouth – Gm

Stokes, Patricia, (801) 537-3320 nrugs.pstokes@state.ut.us,
Utah Geological Survey – On

Stoklosa, Michelle , 503-725-3353 stoklosa@pdx.edu,
Portland State University – GdPiOg

Stolper, Daniel, (609) 258-1052 dstolper@princeton.edu,
Princeton University – Pe

Stolper, Edward M., (626) 395-6504 ems@gps.caltech.edu,
California Institute of Technology – Cp

Stone, Alan T., (410) 516-8476 astone@jhu.edu,
Johns Hopkins University – Cl

Stone, Glenn D., (314) 935-5239 stone@artsci.wustl.edu,
Washington University – On

Stone, Jim, 970-339-6664 jim.stone@aims.edu,
Aims Community College – Og

Stone, John O., 206-221-6332 stn@uw.edu,
University of Washington – Cca

Stone, Loyd, (785) 532-6101 stoner@ksu.edu,
Kansas State University – Sp

Stone, Peter H., (617) 253-2443 phstone@mit.edu,
Massachusetts Institute of Technology – Oa

Stoner, Joseph, 541-737-9002 jstoner@coas.oregonstate.edu,
Oregon State University – Gsr

Stoner, Sherri, (573) 368-2129 sherri.stoner@dnr.mo.gov,
Missouri Dept of Natural Resources – Ge

Storey, Craig, +44 023 92 842245 craig.storey@port.ac.uk,
University of Portsmouth – Gp

Stork, Allen L., (970) 943-3044 astork@western.edu,
Western State Colorado University – Giv

Stormer, Jr., John C., (904) 456-7884 Rice University – Gi

Storrs, Glenn W., (513) 345-8500 University of Cincinnati – Pv

Storrs, Glenn W., (513) 455-7141 gstorrs@cincymuseum.org,
Cincinnati Museum Center – Pv

Stotler, Randy, (785) 864-6048 rstotler@ku.edu,
University of Kansas – Hw

Stott, Lowell D., (213) 740-5120 stott@usc.edu,
University of Southern California – Pm

Stoudt, Emily L., 432 552-2244 stoudt_e@utpb.edu,
University of Texas, Permian Basin – GdPsi

Stout, James H., 612-624-4344 jstout@umn.edu,
University of Minnesota, Twin Cities – Gp

Stover, Susan G., 785-864-2063 sstover@kgs.ku.edu,
University of Kansas – Gg

Stowell, Harold H., 205-348-5098 hstowell@ua.edu,
University of Alabama – Gp

Stowell Gale, Julia, 512-232-7957 julia.gale@beg.utexas.edu,
University of Texas at Austin, Jackson School of Geosciences – Gc

Stoykova, Kristalina C., +35929792213 stoykova@geology.bas.bg,
Bulgarian Academy of Sciences – PsmPe

Strachan, Rob, +44 023 92 842279 rob.strachan@port.ac.uk,
University of Portsmouth – Cc

Strachan, Scotty, strachan@unr.edu,University of Nevada, Reno – Pe

Stracher, Glenn B., (478) 289-2073 stracher@ega.edu,
East Georgia State College – GycEc

Strack, Otto D., (612) 625-3009 strac001@tc.umn.edu,
University of Minnesota, Twin Cities – Hw

Stradford, Todd, (608) 342-1674 stradfot@uwplatt.edu,
University of Wisconsin, Platteville – Or

Straffin, Eric, (814) 732-1574 estraffin@edinboro.edu,
Edinboro University of Pennsylvania – Gm

Strahler, Alan, (617) 353-5984 Boston University – Or

Straight, William, (703) 948-7750 wstraight@nvcc.edu,
Northern Virginia Community College - Loudoun Campus – GgPv

Strain, Priscilla L., 202-633-2481 Smithsonian Institution / National Air & Space
Museum – Or

Stramler, Kirstie L., (415) 452-5046 City College of San Francisco – OagGg

Stramski, Dariusz, (858) 534-3353 dstramski@ucsd.edu,
University of California, San Diego – Op

Strangeway, Robert J., (310) 206-6247 strange@igpp.ucla.edu,
University of California, Los Angeles – On

Strasser, Jeffrey C., (309) 794-7218 JeffreyStrasser@augustana.edu,
Augustana College – Gm

Strasser, Stefan, 089/2180 4340 stefan.strasser@vr-web.de,
Ludwig-Maximilians-Universitaet Muenchen – Gz

Stratton, James F., 217-581-2626 jfstratton@eiu.edu,
Eastern Illinois University – Pg

Straub, David, (514) 398-8995 david.straub@mcgill.ca,
McGill University – Op

Straub, Derek J., 570-372-4767 straubd@susqu.edu,
Susquehanna University – Oa

Surpless, Benjamin E., (210) 999-7110 bsurpless@trinity.edu,
Trinity University – Gcx
Surpless, Kathleen D., (210) 999-7365 ksurpless@trinity.edu,
Trinity University – Gs
Susak, Nicholas J., (506) 453-4803 nsusak@unb.ca,
University of New Brunswick – Cg
Sushama, Laxmi, 514-987-3000 #2414 sushama.laxmi@uqam.ca,
Universite du Quebec a Montreal – Hy
Sussman, Robert W., (314) 935-5264 rwsussma@artsci.wustl.edu,
Washington University – On
Suszek, Thomas J., (920) 424-2268 suszek@uwosh.edu,
University of Wisconsin, Oshkosh – Gg
Sutherland, Bruce, 780-492-0573 bruce.sutherland@ualberta.ca,
University of Alberta – Cm
Sutherland, Mary K., 406.496.4410 msutherland@mtech.edu,
Montana Tech of The University of Montana – Hws
Sutherland, Stuart, (604) 822-0176 ssutherland@eos.ubc.ca,
University of British Columbia – Pg
Sutherland, Wayne, (307) 766-2286 Ext. 247 wayne.sutherland@wyo.gov,
Wyoming State Geological Survey – En
Suttle, Curtis, (604) 822-8610 csuttle@eos.ubc.ca,
University of British Columbia – Ob
Suttner, Lee J., (812) 855-4957 suttner@indiana.edu,
Indiana University, Bloomington – Gd
Sutton, Chris, (360) 650-3581 chris.sutton@wwu.edu,
Western Washington University – On
Sutton, Mark, +44 20 759 47487 m.sutton@imperial.ac.uk,
Imperial College – Pg
Sutton, Paul C., (303) 871-2513 psutton@du.edu,
University of Denver – Oi
Sutton, Sally J., (970) 491-5995 sallys@warnercnr.colostate.edu,
Colorado State University – GdCl
Suyker, Andrew E., asuyker@unl.edu,
University of Nebraska, Lincoln – Oa
Sverdrup, Keith A., 414-229-4017 sverdrup@uwm.edu,
University of Wisconsin, Milwaukee – Ys
Sverjensky, Dimitri A., (410) 516-8568 sver@jhu.edu,
Johns Hopkins University – Cl
Svitra, Zita V., (505) 667-7616 Los Alamos National Laboratory – On
Svoma, Bohumil, svomab@missouri.edu,
University of Missouri, Columbia – Oa
Swain, Geoffrey W., (321) 674-8096 Florida Institute of Technology – Ob
Swanger, Kate, (978) 934-2664 kate_swanger@uml.edu,
University of Massachusetts Lowell – Gl
Swann, Abigail L., 206-616-0486 aswann@atmos.washington.edu,
University of Washington – Oan
Swanson, Basil I., (505) 667-5814 Los Alamos National Laboratory – On
Swanson, Donald A., (808) 967-8863 donswan@usgs.gov,
University of Hawai'i, Manoa – Gv
Swanson, Karen, (201) 595-2589 William Paterson University – Cc
Swanson, R. L., (631) 632-8704 larry.swanson@stonybrook.edu,
SUNY, Stony Brook – Og
Swanson, Sherman, (775) 784-4057 sswanson@agnt1.ag.unr.edu,
University of Nevada, Reno – Hs
Swanson, Susan K., (608) 363-2132 swansons@beloit.edu,
Beloit College – Hw
Swanson, Terry W., tswanson@uw.edu, University of Washington – CcGe
Swap, Robert J., (434) 924-7714 rjs8g@virginia.edu,
University of Virginia – On
Swapp, Susan M., (307) 766-2513 swapp@uwyo.edu,
University of Wyoming – Gp
Swarr, Gretchen, (508) 289-2558 gswarr@whoi.edu,
Woods Hole Oceanographic Institution – Oc
Swart, Peter K., 305 421 4103 pswart@rsmas.miami.edu,
University of Miami – ClPs
Swartwood, Jade L., (570) 389-4108 jswartwo@bloomu.edu,
Bloomsburg University – On
Swaters, Gordon E., (780) 492-7159 gordon.swaters@ualberta.ca,
University of Alberta – Op
Sweeney, Mark D., (509) 373-0703 mark.sweeney@pnl.gov,
Pacific Northwest National Laboratory – Yg
Sweeney, Mark R., (605) 677-6142 Mark.Sweeney@usd.edu,
University of South Dakota – Gs
Sweeny, Daniel, (620) 421-4826 dsweeney@ksu.edu,
Kansas State University – So
Sweet, Alisan C., 806-834-2398 alisan.sweet@ttu.edu,
Texas Tech University – Gs
Sweet, Dustin E., 806-834-8390 dustin.sweet@ttu.edu,
Texas Tech University – Gs
Sweet, Walter C., (614) 292-2326 Ohio State University – Ps
Sweetman, Steve, +44 023 9284 2257 steve.sweetman@port.ac.uk,
University of Portsmouth – Pg
Swennen, Rudy, rudy.swennen@ees.kuleuven.be,
Katholieke Universiteit Leuven – Gso
Swenson, John B., 218-726-6844 jswenso2@d.umn.edu,
University of Minnesota, Duluth – Gr
Swetnam, Thomas W., tswetnam@email.arizona.edu,
University of Arizona – On
Swetnam, Thomas W., (520) 621-2112 tswetnam@ltrr.arizona.edu,
University of Arizona – Pe

Swett, Keene, (319) 351-4644 keene-swett@uiowa.edu,
University of Iowa – Gs
Swift, Donald J. P., (757) 683-4937 dswift@odu.edu,
Old Dominion University – Ou
Swift, Elijah V., (401) 874-6146 lige@gso.uri.edu,
University of Rhode Island – Ob
Swift, Robert P., (505) 665-7871 bswift@lanl.gov,
Los Alamos National Laboratory – Nr
Swift, Stephen A., (508) 289-2626 sswift@whoi.edu,
Woods Hole Oceanographic Institution – Yr
Swihart, George H., (901) 678-2606 gswihart@memphis.edu,
University of Memphis – Gx
Swindle, Timothy, 520-621-4128 tswindle@lpl.arizona.edu,
University of Arizona – Xc
Swisher III, Carl C., 848-445-5363 cswish@rci.rutgers.edu,
Rutgers, The State University of New Jersey – Cc
Switzer, Paul, (650) 723-2879 switzer@stanford.edu,
Stanford University – Gq
Swope, R. J., (317) 278-0132 rjswope@iupui.edu,
Indiana University / Purdue University, Indianapolis – Gz
Swyrtek, Sheila, (810)232-9312 sheila.swyrtek@mcc.edu,
Charles Stewart Mott Community College – Ga
Sydora, Richard D., (780) 492-3624 rsydora@phys.ualberta.ca,
University of Alberta – Xy
Sykes, Lynn R., (845) 365-8880 sykes@ldeo.columbia.edu,
Columbia University – YsGt
Sylva, Sean, 508-289-3546 ssylva@whoi.edu,
Woods Hole Oceanographic Institution – Oc
Sylvan, Jason, 979-845-5105 jasonsylvan@tamu.edu,
Texas A&M University – Ob
Sylvester, Paul J., (709) 737-4736 sylvester@sparky2.esd.mun.ca,
Memorial University of Newfoundland – Ca
Sylvester, Steven, (717) 291-3821 steve.sylvester@fandm.edu,
Franklin and Marshall College – Ca
Sylvia, Elizabeth R., 410 554-5542 elizabeth.sylvia@maryland.gov,
Maryland Department of Natural Resources – Ge
Symbalisty, E.M.D., (505) 667-9670 esymbalisty@lanl.gov,
Los Alamos National Laboratory – On
Symes, William S., (713) 348-5997 symes@caam.rice.edu,
Rice University – On
Symons, David T., 519-253-3000 ext. 2493 dsymons@uwindsor.ca,
University of Windsor – Ym
Syrett, William, (814) 865-6172 Pennsylvania State University, University Park – Ow
Syrup, Krista, 708-974-5615 syrup@morainevalley.edu,
Moraine Valley Community College – Cs
Syverson, Kent M., (715) 836-3676 syverskm@uwec.edu,
University of Wisconsin, Eau Claire – Gl
Syvitski, James P., 303-492-7909 james.syvitski@colorado.edu,
University of Colorado – Gs
Szabo, Csaba, cszabo@elte.hu,
Virginia Polytechnic Institute & State University – Gi
Szecsody, James E., (509) 372-6080 jim.szecsody@pnl.gov,
Pacific Northwest National Laboratory – So
Székely, Balázs, balazs.szekely@ttk.elte.hu,
Eotvos Lorand University – GmOri
Szekielda, Karl H., (212) 772-4019 szekielda@aol.com,
Hunter College (CUNY) – Or
Szeliga, Walter, 509-963-2705 walter@geology.cwu.edu,
Central Washington University – YgsYd
Szente, Istvan, szente@ludens.elte.hu, Eotvos Lorand University – Pig
Szeto, Anthony M. K., (416)736-2100 #77703 szeto@yorku.ca,
York University – Yg
Szidarovszky, Ferenc, (520) 621-6557 ferenc@email.arizona.edu,
University of Arizona – Hq
Szilagyi, Jozsef, jszilagyi@unl.edu, Unversity of Nebraska - Lincoln – Hq
Szlavecz, Katalin, (410) 516-8947 szlavecz@jhu.edu,
Johns Hopkins University – Pi
Szulczewski, Melanie, 540 654-1234 mszulcze@umw.edu,
University of Mary Washington – Osg
Szunyogh, Istvan, (979) 458-0553 szunyogh@tamu.edu,
Texas A&M University – Oa
Szymanski, David, 781-891-2980 dszymanski@bentley.edu,
Bentley University – GvfCg
Szymanski, Jason, 585-292-2423 jszymanski@monroecc.edu,
Monroe Community College – GlPe
Szynkiewicz, Anna, 865-974-6006 aszynkie@utk.edu,
University of Tennessee, Knoxville – Cs
Söllner, Frank, 089/2180 6519 fank.soellner@iaag.geo.uni-muenchen.de,
Ludwig-Maximilians-Universitaet Muenchen – Gg

T

T. A., Vishwanath, +91-832-6519331 tavis@unigoa.ac.in,
Goa University – GpzGg
Tabet, David E., (801) 537-3373 davidtabet@utah.gov,
Utah Geological Survey – Ec
Tabidian, M. Ali, (818) 677-2536 ali.tabidian@csun.edu,
California State University, Northridge – Hw
Taboada Castro, Maria T., 00 34 981 167000 teresat@udc.es,
Coruna University – Sd
Taboga, Karl, (307) 766-2286 Ext. 226 karl.taboga@wyo.gov,

University of Nevada, Reno – Cl

Temples, Tommy, (803) 348-0472 ttemples@sc.rr.com,
  Clemson University – GoYg

Templeton, Alan R., (314) 935-6868 temple_a@wustl.edu,
  Washington University – On

Templeton, Alexis, 303-492-6069 alexis.templeton@colorado.edu,
  University of Colorado – ClGe

Templeton, Jeffrey H., 503-838-8858 templej@wou.edu,
  Western Oregon University – Gv

Ten Brink, Norman W., tenbrinn@gvsu.edu,
  Grand Valley State University – Gm

Tencate, James, (505) 665-6667 tencate@lanl.gov,
  Los Alamos National Laboratory – On

Teng, Fangzhen, 206-543-7615 fteng@uw.edu,
  University of Washington – Cg

Teng, Ta-liang, (213) 740-5838 lteng@usc.edu,
  University of Southern California – Ys

Tenorio, Victor, vtenorio@email.arizona.edu, University of Arizona – Nmx

Teodoriu, Catalin, 405-325-6872 cteodoriu@ou.edu,
  University of Oklahoma – Np

Tepley, III, Frank J., 541-737-2064 ftepley@coas.oregonstate.edu,
  Oregon State University – GiCs

Teplitski, Max, 352-392-1951 maxtep@ufl.edu,
  University of Florida – On

Ter-Simonian, Vardui, (213) 740-6106 tersimon@usc.edu,
  University of Southern California – On

Tera, Fouad, (202) 478-8472 ftera@carnegiescience.edu,
  Carnegie Institution of Washington – Cc

Terkla, David, david.terkla@umb.edu, University of Massachusetts, Boston – On

Terry, Dennis O., (215) 204-8226 doterry@temple.edu,
  Temple University – Gr

Tertyshnikov, Konstantin, +61 8 9266 2297 Konstantin.Tertyshnikov@curtin.edu.au,
  Curtin University – Ye

Terwey, Wes, terwey@southalabama.edu, University of South Alabama – Ow

Tesfaye, Samson, (573) 681-5586 Tesfayes@lincolnU.edu,
  University of Missouri – GtcOr

Tesso, Tesfaye, (785) 532-7238 ttesso@ksu.edu,
  Kansas State University – So

Tester, Jefferson W., 607-254-7211 jwt54@cornell.edu,
  Cornell University – On

Tetrault, Denis, 519-253-3000 ext. 2495 deniskt@uwindsor.ca,
  University of Windsor – Gg

Tett, Simon F., +44 (0) 131 650 5341 Simon.Tett@ed.ac.uk,
  Edinburgh University – Ow

Tettenhorst, Rodney T., 614 247-4246 tettenhorst.2@osu.edu,
  Ohio State University – Gz

Tew , Berry H., 205-247-3679 ntew@gsa.state.al.us,
  Geological Survey of Alabama – GroGs

Tewksbury, Barbara J., (315) 859-4713 btewksbu@hamilton.edu,
  Hamilton College – Gc

Textoris, Daniel A., (919) 962-0690 dtextori@email.unc.edu,
  University of North Carolina, Chapel Hill – Gd

Teyssier, Christian P., 612-624-6801 teyssier@umn.edu,
  University of Minnesota, Twin Cities – Oc

Tezcan, Levent, +90 (312) 2977750 tezcan@hacettepe.edu.tr,
  Hacettepe University – Hw

Thackray, Glenn D., (208) 282-3565 thacglen@isu.edu,
  Idaho State University – Gl

Thaisen, Kevin G., 616-331-9219 thaisenk@gvsu.edu,
  Grand Valley State University – XgGxOi

Thakurta, Joyashish, (269) 387-3667 joyashish.thakurta@wmich.edu,
  Western Michigan University – GiEg

Thale, Paul R., 406-496-4653 pthale@mtech.edu,
  Montana Tech of The University of Montana – Oi

Tharp, Thomas M., (765) 494-8678 ttharp1@purdue.edu,
  Purdue University – Nm

Thatje, Sven, +44 (0)23 80592009 svth@noc.soton.ac.uk,
  University of Southampton – Ob

Thayer, Paul A., (910) 962-3780 thayer@uncw.edu,
  University of North Carolina Wilmington – Gd

Thayn, Jonathan B., 309-438-8112 jthayn@ilstu.edu,
  Illinois State University – Oir

Theis, Karen, +44 0161 275-0407 Karen.Theis@manchester.ac.uk,
  University of Manchester – On

Theissen, Kevin, 651-962-5243 kmtheissen@stthomas.edu,
  University of Saint Thomas – GnOg

Themelis, Nickolas J., (212) 854-2138 njt1@columbia.edu,
  Columbia University – Nx

Thériault, Julie Mireille, 514 987-3000 #4276 theriault.julie@uqam.ca,
  Universite du Quebec a Montreal – On

Therrien, Francois, (403) 823-7707 Royal Tyrrell Museum of Palaeontology – Pv

Therrien, Pierre, therrien@ggl.ulaval.ca, Universite Laval – Gq

Therrien, Rene, (418) 656-5400 rene.therrien@ggl.ulaval.ca,
  Universite Laval – Hw

Thiel, Dr., Volker, +49 (0)551 3914395 vthiel@gwdg.de,
  Georg-August University of Goettingen – CooCo

Thieme, Donald, (229) 333-5752 dmthieme@valdosta.edu,
  Valdosta State University – GaSdGm

Thien, Steve J., (785) 532-7207 sjthien@ksu.edu,
  Kansas State University – Sc

Thigpen, Ryan, 859-2181532 ryan.thigpen@uky.edu,
  University of Kentucky – Gtc

Thirlwall, Matthew, +44 1784 443609 M.Thirlwall@rhul.ac.uk,
  University of London, Royal Holloway & Bedford New College – Cs

Thiruvathukal, John V., (973) 655-4417 Montclair State University – Yg

Thole, Jeffrey T., (651) 696-6426 thole@macalester.edu,
  Macalester College – Gg

Thomas, Christoph, 49-0-921-55-2293 christoph.thomas@uni-bayreuth.de,
  Oregon State University – Owa

Thomas, Debbie, (979) 862-7742 dthomas@ocean.tamu.edu,
  Texas A&M University – Ou

Thomas, Donald M., (808) 956-6482 dthomas@soest.hawaii.edu,
  University of Hawai'i, Manoa – Ca

Thomas, Elizabeth K., ekthomas@buffalo.edu, SUNY, Buffalo – Cos

Thomas, Ellen, (860) 685-2238 Yale University – Pm

Thomas, Florence, (808) 236-7418 fithomas@hawaii.edu,
  University of Hawai'i, Manoa – Ob

Thomas, Helmuth, (902) 494-7177 helmuth.thomas@dal.ca,
  Dalhousie University – Oc

Thomas, Jay, (315)443-7631 jthom102@syr.edu, Syracuse University – Gi

Thomas, Jim, (775) 887-7648 tom_j_smith@usgs.gov ,
  University of Nevada, Reno – Cg

Thomas, John, 352-392-1951 ext 216 thomas@ufl.edu,
  University of Florida – Sp

Thomas, Kimberly W., (505) 667-4379 Los Alamos National Laboratory – Ct

Thomas, Margaret A., (860) 424-3583 margaret.thomas@ct.gov,
  Dept of Energy and Environmental Protection – Gg

Thomas, Mark, +44(0) 113 34 35233 m.e.thomas@leeds.ac.uk,
  University of Leeds – Ng

Thomas, Megan D., 410-293-6574 mdthomas@usna.edu,
  United States Naval Academy – Og

Thomas, Peter, 361749-6768 peter.thomas@utexas.edu,
  University of Texas at Austin – Ob

Thomas, Ray G., (352) 392-7984 rgthomas@ufl.edu,
  University of Florida – Og

Thomas, Robert C., (406) 683-7615 rob.thomas@umwestern.edu,
  University of Montana Western – GsHsOe

Thomas, Roger D. K., (717) 291-4135 roger.thomas@fandm.edu,
  Franklin and Marshall College – PoGh

Thomas, Valerie, (404) 385-7254 valerie.thomas@isye.gatech.edu,
  Georgia Institute of Technology – Ou

Thomas, William A., 205-247-3547 bthomas@gsa.state.al.us,
  Geological Survey of Alabama – Gg

Thomas, William A., (859) 257-3758 geowat@uky.edu,
  University of Kentucky – Gt

Thomason, Jason F., 217-244-2508 jthomaso@illinois.edu,
  University of Illinois, Urbana-Champaign – Hw

Thomasson, Joseph R., (785) 628-5665 Fort Hays State University – Pb

Thompson, Allan M., (302) 831-2585 thompson@udel.edu,
  University of Delaware – Gx

Thompson, Andrew F., 626.395.8345 andrewt@caltech.edu,
  California Institute of Technology – Op

Thompson, Anu, +440151 794 4095 Anu@liverpool.ac.uk ,
  University of Liverpool – Ou

Thompson, Carol A., (254) 968-9739 cthompson@tarleton.edu,
  Tarleton State University – Hy

Thompson, Christopher J., (509) 376-6602 chris.thompson@pnl.gov,
  Pacific Northwest National Laboratory – Ca

Thompson, Curtis, (785) 532-5776 cthompso@ksu.edu,
  Kansas State University – So

Thompson, David W. J., (970) 491-8360 davet@atmos.colostate.edu,
  Colorado State University – Yr

Thompson, Geoffrey, (508) 289-2397 gthompson@whoi.edu,
  Woods Hole Oceanographic Institution – Cm

Thompson, George A., (650) 723-3714 Stanford University – Yg

Thompson, Glennis, (510) 642-7025 University of California, Berkeley – On

Thompson, Jann W. M., (202) 633-1357 Smithsonian Institution / National
  Museum of Natural History – Pg

Thompson, Joel B., (727) 864-8991 thompsjb@eckerd.edu,
  Eckerd College – Py

Thompson, John F., jft66@cornell.edu, Cornell University – EgNx

Thompson, John F. H., (604) 687-1117 University of British Columbia – Em

Thompson, Joseph L., (505) 667-4559 Los Alamos National Laboratory – Ct

Thompson, Keith R., (902) 494-3491 keith.thompson@dal.ca,
  Dalhousie University – Op

Thompson, Kenneth W., 620-341-5985 kthompso@emporia.edu,
  Emporia State University – Oe

Thompson, Lonnie G., (614) 292-6652 thompson.3@osu.edu,
  Ohio State University – Gl

Thompson, LuAnne, 206-543-9965 luanne@ocean.washington.edu,
  University of Washington – Og

Thompson, Margaret D., (781) 283-3029 mthompson@wellesley.edu,
  Wellesley College – Oc

Thompson, Michael D., (630) 252-9269 Argonne National Laboratory – Yg

Thompson, Michael L., (515) 294-2415 mlthomps@iastate.edu,
  Iowa State University of Science & Technology – Sd

Thompson, Tommy B., (775) 327-5146 tommyt@mines.unr.edu,
  University of Nevada, Reno – Eg

Thompson, Wiley C., 845-938-2305 wiley.thompson@usma.edu,
  United States Military Academy – Oy

U

Faculty Index -U

Utgard, Russell O., 614 247-4246 rutgard@regents.state.oh.us,
  Ohio State University – Ge
Utley, Tom, 321-674-8120 tutley@fit.edu, Florida Institute of Technology – Ow
Utter, James M., (914) 251-6642 SUNY, Purchase – On
Uzunlar, Nuri, 605-394-2494 Nuri.Uzunlar@sdsmt.edu,
  South Dakota School of Mines & Technology – Gg

V

Vacher, H. Leonard, (813) 974-5267 vacher@chuma.cas.usf.edu,
  University of South Florida, Tampa – Hw
Vacquier, Victor D., (858) 534-4803 vvacquier@ucsd.edu,
  University of California, San Diego – Ob
Vaezi, Reza, +98 (411) 339 2721 vaezi@tabrizu.ac.ir,
  University of Tabriz – GeHgs
Vaiden, Robert C., 217-244-4299 vaiden@isgs.uiuc.edu,
  Illinois State Geological Survey – Hw
Vail, Lance W., (509) 372-6237 lance.vail@pnl.gov,
  Pacific Northwest National Laboratory – Hg
Vail, Peter R., (713) 348-4888 vail@rice.edu, Rice University – Gr
Vaillancourt, Robert, 717-872-3294 Robert.Vaillancourt@millersville.edu,
  Millersville University – Obc
Valdes, Juan B., (520) 621-2266 jvaldes@email.arizona.edu,
  University of Arizona – Hs
Valencia, Victor, 509-335-9185 victor.valencia@wsu.edu,
  Washington State University – Og
Valenti, Christine, (973) 655-4448 Montclair State University – Gg
Valentine, David, valentine@geol.ucsb.edu,
  University of California, Santa Barbara – Cm
Valentine, Gregory, (716) 645-4295 gav4@buffalo.edu,
  SUNY, Buffalo – Gv
Valentine, James W., (510) 643-5791 University of California, Berkeley – Po
Valentine, Michael , mvalentine@highline.edu, Highline College – Gt
Valentine, Michael, 253-566-5060 mvalentine@tacomacc.edu,
  Tacoma Community College – Og
Valentine, Michael J., (253) 879-3129 mvalentine@pugetsound.edu,
  University of Puget Sound – YmGc
Valentino, David W., (315) 312-2978 dvalenti@oswego.edu,
  State University of New York at Oswego – GtcGp
Valley, John W., (608) 263-5659 valley@geology.wisc.edu,
  University of Wisconsin, Madison – Gp
van Alstine, James, +44(0) 113 34 37531 J.VanAlstine@leeds.ac.uk,
  University of Leeds – Ge
Van Alstine, James B., (320) 589-6313 vanalstj@mrs.umn.edu,
  University of Minnesota, Morris – Pg
Van Arsdale, Roy B., (901) 678-4356 rvanrsdl@memphis.edu,
  University of Memphis – Gc
Van Avendonk, Harm, 512-471-0429 harm@ig.utexas.edu,
  University of Texas at Austin – Yg
Van Buer, Nicholas J., 909-869-3457 njvanbuer@csupomona.edu,
  California State Polytechnic University, Pomona – GxtGz
Van Burgh, Dana P., (307) 268-2536 vbbison@aol.com,
  Casper College – Oe
van de Flierdt, Tina, +44 20 759 41290 tina.vandeflierdt@imperial.ac.uk,
  Imperial College – Cs
van de Gevel, Saskia, (828) 262-7028 gevelsv@appstate.edu,
  Appalachian State University – Og
Van De Poll, Henk W., (506) 453-4804 University of New Brunswick – Gs
Van de Water, Peter, 559-278-2912 pvandewater@csufresno.edu,
  California State University, Fresno – GrPbGf
Van Den Broeke, Matthew S., 402-472-2418 mvandenbroeke2@unl.edu,
  University of Nebraska, Lincoln – Oa
van den Heever, Sue, 970-491-8501 sue@atmos.colostate.edu,
  Colorado State University – Oa
Van Den Hoek, Jamon, 541-737-1229 vandenhj@oregonstate.edu,
  Oregon State University – Our
van der Berg, Stan, +440151 794 4096 Vandenberg@liverpool.ac.uk ,
  University of Liverpool – Em
Van Der Flier-Keller, Eileen, (250) 472-4019 fkeller@uvic.ca,
  University of Victoria – Cl
van der Hilst, Robert, (617) 253-6977 hilst@mit.edu,
  Massachusetts Institute of Technology – Ys
van der Horst, Dan, +44 (0) 131 651 4467 Dan.vanderHorst@ed.ac.uk,
  Edinburgh University – Eg
van der Land, Crees, +44 (0) 191 208 6513 cees.van.der.land@ncl.ac.uk,
  University of Newcastle Upon Tyne – Go
van der Lee, Suzan, 847-491-8183 suzan@earth.northwestern.edu,
  Northwestern University – YsxYg
van der Pluijm, Ben A., (734) 763-0373 vdpluijm@umich.edu,
  University of Michigan – Gc
van der Voo, Rob, (734) 764-8322 voo@umich.edu, University of Michigan – Ym
van der Westhuizen, Willem, +27 (0)51 401 9008 vdwestwa@ufs.ac.za,
  University of the Free State – CgGgv
van Dijk, Deanna, (616) 526-6510 dvandijk@calvin.edu,
  Calvin College – GmOny
van Dongen, Bart, +44 0161 306-7460 Bart.VanDongen@manchester.ac.uk,
  University of Manchester – Co
Van Eerd, Laura, (519) 674-1644 lvaneerd@ridgetownc.uoguelph.ca,
  University of Guelph – On
van Gardingen, Paul R., +44 (0) 131 650 7253 P.Vangardingen@ed.ac.uk,
  Edinburgh University – On

Van Geen, Alexander, (845) 365-8644 Columbia University – Cg
van Hees, Edmond H., (313) 577-9436 midas@wayne.edu,
  Wayne State University – GzxEg
van Hinsberg, Vincent, vincent.vanhinsberg@mcgill.ca,
  McGill University – EgCg
Van Horn, Stephen R., (740) 826-8306 svanhorn@muskingum.edu,
  Muskingum University – GeOiEo
van Hunen, Jeroen, +44 (0) 191 33 42293 jeroen.van-hunen@durham.ac.uk,
  Durham University – Gv
Van Iten, Heyo, (812) 866-7303 vaniten@hanover.edu,
  Hanover College – Pg
van Keken, Peter J., (734) 764-1497 keken@umich.edu,
  University of Michigan – Yg
Van Kooten, Gerald K., (616) 526-6374 gkv2@calvin.edu,
  Calvin College – EgCePi
van Kranendonk, Martin, m.vankranendonk,
  University of New South Wales – GxPeGd
Van Leuven, Judy, (831) 459-4478 judy@ucsc.edu,
  University of California, Santa Cruz – On
Van Mooy, Benjamin, (508) 289-2740 bvanmooy@whoi.edu,
  Woods Hole Oceanographic Institution – Oc
van Nest, Julieann, (518) 474-5814 jvannest@mail.nysed.gov,
  New York State Geological Survey – Ga
Van Niewenhuise, Donald, 713-743-3423 donvann@uh.edu,
  University of Houston – Ps
van Norden, Maxim F., (228) 688-7123 maxim.vannorden@usm.edu,
  University of Southern Mississippi – Op
Van Oostende, Nicolas, 609-258-1052 oostende@princeton.edu,
  Princeton University – Ob
Van Orman, James, jav12@case.edu, Case Western Reserve University – Cg
van Oss, Carel J., 716-829-2900 SUNY, Buffalo – Gy
Van Roosendaal, Susan, (801) 581-8218 University of Utah – On
Van Ry, Michael, mvanry@occ.cccd.edu, Orange Coast College – Gv
Van Ry, Mike, (657) 278-4371 mvanry@fullerton.edu,
  California State University, Fullerton – Og
Van Ryswick, Stephen, 410-554-5544 stephen.vanryswick@maryland.gov,
  Maryland Department of Natural Resources – Ge
Van Schmus, W. Randall, (785) 864-2727 rvschmus@ku.edu,
  University of Kansas – Cc
Van Stan, John, (912) 478-8040 JVanStan@GeorgiaSouthern.edu,
  Georgia Southern University – Oy
Van Straaten, H. Peter, (519) 824-4120 (Ext. 52454) pvanstra@uoguelph.ca,
  University of Guelph – En
Van Tongeren, Jill, (848) 445-5363 jvantongeren@eps.rutgers.edu,
  Rutgers, The State University of New Jersey – GpcGt
Van Vleet, Edward S., (727) 553-1165 vanvleet@usf.edu,
  University of South Florida – Co
van Westrenen, Wim, w.van.westrenen@vu.nl,
  VU University Amsterdam – CpGz
VanAller-Hernick, Linda A., (518) 486-3699 lhernick@mail.nysed.gov,
  New York State Geological Survey – Pgb
VanBrocklin, Matt, (315) 229-5197 mvanbrocklin@stlawu.edu,
  St. Lawrence University – On
Vancas, Tina, (814) 865-2622 tqs5@psu.edu,
  Pennsylvania State University, University Park – On
Vance, R. K., (912) 478-5640 RKvance@GeorgiaSouthern.edu,
  Georgia Southern University – Eg
Vandeberg, Gregory S., gregory.vandeberg@email.und.edu,
  University of North Dakota – GmOi
Vandemark, Douglas C., 603-862-0195 doug.vandemark@unh.edu,
  University of New Hampshire – Or
Vander Auwera, Jacqueline, 32 4 366 22 53 jvdauwera@ulg.ac.be,
  Universite de Liege – Gx
Vanderkluysen, Loyc, (215) 571-4673 loyc@drexel.edu,
  Drexel University – GviGz
Vanderlip, Richard, (785) 532-6101 vanderrl@ksu.edu,
  Kansas State University – So
Vandike, James E., (573) 341-4616 Missouri University of Science and Technol-
  ogy – Hg
VanDorpe, Paul E., Paul.VanDorpe@dnr.iowa.gov,
  Iowa Dept of Natural Resources – Gg
VanGundy, Robert D., (276) 376-4656 rdv4v@uvawise.edu,
  University of Virginia College, Wise – GeHgOg
VanHorn, Jason, (616) 526-7623 jev35@calvin.edu, Calvin College – Oi
Vaniman, David T., (505) 667-1863 vaniman@lanl.gov,
  Los Alamos National Laboratory – Gx
vanKeken, Peter E., pvankeken@carnegiescience.edu,
  Carnegie Institution of Washington – GtYsCg
Vanko, David A., (410) 704-2121 dvanko@towson.edu,
  Towson University – Gx
Vanlandingham, Karen M., (610) 436-2788 kvanlandingham@wcupa.edu,
  West Chester University – On
Vann, David R., (215) 898-4906 drvann@sas.upenn.edu,
  University of Pennsylvania – Py
Vannier, Ryan G., 616-331-3164 vannierr@gvsu.edu,
  Grand Valley State University – CgGn
Vannucchi, Paola, +44 01784 443616 Paola.Vannucchi@rhul.ac.uk,
  University of London, Royal Holloway & Bedford New College – Gu
Vanos, Jennifer K., 806-834-3319 jennifer.vanos@ttu.edu,
  Texas Tech University – Oa

W

Wallace, Janae, (801) 537-3387 nrugs.jwallace@state.ut.us,
   Utah Geological Survey – Hw
Wallace, John M., 206-543-7390 wallace@atmos.washington.edu,
   University of Washington – Oa
Wallace, Laura, lwallace@ig.utexas.edu, University of Texas at Austin – GtYdOr
Wallace, Paul, (541) 346-5985 pwallace@uoregon.edu,
   University of Oregon – GviCg
Wallace, Tim, 662-268-1032 Ext 244 tjw5@msstate.edu,
   Mississippi State University – Ow
Wallace, William G., (718) 982-3876 william.wallace@csi.cuny.edu,
   Graduate School of the City University of New York – Og
Wallace, Jr., Terry C., (505) 667-3644 wallacet@lanl.gov,
   Los Alamos National Laboratory – Ys
Wallender, Wes W., 530.752.0688 wwwallender@ucdavis.edu,
   University of California, Davis – Hg
Waller, Thomas R., (202) 357-2127 Smithsonian Institution / National Museum of
   Natural History – Pi
Walrod, Amanda G., (501) 575-7317 awalrod@comp.uark.edu,
   University of Arkansas, Fayetteville – On
Walsh, Christopher, (301) 405-4351 cswalsh@umd.edu,
   University of Maryland – On
Walsh, Daniel E., (907) 474-6746 dewalsh@alaska.edu,
   University of Alaska, Fairbanks – On
Walsh, Ellen c., (920) 832-6739 ellen.c.walsh@lawrence.edu,
   Lawrence University – On
Walsh, Emily O., (319) 895-4302 EWalsh@cornellcollege.edu,
   Cornell College – GptCc
Walsh, J.P., 252 3285431 walshj@ecu.edu, East Carolina University – Gs
Walsh, John E., (217) 333-7521 walsh@atmos.uiuc.edu,
   University of Illinois, Urbana-Champaign – Oa
Walsh, John J., (727) 553-1164 jwalsh@marine.usf.edu,
   University of South Florida – Ob
Walsh, Maud, 225-578-1211 evwals@lsu.edu,
   Louisiana State University – Ge
Walsh, Tim R., 806-291-1123 Wayland Baptist University – GsPmGo
Walter, Lynn M., (734) 763-4590 lmwalter@umich.edu,
   University of Michigan – Cl
Walter , Michael , 0117 9515007 m.j.walter@bristol.ac.uk,
   University of Bristol – GiCpg
Walter, Nathan A., (678) 839-4070 awalter@westga.edu,
   University of West Georgia – Og
Walter, Robert C., 717 358-7198 robert.walter@fandm.edu,
   Franklin and Marshall College – Cc
Walter, Thomas, (212) 772-5457 twalter@hunter.cuny.edu,
   Hunter College (CUNY) – On
Walter-Shea, Elizabeth A., (402) 472-1553 University of Nebraska, Lincoln – Oa
Walters, James C., james.walters@uni.edu, University of Northern Iowa – Gm
Waltham, Dave, +44 1784 443617 D.Waltham@rhul.ac.uk,
   University of London, Royal Holloway & Bedford New College – Yg
Walther, Ferdinand, 089/2180 4346 macferdi@gmx.org,
   Ludwig-Maximilians-Universitaet Muenchen – Gz
Walther, John V., (214) 768-3174 Southern Methodist University – Cg
Walton, Anthony W., (785) 864-2726 twalton@ku.edu,
   University of Kansas – Gs
Walton, Gabriel, (303) 273-2235 gwalton@mines.edu,
   Colorado School of Mines – NgrYg
Walton, Ian, 801-581-8497 iwalton@egi.utah.edu,
   University of Utah – Gq
Walton, Nick, +44 023 92 842263 nick.walton@port.ac.uk,
   University of Portsmouth – Hw
Walworth, James, (520) 626-3364 walworth@ag.arizona.edu,
   University of Arizona – So
Wampler, J. Marion, kayargon@earthlink.net, Georgia State University – Cc
Wampler, Peter J., 616-331-2834 wamplerp@gvsu.edu,
   Grand Valley State University – HsOiGm
Wanamaker, Alan D., 515-294-5142 adw@iastate.edu,
   Iowa State University of Science & Technology – CsPe
Wang, Alian, (314) 935-5671 alianw@levee.wustl.edu,
   Washington University in St. Louis – Ca
Wang, Bin, wangbin@hawaii.edu, University of Hawai'i, Manoa – Ow
Wang, Chi-Yuen, (510) 642-2288 chiyuen@seismo.berkeley.edu,
   University of California, Berkeley – Yg
Wang, Chien, (617) 253-5432 wangc@mit.edu,
   Massachusetts Institute of Technology – Oa
Wang, Dongmei, (701) 777-6143 dongmei.wang@engr.und.edu,
   University of North Dakota – Ng
Wang, Enru, enru.wang@und.edu, University of North Dakota – Ogi
Wang, Fred P., 512-471-7358 fred.wang@beg.utexas.edu,
   University of Texas at Austin – Np
Wang, Harry, (804) 684-7215 wang@vims.edu,
   College of William & Mary – Op
Wang, Herbert F., (608) 262-5932 wang@geology.wisc.edu,
   University of Wisconsin, Madison – Yx
Wang, Hong, 217-244-7692 hongwang@illinois.edu,
   University of Illinois, Urbana-Champaign – Cg
Wang, Hsiang-Jui, (404) 894-3748 raywang@eas.gatech.edu,
   Georgia Institute of Technology – Oa
Wang, Jeen-Hwa, 886-2-27839910-326 jhwang@earth.sinica.edu.tw,
   Academia Sinica – Ys
Wang, Jianhua, 202-478-8457 jwang@carnegiescience.edu,

Carnegie Institution of Washington – Cs
Wang, Jianwei, (225) 578-5532 jianwei@lsu.edu,
   Louisiana State University – CgGz
Wang, Jim, 225-578-1360 jjwang@agcenter.lsu.edu,
   Louisiana State University – Sc
Wang, Jun, jwang7@unl.edu, University of Nebraska, Lincoln – Oa
Wang, Lillian T., 302-831-1096 lillian@udel.edu,
   University of Delaware – Oi
Wang, Pao-Kuan, (608)263-6479 pao@windy.aos.wisc.edu,
   University of Wisconsin, Madison – Oa
Wang, Qing, 831-656-7716 qwang@nps.edu,
   Naval Postgraduate School – Ow
Wang, Wei-Chyung, (518) 437-8708 wcwang@albany.edu,
   SUNY, Albany – Oa
Wang, Weihong, (801) 863-7607 Weihong.Wang@uvu.edu,
   Utah Valley University – CmGeOi
Wang, Yang, (850) 644-1121 ywang@magnet.fsu.edu,
   Florida State University – Cg
Wang, Yanghua, +44 20 759 41171 yanghua.wang@imperial.ac.uk,
   Imperial College – Yg
Wang, Yuhang, (404) 894-3995 yuhang.wang@eas.gatech.edu,
   Georgia Institute of Technology – Oa
Wang, Yumei, (971) 673-1555 meimei.wang@state.or.us,
   Oregon Dept of Geology & Mineral Industries – Ne
Wang, Yuqing, yuqing@hawaii.edu,
   University of Hawai'i, Manoa – Oa
Wang, Yuxuan, (409) 740-4829 wangyx@tamug.edu,
   Texas A&M University – Oa
Wang, Z. Aleck, (508) 289-3676 zawang@whoi.edu,
   Woods Hole Oceanographic Institution – Cm
Wang, Zhankun, 979 458 3464 zhankunwang@tamu.edu,
   Texas A&M University – Op
Wang, Zhengrong, (203) 432-8461 zhengrong.wang@yale.edu,
   Yale University – Cg
Wang, Zhenming, (859)257-5500(142) zmwang@uky.edu,
   University of Kentucky – Ys
Wang, Zhenming, 859-323-0564 zmwang@uky.edu,
   University of Kentucky – Ys
Wang, Zhi (Luke), (559) 278-4427 zwang@csufresno.edu,
   California State University, Fresno – GeHwOr
Wang, Zhuo, 217-244-4270 zhuowang@illinois.edu,
   University of Illinois, Urbana-Champaign – Oa
Wanke, Ansgar, awanke@unam.na, University of Namibia – GsCl
Wankel, Scott, (508) 289-3944 sdwankel@whoi.edu,
   Woods Hole Oceanographic Institution – Cm
Wanless, Harold R., (305) 284-2697 hwanless@miami.edu,
   University of Miami – Gs
Wannamaker, Phillip E., (801) 581-3547 pewanna@egi.utah.edu,
   University of Utah – Ye
Wannamaker, Phillip E., pewanna@egi.utah.edu, University of Utah – Ye
Warburton, David L., (561) 297-3312 warburto@fau.edu,
   Florida Atlantic University – CgGe
Ward, Bess B., (609) 258-5150 bbw@princeton.edu,
   Princeton University – Ob
Ward, Brent C., (604) 291-4229 bcward@sfu.ca,
   Simon Fraser University – Ge
Ward, Calvin H., (713) 348-4086 wardch@rice.edu,
   Rice University – Og
Ward, Colin R., + 61 2 9385 4807 c.ward@unsw.edu.au,
   University of New South Wales – Gs
Ward, David M., (406) 994-3401 umbdw@montana.edu,
   Montana State University – On
Ward, Dylan, dylan.ward@uc.edu, University of Cincinnati – GmqOi
Ward, J. Evan, 860-405-9073 evan.ward@uconn.edu,
   University of Connecticut – Ob
Ward, James W., (325)486-6767 James.Ward@angelo.edu,
   Angelo State University – HwClOn
Ward, Larry G., (603) 862-5132 larry.ward@unh.edu,
   University of New Hampshire – Gu
Ward, Marie D., (604) 291-4229 University of Alaska, Fairbanks – On
Ward, Peter D., 206-543-2962 swift@ocean.washington.edu,
   University of Washington – Po
Ward, Steven N., (831) 459-2480 sward@es.ucsc.edu,
   University of California, Santa Cruz – Ys
Wardlaw, Norman C., (403) 220-6429 nwardlaw@geo.ucalgary.ca,
   University of Calgary – Go
Waren, Kirk B., 406-496-4866 kwaren@mtech.edu,
   Montana Tech of The University of Montana – HwsOe
Warger, Jane, 909-652-6485 jane.warger@chaffey.edu,
   Chaffey College – OgGg
Warhaft, Zellman, 607-255-3898 zw16@cornell.edu,
   Cornell University – On
Warland, Jon, (519) 824-4120 (Ext. 6374) jwarland@uoguelph.ca,
   University of Guelph – Oa
Warme, John E., jwarme@mines.edu, Colorado School of Mines – Pi
Warner, Mark J., (206) 543-0765 warner@u.washington.edu,
   University of Washington – Op
Warner, Michael, +44 20 759 46535 m.warner@imperial.ac.uk,
   Imperial College – Ys
Warner, Nicholas H., 585-245-5291 warner@geneseo.edu,

SUNY, Geneseo – XgGrHg

Warner, Richard D., (864) 656-5023 wrichar@ces.clemson.edu,
    Clemson University – Gz
Warner, Timothy A., 3042935603x4328 tim.warner@mail.wvu.edu,
    West Virginia University – Or
Warnock, Jonathan P., 724-357-2379 jwarnock@iup.edu,
    Indiana University of Pennsylvania – GsPe
Warny, Sophie, (225) 578-5089 swarny@lsu.edu,
    Louisiana State University – Pl
Warren, Jessica, 302-831-2569 warrenj@udel.edu,
    University of Delaware – GxCpGt
Warren, Joseph, (631) 632-5045 Joe.Warren@stonybrook.edu,
    SUNY, Stony Brook – Ob
Warren, Lesley A., (905) 525-9140 (Ext. 27347) warrenl@mcmaster.ca,
    McMaster University – CgHg
Warren, Linda, (314) 977-3197 lwarren8@slu.edu,
    Saint Louis University – Yg
Warren, Paul, (310) 825-2015 University of California, Los Angeles – Xm
Warren, Rachel, +44 (0)1603 59 3912 r.warren@uea.ac.uk,
    University of East Anglia – Eg
Warren, Richard G., (505) 667-7063 rgw@lanl.gov,
    Los Alamos National Laboratory – Gi
Warren, Richard L., (520) 621-2320 University of Arizona – On
Warren, Stephen G., 206-543-7230 sgw@atmos.washington.edu,
    University of Washington – Yg
Warrick, Arthur W., (520) 621-1516 aww@ag.arizona.edu,
    University of Arizona – Sp
Warter, Marwan A., (907)451-5056 marwan.wartes@alaska.gov,
    Division of Geological & Geophysical Surveys – Gg
Wash, Carlyle H., 831-656-7776 wash@nps.edu,
    Naval Postgraduate School – Ow
Washburn, Robert H., (814) 641-3600 Juniata College – Gs
Washburne, James C., (520) 626-4107 jwash@hwr.arizona.edu,
    University of Arizona – Hs
Wasomi, Charles B., cwasomi@jkuat.ac.ke ,
    Jomo Kenyatta University of Agriculture & Technology – OrrOi
Wassenaar, Len, (306) 239-2270 University of Saskatchewan – Hw
Wasserburg, Gerald J., (626) 395-6139 gjw@gps.caltech.edu,
    California Institute of Technology – Cc
Wassermann, Joachim, 08141/5346762 jowa@geophysik.uni-muenchen.de,
    Ludwig-Maximilians-Universitaet Muenchen – Yg
Wasson, John T., (310) 825-1986 jtwasson@ucla.edu,
    University of California, Los Angeles – Xm
Wasylenki, Laura E., (812) 855-7508 lauraw@indiana.edu,
    Indiana University, Bloomington – Cl
Watanabe, Tohru, 81-76-445-6650 twatnabe@sci.u-toyama.ac.jp,
    University of Toyama – YxsGv
Waters, Dave, +44 (1865) 282457 dave.waters@earth.ox.ac.uk,
    University of Oxford – Gp
Waters, Johnny, 828-262-7820 watersja@appstate.edu,
    University of Tennessee, Knoxville – Pg
Waters, Johnny A., watersja@appstate.edu,
    Appalachian State University – Pi
Waters, Michael R., (979) 845-5246 mwaters@tamu.edu,
    Texas A&M University – Ga
Waters-Tormey, Cheryl, (828) 227-3696 cherylwt@wcu.edu,
    Western Carolina University – Gc
Waterstone, Marvin, marvinw@email.arizona.edu,
    University of Arizona – On
Waterstone, Marvin, (520) 621-1478 marvinw@u.arizona.edu,
    University of Arizona – On
Watkins, David, D.C.Watkins@exeter.ac.uk, Exeter University – Hg
Watkins, David K., (402) 472-2177 dwatkins1@unl.edu,
    University of Nebraska, Lincoln – Pm
Watkinson, A. John, (509) 335-2470 watkinso@mail.wsu.edu,
    Washington State University – Gc
Watkinson, Andrew, +44 (0)1603 59 2267 a.watkinson@uea.ac.uk,
    University of East Anglia – Ge
Watkinson, David H., dwatkson@ccs.carleton.ca, Carleton University – Em
Watkinson, Ian, +44 1784 414046 i.watkinson@es.rhul.ac.uk,
    University of London, Royal Holloway & Bedford New College – Gt
Watkinson, Matthew, +44 1752 584765 M.P.Watkinson@plymouth.ac.uk,
    University of Plymouth – Gs
Watney, Lynn W., (785) 864-2184 lwatney@kgs.ku.edu,
    University of Kansas – Gr
Watson, Alan, (519) 824-4120 Ext.52356 awatson@uoguelph.ca,
    University of Guelph – On
Watson, David B., (865) 241-4749 v6i@ornl.gov,
    Oak Ridge National Laboratory – Hw
Watson, E. Bruce, (518) 276-8838 watsoe@rpi.edu,
    Rensselaer Polytechnic Institute – Cp
Watson, Gerald F., (919) 515-7076 jerry_watson@ncsu.edu,
    North Carolina State University – Oa
Watson, Kelly, 859-622-1419 kelly.watson@eku.edu,
    Eastern Kentucky University – Or
Watson, Michael, +44 (0)131 451 4307 michael.watson@pet.hw.ac.uk,
    Heriot-Watt University – Gb
Watters, Robert J., (775) 784-6069 watters@mines.unr.edu,
    University of Nevada, Reno – Nrg
Watters, Thomas R., 202-633-2483 Smithsonian Institution / National Air &

Space Museum – Xg

Wattrus, Nigel J., (218) 726-7154 nwattrus@d.umn.edu,
    University of Minnesota, Duluth – Yr
Watts, Chester F., (540) 831-5637 cwatts@radford.edu,
    Radford University – NgrHw
Watts, D. Randolph, (401) 874-6507 rwatts@gso.uri.edu,
    University of Rhode Island – Op
Watts, Doyle, 937 775-3455 doyle.watts@wright.edu,
    Wright State University – YeOr
Watts, Tony, +44 (1865) 272032 tony@earth.ox.ac.uk,
    University of Oxford – Gu
Waugh, Darryn W., (410) 516-8344 waugh@jhu.edu,
    Johns Hopkins University – Oa
Waugh, John, 757-822-7436 tcwaugj@tcc.edu,
    Tidewater Community College – Gg
Waugh, Richard A., (608) 342-1386 waugh@uwplatt.edu,
    University of Wisconsin, Platteville – Gc
Waugh, Truman, 785-864-2119 twaugh@ku.edu,
    University of Kansas – Ca
Wauthier, Christelle, 814-865-6711 cuw25@psu.edu,
    Pennsylvania State University, University Park – On
Wax, Charles L., (662) 325-3915 wax@geosci.msstate.edu,
    Mississippi State University – Oa
Wayne, William, wwayne3@unl.edu, University of Nebraska, Lincoln – Gm
Wdowinski, Shimon, 305 421-4730 swdowinski@rsmas.miami.edu,
    University of Miami – Yd
Weaver, Andrew J., (250) 472-4001 weaver@ocean.seos.uvic.ca,
    University of Victoria – Op
Weaver, Barry L., (405) 325-4492 bweaver@ou.edu,
    University of Oklahoma – Ct
Weaver, Douglas J., (702) 295-5916 douglas_weaver@lanl.gov,
    Los Alamos National Laboratory – On
Weaver, John T., (250) 721-6155 weaver@phys.uvic.ca,
    University of Victoria – Ym
Weaver, Justin E., 806-834-4610 justin.e.weaver@ttu.edu,
    Texas Tech University – Oa
Weaver, Robert, (321) 674-7273 Florida Institute of Technology – Oo
Weaver, Stephen G., (719) 389-6954 sweaver@coloradocollege.edu,
    Colorado College – Gx
Weaver, Thomas A., (505) 667-8464 tweaver@lanl.gov,
    Los Alamos National Laboratory – Yg
Weaver Bowman, Kristin, (657) 278-3331 kweaver-bowman@fullerton.edu,
    California State University, Fullerton – Oe
Webb, Amelinda, awebb16@gmu.edu, George Mason University – Gg
Webb, Elizabeth, 5196612111 ext. 80208 ewebb5@uwo.ca,
    Western University – Cs
Webb, Fred, (828) 262-2166 webbfj@appstate.edu,
    Appalachian State University – Or
Webb, John A., +61 3 9479 1273 john.webb@latrobe.edu.au,
    La Trobe University – Ge
Webb, Laura E., 802-656-8136 lewebb@uvm.edu,
    University of Vermont – Gtx
Webb, Nathan D., 217-244-2426 ndwebb2@illinois.edu,
    University of Illinois, Urbana-Champaign – EcGo
Webb, Peter N., (614) 292-7285 webb.3@osu.edu,
    Ohio State University – Pm
Webb, Robert H., (520) 626-3293 rhwebb@usgs.gov,
    University of Arizona – Gm
Webb, Spahr, (845) 365-8439 Columbia University – Yr
Webb, III, Thompson, (401) 863-3128 Thompson_Webb_III@brown.edu,
    Brown University – Ye
Webber, Andrew, (513) 455-7160 Cincinnati Museum Center – Pi
Webber, Karen L., (504) 280-7395 kwebber@uno.edu,
    University of Michigan – Gv
Webber, Karen L., (504) 280-6791 kwebber@uno.edu,
    University of New Orleans – Gv
Weber, Bodo, bweber@cicese.mx,
    Centro de Investigación Científica y de Educación Superior de Ensenada – Gp
Weber, Gerald E., (831) 459-5429 gweber@pmc.ucsc.edu,
    University of California, Santa Cruz – Ng
Weber, John C., 616-331-3191 weberj@gvsu.edu,
    Grand Valley State University – Gc
Weber, Karrie A., 402-472-2720 kweber2@unl.edu,
    University of Nebraska, Lincoln – Py
Weber, Keith, (208) 282-2757 webekeit@isu.edu,
    Idaho State University – Oi
Weber, Rodney J., (404) 894-1750 rweber@eas.gatech.edu,
    Georgia Institute of Technology – Oa
Weber-Diefenbach, Klaus, 089/2180 6549 klaus.diefenbach@iaag.geo.uni-
    muenchen.de, Ludwig-Maximilians-Universitaet Muenchen – Gg
Weborg-Benson, Kimberly, (716) 673-3293 kim.weborg-benson@fredonia.edu,
    SUNY, Fredonia – GgOaPy
Webre, Cherri B., (225) 388-8328 cherri@lgs.bri.lsu.edu,
    Louisiana State University – On
Webster, Ferris, (302) 645-4266 University of Delaware – Op
Webster, Gary D., (509) 335-4369 webster@wsu.edu,
    Washington State University – Pis
Webster, James D., 212-769-5401 jdw@amnh.org,
    American Museum of Natural History – Eg
Webster, John R., (701) 858-3873 jolynn.webster@minotstateu.edu,

Williams, Nancy, 785-532-7257 nkw@ksu.edu, Kansas State University – On
Williams, Paul, +44 0161 306-3905 paul.i.williams@manchester.ac.uk,
 University of Manchester – Oa
Williams, Paul F., (506) 453-5185 pfw@unb.ca,
 University of New Brunswick – Gc
Williams, Quentin, (831) 459-3132 qwilliams@pmc.ucsc.edu,
 University of California, Santa Cruz – Gy
Williams, Ric, +44-151-794-5136 Ric@liverpool.ac.uk,
 University of Liverpool – Og
Williams, Roger T., rtwillia@nps.edu, Naval Postgraduate School – Ow
Williams, Stanley N., (480) 965-1438 stanley.williams@asu.edu,
 Arizona State University – Gv
Williams, Wayne K., (423) 425-4427 wayne-williams@utc.edu,
 University of Tennessee at Chattanooga – Gg
Williams, Wyn, +44 (0) 131 650 4909 Wyn.Williams@ed.ac.uk,
 Edinburgh University – Ym
Williams, II, Richard T., (865) 974-6169 rwilliams@utk.edu,
 University of Tennessee, Knoxville – Yg
Williams-Jones, Anthony E., (514) 398-1676 willyj@eps.mcgill.ca,
 McGill University – Ce
Williams-Jones, Glyn, (604) 291-3306 glynwj@sfu.ca,
 Simon Fraser University – Gv
Williamson, Ben, +44 01326 371856 B.J.Williamson@exeter.ac.uk,
 Exeter University – EmGv
Williamson, Douglas, 212-772-5265 douglas.williamson@hunter.cuny.edu,
 Hunter College (CUNY) – Oi
Willis, Grant C., (801) 537-3355 grantwillis@utah.gov,
 Utah Geological Survey – Gg
Willis, Julie B., 208-496-1905 willisj@byui.edu,
 Brigham Young University - Idaho – GtOri
Willis, Marc, 714-992-7446 mwillis@fullcoll.edu, Fullerton College – Gg
Willoughby, Hugh E., 305-348-0243 hugh.willoughby@fiu.edu,
 Florida International University – Oa
Wills, Christopher J., (415) 557-1668 California Geological Survey – Ng
Wills, William V., 813-253-7809 wwills@hccfl.edu,
 Hillsborough Community College – Og
Willsey, Shawn P., (208) 732-6421 swillsey@csi.edu,
 College of Southern Idaho – GgcGv
Willson, Lee, 713.348.6219 Rice University – On
Wilmut, Michael, (250) 472-4343 University of Victoria – On
Wilson, Alicia M., 803 777-1240 awilson@geol.sc.edu,
 University of South Carolina – Hw
Wilson, Blake, (785) 864-2118 bwilson@kgs.ku.edu,
 University of Kansas – Oi
Wilson, Carol A., carolw@lsu.edu, Louisiana State University – GsOnCc
Wilson, Charlie, +44 (0)1603 59 1386 charlie.wilson@uea.ac.uk,
 University of East Anglia – Ge
Wilson, Clark R., (512) 471-5008 clarkw@maestro.geo.utexas.edu,
 University of Texas at Austin – Yg
Wilson, Fred L., 325-486-6984 fwilson@angelo.edu,
 Angelo State University – Gm
Wilson, Gary S., +64 3 479-7519 gary.wilson@otago.ac.nz,
 University of Otago – GuYmGs
Wilson, Greg C., 616-331-2392 wilsong@gvsu.edu,
 Grand Valley State University – Gm
Wilson, James R., jwilson@weber.edu, Weber State University – Gz
Wilson, Jeffey S., (317) 274-1128 jeswilso@iupui.edu,
 Indiana University, Indianapolis – Oy
Wilson, Jeffrey A., (734) 647-7461 wilsonja@umich.edu,
 University of Michigan – Gg
Wilson, John D., (780) 492-0353 University of Alberta – Ow
Wilson, John L., (575) 835-5308 jwilson@nmt.edu,
 New Mexico Institute of Mining and Technology – Hw
Wilson, John R., 610-330-5197 wilsonj@lafayette.edu,
 Lafayette College – Oi
Wilson, Laura E., (785) 639-6192 lewilson6@fhsu.edu,
 Fort Hays State University – PgGgOn
Wilson, Lorne G., (520) 621-9108 lorne@email.arizona.edu,
 University of Arizona – Hw
Wilson, Lucy A., (506) 648-5607 lwilson@unbsj.ca,
 University of New Brunswick Saint John – Ga
Wilson, Mark A., (330) 263-2247 mwilson@wooster.edu,
 College of Wooster – Pi
Wilson, Merwether, +44 (0) 131 650 8636 Meriwether.Wilson@ed.ac.uk,
 Edinburgh University – Ob
Wilson, Michael C., wilsonmi@douglascollege.ca, Douglas College – GaPgGs
Wilson, P. Christopher, 772-468-3922 ext 119 pcwilson@ufl.edu,
 University of Florida – So
Wilson, Paul A., +44 (0)23 80596164 paul.wilson@noc.soton.ac.uk,
 University of Southampton – GsCg
Wilson, Rick I., (709) 737-8386 California Geological Survey – Ge
Wilson, Robert, +44 01334 463914 rjsw@st-andrews.ac.uk,
 University of St. Andrews – On
Wilson, Robert E., (631) 632-8689 robert.wilson@stonybrook.edu,
 SUNY, Stony Brook – Op
Wilson, Roy R., (860) 465-4370 wilsonr@easternct.edu,
 Eastern Connecticut State University – Oi
Wilson, Sarah, (540) 458-8800 wilsons@wlu.edu,
 Washington & Lee University – On
Wilson, Steven D., (217) 333-0956 Illinois State Water Survey – Hw

Wilson, Terry J., (614) 292-0723 twilson@mps.ohio-state.edu,
 Ohio State University – Gc
Wilson, Thomas, +64 3 3667001 Ext 45511 thomas.wilson@canterbury.ac.nz,
 University of Canterbury – Gv
Wilson, Thomas B., (520) 621-9308 twilson@ag.arizona.edu,
 University of Arizona – On
Wilson, Thomas H., 304 293 6431 tom.wilson@mail.wvu.edu,
 West Virginia University – Ye
Wilton, Derek H., (709) 737-8389 dwilton@sparky2.esd.mun.ca,
 Memorial University of Newfoundland – Eg
Wilton, Robert D., (905) 525-9140 (Ext. 24536) wiltonr@mcmaster.ca,
 McMaster University – On
Wiltshire, John C., (808) 956-6042 johnw@soest.hawaii.edu,
 University of Hawai'i, Manoa – Og
Wimbush, Mark, (401) 874-6515 m.wimbush@gso.uri.edu,
 University of Rhode Island – Op
Winant, Clinton D., (858) 534-2067 cwinant@ucsd.edu,
 University of California, San Diego – On
Winberry, Paul, winberry@geology.cwu.edu,
 Central Washington University – Yg
Winchell, Robert E., (562) 985-4920 California State University, Long Beach – Gz
Winckler, Gisela, 845-365-8756 Columbia University – Cg
Windsor, John G., (321) 674-8096 jwindsor@fit.edu,
 Florida Institute of Technology – Oc
Windsor, Jr., John G., jwindsor@winnie.fit.edu,
 Florida Institute of Technology – Oc
Wine, Paul H., (404) 894-3425 pw7@prism.gatech.edu,
 Georgia Institute of Technology – Oa
Winebrenner, Dale P., 206-543-1393 dpw@apl.washington.edu,
 University of Washington – Olr
Wing, Boswell, 514-398-6772 boswell.wing@mcgill.ca,
 McGill University – Cs
Wing, Scott L., (202) 357-2649 Smithsonian Institution / National Museum of
 Natural History – Pb
Winglee, Robert M., 206-685-8160 winglee@ess.washington.edu,
 University of Washington – XyYx
Winguth, Arne M., 817 272 2987 awinguth@uta.edu,
 University of Texas, Arlington – Opa
Winkler, Dale A., (214) 768-2750 Southern Methodist University – Pv
Winkler, Stefan, +64 3 3667001 Ext 45681 stefan.winkler@canterbury.ac.nz,
 University of Canterbury – Gn
Winklhofer, Michael, 089/2180 4143 michael@geophysik.uni-muenchen.de,
 Ludwig-Maximilians-Universitaet Muenchen – Yg
Winslow, Margaret S., (212) 650-6984 Graduate School of the City University of
 New York – Gc
Winsor, Roger A., (828) 262-7053 winsorra@appstate.edu,
 Appalachian State University – On
Winston, Barbara, (314) 935-7047 Washington University – On
Winterbottom, Wesley, winterbottomw@easternct.edu,
 Eastern Connecticut State University – Og
Winterer, Edward ., (858) 534-2360 jwinterer@ucsd.edu,
 University of California, San Diego – Gd
Winterkamp, Judith L., (505) 667-1264 judyw@lanl.gov,
 Los Alamos National Laboratory – On
Winton, Mary A., 806-834-0497 alison.winton@ttu.edu,
 Texas Tech University – OnnOn
Wintsch, Robert P., (812) 855-4018 wintsch@indiana.edu,
 Indiana University, Bloomington – Gp
Wirth, Karl R., (651) 696-6449 wirth@macalester.edu,
 Macalester College – Gi
Wisdom, Jack, (617) 253-7730 wisdom@mit.edu,
 Massachusetts Institute of Technology – Og
Wise, James A., (850) 644-6265 Washington State University – On
Wise, Michael A., (202) 633-1826 wisem@si.edu,
 Smithsonian Institution / National Museum of Natural History – Gz
Wise, Jr, Sherwood W., (850) 644-6265 wise@gly.fsu.edu,
 Florida State University – Pm
Wishart, De Bonne N., dwishart@centralstate.edu,
 Central State University – YxCt
Wishner, Karen, (401) 874-6402 kwishner@gso.uri.edu,
 University of Rhode Island – Ob
Withers, Kim, 361-825-5907 Kim.Withers@tamucc.edu,
 Texas A&M University, Corpus Christi – On
Withers, Mitchell M., (901) 678-4940 mwithers@memphis.edu,
 University of Memphis – Ys
Withers, Mitchell M., (901) 678-2007 mwithers@memphis.edu,
 University of Memphis – Ys
Withers, Tony, 519-661-2111 x.88627 tony.withers@uwo.ca,
 Western University – Cp
Withjack, Martha O., (848) 445-3445 drmeow3@yahoo.com,
 Rutgers, The State University of New Jersey – Gct
Witkowski, Christine, 860-343-5781 CWitkowski@mxcc.commnet.edu,
 Middlesex Community College – Og
Witt, Emma, emma.witt@stockton.edu, Stockton University – Hgs
Witte, Ronald W., (609) 292-2576 ron.witte@dep.state.nj.us,
 New Jersey Geological Survey – Gl
Witter, Rob, 541-574-7969 rwitter@usgs.gov,
 Oregon Dept of Geology & Mineral Industries – Og
Wittke, James, 9285239565/9044 james.wittke@nau.edu,
 Northern Arizona University – Gi

Wittke, Seth, (307) 766-2286 Ext. 244 seth.wittke@wyo.gov ,
  Wyoming State Geological Survey – Ng
Wittkop, Chad, (507) 389-6929 chad.wittkop@mnsu.edu,
  Minnesota State University – Gsr
Witzke, Brian J., (319) 335-1590 brian-witzke@uiowa.edu,
  University of Iowa – Ps
Wixman, Ronald, (541) 346-4568 rwixman@uoregon.edu,
  University of Oregon – On
Wobus, Reinhard A., (413) 597-2470 reinhard.a.wobus@williams.edu,
  Williams College – Gi
Woerheide, Gert, geobiologie@geo.lmu.de,
  Ludwig-Maximilians-Universitaet Muenchen – Pyo
Wofsy, Steven C., (617) 495-4566 scw@io.harvard.edu,
  Harvard University – Oa
Wogelius, Roy, (+44)-(0)161-275 3841 Roy.Wogelius@manchester.ac.uk,
  University of Manchester – Cg
Wohl, Ellen E., (970) 491-5298 ellenw@warnercnr.colostate.edu,
  Colorado State University – Gm
Wohletz, Kenneth H., (505) 667-9202 wohletz@lanl.gov,
  Los Alamos National Laboratory – Gv
Wojtal, Steven F., (440) 775-8352 steven.wojtal@oberlin.edu,
  Oberlin College – Gc
Wolak, Jeannette, (931) 372-3695 jwolak@tntech.edu,
  Tennessee Tech University – Gsr
Wolaver, Brad, 512-471-1368 brad.wolaver@beg.utexas.edu,
  University of Texas at Austin – HwGe
Wolcott, Donna L., (919) 515-7866 donna_wolcott@ncsu.edu,
  North Carolina State University – Ob
Wolcott, Ray, 6196447454 x3099 rwolcott@palomar.edu,
  Cuyamaca College – Og
Wolcott, Thomas G., (919) 515-7866 tom_wolcott@ncsu.edu,
  North Carolina State University – Ob
WoldeGabriel, Giday, 505-667-8749 wgiday@lanl.gov,
  Los Alamos National Laboratory – Gx
Wolf, Aaron T., (541) 737-2722 wolfa@geo.oregonstate.edu,
  Oregon State University – Hg
Wolf, Lorraine W., (334) 844-4878 wolflor@auburn.edu,
  Auburn University – Ysg
Wolf, Michael B., (309) 794-7304 MichaelWolf@augustana.edu,
  Augustana College – Gi
Wolfe, Ben, (816) 604-6622 ben.wolfe@mcckc.edu,
  Metropolitan Community College-Kansas City – GgOyg
Wolfe, Christopher, christopher.wolfe@stonybrook.edu,
  SUNY, Stony Brook – Op
Wolfe, Karen M., (615)898-2726 Karen.Wolfe@mtsu.edu,
  Middle Tennessee State University – On
Wolfe, Paul J., 937 775-2201 paul.wolfe@wright.edu,
  Wright State University – Ye
Wolff, Eric, +44 (0) 1223 333486 ew428@cam.ac.uk,
  University of Cambridge – Ge
Wolff, George, +44-151-794-4094 Wolff@liverpool.ac.uk,
  University of Liverpool – Og
Wolff, John A., (509) 335-2825 jawolff@mail.wsu.edu,
  Washington State University – Giv
Wolfgram, Diane, 406-496-4353 dwolfgram@mtech.edu,
  Montana Tech of the University of Montana – EgoNm
Wolfsberg, Andrew V., (505) 667-3599 awolf@lanl.gov,
  Los Alamos National Laboratory – Hw
Wolfsberg, Kurt, (505) 667-4464 Los Alamos National Laboratory – Cc
Wolken, Gabriel J., (907) 451-5018 gabriel.wolken@alaska.gov,
  Alaska Division of Geological & Geophysical Surveys – Gm
Wollan, Jacinda, mandy.looser@ndsu.edu,
  North Dakota State University – On
Wolny, Dave, (970) 248-1154 dwolmy@mesastate.edu,
  Colorado Mesa University – Ys
Wolosz, Thomas H., (518) 564-4031 woloszth@plattsburgh.edu,
  Plattsburgh State University (SUNY) – Pe
Woltemade, Christopher J., (717) 477-1143 cjwolt@ship.edu,
  Shippensburg University – Hg
Wolter, Calvin, Calvin.Wolter@dnr.iowa.gov,
  Iowa Dept of Natural Resources – GgOi
Wolverton, Steve, 940-565-4987 steven.wolverton@unt.edu,
  University of North Texas – Ga
Wong, Chi S., (250) 363-6407 WongCS@pac.dfo-mpo.gc.ca,
  University of British Columbia – Cm
Wong, Cindy, (716) 878-6731 solargs@buffalostate.edu,
  Buffalo State College – On
Wong, Corinne I., 617-553-1817 wongcw@bc.edu,
  Boston College – PeCsHw
Wong, George T. F., (757) 683-4932 gwong@odu.edu,
  Old Dominion University – Oc
Wong, Martin, (315) 228-7203 mswong@colgate.edu,
  Colgate University – Gtc
Wong, Teng-fong, 631-632-8212 teng-fong.wong@stonybrook.edu,
  SUNY, Stony Brook – Yx
Woo, David, 510-885-3160 david.woo@csueastbay.edu,
  California State University, East Bay – Or
Woo, Ming-Ko, (905) 525-9140 woo@mcmaster.ca,
  McMaster University – Hg
Wood, Aaron R., 515-294-4477 awood@iastate.edu,

Iowa State University of Science & Technology – Po
Wood, Bernard, +44 (1865) 272014 Bernie.Wood@earth.ox.ac.uk,
  University of Oxford – Gz
Wood, Charles W., (334) 844-3997 woodcha@auburn.edu,
  Auburn University – Sc
Wood, Craig B., 401-865-2585 cbwood@providence.edu,
  Providence College – Pv
Wood, David A., 210-486-0063 dwood30@alamo.edu,
  San Antonio Community College – Onn
Wood, Eric F., (609) 258-4675 efwood@princeton.edu,
  Princeton University – Hg
Wood, Howard , 361-825-3335 Tony.Wood@tamucc.edu,
  Texas A&M University, Corpus Christi – On
Wood, Ian, +44 020 7679 32405 ian.wood@ucl.ac.uk,
  University College London – Gz
Wood, Jacqueline, (504) 671-6485 jwood@lakelandcc.edu,
  Delgado Community College – Gg
Wood, James R., (906) 487-2894 jrw@mtu.edu,
  Michigan Technological University – Cl
Wood, Kim, 662-268-1032 kimberly.wood@msstate.edu,
  Mississippi State University – OawOr
Wood, Lesli, lwood@mines.edu, Colorado School of Mines – Go
Wood, Lesli J., 512-471-0328 lesli.wood@beg.utexas.edu,
  University of Texas at Austin – Eo
Wood, Neill, +44 01326 255163 N.A.Wood@exeter.ac.uk,
  Exeter University – Oo
Wood, Robert, 206-543-1203 robwood@atmos.washington.edu,
  University of Washington – Oa
Wood, Spencer H., (208) 426-3629 swood@boisestate.edu,
  Boise State University – Gmm
Wood, Stephen E., 206-543-0900 sewood@ess.washington.edu,
  University of Washington – On
Wood, Stephen L., (321) 674-8096 swood@fit.edu,
  Florida Institute of Technology – Oo
Wood, Thomas R., (208) 533-8164 twood@uidaho.edu,
  University of Idaho – Hw
Woodall, Debra W., (386) 506-3765 WoodalD@daytonastate.edu,
  Daytona State College – GgOg
Woodard, Gary C., (520) 621-5399 gwoodard@sahra.arizona.edu,
  University of Arizona – On
Woodard, Howard J., (605) 688-4774 Howard.Woodard@sdstate.edu,
  South Dakota State University – ScoGg
Woodburne, Michael O., (909) 787-5028 michael.woodburne@ucr.edu,
  University of California, Riverside – Pv
Woodbury, Randy J., 716 673 3841 randy.woodbury@fredonia.edu,
  SUNY, Fredonia – GeOuGl
Woodcock, Curtis, curtis@bu.edu, Boston University – Or
Woodcock, Nigel, +44 (0) 1223 333430 nhw1@esc.cam.ac.uk,
  University of Cambridge – Gtt
Woodgate, Rebecca A., (206) 221-3268 woodgate@apl.washington.edu,
  University of Washington – Op
Woodhouse, Connie, 520-626-0235 conniew1@email.arizona.edu,
  University of Arizona – Pe
Woodhouse, Iain H., +44 (0) 131 650 2527 i.h.woodhouse@ed.ac.uk,
  Edinburgh University – Oi
Woodhouse, John, +44 (1865) 272021 john.woodhouse@earth.ox.ac.uk,
  University of Oxford – Yg
Woodin, Sarah A., (803) 777-4254 woodin@biol.sc.edu,
  University of South Carolina – Ob
Wooding, Frank B., (508) 289-3334 Woods Hole Oceanographic Institution – Yr
Woodland, Bertram G., (312) 665-7648 Field Museum of Natural History – Gp
Woodley, Teresa, (604) 822-3146 twoodley@eos.ubc.ca,
  University of British Columbia – On
Woodruff, Jonathan D., 413-577-3831 woodruff@geo.umass.edu,
  University of Massachusetts, Amherst – Gs
Woodruff, William H., (505) 665-2557 Los Alamos National Laboratory – On
Woods, Adam D., (657) 278-2921 awoods@fullerton.edu,
  California State University, Fullerton – Gsg
Woods, Andy, +44 (0) 1223 765702 andy@bpi.cam.ac.uk,
  University of Cambridge – YgGt
Woods, Karen M., (409) 880-2251 karen.woods@lamar.edu,
  Lamar University – On
Woods, Rachel A., +44 (0) 131 650 6014 Rachel.Wood@ed.ac.uk,
  Edinburgh University – Gs
Woodward, Lee A., (505) 277-5309 University of New Mexico – Gc
Woodward, Mac B., 501 683-0113 mac.woodward@arkansas.gov,
  Arkansas Geological Survey – Gog
Woodwell, Grant R., (540) 654-1427 gwoodwel@mwc.edu,
  University of Mary Washington – Gc
Wooldridge, C F., wooldridge@cf.ac.uk, Cardiff University – On
Woolery, Edward W., (859) 257-3016 woolery@uky.edu,
  University of Kentucky – Ys
Woolsey, Jamie, 479-575-3355 jwoolse@uark.edu,
  University of Arkansas, Fayetteville – Gg
Worcester, Peter A., (812) 866-7306 worcestr@hanover.edu,
  Hanover College – Gi
Worden, Richard, 0151 794 5184 R.Worden@liverpool.ac.uk ,
  University of Liverpool – Gs
Worrall, Fred, 0191 3742525 fred.worrall@durham.ac.uk,
  Durham University – Cg

Worsley, Thomas R., (740) 593-1101 Ohio University – Og

Wortel, Matthew J., (319) 335-3992 matthew-wortel@uiowa.edu,
University of Iowa – On

Worthington, Lindsay L., 505.277.4204 lworthington@unm.edu,
University of New Mexico – Yg

Wortmann, Ulrich B., 416-978-2084 University of Toronto – Gg

Wraith, Jon M., (406) 994-1997 jean.dixon@montana.edu,
Montana State University – Sp

Wright, Alan, 561-992-1555 alwr@ufl.edu, University of Florida – Sc

Wright, Carrie L., (812) 465-1145 clwright@usieagles.org,
University of Southern Indiana – Oe

Wright, Clay, claywright@cwidaho.cc, College of Western Idaho – Gg

Wright, Eric S., (406) 683-7274 eric.wright@umwestern.edu,
University of Montana Western – Gq

Wright, James D., (848) 445-5722 Rutgers, The State University of New Jersey
– CsOuPm

Wright, James (Jim) E., (706) 542-4394 jwright@gly.uga.edu,
University of Georgia – Gt

Wright, Judith V., (509) 376-2138 Washington State University – On

Wright, Kathyrn, (269) 387-5486 kathyrn.wright@wmich.edu,
Western Michigan University – On

Wright, Stephen F., (802) 656-4479 swright@uvm.edu,
University of Vermont – Gc

Wright, Tim, +44(0) 113 34 35258 t.j.wright@leeds.ac.uk,
University of Leeds – Yd

Wright, V P., wrightVP@cf.ac.uk, Cardiff University – Gs

Wright, Jr., Herbert E., 612-624-5215 hew@umn.edu,
University of Minnesota, Twin Cities – Gl

Wronkiewicz, David J., (630) 252-4385 Argonne National Laboratory – Cg

Wu, Charles T., (519) 661-3791 ctwu@uwo.ca,
Western University – On

Wu, Chin, 608-263-3078 chinwu@engr.wisc.edu,
University of Wisconsin, Madison – Hs

Wu, David T., (303) 273-2066 dwu@mines.edu,
Colorado School of Mines – On

Wu, Francis T., (607) 777-2512 Binghamton University – Ys

Wu, Patrick, (403) 220-7855 ppwu@ucalgary.ca,
University of Calgary – Ys

Wu, Ru-shan, (831) 459-5135 wrs@es.ucsc.edu,
University of California, Santa Cruz – Ys

Wu, Shiliang, (906) 487-2590 slwu@mtu.edu,
Michigan Technological University – OaCg

Wu, Shuang-Ye, (937) 229-1720 Shuang-Ye.Wu@notes.udayton.edu,
University of Dayton – Oy

Wu, Xiaoqing, (515) 294-9872 wuxq@iastate.edu,
Iowa State University of Science & Technology – Oa

Wu, Xingru, xingru.wu@ou.edu,
University of Oklahoma – Np

Wu, Yi-Hwa, (660) 562-1869 ywu@nwmissouri.edu,
Northwest Missouri State University – Oi

Wu, Yutian, (765) 494-8677 wu640@purdue.edu,
Purdue University – Oa

Wuebbles, Donald J., (217) 244-1568 wuebbles@illinois.edu,
University of Illinois, Urbana-Champaign – Oa

Wuerthele, Norman, (412) 622-3265 wuerthelen@carnegiemnh.org,
Carnegie Museum of Natural History – Pv

Wulff, Andrew, (270) 745-5976 andrew.wulff@wku.edu,
Western Kentucky University – Gv

Wulff, Andrew H., (562) 907-4220 Whittier College – Gi

Wunderman, Richard, (202) 633-1827 wunderma@si.edu,
Smithsonian Institution / National Museum of Natural History – Gv

Wunsch, Carl I., (617) 253-5937 cwunsch@mit.edu,
Massachusetts Institute of Technology – Op

Wunsch, David R., 302-831-8258 dwunsch@udel.edu,
University of Delaware – CmNg

Wust-Bloch, Gilles H., (03-) 640-5475 l, Tel Aviv University – Ys

Wyckoff, John W., (303) 556-2590 john.wyckoff@ucdenver.edu,
University of Colorado, Denver – Oy

Wyckoff, William K., (406) 994-6914 ueswww@montana.edu,
Montana State University – On

Wylie, Ann G., (301) 405-4079 awylie@umd.edu,
University of Maryland – Gz

Wyllie, Peter J., (626) 395-6461 wyllie@gps.caltech.edu,
California Institute of Technology – Cp

Wyman, Derek A., (618) 938-0117 University of Saskatchewan – Cg

Wyngaard, John C., wyngaard@ems.psu.edu,
Pennsylvania State University, University Park – Ow

Wynn, Elizabeth Anne, 205-247-3671 awynn@gsa.state.al.us,
Geological Survey of Alabama – Gm

Wynn, Thomas C., (570) 484-2081 twynn@lhup.edu,
Lock Haven University – GsPiEo

Wypych, Alicia, (907)451-5016 alicja.wypych@alaska.gov,
Division of Geological & Geophysical Surveys – Gz

Wypych, Alicja, 907-451-5010 alicja.wypych@alaska.gov,
Alaska Division of Geological & Geophysical Surveys – Gg

Wyse Jackson, Patrick N., + 353-1-8961477 wysjcknp@tcd.ie,
Trinity College – Ob

Wysession, Michael E., (314) 935-5625 michael@wucore.wustl.edu,
Washington University in St. Louis – Ys

Wysocki, Mark, (607) 255-2568 mww3@cornell.edu, Cornell University – Oa

Wysong, Jr., James F., (813) 253-7805 jwysong@hccfl.edu,
Hillsborough Community College – Ow

Wyss, Andre R., (805) 893-8628 wyss@geol.ucsb.edu,
University of California, Santa Barbara – Pv

X

Xia, Renjie, (217) 244-6166 Illinois State Water Survey – Hs

Xiao, Shuhai, 540-231-1366 xiao@vt.edu,
Virginia Polytechnic Institute & State University – Pi

Xie, Feiqin, 361-825-3229 Feiqin.Xie@tamucc.edu,
Texas A&M University, Corpus Christi – Oa

Xie, Lian, (919) 515-1435 xie@ncsu.edu ,
North Carolina State University – Oa

Xie, Xiangyang, (817) 257-4395 x.xie@tcu.edu,
Texas Christian University – GoEog

Xie, Xiao-bi, (831) 459-5094 xie@es.ucsc.edu,
University of California, Santa Cruz – Ys

Xie, Zhixiao, 561 297-2852 xie@fau.edu,
Florida Atlantic University – Oir

Xu, Huifang, 608/265-5587 hfxu@geology.wisc.edu,
University of Wisconsin, Madison – Gz

Xu, Li, (508)289-3673 lxu@whoi.edu,
Woods Hole Oceanographic Institution – Yr

Xu, Shangping, 414-229-6148 xus@uwm.edu,
University of Wisconsin, Milwaukee – Hg

Xu, Wei, wei.xu@uleth.ca, University of Lethbridge – Oi

Xuan, Chuang, +44 (0)23 80596401 C.Xuan@soton.ac.uk,
University of Southampton – Pe

Y

Yabusaki, Steven B., (509) 372-6095 steve.yabusaki@pnl.gov,
Pacific Northwest National Laboratory – Hg

Yacobucci, Peg M., (419) 372-7982 mmyacob@bgsu.edu,
Bowling Green State University – Po

Yacucci, Mark, (309) 268-8640 mark.yacucci@heartland.edu,
Heartland Community College – Og

Yacucci, Mark A., 217-265-0747 yacucci@illinois.edu,
University of Illinois – Oi

Yalcin, Kaplan, (541) 737-1230 yalcink@geo.oregonstate.edu,
Oregon State University – Og

Yalcin, Rebecca, yalcinr@onid.orst.edu, Oregon State University – Gg

Yalda, Sepideh, 717-872-3293 Sepi.Yalda@millersville.edu,
Millersville University – Oa

Yamanaka, Tsuyuko, +44 0151 795 5291 T.Yamanaka@liverpool.ac.uk,
University of Liverpool – Ob

Yan, Eugene, (630) 252-6322 eyan@anl.gov, Argonne National Laboratory – Hw

Yan, Eugene, rgmartin@uic.edu, University of Illinois at Chicago – Hg

Yan, Jun, (270) 745-8952 jun.yan@wku.edu,
Western Kentucky University – Oi

Yan, Xiao-Hai, (302) 831-3694 University of Delaware – Or

Yan, Y E., (630) 252-6322 eyan@anl.gov,
Argonne National Laboratory – Gg

Yancey, Thomas E., (979) 845-0643 yancey@geo.tamu.edu,
Texas A&M University – Pg

Yandle, Tracy, 404 727 5652 tyandle@emory.edu,
Emory University – Ob

Yang, Changbing, 512-471-4364 changbing.yang@beg.utexas.edu,
University of Texas at Austin – Hw

Yang, Gang, (970)-491-3789 gang.yang@colostate.edu,
Colorado State University – Cc

Yang, Jianwen, 519-253-3000 x2181 jianweny@uwindsor.ca,
University of Windsor – HwYg

Yang, Panseok, (204) 474-9452 yangp@cc.umanitoba.ca,
University of Manitoba – Ca

Yang, Ping, (979) 845-7679 pyang@tamu.edu,
Texas A&M University – Oa

Yang, Wan, 316 -978-3140 Wichita State University – Gs

Yang, Y, YangY6@cf.ac.uk, Cardiff University – Hg

Yang, Zong-Liang, (512) 471-3824 liang@mail.utexas.edu,
University of Texas at Austin – Ow

Yanites, Brian J., (208) 885-4704 byanites@uidaho.edu,
University of Idaho – Gm

Yankovsky, Alexander , 803-777-3550 ayankovsky@geol.sc.edu,
University of South Carolina – Opn

Yao, Wensheng, (727) 553-3922 University of South Florida – Oc

Yao, Yon, +27 (0)46-603-7393 y.yao@ru.ac.za, Rhodes University – Eg

Yapp, Crayton J., (214) 768-3897 Southern Methodist University – Csl

Yarbrough, Robert A., 912-478-0846 RYarbrough@GeorgiaSouthern.edu,
Georgia Southern University – On

Yardley, Bruce, +44(0) 113 34 35227 B.W.D.Yardley@leeds.ac.uk,
University of Leeds – Cg

Yarger, Douglas N., doug@iastate.edu,
Iowa State University of Science & Technology – Oa

Yarger, Douglas N., (515) 294-9872 doug@iastate.edu,
Iowa State University of Science & Technology – Oa

Yassin, Barbara E., (601) 961-5571 barbara_yassin@deq.state.ms.us,
Mississippi Office of Geology – Oyi

Yates, Martin G., (207) 581-2154 yates@maine.edu,
University of Maine – Eg

Z